BASEBALL PROSPECTUS

2017

The Essential Guide to the 2017 Season

Edited by Aaron Gleeman and Bret Sayre

Emma Baccellieri, Demetrius Bell, Craig Brown, Russell Carleton, Ben Carsley, Matthew Collins, Patrick Dubuque, Kenny Ducey, James Fegan, Ken Funck, Catherine Garcia, Eric Garcia McKinley, Brendan Gawlowski, Mike Gianella, Craig Goldstein, Bryan Grosnick, Matt Gwin, Joshua Howsam, Bryan Joiner, Wilson Karaman, Matthew Kory, David Lee, Rob Mains, Jack Moore, Ryan P. Morrison, Mauricio Rubio, Dustin Palmateer, Jeffrey Paternostro, Jeff Quinton, Meg Rowley, Jarrett Seidler, Trevor Strunk, Matt Sussman, Matt Trueblood, Ashley Varela, Rian Watt, Jeff Wiser, Nicholas Zettel

Dave Pease and Stephen Reichert, Consultant Editors
Harry Pavlidis and Rob McQuown, Statistics Editors

Turner Publishing Company
Nashville, Tennessee
New York, New York
www.turnerpublishing.com

Copyright © 2017 by Baseball Prospectus, LLC.
All rights reserved

This book or any part thereof may not be reproduced or
transmitted in any form or by any means, electronic or
mechanical, including photocopying, recording, or by any
information storage and retrieval system, without permission
in writing from the publisher.

Team logos and trademarks used with permission of
MLB Advanced Media.

Limit of Liability/Disclaimer of Warranty: While the publisher
and the author have used their best efforts in preparing
this book, they make no representations or warranties with
respect to the accuracy or completeness of the contents of
this book and specifically disclaim any implied warranties of
merchantability or fitness for a particular purpose. No warranty
may be created or extended by sales representatives or written
sales materials. The advice and strategies contained herein
may not be suitable for your situation. You should consult
with a professional where appropriate. Neither the publisher
nor the author shall be liable for any loss of profit or any other
commercial damages, including but not limited to special,
incidental, consequential, or other damages.

Library of Congress Cataloging-in-Publication Data:
paperback
ISBN-10: 1681626403
ISBN-13: 978-1681626406
hardback
ISBN-10: 1681626411
ISBN-13: 978-1681626413

Project Credits
Cover Design: Karen Siatras
Interior design and production: Bryan Davidson
Layout: Misty Horten & Colleen Cunningham

Cover Photos
Front Cover: Mookie Betts. © Kim Klement-USA TODAY Sports
Back Cover: Corey Kluber. © Bill Streicher-USA TODAY Sports
Back Cover: Kris Bryant. © Kamil Krzaczynski-USA TODAY Sports

Manufactured in the United States of America
10 9 8 7 6 5 4 3 2 1

TABLE OF CONTENTS

Foreword

by Glen Perkins

"**I**t's not sustainable."

No, that isn't a quote from the *Farmer's Almanac* about cutting-edge agriculture techniques—it was my introduction to Baseball Prospectus and the wonderful world of sabermetrics.

I stumbled upon BP sometime in early 2009 when I read an article containing the acronym FIP. Advanced statistics, at least from a player's point of view, were not even in the embryonic stage, but that term and its meaning stuck its tentacles in my brain and didn't let go. More on that later.

What makes this book—and the BP website—great is its accessibility to all realms of baseball folk. For kids who yearn for a better understanding of baseball, fantasy gurus, active players such as myself and all the way up to MLB front office executives—Baseball Prospectus has been a resource for statistics, knowledge and analysis since 1996.

BP has earned its reputation through smart writing by some of the brightest minds this game has to offer. Not only is BP represented in nearly every major sports publication, it's becoming increasingly difficult to find MLB teams that don't employ at least one former BP staffer.

The trend toward the acceptance and use of advanced statistics has improved the game and also improved the experience fans can have while watching. The sport actually hasn't changed *that* much since the 1800s, but the lens through which it's seen has evolved more in the past 30 years than it did in the previous 100. BP has played a large role in that.

OK, now let's go back to 2009. I was coming off a season in which I posted a 12-4 record as a starter for the Twins. I thought a dozen wins was not too shabby. Had I known then that the "wins" stat is meaningless for individual pitchers, I would have looked further into my performance and seen a 4.41 ERA with just 74 strikeouts in 151 innings. I also may have noticed a high fly-ball rate and a FIP above 5.00, and realized that I was somewhat lucky to escape with such a nice-looking record.

I began the 2009 season with three straight starts of at least eight innings, allowing a total of four runs. However, those three starts and 24 total innings included just 12 strikeouts and zero home runs allowed, despite allowing tons of fly balls. You can probably see where the word "unsustainable" starts to come in.

From there it was a downward spiral of poor pitching, bad health and ultimately a demotion to Triple-A, but that BP article stuck with me. I continued to research and learn what I could do to improve my performance by relying less on the defense to make plays. By 2010, I had a decent grasp of what needed to be done—it was just a matter of putting the plan in action. I modified my pitching style and, along with a move to the bullpen and the obligatory bump in velocity, my strikeout rate went way up, my walk rate went down and I induced more ground balls.

As the years went on and my FIP improved, the proliferation of advanced metrics within the clubhouse was still as slow as molasses in January. I continued to preach the importance of sabermetrics, finding myself in arguments about the greatness of Barry Bonds that turned into debates about whether a hitter who walked in every plate appearance would be the MVP.

It wasn't until a trip to Costa Rica with some other players that I felt like I actually had people listening to what I was saying. In one of the more baseball-ratty things of all time, I was with a few other players on a catamaran in the waters off Central America, and not snorkeling or swimming with dolphins but holding court about the meaning of FIP and WAR. In Costa Rica! On a boat!

I realized then that the lack of stats and analysis wasn't about a closed mindset but rather a lack of understanding. The mix of people on that boat—10-year veterans and guys with only a year or two under their belts—could not believe that there were people figuring all this stuff out and that it actually applied to what we did. It was a eureka moment for me and a day in my baseball geek life that I won't forget.

Of course, throughout all of my belief in stats and analysis there is still one thing that has always chapped my ass (that's a technical term). I love numbers like FIP and DRA and WARP, but it always seemed like relievers were undervalued in some way. Part of that is simple: counting or bulk stats are always going to value a starter's workload more than a reliever's workload. There's more to being a reliever than the lower inning total.

Stressful, high-leverage innings, back-to-back days, less predictable usage—I felt that relievers were undervalued. When I had an opportunity to sign a four-year contract in the spring of 2014, I didn't hesitate. I saw a trend of relievers getting shorter contracts due to their volatility and couldn't pass up the security, all while thinking that teams just weren't seeing the full value.

Not everyone can be a late-inning reliever. I know from experience. By and large, they are made—rather than born—from mediocre starters (myself included) and that may have also played a part in their being undervalued. But now there are metrics to account for leverage and high-pressure situations, and relievers are getting three-, four- and even five-year contracts as teams realize the impact shortening a game has on the other team.

I'm thrilled to see the claws of sabermetrics dig into our game further and further. It's only a positive when there's new knowledge available and that knowledge is accepted by a larger audience, on and off the field.

Enjoy this baseball season for all it's worth. I know I will. ▩

—Glen Perkins is a three-time All-Star pitcher
for the Minnesota Twins

Baseball Prospectus 2017
Statistical Introduction

Why don't you get your nose out of those numbers and watch a game?

It's a false dilemma, of course. We would wager that Baseball Prospectus readers watch more games than the typical fan. They also probably pay better attention when they watch. The numbers do not replace observation; they supplement it. Having the numbers allows you to learn things not readily seen by mere watching and to keep up on many more players than any one person otherwise could.

This book doesn't ask you to choose between the two. Instead, we combine numerical analysis with the observations of a lot of very bright people. They won't always agree. Just as the eyes don't always see what the numbers do, the reverse can be true. In order to get the most out of this book, however, it helps to understand the numbers we're presenting and why.

Offense

The core of our offense measurements is True Average, which attempts to quantify everything a player does at the plate—hitting for power, taking walks, striking out and even "productive" outs—and scale it to batting average. A player with a TAv of .260 is average, .300 exceptional, .200 rather awful.

True Average also accounts for the context a player performs in. That means we adjust it based on the mix of parks a player plays in. Also, rather than use a blanket park adjustment for every player on a team, a player who plays a disproportionate number of his games at home will see that reflected in his numbers. We also adjust based on league quality: The average player in the AL is better than the average player in the NL, and True Average accounts for this.

Because hitting isn't the entirety of scoring runs, we also look at a player's Baserunning Runs. BRR accounts for the value of a player's ability to steal bases, of course, but also accounts for his ability to go first to third on a single, or advance on a flyball.

Defense

Defense is a much thornier issue. The general move in the sabermetric community has been toward stats based on zone data, where human stringers record the type of batted ball (grounder, liner, flyball) and its presumed landing location. That data is used to compile expected outs for comparing a fielder's actual performance.

The trouble with zone data is twofold. First, unlike the data we use in the calculation of the statistics you see in this book, zone data wasn't made publicly available; it was recorded by commercial providers who kept the raw data private, only disclosing it to a select few who paid for it. Second, as we've seen the field of zone-based defensive analysis open up—more data and more metrics based upon that data coming to light—we see that the conclusions of zone-based defensive metrics don't hold up to outside scrutiny. Different data providers can come to very different conclusions about the same events. Even two metrics based on the same data set can come to radically different conclusions based on their starting assumptions, assumptions that haven't been tested, using methods that can't be duplicated or verified by outside analysts.

The quality of the fielder can bias the data: Zone-based fielding metrics will tend to attribute more expected outs to good fielders than bad fielders, irrespective of the distribution of batted balls. Scorers who work in parks with high press boxes will tend to score more line drives than scorers who work in parks with low press boxes.

Our Field Runs Above Average (FRAA) incorporates play-by-play data, allowing us to study the issue of defense at a granular level without resorting to the sorts of subjective data used in some other fielding metrics. We count how many plays a player made, as well as expected plays for the average player at that position based on a pitcher's estimated groundball tendencies and the handedness of the batter. There are also adjustments for park and base-out situations.

In addition, catchers have different defensive responsibilities than other defensive players, in particular framing pitches to make umpires more likely to call them strikes and blocking errant pitches. We incorporate PITCHf/x data, where available, and adjust for the pitcher, umpire, batter (including handedness) and home-field advantage using a mixed-model approach to determine how many strikes a catcher is adding to or subtracting from his pitchers' ledgers, and then convert those extra or lost strikes to runs using simple linear weights. We use a similar approach to determine how much better or worse than average a catcher is at letting errant pitches past him (regardless of whether the official scorer labels it a passed ball or a wild pitch)—PITCHf/x is a particularly powerful tool in this regard because we can tell which pitches end up in the dirt (and at what angle and speed) even though basic play-by-play data simply records the pitch as a ball or a swinging strike because the catcher successfully blocked it.

These metrics, as well as the catcher's abilities to prevent steals, are incorporated into catchers' FRAA along with their ball-in-play fielding (e.g. popups and bunts near home plate).

Pitching

Of course, how we measure fielding influences how we measure pitching. Most sabermetric analysis of pitching has been inspired by Voros McCracken, who stated, "There is little if any difference among major-league pitchers in their ability to prevent hits on balls hit in the field of play." When first published, this statement was extremely controversial, but later research has, by and large, validated it. McCracken (and others) went forth from that finding to create a variety of defense-independent pitching measures. One that you'll see in the book is FIP, Fielding Independent Pitching, which accounts for walks, strikeouts, hit-by-pitches and homers accumulated by a pitcher and puts them into one number on an ERA scale. Another is cFIP, which takes those FIP inputs, makes a variety of adjustments (including the batter, catcher, umpire, stadium, home-field advantage and handedness) and puts the whole thing on a "100 minus" scale in which the lower the number the better. The standard deviation of cFIP is forced to 15, so you know that a 56 cFIP is nearly three standard deviations from the mean.

The trouble is that many efforts to separate pitching from fielding have ended up separating pitching from pitching—looking at only a handful of variables in isolation from the situation in which they occurred. What we've done instead is take a pitcher's actual results, event by event, and adjust each event based on the environment in which it occurred, including park factor, batter, catcher, umpire, base-out situation, run differential, inning, defense, home-field advantage, whether the pitcher is a starter or reliever and game-time temperature. DRA also considers the pitcher's effect on basestealing (both in terms of likelihood of stealing and likelihood of success) and the pitcher's effect on passed balls and wild pitches. Out of all this comes Deserved Run Average (DRA), our core pitching metric, which is making its first appearance in the Annual this year. It is the rate stat on which pitcher Wins Above Replacement Player is determined.

One key point to note is that DRA is set on the same scale as runs allowed per nine innings, not ERA. Looking only at earned runs tends to overrate three kinds of pitchers:

1. Pitchers who play in parks where scorers hand out more errors. Looking at error rates between parks tells us scorers differ significantly in how likely they are to score any given play as an error (as opposed to an infield hit);
2. Groundball pitchers, because a substantial proportion of errors occurs on groundballs; and
3. Pitchers who aren't very good. Good pitchers tend to allow fewer unearned runs than bad pitchers, because good pitchers have more ways to get out of jams than bad pitchers. They're more likely to get a strikeout to end the inning, and less likely to give up a home run.

Projections

Many of you aren't turning to this book just for a look at what a player has done, but a look at what a player is going to do: the PECOTA projections.

PECOTA, initially developed by Nate Silver (who has moved on to greater fame as a political analyst), consists of three parts:

1. Major-league equivalencies, to allow us to use minor-league stats to project how a player will perform in the majors;
2. Baseline forecasts, which use weighted averages and regression to the mean to produce an estimate of a player's true talent level; and
3. A career-path adjustment, which incorporates information on how comparable players' stats changed over time.

Now that we've gone over the core stats, let's go over what's in the book.

Team Prospectus

The bulk of this book comprises team chapters, with one for each of the 30 major-league franchises. On the first page of each chapter, you will be greeted by a box laying out some key statistics for each team. You can see Milwaukee's box on the facing page.

At the top, 2016 W-L is exactly as it sounds, the unadjusted tally of wins and losses. Pythag presents an adjusted 2016 win percentage by taking the runs scored per game (RS/G) and allowed (RA/G) by the team last season and running them through a version of Bill James' Pythagorean formula refined and developed by David Smyth and Brandon Heipp, called "Pythagenpat."

A team's runs scored is accompanied by True Average (TAv) and Baserunning Runs (BRR), both of which were described above, to give a picture of how a team scores its runs. In terms of run-prevention ability, we present a team's TAv allowed (TAv-P), FIP and Defensive Efficiency Rating (DER), which is simply its rate of balls in play turned into outs.

Then we have several measures not directly related to on-field performance. B-Age and P-Age tell us the average age of a team's batters and pitchers, respectively. Salary tells us how much the team cost to put on the field, and Doug Pappas' Marginal Dollars per Marginal Win (M$/MW) tells us

BREWERS PROSPECTUS
2016 W-L: 73-89, 4TH IN NL CENTRAL

Pythag	.459	23rd	DER	0.700	20th
RS/G	4.03	28th	B-Age	27.4	5th
RA/G	4.84	27th	P-Age	28.1	13th
TAv	.263	12th	Salary	$63.9M	30th
BRR	-0.19	15th	M$/MW	$2.1M	28th
TAv-P	.276	25th	DL Days	1184	23rd
FIP	4.41	23rd	$ on DL	14%	19th

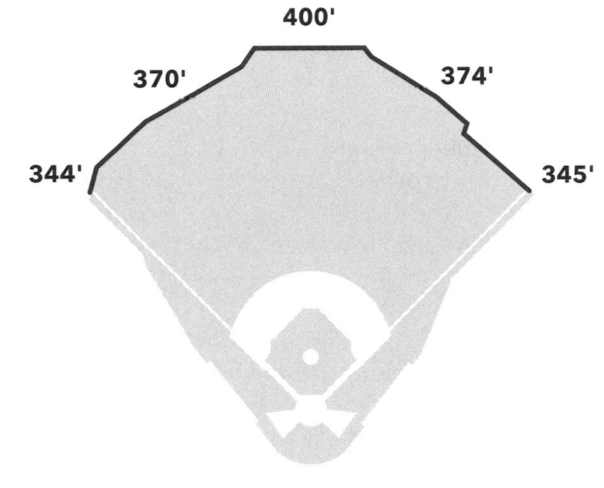

400'

370' **374'**

344' **345'**

Outfield wall profile: **8'**

Three-Year Park Factors

Runs	Runs/RH	Runs/LH	HR/RH	HR/LH
102	99	104	106	124

Top Hitter WARP	4.8	Jonathan Villar
Top Pitcher WARP	3.3	Zach Davies
Top Prospect		Lewis Brinson

how much a team paid above the bare minimum it had to pay and how much production above replacement it received for that money.

Finally, we count up the number of disabled-list days a team had, as well as the amount of salary paid to players while they were on the DL, expressed as a percentage of the total payroll.

Next to each of these stats, you see the team's MLB rank in that category, where 1st signifies a good outcome (e.g. highest TAv, lowest Tav-P) and 30th a bad outcome (highest $ on DL, lowest DER), except for salary, where we make no value judgments—1st is highest.

After the team information comes a variety of data about the home ballpark: a diagram of the park's dimensions showing distances to the outfield wall; a graphic that shows the height of the wall from the left-field pole to the right-field pole, reading left to right; and a table showing the three-year park factors presented in their usual 100-scale fashion, with 100 being average, 110 meaning that the park inflates the stat by 10 percent and 90 meaning the park deflates the stat by 10 percent.

On the second page of each chapter, you will see three graphs. The first graph, titled "2016 Hit List Ranking," shows the Hit List Rank for this team on every day of the 2016 season and is intended to give you an idea of the shape of the season. Hit List Rank is a measure of overall team performance that drives the Prospectus Hit List power ranking at baseballprospectus.com. It is based on team run differential and includes adjustments for park, league and quality of opposition. You can see more about Hit List Ranking at http://bbp.cx/a/4383.

The second graph is entitled "Committed Payroll" and is intended to give you an idea of how this team's player budgets match up with the competition historically and going forward. The payroll figures are current as of January 1, 2017; with several free agents still unsigned as of this writing, keep in mind the final 2016 figure will be significantly different for many teams. You can always find current data at Baseball Prospectus' Cot's Baseball Contracts page. MLB and division averages are also plotted to allow for quick comparison.

The third graph is entitled "Farm System Ranking" and shows the Baseball Prospectus prospect team's ranking of this team's farm system for the last several years.

Following the graphs is the "Personnel" section. Here you'll find some of the important people in the organization, and any former Baseball Prospectus staff who are currently part of the team's front office or scouting staff.

Position Players
After a bylined opening essay about each team, the chapters move to the player comments, which are also bylined, though the vagaries of player movement and the group-project nature of the book means that the names you see at the head of each chapter are more a rough guide than a precise accounting of the division of labor.

Each player is listed with the major-league team by whom he was employed as of mid-December 2016, meaning that players who changed teams via free agency, trade or otherwise later in the offseason will be listed under their previous employer.

Manny Machado   3B

Born: 7/6/92   Age: 24   Bats: R   Throws: R   Height: 6'3"   Weight: 185   Entered Pro Ball: Round 1, 2010 Draft (#3 overall)

YEAR	TEAM	LVL	AGE	PA	R	2B	3B	HR	RBI	BB	K	SB	CS	AVG/OBP/SLG	TAv	VORP	BABIP	BRR	FRAA	WARP
2014	BAL	MLB	21	354	38	14	0	12	32	20	68	2	0	.278/.324/.431	.274	13.7	.317	-1.2	3B(82): 7.7	2.4
2015	BAL	MLB	22	713	102	30	1	35	86	70	111	20	8	.286/.359/.502	.292	47.7	.297	3.4	3B(156): 21.7 • SS(7): -0.8	7.3
2016	BAL	MLB	23	696	105	40	1	37	96	48	120	0	3	.294/.343/.533	.292	46.7	.309	0.0	3B(114): 8.7 • SS(45): -0.4	5.7
2017	BAL	MLB	24	640	78	34	3	25	88	47	105	8	4	.283/.337/.477	.280	32.2	.305	-1.1	3B 16, SS 5	4.7
2018	BAL	MLB	25	602	84	33	2	26	88	49	101	7	4	.288/.350/.498	.281	27.2	.309	0.6	3B 15, SS 0	4.6

Breakout: 2%   Improve: 65%   Collapse: 0%   Attrition: 1%   MLB: 99%   *Comparables: Ryan Zimmerman, Brett Lawrie, Pablo Sandoval*

As an example, take a look at Manny Machado: his stat block is at the top of the page.

The player-specific sections begin with biographical information before moving onto the column headers and actual data. The column headers begin with standard information like year, team, level (majors or level of the minors), and the raw, untranslated tallies found on the back of a baseball card: PA (plate appearances), R (runs), 2B (doubles), 3B (triples), HR (home runs), RBI (runs batted in), BB (walks), K (strikeouts), SB (stolen bases) and CS (caught stealing).

Following those are untranslated "slash" statistics: batting average (AVG), on-base percentage (OBP) and slugging percentage (SLG). The slash line is followed by True Average (TAv), which, as described above, rolls all those things and more into one easy-to-digest number.

BABIP stands for Batting Average on Balls in Play, and is what it sounds like: How often did a ball put in play by the hitter fall for a hit? An especially low or high BABIP may mean a hitter was especially lucky or unlucky. However, hitters who hit the ball hard tend to have especially high BABIPs from season to season; so do speedy hitters who are able to beat out more grounders for base hits.

Next is Baserunning Runs (BRR) which, as mentioned earlier, covers all sorts of baserunning accomplishments, not just stolen bases. Then comes Fielding Runs Above Average (FRAA); for historical stats, we have the number of games played at each position in parenthesis. For multi-position players, we are only able to display the two positions the fielder played most frequently that season.

One of Prospectus' oldest active metrics, Value Over Replacement Player (VORP), considers offensive production, position, and plate appearances. More specifically, it is the number of runs contributed beyond what a replacement-level player at the same position would contribute if given the same percentage of team plate appearances. VORP scores do not consider the quality of a player's defense.

The last column is Wins Above Replacement Player. WARP is our total-value stat that, for a hitter, combines a player's batting runs above average (derived from True Average), BRR, FRAA, an adjustment for positions played and a credit for plate appearances based upon the difference between the "replacement level" (derived by looking at the quality of players added to a team's roster after the start of the season) and the league average.

The final line below the comment is PECOTA data, which is discussed further below.

Catchers

As we debuted last year, there is a separate box for catchers showing some of the defensive metrics that apply particularly to them. As an example, let's check out Yasmani Grandal.

Yasmani Grandal

YEAR	TEAM	P. COUNT	FRM RUNS	BLK RUNS	THRW RUNS	TOT RUNS
2014	SDN	9898	14.5	-1.1	-2.7	10.8
2015	LAN	13767	25.6	-0.8	0.0	24.8
2016	LAN	15887	26.7	0.4	0.4	27.5
2017	LAN	18703	34.2	-0.4	0.0	33.8
2018	LAN	15138	26.7	-0.4	-0.1	26.2

The YEAR and TEAM columns are what you'd expect. P. COUNT is the number of pitches the catcher "received," though really it's the number of pitches thrown by pitchers when the catcher was in the battery; that is, it includes swinging strikes, fouls and balls in play. FRM RUNS is the total runs the catcher added by getting the umpire to call strikes where the average catcher did not (or vice versa). The calculation of this statistic is described above. BLK RUNS, also described above, expresses in runs above or below average the catcher's ability to prevent wild pitches and passed balls. Finally, THRW RUNS sums the catcher's ability to dissuade runners from stealing and to catch them when they do run. This statistic is calculated similarly to the Framing and Blocking stats, and takes into account various factors, including the pitcher (who may have a quick or slow delivery, or a good or bad pickoff move) and the baserunner (who may be Billy Hamilton or Billy Butler). The final column, TOT RUNS, is the sum of the previous three.

Pitchers

Now let's look at how pitchers are presented, using Johnny Cueto. His stat block is at the top of the facing page.

The first line and the YEAR, TEAM, LVL and AGE columns are the same as in the hitters example above. The next set of columns—W (wins), L (losses), SV (saves), G (games pitched), GS (games started), IP (innings pitched), H (hits), HR (home runs), BB9 (walks per nine innings), K/9 (strikeouts per nine innings) and K (strikeouts)—are the actual, unadjusted stats compiled by the pitcher during each season.

Next is GB%, which is the percentage of all batted balls that were hit on the ground, including both outs and hits. As mentioned above, this is based on observation by human stringers and can be skewed based upon a number of factors. We've included the number as a guide, but please approach it skeptically.

Johnny Cueto   RHP

Born: 2/15/86   Age: 31   Bats: R   Throws: R   Height: 5'11"   Weight: 220   Entered Pro Ball: International Free Agent, 2004

YEAR	TEAM	LVL	AGE	W	L	SV	G	GS	IP	H	HR	BB/9	K/9	K	GB%	BABIP	WHIP	ERA	FIP	DRA	VORP	WARP	cFIP	MPH
2014	CIN	MLB	28	20	9	0	34	34	243²	169	22	2.4	8.9	242	48%	.238	0.96	2.25	3.28	2.56	61.6	6.8	86	95.9
2015	CIN	MLB	29	7	6	0	19	19	130²	93	11	2.0	8.3	120	45%	.234	0.93	2.62	3.73	3.22	19.6	2.1	95	95.3
2015	KCA	MLB	29	4	7	0	13	13	81¹	101	10	1.9	6.2	56	43%	.343	1.45	4.76	4.03	3.69	12.6	1.3	95	95.0
2016	SFN	MLB	30	18	5	0	32	32	219²	195	15	1.8	8.1	198	52%	.293	1.09	2.79	3.00	3.54	44.5	4.6	90	94.3
2017	SFN	MLB	31	11	10	0	29	29	174	157	18	2.6	8.6	166	51%	.289	1.17	3.46	3.56	4.08	21.2	2.2	94	
2018	SFN	MLB	32	11	10	0	30	30	192¹	160	19	2.4	8.5	181	51%	.291	1.10	3.29	3.65	3.95	32.2	3.3	88	

Breakout: 8%   Improve: 33%   Collapse: 30%   Attrition: 7%   MLB: 90%   Comparables: *Roy Oswalt, Justin Verlander, Erik Bedard*

BABIP is the same statistic as for batters, but often tells you more in the case of pitchers, because most major-league pitchers have little control over their batting average on balls in play. A high BABIP is often due to a poor defense or bad luck rather than a pitcher's own abilities, and may be a good indicator of a potential rebound. A typical league-average BABIP is around .290–.300.

WHIP and ERA are common to most fans, with the former measuring the number of walks and hits allowed on a per-inning basis while the latter prorates earned runs allowed on a nine-innings basis. Neither is translated or adjusted in any way.

FIP was discussed above: It puts onto an ERA scale a measurement of how the pitcher performed on the events that do not involve the fielders behind him.

Deserved Run Average (DRA) was also described above. It is the basis of pitcher WARP and measures how many runs (not earned runs) the pitcher "deserved" to allow per nine innings. One important point about minor leaguers is that because we do not have all the data we would need to fully calculate minor-league DRA, what is listed under "DRA" for minor leaguers is really a runs-allowed-per-nine figure calculated based on cFIP's components.

Because, as has been true of BP's pitching metrics in the past, neither DRA nor the conversion from DRA to WARP contains a "leverage" multiplier, WARP for relief pitchers (especially closers) may seem lower than you might see elsewhere and may conflict with how we feel about relief aces coming in and "saving" the game. This is by design: Saves give extra credit to the closer for what his teammates did to put him in a save spot to begin with; WARP is incapable of feeling excitement over a successful save, and judges them dispassionately. Furthermore, DRA controls for players who have the benefit of pitching in short durations and at maximum ability.

cFIP, described above, adjusts FIP for a variety of factors and scales it on the familiar 100 scale; because these are pitchers preventing runs, below 100 is good, and above 100 is bad.

MPH is the pitcher's 95th percentile velocity for that season—the goal is to give you a sense of the pitcher's peak fastball velocity, not his average. This comes from PITCHf/x data, and thus is not publicly available for minor leaguers.

PECOTA

Both pitchers and hitters have PECOTA projections for next season, as well as a set of biographical details that describe the performance of that player's comparable players according to PECOTA. The book contains two years of PECOTA projections for every player.

The 2017 and 2018 lines are the PECOTA projection for the player at the date we went to press in late December. The player is projected into the league and park context as indicated by his team abbreviation. All PECOTAs represent a player's projected major-league performance. The numbers beneath the player's stats—Breakout, Improve, Collapse, Attrition—are a part of PECOTA. These estimate the likelihood of changes in performance relative to a player's previously established level of production, based upon the performance of the comparable players:

Breakout Rate is the percent chance that a player's production will improve by at least 20 percent relative to the weighted average of his performance over his most recent seasons.

Improve Rate is the percent chance that a player's production will improve at all relative to his baseline performance. A player who is expected to perform just the same as he has in the recent past will have an Improve Rate of 50 percent.

Collapse Rate is the percent chance that a position player's runs produced per plate appearance will decline by at least 25 percent relative to his baseline performance.

Attrition Rate operates on playing time rather than performance. Specifically, it measures the likelihood that a player's playing time will decrease by at least 50 percent relative to his established level.

Breakout Rate and **Collapse Rate** can sometimes be counterintuitive for players who have already experienced a radical change in performance level. It's also worth noting that the projected decline in a player's rate performances might not be indicative of an expected decline in underlying ability or skill, but rather something of an anticipated correction following a breakout season.

MLB% is the percentage of similar players who played in the major leagues in their relevant season.

The final pieces of information are the player's three highest-scoring comparable players as determined by PECOTA. Occasionally, a player's top comparables will not be representative of the larger sample that PECOTA uses. All comparables represent a snapshot of how the listed player was performing at the same age as the current player, so if a 23-year-old pitcher is compared to Barry Zito, he's actually being compared to a 23-year-old Barry Zito, not the version of Zito the Giants couldn't wait to be rid of, nor to Zito's career as a whole.

A few points about pitcher projections. First, we aren't yet projecting peak velocity, so that column will be blank in the PECOTA lines. Second, projecting DRA is trickier than evaluating past performance, because it is unclear how deserving each pitcher will be of his anticipated outcomes. However, we know that cFIP estimates future run-scoring very well, and that cFIP and DRA are based on a similar structure and model. Thus, the projected DRA figures you see are based on the past cFIPs generated by the pitcher and comparable players over time, along with the other factors described above.

Lineouts

The stats box in the Lineouts section contains all the same information, but only has the 2016 stats for each player.

Managers

After the team chapters end, there is an essay discussing the impact of the modern manager, which replaces the individual comments at the end of each chapter in previous annuals. Though it's often difficult to isolate a manager's contribution to a team, comparing specific data modeled after well-documented plays and styles to the league average helps determine what a manager likes to do, even if we are still unable to translate that information into actual wins and losses. Individual manager statistical profiles follow, with an explanation of those statistics leading off that section of the book.

PECOTA Leaderboards

As a result of the way it weights previous seasons, PECOTA can tend to appear bullish on players coming off a bad year and bearish on players coming off a great year. And because we list the 50th percentile projections—the middle of the range the system thinks this player is capable of producing—it rarely predicts any player will hit 40 home runs or strike out 250 batters. At the end of this book, though, we've ranked the top players according to their projections. It's often as helpful to know who the system thinks will be the top second baseman as what his actual stats are likely to be. ▪

ARIZONA DIAMONDBACKS

Essay by Nick Piecoro

Player comments by Jeff Wiser, Ryan Morrison and BP staff

Mitch Haniger was riding the team bus one spring day when he heard a pair of Diamondbacks players, A.J. Pollock and Nick Ahmed, talking about hitting in a way he'd never considered. What they were saying ran contrary to many of the things he had been taught his entire life, but their ideas were so intriguing and made so much sense that Haniger, then a middling outfield prospect in the organization, couldn't help but interject and ask questions.

That interaction in 2015 eventually led to a wholesale reconstruction of Haniger's swing, a process that took parts of two seasons and culminated in his promotion to the big leagues last year. But for as nice of a story as Haniger is—he went from never posting a minor-league OPS north of .779 to hitting .321/.419/.581 between Double-A and Triple-A last year—perhaps the most interesting aspect of his emergence is how commonplace such transformations have become.

Every year more players reinvent their swings, eschewing old-school philosophies for more modern techniques. Many of them have emerged from relative obscurity to develop into some of the game's more dangerous hitters. It happened first with Jose Bautista, then with Josh Donaldson and J.D. Martinez. Justin Turner did it, following the lead of former teammate Marlon Byrd. Mark Trumbo's adjustments led to 47 homers last year. Haniger was the fourth Diamondbacks player to enjoy success after embracing change, joining Pollock, Jake Lamb and Jean Segura, all of whom saw their power output grow exponentially.

Each of these hitters went outside the slow-moving professional baseball world to find forward-thinking coaches to help them implement change, putting into effect ideas that ran counter to many of the hitting tenets taught within the baseball establishment. They stopped swinging down at the ball. They stopped worrying so much about staying back or getting the bat head out or keeping their head still.

What they started to do is tap into their athleticism, making changes that allowed them to adjust to the variety of repertoires they see in the modern game, pitches that routinely sit in the mid-90s and above or have so much movement they cut through multiple planes—or sometimes both. The hitters made changes that keep their bats in the hitting zone for as long as possible and increase their

DIAMONDBACKS PROSPECTUS
2016 W-L: 69-93, 4TH IN NL WEST

Pythag	.419	26th	DER	.680	30th
RS/G	4.64	10th	B-Age	26.7	2nd
RA/G	5.49	16th	P-Age	26.3	3rd
TAv	.261	18th	Salary	$98.2M	22nd
BRR	19.42	1st	M$/MW	$4.2M	8th
TAv-P	.277	27th	DL Days	660	6th
FIP	4.54	27th	$ on DL	12%	14th

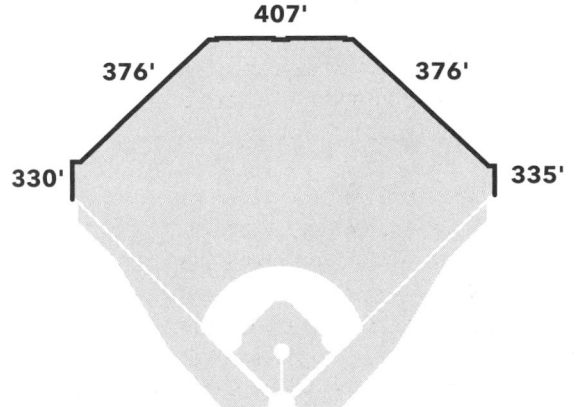

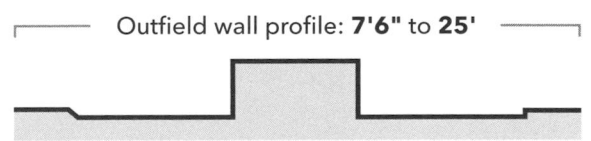

Outfield wall profile: **7'6" to 25'**

Three-Year Park Factors

Runs	Runs/RH	Runs/LH	HR/RH	HR/LH
103	100	106	109	104

Top Hitter WARP	6.3	Paul Goldschmidt
Top Pitcher WARP	4.8	Robbie Ray
Top Prospect		Anthony Banda

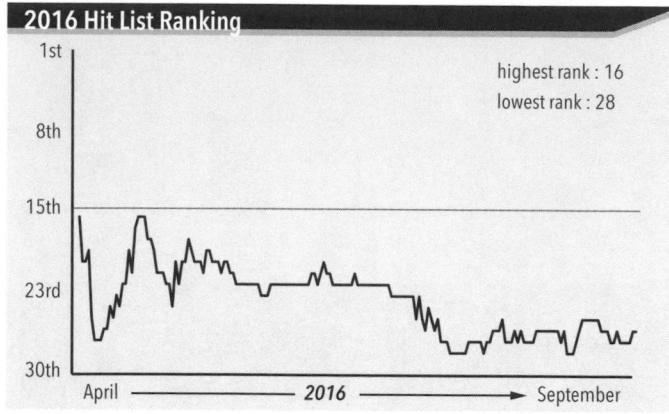

2016 Hit List Ranking

highest rank : 16
lowest rank : 28

April — 2016 → September

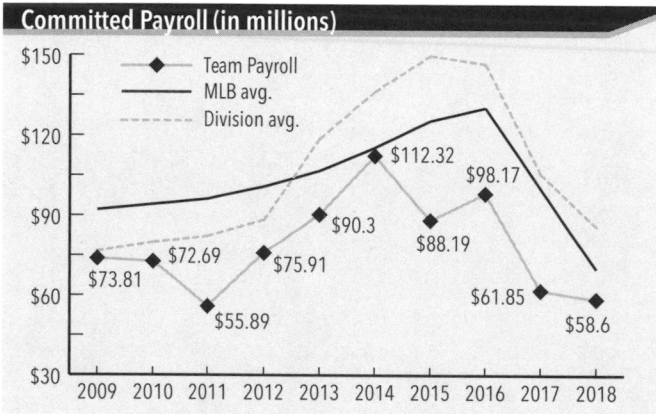

Committed Payroll (in millions)

◆ Team Payroll
— MLB avg.
---- Division avg.

$73.81
$72.69
$55.89
$75.91
$90.3
$112.32
$88.19
$98.17
$61.85
$58.6

2009 2010 2011 2012 2013 2014 2015 2016 2017 2018

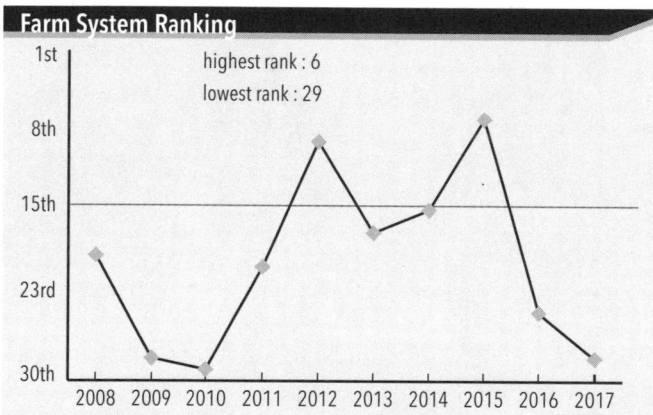

Farm System Ranking

highest rank : 6
lowest rank : 29

2008 2009 2010 2011 2012 2013 2014 2015 2016 2017

Personnel

President:
Derrick Hall

**Executive VP,
General Manager:**
Mike Hazen

**Senior Vice President,
Assistant GM:**
Amiel Sawdaye

**Senior Vice President,
Assistant GM:**
Jared Porter

Manager:
Torey Lovullo

likelihood of driving balls—in the air—to all fields.

"There's a huge trend happening," said Bobby Tewksbary, the coach who helped Donaldson develop into an MVP. "There's a huge movement right now that is changing guys' careers."

Tewksbary said this last March, six months before MLB hitters as a whole turned in their most power-charged season in years. And according to a grassroots network of hitting gurus, many of whom share swing GIFs on Twitter and spend hours online debating the nuances of the ideal bat path, the home run explosion can be traced to the systematic infiltration of proper swing mechanics into the modern game.

"I have never come across more hitters in the game that are talking about the things that you and I are talking about since I started playing when I was 10 years old, and I'm 70 now," said Craig Wallenbrock, who is recognized by many as one of the pioneers of this new philosophy.

"It had to [change] because pitching got so good. All of the [offensive] numbers were going down and the old way wasn't working, and with the technology that was available, the hitters started picking up and using that technology, and they're catching up."

Throughout its history, baseball has relied on word-of-mouth instruction, with veteran hitters or former-players-turned-coaches passing along insights to the next generation. If a player heard from a coach who once talked to Ted Williams about his belief in a short stride, who was he to argue the merits of a 12-inch stride with a leg kick? But the information age has helped level the playing field, to the point that any observant baseball mind can access troves of hitting videos, giving them the ability to break down film and reach their own conclusions about what makes a hitter great.

That's what happened back in 2009 with Tewksbary, a former college and independent league player who began what he calls an accidental obsession with the swing. He remembers digging into the mechanics of Albert Pujols, who at the time was the best hitter in baseball, and noticing Pujols doing things Tewksbary had long believed to be wrong. It forced him to reconsider everything.

"If what I believed to be right was the opposite of what Albert Pujols was doing, then I was the one that was wrong and he was the one that was right," said Tewksbary, who runs a hitting facility out of Nashua, N.H. "I had to forget everything I thought I knew and start over. It just became an obsession."

Years earlier, on the other side of the country, Wallenbrock had been drawing conclusions of his own. After an eight-year scouting career with the White Sox, Athletics and Indians, he began building up a clientele of hitters in Southern California. He said Miguel Cabrera was the first hitter he spent hours deconstructing, and he realized Cabrera was doing something similar to a pair of hitters with whom Wallenbrock had worked in the past.

Wallenbrock remembers once throwing batting practice to Eric Davis and yelling, "Look out!" at a pitch he thought was going to hit Davis on the hip. Instead, Davis lined it up the middle, off the 'L' screen protecting Wallenbrock. A few years later, when tossing flips to Paul Konerko, Wallenbrock recalls Konerko taking a ball that was far inside and lining it to the opposite field. Wallenbrock says both players told him they felt they were at their best when they were letting inside fastballs travel deep—notions that are contrary to traditional hitting philosophies.

"That's the basis to Cabrera's approach to hitting," Wallenbrock said. "If you're in a ready to position to hit the inside fastball the deepest, then anything that moves out over the plate or decreases in velocity, you have more time to adjust to it and you can handle more pitches."

That ties into one of the major tenets of the new-school thinking: keeping the bat in the hitting zone for as long as possible. To understand what it means to be "longer through the zone," imagine taking a knife and cutting through a stick of butter. Rather than starting from the upper corner, moving down to the middle and out the other side, imagine starting the cut closer to the center and going cleanly all the way through.

"With a steep swing you have to have perfect timing," said Lamb, whose changes helped him launch 29 homers for the Diamondbacks in 2016. "You still want good timing, but this swing allows you a bigger margin for error."

Haniger says the changes he made allowed him to finally drive the ball with power to all fields, something he noticed smaller and less athletic players being able to do better than him in the past. He said he was recently watching video of his swing from 2014, and the number of things he was doing wrong made him feel sick to his stomach.

"For me, I was brought up taught to have no stride or barely any stride, stay inside, swing down on the ball," Haniger said. "Those are a lot of keys that can kind of mess your swing up over a long period of time."

More hitters are also beginning to realize something else: the importance of launch angle.

"Hitting the ball in the air is pretty paramount, especially with the way the defensive shifts go and things like that," Trumbo said. "Trying to groove a swing plane that would produce more of that. I don't have the speed to beat anything out. Ground balls are pretty much the enemy for the most part. There are situations when they can benefit the team, but, by and large, I'm at my best when it's on a line or in the air."

✦ ✦ ✦

Many of the game's best hitters practiced—or currently practice—some of these same philosophies. One even wrote a book mentioning a few them. In *The Science of Hitting*, published in 1971, Ted Williams endorsed a slight uppercut in hopes of getting the ball in the air. He also saw it as a way of keeping the bat in the zone longer. He wrote: "A slight upswing—again, led by the hips coming around and up—puts the bat flush in line with the path of the ball for a longer period—that 12- to 18-inch impact zone."

Somewhere along the way, Williams' ideas went out of fashion—or perhaps they were never truly endorsed by the baseball establishment. Either way, some of the best modern hitters still share some of the same swing characteristics he discussed. And not only did many of them get there without reconstructing their swings, some don't even realize the things they're doing.

"I've seen Mike Trout in videos talk about swinging down at the ball, which he doesn't do," said Robert Van Scoyoc, a hitting coach who has worked alongside Wallenbrock for six years. "That's how some of these theories live on. If one Mike Trout says swing down, then it lives on."

Van Scoyoc can rattle off names of hitters he's heard describe their own swings inaccurately, leading him to conclude some of the best natural hitters can be the worst teachers.

"Here's the example that I use," he said. "If you're a person that lost the ability to walk and you had to relearn how to walk, would you want to learn from a person that also lost the ability and had to relearn or would you want to learn from someone who was just naturally a great walker? You'd want to learn from the person who also had to relearn. With some of the great, natural hitters, hitting is just like walking for them."

But Wallenbrock believes most hitters aren't natural hitters. Back when he was a young scout, he remembers reading an anecdote from a book about Ty Cobb, who claimed that despite what many people thought, he wasn't a natural hitter. "I have to work on my swing," Cobb said. "Shoeless Joe taught me how to hit."

"I would say every good hitter," Wallenbrock said, "is a natural athlete, but only about three percent of the hitters are pure, natural hitters. If you look long enough and talk to them long enough, you would find that there was somebody in their past that put the teach on them even if they don't give them credit. I think there are natural hitters, but I think there are more self-made hitters."

✦ ✦ ✦

In August, Donaldson stood in the MLB Network studio with analyst and former big leaguer Mark DeRosa, and the two went frame-by-frame through Donaldson's swing. It was clear from DeRosa's reactions how far outside the professional baseball world some of Donaldson's hitting philosophies resided.

"Where did that come from?" DeRosa asked at one point. "I played 16 years in the big leagues and I never heard a hitting coach one time say to get the weight into your hip."

Then came this exchange a few moments later:

Donaldson: "I never want to think about my hands going

toward the baseball."

DeRosa: *"That's the craziest thing. That's all I thought about was hands."*

Donaldson's appearance was a sort of landmark moment for the new-school hitting movement. Here was a player whose changes had led him to the peak of his profession openly espousing new-school thought—and, indirectly, casting doubt on the old guard. Not only was Donaldson the ultimate example of what a hitter might become, but he'd also taken to championing the cause. The appearance set off a sort of celebration online among many of the new-school believers.

"Everybody who has been fringe on this for so long was rejoicing," Tewksbary said. "They were like, 'Finally, somebody said it on that stage.' Then you had other coaches saying, 'Yeah, but he's a big leaguer. If you're not big and strong and a freak, you can't do that.' But Josh is an interesting case, just like Bautista was. He wasn't a superstar and now he is. He has a lot of clout—he can say things and you kind of have to listen."

Other professional hitters have taken notice. Wallenbrock said that a decade ago he regularly worked with perhaps a half-dozen hitters at a given time. A month into this past offseason Wallenbrock said he, Van Scoyoc and their team of coaches were up to 50 hitters at the major and minor league levels. Tewksbary and other coaches say their client lists are growing, as well.

What all this means for the future of hitting remains to be seen. MLB organizations have layer upon layer of hitting coaches. At the big-league level, many clubs have a hitting coach as well as an assistant hitting coach, and organizations have hitting coaches at every minor-league level as well as roving hitting coaches. And each coach has his own philosophy. It can make change difficult. Wallenbrock and

Van Scoyoc found that out for themselves last year, when both were full-time hitting consultants for the Dodgers.

Wallenbrock said he found the structure of professional baseball too unwieldy. Not only were there too many voices, but those voices often were in competition, either philosophically or politically, and the pressure to produce results made hitters less likely to want to make in-season swing changes. Wallenbrock believes the best way—and, for now at least, the only way—to rebuild swings is to do it in the offseason.

"I just came to the conclusion that that's never going to change," Wallenbrock said. "They tried to bring us in full time and tried to have us rove and make changes year-round, and, in my opinion, it didn't work. It was a noble effort, but it didn't work because the system wouldn't let it work—not just the Dodgers, but the entire system of baseball."

Tewksbary takes a more optimistic view. From his vantage point, change is happening, and it's happening fast. He sees more open-minded front offices, with the Diamondbacks' new regime being a prime example. He sees more hitters seeking out information on their own. He's heard stories of less resistance from coaches in the pro baseball world. And he thinks the more information that's out there—the more hitters begin to understand Statcast data like launch angle, exit velocity and even batted-ball spin rate—the more they'll be willing to change themselves.

"It's really cool to know guys are talking about it in the clubhouse," Tewksbary said. "It's players actively choosing to make adjustments for the betterment of their career. It's becoming more accessible and it's pretty cool to see. A couple of years ago, it was a couple guys on the internet thinking they were seeing stuff. It's becoming more mainstream. It's definitely not there yet, but it's becoming less and less fringe." ▪

—Nick Piecoro covers the Diamondbacks for the Arizona Republic

HITTERS

Nick Ahmed   SS

Born: 3/15/90   Age: 27   Bats: R   Throws: R   Height: 6'2"   Weight: 195   Entered Pro Ball: Round 2, 2011 Draft (#85 overall)

YEAR	TEAM	LVL	AGE	PA	R	2B	3B	HR	RBI	BB	K	SB	CS	AVG/OBP/SLG	TAv	VORP	BABIP	BRR	FRAA	WARP
2014	RNO	AAA	24	452	57	26	4	4	47	37	55	14	6	.312/.373/.425	.272	25.5	.352	0.3	SS(91): 14.6 • 2B(14): -0.8	3.9
2014	ARI	MLB	24	75	9	2	0	1	4	3	10	0	1	.200/.233/.271	.200	-0.5	.220	1.0	SS(18): -1.7 • 2B(2): -0.3	-0.3
2015	ARI	MLB	25	459	49	17	6	9	34	29	81	4	5	.226/.275/.359	.236	12.0	.257	4.6	SS(129): 5.2	1.8
2016	ARI	MLB	26	308	26	9	1	4	20	15	58	5	2	.218/.265/.299	.197	-4.8	.258	2.3	SS(88): 9.5	0.5
2017	*ARI*	*MLB*	*27*	*226*	*23*	*10*	*2*	*4*	*21*	*14*	*41*	*3*	*2*	*.245/.293/.371*	*.225*	*2.5*	*.280*	*-0.2*	*2B 0, SS 1*	*0.0*
2018	*ARI*	*MLB*	*28*	*259*	*28*	*11*	*2*	*6*	*27*	*18*	*48*	*3*	*2*	*.243/.299/.378*	*.236*	*3.9*	*.278*	*2.0*	*2B 0, SS 1*	*0.6*

Breakout: 11%   Improve: 42%   Collapse: 5%   Attrition: 22%   MLB: 97%   Comparables: *Alexi Amarista, Alex Cintron, Daniel Descalso*

Ahmed was persuaded to train with tinier and tinier gloves while playing for UConn and practicing in the offseason since, and you'd be hard pressed to argue with the results—he's been one of the majors' best shortstops, posting 9.5 Fielding Runs Above Average in a half-season of work in 2016. Sadly, Ahmed seems to have believed the same process would work at the plate; his ever-shrinking bat sparking debates about the modern Mendoza line. It could all be a moot point in 2017, with Ahmed ending the season on the shelf with a hip injury. If his hip limits his defense at all, Ahmed may be little more than a utility player going forward.

Socrates Brito   RF

Born: 9/6/92   Age: 24   Bats: L   Throws: L   Height: 6'2"   Weight: 205   Entered Pro Ball: International Free Agent, 2010

YEAR	TEAM	LVL	AGE	PA	R	2B	3B	HR	RBI	BB	K	SB	CS	AVG/OBP/SLG	TAv	VORP	BABIP	BRR	FRAA	WARP
2014	VIS	A+	21	561	82	30	5	10	62	36	109	38	10	.293/.339/.429	.270	24.0	.351	6.8	RF(71): 2.1 • CF(32): -3.6	1.9
2015	MOB	AA	22	522	70	17	15	9	57	29	84	20	6	.300/.339/.451	.286	31.1	.346	5.6	RF(63): 12.2 • CF(48): 3.4	5.1
2015	ARI	MLB	22	34	5	3	1	0	1	1	7	1	0	.303/.324/.455	.268	1.5	.385	0.5	RF(5): 2.0 • CF(1): -0.1	0.4
2016	RNO	AAA	23	317	46	10	8	6	39	13	60	7	6	.294/.322/.439	.265	10.6	.349	1.6	RF(43): -1.2 • CF(31): 1.3	1.1
2016	ARI	MLB	23	97	10	3	1	4	12	2	23	2	0	.179/.196/.358	.188	-3.0	.191	1.6	CF(17): -2.1 • RF(16): -0.3	-0.4
2017	*ARI*	*MLB*	*24*	*205*	*21*	*8*	*3*	*5*	*23*	*8*	*48*	*5*	*2*	*.255/.283/.411*	*.232*	*1.5*	*.311*	*0.6*	*LF 2, CF 0*	*0.2*
2018	*ARI*	*MLB*	*25*	*403*	*45*	*16*	*7*	*11*	*48*	*18*	*95*	*10*	*4*	*.258/.292/.426*	*.247*	*6.4*	*.314*	*1.5*	*LF 3, CF 0*	*1.1*

Breakout: 4%   Improve: 10%   Collapse: 2%   Attrition: 11%   MLB: 16%   Comparables: *Tyler Colvin, Kyle Waldrop, David Lough*

The biggest discussion surrounding Brito in 2016 was how to best make light of his name. The Socrates jokes availed themselves readily while his last name does sound a lot like "burrito." Platonic Mexican food aside, he was rushed to the majors after A.J. Pollock went down and Arizona was caught without a justifiable replacement. He performed like you'd expect an explosive 23-year-old athlete with a lagging hit tool: pretty poorly with a few intriguing flashes along the way. There's still plenty of upside—he's better off in right field than center—and he'll enter spring training as a bonafide 25-man roster candidate as he looks to add polish to his game. Should it all break right, he's got the tools and athleticism to be a difference-maker in the field, on the bases and at the plate.

Jasrado Chisholm   SS

Born: 2/1/98   Age: 19   Bats: L   Throws: R   Height: 5'11"   Weight: 165   Entered Pro Ball: International Free Agent, 2015

YEAR	TEAM	LVL	AGE	PA	R	2B	3B	HR	RBI	BB	K	SB	CS	AVG/OBP/SLG	TAv	VORP	BABIP	BRR	FRAA	WARP
2017	*ARI*	*MLB*	*19*	*250*	*26*	*9*	*1*	*7*	*22*	*12*	*93*	*3*	*1*	*.195/.236/.326*	*.183*	*-8.2*	*.285*	*0.0*	*SS -0, 2B 0*	*-0.9*
2018	*ARI*	*MLB*	*20*	*328*	*35*	*12*	*2*	*10*	*36*	*18*	*117*	*5*	*2*	*.210/.256/.359*	*.214*	*-4.0*	*.298*	*0.2*	*SS 0, 2B 0*	*-0.5*

Breakout: 0%   Improve: 4%   Collapse: 2%   Attrition: 5%   MLB: 9%   Comparables: *Raul Mondesi, Elvis Andrus, Nomar Mazara*

Arizona's mismanagement under Tony La Russa and Dave Stewart may have been most evident when the pair bungled their international signing abilities in 2015 and beyond (all on behalf of Yoan Lopez, nonetheless). While limited in their spending, they seemed to strike gold with the signing of Bahamian prospect "Jazz" Chisholm. On the smaller side physically, the athletic switch-hitter is quick, has a strong arm and has more power than his frame would suggest. A strong debut in the Pioneer League put Chisholm on the map as one of the few exciting, upside-oriented prospects in the Diamondbacks' system. Having a 70-grade name helps, of course.

Brandon Drury   2B/3B/OF

Born: 8/21/92   Age: 24   Bats: R   Throws: R   Height: 6'2"   Weight: 210   Entered Pro Ball: Round 13, 2010 Draft (#404 overall)

YEAR	TEAM	LVL	AGE	PA	R	2B	3B	HR	RBI	BB	K	SB	CS	AVG/OBP/SLG	TAv	VORP	BABIP	BRR	FRAA	WARP
2014	VIS	A+	21	478	73	35	1	19	81	41	76	4	3	.300/.366/.519	.299	30.1	.326	-2.7	3B(84): 1.3 • 3B(4): 1.3	3.3
2014	MOB	AA	21	116	12	7	0	4	14	7	19	0	0	.295/.345/.476	.302	9.4	.321	0.8	3B(28): -1.5 • 2B(2): 0.3	0.9
2015	MOB	AA	22	291	22	14	1	3	36	11	41	4	5	.278/.306/.370	.252	5.1	.312	-0.7	2B(35): 2.1 • 3B(33): 2.0	1.0
2015	RNO	AAA	22	276	43	26	0	2	25	21	35	0	2	.331/.384/.458	.279	13.0	.375	-1.0	3B(28): -2.9 • 2B(27): -1.5	0.9
2015	ARI	MLB	22	59	3	3	0	2	8	2	8	0	0	.214/.254/.375	.205	-3.0	.217	-1.5	3B(11): -0.6 • 2B(6): -0.1	-0.4
2016	ARI	MLB	23	499	59	31	1	16	53	31	100	1	1	.282/.329/.458	.270	18.6	.327	1.9	LF(62): -5.2 • RF(32): -1.6	1.0
2017	*ARI*	*MLB*	*24*	*448*	*47*	*26*	*1*	*13*	*53*	*24*	*90*	*1*	*1*	*.266/.309/.431*	*.249*	*9.9*	*.308*	*-1.2*	*2B -1, 3B -1*	*0.4*
2018	*ARI*	*MLB*	*25*	*534*	*65*	*34*	*1*	*17*	*68*	*30*	*105*	*1*	*1*	*.275/.320/.450*	*.266*	*17.6*	*.316*	*-0.4*	*2B -1, 3B -1*	*1.6*

Breakout: 6%   Improve: 34%   Collapse: 8%   Attrition: 16%   MLB: 68%   Comparables: *Eddie Rosario, Gerardo Parra, Michael Saunders*

Drury played second base, third base and both corner outfield spots as a rookie. Finding a way to get his bat in the lineup proved to be less of a challenge for former Diamondbacks skipper Chip Hale with injuries to David Peralta and others, but he was inconsistent all year long. After a hot start, Drury cooled considerably before some mid-season adjustments to his stance like opening himself up slightly, which helped him get back on track. He finished the year strong but lacks a true defensive position, something that's problematic in the NL. Drury's got the chops to be a useful offensive player as he matures, and guys who can contribute with the bat usually find their way into the lineup one way or another.

Paul Goldschmidt   1B

Born: 9/10/87   Age: 29   Bats: R   Throws: R   Height: 6'3"   Weight: 225   Entered Pro Ball: Round 8, 2009 Draft (#246 overall)

YEAR	TEAM	LVL	AGE	PA	R	2B	3B	HR	RBI	BB	K	SB	CS	AVG/OBP/SLG	TAv	VORP	BABIP	BRR	FRAA	WARP
2014	ARI	MLB	26	479	75	39	1	19	69	64	110	9	3	.300/.396/.542	.332	40.4	.368	3.9	1B(109): 3.1	4.8
2015	ARI	MLB	27	695	103	38	2	33	110	118	151	21	5	.321/.435/.570	.348	68.8	.382	2.4	1B(157): 17.1	9.2
2016	ARI	MLB	28	705	106	33	3	24	95	110	150	32	5	.297/.411/.489	.311	45.3	.358	1.5	1B(157): 15.7	6.3
2017	ARI	MLB	29	634	93	36	2	28	94	90	141	18	5	.295/.397/.525	.309	44.3	.350	1.0	1B 11	5.6
2018	ARI	MLB	30	558	85	32	1	23	82	84	123	14	4	.291/.399/.516	.312	38.0	.345	1.8	1B 10	5.2

Breakout: 4%   Improve: 61%   Collapse: 1%   Attrition: 3%   MLB: 99%   *Comparables: Mark Teixeira, Joey Votto, Miguel Cabrera*

Goldschmidt's 2016 was an epic story of self-restraint. Sure, he finished with "only" 24 home runs, but what about all those other plate appearances? Goldy led the National League in walks after learning from MLB's marketing arm that he could light things on fire simply by focusing his thoughts. Team after team threw around him, and we should be in awe of a man who chose *not* to cause Noah Syndergaard's flowing tresses to burst into flames, who practiced Zen-like patience every time he served as the cutoff man for Yasmany Tomás, only to be wantonly ignored. In a land so dry that urine can turn into hazardous plasma by the time it hits the ground, Goldschmidt has taught us a lesson about the responsibility that comes with great power. Isn't the strength *not* to act the greatest superpower of them all?

Anfernee Grier   CF

Born: 10/13/95   Age: 21   Bats: R   Throws: R   Height: 6'1"   Weight: 180   Entered Pro Ball: Round 1, 2016 Draft (#39 overall)

YEAR	TEAM	LVL	AGE	PA	R	2B	3B	HR	RBI	BB	K	SB	CS	AVG/OBP/SLG	TAv	VORP	BABIP	BRR	FRAA	WARP
2016	YAK	A-	20	79	8	2	0	1	6	3	21	9	2	.240/.278/.307	.221	-2.8	.321	-0.6	CF(2): -0.4	-0.3
2017	ARI	MLB	21	250	32	10	1	6	21	12	81	11	4	.208/.251/.342	.193	-9.6	.284	1.0	CF 0	-1.0
2018	ARI	MLB	22	223	23	10	1	6	24	11	72	10	4	.216/.261/.360	.216	-2.8	.294	1.3	CF 0	-0.3

Breakout: 0%   Improve: 0%   Collapse: 0%   Attrition: 0%   MLB: 0%   *Comparables: Destin Hood, Kyle Waldrop, Tyler Goeddel*

The Diamondbacks lost their 2016 first-round pick by signing Zack Greinke, and plucked Grier in the competitive balance round with the 39th overall pick. After trading away talented young players like Dansby Swanson, Aaron Blair and Touki Toussaint, the Braves were surely excited to see Grier chosen by the D-backs as he's got plus speed, will likely stick in center and should develop plus raw power. If, for some reason, Arizona decides to keep him, there's impact potential, but Grier is raw and hasn't fared particularly well against polished talent. He did much of his damage at Auburn in non-conference play, then scuffled in SEC competition and his pro debut before an injury ended his campaign.

Jeremy Hazelbaker   OF

Born: 8/14/87   Age: 29   Bats: L   Throws: R   Height: 6'3"   Weight: 190   Entered Pro Ball: Round 4, 2009 Draft (#138 overall)

YEAR	TEAM	LVL	AGE	PA	R	2B	3B	HR	RBI	BB	K	SB	CS	AVG/OBP/SLG	TAv	VORP	BABIP	BRR	FRAA	WARP
2014	ABQ	AAA	26	92	12	3	2	4	11	2	27	6	2	.222/.239/.433	.227	-0.9	.271	0.6	LF(14): -2.7 • RF(8): 2.5	-0.1
2014	CHT	AA	26	307	31	9	8	4	33	30	70	15	7	.251/.326/.387	.247	0.8	.325	-1.0	RF(48): 4.0 • LF(27): -1.5	0.4
2015	TUL	AA	27	58	5	2	2	0	2	3	11	6	0	.245/.286/.358	.266	2.0	.310	0.6	LF(8): 0.1 • RF(4): -0.1	0.2
2015	SFD	AA	27	168	30	13	3	3	20	18	33	10	0	.308/.394/.503	.300	12.4	.380	2.9	RF(31): -1.1	1.2
2015	MEM	AAA	27	233	38	10	7	10	46	23	60	8	2	.333/.403/.594	.357	27.4	.428	-0.6	RF(52): -3.8 • CF(3): -0.4	2.4
2016	MEM	AAA	28	50	8	3	0	1	11	6	12	2	1	.325/.438/.475	.299	2.4	.444	-0.9	CF(6): -0.4 • RF(4): 0.2	0.3
2016	SLN	MLB	28	224	35	7	3	12	28	18	64	5	2	.235/.295/.480	.283	9.2	.278	-1.6	LF(52): -1.9 • CF(21): -1.1	0.6
2017	ARI	MLB	29	118	15	4	2	4	14	9	35	4	1	.244/.304/.433	.246	2.3	.317	0.6	LF -0, CF 0	0.3
2018	ARI	MLB	30	318	39	13	5	11	41	26	97	9	3	.241/.307/.439	.254	5.6	.315	-0.5	LF -1, CF 1	0.6

Breakout: 3%   Improve: 13%   Collapse: 6%   Attrition: 11%   MLB: 32%   *Comparables: Trent Oeltjen, Jordan Danks, Michael Restovich*

If you're the sort of hater who regularly checks out Deadspin to read their gleeful summation of each Cardinals loss, you probably couldn't abide ~~Hudsucker's~~ Hazelbaker's work last spring. The kid came out of nowhere (well, Muncie) to earn his first big-league job, and when handed the opportunity to be the injured Tommy Pham's proxy, Hazelbaker ran rings around the Senior Circuit to the tune of a .317/.357/.683 April. His numbers would soon plummet toward the pavement, of course, but the former Boston draftee and Dodgers farmhand showed enough power and resilience to earn a look-see in Arizona this spring. Hazelbaker's a strikeout machine and only average defensively in an outfield corner, but can be a useful platoon or bench bat capable of launching round souvenirs. You know, for kids.

Chris Herrmann   C/OF

Born: 11/24/87 Age: 29 Bats: L Throws: R Height: 6'0" Weight: 200 Entered Pro Ball: Round 6, 2009 Draft (#192 overall)

YEAR	TEAM	LVL	AGE	PA	R	2B	3B	HR	RBI	BB	K	SB	CS	AVG/OBP/SLG	TAv	VORP	BABIP	BRR	FRAA	WARP
2014	ROC	AAA	26	228	31	18	4	5	26	21	45	4	1	.304/.373/.505	.286	15.0	.368	1.0	C(26): 0.9 • RF(23): 1.2	1.7
2014	MIN	MLB	26	79	8	3	0	0	4	4	17	1	0	.213/.253/.253	.194	-2.7	.276	0.7	RF(13): -0.3 • LF(12): -1.2	-0.5
2015	ROC	AAA	27	88	9	3	0	1	6	11	13	3	0	.260/.364/.342	.266	3.3	.295	-0.4	C(17): 1.8 • LF(1): -0.0	0.5
2015	MIN	MLB	27	113	13	5	1	2	10	7	37	0	0	.146/.214/.272	.186	-2.4	.203	1.0	C(38): -4.8 • 1B(2): 0.0	-0.8
2016	RNO	AAA	28	28	3	1	0	0	3	3	8	0	0	.087/.214/.130	.151	-2.1	.125	0.3	C(3): 0.1 • LF(2): -0.0	-0.2
2016	ARI	MLB	28	166	21	5	4	6	28	16	44	4	0	.284/.352/.493	.291	13.0	.364	1.1	C(31): -5.1 • RF(4): 0.4	0.8
2017	*ARI*	*MLB*	*29*	*449*	*46*	*19*	*4*	*10*	*45*	*39*	*112*	*6*	*1*	*.234/.302/.374*	*.230*	*8.5*	*.295*	*0.5*	*C -14, 1B -0*	*-1.3*
2018	*ARI*	*MLB*	*30*	*367*	*41*	*15*	*3*	*9*	*39*	*33*	*94*	*4*	*1*	*.226/.298/.370*	*.236*	*5.1*	*.284*	*1.3*	*C -12, 1B 0*	*-0.8*

Breakout: 4%   Improve: 23%   Collapse: 10%   Attrition: 31%   MLB: 62%   *Comparables: Bobby Wilson, Rob Johnson, Omir Santos*

It was brilliant, really. In the waning days of the 2014 season, the ever-prescient Dave Stewart knew roster troubles would be in the future for client Chris Herrmann, so he did what any self-respecting then-agent would do: he pulled some strings with his former manager, and got himself hired as GM of the Diamondbacks. "Now, to get expectations as low as possible," he said to no one in particular, trading Miguel Montero and patching a season's worth of catching out of Gerald Laird, Tuffy Gosewisch, Jordan Pacheco and Oscar Hernandez. When the Twins called to talk trade in advance of the Rule 5 cutoff in November of 2015, Stewart pounced, completing one of the most notorious heists of the 21st century. After he succeeded in getting Herrmann used as a center fielder in 2016, Stewart wept, for there were no more worlds to conquer.

YEAR	TEAM	P. COUNT	FRM RUNS	BLK RUNS	THRW RUNS	TOT RUNS
2014	MIN	13	0.0	0.0	0.0	0.0
2014	ROC	3555	0.5	0.0	0.2	0.7
2015	MIN	4431	-4.7	-0.5	0.3	-5.0
2015	ROC	2119	1.7	0.1	0.1	1.8
2016	ARI	4304	-5.0	0.1	0.1	-4.9
2017	ARI	15575	-13.6	-0.5	0.4	-13.8
2018	*ARI*	*12725*	*-12.1*	*-0.6*	*0.2*	*-12.4*
2018	*ARI*	*14539*	*-14.4*	*-0.4*	*1.4*	*-13.4*

Jake Lamb   3B

Born: 10/9/90 Age: 26 Bats: L Throws: R Height: 6'3" Weight: 215 Entered Pro Ball: Round 6, 2012 Draft (#213 overall)

YEAR	TEAM	LVL	AGE	PA	R	2B	3B	HR	RBI	BB	K	SB	CS	AVG/OBP/SLG	TAv	VORP	BABIP	BRR	FRAA	WARP
2014	MOB	AA	23	439	60	35	5	14	79	50	99	0	0	.318/.399/.551	.334	45.8	.389	-1.1	3B(97): -3.0	4.6
2014	RNO	AAA	23	21	3	4	0	1	5	3	4	2	0	.500/.571/.889	.471	5.4	.615	0.1	3B(5): -0.5 • 1B(1): -0.1	0.5
2014	ARI	MLB	23	133	15	4	1	4	11	6	37	1	1	.230/.263/.373	.226	0.1	.291	0.4	3B(34): -0.4	0.0
2015	ARI	MLB	24	390	38	15	5	6	34	36	97	3	2	.263/.331/.386	.263	11.2	.344	-1.7	3B(95): 10.0 • 1B(8): 0.4	2.3
2016	ARI	MLB	25	594	81	31	9	29	91	64	154	6	1	.249/.332/.509	.287	37.8	.294	2.3	3B(142): -4.7	3.4
2017	*ARI*	*MLB*	*26*	*577*	*68*	*29*	*6*	*21*	*77*	*56*	*151*	*5*	*2*	*.259/.333/.463*	*.268*	*21.7*	*.323*	*0.0*	*3B 4*	*2.3*
2018	*ARI*	*MLB*	*27*	*524*	*69*	*27*	*6*	*20*	*71*	*51*	*136*	*4*	*2*	*.256/.331/.466*	*.274*	*19.2*	*.316*	*0.3*	*3B 3*	*2.5*

Breakout: 3%   Improve: 49%   Collapse: 6%   Attrition: 13%   MLB: 98%   *Comparables: Ian Stewart, Wilson Betemit, Pedro Alvarez*

In 2015, Statcast verified what Lamb's extreme minor-league BABIPs seemed to promise: the third baseman scorched the ball regularly, even though all of those hard hits didn't show up as home runs. Strikeout rates in the 22-24 percent range are usually hard to stomach without the long balls to match, but in Chase Field's cavernous outfield, Lamb added value with doubles and triples. Before the 2016 season began, Lamb made a subtle change in batting stance, gambling that by lowering his hands in his setup, he'd be able to pull balls inside while still managing to cover pitches low and outside. Let's just say the change worked. Lamb raised his fly-ball percentage to 36.7 percent, and after hitting a home run every 58 at-bats in 2015, he hit one every 18 at-bats last season. It wasn't all good news—an August slump continued into September—but Lamb looks like one of the D-backs' core players.

Domingo Leyba   MI

Born: 9/11/95 Age: 21 Bats: B Throws: R Height: 5'11" Weight: 160 Entered Pro Ball: International Free Agent, 2006

YEAR	TEAM	LVL	AGE	PA	R	2B	3B	HR	RBI	BB	K	SB	CS	AVG/OBP/SLG	TAv	VORP	BABIP	BRR	FRAA	WARP
2014	ONE	A-	18	154	20	1	1	1	17	8	17	1	2	.264/.303/.375	.252	4.8	.294	1.9	2B(35): -5.3 • SS(3): -0.6	-0.1
2014	WMI	A	18	124	20	7	0	1	7	6	13	1	2	.397/.431/.483	.346	16.8	.441	1.0	SS(17): 0.4 • 2B(13): 2.1	2.0
2015	VIS	A+	19	562	60	21	5	2	43	26	90	10	6	.237/.277/.309	.239	14.2	.278	4.2	SS(123): 0.5	1.6
2016	VIS	A+	20	374	48	25	1	6	40	29	62	5	1	.294/.346/.426	.285	26.5	.341	2.1	SS(66): -3.0 • 2B(17): -1.9	2.2
2016	MOB	AA	20	174	21	7	1	4	20	17	22	4	2	.301/.374/.436	.302	14.7	.331	0.8	SS(39): -2.8 • 2B(5): 0.1	1.3
2017	*ARI*	*MLB*	*21*	*250*	*27*	*12*	*1*	*5*	*24*	*14*	*51*	*1*	*1*	*.253/.296/.385*	*.221*	*1.0*	*.298*	*-0.2*	*SS -1, 2B -0*	*0.0*
2018	*ARI*	*MLB*	*22*	*346*	*38*	*18*	*2*	*8*	*38*	*18*	*68*	*2*	*1*	*.261/.302/.401*	*.244*	*5.5*	*.303*	*-0.4*	*SS -1, 2B -1*	*0.4*

Breakout: 4%   Improve: 9%   Collapse: 2%   Attrition: 6%   MLB: 14%   *Comparables: Tyler Pastornicky, Gavin Cecchini, Jose Pirela*

Trevor Bauer turned into Didi Gregorius, and Gregorius turned into Robbie Ray and Domingo Leyba. While the Diamondbacks have watched from afar as Gregorius blossoms in New York and Bauer attempts to amputate his digits while playing with drones, they've already reaped the benefits of Ray and it may not be long before Leyba joins the fray. After a tough 2015 campaign, Leyba rebounded and did more than hold his own following a promotion to Double-A before his 21st birthday. He's a contact-oriented hitter who'll have to slide over to second base sooner than later, but he has a big-league future.

Dawel Lugo   3B

Born: 12/31/94 Age: 22 Bats: R Throws: R Height: 6'0" Weight: 190 Entered Pro Ball: International Free Agent, 2012

YEAR	TEAM	LVL	AGE	PA	R	2B	3B	HR	RBI	BB	K	SB	CS	AVG/OBP/SLG	TAv	VORP	BABIP	BRR	FRAA	WARP
2014	LNS	A	19	498	40	17	2	4	53	18	72	3	3	.259/.286/.329	.224	-4.8	.296	-5.6	SS(110): -17.3	-2.3
2015	DUN	A+	20	276	16	9	2	2	21	9	49	1	3	.219/.258/.292	.207	-7.5	.262	-3.8	SS(67): 2.0	-0.6
2015	LNS	A	20	132	15	6	1	2	23	5	24	3	1	.336/.348/.451	.284	8.4	.386	0.1	SS(29): 2.0	1.1
2015	KNC	A	20	86	12	1	1	0	3	4	13	2	2	.333/.372/.370	.272	2.2	.397	-1.5	SS(14): -0.7 • 2B(2): -0.4	0.1
2016	VIS	A+	21	333	61	14	5	13	42	15	41	2	1	.314/.348/.514	.303	28.6	.328	2.5	3B(60): -3.2 • SS(14): 2.0	2.8
2016	MOB	AA	21	177	24	9	2	4	20	4	15	1	1	.306/.322/.451	.287	13.3	.318	2.7	3B(41): 4.6 • SS(10): 0.4	2.0
2017	*ARI*	*MLB*	*22*	*250*	*23*	*11*	*2*	*7*	*29*	*6*	*53*	*0*	*0*	*.252/.274/.400*	*.218*	*-2.5*	*.294*	*-0.2*	*3B 2, SS -0*	*0.0*
2018	*ARI*	*MLB*	*23*	*294*	*33*	*12*	*2*	*9*	*35*	*10*	*65*	*0*	*0*	*.250/.280/.407*	*.240*	*0.7*	*.294*	*-0.4*	*3B 3, SS 0*	*0.3*

Breakout: 1%   Improve: 9%   Collapse: 2%   Attrition: 14%   MLB: 18%   *Comparables: Giovanny Urshela, Josh Harrison, Josh Vitters*

Lugo was acquired from the Blue Jays for Cliff Pennington in August of 2015. All he's done since is hit, and he displayed greater power in 2016 than at any of his other minor-league stops. A midseason promotion to Double-A challenged Lugo, but he more than held his own, taking well to the Southern League at age 21. He's made the transition from shortstop to third base and profiles as a potentially average defender there. With future plus raw power, a plus arm and an ability to make contact, Lugo looks the part of a big leaguer. What may undo him, however, is an approach at the plate in which he never walks. Lugo scuffled in the AFL, and his 2016 numbers disguise his lack of polish at the plate.

Ketel Marte   SS

Born: 10/12/93 Age: 23 Bats: B Throws: R Height: 6'1" Weight: 165 Entered Pro Ball: International Free Agent, 2010

YEAR	TEAM	LVL	AGE	PA	R	2B	3B	HR	RBI	BB	K	SB	CS	AVG/OBP/SLG	TAv	VORP	BABIP	BRR	FRAA	WARP
2014	WTN	AA	20	472	63	27	6	2	46	19	65	23	10	.302/.329/.404	.265	21.0	.346	0.2	SS(102): -4.5 • 2B(7): 2.0	2.0
2014	TAC	AAA	20	90	16	5	0	2	9	8	13	6	0	.313/.367/.450	.297	8.9	.343	1.2	SS(19): 3.3	1.2
2015	TAC	AAA	21	287	41	12	2	3	29	20	32	20	3	.314/.359/.410	.279	19.5	.345	3.3	SS(49): 0.1 • 2B(14): 0.2	2.1
2015	SEA	MLB	21	247	25	14	3	2	17	24	43	8	4	.283/.351/.402	.289	15.9	.341	-0.5	SS(51): 4.6 • 2B(4): 0.4	2.2
2016	TAC	AAA	22	31	5	2	0	0	2	2	1	2	0	.214/.258/.286	.253	1.2	.214	0.5	SS(5): -0.5	0.1
2016	SEA	MLB	22	466	55	21	2	1	33	18	84	11	5	.259/.287/.323	.219	2.5	.313	2.6	SS(119): -1.2	0.1
2017	*ARI*	*MLB*	*23*	*261*	*27*	*14*	*2*	*3*	*25*	*14*	*46*	*9*	*3*	*.282/.318/.401*	*.242*	*6.1*	*.330*	*0.6*	*2B 3, SS 0*	*0.8*
2018	*ARI*	*MLB*	*24*	*478*	*52*	*25*	*4*	*7*	*50*	*28*	*83*	*16*	*6*	*.285/.327/.412*	*.256*	*14.9*	*.331*	*1.7*	*2B 5, SS 0*	*2.2*

Breakout: 11%   Improve: 49%   Collapse: 9%   Attrition: 22%   MLB: 87%   *Comparables: Everth Cabrera, Jean Segura, Andrelton Simmons*

The most surprising part of Marte's trade wasn't that Seattle would look to upgrade at short, but that such an upgrade somehow didn't result in Marte as the latest Mariners middle-infield figurine in Tampa's curio cabinet. When the conditions are exactly right, Marte is a patient hitter who makes contact and shows plus speed on the basepaths, while playing respectable defense. When conditions aren't exactly right, he's liable to have a year like 2016, where he regressed in almost every way offensively, often looking overmatched at the plate. His defense took a step backward as well and he wasn't quite as potent running the bases as you'd expect from a guy with his natural speed. Just what sort of conditions Arizona's desert clime present is an open question, but Marte is young and has time to develop, a truism that can excuse all manner of sins.

Peter O'Brien   OF

Born: 7/15/90 Age: 26 Bats: R Throws: R Height: 6'4" Weight: 235 Entered Pro Ball: Round 2, 2012 Draft (#94 overall)

YEAR	TEAM	LVL	AGE	PA	R	2B	3B	HR	RBI	BB	K	SB	CS	AVG/OBP/SLG	TAv	VORP	BABIP	BRR	FRAA	WARP
2014	TAM	A+	23	119	19	9	1	10	19	4	29	0	0	.321/.353/.688	.349	16.6	.351	-0.1	C(24): -2.1 • RF(6): 2.2	1.7
2014	TRN	AA	23	294	47	14	1	23	51	16	77	0	0	.245/.296/.555	.291	14.1	.253	-0.9	1B(27): -1.1 • C(19): -3.7	0.8
2015	RNO	AAA	24	534	77	35	9	26	107	31	124	1	3	.284/.332/.551	.293	29.4	.328	-0.1	LF(57): -8.6 • RF(47): 0.0	2.1
2015	ARI	MLB	24	12	1	1	0	1	3	2	5	0	0	.400/.500/.800	.433	2.0	.750	-0.3	LF(3): -0.1	0.2
2016	RNO	AAA	25	434	64	20	5	24	75	23	147	2	0	.254/.295/.505	.269	14.8	.332	2.9	LF(69): -1.4 • 1B(17): -0.2	1.4
2016	ARI	MLB	25	67	6	1	0	5	9	3	27	0	0	.141/.179/.391	.188	-3.6	.125	-0.2	LF(16): -0.4 • 1B(1): 0.0	-0.4
2017	*ARI*	*MLB*	*26*	*250*	*31*	*11*	*2*	*15*	*41*	*13*	*84*	*0*	*0*	*.236/.281/.493*	*.251*	*5.2*	*.296*	*-0.2*	*LF -4, 1B -0*	*0.1*
2018	*ARI*	*MLB*	*27*	*353*	*48*	*16*	*3*	*20*	*56*	*19*	*119*	*0*	*0*	*.234/.282/.487*	*.260*	*7.3*	*.297*	*-0.5*	*LF -6, 1B 0*	*0.1*

Breakout: 6%   Improve: 19%   Collapse: 13%   Attrition: 28%   MLB: 52%   *Comparables: Zach Walters, Cody Decker, Kyle Jensen*

After failing to make the grade at catcher or third base, O'Brien's unsightly metamorphosis seemed to complete itself with him landing in left field. The Diamondbacks had struggled to find a place for O'Brien before he slugged his way into the big-league lineup in June after destroying Triple-A pitching. He flailed miserably at the plate, however, and proved that even left field is a field too far for him. A tough close to the season might suggest that his epic raw power will ultimately be undone by his swing mechanics and approach, leaving him unplayable. O'Brien serves as a fresh reminder for an all-too-familiar theme in Arizona: guys with big raw power, a questionable ability to make contact and no defensive value flaming out in dramatic fashion.

Chris Owings   SS

Born: 8/12/91   Age: 25   Bats: R   Throws: R   Height: 5'10"   Weight: 185   Entered Pro Ball: Round 1, 2009 Draft (#41 overall)

YEAR	TEAM	LVL	AGE	PA	R	2B	3B	HR	RBI	BB	K	SB	CS	AVG/OBP/SLG	TAv	VORP	BABIP	BRR	FRAA	WARP
2014	RNO	AAA	22	40	6	1	0	0	1	0	9	3	0	.250/.250/.275	.178	-1.7	.323	0.8	2B(8): -0.1 • SS(1): -0.0	-0.2
2014	ARI	MLB	22	332	34	15	6	6	26	16	67	8	1	.261/.300/.406	.250	7.4	.314	-0.8	SS(61): -3.7 • 2B(18): -1.3	0.3
2015	ARI	MLB	23	552	59	27	5	4	43	26	144	16	4	.227/.264/.322	.213	-7.5	.305	1.9	2B(115): -5.0 • SS(35): -4.9	-1.9
2016	RNO	AAA	24	21	7	1	1	1	6	3	3	0	1	.611/.667/.944	.477	0.0	.714	0.0	SS(3): 0.0, CF(2): 0.1	0.6
2016	ARI	MLB	24	466	52	24	11	5	49	20	87	21	2	.277/.315/.416	.251	14.7	.334	1.9	SS(70): -3.3 • CF(49): -3.6	0.8
2017	ARI	MLB	25	615	72	31	7	11	55	29	134	20	4	.265/.300/.403	.235	10.8	.322	2.9	SS -9, 2B -1	-0.4
2018	ARI	MLB	26	569	61	28	6	12	61	27	124	18	4	.262/.301/.405	.244	11.0	.317	1.0	SS -8, 2B -1	0.2

Breakout: 1%   Improve: 61%   Collapse: 5%   Attrition: 13%   MLB: 98%   Comparables: Ronny Cedeno, Yuniesky Betancourt, Erick Aybar

Owings was limited in 2015 by the lingering effects of a 2014 shoulder injury that went undiagnosed for much of that season, as he struggled to adopt a two-handed finish on his swing. Things turned around in 2016, when he was selected a few days before the start of the season to play center field in A.J. Pollock's absence. To his credit, Owings held his own at the position, but by midseason he was back to providing below-average defense at shortstop with a below-average bat. It seems Owings has recovered from his injury, and is well on his way to reaching his replacement-level ceiling.

David Peralta   RF

Born: 8/14/87   Age: 29   Bats: L   Throws: L   Height: 6'1"   Weight: 210   Entered Pro Ball: International Free Agent, 2005

YEAR	TEAM	LVL	AGE	PA	R	2B	3B	HR	RBI	BB	K	SB	CS	AVG/OBP/SLG	TAv	VORP	BABIP	BRR	FRAA	WARP
2014	MOB	AA	26	223	33	17	1	6	46	18	21	2	0	.297/.359/.480	.311	18.1	.307	1.8	LF(43): 1.8 • CF(4): -0.6	2.0
2014	ARI	MLB	26	348	40	12	9	8	36	16	60	6	3	.286/.320/.450	.272	10.8	.328	0.1	RF(40): 3.2 • LF(36): -4.5	0.8
2015	ARI	MLB	27	517	61	26	10	17	78	44	107	9	4	.312/.371/.522	.320	39.7	.368	-1.2	LF(124): 4.3 • RF(9): -0.3	4.7
2016	RNO	AAA	28	34	6	4	0	0	2	4	5	0	0	.276/.353/.414	.250	0.2	.320	0.0	RF(9): 0.3	0.1
2016	ARI	MLB	28	183	23	9	5	4	15	8	42	2	0	.251/.295/.433	.253	4.7	.310	2.4	RF(44): 0.1 • CF(8): -0.3	0.5
2017	ARI	MLB	29	551	63	28	9	17	70	38	110	8	3	.280/.334/.470	.268	18.9	.326	0.5	RF 8	2.4
2018	ARI	MLB	30	466	58	22	7	15	60	33	100	5	2	.271/.326/.460	.270	14.7	.320	0.5	RF 6	2.3

Breakout: 4%   Improve: 47%   Collapse: 6%   Attrition: 11%   MLB: 96%   Comparables: Xavier Nady, Nate Schierholtz, Juan Rivera

Peralta established himself as one of the Diamondbacks' best position players in 2015, just two years out of indy ball, even earning playing time against lefties as the season progressed. His claim to fame: supple wrists that let him crush the life out of baseballs with an extremely high-leverage swing, earning him the nickname "Pinball Wizard" in at least three or four Arizona homesteads. Just as shoulder woes ended Peralta's career as a pitching prospect, his wrist injury threatens to deprive him of playing time, as well as an otherwise promising nickname. If he's not back to himself by the end of 2017, his career could depend on whether any team needs a pinch-runner who can scare the living bejeezus out of infielders.

A.J. Pollock   CF

Born: 12/5/87   Age: 29   Bats: R   Throws: R   Height: 6'1"   Weight: 195   Entered Pro Ball: Round 1, 2009 Draft (#17 overall)

YEAR	TEAM	LVL	AGE	PA	R	2B	3B	HR	RBI	BB	K	SB	CS	AVG/OBP/SLG	TAv	VORP	BABIP	BRR	FRAA	WARP
2014	RNO	AAA	26	52	4	1	1	0	9	2	4	0	0	.163/.192/.224	.146	-3.8	.174	1.1	CF(13): 1.6	-0.2
2014	ARI	MLB	26	287	41	19	6	7	24	19	46	14	3	.302/.353/.498	.308	22.8	.344	1.9	CF(68): -2.4 • LF(2): -0.2	2.2
2015	ARI	MLB	27	673	111	39	6	20	76	53	89	39	7	.315/.367/.498	.306	57.9	.338	7.9	CF(151): -7.8	5.4
2016	VIS	A+	28	20	3	1	0	2	4	4	1	1	0	.438/.550/.875	.474	4.7	.385	-0.2	CF(2): 0.1	0.5
2016	RNO	AAA	28	20	6	4	0	1	8	2	1	1	1	.444/.500/.833	.416	4.1	.438	0.2	CF(4): -0.7	0.3
2016	ARI	MLB	28	46	9	0	0	2	4	5	8	4	0	.244/.326/.390	.252	2.8	.258	1.8	CF(12): 1.6	0.4
2017	ARI	MLB	29	628	87	34	6	16	65	47	101	31	6	.285/.339/.450	.265	29.6	.317	4.2	CF -1	2.3
2018	ARI	MLB	30	403	50	22	4	11	50	33	68	18	4	.281/.341/.454	.274	20.3	.314	3.5	CF -1	2.1

Breakout: 4%   Improve: 50%   Collapse: 5%   Attrition: 9%   MLB: 97%   Comparables: Shane Victorino, Charlie Blackmon, Chone Figgins

Pollock's busted elbow (for the second time) was effective in foreshadowing the disappointment the Diamondbacks would experience in 2016. He returned in late August to perform reasonably well at the plate, but was shut down again for a strained groin after just two weeks on the active roster, ending his season. Pollock's defense/power/speed combo still makes him one of the National League's most dynamic talents, and after breaking out for 5.4 WARP in 2015 he should be good to go on Opening Day.

Yasmany Tomas   LF

Born: 11/14/90   Age: 26   Bats: R   Throws: R   Height: 6'2"   Weight: 250   Entered Pro Ball: International Free Agent, 2014

YEAR	TEAM	LVL	AGE	PA	R	2B	3B	HR	RBI	BB	K	SB	CS	AVG/OBP/SLG	TAv	VORP	BABIP	BRR	FRAA	WARP
2015	RNO	AAA	24	23	2	1	0	1	3	2	5	0	0	.190/.261/.381	.172	-2.2	.200	-0.5	RF(5): -1.4	-0.4
2015	ARI	MLB	24	426	40	19	3	9	48	17	110	5	2	.273/.305/.401	.246	3.2	.354	-0.1	RF(57): -1.9 • 3B(31): -2.6	-0.2
2016	ARI	MLB	25	563	72	30	1	31	83	31	136	2	4	.272/.313/.508	.276	19.5	.310	-0.8	RF(91): -14.0 • LF(60): -8.6	-0.3
2017	ARI	MLB	26	567	67	28	2	24	79	31	140	5	3	.267/.309/.467	.259	16.5	.319	-1.0	LF -11, RF	-0.2
2018	ARI	MLB	27	538	71	28	2	23	77	31	132	4	3	.269/.315/.473	.269	17.6	.320	0.1	LF -10, RF	0.6

Breakout: 0%   Improve: 56%   Collapse: 5%   Attrition: 8%   MLB: 98%   Comparables: Tony Conigliaro, Ivan Calderon, Ozzie Timmons

After a rookie year in which he alternated between being too timid and too wild at the plate, Tomás began working out with martial arts fitness guru Mack Newton. The results were impressive: Tomás was consistently aggressive, more than tripling his 2015 homer total while making modest strides in strikeout and walk rates. Word has it that Tomás will be working out with a Boy Scout troop this time around. If he earns his Orienteering badge and MLB allows him to carry a compass on the field, he might become a passable outfielder, too.

PITCHERS

Anthony Banda   LHP

Born: 8/10/93   Age: 23   Bats: L   Throws: L   Height: 6'2"   Weight: 190   Entered Pro Ball: Round 10, 2012 Draft (#335 overall)

YEAR	TEAM	LVL	AGE	W	L	SV	G	GS	IP	H	HR	BB/9	K/9	K	GB%	BABIP	WHIP	ERA	FIP	DRA	VORP	WARP	cFIP	MPH
2014	WIS	A	20	6	6	2	20	14	83²	84	4	4.1	8.9	83	50%	.339	1.46	3.66	3.52	3.99	13.0	1.3	95	
2014	SBN	A	20	3	0	0	6	6	35	32	2	1.8	8.7	34	45%	.303	1.11	1.54	2.97	4.51	3.4	0.4	96	
2015	VIS	A+	21	8	8	0	28	27	151²	150	8	2.3	9.0	152	48%	.336	1.25	3.32	3.31	2.77	38.8	4.2	87	
2016	MOB	AA	22	6	2	0	13	13	76¹	70	4	3.3	9.9	84	50%	.317	1.28	2.12	2.94	1.91	27.0	2.9	78	
2016	RNO	AAA	22	4	4	0	13	13	73²	73	6	3.3	8.3	68	46%	.313	1.36	3.67	4.11	3.68	13.6	1.4	91	
2017	ARI	MLB	23	1	1	0	14	0	14	14	1	3.9	7.9	13	49%	.303	1.47	4.15	3.72	4.28	1.0	0.1	98	
2018	ARI	MLB	24	2	1	0	49	0	52	43	5	5.0	10.6	61	49%	.323	1.38	3.96	4.09	4.36	4.3	0.4	97	

Breakout: 27%   Improve: 39%   Collapse: 16%   Attrition: 41%   MLB: 59%   *Comparables: Wily Peralta, Matt Magill, Nick Tropeano*

Banda's stock has steadily improved since he was acquired from the Brewers (along with Mitch Haniger) at the trade deadline for Gerardo Parra back in 2014. The Texan showed up to spring training with increased velocity, throwing consistently in the mid-90s from the left side. His curve and changeup can be average offerings, making Banda a strong bet to see the big-league rotation at some point in 2017, even if it's just with a no. 4 starter's ceiling.

Jake Barrett   RHP

Born: 7/22/91   Age: 25   Bats: R   Throws: R   Height: 6'2"   Weight: 240   Entered Pro Ball: Round 3, 2012 Draft (#120 overall)

YEAR	TEAM	LVL	AGE	W	L	SV	G	GS	IP	H	HR	BB/9	K/9	K	GB%	BABIP	WHIP	ERA	FIP	DRA	VORP	WARP	cFIP	MPH
2014	MOB	AA	22	1	2	12	25	0	26¹	25	0	4.1	8.2	24	46%	.338	1.41	2.39	2.73	3.92	2.7	0.3	94	
2014	RNO	AAA	22	1	0	16	30	0	29	22	3	4.7	7.1	23	45%	.268	1.28	3.72	5.11	5.01	1.1	0.1	106	
2015	RNO	AAA	23	1	3	11	22	0	23²	27	1	4.7	8.2	21	49%	.371	1.70	5.09	3.90	4.97	-0.1	0.0	104	
2015	MOB	AA	23	0	4		25	0	30	34	2	3.3	9.0	30	47%	.364	1.50	4.20	3.27	3.04	5.6	0.6	90	
2016	ARI	MLB	24	1	2	4	68	0	59¹	47	6	4.2	8.5	56	45%	.261	1.26	3.49	4.18	4.46	3.3	0.3	101	97.3
2017	ARI	MLB	25	3	3	2	56	0	59	61	8	3.9	8.1	53	48%	.307	1.47	4.64	4.51	4.71	1.4	0.1	100	
2018	ARI	MLB	26	1	1	1	30	0	31²	28	4	4.7	10.0	35	48%	.325	1.41	4.33	4.47	4.84	1.0	0.1	107	

Breakout: 23%   Improve: 37%   Collapse: 20%   Attrition: 36%   MLB: 70%   *Comparables: Josh Spence, Jose Mijares, Tommy Kahnle*

Barrett did what almost no other Diamondbacks pitcher accomplished in 2016: he outperformed even the most tepid of expectations on the season. By May, Barrett had established himself as Chip Hale's most reliable non-Brad Ziegler reliever, and given his former pedigree as a "top relief prospect" years before there's some reason to believe he can continue to succeed as a fastball/slider fireman. The gap of nearly a full run between his ERA and his DRA is a reminder that all bullpen life is fragile, but it's hard to write off Barrett's success for a team on which nearly every pitcher finds a way to fail.

Silvino Bracho   RHP

Born: 7/17/92   Age: 24   Bats: R   Throws: R   Height: 5'10"   Weight: 190   Entered Pro Ball: International Free Agent, 2011

YEAR	TEAM	LVL	AGE	W	L	SV	G	GS	IP	H	HR	BB/9	K/9	K	GB%	BABIP	WHIP	ERA	FIP	DRA	VORP	WARP	cFIP	MPH
2014	SBN	A	21	3	2	26	45	0	43¹	25	3	1.7	14.5	70	40%	.275	0.76	2.08	1.85	0.58	21.5	2.2	47	
2015	MOB	AA	22	2	1	16	37	0	44²	34	3	1.8	11.9	59	25%	.295	0.96	1.81	2.21	1.28	17.1	1.9	66	
2015	ARI	MLB	22	0	0	1	13	0	12¹	9	2	2.9	12.4	17	21%	.269	1.05	1.46	3.73	3.94	1.1	0.1	98	94.9
2016	RNO	AAA	23	0	2	15	36	0	33²	34	2	2.1	11.5	43	28%	.352	1.25	4.81	2.65	1.92	11.4	1.2	81	
2016	ARI	MLB	23	0	2	0	26	0	24²	31	7	3.6	6.2	17	29%	.293	1.66	7.30	7.08	7.59	-7.2	-0.7	136	95.0
2017	ARI	MLB	24	2	2	0	37	0	39²	42	6	3.2	8.6	38	57%	.308	1.44	4.77	4.43	4.82	0.4	0.0	100	
2018	ARI	MLB	25	2	1	0	37	0	39	35	6	4.0	10.4	45	57%	.319	1.35	4.52	4.66	5.06	0.3	0.0	115	

Breakout: 26%   Improve: 39%   Collapse: 7%   Attrition: 19%   MLB: 56%   *Comparables: Shae Simmons, Stephen Pryor, Ken Giles*

After an exciting 2015 that saw Bracho make a strong major-league debut, everything went south for the slight-of-stature reliever in 2016. He played the role of Santa Claus, spreading joy to just about every batter he faced in several big-league stints. His strikeout rate dried up and the fly ball-oriented righty gave up hits and homers like they were going out of style. A groin injury in spring training seemed to throw him off and Bracho never recovered. He was fringy to start with and his stock took a serious dive last season, leaving his future in serious jeopardy.

Archie Bradley   RHP

Born: 8/10/92   Age: 24   Bats: R   Throws: R   Height: 6'4"   Weight: 225   Entered Pro Ball: Round 1, 2011 Draft (#7 overall)

YEAR	TEAM	LVL	AGE	W	L	SV	G	GS	IP	H	HR	BB/9	K/9	K	GB%	BABIP	WHIP	ERA	FIP	DRA	VORP	WARP	cFIP	MPH
2014	RNO	AAA	21	1	4	0	5	5	24¹	26	0	4.4	8.5	23	46%	.373	1.56	5.18	3.78	5.19	1.5	0.2	102	
2014	MOB	AA	21	2	3	0	12	12	54²	45	2	5.9	7.6	46	44%	.285	1.48	4.12	4.23	6.66	-8.7	-0.9	120	
2015	ARI	MLB	22	3	0	0	8	8	35²	36	3	5.6	5.8	23	60%	.297	1.63	5.80	4.98	5.13	-0.2	0.0	111	94.4
2015	RNO	AAA	22	1	0	0	4	4	21¹	26	3	2.1	8.4	20	40%	.359	1.45	2.95	4.26	3.53	4.2	0.4	92	
2016	RNO	AAA	23	5	1	0	7	7	40²	26	0	4.0	10.4	47	64%	.289	1.08	1.99	2.88	1.28	18.4	1.9	72	
2016	ARI	MLB	23	8	9	0	26	26	141²	154	16	4.3	9.1	143	47%	.338	1.56	5.02	4.14	4.24	17.6	1.8	98	95.1
2017	ARI	MLB	24	5	6	0	16	16	84	81	10	3.8	8.9	84	48%	.301	1.39	4.18	4.07	4.39	7.4	0.8	100	
2018	ARI	MLB	25	8	9	0	26	26	153	128	18	4.1	10.4	176	48%	.316	1.29	3.97	4.09	4.45	16.8	1.7	100	

Breakout: 25%   Improve: 60%   Collapse: 13%   Attrition: 15%   MLB: 94%   *Comparables: Jarrod Parker, Gio Gonzalez, Daniel Hudson*

Throwing strikes is a prerequisite for MLB success, a prerequisite that seems to have eluded Bradley. His heater has good movement and can touch the mid-90s, and it can paired with a wicked knuckle-curve and a changeup that's been effective at times. Simply put, the former no. 7 overall pick checks off the "quality stuff" box. He finished the season near the worst in baseball in walk rate, however, and if he can't iron out the command problems he may ultimately never reach the high ceiling that was projected just a few years ago. He'll be just 24 in 2017, but should the struggles continue Bradley may wind up in the back of the bullpen long-term.

Enrique Burgos   RHP

Born: 11/23/90   Age: 26   Bats: R   Throws: R   Height: 6'4"   Weight: 250   Entered Pro Ball: International Free Agent, 2007

YEAR	TEAM	LVL	AGE	W	L	SV	G	GS	IP	H	HR	BB/9	K/9	K	GB%	BABIP	WHIP	ERA	FIP	DRA	VORP	WARP	cFIP	MPH
2014	VIS	A+	23	3	3	29	55	0	54²	37	5	4.3	13.7	83	47%	.275	1.15	2.47	3.43	1.57	22.0	2.2	70	
2015	RNO	AAA	24	0	1	5	15	0	15	19	3	7.2	13.8	23	42%	.421	2.07	6.00	5.93	5.21	-0.5	0.0	96	
2015	ARI	MLB	24	2	2	2	30	0	27	27	2	5.0	13.0	39	36%	.385	1.56	4.67	2.90	4.04	2.0	0.2	92	98.3
2016	RNO	AAA	25	3	0	1	24	0	27²	23	1	5.5	9.4	29	49%	.301	1.45	1.95	4.05	4.61	1.1	0.1	97	
2016	ARI	MLB	25	1	2	1	43	0	41¹	38	5	5.0	9.4	43	44%	.311	1.48	5.66	4.42	4.06	4.2	0.4	98	98.5
2017	ARI	MLB	26	2	2	0	42	0	44	44	6	4.2	9.5	47	46%	.308	1.47	4.58	4.37	4.68	1.2	0.1	100	
2018	ARI	MLB	27	3	1	0	54	0	57	45	7	4.4	11.6	73	46%	.318	1.28	3.79	3.91	4.24	5.6	0.6	93	

Breakout: 32%   Improve: 48%   Collapse: 15%   Attrition: 25%   MLB: 74%   *Comparables: Tommy Kahnle, Kevin Quackenbush, Brian Wilson*

Of all the wondrous creatures in the world Dave Stewart helped to create, it was Burgos whom he loved most, for reasons completely unrelated to his being represented by Stewart's wife. Like a modern day Prometheus, Stewart gave Burgos the gift of his splitter, and Burgos enjoyed a whiff rate of nearly 30 percent on the pitch. He also threw just 28 of them among his 714 pitches. Burgos broke out in the minors in 2014 by making unbelievable strides in both walks and strikeouts, but after his control slipped in 2015, his strikeout rate followed suit last year. Now that Stewart has been banished to an eternity of torment, it remains to be seen whether Burgos can keep the fire burning in his absence.

Andrew Chafin   LHP

Born: 6/17/90   Age: 27   Bats: R   Throws: L   Height: 6'2"   Weight: 225   Entered Pro Ball: Round 1, 2011 Draft (#43 overall)

YEAR	TEAM	LVL	AGE	W	L	SV	G	GS	IP	H	HR	BB/9	K/9	K	GB%	BABIP	WHIP	ERA	FIP	DRA	VORP	WARP	cFIP	MPH
2014	MOB	AA	24	4	1	0	9	9	55	49	4	3.1	6.7	41	46%	.280	1.24	1.96	3.73	4.07	7.1	0.8	94	
2014	RNO	AAA	24	5	6	0	17	16	92²	111	11	3.8	7.1	73	52%	.339	1.62	5.34	4.99	3.71	20.8	2.1	97	
2014	ARI	MLB	24	0	1	0	3	3	14	13	0	5.1	6.4	10	56%	.317	1.50	3.86	3.60	3.96	1.4	0.2	103	92.9
2015	ARI	MLB	25	5	1	2	66	0	75	56	3	3.6	7.0	58	60%	.248	1.15	2.76	3.38	3.73	8.2	0.9	97	95.6
2016	ARI	MLB	26	0	1	0	32	0	22²	22	1	4.4	11.1	28	52%	.368	1.46	6.75	2.88	3.30	4.2	0.4	83	96.0
2017	ARI	MLB	27	2	2	0	47	0	49	47	5	3.5	8.1	45	44%	.298	1.35	3.95	3.94	4.18	4.0	0.4	92	
2018	ARI	MLB	28	2	1	0	45	0	47¹	38	5	4.6	10.5	55	44%	.309	1.31	4.01	4.13	4.48	3.4	0.4	97	

Breakout: 23%   Improve: 36%   Collapse: 24%   Attrition: 30%   MLB: 75%   *Comparables: Michael Blazek, Justin Wilson, Randy Wells*

Tapped to join Arizona's bullpen to start 2015 after working as a starter throughout his minor-league career, Chafin seemed to have it all figured out, with a major-league fastball, major-league stirrups and a major-league mustache. In all the comings and goings on the Diamondbacks' pitching merry-go-round to start 2016, somehow manager Chip Hale forgot to tell Chafin to get off the carousel. After appearing in 23 of the first 49 games, Chafin became dizzy and ineffective, landing on his pitching shoulder as he was thrown from the ride and vomiting all over several small children.

Patrick Corbin   LHP

Born: 7/19/89   Age: 27   Bats: L   Throws: L   Height: 6'3"   Weight: 210   Entered Pro Ball: Round 2, 2009 Draft (#80 overall)

YEAR	TEAM	LVL	AGE	W	L	SV	G	GS	IP	H	HR	BB/9	K/9	K	GB%	BABIP	WHIP	ERA	FIP	DRA	VORP	WARP	cFIP	MPH
2015	MOB	AA	25	1	0	0	3	3	16¹	13	1	2.8	6.1	11	44%	.255	1.10	2.76	3.85	4.35	1.3	0.1	102	
2015	ARI	MLB	25	6	5	0	16	16	85	91	9	1.8	8.3	78	48%	.327	1.27	3.60	3.37	3.61	13.9	1.5	89	95.0
2016	ARI	MLB	26	5	13	1	36	24	155²	177	24	3.8	7.6	131	55%	.322	1.56	5.15	4.88	3.89	24.5	2.5	97	94.4
2017	ARI	MLB	27	8	9	0	24	24	144	145	20	3.1	8.5	137	50%	.305	1.37	4.27	4.22	4.48	11.2	1.2	100	
2018	ARI	MLB	28	9	9	0	26	26	151²	141	19	2.8	8.9	151	50%	.317	1.24	3.91	4.03	4.38	19.9	2.1	100	

Breakout: 32%   Improve: 60%   Collapse: 19%   Attrition: 15%   MLB: 95%   *Comparables: Matt Garza, Jose Quintana, Matt Harrison*

Blessed with boyish good looks and a devastating slider, Corbin entered 2016 with a thirst for success. An excellent 2013 campaign gave way to Tommy John surgery, which begat a lost campaign. His 2015 return was quite promising, but 2016 started badly and only got worse. His plan to throw a changeup more revealed what was already known: It's his worst pitch. Corbin struggled to get ahead early in counts, then was demoted in mid-August to the bullpen, where lo and behold, he found his footing and began racking up the strikeouts. He began relying on the slider again en route to finding success over the last month and a half of the season. He's best-served throwing his two fastballs and slider, a breaking pitch that's worthy of being thrown over 30 percent of the time. He's had success with that combination in the past and it should return in 2017 if he wants to avoid another unmitigated disaster.

Rubby De La Rosa   RHP

Born: 3/4/89   Age: 28   Bats: R   Throws: R   Height: 6'0"   Weight: 210   Entered Pro Ball: International Free Agent, 2007

YEAR	TEAM	LVL	AGE	W	L	SV	G	GS	IP	H	HR	BB/9	K/9	K	GB%	BABIP	WHIP	ERA	FIP	DRA	VORP	WARP	cFIP	MPH
2014	PAW	AAA	25	2	4	0	12	12	60	50	1	3.8	8.6	57	55%	.299	1.25	3.45	2.97	4.45	8.7	0.9	96	
2014	BOS	MLB	25	4	8	0	19	18	101²	116	12	3.1	6.6	74	47%	.327	1.49	4.43	4.33	5.45	-7.0	-0.8	107	98.1
2015	ARI	MLB	26	14	9	0	32	32	188²	193	32	3.0	7.2	150	51%	.287	1.36	4.67	4.84	3.98	23.0	2.5	101	97.9
2016	ARI	MLB	27	4	5	0	13	10	50²	43	8	3.6	9.6	54	54%	.257	1.24	4.26	4.53	3.01	13.1	1.4	85	97.5
2017	ARI	MLB	28	4	4	0	14	14	68²	68	10	3.2	8.8	67	42%	.328	1.35	4.33	4.25	4.84	5.5	0.6	112	
2018	ARI	MLB	29	9	10	0	31	31	194¹	177	29	3.3	9.6	206	42%	.315	1.27	4.27	4.40	4.77	13.6	1.4	110	

Breakout: 11%   Improve: 55%   Collapse: 15%   Attrition: 13%   MLB: 86%   *Comparables: Wade Miley, Shaun Marcum, Dave Bush*

After torturing Dodgers, Red Sox *and* Diamondbacks fans for years with brilliant stuff and poor results, De La Rosa appeared to put it all together in 2016. Well, at least until his elbow flared up and he was DL'd for most of the season. The club attempted to bring the Tommy John survivor back late, but more elbow discomfort forced him to the DL yet again. Baseball is a cruel mistress and De La Rosa's campaign is proof, as he'd set a new high in strikeout rate and reduced the painful walks that often haunted him before he was put on the shelf. His capacity is very much in question going forward—can he still start or is he a reliever for good?

Randall Delgado   RHP

Born: 2/9/90   Age: 27   Bats: R   Throws: R   Height: 6'4"   Weight: 220   Entered Pro Ball: International Free Agent, 2006

YEAR	TEAM	LVL	AGE	W	L	SV	G	GS	IP	H	HR	BB/9	K/9	K	GB%	BABIP	WHIP	ERA	FIP	DRA	VORP	WARP	cFIP	MPH
2014	ARI	MLB	24	4	4	0	47	4	77²	71	6	4.1	10.0	86	37%	.311	1.36	4.87	3.36	4.77	-1.8	-0.2	105	95.9
2015	ARI	MLB	25	8	4	1	64	1	72	63	7	4.1	9.1	73	44%	.290	1.33	3.25	3.81	4.58	1.1	0.1	102	96.0
2016	ARI	MLB	26	5	2	0	79	0	75	77	8	4.3	8.2	68	43%	.309	1.51	4.44	4.28	5.20	-1.9	-0.2	110	94.8
2017	*ARI*	*MLB*	*27*	*2*	*3*	*0*	*51*	*0*	*54¹*	*52*	*7*	*4.0*	*9.1*	*55*	*43%*	*.303*	*1.42*	*4.42*	*4.26*	*4.56*	*2.1*	*0.2*	*100*	
2018	*ARI*	*MLB*	*28*	*2*	*1*	*1*	*42*	*0*	*44¹*	*39*	*5*	*3.8*	*9.7*	*48*	*43%*	*.315*	*1.29*	*3.97*	*4.10*	*4.46*	*3.3*	*0.3*	*99*	

Breakout: 31%   Improve: 58%   Collapse: 17%   Attrition: 14%   MLB: 91%   *Comparables: Matt Garza, Sean Marshall, Tommy Hunter*

Delgado is your basic OK reliever, which is pretty underwhelming when you consider he was once the prospect centerpiece of a trade for a 25-year old Justin Upton. He walks too many and doesn't strike enough out, but remains valuable in that he can be deployed in 70-plus games a year as a utility reliever. Delgado will turn 27 before Opening Day and what you see is what you get: a guy who can struggle to throw strikes on occasion, but is effective enough to get the job done most times out, even if it's in unexciting fashion.

Zachary Godley   RHP

Born: 4/21/90   Age: 27   Bats: R   Throws: R   Height: 6'3"   Weight: 240   Entered Pro Ball: Round 10, 2013 Draft (#288 overall)

YEAR	TEAM	LVL	AGE	W	L	SV	G	GS	IP	H	HR	BB/9	K/9	K	GB%	BABIP	WHIP	ERA	FIP	DRA	VORP	WARP	cFIP	MPH
2014	KNC	A	24	1	1	7	11	0	15	9	0	4.2	15.0	25	52%	.310	1.07	1.80	1.55	1.75	5.5	0.6	77	
2014	DAY	A+	24	3	2	8	29	0	40¹	40	3	3.8	11.6	52	56%	.349	1.41	3.57	3.19	2.08	13.9	1.4	81	
2015	VIS	A+	25	8	3	0	14	12	75¹	64	3	2.3	9.3	78	56%	.300	1.10	2.27	3.10	2.55	21.0	2.3	88	
2015	MOB	AA	25	2	1	0	7	5	24¹	21	2	3.7	4.4	12	61%	.260	1.27	4.07	4.99	5.28	-0.6	-0.1	110	
2015	ARI	MLB	25	5	1	0	9	6	36²	29	4	4.2	8.3	34	47%	.272	1.25	3.19	4.36	4.05	3.9	0.4	102	93.8
2016	MOB	AA	26	2	5	0	8	8	49¹	48	4	2.0	5.7	31	56%	.291	1.20	3.83	4.03	3.97	6.2	0.7	95	
2016	RNO	AAA	26	2	1	0	7	6	32²	37	3	4.1	10.5	38	50%	.382	1.59	3.31	4.06	2.17	11.4	1.2	81	
2016	ARI	MLB	26	5	4	0	27	9	74²	86	13	3.0	7.2	60	55%	.313	1.49	6.39	5.01	3.46	14.6	1.5	95	92.8
2017	*ARI*	*MLB*	*27*	*2*	*3*	*0*	*39*	*2*	*49*	*50*	*5*	*3.5*	*7.7*	*42*	*42%*	*.306*	*1.42*	*4.19*	*4.06*	*4.35*	*3.4*	*0.4*	*99*	
2018	*ARI*	*MLB*	*28*	*3*	*2*	*0*	*47*	*2*	*59²*	*53*	*6*	*3.8*	*9.6*	*63*	*42%*	*.326*	*1.31*	*3.81*	*3.91*	*4.22*	*6.3*	*0.7*	*92*	

Breakout: 27%   Improve: 53%   Collapse: 14%   Attrition: 24%   MLB: 80%   *Comparables: Burke Badenhop, Mitchell Boggs, Shawn Hill*

Godley was the poster child for what the D-backs tried to accomplish with their pitching staff in 2015, as an insane ground-ball percentage fueled his improbable rise to the majors. He did it by doggedly throwing below the strike zone with fastballs, and was rewarded with a 3.19 ERA in 37 innings. Were the Diamondbacks onto something? We'll never know, as Godley's "the devil may care" approach to pitching led to a 6.39 ERA over 75 innings in 2016, and the obvious conclusion that he simply wasn't the right man for the job.

Zack Greinke   RHP

Born: 10/21/83   Age: 33   Bats: R   Throws: R   Height: 6'2"   Weight: 200   Entered Pro Ball: Round 1, 2002 Draft (#6 overall)

YEAR	TEAM	LVL	AGE	W	L	SV	G	GS	IP	H	HR	BB/9	K/9	K	GB%	BABIP	WHIP	ERA	FIP	DRA	VORP	WARP	cFIP	MPH
2014	LAN	MLB	30	17	8	0	32	32	202¹	190	19	1.9	9.2	207	50%	.311	1.15	2.71	2.94	2.62	49.8	5.5	78	94.6
2015	LAN	MLB	31	19	3	0	32	32	222²	148	14	1.6	8.1	200	49%	.229	0.84	1.66	2.79	3.26	44.9	4.8	88	94.7
2016	ARI	MLB	32	13	7	0	26	26	158²	161	23	2.3	7.6	134	47%	.294	1.27	4.37	4.16	3.51	32.7	3.4	92	93.8
2017	*ARI*	*MLB*	*33*	*11*	*11*	*0*	*28*	*28*	*187*	*174*	*23*	*2.4*	*9.1*	*189*	*36%*	*.296*	*1.19*	*3.69*	*3.63*	*3.86*	*27.5*	*2.8*	*88*	
2018	*ARI*	*MLB*	*34*	*13*	*11*	*0*	*32*	*32*	*211²*	*187*	*26*	*2.2*	*9.1*	*215*	*36%*	*.309*	*1.13*	*3.60*	*3.70*	*4.01*	*36.6*	*3.8*	*90*	

Breakout: 13%   Improve: 50%   Collapse: 18%   Attrition: 24%   MLB: 96%   *Comparables: Justin Verlander, Chris Carpenter, Roy Oswalt*

Greinke was paid to be Arizona's "ace," but didn't pitch like one in his first season with the Diamondbacks. He walked more batters than he had in recent years and his strikeout rate fell yet again—a concerning trend. The thin desert air seemingly wreaked havoc with Greinke in the long-ball department, as he reached a HR/9 rate that he hadn't experienced since his early days in Kansas City. On top of it all, Greinke also lost a bit of velocity in his age-32 season. With five years left on his massive contract, his ability to reach "ace" status again is in serious doubt as 2016 revealed some pretty typical signs of age-related decline.

Daniel Hudson   RHP

Born: 3/9/87   Age: 30   Bats: R   Throws: R   Height: 6'3"   Weight: 230   Entered Pro Ball: Round 5, 2008 Draft (#150 overall)

YEAR	TEAM	LVL	AGE	W	L	SV	G	GS	IP	H	HR	BB/9	K/9	K	GB%	BABIP	WHIP	ERA	FIP	DRA	VORP	WARP	cFIP	MPH
2014	ARI	MLB	27	0	1	0	3	0	2²	4	0	0.0	6.8	2	46%	.364	1.50	13.50	1.60	4.27	0.1	0.0	102	96.8
2015	ARI	MLB	28	4	3	4	64	1	67²	64	7	3.3	9.4	71	43%	.305	1.32	3.86	3.52	3.70	7.7	0.8	94	98.6
2016	ARI	MLB	29	3	2	5	70	0	60¹	65	6	3.3	8.7	58	41%	.331	1.44	5.22	3.85	4.20	5.2	0.5	100	97.7
2017	*ARI*	*MLB*	*30*	*3*	*1*	*2*	*54*	*0*	*57*	*58*	*8*	*3.0*	*9.6*	*61*	*42%*	*.345*	*1.35*	*3.95*	*3.92*	*4.43*	*4.0*	*0.4*	*99*	
2018	*ARI*	*MLB*	*31*	*2*	*1*	*2*	*47*	*0*	*44¹*	*43*	*6*	*3.0*	*9.8*	*48*	*42%*	*.340*	*1.31*	*3.94*	*4.06*	*4.42*	*3.6*	*0.4*	*98*	

Breakout: 32%   Improve: 48%   Collapse: 18%   Attrition: 11%   MLB: 84%   *Comparables: Jeremy Affeldt, Mark Lowe, Carlos Villanueva*

After two Tommy John surgeries, Hudson returned to the bullpen for good in 2016 and looked like a trade candidate at the dead-line before his 19.29 ERA in July tanked his value. Hudson slowly returned to form and closed the year on a high note. His stuff is as good as ever, with a fastball in the upper 90s, a quality slider and a changeup that's been historically effective, even if the pitch lagged behind his other two offerings in 2016. He's a power arm capable of holding down a high-leverage job, so long as he doesn't face the knife for a third time.

Yoan Lopez   RHP

Born: 1/2/93   Age: 24   Bats: R   Throws: R   Height: 6'3"   Weight: 185   Entered Pro Ball: International Free Agent, 2015

YEAR	TEAM	LVL	AGE	W	L	SV	G	GS	IP	H	HR	BB/9	K/9	K	GB%	BABIP	WHIP	ERA	FIP	DRA	VORP	WARP	cFIP	MPH
2015	MOB	AA	22	1	6	0	10	9	48	46	4	4.5	6.0	32	40%	.290	1.46	4.69	4.55	6.71	-8.8	-1.0	118	
2016	MOB	AA	23	4	7	0	14	14	62	67	10	4.6	5.2	36	42%	.285	1.60	5.52	5.90	9.61	-31.1	-3.4	127	
2017	ARI	MLB	24	3	4	0	12	12	51²	64	9	4.6	5.4	31	64%	.337	1.75	5.98	5.82	6.62	-6.1	-0.6	157	
2018	ARI	MLB	25	3	6	0	16	16	91¹	93	17	5.8	7.9	80	64%	.316	1.66	6.03	6.23	6.67	-8.5	-0.9	156	

Breakout: 4%   Improve: 5%   Collapse: 0%   Attrition: 6%   MLB: 6%   *Comparables: Frank Garces, Luis Atilano, Alfredo Figaro*

The good news: Lopez would be a top-three prospect in virtually any organization, per former chief baseball officer and current chief baseball analyst/advisor Tony La Russa. The bad news: Lopez wouldn't actually be a top-10 prospect in virtually any orga-nization, and most of the time, the D-backs don't even know where he is. After skipping out on his team for a second time, Lopez returned once more to throw three uninspired innings in the AZL to round out his campaign. There's effort in the delivery and he's missed considerable development time, but if moved to a relief role there's still a glimmer of hope that his fastball/curveball pair-ing could be some kind of effective. As of now, it looks like Arizona blew their bonus pool on a guy who'd rather be somewhere else, and it's hard to imagine the organization's patience isn't wearing thin.

Evan Marshall   RHP

Born: 4/18/90   Age: 27   Bats: R   Throws: R   Height: 6'2"   Weight: 225   Entered Pro Ball: Round 4, 2011 Draft (#124 overall)

YEAR	TEAM	LVL	AGE	W	L	SV	G	GS	IP	H	HR	BB/9	K/9	K	GB%	BABIP	WHIP	ERA	FIP	DRA	VORP	WARP	cFIP	MPH
2014	RNO	AAA	24	0	1	1	14	0	16²	10	0	2.7	10.3	19	61%	.303	0.90	0.54	2.32	2.86	4.6	0.5	76	
2014	ARI	MLB	24	4	4	0	57	0	49¹	50	3	3.1	9.9	54	61%	.351	1.36	2.74	2.86	2.29	12.0	1.3	82	95.9
2015	ARI	MLB	25	0	2	0	13	0	13¹	20	3	3.4	4.7	7	51%	.370	1.88	6.07	6.16	5.16	-0.7	-0.1	113	96.3
2015	RNO	AAA	25	3	2	0	31	0	32¹	47	1	3.6	7	25	66%	.380	1.86	6.40	3.94	6.06	-4.1	-0.4	97	
2016	ARI	MLB	26	0	1	0	15	0	15¹	28	2	4.7	5.3	9	57%	.441	2.35	8.80	5.47	5.30	-0.6	-0.1	107	95.7
2016	RNO	AAA	26	1	1	0	33	0	33¹	36	1	4.3	7.6	28	48%	.340	1.56	4.59	4.14	6.55	-5.9	-0.6	105	
2017	ARI	MLB	27	1	2	0	28	0	29	35	4	3.8	7.2	24	43%	.321	1.66	4.94	4.73	4.90	0.1	0.0	100	
2018	ARI	MLB	28	2	1	0	33	0	34²	36	4	4.4	9.3	36	43%	.354	1.53	4.40	4.53	4.86	1.0	0.1	108	

Breakout: 25%   Improve: 34%   Collapse: 15%   Attrition: 23%   MLB: 51%   *Comparables: Franquelis Osoria, Joe Thatcher, Evan Meek*

Marshall was dominant in 2014 as a big-league reliever, but was struck in the head by a comebacker in 2015 while at Triple-A. He initially feared for his life, something *a fractured skull* will do to you, but survived the incident and worked his way back to the mound and the majors in 2016. The results were uninspiring, though he can still touch the mid-90s and has a slider with big horizontal break. A drop in his release point flattened his stuff and he caught more of the plate. It's yet to be seen if Marshall can recapture the form he showed in his rookie season, but perhaps just being on the mound is victory enough.

Jared Miller   LHP

Born: 8/21/93   Age: 23   Bats: L   Throws: L   Height: 6'7"   Weight: 240   Entered Pro Ball: Round 11, 2014 Draft (#330 overall)

YEAR	TEAM	LVL	AGE	W	L	SV	G	GS	IP	H	HR	BB/9	K/9	K	GB%	BABIP	WHIP	ERA	FIP	DRA	VORP	WARP	cFIP	MPH
2014	YAK	A-	20	1	1	0	8	5	27²	21	3	2.9	6.8	21	47%	.232	1.08	3.58	4.68	3.76	4.9	0.5	99	
2015	YAK	A-	21	7	2	0	9	9	59²	42	2	1.8	8.6	57	54%	.248	0.91	1.81	2.93	2.62	17.6	1.8	84	
2015	KNC	A	21	4	5	0	13	12	59²	69	5	4.7	6.3	42	52%	.323	1.68	5.88	4.74	6.80	-10.5	-1.1	113	
2016	KNC	A	22	0	0	2	9	0	14¹	4	0	3.1	13.2	21	85%	.154	0.63	0.00	1.59	2.20	3.9	0.4	82	
2016	VIS	A+	22	0	1	1	12	0	14¹	9	0	1.9	12.6	20	72%	.281	0.84	1.88	1.55	1.77	5.3	0.5	76	
2016	MOB	AA	22	1	2	19	0	26²	18	1	4.4	12.1	36	70%	.283	1.16	3.71	3.13	1.92	8.3	0.9	84		
2017	ARI	MLB	23	3	3	1	24	7	58²	67	9	4.2	6.5	42	58%	.332	1.61	5.35	5.23	5.81	-2.7	-0.3	140	
2018	ARI	MLB	24	5	5	1	36	12	104²	99	16	5.1	9.0	105	58%	.319	1.51	5.16	5.32	5.60	-1.8	-0.2	134	

Breakout: 9%   Improve: 13%   Collapse: 3%   Attrition: 11%   MLB: 19%   *Comparables: Charles Brewer, Anthony Bass, Kyle Hendricks*

Miller was moved from the rotation to the bullpen in 2016 and saw his stock soar as he pitched across four levels, topping out at Triple-A before posting a strong line in the AFL. It's a nice story for an uninspiring minor-league system, but the 6-foot-7 lefty isn't a closer in waiting—he instead looks like a valuable middle-inning arm. There's some deception in the delivery, but his fastball sits in the low 90s and there's nothing left in terms of projection. His secondaries are fringy, fooling minor leaguers, but they may not translate well to the majors. Feel-good stories are great, but minor-league pitchers, and especially relievers, are a volatile bunch.

Shelby Miller   RHP

Born: 10/10/90   Age: 26   Bats: R   Throws: R   Height: 6'3"   Weight: 225   Entered Pro Ball: Round 1, 2009 Draft (#19 overall)

YEAR	TEAM	LVL	AGE	W	L	SV	G	GS	IP	H	HR	BB/9	K/9	K	GB%	BABIP	WHIP	ERA	FIP	DRA	VORP	WARP	cFIP	MPH
2014	SLN	MLB	23	10	9	0	32	31	183	160	22	3.6	6.2	127	42%	.256	1.27	3.74	4.51	5.94	-22.4	-2.5	124	96.0
2015	ATL	MLB	24	6	17	0	33	33	205¹	183	13	3.2	7.5	171	49%	.285	1.25	3.02	3.47	3.85	28.0	3.0	97	96.7
2016	VIS	A+	25	2	0	0	2	2	12	8	0	0.8	14.2	19	46%	.308	0.75	0.75	0.80	1.23	5.7	0.6	66	
2016	RNO	AAA	25	5	1	0	8	8	50²	55	4	1.8	9.8	55	52%	.367	1.28	3.91	3.23	1.07	24.1	2.5	65	
2016	ARI	MLB	25	3	12	0	20	20	101	127	14	3.7	6.2	70	44%	.340	1.67	6.15	4.91	5.86	-5.7	-0.6	117	95.9
2017	ARI	MLB	26	8	10	0	26	26	156	158	22	3.3	8.3	144	49%	.302	1.39	4.40	4.35	4.60	10.0	1.0	100	
2018	ARI	MLB	27	9	10	0	27	27	163¹	153	22	3.1	8.7	159	49%	.312	1.28	4.19	4.32	4.68	15.7	1.6	108	

Breakout: 23%   Improve: 52%   Collapse: 19%   Attrition: 9%   MLB: 90%   *Comparables: Tommy Hanson, Anibal Sanchez, Jarrod Parker*

Dumpster-fire jokes are old and tired, but Miller kept them around in 2016. After tweaking his mechanics early, he never got right and pitched poorly all year. Compounding the matter for the Diamondbacks, trade chip Ender Inciarte thrived in Atlanta and the darling Dansby Swanson acquitted himself well in his big-league debut, making the firing of GM Dave Stewart seem like more than a coincidence. After mixing his three fastballs effectively in Atlanta, Miller altered that approach in Arizona—a perplexing change given the success he'd experienced just the year before. Returning to just a league-average starter would be a clear move in the right direction at this point, and Miller showed some flashes down the stretch of being able to get there.

Robbie Ray   LHP

Born: 10/1/91   Age: 25   Bats: L   Throws: L   Height: 6'2"   Weight: 195   Entered Pro Ball: Round 12, 2010 Draft (#356 overall)

YEAR	TEAM	LVL	AGE	W	L	SV	G	GS	IP	H	HR	BB/9	K/9	K	GB%	BABIP	WHIP	ERA	FIP	DRA	VORP	WARP	cFIP	MPH
2014	TOL	AAA	22	7	6	0	20	19	100¹	106	6	3.9	6.7	75	36%	.326	1.50	4.22	4.05	6.38	-7.0	-0.7	109	
2014	DET	MLB	22	1	4	0	9	6	28²	43	5	3.5	6.0	19	40%	.376	1.88	8.16	5.25	6.37	-5.0	-0.6	118	95.5
2015	RNO	AAA	23	2	3	0	9	9	41²	44	1	5.8	12.3	57	44%	.422	1.70	3.67	3.12	2.16	14.6	1.5	75	
2015	ARI	MLB	23	5	12	0	23	23	127²	121	9	3.5	8.4	119	45%	.311	1.33	3.52	3.55	4.16	13.1	1.4	99	96.4
2016	ARI	MLB	24	8	15	0	32	32	174¹	185	24	3.7	11.3	218	47%	.352	1.47	4.90	3.80	2.95	46.8	4.8	81	97.2
2017	ARI	MLB	25	9	9	0	26	26	148	140	17	3.3	10.3	169	47%	.314	1.35	3.71	3.62	3.89	21.2	2.2	87	
2018	ARI	MLB	26	11	10	0	30	30	190²	159	21	3.6	11.3	239	47%	.328	1.23	3.52	3.62	3.93	30.8	3.2	87	

Breakout: 29%   Improve: 58%   Collapse: 18%   Attrition: 16%   MLB: 90%   *Comparables: Gio Gonzalez, Patrick Corbin, Zack Wheeler*

Ray ranked near the top of the National League in strikeout rate and did so in infuriating fashion. While he's got plus heat from the left side, he routinely fails to put hitters away with anything resembling efficiency. Case in point: he averaged just under 5.5-innings per start while throwing nearly 100 pitches per outing. That all highlights Ray's inability to harness his secondary stuff and command the strike zone. DRA tells the story of a pitcher who was unlucky, so perhaps he'll take a big leap forward in 2017. If his secondaries improve just slightly, that big leap is possible and he can be a very valuable pitcher. If they don't, he'll continue to be classified as a pitcher who doesn't pitch deep into games, limiting his ultimate value.

Fernando Rodney   RHP

Born: 3/18/77   Age: 40   Bats: R   Throws: R   Height: 5'11"   Weight: 230   Entered Pro Ball: International Free Agent, 1997

YEAR	TEAM	LVL	AGE	W	L	SV	G	GS	IP	H	HR	BB/9	K/9	K	GB%	BABIP	WHIP	ERA	FIP	DRA	VORP	WARP	cFIP	MPH
2014	SEA	MLB	37	1	6	48	69	0	66¹	61	3	3.8	10.3	76	51%	.330	1.34	2.85	2.86	3.42	7.9	0.9	89	98.0
2015	SEA	MLB	38	5	5	16	54	0	50²	51	8	4.4	7.6	43	51%	.295	1.50	5.68	5.24	4.25	2.6	0.3	103	98.0
2015	CHN	MLB	38	2	0	0	14	0	12	8	1	3.0	11.2	15	57%	.259	1.00	0.75	3.50	4.24	0.6	0.1	103	97.0
2016	SDN	MLB	39	0	1	17	28	0	28²	13	0	3.8	10.4	33	60%	.210	0.87	0.31	2.35	3.51	4.7	0.5	89	97.3
2016	MIA	MLB	39	2	3	8	39	0	36²	41	5	6.1	10.1	41	54%	.360	1.80	5.89	5.01	3.48	6.1	0.6	90	97.6
2017	ARI	MLB	40	3	3	38	56	0	59	56	8	4.5	10.0	66	57%	.308	1.47	4.35	4.32	4.49	2.8	0.3	99	
2018	ARI	MLB	41	2	1	23	36	0	38¹	35	5	4.5	9.3	40	57%	.317	1.41	4.48	4.62	5.00	0.6	0.1	114	

Breakout: 18%   Improve: 28%   Collapse: 17%   Attrition: 5%   MLB: 55%   *Comparables: Randy Choate, Darren Oliver, Arthur Rhodes*

The dude had fun. Entering his age-40 season, the archer was shaky for Miami, but he was an attraction, and it's safe to say South Florida loves its attractions. He supplanted A.J. Ramos as closer with nothing more than smoke, mirrors and a gimmick, and good for him. Time could be running short for Rodney, but he'll have another crack at a closer gig in 2017. If he's hit a dead end, kudos for doing it with so much flair. There are few near-universally beloved quantities in baseball, but Rodney may have been one of them. We've all been shot through the heart on some level.

Jimmie Sherfy   RHP

Born: 12/27/91   Age: 25   Bats: R   Throws: R   Height: 6'0"   Weight: 175   Entered Pro Ball: Round 10, 2013 Draft (#300 overall)

YEAR	TEAM	LVL	AGE	W	L	SV	G	GS	IP	H	HR	BB/9	K/9	K	GB%	BABIP	WHIP	ERA	FIP	DRA	VORP	WARP	cFIP	MPH
2014	VIS	A+	22	2	0	6	11	0	11	6	2	4.1	18.8	23	53%	.308	1.00	3.27	3.56	1.70	4.3	0.4	72	
2014	MOB	AA	22	3	1	1	37	0	38	34	4	4.3	10.7	45	48%	.316	1.37	4.97	3.92	2.42	10.3	1.1	90	
2015	MOB	AA	23	1	6	2	44	0	49²	50	3	5.1	9.1	50	50%	.336	1.57	6.52	3.95	3.56	6.5	0.7	98	
2016	VIS	A+	24	0	0	8	12	0	12¹	5	0	4.4	15.3	21	68%	.263	0.89	0.00	1.77	1.64	4.7	0.5	76	
2016	MOB	AA	24	2	0	10	16	0	19²	6	1	2.3	14.2	31	51%	.147	0.56	0.46	1.90	0.79	8.6	0.9	63	
2016	RNO	AAA	24	1	4	12	24	0	23¹	20	5	5.0	10.4	27	42%	.288	1.41	6.17	5.86	2.33	6.8	0.7	89	
2017	ARI	MLB	25	1	1	0	19	0	19²	20	3	4.2	8.4	18	51%	.305	1.52	4.78	4.86	4.80	0.3	0.0	100	
2018	ARI	MLB	26	2	1	0	44	0	46¹	38	6	5.4	11.1	57	51%	.320	1.43	4.43	4.57	4.91	1.1	0.1	112	

Breakout: 16%   Improve: 21%   Collapse: 12%   Attrition: 27%   MLB: 37%   *Comparables: Blake Parker, Joe Paterson, Mark Worrell*

Sherfy has been a tough nut to crack since being drafted in the 10th round in 2013. The former Oregon closer had a funky delivery that was hard to pick up for hitters and even tougher to repeat for the pitcher. After a promising debut, he hit a major bump in the road in 2015, walking over five batters per nine at Double-A. Some mechanical tweaks have quieted the delivery and he rebounded to dominate the Southern League in 2016 before a promotion to Triple-A issued yet another blow to his stat line. His fastball can play above average at times, but it's his plus slider that often gets the job done. With better command, he's a big leaguer. Without, he may just stall out at Triple-A.

Braden Shipley   RHP

Born: 2/22/92   Age: 25   Bats: R   Throws: R   Height: 6'1"   Weight: 190   Entered Pro Ball: Round 1, 2013 Draft (#15 overall)

YEAR	TEAM	LVL	AGE	W	L	SV	G	GS	IP	H	HR	BB/9	K/9	K	GB%	BABIP	WHIP	ERA	FIP	DRA	VORP	WARP	cFIP	MPH
2014	SBN	A	22	4	2	0	8	8	45²	46	1	2.2	8.1	41	47%	.336	1.25	3.74	2.83	2.98	12.5	1.3	89	
2014	VIS	A+	22	2	4	0	10	10	60¹	57	7	3.1	10.1	68	48%	.331	1.29	4.03	4.39	3.40	14.7	1.5	86	
2014	MOB	AA	22	1	2	0	4	4	20	14	3	4.5	8.1	18	56%	.216	1.20	3.60	4.84	3.92	2.9	0.3	93	
2015	MOB	AA	23	9	11	0	28	27	156²	147	7	3.2	6.8	118	46%	.294	1.30	3.50	3.55	4.71	6.5	0.7	99	
2016	RNO	AAA	24	8	5	0	19	19	119¹	131	7	1.7	5.8	77	47%	.316	1.28	3.70	3.75	3.68	22.1	2.3	92	
2016	ARI	MLB	24	4	5	0	13	11	70	80	14	3.6	5.5	43	45%	.300	1.54	5.27	5.80	5.82	-3.9	-0.4	125	94.2
2017	ARI	MLB	25	4	5	0	25	11	80	91	11	3.1	6.0	54	51%	.305	1.50	4.89	4.77	5.02	1.0	0.1	100	
2018	ARI	MLB	26	8	10	0	26	26	150²	141	20	4.1	8.3	138	51%	.311	1.39	4.74	4.88	5.28	4.7	0.5	123	

Breakout: 17%   Improve: 35%   Collapse: 34%   Attrition: 43%   MLB: 80%   Comparables: Shairon Martis, Blake Wood, Chad Bettis

After trading Dansby Swanson and his 80-grade hair to Atlanta over the winter, Shipley checked in as Arizona's top prospect for 2016. He debuted in the majors in late July after performing well in the pitching hell hole that is the PCL. That debut didn't go well, as the organization's game plan called for less fastball velocity in favor of more fastball command. This has proven problematic, as Shipley's plus changeup played down when his fastball dipped from 96 to 92 mph. Without the big gap in velocity between the heater and the change, batters whiffed less often, expanding pitch counts and limiting innings in the process. Shipley's third pitch, a curve, is inconsistent but can flash plus at times. Should he put it all together, including adding back more velocity to the fastball without losing his ability to control it, Shipley may be able to emerge as a mid-rotation stalwart.

Taijuan Walker   RHP

Born: 8/13/92   Age: 24   Bats: R   Throws: R   Height: 6'4"   Weight: 235   Entered Pro Ball: Round 1, 2010 Draft (#43 overall)

YEAR	TEAM	LVL	AGE	W	L	SV	G	GS	IP	H	HR	BB/9	K/9	K	GB%	BABIP	WHIP	ERA	FIP	DRA	VORP	WARP	cFIP	MPH
2014	TAC	AAA	21	6	4	0	14	14	73	68	13	3.1	9.1	74	37%	.281	1.27	4.81	5.30	4.22	12.5	1.2	100	
2014	SEA	MLB	21	2	3	0	8	5	38	31	2	4.3	8.1	34	49%	.282	1.29	2.61	3.71	4.28	2.0	0.2	104	98.2
2015	SEA	MLB	22	11	8	0	29	29	169²	163	25	2.1	8.3	157	41%	.291	1.20	4.56	4.04	3.97	21.0	2.2	98	97.2
2016	TAC	AAA	23	1	0	0	3	3	15	12	1	4.8	3.6	6	55%	.220	1.33	3.60	5.59	7.19	-3.1	-0.3	121	
2016	SEA	MLB	23	8	11	0	25	25	134¹	129	27	2.5	8.0	119	45%	.267	1.24	4.22	4.95	3.84	22.7	2.3	97	97.0
2017	ARI	MLB	24	9	11	0	29	29	153²	148	21	2.7	8.9	151	55%	.298	1.27	4.10	4.00	4.30	15.0	1.5	100	
2018	ARI	MLB	25	10	10	0	32	32	207¹	179	28	2.9	9.9	227	55%	.310	1.19	3.92	4.03	4.37	22.3	2.3	99	

Breakout: 31%   Improve: 58%   Collapse: 13%   Attrition: 14%   MLB: 95%   Comparables: Gerrit Cole, David Price, Tommy Hanson

The centerpiece of a blockbuster trade that brought Jean Segura to Seattle, many were surprised the Mariners were willing to trade Walker. It wasn't long ago he was a top prospect with a big, athletic body, a good fastball, and what we'd call a developing secondary offering if we were feeling generous. He was plagued by foot and ankle issues, opting for off-season surgery to remove a bone fragment in his right ankle, and his production was spotty, with glimpses of dominance punctuated by stretches of ineffectiveness. His secondary stuff remained inconsistent and it was hard to tease out what was acting on what. Following a particularly grim September start against the Angels, during which he gave up five earned in less than an inning, he and pitching coach Mel Stottlemyre Jr. worked to retool his mechanics. It worked pretty well considering they were beta testing against big league hitters—Walker closed the season by allowing three or fewer runs in each of his last five starts. A big fastball isn't enough for a starter to live on, and Walker has yet to show the consistency the Mariners hoped for. Now we'll see if the drier air can bring it out.

LINEOUTS

Hitters

NAME	POS	TEAM	LVL	AGE	PA	R	2B	3B	HR	RBI	BB	K	SB	CS	AVG/OBP/SLG	TAv	VORP	BABIP	BRR	FRAA	WARP
Sergio Alcantara	SS	YAK	A-	19	59	12	2	0	0	8	10	10	4	2	.319/.441/.362	.348	7.4	.395	-0.3	SS(15): 2.5	1.0
	SS	KNC	A	19	201	15	6	1	1	16	14	26	3	2	.267/.313/.328	.252	4.2	.299	-1.9	SS(44): 1.7, 3B(5): 0.2	0.6
Phil Gosselin	2B	ARI	MLB	27	240	26	12	1	2	13	15	46	3	0	.277/.324/.368	.248	2.9	.339	-0.3	2B(35): -1.8, 3B(10): -0.6	0.1
Oscar Hernandez	C	VIS	A+	22	133	15	10	0	3	15	18	26	1	0	.295/.402/.464	.305	11.0	.361	-1.2	C(33): 0.6	1.2
	C	MOB	AA	22	150	12	6	0	7	18	5	27	3	0	.194/.227/.382	.218	-0.5	.191	-0.6	C(41): 8.1	0.8
	C	ARI	MLB	22	11	1	0	0	1	1	0	0	0	0	.182/.182/.455	.208	-0.1	.100	0.0	C(4): 0.4	0.0
Jeff Mathis	C	MIA	MLB	33	132	12	4	1	2	15	4	36	0	0	.238/.267/.333	.230	1.9	.318	0.0	C(38): 8.0	1.0
Jack Reinheimer	SS	RNO	AAA	23	560	64	28	7	2	48	48	93	20	11	.288/.353/.384	.268	26.5	.347	-0.9	SS(130): -12.6	1.4
Victor Reyes	OF	VIS	A+	21	509	62	11	12	6	54	33	78	20	8	.303/.341/.416	.284	24.6	.352	1.3	RF(89): -7.6, LF(20): -2.3	1.5
Stryker Trahan	C	VIS	A+	22	155	16	10	0	2	19	15	46	0	2	.201/.277/.317	.207	-6.2	.283	0.4	RF(23): -0.2	-0.7
	C	KNC	A	22	103	7	5	1	2	10	3	30	1	0	.200/.223/.330	.211	-4.1	.265	-0.9	RF(23): -1.6	-0.6
Ildemaro Vargas	INF	MOB	AA	24	351	41	15	2	4	19	24	24	8	0	.276/.325/.372	.260	12.9	.287	-0.7	SS(77): 7.3, 2B(4): -0.1	2.2
	INF	RNO	AAA	24	224	35	13	0	2	18	20	13	13	1	.354/.418/.449	.313	19.9	.372	1.3	2B(45): 3.9, SS(6): 1.5	2.6
Rickie Weeks	PH	ARI	MLB	33	205	29	9	1	9	27	20	54	5	0	.239/.327/.450	.270	8.0	.288	1.3	LF(36): -1.3, RF(2): -0.2	0.7
Jamie Westbrook	2B	MOB	AA	21	473	50	21	1	5	36	26	60	10	5	.262/.312/.349	.239	2.3	.294	0.2	2B(116): 0.6	0.3
Marcus Wilson	CF	YAK	A-	19	177	24	5	2	0	15	38	40	18	3	.252/.418/.319	.306	15.4	.351	1.9	CF(41): -1.7, RF(2): -0.1	1.4
	CF	KNC	A	19	115	11	8	1	1	5	13	32	7	2	.253/.357/.384	.276	6.2	.364	1.0	CF(25): -1.6	0.5

Sergio Alcantara finally hit some in 2016, helping the wiry switch-hitter round out a solid profile at shortstop, where he has a strong arm and can make most of the plays. ❖ **Gabriel Arias** is just 16 years old and has yet to play in recorded games, but he's shown off a strong glove at shortstop and enough with the bat for people to start dreaming on him. ❖ **Phil Gosselin** got by far the most big-league playing time of his career at age 27 and hit enough singles to have some value as a role guy, but that's the extent of his upside. ❖ **Oscar Hernandez** was a rare Rule 5 pick who stuck, thanks to some roster engineering on the part of the Diamondbacks. He's light with the bat, but has the defensive chops to be a solid backup catcher. ❖ The Diamondbacks have found some interesting prospects in Brazil and **Gabriel Maciel** is the latest find. He's a plus-plus runner who should hold down center field easily enough and made plenty of contact in his rookie debut. ❖ A long-ago top prospect turned bust, **Jeff Mathis** is mostly impressive for sustaining a decade-long career in the majors with a TAv of .206. As you'd expect, his FRAA totals are consistently very good and he's got clubhouse popularity in spades. ❖ **Jack Reinheimer** has a quiet, short stroke with gap power to go along with some plate discipline and the ability to make all of the usual plays at shortstop. ❖ There's usually not much desire for light-hitting left fielders, but **Victor Reyes** could make enough contact to dispel that notion. He hit more triples than doubles in 2016 while stealing double-digit bags for the third straight season. ❖ **Stryker Trahan** is built like a brick and can put on the kind of batting practice that will make you take notice. Unfortunately, he's never gotten a feel for the strike zone and his big raw power has never shown up in games. ❖ **Ildemaro Vargas** is the latest indy ball sign for the Diamondbacks to produce something of intrigue. He's not David Peralta, but Vargas has some of the lowest strikeout rates in the minors and the makings of a utility man. ❖ **Rickie Weeks** rode out the 2016 season on Arizona's bench and saw his fair share of pinch-hitting opportunities and spot starts. He showed some pop, but the former All-Star's career outlook continues to slowly dim. ❖ **Jamie Westbrook**'s well-rounded but limited-impact skill set suggests he has a big-league future, though he found rough sledding at Double-A as a 21-year-old. ❖ Drafted as an unpolished athlete, center fielder **Marcus Wilson** has made steady progress. He's a 70-grade runner with a fringy hit tool and limited power, but his ability to get on base shines bright. ❖ **Andy Yerzy** was drafted in the second round as a catcher with big raw power out of a Toronto high school, but probably won't last as a catcher and has trouble making enough contact to use his power.

Pitchers

NAME	TEAM	LVL	AGE	W	L	SV	G	GS	IP	H	HR	BB/9	K/9	K	GB%	BABIP	WHIP	ERA	FIP	DRA	VORP	WARP	cFIP	MPH
Taylor Clarke	KNC	A	23	3	2	0	6	6	28²	24	1	1.6	7.5	24	32%	.277	1.01	2.83	2.78	3.14	6.0	0.7	90	
	VIS	A+	23	1	1	0	4	4	23	19	3	2.7	8.6	22	31%	.262	1.13	2.74	4.80	3.96	3.9	0.4	99	
	MOB	AA	23	8	6	0	17	17	97²	99	9	1.9	6.6	72	38%	.297	1.23	3.59	3.84	5.85	-8.2	-0.9	108	
Daniel Gibson	MOB	AA	24	4	1	0	24	0	22²	22	0	3.2	6.8	17	41%	.324	1.32	0.40	3.14	3.96	1.9	0.2	102	
	RNO	AAA	24	2	0	0	21	0	21	25	4	6.0	7.3	17	56%	.323	1.86	6.86	6.72	6.86	-4.4	-0.5	111	
Steve Hathaway	MOB	AA	25	1	1	0	13	0	15¹	14	1	1.8	5.9	10	49%	.298	1.11	1.17	2.60	3.36	2.3	0.3	96	
	RNO	AAA	25	1	2	1	28	0	29²	21	2	5.8	8.8	29	40%	.260	1.35	3.34	4.66	5.40	-1.4	-0.1	104	
	ARI	MLB	25	0	0	0	24	0	14²	18	1	3.7	9.2	15	50%	.395	1.64	4.91	3.25	4.50	0.8	0.1	100	95.0
Wei-Chieh Huang	VIS	A+	22	1	1	0	6	6	26¹	33	5	4.1	8.5	25	44%	.346	1.71	6.49	5.88	4.88	1.7	0.2	108	
	YAK	A-	22	2	2	0	9	4	30¹	33	4	3.3	12.5	42	39%	.382	1.45	5.34	4.00	1.94	10.4	1.1	81	
Tyler Jones	TRN	AA	26	6	2	11	33	0	45²	45	1	2.2	13.2	67	45%	.379	1.23	2.17	1.50	0.88	19.5	2.1	63	
Matthew Koch	MOB	AA	25	2	4	0	14	14	74²	87	7	1.6	5.9	49	42%	.324	1.34	4.70	3.87	3.39	14.1	1.5	105	
	RNO	AAA	25	4	2	0	7	7	46²	55	3	1.2	4.8	25	55%	.325	1.31	3.09	3.87	3.24	10.9	1.1	97	
	ARI	MLB	25	1	1	1	7	2	18	9	1	2.0	5.0	10	43%	.154	0.72	2.00	3.80	5.48	-0.6	-0.1	115	94.2
Mack Lemieux	YAK	A-	19	1	2	0	7	7	23	24	1	4.7	10.2	26	42%	.359	1.57	3.91	3.90	3.82	3.6	0.4	99	
Yuhei Nakaushiro	VIS	A+	26	0	0	2	13	0	14¹	12	0	5.7	10.0	16	55%	.300	1.47	2.51	3.78	4.47	1.0	0.1	107	
	RNO	AAA	26	0	0	0	13	0	10²	7	0	2.5	11.0	13	46%	.292	0.94	0.00	2.13	2.23	3.2	0.3	87	
Alex Young	KNC	A	22	3	1	0	9	9	50	39	1	2.9	6.7	37	44%	.268	1.10	2.16	3.34	4.53	2.7	0.3	104	
	VIS	A+	22	2	7	0	12	11	68²	79	10	2.8	7.3	56	36%	.324	1.46	4.59	4.98	4.58	6.7	0.7	102	

Taylor Clarke had another solid showing in 2016, reaching Double-A and holding his own. The 2014 third rounder possesses a plus fastball that can touch the mid-90s and an above average slider. ❖ **Jon Duplantier** was drafted in the second round with a first-round arm and a history of injury and overuse at Rice. The ceiling's high, but so is the risk. ❖ **Daniel Gibson** is a polished lefty reliever who's made steady progress in the minors, where the PCL did him no favors in 2016. He's got a solid fastball/slider mix and he's essentially big-league ready. ❖ Lefties who can touch 96 mph don't grow on trees. **Steve Hathaway** reached the majors for the first time at age 25 and acquitted himself well in 24 appearances. ❖ Taiwanese righty **Wei-Chieh Huang** broke out in 2015, his American debut, making an appearance in the Future's Game. Last season was a disappointment, as his control proved problematic. ❖ **Tyler Jones** never got a chance with the Yankees despite a strong season at Double-A Trenton, so the Diamondbacks snagged him in the Rule 5 draft. Now in his fourth pro organization, the fastball/slider right-hander has middle-relief upside. ❖ Acquired from the Mets in the Addison Reed trade, right-hander **Matt Koch** has neither the raw stuff nor the minor-league numbers to create much optimism. ❖ **Mack Lemieux** is a projectable lefty in the low 90s with a potentially plus curveball who pitched well in his debut at just 20. ❖ **Yuhei Nakaushiro** is your typical 27-year old left-handed Japanese rookie reliever who played at four levels, topping out with a brief stint at Triple-A. Despite some solid numbers, scouts see him as a org player. ❖ The D-backs thought they might have quick-mover on their hands when they popped lefty **Alex Young** in the second round of the 2015 draft. Instead, his stuff went backwards after turning pro and a long-term move to the 'pen may be on the horizon.

ATLANTA BRAVES

Essay by Bryan Grosnick

*Player comments by Demetrius Bell, David Lee
and BP staff*

Kid Nichols. Warren Spahn. Greg Maddux. Matt Wisler? It's not crazy to say that the Atlanta Braves and starting pitching go together like biscuits and gravy, and it's certainly not crazy to say that America's Team has lived and died by its hurlers over the past several decades. (No, that's not quite fair to Chipper and Andruw Jones, but that's the way things go.) So when it came time for the front office to embark on a rebuilding project after a disappointing 2014 season, why wouldn't the Braves look to the mound for inspiration? Sure, Theo Epstein and Jeff Luhnow were constructing the Cubs and Astros, respectively, with an eye towards youthful position players. Then again, if there was or is an easy path to building a winner, then we wouldn't need a BP Annual or baseball operations departments or even MLB Network analysts. What we don't know is if the Braves' path of pitching is working. As we enter the first year of the Cobb County era, can we make a little extra sense of how things have gone and where they are going?

Perhaps we should start with a high-level question: *Why did the Braves choose to try and rebuild through pitching?* Make no mistake, the Braves have tried to revamp their team around the acquisition and development of the game's most volatile commodity: the pitching prospect. Of course, the Braves have an absolutely sterling recent history of starting pitching success. Beyond the team's Hall-of-Fame trio of starting pitchers in Maddux, Tom Glavine, and John Smoltz—three pitchers that formed the foundation of nearly two decades of National League dominance—the Braves found a way to acquire or develop other quality starters such as Charlie Liebrandt, Steve Avery, Denny Neagle, Kevin Millwood, Jason Marquis, Mike Hampton and Tim Hudson. Somehow, this team has kept itself rich in righties and loaded with lefties for the better part of 30 years.

There's another smart reason why rebuilding through pitching might have interested the Braves when they were tearing down their team from the early '10s: if teams like the Cubs and Astros were trying to rebuild by acquiring as many young *positional* prospects as possible, then the cost of those position players should have been driven up by the increased demand. Why try to beat them to the punch? If many other teams are looking in one place for talent, then it stands to reason that looking elsewhere

BRAVES PROSPECTUS
2016 W-L: 68-93, 5TH IN NL EAST

Pythag	.413	28th	DER	.707	11th
RS/G	4.01	29th	B-Age	29	23rd
RA/G	4.81	25th	P-Age	26.1	2nd
TAv	.263	12th	Salary	$86.6M	27th
BRR	-8.21	24th	M$/MW	$3.7M	12th
TAv-P	.277	27th	DL Days	1462	27th
FIP	4.36	20th	$ on DL	8%	7th

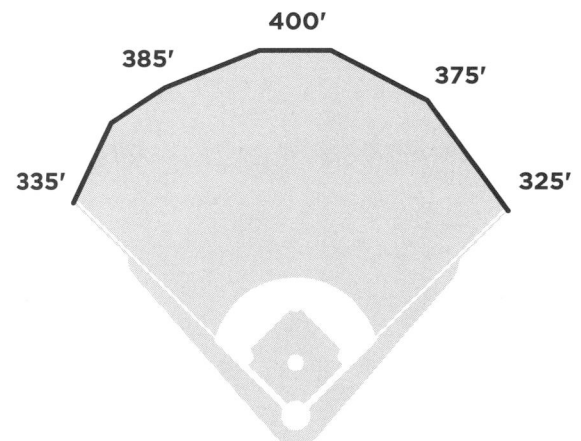

Outfield wall profile: **6′** to **16′**

Three-Year Park Factors

Runs	Runs/RH	Runs/LH	HR/RH	HR/LH
91	86	90	80	86

Top Hitter WARP	6.8	Freddie Freeman
Top Pitcher WARP	3.2	Julio Teheran
Top Prospect		Dansby Swanson

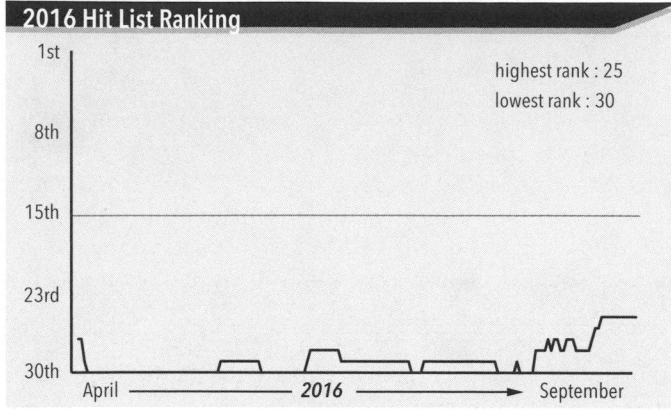

2016 Hit List Ranking

highest rank : 25
lowest rank : 30

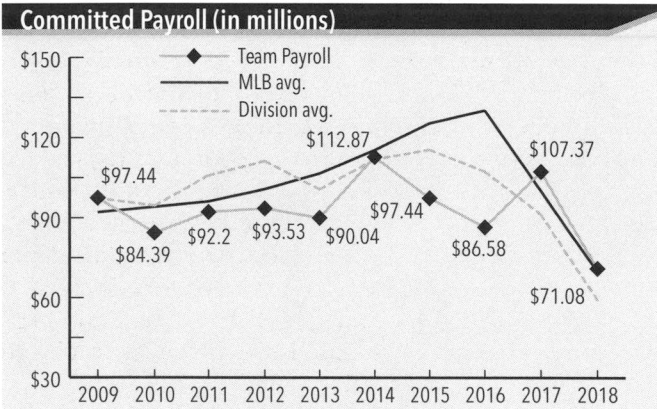

Committed Payroll (in millions)

Legend: Team Payroll ◆ / MLB avg. / Division avg.

$97.44
$84.39
$92.2
$93.53
$112.87
$90.04
$97.44
$86.58
$107.37
$71.08

2009 2010 2011 2012 2013 2014 2015 2016 2017 2018

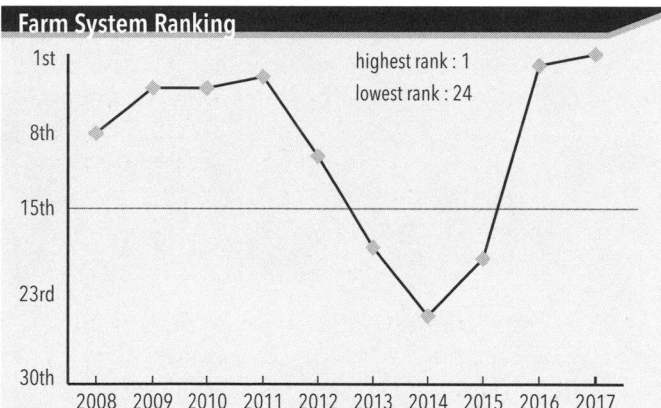

Farm System Ranking

highest rank : 1
lowest rank : 24

2008 2009 2010 2011 2012 2013 2014 2015 2016 2017

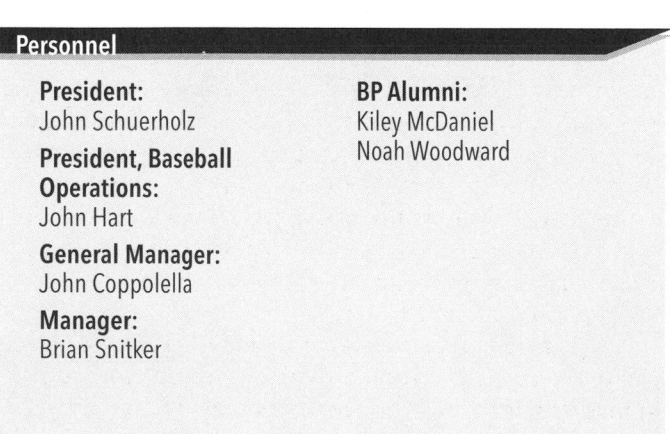

Personnel

President:
John Schuerholz

President, Baseball Operations:
John Hart

General Manager:
John Coppolella

Manager:
Brian Snitker

BP Alumni:
Kiley McDaniel
Noah Woodward

might reap cheaper rewards, finding value that is slipping through the cracks.

Of course, there's also the democratic response: There Is No Such Thing As A Pitching Prospect (TINSTAAPP), Gary Huckabay's oft-acronymed exhortation against relying on the fickle arms of teens. Going into 2017, we think we know the truth—helped along by the recent work of saberists like Jeff Long, Jeff Quinton and others—that while pitching prospects are riskier than position prospects, both types of young players still pan out at a reasonable rate. Make no mistake, betting on young pitchers still feels like staring down the craps table at the tumbling dice, but it's not exactly a complete cipher either.

At the end of 2014, Atlanta was ready for a change. The Braves teams of 2012 and 2013 won 190 games and made the playoffs each season, before their fateful 2014 season: a 79-win disappointment. Despite locking up Andrelton Simmons and Freddie Freeman to the types of long-term deals that fanbases love and franchises long for, the front office chose to dismantle much of the team as it stood, starting with the exceptional Jason Heyward. Within the span of a few months, the team cut ties with several high-value players in Heyward, Jordan Walden, Justin Upton, Evan Gattis and finally Craig Kimbrel. In the return, they received two fistfuls of high-ceiling pitching prospects—you could include young MLB starter Shelby Miller in that group, if you choose—and a handful of secondary position prospects as well. As the next two seasons pushed on, the team collected young pitchers as if it were a middle school student seeking Pokémon. *Gotta catch 'em all.*

There was also what some consider the *coup de grace*, the deal of Miller to Arizona just a year after his acquisition. In return, the Braves picked up pitching prospect Aaron Blair as well as two legitimate position players: underrated and fleet Ender Inciarte and former first-overall pick Dansby Swanson. This deal wasn't exactly like the others in that the team's big-ticket item was a position player, but it was another example of the team targeting young, talented arms—Blair was one of Arizona's top prospects.

When you finally mark it all down in a list, the number of pitching prospects of note that the team acquired in the span of about two and a half years looks very, very substantial.

A Brief History of Braves Pitching Prospect Acquisition (2014-2016)

Tyrell Jenkins	Jason Heyward
Max Fried	Justin Upton
Mike Foltynewicz	Evan Gattis
Matt Wisler	Craig Kimbrel
Manny Banuelos	David Carpenter
Touki Toussaint	Bronson Arroyo's contract/Phil Gosselin
John Gant	Juan Uribe/Kelly Johnson
Rob Whalen	Juan Uribe/Kelly Johnson
Sean Newcomb	Andrelton Simmons
Chris Ellis	Andrelton Simmons

Aaron Blair	Shelby Miller
Casey Kelly	Christian Bethancourt
Sean Radcliffe	Jason Grilli
Akeel Morris	Kelly Johnson, again
Philip Pfeifer	Bud Norris
Caleb Dirks	Bud Norris

That's 16 distinct pitching prospects acquired (17 if you stretch to count Miller, who was entering his age-24 season but had two full seasons of performance under his belt). Yet, the results from these deals haven't actually translated into much MLB value … yet.

This past season, the Braves looked to their young corps of hurlers to fill out the big-league rotation for the first time. It did not go well.

Pitcher	Starts	Innings	ERA	DRA
Matt Wisler	26	156.7	5.00	5.54
Mike Foltynewicz	22	123.3	4.31	4.20
Aaron Blair	15	70	7.59	6.73
Tyrell Jenkins	8	52	5.88	7.42
John Gant	7	50	4.86	3.93
Robert Whalen	5	24.7	6.57	4.91

Wisler improved on his 2015 debut, which is damning with only the faintest whisper of praise. He has solid control, and there's something to like in his slider, but if he could put the ball on the ground instead of in the stands a bit more often, that'd help. Foltynewicz remains one of the league's best post-thoracic outlet syndrome case studies, and finally started tapping into some of his incredible potential. He has a cruiser of a fastball that sits in the mid-90s, and he's able to get many more swings and misses by playing his mid-80s changeup off that pitch. The less said about Blair's rookie season, the better. Left-handed hitters absolutely ate his lunch, brutalizing him to the tune of a .316/.433/.600 slash line. For perspective, imagine that every hitter he faced last year was David Ortiz, the same guy who led all of baseball in doubles, RBI, slugging, and smiles. First guy up: Ortiz. Double. Smile. Next guy up: Ortiz. Homer. Smile. Next guy up: Ortiz. Walk. Smile.

By the close of 2016, John Coppolella lamented his rotation, insisting that the team needed to improve performance. He was certainly right: the Braves had one of the worst DRAs in baseball; their 4.79 team mark was 28th in baseball and that was largely thanks to their awful youngsters. Their cFIP was just slightly better at 27th in the game, which indicates that last season's true talent wasn't very good either. So, at the start of this offseason, Coppolella was moving on. The Braves were bringing in veteran starters on short-term contracts in order to make the team more competitive right away. Gant was paired with fellow traded-for pitching prospect Chris Ellis, and dealt to St. Louis for veteran southpaw Jaime Garcia. Jenkins and Whalen were shipped out for prospects who had faltered in other organizations. And the Braves signed the two oldest starters on the free agent market—Bartolo Colon and R.A. Dickey—to one-year contracts to bridge the gap between now and the uncertain future.

So, TINSTAAPP, right?

The *real* value that the Braves have created thus far was when they flipped Miller for positional prospects later, which was a tremendous deal. So I ask this … do you think that it's possible that the end game isn't necessarily to develop pitching, but rather to develop pitching assets that can perhaps be swapped for positional players? And if that is the case, do you think that the advantage gained by absorbing some risk and playing middle-man outweighs cutting to the chase and dealing directly for the prospects? Is Coppolella Darius from FX's *Atlanta*?

I'll explain. In the other Atlanta, the real-but-surreal version that exists in Donald Glover's head and on our televisions, there's a scene where Glover's Earn—boy, that name's a bit on the nose—hits a pawnshop in order to trade his cell phone for cash. He's at his low point, perhaps like the rebuilding Braves, and he too has become transactional. To meet his needs, to get where he wants to go, he must hustle. Instead of taking the certain cash to make it another week, the philosophical Darius convinces Earn to trade the phone for a katana, promising more money in the end. They trade the sword for a dog, give the dog to a breeder and in the end Earn's left with … nothing. "More money" is coming in October, not when Earn needs it: now.

Could the Braves be taking this same long walk, swapping assets not necessarily for the end pieces, but perhaps the transitional guys? Are they in the market for the guys that get you *the guy*? The Braves sold high on Shelby Miller at exactly the right time, turning his performance into an unparalleled return. Is it possible that guys like Miller, Wisler, Foltynewicz and the like are the katanas and not the cash? If so, would such delayed gratification be worth it? Is the risk and the wait worth the potential gain?

As we venture into 2017, the Braves are moving into their new Cobb County digs and want to give themselves an air of competitiveness. *(Note: we can write a whole second essay about the sketchy stadium deals and middle fingers to taxpayers throughout the south, but there's just no time here.)* The bill has come due; the cash is somewhere out in the future. So the Braves pick up short-term stopgaps, all moves that perhaps add a little value today at the cost of value down the line. Sure, Garcia should be a marked improvement over what Wisler gave the Braves in 2016, but his presence perhaps also prevents the Braves from throwing Wisler out in the rotation again to give him another chance to develop in the majors and turn himself into either a tradeable asset or a present-day contributor.

These moves are possibly a payday loan, or a Walter White-derided half-measure. Unable to completely commit to that long-term outlook, they move towards a short-term fix, albeit one that costs them nothing more than a couple of mid-tier short-term contracts. The big bet on pitching only paid off in the case of Miller and perhaps Foltynewicz so far, and finding out what sticks to the wall works best when the wall is at its largest.

Perhaps the Braves' tolerance for pitching risk is something to be applauded, and they simply have more intestinal fortitude than those who would tread the path of safety. It takes real guts to be willing to shoulder risk, to hold onto your chips through the downturns and the upswings. But I do think that the past two years have taught us a little something about the franchise—that there does not appear to be some outsized institutional advantage towards developing starters in Atlanta anymore. If there

was starting pitching magic in the Atlanta water, that fountain has run dry.

No matter what, the last thing the Braves want is to be three years down the line, still below .500 and looking to trade away Dansby Swanson and Freddie Freeman for prospects so they can rebuild again with an eye towards 2023. With the team they're currently fielding, that option is certainly still in play.

If they ever do fall to that low, maybe it'd be worth it to give up on the exciting young pitchers and start targeting a few more hitters. ■

—Bryan Grosnick is an author of Baseball Prospectus

Hitters

Ronald Acuna   CF

Born: 12/18/97   Age: 19   Bats: R   Throws: R   Height: 6'0"   Weight: 180   Entered Pro Ball: International Free Agent, 2014

YEAR	TEAM	LVL	AGE	PA	R	2B	3B	HR	RBI	BB	K	SB	CS	AVG/OBP/SLG	TAv	VORP	BABIP	BRR	FRAA	WARP
2016	ROM	A	18	171	27	2	2	4	18	18	28	14	7	.311/.387/.432	.326	18.4	.359	2.9	CF(34): 1.2	2.2
2017	ATL	MLB	19	250	32	8	1	6	22	20	69	8	4	.221/.290/.350	.229	0.9	.284	0.0	CF 0, RF -0	0.1
2018	ATL	MLB	20	397	48	14	3	12	46	35	104	14	8	.241/.315/.399	.267	13.8	.300	1.0	CF 0, RF 0	1.5

Breakout: 0%   Improve: 22%   Collapse: 2%   Attrition: 9%   MLB: 31%   Comparables: Mike Trout, Carlos Correa, Jurickson Profar

It's only a matter of time before fans start singing "Hakuna Matata" for Acuna's plate appearances, especially after they see the kid launch a 400-foot blast with a swing that rivals the aggressiveness of Pumbaa's appetite for grubs. Acuna is a full season away from being all over the prospect map, and it would've happened in 2016 if not for a torn thumb ligament that required surgery. He came back late in the season and did more damage as a teenager in the South Atlantic League. Acuna has the reputation of a top-of-the-order hitter with speed, but he shows all five tools, including plus power with even more raw. He shows advanced pitch recognition that should serve him well in the future. Combine all this with the potential to stick in center field and you have a possible All-Star. No worries here.

Ozhaino Albies   SS

Born: 1/7/97   Age: 20   Bats: B   Throws: R   Height: 5'9"   Weight: 160   Entered Pro Ball: International Free Agent, 2013

YEAR	TEAM	LVL	AGE	PA	R	2B	3B	HR	RBI	BB	K	SB	CS	AVG/OBP/SLG	TAv	VORP	BABIP	BRR	FRAA	WARP
2015	ROM	A	18	439	64	21	8	0	37	36	56	29	8	.310/.368/.404	.304	41.5	.358	4.7	SS(93): 5.8	5.0
2016	GWN	AAA	19	247	27	11	3	2	20	19	39	9	4	.248/.307/.351	.242	4.9	.290	1.1	SS(33): 1.5 • 2B(23): 2.1	0.9
2016	MIS	AA	19	371	56	22	7	4	33	33	57	21	9	.321/.391/.467	.339	44.7	.376	4.5	2B(60): 3.1 • SS(22): 2.9	5.5
2017	ATL	MLB	20	250	31	12	2	5	23	18	53	9	4	.258/.318/.393	.250	8.6	.311	0.4	2B 3, SS 2	1.4
2018	ATL	MLB	21	427	50	21	4	9	48	32	86	15	6	.269/.331/.418	.277	22.7	.319	1.5	2B 5, SS 3	3.3

Breakout: 6%   Improve: 22%   Collapse: 0%   Attrition: 7%   MLB: 24%   Comparables: Jonathan Schoop, Rougned Odor, Ronald Torreyes

Albies is such an intense competitor that he expected himself to make the major-league team out of spring training as a 19-year-old and was upset when it didn't happen. He merely responded by winning the Southern League batting title. Albies has a contact-heavy approach that produces consistent line drives to all fields from both sides of the plate. The kid could end up being a plus hitter with plus-plus speed and a plus middle infield glove. That's a lot of pluses. Add his makeup to that list and you have the makings of a reliable everyday player at the top of the lineup. Albies suffered a fractured elbow late in the season and missed fall development time, but the injury shouldn't hinder his future.

Chase d'Arnaud   SS

Born: 1/21/87   Age: 30   Bats: R   Throws: R   Height: 6'2"   Weight: 205   Entered Pro Ball: Round 4, 2008 Draft (#114 overall)

YEAR	TEAM	LVL	AGE	PA	R	2B	3B	HR	RBI	BB	K	SB	CS	AVG/OBP/SLG	TAv	VORP	BABIP	BRR	FRAA	WARP
2014	IND	AAA	27	416	59	16	9	2	23	29	82	30	13	.250/.313/.356	.239	5.8	.312	3.9	CF(38): 2.2 • LF(32): -2.5	0.6
2015	LEH	AAA	28	540	77	18	5	5	35	26	64	28	8	.268/.317/.354	.258	23.7	.298	4.5	SS(87): 2.0 • 3B(34): -1.0	2.5
2015	PHI	MLB	28	18	2	0	1	0	0	1	7	0	1	.176/.222/.294	.185	-1.3	.300	-0.6	SS(3): 0.0 • 3B(1): 0.4	-0.1
2016	GWN	AAA	29	100	11	6	1	1	4	6	16	7	0	.255/.300/.372	.244	2.7	.299	1.8	RF(12): 1.5 • CF(7): -0.4	0.4
2016	ATL	MLB	29	262	24	14	2	1	21	23	50	9	3	.245/.317/.335	.244	4.7	.303	0.4	SS(21): -0.7 • 3B(19): -2.3	0.4
2017	ATL	MLB	30	212	25	8	2	3	15	14	46	9	3	.231/.289/.337	.232	0.3	.286	0.9	3B -1, 1B 0	-0.1
2018	ATL	MLB	31	339	34	13	3	5	31	22	76	13	5	.229/.290/.341	.237	0.1	.284	1.1	3B -1	-0.1

Breakout: 1%   Improve: 11%   Collapse: 9%   Attrition: 18%   MLB: 35%   Comparables: Brian Barden, Chris Valaika, Kris Negron

The frontman of the aptly-named Chase d'Arnaud Band didn't cook up many hits on the field in 2016. d'Arnaud was one of a few players who occasionally replaced Erick Aybar at shortstop during his misadventure of a stint with the Braves and he wasn't much of an improvement. His ceiling is low enough to get kicked off "House Hunters," but on the plus side he's probably the only player in baseball history to play a postgame concert and deliver a walk-off hit within a 24-hour span.

Tyler Flowers C

Born: 1/24/86 Age: 31 Bats: R Throws: R Height: 6'4" Weight: 260 Entered Pro Ball: Round 33, 2005 Draft (#1007 overall)

YEAR	TEAM	LVL	AGE	PA	R	2B	3B	HR	RBI	BB	K	SB	CS	AVG/OBP/SLG	TAv	VORP	BABIP	BRR	FRAA	WARP
2014	CHA	MLB	28	442	42	16	1	15	50	25	159	0	1	.241/.297/.396	.250	13.6	.355	-0.5	C(124): 5.2	2.1
2015	CHA	MLB	29	361	21	12	0	9	39	21	104	0	1	.239/.295/.356	.239	6.2	.320	-1.8	C(110): 14.0 • 1B(2): 0.0	2.2
2016	ATL	MLB	30	325	27	18	0	8	41	29	91	0	0	.270/.357/.420	.295	19.9	.366	-6.4	C(81): 6.7	2.8
2017	ATL	MLB	31	431	41	16	1	12	48	30	140	0	1	.224/.291/.362	.238	8.4	.311	-1.2	C 9	1.2
2018	ATL	MLB	32	378	44	14	0	11	41	28	123	0	0	.221/.293/.359	.244	5.4	.308	-2.2	C 7	1.3

Breakout: 4% Improve: 35% Collapse: 14% Attrition: 20% MLB: 95% *Comparables: Ramon Castro, Ron Karkovice, David Ross*

The plan for Flowers when the Braves signed him to a two-year deal was for him to spend the first year as the more defensive-minded half of a platoon with A.J. Pierzynski. By the time September rolled around, Pierzynski had been usurped by Anthony Recker and Flowers was the only catcher on the roster worthy of starting regularly. It ended up being Flowers' best season at the plate despite a hand injury costing him significant time. His defense took a slight step back, but the Braves weren't complaining too much about that. He's not a good long-term solution, but he's definitely not a bad short-term solution.

YEAR	TEAM	P. COUNT	FRM RUNS	BLK RUNS	THRW RUNS	TOT RUNS
2014	CHA	17840	6.9	-3.5	1.3	4.7
2015	CHA	14504	16.7	-2.8	-0.6	13.4
2016	ATL	11338	12.3	-0.9	-3.7	7.7
2017	ATL	16651	14.3	-2.5	-2.2	9.6
2018	ATL	14611	11.3	-2.4	-2.1	6.9

Freddie Freeman 1B

Born: 9/12/89 Age: 27 Bats: L Throws: R Height: 6'5" Weight: 220 Entered Pro Ball: Round 2, 2007 Draft (#78 overall)

YEAR	TEAM	LVL	AGE	PA	R	2B	3B	HR	RBI	BB	K	SB	CS	AVG/OBP/SLG	TAv	VORP	BABIP	BRR	FRAA	WARP
2014	ATL	MLB	24	708	93	43	4	18	78	90	145	3	4	.288/.386/.461	.315	41.8	.351	-1.4	1B(162): -4.4	4.1
2015	ATL	MLB	25	481	62	27	0	18	66	56	98	3	1	.276/.370/.471	.316	32.5	.321	1.4	1B(117): -9.7	2.4
2016	ATL	MLB	26	693	102	43	6	34	91	89	171	6	1	.302/.400/.569	.350	69.6	.370	-0.9	1B(158): -3.2	6.9
2017	ATL	MLB	27	642	82	33	3	24	88	76	136	3	1	.282/.374/.481	.303	38.8	.330	-0.9	1B -3	3.4
2018	ATL	MLB	28	599	87	34	2	22	83	80	123	2	1	.287/.388/.491	.322	45.2	.336	-0.2	1B -3	4.6

Breakout: 3% Improve: 59% Collapse: 5% Attrition: 5% MLB: 100% *Comparables: Miguel Cabrera, Prince Fielder, John Mayberry*

Going into 2016, the expectations for Freeman were that he'd provide a stabilizing effect on the rest of what figured to be a moribund Braves lineup while also trying to bounce back from two seasons of relative decline. He lived up to those expectations in the first half, hitting .286/.373/.518, and then turned on the jets in the second half. He hit .323/.433/.634 following the break and ended the season with career-bests in most stats. It was a breakout season for the franchise cornerstone and proof that Freeman's ceiling may be higher than most people believed. He did all that mashing while playing through an assortment of ailments (cracked ribs, a cancerous mole removed from his back, a finger injury that bothered him since spring training) and now moves into a new home ballpark that seems tailored to his strengths as a hitter. There's some reason to believe the breakout could be a sign of things to come for Freeman, rather than a fluke. If so, then the Braves will have a bonafide superstar and John Coppolella's promise of trading his own right arm before trading Freeman will look like a a smart move.

Adonis Garcia 3B

Born: 4/12/85 Age: 32 Bats: R Throws: R Height: 5'9" Weight: 205 Entered Pro Ball: International Free Agent, 2012

YEAR	TEAM	LVL	AGE	PA	R	2B	3B	HR	RBI	BB	K	SB	CS	AVG/OBP/SLG	TAv	VORP	BABIP	BRR	FRAA	WARP
2014	SWB	AAA	29	368	58	20	3	9	45	17	51	11	3	.319/.353/.474	.282	23.0	.348	4.3	CF(25): 1.7 • RF(24): 0.7	2.4
2015	GWN	AAA	30	350	43	17	1	3	47	15	41	5	1	.284/.314/.369	.247	8.1	.314	3.4	3B(66): 2.0 • LF(9): 1.0	1.1
2015	ATL	MLB	30	198	20	12	0	10	26	5	35	0	0	.277/.293/.497	.287	11.1	.291	0.1	3B(42): -3.1 • LF(10): 0.4	0.9
2016	GWN	AAA	31	80	14	7	0	4	18	3	12	2	1	.356/.413/.616	.367	8.5	.386	-2.0	LF(17): -0.2	0.9
2016	ATL	MLB	31	563	65	29	0	14	65	24	93	3	2	.273/.311/.406	.258	18.5	.308	1.8	3B(123): -10.7 • LF(4): -0.3	0.8
2017	ATL	MLB	32	610	70	30	1	17	63	24	110	5	2	.265/.300/.408	.254	14.2	.300	-0.9	3B -5	0.3
2018	ATL	MLB	33	545	62	27	1	15	63	23	105	3	1	.262/.298/.410	.260	12.8	.300	0.8	3B -4	0.9

Breakout: 3% Improve: 24% Collapse: 11% Attrition: 23% MLB: 79% *Comparables: Adam Rosales, Greg Dobbs, Don Kelly*

Atlanta sent Garcia to the minors in May of last season because of defense, wanting him to become a left fielder. He ended up returning to the majors at his usual position, third base, and that's where he stayed. His numbers there weren't pretty, but Garcia manned the position capably enough to give the Braves some hope that he can be an asset overall. However, Adonis will probably end up being the Greek God of Bridges, serving as the connection to the next wave of third base talent that will be coming up from the Braves' talent-rich farm system.

Tuffy Gosewisch   C

Born: 8/17/83   Age: 33   Bats: R   Throws: R   Height: 5'11"   Weight: 200   Entered Pro Ball: Round 11, 2005 Draft (#337 overall)

YEAR	TEAM	LVL	AGE	PA	R	2B	3B	HR	RBI	BB	K	SB	CS	AVG/OBP/SLG	TAv	VORP	BABIP	BRR	FRAA	WARP
2014	ARI	MLB	30	132	6	8	0	1	7	3	24	0	0	.225/.242/.310	.211	-0.2	.269	0.5	C(35): -1.1	-0.1
2015	ARI	MLB	31	138	9	6	0	1	13	8	23	2	1	.211/.261/.281	.240	4.7	.248	1.4	C(37): -1.4	0.4
2016	RNO	AAA	32	219	33	13	1	9	26	15	30	0	0	.342/.399/.553	.315	21.0	.369	-1.4	C(57): 0.5	2.2
2016	ARI	MLB	32	99	8	1	1	3	7	7	22	0	0	.156/.224/.289	.183	-2.8	.169	0.5	C(31): -3.3	-0.6
2017	ATL	MLB	33	93	8	4	0	2	9	5	18	0	0	.230/.276/.345	.231	1.7	.267	-0.2	C -1	0.0
2018	ATL	MLB	34	169	17	7	0	3	16	9	35	0	0	.223/.270/.333	.228	0.7	.263	0.6	C -3	-0.2

Breakout: 2%   Improve: 20%   Collapse: 20%   Attrition: 29%   MLB: 71%   Comparables: Shawn Wooten, Wil Nieves, Koyie Hill

Gosewisch is equivalent to an eggplant, in that if it shows up in your food once in a while, you're OK with it. If it's a staple of your everyday lineup, you start to hate life rather quickly. At age 33, his career as a mediocre backup catcher looks set in stone. Gosewisch has never hit in the majors and his framing numbers aren't inspiring. An 80-grade name and too many 30-grade tools, although BP's own Patrick Dubuque is lucky to have him as a muse.

YEAR	TEAM	P. COUNT	FRM RUNS	BLK RUNS	THRW RUNS	TOT RUNS
2014	ARI	4630	-1.7	1.0	0.4	-0.3
2015	ARI	5113	-1.7	0.9	0.3	-0.5
2016	ARI	4045	-2.4	-0.6	0.0	-3.0
2017	ATL	2496	-1.3	0.0	0.1	-1.2
2018	ATL	4548	-2.8	0.0	0.0	-2.8

Ender Inciarte   CF

Born: 10/29/90   Age: 26   Bats: L   Throws: L   Height: 5'11"   Weight: 190   Entered Pro Ball: International Free Agent, 2008

YEAR	TEAM	LVL	AGE	PA	R	2B	3B	HR	RBI	BB	K	SB	CS	AVG/OBP/SLG	TAv	VORP	BABIP	BRR	FRAA	WARP
2014	RNO	AAA	23	120	22	4	2	2	12	10	21	7	2	.312/.367/.440	.276	8.1	.368	2.2	CF(25): -2.1	0.6
2014	ARI	MLB	23	447	54	18	2	4	27	25	53	19	3	.278/.318/.359	.252	10.3	.310	2.3	CF(76): 9.3 • LF(37): 6.9	2.9
2015	MOB	AA	24	23	3	1	1	1	1	3	2	0	0	.300/.391/.600	.369	3.1	.294	0.0	CF(4): 0.5 • RF(1): 0.1	0.4
2015	ARI	MLB	24	561	73	27	5	6	45	26	58	21	10	.303/.338/.408	.277	27.1	.329	6.5	RF(77): 2.7 • LF(47): 7.7	4.1
2016	ATL	MLB	25	578	85	24	7	3	29	45	68	16	7	.291/.351/.381	.274	26.2	.329	0.4	CF(120): 15.5 • LF(10): 3.3	4.6
2017	ATL	MLB	26	636	75	26	4	7	51	43	78	22	8	.280/.329/.379	.259	23.4	.307	1.1	CF 16	3.5
2018	ATL	MLB	27	587	68	26	4	9	60	43	76	19	8	.286/.341/.404	.278	29.5	.313	2.9	CF 15	4.8

Breakout: 2%   Improve: 55%   Collapse: 6%   Attrition: 15%   MLB: 97%   Comparables: Cookie Rojas, Richie Ashburn, Melky Cabrera

Had the Braves received just Inciarte in exchange for Shelby Miller it would've been initially received as a fair trade for both sides. Of course, Inciarte wasn't the only asset in the deal that continues to tilt further and further in Atlanta's favor. He had a rough start to 2016 due to an injury and struggles at the plate, but things turned around by the All-Star break. He hit .341/.396/.440 in the second half and served as a capable leadoff man for a Braves offense that was shockingly good in that span. The second-half resurgence was a nice complement to the always-excellent defense that never wavered. As a result, the Game Ender finished his season on a high and there's still room to develop into an all-around star.

Alex Jackson   RF

Born: 12/25/95   Age: 21   Bats: R   Throws: R   Height: 6'2"   Weight: 215   Entered Pro Ball: Round 1, 2014 Draft (#6 overall)

YEAR	TEAM	LVL	AGE	PA	R	2B	3B	HR	RBI	BB	K	SB	CS	AVG/OBP/SLG	TAv	VORP	BABIP	BRR	FRAA	WARP
2015	CLN	A	19	121	10	6	0	0	13	6	35	1	1	.157/.240/.213	.187	-6.3	.230	0.5	RF(18): -0.2 • LF(10): -2.8	-1.0
2015	EVE	A-	19	197	31	11	1	8	25	21	61	2	4	.239/.365/.466	.290	9.9	.326	0.4	RF(38): 5.4 • CF(3): 1.1	1.7
2016	CLN	A	20	381	43	20	1	11	55	34	103	2	1	.243/.332/.408	.284	18.8	.317	3.4	RF(54): 0.5 • LF(10): 0.5	2.4
2017	ATL	MLB	21	250	23	9	0	7	27	17	87	0	0	.193/.266/.331	.212	-5.3	.273	-0.5	RF 1, LF -0	-0.5
2018	ATL	MLB	22	323	36	12	1	10	35	23	110	0	0	.197/.273/.347	.231	-3.3	.273	-0.7	RF 2, LF 0	-0.3

Breakout: 0%   Improve: 2%   Collapse: 0%   Attrition: 2%   MLB: 4%   Comparables: Marcell Ozuna, Caleb Gindl, Yorman Rodriguez

Accounting for the disappointment he must have felt after being held back in extended spring and then hitting in a pitcher's circuit once he finally arrived in the Midwest League, Jackson's 2016 numbers are actually pretty good. But the power hides some serious deficiencies in his game, most notably his 27 percent strikeout rate. The root causes are easy enough to identify: he still struggles with spin, routinely expands the zone and doesn't cover the outer half of the plate. Moving Jackson off of catcher after being drafted was supposed to speed up his ascent through the minors, but he's plodding along like one anyway. The Braves will now try their luck with Jackson after Jerry Dipoto sacrificed him to the gods of the previous regime, but they're going to be pretty surprised when they realize Jackson isn't a pitcher.

Matt Kemp   LF

Born: 9/23/84   Age: 32   Bats: R   Throws: R   Height: 6'4"   Weight: 210   Entered Pro Ball: Round 6, 2003 Draft (#181 overall)

YEAR	TEAM	LVL	AGE	PA	R	2B	3B	HR	RBI	BB	K	SB	CS	AVG/OBP/SLG	TAv	VORP	BABIP	BRR	FRAA	WARP
2014	LAN	MLB	29	599	77	38	3	25	89	52	145	8	5	.287/.346/.506	.307	37.7	.345	-0.8	RF(59): -0.8 • LF(44): -2.1	3.7
2015	SDN	MLB	30	648	80	31	3	23	100	39	147	12	2	.265/.312/.443	.273	21.2	.311	1.8	RF(149): 4.5	2.8
2016	SDN	MLB	31	431	54	24	0	23	69	16	100	0	0	.262/.285/.489	.269	11.0	.288	-0.4	RF(97): -7.3	0.4
2016	ATL	MLB	31	241	35	15	0	12	39	20	56	1	0	.280/.336/.519	.307	18.3	.316	1.5	LF(54): -1.6	1.7
2017	ATL	MLB	32	593	70	28	2	23	79	44	145	7	2	.261/.316/.447	.269	24.7	.310	-0.2	LF -3	1.8
2018	ATL	MLB	33	525	66	24	1	20	68	39	133	5	1	.253/.309/.432	.270	18.1	.305	0.4	LF -2	1.7

Breakout: 0%   Improve: 33%   Collapse: 5%   Attrition: 12%   MLB: 97%   Comparables: Ryan Ludwick, Cody Ross, Geoff Jenkins

After the grand Hector Olivera experiment crashed and burned in a spectacular manner, the Braves filled their left field hole in mid-August with Kemp. He's made a habit out of surging at the plate in second halves and did it again in Atlanta, hitting .280/.336/.519 with 12 homers in 56 games as the Braves' entire lineup produced surprisingly well. It's a good thing that Kemp is still solid at the plate—abandoning all attempts to work counts in an effort to keep the homer totals up—because his defense has continued to regress. On the wrong side of 30 and with arthritic hips, the FRAAs aren't getting any less ugly, but he'll play as long as the power stays.

Kevin Maitan   INF

Born: 2/12/00 Age: 17 Bats: B Throws: R Height: 6'2" Weight: 190 Entered Pro Ball: International Free Agent, 2016

As is typical with international talent, fans were freaking out about Maitan before they even knew about him. It's usually not that justified, but Maitan could be the exception, so go ahead and freak out now. Scouts sometimes like to mention Miguel Cabrera when comparing a young international prospect, but they usually do so with only specific parts of a kid's game, such as his opposite-field power potential, swing or body. With Maitan, you kinda see it all. He has the potential to be a plus hit/plus power switch-hitter on the left side of the infield (growth could move him to third). He was born in 2000 (we're all getting old), so he's forever and a day away and so much could happen over that span, but this kid has the ingredients to be the real deal.

Nick Markakis   RF

Born: 11/17/83 Age: 33 Bats: L Throws: L Height: 6'1" Weight: 215 Entered Pro Ball: Round 1, 2003 Draft (#7 overall)

YEAR	TEAM	LVL	AGE	PA	R	2B	3B	HR	RBI	BB	K	SB	CS	AVG/OBP/SLG	TAv	VORP	BABIP	BRR	FRAA	WARP
2014	BAL	MLB	30	710	81	27	1	14	50	62	84	4	2	.276/.342/.386	.272	17.4	.299	-1.8	RF(147): 7.1 • 1B(2): -0.2	2.7
2015	ATL	MLB	31	686	73	38	1	3	53	70	83	2	1	.296/.370/.376	.283	25.5	.338	-1.8	RF(153): -8.0	1.9
2016	ATL	MLB	32	684	67	38	0	13	89	71	101	0	2	.269/.346/.397	.275	19.6	.300	-3.1	RF(150): -5.9 • 1B(1): 0.1	1.4
2017	ATL	MLB	33	619	59	27	1	8	60	57	83	2	1	.268/.338/.368	.259	13.2	.299	-1.6	RF 0	0.9
2018	ATL	MLB	34	521	60	21	0	7	48	54	73	0	0	.262/.341/.356	.264	11.4	.296	-1.5	RF 0	1.2

Breakout: 3%   Improve: 24%   Collapse: 8%   Attrition: 22%   MLB: 89%   *Comparables: Willard Marshall, Tony Gwynn, Lee Thomas*

Markakis upped his homer total by more than 300 percent from 2015 to 2016 ... and still slugged below .400. Those numbers are in line with what he put up for most of his time in Baltimore and at age 33 he's regressed as a defender. The fact that Markakis wasn't traded during the first two seasons of a four-year deal with the Braves is a surprise, although perhaps it just means there isn't much market for sub-2.0 WARP corner outfielders with sizable salaries. He's consistent like fast food—you know what you're going to get and there are better options out there, but it'll tide you over for the time being.

Jace Peterson   2B

Born: 5/9/90 Age: 27 Bats: L Throws: R Height: 6'0" Weight: 215 Entered Pro Ball: Round 1, 2011 Draft (#58 overall)

YEAR	TEAM	LVL	AGE	PA	R	2B	3B	HR	RBI	BB	K	SB	CS	AVG/OBP/SLG	TAv	VORP	BABIP	BRR	FRAA	WARP
2014	SAN	AA	24	83	10	3	0	1	7	9	9	4	3	.311/.386/.392	.291	7.2	.344	1.3	SS(17): -0.8 • 3B(1): 0.0	0.7
2014	SDN	MLB	24	58	3	0	0	0	0	2	18	2	0	.113/.161/.113	.107	-6.4	.171	0.3	2B(14): 1.1 • 3B(10): 0.4	-0.5
2014	ELP	AAA	24	299	44	21	6	2	39	42	50	12	6	.306/.406/.464	.356	8.7	.374	0.1	SS(28): -0.5 • 2B(25): 1.8	0.9
2015	ATL	MLB	25	597	55	23	5	6	52	56	120	12	10	.239/.314/.335	.251	12.4	.296	2.3	2B(144): -3.4	1.0
2016	GWN	AAA	26	110	8	3	2	0	6	11	15	2	2	.186/.275/.258	.194	-4.3	.220	0.2	2B(16): 1.8 • CF(10): 0.2	-0.2
2016	ATL	MLB	26	408	45	16	1	7	29	52	69	5	5	.254/.350/.366	.275	16.6	.296	-0.4	2B(87): 3.2 • LF(15): -1.3	1.9
2017	ATL	MLB	27	526	55	21	4	7	45	56	102	10	7	.238/.320/.346	.244	11.7	.284	-0.9	2B 5	1.3
2018	ATL	MLB	28	499	56	19	3	8	47	55	100	9	7	.232/.319/.350	.250	11.5	.276	1.3	2B 5	1.8

Breakout: 10%   Improve: 38%   Collapse: 8%   Attrition: 19%   MLB: 94%   *Comparables: Chris Getz, Alexi Casilla, DJ LeMahieu*

You could say Jace is an ace of all trades and a master of none. He spent most of last season attempting to master the art of second base while taking up side hobbies at third base, left field and center field. He's not the worst defender in the world at second, but might have more value moving around the diamond. Peterson provided solid, walk-heavy production at the plate, looking like a quality regular for the first time since being in the Padres' farm system. Jace is the space where you take a rest in order to get to that place of greener pastures.

A.J. Pierzynski   C

Born: 12/30/76 Age: 40 Bats: L Throws: R Height: 6'3" Weight: 250 Entered Pro Ball: Round 3, 1994 Draft (#71 overall)

YEAR	TEAM	LVL	AGE	PA	R	2B	3B	HR	RBI	BB	K	SB	CS	AVG/OBP/SLG	TAv	VORP	BABIP	BRR	FRAA	WARP
2014	BOS	MLB	37	274	19	10	1	4	31	9	40	0	0	.254/.286/.348	.233	1.6	.282	-2.0	C(64): -4.2	-0.3
2014	SLN	MLB	37	88	6	2	0	1	6	5	14	0	1	.244/.295/.305	.224	-0.5	.284	-1.0	C(23): -5.4	-0.7
2015	ATL	MLB	38	436	38	24	1	9	49	19	37	0	2	.300/.339/.430	.281	25.2	.310	-2.4	C(107): -12.1	1.4
2016	ATL	MLB	39	259	15	15	0	2	23	6	29	1	0	.219/.243/.304	.194	-7.0	.237	-1.0	C(64): -7.8	-1.5
2017	ATL	MLB	40	280	26	12	1	7	31	10	41	1	0	.252/.286/.379	.231	4.6	.272	-1.2	C -12	-0.8
2018	ATL	MLB	41	236	24	10	1	5	23	8	37	0	0	.238/.272/.355	.229	0.2	.262	-1.0	C -11	-1.2

Breakout: 3%   Improve: 20%   Collapse: 10%   Attrition: 28%   MLB: 63%   *Comparables: Sandy Alomar Jr., Ivan Rodriguez, Jose Molina*

Pierzynski bounced back from two years of steep decline to perform at an above-average level in 2015, but whatever magic he conjured up completely evaporated by 2016. At age 39 he went from being in a platoon with Tyler Flowers to eventually sitting third on the depth chart, announcing his retirement after 19 years of hitting .280 and constantly annoying opponents. Despite not becoming a regular until age 24, he ranks sixth all-time in games started at catcher, logging more than 16,000 innings behind the plate.

YEAR	TEAM	P. COUNT	FRM RUNS	BLK RUNS	THRW RUNS	TOT RUNS
2014	BOS	8804	-2.3	-0.7	-0.9	-3.9
2014	SLN	2922	-4.0	-0.4	-1.0	-5.5
2015	ATL	14752	-9.5	-1.3	-1.0	-11.9
2016	ATL	8982	-5.4	-4.1	-0.5	-10.0
2017	ATL	9979	-7.9	-2.6	-0.6	-11.1
2018	ATL	8400	-7.9	-2.2	-0.7	-10.8

ATLANTA BRAVES – 35

Anthony Recker   C

Born: 8/29/83   Age: 33   Bats: R   Throws: R   Height: 6'2"   Weight: 240   Entered Pro Ball: Round 18, 2005 Draft (#551 overall)

YEAR	TEAM	LVL	AGE	PA	R	2B	3B	HR	RBI	BB	K	SB	CS	AVG/OBP/SLG	TAv	VORP	BABIP	BRR	FRAA	WARP
2014	NYN	MLB	30	189	18	9	0	7	27	10	64	1	1	.201/.246/.374	.239	5.2	.267	1.2	C(52): -10.8	-0.6
2015	LVG	AAA	31	108	17	3	1	8	21	12	26	0	0	.245/.343/.553	.287	6.7	.250	-0.3	C(21): 0.5 • 1B(2): -0.1	0.7
2015	NYN	MLB	31	92	6	1	0	2	5	11	35	1	0	.125/.239/.213	.180	-3.5	.186	-0.1	C(28): -4.4 • 3B(1): -0.0	-0.9
2016	COH	AAA	32	76	10	5	0	2	10	14	17	1	0	.246/.395/.426	.302	4.1	.310	-1.7	C(12): -12.8 • P(1): -0.0	-0.9
2016	GWN	AAA	32	154	20	6	0	6	18	16	45	0	0	.243/.325/.419	.268	8.1	.314	0.5	C(34): 0.6 • 1B(1): -0.0	0.9
2016	ATL	MLB	32	112	6	8	0	2	15	16	22	1	0	.278/.394/.433	.317	11.1	.343	-0.3	C(28): -7.9	0.3
2017	*ATL*	*MLB*	*33*	*186*	*20*	*7*	*0*	*6*	*21*	*19*	*57*	*1*	*0*	*.211/.297/.371*	*.243*	*5.6*	*.276*	*-0.3*	*C -9*	*-0.6*
2018	*ATL*	*MLB*	*34*	*180*	*22*	*6*	*0*	*6*	*21*	*18*	*56*	*0*	*0*	*.210/.297/.368*	*.247*	*4.0*	*.275*	*0.1*	*C -9*	*-0.6*

Breakout: 4%   Improve: 22%   Collapse: 13%   Attrition: 23%   MLB: 74%   Comparables: *Chris Snyder, David Ross, Mike Rivera*

It finally happened. After years of twisting in the wind as an unreliable backup catcher, Recker played 33 games for the Braves and became a *reliable* backup catcher in 2016. He was thrust into the role following an injury to Tyler Flowers and finished the season with the best numbers of his career at the plate. Granted, those numbers aren't nearly as handsome as the man himself, but they were good enough that he can probably get another season in the majors under his belt. That's not the worst ceiling to have as a baseball player.

YEAR	TEAM	P. COUNT	FRM RUNS	BLK RUNS	THRW RUNS	TOT RUNS
2014	NYN	6531	-13.0	1.2	0.2	-11.6
2015	LVG	2639	-0.1	-0.1	-0.1	-0.1
2015	NYN	3145	-4.4	0.6	-0.1	-3.8
2016	ATL	3963	-7.1	0.6	-0.5	-6.9
2017	*ATL*	*5814*	*-10.0*	*0.7*	*-0.5*	*-9.7*
2018	*ATL*	*5621*	*-10.2*	*0.6*	*-0.5*	*-10.1*

Austin Riley   3B

Born: 4/2/97   Age: 20   Bats: R   Throws: R   Height: 6'3"   Weight: 220   Entered Pro Ball: Round 1, 2015 Draft (#41 overall)

YEAR	TEAM	LVL	AGE	PA	R	2B	3B	HR	RBI	BB	K	SB	CS	AVG/OBP/SLG	TAv	VORP	BABIP	BRR	FRAA	WARP
2016	ROM	A	19	543	68	39	2	20	80	39	147	3	3	.271/.324/.479	.300	31.9	.341	-2.6	3B(122): 3.6	3.9
2017	*ATL*	*MLB*	*20*	*250*	*25*	*11*	*1*	*9*	*31*	*15*	*87*	*0*	*0*	*.212/.264/.382*	*.224*	*-1.8*	*.290*	*-0.5*	*3B 2*	*0.1*
2018	*ATL*	*MLB*	*21*	*382*	*46*	*17*	*1*	*15*	*48*	*26*	*128*	*0*	*0*	*.223/.280/.404*	*.250*	*3.6*	*.300*	*-0.9*	*3B 4*	*0.8*

Breakout: 4%   Improve: 12%   Collapse: 0%   Attrition: 5%   MLB: 14%   Comparables: *Miguel Sano, Matt Davidson, Matt Olson*

For many, Riley is one of the most difficult players in the minors to peg. Some see the raw power—which borders on plus-plus and sends balls screaming into the next hemisphere—and they want to buy into a power-hitting corner infielder. Some see a strikeout machine who struggled to consistently barrel average velocity in his first full season of the low minors, and they can't write him up higher than Triple-A. The key to unlocking his future is as obvious as his prodigious strength: the hit tool. If Riley can barrel enough pitches to hit .250 in the majors, the power will play at either third or first. If he can't get to fastballs on the inner third while laying off soft stuff away, he's a minor-league bat.

Sean Rodriguez   2B

Born: 4/26/85   Age: 32   Bats: R   Throws: R   Height: 6'0"   Weight: 200   Entered Pro Ball: Round 3, 2003 Draft (#90 overall)

YEAR	TEAM	LVL	AGE	PA	R	2B	3B	HR	RBI	BB	K	SB	CS	AVG/OBP/SLG	TAv	VORP	BABIP	BRR	FRAA	WARP
2014	TBA	MLB	29	259	30	13	3	12	41	10	66	2	1	.211/.258/.443	.260	3.3	.235	-1.4	2B(23): -0.7 • 1B(18): 0.5	0.1
2015	PIT	MLB	30	240	25	12	1	4	17	5	63	2	2	.246/.281/.362	.230	-0.9	.325	2.2	1B(102): -0.8, LF(16): -1.8	-0.4
2016	PIT	MLB	31	342	49	16	1	18	56	33	102	2	1	.270/.349/.510	.296	20.6	.344	-0.9	1B(57): 4.0 • 2B(29): -0.0	2.3
2017	*ATL*	*MLB*	*32*	*383*	*39*	*16*	*2*	*12*	*44*	*26*	*104*	*3*	*2*	*.231/.292/.389*	*.245*	*7.7*	*.288*	*-0.5*	*2B 3, RF 1*	*0.8*
2018	*ATL*	*MLB*	*33*	*288*	*33*	*11*	*1*	*9*	*32*	*21*	*80*	*2*	*1*	*.222/.291/.376*	*.246*	*3.9*	*.278*	*0.0*	*2B 2, RF 1*	*0.6*

Breakout: 12%   Improve: 38%   Collapse: 6%   Attrition: 22%   MLB: 98%   Comparables: *Robby Thompson, Jeff Kent, Ryan Raburn*

After a disastrous first season in Pittsburgh, Rodriguez rebounded nicely, earning the third-most PA of his career and doubling his career WARP. The utility player spent the most time at first base, but appeared at every position save catcher and pitcher, and per usual he hit lefties (.325 TAv) better than righties (.285 TAv). Add it all up, and Rodriguez was pretty much the perfect part-time player. Rodriguez's free agency came at a good time, as versatility and platooning are en vogue. The only problem? Consistency is too, and it requires quite the leap of faith to think Rodriguez's 2016 production will be the norm moving forward.

Rio Ruiz   3B

Born: 5/22/94   Age: 23   Bats: L   Throws: R   Height: 6'1"   Weight: 230   Entered Pro Ball: Round 4, 2012 Draft (#129 overall)

YEAR	TEAM	LVL	AGE	PA	R	2B	3B	HR	RBI	BB	K	SB	CS	AVG/OBP/SLG	TAv	VORP	BABIP	BRR	FRAA	WARP
2014	LNC	A+	20	602	76	37	2	11	77	82	91	4	4	.293/.387/.436	.293	35.5	.335	-3.7	3B(105): -6.1 • 3B(11): -6.1	2.4
2015	MIS	AA	21	489	48	21	1	5	46	63	94	2	2	.233/.333/.324	.259	10.9	.288	-2.8	3B(120): 6.7	1.9
2016	GWN	AAA	22	533	52	24	3	10	62	61	116	1	4	.271/.355/.400	.265	14.8	.337	-3.8	3B(119): -6.6	0.8
2016	ATL	MLB	22	7	1	0	1	0	2	0	2	1	0	.286/.286/.571	.251	0.3	.400	0.2	3B(2): -0.1	0.0
2017	*ATL*	*MLB*	*23*	*27*	*3*	*1*	*0*	*1*	*3*	*3*	*7*	*0*	*0*	*.230/.315/.349*	*.243*	*0.5*	*.292*	*-0.1*		*0.1*
2018	*ATL*	*MLB*	*24*	*292*	*35*	*12*	*1*	*7*	*30*	*32*	*72*	*0*	*0*	*.234/.321/.369*	*.257*	*9.0*	*.296*	*-0.7*	*-*	*1.0*

Breakout: 8%   Improve: 24%   Collapse: 6%   Attrition: 21%   MLB: 33%   Comparables: *Garin Cecchini, Taylor Green, Zelous Wheeler*

After going through some struggles at Double-A in 2015, Ruiz was at a bit of a crossroads. He received a pep talk from John Hart, which amounted to "get in better shape, please" and Ruiz took the advice to heart, emerging as one of the better young players in the International League. Assuming all goes well during spring training, Ruiz should be seeing major-league action right out of the gate this season. As much as he improved most facets of his game in 2016, Rio struggled to make his way up the river at the plate against lefties, so he'll probably be joining a platoon once he gets to the majors. Still, he's clearly in a better place now than he was at this time last year.

Mallex Smith   CF

Born: 5/6/93   Age: 24   Bats: L   Throws: R   Height: 5'9"   Weight: 180   Entered Pro Ball: Round 5, 2012 Draft (#165 overall)

YEAR	TEAM	LVL	AGE	PA	R	2B	3B	HR	RBI	BB	K	SB	CS	AVG/OBP/SLG	TAv	VORP	BABIP	BRR	FRAA	WARP
2014	FTW	A	21	303	56	13	6	0	15	38	55	48	16	.295/.393/.394	.286	21.8	.373	3.9	CF(63): -0.5	2.2
2014	LEL	A+	21	261	43	16	1	5	16	31	48	40	10	.327/.414/.475	.330	27.5	.400	2.1	CF(33): -4.0 • RF(4): -0.8	1.8
2015	MIS	AA	22	241	35	5	2	2	22	27	41	23	6	.340/.418/.413	.335	29.3	.412	4.1	CF(55): -0.5	3.1
2015	GWN	AAA	22	307	49	12	6	0	13	24	44	34	7	.281/.339/.367	.268	16.2	.332	4.4	CF(68): 1.2	1.8
2016	MIS	AA	23	20	4	0	1	0	4	4	5	3	1	.438/.550/.563	.447	4.0	.636	-0.3	CF(5): 1.3	0.6
2016	ATL	MLB	23	215	28	7	4	3	22	20	48	16	8	.238/.316/.365	.255	5.0	.302	0.2	CF(35): 3.1 • LF(22): 0.4	0.9
2017	ATL	MLB	24	246	32	9	3	3	20	22	55	20	7	.257/.324/.370	.255	8.8	.320	2.2	CF 2, LF -2	0.8
2018	ATL	MLB	25	446	51	17	5	7	44	40	99	36	12	.261/.334/.385	.268	19.8	.322	4.9	CF 3, LF -3	2.1

Breakout: 7%   Improve: 37%   Collapse: 8%   Attrition: 15%   MLB: 66%   Comparables: Jacoby Ellsbury, Julio Borbon, Gary Brown

When Smith was actually on the field, the young outfielder provided a thrill a minute. He's a certified burner who proved he smells blood on the basepaths by suffering a nasty cut on his forehead while attempting to swipe his first major-league bag and made full-time work for MLB's replay center sorting out the routine plays his speed turned into close calls. The main issue for Smith was staying healthy. A thumb injury robbed him of a couple months, and when he returned in September he was relegated to the role of fourth outfielder. That might turn out to be his ideal role; he has the defensive tools and speed to be productive, but his bat is holding him back from being an everyday asset.

Dansby Swanson   SS

Born: 2/11/94   Age: 23   Bats: R   Throws: R   Height: 6'1"   Weight: 190   Entered Pro Ball: Round 1, 2015 Draft (#1 overall)

YEAR	TEAM	LVL	AGE	PA	R	2B	3B	HR	RBI	BB	K	SB	CS	AVG/OBP/SLG	TAv	VORP	BABIP	BRR	FRAA	WARP
2015	YAK	A-	21	99	19	7	3	1	11	14	14	0	0	.289/.394/.482	.372	17.9	.333	2.5	SS(22): 1.7	2.1
2016	CAR	A+	22	93	14	12	0	1	10	15	13	7	1	.333/.441/.526	.361	14.9	.391	1.0	SS(21): 1.3	1.7
2016	MIS	AA	22	377	54	13	5	8	45	35	71	6	2	.261/.342/.402	.295	29.9	.309	2.0	SS(83): 16.0	5.0
2016	ATL	MLB	22	145	20	7	1	3	17	13	34	3	0	.302/.361/.442	.303	13.1	.383	0.8	SS(37): -2.2	1.1
2017	ATL	MLB	23	531	59	23	3	14	58	47	121	5	1	.253/.324/.407	.265	25.5	.308	0.0	SS 10	3.3
2018	ATL	MLB	24	512	64	22	3	16	62	46	118	5	1	.257/.330/.424	.281	28.5	.311	0.1	SS 10	4.2

Breakout: 6%   Improve: 43%   Collapse: 9%   Attrition: 18%   MLB: 77%   Comparables: Marcus Semien, Eugenio Suarez, Wilmer Flores

The crown jewel of the Braves' grand heist of Arizona's prospect chest was put on display in mid-August after being molded and cast in Atlanta's minor-league system for a few months. Any worries that the jump from Double-A to the majors would be too much for Swanson were allayed when he displayed a skill set both at the plate and in the field that proved he was ready. He'll still be considered a rookie for the 2017 season, but this year won't be about proving that he belongs. It'll be more about showing that he's worth being considered a cornerstone of the Braves' keystone combination. If he can continue to make strides at the plate and develop his defensive skills, then the Braves will have a beautiful piece of jewelry to display in their case—even if it was acquired in a heist from the desert.

PITCHERS

Kolby Allard   LHP

Born: 8/13/97   Age: 19   Bats: L   Throws: L   Height: 6'1"   Weight: 180   Entered Pro Ball: Round 1, 2015 Draft (#14 overall)

YEAR	TEAM	LVL	AGE	W	L	SV	G	GS	IP	H	HR	BB/9	K/9	K	GB%	BABIP	WHIP	ERA	FIP	DRA	VORP	WARP	cFIP	MPH
2016	ROM	A	18	5	3	0	11	11	60¹	54	5	3.0	9.2	62	38%	.314	1.23	3.73	3.51	3.23	12.0	1.3	96	

Breakout: 0%   Improve: 0%   Collapse: 0%   Attrition: 0%   MLB: 0%   Comparables: Vicente Campos, Roberto Osuna, Manny Banuelos

Allard throws with the conviction of an ace and sometimes has the stuff of one, too. He fell to the 14th overall pick in 2015 because of a stress reaction in his back. The Braves had no problem taking a chance on such a talented arm, and he's now healthy and progressing. Allard can unleash a plus-potential fastball in the low 90s and a plus-potential curveball that's among the best in the minors for a left-hander. His changeup has always been the developing pitch, but he shows glimpses of average ability down the road. The question is, and will continue to be, Allard's health. He'll always be on the wiry side, so he needs to prove he can handle a full starter's workload. If he can, the Braves are going to make a few teams look silly for passing on the pitcher with the silly-good curve.

Ian Anderson   RHP

Born: 5/2/98   Age: 19   Bats: R   Throws: R   Height: 6'3"   Weight: 170   Entered Pro Ball: Round 1, 2016 Draft (#3 overall)

The Braves drafted Anderson third overall despite some ranking him outside of the top 10 entering the draft, and they signed him for $4 million, which was about $2.5 million below slot value. The Braves' scouting department is adamant that Anderson is no under-slot pick and he did his part to back that up in his initial taste of pro ball. He's aggressive around the zone with an athletic motion and projectable frame, tossing a low-90s fastball that bumps mid-90s, a slider that flashes wipeout ability when tight and a developing changeup. Reports are high on Anderson as he enters his first full season, and if everything breaks right he could one day leave big-league hitters spitting out pieces of their broken luck.

Aaron Blair   RHP

Born: 5/26/92   Age: 25   Bats: R   Throws: R   Height: 6'4"   Weight: 250   Entered Pro Ball: Round 1, 2013 Draft (#36 overall)

YEAR	TEAM	LVL	AGE	W	L	SV	G	GS	IP	H	HR	BB/9	K/9	K	GB%	BABIP	WHIP	ERA	FIP	DRA	VORP	WARP	cFIP	MPH
2014	SBN	A	22	1	2	0	6	6	35²	25	2	3.5	11.1	44	42%	.258	1.09	4.04	3.01	2.50	11.7	1.2	86	
2014	VIS	A+	22	4	2	0	13	13	72¹	70	6	2.6	10.1	81	41%	.338	1.26	4.35	3.86	3.17	19.5	2.0	90	
2014	MOB	AA	22	4	1	0	8	8	46¹	30	4	3.1	8.9	46	44%	.228	0.99	1.94	3.49	2.22	15.5	1.7	84	
2015	MOB	AA	23	6	3	0	13	13	83¹	70	8	2.5	6.9	64	55%	.265	1.12	2.70	3.95	2.69	22.2	2.4	87	
2015	RNO	AAA	23	7	2	0	13	12	77	67	5	3.2	6.5	56	48%	.273	1.22	3.16	4.08	3.49	15.4	1.6	93	
2016	GWN	AAA	24	5	4	0	13	13	71²	77	4	4.0	8.9	71	50%	.358	1.52	4.65	3.38	3.62	13.8	1.4	88	
2016	ATL	MLB	24	2	7	0	15	15	70	82	14	4.4	5.9	46	42%	.304	1.66	7.59	6.19	6.73	-10.6	-1.1	128	93.2
2017	ATL	MLB	25	2	2	0	6	6	30	29	3	3.7	7.3	24	51%	.294	1.37	4.21	4.17	4.82	1.2	0.1	100	
2018	ATL	MLB	26	8	10	0	29	29	180¹	143	20	4.6	9.9	198	51%	.294	1.30	3.91	4.37	4.74	13.3	1.4	107	

Breakout: 14%   Improve: 38%   Collapse: 29%   Attrition: 36%   MLB: 78%   Comparables: Shairon Martis, Esmil Rogers, Eddie Butler

When the Braves received Ender Inciarte and Dansby Swanson from the Diamondbacks for Shelby Miller, getting a pitching prospect like Blair was considered the cherry on top of one of the tastiest ice cream sundaes ever made via trade. As far as 2016 is concerned the cherry wasn't exactly sweet and delicious, as Blair ended up being one of many young Braves pitchers who took their lumps. If Blair can remember how to miss bats and cut into his walk rate the Braves could still have a mid-rotation starter on their hands. If not, he'll turn out to be little more than garnish after all.

Mauricio Cabrera   RHP

Born: 9/22/93   Age: 23   Bats: R   Throws: R   Height: 6'3"   Weight: 245   Entered Pro Ball: International Free Agent, 2010

YEAR	TEAM	LVL	AGE	W	L	SV	G	GS	IP	H	HR	BB/9	K/9	K	GB%	BABIP	WHIP	ERA	FIP	DRA	VORP	WARP	cFIP	MPH
2014	LYN	A+	20	1	1	0	19	3	29	24	1	5.9	8.7	28	65%	.295	1.48	5.59	4.41	6.97	-5.2	-0.5	117	
2015	CAR	A+	21	2	2	1	23	0	31	30	1	4.9	8.1	28	61%	.309	1.52	5.52	3.51	6.07	-4.7	-0.5	108	
2015	MIS	AA	21	0	1	0	13	0	17¹	12	1	9.3	13.0	25	46%	.289	1.73	5.71	4.46	6.56	-3.5	-0.4	103	
2016	MIS	AA	22	3	3	4	25	0	33²	20	0	5.9	9.4	35	56%	.233	1.25	3.21	3.47	5.00	-1.0	-0.1	102	
2016	ATL	MLB	22	5	1	6	41	0	38¹	31	0	4.5	7.5	32	51%	.282	1.30	2.82	3.08	4.76	0.9	0.1	106	102.7
2017	ATL	MLB	23	3	3	0	52	0	55	52	5	4.8	7.7	47	45%	.293	1.48	4.45	4.44	4.81	0.7	0.1	100	
2018	ATL	MLB	24	2	1	1	48	0	51	40	4	5.9	9.9	56	45%	.305	1.44	3.93	4.40	4.69	2.5	0.3	105	

Breakout: 25%   Improve: 38%   Collapse: 15%   Attrition: 29%   MLB: 64%   Comparables: Luis Avilan, Alex Burnett, Ian Krol

The flame-throwing reliever made the jump from Double-A to the big leagues, and the same question that stuck with him throughout his journey followed him to the majors: can he get his 100-plus mph fastball under control? Cabrera handed out far too many free passes during his big-league stint, but his overall walk rate last year was his lowest since rookie ball. If this is a trend instead of a fluke, he could very well realize his potential as a feared late-inning reliever.

Jhoulys Chacin   RHP

Born: 1/7/88   Age: 29   Bats: R   Throws: R   Height: 6'3"   Weight: 215   Entered Pro Ball: International Free Agent, 2004

YEAR	TEAM	LVL	AGE	W	L	SV	G	GS	IP	H	HR	BB/9	K/9	K	GB%	BABIP	WHIP	ERA	FIP	DRA	VORP	WARP	cFIP	MPH
2014	CSP	AAA	26	1	1	0	2	2	10²	9	0	4.2	6.8	8	52%	.273	1.31	2.53	3.89	4.18	1.9	0.2	99	
2014	COL	MLB	26	1	7	0	11	11	63¹	63	8	4.0	6.0	42	44%	.285	1.44	5.40	4.79	4.60	1.7	0.2	115	91.4
2015	COH	AAA	27	1	3	0	7	7	42	39	3	3.2	5.4	25	45%	.271	1.29	3.21	3.97	5.06	1.1	0.1	108	
2015	RNO	AAA	27	6	3	0	13	13	86²	79	3	3.1	6.5	63	51%	.292	1.26	3.22	3.81	2.79	24.2	2.5	92	
2015	ARI	MLB	27	2	1	0	5	4	26²	24	4	3.4	7.1	21	51%	.263	1.27	3.38	4.66	4.32	2.1	0.2	101	90.9
2016	ATL	MLB	28	1	2	0	5	5	26²	29	4	2.7	9.1	27	50%	.321	1.39	5.40	4.01	3.87	4.2	0.4	99	92.4
2016	ANA	MLB	28	5	6	0	29	17	117¹	124	10	3.6	7.1	92	52%	.316	1.46	4.68	3.98	3.95	17.4	1.8	99	93.9
2017	SDN	MLB	29	9	12	0	29	29	174	165	21	3.2	7.9	152	48%	.289	1.30	4.06	4.17	4.57	11.8	1.2	100	
2018	SDN	MLB	30	10	11	0	30	30	184	160	22	3.3	8.6	176	48%	.297	1.23	3.79	4.24	4.60	18.6	1.9	106	

Breakout: 21%   Improve: 47%   Collapse: 24%   Attrition: 16%   MLB: 94%   Comparables: Brandon McCarthy, John Maine, Joe Saunders

Dropped by the Rockies (never a good start to a sentence about a pitcher) due to injuries and declining velocity, Chacin signed with Atlanta, who then traded him to the Angels in May. His 2016 season was about the best possible scenario for someone with all that on his resume. Chacin throws six pitches, because none of them are particularly good. Still, the depth of the repertoire allows him to keep batters off balance, something he can't do with stuff alone. His velocity ticked up to pre-health problem levels, allowing him the chance to hold down a spot in the back of a rotation until the health problems from gradually tearing your arm from your body pitch by pitch inevitably pop back up. But hey, on the bright side, maybe the earth will crash into the sun first!

Josh Collmenter   RHP

Born: 2/7/86   Age: 31   Bats: R   Throws: R   Height: 6'3"   Weight: 240   Entered Pro Ball: Round 15, 2007 Draft (#463 overall)

YEAR	TEAM	LVL	AGE	W	L	SV	G	GS	IP	H	HR	BB/9	K/9	K	GB%	BABIP	WHIP	ERA	FIP	DRA	VORP	WARP	cFIP	MPH
2014	ARI	MLB	28	11	9	1	33	28	179¹	163	18	2.0	5.8	115	41%	.267	1.13	3.46	3.84	5.47	-13.0	-1.4	120	88.8
2015	ARI	MLB	29	4	6	1	44	12	121	129	18	1.8	4.7	63	36%	.282	1.26	3.79	4.67	5.52	-8.0	-0.9	130	87.7
2016	ARI	MLB	30	1	0	0	15	0	22¹	21	4	4.4	6.9	17	49%	.270	1.43	4.84	5.74	4.43	1.8	0.2	107	86.6
2016	IOW	AAA	30	1	0	0	4	4	16	13	0	4.5	5.1	9	37%	.255	1.31	2.25	4.10	6.52	-2.1	-0.2	119	
2016	ATL	MLB	30	2	0	0	3	3	19	15	3	2.4	7.6	16	44%	.235	1.05	2.37	4.50	4.39	1.6	0.2	107	87.5
2017	ATL	MLB	31	3	4	0	54	2	66	66	8	3.3	6.7	50	38%	.285	1.34	4.70	4.40	5.08	-0.9	-0.1	100	
2018	ATL	MLB	32	3	1	0	49	2	60	57	7	3.2	6.6	44	38%	.296	1.31	4.22	4.72	5.09	0.7	0.1	116	

Breakout: 22%   Improve: 45%   Collapse: 22%   Attrition: 18%   MLB: 89%   Comparables: Dave Stewart, Alexi Ogando, Jaret Wright

It was inevitable that a player nicknamed "Tomahawk" was going to land with the Braves at some point. Granted, the Braves were Collmenter's third organization in 2016, but he pitched well in a brief Atlanta stint after mostly struggling elsewhere. He's a fly-ball pitcher who's been giving up home runs at a worrisome rate and 2017 figures to be another year in which he'll either be an end-of-rotation starter or a long reliever.

Bartolo Colon RHP

Born: 5/24/73   Age: 44   Bats: R   Throws: R   Height: 5'11"   Weight: 285   Entered Pro Ball: International Free Agent, 1993

YEAR	TEAM	LVL	AGE	W	L	SV	G	GS	IP	H	HR	BB/9	K/9	K	GB%	BABIP	WHIP	ERA	FIP	DRA	VORP	WARP	cFIP	MPH
2014	NYN	MLB	41	15	13	0	31	31	202¹	218	22	1.3	6.7	151	41%	.307	1.23	4.09	3.54	4.59	5.5	0.6	104	93.1
2015	NYN	MLB	42	14	13	0	33	31	194²	217	25	1.1	6.3	136	44%	.307	1.24	4.16	3.87	4.93	3.0	0.3	104	92.8
2016	NYN	MLB	43	15	8	0	34	33	191²	200	24	1.5	6.0	128	45%	.291	1.21	3.43	4.03	5.15	4.4	0.5	111	92.1
2017	ATL	MLB	44	10	12	0	30	30	180	188	23	2.2	7.1	142	44%	.301	1.30	4.04	4.11	4.64	10.8	1.1	100	
2018	ATL	MLB	45	11	11	0	31	31	196¹	195	24	2.2	7.2	157	44%	.313	1.24	3.78	4.25	4.60	19.5	2.0	105	

Breakout: 1%   Improve: 5%   Collapse: 16%   Attrition: 5%   MLB: 46%   Comparables: Greg Maddux, John Smoltz, Kenny Rogers

Roll up for Bartolo's Magical Mystery Tour! Baseball's most interesting pitcher continued to defy age and what we think we know about pitching in 2016 with an All-Star nod, his fourth consecutive 190-inning season in his 40s, and a totally unexpected home run off James Shields—at least as much as any home run off of Shields can be unexpected. In between, he was the stabilizing force in a Mets rotation decimated by injury, taking the ball for much-needed innings nearly every time out. The formula itself is no longer much of a mystery, just a fastball thrown over-and-over again, mostly within a few ticks of 90 in either direction. There's the occasional show-me slider in there too, but this is a heavier one pitch mix than anyone else in baseball. Colon threw a higher percentage of fastballs in 2016 than R.A. Dickey or Steven Wright threw knuckleballs, for example. So how exactly can a portly, short man pitch effectively deep into his forties needing only a fastball?

Colon's fastball command is akin to Billy Hamilton's speed in how far it exceeds the normal measuring scales of the game. When on, Colon is capable of throwing his fastball anywhere he wants it, inside or outside the strike zone, with any shape he wants. His better two-seamers eclipse the movement you'd expect to see on a quality changeup, and almost have a screwball feel. In the 2000 annual, we called Colon "as pure a power pitcher as you're going to find" in marveling at his ability to excel with his fastball alone. Here we are seventeen years later and we're still marveling at Colon as a fastball-only wonder, except that he's now as pure a crafty finesse pitcher as you're going to find, armed with all the tricks learned over a 20-year career.

Colon would almost certainly be on a Hall of Fame track if he hadn't lost so many years in the late-aughts, and he might be there regardless of the lost time were it not for a PED suspension in 2012. He enters 2017 at 233 career wins, within shouting distance of two records he's been very clear he wants to set before retiring: Juan Marichal's 243 wins, most by a Dominican-born pitcher, and Dennis Martinez's 245 wins, most by a Latino pitcher. This may be challenging as he will be backed by an even more putrid offense in Cobb County than he was in Queens, at least for three and a half months, but doubt him at your own peril. Nobody can truly pitch forever—even Jamie Moyer wasn't really effective after 45—but while younger pitchers say goodbye, Bartolo still says hello.

Joel De La Cruz RHP

Born: 6/9/89   Age: 28   Bats: R   Throws: R   Height: 6'1"   Weight: 240   Entered Pro Ball: International Free Agent, 2006

YEAR	TEAM	LVL	AGE	W	L	SV	G	GS	IP	H	HR	BB/9	K/9	K	GB%	BABIP	WHIP	ERA	FIP	DRA	VORP	WARP	cFIP	MPH
2014	SWB	AAA	25	3	5	0	17	12	65²	74	6	2.5	5.2	38	58%	.302	1.40	4.52	4.30	7.05	-10.1	-1.0	109	
2014	TRN	AA	25	4	4	0	11	10	56	60	3	3.1	6.3	39	59%	.322	1.41	4.34	3.84	5.67	-2.9	-0.3	101	
2015	TRN	AA	26	1	2	0	8	2	23¹	24	2	1.9	5	13	64%	.278	1.24	3.47	4.17	5.21	-0.9	-0.1	103	
2015	SWB	AAA	26	7	0	0	15	7	61	59	4	2.5	4.3	29	54%	.281	1.25	3.25	3.99	6.07	-6.4	-0.7	114	
2016	GWN	AAA	27	1	3	0	21	5	57²	62	5	3.7	6.9	44	48%	.333	1.49	4.68	4.28	5.21	-0.4	0.0	107	
2016	ATL	MLB	27	0	7	0	22	9	62²	65	10	3.2	5.3	37	46%	.268	1.39	4.88	5.23	5.91	-4.5	-0.5	122	94.0
2017	ATL	MLB	28	5	5	1	50	12	98²	101	11	3.3	5.9	64	48%	.307	1.38	4.49	4.50	5.45	-2.0	-0.2	128	
2018	ATL	MLB	29	2	2	0	18	6	61²	59	7	4.5	7.6	52	48%	.313	1.45	4.41	4.94	5.35	0.1	0.0	123	

Breakout: 19%   Improve: 25%   Collapse: 16%   Attrition: 27%   MLB: 43%   Comparables: Steven Jackson, Alex Wilson, Eric Stults

A decade-long journey for De La Cruz through multiple organizations eventually landed him in Atlanta, which is where he finally made his major-league debut. That's normally a story reserved for graybeards reaching the end of their career, but De La Cruz is only 27. The low-leverage, low-velo mediocrity we saw from the righty last season is probably what we should continue to expect from him if he sticks around in the bigs. Absent the sudden development of a knuckler or a screwball or four more ticks on his heater, at best he'll fill a role as an innings eater or spot starter/long reliever. Most likely De La Cruz will spend more time in the minors learning to appreciate the journey as much as the destination.

R.A. Dickey RHP

Born: 10/29/74   Age: 42   Bats: R   Throws: R   Height: 6'3"   Weight: 215   Entered Pro Ball: Round 1, 1996 Draft (#18 overall)

YEAR	TEAM	LVL	AGE	W	L	SV	G	GS	IP	H	HR	BB/9	K/9	K	GB%	BABIP	WHIP	ERA	FIP	DRA	VORP	WARP	cFIP	MPH
2014	TOR	MLB	39	14	13	0	34	34	215²	191	26	3.1	7.2	173	45%	.263	1.23	3.71	4.35	4.09	17.8	2.0	106	84.7
2015	TOR	MLB	40	11	11	0	33	33	214¹	195	25	2.6	5.3	126	42%	.257	1.19	3.91	4.45	5.79	-16.9	-1.8	119	84.6
2016	TOR	MLB	41	10	15	0	30	29	169²	169	28	3.3	6.7	126	42%	.279	1.37	4.46	4.99	5.53	-3.2	-0.3	117	85.4
2017	ATL	MLB	42	8	11	0	26	26	156	144	19	3.4	7.8	134	56%	.282	1.28	4.28	4.33	4.89	5.0	0.5	100	
2018	ATL	MLB	43	10	10	0	28	28	167²	143	20	3.0	7.6	141	56%	.279	1.18	3.93	4.38	4.75	14.7	1.5	110	

Breakout: 6%   Improve: 40%   Collapse: 10%   Attrition: 10%   MLB: 72%   Comparables: Tim Wakefield, Tom Glavine, Greg Maddux

Despite no longer being the ace he once was, 2016 must have been a relief for Robert Allen Dickey. In previous seasons with the Blue Jays, a lackluster rotation had forced Dickey to be a focal point. But, with the likes of Aaron Sanchez, J.A. Happ and Marco Estrada all performing above expectations, Dickey could perform like the fourth starter he is and be a valuable contributor. Dickey's last guard will be seeing how long he can make the knuckleball last. He's 42, two years younger than Tim Wakefield was when he retired, and six years younger than Phil Niekro was. And maybe pitching alongside Bartolo Colon will make him feel younger.

Mike Foltynewicz   RHP

Born: 10/7/91   Age: 25   Bats: R   Throws: R   Height: 6'4"   Weight: 220   Entered Pro Ball: Round 1, 2010 Draft (#19 overall)

YEAR	TEAM	LVL	AGE	W	L	SV	G	GS	IP	H	HR	BB/9	K/9	K	GB%	BABIP	WHIP	ERA	FIP	DRA	VORP	WARP	cFIP	MPH
2014	OKL	AAA	22	7	7	0	21	18	102²	98	10	4.6	8.9	102	49%	.322	1.46	5.08	4.79	5.54	2.1	0.2	98	
2014	HOU	MLB	22	0	1	0	16	0	18²	23	3	3.4	6.8	14	29%	.333	1.61	5.30	4.87	6.90	-5.0	-0.6	124	100.0
2015	GWN	AAA	23	1	6	0	10	10	56²	52	7	4.1	10	63	42%	.308	1.38	3.49	3.92	2.07	20.3	2.1	85	
2015	ATL	MLB	23	4	6	0	18	15	86²	112	17	3.0	8.0	77	36%	.349	1.63	5.71	5.08	5.99	-8.9	-1.0	116	99.0
2016	GWN	AAA	24	1	2	0	5	5	27	13	0	4.7	8.3	25	54%	.206	1.00	1.67	3.09	3.42	5.8	0.6	95	
2016	ATL	MLB	24	9	5	0	22	22	123¹	125	18	2.6	8.1	111	43%	.301	1.30	4.31	4.28	4.20	15.8	1.6	101	98.7
2017	ATL	MLB	25	6	7	0	19	19	108¹	102	12	3.2	8.4	101	51%	.296	1.30	3.85	3.94	4.41	9.3	1.0	100	
2018	ATL	MLB	26	10	9	0	28	28	173¹	137	19	3.7	10.0	193	51%	.298	1.20	3.48	3.89	4.22	23.6	2.4	94	

Breakout: 26%   Improve: 52%   Collapse: 20%   Attrition: 22%   MLB: 90%   *Comparables: Drew Pomeranz, Ricky Romero, Wade Davis*

Foltynewicz recovered from a scary ordeal with blood clots in his arm and made his return to the big leagues in early May. There were outings in which he looked like a bonafide starter down the road, and then there were outings in which he'd get through a few innings with relatively few issues before losing control and going off of the rails. Fortunately, the latter became rarer as the season progressed, and he figures to be a decent starter. Foltynewicz's high-octane stuff has never been in question—it was only a matter of getting it under control, and he's taking strides toward utilizing it to the fullest of his capability.

Max Fried   LHP

Born: 1/18/94   Age: 23   Bats: L   Throws: L   Height: 6'4"   Weight: 185   Entered Pro Ball: Round 1, 2012 Draft (#7 overall)

YEAR	TEAM	LVL	AGE	W	L	SV	G	GS	IP	H	HR	BB/9	K/9	K	GB%	BABIP	WHIP	ERA	FIP	DRA	VORP	WARP	cFIP	MPH
2016	ROM	A	22	8	7	0	21	20	103	87	10	4.1	9.8	112	52%	.305	1.30	3.93	3.97	3.92	12.3	1.4	102	
2017	ATL	MLB	23	3	5	0	14	14	67¹	70	8	5.7	6.2	47	52%	.314	1.66	5.30	5.29	6.26	-5.2	-0.5	149	
2018	ATL	MLB	24	6	10	0	26	26	155¹	141	18	6.6	8.6	148	52%	.315	1.65	4.91	5.51	5.80	-3.3	-0.3	137	

Breakout: 4%   Improve: 6%   Collapse: 1%   Attrition: 6%   MLB: 8%   *Comparables: Tyler Wagner, Taylor Rogers, Ricky Romero*

The Braves acquired Fried with the knowledge that it would take time for him to recover from Tommy John surgery and there were uncertainties. Those question marks were still present midway through 2016, but a late-season push was the first promising step forward on the mound since surgery. When he's on, Fried shows No. 2 starter ability between a plus-potential fastball and curveball, and a serviceable changeup. The curve can buckle knees quicker than a first kiss for an awkward teenager. He does tend to cast his pitches and lose his height advantage at times, and a mechanical tweak or two might be necessary to succeed in the upper levels. If he puts it together and stays healthy, he'll be buckling knees all the way to a major-league rotation spot.

Jaime Garcia   LHP

Born: 7/8/86   Age: 30   Bats: L   Throws: L   Height: 6'2"   Weight: 215   Entered Pro Ball: Round 22, 2005 Draft (#680 overall)

YEAR	TEAM	LVL	AGE	W	L	SV	G	GS	IP	H	HR	BB/9	K/9	K	GB%	BABIP	WHIP	ERA	FIP	DRA	VORP	WARP	cFIP	MPH
2014	SLN	MLB	27	3	1	0	7	7	43²	39	6	1.4	8.0	39	54%	.270	1.05	4.12	3.79	3.25	7.7	0.9	87	92.7
2015	SLN	MLB	28	10	6	0	20	20	129²	106	6	2.1	6.7	97	62%	.267	1.05	2.43	3.03	3.17	27.5	2.9	90	92.3
2016	SLN	MLB	29	10	13	0	32	30	171²	179	26	3.0	7.9	150	58%	.305	1.37	4.67	4.53	3.55	34.3	3.5	93	93.1
2017	ATL	MLB	30	8	9	0	24	24	136	131	17	2.9	8.2	125	51%	.296	1.28	3.95	4.06	4.53	9.9	1.0	100	
2018	ATL	MLB	31	11	11	0	32	32	204	181	24	2.5	8.3	187	51%	.302	1.17	3.58	4.01	4.35	23.9	2.5	99	

Breakout: 21%   Improve: 54%   Collapse: 16%   Attrition: 11%   MLB: 92%   *Comparables: Wandy Rodriguez, Justin Masterson, Brett Myers*

Last season the notoriously fragile Garcia managed 30 starts for the first time in five years, but as the season wore on his outings produced diminishing returns. He induced his usual mountain of ground balls with his sinker and copious off-speed whiffle balls, but his command deserted him and patient hitters teed off when he left anything up in the zone. Some of this may have been fatigue and some bad luck (his 20 percent rate of home runs on fly balls was among the highest in the league), so his new employers in Atlanta are betting on a bounce back. If history is any guide, expect Garcia's production to improve significantly on a rate basis but decrease significantly on a volume basis.

Luke Jackson   RHP

Born: 8/24/91   Age: 25   Bats: R   Throws: R   Height: 6'2"   Weight: 210   Entered Pro Ball: Round 1, 2010 Draft (#45 overall)

YEAR	TEAM	LVL	AGE	W	L	SV	G	GS	IP	H	HR	BB/9	K/9	K	GB%	BABIP	WHIP	ERA	FIP	DRA	VORP	WARP	cFIP	MPH
2014	FRI	AA	22	8	2	1	15	14	83¹	58	5	2.6	9.0	83	44%	.242	0.98	3.02	2.92	3.60	14.9	1.6	85	
2014	ROU	AAA	22	1	3	0	11	10	40	56	9	6.3	9.7	43	45%	.395	2.10	10.35	6.72	7.03	-5.7	-0.6	112	
2015	ROU	AAA	23	2	3	0	39	5	66¹	62	3	4.7	10.7	79	54%	.335	1.46	4.34	3.43	4.09	7.0	0.7	93	
2015	TEX	MLB	23	0	0	0	7	0	6¹	5	1	2.8	8.5	6	53%	.222	1.11	4.26	4.21	4.08	0.4	0.0	101	98.8
2016	ROU	AAA	24	1	0	2	16	0	22	13	2	6.1	11.0	27	45%	.244	1.27	2.45	4.63	3.72	3.0	0.3	97	
2016	TEX	MLB	24	0	0	0	8	0	11²	22	4	6.2	2.3	3	33%	.383	2.57	10.80	9.11	10.43	-7.1	-0.7	141	96.6
2016	FRI	AA	24	0	1	1	20	0	24¹	27	4	6.3	11.8	32	43%	.365	1.81	4.81	5.03	4.24	1.3	0.1	97	
2017	ATL	MLB	25	3	3	0	25	8	58	55	7	4.0	8.1	52	54%	.315	1.40	4.27	4.41	5.17	1.7	0.2	120	
2018	ATL	MLB	26	5	5	0	37	12	105	85	14	5.6	11.0	128	54%	.312	1.44	4.30	4.83	5.21	2.2	0.2	120	

Breakout: 15%   Improve: 21%   Collapse: 26%   Attrition: 40%   MLB: 63%   *Comparables: Maikel Cleto, Jimmy Nelson, J.J. Hoover*

Serving as a middle man peddling innings between Arlington, Frisco and Round Rock for most of 2016, Jackson tried to survive while missing a full tick on his fastball. Turns out it was an important tick, as he allowed at least one run in all but one of his eight appearances, and giving up six in his last outing against the Twins for good measure. Jackson's mid-90s fastball, even at N-1, still has velocity and his curve still shows promise. But his command is poor and his change might as well be non-existent, giving him an empty arsenal against lefties—who tattooed him for a .462/.533/.846 line. With an uncertain future at best, the Rangers flipped him to Atlanta in December in a different kind of challenge trade—the Former Prospect Reliever Reclamation Project challenge trade—in exchange for another not-so-great developmental story, Tyrell Jenkins.

Jim Johnson   RHP

Born: 6/27/83   Age: 34   Bats: R   Throws: R   Height: 6'6"   Weight: 250   Entered Pro Ball: Round 5, 2001 Draft (#143 overall)

YEAR	TEAM	LVL	AGE	W	L	SV	G	GS	IP	H	HR	BB/9	K/9	K	GB%	BABIP	WHIP	ERA	FIP	DRA	VORP	WARP	cFIP	MPH
2014	OAK	MLB	31	4	2	2	38	0	40¹	60	5	5.1	6.2	28	60%	.390	2.06	7.14	5.32	4.85	-1.6	-0.2	110	96.2
2014	DET	MLB	31	1	0	0	16	0	13	9	0	8.3	9.7	14	68%	.265	1.62	6.92	4.47	4.83	-0.5	-0.1	111	95.4
2015	ATL	MLB	32	2	3	9	49	0	48	45	2	2.6	6.2	33	64%	.295	1.23	2.25	3.27	3.44	6.8	0.7	95	96.5
2015	LAN	MLB	32	0	3	1	23	0	18²	32	3	2.9	8.2	17	65%	.446	2.04	10.12	5.04	3.00	3.6	0.4	94	96.9
2016	ATL	MLB	33	2	6	20	65	0	64²	57	3	2.8	9.5	68	56%	.314	1.19	3.06	2.75	2.90	14.9	1.5	84	96.1
2017	*ATL*	*MLB*	*34*	*3*	*3*	*30*	*52*	*0*	*55*	*54*	*6*	*3.6*	*8.4*	*52*	*63%*	*.307*	*1.40*	*3.99*	*4.06*	*4.51*	*2.5*	*0.3*	*100*	
2018	*ATL*	*MLB*	*35*	*1*	*0*	*9*	*20*	*0*	*21*	*19*	*2*	*3.2*	*8.0*	*19*	*63%*	*.313*	*1.28*	*3.68*	*4.13*	*4.48*	*1.5*	*0.2*	*99*	

Breakout: 13%   Improve: 30%   Collapse: 34%   Attrition: 9%   MLB: 83%   Comparables: Matt Lindstrom, J.C. Romero, Dennys Reyes

After the Braves successfully used him as a trade chip in 2015, Johnson returned to Atlanta and continued his career resurgence. This time around the Braves resisted trading him, instead signing Johnson to a two-year contract extension. Johnson has always been a ground-ball machine, but at age 33 he struck out more than a batter per inning for the first time, blowing away his previous career-high strikeout rate, and showed that a rough 2014 was an outlier rather than a sign of steep decline.

Ian Krol   LHP

Born: 5/9/91   Age: 26   Bats: L   Throws: L   Height: 6'1"   Weight: 210   Entered Pro Ball: Round 7, 2009 Draft (#213 overall)

YEAR	TEAM	LVL	AGE	W	L	SV	G	GS	IP	H	HR	BB/9	K/9	K	GB%	BABIP	WHIP	ERA	FIP	DRA	VORP	WARP	cFIP	MPH
2014	DET	MLB	23	0	0	1	45	0	32²	42	6	3.6	7.7	28	42%	.343	1.68	4.96	5.21	4.94	-1.6	-0.2	106	94.9
2015	TOL	AAA	24	1	1	1	28	0	31¹	21	0	3.7	9.8	34	56%	.259	1.09	2.30	2.23	3.21	6.0	0.6	91	
2015	DET	MLB	24	2	3	0	33	0	28	31	4	5.5	8.4	26	46%	.338	1.71	5.79	5.14	4.57	0.4	0.0	109	96.5
2016	GWN	AAA	25	1	2	1	12	0	12¹	10	1	4.4	10.2	14	42%	.281	1.30	4.38	3.41	3.28	2.3	0.2	96	
2016	ATL	MLB	25	2	0	0	63	0	51	54	4	2.3	9.9	56	59%	.355	1.31	3.18	2.95	2.85	12.0	1.2	81	96.3
2017	*ATL*	*MLB*	*26*	*3*	*3*	*0*	*52*	*0*	*55*	*53*	*6*	*3.3*	*8.7*	*54*	*55%*	*.304*	*1.34*	*3.78*	*3.88*	*4.34*	*3.5*	*0.4*	*98*	
2018	*ATL*	*MLB*	*27*	*3*	*1*	*0*	*57*	*0*	*60²*	*50*	*6*	*3.5*	*10.0*	*68*	*55%*	*.310*	*1.22*	*3.27*	*3.67*	*3.98*	*7.7*	*0.8*	*85*	

Breakout: 37%   Improve: 51%   Collapse: 16%   Attrition: 20%   MLB: 81%   Comparables: Kris Medlen, Wesley Wright, Aaron Crow

Krol started the season at Triple-A after losing the spring bullpen competition and ended the year as the Braves' top left-handed reliever. He avoided the pratfall appearances that plagued him during his time with the Tigers in 2015, emerging as a fixture in the middle innings. He made a concerted effort to trim down his repertoire and the payoff was substantial. He cut his walk rate in half, improved his strikeout rate and started inducing more ground balls. It's very possible that, after a few years of bouncing around from team to team, Krol may have finally put down permanent stakes as a reliable bullpen arm.

Jacob Lindgren   LHP

Born: 3/12/93   Age: 24   Bats: L   Throws: L   Height: 5'11"   Weight: 210   Entered Pro Ball: Round 2, 2014 Draft (#55 overall)

YEAR	TEAM	LVL	AGE	W	L	SV	G	GS	IP	H	HR	BB/9	K/9	K	GB%	BABIP	WHIP	ERA	FIP	DRA	VORP	WARP	cFIP	MPH
2014	TRN	AA	21	1	1	0	8	0	11²	6	0	6.9	13.9	18	73%	.273	1.29	3.86	2.58	2.71	2.8	0.3	80	
2015	SWB	AAA	22	1	1	3	15	0	22	16	0	4.1	11.9	29	70%	.302	1.18	1.23	1.88	2.63	5.6	0.6	81	
2015	NYA	MLB	22	0	0	0	7	0	7	5	3	5.1	10.3	8	41%	.143	1.29	5.14	8.10	4.31	0.3	0.0	102	91.7
2017	*ATL*	*MLB*	*24*	*2*	*1*	*1*	*34*	*0*	*36¹*	*32*	*4*	*4.4*	*8.9*	*36*	*53%*	*.302*	*1.36*	*4.27*	*4.23*	*5.16*	*-0.1*	*0.0*	*118*	
2018	*ATL*	*MLB*	*25*	*2*	*1*	*2*	*36*	*0*	*46²*	*35*	*5*	*5.1*	*10.7*	*55*	*53%*	*.294*	*1.32*	*3.89*	*4.34*	*4.70*	*2.1*	*0.2*	*106*	

Breakout: 16%   Improve: 25%   Collapse: 4%   Attrition: 19%   MLB: 35%   Comparables: Lester Oliveros, Kevin Quackenbush, Nick Goody

It seemed like just yesterday that Lindgren, at 21, became the first player younger than Bryce Harper to strike the slugger out. It was a better time for everyone—there wasn't a war on headphone jacks and DJ Khaled wasn't a household name—and that's especially true for Lindgren. Since then, the prospect has had a short, mediocre stint in the major leagues and two surgeries, the most recent being Tommy John. That will likely keep him out all of 2017, meaning that by the time he gets a healthy dose of work out of the bullpen, he'll be 25. That would have seemed like blasphemy a couple of years ago.

Sean Newcomb   LHP

Born: 6/12/93   Age: 24   Bats: L   Throws: L   Height: 6'5"   Weight: 255   Entered Pro Ball: Round 1, 2014 Draft (#15 overall)

YEAR	TEAM	LVL	AGE	W	L	SV	G	GS	IP	H	HR	BB/9	K/9	K	GB%	BABIP	WHIP	ERA	FIP	DRA	VORP	WARP	cFIP	MPH
2014	BUR	A	21	0	1	0	4	4	11²	13	1	3.9	11.6	15	28%	.387	1.54	6.94	3.31	3.67	2.3	0.2	94	
2015	BUR	A	22	1	0	0	7	7	34¹	25	1	5.0	11.8	45	66%	.308	1.28	1.83	2.90	2.43	10.6	1.1	90	
2015	INL	A+	22	6	1	0	13	13	65²	50	2	4.5	11.5	84	49%	.300	1.26	2.47	3.17	2.63	17.8	1.9	89	
2015	ARK	AA	22	2	2	0	7	7	36	22	4	6.0	9.8	39	47%	.235	1.28	2.75	3.94	4.60	2.0	0.2	107	
2016	MIS	AA	23	8	7	0	27	27	140	113	4	4.6	9.8	152	46%	.302	1.31	3.86	3.19	4.33	11.9	1.3	97	
2017	*ATL*	*MLB*	*24*	*7*	*8*	*0*	*24*	*24*	*116¹*	*106*	*11*	*4.8*	*8.0*	*104*	*46%*	*.308*	*1.44*	*4.32*	*4.33*	*5.18*	*4.9*	*0.5*	*121*	
2018	*ATL*	*MLB*	*25*	*6*	*8*	*0*	*22*	*22*	*131¹*	*102*	*13*	*6.1*	*10.8*	*158*	*46%*	*.308*	*1.46*	*4.07*	*4.56*	*4.88*	*8.2*	*0.8*	*112*	

Breakout: 12%   Improve: 27%   Collapse: 15%   Attrition: 28%   MLB: 48%   Comparables: Trevor May, Charles Brewer, Chris Withrow

"I may not be a smart man, but I know what command is." Like Forrest's technicolor pursuit of Jenny, Newcomb is engaged in an epic quest to consistently hit his spots, and the coaches who are working to smooth out his stiff lead side and inconsistent halves believe he'll get the girl in the end. If they're right, Newcomb's arsenal makes him a potential No. 2 starter with flashes of front-line ability.

That's the result of a plus-potential fastball that touches 96 mph and an above-average-potential curveball, while his changeup has made strides and should reach average. The stuff is there, but if the command doesn't allow it to play it's a back-end profile.

Eric O'Flaherty   LHP

Born: 2/5/85   Age: 32   Bats: L   Throws: L   Height: 6'2"   Weight: 210   Entered Pro Ball: Round 6, 2003 Draft (#176 overall)

YEAR	TEAM	LVL	AGE	W	L	SV	G	GS	IP	H	HR	BB/9	K/9	K	GB%	BABIP	WHIP	ERA	FIP	DRA	VORP	WARP	cFIP	MPH
2014	OAK	MLB	29	1	0	1	21	0	20	15	3	1.8	6.8	15	56%	.214	0.95	2.25	4.51	3.77	1.6	0.2	99	92.1
2015	OAK	MLB	30	1	2	0	25	0	21¹	29	1	5.5	6.3	15	68%	.354	1.97	5.91	4.14	4.50	0.5	0.1	113	92.3
2015	NYN	MLB	30	0	0	0	16	0	8²	18	1	5.2	6.2	6	47%	.459	2.65	13.50	5.70	4.24	0.5	0.0	113	93.1
2016	ATL	MLB	31	1	4	0	39	0	28²	39	3	3.5	6.9	22	55%	.367	1.74	6.91	4.37	4.63	1.1	0.1	105	92.6
2017	ATL	MLB	32	2	1	0	34	0	36¹	36	5	3.3	7.1	29	58%	.311	1.37	4.44	4.56	5.38	-0.8	-0.1	124	
2018	ATL	MLB	33	2	1	0	37	0	31¹	33	4	3.7	6.9	24	58%	.321	1.46	4.46	4.99	5.40	-0.9	-0.1	123	

Breakout: 27%   Improve: 46%   Collapse: 14%   Attrition: 14%   MLB: 81%   *Comparables: John Grabow, Mike MacDougal, Dennys Reyes*

For the second consecutive season, a major-league team brought in O'Flaherty to (eventually) replace Alex Torres. Someone out there will probably eat their hat if this happens for a third year in a row. O'Flaherty's second time around with the Braves didn't go nearly as well, as injuries and general ineffectiveness made 2016 a season to forget. His season eventually ended due to elbow neuritis—while he'll probably be ready for spring training, there's no guarantee he'll be able to latch onto a major-league squad past March.

Williams Perez   RHP

Born: 5/21/91   Age: 26   Bats: R   Throws: R   Height: 6'0"   Weight: 240   Entered Pro Ball: International Free Agent, 2009

YEAR	TEAM	LVL	AGE	W	L	SV	G	GS	IP	H	HR	BB/9	K/9	K	GB%	BABIP	WHIP	ERA	FIP	DRA	VORP	WARP	cFIP	MPH
2014	MIS	AA	23	7	6	0	26	25	133	119	4	2.6	6.4	94	59%	.283	1.19	2.91	3.29	3.19	29.9	3.2	96	
2015	GWN	AAA	24	3	1	0	8	8	38²	32	1	2.3	8.4	36	52%	.292	1.09	1.16	2.48	2.61	11.6	1.2	78	
2015	ATL	MLB	24	7	6	1	23	20	116²	130	13	3.9	5.6	73	51%	.318	1.55	4.78	4.90	4.90	2.2	0.2	119	93.4
2016	GWN	AAA	25	1	2	0	4	4	24¹	15	2	2.6	8.9	24	63%	.224	0.90	2.59	3.25	2.08	8.8	0.9	78	
2016	ATL	MLB	25	2	3	0	11	11	53²	57	7	2.5	4.5	27	59%	.275	1.34	6.04	4.83	5.77	-2.5	-0.3	109	94.1
2017	ATL	MLB	26	2	3	0	8	8	42	43	4	3.3	6.6	31	61%	.295	1.38	4.21	4.21	4.83	1.6	0.2	100	
2018	ATL	MLB	27	9	10	0	29	29	178	157	19	4.0	8.4	165	61%	.306	1.33	3.99	4.47	4.85	11.9	1.2	111	

Breakout: 25%   Improve: 54%   Collapse: 20%   Attrition: 24%   MLB: 83%   *Comparables: Dillon Gee, Clayton Richard, Justin Germano*

On May 11, 2016, Perez started for the Braves against the Phillies and put together the best eight innings of his career. Unfortunately for Perez, that turned out to be a peak rather than a plateau—he spent the rest of the season scaling down that particular mountain in precarious fashion with a season-ending elbow impingement welcoming him at the base in September. Perez made 11 starts in 2016, but was one of many young Braves starters who took a beating. He'll more than likely be in the midst of a fierce battle for a rotation spot this spring.

Jose Ramirez   RHP

Born: 1/21/90   Age: 27   Bats: R   Throws: R   Height: 6'1"   Weight: 215   Entered Pro Ball: International Free Agent, 2007

YEAR	TEAM	LVL	AGE	W	L	SV	G	GS	IP	H	HR	BB/9	K/9	K	GB%	BABIP	WHIP	ERA	FIP	DRA	VORP	WARP	cFIP	MPH
2014	NYA	MLB	24	0	2	0	8	0	10	11	2	6.3	9.0	10	23%	.321	1.80	5.40	6.46	7.58	-3.4	-0.4	127	97.5
2014	SWB	AAA	24	3	0	1	9	0	12¹	13	2	7.3	11.7	16	48%	.394	1.86	1.46	3.44	4.71	0.9	0.1	96	
2015	NYA	MLB	25	0	0	0	3	0	3	6	0	12.0	6.0	2	46%	.462	3.33	15.00	6.77	8.91	-1.4	-0.1	121	98.2
2015	SWB	AAA	25	3	0	10	32	0	49²	40	1	4.2	10.1	56	46%	.305	1.27	2.90	2.67	2.99	10.7	1.1	88	
2015	TAC	AAA	25	1	1	0	9	0	13	16	5	4.8	6.9	10	32%	.282	1.77	9.00	8.68	5.26	-0.5	0.0	110	
2015	SEA	MLB	25	1	0	0	5	0	4²	9	0	11.6	5.8	3	43%	.429	3.21	11.57	6.96	8.54	-2.0	-0.2	121	98.5
2016	GWN	AAA	26	3	2	6	36	0	41¹	34	3	3.9	9.8	45	51%	.292	1.26	2.18	3.31	3.38	7.2	0.7	87	
2016	ATL	MLB	26	2	2	0	33	0	32²	26	2	5.0	9.1	33	35%	.279	1.35	3.58	3.98	4.95	0.1	0.0	110	97.9
2017	ATL	MLB	27	2	2	0	48	0	50	48	5	4.1	8.5	47	52%	.297	1.40	4.08	4.15	4.58	1.9	0.2	100	
2018	ATL	MLB	28	3	1	0	55	0	58	45	5	4.7	10.6	68	52%	.302	1.30	3.54	3.96	4.29	5.4	0.6	93	

Breakout: 19%   Improve: 39%   Collapse: 13%   Attrition: 30%   MLB: 66%   *Comparables: Carlos Fisher, Chad Qualls, Nick Hagadone*

Ramirez's brief 2015 stint in the majors was calamitous, as he displayed plenty of velocity with very little control. By the time he returned on a permanent basis in July of 2016, he'd managed to rein things in and actually became a viable bullpen option for the Braves. He probably doesn't have the stuff to be a high-leverage end-of-game reliever, but if you have a flame-throwing reliever that you can put in for the seventh inning, then you have a decently valuable piece on your hands. His fastball is still sitting comfortably in the high 90s and he now has a decent idea of where said fastball is going.

Chaz Roe   RHP

Born: 10/9/86   Age: 30   Bats: R   Throws: R   Height: 6'5"   Weight: 190   Entered Pro Ball: Round 1, 2005 Draft (#32 overall)

YEAR	TEAM	LVL	AGE	W	L	SV	G	GS	IP	H	HR	BB/9	K/9	K	GB%	BABIP	WHIP	ERA	FIP	DRA	VORP	WARP	cFIP	MPH
2014	NWO	AAA	27	3	3	14	47	0	64	53	5	3.0	10.1	72	60%	.304	1.16	3.66	3.73	1.81	25.1	2.5	73	
2014	NYA	MLB	27	0	0	0	3	0	2	3	0	13.5	18.0	4	17%	.500	3.00	9.00	3.66	5.40	-0.2	0.0	112	94.1
2015	NOR	AAA	28	3	1	2	17	0	24²	17	0	3.3	8	22	67%	.258	1.05	2.19	2.83	2.47	6.7	0.7	94	
2015	BAL	MLB	28	4	2	0	36	0	41¹	44	4	3.7	8.3	38	55%	.342	1.48	4.14	3.83	4.01	3.2	0.3	96	94.9
2016	NOR	AAA	29	1	2	4	33	0	37²	27	1	2.4	10.8	45	59%	.292	0.98	2.39	2.00	1.50	14.5	1.5	69	
2016	BAL	MLB	29	1	0	0	9	0	9²	8	2	6.5	10.2	11	46%	.250	1.55	3.72	5.69	2.75	2.4	0.2	78	94.2
2016	ATL	MLB	29	1	0	0	21	0	20	14	3	3.2	11.7	26	65%	.304	1.05	3.60	1.79	3.24	3.8	0.4	81	94.8
2017	ATL	MLB	30	2	2	0	48	0	50	47	5	3.7	9.0	50	52%	.298	1.33	3.83	3.85	4.38	3.0	0.3	99	
2018	ATL	MLB	31	2	1	0	43	0	45²	35	4	4.1	10.7	54	52%	.309	1.23	3.29	3.67	4.00	5.7	0.6	84	

Breakout: 23%   Improve: 45%   Collapse: 13%   Attrition: 18%   MLB: 71%   *Comparables: Mitch Stetter, Will Harris, Doug Slaten*

Outside of a couple of disastrous appearances at the end of August/early September, Roe was about as reliable as a middle reliever could be and ended up being a very nifty waiver wire acquisition for the Braves. He gave up eight earned runs after getting picked up by Atlanta, and seven of them came in those two appearances. Roe's newfound effectiveness was the result of a soaring strikeout rate and a walk rate that was cut in half compared to his time in Baltimore. As long as that continues to be the case, he'll have the tools to stick around as a middle reliever.

Shae Simmons RHP

Born: 9/3/90 Age: 26 Bats: R Throws: R Height: 5'11" Weight: 190 Entered Pro Ball: Round 22, 2012 Draft (#689 overall)

YEAR	TEAM	LVL	AGE	W	L	SV	G	GS	IP	H	HR	BB/9	K/9	K	GB%	BABIP	WHIP	ERA	FIP	DRA	VORP	WARP	cFIP	MPH
2014	MIS	AA	23	0	0	14	20	0	23	15	0	2.3	11.7	30	65%	.288	0.91	0.78	1.49	1.17	9.4	1.0	64	
2014	ATL	MLB	23	1	2	1	26	0	21²	15	1	4.6	9.6	23	56%	.259	1.20	2.91	3.10	2.93	3.8	0.4	94	97.2
2016	GWN	AAA	25	0	0	1	12	4	12	7	0	6.8	10.5	14	50%	.250	1.33	1.50	3.58	5.19	-0.1	0.0	99	
2016	ATL	MLB	25	0	0	0	7	0	6²	6	0	0.0	4.1	3	59%	.273	0.90	1.35	2.29	5.16	-0.1	0.0	105	98.3
2017	*ATL*	*MLB*	*26*	*2*	*2*	*0*	*38*	*0*	*40¹*	*40*	*5*	*4.0*	*7.8*	*35*	*49%*	*.298*	*1.44*	*4.58*	*4.55*	*5.02*	*-0.5*	*0.0*	*100*	
2018	*ATL*	*MLB*	*27*	*2*	*1*	*0*	*39*	*0*	*41*	*35*	*5*	*4.5*	*9.7*	*44*	*49%*	*.307*	*1.34*	*3.96*	*4.43*	*4.85*	*1.3*	*0.1*	*109*	

Breakout: 30%   Improve: 41%   Collapse: 13%   Attrition: 26%   MLB: 59%   Comparables: *Dan Runzler, Josh Edgin, Andrew McKirahan*

He only threw a handful of innings in 2016 after returning from Tommy John surgery, but Simmons showed off the big arm and velocity that once had people comparing him to Craig Kimbrel. While the steam on his fastball and slider may still be there after such a long layoff, the injury concerns also linger. He suffered a few setbacks that resulted in his eventual return being delayed and he was shut down in late September due to forearm issues. Simmons has the potential to become a bullpen cornerstone, but he first needs to put together one fully healthy season.

Lucas Sims RHP

Born: 5/10/94 Age: 23 Bats: R Throws: R Height: 6'2" Weight: 220 Entered Pro Ball: Round 1, 2012 Draft (#21 overall)

YEAR	TEAM	LVL	AGE	W	L	SV	G	GS	IP	H	HR	BB/9	K/9	K	GB%	BABIP	WHIP	ERA	FIP	DRA	VORP	WARP	cFIP	MPH
2014	LYN	A+	20	8	11	0	28	28	156²	146	12	3.3	6.1	107	42%	.277	1.30	4.19	4.56	6.41	-14.2	-1.4	114	
2015	CAR	A+	21	3	4	0	9	9	40	39	2	5.2	8.3	37	47%	.325	1.55	5.18	4.00	6.00	-4.1	-0.4	112	
2015	MIS	AA	21	4	2	0	9	9	47²	29	1	5.5	10.6	56	48%	.257	1.22	3.21	3.30	3.59	7.9	0.9	92	
2016	GWN	AAA	22	2	6	0	11	10	50	56	12	6.7	10.4	58	42%	.333	1.86	7.56	6.31	6.49	-6.5	-0.7	108	
2016	MIS	AA	22	5	5	0	17	17	91	64	3	5.4	10.0	101	42%	.276	1.31	2.67	3.70	5.87	-7.9	-0.8	109	
2017	*ATL*	*MLB*	*23*	*1*	*1*	*0*	*2*	*2*	*10*	*10*	*1*	*5.1*	*7.6*	*8*	*53%*	*.295*	*1.52*	*4.66*	*4.98*	*5.23*	*-0.1*	*0.0*	*100*	
2018	*ATL*	*MLB*	*24*	*5*	*6*	*0*	*16*	*16*	*96*	*76*	*10*	*6.3*	*10.4*	*111*	*53%*	*.305*	*1.49*	*4.27*	*4.79*	*5.11*	*4.1*	*0.4*	*118*	

Breakout: 8%   Improve: 18%   Collapse: 12%   Attrition: 19%   MLB: 33%   Comparables: *Alex Colome, Travis Wood, Adalberto Mejia*

Sims has worked under pro instruction for five years now and made considerable strides since being drafted as a raw, strong-armed tyro. At the same time, he continues to create frustration for Atlanta's development staff. Sims is gifted with a borderline plus-plus fastball that can reach upper 90s and a downward-breaking curveball that can be devastating. The issue since the beginning has been his lack of feel brought on by inconsistent timing. He'll give you six innings of scoreless ball with two plus-plus pitches, then stick you behind by six runs next time out. At this point, relief is the stronger possibility. Let him work with those two pitches at max effort over one-inning stints and everyone except opposing hitters would be a happy camper.

Mike Soroka RHP

Born: 8/4/97 Age: 19 Bats: R Throws: R Height: 6'4" Weight: 195 Entered Pro Ball: Round 1, 2015 Draft (#28 overall)

YEAR	TEAM	LVL	AGE	W	L	SV	G	GS	IP	H	HR	BB/9	K/9	K	GB%	BABIP	WHIP	ERA	FIP	DRA	VORP	WARP	cFIP	MPH
2016	ROM	A	18	9	9	0	25	24	143	130	3	2.0	7.9	125	53%	.303	1.13	3.02	2.78	3.25	27.8	3.0	91	

Breakout: 1%   Improve: 1%   Collapse: 0%   Attrition: 0%   MLB: 1%   Comparables: *Manny Banuelos, Tyler Skaggs, Taijuan Walker*

Count the Braves among the best at finding shortstops and quality pitching. Soroka is blossoming into a prime example of the latter. Atlanta nabbed him at the end of the first round despite little pre-draft fanfare, and he has promptly vaulted himself up the prospect ladder as a potential mid-rotation starter. One could argue that his recipe for success starts with a plus-potential fastball and curveball, or perhaps his strong, durable frame, but to talk to the young man is a treat in itself. Soroka is an information sponge who knows exactly what he has to do to succeed and he has the talent to implement it on the mound. He's a safer bet than most teenagers to be a major-league starter, and a big part of that is his aptitude and knowledge.

Julio Teheran RHP

Born: 1/27/91 Age: 26 Bats: R Throws: R Height: 6'2" Weight: 205 Entered Pro Ball: International Free Agent, 2007

YEAR	TEAM	LVL	AGE	W	L	SV	G	GS	IP	H	HR	BB/9	K/9	K	GB%	BABIP	WHIP	ERA	FIP	DRA	VORP	WARP	cFIP	MPH
2014	ATL	MLB	23	14	13	0	33	33	221	188	22	2.1	7.6	186	37%	.267	1.08	2.89	3.46	3.85	24.1	2.7	103	93.8
2015	ATL	MLB	24	11	8	0	33	33	200²	189	27	3.3	7.7	171	42%	.288	1.31	4.04	4.43	4.54	12.1	1.3	107	94.3
2016	ATL	MLB	25	7	10	0	30	30	188	157	22	2.0	8.0	167	41%	.260	1.05	3.21	3.73	3.88	30.9	3.2	99	94.0
2017	*ATL*	*MLB*	*26*	*10*	*11*	*0*	*29*	*29*	*174*	*156*	*21*	*2.7*	*8.8*	*169*	*48%*	*.287*	*1.19*	*3.73*	*3.82*	*4.28*	*17.4*	*1.8*	*100*	
2018	*ATL*	*MLB*	*27*	*11*	*10*	*0*	*30*	*30*	*192²*	*159*	*23*	*2.6*	*8.9*	*191*	*48%*	*.289*	*1.11*	*3.44*	*3.84*	*4.16*	*28.0*	*2.9*	*94*	

Breakout: 21%   Improve: 50%   Collapse: 15%   Attrition: 8%   MLB: 96%   Comparables: *Phil Hughes, Jered Weaver, John Danks*

While he didn't take a quantum leap like fellow Braves cornerstone Freddie Freeman did in 2016, Teheran still managed to bounce back from an inconsistent 2015. The obvious reasoning behind the return to normalcy is that he managed to turn the mechanical tweaks and command gains that appeared during the tail end of his disappointing 2015 into tangible improvement last year. Much of his success hinged on an improved walk rate, and overall Teheran was arguably Atlanta's only reliable starter although it's an open question whether he can keep this up. Many of his numbers from previous seasons suggest that 2015 may have actually been the fluke, and that we should expect more of the 2014/2016-caliber work going forward from a pitcher who's only 26. The man from the land of Magical Realism may not have especially magical stuff up his sleeve, but he'll realistically give you the type of production that you need from a pitcher at the top of a rotation.

Touki Toussaint   RHP

Born: 6/20/96   Age: 21   Bats: R   Throws: R   Height: 6'3"   Weight: 185   Entered Pro Ball: Round 1, 2014 Draft (#16 overall)

YEAR	TEAM	LVL	AGE	W	L	SV	G	GS	IP	H	HR	BB/9	K/9	K	GB%	BABIP	WHIP	ERA	FIP	DRA	VORP	WARP	cFIP	MPH
2015	KNC	A	19	2	2	0	7	7	39	31	4	3.5	6.7	29	38%	.243	1.18	3.69	4.55	5.06	0.7	0.1	106	
2015	ROM	A	19	3	5	0	10	10	48²	40	6	6.1	7.0	38	41%	.252	1.50	5.73	5.74	6.99	-9.5	-1.0	122	
2016	ROM	A	20	4	8	0	27	24	132¹	105	13	4.8	8.7	128	38%	.265	1.33	3.88	4.56	5.15	-2.4	-0.3	110	
2017	*ATL*	*MLB*	*21*	*4*	*9*	*0*	*20*	*20*	*91²*	*100*	*17*	*6.1*	*5.2*	*53*	*77%*	*.299*	*1.77*	*6.55*	*6.61*	*7.75*	*-22.2*	*-2.3*	*184*	
2018	*ATL*	*MLB*	*22*	*4*	*9*	*0*	*20*	*20*	*118*	*116*	*22*	*7.7*	*8.1*	*106*	*77%*	*.306*	*1.84*	*6.30*	*7.07*	*7.46*	*-19.7*	*-2.0*	*175*	

Breakout: 4%   Improve: 5%   Collapse: 0%   Attrition: 3%   MLB: 7%   *Comparables: Robbie Ray, Alex Cobb, Timothy Melville*

Toussaint came out of the Single-A Rome bullpen for a one-inning stint in early September to stay fresh ahead of a playoff run. It was as if the heavens opened, angels came to earth and gave those mere humans in attendance a gift from God in the form of a Touki relief outing. The kid has the appropriate combination of filthy stuff, cool demeanor and 80-grade name to close major-league games, but he's working tirelessly to avoid coming out of the bullpen in the future. His fastball can hit plus-plus in the mid-90s when he needs it and sits low 90s as a starter. His curveball can also hit plus-plus with 12-6 break and extremely tight spin, and his changeup flashes plus but is still developing into a consistently usable offering. Toussaint has made strides developing the command he'll need to remain a starter by improving his timing and syncing his halves better. That needs to continue over a full season, but his positive steps in that direction have helped him maintain an ultra-high ceiling.

Arodys Vizcaino   RHP

Born: 11/13/90   Age: 26   Bats: R   Throws: R   Height: 6'0"   Weight: 230   Entered Pro Ball: International Free Agent, 2007

YEAR	TEAM	LVL	AGE	W	L	SV	G	GS	IP	H	HR	BB/9	K/9	K	GB%	BABIP	WHIP	ERA	FIP	DRA	VORP	WARP	cFIP	MPH
2014	TEN	AA	23	1	1	1	14	0	13²	7	1	2.0	10.5	16	52%	.200	0.73	2.63	2.67	2.21	4.0	0.4	75	
2014	IOW	AAA	23	0	0	0	17	0	18¹	25	1	5.4	7.9	16	47%	.393	1.96	5.40	4.79	6.88	-3.1	-0.3	109	
2014	CHN	MLB	23	0	0	0	5	0	5	5	1	5.4	7.2	4	40%	.286	1.60	5.40	5.90	5.12	-0.4	0.0	109	98.0
2015	ATL	MLB	24	3	1	9	36	0	33²	27	1	3.5	9.9	37	37%	.295	1.19	1.60	2.51	4.00	2.7	0.3	95	100.2
2016	ATL	MLB	25	1	4	10	43	0	38²	37	3	6.1	11.6	50	56%	.333	1.63	4.42	3.70	3.20	7.6	0.8	88	100.1
2017	*ATL*	*MLB*	*26*	*3*	*3*	*0*	*67*	*0*	*70*	*65*	*7*	*4.1*	*9.7*	*76*	*50%*	*.306*	*1.39*	*3.69*	*3.79*	*4.25*	*5.2*	*0.5*	*95*	
2018	*ATL*	*MLB*	*27*	*3*	*1*	*1*	*58*	*0*	*62*	*47*	*5*	*4.2*	*10.5*	*72*	*50%*	*.301*	*1.22*	*3.21*	*3.59*	*3.90*	*8.4*	*0.9*	*83*	

Breakout: 30%   Improve: 52%   Collapse: 21%   Attrition: 16%   MLB: 83%   *Comparables: Sean Doolittle, Cla Meredith, Jordan Walden*

Based on talent alone, Vizcaino is the Braves' best reliever. That's been the case since he became a regular in Atlanta's bullpen following his return to the organization in 2015. In addition to the talent and stuff, the production improved in 2016, as Vizcaino posted career-bests in cFIP and DRA in a late-inning role. Normally that combination of talent and production would result in a rebuilding team like Atlanta trading him, but an injury near the deadline sapped his value. Health issues are still a bit of a concern with Vizcaino. He won't be throwing at all during the offseason, but he'll be free to throw as much as he wants once spring arrives. As usual, if he can stay healthy he's definitely a nice late-inning option.

Patrick Weigel   RHP

Born: 7/8/94   Age: 22   Bats: R   Throws: R   Height: 6'6"   Weight: 220   Entered Pro Ball: Round 7, 2015 Draft (#210 overall)

YEAR	TEAM	LVL	AGE	W	L	SV	G	GS	IP	H	HR	BB/9	K/9	K	GB%	BABIP	WHIP	ERA	FIP	DRA	VORP	WARP	cFIP	MPH
2016	ROM	A	21	10	4	0	22	21	129	92	7	3.3	9.4	135	46%	.256	1.08	2.51	3.41	3.00	28.5	3.1	93	
2016	MIS	AA	21	1	2	0	3	3	20²	9	2	3.5	7.4	17	45%	.143	0.82	2.18	4.67	4.40	1.6	0.2	105	
2017	*ATL*	*MLB*	*22*	*5*	*7*	*0*	*19*	*19*	*95²*	*96*	*13*	*4.7*	*6.1*	*65*	*60%*	*.298*	*1.53*	*5.28*	*5.30*	*6.44*	*-9.3*	*-1.0*	*150*	
2018	*ATL*	*MLB*	*23*	*6*	*10*	*0*	*24*	*24*	*144¹*	*131*	*21*	*6.0*	*8.5*	*136*	*60%*	*.302*	*1.57*	*5.15*	*5.76*	*6.28*	*-10.0*	*-1.0*	*145*	

Breakout: 5%   Improve: 7%   Collapse: 1%   Attrition: 9%   MLB: 13%   *Comparables: Zack Wheeler, Miguel Almonte, Joe Ross*

Weigel emerged from the smoke, cocked his leg and let loose a 97 mph fastball in a hail of fury as sparks flew behind him. OK, it wasn't that dramatic, but he did explode onto the scene after being drafted in the seventh round in 2015. The Braves showed off their scouting ability by popping a major league-quality arm there, and it shouldn't take that long for him to reach the ultimate level. He sits in the low 90s as a starter, but can reach back for 95-97 when he wants, paired with a biting slider. He adds a slow curveball and flashes a usable changeup to get through lineups multiple times. Weigel comes at batters from a tough angle and is a high-energy starter to make things even more difficult on them. The stuff and effort would play up in a high-leverage relief role, but the ceiling is closer to a back-end type.

Matt Wisler   RHP

Born: 9/12/92   Age: 24   Bats: R   Throws: R   Height: 6'3"   Weight: 205   Entered Pro Ball: Round 7, 2011 Draft (#233 overall)

YEAR	TEAM	LVL	AGE	W	L	SV	G	GS	IP	H	HR	BB/9	K/9	K	GB%	BABIP	WHIP	ERA	FIP	DRA	VORP	WARP	cFIP	MPH
2014	SAN	AA	21	1	0	0	6	6	30	26	2	1.8	10.5	35	47%	.312	1.07	2.10	2.25	2.67	8.5	0.9	79	
2014	ELP	AAA	21	9	5	0	22	22	116²	131	19	2.8	7.8	101	44%	.317	1.43	5.01	5.14	4.19	15.7	1.6	92	
2015	GWN	AAA	22	3	4	0	12	12	65	68	5	1.8	6.8	49	40%	.307	1.25	4.29	3.30	3.14	15.6	1.6	93	
2015	ATL	MLB	22	8	8	0	20	19	109	119	16	3.3	5.9	72	35%	.298	1.46	4.71	4.96	6.25	-14.3	-1.5	127	95.6
2016	GWN	AAA	23	2	1	0	4	4	26²	27	3	1.7	7.4	22	52%	.296	1.20	3.71	3.77	3.90	4.3	0.4	91	
2016	ATL	MLB	23	7	13	1	27	26	156²	159	26	2.8	6.6	115	42%	.279	1.33	5.00	4.89	5.54	-3.2	-0.3	116	95.1
2017	ATL	MLB	24	3	4	0	10	10	57	58	7	2.9	7.2	45	53%	.293	1.32	4.16	4.29	4.77	2.6	0.3	100	
2018	ATL	MLB	25	11	11	0	32	32	205¹	174	24	3.3	9.1	208	53%	.299	1.22	3.66	4.10	4.45	21.7	2.2	101	

Breakout: 25%   Improve: 61%   Collapse: 13%   Attrition: 18%   MLB: 92%   *Comparables: Yordano Ventura, Jarrod Parker, Trevor Bauer*

It's a bit rash and maybe even short-sighted to say that a 24-year old is approaching a make-or-break season, but that may be the case for Wisler. Sure, he showed flashes of the potential that made the Braves so intent on acquiring him from the Padres, but he struggled mightily at times and earned his midseason demotion to Triple-A. He made it back into the rotation to close out the season and he'll surely be fighting for a starting role once spring training rolls around. If he can pull it together there's a mid-rotation pitcher here, but it's time to show it.

Chris Withrow   RHP

Born: 4/1/89   Age: 28   Bats: R   Throws: R   Height: 6'3"   Weight: 240   Entered Pro Ball: Round 1, 2007 Draft (#20 overall)

YEAR	TEAM	LVL	AGE	W	L	SV	G	GS	IP	H	HR	BB/9	K/9	K	GB%	BABIP	WHIP	ERA	FIP	DRA	VORP	WARP	cFIP	MPH
2014	LAN	MLB	25	0	0	0	20	0	21¹	10	1	7.6	11.8	28	46%	.214	1.31	2.95	3.76	4.11	0.9	0.1	102	97.7
2016	GWN	AAA	27	0	1	5	11	0	10	7	1	5.4	10.8	12	48%	.250	1.30	4.50	3.87	3.31	1.8	0.2	97	
2016	ATL	MLB	27	3	0	0	46	0	37²	29	5	4.1	6.7	28	46%	.226	1.22	3.58	4.94	5.56	-2.5	-0.3	113	95.8
2017	ATL	MLB	28	2	1	1	35	0	36²	33	5	3.9	8.1	33	47%	.297	1.33	4.35	4.58	5.26	-0.5	0.0	123	
2018	ATL	MLB	29	2	1	1	45	0	46	39	5	4.4	9.3	48	47%	.300	1.33	4.02	4.49	4.86	1.4	0.1	112	

Breakout: 26%   Improve: 45%   Collapse: 22%   Attrition: 23%   MLB: 78%   *Comparables: Blake Wood, Jason Frasor, Santiago Casilla*

Joining a Braves staff that frequently resembled M*A*S*H extras being shipped back to the front, Withrow's return from Tommy John surgery last year helped him fit right in. The main difference compared to the others is that Withrow returned with a normal-looking beard instead of the weird-looking Fu Manchu that he had going on during his final Dodgers days. While he was able to nail down a regular spot in the Braves' bullpen, he wasn't able to reach the levels that he hit in his previous two seasons. He cut down his walk rate, but his strikeout rate also sank. Granted, he did have some injury issues crop up over the course of the season, and command often lags for TJ survivors, so there's hope that a healthy Withrow can return to the form he showed in Los Angeles.

LINEOUTS

Hitters

NAME	POS	TEAM	LVL	AGE	PA	R	2B	3B	HR	RBI	BB	K	SB	CS	AVG/OBP/SLG	TAv	VORP	BABIP	BRR	FRAA	WARP
Emilio Bonifacio	CF	GWN	AAA	31	471	57	14	5	2	40	39	70	37	9	.298/.356/.369	.269	17.8	.349	0.5	CF(77): -3.8, LF(19): -1.8	1.2
	CF	ATL	MLB	31	43	6	0	0	0	3	3	12	1	0	.211/.268/.211	.246	-0.1	.308	-0.6	LF(12): -0.7, CF(1): -0.0	-0.1
Johan Camargo	INF	MIS	AA	22	491	46	26	6	4	43	24	82	1	2	.267/.304/.379	.262	17.3	.317	1.2	2B(64): 2.3, SS(32): -0.5	2.0
Daniel Castro	2B	GWN	AAA	23	229	29	10	0	3	20	8	25	0	1	.257/.279/.346	.240	2.8	.274	-1.5	SS(59): 5.4, 2B(1): -0.0	0.8
	2B	ATL	MLB	23	139	8	1	0	0	7	7	24	1	1	.200/.241/.208	.172	-7.2	.245	0.5	SS(20): 0.9, 2B(16): -0.5	-0.7
Blake Lalli	C	GWN	AAA	33	380	28	22	0	1	36	22	60	1	1	.256/.301/.328	.219	-7.2	.302	-0.8	1B(60): 2.7, C(45): -14.9	-2.0
	C	ATL	MLB	33	13	0	1	0	0	1	0	3	0	0	.154/.154/.231	.109	-1.7	.200	0.0	1B(4): -0.1	-0.2
Dustin Peterson	LF	MIS	AA	21	578	65	38	2	12	88	45	100	4	1	.282/.343/.431	.303	37.1	.327	0.1	LF(125): -6.3, CF(4): -1.1	3.2
Brandon Snyder	3B	GWN	AAA	29	160	19	8	0	3	26	8	35	6	0	.327/.358/.442	.278	7.5	.402	1.5	RF(24): 0.6, LF(10): -0.3	0.7
	3B	ATL	MLB	29	47	8	5	1	4	9	1	16	0	0	.239/.255/.652	.317	2.9	.269	-1.1	3B(2): -0.4, 1B(1): 0.1	0.3

Emilio Bonifacio had a solid year at Triple-A, but none of that success translated to the big leagues and his days as a super-utility man may be over. ❖ He looks like a good player with a smooth line-drive swing from both sides of the plate and plenty of defensive chops, but **Johan Camargo** has yet to hit enough to even enter the picture as a utility man. ❖ **Daniel Castro** was out-played by Erick Aybar, which wasn't a good place to be in 2016, but his topping out as a potential utility man is nothing new. ❖ **Brett Cumberland** has a catcher's build with a long, powerful swing and a mustache that just won't quit. ❖ It was such a strange year for the Braves at the catcher spot that **Blake Lalli** had a few cameo appearances. If that happens in 2017, something went horribly wrong. ❖ **Dustin Peterson** became a Double-A masher overnight and put himself back on radars, but it's still tough to pull the trigger on an impact-role projection based on the bat-carrying profile. ❖ After two full seasons in the minors, **Brandon Snyder** managed to make his return to the majors. Don't expect a repeat in 2017.

Pitchers

NAME	TEAM	LVL	AGE	W	L	SV	G	GS	IP	H	HR	BB/9	K/9	K	GB%	BABIP	WHIP	ERA	FIP	DRA	VORP	WARP	cFIP	MPH
Brandon Cunniff	MIS	AA	27	0	1	2	8	0	12²	6	0	3.6	7.1	10	48%	.182	0.87	0.71	3.16	3.82	1.3	0.1	98	
	GWN	AAA	27	3	3	2	35	0	42²	35	3	4.0	8.2	39	51%	.286	1.27	4.01	3.59	3.39	7.5	0.8	94	
	ATL	MLB	27	2	0	0	15	0	17	14	2	4.8	8.5	16	26%	.267	1.35	4.24	4.77	4.93	0.1	0.0	115	94.9
Jason Hursh	MIS	AA	24	3	2	3	35	0	57	42	0	3.6	6.6	42	69%	.250	1.14	2.05	3.21	4.08	4.1	0.4	101	
	ATL	MLB	24	0	0	0	2	0	1¹	4	0	20.2	6.8	1	100%	.571	5.25	33.75	8.44	5.05	0.0	0.0	106	96.5
	GWN	AAA	24	0	0	0	8	0	16	15	0	4.5	4.5	8	56%	.312	1.44	1.69	4.04	5.11	-0.3	0.0	115	
Casey Kelly	ATL	MLB	26	0	3	0	10	1	21²	30	1	2.9	2.9	7	45%	.341	1.71	5.82	4.39	7.38	-5.6	-0.6	128	92.3
	GWN	AAA	26	3	6	0	15	12	74	64	6	3.4	5.7	47	48%	.266	1.24	3.53	4.21	5.71	-3.4	-0.4	113	
Matt Marksberry	GWN	AAA	25	4	2	0	28	0	34	34	2	4.0	8.5	32	39%	.327	1.44	2.65	3.37	4.79	0.7	0.1	101	
	ATL	MLB	25	0	0	0	4	0	3¹	5	1	2.7	5.4	2	31%	.333	1.80	5.40	7.69	4.72	0.1	0.0	114	94.1
A.J. Minter	MIS	AA	22	1	0	0	18	0	18²	13	0	2.9	14.9	31	46%	.333	1.02	2.41	0.96	1.50	6.7	0.7	67	
Akeel Morris	BIN	AA	23	2	2	6	22	0	25¹	19	4	5.7	12.8	36	39%	.283	1.38	4.62	4.46	2.97	5.0	0.5	90	
	MIS	AA	23	3	1	0	25	0	35²	27	0	5.3	12.6	50	36%	.333	1.35	2.27	2.28	3.91	3.3	0.4	91	
Armando Rivero	IOW	AAA	28	5	3	1	43	0	67²	41	3	4.7	14.0	105	35%	.279	1.12	2.13	2.83	1.44	26.5	2.7	70	
Daniel Winkler	ATL	MLB	26	0	0	0	3	0	2¹	0	0	3.9	15.4	4	100%	.000	0.43	0.00	1.04	4.10	0.2	0.0	96	93.4

Remember **Jesse Biddle**? Did you know the once-promising Phillies prospect spent 2016 in the Braves' organization while rehabbing from Tommy John surgery? You do now, and that fact will likely overwrite the neurons that previously stored your laptop password. You're welcome. ❖ Extremely Ambitious Atlanta Braves Pitching Project No. 94857, aka **Brandon Cunniff**, spent most of 2016 in the minors trying to figure out his control problems. ❖ **Jason Hursh** managed to get a cup of coffee in 2016, but his 2017 figures to involve little more than another cameo in the majors. ❖ Once upon a time, **Casey Kelly** had a reputation for being a strikeout pitcher. That rep slowly disappeared once he made it to the majors, and it completely evaporated last season. ❖ A rough 2016 for **Matt Marksberry** was put into perspective when he suffered a collapsed lung in November. Fortunately he'll make a full recovery and now he can focus on more trivial issues like making it into a major-league bullpen in 2017. ❖ After missing half of 2015 due to a positive test for Ipamorelin, **Andrew McKirahan** missed all of 2016 due to Tommy John surgery, his second such operation. ❖ **A.J. Minter** is a fast-rising, bulldog lefty who only needs to stay healthy to be a high-leverage reliever in the majors. ❖ After a one-game stint with the Mets in 2015, **Akeel Morris** was called up by the Braves last season and sent back down without pitching. Will this be the year he finally gets to stay for longer than a day? ❖ **Kyle Muller** contended for the nationwide high school home run title while refusing to give up long balls on the mound. That makes for a better baseball player than the other way around. ❖ Still stuck in the minors four years after signing with the Cubs out of Cuba, 28-year-old **Armando Rivero** has a mid-90s fastball and horrible control. ❖ If **Paco Rodriguez** comes back from Tommy John surgery fully recovered, he'll serve as a quality lefty option out of the bullpen. ❖ The Braves paid **Joey Wentz** like a top-15 draft pick and, when it's all said and done, his three plus-potential pitches could have him performing better than many popped ahead of him. ❖ Poor **Daniel Winkler**. The guy threw 1.2 innings in 2015 due to recovery from Tommy John surgery and then 2.1 innings in 2016 before suffering a fractured elbow.

BALTIMORE ORIOLES

Essay by Jake Mintz

Player comments by Matthew Trueblood and BP staff

Buck Showalter didn't use baseball's best closer in a tie game on the road in the Wild Card game.

Like every other Orioles fan, I spent the remainder of the playoffs just mumbling that tragic truth to myself over and over and over. Though infinitely less meme-able, those words have become the Orioles' equivalent of blowing a 3-1 lead. If Jeffrey Maier's regrettable catch reach-around was Vesuvius, then the 12th inning of the Wild Card game has to be Krakatoa.

Ask any Orioles fan and they'll tell you that nothing will ever top Jeffrey Maier. Not Raul Ibanez's rampage in the 2012 ALDS. Not the unbearably annoying 1979 "We Are Family" Pittsburgh Pirates. And no, not even trading Jake Arrieta for Steve Clevenger and Scott Feldman. Nothing could be worse than Jeffrey Maier. Nothing. But I'll tell you what: This was pretty damn close.

Putting aside the pain of Ubaldo Jimenez's meatball, let me remind you that last season the Orioles were good. More importantly they were fun good and most importantly they were fun weird good. Despite a pitching staff that hemorrhaged runs, the Orioles led the division for five months, won 89 games and came within one run of the ALDS. As is usually the case with the Birds, it was the bullpen, the Buck Showalter and the long ball that made them competitive.

As bad as BrittonGate was, it seems unfair to allow one managerial decision to define the season. Unfortunately, life isn't always fair. Sometimes an innocent teenager reaches over a fence at the wrong time. Sometimes that apple you thought was firm turns out to be mushy and you get apple stuck in your bottom teeth retainer. Sometimes, a single dinger conceded at the wrong time ruins six months of baseball.

Even-Year Magic But Lamer

By winning the World Series in 2010, 2012 and 2014 the Giants developed a reputation for being beneficiaries of a certain extraterrestrial force known as "Even-Year Magic." Time and time again the team by The Bay exceeded expectations thanks to performances from the unlikeliest of sources. The types of fill-in players you find in the proverbial baseball couch cushions—dudes like Cody Ross, Marco Scutaro and Travis Ishikawa—became playoff

ORIOLES PROSPECTUS
2016 W-L: 89-73, 2ND IN AL EAST

Pythag	.519	11th	DER	.701	17th
RS/G	4.59	12th	B-Age	28.4	13th
RA/G	4.41	16th	P-Age	27.8	9th
TAv	.258	18th	Salary	$147.7M	9th
BRR	1.04	11th	M$/MW	$3.3M	19th
TAv-P	.255	10th	DL Days	709	8th
FIP	4.27	18th	$ on DL	9%	8th

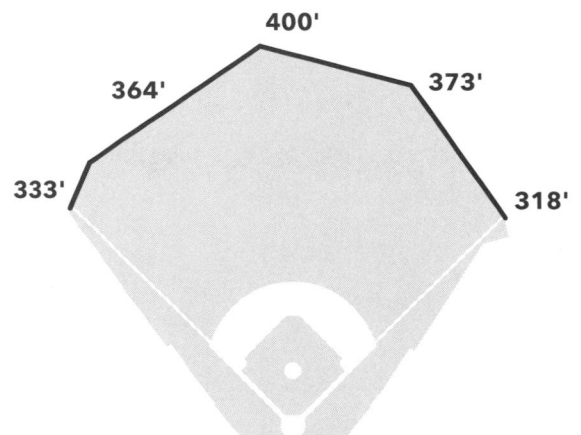

Outfield wall profile: **7'** to **21'**

Three-Year Park Factors

Runs	Runs/RH	Runs/LH	HR/RH	HR/LH
108	111	113	108	106

Top Hitter WARP	5.7	Manny Machado
Top Pitcher WARP	4.5	Kevin Gausman
Top Prospect		Chance Sisco

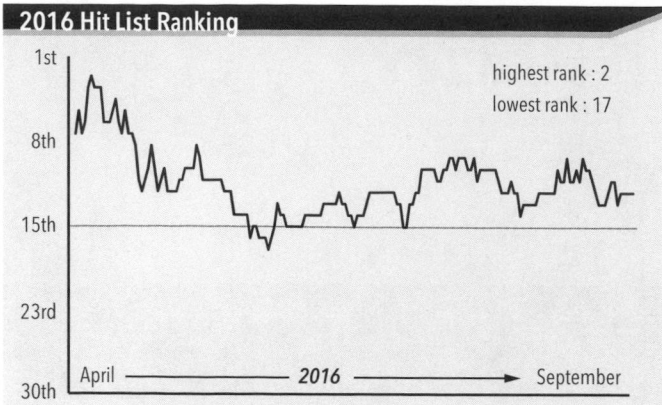

2016 Hit List Ranking

highest rank : 2
lowest rank : 17

April — 2016 → September

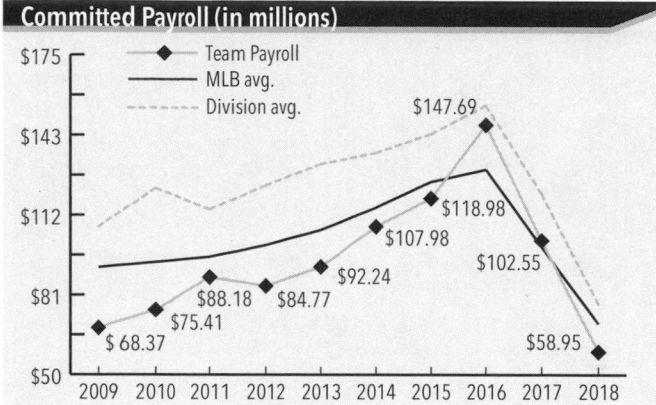

Committed Payroll (in millions)

- ◆ Team Payroll
- — MLB avg.
- --- Division avg.

$147.69

$118.98
$107.98
$102.55
$92.24
$88.18 $84.77
$75.41
$68.37
$58.95

2009 2010 2011 2012 2013 2014 2015 2016 2017 2018

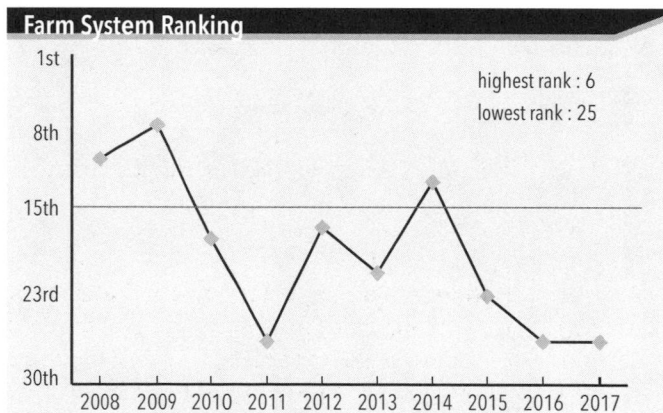

Farm System Ranking

highest rank : 6
lowest rank : 25

2008 2009 2010 2011 2012 2013 2014 2015 2016 2017

Personnel

EVP, Baseball Operations:
Dan Duquette

Director, Player Personnel:
John Stockstill

Director, Scouting:
Gary Rajsich

Director, Player Development:
Brian Graham

Manager:
Buck Showalter

heroes, forever solidified in Giants lore. Though it came to a halt in 2016, the wondrous run of even-year magic was both captivating and unwatchable, frustrating and liberating, complex and innate.

The Orioles seem to be developing some even-year magic of their own—a much lamer and less memorable version of the phenomenon, but even-year magic all the same. In 2012, 2014 and 2016 the Orioles found a way to blast past preseason expectations.

Year	PECOTA Projected Win Total	Actual Win Total
2012	71	93
2014	75	96
2016	72	89

In those three seasons the Orioles beat their PECOTA projections by a combined total of 60 wins. Many people have written about how and why the Orioles have exceeded expectations so consistently. This seemingly repeatable ability to surpass expectations has certainly become part of the identity associated with the current core's run of success. At this point many of those narratives are overwrought. Dan Duquette is adept at finding undervalued pieces. Showalter is a magician in a dugout jacket. Adam Jones is a leader on and off the field. The bullpen makes up for less-than-stellar rotations. Orioles magic is a tangible force that makes Baltimore, Maryland and the world a safer and more prosperous place. You get the idea.

But what exactly made 2016 different? Because for whatever reason, up until Edwin Encarnacion ripped Baltimore asunder, last season felt different. Maybe they were just divinely doomed. If only there was a visual device that we could use to compare and contrast similarities and differences between various phenomena. Oh wait. Did you hear that? On the horizon? A whisper? No. A thundering sound. It's. A. Venn Diagram.

What Made The 2016 Orioles Different, Ranked

131. They played 162 regular-season baseball games. This happens to almost everyone, every year. Who put this on here?

64. J.J. Hardy. He was hurt for a chunk, struck out a lot, hit for a low average and above-average power for a shortstop, good defender.

10. Ubaldo Jimenez's disastrous season. He started spring training off poorly. Here's the second inning of his first spring start:
- HBP
- BB
- Jimenez error
- Wild Pitch
- Fly Out
- Single
- HBP
- Three-Run Homer

Here are some real text conversations I had with my mother, the person who made me an Orioles fan and is the biggest Ubaldo hater I know:

May 17th

Mom: Hmmmm. The Orioles got crushed. I wonder who was pitching.

June 2nd

Me: Mom what do you think of Ubaldo so far?

Mom: He's looked good, but you know it's only the 5th inning. Still time for him to Ubaldo.

*Note: Jimenez allowed five runs in the fifth inning.

5. Ubaldo Jimenez's fantastic end to the season. After being relegated to the bullpen for solidifying himself as a bad pitcher™, Jimenez bounced back in his last six starts by posting a 2.45 ERA in 47.2 innings. My mother, a vulgarly vocal critic, even started to come around.

September 24th

Me: You know Ubaldo's been the O's best pitcher the last month or so?

Mom: Yeah and a broken clock is right twice a day. Just you watch.

They say moms are always right.

3. Mark Trumbo makes contact, sends balls over fences. Yeah, what the hell happened here? At first I thought the Orioles were giving up a cornerstone, franchise-defining piece in Steve Clevenger. Then Mark Trumbo led the majors in homers and Clevenger said some racist stuff. Oh, how the tables turn. Trumbo's season was essentially just a more out-of-nowhere version of Nelson Cruz in 2014. He was very fun to watch. Sometimes baseball analysis is simple.

2. Manny Machado solidifies himself as a generational talent. In any other year this would be no. 1. There's something beautiful about a dude like Machado. Coming up the chain he was hailed as the future of the Orioles. Expectations were through the roof, comparisons to Alex Rodriguez were made and 2030 Hall of Fame trips were planned. He was supposed to be the next big star, a generational player who could transform the game with his glove and his bat. And guess what? He's all that and maybe more. Orioles fans are wary of one-year outliers (looking at you, 2014 Steve Pearce and 1997 Brady Anderson) so

Machado's 2016 was like a warm hug from a motherly figure telling you everything is going to be OK. That is, until your mom takes $200 million to move to a bigger city in a few years. (SORRY.)

1. Zach Britton. ZACH BRITTON ALLOWED FOUR EARNED RUNS IN 2016. FOUR! In baseball, if the circumstances are correct, you can allow that many runs on a single pitch. But Britton, titan of the hump, is not your average pitcher. His hellacious fastball/sinker *thing* that he somehow throws 97 mph is devastating. That pitch defies physics, religion, and the American judicial system. The only home run Britton served up in 2016 was to Mookie Betts, which is actually a legally mandated act for all Orioles pitchers so it barely counts.

It's a super weird feeling for a fan to know that your team's closer is going to get the job done every single time he goes out there. Even Dodgers fans have had to get nervous about Kenley Jansen sometimes. Same thing with fans of the various teams that have employed Aroldis Chapman. Britton was a different beast. By September there was nay a rumble in the tummy, nor trepidation to be found. Britton was the best, plain and simple, which is what made the late innings of the Wild Card game so inexplicable and excruciatingly difficult to watch.

Unpacking the Sadness

There's a scene in *Captain America: Civil War* where the bad guy, a menacing Eastern European dude named Zemo, reveals his dastardly plan to turn the Avengers (the superhero equivalent of the MLBPA) against one another. "An empire toppled by its enemies can rise again," he proclaims to an astonished Chris Pine and Robert Downey Jr. "But one which crumbles from within? That's dead ... forever."

Calling the Orioles an empire is farcical and implying that said pseudo-empire is "dead forever" is irresponsible, but the connection is clear. The Orioles weren't beaten into submission and they weren't toppled by invaders. They imploded internally. In an instant the forces meant to ensure order and prosperity were revealed instead as architects of chaos. The heroes themselves became the iconoclasts. The machine exploded from the inside.

Throughout the Orioles' recent run of success the most meaningful constant has been William Nathaniel Showalter III. Some fans have credited Showalter as the force motivating the Orioles beyond their expectations every year. You can buy shirts that read "Buck Not Luck" and "In Buck We Trust." Beyond the grumpy, introverted exterior there's a genius at work, or so the thinking went. His bullpen management was often mentioned as a particular strong suit. Like I said, the machine exploded from the inside.

Hopefully the 2017 Orioles can put that moment in the past. Maybe they can kick the even-year trend and make a serious run at the postseason. Maybe Machado is only going to get better and Mookie Betts peaked. Maybe Showalter learned from his cataclysmic gaffe and understands why using a closer on the road in a tie game is the best way to go. Maybe Jimenez wins the Cy Young award in the last year of his contract, signs a long-term deal to stay in Baltimore and goes into the Hall of Fame as an Oriole. Maybe Britton can do it all over again. But at the same time, maybe not.

That's the thing about the Orioles as currently constructed. Success relies upon these maybes. They can't utilize a stocked farm system midseason or fall back on the Tempur-Pedic comfort of a deep pitching staff or overcome devastating injuries. The margin for error is small. There's a margin for success too, as the Orioles have shown, but for it to work the baseball gods need to smile down forgivingly upon Camden Yards. In retrospect, 2016 feels like a missed opportunity. A captivating, bizarre, entertaining and unique missed opportunity, but a missed opportunity all the same. I guess all the Orioles can do now is look to the future and hope that 2018 brings more even-year magic, some better luck and a better Buck. ■

—Jake Mintz plays baseball at Washington University and is one half of Cespedes Family BBQ

HITTERS

Dariel Alvarez   RF

Born: 11/7/88   Age: 28   Bats: R   Throws: R   Height: 6'2"   Weight: 180   Entered Pro Ball: International Free Agent, 2013

YEAR	TEAM	LVL	AGE	PA	R	2B	3B	HR	RBI	BB	K	SB	CS	AVG/OBP/SLG	TAv	VORP	BABIP	BRR	FRAA	WARP
2014	BOW	AA	25	381	52	20	1	14	68	13	35	7	4	.309/.332/.487	.286	20.9	.307	-0.7	CF(90): 4.7	2.7
2014	NOR	AAA	25	183	23	17	2	1	19	8	27	1	1	.301/.328/.439	.259	3.0	.347	-0.6	RF(37): -1.0, CF(6): 1.3	0.3
2015	NOR	AAA	26	541	61	24	2	16	72	16	63	7	3	.275/.305/.424	.265	17.5	.285	2.8	RF(95): 10.5, CF(47): -2.2	2.6
2015	BAL	MLB	26	31	3	1	0	1	1	2	8	0	0	.241/.290/.379	.251	0.9	.300	0.6	RF(12): 1.9, CF(1): -0.1	0.3
2016	BAL	MLB	27	4	0	1	0	0	0	1	0	0	0	.333/.500/.667	.566	1.1	.333	-0.2	RF(1): -0.1	0.1
2016	NOR	AAA	27	560	53	38	0	4	49	28	80	7	2	.288/.324/.384	.254	3.8	.331	-2.2	RF(108): -3.6, LF(4): 1.4	0.2
2017	*BAL*	*MLB*	*28*	*101*	*10*	*5*	*0*	*3*	*12*	*4*	*18*	*1*	*0*	*.263/.298/.415*	*.247*	*1.3*	*.293*	*-0.1*	*RF 0, LF -0*	*0.0*
2018	*BAL*	*MLB*	*29*	*273*	*32*	*14*	*1*	*9*	*33*	*12*	*49*	*2*	*1*	*.261/.299/.425*	*.245*	*1.2*	*.290*	*-0.4*	*RF 1, LF -1*	*0.1*

Breakout: 2%   Improve: 10%   Collapse: 7%   Attrition: 19%   MLB: 26%   *Comparables: Matt McBride, Nick Buss, Keith Reed*

If you could pick just one tool around which to build a successful big-league position player, it'd be the hit tool. The sheer ability to put the bat on the ball consistently, and with some authority, is the most valuable skill there is. Unfortunately, it's the *only* one Alvarez has, and it's not enough to carry him to any kind of full-time utility. He won't embarrass himself in right field, but doesn't add value there either. He hit for some power in his first two minor-league seasons, but seems unable to sustain it against advanced pitching. He doesn't draw walks or run well. His only value is as a short-side platoon guy and bench bat.

Pedro Alvarez   DH

Born: 2/6/87   Age: 30   Bats: L   Throws: R   Height: 6'3"   Weight: 250   Entered Pro Ball: Round 1, 2008 Draft (#2 overall)

YEAR	TEAM	LVL	AGE	PA	R	2B	3B	HR	RBI	BB	K	SB	CS	AVG/OBP/SLG	TAv	VORP	BABIP	BRR	FRAA	WARP
2014	PIT	MLB	27	445	46	13	1	18	56	45	113	8	3	.231/.312/.405	.260	11.3	.277	-1.1	3B(99): 8.2, 1B(5): -0.6	2.1
2015	PIT	MLB	28	491	60	18	0	27	77	48	131	2	0	.243/.318/.469	.285	17.4	.279	0.4	1B(124): 3.6	2.2
2016	BAL	MLB	29	376	43	20	0	22	49	37	97	1	0	.249/.322/.504	.273	10.5	.282	1.2	3B(12): -0.6	1.0
2017	BAL	MLB	30	32	4	1	0	2	5	3	9	0	0	.236/.313/.462	.266	1.1	.280	0.0	3B 0	0.1
2018	BAL	MLB	31	205	29	8	0	11	31	21	58	1	0	.233/.315/.458	.258	4.2	.275	0.0	3B 3	0.8

Breakout: 2%   Improve: 49%   Collapse: 9%   Attrition: 19%   MLB: 98%   Comparables: Craig Wilson, Cecil Fielder, Mark Reynolds

Alvarez drifted unwanted to a new home and kept doing what he always does: hitting for tremendous power and drawing plenty of walks. He can't hit left-handed pitchers. Even short stints in the field serve as a stern reminder that he can't play defense at all. He's huge and hulking and doesn't run the bases well. He strikes out a ton. All of that is true, and still the guy hits for tremendous power and he draws plenty of walks. He's one of the best platoon DHs in baseball. Why are you laughing? That's a real thing!!

Michael Bourn   CF

Born: 12/27/82   Age: 34   Bats: L   Throws: R   Height: 5'11"   Weight: 190   Entered Pro Ball: Round 4, 2003 Draft (#115 overall)

YEAR	TEAM	LVL	AGE	PA	R	2B	3B	HR	RBI	BB	K	SB	CS	AVG/OBP/SLG	TAv	VORP	BABIP	BRR	FRAA	WARP
2014	AKR	AA	31	25	0	0	0	0	0	0	2	10	1	0	.087/.160/.087	.120	-3.8	.154	-1.0	CF(6): -0.0	-0.4
2014	COH	AAA	31	20	1	1	0	0	2	0	3	0	0	.150/.150/.200	.118	-3.3	.176	-0.6	CF(3): 0.3	-0.3
2014	CLE	MLB	31	487	57	17	10	3	28	35	114	10	6	.257/.314/.360	.246	9.2	.337	1.8	CF(105): -6.6	0.3
2015	CLE	MLB	32	326	29	12	1	0	19	29	76	13	5	.246/.313/.294	.224	0.3	.332	2.1	CF(88): 0.6 • LF(1): -0.0	0.1
2015	ATL	MLB	32	156	10	3	1	0	11	17	31	4	2	.221/.303/.257	.229	-1.3	.280	-0.3	LF(28): 2.8 • CF(18): 1.7	0.4
2016	DUN	A+	33	41	2	2	1	0	4	5	8	1	0	.257/.366/.371	.261	1.3	.333	0.2	CF(5): -0.7 • LF(4): 0.0	0.1
2016	MOB	AA	33	23	1	1	0	0	1	0	5	1	0	.273/.261/.318	.259	1.3	.333	0.7	CF(5): -0.6	0.1
2016	ARI	MLB	33	358	43	12	6	3	30	22	83	13	5	.261/.307/.362	.231	0.5	.340	0.7	CF(74): -0.1 • LF(8): 1.4	0.1
2016	BAL	MLB	33	55	5	1	0	2	8	6	9	2	0	.283/.358/.435	.282	2.9	.306	0.5	RF(13): -0.5 • LF(13): 1.0	0.3
2017	BAL	MLB	34	412	49	13	4	5	32	35	94	13	6	.248/.315/.348	.226	1.4	.312	0.9	CF 0, LF -0	0.1
2018	BAL	MLB	35	373	39	13	4	5	33	32	89	10	5	.238/.306/.345	.225	-2.5	.303	1.3	CF 0, LF 0	-0.3

Breakout: 3%   Improve: 31%   Collapse: 16%   Attrition: 25%   MLB: 92%   Comparables: Darin Erstad, Jerry Morales, Jim Busby

Bourn's four-year contract with the Indians saw him accumulate just 2.5 WARP, or half a win for every organization to which he belonged during that span. Now that he's no longer attached to that $50 million albatross, it's easy to see him as a role player with a little bit of utility. He still runs well and steals bases efficiently. He can still fill in at a corner outfield spot without hurting the club. He's probably never going to provide value as a hitter again, but as a non-roster invitee, he doesn't need to.

Welington Castillo   C

Born: 4/24/87   Age: 30   Bats: R   Throws: R   Height: 5'10"   Weight: 220   Entered Pro Ball: International Free Agent, 2004

YEAR	TEAM	LVL	AGE	PA	R	2B	3B	HR	RBI	BB	K	SB	CS	AVG/OBP/SLG	TAv	VORP	BABIP	BRR	FRAA	WARP
2014	CHN	MLB	27	417	28	19	0	13	46	26	102	0	0	.237/.296/.389	.261	15.5	.288	-1.9	C(106): -15.1	0.0
2015	CHN	MLB	28	47	5	2	0	2	5	3	12	0	0	.163/.234/.349	.233	0.6	.172	0.0	C(9): 0.2	0.1
2015	SEA	MLB	28	28	3	0	0	0	2	1	5	0	0	.160/.179/.160	.134	-2.4	.182	0.0	C(5): -0.9	-0.4
2015	ARI	MLB	28	303	34	13	1	17	50	21	75	0	0	.255/.317/.496	.284	19.2	.286	-0.9	C(74): -10.1	1.0
2016	ARI	MLB	29	457	41	24	0	14	68	33	121	0	0	.264/.322/.423	.266	18.6	.337	-4.5	C(107): -9.7	0.9
2017	ARI	MLB	30	414	48	20	1	15	54	33	105	1	0	.256/.326/.434	.252	15.5	.315	-2.0	C -12	0.3
2018	ARI	MLB	31	406	51	20	1	14	50	32	106	0	0	.251/.319/.419	.257	11.5	.313	-2.2	C -13	-0.2

Breakout: 1%   Improve: 36%   Collapse: 6%   Attrition: 11%   MLB: 90%   Comparables: Ryan Doumit, Nick Hundley, Geovany Soto

"Beef" Welington Castillo saw his power dry up some in 2016, though he appeared to make some small strides in the framing department, going from terrible to simply very bad. He shouldn't be a primary catcher based on advanced metrics, but made perfect sense for Arizona to run out there every day given their longtime bent for traditional performance indicators. Castillo has undoubtedly exacted his own toll on Diamondbacks pitchers, a group that could have used every extra strike they can get. He's still an above-average hitter for the catching crowd, but the trade-off behind the plate sucks up much of the value produced by the bat.

YEAR	TEAM	P. COUNT	FRM RUNS	BLK RUNS	THRW RUNS	TOT RUNS
2014	CHN	15118	-15.6	1.5	1.0	-13.1
2014	IOW	140	0.0	0.0	0.0	0.0
2015	CHN	1119	0.3	0.3	0.0	0.6
2015	SEA	860	-0.9	0.4	0.0	-0.5
2015	ARI	10394	-10.6	1.1	0.0	-9.5
2016	ARI	15918	-9.8	-1.7	2.8	-8.7
2017	ARI	14829	-13.4	-0.2	1.6	-12.0
2018	ARI	14539	-14.4	-0.4	1.4	-13.4

Chris Davis   1B

Born: 3/17/86   Age: 31   Bats: L   Throws: R   Height: 6'3"   Weight: 230   Entered Pro Ball: Round 5, 2006 Draft (#148 overall)

YEAR	TEAM	LVL	AGE	PA	R	2B	3B	HR	RBI	BB	K	SB	CS	AVG/OBP/SLG	TAv	VORP	BABIP	BRR	FRAA	WARP
2014	BAL	MLB	28	525	65	16	0	26	72	60	173	2	1	.196/.300/.404	.272	9.0	.242	-3.1	1B(115): -3.1 • 3B(21): 0.6	0.7
2015	BAL	MLB	29	670	100	31	0	47	117	84	208	2	3	.262/.361/.562	.316	43.4	.319	-0.9	1B(111): -5.0 • RF(30): -2.4	3.9
2016	BAL	MLB	30	665	99	21	0	38	84	88	219	1	0	.221/.332/.459	.271	14.6	.279	0.3	1B(152): 5.3 • RF(3): -0.1	2.0
2017	BAL	MLB	31	592	82	23	1	35	96	67	185	2	1	.242/.337/.497	.285	24.2	.300	-1.4	1B -2	2.0
2018	BAL	MLB	32	547	82	22	0	32	87	62	176	1	0	.235/.331/.484	.270	11.3	.294	-1.0	1B -2	1.1

Breakout: 4%   Improve: 48%   Collapse: 8%   Attrition: 9%   MLB: 99%   Comparables: Ryan Howard, Adam Dunn, Danny Tartabull

He continues to provide above-average offensive production while striking out at historic rates. But for Davis to be worth his salary, given his relative lack of defensive value, he needs to hit for overwhelming power. There's some evidence—beyond the empirical evidence about aging that has piled up over the decades—that he's going to find that increasingly difficult. Davis swung much less often than he ever had before in 2016, but still made less contact. He pulled the ball less often than he had since 2011, and had less success when he did pull it. He should keep hitting for power and drawing walks for another few years, but that doesn't guarantee he'll be more than an average player.

Ryan Flaherty   UT

Born: 7/27/86   Age: 30   Bats: L   Throws: R   Height: 6'3"   Weight: 220   Entered Pro Ball: Round 1, 2008 Draft (#41 overall)

YEAR	TEAM	LVL	AGE	PA	R	2B	3B	HR	RBI	BB	K	SB	CS	AVG/OBP/SLG	TAv	VORP	BABIP	BRR	FRAA	WARP
2014	BAL	MLB	27	312	33	15	1	7	32	22	68	1	0	.221/.288/.356	.242	4.7	.266	0.8	3B(43): 1.7, 2B(30): 1.5	0.6
2015	BAL	MLB	28	301	34	8	3	9	31	26	81	0	0	.202/.281/.356	.220	-3.3	.251	0.7	2B(56): -1.8 • SS(15): -0.8	-0.6
2016	NOR	AAA	29	22	3	1	0	0	1	3	5	0	0	.421/.500/.474	.361	2.7	.571	-0.2	2B(3): -0.5 • 3B(2): -0.1	0.2
2016	BAL	MLB	29	176	16	7	0	3	15	17	48	2	0	.217/.291/.318	.219	-0.7	.290	1.0	3B(40): 1.0 • SS(13): -0.4	-0.1
2017	BAL	MLB	30	216	23	8	1	6	23	17	53	1	0	.225/.294/.373	.233	2.3	.271	-0.2	2B -1, 3B 1	-0.1
2018	BAL	MLB	31	210	25	7	1	6	23	18	53	0	0	.218/.297/.365	.227	-0.6	.265	0.3	2B -1, 3B 1	-0.2

Breakout: 4%   Improve: 44%   Collapse: 8%   Attrition: 13%   MLB: 92%   Comparables: Brandon Inge, Bobby Crosby, Mark Teahen

He's big and he bats left-handed and he hits for a little bit of power. He plays wherever you put him, though not necessarily well. That's how Flaherty has survived five seasons as a utility player for one team and has consistently gotten a fair bit of playing time, despite not being any good. His strikeout rate keeps climbing and his defensive value keeps eroding, so the gravy train is bound to come to a stop soon, but Rule 5 draftees rarely make it even this far.

J.J. Hardy   SS

Born: 8/19/82   Age: 34   Bats: R   Throws: R   Height: 6'1"   Weight: 200   Entered Pro Ball: Round 2, 2001 Draft (#56 overall)

YEAR	TEAM	LVL	AGE	PA	R	2B	3B	HR	RBI	BB	K	SB	CS	AVG/OBP/SLG	TAv	VORP	BABIP	BRR	FRAA	WARP
2014	BAL	MLB	31	569	56	28	0	9	52	29	104	0	0	.268/.309/.372	.256	18.2	.317	-0.9	SS(141): 1.9	2.2
2015	BAL	MLB	32	437	45	14	0	8	37	20	88	0	0	.219/.253/.311	.209	-6.7	.257	-2.1	SS(114): -2.0	-0.9
2016	BAL	MLB	33	438	43	29	0	9	48	26	68	0	0	.269/.309/.407	.246	11.6	.299	-0.4	SS(115): 5.5	1.8
2017	BAL	MLB	34	550	53	24	1	13	56	32	89	0	0	.248/.291/.373	.234	7.8	.275	-1.3	SS 0	0.2
2018	BAL	MLB	35	378	41	16	0	9	40	22	63	0	0	.247/.293/.372	.231	0.6	.274	-1.0	SS 0	0.1

Breakout: 2%   Improve: 26%   Collapse: 8%   Attrition: 15%   MLB: 85%   Comparables: Willie Bloomquist, Geoff Blum, Alexei Ramirez

Of the 302 players who saw at least 1,000 pitches last season, only Ben Zobrist and Joe Mauer swung at a lower percentage than Hardy (36.3). That's a telling stat for anyone, but particularly staggering in Hardy's case because 53.3 percent of the pitches he saw were in the strike zone. Only the Rays' Logan Forsythe swung at fewer than 40 percent of his pitches and saw more than 51 percent strikes. When healthy, the aging Hardy is still a good shortstop, and he righted the ship after an uptick in strikeouts in 2015. It's clear that he has simply acknowledged his sharp decline as a pure hitter and is determined to make the most of his limited offensive skill set.

Adam Jones   CF

Born: 8/1/85   Age: 31   Bats: R   Throws: R   Height: 6'2"   Weight: 215   Entered Pro Ball: Round 1, 2003 Draft (#37 overall)

YEAR	TEAM	LVL	AGE	PA	R	2B	3B	HR	RBI	BB	K	SB	CS	AVG/OBP/SLG	TAv	VORP	BABIP	BRR	FRAA	WARP
2014	BAL	MLB	28	682	88	30	2	29	96	19	133	7	1	.281/.311/.469	.291	40.7	.311	2.1	CF(155): -1.5	4.3
2015	BAL	MLB	29	581	74	25	3	27	82	24	102	3	1	.269/.308/.474	.259	17.8	.286	1.4	CF(134): 7.6	2.7
2016	BAL	MLB	30	672	86	19	0	29	83	39	115	2	0	.265/.310/.436	.251	17.4	.280	2.7	CF(152): 2.4	2.0
2017	BAL	MLB	31	707	95	30	2	30	90	34	131	5	1	.272/.315/.463	.268	31.7	.297	-0.5	CF -2	2.2
2018	BAL	MLB	32	575	76	25	1	26	82	28	110	3	1	.272/.316/.467	.261	17.5	.297	1.3	CF -1	1.8

Breakout: 0%   Improve: 53%   Collapse: 1%   Attrition: 2%   MLB: 98%   Comparables: Aaron Rowand, Torii Hunter, Joe Carter

From late May through the end of the season Buck Showalter made Jones the Orioles' primary leadoff hitter. Jones swung at a higher percentage of all pitches than any other qualifying big-league batter and finished with an OBP south of .315 for the third straight season. That's the bad news. The worse news is that in a season that saw a league-wide sonic boom of offensive thunder, Jones' power ran dry. Only 7.1 percent of his plate appearances resulted in extra-base hits, a career-worst. At 31, Jones can hold his own in center field, but no longer profiles as a dynamic offensive force. He'll need to rediscover his pop in order to earn what's left of his contract.

Caleb Joseph   C

Born: 6/18/86   Age: 31   Bats: R   Throws: R   Height: 6'3"   Weight: 180   Entered Pro Ball: Round 7, 2008 Draft (#206 overall)

YEAR	TEAM	LVL	AGE	PA	R	2B	3B	HR	RBI	BB	K	SB	CS	AVG/OBP/SLG	TAv	VORP	BABIP	BRR	FRAA	WARP
2014	NOR	AAA	28	95	8	7	0	2	11	3	22	0	0	.261/.284/.402	.254	4.4	.324	0.6	C(21): 4.2	0.9
2014	BAL	MLB	28	275	22	9	0	9	28	17	69	0	1	.207/.264/.354	.231	2.4	.246	-1.4	C(78): 16.1 • 1B(4): -0.0	2.0
2015	BAL	MLB	29	355	38	16	1	11	49	27	72	0	0	.234/.299/.394	.242	7.3	.269	-1.5	C(94): 11.0 • 1B(1): 0.1	2.0
2016	BOW	AA	30	23	2	1	0	1	2	1	7	0	1	.286/.348/.476	.276	0.0	.385	-0.6		0.0
2016	FRD	A+	30	23	4	1	0	1	5	2	4	0	0	.294/.348/.529	.292	1.3	.267	-0.1	C(3): 0.0	0.1
2016	NOR	AAA	30	42	2	0	0	0	4	2	5	0	0	.250/.286/.250	.183	-2.5	.286	-0.6	C(7): 0.2	-0.2
2016	BAL	MLB	30	141	7	3	0	0	0	7	28	0	0	.174/.216/.197	.147	-9.4	.221	0.4	C(48): 7.1 • 1B(2): -0.0	-0.2
2017	*BAL*	*MLB*	*31*	*422*	*41*	*17*	*1*	*11*	*43*	*29*	*96*	*1*	*0*	*.226/.282/.359*	*.226*	*4.8*	*.267*	*-1.0*	*C 16*	*1.2*
2018	*BAL*	*MLB*	*32*	*286*	*32*	*12*	*0*	*8*	*31*	*20*	*68*	*0*	*0*	*.225/.284/.362*	*.223*	*-0.9*	*.268*	*-0.7*	*C 10*	*1.0*

Breakout: 1%   Improve: 34%   Collapse: 14%   Attrition: 28%   MLB: 90%   *Comparables: Yorvit Torrealba, Jose Lobaton, Miguel Ojeda*

RBI is a meaningless stat and you'll rarely have to read about it in these pages. But we have to talk about this. How could we not talk about this? Joseph is the only position player since 1910 to bat at least 100 times in a season without driving in a run. That may not be the most direct way to say that he's a terrible hitter because it doesn't capture that he walked just five percent of the time, but it *does* help highlight his utter lack of power. It may not tell you the full story of his value—he's a really good catcher—but it gives you an idea of the ceiling. If you can go 141 plate appearances without driving in a run, you can't be good.

YEAR	TEAM	P. COUNT	FRM RUNS	BLK RUNS	THRW RUNS	TOT RUNS
2014	BAL	10859	13.0	-0.7	2.2	14.5
2014	NOR	3082	4.0	0.1	0.3	4.3
2015	BAL	13197	9.8	0.4	1.1	11.3
2016	BAL	6127	6.7	1.5	0.2	8.3
2017	*BAL*	*16569*	*12.9*	*0.9*	*1.0*	*14.8*
2018	*BAL*	*11233*	*7.8*	*0.5*	*0.5*	*8.8*

Hyun-Soo Kim   OF

Born: 1/12/88   Age: 29   Bats: L   Throws: R   Height: 6'2"   Weight: 210   Entered Pro Ball: International Free Agent, 2015

YEAR	TEAM	LVL	AGE	PA	R	2B	3B	HR	RBI	BB	K	SB	CS	AVG/OBP/SLG	TAv	VORP	BABIP	BRR	FRAA	WARP
2016	BAL	MLB	28	346	36	16	1	6	22	36	51	1	3	.302/.382/.420	.284	13.7	.345	-2.3	LF(91): -8.7	0.5
2017	*BAL*	*MLB*	*29*	*547*	*68*	*25*	*2*	*13*	*55*	*56*	*87*	*4*	*3*	*.278/.358/.416*	*.275*	*23.9*	*.315*	*-1.3*	*LF -11*	*1.0*
2018	*BAL*	*MLB*	*30*	*449*	*58*	*22*	*1*	*11*	*52*	*46*	*74*	*2*	*2*	*.276/.357/.421*	*.268*	*12.9*	*.312*	*-1.3*	*LF -9*	*0.4*

Breakout: 2%   Improve: 34%   Collapse: 8%   Attrition: 13%   MLB: 98%   *Comparables: Conor Jackson, Martin Prado, Brady Clark*

Boy, do humans make terrible judgments when they operate with incomplete information. The Orioles tried to get out of a two-year, $7 million commitment to Kim last spring because he started 0-for-23 in the Grapefruit League. They were lucky they weren't able to do so. Kim figured it out, because a good hitter with a long track record (no matter where that track record was compiled) does not suddenly and permanently forget how to play baseball. He didn't hit for power, and like virtually all of his teammates he was a moderate liability both in the field and on the bases. His ability to draw walks and hit singles made him a vital part of the Baltimore offense, and between that steady approach and his excellent contact skills there's every reason to expect him to remain an OBP threat in 2017.

Manny Machado   3B

Born: 7/6/92   Age: 24   Bats: R   Throws: R   Height: 6'3"   Weight: 185   Entered Pro Ball: Round 1, 2010 Draft (#3 overall)

YEAR	TEAM	LVL	AGE	PA	R	2B	3B	HR	RBI	BB	K	SB	CS	AVG/OBP/SLG	TAv	VORP	BABIP	BRR	FRAA	WARP
2014	BAL	MLB	21	354	38	14	0	12	32	20	68	2	0	.278/.324/.431	.274	13.7	.317	-1.2	3B(82): 7.7	2.4
2015	BAL	MLB	22	713	102	30	1	35	86	70	111	20	8	.286/.359/.502	.292	47.7	.297	3.4	3B(156): 21.7 • SS(7): -0.8	7.3
2016	BAL	MLB	23	696	105	40	1	37	96	48	120	0	3	.294/.343/.533	.292	46.7	.309	0.0	3B(114): 8.7 • SS(45): -0.4	5.7
2017	*BAL*	*MLB*	*24*	*640*	*78*	*34*	*3*	*25*	*88*	*47*	*105*	*8*	*4*	*.283/.337/.477*	*.280*	*32.2*	*.305*	*-1.1*	*3B 16, SS -0*	*4.7*
2018	*BAL*	*MLB*	*25*	*602*	*84*	*33*	*2*	*26*	*88*	*49*	*101*	*7*	*4*	*.288/.350/.498*	*.281*	*27.2*	*.309*	*0.6*	*3B 15, SS 0*	*4.6*

Breakout: 2%   Improve: 65%   Collapse: 0%   Attrition: 1%   MLB: 99%   *Comparables: Ryan Zimmerman, Brett Lawrie, Pablo Sandoval*

Machado remains one of baseball's best and most exciting young players, but his 2016 was sort of a weird season. His unintentional walk rate fell from 9.6 percent in 2015 to 5.6 percent. After stealing 20 bases (admittedly, at a poor success rate) in 2015, he stole zero last year. No 22-year-old has stolen 20 bases in a season only to come back and be shut out in the category at 23 since Rick Auerbach in 1973 (and Rick played six games that year). Forced into about seven weeks of action at shortstop, Machado proved that he can provide plus defense there in addition to being a wizard at third base. The signs all point toward continued stardom even if the shape of his overall production isn't set in stone yet.

Trey Mancini   1B

Born: 3/18/92   Age: 25   Bats: R   Throws: R   Height: 6'4"   Weight: 215   Entered Pro Ball: Round 8, 2013 Draft (#249 overall)

YEAR	TEAM	LVL	AGE	PA	R	2B	3B	HR	RBI	BB	K	SB	CS	AVG/OBP/SLG	TAv	VORP	BABIP	BRR	FRAA	WARP
2014	DEL	A	22	291	30	13	3	3	42	14	52	1	1	.317/.357/.422	.292	11.7	.378	-1.1	1B(66): 1.8	1.4
2014	FRD	A+	22	295	37	19	0	7	41	14	43	0	1	.251/.295/.396	.243	-2.8	.273	-0.4	1B(69): -6.7	-1.0
2015	FRD	A+	23	217	28	14	3	8	32	9	35	4	2	.314/.341/.527	.299	10.6	.345	-0.1	1B(51): 2.8	1.4
2015	BOW	AA	23	354	60	29	3	13	57	22	58	2	1	.359/.395/.586	.340	32.5	.400	0.2	1B(75): -0.8	3.4
2016	BOW	AA	24	75	18	4	0	7	14	10	17	0	0	.302/.413/.698	.346	7.8	.308	0.6	1B(15): 0.4	0.9
2016	NOR	AAA	24	536	60	22	5	13	54	48	123	2	2	.280/.349/.427	.281	15.4	.351	-1.9	1B(121): 6.4	2.2
2016	BAL	MLB	24	15	3	1	0	3	5	0	4	0	0	.357/.400/1.071	.435	2.7	.286	-0.1		0.3
2017	*BAL*	*MLB*	*25*	*568*	*62*	*26*	*3*	*21*	*76*	*37*	*137*	*1*	*0*	*.262/.315/.445*	*.263*	*11.3*	*.314*	*-1.0*	*1B 0*	*1.2*
2018	*BAL*	*MLB*	*26*	*545*	*69*	*26*	*3*	*21*	*72*	*37*	*138*	*0*	*0*	*.256/.312/.443*	*.255*	*9.4*	*.311*	*-1.0*	*1B 0*	*1.0*

Breakout: 6%   Improve: 25%   Collapse: 8%   Attrition: 25%   MLB: 45%   *Comparables: Mark Trumbo, Christian Walker, Steve Pearce*

There used to be more players like Mancini in the majors. He's a tall, right-handed-hitting first baseman with a good glove, a solid approach and a modicum of power. Even the guys who come close to matching his profile in today's MLB (like, say, C.J. Cron) tend to have reverse platoon splits. That lets them provide value as everyday starters at a position where offense matters, so struggling to hit 70 percent of the pitchers they face isn't a problem. Mancini will have to prove he can hang in there against big-league righties if he wants to win a regular role.

Ryan Mountcastle   SS

Born: 2/18/97   Age: 20   Bats: R   Throws: R   Height: 6'3"   Weight: 195   Entered Pro Ball: Round 1, 2015 Draft (#36 overall)

YEAR	TEAM	LVL	AGE	PA	R	2B	3B	HR	RBI	BB	K	SB	CS	AVG/OBP/SLG	TAv	VORP	BABIP	BRR	FRAA	WARP
2015	ABE	A-	18	34	2	0	0	1	5	0	10	0	1	.212/.206/.303	.193	-2.0	.261	-0.5	SS(6): -1.0	-0.3
2016	DEL	A	19	489	53	28	4	10	51	25	95	5	4	.281/.319/.426	.287	28.5	.331	-1.7	SS(105): -21.0	0.8
2017	BAL	MLB	20	250	27	11	1	8	26	10	68	0	0	.231/.265/.377	.215	-0.7	.288	-0.4	SS -6	-0.7
2018	BAL	MLB	21	363	41	16	1	12	43	16	95	0	0	.241/.277/.400	.229	0.2	.295	-0.8	SS -8	-0.9

Breakout: 2%   Improve: 10%   Collapse: 0%   Attrition: 5%   MLB: 16%   Comparables: Raul Mondesi, Alen Hanson, Tim Beckham

The only reason Mountcastle is listed as a shortstop is that the Orioles stashed him there for an entire year in the South Atlantic League. That's OK—it relieves the pressure to be funny in the rest of his write-up. Mountcastle is a future corner guy and it might not be the hot corner. Given that, it would be nice if he walked a bit more or hit for a bit more power. The hit tool plays, though, and he's enough of an athlete that whenever someone decides the joke is stale and moves him to left field, he won't hurt the team there. If his power matures the way scouts project it will, he'll have a future in the majors regardless of his position.

Alex Murphy   C

Born: 10/5/94   Age: 22   Bats: R   Throws: R   Height: 5'11"   Weight: 210   Entered Pro Ball: Round 6, 2013 Draft (#189 overall)

YEAR	TEAM	LVL	AGE	PA	R	2B	3B	HR	RBI	BB	K	SB	CS	AVG/OBP/SLG	TAv	VORP	BABIP	BRR	FRAA	WARP
2014	ABE	A-	19	215	21	12	0	3	25	15	42	2	1	.277/.330/.385	.286	13.3	.333	0.2	C(35): 1.6	1.6
2015	DEL	A	20	134	17	8	2	2	28	11	31	0	0	.258/.328/.408	.288	6.6	.330	-0.3	C(13): -1.0	0.6
2015	ABE	A-	20	62	8	7	0	2	8	7	10	0	0	.291/.371/.527	.334	7.2	.326	0.1	C(12): 0.1	0.8
2016	DEL	A	21	516	54	28	1	16	63	49	138	0	0	.252/.343/.423	.275	16.0	.326	-3.8	C(57): -0.5 • 1B(42): 0.1	1.7
2017	BAL	MLB	22	250	24	10	0	8	29	18	78	0	0	.211/.277/.363	.217	-2.3	.281	-0.4	C -0, 1B -0	-0.3
2018	BAL	MLB	23	301	35	13	1	11	36	22	92	0	0	.217/.282/.383	.227	-2.9	.281	-0.7	C 0, 1B -1	-0.4

Breakout: 2%   Improve: 5%   Collapse: 5%   Attrition: 10%   MLB: 12%   Comparables: Christian Vazquez, Jorge Alfaro, Kyle Skipworth

Murphy's progress through the low minors has been slow but steady. He has better than average power, for a catcher at least. He works the count. There's too much swing-and-miss in his game right now, but the plan seems to be to bring him along slowly anyway, so he'll have ample opportunity to make adjustments at the plate while he hones his craft behind it. He has some natural receiving skills, though not the athletic defensive tools of a model 22-year-old backstop. Catcher development is fraught with risk because one injury can throw a wrench into the works. So can a sudden adjustment deficit. If Murphy can avoid both, he has potential.

YEAR	TEAM	P. COUNT	FRM RUNS	BLK RUNS	THRW RUNS	TOT RUNS
2015	ABE	1594	0.1	0.1	-0.1	0.1
2017	BAL	4951	0.0	0.0	0.0	0.0
2018	BAL	5952	0.0	0.0	0.0	0.0

Jomar Reyes   3B

Born: 2/20/97   Age: 20   Bats: R   Throws: R   Height: 6'3"   Weight: 220   Entered Pro Ball: International Free Agent, 2014

YEAR	TEAM	LVL	AGE	PA	R	2B	3B	HR	RBI	BB	K	SB	CS	AVG/OBP/SLG	TAv	VORP	BABIP	BRR	FRAA	WARP
2015	DEL	A	18	335	36	27	4	5	44	18	73	1	0	.278/.334/.440	.309	23.1	.351	-3.4	3B(74): -6.5	1.8
2016	FRD	A+	19	498	53	16	2	10	51	25	102	3	0	.228/.271/.336	.214	-7.8	.269	0.8	3B(122): -3.9	-1.2
2017	BAL	MLB	20	250	22	10	1	7	27	10	69	0	0	.219/.258/.353	.208	-5.8	.278	-0.3	3B -3	-1.0
2018	BAL	MLB	21	411	44	18	1	12	46	18	106	0	0	.226/.269/.371	.222	-7.7	.279	-0.8	3B -5	-1.4

Breakout: 1%   Improve: 3%   Collapse: 0%   Attrition: 1%   MLB: 4%   Comparables: Jefry Marte, Maikel Franco, Alex Liddi

Giving up on a player born after the publication of the first BP Annual would be silly. Pushed into full-season ball at 18, Reyes looked great. That he went miles backward as a teenager in High-A last season doesn't erase his potential plus hit and power tools. Here's the thing, though: Reyes doesn't run or field well. He's going to be a first baseman or a DH before he reaches the big leagues. He can't afford to have his power dry up and he definitely can't afford to walk just five percent of the time. Given his skill set, he'll be on the doorstep of the big leagues or on the verge of a flameout by the time he can legally drink.

Joey Rickard   OF

Born: 5/21/91   Age: 26   Bats: R   Throws: L   Height: 6'1"   Weight: 185   Entered Pro Ball: Round 9, 2012 Draft (#302 overall)

YEAR	TEAM	LVL	AGE	PA	R	2B	3B	HR	RBI	BB	K	SB	CS	AVG/OBP/SLG	TAv	VORP	BABIP	BRR	FRAA	WARP
2014	MNT	AA	23	247	33	8	0	1	17	28	39	9	4	.243/.337/.296	.256	4.6	.287	-0.5	CF(40): -3.7 • RF(23): 5.8	0.6
2015	PCH	A+	24	94	8	3	0	0	12	20	13	3	2	.268/.436/.310	.308	6.0	.322	-0.5	LF(11): -1.8 • RF(6): 1.2	0.6
2015	MNT	AA	24	282	38	19	6	2	32	39	42	19	4	.322/.420/.479	.327	26.4	.379	1.5	LF(24): -1.7 • RF(19): 2.9	2.8
2015	DUR	AAA	24	104	16	6	2	0	11	10	20	1	0	.360/.437/.472	.334	8.8	.457	-1.3	LF(13): -0.2 • RF(11): -0.6	0.8
2016	BAL	MLB	25	282	32	13	0	5	19	18	54	4	1	.268/.319/.377	.241	0.6	.320	0.3	RF(51): -0.6 • LF(31): 1.1	0.0
2017	BAL	MLB	26	512	56	23	2	8	48	49	101	11	3	.259/.335/.378	.252	9.2	.311	0.6	RF 4, LF 0	1.0
2018	BAL	MLB	27	503	59	22	2	9	51	49	102	11	3	.256/.337/.379	.247	4.2	.307	0.5	RF 4, LF 0	0.9

Breakout: 4%   Improve: 40%   Collapse: 10%   Attrition: 21%   MLB: 64%   Comparables: L.J. Hoes, Jon Jay, Clete Thomas

For all of a week, Rickard looked like Dan Duquette's greatest Rule 5 find to date. He started his career on a seven-game hitting streak, during which he had a .922 OPS. Then the league took a deep breath, resolved to stop throwing him thigh-high fastballs down the middle and started getting Rickard out regularly. His speed is visible in the way he plays, but it provides no tangible value. He's not a good baserunner or a good center fielder. He's a fifth outfielder named Joey.

Jonathan Schoop   2B

Born: 10/16/91 Age: 25   Bats: R   Throws: R   Height: 6'1"   Weight: 225   Entered Pro Ball: International Free Agent, 2008

YEAR	TEAM	LVL	AGE	PA	R	2B	3B	HR	RBI	BB	K	SB	CS	AVG/OBP/SLG	TAv	VORP	BABIP	BRR	FRAA	WARP
2014	BAL	MLB	22	481	48	18	0	16	45	13	122	2	0	.209/.244/.354	.220	-5.4	.249	0.3	2B(123): 1.8, 3B(17): -1.5	-0.6
2015	BOW	AA	23	26	3	2	0	3	6	1	6	0	0	.240/.269/.680	.308	1.1	.188	-0.8	2B(7): 0.3	0.1
2015	BAL	MLB	23	321	34	17	0	15	39	9	79	2	0	.279/.306/.482	.271	8.9	.329	-2.9	2B(84): -0.0	1.0
2016	BAL	MLB	24	647	82	38	1	25	82	21	137	1	2	.267/.298/.454	.250	12.3	.305	1.5	2B(162): -2.0	1.1
2017	BAL	MLB	25	585	64	28	1	24	78	23	132	2	1	.253/.291/.436	.251	15.8	.290	-1.2	2B 0	1.2
2018	BAL	MLB	26	572	72	29	0	25	79	23	126	2	1	.255/.294/.446	.249	10.6	.287	-0.4	2B 0	1.2

Breakout: 4%   Improve: 54%   Collapse: 5%   Attrition: 15%   MLB: 98%   *Comparables: Jorge Cantu, Howie Kendrick, Bret Boone*

Of the 140-plus seasons that make up baseball history, there have been only 16 in which a player had at least 60 extra-base hits but an OBP south of .300. The thing has only been done 21 total times. Yet, four players did it in 2016 alone. Schoop was among them. His extreme impatience at the plate actually helped hold down his previously problematic strikeout rate, but it still put a ceiling on his offensive value. It's hard to say how viable his hitting profile is. He relies on power for value, but doesn't hit the ball that hard (171st of 213 qualifiers in average exit velocity). He doesn't pull the ball or hit it in the air at an exceptional rate. Any time now, he could go from a hair above average for a second baseman to below average for just about anyone.

Chance Sisco   C

Born: 2/24/95 Age: 22   Bats: L   Throws: R   Height: 6'2"   Weight: 195   Entered Pro Ball: Round 2, 2013 Draft (#61 overall)

YEAR	TEAM	LVL	AGE	PA	R	2B	3B	HR	RBI	BB	K	SB	CS	AVG/OBP/SLG	TAv	VORP	BABIP	BRR	FRAA	WARP
2014	DEL	A	19	478	56	27	2	5	63	42	79	1	2	.340/.406/.448	.312	41.1	.406	-1.2	C(74): -6.4	3.6
2015	FRD	A+	20	300	30	12	3	4	26	33	41	8	1	.308/.387/.422	.299	21.3	.350	-0.7	C(57): -1.3	2.2
2015	BOW	AA	20	84	9	4	0	2	8	9	14	0	1	.257/.337/.392	.268	2.0	.293	-1.9	C(17): -0.1	0.2
2016	BOW	AA	21	479	53	28	1	4	44	59	83	2	2	.320/.406/.422	.297	28.8	.387	-5.7	C(83): -10.9	1.9
2017	BAL	MLB	22	60	6	3	0	1	6	6	13	0	0	.259/.332/.382	.252	2.2	.322	-0.1	C -3	-0.1
2018	BAL	MLB	23	299	38	14	1	8	34	30	66	0	0	.267/.345/.414	.258	9.7	.325	-0.7	C -14	-0.5

Breakout: 10%   Improve: 24%   Collapse: 9%   Attrition: 30%   MLB: 45%   *Comparables: Travis d'Arnaud, Gary Sanchez, Hank Conger*

It's not hard to imagine Sisco growing into a star catcher. He consistently puts the good part of the bat on the ball despite below-average power. He controls the strike zone well. In many ways he feels like a polished product on the verge of big-league readiness. He could probably find success in an outfield corner or even at second base. Instead, the Orioles have tried to coach him up as a catcher—a position at which his fluid athleticism doesn't serve him as well. Early statistical returns on his framing match the eye test, which is never a good sign.

YEAR	TEAM	P. COUNT	FRM RUNS	BLK RUNS	THRW RUNS	TOT RUNS
2015	BOW	2140	0.1	-0.2	0.1	0.0
2017	BAL	2194	-2.0	-0.4	-0.3	-2.7
2018	BAL	10937	-10.0	-1.9	-1.3	-13.2

D.J. Stewart   OF

Born: 11/30/93 Age: 23   Bats: L   Throws: R   Height: 6'0"   Weight: 230   Entered Pro Ball: Round 1, 2015 Draft (#25 overall)

YEAR	TEAM	LVL	AGE	PA	R	2B	3B	HR	RBI	BB	K	SB	CS	AVG/OBP/SLG	TAv	VORP	BABIP	BRR	FRAA	WARP
2015	ABE	A-	21	268	25	8	2	6	24	23	52	4	1	.218/.288/.345	.247	1.1	.250	-0.3	LF(52): -0.2	0.1
2016	DEL	A	22	262	27	12	1	4	25	42	58	16	6	.230/.366/.352	.274	7.6	.294	-1.2	LF(58): 0.8	0.9
2016	FRD	A+	22	240	41	12	2	6	30	36	46	10	3	.279/.389/.448	.282	10.7	.333	0.0	LF(51): 1.3 • CF(2): -0.1	1.2
2017	BAL	MLB	23	250	29	9	1	7	27	29	67	6	2	.213/.309/.358	.229	0.7	.270	0.1	LF 3, CF -0	0.4
2018	BAL	MLB	24	269	33	10	1	8	29	31	73	7	3	.212/.313/.364	.234	-0.2	.269	0.4	LF 3, CF 0	0.3

Breakout: 1%   Improve: 5%   Collapse: 2%   Attrition: 6%   MLB: 9%   *Comparables: Tyler Collins, Jake Smolinski, Chad Huffman*

Stewart has a fluid and athletic swing, and every move on the diamond looks natural for him. He has great plate discipline, partially because he has such smooth early swing mechanics that he gets it going on every pitch without getting off balance. He got on base consistently at both levels of Single-A in 2016 and then did the same in the Arizona Fall League. He's a below-average runner and thrower, confined to the corner outfield spots and unlikely to win any Gold Gloves there. If he wants to climb all the way up the ladder, he'll need to find some power and a sustainable on-base percentage.

Drew Stubbs CF

Born: 10/4/84 Age: 32 Bats: R Throws: R Height: 6'4" Weight: 205 Entered Pro Ball: Round 1, 2006 Draft (#8 overall)

YEAR	TEAM	LVL	AGE	PA	R	2B	3B	HR	RBI	BB	K	SB	CS	AVG/OBP/SLG	TAv	VORP	BABIP	BRR	FRAA	WARP
2014	COL	MLB	29	424	67	22	4	15	43	30	136	20	3	.289/.339/.482	.269	17.7	.404	2.1	CF(113): -6.5	1.2
2015	ABQ	AAA	30	165	22	4	3	2	20	24	39	6	3	.263/.376/.380	.264	4.3	.347	-1.1	CF(34): 0.5	0.5
2015	COL	MLB	30	114	14	3	2	5	10	9	50	2	1	.216/.286/.431	.230	-0.3	.362	0.1	CF(25): 1.1 • LF(13): -1.1	-0.1
2015	ROU	AAA	30	30	6	1	0	0	0	3	7	4	0	.222/.300/.259	.260	1.8	.300	1.0	LF(3): -0.1 • CF(3): -0.4	0.1
2015	TEX	MLB	30	26	6	1	0	0	0	5	10	3	0	.095/.269/.143	.166	-0.8	.182	0.9	CF(17): -1.2 • LF(8): -0.6	-0.3
2016	ATL	MLB	31	42	6	0	0	1	3	4	20	4	0	.237/.310/.316	.241	1.9	.471	1.4	CF(10): -1.5 • LF(4): -0.6	0.0
2016	ROU	AAA	31	51	10	4	0	2	10	10	8	2	1	.231/.373/.487	.358	6.5	.226	0.0	CF(7): 0.8 • RF(3): -0.1	0.7
2016	TEX	MLB	31	25	6	0	0	2	3	4	7	4	0	.300/.400/.600	.341	1.5	.333	-1.0	LF(9): -0.7 • RF(4): -0.4	0.0
2016	BAL	MLB	31	27	1	0	0	0	1	4	11	1	1	.136/.296/.136	.189	-1.8	.273	-0.4	RF(13): -0.9 • LF(6): -0.1	-0.3
2017	*BAL*	*MLB*	*32*	*250*	*34*	*8*	*1*	*7*	*24*	*24*	*79*	*11*	*2*	*.225/.303/.368*	*.232*	*1.9*	*.310*	*0.7*	*CF -1, RF -0*	*-0.1*
2018	*BAL*	*MLB*	*33*	*98*	*11*	*3*	*0*	*3*	*10*	*9*	*32*	*4*	*1*	*.213/.291/.345*	*.224*	*-0.9*	*.297*	*0.3*	*CF 0, RF 0*	*-0.2*

Breakout: 5% Improve: 37% Collapse: 11% Attrition: 22% MLB: 87% *Comparables: Devon White, Justin Maxwell, Gary Matthews*

Stubbs used to be the kind of player you'd pay to see for the sheer athletic spectacle. He was never quite as elite a defender as he should have been given his speed, but he made some highlight-reel plays. He had surprising and impressive raw power. He worked counts, got on base and stole bases efficiently. He always struck out more than you'd have liked, but for a while he made it work. Now, the power has been swallowed by his inability to make contact on anything with movement. He's walking more, but only by changing his approach from patient to passive. He's a below-average defender even in the corners. He's become a spare part.

Mark Trumbo 1B

Born: 1/16/86 Age: 31 Bats: R Throws: R Height: 6'4" Weight: 225 Entered Pro Ball: Round 18, 2004 Draft (#533 overall)

YEAR	TEAM	LVL	AGE	PA	R	2B	3B	HR	RBI	BB	K	SB	CS	AVG/OBP/SLG	TAv	VORP	BABIP	BRR	FRAA	WARP
2014	ARI	MLB	28	362	37	15	1	14	61	28	89	2	3	.235/.293/.415	.254	0.8	.274	-2.2	1B(43): -4.6 • LF(41): -0.2	-0.4
2015	ARI	MLB	29	184	23	10	3	9	23	10	39	0	0	.259/.299/.506	.282	5.6	.286	-1.5	RF(42): -2.1 • 1B(1): 0.0	0.4
2015	SEA	MLB	29	361	39	13	0	13	41	26	93	0	0	.263/.316/.419	.274	11.8	.328	1.9	RF(34): -3.0 • 1B(22): 0.1	0.9
2016	BAL	MLB	30	667	94	27	1	47	108	51	170	2	0	.256/.316/.533	.276	18.5	.278	-2.6	RF(95): 0.4 • 1B(6): 0.1	2.0
2017	*BAL*	*MLB*	*31*	*603*	*78*	*24*	*2*	*33*	*94*	*48*	*154*	*2*	*1*	*.251/.313/.479*	*.265*	*18.3*	*.288*	*-1.3*	*RF -7, 1B -1*	*1.2*
2018	*BAL*	*MLB*	*32*	*534*	*73*	*20*	*1*	*28*	*80*	*42*	*141*	*1*	*0*	*.244/.305/.462*	*.258*	*8.4*	*.283*	*-1.4*	*RF -6, 1B -1*	*0.2*

Breakout: 1% Improve: 40% Collapse: 6% Attrition: 5% MLB: 96% *Comparables: Geoff Jenkins, Matt Kemp, Jay Buhner*

Trumbo made exactly the right adjustment to suit his skill set in 2016. He'd spent too much of his career chasing pitches down, in and below the strike zone, trying to drive the ball to all fields and trying not to be the one-dimensional slugger everyone said he was. He *is* that one-dimensional slugger. Embracing that reality made him a much better one. In 2016, Trumbo laid off more of those pitches down in the zone and looked to turn on and hammer high fastballs. He pulled the ball more, hit it in the air more often when he did pull it and hit it much harder when he pulled it in the air. Maybe the ball was juiced. Maybe the strike zone subtly rose. To whatever extent either of those things are true, they certainly helped Trumbo. In any event, give the lion's share of the credit for his 47-homer barrage to the player himself. As long as he remains committed to his altered approach, he'll remain a dangerous power hitter.

Adam Walker RF

Born: 10/18/91 Age: 25 Bats: R Throws: R Height: 6'5" Weight: 225 Entered Pro Ball: Round 3, 2012 Draft (#97 overall)

YEAR	TEAM	LVL	AGE	PA	R	2B	3B	HR	RBI	BB	K	SB	CS	AVG/OBP/SLG	TAv	VORP	BABIP	BRR	FRAA	WARP
2014	FTM	A+	22	555	78	19	1	25	94	44	156	9	5	.246/.307/.436	.267	14.6	.303	0.6	RF(110): 0.9	1.6
2015	CHT	AA	23	560	75	31	3	31	106	51	195	13	4	.239/.309/.498	.283	24.2	.317	0.5	LF(110): -22.5 • RF(6): -0.7	0.1
2016	ROC	AAA	24	531	61	22	5	27	75	44	202	7	4	.243/.305/.479	.279	18.5	.348	-2.0	LF(97): -3.3 • CF(1): -0.0	1.6
2017	*BAL*	*MLB*	*25*	*60*	*8*	*2*	*0*	*3*	*8*	*4*	*23*	*1*	*0*	*.214/.273/.433*	*.241*	*0.5*	*.295*	*0.0*	*RF 0, LF -1*	*-0.1*
2018	*BAL*	*MLB*	*26*	*257*	*34*	*10*	*1*	*14*	*38*	*20*	*97*	*3*	*1*	*.217/.281/.445*	*.242*	*0.9*	*.295*	*-0.1*	*RF 0, LF -3*	*-0.2*

Breakout: 2% Improve: 14% Collapse: 9% Attrition: 25% MLB: 42% *Comparables: Peter O'Brien, Carlos Peguero, Brad Eldred*

The highest career strikeout rate in MLB history is 33 percent, an honor shared by Chris Carter and Russell Branyan. Most of the modern hitters known for astronomical strikeout rates—Adam Dunn, Rob Deer, Bo Jackson, Jack Cust, Mark Reynolds, Ryan Howard, Chris Davis—are around 28-32 percent. Adam Walker has struck out in 30 percent of his pro plate appearances, including 35 percent at Double-A in 2015 and 38 percent at Triple-A last year. Walker has the exceptional power to match, but his walk rates have been below average and he's destined to be either a poor, weak-armed corner outfielder or a designated hitter. If you're going to ride or die with just one skill, upper-deck power isn't a bad choice, but there's no way he can succeed long term without at least some progress making contact and so far Walker has been going in the wrong direction.

Matt Wieters   C

Born: 5/21/86   Age: 31   Bats: B   Throws: R   Height: 6'5"   Weight: 230   Entered Pro Ball: Round 1, 2007 Draft (#5 overall)

YEAR	TEAM	LVL	AGE	PA	R	2B	3B	HR	RBI	BB	K	SB	CS	AVG/OBP/SLG	TAv	VORP	BABIP	BRR	FRAA	WARP
2014	BAL	MLB	28	112	13	5	0	5	18	6	19	0	1	.308/.339/.500	.314	9.5	.329	-0.2	C(22): -2.6	0.8
2015	BAL	MLB	29	282	24	14	1	8	25	21	67	0	0	.267/.319/.422	.257	8.0	.328	-1.3	C(55): -1.3, • 1B(3): -0.1	0.7
2016	BAL	MLB	30	464	48	17	1	17	66	32	85	1	0	.243/.302/.409	.245	12.0	.265	-1.4	C(117): -2.3	1.0
2017	BAL	MLB	31	402	45	18	1	15	53	34	78	1	0	.252/.317/.428	.251	15.6	.278	-0.9	C -4	1.3
2018	BAL	MLB	32	380	47	16	1	13	46	32	78	0	0	.241/.307/.407	.242	6.0	.271	-1.0	C -4	0.2

Breakout: 1%   Improve: 32%   Collapse: 15%   Attrition: 22%   MLB: 97%   *Comparables: Ramon Hernandez, Michael Barrett, Matt Nokes*

Wieters never developed into the superstar expected of the former stud prospect, but he's still a four-time All-Star at age 31. His future outlook is murky, however. Wieters racked up heavy workloads behind the plate early in his career and then missed most of 2014 and half of 2015 following Tommy John surgery. His rebuilt arm is still capable of controlling the running game, but pitch-framing data casts his overall defense in a poor light and his offense is lacking beyond 20-homer power. He's never topped a .265 TAv in a full season and has struggled to look like an average regular since blowing out his elbow. Viewing everything through the lens of long-expired hype overshadows what has been a perfectly solid career, but Wieters seems unlikely to age well and doesn't have much room for error to remain an everyday asset.

YEAR	TEAM	P. COUNT	FRM RUNS	BLK RUNS	THRW RUNS	TOT RUNS
2014	BAL	3357	-2.2	0.8	-0.3	-1.7
2015	BAL	8132	-3.6	-0.6	0.2	-4.0
2015	BOW	405	0.0	0.0	0.0	0.0
2015	NOR	109	0.0	0.0	0.0	0.0
2016	BAL	16454	-4.4	1.1	1.7	-1.6
2017	BAL	14612	-6.3	0.4	1.1	-4.9
2018	BAL	13801	-7.2	0.1	0.9	-6.1

PITCHERS

Keegan Akin   LHP

Born: 4/1/95   Age: 22   Bats: L   Throws: L   Height: 6'0"   Weight: 225   Entered Pro Ball: Round 2, 2016 Draft (#54 overall)

YEAR	TEAM	LVL	AGE	W	L	SV	G	GS	IP	H	HR	BB/9	K/9	K	GB%	BABIP	WHIP	ERA	FIP	DRA	VORP	WARP	cFIP	MPH
2016	ABE	A-	21	0	1	0	9	9	26	15	0	2.4	10.0	29	57%	.150	0.85	1.04	1.85	2.69	7.4	0.8	84	
2017	BAL	MLB	22	2	3	0	9	9	32²	38	6	4.5	6.7	24	57%	.310	1.65	5.67	5.70	5.77	-1.1	-0.1	137	
2018	BAL	MLB	23	5	8	0	28	28	168²	170	27	4.4	8.3	155	57%	.298	1.49	5.20	4.98	5.29	2.1	0.2	126	

Breakout: 3%   Improve: 3%   Collapse: 1%   Attrition: 2%   MLB: 4%   *Comparables: Wilking Rodriguez, Tyler Wilson, Marco Gonzales*

The Orioles grabbed Akin in the second round last June after his stock rose steadily throughout his season at Western Michigan. He's built a bit like Dylan Bundy: shorter than the prototypical starter but thick and powerful, especially through the lower half. His fastball can reach the high 90s when he reaches for it, but as a starter he sits 92-93 with sink and solid command. His slider is a developed pitch with plus potential and his changeup showed improvement. There are multiple paths to success from here, in the rotation or in the bullpen. Akin has positioned himself for a full-season assignment in 2017 and could move quickly if all goes well.

Brad Brach   RHP

Born: 4/12/86   Age: 31   Bats: R   Throws: R   Height: 6'6"   Weight: 215   Entered Pro Ball: Round 42, 2008 Draft (#1275 overall)

YEAR	TEAM	LVL	AGE	W	L	SV	G	GS	IP	H	HR	BB/9	K/9	K	GB%	BABIP	WHIP	ERA	FIP	DRA	VORP	WARP	cFIP	MPH
2014	NOR	AAA	28	3	1	1	17	0	23¹	26	1	2.3	16.6	43	31%	.490	1.37	3.47	1.00	0.67	12.1	1.2	45	
2014	BAL	MLB	28	7	1	0	46	0	62¹	48	6	3.6	7.8	54	41%	.250	1.17	3.18	3.93	4.53	-0.3	0.0	109	96.0
2015	BAL	MLB	29	5	3	1	62	0	79¹	57	7	4.3	10.1	89	46%	.263	1.20	2.72	3.44	3.83	7.7	0.8	89	96.5
2016	BAL	MLB	30	10	4	2	71	0	79	57	7	2.8	10.5	92	43%	.267	1.04	2.05	2.88	3.16	15.9	1.6	83	96.8
2017	BAL	MLB	31	2	3	3	53	0	56	50	7	3.8	9.9	62	36%	.294	1.31	3.84	3.97	4.06	5.7	0.6	89	
2018	BAL	MLB	32	2	1	2	42	0	44	39	6	4.1	9.9	48	36%	.293	1.34	4.31	4.11	4.46	2.9	0.3	99	

Breakout: 26%   Improve: 38%   Collapse: 26%   Attrition: 16%   MLB: 88%   *Comparables: John Axford, Jason Motte, Jose Veras*

Brach belongs to the growing fraternity of high-leverage, high-profile relief pitchers drafted in rounds that have since been eliminated from the draft itself (42nd, in 2008), along with Tony Sipp, Kevin Siegrist and Carl Edwards Jr. He might be the best of the bunch, and despite being on the wrong side of 30 already he's only getting better. His average fastball velocity has increased in recent seasons and he now sits comfortably at 96. Long a two-pitch pitcher, Brach started throwing his slider as often as his change last June, with terrific results.

Parker Bridwell   RHP

Born: 8/2/91   Age: 25   Bats: R   Throws: R   Height: 6'4"   Weight: 185   Entered Pro Ball: Round 9, 2010 Draft (#268 overall)

YEAR	TEAM	LVL	AGE	W	L	SV	G	GS	IP	H	HR	BB/9	K/9	K	GB%	BABIP	WHIP	ERA	FIP	DRA	VORP	WARP	cFIP	MPH
2014	FRD	A+	22	7	10	0	26	26	141²	123	11	4.4	9.0	142	41%	.299	1.36	4.45	4.20	3.73	29.3	3.0	101	
2015	BOW	AA	23	4	5	0	18	18	97	96	7	3.5	8.6	93	40%	.320	1.38	3.99	3.53	5.06	0.4	0.0	97	
2016	BOW	AA	24	1	1	1	18	7	55²	56	7	4.5	6.1	38	43%	.283	1.51	4.53	5.10	6.60	-10.1	-1.1	120	
2016	BAL	MLB	24	0	0	0	2	0	3¹	5	2	2.7	8.1	3	27%	.333	1.80	13.50	10.01	4.31	0.2	0.0	109	94.6
2016	NOR	AAA	24	1	0	0	4	0	10	4	1	0.9	12.6	14	47%	.167	0.50	1.80	1.97	2.42	2.8	0.3	71	
2017	BAL	MLB	25	1	1	0	14	0	15¹	16	2	4.8	6.5	11	56%	.293	1.56	5.23	5.20	5.06	-0.1	0.0	100	
2018	BAL	MLB	26	1	0	0	19	0	20²	19	3	6.1	9.5	22	56%	.292	1.58	5.23	5.01	5.33	-0.6	-0.1	123	

Breakout: 9%   Improve: 10%   Collapse: 4%   Attrition: 12%   MLB: 15%   *Comparables: Thad Weber, Justin Marks, Erik Goeddel*

A ninth-round pick in 2010, Bridwell has had to fight for every handhold on the long climb to the big leagues. It's not hard to imagine why a guy with that background—a pitcher going on 25, assigned to pitch at Double-A for a second season—would be reticent to report an injury. Thus, Bridwell pitched the first month and a half of the season with a broken rib, and in his compromised state he ran up a 5.13 ERA. When he finally fessed up, and after nearly two months of recovery, he moved to the bullpen and everything clicked. Bridwell faced 104 batters over 28 innings from July 20 onward, fanning 35, walking five and holding opponents to a .240 OBP. He even made it (briefly) to the majors. The move to relief work might be a permanent but beneficial one.

Zach Britton   LHP

Born: 12/22/87 Age: 29   Bats: L   Throws: L   Height: 6'3"   Weight: 195   Entered Pro Ball: Round 3, 2006 Draft (#85 overall)

YEAR	TEAM	LVL	AGE	W	L	SV	G	GS	IP	H	HR	BB/9	K/9	K	GB%	BABIP	WHIP	ERA	FIP	DRA	VORP	WARP	cFIP	MPH
2014	BAL	MLB	26	3	2	37	71	0	76¹	46	4	2.7	7.3	62	76%	.215	0.90	1.65	3.16	2.40	17.7	2.0	82	97.8
2015	BAL	MLB	27	4	1	36	64	0	65²	51	3	1.9	10.8	79	81%	.308	0.99	1.92	1.98	1.40	24.2	2.6	52	98.7
2016	BAL	MLB	28	2	1	47	69	0	67	38	1	2.4	9.9	74	80%	.230	0.84	0.54	1.90	2.17	20.9	2.2	61	98.6
2017	BAL	MLB	29	3	3	35	58	0	61	50	5	2.9	9.8	67	51%	.290	1.14	2.73	3.16	3.02	13.3	1.4	58	
2018	BAL	MLB	30	2	1	23	44	0	46²	35	3	3.2	10.4	54	51%	.281	1.10	3.12	2.95	3.20	9.4	1.0	63	

Breakout: 29%   Improve: 57%   Collapse: 22%   Attrition: 19%   MLB: 97%   *Comparables: Brandon Webb, Mark Melancon, Jim Johnson*

Relievers are inevitably defined by the innings they don't throw. They're made heroes or rendered irrelevant in the innings leading up to their dramatic entrance. In sabermetric terms, they're prevented from matching the value of their starting counterparts by their sheer lack of outs recorded. Britton had his otherwise brilliant season defined by an inning he didn't throw, even though he inarguably should have thrown it. And therein, as the bard would tell us, lies the rub. October showed us that, at least under certain circumstances, relievers are capable of handling heavier workloads than their managers believe, especially within a given game. The pre-closer model of bullpen usage suggests the same. So, open your mind about guys like Britton. Evaluate him on the merits of his 98 mph sinker, extraordinary ground-ball and weak contact rates, and command.

Dylan Bundy   RHP

Born: 11/15/92 Age: 24   Bats: B   Throws: R   Height: 6'1"   Weight: 200   Entered Pro Ball: Round 1, 2011 Draft (#4 overall)

YEAR	TEAM	LVL	AGE	W	L	SV	G	GS	IP	H	HR	BB/9	K/9	K	GB%	BABIP	WHIP	ERA	FIP	DRA	VORP	WARP	cFIP	MPH
2014	ABE	A-	21	0	1	0	3	3	15	10	0	1.8	13.2	22	55%	.323	0.87	0.60	1.11	1.75	6.0	0.6	75	
2014	FRD	A+	21	1	2	0	6	6	26¹	28	0	4.4	5.1	15	47%	.318	1.56	4.78	3.97	6.79	-3.5	-0.4	115	
2015	BOW	AA	22	0	3	0	8	8	22	21	0	2	10.2	25	42%	.356	1.18	3.68	1.81	2.77	5.7	0.6	81	
2016	BAL	MLB	23	10	6	0	36	14	109²	109	18	3.4	8.5	104	37%	.299	1.38	4.02	4.66	4.81	5.1	0.5	107	97.0
2017	BAL	MLB	24	6	7	0	19	19	100²	100	15	3.5	8.2	92	50%	.297	1.40	4.55	4.63	4.71	6.0	0.6	100	
2018	BAL	MLB	25	9	10	0	29	29	175	165	26	3.7	9.2	179	50%	.296	1.35	4.62	4.40	4.76	11.8	1.2	110	

Breakout: 34%   Improve: 64%   Collapse: 10%   Attrition: 14%   MLB: 92%   *Comparables: Josh Johnson, Sean Gallagher, Drew Smyly*

Sometimes roster rules can derail promising careers, forcing development to be rushed or spurring a change of scenery the player didn't need. Then there are cases like Bundy's. The injury-riddled former elite prospect had to fit onto Baltimore's roster in 2016 or the franchise was going to lose him on a waiver claim. They shifted him into medium-length, medium-leverage relief, hoping to keep his workload low as he continued to build toward a healthy future. Then, life got in the way. Bundy dominated in relief, including an appearance at Dodger Stadium in which he struck out seven batters in 2.1 innings. The contending Orioles had holes in their rotation all year and Bundy turned out to be the best stopgap on hand. Over the final six weeks he showed fatigue and struggled to keep his fastball from straightening out. His future might still be in the bullpen, but he answered a lot of questions and put himself firmly back on the map in 2016.

Oliver Drake   RHP

Born: 1/13/87 Age: 30   Bats: R   Throws: R   Height: 6'4"   Weight: 215   Entered Pro Ball: Round 43, 2008 Draft (#1286 overall)

YEAR	TEAM	LVL	AGE	W	L	SV	G	GS	IP	H	HR	BB/9	K/9	K	GB%	BABIP	WHIP	ERA	FIP	DRA	VORP	WARP	cFIP	MPH
2014	BOW	AA	27	2	4	31	50	0	52²	41	2	2.9	12.1	71	44%	.325	1.10	3.08	2.12	1.02	22.4	2.4	63	
2015	NOR	AAA	28	1	2	23	42	0	44	23	1	3.3	13.5	66	47%	.256	0.89	0.82	1.54	1.06	18.9	1.9	56	
2015	BAL	MLB	28	0	0	0	13	0	15²	16	1	5.2	9.8	17	50%	.333	1.60	2.87	3.49	3.65	1.8	0.2	100	93.0
2016	NOR	AAA	29	1	4	10	47	1	56¹	44	5	4.0	12.6	79	46%	.322	1.22	2.72	2.90	1.93	19.1	2.0	76	
2016	BAL	MLB	29	1	0	0	14	0	18	11	2	3.5	10.5	21	52%	.205	1.00	4.00	3.38	4.05	1.8	0.2	92	92.3
2017	BAL	MLB	30	2	2	0	43	0	45	42	6	4.0	9.4	48	41%	.293	1.36	4.24	4.21	4.40	3.0	0.3	100	
2018	BAL	MLB	31	1	0	0	12	0	12²	10	2	5.3	11.8	17	41%	.285	1.37	4.37	4.16	4.54	0.7	0.1	103	

Breakout: 22%   Improve: 28%   Collapse: 15%   Attrition: 17%   MLB: 48%   *Comparables: Jason Bulger, Clay Rapada, Jose Valdez*

The entire baseball world's skepticism about Drake (the relief pitcher) is as inscrutable as the rest of the world's adulation for Drake (the rapper). Drake (the relief pitcher) has been outright dominant at every level since moving from the rotation to the bullpen in 2013. His fastball barely tops 90, but it plays much faster, especially up in the zone, because Drake gets great extension and even better deception from his wacky over-the-top delivery. That same delivery makes his splitter play really well off that fastball. He piles up strikeouts, gets plenty of ground balls and yet seems to have convinced no one.

Yovani Gallardo   RHP

Born: 2/27/86   Age: 31   Bats: R   Throws: R   Height: 6'2"   Weight: 205   Entered Pro Ball: Round 2, 2004 Draft (#46 overall)

YEAR	TEAM	LVL	AGE	W	L	SV	G	GS	IP	H	HR	BB/9	K/9	K	GB%	BABIP	WHIP	ERA	FIP	DRA	VORP	WARP	cFIP	MPH
2014	MIL	MLB	28	8	11	0	32	32	192¹	195	21	2.5	6.8	146	54%	.294	1.29	3.51	3.91	3.51	28.3	3.1	104	93.7
2015	TEX	MLB	29	13	11	0	33	33	184¹	193	15	3.3	5.9	121	51%	.303	1.42	3.42	3.97	4.50	11.8	1.3	107	93.2
2016	NOR	AAA	30	1	0	0	2	2	10	5	2	3.6	9.0	10	32%	.130	0.90	3.60	4.97	4.34	1.1	0.1	105	
2016	BAL	MLB	30	6	8	0	23	23	118	126	16	4.7	6.5	85	44%	.304	1.58	5.42	5.00	5.60	-3.2	-0.3	122	92.9
2017	BAL	MLB	31	9	12	0	30	30	171	181	25	4.0	6.7	128	38%	.296	1.51	5.03	5.02	5.23	0.3	0.0	100	
2018	BAL	MLB	32	8	11	0	28	28	168	181	26	4.1	6.6	124	38%	.299	1.53	5.34	5.11	5.54	-1.2	-0.1	130	

Breakout: 15%   Improve: 39%   Collapse: 24%   Attrition: 14%   MLB: 90%   Comparables: Carlos Zambrano, Doug Fister, Justin Masterson

He started losing velocity in 2012. He stopped missing bats in 2013. He turned into a kitchen-sink junkballer in 2014. He stopped being able to work deep into games in 2015. Finally, in 2016, Gallardo ran out of ways to fake it, and imploded. Unless he learns a cutter, starts pitching left-handed or procures compromising photos of a general manager, Gallardo is likely nearing the end of the line.

Jason Garcia   RHP

Born: 11/21/92   Age: 24   Bats: R   Throws: R   Height: 6'0"   Weight: 185   Entered Pro Ball: Round 17, 2010 Draft (#533 overall)

YEAR	TEAM	LVL	AGE	W	L	SV	G	GS	IP	H	HR	BB/9	K/9	K	GB%	BABIP	WHIP	ERA	FIP	DRA	VORP	WARP	cFIP	MPH
2014	LOW	A-	21	1	1	0	5	4	20²	19	0	3.0	9.6	22	50%	.328	1.26	3.48	2.76	3.47	4.2	0.4	90	
2014	GRN	A	21	2	1	3	9	3	35²	31	0	4.3	9.3	37	54%	.326	1.35	3.79	3.14	5.58	5.5	0.6	99	
2015	BOW	AA	22	1	2	0	9	0	15	12	2	5.4	8.4	14	57%	.250	1.40	4.20	5.14	7.61	-4.8	-0.5	106	
2015	BAL	MLB	22	1	0	0	21	0	29²	25	3	5.2	6.7	22	44%	.250	1.42	4.25	4.86	5.56	-2.8	-0.3	115	95.7
2016	BOW	AA	23	6	10	0	24	24	123²	137	5	3.9	5.2	71	45%	.325	1.54	4.73	4.26	8.27	-43.6	-4.7	124	
2017	BAL	MLB	24	1	1	0	19	0	20	23	3	4.7	5.1	12	52%	.298	1.67	5.82	5.70	5.53	-1.2	-0.1	100	
2018	BAL	MLB	25	2	0	0	32	0	34¹	34	5	6.4	7.8	30	52%	.299	1.71	5.76	5.53	5.88	-3.1	-0.3	137	

Breakout: 5%   Improve: 6%   Collapse: 3%   Attrition: 6%   MLB: 10%   Comparables: Colin Rea, Jeff Karstens, Jeremy Horst

Thanks to the Rule 5 draft Garcia went from the Red Sox's system (where he'd never pitched above Low-A) to the Orioles' 25-man roster in 2015. The Orioles had to keep him in the majors in order to keep him, so they did and he stunk there. And then they sent him to the Eastern League in 2016, a year gone and his development derailed. The Orioles ventured virtually nothing to acquire him. They threw him into the deep end of the pool, knowing they'd reap the benefits if he swam and realize very little loss if he sank. There are certainly some Rule 5 success stories, but Garcia isn't one of them and the system didn't do him any favors.

Kevin Gausman   RHP

Born: 1/6/91   Age: 26   Bats: L   Throws: R   Height: 6'3"   Weight: 190   Entered Pro Ball: Round 1, 2012 Draft (#4 overall)

YEAR	TEAM	LVL	AGE	W	L	SV	G	GS	IP	H	HR	BB/9	K/9	K	GB%	BABIP	WHIP	ERA	FIP	DRA	VORP	WARP	cFIP	MPH
2014	NOR	AAA	23	1	3	0	11	11	43¹	41	5	3.7	9.1	44	47%	.298	1.36	3.32	4.07	3.57	10.5	1.0	91	
2014	BAL	MLB	23	7	7	0	20	20	113¹	111	7	3.0	7.0	88	44%	.304	1.31	3.57	3.44	4.31	6.6	0.7	106	98.2
2015	NOR	AAA	24	0	1	0	3	3	14	10	2	3.9	9	14	51%	.242	1.14	1.29	4.30	4.23	1.7	0.2	98	
2015	BAL	MLB	24	4	7	0	25	17	112¹	109	17	2.3	8.3	103	46%	.288	1.23	4.25	4.07	3.58	18.2	1.9	90	98.7
2016	BAL	MLB	25	9	12	0	30	30	179²	183	28	2.4	8.7	174	46%	.308	1.28	3.61	4.06	3.16	43.9	4.5	86	98.2
2017	BAL	MLB	26	9	10	0	29	29	165¹	164	24	3.0	8.6	159	52%	.300	1.34	4.23	4.24	4.38	15.9	1.6	100	
2018	BAL	MLB	27	10	9	0	28	28	170¹	165	24	3.1	9.5	180	52%	.307	1.31	4.17	3.97	4.30	20.5	2.1	98	

Breakout: 22%   Improve: 65%   Collapse: 13%   Attrition: 8%   MLB: 97%   Comparables: Derek Holland, Matt Garza, Jon Niese

Gausman had a 2.83 ERA after August 1, pushing himself to the top of the Baltimore rotation and pushing the team into the Wild Card game. Despite high-end stuff—his fastball works in the upper 90s and his splitter can be devastating—he hasn't yet figured out how to avoid hard contact consistently enough to really dominate. Chalk that up to a deleterious reliance on his fastball. More than anything, the future of pitching involves fewer fastballs and more of whatever other pitch a hurler trusts most. The problem with that formula is that the splitter is a tough pitch to throw very often without inviting arm trouble, and Gausman's curveball just isn't good enough to be his primary weapon. Unless and until he finds a way around that, Gausman will continue to give up too many homers and have trouble getting right-handed batters out.

Mychal Givens   RHP

Born: 5/13/90   Age: 27   Bats: R   Throws: R   Height: 6'0"   Weight: 210   Entered Pro Ball: Round 2, 2009 Draft (#54 overall)

YEAR	TEAM	LVL	AGE	W	L	SV	G	GS	IP	H	HR	BB/9	K/9	K	GB%	BABIP	WHIP	ERA	FIP	DRA	VORP	WARP	cFIP	MPH
2014	FRD	A+	24	1	2	3	18	0	33¹	21	2	4.3	7.3	27	62%	.202	1.11	3.24	4.30	5.68	-1.8	-0.2	109	
2014	BOW	AA	24	0	0	0	18	0	25¹	19	0	8.2	9.9	28	66%	.292	1.66	3.91	4.58	6.18	-3.7	-0.4	105	
2015	BOW	AA	25	4	2	15	35	0	57¹	38	1	2.5	12.4	79	42%	.289	0.94	1.73	1.73	1.15	22.8	2.5	63	
2015	BAL	MLB	25	2	0	0	22	0	30	20	1	1.8	11.4	38	42%	.268	0.87	1.80	1.70	3.04	5.6	0.6	80	97.1
2016	BAL	MLB	26	8	2	0	66	0	74²	59	6	4.3	11.6	96	38%	.314	1.27	3.13	3.27	3.63	11.2	1.2	90	97.3
2017	BAL	MLB	27	2	3	0	48	0	51	45	6	4.1	10.0	56	50%	.293	1.34	4.01	3.97	4.20	4.4	0.5	95	
2018	BAL	MLB	28	3	1	0	51	0	54¹	43	7	4.7	11.8	71	50%	.291	1.32	4.04	3.85	4.18	5.2	0.5	94	

Breakout: 29%   Improve: 44%   Collapse: 27%   Attrition: 25%   MLB: 86%   Comparables: Rich Thompson, Greg Holland, Fernando Salas

It took Givens until 2015 to find real comfort on the mound. He started in pro ball as a shortstop and, although he transitioned to the mound in 2013, he didn't pitch with conviction or command for a couple years. When he finally found that comfort, everything took off. His fastball runs to his arm side and rides high. The command of his slider has tightened up nicely. He doesn't have a good answer for left-handed batters yet, but righties have no chance, and on the way to striking out they often look really bad on at least one swing.

Joe Gunkel   RHP

Born: 12/30/91 Age: 25   Bats: R   Throws: R   Height: 6'5"   Weight: 225   Entered Pro Ball: Round 18, 2013 Draft (#533 overall)

YEAR	TEAM	LVL	AGE	W	L	SV	G	GS	IP	H	HR	BB/9	K/9	K	GB%	BABIP	WHIP	ERA	FIP	DRA	VORP	WARP	cFIP	MPH
2014	GRN	A	22	3	0	2	17	5	51¹	26	3	1.9	10.9	62	48%	.204	0.72	2.28	2.92	1.52	21.3	2.2	70	
2014	SLM	A+	22	3	5	0	10	10	52¹	62	3	2.2	6.7	39	45%	.339	1.43	4.64	3.63	4.26	7.8	0.8	97	
2015	SLM	A+	23	1	1	2	8	2	22	16	2	1.6	9.0	22	47%	.250	0.91	2.05	2.98	2.12	6.7	0.7	78	
2015	PME	AA	23	2	1	0	4	3	18¹	26	1	3.9	10.8	22	40%	.481	1.85	3.93	2.89	3.20	3.8	0.4	87	
2015	BOW	AA	23	8	4	0	17	17	104¹	85	7	1.3	6	69	40%	.250	0.96	2.59	3.39	3.39	19.6	2.1	87	
2016	BOW	AA	24	0	3	0	4	4	19²	26	2	1.4	6.9	15	47%	.353	1.47	3.66	3.92	2.57	5.5	0.6	95	
2016	NOR	AAA	24	8	11	0	24	24	141¹	156	14	1.1	6.0	94	42%	.313	1.23	4.08	3.61	3.19	33.8	3.5	105	
2017	*BAL*	*MLB*	*25*	*7*	*8*	*1*	*37*	*20*	*128²*	*149*	*20*	*2.7*	*5.1*	*73*	*55%*	*.299*	*1.45*	*5.05*	*5.04*	*5.21*	*2.7*	*0.3*	*122*	
2018	*BAL*	*MLB*	*26*	*4*	*5*	*0*	*19*	*12*	*85²*	*85*	*14*	*4.6*	*7.9*	*75*	*55%*	*.288*	*1.51*	*5.52*	*5.28*	*5.70*	*-2.6*	*-0.3*	*134*	

Breakout: 15%   Improve: 20%   Collapse: 20%   Attrition: 31%   MLB: 44%   *Comparables: Gus Schlosser, Phil Irwin, Hiram Burgos*

Scouting the stat line won't tell you everything about a prospect, but over a big enough sample there are some numbers that inevitably tell you *something*. In Gunkel's case, what the numbers say is this: he pounds the strike zone. He's not going to walk anyone. He's also good at inviting weak contact. Here's the other thing, though: it's pretty clear that advanced hitters aren't as fooled by him as younger ones. Gunkel gave up 16 home runs in his first 270 professional innings through 2015 and then doubled that number in 160 innings in 2016. What the stat line can't see: he's deceptive but lacking for raw stuff. He might have to shift into relief, where he'd be less exposed to left-handed batters, in order to succeed at all in the majors.

Donnie Hart   LHP

Born: 9/6/90   Age: 26   Bats: L   Throws: L   Height: 5'11"   Weight: 180   Entered Pro Ball: Round 27, 2013 Draft (#819 overall)

YEAR	TEAM	LVL	AGE	W	L	SV	G	GS	IP	H	HR	BB/9	K/9	K	GB%	BABIP	WHIP	ERA	FIP	DRA	VORP	WARP	cFIP	MPH
2014	DEL	A	23	1	3	4	24	0	29¹	25	2	3.4	9.5	31	50%	.295	1.23	3.68	3.59	3.71	4.4	0.5	95	
2015	DEL	A	24	1	1	10	19	0	17	14	0	2.1	9.0	17	68%	.280	1.06	2.12	2.37	2.85	3.8	0.4	87	
2015	FRD	A+	24	5	1	3	27	0	35	26	0	2.6	7.5	29	61%	.265	1.03	1.03	2.62	2.88	7.1	0.8	91	
2016	BOW	AA	25	3	1	4	40	0	46¹	41	1	1.4	9.7	50	50%	.325	1.04	2.72	2.19	1.45	16.9	1.8	70	
2016	BAL	MLB	25	0	0	0	22	0	18¹	12	1	2.9	5.9	12	60%	.212	0.98	0.49	3.49	4.45	1.1	0.1	102	89.7
2017	*BAL*	*MLB*	*26*	*2*	*3*	*0*	*48*	*0*	*51*	*55*	*6*	*3.3*	*6.4*	*36*	*45%*	*.299*	*1.45*	*4.76*	*4.53*	*4.76*	*1.3*	*0.1*	*100*	
2018	*BAL*	*MLB*	*27*	*1*	*0*	*0*	*19*	*0*	*19²*	*18*	*2*	*4.6*	*9.3*	*20*	*45%*	*.302*	*1.44*	*4.50*	*4.30*	*4.64*	*0.9*	*0.1*	*104*	

Breakout: 20%   Improve: 27%   Collapse: 5%   Attrition: 18%   MLB: 40%   *Comparables: Josh Edgin, Ryan Braun, Fernando Abad*

Many sidearm hurlers drop low and stride long to ensure that they get their arm moving downhill or to maximize extension. They're worried about leaving the ball up, which no sidearmer can afford to do. Hart doesn't worry about that. He stabs the ball behind his back hip as he starts his delivery, then strides fairly short and lands on a relatively stiff leg. He fully trusts his arm slot to create sink. His finish is quiet. Everything looks easy. That helps explain his unusually good control and the difficulty batters have hitting his tepid fastball. Everything Hart throws seems to have batters off-balance, perhaps because he mixes his fastball and his slurvy slider so evenly.

Hunter Harvey   RHP

Born: 12/9/94   Age: 22   Bats: R   Throws: R   Height: 6'3"   Weight: 175   Entered Pro Ball: Round 1, 2013 Draft (#22 overall)

YEAR	TEAM	LVL	AGE	W	L	SV	G	GS	IP	H	HR	BB/9	K/9	K	GB%	BABIP	WHIP	ERA	FIP	DRA	VORP	WARP	cFIP	MPH
2014	DEL	A	19	7	5	0	17	17	87²	66	5	3.4	10.9	106	46%	.290	1.13	3.18	3.42	1.96	33.9	3.5	80	
2017	*BAL*	*MLB*	*22*	*2*	*3*	*0*	*7*	*7*	*32*	*36*	*6*	*5.4*	*7.3*	*26*	*61%*	*.309*	*1.72*	*5.88*	*5.91*	*5.95*	*-1.7*	*-0.2*	*142*	
2018	*BAL*	*MLB*	*23*	*5*	*8*	*0*	*23*	*23*	*137¹*	*133*	*22*	*6.2*	*10.1*	*154*	*61%*	*.310*	*1.65*	*5.49*	*5.28*	*5.56*	*-1.0*	*-0.1*	*132*	

Breakout: 13%   Improve: 19%   Collapse: 3%   Attrition: 17%   MLB: 26%   *Comparables: Matt Moore, Aaron Nola, David Paulino*

In late May of 2014 there were rumors that the Orioles were the leading team in the Jeff Samardzija sweepstakes, with Harvey at the top of the list of potential Cubs targets. In July, they were close to a deal for Jon Lester—how close, no one ever knew, because the deal fell apart when Harvey reported elbow trouble a week before the deadline. In the two-and-a-half years since, Harvey has made five appearances, and because he underwent Tommy John surgery in July that's unlikely to change this season. It's not entirely clear that the Orioles had a real chance to deal him, given the timing of it all, but the lesson remains: TINSTAAPP.

Ubaldo Jimenez   RHP

Born: 1/22/84   Age: 33   Bats: R   Throws: R   Height: 6'5"   Weight: 210   Entered Pro Ball: International Free Agent, 2001

YEAR	TEAM	LVL	AGE	W	L	SV	G	GS	IP	H	HR	BB/9	K/9	K	GB%	BABIP	WHIP	ERA	FIP	DRA	VORP	WARP	cFIP	MPH
2014	BAL	MLB	30	6	9	0	25	22	125¹	113	14	5.5	8.3	116	43%	.289	1.52	4.81	4.70	4.93	-1.5	-0.2	115	93.7
2015	BAL	MLB	31	12	10	0	32	32	184	182	20	3.3	8.2	168	50%	.309	1.36	4.11	3.98	3.19	38.6	4.1	94	93.7
2016	BAL	MLB	32	8	12	1	29	25	142¹	150	16	4.6	7.9	125	50%	.318	1.56	5.44	4.39	4.14	18.8	1.9	106	92.9
2017	*BAL*	*MLB*	*33*	*4*	*5*	*0*	*47*	*8*	*86*	*84*	*12*	*4.7*	*8.8*	*85*	*50%*	*.298*	*1.49*	*4.74*	*4.72*	*4.81*	*3.0*	*0.3*	*100*	
2018	*BAL*	*MLB*	*34*	*4*	*4*	*0*	*47*	*8*	*88*	*87*	*13*	*4.7*	*8.9*	*87*	*50%*	*.301*	*1.51*	*5.04*	*4.82*	*5.22*	*0.5*	*0.0*	*120*	

Breakout: 8%   Improve: 45%   Collapse: 20%   Attrition: 19%   MLB: 86%   *Comparables: Jason Vargas, Josh Beckett, Vicente Padilla*

Maybe we need to seriously consider that Jimenez has an evil twin or is having his talent periodically stolen by the Monstars and then returned by Tim Tebow a few weeks later. There might be a 74-year-old cricket bowler living inside him somewhere, taking over when the right trigger word falls into conversation. These are the most plausible explanations possible for Jimenez's uncanny ability to look entirely alien to the art of pitching for long periods, yet end most seasons with a roughly average (or better!) line. He's as talented as he is inconsistent, which is saying something.

Jesus Liranzo   RHP

Born: 3/7/95   Age: 22   Bats: R   Throws: R   Height: 6'2"   Weight: 175   Entered Pro Ball: International Free Agent, 2012

YEAR	TEAM	LVL	AGE	W	L	SV	G	GS	IP	H	HR	BB/9	K/9	K	GB%	BABIP	WHIP	ERA	FIP	DRA	VORP	WARP	cFIP	MPH
2016	DEL	A	21	0	0	0	16	0	34¹	12	0	3.9	12.1	46	36%	.180	0.79	1.05	2.20	2.15	9.5	1.0	84	
2016	BOW	AA	21	1	1	0	11	0	18²	8	3	5.8	9.6	20	38%	.119	1.07	3.38	5.39	7.19	-5.1	-0.6	110	
2017	BAL	MLB	22	1	0	1	34	0	35²	37	6	5.6	7.0	27	59%	.291	1.68	5.86	5.82	6.35	-8.1	-0.8	142	
2018	BAL	MLB	23	1	0	1	20	0	36¹	31	5	6.4	10.3	41	59%	.284	1.57	5.32	5.11	5.77	-2.7	-0.3	128	

Breakout: 23%   Improve: 24%   Collapse: 1%   Attrition: 3%   MLB: 24%   Comparables: Stephen Pryor, Shawn Armstrong, Trevor Gott

In two mostly healthy seasons since a broken elbow healed, Liranzo's career has taken off. He's fanned more than a batter per inning at each stop, largely because he has mid-90s heat and can change eye levels with his fastball alone, touching the top and the bottom of the zone as needed. His slider works, though it won't corkscrew anyone into the ground. He's likely to continue rising fast, but find his ceiling in a big-league bullpen to be pretty low.

Wade Miley   LHP

Born: 11/13/86   Age: 30   Bats: L   Throws: L   Height: 6'0"   Weight: 220   Entered Pro Ball: Round 1, 2008 Draft (#43 overall)

YEAR	TEAM	LVL	AGE	W	L	SV	G	GS	IP	H	HR	BB/9	K/9	K	GB%	BABIP	WHIP	ERA	FIP	DRA	VORP	WARP	cFIP	MPH
2014	ARI	MLB	27	8	12	0	33	33	201¹	207	23	3.4	8.2	183	52%	.317	1.40	4.34	3.95	3.36	33.1	3.7	97	94.0
2015	BOS	MLB	28	11	11	0	32	32	193²	201	17	3.0	6.8	147	50%	.307	1.37	4.46	3.78	3.54	33.0	3.5	97	93.8
2016	SEA	MLB	29	7	8	0	19	19	112	117	18	2.7	6.6	82	48%	.298	1.35	4.98	4.72	3.65	21.3	2.2	97	93.3
2016	BAL	MLB	29	2	5	0	11	11	54	70	7	2.5	9.2	55	50%	.389	1.57	6.17	3.75	3.35	12.1	1.2	97	92.8
2017	BAL	MLB	22	1	0	1	34	0	35²	37	6	5.6	7.0	27	59%	.291	1.68	5.86	5.82	6.35	-8.1	-0.8	142	
2018	BAL	MLB	23	1	0	1	20	0	36¹	31	5	6.4	10.3	41	59%	.284	1.57	5.32	5.11	5.77	-2.7	-0.3	128	

Breakout: 15%   Improve: 40%   Collapse: 28%   Attrition: 12%   MLB: 94%   Comparables: Yovani Gallardo, Gavin Floyd, Jason Hammel

DRA is looking at you while you offer your "Wade Miley is bad" take, but he's not listening to you. He's just waiting for your mouth to stop moving so he can crash into the silence at full speed with "well actually, a lot of Miley's apparent home run problems had to do with parks and opponents" or "well actually, only 11 pitchers were hurt more by poor framing in 2016 than Miley" or "well actually, he was really poorly supported by his defense, according to our model of expected outs on balls in play." That's all true. Miley has still allowed more runs than all but one other pitcher over the last three seasons.

Darren O'Day   RHP

Born: 10/22/82   Age: 34   Bats: R   Throws: R   Height: 6'4"   Weight: 220   Entered Pro Ball: Undrafted Free Agent, 2006

YEAR	TEAM	LVL	AGE	W	L	SV	G	GS	IP	H	HR	BB/9	K/9	K	GB%	BABIP	WHIP	ERA	FIP	DRA	VORP	WARP	cFIP	MPH
2014	BAL	MLB	31	5	2	4	68	0	68²	42	6	2.5	9.6	73	47%	.218	0.89	1.70	3.35	2.64	14.1	1.6	84	89.6
2015	BAL	MLB	32	6	2	6	68	0	65¹	47	5	1.9	11.3	82	36%	.278	0.93	1.52	2.46	2.93	12.9	1.4	80	89.1
2016	BAL	MLB	33	3	1	3	34	0	31	25	6	3.8	11.0	38	34%	.260	1.23	3.77	4.53	3.69	4.4	0.5	96	88.3
2017	BAL	MLB	34	2	2	2	39	0	40	35	6	3.2	9.9	45	61%	.285	1.20	3.85	4.13	4.06	4.2	0.4	90	
2018	BAL	MLB	35	3	1	2	55	0	58	49	9	3.3	9.4	61	61%	.270	1.21	4.46	4.24	4.59	2.9	0.3	104	

Breakout: 18%   Improve: 33%   Collapse: 38%   Attrition: 12%   MLB: 92%   Comparables: J.J. Putz, Damaso Marte, Jose Valverde

O'Day never threw hard and his velocity is fading with age. So, too, is his health. He missed seven weeks with a hamstring strain in 2016 and then was sidelined again by a shoulder strain in August. In each case, he tried to pitch through the injury for a couple outings and the ugly results of those efforts perhaps leave a misleading season line. O'Day can still dominate in short relief. He was very good when he was fully healthy. Going forward, though, he can't afford to keep seeing his stuff soften, nor to have ongoing health problems.

Ofelky Peralta   RHP

Born: 4/20/97   Age: 20   Bats: R   Throws: R   Height: 6'5"   Weight: 195   Entered Pro Ball: International Free Agent, 2013

YEAR	TEAM	LVL	AGE	W	L	SV	G	GS	IP	H	HR	BB/9	K/9	K	GB%	BABIP	WHIP	ERA	FIP	DRA	VORP	WARP	cFIP	MPH
2016	DEL	A	19	8	5	0	23	23	103¹	87	3	5.2	8.8	101	40%	.298	1.42	4.01	3.77	7.98	-34.1	-3.7	124	
2017	BAL	MLB	20	2	7	0	16	16	61²	83	15	7.9	4.3	29	79%	.309	2.22	8.27	8.16	8.49	-20.7	-2.1	195	
2018	BAL	MLB	21	3	9	0	19	19	112²	136	25	9.0	6.7	84	79%	.310	2.21	8.05	7.77	8.26	-23.5	-2.4	189	

Breakout: 0%   Improve: 0%   Collapse: 0%   Attrition: 0%   MLB: 0%   Comparables: Shawn Morimando, Raul Alcantara, Tyler Chatwood

It's wildly impressive that Peralta managed to miss a bunch of bats, as well as the strike zone, for Class-A Delmarva. He's a hard thrower with long levers, and his delivery is not a classic, compact affair. Nor is it unduly messy. As a teenager challenged by his organization to dominate older hitters while still learning his mechanics, Peralta needed only to stay healthy and demonstrate progress in order to call the season a success. He did both of those things, and seemed more comfortable and composed as the season wore on.

Tanner Scott   LHP

Born: 7/22/94   Age: 22   Bats: R   Throws: L   Height: 6'2"   Weight: 220   Entered Pro Ball: Round 6, 2014 Draft (#181 overall)

YEAR	TEAM	LVL	AGE	W	L	SV	G	GS	IP	H	HR	BB/9	K/9	K	GB%	BABIP	WHIP	ERA	FIP	DRA	VORP	WARP	cFIP	MPH
2015	ABE	A-	20	4	0	0	9	1	21¹	16	0	5.1	13.1	31	64%	.340	1.31	3.38	2.72	4.15	1.9	0.2	96	
2015	DEL	A	20	0	3	2	9	2	21	19	0	4.3	12.4	29	57%	.373	1.38	4.29	2.15	2.67	5.3	0.6	88	
2016	FRD	A+	21	4	2	5	29	0	48¹	22	1	7.8	11.7	63	59%	.198	1.32	4.47	3.94	5.69	-3.3	-0.3	117	
2016	BOW	AA	21	1	2	0	14	0	16	18	0	8.4	10.1	18	64%	.429	2.06	5.62	4.11	7.37	-4.7	-0.5	103	
2017	BAL	MLB	22	2	1	1	39	3	48	52	7	7.0	7.2	39	48%	.307	1.86	5.92	5.96	6.00	-6.6	-0.7	142	
2018	BAL	MLB	23	1	0	0	11	1	22¹	21	3	8.3	9.5	24	48%	.304	1.88	6.05	5.82	6.13	-2.2	-0.2	144	

Breakout: 0%   Improve: 1%   Collapse: 1%   Attrition: 1%   MLB: 2%   *Comparables: Hector Santiago, Steven Geltz, Michael Lorenzen*

It's hard to say what everyone hopes will happen with guys like Scott. It's fairly clear that, whatever the needed transformation might be, it's probably not forthcoming. Yet here we sit, waiting. If you were writing a baseball novel centered around a guy named Tanner Scott, he'd be a burly knucklehead with a triple-digit fastball, but no command of it and no complementary skill—in baseball or in life. The real Scott broke his finger punching a wall last spring, has walked 16 percent of the batters he's faced in his pro career and occasionally flashes an average slider. The velocity will keep everyone interested for one more year.

Cody Sedlock   RHP

Born: 6/19/95   Age: 21   Bats: R   Throws: R   Height: 6'3"   Weight: 190   Entered Pro Ball: Round 1, 2016 Draft (#27 overall)

YEAR	TEAM	LVL	AGE	W	L	SV	G	GS	IP	H	HR	BB/9	K/9	K	GB%	BABIP	WHIP	ERA	FIP	DRA	VORP	WARP	cFIP	MPH
2016	ABE	A-	21	0	1	0	9	9	27	16	1	4.3	8.3	25	60%	.163	1.07	3.00	3.35	4.51	2.2	0.2	108	
2017	BAL	MLB	22	2	3	0	8	8	30²	38	6	6.0	5.1	18	53%	.309	1.90	6.54	6.65	6.62	-3.9	-0.4	157	
2018	BAL	MLB	23	3	6	0	18	18	104¹	114	16	7.1	7.0	81	53%	.303	1.88	6.46	6.21	6.54	-8.1	-0.8	154	

Breakout: 0%   Improve: 0%   Collapse: 0%   Attrition: 0%   MLB: 0%   *Comparables: Duke Welker, Trevor Williams, Jason Hursh*

He throws right-handed, but in most other ways Sedlock's story shares a lot with Twins prospect Tyler Jay's narrative two years ago. He pitched in relief for most of his college career at Illinois, but showed scouts enough to be drafted as a starter. He throws hard and has a slider with undeniable plus potential, but his arm path is a bit long and unusual, which poses some problems for command projection. Unlike Jay, Sedlock started throughout his two-month pro debut, but (also unlike Jay) it was in a short-season league and he got hit a bit there. It's not clear that Sedlock can stick in the rotation, but he should have value in the bullpen if it comes to that..

Chris Tillman   RHP

Born: 4/15/88   Age: 29   Bats: R   Throws: R   Height: 6'5"   Weight: 200   Entered Pro Ball: Round 2, 2006 Draft (#49 overall)

YEAR	TEAM	LVL	AGE	W	L	SV	G	GS	IP	H	HR	BB/9	K/9	K	GB%	BABIP	WHIP	ERA	FIP	DRA	VORP	WARP	cFIP	MPH
2014	BAL	MLB	26	13	6	0	34	34	207¹	189	21	2.9	6.5	150	42%	.267	1.23	3.34	4.04	4.29	12.7	1.4	110	94.0
2015	BAL	MLB	27	11	11	0	31	31	173	176	20	3.3	6.2	120	46%	.294	1.39	4.99	4.42	5.22	-2.7	-0.3	111	94.4
2016	BAL	MLB	28	16	6	0	30	30	172	155	19	3.5	7.3	140	42%	.282	1.28	3.77	4.19	4.58	15.0	1.5	109	94.6
2017	BAL	MLB	29	9	12	0	29	29	174	174	28	3.7	7.5	145	43%	.287	1.39	4.94	4.95	5.14	2.1	0.2	100	
2018	BAL	MLB	30	8	11	0	27	27	162²	165	29	4.2	7.6	138	43%	.288	1.48	5.48	5.25	5.68	-3.7	-0.4	135	

Breakout: 17%   Improve: 37%   Collapse: 25%   Attrition: 10%   MLB: 91%   *Comparables: Gavin Floyd, Andrew Cashner, Wade Miley*

Failure forces adjustments. Tillman's brutal 2015 led him to three vital ones. In the middle of that season he developed a sinker, a pitch that matches his four-seamer for velocity but mimics his changeup in its movement. That pitch has served him well because his lower arm slot lets it and the changeup run more to his arm side. He also started moving across the rubber, from the first-base side to the third-base side, which is where he was almost all the time by the end of 2016. That change of position gave him more good angles at which to throw his good cutter, so he roughly doubled his use of that pitch and his strikeout rate bounced back. Tillman is still no darling of advanced metrics, but he's a credible, high-volume third or fourth starter, and his adjustments over the last year and a half have solidified that status.

Alex Wells   LHP

Born: 6/19/95   Age: 21   Bats: R   Throws: R   Height: 6'3"   Weight: 190   Entered Pro Ball: Round 1, 2016 Draft (#27 overall)

YEAR	TEAM	LVL	AGE	W	L	SV	G	GS	IP	H	HR	BB/9	K/9	K	GB%	BABIP	WHIP	ERA	FIP	DRA	VORP	WARP	cFIP	MPH
2016	ABE	A-	19	4	5	0	13	13	62²	48	1	1.3	7.2	50	45%	.265	0.91	2.15	2.36	2.50	19.1	2.0	80	
2017	BAL	MLB	20	2	3	0	7	7	36¹	45	8	3.6	5.4	22	69%	.309	1.65	6.14	6.10	6.20	-2.9	-0.3	151	
2018	BAL	MLB	21	6	9	0	22	22	131	141	27	3.9	7.3	106	69%	.293	1.51	5.85	5.62	5.91	-5.3	-0.5	145	

Breakout: 1%   Improve: 1%   Collapse: 0%   Attrition: 0%   MLB: 1%   *Comparables: Jayson Aquino, Robert Stephenson, Kyle Lobstein*

He's a twin, but while his brother pitches for the Twins, he doesn't. He's from Down Under, but he throws nearly over the top. Wells' bio is always throwing you curves like that. Unfortunately, the man himself throws few breaking pitches at all, and when he does they don't do anything terribly impressive. He has a fastball that can touch 90 mph, but only touch it. And while his command of both that pitch and his changeup are good for his age, he's unlikely to bewilder big-league hitters with that mix. On the positive side, the change does have good movement and his delivery is just deceptive enough to help it play. Also, that Aussie accent really plays in minor-league towns.

Vance Worley   RHP

Born: 9/25/87   Age: 29   Bats: R   Throws: R   Height: 6'2"   Weight: 250   Entered Pro Ball: Round 3, 2008 Draft (#102 overall)

YEAR	TEAM	LVL	AGE	W	L	SV	G	GS	IP	H	HR	BB/9	K/9	K	GB%	BABIP	WHIP	ERA	FIP	DRA	VORP	WARP	cFIP	MPH
2014	IND	AAA	26	3	2	0	7	7	46	47	3	0.8	8.4	43	57%	.331	1.11	4.30	2.73	1.50	21.8	2.2	74	
2014	PIT	MLB	26	8	4	0	18	17	110²	112	9	1.8	6.4	79	53%	.299	1.21	2.85	3.41	4.02	10.0	1.1	102	92.4
2015	IND	AAA	27	3	1	0	5	5	34	30	4	1.3	5.6	21	53%	.255	1.03	2.38	4.07	3.44	7.0	0.7	94	
2015	PIT	MLB	27	4	6	0	23	8	71²	81	6	2.6	6.2	49	48%	.323	1.42	4.02	3.85	5.30	-3.0	-0.3	115	92.0
2016	BAL	MLB	28	2	2	1	35	4	86²	84	11	3.6	5.8	56	49%	.283	1.37	3.53	4.78	4.98	0.9	0.1	114	92.4
2017	*BAL*	*MLB*	*29*	*4*	*4*	*0*	*25*	*10*	*74²*	*87*	*13*	*3.6*	*6.6*	*55*	*47%*	*.316*	*1.56*	*5.25*	*5.24*	*5.44*	*-1.0*	*-0.1*	*127*	
2018	*BAL*	*MLB*	*30*	*7*	*8*	*0*	*34*	*19*	*141²*	*160*	*25*	*3.8*	*7.1*	*111*	*47%*	*.312*	*1.56*	*5.51*	*5.27*	*5.71*	*-5.0*	*-0.5*	*134*	

Breakout: 34%   Improve: 50%   Collapse: 27%   Attrition: 21%   MLB: 91%   *Comparables: Charlie Morton, Sergio Mitre, Jason Vargas*

Worley keeps the ball on the ground pretty well and has managed to keep the ball off opposing hitters' barrels better since his sojourn to Pittsburgh, where he switched to a two-seam, fastball-heavy approach. He really, really needs to have fine command in order to succeed, because he has no way to reliably miss bats. Sometimes walks are his way of avoiding giving up hard contact. It's not walks of which he needs to steer clear. It's mistakes. Such a pitcher lives a little longer in the bullpen, but most managers (rightly) won't trust that kind of pitcher in tight spots.

LINEOUTS

Hitters

NAME	POS	TEAM	LVL	AGE	PA	R	2B	3B	HR	RBI	BB	K	SB	CS	AVG/OBP/SLG	TAv	VORP	BABIP	BRR	FRAA	WARP
Steve Clevenger	C	SEA	MLB	30	76	7	3	0	1	7	8	14	0	0	.221/.303/.309	.207	-0.5	.264	0.1	C(20): -5.5	-0.6
Austin Hays	RF	ABE	A-	20	153	14	9	2	4	21	11	32	4	3	.336/.386/.514	.346	14.6	.410	-1.1	RF(19): 0.3, CF(5): -1.0	1.5
Paul Janish	3B	BAL	MLB	33	35	3	1	0	0	0	3	3	0	0	.194/.286/.226	.191	-1.1	.214	0.2	3B(9): -0.5, SS(6): 0.0	-0.2
	3B	NOR	AAA	33	283	26	8	0	0	18	28	33	1	3	.248/.333/.280	.232	2.2	.285	-1.3	SS(76): -2.9	-0.1
Francisco Pena	C	NOR	AAA	26	208	17	11	1	4	23	15	25	0	1	.246/.298/.377	.237	4.2	.262	0.2	C(51): 8.9	1.3
	C	BAL	MLB	26	43	5	0	0	1	3	2	14	0	0	.200/.238/.275	.167	-1.7	.280	0.4	C(14): -0.9	-0.3
Nolan Reimold	RF	BAL	MLB	32	227	25	9	1	6	15	22	62	1	2	.222/.300/.365	.228	-3.8	.287	-1.3	LF(62): -0.4, RF(32): -1.0	-0.6
Aderlin Rodriguez	1B	FRD	A+	24	542	71	23	6	26	93	36	112	3	3	.304/.359/.532	.296	26.7	.345	-1.5	1B(102): -4.0, 3B(17): 0.0	2.3
Anthony Santander	OF	LYN	A+	21	574	90	42	0	20	95	54	118	10	5	.290/.368/.494	.305	35.2	.339	-1.8	LF(67): -8.4, 1B(9): -0.2	2.7
Logan Schafer	RF	ROC	AAA	29	245	29	7	1	4	19	22	35	5	2	.264/.340/.361	.262	7.6	.299	1.5	RF(32): -1.6, CF(24): 1.4	1.0
	RF	MIN	MLB	29	74	8	3	1	0	1	8	16	0	0	.238/.342/.317	.231	-0.7	.319	-0.1	LF(12): -0.7, RF(8): 0.6	0.0
Aneury Tavarez	OF	PME	AA	24	425	59	19	13	7	47	29	64	18	11	.335/.379/.506	.312	32.3	.381	2.5	RF(61): 0.9, LF(36): 0.1	3.6
Christian Walker	1B	NOR	AAA	25	552	64	29	2	18	64	40	138	1	3	.264/.321/.437	.263	11.4	.327	-0.5	LF(90): -8.0, 1B(5): 0.2	0.4
David Washington	1B	SFD	AA	25	92	15	4	1	5	15	16	27	0	1	.276/.402/.553	.347	9.9	.364	0.3	RF(19): -4.6, 1B(1): -0.1	0.6
	1B	MEM	AAA	25	401	52	17	1	25	62	51	142	4	5	.255/.349/.528	.308	24.0	.346	-1.9	1B(43): 3.0, RF(39): -5.2	2.3
Austin Wynns	C	BOW	AA	25	82	11	7	0	0	10	7	12	1	0	.247/.309/.342	.238	1.8	.290	0.1	C(20): 0.8	0.3
	C	FRD	A+	25	206	23	10	0	5	20	13	32	0	0	.303/.351/.436	.263	8.4	.340	0.4	C(36): 1.8	1.0
Mike Yastrzemski	OF	BOW	AA	25	147	27	5	0	6	27	19	20	4	0	.268/.361/.449	.295	10.3	.275	2.5	RF(29): 0.0, LF(3): -0.4	1.1
	OF	NOR	AAA	25	385	41	21	4	7	32	42	98	10	3	.221/.312/.369	.254	5.4	.289	-1.6	CF(42): 2.5, LF(27): 3.2	1.3

Years from now, **Steve Clevenger's** legacy will be one of bad trades and worse tweets, which considering we probably wouldn't remember him much at all otherwise, is a rather mixed blessing. ❖ **Austin Hays** raked in a short pro debut. He'll have to hit and hit for power to make it as an everyday player, but he might just do it. ❖ **Paul Janish** has played just long enough in the majors to be expected to tip Triple-A clubbies like a big leaguer. ❖ **Francisco Pena** is a good defensive catcher, but for his bat to be viable he's going to need to slide 60 feet, six inches up the defensive spectrum from there. ❖ A formerly injury-prone but promising slugging corner outfielder walks into a bar, with a healthy sub-replacement season hanging around his neck. The bartender looks up, startled, and says: "Geez, **Nolan**, you look like you've seen better days. What happened to that plus hit tool?" The outfielder grimaces and says: "**Arr, I'm old**." ❖ **Aderlin Rodriguez** hit like crazy in the Carolina League in 2016, which would be impressive if he hadn't been a level higher the year before and fallen flat. ❖ On the comeback trail from shoulder surgery, outfielder/first baseman **Anthony Santander** has plus power and zero experience above Single-A. ❖ Given regular playing time in September because the Twins were sick of looking at rookies, **Logan Schafer** hasn't even been a good Triple-A regular in recent years. ❖ 2016 Portland Sea Dogs MVP **Aneury Tavarez** lacks a standout tool but offered across-the-board production in Double-A. He's never been a top prospect, but he's hit at every level. ❖ **Christian Walker**'s an average hitter / Not a true slugger; just a gap-splitter / His hometown's Limerick / Which explains this brief shtick / He's a Quad-A guy, or perhaps a bench-sitter ❖ Very large human **David Washington** matched top prospect Joey Gallo's home run and slugging numbers last year in the Pacific Coast League. Unfortunately, he also struck out more often(!), walked less and is three years older. ❖ Did you know that one day of big-league service time guarantees a player lifetime medical benefits? **Austin Wynns** does. ❖ **Mike Yastrzemski** has plate discipline, but he doesn't make contact or hit for power the way he'll need to if he wants to be an everyday corner outfielder.

Pitchers

NAME	TEAM	LVL	AGE	W	L	SV	G	GS	IP	H	HR	BB/9	K/9	K	GB%	BABIP	WHIP	ERA	FIP	DRA	VORP	WARP	cFIP	MPH
Jayson Aquino	BOW	AA	23	5	10	0	20	19	115¹	130	7	2.6	6.0	77	54%	.325	1.41	3.90	3.80	3.79	16.5	1.8	93	
	NOR	AAA	23	2	0	0	5	0	13	12	0	2.1	8.3	12	69%	.333	1.15	2.08	2.01	2.85	3.0	0.3	83	
	BAL	MLB	23	0	0	0	3	0	2¹	1	0	0.0	11.6	3	0%	.200	0.43	0.00	0.53	4.27	0.2	0.0	103	90.9
Pedro Beato	NOR	AAA	29	5	5	4	65	0	68	59	6	3.2	8.2	62	45%	.279	1.22	2.65	3.64	4.89	0.5	0.1	101	
Jed Bradley	BLX	AA	26	3	2	0	17	0	24²	33	2	2.2	7.3	20	60%	.360	1.58	6.20	3.97	2.83	5.8	0.6	86	
	MIS	AA	26	4	3	0	15	10	65	59	0	3.2	9.6	69	57%	.328	1.26	2.35	2.30	2.34	18.9	2.0	86	
	GWN	AAA	26	2	0	0	3	3	18	14	0	5.5	9.5	19	53%	.311	1.39	1.50	2.89	3.93	2.8	0.3	93	
	ATL	MLB	26	1	1	0	6	0	7	7	0	7.7	5.1	4	44%	.304	1.86	5.14	4.61	6.13	-0.9	-0.1	116	91.9
Garrett Cleavinger	DEL	A	22	5	0	4	17	0	39	25	3	2.5	12.2	53	51%	.278	0.92	1.38	2.60	1.60	13.2	1.5	76	
	FRD	A+	22	2	3	0	20	0	37¹	35	2	5.5	11.8	49	37%	.367	1.55	4.82	3.71	3.25	7.6	0.8	96	
Matthias Dietz	ABE	A-	20	0	3	0	7	7	18²	22	0	4.8	3.9	8	45%	.344	1.71	4.82	4.02	8.17	-6.1	-0.6	122	
David Hale	COL	MLB	28	0	0	0	2	0	2	4	1	9.0	4.5	1	33%	.375	3.00	13.50	11.69	7.33	-0.5	-0.1	119	92.1
	NOR	AAA	28	4	7	0	20	20	94	133	10	2.2	5.4	56	52%	.362	1.66	5.84	4.16	5.97	-6.5	-0.7	107	
Tommy Hunter	CLE	MLB	29	2	2	0	21	0	21²	21	1	2.1	7.1	17	53%	.308	1.20	3.74	3.11	4.89	0.2	0.0	105	96.7
	COH	AAA	29	2	1	1	14	2	15	14	2	1.2	6.0	10	46%	.261	1.07	3.00	3.97	3.32	2.8	0.3	99	
	BAL	MLB	29	0	0	0	12	0	12¹	14	0	2.2	4.4	6	45%	.350	1.38	2.19	2.86	4.96	0.0	0.0	106	96.9
Chris Lee	BOW	AA	23	5	0	0	8	7	51¹	41	4	2.3	3.3	19	60%	.226	1.05	2.98	4.57	4.50	3.1	0.3	104	
T.J. McFarland	BAL	MLB	27	2	2	0	16	0	24²	33	3	3.6	2.6	7	60%	.333	1.74	6.93	5.58	6.17	-3.3	-0.3	120	93.9
	NOR	AAA	27	1	1	0	8	4	26¹	33	3	2.4	3.8	11	63%	.330	1.52	4.44	4.84	5.34	-0.3	0.0	103	
Andy Oliver	NOR	AAA	28	3	2	0	28	14	86²	85	6	3.7	8.7	84	47%	.325	1.40	3.43	3.45	4.47	6.9	0.7	95	
Logan Verrett	LVG	AAA	26	2	0	0	2	2	12	8	1	6.0	3.8	5	40%	.189	1.33	1.50	5.97	7.59	-3.0	-0.3	128	
	NYN	MLB	26	3	8	0	35	12	91²	100	16	4.2	6.5	66	46%	.303	1.56	5.20	5.55	6.28	-10.8	-1.1	124	93.5
Tyler Wilson	NOR	AAA	26	2	0	0	6	6	23²	26	1	1.1	7.6	20	54%	.357	1.23	4.56	2.41	3.22	5.6	0.6	87	
	BAL	MLB	26	4	6	0	24	13	94	110	15	2.3	5.3	55	46%	.301	1.43	5.27	4.90	5.23	0.5	0.0	116	92.7
Mike Wright	NOR	AAA	26	4	4	0	13	13	76¹	72	8	1.7	5.7	48	45%	.272	1.13	3.07	3.86	4.74	5.2	0.5	107	
	BAL	MLB	26	3	4	0	18	12	74²	81	12	3.1	6.0	50	43%	.299	1.43	5.79	5.26	5.46	-1.3	-0.1	115	96.5

A starter almost his entire pro career, **Jayson Aquino** fanned 15 and walked three in seven games after moving to the bullpen late in 2016. ❖ **Pedro Beato** has thrown 140-plus innings of unbelievably consistent, perfectly average relief at Triple-A since his last stint in the majors (in 2014). ❖ Five years after being drafted out of Georgia Tech, **Jed Bradley** returned to Atlanta and finally made it to the big leagues. ❖ With 102 strikeouts as a multi-inning reliever last season, **Garrett Cleavinger** put himself on the fast track toward a big-league roster spot. ❖ **Matthias Dietz** was a nice pick in the 2016 draft, but probably doesn't have the command or feel for his changeup to start. He might be a solid setup man. ❖ **Gray Fenter** had Tommy John surgery in April of what should have been his first full season as a pro, and now has to hope his mid-90s fastball is still there one spring later. ❖ Ted Williams always said, "The hardest thing to do in all of sports is to hit a round baseball with a round bat, squarely, unless **David Hale** threw it, apparently." ❖ Injuries to his core have robbed **Tommy Hunter** of the velocity bump that briefly made him a real weapon in the bullpen. He's still a nice spare arm. ❖ Only a shoulder injury stopped **Chris Lee** from getting a shot in the majors last year, but his strikeout rate is a bigger impediment to his long-term prospects for success. ❖ A season lost to injuries sustained in a spring training car accident will force **Lazaro Leyva** to resurrect the hype his live arm created in 2015. [baseball] In four seasons opponents' contact percent on swings have risen from 78 to 81 to 84 to 87. The first two numbers work. The third is a problem. The fourth might mean the end of **T.J. McFarland**'s tenure in the big leagues. ❖ **Andy Oliver** held opponents to a .550 OPS as a reliever at Triple-A last season, but isn't an ideal LOOGY. ❖ Mets fans often theorized that **Logan Verrett**, an adequate long reliever and emergency starter, was destined to be the next good Met starter to come out of nowhere; however, a 7.18 ERA over seven starts in place of Matt Harvey offered another theory. ❖ "Average stuff" is sometimes a back-handed compliment and sometimes an outright insult. For **Tyler Wilson**, it leans toward the latter. ❖ **Mike Wright** throws hard, but can't miss bats or keep the ball in the park as a starter.

BOSTON RED SOX

Essay by Michael Schur

Player comments by Ben Carsley and BP staff

Dear William,

When the history of your baseball fandom is written, the defining event will have been a meaningless Dodgers-Diamondbacks game in 2014. Your love for the sport was nascent but ascendant, and the suggestion that I take you to Dodger Stadium seemed entirely reasonable. In fact, as your mother put it at the time, it seemed oddly cruel *not* to take you.

Why wouldn't you do this? All he wants is to see a live baseball game.

Okay. It's just…the first game matters. My first live game was at Fenway and it made me a Red Sox fan, and I wanted his first live game to be at Fenway.

It's September. We won't be in Boston until next year. You really want to deny your son seeing a live game until next year?

I nodded sadly. The logic was sound. But I knew what it meant. I was going to lose you to West Coast baseball.

We parked in the endless Dodger Stadium parking lot, and walked up those endless Dodger Stadium stairs. I watched as you took in the crowd and the sight of the field. I bought you a t-shirt with Clayton Kershaw's name and number and a foam #1 finger and you were gone.

My first chance to stop you from abandoning the Boston Red Sox, the team of your father and his father before him, was that day. I could have just refused to take you, maybe claimed all the games were sold out. (You would've believed me. You were six.) My second chance to stop you from abandoning the Red Sox was on the car ride home when, as you were buzzing about Adrian Gonzalez's home run, I told you that he had recently played for the Red Sox who, remember, are the reigning World Champions! You were momentarily interested, but then you asked why he had been traded to the Dodgers if he was so good, and I tried to explain the concept of payroll flexibility and your brain shut off like a tap. (You'll understand someday—it was a great trade.)

My third and best chance to stop you was our first actual trip to Fenway Park, almost exactly a year later. By then your Dodgers fandom was all but calcified. You'd seen who

RED SOX PROSPECTUS
2016 W-L: 93-69, 1ST IN AL EAST

Pythag	.611	2nd	DER	.707	11th
RS/G	5.42	1st	B-Age	28.5	14th
RA/G	4.28	9th	P-Age	28.7	21st
TAv	.269	6th	Salary	$197.9M	4th
BRR	0.63	13th	M$/MW	$4.2M	7th
TAv-P	.241	3rd	DL Days	1018	16th
FIP	3.96	9th	$ on DL	13%	17th

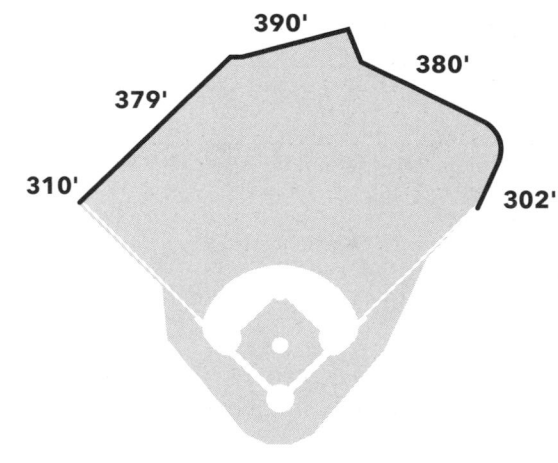

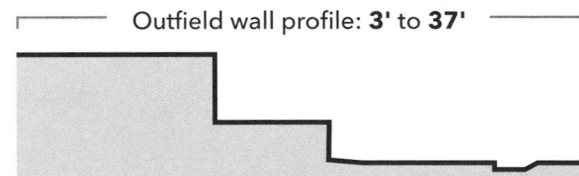

Outfield wall profile: **3'** to **37'**

Three-Year Park Factors

Runs	Runs/RH	Runs/LH	HR/RH	HR/LH
112	115	120	108	95

Top Hitter WARP	6.9	Mookie Betts
Top Pitcher WARP	6.5	David Price
Top Prospect		Andrew Benintendi

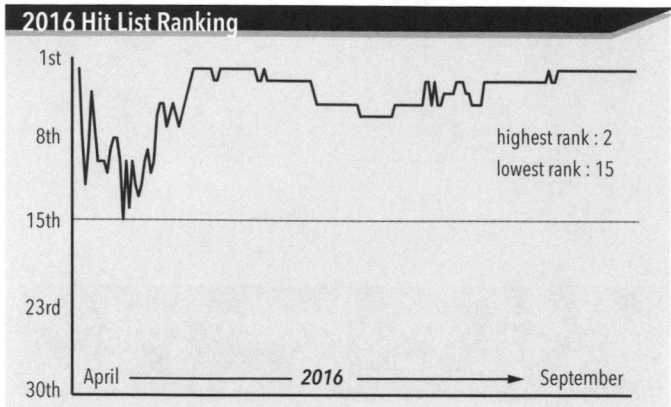

2016 Hit List Ranking

highest rank : 2
lowest rank : 15

April — 2016 → September

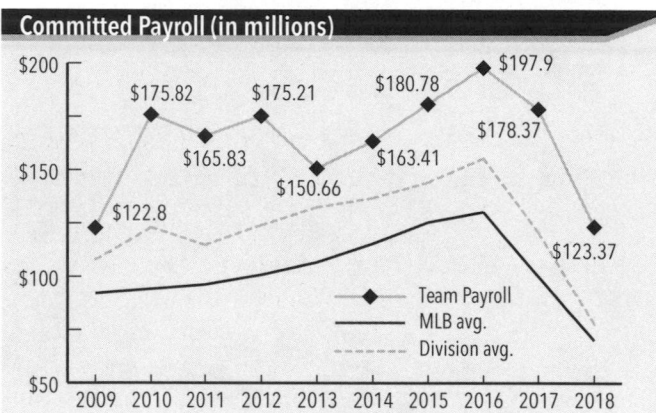

Committed Payroll (in millions)

$197.9
$180.78
$175.82
$175.21
$178.37
$165.83
$163.41
$150.66
$122.8
$123.37

◆ Team Payroll
— MLB avg.
--- Division avg.

2009 2010 2011 2012 2013 2014 2015 2016 2017 2018

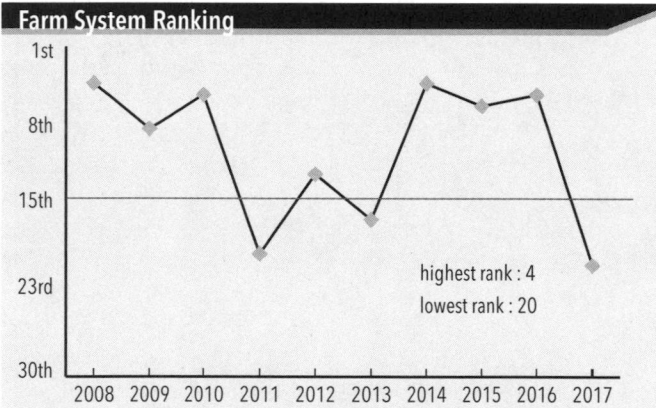

Farm System Ranking

highest rank : 4
lowest rank : 20

2008 2009 2010 2011 2012 2013 2014 2015 2016 2017

Personnel

**President,
Baseball Operations:**
Dave Dombrowski

**Senior VP/
Assistant General Manager:**
Brian O'Halloran

**Senior VP/Assistant General
Manager:**
Eddie Romero

Manager:
John Farrell

BP Alumni:
Todd Gold

knows how many Dodgers games by then—six? ten?—but I felt like Fenway might get you to switch. Fenway would save me. I spent a small fortune (sixth row, behind the dugout) and you, Grandpa Kip and I settled in to let Fenway work its magic. Got there early. Hit the gift shop on Yawkey Way with a mandate straight out of the Terrible Parenting Playbook: get whatever you want. I do not care how many objects you desire. You shall have them all! Three jerseys, two hats, team card set, books, batting glove and foam #1 finger? Is that all? Sure you don't want to take another loop around?

The problem was the Red Sox were playing the Mariners that afternoon, and King Felix was pitching. My fitful sleep the night before was riddled with visions of a 2-0 Mariners win, a three-hitter where the Sox don't get a runner past second, a dead crowd wilting in August heat. Someday you'll love watching 1-0 games, but at seven years old, it would've been a death knell.

But that is not what happened. The Sox scored twenty-two runs that day. Twenty-two! Alejandro De Aza hit a home run. Pablo Sandoval hit a home run! (By now you know how rare an event that truly was.) They knocked Felix out of the game in the second inning. Jackie Bradley went 5-for-6 with two homers and three doubles. It was a joyous cartoon explosion that we saw, in person, and the spark was reignited. I saw it flare up, every time you leapt to your feet and laughed, incredulous, at what we were seeing. The Red Sox were... something to you. Anxious to fan the flame, a second stop at the gift shop for a celebratory Jackie Bradley jersey was hastily arranged, despite the slightly disapproving look from Grandpa Kip that said, Really? More? Yes, Grandpa Kip, more, leave me alone. I'm trying something, here.

There was, that day, a glimmer of hope. But Boston is 3000 miles from your house. Dodger Stadium is five. And day after day, game after game, in the year that has since passed, you've followed the Dodgers, and watched them play—though not on TV very often because of that insane cable deal that makes the Dodgers inaccessible to 70 percent of their fanbase. (Someday you'll learn about TV rights deals in local markets and you will be *incensed*.) Day by day, game by game, I have watched the Dodgers take hold and the Red Sox recede.

I have made my peace with all of this, William. I have reasons to support it, even. The Dodgers are the team of Jackie Robinson, whose importance to the game and the country transcends the sport itself. (Some day you will learn about the Red Sox franchise's shameful history of racism. How there was a chance they could've had both Jackie and Willie Mays on the same team but signed neither because their owner was a retrogressive drunk, and you will feel like you definitely made the right choice.) There is also a shared institutional history of hating the Yankees—very important. A stadium that, despite only being 60ish years old, is the third oldest still standing. Vin Scully. Sandy Koufax. The

Brooklyn Dodger "B" on a hat looks almost exactly like the Red Sox "B," if you squint. A lot of solid stuff here for me to cling to.

And the Red Sox are, as you are fond of telling me, in the tone good children use to make their parents feel better, definitely your second-favorite team. Second-Favorite Team is a real thing when you're a kid. My second favorite team was the Astros because your great-grandparents settled in Houston the year I was born, and I went to the Astrodome and saw Nolan Ryan pitch. Your great-uncle Steve bought me a foam "K" to wave every time he struck someone out, and they were far enough away from Boston that I felt like I was not betraying my real favorite team by rooting for them. But second-favorite teams have a way of burning off in adulthood—they're booster rockets that fuel your youthful passion then fall away as life gets more complicated and the number of things you can reasonably pay attention to gets necessarily whittled down. I fear that today the Red Sox are your second-favorite team, and in ten years, they will be only your dad's favorite team. A big difference.

So. This might be my last chance to make you care—really care—about the Boston Red Sox.

This is a fun team to root for, buddy. And it's fun in a way that Red Sox teams haven't always been fun—even during their recent run of success. The 2004 team will own my heart forever for what they did. On the field, I mean. (Some day you will watch Curt Schilling get interviewed about any aspect of our society, and the realization that these guys exist outside of their uniforms will further taint the purity of their on-field accomplishments. I'm sorry for that. Sports will give you a lot of joy and a lot of moral angst. It's just sort of the deal.) The 2007 and 2013 teams each had great stories, especially the latter, which healed a city and turned David Ortiz from a hero into a deity. But the 2017 team, the first without Ortiz since long before your mom and I were married…this team is just fun.

You know most of these guys already because you keep up on every team, and like a good kid who can read desperation in his father's eyes, you keep a close watch on *this* team, specifically. But let's go over it again.

Mookie Betts is—like you, right now—undersized. He is also—like you—utterly joyous when he plays. I'm not sure anyone has more fun playing the game than he does. He's 5'9" and hits the ball harder than guys twice his size. You want to know how to play the game—every part of the game—correctly and with maximum fun? Watch Mookie Betts.

Xander Bogaerts has gotten better as a hitter every year. Scouts thought he couldn't field the shortstop position, that he'd have to move to third, but he has become an adequate fielder. He's from Aruba. He speaks Dutch. His last name has a diphthong! (You don't understand why that's cool and interesting, but it's cool and interesting.)

Dustin Pedroia, when he's not hurt, is the team's beating heart, or at least its femoral artery or something, and he's wonderful. Sadly, he's almost always hurt because he plays like a maniac but that's exactly why he's the team's beating heart. And he's more undersized than Mookie. He was the first guy I pointed to as a reason you should love the team. Your first jersey was a Pedroia jersey, remember? (I got one for your sister, too. You guys both wore them one day and then Ivy asked me why I was crying and it was hard to explain, but you'll both understand someday.) Now that Ortiz is gone, this is Pedroia's team, and he won't let you down.

Jackie Bradley can throw a baseball from home plate over the centerfield fence at Fenway. Jackie Bradley is a freak of nature. Jackie Bradley is the best defensive centerfielder this team has ever had, and he can hit too. He might be my favorite player, though I say that about a different guy every week.

Andrew Benintendi was the best hitter in collegiate baseball, miraculously fell to the Sox in the draft and seemed major-league ready the day he graduated. Blake Swihart was hurt all last year and he doesn't even really have a position on this team, but he can hit, catch and run. If he becomes the everyday catcher, this lineup officially gets ridiculous.

These guys are young and great and fun, and the team drafted every one of them. They also now have some important players who were not drafted by the team because Dave Dombrowski did what Dave Dombrowski does, and traded about thirty of their minor leaguers to get Chris Sale, Craig Kimbrel, and Drew Pomeranz—in the process, compiling a starting five who were more valuable, in aggregate, than the Cubs starting five last year. The pain of trading away those prospects is very real and may get more real in a few years, but you have to admit it's a really good staff. And on Opening Day, if all goes well, they may start homegrown players at catcher, first (I'm counting Hanley as homegrown), second, short, right, center and left. That's awesome.

Someday you will learn about salary cap flexibility and free agency and arbitration rules and Scott Boras, and you will understand how rare and glorious it is to have a team's core be drafted, homegrown and arriving all at once—like a band with a debut album loaded with nine perfect singles. It's always fun when your team is good, but when they are good and young, it's something else entirely. It's five years, or more, of a very specific promise: that your team will bring you happiness, deep into the summer.

I am the parent of a Dodger fan. I accept that. I will brave as many Los Angeles September Sunday day games as you care to attend, and I will not forget the sunscreen because dear lord those day games are miserable. I will sit with you every night from April to October, in our living room, and we will watch highlights of Corey Seager and Clayton Kershaw until way past bedtime. But in exchange, I hope you follow and care about this Red Sox team because they are loose and fun and young and talented and multicultural in a way that previous iterations have not been, and I want you to enjoy them along with me.

Deal?

Love always,
Dad

P.S. Their bullpen is a little shaky. I glossed over that. Whatever. Relievers are very hard to predict year-to-year because of something called "regression toward the mean." I'll teach you about that someday. It's super nerdy. ■

—Michael Schur is a television writer and producer in Los Angeles

HITTERS

Andrew Benintendi   LF

Born: 7/6/94   Age: 22   Bats: L   Throws: L   Height: 5'10"   Weight: 170   Entered Pro Ball: Round 1, 2015 Draft (#7 overall)

YEAR	TEAM	LVL	AGE	PA	R	2B	3B	HR	RBI	BB	K	SB	CS	AVG/OBP/SLG	TAv	VORP	BABIP	BRR	FRAA	WARP
2015	LOW	A-	20	153	19	2	4	7	15	25	15	7	1	.290/.408/.540	.317	15.0	.279	1.6	CF(31): 8.6	2.5
2015	GRN	A	20	86	17	5	0	4	16	10	9	3	2	.351/.430/.581	.374	13.5	.355	1.0	CF(18): -2.5	1.2
2016	SLM	A+	21	155	30	13	7	1	32	15	9	8	2	.341/.413/.563	.343	18.0	.354	-0.2	CF(30): 4.5	2.3
2016	PME	AA	21	263	40	18	5	8	44	24	30	8	7	.295/.357/.515	.304	19.4	.308	0.7	CF(53): 0.3 • LF(4): 1.0	2.2
2016	BOS	MLB	21	118	16	11	1	2	14	10	25	1	0	.295/.359/.476	.284	5.0	.367	-0.6	LF(29): 0.8 • CF(5): -0.2	0.6
2017	*BOS*	*MLB*	*22*	*583*	*79*	*33*	*6*	*18*	*66*	*49*	*103*	*12*	*7*	*.273/.338/.464*	*.272*	*25.1*	*.306*	*-0.1*	*LF 17, CF 1*	*4.3*
2018	*BOS*	*MLB*	*23*	*556*	*73*	*33*	*6*	*19*	*75*	*48*	*99*	*12*	*6*	*.278/.345/.480*	*.270*	*19.5*	*.311*	*0.5*	*LF 16, CF 1*	*4.0*

Breakout: 6%   Improve: 43%   Collapse: 2%   Attrition: 13%   MLB: 71%   Comparables: *Mookie Betts, Joc Pederson, Colby Rasmus*

You gotta love when the rich get richer. Benintendi made the journey from seventh overall pick to MLB starter in a little over 13 months, dominating at every level. Despite a slender frame, Benintendi produces solid power thanks to a sweet, compact lefty swing. He's capable in center, a genuine defensive asset in left and a threat to swipe double-digit bases. But the real stars of the show are Benintendi's hit tool and approach at the plate. Benny With The Good Hair was a career .312/.392/.540 hitter in the minors, and followed suit by flirting with .300 in Boston. His potent, all-around game makes him a front-runner for 2017 AL Rookie of the Year, and his ascension gives the Red Sox the most talented group of homegrown hitters this side of the North Side. He really should regrow those luscious locks, though.

Mookie Betts   RF

Born: 10/7/92   Age: 24   Bats: R   Throws: R   Height: 5'9"   Weight: 180   Entered Pro Ball: Round 5, 2011 Draft (#172 overall)

YEAR	TEAM	LVL	AGE	PA	R	2B	3B	HR	RBI	BB	K	SB	CS	AVG/OBP/SLG	TAv	VORP	BABIP	BRR	FRAA	WARP
2014	PME	AA	21	253	56	18	3	6	34	35	20	22	3	.355/.443/.551	.346	35.2	.366	6.2	2B(40): 1.7 • CF(12): -0.7	3.9
2014	PAW	AAA	21	211	31	12	2	5	31	26	30	11	4	.335/.417/.503	.314	21.7	.380	2.4	CF(33): -0.5 • 2B(6): -0.5	2.0
2014	BOS	MLB	21	213	34	12	1	5	18	21	31	7	3	.291/.368/.444	.300	16.7	.327	3.2	CF(28): 0.2 • 2B(14): -0.8	1.8
2015	BOS	MLB	22	654	92	42	8	18	77	46	82	21	6	.291/.341/.479	.291	40.4	.310	2.3	CF(133): 12.0 • RF(11): -0.9	5.5
2016	BOS	MLB	23	730	122	42	5	31	113	49	80	26	4	.318/.363/.534	.296	48.3	.322	8.7	RF(157): 18.8	6.9
2017	*BOS*	*MLB*	*24*	*603*	*80*	*36*	*5*	*20*	*80*	*50*	*74*	*23*	*5*	*.308/.366/.503*	*.296*	*42.2*	*.323*	*2.4*	*RF 9, CF 0*	*4.9*
2018	*BOS*	*MLB*	*25*	*599*	*83*	*35*	*5*	*22*	*85*	*51*	*75*	*22*	*5*	*.311/.371/.514*	*.290*	*36.5*	*.326*	*5.4*	*RF 9, CF 0*	*5.0*

Breakout: 0%   Improve: 58%   Collapse: 5%   Attrition: 5%   MLB: 100%   Comparables: *Al Kaline, Nick Markakis, Pablo Sandoval*

Ask someone what makes Betts special on a Monday and you may hear about his hit tool after he goes 3-for-4 with a walk. On Wednesday, they'll marvel at his power and how he generates it with lightning-quick wrists. On Friday, you'll hear about Betts' glove, which truly shines in Fenway's spacious right field. On Sunday, it will all be about his speed and efficiency on the bases. Ask Frank Thomas about Betts' best tools, and he'll smile, look you straight in the eyes and say "hardware." It's tough to blame him; Betts' abilities defy explanation. He would've won the AL MVP if players named for fish were outlawed. He only just turned 24. We're just getting started.

Xander Bogaerts   SS

Born: 10/1/92   Age: 24   Bats: R   Throws: R   Height: 6'1"   Weight: 210   Entered Pro Ball: International Free Agent, 2009

YEAR	TEAM	LVL	AGE	PA	R	2B	3B	HR	RBI	BB	K	SB	CS	AVG/OBP/SLG	TAv	VORP	BABIP	BRR	FRAA	WARP
2014	BOS	MLB	21	594	60	28	1	12	46	39	138	2	3	.240/.297/.362	.247	16.7	.296	3.0	SS(99): -8.2 • 3B(44): -1.9	0.7
2015	BOS	MLB	22	654	84	35	3	7	81	32	101	10	2	.320/.355/.421	.266	34.3	.372	4.8	SS(156): -1.4	3.5
2016	BOS	MLB	23	719	115	34	1	21	89	58	123	13	4	.294/.356/.446	.267	38.4	.335	3.3	SS(157): -11.5	2.8
2017	*BOS*	*MLB*	*24*	*617*	*68*	*30*	*2*	*15*	*71*	*46*	*113*	*9*	*3*	*.287/.344/.428*	*.267*	*33.8*	*.334*	*-0.3*	*SS -7*	*1.8*
2018	*BOS*	*MLB*	*25*	*607*	*79*	*31*	*2*	*18*	*76*	*46*	*114*	*9*	*3*	*.294/.352/.454*	*.268*	*29.0*	*.340*	*3.0*	*SS -7*	*2.4*

Breakout: 3%   Improve: 60%   Collapse: 0%   Attrition: 4%   MLB: 100%   Comparables: *Troy Tulowitzki, Jose Reyes, Starlin Castro*

You're pretty greedy if you see Bogaerts' 2016 performance and demand more, yet it was impossible to watch Bogey in the second half and ignore the untapped potential. Overall, Bogaerts was excellent last season. He finished second in hits and eighth in OBP among qualified shortstops, and continued to look adequate (and very handsome) in the field. He was an All-Star, won a Silver Slugger and reached career highs in almost every counting stat, all during his age-23 season. Still, Bogaerts' .253/.317/.412 line in the second half was a let-down and helped put the Bogaerts vs. Mookie Betts debate to bed...for now. Bogaerts is still so young and talented that it's easy to envision him learning to turn those months-long slumps into just week-long slumps, emerging as a bonafide MVP candidate in the not-so-distant future. It's not his fault that anything less will feel like a disappointment, but such is life when you starve a city hungry for shortstop talent for nearly a decade.

Jackie Bradley   CF

Born: 4/19/90   Age: 27   Bats: L   Throws: R   Height: 5'10"   Weight: 200   Entered Pro Ball: Round 1, 2011 Draft (#40 overall)

YEAR	TEAM	LVL	AGE	PA	R	2B	3B	HR	RBI	BB	K	SB	CS	AVG/OBP/SLG	TAv	VORP	BABIP	BRR	FRAA	WARP
2014	PAW	AAA	24	69	6	1	0	1	5	3	18	0	1	.212/.246/.273	.185	-3.3	.277	0.3	CF(14): 1.6	-0.2
2014	BOS	MLB	24	423	45	19	2	1	30	31	121	8	0	.198/.265/.266	.198	-12.5	.284	0.4	CF(113): 21.0 • RF(12): -0.8	0.8
2015	PAW	AAA	25	318	38	18	1	9	29	30	44	4	4	.305/.382/.472	.320	29.1	.336	-0.2	CF(67): -3.3 • RF(2): 0.1	2.6
2015	BOS	MLB	25	255	43	17	4	10	43	27	69	3	0	.249/.335/.498	.280	12.8	.310	2.0	RF(32): 3.6 • CF(27): -1.7	2.1
2016	BOS	MLB	26	636	94	30	7	26	87	63	143	9	2	.267/.349/.486	.273	31.1	.312	3.0	CF(156): 4.9	3.7
2017	*BOS*	*MLB*	*27*	*557*	*65*	*29*	*4*	*17*	*64*	*51*	*132*	*7*	*2*	*.251/.329/.427*	*.260*	*20.0*	*.307*	*0.0*	*CF 3*	*1.8*
2018	*BOS*	*MLB*	*28*	*498*	*63*	*25*	*3*	*15*	*60*	*49*	*118*	*6*	*2*	*.247/.331/.420*	*.253*	*10.7*	*.302*	*1.0*	*CF 3*	*1.5*

Breakout: 5%   Improve: 49%   Collapse: 8%   Attrition: 11%   MLB: 94%   *Comparables: Michael Saunders, Franklin Gutierrez, Desmond Jennings*

Bradley hit .381 in May and .218 in June, and that's a feature, not a bug. He's got more streaks than a zebra, more momentum shifts than a pendulum. He's hotter and colder than a Katy Perry song. When Bradley is on, like during his 29-game hitting streak, he is one of the best players in the majors, combining a patient approach and plus power at the plate with all-world defense in center. When Bradley is off, he barely belongs in a lineup, marrying strikeouts and weak contact with, well, all-world defense in center, but let's nitpick and mention some airmailed throws. Watching Bradley is a joy, and watching Bradley is incredibly frustrating. Watching Bradley is witnessing a down-ballot MVP candidate one moment and a ninth-place hitter the next. Watching Bradley is...oh god, watching Bradley is like watching Clay Buchholz.

Rusney Castillo   CF

Born: 7/9/87   Age: 29   Bats: R   Throws: R   Height: 5'9"   Weight: 195   Entered Pro Ball: International Free Agent, 2014

YEAR	TEAM	LVL	AGE	PA	R	2B	3B	HR	RBI	BB	K	SB	CS	AVG/OBP/SLG	TAv	VORP	BABIP	BRR	FRAA	WARP
2014	BOS	MLB	26	40	6	1	0	2	6	3	6	3	0	.333/.400/.528	.319	4.0	.357	0.7	CF(10): 1.3	0.6
2015	PAW	AAA	27	172	17	7	0	3	17	14	28	10	2	.282/.337/.385	.291	9.2	.323	0.0	CF(17): 1.6 • RF(16): -1.6	0.9
2015	BOS	MLB	27	289	35	10	2	5	29	13	54	4	5	.253/.288/.359	.213	-6.4	.298	1.3	RF(48): 4.3 • LF(24): 4.6	0.3
2016	BOS	MLB	28	8	4	1	0	0	0	0	3	0	0	.250/.250/.375	.214	0.2	.400	0.4	LF(2): -0.6 • RF(1): -0.0	0.0
2016	PAW	AAA	28	429	55	20	5	2	34	24	68	9	3	.263/.309/.354	.252	13.1	.310	4.6	CF(86): 9.1 • LF(8): -1.9	2.0
2017	*BOS*	*MLB*	*29*	*250*	*31*	*12*	*2*	*5*	*24*	*16*	*49*	*5*	*2*	*.266/.316/.401*	*.240*	*5.0*	*.313*	*1.1*	*CF 3, LF -0*	*0.9*
2018	*BOS*	*MLB*	*30*	*253*	*28*	*11*	*1*	*5*	*26*	*16*	*51*	*5*	*2*	*.257/.309/.386*	*.236*	*1.8*	*.306*	*1.3*	*CF 3, LF 0*	*0.6*

Breakout: 2%   Improve: 28%   Collapse: 16%   Attrition: 22%   MLB: 65%   *Comparables: Julio Borbon, Craig Gentry, Ezequiel Carrera*

On March 10th, Hillsborough, Florida County police seized more than 800 pounds of marijuana and arrested 22 Cuban nationals in, what we kid you not, was called "Operation Hydro Hustlers." Thanks to Rusney Castillo, that was only the second-biggest Cuban bust of the year. T'was a season of no highs and extreme lows for Castillo, who saw just nine games in the majors and whose chronic issues at the plate continued even when facing Triple-A pitching. He is now 29, buried behind a talented outfield and still owed $46 million over the next four seasons. To be blunt, his career in Boston is probably over, but it's not clear any other team will take the hit financially to acquire him.

Michael Chavis   3B

Born: 8/11/95   Age: 21   Bats: R   Throws: R   Height: 5'10"   Weight: 190   Entered Pro Ball: Round 1, 2014 Draft (#26 overall)

YEAR	TEAM	LVL	AGE	PA	R	2B	3B	HR	RBI	BB	K	SB	CS	AVG/OBP/SLG	TAv	VORP	BABIP	BRR	FRAA	WARP
2015	GRN	A	19	471	56	29	1	16	58	29	144	8	5	.223/.277/.405	.244	2.2	.293	-1.2	3B(68): 3.6 • SS(1): -0.1	0.6
2016	GRN	A	20	312	30	11	3	8	35	22	74	3	1	.244/.321/.391	.267	11.7	.303	1.3	3B(68): -0.3	1.2
2016	SLM	A+	20	27	5	0	0	0	1	2	7	1	0	.160/.222/.160	.180	-0.8	.222	1.1	3B(2): -0.7	-0.1
2017	*BOS*	*MLB*	*21*	*250*	*24*	*10*	*1*	*8*	*29*	*13*	*86*	*1*	*0*	*.205/.255/.357*	*.205*	*-6.7*	*.282*	*-0.3*	*3B 2*	*-0.5*
2018	*BOS*	*MLB*	*22*	*364*	*41*	*16*	*1*	*13*	*43*	*21*	*122*	*1*	*1*	*.210/.265/.374*	*.218*	*-8.2*	*.286*	*-0.6*	*3B 3*	*-0.6*

Breakout: 0%   Improve: 0%   Collapse: 0%   Attrition: 3%   MLB: 3%   *Comparables: Josh Bell, Alex Liddi, Renato Nunez*

Everything was going well for Chavis in April. The former first-rounder was hitting .356/.415/.576 in 65 PA in Greenville, an environment in which a 20-year-old with Chavis' pedigree should dominate. Unfortunately, Chavis tore a ligament in his thumb late in the season's first month, and after he returned he was never the same. From June 7 through August 22, Chavis hit just .214/.296/.341. When the Sox gave him an "eh, what the hell" promotion to Salem, he struggled in his seven games there, too. If you squint, you can still see the power, athleticism and bat speed that made Chavis a first rounder, and he did improve his approach at the plate. Those desperate caveats aside, Chavis is one more bad season away from joining Jason Place, Kolbrin Vitek and Trey Ball as a Red Sox trivia answer to a question no one wants to ask.

Rafael Devers   3B

Born: 10/24/96   Age: 20   Bats: L   Throws: R   Height: 6'0"   Weight: 195   Entered Pro Ball: International Free Agent, 2013

YEAR	TEAM	LVL	AGE	PA	R	2B	3B	HR	RBI	BB	K	SB	CS	AVG/OBP/SLG	TAv	VORP	BABIP	BRR	FRAA	WARP
2015	GRN	A	18	508	71	38	1	11	70	24	84	3	1	.288/.329/.443	.282	25.1	.326	1.6	3B(72): -9.0	1.7
2016	SLM	A+	19	546	64	32	8	11	71	40	94	18	6	.282/.335/.443	.276	25.1	.328	-1.2	3B(117): 21.0	4.7
2017	*BOS*	*MLB*	*20*	*250*	*26*	*13*	*1*	*7*	*30*	*11*	*61*	*3*	*1*	*.245/.283/.405*	*.227*	*-0.9*	*.298*	*-0.1*	*3B 4*	*0.3*
2018	*BOS*	*MLB*	*21*	*435*	*51*	*25*	*2*	*15*	*54*	*20*	*101*	*5*	*2*	*.254/.293/.429*	*.240*	*0.7*	*.302*	*-0.2*	*3B 7*	*0.8*

Breakout: 2%   Improve: 9%   Collapse: 0%   Attrition: 5%   MLB: 12%   *Comparables: Josh Vitters, Matt Dominguez, Maikel Franco*

Despite being younger for his levels than a Chinese gymnast at the 2008 Olympic Games (topical, no?), Devers continues to mash. Thanks to his sweet, lefty swing and continually developing power, Devers can get by on natural ability in the mid-minors. As he advances he'll need to refine his approach, but Devers' bat should play even at first base. That's good, because while Devers has a strong arm and decent hands, his thick lower half and lack of elite athleticism could eventually give him as much range as Sanjaya Malakar (even more topical, no?). That said, he did post the best FRAA of any third baseman in the minors this year. Devers could camp out in Portland for two seasons and still be young for his level. He's as good a bet as any to enter 2018 as Boston's [DD note: or some other team's] top prospect.

Ryan Hanigan   C

Born: 8/16/80   Age: 36   Bats: R   Throws: R   Height: 6'0"   Weight: 220   Entered Pro Ball: Undrafted Free Agent, 2002

YEAR	TEAM	LVL	AGE	PA	R	2B	3B	HR	RBI	BB	K	SB	CS	AVG/OBP/SLG	TAv	VORP	BABIP	BRR	FRAA	WARP
2014	PCH	A+	33	24	4	0	0	1	2	2	3	0	0	.250/.375/.400	.294	1.4	.250	-0.1	C(3): 0.0	0.1
2014	TBA	MLB	33	263	18	9	0	5	34	31	39	1	0	.218/.318/.324	.251	7.1	.240	-1.6	C(79): 5.7	1.4
2015	BOS	MLB	34	201	28	8	0	2	16	20	39	0	0	.247/.337/.328	.242	3.1	.306	-1.9	C(53): 0.5	0.4
2016	PAW	AAA	35	31	2	1	0	0	3	3	7	0	0	.200/.323/.240	.244	0.0	.263	-0.5	C(6): 0.1	0.0
2016	BOS	MLB	35	113	9	4	0	1	14	7	27	0	0	.171/.230/.238	.161	-7.0	.221	-0.6	C(34): -4.6	-1.2
2017	BOS	MLB	36	250	25	11	0	3	22	27	38	0	0	.243/.336/.337	.232	4.3	.278	-1.2	C -4	0.0
2018	BOS	MLB	37	94	10	4	0	1	8	10	15	0	0	.235/.327/.320	.228	-0.2	.272	-0.5	C -2	-0.2

Breakout: 0%   Improve: 23%   Collapse: 13%   Attrition: 29%   MLB: 73%   Comparables: Jason Kendall, Del Crandall, Bob Boone

How differently would we look back on Hanigan's career if he could just stay healthy? The perennial backup missed a ton of time once again in 2016, dealing with neck and ankle injuries en route to playing in his fewest games since 2008. He's averaged just 71 games per season over his career, and while that's partially a function of his role, it's also due to a medical record that makes *Infinite Jest* seem succinct. Our catching metrics suggest that Hanigan was a below-average defender for the first time in his career, which could be a sample size issue were it not for the litany of 36-year-old backstops who follow a rational aging curve. Odds are Hanigan will latch on again as a backup somewhere, but whatever team takes the plunge will need a backup for him, too.

YEAR	TEAM	P. COUNT	FRM RUNS	BLK RUNS	THRW RUNS	TOT RUNS
2014	TBA	10071	6.1	1.4	-0.5	7.1
2015	BOS	7692	1.0	-0.9	0.2	0.4
2015	PAW	183	0.0	0.0	0.0	0.0
2015	PME	323	0.0	0.0	0.0	-0.1
2016	BOS	4507	-4.5	-2.1	-0.3	-6.9
2017	BOS	9402	-2.4	-1.6	-0.2	-4.2
2018	BOS	3536	-1.3	-0.6	-0.1	-2.1

Marco Hernandez   SS

Born: 9/6/92   Age: 24   Bats: L   Throws: R   Height: 6'0"   Weight: 200   Entered Pro Ball: International Free Agent, 2009

YEAR	TEAM	LVL	AGE	PA	R	2B	3B	HR	RBI	BB	K	SB	CS	AVG/OBP/SLG	TAv	VORP	BABIP	BRR	FRAA	WARP
2014	DAY	A+	21	486	61	13	7	3	55	30	90	22	8	.270/.315/.351	.246	13.3	.328	0.0	SS(122): 4.3	1.8
2015	PME	AA	22	294	30	21	4	5	31	9	49	4	2	.326/.349/.482	.289	18.1	.382	-1.9	SS(67): -3.0	1.6
2015	PAW	AAA	22	190	27	9	2	4	22	8	39	1	0	.271/.300/.409	.266	6.1	.324	-1.2	SS(22): -4.2 • 2B(15): -0.5	0.1
2016	PAW	AAA	23	237	26	7	4	5	29	12	51	4	2	.309/.343/.444	.291	14.8	.381	-0.5	SS(22): -2.4 • 2B(20): 0.7	1.1
2016	BOS	MLB	23	56	11	1	0	1	5	5	10	1	0	.294/.357/.373	.246	0.7	.350	-0.2	2B(14): -0.6 • 3B(10): -0.1	0.0
2017	BOS	MLB	24	70	8	3	1	2	7	3	17	1	0	.269/.301/.408	.241	0.9	.332	0.0	3B -1, 2B 0	0.0
2018	BOS	MLB	25	261	29	12	3	6	29	14	63	3	1	.265/.307/.414	.240	1.5	.330	0.1	3B -2, 2B 0	0.0

Breakout: 2%   Improve: 22%   Collapse: 5%   Attrition: 22%   MLB: 46%   Comparables: Cory Spangenberg, Ryan Brett, Jimmy Paredes

I mean, sure, Theo Epstein won another ring in Chicago, but before you heap too much praise on him remember that he basically gave Hernandez to the Red Sox for free. For the third-straight season, Hernandez hit well wherever he played. That included a cup of coffee in the majors, in which Hernandez held his own at the plate as a 23-year-old rookie. There's nothing special about Hernandez's game, but he can hit for average, run a bit and serve as a reasonable defender in the middle infield. He's got Brock Holt in front of him, but Hernandez is good enough to be on an MLB bench right now. Take that, Theo.

Aaron Hill   2B

Born: 3/21/82   Age: 35   Bats: R   Throws: R   Height: 5'11"   Weight: 200   Entered Pro Ball: Round 1, 2003 Draft (#13 overall)

YEAR	TEAM	LVL	AGE	PA	R	2B	3B	HR	RBI	BB	K	SB	CS	AVG/OBP/SLG	TAv	VORP	BABIP	BRR	FRAA	WARP
2014	ARI	MLB	32	541	52	26	3	10	60	28	92	4	3	.244/.287/.367	.234	-2.3	.276	-2.6	2B(116): 4.2, 3B(7): -0.1	0.2
2015	ARI	MLB	33	353	32	18	0	6	39	31	54	7	2	.230/.295/.345	.241	5.2	.253	2.1	2B(47): 2.4 • 3B(38): -1.1	0.7
2016	MIL	MLB	34	292	34	11	0	8	29	30	43	4	1	.283/.359/.421	.287	15.6	.309	-1.3	3B(59): 1.8 • 2B(20): 0.5	1.9
2016	BOS	MLB	34	137	14	3	0	2	9	11	16	0	0	.218/.287/.290	.226	-3.0	.236	-2.5	3B(44): -0.9 • 2B(4): 0.1	-0.4
2017	BOS	MLB	35	386	42	20	1	10	45	31	58	4	2	.266/.328/.415	.247	6.3	.291	-1.2	3B -2, 2B 1	0.6
2018	BOS	MLB	36	296	34	14	1	7	32	23	47	3	1	.255/.315/.392	.239	-0.4	.282	-0.9	3B -2, 2B 1	-0.1

Breakout: 1%   Improve: 27%   Collapse: 5%   Attrition: 17%   MLB: 75%   Comparables: Buddy Bell, George Kell, Scott Rolen

On paper, Hill was pretty much the perfect under-the-radar acquisition for the Red Sox last July. He was hitting lefties well (and hitting well in general), the Sox needed a platoon partner for Travis Shaw and Hill was available for the low, low price of Wendell Rijo and Aaron Wilkerson. Unfortunately, much like the Sand Snakes or The Hobbit or any adaptation starring Jim Carrey, paper is where this idea should've stayed. Hill was abysmal in Boston, posting a TAv that'd make Pablo Sandoval blush and playing third base with all the quickness of an Ent. He had a few big base knocks, including a key late RBI in his Boston debut, but those were his only hits to speak of. Given his first-half productivity and nominal ability as an infielder, odds are Hill will catch on as a platoon or bench bat somewhere, but man did he look over his last name from July onward.

Brock Holt 3B

Born: 6/11/88   Age: 29   Bats: L   Throws: R   Height: 5'10"   Weight: 180   Entered Pro Ball: Round 9, 2009 Draft (#265 overall)

YEAR	TEAM	LVL	AGE	PA	R	2B	3B	HR	RBI	BB	K	SB	CS	AVG/OBP/SLG	TAv	VORP	BABIP	BRR	FRAA	WARP
2014	PAW	AAA	26	121	21	8	2	1	7	8	12	7	1	.315/.380/.454	.302	11.0	.344	0.5	SS(19): -0.2 • 3B(4): -0.1	1.2
2014	BOS	MLB	26	492	68	23	5	4	29	33	98	12	2	.281/.331/.381	.261	16.2	.349	3.8	3B(39): -1.5 • RF(35): -0.4	1.5
2015	BOS	MLB	27	509	56	27	6	2	45	46	97	8	1	.280/.349/.379	.256	14.5	.350	3.8	2B(58): 0.8 • 3B(33): -1.4	1.6
2016	PAW	AAA	28	30	2	2	0	0	2	5	5	0	0	.320/.433/.400	.302	2.3	.400	0.2	LF(6): 1.5 • SS(2): 0.1	0.4
2016	BOS	MLB	28	324	45	16	0	7	34	27	58	4	3	.255/.322/.383	.246	5.1	.294	1.7	LF(64): 2.6 • 3B(17): 1.9	0.9
2017	*BOS*	*MLB*	*29*	*296*	*33*	*14*	*2*	*3*	*24*	*24*	*52*	*5*	*2*	*.276/.335/.383*	*.249*	*7.2*	*.326*	*0.2*	*3B -0, LF 2*	*0.7*
2018	*BOS*	*MLB*	*30*	*340*	*38*	*16*	*3*	*4*	*32*	*29*	*62*	*5*	*2*	*.268/.334/.380*	*.241*	*3.4*	*.316*	*1.8*	*3B 0, LF 2*	*0.7*

Breakout: 2%   Improve: 33%   Collapse: 18%   Attrition: 26%   MLB: 90%   *Comparables: Jeremy Reed, Tony Gwynn, Nyjer Morgan*

Is Holt a *Westworld* host? There's substantial evidence to suggest so. Like all creations of Ford and Arnold, Holt looks natural in a variety of settings and storylines. He's been the scrappy utility player, the sparkplug, the relative unknown and the All-Star. Look, there he is flashing decent leather at third base! And now he's playing an adequate left field! But just like hosts can melt down when pushed too far outside of their loops, Holt short-circuits when pressed into everyday duty. He only played in 94 games last season, but that was due more to a concussion than any effort to limit his playing time. For the third season in a row, Holt's second-half performance was noticeably worse than his first. Holt is still a luxury for a Red Sox team that plans to start Pablo Sandoval at third and Andrew Benintendi in left field, and he's great Dustin Pedroia insurance to boot. But much like Teddy or Delores, Holt is at his best when his role is well-defined and not when memories of past triumphs and trials cause him to take on more than he's designed to handle.

Sandy Leon C

Born: 3/13/89   Age: 28   Bats: B   Throws: R   Height: 5'10"   Weight: 225   Entered Pro Ball: International Free Agent, 2007

YEAR	TEAM	LVL	AGE	PA	R	2B	3B	HR	RBI	BB	K	SB	CS	AVG/OBP/SLG	TAv	VORP	BABIP	BRR	FRAA	WARP
2014	SYR	AAA	25	193	26	9	0	5	25	23	36	1	0	.229/.321/.371	.237	2.5	.264	-0.7	C(42): 12.3	
2014	WAS	MLB	25	70	7	1	0	1	3	6	20	0	0	.156/.229/.219	.184	-2.1	.209	0.0	C(20): -0.4	
2015	PAW	AAA	26	111	8	4	0	1	13	10	23	0	1	.263/.342/.333	.258	4.6	.333	0.6	C(21): 2.2	
2015	BOS	MLB	26	128	8	2	0	0	3	7	28	0	1	.184/.238/.202	.170	-6.3	.244	-0.5	C(37): -3.4 • 3B(1): -0.0	
2016	PAW	AAA	27	130	12	3	1	2	13	11	24	0	0	.243/.315/.339	.234	1.4	.286	-0.1	C(29): 6.6 • 1B(1): -0.0	
2016	BOS	MLB	27	283	36	17	2	7	35	23	66	0	0	.310/.369/.476	.293	20.7	.392	-1.5	C(74): -3.8	
2017	*BOS*	*MLB*	*28*	*388*	*37*	*18*	*1*	*7*	*37*	*36*	*85*	*0*	*0*	*.240/.313/.356*	*.236*	*-0.9*	*.293*	*-0.9*	*C -1*	*0.5*
2018	*BOS*	*MLB*	*29*	*417*	*46*	*18*	*1*	*8*	*41*	*37*	*93*	*0*	*0*	*.234/.309/.353*	*.229*	*1.0*	*.286*	*-1.0*	*C -1*	*0.0*

Breakout: 6%   Improve: 29%   Collapse: 16%   Attrition: 36%   MLB: 75%   *Comparables: Rob Johnson, Jason Jaramillo, JD Closser*

Where were you when Sandy Leon turned into Johnny Bench for six weeks? From June 7 through August 16, a 42-game span in which Leon logged 145 plate appearances, he hit .380/.434/.620. No one expected the man who entered the season with a .187 average to stay hotter than a PFT Commenter take, but his regression was as sad and sudden as it was predictable. From August 17 onward, a 36-game stretch in which Leon logged 138 plate appearances, even occupying the DH spot once, he hit just .236/.301/.325. For a Red Sox team getting nothing behind the plate thanks to Blake Swihart (broken ankle), Christian Vazquez (lack of bat) and Ryan Hanigan (looks too much like Droopy Dog), Leon was a smiley, bearded, run-defending (+1.1 throwing runs) godsend. Alas, the flame that burns twice as bright burns half as long. But even if he never hits again, it's better to have Leoned and lost than to never have Leoned at all.

YEAR	TEAM	P. COUNT	FRM RUNS	BLK RUNS	THRW RUNS	TOT RUNS
2014	SYR	5751	11.4	0.1	1.2	12.7
2014	WAS	2453	-0.4	0.2	0.1	0.0
2015	BOS	4770	-5.1	-0.2	0.4	-5.0
2015	PAW	2961	2.3	0.0	0.1	2.4
2016	BOS	9517	-4.7	-0.6	1.1	-4.2
2017	*BOS*	*14076*	*-2.0*	*-0.7*	*1.2*	*-1.6*
2018	*BOS*	*15137*	*-3.1*	*-0.9*	*1.2*	*-2.8*

Deven Marrero SS

Born: 8/25/90   Age: 26   Bats: R   Throws: R   Height: 6'1"   Weight: 195   Entered Pro Ball: Round 1, 2012 Draft (#24 overall)

YEAR	TEAM	LVL	AGE	PA	R	2B	3B	HR	RBI	BB	K	SB	CS	AVG/OBP/SLG	TAv	VORP	BABIP	BRR	FRAA	WARP
2014	PME	AA	23	307	42	19	2	5	39	34	57	12	7	.291/.371/.433	.290	20.2	.349	-1.3	SS(66): -2.5	
2014	PAW	AAA	23	202	23	11	0	1	20	12	37	4	1	.210/.260/.285	.189	-6.8	.255	0.7	SS(50): -0.8	
2015	PAW	AAA	24	419	49	13	1	6	29	33	87	12	5	.256/.316/.344	.257	17.9	.315	2.7	SS(90): 6.1 • 2B(8): -1.1	
2015	BOS	MLB	24	56	8	0	0	1	3	3	19	2	1	.226/.268/.283	.202	-0.7	.333	0.8	3B(13): 0.3 • SS(6): 0.3	
2016	PAW	AAA	25	388	30	11	1	1	27	22	90	10	3	.198/.245/.242	.184	-15.1	.259	-0.2	SS(92): 3.0 • 3B(2): 0.1	
2016	BOS	MLB	25	14	0	0	0	0	0	2	5	0	0	.083/.143/.083	.134	-1.4	.143	0.0	2B(6): -0.5 • SS(4): -0.1	
2017	*BOS*	*MLB*	*26*	*32*	*3*	*1*	*0*	*1*	*3*	*2*	*8*	*1*	*0*	*.234/.292/.343*	*.223*	*0.2*	*.299*	*0.0*	*SS 0*	*0.0*
2018	*BOS*	*MLB*	*27*	*220*	*23*	*9*	*1*	*4*	*21*	*16*	*56*	*5*	*2*	*.231/.291/.347*	*.220*	*-1.3*	*.295*	*0.1*	*SS 0*	*-0.1*

Breakout: 3%   Improve: 13%   Collapse: 7%   Attrition: 12%   MLB: 28%   *Comparables: Gregorio Petit, Sean Kazmar, Jeff Bianchi*

For as much praise as the Red Sox have received over the past decade-plus for their farm system and player development, they've missed pretty badly on a few first-round picks. Marrero is chief among them. We've known for years now that Marrero can pick it at short. The questions have always been about his bat. He answered them in the least-satisfactory way imaginable last season: his TAv in Triple-A was worse than Christian Vazquez's in the majors. As recently as 2014, it seemed like Marrero might possess the skills to be a second-division starter or solid utility player—or, as Red Sox Twitter would call it, "the main piece going back to the White Sox for Chris Sale." Instead, it seems more likely that the Red Sox spent a 24th overall pick on a slower Brendan Ryan.

Mitch Moreland 1B

Born: 9/6/85   Age: 31   Bats: L   Throws: L   Height: 6'2"   Weight: 230   Entered Pro Ball: Round 17, 2007 Draft (#530 overall)

YEAR	TEAM	LVL	AGE	PA	R	2B	3B	HR	RBI	BB	K	SB	CS	AVG/OBP/SLG	TAv	VORP	BABIP	BRR	FRAA	WARP
2014	TEX	MLB	28	184	18	9	1	2	23	12	43	0	0	.246/.297/.347	.237	-3.1	.315	-0.9	1B(22): -0.8 • LF(2): 0.0	-0.4
2015	TEX	MLB	29	515	51	27	0	23	85	32	112	1	0	.278/.330/.482	.284	15.4	.317	-2.1	1B(120): -7.8	0.8
2016	TEX	MLB	30	503	49	21	0	22	60	35	118	1	0	.233/.298/.422	.243	-6.2	.266	-3.0	1B(139): 3.5	-0.3
2017	BOS	MLB	31	491	57	25	1	19	62	37	110	1	0	.253/.314/.438	.255	3.7	.293	-1.1	1B -2	0.0
2018	BOS	MLB	32	501	65	25	0	20	67	40	116	0	0	.249/.315/.439	.250	-1.4	.289	-2.4	1B -2	-0.4

Breakout: 3%   Improve: 44%   Collapse: 13%   Attrition: 17%   MLB: 89%   Comparables: Ben Broussard, John Wockenfuss, Wes Helms

Think of Moreland as a sitcom. It shouldn't be a stretch, since he comes with his own bad intro music. Perhaps, even, think of him as Friends (which, we must admit, had good intro music*). There was promise early on thanks to a balanced approach, supported by the depth of the profile, but the middle years fluctuated more than Chandler's weight. Fans grew tired of wondering whether he'd finally put it together, and an underwhelming final season was done in by a formulaic approach that was easily taken advantage of, and resulted in far too many swings and misses. Now with the Red Sox, Moreland sits at the end of a bar where few will know his name and Texas, much like NBC, will be relying on a one-dimensional Joey spinoff that might crater under its own expectations.

   *Editor's note: The opinions of this author with respect to television show theme music do not reflect the views of Baseball Prospectus or its constituents.

David Ortiz DH

Born: 11/18/75   Age: 41   Bats: L   Throws: L   Height: 6'3"   Weight: 230   Entered Pro Ball: International Free Agent, 1992

YEAR	TEAM	LVL	AGE	PA	R	2B	3B	HR	RBI	BB	K	SB	CS	AVG/OBP/SLG	TAv	VORP	BABIP	BRR	FRAA	WARP
2014	BOS	MLB	38	602	59	27	0	35	104	75	95	0	0	.263/.355/.517	.307	24.4	.256	-7.7	1B(5): 0.0	2.7
2015	BOS	MLB	39	614	73	37	0	37	108	77	95	0	1	.273/.360/.553	.304	25.9	.264	-6.6	1B(9): -0.0	2.8
2016	BOS	MLB	40	626	79	48	1	38	127	80	86	2	0	.315/.401/.620	.317	37.6	.312	-5.1	1B(1): 0.0	3.9
2017	BOS	MLB	41	586	82	33	1	31	95	73	93	1	0	.280/.369/.531	.293	26.7	.286	-5.3	1B 0	2.9
2018	BOS	MLB	42	457	66	24	1	22	68	54	77	0	0	.261/.346/.488	.270	12.1	.270	-4.4	1B 0	1.3

Breakout: 0%   Improve: 17%   Collapse: 10%   Attrition: 17%   MLB: 64%   Comparables: Frank Thomas, Hank Aaron, Jason Giambi

We've told you for years to throw out anything you thought you knew about aging curves or the rules of baseball; they never applied to Ortiz. Since the last Annual publication, Ortiz conducted the best walk-off season in recent memory and posted his best WARP since 2013. He passed legends like Mickey Mantle, Willie McCovey and Ted Williams on the all-time home run list. He made his 10th All-Star Game, finished sixth in AL MVP voting, furthered his Hall of Fame case and wrote the first interesting article in the history of The Players' Tribune. Upon his final homestand of the regular season, Ortiz was showered with the types of gifts reserved not just for great athletes, but for great humanitarians. Boston named a bridge and a street after him. The Red Sox already agreed to retire his number. The President of the Dominican Republic flew in to watch him play. And everyone—even most Yankees fans—saluted a man who's left an indelible mark on not just Boston, but the entire sport. We hope you enjoyed the ride while it lasted because there will never be anyone quite like Ortiz again. And if Ortiz made one thing clear in 2016, it's that he sure as hell enjoyed the ride, too.

Dustin Pedroia 2B

Born: 8/17/83   Age: 33   Bats: R   Throws: R   Height: 5'9"   Weight: 175   Entered Pro Ball: Round 2, 2004 Draft (#65 overall)

YEAR	TEAM	LVL	AGE	PA	R	2B	3B	HR	RBI	BB	K	SB	CS	AVG/OBP/SLG	TAv	VORP	BABIP	BRR	FRAA	WARP
2014	BOS	MLB	30	609	72	33	0	7	53	51	75	6	6	.278/.337/.376	.268	22.6	.307	2.9	2B(135): 10.0	3.6
2015	BOS	MLB	31	425	46	19	1	12	42	38	51	2	2	.291/.356/.441	.271	14.9	.308	-0.4	2B(92): 2.5	1.9
2016	BOS	MLB	32	698	105	36	1	15	74	61	73	7	4	.318/.376/.449	.273	26.4	.339	-2.0	2B(152): -2.4	2.5
2017	BOS	MLB	33	679	82	35	2	13	65	60	78	7	4	.291/.354/.416	.268	30.2	.314	-1.5	2B 4	3.1
2018	BOS	MLB	34	546	66	27	1	11	59	47	69	4	3	.285/.347/.411	.258	15.6	.310	0.4	2B 3	2.0

Breakout: 1%   Improve: 20%   Collapse: 7%   Attrition: 10%   MLB: 94%   Comparables: Placido Polanco, Ian Kinsler, Skip Schumaker

Pedroia has probably never heard of the typical aging curve for second basemen, but if you told him about it, he'd most definitely recommend sticking it up your you-know-where. In his age-32 season, the personification of all things grit posted his best offensive season since 2013, produced the second-highest batting average of his illustrious career and hit the ball harder than in any season since he won Rookie of the Year. Pedroia is no longer a force on the basepaths and his defense has declined from legendary to just good. However, by learning to hit leadoff—a role he's admitted he hates—he's reinvented himself to fit in perfectly with the new Killer Bs-led Red Sox. He's got five years left on his contract, but maybe that's not such a bad thing because Pedroia proved last season that when healthy (yes, that's a big when) he's still one of the game's better middle infielders.

Hanley Ramirez 1B

Born: 12/23/83   Age: 33   Bats: R   Throws: R   Height: 6'2"   Weight: 235   Entered Pro Ball: International Free Agent, 2000

YEAR	TEAM	LVL	AGE	PA	R	2B	3B	HR	RBI	BB	K	SB	CS	AVG/OBP/SLG	TAv	VORP	BABIP	BRR	FRAA	WARP
2014	LAN	MLB	30	512	64	35	0	13	71	56	84	14	5	.283/.369/.448	.305	41.1	.323	0.9	SS(115): -16.2	2.8
2015	BOS	MLB	31	430	59	12	1	19	53	21	71	6	3	.249/.291/.426	.252	5.0	.257	0.0	LF(92): -15.7 • 3B(1): -0.0	-1.1
2016	BOS	MLB	32	620	81	28	1	30	111	60	120	9	3	.286/.361/.505	.280	16.2	.315	-2.8	1B(133): -10.5	0.6
2017	BOS	MLB	33	591	75	29	2	23	81	51	108	11	4	.276/.345/.470	.280	22.4	.305	0.0	1B -3	2.1
2018	BOS	MLB	34	500	68	24	1	20	68	43	95	8	3	.274/.343/.463	.269	15.6	.308	-0.3	1B -2	1.5

Breakout: 2%   Improve: 33%   Collapse: 4%   Attrition: 10%   MLB: 98%   Comparables: Kendrys Morales, Justin Morneau, Derrek Lee

That's more like it. One year after looking like the most mismanaged asset in New England since Curt Schilling's gaming startup, Ramirez became the player the Red Sox needed him to be. He finished seventh in slugging, seventh in homers and ninth in OBP among qualified first basemen. A hot start gave way to a cold June (.229/.324/.396) and plenty of "here we go again" talk-radio rants, but Ramirez caught fire once more in July and burned brighter than the sun in September, hitting .307/.391/.653 when it felt like the Red Sox needed it most. More surprisingly, Ramirez became a serviceable first baseman (FRAA disagrees), committing just four errors—that would've been a solid week for Ramirez in left field—and providing more evidence that Brian Bannister is a warlock. If Season 2 of Hanley Ramirez: First Baseman goes as well as the inaugural edition, his contract will look more like an asset than an albatross. Now if he could just get some of that rebound magic to rub off on Pablo Sandoval...

Pablo Sandoval   3B

Born: 8/11/86   Age: 30   Bats: B   Throws: R   Height: 5'11"   Weight: 255   Entered Pro Ball: International Free Agent, 2003

YEAR	TEAM	LVL	AGE	PA	R	2B	3B	HR	RBI	BB	K	SB	CS	AVG/OBP/SLG	TAv	VORP	BABIP	BRR	FRAA	WARP
2014	SFN	MLB	27	638	68	26	3	16	73	39	85	0	0	.279/.324/.415	.283	27.7	.300	-4.7	3B(151): -0.1	3.0
2015	BOS	MLB	28	505	43	25	1	10	47	25	73	0	0	.245/.292/.366	.229	-5.1	.270	-5.5	3B(123): -7.8	-1.4
2016	BOS	MLB	29	7	0	0	0	0	0	1	4	0	0	.000/.143/.000	.089	-1.0	.000	0.0	3B(2): 0.1	-0.1
2017	BOS	MLB	30	580	61	29	1	16	70	41	81	0	0	.274/.330/.426	.260	11.0	.295	-1.3	3B -2	0.9
2018	BOS	MLB	31	345	43	17	1	10	42	25	51	0	0	.270/.328/.427	.253	2.7	.291	-2.6	3B -1	0.1

Breakout: 2%   Improve: 44%   Collapse: 5%   Attrition: 10%   MLB: 96%   *Comparables: Martin Prado, Chip Hale, Lou Klimchock*

Female pandas are in heat just once a year, yet they're still more productive than Pablo Sandoval. As far as pandas go, Jia Jia had a better year. Folks, the last time this many people were annoyed with a Panda, Desiinger made millions. Ok, we'll stop bamboozling you with panda puns. Sandoval played in three games last season before undergoing shoulder surgery, yet Sox fans generally considered his absence an improvement over his 2015 campaign (and by WARP, they likely don't realize how right they were). Red Sox third basemen conspired to hit just .242/.306/.380, but there were no calls for Sandoval to come save the day and no hopes for a Hanley Ramirez-like rebound. A productive Sandoval would go a long way toward recovering some of the offense the Sox will lose with David Ortiz retiring. If he struggles again, well, someone get this man Carl Crawford's number.

Blake Swihart   C

Born: 4/3/92   Age: 25   Bats: B   Throws: R   Height: 6'1"   Weight: 200   Entered Pro Ball: Round 1, 2011 Draft (#26 overall)

YEAR	TEAM	LVL	AGE	PA	R	2B	3B	HR	RBI	BB	K	SB	CS	AVG/OBP/SLG	TAv	VORP	BABIP	BRR	FRAA	WARP
2014	PME	AA	22	380	47	23	3	12	55	29	65	7	1	.300/.353/.487	.303	34.4	.337	2.2	C(81): 22.2	6.0
2014	PAW	AAA	22	71	6	3	1	1	9	2	15	1	0	.261/.282/.377	.212	-0.6	.321	0.1	C(16): 0.8	0.0
2015	PAW	AAA	23	80	7	3	0	0	11	6	14	1	1	.311/.363/.351	.270	2.5	.383	-1.4	C(16): 1.8	0.4
2015	BOS	MLB	23	309	47	17	1	5	31	18	77	4	2	.274/.319/.392	.241	10.1	.359	2.4	C(83): -6.2	0.4
2016	PAW	AAA	24	122	13	4	0	1	8	17	17	2	1	.243/.344/.311	.247	2.1	.276	-0.2	C(15): 0.3 • LF(11): 1.4	0.4
2016	BOS	MLB	24	74	9	0	3	0	5	11	17	0	1	.258/.365/.355	.247	0.5	.348	-0.6	LF(13): 0.9 • C(6): -0.8	0.1
2017	BOS	MLB	25	90	10	4	1	2	9	7	20	1	0	.264/.323/.400	.250	3.6	.327	-0.1	C -1	0.2
2018	BOS	MLB	26	251	30	13	1	6	29	20	56	2	1	.268/.329/.422	.252	7.9	.327	0.8	C -3	0.5

Breakout: 6%   Improve: 42%   Collapse: 14%   Attrition: 29%   MLB: 82%   *Comparables: Andre Ethier, J.D. Martinez, Robbie Grossman*

The Red Sox have done a good job developing homegrown, everyday players in recent seasons, but when it comes to Swihart they may have screwed the pooch. The Sox rushed Swihart into MLB playing time in 2015, but he hit well for a catcher and served as a tolerable defensive option. How was Swihart thanked in 2016? The new Dave Dombrowski-led front office yanked him from starting duties after just seven games, had him learn to play the outfield in the minors and then forced him to stand adjacent to the Monster just six weeks later. Swihart promptly broke his ankle and missed the remainder of the season. That injury isn't the front office's fault, of course, but the overall mismanagement of this talented young asset is. If you read the Boston beats, it seems that Dombrowski and crew don't believe Swihart is going to develop defensively and is destined to forever linger as trade bait. Agree or disagree with that assessment as you see fit, but it's clear the Sox need a better plan behind the plate than Sandy Leon and Christian Vazquez.

YEAR	TEAM	P. COUNT	FRM RUNS	BLK RUNS	THRW RUNS	TOT RUNS
2014	PAW	2329	0.8	0.0	-0.1	0.7
2014	PME	10418	18.3	0.4	2.2	20.9
2015	BOS	11445	-6.0	-3.5	0.2	-9.3
2015	PAW	2261	0.5	0.1	0.0	0.6
2015	PME	133	0.0	0.0	0.0	0.0
2016	BOS	908	-0.7	-0.7	0.0	-1.5
2017	BOS	3352	-0.8	-0.8	0.1	-1.5
2018	BOS	9345	-2.5	-2.1	0.3	-4.3

Sam Travis   1B

Born: 8/27/93   Age: 23   Bats: R   Throws: R   Height: 6'0"   Weight: 205   Entered Pro Ball: Round 2, 2014 Draft (#67 overall)

YEAR	TEAM	LVL	AGE	PA	R	2B	3B	HR	RBI	BB	K	SB	CS	AVG/OBP/SLG	TAv	VORP	BABIP	BRR	FRAA	WARP
2014	LOW	A-	20	174	28	5	1	4	30	4	18	5	1	.333/.364/.448	.291	6.7	.357	-0.7	1B(33): -1.7	0.5
2014	GRN	A	20	115	12	11	1	3	14	7	14	0	1	.290/.330/.495	.276	1.8	.308	-1.3	1B(23): 0.3	0.2
2015	SLM	A+	21	278	35	15	4	5	40	26	43	10	6	.313/.378/.467	.306	17.6	.356	2.0	1B(46): 2.3	2.2
2015	PME	AA	21	281	35	17	2	4	38	33	34	9	6	.300/.384/.436	.297	15.9	.332	2.7	1B(63): 8.7	2.7
2016	PAW	AAA	22	190	26	10	0	6	29	15	40	1	0	.272/.332/.434	.283	7.8	.320	1.4	1B(34): 2.0	1.0
2017	BOS	MLB	23	32	4	2	0	1	4	3	7	0	0	.264/.325/.422	.257	0.4	.314	0.0	1B: 0	0.0
2018	BOS	MLB	24	279	35	15	1	9	35	23	60	3	2	.269/.332/.446	.259	4.5	.317	-0.3	1B: 0	0.5

Breakout: 10%   Improve: 27%   Collapse: 6%   Attrition: 20%   MLB: 38%   *Comparables: Max Kepler, Mike Carp, Josh Bell*

It's no secret that Travis has a tough profile as a prospect. He lacks big-time power, he's not a premium athlete and he's confined to first base, where he's still a work in progress. But a good hit tool will cover up lots of sins, and Travis has mashed at every professional level he's seen thus far. That continued through his first brief stint in Pawtucket, at least until he tore his ACL in a rundown just before Memorial Day and missed the rest of the season. Travis began to show a bit more power as a Paw Sox, and if that continues, he could yet force his way into regular MLB at-bats. If not, he profiles as a useful bench bat or second-division starter, but one whose limited paths to value place tremendous pressure on his hit tool and pop.

Christian Vazquez   C

Born: 8/21/90   Age: 26   Bats: R   Throws: R   Height: 5'9"   Weight: 195   Entered Pro Ball: Round 9, 2008 Draft (#292 overall)

YEAR	TEAM	LVL	AGE	PA	R	2B	3B	HR	RBI	BB	K	SB	CS	AVG/OBP/SLG	TAv	VORP	BABIP	BRR	FRAA	WARP
2014	PAW	AAA	23	270	35	17	0	3	20	21	52	0	1	.279/.336/.385	.252	9.4	.340	0.8	C(52): 7.7	1.7
2014	BOS	MLB	23	201	15	9	0	1	20	19	33	0	0	.240/.308/.309	.239	2.5	.283	-1.8	C(54): 14.9	1.9
2016	PAW	AAA	25	171	19	9	0	2	16	15	31	2	0	.270/.345/.368	.269	9.4	.325	0.3	C(41): 5.5	1.5
2016	BOS	MLB	25	184	21	9	1	1	12	10	39	0	0	.227/.277/.308	.198	-4.0	.288	-0.7	C(56): 7.1	0.3
2017	BOS	MLB	26	119	11	6	0	2	11	9	24	0	0	.256/.317/.366	.239	2.6	.309	-0.3	C 3	0.6
2018	BOS	MLB	27	183	21	9	1	3	19	15	38	0	0	.252/.320/.379	.238	2.0	.304	-0.7	C 5	0.7

Breakout: 11%   Improve: 44%   Collapse: 15%   Attrition: 29%   MLB: 90%   *Comparables: Jonathan Lucroy, Lou Marson, Hector Sanchez*

If you thought *The Walking Dead* had 2016's ugliest moment with a bat, you didn't catch much of Vazquez as a hitter. The defensive wunderkind finished 51st in TAv among catchers with at least 150 plate appearances, behind Juan Centeno, Kevin Plawecki and the sentient remains of A.J. Ellis. Seriously, Vazquez's at-bats were so lifeless, Peter King kept asking baristas if they'd heard about them. Our catching metrics still love Vazquez as a framer, but his arm looked more good than legendary in his first post-Tommy John season. And his much-ballyhooed rapport with the pitching staff? It mattered so much in April that the Sox screwed with Blake Swihart, but so little by July that Vazquez lost playing time to Ryan Hanigan and Bryan frickin Holaday. In the era of three-year contracts for Jason Castro, players like Vazquez have value. But his bat needs some quality alone time with Melisandre if Vazquez is to be anything more than a backup.

YEAR	TEAM	P. COUNT	FRM RUNS	BLK RUNS	THRW RUNS	TOT RUNS
2014	BOS	7331	13.7	-0.8	1.2	14.1
2014	PAW	7253	7.6	0.0	1.6	9.3
2016	BOS	7176	7.0	-0.9	0.0	6.1
2017	BOS	4477	3.6	-0.4	0.2	3.3
2018	BOS	6903	5.3	-0.6	0.2	4.8

Chris Young   LF

Born: 9/5/83   Age: 33   Bats: R   Throws: R   Height: 6'2"   Weight: 200   Entered Pro Ball: Round 16, 2001 Draft (#493 overall)

YEAR	TEAM	LVL	AGE	PA	R	2B	3B	HR	RBI	BB	K	SB	CS	AVG/OBP/SLG	TAv	VORP	BABIP	BRR	FRAA	WARP
2014	NYN	MLB	30	287	31	12	0	8	28	25	54	7	3	.205/.283/.346	.252	5.3	.226	1.1	LF(55): 3.3 • CF(27): -1.8	0.7
2014	NYA	MLB	30	79	9	8	0	3	10	7	16	1	0	.282/.354/.521	.311	5.8	.327	0.6	LF(18): 1.4 • RF(1): 0.0	0.8
2015	NYA	MLB	31	356	53	20	1	14	42	30	73	3	1	.252/.320/.453	.272	9.4	.283	-2.0	RF(76): -3.0 • LF(55): -2.2	0.4
2016	PAW	AAA	32	25	2	2	0	0	2	1	7	0	0	.217/.280/.304	.205	-1.1	.313	-0.1	LF(4): 0.6	-0.1
2016	BOS	MLB	32	227	29	18	0	9	24	21	50	4	2	.276/.352/.498	.280	9.6	.326	-0.2	LF(63): -1.0 • CF(3): -0.5	0.9
2017	BOS	MLB	33	267	31	15	1	9	33	25	59	4	2	.241/.317/.423	.255	5.7	.282	-0.2	RF -1, LF 1	0.4
2018	BOS	MLB	34	205	25	12	0	6	24	19	48	3	1	.229/.308/.398	.241	0.5	.275	-0.1	RF -1, LF 1	0.0

Breakout: 0%   Improve: 25%   Collapse: 11%   Attrition: 15%   MLB: 95%   *Comparables: Cody Ross, Eric Byrnes, Rickie Weeks*

Young did his job in 2016, hitting .329/.410/.589 against left-handed pitching. Young also did more than his job required, batting a passable .246/.319/.446 against same-side pitching. The only problem? Young missed the better part of two months after suffering a serious hamstring injury in late June, and the Red Sox had to turn to noted firearms enthusiast Bryce Brentz in his absence. Still, when on the field Young served as the perfect veteran complement to an outfield that otherwise boasted the average age of a first-time career fair attendee. With two lefties in Jackie Bradley Jr. and Andrew Benintendi poised to start in the outfield and the DH spot now vacant, Young should get plenty of opportunities next season. Odds are he'll do his job again.

PITCHERS

Fernando Abad   LHP

Born: 12/17/85   Age: 31   Bats: L   Throws: L   Height: 6'1"   Weight: 220   Entered Pro Ball: International Free Agent, 2002

YEAR	TEAM	LVL	AGE	W	L	SV	G	GS	IP	H	HR	BB/9	K/9	K	GB%	BABIP	WHIP	ERA	FIP	DRA	VORP	WARP	cFIP	MPH
2014	OAK	MLB	28	2	4	0	69	0	57¹	34	4	2.4	8.0	51	42%	.211	0.85	1.57	3.28	3.62	5.5	0.6	96	95.4
2015	OAK	MLB	29	2	2	0	62	0	47²	45	11	3.6	8.5	45	41%	.264	1.34	4.15	5.48	4.91	-1.1	-0.1	105	94.5
2016	MIN	MLB	30	1	4	1	39	0	34	27	2	3.7	7.7	29	46%	.269	1.21	2.65	3.40	4.75	0.8	0.1	109	94.5
2016	BOS	MLB	30	0	2	0	18	0	12²	13	2	5.7	8.5	12	38%	.297	1.66	6.39	5.40	5.09	-0.2	0.0	109	95.4
2017	BOS	MLB	31	2	2	0	37	0	39	41	6	3.8	7.8	34	53%	.302	1.48	5.03	4.80	5.12	-0.6	-0.1	100	
2018	BOS	MLB	32	2	1	0	41	0	43²	45	6	3.8	8.1	39	53%	.306	1.46	4.68	4.71	5.08	-0.1	0.0	116	

Breakout: 36%   Improve: 48%   Collapse: 23%   Attrition: 27%   MLB: 86%   *Comparables: Tyler Yates, Matt Lindstrom, Santiago Casilla*

The posterboy for Reliever Name Foreshadowing syndrome (RNF), Abad lived up to his last name after the Red Sox traded for him at the 2016 deadline. In Minnesota, he allowed just 11 earned runs in 34 innings, holding hitters to a .218 average. Once he was a Red Sox, Abad allowed nine runs in just 12 innings, blowing three saves and earning the ire of everyone with Dunkin Donuts coursing through their veins. To be fair to Abad, he held southpaws to a .151/.195/.264 line on the season. To be fair to the puns, he allowed a .339/.429/.559 line in high-leverage situations, prompting Boston to leave him off their postseason roster. This deal looks even worse when you remember that the Red Sox had to trade reliever prospect Pat Light to get the should-be LOOGY, meaning the Twins *literally* made Light of Abad trade.

Trey Ball   LHP

Born: 6/27/94   Age: 23   Bats: L   Throws: L   Height: 6'6"   Weight: 185   Entered Pro Ball: Round 1, 2013 Draft (#7 overall)

YEAR	TEAM	LVL	AGE	W	L	SV	G	GS	IP	H	HR	BB/9	K/9	K	GB%	BABIP	WHIP	ERA	FIP	DRA	VORP	WARP	cFIP	MPH
2014	GRN	A	20	5	10	0	22	22	100	111	9	3.5	6.1	68	38%	.309	1.50	4.68	4.66	6.94	-16.6	-1.7	116	
2015	SLM	A+	21	9	13	0	25	25	129¹	129	16	4.2	5.4	77	40%	.277	1.46	4.73	5.13	8.25	-45.6	-4.9	124	
2016	SLM	A+	22	8	6	0	23	23	117¹	121	8	5.2	6.6	86	49%	.311	1.61	3.84	4.91	7.68	-28.8	-3.0	119	
2017	BOS	MLB	23	5	8	0	20	20	94¹	127	20	5.6	3.7	39	75%	.310	1.96	7.00	7.09	7.38	-20.0	-2.1	176	
2018	BOS	MLB	24	3	7	0	16	16	94	110	18	7.3	7.2	75	75%	.315	1.98	6.75	6.75	7.12	-13.8	-1.4	167	

Breakout: 6%   Improve: 7%   Collapse: 0%   Attrition: 5%   MLB: 7%   *Comparables: Kris Johnson, Josh Butler, Deunte Heath*

Drafted as a two-way prospect out of high school in 2013, Ball was projected by many to be a better pitcher than hitter. Fortunately, the Red Sox saw that Ball's true talent lied in his bat, something the 22-year-old proved in High-A last season, hitting .271/.341/.381 in 533 PA. Now that he profiles as a corner outfielder with a great arm and a good hit tool, Ball ... wait, what? Ball is still a pitcher, and that slash line is actually what hitters did to him in Salem last season? *Extremely Michael Scott voice* Nooooo, God, No, Please, No.

Matt Barnes   RHP

Born: 6/17/90   Age: 27   Bats: R   Throws: R   Height: 6'4"   Weight: 210   Entered Pro Ball: Round 1, 2011 Draft (#19 overall)

YEAR	TEAM	LVL	AGE	W	L	SV	G	GS	IP	H	HR	BB/9	K/9	K	GB%	BABIP	WHIP	ERA	FIP	DRA	VORP	WARP	cFIP	MPH
2014	PAW	AAA	24	8	9	0	23	22	127²	119	8	3.2	7.3	103	44%	.294	1.29	3.95	3.71	5.15	8.5	0.8	100	
2014	BOS	MLB	24	0	0	0	5	0	9	11	1	2.0	8.0	8	34%	.357	1.44	4.00	3.49	4.68	-0.2	0.0	106	96.5
2015	PAW	AAA	25	1	1	0	17	5	37²	36	3	5.3	9.8	41	42%	.320	1.54	4.06	3.85	4.62	2.1	0.2	102	
2015	BOS	MLB	25	3	4	0	32	2	43	56	9	3.1	8.2	39	42%	.351	1.65	5.44	5.20	4.91	-0.5	-0.1	106	97.7
2016	BOS	MLB	26	4	3	1	62	0	66²	62	6	4.2	9.6	71	46%	.318	1.39	4.05	3.68	4.05	6.8	0.7	98	99.1
2017	BOS	MLB	27	2	3	2	46	0	48	48	5	4.0	8.5	46	47%	.308	1.47	3.91	4.10	4.27	3.8	0.4	96	
2018	BOS	MLB	28	2	1	1	45	0	48	43	5	5.3	10.7	57	47%	.308	1.48	4.03	4.07	4.41	3.4	0.3	97	

Breakout: 25%   Improve: 52%   Collapse: 20%   Attrition: 28%   MLB: 81%   *Comparables: Adam Warren, Alex Torres, David Purcey*

Barnes has three things going for him: size, velocity and pedigree. The big right-hander routinely reaches 97 with his fastball, and while his curveball is inconsistent it flashes plus often enough for you to understand why the Red Sox popped him 19th overall back in 2011. Barnes also has three things working against him: the lack of a third pitch, spotty command and a heater that's more about speed than movement. Seriously, Barnes' fastball is so straight it could hold a Senate seat in North Carolina. Add it all together and you have a middle reliever who's sometimes dominant and sometimes dominated, making Barnes more likely to stay a seventh-inning guy than ascend to something greater.

Roenis Elias   LHP

Born: 8/1/88   Age: 28   Bats: L   Throws: L   Height: 6'1"   Weight: 205   Entered Pro Ball: International Free Agent, 2011

YEAR	TEAM	LVL	AGE	W	L	SV	G	GS	IP	H	HR	BB/9	K/9	K	GB%	BABIP	WHIP	ERA	FIP	DRA	VORP	WARP	cFIP	MPH
2014	SEA	MLB	25	10	12	0	29	29	163²	151	16	3.5	7.9	143	48%	.294	1.31	3.85	4.06	3.86	17.8	2.0	104	94.3
2015	TAC	AAA	26	4	2	0	12	12	61¹	80	9	2.6	6.9	47	43%	.350	1.60	7.34	5.05	3.95	9.2	0.9	99	
2015	SEA	MLB	26	5	8	0	22	20	115¹	106	15	3.4	7.6	97	45%	.280	1.30	4.14	4.49	4.13	12.2	1.3	105	94.5
2016	BOS	MLB	27	0	1	0	3	1	7²	15	2	5.9	3.5	3	36%	.419	2.61	12.91	7.67	7.64	-2.1	-0.2	126	94.9
2016	PAW	AAA	27	10	5	0	21	19	125	115	10	4.1	8.1	113	42%	.303	1.38	3.60	3.91	4.52	11.1	1.1	107	
2017	BOS	MLB	28	2	2	0	24	3	37	37	4	4.2	7.8	33	46%	.298	1.46	4.27	4.39	4.56	2.2	0.2	100	
2018	BOS	MLB	29	3	2	0	43	5	69	63	8	5.0	9.6	74	46%	.305	1.47	4.29	4.32	4.65	4.1	0.4	105	

Breakout: 21%   Improve: 38%   Collapse: 19%   Attrition: 31%   MLB: 78%   *Comparables: J.A. Happ, Brad Peacock, Justin Germano*

You know that scene in the movie where the supporting character says "hey, it can't get worse, right?" and then it promptly starts raining? That's what swapping Wade Miley for Elias felt like. After providing some value for Seattle over the past two seasons, Elias was pedestrian as a Paw Sox and ravaged as a Red Sox. Boston opted to start Sean O'Sullivan and Henry Owens over him a combined nine times, which is a more stinging indictment than the one the Feds slapped on Nick's Roast Beef. The Red Sox have more starting depth now, so maybe they'll transition Elias to relief and see how he fares there. Hey, it can't get worse, right?

Jason Groome   LHP

Born: 8/23/98   Age: 18   Bats: L   Throws: L   Height: 6'6"   Weight: 220   Entered Pro Ball: Round 1, 2016 Draft (#12 overall)

YEAR	TEAM	LVL	AGE	W	L	SV	G	GS	IP	H	HR	BB/9	K/9	K	GB%	BABIP	WHIP	ERA	FIP	DRA	VORP	WARP	cFIP	MPH
2017	BOS	MLB	18	3	2	0	8	8	34¹	48	1	0.4	0.1	0	47%	.320	1.43	3.43	3.59	3.78	6.5	0.7	83	

Breakout: 0%   Improve: 0%   Collapse: 0%   Attrition: 0%   MLB: 0%   *Comparables: Jordan Lyles, Roberto Osuna, German Marquez*

Many scouts thought Groome was the best man in the 2016 draft, but he fell to the Red Sox at no. 12 overall due to signability concerns (commitment issues) and whispers about his makeup (rumors he wasn't made of honor). A big, powerful lefty, Groome marries his mid-90s heat with an advanced curveball that hitters find tough to engage. He boasts a repeatable delivery that the Sox shouldn't have to altar, and his scouting reports are bursting with unbride-eled enthusiasm. It's easy to fall in love with Groome, who is already one of the best southpaw prospects in the game. A few years down the line, perhaps he'll be the latest Red Sox ring-bearer. Also, it's pronounced "Grom," but what were we going to do with that?

Heath Hembree   RHP

Born: 1/13/89   Age: 28   Bats: R   Throws: R   Height: 6'4"   Weight: 210   Entered Pro Ball: Round 5, 2010 Draft (#168 overall)

YEAR	TEAM	LVL	AGE	W	L	SV	G	GS	IP	H	HR	BB/9	K/9	K	GB%	BABIP	WHIP	ERA	FIP	DRA	VORP	WARP	cFIP	MPH
2014	FRE	AAA	25	1	3	18	41	0	39¹	40	5	3.0	10.5	46	31%	.337	1.35	3.89	4.16	3.23	9.2	0.9	95	
2014	BOS	MLB	25	0	0	0	6	0	10	11	1	4.5	5.4	6	28%	.323	1.60	4.50	4.76	5.83	-1.5	-0.2	121	94.7
2015	PAW	AAA	26	0	5	8	29	0	31²	23	1	2.8	9.1	32	36%	.265	1.04	2.27	2.68	2.28	9.3	0.9	86	
2015	BOS	MLB	26	2	0	0	22	0	25¹	25	5	3.2	5.3	15	30%	.260	1.34	3.55	5.55	6.42	-4.8	-0.5	128	97.7
2016	PAW	AAA	27	0	0	8	13	0	13¹	6	0	2.0	14.9	22	38%	.250	0.68	0.68	0.54	1.42	5.2	0.5	68	
2016	BOS	MLB	27	4	1	0	38	0	51	51	6	3.0	8.3	47	38%	.294	1.33	2.65	3.79	4.97	0.0	0.0	110	96.5
2017	*BOS*	*MLB*	*28*	*1*	*1*	*0*	*25*	*0*	*26¹*	*28*	*4*	*3.3*	*7.3*	*21*	*52%*	*.297*	*1.42*	*4.57*	*4.81*	*4.81*	*0.5*	*0.1*	*100*	
2018	*BOS*	*MLB*	*29*	*2*	*1*	*0*	*38*	*0*	*39²*	*38*	*6*	*4.0*	*9.5*	*42*	*52%*	*.295*	*1.39*	*4.46*	*4.49*	*4.89*	*0.7*	*0.1*	*112*	

Breakout: 19%   Improve: 33%   Collapse: 16%   Attrition: 20%   MLB: 58%   *Comparables:* Edgmer Escalona, Cory Wade, Pedro Beato

You don't hear much about ROOGYs, but Hembree would be best served in that role. Righties hit just .200/.225/.336 against him—essentially Christian Vazquez's slash line. On the other hand, southpaws feasted to the tune of .338/.397/.493—he made them all First-Half Xander. That may seem like a disappointing outcome for a former "closer of the future," but in today's world of specialized bullpen roles, a guy like Hembree can be valuable if used correctly. Whether you trust John Farrell to use him correctly is a different story, but Hembree is out of options, so the Sox will need to play him or trade him.

Brian Johnson   LHP

Born: 12/7/90   Age: 26   Bats: L   Throws: L   Height: 6'4"   Weight: 235   Entered Pro Ball: Round 1, 2012 Draft (#31 overall)

YEAR	TEAM	LVL	AGE	W	L	SV	G	GS	IP	H	HR	BB/9	K/9	K	GB%	BABIP	WHIP	ERA	FIP	DRA	VORP	WARP	cFIP	MPH
2014	SLM	A+	23	3	1	0	5	5	25²	23	0	2.5	11.6	33	41%	.333	1.17	3.86	1.76	2.08	10.0	1.0	78	
2014	PME	AA	23	10	2	0	20	20	118	78	6	2.4	7.6	99	48%	.229	0.93	1.75	3.15	1.97	42.7	4.5	83	
2015	BOS	MLB	24	0	1	0	1	1	4¹	3	0	8.3	6.2	3	33%	.250	1.62	8.31	4.49	5.43	-0.2	0.0	118	91.7
2015	PAW	AAA	24	9	6	0	18	18	96	74	6	3	8.4	90	47%	.264	1.10	2.53	3.22	2.24	32.7	3.3	86	
2016	LOW	A-	25	0	0	0	2	2	11	7	0	1.6	9.0	11	37%	.259	0.82	0.00	1.82	2.39	3.5	0.4	84	
2016	PAW	AAA	25	5	6	0	15	15	77	74	9	4.2	6.3	54	36%	.284	1.43	4.09	4.73	7.25	-16.3	-1.7	130	
2017	*BOS*	*MLB*	*26*	*2*	*2*	*0*	*20*	*3*	*33*	*33*	*4*	*4.0*	*6.6*	*25*	*55%*	*.290*	*1.43*	*4.66*	*4.68*	*4.92*	*0.7*	*0.1*	*100*	
2018	*BOS*	*MLB*	*27*	*3*	*3*	*0*	*42*	*6*	*73*	*64*	*9*	*5.6*	*9.2*	*75*	*55%*	*.282*	*1.50*	*4.78*	*4.81*	*5.22*	*0.2*	*0.0*	*119*	

Breakout: 7%   Improve: 19%   Collapse: 15%   Attrition: 29%   MLB: 41%   *Comparables:* Tyler Anderson, Rudy Owens, Charles Brewer

Since being drafted, Johnson has missed time with a broken face, a shoulder injury, elbow soreness and, most recently, anxiety issues. That collection of maladies has limited him to just 430 innings pitched in more than four years as a professional. Yet Johnson is an advanced enough arm that he still sits on the precipice of a return to the majors. When he felt well enough to climb back on a Pawtucket mound late in the season, he posted a 3.68 ERA, logged at least six innings in more than half his starts and looked like his old self. Of course, looking like his old self means looking like a back-of-the-rotation, crafty lefty but that's still good news for a Red Sox team that could use some non-Henry Owens starting depth.

Joe Kelly   RHP

Born: 6/9/88   Age: 29   Bats: R   Throws: R   Height: 6'1"   Weight: 190   Entered Pro Ball: Round 3, 2009 Draft (#98 overall)

YEAR	TEAM	LVL	AGE	W	L	SV	G	GS	IP	H	HR	BB/9	K/9	K	GB%	BABIP	WHIP	ERA	FIP	DRA	VORP	WARP	cFIP	MPH
2014	MEM	AAA	26	0	0	0	3	3	10¹	8	1	5.2	3.5	4	56%	.226	1.35	2.61	5.93	5.92	-0.2	0.0	114	
2014	SLN	MLB	26	2	2	0	7	7	35	41	3	2.6	6.4	25	55%	.330	1.46	4.37	3.90	4.59	0.9	0.1	112	97.8
2014	BOS	MLB	26	4	2	0	10	10	61¹	47	5	4.7	6.0	41	57%	.237	1.29	4.11	4.64	4.63	1.4	0.2	111	98.3
2015	PAW	AAA	27	1	1	0	4	4	19	14	1	2.8	8.5	18	58%	.265	1.05	2.84	3.05	3.10	4.6	0.5	90	
2015	BOS	MLB	27	10	6	0	25	25	134¹	145	15	3.3	7.4	110	46%	.319	1.44	4.82	4.15	4.68	6.0	0.6	104	98.6
2016	PAW	AAA	28	1	1	2	17	4	35	29	1	1.5	11.8	46	57%	.341	1.00	1.54	1.51	1.08	15.9	1.6	59	
2016	BOS	MLB	28	4	0	0	20	6	40	44	5	5.4	10.8	48	48%	.358	1.70	5.18	4.28	3.69	6.7	0.7	96	100.4
2017	*BOS*	*MLB*	*29*	*2*	*2*	*0*	*41*	*0*	*43*	*41*	*4*	*4.0*	*8.9*	*43*	*54%*	*.300*	*1.37*	*3.64*	*3.83*	*4.04*	*4.6*	*0.5*	*90*	
2018	*BOS*	*MLB*	*30*	*3*	*1*	*0*	*50*	*0*	*53¹*	*48*	*5*	*4.3*	*9.6*	*57*	*54%*	*.304*	*1.38*	*3.80*	*3.83*	*4.14*	*5.3*	*0.5*	*91*	

Breakout: 31%   Improve: 48%   Collapse: 29%   Attrition: 17%   MLB: 94%   *Comparables:* Tyson Ross, Sergio Mitre, Roberto Hernandez

We've always known that Joe Kelly has Great Stuff™. Now he's finally putting it to good use. After yet another disastrous stint as a starter, the Red Sox finally, mercifully moved Kelly to the bullpen in July. He responded by allowing just two earned runs in 17.2 innings, striking out 21 while walking just five. Kelly's fastball routinely touched the upper-90s in relief, and hitters had a bear of a time trying to pull the ball against him. Couple Kelly's hotter heat with his improved command out of the pen, and he certainly looks the part of a high-leverage, late-inning reliever. He's unlikely to get many Cy Young votes in such a role, it's true, but perhaps no less likely than if he'd remained a starter.

Craig Kimbrel   RHP

Born: 5/28/88   Age: 29   Bats: R   Throws: R   Height: 6'0"   Weight: 210   Entered Pro Ball: Round 3, 2008 Draft (#96 overall)

YEAR	TEAM	LVL	AGE	W	L	SV	G	GS	IP	H	HR	BB/9	K/9	K	GB%	BABIP	WHIP	ERA	FIP	DRA	VORP	WARP	cFIP	MPH
2014	ATL	MLB	26	0	3	47	63	0	61²	30	2	3.8	13.9	95	43%	.237	0.91	1.61	1.81	1.79	18.5	2.0	67	99.6
2015	SDN	MLB	27	4	2	39	61	0	59¹	40	6	3.3	13.2	87	46%	.276	1.04	2.58	2.71	2.24	16.3	1.7	68	99.5
2016	BOS	MLB	28	2	6	31	57	0	53	28	4	5.1	14.1	83	31%	.242	1.09	3.40	2.88	3.01	11.5	1.2	83	99.7
2017	*BOS*	*MLB*	*29*	*2*	*2*	*38*	*46*	*0*	*48*	*36*	*5*	*4.1*	*12.3*	*66*	*50%*	*.291*	*1.20*	*2.88*	*3.26*	*3.37*	*8.6*	*0.9*	*70*	
2018	*BOS*	*MLB*	*30*	*3*	*1*	*53*	*63*	*0*	*66²*	*50*	*7*	*4.0*	*12.1*	*89*	*50%*	*.283*	*1.20*	*3.35*	*3.38*	*3.65*	*10.2*	*1.1*	*80*	

Breakout: 23%   Improve: 51%   Collapse: 32%   Attrition: 9%   MLB: 98%   *Comparables:* Carlos Marmol, Francisco Rodriguez, David Robertson

The problem with being labeled "the best" at something is that the expectations become sky-high. After a four-year stretch from 2011-2014 in which Kimbrel was historically dominant, he took a slight step back in 2015. That didn't stop Dave Dombrowski from backing up the prospect truck for him last offseason, which raised the stakes even more. Kimbrel responded by taking another step backward, walking a whopping 13.6 percent of batters faced en route to posting the highest DRA and ERA marks of his career. However, Kimbrel was still dominant for stretches, still averaged 98 mph on his fastball and still struck out well over a third of opposing hitters. He should also be commended for recovering from a torn meniscus in just three weeks. But he looked awfully mortal at times, especially when the two losses he suffered in the season's final five days helped cost the Red Sox the two-seed. Kimbrel clearly still has the talent to be an elite reliever, but if he's just good instead of special moving forward, he'll look a lot like an overpay.

Sean O'Sullivan   RHP

Born: 9/1/87   Age: 29   Bats: R   Throws: R   Height: 6'1"   Weight: 245   Entered Pro Ball: Round 3, 2005 Draft (#103 overall)

YEAR	TEAM	LVL	AGE	W	L	SV	G	GS	IP	H	HR	BB/9	K/9	K	GB%	BABIP	WHIP	ERA	FIP	DRA	VORP	WARP	cFIP	MPH
2014	LEH	AAA	26	6	10	0	25	25	148²	154	17	3.0	5.7	94	43%	.292	1.37	4.30	4.65	5.17	9.7	1.0	111	
2014	PHI	MLB	26	0	1	0	3	2	12²	15	3	1.4	5.0	7	42%	.300	1.34	6.39	5.55	5.55	-1.0	-0.1	115	94.2
2015	PHI	MLB	27	1	6	0	13	13	71	94	16	2.5	4.4	35	44%	.312	1.61	6.08	6.20	6.58	-11.9	-1.3	126	92.5
2015	LEH	AAA	27	5	2	0	9	9	56¹	48	3	3	6.6	41	39%	.266	1.19	3.20	3.46	5.20	0.6	0.1	106	
2016	BOS	MLB	28	2	0	0	5	4	21¹	30	3	2.5	5.5	13	39%	.365	1.69	6.75	4.84	5.92	-1.4	-0.1	117	93.0
2016	PAW	AAA	28	9	6	0	19	19	105¹	112	7	2.3	7.3	85	40%	.334	1.32	4.02	3.42	3.50	21.6	2.2	110	
2017	*BOS*	*MLB*	*29*	*6*	*6*	*0*	*18*	*18*	*104*	*123*	*16*	*3.4*	*5.8*	*67*	*54%*	*.314*	*1.56*	*5.00*	*5.11*	*5.45*	*0.2*	*0.0*	*127*	
2018	*BOS*	*MLB*	*30*	*5*	*7*	*0*	*17*	*17*	*98²*	*117*	*18*	*4.7*	*8.0*	*88*	*54%*	*.331*	*1.70*	*5.47*	*5.50*	*5.96*	*-5.2*	*-0.5*	*138*	

Breakout: 9%   Improve: 20%   Collapse: 8%   Attrition: 21%   MLB: 35%   *Comparables: Billy Buckner, Doug Mathis, Eric Stults*

Raise your hand if you had O'Sullivan pegged to start four games for a playoff team in 2016? Either your hand stayed down and you were wrong or your hand went up and you're a liar. Everyone's favorite no. 8 starter took on the A's and Astros in May and then the Angels and Rays in July as a Red Sox. He failed to log a quality start, but he did spare Red Sox Nation from more Henry Owens or Roenis Elias starts. Quite frankly, no stat can measure the value therein. O'Sullivan has now cost his teams in excess of four wins in his career, but he remains among the ~.000000193% of the population who physically has the ability to pitch in the majors, and odds are some team will be desperate enough to take the plunge again this season.

Edgar Olmos   LHP

Born: 4/12/90   Age: 27   Bats: L   Throws: L   Height: 6'4"   Weight: 220   Entered Pro Ball: Round 3, 2008 Draft (#83 overall)

YEAR	TEAM	LVL	AGE	W	L	SV	G	GS	IP	H	HR	BB/9	K/9	K	GB%	BABIP	WHIP	ERA	FIP	DRA	VORP	WARP	cFIP	MPH
2014	JAX	AA	24	1	0	2	18	0	26¹	22	5	4.4	5.5	16	47%	.218	1.33	4.44	6.03	7.79	-8.6	-0.9	119	
2014	NWO	AAA	24	2	3	1	33	0	51¹	49	4	3.0	7.7	44	53%	.312	1.29	3.86	4.11	4.31	5.9	0.6	93	
2015	TAC	AAA	25	1	1	1	20	2	33	32	0	3.5	9.3	34	40%	.344	1.36	3.55	3.27	4.66	1.3	0.1	99	
2015	SEA	MLB	25	1	0	0	6	2	14	16	1	5.1	2.6	4	50%	.283	1.71	4.50	5.39	5.80	-1.4	-0.2	120	95.4
2016	NOR	AAA	26	4	4	0	42	0	68²	63	4	3.7	10.0	76	51%	.339	1.33	2.88	3.02	3.06	14.5	1.5	85	
2017	*BOS*	*MLB*	*27*	*2*	*1*	*1*	*50*	*0*	*52¹*	*56*	*7*	*4.1*	*7.5*	*44*	*54%*	*.313*	*1.52*	*4.53*	*4.73*	*4.95*	*0.8*	*0.1*	*113*	
2018	*BOS*	*MLB*	*28*	*1*	*0*	*0*	*21*	*0*	*31²*	*31*	*4*	*5.5*	*9.8*	*35*	*54%*	*.318*	*1.58*	*4.68*	*4.71*	*5.11*	*-0.2*	*0.0*	*116*	

Breakout: 13%   Improve: 20%   Collapse: 12%   Attrition: 33%   MLB: 39%   *Comparables: Chuckie Fick, Danny Burawa, Jake Dunning*

In some ways, MLB players are still treated like chattel, and it's wrong. It's wrong that Olmos, a pitcher with a spotty minor-league track record but plenty of promise, was wanted by multiple teams in need of left-handed relief depth in the winter of 2015-16, but was doomed by the league's roster rules to bounce among them without self-determination or any ability to leverage that wantedness into more money. Instead, he was designated for assignment four times, eventually stashed at Triple-A by Baltimore, and then dropped into free agency without big-league innings on his 2016 resume. This could be the year he provides crucial situational help in a big-league bullpen, but he'll do it on a minor-league deal.

Henry Owens   LHP

Born: 7/21/92   Age: 24   Bats: L   Throws: L   Height: 6'6"   Weight: 220   Entered Pro Ball: Round 1, 2011 Draft (#36 overall)

YEAR	TEAM	LVL	AGE	W	L	SV	G	GS	IP	H	HR	BB/9	K/9	K	GB%	BABIP	WHIP	ERA	FIP	DRA	VORP	WARP	cFIP	MPH
2014	PME	AA	21	14	4	0	20	20	121	89	6	3.5	9.4	126	48%	.267	1.12	2.60	3.16	2.73	33.5	3.6	81	
2014	PAW	AAA	21	3	1	0	6	6	38	32	4	2.8	10.4	44	44%	.301	1.16	4.03	3.59	2.27	14.7	1.5	78	
2015	PAW	AAA	22	3	8	0	21	21	122¹	84	7	4.1	7.6	103	41%	.233	1.14	3.16	3.66	4.84	6.3	0.6	106	
2015	BOS	MLB	22	4	4	0	11	11	63	62	7	3.4	7.1	50	37%	.293	1.37	4.57	4.25	5.13	-0.4	-0.1	114	92.5
2016	PAW	AAA	23	10	7	0	24	24	137²	107	13	5.3	8.8	135	36%	.266	1.37	3.53	4.48	7.36	-30.9	-3.2	123	
2016	BOS	MLB	23	0	2	0	5	5	22	23	5	8.2	8.6	21	31%	.321	1.95	6.95	7.02	5.59	-0.6	-0.1	123	92.6
2017	*BOS*	*MLB*	*24*	*2*	*2*	*0*	*20*	*3*	*34*	*32*	*4*	*4.9*	*8.0*	*31*	*49%*	*.290*	*1.47*	*4.55*	*4.71*	*4.82*	*1.1*	*0.1*	*100*	
2018	*BOS*	*MLB*	*25*	*5*	*4*	*0*	*51*	*8*	*90²*	*75*	*11*	*6.0*	*10.3*	*104*	*49%*	*.285*	*1.50*	*4.57*	*4.60*	*4.99*	*2.5*	*0.3*	*113*	

Breakout: 10%   Improve: 28%   Collapse: 28%   Attrition: 35%   MLB: 74%   *Comparables: Eric Hurley, Rafael Montero, Garrett Olson*

For a few seasons it looked like Owens would break Boston's trend of pitching prospect busts. Now, it's Owens who looks broken. The lanky lefty missed bats, but allowed too many free passes in Pawtucket, averaging under six innings per start as a result. In five MLB outings, Owens was atrocious, recording just one quality start and walking nearly a batter per inning. It's easy to keep making excuses for Owens, and it's easy to harp on the positives: he's tall, he's young, he's left-handed and he looks like a *Point Break* extra. It's also pretty easy to hit Owens, apparently, and it's even easier to work a walk against him. As Bane tells us in *The Dark Knight Rises*, deception and theatricality are powerful agents against the uninitiated. But MLB hitters *are* initiated, and Owens is only going to sneak high-80s fastballs and average curveballs by them so often. He still has a little time to figure it all out, but when your team would rather hand the ball to Sean O'Sullivan than let you near an MLB lineup, the clock is ticking.

Drew Pomeranz   LHP

Born: 11/22/88 Age: 28 Bats: R Throws: L Height: 6'6" Weight: 240 Entered Pro Ball: Round 1, 2010 Draft (#5 overall)

YEAR	TEAM	LVL	AGE	W	L	SV	G	GS	IP	H	HR	BB/9	K/9	K	GB%	BABIP	WHIP	ERA	FIP	DRA	VORP	WARP	cFIP	MPH
2014	SAC	AAA	25	3	1	0	8	8	46¹	45	6	3.3	10.5	54	42%	.325	1.34	3.69	4.15	2.29	17.9	1.8	77	
2014	OAK	MLB	25	5	4	0	20	10	69	51	7	3.4	8.3	64	48%	.244	1.12	2.35	3.80	3.40	10.4	1.1	93	94.0
2015	OAK	MLB	26	5	6	3	53	9	86	71	8	3.2	8.6	82	43%	.266	1.19	3.66	3.59	4.00	8.6	0.9	98	94.5
2016	SDN	MLB	27	8	7	0	17	17	102	67	8	3.6	10.1	115	50%	.240	1.06	2.47	3.19	3.12	25.4	2.6	84	93.5
2016	BOS	MLB	27	3	5	0	14	13	68²	70	14	3.1	9.3	71	47%	.306	1.37	4.59	4.74	2.90	18.7	1.9	84	94.0
2017	BOS	MLB	28	10	8	0	26	26	148	136	16	3.6	9.5	156	49%	.299	1.32	3.72	3.78	4.06	19.6	2.0	93	
2018	BOS	MLB	29	8	8	0	23	23	138	132	16	3.9	10.2	157	49%	.319	1.39	3.88	3.92	4.25	17.9	1.8	96	

Breakout: 17%   Improve: 53%   Collapse: 22%   Attrition: 12%   MLB: 94%   *Comparables:* Garrett Richards, Tyson Ross, Kyle Gibson

You think *you* had an up-and-down 2016? After getting shipped to the Padres last offseason, Pomeranz finally put on display the talent so many saw in him when he was drafted fifth overall back in 2010. Using a dominant curveball and a rediscovered cutter, Pomeranz carved up opponents in the NL West, posting the highest strikeout rate and lowest FIP of his career. The southpaw transformed himself from Rockies castoff to A's reliever to Padres All-Star in just 18 months, which is a pretty neat trick. So neat that the Padres were able to flip him to the Red Sox in advance of the trade deadline, acquiring blue-chip prospect Anderson Espinoza in return.

They say you only get one chance to make a first impression, and by that measure Pomeranz looked like the Ghost of Henry Owens Future, angering a fan base already suspicious of trading the uber-hyped Espinoza. He was quite good in August, but his first few and last several starts with the Sox left a sour taste in many mouths, as did his postseason move to the bullpen. Through no fault of his own, Pomeranz also found himself in the midst of the A.J. Preller scandal, and was subsequently labeled as damaged goods. In fact, reports surfaced in October that MLB gave the Red Sox the chance to reverse the Pomeranz trade, but Dave Dombrowski and company declined.

So why did the Sox opt to keep Pomeranz despite his medical history and so-so performance in Boston? Because they can't develop pitching, and because the 2017 free-agent market for starters was less inspiring than the Padres' new uniforms. Pomeranz is under control through 2018, made tangible changes to his repertoire and still missed plenty of bats as a Red Sox. Is he the ace he looked like through the first half of 2016? Probably not. But if Pomeranz can stay healthy he should serve as a mid-rotation starter with upside, and that's something the Sox sorely lacked. Yes, losing Espinoza hurts, but as Pomeranz himself proves you never know how pitching prospects are going to turn out.

Rick Porcello   RHP

Born: 12/27/88 Age: 28 Bats: R Throws: R Height: 6'5" Weight: 205 Entered Pro Ball: Round 1, 2007 Draft (#27 overall)

YEAR	TEAM	LVL	AGE	W	L	SV	G	GS	IP	H	HR	BB/9	K/9	K	GB%	BABIP	WHIP	ERA	FIP	DRA	VORP	WARP	cFIP	MPH
2014	DET	MLB	25	15	13	0	32	31	204²	211	18	1.8	5.7	129	51%	.298	1.23	3.43	3.70	3.75	24.7	2.7	94	93.2
2015	BOS	MLB	26	9	15	0	28	28	172	196	25	2.0	7.8	149	47%	.332	1.36	4.92	4.10	4.14	18.0	1.9	93	94.2
2016	BOS	MLB	27	22	4	0	33	33	223	193	23	1.3	7.6	189	44%	.269	1.01	3.15	3.36	3.45	47.4	4.9	89	93.9
2017	BOS	MLB	28	12	9	0	29	29	182²	188	25	2.1	8.0	162	55%	.306	1.28	3.94	4.01	4.29	19.5	2.0	100	
2018	BOS	MLB	29	10	10	0	28	28	172¹	183	25	2.0	8.0	154	55%	.314	1.29	4.06	4.10	4.44	19.9	2.1	102	

Breakout: 24%   Improve: 55%   Collapse: 26%   Attrition: 10%   MLB: 94%   *Comparables:* Johnny Cueto, John Danks, Hyun-jin Ryu

Apparently Porcello read his 2016 Annual comment (set to the tune of TLC's "Waterfalls") and set out to prove he was No Scrub. One year after his play said "I'm Good At Being Bad," Porcello won the AL Comeback Player of the Year award and, more notably, the AL Cy Young. You can make a big Whoop De Woo about Justin Verlander or Corey Kluber deserving it more, but Porcello certainly belonged in the conversation. The right-hander set career-best marks in innings pitched, strikeouts, walk rate, ERA and WARP. He challenged hitters to Come Get Some, throwing his fastball higher in the zone than early in his career, but locating it much better than in 2015. As a result, batters couldn't Get It Up like in years past and Porcello posted a personal-best 9.3 HR/FB percentage. When opponents tried to Creep on base, Porcello wasn't Damaged; he produced a 3.18 FIP with runners on. And when the ever-vociferous Manny Machado barked at Porcello for hitting him with a Perfect Game going in September, Rick barked back, suggesting Machado was, well, Unpretty. So if you're reading again, Mr. Porcello, know that while not everyone in the saber community is Diggin' On You, we also Ain't 2 Proud 2 Beg to watch you dominate again. Because what you did in 2016 was straight CrazySexyCool.

David Price   LHP

Born: 8/26/85 Age: 31 Bats: L Throws: L Height: 6'5" Weight: 215 Entered Pro Ball: Round 1, 2007 Draft (#1 overall)

YEAR	TEAM	LVL	AGE	W	L	SV	G	GS	IP	H	HR	BB/9	K/9	K	GB%	BABIP	WHIP	ERA	FIP	DRA	VORP	WARP	cFIP	MPH
2014	TBA	MLB	28	11	8	0	23	23	170²	156	20	1.2	10.0	189	42%	.301	1.05	3.11	2.96	2.17	50.5	5.6	73	95.9
2014	DET	MLB	28	4	4	0	11	11	77²	74	5	1.7	9.5	82	45%	.317	1.15	3.59	2.46	2.33	21.6	2.4	73	96.3
2015	DET	MLB	29	9	4	0	21	21	146	133	13	1.8	8.5	138	41%	.293	1.11	2.53	3.03	2.70	38.6	4.1	76	96.5
2015	TOR	MLB	29	9	1	0	11	11	74¹	57	4	2.2	10.5	87	44%	.283	1.01	2.30	2.19	2.66	20.0	2.1	75	97.2
2016	BOS	MLB	30	17	9	0	35	35	230	227	30	2.0	8.9	228	45%	.310	1.20	3.99	3.56	2.90	62.4	6.5	84	95.5
2017	BOS	MLB	31	14	9	0	30	30	201	191	24	2.2	9.4	210	42%	.305	1.21	3.40	3.46	3.71	34.4	3.5	83	
2018	BOS	MLB	32	13	11	0	31	31	197	190	25	2.2	9.2	202	42%	.307	1.21	3.58	3.62	3.93	34.7	3.6	88	

Breakout: 10%   Improve: 36%   Collapse: 25%   Attrition: 6%   MLB: 80%   *Comparables:* Erik Bedard, Adam Wainwright, Justin Verlander

Life can be tough for players who don't live up to their contracts in Boston, but even if Price had dominated in 2016, he was going to be a tough sell for many Sox fans. After all, Price served as one of their chief antagonists for years. He shut them down in the 2008 postseason, was a sore loser when Boston returned the favor in 2013 and took more shots at David Ortiz than your average Yankees fan along the way. There was always going to be an adjustment period, but Price didn't endear himself to Massholes by carrying an an ERA that started with a four for most of the year and submitting yet another bad playoff start. Seriously, the only way Price could be less popular in Boston right now is if you stitched "Drew" on the back of his uniform. Advanced metrics suggest Price was actually quite good last season, and the $217 million man did lead all of baseball in innings pitched. Good luck bringing those points up to your standard Red Sox fan who just watched Jon Lester win another ring, though. All Price can do is hope his ERA matches his DRA next season as he waits for another shot at October redemption. Until then, Price will remain the ire of Sox fans with long memories, medium iced coffees, short tempers and no patience.

Eduardo Rodriguez   LHP

Born: 4/7/93   Age: 24   Bats: L   Throws: L   Height: 6'2"   Weight: 220   Entered Pro Ball: International Free Agent, 2010

YEAR	TEAM	LVL	AGE	W	L	SV	G	GS	IP	H	HR	BB/9	K/9	K	GB%	BABIP	WHIP	ERA	FIP	DRA	VORP	WARP	cFIP	MPH
2014	BOW	AA	21	3	7	0	16	16	82²	90	5	3.2	7.5	69	46%	.328	1.44	4.79	3.52	2.68	23.4	2.5	87	
2014	PME	AA	21	3	1	0	6	6	37¹	30	1	1.9	9.4	39	47%	.299	1.02	0.96	2.42	2.55	11.1	1.2	88	
2015	PAW	AAA	22	4	3	0	8	8	48¹	46	2	1.3	8.2	44	50%	.321	1.10	2.98	2.31	1.82	18.7	1.9	74	
2015	BOS	MLB	22	10	6	0	21	21	121²	120	13	2.7	7.2	98	45%	.290	1.29	3.85	3.89	4.60	6.4	0.7	101	96.8
2016	PAW	AAA	23	0	4	0	7	7	38	33	6	1.7	5.7	24	43%	.233	1.05	3.08	4.59	4.67	2.8	0.3	107	
2016	BOS	MLB	23	3	7	0	20	20	107	99	16	3.4	8.4	100	33%	.278	1.30	4.71	4.39	5.11	3.0	0.3	115	96.1
2017	BOS	MLB	24	10	8	0	26	26	148	151	17	3.2	7.5	124	48%	.300	1.39	4.12	4.18	4.49	12.5	1.3	100	
2018	BOS	MLB	25	10	10	0	30	30	189²	180	22	3.8	9.1	192	48%	.304	1.37	3.99	4.03	4.37	20.7	2.1	99	

Breakout: 24%   Improve: 54%   Collapse: 22%   Attrition: 19%   MLB: 93%   *Comparables: Vin Mazzaro, Martin Perez, Homer Bailey*

Rodriguez's 2016 is a play that can be told in two acts. A knee injury suffered in spring training prevented him from joining Boston's rotation until late May. In his first six starts, he was atrocious, posting an 8.59 ERA and allowing a .315/.372/.621 (yes, .621) line against. Rodriguez was still tipping pitches like he was trying to get their number, and he was banished to Rhode Island to iron out the kinks. It worked. The talented lefty resurfaced in mid-July and was a viable mid-rotation starter from there on out, posting a 3.24 ERA and a .210/.284/.329 line against in 14 starts. Assuming Rodriguez stops telegraphing his pitches, he's well on his way to becoming Boston's best home-grown(ish) starter since Clay Buchholz. If he keeps letting hitters know what's coming, well, Pawtucket is nice in the spring.

Robbie Ross   LHP

Born: 6/24/89   Age: 28   Bats: L   Throws: L   Height: 5'11"   Weight: 215   Entered Pro Ball: Round 2, 2008 Draft (#57 overall)

YEAR	TEAM	LVL	AGE	W	L	SV	G	GS	IP	H	HR	BB/9	K/9	K	GB%	BABIP	WHIP	ERA	FIP	DRA	VORP	WARP	cFIP	MPH
2014	ROU	AAA	25	5	4	0	12	9	60¹	66	7	2.4	6.4	43	58%	.319	1.36	4.33	4.73	5.17	3.6	0.4	92	
2014	TEX	MLB	25	3	6	0	27	12	78¹	103	9	3.4	5.9	51	54%	.352	1.70	6.20	4.77	4.83	-0.7	-0.1	110	92.9
2015	BOS	MLB	26	0	2	6	54	0	60²	59	7	3.0	7.9	53	51%	.295	1.30	3.86	3.99	4.10	4.1	0.4	97	95.1
2016	BOS	MLB	27	3	2	0	54	0	55¹	47	2	3.7	9.1	56	51%	.302	1.27	3.25	3.23	3.79	7.2	0.7	98	96.0
2017	BOS	MLB	28	2	3	0	46	0	48	48	5	3.6	7.8	42	67%	.304	1.43	4.28	4.14	4.58	2.1	0.2	100	
2018	BOS	MLB	29	2	1	0	42	0	44²	46	6	3.8	8.2	41	67%	.311	1.44	4.35	4.39	4.77	1.4	0.1	107	

Breakout: 21%   Improve: 50%   Collapse: 25%   Attrition: 17%   MLB: 93%   *Comparables: Joe Smith, Neftali Feliz, Bryan Shaw*

Ross is like your backup pair of dress shoes or your favorite shirt that has a little hole under the armpit: You don't want to trot him out for special occasions, but more often than not he gets the job done. Ross can miss bats, can throw often and he's very good against southpaws—they hit just .185/.320/.225 against him. He also improved against right-handers (.233 TAv) and succeeded in keeping the ball in the park like never before. The caveats? Ross walked more batters than ever and, while he threw his slider more and his fastball less, there's no real evidence that he has found a permanent recipe for successfully limiting righties or homers. Just like that comfy, oversized sweater has a place in your closet, Ross definitely belongs in a good big league bullpen. He just shouldn't be the second- or third-best option in it.

Chris Sale   LHP

Born: 3/30/89   Age: 28   Bats: L   Throws: L   Height: 6'6"   Weight: 180   Entered Pro Ball: Round 1, 2010 Draft (#13 overall)

YEAR	TEAM	LVL	AGE	W	L	SV	G	GS	IP	H	HR	BB/9	K/9	K	GB%	BABIP	WHIP	ERA	FIP	DRA	VORP	WARP	cFIP	MPH
2014	CHA	MLB	25	12	4	0	26	26	174	129	13	2.0	10.8	208	43%	.280	0.97	2.17	2.60	2.25	50.1	5.5	64	97.5
2015	CHA	MLB	26	13	11	0	31	31	208²	185	23	1.8	11.8	274	43%	.323	1.09	3.41	2.70	2.40	62.0	6.6	68	98.4
2016	CHA	MLB	27	17	10	0	32	32	226²	190	27	1.8	9.3	233	42%	.279	1.04	3.34	3.42	2.69	67.3	6.7	77	97.0
2017	BOS	MLB	28	14	8	0	29	29	203	179	24	2.2	10.6	238	66%	.303	1.14	3.18	3.25	3.47	40.1	4.1	76	
2018	BOS	MLB	29	14	10	0	31	31	198¹	182	26	2.1	10.6	234	66%	.310	1.15	3.35	3.39	3.67	42.5	4.4	80	

Breakout: 23%   Improve: 48%   Collapse: 29%   Attrition: 7%   MLB: 97%   *Comparables: Rich Harden, Felix Hernandez, Tim Lincecum*

In 2015, Sale posted the 11th-best strikeout rate by any starter in history. Last year, that strikeout rate dipped by 2.5 batters per full game, as did his fastball by two mph, and all that really suffered was his FIP and a set of throwbacks. This was intentional: he wanted to work deeper into games and did so, averaging an additional two outs per start. He finished games six times, a career-best, finally resembling a Felix Hernandez-style ace instead of a good and promising left-handed Gumby. He has a team-friendly contract through 2019, which along with Sale's overall greatness is how the White Sox turned him into a big package of Red Sox prospects in December.

Robby Scott   LHP

Born: 8/29/89   Age: 27   Bats: B   Throws: L   Height: 6'3"   Weight: 220   Entered Pro Ball: International Free Agent, 2011

YEAR	TEAM	LVL	AGE	W	L	SV	G	GS	IP	H	HR	BB/9	K/9	K	GB%	BABIP	WHIP	ERA	FIP	DRA	VORP	WARP	cFIP	MPH
2014	PME	AA	24	8	2	3	35	1	59²	55	3	2.3	7.7	51	44%	.301	1.17	1.96	3.05	3.19	11.2	1.2	89	
2015	PME	AA	25	1	1	0	25	2	43²	32	3	2.7	8.5	41	37%	.240	1.03	2.06	3.25	3.24	7.5	0.8	90	
2015	PAW	AAA	25	1	1	1	13	1	31²	47	5	2.6	7.7	27	45%	.385	1.77	7.67	4.36	4.05	3.1	0.3	97	
2016	PAW	AAA	26	4	3	0	32	6	78	57	9	1.6	8.4	73	31%	.240	0.91	2.54	3.49	2.68	20.7	2.1	95	
2016	BOS	MLB	26	1	0	0	7	0	6	6	0	3.0	7.5	5	50%	.333	1.33	0.00	2.44	4.57	0.3	0.0	103	89.9
2017	BOS	MLB	27	3	2	2	56	2	64²	68	8	3.1	7.1	51	53%	.302	1.39	4.33	4.32	4.71	4.4	0.5	109	
2018	BOS	MLB	28	1	1	1	26	1	53	51	7	4.1	10.0	59	53%	.312	1.42	4.16	4.19	4.52	3.1	0.3	103	

Breakout: 11%   Improve: 18%   Collapse: 13%   Attrition: 23%   MLB: 33%   Comparables: Pedro Viola, Alex Serrano, Daniel Stange

Do yourself a favor and Google Tim Britton's story about getting to know Robby Scott. In summary, Scott signed with the Yuma Scorpions after going undrafted out of FSU in 2011. Jose Canseco was his manager, Joey Gathright and his 20 steals patrolled center and a 52-year-old Tony Phillips was the team's third baseman. Former Red Sox pitcher and scout Al Nipper saw Scott pitch in Yuma and the Sox signed him, apparently so abruptly that Scott was pulled just one inning into a start. Since 2011, Scott has made slow and steady progress through the minor leagues, culminating in his first-ever appearance in the majors last season. His future is likely as a LOOGY—he held southpaws to a .147/.206/.253 line in Pawtucket—but he's used to pitching in a variety of roles, including as a swingman. That's not a very exciting ending to the story, but, uh, Phillips hit .269 for Yuma that year.

Carson Smith   RHP

Born: 10/19/89   Age: 27   Bats: R   Throws: R   Height: 6'6"   Weight: 215   Entered Pro Ball: Round 8, 2011 Draft (#243 overall)

YEAR	TEAM	LVL	AGE	W	L	SV	G	GS	IP	H	HR	BB/9	K/9	K	GB%	BABIP	WHIP	ERA	FIP	DRA	VORP	WARP	cFIP	MPH
2014	TAC	AAA	24	1	3	10	39	0	43	44	1	2.7	9.4	45	70%	.352	1.33	2.93	2.89	2.14	15.3	1.5	71	
2014	SEA	MLB	24	1	0	0	9	0	8¹	2	0	3.2	10.8	10	81%	.125	0.60	0.00	1.84	2.86	1.5	0.2	82	96.2
2015	SEA	MLB	25	2	5	13	70	0	70	49	2	2.8	11.8	92	66%	.292	1.01	2.31	2.09	1.79	22.7	2.4	61	95.9
2016	BOS	MLB	26	0	0	0	3	0	2²	2	0	3.4	6.8	2	75%	.250	1.12	0.00	2.73	4.12	0.3	0.0	100	94.5
2017	BOS	MLB	27	1	1	0	21	0	21	19	2	3.4	10.2	25	38%	.303	1.30	3.13	3.29	3.62	3.3	0.3	77	
2018	BOS	MLB	28	3	1	0	59	0	62	50	6	3.9	12.3	85	38%	.312	1.24	3.14	3.18	3.45	10.8	1.1	71	

Breakout: 35%   Improve: 53%   Collapse: 22%   Attrition: 16%   MLB: 85%   Comparables: Mark Melancon, Kevin Quackenbush, Steve Cishek

If the 2016 Red Sox were a jigsaw puzzle, Smith was the border piece that fell onto the floor and ended up under your couch; everything looked fine from afar, but you knew it was somehow incomplete. The Smart Guy Baseball Community has come so far around on relievers that when Dave Dombrowski traded World's Most Boring Starter Wade Miley for Smith (and Roenis Elias) last offseason, most people praised Boston despite their spotty rotation. Unfortunately, no one knew at the time that Smith's right UCL had just four professional innings remaining, and his stop-and-start season came to an abrupt end in late May. Assuming all goes well with his Tommy John recovery, Smith should establish himself in a late-inning role with the Sox during the second half of this season. Then again, Smith is a 27-year-old reliever with one full season under his belt, and you know what happens when you assume...

Tyler Thornburg   RHP

Born: 9/29/88   Age: 28   Bats: R   Throws: R   Height: 5'11"   Weight: 190   Entered Pro Ball: Round 3, 2010 Draft (#96 overall)

YEAR	TEAM	LVL	AGE	W	L	SV	G	GS	IP	H	HR	BB/9	K/9	K	GB%	BABIP	WHIP	ERA	FIP	DRA	VORP	WARP	cFIP	MPH
2014	MIL	MLB	25	3	1	0	27	0	29²	24	4	6.4	8.5	28	37%	.284	1.52	4.25	3.78	6.27	-5.9	-0.6	123	96.3
2015	CSP	AAA	26	2	7	0	17	17	88²	106	16	3.7	5.8	57	42%	.315	1.60	5.28	5.91	4.91	3.9	0.4	112	
2015	MIL	MLB	26	0	2	0	24	0	34¹	31	7	3.1	8.9	34	35%	.253	1.25	3.67	5.14	5.35	-2.5	-0.3	113	95.2
2016	MIL	MLB	27	8	5	13	67	0	67	38	6	3.4	12.1	90	36%	.229	0.94	2.15	2.87	2.89	15.5	1.6	80	96.4
2017	BOS	MLB	28	2	2	5	46	0	48	44	5	3.8	9.4	50	49%	.296	1.33	3.62	3.81	4.01	5.2	0.5	90	
2018	BOS	MLB	29	3	1	3	55	0	58²	48	6	4.3	11.2	73	49%	.296	1.29	3.59	3.62	3.90	7.4	0.8	85	

Breakout: 24%   Improve: 50%   Collapse: 17%   Attrition: 26%   MLB: 87%   Comparables: Alfredo Aceves, Joe Saunders, Wade LeBlanc

After several up-and-down, injury riddled seasons, Thornburg was the Phoenix to the ashes of the Jeremy Jeffress trade. Rather than shaking up the Brewers' bullpen, losing Jeffress opened a spot for the dominant Thornburg to prove his way as a closer. It's almost like an assembly line: depth RHP-in, closer RHP-out. And then just as quickly, Thornburg became the next closer reclamation project traded out of Milwaukee, heading to Boston in a setup role.

Steven Wright   RHP

Born: 8/30/84   Age: 32   Bats: R   Throws: R   Height: 6'2"   Weight: 215   Entered Pro Ball: Round 2, 2006 Draft (#56 overall)

YEAR	TEAM	LVL	AGE	W	L	SV	G	GS	IP	H	HR	BB/9	K/9	K	GB%	BABIP	WHIP	ERA	FIP	DRA	VORP	WARP	cFIP	MPH
2014	PAW	AAA	29	5	5	0	15	15	95	86	9	2.1	6.4	68	48%	.269	1.14	3.41	3.88	3.67	22.0	2.2	94	
2014	BOS	MLB	29	0	1	0	6	1	21	21	2	1.7	9.4	22	57%	.328	1.19	2.57	2.87	2.72	4.3	0.5	86	87.2
2015	PAW	AAA	30	2	5	0	8	8	52	55	2	2.6	7.3	42	51%	.331	1.35	3.81	3.02	3.96	7.7	0.8	91	
2015	BOS	MLB	30	5	4	0	16	9	72²	67	12	3.3	6.4	52	45%	.252	1.29	4.09	4.98	4.76	1.7	0.2	108	88.2
2016	BOS	MLB	31	13	6	0	24	24	156²	138	12	3.3	7.3	127	46%	.279	1.24	3.33	3.73	3.92	25.1	2.6	103	87.7
2017	BOS	MLB	32	6	6	0	42	13	104	101	9	3.5	7.3	85	50%	.293	1.34	3.87	3.95	4.24	10.8	1.1	97	
2018	BOS	MLB	33	4	4	0	31	9	78²	71	9	4.5	9.0	78	50%	.292	1.40	4.20	4.25	4.60	6.2	0.6	105	

Breakout: 13%   Improve: 20%   Collapse: 20%   Attrition: 18%   MLB: 47%   Comparables: Dana Eveland, Matt Palmer, Justin Germano

Through June, Wright was one of the best pitchers in the game. In 15 starts he posted a 2.18 ERA and held batters to a .207/.289/.290 line, all while throwing his knuckleball 70 percent of the time. That performance made Wright one of 2016's most surprising All-Stars, but—like a five-year high school quarterback or Pokemon Go—Wright peaked too soon. In his nine July and August starts, he allowed a 5.53 ERA and admitted to struggling when it got too hot. He also struggles when it rains and when it's humid, which means Wright… can't really pitch outside in the summer? Seems less than ideal for a baseball player. Nonetheless, he was robbed of a chance at autumn redemption after injuring his shoulder while diving back to the bag as a pinch-runner in August. The heir apparent to Tim Wakefield certainly deserves a chance to start again next season, though we suspect his baserunning days are over.

LINEOUTS

Hitters

NAME	POS	TEAM	LVL	AGE	PA	R	2B	3B	HR	RBI	BB	K	SB	CS	AVG/OBP/SLG	TAv	VORP	BABIP	BRR	FRAA	WARP
Bryce Brentz	LF	PME	AA	27	48	5	2	0	1	3	7	14	1	0	.200/.333/.325	.238	0.6	.280	1.0	RF(8): -1.6, LF(1): -0.1	-0.1
	LF	BOS	MLB	27	64	8	3	0	1	7	3	17	0	0	.279/.313/.377	.253	0.2	.372	-0.7	LF(22): -0.5	0.0
	LF	PAW	AAA	27	212	16	17	1	4	21	8	52	2	0	.250/.278/.402	.239	0.6	.318	1.3	LF(33): 1.6, RF(18): 0.7	0.3
C.J. Chatham	SS	LOW	A-	21	121	19	4	1	4	19	8	20	0	1	.259/.319/.426	.268	5.0	.282	-0.7	SS(26): 0.5	0.6
Allen Craig	RF	LOW	A-	31	27	2	1	0	0	3	6	4	0	0	.250/.407/.300	.280	1.0	.294	0.1	RF(2): 0.3, LF(1): -0.1	0.1
	RF	PAW	AAA	31	84	5	3	1	1	6	7	16	0	0	.173/.250/.280	.216	-2.1	.203	0.8	1B(11): -0.5, RF(2): -0.0	-0.3
Bobby Dalbec	3B	LOW	A-	21	143	25	13	2	7	33	9	33	2	2	.386/.427/.674	.356	17.8	.473	1.3	3B(22): 2.6	2.2
Bryan Holaday	C	TEX	MLB	28	94	14	6	1	2	13	5	16	0	1	.238/.290/.405	.235	3.4	.265	1.7	C(27): -5.4, LF(1): -0.0	-0.2
	C	ROU	AAA	28	38	6	1	1	2	8	3	9	0	0	.324/.395/.588	.359	4.8	.391	-0.2	C(5): -1.6	0.3
	C	BOS	MLB	28	35	3	1	0	0	1	2	12	0	0	.212/.257/.242	.173	-0.4	.333	1.1	C(13): -0.6, 3B(1): 0.0	-0.1
Nick Longhi	1B	SLM	A+	20	535	56	40	3	2	77	50	106	2	3	.282/.349/.393	.266	5.5	.352	-3.9	1B(99): 2.6, RF(12): 0.6	0.9
Josh Ockimey	1B	GRN	A	20	499	60	25	1	18	62	88	129	3	1	.226/.367/.425	.287	18.9	.284	1.8	1B(101): -3.7	1.7
Henry Ramos	OF	PAW	AAA	24	209	18	8	3	5	29	11	44	4	2	.247/.285/.400	.253	0.2	.288	-2.1	RF(41): 0.8, CF(7): 0.7	0.2
	OF	PME	AA	24	189	20	6	3	3	11	11	25	3	3	.281/.330/.404	.271	5.6	.313	-1.0	CF(27): -0.4, RF(13): -0.9	0.5
Austin Rei	C	GRN	A	22	369	50	13	1	6	33	41	82	1	4	.212/.331/.318	.248	10.3	.267	0.5	C(81): 1.3	1.3
Josh Rutledge	SS	PAW	AAA	27	20	3	2	0	0	0	1	4	1	0	.316/.350/.421	.285	1.4	.400	0.3	3B(3): -0.1, 2B(2): 0.1	0.1
	SS	BOS	MLB	27	56	9	6	0	0	3	6	19	2	0	.265/.345/.388	.235	2.0	.433	1.7	3B(17): -0.2, 2B(5): -0.1	0.2

Bryce Brentz hit .295/.343/.453 against lefties in Triple-A, appeared in 25 games in the majors and did not shoot himself. That's a really good year by his standards. ❖ The 51st pick in the 2016 draft, **C.J. Chatham** has good defensive skills, a questionable bat and a name Cape Codders will love. The Sox signed him to an under-slot contract, marking the first time anyone's gotten a good deal on Chatham property in decades. ❖ Enron had a gentler decline than **Allen Craig**, who's gone from All-Star to Triple-A scrub in remarkably little time. He's been either hurt, bad or both for three full seasons now. ❖ Fourth-rounder **Bobby Dalbec** has big power, a big arm and a big body, but he'd manage to swing and miss at a piñata even without a blindfold. If he strikes out as a position player, he's got a potential future on the mound. ❖ Ernie Banks played for 19 seasons and never made the postseason. **Bryan Holaday** has played for five playoff teams in his five-year career, including the Rangers and Red Sox last year. Eat at Arby's. ❖ Springfield, MA, native **Nick Longhi** hit well and reached base often as a 20-year-old in High-A, but he stopped hitting for power and saw more time at first base, which is an unfortunate confluence of events. ❖ Pop-up prospect **Josh Ockimey**'s brother is a college linebacker and his sister is a Ph.D. candidate, but neither of them hit 18 homers and posted a .199 ISO in Greenville as a 20-year-old. ❖ **Henry Ramos** celebrated Independence Day by becoming the first Paw Sox to hit for the cycle since 1999. "Why can't Colin Kaepernick make a statement like *that*," your uncle asks. ❖ To say that **Austin Rei** is a glove-only catching prospect is entirely too kind to his bat. ❖ Handsome backup infielder **Josh Rutledge** suffered from patellar tendonitis all season long, managing just 76 PA between Boston and Pawtucket. He went under the knife in late August, so he should be ready to battle for a backup spot come the spring.

Pitchers

NAME	TEAM	LVL	AGE	W	L	SV	G	GS	IP	H	HR	BB/9	K/9	K	GB%	BABIP	WHIP	ERA	FIP	DRA	VORP	WARP	cFIP	MPH
Jake Cosart	GRN	A	22	4	1	2	29	0	52²	36	2	4.3	13.0	76	43%	.288	1.16	2.05	2.49	1.96	15.7	1.7	83	
	SLM	A+	22	0	0	0	8	0	18	7	0	5.5	14.0	28	26%	.200	1.00	1.00	2.44	2.33	5.5	0.6	88	
Williams Jerez	PME	AA	24	1	6	0	40	0	65	70	6	4.2	9.0	65	46%	.350	1.54	4.71	4.04	4.84	-0.8	-0.1	96	
Travis Lakins	SLM	A+	22	6	3	0	19	18	91	111	8	3.6	7.8	79	38%	.354	1.62	5.93	4.30	4.81	6.5	0.7	104	
Kyle Martin	PAW	AAA	25	3	4	6	36	0	66²	58	5	2.8	10.5	78	46%	.329	1.18	3.38	3.02	2.26	20.0	2.1	78	
Noe Ramirez	PAW	AAA	26	2	3	7	30	0	43²	39	3	2.3	11.1	54	44%	.333	1.15	1.85	2.41	1.83	15.2	1.6	77	
	BOS	MLB	26	0	0	0	14	0	13	16	4	5.5	10.4	15	36%	.375	1.85	6.23	7.11	4.89	0.1	0.0	108	91.9
Roniel Raudes	GRN	A	18	11	6	0	24	24	113¹	112	8	1.8	8.3	104	34%	.314	1.19	3.65	3.12	2.71	29.0	3.2	86	
Teddy Stankiewicz	PME	AA	22	5	9	0	25	25	135²	142	16	2.6	6.4	97	43%	.307	1.33	4.71	4.48	4.04	15.8	1.7	102	
Ben Taylor	SLM	A+	23	0	2	3	15	3	45	35	0	2.0	11.2	56	49%	.318	1.00	2.60	1.92	1.20	20.0	2.1	67	
	PME	AA	23	1	0	5	21	0	34	28	4	3.2	11.1	42	30%	.300	1.18	3.44	3.56	2.05	10.1	1.1	90	
Brandon Workman	PME	AA	27	0	0	0	4	0	10	15	4	6.3	4.5	5	48%	.324	2.20	9.00	8.36	5.52	-0.9	-0.1	120	
Luis Ysla	PME	AA	24	2	5	3	39	0	55¹	54	4	4.4	9.8	60	38%	.333	1.46	4.07	3.70	4.25	3.0	0.3	101	

Jake Cosart—yes, Jarred's little brother—blew away hitters as a reliever in the low- and mid-minors, but needs to improve his command as he climbs the ladder. Does anyone else miss Daniel Bard? ❖ **Williams Jerez**'s parents may not have understood the whole LAST NAME, FIRST NAME part of his birth certificate, but they sure knew how to make a kid with a live arm. So live, in fact, that he held on to his 40-man roster spot despite a lackluster repeat engagement in Portland. ❖ **Travis Lakins** is the ever-rare projectable right-hander with college experience. His first go-around in Salem didn't inspire much confidence, but that first year out of school is rough for a lot of us. ❖ **Kyle Martin** is a tall drink of fastball who pitched well as a middle reliever in Triple-A last season. He's well-positioned to challenge for the league-lead in miles logged between Boston and Pawtucket. ❖ **Noe Ramirez** was dominant in Triple-A and terrible in the majors once again, but at least he went a perfect one-for-one in fielding chances, making his first name literally correct. ❖ The 2016 Red Sox Minor League Pitcher of the Year, **Roniel Raudes** carved up Sally League hitters as an 18-year-old but lacks top-shelf upside. His future as the fourth piece in a megatrade Dave Dombrowski makes for an aging slugger remains intact. ❖ Former second-rounder **Teddy Stankiewicz** posted an odorous 4.71 ERA as a starter in Portland. A shift to the bullpen may soon be in order if he wants to continue his a-scent. ❖ **Ben Taylor** has middle relief upside at best, but he reached Portland and succeeded there just 12 months after being drafted, proving that not all recent grads are underemployed. ❖ **Brandon Workman** has now thrown just 20 innings over the past two seasons thanks to Tommy John surgery, giving him the most ironic reliever name since Josh Outman. ❖ The Red Sox think highly enough of **Luis Ysla** that they added him to the 40-man roster this winter despite his so-so season in Double-A. His future as a potential LOOGY remains intact.

CHICAGO CUBS

Essay by Sahadev Sharma

Player comments by Rian Watt and BP staff

There's a common misperception in sports; a belief that games that occurred generations ago somehow impact the current team on the field. The idea suggests that the very clothing an organization dons, often emblazoned with a crest that bears some vague resemblance to that seen decades ago, still carries the weight of expectations unmet from years earlier.

But David Ortiz didn't allow the failures of Bill Buckner, John McNamara and Grady Little to sink the Red Sox in 2004. Paul Konkero and Mark Buehrle weren't around for a gambling scandal that rocked the baseball world and didn't see their organization get labeled the Black Sox; it mattered not to them as they swept away the Houston Astros a little over a decade ago. Years of incompetence for the Royals didn't keep Lorenzo Cain, Alex Gordon and Eric Hosmer from bringing a championship to Kansas City.

And finally, on the North Side of Chicago, it's over. No more talk about curses, black cats or goats. Whatever you want to call it—let's go with decades of ineptitude—as a champagne-drenched Miguel Montero told me: "It's dead. We killed it."

The Cubs were never threatened in their division and rarely in the league; it was a summer during which they ran away from the competition. They proved to be the best team not just in one area, but a multi-faceted group that possessed one of the greatest defensive units of all time, a starting rotation that was the best in baseball, a bullpen that stabilized as the season progressed and an offense that was near the top in the league and actually got better in the World Series with the unexpected return of Kyle Schwarber.

But it was in October when they truly showed their mettle. Some questioned the fact that the group was front-running all regular season; could they come through if faced with adversity? In the NLDS they vanquished those even-year wonders, the Giants. In the fourth and decisive game, the Cubs' offense looked lost, trailing 5-2 heading into the ninth inning. Angst-ridden fans were sure the team was on the verge of blowing a 2-0 series lead, especially with Johnny Cueto and Madison Bumgarner lurking in Game 5. Heck, even manager Joe Maddon admitted he wasn't looking forward to that matchup. Then they roared back for four runs in the frame and headed to the NLCS in impressive fashion.

CUBS PROSPECTUS
2016 W-L: 103-58, 1st in NL Central

Pythag	.666	1st	DER	.745	1st
RS/G	5.02	3rd	B-Age	27.4	5th
RA/G	3.45	1st	P-Age	30.3	30th
TAv	.287	1st	Salary	$171.6M	6th
BRR	0.74	12th	M$/MW	$2.9M	24th
TAv-P	.238	1st	DL Days	1123	20th
FIP	3.81	5th	$ on DL	6%	3rd

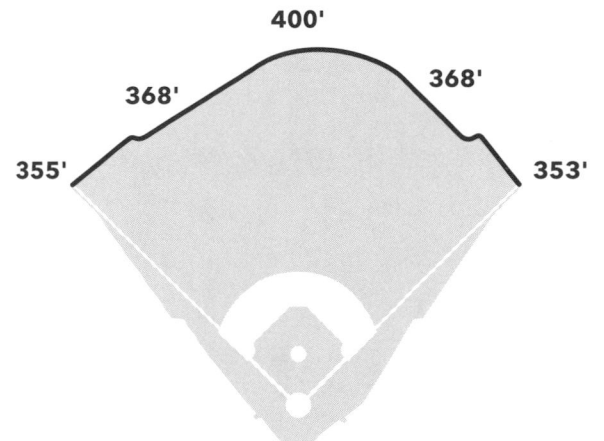

Outfield wall profile: **11'6"** to **15'**

Three-Year Park Factors

Runs	Runs/RH	Runs/LH	HR/RH	HR/LH
92	93	84	105	80

Top Hitter WARP	9.1	Kris Bryant
Top Pitcher WARP	5.3	Jon Lester
Top Prospect	Eloy Jimenez	

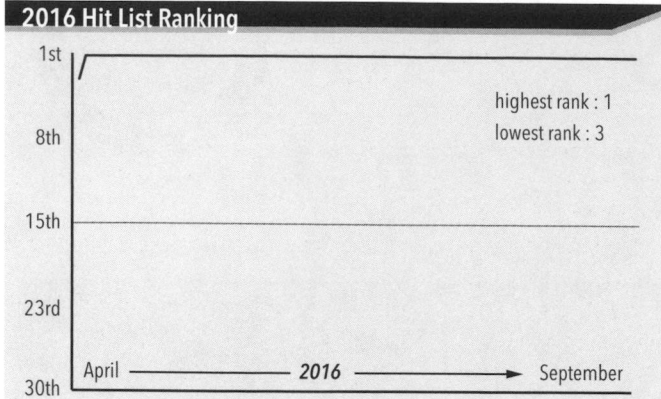

2016 Hit List Ranking

highest rank : 1
lowest rank : 3

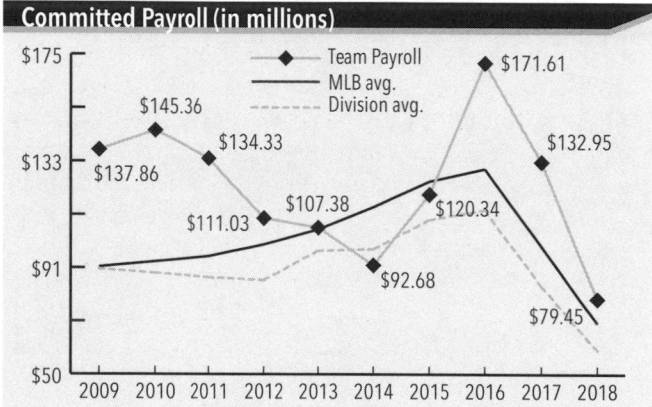

Committed Payroll (in millions)

Team Payroll
MLB avg.
Division avg.

$137.86
$145.36
$134.33
$111.03
$107.38
$92.68
$120.34
$171.61
$132.95
$79.45

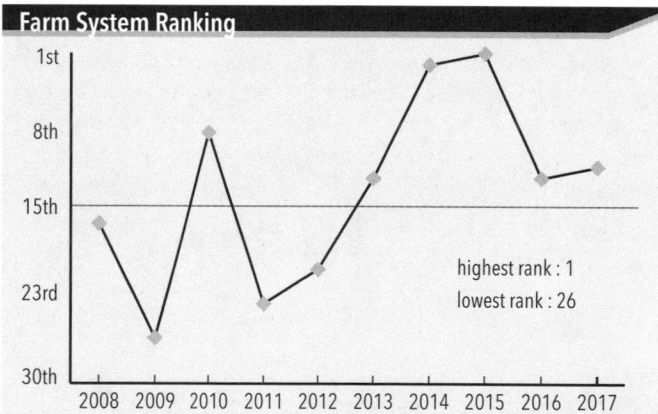

Farm System Ranking

highest rank : 1
lowest rank : 26

Personnel

President:
Theo Epstein

General Manager:
Jed Hoyer

Senior Vice President:
Jason McLeod

Manager:
Joe Maddon

BP Alumni:
Jeremy Greenhouse
Jason Karegeannes
Jason Parks

In the next series they went down 2-1 to the Dodgers, getting blanked in back-to-back games and failing to score for 21 consecutive innings. Then the Cubs ran off three straight wins, scoring 23 runs in their final 23 innings of the series. Then came the World Series, where once again the offense seemed listless as it stared down a 3-1 deficit to the Indians and what seemed like another October disappointment. It appeared that once again, regardless of how talented the team was, the Cubs had exited their season with a whimper.

But if there was anything learned from October, it's that those Cubs—the team that always ends their season in disappointment—no longer exist. These young Cubs were almost too naïve to allow the past to overwhelm them. As the Cubs' kids often said, not only were they not a part of previous teams' failures, they weren't even alive for many of them.

"We're looking to make our own history" was a common refrain in October. So when many panicked at each tough moment along the way, the players on the field never did. There was never any doubt that they were the best team in baseball, and it was only a matter of that team showing up. At times it took a little cajoling—Jason Heyward's weight-room speech during a rain delay in Game 7 of the World Series is the type of moment of which legends are made—but the group everyone had grown accustomed to seeing eventually rose to the top.

The Cubs are World Champions. It's a phrase many had dreamt of saying and now they finally can. Even weeks after the goal had been accomplished, it was nearly impossible to walk the streets of Chicago and not be reminded by a T-shirt, hat or billboard. Once a laughingstock, the North Siders are now the pride of the sports-obsessed city.

But it's not enough. Not with this group. They have the talent on the field, minds in the dugout and vision in the front office to take this a step further. When Theo Epstein and company took over an organization that seemed a generation away from competing and appeared to lack talent from top to bottom, Epstein's stated goal was to build a foundation for sustained success. He's done exactly that.

The Cubs have youth on their side, especially on offense. At 27, Heyward and Anthony Rizzo are actually two of the elder statesmen. Questioning the future of their pitching staff wouldn't be out of line, but the front office has repeatedly managed to put together strong rotations and piece together bullpens with its ability to identify overlooked talent in both the trade market and free agency. The fact that it's wield a mighty bank account doesn't hurt either.

They have all of this on their side, and they're coming off a season in which they were unquestionably the best in baseball. And the one thing the Cubs may have lacked, experience, they now possess in spades. They already had veterans like Jon Lester, John Lackey and Ben Zobrist, but now Rizzo, Kris Bryant and Addison Russell have gone through the rigors of multiple Octobers as well.

The offensive core is around for numerous seasons, and it might even be better going forward. Rizzo is just entering his theoretical prime, and Bryant is coming off an MVP year at age 24 while proving to be a master at adjusting his approach. Russell started tapping into his power, Javy Baez impressed in October and the Cubs seem to have found their long-term catcher in Willson Contreras. And it only gets scarier for opponents when reminded of the presence of Schwarber.

The slugging Indiana product missed all but three games of the regular season and wasn't expected back until 2017. However, in a movie-like story Schwarber made a near-miraculous return to the field to be the designated hitter for all four games in Cleveland. And he wasn't just there to hold a bat in an attempt to intimidate the opponent. Schwarber looked impressive against high-level pitching after missing six months and having been cleared to take batting practice just a week before his return.

He was so good that expectations for his offense in 2017—assuming health, a caveat we can place on all players—have risen to the point that some believe it will compensate enough for his suspect defense to put him in MVP consideration. For those concerned about Schwarber's defense, keep in mind that the Cubs got 98 games from below-average defenders in left field last season and still managed to put together a historically elite defensive unit.

In late September of 2016, five years after he'd first started the Cubs rebuild, Epstein was days away from becoming a free agent. There were some rumors that if the Cubs were to win a World Series, perhaps Epstein would move on. Maybe for another great challenge? Or a different sport altogether? Or perhaps just retirement to a beach island or trekking the Himalayas?

In the end, it was nothing but uninformed speculation, a little too far-fetched for reality. Epstein signed a five-year contract extension just prior to the playoffs, and when asked about the idea that he may have left, he couldn't help but laugh. "I know I've made some odd decisions, but going through the building process to bolt right when we have an opportunity to do what we came here to do?" Epstein posited. "That would be an all-timer."

Epstein and his top lieutenants, Jed Hoyer and Jason McLeod, were able to come to Chicago and essentially start from scratch (though Epstein was quick to credit Jim Hendry, the man in charge before him, for bringing in both Baez and Contreras), rebuilding an organization from the ground up using their own vision. It was a slow process that included upgrading their facilities in the Dominican Republic, Arizona and even at home at Wrigley Field.

They reshaped player development, brought in more scouts, kick-started a research and development group and upgraded and expanded an information management system that was badly outdated upon their arrival. They instilled confidence throughout the organization, and players at all levels bought into a new "Cubs Way." When they'd accomplish a feat, whether it was as small as beating out an infield grounder or as large as winning a minor-league championship, there was a common refrain: "That's Cub."

A term that once was almost taken as an insult permeated throughout the organization to become the ultimate compliment. To them, it had no other meaning than doing your best to get the results you desire. Outwork-, outhustle- and outsmart the competition until you come out on top. It's not that previous regimes didn't want to win, but with these Cubs expectations have been raised. With lofty goals in mind and a clear vision, the Cubs took a team that was once derided every step of the way, often mocked and made the butt of jokes, and made them they envy of the league.

But don't assume their work is done. That would be misjudging Epstein—underestimating his desire to not only get to the top but stay there. Many assumed that what Epstein came to the North Side to do was end another curse and solidify his legacy as one of the greatest front office minds the game has seen. However, it's much grander than that. Ending 108 years of misery for the Cubs is certainly a lofty goal, but this experiment can go beyond that. The Cubs can finally say they're champions, but the reality is they're gunning for another target: a dynasty. ■

—Sahadev Sharma covers the Cubs and White Sox for The Athletic Chicago

HITTERS

Albert Almora   CF

Born: 4/16/94   Age: 23   Bats: R   Throws: R   Height: 6'2"   Weight: 190   Entered Pro Ball: Round 1, 2012 Draft (#6 overall)

YEAR	TEAM	LVL	AGE	PA	R	2B	3B	HR	RBI	BB	K	SB	CS	AVG/OBP/SLG	TAv	VORP	BABIP	BRR	FRAA	WARP
2014	DAY	A+	20	385	55	20	2	7	50	12	46	6	3	.283/.306/.406	.254	10.5	.305		CF(87): 5.9	1.7
2014	TEN	AA	20	144	20	7	2	2	10	2	23	0	1	.234/.250/.355	.212	-3.0	.267	-0.1	CF(32): -1.8	-0.5
2015	TEN	AA	21	452	69	26	4	6	46	32	47	8	4	.272/.327/.400	.271	17.8	.291	1.2	CF(69): 3.4 • LF(18): -0.4	2.3
2016	IOW	AAA	22	336	46	18	3	4	43	9	44	10	3	.303/.317/.416	.285	22.5	.336	3.8	CF(69): -4.6 • LF(6): -0.1	1.8
2016	CHN	MLB	22	117	14	9	1	3	14	5	20	0	0	.277/.308/.455	.267	5.1	.315	0.9	CF(33): 0.2 • LF(8): -0.5	0.5
2017	CHN	MLB	23	207	20	10	1	5	21	7	35	2	1	.250/.277/.386	.239	2.7	.279	-0.1	CF 1	0.2
2018	CHN	MLB	24	417	45	21	2	11	47	15	70	4	2	.253/.283/.400	.250	6.9	.278	-0.1	CF 3	1.0

Breakout: 5%   Improve: 15%   Collapse: 3%   Attrition: 12%   MLB: 32%   *Comparables: Logan Schafer, Charlie Blackmon, Matt Szczur*

Almora was sold, all the way up the system, as an elite defender with superb bat-to-ball skills, 80-grade makeup and little patience for such trivialities as walks. He arrived on the big-league scene in 2016 and that's pretty much exactly what he was. Unless he can separate his OBP more noticeably from his AVG, or add a little pop, he'll probably be stuck where his glove is too good to keep off the field, but his bat might have to sit at the bottom of a lineup. That can work on strong teams, but it's a hard profile to maintain and certainly a difficult one to get offensive reps in. Almora has a big-league future, but his plate discipline will go a long way toward determining what kind.

Javier Baez   SS

Born: 12/1/92   Age: 24   Bats: R   Throws: R   Height: 6'0"   Weight: 190   Entered Pro Ball: Round 1, 2011 Draft (#9 overall)

YEAR	TEAM	LVL	AGE	PA	R	2B	3B	HR	RBI	BB	K	SB	CS	AVG/OBP/SLG	TAv	VORP	BABIP	BRR	FRAA	WARP
2014	IOW	AAA	21	434	64	24	2	23	80	34	130	16	8	.260/.323/.510	.285	32.8	.322	2.8	SS(85): -3.8 • 2B(16): 0.5	2.9
2014	CHN	MLB	21	229	25	6	0	9	20	15	95	5	1	.169/.227/.324	.197	-5.1	.248	1.2	SS(30): 0.3 • 2B(25): -4.4	-1.0
2015	IOW	AAA	22	313	49	14	2	13	61	21	76	17	3	.324/.385/.527	.330	35.5	.402	1.7	SS(40): 2.3 • 2B(19): 1.6	4.0
2015	CHN	MLB	22	80	4	6	0	1	4	4	24	1	2	.289/.325/.408	.268	2.0	.412	-1.1	2B(17): -0.5 • 3B(11): 1.9	0.4
2016	CHN	MLB	23	450	50	19	1	14	59	15	108	12	3	.273/.314/.423	.275	20.2	.336	-0.7	3B(62): 1.1 • 2B(59): 2.7	2.5
2017	*CHN*	*MLB*	*24*	*438*	*56*	*18*	*1*	*18*	*53*	*24*	*128*	*13*	*4*	*.243/.295/.422*	*.254*	*12.7*	*.309*	*0.8*	*3B 4, 2B 0*	*1.6*
2018	*CHN*	*MLB*	*25*	*500*	*64*	*20*	*1*	*21*	*67*	*31*	*147*	*14*	*5*	*.243/.302/.428*	*.266*	*17.2*	*.308*	*0.1*	*3B 4, 2B 0*	*2.3*

Breakout: 3%   Improve: 40%   Collapse: 17%   Attrition: 23%   MLB: 93%   *Comparables: Jonathan Schoop, Travis Snider, Mark Reynolds*

Well, he did it. He cut his strikeouts by enough to be a valuable big-league player. He also, impressively for a man who can hit the ball to San Juan and back, made more noise for what he did outside the batters' box than what he did inside it. Báez is a man of tremendous talent but even greater smarts and instincts, and those latter two qualities were on full display throughout the regular season and postseason. He runs. He slides. He tags. He believes he can hit anything, and sometimes he can. If he wants to stay valuable, though, he'll have to keep his head in the game while at the plate. Too often last year, he let his hands get ahead of his head and swung through two-strike pitches he'd have been better off taking. It was a year of tremendous improvements for Báez, and 2017 will be a test of whether he can keep them up.

Kris Bryant   3B

Born: 1/4/92   Age: 25   Bats: R   Throws: R   Height: 6'5"   Weight: 230   Entered Pro Ball: Round 1, 2013 Draft (#2 overall)

YEAR	TEAM	LVL	AGE	PA	R	2B	3B	HR	RBI	BB	K	SB	CS	AVG/OBP/SLG	TAv	VORP	BABIP	BRR	FRAA	WARP
2014	TEN	AA	22	297	61	20	0	22	58	43	77	8	2	.355/.458/.702	.397	50.5	.440	0.1	3B(62): 3.7	5.8
2014	IOW	AAA	22	297	57	14	1	21	52	43	85	7	2	.295/.418/.619	.363	42.4	.367	-2.2	3B(67): 3.5	4.6
2015	IOW	AAA	23	33	7	1	0	3	10	2	9	2	0	.321/.364/.679	.408	6.6	.333	0.5	3B(7): -1.0	0.6
2015	CHN	MLB	23	650	87	31	5	26	99	77	199	13	4	.275/.369/.488	.317	58.0	.378	2.3	3B(144): -2.7 • LF(8): -0.3	5.9
2016	CHN	MLB	24	699	121	35	3	39	102	75	154	8	5	.292/.385/.554	.350	86.5	.332	3.4	3B(107): 1.6 • LF(60): 1.4	9.1
2017	*CHN*	*MLB*	*25*	*606*	*88*	*27*	*2*	*33*	*96*	*69*	*164*	*10*	*4*	*.273/.384/.522*	*.312*	*51.1*	*.334*	*-0.3*	*3B 1, LF 1*	*5.0*
2018	*CHN*	*MLB*	*26*	*587*	*93*	*26*	*2*	*32*	*96*	*70*	*159*	*9*	*4*	*.273/.373/.523*	*.326*	*54.5*	*.333*	*2.3*	*3B 1, LF 1*	*6.1*

Breakout: 3%   Improve: 65%   Collapse: 2%   Attrition: 5%   MLB: 98%   *Comparables: Giancarlo Stanton, Dick Allen, Eddie Mathews*

Bryant is God's way of telling us that life isn't fair. The man is an underwear model and a millionaire to boot, for crying out loud, and he still managed to get away with spending his age-24 summer playing baseball for a living. He was good at it, too: His 9.1 WARP was, by a large margin, the best in the majors, as a new swing path (flatter through the zone) helped drive increases in contact rate across the board without sacrificing any of the power that helped make him Theo Epstein's second first-round draft pick. He's a plus defender at multiple positions and, as we saw in Game 7 of the World Series, even a good baserunner. Unless the moral balance of the universe swings wildly in 2017, expect Bryant to be at or near the top of most offensive leaderboards again this year.

Jeimer Candelario   3B

Born: 11/24/93   Age: 23   Bats: B   Throws: R   Height: 6'1"   Weight: 210   Entered Pro Ball: International Free Agent, 2010

YEAR	TEAM	LVL	AGE	PA	R	2B	3B	HR	RBI	BB	K	SB	CS	AVG/OBP/SLG	TAv	VORP	BABIP	BRR	FRAA	WARP
2014	DAY	A+	20	244	24	10	2	5	26	23	44	0	3	.193/.275/.326	.224	-4.0	.218	-2.1	3B(57): 8.1	0.4
2014	KNC	A	20	263	32	19	3	6	37	18	45	0	1	.250/.300/.426	.264	8.9	.284	-0.6	3B(62): 5.7	1.5
2015	MYR	A+	21	343	42	25	3	5	39	20	62	0	1	.270/.318/.415	.270	13.2	.320	-0.5	3B(77): -8.3	0.5
2015	TEN	AA	21	182	21	10	1	5	25	22	21	0	0	.291/.379/.462	.306	14.1	.308	0.2	3B(44): -3.6	1.1
2016	TEN	AA	22	244	30	17	1	4	23	32	46	0	0	.219/.324/.367	.247	4.2	.261	0.0	3B(54): 2.7 • 1B(2): -0.3	0.7
2016	CHN	MLB	22	14	0	0	0	0	0	2	5	0	0	.091/.286/.091	.178	-0.5	.167	0.2	3B(3): -0.4	-0.1
2016	IOW	AAA	22	309	44	22	3	9	54	38	53	0	2	.333/.417/.542	.353	40.9	.383	1.7	3B(67): -0.8 • 1B(10): 1.1	4.2
2017	*CHN*	*MLB*	*23*	*123*	*12*	*6*	*1*	*3*	*14*	*10*	*27*	*0*	*0*	*.232/.301/.391*	*.248*	*1.6*	*.274*	*-0.3*	*3B -0, 1B 0*	*0.1*
2018	*CHN*	*MLB*	*24*	*367*	*44*	*19*	*2*	*12*	*44*	*32*	*82*	*0*	*0*	*.239/.310/.412*	*.263*	*7.8*	*.281*	*-0.9*	*3B 0, 1B 1*	*0.9*

Breakout: 5%   Improve: 25%   Collapse: 8%   Attrition: 20%   MLB: 38%   *Comparables: Colin Moran, Taylor Green, Jedd Gyorko*

It's a bit of a shame that Candelario made his big-league debut last year, hitting just .091 in the process, because it'll give people the wrong impression about his many skills. He doesn't have all that much pop now, but he's got an excellent eye at the plate, gap power and youth. If things break the right way, you've got yourself a big-league regular.

Chris Coghlan   LF

Born: 6/18/85   Age: 32   Bats: L   Throws: R   Height: 6'0"   Weight: 195   Entered Pro Ball: Round 1, 2006 Draft (#36 overall)

YEAR	TEAM	LVL	AGE	PA	R	2B	3B	HR	RBI	BB	K	SB	CS	AVG/OBP/SLG	TAv	VORP	BABIP	BRR	FRAA	WARP
2014	IOW	AAA	29	88	9	5	0	0	6	13	18	6	1	.243/.379/.314	.267	2.7	.321	0.5	RF(16): -0.7 • 1B(5): -0.0	0.2
2014	CHN	MLB	29	432	50	28	5	9	41	39	81	7	4	.283/.352/.452	.292	23.8	.337	2.4	LF(101): 4.5 • RF(4): 0.2	3.2
2015	CHN	MLB	30	503	64	25	6	16	41	58	94	11	2	.250/.341/.443	.279	21.4	.284	1.4	LF(99): 2.2 • RF(21): 0.3	2.5
2016	OAK	MLB	31	172	14	5	0	5	14	13	47	1	1	.146/.215/.272	.167	-11.1	.170	0.7	2B(20): -0.5 • 3B(17): -0.4	-1.5
2016	TEN	AA	31	21	3	4	0	0	6	5	1	0	0	.500/.619/.750	.464	4.1	.533	-0.6	RF(4): -0.4 • LF(1): -0.1	0.4
2016	CHN	MLB	31	128	21	7	2	1	16	22	26	1	0	.252/.391/.388	.295	7.0	.325	-0.2	LF(25): 1.5 • 1B(6): -0.2	0.8
2017	*CHN*	*MLB*	*32*	*328*	*36*	*15*	*2*	*8*	*36*	*35*	*64*	*5*	*2*	*.238/.323/.388*	*.247*	*7.6*	*.277*	*1.0*	*LF 1, 2B 0*	*1.0*
2018	*CHN*	*MLB*	*33*	*302*	*36*	*14*	*2*	*7*	*32*	*32*	*60*	*4*	*1*	*.233/.320/.383*	*.258*	*7.6*	*.272*	*0.9*	*LF 0, 2B 0*	*1.0*

Breakout: 5%   Improve: 30%   Collapse: 6%   Attrition: 25%   MLB: 88%   *Comparables: Ben Francisco, Nate McLouth, Alejandro De Aza*

In 2015, Coghlan rode an increasingly leveraged swing into one of the best seasons of his career. In 2016, the league caught up to him, and even a midseason return to Chicago couldn't save the full-season numbers. He's got a strong enough approach at the plate to put up good numbers for a few years more if used situationally, but at age 32 don't look for him to be a starting outfielder on a contending team.

Willson Contreras   C

Born: 5/13/92   Age: 25   Bats: R   Throws: R   Height: 6'1"   Weight: 210   Entered Pro Ball: International Free Agent, 2009

YEAR	TEAM	LVL	AGE	PA	R	2B	3B	HR	RBI	BB	K	SB	CS	AVG/OBP/SLG	TAv	VORP	BABIP	BRR	FRAA	WARP
2014	DAY	A+	22	317	40	14	2	5	37	28	66	5	5	.242/.320/.359	.255	10.3	.297	-1.9	C(73): -2.0 • 1B(2): -0.0	0.8
2015	TEN	AA	23	521	71	34	4	8	75	57	62	4	4	.333/.413/.478	.322	48.6	.370	-0.6	C(75): -7.1 • 3B(8): -0.5	4.4
2016	IOW	AAA	24	240	40	16	3	9	43	28	32	4	4	.353/.442/.593	.378	38.1	.382	-0.9	C(45): -4.7	3.4
2016	CHN	MLB	24	283	33	14	1	12	35	26	67	2	2	.282/.357/.488	.302	21.5	.339	-0.9	C(57): 5.2 • LF(24): -2.3	2.5
2017	CHN	MLB	25	516	59	24	2	17	65	46	105	3	3	.268/.343/.440	.281	34.9	.313	-1.2	C -8	0.5
2018	CHN	MLB	26	522	69	25	2	19	68	47	109	3	3	.266/.343/.447	.292	35.8	.309	-0.4	C -9	2.9

Breakout: 3%   Improve: 40%   Collapse: 5%   Attrition: 21%   MLB: 93%   *Comparables: Devin Mesoraco, Travis d'Arnaud, Ryan Lavarnway*

Assembled in a Chicago system from raw Latin American materials, he spent most of his early years languishing in thankless obscurity—not even accepted as a gift when offered around—before finding success and purpose in Tennessee, getting on an airplane and becoming part of a story bigger than himself. He caught some hard breaks over the course of his first year in his new environment, to be sure, but through it all he held strong—an untested, just-washed-up-on-shore product onto which his companions could project their dreams and fevered visions during a trip to the loneliest place on earth: a big-league pitcher's mound. Which Willson did you think I was talking about?

YEAR	TEAM	P. COUNT	FRM RUNS	BLK RUNS	THRW RUNS	TOT RUNS
2015	TEN	10381	-6.4	1.3	-0.8	-5.9
2016	CHN	6569	4.5	1.5	0.7	6.7
2017	CHN	18950	-9.3	1.7	-0.3	-7.9
2018	CHN	19160	-9.9	1.8	-0.4	-8.5

Ian Happ   2B

Born: 8/12/94   Age: 22   Bats: B   Throws: R   Height: 6'0"   Weight: 205   Entered Pro Ball: Round 1, 2015 Draft (#9 overall)

YEAR	TEAM	LVL	AGE	PA	R	2B	3B	HR	RBI	BB	K	SB	CS	AVG/OBP/SLG	TAv	VORP	BABIP	BRR	FRAA	WARP
2015	EUG	A-	20	130	26	8	1	4	11	23	28	9	0	.283/.408/.491	.355	19.4	.347	2.7	CF(28): -4.9	1.5
2015	SBN	A	20	165	24	9	3	5	22	17	39	1	1	.241/.315/.448	.277	6.1	.288	-0.1	LF(14): 0.7 • RF(12): -1.2	0.7
2016	MYR	A+	21	293	37	16	3	7	42	48	69	10	3	.296/.410/.475	.320	26.1	.381	0.2	2B(50): -3.1 • LF(6): 0.1	2.4
2016	TEN	AA	21	274	35	14	0	8	31	20	60	6	2	.262/.318/.415	.271	9.8	.310	0.4	2B(42): -0.7 • RF(7): -1.7	0.9
2017	CHN	MLB	22	250	28	10	1	9	31	24	71	3	1	.227/.303/.397	.242	5.0	.287	0.0	2B -1, LF 0	0.4
2018	CHN	MLB	23	347	43	14	2	12	43	32	100	4	1	.225/.300/.401	.256	8.7	.287	0.0	2B -2, LF 1	0.8

Breakout: 2%   Improve: 23%   Collapse: 4%   Attrition: 19%   MLB: 43%   *Comparables: Matt Davidson, Eddie Rosario, Dilson Herrera*

A Sean Casey protege, Happ was billed as a infielder/outfielder combo with a sweet swing from both sides of the plate and 20-homer power. Well, the bat has been there. About second base, though: His defense at the position has been less than convincing, but not outright terrible, and if he can't play competently there the bat has a higher burden to bear as Happ advances up the system and onward to the majors.

Jason Heyward   RF

Born: 8/9/89   Age: 27   Bats: L   Throws: L   Height: 6'5"   Weight: 240   Entered Pro Ball: Round 1, 2007 Draft (#14 overall)

YEAR	TEAM	LVL	AGE	PA	R	2B	3B	HR	RBI	BB	K	SB	CS	AVG/OBP/SLG	TAv	VORP	BABIP	BRR	FRAA	WARP
2014	ATL	MLB	24	649	74	26	3	11	58	67	98	20	4	.271/.351/.384	.288	28.6	.308	1.0	RF(149): 27.6	6.2
2015	SLN	MLB	25	610	79	33	4	13	60	56	90	23	3	.293/.359/.439	.294	37.0	.329	6.1	RF(144): 16.0 • CF(10): 2.1	5.9
2016	CHN	MLB	26	592	61	27	1	7	49	54	93	11	4	.230/.306/.325	.237	-2.6	.266	-0.4	RF(131): -2.6 • CF(24): 2.9	-0.2
2017	CHN	MLB	27	608	74	27	3	17	66	61	102	15	4	.257/.336/.410	.270	23.0	.287	0.9	RF 15	3.6
2018	CHN	MLB	28	513	65	24	2	15	61	53	87	11	3	.258/.339/.419	.281	23.1	.288	1.3	RF 13	3.9

Breakout: 3%   Improve: 46%   Collapse: 5%   Attrition: 15%   MLB: 98%   *Comparables: Terry Puhl, Carl Taylor, Jody Gerut*

Just about everything that could go wrong did go wrong for Heyward in 2016, save for his defense. Although it's hard to fault the Cubs for the deal they struck with him in December 2015, given what they knew at the time, it's also fair to say the first year gave them legitimate reason for concern. Heyward's constant swing tinkering finally caught up with him, as his hard-hit balls were increasingly hit into the ground. A nagging wrist injury sapped what little power his swing initially had. He'll spend the offseason licking his wounds and will come back with a plan of attack for 2017. Will it work? Hard to say. Heyward was mired in a months-long stretch during which he seemed utterly lost at the plate, but his baseline talent is high enough that he looked all-world once in a while. If he finds a consistent approach, and becomes even an average offensive player again, his defense will carry him through the contract.

Jon Jay   CF

Born: 3/15/85   Age: 32   Bats: L   Throws: L   Height: 5'11"   Weight: 195   Entered Pro Ball: Round 2, 2006 Draft (#74 overall)

YEAR	TEAM	LVL	AGE	PA	R	2B	3B	HR	RBI	BB	K	SB	CS	AVG/OBP/SLG	TAv	VORP	BABIP	BRR	FRAA	WARP
2014	SLN	MLB	29	468	52	16	3	3	46	28	78	6	3	.303/.372/.378	.277	18.1	.363	-1.6	CF(98): -3.9 • RF(33): -3.7	1.1
2015	SLN	MLB	30	245	25	5	1	1	10	19	36	0	2	.210/.306/.257	.214	-4.3	.246	-0.1	CF(54): 1.3 • LF(17): -0.0	-0.3
2016	SDN	MLB	31	373	49	26	1	2	26	19	78	2	0	.291/.339/.389	.271	18.0	.371	3.1	CF(72): -3.4 • RF(9): 0.2	1.6
2017	CHN	MLB	32	437	43	17	2	5	38	31	77	4	2	.262/.330/.354	.253	12.1	.308	-0.6	CF -0	0.7
2018	CHN	MLB	33	355	39	13	1	4	32	26	65	2	1	.255/.329/.346	.254	8.0	.302	0.4	CF 0	0.8

Breakout: 2%   Improve: 36%   Collapse: 4%   Attrition: 12%   MLB: 84%   *Comparables: Eddie Milner, Brian McRae, Mike Hershberger*

One can only imagine the culture shock that came to Jay after being sent from St. Louis to San Diego, both in terms of baseball culture and city culture. You wouldn't know it with the way he performed on the field, though, as he got right back to the player he was before a hurt wrist derailed any hope he had of being productive in 2015. Unfortunately, the one part of that season which did carry over was the injuries, as a broken forearm forced him to miss about 10 weeks. On the bright side, The Federalist reminded people of his contact-oriented skill set that can play everyday on a bad team but is better suited in a bench role for a playoff contender like the Cubs.

Eloy Jimenez   RF

Born: 11/27/96   Age: 20   Bats: R   Throws: R   Height: 6'4"   Weight: 205   Entered Pro Ball: International Free Agent, 2013

YEAR	TEAM	LVL	AGE	PA	R	2B	3B	HR	RBI	BB	K	SB	CS	AVG/OBP/SLG	TAv	VORP	BABIP	BRR	FRAA	WARP
2015	EUG	A-	18	250	36	10	0	7	33	15	43	3	2	.284/.328/.418	.300	15.1	.321	-0.2	LF(46): -4.8 • RF(8): 3.1	1.4
2016	SBN	A	19	464	65	40	3	14	81	25	94	8	3	.329/.369/.532	.320	35.4	.391	-0.3	LF(86): -4.0 • RF(11): 0.4	3.5
2017	CHN	MLB	20	250	26	12	1	9	32	10	66	0	0	.241/.274/.415	.234	1.1	.291	-0.4	LF -1, RF 0	0.1
2018	CHN	MLB	21	399	48	19	1	15	52	16	102	1	0	.249/.285/.428	.255	6.4	.299	-0.9	LF -1, RF 1	0.6

Breakout: 5%   Improve: 15%   Collapse: 0%   Attrition: 6%   MLB: 18%   *Comparables: Chris Marrero, Nomar Mazara, Gary Sanchez*

Jimenez makes grown men and women stop what they're doing to watch him play baseball. He's big. He's strong. He hits for power. He hits for average. He's only 20 years old. If there's one player in the Cubs' farm system who could be a multi-time All-Star, it's Jimenez. The Cubs rave about his makeup, and his arm in right field is one of the best in the system. This season should see Jimenez get his first taste of the high minors, and a September call-up to Wrigley Field isn't out of the question if he performs well.

Munenori Kawasaki   2B

Born: 6/3/81   Age: 36   Bats: L   Throws: R   Height: 5'11"   Weight: 175   Entered Pro Ball: International Free Agent, 2012

YEAR	TEAM	LVL	AGE	PA	R	2B	3B	HR	RBI	BB	K	SB	CS	AVG/OBP/SLG	TAv	VORP	BABIP	BRR	FRAA	WARP
2014	BUF	AAA	33	129	12	11	1	0	9	8	17	1	1	.276/.320/.388	.253	3.6	.320	-0.3	SS(28): -0.8 • 2B(13): 1.7	0.4
2014	TOR	MLB	33	274	31	7	1	0	17	22	49	1	0	.258/.327/.296	.240	3.3	.323	1.3	2B(64): 2.9 • 3B(19): 2.0	0.9
2015	BUF	AAA	34	227	18	8	0	0	8	24	32	8	4	.245/.332/.286	.258	5.3	.291	-1.4	2B(34): 0.6 • SS(26): 2.8	0.9
2015	TOR	MLB	34	34	6	2	0	0	2	4	6	0	1	.214/.313/.286	.214	-0.5	.273	0.1	2B(17): 1.0 • 3B(3): -0.0	0.0
2016	IOW	AAA	35	378	42	11	2	1	39	49	61	20	8	.255/.332/.312	.254	18.1	.307	4.9	SS(100): -3.9	1.5
2016	CHN	MLB	35	26	3	2	0	1	4	5	2	0	1	.333/.462/.429	.339	3.1	.438	0.3	2B(10): -0.3	0.3
2017	CHN	MLB	36	250	25	8	1	2	18	25	45	7	3	.231/.316/.304	.223	2.2	.272	0.4	SS -1, 2B 0	0.1
2018	CHN	MLB	37	69	7	2	0	1	5	7	13	2	1	.226/.312/.297	.231	0.5	.266	0.2	SS 0, 2B 0	0.0

Breakout: 3%   Improve: 32%   Collapse: 10%   Attrition: 19%   MLB: 74%   *Comparables: Miguel Cairo, Bill Russell, Craig Counsell*

Kawasaki works a better at-bat than you think he does. For the bajillionth consecutive season, the differential between his batting average and his on-base percentage hovered right around 100 points, which is excellent for any player and particularly impressive for a guy who doesn't present a threat of hitting the ball out of the ballpark. As he ages that skill will probably maintain itself, which alongside his clubhouse reputation will probably get him a couple more random stints in the big leagues.

Tommy La Stella   2B

Born: 1/31/89   Age: 28   Bats: L   Throws: R   Height: 5'11"   Weight: 180   Entered Pro Ball: Round 8, 2011 Draft (#266 overall)

YEAR	TEAM	LVL	AGE	PA	R	2B	3B	HR	RBI	BB	K	SB	CS	AVG/OBP/SLG	TAv	VORP	BABIP	BRR	FRAA	WARP
2014	GWN	AAA	25	199	18	6	1	1	23	25	14	1	1	.293/.384/.359	.271	7.7	.308	0.0	2B(40): 2.8	1.1
2014	ATL	MLB	25	360	22	16	1	1	31	36	40	2	1	.251/.328/.317	.240	1.8	.283	-0.2	2B(88): -0.0	0.2
2015	TEN	AA	26	41	9	3	0	0	3	3	1	0	0	.250/.325/.333	.261	0.4	.257	-0.7	2B(5): 0.4 • 3B(4): 0.9	0.2
2015	IOW	AAA	26	38	3	2	1	1	6	4	3	0	0	.333/.395/.545	.313	2.2	.333	-0.7	2B(5): 0.1	0.2
2015	CHN	MLB	26	75	4	6	0	1	11	5	7	2	0	.269/.324/.403	.269	2.2	.283	-0.4	2B(14): 0.5 • 3B(12): -0.7	0.2
2016	IOW	AAA	27	46	6	2	0	1	3	2	9	0	0	.273/.304/.386	.223	-0.2	.324	0.4	3B(6): 0.9 • 2B(4): -0.5	0.0
2016	CHN	MLB	27	169	17	12	1	2	11	18	27	0	1	.270/.357/.405	.287	8.0	.319	-1.8	3B(33): -3.2 • 2B(9): -0.9	0.4
2017	CHN	MLB	28	152	15	7	1	2	14	15	19	1	0	.254/.333/.363	.255	4.6	.278	-0.2	2B 0	0.5
2018	CHN	MLB	29	167	19	8	0	3	16	18	21	0	0	.248/.333/.363	.260	4.3	.270	-0.4	2B 0	0.5

Breakout: 3%   Improve: 40%   Collapse: 4%   Attrition: 13%   MLB: 92%   *Comparables: Yangervis Solarte, Luis Rodriguez, Alberto Callaspo*

La Stella's existence makes you wonder if you should be reading this book at all. Midway through the 2016 campaign, the Cubs assigned him to Triple-A Iowa, and he just … didn't go. When asked about it later, he said that he'd been thinking about his life and the way he wanted to live it, and playing baseball wasn't the only thing important to him. Did he want to play for the big-league Cubs? Sure. Did he want to head to Des Moines to play there? Not really, no. He'd rather go home to New Jersey and spend time with his family. Maybe we should all go spend some time with our families. Maybe you should stop reading right now. Maybe we should stop writing these comme

Miguel Montero   C

Born: 7/9/83   Age: 33   Bats: L   Throws: R   Height: 5'11"   Weight: 210   Entered Pro Ball: International Free Agent, 2001

YEAR	TEAM	LVL	AGE	PA	R	2B	3B	HR	RBI	BB	K	SB	CS	AVG/OBP/SLG	TAv	VORP	BABIP	BRR	FRAA	WARP
2014	ARI	MLB	30	560	40	23	0	13	72	56	97	0	4	.243/.329/.370	.260	18.3	.275	-4.6	C(131): 11.3	3.3
2015	CHN	MLB	31	403	36	11	0	15	53	49	103	1	1	.248/.345/.409	.279	23.4	.306	-1.1	C(109): 13.3	3.9
2016	CHN	MLB	32	284	33	8	1	8	33	38	58	1	0	.216/.327/.357	.257	10.0	.249	-1.7	C(71): 10.8 • P(1): -0.0	2.1
2017	CHN	MLB	33	164	17	5	0	4	18	19	36	0	0	.232/.329/.365	.254	6.0	.279	-0.4	C 5	0.7
2018	CHN	MLB	34	182	23	6	0	5	20	21	42	0	0	.231/.327/.368	.260	5.6	.277	-0.7	C 5	1.2

Breakout: 1%   Improve: 43%   Collapse: 5%   Attrition: 14%   MLB: 94%   *Comparables: Chris Iannetta, Ernie Whitt, Russell Martin*

Time comes and gets all of us eventually, but it gets old catchers faster. Montero actually didn't have that bad of a season at the plate in 2016, although a very poor start depressed his overall numbers. A lingering bad back kept him from being the solid offensive contributor he's been in previous years. The plate discipline was still pretty much intact—he's great at working counts, and waiting for his pitch—and he still has the ability to knock the ball out of the park when the occasion calls for it. Still, the question for Montero is not whether he declines in 2017, but by how much.

YEAR	TEAM	P. COUNT	FRM RUNS	BLK RUNS	THRW RUNS	TOT RUNS
2014	ARI	18483	11.2	0.2	-0.1	11.3
2015	CHN	13007	16.0	1.4	-2.6	14.8
2015	TEN	192	0.1	0.0	0.0	0.1
2016	CHN	8698	15.2	-2.0	-2.9	10.3
2017	CHN	4648	6.1	-0.3	-0.7	5.1
2018	CHN	5149	6.2	-0.4	-0.8	5.0

Anthony Rizzo   1B

Born: 8/8/89   Age: 27   Bats: L   Throws: L   Height: 6'3"   Weight: 240   Entered Pro Ball: Round 6, 2007 Draft (#204 overall)

YEAR	TEAM	LVL	AGE	PA	R	2B	3B	HR	RBI	BB	K	SB	CS	AVG/OBP/SLG	TAv	VORP	BABIP	BRR	FRAA	WARP
2014	CHN	MLB	24	616	89	28	1	32	78	73	116	5	4	.286/.386/.527	.335	51.0	.311	2.1	1B(140): -0.9	5.5
2015	CHN	MLB	25	701	94	38	3	31	101	78	105	17	6	.278/.387/.512	.328	48.4	.289	-5.1	1B(160): 1.5	5.3
2016	CHN	MLB	26	676	94	43	4	32	109	74	108	3	5	.292/.385/.544	.334	56.5	.309	-1.2	1B(154): 11.1 • 2B(1): -0.2	7.0
2017	CHN	MLB	27	657	90	32	2	31	98	70	112	8	4	.270/.362/.499	.302	38.0	.284	-1.2	1B 2	4.0
2018	CHN	MLB	28	604	91	32	1	28	90	73	101	7	4	.273/.375/.501	.318	42.3	.289	-1.0	1B 2	4.8

Breakout: 5%   Improve: 56%   Collapse: 4%   Attrition: 5%   MLB: 100%   Comparables: Prince Fielder, Ron Blomberg, Billy Butler

A few years ago, Rizzo started holding the bat lower down in the zone and much closer into his body. Also a few years ago, Rizzo became one of the best hitters in the game. It's not all down to that change, of course—Rizzo still tinkers plenty, his selectivity at the plate has gotten way better and he's grown into his "man strength"—but you've got to admire a slugger who realized he was strong enough to be short and quick to the ball as the default setting. He's absolutely unafraid to loom over the inside half of the plate and dare the opposing guy to sneak one inside on him. Rizzo had his most complete season as a big leaguer last year, winning a Gold Glove award and finishing fourth in the MVP voting. He doesn't have to change much to retain his place near the front of the class.

Addison Russell   SS

Born: 1/23/94   Age: 23   Bats: R   Throws: R   Height: 6'0"   Weight: 200   Entered Pro Ball: Round 1, 2012 Draft (#11 overall)

YEAR	TEAM	LVL	AGE	PA	R	2B	3B	HR	RBI	BB	K	SB	CS	AVG/OBP/SLG	TAv	VORP	BABIP	BRR	FRAA	WARP
2014	MID	AA	20	57	7	3	1	1	8	8	8	3	2	.333/.439/.500	.304	4.3	.385	-0.3	SS(11): -0.9	0.4
2014	TEN	AA	20	205	32	11	0	12	36	9	35	2	2	.294/.332/.536	.304	17.4	.306	0.2	SS(47): 5.7	2.5
2015	IOW	AAA	21	46	7	4	0	1	9	1	7	1	0	.318/.326/.477	.298	2.7	.351	-0.8	SS(6): -1.0 • 2B(5): 0.3	0.2
2015	CHN	MLB	21	523	60	29	1	13	54	42	149	4	3	.242/.307/.389	.252	10.3	.324	-1.7	2B(86): 6.8 • SS(61): -2.5	1.6
2016	CHN	MLB	22	598	67	25	3	21	95	55	135	5	1	.238/.321/.417	.275	28.5	.277	-0.4	SS(148): 3.7	3.9
2017	CHN	MLB	23	597	67	27	2	21	74	48	145	5	2	.242/.311/.415	.258	23.5	.291	-0.7	SS 4	2.3
2018	CHN	MLB	24	568	73	26	1	22	74	49	137	5	2	.244/.318/.429	.272	25.6	.289	-0.9	SS 4	3.2

Breakout: 11%   Improve: 60%   Collapse: 1%   Attrition: 1%   MLB: 97%   Comparables: Troy Tulowitzki, Xander Bogaerts, Ryan Zimmerman

Russell is maybe the fourth- or fifth-best young shortstop in the game today, and possibly not even the best shortstop on his own team, but he's still pretty damn good: brilliant on defense and above-average at the plate, with pop. Still, you don't hear too much about him because a) this era's shortstop class is ridiculously loaded, and b) his bat may be his weakest tool. After whiffing nearly 30 percent of the time in 2015, Russell dropped his K rate by about one-fifth, while adding power and walking a bit more. He's a big boy and just 23 in 2017, so there's probably more room for growth. Look for an improved ability to foul off tough pitches at the upper and lower extremes of the strike zone and hands tucked tighter inside his body to muscle more inside pitches to right.

Kyle Schwarber   C

Born: 3/5/93   Age: 24   Bats: L   Throws: R   Height: 6'0"   Weight: 235   Entered Pro Ball: Round 1, 2014 Draft (#4 overall)

YEAR	TEAM	LVL	AGE	PA	R	2B	3B	HR	RBI	BB	K	SB	CS	AVG/OBP/SLG	TAv	VORP	BABIP	BRR	FRAA	WARP
2014	BOI	A-	21	24	7	1	1	4	10	2	2	0	1	.600/.625/1.350	.612	0.0	.533	0.0		0.0
2014	KNC	A	21	96	17	8	0	4	15	11	17	1	1	.361/.448/.602	.297	1.2	.419	-0.1	LF(2): 0.0 • C(1): 0.0	0.1
2014	DAY	A+	21	191	31	9	1	10	28	26	38	4	0	.302/.393/.560	.324	17.6	.328	-0.7	LF(26): 1.9 • C(9): -0.5	1.9
2015	TEN	AA	22	243	39	10	1	13	39	42	49	1	0	.320/.438/.579	.371	35.5	.365	0.3	C(37): 4.2	4.3
2015	IOW	AAA	22	67	7	7	1	3	10	7	23	0	0	.333/.403/.633	.385	11.5	.500	0.1	C(15): 0.1	1.2
2015	CHN	MLB	22	273	52	6	1	16	43	36	77	3	3	.246/.355/.487	.307	23.0	.293	3.4	LF(41): -3.1 • C(21): -1.4	2.0
2016	CHN	MLB	23	5	0	0	0	0	0	1	2	0	0	.000/.200/.000	.099	-0.7	.000	0.0	LF(2): 0.0	-0.1
2017	CHN	MLB	24	597	89	21	2	31	83	74	162	4	2	.248/.347/.477	.288	40.0	.297	-0.9	LF -5	2.8
2018	CHN	MLB	25	466	71	17	2	25	72	59	128	3	2	.249/.351/.486	.303	34.6	.298	3.2	LF -4	3.3

Breakout: 1%   Improve: 47%   Collapse: 14%   Attrition: 17%   MLB: 88%   Comparables: Joc Pederson, Brandon Belt, Pedro Alvarez

The thing about Schwarber is that it matters whether he can catch. The other thing about Schwarber is that we're really not sure whether he can catch. A horrific knee injury sustained in his second game of the 2016 campaign kept the young slugger out for the remainder of the regular season and cast increasingly deep shadows over what was already a fairly murky exercise for Schwarber. He's got the work ethic to be a first-tier backstop, and the Cubs' catching infrastructure—led by Mike Borzello and the coaching staff—shouldn't be second-guessed, but with knees being the way they are and his bat being as valuable as it is, it might not be worth it to force the issue. If they do and it works, he'll be an MVP candidate. If they don't, he'll still be a very good big-league hitter.

YEAR	TEAM	P. COUNT	FRM RUNS	BLK RUNS	THRW RUNS	TOT RUNS
2015	CHN	2400	-0.9	-0.2	-0.2	-1.4
2015	IOW	1863	0.8	-0.1	0.0	0.6
2015	TEN	4884	5.9	-1.1	-1.2	3.7

Matt Szczur   RF

Born: 7/20/89   Age: 27   Bats: R   Throws: R   Height: 6'0"   Weight: 200   Entered Pro Ball: Round 5, 2010 Draft (#160 overall)

YEAR	TEAM	LVL	AGE	PA	R	2B	3B	HR	RBI	BB	K	SB	CS	AVG/OBP/SLG	TAv	VORP	BABIP	BRR	FRAA	WARP
2014	IOW	AAA	24	457	52	16	1	1	24	30	78	30	7	.261/.315/.312	.230	-0.1	.318	2.1	CF(79): 4.2 • LF(20): 4.3	0.8
2014	CHN	MLB	24	66	6	2	0	2	5	4	11	0	0	.226/.273/.355	.216	-1.3	.245	0.0	RF(13): 1.3 • CF(9): -0.3	0.0
2015	IOW	AAA	25	305	40	12	2	8	31	22	51	20	5	.292/.355/.442	.305	22.3	.330	-0.3	CF(50): -0.0 • LF(10): -0.5	2.2
2015	CHN	MLB	25	80	5	5	0	1	8	6	15	2	0	.222/.278/.333	.229	0.1	.263	0.5	LF(26): -1.0 • CF(6): -0.9	-0.2
2016	CHN	MLB	26	200	30	9	1	5	24	13	39	2	4	.259/.312/.400	.265	6.2	.305	0.4	LF(50): -1.3 • CF(15): 1.9	0.8
2017	*CHN*	*MLB*	*27*	*121*	*13*	*5*	*0*	*2*	*11*	*8*	*24*	*4*	*1*	*.241/.291/.357*	*.234*	*1.3*	*.279*	*0.3*	*RF 1, CF 0*	*0.2*
2018	*CHN*	*MLB*	*28*	*274*	*30*	*10*	*1*	*6*	*28*	*18*	*57*	*9*	*3*	*.241/.295/.362*	*.239*	*2.2*	*.282*	*1.3*	*RF 2, CF 1*	*0.5*

Breakout: 4%   Improve: 23%   Collapse: 9%   Attrition: 31%   MLB: 60%   *Comparables: Logan Schafer, Josh Anderson, Eric Young*

Szczur's solid 2015 season at Triple-A got him the first extended big-league shot of his career in 2016 and he stuck with the Cubs all year as a backup outfielder. Speed and defense are his calling cards, but Szczur hit adequately enough to potentially be more than a once-a-week starter for a team that isn't overflowing in outfield depth like the Cubs are. More than anything, it's important that everyone reading this knows the effort required not to make a Caesar-related pun of some sort. When in Rome, ya know?

Mark Zagunis   OF

Born: 2/5/93   Age: 24   Bats: R   Throws: R   Height: 6'0"   Weight: 205   Entered Pro Ball: Round 3, 2014 Draft (#78 overall)

YEAR	TEAM	LVL	AGE	PA	R	2B	3B	HR	RBI	BB	K	SB	CS	AVG/OBP/SLG	TAv	VORP	BABIP	BRR	FRAA	WARP
2014	BOI	A-	21	191	32	9	2	2	27	31	31	11	2	.299/.429/.422	.250	2.2	.361	1.3	C(4): -0.1 • LF(3): -0.5	0.1
2014	KNC	A	21	62	11	6	1	0	4	10	9	5	0	.280/.419/.440	.320	6.3	.341	0.9	RF(4): 0.2 • LF(3): -0.1	0.7
2015	MYR	A+	22	512	78	24	5	8	54	80	86	12	10	.271/.406/.412	.317	39.2	.323	1.4	RF(80): -10.2 • LF(13): 1.5	3.2
2016	TEN	AA	23	211	30	13	1	4	24	30	36	1	2	.302/.408/.453	.306	11.2	.360	-2.7	LF(40): 4.2 • RF(8): -1.2	1.5
2016	IOW	AAA	23	211	31	12	4	6	25	22	42	4	0	.274/.360/.486	.301	13.5	.316	0.4	RF(33): -0.4 • LF(17): 0.1	1.4
2017	*CHN*	*MLB*	*24*	*250*	*29*	*11*	*2*	*7*	*30*	*30*	*57*	*2*	*1*	*.241/.346/.405*	*.265*	*9.0*	*.293*	*-0.2*	*LF 4, RF -1*	*1.2*
2018	*CHN*	*MLB*	*25*	*294*	*38*	*13*	*2*	*8*	*34*	*35*	*70*	*2*	*1*	*.242/.347/.408*	*.282*	*12.8*	*.300*	*-0.3*	*LF 4, RF -2*	*1.7*

Breakout: 1%   Improve: 11%   Collapse: 14%   Attrition: 19%   MLB: 40%   *Comparables: Alex Hassan, Chad Huffman, Khris Davis*

For a while Zagunis was among a handful of guys—along with Willson Contreras and Victor Caratini—whom the Cubs thought might one day be catching full time if everything broke the right way. Contreras made it to the majors as a catcher and he's staying there, but Zagunis hasn't caught since 2014 and is now a full-time outfielder. His bat has been solid to above average at every level, featuring good strike zone control and tons of walks, but at age 24 he's no longer young for his level.

Ben Zobrist   2B

Born: 5/26/81   Age: 36   Bats: B   Throws: R   Height: 6'3"   Weight: 210   Entered Pro Ball: Round 6, 2004 Draft (#184 overall)

YEAR	TEAM	LVL	AGE	PA	R	2B	3B	HR	RBI	BB	K	SB	CS	AVG/OBP/SLG	TAv	VORP	BABIP	BRR	FRAA	WARP
2014	TBA	MLB	33	654	83	34	3	10	52	75	84	10	5	.272/.354/.395	.288	35.8	.301	2.4	2B(79): 4.6 • LF(38): 2.6	4.7
2015	OAK	MLB	34	271	39	20	2	6	33	33	26	1	1	.268/.354/.447	.298	15.9	.277	-0.2	2B(34): -0.1 • LF(27): -0.9	1.6
2015	KCA	MLB	34	264	37	16	1	7	23	29	30	2	3	.284/.364/.453	.293	16.0	.299	1.2	2B(35): -2.3 • LF(18): -1.3	1.3
2016	CHN	MLB	35	631	94	31	3	18	76	96	82	6	4	.272/.386/.446	.306	49.2	.290	3.9	2B(119): -6.9 • LF(27): -1.3	4.1
2017	*CHN*	*MLB*	*36*	*645*	*81*	*32*	*3*	*14*	*63*	*79*	*88*	*7*	*4*	*.260/.353/.407*	*.275*	*35.0*	*.283*	*-1.2*	*2B -1, LF 0*	*2.9*
2018	*CHN*	*MLB*	*37*	*517*	*64*	*26*	*2*	*11*	*56*	*62*	*78*	*4*	*3*	*.255/.347/.400*	*.278*	*26.6*	*.282*	*1.9*	*2B -1, LF 0*	*2.9*

Breakout: 0%   Improve: 21%   Collapse: 10%   Attrition: 15%   MLB: 85%   *Comparables: Chase Utley, Barry Larkin, Lou Whitaker*

By the time the Cubs put the finishing touches on their 2016 season, Zobrist had been largely supplanted at second base by Javier Báez, but that didn't stop the 35-year-old jack-of-all-trades from making an impact in his first year in Chicago. Zobrist's elite contact and pitch-recognition skills showed no signs of decline, even as his still-strong positional flexibility shrunk a bit. As he continues to age and probably spends more and more time in the outfield, that defensive "decline" will continue, but remember that it's more a decline relative to our expectations of Zobrist than any real slide. That slide will come—36 is not an age at which upside starts to manifest—but Zobrist's offensive profile and value propositions are such that it might not become apparent for a few years yet.

PITCHERS

Jake Arrieta   RHP

Born: 3/6/86   Age: 31   Bats: R   Throws: R   Height: 6'4"   Weight: 225   Entered Pro Ball: Round 5, 2007 Draft (#159 overall)

YEAR	TEAM	LVL	AGE	W	L	SV	G	GS	IP	H	HR	BB/9	K/9	K	GB%	BABIP	WHIP	ERA	FIP	DRA	VORP	WARP	cFIP	MPH
2014	TEN	AA	28	1	1	0	4	4	14¹	8	0	3.1	6.9	11	62%	.200	0.91	1.26	2.70	3.83	2.2	0.2	92	
2014	CHN	MLB	28	10	5	0	25	25	156²	114	5	2.4	9.6	167	51%	.272	0.99	2.53	2.23	2.42	42.0	4.6	75	95.9
2015	CHN	MLB	29	22	6	0	33	33	229	150	10	1.9	9.3	236	58%	.246	0.86	1.77	2.38	2.89	55.8	6.0	73	97.0
2016	CHN	MLB	30	18	8	0	31	31	197¹	138	16	3.5	8.7	190	54%	.241	1.08	3.10	3.56	4.02	29.4	3.0	94	96.3
2017	*CHN*	*MLB*	*31*	*13*	*9*	*0*	*29*	*29*	*194¹*	*158*	*20*	*3.3*	*9.1*	*197*	*44%*	*.275*	*1.15*	*3.65*	*3.69*	*3.89*	*27.8*	*2.9*	*88*	
2018	*CHN*	*MLB*	*32*	*13*	*11*	*0*	*33*	*33*	*212¹*	*158*	*20*	*3.2*	*9.1*	*215*	*44%*	*.275*	*1.09*	*3.49*	*3.70*	*4.01*	*36.7*	*3.8*	*90*	

Breakout: 11%   Improve: 39%   Collapse: 25%   Attrition: 8%   MLB: 91%   *Comparables: Roy Halladay, Bob Gibson, Mike Fiers*

Arrieta rode his cut fastball to the Cy Young award in 2015, but he didn't have it in 2016. His usage of the pitch dropped by nearly a third, and his overall numbers suffered accordingly. He was still good, sure, even after accounting for the Cubs' transcendent defense, but without that cut fastball in the back of hitters' minds and the front of their strike zones, Arrieta transformed from league-wide ace to merely the third- or fourth-best pitcher on a very good starting staff. Meanwhile, his mechanics are high-energy enough that he'll need peak conditioning to stay on top; as he grows older, that'll be increasingly difficult to do. Bottom line: the present still looks good for Arrieta, but his future is increasingly murky.

Trevor Cahill   RHP

Born: 3/1/88   Age: 29   Bats: R   Throws: R   Height: 6'4"   Weight: 240   Entered Pro Ball: Round 2, 2006 Draft (#66 overall)

YEAR	TEAM	LVL	AGE	W	L	SV	G	GS	IP	H	HR	BB/9	K/9	K	GB%	BABIP	WHIP	ERA	FIP	DRA	VORP	WARP	cFIP	MPH
2014	RNO	AAA	26	2	2	0	6	6	28¹	21	4	6.4	8.6	27	63%	.254	1.45	3.49	5.75	3.21	8.0	0.8	92	
2014	ARI	MLB	26	3	12	1	32	17	110²	123	9	4.5	8.5	105	50%	.350	1.61	5.61	3.86	5.14	-4.6	-0.5	108	93.0
2015	ATL	MLB	27	0	3	0	15	3	26¹	36	2	3.8	4.8	14	64%	.354	1.78	7.52	4.45	3.95	2.5	0.3	98	94.1
2015	OKL	AAA	27	1	3	0	6	6	28²	32	3	4.4	5.3	17	51%	.299	1.60	6.28	5.24	5.22	0.0	0.0	109	
2015	CHN	MLB	27	1	0	0	11	0	17	8	2	2.6	11.6	22	63%	.182	0.76	2.12	3.16	3.86	1.8	0.2	97	95.2
2016	IOW	AAA	28	0	3	0	6	6	19²	25	3	5.5	11.4	25	53%	.407	1.88	4.58	5.14	4.41	2.0	0.2	95	
2016	CHN	MLB	28	4	4	0	50	1	65²	49	7	4.8	9.0	66	51%	.246	1.28	2.74	4.39	3.80	8.8	0.9	101	95.1
2017	CHN	MLB	29	5	4	0	31	11	78¹	64	9	4.0	8.0	70	51%	.280	1.26	4.22	4.33	4.87	5.2	0.5	112	
2018	CHN	MLB	30	3	3	0	22	9	69²	62	8	4.4	8.4	65	51%	.304	1.38	4.40	4.69	5.08	2.5	0.3	118	

Breakout: 25%   Improve: 46%   Collapse: 29%   Attrition: 19%   MLB: 90%   *Comparables: Tyson Ross, Edinson Volquez, David Phelps*

When his stuff is on it makes you wonder why Cahill isn't the first reliever out of the bullpen every night. His curve curves. His changeup drops way out of the zone. All of his pitches generate high rates of swings and misses and ground balls. Those are all good things! And then he goes and puts up numbers that say he's merely an adequate relief arm. Which is what he is. Something about his sequencing hasn't quite clicked. Something about his command hasn't quite come together.

Dylan Cease   RHP

Born: 12/28/95   Age: 21   Bats: R   Throws: R   Height: 6'2"   Weight: 190   Entered Pro Ball: Round 6, 2014 Draft (#169 overall)

YEAR	TEAM	LVL	AGE	W	L	SV	G	GS	IP	H	HR	BB/9	K/9	K	GB%	BABIP	WHIP	ERA	FIP	DRA	VORP	WARP	cFIP	MPH
2016	EUG	A-	20	2	0	0	12	12	44²	27	1	5.0	13.3	66	55%	.295	1.16	2.22	2.92	2.14	15.4	1.6	84	
2017	CHN	MLB	21	2	3	0	10	10	35²	29	3	5.6	8.2	33	33%	.291	1.45	4.42	4.39	4.98	2.3	0.2	116	
2018	CHN	MLB	22	6	8	0	30	30	185	141	15	5.8	10.2	209	33%	.302	1.41	4.01	4.29	4.52	12.6	1.3	105	

Breakout: 1%   Improve: 1%   Collapse: 0%   Attrition: 1%   MLB: 1%   *Comparables: Vincent Velasquez, T.J. McFarland, Alex Colome*

Cease may have been drafted in the first round had he not undergone Tommy John surgery as a high school senior. He fell to the Cubs in the sixth round and has performed very well since. His command has been somewhat iffy at age 21, but his fastball and power curve stand out. He's still in the lower reaches of the Cubs' system but might be the best bet of any arm they have to eventually become a star in the majors.

Wade Davis   RHP

Born: 9/7/85   Age: 31   Bats: R   Throws: R   Height: 6'5"   Weight: 225   Entered Pro Ball: Round 3, 2004 Draft (#75 overall)

YEAR	TEAM	LVL	AGE	W	L	SV	G	GS	IP	H	HR	BB/9	K/9	K	GB%	BABIP	WHIP	ERA	FIP	DRA	VORP	WARP	cFIP	MPH
2014	KCA	MLB	28	9	2	3	72	0	72	38	0	2.9	13.6	109	49%	.264	0.85	1.00	1.22	1.44	24.4	2.7	57	98.5
2015	KCA	MLB	29	8	1	17	69	0	67¹	33	3	2.7	10.4	78	39%	.200	0.79	0.94	2.26	3.23	11.1	1.2	80	98.4
2016	KCA	MLB	30	2	1	27	45	0	43¹	33	0	3.3	9.8	47	48%	.300	1.13	1.87	2.25	3.73	6.0	0.6	90	97.8
2017	CHN	MLB	31	3	2	41	50	0	53	43	6	3.4	11.0	65	50%	.290	1.18	3.11	3.42	3.51	8.3	0.9	73	
2018	CHN	MLB	32	3	1	55	65	0	69¹	53	8	3.1	10.7	83	50%	.297	1.11	3.33	3.51	3.81	10.1	1.0	82	

Breakout: 16%   Improve: 31%   Collapse: 33%   Attrition: 9%   MLB: 87%   *Comparables: Sean Marshall, C.J. Wilson, Ryan Madson*

Who knew even cyborgs can break down? The warning signs were there from the start, namely a decline in velocity of his fastball and cutter. Was it fatigue from the extra mileage of back-to-back postseason runs? Or something more sinister? Davis' velocity peaked in June, but a strained forearm landed the Royals' closer on the disabled list twice—the first time just ahead of the All-Star break and then again for the entire month of August. Despite the arm worries, he was still dominant, just not as dominant as we've come to expect. Traded to Chicago in the final year of a contract extension signed while still in Tampa Bay, he'll take over for Aroldis Chapman as the Cubs' closer and try to re-establish his cyborg bonafides.

Carl Edwards Jr   RHP

Born: 9/3/91   Age: 25   Bats: R   Throws: R   Height: 6'3"   Weight: 170   Entered Pro Ball: Round 48, 2011 Draft (#1464 overall)

YEAR	TEAM	LVL	AGE	W	L	SV	G	GS	IP	H	HR	BB/9	K/9	K	GB%	BABIP	WHIP	ERA	FIP	DRA	VORP	WARP	cFIP	MPH
2014	TEN	AA	22	1	2	0	10	10	48	30	1	3.9	8.6	46	47%	.234	1.06	2.44	2.92	4.36	4.6	0.5	89	
2015	TEN	AA	23	2	2	4	13	0	23²	11	1	6.5	13.7	36	67%	.222	1.18	2.66	2.96	2.34	6.3	0.7	74	
2015	IOW	AAA	23	3	1	2	23	0	31²	15	0	6.8	11.1	39	44%	.221	1.23	2.84	3.50	2.92	7.0	0.7	94	
2015	CHN	MLB	23	0	0	0	5	0	4²	3	0	5.8	7.7	4	58%	.250	1.29	3.86	3.38	4.46	0.1	0.0	104	96.0
2016	IOW	AAA	24	1	1	1	24	0	25¹	17	1	6.0	12.4	35	40%	.286	1.34	4.26	3.60	3.37	4.5	0.5	93	
2016	CHN	MLB	24	0	1	2	36	0	36	15	4	3.5	13.0	52	51%	.162	0.81	3.75	2.91	2.46	10.1	1.0	70	97.6
2017	CHN	MLB	25	2	2	0	46	0	49	37	4	4.2	9.9	54	45%	.274	1.20	3.55	3.56	3.90	5.5	0.6	86	
2018	CHN	MLB	26	3	1	0	50	0	52²	32	5	4.9	12.1	71	45%	.275	1.15	3.36	3.55	3.86	7.4	0.8	83	

Breakout: 21%   Improve: 44%   Collapse: 21%   Attrition: 23%   MLB: 79%   *Comparables: Rafael Montero, Jess Todd, Nick Tropeano*

Edwards, picked out of the literal bush league in the 48th round of 2011's draft, can pitch a little. The String Bean Slinger leveraged his 6-foot-3 frame and unnaturally long fingers to enormous success at every minor-league level before finally debuting with the Cubs late in 2015. His command is still a work in progress, and he's still struggling to keep on weight even as he gobbles up every pasta plate and fried egg sandwich in sight, but the basic formula he executes—tall man throws ball fast—is still likely to render him at least a few more years of big-league success out of the bullpen. The upside could give him far more than that.

Justin Grimm   RHP

Born: 8/16/88   Age: 28   Bats: R   Throws: R   Height: 6'3"   Weight: 210   Entered Pro Ball: Round 5, 2010 Draft (#166 overall)

YEAR	TEAM	LVL	AGE	W	L	SV	G	GS	IP	H	HR	BB/9	K/9	K	GB%	BABIP	WHIP	ERA	FIP	DRA	VORP	WARP	cFIP	MPH
2014	CHN	MLB	25	5	2	0	73	0	69	59	4	3.5	9.1	70	51%	.294	1.25	3.78	3.18	3.47	7.8	0.9	93	96.8
2015	CHN	MLB	26	3	5	3	62	0	49²	31	4	4.7	12.1	67	46%	.255	1.15	1.99	3.14	3.31	7.8	0.8	89	97.8
2016	CHN	MLB	27	2	1	0	68	0	52²	47	5	3.9	11.1	65	42%	.321	1.33	4.10	3.32	3.52	8.5	0.9	95	96.5
2017	*CHN*	*MLB*	*28*	*2*	*2*	*0*	*46*	*0*	*49*	*42*	*4*	*3.9*	*9.9*	*54*	*54%*	*.296*	*1.30*	*3.45*	*3.43*	*3.81*	*6.0*	*0.6*	*84*	
2018	*CHN*	*MLB*	*29*	*3*	*1*	*0*	*51*	*0*	*53²*	*42*	*5*	*3.9*	*10.7*	*64*	*54%*	*.307*	*1.21*	*3.40*	*3.61*	*3.91*	*7.2*	*0.7*	*85*	

Breakout: 16%   Improve: 60%   Collapse: 14%   Attrition: 12%   MLB: 88%   *Comparables: Carlos Carrasco, Zach McAllister, Angel Guzman*

Grimm is the Jeff Samardzija of relievers. Every time you see him throw a bullpen session, you're sure he's going to be something special once he gets out on the mound. And indeed, sometimes he's brilliant—his stuff is just too good for him not to be. But it's never fully come together for Grimm, even after a 1.99 ERA in 2015, and it's not entirely evident why. Some of the inconsistency is due to injuries, but some probably comes down to there not being one single Grimm arsenal or one single Grimm approach. To wit: he ditched his slider entirely in 2016, after throwing it as much as a quarter of the time in prior years, and may yet have an entirely different look in 2017. Heck, maybe that version will dominate.

Jason Hammel   RHP

Born: 9/2/82   Age: 34   Bats: R   Throws: R   Height: 6'6"   Weight: 225   Entered Pro Ball: Round 10, 2002 Draft (#284 overall)

YEAR	TEAM	LVL	AGE	W	L	SV	G	GS	IP	H	HR	BB/9	K/9	K	GB%	BABIP	WHIP	ERA	FIP	DRA	VORP	WARP	cFIP	MPH
2014	CHN	MLB	31	8	5	0	17	17	108²	88	10	1.9	8.6	104	41%	.272	1.02	2.98	3.16	3.72	13.5	1.5	101	94.7
2014	OAK	MLB	31	2	6	0	13	12	67²	66	13	2.8	7.2	54	38%	.272	1.29	4.26	5.13	4.08	5.7	0.6	102	94.9
2015	CHN	MLB	32	10	7	0	31	31	170²	158	23	2.1	9.1	172	41%	.288	1.16	3.74	3.71	4.15	17.7	1.9	98	94.4
2016	CHN	MLB	33	15	10	0	30	30	166²	148	25	2.9	7.8	144	44%	.267	1.21	3.83	4.52	4.97	7.1	0.7	111	94.3
2017	*CHN*	*MLB*	*34*	*9*	*8*	*0*	*25*	*25*	*141¹*	*117*	*21*	*3.0*	*8.1*	*126*	*52%*	*.273*	*1.16*	*4.35*	*4.41*	*5.02*	*8.5*	*0.9*	*118*	
2018	*CHN*	*MLB*	*35*	*10*	*12*	*0*	*31*	*31*	*197¹*	*184*	*32*	*2.9*	*8.2*	*179*	*52%*	*.299*	*1.25*	*4.53*	*4.83*	*5.23*	*6.4*	*0.7*	*124*	

Breakout: 19%   Improve: 44%   Collapse: 19%   Attrition: 10%   MLB: 86%   *Comparables: A.J. Burnett, James Shields, Ted Lilly*

The question with Hammel coming into 2016 was whether he could thrive in the second half. There was no reason he shouldn't be able to, except he hadn't. Not in 2014, when he was traded to Oakland midseason in the Addison Russell deal. And not in 2015, when a lower-half injury had him fading fast down the stretch. He pitched much better in the second half of 2016—although his 4.35 ERA still wasn't what you'd call brilliant—and was left off the postseason roster in favor of a four-man rotation. Hammel can look outright dominant when his heavy stuff is working but he's not been able to put that together into a full season's worth of work yet. At age 34, he doesn't have many more chances to prove it.

Kyle Hendricks   RHP

Born: 12/7/89   Age: 27   Bats: R   Throws: R   Height: 6'3"   Weight: 190   Entered Pro Ball: Round 8, 2011 Draft (#264 overall)

YEAR	TEAM	LVL	AGE	W	L	SV	G	GS°	IP	H	HR	BB/9	K/9	K	GB%	BABIP	WHIP	ERA	FIP	DRA	VORP	WARP	cFIP	MPH
2014	IOW	AAA	24	10	5	0	17	17	102²	98	5	2.0	8.5	97	56%	.322	1.18	3.59	3.17	1.26	51.3	5.1	71	
2014	CHN	MLB	24	7	2	0	13	13	80¹	72	4	1.7	5.3	47	51%	.271	1.08	2.46	3.29	3.96	7.9	0.9	102	90.6
2015	CHN	MLB	25	8	7	0	32	32	180	166	17	2.2	8.4	167	54%	.296	1.16	3.95	3.38	3.13	38.9	4.2	89	90.7
2016	CHN	MLB	26	16	8	0	31	30	190	142	15	2.1	8.1	170	50%	.250	0.98	2.13	3.24	3.34	42.5	4.4	92	90.2
2017	*CHN*	*MLB*	*27*	*11*	*9*	*0*	*29*	*29*	*165¹*	*149*	*18*	*2.6*	*8.0*	*147*	*49%*	*.283*	*1.17*	*3.83*	*3.81*	*4.08*	*20.2*	*2.1*	*93*	
2018	*CHN*	*MLB*	*28*	*11*	*10*	*0*	*31*	*31*	*197²*	*152*	*21*	*3.0*	*9.3*	*204*	*49%*	*.281*	*1.10*	*3.60*	*3.81*	*4.13*	*27.8*	*2.9*	*93*	

Breakout: 25%   Improve: 48%   Collapse: 21%   Attrition: 17%   MLB: 92%   *Comparables: Garrett Richards, Jeff Niemann, Drew Pomeranz*

Hendricks is a weird mix of real-world privilege—a SoCal white boy educated at Dartmouth—and whatever is the baseball equivalent of the University of Phoenix. Like Phoenix graduates all around the country (at least relative to Big Green alums), Hendricks has had to work a little harder to prove himself at every level. He never had a wipeout pitch. He never threw much faster than your average D1 Friday night starter. All he had to go on were his results, and his results were always excellent. He put up a 1.93 ERA at A-ball in 2011, at age 21. OK, but Double-A is the big talent jump. Let's see how he does there. That took a little longer, but Hendricks had a 1.88 ERA in 129 Double-A innings, finally leaving the level behind for good in 2013. OK, but at Triple-A hitters have finally learned to hit the changeup and that's Hendricks's bread and butter. Hendricks had a 3.28 ERA in 143 innings there. And now Hendricks has a 2.92 ERA in 450 big-league innings. Hendricks' numbers will probably never look as good again as they did in 2016 and the comparisons to Greg Maddux are still way overblown, but Hendricks is a top-tier major-league starter, and that's a hell of a lot more than the league believed of him just 18 months ago.

Pierce Johnson   RHP

Born: 5/10/91   Age: 26   Bats: R   Throws: R   Height: 6'3"   Weight: 200   Entered Pro Ball: Round 1, 2012 Draft (#43 overall)

YEAR	TEAM	LVL	AGE	W	L	SV	G	GS	IP	H	HR	BB/9	K/9	K	GB%	BABIP	WHIP	ERA	FIP	DRA	VORP	WARP	cFIP	MPH
2014	KNC	A	23	0	1	0	2	2	11	4	1	2.5	6.5	8	63%	.115	0.64	2.45	4.30	4.35	1.3	0.1	100	
2014	TEN	AA	23	5	4	0	18	17	91²	60	8	5.3	8.9	91	44%	.242	1.24	2.55	4.27	4.02	12.2	1.3	103	
2015	TEN	AA	24	6	2	0	16	16	95	76	4	3.0	6.8	72	42%	.266	1.14	2.08	3.47	3.23	19.6	2.1	101	
2016	IOW	AAA	25	4	6	0	22	11	63	60	8	6.1	10.7	75	47%	.331	1.63	6.14	5.28	3.10	14.8	1.5	101	
2017	*CHN*	*MLB*	*26*	*2*	*2*	*0*	*5*	*5*	*25*	*24*	*3*	*4.4*	*7.4*	*20*	*50%*	*.293*	*1.43*	*4.62*	*4.70*	*4.92*	*0.7*	*0.1*	*100*	
2018	*CHN*	*MLB*	*27*	*9*	*11*	*0*	*31*	*31*	*198*	*149*	*24*	*5.3*	*10.3*	*226*	*50%*	*.288*	*1.34*	*4.37*	*4.67*	*5.04*	*9.0*	*0.9*	*118*	

Breakout: 3%   Improve: 18%   Collapse: 5%   Attrition: 24%   MLB: 33%   *Comparables: Sam LeCure, Yohan Pino, Hector Ambriz*

Johnson—whose name is a regrettable concatenation of the surnames of two forgettable Democratic presidents of the mid-19th century—looked for a little while like he might be the first Epstein-era pitching prospect to reach Wrigley Field. Then he had a stinker of an Arizona Fall League in 2015 and followed it with an even uglier run through Triple-A last year. He'll need to get his command right in 2017—and get some more movement on his pitches, which are looking flat—if he wants to hurdle that last barrier. Triple-A hitters are ready for your mid-count pitches in the zone if you're constantly getting to 2-0 on them, and they don't miss often.

John Lackey   RHP

Born: 10/23/78   Age: 38   Bats: R   Throws: R   Height: 6'6"   Weight: 235   Entered Pro Ball: Round 2, 1999 Draft (#68 overall)

YEAR	TEAM	LVL	AGE	W	L	SV	G	GS	IP	H	HR	BB/9	K/9	K	GB%	BABIP	WHIP	ERA	FIP	DRA	VORP	WARP	cFIP	MPH
2014	BOS	MLB	35	11	7	0	21	21	137¹	137	15	2.1	7.6	116	49%	.298	1.23	3.60	3.59	3.59	19.0	2.1	94	94.8
2014	SLN	MLB	35	3	3	0	10	10	60²	69	9	2.2	7.1	48	43%	.319	1.38	4.30	4.24	3.46	9.3	1.0	94	93.6
2015	SLN	MLB	36	13	10	0	33	33	218	211	21	2.2	7.2	175	48%	.295	1.21	2.77	3.59	4.24	20.3	2.2	101	94.4
2016	CHN	MLB	37	11	8	0	29	29	188¹	146	23	2.5	8.6	180	44%	.255	1.06	3.35	3.85	3.99	28.6	3.0	98	94.4
2017	*CHN*	*MLB*	*38*	*13*	*10*	*0*	*29*	*29*	*194¹*	*176*	*25*	*2.9*	*8.3*	*179*	*43%*	*.283*	*1.21*	*4.09*	*4.07*	*4.37*	*17.5*	*1.8*	*100*	
2018	*CHN*	*MLB*	*39*	*13*	*12*	*0*	*32*	*32*	*211¹*	*175*	*25*	*2.8*	*8.2*	*192*	*43%*	*.283*	*1.14*	*3.89*	*4.13*	*4.48*	*25.5*	*2.6*	*104*	

Breakout: 13%   Improve: 37%   Collapse: 14%   Attrition: 11%   MLB: 73%   *Comparables: Andy Pettitte, Derek Lowe, Chris Carpenter*

Some pitchers pitch to batters, as is traditional. Lackey snarls batters into submission. Lackey once killed a squirrel by throwing another squirrel directly at it from 300 yards away. (It was a clean kill, although the thrown squirrel died, too.) Lackey once scared a reporter out of the industry just by holding his gaze a little longer than usual after hearing a question he didn't like. Lackey once ordered liver and onions at a French restaurant, then sent the plate back because the chef cooked the food first. Lackey once fished for sharks barehanded. And in 2016, Lackey snarled at batters. He dropped his sinker too—in favor of his four-seam fastball, slider and curve—and had one of the best seasons of his career at age 37.

Jon Lester   LHP

Born: 1/7/84   Age: 33   Bats: L   Throws: L   Height: 6'4"   Weight: 240   Entered Pro Ball: Round 2, 2002 Draft (#57 overall)

YEAR	TEAM	LVL	AGE	W	L	SV	G	GS	IP	H	HR	BB/9	K/9	K	GB%	BABIP	WHIP	ERA	FIP	DRA	VORP	WARP	cFIP	MPH
2014	BOS	MLB	30	10	7	0	21	21	143	128	9	2.0	9.4	149	46%	.308	1.12	2.52	2.65	2.27	40.8	4.5	79	94.4
2014	OAK	MLB	30	6	4	0	11	11	76²	66	7	1.9	8.3	71	43%	.281	1.07	2.35	3.16	2.61	18.9	2.1	79	93.7
2015	CHN	MLB	31	11	12	0	32	32	205	183	16	2.1	9.1	207	50%	.304	1.12	3.34	2.95	2.85	50.7	5.4	82	94.3
2016	CHN	MLB	32	19	5	0	32	32	202²	154	21	2.3	8.7	197	48%	.256	1.02	2.44	3.45	3.10	51.0	5.3	90	94.4
2017	*CHN*	*MLB*	*33*	*14*	*10*	*0*	*29*	*29*	*203*	*176*	*23*	*2.7*	*9.3*	*210*	*50%*	*.288*	*1.15*	*3.60*	*3.60*	*3.82*	*30.7*	*3.2*	*87*	
2018	*CHN*	*MLB*	*34*	*14*	*12*	*0*	*32*	*32*	*211¹*	*177*	*26*	*2.6*	*9.2*	*216*	*50%*	*.297*	*1.12*	*3.69*	*3.90*	*4.22*	*33.0*	*3.4*	*97*	

Breakout: 12%   Improve: 42%   Collapse: 32%   Attrition: 30%   MLB: 94%   *Comparables: CC Sabathia, A.J. Burnett, Adam Wainwright*

Lester never seemed particularly comfortable being the $155 million man during his first year in Chicago. Last year—with a season's worth of success under his belt and Jason Heyward's contract sucking up much of the media oxygen—Lester raised the level of his game from its already high starting point. The change was especially noticeable in the second half, when the big lefty posted a 1.76 ERA in nearly 100 innings. He learned to ignore runners dancing off first base, which will matter a great deal this year without a now-retired David Ross around to help him manage the running game. Look for another solid season from Lester in 2017, but don't count on his caught-stealing rate to stay quite as high.

Mike Montgomery   LHP

Born: 7/1/89   Age: 27   Bats: L   Throws: L   Height: 6'5"   Weight: 215   Entered Pro Ball: Round 1, 2008 Draft (#36 overall)

YEAR	TEAM	LVL	AGE	W	L	SV	G	GS	IP	H	HR	BB/9	K/9	K	GB%	BABIP	WHIP	ERA	FIP	DRA	VORP	WARP	cFIP	MPH
2014	DUR	AAA	24	10	5	0	25	25	126	117	9	3.4	7.0	98	51%	.285	1.31	4.29	3.99	5.98	-3.1	-0.3	105	
2015	SEA	MLB	25	4	6	0	16	16	90	92	11	3.7	6.4	64	53%	.291	1.43	4.60	4.64	4.43	6.5	0.7	105	93.4
2015	TAC	AAA	25	4	3	0	11	11	65¹	59	3	2.6	8	58	51%	.299	1.19	4.13	3.43	3.28	14.7	1.5	90	
2016	SEA	MLB	26	3	4	0	32	2	61²	49	3	2.6	7.9	54	59%	.272	1.09	2.34	3.15	3.94	8.0	0.8	91	96.4
2016	CHN	MLB	26	1	1	0	17	5	38¹	30	5	4.7	8.9	38	61%	.258	1.30	2.82	4.78	3.81	5.5	0.6	91	95.5
2017	*CHN*	*MLB*	*27*	*8*	*8*	*0*	*24*	*24*	*127*	*118*	*13*	*3.2*	*7.6*	*107*	*64%*	*.287*	*1.27*	*4.02*	*4.07*	*4.29*	*12.6*	*1.3*	*100*	
2018	*CHN*	*MLB*	*28*	*9*	*10*	*0*	*29*	*29*	*175²*	*138*	*19*	*3.9*	*9.2*	*180*	*64%*	*.287*	*1.22*	*3.96*	*4.21*	*4.56*	*16.7*	*1.7*	*105*	

Breakout: 35%   Improve: 53%   Collapse: 19%   Attrition: 34%   MLB: 87%   *Comparables: Joe Saunders, Alex Colome, David Phelps*

Montgomery is now the answer to a trivia question. But he already would have been. Promise. Seems like every generation has a dozen or so of this type of pitcher out there, stuck halfway between starter and reliever. Montgomery did a bit more than that in 2016, going on the best run of his short big-league career in Chicago at the end of the season, and he'll probably have a shot to try his pitch mix in the starting rotation this year. The Cubs are confident he'll be able to do it, but the history of this type of pitcher is not on Montgomery's side.

Hector Rondon   RHP

Born: 2/26/88   Age: 29   Bats: R   Throws: R   Height: 6'3"   Weight: 230   Entered Pro Ball: International Free Agent, 2004

YEAR	TEAM	LVL	AGE	W	L	SV	G	GS	IP	H	HR	BB/9	K/9	K	GB%	BABIP	WHIP	ERA	FIP	DRA	VORP	WARP	cFIP	MPH
2014	CHN	MLB	26	4	4	29	64	0	63¹	52	2	2.1	9.0	63	50%	.286	1.06	2.42	2.23	3.10	9.7	1.1	85	98.7
2015	CHN	MLB	27	6	4	30	72	0	70	55	4	1.9	8.9	69	53%	.268	1.00	1.67	2.70	3.51	9.3	1.0	87	99.0
2016	CHN	MLB	28	2	3	18	54	0	51	42	8	1.4	10.2	58	49%	.274	0.98	3.53	3.53	2.71	12.8	1.3	81	98.5
2017	*CHN*	*MLB*	*29*	*3*	*3*	*2*	*50*	*0*	*53*	*49*	*7*	*2.8*	*9.1*	*54*	*45%*	*.288*	*1.22*	*3.94*	*3.87*	*4.22*	*4.1*	*0.4*	*96*	
2018	*CHN*	*MLB*	*30*	*3*	*1*	*2*	*62*	*0*	*66*	*54*	*8*	*2.6*	*9.0*	*66*	*45%*	*.285*	*1.11*	*3.70*	*3.91*	*4.24*	*6.5*	*0.7*	*96*	

Breakout: 27%   Improve: 53%   Collapse: 27%   Attrition: 15%   MLB: 96%   *Comparables: Bobby Jenks, Jeff Nelson, Francisco Rodriguez*

By DRA, last season was the best of Rondon's career, but you wouldn't know it by the press he got. After emerging as one of the league's better closers in 2015, Rondon was supplanted midseason by Chicago's deadline acquisition of Aroldis Chapman. He spent some time on the disabled list and generally flew well under the radar for much of the season. Don't let that fool you. Rondon can throw nearly as fast as anyone but Chapman, with somewhat better control and a much better ground-ball rate. His slider, when it's on, is devastating. And he's proven, over the last three seasons, that he isn't afraid of big moments. Not many relievers are consistently great year over year. Rondon may be one of them.

Zac Rosscup   LHP

Born: 6/9/88   Age: 29   Bats: R   Throws: L   Height: 6'2"   Weight: 220   Entered Pro Ball: Round 28, 2009 Draft (#859 overall)

YEAR	TEAM	LVL	AGE	W	L	SV	G	GS	IP	H	HR	BB/9	K/9	K	GB%	BABIP	WHIP	ERA	FIP	DRA	VORP	WARP	cFIP	MPH
2014	IOW	AAA	26	2	0	4	29	0	30	18	0	4.5	11.4	38	29%	.265	1.10	2.10	2.67	4.91	1.4	0.1	89	
2014	CHN	MLB	26	1	0	0	18	0	13¹	14	2	8.1	14.2	21	30%	.387	1.95	9.45	4.60	4.05	0.6	0.1	101	94.6
2015	IOW	AAA	27	0	0	0	11	0	11¹	8	1	3.2	15.9	20	30%	.318	1.06	4.76	2.54	1.61	4.2	0.4	78	
2015	CHN	MLB	27	2	1	0	33	0	26²	26	5	4.4	9.8	29	38%	.296	1.46	4.39	4.89	4.68	0.1	0.0	106	95.5
2017	CHN	MLB	29	2	1	1	35	0	37¹	30	5	3.7	9.3	38	50%	.287	1.22	3.99	4.20	4.59	2.1	0.2	104	
2018	CHN	MLB	30	3	1	1	59	0	55²	44	7	4.3	10.3	63	50%	.293	1.27	4.02	4.28	4.63	3.2	0.3	105	

Breakout: 14%   Improve: 33%   Collapse: 12%   Attrition: 24%   MLB: 63%   Comparables: Brian Falkenborg, Henry Owens, Chris Schroder

There was a time—2013, to be precise—when it looked like Rosscup would be a big part of the Cubs' next championship bullpen. He wasn't, undergoing shoulder surgery and sitting out the entire 2016 season at the big-league level. Even before his injury, things weren't quite right, as the fastball/slider mix that carried him to success through the high minors and into the big leagues never really worked. With that kind of pitch mix, you need either a) really good pitches, or b) perfect execution. Rosscup had neither. If he's honestly and truly back to form in 2017, he could be a nice bullpen arm.

Pedro Strop   RHP

Born: 6/13/85   Age: 32   Bats: R   Throws: R   Height: 6'1"   Weight: 220   Entered Pro Ball: International Free Agent, 2002

YEAR	TEAM	LVL	AGE	W	L	SV	G	GS	IP	H	HR	BB/9	K/9	K	GB%	BABIP	WHIP	ERA	FIP	DRA	VORP	WARP	cFIP	MPH
2014	CHN	MLB	29	2	4	2	65	0	61	40	2	3.7	10.5	71	56%	.268	1.07	2.21	2.63	2.56	13.0	1.4	79	97.3
2015	CHN	MLB	30	2	6	3	76	0	68	39	5	3.8	10.7	81	53%	.225	1.00	2.91	3.19	3.10	12.2	1.3	83	97.5
2016	CHN	MLB	31	2	2	0	54	0	47¹	27	4	2.9	11.4	60	61%	.221	0.89	2.85	2.95	2.39	13.6	1.4	71	97.0
2017	CHN	MLB	32	2	2	0	42	0	44	35	5	3.6	10.6	52	57%	.281	1.17	3.48	3.64	3.83	5.4	0.6	84	
2018	CHN	MLB	33	3	1	0	60	0	63²	46	7	3.8	9.8	69	57%	.271	1.14	3.84	4.03	4.37	5.3	0.5	98	

Breakout: 22%   Improve: 46%   Collapse: 20%   Attrition: 9%   MLB: 94%   Comparables: Scot Shields, Luke Gregerson, Sean Marshall

At this point, you sort of know what you're going to get with Strop. Opponents will hit him to a TAv of about .260 (that's good!), he'll strike out about 30 percent of the batters he faces (that's better!) and he'll get them to hit the ball on the ground about 55 percent of the time (that's very solid!). Put it all together, and you have a picture of one of the more consistent relief pitchers in baseball, now five years into a run of success. If his arm doesn't fall off—he looked gassed at the end of the Cubs' postseason run—there's no particular reason to suspect he won't be roughly as effective again in 2017. If the arm does fall off, well, there's a recipe for disaster waiting here.

Koji Uehara   RHP

Born: 4/3/75   Age: 42   Bats: R   Throws: R   Height: 6'2"   Weight: 195   Entered Pro Ball: International Free Agent, 2009

YEAR	TEAM	LVL	AGE	W	L	SV	G	GS	IP	H	HR	BB/9	K/9	K	GB%	BABIP	WHIP	ERA	FIP	DRA	VORP	WARP	cFIP	MPH
2014	BOS	MLB	39	6	5	26	64	0	64¹	51	10	1.1	11.2	80	35%	.273	0.92	2.52	3.11	2.33	15.4	1.7	73	90.3
2015	BOS	MLB	40	2	4	25	43	0	40¹	28	3	2.0	10.5	47	29%	.248	0.92	2.23	2.41	4.22	2.2	0.2	92	89.1
2016	BOS	MLB	41	2	3	7	50	0	47	34	8	2.1	12.1	63	27%	.260	0.96	3.45	3.47	2.80	11.3	1.2	84	88.8
2017	CHN	MLB	42	2	2	3	38	0	40	32	6	2.6	10.6	47	37%	.279	1.07	3.41	3.75	3.76	5.1	0.5	83	
2018	CHN	MLB	43	3	1	3	51	0	54¹	39	7	2.2	10.1	61	37%	.268	0.96	3.48	3.52	3.80	7.9	0.8	84	

Breakout: 7%   Improve: 22%   Collapse: 27%   Attrition: 15%   MLB: 64%   Comparables: Takashi Saito, Trevor Hoffman, Arthur Rhodes

When Uehara hit the DL with a pectoral strain on July 19th, it looked like his career was over. After years of dominance, Uehara appeared frighteningly mortal in 2016, coughing up a 4.50 ERA and allowing a .448 slugging percentage in the 36 innings preceding his injury. But Uehara wasn't done giving high-fives. The 41-year-old returned on September 7th and looked like his old self rather than his elderly self, holding opponents to a .167/.231/.222 line and refusing to allow an earned run in 11 innings. Many assumed Uehara would retire this offseason, but despite Uehara's age, 86-mph fastball and obvious limitations—he can't pitch on back-to-back days—the Cubs added him to their ex-Red Sox collection on a one-year deal.

Travis Wood   LHP

Born: 2/6/87   Age: 30   Bats: R   Throws: L   Height: 5'11"   Weight: 175   Entered Pro Ball: Round 2, 2005 Draft (#60 overall)

YEAR	TEAM	LVL	AGE	W	L	SV	G	GS	IP	H	HR	BB/9	K/9	K	GB%	BABIP	WHIP	ERA	FIP	DRA	VORP	WARP	cFIP	MPH
2014	CHN	MLB	27	8	13	0	31	31	173²	190	20	3.9	7.6	146	37%	.320	1.53	5.03	4.35	6.35	-29.3	-3.2	117	91.1
2015	CHN	MLB	28	5	4	4	54	9	100²	86	11	3.5	10.5	118	37%	.300	1.24	3.84	3.43	4.04	9.3	1.0	98	93.3
2016	CHN	MLB	29	4	0	0	77	0	61	45	8	3.5	6.9	47	38%	.215	1.13	2.95	4.58	5.75	-5.3	-0.5	122	93.1
2017	CHN	MLB	30	4	3	0	21	8	60¹	49	9	3.5	8.3	55	46%	.266	1.20	4.50	4.54	5.20	1.8	0.2	122	
2018	CHN	MLB	31	7	8	1	51	19	142²	128	23	3.5	8.3	132	46%	.290	1.28	4.72	5.02	5.45	0.2	0.0	129	

Breakout: 11%   Improve: 36%   Collapse: 31%   Attrition: 17%   MLB: 88%   Comparables: Shaun Marcum, Daisuke Matsuzaka, Clay Buchholz

As a starter, Wood was never particularly effective, mostly because he never seemed to have a good idea of when to use any of his three fastballs (a four-seamer, a sinker and a cutter). Since transitioning to the bullpen full-time, Wood has ditched the sinker almost entirely and diminished his use of the cutter, instead relying on the four-seam to set up an increasingly effective slider. It's worked and Wood's become a bullpen jack-of-all-trades, hovering somewhere between a long man and a LOOGY. He's been good, although last year's sparkling ERA (2.95) may be a bit deceiving: Wood played in front of the best defense in baseball history, gave up more than his share of hard contact and had to be shielded from right-handed sluggers. Heading into his age-30 season, he doesn't have a ton of upside left, and the end may be closer than it seems.

Rob Zastryzny   LHP

Born: 3/26/92   Age: 25   Bats: R   Throws: L   Height: 6'3"   Weight: 205   Entered Pro Ball: Round 2, 2013 Draft (#41 overall)

YEAR	TEAM	LVL	AGE	W	L	SV	G	GS	IP	H	HR	BB/9	K/9	K	GB%	BABIP	WHIP	ERA	FIP	DRA	VORP	WARP	cFIP	MPH
2014	DAY	A+	22	4	6	0	23	23	110	121	10	2.7	9.0	110	48%	.348	1.40	4.66	3.66	3.10	30.5	3.1	91	
2015	TEN	AA	23	2	5	0	14	14	60²	77	9	4.2	7.1	48	42%	.345	1.73	6.23	5.03	8.09	-20.2	-2.2	114	
2016	TEN	AA	24	3	2	0	9	9	54²	50	6	3.3	6.9	42	43%	.282	1.28	4.28	4.36	5.17	-0.4	0.0	108	
2016	IOW	AAA	24	7	3	0	15	14	81	67	7	3.4	8.6	77	50%	.270	1.21	4.33	4.17	3.90	12.9	1.3	88	
2016	CHN	MLB	24	1	0	0	8	1	16	12	0	2.8	9.6	17	58%	.279	1.06	1.12	2.19	3.75	2.3	0.2	90	92.5
2017	CHN	MLB	25	2	2	0	31	2	41	41	4	3.9	6.9	32	50%	.293	1.42	4.50	4.33	4.66	1.5	0.2	100	
2018	CHN	MLB	26	2	1	0	40	2	52¹	41	6	4.6	9.6	56	50%	.287	1.29	4.16	4.44	4.77	2.5	0.3	109	

Breakout: 13%   Improve: 26%   Collapse: 23%   Attrition: 49%   MLB: 63%   *Comparables: Brad Mills, David Pauley, Joel Carreno*

The last name on the World Championship T-shirt—and on every list he's ever been on, probably—Zastryzny has a chance to avoid making 2016 the highlight of his nascent big-league career. He's got a solid four-pitch mix, has demonstrated reasonable durability over four minor-league seasons and should be in line for a shot in the rotation sometime soon (although maybe not in 2017). When he gets there, he'll probably want to add depth to his curveball, which is a little flat at the moment, but he otherwise has a good shot at a few solid years at the back of somebody's rotation.

LINEOUTS

Hitters

NAME	POS	TEAM	LVL	AGE	PA	R	2B	3B	HR	RBI	BB	K	SB	CS	AVG/OBP/SLG	TAv	VORP	BABIP	BRR	FRAA	WARP
Victor Caratini	C	TEN	AA	22	480	57	25	2	6	47	54	80	2	1	.291/.375/.405	.290	29.3	.341	-1.5	C(82): -10.1, 1B(30): -0.1	2.1
Donnie Dewees	OF	SBN	A	22	410	65	15	12	3	54	29	51	17	5	.282/.337/.414	.293	31.9	.316	7.7	CF(74): -0.8, LF(15): 1.7	3.6
	OF	MYR	A+		167	25	10	2	2	19	10	36	14	0	.289/.339/.423	.289	13.5	.360	3.2	CF(33): 3.9	1.8
Tim Federowicz	C	IOW	AAA	28	253	25	12	0	8	39	18	51	3	0	.293/.352/.450	.283	12.8	.343	-2.0	C(42): 1.6, 1B(10): 0.1	1.5
	C	CHN	MLB	28	33	3	2	0	0	3	1	12	0	0	.194/.212/.258	.204	-0.9	.300	-0.4	C(12): -0.6	-0.2
Jacob Hannemann	OF	TEN	AA	25	327	37	14	4	10	30	25	55	26	8	.247/.326/.426	.270	13.8	.274	1.2	CF(71): -3.8, RF(2): -0.2	1.1
Eddy Martinez	OF	SBN	A	21	517	72	24	2	10	67	50	113	8	5	.254/.331/.380	.272	11.9	.315	-1.3	RF(97): 1.5, CF(5): 0.7	1.5
Bijan Rademacher	OF	TEN	AA	25	294	43	17	0	9	36	35	49	0	0	.313/.395/.484	.323	23.5	.355	0.0	LF(27): -1.2, RF(20): 2.3	2.8
	OF	IOW	AAA	25	81	10	5	0	1	8	7	14	0	0	.286/.350/.400	.310	6.0	.333	0.3	RF(13): -0.6, LF(7): -1.1	0.5
David Ross	C	CHN	MLB	39	205	24	6	0	10	32	30	54	0	1	.229/.338/.446	.292	17.2	.262	1.4	C(58): 5.7	2.4
Chesny Young	INF	TEN	AA	23	553	60	25	2	4	37	57	64	16	14	.303/.376/.387	.282	24.2	.340	-2.9	2B(58): -0.2, 3B(35): -1.8	2.3

Pretty much everything **Victor Caratini** does, someone else in the system does better. A backup catching spot in Chicago is a possibility late in 2017, but a 2018 arrival is more likely. ❖ If **Donnie Dewees** proves he can recognize pitches out of the zone as effectively as he can barrel up those inside it, he could be a .280 hitter with power. See ball, hit ball has worked so far, but Dewees will need a more thoughtful approach. ❖ **Tim Federowicz** is entering his sixth season as a backup catcher in the major leagues. Get to know him now: he'll probably get you a good discount on the Chevy Camaros he'll be selling in a few years. ❖ **Jacob Hanneman** was finally added to the 40-man roster, a nod more to his extraordinary athleticism than any particular skills he's demonstrated on the field. ❖ **Eddy Martinez** hasn't broken out in quite the same way as, say, Eloy Jimenez, but he performed competently as a 21-year-old at A-ball. His arm is strong and his speed makes him dangerous, but the bat needs to come around. ❖ Overlooked for most of his first few years in the Chicago system, **Bijan Rademacher** should be a nice fourth outfielder sooner rather than later. ❖ World's Best Grandpa™ **David Ross** got a giant ring for a retirement gift after 15 years of giving pitchers strikes for presents. ❖ At 25, it's go time for **Christian Villanueva**. He's worked his way steadily up the system, showcasing a great glove and moderate pop, giving him a chance to provide value at the hot corner or as a bench bat. ❖ **Chesny Young** has tremendous bat-to-ball ability and can line drives into the gaps, but doesn't have enough power to make it matter yet.

Pitchers

NAME	TEAM	LVL	AGE	W	L	SV	G	GS	IP	H	HR	BB/9	K/9	K	GB%	BABIP	WHIP	ERA	FIP	DRA	VORP	WARP	cFIP	MPH
Corey Black	TEN	AA	24	0	3	8	20	0	22^2	18	0	6.0	9.9	25	39%	.316	1.46	3.18	3.36	4.18	1.4	0.2	106	
	IOW	AAA	24	0	3	6	28	0	30^1	30	1	6.2	11.0	37	49%	.363	1.68	5.04	3.89	4.38	2.0	0.2	97	
Aaron Brooks	IOW	AAA	26	1	1	0	5	4	16^1	23	5	2.2	6.6	12	48%	.333	1.65	7.71	6.97	5.28	0.0	0.0	105	
Jake Buchanan	IOW	AAA	26	12	8	0	24	22	141	154	6	2.4	6.7	105	61%	.329	1.36	4.34	3.78	3.09	34.9	3.6	91	
	CHN	MLB	26	1	0	0	2	1	6	3	1	1.5	6.0	4	50%	.133	0.67	1.50	4.52	4.17	0.8	0.1	104	91.5
Trevor Clifton	MYR	A+	21	7	7	0	23	23	119	97	4	3.1	9.8	129	37%	.300	1.16	2.72	3.05	2.63	37.7	3.9	86	
Gerardo Concepcion	TEN	AA	24	1	0	0	10	0	17^2	5	0	2.0	8.7	17	54%	.128	0.51	0.00	2.41	2.53	4.3	0.5	83	
	CHN	MLB	24	0	0	0	3	0	2^1	2	0	3.9	7.7	2	14%	.286	1.29	3.86	2.76	4.88	0.0	0.0	108	93.2
	IOW	AAA	24	2	4	1	32	0	42	57	6	5.1	7.5	35	42%	.378	1.93	7.29	5.77	8.80	-17.9	-1.8	121	
Oscar De La Cruz	SBN	A	21	1	2	0	6	6	27^2	22	0	2.6	11.4	35	43%	.328	1.08	3.25	2.14	2.03	9.2	1.0	81	
Brian Duensing	OMA	AAA	33	1	0	2	12	0	20^1	16	0	2.2	8.4	19	50%	.276	1.03	3.10	2.59	3.57	3.2	0.3	92	
	BAL	MLB	33	1	0	0	14	0	13^1	13	2	2.0	6.8	10	26%	.275	1.20	4.05	4.23	4.89	0.1	0.0	117	94.4
Jack Leathersich	TEN	AA	25	0	0	0	11	0	10^1	11	0	3.5	10.5	12	43%	.393	1.45	3.48	2.45	3.42	1.5	0.2	93	
Brian Matusz	BAL	MLB	29	0	0	0	7	0	6	11	3	10.5	1.5	1	41%	.333	3.00	12.00	12.77	8.53	-2.3	-0.2	135	92.4
	CHN	MLB	29	0	0	0	1	1	3	6	3	6.0	6.0	2	38%	.300	2.67	18.00	17.85	10.71	-1.9	-0.2	147	92.1
	IOW	AAA	29	0	1	0	4	3	13^1	12	1	2.7	11.5	17	29%	.333	1.20	3.38	3.05	2.29	4.4	0.5	86	
Conor Mullee	NYA	MLB	28	0	0	0	3	0	3	0	0	12.0	12.0	4	60%	.000	1.33	3.00	5.44	4.48	0.2	0.0	104	94.2
	SWB	AAA	28	4	0	6	25	0	36^1	21	1	2.7	11.1	45	47%	.250	0.88	0.99	1.96	2.28	10.8	1.1	75	
Spencer Patton	IOW	AAA	28	1	0	11	35	0	36	21	0	3.8	14.8	59	40%	.313	1.00	0.75	1.86	1.08	15.5	1.6	60	
	CHN	MLB	28	1	1	0	16	0	21^1	20	3	5.9	9.3	22	42%	.279	1.59	5.48	5.06	5.87	-2.1	-0.2	114	94.6
Felix Pena	IOW	AAA	26	3	4	3	36	0	63^1	46	4	3.3	11.5	81	35%	.288	1.09	3.41	3.17	2.41	17.9	1.8	76	
	CHN	MLB	26	0	0	1	11	0	9	5	1	3.0	13.0	13	42%	.222	0.89	4.00	2.74	3.41	1.6	0.2	91	95.3
Jose Rosario	MYR	A+	25	0	0	5	12	0	16^1	15	0	4.4	7.7	14	57%	.306	1.41	1.65	3.30	4.97	0.2	0.0	105	
	TEN	AA	25	0	0	4	11	0	16^1	11	1	1.7	8.3	15	51%	.227	0.86	2.76	2.83	2.16	4.7	0.5	86	
	IOW	AAA	25	1	1	5	22	0	21^1	26	0	2.5	7.6	18	54%	.377	1.50	2.95	2.88	3.48	3.5	0.4	97	
Caleb Smith	TRN	AA	24	3	5	3	27	7	63^2	66	4	2.8	9.9	70	45%	.344	1.35	3.96	3.15	3.38	10.7	1.2	91	
Joe Smith	ANA	MLB	32	1	4	6	38	0	37^2	36	4	3.1	6.0	25	57%	.283	1.30	3.82	4.59	4.24	3.1	0.3	104	90.6
	CHN	MLB	32	1	1	0	16	0	14^1	11	4	3.1	9.4	15	36%	.219	1.12	2.51	5.98	4.01	1.5	0.2	104	90.6
Jake Stinnett	MYR	A+	24	9	4	0	20	20	116	114	7	3.1	7.5	97	48%	.311	1.33	4.27	3.87	3.92	20.0	2.1	100	
Daury Torrez	MYR	A+	23	2	2	2	42	0	68^1	74	6	2.5	9.1	69	43%	.343	1.36	3.56	3.63	2.57	19.0	2.0	84	
Jen-Ho Tseng	TEN	AA	21	6	8	0	22	22	113^1	138	12	2.5	5.5	69	49%	.327	1.50	4.29	4.43	5.17	-0.9	-0.1	108	
Duane Underwood	TEN	AA	21	0	5	0	13	13	58^2	66	7	4.8	7.1	46	48%	.317	1.65	4.91	5.09	7.14	-13.3	-1.4	112	
Ryan Williams	IOW	AAA	24	4	1	0	9	9	44	43	4	2.5	6.1	30	58%	.291	1.25	3.27	4.43	2.65	13.2	1.4	94	

Dallas Beeler pitched for Oral Roberts before turning pro, which is good because he'll need some help from the man upstairs to get his career back on track after injuries. ❖ **Corey Black** is a small man and throws crossfire, which is hard to do with any consistency if you don't have the conditioning of, say, a Jake Arrieta. Neither barrier is insurmountable, but Black's lack of consistency has lowered the effectiveness of his occasionally electric stuff. ❖ So far, the most notable thing about **Aaron Brooks** is that he played 2016 in the same organization as two men he was once traded for: Ben Zobrist and Chris Coghlan. ❖ **Jake Buchanan** has an unusually high ground-ball rate, reasonable command and not much else going for him at age 27. ❖ The Carolina League pitcher of the year, **Trevor Clifton** is a name watch going into 2017 thanks to improved command and above-average stuff. ❖ **Gerardo Concepción** is a leap-year baby, and that's perhaps the most interesting thing about him. He has pretty good stuff, but the command has never been there, and he'll need it to stick in the majors. ❖ A converted infielder, **Oscar De La Cruz** hasn't had a full season of brilliance yet, but 2017 might be the year. He's a big man with a big fastball and tons of upside. ❖ Unless all you need is someone to sit to your left at dinner, **Brian Duensing** is not the lefty you're looking for. ❖ From an engineering standpoint, it's a terrible idea to make a rocket out of leather, but it's a great idea to make a left-handed pitcher out of velocity. Fortunately, **Jack Leathersich** is figuratively the former and literally the latter, and will return from Tommy John surgery in 2017. ❖ **Brian Matusz** found a useful niche as a middle reliever after failing to pan out as a highly touted starter prospect, but now even that seems like a lofty goal following a rough 2016. ❖ **Conor Mullee** has quietly pieced together five great seasons in the minors, striking out hitters at a healthy clip. On second thought, for a guy who's had three elbow surgeries, perhaps that's the wrong adjective. Don't want to jinx him. ❖ **Spencer Patton** can't seem to translate his minor-league success to the majors, which is often the sign of a missing "out" pitch. ❖ **Felix Peña** is from the same hometown as Sammy Sosa, Alfonso Soriano and half of the Dominican stars of yesteryear. He isn't quite at that level, though: Being a fly-ball starter with just two pitches will do that to you. ❖ After his career as a starter and his original UCL ended in 2014, **Jose Rosario** returned with a near-triple-digit fastball out of the pen and shot through the minors, ending the season in Iowa and on the 40-man roster. ❖ **Caleb Smith** had a bad ERA and good secondary numbers as a starter/reliever at Double-A Trenton last season, but the Yankees left him unprotected and he was plucked in the Rule 5 draft despite a lack of upside. ❖ BP regrets to inform you that, after an extensive search of our records, we're unable to locate even a single piece of information about "**Joe Smith**." Please report to our headquarters at the J. Edgar Hoover federal building in Washington, D.C. for further updates. ❖ **Jake Stinnett** largely stopped the bleeding from 2015 and will have a chance to move quickly up the system if he regained the form that made him a second-round pick. ❖ **Daury Torrez** has struck out way more batters than he's walked as a pro, and his first full season as a reliever suggests he could move quickly. None of his pitches grade out as plus-plus, but he can command all of them effectively. ❖ **Jen-Ho Tseng** put himself on the map with a dominant 2014, but has struggled since to make best use of his below-average stuff. Without a truly dominant pitch, he'll have little room for error as he navigates the upper reaches of the minor leagues. ❖ **Duane Underwood**'s prospects collapsed like a house of cards in 2016 as his walk rate spiked and he showed an inability to sequence. His late movement and developing curveball keep scouts interested and gave the Cubs enough hope to add him to the 40-man roster. ❖ Chicago's minor league pitcher of the year at Double-A in 2015, **Ryan Williams** performed adequately at Triple-A in 2016, but there were warning signs: his walk rate more than doubled, with no attendant increase in strikeouts. His big-league future is probably as a reliever.

CHICAGO WHITE SOX

Essay by James Fegan

Player comments by Matt Sussman, Mauricio Rubio and BP staff

Imagine where the White Sox would be if anything they tried went right.

When an organization goes eight years without a playoff appearance like the White Sox have, there is no one simple failure that can account for all of it. The greatest organization in baseball could probably have endured the Adam Dunn contract, or not placed themselves in the position to rely on Jeff Keppinger, and the Sox are most certainly not that. But a theme as consistent as the threadbare nature of all their leaps to join the stratosphere of contenders is the parade of gambits on veteran contributors that went so devilishly wrong.

It's not the most important factor in recent franchise history, and may not be even the most colorful issue, since for their part the White Sox are immaculately thorough in the menagerie of disasters they have collected to limit their upward trajectory.

The big attention-grabber will always be Dave Wilder, their former director of player personnel, destroying their international operations in the mid-aughts by setting up an operation to skim bonuses from prospects so that he in turn could fund a nightclub in Arizona. But that scandal might be matched in impact by more boring deficiencies like the Sox's aversion to high school talent and abstaining from the draft-spending arms race that peaked just before they pushed to make hard-slotting rules the law of the land.

The no. 18 ranking BP gave the White Sox's farm system in 2015 was a recent high-water mark for the franchise, and Tim Anderson could wind up being their first drafted-and-developed above-average position player since Aaron Rowand. Anderson just wrapped his rookie season and Rowand has been retired since 2011, so that should be a decent hint of how things went in the interim. One of the few organizations left that has never handed out a $100 million contract, the White Sox have also retreated to below-median payrolls the last three seasons despite ostensibly being in win-now mode for the last two.

All of which is to say the White Sox have choked off many of their avenues for adding talent to their organization and have put added pressure on themselves to make every player personnel decision a home run. Instead, they have had unmitigated disaster. They finished 11 games out of the

WHITE SOX PROSPECTUS
2016 W-L: 78-84, 4TH IN AL CENTRAL

Pythag	.481	19th	DER	.702	14th
RS/G	4.23	20th	B-Age	28.3	12th
RA/G	4.41	16th	P-Age	28.2	15th
TAv	.254	23rd	Salary	$114.5M	16th
BRR	-2.29	18th	M$/MW	$3.4M	17th
TAv-P	.259	13th	DL Days	950	14th
FIP	4.23	16th	$ on DL	6%	3rd

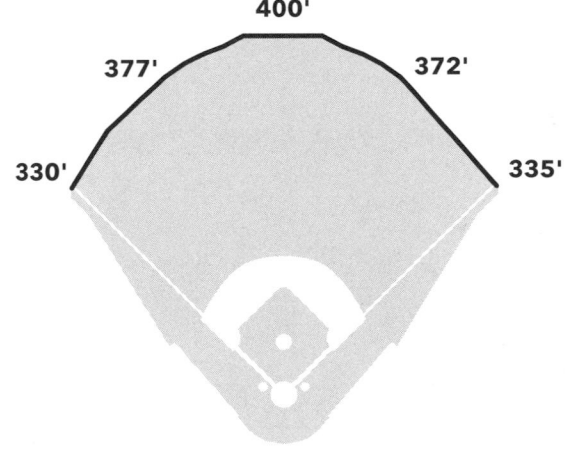

Outfield wall profile: 8'

Three-Year Park Factors

Runs	Runs/RH	Runs/LH	HR/RH	HR/LH
103	109	100	104	104

Top Hitter WARP	6.4	Adam Eaton
Top Pitcher WARP	6.9	Chris Sale
Top Prospect		Yoan Moncada

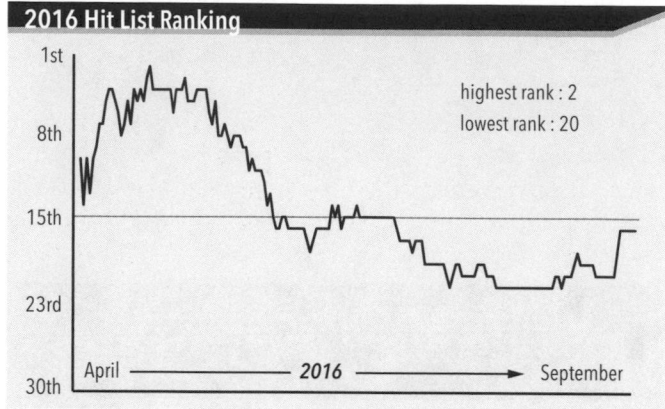

2016 Hit List Ranking

highest rank : 2
lowest rank : 20

April — *2016* → September

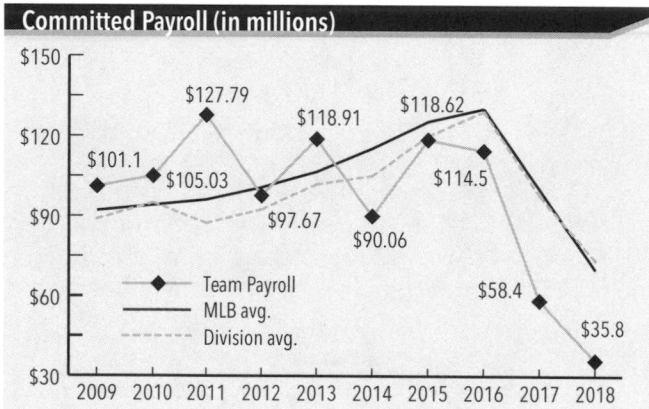

Committed Payroll (in millions)

$127.79
$118.91
$118.62
$101.1
$105.03
$97.67
$90.06
$114.5
$58.4
$35.8

◆ Team Payroll
— MLB avg.
‑‑‑ Division avg.

2009 2010 2011 2012 2013 2014 2015 2016 2017 2018

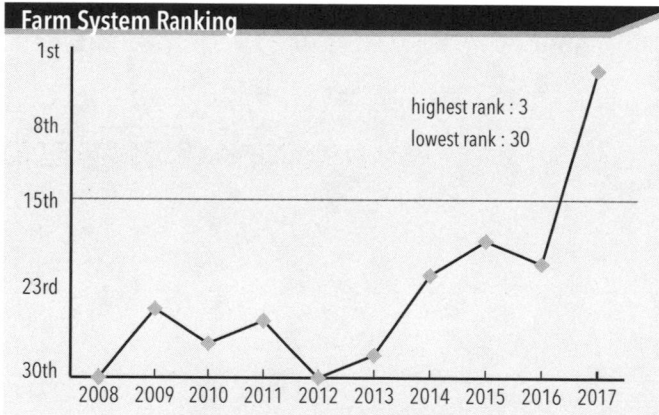

Farm System Ranking

highest rank : 3
lowest rank : 30

2008 2009 2010 2011 2012 2013 2014 2015 2016 2017

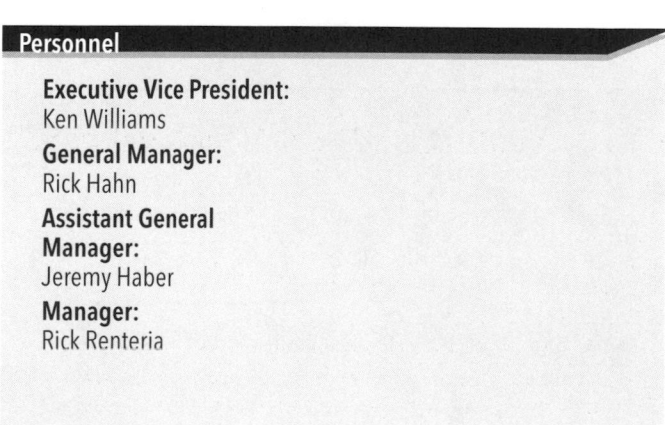

Personnel

Executive Vice President:
Ken Williams

General Manager:
Rick Hahn

Assistant General Manager:
Jeremy Haber

Manager:
Rick Renteria

second Wild Card slot and not even the salad days of James Shields could have rescued them from their fate. But what if he wasn't a shortlist contender for the worst starter in baseball?

There were warning signs that Shields was not what he once was before he became the White Sox's "big" acquisition of the 2016 trade season. He'd been annihilated for 10 runs in his final start in San Diego before the trade, getting called out publicly by his owner while sporting a homer rate of 1.4 per nine innings despite calling Petco Park home. He probably wasn't destined to start Game 1 of the World Series for the White Sox.

Yet there was still some shock to be extended when only six pitchers finished with a lower WARP than Shields, and most of those guys were fringe major leaguers getting shelled in smaller samples. The rare exception was Jered Weaver, who was in the same boat as Shields, trying to work through a full season with the ghost of his long-dead stuff. Shields' 3.1 WARP in 2015 was his lowest total since his rookie season in 2006 … and his WARP dropped by 4.5 in 2016.

He was just one bad player in a 78-win season, but the White Sox traded for Shields (and his contract) at the start of June and were essentially dead in the water six weeks later. They did not buy at the deadline, they didn't even lift a hand when half of the bullpen went down with injuries, and there's something to be said for not making any more steps to shore up a contention run when the first step is onto a landmine. At the very least, it could have changed the perception of how far away they were from being contenders *after* 2016 and perhaps altered their plans to eventually trade Chis Sale and Adam Eaton in a full-scale rebuild.

There were similarly disappointing performances in 2015 from Adam LaRoche and Jeff Samardzija. The latter's ramshackle mechanics did not meld with pitching coach Don Cooper's rigidly uniform approach and the former was just done at age 35. When the White Sox played the percentages—or just saved money—and stayed with LaRoche for 2016, he retired over a dispute about having his son in the clubhouse, which given their history isn't less believable than anything else that has happened to this franchise.

Name a recent disappointing White Sox season and there's at least one awful acquisition. Since 2010, they've acquired 43 major-league veterans via free agency, trade or waiver claim. Based on PECOTA, the projected WARP for that group in their first year with the White Sox was a combined 32.5. The actual production for that group in their first year was 13.4. While Dunn's infamous first year is the headliner, the White Sox have mostly been done in by the LaRoches, Keppingers, Mark Teahens and Dioner Navarros—players who were counted on to be no more than solid regulars and wound up collapsing into lineup-dragging weaknesses. Nearly 40 percent of new veteran acquisitions provided negative WARP in their first season in Chicago.

The White Sox have been mostly invisible since winning the World Series—and even that triumph has been literally forgotten by national media at times—but it's worth noting that they have not been completely terrible. The end of the Ozzie Guillen era saw him pilot an 88-win 2010 team to the doorstep of a playoff berth before the expected upgrades to that same core all tanked and Guillen bolted from an increasingly contentious workplace in 2011. Robin Ventura was considered a Manager of the Year candidate in 2012 until the Sox crashed in the final week and fumbled away the AL Central. The 2015 and 2016 teams did not finish close to the playoffs but were considered preseason dark horses that could make noise if everything broke right for them.

Despite all of their systemic oddness, it's not hard to see how a successful veteran infusion over the past seven years would have produced a playoff berth and significantly altered our collective perception of the franchise. Instead we have this.

Assuming that the current rebuilding effort eventually produces some decent homegrown building blocks, the White Sox cannot simply write off ever supplementing the roster by acquiring major-league talent from outside the organization. To some degree the lower-budget model of chasing mid-tier free agents means they are always ripe for acquiring busts, but trading for Shields to shore up a fractured rotation only to have him break it further is the sort of disaster that should send ripples through the franchise's entire pro scouting framework even if they weren't already saddled with the brutal history that preceded it.

Changes in scouting and player development are carried out as quietly as their construction and as secretly as their actual work. Even the White Sox hiring Chris Getz away from the Royals as a new head of player development barely caused waves during an otherwise dead period for baseball news. The White Sox could overhaul their entire scouting operation, a shift in power between their burgeoning analytics department and their traditional old guard could occur and barely a whisper of it would make it to public knowledge unless they chose to announce it. Any problem with the White Sox's infrastructure could thus already be on the path to getting fixed, but also the only real way to judge it would be through the results they produce.

All of which could take a while. Wilder was sent to prison in 2013 for the skimming scandal and it's possible the White Sox's international operation still hasn't fully regained its credibility. It took rule changes on draft spending to stop being an annual calamity and Tim Anderson is being hailed as a success story despite not proving much yet. Even a long-desired rebuild only offers the illusion of retreat from the regular torment of free agency and trade misfires, because when the White Sox deal from their strength—the ability to generate a wealth of viable starting pitching—all of their talent will never help push them forward until they can match it to the league around them. ■

—James Fegan is an author of Baseball Prospectus

HITTERS

Jose Abreu   1B

Born: 1/29/87   Age: 30   Bats: R   Throws: R   Height: 6'3"   Weight: 255   Entered Pro Ball: International Free Agent, 2013

YEAR	TEAM	LVL	AGE	PA	R	2B	3B	HR	RBI	BB	K	SB	CS	AVG/OBP/SLG	TAv	VORP	BABIP	BRR	FRAA	WARP
2014	CHA	MLB	27	622	80	35	2	36	107	51	131	3	1	.317/.383/.581	.343	53.3	.356	-1.0	1B(109): -2.0	5.7
2015	CHA	MLB	28	668	88	34	3	30	101	39	140	0	0	.290/.347/.502	.291	23.7	.333	-2.9	1B(115): 6.3	3.2
2016	CHA	MLB	29	695	67	32	1	25	100	47	125	0	2	.293/.353/.468	.283	21.8	.327	-1.7	1B(152): 6.8	2.9
2017	CHA	MLB	30	629	78	31	2	28	92	44	129	1	1	.287/.349/.495	.295	31.5	.326	-1.4	1B 4	3.5
2018	CHA	MLB	31	574	81	26	1	25	83	43	119	0	0	.286/.352/.489	.288	21.8	.326	-1.6	1B 4	2.8

Breakout: 1%   Improve: 46%   Collapse: 5%   Attrition: 14%   MLB: 97%   *Comparables: Ted Kluszewski, Glenn Davis, Derrek Lee*

Teams are finally starting to figure out how to pitch Abreu. Last year's early-season slump indicated a tendency to chase up and in, although his second-half power surge indicated an ability to adjust. We're probably not going to see those monstrous numbers from his rookie season repeated. In an era when many of the most intimidating hitters are shortstops too young to rent a car, Abreu still has that fear factor when stepping to the plate, despite himself possessing no fear of swinging at anything. He might be the top American League first baseman not named Miguel Cabrera.

Tim Anderson   SS

Born: 6/23/93   Age: 24   Bats: R   Throws: R   Height: 6'1"   Weight: 185   Entered Pro Ball: Round 1, 2013 Draft (#17 overall)

YEAR	TEAM	LVL	AGE	PA	R	2B	3B	HR	RBI	BB	K	SB	CS	AVG/OBP/SLG	TAv	VORP	BABIP	BRR	FRAA	WARP
2014	WNS	A+	21	300	48	18	7	6	31	7	68	10	3	.297/.323/.472	.267	18.5	.369	3.6	SS(66): -1.1	1.8
2014	BIR	AA	21	45	7	3	0	1	7	0	9	0	1	.364/.364/.500	.322	4.6	.441	-0.1	SS(10): 0.3	0.5
2015	BIR	AA	22	550	79	21	12	5	46	24	114	49	13	.312/.350/.429	.289	46.9	.391	10.9	SS(110): 0.6	5.1
2016	CHR	AAA	23	256	39	10	2	4	20	8	58	11	4	.304/.325/.409	.262	10.9	.384	0.1	SS(52): -1.4	1.0
2016	CHA	MLB	23	431	57	22	6	9	30	13	117	10	2	.283/.306/.432	.248	16.6	.375	4.0	SS(98): -4.5	1.3
2017	CHA	MLB	24	623	76	26	7	14	58	17	169	23	6	.267/.288/.404	.244	19.2	.345	3.1	SS -2	1.2
2018	CHA	MLB	25	580	63	26	7	13	65	21	160	21	6	.270/.301/.416	.245	14.8	.353	3.6	SS -1	1.4

Breakout: 4%   Improve: 34%   Collapse: 14%   Attrition: 24%   MLB: 73%   *Comparables: Josh Rutledge, Stephen Drew, Michael Morse*

Anderson's toolsy athleticism was put to the test for two-thirds of the season and he emerged at the other end as a capable two-way player, even though he struck out 27 times before drawing his first walk. The 9-to-1 strikeout-to-walk-ratio stands out, but isn't unprecedented—Orioles infielder Jonathan Schoop had worse in his rookie year—and he clobbered enough extra-base hits to to avoid being a lineup liability. In the field, however, at some point he may need to run to a position other than shortstop; we know he won't walk there.

Alex Avila   C

Born: 1/29/87   Age: 30   Bats: L   Throws: R   Height: 5'11"   Weight: 210   Entered Pro Ball: Round 5, 2008 Draft (#163 overall)

YEAR	TEAM	LVL	AGE	PA	R	2B	3B	HR	RBI	BB	K	SB	CS	AVG/OBP/SLG	TAv	VORP	BABIP	BRR	FRAA	WARP
2014	DET	MLB	27	457	44	22	0	11	47	61	151	0	3	.218/.327/.359	.250	8.9	.322	-5.5	C(122): -1.5 • 1B(1): -0.0	0.8
2015	TOL	AAA	28	22	2	0	0	1	5	0	8	0	0	.300/.273/.450	.253	0.5	.385	0.0	C(4): -0.1	
2015	DET	MLB	28	219	21	5	0	4	13	40	66	0	1	.191/.339/.287	.235	-1.0	.278	-3.3	C(44): -9.5 • 1B(23): -0.1	-1.1
2016	CHR	AAA	29	30	4	1	0	1	3	6	7	0	0	.333/.467/.500	.325	2.7	.438	-0.1	C(5): -0.1	0.3
2016	CHA	MLB	29	209	19	6	0	7	11	38	78	0	0	.213/.359/.373	.266	8.3	.341	-2.2	C(54): -8.1	0.0
2017	DET	MLB	30	160	17	6	0	4	17	23	49	0	0	.217/.330/.360	.247	3.3	.302	-0.4	C -5, 1B -0	-0.1
2018	DET	MLB	31	134	16	5	0	3	13	19	43	0	0	.210/.326/.342	.239	0.3	.302	-1.0	C -4, 1B 0	-0.4

Breakout: 3%   Improve: 38%   Collapse: 4%   Attrition: 17%   MLB: 90%   *Comparables: Chris Snyder, Geovany Soto, Rick Wilkins*

Avila is a 30-year-old man with a 50-year-old baseball body, but last year's stint with the White Sox produced his first above-average OPS since that bizarre 2011 season in which he started the All-Star game. He has a gilded future in his post-baseball career, with his dad being a general manager and his grandfather a pioneering scout. ("References? Take a look at our Christmas newsletter from 1995.") Given the pedigree, he can probably play a while longer and leave on his own terms, provided he's down with staying a backup catcher. All he can really do is draw a walk and occasionally demolish the ball, usually directly into the shift.

YEAR	TEAM	P. COUNT	FRM RUNS	BLK RUNS	THRW RUNS	TOT RUNS
2014	DET	16914	-3.4	3.6	2.6	2.8
2015	DET	5969	-8.5	-1.2	0.1	-9.5
2015	TOL	361	-0.1	0.0	0.0	-0.1
2016	CHA	7394	-6.8	0.0	-0.5	-7.3
2017	CHA	4745	-4.2	0.0	0.1	-4.1
2018	CHA	3988	-3.8	0.0	0.0	-3.8

Luis Alexander Basabe   CF

Born: 8/26/96   Age: 20   Bats: B   Throws: R   Height: 6'0"   Weight: 160   Entered Pro Ball: International Free Agent, 2012

YEAR	TEAM	LVL	AGE	PA	R	2B	3B	HR	RBI	BB	K	SB	CS	AVG/OBP/SLG	TAv	VORP	BABIP	BRR	FRAA	WARP
2015	LOW	A-	18	256	36	8	3	7	23	32	67	15	4	.243/.340/.401	.273	13.5	.315	4.1	CF(28): 4.9 • RF(25): 5.9	2.9
2016	GRN	A	19	451	61	24	8	12	52	40	116	25	5	.258/.325/.447	.290	27.4	.330	2.7	CF(98): 12.7	4.4
2016	SLM	A+	19	23	5	2	1	0	1	1	3	0	0	.364/.391/.545	.320	2.8	.421	0.8	CF(2): 0.2 • RF(2): 0.4	0.3
2017	CHA	MLB	20	250	31	9	2	8	25	17	81	7	2	.211/.269/.367	.219	-0.5	.286	0.7	CF 6, RF 0	0.6
2018	CHA	MLB	21	391	45	15	3	13	46	31	121	11	3	.222/.286/.391	.235	2.0	.293	1.6	CF 9, RF 0	1.2

Breakout: 3%   Improve: 10%   Collapse: 0%   Attrition: 5%   MLB: 12%   *Comparables: Nomar Mazara, Caleb Gindl, Chris Parmelee*

On July 8th, the Red Sox traded Luis Alejandro Basabe and Jose Almonte to the Diamondbacks for Brad Ziegler. Arizona must have gotten their Basabes confused, because Luis Alexander is the real prize. A switch-hitting center fielder with plus speed and emerging power, Basabe is a toolsy 20-year-old who hit .301/.370/.489 over his last two months in Greenville, leading to a late-season promotion to Salem. There's some swing-and-miss to his game, but Basabe has a solid approach at the plate, can fly down the line and added 40 points of ISO while climbing the minor league ladder. It's possible that the more advanced arms in the mid-minors stay Basabe's progress, but if not, the White Sox will have another elite outfield prospect on their hands.

Melky Cabrera   LF

Born: 8/11/84   Age: 32   Bats: B   Throws: L   Height: 5'10"   Weight: 210   Entered Pro Ball: International Free Agent, 2001

YEAR	TEAM	LVL	AGE	PA	R	2B	3B	HR	RBI	BB	K	SB	CS	AVG/OBP/SLG	TAv	VORP	BABIP	BRR	FRAA	WARP
2014	TOR	MLB	29	621	81	35	3	16	73	43	67	6	2	.301/.351/.458	.293	29.4	.316	-1.8	LF(133): 2.7 • RF(4): -0.2	3.5
2015	CHA	MLB	30	683	70	36	2	12	77	40	88	3	0	.273/.314/.394	.253	6.3	.297	-2.6	LF(150): -7.6	-0.1
2016	CHA	MLB	31	646	70	42	5	14	86	47	69	2	0	.296/.345/.455	.269	15.7	.314	-4.3	LF(147): -6.7	0.9
2017	CHA	MLB	32	607	61	30	4	12	67	40	79	3	1	.288/.333/.422	.268	20.1	.313	-0.4	LF -3	1.6
2018	CHA	MLB	33	527	62	25	3	12	60	35	70	1	0	.284/.331/.424	.261	10.9	.306	-2.4	LF -3	0.9

Breakout: 4%   Improve: 40%   Collapse: 2%   Attrition: 16%   MLB: 97%   *Comparables: Shannon Stewart, Frank Catalanotto, Mike Greenwell*

Cabrera's defining strength is that he consistently stays OK, even if he isn't one of the top left fielders in the game. A high average, a high contact rate and double-digit dingers make him a decent selection anywhere in the lineup. Now on the gentle downward slope of his career, a corresponding dropoff may occur, but one may not notice, especially given that he's already a second-division starter.

Zack Collins   C

Born: 2/6/95   Age: 22   Bats: L   Throws: R   Height: 6'3"   Weight: 220   Entered Pro Ball: Round 1, 2016 Draft (#10 overall)

YEAR	TEAM	LVL	AGE	PA	R	2B	3B	HR	RBI	BB	K	SB	CS	AVG/OBP/SLG	TAv	VORP	BABIP	BRR	FRAA	WARP
2016	WNS	A+	21	153	24	7	0	6	18	33	39	0	0	.258/.418/.467	.302	10.8	.333	-0.4	C(18): -0.6	1.0
2017	CHA	MLB	22	250	27	9	1	8	29	32	80	1	0	.210/.316/.369	.241	6.5	.286	-0.4	C -0	0.7
2018	CHA	MLB	23	254	32	9	1	9	30	33	80	1	0	.213/.318/.379	.246	4.8	.288	-0.5	C 0	0.5

Breakout: 2%   Improve: 16%   Collapse: 4%   Attrition: 16%   MLB: 33%   *Comparables: Derek Norris, Jon Singleton, Chris Parmelee*

Power, walks and whiffs were the hallmarks of his draft profile and and Collins didn't disappoint when he came to pro ball. He has a ton of natural strength and a swing geared for long, hard contact, but it opens him up to a lot of strikeouts. Collins mitigates the swing-and-miss with an intelligent approach at the plate. The Kyle Schwarber comps were cute, but Collins has even less of the required athleticism to stick at

YEAR	TEAM	P. COUNT	FRM RUNS	BLK RUNS	THRW RUNS	TOT RUNS
2017	CHA	7794	0.0	0.0	0.0	0.0
2018	CHA	7927	0.0	0.0	0.0	0.0

catcher. His mechanics getting up the chute and throwing to second base are rigid and slow. Collins profiles as a low-average hitter with on-base skills who can mash long home runs. There's a lot of pressure on the bat, but so long as the power shows up it should profile just fine at DH.

Adam Engel OF

Born: 12/9/91   Age: 25   Bats: R   Throws: R   Height: 6'2"   Weight: 210   Entered Pro Ball: Round 19, 2013 Draft (#573 overall)

YEAR	TEAM	LVL	AGE	PA	R	2B	3B	HR	RBI	BB	K	SB	CS	AVG/OBP/SLG	TAv	VORP	BABIP	BRR	FRAA	WARP
2014	KAN	A	22	341	54	14	7	6	30	29	86	28	11	.261/.334/.410	.272	18.1	.344	3.3	CF(74): -0.7	1.8
2014	WNS	A+	22	100	11	0	0	0	5	6	21	9	1	.239/.296/.239	.208	-1.3	.304	1.5	CF(18): 3.1	0.2
2015	WNS	A+	23	608	90	23	9	7	43	62	132	65	11	.251/.335/.369	.259	27.6	.321	10.3	CF(136): -0.3	3.0
2016	WNS	A+	24	64	15	6	1	0	5	7	11	6	0	.327/.413/.473	.319	9.6	.409	3.6	CF(12): -1.6 • LF(2): -0.2	0.8
2016	BIR	AA	24	357	56	18	9	4	25	39	70	31	9	.255/.352/.412	.288	26.1	.319	5.8	CF(71): -1.5	2.7
2016	CHR	AAA	24	161	19	6	2	3	16	10	50	8	5	.242/.298/.369	.235	-0.1	.344	-0.1	CF(25): 5.3 • LF(16): -2.3	0.3
2017	*CHA*	*MLB*	*25*	*63*	*8*	*2*	*1*	*1*	*5*	*5*	*18*	*4*	*1*	*.218/.285/.346*	*.227*	*0.5*	*.294*	*0.5*	*CF 0*	*0.0*
2018	*CHA*	*MLB*	*26*	*271*	*29*	*10*	*3*	*6*	*28*	*22*	*80*	*16*	*5*	*.221/.292/.359*	*.227*	*0.7*	*.296*	*2.5*	*CF 1*	*0.2*

Breakout: 7%   Improve: 23%   Collapse: 5%   Attrition: 27%   MLB: 33%   *Comparables: Brian Goodwin, Ryan LaMarre, Roger Bernadina*

An impressive 2015 performance in the Arizona Fall League put Engel on the map and he proceeded to follow it up by slugging just .369 and striking out 31 percent of the time at Triple-A Charlotte. Engel has average strength and flashes barrel ability with a competent approach, so there's hope that his 2016 was a major outlier on his otherwise solid prospect past. If he wants to avoid the Rich Boy path and be more than a one-hit wonder Engel will have to regain his approach at the plate. While the upside here isn't insanely high, Engel's profile suggests he could be a fourth outfielder if everything clicks.

Todd Frazier 3B

Born: 2/12/86   Age: 31   Bats: R   Throws: R   Height: 6'3"   Weight: 220   Entered Pro Ball: Round 1, 2007 Draft (#34 overall)

YEAR	TEAM	LVL	AGE	PA	R	2B	3B	HR	RBI	BB	K	SB	CS	AVG/OBP/SLG	TAv	VORP	BABIP	BRR	FRAA	WARP
2014	CIN	MLB	28	660	88	22	1	29	80	52	139	20	8	.273/.336/.459	.297	42.1	.309	3.2	3B(124): -3.3 • 1B(43): 0.6	4.4
2015	CIN	MLB	29	678	82	43	1	35	89	44	137	13	8	.255/.309/.498	.293	41.7	.271	-1.1	3B(155): 2.5	4.7
2016	CHA	MLB	30	666	89	21	0	40	98	64	163	15	5	.225/.302/.464	.266	27.2	.236	2.4	3B(149): -2.1 • 1B(7): -1.1	2.5
2017	*CHA*	*MLB*	*31*	*610*	*77*	*27*	*2*	*27*	*83*	*48*	*137*	*13*	*5*	*.246/.312/.449*	*.269*	*23.2*	*.278*	*0.0*	*3B -2*	*1.8*
2018	*CHA*	*MLB*	*32*	*546*	*70*	*24*	*2*	*22*	*72*	*41*	*127*	*10*	*5*	*.244/.308/.431*	*.257*	*12.1*	*.281*	*1.3*	*3B -2*	*1.1*

Breakout: 0%   Improve: 32%   Collapse: 12%   Attrition: 12%   MLB: 94%   *Comparables: Eric Chavez, Chase Headley, Vern Stephens*

In 2000, Tony Batista set the record for lowest OPS in a 40-homer season with .827. In 2012, Adam Dunn and Curtis Granderson broke that threshold. Two years ago, Albert Pujols sunk the bar with a .787 campaign. And last year Frazier became the aluminum standard with a .767 OPS. Despite the one-dimensional approach at the plate, that one dimension is still a crazy amount of home runs—the best outcome in baseball—and he can hold his own at third base defensively. In an era when home runs and strikeouts are up, what's the point of putting the ball in play when they're just going to catch it? This is a perfect time in history to be Todd Frazier.

Avisail Garcia RF

Born: 6/12/91   Age: 26   Bats: R   Throws: R   Height: 6'4"   Weight: 240   Entered Pro Ball: International Free Agent, 2007

YEAR	TEAM	LVL	AGE	PA	R	2B	3B	HR	RBI	BB	K	SB	CS	AVG/OBP/SLG	TAv	VORP	BABIP	BRR	FRAA	WARP
2014	CHR	AAA	23	53	9	3	0	1	3	1	16	0	0	.340/.377/.460	.280	2.8	.485	0.8	RF(7): 0.2	0.3
2014	CHA	MLB	23	190	19	8	0	7	29	14	44	4	1	.244/.305/.413	.257	0.8	.285	-1.8	RF(46): -1.0	0.0
2015	CHA	MLB	24	601	66	17	2	13	59	36	141	7	7	.257/.309/.365	.245	0.6	.320	-0.3	RF(130): 3.5	0.4
2016	CHA	MLB	25	453	59	18	2	12	51	34	115	4	4	.245/.307/.385	.247	2.3	.309	2.0	RF(46): 4.4 • LF(11): 0.0	0.7
2017	*CHA*	*MLB*	*26*	*448*	*49*	*16*	*3*	*12*	*49*	*25*	*107*	*5*	*4*	*.263/.311/.404*	*.256*	*7.6*	*.325*	*-0.6*	*RF -1*	*0.6*
2018	*CHA*	*MLB*	*27*	*454*	*55*	*17*	*3*	*14*	*54*	*29*	*110*	*5*	*4*	*.268/.321/.420*	*.258*	*10.1*	*.332*	*0.0*	*RF -1*	*1.0*

Breakout: 5%   Improve: 62%   Collapse: 8%   Attrition: 14%   MLB: 93%   *Comparables: Jorge Cantu, Peter Bourjos, Cameron Maybin*

Once dubbed "Mini Miggy" in his Detroit tenure, the nickname still holds true for Garcia as long as we're referring to Olivo. He's in a precarious situation: for much of the first half, he DHed and looked uncomfortable doing it. When he plays in right field he looks even more uncomfortable, although last August when this happened he finally began wrecking the ball at the plate. Defensively the ball wrecks him, as his plus throwing arm is the only reason a team would bother penciling a "9" next to his name. If he can't pair the best of both worlds, Garcia will spend the rest of his career like Olivo—a different city every year in a backup role.

Austin Jackson CF

Born: 2/1/87   Age: 30   Bats: R   Throws: R   Height: 6'1"   Weight: 205   Entered Pro Ball: Round 8, 2005 Draft (#259 overall)

YEAR	TEAM	LVL	AGE	PA	R	2B	3B	HR	RBI	BB	K	SB	CS	AVG/OBP/SLG	TAv	VORP	BABIP	BRR	FRAA	WARP
2014	DET	MLB	27	420	52	25	5	4	33	35	85	9	4	.273/.332/.398	.265	16.0	.334	2.4	CF(100): -5.9	1.1
2014	SEA	MLB	27	236	19	5	1	0	14	12	59	11	2	.229/.267/.260	.195	-7.2	.309	0.4	CF(56): 0.1	-0.8
2015	TAC	AAA	28	42	4	1	0	0	1	4	12	1	0	.263/.333/.289	.229	-0.2	.385	0.4	CF(4): -1.2	-0.1
2015	SEA	MLB	28	448	46	18	3	8	38	24	107	15	9	.272/.312/.387	.255	8.3	.348	-2.6	CF(107): 4.9	1.4
2015	CHN	MLB	28	79	10	7	0	1	10	5	19	2	1	.236/.304/.375	.247	0.9	.308	0.2	RF(22): 1.2 • CF(8): -0.6	0.1
2016	CHA	MLB	29	203	24	12	2	0	18	17	39	2	1	.254/.318/.343	.234	0.4	.319	-0.4	CF(54): -4.0	-0.4
2017	*CHA*	*MLB*	*30*	*260*	*32*	*12*	*2*	*5*	*23*	*22*	*61*	*7*	*3*	*.262/.327/.393*	*.250*	*6.8*	*.329*	*-0.2*	*CF -0*	*0.7*
2018	*CHA*	*MLB*	*31*	*250*	*28*	*12*	*2*	*5*	*26*	*21*	*59*	*6*	*3*	*.256/.320/.386*	*.247*	*3.5*	*.322*	*0.1*	*CF 0*	*0.3*

Breakout: 2%   Improve: 48%   Collapse: 7%   Attrition: 10%   MLB: 99%   *Comparables: Franklin Gutierrez, Jacob Brumfield, Dave May*

Jackson spent the entire year with one team for the first time since 2013, but in fairness nobody will acquire a center fielder with a torn meniscus at the deadline. The malady usually keeps a player out for 6-8 weeks, but for him it wiped out four months. Once he's healthy he'll still provide value for a contender. He's a center fielder first, and there is little value in placing him at the corners given his perfectly vanilla offensive production. There's enough speed in those legs to chase down doubles and his Jon Lesterly refusal to dive for balls should further extend his career. That breakout year hasn't happened yet, and now in his 30s might never come, but he can still finish his career in a steady Mark Kotsay-like trajectory.

Brett Lawrie   2B

Born: 1/18/90   Age: 27   Bats: R   Throws: R   Height: 6'0"   Weight: 210   Entered Pro Ball: Round 1, 2008 Draft (#16 overall)

YEAR	TEAM	LVL	AGE	PA	R	2B	3B	HR	RBI	BB	K	SB	CS	AVG/OBP/SLG	TAv	VORP	BABIP	BRR	FRAA	WARP
2014	TOR	MLB	24	282	27	9	0	12	38	16	49	0	0	.247/.301/.421	.264	8.6	.260	-0.2	3B(63): 1.1 • 2B(32): 1.7	1.3
2015	OAK	MLB	25	602	64	29	3	16	60	28	144	5	2	.260/.299/.407	.266	17.9	.320	-2.9	3B(109): 3.6 • 2B(42): -3.4	1.9
2016	CHA	MLB	26	384	35	22	0	12	36	30	109	7	3	.248/.310/.413	.253	6.6	.325	-1.0	2B(92): 6.5	1.4
2017	*CHA*	*MLB*	*27*	*511*	*55*	*23*	*2*	*14*	*59*	*33*	*108*	*6*	*3*	*.258/.312/.408*	*.256*	*14.1*	*.304*	*-0.3*	*2B 5*	*1.9*
2018	*CHA*	*MLB*	*28*	*449*	*53*	*20*	*2*	*13*	*53*	*31*	*96*	*5*	*2*	*.252/.310/.407*	*.251*	*8.0*	*.296*	*-1.3*	*2B 4*	*1.3*

Breakout: 2%   Improve: 54%   Collapse: 1%   Attrition: 8%   MLB: 99%   Comparables: Ryne Sandberg, Frank Catalanotto, Jorge Orta

The biggest question surrounding the eighth-best British Columbian ballplayer in history is the injury that ended his White Sox season on July 21. For starters, was it a hamstring injury? Knee? Calf? Leg? General undisclosed extremity? And of course, is he healthy for Opening Day? Prior to the mysterious malady he was his typical full-energy, overaggressive but league-average hitter. Assuming the leg cooperates that's the player you're getting, and it's more fan favorite than fantasy favorite. And that's what you have to tell yourself if you're getting 140 more games of Brett Lawrie, Second Baseman.

Trey Michalczewski   3B

Born: 2/27/95   Age: 22   Bats: B   Throws: R   Height: 6'3"   Weight: 210   Entered Pro Ball: Round 7, 2013 Draft (#213 overall)

YEAR	TEAM	LVL	AGE	PA	R	2B	3B	HR	RBI	BB	K	SB	CS	AVG/OBP/SLG	TAv	VORP	BABIP	BRR	FRAA	WARP
2014	KAN	A	19	495	57	25	7	10	70	45	140	6	3	.273/.348/.433	.278	26.2	.375	0.9	3B(114): -7.7	1.9
2014	WNS	A+	19	84	5	2	0	0	5	9	21	1	0	.194/.293/.222	.222	-1.6	.275	-0.7	3B(17): -0.9	-0.3
2015	WNS	A+	20	532	59	35	4	7	75	50	114	4	3	.259/.335/.395	.256	15.0	.326	0.9	3B(127): 3.5	2.0
2016	BIR	AA	21	557	62	24	5	11	59	56	153	4	0	.226/.314/.363	.264	19.9	.304	0.4	3B(118): 10.1 • SS(12): -2.0	3.0
2017	*CHA*	*MLB*	*22*	*250*	*23*	*10*	*1*	*6*	*27*	*20*	*81*	*0*	*0*	*.212/.282/.352*	*.220*	*-2.3*	*.297*	*-0.3*	*3B 2, SS -0*	*-0.1*
2018	*CHA*	*MLB*	*23*	*376*	*43*	*16*	*2*	*11*	*42*	*31*	*121*	*0*	*0*	*.219/.290/.377*	*.232*	*-2.7*	*.302*	*-0.6*	*3B 2, SS 0*	*-0.1*

Breakout: 4%   Improve: 13%   Collapse: 3%   Attrition: 16%   MLB: 19%   Comparables: Mat Gamel, Will Middlebrooks, Kyle Kubitza

He danced around a strikeout rate that was approaching danger levels in his first three years, but Michalczewski was always able to prop up his production by making enough contact to tease at above-average power. His contact collapsed in 2016, which cut deep into his power production. His defense improved some over the course of the year, but his play at third can still get a bit adventurous.

Yoan Moncada   2B

Born: 5/27/95   Age: 22   Bats: B   Throws: R   Height: 6'2"   Weight: 205   Entered Pro Ball: International Free Agent, 2015

YEAR	TEAM	LVL	AGE	PA	R	2B	3B	HR	RBI	BB	K	SB	CS	AVG/OBP/SLG	TAv	VORP	BABIP	BRR	FRAA	WARP
2015	GRN	A	20	363	61	19	3	8	38	42	83	49	3	.278/.380/.438	.312	35.7	.353	7.6	2B(71): -5.6	3.2
2016	SLM	A+	21	284	57	25	3	4	34	45	60	36	8	.307/.427/.496	.320	31.9	.395	6.2	2B(58): -1.4	3.1
2016	PME	AA	21	207	37	6	3	11	28	27	64	9	4	.277/.379/.531	.309	16.4	.373	0.6	2B(34): -4.6 • 3B(10): 0.7	1.3
2016	BOS	MLB	21	20	3	1	0	0	1	1	12	0	0	.211/.250/.263	.189	-0.5	.571	0.3	3B(5): 0.2	0.0
2017	*CHA*	*MLB*	*22*	*130*	*17*	*5*	*1*	*4*	*14*	*14*	*42*	*7*	*2*	*.223/.312/.388*	*.250*	*2.8*	*.310*	*0.9*	*3B 1, 2B -1*	*0.3*
2018	*CHA*	*MLB*	*23*	*361*	*46*	*14*	*2*	*13*	*44*	*39*	*119*	*20*	*5*	*.224/.317/.402*	*.250*	*8.5*	*.308*	*2.9*	*3B 2, 2B -2*	*1.0*

Breakout: 2%   Improve: 24%   Collapse: 4%   Attrition: 14%   MLB: 47%   Comparables: Chris Carter, Matt Davidson, Andy Marte

Moncada could be the best prospect in baseball, but he has two glaring flaws; he's not perfect and he's already been paid a lot of money. Moncada destroyed Salem and held his own in Portland as a 20-year-old, showcasing explosive speed, emerging power and a willingness to walk. Things didn't go as well in the majors, where Moncada struck out nine straight times and got burned during his baptism by fire at the hot corner. Expectations are always unreasonable in Boston, but add $63 million to the top prospect billing and things can get ugly faster than a Curt Schilling Facebook post. Case in point: On September 10th Moncada pinch-ran for David Ortiz in the eighth inning of a nationally-televised game against the Blue Jays. Moncada seemed to forget how many outs there were and Tom Verducci hit America with the type of moral outrage not seen in a broadcast booth since Joe Buck was red and nude and mad at Randy Moss's fake butt. Moncada's going to have to get used to that type of unreasonable reaction whenever he fails because the expectations couldn't be higher. The good news for the Red Sox? He looks to have the talent to meet them anyway.

Justin Morneau   1B

Born: 5/15/81   Age: 36   Bats: L   Throws: R   Height: 6'4"   Weight: 220   Entered Pro Ball: Round 3, 1999 Draft (#89 overall)

YEAR	TEAM	LVL	AGE	PA	R	2B	3B	HR	RBI	BB	K	SB	CS	AVG/OBP/SLG	TAv	VORP	BABIP	BRR	FRAA	WARP
2014	COL	MLB	33	550	62	32	3	17	82	34	60	0	3	.319/.364/.496	.297	23.6	.330	-0.7	1B(131): 3.6	3.0
2015	COL	MLB	34	182	19	10	3	3	15	13	25	0	0	.310/.363/.458	.279	5.4	.350	0.2	1B(44): -1.7	0.4
2016	CHA	MLB	35	218	16	14	1	6	25	12	52	0	0	.261/.303/.429	.252	-0.5	.320	-0.9		0.0
2017	*CHA*	*MLB*	*36*	*250*	*26*	*12*	*1*	*7*	*30*	*18*	*47*	*0*	*0*	*.260/.319/.415*	*.252*	*3.2*	*.295*	*-0.1*		*0.3*
2018	*CHA*	*MLB*	*37*	*171*	*20*	*8*	*1*	*5*	*19*	*13*	*33*	*0*	*0*	*.250/.311/.395*	*.245*	*0.5*	*.286*	*-0.1*	*-*	*0.1*

Breakout: 1%   Improve: 27%   Collapse: 13%   Attrition: 20%   MLB: 74%   Comparables: Mike Sweeney, Michael Young, Ty Wigginton

Morneau's defining value is that he used to be Justin Morneau, something to which no other baseball player can lay claim. His MVP season is now 11 years ago, and today he's just a solid left-handed bat used to fill out the first base/DH situation. He played just three months for the White Sox last year after getting an elbow tendon fixed in the offseason. Even if he's ready for a full season this time, you're not going to want to see him out there every day, because you can only take so many stories about what Brad Radke and Lew Ford are up to these days.

Tyler Saladino   IF

Born: 7/20/89   Age: 27   Bats: R   Throws: R   Height: 6'0"   Weight: 200   Entered Pro Ball: Round 7, 2010 Draft (#218 overall)

YEAR	TEAM	LVL	AGE	PA	R	2B	3B	HR	RBI	BB	K	SB	CS	AVG/OBP/SLG	TAv	VORP	BABIP	BRR	FRAA	WARP
2014	CHR	AAA	24	325	41	16	4	9	43	27	50	7	1	.310/.367/.483	.275	17.9	.346	1.3	SS(50): 3.4 • 1B(10): 0.3	2.2
2015	CHR	AAA	25	231	28	7	2	4	29	22	33	25	2	.255/.332/.372	.256	7.9	.277	1.7	SS(34): 2.3 • 3B(2): -0.3	1.0
2015	CHA	MLB	25	254	33	6	4	4	20	12	51	8	2	.225/.267/.335	.210	-3.3	.269	1.1	3B(60): 5.4 • SS(11): -0.7	0.2
2016	CHA	MLB	26	319	33	14	0	8	38	13	62	11	5	.282/.315/.409	.251	8.5	.329	1.1	2B(41): 1.9 • SS(32): 0.5	1.4
2017	CHA	MLB	27	332	37	13	3	8	35	20	65	13	3	.257/.305/.392	.249	8.5	.298	1.7	2B 0, 3B 2	1.1
2018	CHA	MLB	28	360	41	14	3	9	41	24	74	13	3	.253/.308/.402	.246	6.2	.295	1.8	2B 0, 3B 2	1.1

Breakout: 7%   Improve: 36%   Collapse: 12%   Attrition: 25%   MLB: 90%   Comparables: Brian Dozier, Brandon Phillips, Chris Burke

In the frenetic, dog-eat-dog world of utility players, Saladino needed to prove he could hit and blew away expectations by hitting exactly league average. Given that he can also play every position (although technically anyone *can* play any position, even Billy Butler), the man with the name of a vegetarian magician has enough all-around baseball skills to round out a roster.

Carlos Sanchez   2B

Born: 6/29/92   Age: 25   Bats: B   Throws: R   Height: 5'11"   Weight: 195   Entered Pro Ball: International Free Agent, 2009

YEAR	TEAM	LVL	AGE	PA	R	2B	3B	HR	RBI	BB	K	SB	CS	AVG/OBP/SLG	TAv	VORP	BABIP	BRR	FRAA	WARP
2014	CHR	AAA	22	494	60	19	6	7	57	36	84	16	4	.293/.349/.412	.249	12.6	.344	1.8	2B(64): -0.2 • SS(44): 0.1	1.2
2014	CHA	MLB	22	104	6	5	0	0	5	3	25	1	1	.250/.269/.300	.221	-2.7	.329	-1.5	2B(27): -3.4 • SS(1): -0.1	-0.7
2015	CHR	AAA	23	137	17	10	0	2	17	4	28	5	2	.344/.368/.466	.281	7.4	.426	0.6	2B(26): -0.6 • SS(3): 1.2	0.8
2015	CHA	MLB	23	420	40	23	1	5	31	19	81	2	2	.224/.268/.326	.218	-5.0	.270	1.5	2B(117): -2.2	-0.8
2016	CHR	AAA	24	260	31	11	2	8	29	17	55	10	4	.255/.309/.421	.244	1.8	.299	-1.5	2B(45): -0.4 • SS(16): 1.8	0.3
2016	CHA	MLB	24	163	15	9	1	4	21	5	42	0	1	.208/.236/.357	.210	-4.9	.257	-1.2	2B(33): -1.7 • 3B(6): 0.3	-0.7
2017	CHA	MLB	25	88	9	4	1	2	8	4	19	1	1	.246/.286/.371	.233	0.8	.296	0.0	2B -1	-0.1
2018	CHA	MLB	26	272	30	13	1	6	28	17	62	4	2	.247/.299/.380	.235	1.3	.299	-0.1	2B -2	-0.1

Breakout: 5%   Improve: 27%   Collapse: 14%   Attrition: 30%   MLB: 79%   Comparables: DJ LeMahieu, Ruben Gotay, Scooter Gennett

When the White Sox were caught on the Brett Lawrie end of a trade, Sanchez saw only marginal playing time, "hitting" .132/.175/.171 through August. But in a month of auditioning for 2017, Sanchez may well have earned some type of roster presence with a .282/.296/.538 mark the rest of the way. No matter the situation, walks and home runs are as likely as scratch-off payouts. More likely, he's going to turn his decent contact rate into doubles power. Failing that, he's trying to show he can also spell players around the infield to make an argument for staying on the 25-man beyond "well, you already signed me and Brett Lawrie isn't here anymore."

Charlie Tilson   CF

Born: 12/2/92   Age: 24   Bats: L   Throws: L   Height: 5'11"   Weight: 195   Entered Pro Ball: Round 2, 2011 Draft (#79 overall)

YEAR	TEAM	LVL	AGE	PA	R	2B	3B	HR	RBI	BB	K	SB	CS	AVG/OBP/SLG	TAv	VORP	BABIP	BRR	FRAA	WARP
2014	PMB	A+	21	402	54	8	8	5	36	24	76	10	7	.308/.357/.414	.281	25.3	.377	3.8	CF(83): -10.8	1.5
2014	SFD	AA	21	145	19	4	1	2	17	6	28	2	3	.237/.269/.324	.221	1.2	.284	2.8	CF(26): -3.2 • LF(6): 1.2	-0.1
2015	SFD	AA	22	594	85	20	9	4	32	46	72	46	19	.295/.351/.388	.276	31.4	.333	4.8	CF(128): 2.6	3.7
2016	MEM	AAA	23	395	53	16	8	4	34	33	51	15	3	.282/.345/.407	.270	15.8	.317	0.9	CF(65): -7.9 • LF(35): -4.1	0.4
2016	CHA	MLB	23	2	0	0	0	0	0	0	0	0	0	.500/.500/.500	.337	0.2	.500	-0.1	CF(1): -0.1	0.0
2017	CHA	MLB	24	448	53	15	6	7	37	26	90	16	6	.255/.300/.370	.239	7.2	.305	1.7	CF -5	-0.2
2018	CHA	MLB	25	539	60	18	7	11	57	35	107	20	8	.263/.315/.396	.245	9.1	.310	2.7	CF -6	0.4

Breakout: 12%   Improve: 22%   Collapse: 6%   Attrition: 23%   MLB: 47%   Comparables: Matt Szczur, Denard Span, Ezequiel Carrera

He's faster than a Twista lyric, but he packs about as much punch as Macklemore. Tilson shows some barrel ability with a short, compact, contact-oriented swing, which helps him utilize his impressive speed. Players with well-below-average strength don't typically start at the major-league level and he's already working at a detriment defensively thanks to a fringe arm. Tilson will have to maximize his hit tool and play the hell out of center field to earn a starting role.

PITCHERS

Spencer Adams   RHP

Born: 4/13/96   Age: 21   Bats: R   Throws: R   Height: 6'3"   Weight: 171   Entered Pro Ball: Round 2, 2014 Draft (#44 overall)

YEAR	TEAM	LVL	AGE	W	L	SV	G	GS	IP	H	HR	BB/9	K/9	K	GB%	BABIP	WHIP	ERA	FIP	DRA	VORP	WARP	cFIP	MPH
2015	KAN	A	19	9	5	0	19	19	100	111	7	1.0	6.6	73	52%	.311	1.22	3.24	3.29	2.80	26.9	2.9	81	
2015	WNS	A+	19	3	0	0	5	5	29¹	31	1	2.1	7.1	23	49%	.323	1.30	2.15	2.95	3.56	4.9	0.5	95	
2016	WNS	A+	20	8	7	0	18	18	107²	120	7	1.8	6.2	74	55%	.313	1.31	4.01	3.69	3.55	23.1	2.4	92	
2016	BIR	AA	20	2	5	0	9	9	55¹	59	2	1.6	4.2	26	42%	.298	1.25	3.90	3.45	5.95	-5.3	-0.6	111	
2017	*CHA*	*MLB*	*21*	*7*	*9*	*0*	*23*	*23*	*127¹*	*160*	*19*	*2.9*	*4.5*	*63*	*54%*	*.312*	*1.58*	*5.17*	*5.16*	*5.65*	*-2.5*	*-0.3*	*134*	
2018	*CHA*	*MLB*	*22*	*6*	*7*	*0*	*19*	*19*	*111²*	*118*	*16*	*4.0*	*7.8*	*96*	*54%*	*.306*	*1.50*	*4.69*	*4.80*	*5.12*	*4.0*	*0.4*	*121*	

Breakout: 8%   Improve: 9%   Collapse: 3%   Attrition: 13%   MLB: 16%   *Comparables: Jon Niese, Wilfredo Boscan, Tyler Danish*

It still hasn't quite come together for Adams, whose stuff remains erratic. Adams' control numbers have been comparable to Janet Jackson's "Control" numbers in terms of success, but he's working more in the 88-92 mph range rather than the 92-96 range he was in as a prep. He still has ingredients: he's young and he flashes feel for his slider and shows promise with his curve. Adams might be well served by repeating Double-A and taking it slowly until he starts missing bats.

Matt Albers   RHP

Born: 1/20/83   Age: 34   Bats: L   Throws: R   Height: 6'1"   Weight: 225   Entered Pro Ball: Round 23, 2001 Draft (#686 overall)

YEAR	TEAM	LVL	AGE	W	L	SV	G	GS	IP	H	HR	BB/9	K/9	K	GB%	BABIP	WHIP	ERA	FIP	DRA	VORP	WARP	cFIP	MPH
2014	HOU	MLB	31	0	0	0	8	0	10	10	0	2.7	7.2	8	53%	.333	1.30	0.90	2.76	4.15	0.4	0.0	101	96.2
2015	CHA	MLB	32	2	0	0	30	0	37¹	31	3	2.2	6.8	28	59%	.259	1.07	1.21	3.45	3.60	4.6	0.5	97	93.0
2016	CHA	MLB	33	2	6	0	58	1	51¹	67	10	3.3	5.3	30	50%	.328	1.68	6.31	5.76	5.72	-4.2	-0.4	115	95.1
2017	*CHA*	*MLB*	*34*	*2*	*1*	*1*	*43*	*0*	*45¹*	*46*	*6*	*3.4*	*6.9*	*35*	*52%*	*.293*	*1.40*	*4.68*	*4.56*	*5.21*	*-0.8*	*-0.1*	*120*	
2018	*CHA*	*MLB*	*35*	*2*	*1*	*0*	*35*	*0*	*38*	*39*	*5*	*3.2*	*6.6*	*28*	*52%*	*.289*	*1.38*	*4.51*	*4.63*	*5.02*	*0.1*	*0.0*	*114*	

Breakout: 15%   Improve: 31%   Collapse: 29%   Attrition: 9%   MLB: 79%   *Comparables: Joe Beimel, Matt Lindstrom, Dennys Reyes*

After a couple of sneaky good years of middle relief, Albers' peripherals came crashing down like the engine from *Donnie Darko*. Despite that, his finest moment from the 2016 campaign came on the other side of ball, drilling a 13th-inning gapper and motoring like a gazelle on anesthesia for a double and ultimately the go-ahead run. He shouldn't quit his day job, although if he can't command his two-seamer he may have no choice.

Zack Burdi   RHP

Born: 3/9/95   Age: 22   Bats: R   Throws: R   Height: 6'3"   Weight: 205   Entered Pro Ball: Round 1, 2016 Draft (#26 overall)

YEAR	TEAM	LVL	AGE	W	L	SV	G	GS	IP	H	HR	BB/9	K/9	K	GB%	BABIP	WHIP	ERA	FIP	DRA	VORP	WARP	cFIP	MPH
2016	BIR	AA	21	0	0	0	12	0	16	7	2	5.1	13.5	24	63%	.179	1.00	3.94	3.82	3.10	2.9	0.3	80	
2016	CHR	AAA	21	1	0	1	9	0	16	9	0	6.2	12.4	22	47%	.265	1.25	2.25	2.48	3.46	2.7	0.3	83	
2017	*CHA*	*MLB*	*22*	*1*	*1*	*0*	*23*	*0*	*23*	*23*	*3*	*4.5*	*9.0*	*24*	*55%*	*.295*	*1.44*	*4.78*	*4.42*	*4.94*	*0.1*	*0.0*	*100*	
2018	*CHA*	*MLB*	*23*	*2*	*1*	*1*	*44*	*0*	*46¹*	*36*	*6*	*5.5*	*11.4*	*58*	*55%*	*.284*	*1.39*	*4.11*	*4.21*	*4.55*	*2.5*	*0.3*	*103*	

Breakout: 16%   Improve: 16%   Collapse: 4%   Attrition: 10%   MLB: 22%   *Comparables: Danny Barnes, Alex Claudio, Akeel Morris*

The Burdi brothers specialize in heat, and while Zack clocks in slightly behind Nick his fastball is still at the top of the scale in terms of velocity. Burdi the younger can touch triple digits, but he works more comfortably in the upper 90s by generating late life on a hard fastball. Burdi's mechanics don't inspire much hope for a starter's role and the White Sox used him exclusively as a reliever in 2016. He has a great shot to pitch in a high-leverage role thanks to the heater and bat-missing slider.

Tyler Danish   RHP

Born: 9/12/94   Age: 22   Bats: R   Throws: R   Height: 6'0"   Weight: 200   Entered Pro Ball: Round 2, 2013 Draft (#55 overall)

YEAR	TEAM	LVL	AGE	W	L	SV	G	GS	IP	H	HR	BB/9	K/9	K	GB%	BABIP	WHIP	ERA	FIP	DRA	VORP	WARP	cFIP	MPH
2014	KAN	A	19	3	0	0	7	7	38	28	0	2.4	5.9	25	66%	.252	1.00	0.71	3.06	4.14	5.5	0.6	97	
2014	WNS	A+	19	5	3	0	18	18	91²	87	7	2.3	7.7	78	62%	.301	1.20	2.65	3.69	3.29	23.5	2.4	91	
2015	BIR	AA	20	8	12	0	26	26	142	175	13	3.8	5.7	90	56%	.347	1.65	4.50	4.60	4.75	5.4	0.6	107	
2016	BIR	AA	21	3	7	0	12	12	75¹	71	3	1.9	5.6	47	57%	.281	1.15	4.42	3.23	4.15	7.9	0.9	98	
2016	CHA	MLB	21	0	0	0	3	0	1²	6	0	16.2	0.0	0	44%	.667	5.40	10.80	8.51	4.41	0.1	0.0	116	93.8
2016	CHR	AAA	21	1	3	0	7	5	29¹	39	0	3.1	6.4	21	54%	.382	1.67	5.83	2.86	5.40	-0.4	0.0	104	
2017	*CHA*	*MLB*	*22*	*5*	*7*	*0*	*17*	*17*	*93*	*114*	*13*	*3.5*	*4.9*	*51*	*53%*	*.317*	*1.61*	*5.14*	*5.14*	*5.64*	*-1.7*	*-0.2*	*133*	
2018	*CHA*	*MLB*	*23*	*5*	*7*	*0*	*18*	*18*	*107*	*114*	*16*	*5.0*	*8.0*	*95*	*53%*	*.313*	*1.62*	*5.09*	*5.22*	*5.59*	*-1.3*	*-0.1*	*131*	

Breakout: 13%   Improve: 23%   Collapse: 7%   Attrition: 19%   MLB: 32%   *Comparables: Daniel Corcino, Greg Reynolds, Eduardo Rodriguez*

Danish's stock has been in a downturn since a strong 2014 season put him on the map. His stuff has been walking backward; his slider lacks bite and his fastball, which was middling to begin with, doesn't have anything outside of a changeup to play off of, so hitters jump all over it. Danish will likely have to ply his fastball/changeup combination in a bullpen role.

John Danks   LHP

Born: 4/15/85   Age: 32   Bats: L   Throws: L   Height: 6'1"   Weight: 210   Entered Pro Ball: Round 1, 2003 Draft (#9 overall)

YEAR	TEAM	LVL	AGE	W	L	SV	G	GS	IP	H	HR	BB/9	K/9	K	GB%	BABIP	WHIP	ERA	FIP	DRA	VORP	WARP	cFIP	MPH
2014	CHA	MLB	29	11	11	0	32	32	193²	205	25	3.4	6.0	129	44%	.291	1.44	4.74	4.79	4.91	-1.6	-0.2	112	91.3
2015	CHA	MLB	30	7	15	0	30	30	177²	195	24	2.8	6.3	124	40%	.305	1.41	4.71	4.46	4.92	3.1	0.3	117	92.2
2016	CHA	MLB	31	0	4	0	4	4	22¹	28	5	4.4	6.4	16	32%	.338	1.75	7.25	6.06	5.56	-0.5	-0.1	123	89.9
2017	CHA	MLB	32	2	3	0	7	7	44	46	7	3.3	7.7	38	43%	.299	1.41	4.82	4.70	5.34	0.6	0.1	126	
2018	CHA	MLB	33	9	11	0	29	29	178¹	187	32	3.2	7.8	155	43%	.299	1.41	4.77	4.89	5.29	3.5	0.4	125	

Breakout: 20%   Improve: 48%   Collapse: 16%   Attrition: 11%   MLB: 81%   Comparables: Kevin Correia, Nate Robertson, Kip Wells

Danks has the career numbers of a journeyman fifth starter, but he's one of the few pitchers who (so far) spent his entire career with one franchise. The complete list of pitchers with 1,500 or more career innings and a below-average ERA+ for one team is compact: Danks, Scott McGregor, Steve Blass and someone named "Grunting" Jim Shaw of the Washington Senators. With his already average stuff fading into the high 80s, the White Sox cut ties with him in June, along with every veteran within a 10-mile radius. If this is it for his career, he should have no regrets (especially as a back-end starter who once hooked a $65 million extension) except perhaps that nobody called him "Grunting" John Danks.

Dane Dunning   RHP

Born: 12/20/94   Age: 22   Bats: R   Throws: R   Height: 6'4"   Weight: 200   Entered Pro Ball: Round 1, 2016 Draft (#29 overall)

YEAR	TEAM	LVL	AGE	W	L	SV	G	GS	IP	H	HR	BB/9	K/9	K	GB%	BABIP	WHIP	ERA	FIP	DRA	VORP	WARP	cFIP	MPH
2016	AUB	A-	21	3	2	0	7	7	33²	26	1	1.9	7.8	29	62%	.279	0.98	2.14	2.56	2.93	8.6	0.9	87	
2017	CHA	MLB	22	2	3	0	7	7	32²	39	5	4.2	5.9	21	50%	.313	1.65	5.38	5.30	5.80	-1.2	-0.1	139	
2018	CHA	MLB	23	6	8	0	24	24	139²	146	19	4.3	7.6	118	50%	.307	1.52	4.69	4.80	5.06	5.0	0.5	121	

Breakout: 1%   Improve: 1%   Collapse: 0%   Attrition: 1%   MLB: 2%   Comparables: Wilking Rodriguez, Tyler Wilson, Braden Shipley

A victim of the Florida Gators' excess, Dunning was pushed to a relief role for much of his draft season. That didn't stop Washington from tapping him 29th overall in June, however, and the organization wasted no time dropping him into its short-season rotation. He made notable strides refining his command while in college and the improvements carried over through his first eight professional appearances after signing. With good size, a plus fastball, and a couple solid secondaries behind it, Dunning boasts a prototypical fourth starter's profile.

Carson Fulmer   RHP

Born: 12/13/93   Age: 23   Bats: R   Throws: R   Height: 6'0"   Weight: 195   Entered Pro Ball: Round 1, 2015 Draft (#8 overall)

YEAR	TEAM	LVL	AGE	W	L	SV	G	GS	IP	H	HR	BB/9	K/9	K	GB%	BABIP	WHIP	ERA	FIP	DRA	VORP	WARP	cFIP	MPH
2015	WNS	A+	21	0	0	0	8	8	22	16	2	3.7	10.2	25	43%	.269	1.14	2.05	3.66	3.22	4.5	0.5	94	
2016	BIR	AA	22	4	9	0	17	17	87	82	7	5.3	9.3	90	45%	.310	1.53	4.76	4.16	6.09	-9.6	-1.0	109	
2016	CHA	MLB	22	0	2	0	8	0	11²	12	2	5.4	7.7	10	44%	.312	1.63	8.49	5.93	4.90	0.1	0.0	110	95.3
2016	CHR	AAA	22	2	1	0	4	4	16	14	1	2.8	7.9	14	61%	.289	1.19	3.94	3.17	3.08	4.0	0.4	87	
2017	CHA	MLB	23	1	2	0	20	2	29	29	3	4.9	7.4	24	52%	.296	1.55	5.08	4.63	5.21	-0.4	0.0	100	
2018	CHA	MLB	24	2	2	0	33	3	49¹	43	6	6.0	9.9	55	52%	.296	1.54	4.43	4.54	4.89	1.5	0.2	111	

Breakout: 7%   Improve: 13%   Collapse: 4%   Attrition: 14%   MLB: 18%   Comparables: Tyler Clippard, Nick Maronde, Anthony Lerew

A standout starter at Vanderbilt and the No. 8 overall pick in the 2015 draft, Fulmer made his big-league debut as a reliever and struggled. Even in college many scouting reports pegged him as a better fit in the bullpen long term, so the only surprise would be if the White Sox shifted him to relief work before giving him a chance to start. Fulmer has big-time raw stuff, including a mid-90s fastball and a power curveball that both play up even more in short stints, but his command needs serious work and his minor-league numbers as a starter were mostly underwhelming.

Lucas Giolito   RHP

Born: 7/14/94   Age: 22   Bats: R   Throws: R   Height: 6'6"   Weight: 255   Entered Pro Ball: Round 1, 2012 Draft (#16 overall)

YEAR	TEAM	LVL	AGE	W	L	SV	G	GS	IP	H	HR	BB/9	K/9	K	GB%	BABIP	WHIP	ERA	FIP	DRA	VORP	WARP	cFIP	MPH
2014	HAG	A	19	10	2	0	20	20	98	70	7	2.6	10.1	110	51%	.262	1.00	2.20	3.16	1.60	41.9	4.3	73	
2015	POT	A+	20	3	5	0	13	11	69²	65	1	2.6	11.1	86	54%	.352	1.22	2.71	1.96	1.19	29.6	3.2	68	
2015	HAR	AA	20	4	2	0	8	8	47¹	48	2	3.2	8.6	45	56%	.341	1.37	3.80	3.18	3.00	11.0	1.2	87	
2016	HAR	AA	21	5	3	0	14	14	71	67	2	4.3	9.1	72	53%	.323	1.42	3.17	3.30	3.71	11.0	1.2	91	
2016	SYR	AAA	21	1	2	0	7	7	37¹	31	3	2.4	9.6	40	56%	.298	1.10	2.17	2.95	2.42	12.1	1.3	73	
2016	WAS	MLB	21	0	1	0	6	4	21¹	26	7	5.1	4.6	11	42%	.271	1.78	6.75	8.25	7.87	-6.2	-0.6	136	96.1
2017	CHA	MLB	22	5	6	0	16	16	91	96	11	4.0	7.2	72	49%	.302	1.52	4.68	4.61	5.05	2.0	0.2	100	
2018	CHA	MLB	23	9	10	0	29	29	176¹	163	22	5.2	9.8	192	49%	.304	1.50	4.39	4.51	4.85	11.0	1.1	112	

Breakout: 21%   Improve: 37%   Collapse: 3%   Attrition: 19%   MLB: 48%   Comparables: Jon Niese, Arodys Vizcaino, Wade Davis

If the quickest path from Point A to B is a straight line, the one your average pitching prospect travels more closely resembles a pine tree in Nowe Czarnowo. To wit, the Nationals' former top prospect, who remains a really, really good prospect, lost a few ticks of shine after an inconsistent-at-best season. Reported mechanical tweaks may have contributed to his bugaboo command stagnating, but the stuff seemed to follow suit. The triple-digit amateur showcase heat of yore continued to drift closer to the memory dump, and what remains was battered to the tune of a .742 slugging percentage in an erratic six-game debut in The Show. The curve continued to show elite downer action, but he struggled to keep it in the zone long enough to tantalize the best hitters in the world. He'll certainly get another crack at big-league bats in 2017 (health permitting), and will enter the season as the largest of X-factors in the Washington rotation.

Miguel Gonzalez   RHP

Born: 5/27/84   Age: 33   Bats: R   Throws: R   Height: 6'1"   Weight: 170   Entered Pro Ball: International Free Agent, 2004

YEAR	TEAM	LVL	AGE	W	L	SV	G	GS	IP	H	HR	BB/9	K/9	K	GB%	BABIP	WHIP	ERA	FIP	DRA	VORP	WARP	cFIP	MPH
2014	BAL	MLB	30	10	9	0	27	26	159	155	25	2.9	6.3	111	39%	.273	1.30	3.23	4.92	5.60	-13.5	-1.5	120	93.3
2015	BAL	MLB	31	9	12	0	26	26	144²	151	24	3.2	6.8	109	42%	.295	1.40	4.91	4.98	4.83	4.0	0.4	114	93.8
2016	CHR	AAA	32	1	1	0	5	5	21¹	27	5	1.7	10.5	25	42%	.386	1.45	4.64	4.57	1.74	8.5	0.9	80	
2016	CHA	MLB	32	5	8	0	24	23	135	132	11	2.3	6.3	95	42%	.289	1.24	3.73	3.67	4.65	10.6	1.1	105	94.0
2017	CHA	MLB	33	9	11	0	28	28	168	164	24	2.9	7.5	139	52%	.288	1.29	4.48	4.46	4.86	7.2	0.7	100	
2018	CHA	MLB	34	9	10	0	27	27	160	165	26	2.9	7.3	130	52%	.292	1.35	4.63	4.75	5.13	6.0	0.6	121	

Breakout: 8%   Improve: 39%   Collapse: 19%   Attrition: 17%   MLB: 87%   Comparables: Scott Feldman, Chris Young, Justin Duchscherer

Gonzalez knows how to pitch, and does. Released by the Orioles during spring training when his velocity faded, Gonzalez joined the White Sox and had a solid season while consistently throwing 92 mph with great command around the corners. He pitches to weak contact and his Achilles' heel of home runs was mostly slayed in classic Greek fashion by moving to Guaranteed Rate Field, of all places. Toss in a smoothed-up walk rate and for once Gonzalez posted a good FIP. Another satisfied Don Cooper customer.

Jordan Guerrero   LHP

Born: 5/31/94   Age: 23   Bats: L   Throws: L   Height: 6'3"   Weight: 195   Entered Pro Ball: Round 15, 2012 Draft (#471 overall)

YEAR	TEAM	LVL	AGE	W	L	SV	G	GS	IP	H	HR	BB/9	K/9	K	GB%	BABIP	WHIP	ERA	FIP	DRA	VORP	WARP	cFIP	MPH
2014	KAN	A	20	6	2	0	27	9	78	81	5	3.1	9.2	80	48%	.344	1.38	3.46	3.52	2.88	20.6	2.1	92	
2015	KAN	A	21	6	1	0	9	9	55¹	42	1	1.6	9.8	60	44%	.293	0.94	2.28	2.20	1.45	23.2	2.5	70	
2015	WNS	A+	21	7	3	0	16	16	93²	82	6	2.0	8.5	88	45%	.298	1.10	3.56	3.04	1.72	34.9	3.8	80	
2016	BIR	AA	22	7	8	0	25	25	136	133	13	4.8	7.1	108	45%	.302	1.51	4.83	4.70	6.32	-18.4	-2.0	121	
2017	CHA	MLB	23	6	8	0	20	20	110¹	130	17	4.7	5.8	71	57%	.310	1.70	5.56	5.56	6.05	-7.1	-0.7	143	
2018	CHA	MLB	24	5	7	0	18	18	105²	106	16	6.0	8.6	101	57%	.302	1.67	5.28	5.40	5.74	-2.9	-0.3	136	

Breakout: 7%   Improve: 10%   Collapse: 2%   Attrition: 9%   MLB: 14%   Comparables: Jeff Manship, Michael Stutes, Michael Kirkman

The fastball velocity never got to the heights he teased as a high schooler, but Guerrero's heater has climbed back into the above-average range and he's pairing it with a plus changeup. Guerrero can manipulate the baseball by showing cutting action on the fastball and he pounds the lower quadrants of the zone to keep the ball in the park. He's lacking a breaking ball, which has created issues as he climbs the ladder. Guerrero's command took a curious step backward in 2016, so that's something to keep an eye on.

Alec Hansen   RHP

Born: 10/10/94   Age: 22   Bats: R   Throws: R   Height: 6'7"   Weight: 235   Entered Pro Ball: Round 2, 2016 Draft (#49 overall)

YEAR	TEAM	LVL	AGE	W	L	SV	G	GS	IP	H	HR	BB/9	K/9	K	GB%	BABIP	WHIP	ERA	FIP	DRA	VORP	WARP	cFIP	MPH
2016	KAN	A	21	0	1	0	2	2	11	11	0	3.3	9.0	11	54%	.346	1.36	2.45	2.76	3.71	1.6	0.2	99	
2017	CHA	MLB	22	2	2	0	7	7	32²	34	5	5.4	8.6	31	54%	.311	1.62	5.06	5.24	5.45	0.1	0.0	130	
2018	CHA	MLB	23	8	9	0	29	29	180²	167	25	4.9	9.9	198	54%	.304	1.47	4.42	4.52	4.76	10.8	1.1	113	

Breakout: 4%   Improve: 4%   Collapse: 2%   Attrition: 3%   MLB: 7%   Comparables: Tyler Wilson, Andrew Heaney, T.J. McFarland

At one point Hansen was in the mix to go in the top 10 of the 2016 draft, but like Nas he followed up the initial hype with a long and drawn out battle with mediocrity and disastrous command. Also like Nas, he experienced a revival of sorts as soon as he hit pro ball, dramatically cutting his out-of-control walk rates from college, albeit against rookie-ball hitters. Hansen pumps absolute gas and pairs it with a plus-potential slider. Sometimes he shows feel for a changeup. If he can hold his command gains he'll be drinkin Moets and makin sure the cash came correct.

Dan Jennings   LHP

Born: 4/17/87   Age: 30   Bats: L   Throws: L   Height: 6'3"   Weight: 210   Entered Pro Ball: Round 9, 2008 Draft (#268 overall)

YEAR	TEAM	LVL	AGE	W	L	SV	G	GS	IP	H	HR	BB/9	K/9	K	GB%	BABIP	WHIP	ERA	FIP	DRA	VORP	WARP	cFIP	MPH
2014	MIA	MLB	27	0	2	0	47	0	40¹	45	3	3.8	8.5	38	50%	.339	1.54	1.34	3.45	3.90	2.6	0.3	101	94.5
2015	CHA	MLB	28	2	3	0	53	0	56¹	55	3	3.8	7.3	46	65%	.304	1.40	3.99	3.44	3.33	8.6	0.9	95	95.0
2016	CHA	MLB	29	4	3	1	64	0	60²	57	1	4.2	6.8	46	56%	.309	1.40	2.08	3.34	4.58	2.6	0.3	101	93.3
2017	CHA	MLB	30	2	3	0	50	0	52	52	6	3.8	7.7	45	50%	.301	1.44	4.50	4.31	4.74	1.4	0.1	100	
2018	CHA	MLB	31	2	1	1	40	0	42	41	5	3.9	8.5	40	50%	.304	1.41	4.08	4.19	4.53	2.4	0.2	101	

Breakout: 30%   Improve: 56%   Collapse: 18%   Attrition: 23%   MLB: 85%   Comparables: Jared Burton, Pedro Strop, Jared Hughes

Jennings will never be mistaken for Zach Britton, even though they were the only two left-handers last season who pitched 60 or more innings and gave up just one home run. (Also: neither pitched in the postseason.) The difference, of course, is that Jennings is such a middle reliever that he doesn't even have his own inning. How gauche. The sinker/slider lefty has home run limiting powers, no tiny task in Guaranteed Rate Field, and in fact the lone homer was a walk-off in Seattle (a hanging slider on an 0-2 pitch against a lefty). Beyond that one mistake, he's still a lefty specialist profile, but he's daft enough to go a full inning, especially since he locates the sinker so well even if you can't locate him on a team photo.

Nate Jones   RHP

Born: 1/28/86   Age: 31   Bats: R   Throws: R   Height: 6'5"   Weight: 220   Entered Pro Ball: Round 5, 2007 Draft (#179 overall)

YEAR	TEAM	LVL	AGE	W	L	SV	G	GS	IP	H	HR	BB/9	K/9	K	GB%	BABIP	WHIP	ERA	FIP	DRA	VORP	WARP	cFIP	MPH
2014	CHA	MLB	28	0	0	0	2	0	0	2	0			0	0%	1.000								98.3
2015	CHA	MLB	29	2	2	0	19	0	19	12	5	2.8	12.8	27	49%	.206	0.95	3.32	4.63	2.95	3.7	0.4	76	100.0
2016	CHA	MLB	30	5	3	3	71	0	70²	48	7	1.9	10.2	80	47%	.243	0.89	2.29	2.89	2.59	18.7	1.9	70	99.2
2017	CHA	MLB	31	3	3	0	54	0	57¹	48	6	2.3	10.5	67	50%	.295	1.10	3.05	3.07	3.52	9.3	1.0	75	
2018	CHA	MLB	32	3	1	1	63	0	66²	56	8	2.4	10.6	78	50%	.296	1.11	3.13	3.23	3.51	11.3	1.2	73	

Breakout: 23%   Improve: 36%   Collapse: 34%   Attrition: 10%   MLB: 91%   Comparables: *Rafael Soriano, Sergio Romo, Luke Gregerson*

It's easy to get mesmerized by Jones' arm delivery. Out of the stretch, the pitching arm is flailed behind him like a fishing lure. Ah, fishing. A hobby most often associated with inner peace, and with humankind connecting with nature in a deeply personal way. Of course, once you hook your prey, then it's a mad dash to reel it in. Maybe that's what makes his delivery so deceptively dangerous. He makes no attempt the hide the ball, but then again he brandishes two plus gambits—upper-90s heat and one of the league's hardest sliders—so you have a 50-50 chance of being right. He'll hook many a guppy with both offerings, and if it's the slider, don't bother—batters hit .094 against it. By comparison, batters hit .170 off Andrew Miller. And like Miller, it took Jones some time to reach his current position. It took him until age 25 to reach Double-A and also a year for his body to work in a new UCL. He's locked into a team-friendly contract with club options through 2021, so if he does become a closer, somebody in the front office is getting a gold star. Or at least a new fishing boat.

Tommy Kahnle   RHP

Born: 8/7/89   Age: 27   Bats: R   Throws: R   Height: 6'1"   Weight: 235   Entered Pro Ball: Round 5, 2010 Draft (#175 overall)

YEAR	TEAM	LVL	AGE	W	L	SV	G	GS	IP	H	HR	BB/9	K/9	K	GB%	BABIP	WHIP	ERA	FIP	DRA	VORP	WARP	cFIP	MPH
2014	COL	MLB	24	2	1	0	54	0	68²	51	7	4.1	8.3	63	48%	.240	1.19	4.19	3.99	3.48	7.7	0.8	98	97.5
2015	COL	MLB	25	0	1	2	36	0	33¹	31	3	7.6	10.5	39	59%	.329	1.77	4.86	4.51	3.20	5.6	0.6	94	99.1
2015	ABQ	AAA	25	1	3	6	21	0	27	19	3	4	9.3	28	38%	.235	1.15	4.67	4.41	5.02	-0.3	0.0	99	
2016	CHR	AAA	26	1	1	7	23	0	27	17	0	4.0	12.0	36	48%	.283	1.07	3.00	1.95	1.62	10.0	1.0	74	
2016	CHA	MLB	26	0	1	1	29	0	27¹	21	2	6.6	8.2	25	50%	.264	1.50	2.63	4.42	4.99	-0.1	0.0	107	99.3
2017	CHA	MLB	27	1	1	0	23	0	23	22	3	4.3	8.8	23	49%	.286	1.35	4.61	4.38	4.82	0.4	0.0	100	
2018	CHA	MLB	28	3	1	1	51	0	53²	43	7	4.6	10.7	64	49%	.278	1.31	4.04	4.13	4.47	3.4	0.4	101	

Breakout: 35%   Improve: 52%   Collapse: 19%   Attrition: 15%   MLB: 83%   Comparables: *Kevin Quackenbush, Steve Cishek, Brian Wilson*

When you first think of Kahnle you might say "who?" when in reality it should be "The Who." (Tommy Kahnle hear me? Can you feel me near you?) Initially thought to be a bargain last offseason, Kahnle's walk rate makes you think the umpire's putting a squeeze box on him. Instead he rode the magic bus between Charlotte and Chicago, trying to be the seeker of the strike zone. Otherwise, he'll constantly change uniforms anyway, anyhow anywhere they choose. In conclusion … pinball wizard.

Michael Kopech   RHP

Born: 4/30/96   Age: 21   Bats: R   Throws: R   Height: 6'3"   Weight: 205   Entered Pro Ball: Round 1, 2014 Draft (#33 overall)

YEAR	TEAM	LVL	AGE	W	L	SV	G	GS	IP	H	HR	BB/9	K/9	K	GB%	BABIP	WHIP	ERA	FIP	DRA	VORP	WARP	cFIP	MPH
2015	GRN	A	19	4	5	0	16	15	65	53	2	3.7	9.7	70	47%	.313	1.23	2.63	3.35	3.40	13.0	1.4	97	
2016	SLM	A+	20	4	1	0	11	11	52	25	1	5.0	14.2	82	45%	.273	1.04	2.25	2.60	1.22	24.6	2.5	77	
2017	CHA	MLB	21	3	4	0	11	11	44¹	43	6	5.7	8.9	44	54%	.306	1.61	5.00	5.00	5.50	-0.1	0.0	128	
2018	CHA	MLB	22	5	8	0	25	25	145	122	20	6.5	11.2	181	54%	.300	1.56	4.66	4.78	5.13	3.6	0.4	120	

Breakout: 14%   Improve: 18%   Collapse: 2%   Attrition: 9%   MLB: 20%   Comparables: *Keyvius Sampson, Luis Severino, Alex Reyes*

For a player who's not even close to the majors, Kopech sure does find himself in the news a lot. Sometimes it's for good reasons, like when he hits triple-digits on the radar gun in the AFL All-Star game. Other times it's because he's just broken his hand after punching a teammate (these violent deliveries have violent ends), or because he's dating a bit player on Bravo's *Don't Be Tardy*—advice those who face his fastball have trouble following. When he's on the mound, Kopech dazzles. He blew High-A hitters away with his fastball and a sharp slider, but he also walked 14 percent of batters faced and threw more than five innings just three times in 19 starts. His command issues and high-effort delivery have many scouts projecting a future closer, but if he does remain in the rotation there's some Baby Thor potential here, right down to the Norse god's immaturity issues.

Reynaldo Lopez   RHP

Born: 1/4/94   Age: 23   Bats: R   Throws: R   Height: 6'0"   Weight: 185   Entered Pro Ball: International Free Agent, 2012

YEAR	TEAM	LVL	AGE	W	L	SV	G	GS	IP	H	HR	BB/9	K/9	K	GB%	BABIP	WHIP	ERA	FIP	DRA	VORP	WARP	cFIP	MPH
2014	AUB	A-	20	3	2	0	7	7	36	15	0	3.8	7.8	31	62%	.167	0.83	0.75	3.14	3.39	7.8	0.8	100	
2014	HAG	A	20	4	1	0	9	9	47¹	27	1	2.1	7.4	39	65%	.211	0.80	1.33	2.91	3.09	12.4	1.3	89	
2015	POT	A+	21	6	7	0	19	19	99	93	5	2.5	8.5	94	47%	.321	1.22	4.09	2.95	2.44	29.0	3.1	83	
2016	HAR	AA	22	3	5	0	14	14	76¹	69	7	2.9	11.8	100	43%	.320	1.23	3.18	3.03	1.50	30.5	3.3	68	
2016	SYR	AAA	22	2	2	0	5	5	33	21	6	2.7	7.1	26	33%	.174	0.94	3.27	4.96	7.09	-6.4	-0.7	118	
2016	WAS	MLB	22	5	3	0	11	6	44	47	4	4.5	8.6	42	43%	.326	1.57	4.91	3.96	4.58	3.2	0.3	105	98.7
2017	CHA	MLB	23	3	3	0	25	7	56	55	6	3.6	8.0	50	47%	.295	1.37	4.18	4.11	4.46	4.4	0.4	100	
2018	CHA	MLB	24	8	6	0	62	16	144¹	123	17	4.7	10.4	167	47%	.293	1.37	3.96	4.06	4.34	14.3	1.5	99	

Breakout: 24%   Improve: 44%   Collapse: 12%   Attrition: 22%   MLB: 75%   Comparables: *Daniel Hudson, Andy Oliver, Robbie Erlin*

Lopez's strengths and weaknesses were both on display after the Washington's third-ranked prospect forced an audition with the big club in August and September. He whiffed nine in less than five innings in his Nationals debut, though he got pounded for six runs and 10 hits in the process. Then a month later, he whiffed 11 in one start before failing to make it out of the third in his next. So it goes for rookie starters, especially those with Lopez's boom-and-bust profile. His high-octane heater plays fairly straight, while his secondaries still lack consistent shape and effectiveness. The premium velocity and a curve that flashes plus all but guarantee a whole bunch of big-league innings in his future, though the bullpen gate still sits ajar, beckoning sooner than later if the command and secondary stability don't materialize quickly enough for his new organization's liking.

Jose Quintana   LHP

Born: 1/24/89   Age: 28   Bats: R   Throws: L   Height: 6'1"   Weight: 220   Entered Pro Ball: International Free Agent, 2006

YEAR	TEAM	LVL	AGE	W	L	SV	G	GS	IP	H	HR	BB/9	K/9	K	GB%	BABIP	WHIP	ERA	FIP	DRA	VORP	WARP	cFIP	MPH
2014	CHA	MLB	25	9	11	0	32	32	200¹	197	10	2.3	8.0	178	47%	.318	1.24	3.32	2.84	2.80	45.4	5.0	85	93.9
2015	CHA	MLB	26	9	10	0	32	32	206¹	218	16	1.9	7.7	177	48%	.327	1.27	3.36	3.15	3.53	35.4	3.8	91	94.1
2016	CHA	MLB	27	13	12	0	32	32	208	192	22	2.2	7.8	181	41%	.293	1.16	3.20	3.52	3.48	43.6	4.5	91	94.6
2017	CHA	MLB	28	12	11	0	31	31	195¹	186	23	2.3	8.8	190	46%	.301	1.22	3.70	3.64	4.02	26.7	2.7	91	
2018	CHA	MLB	29	12	10	0	31	31	196²	192	25	2.3	8.9	195	46%	.307	1.23	3.59	3.68	4.00	31.2	3.2	89	

Breakout: 27%   Improve: 54%   Collapse: 26%   Attrition: 9%   MLB: 95%   Comparables: Johnny Cueto, David Price, Adam Wainwright

The solid no. 2 lefty who slipped through the hands of both New York teams' minor-league systems is now "Jose Quintana, All-Star" on his business cards. Consistency is never sexy unless the ERA begins with a 1 or 2, so he's still an underappreciated arm on a relatively cheap contract with team options through 2020. Ergo, he's a general manager's dream pitcher. There's no reason to believe the Colombian isn't good for a fifth straight season of 200-plus innings of a 3.50 or so ERA. Unless, of course, Quintana is nothing but a concurrent lucid dream between Brian Cashman and Omar Minaya. In which case they're bound to wake up soon.

Anthony Ranaudo   RHP

Born: 9/9/89   Age: 27   Bats: R   Throws: R   Height: 6'7"   Weight: 240   Entered Pro Ball: Round 1, 2010 Draft (#39 overall)

YEAR	TEAM	LVL	AGE	W	L	SV	G	GS	IP	H	HR	BB/9	K/9	K	GB%	BABIP	WHIP	ERA	FIP	DRA	VORP	WARP	cFIP	MPH
2014	PAW	AAA	24	14	4	0	24	24	138	112	9	3.5	7.2	111	37%	.264	1.20	2.61	3.86	3.38	36.5	3.6	103	
2014	BOS	MLB	24	4	3	0	7	7	39¹	39	10	3.7	3.4	15	35%	.225	1.40	4.81	6.92	8.28	-15.1	-1.7	140	94.0
2015	TEX	MLB	25	0	1	0	4	2	15¹	18	2	4.7	6.5	11	30%	.314	1.70	7.63	5.13	6.46	-2.6	-0.3	126	93.2
2015	ROU	AAA	25	7	6	0	21	21	118	124	14	3.5	6.9	90	37%	.306	1.44	4.58	4.89	4.06	16.3	1.7	102	
2016	ROU	AAA	26	1	1	0	3	3	13¹	6	0	2.7	12.1	18	59%	.207	0.75	2.03	2.37	0.04	7.9	0.8	74	
2016	TEX	MLB	26	1	0	0	2	0	3²	2	1	19.6	4.9	2	36%	.100	2.73	17.18	12.11	7.87	-1.0	-0.1	133	94.0
2016	CHR	AAA	26	6	5	0	16	16	96²	92	15	1.0	6.1	65	44%	.266	1.07	3.35	4.28	4.10	13.4	1.4	96	
2016	CHA	MLB	26	0	1	0	7	5	27²	34	9	3.9	5.2	16	41%	.269	1.66	8.46	7.48	7.65	-7.3	-0.7	136	93.6
2017	CHA	MLB	27	7	8	0	21	21	117¹	119	17	3.2	6.3	83	48%	.282	1.37	4.77	4.80	5.29	2.4	0.2	125	
2018	CHA	MLB	28	6	8	0	21	21	124	112	20	5.1	8.6	119	48%	.273	1.47	5.06	5.19	5.61	-1.8	-0.2	133	

Breakout: 14%   Improve: 26%   Collapse: 21%   Attrition: 40%   MLB: 58%   Comparables: Chris Rusin, Jeremy Hefner, Stephen Fife

Being a top prospect is a little like being a politician; years after you are one, you are still called one. Ranaudo didn't put himself on the prospect rankings, we did—five years ago. However he did pitch himself out of a spot on the Texas roster, then was flipped to the White Sox in an act we'll call Former Top Prospect Second Chance #2, splitting time between Chicago and Charlotte. A month-long tryout in the rotation went about how you'd expect, but hey, he's a former top prospect, so he's going to get another chance somewhere, or try his hand at long reliever, and you can't rule out a trade to yet another team, and on and on, until the scenery is just right.

David Robertson   RHP

Born: 4/9/85   Age: 32   Bats: R   Throws: R   Height: 5'11"   Weight: 195   Entered Pro Ball: Round 17, 2006 Draft (#524 overall)

YEAR	TEAM	LVL	AGE	W	L	SV	G	GS	IP	H	HR	BB/9	K/9	K	GB%	BABIP	WHIP	ERA	FIP	DRA	VORP	WARP	cFIP	MPH
2014	NYA	MLB	29	4	5	39	63	0	64¹	45	7	3.2	13.4	96	47%	.288	1.06	3.08	2.71	2.03	17.6	1.9	66	94.4
2015	CHA	MLB	30	6	5	34	60	0	63¹	46	7	1.8	12.2	86	38%	.275	0.93	3.41	2.49	2.68	14.3	1.5	74	94.7
2016	CHA	MLB	31	5	3	37	62	0	62¹	53	6	4.6	10.8	75	47%	.307	1.36	3.47	3.54	2.78	15.2	1.6	86	94.5
2017	CHA	MLB	32	3	3	37	59	0	62	52	6	3.4	10.9	75	42%	.298	1.22	3.09	3.25	3.55	9.9	1.0	74	
2018	CHA	MLB	33	3	1	34	61	0	64¹	52	7	3.4	10.6	76	42%	.289	1.20	3.30	3.41	3.69	9.6	1.0	79	

Breakout: 22%   Improve: 40%   Collapse: 23%   Attrition: 8%   MLB: 90%   Comparables: Jonathan Papelbon, Michael Gonzalez, Francisco Rodriguez

Yes, strikeouts are as prevalent as they've ever been in the league. Given the current era, this is still impressive: the only three pitchers to have nine straight seasons of at least 10.0 strikeouts per nine innings are Randy Johnson (12), Billy Wagner (10) and this guy. Having a natural cut fastball, years of Mariano Rivera mentorship and an extra-bendy curveball really helps pad those numbers. Most great closers can't keep the high-velocity readings forever, but since Robertson never really had them it's a safe bet that he'll still be a closer for years.

Carlos Rodon   LHP

Born: 12/10/92   Age: 24   Bats: L   Throws: L   Height: 6'3"   Weight: 235   Entered Pro Ball: Round 1, 2014 Draft (#3 overall)

YEAR	TEAM	LVL	AGE	W	L	SV	G	GS	IP	H	HR	BB/9	K/9	K	GB%	BABIP	WHIP	ERA	FIP	DRA	VORP	WARP	cFIP	MPH
2014	CHR	AAA	21	0	0	0	3	3	12	9	0	6.0	13.5	18	42%	.346	1.42	3.00	2.61	2.84	3.9	0.4	85	
2015	CHR	AAA	22	1	0	0	2	2	10	8	0	3.6	11.7	13	42%	.333	1.20	3.60	2.36	2.67	2.9	0.3	85	
2015	CHA	MLB	22	9	6	0	26	23	139¹	130	11	4.6	9.0	139	49%	.315	1.44	3.75	3.84	4.23	12.8	1.4	102	97.1
2016	CHA	MLB	23	9	10	0	28	28	165	176	23	2.9	9.2	168	44%	.330	1.39	4.04	3.97	3.44	35.2	3.6	88	97.5
2017	CHA	MLB	24	10	11	0	31	31	176²	168	23	3.2	9.6	189	46%	.307	1.33	3.97	3.94	4.33	18.0	1.9	100	
2018	CHA	MLB	25	10	9	0	28	28	173²	167	23	3.1	9.7	186	46%	.313	1.31	3.77	3.89	4.22	22.2	2.3	95	

Breakout: 28%   Improve: 63%   Collapse: 13%   Attrition: 6%   MLB: 97%   Comparables: Madison Bumgarner, Scott Kazmir, Mike Leake

The standout sophomore needed to shatter his walk rate and did that by nearly one-third. His reward: a slightly higher FIP. Hey, sometimes a good deed has to be its own reward. Better command resulted in right-handers sitting on Rodon's fastball and slugging .570 against it. According to FanGraphs' pitch values, his was the seventh-worst fastball in the league—just barely worse than James Shields, who is probably no longer allowed to mentor him. But by no means did he limp to the finish line, as his penultimate start was eight shutout innings and 11 strikeouts at Cleveland. Not unlike surviving in an ice fishing shanty, heater location is going to be crucial for him this year.

James Shields   RHP

Born: 12/20/81   Age: 35   Bats: R   Throws: R   Height: 6'3"   Weight: 215   Entered Pro Ball: Round 16, 2000 Draft (#466 overall)

YEAR	TEAM	LVL	AGE	W	L	SV	G	GS	IP	H	HR	BB/9	K/9	K	GB%	BABIP	WHIP	ERA	FIP	DRA	VORP	WARP	cFIP	MPH
2014	KCA	MLB	32	14	8	0	34	34	227	224	23	1.7	7.1	180	47%	.295	1.18	3.21	3.62	3.37	37.1	4.1	93	94.7
2015	SDN	MLB	33	13	7	0	33	33	202¹	189	33	3.6	9.6	216	47%	.299	1.33	3.91	4.48	3.79	29.0	3.1	95	93.6
2016	SDN	MLB	34	2	7	0	11	11	67¹	69	9	3.6	7.6	57	48%	.316	1.43	4.28	4.48	5.73	-2.8	-0.3	122	92.5
2016	CHA	MLB	34	4	12	0	22	22	114¹	139	31	4.3	6.1	78	38%	.296	1.70	6.77	6.89	6.20	-10.7	-1.1	124	93.1
2017	*CHA*	*MLB*	*35*	*10*	*12*	*0*	*28*	*28*	*187*	*190*	*30*	*3.5*	*8.1*	*169*	*50%*	*.298*	*1.41*	*4.76*	*4.75*	*5.18*	*1.4*	*0.1*	*100*	
2018	*CHA*	*MLB*	*36*	*11*	*12*	*0*	*29*	*29*	*177²*	*182*	*31*	*3.3*	*8.1*	*160*	*50%*	*.297*	*1.40*	*4.72*	*4.83*	*5.23*	*5.1*	*0.5*	*123*	

Breakout: 15%   Improve: 36%   Collapse: 15%   Attrition: 12%   MLB: 75%   *Comparables: Johan Santana, A.J. Burnett, Erik Bedard*

Big ERA James didn't benefit from a change of scenery after the Padres mashed the reset button to stop the pain and paid half of his contract to make him leave, too. The White Sox saw their former division rival allow six-plus runs in starts eight times, and the fly-ball pitcher was ill-suited for Guaranteed Rate Park—the 40 homers allowed was the most by any pitcher in five years. Never a big strikeout specialist, Shields suffered the worst K/9 rate of his career, and with two more guaranteed years on his contract he's going to survive on a major-league roster on name recognition alone. "Hey, didn't you use to be ... wait, don't tell me ... the guy from Tampa Bay who was traded with the other guy who turned out to be really good? What's he up to, anyway?"

Blake Smith   RHP

Born: 12/9/87   Age: 29   Bats: L   Throws: R   Height: 6'2"   Weight: 220   Entered Pro Ball: Round 2, 2009 Draft (#56 overall)

YEAR	TEAM	LVL	AGE	W	L	SV	G	GS	IP	H	HR	BB/9	K/9	K	GB%	BABIP	WHIP	ERA	FIP	DRA	VORP	WARP	cFIP	MPH
2014	RCU	A+	26	1	3	9	22	0	28	23	2	4.2	9.0	28	48%	.312	1.29	3.54	4.28	5.13	0.2	0.0	103	
2014	CHT	AA	26	1	4	2	26	0	33¹	35	2	4.3	8.9	33	42%	.333	1.53	4.05	3.70	2.82	7.5	0.8	94	
2015	TUL	AA	27	0	3	3	16	0	16²	8	1	4.9	8.6	16	66%	.163	1.02	1.62	4.14	3.55	2.2	0.2	94	
2015	CHR	AAA	27	1	2	0	24	0	30	29	1	4.5	12.6	42	53%	.368	1.47	3.30	2.29	1.90	10.1	1.0	78	
2016	CHR	AAA	28	3	1	1	39	0	71¹	64	6	3.0	9.5	75	44%	.309	1.23	3.53	3.17	2.09	22.7	2.3	85	
2016	CHA	MLB	28	0	0	0	5	0	4¹	7	1	0.0	2.1	1	47%	.333	1.62	6.23	6.34	5.49	-0.2	0.0	110	95.0
2017	*CHA*	*MLB*	*29*	*3*	*1*	*1*	*55*	*0*	*58*	*61*	*8*	*3.8*	*8.2*	*53*	*49%*	*.310*	*1.47*	*4.45*	*4.54*	*4.95*	*0.8*	*0.1*	*112*	
2018	*CHA*	*MLB*	*30*	*1*	*0*	*0*	*16*	*0*	*21²*	*19*	*3*	*5.2*	*10.8*	*26*	*49%*	*.303*	*1.47*	*4.24*	*4.35*	*4.72*	*0.8*	*0.1*	*105*	

Breakout: 15%   Improve: 17%   Collapse: 12%   Attrition: 17%   MLB: 32%   *Comparables: Neil Wagner, Dane De La Rosa, Jose Valdez*

When we last saw Smith in this book (2013), he was a Dodgers outfielder with an all-or-nothing swing that had too much nothing even at Double-A. We said he could potentially pitch (as he did in college at Berkeley), so maybe the Dodgers read that and said, "Sure, why not." He worked up enough value to be traded for Eric Surkamp, then was Rule 5'd by the Padres for an unsuccessful spring training tryout. His September call-up went well in that he became a big leaguer after a position change, but that's about it. Both the low-90s fastball and mid-70s curveball need to improve if he's going to win a job, because in this business he's basically out of career changes.

Michael Ynoa   RHP

Born: 9/24/91   Age: 25   Bats: R   Throws: R   Height: 6'7"   Weight: 210   Entered Pro Ball: International Free Agent, 2008

YEAR	TEAM	LVL	AGE	W	L	SV	G	GS	IP	H	HR	BB/9	K/9	K	GB%	BABIP	WHIP	ERA	FIP	DRA	VORP	WARP	cFIP	MPH
2014	STO	A+	22	4	2	0	31	0	45²	42	5	4.1	12.6	64	41%	.352	1.38	5.52	4.07	2.42	14.1	1.4	84	
2015	WNS	A+	23	0	2	6	28	0	38	37	2	3.8	9.5	40	44%	.337	1.39	2.61	3.65	3.38	5.6	0.6	98	
2016	CHR	AAA	24	1	3	4	18	0	23²	25	2	4.6	7.6	20	33%	.324	1.56	4.56	4.48	7.27	-6.1	-0.6	118	
2016	CHA	MLB	24	1	0	0	23	0	30	20	0	5.1	9.0	30	40%	.241	1.23	3.00	3.31	4.43	1.8	0.2	107	97.0
2017	*CHA*	*MLB*	*25*	*2*	*2*	*0*	*36*	*0*	*38*	*39*	*5*	*4.1*	*7.7*	*33*	*52%*	*.298*	*1.47*	*4.85*	*4.64*	*4.97*	*0.0*	*0.0*	*100*	
2018	*CHA*	*MLB*	*26*	*2*	*1*	*0*	*44*	*0*	*47*	*42*	*6*	*5.1*	*10.1*	*53*	*52%*	*.301*	*1.47*	*4.34*	*4.44*	*4.77*	*1.5*	*0.2*	*108*	

Breakout: 31%   Improve: 41%   Collapse: 16%   Attrition: 31%   MLB: 62%   *Comparables: Phillippe Aumont, Mayckol Guaipe, Jeremy Jeffress*

Ynoa's first Annual comment was in 2009 as an extravagant A's signing out of the Dominican Republic. Since then it's been setback after setback, and last year was his first appearance past High-A. As fortune would have it, his first promotion was due to the birth of Adam Eaton's son, who will now grow up in a world thinking Ynoa was always a major leaguer. The 6-foot-7 righty's debut came months later after a "real" call-up and in true raw pitcher fashion: two innings, two strikeouts, two walks, no runs or hits. Despite the wild mid-90s fastball, he was there to stay in the White Sox's bullpen. He's 25, but in baseball years it's an old 25. He's seen some things, mostly minor-league lockers, but not for much longer.

LINEOUTS

Hitters

NAME	POS	TEAM	LVL	AGE	PA	R	2B	3B	HR	RBI	BB	K	SB	CS	AVG/OBP/SLG	TAv	VORP	BABIP	BRR	FRAA	WARP
Micker Adolfo	OF	KAN	A	19	265	30	13	1	5	21	14	88	0	1	.219/.269/.340	.246	1.0	.318	0.0	RF(61): 6.5, CF(2): -0.2	0.8
Jason Coats	OF	CHR	AAA	26	332	44	22	2	10	38	25	69	1	3	.330/.394/.519	.317	25.6	.402	0.2	RF(61): -2.3, LF(11): -0.6	2.3
	OF	CHA	MLB	26	58	8	4	0	1	4	5	12	1	0	.200/.298/.340	.239	0.0	.243	0.2	RF(11): -0.9, LF(7): -1.0	-0.2
Matt Davidson	3B	CHR	AAA	25	326	35	20	0	10	46	32	86	0	0	.268/.349/.444	.271	10.7	.346	-2.6	3B(66): 6.3, 1B(6): 0.1	1.8
	3B	CHA	MLB	25	2	1	0	0	0	1	0	1	0	0	.500/.500/.500	.352	0.1	1.000	-0.1		0.0
Leury Garcia	3B	CHR	AAA	25	342	45	9	4	6	35	24	64	18	8	.313/.367/.426	.275	16.9	.378	1.3	LF(28): 1.1, SS(25): -1.0	2.1
	3B	CHA	MLB	25	50	6	1	1	1	5	1	13	2	1	.229/.260/.354	.214	-0.4	.294	0.4	CF(16): -0.9	-0.1
Alfredo Gonzalez	C	CCH	AA	23	162	14	5	1	0	7	14	40	0	0	.158/.236/.205	.179	-9.4	.217	-3.2	C(44): 10.6	0.1
	C	BIR	AA	23	152	13	6	0	0	8	10	22	2	0	.296/.358/.341	.270	6.3	.348	-1.3	C(35): 3.9	1.1
Courtney Hawkins	CF	BIR	AA	22	455	35	25	0	12	60	28	137	0	3	.203/.255/.349	.232	-3.0	.265	1.3	LF(81): -11.2, RF(8): -0.2	-1.6
Slade Heathcott	DH	SWB	AAA	25	97	14	5	1	0	7	5	31	2	1	.230/.271/.310	.233	0.4	.339	0.6	CF(16): -1.2, LF(5): 0.1	-0.1
	DH	CHR	AAA	25	119	19	2	1	2	7	22	30	1	1	.258/.407/.366	.276	3.8	.355	0.1	RF(15): 0.1, LF(5): 0.4	0.4
Jacob May	OF	CHR	AAA	24	321	38	19	2	1	24	15	72	19	8	.266/.309/.352	.234	-0.3	.346	-1.0	CF(78): 1.4, LF(4): -0.0	0.1
Omar Narvaez	C	BIR	AA	24	49	4	2	0	0	5	4	8	0	0	.222/.286/.267	.208	-1.6	.270	-1.1	C(13): -0.2	-0.2
	C	CHR	AAA	24	156	14	6	0	2	11	9	17	0	0	.245/.292/.329	.210	0.1	.264	1.5	C(39): -4.7	-0.5
	C	CHA	MLB	24	117	13	4	0	1	10	14	14	0	0	.267/.350/.337	.261	5.0	.295	-0.5	C(34): -3.5	0.2
Jake Peter	INF	BIR	AA	23	291	27	14	0	4	29	31	52	5	1	.304/.378/.407	.309	19.3	.361	-0.1	1B(25): 0.7, LF(17): -3.9	1.6
	INF	CHR	AAA	23	250	30	13	0	2	24	17	44	3	1	.259/.317/.342	.243	4.3	.311	0.9	2B(34): 2.7, SS(19): -2.1	0.6
Jimmy Rollins	SS	CHA	MLB	37	166	25	8	1	2	8	16	33	5	2	.221/.295/.329	.223	-0.6	.270	-0.6	SS(35): -3.0	-0.4
Jerry Sands	DH	CHA	MLB	28	58	2	0	0	1	7	3	24	0	0	.236/.276/.291	.188	-3.5	.400	-0.4	1B(4): 0.2, LF(3): -0.4	-0.4
	DH	CHR	AAA	28	301	32	12	1	8	37	26	62	0	1	.252/.318/.393	.246	-1.5	.297	-0.1	1B(61): -2.6, RF(1): -0.4	-0.5
J.B. Shuck	LF	CHR	AAA	29	170	20	9	2	2	17	11	13	4	2	.299/.339/.422	.256	2.6	.310	0.3	LF(19): 0.8, 1B(8): -0.6	0.4
	LF	CHA	MLB	29	241	27	5	2	4	14	12	21	3	3	.205/.248/.299	.196	-1.2	.210	-1.4	CF(60): -4.3, LF(3): 1.0	-1.4
Kevan Smith	C	CHR	AAA	28	205	18	9	0	8	24	16	36	0	0	.219/.291/.399	.225	-0.2	.229	-1.1	C(43): -2.2	-0.2
	C	CHA	MLB	28	16	2	0	0	0	0	0	6	0	0	.125/.125/.125	.121	-1.0	.200	0.7	C(6): -0.3	-0.1
Corey Zangari	1B	KAN	A	19	248	22	9	0	8	24	20	106	0	2	.166/.247/.314	.213	-7.0	.266	1.3	1B(51): -2.1	-1.0

Micker Adolfo presents a lot of tools. He's physically yoked and has tremendous arm strength, but concerns over his contact issues weren't assuaged in a troublesome 2016 season. ❖ A middling prospect heading into 2016, outfielder **Jason Coats** bashed Triple-A pitching for 78 games to earn his first call-up to the majors at age 26. There's little to suggest he's an impact bat, but he could be a useful role player. ❖ After two brutal Triple-A seasons, the hapless **Matt Davidson** returned to the majors and broke his foot rounding the bases in his White Sox debut. Once healthy he'll be perfectly fine corner infield depth. ❖ **Jameson Fisher** came in and wrecked the Pioneer League, which is to be expected of college-age hitters facing much younger competition. He's a below-average athlete without the arm to play in right field. ❖ **Leury Garcia** plays five different premium defensive positions, but has just three offensive positions: whoops, uh-oh, and soft groundout. ❖ Acquired from the Astros at midseason for a small pile of cash, **Alfredo Gonzalez** has the defensive chops to reach the majors despite a punchless bat. ❖ Noted White Sox fan Chance the Rapper did **Courtney Hawkins** a solid by making 3 merchandise a pretty popular item in Chicago. ❖ A former Yankees first-round pick and top-100 prospect, **Slade Heathcott** now looks like little more than organizational depth after repeatedly being derailed by injuries. ❖ The worst-case injury and "what could be?" prospect scenario in 2016 converge: seeing Keon Broxton's breakout thanks to regular playing time amplifies that imagination about what **Rymer Liriano** could have done. ❖ The grandson of Lee, **Jacob May** has a double-plus run tool and little to no power, which is almost the exact opposite skill set his gramps had. ❖ **Omar Narvaez** made his MLB debut filling in for an injured Alex Avila and stuck around longer than expected, showing the strike-zone control that could earn him a backup role despite nonexistent power. ❖ A two-way college player at Creighton, **Jake Peter** became a full-time hitter as a pro and has struggled to produce enough power to be more than a role player. ❖ **Jimmy Rollins** never played for the Dodgers or the White Sox. Nope. That was a hoax. He began and retired as a Phillie, and that's what you should choose to believe even if he latches on with the Giants for another forgettable season. ❖ There's always been the sense that **Jerry Sands** could be a productive, power-hitting platoon 1B/OF if given a chance, but he's never really taken advantage and that's not exactly a difficult-to-fill role. ❖ **J.B. Shuck**'s speed doesn't quite translate to center field-caliber range and his power is lacking for a corner spot, making him a tweener. ❖ At age 29 and coming off back-to-back poor seasons at Triple-A, catcher **Kevan Smith** will need some good fortune just to latch on as a backup. ❖ **Corey Zangari** came into 2016 teasing at some serious power potential and a double-plus arm behind the plate. That all collapsed along with his contact rates and he was sent down to the Pioneer league to find some success.

Pitchers

NAME	TEAM	LVL	AGE	W	L	SV	G	GS	IP	H	HR	BB/9	K/9	K	GB%	BABIP	WHIP	ERA	FIP	DRA	VORP	WARP	cFIP	MPH
Chris Beck	CHR	AAA	25	5	4	0	22	7	66¹	77	5	3.4	6.8	50	50%	.348	1.54	4.21	3.91	4.82	2.6	0.3	99	
	CHA	MLB	25	2	2	0	25	0	25¹	31	3	6.0	7.1	20	48%	.346	1.89	6.39	5.32	5.54	-1.6	-0.2	118	96.9
Dylan Covey	MID	AA	24	2	1	0	6	6	29¹	21	2	5.2	8.0	26	61%	.247	1.30	1.84	4.13	4.27	2.7	0.3	97	
Brad Goldberg	CHR	AAA	26	3	5	10	43	0	50²	42	3	4.1	7.8	44	55%	.275	1.28	2.84	3.68	5.32	-2.0	-0.2	98	
Javy Guerra	ANA	MLB	30	0	0	0	7	0	6¹	5	1	9.9	5.7	4	56%	.235	1.89	5.68	7.69	5.66	-0.5	-0.1	116	95.5
	SLC	AAA	30	3	2	12	43	1	51²	48	5	5.4	9.9	57	50%	.303	1.53	4.35	4.57	3.97	5.8	0.6	98	
Thad Lowry	WNS	A+	21	8	8	0	24	23	135¹	143	8	2.5	6.0	90	48%	.305	1.34	4.06	4.00	4.80	9.9	1.0	103	
	BIR	AA	21	0	3	0	4	4	24	23	0	1.5	4.1	11	41%	.267	1.12	4.12	3.03	7.37	-6.1	-0.7	114	
Luis Martinez	KAN	A	21	8	9	0	28	28	137	126	9	3.4	9.3	141	46%	.312	1.29	3.81	3.49	3.07	29.6	3.2	93	
Juan Minaya	FRE	AAA	25	1	3	0	17	0	25¹	25	1	3.6	6.8	19	51%	.308	1.38	3.91	4.04	4.95	0.0	0.0	102	
	CHR	AAA	25	4	3	1	17	0	26²	23	2	3.4	9.4	28	48%	.288	1.24	3.38	3.28	2.36	7.7	0.8	87	
	CHA	MLB	25	1	0	0	11	0	10¹	10	0	4.4	5.2	6	24%	.294	1.45	4.35	3.98	6.43	-1.7	-0.2	128	96.6
Jake Petricka	CHA	MLB	28	0	0	0	9	0	8	8	1	9.0	7.9	7	71%	.304	2.00	4.50	5.98	4.42	0.5	0.1	101	97.4
Matt Purke	CHA	MLB	25	0	1	0	12	0	18	20	0	6.0	7.5	15	53%	.351	1.78	5.50	3.44	4.76	0.4	0.0	106	94.5
	CHR	AAA	25	0	0	2	26	1	38¹	30	4	5.4	8.9	38	48%	.252	1.38	3.52	4.42	4.98	0.1	0.0	102	
Zach Putnam	CHA	MLB	28	1	0	0	25	0	27¹	25	3	3.6	9.9	30	41%	.324	1.32	2.30	3.07	3.93	3.2	0.3	93	92.5
Giovanni Soto	IOW	AAA	25	1	3	0	33	0	49	51	3	5.7	10.1	55	57%	.361	1.67	5.14	4.48	4.51	2.5	0.3	98	
Jordan Stephens	WNS	A+	23	7	10	0	27	27	141	129	12	3.1	9.9	155	46%	.319	1.26	3.45	3.60	1.99	54.6	5.6	79	
Jacob Turner	CHR	AAA	25	4	7	0	18	18	107	125	10	2.4	7.1	85	49%	.342	1.44	4.71	3.69	2.92	28.8	3.0	92	
	CHA	MLB	25	1	2	0	18	2	24²	33	5	5.8	6.6	18	49%	.346	1.99	6.57	6.47	6.21	-3.1	-0.3	117	98.0
Chris Volstad	CHR	AAA	29	8	11	0	29	27	176²	193	16	1.7	4.3	84	55%	.297	1.28	4.79	4.06	4.77	10.8	1.1	101	
Daniel Webb	CHR	AAA	26	2	1	2	7	0	10²	12	1	0.0	4.2	5	56%	.289	1.12	3.38	3.45	4.81	0.2	0.0	98	
	CHA	MLB	26	0	0	0	1	0	1	2	0	9.0	27.0	3	0%	1.000	3.00	0.00	0.11	3.63	0.1	0.0	95	94.3
Ryan Webb	TBA	MLB	30	0	0	0	18	0	17¹	27	2	1.6	5.7	11	50%	.417	1.73	5.19	3.86	5.31	-0.6	-0.1	107	93.4

Converted starter **Chris Beck** has a fastball lively enough for the bullpen, but the walk rate of an insomniac canine babysitter. ❖ Oakland had a long to-do list for **Dylan Covey** when he reported to Double-A Midland in the spring, but a strained oblique sidelined any progress he was scheduled to make in 2016. ❖ **Brad Goldberg** was supposed to move quickly coming out of college, but instead he was 26 years old by the time he reached Triple-A. He has plenty of velocity, but doesn't generate enough missed bats to make up for poor control. ❖ A former Dodgers closer, **Javy Guerra** doesn't rate a 40-man spot, and as such he'll be lucky to find himself listed here next season. ❖ **Thaddius Lowry** has yet to post a sub-4.00 ERA in four pro seasons, but the former fifth-round pick has back-end starter potential with a low-90s fastball. ❖ Chicago continues to develop **Luis Martinez** as a starter, but he may eventually find a better fit for his mid-90s fastball in the bullpen. ❖ Claimed off waivers from the Astros in June, **Juan Minaya** made his MLB debut as a September call-up despite a 4.65 career ERA and equally underwhelming secondary numbers in the minors. ❖ **Jake Petricka** had problems with his hip like sportswriters had with his last name, and surgery to fix an impingement wiped out most of the ground-balling ROOGY's season. ❖ **Matt Purke** didn't sign with the Rangers as a top-15 pick, later signed with the Nationals as a third-round pick, and finally arrived in the majors last season as a marginal reliever after multiple injuries. ❖ **Zach Putnam** missed yet another half-season, this time due to bone spurs. The good news for this split-finger reliever is that, according to his punch card, his next elbow operation is 50 percent off. ❖ This **Giovanni Soto** is not the Cubs catcher you remember. This is another person. The other one probably had a better arm, though. ❖ As a diminutive Tommy John survivor **Jordan Stephens** may have trouble with a starter's workload long term, but for now the results are promising. ❖ **Jacob Turner** is still young enough for front offices to remember those dreamy scouting reports when he was a top prospect, but they've also seen him constantly fail to execute since then. ❖ Imagine your career peaking at age 21. But the difference between **Chris Volstad** and Daniel Radcliffe is that the latter didn't lead the International League in earned runs allowed last year. ❖ Erratic reliever **Daniel Webb** found a foolproof way to cut down his walk rate all the way to zero! The bad news: it involved the surgery with a 14-month timetable. ❖ **Ryan Webb** struggled and suffered injuries last year with the Rays and White Sox, both of whom released him. Not at the same time, of course, although the thought of a pitcher moonlighting as a pitcher for another team would be both cause for termination and the premise of a hilarious sitcom.

CINCINNATI REDS

Essay by Zach Buchanan

Player comments by Matthew Trueblood and BP staff

Reds general manager and president of baseball operations Dick Williams is never going to work for another team. No one is going to hire him away even if he resuscitates baseball's oldest franchise back into relevancy. He has no desire—it'd make for awkward family reunions.

The 46-year-old Williams is unique in his role because his family has an ownership stake in the team and has for much of the past 50 years. His grandfather was a minority owner from 1966, took a controlling interest in 1980 and sold to Marge Schott in 1984. In 2006, Williams' father and uncle joined a group led by Bob Castellini that purchased the Reds from Carl Lindner.

His family is the entire reason Williams works for the Reds in the first place and why he left careers in finance and politics in his mid-30s to start over at the bottom of the baseball operations department 12 seasons ago. (He can hear you screaming "nepotism!" already, although forcing your 30-something son to spend more than a decade learning the ropes before finally letting him make decisions would be an odd way for a father to shower his offspring with preferential treatment.)

It's why, after being handed final say over baseball decisions last offseason in the wake of the semi-retirement of Walt Jocketty, Williams knows his first chance to run a team is likely his only one. He wants to get it right.

"I've been the first one to admit that knowing the right people played a part in ending up where I was," Williams said. "I believe this is such an important asset in such an important business that I don't think Bob Castellini would turn a job over like this to someone for reasons of nepotism and not ability. There's just too much at stake for all of us."

"Dick Williams" is a pretty boring name. (Sorry, Dick.) It doesn't reveal much about the person to whom it's affixed, and a quick scan of Williams' background doesn't exactly pop and crackle with excitement.

He attended the University of Virginia, and then went to work as an investment banker in New York and Atlanta. Later, he opened and operated a venture capital fund, and starting in 2003 he worked full time for the reelection campaign of President George W. Bush. A lot of things you'd expect a Dick Williams to have done.

But then his dad joined the new Reds ownership group, and Williams assisted in the financial due-diligence of the

REDS PROSPECTUS
2016 W-L: 68-94, 5TH IN NL CENTRAL

Pythag	.416	27th	DER	.710	7th
RS/G	4.42	18th	B-Age	27.8	7th
RA/G	5.27	27th	P-Age	26.9	5th
TAv	.258	18th	Salary	$90.4M	24th
BRR	5.52	7th	M$/MW	$4M	10th
TAv-P	.288	30th	DL Days	1096	18th
FIP	5.28	30th	$ on DL	22%	25th

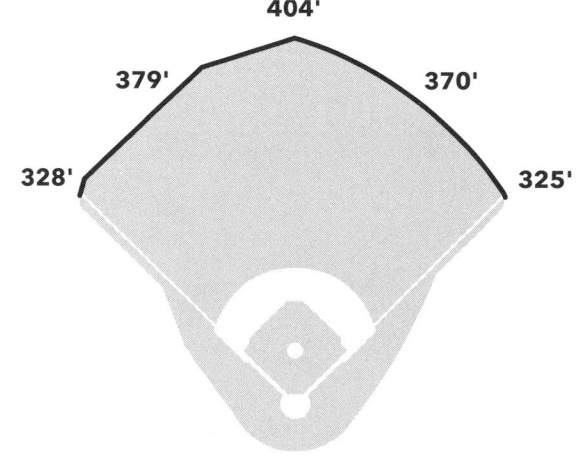

Outfield wall profile: **8'** to **12'**

Three-Year Park Factors

Runs	Runs/RH	Runs/LH	HR/RH	HR/LH
97	93	98	107	115

Top Hitter WARP	5.9	Joey Votto
Top Pitcher WARP	1.6	Anthony DeSclafani
Top Prospect		Nick Senzel

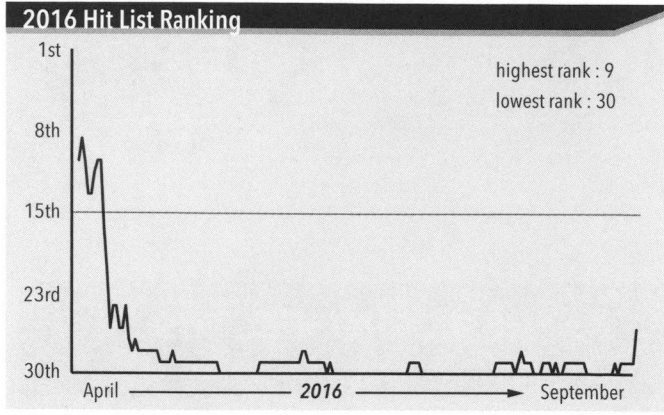

2016 Hit List Ranking

highest rank : 9
lowest rank : 30

April — *2016* → September

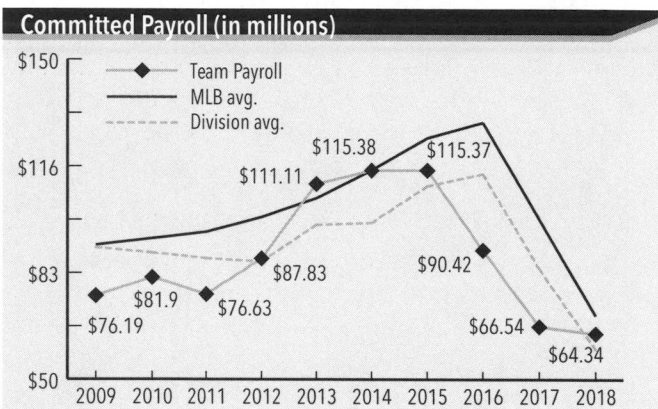

Committed Payroll (in millions)

◆ Team Payroll
— MLB avg.
--- Division avg.

$115.38
$111.11
$115.37
$87.83
$90.42
$81.9
$76.63
$76.19
$66.54
$64.34

2009 2010 2011 2012 2013 2014 2015 2016 2017 2018

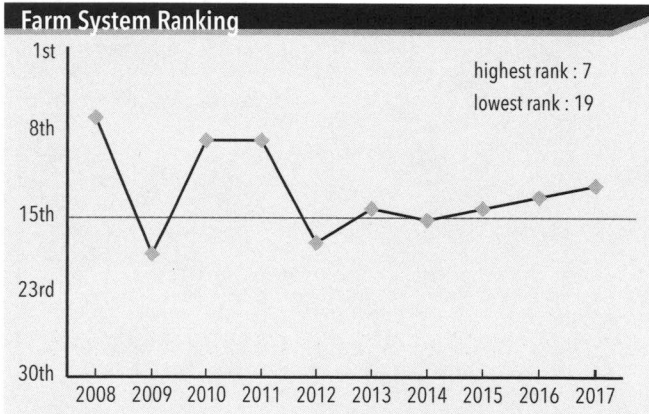

Farm System Ranking

highest rank : 7
lowest rank : 19

2008 2009 2010 2011 2012 2013 2014 2015 2016 2017

Personnel

**Executive Advisor
to the CEO:**
Walt Jocketty

**President, Baseball
Operations & GM:**
Dick Williams

**VP, Assistant General
Managers:**
Nick Krall
Sam Grossman

Manager:
Bryan Price

purchase. The closer he looked at the business the more he considered a career change, and in 2006 he joined the organization as a director of baseball operations, answering to then-general manager Wayne Krivsky.

"I didn't care what the title was," Williams said. "I just wanted to be on the baseball operations team and observe and learn what I could learn. That's how the first five years at least were spent, just soaking up how the business worked."

Promotions to vice president of baseball operations and then assistant GM followed as Williams dug more into the business of baseball. After the 2015 season—10 years into his apprenticeship—came a surprise jump to GM, although Jocketty retained final decision-making power as president of baseball ops. With Jocketty moving into an advisory role following the 2016 season, Williams now has full command over the baseball side of things.

He brings a style shaped by Jocketty's tutelage but also by his own experiences. He entered the game just as advanced statistics began gaining a foothold throughout front offices and his experience on Wall Street made him predisposed to an analytical approach to the game, helping to grow that department from one person in 2007 to what he expects to be double digits by the start of the 2017 season.

Like all teams, the Reds have always tried to project the future of their prospects, but now try to do so with more certainty with a proprietary statistical model. They've also invested in the area of sports science, making three hires in that fledgling department before last season. Of course, all those things happened under Jocketty as well, and it will be interesting to see in what ways Williams differs from his mentor.

Not being on the verge of retirement should help. In his last few years at the helm Jocketty more and more eagerly looked forward to winding down from the daily grind of running a team after decades calling the shots. He irked some rival executives before last season's trade deadline by not responding in a particularly timely fashion to trade inquiries.

There's also a sense that Williams will follow the rebuilding roadmap more fervently, resisting the urge to shortcut the process by making a splash in the free agent market or spending his prospect capital on an upgrade before the team is truly ready to compete. (That may be more of a criticism of Castellini's admirably competitive nature, although those in the organization say the owner has been supportive of the painful rebuilding process since that course was decided upon fully after the 2015 season.)

Williams is more likely to avoid big contracts that hamper the team's ability to compete in such a small market. As currently constituted, the Reds are weighed down by expensive, immovable deals that Jocketty handed to Brandon Phillips, Homer Bailey, Devin Mesoraco and Joey Votto, although Williams maintains that the Votto deal won't be an albatross the closer the first baseman gets to 40.

"Some of the other big-market teams have the luxury of

being able to sign players they don't intend to keep because they have more capacity to sign players," Williams said. "They can sign them and then look at those contracts as tradable assets more so than we can, just because those contracts are a higher percentage of our payroll. We have to be more prudent about when we make those commitments. We can't always assume we're going to be able to move them along if needed."

(Big-market teams like the Cubs, of course, are doing things just as intelligently as the Reds *and* with bigger budgets, but Williams promises Cincinnati will gain an edge somehow: "If you didn't think you had a way to outsmart the competition, then you're in the wrong business. You're in for a long haul.")

Some things will stay the same. Just like under Jocketty, Williams' Reds primarily will rely on scouting and development to make their mark. By that measure—and not the team's 68-94 record—the 2016 season was quite the success. The Reds arguably added more talent to their system than in any year in recent memory.

The team's trade acquisitions from the 2015 deadline to the 2016 deadline were a mixed bag, but offer plenty of reasons for optimism. Adam Duvall wilted after making a surprising All-Star appearance, but still hit 33 home runs and racked up 3.7 WARP thanks in large part to strong defensive numbers. Jose Peraza slashed .366/.387/.484 after manager Bryan Price finally was able to use the Jaws of Life to separate the young Venezuelan from the bench over the last month-plus of the season.

Left-hander Brandon Finnegan surprised his doubters (and defied DRA) by posting a 3.98 ERA in 172 innings as a starter, and by at long last throwing a goddamn changeup with any goddamn regularity. Scott Schebler posted a .357 on-base percentage and an .818 OPS in the final two months after being summoned from the minors to replace Jay Bruce. Left-hander Cody Reed took his lumps in his first taste of the majors, but still offers tantalizing potential. The addition of former top prospect Dilson Herrera gives the Reds a successor to Phillips at second base.

The successes on the amateur side are even greater. Second overall pick Nick Senzel looks like a monster, and leads a draft class that *Baseball America* called the best out of all 30 teams. That includes outfielder T.J. Friedl, a second- or third-round talent the Reds landed after discovering he had double-secret draft eligibility and that they had more than $700,000 left to throw at him. Internationally, the Reds added two high-profile Cuban amateurs in shortstop Alfredo Rodriguez and pitcher Vladimir Gutierrez, at a cost of around $18.5 million.

If the Reds' rebuild succeeds, the period between those two deadlines may be the reason. The upcoming year will be tantalizing as well—the Reds again have the no. 2 pick in the draft—but they have fewer veteran assets to move via trade and will face spending limits internationally.

"I can't remember a year where we had this much positive impact," Williams said. "Where that takes us, I'm excited to see. But it certainly was the most impactful year that I can remember." ▪

—Zach Buchanan covers the Reds for the Cincinnati Enquirer

HITTERS

Arismendy Alcantara CF

Born: 10/29/91 Age: 25 Bats: B Throws: R Height: 5'10" Weight: 170 Entered Pro Ball: International Free Agent, 2008

YEAR	TEAM	LVL	AGE	PA	R	2B	3B	HR	RBI	BB	K	SB	CS	AVG/OBP/SLG	TAv	VORP	BABIP	BRR	FRAA	WARP
2014	IOW	AAA	22	366	62	25	11	10	41	25	83	21	3	.307/.353/.537	.303	32.7	.380	3.8	2B(70): -4.5 • CF(11): -1.0	2.7
2014	CHN	MLB	22	300	31	11	2	10	29	17	93	8	5	.205/.254/.367	.227	-0.7	.266	0.7	CF(48): -4.2 • 2B(25): -1.3	-0.4
2015	CHN	MLB	23	32	5	0	0	0	1	5	11	1	0	.077/.226/.077	.161	-1.8	.133	0.4	2B(8): 0.1 • 3B(2): 0.4	-0.1
2015	IOW	AAA	23	499	72	20	10	12	36	35	125	16	6	.231/.285/.399	.249	11.6	.291	4.3	2B(74): 6.3 • CF(16): -0.9	1.7
2016	IOW	AAA	24	214	32	9	5	5	21	15	61	21	0	.263/.313/.434	.277	11.7	.353	2.3	2B(51): 2.9	1.5
2016	NAS	AAA	24	219	28	10	5	6	27	14	57	11	6	.290/.336/.480	.295	14.3	.374	0.4	CF(14): -0.6 • SS(12): -0.3	1.5
2016	STO	A+	24	27	4	3	1	1	8	1	9	0	0	.308/.333/.615	.349	3.4	.438	0.0	2B(3): 0.2 • CF(2): 0.1	0.4
2016	OAK	MLB	24	19	2	1	0	0	2	0	8	3	3	.211/.211/.263	.144	-2.2	.364	-0.5	CF(4): -0.0 • 2B(3): -0.3	-0.2
2017	*CIN*	*MLB*	*25*	*218*	*27*	*9*	*3*	*7*	*24*	*13*	*62*	*9*	*3*	*.232/.279/.409*	*.237*	*3.0*	*.293*	*1.3*	*LF 1, 2B 0*	*0.2*
2018	*CIN*	*MLB*	*26*	*343*	*40*	*14*	*4*	*12*	*43*	*24*	*95*	*14*	*5*	*.235/.290/.419*	*.250*	*7.0*	*.293*	*1.8*	*LF 1, 2B 0*	*0.8*

Breakout: 7%   Improve: 26%   Collapse: 17%   Attrition: 33%   MLB: 65%   *Comparables: Ryan Adams, Jordany Valdespin, Taylor Featherston*

Some prospects are launched on the track from the minors to the majors. Others are pulled, sub par batting average and all, along the lift hill until they reach the top. Alcantara peaked in 2014 during his first full season in the Cubs' system, then plunged in 2015, braking on a .167 ISO at Triple-A that didn't stabilize quickly enough for another second-half call-up. His 2016 season with the A's followed much of the same route, riding a .290 AVG at Triple-A and nearly dipping below the Mendoza line in three brief bursts as an under-utilized utility player in the majors. Is he on a trick hill, a temporary plateau that precedes another drop? Is he approaching a career-flattening brake run? Or is this just the first tick in another lift hill to a stable role? Maybe the Athletics were lucky to get off the ride when they did.

Aristides Aquino   RF

Born: 4/22/94   Age: 23   Bats: R   Throws: R   Height: 6'4"   Weight: 190   Entered Pro Ball: International Free Agent, 2011

YEAR	TEAM	LVL	AGE	PA	R	2B	3B	HR	RBI	BB	K	SB	CS	AVG/OBP/SLG	TAv	VORP	BABIP	BRR	FRAA	WARP
2015	DYT	A	21	249	25	9	3	5	27	11	53	6	1	.234/.281/.364	.236	0.1	.280	2.0	RF(60): 1.1	0.1
2016	DAY	A+	22	526	69	26	12	23	79	34	104	11	7	.273/.327/.519	.282	22.9	.304	1.3	RF(123): 21.3	4.5
2017	CIN	MLB	23	250	28	10	2	11	34	12	68	2	1	.228/.272/.428	.232	0.0	.272	0.0	RF 3	0.3
2018	CIN	MLB	24	293	36	12	3	13	40	14	78	3	2	.233/.279/.436	.251	3.5	.278	0.1	RF 3	0.8

Breakout: 1%   Improve: 8%   Collapse: 2%   Attrition: 5%   MLB: 14%   Comparables: Bryce Brentz, Yorman Rodriguez, Scott Schebler

His first name sounds like it ought to belong to the hero of a Greek tragedy and for a while it looked like his career would follow that kind of arc. Despite huge tools, Aquino was held back by injuries and a hyper-aggressive approach. Then 2016 happened. Call it a reminder that guys with plus tools all over the scouting report don't need that many things to break right in order to break out. Despite remaining a free swinger, Aquino flashed too much power for even the Florida State League to swallow up, made plays with his legs and made enough contact to have an impact. Now, he has to prove he can do the same thing at Double-A.

Tucker Barnhart   C

Born: 1/7/91   Age: 26   Bats: B   Throws: R   Height: 5'11"   Weight: 190   Entered Pro Ball: Round 10, 2009 Draft (#299 overall)

YEAR	TEAM	LVL	AGE	PA	R	2B	3B	HR	RBI	BB	K	SB	CS	AVG/OBP/SLG	TAv	VORP	BABIP	BRR	FRAA	WARP
2014	LOU	AAA	23	292	18	9	3	1	29	28	34	0	1	.246/.319/.316	.230	0.9	.277	-3.0	C(75): -7.9	-0.7
2014	CIN	MLB	23	60	3	0	0	1	1	4	10	0	0	.185/.241/.241	.206	-0.9	.209	-0.4	C(20): -1.3	-0.2
2015	CIN	MLB	24	274	23	9	0	3	18	25	45	0	1	.252/.324/.326	.245	10.1	.294	2.4	C(73): 3.4 • RF(1): 0.2	1.5
2016	CIN	MLB	25	420	34	23	1	7	51	36	72	1	0	.257/.323/.379	.254	14.6	.299	-1.7	C(108): -0.6	1.4
2017	CIN	MLB	26	282	28	12	1	5	28	24	47	1	0	.248/.313/.367	.241	7.8	.280	-0.6	C -0	-0.5
2018	CIN	MLB	27	333	39	14	1	7	35	30	57	0	0	.248/.320/.375	.252	9.2	.278	-0.2	C -1	0.9

Breakout: 9%   Improve: 48%   Collapse: 9%   Attrition: 25%   MLB: 95%   Comparables: Dioner Navarro, Josh Thole, Jason Castro

Look, we're as surprised as you are. Barnhart has the pedigree, the minor-league career arc and definitely—definitely—the name to be a career backup. Yet he's spent most of the last two seasons proving he can and should be something closer to a regular. His arm is a weapon, he won't kill you as a pitch framer or a game caller, and the guy can hit right-handed pitching. He'll never be first-division, but he's a legitimate big-league catcher, and his best season might be ahead of him.

YEAR	TEAM	P. COUNT	FRM RUNS	BLK RUNS	THRW RUNS	TOT RUNS
2014	CIN	2291	-2.0	0.2	0.5	-1.4
2014	LOU	10597	-7.9	0.6	0.6	-6.7
2015	CIN	10131	2.0	0.4	0.2	2.6
2015	LOU	676	0.0	0.0	0.1	0.0
2016	CIN	16074	-4.4	2.6	1.4	-0.5
2017	CIN	10800	-3.1	1.2	0.6	-1.4
2018	CIN	12758	-4.1	1.4	0.6	-2.1

Alex Blandino   SS

Born: 11/6/92   Age: 24   Bats: R   Throws: R   Height: 6'0"   Weight: 190   Entered Pro Ball: Round 1, 2014 Draft (#29 overall)

YEAR	TEAM	LVL	AGE	PA	R	2B	3B	HR	RBI	BB	K	SB	CS	AVG/OBP/SLG	TAv	VORP	BABIP	BRR	FRAA	WARP
2014	DYT	A	21	152	20	10	1	4	16	13	42	1	2	.261/.329/.440	.291	11.6	.341	0.3	SS(34): 5.1	1.7
2015	DAY	A+	22	342	46	18	2	7	35	31	56	7	10	.294/.370/.438	.317	32.3	.338	0.5	SS(68): -0.2 • 2B(6): 0.1	3.5
2015	PEN	AA	22	138	15	7	0	3	18	18	21	2	2	.235/.350/.374	.283	8.5	.261	0.3	SS(24): 1.9 • 2B(6): -0.4	1.1
2016	PEN	AA	23	465	52	18	0	8	37	55	114	14	5	.232/.333/.337	.262	12.2	.302	-2.0	2B(74): -4.8 • 3B(30): 1.2	0.9
2017	CIN	MLB	24	250	32	11	0	8	26	24	65	4	2	.233/.315/.393	.242	4.6	.289	-0.4	2B -3, 3B 0	0.3
2018	CIN	MLB	25	331	41	14	0	11	40	32	86	5	3	.234/.316/.400	.258	8.4	.288	-0.4	2B -3, 3B 0	0.6

Breakout: 2%   Improve: 14%   Collapse: 2%   Attrition: 23%   MLB: 32%   Comparables: Carlos Asuaje, Colin Walsh, Corban Joseph

He's still got a nice plate approach. His instincts serve him well all over the field. He'll make the most of his (mostly average) tools. Shortstop probably isn't his long-term home, but he has the chops for second base. The problem is, he never found any pop in Pensacola, and he doesn't make enough contact to work around that. Last season really saw his profile flatten out. He's uninspiring, man. A real Blandino.

Ramon Cabrera   C

Born: 11/5/89   Age: 27   Bats: B   Throws: R   Height: 5'8"   Weight: 195   Entered Pro Ball: International Free Agent, 2008

YEAR	TEAM	LVL	AGE	PA	R	2B	3B	HR	RBI	BB	K	SB	CS	AVG/OBP/SLG	TAv	VORP	BABIP	BRR	FRAA	WARP
2014	ERI	AA	24	431	42	17	0	5	47	33	37	1	0	.277/.329/.358	.247	7.6	.292	-1.1	C(73): -17.1	-1.0
2014	ALT	AA	24	49	5	5	0	1	5	3	6	0	1	.239/.286/.413	.266	0.5	.256	-1.8	C(11): -6.8	-0.7
2015	LOU	AAA	25	351	29	14	0	2	35	27	44	1	1	.290/.343/.353	.258	12.7	.328	-2.3	C(84): -14.7	-0.2
2015	CIN	MLB	25	30	4	1	0	1	3	0	5	0	0	.367/.367/.500	.362	3.2	.417	-1.0	C(8): -1.3	0.2
2016	LOU	AAA	26	56	3	1	0	0	2	1	6	0	1	.259/.286/.278	.184	-1.6	.286	0.3	C(14): 1.2	0.0
2016	CIN	MLB	26	185	11	10	0	3	23	8	30	1	1	.246/.279/.357	.236	2.1	.277	-1.4	C(48): -17.4	-1.6
2017	CIN	MLB	27	250	24	11	0	6	27	16	41	1	0	.255/.303/.378	.230	4.0	.284	-1.1	C -18	-1.5
2018	CIN	MLB	28	247	27	11	0	5	26	16	44	0	0	.254/.303/.377	.245	4.0	.288	-1.2	C -18	-1.5

Breakout: 8%   Improve: 18%   Collapse: 22%   Attrition: 32%   MLB: 61%   Comparables: Drew Butera, Bryan Holaday, Rob Johnson

Cabrera's bat is poor, even for a backup backstop. Fortunately for him, few teams select their backup catchers for their offensive skill set. Cabrera is short and squat, and he's a switch-hitter. He's just headed into his prime and is the kind of guy teams want to pan out. Unfortunately, he's a dreadful framer and a so-so thrower. Can't hit, can't catch, can't control the running game. There's still a place for the kind of catcher we're talking about now, but it's in the bullpen, and the per diem isn't as good.

YEAR	TEAM	P. COUNT	FRM RUNS	BLK RUNS	THRW RUNS	TOT RUNS
2014	ERI	10284	-15.6	1.1	-1.8	-16.2
2014	ALT	1491	-7.0	0.1	0.4	-6.5
2015	CIN	836	-1.4	-0.3	0.1	-1.7
2015	LOU	12245	-12.4	0.4	-1.4	-13.4
2016	CIN	6572	-16.3	-0.8	-0.6	-17.8
2017	CIN	9340	-15.7	-0.5	-0.9	-17.2
2018	CIN	9214	-16.0	-0.5	-0.9	-17.4

Zack Cozart   SS

Born: 8/12/85   Age: 31   Bats: R   Throws: R   Height: 6'0"   Weight: 195   Entered Pro Ball: Round 2, 2007 Draft (#79 overall)

YEAR	TEAM	LVL	AGE	PA	R	2B	3B	HR	RBI	BB	K	SB	CS	AVG/OBP/SLG	TAv	VORP	BABIP	BRR	FRAA	WARP
2014	CIN	MLB	28	543	48	18	5	4	38	25	79	7	0	.221/.268/.300	.212	-1.8	.255	2.0	SS(147): 9.1	0.8
2015	CIN	MLB	29	214	28	10	1	9	28	14	29	3	3	.258/.310/.459	.288	15.1	.258	0.8	SS(52): 0.8	1.7
2016	CIN	MLB	30	508	67	28	2	16	50	37	84	4	1	.252/.308/.425	.253	20.3	.274	3.1	SS(111): 2.7	2.4
2017	CIN	MLB	31	618	69	28	3	15	60	35	101	5	2	.243/.288/.385	.235	12.5	.266	-0.4	SS 4	0.8
2018	CIN	MLB	32	459	50	21	2	11	49	28	82	3	1	.239/.291/.379	.240	7.8	.267	1.5	SS 3	1.2

Breakout: 0%   Improve: 30%   Collapse: 8%   Attrition: 13%   MLB: 91%   Comparables: Jack Wilson, Bobby Crosby, Brendan Ryan

Some players have a special proclivity for bashing the first pitch, or for hitting from behind in the count, or for sitting fastball and doing damage. Cozart is not such a player. He's a slightly-above-average hitter when ahead in the count, and a slightly-below-average hitter when behind, and he falls behind more often than he gets ahead, so he's a slightly-below-average hitter. It looked, for a spell, like he could be more. Coming off of a knee injury that halved a promising 2015, Cozart raked to a .513 slugging percentage as late as the summer solstice. From then on, his strikeout rate rose, his power fell and nagging injuries nagged. He batted .220/.290/.336 in the second half of his plate appearances, beginning June 22. Another injury to his right knee ended his season in mid-September. Being a plus defensive shortstop is the skill that made the tepid offensive value play up, but after two knee injuries it's hard to envision the 31-year-old maintaining his carrying tool.

Calten Daal   SS

Born: 8/1/93   Age: 23   Bats: R   Throws: R   Height: 6'1"   Weight: 180   Entered Pro Ball: International Free Agent, 2012

YEAR	TEAM	LVL	AGE	PA	R	2B	3B	HR	RBI	BB	K	SB	CS	AVG/OBP/SLG	TAv	VORP	BABIP	BRR	FRAA	WARP
2014	DYT	A	20	370	46	10	3	1	29	19	60	13	3	.296/.334/.351	.261	17.7	.356	2.1	SS(93): -8.8	0.9
2015	DAY	A+	21	415	38	6	0	0	30	21	61	21	5	.270/.311/.286	.231	4.9	.318	3.4	2B(59): -1.2 • SS(53): 5.9	1.0
2016	PEN	AA	22	127	15	3	1	1	6	9	26	5	1	.310/.365/.379	.284	9.3	.393	1.5	SS(31): -2.5	0.7
2017	CIN	MLB	23	250	25	8	1	5	23	12	55	5	1	.248/.287/.351	.216	0.5	.300	0.3	SS 0, 2B 0	0.1
2018	CIN	MLB	24	248	26	8	1	5	24	14	55	5	1	.245/.293/.353	.234	2.4	.297	0.5	SS 0, 2B 0	0.3

Breakout: 23%   Improve: 39%   Collapse: 10%   Attrition: 23%   MLB: 57%   Comparables: Dee Gordon, Jonathan Herrera, Eduardo Escobar

With no power whatsoever, Daal has a relatively low ceiling. On the other hand, with an excellent glove at shortstop, he has a relatively high floor. Injuries stopped him from developing much in 2016 and stopped everyone from gaining needed insight into his ability not to have the bat knocked out of his hands. He's quick to the ball, makes a lot of contact and has a chance to provide non-zero offensive value. He can really run, too. When a guy this small has trouble staying healthy, it's a bit of a red flag. If he can stay in the lineup and proves able to make hard contact—even if it's singles power— he has a big-league future.

Adam Duvall   LF

Born: 9/4/88   Age: 28   Bats: R   Throws: R   Height: 6'1"   Weight: 220   Entered Pro Ball: Round 11, 2010 Draft (#348 overall)

YEAR	TEAM	LVL	AGE	PA	R	2B	3B	HR	RBI	BB	K	SB	CS	AVG/OBP/SLG	TAv	VORP	BABIP	BRR	FRAA	WARP
2014	FRE	AAA	25	394	67	21	3	27	90	30	82	2	0	.298/.360/.599	.326	40.2	.320	1.7	3B(52): 2.1 • 1B(41): 2.0	4.4
2014	SFN	MLB	25	77	8	2	0	3	5	3	20	0	0	.192/.234/.342	.222	-1.5	.220	0.4	1B(21): -1.0 • 3B(1): -0.0	-0.3
2015	SAC	AAA	26	437	60	25	2	26	80	25	91	4	1	.281/.325/.547	.304	30.4	.299	1.1	3B(46): -5.1 • 1B(45): 2.1	2.7
2015	LOU	AAA	26	104	11	4	0	4	7	6	23	1	0	.189/.260/.358	.212	-4.6	.206	-1.1	LF(16): 0.3 • 1B(8): 2.1	-0.2
2015	CIN	MLB	26	72	6	2	0	5	9	6	26	0	0	.219/.306/.484	.286	3.7	.273	0.4	LF(15): -0.7 • 1B(4): -0.0	0.3
2016	CIN	MLB	27	608	85	31	6	33	103	41	164	6	5	.241/.297/.498	.285	24.5	.275	-3.8	LF(137): 11.4 • RF(6): -1.1	3.7
2017	CIN	MLB	28	588	75	29	3	34	93	38	155	4	2	.240/.297/.486	.266	19.9	.270	-0.9	LF 4, 1B 0	2.2
2018	CIN	MLB	29	576	79	24	2	32	89	38	154	3	2	.234/.292/.471	.268	16.5	.265	-1.2	LF 4, 1B 0	2.2

Breakout: 4%   Improve: 43%   Collapse: 11%   Attrition: 19%   MLB: 85%   Comparables: Scott Hairston, Casper Wells, Darin Ruf

When Cincinnati got Duvall in the Mike Leake trade in mid-2015, there were some passing comparisons to a notable former inhabitant of the same outfield pastures: Adam Dunn. Right away, wise observers noted that that comp was an insult to Dunn's plate approach: Duvall doesn't draw walks at even an average rate. His OBP was, is and probably always will be poor. As it turned out, though, it was just as great an insult to Duvall's glove work. He's an above-average left fielder, and that might understate the case. An ancient rookie in 2016, Duvall may already be passing his prime, but unless he loses a step or is made to play the field blindfolded, he should be about as good a player in 2017 as Dunn ever was—albeit in a dramatically different way.

Phil Ervin   OF

Born: 7/15/92   Age: 24   Bats: R   Throws: R   Height: 5'10"   Weight: 205   Entered Pro Ball: Round 1, 2013 Draft (#27 overall)

YEAR	TEAM	LVL	AGE	PA	R	2B	3B	HR	RBI	BB	K	SB	CS	AVG/OBP/SLG	TAv	VORP	BABIP	BRR	FRAA	WARP
2014	DYT	A	21	562	68	34	7	7	68	46	110	30	5	.237/.305/.376	.264	19.5	.284	3.1	CF(68): -4.9 • LF(38): -2.8	1.2
2015	DAY	A+	22	475	68	18	0	12	63	53	83	30	7	.242/.338/.375	.277	23.1	.271	4.2	LF(83): 10.3 • CF(26): 1.3	3.8
2015	PEN	AA	22	66	7	3	0	2	8	13	15	4	3	.235/.409/.412	.296	2.5	.294	-1.5	LF(12): -0.2 • CF(5): 1.1	0.4
2016	PEN	AA	23	505	71	22	3	13	45	65	88	36	10	.239/.362/.399	.311	38.7	.271	1.2	LF(76): 2.1 • CF(31): -1.0	4.3
2017	CIN	MLB	24	250	32	11	1	8	29	25	58	11	3	.226/.317/.394	.245	5.6	.266	0.8	LF 1, CF 0	0.8
2018	CIN	MLB	25	310	39	13	1	10	37	31	74	14	4	.230/.321/.403	.263	10.0	.274	1.5	LF 1, CF 0	1.3

Breakout: 0%   Improve: 4%   Collapse: 7%   Attrition: 14%   MLB: 22%   Comparables: Chad Huffman, Cole Gillespie, Shane Peterson

It would be really easy to overlook Ervin's 2016. He was a 23-year-old at Double-A. He batted .239 with 13 home runs. He's clearly not a center fielder in the long run. In truth, though, last season was an emphatic announcement that Ervin is a legitimate prospect. He posted a .160 isolated power in a league that had a .114 aggregate ISO. He walked 65 times and got hit by 18 pitches in 505 plate appearances. We already knew he could run. Ervin has a real shot to be a solid-average regular, and soon.

Billy Hamilton   CF

Born: 9/9/90   Age: 26   Bats: B   Throws: R   Height: 6'0"   Weight: 160   Entered Pro Ball: Round 2, 2009 Draft (#57 overall)

YEAR	TEAM	LVL	AGE	PA	R	2B	3B	HR	RBI	BB	K	SB	CS	AVG/OBP/SLG	TAv	VORP	BABIP	BRR	FRAA	WARP
2014	CIN	MLB	23	611	72	25	8	6	48	34	117	56	23	.250/.292/.355	.243	12.6	.304	5.4	CF(144): 16.3	3.2
2015	CIN	MLB	24	454	56	8	3	4	28	28	75	57	8	.226/.274/.289	.215	4.2	.264	10.9	CF(110): 1.5	0.6
2016	CIN	MLB	25	460	69	19	3	3	17	36	93	58	8	.260/.321/.343	.236	13.4	.329	10.5	CF(115): 3.9	1.8
2017	CIN	MLB	26	626	92	22	5	9	42	42	117	71	14	.249/.294/.354	.226	9.2	.288	11.1	CF 8	1.3
2018	CIN	MLB	27	544	58	19	4	9	52	39	101	61	13	.248/.303/.358	.235	10.8	.284	10.1	CF 7	1.9

Breakout: 4%   Improve: 56%   Collapse: 11%   Attrition: 20%   MLB: 96%   *Comparables: Willy Taveras, Michael Bourn, Joey Gathright*

It was Alexander Hamilton who said, "I never expect to see a perfect work from an imperfect man." That quote is about evaluating people's endeavors based on the degree to which they realize their potential, not by the magnitude of that potential, and about keeping in mind how hard life is before judging the way anyone endures it. We've seen enough of Billy Hamilton now to understand his imperfections. We need not dwell on his inability to hit much (or to hit left-handed pitchers at all). From June 1 until an oblique injury that ended his season on Labor Day weekend, Hamilton hit plenty (.269/.336/.338; that's plenty for him, really!), stole 48 bases in 53 tries and consistently made a positive impact. In center field and on the bases, Hamilton's speed changes the game. His challenge is to stay healthy and keep improving his on-base skills. If he can do it, he can consistently be the most exciting average regular in baseball.

Dilson Herrera   2B

Born: 3/3/94   Age: 23   Bats: R   Throws: R   Height: 5'10"   Weight: 205   Entered Pro Ball: International Free Agent, 2010

YEAR	TEAM	LVL	AGE	PA	R	2B	3B	HR	RBI	BB	K	SB	CS	AVG/OBP/SLG	TAv	VORP	BABIP	BRR	FRAA	WARP
2014	SLU	A+	20	309	48	16	2	3	23	18	44	14	3	.307/.355/.410	.272	13.7	.353	0.3	2B(43): -3.5 • SS(19): 1.5	1.2
2014	BIN	AA	20	278	50	17	3	10	48	29	52	9	4	.340/.406/.560	.330	28.7	.389	0.9	2B(55): -1.4 • SS(8): -1.1	2.8
2014	NYN	MLB	20	66	6	0	1	3	11	7	17	0	0	.220/.303/.407	.254	0.4	.256	-0.9	2B(17): -0.1	0.0
2015	LVG	AAA	21	364	68	23	2	11	50	28	59	13	9	.327/.382/.511	.294	25.1	.369	2.7	2B(78): 2.1	2.8
2015	NYN	MLB	21	103	7	3	1	3	6	11	23	2	0	.211/.311/.367	.259	2.7	.250	0.2	2B(29): 2.0	0.5
2016	LVG	AAA	22	389	61	24	2	13	55	27	72	6	7	.276/.327/.462	.261	11.0	.313	0.5	2B(75): -4.5	0.7
2016	LOU	AAA	22	80	10	0	2	2	9	11	15	1	2	.266/.372/.422	.312	6.4	.306	0.1	2B(16): -0.1	0.6
2017	CIN	MLB	23	94	11	4	0	3	11	7	21	2	1	.255/.316/.429	.258	3.1	.299	-0.1	2B 0	0.3
2018	CIN	MLB	24	301	38	13	2	11	39	23	69	5	4	.255/.317/.436	.266	10.6	.298	-0.1	2B 0	1.1

Breakout: 3%   Improve: 27%   Collapse: 13%   Attrition: 19%   MLB: 56%   *Comparables: Travis Denker, Nick Franklin, Arismendy Alcantara*

Herrera traced a short, low arc across the starscape of the national prospect scene. He's not going to be the kind of player it appeared he might be in that short window. He's a right-handed hitter without much speed or power, he's stuck at second base and he has only just enough hit tool to make that viable. If he's a regular, he's a bottom-of-the-order bat on a good team and he gets his value from fielding his position well. If he's not a regular, he's probably not a big leaguer, because everyone's backup second baseman now plays relief pitcher.

Devin Mesoraco   C

Born: 6/19/88   Age: 29   Bats: R   Throws: R   Height: 6'1"   Weight: 220   Entered Pro Ball: Round 1, 2007 Draft (#15 overall)

YEAR	TEAM	LVL	AGE	PA	R	2B	3B	HR	RBI	BB	K	SB	CS	AVG/OBP/SLG	TAv	VORP	BABIP	BRR	FRAA	WARP
2014	CIN	MLB	26	440	54	25	0	25	80	41	103	1	3	.273/.359/.534	.333	41.9	.309	-6.2	C(109): -6.0	4.0
2015	CIN	MLB	27	51	2	1	1	0	2	5	9	1	0	.178/.275/.244	.203	-0.7	.222	0.3	C(6): -0.7	-0.2
2016	CIN	MLB	28	55	2	1	0	0	1	5	10	0	1	.140/.218/.160	.146	-4.6	.175	-0.6	C(13): -2.3	-0.7
2017	CIN	MLB	29	337	40	15	0	13	42	30	66	2	2	.245/.318/.424	.259	13.1	.271	-1.1	C -8	0.1
2018	CIN	MLB	30	234	31	10	0	9	31	21	48	1	1	.245/.319/.428	.268	8.7	.273	-1.7	C -6	0.3

Breakout: 2%   Improve: 38%   Collapse: 8%   Attrition: 17%   MLB: 99%   *Comparables: John Wockenfuss, Matt Wieters, Del Crandall*

The injury issues Mesoraco has been forced to deal with over the last two years would be devastating to anyone. The timing is particularly painful, since the last time he was healthy, Mesoraco lit up the league to the tune of the sixth-best TAv in baseball. That's not an accurate reflection of his true talent, though, and it's not the worst thing about his injuries. The worst thing about his injuries (severe ones, requiring surgery to his hip and shoulder) is that a lot of Mesoraco's value was tied up in simply squatting behind the plate. He was always a poor defensive catcher, but his bat was more than worth the trade off as long as he was playable back there. It's an open question whether he can still catch, and if he can't catch, he's without a position.

YEAR	TEAM	P. COUNT	FRM RUNS	BLK RUNS	THRW RUNS	TOT RUNS
2014	CIN	14953	-5.8	1.6	-0.6	-4.8
2014	LOU	306	0.0	0.0	0.0	0.0
2014	PEN	212	-0.1	0.0	-0.1	-0.1
2015	CIN	777	-0.5	-0.2	0.0	-0.8
2016	CIN	2035	-1.9	-0.3	0.0	-2.3
2017	CIN	12056	-8.0	0.0	-0.6	-8.6
2018	CIN	8375	-6.2	-0.1	-0.5	-6.7

Chris Okey C

Born: 12/29/94 Age: 22 Bats: R Throws: R Height: 5'11" Weight: 195 Entered Pro Ball: Round 2, 2016 Draft (#43 overall)

YEAR	TEAM	LVL	AGE	PA	R	2B	3B	HR	RBI	BB	K	SB	CS	AVG/OBP/SLG	TAv	VORP	BABIP	BRR	FRAA	WARP
2016	DYT	A	21	169	21	8	1	6	21	14	49	5	0	.243/.323/.432	.272	12.1	.319	3.0	C(39): 1.0	1.4
2017	CIN	MLB	22	250	25	9	1	9	29	15	81	2	0	.204/.262/.361	.209	-0.6	.269	-0.1	C 1	0.0
2018	CIN	MLB	23	209	24	8	0	8	25	13	66	2	0	.211/.269/.379	.230	1.1	.273	-0.2	C 0	0.2

Breakout: 1%   Improve: 3%   Collapse: 4%   Attrition: 6%   MLB: 8%   Comparables: Jorge Alfaro, Kyle Skipworth, Christian Vazquez

A second-round pick out of Clemson, Okey ran into some contact issues in his debut, partially because of an aggressive assignment that had him in the Midwest League. Those issues might persist. His bat speed is no more than average, and it remains to be seen to what extent he can port his power—which steadily improved throughout his college career—to pro ball. He's built to catch and to drive the ball on occasion, though. He's also patient at the plate and a bit more athletic than an average college catcher. His biggest asset might be his makeup. He's a leader, his instincts serve him well on the bases and behind the plate, and failure won't put him on tilt.

YEAR	TEAM	P. COUNT	FRM RUNS	BLK RUNS	THRW RUNS	TOT RUNS
2017	CIN	8895	0.0	0.0	0.0	0.0
2018	CIN	7445	0.0	0.0	0.0	0.0

Jose Peraza SS

Born: 4/30/94 Age: 23 Bats: R Throws: R Height: 6'0" Weight: 180 Entered Pro Ball: International Free Agent, 2010

YEAR	TEAM	LVL	AGE	PA	R	2B	3B	HR	RBI	BB	K	SB	CS	AVG/OBP/SLG	TAv	VORP	BABIP	BRR	FRAA	WARP
2014	LYN	A+	20	304	44	13	8	1	27	10	32	35	7	.342/.365/.454	.308	29.7	.376	5.0	2B(58): -6.1 • SS(7): 0.6	2.4
2014	MIS	AA	20	195	35	7	3	1	17	7	15	25	8	.335/.363/.422	.291	16.4	.361	5.2	2B(41): -3.7	1.3
2015	GWN	AAA	21	427	52	10	7	3	37	15	35	26	5	.294/.318/.379	.253	9.6	.311	0.9	2B(81): -1.2 • CF(13): -2.7	0.5
2015	OKL	AAA	21	94	11	3	1	1	5	2	10	7	0	.289/.304/.378	.263	4.7	.316	1.6	2B(14): 0.2 • SS(4): -0.4	0.4
2015	LAN	MLB	21	25	3	1	1	0	1	2	2	3	0	.182/.250/.318	.224	0.4	.200	0.7	2B(6): 0.6 • CF(1): -0.0	0.1
2016	LOU	AAA	22	322	40	15	3	2	21	21	43	10	7	.281/.333/.375	.263	14.8	.324	1.5	SS(58): -3.5 • CF(6): -0.1	1.2
2016	CIN	MLB	22	256	25	8	2	3	25	7	33	21	10	.324/.352/.411	.271	10.9	.361	-0.8	SS(31): -0.9 • CF(13): -1.2	0.8
2017	CIN	MLB	23	342	42	13	4	7	33	13	49	19	6	.283/.309/.413	.248	8.3	.307	2.1	SS -1, 2B -0	0.6
2018	CIN	MLB	24	490	56	17	5	12	56	21	70	27	9	.280/.316/.421	.258	14.4	.301	1.1	SS -2, 2B 0	1.1

Breakout: 10%   Improve: 52%   Collapse: 13%   Attrition: 23%   MLB: 81%   Comparables: Andrelton Simmons, Tyler Pastornicky, Daniel Castro

The path to playing time for a player without power or patience at the plate is considerably rockier than it used to be. Even an athletic infielder with top-end speed needs to prove he can turn those tools into actual on-field value, rather than getting the benefit of the doubt. That's why Peraza has been traded twice in two years. In 2016, though, he made strides toward proving that he can make his skill set work. In a season split between Triple-A and MLB, he maintained a high contact rate and stroked line drives with some consistency. He doesn't hit the ball hard and probably can't stick at shortstop, so he has to keep those things up. That's a tall task, which is why the path to playing time for a player without power or patience at the plate is considerably rockier than it used to be.

Brandon Phillips 2B

Born: 6/28/81 Age: 36 Bats: R Throws: R Height: 6'0" Weight: 210 Entered Pro Ball: Round 2, 1999 Draft (#57 overall)

YEAR	TEAM	LVL	AGE	PA	R	2B	3B	HR	RBI	BB	K	SB	CS	AVG/OBP/SLG	TAv	VORP	BABIP	BRR	FRAA	WARP
2014	CIN	MLB	33	499	44	25	0	8	51	23	74	2	3	.266/.306/.372	.253	6.7	.298	-2.2	2B(121): -7.4	-0.1
2015	CIN	MLB	34	623	69	19	2	12	70	27	68	23	3	.294/.328/.395	.270	24.7	.315	2.3	2B(141): 0.2 • SS(1): -0.0	2.7
2016	CIN	MLB	35	584	74	34	1	11	64	18	68	14	8	.291/.320/.416	.266	17.5	.312	-1.4	2B(138): -4.0	1.4
2017	CIN	MLB	36	514	53	22	1	12	55	23	69	10	4	.268/.305/.389	.245	10.4	.288	-0.3	2B -2	0.6
2018	CIN	MLB	37	453	50	18	0	10	47	21	66	7	3	.256/.298/.373	.246	6.8	.278	-0.4	2B -2	0.6

Breakout: 0%   Improve: 31%   Collapse: 13%   Attrition: 19%   MLB: 82%   Comparables: Willie Bloomquist, Cookie Rojas, Mark Ellis

Arguably the MVP of the 2016 NL East champion Nationals, Phillips toiled in frustrating irrelevance after rejecting a trade to Washington and sending that club running after free agent Daniel Murphy. He had a minor late-season offensive renaissance, but only after wandering up to the very cusp of obsolescence. He can still pick it at second base, though his range has diminished a great deal, and he found the gaps more often in 2016 than in previous years—though the above-average power he once boasted has been missing since Scott Rolen shared the Cincinnati infield. His atrocious plate discipline—he puts the ball in play a ton, but never walks—seems poised to give him the final push out of regular playing time, be it this year or next.

Tony Renda 2B

Born: 1/24/91 Age: 26 Bats: R Throws: R Height: 5'8" Weight: 175 Entered Pro Ball: Round 2, 2012 Draft (#80 overall)

YEAR	TEAM	LVL	AGE	PA	R	2B	3B	HR	RBI	BB	K	SB	CS	AVG/OBP/SLG	TAv	VORP	BABIP	BRR	FRAA	WARP
2014	POT	A+	23	472	75	21	4	0	47	43	59	19	5	.307/.381/.377	.290	33.1	.353	4.7	2B(91): -2.2 • SS(8): -1.3	3.0
2015	HAR	AA	24	228	31	10	1	1	23	19	15	13	3	.267/.333/.340	.253	9.2	.283	4.8	2B(52): -0.9 • SS(2): -0.0	0.9
2015	TRN	AA	24	304	42	20	1	2	21	24	24	10	3	.270/.328/.372	.269	10.0	.287	-0.1	2B(64): 0.6	1.1
2016	PEN	AA	25	282	36	25	3	2	28	14	20	15	1	.326/.369/.467	.323	26.2	.344	2.1	LF(46): 0.2 • 3B(11): -0.2	2.8
2016	LOU	AAA	25	121	13	3	1	1	9	10	16	2	3	.276/.350/.352	.268	4.0	.318	-0.3	2B(17): 0.1 • LF(7): 1.3	0.6
2016	CIN	MLB	25	67	4	2	0	0	3	5	11	0	0	.183/.246/.217	.155	-4.2	.224	1.3	2B(9): 0.5 • LF(4): 0.3	-0.4
2017	CIN	MLB	26	104	11	5	0	2	10	7	15	3	1	.260/.315/.383	.247	2.3	.288	0.2	3B 0	0.2
2018	CIN	MLB	27	334	39	17	1	7	36	24	50	8	2	.262/.321/.398	.260	8.8	.289	0.6	3B 0	1.0

Breakout: 1%   Improve: 12%   Collapse: 6%   Attrition: 15%   MLB: 25%   Comparables: Brian Horwitz, Matt Young, Cedric Hunter

Can we drop the BS about grit for a second? Awesome. Thanks. Because that stuff really gets in the way of good player evaluation sometimes. You either overvalue "grit" because you define that word in a baseball context by loading it up with implications about character and perseverance, or you undervalue it, because you focus solely on the guys to whom scouts usually attach it (short, weak white dudes). Here's Renda in a nutshell: makes a ton of contact. Can work a walk. Both fast and smart on the bases. Not enough power to play every day at second, third or in the outfield corners, not enough arm or raw athleticism to play short or center field. Utility profile all the way, but a pretty good one.

Scott Schebler   LF

Born: 10/6/90   Age: 26   Bats: L   Throws: R   Height: 6'0"   Weight: 225   Entered Pro Ball: Round 26, 2010 Draft (#802 overall)

YEAR	TEAM	LVL	AGE	PA	R	2B	3B	HR	RBI	BB	K	SB	CS	AVG/OBP/SLG	TAv	VORP	BABIP	BRR	FRAA	WARP
2014	CHT	AA	23	560	82	23	14	28	73	45	110	10	4	.280/.365/.556	.307	39.3	.308	0.8	LF(87): 2.2 • RF(45): -2.8	4.1
2015	OKL	AAA	24	485	57	16	9	13	50	40	93	15	2	.241/.322/.410	.275	21.0	.278	2.3	RF(48): -5.3 • CF(38): 2.3	1.8
2015	LAN	MLB	24	40	6	0	0	3	4	3	13	2	1	.250/.325/.500	.325	3.8	.300	0.4	LF(7): -0.2 • RF(6): -0.0	0.4
2016	LOU	AAA	25	319	40	18	8	13	43	19	59	2	0	.311/.370/.564	.329	29.9	.352	-1.7	CF(49): 3.4 • LF(16): -1.1	3.3
2016	CIN	MLB	25	282	36	12	2	9	40	19	59	2	4	.265/.330/.432	.267	10.0	.312	1.7	RF(41): 4.3 • CF(18): -2.5	1.2
2017	CIN	MLB	26	483	62	18	6	21	65	33	113	6	2	.250/.318/.463	.268	18.9	.289	0.5	RF 1	1.5
2018	CIN	MLB	27	518	69	20	6	22	73	38	123	6	3	.250/.323/.464	.277	22.7	.292	3.0	RF 1	2.6

Breakout: 6%   Improve: 34%   Collapse: 16%   Attrition: 25%   MLB: 75%   *Comparables: Ben Johnson, Casper Wells, Mike Carp*

The Reds caught a lot of flak for the deal that sent Todd Frazier to the White Sox and brought them a trio of Dodgers prospects with imperfect profiles. A season later, though, the move looks pretty wise. Schebler had great numbers (usually at slightly old ages for his levels) in the minors, but the industry didn't trust them. That great minor-league production continued in 2016, and when he got the call to the parent club Schebler continued to put together good at-bats. He's stretched in center field but fine in either corner. He might have occasional contact issues, but Schebler has the potential to be an average regular in 2017.

Nick Senzel   3B

Born: 6/29/95   Age: 22   Bats: R   Throws: R   Height: 6'1"   Weight: 205   Entered Pro Ball: Round 1, 2016 Draft (#2 overall)

YEAR	TEAM	LVL	AGE	PA	R	2B	3B	HR	RBI	BB	K	SB	CS	AVG/OBP/SLG	TAv	VORP	BABIP	BRR	FRAA	WARP
2016	DYT	A	21	251	38	23	3	7	36	32	49	15	7	.329/.415/.567	.364	34.2	.392	1.6	3B(56): 3.2	4.1
2017	CIN	MLB	22	250	31	11	1	9	30	23	66	7	3	.234/.309/.406	.243	3.4	.288	-0.1	3B 2	0.6
2018	CIN	MLB	23	268	33	12	1	10	33	24	71	7	4	.230/.303/.407	.254	4.7	.282	0.3	3B 3	0.8

Breakout: 5%   Improve: 30%   Collapse: 3%   Attrition: 29%   MLB: 48%   *Comparables: Matt Davidson, Alex Liddi, Lonnie Chisenhall*

Unlike fellow college third baseman-turned-second overall pick Kris Bryant, Senzel doesn't have a top-of-the-scale tool in the box. At this point he seems to be an average runner and to be above average in every other respect. He won't hit for enormous power, but what power he has will flow naturally out of his exceptionally polished approach and finely honed swing. No right-handed hitter has come out of the draft more ready for the big leagues than Senzel since Bryant. That Senzel only surprised pro scouts in a good way during an extended assignment to the Midwest League is a great omen. Bryant could have played well in the majors the year after he was drafted. Senzel could too, though like Bryant he probably won't.

Eugenio Suarez   SS

Born: 7/18/91   Age: 25   Bats: R   Throws: R   Height: 5'11"   Weight: 205   Entered Pro Ball: International Free Agent, 2008

YEAR	TEAM	LVL	AGE	PA	R	2B	3B	HR	RBI	BB	K	SB	CS	AVG/OBP/SLG	TAv	VORP	BABIP	BRR	FRAA	WARP
2014	ERI	AA	22	170	26	14	1	6	29	15	38	7	2	.284/.347/.503	.293	12.0	.342	-0.5	SS(42): -0.7	1.2
2014	TOL	AAA	22	52	6	4	0	2	7	6	9	2	0	.302/.404/.535	.300	5.3	.333	0.6	SS(12): -0.8	0.5
2014	DET	MLB	22	277	33	9	1	4	23	22	67	3	2	.242/.316/.336	.247	8.0	.316	1.1	SS(81): 0.5 • 3B(2): -0.1	0.9
2015	LOU	AAA	23	238	30	9	2	8	25	26	40	3	4	.256/.348/.438	.285	16.1	.282	0.5	SS(55): -2.8	1.4
2015	CIN	MLB	23	398	42	19	2	13	48	17	94	4	1	.280/.315/.446	.283	24.9	.341	0.3	SS(96): -2.6 • 3B(1): -0.0	2.4
2016	CIN	MLB	24	627	78	25	2	21	70	51	155	11	5	.248/.317/.411	.258	19.8	.304	0.7	3B(151): 2.2 • SS(2): -0.3	2.2
2017	CIN	MLB	25	573	66	25	2	20	72	44	137	8	4	.252/.315/.424	.257	15.2	.300	-0.6	3B 2	1.3
2018	CIN	MLB	26	542	70	24	2	20	70	46	133	7	4	.251/.323/.433	.269	17.9	.300	0.8	3B 2	2.2

Breakout: 4%   Improve: 59%   Collapse: 1%   Attrition: 9%   MLB: 99%   *Comparables: Alex Gordon, Edwin Encarnacion, Hank Blalock*

Here's the value of power in a nutshell. Suarez swung at pitches inside the zone at nearly identical rates in 2015 and 2016. Ditto for pitches outside the zone. Because he showed pitchers—somewhat unexpectedly, given his scouting report—that he could consistently put mistakes on the other side of the wall, Suarez saw fewer pitches in the zone (51.8 percent in 2015, 47.5 percent in 2016), and since he didn't expand his zone, he started walking consistently for the first time in his career. He also moved from shortstop to third base, where he's a better defensive fit. Stardom is a long way off, but Suarez has a credible everyday profile and is young enough to stay this good until the real money starts coming.

Blake Trahan   SS

Born: 9/5/93   Age: 23   Bats: R   Throws: R   Height: 5'9"   Weight: 180   Entered Pro Ball: Round 3, 2015 Draft (#84 overall)

YEAR	TEAM	LVL	AGE	PA	R	2B	3B	HR	RBI	BB	K	SB	CS	AVG/OBP/SLG	TAv	VORP	BABIP	BRR	FRAA	WARP
2015	DAY	A+	21	36	1	0	0	0	0	0	5	0	0	.114/.139/.114	.097	-4.3	.133	0.2	SS(11): 0.1	-0.5
2016	DAY	A+	22	587	90	21	9	4	47	49	73	25	8	.263/.325/.361	.244	21.0	.297	7.6	SS(124): 15.1	3.7
2017	CIN	MLB	23	250	29	10	2	6	23	17	50	5	2	.233/.287/.363	.219	1.2	.268	0.3	SS 2, 2B 0	0.4
2018	CIN	MLB	24	286	31	10	2	7	30	20	57	6	2	.235/.291/.369	.236	3.3	.268	0.6	SS 2, 3B 0	0.6

Breakout: 5%   Improve: 20%   Collapse: 7%   Attrition: 25%   MLB: 34%   *Comparables: Ramiro Pena, Justin Sellers, Cristhian Adames*

Trahan's scouting report reads like a Mad Lib, so let's make it one. [Any shortstop prospect] could be an average regular at the position, or even a bit more. Ever since he was in [his home nation in the Caribbean, or college in Louisiana, Arizona or California], we've known he could pick it with the best of them. He's an above-average runner and has a plus arm for the position. He's held his own at the plate at [any level above rookie-ball but below the majors] at age [neither especially young nor especially old for that level], but with his lack of power and his reliance on speed, he has only a [number between 20 and 40] percent chance to hold down an everyday job. (Trahan is from Lafayette University in Louisiana, hit as a 22-year-old at High-A, and has, let's say, a 30 percent chance.)

Taylor Trammell   OF

Born: 9/13/97   Age: 19   Bats: L   Throws: L   Height: 6'2"   Weight: 195   Entered Pro Ball: Round 1, 2016 Draft (#35 overall)

YEAR	TEAM	LVL	AGE	PA	R	2B	3B	HR	RBI	BB	K	SB	CS	AVG/OBP/SLG	TAv	VORP	BABIP	BRR	FRAA	WARP
2017	CIN	MLB	19	250	24	8	1	5	22	14	86	7	3	.191/.240/.300	.184	-10.4	.274	0.4	LF 1, CF 0	-1.0
2018	CIN	MLB	20	327	33	11	2	8	32	21	106	11	5	.208/.262/.333	.215	-6.0	.289	1.1	LF 2, CF 0	-0.4

Breakout: 0%   Improve: 6%   Collapse: 2%   Attrition: 5%   MLB: 11%   *Comparables: Engel Beltre, Nomar Mazara, Francisco Pena*

When the Reds drafted Nick Senzel higher than expected last June, it was with an eye toward spending less than the bonus pool system allotted to that pick and nabbing big talent later on. With the first pick in the competitive-balance round (35th overall), Cincinnati took Trammell, then paid him $3.2 million—or roughly the slot value of the 12th pick. He spent the summer raking in the Pioneer League. He's a tremendous athlete with a sound approach at the plate, and there's power projection in his swing and his frame. There's work to do, but the upside is huge. It's not so much that the Reds got a steal by drafting Trammell where they did, as that the broken system that is the draft dropped him into their laps.

Zach Vincej   SS

Born: 5/1/91   Age: 26   Bats: R   Throws: R   Height: 5'11"   Weight: 177   Entered Pro Ball: Round 37, 2012 Draft (#1132 overall)

YEAR	TEAM	LVL	AGE	PA	R	2B	3B	HR	RBI	BB	K	SB	CS	AVG/OBP/SLG	TAv	VORP	BABIP	BRR	FRAA	WARP
2014	BAK	A+	23	481	72	23	1	1	40	44	73	11	8	.271/.342/.336	.248	17.2	.323	3.2	SS(108): -6.8 • SS(3): -6.8	0.4
2015	PEN	AA	24	339	39	10	0	5	22	44	48	7	7	.241/.347/.329	.260	13.1	.271	1.0	SS(68): -10.3 • 2B(21): 1.1	0.4
2016	PEN	AA	25	438	45	24	3	3	47	25	85	7	6	.281/.329/.378	.282	26.9	.346	0.6	SS(105): 3.9 • 2B(11): 0.4	3.4
2017	CIN	MLB	26	250	28	10	1	5	23	19	54	3	2	.239/.302/.360	.226	2.0	.286	-0.6	SS -1, 2B 0	0.1
2018	CIN	MLB	27	245	27	10	1	6	25	18	53	2	2	.239/.300/.363	.239	2.7	.284	-0.5	SS -1, 2B 0	0.2

Breakout: 3%   Improve: 9%   Collapse: 5%   Attrition: 9%   MLB: 19%   *Comparables: Sean Kazmar, Angel Sanchez, Ryan Jackson*

Vincej was a good-glove, no-hit shortstop from the time he was in college until last June. He was 25, taking his second tour of the Southern League, and woke up June 1 batting .207/.270/.234. "Adapt or die" is much more than Brad Pitt dialogue at a moment like that. So Vincej adapted. He'd always done one thing well at the plate: make contact. Through May, he'd fanned just 19 times in 125 plate appearances. Starting in June, he traded some of that contact for a lot more punch. He batted .309/.353/.434 from June 1 through the end of Pensacola's season. Cincinnati sent Vincej to the Arizona Fall League, where he kept trading contact for power and the breakout became real. It's unlikely to keep happening if and when he reaches MLB, but the chances are no longer slim and none.

Joey Votto   1B

Born: 9/10/83   Age: 33   Bats: L   Throws: R   Height: 6'2"   Weight: 220   Entered Pro Ball: Round 2, 2002 Draft (#44 overall)

YEAR	TEAM	LVL	AGE	PA	R	2B	3B	HR	RBI	BB	K	SB	CS	AVG/OBP/SLG	TAv	VORP	BABIP	BRR	FRAA	WARP
2014	CIN	MLB	30	272	32	16	0	6	23	47	49	1	1	.255/.390/.409	.303	12.8	.299	-0.7	1B(61): 2.6	1.7
2015	CIN	MLB	31	695	95	33	2	29	80	143	135	11	3	.314/.459/.541	.360	69.2	.371	-5.7	1B(156): 1.4	7.6
2016	CIN	MLB	32	677	101	34	2	29	97	108	120	8	1	.326/.434/.550	.341	58.6	.366	-4.1	1B(154): -1.4	5.9
2017	CIN	MLB	33	639	90	31	1	23	88	115	121	8	2	.294/.424/.495	.317	44.5	.342	-0.6	1B 1	4.9
2018	CIN	MLB	34	552	84	26	1	20	74	98	112	4	1	.281/.412/.475	.315	34.9	.332	-3.1	1B 1	3.9

Breakout: 1%   Improve: 22%   Collapse: 7%   Attrition: 11%   MLB: 99%   *Comparables: Lance Berkman, Jason Giambi, Miguel Cabrera*

Time marches like Sherman to the sea, not merely unstoppable, but ruthlessly destructive. One of its most recent victims, if you consider the broad sweep of history, is the joyful fun fact that Votto never hit pop-ups. He's still less likely to hit a pop-up than most hitters, but that tidbit neatly encapsulated what made the 2010 MVP special, and now it doesn't apply. Here's a new fact to fill some portion of the hole in your heart: Since Votto's debut, no MLB player has seen as many full counts as he has, and no player with at least 4,000 plate appearances over that span has as high an OBP in full counts. Votto is a churlish chip off the Splendid Splinter's block. At bat, he wages a precise, finely choreographed form of mental and physical war on the pitcher, and no one wins more of those battles. It seemed improbable two years ago, but PECOTA now projects Votto to more than earn his remaining contract obligations.

Jesse Winker   LF

Born: 8/17/93   Age: 23   Bats: L   Throws: L   Height: 6'3"   Weight: 215   Entered Pro Ball: Round 1, 2012 Draft (#49 overall)

YEAR	TEAM	LVL	AGE	PA	R	2B	3B	HR	RBI	BB	K	SB	CS	AVG/OBP/SLG	TAv	VORP	BABIP	BRR	FRAA	WARP
2014	BAK	A+	20	249	42	15	0	13	49	40	46	5	1	.317/.426/.580	.319	19.3	.349	-2.2	LF(46): -2.2 • LF(2): -2.2	1.5
2014	PEN	AA	20	92	15	5	0	2	8	14	22	0	0	.208/.326/.351	.256	1.9	.259	0.4	LF(20): 1.8	0.4
2015	PEN	AA	21	526	69	24	2	13	55	74	83	8	4	.282/.390/.433	.308	33.7	.320	-2.0	LF(83): -4.8 • RF(40): -2.9	2.8
2016	LOU	AAA	22	448	39	22	0	3	45	59	59	0	0	.303/.397/.384	.288	20.4	.347	-1.0	RF(52): 0.7 • LF(46): -2.4	1.9
2017	CIN	MLB	23	165	19	7	0	5	20	20	33	0	0	.259/.352/.420	.270	5.8	.300	-0.4	RF -1, LF -0	0.4
2018	CIN	MLB	24	359	48	17	0	12	45	44	74	1	0	.262/.355/.432	.282	14.9	.305	-0.9	RF -1, LF 0	1.4

Breakout: 4%   Improve: 22%   Collapse: 11%   Attrition: 20%   MLB: 42%   *Comparables: Adam Eaton, Caleb Gindl, Jaff Decker*

Winker's approach is terrific. He looks to get ahead in counts, and when he falls behind, he can stay in the at-bat. He has tremendous hands, can adjust mid-swing and puts the ball in play all the time. That's the good news. Here's the bad news: Winker is a corner outfielder all the way, and not the Alex Gordon or Starling Marte kind. He's a below-average athlete, so his entire value lives in his bat. And while the bat is nice, it's missing something: power. Winker did have a wrist injury that probably affected him in 2016, but the truth is that he never had above-average power in the first place.

PITCHERS

Homer Bailey   RHP

Born: 5/3/86   Age: 31   Bats: R   Throws: R   Height: 6'4"   Weight: 225   Entered Pro Ball: Round 1, 2004 Draft (#7 overall)

YEAR	TEAM	LVL	AGE	W	L	SV	G	GS	IP	H	HR	BB/9	K/9	K	GB%	BABIP	WHIP	ERA	FIP	DRA	VORP	WARP	cFIP	MPH
2014	CIN	MLB	28	9	5	0	23	23	145²	134	16	2.8	7.7	124	52%	.286	1.23	3.71	3.90	3.41	23.0	2.5	96	96.8
2015	CIN	MLB	29	0	1	0	2	2	11¹	16	3	3.2	2.4	3	59%	.317	1.76	5.56	7.13	5.45	-0.5	0.0	112	94.5
2016	LOU	AAA	30	1	2	0	7	7	24	31	7	3.4	7.1	19	54%	.312	1.67	5.62	6.63	4.74	1.6	0.2	104	
2016	CIN	MLB	30	2	3	0	6	6	23	35	2	2.7	10.6	27	47%	.452	1.83	6.65	3.14	3.69	4.3	0.4	92	96.0
2017	CIN	MLB	31	9	11	0	28	28	168	166	24	3.2	7.9	147	51%	.294	1.34	4.56	4.48	4.58	11.2	1.2	100	
2018	CIN	MLB	32	10	11	0	29	29	176¹	163	25	3.0	7.8	153	51%	.298	1.26	4.56	4.64	4.98	10.9	1.1	118	

Breakout: 14%   Improve: 43%   Collapse: 26%   Attrition: 16%   MLB: 89%   Comparables: Scott Feldman, Doug Fister, Carlos Zambrano

When he's right, Bailey still looks like the guy who convinced the Reds to shell out $105 million to keep him for six years, three years ago. At least, we'll give him the benefit of the doubt and say so. A fully healthy Bailey is some mixture of memory and myth by now, a real piece of the recent past that nonetheless feels like it belongs to another century, if not another dimension. Two surgeries and a nebulous biceps injury have limited him to 31 starts since the beginning of his deal. He might stay healthier doing stunt work for Christian Bale. Gig doesn't pay as well, though.

Tony Cingrani   LHP

Born: 7/5/89   Age: 27   Bats: L   Throws: L   Height: 6'4"   Weight: 210   Entered Pro Ball: Round 3, 2011 Draft (#114 overall)

YEAR	TEAM	LVL	AGE	W	L	SV	G	GS	IP	H	HR	BB/9	K/9	K	GB%	BABIP	WHIP	ERA	FIP	DRA	VORP	WARP	cFIP	MPH
2014	CIN	MLB	24	2	8	0	13	11	63¹	62	12	5.0	8.7	61	37%	.292	1.53	4.55	5.34	5.52	-4.9	-0.5	117	94.4
2015	LOU	AAA	25	0	1	0	9	6	24²	20	2	4	11.7	32	45%	.310	1.26	1.82	3.20	2.08	8.6	0.9	72	
2015	CIN	MLB	25	0	3	0	35	1	33¹	31	3	6.8	10.5	39	41%	.329	1.68	5.67	4.51	4.20	2.0	0.2	107	94.7
2016	CIN	MLB	26	2	5	17	65	0	63	54	5	5.3	7.0	49	48%	.277	1.44	4.14	4.57	5.24	-1.9	-0.2	114	96.7
2017	CIN	MLB	27	3	3	25	58	0	61¹	56	9	4.6	8.5	58	50%	.282	1.41	5.01	4.86	4.88	0.2	0.0	100	
2018	CIN	MLB	28	2	1	15	50	0	52²	42	7	4.7	9.6	56	50%	.283	1.31	4.71	4.81	5.22	-0.5	0.0	120	

Breakout: 22%   Improve: 49%   Collapse: 17%   Attrition: 9%   MLB: 81%   Comparables: Tom Gorzelanny, Wade Davis, Brandon Beachy

Bringing him in was usually a tactical Sin-grani. From the faithful Reds fans who showed up to slog side-along through a miserable season, his appearances drew many a Cin-groani. He probably drove Bryan Price to the bottom of one or two bottles of Sangria-ni. That, right there. Those three puns. The horrible feeling they're giving you. That was Cingrani's season. He threw harder than ever, averaging 95 mph on that string-straight barrel-seeker of a four-seam fastball, but it was hardly enough to get by. As spring turned to summer and life flowered all around, Cingrani's slider died. He replaced the slider with a changeup, but very rarely threw it, because what's the point? He had a 6.88 ERA from the trade deadline onward, which is as close as the Reds came to getting anything nice out of their former prized prospect.

Anthony DeSclafani   RHP

Born: 4/18/90   Age: 27   Bats: R   Throws: R   Height: 6'1"   Weight: 200   Entered Pro Ball: Round 6, 2011 Draft (#199 overall)

YEAR	TEAM	LVL	AGE	W	L	SV	G	GS	IP	H	HR	BB/9	K/9	K	GB%	BABIP	WHIP	ERA	FIP	DRA	VORP	WARP	cFIP	MPH
2014	JAX	AA	24	3	4	0	8	8	43	45	4	2.1	8.0	38	46%	.333	1.28	4.19	3.33	3.52	8.2	0.9	87	
2014	NWO	AAA	24	3	3	0	12	11	59¹	48	2	3.2	8.9	59	44%	.284	1.16	3.49	3.41	2.60	20.6	2.1	90	
2014	MIA	MLB	24	2	2	0	13	5	33	40	4	1.4	7.1	26	42%	.330	1.36	6.27	3.74	4.69	0.2	0.0	104	95.5
2015	CIN	MLB	25	9	13	0	31	31	184²	194	17	2.7	7.4	151	47%	.318	1.35	4.05	3.70	4.24	17.1	1.8	101	95.3
2016	LOU	AAA	26	0	1	0	3	3	13	12	4	0.0	7.6	11	46%	.229	0.92	5.54	5.48	2.78	3.7	0.4	86	
2016	CIN	MLB	26	9	5	0	20	20	123¹	120	16	2.2	7.7	105	44%	.295	1.22	3.28	4.00	4.22	15.7	1.6	95	95.3
2017	CIN	MLB	27	10	11	0	29	29	174	174	22	2.6	7.9	154	46%	.300	1.29	4.07	4.01	4.10	20.9	2.2	94	
2018	CIN	MLB	28	11	10	0	30	30	188²	165	23	2.9	9.3	196	46%	.310	1.20	3.92	3.96	4.30	24.8	2.6	98	

Breakout: 26%   Improve: 53%   Collapse: 12%   Attrition: 11%   MLB: 85%   Comparables: Wade Miley, Tyson Ross, Sergio Mitre

Being a pitching coach doesn't seem that hard. Lately, it seems mostly to consist of saying to struggling but talented starters in their mid-20s: "Hey, dude, you know the pitch in your repertoire that doesn't work? Stop throwing that one. Yeah. Just quit." Someone got into DeSclafani's ear with just that message last summer. Out went the changeup, which he'd always thrown to lefties because that's what a righty throws to a lefty, if he doesn't have a blessed clue what he's doing. Instead, DeSclafani threw them his slider and his curve more often and he looked more comfortable, lowered his walk rate and solidified his future as a mid-rotation starter.

Jumbo Diaz   RHP

Born: 2/27/84   Age: 33   Bats: R   Throws: R   Height: 6'4"   Weight: 280   Entered Pro Ball: International Free Agent, 2001

YEAR	TEAM	LVL	AGE	W	L	SV	G	GS	IP	H	HR	BB/9	K/9	K	GB%	BABIP	WHIP	ERA	FIP	DRA	VORP	WARP	cFIP	MPH
2014	LOU	AAA	30	2	2	18	30	0	33¹	25	1	2.7	8.4	31	48%	.267	1.05	1.35	2.97	3.29	7.6	0.8	88	
2014	CIN	MLB	30	0	1	0	36	0	34²	29	3	3.6	9.6	37	41%	.295	1.24	3.38	3.30	3.40	4.2	0.5	95	99.6
2015	LOU	AAA	31	0	1	8	13	0	16	11	0	2.2	6.8	12	42%	.229	0.94	1.12	2.59	4.41	0.9	0.1	98	
2015	CIN	MLB	31	2	1	1	61	0	60¹	58	9	2.7	10.4	70	47%	.316	1.26	4.18	3.82	3.25	9.8	1.1	82	100.0
2016	LOU	AAA	32	1	1	11	22	0	24	16	0	2.6	10.5	28	49%	.271	0.96	0.75	1.71	1.97	8.0	0.8	78	
2016	CIN	MLB	32	1	1	0	45	0	43	36	8	4.0	7.7	37	49%	.239	1.28	3.14	5.28	4.57	1.9	0.2	104	98.4
2017	CIN	MLB	33	2	3	0	53	0	55²	54	8	3.5	8.2	51	46%	.288	1.34	4.69	4.51	4.65	1.6	0.2	100	
2018	CIN	MLB	34	2	1	0	47	0	50	44	9	3.9	9.3	52	46%	.289	1.31	5.07	5.15	5.60	-2.5	-0.3	129	

Breakout: 16%   Improve: 21%   Collapse: 41%   Attrition: 11%   MLB: 65%   Comparables: Jean Machi, Jason Bulger, Dale Thayer

His fastball kept humming in at its customary speed, but Diaz wasn't able to miss bats with it in 2016. That derailed his season. His slider induced more whiffs than ever. He kept the ball on the ground. With his sinker essentially scrapped and his changeup bereft of movement, though, he couldn't get batters to chase often enough, and when he had to come into the zone with his heat something was missing. Diaz's career has been on life support before. He's been through more than a decade in the minors and carved out a relief career with an unusual four-pitch mix. Now he's one more good adjustment from reaching arbitration and making a little real money.

Brandon Finnegan   LHP

Born: 4/14/93   Age: 24   Bats: L   Throws: L   Height: 5'11"   Weight: 200   Entered Pro Ball: Round 1, 2014 Draft (#17 overall)

YEAR	TEAM	LVL	AGE	W	L	SV	G	GS	IP	H	HR	BB/9	K/9	K	GB%	BABIP	WHIP	ERA	FIP	DRA	VORP	WARP	cFIP	MPH
2014	WIL	A+	21	0	1	0	5	5	15	5	1	1.2	7.8	13	50%	.121	0.47	0.60	3.05	3.10	4.2	0.4	87	
2014	NWA	AA	21	0	3	0	8	0	12	15	2	1.5	9.8	13	52%	.342	1.42	2.25	3.87	3.07	2.4	0.3	85	
2014	KCA	MLB	21	0	1	0	7	0	7	6	0	1.3	12.9	10	59%	.353	1.00	1.29	0.73	2.63	1.4	0.2	82	95.3
2015	NWA	AA	22	0	1	1	5	3	13	10	1	8.3	9.0	13	42%	.257	1.69	2.77	5.07	8.44	-5.0	-0.5	120	
2015	KCA	MLB	22	3	0	0	14	0	24¹	16	3	4.8	7.8	21	59%	.213	1.19	2.96	4.71	3.62	3.4	0.4	96	96.0
2015	OMA	AAA	22	0	2	0	6	4	14	17	1	4.5	12.2	19	46%	.421	1.71	7.07	3.31	3.15	3.3	0.3	91	
2015	LOU	AAA	22	0	3	0	8	8	30¹	31	3	5	8.9	30	45%	.318	1.58	6.23	4.34	3.87	4.7	0.5	97	
2015	CIN	MLB	22	2	2	0	6	4	23²	21	5	3.0	9.1	24	52%	.262	1.23	4.18	4.89	3.69	3.1	0.3	96	94.6
2016	CIN	MLB	23	10	11	0	31	31	172	150	29	4.4	7.6	145	41%	.256	1.36	3.98	5.23	5.43	-1.4	-0.1	115	94.6
2017	CIN	MLB	24	7	10	0	26	26	130	123	20	3.7	8.3	119	51%	.287	1.35	4.72	4.69	4.79	5.6	0.6	100	
2018	CIN	MLB	25	9	11	0	31	31	196	167	27	3.8	8.7	190	51%	.288	1.27	4.55	4.64	5.02	9.3	1.0	118	

Breakout: 26%   Improve: 62%   Collapse: 14%   Attrition: 11%   MLB: 98%   Comparables: Andrew Miller, Brian Matusz, Chad Billingsley

Finnegan answered some of the questions about his ability to stick in the rotation, but not always the way he might have hoped. He largely held up under the physical demands of a starter's workload and added a four-seam fastball to play off his sinker—throwing the former more against left-handed batters and the latter more against righties. His ground-ball rate suffered and long-standing command issues seemed to worsen. He had an ERA pushing 5.00 into late July. Over his final 11 starts, Finnegan found something. He started trusting his changeup again after teammate Dan Straily showed him a new grip, and fanned more than a quarter of opposing batters. Walks will always be a problem. Finnegan is going to have to keep the ball down and keep throwing his secondary pitches at an increased frequency if he's going to remain a starter.

Amir Garrett   LHP

Born: 5/3/92   Age: 25   Bats: R   Throws: L   Height: 6'5"   Weight: 210   Entered Pro Ball: Round 22, 2011 Draft (#685 overall)

YEAR	TEAM	LVL	AGE	W	L	SV	G	GS	IP	H	HR	BB/9	K/9	K	GB%	BABIP	WHIP	ERA	FIP	DRA	VORP	WARP	cFIP	MPH
2014	DYT	A	22	7	8	0	27	27	133¹	115	11	3.4	8.6	127	50%	.282	1.25	3.64	3.87	3.99	21.5	2.2	100	
2015	DAY	A+	23	9	7	0	26	26	140¹	117	4	3.5	8.5	133	45%	.298	1.23	2.44	2.90	3.09	31.0	3.4	94	
2016	PEN	AA	24	5	3	0	13	12	77	51	0	3.3	9.1	78	50%	.252	1.03	1.75	2.50	3.33	14.9	1.6	89	
2016	LOU	AAA	24	2	5	0	12	11	67²	48	6	4.1	7.2	54	49%	.231	1.17	3.46	4.14	4.51	6.0	0.6	100	
2017	CIN	MLB	25	2	2	0	24	3	37¹	37	4	4.5	6.8	28	51%	.289	1.47	5.10	4.76	4.96	0.3	0.0	100	
2018	CIN	MLB	26	4	3	0	60	7	95¹	73	11	5.8	9.5	101	51%	.283	1.41	4.89	4.99	5.35	-0.5	-0.1	124	

Breakout: 11%   Improve: 19%   Collapse: 14%   Attrition: 26%   MLB: 36%   Comparables: George Kontos, Gus Schlosser, Josh Smith

This is one of those things that always sounds good, but never works. Former basketball player commits himself to baseball, the arm action is really loose, the body fluid, the slider can look great when it's right, there's a changeup in the arm and the delivery. This never works. The kid will have too much trouble repeating the delivery, or never find command of the heat, or get hurt. Only here's the thing: Garrett keeps climbing the ladder and slowly adding to his seasonal workloads. He keeps dominating hitters with a fastball that can touch 97, that slider (it still comes and goes, but he has a deceptive delivery) and the maybe-decent changeup. Unless injury strikes (and there are zero red flags, but there never are), Garrett is going to arrive in 2017, and has a great chance to be good, even if it ends up being in the bullpen.

Ariel Hernandez   RHP

Born: 3/2/92   Age: 25   Bats: R   Throws: R   Height: 6'3"   Weight: 180   Entered Pro Ball: International Free Agent, 2009

YEAR	TEAM	LVL	AGE	W	L	SV	G	GS	IP	H	HR	BB/9	K/9	K	GB%	BABIP	WHIP	ERA	FIP	DRA	VORP	WARP	cFIP	MPH
2015	YAK	A-	23	1	1	2	22	0	22¹	18	1	8.5	12.9	32	40%	.327	1.75	6.04	4.41	7.01	-5.2	-0.5	114	
2016	DYT	A	24	0	1	2	18	0	31¹	11	0	5.7	11.5	40	55%	.164	0.99	2.59	2.93	3.78	3.1	0.3	104	
2016	DAY	A+	24	3	1	3	25	0	30²	18	1	5.6	10.0	34	50%	.227	1.21	1.76	3.41	4.28	2.7	0.3	105	
2017	CIN	MLB	25	2	1	2	43	0	45¹	45	7	6.1	6.9	35	51%	.299	1.67	5.83	5.78	6.34	-6.8	-0.7	151	
2018	CIN	MLB	26	1	0	1	23	0	28²	23	4	7.0	10.6	34	51%	.298	1.57	5.22	5.40	5.68	-1.7	-0.2	134	

Breakout: 3%   Improve: 3%   Collapse: 0%   Attrition: 0%   MLB: 3%   *Comparables: Mychal Givens, Leyson Septimo, Taylor Thompson*

Hernandez signed with the Giants a presidency ago, never managed to command his combination of mid-90s heat and a power curve, then hurt his shoulder, lost that velocity and should have been done in pro baseball. Instead, he found the right pair of eyes and hands, fixed his delivery in indy ball, fell into the right minor-league pitching coach's hands, started throwing the curveball more and is suddenly, at 25, a genuine relief prospect with a clear, short path to the big leagues.

Raisel Iglesias   RHP

Born: 1/4/90   Age: 27   Bats: R   Throws: R   Height: 6'2"   Weight: 185   Entered Pro Ball: International Free Agent, 2014

YEAR	TEAM	LVL	AGE	W	L	SV	G	GS	IP	H	HR	BB/9	K/9	K	GB%	BABIP	WHIP	ERA	FIP	DRA	VORP	WARP	cFIP	MPH
2015	LOU	AAA	25	1	3	0	6	6	29	26	4	2.5	6.5	21	53%	.250	1.17	3.41	4.33	4.25	3.4	0.3	92	
2015	CIN	MLB	25	3	7	0	18	16	95¹	81	11	2.6	9.8	104	48%	.286	1.14	4.15	3.58	2.96	22.3	2.4	82	95.4
2016	CIN	MLB	26	3	2	6	37	6	78¹	63	7	3.0	9.5	83	43%	.275	1.14	2.53	3.42	3.47	14.3	1.5	89	97.9
2017	CIN	MLB	27	3	3	10	58	0	61¹	52	7	3.0	9.7	66	46%	.284	1.17	3.56	3.68	3.74	8.0	0.8	81	
2018	CIN	MLB	28	3	1	6	67	0	70²	53	8	2.7	10.0	79	46%	.283	1.05	3.58	3.61	3.91	9.5	1.0	86	

Breakout: 28%   Improve: 59%   Collapse: 16%   Attrition: 13%   MLB: 94%   *Comparables: Brandon Morrow, Jered Weaver, Adam Wainwright*

Baseball needs a relief ace capable of pitching more than 100 innings in a season. In 2016, Iglesias quietly took steps toward becoming that kind of pioneer. Firstly, he proved unable to handle a starter's workload. Five starts into his season Iglesias hit the DL with a shoulder injury after being shut down in 2015 for essentially the same reason. He returned in mid-June as a reliever, and one barred from pitching on consecutive days, to boot. The Reds found a creative way to get their money's worth from him, as Iglesias threw at least 25 pitches in 18 of his 32 appearances after coming off the DL. He got at least six outs in 16 of the 32. He also dominated opposing batters in that role, holding them to a .165/.264/.250 line in 50 innings. His spotty command keeps him from being elite, but his stuff is good enough to more than outweigh that shortcoming. If he continues to be used this way, look out world.

Michael Lorenzen   RHP

Born: 1/4/92   Age: 25   Bats: R   Throws: R   Height: 6'3"   Weight: 215   Entered Pro Ball: Round 1, 2013 Draft (#38 overall)

YEAR	TEAM	LVL	AGE	W	L	SV	G	GS	IP	H	HR	BB/9	K/9	K	GB%	BABIP	WHIP	ERA	FIP	DRA	VORP	WARP	cFIP	MPH
2014	PEN	AA	22	4	6	0	24	24	120²	112	9	3.3	6.3	84	53%	.285	1.29	3.13	4.01	4.63	8.1	0.9	99	
2015	LOU	AAA	23	4	2	0	6	6	43	34	3	1.7	4	19	49%	.231	0.98	1.88	3.74	4.20	5.3	0.5	102	
2015	CIN	MLB	23	4	9	0	27	21	113¹	131	18	4.5	6.6	83	42%	.322	1.66	5.40	5.43	6.77	-21.7	-2.3	127	97.1
2016	CIN	MLB	24	2	1	0	35	0	50	41	5	2.3	8.6	48	64%	.277	1.08	2.88	3.71	3.05	10.7	1.1	76	98.6
2017	CIN	MLB	25	2	3	0	53	0	55²	53	7	3.6	7.5	46	56%	.291	1.35	4.52	4.51	4.52	2.4	0.3	100	
2018	CIN	MLB	26	3	1	0	53	0	56²	47	7	3.8	8.7	55	56%	.291	1.26	4.37	4.44	4.82	2.0	0.2	110	

Breakout: 22%   Improve: 47%   Collapse: 18%   Attrition: 22%   MLB: 87%   *Comparables: Nick Martinez, Greg Smith, Chad Gaudin*

A sprained elbow kept Lorenzen off MLB mounds until late June, but when he returned, he was a revelation. Formerly a flame-throwing starter with a straight four-seam fastball and a bunch of other, undistinguished stuff, Lorenzen transformed into a multi-inning relief weapon with a wrinkle on almost everything he threw. He threw his four-seamer, a sinker with good fade and a mid-90s cutter that often achieved real slider action, all in pretty equal measures. His curveball worked better off that power trio than it ever had as a predictable secondary pitch off the four-seam heat alone. If he can stay healthy and keep that cutter working the way it did in 2016, Lorenzen is a legitimate asset in the bullpen.

Tyler Mahle   RHP

Born: 9/29/94   Age: 22   Bats: R   Throws: R   Height: 6'4"   Weight: 200   Entered Pro Ball: Round 7, 2013 Draft (#225 overall)

YEAR	TEAM	LVL	AGE	W	L	SV	G	GS	IP	H	HR	BB/9	K/9	K	GB%	BABIP	WHIP	ERA	FIP	DRA	VORP	WARP	cFIP	MPH
2015	DYT	A	20	13	8	0	27	26	152	145	7	1.5	8.0	135	53%	.313	1.12	2.43	2.93	2.11	52.3	5.6	81	
2016	DAY	A+	21	8	3	0	13	13	79¹	58	6	1.9	8.6	76	48%	.255	0.95	2.50	3.15	1.99	30.7	3.2	79	
2016	PEN	AA	21	6	3	0	14	14	71¹	78	12	2.5	8.2	65	42%	.320	1.37	4.92	4.78	2.94	17.1	1.8	100	
2017	CIN	MLB	22	7	9	0	23	23	126	131	19	3.2	6.1	85	54%	.307	1.40	4.90	4.96	5.39	2.4	0.2	126	
2018	CIN	MLB	23	7	9	0	24	24	141	126	20	4.3	8.5	133	54%	.300	1.37	4.88	4.98	5.37	2.7	0.3	127	

Breakout: 15%   Improve: 25%   Collapse: 2%   Attrition: 20%   MLB: 36%   *Comparables: Derek Holland, Kyle Drabek, Rafael Montero*

Everywhere on the scouting sheet, Mahle seems to be a little too polished to properly evaluate. He throws pretty hard and can get to 96 mph when he really needs it, sitting 92-94. But what stands out is that in his early 20s, he's already figured out how to use that power against hitters. He doesn't have a breaking ball that can get him to two strikes or consistently put hitters away, but he's learned to use both a curve and a slider to keep hitters off balance. What's missing now is a changeup that really does something. Then it will all be about whether he can respond once he encounters hitters who quickly and lethally adjust to good command and sequencing.

Keury Mella RHP

Born: 8/2/93 Age: 23 Bats: R Throws: R Height: 6'2" Weight: 200 Entered Pro Ball: International Free Agent, 2012

YEAR	TEAM	LVL	AGE	W	L	SV	G	GS	IP	H	HR	BB/9	K/9	K	GB%	BABIP	WHIP	ERA	FIP	DRA	VORP	WARP	cFIP	MPH
2014	AUG	A	20	3	3	0	12	12	66¹	69	1	1.8	8.5	63	62%	.337	1.24	3.93	2.79	3.01	17.9	1.9	84	
2014	SLO	A-	20	1	1	0	6	6	19²	16	0	2.7	9.2	20	47%	.302	1.12	1.83	3.00	3.65	3.7	0.4	95	
2015	SJO	A+	21	5	3	0	16	16	81²	66	5	2.9	9.1	83	44%	.272	1.13	3.31	3.79	3.74	12.2	1.3	97	
2015	DAY	A+	21	3	1	0	4	4	21¹	11	2	6.3	9.7	23	41%	.184	1.22	2.95	4.62	4.82	0.6	0.1	109	
2016	DAY	A+	22	8	9	0	25	24	131²	150	7	3.8	6.5	95	40%	.340	1.56	3.90	3.98	5.55	-1.3	-0.1	109	
2017	*CIN*	*MLB*	*23*	*6*	*9*	*0*	*23*	*23*	*114²*	*129*	*19*	*4.3*	*5.3*	*68*	*58%*	*.312*	*1.61*	*5.67*	*5.70*	*6.18*	*-7.9*	*-0.8*	*147*	
2018	*CIN*	*MLB*	*24*	*4*	*7*	*0*	*16*	*16*	*95²*	*93*	*15*	*6.0*	*8.6*	*91*	*58%*	*.318*	*1.64*	*5.74*	*5.91*	*6.26*	*-6.2*	*-0.6*	*148*	

Breakout: 9%   Improve: 13%   Collapse: 0%   Attrition: 12%   MLB: 15%   Comparables: *Michael Stutes, Donnie Veal, Daniel Corcino*

It's not terribly hard to see what Mella was trying to do in 2016. He stopped throwing 97, preferring to lean more on his two-seam heat and work in the low-to-mid-90s with better command. The problem was that neither fastball could miss bats at that speed and he still had just an ill-defined slurve for a breaking ball. It's time to dispense with cuteness and the dream of a mid-rotation workhorse and see whether short bursts and his hottest heat can turn Mella into a dominant reliever.

Cody Reed LHP

Born: 4/15/93 Age: 24 Bats: L Throws: L Height: 6'5" Weight: 225 Entered Pro Ball: Round 2, 2013 Draft (#46 overall)

YEAR	TEAM	LVL	AGE	W	L	SV	G	GS	IP	H	HR	BB/9	K/9	K	GB%	BABIP	WHIP	ERA	FIP	DRA	VORP	WARP	cFIP	MPH
2014	LEX	A	21	3	9	0	19	19	84	105	4	3.9	6.2	58	59%	.351	1.68	5.46	4.37	7.68	-20.9	-2.2	115	
2015	WIL	A+	22	5	5	1	13	10	67¹	62	3	2.4	8.7	65	46%	.309	1.19	2.14	2.75	2.58	18.2	2.0	87	
2015	NWA	AA	22	2	2	0	5	5	28²	26	3	2.5	6.0	19	45%	.258	1.19	3.45	4.27	4.54	1.8	0.2	104	
2015	PEN	AA	22	6	2	0	8	8	49²	39	1	2.9	10.9	60	50%	.311	1.11	2.17	2.24	1.85	17.9	1.9	67	
2016	CIN	MLB	23	0	7	0	10	10	47²	67	12	3.6	8.1	43	54%	.364	1.80	7.36	6.10	3.93	7.6	0.8	96	95.8
2016	LOU	AAA	23	6	4	0	13	13	73	71	6	2.5	8.0	65	52%	.314	1.25	3.08	3.40	2.12	26.2	2.7	78	
2017	*CIN*	*MLB*	*24*	*5*	*7*	*0*	*32*	*16*	*96²*	*104*	*12*	*3.4*	*7.2*	*77*	*47%*	*.306*	*1.47*	*4.62*	*4.43*	*4.63*	*5.4*	*0.6*	*100*	
2018	*CIN*	*MLB*	*25*	*5*	*7*	*0*	*19*	*19*	*112¹*	*99*	*14*	*4.2*	*9.3*	*116*	*47%*	*.314*	*1.35*	*4.45*	*4.51*	*4.87*	*7.3*	*0.8*	*112*	

Breakout: 26%   Improve: 46%   Collapse: 13%   Attrition: 27%   MLB: 71%   Comparables: *Marco Gonzales, Felipe Rivero, Burch Smith*

No getting around it: Reed had an ugly big-league debut. Except, wait, maybe there is some getting around it. The tall and solid southpaw gave up a homer for every 12 outs he recorded, but still showed plenty of the things that made him a legitimate mid-rotation prospect entering the season. His fastball moves like mad. His slider works even as a back-foot offering against righties. Despite the ugly results, the advanced numbers see a pitcher who did his best to hold his own under tough circumstances. Close observers of his starts saw the same thing. Reed remains a pretty good bet to figure it out.

Salvatore Romano RHP

Born: 10/12/93 Age: 23 Bats: L Throws: R Height: 6'5" Weight: 260 Entered Pro Ball: Round 23, 2011 Draft (#715 overall)

YEAR	TEAM	LVL	AGE	W	L	SV	G	GS	IP	H	HR	BB/9	K/9	K	GB%	BABIP	WHIP	ERA	FIP	DRA	VORP	WARP	cFIP	MPH
2014	DYT	A	20	8	11	0	28	28	148²	169	9	2.5	7.7	128	54%	.352	1.42	4.12	3.56	4.43	16.7	1.7	99	
2015	DAY	A+	21	6	5	0	19	18	104	103	2	2.9	6.8	79	59%	.318	1.31	3.46	2.91	4.13	10.7	1.2	99	
2015	PEN	AA	21	0	4	0	7	7	23	35	4	4.7	3.5	9	47%	.348	2.04	10.96	6.35	8.86	-9.6	-1.0	126	
2016	PEN	AA	22	6	11	0	27	27	156	157	10	2.0	8.3	144	49%	.320	1.22	3.52	3.06	2.78	40.2	4.3	85	
2017	*CIN*	*MLB*	*23*	*1*	*1*	*0*	*26*	*0*	*27*	*30*	*3*	*3.5*	*6.2*	*19*	*48%*	*.305*	*1.49*	*4.49*	*4.49*	*4.40*	*1.6*	*0.2*	*100*	
2018	*CIN*	*MLB*	*24*	*2*	*1*	*0*	*44*	*0*	*46¹*	*42*	*4*	*4.4*	*8.8*	*45*	*48%*	*.322*	*1.40*	*4.23*	*4.30*	*4.56*	*2.9*	*0.3*	*104*	

Breakout: 7%   Improve: 14%   Collapse: 10%   Attrition: 24%   MLB: 30%   Comparables: *Scott Diamond, Brian Flynn, Dallas Beeler*

His name makes it feel like Romano should have played for the 1950s Brooklyn Dodgers, but back then they didn't make them this big. He's not much of an athlete on the mound, but Romano manages to repeat his delivery well enough to keep his walks down. He also gets the ball moving downhill and induces lots of grounders. His fastball reaches the mid-90s. Unless his body gets out of control, his size should work in his favor, allowing him to pile up innings. More consistency with the curveball could really change the conversation, but in the meantime he's a possible back-end starter.

Antonio Santillan RHP

Born: 4/15/97 Age: 20 Bats: R Throws: R Height: 6'3" Weight: 240 Entered Pro Ball: Round 2, 2015 Draft (#49 overall)

YEAR	TEAM	LVL	AGE	W	L	SV	G	GS	IP	H	HR	BB/9	K/9	K	GB%	BABIP	WHIP	ERA	FIP	DRA	VORP	WARP	cFIP	MPH
2016	DYT	A	19	2	3	0	7	7	30¹	27	3	7.1	11.3	38	38%	.338	1.68	6.82	4.83	4.64	1.3	0.1	108	
2017	*CIN*	*MLB*	*20*	*2*	*5*	*0*	*12*	*12*	*50¹*	*55*	*10*	*6.3*	*6.6*	*37*	*69%*	*.314*	*1.79*	*6.50*	*6.51*	*7.10*	*-8.6*	*-0.9*	*168*	
2018	*CIN*	*MLB*	*21*	*5*	*10*	*0*	*26*	*26*	*154²*	*149*	*29*	*6.6*	*9.2*	*158*	*69%*	*.316*	*1.70*	*6.15*	*6.38*	*6.72*	*-14.0*	*-1.4*	*161*	

Breakout: 0%   Improve: 0%   Collapse: 0%   Attrition: 2%   MLB: 2%   Comparables: *Miguel Castro, Alex Reyes, Kyle Lobstein*

At some point during his development, Santillan will need to show better command. He'll also need to improve his changeup by a mile, if he wants to make it as a starter. In the meantime, the huge Texan is dominating hitters in the low minors with a fastball that reaches the high 90s and a sharp, plus curveball. That's damn good, and given that Santillan pitched all of last season at age 19, it's probably just the beginning. He has the body and the stuff to be a mid-rotation starter—and maybe more—and his delivery doesn't disqualify him from that role, nor from seeing his command really tighten up as he grows fully into his body. He could take off anytime, though the smart money says it'll be a year or two before he comes knocking at the door of the big leagues.

Robert Stephenson   RHP

Born: 2/24/93   Age: 24   Bats: R   Throws: R   Height: 6'2"   Weight: 200   Entered Pro Ball: Round 1, 2011 Draft (#27 overall)

YEAR	TEAM	LVL	AGE	W	L	SV	G	GS	IP	H	HR	BB/9	K/9	K	GB%	BABIP	WHIP	ERA	FIP	DRA	VORP	WARP	cFIP	MPH
2014	PEN	AA	21	7	10	0	27	26	136²	114	18	4.9	9.2	140	38%	.264	1.38	4.74	4.58	6.54	-20.1	-2.1	104	
2015	PEN	AA	22	4	7	0	14	14	78¹	53	8	4.9	10.2	89	39%	.249	1.23	3.68	4.16	3.48	14.1	1.5	92	
2015	LOU	AAA	22	4	4	0	11	11	55²	51	2	4.4	8.2	51	41%	.306	1.40	4.04	3.35	6.32	-6.3	-0.6	104	
2016	LOU	AAA	23	8	9	0	24	24	136²	115	17	4.7	7.9	120	42%	.259	1.36	4.41	4.65	8.72	-51.3	-5.3	115	
2016	CIN	MLB	23	2	3	0	8	8	37	41	9	4.6	7.5	31	35%	.299	1.62	6.08	6.54	6.34	-4.0	-0.4	126	95.7
2017	CIN	MLB	24	5	7	0	19	19	95	92	12	4.3	7.6	80	51%	.287	1.42	4.79	4.72	4.86	3.4	0.3	100	
2018	CIN	MLB	25	9	11	0	31	31	198²	143	24	5.5	10.5	233	51%	.275	1.33	4.52	4.61	4.98	10.1	1.0	116	

Breakout: 16%   Improve: 29%   Collapse: 22%   Attrition: 33%   MLB: 64%   Comparables: Michael Bowden, Neil Ramirez, Daryl Thompson

In baseball, you can fail without learning, but you can't learn without failing. Stephenson failed spectacularly in 2016. If he's made of the right stuff, he'll learn from that failure and turn it around in 2017. Step one: fall out of love with the fastball. Stephenson threw his heat nearly 75 percent of the time in 2016, and doesn't have the command to make that work. Moreover, there's no earthly reason why he should try to make it work. In his curveball and changeup, he has two plus pitches to which to turn. If he gains in wisdom, experience and maturity, and figures out how to better use his secondary weapons, Stephenson could be at the top of the Reds' rotation by season's end.

Dan Straily   RHP

Born: 12/1/88   Age: 28   Bats: R   Throws: R   Height: 6'2"   Weight: 220   Entered Pro Ball: Round 24, 2009 Draft (#723 overall)

YEAR	TEAM	LVL	AGE	W	L	SV	G	GS	IP	H	HR	BB/9	K/9	K	GB%	BABIP	WHIP	ERA	FIP	DRA	VORP	WARP	cFIP	MPH
2014	OAK	MLB	25	1	2	0	7	7	38¹	33	9	3.5	8.0	34	36%	.240	1.25	4.93	5.69	5.61	-3.5	-0.4	113	90.9
2014	SAC	AAA	25	4	3	0	10	10	63	54	9	3.7	9.6	67	33%	.296	1.27	4.71	4.76	4.13	11.4	1.1	104	
2014	IOW	AAA	25	3	5	0	10	10	55	59	7	3.3	9.2	56	34%	.327	1.44	4.09	4.57	4.85	5.5	0.5	105	
2014	CHN	MLB	25	0	1	0	7	1	13²	20	1	5.9	8.6	13	35%	.396	2.12	11.85	4.35	5.75	-1.5	-0.2	112	92.2
2015	FRE	AAA	26	10	9	0	22	22	122²	147	13	1.8	9.1	124	33%	.356	1.40	4.77	3.66	2.18	42.6	4.3	77	
2015	HOU	MLB	26	0	1	0	4	3	16²	16	2	4.3	7.6	14	42%	.275	1.44	5.40	4.60	4.91	0.3	0.0	105	91.3
2016	CIN	MLB	27	14	8	0	34	31	191¹	154	31	3.4	7.6	162	36%	.239	1.19	3.76	4.92	4.61	15.5	1.6	119	91.8
2017	CIN	MLB	28	8	11	0	28	28	159	150	24	3.2	8.3	148	55%	.285	1.28	4.50	4.44	4.56	11.0	1.1	100	
2018	CIN	MLB	29	10	11	0	31	31	200	161	28	3.5	10.0	223	55%	.290	1.19	4.17	4.25	4.60	18.8	1.9	106	

Breakout: 18%   Improve: 43%   Collapse: 16%   Attrition: 26%   MLB: 80%   Comparables: Anthony Reyes, David Phelps, Chase Anderson

Straily got only a lineout in the 2015 version of this tome, and didn't appear at all in the 2016 book. When his velocity plunged into the mid-80s, he seemed unlikely to survive as a big-league arm. Then he went to work at Driveline Baseball, rediscovered his (below-average) full velocity, and ended up as the Reds' most reliable and durable starter. Funny thing, though: hardly anything actually changed. Straily still doesn't throw hard, still doesn't miss bats, still can't keep the ball on the ground. He got lucky on balls in play and with runners on base, leading to a solid ERA. Nothing else suggests he's a long-term solution to anyone's rotation problems. He's figured out how to play on batters' expectations with pitch selection and how to pose perceptual problems with his mechanics.

Nick Travieso   RHP

Born: 1/31/94   Age: 23   Bats: R   Throws: R   Height: 6'2"   Weight: 225   Entered Pro Ball: Round 1, 2012 Draft (#14 overall)

YEAR	TEAM	LVL	AGE	W	L	SV	G	GS	IP	H	HR	BB/9	K/9	K	GB%	BABIP	WHIP	ERA	FIP	DRA	VORP	WARP	cFIP	MPH
2014	DYT	A	20	14	5	0	26	26	142²	123	10	2.8	7.2	114	50%	.272	1.17	3.03	3.93	4.59	13.5	1.4	105	
2015	DAY	A+	21	6	6	0	19	19	93¹	82	4	2.9	7.3	76	44%	.282	1.20	2.70	3.32	4.89	2.0	0.2	104	
2016	PEN	AA	22	5	7	0	23	23	117¹	109	11	4.1	7.0	91	44%	.282	1.38	3.84	4.52	8.54	-45.0	-4.9	118	
2017	CIN	MLB	23	5	7	0	18	18	93²	99	15	4.4	5.2	54	59%	.298	1.55	5.71	5.69	6.23	-6.9	-0.7	149	
2018	CIN	MLB	24	4	8	0	18	18	106²	101	18	6.0	8.1	96	59%	.303	1.62	6.01	6.17	6.56	-10.2	-1.1	156	

Breakout: 12%   Improve: 19%   Collapse: 3%   Attrition: 16%   MLB: 22%   Comparables: James Houser, Adam Ottavino, Josh Outman

Travieso has three pitches he can throw for strikes and none of them are threatening to fall off the bottom end of the scouting scale. Unfortunately, they're also not threatening to start missing bats. Travieso's stuff has backed up considerably since being drafted. To succeed, he needs to make fewer mistakes than most pitchers and stay off the barrels of opponents' bats. His first taste of Double-A didn't inspire confidence that he can manage that.

Blake Wood   RHP

Born: 8/8/85   Age: 31   Bats: R   Throws: R   Height: 6'5"   Weight: 240   Entered Pro Ball: Round 3, 2006 Draft (#77 overall)

YEAR	TEAM	LVL	AGE	W	L	SV	G	GS	IP	H	HR	BB/9	K/9	K	GB%	BABIP	WHIP	ERA	FIP	DRA	VORP	WARP	cFIP	MPH
2014	CLE	MLB	28	0	1	0	7	0	6¹	4	0	9.9	9.9	7	47%	.267	1.74	7.11	4.74	4.07	0.3	0.0	105	98.7
2014	OMA	AAA	28	0	0	0	14	0	18¹	18	2	7.9	10.3	21	60%	.348	1.85	6.38	5.44	5.04	0.6	0.1	88	
2015	IND	AAA	29	2	5	29	57	0	58²	52	2	3.8	10.7	70	50%	.327	1.31	3.53	2.54	2.66	14.7	1.5	86	
2016	CIN	MLB	30	6	5	1	70	0	76²	72	9	4.5	9.5	81	53%	.315	1.43	3.99	4.16	3.50	12.5	1.3	88	98.5
2017	CIN	MLB	31	3	3	0	58	0	61¹	60	8	4.0	9.0	61	45%	.307	1.44	4.49	4.30	4.49	2.9	0.3	100	
2018	CIN	MLB	32	2	1	1	50	0	52²	44	7	4.4	10.2	60	45%	.304	1.31	4.47	4.53	4.92	1.3	0.1	113	

Breakout: 14%   Improve: 20%   Collapse: 7%   Attrition: 7%   MLB: 35%   Comparables: Wil Ledezma, Mike Zagurski, Greg Aquino

The Reds' bullpen was an almost unprecedented disaster in 2016, but it wasn't an unmitigated one. Meet Blake "The Mitigator" Wood. He made a weapon out of an every-now-and-then splitter that induced a ton of swings and misses. Wood can graze triple digits with his sinker and has a vicious slider that hums in at around 90 mph. Both of those primary pitches posed plenty of problems for opposing batters, even when Wood's command faltered. That third pitch really turned them inside out. Barring injury, Wood is a valuable relief arm.

Max Wotell   LHP

Born: 9/13/96   Age: 20   Bats: R   Throws: L   Height: 6'3"   Weight: 195   Entered Pro Ball: Round 3, 2015 Draft (#88 overall)

YEAR	TEAM	LVL	AGE	W	L	SV	G	GS	IP	H	HR	BB/9	K/9	K	GB%	BABIP	WHIP	ERA	FIP	DRA	VORP	WARP	cFIP	MPH
2017	CIN	MLB	20	1	3	0	13	6	32²	39	8	5.9	5.6	20	76%	.317	1.85	7.13	7.20	7.81	-8.5	-0.9	185	
2018	CIN	MLB	21	4	7	1	39	16	119²	131	26	5.7	7.5	99	76%	.321	1.74	6.66	6.94	7.30	-19.0	-2.0	175	

Breakout: 0%   Improve: 0%   Collapse: 0%   Attrition: 0%   MLB: 0%   Comparables: Jose Ramirez, Matt Magill, Jorge Lopez

All the pieces of a back-end starter, and maybe even a bit more, are here. There's a ton of assembly required, though. Wotell entered pro ball with a weird windup that involved his back foot stepping from the first-base side of the rubber to the third-base side, then found him coming slightly across his body to get the ball to the third-base side of the plate. He's cleaner out of the stretch, but still has trouble repeating his mechanics, which has slowed any development of his changeup. He throws fairly hard and his curveball flashes above average.

LINEOUTS

Hitters

NAME	POS	TEAM	LVL	AGE	PA	R	2B	3B	HR	RBI	BB	K	SB	CS	AVG/OBP/SLG	TAv	VORP	BABIP	BRR	FRAA	WARP
Ivan De Jesus	UT	CIN	MLB	29	243	21	10	0	1	20	17	51	3	1	.253/.311/.312	.232	-0.4	.324	-1.3	SS(30): 3.1, 2B(22): 0.0	0.4
Juan Graterol	C	SLC	AAA	27	246	24	10	0	2	23	10	27	2	1	.300/.340/.370	.235	2.3	.330	-1.7	C(61): 0.9	0.3
	C	ANA	MLB	27	15	2	2	0	0	3	0	3	0	0	.286/.286/.429	.243	-0.5	.364	-0.9	C(9): -0.2	-0.1
Gabriel Guerrero	RF	RNO	AAA	22	110	10	5	1	1	9	9	25	0	0	.212/.273/.313	.211	-2.2	.267	1.4	RF(29): 2.2, LF(3): -0.3	0.0
	RF	MOB	AA	22	342	39	18	5	8	45	20	76	6	3	.241/.284/.404	.255	5.1	.290	0.8	RF(80): 5.4, CF(6): -0.2	1.1
Tyler Holt	OF	CIN	MLB	27	208	21	5	3	0	13	23	48	4	3	.235/.327/.296	.229	1.2	.318	2.3	CF(32): -0.3, RF(23): -3.1	-0.3
Hernan Iribarren	2B	LOU	AAA	32	410	46	20	1	3	35	33	60	3	5	.327/.380/.410	.284	22.0	.381	1.5	CF(25): 2.6, 1B(20): 1.6	2.6
	2B	CIN	MLB	32	45	6	0	3	0	2	0	11	0	0	.311/.311/.444	.262	1.3	.412	0.0	CF(6): -0.3, 2B(5): -0.2	0.1
Eric Jagielo	SS	PEN	AA	24	420	26	15	1	7	26	44	128	0	0	.205/.305/.310	.233	-8.0	.294	-5.1	3B(49): -2.8, 1B(46): 0.7	-1.1
Patrick Kivlehan	OF	ROU	AAA	26	155	17	8	0	1	16	11	36	2	2	.184/.252/.262	.195	-6.6	.238	0.9	3B(17): -1.8, 1B(16): -0.1	-0.9
	OF	TAC	AAA	26	166	21	8	2	8	25	8	49	2	2	.293/.327/.522	.318	14.3	.380	0.2	3B(24): -0.6, RF(7): -0.1	1.4
	OF	SDN	MLB	26	19	5	0	0	1	2	2	9	0	0	.250/.368/.438	.301	1.0	.500	-0.1	RF(4): -0.8, LF(1): -0.1	0.0
	OF	ELP	AAA	26	78	8	2	1	3	8	5	23	1	0	.306/.351/.486	.287	4.6	.413	1.1	1B(11): -0.2, LF(7): -1.2	0.3
	OF	CIN	MLB	26	5	0	0	0	0	0	0	2	0	0	.000/.000/.000	.000	-1.2	.000	0.0	RF(2): 0.6	-0.1
Rafael Lopez	C	LOU	AAA	28	169	12	10	0	1	17	9	39	1	0	.213/.262/.297	.203	-6.7	.274	-4.2	C(46): 0.1	-0.7
	C	CIN	MLB	28	7	0	0	0	0	0	0	3	0	0	.000/.000/.000	.009	-1.6	.000	0.0	C(4): -0.0, 1B(1): -0.0	-0.2
Yorman Rodriguez	RF	DAY	A+	23	27	3	1	0	0	1	1	8	0	0	.346/.370/.385	.281	0.3	.500	-0.7	LF(5): -0.4	0.0
Steve Selsky	OF	LOU	AAA	26	339	40	24	1	9	37	29	74	2	1	.280/.363/.459	.293	14.1	.343	-2.5	1B(36): 4.7, RF(27): 0.4	2.1
	OF	CIN	MLB	26	54	9	2	0	2	7	2	22	1	0	.314/.340/.471	.284	3.5	.519	1.0	RF(11): 1.0, LF(3): -0.1	0.5
Tyler Stephenson	C	DYT	A	19	153	17	4	1	3	16	12	45	0	0	.216/.278/.324	.225	0.8	.297	0.9	C(27): -1.2	0.0
Stuart Turner	C	CHT	AA	24	370	40	22	0	6	41	35	72	5	3	.239/.322/.363	.263	14.0	.285	-1.4	C(83): -0.4	1.5
Josh Van Meter	INF	LEL	A+	21	401	51	21	2	12	51	48	64	9	2	.267/.355/.443	.294	26.2	.295	0.7	3B(61): -1.0, 2B(17): -1.0	2.5
	INF	SAN	AA	21	114	10	2	0	2	5	7	18	2	1	.198/.248/.274	.199	-3.0	.221	0.5	3B(29): -2.8	-0.6

Punchless at the plate and heavier in the legs than he used to be, **Ivan De Jesus** earns his keep by playing wherever you put him and going down to the desk to ask for takeout menus. ❖ Congratulations to **Juan Graterol** for defining a new position: the emergency backup to the emergency backup backup catcher. ❖ **Gabriel Guerrero** has a plus arm in right field and easy raw power, but struggles to make enough contact to use it. ❖ **Tyler Holt** has a patient approach at the plate, but no other tools that accredit him as a big leaguer. ❖ **Hernan Iribarren** got his first cup of coffee in seven years. Not literally. ❖ **Eric Jagielo** went to Notre Dame, but he's had only the luck o' the mid-19th century Irish immigrant during his pro career so far. ❖ **Patrick Kivlehan** bats right, throws right, plays right and is right on the line between useful bench bat and high-school baseball coach. ❖ For the first time in his pro career, **Rafael Lopez** was an average framer in 2016. Alas, he traded his OBP to whoever it is that gives out framing skills. ❖ The best we can say about the Reds' signing of **Alfredo Rodriguez**, so far, is that it doesn't seem to have lived up to the Yoan Lopez comps. ❖ A hamstring injury stole **Yorman Rodriguez**'s season, derailing a career that promised to be full of waiver claims and weeks spent in DFA limbo. ❖ Two injury-plagued seasons have stopped **Steve Selsky** from getting any buzz out of his solid, steady hitting. ❖ Concussions and wrist surgery, plus an inability to hit in the Midwest League, made 2016 a lost season for 2015 first rounder **Tyler Stephenson**. ❖ **Stuart Turner**'s bat never developed as hoped after the Twins picked him in the third round of the 2013 draft, but his strong defensive reputation could be his ticket to the big leagues. ❖ **Josh Van Meter** showed plus power and strong plate discipline at High-A, but then fell below the Mendoza Line at Double-A and was traded to the Reds in a Rule 5 swap.

Pitchers

NAME	TEAM	LVL	AGE	W	L	SV	G	GS	IP	H	HR	BB/9	K/9	K	GB%	BABIP	WHIP	ERA	FIP	DRA	VORP	WARP	cFIP	MPH
Tim Adleman	LOU	AAA	28	3	1	0	10	10	56²	52	4	1.6	6.0	38	47%	.277	1.09	2.38	3.38	3.54	11.3	1.2	99	
	CIN	MLB	28	4	4	0	13	13	69²	64	13	2.6	6.1	47	40%	.252	1.21	4.00	5.34	5.36	0.0	0.0	119	93.5
Barrett Astin	PEN	AA	24	9	3	0	37	11	103¹	74	8	2.2	8.4	96	64%	.246	0.96	2.26	3.37	3.25	19.3	2.1	80	
Caleb Cotham	CIN	MLB	28	0	3	0	23	0	24¹	32	3	4.4	7.8	21	46%	.372	1.81	7.40	4.91	4.83	0.4	0.0	108	95.1
William Davis	LOU	AAA	23	0	2	0	5	4	24	38	3	2.6	5.6	15	43%	.389	1.88	7.50	4.42	6.46	-3.2	-0.3	113	
	PEN	AA	23	10	3	0	19	19	101	88	10	2.7	5.5	62	49%	.254	1.17	2.94	4.42	5.80	-7.9	-0.9	115	
J.J. Hoover	CIN	MLB	28	1	2	1	18	0	18²	29	9	5.8	7.2	15	33%	.333	2.20	13.50	9.94	7.54	-5.3	-0.5	128	94.1
	LOU	AAA	28	4	2	4	32	0	38¹	39	2	2.6	11.7	50	35%	.370	1.30	3.52	2.18	1.56	14.5	1.5	78	
Matt Magill	LOU	AAA	26	4	1	0	29	0	42¹	40	6	4.5	9.1	43	44%	.306	1.44	4.46	4.47	3.49	6.9	0.7	100	
	CIN	MLB	26	0	0	0	5	0	4¹	5	1	10.4	2.1	1	29%	.308	2.31	6.23	9.19	6.38	-0.7	-0.1	125	94.9
Jon Moscot	CIN	MLB	24	0	3	0	5	5	21¹	26	10	4.2	4.2	10	41%	.219	1.69	8.02	9.89	8.19	-6.7	-0.7	134	93.2
	LOU	AAA	24	4	4	0	9	9	49²	58	9	2.9	5.6	31	39%	.306	1.49	5.26	5.48	7.25	-10.5	-1.1	121	
Ross Ohlendorf	CIN	MLB	33	5	7	2	64	0	65²	59	14	4.4	9.3	68	34%	.265	1.39	4.66	5.62	4.74	1.7	0.2	113	96.4
Wandy Peralta	PEN	AA	24	0	1	0	13	0	17²	17	1	1.5	10.2	20	50%	.327	1.13	3.06	2.30	3.08	3.2	0.4	84	
	LOU	AAA	24	4	1	3	37	2	58	44	2	3.6	5.9	38	61%	.249	1.16	2.33	3.60	4.46	3.6	0.4	98	
	CIN	MLB	24	0	0	0	10	0	7¹	11	1	8.6	6.1	5	46%	.400	2.45	8.59	6.87	6.10	-0.9	-0.1	118	97.5
Keyvius Sampson	LOU	AAA	25	3	3	0	18	9	62¹	38	3	3.0	9.0	62	46%	.226	0.95	1.88	2.86	2.30	20.5	2.1	85	
	CIN	MLB	25	0	1	0	18	2	39¹	40	9	6.2	9.6	42	39%	.287	1.70	4.35	6.24	4.94	0.5	0.1	118	95.8
Alfredo Simon	LOU	AAA	35	0	2	0	5	5	15	17	1	3.6	4.2	7	34%	.296	1.53	4.80	4.30	8.30	-4.9	-0.5	125	
	CIN	MLB	35	2	7	0	15	11	58²	89	15	4.8	6.0	39	51%	.361	2.05	9.36	7.17	5.92	-4.0	-0.4	119	95.4
Jackson Stephens	PEN	AA	22	8	11	0	27	26	151¹	148	7	2.4	7.8	131	46%	.312	1.25	3.33	3.14	3.42	28.0	3.0	97	

Tim Adleman might not hold up physically in the big leagues. He's tall and thick, and twisting around that often to watch well-struck fly balls is hard on the spinal column. ❖ **Barrett Astin** may not be a brand of luxury yachts, but he sailed back into potential starter territory during a repeat voyage at Double-A Pensacola. ❖ **Caleb Cotham** sounds like a superhero's secret identity, but if he has superhuman powers he hides them too well. ❖ **Rookie Davis** is going to end up a minor-league veteran, so he'd better get ready to trade in his nickname for another tired baseball sobriquet. He's a big guy from North Carolina. Bubba? ❖ Signed out of Cuba last August for $4.75 million, 21-year-old right-hander **Vladimir Gutierrez** is a tall, skinny starter with a mid-90s fastball who could begin paying big dividends in a couple years. ❖ **Nick Hanson** has power stuff, poor command, time to fix that and a very common name that has, nonetheless, never belonged to any other professional baseball player. (If more players were from Minnesota like he is, that wouldn't be so.) ❖ There's no evidence that **J.J. Hoover** is the rebellious would-be heir to a vacuum empire, but if he is, his frustrated father can take solace in knowing that even in this alternative career his son is devoted to sucking. ❖ Only six pitchers in MLB history have pitched more innings than **Matt Magill** over their careers and walked more than a batter per inning. ❖ That **Jon Moscot** amassed an even 10 strikeouts, walks and home runs allowed is fun trivia, as long as you aren't Jon Moscot. ❖ A Princeton degree and a funny, old-fashioned delivery make **Ross Ohlendorf** more interesting than an ordinary mop-up man, but not better. ❖ If you look up "org arm" in the *Oxford English Dictionary*, you won't find **Wandy Peralta**'s picture. In fact, you won't find anything, because "org arm" is obscure baseball jargon and the *Oxford English Dictionary* doesn't contain that kind of information. ❖ **Keyvius Sampson** could throw a baseball through a brick wall, as long as he wasn't aiming at it. ❖ Batters facing **Alfredo Simon** in 2016 hit like Joey Votto, only better. ❖ The Reds added **Jackson Stephens** to the 40-man roster in November, and when reached for comment he just screamed "ROLL TIDE!" ❖

CLEVELAND INDIANS

Essay by David Brown

Player comments by Emma Baccellieri and BP staff

Rajai Davis said he never dreamed of something so wild in his 36 years on earth.

With his team down two runs in the eighth inning and four outs from elimination in the World Series, Davis worked the count to 2-2 against Cubs closer Aroldis Chapman. It was true that Davis stood in the batters' box as the tying run in Game 7, but odds of success were not with him. Chicago's win expectancy was 86 percent.

Still, Cubs manager Joe Maddon was using his closer for the fifth time in eight days, and instead of reaching 102, 103, 104 on the radar gun with each heave, Chapman was showing slight-yet-perceptible signs of fatigue. He threw 101 mph on pitches five and six to Davis, who stayed alive by spoiling the latter for a foul ball. On pitch seven, Chapman followed with a poorly located 98 mph fastball, down in the zone and just left to the center of home plate.

Davis, noticeably choking up on the bat handle like a small-ball batter from a bygone era, connected for an exit velocity of 101.5 mph and a 22-degree launch angle—hard enough and barely high enough to propel the ball over the 19-foot fence, perhaps six or seven feet fair, for a two-run homer. Progressive Field went out of its collective mind because Cleveland had life with a 6-6 tie. Davis, who came into the game with 55 homers in 4,000-odd career plate appearances, had gone deep at the damnedest time.

"I definitely thought it had a good shot because I know I squared it up pretty good," Davis told the media later. "I was just hoping it would get over that tall wall over there. Beyond my wildest dreams, it was incredible, that feeling."

The greatest feeling ever was fleeting. In the top of the 10th, after a 17-minute rain delay that gave the Cubs enough time to regroup mentally and emotionally, Chicago took back the lead 8-6. Davis again came up as the tying run in the bottom half of the inning, and he again came through with an RBI single to center field, but that was as close as Cleveland got. One batter later, Michael Martinez grounded to third baseman Kris Bryant, who threw to Anthony Rizzo at first base for the final out. For the 68th straight year, Cleveland awoke before finishing its dream of winning the World Series.

✦✦✦

INDIANS PROSPECTUS
2016 W-L: 94-67, 1ST IN AL CENTRAL

Pythag	.562	4th	DER	.711	6th
RS/G	4.83	4th	B-Age	29	23rd
RA/G	4.2	7th	P-Age	28.1	13th
TAv	.254	23rd	Salary	$96.3M	23rd
BRR	13.12	4th	M$/MW	$1.8M	30th
TAv-P	.239	2nd	DL Days	500	3rd
FIP	3.87	7th	$ on DL	11%	11th

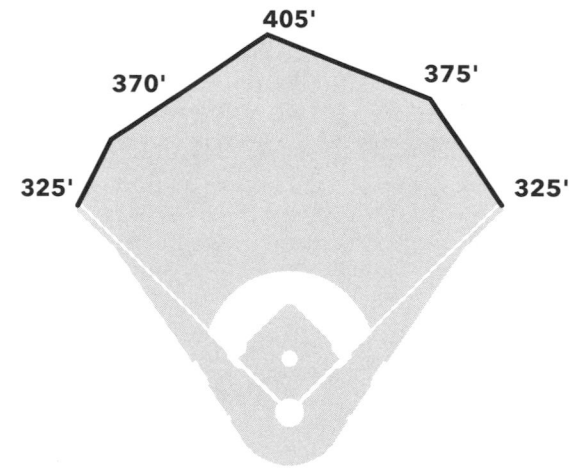

Outfield wall profile: **9'** to **19'**

Three-Year Park Factors

Runs	Runs/RH	Runs/LH	HR/RH	HR/LH
112	110	120	107	121

Top Hitter WARP	6.2	Francisco Lindor
Top Pitcher WARP	5.9	Corey Kluber
Top Prospect		Francisco Mejia

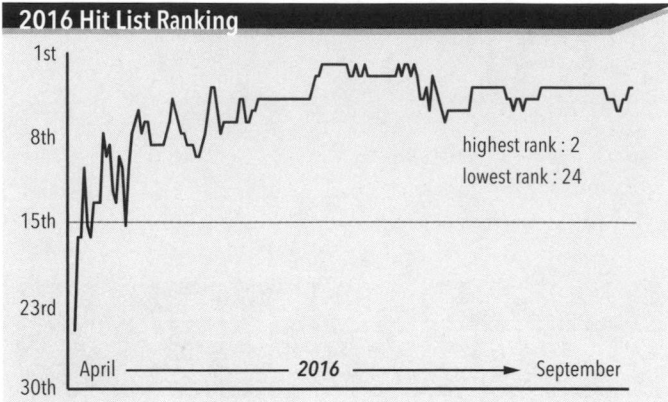

2016 Hit List Ranking

highest rank : 2
lowest rank : 24

April — *2016* → September

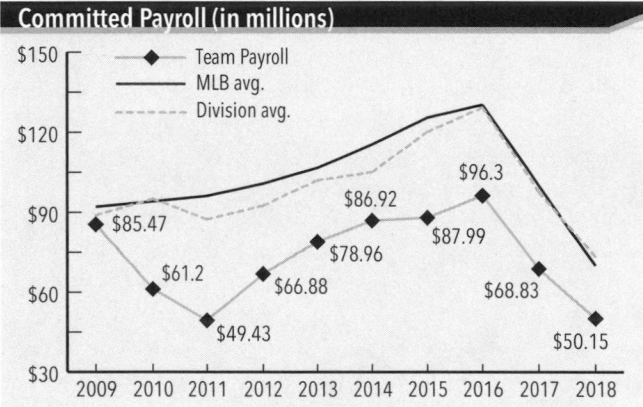

Committed Payroll (in millions)

◆ Team Payroll
— MLB avg.
--- Division avg.

$85.47
$61.2
$49.43
$66.88
$78.96
$86.92
$87.99
$96.3
$68.83
$50.15

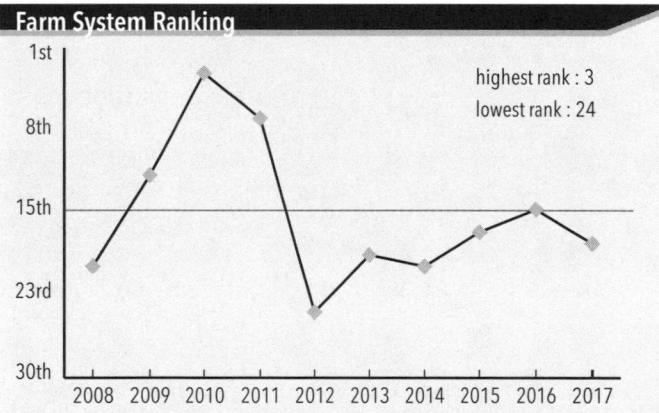

Farm System Ranking

highest rank : 3
lowest rank : 24

Personnel

President:
Chris Antonetti

General Manager:
Mike Chernoff

Assistant General Manager:
Carter Hawkins

Manager:
Terry Francona

BP Alumni:
Max Marchi
Ethan Purser
Steffan Segui
Keith Woolner

Weeks earlier, Indians manager Terry Francona had discussed a broad range of topics with reporters before the first game of the ALDS against the Red Sox. Francona talked about what, if anything, his time as the Red Sox's manager—having won the World Series twice with Boston—had to do with him managing the Indians now. Reporters also asked his feelings on Tito Francona, his father and a popular Cleveland player in the 1950s and 1960s, throwing out a ceremonial first pitch. Tito Francona played on a good Cleveland team, the 1959 squad that finished second to the Go-Go White Sox, but mostly they were mediocre.

But it was in response to questions about Cleveland possibly benefiting emotionally from the Cavaliers winning the NBA title in June—did that take any pressure off the baseball team, considering the city's championship drought was over?—that Francona thought of his father and the disappointing history of baseball in Cleveland. Champions in 1920 and 1948, but feelers of World Series heartbreak in 1954, 1995 and 1997, along with numerous other disappointments.

None of it should prevent the 2016 team from doing its best, Francona said:

"I mean, we can't play for—I was telling the group a couple of weeks ago—it's not my fault my dad didn't win. This is hard enough to win when you're playing good teams. But to go back 50, 60, 70 years, it's not fair to anybody. Being a fan, I understand that it's been a while. For the city I was thrilled when the Cavs won. It was hard not to get caught up in all of that. And then the timing was kind of unique where we went on that 14-game run right after that. But other than that, I just think—I don't think it's fair to the players to go back 60, 70 years. We try to not even go back much past yesterday. We're trying to stay in the moment because that's the best way to go about doing good things."

That day Francona also talked about the return of catcher Yan Gomes from a shoulder injury after it was thought his season had ended in July. The Indians sustained a number of injuries during the 2016 season, including to All-Star outfielder Michael Brantley. They also were dealing with the losses of Gomes and right-handers Carlos Carrasco and Danny Salazar. As of then both were expected to miss the playoffs, though Salazar was angling to return as a reliever if Cleveland's postseason run lasted until the World Series. Fat chance of that, many prognosticators figured, once Carrasco sustained a broken hand on September 17.

It was put most bluntly that day by Paul Hoynes of the *Cleveland Plain Dealer*. Hoynes has covered the Indians for 34 years, so he's seen some shit. And once Carrasco was lost for the season—which happened shortly after Salazar fell to arm problems—Hoynes thought for sure he'd seen the end of Cleveland's chances in 2016, writing:

"The Indians won a ballgame Saturday afternoon, but their postseason dreams ended.

Write it down. On Sept. 17, the Indians were eliminated from serious postseason advancement before they even got there.

They have 14 regular season games left and they'll eventually clinch their first AL Central title in nine years. But that's where it ends, because no team can withstand the losses the Indians have suffered over the last nine days."

Nearly four weeks after Hoynes' proclamation, with Cleveland having swept Boston in the ALDS, players were pouring beer over the reporter's head, and he was writing an apology for being incorrect on a legendary scale:

"As you can imagine, the Indians weren't pleased with what I wrote. Some of them still aren't. Near the end of Monday's celebration, Jason Kipnis said, "Will you at least admit you were wrong?" I told him I was wrong."

Not out of the woods yet, Cleveland appeared to lose another starting pitcher when drone enthusiast Trevor Bauer bled profusely from his right thumb early in Game 3 of the ALCS. He had injured himself repairing his pet robot, and while he made three appearances in the World Series his availability and effectiveness was compromised. No matter. Bauer's teammates—notably Josh Tomlin, rookie Ryan Merritt and the bullpen—picked him up.

✦ ✦ ✦

In the previous BP Annual, Pete Beatty wrote that Cleveland's 2015 team could have finished where the 2016 team did—in the World Series—had a few things broken their way. *Sports Illustrated* had predicted that the 2015 team would win the World Series, although that publication's judgment regarding Cleveland baseball has been in question since Cory Snyder appeared on the cover in 1987.

The 2015 Indians had more than predictions based in the heart. It had a third-order winning percentage pegging them as a 93-win team. Cleveland seemed close and the front office leadership of Chris Antonetti and Mike Chernoff helped to make the World Series happen in 2016 by way of several complementary changes.

During the offseason they signed first baseman Mike Napoli and outfielder Rajai Davis, and purchased reliever Dan Otero. In the middle of the season they called up Tyler Naquin, dumped Juan Uribe and let Jose Ramirez play third base every day. Down the stretch they traded for Brandon Guyer and Coco Crisp.

One or two other moves didn't work out—notably the acquisition of Marlon Byrd and the non-acquisition of Jonathan Lucroy—but the most transformative change occurred when they sent prospects to the Yankees for left-hander Andrew Miller on July 31. Cleveland already had

Cody Allen closing games, but adding Miller to the bullpen mix gave Francona and pitching coach Mickey Callaway two of the top 10 relievers in baseball.

Cleveland frequently used Miller in middle relief during his 26 regular-season appearances and four times in 10 postseason appearances he came on during the fifth or sixth innings. Miller's effectiveness as a midgame weapon was unmatched in baseball history and he was named MVP of the ALCS. And it was all made possible by Allen continuing to dominate in a more traditional eighth- and ninth-inning role.

How the Indians use Miller and Allen over the course of a full season will be fascinating to watch. It's safe to expect that it will not look like the 2016 postseason, given the expanse of the schedule, how starting pitchers tend to be used over 162 games and the different demands usage puts on the respective arms. Miller and Chapman looked a bit raggedy by the end of the 2016 postseason. If Francona loses confidence for any reason in either Miller or Allen, or even if there's no third man like Bryan Shaw, Cleveland's relief picture will look a lot more conventional in 2017.

✦ ✦ ✦

Cleveland has been short on championships, but not on fantastic individual players. Jim Thome, Albert Belle, Carlos Baerga, Kenny Lofton, Manny Ramirez, CC Sabathia, Roberto Alomar and Omar Vizquel--great players, many Hall-of-Fame caliber. Shortstop Francisco Lindor seems poised to join that list of Indians greatness.

If someone could calculate a joy created/run production metric, Lindor would have to be at the top of the list. It's easy to envision an AL MVP, or a string of them, considering the WARP he has accumulated through age 22. Nobody covered more ground on defense in the AL (except maybe Andrelton Simmons) and only a few MLB shortstops hit better than Lindor, who also appeared to be happier in his work than anyone else.

"Shoot, if I had his ability I'd feel confident, too," Francona said. "But, I mean, on the baseball field that's where he's most comfortable. And you can tell he's enjoying himself. And what's probably even better is as good a player he is, he's probably a better kid. That's saying something."

Lindor stands poised to lead Cleveland back to the playoffs on a regular basis in search of that elusive championship. When he was still in the minors three years ago, Lindor tweeted out a dream he'd had:

Last night I dreamed that I was playing shortstop 4 the @Indians in the World Series and we won #cantwait #WinningisEverything #Lindor12BC

It's hard to imagine how happy seeing that dream come true would make Lindor and Cleveland. ■

—David Brown is a freelance writer and BBWAA member

HITTERS

Abraham Almonte CF

Born: 6/27/89   Age: 28   Bats: B   Throws: R   Height: 5'9"   Weight: 210   Entered Pro Ball: International Free Agent, 2005

YEAR	TEAM	LVL	AGE	PA	R	2B	3B	HR	RBI	BB	K	SB	CS	AVG/OBP/SLG	TAv	VORP	BABIP	BRR	FRAA	WARP
2014	SEA	MLB	25	113	10	5	1	1	8	6	40	3	1	.198/.248/.292	.218	-0.2	.308	1.1	CF(26): 0.3	0.0
2014	TAC	AAA	25	312	42	10	3	6	31	28	66	7	4	.267/.333/.390	.261	10.4	.330	-0.2	CF(69): 1.7	1.2
2014	SDN	MLB	25	107	9	5	0	2	7	6	20	1	2	.265/.305/.378	.257	0.7	.312	-1.7	LF(16): -0.4 • CF(15): 7.4	0.9
2015	ELP	AAA	26	282	43	18	2	4	35	33	46	11	4	.275/.361/.414	.285	17.0	.325	1.3	CF(59): -11.3 • LF(3): -0.5	0.5
2015	SDN	MLB	26	62	6	3	0	0	4	5	19	1	1	.204/.271/.259	.215	-3.0	.314	-1.8	LF(6): -1.0 • CF(6): -0.5	-0.5
2015	CLE	MLB	26	196	30	9	5	5	20	16	33	6	0	.264/.321/.455	.264	7.7	.296	1.2	CF(50): 3.7	1.2
2016	COH	AAA	27	33	6	2	1	1	4	5	4	2	0	.444/.545/.704	.413	5.7	.500	-0.5	CF(6): -0.2	0.6
2016	CLE	MLB	27	194	24	20	1	1	22	8	42	8	0	.264/.294/.401	.229	-2.4	.331	-0.2	RF(36): 2.4 • LF(34): -2.2	-0.3
2017	*CLE*	*MLB*	*28*	*429*	*53*	*22*	*3*	*9*	*40*	*37*	*95*	*12*	*3*	*.256/.317/.403*	*.249*	*7.0*	*.309*	*1.0*	*RF -0, CF -1*	*0.2*
2018	*CLE*	*MLB*	*29*	*430*	*50*	*22*	*3*	*11*	*49*	*35*	*99*	*10*	*3*	*.252/.314/.410*	*.243*	*2.0*	*.303*	*-0.7*	*RF 0, CF -1*	*-0.2*

Breakout: 1%   Improve: 34%   Collapse: 11%   Attrition: 27%   MLB: 72%   *Comparables: Matt Murton, Travis Buck, Russ Adams*

In this book last year, we wrote: "Almonte is no team's first choice as an everyday center fielder, but in Cleveland all he had to do to win over the fanbase was not be Michael Bourn." This was and is true, but it missed a little something. A more accurate version: "… not be Michael Bourn and not get suspended 80 games for performance-enhancing drugs when the outfield is already a weak spot." Almonte continued to excel at being a human who is not Michael Bourn in 2016, but he failed at that second task. In the half of the season he *did* play, he regressed from his hot 2015 and was the solidly middle-of-the-road accessory option he was expected to be. And that is just about what he should be in 2017.

Will Benson RF

Born: 6/16/98   Age: 19   Bats: L   Throws: L   Height: 6'5"   Weight: 225   Entered Pro Ball: Round 1, 2016 Draft (#14 overall)

YEAR	TEAM	LVL	AGE	PA	R	2B	3B	HR	RBI	BB	K	SB	CS	AVG/OBP/SLG	TAv	VORP	BABIP	BRR	FRAA	WARP
2017	*CLE*	*MLB*	*19*	*250*	*24*	*9*	*1*	*7*	*26*	*17*	*93*	*4*	*1*	*.188/.249/.322*	*.192*	*-10.2*	*.277*	*0.1*	*RF -0*	*-1.1*
2018	*CLE*	*MLB*	*20*	*337*	*38*	*13*	*1*	*11*	*38*	*25*	*117*	*6*	*2*	*.209/.273/.365*	*.217*	*-7.5*	*.293*	*0.4*	*RF 0*	*-0.8*

Breakout: 0%   Improve: 5%   Collapse: 1%   Attrition: 4%   MLB: 9%   *Comparables: Nomar Mazara, Domingo Santana, Engel Beltre*

Benson chose to sign below slot as a first-round pick, choosing a future with Cleveland over the opportunity to play at Duke. This means he'll miss out on the Gothic Wonderland of the campus architecture and the fact that the school holds the largest lemur population outside of Madagascar, but he could have one hell of a future regardless. The toolsy outfielder has a ton of upside, thanks to plenty of raw power and a strong arm. Plus the kid is 6-foot-6 and *built*. Who needs lemurs when you've got potential like this?

Bobby Bradley 1B

Born: 5/29/96   Age: 21   Bats: L   Throws: R   Height: 6'1"   Weight: 225   Entered Pro Ball: Round 3, 2014 Draft (#97 overall)

YEAR	TEAM	LVL	AGE	PA	R	2B	3B	HR	RBI	BB	K	SB	CS	AVG/OBP/SLG	TAv	VORP	BABIP	BRR	FRAA	WARP
2015	LKC	A	19	465	62	15	4	27	92	56	148	3	0	.269/.361/.529	.314	28.1	.352	-2.1	1B(101): 4.8	3.5
2016	LYN	A+	20	572	82	23	1	29	102	75	170	3	0	.235/.344/.466	.288	23.4	.293	0.2	1B(116): -5.6	1.8
2017	*CLE*	*MLB*	*21*	*250*	*31*	*9*	*1*	*13*	*37*	*25*	*90*	*0*	*0*	*.217/.299/.441*	*.245*	*0.9*	*.289*	*-0.3*	*1B -1*	*0.0*
2018	*CLE*	*MLB*	*22*	*430*	*61*	*17*	*1*	*23*	*65*	*44*	*152*	*0*	*0*	*.226/.311/.459*	*.253*	*1.4*	*.301*	*-0.9*	*1B -1*	*0.0*

Breakout: 4%   Improve: 19%   Collapse: 8%   Attrition: 12%   MLB: 34%   *Comparables: Miguel Sano, Matt Olson, Travis Snider*

Bradley was the Carolina League's Three True Outcomes poster child in 2016. First in home runs, first in walks and tied for second in strikeouts; nearly half of his plate appearances (48 percent) ended in one of the three. His own true outcome will likely be hindered by limited defensive ability (he improved his play at first last year, but it's still not a pretty sight) and those many, many strikeouts. But those red flags aside, the power is real and so is the plate discipline, and the kid's still not even 21.

Michael Brantley LF

Born: 5/15/87   Age: 30   Bats: L   Throws: L   Height: 6'2"   Weight: 200   Entered Pro Ball: Round 7, 2005 Draft (#205 overall)

YEAR	TEAM	LVL	AGE	PA	R	2B	3B	HR	RBI	BB	K	SB	CS	AVG/OBP/SLG	TAv	VORP	BABIP	BRR	FRAA	WARP
2014	CLE	MLB	27	676	94	45	2	20	97	52	56	23	1	.327/.385/.506	.320	57.7	.333	5.1	LF(107): -2.4 • CF(46): -0.1	6.1
2015	CLE	MLB	28	596	68	45	0	15	84	60	51	15	1	.310/.379/.480	.294	28.9	.318	-3.2	LF(101): 3.3 • CF(28): -3.9	3.0
2016	CLE	MLB	29	43	5	2	0	0	7	3	6	1	0	.231/.279/.282	.207	-1.0	.265	0.4	LF(11): 0.3	-0.1
2016	AKR	AA	29	21	1	1	0	0	1	2	1	0	0	.211/.286/.263	.244	-0.1	.222	-0.2	LF(6): 1.1	0.1
2017	*CLE*	*MLB*	*30*	*495*	*59*	*31*	*2*	*12*	*58*	*42*	*48*	*13*	*1*	*.301/.360/.455*	*.277*	*23.4*	*.312*	*1.5*	*LF 0*	*2.4*
2018	*CLE*	*MLB*	*31*	*287*	*36*	*18*	*1*	*8*	*35*	*23*	*29*	*7*	*1*	*.295/.353/.458*	*.267*	*9.1*	*.305*	*0.1*	*LF 0*	*1.0*

Breakout: 0%   Improve: 36%   Collapse: 2%   Attrition: 6%   MLB: 98%   *Comparables: Gregg Jefferies, Mike Greenwell, Dale Mitchell*

Two months after Brantley had shoulder surgery in the winter of 2016, an exhibit on suspended animation opened at the Smithsonian Institution's Hirshhorn Museum: art exploring the subject of dormancy without death. Brantley's season entered suspended animation shortly thereafter. He began the season on the disabled list, but was supposed to be back in just a few weeks. Then a few weeks more. Then he *was* back, but only briefly, and a far cry from the well-rounded talent that made him Cleveland's best position player in years prior. He went back to the DL for what was meant to be just a little more rest, but then came a diagnosis of biceps tendonitis, followed by a surgery to clean up scar tissue in July—with promises that his season wasn't over. At least until another shoulder surgery in August officially ended his year and saddled him with several months of recovery to come. The museum's suspended animation exhibit is set to close in March. Whether Brantley's 2017 escapes the suspended animation of 2016 and allows him to return to form is still in question, but Cleveland hopes his talent was only dormant.

Ulysses Cantu   1B

Born: 5/1/98   Age: 19   Bats: R   Throws: R   Height: 5'11"   Weight: 220   Entered Pro Ball: Round 6, 2016 Draft (#182 overall)

YEAR	TEAM	LVL	AGE	PA	R	2B	3B	HR	RBI	BB	K	SB	CS	AVG/OBP/SLG	TAv	VORP	BABIP	BRR	FRAA	WARP
2017	CLE	MLB	19	250	20	9	0	5	24	15	92	1	0	.187/.240/.301	.181	-15.4	.276	-0.4	1B -0, 3B 0	-1.7
2018	CLE	MLB	20	302	31	11	1	8	30	20	106	1	0	.204/.261/.333	.204	-13.8	.292	-0.5	1B 0, 3B 0	-1.5

Breakout: 0%   Improve: 6%   Collapse: 2%   Attrition: 5%   MLB: 11%   *Comparables: Nomar Mazara, Francisco Pena, Raul Mondesi*

I was committed to Texas Tech yes when they thought I might not sign and how Cleveland drafted me in the sixth round and I thought well as well them as another and then they asked me yes to say yes to convert from third base to first (though my bat and power potential were why they'd wanted me, anyways) and first I went to the Arizona League and struggled a bit but yes I said yes I will Yes

Yu-Cheng Chang   SS

Born: 8/18/95   Age: 21   Bats: R   Throws: R   Height: 6'1"   Weight: 175   Entered Pro Ball: International Free Agent, 2013

YEAR	TEAM	LVL	AGE	PA	R	2B	3B	HR	RBI	BB	K	SB	CS	AVG/OBP/SLG	TAv	VORP	BABIP	BRR	FRAA	WARP
2015	LKC	A	19	440	52	16	4	9	52	27	103	5	6	.232/.293/.361	.260	20.1	.288	2.8	SS(99): 11.2	3.3
2016	LYN	A+	20	477	78	30	8	13	70	45	110	11	3	.259/.332/.463	.285	35.1	.316	2.9	SS(104): 0.2	3.6
2017	CLE	MLB	21	250	25	11	2	8	30	15	73	2	1	.224/.276/.392	.222	1.5	.284	-0.2	SS 3, 2B 0	0.4
2018	CLE	MLB	22	408	48	19	3	14	51	28	116	3	1	.232/.291/.415	.236	3.6	.291	-0.4	SS 4	0.8

Breakout: 3%   Improve: 7%   Collapse: 1%   Attrition: 8%   MLB: 12%   *Comparables: Nick Franklin, Trevor Story, Eugenio Suarez*

Chang doesn't have a great chance of sticking at shortstop. He's not bad there, but Cleveland has plenty of minor-league talent at the position and an (exceptionally) attractive long-term option already with the club. But he *does* have a great chance of becoming the first Taiwanese position player to get more than a pot of coffee in the major leagues (Chin-Feng Chen played 19 games across four seasons with the Dodgers a decade ago). After struggling a bit in the Midwest League during his first full season, Chang moved up to High-A in 2016 and flourished. He profiles just fine at third, though his bat fits the expectations of short better than those of the hot corner, and it's likely that's where he ends up sticking long term.

Lonnie Chisenhall   RF

Born: 10/4/88   Age: 28   Bats: L   Throws: R   Height: 6'2"   Weight: 190   Entered Pro Ball: Round 1, 2008 Draft (#29 overall)

YEAR	TEAM	LVL	AGE	PA	R	2B	3B	HR	RBI	BB	K	SB	CS	AVG/OBP/SLG	TAv	VORP	BABIP	BRR	FRAA	WARP
2014	CLE	MLB	25	533	62	29	1	13	59	39	99	3	1	.280/.343/.427	.278	21.3	.328	-1.8	3B(114): -9.3 • 1B(11): -0.7	1.3
2015	COH	AAA	26	171	18	13	0	3	21	11	35	1	0	.280/.329/.420	.256	2.0	.342	-2.0	3B(32): -1.4 • RF(4): 1.2	0.2
2015	CLE	MLB	26	362	38	19	1	7	44	23	69	4	1	.246/.294/.372	.238	2.5	.288	1.6	RF(51): 5.6 • 3B(50): 2.6	1.1
2016	CLE	MLB	27	418	43	25	5	8	57	23	70	6	0	.286/.328/.439	.260	7.5	.328	-0.3	RF(118): 0.4 • 1B(3): -0.0	0.8
2017	CLE	MLB	28	369	41	21	2	10	43	24	70	3	1	.268/.319/.433	.255	7.0	.305	-0.1	RF 5	1.0
2018	CLE	MLB	29	403	50	23	1	13	51	27	78	3	1	.270/.324/.445	.253	5.0	.307	-0.4	RF 5	1.1

Breakout: 1%   Improve: 49%   Collapse: 9%   Attrition: 20%   MLB: 90%   *Comparables: Domonic Brown, Xavier Nady, Angel Pagan*

To use the framework set by Oscar Wilde when he wrote "consistency is the hallmark of the unimaginative," Chisenhall has a remarkable imagination—though it was a little less remarkable than usual in 2016. After back-to-back seasons in which his OPS swung by several hundred points between the first and second halves, Chisenhall saw a comparatively moderate change between his hot first half (.819 OPS) and cooler second (.703). The result was stronger offense in 2015, but not quite as strong as in 2014, fitting an imaginatively inconsistent big picture. Defense only helped sketch in the details there. Chisenhall was still far more valuable in right field than he'd been in his years as a third baseman, but wasn't quite as dazzling as he'd initially looked when switching to the outfield in the summer of 2015. That it's not his natural position was occasionally clear (see: tripping and falling in a sad misplay in Game 2 of the World Series), but he was a perfectly solid option for an outfield that didn't have many of those.

Coco Crisp   CF

Born: 11/1/79   Age: 37   Bats: B   Throws: R   Height: 5'10"   Weight: 185   Entered Pro Ball: Round 7, 1999 Draft (#222 overall)

YEAR	TEAM	LVL	AGE	PA	R	2B	3B	HR	RBI	BB	K	SB	CS	AVG/OBP/SLG	TAv	VORP	BABIP	BRR	FRAA	WARP
2014	OAK	MLB	34	536	68	21	3	9	47	66	66	19	5	.246/.336/.363	.282	25.7	.266	0.4	CF(111): -19.2	0.7
2015	STO	A+	35	31	6	1	0	2	4	4	3	0	0	.222/.323/.481	.277	1.7	.182	0.6	LF(5): 0.2	0.2
2015	OAK	MLB	35	139	11	6	0	0	6	13	25	2	0	.175/.252/.222	.176	-7.0	.218	1.5	LF(37): -2.8	-1.0
2016	OAK	MLB	36	434	45	24	4	11	47	37	65	7	5	.234/.299/.399	.253	7.4	.254	0.0	LF(58): -2.4 • CF(36): -2.9	0.2
2016	CLE	MLB	36	64	9	3	0	2	8	9	13	3	0	.208/.323/.377	.255	1.7	.237	0.7	LF(13): -0.6	0.1
2017	CLE	MLB	37	400	54	19	2	11	42	41	59	10	4	.255/.330/.422	.250	10.2	.271	0.4	LF -0, CF -4	0.7
2018	CLE	MLB	38	336	41	16	2	9	38	37	51	8	3	.249/.329/.401	.247	4.4	.269	0.6	LF 0, CF -3	0.1

Breakout: 1%   Improve: 34%   Collapse: 12%   Attrition: 20%   MLB: 79%   *Comparables: Tim Raines, Dave Roberts, Mark Kotsay*

Oakland seemed ready to put Crisp behind them for the last year of his contract after an atrociously bad 2015. There was just one problem: Crisp rebounded pretty nicely, enough so that he accused the A's of benching him just to keep him from milestones that were in his contract as extra-pay incentives. But the story had a happy ending, or at least as happy an ending as a 36-year-old outfielder can get. Traded to Cleveland for the last month of the season, Crisp bolstered an outfield that had been seriously lacking in depth, and even notched the game-winning single in Game 3 of the World Series. Meanwhile, as Crisp enjoyed October baseball, the A's were at home in a Twitter feud with 90s band Smash Mouth that started with a snide remark about Crisp's contract. Certainly no longer an All-Star, but he got his game on and got paid all the same.

Rajai Davis   LF

Born: 10/19/80 Age: 36 Bats: R Throws: R Height: 5'10" Weight: 195 Entered Pro Ball: Round 38, 2001 Draft (#1134 overall)

YEAR	TEAM	LVL	AGE	PA	R	2B	3B	HR	RBI	BB	K	SB	CS	AVG/OBP/SLG	TAv	VORP	BABIP	BRR	FRAA	WARP
2014	DET	MLB	33	494	64	27	2	8	51	22	75	36	11	.282/.320/.401	.263	17.4	.320	4.8	LF(99): 0.8 • CF(48): -1.5	1.9
2015	DET	MLB	34	370	55	16	11	8	30	22	76	18	8	.258/.306/.440	.263	11.0	.308	0.9	CF(46): -1.0 • LF(39): -2.0	0.8
2016	CLE	MLB	35	495	74	23	2	12	48	33	106	43	6	.249/.306/.388	.238	6.3	.299	3.7	CF(80): 0.5 • LF(66): 1.5	0.9
2017	CLE	MLB	36	440	61	21	3	9	38	26	90	31	7	.256/.306/.391	.233	6.0	.305	2.4	CF 1, LF 2	1.0
2018	CLE	MLB	37	400	42	19	2	8	40	24	83	26	7	.246/.297/.372	.228	0.0	.294	2.9	CF 1, LF 1	0.3

Breakout: 2%   Improve: 30%   Collapse: 7%   Attrition: 23%   MLB: 77%   *Comparables: Frank Baumholtz, Bill Bruton, Reed Johnson*

Davis was nearly a hero. Game 7 of the World Series, down three in the bottom of the eighth, two on and two outs with one of baseball's most dominant closers on the mound—and he delivered, with a three-run shot to tie the game. But Cleveland went on to lose in extra innings, and so Davis became a footnote rather than a headliner. Whether acts of greatness like this get to retain any of that greatness in a vacuum, future events notwithstanding, is maybe a little too deep of a philosophical question to get into here. Either way, Davis showed that he's aging fairly gracefully, playing capable defense in the outfield and becoming only the eighth 35-year-old ever to steal more bases than his age.

Yandy Diaz   3B

Born: 8/8/91 Age: 25 Bats: R Throws: R Height: 6'2" Weight: 185 Entered Pro Ball: International Free Agent, 2013

YEAR	TEAM	LVL	AGE	PA	R	2B	3B	HR	RBI	BB	K	SB	CS	AVG/OBP/SLG	TAv	VORP	BABIP	BRR	FRAA	WARP
2014	CAR	A+	22	338	42	7	5	2	37	49	35	3	3	.286/.396/.367	.293	24.0	.320	0.6	3B(74): -2.3	2.2
2015	AKR	AA	23	564	61	13	5	7	55	78	65	8	7	.315/.412/.408	.306	40.2	.350	-2.3	3B(122): -9.8	3.3
2016	AKR	AA	24	110	13	0	1	2	14	24	16	6	2	.286/.445/.381	.324	9.5	.328	-0.7	3B(22): -1.0 • 2B(1): -0.0	0.9
2016	COH	AAA	24	416	53	22	3	7	44	47	70	5	1	.325/.399/.461	.300	28.9	.381	2.1	3B(30): -0.8 • RF(28): 2.1	3.4
2017	CLE	MLB	25	34	4	1	0	1	4	4	6	0	0	.275/.366/.415	.273	1.4	.323	0.0	3B -1	0.1
2018	CLE	MLB	26	238	31	9	2	6	27	30	44	2	1	.276/.367/.423	.266	6.4	.322	-0.2	3B -4	0.3

Breakout: 1%   Improve: 13%   Collapse: 13%   Attrition: 34%   MLB: 53%   *Comparables: Brad Emaus, Zelous Wheeler, Jermaine Curtis*

After his 2015 debut at Triple-A was a fairly underwhelming cup of coffee, Diaz answered in 2016 with the equivalent of a very good pot of coffee and some nice hearty breakfasts to match. Like bacon, and biscuits and perfectly poached eggs that ooze in the most glorious way when you cut into them with your fork. Not award-winning brunches at a fancy restaurant or anything, but the added power and improvements at the plate nicely complemented his outstanding defense, and chances are good that the Cuban-born prospect shows up in Cleveland this year.

Edwin Encarnacion   1B

Born: 1/7/83 Age: 34 Bats: R Throws: R Height: 6'1" Weight: 230 Entered Pro Ball: Round 9, 2000 Draft (#274 overall)

YEAR	TEAM	LVL	AGE	PA	R	2B	3B	HR	RBI	BB	K	SB	CS	AVG/OBP/SLG	TAv	VORP	BABIP	BRR	FRAA	WARP
2014	TOR	MLB	31	542	75	27	2	34	98	62	82	2	0	.268/.354/.547	.310	30.4	.260	-0.1	1B(80): -5.3 • LF(2): -0.1	2.8
2015	TOR	MLB	32	624	94	31	0	39	111	77	98	3	2	.277/.372/.557	.324	43.5	.267	-1.6	1B(59): 0.1	4.7
2016	TOR	MLB	33	702	99	34	0	42	127	87	138	2	0	.263/.357/.529	.291	28.7	.270	-0.4	1B(75): -2.9	2.7
2017	CLE	MLB	34	608	87	28	1	35	99	76	97	3	1	.268/.363/.523	.302	36.3	.265	-1.0	1B -1	3.6
2018	CLE	MLB	35	581	91	25	1	33	96	71	95	1	0	.266/.361/.522	.290	29.2	.264	-0.6	1B -1	3.0

Breakout: 1%   Improve: 28%   Collapse: 2%   Attrition: 2%   MLB: 96%   *Comparables: Lance Berkman, Albert Pujols, Mark Teixeira*

Only 142 players in baseball history have had a season in which they hit 40 or more home runs, and only 32 of those players had one of those seasons at age 33 or older. After surpassing the 40-homer mark in 2016, Encarnacion is now one of the 32. Home Run Tracker on-line labelled 20 of his 42 home runs as no doubters, meaning they didn't just clear the fence, they flew way beyond it. Edwin had five more no-doubt home runs than Nelson Cruz and Mark Trumbo; the two next best hitters in that category. He's also now led the league in that statistic three years running. Yet, there's this aura around Encarnacion and other DHs; there seems to be a subconscious feeling that they could crash and burn at any moment. It makes some sense, as they only contribute on one side of the ball, but Encarnacion has also been one of the most consistent hitters over the last five seasons. It's hard to imagine him flailing anytime soon.

Chris Gimenez   C

Born: 12/27/82 Age: 34 Bats: R Throws: R Height: 6'2" Weight: 230 Entered Pro Ball: Round 19, 2004 Draft (#557 overall)

YEAR	TEAM	LVL	AGE	PA	R	2B	3B	HR	RBI	BB	K	SB	CS	AVG/OBP/SLG	TAv	VORP	BABIP	BRR	FRAA	WARP
2014	TEX	MLB	31	118	13	10	0	0	11	11	26	0	1	.262/.331/.355	.248	3.1	.346	0.0	C(26): 2.5 • 1B(5): -0.2	0.6
2014	ROU	AAA	31	156	18	4	2	6	22	19	30	0	1	.284/.365/.478	.293	10.5	.317	0.0	C(18): -1.5 • 1B(14): -0.5	0.9
2014	CLE	MLB	31	10	0	0	0	0	0	1	3	0	0	.000/.100/.000	.068	-1.7	.000	0.0	1B(5): -0.2 • C(2): -0.1	-0.2
2015	ROU	AAA	32	277	28	10	0	6	33	24	62	2	0	.243/.315/.356	.254	3.0	.298	-2.3	C(26): 0.5 • 1B(20): -1.1	0.3
2015	TEX	MLB	32	113	19	6	1	5	14	10	19	2	0	.255/.330/.490	.279	7.1	.270	0.1	C(36): 0.3	0.8
2016	FRI	AA	33	29	3	0	0	1	4	3	8	0	0	.240/.345/.360	.244	0.2	.313	-0.3	C(5): 0.2	0.0
2016	CLE	MLB	33	155	17	4	0	4	11	10	41	0	0	.216/.272/.331	.206	-2.4	.274	-1.0	C(59): -2.6 • 1B(4): -0.0	-0.6
2017	CLE	MLB	34	250	27	11	0	6	26	24	58	1	0	.240/.317/.375	.233	5.0	.291	-0.2	C -3, 1B -0	0.2
2018	CLE	MLB	35	221	25	9	0	4	21	23	50	0	0	.225/.313/.343	.226	-0.3	.273	-0.3	C -3, 1B 0	-0.4

Breakout: 2%   Improve: 21%   Collapse: 7%   Attrition: 33%   MLB: 66%   *Comparables: Corky Miller, Shawn Wooten, Chris Coste*

The very dumb, very human phenomenon of returning again and again to things that are bad for you is well-documented. A little less well-documented is the equally dumb and equally human phenomenon of returning again and again to things that aren't quite bad for you, but certainly aren't good for you; not out of desire or devotion but out of simple convenience and familiarity. This is the sandwich place you keep going to not because you like it but because it is cheap and you know what to order or the old acquaintance you keep getting drinks with not because you enjoy their company but because you know exactly what to expect and you do not have to try. Cleveland signed Gimenez for the third time in six years in May after he was designated for assignment by Texas.

YEAR	TEAM	P. COUNT	FRM RUNS	BLK RUNS	THRW RUNS	TOT RUNS
2014	ROU	2563	-2.2	0.0	1.1	-1.1
2014	TEX	3591	2.9	-1.1	-0.1	1.7
2014	TEX	3591	2.9	-1.1	-0.1	1.7
2014	CLE	61	0.0	0.0	0.0	0.0
2015	ROU	3578	0.4	0.1	0.1	0.6
2015	TEX	4512	0.4	-0.5	-0.6	-0.6
2016	CLE	6271	-3.1	0.4	-0.2	-2.9
2016	CLE	6271	-3.1	0.4	-0.2	-2.9
2017	CLE	9021	-3.1	-0.4	-0.4	-3.8
2018	CLE	7987	-3.6	-0.4	-0.4	-4.4

Yan Gomes C

Born: 7/19/87   Age: 29   Bats: R   Throws: R   Height: 6'2"   Weight: 215   Entered Pro Ball: Round 10, 2009 Draft (#310 overall)

YEAR	TEAM	LVL	AGE	PA	R	2B	3B	HR	RBI	BB	K	SB	CS	AVG/OBP/SLG	TAv	VORP	BABIP	BRR	FRAA	WARP
2014	CLE	MLB	26	518	61	25	3	21	74	24	120	0	0	.278/.313/.472	.281	30.4	.326	-0.1	C(126): 13.2	4.8
2015	CLE	MLB	27	389	38	22	0	12	45	13	104	0	0	.231/.267/.391	.237	6.7	.285	-0.7	C(91): -3.1	0.4
2016	CLE	MLB	28	264	22	11	1	9	34	9	69	0	0	.167/.201/.327	.179	-7.4	.189	2.3	C(73): -6.9	-1.5
2017	CLE	MLB	29	375	41	20	1	14	47	20	92	0	0	.253/.298/.435	.249	14.1	.302	-0.7	C -3	1.3
2018	CLE	MLB	30	334	41	17	1	13	44	18	84	0	0	.253/.300/.438	.245	7.2	.302	0.2	C -3	0.4

Breakout: 3%   Improve: 37%   Collapse: 5%   Attrition: 11%   MLB: 97%   *Comparables: Nick Hundley, Ryan Doumit, J.P. Arencibia*

"We have prepared this exorcism to honor thy holiness and to absolve Yan Gomes of any wrongdoing that he may have committed towards thee. We urge you to forgive his obsession with the octagon and bestow him with your guidance and grace on the diamond." This was read in Cleveland's locker room in July, part of a team ceremony designed to turn around Gomes' dreadful season by asking forgiveness from Jobu, the voodoo doll in *Major League*. A sacrificial rotisserie chicken was purchased, as were maracas, flowers, costumes and a piñata. And the very next day, Gomes got what looked like his first hit in two weeks——then he tripped and fell while running to first, separating his shoulder and sidelining him for more than two months. That moment represents the misery of Gomes' year better than any number can, but the sub-.190 TAv and sharp decline in his catching metrics help prove the point.

YEAR	TEAM	P. COUNT	FRM RUNS	BLK RUNS	THRW RUNS	TOT RUNS
2014	CLE	17511	9.8	3.6	2.4	15.8
2015	CLE	12205	-2.6	-0.5	0.0	-3.1
2015	COH	303	0.1	0.0	0.0	0.1
2016	CLE	9256	-5.6	-0.4	0.1	-5.9
2017	CLE	13229	-3.4	0.2	0.5	-2.7
2018	CLE	11781	-3.9	0.0	0.3	-3.6

Erik Gonzalez   SS

Born: 8/31/91   Age: 25   Bats: R   Throws: R   Height: 6'3"   Weight: 195   Entered Pro Ball: International Free Agent, 2008

YEAR	TEAM	LVL	AGE	PA	R	2B	3B	HR	RBI	BB	K	SB	CS	AVG/OBP/SLG	TAv	VORP	BABIP	BRR	FRAA	WARP
2014	CAR	A+	22	336	44	14	7	3	46	23	65	15	6	.289/.336/.409	.265	17.6	.355	1.3	SS(74): -3.2	1.5
2014	AKR	AA	22	136	21	6	3	1	16	7	23	6	1	.357/.390/.473	.292	12.8	.429	2.9	SS(30): -3.9	0.9
2015	AKR	AA	23	327	38	18	4	6	46	11	56	10	5	.280/.304/.421	.263	14.2	.321	0.5	SS(71): 4.1	2.0
2015	COH	AAA	23	261	32	6	3	3	23	15	47	8	2	.223/.277/.311	.221	2.3	.266	2.7	SS(62): 8.5	1.1
2016	COH	AAA	24	460	62	31	1	11	53	19	88	12	10	.296/.329/.450	.279	27.3	.349	0.5	SS(90): 0.3 • 2B(8): -1.5	2.7
2016	CLE	MLB	24	17	2	0	0	0	0	1	8	0	1	.313/.353/.313	.235	0.2	.625	0.1	SS(8): -0.0 • 2B(5): -0.1	0.0
2017	CLE	MLB	25	60	7	3	0	2	6	3	14	1	1	.259/.292/.408	.241	1.4	.316	0.0	SS 0	0.1
2018	CLE	MLB	26	319	37	16	2	9	38	16	75	7	4	.264/.302/.424	.243	5.6	.318	0.2	SS 2	0.9

Breakout: 3%   Improve: 21%   Collapse: 9%   Attrition: 28%   MLB: 46%   *Comparables: Trevor Plouffe, Charlie Culberson, Josh Wilson*

After faltering a bit during his transition to Triple-A in 2015, Gonzalez answered any questions about his talent by hitting the ball better than ever to start 2016. Unfortunately, there's still a question with the same answer it's always had: does he have a chance on a team that already employs Francisco Lindor? (Answer: LOL.) The glove-first prospect got his taste of the majors in late July and returned as a September call-up, but long-term opportunities for him in Cleveland look scarce. He did, however, finish his 21 games in the big leagues just one walk away from a perfect .312/.312/.312 line—which would have made him about 31.2 percent more interesting than he actually is.

Brandon Guyer   LF

Born: 1/28/86   Age: 31   Bats: R   Throws: R   Height: 6'2"   Weight: 200   Entered Pro Ball: Round 5, 2007 Draft (#157 overall)

YEAR	TEAM	LVL	AGE	PA	R	2B	3B	HR	RBI	BB	K	SB	CS	AVG/OBP/SLG	TAv	VORP	BABIP	BRR	FRAA	WARP
2014	DUR	AAA	28	26	8	2	2	0	1	6	4	0	0	.400/.538/.700	.395	4.5	.500	0.2	RF(1): 0.2 • LF(1): -0.0	0.5
2014	TBA	MLB	28	294	37	15	1	3	26	16	52	6	1	.266/.334/.367	.276	13.8	.322	3.5	LF(62): 0.2 • CF(11): -0.8	1.5
2015	TBA	MLB	29	385	51	21	2	8	28	25	61	10	4	.265/.359/.413	.279	17.1	.303	1.6	LF(60): 4.8 • RF(41): -3.8	1.8
2016	TBA	MLB	30	249	27	12	1	7	18	12	42	2	1	.241/.347/.406	.280	9.7	.268	-0.8	LF(25): 0.1 • CF(18): -0.4	0.9
2016	CLE	MLB	30	96	12	5	0	2	14	7	13	1	1	.333/.438/.469	.302	6.4	.379	0.2	LF(26): 2.1 • RF(7): 0.2	0.9
2017	CLE	MLB	31	263	31	14	1	6	29	17	44	4	2	.272/.352/.426	.271	11.8	.307	0.0	LF 3, RF -1	1.2
2018	CLE	MLB	32	219	27	11	1	5	24	15	38	3	1	.258/.347/.405	.257	5.1	.293	0.7	LF 3, RF 0	0.8

Breakout: 0%   Improve: 41%   Collapse: 5%   Attrition: 14%   MLB: 88%   *Comparables: Nate McLouth, Brett Gardner, Dale Mitchell*

Guyer is never going to lead baseball in hits. The career fourth outfielder presumably knows this, which is why he appears to have set his eyes on a different goal—leading baseball in *getting* hit. From 2014 to 2015, he more than doubled the times he was hit by a pitch, but those 24 HBPs left him in second place on the leaderboard at the end of the season. In 2016, Guyer blew everyone else away. He'd nearly matched last year's HBP total by the time he was traded to Cleveland at the deadline, and not only hit better than he had in Tampa, he got hit more. The result was 31 HBPs, the most baseball had seen in 20 years, even though his status as a backup meant less than a full season of play. This is what life coaches talk about when they say "effective goal setting."

Nolan Jones   3B

Born: 5/7/98   Age: 19   Bats: L   Throws: R   Height: 6'4"   Weight: 185   Entered Pro Ball: Round 2, 2016 Draft (#55 overall)

YEAR	TEAM	LVL	AGE	PA	R	2B	3B	HR	RBI	BB	K	SB	CS	AVG/OBP/SLG	TAv	VORP	BABIP	BRR	FRAA	WARP
2017	CLE	MLB	19	250	20	9	1	5	23	20	94	0	0	.183/.251/.291	.184	-11.3	.281	-0.4	3B 3, SS 0	-1.0
2018	CLE	MLB	20	315	33	11	1	7	30	28	113	1	0	.199/.272/.324	.206	-10.2	.296	-0.5	3B 3, SS 0	-0.8

Breakout: 0%   Improve: 7%   Collapse: 3%   Attrition: 7%   MLB: 13%   Comparables: Nomar Mazara, Raul Mondesi, Francisco Pena

Jones and his older brother Peyton were projected to be drafted in the same month: the former for baseball, the latter for hockey. But Nolan beat out his big brother here, as he was taken in MLB's second round while Peyton tumbled down the NHL boards and was forced to wait for next year. After being drafted, Jones converted from short to third (not too surprising, at 6-foot-4 and having recently bulked up a bit) and showed that his ceiling is high, with projectability both in the field and at the plate.

Jason Kipnis   2B

Born: 4/3/87   Age: 30   Bats: L   Throws: R   Height: 5'11"   Weight: 195   Entered Pro Ball: Round 2, 2009 Draft (#63 overall)

YEAR	TEAM	LVL	AGE	PA	R	2B	3B	HR	RBI	BB	K	SB	CS	AVG/OBP/SLG	TAv	VORP	BABIP	BRR	FRAA	WARP
2014	CLE	MLB	27	555	61	25	1	6	41	50	100	22	3	.240/.310/.330	.238	6.3	.288	4.6	2B(123): 11.8	2.0
2015	CLE	MLB	28	641	86	43	7	9	52	57	107	12	8	.303/.372/.451	.290	35.3	.356	0.9	2B(124): -5.6	3.2
2016	CLE	MLB	29	688	91	41	4	23	82	60	146	15	3	.275/.343/.469	.264	24.1	.324	3.0	2B(151): 10.7	3.6
2017	CLE	MLB	30	677	88	35	4	16	68	66	129	17	5	.271/.344/.424	.264	30.1	.316	0.8	2B 6	3.3
2018	CLE	MLB	31	558	70	29	3	15	66	57	111	12	4	.268/.346/.429	.259	18.2	.313	2.0	2B 5	2.5

Breakout: 0%   Improve: 52%   Collapse: 2%   Attrition: 4%   MLB: 92%   Comparables: Marcus Giles, Orlando Hudson, Neil Walker

Don't be fooled by the casual bro-y nature Kipnis projects on social media: the man is a master-level chess player. His 2016 power surge was no random spike, he claims; it was the result of carefully studying opposing pitchers and adjusting to their adjustments to him. "I use your guys' adjustments to my advantage and set up all of you over-thinkers," he boasted to the Cleveland Plain Dealer in August. Whatever he did, it seemed to work—he recorded a new career-high ISO and homered more in 2016 than he had in the previous two seasons combined. He's still among the best second basemen in baseball, and that's unlikely to change any time soon.

Francisco Lindor   SS

Born: 11/14/93   Age: 23   Bats: B   Throws: R   Height: 5'11"   Weight: 190   Entered Pro Ball: Round 1, 2011 Draft (#8 overall)

YEAR	TEAM	LVL	AGE	PA	R	2B	3B	HR	RBI	BB	K	SB	CS	AVG/OBP/SLG	TAv	VORP	BABIP	BRR	FRAA	WARP
2014	AKR	AA	20	387	51	12	4	6	48	40	61	25	9	.278/.352/.389	.273	20.9	.320	0.1	SS(88): 7.3	3.0
2014	COH	AAA	20	180	24	4	0	5	14	9	36	3	7	.273/.307/.388	.230	2.4	.317	0.7	SS(38): 2.5	0.5
2015	COH	AAA	21	262	26	11	5	2	22	25	38	9	7	.284/.350/.402	.271	13.6	.328	0.4	SS(56): -1.1	1.3
2015	CLE	MLB	21	438	50	22	4	12	51	27	69	12	2	.313/.353/.482	.286	27.7	.348	-0.6	SS(98): 3.4	3.3
2016	CLE	MLB	22	684	99	30	3	15	78	57	88	19	5	.301/.358/.435	.270	40.4	.324	5.5	SS(155): 19.4	6.2
2017	CLE	MLB	23	663	77	29	5	17	76	51	108	18	7	.286/.338/.434	.265	32.4	.316	0.8	SS 10	3.8
2018	CLE	MLB	24	609	79	27	4	18	76	52	99	17	7	.292/.353/.454	.267	26.6	.321	1.6	SS 9	3.9

Breakout: 5%   Improve: 52%   Collapse: 4%   Attrition: 15%   MLB: 98%   Comparables: J.J. Hardy, Xander Bogaerts, Ruben Tejada

If Francisco Lindor were your boyfriend, he would write down what he loved about you on little scraps of paper that he'd hide around the house for you to find. Tiny notes in his boyish scrawl, folded up in cabinets or desk drawers or under your pillow. You'd bring them up, and he'd grin and say that he didn't know what you were talking about. If Francisco Lindor were your doctor, you'd find yourself wishing to get sick just so you could see him. If Francisco Lindor were your coworker, he'd make you want to care about work. He wouldn't take anything too seriously, but he'd be earnest without being cheesy, and he'd always find something interesting in even the most mundane projects. Sometimes, while talking on the phone or filling out a spreadsheet, he'd twirl a pencil between his fingers in smooth figure-eights. You'd try it once and drop the pencil and look like an idiot. If Francisco Lindor were your neighbor, he'd always know the perfect time to invite you over for a beer. He would never be unnecessarily loud, and he would always stay home to sign for your UPS packages. If Francisco Lindor were your shortstop, he would be perfect.

Michael Martinez   UT

Born: 9/16/82   Age: 34   Bats: B   Throws: R   Height: 5'9"   Weight: 180   Entered Pro Ball: International Free Agent, 2005

YEAR	TEAM	LVL	AGE	PA	R	2B	3B	HR	RBI	BB	K	SB	CS	AVG/OBP/SLG	TAv	VORP	BABIP	BRR	FRAA	WARP
2014	PIT	MLB	31	44	2	1	0	0	2	4	13	0	0	.128/.209/.154	.148	-4.3	.192	-0.8	2B(6): -0.7 • LF(6): -0.4	-0.6
2014	IND	AAA	31	361	34	6	6	1	32	29	46	7	4	.244/.303/.311	.219	-2.9	.275	2.1	2B(55): 0.2 • SS(22): 0.9	-0.2
2015	COH	AAA	32	401	53	24	5	5	42	32	60	11	3	.289/.344/.424	.270	17.7	.332	2.3	2B(66): -4.6 • CF(19): -0.6	1.7
2015	CLE	MLB	32	32	7	2	0	0	2	1	12	0	1	.267/.290/.333	.255	0.1	.444	-0.4	LF(9): 0.3 • CF(2): 0.0	0.0
2016	COH	AAA	33	114	12	8	1	2	12	9	21	2	2	.288/.351/.442	.270	4.7	.346	0.0	2B(14): -0.1 • SS(6): 0.8	0.5
2016	BOS	MLB	33	7	1	0	0	0	0	1	2	0	0	.167/.286/.167	.175	-1.4	.250	-0.9	RF(2): -0.3 • SS(1): -0.0	-0.2
2016	CLE	MLB	33	99	15	4	0	1	4	3	21	0	2	.242/.265/.316	.196	-3.3	.301	0.4	2B(21): -0.7 • CF(11): -0.7	-0.6
2017	CLE	MLB	34	60	6	2	0	1	5	4	12	1	1	.241/.284/.351	.218	-0.4	.286	-0.1	2B -0	-0.1
2018	CLE	MLB	35	168	17	7	1	3	16	10	35	2	1	.240/.286/.352	.217	-2.4	.285	-0.1	2B -1	-0.4

Breakout: 2%   Improve: 22%   Collapse: 8%   Attrition: 29%   MLB: 52%   Comparables: Matt Kata, Nick Green, Keith Ginter

Martinez's selling point has always been that he can play just about every position; the catch is that he can play none of them particularly well, and this has only become truer as he's grown older. But a funny thing happened on the way to what seemed a certain descent into total irrelevance and out of the major leagues. Terry Francona fell for the utility man's sheer versatility, with a love apparently unconditional enough to forgive his sins at the plate and mediocrity in the field—and Martinez ended up seeing more game action than he had since his rookie year in 2011. Traded to the Red Sox at midseason for cash, he languished on the bench before being designated for assignment a month later, and Cleveland snapped him right back up. And that's the story of how Martinez and his sub-.200 TAv came to the plate in the extra innings of Game 7 of the World Series.

Francisco Mejia   C

Born: 10/27/95 Age: 21   Bats: B   Throws: R   Height: 5'10"   Weight: 175   Entered Pro Ball: International Free Agent, 2012

YEAR	TEAM	LVL	AGE	PA	R	2B	3B	HR	RBI	BB	K	SB	CS	AVG/OBP/SLG	TAv	VORP	BABIP	BRR	FRAA	WARP
2014	MHV	A-	18	274	32	17	4	2	36	18	47	2	4	.282/.339/.407	.277	15.3	.337	0.0	C(52): 2.2	1.8
2015	LKC	A	19	446	45	13	0	9	53	38	78	4	1	.243/.324/.345	.259	15.1	.281	-1.8	C(94): 4.5	2.1
2016	LKC	A	20	259	41	17	3	7	51	15	39	1	0	.347/.384/.531	.328	29.7	.388	2.3	C(52): 1.3	3.4
2016	LYN	A+	20	184	22	12	1	4	29	13	24	1	2	.333/.380/.488	.308	16.8	.366	-0.1	C(35): 0.5	1.8
2017	CLE	MLB	21	250	25	12	1	8	30	14	57	0	0	.250/.296/.405	.232	4.7	.297	-0.4	C 0	0.6
2018	CLE	MLB	22	320	38	15	1	10	39	18	72	0	0	.258/.307/.419	.242	5.2	.306	-0.7	C 0	0.6

Breakout: 3%   Improve: 9%   Collapse: 0%   Attrition: 9%   MLB: 16%   Comparables: Travis d'Arnaud, Austin Romine, Christian Vazquez

Prior editions of this book have warned you not to fall in love with Mejia. A catcher who graduates rookie-ball as a teenager is alluring ("sure looks like a dime," we said in 2014), but pinning your affections on him is just too risky (gird your inflamed "prospect loins," we said in 2015). But Mejia's 2016 season made it impossible for you *not* to love him, and in the process of doing so, took away essentially all risk involved in falling for him. The switch-hitter showed more power than he ever has, continued to show off his strong arm behind the plate and oh, yeah, put together a 50-game hitting streak. He might not be in Cleveland for a while yet, but go ahead and buy that Valentine's Day card.

YEAR	TEAM	P. COUNT	FRM RUNS	BLK RUNS	THRW RUNS	TOT RUNS
2017	CLE	8812	0.0	0.0	0.0	0.0
2018	CLE	11288	0.0	0.0	0.0	0.0

Mike Napoli   1B

Born: 10/31/81 Age: 35   Bats: R   Throws: R   Height: 6'1"   Weight: 225   Entered Pro Ball: Round 17, 2000 Draft (#500 overall)

YEAR	TEAM	LVL	AGE	PA	R	2B	3B	HR	RBI	BB	K	SB	CS	AVG/OBP/SLG	TAv	VORP	BABIP	BRR	FRAA	WARP
2014	BOS	MLB	32	500	49	20	0	17	55	78	133	3	2	.248/.370/.419	.295	19.2	.321	-1.8	1B(110): -0.1	2.1
2015	BOS	MLB	33	378	37	18	1	13	40	45	99	3	1	.207/.307/.386	.247	-1.1	.252	-0.1	1B(96): 5.2	0.4
2015	TEX	MLB	33	91	9	2	0	5	10	12	19	0	2	.295/.396/.513	.318	6.3	.333	-0.3	1B(15): 0.6 • LF(11): -1.2	0.6
2016	CLE	MLB	34	645	92	22	1	34	101	78	194	5	1	.239/.335/.465	.262	4.7	.296	-3.4	1B(98): 3.4	0.8
2017	CLE	MLB	35	571	73	23	1	25	80	74	170	4	2	.236/.341/.442	.265	12.8	.303	-1.6	1B 2	1.6
2018	CLE	MLB	36	423	57	16	0	18	55	50	124	2	1	.223/.321/.415	.249	-0.3	.282	-1.2	1B 1	0.1

Breakout: 1%   Improve: 22%   Collapse: 9%   Attrition: 10%   MLB: 90%   Comparables: Carlos Pena, Ryan Howard, Mickey Tettleton

"Party at Napoli's" became a rallying cry for Cleveland last year, emblazoned on t-shirts and scattered across social media. But like many a party Napoli's year had far more flash than substance, as a career-high and team-leading 34 home runs came with an otherwise mediocre year at the plate. The health problems that have dogged him in the past didn't play much of a role, but that degenerative hip condition of his is not something that just goes away on its own. Napoli's now in the back half of his 30s, and so the party's closer to cleaning up than setting up. But while it lasts, it can still be a hell of a lot of fun to watch. Who, after all, can forget Napoli pleading with Cleveland's GM for a little detour to Vegas after winning the pennant?

Tyler Naquin   CF

Born: 4/24/91 Age: 26   Bats: L   Throws: R   Height: 6'2"   Weight: 195   Entered Pro Ball: Round 1, 2012 Draft (#15 overall)

YEAR	TEAM	LVL	AGE	PA	R	2B	3B	HR	RBI	BB	K	SB	CS	AVG/OBP/SLG	TAv	VORP	BABIP	BRR	FRAA	WARP
2014	AKR	AA	23	341	54	12	5	4	30	29	71	14	3	.313/.371/.424	.290	20.6	.389	-0.1	CF(73): 4.0 • RF(1): 0.1	2.6
2015	AKR	AA	24	160	16	12	1	1	10	15	24	7	1	.348/.419/.468	.336	15.5	.410	-1.4	CF(33): 1.6	1.9
2015	COH	AAA	24	218	34	13	0	6	17	25	49	6	2	.263/.353/.430	.269	9.2	.323	0.8	CF(47): 2.2	1.2
2016	COH	AAA	25	79	6	3	1	1	8	8	15	1	2	.286/.354/.400	.288	3.1	.345	-1.6	CF(15): 1.2 • RF(2): -0.1	0.4
2016	CLE	MLB	25	365	52	18	5	14	43	36	112	6	3	.296/.372/.514	.285	18.0	.411	-2.3	CF(105): -7.5 • RF(4): -0.3	1.1
2017	CLE	MLB	26	490	59	23	4	14	55	45	133	9	4	.264/.336/.428	.261	14.9	.344	0.1	CF -2, RF -1	0.9
2018	CLE	MLB	27	497	63	24	3	14	60	49	133	9	4	.264/.342/.433	.256	9.7	.343	-1.5	CF -2, RF -1	0.7

Breakout: 9%   Improve: 46%   Collapse: 12%   Attrition: 21%   MLB: 79%   Comparables: Curtis Granderson, Kirk Nieuwenhuis, Wladimir Balentie

Expectations for Naquin before his major-league debut were nothing extreme, as most accounts had him pegged as a proto-typically boring fourth outfielder. Yet the story of his season is most clear only through extremes. An incredibly hot summer (.343/.425/.731 in June and July, even though he'd never been known for his bat) was strong enough to put him in the Rookie of the Year conversation. And then a cool descent into the fall crystallized in not one, but two heart-wrenching moments in the World Series—a terrible outfield misplay, followed by a strikeout with the bases loaded that effectively killed Cleveland's chances of taking Game 6. Naquin ended up on the bench for Game 7, maybe a lower extreme than his very public failings the night before. So what's next? Cleveland would settle for something between the poles, and that's likely what's coming.

Roberto Perez   C

Born: 12/23/88   Age: 28   Bats: R   Throws: R   Height: 5'11"   Weight: 220   Entered Pro Ball: Round 33, 2008 Draft (#1011 overall)

YEAR	TEAM	LVL	AGE	PA	R	2B	3B	HR	RBI	BB	K	SB	CS	AVG/OBP/SLG	TAv	VORP	BABIP	BRR	FRAA	WARP
2014	COH	AAA	25	209	29	11	1	8	43	29	51	1	0	.305/.405/.517	.296	17.3	.388	-1.2	C(53): 17.0	3.4
2014	CLE	MLB	25	95	10	5	0	1	4	5	26	0	0	.271/.311/.365	.244	1.0	.379	-1.5	C(29): 2.3	0.4
2015	CLE	MLB	26	226	30	9	1	7	21	33	64	0	0	.228/.348/.402	.257	8.4	.304	-0.8	C(69): 5.2	1.5
2016	CLE	MLB	27	184	14	6	1	3	17	23	44	0	0	.183/.285/.294	.218	0.2	.229	-0.2	C(61): 9.3	1.0
2017	*CLE*	*MLB*	*28*	*216*	*24*	*9*	*1*	*6*	*24*	*26*	*57*	*0*	*0*	*.238/.327/.394*	*.249*	*7.2*	*.297*	*-0.4*	*C 10*	*1.2*
2018	*CLE*	*MLB*	*29*	*242*	*31*	*10*	*1*	*8*	*29*	*31*	*65*	*0*	*0*	*.237/.339/.405*	*.246*	*4.7*	*.295*	*-0.8*	*C 10*	*1.6*

Breakout: 4%   Improve: 46%   Collapse: 7%   Attrition: 17%   MLB: 89%   *Comparables: Hank Conger, Chris Snyder, Devin Mesoraco*

In this space last year, we wrote that Perez had a chance to be baseball's best backup catcher in 2016. Given the injury-riddled catastrophe that was Yan Gomes last season, Perez had a perfect opportunity to step up and prove his value. Defensively, he more than answered the call, with a killer ability to throw out runners and solid framing that placed him in baseball's top 10 for adjusted catcher FRAA. Offensively ... about all you can say is that he was an improvement over Gomes, which is saying nothing, as Gomes had the worst TAv in baseball and Perez watched his own plummet more than 30 points from 2015. But, hey, there's a reason we called him the best backup catcher and not the best should-be-starting catcher

YEAR	TEAM	P. COUNT	FRM RUNS	BLK RUNS	THRW RUNS	TOT RUNS
2014	CLE	3667	1.9	1.8	0.4	4.1
2014	COH	7159	14.8	0.3	1.2	16.3
2015	CLE	8759	4.7	2.0	1.2	7.9
2016	CLE	7261	8.0	1.4	1.1	10.5
2016	CLE	7261	8.0	1.4	1.1	10.5
2017	*CLE*	*8296*	*6.8*	*1.6*	*1.1*	*9.6*
2018	*CLE*	*9282*	*7.1*	*1.8*	*1.2*	*10.0*

Jose Ramirez   3B

Born: 9/17/92   Age: 24   Bats: B   Throws: R   Height: 5'9"   Weight: 180   Entered Pro Ball: International Free Agent, 2009

YEAR	TEAM	LVL	AGE	PA	R	2B	3B	HR	RBI	BB	K	SB	CS	AVG/OBP/SLG	TAv	VORP	BABIP	BRR	FRAA	WARP
2014	COH	AAA	21	277	37	15	2	5	29	25	30	19	11	.302/.360/.441	.268	9.7	.321	-1.8	2B(35): 6.0 • SS(21): 1.3	1.7
2014	CLE	MLB	21	266	27	10	2	2	17	13	35	10	1	.262/.300/.346	.233	5.0	.297	2.1	SS(56): 1.8 • 2B(11): -0.5	0.7
2015	COH	AAA	22	195	29	13	2	1	12	17	9	15	4	.293/.354/.408	.268	9.1	.303	1.6	2B(28): 1.8 • SS(10): -0.5	1.0
2015	CLE	MLB	22	355	50	14	3	6	27	32	39	10	4	.219/.291/.340	.238	5.2	.232	1.0	SS(46): -4.2 • 2B(33): 2.5	0.5
2016	CLE	MLB	23	618	84	46	3	11	76	44	62	22	7	.312/.363/.462	.274	31.4	.333	4.7	3B(117): -2.4 • LF(48): -0.7	2.9
2017	*CLE*	*MLB*	*24*	*586*	*65*	*31*	*4*	*11*	*60*	*42*	*65*	*23*	*8*	*.276/.325/.410*	*.251*	*12.7*	*.291*	*1.6*	*3B -4*	*0.5*
2018	*CLE*	*MLB*	*25*	*584*	*69*	*31*	*4*	*13*	*66*	*43*	*66*	*22*	*8*	*.279/.332/.429*	*.252*	*11.3*	*.291*	*3.1*	*3B -4*	*0.8*

Breakout: 2%   Improve: 51%   Collapse: 5%   Attrition: 6%   MLB: 92%   *Comparables: Ruben Tejada, Andrelton Simmons, Matt Dominguez*

According to the *Cleveland Plain Dealer*'s (very observant) Zack Meisel, Ramirez's helmet flew off his head an incredible 62 times during the season. Showing off the energetic baserunning implied by his nickname of Angry Hamster? So excited about his break-out season that he couldn't bother with cranium protection? Simply too full of childlike joy to be contained? A little of all three, perhaps. The helmet mishaps certainly didn't do anything to delay him on the basepaths, as he took the extra base 60 percent of the time. And the flexible attitude toward headgear may have represented his flexibility on defense, gamely transitioning away from his usual third base to fill a void in left field for a few months. Cleveland hopes that the speed, versatility and general energy keep the helmet flying in 2017.

Carlos Santana   1B

Born: 4/8/86   Age: 31   Bats: B   Throws: R   Height: 5'11"   Weight: 210   Entered Pro Ball: International Free Agent, 2004

YEAR	TEAM	LVL	AGE	PA	R	2B	3B	HR	RBI	BB	K	SB	CS	AVG/OBP/SLG	TAv	VORP	BABIP	BRR	FRAA	WARP
2014	CLE	MLB	28	660	68	25	0	27	85	113	124	5	2	.231/.365/.427	.292	27.8	.249	-1.8	1B(94): 5.0 • 3B(26): -0.9	3.1
2015	CLE	MLB	29	666	72	29	2	19	85	108	122	11	3	.231/.357/.395	.265	7.4	.261	-2.3	1B(132): -3.5	0.4
2016	CLE	MLB	30	688	89	31	3	34	87	99	99	5	2	.259/.366/.498	.280	20.3	.258	-0.9	1B(64): 4.5	2.6
2017	*CLE*	*MLB*	*31*	*714*	*102*	*33*	*2*	*26*	*85*	*109*	*124*	*8*	*3*	*.251/.367/.445*	*.281*	*26.3*	*.273*	*-0.8*	*1B 1*	*2.8*
2018	*CLE*	*MLB*	*32*	*580*	*81*	*26*	*1*	*21*	*74*	*90*	*107*	*4*	*2*	*.239/.360/.430*	*.266*	*12.4*	*.261*	*-1.5*	*1B 1*	*1.4*

Breakout: 0%   Improve: 44%   Collapse: 2%   Attrition: 12%   MLB: 96%   *Comparables: John Olerud, Nick Johnson, Ferris Fain*

Man, Santana rebounded from his struggles in 2015. It's easy to see, with a career-high 34 home runs serving as a reminder that the guy really does have power to go with his patience. A new test of his talent was the chance to bat leadoff for the first time, where he demonstrated that while he may not look like the archetypical leadoff hitter, he sure can get on base like one. Hot stuff, even as a more aggressive approach at the plate had him swinging a bit more and bringing his walk rate slightly down from its typically lofty mark. One season now stands between him and free agency—and assuming he keeps everything up, signing a new contract this winter should be smooth.

YEAR	TEAM	P. COUNT	FRM RUNS	BLK RUNS	THRW RUNS	TOT RUNS
2014	CLE	3667	1.9	1.8	0.4	4.1

Bradley Zimmer   OF

Born: 11/27/92   Age: 24   Bats: L   Throws: R   Height: 6'4"   Weight: 185   Entered Pro Ball: Round 1, 2014 Draft (#21 overall)

YEAR	TEAM	LVL	AGE	PA	R	2B	3B	HR	RBI	BB	K	SB	CS	AVG/OBP/SLG	TAv	VORP	BABIP	BRR	FRAA	WARP
2014	MHV	A-	21	197	32	11	2	4	30	19	30	11	4	.304/.401/.464	.327	21.9	.348	2.4	CF(42): 1.4	2.4
2015	LYN	A+	22	335	60	17	3	10	39	37	77	32	5	.308/.403/.493	.322	31.3	.388	3.1	CF(41): 7.5 • RF(22): 0.2	4.2
2015	AKR	AA	22	214	24	9	1	6	24	18	54	12	2	.219/.313/.374	.257	4.8	.273	-0.2	CF(42): 0.7	0.6
2016	AKR	AA	23	407	58	20	6	14	53	56	115	33	13	.253/.371/.471	.304	30.6	.341	1.8	CF(76): -0.1 • RF(9): 2.0	3.5
2016	COH	AAA	23	150	18	5	0	1	9	21	56	5	1	.242/.349/.305	.245	1.4	.423	-0.7	CF(36): -0.6	0.1
2017	*CLE*	*MLB*	*24*	*66*	*9*	*3*	*0*	*2*	*7*	*7*	*21*	*3*	*1*	*.230/.324/.406*	*.255*	*2.2*	*.317*	*0.3*	*CF 1*	*0.3*
2018	*CLE*	*MLB*	*25*	*309*	*40*	*13*	*1*	*11*	*38*	*32*	*100*	*15*	*5*	*.232/.326/.414*	*.249*	*6.8*	*.321*	*1.8*	*CF 4*	*1.2*

Breakout: 5%   Improve: 13%   Collapse: 8%   Attrition: 15%   MLB: 28%   *Comparables: Joe Benson, Brett Jackson, Jabari Blash*

From the time Zimmer was drafted in 2014, it was hard to find a mention of him without one of fellow prospect Clint Frazier close by. Together they were the future of Cleveland's outfield, endlessly paired and compared to one another in a constant game of "Who Would You Rather?" And then, with Cleveland's deadline deal for Andrew Miller, Frazier was sent packing, leaving Zimmer to anchor the franchise's outfield hopes by himself. The transition to Triple-A wasn't an easy one for him, with a ton of strikeouts and his inability to hit lefties exploited. But his power and speed still leave him with one of the highest outfielder ceilings around, and there's a good chance he'll be seen in Cleveland this year.

PITCHERS

Brady Aiken   LHP

Born: 8/16/96   Age: 20   Bats: L   Throws: L   Height: 6'4"   Weight: 205   Entered Pro Ball: Round 1, 2015 Draft (#17 overall)

YEAR	TEAM	LVL	AGE	W	L	SV	G	GS	IP	H	HR	BB/9	K/9	K	GB%	BABIP	WHIP	ERA	FIP	DRA	VORP	WARP	cFIP	MPH
2016	MHV	A-	19	2	1	0	5	5	22¹	20	3	3.2	8.9	22	0%	.266	1.25	4.43	4.26					
2017	CLE	MLB	20	2	3	0	8	8	31¹	40	8	5.6	6.1	21	67%	.318	1.91	6.82	7.12	7.16	-5.9	-0.6	170	
2018	CLE	MLB	21	4	9	0	23	23	135	153	30	5.9	7.6	115	67%	.305	1.79	6.54	6.50	6.87	-14.1	-1.5	165	

Breakout: 2%   Improve: 2%   Collapse: 0%   Attrition: 0%   MLB: 2%   *Comparables: Jordan Walden, Severino Gonzalez, Wilking Rodriguez*

For the first few years that Aiken was in baseball's public consciousness, it was most often as a stand-in for a larger topic: the rise of Tommy John surgery, the changes to the draft bonus rules, a player's relationship to his medical information. He's still all of those things, but mostly he's just a pitching prospect. And still a very good one, albeit one that struggled a bit as he continued recovering from TJS. He battled control problems throughout the year and didn't look exactly like the pitcher he was when he dazzled as a high schooler, but he has plenty of time to adjust and move toward his ridiculously high ceiling.

Cody Allen   RHP

Born: 11/20/88   Age: 28   Bats: R   Throws: R   Height: 6'1"   Weight: 210   Entered Pro Ball: Round 23, 2011 Draft (#698 overall)

YEAR	TEAM	LVL	AGE	W	L	SV	G	GS	IP	H	HR	BB/9	K/9	K	GB%	BABIP	WHIP	ERA	FIP	DRA	VORP	WARP	cFIP	MPH
2014	CLE	MLB	25	6	4	24	76	0	69²	48	7	3.4	11.8	91	40%	.266	1.06	2.07	3.02	2.47	15.6	1.7	79	97.4
2015	CLE	MLB	26	2	5	34	70	0	69¹	56	2	3.2	12.9	99	35%	.342	1.17	2.99	1.79	2.76	15.0	1.6	76	97.1
2016	CLE	MLB	27	3	5	32	67	0	68	41	8	3.6	11.5	87	48%	.232	1.00	2.51	3.27	2.50	18.7	1.9	75	96.5
2017	CLE	MLB	28	3	3	30	58	0	61¹	50	7	3.6	11.3	77	39%	.295	1.21	3.02	3.40	3.45	10.4	1.1	71	
2018	CLE	MLB	29	2	1	19	45	0	48¹	38	6	3.6	11.5	62	39%	.286	1.18	3.46	3.44	3.73	7.0	0.7	80	

Breakout: 28%   Improve: 49%   Collapse: 30%   Attrition: 14%   MLB: 91%   *Comparables: David Robertson, Carlos Marmol, Drew Storen*

The buzz around Cleveland's late-season bullpen use centered on Andrew Miller and the fact that the team was willing to use its best reliever in its highest-leverage situations, inning be damned. But that setup only worked so well because Cleveland could back it up with a pitcher as good as Allen. For several seasons now, he's been used flexibly and somewhat creatively as closer, logging more innings in the role than all but two other designated closers from 2014–2016. The team's bullpen usage got even more creative after Cleveland acquired Miller, but it only worked because Allen was as productive as ever, coming up just a few decimal points shy of a career-low DRA. He may not be the bullpen's biggest star, but his talent is still key to the bullpen's success. Somewhat related: the Oscars originally awarded winners for best supporting actor with a plaque, rather than the famous statuette. But they soon realized that secondary roles can require just as much talent as their headlining counterparts and upgraded the winners to the little gold men they deserve. Allen's in a supporting role, but he's been worthy of the statue all along.

Cody Anderson   RHP

Born: 9/14/90   Age: 26   Bats: R   Throws: R   Height: 6'4"   Weight: 240   Entered Pro Ball: Round 14, 2011 Draft (#428 overall)

YEAR	TEAM	LVL	AGE	W	L	SV	G	GS	IP	H	HR	BB/9	K/9	K	GB%	BABIP	WHIP	ERA	FIP	DRA	VORP	WARP	cFIP	MPH
2014	AKR	AA	23	4	11	0	25	25	125²	141	17	3.2	5.8	81	46%	.312	1.48	5.44	4.99	8.03	-39.2	-4.2	119	
2015	AKR	AA	24	3	2	0	10	10	52	46	3	1.6	6.2	36	46%	.273	1.02	1.73	2.96	3.02	12.0	1.3	95	
2015	COH	AAA	24	1	1	0	3	3	19¹	17	0	2.3	8.4	18	41%	.315	1.14	2.33	2.23	3.50	3.9	0.4	89	
2015	CLE	MLB	24	7	3	0	15	15	91¹	77	9	2.4	4.3	44	47%	.237	1.11	3.05	4.24	5.30	-2.3	-0.2	119	94.8
2016	COH	AAA	25	0	2	1	13	6	32¹	32	4	2.8	11.1	40	56%	.329	1.30	3.62	3.42	1.62	13.1	1.3	69	
2016	CLE	MLB	25	2	5	0	19	9	60²	85	13	1.9	8.0	54	40%	.381	1.62	6.68	4.80	4.73	3.4	0.4	104	96.7
2017	CLE	MLB	26	4	4	0	30	8	71	76	10	3.1	6.6	52	53%	.299	1.42	4.55	4.63	4.78	3.0	0.3	100	
2018	CLE	MLB	27	5	5	0	43	12	102	99	15	3.9	8.5	96	53%	.295	1.41	4.73	4.69	5.10	2.6	0.3	118	

Breakout: 21%   Improve: 43%   Collapse: 28%   Attrition: 33%   MLB: 81%   *Comparables: Justin Germano, Billy Buckner, Trevor Bell*

Peripheral measures showed that Anderson's dazzling September in 2015 wasn't something he was likely to repeat. His 2016 showed that this was true. While he added a bit of velocity to his fastball and was significantly better with two of the three true outcomes, he was significantly worse on the third (that HR total is a bit HoRrendous) and allowed far more hard contact. He improved after shifting to the bullpen, but not enough to make him look any better than the fringy fifth starter he seems destined to be. The fact that his offseason kicked off with elbow surgery probably won't help, either.

Shawn Armstrong   RHP

Born: 9/11/90   Age: 26   Bats: R   Throws: R   Height: 6'2"   Weight: 225   Entered Pro Ball: Round 18, 2011 Draft (#548 overall)

YEAR	TEAM	LVL	AGE	W	L	SV	G	GS	IP	H	HR	BB/9	K/9	K	GB%	BABIP	WHIP	ERA	FIP	DRA	VORP	WARP	cFIP	MPH
2014	AKR	AA	23	6	2	15	44	0	51	39	3	3.4	12.0	68	41%	.310	1.14	2.12	2.63	1.47	19.1	2.0	70	
2015	COH	AAA	24	1	2	16	46	0	49²	37	0	4.7	14.5	80	43%	.363	1.27	2.36	1.63	1.87	16.9	1.7	66	
2015	CLE	MLB	24	0	0	0	8	0	8	5	1	2.2	12.4	11	35%	.250	0.88	2.25	2.73	3.54	1.0	0.1	91	96.5
2016	COH	AAA	25	3	1	9	47	0	49	27	0	5.3	13.2	72	43%	.270	1.14	1.84	2.19	1.63	18.1	1.9	79	
2016	CLE	MLB	25	0	0	0	10	0	10²	9	1	4.2	5.9	7	53%	.258	1.31	2.53	4.42	5.05	-0.1	0.0	108	95.3
2017	CLE	MLB	26	1	1	0	18	0	18	18	2	4.5	9.9	21	50%	.300	1.45	4.20	3.90	4.47	1.1	0.1	100	
2018	CLE	MLB	27	2	1	0	38	0	40²	34	5	6.1	12.4	56	50%	.312	1.51	4.22	4.20	4.59	2.0	0.2	101	

Breakout: 33%   Improve: 44%   Collapse: 20%   Attrition: 27%   MLB: 65%   *Comparables: Cory Burns, Ryan Dull, Donnie Joseph*

The question with Armstrong has never been whether he can live up to his name—he definitely can with that fastball—but whether he can maintain the command he needs to complement it. The answer he offered last season was a resounding "maybe, kind of." For the second straight year, Armstrong spent most of his time at Triple-A. But 2016 was not quite as sharp or strikeout-filled as 2015 in either Columbus or in Cleveland. An adjustment to which part of the rubber he pitches from was supposed to be a breakthrough, but it didn't reflect particularly well in his results. Armstrong, sure, but being a quality bullpen arm takes a bit more than that.

Trevor Bauer   RHP

Born: 1/17/91   Age: 26   Bats: R   Throws: R   Height: 6'1"   Weight: 200   Entered Pro Ball: Round 1, 2011 Draft (#3 overall)

YEAR	TEAM	LVL	AGE	W	L	SV	G	GS	IP	H	HR	BB/9	K/9	K	GB%	BABIP	WHIP	ERA	FIP	DRA	VORP	WARP	cFIP	MPH
2014	COH	AAA	23	4	1	0	7	7	46	36	5	2.7	8.6	44	40%	.263	1.09	2.15	3.84	3.50	11.5	1.1	88	
2014	CLE	MLB	23	5	8	0	26	26	153	151	16	3.5	8.4	143	37%	.312	1.38	4.18	4.04	4.94	-1.7	-0.2	110	96.5
2015	CLE	MLB	24	11	12	0	31	30	176	152	23	4.0	8.7	170	41%	.276	1.31	4.55	4.30	3.88	23.4	2.5	106	95.6
2016	CLE	MLB	25	12	8	0	35	28	190	179	20	3.3	8.0	168	49%	.292	1.31	4.26	3.95	4.12	25.5	2.6	100	96.2
2017	CLE	MLB	26	9	7	0	24	24	136	132	18	3.9	8.5	129	56%	.295	1.40	4.29	4.42	4.59	10.0	1.0	100	
2018	CLE	MLB	27	10	11	0	30	30	187²	174	26	4.0	9.5	198	56%	.298	1.38	4.32	4.30	4.66	15.1	1.6	107	

Breakout: 26%   Improve: 56%   Collapse: 15%   Attrition: 10%   MLB: 89%   *Comparables: Brandon McCarthy, Michael Pineda, Edinson Volquez*

A boy and his drone, selected highlights, 2016:

February—while in Arizona for spring training, Bauer takes his beloved drone to a park. He encounters a man who suggests he should use the drone in a comedy film about a bank robbery, to which Bauer responds that drone-users already have a stigma and so a drone movie should not include robbery. He films the conversation and uploads it to YouTube, with flight footage from the drone set to "A Little Less Conversation" by Elvis.

April—The *Chicago Tribune* reports that "a Cleveland Indians player" has crashed a drone into the White Sox video scoreboard. Bauer claims he did not do it.

July—"Trevor Bauer and friends recover treed drone in dead of night" is a headline in the *Cleveland Plain Dealer*.

October—Bauer tries to repair his drone before a playoff start and cuts his finger badly enough that his start must be pushed back. When he *does* start, he bleeds so profusely on the mound that he must be removed in the first inning.

Conclusion: Bauer continued to be maddeningly inconsistent, and even at his best is more fascinating than he is productive.

Carlos Carrasco   RHP

Born: 3/21/87   Age: 30   Bats: R   Throws: R   Height: 6'4"   Weight: 210   Entered Pro Ball: International Free Agent, 2003

YEAR	TEAM	LVL	AGE	W	L	SV	G	GS	IP	H	HR	BB/9	K/9	K	GB%	BABIP	WHIP	ERA	FIP	DRA	VORP	WARP	cFIP	MPH
2014	CLE	MLB	27	8	7	1	40	14	134	103	7	1.9	9.4	140	54%	.274	0.99	2.55	2.47	2.43	34.1	3.8	73	98.4
2015	CLE	MLB	28	14	12	0	30	30	183²	154	18	2.1	10.6	216	53%	.304	1.07	3.63	2.81	2.22	58.4	6.3	62	97.5
2016	CLE	MLB	29	11	8	0	25	25	146¹	134	21	2.1	9.2	150	50%	.289	1.15	3.32	3.68	2.69	43.4	4.5	76	96.8
2017	CLE	MLB	30	13	8	0	30	30	180	163	23	2.7	10.0	201	44%	.301	1.22	3.44	3.58	3.68	31.4	3.2	82	
2018	CLE	MLB	31	11	9	0	29	29	182	165	23	2.5	10.2	205	44%	.303	1.18	3.47	3.44	3.73	33.5	3.5	82	

Breakout: 16%   Improve: 50%   Collapse: 22%   Attrition: 9%   MLB: 92%   *Comparables: Felix Hernandez, David Price, Doug Fister*

Carrasco's year was bookended by frustration—a strained hamstring that sidelined him for the entire month of May and a hand injury that kept him watching from the dugout for the entirety of Cleveland's playoff run. But the book in between was a great read. Not a classic—after all, you can't set the franchise record for starter strikeout rate every season, and Carrasco took care of that in 2015—but solid reviews and worth the hype. It was Carrasco's worst season since his breakout year in 2014, but the high bar he set there has left plenty of space for the "worst" to still read like a pretty damn good edition. And that should be true in 2017, provided he doesn't suffer a debilitating paper cut while turning the page.

Michael Clevinger   RHP

Born: 12/21/90 Age: 26 Bats: R Throws: R Height: 6'4" Weight: 210 Entered Pro Ball: Round 4, 2011 Draft (#135 overall)

YEAR	TEAM	LVL	AGE	W	L	SV	G	GS	IP	H	HR	BB/9	K/9	K	GB%	BABIP	WHIP	ERA	FIP	DRA	VORP	WARP	cFIP	MPH
2014	INL	A+	23	1	3	0	13	13	55¹	58	8	4.4	9.4	58	0%	.331	1.54	5.37	5.20					
2014	BUR	A	23	3	0	0	5	5	24	16	2	1.9	10.1	27	48%	.241	0.88	1.88	2.94	2.47	7.9	0.8	82	
2014	CAR	A+	23	0	1	0	5	4	20²	20	1	4.8	6.5	15	41%	.328	1.50	4.79	4.73	7.91	-5.4	-0.5	115	
2015	AKR	AA	24	9	8	0	27	26	158	127	8	2.3	8.3	145	37%	.272	1.06	2.73	3.02	2.94	37.5	4.1	85	
2016	COH	AAA	25	11	1	0	17	17	93	78	8	3.4	9.4	97	40%	.293	1.22	3.00	3.36	2.50	29.4	3.0	90	
2016	CLE	MLB	25	3	3	0	17	10	53	50	8	4.9	8.5	50	40%	.288	1.49	5.26	4.82	4.79	2.8	0.3	113	96.1
2017	CLE	MLB	26	7	6	0	29	16	105¹	106	15	4.0	7.9	92	54%	.296	1.46	4.60	4.73	4.88	3.9	0.4	100	
2018	CLE	MLB	27	5	6	0	15	15	88²	81	14	5.3	10.3	101	54%	.294	1.50	4.88	4.85	5.26	2.0	0.2	122	

Breakout: 19%   Improve: 31%   Collapse: 30%   Attrition: 42%   MLB: 76%   Comparables: Tyler Lyons, Steve Johnson, Neil Ramirez

Comparisons to Jake deGrom are almost inevitable for all right-handed pitchers with shoulder-length hair, but Clevinger's first go-round in the majors was hardly deGromesque. He struggled with his command and had to spend time in the bullpen as a result. You might wonder if that's where he'll end up when all is said and done, but it's too early to give up on his starting career. Just know the Angels would still probably like to take back the deal that sent Clevinger to Cleveland for Vinnie Pestano.

Kyle Crockett   LHP

Born: 12/15/91 Age: 25 Bats: L Throws: L Height: 6'2" Weight: 175 Entered Pro Ball: Round 4, 2013 Draft (#111 overall)

YEAR	TEAM	LVL	AGE	W	L	SV	G	GS	IP	H	HR	BB/9	K/9	K	GB%	BABIP	WHIP	ERA	FIP	DRA	VORP	WARP	cFIP	MPH
2014	AKR	AA	22	0	0	6	15	0	15²	8	0	1.7	9.8	17	60%	.211	0.70	0.57	1.95	1.37	6.1	0.6	77	
2014	CLE	MLB	22	4	1	0	43	0	30	26	2	2.4	8.4	28	57%	.296	1.13	1.80	3.26	3.15	4.5	0.5	93	92.1
2015	COH	AAA	23	3	1	0	29	0	28²	42	3	3.5	8.5	27	50%	.406	1.85	5.97	3.89	3.79	3.6	0.4	101	
2015	CLE	MLB	23	0	0	0	31	0	17²	17	1	3.6	7.6	15	55%	.320	1.36	4.08	3.50	4.15	1.1	0.1	101	92.5
2016	COH	AAA	24	1	1	0	29	0	30	29	2	3.3	7.8	26	42%	.300	1.33	3.90	3.50	2.80	7.2	0.7	97	
2016	CLE	MLB	24	0	0	0	29	0	16	16	0	3.9	9.6	17	48%	.348	1.44	5.06	2.29	3.81	2.1	0.2	97	91.7
2017	CLE	MLB	25	1	1	0	27	0	28¹	30	4	3.5	7.3	23	51%	.304	1.50	4.88	4.66	4.94	0.1	0.0	100	
2018	CLE	MLB	26	2	1	0	36	0	37²	39	6	4.4	8.5	35	51%	.313	1.54	4.85	4.81	5.18	-0.5	-0.1	118	

Breakout: 32%   Improve: 45%   Collapse: 26%   Attrition: 41%   MLB: 84%   Comparables: Wes Littleton, Ian Krol, Bruce Rondon

As Cleveland's bullpen became one of the team's greatest strengths with the deadline trade for Andrew Miller, it became clear that Crockett didn't have a secure place there. He has spent less and less time in the majors each season since debuting in 2014, and the future doesn't look particularly bright for the lefty specialist as he runs out of minor-league options. Particularly as the Davy Crockett quote "always be sure you are right, then go ahead" continues to apply to righties facing Kyle.

Edwin Escobar   LHP

Born: 4/22/92 Age: 25 Bats: L Throws: L Height: 6'2" Weight: 225 Entered Pro Ball: International Free Agent, 2008

YEAR	TEAM	LVL	AGE	W	L	SV	G	GS	IP	H	HR	BB/9	K/9	K	GB%	BABIP	WHIP	ERA	FIP	DRA	VORP	WARP	cFIP	MPH
2014	FRE	AAA	22	3	8	0	20	20	111	128	16	3.0	7.8	96	44%	.326	1.49	5.11	5.01	4.84	11.3	1.1	99	
2014	PAW	AAA	22	0	2	0	5	5	27¹	33	3	2.6	6.6	20	40%	.337	1.50	4.28	4.20	6.22	-1.4	-0.1	98	
2014	BOS	MLB	22	0	0	0	2	0	2	1	0	0.0	9.0	2	20%	.200	0.50	4.50	2.66	4.56	0.0	0.0	103	96.1
2015	PAW	AAA	23	3	3	0	19	6	49²	52	8	4.5	4.3	24	38%	.272	1.55	5.07	5.92	12.13	-38.5	-3.9	131	
2016	RNO	AAA	24	6	3	0	16	16	91	99	8	3.6	6.2	63	46%	.318	1.48	4.25	4.76	5.84	-5.2	-0.5	110	
2016	ARI	MLB	24	1	2	0	25	0	23²	33	4	4.6	6.5	17	36%	.367	1.90	7.23	5.98	7.06	-5.2	-0.5	123	94.3
2017	CLE	MLB	25	5	6	0	24	15	89	102	13	3.7	5.8	57	54%	.305	1.56	4.98	5.13	5.34	0.9	0.1	123	
2018	CLE	MLB	26	5	6	0	25	15	101¹	108	17	5.5	8.6	96	54%	.314	1.67	5.46	5.41	5.85	-4.3	-0.4	135	

Breakout: 19%   Improve: 29%   Collapse: 15%   Attrition: 34%   MLB: 55%   Comparables: Tyler Wagner, Lance Broadway, Zeke Spruill

Escobar's *best* attributes are that he's left-handed and inexpensive. His *worst* attributes are tied to the fact that he's a below-average pitcher. Escobar doesn't own an elite pitch, which is perhaps why he threw his four-seamer nearly 70 percent of the time in 2016. That heater isn't terrible, as it has good arm-side run and sits at 93 mph. Unfortunately his curveball lacks depth and his changeup is so bad that he only threw it eight times in 25 appearances. That was good enough to get him action in the desert in 2016, which reveals plenty about Arizona's pitching issues last season.

Perci Garner   RHP

Born: 12/13/88 Age: 28 Bats: R Throws: R Height: 6'3" Weight: 225 Entered Pro Ball: Round 2, 2010 Draft (#77 overall)

YEAR	TEAM	LVL	AGE	W	L	SV	G	GS	IP	H	HR	BB/9	K/9	K	GB%	BABIP	WHIP	ERA	FIP	DRA	VORP	WARP	cFIP	MPH
2014	REA	AA	25	4	5	0	19	16	81²	79	3	6.8	6.8	62	59%	.308	1.73	4.85	4.74	10.60	-48.9	-5.2	121	
2014	CLR	A+	25	0	0	0	7	0	12	9	0	11.2	9.8	13	60%	.300	2.00	3.00	4.97	8.12	-3.9	-0.4	126	
2015	LYN	A+	26	3	1	1	18	1	30²	27	0	3.5	9.7	33	65%	.329	1.27	2.93	2.37	3.50	4.3	0.5	92	
2016	AKR	AA	27	5	1	2	23	0	51	37	1	1.9	8.3	47	70%	.263	0.94	1.94	2.53	2.29	13.8	1.5	74	
2016	COH	AAA	27	2	0	5	18	0	27²	15	1	3.6	7.5	23	73%	.192	0.94	1.63	3.17	3.43	4.7	0.5	88	
2016	CLE	MLB	27	0	0	0	8	0	9¹	12	0	4.8	11.6	12	59%	.444	1.82	4.82	2.78	3.98	1.0	0.1	92	96.5
2017	CLE	MLB	28	1	1	0	22	0	23	25	2	4.4	6.9	18	46%	.298	1.53	4.63	4.39	4.76	0.6	0.1	100	
2018	CLE	MLB	29	1	0	0	25	0	27	25	4	5.8	10.1	30	46%	.306	1.56	4.74	4.70	5.07	0.0	0.0	115	

Breakout: 10%   Improve: 18%   Collapse: 2%   Attrition: 13%   MLB: 21%   Comparables: Heath Phillips, Andy Oliver, Jake Brigham

Garner is the first major leaguer named Perci since 1973, when Percival Wentworth Ford pitched in a few games for the Braves. Ford then languished in the minors for a few years before returning home to the Bahamas and dying in a car crash at the age of 33. Hopefully a better future awaits Garner, but the chances that said future will be in baseball aren't so great. After a series of injuries and a move to the bullpen in 2015, Garner lost any potential for prospect shine well before he finally debuted in the majors as a wholly unremarkable relief arm at age 27.

Juan Hillman   LHP

Born: 5/15/97   Age: 20   Bats: L   Throws: L   Height: 6'2"   Weight: 185   Entered Pro Ball: Round 2, 2015 Draft (#59 overall)

YEAR	TEAM	LVL	AGE	W	L	SV	G	GS	IP	H	HR	BB/9	K/9	K	GB%	BABIP	WHIP	ERA	FIP	DRA	VORP	WARP	cFIP	MPH
2016	MHV	A-	19	3	4	0	15	15	63	66	5	3.4	6.7	47	38%	.308	1.43	4.43	4.24	4.85	2.7	0.3	105	
2017	CLE	MLB	20	2	5	0	11	11	43¹	62	13	5.1	3.9	19	95%	.315	2.00	7.81	7.95	8.15	-12.9	-1.3	194	
2018	CLE	MLB	21	2	6	0	13	13	77¹	103	22	5.1	6.0	52	95%	.318	1.90	7.53	7.46	7.86	-14.0	-1.4	189	

Breakout: 0%   Improve: 0%   Collapse: 0%   Attrition: 0%   MLB: 0%   Comparables: Jose Urena, Adrian Houser, Jose Torres

If you say Juan Hillman's name really first, it sounds kind of like "One Hill Man"—which is basically exactly what he is. ("One Hill Man" could perhaps also be used to describe a *One Tree Hill* fan, which was on television just a bit before Hillman's time but is timeless enough that he should be a fan regardless, preferably of Team Leyton.) The most interesting thing about Hillman is that he's a projectable southpaw with the chance for three average-or-better pitches. Second-most interesting? Tom Gordon is his legal guardian.

Rob Kaminsky   LHP

Born: 9/2/94   Age: 22   Bats: R   Throws: L   Height: 5'11"   Weight: 190   Entered Pro Ball: Round 1, 2013 Draft (#28 overall)

YEAR	TEAM	LVL	AGE	W	L	SV	G	GS	IP	H	HR	BB/9	K/9	K	GB%	BABIP	WHIP	ERA	FIP	DRA	VORP	WARP	cFIP	MPH
2014	PEO	A	19	8	2	0	18	18	100²	71	2	2.8	7.1	79	53%	.239	1.01	1.88	3.28	4.46	11.0	1.1	103	
2015	PMB	A+	20	6	5	0	17	17	94²	82	0	2.7	7.5	79	63%	.291	1.16	2.09	2.51	4.31	8.1	0.9	99	
2016	AKR	AA	21	11	7	0	25	25	137	122	7	3.2	6.0	92	55%	.277	1.24	3.28	3.91	4.95	2.3	0.2	102	
2017	CLE	MLB	22	6	8	0	20	20	104²	120	16	3.9	4.8	55	54%	.294	1.58	5.46	5.50	5.80	-3.8	-0.4	138	
2018	CLE	MLB	23	6	10	0	23	23	136²	141	23	5.7	8.0	122	54%	.302	1.67	5.67	5.63	6.02	-7.5	-0.8	143	

Breakout: 8%   Improve: 20%   Collapse: 10%   Attrition: 23%   MLB: 41%   Comparables: Will Smith, Carlos Carrasco, David Holmberg

Kaminsky's hype has faded a bit each year since he was a first-round pick in 2013. This doesn't mean the hype is gone, but the buzz around the undersized lefty and his killer curve has settled down to leave focus on the fact that a) he's undersized and b) everything other than the curve is kind of underwhelming. But his command is strong, he still projects as a solidly back-of-the-rotation guy even after struggling a bit at Double-A last year. And no matter what, he's almost absolutely still a steal when you consider that Cleveland got him from St. Louis for a season-and-a-half of Brandon Moss.

Corey Kluber   RHP

Born: 4/10/86   Age: 31   Bats: R   Throws: R   Height: 6'4"   Weight: 215   Entered Pro Ball: Round 4, 2007 Draft (#134 overall)

YEAR	TEAM	LVL	AGE	W	L	SV	G	GS	IP	H	HR	BB/9	K/9	K	GB%	BABIP	WHIP	ERA	FIP	DRA	VORP	WARP	cFIP	MPH
2014	CLE	MLB	28	18	9	0	34	34	235²	207	14	1.9	10.3	269	50%	.316	1.09	2.44	2.37	1.96	75.4	8.3	67	95.7
2015	CLE	MLB	29	9	16	0	32	32	222	189	22	1.8	9.9	245	44%	.297	1.05	3.49	2.94	3.05	50.0	5.4	73	95.2
2016	CLE	MLB	30	18	9	0	32	32	215	170	22	2.4	9.5	227	46%	.271	1.06	3.14	3.22	2.97	57.2	5.9	78	94.8
2017	CLE	MLB	31	14	8	0	29	29	194¹	176	25	2.7	10.2	220	49%	.303	1.22	3.48	3.59	3.71	33.2	3.4	83	
2018	CLE	MLB	32	12	11	0	30	30	191²	176	26	2.8	10.0	213	49%	.304	1.23	3.77	3.74	4.05	31.4	3.2	91	

Breakout: 17%   Improve: 44%   Collapse: 28%   Attrition: 11%   MLB: 92%   Comparables: Erik Bedard, John Lackey, Justin Verlander

First is a two-seam fastball, starting a few inches off the plate before breaking to catch a bit of black at the last second. It is beautiful; the hitter has no chance; strike one, called. Next is a breaking ball, equally nasty whether you choose to classify it as a slider or a curve. The hitter swings, misses wildly, strike two. The breaking ball again, but a little further off this time and the hitter lays off. (The pitcher may be robotic, but he isn't perfect.) And finally that two-seamer again, just ever so barely on the edge of the strike zone. Strike three, called. The corners of the pitcher's mouth twitch upwards ever so briefly. He does not smile, but he is satisfied. Now imagine slight variations of this over 200-plus innings, and you have Kluber.

Jeff Manship   RHP

Born: 1/16/85   Age: 32   Bats: R   Throws: R   Height: 6'2"   Weight: 205   Entered Pro Ball: Round 14, 2006 Draft (#426 overall)

YEAR	TEAM	LVL	AGE	W	L	SV	G	GS	IP	H	HR	BB/9	K/9	K	GB%	BABIP	WHIP	ERA	FIP	DRA	VORP	WARP	cFIP	MPH
2014	PHI	MLB	29	1	2	0	20	0	23	24	1	5.5	6.3	16	45%	.311	1.65	6.65	4.10	5.72	-3.2	-0.3	119	94.2
2014	LEH	AAA	29	0	1	0	8	5	25¹	29	1	6.4	7.5	21	54%	.354	1.86	4.62	4.34	5.30	1.1	0.1	110	
2015	COH	AAA	30	2	2	2	23	0	31²	25	3	2.6	8.8	31	57%	.262	1.07	1.99	3.28	2.94	7.0	0.7	85	
2015	CLE	MLB	30	1	0	0	32	0	39¹	20	1	2.3	7.6	33	52%	.192	0.76	0.92	2.60	3.61	4.8	0.5	93	94.5
2016	CLE	MLB	31	2	1	0	53	0	43¹	40	7	4.6	7.5	36	53%	.266	1.43	3.12	5.07	4.70	1.3	0.1	108	93.3
2017	CLE	MLB	32	2	2	0	24	4	40	41	5	4.0	7.4	33	47%	.298	1.46	4.58	4.60	4.96	1.3	0.1	112	
2018	CLE	MLB	33	4	3	0	49	7	86²	80	12	4.7	9.4	90	47%	.298	1.44	4.58	4.54	4.96	2.4	0.2	112	

Breakout: 19%   Improve: 23%   Collapse: 11%   Attrition: 21%   MLB: 46%   Comparables: David Purcey, Rick Bauer, Evan Meek

A few years ago, the Manship looked kind of like the *Titanic*: three teams in five seasons, with a 6.46 ERA and 1.55 strikeout-to-walk ratio. Now? It's a sturdy and dependable rowboat—no frills or anything, but it can certainly get the job done—with a 2.07 ERA and 2.16 strikeout-to-walk ratio in his two years in Cleveland. Manship is yet another entry in the endless encyclopedia of relievers with weird career arcs, so you'd be forgiven for wanting to keep your life vest on, but it's safe to climb aboard now.

Zach McAllister   RHP

Born: 12/8/87   Age: 29   Bats: R   Throws: R   Height: 6'6"   Weight: 240   Entered Pro Ball: Round 3, 2006 Draft (#104 overall)

YEAR	TEAM	LVL	AGE	W	L	SV	G	GS	IP	H	HR	BB/9	K/9	K	GB%	BABIP	WHIP	ERA	FIP	DRA	VORP	WARP	cFIP	MPH
2014	COH	AAA	26	7	1	0	11	11	69	57	3	1.8	7.7	59	44%	.276	1.03	2.09	2.86	2.00	28.8	2.9	85	
2014	CLE	MLB	26	4	7	0	22	15	86	96	7	2.9	7.7	74	43%	.332	1.44	5.23	3.47	4.37	3.9	0.4	104	97.1
2015	CLE	MLB	27	4	4	1	61	1	69	70	7	3.0	11.0	84	46%	.346	1.35	3.00	3.12	3.07	12.8	1.4	85	97.9
2016	CLE	MLB	28	3	2	0	53	2	52¹	53	6	4.0	9.3	54	35%	.318	1.45	3.44	3.97	4.92	0.4	0.0	110	96.6
2017	*CLE*	*MLB*	*29*	*2*	*3*	*0*	*49*	*0*	*51*	*50*	*7*	*3.5*	*8.9*	*52*	*46%*	*.299*	*1.35*	*4.08*	*4.19*	*4.35*	*3.6*	*0.4*	*98*	
2018	*CLE*	*MLB*	*30*	*2*	*1*	*0*	*32*	*0*	*34*	*32*	*5*	*3.9*	*9.6*	*36*	*46%*	*.301*	*1.38*	*4.27*	*4.24*	*4.61*	*1.7*	*0.2*	*103*	

Breakout: 33%   Improve: 50%   Collapse: 24%   Attrition: 15%   MLB: 91%   Comparables: *David Phelps, Robinson Tejeda, Brian Bannister*

McAllister's 2015 move from the rotation to the bullpen looked like it could be a career changer, perhaps even a career saver. Now, it looks like it might just be a blip on the winding road to irrelevance. In his second year in relief, McAllister was meaningfully worse by every metric and peripheral. The cutter he'd unveiled in 2015 took a backseat to his curveball as his top secondary pitch, and the results were not encouraging. In a Cleveland relief corps that has significantly more competitive options than was the case when McAllister first converted to the pen, the margin for continued error is not so great—but the chances of avoiding it don't look so good.

Triston McKenzie   RHP

Born: 8/2/97   Age: 19   Bats: R   Throws: R   Height: 6'5"   Weight: 165   Entered Pro Ball: Round 1, 2015 Draft (#42 overall)

YEAR	TEAM	LVL	AGE	W	L	SV	G	GS	IP	H	HR	BB/9	K/9	K	GB%	BABIP	WHIP	ERA	FIP	DRA	VORP	WARP	cFIP	MPH
2016	MHV	A-	18	4	3	0	9	9	49¹	31	2	2.9	10.0	55	37%	.248	0.95	0.55	2.66	1.78	19.0	2.0	77	
2016	LKC	A	18	2	2	0	6	6	34	27	2	1.6	13.0	49	40%	.333	0.97	3.18	1.98	1.14	14.6	1.6	65	
2017	*CLE*	*MLB*	*19*	*4*	*3*	*0*	*11*	*11*	*55¹*	*74*	*2*	*0.3*	*0.2*	*1*	*47%*	*.309*	*1.37*	*3.57*	*3.67*	*3.77*	*10.5*	*1.1*	*83*	
2018	*CLE*	*MLB*	*20*	*6*	*5*	*0*	*17*	*17*	*102²*	*121*	*3*	*0.3*	*2.5*	*29*		*.303*	*1.22*	*3.17*	*3.11*	*3.35*	*20.8*	*2.1*	*70*	

Breakout: 3%   Improve: 3%   Collapse: 0%   Attrition: 2%   MLB: 3%   Comparables: *Roberto Osuna, Jordan Lyles, Vicente Campos*

"Rail-thin" is a generous descriptor for McKenzie. Stick-thin, wafer-thin, piece-of-straw thin—these are closer to the truth. But that skinniness just leaves more space around him for projection, and McKenzie is a teenage prep arm with a lot of projection. In his first full season in the minors, he started to make that projection look like a good idea. With plenty of strikeouts on a low-90s fastball, and both a curveball and changeup that are nicely developed and improving still, McKenzie exceeded expectations in 2016. And he has a chance to keep doing so in 2017.

Ryan Merritt   LHP

Born: 2/21/92   Age: 25   Bats: L   Throws: L   Height: 6'0"   Weight: 180   Entered Pro Ball: Round 16, 2011 Draft (#488 overall)

YEAR	TEAM	LVL	AGE	W	L	SV	G	GS	IP	H	HR	BB/9	K/9	K	GB%	BABIP	WHIP	ERA	FIP	DRA	VORP	WARP	cFIP	MPH
2014	CAR	A+	22	13	3	0	25	25	160¹	128	12	1.4	7.1	127	47%	.251	0.95	2.58	3.47	2.21	60.4	6.1	80	
2015	AKR	AA	23	10	7	0	22	22	141	145	8	1	5.7	89	44%	.304	1.14	3.51	3.25	1.71	53.0	5.7	87	
2015	COH	AAA	23	2	0	0	5	5	30	38	1	1.8	4.8	16	49%	.343	1.47	4.20	3.22	3.99	4.4	0.4	103	
2016	COH	AAA	24	11	8	0	24	24	143¹	156	15	1.4	5.8	92	40%	.307	1.25	3.70	3.85	3.68	26.5	2.7	103	
2016	CLE	MLB	24	1	0	0	4	1	11	6	0	0.0	4.9	6	55%	.194	0.55	1.64	2.02	4.08	1.3	0.1	99	90.1
2017	*CLE*	*MLB*	*25*	*2*	*2*	*0*	*31*	*0*	*33*	*35*	*4*	*2.5*	*5.9*	*21*	*54%*	*.294*	*1.33*	*4.14*	*4.38*	*4.37*	*2.2*	*0.2*	*100*	
2018	*CLE*	*MLB*	*26*	*2*	*1*	*0*	*40*	*0*	*42²*	*40*	*6*	*4.0*	*8.7*	*41*	*54%*	*.291*	*1.38*	*4.47*	*4.43*	*4.78*	*1.3*	*0.1*	*108*	

Breakout: 27%   Improve: 34%   Collapse: 15%   Attrition: 38%   MLB: 57%   Comparables: *Ty Blach, Chris Beck, David Phelps*

Being up three games to one in the ALCS is generally pretty great. Being up three games to one in the ALCS with a rotation so ravaged by injury and fatigue that the only option for Game 5 is a rookie making one of his first career starts? Less great, particularly when said rookie is a crafty lefty still mastering his craft. But this was the situation for Cleveland and Merrit, and the anonymous southpaw rose to the challenge. In four-plus innings of work, he kept things scoreless with a fastball that maxed out at 88 mph and a slow curve that baffled. Cleveland fans responded by finding his online wedding registry and buying everything he and his bride-to-be needed. Awww. Is there serious reason to expect him to evolve beyond a back-end starter? Not particularly. But it's a hell of a way to start a career.

Andrew Miller   LHP

Born: 5/21/85   Age: 32   Bats: L   Throws: L   Height: 6'7"   Weight: 205   Entered Pro Ball: Round 1, 2006 Draft (#6 overall)

YEAR	TEAM	LVL	AGE	W	L	SV	G	GS	IP	H	HR	BB/9	K/9	K	GB%	BABIP	WHIP	ERA	FIP	DRA	VORP	WARP	cFIP	MPH
2014	BOS	MLB	29	3	5	0	50	0	42¹	25	2	2.8	14.7	69	55%	.280	0.90	2.34	1.72	1.27	15.1	1.7	49	96.7
2014	BAL	MLB	29	2	0	1	23	0	20	8	1	1.8	15.3	34	36%	.219	0.60	1.35	1.16	1.30	7.1	0.8	47	96.9
2015	NYA	MLB	30	3	2	36	60	0	61²	33	5	2.9	14.6	100	50%	.241	0.86	2.04	2.13	1.84	19.7	2.1	51	97.6
2016	NYA	MLB	31	6	1	9	44	0	45¹	28	5	1.4	15.3	77	50%	.284	0.77	1.39	1.74	1.17	19.2	2.0	31	98.2
2016	CLE	MLB	31	4	0	3	26	0	29	14	3	0.6	14.3	46	58%	.212	0.55	1.55	1.49	1.31	11.8	1.2	35	97.5
2017	*CLE*	*MLB*	*32*	*3*	*3*	*8*	*58*	*0*	*61¹*	*43*	*7*	*2.5*	*13.8*	*94*	*59%*	*.293*	*0.97*	*2.11*	*2.55*	*2.44*	*17.3*	*1.8*	*42*	
2018	*CLE*	*MLB*	*33*	*4*	*2*	*6*	*78*	*0*	*82¹*	*56*	*9*	*2.5*	*13.4*	*122*	*59%*	*.279*	*0.95*	*2.50*	*2.49*	*2.70*	*21.2*	*2.2*	*49*	

Breakout: 22%   Improve: 43%   Collapse: 23%   Attrition: 7%   MLB: 92%   Comparables: *Jonathan Papelbon, Brad Lidge, J.J. Putz*

There came a point last postseason when Miller seemed not so much a relief pitcher as the perfect symbol for an Official Bullpen Revolution. (Or, at least, the perfect symbol for all the debates over whether or not Miller really represented said revolution.) It was almost easy to believe that he was somehow immune to all the quirks of ability and fate that make pitchers *pitchers* rather than simple symbols of classical perfection. Those strikeouts—27 in his first 15 postseason innings!—that flexibility—able to perform in any inning, no matter the circumstances!—that slider—that *slider*! Add it all together and you have, well, not quite the dominance of Mariano Rivera, because Miller went multiple innings more often than Rivera ever did. Unreal. But Miller's not an unreal symbol, he's just a relief pitcher. A really, really damn good one at that.

Dan Otero   RHP

Born: 2/19/85   Age: 32   Bats: R   Throws: R   Height: 6'3"   Weight: 205   Entered Pro Ball: Round 21, 2007 Draft (#644 overall)

YEAR	TEAM	LVL	AGE	W	L	SV	G	GS	IP	H	HR	BB/9	K/9	K	GB%	BABIP	WHIP	ERA	FIP	DRA	VORP	WARP	cFIP	MPH
2014	OAK	MLB	29	8	2	1	72	0	86²	80	4	1.6	4.7	45	58%	.269	1.10	2.28	3.31	3.61	8.4	0.9	100	92.7
2015	NAS	AAA	30	2	0	0	15	2	27²	23	1	1.3	6.2	19	60%	.262	0.98	1.95	3.13	3.02	6.1	0.6	93	
2015	OAK	MLB	30	2	4	0	41	0	46²	64	7	1.2	5.4	28	50%	.354	1.50	6.75	4.37	4.53	0.9	0.1	105	92.1
2016	CLE	MLB	31	5	1	1	62	0	70²	54	2	1.3	7.3	57	64%	.260	0.91	1.53	2.29	3.06	15.0	1.5	80	92.9
2017	*CLE*	*MLB*	*32*	*2*	*3*	*0*	*49*	*0*	*51*	*56*	*7*	*2.5*	*6.6*	*38*	*47%*	*.300*	*1.35*	*4.33*	*4.38*	*4.53*	*2.6*	*0.3*	*100*	
2018	*CLE*	*MLB*	*33*	*2*	*1*	*0*	*44*	*0*	*46¹*	*48*	*6*	*2.7*	*6.8*	*35*	*47%*	*.297*	*1.34*	*4.43*	*4.39*	*4.74*	*1.6*	*0.2*	*108*	

Breakout: 23%   Improve: 40%   Collapse: 27%   Attrition: 21%   MLB: 83%   *Comparables: Brad Ziegler, Ryan Mattheus, Saul Rivera*

Otero comes from a family of competitive swimmers, but he doesn't share the talent. When his father, who swam at Princeton, first put young Dan in the pool, "I sank to the bottom," he told the *Cleveland Plain Dealer*. This was a harbinger of Otero's athletic ability, and not just the fact that he apparently lacks any when it comes to swimming: he grew up to be a sinkerballer. The only problem was that he was a sinkerballer whose sinker didn't always sink—an issue he fixed in 2016, when the pitch obediently followed the example set by Otero's attempts to swim. Otero got more ground balls than ever in his first year in Cleveland, and had the best year of career as a result. He can keep swimming in the big-league pool so long as the sinker stays sunk.

Danny Salazar   RHP

Born: 1/11/90   Age: 27   Bats: R   Throws: R   Height: 6'0"   Weight: 195   Entered Pro Ball: International Free Agent, 2006

YEAR	TEAM	LVL	AGE	W	L	SV	G	GS	IP	H	HR	BB/9	K/9	K	GB%	BABIP	WHIP	ERA	FIP	DRA	VORP	WARP	cFIP	MPH
2014	COH	AAA	24	4	6	0	11	11	60²	58	7	4.2	11.3	76	38%	.323	1.42	3.71	3.79	2.71	20.5	2.0	79	
2014	CLE	MLB	24	6	8	0	20	20	110	117	13	2.9	9.8	120	36%	.343	1.38	4.25	3.55	3.47	16.6	1.8	96	97.8
2015	CLE	MLB	25	14	10	0	30*	30	185	156	23	2.6	9.5	195	45%	.278	1.13	3.45	3.59	3.22	38.2	4.1	83	97.9
2016	CLE	MLB	26	11	6	0	25	25	137¹	121	16	4.1	10.6	161	49%	.307	1.34	3.87	3.70	3.12	34.2	3.5	83	97.5
2017	*CLE*	*MLB*	*27*	*11*	*7*	*0*	*26*	*26*	*148*	*136*	*20*	*3.8*	*10.2*	*167*	*42%*	*.302*	*1.36*	*3.91*	*4.04*	*4.19*	*17.4*	*1.8*	*95*	
2018	*CLE*	*MLB*	*28*	*9*	*9*	*0*	*27*	*27*	*163*	*153*	*24*	*4.1*	*10.9*	*197*	*42%*	*.315*	*1.39*	*4.16*	*4.14*	*4.50*	*16.4*	*1.7*	*102*	

Breakout: 22%   Improve: 46%   Collapse: 19%   Attrition: 10%   MLB: 86%   *Comparables: Alex Cobb, Drew Smyly, Francisco Liriano*

Salazar carried his improvements from 2015 into 2016—he just did so inconsistently, erratically and between injuries. His command had a way of coming and going, but when it was there things were good. Great, even! The 97 mph fastball was hot as ever, the changeup was strong and the sinker he'd worked into his arsenal in 2015 was still used to great effect. But the conditional "when his command was there" was key, and that certainly wasn't always the case, sometimes disappearing even when he seemed to be cruising. He was also sidelined at different points by an elbow issue and a forearm strain. Salazar has the potential to be one of the most dynamic starters in baseball. He also has a chance to be one of the most frustrating teases.

Bryan Shaw   RHP

Born: 11/8/87   Age: 29   Bats: B   Throws: R   Height: 6'1"   Weight: 220   Entered Pro Ball: Round 2, 2008 Draft (#73 overall)

YEAR	TEAM	LVL	AGE	W	L	SV	G	GS	IP	H	HR	BB/9	K/9	K	GB%	BABIP	WHIP	ERA	FIP	DRA	VORP	WARP	cFIP	MPH
2014	CLE	MLB	26	5	5	2	80	0	76¹	61	6	2.6	7.5	64	50%	.251	1.09	2.59	3.45	3.92	4.8	0.5	98	95.5
2015	CLE	MLB	27	3	3	2	74	0	64	59	8	2.7	7.6	54	47%	.279	1.22	2.95	3.98	4.18	3.8	0.4	101	94.3
2016	CLE	MLB	28	2	5	1	75	0	66²	56	8	3.8	9.3	69	56%	.284	1.26	3.24	3.90	3.71	9.3	1.0	87	95.9
2017	*CLE*	*MLB*	*29*	*3*	*3*	*5*	*53*	*0*	*56*	*54*	*8*	*3.5*	*8.4*	*53*	*40%*	*.293*	*1.35*	*4.30*	*4.40*	*4.52*	*2.9*	*0.3*	*100*	
2018	*CLE*	*MLB*	*30*	*2*	*1*	*2*	*33*	*0*	*35*	*35*	*5*	*4.0*	*8.5*	*33*	*40%*	*.302*	*1.44*	*4.49*	*4.47*	*4.84*	*0.8*	*0.1*	*110*	

Breakout: 34%   Improve: 55%   Collapse: 27%   Attrition: 20%   MLB: 96%   *Comparables: Eric O'Flaherty, Peter Moylan, Jonathan Broxton*

During an April game, the Tigers called umpires in to see if Shaw was using his wedding ring to illegally scuff the ball. He wasn't—he was wearing his ring on the mound just as he had for years, he said, happily married as ever. But the incident was perhaps foreshadowing for a shake-up in another contractual relationship in Shaw's life. Since he was traded to Cleveland in 2013, no pitcher had logged more innings from the team's bullpen. In 2016 that started to shift: Cleveland had a stronger bullpen with more options, Shaw had a few rough outings that stung and the result was finishing third on the list of bullpen innings. It wasn't that Shaw was overall worse as a pitcher—by most metrics, he was better!—it was simply that the situation was different. And really, what is marriage about if not staying faithful while the relationship evolves?

Josh Tomlin   RHP

Born: 10/19/84   Age: 32   Bats: R   Throws: R   Height: 6'1"   Weight: 190   Entered Pro Ball: Round 19, 2006 Draft (#581 overall)

YEAR	TEAM	LVL	AGE	W	L	SV	G	GS	IP	H	HR	BB/9	K/9	K	GB%	BABIP	WHIP	ERA	FIP	DRA	VORP	WARP	cFIP	MPH
2014	COH	AAA	29	2	1	0	6	6	40	26	5	2.2	7.4	33	37%	.210	0.90	2.25	4.08	3.05	12.0	1.2	91	
2014	CLE	MLB	29	6	9	0	25	16	104	120	18	1.2	8.1	94	39%	.320	1.29	4.76	4.03	3.58	14.1	1.6	93	91.3
2015	COH	AAA	30	1	2	0	4	4	21¹	25	3	0.4	7.2	17	43%	.328	1.22	4.22	3.53	2.59	6.4	0.7	83	
2015	CLE	MLB	30	7	2	0	10	10	65²	47	13	1.1	7.8	57	39%	.199	0.84	3.02	4.40	3.94	8.3	0.9	94	91.2
2016	CLE	MLB	31	13	9	0	30	29	174	186	36	1.0	6.1	118	44%	.276	1.19	4.40	4.84	4.17	23.0	2.4	105	89.9
2017	*CLE*	*MLB*	*32*	*12*	*9*	*0*	*29*	*29*	*174*	*185*	*30*	*2.0*	*6.9*	*133*	*43%*	*.291*	*1.28*	*4.53*	*4.67*	*4.84*	*7.9*	*0.8*	*100*	
2018	*CLE*	*MLB*	*33*	*9*	*10*	*0*	*27*	*27*	*164*	*174*	*30*	*2.1*	*7.2*	*131*	*43%*	*.292*	*1.29*	*4.74*	*4.71*	*5.09*	*6.8*	*0.7*	*120*	

Breakout: 18%   Improve: 45%   Collapse: 22%   Attrition: 15%   MLB: 83%   *Comparables: Jeff Francis, Claudio Vargas, Chris Capuano*

From a cursory glance at the simplest figures, Tomlin's spring appeared to put him on track for the best year of his career—through the end of June, he had a 9-1 record with a 3.32 ERA. But the peripherals behind those numbers were not nearly so encouraging, and that hot spring melted into a so-so summer. It soon became clear that 2016 would not be Tomlin's best year, but it would be the year in which Tomlin was the best at being himself. The two factors that have always defined him are walks (of which there are very few) and home runs (of which there are very many). With his precision more freakish than ever and even more time spent watching balls sail over the fence, he became the first pitcher in history with more home runs than walks over the course of a full career. Kind of a depressing way to reach the peak version of yourself, maybe, but self-actualization isn't always everything it's cracked up to be.

LINEOUTS

Hitters

NAME	POS	TEAM	LVL	AGE	PA	R	2B	3B	HR	RBI	BB	K	SB	CS	AVG/OBP/SLG	TAv	VORP	BABIP	BRR	FRAA	WARP
Jesus Aguilar	1B	COH	AAA	26	578	62	26	0	30	92	53	110	0	0	.247/.319/.472	.268	7.8	.255	-3.0	1B(120): -1.0, 3B(2): 0.3	0.7
	1B	CLE	MLB	26	6	0	0	0	0	0	0	1	0	0	.000/.000/.000	-.027	-1.7	.000	0.0	1B(7): -0.3	-0.2
Greg Allen	CF	LYN	A+	23	432	93	16	4	4	31	58	51	38	7	.298/.424/.402	.309	49.4	.338	13.1	CF(92): 12.9	6.4
	CF	AKR	AA	23	174	26	7	3	3	13	19	27	7	6	.290/.399/.441	.310	16.1	.336	2.3	CF(36): 0.3	1.8
Joey Butler	LF	COH	AAA	30	465	54	15	2	8	42	45	106	4	1	.240/.318/.344	.240	-0.4	.303	0.9	LF(60): 4.7, RF(37): 2.6	0.7
Marlon Byrd	RF	CLE	MLB	38	129	11	6	0	5	19	11	38	0	0	.270/.326/.452	.264	3.6	.347	0.6	RF(21): -1.3, LF(14): -0.3	0.2
Willi Castro	SS	LKC	A	19	548	68	21	8	7	49	19	96	16	11	.259/.286/.371	.249	13.6	.302	-1.8	SS(119): 0.2	1.2
Collin Cowgill	RF	CLE	MLB	30	14	0	0	0	0	0	2	7	0	0	.083/.214/.083	.088	-2.1	.200	0.1	RF(8): -0.2	-0.2
	RF	COH	AAA	30	407	46	17	1	4	30	34	85	7	2	.234/.311/.320	.229	-2.2	.294	0.6	CF(56): 0.1, RF(29): 5.2	0.4
Logan Ice	C	MHV	A-	21	154	13	7	0	2	8	23	38	0	0	.198/.329/.302	.257	5.9	.264	0.5	C(33): -0.3	0.6
Erik Kratz	C	HOU	MLB	36	30	0	1	0	0	0	1	14	0	0	.069/.100/.103	.064	-4.8	.133	-0.1	C(13): 0.5, P(1): -0.0	-0.5
	C	SLC	AAA	36	41	6	3	0	0	7	1	12	0	0	.231/.268/.308	.218	0.4	.333	0.6	C(8): 0.3	0.1
	C	PIT	MLB	36	57	3	1	0	1	4	0	18	0	0	.107/.107/.179	.098	-6.5	.135	0.3	C(17): -0.2, 1B(1): -0.0	-0.7
	C	BUF	AAA	36	68	6	1	0	0	1	7	11	0	0	.155/.269/.172	.162	-4.5	.191	-0.5	C(19): 3.4	-0.1
Tyler Krieger	2B	LKC	A	22	299	51	13	4	3	35	29	66	15	8	.313/.385/.427	.293	14.7	.401	0.3	2B(52): -4.7	1.1
	2B	LYN	A+	22	257	33	13	4	2	23	28	52	6	7	.282/.369/.405	.287	14.2	.355	-0.1	2B(56): -2.0	1.3
Mark Mathias	2B	LYN	A+	21	490	70	39	1	5	60	48	87	9	1	.274/.359/.405	.281	30.1	.331	4.3	2B(69): 4.3, 3B(26): 1.9	3.8
Adam Moore	C	COH	AAA	32	329	35	14	0	7	31	26	63	0	0	.247/.316/.365	.239	5.3	.293	-1.3	C(77): -3.7, 1B(1): -0.0	0.2
	C	CLE	MLB	32	5	0	0	0	0	0	0	4	0	0	.000/.000/.000	.014	-1.0	.000	0.0	C(9): -0.3	-0.1
Mike Papi	DH	LYN	A+	23	173	22	9	0	7	18	30	42	0	1	.236/.370/.450	.295	8.5	.280	-0.9	RF(18): -4.0, LF(11): 1.0	0.6
	DH	AKR	AA	23	306	33	16	2	8	40	41	72	4	0	.228/.340/.398	.279	9.0	.282	-2.2	LF(40): 11.4, RF(23): -3.8	1.8
Guillermo Quiroz	C	COH	AAA	34	297	41	17	0	11	38	16	68	0	0	.264/.314/.447	.266	9.5	.311	-2.8	C(55): -12.2, 1B(12): -0.9	-0.4
Daniel Robertson	LF	SEA	MLB	30	21	1	1	0	0	1	1	3	0	1	.263/.300/.316	.193	-0.7	.313	-0.1	LF(6): -0.1, RF(3): 0.1	-0.1
	LF	TAC	AAA	30	460	50	19	7	6	46	42	41	13	2	.287/.357/.412	.293	27	.305	-0.7	2B(38): -1.6, LF(35): 1.8	3.4
Nellie Rodriguez	1B	AKR	AA	22	579	66	28	2	26	85	75	186	1	0	.250/.352/.474	.299	25.6	.339	-2.6	1B(123): 0.7	2.8
Giovanny Urshela	3B	COH	AAA	24	491	54	24	1	8	57	15	58	0	0	.274/.294/.380	.236	-1.6	.294	-4.3	3B(104): 6.1, SS(5): -0.3	0.4
Luke Wakamatsu	SS	MHV	A-	19	77	4	5	0	0	9	6	12	1	1	.232/.312/.304	.242	1.2	.281	-0.5	SS(17): 0.4	0.2

"I'm 27 years old, I've no money and no prospects, I'm already a burden." That's Charlotte in Jane Austen's *Pride and Prejudice*, but maybe also **Jesus Aguilar**, if you swap "money" for "money tool." Being a Quad-A first baseman nearing your 27th birthday isn't really so different from being an unmarried woman of the same age in nineteenth-century England. ❖ Glove-first outfielder **Greg Allen** took his midseason promotion to Double-A like he takes most balls hit his way—smoothly and in stride. ❖ **Joey Butler** spent the entirety of his age-30 season at Triple-A, and his raw numbers were still worse than any he'd posted during his brief time in the majors in years prior. ❖ "You have to be an idiot to test positive for PEDs, and I was one of those idiots," **Marlon Byrd** said in 2013. It's unclear what he thinks of people who test positive for PEDs *twice*, but Byrd became one of those people in 2016, with a 162-game suspension that likely signaled the end of his career. ❖ **Willi Castro** offers organizational depth at shortstop to an organization that already has depth at shortstop, and the depth he offers is kind of shallow, anyway. ❖ The bad news for **Collin Cowgill** is that he struck out in half of his 2016 plate appearances. But because of how little time he spent in the majors, that was only seven strikeouts, which is … also bad news. Mobius strip! ❖ "Cold as fire, baby / Hot as (**Logan) Ice** / If you've ever been to heaven, this is twice as nice." Britney Spears was a little overzealous in this scouting report of the switch-hitting catcher, but given how he hit in his final season at Oregon State you can kind of see where she's coming from. ❖ Teams always need catching depth, and that often seems to mean they need **Erik Kratz**. Three of them in 2016, to be exact. ❖ Bouncing back from 2015 shoulder surgery, **Tyler Krieger** showed off the offensive polish that was a selling point of his game in college. But there's no power there at all, and he might remind some of Joey Wendle … take that as you will. ❖ Last year, we wrote that **Mark Mathias** would have to rake in full-season ball to earn a whole comment and not a lineout; he was solidly above average, but not quite strong enough to earn that comment. ❖ For several years and several teams now, **Adam Moore** has been nothing but organizational filler. If there was ever a situation to give him a chance to change that it was the disaster zone that was Cleveland at catcher in 2016, but Moore couldn't make anything happen. ❖ The retirement of David Ortiz means **Mike** is now baseball's biggest **Papi**, but being a bat-first guy who had long cool stretches at the plate last year presents its own set of difficulties. ❖ With eight more round-trippers in 2017, **Guillermo Quiroz**—who hits like a backup and frames like an emergency catcher—will have more Triple-A homers than major league hits. ❖ After flipping his calendar to 2017, **Daniel Robertson** realized this was the year he would not be alone, as his namesake in the Rays organization is on the verge of the majors. Of course, with only two weeks of MLB time last season and a career .325 slugging percentage, this Robertson might find himself alone anyway. ❖ In his first season at Double-A, **Nellie Rodriguez** set career-highs in each of the the Three True Outcomes, and if he could just lower that strikeout rate he could be worth getting excited about. ❖ In 2015 **Giovanny Urshela**'s sharp defense earned him a chance in the majors; in 2016 his hapless bat showed there are some offensive sins simply too great to be atoned for by any defense. ❖ A shoulder injury sidelined **Luke Wakamatsu** for much of 2016; he'll hope to leave the dugout more often than his father, Don, in 2017.

Pitchers

NAME	TEAM	LVL	AGE	W	L	SV	G	GS	IP	H	HR	BB/9	K/9	K	GB%	BABIP	WHIP	ERA	FIP	DRA	VORP	WARP	cFIP	MPH
Austin Adams	COH	AAA	29	2	4	8	34	0	37²	44	1	2.2	9.8	41	50%	.384	1.41	4.54	2.13	2.91	8.6	0.9	80	
	CLE	MLB	29	0	0	0	19	0	18¹	27	5	3.4	8.3	17	45%	.373	1.85	9.82	5.94	4.57	0.8	0.1	105	98.4
Shane Bieber	MHV	A-	21	0	0	0	9	8	24	10	0	0.8	7.9	21	56%	.164	0.50	0.38	1.90	2.32	7.7	0.8	79	
Joseph Colon	COH	AAA	26	0	1	0	20	0	22	8	0	4.9	8.6	21	53%	.157	0.91	0.82	3.03	4.36	1.5	0.2	96	
	CLE	MLB	26	1	3	0	11	0	10	12	2	6.3	9.0	10	33%	.323	1.90	7.20	5.81	5.37	-0.4	0.0	114	96.9
T.J. House	CLE	MLB	26	0	0	0	4	0	2²	6	0	0.0	6.8	2	27%	.545	2.25	3.38	2.73	4.65	0.1	0.0	108	93.0
	COH	AAA	26	5	3	1	33	12	72¹	89	6	5.4	6.2	50	52%	.344	1.82	3.98	4.73	7.59	-18.9	-1.9	117	
Hoby Milner	REA	AA	25	5	3	5	38	0	49	41	3	2.2	9.9	54	48%	.292	1.08	1.84	2.93	1.38	18.3	2.0	81	
	LEH	AAA	25	0	1	1	11	0	16	16	2	1.7	12.4	22	36%	.350	1.19	4.50	2.61	1.23	6.6	0.7	77	
Shawn Morimando	AKR	AA	23	10	3	0	16	16	93¹	77	5	3.5	7.0	73	48%	.270	1.21	3.09	3.74	3.15	20.2	2.2	100	
	CLE	MLB	23	0	0	0	2	0	4²	9	2	9.6	9.6	5	41%	.467	3.00	11.57	9.75	4.99	0.0	0.0	108	94.6
	COH	AAA	23	5	2	0	11	11	59	64	5	3.2	7.0	46	39%	.330	1.44	3.51	3.88	4.61	4.8	0.5	109	
Adam Plutko	AKR	AA	24	3	3	0	13	13	71²	64	5	1.5	7.9	63	35%	.289	1.06	3.27	3.01	2.38	21.6	2.3	89	
	COH	AAA	24	6	5	0	15	15	90	87	8	3.4	6.7	67	34%	.293	1.34	4.10	3.97	6.64	-12.9	-1.3	122	
	CLE	MLB	24	0	0	0	2	0	3²	5	1	4.9	7.4	3	23%	.333	1.91	7.36	6.65	5.55	-0.2	0.0	114	92.9

Austin Adams and his high-90s fastball have gotten clobbered in the majors, but the 30-year-old will probably get at least a couple more chances to stick. ❖ **Dylan Baker** has now been sidelined by ankle surgery, Tommy John surgery and complications from Tommy John surgery, but the Indians believed in him enough to protect him from the Rule 5 draft with a 40-man roster spot. ❖ Baby, baby, baby, oh / Like baby, baby, baby, no / Thought **Shane Bieber**'s high floor and low ceiling would always be mine. (And they are for now, if you're Cleveland, with his solid command and otherwise generic stuff.) ❖ **Joseph Colon** is like a semicolon in that he only pitched a portion of the season due to drug suspension and is only a portion of Bartolo, both in ability and in size. ❖ Shoulder woes kept lefty **Tim Cooney** off the mound entirely last season, but if he's healthy this spring solid fastball command and an effective changeup will make him a viable candidate to eat innings at the end of a rotation. ❖ A step back to Triple-A that didn't go so well has **T.J. House** looking homeless in terms of major-league opportunities. ❖ **Hoby Milner** stopped starting, moved to the bullpen and began throwing his fastball/slider combo sidearm, which has given him a chance to develop into a useful LOOGY. ❖ The more a man do, the better his chances of sticking as a starter: a lesson for **Shawn Morimando**, whose future is looking more and more like it will be the bullpen. ❖ Pluto: a dwarf planet on the fringes of the solar system. **Adam Plutko**: an archetypical fifth starter destined for the fringes of the rotation.

COLORADO ROCKIES

Essay by Patrick Dubuque

Player comments by Eric Garcia-McKinley and BP staff

It's a strange thing, being a baseball fan. We live in a postmodern marketing age where companies no longer just attempt to seize our time and attention; waning are the days of the billboard-flecked highway and the mid-dinner telemarketing call. Instead what corporations most want is for people to care, to create user-based content and join crusades, to graft the product directly onto one's identity. And yet baseball has been doing this forever, getting people to pay to wear advertising for the local franchise. The caring came first, of course, but the integration has been seamless. People have been happy to concede it.

Imagine it: Tens of thousands of people fight traffic and parking to assemble in a concrete building, pay money for the right to fade into a muddy watercolor background and sip beer five times the price of the same stuff sitting in their fridge at home. There, they voluntarily place their happiness into the hands of 25 young men who do not know them. They make appropriate noises to appropriate stimuli, boo the pickoff moves and cry lustily at the entreaties of fake pipe organs, largely to no effect. They create little home field advantage for their heroes, wound their cable-bolstered owners little with the threat of non-attendance. The team does not listen to their talk-radio demands regarding bullpen usage. They are powerless. All they can do is be happy if their chosen team wins, or sad if they lose.

But fans aren't alone in being buffeted by the winds of fate. Among all the team sports, baseball is a universe of chance. The sharp line drive finds or flees the outstretched glove; the bunt catches the invisible berm of the chalk and rolls fair; a cell in the tendon separates from that of the bone, and then another. The best laid plans of player, manager, president all can be torn apart by the force of a batter's swing, three thousand miles away.

Nowhere is this powerlessness more on display than in the city of Denver, where the Colorado Rockies have—for seven post-World Series years—beat against the current of their own mediocrity. Owners Dick and Charlie Monfort have implemented one plan after another in an attempt to conquer the cold, thin air of the mountains, chasing power, outfield defense, strikeout pitchers, wormburners, free agents, farm systems, Juan Pierre and Dante Bichette. Their inconsistency in approach is rivaled only by their consistency in culture, matched perhaps only by the Minnesota Twins, in

ROCKIES PROSPECTUS
2016 W-L: 75-87, 3RD IN NL WEST

Pythag	.491	16th	DER	.683	28th
RS/G	5.22	2nd	B-Age	27.8	7th
RA/G	5.31	28th	P-Age	27.5	7th
TAv	.264	11th	Salary	$112.6M	17th
BRR	11.12	6th	M$/MW	$3.8M	11th
TAv-P	.268	19th	DL Days	1177	22nd
FIP	4.42	24th	$ on DL	11%	11th

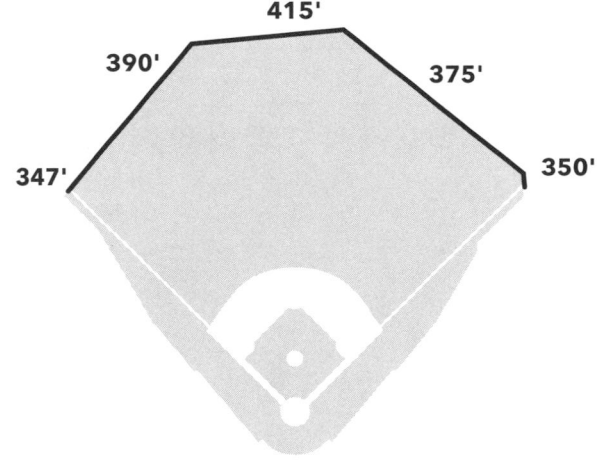

Outfield wall profile: **8'** to **14'**

Three-Year Park Factors

Runs	Runs/RH	Runs/LH	HR/RH	HR/LH
114	116	112	112	107

Top Hitter WARP	7.8	Nolan Arenado
Top Pitcher WARP	3.7	Jon Gray
Top Prospect		Brendan Rodgers

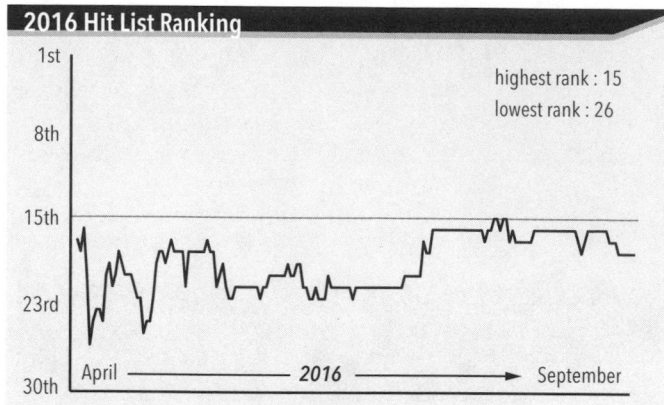

2016 Hit List Ranking

highest rank : 15
lowest rank : 26

April — 2016 → September

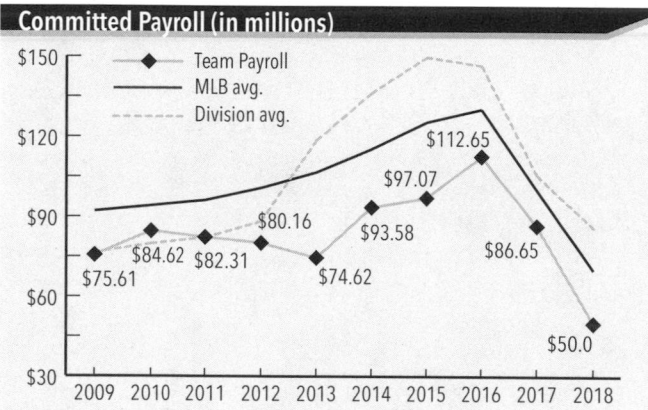

Committed Payroll (in millions)

◆ Team Payroll
— MLB avg.
---- Division avg.

$75.61 $84.62 $82.31 $80.16 $74.62 $93.58 $97.07 $112.65 $86.65 $50.0

2009 2010 2011 2012 2013 2014 2015 2016 2017 2018

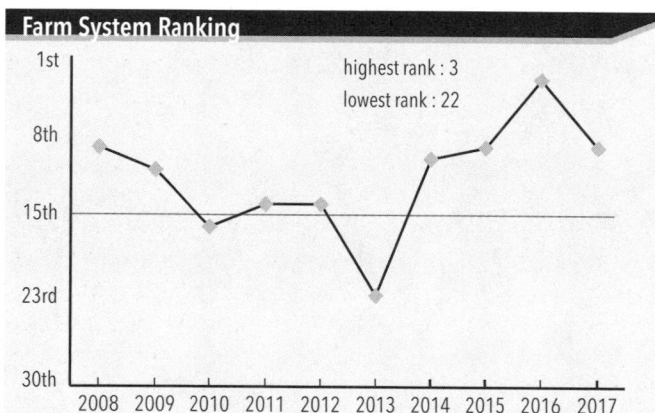

Farm System Ranking

highest rank : 3
lowest rank : 22

2008 2009 2010 2011 2012 2013 2014 2015 2016 2017

Personnel

General Manager:
Jeff Bridich

Senior Director, Player Development:
Zach Wilson

Assistant General Manager:
Zach Rosenthal

Manager:
Bud Black

BP Alumni:
Marat Biyashev

assembling front office personnel and imposing a rigid, top-down set of corporate values.

The team's latest Master Plan has not fully congealed as this essay went to press, but we can surmise it. It began with signing Ian Desmond, a shortstop converted to outfield being converted yet again to first base, to a generous five-year deal. His plunge down the defensive spectrum, combined with a bat above average only at its very top, marks the rare example of a baseball team forsaking half a contract's value the moment it's driven off the lot. Due next is another eventual middling free agent of the Gerardo Parra or Justin Morneau mold, which will end terribly if the Desmond contract doesn't first. A few role players, guys like Ryan Raburn and John Axford, signed as stopgaps and providing replacement value. For the rest: kind words and hopes, an ad campaign based on young men being extraordinarily genial. No change in course, no overarching vision that provides the skeleton to a good essay for a Baseball Prospectus annual. Just a quiet, unswerving march into fourth place.

Fans of the Rockies have watched this with the same tired, grim acceptance of the farmer watching their crops drown in a monsoon. Despite chafing with an uncaring ownership group and an unreflective front office, they abide. The team, despite finishing well-below .500 for the sixth consecutive season, finished eleventh in the majors in attendance.

But not this year, the learned fan might cry: this year is different. The Monforts have sworn that they will increase payroll, which ranked 19th in the league, and is buoyed by the impending departure of Jorge De La Rosa's $12.5 million salary. They do this because the team's young nucleus has begun to form: joining All-Star Nolan Arenado and former All-Star Carlos Gonzalez are Trevor Story, David Dahl, and sudden batting champ DJ LeMahieu. The farm system, for years a source of cautious optimism, is ripening.

And on the mound, the Rockies showed a level of promise unthinkable since the days of Ubaldo. Jon Gray proved that there could be such a thing as a Rockies pitching prospect, striking out more than a batter an inning. Chad Bettis, Tyler Anderson and Tyler Chatwood provided the sort of reliable, groundball-oriented pitching that always should have worked in Coors and never did. Between them they allowed less than a homer per nine innings, a moral victory of the first degree. The bullpen... well, you can never predict bullpens anyway. But the names on the roster are by no means demoralizing.

So it goes. Passages like these are the benediction of every baseball season, its opening sales pitch: hope. Hope is what baseball sells better than nearly anyone: *This could be the year. You could be here for the beginning of it. The story won't restart for the latecomers.* And its reward: the World Series Championship, the taste of champagne savored vicariously. It's this chase for success, and particularly a success so clearly defined, that makes baseball the great American pastime. People spend their whole lives chasing that moment of euphoria, aligning themselves with anything—a political party, a corporate conglomerate, a number on a roulette wheel, a bunch of people wearing blue shirts on a television screen—in order to feel it. Sometimes they do. Often, they do not.

What they could really use, whether they know it or not, are the Colorado Rockies. The existence of the Rockies is a rejection of the traditional Western mores regarding purpose and success. Within them lies something deeper, something more tranquil. To learn to be a Rockies fan is to learn how to live—as much as one can—a peaceful, happy life. There is a Rockies Way which is really just The Way, as best as anything can approximate it: It is the Tao.

I will try to explain.

The Tao, or the Way, is named as such because it cannot be named. The Tao is everything; it is beyond our abilities to describe. So we use the word Tao as kind of a placeholder for it, although you can use "the Rockies." The goal of its primary thinker, Lao-tzu, was to create a philosophy not designed for the heavens, but for the rice fields; it is a model for survival. Its focus is not to achieve some arbitrary definition of success, or to create some legacy. The legacy already exists; it is the natural way of things. Like Rousseau got credit for speculating two thousand years later, Lao-tzu claimed that the majority of human effort, the things we try to create and to foster in our lives and our societies, are actually interfering with that natural order. The happy person is not someone who fights against the external world, but allows themselves to be carried along by it, to accept it.

Powerlessness and uselessness are, in such a philosophy, not weaknesses but virtues; they can only help one become independent of the futile worries that are the endless die rolls of existence. Power would appear to be a valuable tool, to be used with restraint and righteousness; and yet, according to the Taoists, such noble attempts have historically only led to selfishness, want and war. The Rockies offer that unique opportunity for disempowerment. Their exclusivity and dismissal make a cleaner break for the fan than any other franchise. Fans can still empathize with players when they fail, but it's harder for them to take it on as their own failing, their own deserved sadness, even if it also detaches them from the ecstasy. This is a net benefit; the avoidance of unhappiness is, on the whole, of far greater importance than obtaining happiness, especially in a sport where it blesses only one city out of thirty. Moderation in emotions is the ultimate goal, and no team is more moderate than the Rockies.

It's not easy, of course, to abandon one's pride and accept The Way. One of the most difficult pursuits to give up, particularly for the purchaser of this book, is wisdom for its own sake. Intellectualism can often be its own form of a thirst for power, to understand and then control the forces that are beyond us. It would seem like understanding and wisdom would be innocent at worst and incredibly helpful at best; the Taoists would counter that the drive for knowledge, much like political power, has had its share of disastrous consequences. More than anything, they mistrusted intellectuals, who hoarded knowledge and then made it inaccessible by clouding it in impenetrable language. It's when this knowledge serves no practical purpose, when it pretends at wisdom while failing to actually offer solutions for the problems of life, that the Taoists dislike it.

In our example, the fault of this quest for knowledge lies in advanced statistics. Here, knowledge can only bring stress and dissatisfaction. To Lao-tzu, all knowledge led one only to unattainable happiness; he considers ignorance to be a virtue, akin to the innocence of childhood. In order to fulfill his anti-intellectual standard, we'd have to go back in time and throw Henry Chadwick and his box scores onto an ocean liner for England. A compromise: There's nothing wrong with learning for the sake of adding to one's own enjoyment, and refining one's understanding of the game to achieve that end. Where it becomes problematic is when that knowledge makes it more difficult to accept powerlessness; it's never easy to watch someone who seems less wise obtain a position of authority.

Nor do the Rockies offer the casual fan another common pitfall toward happiness: action. The Rockies do not confuse motion with progress; they do not tend to make moves for the sake of moves. Their underwhelming offseasons give fans little kindling for the hot stove and its corresponding industry of Baseball Analysis. Baseball is not built for this sort of unhealthy myopia, really: seasons are designed to crawl, for no one moment to be particularly important in their grand scheme. Worrying and overreacting about every little detail in life leads to conflict with The Way and, with it, misery. Far better to act slowly, or even not at all, rather than to work against one's self.

Instead of worrying, or getting angry, or getting hopeless—those typical activities of the sports fan—The Way encourages a different reaction to the constant misery that is Rockies Baseball and also the rest of life: to laugh. Don't fight fire with fire, the Tao Te Ching warns: fight fire with water, reverse or disperse. Baseball is such an effective palliative to life's repetitive woes specifically because of its absurdity; it's the perfect example of the catharsis of Greek tragedy without sticking to the soul for days. Finding light within darkness is probably the single greatest trait of Taoism in a post-existential world, and this trait is why it's built to be so flexible and (at times) nonsensical. Finding meaning in tragedy is fruitless and often destructive; so it is with bad baseball teams.

In fact, though the Taoists are shy when it comes to social functions, preferring to avoid governments, instead hanging out in the wilderness and standing beneath waterfalls for fun, their vision for a powerless collective comes very close to the ideal conceptualization of what Rockies fans could really use: a support network. Avoiding desire doesn't prevent people from helping each other. After all, Taoism was designed to help people stay steady and be there for each other. Along with frugality and humility, the third of the Three Treasures of Taoism is compassion. Compassion fosters empathy, and sets up the practicality of wisdom; we can only be wise if we understand how our actions affect other people. But while baseball tries to pull us onto the field, to empathize with the players, it's really the other fans that form the community of the game.

And so the first half of this essay was a bit of a feint. All of it is true: the Colorado Rockies of 2018, if not 2017, portend to be a better-than-average baseball team. But that's not important, according to Lao-tzu. Winning (and its inextricable twin, caring about winning) is the ultimate distraction, and its pursuit will end in each fan losing their soul. "There is no disaster greater," he writes in the Tao Te

Ching, "than not knowing contentment with what one has; no greater sin than the desire for acquisition." So count up your prospects, add up their future WARP if you find it diverting. But do not borrow happiness against this conjured future. Enjoy baseball as it is, no matter what it proves to be, rather than what you want it to be. Because the game, especially the mild variant that the Rockies have mastered, is itself The Way. Find happiness in it, and in the people who share it with you. And when Jeff Hoffman gives up a HR/9 over two, be like water. ∎

—Patrick Dubuque is an author
of Baseball Prospectus

HITTERS

Nolan Arenado   3B

Born: 4/16/91   Age: 26   Bats: R   Throws: R   Height: 6'2"   Weight: 205   Entered Pro Ball: Round 2, 2009 Draft (#59 overall)

YEAR	TEAM	LVL	AGE	PA	R	2B	3B	HR	RBI	BB	K	SB	CS	AVG/OBP/SLG	TAv	VORP	BABIP	BRR	FRAA	WARP
2014	CSP	AAA	23	20	2	2	0	0	3	0	3	0	0	.350/.350/.450	.246	0.5	.412	0.1	3B(4): -0.0	0.0
2014	COL	MLB	23	467	58	34	2	18	61	25	58	2	1	.287/.328/.500	.273	20.5	.294	1.3	3B(111): 18.5	4.3
2015	COL	MLB	24	665	97	43	4	42	130	34	110	2	5	.287/.323/.575	.299	47.1	.284	1.5	3B(157): 22.6	7.5
2016	COL	MLB	25	696	116	35	6	41	133	68	103	2	3	.294/.362/.570	.304	52.4	.293	-0.9	3B(160): 22.9	7.8
2017	*COL*	*MLB*	*26*	*583*	*74*	*36*	*3*	*29*	*91*	*38*	*86*	*2*	*2*	*.288/.334/.528*	*.277*	*26.8*	*.293*	*-1.5*	*3B 16*	*4.0*
2018	*COL*	*MLB*	*27*	*570*	*83*	*36*	*2*	*31*	*94*	*41*	*85*	*2*	*2*	*.289/.341/.544*	*.288*	*29.7*	*.292*	*0.6*	*3B 15*	*4.9*

Breakout: 1%   Improve: 47%   Collapse: 1%   Attrition: 5%   MLB: 100%   *Comparables: Puddin Head Jones, Richie Hebner, Eric Chavez*

He got better. In his first three seasons, Arenado was what might be called effectively impatient. He swung a bunch and didn't walk much, but he was still able to put the barrel on the ball and limit strikeouts. Arenado changed in 2016. From 2013–2015, he swung at 54.1 percent of the pitches he saw. In 2016, he swung at 48.1 percent. The result was a walk rate that nearly doubled to 9.8 percent and an OBP that rose about 40 points. Arenado was also able to make contact just as much as before while replicating the power he exhibited in 2015. His defense was also excellent, as usual. The problem now—and it's not much of a problem—is that Arenado doesn't have any more flaws left to improve upon.

Brandon Barnes   PH

Born: 5/15/86   Age: 31   Bats: R   Throws: R   Height: 6'2"   Weight: 210   Entered Pro Ball: Round 6, 2005 Draft (#194 overall)

YEAR	TEAM	LVL	AGE	PA	R	2B	3B	HR	RBI	BB	K	SB	CS	AVG/OBP/SLG	TAv	VORP	BABIP	BRR	FRAA	WARP
2014	COL	MLB	28	313	37	17	4	8	27	15	100	5	4	.257/.293/.425	.235	-1.1	.364	0.2	RF(55): 0.6 • LF(18): -2.1	-0.4
2015	ABQ	AAA	29	143	19	6	0	5	12	10	34	7	3	.205/.266/.364	.215	-2.1	.237	0.4	CF(28): -0.2 • LF(1): -0.1	-0.3
2015	COL	MLB	29	281	30	13	2	2	17	21	67	4	2	.251/.314/.341	.229	-1.0	.332	1.7	LF(75): 1.2 • RF(21): -1.1	0.0
2016	COL	MLB	30	109	10	6	2	0	8	3	30	1	2	.220/.250/.320	.198	-2.5	.314	1.7	LF(29): 1.4 • CF(13): -0.5	-0.2
2016	ABQ	AAA	30	255	30	13	2	5	32	15	58	11	5	.282/.323/.416	.243	1.9	.352	0.9	RF(30): -0.1 • LF(15): 2.1	0.3
2017	*COL*	*MLB*	*31*	*250*	*28*	*13*	*1*	*6*	*25*	*15*	*68*	*6*	*4*	*.251/.300/.391*	*.221*	*-1.0*	*.325*	*0.6*	*LF 0, RF -1*	*-0.2*
2018	*COL*	*MLB*	*32*	*250*	*27*	*13*	*1*	*5*	*26*	*15*	*70*	*5*	*3*	*.243/.294/.378*	*.231*	*-0.7*	*.320*	*0.9*	*LF 0, RF -1*	*-0.2*

Breakout: 0%   Improve: 28%   Collapse: 12%   Attrition: 22%   MLB: 69%   *Comparables: Elliot Johnson, Cory Sullivan, Corey Patterson*

The energy that showed itself on the field and in the clubhouse made Barnes an effective fourth outfielder—one that could fill in at each of the three grassy spots. But the incremental gains Barnes made in his plate discipline during 2015 disappeared last season. In addition to his dreadful OBP, he's never exhibited power and what has shown up on his stat page is overstated: Two of the 10 home runs Barnes has hit over the last three years were of the inside-the-park persuasion. Barnes lost his spot on the 40-man roster in August and received his release in September. With his 20s behind him and deteriorating skills at the plate, success now means turning an invitation to spring training into a job as a fifth outfielder.

Charlie Blackmon   RF

Born: 7/1/86   Age: 30   Bats: L   Throws: L   Height: 6'3"   Weight: 210   Entered Pro Ball: Round 2, 2008 Draft (#72 overall)

YEAR	TEAM	LVL	AGE	PA	R	2B	3B	HR	RBI	BB	K	SB	CS	AVG/OBP/SLG	TAv	VORP	BABIP	BRR	FRAA	WARP
2014	COL	MLB	27	648	82	27	3	19	72	31	96	28	10	.288/.335/.440	.260	14.1	.315	0.0	RF(73): -4.6 • CF(69): -0.9	1.2
2015	COL	MLB	28	682	93	31	9	17	58	46	112	43	13	.287/.347/.450	.272	31.1	.325	3.4	CF(147): -5.1 • LF(14): -1.1	2.7
2016	COL	MLB	29	641	111	35	5	29	82	43	102	17	9	.324/.381/.552	.311	57.3	.350	4.2	CF(138): -6.7	5.2
2017	*COL*	*MLB*	*30*	*624*	*88*	*31*	*5*	*19*	*72*	*40*	*105*	*25*	*9*	*.286/.339/.458*	*.260*	*23.0*	*.317*	*2.0*	*CF -1*	*1.7*
2018	*COL*	*MLB*	*31*	*558*	*71*	*28*	*4*	*18*	*72*	*37*	*99*	*21*	*8*	*.283/.340/.461*	*.267*	*21.1*	*.315*	*2.3*	*CF -1*	*2.2*

Breakout: 0%   Improve: 40%   Collapse: 9%   Attrition: 7%   MLB: 96%   *Comparables: Angel Pagan, Lorenzo Cain, Marlon Byrd*

It was easy to pinpoint the reasons for Blackmon's improvement in 2015: he didn't swing as much. The patience that edged into passivity led to more pitches seen and a higher on-base percentage. Easy peasy, at least from the analyst's point of view. It's a bit more difficult to identify what led to his 2016 results, which have him as perhaps the best centerfielder in the National League and a top-five centerfielder in baseball by WARP. He finished the year with the exact same walk rate as 2015, but he was more aggressive at the plate. Rather than mere passivity, Blackmon seems to have learned zone awareness. Couple this with his hit tendencies—he hit more line drives off fastballs and more fly balls off secondary pitches—and we get a pretty good idea of Blackmon's growth. He's no longer a Coors Field creation, but a centerfielder almost any contender would welcome, which is good timing as he progresses through his arbitration years and the Rockies' outfield situation gets more crowded.

Stephen Cardullo   UT

Born: 8/31/87 Age: 29 Bats: R Throws: R Height: 6'0" Weight: 215 Entered Pro Ball: Round 24, 2010 Draft (#721 overall)

YEAR	TEAM	LVL	AGE	PA	R	2B	3B	HR	RBI	BB	K	SB	CS	AVG/OBP/SLG	TAv	VORP	BABIP	BRR	FRAA	WARP
2016	ABQ	AAA	28	452	71	26	5	17	72	37	58	6	3	.308/.367/.522	.295	27.1	.321	1.7	LF(79): 2.8 • RF(11): -0.3	3.1
2016	COL	MLB	28	59	5	3	1	2	6	3	12	0	0	.214/.254/.411	.206	-2.7	.238	-0.3	1B(15): 0.2 • RF(3): -0.1	-0.3
2017	*COL*	*MLB*	*29*	*65*	*8*	*3*	*0*	*2*	*9*	*5*	*11*	*1*	*0*	*.276/.335/.475*	*.266*	*1.4*	*.302*	*-0.1*	*1B -0*	*0.1*
2018	*COL*	*MLB*	*30*	*213*	*28*	*11*	*1*	*9*	*30*	*16*	*39*	*1*	*1*	*.274/.335/.477*	*.272*	*5.0*	*.301*	*-0.3*	*1B -1*	*0.4*

Breakout: 0%   Improve: 13%   Collapse: 10%   Attrition: 16%   MLB: 35%   *Comparables: Daniel Nava, Chris Denorfia, Jamie Hoffmann*

A 24th round draft pick out of Florida State in 2010, Cardullo played a season and a half of rookie ball in Missoula before exiting to that liminal space called unaffiliated baseball. Cardullo began the summer of 2012 playing for the Frontier League's London Rippers, and he played for them until they folded in the middle of the season. (The league's owners decided to fill the violent sobriquet void by creating a traveling team called the Road Warriors.) Cardullo filled out 2012 with the league's Florence Freedom. After that, Cardullo found some welcome stability. He played the next three seasons for the Canadian-American Association's Rockland Boulders, and well enough to earn a minor-league contract from the Rockies prior to the 2016 season. In late August, with the need for someone to play first base and the inclination to acknowledge a consistently good season, the Rockies brought him 450 miles up Interstate 25 to Denver. He hit a couple of dingers—both on the same day, no less—but that's clearly not the important part of this story.

David Dahl   CF

Born: 4/1/94 Age: 23 Bats: L Throws: R Height: 6'2" Weight: 195 Entered Pro Ball: Round 1, 2012 Draft (#10 overall)

YEAR	TEAM	LVL	AGE	PA	R	2B	3B	HR	RBI	BB	K	SB	CS	AVG/OBP/SLG	TAv	VORP	BABIP	BRR	FRAA	WARP
2014	MOD	A+	20	125	14	8	2	4	14	5	27	3	0	.267/.296/.467	.269	6.9	.315	1.7	CF(25): 3.3 • CF(4): 3.3	1.4
2014	ASH	A	20	422	69	33	6	10	41	23	65	18	5	.309/.347/.500	.279	23.6	.348	3.3	CF(70): 11.8 • LF(7): 0.5	3.7
2015	BOI	A-	21	24	1	1	0	0	1	0	9	0	0	.125/.125/.167	.113	-2.8	.200	0.2	CF(6): 0.5	-0.2
2015	NBR	AA	21	302	46	16	3	6	24	11	72	22	7	.278/.304/.417	.265	14.8	.352	5.0	CF(62): -4.5 • RF(3): -0.4	1.1
2016	NBR	AA	22	332	53	21	2	13	45	39	85	16	5	.278/.367/.500	.311	28.6	.351	3.7	CF(38): -1.8 • RF(19): 0.2	2.8
2016	ABQ	AAA	22	68	17	6	2	5	16	6	11	1	2	.484/.529/.887	.426	14.4	.543	0.8	CF(11): -1.5 • LF(3): -0.2	1.3
2016	COL	MLB	22	237	42	12	4	7	24	15	59	5	0	.315/.359/.500	.289	14.5	.404	2.1	LF(54): -2.3 • CF(6): 0.3	1.3
2017	*COL*	*MLB*	*23*	*558*	*67*	*30*	*5*	*19*	*70*	*33*	*146*	*17*	*5*	*.272/.315/.458*	*.253*	*14.9*	*.341*	*1.8*	*LF -6, CF 0*	*0.5*
2018	*COL*	*MLB*	*24*	*567*	*71*	*32*	*6*	*19*	*75*	*38*	*146*	*18*	*5*	*.276/.327/.468*	*.265*	*18.8*	*.346*	*2.2*	*LF -6, CF 0*	*1.4*

Breakout: 4%   Improve: 27%   Collapse: 5%   Attrition: 11%   MLB: 45%   *Comparables: Randal Grichuk, Michael Saunders, Marcell Ozuna*

Talk about making an entrance. Dahl debuted on July 25 and notched a hit in 34 out of his first 37 games, including his first 17 in a row. His athleticism and glove played well in left field, although Dahl is underutilized at any outfield spot other than center because of his speed—which also allows him to be a plus baserunner. The highlight of his season, and the moment that shouted "I belong here," came during the penultimate weekend when he took a 96-mph cutter from Kenley Jansen and lifted it over Dodger Stadium's right-field fence to tie a game that was down to its final out. For those counting along, that makes five tools, but there is development needed ahead. Even shallow digging into his BABIP and plate discipline suggest that he'll still be going through some growing pains in 2017, at least at the plate. The rest of his repertoire can compensate in the meantime.

Daniel Descalso   PH

Born: 10/19/86 Age: 30 Bats: L Throws: R Height: 5'10" Weight: 190 Entered Pro Ball: Round 3, 2007 Draft (#112 overall)

YEAR	TEAM	LVL	AGE	PA	R	2B	3B	HR	RBI	BB	K	SB	CS	AVG/OBP/SLG	TAv	VORP	BABIP	BRR	FRAA	WARP
2014	SLN	MLB	27	184	20	11	0	0	10	20	33	1	3	.242/.333/.311	.244	1.7	.305	-0.6	2B(21): 2.7 • SS(19): -2.1	0.1
2015	COL	MLB	28	209	22	3	2	5	22	20	45	1	2	.205/.283/.324	.225	-1.3	.244	-0.6	SS(33): 0.8 • 2B(15): -1.2	-0.2
2016	COL	MLB	29	289	38	12	2	8	38	34	56	3	0	.264/.349/.424	.272	15.4	.305	3.4	SS(31): -5.9 • 1B(16): 0.2	1.1
2017	*COL*	*MLB*	*30*	*258*	*28*	*12*	*2*	*6*	*27*	*24*	*49*	*2*	*2*	*.254/.329/.399*	*.234*	*3.3*	*.294*	*0.5*	*SS -1, 2B 0*	*0.2*
2018	*COL*	*MLB*	*31*	*192*	*22*	*8*	*1*	*4*	*20*	*18*	*37*	*1*	*1*	*.247/.324/.385*	*.243*	*2.5*	*.287*	*0.4*	*SS -1, 2B 0*	*0.2*

Breakout: 0%   Improve: 39%   Collapse: 6%   Attrition: 16%   MLB: 96%   *Comparables: Larry Brown, Chris Speier, Billy Klaus*

Descalso started games at five different positions for the Rockies in 2016. That's what utility players do. But 11 of those were at first base, and he also added four starts as designated hitter. That's what utility players should not do. Of course, Descalso didn't hit like one—posting career highs in TAv, OBP and SLG—and there was even a modicum of substance to it. He laid off pitches outside the zone better than he ever has before, but that's a weak peg on which to hang a dramatic difference. Nevertheless, the anomalous season should at least work to extend his career as a utility player, if not as a first baseman or DH.

Ian Desmond SS

Born: 9/20/85 Age: 31 Bats: R Throws: R Height: 6'3" Weight: 215 Entered Pro Ball: Round 3, 2004 Draft (#84 overall)

YEAR	TEAM	LVL	AGE	PA	R	2B	3B	HR	RBI	BB	K	SB	CS	AVG/OBP/SLG	TAv	VORP	BABIP	BRR	FRAA	WARP
2014	WAS	MLB	28	648	73	26	3	24	91	46	183	24	5	.255/.313/.430	.271	32.9	.326	1.8	SS(154): 6.6	4.4
2015	WAS	MLB	29	641	69	27	2	19	62	45	187	13	5	.233/.290/.384	.254	23.7	.307	2.5	SS(155): -1.4	2.4
2016	TEX	MLB	30	677	107	29	3	22	86	44	160	21	6	.285/.335/.446	.261	26.2	.350	5.5	CF(130): -8.0 • LF(29): -1.1	1.8
2017	COL	MLB	31	538	67	28	3	20	70	36	133	15	4	.274/.326/.461	.258	10.0	.334	1.2	1B 0	0.7
2018	COL	MLB	32	525	65	24	2	18	66	37	136	13	4	.256/.314/.429	.253	4.8	.317	2.1	-	0.5

Breakout: 0%   Improve: 45%   Collapse: 6%   Attrition: 9%   MLB: 96%   *Comparables: Torii Hunter, Ellis Burks, Aaron Rowand*

There's a certain amount of anguish in watching a player destroy his free agent stock in a walk year, and that's exactly what Desmond did in 2015. He settled for a one-year, $8 million deal three months after declining nearly twice that in the form of the qualifying offer. The Rangers immediately rewarded him by shifting him to center field, a position he'd played for five innings, in 2009, in the Dominican Winter League. Of course, it worked. Desmond has now proved to be a useful body in multiple outfield spots, as well as maintaining his shortstop registration, which gives him a nice bump in value during this period of 12- and 13-man bullpens. Unfortunately, he didn't bounce back to his previous offensive heights despite a fourth hand stamp at the 20/20 club and some strides in lowering his strikeout rate. The Rockies looked at all this and decided to sign him to a five-year, $70 million contract, potentially to start at first base. Before you go check: Desmond has never played first base, even in the Dominican Winter League.

Jose Gomez SS

Born: 12/10/96 Age: 20 Bats: R Throws: R Height: 5'11" Weight: 175 Entered Pro Ball: International Free Agent, 2013

YEAR	TEAM	LVL	AGE	PA	R	2B	3B	HR	RBI	BB	K	SB	CS	AVG/OBP/SLG	TAv	VORP	BABIP	BRR	FRAA	WARP
2017	COL	MLB	20	250	25	11	1	5	26	11	61	5	3	.239/.281/.364	.203	-3.7	.293	-0.5	SS 1, 2B 0	-0.3
2018	COL	MLB	21	354	39	16	2	8	38	16	84	7	5	.248/.292/.384	.229	0.7	.301	-0.2	SS 1, 2B 0	0.2

Breakout: 1%   Improve: 8%   Collapse: 0%   Attrition: 2%   MLB: 10%   *Comparables: Ruben Tejada, Jose Peraza, Tim Beckham*

After an 0-for-5 night in his 26th Pioneer League game, Gomez's batting line fell to .400/.449/.486. Over the course of the season, his batting average never fell below .349 and his on base percentage never below .400. He certainly made an impression. Players like Gomez will always carry questions about position (a move to the keystone could be in his future) and handling full-season ball (at least until he does it), but those concerns are only there because of the intrigue.

Carlos Gonzalez LF

Born: 10/17/85 Age: 31 Bats: L Throws: L Height: 6'1" Weight: 220 Entered Pro Ball: International Free Agent, 2002

YEAR	TEAM	LVL	AGE	PA	R	2B	3B	HR	RBI	BB	K	SB	CS	AVG/OBP/SLG	TAv	VORP	BABIP	BRR	FRAA	WARP
2014	COL	MLB	28	281	35	15	1	11	38	19	70	3	0	.238/.292/.431	.233	-0.6	.283	1.2	LF(48): -5.5 • RF(17): 0.1	-0.7
2015	COL	MLB	29	608	87	25	2	40	97	46	133	2	0	.271/.325/.540	.284	24.4	.284	-0.1	RF(151): -4.2	2.2
2016	COL	MLB	30	632	87	42	2	25	100	46	129	2	2	.298/.350/.505	.276	22.9	.346	1.4	RF(148): -4.3	1.9
2017	COL	MLB	31	596	77	31	3	29	91	47	136	5	1	.276/.335/.505	.271	22.6	.317	-0.4	RF -3	1.4
2018	COL	MLB	32	526	73	27	2	25	79	41	126	3	1	.270/.328/.492	.271	17.1	.315	0.6	RF -3	1.5

Breakout: 1%   Improve: 41%   Collapse: 4%   Attrition: 3%   MLB: 96%   *Comparables: Matt Kemp, Geoff Jenkins, Jay Buhner*

On January 1, 2015, the "Injury History" portion of each player's Baseball Prospectus page ceased updating. Against all expectations, Gonzalez's lengthy entry—it requires multiple screen captures and stitching to get it all in a single image—remains mostly accurate. There were a couple day-to-days sprinkled in, but he hasn't seen the 15-day DL in two full seasons and because of that, we have a sense of what can be expected from him as he progresses into his early 30s. Gonzalez is consistent at the plate, and while he's not nearly as fleet of foot on the grass as he used to be, his arm remains well-suited for right field. If that reads like an almost squarely average regular, it's because that is precisely what he is now. Still, the thought of that scary, sweet swing and bat drop remains enough to elicit unease from opposing pitchers—as he saw the sixth-fewest strikes among all qualified hitters in 2016.

Pedro Gonzalez INF

Born: 10/27/97 Age: 19 Bats: R Throws: R Height: 6'5" Weight: 190 Entered Pro Ball: International Free Agent, 2014

YEAR	TEAM	LVL	AGE	PA	R	2B	3B	HR	RBI	BB	K	SB	CS	AVG/OBP/SLG	TAv	VORP	BABIP	BRR	FRAA	WARP
2017	COL	MLB	19	250	26	10	1	6	22	9	96	3	3	.195/.230/.323	.176	-12.6	.293	-0.5	CF -0	-1.4
2018	COL	MLB	20	363	37	14	3	10	39	15	132	4	5	.211/.252/.356	.209	-9.4	.307	-0.4	CF -1	-1.1

Breakout: 0%   Improve: 6%   Collapse: 2%   Attrition: 5%   MLB: 11%   *Comparables: Engel Beltre, Nomar Mazara, Raul Mondesi*

Pedro Gonzalez sprouted two inches in between Annuals and is now listed as 6'5". The 18-year-old also moved from the infield to the outfield for his stateside debut, which was disappointing overall and might cause him to repeat Rookie ball. Some portion of the rough transition can be attributed to the demands of adapting to a new environment, as well as having to manage the literal elongation of arms and legs.

Nick Hundley C

Born: 9/8/83   Age: 33   Bats: R   Throws: R   Height: 6'1"   Weight: 205   Entered Pro Ball: Round 2, 2005 Draft (#76 overall)

YEAR	TEAM	LVL	AGE	PA	R	2B	3B	HR	RBI	BB	K	SB	CS	AVG/OBP/SLG	TAv	VORP	BABIP	BRR	FRAA	WARP
2014	SDN	MLB	30	59	1	3	0	1	3	0	13	0	0	.271/.271/.373	.238	0.3	.333	-0.6	C(14): 1.9	0.2
2014	BAL	MLB	30	174	17	4	0	5	19	10	50	1	0	.233/.273/.352	.245	4.3	.299	-0.4	C(49): -0.7	0.4
2015	COL	MLB	31	389	45	21	5	10	43	21	76	5	6	.301/.339/.467	.268	20.3	.356	0.5	C(102): -12.6	0.8
2016	COL	MLB	32	317	30	20	1	10	48	25	65	0	0	.260/.320/.439	.256	12.8	.302	-0.3	C(79): -14.3	-0.2
2017	COL	MLB	33	314	34	15	1	9	36	20	72	2	1	.254/.304/.413	.230	5.9	.304	-0.3	C -11	-0.6
2018	COL	MLB	34	342	40	16	2	10	40	22	81	1	1	.245/.297/.402	.239	4.9	.295	-0.2	C -13	-0.9

Breakout: 0%   Improve: 33%   Collapse: 15%   Attrition: 24%   MLB: 89%   *Comparables: Yorvit Torrealba, Mike Heath, Terry Steinbach*

Hundley was the third-most valuable catcher on the Rockies in 2016, according to WARP, behind even Tom Murphy, who only started nine games. While that says something positive about the state of catcher for the Rockies, it says something not so positive about Hundley. The magic Hundley wielded to a fine 2015 season at the plate faded away and he finished 2016 as the third-worst receiver (minimum 5,000 CSAA chances) in the majors. He was on a team with two better options at backstop in 2016. Now Hundley's best bet will be to search for a suitor with just one.

YEAR	TEAM	P. COUNT	FRM RUNS	BLK RUNS	THRW RUNS	TOT RUNS
2014	SDN	1462	1.8	0.4	0.0	2.2
2014	BAL	6605	-0.3	2.1	-1.1	0.7
2015	COL	14669	-14.8	1.6	0.5	-12.7
2016	COL	11523	-11.4	0.0	-2.7	-14.0
2017	COL	11740	-11.5	0.7	-1.4	-12.2
2018	COL	12805	-13.8	0.6	-1.6	-14.8

DJ LeMahieu 2B

Born: 7/13/88   Age: 28   Bats: R   Throws: R   Height: 6'4"   Weight: 215   Entered Pro Ball: Round 2, 2009 Draft (#79 overall)

YEAR	TEAM	LVL	AGE	PA	R	2B	3B	HR	RBI	BB	K	SB	CS	AVG/OBP/SLG	TAv	VORP	BABIP	BRR	FRAA	WARP
2014	COL	MLB	25	538	59	15	5	5	42	33	97	10	10	.267/.315/.348	.226	-0.3	.322	3.7	2B(144): 2.7 • 3B(7): -0.8	0.2
2015	COL	MLB	26	620	85	21	5	6	61	50	107	23	3	.301/.358/.388	.253	16.9	.362	4.9	2B(149): -0.9	1.7
2016	COL	MLB	27	635	104	32	8	11	66	80	80	11	7	.348/.416/.495	.298	44.1	.388	2.0	2B(146): -0.9	4.5
2017	COL	MLB	28	611	73	27	5	8	53	45	98	14	6	.294/.344/.406	.249	18.3	.338	0.4	2B 2	1.5
2018	COL	MLB	29	592	68	27	5	9	61	44	96	12	6	.296/.348/.413	.258	20.1	.340	3.4	2B 2	2.4

Breakout: 0%   Improve: 39%   Collapse: 10%   Attrition: 15%   MLB: 94%   *Comparables: Gordon Beckham, Jim Gantner, Mike Lansing*

You can say that LeMahieu's batting title can be attributed to Coors Field, and you'd be right. You'd also miss the point. LeMahieu had one hell of a year that deserves more than a smirk and a "yeah but Coors" proclamation. First, he held the gains he made during 2015 in his ability to either take the ball up the middle or go the other way. It's an intentional approach. For the second consecutive season, he had the lowest pull rate among qualified hitters by a whopping nine percentage points and he led qualified batters in batted balls to the opposite field. LeMahieu went the other way 37.9 percent of the time. A look at LeMahieu's spray chart shows that he spread his singles around pretty consistently, but most of his doubles and triples went to the opposite field.

Of course, he didn't do everything similarly between 2015 and 2016. His 90.2 percent contact rate led baseball, and as a result he struck out just 12.6 percent of the time. Couple that with a walk rate that jumped two percentage points for the second consecutive season, and it makes for a plate approach you can believe in. But it wasn't just the quantitative aspect of his contact that he improved. His batting average was no longer empty. He hit as many doubles as Josh Donaldson. His hard hit rate went from 26.6 percent in 2015 to 35.2 in 2016. And according to Statcast's average exit velocity, LeMahieu's 92.5 mph average, two mph higher than the year before, equaled that of Paul Goldschmidt. To put too fine a point on it deliberately, LeMahieu hit the ball harder than teammates Nolan Arenado and Carlos Gonzalez on average.

Everything about LeMahieu's 2016 season indicates that he made real and significant improvements at the plate. And yet, it was likely the best season he'll ever have. Simply by virtue of getting a year older and a year slower, it's harder to maintain these outcomes than it is to get there in the first place. But, like the assist his home field had in winning the batting title, that's not really the point.

Ryan McMahon 3B

Born: 12/14/94   Age: 22   Bats: L   Throws: R   Height: 6'2"   Weight: 185   Entered Pro Ball: Round 2, 2013 Draft (#42 overall)

YEAR	TEAM	LVL	AGE	PA	R	2B	3B	HR	RBI	BB	K	SB	CS	AVG/OBP/SLG	TAv	VORP	BABIP	BRR	FRAA	WARP
2014	ASH	A	19	552	93	46	3	18	102	54	143	8	5	.282/.358/.502	.284	30.7	.360	-0.3	3B(118): 7.9	4.0
2015	MOD	A+	20	556	85	43	6	18	75	49	153	6	13	.300/.372/.520	.358	72.9	.401	1.5	3B(129): 25.2	10.6
2016	NBR	AA	21	535	49	27	5	12	75	55	161	11	6	.242/.325/.399	.265	14.7	.338	1.3	1B(67): -3.2 • 3B(67): 5.9	1.9
2017	COL	MLB	22	250	28	14	1	8	31	21	81	2	2	.244/.312/.420	.238	0.2	.338	-0.4	1B -1, 3B 3	0.3
2018	COL	MLB	23	397	49	21	2	14	50	32	128	3	3	.242/.309/.428	.249	1.7	.332	-0.6	1B -2, 3B 5	0.6

Breakout: 2%   Improve: 21%   Collapse: 3%   Attrition: 18%   MLB: 36%   *Comparables: Matt Davidson, Chris Carter, Alex Liddi*

It took the power-hitting McMahon 37 games to slug his first Double-A dinger, and on June 26, he was hitting just .209/.309/.319. It looked like a lost year, which certainly wouldn't have been career-crushing considering he was one of the youngest position players in the Eastern League. But McMahon was able to turn the season into a relative success. He finished up with a roughly league average batting line (though the strikeouts—even in his improved second half—are worrisome). McMahon has the defensive skillset to stick at third base, but because of the Arenado-shaped barrier in front of him, he logged just as many games at the cold corner in 2016 as he did the hot one. No such barrier exists over there.

Tom Murphy   C

Born: 4/3/91   Age: 26   Bats: R   Throws: R   Height: 6'1"   Weight: 220   Entered Pro Ball: Round 3, 2012 Draft (#105 overall)

YEAR	TEAM	LVL	AGE	PA	R	2B	3B	HR	RBI	BB	K	SB	CS	AVG/OBP/SLG	TAv	VORP	BABIP	BRR	FRAA	WARP
2014	TUL	AA	23	109	16	4	0	5	15	14	27	0	0	.213/.321/.415	.261	3.8	.242	-0.6	C(23): 1.3	0.5
2015	NBR	AA	24	294	36	17	1	13	44	23	80	5	2	.249/.320/.468	.272	14.8	.306	0.1	C(58): -1.7	1.4
2015	ABQ	AAA	24	136	19	9	2	7	19	5	43	0	1	.271/.301/.535	.266	6.9	.350	0.8	C(27): -1.3	0.6
2015	COL	MLB	24	39	5	1	0	3	9	4	10	0	0	.257/.333/.543	.281	3.0	.273	0.5	C(11): -2.3	0.1
2016	ABQ	AAA	25	322	53	26	7	19	59	16	78	1	1	.327/.361/.647	.321	31.6	.386	-2.2	C(69): 2.1	3.5
2016	COL	MLB	25	49	8	2	0	5	13	4	19	1	0	.273/.347/.659	.290	2.8	.350	-0.7	C(12): 0.4	0.3
2017	COL	MLB	26	393	51	20	3	21	60	25	119	1	1	.256/.309/.504	.262	19.3	.318	-0.5	C -7	0.0
2018	COL	MLB	27	438	61	23	3	24	70	29	133	1	1	.256/.311/.505	.269	19.3	.321	-0.6	C -9	1.2

Breakout: 2%   Improve: 21%   Collapse: 3%   Attrition: 18%   MLB: 36%   *Comparables: Matt Davidson, Chris Carter, Alex Liddi*

While he made the most out of his 2015 cup of coffee, the Rockies made the confounding decision to keep Murphy in Triple-A until September again in 2016. By the end of his five months in Albuquerque, he was playing like someone with nothing left to prove, and once he returned to the majors, he displayed the power and sound defense everyone expected. His poor plate discipline has been an issue in the past, and all those September strikeouts won't do much to quiet those concerns. However, that doesn't detract from the whole of what Murphy can offer, and the lessons he's yet to learn are not going to be learned down on the farm.

YEAR	TEAM	P. COUNT	FRM RUNS	BLK RUNS	THRW RUNS	TOT RUNS
2014	TUL	2740	1.9	-0.1	-0.4	1.4
2015	ABQ	4087	-0.7	-0.3	-0.3	-1.3
2015	COL	1584	-2.1	-0.2	-0.1	-2.4
2015	NBR	7358	0.3	-1.4	0.5	-0.6
2016	COL	1415	0.3	0.1	0.1	0.4
2017	COL	14630	-4.8	-1.9	0.0	-6.7
2018	COL	16303	-6.0	-2.0	-0.1	-8.1

Dom Nunez   C

Born: 1/17/95   Age: 22   Bats: L   Throws: R   Height: 6'0"   Weight: 175   Entered Pro Ball: Round 6, 2013 Draft (#169 overall)

YEAR	TEAM	LVL	AGE	PA	R	2B	3B	HR	RBI	BB	K	SB	CS	AVG/OBP/SLG	TAv	VORP	BABIP	BRR	FRAA	WARP
2015	ASH	A	20	441	61	23	0	13	53	53	55	7	7	.282/.373/.448	.281	27.3	.298	-0.8	C(99): -1.4	2.8
2016	MOD	A+	21	450	44	13	2	10	51	49	91	8	1	.241/.321/.362	.261	20.7	.284	1.6	C(93): 5.1	2.7
2017	COL	MLB	22	250	27	11	1	8	31	22	55	1	0	.243/.312/.409	.228	3.8	.280	-0.4	C 0	0.5
2018	COL	MLB	23	307	40	14	1	11	40	28	67	1	0	.253/.325/.434	.253	8.3	.289	-0.6	C 0	0.9

Breakout: 8%   Improve: 16%   Collapse: 7%   Attrition: 21%   MLB: 27%   *Comparables: Christian Vazquez, J.R. Murphy, Bryan Anderson*

It's becoming a pattern for Nunez. He arrives at a new level and acclimates first as a catcher—getting to know the pitchers, sharpening his skills behind the plate—and only later as a hitter. It's as if he's mature enough to know that catcher development is a slog that won't be expedited by worrying about trouble at the plate. And yet, the bat arrives eventually. Nunez slugged just .295 and didn't have a home run in the first two months of 2016. In the final three-plus months, he slugged .395 and hit 10 home runs, six of which came in August. Double-A baseball will pose a new challenge, but so far there's little evidence to suggest he's not equipped to meet it.

YEAR	TEAM	P. COUNT	FRM RUNS	BLK RUNS	THRW RUNS	TOT RUNS
2017	COL	8835	0.0	0.0	0.0	0.0
2018	COL	10860	0.0	0.0	0.0	0.0

Gerardo Parra   RF

Born: 5/6/87   Age: 30   Bats: L   Throws: L   Height: 5'11"   Weight: 210   Entered Pro Ball: International Free Agent, 2004

YEAR	TEAM	LVL	AGE	PA	R	2B	3B	HR	RBI	BB	K	SB	CS	AVG/OBP/SLG	TAv	VORP	BABIP	BRR	FRAA	WARP
2014	ARI	MLB	27	440	51	18	3	6	30	24	72	5	5	.259/.305/.362	.248	3.2	.300	1.1	RF(102): 0.8 • CF(3): 0.8	0.5
2014	MIL	MLB	27	134	13	4	1	3	10	8	28	4	2	.268/.318/.390	.249	1.5	.326	0.1	LF(27): 0.1 • CF(9): -0.1	0.5
2015	MIL	MLB	28	351	53	24	5	9	31	20	57	9	3	.328/.369/.517	.309	23.1	.372	-1.8	LF(46): -2.2 • CF(31): 0.1	2.3
2015	BAL	MLB	28	238	30	12	0	5	20	8	35	5	1	.237/.268/.357	.218	-5.3	.259	-0.1	RF(47): -0.4 • CF(10): 1.1	-0.4
2016	ABQ	AAA	29	20	2	0	0	0	3	0	5	0	0	.150/.150/.150	.061	-3.8	.200	0.0	RF(2): -0.2 • CF(1): -0.2	-0.4
2016	COL	MLB	29	381	45	27	3	7	39	9	73	6	4	.253/.271/.399	.215	-1.7	.297	-1.1	LF(60): 1.6 • 1B(19): 0.4	-1.1
2017	COL	MLB	30	253	27	15	2	5	27	15	42	5	3	.278/.320/.421	.241	2.9	.314	-0.2	RF -1, CF -1	0.0
2018	COL	MLB	31	277	31	16	1	6	30	17	49	5	3	.267/.316/.412	.247	2.8	.305	-0.2	RF -1, CF -1	0.1

Breakout: 2%   Improve: 33%   Collapse: 22%   Attrition: 28%   MLB: 96%   *Comparables: Derrick May, Hal Rice, Terrence Long*

The Rockies signed Parra to a three-year contract worth $26 million prior to the 2016 season. It started well. After his 3-5 Rockies debut on Opening Day, Rockies players handed out t-shirts with "Parra for President" emblazoned on them. *Denver Post* reporter Patrick Saunders asked Parra what sort of presidential office he sought after the game. "President of something," he responded. In one fanciful version of Parra's 2016, he couldn't shake this question. "The president of what, exactly?" he thought, as poor pitch recognition manifested and he limped along. "Is 'president of baseball' a thing?" he contemplated as he swung at a career-high rate and walked at a career-low. Whatever the cause, Parra dropped below replacement level in 2016 and now appears to be either a sunk cost or a prohibitively expensive fourth outfielder on a team with strong depth at the position.

Ryan Raburn   DH

Born: 4/17/81   Age: 36   Bats: R   Throws: R   Height: 6'0"   Weight: 185   Entered Pro Ball: Round 5, 2001 Draft (#147 overall)

YEAR	TEAM	LVL	AGE	PA	R	2B	3B	HR	RBI	BB	K	SB	CS	AVG/OBP/SLG	TAv	VORP	BABIP	BRR	FRAA	WARP
2014	CLE	MLB	33	212	18	7	0	4	22	13	51	0	0	.200/.250/.297	.198	-9.6	.245	-0.4	RF(25): -0.3 • LF(20): 0.1	-1.1
2015	CLE	MLB	34	201	22	16	1	8	29	23	44	0	0	.301/.393/.543	.320	15.0	.361	0.2	LF(18): 0.7 • RF(17): -0.7	1.6
2016	COL	MLB	35	256	30	10	2	9	30	28	80	0	0	.220/.309/.404	.243	2.3	.292	1.4	LF(47): -2.7 • 1B(5): -0.3	-0.1
2017	COL	MLB	36	250	27	13	1	9	32	22	63	0	0	.243/.317/.425	.238	2.8	.297	0.3	LF -2, RF -0	0.1
2018	COL	MLB	37	181	22	9	1	6	22	16	46	0	0	.236/.311/.410	.245	1.5	.289	0.1	LF -1, RF 0	0.0

Breakout: 0%   Improve: 23%   Collapse: 8%   Attrition: 15%   MLB: 57%   *Comparables: Andres Torres, David Dellucci, Ryan Ludwick*

Having logged more than 400 plate appearances just twice in his 11-year career, Raburn has never been an everyday player. He first claimed roster spots by demonstrating infield/outfield versatility with secondary contributions from the bat, then by relying on offense to make up for the declining utility of his defense. His most recent trick was to crush left-handed pitching, but a 170-point drop in OPS against southpaws, even with Coors at his back, isn't the impression he wanted to make with the Rockies. At 36 and running out of space to maneuver and places to stand on the field, his last best hope is a minor-league contract.

Mark Reynolds   1B

Born: 8/3/83   Age: 33   Bats: R   Throws: R   Height: 6'2"   Weight: 220   Entered Pro Ball: Round 16, 2004 Draft (#476 overall)

YEAR	TEAM	LVL	AGE	PA	R	2B	3B	HR	RBI	BB	K	SB	CS	AVG/OBP/SLG	TAv	VORP	BABIP	BRR	FRAA	WARP
2014	MIL	MLB	30	433	47	9	0	22	45	47	122	5	1	.196/.287/.394	.256	6.4	.218	1.0	1B(91): 1.7 • 3B(42): 1.7	1.1
2015	SLN	MLB	31	432	35	21	2	13	48	44	121	2	3	.230/.315/.398	.253	-1.2	.300	-4.5	1B(100): 1.6 • 3B(22): -0.8	-0.1
2016	COL	MLB	32	441	61	24	0	14	53	42	112	1	2	.282/.356/.450	.275	8.9	.361	-2.6	1B(115): 1.4 • 2B(1): -0.0	1.1
2017	COL	MLB	33	413	50	17	1	17	55	45	117	2	2	.239/.327/.429	.247	1.3	.303	-1.6	1B 3, LF 0	0.5
2018	COL	MLB	34	355	46	14	1	13	44	42	104	1	1	.227/.324/.402	.252	0.0	.295	-1.3	1B 3, LF 0	0.3

Breakout: 3%   Improve: 32%   Collapse: 5%   Attrition: 16%   MLB: 84%   Comparables: Glenn Davis, Andruw Jones, Cecil Fielder

The easy explanation for Reynolds' career high .282 batting average in 2016, which is about 50 points higher than his career mark, is having the privilege of playing home games at Coors Field and the .361 BABIP for which it was partially responsible. But Reynolds also posted a career-high line drive rate of 25.8 percent. He seems to have traded fly balls for them, however, which he hit at a career-low 32.5 percent. And yet, he knocked one more dinger in 2015 than he did in 2016—sailing on a platform of contact and elevation. This is unlikely to be a full-scale reinvention, but it will keep Reynolds employed—for now.

Brendan Rodgers   SS

Born: 8/9/96   Age: 20   Bats: R   Throws: R   Height: 6'0"   Weight: 180   Entered Pro Ball: Round 1, 2015 Draft (#3 overall)

YEAR	TEAM	LVL	AGE	PA	R	2B	3B	HR	RBI	BB	K	SB	CS	AVG/OBP/SLG	TAv	VORP	BABIP	BRR	FRAA	WARP
2016	ASH	A	19	491	73	31	0	19	73	35	98	6	3	.281/.342/.480	.287	22.4	.319	-2.5	SS(56): -0.1 • 2B(24): 0.7	2.5
2017	COL	MLB	20	250	30	12	1	9	29	14	67	0	0	.242/.290/.419	.225	1.1	.296	-0.4	SS 1, 2B -0	0.3
2018	COL	MLB	21	356	45	18	1	14	48	21	96	0	0	.251/.303/.443	.250	7.2	.309	-0.8	SS 2, 2B 0	1.0

Breakout: 3%   Improve: 11%   Collapse: 0%   Attrition: 6%   MLB: 13%   Comparables: Trevor Story, Alen Hanson, Addison Russell

Some might be inclined to qualify Rodgers' first full-season of professional baseball with a reference to his home/road splits. Calling Asheville's McCormick field home, Rodgers had a home ISO of .279 and a road one of .125. But his adjusted batting line still has him well above average. While there appears to be neither a plan nor a need to move Rodgers from shortstop, he did start 24 games at second base in 2016. The purpose, however, was to broaden his world rather than to reorder it. Rodgers will enter the Rockies' new California League affiliate in Lancaster as one of the premier shortstop prospects in the game, and no matter how he performs, those focused on his splits will again have reason to release their cold water.

Trevor Story   SS

Born: 11/15/92   Age: 24   Bats: R   Throws: R   Height: 6'1"   Weight: 180   Entered Pro Ball: Round 1, 2011 Draft (#45 overall)

YEAR	TEAM	LVL	AGE	PA	R	2B	3B	HR	RBI	BB	K	SB	CS	AVG/OBP/SLG	TAv	VORP	BABIP	BRR	FRAA	WARP
2014	MOD	A+	21	218	38	17	7	5	28	31	59	20	4	.332/.436/.582	.341	30.7	.467	2.8	SS(39): -0.1 • 3B(8): -0.9	3.0
2014	TUL	AA	21	237	29	8	1	9	20	28	82	3	1	.200/.302/.380	.255	8.5	.281	0.8	SS(43): -8.9 • 3B(6): 0.7	0.0
2015	NBR	AA	22	300	46	20	6	10	40	35	73	15	2	.281/.373/.523	.330	35.3	.350	3.4	SS(50): 3.3 • 2B(12): -0.2	4.3
2015	ABQ	AAA	22	275	37	20	4	10	40	16	68	7	1	.277/.324/.504	.282	18.5	.341	2.4	SS(35): 2.2 • 3B(14): -0.2	2.1
2016	COL	MLB	23	415	67	21	4	27	72	35	130	8	5	.272/.341/.567	.288	31.1	.343	2.1	SS(96): 1.0	3.3
2017	COL	MLB	24	557	76	28	5	26	77	48	173	13	4	.252/.323/.484	.264	28.3	.330	1.1	SS -1	2.1
2018	COL	MLB	25	541	75	27	5	26	81	48	171	12	4	.249/.323/.486	.269	25.8	.325	2.6	SS -1	2.7

Breakout: 2%   Improve: 35%   Collapse: 21%   Attrition: 29%   MLB: 74%   Comparables: Pedro Alvarez, Mark Reynolds, Brandon Wood

One of the persistent trends Story carried with him throughout his time in the minor leagues was that he had power, but had problems making contact. He demonstrated both in his first run through the majors. Story's home run count in an injury-shortened season equaled his jersey number, 27, and he struck out nearly as often as Chrises Carter and Davis. Another minor-league trend was that it took him a little while to adjust to new levels. Story showed that off as well, despite the splash he made during the first week of the season. His strikeout rates by month were 36.3, 32.2, 27.7 and 28.6. Story's power absolves the strikeouts, and the fact that he's likely to stick at shortstop for at least the next few seasons all but guarantees egregious punning of his name for a while. There's no absolution for that, however.

Raimel Tapia   RF

Born: 2/4/94   Age: 23   Bats: L   Throws: L   Height: 6'2"   Weight: 160   Entered Pro Ball: International Free Agent, 2010

YEAR	TEAM	LVL	AGE	PA	R	2B	3B	HR	RBI	BB	K	SB	CS	AVG/OBP/SLG	TAv	VORP	BABIP	BRR	FRAA	WARP
2014	ASH	A	20	539	93	32	1	9	72	35	90	33	16	.326/.382/.453	.288	31.8	.383	3.1	LF(43): -4.7 • CF(42): -2.4	2.1
2015	MOD	A+	21	593	74	34	9	12	71	24	105	26	10	.305/.333/.467	.317	47.6	.350	-0.7	CF(74): 3.3 • LF(46): 0.4	5.6
2016	NBR	AA	22	457	79	20	5	8	34	25	49	17	14	.323/.363/.450	.287	25.2	.349	1.4	CF(60): 2.7 • RF(22): 5.3	3.6
2016	ABQ	AAA	22	110	14	5	5	0	14	2	12	6	3	.346/.355/.490	.261	2.9	.379	0.0	CF(12): 2.2 • LF(8): 1.3	0.6
2016	COL	MLB	22	41	4	0	0	0	3	2	11	3	0	.263/.293/.263	.191	-0.4	.357	1.2	CF(9): -0.1 • LF(2): -0.1	-0.2
2017	COL	MLB	23	92	10	4	1	2	10	4	18	3	2	.284/.313/.428	.241	1.2	.330	0.0	LF -0	0.1
2018	COL	MLB	24	356	42	17	3	9	43	15	68	11	6	.287/.320/.443	.254	7.2	.329	0.7	LF -1	0.7

Breakout: 3%   Improve: 13%   Collapse: 1%   Attrition: 10%   MLB: 24%   Comparables: Logan Schafer, Matt Szczur, Gary Brown

Two adjectives are frequently attached to Tapia. The first is "unorthodox." It's in reference to his mechanics at the plate, and in particular his two-strike crouch. The second is "preternatural," and that one's used because the approach has worked at every level he's played. Tapia simply knows how to put the barrel to the ball, regardless of how strange the process of doing so might seem. Another adjective that should be used more often with Tapia is "adaptable." He's modified his approach, as well as his crouch, along the way, which is a much more significant reason for his minor-league success than a mystical ability to hit. He studies himself as much as his opponent.

Tapia's 10 hits during his September call-up gave him a .263 batting average. Once he climbs and steadies above .300—and it's a decent bet he will—Tapia might never fall below it again. Call it Ichiro-esque.

Tony Wolters   C

Born: 6/9/92   Age: 25   Bats: L   Throws: R   Height: 5'10"   Weight: 200   Entered Pro Ball: Round 3, 2010 Draft (#87 overall)

YEAR	TEAM	LVL	AGE	PA	R	2B	3B	HR	RBI	BB	K	SB	CS	AVG/OBP/SLG	TAv	VORP	BABIP	BRR	FRAA	WARP
2014	AKR	AA	22	387	36	15	2	1	34	35	74	3	2	.249/.319/.314	.241	10.2	.309	2.9	C(66): 23.5 • 2B(10): -0.7	3.5
2015	AKR	AA	23	271	23	7	2	2	17	21	63	3	2	.209/.290/.280	.219	1.3	.273	1.8	C(56): 14.4 • SS(3): 0.2	1.7
2016	COL	MLB	24	230	27	15	2	3	30	21	53	4	1	.259/.327/.395	.249	8.4	.336	0.7	C(59): 7.8 • 2B(7): -0.1	1.7
2017	COL	MLB	25	210	20	9	1	3	19	17	51	2	1	.238/.303/.351	.220	1.4	.305	-0.1	C 7	0.4
2018	COL	MLB	26	296	32	13	2	5	29	23	76	2	1	.234/.302/.356	.228	0.8	.301	0.1	C 10	1.1

Breakout: 5%   Improve: 19%   Collapse: 10%   Attrition: 25%   MLB: 55%   *Comparables: Austin Romine, Rob Brantly, Carlos Perez*

You might know what you want, but not find it in the expected places. Maybe you, like so many, are searching for that perfect partner with the perfect disposition. You might go searching at all those wells of familiarity: the bar, the internet, friends and family networks or the dog park. And perhaps in one of those places, that person will be found. Perhaps not. Maybe it will happen somewhere unforeseen: the dentist's office, the DMV, the ear and eye aisle at the local pharmacy, Radio Shack (assuming yours didn't close down last year). It's unanticipated and possibly all the more delightful for it. The Rockies claimed Wolters—an infielder-cum-catcher with plus defense who calls a great game on account of his rapport with pitchers and also hits just enough—off of waivers in February 2016.

YEAR	TEAM	P. COUNT	FRM RUNS	BLK RUNS	THRW RUNS	TOT RUNS
2014	AKR	8491	21.5	0.3	2.6	24.4
2015	AKR	7755	11.4	-0.1	2.7	14.0
2016	COL	8341	9.1	-0.2	0.4	9.3
2017	COL	6869	6.6	-0.2	0.6	7.0
2018	COL	9683	9.0	-0.2	0.9	9.7

PITCHERS

Yency Almonte   RHP

Born: 6/4/94   Age: 23   Bats: B   Throws: R   Height: 6'3"   Weight: 205   Entered Pro Ball: Round 17, 2012 Draft (#537 overall)

YEAR	TEAM	LVL	AGE	W	L	SV	G	GS	IP	H	HR	BB/9	K/9	K	GB%	BABIP	WHIP	ERA	FIP	DRA	VORP	WARP	cFIP	MPH
2014	BUR	A	20	2	5	0	9	9	42	40	5	3.0	6.9	32	46%	.280	1.29	4.93	4.65	5.00	2.1	0.2	104	
2015	KAN	A	21	8	4	0	17	16	92²	92	8	2.5	6.9	71	45%	.295	1.27	3.88	4.17	4.38	8.6	0.9	98	
2015	WNS	A+	21	3	3	0	7	6	44²	28	1	2.4	7.9	39	52%	.231	0.90	2.42	2.67	2.56	12.2	1.3	86	
2016	MOD	A+	22	8	9	0	22	22	138¹	124	14	2.5	8.7	134	47%	.285	1.18	3.71	4.13	2.69	42.8	4.4	89	
2016	NBR	AA	22	3	1	0	5	5	30	22	4	4.8	6.6	22	37%	.212	1.27	3.00	5.22	7.40	-7.7	-0.8	118	
2017	COL	MLB	23	8	9	0	24	24	134	161	23	3.9	5.4	81	62%	.330	1.63	5.55	5.59	5.98	-6.2	-0.6	144	
2018	COL	MLB	24	4	7	0	15	15	91	94	16	5.4	8.1	82	62%	.323	1.64	5.89	5.97	6.35	-7.4	-0.8	150	

Breakout: 9%   Improve: 26%   Collapse: 12%   Attrition: 28%   MLB: 43%   *Comparables: Anthony Swarzak, Adrian Sampson, Travis Wood*

On the strength of his mid-90s fastball and above average slider, Almonte earned a late season promotion to Double-A. His next act will be the one where we find out if he adds a workable third pitch to keep more advanced hitters at bay. He used a changeup sparingly, so it's not clear whether it will be that or some other pitch that will determine Almonte's fate as a starter or reliever.

Tyler Anderson   LHP

Born: 12/30/89   Age: 27   Bats: L   Throws: L   Height: 6'4"   Weight: 210   Entered Pro Ball: Round 1, 2011 Draft (#20 overall)

YEAR	TEAM	LVL	AGE	W	L	SV	G	GS	IP	H	HR	BB/9	K/9	K	GB%	BABIP	WHIP	ERA	FIP	DRA	VORP	WARP	cFIP	MPH
2014	TUL	AA	24	7	4	0	23	23	118¹	91	3	3.0	8.1	106	52%	.274	1.11	1.98	2.77	2.80	32.0	3.4	83	
2016	NBR	AA	26	1	1	0	2	2	10	6	0	1.8	9.9	11	59%	.222	0.80	1.80	1.76	2.99	2.3	0.3	82	
2016	ABQ	AAA	26	1	1	0	3	3	17	15	1	3.2	6.9	13	48%	.286	1.24	2.12	4.01	4.50	1.6	0.2	100	
2016	COL	MLB	26	5	6	0	19	19	114¹	119	12	2.2	7.8	99	53%	.319	1.29	3.54	3.63	3.29	26.3	2.7	90	93.7
2017	COL	MLB	27	10	10	0	28	28	168	172	20	2.7	7.4	139	43%	.300	1.33	4.14	4.08	4.22	17.9	1.8	97	
2018	COL	MLB	28	10	10	0	28	28	171	147	22	3.7	9.3	177	43%	.301	1.27	4.31	4.35	4.73	15.3	1.6	108	

Breakout: 28%   Improve: 46%   Collapse: 24%   Attrition: 33%   MLB: 86%   *Comparables: Jimmy Nelson, Joe Saunders, David Purcey*

By Baseball Reference's WAR model, Anderson had the best rookie season for a pitcher in Colorado Rockies history. By ours, it wasn't even the best rookie season in the Rockies' 2016 rotation. Regardless of the alt-WAR you worship at (sorry not sorry), that's a huge success considering he missed the entire 2015 season due to a stress fracture in his pitching elbow. Anderson is able to generate grounders with his four-seam fastball, as well as his cutter and changeup—this trio accounted for 97 percent of his repertoire in 2016. The rest of Anderson's statistics, both descriptive and predictive, support his middle of the rotation profile. His sophomore season will test how well his body can handle pitching a full season in the majors.

Christian Bergman RHP

Born: 5/4/88   Age: 29   Bats: R   Throws: R   Height: 6'1"   Weight: 195   Entered Pro Ball: Round 24, 2010 Draft (#740 overall)

YEAR	TEAM	LVL	AGE	W	L	SV	G	GS	IP	H	HR	BB/9	K/9	K	GB%	BABIP	WHIP	ERA	FIP	DRA	VORP	WARP	cFIP	MPH
2014	CSP	AAA	26	5	5	0	15	15	92¹	96	11	1.8	5.8	60	43%	.287	1.23	4.19	4.60	2.69	31.5	3.1	105	
2014	COL	MLB	26	3	5	0	10	10	54²	75	9	1.6	5.1	31	33%	.333	1.55	5.93	4.71	7.48	-16.0	-1.8	129	91.6
2015	COL	MLB	27	3	1	0	30	4	68¹	82	8	2.0	4.9	37	41%	.327	1.42	4.74	4.26	5.71	-7.0	-0.7	121	92.3
2016	ABQ	AAA	28	3	3	0	10	10	51²	52	8	2.1	5.7	33	36%	.275	1.24	3.66	5.27	5.38	-0.2	0.0	117	
2016	COL	MLB	28	1	3	0	15	1	24²	39	7	2.2	8.0	22	41%	.381	1.82	8.39	5.82	4.61	1.2	0.1	110	91.7
2017	*COL*	*MLB*	*29*	*4*	*3*	*0*	*19*	*10*	*65*	*75*	*10*	*2.6*	*6.0*	*43*	*41%*	*.332*	*1.45*	*4.80*	*4.78*	*5.25*	*1.7*	*0.2*	*124*	
2018	*COL*	*MLB*	*30*	*7*	*9*	*0*	*35*	*22*	*155*	*165*	*26*	*3.8*	*8.2*	*142*	*41%*	*.336*	*1.48*	*5.19*	*5.24*	*5.68*	*-2.9*	*-0.3*	*132*	

Breakout: 9%   Improve: 21%   Collapse: 10%   Attrition: 14%   MLB: 39%   Comparables: Eddie Bonine, J.D. Martin, David Pauley

Christian Bergman is a mop-up guy who looks like the vocalist for a 90s rock cover band named Mop-Up Guy. He's called upon either when the game appears Dead and Bloated or the starting rotation has Fell on Black Days (a more sound depth chart would have a Better Man for the job). Sometimes it Hurts to acknowledge the reality that the likeliest future has him traversing the road between the major leagues and Triple-A—Counting Blue Cars while working on that Interstate Love Song.

Chad Bettis RHP

Born: 4/26/89   Age: 28   Bats: R   Throws: R   Height: 6'1"   Weight: 200   Entered Pro Ball: Round 2, 2010 Draft (#76 overall)

YEAR	TEAM	LVL	AGE	W	L	SV	G	GS	IP	H	HR	BB/9	K/9	K	GB%	BABIP	WHIP	ERA	FIP	DRA	VORP	WARP	cFIP	MPH
2014	COL	MLB	25	0	2	0	21	0	24²	42	4	3.6	4.7	13	53%	.384	2.11	9.12	5.49	5.33	-2.3	-0.3	114	96.4
2014	CSP	AAA	25	3	4	3	20	5	55¹	45	1	3.4	8.9	55	60%	.303	1.19	3.09	3.25	3.57	12.0	1.2	85	
2015	ABQ	AAA	26	3	2	0	7	7	39	41	5	2.3	7.6	33	47%	.319	1.31	3.46	4.42	3.05	9.8	1.0	90	
2015	COL	MLB	26	8	6	0	20	20	115	120	11	3.3	7.7	98	53%	.313	1.41	4.23	3.87	4.00	13.7	1.5	94	95.7
2016	COL	MLB	27	14	8	0	32	32	186	204	22	2.9	6.7	138	54%	.310	1.41	4.79	4.30	4.23	23.3	2.4	100	94.8
2017	*COL*	*MLB*	*28*	*9*	*11*	*0*	*28*	*28*	*168*	*185*	*24*	*2.9*	*7.3*	*137*	*45%*	*.309*	*1.45*	*4.54*	*4.49*	*4.64*	*10.1*	*1.0*	*100*	
2018	*COL*	*MLB*	*29*	*10*	*11*	*0*	*30*	*30*	*192²*	*196*	*27*	*2.8*	*8.3*	*177*	*45%*	*.326*	*1.33*	*4.42*	*4.46*	*4.85*	*14.2*	*1.5*	*111*	

Breakout: 14%   Improve: 57%   Collapse: 14%   Attrition: 12%   MLB: 87%   Comparables: Shaun Marcum, Dustin McGowan, Dillon Gee

In 2014, Twitter discovered that a spoonerized Chad Bettis resulted in an accurate description of his pitching performance. That year, Bad Chettis yo-yoed between Triple-A and the majors, as well as between the bullpen and the rotation. With a firm role out of the rotation in 2015, the Rockies found Pretty Good Chettis, and there was a lot of hope among fans and the front office that he'd be a featured part of the 2016 rotation. That year, Reliable Chettis started 32 games and ended up with an ERA below 5.00 and park-adjusted metrics hovering around league average. Performance and expectations have now, it seems, struck equilibrium. The 28-year-old right-hander will enter 2017 as Fourth Starter Chettis, and that's more palatable than spoonerisms have become.

Eddie Butler RHP

Born: 3/13/91   Age: 26   Bats: R   Throws: R   Height: 6'2"   Weight: 180   Entered Pro Ball: Round 1, 2012 Draft (#46 overall)

YEAR	TEAM	LVL	AGE	W	L	SV	G	GS	IP	H	HR	BB/9	K/9	K	GB%	BABIP	WHIP	ERA	FIP	DRA	VORP	WARP	cFIP	MPH
2014	TUL	AA	23	6	9	0	18	18	108	104	10	2.7	5.2	63	47%	.274	1.26	3.58	4.10	6.14	-10.9	-1.2	111	
2014	COL	MLB	23	1	1	0	3	3	16	23	2	3.9	1.7	3	56%	.328	1.88	6.75	5.67	5.96	-2.0	-0.2	120	96.7
2015	COL	MLB	24	3	10	0	16	16	79¹	102	13	4.8	5.0	44	51%	.333	1.82	5.90	5.92	6.20	-9.9	-1.1	122	96.2
2015	ABQ	AAA	24	2	6	0	11	11	63¹	71	6	3.6	5.3	37	54%	.314	1.52	5.40	4.99	4.52	5.5	0.6	103	
2016	ABQ	AAA	25	8	3	0	15	15	89	93	9	2.6	3.5	35	50%	.271	1.34	4.45	5.13	8.12	-27.4	-2.8	122	
2016	COL	MLB	25	2	5	0	17	9	64	87	13	3.0	6.6	47	48%	.354	1.69	7.17	5.48	5.45	-1.4	-0.1	110	96.2
2017	*COL*	*MLB*	*26*	*4*	*6*	*0*	*28*	*13*	*81*	*95*	*11*	*3.4*	*4.9*	*44*	*50%*	*.301*	*1.56*	*5.28*	*5.11*	*5.29*	*-1.5*	*-0.2*	*100*	
2018	*COL*	*MLB*	*27*	*7*	*8*	*0*	*51*	*21*	*156²*	*156*	*21*	*3.8*	*6.8*	*119*	*50%*	*.308*	*1.42*	*5.04*	*5.10*	*5.52*	*-0.8*	*-0.1*	*128*	

Breakout: 20%   Improve: 38%   Collapse: 22%   Attrition: 35%   MLB: 73%   Comparables: Trevor Bell, Kyle Drabek, Anthony Swarzak

Sometimes, the first impression is the most accurate. Butler's 2013 player comment, his first, reads: "Eddie Butler . . . pitched well in an offense-enhanced league in his debut, but he hasn't shown the ability to strike out batters despite good velocity and may eventually move to the bullpen." Intermittent years saw his prospect status flourish and fade. He found the ability to strike batters out as a starter across three minor-league levels in 2013, but it disappeared shortly after that. Butler eventually added walks to his repertoire of problems, and when he did manage to stay in the zone he was extremely hittable. Butler's fastball still sits in the mid-90s and it hasn't yet lost all of its life. If he can manage to get more whiffs from his slider, the secondary offering that still shows any promise, he really could be an effective arm out of the bullpen.

Ryan Castellani RHP

Born: 4/1/96   Age: 21   Bats: R   Throws: R   Height: 6'3"   Weight: 193   Entered Pro Ball: Round 2, 2014 Draft (#48 overall)

YEAR	TEAM	LVL	AGE	W	L	SV	G	GS	IP	H	HR	BB/9	K/9	K	GB%	BABIP	WHIP	ERA	FIP	DRA	VORP	WARP	cFIP	MPH
2014	TRI	A-	18	1	2	0	10	10	37	35	2	2.2	6.1	25	56%	.282	1.19	3.65	4.22	3.36	8.2	0.9	95	
2015	ASH	A	19	2	7	0	27	27	113¹	134	5	2.3	7.5	94	49%	.348	1.44	4.45	3.27	3.62	20.2	2.1	95	
2016	MOD	A+	20	7	8	0	26	26	167²	156	8	2.7	7.6	142	55%	.302	1.23	3.81	3.61	3.71	32.8	3.4	96	
2017	*COL*	*MLB*	*21*	*8*	*9*	*0*	*25*	*25*	*128*	*168*	*19*	*3.9*	*4.9*	*70*	*53%*	*.351*	*1.74*	*5.42*	*5.35*	*5.78*	*-3.1*	*-0.3*	*139*	
2018	*COL*	*MLB*	*22*	*5*	*7*	*0*	*18*	*18*	*106²*	*115*	*16*	*5.1*	*7.8*	*93*	*53%*	*.340*	*1.64*	*5.40*	*5.47*	*5.76*	*-2.0*	*-0.2*	*137*	

Breakout: 9%   Improve: 10%   Collapse: 6%   Attrition: 17%   MLB: 20%   Comparables: Tyler Danish, Wilfredo Boscan, Zach Eflin

Once again, Castellani advanced a level and faced competition on average three years older. And once again, Castellani acquitted himself well. He complements his two-seam fastball with a changeup and a slider. Scouting reports indicate that each one projects to be at least average, giving him the profile of a worm-hurting backend starter. He'll turn 21 in April, and if Castellani once again performs well with the "young-for-his-level" prefix against more advanced hitters, his stock could rise.

Miguel Castro   RHP

Born: 12/24/94 Age: 22   Bats: R Throws: R   Height: 6'5"   Weight: 190 Entered Pro Ball: International Free Agent, 2012

YEAR	TEAM	LVL	AGE	W	L	SV	G	GS	IP	H	HR	BB/9	K/9	K	GB%	BABIP	WHIP	ERA	FIP	DRA	VORP	WARP	cFIP	MPH
2014	VAN	A-	19	6	2	0	10	10	50¹	36	2	3.6	9.5	53	49%	.272	1.11	2.15	3.48	3.06	12.8	1.3	93	
2014	LNS	A	19	1	1	0	4	4	21²	10	2	2.9	8.3	20	55%	.151	0.78	3.74	3.95	3.37	5.0	0.5	92	
2015	TOR	MLB	20	0	2	4	13	0	12¹	15	2	4.4	8.8	12	41%	.351	1.70	4.38	4.73	5.27	-0.8	-0.1	108	99.5
2015	BUF	AAA	20	1	3	0	13	5	19²	26	4	5.5	9.6	21	42%	.367	1.93	4.58	5.80	4.84	0.5	0.0	106	
2015	ABQ	AAA	20	2	0	0	11	0	13²	6	0	4.6	6.6	10	57%	.162	0.95	1.32	3.89	4.51	0.8	0.1	103	
2015	COL	MLB	20	0	1	0	5	0	5¹	6	1	6.8	10.1	6	25%	.286	1.88	10.12	8.04	5.25	-0.3	0.0	110	99.0
2016	COL	MLB	21	0	0	0	19	0	14²	18	3	3.1	7.4	12	55%	.326	1.57	6.14	5.44	4.53	0.7	0.1	101	98.9
2016	ABQ	AAA	21	2	3	0	16	0	15²	21	5	4.0	8.6	15	49%	.364	1.79	10.34	7.49	4.15	1.4	0.1	100	
2017	*COL*	*MLB*	*22*	*1*	*2*	*0*	*31*	*0*	*32*	*35*	*4*	*4.0*	*7.1*	*26*	*50%*	*.302*	*1.53*	*4.99*	*4.56*	*4.83*	*0.3*	*0.0*	*100*	
2018	*COL*	*MLB*	*23*	*2*	*1*	*0*	*35*	*0*	*36²*	*32*	*4*	*4.3*	*9.1*	*37*	*50%*	*.309*	*1.36*	*4.34*	*4.39*	*4.69*	*1.8*	*0.2*	*107*	

Breakout: 26%   Improve: 39%   Collapse: 8%   Attrition: 18%   MLB: 54%   *Comparables: Mat Latos, Dana Eveland, Jose Garcia*

The 2016 season answered one question about Castro: it looks like his future will be in the bullpen. He has the stuff to make the best out of that future—a high-velocity, lively fastball and a whiff-generating slider. The question he'll set out to answer in 2017 is whether or not more Triple-A seasoning is in order for the 22-year-old, or if he's finally ready to make it all work in the majors.

Tyler Chatwood   RHP

Born: 12/16/89 Age: 27   Bats: R Throws: R   Height: 6'0"   Weight: 185 Entered Pro Ball: Round 2, 2008 Draft (#74 overall)

YEAR	TEAM	LVL	AGE	W	L	SV	G	GS	IP	H	HR	BB/9	K/9	K	GB%	BABIP	WHIP	ERA	FIP	DRA	VORP	WARP	cFIP	MPH
2014	COL	MLB	24	1	0	0	4	4	24	21	4	3.0	7.5	20	46%	.254	1.21	4.50	4.85	4.35	1.3	0.1	102	95.5
2016	COL	MLB	26	12	9	0	27	27	158	147	15	4.0	6.7	117	58%	.286	1.37	3.87	4.36	4.15	21.3	2.2	104	94.8
2017	*COL*	*MLB*	*27*	*7*	*10*	*0*	*26*	*26*	*130*	*135*	*18*	*3.9*	*7.3*	*106*	*44%*	*.301*	*1.49*	*4.77*	*4.76*	*4.88*	*4.3*	*0.4*	*100*	
2018	*COL*	*MLB*	*28*	*9*	*10*	*0*	*30*	*30*	*188¹*	*179*	*24*	*3.9*	*8.3*	*175*	*44%*	*.319*	*1.38*	*4.57*	*4.62*	*5.02*	*9.0*	*0.9*	*116*	

Breakout: 16%   Improve: 39%   Collapse: 27%   Attrition: 12%   MLB: 89%   *Comparables: Brandon McCarthy, Ian Kennedy, Ubaldo Jimenez*

De-funning a splits-based fun fact often just means looking at another component of the split. Take, for example, Chatwood and his *best-in-team-history 1.69 road ERA (min. 75 road IP)*. The last time a pitcher had a road ERA that low was all the way back in 2015, when Jake Arrieta posted a 1.60 mark. But nobody talked about that because his home ERA was 1.97, and they combined for a tidy 1.77. Conversely, Chatwood's home ERA was 6.12. That's where we find this fun fact's genesis and untruth.

Still, he demonstrated real progress in 2016, highlighted by pitching a career-high 158 innings after losing almost two full seasons to Tommy John surgery. He relied more on his four-seam fastball as opposed to his sinker, but Chatwood still posted the third-highest groundball rate among pitchers with at least 150 innings. It might not be fun to say "the truth lies in the middle," but that seems to be the case for the California native.

Jorge De La Rosa   LHP

Born: 4/5/81   Age: 36   Bats: L   Throws: L   Height: 6'1"   Weight: 215 Entered Pro Ball: International Free Agent, 1998

YEAR	TEAM	LVL	AGE	W	L	SV	G	GS	IP	H	HR	BB/9	K/9	K	GB%	BABIP	WHIP	ERA	FIP	DRA	VORP	WARP	cFIP	MPH
2014	COL	MLB	33	14	11	0	32	32	184¹	161	21	3.3	6.8	139	53%	.264	1.24	4.10	4.31	3.30	31.5	3.5	98	94.7
2015	COL	MLB	34	9	7	0	26	26	149	137	17	3.9	8.1	134	54%	.289	1.36	4.17	4.22	3.74	22.1	2.4	96	94.6
2016	ABQ	AAA	35	0	0	0	3	3	14²	14	0	4.9	6.8	11	56%	.311	1.50	4.30	4.27	6.36	-1.7	-0.2	105	
2016	COL	MLB	35	8	9	0	27	24	134	157	23	4.2	7.3	108	49%	.325	1.64	5.51	5.40	5.16	2.6	0.3	111	92.1
2017	*COL*	*MLB*	*36*	*8*	*8*	*0*	*24*	*24*	*131²*	*137*	*18*	*3.7*	*7.9*	*116*	*49%*	*.333*	*1.45*	*4.54*	*4.49*	*4.97*	*8.7*	*0.9*	*116*	
2018	*COL*	*MLB*	*37*	*6*	*8*	*0*	*21*	*21*	*120²*	*119*	*16*	*3.7*	*7.8*	*105*	*49%*	*.321*	*1.40*	*4.67*	*4.72*	*5.11*	*5.7*	*0.6*	*117*	

Breakout: 14%   Improve: 41%   Collapse: 16%   Attrition: 13%   MLB: 75%   *Comparables: Freddy Garcia, Josh Beckett, Kevin Millwood*

De La Rosa spent nine seasons as one of the best and most successful starting pitchers the Rockies have ever had. It's an admittedly low bar, but being one of two pitchers in team history to throw 1,000 innings and start 200 games, and to be better than average while doing so, is an undeniable success. Yet, chronicling the past is a great foreshadower of present struggles, and De La Rosa finally showed his age in 2016. Opponents hit his four-seam fastball and split-change—which he combined to throw about 65 percent of the time in 2016—both harder and more often than ever during his Rockies' tenure. And it's not like his command is a point of strength either. This may not be the end of the line for the player who was once named later, but it's getting close.

Mike Dunn   LHP

Born: 5/23/85   Age: 32   Bats: L   Throws: L   Height: 6'0"   Weight: 215 Entered Pro Ball: Round 33, 2004 Draft (#999 overall)

YEAR	TEAM	LVL	AGE	W	L	SV	G	GS	IP	H	HR	BB/9	K/9	K	GB%	BABIP	WHIP	ERA	FIP	DRA	VORP	WARP	cFIP	MPH
2014	MIA	MLB	29	10	6	1	75	0	57	47	4	3.5	10.6	67	37%	.291	1.21	3.16	3.03	4.19	1.9	0.2	95	97
2015	MIA	MLB	30	2	5	0	72	0	54	46	6	4.8	10.8	65	40%	.301	1.39	4.50	3.92	3.80	5.4	0.6	97	96.7
2016	MIA	MLB	31	6	1	0	51	0	42²	43	5	2.3	8.1	38	30%	.319	1.28	3.40	3.92	5.56	-2.8	-0.3	112	95.8
2017	*COL*	*MLB*	*32*	*3*	*3*	*3*	*57*	*0*	*60*	*64*	*10*	*3.7*	*9.2*	*62*	*55%*	*.317*	*1.51*	*4.70*	*4.67*	*4.66*	*1.7*	*0.2*	*100*	
2018	*COL*	*MLB*	*33*	*1*	*0*	*1*	*27*	*0*	*28²*	*29*	*4*	*3.4*	*9*	*28*	*55%*	*.340*	*1.42*	*4.19*	*4.64*	*5.03*	*0.3*	*0.0*	*113*	

Breakout: 19%   Improve: 35%   Collapse: 25%   Attrition: 10%   MLB: 78%   *Comparables: J.P. Howell, Tyler Yates, Frank Francisco*

As a fly-ball lefty with plus velocity and bad control there's nothing particularly special about Dunn, but that didn't stop the Rockies from handing him a three-year, $19 million deal as a free agent. It'll probably work out better for Colorado than a similarly eyebrow-raising investment in lefty reliever Logan Boone several offseasons ago, but Dunn is best suited for a middle relief role in which he can be spotted mostly versus left-handed hitters.

Carlos Estevez   RHP

Born: 12/28/92 Age: 24 Bats: R Throws: R Height: 6'4" Weight: 210 Entered Pro Ball: International Free Agent, 2011

YEAR	TEAM	LVL	AGE	W	L	SV	G	GS	IP	H	HR	BB/9	K/9	K	GB%	BABIP	WHIP	ERA	FIP	DRA	VORP	WARP	cFIP	MPH
2014	ASH	A	21	1	3	0	33	0	53¹	62	4	1.9	8.4	50	51%	.363	1.37	4.72	3.36	3.06	11.8	1.2	85	
2015	MOD	A+	22	5	0	5	14	0	19²	12	0	2.3	11.4	25	55%	.286	0.86	1.37	2.00	1.85	6.3	0.7	76	
2015	NBR	AA	22	0	3	13	34	0	36	39	2	2.2	10.8	43	42%	.363	1.33	4.50	2.44	1.76	11.9	1.3	79	
2016	COL	MLB	23	3	7	11	63	0	55	50	6	4.6	9.7	59	45%	.297	1.42	5.24	4.26	4.43	3.3	0.3	99	100.0
2017	*COL*	*MLB*	*24*	*2*	*2*	*0*	*41*	*0*	*43*	*49*	*7*	*3.8*	*8.1*	*39*	*53%*	*.318*	*1.59*	*5.03*	*4.92*	*4.90*	*0.1*	*0.0*	*100*	
2018	*COL*	*MLB*	*25*	*2*	*1*	*0*	*32*	*0*	*34*	*33*	*5*	*4.4*	*10.1*	*38*	*53%*	*.334*	*1.45*	*4.75*	*4.80*	*5.19*	*-0.2*	*0.0*	*118*	

Breakout: 38%   Improve: 54%   Collapse: 6%   Attrition: 23%   MLB: 73%   Comparables: Ken Giles, Stephen Pryor, Cody Allen

The essence of Estevez's 2017 season should have the same ingredients as his 2016—questions about role and control along with leverage as high as his heat. The rookie had a brief stint as closer, and he earned that spot on the strength of his triple-digit fastball and the promise found in his ability to limit walks. The velocity, if not terminal, was there, but walks ended up being an issue for the first time in his professional career, and they didn't help upon arrival in high-leverage situations. In fact, Estevez ended up with the fourth worst Win Probability Added among relievers in 2016—highlighted by some spectacularly bad outings. We'll learn soon enough how those essential elements combine in 2017, frame by frame.

Kyle Freeland   LHP

Born: 5/14/93 Age: 24 Bats: L Throws: L Height: 6'3" Weight: 170 Entered Pro Ball: Round 1, 2014 Draft (#8 overall)

YEAR	TEAM	LVL	AGE	W	L	SV	G	GS	IP	H	HR	BB/9	K/9	K	GB%	BABIP	WHIP	ERA	FIP	DRA	VORP	WARP	cFIP	MPH
2014	ASH	A	21	2	0	0	5	5	21²	14	1	1.7	7.5	18	52%	.220	0.83	0.83	3.08	3.32	5.1	0.5	91	
2015	MOD	A+	22	3	2	0	7	7	39²	48	5	1.8	4.3	19	49%	.314	1.41	4.76	5.06	5.52	-1.9	-0.2	107	
2016	NBR	AA	23	5	7	0	14	14	88¹	84	9	2.5	5.2	51	55%	.268	1.23	3.87	4.41	3.83	12.4	1.3	102	
2016	ABQ	AAA	23	6	3	0	12	12	73²	81	7	2.3	7.0	57	55%	.330	1.36	3.91	4.22	4.09	10.2	1.1	90	
2017	*COL*	*MLB*	*24*	*7*	*7*	*0*	*21*	*21*	*115*	*136*	*15*	*3.0*	*5.3*	*67*	*45%*	*.334*	*1.52*	*4.75*	*4.78*	*5.16*	*5.1*	*0.5*	*121*	
2018	*COL*	*MLB*	*25*	*5*	*7*	*0*	*18*	*18*	*105²*	*108*	*14*	*4.5*	*8.0*	*94*	*45%*	*.330*	*1.52*	*5.05*	*5.11*	*5.49*	*0.8*	*0.1*	*128*	

Breakout: 17%   Improve: 29%   Collapse: 12%   Attrition: 38%   MLB: 51%   Comparables: John Gast, Simon Castro, Edwin Escobar

A polished college lefty with advanced command, Freeland looked to be on the fast track to the major leagues. But shoulder fatigue and surgery to remove bone chips from his elbow kept him sidelined for almost the entire 2015 season. He split a healthy 2016 between Double- and Triple-A, posting nearly identical lines in both environments. Freeland relies on commanding the fastball low in the zone to generate grounders and complements it with a plus slider and a changeup. He's also working on a curveball. Freeland profiles as a back-end starter in a good rotation, but if pitches three and four don't progress, taking the fast track to the bullpen would be a fine fit.

Jon Gray   RHP

Born: 11/5/91 Age: 25 Bats: R Throws: R Height: 6'4" Weight: 235 Entered Pro Ball: Round 1, 2013 Draft (#3 overall)

YEAR	TEAM	LVL	AGE	W	L	SV	G	GS	IP	H	HR	BB/9	K/9	K	GB%	BABIP	WHIP	ERA	FIP	DRA	VORP	WARP	cFIP	MPH
2014	TUL	AA	22	10	5	0	24	24	124¹	107	10	3.0	8.2	113	40%	.285	1.19	3.91	3.43	3.12	29.1	3.1	93	
2015	ABQ	AAA	23	6	6	0	21	20	114¹	129	9	3.2	8.7	110	44%	.350	1.49	4.33	3.88	3.77	19.3	2.0	85	
2015	COL	MLB	23	0	2	0	9	9	40²	52	4	3.1	8.9	40	46%	.384	1.62	5.53	3.65	4.44	2.9	0.3	97	97.4
2016	COL	MLB	24	10	10	0	29	29	168	153	18	3.2	9.9	185	45%	.309	1.26	4.61	3.64	3.45	35.7	3.7	88	97.9
2017	*COL*	*MLB*	*25*	*10*	*10*	*0*	*29*	*29*	*165¹*	*166*	*20*	*3.2*	*9.1*	*166*	*48%*	*.311*	*1.38*	*4.00*	*3.92*	*4.06*	*20.6*	*2.1*	*93*	
2018	*COL*	*MLB*	*26*	*10*	*9*	*0*	*28*	*28*	*173¹*	*152*	*20*	*3.4*	*10.4*	*201*	*48%*	*.326*	*1.25*	*3.76*	*3.80*	*4.12*	*25.5*	*2.6*	*92*	

Breakout: 26%   Improve: 57%   Collapse: 19%   Attrition: 20%   MLB: 91%   Comparables: Gio Gonzalez, Edinson Volquez, Michael Pineda

By Baseball Prospectus' WARP model, Gray had the best rookie season for a pitcher in Colorado Rockies history. His season's masterpiece was possibly the best-pitched game the in the history of the club. He needed only 113 pitches to strike out 16 Padres during a complete-game shutout on September 17. Gray gave up four hits without walking a batter, thereby allowing two fewer baserunners than Ubaldo Jimenez did in his 2010 no-hitter. Beyond the Rockies, Gray placed among the top-25 pitchers in DRA and cFIP. His fastball velocity sat a couple of ticks higher in 2016 than the previous year, and his slider remained tough to hit. Gray also added a locatable curveball, which is a more effective third pitch than his changeup was. In all, the man who calls himself "Gray Wolf" is in the midst of realizing his front-of-the-rotation potential.

Jeff Hoffman   RHP

Born: 1/8/93 Age: 24 Bats: R Throws: R Height: 6'5" Weight: 225 Entered Pro Ball: Round 1, 2014 Draft (#9 overall)

YEAR	TEAM	LVL	AGE	W	L	SV	G	GS	IP	H	HR	BB/9	K/9	K	GB%	BABIP	WHIP	ERA	FIP	DRA	VORP	WARP	cFIP	MPH
2015	DUN	A+	22	3	3	0	11	11	56	59	4	2.4	6.1	38	53%	.329	1.32	3.21	3.70	5.03	0.3	0.0	102	
2015	NHP	AA	22	0	0	0	2	2	11²	9	0	1.5	6.2	8	43%	.257	0.94	1.54	2.41	3.09	2.6	0.3	86	
2015	NBR	AA	22	2	2	0	7	7	36¹	27	3	2.5	7.2	29	58%	.242	1.02	3.22	3.74	3.18	7.7	0.8	85	
2016	ABQ	AAA	23	6	9	0	22	22	118²	117	11	3.3	9.4	124	44%	.325	1.36	4.02	4.13	3.32	26.7	2.8	89	
2016	COL	MLB	23	0	4	0	8	6	31¹	37	7	4.9	6.3	22	51%	.297	1.72	4.88	6.31	6.27	-3.3	-0.3	114	96.8
2017	*COL*	*MLB*	*24*	*6*	*8*	*0*	*21*	*21*	*111¹*	*116*	*13*	*3.4*	*7.3*	*90*	*45%*	*.304*	*1.44*	*4.36*	*4.34*	*4.43*	*9.3*	*1.0*	*100*	
2018	*COL*	*MLB*	*25*	*7*	*8*	*0*	*22*	*22*	*132²*	*116*	*15*	*4.5*	*9.7*	*142*	*45%*	*.320*	*1.38*	*4.32*	*4.37*	*4.72*	*11.1*	*1.1*	*108*	

Breakout: 26%   Improve: 48%   Collapse: 12%   Attrition: 22%   MLB: 74%   Comparables: Mike Foltynewicz, Marco Gonzales, Jon Gray

Like Jon Gray before him, Hoffman's first few major-league starts contained more shellacking than not. Unlike Gray, Hoffman can't point to an extreme BABIP against and an "ability to miss bats" as a means of explaining it away. Hoffman allowed seven runs in three out of his first five starts before moving to the bullpen due to an innings limit. However, he finished the season on a high note. The Rockies called upon Hoffman to make a start in the final weekend of the season, and he struck out seven Brewers in five innings while giving up just two hits. All four of his pitches were working for him that day, and it put a hopeful bow on an otherwise forgettable first foray into the majors. He'll still have his rookie status intact heading into the 2017 season, which is possibly more than we can say about his confidence.

Boone Logan   LHP

Born: 8/13/84   Age: 32   Bats: R   Throws: L   Height: 6'5"   Weight: 215   Entered Pro Ball: Round 20, 2002 Draft (#600 overall)

YEAR	TEAM	LVL	AGE	W	L	SV	G	GS	IP	H	HR	BB/9	K/9	K	GB%	BABIP	WHIP	ERA	FIP	DRA	VORP	WARP	cFIP	MPH
2014	COL	MLB	29	2	3	0	35	0	25	31	6	4.0	11.5	32	54%	.379	1.68	6.84	5.10	2.59	5.3	0.6	83	95.0
2015	COL	MLB	30	0	3	0	60	0	35¹	40	3	4.3	11.2	44	45%	.374	1.61	4.33	3.64	3.12	6.3	0.7	94	95.5
2016	COL	MLB	31	2	5	1	66	0	46¹	27	4	3.9	11.1	57	51%	.221	1.01	3.69	3.27	2.60	12.2	1.3	77	95.5
2017	COL	MLB	32	2	1	1	37	0	39¹	37	5	3.6	10.5	46	60%	.340	1.33	3.77	3.74	4.13	2.9	0.3	88	
2018	COL	MLB	33	3	1	1	61	0	40²	36	5	3.5	10.1	45	60%	.320	1.28	4.07	4.10	4.46	3.2	0.3	96	

Breakout: 19%   Improve: 38%   Collapse: 26%   Attrition: 6%   MLB: 85%   Comparables: Francisco Rodriguez, Joel Hanrahan, Brad Lidge

On the one hand, Logan was remarkably consistent during his three years with the Rockies. He struck out between 11.07 and 11.52 batters per nine in his three seasons and walked between 3.88 and 4.33. The results reflected in his ERA, on the other hand, were all over the place. Logan went from regrettable signing in year one on account of his near-7 ERA to the team's best reliever in year three. There's something real to account for the change over time though: he progressively faced fewer right-handed batters, and doing so allowed his slider to thrive. No longer a set-up or late-inning reliever, he should have no trouble continuing to find work as a lefty specialist.

Jordan Lyles   RHP

Born: 10/19/90   Age: 26   Bats: R   Throws: R   Height: 6'4"   Weight: 230   Entered Pro Ball: Round 1, 2008 Draft (#38 overall)

YEAR	TEAM	LVL	AGE	W	L	SV	G	GS	IP	H	HR	BB/9	K/9	K	GB%	BABIP	WHIP	ERA	FIP	DRA	VORP	WARP	cFIP	MPH
2014	COL	MLB	23	7	4	0	22	22	126²	127	12	3.3	6.4	90	53%	.295	1.37	4.33	4.19	4.89	-0.8	-0.1	107	94.1
2015	COL	MLB	24	2	5	0	10	10	49	54	2	3.5	5.5	30	51%	.329	1.49	5.14	3.81	5.14	-0.4	0.0	111	95.2
2016	ABQ	AAA	25	4	2	0	8	8	44²	57	4	3.6	5.8	29	42%	.361	1.68	5.44	5.29	8.83	-17.3	-1.8	117	
2016	COL	MLB	25	4	5	1	40	5	58²	69	4	4.3	4.9	32	52%	.319	1.65	5.83	4.62	7.77	-17.4	-1.8	123	95.7
2017	COL	MLB	26	2	2	0	41	0	43	48	5	3.8	6.6	32	57%	.308	1.55	4.95	4.65	4.84	0.4	0.0	100	
2018	COL	MLB	27	1	0	0	23	0	24²	25	3	3.6	7.7	21	57%	.323	1.41	4.47	4.52	4.88	0.7	0.1	110	

Breakout: 27%   Improve: 60%   Collapse: 15%   Attrition: 12%   MLB: 96%   Comparables: John Lannan, Mike Pelfrey, Chris Volstad

In a final attempt to show that he debuted at age 20 because he was a promising starter rather than an available one, he began the year in the rotation. It didn't go well, and the Rockies demoted him after four uninspiring starts. He made one more spot start in May, but the fastball that hit opposing pitcher Ryan Vogelsong in the head overshadowed that awful outing (Vogelsong later called Lyles out for waiting too long to contact him after a pitch that, according to him, "could have killed me"). Lyles moved to the bullpen upon his return to the majors in June. The results were better, but advanced pitching metrics are extremely skeptical that he was any different in the bullpen than he was in the rotation. Regardless, Lyles is inspiring hope that he can find a second life as a reliever, but he'll only be in that position because of his eminent availability.

German Marquez   RHP

Born: 2/22/95   Age: 22   Bats: R   Throws: R   Height: 6'1"   Weight: 185   Entered Pro Ball: International Free Agent, 2011

YEAR	TEAM	LVL	AGE	W	L	SV	G	GS	IP	H	HR	BB/9	K/9	K	GB%	BABIP	WHIP	ERA	FIP	DRA	VORP	WARP	cFIP	MPH
2014	BGR	A	19	5	7	0	22	18	98	83	5	2.7	8.7	95	53%	.294	1.14	3.21	3.22	3.56	19.7	2.0	93	
2015	PCH	A+	20	7	13	0	26	23	139	147	6	1.9	6.7	104	41%	.320	1.27	3.56	3.14	3.64	21.9	2.4	94	
2016	NBR	AA	21	9	6	0	21	21	135²	124	9	2.2	8.4	126	48%	.304	1.16	2.85	3.25	1.96	47.2	5.1	79	
2016	ABQ	AAA	21	2	0	0	5	5	31	30	5	1.7	8.4	29	45%	.298	1.16	4.35	4.53	2.78	8.8	0.9	85	
2016	COL	MLB	21	1	1	0	6	3	20²	28	2	2.6	6.5	15	55%	.361	1.65	5.23	4.30	4.62	1.5	0.2	105	96.8
2017	COL	MLB	22	3	4	0	23	8	56	65	7	3.1	6.4	40	51%	.310	1.55	4.80	4.60	4.75	2.2	0.2	100	
2018	COL	MLB	23	7	7	0	57	18	145¹	138	19	4.3	9.0	146	51%	.325	1.42	4.69	4.73	5.05	5.4	0.6	118	

Breakout: 23%   Improve: 43%   Collapse: 10%   Attrition: 28%   MLB: 62%   Comparables: Jon Niese, Zach Davies, Jameson Taillon

The prospect that came to the Rockies along with Jake McGee in the trade that sent major-leaguer Corey Dickerson and prospect Kevin Padlo to the Rays, Marquez earned Eastern League Pitcher of the Year honors in 2016. He spent a bit of time in Triple-A before a September cup of coffee. Stamina and whether or not Marquez's changeup can develop into a viable third pitch remain persistent questions. With affirmative answers, Marquez could be a fifth starter as soon as 2017.

Tyler Matzek   LHP

Born: 10/19/90   Age: 26   Bats: L   Throws: L   Height: 6'3"   Weight: 230   Entered Pro Ball: Round 1, 2009 Draft (#11 overall)

YEAR	TEAM	LVL	AGE	W	L	SV	G	GS	IP	H	HR	BB/9	K/9	K	GB%	BABIP	WHIP	ERA	FIP	DRA	VORP	WARP	cFIP	MPH
2014	CSP	AAA	23	5	4	0	12	12	66²	70	8	4.2	8.2	61	51%	.302	1.51	4.05	4.82	4.42	9.9	1.0	92	
2014	COL	MLB	23	6	11	0	20	19	117²	120	9	3.4	7.0	91	52%	.312	1.39	4.05	3.75	4.33	6.6	0.7	101	95.4
2015	COL	MLB	24	2	1	0	5	5	22	21	2	7.8	6.1	15	43%	.302	1.82	4.09	5.98	6.16	-2.6	-0.3	126	95.0
2015	ABQ	AAA	24	0	1	1	10	1	11¹	5	1	13.5	11.9	15	54%	.174	1.94	8.74	6.86	9.08	-5.2	-0.5	125	
2016	MOD	A+	25	0	3	0	25	0	21	17	1	8.1	12.0	28	46%	.356	1.71	4.71	4.95	5.42	-0.8	-0.1	112	
2017	COL	MLB	26	2	2	0	9	6	34²	39	5	4.2	7.5	29	48%	.348	1.60	4.76	4.81	5.12	1.5	0.2	121	
2018	COL	MLB	27	6	7	1	31	18	115²	114	16	5.2	9.2	118	48%	.337	1.56	4.99	5.07	5.37	1.8	0.2	126	

Breakout: 25%   Improve: 43%   Collapse: 23%   Attrition: 33%   MLB: 75%   Comparables: Mitchell Boggs, Trevor Bell, Nathan Adcock

It's hard, sometimes, to remember Matzek. He hasn't pitched a major-league game since May 6, 2015, when he walked six in two innings. It's also getting hard to imagine remembering Matzek for anything other than his dueling demons of anxiety and mechanical issues that have repeatedly led to his ineffective wildness. In 2016, the Rockies attempted to ease Matzek into game action. They started by assigning him to face one batter at a time for High-A Modesto. In his first three outings of the season in early May, Matzek threw 16 balls and zero strikes. Things improved for Matzek in that he didn't walk *every* batter he faced in 2016. Still, the club outrighted him in June because they needed his roster spot and, after clearing waivers, it's getting hard to see a path back to the major leagues for the once-promising lefty.

Jake McGee   LHP

Born: 8/6/86   Age: 30   Bats: L   Throws: L   Height: 6'3"   Weight: 230   Entered Pro Ball: Round 5, 2004 Draft (#135 overall)

YEAR	TEAM	LVL	AGE	W	L	SV	G	GS	IP	H	HR	BB/9	K/9	K	GB%	BABIP	WHIP	ERA	FIP	DRA	VORP	WARP	cFIP	MPH
2014	TBA	MLB	27	5	2	19	73	0	71¹	48	2	2.0	11.4	90	38%	.280	0.90	1.89	1.76	2.69	14.2	1.6	73	99.1
2015	TBA	MLB	28	1	2	6	39	0	37¹	27	3	1.9	11.6	48	39%	.276	0.94	2.41	2.30	2.97	7.2	0.8	78	98.1
2016	COL	MLB	29	2	3	15	57	0	45²	56	9	3.2	7.5	38	41%	.338	1.58	4.73	5.33	5.61	-3.2	-0.3	112	96.5
2017	COL	MLB	30	2	3	5	52	0	54²	59	10	3.1	8.6	52	53%	.308	1.44	5.11	4.81	4.96	-0.3	0.0	100	
2018	COL	MLB	31	2	1	2	39	0	41²	42	8	3.1	8.2	38	53%	.313	1.35	5.09	5.14	5.56	-1.9	-0.2	129	

Breakout: 31%   Improve: 44%   Collapse: 28%   Attrition: 11%   MLB: 87%   *Comparables: Joakim Soria, Andrew Bailey, Antonio Bastardo*

There are no good signs here. McGee was known for his heavy fastball usage, which some observers thought would make him a good fit for the Rockies and Coors Field. But McGee threw his fastball just 84 percent of the time, the lowest since his rookie season and 12 percentage points lower than his most successful season. The change seems to have been due to ineffectiveness and a decline in velocity. He could still find a bullpen role, but what made him one of the best relievers in baseball a short while ago has gone missing.

Scott Oberg   RHP

Born: 3/13/90   Age: 27   Bats: R   Throws: R   Height: 6'2"   Weight: 205   Entered Pro Ball: Round 15, 2012 Draft (#468 overall)

YEAR	TEAM	LVL	AGE	W	L	SV	G	GS	IP	H	HR	BB/9	K/9	K	GB%	BABIP	WHIP	ERA	FIP	DRA	VORP	WARP	cFIP	MPH
2014	TUL	AA	24	0	1	15	27	0	27¹	22	1	2.0	6.9	21	52%	.262	1.02	2.63	2.83	3.69	3.5	0.4	94	
2015	COL	MLB	25	3	4	1	64	0	58¹	58	10	4.8	6.8	44	56%	.286	1.53	5.09	5.78	4.26	2.9	0.3	109	97.7
2016	ABQ	AAA	26	1	0	9	27	0	29²	16	1	3.3	10.9	36	54%	.234	0.91	2.43	2.95	1.79	10.5	1.1	76	
2016	COL	MLB	26	1	1	1	24	0	26	26	3	3.8	6.9	20	56%	.295	1.42	5.19	4.53	4.29	2.0	0.2	102	97.2
2017	COL	MLB	27	1	1	0	26	0	27	29	4	3.8	7.3	22	48%	.302	1.50	5.07	4.90	4.95	-0.1	0.0	100	
2018	COL	MLB	28	2	1	0	46	0	48²	45	6	3.9	9.1	49	48%	.317	1.35	4.43	4.48	4.87	1.4	0.1	111	

Breakout: 28%   Improve: 40%   Collapse: 19%   Attrition: 21%   MLB: 72%   *Comparables: Rich Thompson, Steve Cishek, Tanner Scheppers*

Oberg has a live arm and two workable secondary pitches that missed more bats in 2016 than 2015, so late relief is not an entirely misplaced hope. But he was no less hittable in 2016 than the year prior and still had trouble with his command. He was diagnosed with axillary artery thrombosis, or blood clots, in his pitching arm in August, which ended his season. Assuming he returns fully healthy, Oberg could still find his way to a middle innings role.

Adam Ottavino   RHP

Born: 11/22/85   Age: 31   Bats: B   Throws: R   Height: 6'5"   Weight: 220   Entered Pro Ball: Round 1, 2006 Draft (#30 overall)

YEAR	TEAM	LVL	AGE	W	L	SV	G	GS	IP	H	HR	BB/9	K/9	K	GB%	BABIP	WHIP	ERA	FIP	DRA	VORP	WARP	cFIP	MPH
2014	COL	MLB	28	1	4	1	75	0	65	67	6	2.2	9.7	70	47%	.347	1.28	3.60	3.07	2.67	13.1	1.4	81	98.2
2015	COL	MLB	29	1	0	3	10	0	10¹	3	0	1.7	11.3	13	63%	.158	0.48	0.00	1.52	3.26	1.7	0.2	81	98.1
2016	COL	MLB	30	1	3	7	34	0	27	18	3	2.3	11.7	35	62%	.250	0.93	2.67	3.04	2.51	7.4	0.8	67	96.3
2017	COL	MLB	31	3	3	30	57	0	60	61	9	3.1	9.8	65	48%	.314	1.38	4.12	4.10	4.20	4.8	0.5	92	
2018	COL	MLB	32	2	1	15	36	0	38²	38	6	3.2	9.6	41	48%	.334	1.34	4.41	4.44	4.80	1.4	0.1	108	

Breakout: 28%   Improve: 41%   Collapse: 26%   Attrition: 12%   MLB: 89%   *Comparables: Michael Wuertz, Ryan Madson, Jesse Crain*

Between September 7, 2014 and August 24, 2016, Ottavino struck out 34 batters and walked five in 31 innings of work without allowing a run. The Tommy John surgery he had in 2015 accounts for the limited work. After the scoreless run ended, he gave up nine runs in his next 10 2/3 innings, with five coming in a single disastrous outing. That said, he also struck out 18 batters and walked just four in that rough patch. Ottavino didn't seem to be hampered at all upon his return to baseball, but further distance from surgery will be welcome. That's just one reason to believe he'll be an elite late-inning reliever in 2017.

Riley Pint   RHP

Born: 11/6/97   Age: 19   Bats: R   Throws: R   Height: 6'4"   Weight: 195   Entered Pro Ball: Round 1, 2016 Draft (#4 overall)

The right-hander stood out during the spring due to a fastball that regularly touched 100 mph and an excellent changeup. His maturity separated him from the rest of his draft class as well. Jeff Passan featured him in his recent book *The Arm*, which showed Pint to be arm-health conscious. He didn't pitch year-round and made sure to give his arm rest by not committing to too many showcases. Pint's velocity was there in his professional debut, although his command was not. He's got a long way to go, but the limit of Pint's potential resides in the clouds.

Chad Qualls RHP

Born: 8/17/78 Age: 38 Bats: R Throws: R Height: 6'4" Weight: 235 Entered Pro Ball: Round 2, 2000 Draft (#67 overall)

YEAR	TEAM	LVL	AGE	W	L	SV	G	GS	IP	H	HR	BB/9	K/9	K	GB%	BABIP	WHIP	ERA	FIP	DRA	VORP	WARP	cFIP	MPH
2014	HOU	MLB	35	1	5	19	58	0	51¹	54	5	0.9	7.5	43	58%	.310	1.15	3.33	3.16	2.78	9.7	1.1	83	95.3
2015	HOU	MLB	36	3	5	4	60	0	49¹	46	6	1.6	8.4	46	61%	.288	1.11	4.38	3.49	3.32	7.6	0.8	85	94.2
2016	COL	MLB	37	2	0	0	44	0	32²	43	5	2.5	6.1	22	55%	.328	1.59	5.23	4.66	4.52	1.6	0.2	107	92.5
2017	COL	MLB	38	2	3	0	52	0	54²	63	8	3.0	6.9	42	49%	.316	1.53	4.98	4.65	4.85	0.4	0.0	100	
2018	COL	MLB	39	1	0	0	30	0	31²	36	5	2.9	6.8	24	49%	.335	1.46	4.98	5.02	5.43	-1.0	-0.1	123	

Breakout: 18% Improve: 32% Collapse: 23% Attrition: 8% MLB: 75% Comparables: Alan Embree, Matt Thornton, Kyle Farnsworth

It makes sense to take a chance on an aging reliever with an ostensibly sturdy arm and a decent run of success. It makes less sense to commit more than one year to such a pitcher, but that's what the Rockies did prior to the 2016 season, when they signed Qualls to a two-year, $6 million contract. The first year saw Qualls' fastball velocity drop for the third consecutive season, but on the bright side, it was another year in the books without tripping while pumping his fist. The 2017 season could close the book on Qualls, and it's no sure thing he'll even make it all the way through.

Chris Rusin LHP

Born: 10/22/86 Age: 30 Bats: L Throws: L Height: 6'2" Weight: 195 Entered Pro Ball: Round 4, 2009 Draft (#140 overall)

YEAR	TEAM	LVL	AGE	W	L	SV	G	GS	IP	H	HR	BB/9	K/9	K	GB%	BABIP	WHIP	ERA	FIP	DRA	VORP	WARP	cFIP	MPH
2014	CHN	MLB	27	0	0	0	4	0	12²	16	1	3.6	5.7	8	49%	.341	1.66	7.11	4.05	4.04	0.6	0.1	107	90.5
2014	IOW	AAA	27	8	13	0	23	23	146¹	163	15	2.3	6.0	97	55%	.320	1.37	4.31	4.63	4.16	25.9	2.6	100	
2015	ABQ	AAA	28	3	2	0	7	6	34¹	47	6	2.9	4.7	18	54%	.325	1.69	6.29	5.78	5.88	-2.3	-0.2	107	
2015	COL	MLB	28	6	10	0	24	22	131²	170	19	2.8	5.9	86	53%	.339	1.60	5.33	4.73	4.57	7.1	0.8	103	91.9
2016	COL	MLB	29	3	5	0	29	7	84¹	82	5	2.5	7.4	69	61%	.308	1.25	3.74	3.25	3.16	18.7	1.9	89	91.7
2017	COL	MLB	30	4	4	0	47	6	78	86	9	3.0	6.6	57	47%	.310	1.46	4.45	4.33	4.49	4.7	0.5	100	
2018	COL	MLB	31	3	2	0	30	4	49²	49	7	3.3	8.4	46	47%	.321	1.34	4.48	4.51	4.89	2.3	0.2	110	

Breakout: 7% Improve: 20% Collapse: 21% Attrition: 20% MLB: 48% Comparables: Luis Mendoza, Philip Humber, Justin Germano

There is some value in Rusin's ability to step in and start when needed, but going to him in the first place is an admittance that your organizational depth is lacking. In relief, he notched appearances anywhere from one batter to 4.2 innings, and he did so with a 5.13 strikeout-to-walk ratio and a 2.58 ERA. This remains a vast improvement over his 1.87 K/BB and 5.08 ERA as a starter. On the whole, and from ERA to DRA, Rusin had a fine 2016. Whether or not he has to start going forward, and what that does to his player card, says more about the team he's playing for than it does him.

Robert Tyler RHP

Born: 6/18/95 Age: 21 Bats: R Throws: R Height: 6'4" Weight: 226 Entered Pro Ball: Round 1, 2016 Draft (#38 overall)

YEAR	TEAM	LVL	AGE	W	L	SV	G	GS	IP	H	HR	BB/9	K/9	K	GB%	BABIP	WHIP	ERA	FIP	DRA	VORP	WARP	cFIP	MPH
2017	COL	MLB	22	1	4	0	7	7	27²	40	7	11.4	4.1	13	68%	.353	2.72	9.50	9.48	10.34	-14.7	-1.5	226	

Breakout: 3% Improve: 3% Collapse: 1% Attrition: 3% MLB: 4% Comparables: Wilking Rodriguez, Tyler Wilson, Daniel Hudson

A supplemental first round pick out of the University of Georgia, Tyler has a mid- to high-90s fastball with movement and sink. He has a workable changeup, but no current third pitch to support a run as a starter—which was a big part of why he did not go towards the top of the first round as projected by some heading into the spring. An accelerated path to a major-league bullpen seems to be a pretty likely outcome here.

LINEOUTS

Hitters

NAME	POS	TEAM	LVL	AGE	PA	R	2B	3B	HR	RBI	BB	K	SB	CS	AVG/OBP/SLG	TAv	VORP	BABIP	BRR	FRAA	WARP
Cristhian Adames	SS	COL	MLB	24	256	25	7	3	2	17	24	47	2	3	.218/.304/.302	.209	-3.8	.267	0.3	SS(47): 0.2, 3B(11): -0.1	-0.4
Dustin Garneau	C	ABQ	AAA	28	211	31	11	0	15	35	16	43	2	0	.292/.367/.595	.312	20.4	.302	0.2	C(47): -0.1	2.1
	C	COL	MLB	28	75	7	6	0	1	6	6	22	0	0	.235/.293/.368	.235	0.0	.326	-1.4	C(23): -2.8	-0.3
Jordan Patterson	OF	ABQ	AAA	24	495	75	24	7	14	61	47	118	10	0	.293/.376/.480	.281	19.6	.370	1.5	RF(76): 10.9, 1B(38): 0.5	3.2
	OF	COL	MLB	24	19	1	1	0	0	2	1	1	0	1	.444/.474/.500	.323	0.9	.471	-0.6	RF(5): -0.2, 1B(2): 0.1	0.1
Ben Paulsen	1B	COL	MLB	28	97	8	5	0	1	11	5	27	0	0	.217/.258/.304	.189	-4.7	.297	1.0	1B(23): -1.1, LF(7): -0.2	-0.6
	1B	ABQ	AAA	28	314	44	17	5	6	40	24	64	1	0	.278/.331/.434	.263	4.3	.336	-0.1	1B(64): 0.3, LF(4): 0.7	0.5
Patrick Valaika	INF	NBR	AA	23	474	66	33	3	13	67	28	95	8	9	.269/.314/.450	.275	25.9	.315	2.1	SS(65): -5.3, 3B(29): 1.6	2.2
	INF	ABQ	AAA	23	115	8	8	1	1	13	2	28	2	0	.209/.226/.327	.194	-3.3	.265	0.6	SS(15): 0.7, 2B(9): 1.4	-0.1
	INF	COL	MLB	23	19	3	1	0	1	2	0	8	0	0	.263/.263/.474	.274	0.5	.400	-0.4	3B(6): 0.1, 2B(5): -0.1	0.0
Forrest Wall	2B	MOD	A+	20	521	57	16	4	6	56	41	97	22	11	.264/.329/.355	.266	18.2	.319	0.6	2B(117): -4.6	1.4

Cristhian Adames owns a glove that makes him a useful utility infielder capable of filling in at shortstop in a pinch. Unfortunately, he doesn't appear to own a bat. ❖ **Dustin Garneau** is a human being capable of playing baseball's catcher position both in Triple-A and in the major leagues of baseball if the need should arise. He's also three letters away from being a former MVP. ❖ After hitting well in an unforgiving environment as a 17-year-old, a similar stateside debut could see **Daniel Montano** shoot up prospect rankings by this time next year. ❖ A platoonable lefty that can play the outfield corners and first base, **Jordan Patterson** is a player that teams like to have around, as long as they don't have to rely on him. ❖ **Ben Paulsen** lost his bat speed and, along with it, any semblance of being a major-leaguer. He gave back more than half his career WARP in 2016 and was unceremoniously outrighted to Triple-A in September. ❖ Like his brother Chris, **Pat Valaika** should wrap up his career having played four defensive positions, making seat assignments at the Valaika family Thanksgiving much easier to figure out. ❖ **Forrest Wall**'s bat, especially the distinct gap power he previously demonstrated, stalled in the California League. For now, it's a part of his development and not a reason to worry about the keystoner.

Pitchers

NAME	TEAM	LVL	AGE	W	L	SV	G	GS	IP	H	HR	BB/9	K/9	K	GB%	BABIP	WHIP	ERA	FIP	DRA	VORP	WARP	cFIP	MPH
Matthew Carasiti	NBR	AA	24	0	2	29	38	0	39	28	5	1.6	9.9	43	41%	.245	0.90	2.31	3.44	1.69	13.2	1.4	73	
	COL	MLB	24	1	0	0	19	0	15²	25	1	6.3	9.8	17	36%	.471	2.30	9.19	4.53	5.63	-1.1	-0.1	116	96.9
Shane Carle	ABQ	AAA	24	5	8	0	27	19	111¹	147	9	2.6	7.1	88	48%	.375	1.61	5.42	4.19	5.23	0.8	0.1	98	
Yohan Flande	ABQ	AAA	30	3	3	0	18	1	42¹	52	2	3.0	5.7	27	51%	.352	1.56	4.25	4.05	5.24	-1.2	-0.1	110	
	COL	MLB	30	0	0	0	2	0	3²	8	0	7.4	0.0	0	53%	.471	3.00	12.27	5.64	5.81	-0.3	0.0	115	92.0
Gonzalez Germen	COL	MLB	28	2	1	1	40	0	40²	41	5	5.5	7.1	32	41%	.303	1.62	5.31	5.13	6.31	-6.1	-0.6	122	95.6
	ABQ	AAA	28	1	0	3	11	0	13²	11	0	3.3	10.5	16	38%	.297	1.17	0.66	2.48	3.79	1.8	0.2	93	
Rayan Gonzalez	NBR	AA	25	2	2	1	46	0	52	44	2	4.0	8.5	49	55%	.302	1.29	3.12	3.47	4.39	2.0	0.2	93	
Zachary Jemiola	NBR	AA	22	8	10	0	27	27	162	186	15	2.6	5.1	92	42%	.317	1.43	4.39	4.44	6.39	-23.2	-2.5	117	
Peter Lambert	ASH	A	19	5	8	0	26	26	126	125	7	2.4	7.7	108	47%	.316	1.25	3.93	3.31	2.90	29.6	3.2	88	
Justin Miller	ABQ	AAA	29	0	0	0	12	0	12	15	0	3.0	6.0	8	40%	.349	1.58	6.75	3.39	6.78	-2.4	-0.2	111	
	COL	MLB	29	1	1	0	40	0	42²	50	6	4.2	9.5	45	35%	.367	1.64	5.70	4.45	5.13	-0.8	-0.1	109	95.2
Sam Moll	ABQ	AAA	24	3	5	2	42	0	47¹	55	5	3.6	7.4	39	55%	.345	1.56	4.94	4.71	5.74	-4.1	-0.4	100	
Jason Motte	COL	MLB	34	0	1	0	30	0	23²	28	6	3.0	9.1	24	43%	.319	1.52	4.94	5.72	4.27	1.8	0.2	101	96.1
Harrison Musgrave	NBR	AA	24	5	1	0	6	6	40¹	20	1	1.8	6.7	30	51%	.174	0.69	1.79	2.86	3.34	7.9	0.9	87	
	ABQ	AAA	24	8	7	0	19	19	113	118	17	3.2	6.3	79	43%	.292	1.40	4.30	5.39	5.77	-5.3	-0.5	111	
Antonio Senzatela	NBR	AA	21	4	1	0	7	7	34²	27	1	2.3	7.0	27	44%	.265	1.04	1.82	3.13	3.67	5.5	0.6	94	
Jesus Tinoco	MOD	A+	21	0	3	0	4	4	13¹	37	3	2.0	5.4	8	44%	.586	3.00	14.85	6.34	6.32	-1.3	-0.1	106	
	ASH	A	21	3	8	0	16	16	86¹	118	10	2.6	5.5	53	48%	.345	1.66	5.63	4.62	5.55	-5.1	-0.6	107	
Jerry Vasto	MOD	A+	24	0	1	10	23	0	26	17	0	2.4	12.5	36	51%	.288	0.92	1.38	1.87	1.33	10.8	1.1	70	
	NBR	AA	24	4	3	10	31	0	29²	28	2	4.6	10.3	34	38%	.333	1.45	3.03	3.46	4.55	0.6	0.1	97	
Jack Wynkoop	ASH	A	22	6	3	0	14	14	93¹	107	12	0.7	7.0	73	50%	.337	1.22	3.47	3.76	2.34	27.8	3.0	79	
	MOD	A+	22	7	2	0	14	14	77¹	80	5	0.6	8.3	71	56%	.338	1.10	2.68	3.03	1.98	30.0	3.1	74	

Matt Carasiti made his major-league debut on August 12, and it quickly became clear the reliever should have debuted at some later date. At 25, he has a small, yet very much open, window to fulfill his middle-relief destiny. ❖ A big frame and multiple off-speed pitches provide the glimmer of a starter, but multi-inning middle relief appears to be where **Shane Carle** is headed instead. ❖ **Jairo Diaz**'s fastball velocity dipped all the way down to 94 mph in the spring, portending Tommy John surgery and a missed season. Upon return, he could play a significant bullpen role in 2017. ❖ **Yohan Flande** is the cold sore that returns once a year for a couple of weeks at the most inopportune time, yet after landing with the Samsung Lions of the KBO, at least we'll have more notice next time. ❖ Let's remember **Gonzalez** German **Germen** for his middle name instead of the fact that he was once DFA'd four times in about a month. ❖ A team could do worse than having a depth reliever with a groundball rate higher than 50 percent; a team could do worse than **Rayan Gonzalez**. ❖ **Zach Jemiola** already looks like a rubber-armed pitcher who will have to take the good and the bad of being a pitch-to-contact starter. ❖ **Peter Lambert** is advanced for his age, yet looks like he's 12 years old. Despite that dichotomy, he could see the back-end of a rotation in a few years. ❖ Thought to be a darkhorse candidate for late-inning relief due to his ability to strike guys out, **Justin Miller** couldn't stop walking them in 2016, and now he's not thought of much at all. ❖ Animal, benign skin growth, jetty, unit of measurement, spy, sauce made from chili peppers and chocolate (pronounced "MO-lay"), LOOGY (spelled "**Sam Moll**"). ❖ After barely throwing 20 innings in 2016, **Jason Motte** exhibited almost all of the risk involved in signing a mid-30s reliever as a free agent and not a lot of the reward. Fortunately, he's signed through 2017, so they can learn this lesson all over again this season. ❖ According to wordsmith.org, "**Harrison Musgrave**" has 93,751 anagrams. None of them are "emergency starter," but orange ravish rums overhang Russia, Mr. ❖ Wondering how **Mike Nikorak** is doing? Look first to the BB/9. Almost six is better than over 16, but that's damning with the faintest of praise. The big righty has a long way to go. ❖ **Luis Noguera** was a top-20 international free agent out of Venezuela whose future tense relies on the shape of his frame and his four pitches. ❖ A couple of bouts with shoulder inflammation limited **Antonio Senzatela** to seven starts, but it shouldn't keep him off top prospect lists. ❖ Any notion that **Jesus Tinoco** is a prospect instead of a project has been muted. ❖ Pressed to invent a player—say, a lefty with a fastball/slider combo with a decent shot to be a bullpen option in 2017—one might come up with the name "**Jerry Vasto**." ❖ Don't scout the statline, but lefty **Jack Wynkoop** slung a Buehrle-esque mid-80s fastball and struck out 144 batters while walking just 12 in 170.2 innings across two levels.

DETROIT TIGERS

Essay by Matthew Trueblood

Player comments by Matt Sussman, David Lee and BP staff

In Greek mythology, Dionysus, god of wine, runs into some trouble with Pentheus, an Athenian king. Pentheus doubts Dionysus' divinity, accuses him of being a mortal and a bastard and tries (twice) to imprison him. Dionysus gives him a few chances and tries to reason with him. But Pentheus keeps pressing the issue, really disrespecting Dionysus now, so Dionysus drives the king insane with his gift of wine, gets him to don a woman's dress and charge into the woods where the rabid worshippers of Dionysus are suckling wild beasts. Long story short, the mortal who tried to wrestle the god of wine into submission gets torn to pieces by a pack of revelers led by his own mother. That's one fable, but there are two morals:

1. Don't try to outsmart the gods.
2. When the party goes on for too long, the hangover can get pretty ugly.

The Tigers have been slowly learning these lessons since 2015, when their profoundly Midwestern imitation of a dynasty—smaller than a full-fledged East Coast string of titles, rougher at the edges than a West Coast one, a bit insecure at its foundation—collapsed in on itself. Gone was an entire crucial season, one fewer year in which Mike Ilitch might fairly hope for this core of Miguel Cabrera, Justin Verlander and Victor Martinez to deliver the World Series ring he's wanted so badly for so long. Soon, gone too was Dave Dombrowski, leaving his right-hand man Al Avila in charge but with the unmistakable whiff of gunsmoke in the air.

The position in which Dombrowski left Avila was unenviable, so we should consider the new GM's first season at the helm a qualified success. He did shore up the obvious holes on the roster last winter, adding Cameron Maybin, Francisco Rodriguez and Justin Wilson via trades and signing Jordan Zimmermann and Mark Lowe (and inexplicably Mike Pelfrey). Then, in a surprise move late in the offseason, the Tigers splurged on Justin Upton to seemingly solidify one of the AL's best lineups.

Upton was to be the first sign of the revenge of Dionysus for the 2016 Tigers. In his first 177 plate appearances spanning a quarter of the season, Upton hit .233/.266/.319 with 66 strikeouts and 10 walks. At that point, manager Brad Ausmus sat Upton for almost a full week and thereafter, although slowly, Upton came around. He hit .255/.326/.525 the rest of

TEAM PROSPECTUS
2016 W-L: 86-75, 2ND IN AL CENTRAL

Pythag	.515	12th	DER	.701	17th
RS/G	4.66	10th	B-Age	30	27th
RA/G	4.48	17th	P-Age	28.8	24th
TAv	.262	14th	Salary	$198.6M	3rd
BRR	-18.2	30th	M$/MW	$4.9M	5th
TAv-P	.253	8th	DL Days	887	12th
FIP	4.12	12th	$ on DL	6%	3rd

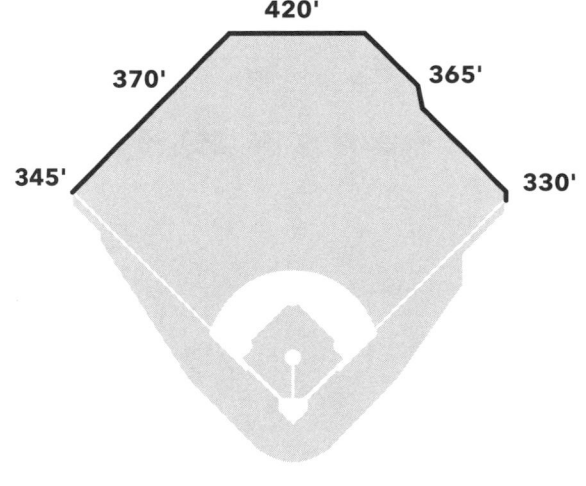

Outfield wall profile: 6'10" to 14'

Three-Year Park Factors

Runs	Runs/RH	Runs/LH	HR/RH	HR/LH
107	111	103	107	117

Top Hitter WARP	4.5	Ian Kinsler
Top Pitcher WARP	6.8	Justin Verlander
Top Prospect		Matt Manning

2016 Hit List Ranking

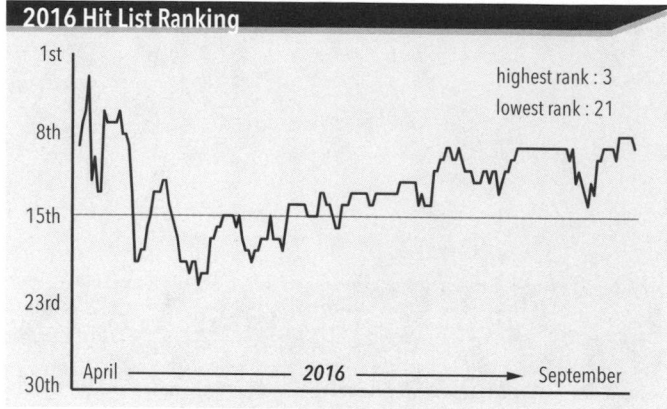

highest rank : 3
lowest rank : 21

April — 2016 → September

Committed Payroll (in millions)

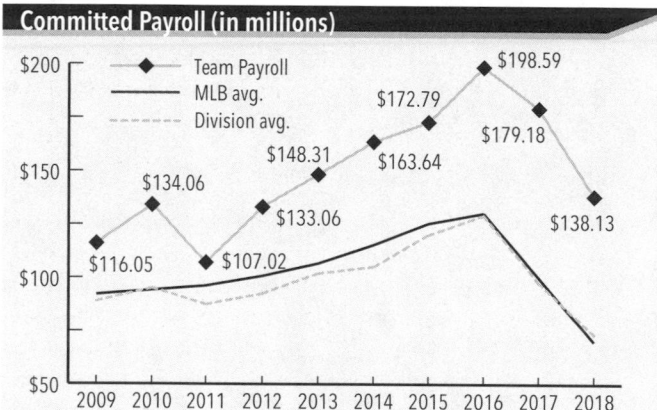

- ◆ Team Payroll
- — MLB avg.
- - - Division avg.

$198.59
$172.79
$179.18
$148.31
$163.64
$134.06
$133.06
$138.13
$116.05
$107.02

2009 2010 2011 2012 2013 2014 2015 2016 2017 2018

Farm System Ranking

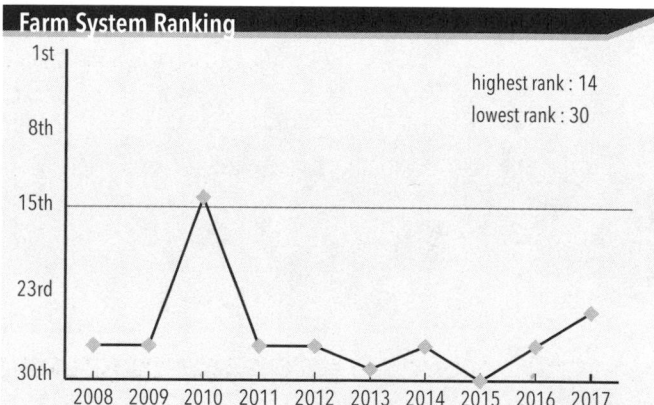

highest rank : 14
lowest rank : 30

2008 2009 2010 2011 2012 2013 2014 2015 2016 2017

Personnel

EVP, General Manager:
Al Avila

VP, Assistant General Manager:
David Chadd

VP, Assistant General Manager:
John Westhoff

Manager:
Brad Ausmus

BP Alumni:
Andrew Koo
Nick Wheatley-Schaller

---

the way, matching his recent track record. Some damage was already done, but his outlook looks positive going forward.

Unfortunately for Detroit, the same may not be true of Zimmermann. He earned AL Pitcher of the Month honors in his first month with the Tigers, but spent the rest of the season battling injuries and an inability to miss bats. Those things would be unwelcome but acceptable bumps in the road, except Zimmermann has encountered one or both of those problems in the majority of his seasons. That the contact issues were exacerbated by a move to the AL might be coincidence—maybe he was simply not at full strength for longer than anyone knew, a plausible theory—but there seems to be trouble ahead.

Despite Zimmermann's misfortune, the Tigers' pitching staff improved dramatically over the course of the season as Verlander rediscovered his former ace-caliber glory and Michael Fulmer emerged as a credible second starter on the way to being named Rookie of the Year. Three pitchers upon whom the team relied entering the season got torched during the first half:

- Anibal Sanchez: 373 batters faced, .889 OPS allowed
- Mike Pelfrey: 442 batters faced, .871 OPS allowed
- Mark Lowe: 137 batters faced, 1.094 OPS allowed

The team's aggregate first-half ERA was 4.60. From July 1 onward, however:

- Sanchez: 295 batters faced, .754 OPS allowed
- Pelfrey: 99 batters faced, .862 OPS allowed
- Lowe: 87 batters faced, .656 OPS allowed

In addition to getting modest improvements from each of these three, Ausmus and his staff were able to shift a lot of work away from them. Daniel Norris had some strong starts. Bruce Rondon came up in late June, stayed healthy and dominated in middle relief. Both Justin and Alex Wilson proved capable setup men for Rodriguez. The Tigers' second-half ERA was 3.88, despite their rotation remaining in flux for much of the stretch run.

Upton's resurgence and the team's newly formidable pitching staff spelled trouble for the rest of the American League. The Tigers won on July 31 to climb to 57-48. They were 4.5 games behind the Indians in the AL Central and just one game out of a Wild Card spot. However, over the final two months the places in which the roster had been worn thin by the team's years of win-now moves became obvious. They finished 29-27, fading to a final weekend elimination from playoff contention.

Here's how it happened.

- Jose Iglesias started 93 of 105 games through July 31. Thereafter, he started 38 of 56. Iglesias was worth 2.4 WARP in 516 plate appearances as the team's shortstop. All other Tigers shortstops combined for 117 plate appearances and -0.1 WARP.
- Nick Castellanos started 100 of the first 105 games, but just eight of the final 56. Castellanos was worth

1.8 WARP at third base, in 444 PAs. All other Tigers third basemen were worth -0.8 WARP in 218 PAs.

- Cameron Maybin started 57 of the first 105 games and 32 of the final 56. He was worth 3.2 WARP in 389 PAs in center field. All other Tigers center fielders were worth -0.1 WARP in 290 PAs.
- J.D. Martinez started 65 of the first 105 games and 54 of the final 56. He finished the season on a tear, batting .332/.392/.553 after August 1. Martinez was worth 1.7 WARP in 509 PAs as the team's right fielder. All other Tigers right fielders were worth -0.9 WARP in 183 PAs.

Though Martinez getting healthy helped, it couldn't offset the simultaneous losses of three of the Tigers' most important supporting cast members for long periods down the stretch. The injuries exposed a glaring lack of depth, a problem created by the Tigers' previous years of wheeling and dealing to stay on top the division. Eugenio Suarez might have been a perfect candidate to step into the breach when Iglesias got hurt, but he'd been traded two winters before to patch up a thin pitching staff. Devon Travis would have been a more viable replacement than Casey McGehee for Castellanos, but he'd been swapped for Anthony Gose that same winter.

The farm system, depleted by trades and surrendered draft picks (the cost of buying top-end free agents), was too thin to offer either direct solutions or the currency to fill holes. And yet the Tigers ended the 2016 season as a good team. They could, with just one or two better breaks, have made the playoffs for the fifth time in six years. But those better breaks didn't happen and now the team appears to be cutting back rather than gearing up. Whether Avila convinced

Ilitch to stop spending lavishly or was convinced to stop, he became an evangelist for a new modus operandi in Detroit.

It's easy to picture a Venn Diagram of the Tigers' roster, with circles for good players, young players and expensive players. According to the organization's new apparent vision, the core of the team—its power center—is shifting from the intersection of "good" and "expensive" (where Cabrera, Verlander and several other established stars sit) to the intersection of "good" and "young" (where Castellanos, Iglesias, Fulmer and Norris are among the names to know). The future of these Cabrera-Verlander Tigers is suddenly, urgently uncertain.

Given that fact, it's worth asking if Avila should have done more in 2016. There was a legitimate chance for two all-time great Tigers to get back to the playoffs together, maybe for the last time. It wouldn't have been an especially clean shot at a title, but it might have been their best one between now and 2020, especially if they follow the course Avila seemed determined to trace going forward. Avila had the aforementioned tepidness of his minor-league system hindering him at the trade deadline, but might he have been more creative? Perhaps he failed by not proactively addressing depth shortfalls that hardly came out of nowhere.

One way or another, a ton of money comes off the Tigers' books at the end of the 2017 season. They'll officially be rebuilding at that point, no matter what shape that rebuild takes. They could have more earnestly raged against the dying of the light last season, but there remains a path forward from here, for one last season. ■

—*Matthew Trueblood is an author*
of Baseball Prospectus

HITTERS

Erick Aybar   SS

Born: 1/14/84   Age: 33   Bats: B   Throws: R   Height: 5'10"   Weight: 195   Entered Pro Ball: International Free Agent, 2002

YEAR	TEAM	LVL	AGE	PA	R	2B	3B	HR	RBI	BB	K	SB	CS	AVG/OBP/SLG	TAv	VORP	DADIP	BRR	FRAA	WARP
2014	ANA	MLB	30	641	77	30	4	7	68	36	62	16	9	.278/.321/.379	.270	35.5	.297	5.5	SS(155): -14.6	2.3
2015	ANA	MLB	31	638	74	30	1	3	44	25	73	15	6	.270/.301/.338	.237	13.8	.300	3.2	SS(154): -13.2	0.1
2016	GWN	AAA	32	31	3	1	0	0	2	2	2	2	0	.172/.226/.207	.148	-2.3	.185	0.2	SS(6): -0.2	-0.3
2016	ATL	MLB	32	368	27	14	2	2	26	20	59	3	5	.242/.293/.313	.232	5.3	.284	0.9	SS(93): -0.4 • 2B(1): 0.8	0.6
2016	DET	MLB	32	91	7	5	0	1	8	11	11	0	0	.250/.341/.350	.246	1.4	.279	-0.5	3B(12): -1.5 • SS(11): -0.6	-0.1
2017	DET	MLB	33	472	47	23	3	7	47	25	57	9	5	.271/.313/.387	.237	11.8	.292	2.0	SS -6, 3B -1	0.5
2018	DET	MLB	34	467	47	21	3	6	43	23	58	7	5	.256/.296/.362	.229	3.0	.279	2.4	SS -6, 3B -1	-0.4

Breakout: 0%   Improve: 24%   Collapse: 9%   Attrition: 15%   MLB: 94%   *Comparables: Luis Aparicio, Jack Wilson, Orlando Cabrera*

The memories of Aybar being a feisty out in a hellacious Angels lineup are still fresh, but he's now the slap hitter who bookends the lineup on the other side. His role in Atlanta was to keep the shortstop dirt warm until Dansby Swanson was ready. Aybar then drummed up enough value to be sent to Detroit, where he tended to the 6.5 hole while Jose Iglesias was on the mend. If you need someone to plug a middle-infield vacancy here and there, you could certainly do worse, but if he's starting 120 games on purpose it might be time to check your minor-league coordinator's pulse.

Jose Azocar   OF

Born: 5/11/96   Age: 21   Bats: R   Throws: R   Height: 5'11"   Weight: 165   Entered Pro Ball: International Free Agent, 2012

YEAR	TEAM	LVL	AGE	PA	R	2B	3B	HR	RBI	BB	K	SB	CS	AVG/OBP/SLG	TAv	VORP	BABIP	BRR	FRAA	WARP
2015	ONE	A-	19	24	1	1	0	0	0	1	7	0	0	.087/.125/.130	.105	-3.0	.125	0.1	CF(7): 1.4	-0.2
2016	WMI	A	20	532	56	11	8	0	51	25	119	14	5	.281/.315/.335	.245	6.0	.366	1.4	RF(68): 2.5 • CF(61): -5.0	0.4
2017	DET	MLB	21	250	20	8	2	5	25	8	73	1	1	.224/.250/.338	.198	-7.5	.297	0.1	RF 0, CF -0	-0.8
2018	DET	MLB	22	305	30	10	3	6	30	10	87	1	1	.232/.260/.352	.211	-7.9	.303	0.1	RF 0, CF 0	-0.9

Breakout: 3%   Improve: 3%   Collapse: 1%   Attrition: 5%   MLB: 5%   Comparables: Destin Hood, Socrates Brito, Avisail Garcia

Azocar entered 2016 as perhaps the most exciting Tigers prospect yet to make a full-season debut. He checked that off the list in the Midwest League and held his own while giving scouts a thrill or two along the way. Azocar likely won't develop serviceable power, but the rest of his tools at least flash and should serve him well. That includes plus speed and the ability to play center field in an above-average way. He shows barrel skills, but likes to take a bite out of that tasty breaking ball away. If he can learn to subdue his appetite at the plate, the contact says he can be a fringe-or-better hitter. That might be enough to start in the majors.

Miguel Cabrera   1B

Born: 4/18/83   Age: 34   Bats: R   Throws: R   Height: 6'4"   Weight: 240   Entered Pro Ball: International Free Agent, 1999

YEAR	TEAM	LVL	AGE	PA	R	2B	3B	HR	RBI	BB	K	SB	CS	AVG/OBP/SLG	TAv	VORP	BABIP	BRR	FRAA	WARP
2014	DET	MLB	31	685	101	52	1	25	109	60	117	1	1	.313/.371/.524	.308	40.8	.346	3.0	1B(126): 2.8 • 3B(10): 0.3	5.5
2015	DET	MLB	32	511	64	28	1	18	76	77	82	1	1	.338/.440/.534	.333	38.2	.384	-3.0	1B(107): 7.0	4.8
2016	DET	MLB	33	679	92	31	1	38	108	75	116	0	0	.316/.393/.563	.308	36.2	.336	-3.8	1B(147): 3.1 • 3B(1): -0.1	4.0
2017	DET	MLB	34	648	91	32	2	32	104	73	110	1	1	.310/.389/.543	.316	47.1	.333	-1.4	1B 4	5.1
2018	DET	MLB	35	583	90	27	1	29	92	65	100	0	0	.306/.385/.533	.302	31.9	.329	-0.9	1B 3	3.8

Breakout: 1%   Improve: 27%   Collapse: 4%   Attrition: 6%   MLB: 97%   Comparables: David Ortiz, Lance Berkman, Albert Pujols

Detroit's lack of recent success has predictably led to some blame being tossed Cabrera's way, but it's not his fault that the rest of the Tigers' core got old in a hurry. At age 33 he remained one of the best, most-feared hitters in baseball, topping a .300 True Average in 2016 for the eighth consecutive season and the 13th time in 14 full seasons in the majors. His production has dipped somewhat from his 2010-2013, MVP-winning peak, but that's to be expected on the wrong side of 30 and Cabrera still ranked sixth among AL hitters in TAv, sandwiched between Josh Donaldson and Robinson Cano. He's already a first-ballot Hall of Famer, ranking among the top dozen in MLB history for hits, homers, RBIs, total bases and Runs Created through age 33. However, he's also due an average of $30 million per season in a contract that stretches until at least 2023. Cabrera has staved off a significant decline thus far, but if the Tigers slip further and his bat goes from "great" to "very good" he'll be under increased scrutiny.

Nick Castellanos   3B

Born: 3/4/92   Age: 25   Bats: R   Throws: R   Height: 6'4"   Weight: 210   Entered Pro Ball: Round 1, 2010 Draft (#44 overall)

YEAR	TEAM	LVL	AGE	PA	R	2B	3B	HR	RBI	BB	K	SB	CS	AVG/OBP/SLG	TAv	VORP	BABIP	BRR	FRAA	WARP
2014	DET	MLB	22	579	50	31	4	11	66	36	140	2	2	.259/.306/.394	.254	10.5	.326	-3.0	3B(145): -1.9	1.0
2015	DET	MLB	23	595	42	33	6	15	73	39	152	0	3	.255/.303/.419	.251	10.3	.322	-2.4	3B(145): 2.2	1.3
2016	DET	MLB	24	447	54	25	4	18	58	28	111	1	1	.285/.331/.496	.278	18.4	.345	-3.9	3B(108): -3.1	1.6
2017	DET	MLB	25	562	61	29	4	18	67	38	132	2	2	.261/.313/.434	.257	11.8	.314	-1.1	3B -2	0.8
2018	DET	MLB	26	509	63	27	3	18	65	39	122	1	1	.260/.318/.445	.257	7.2	.313	-2.4	3B -1	0.6

Breakout: 4%   Improve: 60%   Collapse: 3%   Attrition: 8%   MLB: 99%   Comparables: Alex Gordon, Wilson Betemit, Edwin Encarnacion

The hope for Castellanos is that he becomes Evan Longoria, and for four months he really pulled off the impression until he broke his hand. His line-drive rate is among the league's best and he has an aggressive approach, so while the spacious Comerica Park outfield has helped him crack doubles, his power beyond the fence is far better in other parks. He should still move to first base (or maybe left field) when he has the chance, because right now balls hit to third base are eating him up as if he were Link's shield inside of a *Legend of Zelda* Like-Like.

Tyler Collins   OF

Born: 6/6/90   Age: 27   Bats: L   Throws: L   Height: 5'11"   Weight: 215   Entered Pro Ball: Round 6, 2011 Draft (#197 overall)

YEAR	TEAM	LVL	AGE	PA	R	2B	3B	HR	RBI	BB	K	SB	CS	AVG/OBP/SLG	TAv	VORP	BABIP	BRR	FRAA	WARP
2014	TOL	AAA	24	526	63	17	2	18	62	49	116	12	4	.263/.335/.423	.259	9.6	.310	-1.8	LF(92): -0.8 • RF(22): 2.5	1.0
2014	DET	MLB	24	25	3	0	0	1	4	1	4	0	0	.250/.280/.375	.229	-0.6	.263	-0.4	RF(5): -0.3 • LF(5): -0.1	-0.1
2015	TOL	AAA	25	218	21	10	0	2	20	22	40	9	2	.247/.330/.332	.243	2.0	.298	1.1	RF(17): 1.4 • LF(17): 0.8	0.2
2015	DET	MLB	25	207	18	11	3	4	25	13	43	2	1	.266/.316/.417	.255	2.8	.324	0.0	LF(37): 1.9 • RF(7): -1.2	0.4
2016	TOL	AAA	26	281	29	7	0	7	30	20	69	4	1	.214/.274/.323	.208	-8.7	.262	0.4	LF(38): -1.5 • RF(16): 4.1	-0.4
2016	DET	MLB	26	151	14	2	3	4	15	13	38	1	1	.235/.305/.382	.238	0.1	.295	-0.5	CF(29): -0.2 • LF(13): 0.3	-0.2
2017	DET	MLB	27	369	45	12	2	12	38	28	90	5	2	.236/.300/.390	.241	4.4	.287	0.2	CF -1, RF 0	0.1
2018	DET	MLB	28	440	54	15	3	14	52	38	112	6	2	.237/.309/.397	.241	2.6	.293	-0.3	CF -1, RF 0	0.2

Breakout: 5%   Improve: 28%   Collapse: 11%   Attrition: 26%   MLB: 63%   Comparables: Alejandro De Aza, Daniel Ortmeier, Ryan Langerhans

Sir Topham Hatt loves a Really Useful Engine, and a manager loves a Really Useful Ballplayer, even if he's not all that good. That's Collins: the play-doh mold of an outfielder that can sort of do everything but nothing spectacularly. If he reminds you of Andy Dirks—and who doesn't remember Andy Dirks—then you're not imagining things. He did have to overcome an embarrassing early-season spat in which he brandished the bird toward some home fans booing him for losing a routine ball in the lights. After a demotion (for slumping, not for that) he re-emerged as a Really Useful Ballplayer, mostly in part-time duty, by controlling his overaggressive tendencies and not falling off the tracks.

Michael Gerber   OF

Born: 7/8/92   Age: 24   Bats: L   Throws: R   Height: 6'0"   Weight: 190   Entered Pro Ball: Round 15, 2014 Draft (#460 overall)

YEAR	TEAM	LVL	AGE	PA	R	2B	3B	HR	RBI	BB	K	SB	CS	AVG/OBP/SLG	TAv	VORP	BABIP	BRR	FRAA	WARP
2014	ONE	A-	21	243	40	16	4	7	37	17	48	8	4	.286/.354/.493	.309	18.2	.335	1.5	RF(52): 0.1 • CF(1): -0.0	1.9
2014	WMI	A	21	35	4	3	0	0	5	4	3	1	0	.387/.457/.484	.298	2.3	.429	0.2	RF(6): 1.1 • LF(2): -0.5	0.3
2015	WMI	A	22	583	74	31	10	13	76	49	97	16	4	.292/.355/.468	.301	32.7	.330	-0.2	RF(80): -1.1 • LF(3): -0.7	3.4
2016	LAK	A+	23	388	52	22	3	14	60	32	111	2	3	.282/.343/.481	.275	13.3	.371	-0.6	RF(61): 1.4 • CF(16): -0.8	1.5
2016	ERI	AA	23	175	17	8	3	4	20	20	41	6	0	.261/.349/.431	.277	7.9	.330	0.8	CF(20): -2.1 • RF(19): -0.3	0.6
2017	*DET*	*MLB*	*24*	*250*	*27*	*11*	*2*	*8*	*31*	*17*	*71*	*2*	*0*	*.234/.292/.411*	*.235*	*1.4*	*.298*	*0.1*	*RF 1, CF -0*	*0.3*
2018	*DET*	*MLB*	*25*	*300*	*36*	*13*	*3*	*11*	*38*	*21*	*86*	*2*	*1*	*.239/.298/.422*	*.243*	*1.7*	*.303*	*0.0*	*RF 1, CF 0*	*0.3*

Breakout: 11%   Improve: 16%   Collapse: 2%   Attrition: 18%   MLB: 22%   *Comparables: Jordan Patterson, Hunter Renfroe, Zoilo Almonte*

Gerber can do it all. He has a plan at the plate and barrels balls consistently. He can pop double-digit home runs. He can run a little bit. He can play all three outfield positions in a pinch and is an average defender in the corners. He has enough arm strength for any outfield spot. He's an overachiever after getting drafted in the 15th round. He even posts adorable dog photos and picks up strays off the side of the road. What more could you want from a prospect? Sure, he doesn't have a standout tool and might be best suited as a fourth outfielder, but the guy loves dogs.

Anthony Gose   CF

Born: 8/10/90   Age: 26   Bats: L   Throws: L   Height: 6'1"   Weight: 190   Entered Pro Ball: Round 2, 2008 Draft (#51 overall)

YEAR	TEAM	LVL	AGE	PA	R	2B	3B	HR	RBI	BB	K	SB	CS	AVG/OBP/SLG	TAv	VORP	BABIP	BRR	FRAA	WARP
2014	BUF	AAA	23	224	29	5	2	4	25	17	65	21	8	.244/.305/.346	.222	-2.2	.338	1.4	CF(31): 2.2 • RF(18): -0.1	0.0
2014	TOR	MLB	23	274	31	8	1	2	13	25	74	15	5	.226/.311/.293	.227	2.6	.317	4.3	CF(65): -1.5 • RF(14): 0.3	0.2
2015	DET	MLB	24	535	73	24	8	5	26	45	145	23	11	.254/.321/.367	.248	12.2	.352	2.6	CF(137): 1.7	1.5
2016	DET	MLB	25	101	11	2	2	2	7	9	38	0	1	.209/.287/.341	.226	-0.8	.333	-0.4	CF(30): -1.9	-0.3
2016	TOL	AAA	25	206	22	8	2	1	13	15	75	6	1	.185/.255/.266	.195	-6.4	.300	2.4	CF(30): 1.5 • RF(20): -1.6	-0.7
2016	ERI	AA	25	173	16	4	0	6	27	17	54	11	4	.224/.301/.365	.237	0.8	.302	0.7	CF(23): -2.7 • RF(11): 0.8	-0.1
2017	*DET*	*MLB*	*26*	*149*	*18*	*5*	*2*	*2*	*11*	*12*	*44*	*6*	*3*	*.230/.296/.344*	*.228*	*0.9*	*.318*	*0.5*	*CF 0*	*-0.1*
2018	*DET*	*MLB*	*27*	*278*	*30*	*9*	*3*	*5*	*27*	*24*	*83*	*11*	*5*	*.229/.304/.350*	*.227*	*0.1*	*.317*	*1.8*	*CF 1*	*0.1*

Breakout: 4%   Improve: 47%   Collapse: 11%   Attrition: 23%   MLB: 76%   *Comparables: Brian Anderson, Luis Terrero, Jason Repko*

After a punchless 2015, Gose managed to pull even more punches and was out of a job by mid-May. He can run to 20-plus steals and play solid defense in center field, but at some point you have to hit to stay on the field and Gose was all the way down to the Eastern League's outfields by July. Speed and defense will always have a place in the game as long as players aren't reaching base or running down balls by motorized scooter.

Derek Hill   CF

Born: 12/30/95   Age: 21   Bats: R   Throws: R   Height: 6'2"   Weight: 195   Entered Pro Ball: Round 1, 2014 Draft (#23 overall)

YEAR	TEAM	LVL	AGE	PA	R	2B	3B	HR	RBI	BB	K	SB	CS	AVG/OBP/SLG	TAv	VORP	BABIP	BRR	FRAA	WARP
2014	ONE	A-	18	78	8	1	1	0	3	2	26	2	1	.203/.244/.243	.178	0.0	.313	0.0		0.0
2015	WMI	A	19	235	33	6	5	0	16	20	44	25	7	.238/.305/.314	.258	7.6	.298	1.2	CF(51): 2.7	1.1
2016	WMI	A	20	415	66	17	6	1	31	24	105	35	6	.266/.312/.349	.263	-6.7	.361	6.6	CF(54): -6.7 • RF(33): 5.0	1.8
2017	*DET*	*MLB*	*21*	*250*	*30*	*9*	*2*	*5*	*19*	*13*	*75*	*12*	*3*	*.216/.258/.332*	*.203*	*-4.5*	*.290*	*1.5*	*CF -2, RF 2*	*-0.5*
2018	*DET*	*MLB*	*22*	*319*	*33*	*11*	*3*	*7*	*32*	*19*	*95*	*16*	*4*	*.222/.271/.352*	*.218*	*-3.2*	*.296*	*2.7*	*CF -2, RF 2*	*-0.4*

Breakout: 3%   Improve: 3%   Collapse: 0%   Attrition: 3%   MLB: 5%   *Comparables: Xavier Avery, Abraham Almonte, Joe Benson*

Hill has bloodlines, double-plus speed and plays center field at a high level, so you tend to excuse the kid when he has initial pro struggles and repeats a low level. His second go-round in the Midwest League at age 20 included a lot more time on the field because he was healthier. The more he does that, the more you'll see a speedy table-setter who steals 30-plus bags, is an asset up the middle and makes enough contact for a potentially average bat. Patience is a virtue in life, specifically with high school draft picks with plus tools.

Jose Iglesias   SS

Born: 1/5/90   Age: 27   Bats: R   Throws: R   Height: 5'11"   Weight: 185   Entered Pro Ball: International Free Agent, 2009

YEAR	TEAM	LVL	AGE	PA	R	2B	3B	HR	RBI	BB	K	SB	CS	AVG/OBP/SLG	TAv	VORP	BABIP	BRR	FRAA	WARP
2015	DET	MLB	25	454	44	17	3	2	23	25	44	11	8	.300/.347/.370	.252	10.1	.330	-4.3	SS(119): -6.6	0.4
2016	DET	MLB	26	513	57	26	0	4	32	28	50	7	4	.255/.306/.336	.234	8.6	.276	1.2	SS(136): 14.3	2.4
2017	*DET*	*MLB*	*27*	*504*	*51*	*20*	*3*	*7*	*45*	*28*	*63*	*8*	*5*	*.271/.317/.370*	*.243*	*11.8*	*.294*	*-0.7*	*SS 3*	*1.1*
2018	*DET*	*MLB*	*28*	*468*	*51*	*18*	*2*	*8*	*46*	*26*	*60*	*7*	*4*	*.267/.316/.374*	*.238*	*4.9*	*.287*	*-0.6*	*SS 3*	*0.9*

Breakout: 4%   Improve: 51%   Collapse: 5%   Attrition: 10%   MLB: 98%   *Comparables: Erick Aybar, Alexi Casilla, Eduardo Nunez*

We are in the golden age of shortstops. Much like in 1996, when we had Jeter, A-Rod, Garciaparra, Tejada, Ripken and Larkin; today we're enjoying Lindor, Correa, Seager, Russell, Machado and Bogaerts. Iglesias is basically Omar Vizquel, which is convenient since Vizquel is the Tigers' infield coach. Vizquel is not remembered as one of his generation's greatest shortstops, but when someone brings up the name, you immediately think, "oh yeah, little guy with Cleveland … he was good." And you're referring strictly to his defense. Images of slick highlights appear in your head out of nowhere. The same works for Iglesias. Great instincts, strong wrists and can throw the ball powerfully no matter which direction his body is moving. He's a delight to have on your team, unless it's a fantasy team.

JaCoby Jones   SS

Born: 5/10/92   Age: 25   Bats: R   Throws: R   Height: 6'2"   Weight: 205   Entered Pro Ball: Round 3, 2013 Draft (#87 overall)

YEAR	TEAM	LVL	AGE	PA	R	2B	3B	HR	RBI	BB	K	SB	CS	AVG/OBP/SLG	TAv	VORP	BABIP	BRR	FRAA	WARP
2014	WVA	A	22	501	72	21	3	23	70	33	132	17	9	.288/.347/.503	.291	40.7	.352	5.7	SS(99): 4.1	4.6
2015	BRD	A+	23	423	48	18	3	10	58	31	113	14	4	.253/.313/.396	.261	14.3	.330	-1.8	SS(84): 10.8	2.7
2015	ERI	AA	23	160	26	7	2	6	20	17	52	10	3	.250/.331/.463	.282	11.4	.337	1.5	SS(37): 3.6	1.6
2016	ERI	AA	24	89	11	6	2	4	20	10	23	2	1	.312/.393/.597	.338	9.2	.392	-0.3	3B(9): -0.5 • CF(9): 1.0	1.1
2016	TOL	AAA	24	324	33	14	5	3	23	25	97	11	4	.243/.309/.356	.246	6.9	.349	1.8	CF(57): -5.6 • 3B(22): -1.2	0.0
2016	DET	MLB	24	28	3	3	0	0	2	0	12	0	0	.214/.214/.321	.171	-1.2	.375	0.5	3B(6): -0.0 • CF(5): -0.2	-0.1
2017	DET	MLB	25	286	36	11	2	9	29	19	95	7	2	.224/.281/.389	.233	2.4	.308	0.6	CF 1	0.0
2018	DET	MLB	26	411	49	16	3	14	50	29	134	10	4	.234/.295/.408	.239	3.2	.319	1.0	CF 1	0.4

Breakout: 8%   Improve: 13%   Collapse: 9%   Attrition: 32%   MLB: 37%   Comparables: *Matt Den Dekker, Melky Mesa, Brett Eibner*

You hate to say it, but Jones' situation is starting to reach that make-or-break stage at which he needs to establish his role. He was traded to the Tigers in July of 2015, but was hit with a 50-game suspension for a drug of abuse during the Arizona Fall League. He returned last May and was in the majors by September. Detroit, and many others, like Jones for his power/speed combo that could touch 15/25 in his prime, but a lengthy swing geared for extra bases and a lack of recognition are like anchors to his ship. The more likely outcome at this point is a super-utility type who pops the occasional homer and steals a bag or two.

Ian Kinsler   2B

Born: 6/22/82   Age: 35   Bats: R   Throws: R   Height: 6'0"   Weight: 200   Entered Pro Ball: Round 17, 2003 Draft (#496 overall)

YEAR	TEAM	LVL	AGE	PA	R	2B	3B	HR	RBI	BB	K	SB	CS	AVG/OBP/SLG	TAv	VORP	BABIP	BRR	FRAA	WARP
2014	DET	MLB	32	726	100	40	4	17	92	29	79	15	4	.275/.307/.420	.256	18.4	.288	3.0	2B(160): 3.1	2.4
2015	DET	MLB	33	675	94	35	7	11	73	43	80	10	6	.296/.342/.428	.269	25.1	.323	2.1	2B(153): -0.2	2.7
2016	DET	MLB	34	679	117	29	4	28	83	45	115	14	6	.288/.348/.484	.285	40.2	.314	4.7	2B(151): 3.2	4.5
2017	DET	MLB	35	641	79	30	4	16	64	42	87	12	6	.268/.321/.415	.258	24.0	.288	0.0	2B 3	2.3
2018	DET	MLB	36	517	60	23	3	12	57	35	76	9	4	.262/.318/.402	.248	11.2	.286	2.0	2B 2	1.5

Breakout: 1%   Improve: 30%   Collapse: 7%   Attrition: 13%   MLB: 82%   Comparables: *Brandon Phillips, Mark Ellis, Orlando Hudson*

While second basemen age about as well as dollar store organic bananas, Kinsler must have invented some kind of special rind preservative. All he did at age 35 was post his third-best career TAv and tie Lou Whitaker for the most home runs in a season by a Tigers second baseman. He's still fielding at a high level and his overaggressive baserunning still triggers the *Price is Right* trombones, but that's what grit do. Worst case, he earned his eight-figure salary through its final year (which is this one, plus a $12 million salary or $5 million buy-out in 2018). Best case, he has three more seasons like the last four and becomes as good a new-age Hall of Fame case as Whitaker.

Dixon Machado   SS

Born: 2/22/92   Age: 25   Bats: R   Throws: R   Height: 6'1"   Weight: 170   Entered Pro Ball: International Free Agent, 2008

YEAR	TEAM	LVL	AGE	PA	R	2B	3B	HR	RBI	BB	K	SB	CS	AVG/OBP/SLG	TAv	VORP	BABIP	BRR	FRAA	WARP
2014	LAK	A+	22	187	30	8	1	1	8	23	34	2	1	.252/.348/.333	.253	7.4	.312	0.8	SS(41): -3.4	0.4
2014	ERI	AA	22	342	45	23	1	5	32	40	36	8	5	.305/.391/.442	.294	28.2	.331	2.4	SS(90): 0.1	3.0
2015	TOL	AAA	23	567	61	22	1	4	48	36	85	15	3	.261/.313/.332	.230	6.7	.305	2.0	SS(125): -5.4 • 3B(2): -0.1	0.1
2015	DET	MLB	23	78	6	3	0	0	5	7	14	1	0	.235/.307/.279	.208	-1.6	.296	-0.7	SS(24): -0.8	-0.3
2016	TOL	AAA	24	569	59	28	2	4	48	58	75	17	5	.266/.349/.356	.259	23.1	.305	0.7	SS(130): 12.6 • 2B(4): 0.2	3.7
2016	DET	MLB	24	13	1	0	0	0	0	3	4	0	0	.100/.308/.100	.183	0.1	.167	0.6	SS(6): 0.5 • 2B(2): -0.0	0.1
2017	DET	MLB	25	92	10	4	0	2	9	8	17	2	1	.249/.313/.368	.240	1.5	.284	0.0	SS 0, 3B -0	0.1
2018	DET	MLB	26	329	39	15	1	8	36	28	62	6	2	.255/.323/.395	.243	4.2	.290	0.2	SS 0, 3B -1	0.5

Breakout: 2%   Improve: 22%   Collapse: 12%   Attrition: 27%   MLB: 53%   Comparables: *Jace Peterson, Justin Sellers, Brian Dozier*

Machado is capable of producing lasers across the field. The problem is, they don't come off his bat, just out of his hand from shortstop. Once described as like a clumsy baby deer because of his slight, lanky frame, Machado has filled out some and lost a tick off his speed. That hasn't prevented his defense from being quite the positive at short. He has a reliable glove, makes the routine plays and has first-step quickness to get to his share of ground balls. He also has a borderline plus-plus arm as a standout tool. At the plate he grades below average with little power to speak of, which prevents an everyday role. His defense can keep him in the majors, though.

J.D. Martinez   RF

Born: 8/21/87   Age: 29   Bats: R   Throws: R   Height: 6'3"   Weight: 220   Entered Pro Ball: Round 20, 2009 Draft (#611 overall)

YEAR	TEAM	LVL	AGE	PA	R	2B	3B	HR	RBI	BB	K	SB	CS	AVG/OBP/SLG	TAv	VORP	BABIP	BRR	FRAA	WARP
2014	TOL	AAA	26	71	16	3	1	10	22	3	17	2	0	.308/.366/.846	.349	8.0	.263	-0.5	LF(12): -0.2	0.8
2014	DET	MLB	26	480	57	30	3	23	76	30	126	6	3	.315/.358/.553	.319	36.0	.389	0.6	LF(83): -2.1 • RF(34): -1.4	3.6
2015	DET	MLB	27	657	93	33	2	38	102	53	178	3	2	.282/.344/.535	.304	35.1	.339	-3.9	RF(148): -7.7	2.9
2016	TOL	AAA	28	38	3	3	0	0	5	1	11	1	0	.278/.316/.361	.248	0.4	.400	0.5	RF(2): 0.4	0.1
2016	DET	MLB	28	517	69	35	2	22	68	49	128	1	2	.307/.373/.535	.302	24.0	.378	-7.3	RF(118): -10.7	1.4
2017	DET	MLB	29	587	72	29	3	26	84	44	151	3	2	.271/.328/.480	.278	22.5	.328	-0.8	RF -10	1.0
2018	DET	MLB	30	519	71	26	2	24	76	41	136	2	1	.268/.329/.485	.272	14.7	.325	-2.6	RF -9	0.6

Breakout: 5%   Improve: 59%   Collapse: 0%   Attrition: 1%   MLB: 98%   Comparables: *Richie Zisk, Kirk Gibson, Larry Walker*

While the Tigers struck gold on this homeriffic corner outfielder for cheap, it's the "outfielder" part that gives long-term concern in Martinez's walk year. He has a fabulous arm, but otherwise struggled mightily on batted balls in his fiefdom. His attempt at a running catch in June resulted in a wall collision that broke his wrist, sidelining him for 40 games. But his very next at-bat was the stuff of legends: tie-game, pinch-hitter, Chris Sale on the mound and the first pitch went 440 feet into the center field shrubbery.

All discussions of Martinez come back to his power. He led all right fielders in OPS, but if his right fielding is a liability, he can easily pass as one of the league's top first basemen.

Victor Martinez   DH

Born: 12/23/78 Age: 38 Bats: B Throws: R Height: 6'2" Weight: 210 Entered Pro Ball: International Free Agent, 1996

YEAR	TEAM	LVL	AGE	PA	R	2B	3B	HR	RBI	BB	K	SB	CS	AVG/OBP/SLG	TAv	VORP	BABIP	BRR	FRAA	WARP
2014	DET	MLB	35	641	87	33	0	32	103	70	42	3	2	.335/.409/.565	.335	45.3	.316	-5.9	1B(35): -2.8 • C(2): -0.2	4.7
2015	DET	MLB	36	485	39	20	0	11	64	31	52	0	0	.245/.301/.366	.232	-11.9	.253	-3.5	1B(10): 0.5	-1.2
2016	DET	MLB	37	610	65	22	0	27	86	50	90	0	0	.289/.351/.476	.274	5.6	.303	-9.6	1B(5): -0.0	0.6
2017	DET	MLB	38	598	67	25	1	19	76	48	70	1	1	.278/.339/.437	.268	9.9	.286	-1.3		1.6
2018	DET	MLB	39	475	61	19	1	16	59	36	60	0	0	.272/.331/.429	.257	2.7	.283	-4.6	-	0.3

Breakout: 0%   Improve: 15%   Collapse: 19%   Attrition: 23%   MLB: 69%   *Comparables: Carlos Lee, Rusty Staub, Todd Helton*

With David Ortiz enjoying designated retirement, Martinez is now the dean of DHs, and he's still successful despite having exactly zero good knees. Perhaps a concern, he saw his strikeout rate spike to a career-high of—gasp—14.8 percent! (Still far below the league average of 21 percent.) Maybe it's a statistical outlier, as he's still stinging the ball hard enough to generate tons of extra bases in the gaps and over the fence. With two years remaining on his contract at $18 million per calendar, Martinez is a pricey bat and a fragile one—anything this side of wind shear might cause a series of spiraling and nagging injuries, frustrating the veteran into an even more marginalized role: the dean of pinch-hitters, which used to be John Vernon's gig.

James McCann   C

Born: 6/13/90 Age: 27 Bats: R Throws: R Height: 6'2" Weight: 210 Entered Pro Ball: Round 2, 2011 Draft (#76 overall)

YEAR	TEAM	LVL	AGE	PA	R	2B	3B	HR	RBI	BB	K	SB	CS	AVG/OBP/SLG	TAv	VORP	BABIP	BRR	FRAA	WARP
2014	TOL	AAA	24	460	49	34	0	7	54	25	90	9	2	.295/.343/.427	.262	22.4	.355	0.7	C(98): 0.4 • 3B(1): 0.0	2.3
2014	DET	MLB	24	12	2	1	0	0	0	0	2	1	0	.250/.250/.333	.211	-0.1	.300	0.1	C(6): -0.3	0.0
2015	DET	MLB	25	425	32	18	5	7	41	16	90	0	1	.264/.297/.387	.230	1.2	.325	-4.7	C(112): -17.4	-1.7
2016	TOL	AAA	26	27	2	0	0	0	2	5	6	0	0	.091/.259/.091	.206	-0.5	.125	0.2	C(4): -0.3	-0.1
2016	DET	MLB	26	373	31	9	1	12	48	23	109	0	1	.221/.272/.358	.210	-4.3	.283	-2.0	C(99): 1.6	-0.3
2017	DET	MLB	27	485	48	20	3	12	51	26	118	2	1	.246/.291/.384	.235	7.8	.303	-0.7	C -7	-1.5
2018	DET	MLB	28	494	55	20	3	13	54	27	125	1	1	.239/.287/.382	.227	-1.5	.296	-3.1	C -8	-1.0

Breakout: 8%   Improve: 42%   Collapse: 6%   Attrition: 22%   MLB: 91%   *Comparables: Yorvit Torrealba, Tony Cruz, Miguel Olivo*

The "McCannon" nickname is well earned; for the second straight year he thwarted over 40 percent of base heists. But like most cannons, it was too clunky to be worthwhile on offense. He simply cannot and should not hit against righties, as he struck out more than he reached base. He does, at least, resemble Buster Posey against lefties, though he still whiffs about a third of the time no matter who's pitching. One bright spot is massively improved pitch framing, going from one of the worst in the league to replacement level. But if he can't get his work inside the batter's box to the same passing grade, then we're going to start calling him McPlatoon or McCantHitRighties, and those nicknames are even worse than his splits.

YEAR	TEAM	P. COUNT	FRM RUNS	BLK RUNS	THRW RUNS	TOT RUNS
2014	DET	356	-0.2	-0.1	0.0	-0.4
2014	TOL	13647	-4.9	0.4	5.4	1.0
2015	DET	15395	-16.6	0.9	1.8	-13.9
2016	DET	13823	0.1	1.2	3.1	4.4
2017	DET	18052	-9.9	1.2	3.4	-5.3
2018	DET	18383	-10.9	1.2	3.4	-6.4

Steven Moya   RF

Born: 8/9/91 Age: 25 Bats: L Throws: R Height: 6'7" Weight: 260 Entered Pro Ball: Undrafted Free Agent, 2008

YEAR	TEAM	LVL	AGE	PA	R	2B	3B	HR	RBI	BB	K	SB	CS	AVG/OBP/SLG	TAv	VORP	BABIP	BRR	FRAA	WARP
2014	ERI	AA	22	549	81	33	3	35	105	23	161	16	4	.276/.306/.555	.295	30.5	.327	1.4	RF(131): 2.0	3.5
2014	DET	MLB	22	8	2	0	0	0	0	0	2	0	0	.375/.375/.375	.284	0.4	.500	0.0	RF(5): -0.2	0.0
2015	LAK	A+	23	42	3	3	0	3	8	1	13	0	0	.275/.286/.575	.291	2.1	.320	0.1	RF(9): 0.1	0.2
2015	TOL	AAA	23	535	53	30	0	20	74	27	162	5	4	.240/.283/.420	.242	-1.8	.312	-0.5	RF(97): -11.7 • LF(13): -0.0	-1.4
2015	DET	MLB	23	25	1	0	1	0	0	3	10	0	0	.182/.280/.273	.199	-1.4	.333	-0.3	RF(5): 0.3 • LF(2): 1.7	0.1
2016	TOL	AAA	24	426	60	23	3	20	66	15	96	3	0	.284/.310/.501	.277	15.2	.327	-0.3	RF(72): -4.5 • LF(21): -4.2	0.7
2016	DET	MLB	24	100	9	4	2	5	11	5	38	0	1	.255/.290/.500	.249	-0.3	.365	-1.5	RF(18): -1.8 • LF(8): -0.2	-0.3
2017	DET	MLB	25	196	24	9	1	10	28	8	63	1	1	.240/.272/.461	.248	2.9	.302	-0.1	LF -0, RF -0	0.1
2018	DET	MLB	26	370	48	17	2	20	56	18	118	3	1	.243/.283/.471	.250	4.3	.306	-0.3	LF -1, RF -1	0.3

Breakout: 3%   Improve: 21%   Collapse: 10%   Attrition: 25%   MLB: 44%   *Comparables: Peter O'Brien, Bryce Brentz, Carlos Peguero*

Moya's 2016 season was probably forecast before he was even born. He's a hulk of a human with plus power from the left side. He's also forever stuck around .250 with a sub-.300 on-base percentage, and that 38 percent strikeout rate in 100 big-league plate appearances is a pretty solid indicator going forward. Maybe there's enough here to latch on as a power-hitting platoon mate, but his days of middle-of-the-order projections are likely over and his floor remains a Quad-A player.

Andrew Romine   UT

Born: 12/24/85 Age: 31 Bats: B Throws: R Height: 6'1" Weight: 200 Entered Pro Ball: Round 5, 2007 Draft (#178 overall)

YEAR	TEAM	LVL	AGE	PA	R	2B	3B	HR	RBI	BB	K	SB	CS	AVG/OBP/SLG	TAv	VORP	BABIP	BRR	FRAA	WARP
2014	DET	MLB	28	273	30	6	0	2	12	18	60	12	2	.227/.279/.275	.215	1.9	.291	3.3	SS(83): 1.0 • 2B(12): -0.8	0.2
2015	DET	MLB	29	203	25	5	0	2	15	11	46	10	5	.255/.307/.315	.227	-1.3	.328	-1.0	3B(59): 1.2 • SS(27): 1.5	0.1
2016	DET	MLB	30	194	21	5	2	2	16	13	38	8	0	.236/.304/.322	.224	-0.7	.291	0.4	3B(44): 1.6 • CF(22): 0.3	0.1
2017	DET	MLB	31	265	27	7	2	3	20	18	55	10	3	.240/.294/.322	.224	-0.9	.291	1.2	2B -1, 1B -0	-0.2
2018	DET	MLB	32	303	31	8	2	4	25	22	65	10	3	.231/.295/.317	.217	-4.8	.282	0.9	2B -1, 1B 0	-0.5

Breakout: 3%   Improve: 27%   Collapse: 12%   Attrition: 24%   MLB: 70%   *Comparables: Jason Ellison, Jarrod Dyson, Tike Redman*

With just over 200 career starts in seven seasons, it feels like Romine was born to be a utility player, crawling around the playroom spending about five minutes on each toy. Last year he saw time at every position except catcher, and was written into the lineup at least thrice at six different positions. He also hits from both sides of the plate equally well (which is to say, like a utility player) and if there was a new baseball position discovered in the next calendar year, you can bet your sweet Don Kelly that Romine would find a way to start five games there.

Jarrod Saltalamacchia   C

Born: 5/2/85   Age: 32   Bats: B   Throws: R   Height: 6'4"   Weight: 235   Entered Pro Ball: Round 1, 2003 Draft (#36 overall)

YEAR	TEAM	LVL	AGE	PA	R	2B	3B	HR	RBI	BB	K	SB	CS	AVG/OBP/SLG	TAv	VORP	BABIP	BRR	FRAA	WARP
2014	MIA	MLB	29	435	43	20	0	11	44	55	143	0	1	.220/.320/.362	.258	17.2	.317	0.1	C(107): -37.7	-2.3
2015	MIA	MLB	30	33	3	1	0	1	1	4	12	0	0	.069/.182/.207	.140	-2.7	.063	-0.2	C(9): -0.9	-0.4
2015	RNO	AAA	30	36	2	0	0	2	7	2	13	0	0	.188/.222/.375	.227	-0.2	.211	-0.1	C(5): 0.1	0.0
2015	ARI	MLB	30	194	23	14	0	8	23	19	57	0	0	.251/.332/.474	.280	10.5	.327	-0.6	C(38): -7.8 • 1B(4): -0.1	0.3
2016	DET	MLB	31	292	30	5	1	12	38	41	104	0	0	.171/.284/.346	.237	3.1	.222	-2.1	C(68): -11.2 • 1B(11): 0.1	-0.8
2017	DET	MLB	32	267	31	11	1	11	34	29	86	0	0	.221/.307/.411	.243	7.6	.294	-0.6	C -16, 1B 0	-0.9
2018	DET	MLB	33	237	29	10	1	8	28	26	75	0	0	.214/.301/.387	.236	1.8	.286	-0.6	C -14, 1B 0	-1.4

Breakout: 3%   Improve: 38%   Collapse: 12%   Attrition: 19%   MLB: 93%   Comparables: Ramon Castro, Kelly Shoppach, John Buck

Think Chris Iannetta but even harder to spell. The Marlins finally stopped paying Salty to "hit" for other teams after stints with the Diamondbacks and Tigers, which means he's going to spend the rest of his days as a backup catcher/pinch-hitter. He has plus power and his walk rate will slightly atone for the awful contact rate, but Saltalamacchia is a switch-hitter who only contributes from one side of the plate and his defense is tough to stomach.

YEAR	TEAM	P. COUNT	FRM RUNS	BLK RUNS	THRW RUNS	TOT RUNS
2014	MIA	14700	-34.0	-1.5	-2.6	-38.2
2015	MIA	1187	-1.1	0.2	0.0	-1.0
2015	RNO	659	0.2	0.0	0.0	0.2
2015	ARI	5288	-7.4	0.3	-0.3	-7.4
2016	DET	9179	-8.8	0.0	-1.0	-9.8
2017	DET	8617	-13.6	-0.2	-1.2	-15.0
2018	DET	7647	-12.8	-0.3	-1.1	-14.2

A.J. Simcox   SS

Born: 6/22/94   Age: 23   Bats: R   Throws: R   Height: 6'3"   Weight: 185   Entered Pro Ball: Round 14, 2015 Draft (#430 overall)

YEAR	TEAM	LVL	AGE	PA	R	2B	3B	HR	RBI	BB	K	SB	CS	AVG/OBP/SLG	TAv	VORP	BABIP	BRR	FRAA	WARP
2015	ONE	A-	21	108	14	5	1	0	12	5	14	5	2	.270/.306/.340	.255	5.8	.307	2.0	SS(25): 4.9	1.1
2015	WMI	A	21	91	11	3	0	1	8	5	11	4	2	.400/.440/.471	.323	10.5	.452	1.0	SS(20): -0.3	1.1
2016	LAK	A+	22	568	76	19	5	5	51	28	108	7	5	.262/.298/.345	.230	8.8	.316	3.8	SS(120): 0.6	1.0
2017	DET	MLB	23	250	25	9	2	5	23	9	62	1	1	.238/.267/.362	.210	-1.4	.295	-0.2	SS 1	0.0
2018	DET	MLB	24	353	37	14	3	8	37	14	86	2	1	.240/.275/.372	.221	-2.4	.296	-0.3	SS 2	-0.1

Breakout: 9%   Improve: 22%   Collapse: 18%   Attrition: 32%   MLB: 44%   Comparables: Yadiel Rivera, Erik Gonzalez, Jordy Mercer

Coaches' sons often get the "gym rat" tag whether they've earned it or not. Simcox earns his tag. The son of a Tennessee assistant coach, he's known as a smart player with instincts on the field and a strong work ethic. The Tigers signed him away from his father at the price of $600,000 in the 14th round in 2015, and the move could prove as savvy as Simcox's on-field skills. He doesn't have the flashy range of some shortstops, but is expected to stick at the position with steady play and an above-average arm. He doesn't project for power, but shows the contact skills to work in the upper levels and let his glove carry the profile.

Christin Stewart   OF

Born: 12/10/93   Age: 23   Bats: L   Throws: R   Height: 6'0"   Weight: 205   Entered Pro Ball: Round 1, 2015 Draft (#34 overall)

YEAR	TEAM	LVL	AGE	PA	R	2B	3B	HR	RBI	BB	K	SB	CS	AVG/OBP/SLG	TAv	VORP	BABIP	BRR	FRAA	WARP
2015	ONE	A-	21	59	7	2	2	2	11	5	18	0	0	.245/.322/.490	.315	4.0	.313	-0.6	LF(13): -0.2	0.4
2015	WMI	A	21	216	29	9	4	7	31	18	45	3	2	.286/.375/.492	.316	15.9	.338	-0.5	LF(39): -5.7	1.1
2016	LAK	A+	22	442	60	22	1	24	68	74	105	3	1	.264/.403/.534	.323	32.4	.306	-6.6	LF(94): -15.6	1.7
2016	ERI	AA	22	100	17	2	0	6	19	12	26	0	0	.218/.310/.448	.275	4.1	.232	0.7	LF(22): 1.0	0.5
2017	DET	MLB	23	250	31	9	1	12	37	27	74	0	0	.228/.326/.452	.263	8.9	.281	-0.2	LF -5	0.4
2018	DET	MLB	24	346	48	13	2	16	48	37	102	0	0	.228/.323/.442	.260	7.6	.285	-0.5	LF -7, RF 0	0.1

Breakout: 3%   Improve: 21%   Collapse: 6%   Attrition: 14%   MLB: 48%   Comparables: Jerry Sands, Chris Carter, Joc Pederson

The Tigers drafted something other than a right-handed power pitcher for the first time in eleventy billion years, and Stewart is quickly turning into a legitimate power hitter. Go figure. He mashed in high school, he mashed at Tennessee and he's mashing pro pitching so far. He projects for plus power to all fields and has enough plate discipline and barrel ability to reach that coveted 50-hit tool. He'll always strike out, but not as often as that college kid who's at the bar every night like clockwork. Defense is an adventure, but he's in left field for a reason and the bat will play somewhere.

Justin Upton   LF

Born: 8/25/87   Age: 29   Bats: R   Throws: R   Height: 6'2"   Weight: 205   Entered Pro Ball: Round 1, 2005 Draft (#1 overall)

YEAR	TEAM	LVL	AGE	PA	R	2B	3B	HR	RBI	BB	K	SB	CS	AVG/OBP/SLG	TAv	VORP	BABIP	BRR	FRAA	WARP
2014	ATL	MLB	26	641	77	34	2	29	102	60	171	8	4	.270/.342/.491	.314	45.3	.332	0.4	LF(150): -6.3	4.3
2015	SDN	MLB	27	620	85	26	3	26	81	68	159	19	5	.251/.336/.454	.294	37.3	.304	3.8	LF(146): -6.9	3.2
2016	DET	MLB	28	626	81	28	2	31	87	50	179	9	4	.246/.310/.465	.260	16.3	.301	2.4	LF(146): -5.6 • CF(6): 0.1	1.1
2017	DET	MLB	29	581	76	24	3	25	81	59	144	12	3	.258/.336/.463	.276	29.5	.307	0.6	LF -2	2.4
2018	DET	MLB	30	545	71	22	2	25	79	60	134	10	3	.257/.341/.470	.273	21.9	.302	1.8	LF -1	2.2

Breakout: 2%   Improve: 46%   Collapse: 0%   Attrition: 1%   MLB: 93%   Comparables: Ron Gant, Colby Rasmus, Pat Burrell

If Upton were any streakier, Windex would cast him as a supervillain. Here were his OPS totals by month in the first year of his mega-deal: .569, .612, .765, .842, .713, 1.132. That last month jumps out at you just like the 13 baseballs off his bat jumped out of ballparks in September. A disappointing year turned into a 30-homer season and the first batter to slug a baker's dozen dingers in September in six years. But it wasn't just a different month that triggered the outbreak: manager Brad Ausmus sat him for a few games to reset his psyche. That endpoint was the beginning of the true streak. He's probably not opting out of $22.125 million a year (though he could after this season) unless he lands that coveted window cleaning endorsement deal and doesn't need the cash.

PITCHERS

Tyler Alexander   LHP

Born: 7/14/94   Age: 22   Bats: R   Throws: L   Height: 6'2"   Weight: 200   Entered Pro Ball: Round 2, 2015 Draft (#65 overall)

YEAR	TEAM	LVL	AGE	W	L	SV	G	GS	IP	H	HR	BB/9	K/9	K	GB%	BABIP	WHIP	ERA	FIP	DRA	VORP	WARP	cFIP	MPH
2015	ONE	A-	20	0	2	0	12	12	37	17	3	1.2	8.0	33	67%	.151	0.59	0.97	3.27	2.38	11.9	1.2	82	
2016	LAK	A+	21	6	7	0	19	18	102	87	7	1.4	7.2	82	57%	.268	1.01	2.21	3.10	2.77	30.4	3.1	85	
2016	ERI	AA	21	2	1	0	6	6	34¹	36	4	1.0	6.0	23	49%	.302	1.17	3.15	3.97	3.25	7.0	0.8	94	
2017	*DET*	*MLB*	*22*	*6*	*6*	*0*	*20*	*20*	*93*	*105*	*12*	*2.7*	*5.1*	*53*	*46%*	*.298*	*1.44*	*4.83*	*4.70*	*5.00*	*4.9*	*0.5*	*118*	
2018	*DET*	*MLB*	*23*	*8*	*10*	*0*	*28*	*28*	*173¹*	*165*	*24*	*4.1*	*7.7*	*148*	*46%*	*.285*	*1.41*	*4.86*	*4.74*	*5.03*	*6.5*	*0.7*	*120*	

Breakout: 15%   Improve: 24%   Collapse: 3%   Attrition: 19%   MLB: 32%   *Comparables: Nick Tropeano, Kyle Drabek, Edwin Escobar*

The Tigers drafted Alexander twice, the first time out of a Texas high school and the second time out of TCU in the second round in 2015. He only has 173 innings of work on a professional mound, but he's not far from the show. Detroit knew what it had in Alexander from the beginning. He tosses average stuff across the board from the left side, mainly a fastball around 90, a sinking changeup with good arm action and slurvy breaking pitches that play enough to work in the upper levels. Alexander's calling card is plus control and an excellent idea of what he's doing on the mound. His strong pitchability and command will get him to the majors and help the average arsenal work at the back end of a rotation.

Sandy Baez   RHP

Born: 11/25/93   Age: 23   Bats: R   Throws: R   Height: 6'2"   Weight: 180   Entered Pro Ball: International Free Agent, 2011

YEAR	TEAM	LVL	AGE	W	L	SV	G	GS	IP	H	HR	BB/9	K/9	K	GB%	BABIP	WHIP	ERA	FIP	DRA	VORP	WARP	cFIP	MPH
2015	ONE	A-	21	3	4	0	14	14	65¹	73	4	3.0	7.2	52	41%	.343	1.45	4.13	3.96	3.99	9.4	1.0	100	
2016	WMI	A	22	7	9	0	21	21	113¹	125	7	2.2	7.0	88	40%	.337	1.35	3.81	3.63	4.41	7.6	0.8	100	
2017	*DET*	*MLB*	*23*	*4*	*7*	*0*	*15*	*15*	*78²*	*112*	*19*	*4.5*	*3.6*	*32*	*79%*	*.322*	*1.92*	*7.16*	*7.09*	*7.39*	*-16.8*	*-1.7*	*177*	
2018	*DET*	*MLB*	*24*	*6*	*11*	*0*	*25*	*25*	*146²*	*176*	*34*	*5.6*	*6.6*	*108*	*79%*	*.310*	*1.82*	*6.85*	*6.72*	*7.07*	*-22.6*	*-2.3*	*170*	

Breakout: 1%   Improve: 1%   Collapse: 0%   Attrition: 1%   MLB: 1%   *Comparables: Chris Stratton, Sugar Ray Marimon, Mike Kickham*

Seems a bit early to give up on Baez as a starter, doesn't it? He was a little old for the Midwest League in 2016, but not overly so, and he succeeded in his first full-season assignment. Not only that, some turned in positive reports in the direction of a starter's future. He has a plus fastball and flashes two average secondaries, and he remains a projectable guy with the chance to round out a starter's arsenal. It's not a sexy profile and is limited to a back-end ceiling, but don't count out a lengthy kid with three potential major-league offerings. Plus, we need another Sandy in the majors.

Matt Boyd   LHP

Born: 2/2/91   Age: 26   Bats: L   Throws: L   Height: 6'3"   Weight: 215   Entered Pro Ball: Round 6, 2013 Draft (#175 overall)

YEAR	TEAM	LVL	AGE	W	L	SV	G	GS	IP	H	HR	BB/9	K/9	K	GB%	BABIP	WHIP	ERA	FIP	DRA	VORP	WARP	cFIP	MPH
2014	NHP	AA	23	1	4	0	10	10	42²	55	5	2.7	9.3	44	31%	.379	1.59	6.96	3.94	3.42	8.6	0.9	98	
2014	DUN	A+	23	5	3	0	16	16	90²	65	4	2.0	10.2	103	42%	.270	0.94	1.39	2.49	1.55	40.7	4.1	74	
2015	NHP	AA	24	6	1	0	12	12	73²	39	3	2.2	8.6	70	24%	.199	0.77	1.10	2.67	2.27	23.1	2.5	80	
2015	TOR	MLB	24	0	2	0	2	2	6²	15	5	1.4	9.4	7	43%	.435	2.40	14.85	11.20	6.29	-0.9	-0.1	119	94.8
2015	BUF	AAA	24	3	1	0	6	6	39	32	5	1.4	8.5	37	41%	.260	0.97	2.77	3.46	3.06	9.7	1.0	84	
2015	DET	MLB	24	1	4	0	11	10	50²	56	12	3.4	6.4	36	32%	.297	1.48	6.57	5.95	5.87	-4.5	-0.5	119	94.6
2016	TOL	AAA	25	2	5	0	11	11	64	53	5	2.5	8.0	57	42%	.271	1.11	2.25	3.34	2.63	19.3	2.0	89	
2016	DET	MLB	25	6	5	0	20	18	97¹	97	17	2.7	7.6	82	39%	.286	1.29	4.53	4.71	4.67	7.2	0.7	105	94.3
2017	*DET*	*MLB*	*26*	*6*	*7*	*0*	*19*	*19*	*100²*	*100*	*15*	*3.0*	*7.6*	*85*	*48%*	*.290*	*1.31*	*4.67*	*4.53*	*4.83*	*4.7*	*0.5*	*100*	
2018	*DET*	*MLB*	*27*	*8*	*10*	*0*	*28*	*28*	*169*	*153*	*27*	*3.8*	*9.6*	*180*	*48%*	*.286*	*1.33*	*4.67*	*4.54*	*4.94*	*8.6*	*0.9*	*115*	

Breakout: 22%   Improve: 53%   Collapse: 18%   Attrition: 23%   MLB: 91%   *Comparables: Roenis Elias, Wade LeBlanc, Dan Straily*

Boyd does not have a great fastball, but he used it far too often in two-strike situations and didn't locate it well. He has a wealth of other decent pitches (change, curve, slider), but most of the league, and especially righties, just wreck his bacon when he's throwing heat. Then again he's a fly-ball pitcher, so he's going to live and die in low orbit. Therefore Comerica Park is a terrific fit, provided he can force the batter to guess wrong on the changeup. For a couple months in the rotation last year, he did this far better than his nightmarish rookie campaign. He's a back-end starter with an Eric Milton-style career as his best-case scenario.

Beau Burrows   RHP

Born: 9/18/96   Age: 20   Bats: R   Throws: R   Height: 6'2"   Weight: 200   Entered Pro Ball: Round 1, 2015 Draft (#22 overall)

YEAR	TEAM	LVL	AGE	W	L	SV	G	GS	IP	H	HR	BB/9	K/9	K	GB%	BABIP	WHIP	ERA	FIP	DRA	VORP	WARP	cFIP	MPH
2016	WMI	A	19	6	4	0	21	20	97	87	2	2.8	6.2	67	42%	.283	1.21	3.15	3.48	5.69	-7.5	-0.8	112	
2017	*DET*	*MLB*	*20*	*3*	*6*	*0*	*15*	*15*	*62¹*	*85*	*15*	*5.0*	*3.0*	*21*	*75%*	*.303*	*1.92*	*7.38*	*7.46*	*7.66*	*-15.2*	*-1.6*	*183*	
2018	*DET*	*MLB*	*21*	*3*	*8*	*0*	*19*	*19*	*113*	*138*	*25*	*6.4*	*5.7*	*72*	*75%*	*.304*	*1.93*	*7.27*	*7.14*	*7.55*	*-18.5*	*-1.9*	*179*	

Breakout: 0%   Improve: 0%   Collapse: 0%   Attrition: 0%   MLB: 0%   *Comparables: Jeurys Familia, T.J. House, Alex Sanabia*

Burrows has two quality pitches and a great name. Luckily for him, his initials aren't a precursor to control problems. His delivery has slight effort but is generally repeatable, and he showed solid command and control in his first taste of full-season ball. Burrows has a heavy fastball in the low 90s that can hit 95, and pairs it with a potentially above-average curveball. His changeup is still developing, but flashes average ability. He doesn't have height or length as an advantage, but it's a strong, compact build that can log innings. Depending on who you ask, Burrows can be a solid mid-rotation starter or back-end type.

Buck Farmer   RHP

Born: 2/20/91   Age: 26   Bats: L   Throws: R   Height: 6'4"   Weight: 225   Entered Pro Ball: Round 5, 2013 Draft (#156 overall)

YEAR	TEAM	LVL	AGE	W	L	SV	G	GS	IP	H	HR	BB/9	K/9	K	GB%	BABIP	WHIP	ERA	FIP	DRA	VORP	WARP	cFIP	MPH
2014	WMI	A	23	10	5	0	18	18	103²	91	6	2.1	10.1	116	48%	.314	1.11	2.60	2.78	1.73	42.8	4.4	74	
2014	ERI	AA	23	1	0	0	2	2	12	10	1	3.0	8.2	11	50%	.273	1.17	3.00	3.60	3.53	2.3	0.2	93	
2014	DET	MLB	23	0	1	0	4	2	9¹	12	2	4.8	10.6	11	32%	.385	1.82	11.57	5.84	4.57	0.2	0.0	105	95.8
2015	TOL	AAA	24	7	3	0	16	16	86²	85	6	2.6	7.9	76	44%	.306	1.27	4.15	3.27	2.56	26.4	2.7	88	
2015	DET	MLB	24	0	4	0	14	5	40¹	53	10	3.8	5.4	24	48%	.326	1.74	7.36	6.63	5.62	-3.1	-0.3	114	95.2
2016	TOL	AAA	25	5	6	0	20	20	100	106	11	2.5	8.4	93	47%	.326	1.34	3.96	3.67	2.79	28.3	2.9	92	
2016	DET	MLB	25	0	1	0	14	1	29¹	25	4	6.1	8.3	27	52%	.266	1.53	4.60	5.19	4.01	3.3	0.3	106	95.5
2017	DET	MLB	26	4	5	0	35	10	76²	81	10	3.6	7.1	60	48%	.302	1.47	4.86	4.64	4.90	2.2	0.2	100	
2018	DET	MLB	27	6	6	0	58	15	132²	127	18	4.7	9.5	141	48%	.306	1.47	4.65	4.54	4.91	5.3	0.5	112	

Breakout: 24%   Improve: 44%   Collapse: 24%   Attrition: 40%   MLB: 79%   *Comparables: Charlie Furbush, Andre Rienzo, Taylor Jordan*

The "replacement-level player" is a well-defined concept, a theory, a set of numbers by which all other players are measured. But it's time to put a face to the label: it's Buck Farmer. He's the replacement-level player. Time to change WARP to WABF, is what we're saying. He's a guy who pitches like a fifth starter on his best days, and might have a good enough fastball and secondary pitch (in this case, a changeup) to earn a bullpen spot. But he's always caught in between, so in reality he's your 26th man.

Michael Fulmer   RHP

Born: 3/15/93   Age: 24   Bats: R   Throws: R   Height: 6'3"   Weight: 210   Entered Pro Ball: Round 1, 2011 Draft (#44 overall)

YEAR	TEAM	LVL	AGE	W	L	SV	G	GS	IP	H	HR	BB/9	K/9	K	GB%	BABIP	WHIP	ERA	FIP	DRA	VORP	WARP	cFIP	MPH
2014	SLU	A+	21	6	10	0	19	19	95¹	112	7	2.9	8.1	86	50%	.347	1.50	3.97	3.77	3.72	19.9	2.0	96	
2015	BIN	AA	22	6	2	0	15	15	86	73	3	2.4	8.7	83	52%	.293	1.12	1.88	2.63	2.43	25.5	2.8	70	
2015	ERI	AA	22	4	1	0	6	6	31²	27	4	2	9.4	33	48%	.287	1.07	2.84	3.49	2.36	9.6	1.0	69	
2016	TOL	AAA	23	1	1	0	3	3	15¹	16	3	2.9	11.7	20	49%	.325	1.37	4.11	4.28	2.30	5.2	0.5	79	
2016	DET	MLB	23	11	7	0	26	26	159	136	16	2.4	7.5	132	51%	.268	1.12	3.06	3.72	3.49	33.1	3.4	86	97.3
2017	DET	MLB	24	8	8	0	26	26	130	127	16	2.9	7.9	115	48%	.295	1.30	4.21	4.11	4.31	13.6	1.4	100	
2018	DET	MLB	25	8	8	0	25	25	145²	129	18	3.6	9.8	158	48%	.296	1.29	4.08	3.98	4.30	16.1	1.7	98	

Breakout: 26%   Improve: 54%   Collapse: 18%   Attrition: 16%   MLB: 93%   *Comparables: Max Scherzer, Gio Gonzalez, Erasmo Ramirez*

The Rookie of the Year was six outs from qualifying for the ERA title and nine outs from tying Aaron Sanchez for it. His known slider ruined rallies and his iffy changeup was probably the breakout pitch in his arsenal. His mechanics started to buckle a bit in the second half as Fulmer had no idea he'd be the co-ace of a Justin Verlander-led team, and the Tigers pumped the brakes on his workload by pushing him back with every available off day. One day the Mets may kick themselves in the cranium for letting this guy go, although the trade brought Yoenis Cespedes into their lives. For now, Fulmer has three plus pitches and is a no. 2 or no. 3 starter for anyone.

Kyle Funkhouser   RHP

Born: 3/16/94   Age: 23   Bats: R   Throws: R   Height: 6'2"   Weight: 220   Entered Pro Ball: Round 4, 2016 Draft (#115 overall)

YEAR	TEAM	LVL	AGE	W	L	SV	G	GS	IP	H	HR	BB/9	K/9	K	GB%	BABIP	WHIP	ERA	FIP	DRA	VORP	WARP	cFIP	MPH
2016	ONE	A-	22	0	2	0	13	13	37¹	34	0	1.9	8.2	34	53%	.324	1.12	2.65	2.17	2.59	11.0	1.2	85	
2017	DET	MLB	23	2	3	0	9	9	32¹	40	6	4.1	5.9	21	58%	.315	1.69	5.82	5.82	5.99	-1.9	-0.2	144	
2018	DET	MLB	24	5	8	0	27	27	161²	170	27	4.2	7.8	140	58%	.301	1.52	5.24	5.12	5.39	0.9	0.1	130	

Breakout: 1%   Improve: 1%   Collapse: 2%   Attrition: 3%   MLB: 3%   *Comparables: Jesse Hahn, Alex Wilson, Wilking Rodriguez*

Funkhouser will get tagged as the guy who was once drafted in the first round but returned to Louisville and ended up being taken in the fourth. It's not meant as an insult. These are facts. But these facts can begin to take a backseat if Funkhouser puts them in the past with good pro performances. As a polished college product, Double-A is usually the test. Funkhouser will face that test soon, and he'll be approaching it with only OK stuff unless it rebounds by then. Right now, he fits the profile of a back-end college dude. There's the chance for more, though. That's why he's a prospect.

Shane Greene   RHP

Born: 11/17/88   Age: 28   Bats: R   Throws: R   Height: 6'4"   Weight: 210   Entered Pro Ball: Round 15, 2009 Draft (#465 overall)

YEAR	TEAM	LVL	AGE	W	L	SV	G	GS	IP	H	HR	BB/9	K/9	K	GB%	BABIP	WHIP	ERA	FIP	DRA	VORP	WARP	cFIP	MPH
2014	SWB	AAA	25	5	2	0	15	13	66¹	79	3	3.5	7.7	57	52%	.360	1.58	4.61	3.40	4.24	11.0	1.1	99	
2014	NYA	MLB	25	5	4	0	15	14	78²	81	8	3.3	9.3	81	51%	.330	1.40	3.78	3.76	3.33	13.2	1.5	91	95.3
2015	DET	MLB	26	4	8	0	18	16	83²	103	13	2.9	5.4	50	45%	.325	1.55	6.88	5.11	5.32	-2.4	-0.3	113	94.2
2015	TOL	AAA	26	1	1	0	7	7	35	37	2	2.8	5.4	21	44%	.304	1.37	3.86	3.90	5.65	-1.4	-0.1	107	
2016	DET	MLB	27	5	4	2	50	3	60¹	58	3	3.3	8.8	59	48%	.327	1.33	5.82	3.09	4.28	5.2	0.5	93	96.2
2017	DET	MLB	28	2	3	2	51	0	53	53	5	3.5	8.3	49	46%	.307	1.40	3.96	3.89	4.10	5.2	0.5	90	
2018	DET	MLB	29	1	0	1	24	0	25¹	23	3	4.2	9.8	28	46%	.307	1.38	4.06	3.95	4.27	2.2	0.2	93	

Breakout: 22%   Improve: 42%   Collapse: 21%   Attrition: 34%   MLB: 76%   *Comparables: Mitch Talbot, Jason Berken, Yusmeiro Petit*

To say Greene underperformed according to his FIP and DRA is like saying Animal underperformed next to Buddy Rich. He's a failed starter who's relishing a bullpen opportunity, and seems to have the adrenaline (as well as the two pitches) for it. The difference between the ERA and everything else is pretty obvious: 20 inherited runners, 20 stranded runners. That's the second-best strand rate in history behind Randy Myers, when he went 22-for-22 in his final season. Stranding inherited runners isn't a projectable skill, so this speaks to condoning last year's ERA and trusting his reliability in the middle-to-late innings.

Blaine Hardy   LHP

Born: 3/14/87   Age: 30   Bats: L   Throws: L   Height: 6'2"   Weight: 215   Entered Pro Ball: Round 22, 2008 Draft (#655 overall)

YEAR	TEAM	LVL	AGE	W	L	SV	G	GS	IP	H	HR	BB/9	K/9	K	GB%	BABIP	WHIP	ERA	FIP	DRA	VORP	WARP	cFIP	MPH
2014	TOL	AAA	27	3	2	0	20	6	47	35	2	2.5	10.1	53	50%	.284	1.02	2.68	2.55	2.16	17.8	1.8	73	
2014	DET	MLB	27	2	1	0	38	0	39	34	1	4.6	7.2	31	54%	.289	1.38	2.54	3.52	3.99	2.1	0.2	104	91.3
2015	DET	MLB	28	5	3	0	70	0	61¹	61	2	3.2	8.1	55	42%	.319	1.35	3.08	2.86	4.23	3.3	0.4	101	91.0
2016	TOL	AAA	29	1	0	1	32	0	31¹	20	1	1.4	5.5	19	56%	.213	0.80	1.72	2.94	4.07	3.1	0.3	92	
2016	DET	MLB	29	1	0	0	21	0	25²	25	2	4.2	7.0	20	49%	.295	1.44	3.51	3.96	5.50	-1.5	-0.2	108	91.1
2017	DET	MLB	30	2	3	0	45	0	48	46	6	3.5	7.3	39	47%	.287	1.34	4.53	4.48	4.57	2.2	0.2	100	
2018	DET	MLB	31	2	1	0	43	0	46	40	6	4.3	9.3	47	47%	.286	1.36	4.35	4.24	4.60	2.3	0.2	103	

Breakout: 15%   Improve: 29%   Collapse: 10%   Attrition: 13%   MLB: 48%   *Comparables: Brian Tallet, Blake Parker, George Kontos*

Hopefully you're reading this book sitting down, but Hardy was one of the Tigers' relievers who struggled much of the year. Having the pedigree of a well-commanded southpaw, Hardy saw his walk rate swell up and spent more than half the season in the minors. His strong September should keep him in the middle innings conversation as a left-hander with a hard-looping curve that often avoids the outfield, let alone the seating area behind it. One of his main downfalls, however: that mustache. Some baseballers have been able to pull off the dapper look, but Hardy falls squarely in the "guy who hangs around college long after he graduates" heap.

Joe Jimenez   RHP

Born: 1/17/95   Age: 22   Bats: R   Throws: R   Height: 6'3"   Weight: 220   Entered Pro Ball: Undrafted Free Agent, 2013

YEAR	TEAM	LVL	AGE	W	L	SV	G	GS	IP	H	HR	BB/9	K/9	K	GB%	BABIP	WHIP	ERA	FIP	DRA	VORP	WARP	cFIP	MPH
2014	ONE	A-	19	3	2	4	23	0	26²	22	1	2.0	13.8	41	44%	.350	1.05	2.70	1.75	0.91	12.0	1.3	63	
2015	WMI	A	20	5	1	17	40	0	43	23	2	2.3	12.8	61	34%	.239	0.79	1.47	1.93	1.05	18.1	1.9	62	
2016	LAK	A+	21	0	0	10	17	0	17¹	5	0	2.6	14.5	28	36%	.179	0.58	0.00	1.23	1.25	7.4	0.8	68	
2016	ERI	AA	21	3	2	12	21	0	20²	12	0	3.5	14.8	34	24%	.316	0.97	2.18	1.23	2.23	5.7	0.6	73	
2016	TOL	AAA	21	0	1	8	17	0	15²	9	1	2.3	9.2	16	38%	.205	0.83	2.30	2.72	4.57	0.7	0.1	92	
2017	DET	MLB	22	2	1	2	37	0	38²	37	6	3.9	8.8	38	57%	.297	1.40	4.58	4.65	4.72	1.5	0.2	111	
2018	DET	MLB	23	2	1	2	41	0	45²	38	7	5.1	11.3	58	57%	.289	1.39	4.48	4.37	4.62	2.2	0.2	107	

Breakout: 26%   Improve: 30%   Collapse: 4%   Attrition: 9%   MLB: 36%   *Comparables: Eduardo Sanchez, Alex Claudio, Joe Ortiz*

Relievers are as volatile as it comes in baseball. We all know it. We see it all the time. But if you're willing to put a bet down on a relief prospect fulfilling his destiny as an impact, late-innings arm, go with Jimenez. He turned himself into a potential closer in a matter of a couple years after going undrafted out of Puerto Rico. Now he's knocking on the door to a late-inning role in the majors. Jimenez does it with elite velocity and a swing-and-miss slider while keeping the ball around the plate, all coming from a big, strong frame. Relief prospects don't get the same attention as their mates who start in front of them, but Jimenez is one of the best relievers in the minors. Bet on that.

Mark Lowe   RHP

Born: 6/7/83   Age: 34   Bats: L   Throws: R   Height: 6'3"   Weight: 210   Entered Pro Ball: Round 5, 2004 Draft (#153 overall)

YEAR	TEAM	LVL	AGE	W	L	SV	G	GS	IP	H	HR	BB/9	K/9	K	GB%	BABIP	WHIP	ERA	FIP	DRA	VORP	WARP	cFIP	MPH
2014	CLE	MLB	31	0	1	0	7	0	7	10	2	7.7	7.7	6	30%	.320	2.29	3.86	7.73	6.33	-1.4	-0.2	118	94.6
2014	COH	AAA	31	4	3	17	41	0	41²	46	4	3.7	10.2	47	48%	.368	1.51	5.62	3.65	3.05	10.6	1.1	85	
2015	SEA	MLB	32	0	1	0	34	0	36	31	1	2.8	11.8	47	38%	.357	1.17	1.00	1.85	2.86	7.4	0.8	83	97.8
2015	TOR	MLB	32	1	2	1	23	0	19	15	3	0.5	6.6	14	47%	.231	0.84	3.79	3.84	2.99	3.6	0.4	84	98.8
2016	DET	MLB	33	1	5	0	54	0	49¹	57	12	3.8	8.9	49	37%	.319	1.58	7.11	5.62	4.49	2.6	0.3	110	95.5
2017	DET	MLB	34	2	3	0	56	0	58	61	9	3.6	8.6	56	43%	.306	1.45	4.91	4.59	4.87	0.7	0.1	100	
2018	DET	MLB	35	2	1	0	40	0	42¹	44	7	4.1	8.8	41	43%	.307	1.49	4.94	4.81	5.24	-0.9	-0.1	119	

Breakout: 25%   Improve: 38%   Collapse: 13%   Attrition: 7%   MLB: 65%   *Comparables: Oliver Perez, Randy Flores, Esteban Yan*

It's easy to confuse "daft" (silly and foolish) with "deft" (skillful and adept), so here's a primer: Lowe was a *deft* reliever in 2015, making batters look *daft* when his fastball jumped to 96 and it made his slider that much better. Last year Lowe's fastball dipped to 93, at which point Brad Ausmus realized he would have to be *daft* to still use him as a setup man. So he basically lost all playing time down the stretch. But the team's on the hook for over $5 million (thanks to his deft agent), so he'll need to figure out, at age 34, how to throw it much harder.

Matt Manning   RHP

Born: 1/28/98   Age: 19   Bats: R   Throws: R   Height: 6'6"   Weight: 190   Entered Pro Ball: Round 1, 2016 Draft (#9 overall)

The sky is the limit for Manning, which is fitting considering he's 6-foot-6 and the son of a former NBA player. Rich's son signed for more than $3.5 million as the ninth overall pick in 2016 and basically became Detroit's top prospect with the stroke of a pen. He has everything a team covets in a pitching prospect, from the projectable frame and clean arm action to explosive life on a plus-plus fastball, a reliable secondary in a strong curveball and a deep enough arsenal to start. He also commands his stuff at an advanced level for a teenager.

Daniel Norris   LHP

Born: 4/25/93   Age: 24   Bats: L   Throws: L   Height: 6'2"   Weight: 195   Entered Pro Ball: Round 2, 2011 Draft (#74 overall)

YEAR	TEAM	LVL	AGE	W	L	SV	G	GS	IP	H	HR	BB/9	K/9	K	GB%	BABIP	WHIP	ERA	FIP	DRA	VORP	WARP	cFIP	MPH
2014	DUN	A+	21	6	0	0	13	13	66¹	50	0	2.4	10.3	76	48%	.298	1.03	1.22	1.91	2.04	26.2	2.6	79	
2014	NHP	AA	21	3	1	0	8	8	35²	32	5	4.3	12.4	49	39%	.329	1.37	4.54	4.03	2.25	11.8	1.3	82	
2014	BUF	AAA	21	3	1	0	5	4	22²	14	2	3.2	15.1	38	51%	.324	0.97	3.18	2.21	1.36	11.0	1.1	56	
2014	TOR	MLB	21	0	0	0	5	1	6²	5	1	6.8	5.4	4	38%	.200	1.50	5.40	6.16	5.97	-1.0	-0.1	122	94.8
2015	TOR	MLB	22	1	1	0	5	5	23¹	23	3	4.6	6.9	18	32%	.294	1.50	3.86	5.03	4.41	1.7	0.2	106	94.6
2015	BUF	AAA	22	3	10	0	16	16	90²	96	5	4.1	7.7	78	46%	.325	1.51	4.27	3.54	5.50	-2.0	-0.2	106	
2015	DET	MLB	22	2	1	0	8	8	36²	30	6	1.7	6.6	27	47%	.222	1.01	3.68	4.33	4.54	2.2	0.2	108	95.6
2016	TOL	AAA	23	5	7	0	14	14	73¹	78	2	3.4	9.4	77	57%	.358	1.45	4.54	2.61	2.32	24.6	2.5	75	
2016	DET	MLB	23	4	2	0	14	13	69¹	75	10	2.9	9.2	71	38%	.327	1.40	3.38	3.89	4.53	6.3	0.7	99	96.0
2017	*DET*	*MLB*	*24*	*7*	*8*	*0*	*23*	*23*	*115*	*120*	*16*	*3.6*	*8.2*	*105*	*51%*	*.305*	*1.47*	*4.53*	*4.45*	*4.64*	*7.8*	*0.8*	*100*	
2018	*DET*	*MLB*	*25*	*8*	*9*	*0*	*28*	*28*	*170²*	*158*	*23*	*4.1*	*9.9*	*187*	*51%*	*.301*	*1.39*	*4.35*	*4.23*	*4.58*	*13.9*	*1.4*	*105*	

Breakout: 32%   Improve: 56%   Collapse: 11%   Attrition: 17%   MLB: 83%   *Comparables: Jon Niese, Danny Duffy, Burch Smith*

With his season slowed by back and oblique injuries, Norris still churned out two good pennant-chase months with a 3.04 ERA and nearly a strikeout per inning. The Triple-A numbers are ghastly, but his major-league starts are sort of the important ones, and he never allowed more than three earned runs in any Detroit game. The serendipitous van resident completed at least five innings in all 12 starts and partially completed the seventh inning three times. Watch for him to work on going deeper into games, solidifying his place as a no. 3 starter. Barring multiple DL trips and any unforeseen leprechaun hexes, this is a likely outcome for the former David Price trade centerpiece.

Mike Pelfrey   RHP

Born: 1/14/84   Age: 33   Bats: R   Throws: R   Height: 6'7"   Weight: 240   Entered Pro Ball: Round 1, 2005 Draft (#9 overall)

YEAR	TEAM	LVL	AGE	W	L	SV	G	GS	IP	H	HR	BB/9	K/9	K	GB%	BABIP	WHIP	ERA	FIP	DRA	VORP	WARP	cFIP	MPH
2014	MIN	MLB	30	0	3	0	5	5	23²	29	5	6.8	3.8	10	45%	.286	1.99	7.99	7.60	7.30	-6.5	-0.7	128	93.5
2014	ROC	AAA	30	1	0	0	2	2	10	9	0	2.7	2.7	3	41%	.250	1.20	0.90	3.96	5.51	0.3	0.0	112	
2015	MIN	MLB	31	6	11	0	30	30	164²	198	11	2.5	4.7	86	53%	.334	1.48	4.26	3.97	4.78	5.5	0.6	109	96.0
2016	DET	MLB	32	4	10	0	24	22	119	160	15	3.5	4.2	56	52%	.347	1.73	5.07	5.11	6.73	-18.4	-1.9	121	95.3
2017	*DET*	*MLB*	*33*	*4*	*5*	*0*	*46*	*6*	*74*	*83*	*9*	*3.5*	*6.0*	*50*	*60%*	*.309*	*1.53*	*5.01*	*4.73*	*5.00*	*0.8*	*0.1*	*100*	
2018	*DET*	*MLB*	*34*	*4*	*3*	*0*	*57*	*7*	*93*	*110*	*13*	*3.7*	*6.2*	*64*	*60%*	*.323*	*1.59*	*5.12*	*5.00*	*5.43*	*-2.0*	*-0.2*	*126*	

Breakout: 8%   Improve: 34%   Collapse: 13%   Attrition: 15%   MLB: 80%   *Comparables: Jason Marquis, Jake Westbrook, Vicente Padilla*

It's high time for Pelfrey to reinvent his career in the bullpen. It was high time three years ago, but the Twins were desperate and the Tigers were maybe just flat out thinking of someone else and were too kind to correct it. He could probably pull this off with a fastball and one other pitch, with the difficulty being it has to be a pitch that Pelfrey knows. To go out on a limb, he's never been a big curveball guy, but over the years it's the one pitch that's consistently vexed batters. If he's still in the rotation, then you're going to wish you were in the lineup.

Francisco Rodriguez   RHP

Born: 1/7/82   Age: 35   Bats: R   Throws: R   Height: 6'0"   Weight: 195   Entered Pro Ball: International Free Agent, 1998

YEAR	TEAM	LVL	AGE	W	L	SV	G	GS	IP	H	HR	BB/9	K/9	K	GB%	BABIP	WHIP	ERA	FIP	DRA	VORP	WARP	cFIP	MPH
2014	MIL	MLB	32	5	5	44	69	0	68	49	14	2.4	9.7	73	46%	.216	0.99	3.04	4.47	2.99	11.3	1.2	89	93.0
2015	MIL	MLB	33	1	3	38	60	0	57	38	6	1.7	9.8	62	48%	.235	0.86	2.21	2.93	2.83	11.9	1.3	79	91.5
2016	DET	MLB	34	3	4	44	61	0	58¹	45	6	3.2	8.0	52	55%	.252	1.13	3.24	3.79	3.56	9.1	0.9	91	91.5
2017	*DET*	*MLB*	*35*	*3*	*3*	*39*	*56*	*0*	*58*	*54*	*9*	*3.2*	*8.7*	*57*	*38%*	*.284*	*1.26*	*4.35*	*4.39*	*4.43*	*3.6*	*0.4*	*100*	
2018	*DET*	*MLB*	*36*	*3*	*1*	*33*	*52*	*0*	*55²*	*49*	*9*	*3.1*	*8.6*	*53*	*38%*	*.269*	*1.23*	*4.54*	*4.43*	*4.80*	*1.5*	*0.2*	*112*	

Breakout: 23%   Improve: 45%   Collapse: 26%   Attrition: 15%   MLB: 89%   *Comparables: Rafael Betancourt, Joaquin Benoit, J.J. Putz*

K-Rod had the lowest strikeout rate of his career, so it's time to seek out a new nickname. But first let's also dispel the notion that the Tigers had such a tough time locating a good closer. For beginners, in seven of the last eight years the Tigers' primary closer sported a better-than-average ERA and OPS+ against. The exception to both was the Joe Nathan year. In that time, all of their closers were, at some point in their careers, an All-Star, with the exception of Joaquin Benoit, who darn well could have been. Having said all that, Rodriguez was a sound if unspectacular acquisition, as he's by no means a first-division closer—and hasn't been in almost a decade—but there is he, first in active saves and the fourth ever to reach 400. What helps him close 90 percent of games is that he works off his changeup nearly half the time, and despite batters knowing this they're still left guessing. That's not just because he's a veteran with 400 career saves, but also because it's a really good pitch. Bill James' "Favorite Toy" gives Rodriguez a 25 percent chance to surpass Mariano Rivera in career saves. With all the sturm und drang about reliever value, there has to be something to a pitcher getting the final high-leverage outs as an acquired skill set, especially since his peripherals place him on the hefty portion of the bell curve. Longevity is (and will be) the keystone of his career, but on the whole, compared to the Kimbrels of our day, on paper he's just OK. Wait, there it is. OK-Rod.

Bruce Rondon RHP

Born: 12/9/90   Age: 26   Bats: R   Throws: R   Height: 6'3"   Weight: 275   Entered Pro Ball: International Free Agent, 2007

YEAR	TEAM	LVL	AGE	W	L	SV	G	GS	IP	H	HR	BB/9	K/9	K	GB%	BABIP	WHIP	ERA	FIP	DRA	VORP	WARP	cFIP	MPH
2015	TOL	AAA	24	2	2	1	13	0	12²	16	1	4.3	9.9	14	44%	.375	1.74	7.11	3.39	3.60	1.9	0.2	97	
2015	DET	MLB	24	1	0	5	35	0	31	31	3	5.5	10.5	36	44%	.329	1.61	5.81	4.07	4.32	1.3	0.1	99	101.1
2016	TOL	AAA	25	2	2	9	22	0	21²	23	1	6.6	12.5	30	44%	.407	1.80	3.74	3.35	4.59	0.9	0.1	93	
2016	DET	MLB	25	5	2	0	37	0	36¹	23	5	3.0	11.1	45	34%	.228	0.96	2.97	3.66	3.57	5.6	0.6	90	100.8
2017	DET	MLB	26	2	2	0	40	0	42	40	5	3.8	9.5	45	50%	.296	1.34	4.21	3.99	4.30	3.2	0.3	98	
2018	DET	MLB	27	3	1	0	52	0	54²	46	6	4.3	10.5	64	50%	.292	1.33	4.05	3.94	4.26	4.7	0.5	94	

Breakout: 31%   Improve: 45%   Collapse: 21%   Attrition: 21%   MLB: 78%   Comparables: Jose Mijares, Kevin Jepsen, Alex Hinshaw

It took a few years of youth, UCL repair and literal apathy, but Rondon's stuff is finally turning into results. The fastball still burns at triple digits and the plus slider keeps them honest. The Closer Of The Future™ cleaned up his mechanics, lost a bit of weight, struck out more batters, cleaved the walk rate nearly in half—all the returns are positive on the big boy. It's taken relievers with lesser stuff less time to get the ninth-inning job and keep it, but Rondon's patience is about to pay off as he could step in at any time and menace enough late rallies to begin racking up saves.

Kyle Ryan LHP

Born: 9/25/91   Age: 25   Bats: L   Throws: L   Height: 6'5"   Weight: 215   Entered Pro Ball: Round 12, 2010 Draft (#373 overall)

YEAR	TEAM	LVL	AGE	W	L	SV	G	GS	IP	H	HR	BB/9	K/9	K	GB%	BABIP	WHIP	ERA	FIP	DRA	VORP	WARP	cFIP	MPH
2014	ERI	AA	22	7	10	0	21	21	126²	140	15	2.3	5.5	78	49%	.309	1.36	4.55	4.44	3.43	25.3	2.7	97	
2014	TOL	AAA	22	3	0	0	5	5	33	21	0	1.4	5.5	20	52%	.221	0.79	1.64	2.60	3.23	9.3	0.9	94	
2014	DET	MLB	22	2	0	0	6	1	10¹	10	4	1.7	3.5	4	77%	.286	1.16	2.61	2.97	3.55	1.3	0.1	96	92.8
2015	TOL	AAA	23	4	9	0	17	17	103	117	3	2.9	5.5	63	61%	.335	1.46	4.19	3.30	5.39	-1.1	-0.1	105	
2015	DET	MLB	23	2	4	0	16	6	56¹	60	9	3.2	4.8	30	49%	.288	1.42	4.47	5.23	5.25	-2.1	-0.2	113	90.8
2016	DET	MLB	24	4	2	0	56	0	55²	48	2	2.4	5.7	35	57%	.269	1.13	3.07	3.29	4.69	1.7	0.2	101	91.7
2017	DET	MLB	25	2	2	0	28	3	41²	43	5	3.0	5.9	27	48%	.293	1.38	4.69	4.59	4.71	1.7	0.2	100	
2018	DET	MLB	26	5	3	0	64	6	97	84	11	4.1	8.9	96	48%	.285	1.33	4.32	4.21	4.56	6.3	0.7	104	

Breakout: 13%   Improve: 33%   Collapse: 24%   Attrition: 33%   MLB: 82%   Comparables: Dallas Keuchel, Kyle Hendricks, Nick Tropeano

Ryan can barely throw 90 mph and lacks an out pitch, but he's left-handed and has enough variance in his pitches to stick on the major-league roster and get anywhere between one and nine outs, assuming the game is already in hand. He still profiles best as a Triple-A starter, which isn't much of a compliment, but also means he could grow into a no. 5 starter with enough patience. If he's caught in between, then he's stuck with low-leverage innings and is therefore dependable but expendable.

Anibal Sanchez RHP

Born: 2/27/84   Age: 33   Bats: R   Throws: R   Height: 6'0"   Weight: 205   Entered Pro Ball: International Free Agent, 2001

YEAR	TEAM	LVL	AGE	W	L	SV	G	GS	IP	H	HR	BB/9	K/9	K	GB%	BABIP	WHIP	ERA	FIP	DRA	VORP	WARP	cFIP	MPH
2014	DET	MLB	30	8	5	0	22	21	126	108	4	2.1	7.3	102	48%	.277	1.10	3.43	2.74	3.24	22.3	2.5	87	94.8
2015	DET	MLB	31	10	10	0	25	25	157	152	29	2.8	7.9	138	41%	.278	1.28	4.99	4.70	4.09	17.2	1.8	99	94.5
2016	DET	MLB	32	7	13	0	35	26	153¹	171	30	3.1	7.9	135	41%	.317	1.46	5.87	5.02	5.07	4.3	0.4	109	93.8
2017	DET	MLB	33	6	7	0	19	19	114	116	19	3.1	8.3	106	41%	.297	1.38	4.77	4.64	4.92	4.2	0.4	100	
2018	DET	MLB	34	8	10	0	24	24	142²	150	27	3.3	8.3	132	41%	.301	1.42	5.08	4.95	5.36	1.8	0.2	127	

Breakout: 9%   Improve: 43%   Collapse: 26%   Attrition: 19%   MLB: 90%   Comparables: Johan Santana, Josh Beckett, A.J. Burnett

Imagine a grocery store. Three years ago it was the best place in the neighborhood to buy groceries. It wasn't the most popular, but you knew about it and everyone else didn't. Then suddenly the prices shot up. You tolerated it, because you knew a good grocery store with high quality items was hard to find. Then suddenly the bananas were always rotted; the meat looked suspect. The only snacks they offered were those blue corn chips. The expiration date on all the milk jugs said "soon-ish." The loudspeaker kept playing the same Hall and Oates song over and over. And no other grocery store was within reasonable driving distance. Spoiler alert: Sanchez is that grocery store. And it's going to take the city at least $21 million to sell the building.

Spencer Turnbull RHP

Born: 9/18/92   Age: 24   Bats: R   Throws: R   Height: 6'3"   Weight: 215   Entered Pro Ball: Round 2, 2014 Draft (#63 overall)

YEAR	TEAM	LVL	AGE	W	L	SV	G	GS	IP	H	HR	BB/9	K/9	K	GB%	BABIP	WHIP	ERA	FIP	DRA	VORP	WARP	cFIP	MPH
2014	ONE	A-	21	0	2	0	11	11	28¹	31	1	4.4	6.0	19	68%	.347	1.59	4.45	4.15	4.78	1.8	0.2	107	
2015	WMI	A	22	11	3	0	22	22	116²	106	0	4.0	8.2	106	53%	.314	1.35	3.01	3.10	5.65	-5.6	-0.6	109	
2016	LAK	A+	23	1	1	0	6	6	30	24	1	3.0	8.1	27	56%	.274	1.13	3.00	2.99	3.74	5.8	0.6	98	
2017	DET	MLB	24	2	3	0	8	8	37	45	6	5.5	5.1	21	54%	.310	1.83	6.17	6.13	6.36	-3.7	-0.4	151	
2018	DET	MLB	25	4	7	0	19	19	112	121	18	6.3	7.5	93	54%	.306	1.78	6.00	5.87	6.18	-7.0	-0.7	148	

Breakout: 2%   Improve: 2%   Collapse: 1%   Attrition: 3%   MLB: 3%   Comparables: Jake Petricka, Brad Lincoln, Cory Luebke

A big right-hander who throws hard, a product of the SEC and on the fence between starting and relieving? Sounds like a pitcher the Tigers would draft. Turnbull is a strong-bodied righty with a fastball that has a history of hitting upper 90s but sits 92-94 with sink. He adds a slider that occasionally wipes out and misses bats, but lacks the consistency to rack up big strikeout totals, while his curveball and changeup are fringe level. Turnbull missed a large chunk of 2016 because of a shoulder impingement and needs to start moving up the ladder to avoid falling behind in development. He flashes the arsenal of a mid-rotation starter, but the safe bet is a late-inning reliever.

Justin Verlander RHP

Born: 2/20/83 Age: 34 Bats: R Throws: R Height: 6'5" Weight: 225 Entered Pro Ball: Round 1, 2004 Draft (#2 overall)

YEAR	TEAM	LVL	AGE	W	L	SV	G	GS	IP	H	HR	BB/9	K/9	K	GB%	BABIP	WHIP	ERA	FIP	DRA	VORP	WARP	cFIP	MPH
2014	DET	MLB	31	15	12	0	32	32	206	223	18	2.8	6.9	159	41%	.317	1.40	4.54	3.77	3.75	24.8	2.7	104	96.1
2015	DET	MLB	32	5	8	0	20	20	133¹	113	13	2.2	7.6	113	37%	.267	1.09	3.38	3.46	3.65	21.2	2.3	96	96.5
2016	DET	MLB	33	16	9	0	34	34	227²	171	30	2.3	10.0	254	35%	.255	1.00	3.04	3.44	2.75	66.1	6.8	84	96.8
2017	DET	MLB	34	12	10	0	30	30	189	169	26	2.7	9.8	205	44%	.292	1.20	3.91	3.80	4.00	26.2	2.7	91	
2018	DET	MLB	35	11	10	0	30	30	185²	173	28	2.7	9.9	203	44%	.299	1.24	4.02	3.90	4.23	25.3	2.6	96	

Breakout: 19% Improve: 39% Collapse: 38% Attrition: 8% MLB: 94% *Comparables: Adam Wainwright, Chris Carpenter, Ryan Dempster*

Verlander is the poster boy for why premium pitching costs a king's ransom. After all, if Mike Leake and Ian Kennedy bring home eight figures a year, then get a load of this guy, right? JV is always one bad month from the fan base pointing at the paycheck like it's a handout, but he's a franchise face and, after a couple years of doubt, pitching like it again. Like most 34-year-olds, his velocity isn't what it was when he was in his mid-20s, but unlike most 34-year-olds he's still a threat to win the Cy Young or finish nine innings on any given night. He's the type of throwback ace that doesn't have the throwback numbers making him a lock for the Hall of Fame, but considering there are three years left on the mega-deal, that's for him to decide.

Alex Wilson RHP

Born: 11/3/86 Age: 30 Bats: R Throws: R Height: 6'0" Weight: 215 Entered Pro Ball: Round 2, 2009 Draft (#77 overall)

YEAR	TEAM	LVL	AGE	W	L	SV	G	GS	IP	H	HR	BB/9	K/9	K	GB%	BABIP	WHIP	ERA	FIP	DRA	VORP	WARP	cFIP	MPH
2014	PAW	AAA	27	6	1	5	35	0	41¹	38	2	5.0	8.7	40	38%	.316	1.48	4.35	3.87	4.69	3.0	0.3	103	
2014	BOS	MLB	27	1	0	0	18	0	28¹	20	3	1.6	6.0	19	45%	.213	0.88	1.91	3.94	4.18	1.0	0.1	106	94.7
2015	DET	MLB	28	3	3	2	59	1	70	61	5	1.4	4.9	38	53%	.258	1.03	2.19	3.50	4.61	0.9	0.1	101	94.5
2016	DET	MLB	29	4	0	0	62	0	73	68	5	2.6	6.0	49	45%	.285	1.22	2.96	3.56	4.71	2.1	0.2	108	93.9
2017	DET	MLB	30	2	3	0	51	0	53	58	8	2.9	6.5	39	46%	.301	1.42	4.96	4.78	4.89	0.5	0.1	100	
2018	DET	MLB	31	2	1	0	33	0	34²	37	5	3.4	7.8	30	46%	.314	1.45	4.69	4.56	4.95	0.4	0.0	112	

Breakout: 19% Improve: 43% Collapse: 18% Attrition: 20% MLB: 72% *Comparables: Saul Rivera, Ramon Troncoso, Sean Green*

It's difficult to find relievers to shorten the game in the fifth and sixth innings. Typically they just sprout from the ground and once in a while will become a cash crop that saves games. This type of bailout is what made Brad Brach an All-Star, which he parlayed into a setup role. No such thing is likely to happen for Wilson, who relishes pitching any inning, any time. Relying mostly on a high-80s cut fastball and a slightly quicker sinker, he shows no real platoon splits and pitches more to contact than most relievers. For a bullpen-challenged franchise like Detroit, Wilson was exactly what they've needed since acquiring him as a door prize for Rick Porcello, so don't expect him slotted into a specific inning any time soon.

Justin Wilson LHP

Born: 8/18/87 Age: 29 Bats: L Throws: L Height: 6'2" Weight: 205 Entered Pro Ball: Round 5, 2008 Draft (#144 overall)

YEAR	TEAM	LVL	AGE	W	L	SV	G	GS	IP	H	HR	BB/9	K/9	K	GB%	BABIP	WHIP	ERA	FIP	DRA	VORP	WARP	cFIP	MPH
2014	PIT	MLB	26	3	4	0	70	0	60	49	4	4.5	9.1	61	52%	.285	1.32	4.20	3.59	3.52	6.4	0.7	96	97.9
2015	NYA	MLB	27	5	0	0	74	0	61	49	3	3.0	9.7	66	46%	.301	1.13	3.10	2.66	3.67	7.1	0.8	86	97.6
2016	DET	MLB	28	4	5	1	66	0	58²	61	6	2.6	10.0	65	56%	.340	1.33	4.14	3.14	3.13	12.0	1.2	79	97.7
2017	DET	MLB	29	2	3	0	51	0	53	47	7	3.1	9.1	54	51%	.287	1.23	3.98	4.02	4.13	5.1	0.5	94	
2018	DET	MLB	30	3	1	1	59	0	62²	50	7	3.2	10.1	70	51%	.275	1.15	3.80	3.68	4.00	7.2	0.7	88	

Breakout: 38% Improve: 56% Collapse: 23% Attrition: 18% MLB: 96% *Comparables: Darren O'Day, Andrew Bailey, Jim Johnson*

When you're trying to figure out what to watch on Netflix, Justin Wilson is like *Scrubs*—a quirky fallback option, not your first choice but probably one you can agree upon with others. (Which explains three different teams over three seasons.) For one, he's a lefty with reverse splits, so what's even the point of picking up the ball with that hand? But his ability to mow down righties with a mid-90s fastball means he will eventually lock down a late-inning role. Until then, his name is called early and often, and the manager isn't burned for it.

Jordan Zimmermann RHP

Born: 5/23/86 Age: 31 Bats: R Throws: R Height: 6'2" Weight: 225 Entered Pro Ball: Round 2, 2007 Draft (#67 overall)

YEAR	TEAM	LVL	AGE	W	L	SV	G	GS	IP	H	HR	BB/9	K/9	K	GB%	BABIP	WHIP	ERA	FIP	DRA	VORP	WARP	cFIP	MPH
2014	WAS	MLB	28	14	5	0	32	32	199²	185	13	1.3	8.2	182	42%	.302	1.07	2.66	2.65	3.42	31.4	3.5	90	95.9
2015	WAS	MLB	29	13	10	0	33	33	201²	204	24	1.7	7.3	164	44%	.302	1.20	3.66	3.78	4.75	7.3	0.8	103	95.2
2016	TOL	AAA	30	0	1	0	5	5	20¹	19	2	1.8	4.9	11	46%	.270	1.13	1.33	4.10	4.67	1.5	0.2	109	
2016	DET	MLB	30	9	7	0	19	18	105¹	118	14	2.2	5.6	66	44%	.304	1.37	4.87	4.38	4.94	4.8	0.5	114	94.3
2017	DET	MLB	31	9	10	0	26	26	163	170	25	2.5	7.0	128	46%	.293	1.32	4.70	4.55	4.83	7.6	0.8	100	
2018	DET	MLB	32	9	10	0	26	26	157²	161	25	2.6	6.7	118	46%	.286	1.31	4.80	4.67	5.05	7.6	0.8	120	

Breakout: 12% Improve: 33% Collapse: 29% Attrition: 14% MLB: 93% *Comparables: Jered Weaver, Shaun Marcum, Ben Sheets*

Other than a great April, the big-budget acquisition was pretty much a nightmare. But enough about Michael Bay's rendition of *Teenage Mutant Ninja Turtles*. Zimmermann's 5-0, 0.55 ERA April was the only bright spot of a season that unraveled and ended with an ERA of nearly 7.00 the rest of the way. A neck strain decimated his second half and by the time he healed for the Tigers' postseason run, he only had the endurance for a few innings and was basically pining for *tabula rasa* in 2017. Only $92 million left on the contract, dudes.

Kevin Ziomek   LHP

Born: 3/21/92   Age: 25   Bats: R   Throws: L   Height: 6'3"   Weight: 200   Entered Pro Ball: Round 2, 2013 Draft (#58 overall)

YEAR	TEAM	LVL	AGE	W	L	SV	G	GS	IP	H	HR	BB/9	K/9	K	GB%	BABIP	WHIP	ERA	FIP	DRA	VORP	WARP	cFIP	MPH
2014	WMI	A	22	10	6	0	23	23	123	89	5	3.9	11.1	152	47%	.286	1.15	2.27	2.98	2.30	42.9	4.4	87	
2015	LAK	A+	23	9	11	0	27	27	154²	142	3	2.0	8.3	143	54%	.312	1.14	3.43	2.38	2.56	43.3	4.7	81	
2017	DET	MLB	31	9	10	0	26	26	163	170	25	2.5	7.0	128	46%	.293	1.32	4.70	4.55	4.83	7.6	0.8	100	
2018	DET	MLB	32	9	10	0	26	26	157²	161	25	2.6	6.7	118	46%	.286	1.31	4.80	4.67	5.05	7.6	0.8	120	

Breakout: 8%   Improve: 11%   Collapse: 14%   Attrition: 24%   MLB: 31%   *Comparables: Cory Mazzoni, Charlie Furbush, Corey Kluber*

Ziomek was on his way to the doorstep of the majors after being assigned to Double-A Erie to start 2016, but injuries pushed him back into the yard and surgery had him waving from the street. The left-hander out of Vanderbilt had two successful seasons in the lower levels to open his pro career and was set to get his first real test before undergoing surgery in June for thoracic outlet syndrome. Despite positive early returns as a pro, there were rumblings of the stuff and command not matching the numbers, and the ceiling is closer to that of a back-end starter or reliever. The path back to the doorstep got a little longer after surgery, but if his present stuff returns, it's enough to get in the door.

LINEOUTS

Hitters

NAME	POS	TEAM	LVL	AGE	PA	R	2B	3B	HR	RBI	BB	K	SB	CS	AVG/OBP/SLG	TAv	VORP	BABIP	BRR	FRAA	WARP
Grayson Greiner	C	LAK	A+	23	123	14	6	0	0	12	12	26	0	0	.312/.385/.367	.283	5.1	.410	-3.0	C(27): -1.6	0.4
	C	ERI	AA	23	225	20	9	3	7	30	10	55	1	0	.288/.320/.462	.260	9.7	.351	0.5	C(56): 5.8	1.7
John Hicks	C	ROC	AAA	26	34	1	2	0	1	1	1	5	0	0	.242/.265/.394	.211	-0.3	.259	-0.1	C(9): 2.4	0.2
	C	ERI	AA	26	54	7	1	1	1	4	4	9	1	0	.388/.426/.510	.322	5.7	.450	0.4	C(11): 0.7, 1B(2): 0.2	0.7
	C	TOL	AAA	26	264	38	20	0	8	42	17	59	3	1	.303/.356/.485	.296	20.2	.374	-1.3	C(66): -1.0, 3B(1): -0.0	2.0
	C	DET	MLB	26	2	1	1	0	0	0	0	0	0	0	.500/.500/1.000	.456	0.2	.500	-0.2	1B(1): 0.0	0.0
Casey McGehee	3B	TOL	AAA	33	480	56	37	0	6	50	38	73	6	3	.317/.373/.443	.295	31.0	.368	-0.5	3B(100): -10.8, 1B(10): 0.3	2.1
	3B	DET	MLB	33	96	4	1	0	0	1	3	14	0	0	.228/.260/.239	.184	-5.3	.269	-1.0	3B(27): -1.1, 1B(1): -0.0	-0.7
Zach Shepherd	3B	LAK	A+	20	481	62	20	1	15	50	64	159	0	0	.186/.301/.350	.229	-4.6	.257	-4.1	3B(115): 2.2	-0.3
Jordany Valdespin	INF	TOL	AAA	28	321	31	11	2	3	25	20	59	10	4	.239/.292/.321	.226	-3.5	.286	0.8	2B(42): -1.8, 1B(25): 1.4	-0.1

For some reason, people wrote off **Grayson Greiner** after he broke his hamate bone in 2014 and struggled in an initial return. He's better than that. You're better than that. ❖ **John Hicks**, a backup catcher at best, is on pace to be claimed off waivers by every major-league team in roughly 3-4 years. ❖ If you wish for a right-handed third baseman, a lazy genie might give you **Casey McGehee** for the season. Please try to be more specific in the future. ❖ **Zach Shepherd**'s pro honeymoon ended abruptly when his hit tool didn't play in full-season ball, but there's time for the young Aussie to adjust and raise his batting average from down under. ❖ Peak **Jordany Valdespin** occurred in a midseason Triple-A game: as a defensive sub, he cracked a game-tying, ninth-inning, two-out grand slam, re-tied the game in the 11th on a sac fly and then pitched two-thirds of an inning in the 13th, where his balk resulted in the manager's ejection. They lost, 16-11.

Pitchers

NAME	TEAM	LVL	AGE	W	L	SV	G	GS	IP	H	HR	BB/9	K/9	K	GB%	BABIP	WHIP	ERA	FIP	DRA	VORP	WARP	cFIP	MPH
Victor Alcantara	ARK	AA	23	3	7	0	29	20	111	106	9	4.6	6.4	79	55%	.289	1.47	4.30	4.49	7.30	-27.7	-3.0	114	
Chad Bell	ROU	AAA	27	1	0	0	5	2	18	12	0	2.5	9.5	19	56%	.279	0.94	1.50	2.44	5.43	-0.5	0.0	82	
	TOL	AAA	27	10	4	0	28	10	80¹	79	4	4.3	7.7	69	51%	.321	1.46	3.70	3.55	3.80	12.4	1.3	97	
Mark Ecker	ONE	A-	21	2	0	4	11	0	18	7	0	1.5	10.5	21	33%	.179	0.56	0.50	1.44	1.90	5.9	0.6	76	
Matt Hall	WMI	A	22	8	0	0	12	12	66¹	49	0	2.8	9.8	72	40%	.285	1.06	1.09	2.35	2.22	20.6	2.3	84	
	LAK	A+	22	3	2	0	12	11	60²	61	6	4.2	8.0	54	49%	.318	1.47	4.15	4.24	4.98	3.3	0.3	107	
Myles Jaye	ERI	AA	24	4	8	0	21	21	122²	127	11	2.1	7.6	104	53%	.311	1.27	4.04	3.61	3.35	23.8	2.6	83	
	TOL	AAA	24	1	4	0	7	7	39	30	2	2.8	7.2	31	51%	.248	1.08	3.69	3.32	4.85	2.1	0.2	99	
Austin Kubitza	ERI	AA	24	2	3	0	7	4	20	22	1	7.2	4.9	11	61%	.300	1.90	5.40	5.31	9.11	-9.1	-1.0	121	
	LAK	A+	24	2	1	1	22	0	43	46	3	5.4	7.3	35	57%	.314	1.67	4.60	4.76	8.34	-15.6	-1.6	121	
Jairo Labourt	LAK	A+	22	7	9	1	30	12	87¹	65	3	7.2	8.3	81	52%	.253	1.55	5.26	4.52	9.86	-44.5	-4.6	135	
Joseph Mantiply	ERI	AA	25	3	1	1	49	0	51	40	1	1.9	10.9	62	48%	.302	1.00	2.47	1.95	1.24	19.8	2.1	71	
	DET	MLB	25	0	0	0	5	0	2²	7	1	6.8	6.8	2	58%	.545	3.38	16.88	8.73	4.37	0.2	0.0	104	89.4
Timothy Melville	CIN	MLB	26	0	1	0	3	2	9	16	5	9.0	8.0	8	39%	.355	2.78	11.00	11.96	6.06	-0.8	-0.1	119	93.8
Dustin Molleken	DET	MLB	31	0	0	0	4	0	8¹	12	0	5.4	8.6	8	59%	.414	2.04	4.32	2.99	4.55	0.4	0.0	102	96.6
	TOL	AAA	31	2	4	1	42	5	60¹	49	4	4.5	8.4	56	41%	.281	1.31	3.58	3.76	6.84	-11.9	-1.2	112	
Gerson Moreno	WMI	A	20	1	1	11	23	0	25	19	0	2.9	9.7	27	48%	.297	1.08	1.08	2.40	3.39	3.5	0.4	95	
	LAK	A+	20	0	3	3	21	0	24²	22	4	7.3	9.9	27	51%	.277	1.70	6.93	5.97	6.67	-4.4	-0.4	118	
Angel Nesbitt	ERI	AA	25	1	1	0	11	0	12¹	13	1	1.5	9.5	13	46%	.333	1.22	3.65	2.79	3.29	2.0	0.2	88	
	TOL	AAA	25	1	1	0	28	0	31²	48	2	4.0	6.8	24	44%	.407	1.96	5.68	3.89	7.43	-8.7	-0.9	116	
Bobby Parnell	DET	MLB	31	0	0	0	6	0	5¹	7	1	8.4	6.8	4	50%	.353	2.25	6.75	6.86	4.29	0.4	0.0	108	97.0
	TOL	AAA	31	2	1	12	44	0	43¹	43	2	3.7	6.2	30	45%	.299	1.41	3.95	3.63	6.61	-7.9	-0.8	117	
Adam Ravenelle	LAK	A+	23	2	1	3	23	0	28¹	17	3	5.4	10.8	34	57%	.219	1.20	2.86	4.24	4.07	3.2	0.3	102	
	ERI	AA	23	1	1	1	27	0	29²	30	4	4.9	7.0	23	60%	.292	1.55	4.85	5.18	6.41	-5.5	-0.6	108	
Warwick Saupold	DET	MLB	26	1	1	0	6	0	9²	17	0	2.8	9.3	10	54%	.486	2.07	7.45	2.28	4.11	0.9	0.1	98	94.7
	TOL	AAA	26	7	2	0	18	11	74¹	64	3	2.7	6.1	50	55%	.277	1.16	2.30	3.32	4.65	5.1	0.5	101	
Drew Smith	WMI	A	22	1	2	4	35	0	48²	34	0	4.3	11.5	62	39%	.309	1.17	2.96	2.59	2.73	10.4	1.1	92	
Daniel Stumpf	PHI	MLB	25	0	0	0	7	0	5	9	1	3.6	3.6	2	38%	.400	2.20	10.80	6.19	6.03	-0.6	-0.1	119	95.1
	NWA	AA	25	2	0	1	14	0	21¹	14	0	1.7	11.0	26	55%	.264	0.84	2.11	1.59	2.01	6.4	0.7	74	
Drew VerHagen	DET	MLB	25	1	0	0	19	0	19	28	3	3.3	4.7	10	60%	.362	1.84	7.11	5.37	4.61	0.8	0.1	108	97.0

The higher he gets in the Angels' system, the lower his strikeout rate drops. Generally speaking this might be typical, but considering **Victor Alcantara**'s calling card is his elite velocity, it's not promising. ❖ **Chad Bell** was Detroit's return for journeyman catcher Bobby Wilson in a midseason trade with Texas and stayed in the minors all year, which is where he belongs. ❖ **Mark Ecker** was drafted in the fifth round in 2016 as a safe-bet reliever. The arsenal doesn't pop like a closer's would, but there's no shame in picking a solid middle reliever who could contribute soon. ❖ **Matt Hall** gets by on a fringe fastball, plus curve, deep arsenal and excellent command. Crafty lefty. It's a ceiling limited to the back-end or bullpen. ❖ Acquired from the Rangers in spring training for catcher Bryan Holaday, the well-traveled **Myles Jaye** has back-end rotation potential but may wind up in the bullpen. ❖ Similar to his brother, fringy Kyle, **Austin Kubitza** felt the effects of a limited profile as the Tigers moved him to relief and he still struggled to get outs with basically one-and-a-half pitches. ❖ It's taking a considerable amount of time for **Jairo Labourt** to get out of the lower levels because he usually doesn't know where his pitches are going, but fortunately the Tigers started to realize he's a potential high-leverage reliever and not a starter. ❖ You tend to take notice when a big, left-handed, 27th rounder named **Joseph Mantiply** makes the majors in three-plus years. Long live the left arm. ❖ **Tim Melville**'s listed nicknames on Baseball-Reference.com are "Woody" and "Smellville," so clearly he's the 12th man even on the metaphorical pitching staff that is his friend group. ❖ **Dustin Molleken**'s story is one of perseverance: 12 minor-league seasons, a trip to Japan and multiple arm injuries before his first major-league appearance at age 31 in 2016. ❖ **Gerson Moreno** has a cannon attached to his shoulder and it fires upper-90s missiles and hard sliders. If he can guide it over the plate, there's late-innings potential. ❖ **Angel Nesbitt** didn't do himself any favors by getting tagged for a 5.40 ERA in his 2015 major-league stint, and not much changed at Toledo in 2016. ❖ Here's your annual reminder (and Annual reminder) that Tommy John surgery recovery is not absolute metaphysical certitude. **Bobby Parnell** was a late-inning reliever before it, and bullpen filler after it. ❖ **Adam Ravenelle** is a couple years removed from the possibility of being a fast-rising reliever because of injuries and control issues, but scouts love the big fastball/slider combo. ❖ A South African, a Lithuanian and an Australian walk into a bar and leave starting a fight with another patron outside a Triple-A ballpark. There is no punch line, save for **Warwick Saupold**'s uppercut, which ended his season with an arrest and suspension. ❖ After a successful full-season debut that proved he left much of his command issues in college, **Drew Smith** could move quickly as a hard-throwing reliever with a setup-type future. ❖ Picked in the Rule 5 draft for the second season in a row, **Daniel Stumpf** was suspended 80 games for PEDs the first time around and the Phillies decided not to bother with him. ❖ **Drew VerHagen**, a middle-inning power sinkerballer, missed most of the season following thoracic outlet syndrome surgery.

HOUSTON ASTROS

Essay by Zachary Levine

Player comments by Jack Moore and BP staff

Ten years can never constitute a drought. If you're coming off a title, you're still in that honeymoon period. If you're a franchise starting from scratch, you're not even allowed to use the word drought—three expansion teams have done it in a decade, and one of them had the word "Miracle" in their name.

Down by a run with nobody out and a man on second base in the top of the eighth inning of the first game of the 2005 World Series—if enough prepositional phrases can build a proper stage for this moment—Lance Berkman singled to left field, and Willy Taveras went to third.

Joe Buck, albeit never one to be overly excitable, didn't think much of it, nor raise his voice. It was a single off the bat with no drama, and despite Taveras' speed there was never going to be a play at the plate. Buck and Tim McCarver went lefty-righty through the rest of the lineup, dissecting some minor strategy nuance. The road grays in the dugout were perfectly settled and the game rolled right on to the next batter.

Other than it being a World Series game, maybe one person at the time would have recognized the significance of that moment, and certainly nobody would now.

When Berkman and Taveras took their leads, and before a first-pitch strike to Morgan Ensberg, that moment was the closest the Astros have ever come to being champions. Three strikeouts to end the eighth, three outs in the ninth, three more losses and a mostly sad decade later, it still is.

At **twenty** *years, you're still being kind of a jerk for calling it a drought. There is an element to that passage of time that keeps it from being a dynasty—a twenty-year wait means no players, no manager, and no GM would be the same. And if Texas and Atlanta start a trend, they wouldn't even be celebrating in the same building. But dynasty and drought aren't mutually exhaustive, and plenty of teams would kill for this frequency. Stop being a jerk.*

According to Dan Hirsch, who keeps championship probability statistics at the Baseball Gauge, that moment in Chicago was the all-time peak for the Astros at 50.9 percent. It's not particularly interesting that the Astros didn't win that World Series—51-49 shots lose all the time. Nor is it interesting that they didn't win it all in their next-closest flirtation in 1980 (peaked at 48 percent) or in 2004 (peaked

ASTROS PROSPECTUS
2016 W-L: 84-78, 3RD IN AL WEST

Pythag	.515	12th	DER	.693	25th
RS/G	4.47	15th	B-Age	26.4	1st
RA/G	4.33	10th	P-Age	28.6	19th
TAv	.259	17th	Salary	$98.8M	21st
BRR	3.95	9th	M$/MW	$2.4M	27th
TAv-P	.257	11th	DL Days	413	1st
FIP	3.81	5th	$ on DL	7%	6th

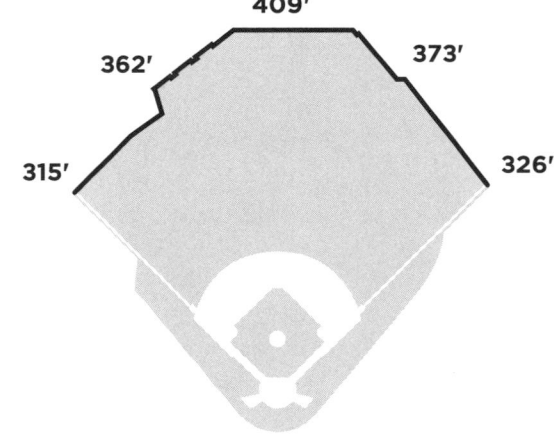

Outfield wall profile: **5'** to **25'**

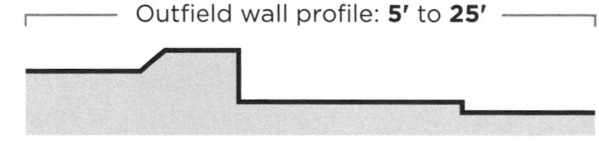

Three-Year Park Factors

Runs	Runs/RH	Runs/LH	HR/RH	HR/LH
97	96	97	101	104

Top Hitter WARP	6.1	Jose Altuve
Top Pitcher WARP	3.5	Dallas Keuchel
Top Prospect	Francis Martes	

2016 Hit List Ranking

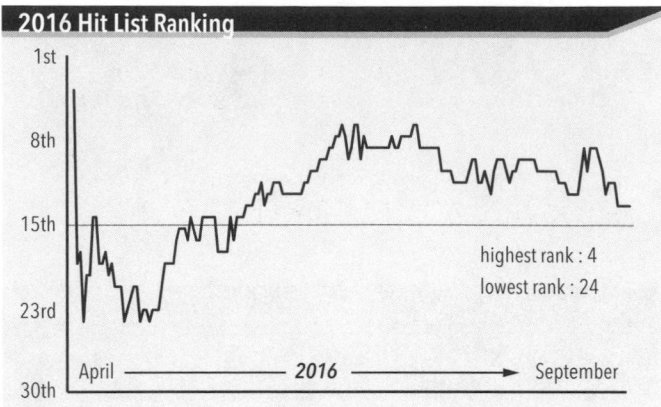

highest rank : 4

lowest rank : 24

April — 2016 → September

Committed Payroll (in millions)

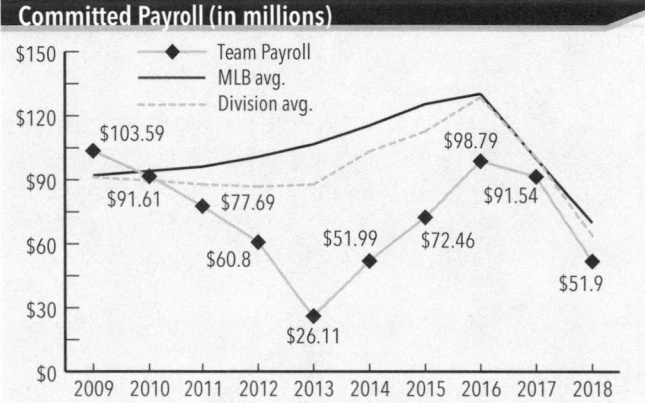

Farm System Ranking

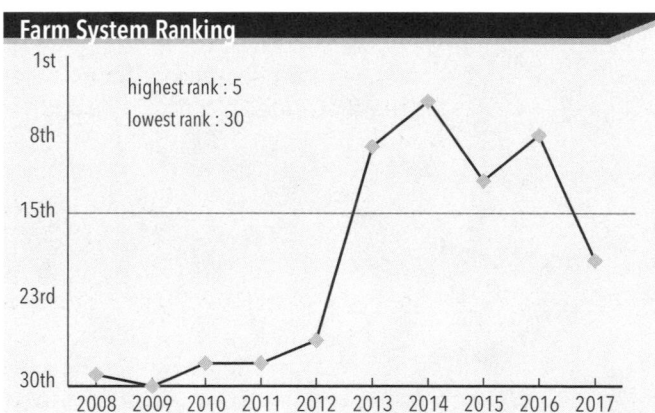

highest rank : 5

lowest rank : 30

Personnel

General Manager:
Jeff Luhnow

**AGM, Scouting and
Player Development:**
Mike Elias

**Special Assistant,
Process Improvement:**
Sig Mejdal

Director, International:
Oz Ocampo

Manager: A.J. Hinch

BP Alumni:
Tucker Blair
Mike Fast
Kevin Goldstein
Ronit Shah
Colin Wyers

at 38 percent), when they didn't make the World Series at all.

But as the Astros begin the 2017 season as a legitimate threat to lift a trophy, it feels somewhat remarkable that in their first 55 years, they have never won it all. Starting at the simplest level, the average team has a 1-in-30 chance to win the World Series (down from 1-in-28 when there were 28 teams, and so on). Accounting for uneven league sizes, there would be an 11 percent chance that a team born in 1962 still would be without a piece of hardware.

The Astros have achieved that 11 percent, in part because they haven't been very good. According to the Baseball Gauge, taking a freeze frame on July 7 of every season, the chance of not winning it all in any of their 54 seasons jumps to 22 percent instead of 11. But there is plenty of postseason bad luck involved. If they were 50-50 to win every series, including their ultimately successful Wild Card game in 2015, there would only be a 21 percent chance of being blanked to date.

Thirty *years in, you start getting generational. The 7-year-old who stayed up super extra late to watch Sundberg dash home let her 7-year-old stay up super extra late to watch Hosmer dash home. Thirty is also exactly what it's supposed to take in baseball's steady equilibrium of thirty teams. The first is why they want you to think thirty is a drought. The second is why it's not a drought.*

So when does this become interesting? When does it become less of a fun fact and more a part of the Astros' identity? According to MLB's official historian John Thorn, the Red Sox weren't an officially cursed team until the World Series drought rolled into its sixth or seventh decade.

"I think we must credit [*Boston Globe* columnist] Dan Shaughnessy for the phrase 'Curse of the Bambino' if not necessarily Boston's Gothic sense of a seven-gabled curse," Thorn said. "Certainly there was talk of a cursed franchise in 1986, but maybe not in 1975 … and surely not in 1967."

For the Cubs, it was acknowledged and sourced much quicker. Per the *Chicago Tribune*, the Billy Goat incident of 1945 (37 years after the last title) prompted a response from owner P.K. Wrigley five years later apologizing for giving the bovid the boot and asking forgiveness. Meaning the team officially recognized it at just 42 years.

As for the Astros, the nation outside of Beltway 8 doesn't really think of them the same way we thought of the Red Sox and Cubs. It makes one wonder what can retroactively be blamed. The curse of the air-conditioner? The curse of the Colt .45? The curse of Joe Morgan?

When it's been **forty** *years, you start to wonder. Six of the 14 expansion teams have broken through and won the World Series. Five did it in their first two decades; the other, the Angels, took 41 years. Five of the other babies of the 1960s have rolled past this point with no signs of slowing down, although just two of them have done it in one city.*

Whether you think they are cursed or not, they're running

out of time before something starts to develop. Even the most level-headed believe that. For a view into the fan psyche, I asked James Yasko, proprietor of the thoughtful Astros County blog and representative of the majority of Astros fans who have not lived through all 55.

"Never having won a World Series doesn't define my status as a fan," Yasko said. "I—as well as most fans, I think—realize that it takes a decent amount of luck in addition to talent to be the last team standing. Had the Astros been in a position to win the 2005 series, you can bet I would have 15 different shirts proclaiming that success. Still, most every logical/sane Astros fan can admit that Randy Johnson and the 1998 Astros should have at least won the pennant."

He continued through their several close calls and then got to the part about the not-so-close calls.

*If you have to wait **fifty** years, you may never see your team win. Not because you're going anywhere, let's hope, but because the team might be. That was the case with the St. Louis Browns, who did the rare eastward move to Baltimore after fifty World Series were played without their winning any of them. The Expos didn't even make it to fifty before they packed up and headed to Washington. They might win some day, but they're probably not your team anymore.*

Let's talk for a minute about those not-so-close calls, because that's a big part of this, too.

When Jeff Luhnow was hired as general manager of the Astros, he presented a five-year plan to work them into a force in the American League West. April will begin Year 6, and there has been mild success. The Astros enter every season—and appear to be set up to do so for the foreseeable future—as a legitimate threat to win the division.

However, the wait in Southeast Texas may have taken its toll. Despite a competitive team and coming off a playoff appearance, the Astros' attendance has not yet caught up to the levels from even 2009 and 2010. It is 17 percent below what it was in 2008—a third straight non-playoff year and the immediate aftermath of a 73-win season.

"Fifty-five years of not winning hasn't been as psychologically damaging to me as much as 2011-2014," Yasko said, referring to a four-year stretch of 232 wins and 416 losses. "But if the Astros don't win a World Series in the next five years, and the Luhnow Gambit doesn't pay off with a ring, then the angst might get kicked up to cursed status."

***Sixty** years makes two generations, and that's when decisions start to be made. You didn't grow up with any parades, and your parents don't remember any either. Now you have a kid, and there are so many other teams out there. Or have you considered musical theater for him? You're strong enough to handle this; you're an adult. But why subject your kid to this?*

For years, even dating back before the Luhnow era, the Astros have been a place of opportunity for those not exactly ready for the majors, so you'll forgive a little bit of skepticism

when presented with facts like this: The Astros led the major leagues in WARP for 22-and-under players in 2016.

This one is a good one. I promise. First of all, look at the teams on this list:

Top 2016 WARP from 22-and-under players

Team	WARP	Contributors*
Astros	8.8	Correa, McCullers, Bregman
Dodgers	7.8	Seager, Urias
Indians	6.2	Lindor
Cubs	4.3	Russell, Almora
Rangers	3.5	Odor, Mazara

22-and-under players with positive WARP

It's the Astros and four playoff teams, including both World Series participants. The Astros also have other markings of a team on the rise. Nobody in the American League got more WARP from players under 27, nor did anybody in the AL get more from players in their 20s—period.

Almost that entire core remains intact for 2017—a year older, and in a lot of cases in this region of the aging curve, a year better. It's also a full season of seemingly permanent solutions where before there was chaos. A full season of Alex Bregman and a full season of Yuli Gurriel, both of whom debuted with some promise and both of whom should take their first Opening Day starts at one position or another.

*The average life expectancy of an American born in 1950 was approximately **seventy** years–a little higher for women, a little lower for men.*

Year 6 for Luhnow will be Year 7 for owner Jim Crane, who after a flurry of moves to begin the offseason was praised for opening his wallet for the first time. The Astros traded for Brian McCann and laid out $82 million for free agents Josh Reddick, Carlos Beltran, and Charlie Morton.

The wave was unprecedented, but to describe it as where the investment started flowing in feels incorrect. The Astros' payroll has been steadily rising, though not to the point of reflecting their market size nor yet in line with Crane's initial comments upon buying the team. However, this is much more gradual an increase as the team has entered what looks like a sustained stretch of putting together potential drought-busters. Either way, what's relatively clear is that the holes in the lineup are mostly filled.

What's even clearer is that the pitching will be what decides this. The rotation went three deep with two-WARP pitchers—Dallas Keuchel, McCullers and Collin McHugh—but was a bit of a mess at the back end, and solidifying that by the end of March or the end of July with a fourth playoff quality starter from within or outside will be crucial.

*At **eighty** years, they make movies. And good for them, because really all that's left of the connections are cinematic ones. The olds have the memories of their childhoods, the rest of us only visions of what it must have been like. There's a hope at eighty years because we still have a few people through which we can experience the full magnitude of the wait, and* *everything is more magical if you've never ever seen it yourself.*

Everyone remembers that *Sports Illustrated* cover from 2014, and if you don't, you'll be reminded of it plenty of times should the Astros start slowly. Inside the issue of *SI* that declared the Astros 2017 World Series champions was a thoughtful article by Ben Reiter, framed at a blackjack table near Lake Tahoe.

"When you're in 2017, you don't really care that much about whether you lost 98 or 107 in 2012," Luhnow told Reiter. "You care about how close we are to winning a championship in 2017."

*At **ninety** years, you devolve into the Stanford Prison Experiment, and the drought is the prison. You start to turn on each other. Blame of abstract concepts and the unknown turns to blame of what's very real and very known.*

Everyone remembers that cover from 2014, but what you may not remember is the little sidebar that ran inside. Coming in just north of 800 words, the sidebar reported from the future on the Astros' victory in 2017, a victory led by ace Mark Appel and closer Brady Aiken. OK, so the path to 2017 has taken some strange turns.

Breaking these things is never easy. Remember the Astros' 48.2 percent chance in 1980? Since championship probability starts from scratch every series, they were 96.4 percent to make the World Series when that snapshot was snapped.

They still would have had to beat the Royals once they got there, but look at it from the other side—down multiple runs with six outs to go in two straight elimination games. That's how close the Phillies were to entering this century and a new century of their drought without *ever* having won it all.

The worst part about these droughts goes back to that chance of the Astros going 55 years without a title. The 11 percent figure was actually cheating—that assumes all years are independent, which they're not. Win one year and you're more likely than 1-in-30 to win the next, so it's not quite as extreme as the 11 percent.

But the flip side is that when you lose one year, you're more likely to lose the next. In probability, a memory-less distribution is one where, if the event doesn't happen at a given time period, the distribution of likelihood for the next "success" looks exactly the same after that time period than it did before. Given the year-to-year correlation, this is actually worse than a memory-less distribution, but only slightly.

The only thing that really changes is you.

*We've seen a **hundred** years before. Just once. We saw how it ended, too. A team that was intentionally bad for years took advantage of that, built the farm system and added major players at the right time. There was a lot of pain in getting to that point and a lot of people who never got to see it. No fan base would ever wish that on anybody. Well, maybe some fan bases would wish it on somebody, but they wouldn't be invited to the party. And after anything approaching that length of time, you wouldn't want to miss the party.* ■

—Zachary Levine is a Baseball Prospectus contributor and covered the Astros for the Houston Chronicle *from 2009-2012*

HITTERS

Jose Altuve 2B

Born: 5/6/90   Age: 27   Bats: R   Throws: R   Height: 5'6"   Weight: 165   Entered Pro Ball: International Free Agent, 2007

YEAR	TEAM	LVL	AGE	PA	R	2B	3B	HR	RBI	BB	K	SB	CS	AVG/OBP/SLG	TAv	VORP	BABIP	BRR	FRAA	WARP
2014	HOU	MLB	24	707	85	47	3	7	59	36	53	56	9	.341/.377/.453	.302	51.0	.360	5.9	2B(156): -7.5	4.8
2015	HOU	MLB	25	689	86	40	4	15	66	33	67	38	13	.313/.353/.459	.285	32.6	.329	-2.0	2B(153): -3.1	3.2
2016	HOU	MLB	26	717	108	42	5	24	96	60	70	30	10	.338/.396/.531	.321	66.3	.347	3.2	2B(148): -6.8 • SS(1): 0.0	6.1
2017	HOU	MLB	27	672	90	38	4	12	62	41	71	35	9	.307/.350/.438	.283	41.3	.327	3.3	2B -6	3.7
2018	HOU	MLB	28	625	76	35	3	12	71	41	66	32	9	.307/.356/.445	.281	34.3	.325	2.1	2B -5	3.2

Breakout: 4%   Improve: 57%   Collapse: 2%   Attrition: 3%   MLB: 100%   Comparables: Nellie Fox, Roberto Alomar, Ted Sizemore

At this point, we can dispense with any height qualifiers when discussing Altuve's astonishing abilities. He had arguably the best MVP case in the American League this side of Mike Trout and may have won the award had his Astros made the postseason. He earned his second AL batting title in three seasons and led the league in hits for the third straight campaign. At 26 years old, he set career highs in home runs, on-base percentage and slugging percentage. The little hit tool that could has evolved into a complete player. Consider him a favorite to make the All-Star team and a contender for MVP for now and the foreseeable future.

Yordan Alvarez OF

Born: 6/27/97   Age: 19   Bats: L   Throws: L   Height: 6'5"   Weight: 225   Entered Pro Ball: International Free Agent, 2016

YEAR	TEAM	LVL	AGE	PA	R	2B	3B	HR	RBI	BB	K	SB	CS	AVG/OBP/SLG	TAv	VORP	BABIP	BRR	FRAA	WARP
2017	HOU	MLB	20	250	22	9	1	5	24	15	82	3	1	.193/.246/.309	.196	-11.2	.269	-0.1	1B 0	-1.2

Breakout: 1%   Improve: 4%   Collapse: 0%   Attrition: 3%   MLB: 6%   Comparables: Alex Liddi, Brandon Drury, Ramon Flores

A hulking outfielder, Alvarez was acquired by the Astros for reliever Josh Fields before he could even play a game in the Dodgers' system. Even though the Dodgers were willing to part with him, they liked what they saw, as they ponied up $2 million signing bonus plus a $2 million bonus pool penalty to acquire the 18-year-old. Given his size—6-foot-5, 225 pounds—Alvarez will likely find himself moved to first base by the time he climbs the organizational ladder to Houston. He has clear raw power, but has lived more on good strike zone recognition in his career thus far. That said, if Alvarez can tap into his body and unleash his full strength against live pitching, he can become a big-time power hitter in the major leagues.

Nori Aoki RF

Born: 1/5/82   Age: 35   Bats: L   Throws: R   Height: 5'9"   Weight: 180   Entered Pro Ball: International Free Agent, 2012

YEAR	TEAM	LVL	AGE	PA	R	2B	3B	HR	RBI	BB	K	SB	CS	AVG/OBP/SLG	TAv	VORP	BABIP	BRR	FRAA	WARP
2014	KCA	MLB	32	549	63	22	6	1	43	43	49	17	8	.285/.349/.360	.267	16.0	.314	3.6	RF(119): -6.9 • LF(5): -0.2	1.0
2015	SFN	MLB	33	392	42	12	3	5	26	30	25	14	5	.287/.353/.380	.272	11.2	.298	-1.3	LF(86): -0.4 • RF(2): -0.4	1.1
2016	TAC	AAA	34	108	17	5	0	1	7	8	13	4	0	.323/.374/.406	.305	8.9	.357	1.5	LF(21): -3.6 • CF(3): -0.1	0.5
2016	SEA	MLB	34	467	63	24	4	4	28	34	45	7	9	.283/.349/.388	.269	14.8	.309	0.1	LF(99): 2.0 • CF(15): -1.0	1.6
2017	HOU	MLB	35	420	43	18	3	3	34	31	43	11	6	.267/.328/.356	.256	11.8	.288	-0.4	LF 1	1.0
2018	HOU	MLB	36	307	33	13	2	3	27	24	35	7	4	.256/.326/.350	.247	3.8	.278	0.7	LF 1	0.5

Breakout: 0%   Improve: 24%   Collapse: 10%   Attrition: 15%   MLB: 84%   Comparables: Juan Pierre, Dave Roberts, Luis Castillo

If one were scoring the soundtrack of The Nori Aoki Show, it would be equal parts "Yakety Sax" and the theme from Curb Your Enthusiasm, with a soupçon of the Inception claxon for the darker moments when, as if propelled by the ballpark flipping on its side, he throws his body out of the path of an incoming fastball. Seattle signed Aoki and his contact-heavy approach to be a "catalyst" in the leadoff spot and a threat on the basepaths and, well, they'd live with the outfield circus. But a .245/.323/.313 line in the early going—with outfield routes and baserunning befitting his audio track—proved unplayable and he was sent to the minors. He was his old self when he returned in a platoon role and the Mariners seemed interested in bringing him back, but the Astros scooped him up off waivers. Sadly, fans will be denied Aoki attempting to summit Tal's Hill; disaster flicks don't really go with Benny Hill anyway.

Carlos Beltran DH

Born: 4/24/77   Age: 40   Bats: B   Throws: R   Height: 6'1"   Weight: 215   Entered Pro Ball: Round 2, 1995 Draft (#49 overall)

YEAR	TEAM	LVL	AGE	PA	R	2B	3B	HR	RBI	BB	K	SB	CS	AVG/OBP/SLG	TAv	VORP	BABIP	BRR	FRAA	WARP
2014	NYA	MLB	37	449	46	23	0	15	49	37	80	3	1	.233/.301/.402	.260	2.3	.252	-2.8	RF(32): -0.5 • 1B(1): -0.0	0.2
2015	NYA	MLB	38	531	57	34	1	19	67	45	85	0	0	.276/.337/.471	.280	18.9	.297	-0.4	RF(123): -15.4	0.4
2016	NYA	MLB	39	387	50	21	0	22	64	22	70	0	0	.304/.344/.546	.293	16.3	.321	-2.6	RF(60): -3.5	1.3
2016	TEX	MLB	39	206	23	12	0	7	29	13	31	1	0	.280/.325/.451	.252	-1.2	.303	-2.0	RF(9): -0.4	-0.2
2017	HOU	MLB	40	535	57	26	2	19	69	39	103	1	0	.252/.307/.428	.261	8.0	.281	-1.0		1.1
2018	HOU	MLB	41	389	47	18	1	14	48	29	82	0	0	.238/.295/.408	.246	-0.2	.269	-1.8	-	0.0

Breakout: 1%   Improve: 16%   Collapse: 15%   Attrition: 20%   MLB: 71%   Comparables: Ken Griffey, Hal McRae, Rico Carty

When Beltran made his major league debut in 1998, Google was 10 days old, J.K Rowling introduced us to the Hogwarts School of Witchcraft and Wizardry, and I was taking home my first iMac computer. 19 years later, Google owns half our souls, the Harry Potter series has sold over 400 million copies, and my iMac is a broken down display piece in my house. Beltran is still playing baseball though, and posting a slash line that, while not spectacular for a designated hitter—the final act of every AL power hitter's career—proves that he's still kickin'. After a very poor 2014 in the Bronx, Beltran took advantage of being a switch hitter and made the Yankee Stadium short porch his age-defying elixir. The problem with that, which was showcased in Texas, is that not every ballpark has a short porch for him to ward off father time with.

Alex Bregman   SS

Born: 3/30/94 Age: 23 Bats: R Throws: R Height: 6'0" Weight: 180 Entered Pro Ball: Round 1, 2015 Draft (#2 overall)

YEAR	TEAM	LVL	AGE	PA	R	2B	3B	HR	RBI	BB	K	SB	CS	AVG/OBP/SLG	TAv	VORP	BABIP	BRR	FRAA	WARP
2015	QUD	A	21	133	18	5	0	1	13	17	13	5	2	.259/.368/.330	.263	7.9	.283	2.4	SS(26): 3.1	1.2
2015	LNC	A+	21	178	19	8	4	3	21	12	17	8	4	.319/.364/.475	.289	10.3	.336	-2.0	SS(37): -1.9	0.9
2016	CCH	AA	22	285	54	16	2	14	46	42	26	5	3	.297/.415/.559	.353	38.9	.286	1.6	SS(51): -3.5 • 3B(11): 1.4	4.0
2016	FRE	AAA	22	83	17	6	0	6	15	5	12	2	1	.333/.373/.641	.353	10.0	.333	-1.2	SS(14): 2.1 • LF(3): -0.1	1.2
2016	HOU	MLB	22	217	31	13	3	8	34	15	52	2	0	.264/.313/.478	.270	9.6	.317	0.5	3B(40): 1.0 • SS(6): -0.0	1.1
2017	HOU	MLB	23	551	66	26	4	21	73	49	103	6	3	.260/.331/.457	.281	27.2	.288	-0.1	3B 10	3.6
2018	HOU	MLB	24	501	68	23	4	21	70	46	95	6	2	.260/.334/.467	.279	20.8	.285	0.1	3B 9	3.3

Breakout: 5%   Improve: 46%   Collapse: 8%   Attrition: 17%   MLB: 84%   *Comparables: Michael Conforto, Marcus Semien, Maikel Franco*

Bregman was arguably the most polished prospect to come out of the 2015 draft after his college career at LSU. He made the competition in the high minors look like child's play in 2016. The plate discipline and contact ability he showcased against minor-league hurlers didn't translate to the show in his first crack at major-league pitching, but Bregman showed excellent power and a solid line-drive stroke before a hamstring injury shut him down for most of September. Bregman has the chops to play shortstop, but that won't be happening in Houston as long as Carlos Correa is around. He can play third base just fine, but he would be most valuable at shortstop. As such, Houston could choose to shop Bregman around, but don't expect a deal unless they get an astronomical return.

Carlos Correa   SS

Born: 9/22/94 Age: 22 Bats: R Throws: R Height: 6'4" Weight: 215 Entered Pro Ball: Round 1, 2012 Draft (#1 overall)

YEAR	TEAM	LVL	AGE	PA	R	2B	3B	HR	RBI	BB	K	SB	CS	AVG/OBP/SLG	TAv	VORP	BABIP	BRR	FRAA	WARP
2014	LNC	A+	19	293	50	16	6	6	57	36	45	20	4	.325/.416/.510	.319	29.6	.373	0.7	SS(48): 5.1 • SS(7): 5.1	4.0
2015	CCH	AA	20	133	25	15	2	7	32	15	25	15	0	.385/.459/.726	.387	22.2	.447	0.0	SS(28): 4.5	2.9
2015	FRE	AAA	20	113	19	6	1	3	12	12	14	3	1	.276/.345/.449	.281	4.8	.286	-2.3	SS(24): -4.7	0.0
2015	HOU	MLB	20	432	52	22	1	22	68	40	78	14	4	.279/.345/.512	.295	32.1	.296	0.4	SS(99): -7.3	2.7
2016	HOU	MLB	21	660	76	36	3	20	96	75	139	13	3	.274/.361/.451	.297	53.7	.328	1.8	SS(153): -4.2	5.1
2017	HOU	MLB	22	618	79	32	4	22	81	62	123	17	4	.272/.348/.465	.294	48.9	.313	1.5	SS -1	4.6
2018	HOU	MLB	23	601	85	32	3	25	86	62	117	17	4	.280/.358/.491	.299	46.1	.316	1.4	SS -1	4.9

Breakout: 4%   Improve: 70%   Collapse: 1%   Attrition: 1%   MLB: 97%   *Comparables: Jason Heyward, Ryan Zimmerman, Justin Upton*

On July 23, at the ripe age of 21 years, 10 months and 1 day, Correa connected for his 36th home run as an Astros shortstop, surpassing the previous franchise record holder, Adam Everett. This has been the story of Correa's early career: setting records, shattering even the highest of expectations and continuing to establish himself as a perennial All-Star and MVP candidate. His game lacks any major flaws. He hits for average and power, he draws walks, he steals bases and does so efficiently, and he plays solid defense at arguably the game's toughest position. And that's the thing about shortstop—it's supposed to be too difficult a position for somebody to have as refined a glove and bat as Correa has shown before even turning 22. Correa became just the ninth shortstop to appear in at least 250 games through his age-21 campaign. Of those nine players, only one recorded a superior OPS to Correa's .829: Alex Rodriguez. But as great as Correa's talent is, what makes him so fantastic to watch is the clear joy he takes in playing the game. His ability and personality both shine every time he takes the diamond, making him a player fans can treasure whether they cheer for the Astros or not.

J.D. Davis   3B

Born: 4/27/93 Age: 24 Bats: R Throws: R Height: 6'3" Weight: 225 Entered Pro Ball: Round 3, 2014 Draft (#75 overall)

YEAR	TEAM	LVL	AGE	PA	R	2B	3B	HR	RBI	BB	K	SB	CS	AVG/OBP/SLG	TAv	VORP	BABIP	BRR	FRAA	WARP
2014	TCV	A-	21	131	18	7	1	5	20	15	25	1	0	.279/.382/.495	.320	11.9	.317	-0.3	3B(27): 3.9 • RF(1): 0.0	1.6
2014	QUD	A	21	171	20	9	0	8	32	13	41	4	0	.303/.363/.516	.312	15.3	.364	0.5	3B(41): -1.9	1.4
2015	LNC	A+	22	552	93	28	3	26	101	54	157	5	2	.289/.370/.520	.294	34.1	.374	-1.3	3B(117): -1.5	3.5
2016	CCH	AA	23	539	61	34	4	23	81	45	143	1	3	.268/.334/.485	.301	34.0	.331	-2.6	3B(101): -6.0 • LF(4): 0.3	3.1
2017	HOU	MLB	24	250	27	11	1	10	34	19	80	0	0	.231/.297/.420	.250	4.6	.305	-0.5	3B -2, LF -0	0.3
2018	HOU	MLB	25	327	41	14	1	13	42	26	106	0	0	.224/.295/.413	.248	2.4	.298	-0.8	3B -2, LF 0	0.0

Breakout: 3%   Improve: 15%   Collapse: 17%   Attrition: 28%   MLB: 45%   *Comparables: Alex Liddi, Mat Gamel, Matt Davidson*

After 49 home runs in the past two seasons, the Astros are looking pretty smart for shifting Davis, a two-way player in college, to hitting full time. Power is his only standout tool at the plate, though, so whether Davis can stick at third base will be a huge question in determining if his future is one as a major-league regular or a Quadruple-A stalwart. Davis has a big-time arm, but lacks the athleticism necessary to make some of the plays demanded at the hot corner. Mashing taters is fun and all, but Davis is going to have to add to his game before he can carve out a niche for himself at the top level.

Derek Fisher   OF

Born: 8/21/93 Age: 23 Bats: L Throws: R Height: 6'3" Weight: 205 Entered Pro Ball: Round 1, 2014 Draft (#37 overall)

YEAR	TEAM	LVL	AGE	PA	R	2B	3B	HR	RBI	BB	K	SB	CS	AVG/OBP/SLG	TAv	VORP	BABIP	BRR	FRAA	WARP
2014	TCV	A-	20	172	31	4	3	2	18	16	35	17	4	.303/.378/.408	.299	10.0	.379	-0.6	LF(38): -1.1 • CF(1): -0.1	0.9
2015	QUD	A	21	171	32	11	1	6	24	19	37	8	2	.305/.386/.510	.326	15.7	.370	-0.5	CF(30): -2.8 • LF(3): -0.8	1.3
2015	LNC	A+	21	398	74	10	7	16	63	47	95	23	5	.262/.354/.471	.295	27.7	.314	4.3	LF(43): -1.5 • CF(35): -1.4	2.7
2016	CCH	AA	22	448	54	13	4	16	59	74	128	23	7	.245/.373/.431	.303	30.0	.329	-0.5	CF(70): -7.3 • RF(19): -1.2	2.3
2016	FRE	AAA	22	118	17	8	0	5	17	9	26	5	0	.290/.347/.505	.308	8.2	.338	-0.6	RF(13): -1.7 • CF(13): -0.9	0.6
2017	HOU	MLB	23	250	31	8	2	9	30	29	77	8	2	.223/.317/.398	.253	7.7	.299	0.8	CF -2, RF -1	0.6
2018	HOU	MLB	24	387	47	13	3	12	45	44	122	12	3	.216/.308/.380	.247	6.2	.294	1.8	CF -3, RF -2	0.2

Breakout: 3%   Improve: 22%   Collapse: 6%   Attrition: 21%   MLB: 58%   *Comparables: Brett Jackson, Joe Benson, Chris Young*

No, not the former Los Angeles Lakers point guard who was dragged to five titles by his supporting cast. This Derek Fisher made it all the way to Triple-A at just 22 thanks to his continually excellent plate discipline and strong raw power. Following two consecutive 20-homer seasons, the Astros are feeling vindicated in giving Fisher a $1.5 million bonus after nabbing him in the 2014 supplemental first round. Fisher mashed in the Pacific Coast League to end the season despite being four years younger than his average opponent. That's where he'll likely start 2017, but at this rate it won't take him long to get to Houston.

Evan Gattis   C

Born: 8/18/86   Age: 30   Bats: R   Throws: R   Height: 6'4"   Weight: 270   Entered Pro Ball: Round 23, 2010 Draft (#704 overall)

YEAR	TEAM	LVL	AGE	PA	R	2B	3B	HR	RBI	BB	K	SB	CS	AVG/OBP/SLG	TAv	VORP	BABIP	BRR	FRAA	WARP
2014	ATL	MLB	27	401	41	17	1	22	52	22	97	0	0	.263/.317/.493	.298	25.1	.298	-5.1	C(93): 0.2	2.8
2015	HOU	MLB	28	604	66	20	11	27	88	30	119	0	1	.246/.285/.463	.262	7.7	.264	0.0	LF(11): -1.7	0.6
2016	CCH	AA	29	42	8	2	0	5	10	1	4	0	0	.375/.405/.800	.432	8.2	.323	0.1	C(4): 0.2	0.9
2016	HOU	MLB	29	499	58	19	0	32	72	43	127	2	1	.251/.319/.508	.290	27.6	.273	-0.1	C(55): 1.6	3.0
2017	HOU	MLB	30	242	29	10	1	12	37	15	55	1	0	.249/.302/.475	.276	12.6	.274	-0.3	C -2	1.2
2018	HOU	MLB	31	380	51	15	2	19	56	26	88	0	0	.246/.303/.466	.269	14.9	.273	-1.1	C -3	1.3

Breakout: 2%   Improve: 41%   Collapse: 6%   Attrition: 19%   MLB: 97%   Comparables: Adam LaRoche, Benny Ayala, Glenn Davis

You don't get the nickname El Oso Blanco by hitting for average. That said, Gattis developed some much-needed plate discipline in 2016. He walked in 8.6 percent of plate appearances, a career high by more than three full points, and set a career-high .319 OBP as a result. Underwhelming as that mark might be for a designated hitter who is occasionally called on to fake it at catcher or in a corner outfield spot, it's good enough to make his bear-like power play. His newfound ability to spit on pitches out of the zone should only enhance his power production as it forces pitchers to challenge him with strikes on a more regular basis.

YEAR	TEAM	P. COUNT	FRM RUNS	BLK RUNS	THRW RUNS	TOT RUNS
2014	ATL	12794	3.5	-2.7	-1.5	-0.7
2014	GWN	180	0.1	0.0	0.0	0.1
2016	HOU	7151	2.2	-4.9	1.1	-1.6
2017	HOU	5898	1.4	-3.2	0.5	-1.4
2018	HOU	9269	1.3	-5.2	0.7	-3.2

Marwin Gonzalez   INF

Born: 3/14/89   Age: 28   Bats: B   Throws: R   Height: 6'1"   Weight: 205   Entered Pro Ball: International Free Agent, 2005

YEAR	TEAM	LVL	AGE	PA	R	2B	3B	HR	RBI	BB	K	SB	CS	AVG/OBP/SLG	TAv	VORP	BABIP	BRR	FRAA	WARP
2014	HOU	MLB	25	310	33	15	1	6	23	17	58	2	4	.277/.327/.400	.261	10.6	.330	-0.6	SS(71): 1.0 • 2B(11): 1.5	1.4
2015	HOU	MLB	26	370	44	18	1	12	34	16	74	4	5	.279/.317/.442	.261	10.8	.326	0.7	1B(43): 2.0 • SS(32): -1.3	1.4
2016	HOU	MLB	27	518	55	26	3	13	51	22	118	12	6	.254/.293/.401	.245	0.1	.311	-1.4	1B(92): 0.5 • 3B(22): 0.6	0.2
2017	HOU	MLB	28	279	32	14	1	6	26	14	55	5	3	.252/.291/.383	.244	5.1	.292	-0.5	SS -0, 2B 0	0.2
2018	HOU	MLB	29	380	42	19	1	9	41	21	75	6	4	.253/.300/.389	.243	4.9	.293	0.3	SS 0, 2B 0	0.5

Breakout: 1%   Improve: 40%   Collapse: 7%   Attrition: 16%   MLB: 90%   Comparables: Tony Muser, Ron Jackson, Ray Webster

Gonzalez's weaknesses at the plate—poor discipline combined with a major contact issue—showed in 2016, but he was able to remain valuable to the Astros thanks to his versatility. Even as the Astros have promoted talented infielder after talented infielder in recent seasons, Gonzalez has found ways to keep himself in the lineup, even donning an outfielder's glove and playing a career-high 111 innings in the outfield in 2016. Gonzalez may not have starter-quality numbers, but he is evolving into the ideal super-utility player to keep a team fresh over the grind of a 162-game season.

Yulieski Gurriel   1B/3B

Born: 6/9/84   Age: 33   Bats: R   Throws: R   Height: 6'0"   Weight: 190   Entered Pro Ball: International Free Agent, 2016

YEAR	TEAM	LVL	AGE	PA	R	2B	3B	HR	RBI	BB	K	SB	CS	AVG/OBP/SLG	TAv	VORP	BABIP	BRR	FRAA	WARP
2016	HOU	MLB	32	137	13	7	0	3	15	5	12	1	1	.262/.292/.385	.223	-3.0	.267	-1.2	3B(21): -0.8 • 1B(5): 0.1	-0.4
2017	HOU	MLB	33	535	56	26	2	13	56	29	86	7	3	.253/.297/.393	.249	3.5	.280	-0.5	1B 2, 3B -2	0.1
2018	HOU	MLB	34	279	31	13	1	7	30	16	47	3	2	.252/.299/.385	.242	-1.5	.281	-0.3	1B 1, 3B -1	-0.2

Breakout: 1%   Improve: 35%   Collapse: 10%   Attrition: 20%   MLB: 83%   Comparables: Don Kelly, Ryan Roberts, Ray Knight

When he was 17, all the way back in 2001, Gurriel was a star in Cuba's Serie Nacional. He hit .300 in his rookie season, managed a 20-homer campaign by age 20—in the shorter Cuban season no less—and had six seasons of a 1.000 OPS or better by age 27. His introduction to American baseball, then, was a rude awakening, as major-league pitchers shut down Gurriel after he took over Houston's third base job in August. Gurriel had no problem making contact, but his bat was utterly devoid of the power that defined his later years in Cuba. Injuries in the Astros' infield forced the club to rush him into a playoff race, so Gurriel deserves another chance to prove himself, but his first major-league season was surely a jarring experience for a man so used to dominating the opposition.

Teoscar Hernandez   OF

Born: 10/15/92   Age: 24   Bats: R   Throws: R   Height: 6'2"   Weight: 180   Entered Pro Ball: International Free Agent, 2011

YEAR	TEAM	LVL	AGE	PA	R	2B	3B	HR	RBI	BB	K	SB	CS	AVG/OBP/SLG	TAv	VORP	BABIP	BRR	FRAA	WARP
2014	LNC	A+	21	455	72	33	8	17	75	49	117	31	6	.294/.376/.550	.327	49.3	.374	3.2	CF(82): 4.7, CF(10): 4.7	5.9
2014	CCH	AA	21	98	12	4	1	4	10	2	36	2	3	.284/.299/.474	.291	4.9	.418	-1.0	CF(21): 0.4, RF(2): 0.1	0.6
2015	CCH	AA	22	514	92	12	2	17	48	33	126	33	7	.219/.275/.362	.237	8.6	.261	7.4	CF(80): -1.1, RF(39): 3.9	1.2
2016	CCH	AA	23	322	53	19	0	6	30	32	55	29	11	.305/.384/.437	.304	25.6	.359	4.2	RF(37): -1.1, CF(30): 0.1	2.7
2016	FRE	AAA	23	160	20	9	3	4	23	13	25	5	4	.313/.365/.500	.306	8.7	.350	-2.4	RF(26): 1.7, CF(11): -2.0	0.9
2016	HOU	MLB	23	112	15	7	0	4	11	11	28	0	2	.230/.304/.420	.246	0.6	.275	-0.6	LF(22): -1.4, CF(15): -1.2	-0.2
2017	HOU	MLB	24	34	4	1	0	1	4	2	9	1	1	.234/.287/.392	.247	0.7	.297	0.1	LF -0	0.0
2018	HOU	MLB	25	319	37	15	2	10	38	22	87	13	5	.242/.297/.412	.250	5.8	.304	1.4	LF 0	0.6

Breakout: 6%   Improve: 28%   Collapse: 5%   Attrition: 20%   MLB: 41%   Comparables: Aaron Cunningham, Moises Sierra, Zoilo Almonte

With his appearance as Houston's starting center fielder on August 12, Hernandez officially became MLB's first Teoscar. He bounced back from a brutal 2015 season to show improved plate discipline and good enough defense for the Astros to trust him in center field. He'll likely need to show he can hack it in center if he's to carve out a lengthy MLB career, as his swing has too many holes and not enough pop to play as a corner outfielder. Hernandez's plate discipline and power translated well in his first stint in the show, though, a good sign for the future of Teoscars in baseball.

Tony Kemp   2B/OF

Born: 10/31/91 Age: 25   Bats: L   Throws: R   Height: 5'6"   Weight: 165   Entered Pro Ball: Round 5, 2013 Draft (#137 overall)

YEAR	TEAM	LVL	AGE	PA	R	2B	3B	HR	RBI	BB	K	SB	CS	AVG/OBP/SLG	TAv	VORP	BABIP	BRR	FRAA	WARP
2014	LNC	A+	22	356	79	19	4	4	37	45	35	28	7	.336/.433/.468	.318	37.0	.367	7.0	2B(54): -1.6 • 2B(7): -1.6	3.4
2014	CCH	AA	22	275	42	11	4	4	21	28	32	13	6	.292/.381/.425	.293	22.2	.322	5.7	2B(56): -2.3 • LF(3): -0.1	2.1
2015	CCH	AA	23	230	36	10	1	0	19	35	28	15	8	.358/.457/.420	.303	17.8	.416	2.0	2B(40): -3.5 • CF(7): -1.6	1.3
2015	FRE	AAA	23	311	42	9	3	3	29	21	37	20	6	.273/.334/.362	.254	8.3	.305	1.8	2B(51): 0.2 • CF(20): -0.7	0.8
2016	FRE	AAA	24	301	36	9	4	2	24	34	34	10	8	.306/.389/.396	.275	12.7	.344	0.2	2B(39): -0.1 • LF(19): 2.3	1.4
2016	HOU	MLB	24	136	15	4	3	1	7	14	27	2	1	.217/.296/.325	.224	-2.5	.269	-0.4	LF(37): -2.2 • 2B(5): -0.0	-0.5
2017	*HOU*	*MLB*	*25*	*76*	*9*	*3*	*1*	*1*	*6*	*7*	*13*	*3*	*1*	*.255/.326/.351*	*.250*	*1.4*	*.296*	*0.1*	*LF -0, RF -0*	*0.0*
2018	*HOU*	*MLB*	*26*	*331*	*37*	*11*	*3*	*4*	*31*	*31*	*57*	*11*	*5*	*.256/.335/.366*	*.248*	*4.1*	*.295*	*0.9*	*LF -2, RF 0*	*0.2*

Breakout: 3%   Improve: 12%   Collapse: 11%   Attrition: 25%   MLB: 41%   *Comparables: Cole Figueroa, Callix Crabbe, Adrian Cardenas*

After Jose Altuve, nobody in their right mind is going to count out an Astros second base prospect just because he's short. But Kemp's first season in the big leagues suggests there just isn't enough power in his 5-foot-6 frame to generate the kind of batting results he'll need to stick around. Despite continuing to exhibit the excellent plate discipline that carried him throughout his minor-league career, Kemp had nothing against the big fastballs of major-league pitchers. Even if he can cut down his strikeouts, his utter lack of power limits his ceiling to that of a utility man.

Jake Marisnick   CF

Born: 3/30/91   Age: 26   Bats: R   Throws: R   Height: 6'4"   Weight: 220   Entered Pro Ball: Round 3, 2009 Draft (#104 overall)

YEAR	TEAM	LVL	AGE	PA	R	2B	3B	HR	RBI	BB	K	SB	CS	AVG/OBP/SLG	TAv	VORP	BABIP	BRR	FRAA	WARP
2014	MIA	MLB	23	51	3	0	0	0	3	19	5	0	.167/.216/.167	.151	-3.7	.276	0.1	CF(13): 3.3	0.0
2014	NWO	AAA	23	377	50	16	4	10	40	17	64	24	6	.277/.326/.434	.276	20.8	.314	1.7	CF(81): 4.7 • RF(4): 2.9	2.2
2014	HOU	MLB	23	186	18	8	0	3	19	5	48	6	3	.272/.299/.370	.246	2.6	.352	1.1	RF(31): 3.3 • CF(17): 1.7	0.9
2015	HOU	MLB	24	372	46	15	4	9	36	18	105	24	9	.236/.281/.383	.243	7.3	.310	3.1	CF(99): 5.6 • LF(16): 2.2	1.7
2016	FRE	AAA	25	28	3	2	0	0	1	1	10	1	1	.185/.214/.259	.168	-2.0	.294	-0.1	CF(6): 0.5 • RF(2): 0.1	-0.1
2016	HOU	MLB	25	311	40	18	1	5	21	16	83	10	5	.209/.257/.331	.216	-6.2	.275	-1.1	CF(74): 7.9 • LF(26): 1.5	0.3
2017	*HOU*	*MLB*	*26*	*220*	*25*	*9*	*1*	*5*	*20*	*10*	*58*	*10*	*4*	*.232/.274/.363*	*.231*	*1.2*	*.292*	*0.9*	*CF 4*	*0.4*
2018	*HOU*	*MLB*	*27*	*308*	*33*	*13*	*2*	*7*	*33*	*16*	*80*	*14*	*6*	*.235/.287/.377*	*.232*	*0.5*	*.292*	*1.0*	*CF 6*	*0.7*

Breakout: 9%   Improve: 59%   Collapse: 12%   Attrition: 24%   MLB: 94%   *Comparables: Juan Lagares, Jordan Schafer, Jason Repko*

Marisnick is quickly playing his way into a career as a defensive replacement—and not much else. After striking out in over a quarter of his at-bats for the third straight season, Marisnick is running out of chances to prove his bat is major-league quality. Given his speed and ability to play all three outfield positions with proficiency, Marisnick's skill set will still be desired, but he has taken a mighty fall since his days as a top-100 prospect.

Brian McCann   C

Born: 2/20/84   Age: 33   Bats: L   Throws: R   Height: 6'3"   Weight: 225   Entered Pro Ball: Round 2, 2002 Draft (#64 overall)

YEAR	TEAM	LVL	AGE	PA	R	2B	3B	HR	RBI	BB	K	SB	CS	AVG/OBP/SLG	TAv	VORP	BABIP	BRR	FRAA	WARP
2014	NYA	MLB	30	538	57	15	1	23	75	32	77	0	0	.232/.286/.406	.258	14.1	.231	-3.6	C(108): 15.9 • 1B(16): -1.1	3.2
2015	NYA	MLB	31	535	68	15	1	26	94	52	97	0	0	.232/.320/.437	.270	23.3	.235	-4.5	C(126): -0.8 • 1B(10): -0.1	2.4
2016	NYA	MLB	32	492	56	13	0	20	58	54	99	1	0	.242/.335/.413	.256	11.7	.269	-3.9	C(92): 9.7 • 1B(3): -0.6	2.1
2017	*HOU*	*MLB*	*33*	*595*	*67*	*19*	*1*	*24*	*77*	*52*	*109*	*1*	*0*	*.232/.307/.406*	*.257*	*19.5*	*.247*	*-1.2*	*C 10, 1B -1*	*2.2*
2018	*HOU*	*MLB*	*34*	*496*	*63*	*15*	*1*	*19*	*62*	*43*	*93*	*0*	*0*	*.230/.304/.399*	*.249*	*7.3*	*.246*	*-3.6*	*C 7, 1B -1*	*1.5*

Breakout: 2%   Improve: 42%   Collapse: 4%   Attrition: 11%   MLB: 95%   *Comparables: Ramon Hernandez, Yadier Molina, Del Crandall*

Catchers who can hit aren't very easy to find these days, and impossibly, the Yankees had two. The younger, Gary Sanchez, supplanted McCann as the team's everyday backstop, moving McCann into the DH role and then to Houston. The 33-year-old is still hitting better than more than half of the catchers in the majors, and if he continues to split time between catcher and DH moving forward his offensive production may even go up, based on his late-season improvement upon Sanchez's call-up. And his defense, which was popular to critique in 2015, was great, too. He led the league in blocking runs, and his framing numbers improved dramatically There are better DHs out there, but there still aren't too many better all-around catchers, which is remarkable when you consider the mileage on McCann's legs after 12 seasons.

YEAR	TEAM	P. COUNT	FRM RUNS	BLK RUNS	THRW RUNS	TOT RUNS
2014	NYA	14665	9.7	1.6	1.9	13.2
2015	NYA	17347	-3.9	0.7	1.2	-2.0
2016	NYA	12380	9.6	3.0	-0.4	12.2
2017	*HOU*	*17082*	*5.1*	*2.3*	*0.6*	*8.0*
2018	*HOU*	*14236*	*2.8*	*1.7*	*0.3*	*4.8*

Colin Moran　3B

Born: 10/1/92　Age: 24　Bats: L　Throws: R　Height: 6'4"　Weight: 204　Entered Pro Ball: Round 1, 2013 Draft (#6 overall)

YEAR	TEAM	LVL	AGE	PA	R	2B	3B	HR	RBI	BB	K	SB	CS	AVG/OBP/SLG	TAv	VORP	BABIP	BRR	FRAA	WARP
2014	JUP	A+	21	392	34	21	0	5	33	28	53	1	2	.294/.342/.393	.271	15.3	.330	-2.2	3B(86): -4.0	1.1
2014	CCH	AA	21	123	12	6	0	2	22	9	23	0	1	.304/.350/.411	.276	5.2	.360	-0.7	3B(28): -0.1	0.5
2015	CCH	AA	22	417	47	25	2	9	67	43	79	1	0	.306/.381/.459	.293	24.9	.365	-0.6	3B(78): 0.4	2.7
2016	FRE	AAA	23	511	50	18	1	10	69	47	124	3	2	.259/.329/.368	.248	5.0	.332	-4.6	3B(109): 4.9 • 1B(2): -0.1	1.0
2016	HOU	MLB	23	25	1	1	0	0	2	1	8	0	0	.130/.200/.174	.089	-3.4	.200	0.1	3B(8): 0.8	-0.3
2017	*HOU*	*MLB*	*24*	*250*	*24*	*11*	*1*	*6*	*27*	*19*	*65*	*0*	*0*	*.239/.299/.368*	*.234*	*0.9*	*.306*	*-0.4*	*3B -0, SS -0*	*0.1*
2018	*HOU*	*MLB*	*25*	*413*	*46*	*19*	*1*	*10*	*43*	*31*	*110*	*0*	*0*	*.239/.300/.373*	*.238*	*-1.0*	*.309*	*-0.9*	*3B 0, SS 0*	*-0.1*

Breakout: 2%　Improve: 8%　Collapse: 5%　Attrition: 12%　MLB: 16%　*Comparables: Matthew Duffy, Andrew Burns, Neil Walker*

The power development many saw as inevitable for Moran has yet to be realized. Triple-A pitching ate him alive in 2016. Moran hasn't shown the ability to elevate the ball for home runs, and he has become more of a line-drive and ground-ball hitter whose power will mostly come in the form of doubles. That might still play at third base if Moran can rediscover his contact skills, but more was expected out of him when he was drafted sixth overall in 2013.

Colby Rasmus　OF

Born: 8/11/86　Age: 30　Bats: L　Throws: L　Height: 6'2"　Weight: 195　Entered Pro Ball: Round 1, 2005 Draft (#28 overall)

YEAR	TEAM	LVL	AGE	PA	R	2B	3B	HR	RBI	BB	K	SB	CS	AVG/OBP/SLG	TAv	VORP	BABIP	BRR	FRAA	WARP
2014	BUF	AAA	27	24	0	0	0	0	2	1	9	0	0	.130/.167/.130	.126	-3.0	.214	0.0	CF(4): 0.3	-0.3
2014	TOR	MLB	27	376	45	21	1	18	40	29	124	4	0	.225/.287/.448	.270	12.8	.294	-0.5	CF(87): 1.7	1.6
2015	HOU	MLB	28	485	67	23	2	25	61	47	154	2	1	.238/.314/.475	.283	23.2	.305	1.9	LF(72): -3.5 • CF(43): 1.0	3.0
2016	HOU	MLB	29	417	38	10	0	15	54	43	121	4	1	.206/.286/.355	.232	-2.8	.257	-0.3	LF(87): 0.8 • CF(21): 1.7	0.1
2017	*HOU*	*MLB*	*30*	*406*	*47*	*16*	*2*	*17*	*54*	*36*	*122*	*3*	*1*	*.229/.299/.420*	*.250*	*9.9*	*.290*	*0.2*	*LF -2, CF 1*	*1.1*
2018	*HOU*	*MLB*	*31*	*380*	*48*	*15*	*1*	*15*	*49*	*34*	*115*	*2*	*1*	*.224/.295/.410*	*.247*	*3.9*	*.285*	*0.0*	*LF -2, CF 1*	*0.4*

Breakout: 4%　Improve: 58%　Collapse: 6%　Attrition: 6%　MLB: 98%　*Comparables: Brad Wilkerson, Don Lenhardt, Geoff Jenkins*

Rasmus was on top of the world on April 24. He had just crushed his seventh home run in 17 starts and owned a .293/.440/.707 batting line. It looked like Rasmus could cruise to an All-Star appearance. Instead, he came crashing down to earth, batting .190 for the rest of the year. From May through the end of the season, Rasmus managed just one month with an OPS better than .600. After drawing 18 walks against 22 strikeouts in April, Rasmus managed just 25 walks the rest of the season and continued to whiff, striking out 99 times in the final five months. Rasmus has always had problems making contact, and he couldn't replicate the power that made him a success in his first year in Houston. The first player ever to accept a qualifying offer in 2015, he didn't receive one in 2016.

Josh Reddick　RF

Born: 2/19/87　Age: 30　Bats: L　Throws: R　Height: 6'2"　Weight: 195　Entered Pro Ball: Round 17, 2006 Draft (#523 overall)

YEAR	TEAM	LVL	AGE	PA	R	2B	3B	HR	RBI	BB	K	SB	CS	AVG/OBP/SLG	TAv	VORP	BABIP	BRR	FRAA	WARP
2014	STO	A+	27	22	6	2	0	3	8	1	6	0	0	.429/.455/.952	.502	4.0	.500	0.0	RF(3): -0.8	0.3
2014	OAK	MLB	27	396	53	16	7	12	54	28	63	1	1	.264/.316/.446	.294	19.6	.289	0.4	RF(107): 3.0 • CF(1): -0.0	2.5
2015	OAK	MLB	28	582	67	25	4	20	77	49	65	10	2	.272/.333/.449	.287	24.9	.278	-0.1	RF(143): -6.7 • CF(1): -0.0	1.9
2016	NAS	AAA	29	26	2	1	0	1	1	1	6	0	0	.120/.154/.280	.138	-2.9	.111	0.0	RF(3): 0.2	-0.3
2016	OAK	MLB	29	272	33	11	1	8	28	28	34	5	0	.296/.368/.449	.300	18.0	.317	2.1	RF(68): 2.2	2.1
2016	LAN	MLB	29	167	20	6	0	2	9	11	22	3	3	.258/.307/.335	.240	-0.7	.290	-0.3	RF(42): 1.0	0.0
2017	*HOU*	*MLB*	*30*	*518*	*61*	*22*	*4*	*17*	*62*	*45*	*93*	*7*	*2*	*.254/.319/.429*	*.270*	*19.3*	*.281*	*0.3*	*RF 1*	*1.8*
2018	*HOU*	*MLB*	*31*	*500*	*63*	*21*	*3*	*17*	*62*	*47*	*93*	*5*	*2*	*.252/.323/.427*	*.265*	*13.9*	*.282*	*0.6*	*RF 1, LF 0*	*1.6*

Breakout: 1%　Improve: 43%　Collapse: 8%　Attrition: 14%　MLB: 99%　*Comparables: Nate Schierholtz, John Wockenfuss, Moises Alou*

Reddick built upon his relatively new profile in 2016, upping his walk rate and retaining a low whiff rate—especially in this era of ever-rising strikeout totals. What did this growth get him? A trip down I-5 to Los Angeles with teammate Rich Hill at the deadline. Reddick cratered in August, posting a .396 OPS (yes, OPS). His struggles began right after his arrival—and, resultingly, Yasiel Puig's demotion—tainting fans who all but ignored his stellar September (.961 OPS). They do remember his postseason, though, where his .308 average belied a total power outage (no extra-base hits), and surprisingly poor defense in right field. The Astros liked what they saw in the big picture and inked Reddick to a four-year, $52 million deal shortly after the season ended. He should patrol the outfield and only see left-handers in photographs.

A.J. Reed　1B

Born: 5/10/93　Age: 24　Bats: L　Throws: L　Height: 6'4"　Weight: 275　Entered Pro Ball: Round 2, 2014 Draft (#42 overall)

YEAR	TEAM	LVL	AGE	PA	R	2B	3B	HR	RBI	BB	K	SB	CS	AVG/OBP/SLG	TAv	VORP	BABIP	BRR	FRAA	WARP
2014	TCV	A-	21	150	22	11	0	5	30	22	22	2	0	.306/.420/.516	.349	13.7	.337	-1.8	1B(31): -1.2	1.3
2014	QUD	A	21	135	21	9	1	7	24	8	32	0	0	.272/.326/.528	.298	4.5	.314	-2.3	1B(18): -1.0	0.4
2015	LNC	A+	22	385	75	16	4	23	81	59	73	0	0	.346/.449/.638	.360	43.5	.385	1.2	1B(64): 3.2	5.1
2015	CCH	AA	22	237	38	14	1	11	46	27	49	0	0	.332/.405/.571	.334	15.5	.383	-4.5	1B(32): -1.7	1.5
2016	FRE	AAA	23	296	42	22	1	15	50	32	67	0	0	.291/.368/.556	.323	20.1	.337	-2.4	1B(46): 2.2	2.3
2016	HOU	MLB	23	141	11	3	0	3	8	18	48	0	0	.164/.270/.262	.200	-7.2	.236	-0.2	1B(35): -2.1	-1.0
2017	*HOU*	*MLB*	*24*	*68*	*8*	*3*	*0*	*3*	*9*	*7*	*19*	*0*	*0*	*.244/.324/.446*	*.275*	*2.1*	*.301*	*-0.1*	*1B -0*	*0.2*
2018	*HOU*	*MLB*	*25*	*371*	*51*	*17*	*1*	*16*	*52*	*42*	*104*	*0*	*0*	*.245/.332/.454*	*.276*	*9.7*	*.305*	*-0.8*	*1B -1*	*1.0*

Breakout: 1%　Improve: 21%　Collapse: 22%　Attrition: 25%　MLB: 57%　*Comparables: Chris Carter, Paul Goldschmidt, Kennys Vargas*

Reed is a big boy who reliably turned his mass into power at every level before his call-up to the majors in August. Once there, though, the 23-year-old had every hole in his swing exploited by the veterans of The Show. He was never a great contact hitter, but the whiffs Reed generated in his short stint with the Astros could impact weather patterns around the Houston area for years. Even when he was mashing taters in the minors, scouts noted Reed's swing was slow and considerably long. The sheer force of his swing was enough to punish the inevitable mistakes of minor-league pitching, but he's going to need to tighten things up if he's to hit enough to stick at first base in the bigs.

George Springer   RF

Born: 9/19/89   Age: 27   Bats: R   Throws: R   Height: 6'3"   Weight: 215   Entered Pro Ball: Round 1, 2011 Draft (#11 overall)

YEAR	TEAM	LVL	AGE	PA	R	2B	3B	HR	RBI	BB	K	SB	CS	AVG/OBP/SLG	TAv	VORP	BABIP	BRR	FRAA	WARP
2014	OKL	AAA	24	61	17	4	1	3	9	9	15	4	0	.353/.459/.647	.372	10.7	.455	1.4	RF(7): 0.1 • CF(6): -0.5	1.0
2014	HOU	MLB	24	345	45	8	1	20	51	39	114	5	2	.231/.336/.468	.304	20.8	.294	0.5	RF(71): 2.0 • CF(8): 0.3	2.6
2015	CCH	AA	25	20	4	1	0	0	0	2	6	1	0	.278/.350/.333	.232	0.0	.417	0.2	RF(3): -0.2	0.0
2015	HOU	MLB	25	451	59	19	2	16	41	50	109	16	4	.276/.367/.459	.299	27.7	.342	2.3	RF(93): 5.6 • CF(10): 0.6	3.6
2016	HOU	MLB	26	744	116	29	5	29	82	88	178	9	10	.261/.359/.457	.280	29.3	.317	1.2	RF(147): 16.6 • CF(1): -0.0	4.7
2017	*HOU*	*MLB*	*27*	*648*	*94*	*25*	*4*	*26*	*78*	*75*	*170*	*13*	*7*	*.253/.351/.449*	*.288*	*40.1*	*.315*	*-0.4*	*CF 13, RF 3*	*5.3*
2018	*HOU*	*MLB*	*28*	*567*	*80*	*23*	*3*	*23*	*77*	*68*	*147*	*11*	*6*	*.253/.354/.453*	*.286*	*30.5*	*.314*	*1.4*	*CF 11, RF 2*	*4.8*

Breakout: 2%   Improve: 57%   Collapse: 4%   Attrition: 6%   MLB: 100%   *Comparables: Jay Bruce, Jack Clark, Roger Maris*

Springer bounced back from an injury-ridden 2015 to be an iron man in 2016 and managed to finally complete his first full major-league season at age 26. He continued to deliver the big-time power and solid plate discipline we've come to expect through his first two campaigns. He has become one of the best in the league at hitting with power to all fields, spreading his home runs nearly evenly around the yard—11 to left field, eight to center and 10 to right. Springer sells out a bit for contact and his ability to hit for average remains limited by his high strikeout rate, but the reward is undeniable. He has a dynamic, game-changing swing and should be one of the most feared batters in the American League for the near future.

Kyle Tucker   OF

Born: 1/17/97   Age: 20   Bats: L   Throws: R   Height: 6'4"   Weight: 190   Entered Pro Ball: Round 1, 2015 Draft (#5 overall)

YEAR	TEAM	LVL	AGE	PA	R	2B	3B	HR	RBI	BB	K	SB	CS	AVG/OBP/SLG	TAv	VORP	BABIP	BRR	FRAA	WARP
2016	QUD	A	19	428	43	19	5	6	56	40	75	31	9	.276/.348/.402	.281	20.6	.322	1.3	CF(61): -4.4 • LF(17): -0.0	1.8
2016	LNC	A+	19	69	13	6	2	3	13	10	6	1	3	.339/.435/.661	.347	8.0	.340	0.2	RF(6): -0.1 • LF(4): 0.2	0.8
2017	*HOU*	*MLB*	*20*	*250*	*28*	*10*	*2*	*6*	*26*	*17*	*62*	*8*	*4*	*.226/.284/.369*	*.229*	*1.2*	*.277*	*0.3*	*CF -2, LF 0*	*0.0*
2018	*HOU*	*MLB*	*21*	*389*	*44*	*17*	*3*	*11*	*43*	*29*	*90*	*13*	*6*	*.235/.296/.388*	*.242*	*4.0*	*.283*	*1.2*	*CF -3, LF 0*	*0.2*

Breakout: 2%   Improve: 12%   Collapse: 0%   Attrition: 4%   MLB: 14%   *Comparables: Cedric Hunter, Jose Tabata, Anthony Gose*

Tucker already has a quick bat and a swing made to hit for average, something very few 19-year-olds can boast. He is making the Astros look smart for popping him fifth overall in the 2015 draft, as he handled full-season ball with aplomb in his first shot at it. Despite his young age, Tucker didn't slow down a beat upon promotion to the High-A California League. At 6-foot-4, he has the frame to fill out and hit for 15-20 homer power, plus the arm to play a competent right field. For now, he's more of a line-drive hitter, but if his development continues on this path, he will wind out far outpacing his brother, fellow Astros outfielder Preston.

Preston Tucker   LF

Born: 7/6/90   Age: 26   Bats: L   Throws: L   Height: 6'0"   Weight: 215   Entered Pro Ball: Round 7, 2012 Draft (#219 overall)

YEAR	TEAM	LVL	AGE	PA	R	2B	3B	HR	RBI	BB	K	SB	CS	AVG/OBP/SLG	TAv	VORP	BABIP	BRR	FRAA	WARP
2014	CCH	AA	23	290	41	17	0	17	43	26	46	3	3	.276/.348/.536	.314	19.1	.278	-1.5	RF(34): 1.6 • LF(15): 0.2	2.2
2014	OKL	AAA	23	309	38	18	0	7	51	31	74	2	0	.287/.356/.429	.271	9.1	.365	-0.8	LF(44): -0.8 • RF(12): -0.7	0.7
2015	FRE	AAA	24	143	20	4	0	11	35	12	25	1	0	.295/.357/.581	.310	10.2	.287	0.4	LF(17): 2.6 • RF(5): 0.5	1.4
2015	HOU	MLB	24	323	35	19	0	13	33	20	68	0	2	.243/.297/.437	.261	5.7	.274	-1.2	LF(79): -2.2 • RF(14): -0.8	0.3
2016	FRE	AAA	25	229	35	14	3	8	29	15	49	1	1	.301/.349/.512	.311	16.9	.355	0.5	RF(25): -4.3 • LF(23): -0.4	1.3
2016	HOU	MLB	25	144	11	8	1	4	8	8	40	0	0	.164/.222/.328	.202	-6.0	.200	0.2	LF(19): -1.3 • RF(3): -0.2	-0.8
2016	CCH	AA	25	24	1	0	0	0	3	2	9	0	0	.095/.167/.095	.120	-3.0	.154	0.1	LF(3): 0.0	-0.3
2017	*HOU*	*MLB*	*26*	*34*	*4*	*2*	*0*	*1*	*4*	*2*	*8*	*0*	*0*	*.239/.297/.423*	*.257*	*0.9*	*.283*	*-0.1*	*LF -0*	*0.1*
2018	*HOU*	*MLB*	*27*	*181*	*22*	*9*	*0*	*7*	*23*	*14*	*45*	*0*	*0*	*.240/.301/.424*	*.253*	*2.9*	*.287*	*-0.1*	*LF -1*	*0.2*

Breakout: 9%   Improve: 41%   Collapse: 7%   Attrition: 17%   MLB: 76%   *Comparables: Eric Thames, Scott Hairston, Ryan Rua*

Tucker had his season ended by a shoulder injury suffered in mid-August that lingered and eventually required surgery, and it's easy to wonder if that injury contributed to his struggles in his limited playing time in 2016. After showing 20-homer power in 2015, Tucker struggled mightily to make contact in a way he never had in the minor leagues. His brother Kyle is rapidly approaching the majors, but if Preston can't figure out his strikeout woes, he may be out of the league by the time Kyle makes it.

Luis Valbuena   3B

Born: 11/30/85   Age: 31   Bats: L   Throws: R   Height: 5'10"   Weight: 215   Entered Pro Ball: International Free Agent, 2002

YEAR	TEAM	LVL	AGE	PA	R	2B	3B	HR	RBI	BB	K	SB	CS	AVG/OBP/SLG	TAv	VORP	BABIP	BRR	FRAA	WARP
2014	CHN	MLB	28	547	68	33	4	16	51	65	113	1	2	.249/.341/.435	.292	31.9	.294	-0.2	3B(124): -11.1 • 2B(21): -1.3	2.2
2015	HOU	MLB	29	493	62	18	0	25	56	50	106	1	0	.224/.310/.438	.267	18.2	.235	1.9	3B(99): -6.3 • 1B(31): 1.9	1.5
2016	HOU	MLB	30	342	38	17	1	13	40	44	81	1	1	.260/.357/.459	.290	19.4	.315	-1.4	3B(81): 6.0 • 1B(8): 0.3	2.6
2017	*HOU*	*MLB*	*31*	*352*	*40*	*17*	*1*	*12*	*44*	*41*	*76*	*1*	*1*	*.235/.328/.413*	*.261*	*11.0*	*.272*	*0.0*	*3B -3, 1B 0*	*0.9*
2018	*HOU*	*MLB*	*32*	*339*	*42*	*15*	*1*	*11*	*40*	*39*	*76*	*0*	*0*	*.226/.319/.396*	*.255*	*5.6*	*.265*	*0.0*	*3B -3, 1B 0*	*0.4*

Breakout: 1%   Improve: 33%   Collapse: 7%   Attrition: 9%   MLB: 86%   *Comparables: Morgan Ensberg, Justin Turner, Eric Chavez*

Much like the "three-and-D" role player in basketball, Valbuena makes up for the holes in his skill set by providing a few premium attributes, at a semi-premium position no less. Valbuena's patience and power have been enough to make him an average or better third baseman over the past three seasons, and he was on his way to a career year before a hamstring injury ended his season after just 90 games. Just four third basemen have managed an ISO over .180 and a walk rate over 10 percent dating back to 2014: Josh Donaldson, Kris Bryant, Matt Carpenter, and Valbuena. Even if Valbuena's overall skill level falls far below those three, that's mighty fine company, and proof that what Valbuena does bring to the table is worthy of a spot somewhere.

Tyler White   1B

Born: 10/29/90 Age: 26   Bats: R   Throws: R   Height: 5'11"   Weight: 225   Entered Pro Ball: Round 33, 2013 Draft (#977 overall)

YEAR	TEAM	LVL	AGE	PA	R	2B	3B	HR	RBI	BB	K	SB	CS	AVG/OBP/SLG	TAv	VORP	BABIP	BRR	FRAA	WARP
2014	QUD	A	23	290	41	20	1	7	41	35	40	0	1	.305/.414/.485	.335	27.9	.337	-3.6	3B(62): -3.6 • 1B(2): 0.4	2.6
2014	LNC	A+	23	186	28	13	1	8	23	28	27	0	0	.267/.403/.527	.313	9.6	.276	-2.5	1B(31): -0.2 • 1B(4): -0.2	0.9
2015	CCH	AA	24	236	33	6	0	7	40	42	35	1	0	.284/.415/.426	.297	14.9	.313	0.2	3B(45): -2.6 • 1B(3): -0.2	1.3
2015	FRE	AAA	24	259	37	19	1	7	59	42	38	0	1	.362/.467/.559	.354	25.5	.412	-3.0	1B(25): -1.5 • 3B(3): -0.1	2.4
2016	FRE	AAA	25	190	28	4	1	13	29	16	30	1	1	.241/.305/.500	.282	5.8	.221	-1.2	1B(24): 0.9 • LF(3): -0.2	0.7
2016	HOU	MLB	25	276	24	16	0	8	28	23	65	1	0	.217/.286/.378	.236	-3.7	.258	-0.1	1B(58): -2.5 • 3B(3): -0.0	-0.7
2017	*HOU*	*MLB*	*26*	*99*	*12*	*5*	*0*	*3*	*12*	*11*	*21*	*0*	*0*	*.245/.333/.421*	*.272*	*2.9*	*.283*	*-0.2*	*1B -0*	*0.2*
2018	*HOU*	*MLB*	*27*	*325*	*42*	*15*	*1*	*11*	*40*	*37*	*71*	*0*	*0*	*.240/.333/.417*	*.266*	*7.0*	*.280*	*-0.3*	*1B -1*	*0.6*

Breakout: 1%   Improve: 17%   Collapse: 14%   Attrition: 23%   MLB: 62%   *Comparables: Ryan Garko, Travis Shaw, Jeff Clement*

White is one of the players who perfectly illustrates the massive skill gap between Triple-A and the majors. Despite a hot start at the major-league level, the game's best pitchers quickly figured him out. The result was a bat that simply won't be able to play at first base. White has excellent plate discipline, but he wasn't able to show the kind of power necessary to force MLB pitchers into handling him with the same level of care he was treated with in the minors. His approach is wonderful and may earn him more shots at The Show, but he just doesn't look like he has the pop for first base at the top level.

PITCHERS

Guadalupe Chavez   RHP

Born: 12/3/97   Age: 19   Bats: R   Throws: R   Height: 6'2"   Weight: 150   Entered Pro Ball: International Free Agent, 2014

Lupe for short, Chavez was the prospect return from the Blue Jays in the Scott Feldman trade this past August. Chavez tore up short-season ball at age 17 and 18, and he has done enough to get his first crack at the full-season leagues at just 19. Chavez is thin as a rail—just 150 pounds at 6-foot-2—and has lots of projection left on that frame. Even so, he's already showing a low-to-mid-90s fastball and a sharp changeup to go with a curveball that remains a work in progress. If he can bulk up and add even more life to his pitches, Chavez could go far in the Astros' system.

Chris Devenski   RHP

Born: 11/13/90   Age: 26   Bats: R   Throws: R   Height: 6'3"   Weight: 210   Entered Pro Ball: Round 25, 2011 Draft (#771 overall)

YEAR	TEAM	LVL	AGE	W	L	SV	G	GS	IP	H	HR	BB/9	K/9	K	GB%	BABIP	WHIP	ERA	FIP	DRA	VORP	WARP	cFIP	MPH
2014	LNC	A+	23	5	5	2	17	11	76²	70	8	1.4	9.0	77	44%	.293	1.07	4.11	3.67	2.11	28.8	2.9	85	
2014	CCH	AA	23	5	3	0	10	5	41¹	33	7	3.9	8.1	37	40%	.232	1.23	3.92	4.84	5.49	-1.8	-0.2	112	
2015	CCH	AA	24	7	4	2	24	17	119²	117	12	2.5	7.8	104	34%	.300	1.25	3.01	3.74	1.80	42.6	4.6	87	
2016	HOU	MLB	25	4	4	1	48	5	108¹	79	4	1.7	8.6	104	34%	.271	0.91	2.16	2.30	3.72	16.1	1.7	95	95.6
2017	*HOU*	*MLB*	*26*	*5*	*4*	*0*	*48*	*8*	*81*	*78*	*8*	*2.7*	*8.2*	*75*	*47%*	*.297*	*1.25*	*3.53*	*3.59*	*4.12*	*9.0*	*0.9*	*94*	
2018	*HOU*	*MLB*	*27*	*6*	*4*	*0*	*62*	*9*	*109*	*90*	*12*	*3.8*	*10.8*	*130*	*47%*	*.293*	*1.25*	*3.38*	*3.61*	*3.90*	*14.9*	*1.5*	*86*	

Breakout: 21%   Improve: 34%   Collapse: 28%   Attrition: 31%   MLB: 81%   *Comparables: Michael Bowden, Ryan Cook, Michael Kirkman*

Few pitchers were farther off the prospect radar two years ago than Devenski. He slowly worked his way up the minor-league ladder until he finally broke out with an excellent campaign in 2015 at Double-A Corpus Christi. It was enough to earn him a shot at the major-league roster in spring training, and Devenski came through and earned a surprise spot on Houston's Opening Day roster. Not only did Devenski pitch exceptionally well for the Astros, he was also one of the most versatile pitchers in MLB last year. He started five games, lasting as long as 6.2 innings in one start, and also regularly served as a multi-inning reliever. In only 16 of Devenski's 43 relief appearances did he pitch just one inning; he went at least three innings on 10 different occasions and even threw four-plus shutout innings on two occasions. Devenski doesn't have big-time closer stuff, but his ability to effectively pitch multiple innings gives the Astros a big weapon out of the bullpen, one that keeps the rest of their relievers fresh as well.

Michael Feliz   RHP

Born: 6/28/93   Age: 24   Bats: R   Throws: R   Height: 6'4"   Weight: 230   Entered Pro Ball: International Free Agent, 2010

YEAR	TEAM	LVL	AGE	W	L	SV	G	GS	IP	H	HR	BB/9	K/9	K	GB%	BABIP	WHIP	ERA	FIP	DRA	VORP	WARP	cFIP	MPH
2014	QUD	A	21	8	6	0	25	19	102²	104	6	3.2	9.7	111	41%	.348	1.37	4.03	3.31	3.24	24.5	2.5	91	
2015	LNC	A+	22	1	1	0	8	5	32²	30	2	3.3	9.1	33	48%	.298	1.29	4.41	3.84	4.03	3.3	0.4	100	
2015	CCH	AA	22	6	3	1	15	12	78²	52	5	2.3	8.0	70	43%	.228	0.92	2.17	3.11	3.23	15.8	1.7	89	
2015	HOU	MLB	22	0	0	0	5	0	8	9	2	4.5	7.9	7	38%	.292	1.62	7.88	6.48	5.76	-0.9	-0.1	107	96.7
2016	HOU	MLB	23	8	1	0	47	0	65	55	10	3.0	13.2	95	42%	.315	1.18	4.43	3.20	2.65	16.8	1.7	74	98.1
2017	*HOU*	*MLB*	*24*	*3*	*3*	*0*	*55*	*0*	*57²*	*49*	*6*	*3.6*	*9.8*	*63*	*56%*	*.290*	*1.25*	*3.58*	*3.64*	*4.15*	*5.3*	*0.5*	*95*	
2018	*HOU*	*MLB*	*25*	*1*	*1*	*0*	*25*	*0*	*26²*	*20*	*3*	*4.7*	*12.1*	*36*	*56%*	*.282*	*1.25*	*3.34*	*3.56*	*3.82*	*3.6*	*0.4*	*83*	

Breakout: 34%   Improve: 62%   Collapse: 10%   Attrition: 17%   MLB: 86%   *Comparables: Vincent Velasquez, Kris Medlen, Edinson Volquez*

When Feliz throws his slider for a strike, good luck hitting it. Over 40 percent of swings against Feliz's slider resulted in whiffs, ranking him in the top third of relievers to throw at least 200 sliders in 2016. But Feliz's control simply isn't good enough for him to take advantage of his nastiness. Feliz struggled with walks throughout his minor-league career, and until he can figure out how to spot his slider for a strike, he's going to struggle to realize his full potential. That potential is so tantalizing, though—at 13.2, Feliz posted the ninth-highest strikeout rate among qualified relievers, right after Dodgers relief ace Kenley Jansen. Such excellent company will almost certainly earn Feliz plenty of chances to work through his issues.

Mike Fiers   RHP

Born: 6/15/85   Age: 32   Bats: R   Throws: R   Height: 6'2"   Weight: 200   Entered Pro Ball: Round 22, 2009 Draft (#676 overall)

YEAR	TEAM	LVL	AGE	W	L	SV	G	GS	IP	H	HR	BB/9	K/9	K	GB%	BABIP	WHIP	ERA	FIP	DRA	VORP	WARP	cFIP	MPH
2014	NAS	AAA	29	8	5	0	17	17	102¹	80	8	1.5	11.3	129	46%	.289	0.95	2.55	2.90	0.51	59.7	5.9	53	
2014	MIL	MLB	29	6	5	0	14	10	71²	46	7	2.1	9.5	76	36%	.224	0.88	2.13	2.96	3.39	11.3	1.2	93	92.0
2015	MIL	MLB	30	5	9	0	21	21	118	117	14	3.3	9.2	121	41%	.316	1.36	3.89	3.87	3.87	15.7	1.7	99	91.8
2015	HOU	MLB	30	2	1	0	10	9	62¹	45	10	3.0	8.5	59	39%	.217	1.06	3.32	4.36	3.95	7.7	0.8	100	92.2
2016	HOU	MLB	31	11	8	0	31	30	168²	187	26	2.2	7.2	134	44%	.313	1.36	4.48	4.39	4.51	15.7	1.6	105	91.9
2017	*HOU*	*MLB*	*32*	*10*	*8*	*0*	*26*	*26*	*148*	*145*	*22*	*2.9*	*8.4*	*138*	*47%*	*.293*	*1.30*	*4.20*	*4.29*	*4.83*	*6.9*	*0.7*	*100*	
2018	*HOU*	*MLB*	*33*	*8*	*9*	*0*	*24*	*24*	*141*	*143*	*24*	*3.2*	*8.5*	*132*	*47%*	*.298*	*1.36*	*4.34*	*4.61*	*5.00*	*7.0*	*0.7*	*116*	

Breakout: 34%   Improve: 62%   Collapse: 10%   Attrition: 17%   MLB: 86%   *Comparables: Vincent Velasquez, Kris Medlen, Edinson Volquez*

Despite a fastball averaging under 90 mph, Fiers had held opponents under a hit per inning over his first four MLB campaigns. But MLB hitters are a sharp bunch, and it looks like they're finally deciphering the deception Fiers brings every time he steps on the mound. In his first full season as an American Leaguer, Fiers gave up more hits and home runs than ever before. Fiers has been capable of brilliance, as he showed with a no-hitter in 2015, and he did have six starts of at least six innings with one or fewer earned runs allowed. But with his soft arsenal, his margin for error is razor thin, and when he's off, he gets hammered. Fiers served up multiple home runs on six different occasions in 2016, and at 32 years old, it's hard to imagine this is an issue Fiers will be able to resolve.

Doug Fister   RHP

Born: 2/4/84   Age: 33   Bats: L   Throws: R   Height: 6'8"   Weight: 210   Entered Pro Ball: Round 7, 2006 Draft (#201 overall)

YEAR	TEAM	LVL	AGE	W	L	SV	G	GS	IP	H	HR	BB/9	K/9	K	GB%	BABIP	WHIP	ERA	FIP	DRA	VORP	WARP	cFIP	MPH
2014	WAS	MLB	30	16	6	0	25	25	164	153	18	1.3	5.4	98	51%	.262	1.08	2.41	3.90	3.59	22.8	2.5	104	90.5
2015	WAS	MLB	31	5	7	1	25	15	103	120	14	2.1	5.5	63	47%	.310	1.40	4.19	4.58	5.88	-9.9	-1.1	117	88.9
2016	HOU	MLB	32	12	13	0	32	32	180¹	195	24	3.1	5.7	115	47%	.300	1.43	4.64	4.71	5.34	0.4	0.0	117	89.7
2017	*HOU*	*MLB*	*33*	*8*	*9*	*0*	*23*	*23*	*141¹*	*155*	*22*	*3.2*	*6.8*	*107*	*55%*	*.305*	*1.45*	*4.83*	*4.80*	*5.51*	*-0.6*	*-0.1*	*130*	
2018	*HOU*	*MLB*	*34*	*7*	*9*	*0*	*22*	*22*	*131*	*147*	*23*	*3.3*	*6.8*	*98*	*55%*	*.306*	*1.48*	*4.86*	*5.13*	*5.54*	*-1.0*	*-0.1*	*131*	

Breakout: 8%   Improve: 43%   Collapse: 16%   Attrition: 17%   MLB: 90%   *Comparables: Mark Buehrle, Jason Marquis, Jered Weaver*

Fister stayed healthy for the first time in three years, but he remains in search of the form that earned him Cy Young votes in 2014. He previously thrived by keeping the ball in the yard and by keeping runners off the bases, but he could do neither of those things last season. His one-year, $7 million deal with the Astros was meant to be a pillow contract, but Fister couldn't stick the landing.

Ken Giles   RHP

Born: 9/20/90   Age: 26   Bats: R   Throws: R   Height: 6'2"   Weight: 205   Entered Pro Ball: Round 7, 2011 Draft (#241 overall)

YEAR	TEAM	LVL	AGE	W	L	SV	G	GS	IP	H	HR	BB/9	K/9	K	GB%	BABIP	WHIP	ERA	FIP	DRA	VORP	WARP	cFIP	MPH
2014	REA	AA	23	0	0	7	13	0	15	8	0	3.0	17.4	29	44%	.348	0.87	1.20	0.49	1.00	6.4	0.7	53	
2014	LEH	AAA	23	2	0	5	11	0	13²	10	0	5.3	5.9	9	31%	.256	1.32	2.63	4.02	5.42	-0.1	0.0	110	
2014	PHI	MLB	23	3	1	1	44	0	45²	25	1	2.2	12.6	64	46%	.267	0.79	1.18	1.31	1.80	13.6	1.5	59	100.3
2015	PHI	MLB	24	6	3	15	69	0	70	59	2	3.2	11.2	87	41%	.311	1.20	1.80	2.16	2.52	17.1	1.9	78	99.8
2016	HOU	MLB	25	2	5	15	69	0	65²	60	8	3.4	14.0	102	41%	.349	1.29	4.11	2.82	2.41	18.7	1.9	71	100.0
2017	*HOU*	*MLB*	*26*	*3*	*2*	*30*	*55*	*0*	*57²*	*48*	*6*	*3.2*	*11.8*	*76*	*44%*	*.301*	*1.18*	*2.72*	*3.02*	*3.40*	*10.1*	*1.0*	*71*	
2018	*HOU*	*MLB*	*27*	*3*	*1*	*28*	*62*	*0*	*65¹*	*49*	*6*	*3.7*	*12.4*	*90*	*44%*	*.295*	*1.17*	*2.79*	*3.00*	*3.25*	*12.9*	*1.3*	*66*	

Breakout: 36%   Improve: 61%   Collapse: 20%   Attrition: 12%   MLB: 89%   *Comparables: Rex Brothers, David Robertson, Manny Delcarmen*

Giles' season hardly could have had a worse beginning, as he gave up 10 runs in as many innings in April. Over his next 55.2 innings, Giles held opponents to a 3.23 ERA and struck out 88 batters—much more like the closer understudy (he moved into the lead role in Augsut) the Astros thought they had acquired from the Phillies over the offseason. Giles' slider is a contender for the nastiest pitch in baseball. Hitters swung and missed at more than one-third of them in 2016, and his 62.2 percent whiffs-per-swing ratio was the best of any reliever to throw 200 sliders. Pair it with Giles' triple-digit-teasing fastball and the recipe is there for him to become one of baseball's most dominant relievers on a more consistent basis.

Luke Gregerson   RHP

Born: 5/14/84   Age: 33   Bats: L   Throws: R   Height: 6'3"   Weight: 205   Entered Pro Ball: Round 28, 2006 Draft (#856 overall)

YEAR	TEAM	LVL	AGE	W	L	SV	G	GS	IP	H	HR	BB/9	K/9	K	GB%	BABIP	WHIP	ERA	FIP	DRA	VORP	WARP	cFIP	MPH
2014	OAK	MLB	30	5	5	3	72	0	72¹	58	6	1.9	7.3	59	54%	.256	1.01	2.12	3.27	3.07	11.4	1.3	89	90.3
2015	HOU	MLB	31	7	3	31	64	0	61	48	5	1.5	8.7	59	62%	.264	0.95	3.10	2.83	2.74	13.4	1.4	76	91.4
2016	HOU	MLB	32	4	3	15	59	0	57²	38	5	2.8	10.5	67	62%	.239	0.97	3.28	2.95	2.75	14.2	1.5	71	91.4
2017	HOU	MLB	33	3	3	5	59	0	62	53	7	2.8	9.5	66	49%	.283	1.14	3.25	3.52	3.88	7.7	0.8	85	
2018	HOU	MLB	34	3	1	3	58	0	61¹	52	7	3.1	9.0	61	49%	.275	1.20	3.63	3.87	4.19	5.8	0.6	92	

Breakout: 21%   Improve: 45%   Collapse: 33%   Attrition: 15%   MLB: 95%   Comparables: Scot Shields, Jonathan Papelbon, Heath Bell

Gregerson cannot escape fate. His year-and-a-half run as Astros closer ended in ignominy in early June after he blew consecutive saves against the Diamondbacks and Athletics, his fourth and fifth blown saves in just 18 chances to that point. Back in a setup role, Gregerson settled into his old niche very nicely, as he held opponents to a .498 OPS and recorded a 2.25 ERA in 32 innings. As a righty without big-time strikeout stuff, Gregerson never fit the closer mold particularly well. But he fits in middle relief: only Tyler Clippard, Joaquin Benoit, and Tony Watson have more holds in the 2010s than Gregerson's 142, a testament to his longevity in a role known for its fungibility.

Jandel Gustave   RHP

Born: 10/12/92   Age: 24   Bats: R   Throws: R   Height: 6'2"   Weight: 210   Entered Pro Ball: International Free Agent, 2010

YEAR	TEAM	LVL	AGE	W	L	SV	G	GS	IP	H	HR	BB/9	K/9	K	GB%	BABIP	WHIP	ERA	FIP	DRA	VORP	WARP	cFIP	MPH
2014	QUD	A	21	5	5	2	23	14	79	94	3	3.3	9.3	82	48%	.374	1.56	5.01	3.50	5.45	-1.1	-0.1	102	
2015	CCH	AA	22	5	2	20	46	0	58²	51	2	3.8	7.5	49	57%	.290	1.30	2.15	3.45	4.77	-0.3	0.0	107	
2016	FRE	AAA	23	3	3	3	47	0	57	46	1	3.6	8.7	55	54%	.281	1.21	3.79	3.65	3.22	11.0	1.1	98	
2016	HOU	MLB	23	1	0	0	14	0	15¹	12	2	2.3	9.4	16	40%	.289	1.11	3.52	3.50	3.92	1.8	0.2	96	99.4
2017	HOU	MLB	24	2	2	0	35	0	36²	39	4	3.9	6.9	28	55%	.299	1.49	4.90	4.54	5.22	-1.0	-0.1	100	
2018	HOU	MLB	25	2	1	0	39	0	41	36	5	5.4	9.7	44	55%	.292	1.48	4.33	4.56	4.92	0.6	0.1	111	

Breakout: 21%   Improve: 32%   Collapse: 8%   Attrition: 24%   MLB: 44%   Comparables: Frankie De La Cruz, Cesar Vargas, Arnold Leon

Gustave's upper-90s fastball and swing-and-miss slider was enough for the Astros to protect him on the 40-man roster despite his lack of reliable command. That still hasn't changed, but he handled Triple-A hitters and held his own upon promotion to the majors in August with more than a strikeout per inning. He'll need to develop more feel for his slider if he's ever going to be a true back-end relief option, but that Gustave has already shown a 100 mph heater is a great place to start.

Will Harris   RHP

Born: 8/28/84   Age: 32   Bats: R   Throws: R   Height: 6'4"   Weight: 250   Entered Pro Ball: Round 9, 2006 Draft (#258 overall)

YEAR	TEAM	LVL	AGE	W	L	SV	G	GS	IP	H	HR	BB/9	K/9	K	GB%	BABIP	WHIP	ERA	FIP	DRA	VORP	WARP	cFIP	MPH
2014	RNO	AAA	29	3	2	1	43	0	45²	34	3	3.9	8.7	44	45%	.259	1.18	0.99	4.27	4.47	4.4	0.4	99	
2014	ARI	MLB	29	0	3	0	29	0	29	27	3	2.8	10.9	35	36%	.338	1.24	4.34	3.17	3.43	3.4	0.4	92	93.6
2015	HOU	MLB	30	5	5	2	68	0	71	42	8	2.8	8.6	68	52%	.192	0.90	1.90	3.63	3.58	8.9	1.0	90	94.2
2016	HOU	MLB	31	1	2	12	66	0	64	52	3	2.1	9.7	69	59%	.293	1.05	2.25	2.31	2.48	17.7	1.8	77	94.6
2017	HOU	MLB	32	3	2	5	55	0	57²	50	6	3.1	9.2	59	46%	.290	1.21	3.29	3.62	3.94	6.7	0.7	87	
2018	HOU	MLB	33	3	1	3	60	0	63¹	54	6	3.4	9.2	65	46%	.281	1.22	3.39	3.61	3.94	7.7	0.8	85	

Breakout: 29%   Improve: 47%   Collapse: 24%   Attrition: 18%   MLB: 90%   Comparables: Brad Ziegler, Mike Adams, Jared Burton

Ever since he was freed from the unfortunate life that is pitching in the Rockies organization, Harris has thrived. He reached an un-likely summit in 2016, earning an All-Star berth with an incredible first half that saw him hold opponents to a .493 OPS, recording a 1.62 ERA in 39 innings, and even snagging the Astros' closer role for a brief time. Reality set in a bit during the second half, as Harris surrendered a 3.24 ERA in his final 25 innings, but he still struck out 30 batters in that span. It took until his age-27 season to reach the majors, but Harris has become a consistently productive reliever in his 30s.

James Hoyt   RHP

Born: 9/30/86   Age: 30   Bats: R   Throws: R   Height: 6'6"   Weight: 230   Entered Pro Ball: Undrafted Free Agent, 2013

YEAR	TEAM	LVL	AGE	W	L	SV	G	GS	IP	H	HR	BB/9	K/9	K	GB%	BABIP	WHIP	ERA	FIP	DRA	VORP	WARP	cFIP	MPH
2014	GWN	AAA	27	1	1	1	24	0	28	38	4	4.5	10.9	34	44%	.395	1.86	5.46	4.50	5.02	1.0	0.1	91	
2014	MIS	AA	27	2	2	6	28	0	31²	19	1	2.8	12.2	43	47%	.250	0.92	1.14	1.83	1.58	11.5	1.2	69	
2015	FRE	AAA	28	0	1	9	47	0	49	48	1	2	12.1	66	40%	.362	1.20	3.49	2.03	1.91	16.4	1.7	70	
2016	FRE	AAA	29	4	3	29	49	0	55	29	2	3.1	15.2	93	67%	.276	0.87	1.64	1.85	0.68	26.1	2.7	32	
2016	HOU	MLB	29	1	1	0	22	0	22	16	5	3.7	11.5	28	55%	.229	1.14	4.50	4.88	3.24	4.2	0.4	84	95.7
2017	HOU	MLB	30	2	2	0	45	0	47	40	5	3.3	10.7	56	48%	.297	1.21	3.02	3.37	3.69	6.8	0.7	80	
2018	HOU	MLB	31	1	1	0	25	0	26	19	3	4.8	13.2	38	48%	.292	1.24	3.10	3.32	3.61	4.1	0.4	76	

Breakout: 27%   Improve: 33%   Collapse: 13%   Attrition: 17%   MLB: 51%   Comparables: Jason Bulger, Jose Valdez, Warner Madrigal

On the surface, Hoyt is an undrafted 30-year-old reliever who just had a mediocre rookie season—not much to get excited about there. But Hoyt flashed what might be one of the game's best sliders. It was his primary pitch, thrown more often than his fastball by a solid 210-143 margin, and despite the fact that hitters saw it over and over again, the pitch induced a swing-and-a-miss 23.8 percent of the time and a 68 percent ground-ball rate on contact. The problems came when Hoyt fell behind and was forced to rely on his fastball. Velocity isn't the problem—it averaged 94 mph—but it's simply too hittable, as opponents owned a ridiculous .320 average and .700 slugging percentage against the fastball. Considering Hoyt was able to pile on the strikeouts behind that vicious slider, he's worth another look in a major-league bullpen.

Dallas Keuchel   LHP

Born: 1/1/88   Age: 29   Bats: L   Throws: L   Height: 6'3"   Weight: 205   Entered Pro Ball: Round 7, 2009 Draft (#221 overall)

YEAR	TEAM	LVL	AGE	W	L	SV	G	GS	IP	H	HR	BB/9	K/9	K	GB%	BABIP	WHIP	ERA	FIP	DRA	VORP	WARP	cFIP	MPH
2014	HOU	MLB	26	12	9	0	29	29	200	187	11	2.2	6.6	146	65%	.296	1.17	2.92	3.24	1.94	64.3	7.1	83	92.0
2015	HOU	MLB	27	20	8	0	33	33	232	185	17	2.0	8.4	216	62%	.269	1.02	2.48	2.88	2.14	75.6	8.1	69	91.8
2016	HOU	MLB	28	9	12	0	26	26	168	168	20	2.6	7.7	144	58%	.304	1.29	4.55	3.83	3.53	34.2	3.5	89	90.6
2017	HOU	MLB	29	13	9	0	31	31	186	169	20	2.7	8.5	175	42%	.294	1.21	3.57	3.67	4.12	23.3	2.4	95	
2018	HOU	MLB	30	11	10	0	30	30	191¹	170	20	2.6	8.8	187	42%	.294	1.18	3.29	3.51	3.80	33.2	3.4	84	

Breakout: 17%   Improve: 44%   Collapse: 27%   Attrition: 14%   MLB: 95%   Comparables: Tyson Ross, Justin Masterson, CC Sabathia

The Cy Young hangover was as real for Keuchel as it was for Corey Kluber the year before (or prior). Keuchel missed time due to injury, saw his strikeout rate dip while his walk and home run rates increased, and couldn't sustain 2015's career-low BABIP. All that said, Keuchel was so incredible in 2014 and 2015 that even with this major dip in performance, he still finished in the top 35 in WARP among major-league pitchers. Keuchel may be a ground-ball machine, but it's awfully hard for anybody with a fastball that averages under 90 mph like his to maintain the minuscule home run rates he posted over the previous two seasons. At 29 years old, Keuchel should still have a few years of solidly above-average performance left in the tank, even if he doesn't ever compete for a Cy Young award again.

Francis Martes   RHP

Born: 11/24/95   Age: 21   Bats: R   Throws: R   Height: 6'1"   Weight: 225   Entered Pro Ball: International Free Agent, 2012

YEAR	TEAM	LVL	AGE	W	L	SV	G	GS	IP	H	HR	BB/9	K/9	K	GB%	BABIP	WHIP	ERA	FIP	DRA	VORP	WARP	cFIP	MPH
2015	QUD	A	19	3	2	2	10	8	52	33	1	2.2	7.8	45	48%	.229	0.88	1.04	2.78	3.35	10.5	1.1	93	
2015	LNC	A+	19	4	1	0	6	5	35	31	1	2.1	9.5	37	55%	.309	1.11	2.31	2.81	2.55	9.7	1.1	86	
2015	CCH	AA	19	1	0	0	3	3	14²	19	2	4.3	9.8	16	30%	.386	1.77	4.91	4.32	4.49	1.0	0.1	100	
2016	CCH	AA	20	9	6	0	25	22	125¹	104	4	3.4	9.4	131	45%	.296	1.20	3.30	2.73	3.72	18.8	2.0	89	
2017	HOU	MLB	21	5	6	0	27	16	96²	103	13	4.3	7.3	78	56%	.304	1.54	4.82	4.84	5.55	-2.1	-0.2	128	
2018	HOU	MLB	22	7	9	0	29	23	156	145	22	5.7	10.1	175	56%	.304	1.56	4.54	4.79	5.23	3.0	0.3	119	

Breakout: 7%   Improve: 13%   Collapse: 2%   Attrition: 13%   MLB: 19%   Comparables: Jameson Taillon, John Lamb, Carlos Martinez

Martes has been a quick riser, reaching Double-A at just age 19 in 2015. In a full crack at the Texas League in 2016, Martes sure didn't look like he was more than four years younger than his average opponent. He struck out over a batter per inning behind a nasty fastball-curveball combo and a changeup that continues to develop. At 6-foot-1 and 225 pounds with what one BP prospect analyst called a "thick middle," there are questions about his body's ability to handle a full starter's workload. His fastball-curveball combo could play up enough in the bullpen to make him a front-line closer, but if he can keep refining his changeup, Martes has a future in the top half of Houston's starting rotation.

Lance McCullers   RHP

Born: 10/2/93   Age: 23   Bats: L   Throws: R   Height: 6'1"   Weight: 205   Entered Pro Ball: Round 1, 2012 Draft (#41 overall)

YEAR	TEAM	LVL	AGE	W	L	SV	G	GS	IP	H	HR	BB/9	K/9	K	GB%	BABIP	WHIP	ERA	FIP	DRA	VORP	WARP	cFIP	MPH
2014	LNC	A+	20	3	6	4	25	18	97	95	18	5.2	10.7	115	48%	.311	1.56	5.47	5.73	3.49	21.6	2.2	100	
2015	CCH	AA	21	3	1	1	7	5	32	16	1	3.9	13.5	48	42%	.234	0.94	0.56	2.20	2.08	10.4	1.1	76	
2015	HOU	MLB	21	6	7	0	22	22	125²	106	10	3.1	9.2	129	48%	.288	1.19	3.22	3.23	2.97	29.5	3.2	85	97.4
2016	HOU	MLB	22	6	5	0	14	14	81	80	5	5.0	11.8	106	59%	.383	1.54	3.22	2.96	2.80	23.1	2.4	76	97.0
2017	HOU	MLB	23	11	7	0	26	26	148	124	12	4.2	10.5	172	35%	.300	1.32	3.37	3.43	3.90	22.2	2.3	87	
2018	HOU	MLB	24	11	9	0	31	31	193	156	17	4.4	11.3	242	35%	.305	1.30	3.14	3.35	3.63	35.1	3.6	78	

Breakout: 32%   Improve: 69%   Collapse: 15%   Attrition: 12%   MLB: 97%   Comparables: Alex Wood, Jair Jurrjens, Mat Latos

Even though his season debut was delayed by a shoulder injury, McCullers came out of the gates with the same kind of fire he displayed in his rookie season, racking up strikeouts and keeping runs off the board despite wildness. Unfortunately, he was able to make only 14 starts before an elbow injury ended his season in August. McCullers continues to dominate hitters with his curveball—the pitch finished off 89 of his 106 strikeouts and held hitters to a ludicrously low .192 slugging percentage on contact. His fastball remains vulnerable, however—hitters managed a .606 slugging percentage and 10 extra-base hits against it. That's the key for McCullers. When he gets into pitchers' counts and can utilize his curveball to its maximum, he's near unhittable. McCullers' elbow injury wasn't serious enough to rule him out of playoff action, so expect him to be ready for spring training.

Brendan McCurry   RHP

Born: 1/7/92   Age: 25   Bats: R   Throws: R   Height: 5'10"   Weight: 170   Entered Pro Ball: Round 22, 2014 Draft (#672 overall)

YEAR	TEAM	LVL	AGE	W	L	SV	G	GS	IP	H	HR	BB/9	K/9	K	GB%	BABIP	WHIP	ERA	FIP	DRA	VORP	WARP	cFIP	MPH
2014	BLT	A	22	2	0	2	15	0	26¹	12	1	1.0	11.6	34	65%	.192	0.57	0.34	1.97	3.10	5.7	0.6	76	
2015	STO	A+	23	1	2	21	36	0	46¹	30	3	2.1	10.9	56	47%	.252	0.88	1.94	3.17	1.81	15.0	1.6	76	
2015	MID	AA	23	0	1	6	14	0	16²	9	1	3.2	14.0	26	36%	.250	0.90	1.62	2.04	2.11	4.9	0.5	75	
2016	CCH	AA	24	2	4	13	28	0	39²	28	4	1.8	11.3	50	58%	.273	0.91	2.27	2.80	1.73	13.2	1.4	69	
2016	FRE	AAA	24	1	1	3	28	1	42¹	47	2	2.8	9.4	44	46%	.366	1.42	3.83	3.67	3.31	7.9	0.8	93	
2017	HOU	MLB	25	3	1	3	61	0	64¹	65	8	3.4	8.0	57	52%	.305	1.39	4.27	4.28	4.89	1.5	0.2	112	
2018	HOU	MLB	26	2	1	1	30	0	41	34	5	4.7	11.0	50	52%	.294	1.35	3.82	4.05	4.37	3.0	0.3	97	

Breakout: 24%   Improve: 29%   Collapse: 21%   Attrition: 35%   MLB: 54%   Comparables: Nick Wittgren, Rob Delaney, Louis Coleman

With every passing season it looks more and more like McCurry can overcome the odds and make the majors as a 22nd-round pick. McCurry has struck out a batter per inning at every stop and continued that streak upon his midseason promotion to Triple-A.

Critically, his control showed improvement in 2016, as he walked just four more batters than he did in 2015 despite hurling 19 more innings. McCurry doesn't have the high-90s fastball we expect out of today's relievers, but he has the diverse repertoire to keep hitters off balance and make it work. If he can put together a solid start to the season at Triple-A, it wouldn't surprise to see McCurry in Houston come the second half.

Collin McHugh   RHP

Born: 6/19/87   Age: 30   Bats: R   Throws: R   Height: 6'2"   Weight: 190   Entered Pro Ball: Round 18, 2008 Draft (#554 overall)

YEAR	TEAM	LVL	AGE	W	L	SV	G	GS	IP	H	HR	BB/9	K/9	K	GB%	BABIP	WHIP	ERA	FIP	DRA	VORP	WARP	cFIP	MPH
2014	OKL	AAA	27	0	0	0	5	3	19	15	0	2.8	6.2	13	33%	.263	1.11	3.79	3.28	6.47	-1.7	-0.2	120	
2014	HOU	MLB	27	11	9	0	25	25	154²	117	13	2.4	9.1	157	45%	.259	1.02	2.73	3.13	2.73	36.2	4.0	80	93.8
2015	HOU	MLB	28	19	7	0	32	32	203²	207	19	2.3	7.6	171	47%	.310	1.28	3.89	3.55	4.40	15.4	1.7	96	92.7
2016	HOU	MLB	29	13	10	0	33	33	184²	206	25	2.6	8.6	177	43%	.339	1.41	4.34	3.91	4.35	20.8	2.1	97	92.6
2017	HOU	MLB	30	12	8	0	29	29	174	164	19	2.9	8.8	169	50%	.298	1.27	3.65	3.73	4.21	20.1	2.1	97	
2018	HOU	MLB	31	11	10	0	29	29	178¹	157	23	3.1	9.8	193	50%	.291	1.23	3.58	3.81	4.13	25.4	2.6	93	

Breakout: 13%   Improve: 39%   Collapse: 23%   Attrition: 16%   MLB: 80%   Comparables: Rich Hill, Corey Kluber, Miguel Gonzalez

McHugh may never recapture the magic of his rookie season, but he continues to craft a nifty career despite his humble beginnings as an 18th-round draft pick out of Berry College. His lack of top-end stuff was exposed in 2016, as he allowed a career-high 25 home runs, 17 of which came off one of his two fastballs (four-seam and cutter). McHugh's curveball is the main event, as it polished off more than half of his strikeouts and limited hitters to just a .365 slugging percentage on contact. He has made a living off of that pitch, and while his fastball is too meaty for him to be a top-of-the-rotation pitcher, it should be enough for the 29-year-old to hold a starting job for the next few years.

Charlie Morton   RHP

Born: 11/12/83   Age: 33   Bats: R   Throws: R   Height: 6'5"   Weight: 235   Entered Pro Ball: Round 3, 2002 Draft (#95 overall)

YEAR	TEAM	LVL	AGE	W	L	SV	G	GS	IP	H	HR	BB/9	K/9	K	GB%	BABIP	WHIP	ERA	FIP	DRA	VORP	WARP	cFIP	MPH
2014	PIT	MLB	30	6	12	0	26	26	157¹	143	9	3.3	7.2	126	58%	.295	1.27	3.72	3.69	3.89	16.5	1.8	103	93.6
2015	IND	AAA	31	1	1	0	2	2	13¹	13	0	2.7	11.5	17	60%	.371	1.27	2.03	1.51	1.90	5.0	0.5	80	
2015	PIT	MLB	31	9	9	0	23	23	129	137	13	2.9	6.7	96	60%	.309	1.38	4.81	4.22	4.04	14.8	1.6	101	94.4
2016	PHI	MLB	32	1	1	0	4	4	17¹	15	1	4.2	9.9	19	66%	.326	1.33	4.15	3.13	3.53	3.5	0.4	92	96.5
2017	HOU	MLB	33	7	6	0	19	19	108¹	106	12	3.6	7.6	91	81%	.298	1.39	4.19	4.31	4.80	5.4	0.6	100	
2018	HOU	MLB	34	7	8	0	22	22	131²	132	16	3.7	7.8	114	81%	.305	1.41	4.16	4.40	4.76	9.9	1.0	109	

Breakout: 6%   Improve: 38%   Collapse: 15%   Attrition: 18%   MLB: 80%   Comparables: Jake Westbrook, Doug Davis, Carlos Zambrano

Never let it be said that the universe doesn't have a sense of humor. When Morton was traded to the Phillies—the team that once employed Roy Halladay, the pitcher who Morton based his delivery on—it led to some patently unfair comparisons between the two. This is unfortunate, because while Morton was never going to be anything close to what Halladay was, this is true for all but a very small handful of pitchers in the history of the game. Morton's problem isn't that he won't be Roy Halladay, it is that he gets hurt so often that he doesn't even get the chance to be Charlie Morton. Four starts into his 2016 campaign, Morton blew out his hamstring running out a bunt and lost his entire season due to surgery. Somewhere out there, perhaps there's a multiverse where a healthy Charlie Morton consistently throws 190-200 innings, is a 3-4 WARP pitcher and is appreciated on his own merits.

Joe Musgrove   RHP

Born: 12/4/92   Age: 24   Bats: R   Throws: R   Height: 6'5"   Weight: 265   Entered Pro Ball: Round 1, 2011 Draft (#46 overall)

YEAR	TEAM	LVL	AGE	W	L	SV	G	GS	IP	H	HR	BB/9	K/9	K	GB%	BABIP	WHIP	ERA	FIP	DRA	VORP	WARP	cFIP	MPH
2014	TCV	A-	21	7	1	0	15	13	77	64	4	1.2	7.8	67	53%	.275	0.96	2.81	2.84	2.21	26.6	2.8	78	
2015	QUD	A	22	4	1	0	5	3	25²	22	0	0.4	8.1	23	51%	.293	0.90	0.70	1.84	2.34	7.8	0.8	81	
2015	LNC	A+	22	4	0	0	6	4	30	28	2	0.3	12.9	43	52%	.366	0.97	2.40	2.08	1.46	11.7	1.3	61	
2015	CCH	AA	22	4	0	1	8	7	45	35	7	1.2	6.6	33	45%	.219	0.91	2.20	4.25	3.78	6.4	0.7	84	
2016	CCH	AA	23	2	1	0	6	4	26¹	19	1	1.0	10.3	30	49%	.265	0.84	0.34	1.74	0.94	11.9	1.3	68	
2016	FRE	AAA	23	5	3	0	10	10	59	60	8	1.1	8.7	57	55%	.317	1.14	3.81	3.96	1.80	23.2	2.4	69	
2016	HOU	MLB	23	4	4	0	11	10	62	59	9	2.3	8.0	55	43%	.289	1.21	4.06	4.14	4.97	2.5	0.3	103	94.6
2017	HOU	MLB	24	6	5	0	46	11	91²	88	10	2.8	7.6	78	53%	.291	1.26	3.89	3.90	4.38	7.8	0.8	100	
2018	HOU	MLB	25	5	4	0	43	9	89¹	78	11	3.8	9.9	98	53%	.291	1.29	3.76	3.99	4.23	9.5	1.0	98	

Breakout: 25%   Improve: 56%   Collapse: 16%   Attrition: 20%   MLB: 89%   Comparables: Vincent Velasquez, Jon Gray, Edinson Volquez

Musgrove emerged from off the prospect radar to earn 10 starts for the Astros following a season-ending injury to Lance McCullers. While his stuff is by no means soft—Musgrove features a fastball that averaged 92 mph and a slider, cutter, changeup and curveball—he has made his living off of plus control and command. Keeping runners off the bases will be imperative in the majors because his arsenal doesn't give him much margin for error. He struggled with home runs in the upper minors and was punished hard for his mistakes in the majors as well. Even with a big-league home run problem, though, Musgrove held his own, and he has worked his way into consideration for Houston's rotation heading into 2017.

David Paulino   RHP

Born: 2/6/94   Age: 23   Bats: R   Throws: R   Height: 6'7"   Weight: 215   Entered Pro Ball: International Free Agent, 2010

YEAR	TEAM	LVL	AGE	W	L	SV	G	GS	IP	H	HR	BB/9	K/9	K	GB%	BABIP	WHIP	ERA	FIP	DRA	VORP	WARP	cFIP	MPH
2015	QUD	A	21	3	2	0	5	5	28²	21	0	2.2	10.0	32	47%	.292	0.98	1.57	2.00	2.18	9.7	1.0	81	
2015	LNC	A+	21	1	1	1	6	5	29¹	24	1	3.1	9.2	30	40%	.295	1.16	4.91	3.40	3.39	5.3	0.6	95	
2016	CCH	AA	22	5	2	1	14	9	64	47	3	1.5	10.1	72	40%	.280	0.91	1.83	2.20	2.17	20.1	2.2	76	
2016	FRE	AAA	22	0	2	0	3	3	14	16	1	3.9	12.9	20	45%	.385	1.57	3.86	3.08	2.33	4.7	0.5	81	
2016	HOU	MLB	22	0	1	0	3	1	7	6	0	3.9	2.6	2	44%	.261	1.29	5.14	4.25	6.31	-0.9	-0.1	119	94.8
2017	*HOU*	*MLB*	*23*	*4*	*4*	*0*	*22*	*13*	*72²*	*75*	*10*	*3.5*	*7.9*	*64*	*57%*	*.305*	*1.42*	*4.42*	*4.43*	*5.03*	*3.1*	*0.3*	*118*	
2018	*HOU*	*MLB*	*24*	*7*	*7*	*0*	*28*	*21*	*146²*	*129*	*20*	*4.4*	*10.6*	*173*	*57%*	*.299*	*1.37*	*3.98*	*4.20*	*4.53*	*11.9*	*1.2*	*104*	

Breakout: 32%   Improve: 41%   Collapse: 8%   Attrition: 25%   MLB: 57%   Comparables: *Frankie Montas, Macay McBride, Matt Harvey*

A giant with an aptly huge fastball, Paulino dominated the upper minors and rocketed his way to the big leagues in 2016. After Tommy John surgery in 2013, Paulino understandably dropped off the prospect radar, but he has only looked stronger and stronger as the injury recedes into the past. His fastball reached as high as 94 and has exceptional movement aided by Paulino's height, which gives the pitch a nasty downward plane and creates ground balls. That pitch alone could be enough for Paulino to carve out a fine career as a back-end starter or in the bullpen. If he can develop his secondary pitches—he mostly used a curveball but also flashed a changeup and slider—Paulino could work his way into the middle of Houston's rotation.

Brad Peacock   RHP

Born: 2/2/88   Age: 29   Bats: R   Throws: R   Height: 6'1"   Weight: 210   Entered Pro Ball: Round 41, 2006 Draft (#1231 overall)

YEAR	TEAM	LVL	AGE	W	L	SV	G	GS	IP	H	HR	BB/9	K/9	K	GB%	BABIP	WHIP	ERA	FIP	DRA	VORP	WARP	cFIP	MPH
2014	HOU	MLB	26	4	9	0	28	24	131²	136	20	4.8	8.1	119	40%	.309	1.56	4.72	5.01	5.27	-6.7	-0.7	116	94.6
2015	HOU	MLB	27	0	1	0	1	1	5	5	0	3.6	5.4	3	31%	.312	1.40	5.40	3.70	4.88	0.1	0.0	107	92.3
2016	FRE	AAA	28	5	6	0	22	21	117	122	11	3.1	9.2	119	44%	.335	1.38	4.23	4.09	2.77	33.3	3.4	89	
2016	HOU	MLB	28	0	1	0	10	5	31²	21	6	4.0	8.0	28	41%	.190	1.11	3.69	5.13	5.01	0.9	0.1	107	94.1
2017	*HOU*	*MLB*	*29*	*3*	*3*	*0*	*10*	*10*	*50*	*49*	*7*	*4.0*	*8.2*	*46*	*47%*	*.295*	*1.42*	*4.45*	*4.60*	*5.08*	*0.9*	*0.1*	*100*	
2018	*HOU*	*MLB*	*30*	*7*	*10*	*0*	*27*	*27*	*159*	*148*	*25*	*4.9*	*9.7*	*172*	*47%*	*.296*	*1.47*	*4.55*	*4.81*	*5.19*	*4.2*	*0.4*	*120*	

Breakout: 18%   Improve: 42%   Collapse: 14%   Attrition: 16%   MLB: 72%   Comparables: *Tom Koehler, Darrell Rasner, Brian Burres*

Peacock still has the sharp stuff that made him an intriguing prospect earlier in the decade, and at just 29 years old that will be enough to keep earning him chances to prove he belongs in a rotation. But when he did get a chance with the Astros in 2016, it was more of the same: iffy control, poor command and simply too many walks and home runs allowed to be a productive major leaguer. For now, Peacock serves as perhaps the perfect example of the Quad-A pitcher.

Franklin Perez   RHP

Born: 12/6/97   Age: 19   Bats: R   Throws: R   Height: 6'3"   Weight: 197   Entered Pro Ball: International Free Agent, 2014

YEAR	TEAM	LVL	AGE	W	L	SV	G	GS	IP	H	HR	BB/9	K/9	K	GB%	BABIP	WHIP	ERA	FIP	DRA	VORP	WARP	cFIP	MPH
2016	QUD	A	18	3	3	1	15	10	66²	63	1	2.6	10.1	75	39%	.344	1.23	2.84	2.37	2.17	20.3	2.2	81	
2017	*HOU*	*MLB*	*19*	*3*	*2*	*1*	*25*	*9*	*53²*	*73*	*1*	*0.2*	*0.6*	*3*	*47%*	*.320*	*1.39*	*3.23*	*3.31*	*3.78*	*12.8*	*1.3*	*83*	
2018	*HOU*	*MLB*	*20*	*4*	*3*	*0*	*22*	*12*	*103*	*120*	*2*	*0.2*	*2.9*	*33*		*.307*	*1.20*	*2.58*	*2.80*	*3.02*	*19.1*	*2.0*	*60*	

Breakout: 0%   Improve: 0%   Collapse: 0%   Attrition: 0%   MLB: 0%   Comparables: *Roberto Osuna, Jordan Lyles, Vicente Campos*

At just 19 years old, Perez is already showing remarkable feel for pitching. Perez doesn't have just a 95 mph fastball, an average curveball with plus potential and a nasty changeup. Most impressively, he is already showing the ability to use those off-speed pitches, primarily his already-plus changeup, outside of pitchers' counts. At 6-foot-3, Perez has both the body and the stuff to become a mid-rotation starter. The real tests will begin for Perez now, as he has thrown just 66 innings above rookie ball. If he can maintain his control and continue to improve the feel of his off-speed stuff, the big righty could become a top-of-the-rotation starter down the line. Perhaps the best news for Houston, though? Perez's arsenal is already good enough to see him as a successful starter even if he never develops better than mediocre command.

Tony Sipp   LHP

Born: 7/12/83   Age: 33   Bats: L   Throws: L   Height: 6'0"   Weight: 190   Entered Pro Ball: Round 45, 2004 Draft (#1333 overall)

YEAR	TEAM	LVL	AGE	W	L	SV	G	GS	IP	H	HR	BB/9	K/9	K	GB%	BABIP	WHIP	ERA	FIP	DRA	VORP	WARP	cFIP	MPH
2014	ELP	AAA	30	1	1	0	11	0	14²	14	1	1.2	12.9	21	38%	.361	1.09	4.30	2.34	4.24	1.8	0.2	101	
2014	HOU	MLB	30	4	3	4	56	0	50²	28	5	3.0	11.2	63	35%	.205	0.89	3.38	2.96	2.53	11.0	1.2	82	94.9
2015	HOU	MLB	31	3	4	0	60	0	54¹	41	5	2.5	10.3	62	41%	.271	1.03	1.99	2.90	3.15	9.4	1.0	87	93.2
2016	HOU	MLB	32	1	2	1	60	0	43²	52	12	3.7	8.2	40	37%	.323	1.60	4.95	6.15	5.49	-2.5	-0.3	119	93.2
2017	*HOU*	*MLB*	*33*	*3*	*3*	*0*	*55*	*0*	*57²*	*52*	*8*	*3.5*	*9.1*	*58*	*42%*	*.288*	*1.29*	*4.23*	*4.21*	*4.72*	*1.7*	*0.2*	*100*	
2018	*HOU*	*MLB*	*34*	*2*	*1*	*0*	*35*	*0*	*37¹*	*35*	*6*	*3.8*	*9.4*	*39*	*42%*	*.292*	*1.36*	*4.13*	*4.38*	*4.75*	*1.2*	*0.1*	*107*	

Breakout: 17%   Improve: 36%   Collapse: 19%   Attrition: 16%   MLB: 79%   Comparables: *Joe Thatcher, Frank Francisco, Jason Motte*

Nothing seemed particularly different about Sipp's pitches from a velocity standpoint in 2016—at least, not on the way in. But after being one of baseball's most reliable left-handed setup men in 2015, Sipp found himself battered by opposing hitters. He served up 12 home runs in 2016, more than he surrendered in 2014 and 2015 combined, and he failed to strike out a batter per inning for the first time since 2012, his last season with Cleveland. Luckily for Sipp, he'll be well-paid while he tries to figure things out; 2016 was the first year of a three-year, $18 million contract.

Ashur Tolliver LHP

Born: 1/24/88 Age: 29 Bats: L Throws: L Height: 6'0" Weight: 170 Entered Pro Ball: Round 5, 2009 Draft (#146 overall)

YEAR	TEAM	LVL	AGE	W	L	SV	G	GS	IP	H	HR	BB/9	K/9	K	GB%	BABIP	WHIP	ERA	FIP	DRA	VORP	WARP	cFIP	MPH
2014	FRD	A+	26	0	1	2	9	0	14²	14	1	1.2	9.2	15	50%	.302	1.09	2.45	2.77	2.43	4.5	0.5	83	
2014	BOW	AA	26	3	1	0	18	1	22²	27	1	2.0	9.9	25	43%	.394	1.41	3.18	2.38	2.45	6.1	0.7	82	
2015	BOW	AA	27	1	2	1	39	2	58²	51	2	4.4	9.4	61	40%	.312	1.36	2.91	3.12	5.76	-6.6	-0.7	102	
2016	BOW	AA	28	1	1	2	18	0	26	22	4	2.8	8.7	25	46%	.273	1.15	2.42	4.36	2.47	6.5	0.7	85	
2016	BAL	MLB	28	1	0	0	5	0	4²	5	1	5.8	9.6	5	36%	.308	1.71	5.79	5.68	5.03	0.0	0.0	110	96.0
2016	NOR	AAA	28	0	0	0	11	0	12²	11	0	4.3	11.4	16	39%	.355	1.34	1.42	2.30	3.24	2.4	0.3	94	
2017	HOU	MLB	29	1	1	0	25	0	26	27	3	3.9	7.4	21	53%	.301	1.49	4.72	4.42	5.11	-0.4	0.0	100	
2018	HOU	MLB	30	1	0	0	25	0	26	25	3	5.2	10.0	29	53%	.313	1.53	4.20	4.43	4.81	0.7	0.1	109	

Breakout: 9% Improve: 9% Collapse: 6% Attrition: 10% MLB: 15% *Comparables: Tyler Sturdevant, Juan Perez, Pedro Viola*

It's usually difficult to learn anything about a player from 4.2 innings, and that's all Tolliver has given us at the major-league level. However, it was enough for the Orioles, and they waived him. Claimed by the Angels in September, the lefty offers a mid-90s fastball and an impressive minor-league strikeout rate. Right now he's organizational filler, but for the price of a spot on the 40-man roster Tolliver's fastball is exactly the kind of no-downside addition the Angels needed to make.

Forrest Whitley RHP

Born: 9/15/97 Age: 19 Bats: R Throws: R Height: 6'7" Weight: 240 Entered Pro Ball: Round 1, 2016 Draft (#17 overall)

The top right-handed high school arm in Texas, Whitley remained in his home state after the Astros used the 17th overall pick of the 2016 draft to secure his rights. A cool $3.148 million signing bonus made spurning an offer from Florida State an easy decision. Whitley already owns a fastball that touches 97 mph and has the potential to develop into a front-line starter. Ironically enough, the 6-foot-7 Whitley calls Tim Lincecum his favorite pitcher. Despite their polar opposite statures, Whitley considers himself a changeup artist like Lincecum. If Whitley can develop a changeup anything like The Freak's to go with that huge fastball? Look out.

LINEOUTS

Hitters

NAME	POS	TEAM	LVL	AGE	PA	R	2B	3B	HR	RBI	BB	K	SB	CS	AVG/OBP/SLG	TAv	VORP	BABIP	BRR	FRAA	WARP
Andrew Aplin	CF	FRE	AAA	25	447	61	15	4	5	32	42	98	21	9	.223/.300/.318	.228	4.1	.284	6.0	CF(103): 5.8, RF(11): 0.6	1.1
Daz Cameron	OF	QUD	A	19	87	5	2	2	0	6	8	33	4	3	.143/.221/.221	.170	-5.4	.244	0.1	CF(10): -0.4, LF(6): -0.3	-0.7
	OF	TCV	A-	19	89	13	3	1	2	14	6	26	8	2	.278/.352/.418	.285	4.7	.392	0.0	CF(15): 0.4, LF(2): -0.3	0.5
Ronnie Dawson	OF	TCV	A-	21	291	41	13	1	7	36	41	66	12	6	.225/.351/.373	.257	3.6	.281	-0.5	LF(44): 3.4, RF(12): -1.1	0.6
Jon Kemmer	OF	FRE	AAA	25	452	53	24	4	18	69	38	128	8	10	.265/.334/.477	.292	20.5	.342	-3.1	RF(59): -4.3, LF(48): -2.9	1.4
Ramon Laureano	RF	LNC	A+	21	357	69	19	5	10	60	50	86	33	11	.317/.426/.519	.327	35.1	.411	1.2	CF(30): 4.4, RF(23): 1.7	4.6
	RF	CCH	AA	21	148	20	9	2	5	13	20	33	10	3	.323/.432/.548	.356	18.9	.407	1	CF(20): 3.6, RF(15): 1.3	2.6
Jason Martin	OF	LNC	A+	20	462	74	22	7	23	75	55	108	20	12	.270/.357/.533	.290	27.8	.310	1.2	CF(54): -7.9, LF(26): -5.2	0.9
Miguelangel Sierra	SS	TCV	A-	18	102	6	2	1	0	5	7	34	0	0	.140/.216/.183	.172	-6.2	.220	-0.9	SS(24): -3.2	-1.0
Jon Singleton	1B	FRE	AAA	24	501	62	17	0	20	66	83	124	0	0	.202/.337/.390	.271	3.8	.232	-7.3	1B(63): -6.0, LF(7): -0.4	-0.3
Max Stassi	C	FRE	AAA	25	266	21	12	1	7	32	20	65	1	0	.230/.294/.374	.233	5.1	.287	1.1	C(66): 8.9	1.4
	C	HOU	MLB	25	13	1	0	0	0	0	0	5	0	0	.077/.077/.077	.047	-2.3	.125	-0.1	C(8): -0.5	-0.3
Garrett Stubbs	C	LNC	A+	23	244	35	13	0	6	38	29	37	10	3	.291/.385/.442	.279	14.2	.323	1.0	C(37): 1.1	1.6
	C	CCH	AA	23	137	23	9	1	4	16	14	11	5	0	.325/.401/.517	.338	17.9	.330	1.4	C(30): -3.2	1.6
Stephen Wrenn	OF	TCV	A-	21	171	30	8	2	9	27	18	40	8	1	.282/.365/.544	.315	11.4	.327	0.2	CF(20): 0.3, LF(10): -0.1	1.2
	OF	QUD	A	21	150	16	7	3	3	12	7	38	7	2	.236/.277/.393	.259	5.2	.303	1.4	CF(23): 1.7, LF(9): 0.2	0.8

Excellent plate discipline numbers made **Andrew Aplin** a favorite of stat-based scouting systems, but after stalling out at Triple-A the 25-year-old outfielder is once again looking like nothing more than an org guy. ❖ Part of the Ken Giles trade, the young **Jonathan Arauz** has a nifty glove at shortstop. That glove will have to carry him, because his bat looks mediocre at best. ❖ **Daz Cameron**, son of former big leaguer Mike, had his 2016 season ended prematurely when his left index finger was broken by a pitch in July. His tools are excellent, but he has played just 40 games above rookie ball. ❖ The fantastically named **Gilberto Celestino** was considered one of the most polished of last year's July 2 international class. He'll try to turn his athleticism and excellent makeup into a star career in center field. ❖ Venezuelan shortstop **Yorbin Ceuta** was part of Houston's 2016 international spending spree, earning a $2 million bonus. His pop isn't expecrted to be much, but strong discipline and fielding could carry him to the majors. ❖ **Ronnie Dawson** was a true five-tool talent for Ohio State, where he hit for average and power, stole bases with regularity and efficiency, and exhibited excellent plate discipline. He had a slow start at Low-A, but still took his walks and showed occasional power. ❖ Despite little to no prospect hype, lefty outfielder **Jon Kemmer** has kept plugging away, as he mashed 18 homers in a modestly successful campaign in his first crack at Triple-A. A southpaw with a bit of pop but no glove for center field, his profile screams fourth outfielder. ❖ **Ramon Laureano**, a generic 16th round pick in 2014, went supernova offensively last season, leading the minors in on-base percentage with a .428 mark across High-A and Double-A. He makes the most of his size and speed, giving the Astros yet another potential everyday outfielder. ❖ **Jason Martin** mashed 52 extra-base hits in the California League—sure, it's a hitter's paradise, but thats still impressive for a 20-year-old eighth-round draft pick. ❖ He smacked 11 home runs in just 31 rookie ball games, but reality hit **Miguelangel Sierra** hard upon elevation to full-season ball. The power is nice, but Sierra has to figure out how to make consistent contact. ❖ The life has departed from **Jon Singleton**'s bat. After a merely pedestrian season at Triple-A, Singleton will have to fight an uphill battle to make the Opening Day roster despite the fact that he remains under contract through 2018. ❖ The promise **Max Stassi** showed as a 22-year-old has never been realized. After 69 more exceptionally mediocre games at the Triple-A level, Stassi's prospect stock is firmly at rock bottom. ❖ The undersized **Garrett Stubbs** didn't let his 5-foot-

10 frame stop him in 2016, as he used his sharp hitter's mind and contact abilities to shoot through the low minors. The question is if his body can handle 100-plus games of catching, as his bat may not have enough pop to play anywhere else. ❖ **Stephen Wrenn** slipped to the sixth round because injuries wracked the end of his college career. His first pro season went excellently, and with 32 extra-base hits in just 71 games he's making scouts look silly for doubting his recovery skills.

Pitchers

NAME	TEAM	LVL	AGE	W	L	SV	G	GS	IP	H	HR	BB/9	K/9	K	GB%	BABIP	WHIP	ERA	FIP	DRA	VORP	WARP	cFIP	MPH
Rogelio Armenteros	QUD	A	22	0	2	0	4	3	18²	12	0	1.4	9.6	20	67%	.245	0.80	1.93	1.98	2.15	5.8	0.6	79	
	LNC	A+	22	6	4	1	19	16	90¹	87	13	3.7	10.7	107	39%	.323	1.37	4.18	4.58	2.41	30.4	3.1	88	
	CCH	AA	22	2	0	0	3	3	18¹	17	1	2.0	6.4	13	36%	.308	1.15	1.96	3.13	4.73	0.7	0.1	104	
Akeem Bostick	TCV	A-	21	1	1	0	2	2	11	10	1	0.0	5.7	7	43%	.265	0.91	3.27	3.45	3.75	1.8	0.2	94	
	LNC	A+	21	5	3	0	14	13	68²	79	7	5.5	6.3	48	40%	.327	1.76	4.98	5.69	9.44	-30.4	-3.1	131	
Kevin Chapman	FRE	AAA	28	3	4	0	51	0	61	68	5	4.0	11.2	76	46%	.364	1.56	4.87	3.97	2.17	18.9	1.9	93	
	HOU	MLB	28	0	0	0	9	0	8	15	0	4.5	6.8	6	47%	.469	2.38	9.00	3.11	5.84	-0.8	-0.1	112	93.0
Riley Ferrell	LNC	A+	22	0	1	4	8	0	10	9	1	1.8	12.6	14	62%	.348	1.10	1.80	2.81	2.19	3.2	0.3	81	
Reymin Guduan	CCH	AA	24	1	0	2	9	0	13	7	1	2.1	13.2	19	62%	.240	0.77	0.69	1.95	1.46	4.7	0.5	62	
	FRE	AAA	24	2	3	0	34	0	43	43	2	7.1	9.2	44	52%	.333	1.79	5.23	4.65	6.13	-5.6	-0.6	112	
Brady Rodgers	FRE	AAA	25	12	4	0	22	22	132	129	7	1.6	7.9	116	48%	.319	1.15	2.86	3.20	1.62	54.6	5.6	78	
	HOU	MLB	25	0	1	0	5	1	8¹	15	0	7.6	3.2	3	24%	.405	2.64	15.12	5.27	8.46	-3.1	-0.3	136	92.9

Cuban international free agent **Rogelio Armenteros** has three pitches with plus potential, but will need to improve his command to become more than a back-end starter. ❖ **Akeem Bostick** scuffled at High-A, but the lanky right-hander has enough raw projection in his fastball-curveball combo that there's room to dream if he can just iron out his mechanics. ❖ **Kevin Chapman** continues to get chances thanks to his elite strikeout ability, but he lacks the control he'll need to stick for more than few games at a time. ❖ Plans for **Riley Ferrell** to get fast-tracked to the big leagues were cut short when he needed season-ending surgery in May to repair an aneurysm in his throwing shoulder. Ferrell's big fastball-slider combo and lack of command suggests his future is in the bullpen. ❖ If **Reymin Guduan** could find a semblance of control, he could find himself in the Astros' bullpen in a hurry. Unfortunately, with a career 7.1 BB/9 in the minors, Guduan may have to dig all the way to Hades to find that apple. ❖ **Cionel Perez** became a Cuban Serie Nacional star as a teenager and earned over $5 million as an international free agent from the Astros as a result. His off-speed stuff is raw, but Houston believed in his projection enough to eat significant bonus pool penalties to sign him. ❖ **Brady Rodgers** exhibited stellar control and improved his strikeout rate at Triple-A in 2016, earning himself five games in Houston. He's a precise enough pitcher that we should expect him to hit the Astros' rotation at some point, but his stuff may not be good enough to handle The Show.

KANSAS CITY ROYALS

Essay by Trevor Strunk

Player comments by Craig Brown and BP staff

If ever there was a group of people who wanted to understand the ins and outs of futility and disillusionment, it was 18th- and 19th-century German philosophers. Ah, you thought I was going to say "Kansas City Royals fans." We'll get there eventually, but first I want to take a quick detour into the world of the grim perspectives of Arthur Schopenhauer and the decidedly less grim but equally depressing visions of Friedrich Schiller.

Schopenhauer was largely committed to describing the world through a phenomenology of pessimism, arguing (as the *Stanford Encyclopedia of Philosophy* helpfully puts it) that "in the face of a world filled with endless strife, we ought to minimize our natural desires for the sake of achieving a more tranquil frame of mind and a disposition towards universal beneficence." Schiller, far from a pessimist and who hoped we might make the best of things, argued most famously in the realm of the aesthetic, connecting truth and beauty as Germans so famously do. So where do a crusty pragmatic pessimistic and an aesthetician meet to chat? Why, the clown responded, at the hospital of course.

Schopenhauer writes in his *Psychological Observations* that "it is a curious fact that in bad days we can very vividly recall the good time that is now no more; but that in good days, we have only a very cold and imperfect memory of the bad." When we're happy and well, Schopenhauer tells us, we barely make a note of it, but when we are miserable or sick, that past moment is all we can remember. Schiller, coming at this from the opposite angle in his *On Naive And Sentimental Poetry*, argues that the contemporary reader has lost the sense of the natural that the ancients had, that our feeling for the natural as compared to, say, Homer is "the feeling of the sick for health." Again, we get a feeling for something past, never to return, only by feeling its absence: you never knew how good you had it.

And this, of course, is where the Royals come in. In 2015, as you might already know, the Royals won the World Series and broke one of the more persistent droughts in contemporary MLB. While the 30 years between 1985 and 2015 were certainly no 108-year Cubsian walk in the desert, the Royals had to suffer through botched first-round picks, terrible ownership and leadership decisions and decades of some of the worst baseball that you could wish upon friends or enemies. Between 1985-2015, the Royals lost

ROYALS PROSPECTUS
2016 W-L: 81-81, 3RD IN AL CENTRAL

Pythag	.475	21st	DER	.702	14th
RS/G	4.17	23rd	B-Age	28.5	14th
RA/G	4.4	13th	P-Age	29.9	28th
TAv	.248	30th	Salary	$131.5M	15th
BRR	-1.27	17th	M$/MW	$3.6M	13th
TAv-P	.262	15th	DL Days	937	13th
FIP	4.38	21st	$ on DL	21%	23rd

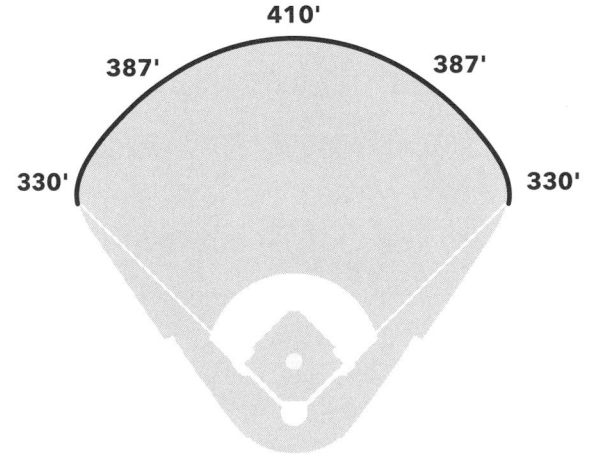

Outfield wall profile: **8'**

Three-Year Park Factors

Runs	Runs/RH	Runs/LH	HR/RH	HR/LH
103	106	105	92	101

Top Hitter WARP	2.2	Lorenzo Cain
Top Pitcher WARP	3.8	Danny Duffy
Top Prospect		Hunter Dozier

2016 Hit List Ranking

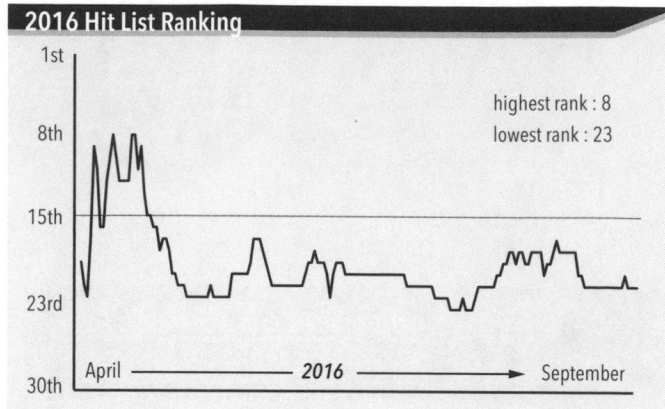

highest rank : 8
lowest rank : 23

April — 2016 → September

Committed Payroll (in millions)

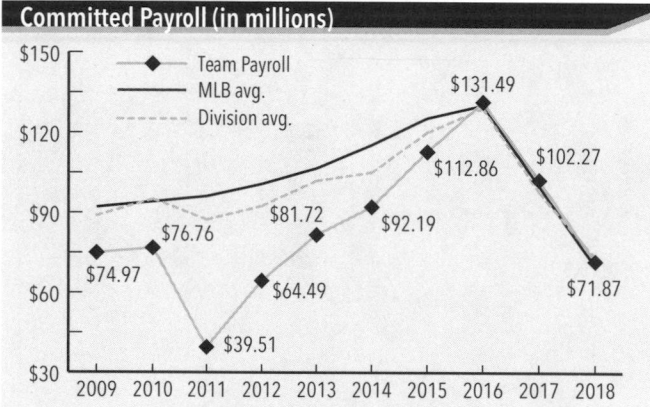

- ◆ Team Payroll
- — MLB avg.
- --- Division avg.

$131.49
$112.86
$102.27
$92.19
$81.72
$76.76
$74.97
$71.87
$64.49
$39.51

2009 2010 2011 2012 2013 2014 2015 2016 2017 2018

Farm System Ranking

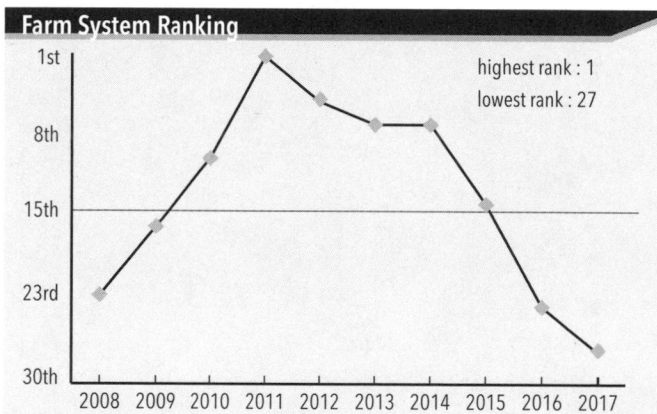

highest rank : 1
lowest rank : 27

2008 2009 2010 2011 2012 2013 2014 2015 2016 2017

Personnel

General Manager:
Dayton Moore

AGM, Player Personnel:
J.J. Picollo

AGM, MLB and International Ops:
Rene Francisco

Assistant General Manager:
Scott Sharp

Manager:
Ned Yost

BP Alumni:
Mike Groopman
Daniel Mack

100 games four times (2002, 2004, 2005, 2006) and finished above .500 nine times. That means there were 21 seasons of losing baseball for the Royals before they won their World Series. Basically the lifespan of the most hard-luck and downtrodden adult you can imagine.

And then they won! They won the World Series after being Giantsed out of it the year before and finally every fan let out a deep sigh of relief, as the Carlos Beltrans and Johnny Damons and Zack Greinkes of the past had been exorcised (not to mention the Brian Bannister- and Gil Meche-shaped ghosts haunting the clubhouse). There were lots of Royals fans who felt a deep sense of joy, fulfillment and health after three decades of fan sickness. Like Schopenhauer and Schiller suggest, that first feeling of health is memorable and impactful. In no way do I wish to take that away from the 2015 Royals. But, let's remember that 2016 came next.

The hangover year. This is the year every fan bakes into their World Series joy, the year that's supposed to be the "defense" of the title, but (particularly for fans who haven't had the chance to savor a championship in a while) basically serves as the one unassailable year for the players and coaches. "Ah well," a Royals fan might say wistfully, "the team finished exactly .500 and we got some bad luck and worse performances, but flags fly forever." And indeed, injuries to bullpen studs Wade Davis and Greg Holland, the rotation regressions of Yordano Ventura and Edinson Volquez and the almost lineup-wide offensive slump put all of the ingredients together for a hangover stew.

There were also some bright spots. Ian Kennedy put together a credible year and perma-prospect Danny Duffy finally came into his own. Prospects debuted at improbably young ages and the team was certainly more fun than its early 2000s iterations. But the Royals did not follow up 2015 with anything particularly inspiring, leaning hard into their post-championship gap year as the Indians played the role of 2014 Royals. Every party comes to an end, though.

We don't feel health when we have it, Schopenhauer tells us, and when we have a sickness, Schiller might chime in, health can feel so far away as to feel beyond memory. And so the immortality of the World Series trophy, the parade, the endless string of player reaction GIFs all begins to feel like a movie that happened to some other, distant version of yourself. When you're left with an uncertain rotation, a volatile lineup and a tapped-out farm system, the joy of yesteryear can feel as far off as Homer to a German living through the Industrial Revolution.

There are positives and 2017 need not turn into the preface to another three decades in the desert, but a fairly dramatic stop is in the not-so-distant future with many prominent Royals entering their final seasons of team control and Davis already traded away to the Cubs. They won't be able to keep everyone, and the makeup and personality of the club is going to dramatically change. If they're winning in July, this could mean that they make one last push as a group to win a second championship and cement their legacy. Or it could mean a massive firesale. Either way, 2017 is laden with significance for the Royals in a way that they could not have expected in 2015.

If 2015 is the party where you feel so good and well and loved that you order everyone the exact rare whiskey and top-shelf liquor they want, 2017 is the moment you get the bill and you have to ask yourself if the whole thing was worth it. It's distasteful and certainly not the kind of thing you should be thinking about in the throes of victory, but there's a hard cost to pay at the end of any moment of ecstatic joy and the Royals are staring that in the face. Despite our best intentions, we never really celebrate as much as we should in the moment, before the moment becomes another frame in the patina of team-based nostalgia, as ineffable and ghostly as George Brett's pine tar or Don Denkinger's blown call.

And so we see the Royals in the unenviable position of Schopenhauer's sad man or Schiller's sick one: longing for something they had and realizing that the absence of that thing is the only way they could realize what they're missing. Take heart, however, Royals fans—your team is certainly a contender this year. If the pitching holds up in some places and improves in others, and if the team starts hitting a bit more like its 2015 self, the Royals could push the Indians for the AL Central and certainly contend for a Wild Card. I truly would not be shocked if they won 90 games, a fairly modest improvement over their 81 wins last year. This could absolutely be that final, group-defining push.

But don't get *too* excited, because there are two dire truths that I must leave you with: First, even if they win it all in 2017, 2019 is waiting for you like the dour waiter at the end of the hall holding the bill. This is the curse of baseball, after all—that you're left wanting more even after being filled to the brim with agony, happiness or boredom. Two championships won't actually be enough, even if it makes for a more satisfying narrative ending. You still have the three-year cycle if you're a Royal or a Yankee.

And the second dour truth? Even at the next championship—and there will be one, despite the negative immediate outlook—you won't be able to really appreciate it enough to bottle up the feeling for the droughts. That's the lesson we have to take from Schopenhauer and Schiller, who many see as overly pessimistic or harsh. Neither of them is saying that the strong person can maintain a feeling for the happy times when they're happening, there's no positive account of the problem of health and sickness for either writer. The moral of their story is that the inability to really enjoy health or good fortune in its moment is a human failing, unavoidable and impossible to fight against.

In a way the Royals are the perfect exemplar of this problem, a problem that is true to baseball at its very core. We are pessimists as fans, always at our best when our team is at our worst and we can live in angry recrimination of the club or far-flung hope for a distant prospect-fueled future. The 2015 Royals may have the storybook ending, but as the philosophers will tell us, the 2017 Royals have the truth of their situation more fully in view. And that, even if not quite as tangible as a World Series trophy, is worthy of deep and serious consideration as a fan of the sport in general. ◾

—Trevor Strunk is an author
of Baseball Prospectus

HITTERS

Jorge Bonifacio　RF

Born: 6/4/93　Age: 24　Bats: R　Throws: R　Height: 6'1"　Weight: 195　Entered Pro Ball: International Free Agent, 2009

YEAR	TEAM	LVL	AGE	PA	R	2B	3B	HR	RBI	BB	K	SB	CS	AVG/OBP/SLG	TAv	VORP	BABIP	BRR	FRAA	WARP
2014	NWA	AA	21	566	49	20	4	4	51	50	127	8	3	.230/.302/.309	.232	-3.3	.295	3.3	RF(125): -12.5 • LF(2): -0.1	-1.7
2015	NWA	AA	22	536	60	30	2	17	64	42	126	3	2	.240/.305/.416	.256	7.1	.287	0.1	RF(97): -6.2 • LF(18): -1.3	0.0
2016	OMA	AAA	23	558	82	22	6	19	86	51	130	6	2	.277/.351/.461	.290	29.3	.339	1.2	RF(72): 10.3 • LF(50): 2.6	4.3
2017	KCA	MLB	24	250	25	11	2	7	28	18	66	1	0	.233/.294/.382	.233	0.5	.295	-0.2	RF -2, LF -0	-0.2
2018	KCA	MLB	25	344	41	15	2	10	40	26	90	1	1	.240/.305/.399	.245	1.9	.302	-0.4	RF -2, LF 0	-0.1

Breakout: 4%　Improve: 13%　Collapse: 5%　Attrition: 19%　MLB: 21%　*Comparables: Scott Van Slyke, Tyler Austin, Chris Pettit*

From top-10 prospect lists to off the radar in a flash, Bonifacio reestablished his prospect cred with his best offensive season since 2013. His bat speed and solid mechanics can translate into pop and improved patience meant he saw better pitches he could crush. When he arrived in the organization, he was more apt to take the ball to the opposite field. The power has developed as he's become more of a pull hitter. However, questions remain about his ability to consistently reach base. The younger brother of Emilio, his best tool is his right arm, which he pairs with solid outfield instincts. Welcome back.

Billy Burns OF

Born: 8/30/89   Age: 27   Bats: B   Throws: R   Height: 5'9"   Weight: 170   Entered Pro Ball: Round 32, 2011 Draft (#967 overall)

YEAR	TEAM	LVL	AGE	PA	R	2B	3B	HR	RBI	BB	K	SB	CS	AVG/OBP/SLG	TAv	VORP	BABIP	BRR	FRAA	WARP
2014	MID	AA	24	421	57	20	3	1	23	44	65	51	5	.250/.333/.330	.253	14.2	.298	4.9	CF(81): 7.0 • LF(6): -1.8	2.1
2014	SAC	AAA	24	121	17	2	0	0	5	9	19	3	1	.193/.254/.211	.174	-7.4	.233	0.5	CF(28): 2.0	-0.5
2014	OAK	MLB	24	6	4	0	0	0	0	0	0	3	1	.167/.167/.167	.158	-1.0	.167	-0.6	CF(1): -0.2	-0.1
2015	NAS	AAA	25	101	18	2	3	0	3	9	17	5	2	.308/.370/.396	.295	7.3	.378	0.5	CF(21): 0.3	0.8
2015	OAK	MLB	25	555	70	18	9	5	42	26	81	26	8	.294/.334/.392	.265	21.4	.339	2.4	CF(125): -13.0	0.9
2016	OAK	MLB	26	292	32	11	4	0	12	10	30	14	3	.234/.270/.303	.206	-2.6	.261	4.6	CF(69): -2.3 • RF(4): -0.2	-0.5
2016	NAS	AAA	26	44	7	1	0	0	4	2	12	4	0	.293/.326/.317	.246	1.5	.414	0.8	CF(10): -0.6	0.1
2016	KCA	MLB	26	40	7	0	0	0	1	0	7	3	2	.243/.275/.243	.203	-0.9	.290	0.4	CF(11): -1.2 • LF(6): 0.1	-0.2
2017	KCA	MLB	27	91	10	3	1	1	7	5	15	5	1	.259/.305/.351	.234	0.9	.302	0.7	LF -2	-0.2
2018	KCA	MLB	28	268	28	10	3	3	25	16	46	14	3	.260/.309/.364	.231	0.6	.302	2.1	LF -6	-0.5

Breakout: 2%   Improve: 34%   Collapse: 6%   Attrition: 15%   MLB: 80%   Comparables: *Joey Gathright, Nook Logan, Tony Gwynn*

Have you ever gone to the grocery store, walked down the peanut butter aisle and grabbed a jumbo-sized container of creamy only to get home and realize you already have four unopened jars in your pantry? That's what happened to Dayton Moore when he acquired Burns from the A's. On a roster built around plenty of outfield speed, the Royals general manager spun Brett Eibner for another wheels guy who lacks the plate discipline gene. Mmmmm … peanut butter.

Drew Butera C

Born: 8/9/83   Age: 33   Bats: R   Throws: R   Height: 6'1"   Weight: 200   Entered Pro Ball: Round 5, 2005 Draft (#149 overall)

YEAR	TEAM	LVL	AGE	PA	R	2B	3B	HR	RBI	BB	K	SB	CS	AVG/OBP/SLG	TAv	VORP	BABIP	BRR	FRAA	WARP
2014	LAN	MLB	30	192	16	6	1	3	14	17	41	0	0	.188/.267/.288	.214	-0.6	.227	-0.2	C(57): 5.6 • P(2): -0.0	0.6
2015	ANA	MLB	31	21	3	0	0	0	0	0	2	0	1	.190/.190/.190	.180	-1.0	.211	-0.2	C(7): -0.8 • 1B(3): -0.0	-0.2
2015	KCA	MLB	31	99	6	3	0	1	5	6	24	0	0	.198/.266/.267	.202	-2.6	.262	-1.0	C(42): -2.1 • 1B(5): 0.0	-0.5
2016	KCA	MLB	32	133	18	10	1	4	16	8	36	0	0	.285/.328/.480	.268	6.0	.373	-1.1	C(51): 0.3 • P(2): -0.0	0.7
2017	KCA	MLB	33	124	11	5	1	2	11	8	29	0	0	.218/.271/.325	.214	-0.3	.269	-0.2	C -0	-0.3
2018	KCA	MLB	34	153	15	6	1	3	14	9	37	0	0	.213/.265/.320	.205	-3.5	.263	-0.5	C -1	-0.5

Breakout: 1%   Improve: 33%   Collapse: 17%   Attrition: 30%   MLB: 86%   Comparables: *Humberto Quintero, Vance Wilson, Wil Nieves*

Butera is the Royals' glue guy. A defense-first backup catcher with a glorious head of hair, he's known more for his celebratory hair flips when he reaches base than actually, you know, reaching base. Seriously. A cursory Google search of "Drew Butera hair flip" returns 11,000 results. If this backup-catching thing doesn't work out, he's plenty adept at toeing the slab in blowouts, working a fastball that averages 88 mph along with a clever changeup in a pair of mop-up appearances. And if this backup-catching or relief-pitching thing doesn't work out, maybe a shampoo commercial is in his future.

YEAR	TEAM	P. COUNT	FRM RUNS	BLK RUNS	THRW RUNS	TOT RUNS
2014	LAN	7366	4.9	-0.7	0.4	4.6
2014	LAN	7366	4.9	-0.7	0.4	4.6
2015	ANA	933	-0.7	0.3	0.0	-0.4
2015	KCA	3765	-3.1	-0.2	0.2	-3.0
2016	KCA	5369	1.4	-0.4	-0.1	0.9
2016	KCA	5369	1.4	-0.4	-0.1	0.9
2017	KCA	4894	-0.2	-0.3	0.0	-0.4
2018	KCA	6055	-0.8	-0.4	0.0	-1.2

Lorenzo Cain CF

Born: 4/13/86   Age: 31   Bats: R   Throws: R   Height: 6'2"   Weight: 205   Entered Pro Ball: Round 17, 2004 Draft (#496 overall)

YEAR	TEAM	LVL	AGE	PA	R	2B	3B	HR	RBI	BB	K	SB	CS	AVG/OBP/SLG	TAv	VORP	BABIP	BRR	FRAA	WARP
2014	KCA	MLB	28	502	55	29	4	5	53	24	108	28	5	.301/.339/.412	.269	19.7	.380	3.2	CF(93): 2.5 • RF(77): 4.1	2.9
2015	KCA	MLB	29	604	101	34	6	16	72	37	98	28	6	.307/.361/.477	.301	45.4	.347	4.0	CF(136): 17.5 • RF(5): -0.3	6.7
2016	KCA	MLB	30	434	56	19	1	9	56	31	84	14	5	.287/.339/.408	.258	13.1	.341	2.2	CF(72): 8.2 • RF(29): 0.5	2.2
2017	KCA	MLB	31	603	67	29	4	11	61	39	124	24	6	.274/.326/.400	.259	20.1	.332	2.3	CF 10, RF 1	2.9
2018	KCA	MLB	32	441	50	20	2	9	46	28	94	15	5	.267/.319/.393	.249	8.5	.324	2.1	CF 7, RF 1	1.8

Breakout: 0%   Improve: 52%   Collapse: 2%   Attrition: 6%   MLB: 97%   Comparables: *Michael Bourn, Aaron Rowand, Angel Pagan*

Thanks to Salvador Perez, Cain is a reluctant Instagram star. He's a star on the diamond as well, emerging as an offensive force in the middle of the Royals' lineup and a defensive stalwart in the center of their outfield. However, a year removed from shedding the injury-prone tag and snagging a third-place finish in the MVP voting, Cain stumbled. The disabled list beckoned in late June when he suffered a hamstring injury attempting to beat out a ground ball at first base. Upon his return the Royals shifted him to right field to protect his legs. The legs stayed healthy through August, but a wrist sprain shut him down for all but one game in September. While his Instagram appearances are always enjoyable, the Royals need him to remain healthy if they hope to remain competitive.

Christian Colon   IF

Born: 5/14/89   Age: 28   Bats: R   Throws: R   Height: 5'10"   Weight: 185   Entered Pro Ball: Round 1, 2010 Draft (#4 overall)

YEAR	TEAM	LVL	AGE	PA	R	2B	3B	HR	RBI	BB	K	SB	CS	AVG/OBP/SLG	TAv	VORP	BABIP	BRR	FRAA	WARP
2014	OMA	AAA	25	388	55	18	0	8	47	30	29	15	4	.311/.366/.433	.278	21.9	.317	0.6	SS(35): 2.0 • 2B(35): 0.6	2.4
2014	KCA	MLB	25	49	8	5	1	0	6	3	4	2	0	.333/.375/.489	.316	4.6	.366	0.8	2B(11): 0.4 • 3B(5): 0.2	0.6
2015	OMA	AAA	26	217	19	9	0	1	17	21	18	8	2	.281/.353/.344	.248	3.5	.305	-1.2	SS(26): 3.2 • 2B(16): 0.1	0.6
2015	KCA	MLB	26	119	8	5	0	0	6	11	17	3	2	.290/.356/.336	.249	1.4	.344	-1.3	SS(21): 0.4 • 2B(14): -0.3	0.3
2016	OMA	AAA	27	85	9	5	0	1	5	6	11	2	0	.273/.333/.377	.240	2.0	.308	0.9	SS(11): 1.1 • 2B(6): -0.4	0.3
2016	KCA	MLB	27	161	13	6	0	1	13	11	31	0	1	.231/.294/.293	.217	-4.1	.287	-1.6	2B(32): 4.6 • 3B(15): 1.0	0.2
2017	*KCA*	*MLB*	*28*	*219*	*22*	*10*	*1*	*2*	*18*	*16*	*31*	*4*	*2*	*.261/.317/.352*	*.241*	*3.0*	*.294*	*0.0*	*2B 2, SS 1*	*0.5*
2018	*KCA*	*MLB*	*29*	*288*	*31*	*13*	*1*	*4*	*26*	*22*	*42*	*5*	*2*	*.258/.320/.356*	*.236*	*0.7*	*.290*	*-0.7*	*2B 2, SS 1*	*0.5*

Breakout: 2%   Improve: 21%   Collapse: 14%   Attrition: 25%   MLB: 68%   *Comparables: Johnny Giavotella, Eric Sogard, Matt Tolbert*

How many utility guys can claim to have driven home the game-tying run in the 12th inning of a Wild Card game and then followed that up a year later by knocking in the go-ahead run in the 12th inning of the deciding game of the World Series? We know of only one. You're reading his profile. Colon's versatility on the infield plays, but despite the postseason heroics the Royals remain wary of overexposing the former first-round pick. His contact rate is above average, but if he's ever going to spend a full season on a major-league roster it will be because his steady defensive plays around the horn. In fewer than 250 innings at second base, his 4.6 FRAA was the sixth-best among all American League defenders at the keystone.

Cheslor Cuthbert   3B

Born: 11/16/92   Age: 24   Bats: R   Throws: R   Height: 6'1"   Weight: 190   Entered Pro Ball: International Free Agent, 2009

YEAR	TEAM	LVL	AGE	PA	R	2B	3B	HR	RBI	BB	K	SB	CS	AVG/OBP/SLG	TAv	VORP	BABIP	BRR	FRAA	WARP
2014	NWA	AA	21	395	35	19	1	10	48	36	67	9	5	.276/.342/.420	.275	13.5	.313	-2.1	3B(60): -1.8 • 1B(28): 1.6	1.3
2014	OMA	AAA	21	100	12	5	0	2	16	9	12	1	1	.264/.330/.385	.232	-0.6	.286	0.3	3B(15): -0.8 • 1B(9): -0.9	-0.2
2015	OMA	AAA	22	438	55	22	1	11	51	37	60	5	2	.277/.339/.421	.275	16.4	.302	-1.8	3B(75): 4.5 • 1B(25): 0.5	2.2
2015	KCA	MLB	22	50	6	2	1	1	8	4	9	0	0	.217/.280/.370	.236	0.1	.250	-0.2	3B(17): 1.1 • 1B(1): -0.0	0.1
2016	OMA	AAA	23	107	15	4	1	7	28	11	14	0	1	.333/.402/.624	.377	14.8	.324	-1.4	3B(21): -2.0 • 1B(3): -0.0	1.3
2016	KCA	MLB	23	510	49	28	1	12	46	32	96	2	0	.274/.318/.413	.250	5.9	.320	-5.1	3B(127): -1.9	0.4
2017	*KCA*	*MLB*	*24*	*409*	*44*	*20*	*1*	*11*	*45*	*29*	*76*	*2*	*1*	*.261/.314/.408*	*.256*	*4.1*	*.299*	*-0.7*	*3B 0, 1B 0*	*0.7*
2018	*KCA*	*MLB*	*25*	*511*	*62*	*25*	*2*	*15*	*61*	*37*	*94*	*2*	*1*	*.264/.320/.422*	*.257*	*7.0*	*.300*	*-3.6*	*3B 0, 1B 0*	*0.8*

Breakout: 3%   Improve: 42%   Collapse: 8%   Attrition: 13%   MLB: 80%   *Comparables: Blake DeWitt, Lonnie Chisenhall, Willy Aybar*

Called into action when regular third baseman Mike Moustakas twice landed on the disabled list—the second time with a season-ending knee injury—Cuthbert acquitted himself well in his first extended taste of the big leagues. Offensively, he flashed a league-average contact rate with adequate pop. Defensively, he was a mixed bag. His reflexes play at the hot corner, but as the season continued, his arm seemed to falter and he seemed to have difficulty with his footwork. The Royals sent him to the instructional league for some reps at second base, but the consensus among talent evaluators is that he lacks the foot speed and range to stick. He's out of options and looks to be without a position, which presents a conundrum for the Royals.

Hunter Dozier   3B

Born: 8/22/91   Age: 25   Bats: R   Throws: R   Height: 6'4"   Weight: 220   Entered Pro Ball: Round 1, 2013 Draft (#8 overall)

YEAR	TEAM	LVL	AGE	PA	R	2B	3B	HR	RBI	BB	K	SB	CS	AVG/OBP/SLG	TAv	VORP	BABIP	BRR	FRAA	WARP
2014	WIL	A+	22	267	36	18	0	4	39	35	56	7	3	.295/.397/.429	.324	29.4	.371	2.2	3B(62): -7.8	2.2
2014	NWA	AA	22	267	33	12	0	4	21	31	70	3	2	.209/.303/.312	.222	-1.4	.280	0.9	3B(61): -6.2	-0.8
2015	NWA	AA	23	523	65	27	1	12	53	45	151	6	2	.213/.281/.349	.241	3.8	.283	-0.7	3B(115): -4.2	0.0
2016	NWA	AA	24	110	14	8	0	8	21	14	23	4	0	.305/.400/.642	.365	14.5	.328	0.1	3B(19): -0.3 • LF(6): -1.2	1.4
2016	OMA	AAA	24	434	65	36	1	15	54	40	100	3	1	.294/.357/.506	.304	31.6	.358	0.9	3B(63): -6.3 • RF(14): 1.1	2.6
2016	KCA	MLB	24	21	4	1	0	0	1	2	8	0	0	.211/.286/.263	.236	-0.2	.364	0.0	RF(7): -0.2	0.0
2017	*KCA*	*MLB*	*25*	*250*	*26*	*13*	*1*	*7*	*30*	*21*	*72*	*1*	*0*	*.233/.301/.393*	*.241*	*2.3*	*.305*	*-0.3*	*3B -3, RF 1*	*0.1*
2018	*KCA*	*MLB*	*26*	*381*	*44*	*20*	*1*	*11*	*43*	*33*	*110*	*2*	*1*	*.229/.299/.388*	*.241*	*0.1*	*.300*	*-0.6*	*3B -4, RF 2*	*-0.3*

Breakout: 10%   Improve: 16%   Collapse: 13%   Attrition: 32%   MLB: 37%   *Comparables: Matthew Brown, Luke Hughes, Russ Canzler*

Sometimes, prospects seem to get stuck on repeat. It took two-plus seasons, but Dozier finally solved the Double-A riddle and earned a long awaited promotion to Triple-A. Once in Omaha he didn't miss a beat, restoring some of the prospect luster that had dulled thanks to those extended struggles in the Texas League. With outstanding barrel control and plus bat speed, the hit tool is blossoming. Trying to pull the ball and swing for the fences is probably what held him back the last couple of seasons, but with his build and the loft his swing generates, the power is coming. Originally drafted as a shortstop, he's blocked at third base by Mike Moustakas and Cheslor Cuthbert, so the Royals have worked on shifting him to right field.

Jarrod Dyson CF

Born: 8/15/84 Age: 32 Bats: L Throws: R Height: 5'10" Weight: 165 Entered Pro Ball: Round 50, 2006 Draft (#1475 overall)

YEAR	TEAM	LVL	AGE	PA	R	2B	3B	HR	RBI	BB	K	SB	CS	AVG/OBP/SLG	TAv	VORP	BABIP	BRR	FRAA	WARP
2014	KCA	MLB	29	290	33	4	4	1	24	22	52	36	7	.269/.324/.327	.242	7.9	.330	4.7	CF(106): 4.2 • LF(3): 0.1	1.3
2015	KCA	MLB	30	225	31	8	6	2	18	14	37	26	3	.250/.311/.380	.249	7.7	.296	4.7	CF(37): 4.0 • LF(27): 5.9	1.9
2016	OMA	AAA	31	29	7	0	0	0	1	4	4	4	0	.318/.464/.318	.352	5.5	.389	2.1	RF(4): 0.3 • CF(3): -0.3	0.6
2016	KCA	MLB	31	337	46	14	8	1	25	26	39	30	7	.278/.340/.388	.250	7.1	.315	1.7	CF(57): 0.7 • RF(21): 3.9	1.3
2017	*KCA*	*MLB*	*32*	*222*	*28*	*7*	*4*	*1*	*15*	*17*	*39*	*24*	*5*	*.255/.313/.344*	*.237*	*4.3*	*.301*	*3.9*	*CF 2, RF -0*	*0.5*
2018	*KCA*	*MLB*	*33*	*278*	*28*	*9*	*4*	*2*	*23*	*23*	*52*	*28*	*6*	*.250/.317/.344*	*.232*	*2.9*	*.298*	*3.5*	*CF 2, RF 0*	*0.5*

Breakout: 3%   Improve: 30%   Collapse: 8%   Attrition: 21%   MLB: 82%   *Comparables: Alfredo Amezaga, Ryan Freel, Nyjer Morgan*

If there were a subset of baseball player labeled "Kansas City Fourth Outfielder" Dyson would perfectly fit the bill. Speed for days and plus defense make him a cherished asset covering the acreage at The K. The bat has always been suspect, but plays better against right-handed pitching. This is Dyson we're discussing, so let's turn back to his asset: speed. At 32, he may have lost a step, but that's like complaining your finely-tuned Ferrari isn't as finely-tuned as it was last year. Come on, it's a damn Ferrari! He's still one of the fastest guys in the league and still a disruptive presence on the bases when deployed as a pinch-runner late in games. He's as Royal as Royal could be. No profile is complete without his catchphrase: "That's what speed do."

Alcides Escobar SS

Born: 12/16/86 Age: 30 Bats: R Throws: R Height: 6'1" Weight: 185 Entered Pro Ball: International Free Agent, 2003

YEAR	TEAM	LVL	AGE	PA	R	2B	3B	HR	RBI	BB	K	SB	CS	AVG/OBP/SLG	TAv	VORP	BABIP	BRR	FRAA	WARP
2014	KCA	MLB	27	620	74	34	5	3	50	23	83	31	6	.285/.317/.377	.255	25.6	.326	5.3	SS(162): -3.3	2.5
2015	KCA	MLB	28	662	76	20	5	3	47	26	75	17	5	.257/.293/.320	.224	8.4	.286	5.3	SS(148): 7.2	1.7
2016	KCA	MLB	29	682	57	24	6	7	55	27	96	17	4	.261/.292/.350	.227	5.8	.295	0.4	SS(162): 1.1	0.7
2017	*KCA*	*MLB*	*30*	*667*	*70*	*26*	*5*	*5*	*48*	*27*	*97*	*21*	*5*	*.261/.293/.346*	*.229*	*10.1*	*.295*	*2.6*	*SS 2*	*0.5*
2018	*KCA*	*MLB*	*31*	*571*	*56*	*22*	*4*	*6*	*49*	*25*	*88*	*16*	*4*	*.258/.295/.346*	*.224*	*1.3*	*.291*	*2.9*	*SS 2*	*0.4*

Breakout: 2%   Improve: 35%   Collapse: 5%   Attrition: 21%   MLB: 97%   *Comparables: Bill Russell, Eddie Kasko, Alfredo Griffin*

Square peg, meet round hole. Despite a mountain of evidence against deploying Escobar at the top of the batting order, Ned Yost hit his shortstop first more than any other Royal in 2016. Royals Devil Magic may have been enough to compensate in the past, but it had to run out sometime, helped no doubt by the lowest TAv in the AL among qualified hitters. What's alarming is that his abysmal offensive performance is nothing new. It was the third time in the last four seasons Escobar posted the worst TAv in the junior circuit. When a player struggles like that on offense, maybe you can point to his defense as a reason to keep him in the lineup. However, he seems to have lost a step, especially moving to his left. With one year left on a contract extension signed back in 2012, we're edging closer to the Raul Mondesi era at shortstop in KC.

Alex Gordon LF

Born: 2/10/84 Age: 33 Bats: L Throws: R Height: 6'1" Weight: 220 Entered Pro Ball: Round 1, 2005 Draft (#2 overall)

YEAR	TEAM	LVL	AGE	PA	R	2B	3B	HR	RBI	BB	K	SB	CS	AVG/OBP/SLG	TAv	VORP	BABIP	BRR	FRAA	WARP
2014	KCA	MLB	30	643	87	34	1	19	74	65	126	12	3	.266/.351/.432	.287	32.9	.310	4.2	LF(156): 15.7	5.4
2015	OMA	AAA	31	37	6	2	0	1	5	8	6	0	0	.429/.568/.607	.428	5.9	.524	-1.1	LF(4): 1.0	0.7
2015	KCA	MLB	31	422	40	18	0	13	48	49	92	2	5	.271/.377/.432	.299	23.2	.327	-1.7	LF(101): 4.0	2.9
2016	KCA	MLB	32	506	62	16	2	17	40	52	148	8	1	.220/.312/.380	.240	1.6	.288	1.2	LF(126): -4.5	-0.3
2017	*KCA*	*MLB*	*33*	*565*	*63*	*25*	*3*	*15*	*64*	*56*	*130*	*7*	*3*	*.255/.338/.405*	*.264*	*20.5*	*.314*	*-0.4*	*LF 4*	*2.1*
2018	*KCA*	*MLB*	*34*	*482*	*59*	*21*	*2*	*12*	*53*	*49*	*115*	*5*	*2*	*.249/.334/.391*	*.254*	*9.5*	*.311*	*0.9*	*LF 3*	*1.4*

Breakout: 1%   Improve: 29%   Collapse: 7%   Attrition: 13%   MLB: 96%   *Comparables: Seth Smith, Rickie Weeks, Jose Cruz Jr.*

Injuries and age can be a toxic combination. Gordon, the all-around star of the Royals, missed considerable time for the second consecutive season, and when he was healthy, failed to contribute in a meaningful way. The result was his first season without either an All-Star appearance or a Gold Glove to his name since 2010 (which was, by the way, the last time he posted a WARP lower than 1.0). His .240 TAv matched the lowest rate of his career. It was a true *annus mirabilis* for the Royals left fielder. He was hitting .211/.319/.331 when he collided with Mike Moustakas, running down a foul pop that landed both on the disabled list. When he returned from a broken wrist a month later, he hit just .224/.309/.403 the rest of the way. Along with the woeful performance at the plate, the range seemed to diminish in the outfield. Father Time catches up with everyone, but this felt premature. A return to the Gordon of old instead of another version of Old Gordon will be needed if this team is to contend again.

Terrance Gore LF

Born: 6/8/91 Age: 26 Bats: R Throws: R Height: 5'7" Weight: 165 Entered Pro Ball: Round 20, 2011 Draft (#606 overall)

YEAR	TEAM	LVL	AGE	PA	R	2B	3B	HR	RBI	BB	K	SB	CS	AVG/OBP/SLG	TAv	VORP	BABIP	BRR	FRAA	WARP
2014	WIL	A+	23	287	34	8	1	0	15	20	66	36	4	.218/.284/.258	.242	5.3	.293	4.3	LF(81): 17.7 • CF(8): -1.4	2.2
2014	OMA	AAA	23	26	8	0	0	0	0	2	4	11	3	.250/.348/.250	.231	1.6	.313	1.9	LF(7): -0.7	0.1
2014	KCA	MLB	23	2	5	0	0	0	0	0	0	5	0	.000/.500/.000	.296	1.1	.000	1.0	LF(2): -0.0	0.1
2015	NWA	AA	24	259	42	4	1	0	16	26	50	39	2	.284/.367/.311	.256	8.8	.366	4.1	LF(51): 0.4 • CF(21): -2.9	0.7
2015	KCA	MLB	24	4	1	0	0	0	0	0	1	3	0	.000/.250/.000	.147	0.6	.000	0.9	LF(4): -0.4	0.0
2016	NWA	AA	25	302	31	2	1	0	11	26	58	44	5	.233/.314/.249	.233	5.7	.303	5.4	CF(70): 5.4 • LF(15): 0.1	1.2
2016	KCA	MLB	25	3	6	0	0	0	0	0	1	11	2	.000/.000/.000	.025	-0.5	.000	0.1	LF(2): 0.0	-0.1
2017	*KCA*	*MLB*	*26*	*250*	*31*	*7*	*1*	*2*	*17*	*18*	*61*	*26*	*3*	*.231/.299/.304*	*.210*	*0.5*	*.291*	*4.2*	*CF 3, LF 2*	*0.6*
2018	*KCA*	*MLB*	*27*	*203*	*20*	*5*	*1*	*2*	*16*	*14*	*49*	*21*	*2*	*.227/.294/.300*	*.209*	*-1.3*	*.284*	*3.9*	*CF 2, LF 2*	*0.3*

Breakout: 6%   Improve: 16%   Collapse: 6%   Attrition: 14%   MLB: 24%   *Comparables: Rico Noel, Quintin Berry, Jose Constanza*

You start with a bowl. Drop in a couple scoops of ice cream. A little hot fudge. Maybe some butterscotch or caramel. Some whipped cream. Sprinkles. Brownie bites? Sure. Chopped nuts would be nice. Maybe an extra drizzle of chocolate sauce. You've got yourself an ice cream sundae. So good. But wait! You're missing something. Crushed Oreos! Yes, it may be unnecessary and even a bit excessive. Yet it turns out to be so much improved and dare we say, even a little useful. Gore on the 25-man roster is the Royals' version of crushed Oreos. Unnecessary, and maybe even a little excessive, but when deployed at the proper moment, like say in as a pinch-runner with the Royals trailing by one in the late innings, imminently perfect.

Eric Hosmer   1B

Born: 10/24/89   Age: 27   Bats: L   Throws: L   Height: 6'4"   Weight: 225   Entered Pro Ball: Round 1, 2008 Draft (#3 overall)

YEAR	TEAM	LVL	AGE	PA	R	2B	3B	HR	RBI	BB	K	SB	CS	AVG/OBP/SLG	TAv	VORP	BABIP	BRR	FRAA	WARP
2014	KCA	MLB	24	547	54	35	1	9	58	35	93	4	2	.270/.318/.398	.262	4.4	.312	-1.9	1B(130): 8.1	1.4
2015	KCA	MLB	25	667	98	33	5	18	93	61	108	7	3	.297/.363/.459	.289	28.1	.336	2.7	1B(154): 3.7 • RF(1): 0.0	3.4
2016	KCA	MLB	26	667	80	24	1	25	104	57	132	5	3	.266/.328/.433	.261	7.6	.301	0.1	1B(154): -2.4	0.5
2017	KCA	MLB	27	662	73	31	3	18	78	56	115	6	3	.273/.335/.424	.268	17.1	.308	-0.9	1B 2	1.6
2018	KCA	MLB	28	569	73	26	2	17	69	55	100	5	2	.274/.344/.431	.269	12.4	.309	0.3	1B 2	1.6

Breakout: 3%   Improve: 47%   Collapse: 0%   Attrition: 2%   MLB: 98%   Comparables: Ray Webster, Mike Sweeney, Pete O'Brien

Those who cling to the idea of "clutch" as a skill have an example in Hosmer. Understandable. From postseason heroics to his RBI tally in 2016, he does have a knack of coming through. Yet the underlying reality is he remains one of the more frustratingly inconsistent offensive performers in the game. A torrid first 60 games where he hit .324/.382/.547 got fans thinking a breakout season was in the making. Then he didn't so much pump the brakes as he slammed down on them with both feet, hitting a meager .232/.297/.366 the rest of the way. It certainly doesn't help when your first baseman with modest power potential posts a 59 percent ground-ball rate, the highest in the AL among qualified hitters. He's a much better hitter when he uses the whole field. The grounders come when he tries to pull. In fact, in the time it took to write this comment he probably rolled his wrists and topped another weak grounder to second.

Khalil Lee   OF

Born: 6/26/98   Age: 19   Bats: L   Throws: L   Height: 5'10"   Weight: 170   Entered Pro Ball: Round 3, 2016 Draft (#103 overall)

YEAR	TEAM	LVL	AGE	PA	R	2B	3B	HR	RBI	BB	K	SB	CS	AVG/OBP/SLG	TAv	VORP	BABIP	BRR	FRAA	WARP
2017	KCA	MLB	19	250	22	8	1	6	25	20	88	1	1	.190/.262/.314	.202	-6.6	.276	-0.2	CF -0, RF -0	-0.8
2018	KCA	MLB	20	341	38	11	2	10	36	30	113	2	1	.208/.284/.352	.224	-4.6	.291	-0.3	CF -1, RF 0	-0.6

Breakout: 0%   Improve: 8%   Collapse: 2%   Attrition: 7%   MLB: 15%   Comparables: Nomar Mazara, Domingo Santana, Engel Beltre

The Royals drafted Lee, an athletic two-way player, in the third round last June. Despite a fastball that touches 94 mph, a slider and a developing change, scouting director Lonnie Goldberg said the plan was always for Lee to start his professional career in the outfield. There may be some concerns about his ability to make consistent contact, but the Royals love them some athletic outfielders with upside, and the left-hander totally fits the bill. Joining the rookie league team in Arizona, he did struggle with a 25 percent strikeout rate, but the Royals were encouraged as he actually improved his contact rate during the course of the summer. The 15 percent walk rate, a hit tool that produces line drives, and developing power make him one to watch going forward.

Whit Merrifield   UT

Born: 1/24/89   Age: 28   Bats: R   Throws: R   Height: 6'0"   Weight: 195   Entered Pro Ball: Round 9, 2010 Draft (#269 overall)

YEAR	TEAM	LVL	AGE	PA	R	2B	3B	HR	RBI	BB	K	SB	CS	AVG/OBP/SLG	TAv	VORP	BABIP	BRR	FRAA	WARP
2014	NWA	AA	25	190	22	13	1	5	20	22	27	5	4	.278/.366/.463	.311	14.7	.305	-0.2	LF(21): 2.3 • 2B(14): -1.0	1.7
2014	OMA	AAA	25	345	57	28	3	3	29	17	52	11	7	.340/.373/.474	.298	25.3	.394	2.9	LF(56): -0.8 • RF(17): -1.5	2.3
2015	OMA	AAA	26	594	83	29	5	8	38	39	66	32	9	.265/.317/.364	.241	8.4	.292	6.0	2B(57): 4.8 • LF(39): 3.1	1.8
2016	OMA	AAA	27	304	46	19	0	8	29	22	55	20	2	.266/.321/.423	.278	14.4	.302	1.5	2B(40): 1.5 • 1B(9): -0.5	1.5
2016	KCA	MLB	27	332	44	22	3	2	29	19	72	8	3	.283/.323/.392	.253	6.0	.361	-0.2	2B(65): 2.2 • LF(13): 0.3	0.8
2017	KCA	MLB	28	111	13	6	1	1	9	6	21	4	1	.256/.300/.370	.238	1.4	.305	0.3	2B 1, 3B -0	0.1
2018	KCA	MLB	29	325	34	18	2	5	31	20	63	10	3	.251/.301/.372	.234	0.7	.299	0.5	2B 2, 3B -1	0.2

Breakout: 2%   Improve: 20%   Collapse: 16%   Attrition: 26%   MLB: 53%   Comparables: Rafael Ynoa, Matt Tolbert, Mike Fontenot

Sometimes, all it takes is opportunity. Toiling in the Royals' organization since 2010, injuries got Merrifield his call to the show. The entirely predictable crash and burn of Omar Infante got him a semi-regular spot. A week after his debut, he strung together five consecutive starts in which he collected a pair of hits in each. Thus, the legend of "Two-Hit" Whit was born. He was farmed back out for a bit at the end of July, but finished with a respectable batting line and accomplished it while appearing at first, second, third and both corner outfield spots. The bat remains below average, but his versatility afield can keep him on the 25-man roster. Quite a journey for the former ninth-round selection.

Raul Mondesi   2B/SS

Born: 7/27/95   Age: 21   Bats: B   Throws: R   Height: 6'1"   Weight: 185   Entered Pro Ball: International Free Agent, 2011

YEAR	TEAM	LVL	AGE	PA	R	2B	3B	HR	RBI	BB	K	SB	CS	AVG/OBP/SLG	TAv	VORP	BABIP	BRR	FRAA	WARP
2014	WIL	A+	18	472	54	14	12	8	33	24	122	17	4	.211/.256/.354	.232	6.8	.274	1.4	SS(106): 2.2	0.9
2015	NWA	AA	19	338	36	11	5	6	33	17	88	19	6	.243/.279/.372	.239	5.7	.316	0.8	SS(63): -2.0 • 2B(18): -3.2	0.0
2016	WIL	A+	20	39	5	2	1	1	4	2	11	2	0	.243/.282/.432	.246	1.5	.320	0.9	SS(6): 0.5	0.2
2016	NWA	AA	20	131	20	5	1	5	17	13	30	17	1	.259/.331/.448	.297	10.5	.305	1.0	SS(21): 2.1 • 2B(6): 0.4	1.4
2016	OMA	AAA	20	61	9	2	4	1	9	2	19	5	0	.304/.328/.536	.312	7.1	.444	1.4	SS(12): 0.6 • 2B(2): 0.1	0.8
2016	KCA	MLB	20	149	16	1	3	2	13	6	48	9	1	.185/.231/.281	.190	-5.1	.271	1.5	2B(42): -4.2 • SS(7): -0.1	-1.0
2017	KCA	MLB	21	448	49	14	7	10	40	18	135	22	4	.218/.247/.355	.213	-0.7	.284	4.8	2B -9	-1.4
2018	KCA	MLB	22	522	54	17	8	13	56	25	154	27	5	.227/.269/.379	.221	1.3	.293	6.1	2B -11	-1.0

Breakout: 4%   Improve: 5%   Collapse: 1%   Attrition: 8%   MLB: 10%   Comparables: Jonathan Villar, Junior Lake, Chris Owings

It was quite the whirlwind 2016 for the Royals' top prospect. In May, Mondesi was suspended 50 games after testing positive for an over-the-counter cold remedy purchased in his native Dominican Republic. He returned to Double-A in July, but was promptly promoted to Triple-A. After just 14 games there, he was summoned to the majors. Premature? Definitely. Although not entirely surprising, as the Royals have always been aggressive with the young shortstop. We're talking about a guy who made his MLB debut pinch-hitting in the World Series, for crying out loud. Predictably, in his first extended taste of big-league action he failed at the dish but played well in the field, manning the keystone in Kansas City. Still, he possesses strong bat speed and tantalizes with some power potential. Signed for $2 million in 2011, it seems as though he's been in the system forever so it can be difficult to remember he will be playing his age-21 season and has been among the younger players in every league he's played. The heir apparent to Alcides Escobar at short, he will likely return to Triple-A for a little more seasoning.

Mike Moustakas 3B

Born: 9/11/88 Age: 28 Bats: L Throws: R Height: 6'0" Weight: 215 Entered Pro Ball: Round 1, 2007 Draft (#2 overall)

YEAR	TEAM	LVL	AGE	PA	R	2B	3B	HR	RBI	BB	K	SB	CS	AVG/OBP/SLG	TAv	VORP	BABIP	BRR	FRAA	WARP
2014	OMA	AAA	25	34	3	3	0	1	5	3	6	0	0	.355/.412/.548	.328	3.8	.417	0.1	3B(7): 1.6	0.5
2014	KCA	MLB	25	500	45	21	1	15	54	35	74	1	0	.212/.271/.361	.233	3.6	.220	1.7	3B(138): 7.1	1.2
2015	KCA	MLB	26	614	73	34	1	22	82	43	76	1	2	.284/.348/.470	.291	35.9	.294	-1.3	3B(146): 7.5	4.7
2016	KCA	MLB	27	113	12	6	0	7	13	9	13	0	1	.240/.301/.500	.281	5.4	.214	-0.7	3B(26): -0.4	0.5
2017	KCA	MLB	28	545	65	27	1	17	60	38	90	1	2	.247/.307/.413	.254	11.5	.267	-1.6	3B 4	1.1
2018	KCA	MLB	29	375	46	18	0	13	46	28	64	1	1	.246/.310/.417	.251	4.9	.265	-0.1	3B 2	0.8

Breakout: 2% Improve: 50% Collapse: 2% Attrition: 6% MLB: 94% Comparables: Puddin Head Jones, Chad Tracy, Mike Lowell

This one, quite literally, hurt. Coming off a breakout 2015 season during which the fan favorite learned to beat the shift by hitting the ball to the opposite field, big things were expected from Moustakas. Then, a broken thumb sidelined him for most of May. When he returned, he played only two games before a collision with Alex Gordon resulted in a torn meniscus, ending his season. The opposite-field approach in 2015 was real and it was spectacular. He hit .436 on balls in play to the left side, earning him yet another nickname among the Kansas City faithful: Moustoppo. The small sample from last year wasn't as promising, as a lower percentage of balls in play went the opposite way and for a .294 AVG, but there simply weren't enough plate appearances to draw a definitive conclusion. So now we wait until this year to see if the opposite-field lessons learned have true staying power.

Daniel Nava RF

Born: 2/22/83 Age: 34 Bats: B Throws: L Height: 5'11" Weight: 200 Entered Pro Ball: Undrafted Free Agent, 2007

YEAR	TEAM	LVL	AGE	PA	R	2B	3B	HR	RBI	BB	K	SB	CS	AVG/OBP/SLG	TAv	VORP	BABIP	BRR	FRAA	WARP
2014	PAW	AAA	31	98	12	3	0	3	14	12	21	2	1	.253/.347/.398	.259	-0.3	.295	-2.2	LF(8): -0.5 • RF(6): -0.3	-0.2
2014	BOS	MLB	31	408	41	21	0	4	37	33	81	4	2	.270/.346/.361	.272	13.2	.336	1.7	RF(69): 8.5 • LF(38): -0.5	2.4
2015	PAW	AAA	32	42	4	1	0	1	8	4	11	2	0	.250/.357/.361	.269	0.9	.333	0.0	RF(6): -0.1 • 1B(3): 0.1	0.1
2015	BOS	MLB	32	78	6	2	0	0	7	8	17	0	0	.152/.260/.182	.194	-2.2	.200	1.6	RF(15): 0.5 • LF(7): -0.1	-0.2
2015	TBA	MLB	32	88	7	2	0	1	3	12	19	1	0	.233/.364/.301	.269	1.5	.302	-0.7	RF(19): 0.5 • 1B(7): 0.0	0.2
2016	ANA	MLB	33	136	10	5	0	1	13	9	26	0	0	.235/.309/.303	.240	-0.7	.284	-0.9	LF(37): -0.1 • RF(2): 0.1	-0.1
2016	SLC	AAA	33	92	5	6	0	1	13	6	10	1	1	.365/.413/.471	.298	2.2	.405	-2.7	LF(8): 0.6 • 1B(5): 0.4	0.3
2016	KCA	MLB	33	12	1	1	0	0	0	0	1	4	0	0	.091/.167/.182	.145	-0.8	.143	0.4	1B(6): -0.1	-0.1
2017	PHI	MLB	34	352	35	15	0	7	36	32	74	2	1	.248/.332/.364	.259	9.9	.301	-0.7	LF 1, 1B 0	1.0
2018	PHI	MLB	35	188	22	8	0	3	18	18	39	1	0	.250/.340/.358	.251	2.4	.306	0.3	LF 1, 1B 0	0.4

Breakout: 0% Improve: 35% Collapse: 16% Attrition: 24% MLB: 88% Comparables: Willie Harris, Scott Spiezio, Roy White

The Legend Of Daniel Nava was born in Boston. However, it deserves an honorable mention in Kansas City. It was his grand slam against Royals reliever Aaron Crow in mid-September of 2014 that provided a necessary re-think by manager Ned Yost about how to best deploy his bullpen entering the postseason. Acquired just ahead of the trade deadline in one of those deals that makes you wonder exactly what information the Royals have that is exclusive to their organization, he lacks the range to cover the acreage at The K and has seen his offensive output tumble. Now, he's not so much Legend as much as fringe fourth outfielder or platoon bat.

Paulo Orlando RF

Born: 11/1/85 Age: 31 Bats: R Throws: R Height: 6'2" Weight: 210 Entered Pro Ball: International Free Agent, 2005

YEAR	TEAM	LVL	AGE	PA	R	2B	3B	HR	RBI	BB	K	SB	CS	AVG/OBP/SLG	TAv	VORP	BABIP	BRR	FRAA	WARP
2014	OMA	AAA	28	554	61	21	9	6	63	39	86	34	9	.301/.355/.415	.277	29.1	.351	3.6	CF(80): 12.4 • RF(42): 4.7	4.5
2015	OMA	AAA	29	182	20	11	0	3	17	8	32	9	0	.276/.309/.394	.256	5.5	.321	2.1	CF(18): -1.2 • RF(11): 0.4	0.8
2015	KCA	MLB	29	251	31	14	6	7	27	5	53	3	3	.249/.269/.444	.254	3.4	.291	0.1	RF(45): -1.7 • LF(37): 2.1	0.5
2016	KCA	MLB	30	484	52	24	4	5	43	13	105	14	3	.302/.329/.405	.257	10.0	.380	1.0	RF(89): -2.4 • CF(37): -2.4	0.5
2017	KCA	MLB	31	227	22	10	2	3	21	9	48	7	2	.262/.294/.370	.237	1.5	.322	0.8	RF 1, CF 0	0.1
2018	KCA	MLB	32	426	43	20	4	6	41	17	95	11	3	.261/.297/.375	.234	-0.5	.324	1.0	RF 1, CF 0	0.2

Breakout: 1% Improve: 28% Collapse: 12% Attrition: 17% MLB: 67% Comparables: Chris Denorfia, Eugenio Velez, Cory Sullivan

As the right-handed half of an outfield platoon to open the season, Orlando slowly gained the trust of the Royals' staff and a subsequent increase in playing time. The Brazilian rode the BABIP train to success, but actually made a lower rate of hard contact than in his rookie season, which is probably why you see a decline in his slugging. Defensively, he's a mixed bag, looking much more comfortable in center field than in right. The combination of bat and glove make him a low-cost fourth-outfield option. His plate appearance totals can perform a barometer of the Royals' fortunes going forward. If he's around 250, as he was in 2015, that means the Royals have better options in place and the team is probably doing well. If above 400, that means the Royals failed to solve their right field riddle and the team is failing to meet expectations for the second consecutive season.

Salvador Perez   C

Born: 5/10/90   Age: 27   Bats: R   Throws: R   Height: 6'3"   Weight: 240   Entered Pro Ball: International Free Agent, 2006

YEAR	TEAM	LVL	AGE	PA	R	2B	3B	HR	RBI	BB	K	SB	CS	AVG/OBP/SLG	TAv	VORP	BABIP	BRR	FRAA	WARP
2014	KCA	MLB	24	606	57	28	2	17	70	22	85	1	0	.260/.289/.403	.251	16.2	.278	-3.6	C(146): -14.4	0.2
2015	KCA	MLB	25	553	52	25	0	21	70	13	82	1	0	.260/.280/.426	.251	16.0	.270	-2.5	C(139): -8.5 • 1B(1): -0.0	0.8
2016	KCA	MLB	26	546	57	28	2	22	64	22	119	0	0	.247/.288/.438	.245	12.7	.280	-2.7	C(128): -8.5 • 1B(1): -0.0	0.4
2017	KCA	MLB	27	556	60	27	2	18	68	22	87	1	0	.269/.302/.432	.259	21.5	.289	-1.0	C -9	0.6
2018	KCA	MLB	28	521	64	23	1	20	68	25	86	0	0	.262/.302/.437	.255	13.0	.280	-2.5	C -9	0.4

Breakout: 5%   Improve: 41%   Collapse: 7%   Attrition: 16%   MLB: 97%   Comparables: Hal Smith, Keith Moreland, John Ellis

In this iteration of the Royals, Eric Hosmer may be the face of the franchise. Alex Gordon can be the guts. But Perez is the heart and the soul. The recipient of four consecutive Gold Gloves for his work behind the dish, his framing skill still leaves something to be desired. However, his footwork showed amazing improvement in 2016. The quick feet led to improved catch-and-release times, which translated to a career-best 48 percent caught-stealing rate that was almost a full 20 percentage points above the league average. Offensively, it's like you tell your kids, "You get what you get, so don't throw a fit." He will never be able to lay off the low-and-away slider, but he did trade some of his contact rate on pitches out of the zone (which all too frequently go for outs) for a little more pop that netted him his first Silver Slugger. Though it still wasn't enough to get the TAv to where you think it should be. Maybe a day off or two would help the offensive cause? But the heart never stops beating.

YEAR	TEAM	P. COUNT	FRM RUNS	BLK RUNS	THRW RUNS	TOT RUNS
2014	KCA	20329	-13.5	1.3	0.6	-11.6
2015	KCA	19339	-8.3	0.6	0.5	-7.2
2016	KCA	18379	-13.4	3.2	4.9	-5.3
2017	KCA	17358	-12.3	2.0	2.7	-7.6
2018	KCA	16269	-12.4	1.8	2.5	-8.1

Jorge Soler   RF

Born: 2/25/92   Age: 25   Bats: R   Throws: R   Height: 6'4"   Weight: 215   Entered Pro Ball: International Free Agent, 2012

YEAR	TEAM	LVL	AGE	PA	R	2B	3B	HR	RBI	BB	K	SB	CS	AVG/OBP/SLG	TAv	VORP	BABIP	BRR	FRAA	WARP
2014	TEN	AA	22	79	13	9	1	6	22	12	15	0	0	.415/.494/.862	.450	16.4	.457	-0.3	RF(16): -2.8	1.4
2014	IOW	AAA	22	127	22	11	1	8	29	17	26	0	0	.282/.378/.618	.324	11.5	.303	-0.1	RF(27): -1.2	1.0
2014	CHN	MLB	22	97	11	8	1	5	20	6	24	1	0	.292/.330/.573	.324	7.2	.339	-0.2	RF(24): -0.7	0.7
2015	CHN	MLB	23	404	39	18	1	10	47	32	121	3	1	.262/.324/.399	.263	7.7	.361	-0.2	RF(95): -8.7	-0.1
2016	TEN	AA	24	42	4	0	0	0	2	11	11	0	0	.167/.381/.167	.246	0.1	.250	0.0	LF(6): -0.5	0.0
2016	CHN	MLB	24	264	37	9	0	12	31	31	66	0	0	.238/.333/.436	.293	13.9	.276	-0.4	LF(53): -2.5 • RF(7): -1.0	1.1
2017	KCA	MLB	25	578	67	27	2	22	76	56	155	2	1	.254/.329/.440	.271	19.6	.318	-0.9	RF -8	0.8
2018	KCA	MLB	26	449	60	21	1	17	59	46	119	2	1	.255/.334/.444	.269	13.3	.318	-0.6	RF -6	0.8

Breakout: 1%   Improve: 57%   Collapse: 1%   Attrition: 3%   MLB: 99%   Comparables: Carlos Gonzalez, Chris Young, Travis Snider

Soler would probably be a pretty good big-league player if he ever spent more than 30 seconds on the field without straining one or both of his hamstrings. In the short bursts of big-league action he's seen since making his debut late in 2014, he's shown the ability to work counts and force the pitcher into his hitting zone. And once the pitch is there, he can crush it with the best of 'em. The problem is that a) he gets injured a lot, b) he's not an especially good defender and c) he occasionally forgets about the plate discipline entirely and extends his arms over the plate at a slider 10 feet out of the zone. That last issue can probably be fixed, but the other two mean he has to hit really well to be a big net positive.

Bubba Starling   CF

Born: 8/3/92   Age: 24   Bats: R   Throws: R   Height: 6'4"   Weight: 210   Entered Pro Ball: Round 1, 2011 Draft (#5 overall)

YEAR	TEAM	LVL	AGE	PA	R	2B	3B	HR	RBI	BB	K	SB	CS	AVG/OBP/SLG	TAv	VORP	BABIP	BRR	FRAA	WARP
2014	WIL	A+	21	549	67	23	4	9	54	49	150	17	2	.218/.304/.338	.260	22.2	.293	4.9	CF(130): 1.8	2.4
2015	WIL	A+	22	51	6	4	0	2	12	7	17	2	1	.386/.471/.614	.388	7.9	.600	-0.1	CF(11): -2.5	0.8
2015	NWA	AA	22	367	51	19	4	10	32	30	91	4	5	.254/.318/.426	.272	15.0	.319	0.9	CF(75): -3.4 • RF(9): -0.4	1.2
2016	NWA	AA	23	255	28	15	1	5	23	15	81	10	1	.185/.251/.322	.219	-2.4	.257	1.3	CF(51): 1.7 • RF(8): 0.9	0.0
2016	OMA	AAA	23	176	14	8	0	2	17	7	64	1	0	.181/.213/.265	.180	-1.9	.277	-1.2	CF(44): 1.4 • RF(1): -0.2	-1.0
2017	KCA	MLB	24	250	24	11	1	6	26	15	82	3	1	.207/.264/.343	.211	-3.2	.289	0.1	CF -1, RF 1	-0.5
2018	KCA	MLB	25	293	31	12	2	7	30	19	95	4	1	.211/.271/.351	.220	-4.0	.293	0.3	CF -2, RF 1	-0.5

Breakout: 9%   Improve: 10%   Collapse: 1%   Attrition: 5%   MLB: 12%   Comparables: Jordan Danks, Aaron Altherr, Matt Den Dekker

A year removed from restoring some of his prospect luster, Starling saw it all washed away, drowned in a strikeout rate that rose above 35 percent. Despite his struggles in the Texas League, the Royals pushed him to Triple-A. Bold strategy or just misguided? We'll settle on the latter. Time is running short for the former first rounder. Not even his superior defensive tools can survive the issues with pitch recognition and the wretched performance at the plate.

PITCHERS

Scott Alexander LHP

Born: 7/10/89 Age: 27 Bats: L Throws: L Height: 6'2" Weight: 190 Entered Pro Ball: Round 6, 2010 Draft (#179 overall)

YEAR	TEAM	LVL	AGE	W	L	SV	G	GS	IP	H	HR	BB/9	K/9	K	GB%	BABIP	WHIP	ERA	FIP	DRA	VORP	WARP	cFIP	MPH
2014	NWA	AA	24	1	2	3	35	0	48²	42	3	3.0	6.7	36	60%	.267	1.19	3.88	3.61	4.83	0.1	0.0	95	
2014	OMA	AAA	24	1	2	0	11	0	19	23	4	4.7	6.2	13	63%	.328	1.74	6.16	6.65	5.75	-0.9	-0.1	104	
2015	OMA	AAA	25	2	3	14	41	0	63¹	48	5	2.4	7.1	50	64%	.243	1.03	2.56	3.90	4.10	5.8	0.6	96	
2015	KCA	MLB	25	0	0	0	4	0	6	5	0	4.5	4.5	3	72%	.278	1.33	4.50	4.10	3.52	0.8	0.1	104	95.0
2016	OMA	AAA	26	2	0	1	22	0	30	32	2	3.0	7.2	24	67%	.323	1.40	3.00	4.09	3.80	3.9	0.4	92	
2016	KCA	MLB	26	0	0	0	17	0	19	24	1	3.3	7.6	16	69%	.383	1.63	3.32	3.21	3.91	2.2	0.2	94	94.1
2017	KCA	MLB	27	2	3	0	55	0	58	63	7	3.4	6.0	39	50%	.302	1.47	4.86	4.68	5.07	-0.6	-0.1	100	
2018	KCA	MLB	28	1	0	0	21	0	22¹	22	2	4.6	9.0	22	50%	.316	1.50	4.13	4.30	4.69	0.9	0.1	105	

Breakout: 14% Improve: 19% Collapse: 17% Attrition: 32% MLB: 43% *Comparables: Zach Phillips, Andrew Triggs, Danny Burawa*

He's not your garden variety LOOGY, but Alexander is certainly useful against same-siders. His .627 OPS allowed versus left-handed bats was 200 points better than he fared with righties across all levels in 2016. Even better, he surrendered just four extra-base hits against those lefties in 85 plate appearances. His bread-and-butter pitch is the sinker. He induced a grounder on 81 percent of all two-seamers put in play. In the days of the eight-man bullpen, Alexander can certainly find a place as a second southpaw.

Miguel Almonte RHP

Born: 4/4/93 Age: 24 Bats: R Throws: R Height: 6'2" Weight: 210 Entered Pro Ball: International Free Agent, 2010

YEAR	TEAM	LVL	AGE	W	L	SV	G	GS	IP	H	HR	BB/9	K/9	K	GB%	BABIP	WHIP	ERA	FIP	DRA	VORP	WARP	cFIP	MPH
2014	WIL	A+	21	6	8	0	23	22	110¹	107	9	2.6	8.2	101	48%	.316	1.26	4.49	3.92	3.75	22.4	2.3	95	
2015	NWA	AA	22	4	4	0	17	17	67	65	4	3.6	7.4	55	43%	.307	1.37	4.03	4.00	5.11	-0.1	0.0	103	
2015	OMA	AAA	22	2	2	0	11	6	36²	33	3	3.7	10.1	41	43%	.323	1.31	5.40	3.90	3.77	5.9	0.6	91	
2015	KCA	MLB	22	0	2	0	9	0	8²	7	4	7.3	10.4	10	52%	.158	1.62	6.23	9.57	4.20	0.5	0.1	103	98.9
2016	OMA	AAA	23	3	7	0	21	12	60	63	5	6.3	8.6	57	43%	.335	1.75	5.55	5.15	7.67	-16.1	-1.7	113	
2016	NWA	AA	23	2	1	0	11	0	16	24	4	2.2	8.4	15	41%	.400	1.75	7.31	5.31	5.44	-1.3	-0.1	103	
2017	KCA	MLB	24	4	5	0	38	8	77	84	9	4.4	6.4	55	53%	.303	1.58	5.08	4.89	5.29	-1.3	-0.1	100	
2018	KCA	MLB	25	5	4	0	48	10	98²	96	12	6.0	9.3	101	53%	.311	1.65	4.78	4.96	5.32	-0.3	0.0	122	

Breakout: 13% Improve: 24% Collapse: 20% Attrition: 33% MLB: 53% *Comparables: Esmil Rogers, Daniel Wright, Charles Brewer*

From September call-up in the thick of a pennant race in 2015 to a demotion to Double-A in the middle of the following season, Almonte suffered through a miserable 2016. The uptick in his walk rate—nearly two free passes per nine above his minor-league career average—pulled back the curtain on his below-average command of the strike zone and was the root of myriad issues. The fastball will play in the mid-90s and his curve grades out as average, but it's the change that really shines. However, none of the previous sentence matters much if he can't locate. Moved to the bullpen prior to his demotion, the struggle with command continued. Under Dayton Moore, the Royals have a history of highly-rated pitching prospects topping out at Triple-A. Is he the next? TINSTAAPP indeed.

Scott Blewett RHP

Born: 4/10/96 Age: 21 Bats: R Throws: R Height: 6'6" Weight: 210 Entered Pro Ball: Round 2, 2014 Draft (#56 overall)

YEAR	TEAM	LVL	AGE	W	L	SV	G	GS	IP	H	HR	BB/9	K/9	K	GB%	BABIP	WHIP	ERA	FIP	DRA	VORP	WARP	cFIP	MPH
2015	LEX	A	19	3	5	0	18	18	81¹	88	6	2.7	6.6	60	48%	.317	1.38	5.20	3.96	3.81	12.8	1.4	95	
2016	LEX	A	20	8	11	0	25	25	129¹	138	10	3.5	8.4	121	47%	.338	1.46	4.31	3.90	3.93	15.5	1.7	99	
2017	KCA	MLB	21	4	8	0	19	19	91	120	16	5.1	4.6	46	65%	.322	1.89	6.25	6.28	6.79	-13.3	-1.4	162	
2018	KCA	MLB	22	4	8	0	19	19	112¹	124	19	6.2	7.6	95	65%	.312	1.80	5.70	5.88	6.19	-7.2	-0.7	147	

Breakout: 4% Improve: 4% Collapse: 1% Attrition: 5% MLB: 6% *Comparables: Edwin Diaz, Joe Wieland, Jose Urena*

With a plus fastball that reaches the mid-90s and a solid curve, what's holding Blewett back as a starter is a third pitch and consistency. Searching for that third pitch, he's still working on a changeup that shows a moderate amount of promise. Now about that consistency. Early in the season it was so elusive for the young right-hander, his Game Scores resembled an EKG of someone under an inordinate amount of stress. He seemed to find equilibrium and gained strength as the season progressed, posting a 10.5 K/9 and a 2.6 BB/9 over his final 11 starts. Small sample size be damned, it was his best stretch as a professional.

Danny Duffy LHP

Born: 12/21/88 Age: 28 Bats: L Throws: L Height: 6'3" Weight: 205 Entered Pro Ball: Round 3, 2007 Draft (#96 overall)

YEAR	TEAM	LVL	AGE	W	L	SV	G	GS	IP	H	HR	BB/9	K/9	K	GB%	BABIP	WHIP	ERA	FIP	DRA	VORP	WARP	cFIP	MPH
2014	KCA	MLB	25	9	12	0	31	25	149¹	113	12	3.2	6.8	113	38%	.239	1.11	2.53	3.86	5.06	-4.0	-0.4	113	96.7
2015	KCA	MLB	26	7	8	1	30	24	136²	137	15	3.5	6.7	102	41%	.298	1.39	4.08	4.40	5.08	-0.4	0.0	112	97.0
2016	KCA	MLB	27	12	3	0	42	26	179²	163	27	2.1	9.4	188	37%	.291	1.14	3.51	3.79	3.46	37.1	3.8	91	97.8
2017	KCA	MLB	28	8	11	0	29	29	153²	146	21	2.7	8.8	150	53%	.295	1.25	4.05	4.05	4.43	14.0	1.4	100	
2018	KCA	MLB	29	8	8	0	25	25	148	145	21	3.0	9.0	148	53%	.303	1.31	3.99	4.17	4.51	14.1	1.5	103	

Breakout: 21% Improve: 47% Collapse: 29% Attrition: 14% MLB: 89% *Comparables: Brandon Morrow, Homer Bailey, Chris Tillman*

"It's a bear suit, Joel." Duffy famously informed Fox Sports Kansas City reporter Joel Goldberg of his celebratory attire following the Royals' championship. Duffy brings a laid-back SoCal vibe to the clubhouse. On the mound, it's been a bit of a different tale as he's struggled to find his role, bouncing between the rotation and the relief corps. Opening last year in his preferred bullpen role, he was pushed to the rotation when injuries created an opening. There, he flourished, posting the highest WARP of his career while setting positive milestones in walk and strikeout rates. In the past when Duffy got ahead of hitters, he would pump the brakes and nibble, letting them off the hook while leading to elevated pitch counts. Not anymore. He got more swings and, trusting his stuff, got more misses as well. His resurgence culminated with a tour de force in Tampa in which he struck out a career-high 16 and generated an astounding 35 swings and misses. As they say in Cali, his performance was totally gnar, braj.

Brian Flynn   LHP

Born: 4/19/90   Age: 27   Bats: L   Throws: L   Height: 6'7"   Weight: 250   Entered Pro Ball: Round 7, 2011 Draft (#227 overall)

YEAR	TEAM	LVL	AGE	W	L	SV	G	GS	IP	H	HR	BB/9	K/9	K	GB%	BABIP	WHIP	ERA	FIP	DRA	VORP	WARP	cFIP	MPH
2014	MIA	MLB	24	0	1	0	2	1	7	12	0	3.9	7.7	6	50%	.462	2.14	9.00	2.67	4.40	0.2	0.0	105	92.6
2014	NWO	AAA	24	8	10	0	25	25	139²	169	13	3.2	6.7	104	47%	.342	1.57	4.06	4.62	7.83	-32.2	-3.2	105	
2016	OMA	AAA	26	2	1	0	9	4	23²	22	1	4.6	10.6	28	66%	.350	1.44	3.04	3.43	2.59	6.8	0.7	80	
2016	KCA	MLB	26	1	2	0	36	1	55¹	38	5	3.7	7.2	44	57%	.223	1.10	2.60	3.99	4.20	4.8	0.5	102	95.4
2017	*KCA*	*MLB*	*27*	*3*	*3*	*3*	*55*	*0*	*58*	*58*	*5*	*3.7*	*7.5*	*49*	*50%*	*.305*	*1.42*	*3.93*	*3.99*	*4.32*	*4.3*	*0.4*	*96*	
2018	*KCA*	*MLB*	*28*	*2*	*1*	*2*	*47*	*0*	*50*	*45*	*5*	*5.1*	*9.8*	*55*	*50%*	*.307*	*1.45*	*3.87*	*4.03*	*4.38*	*3.7*	*0.4*	*96*	

Breakout: 21%   Improve: 38%   Collapse: 21%   Attrition: 37%   MLB: 66%   *Comparables: Doug Mathis, Brandon Cumpton, Blake Treinen*

Acquired in a trade for former first rounder Aaron Crow, the Royals were counting on Flynn to contribute to the bullpen upon his arrival in 2015. Sometimes, the best laid plans are delayed. A torn lat muscle pushed the timetable back a year, but he was certainly able to provide valuable innings in relief in '16. His fastball lives on the lower side of the mid-90s, and both his four- and two-seam offerings generate ground balls. The fastballs pair well with an above-average change, which hitters from both sides of the plate struggle against. In fact, he generates almost an identical percentage of swing-and-miss stuff against both left- and right-handed bats. He still struggles with finding a consistent release point and the walks continue to be an issue, but the grounders help dodge the potential for flameouts.

Dillon Gee   RHP

Born: 4/28/86   Age: 31   Bats: R   Throws: R   Height: 6'1"   Weight: 205   Entered Pro Ball: Round 21, 2007 Draft (#663 overall)

YEAR	TEAM	LVL	AGE	W	L	SV	G	GS	IP	H	HR	BB/9	K/9	K	GB%	BABIP	WHIP	ERA	FIP	DRA	VORP	WARP	cFIP	MPH
2014	NYN	MLB	28	7	8	0	22	22	137¹	128	18	2.8	6.2	94	45%	.268	1.25	4.00	4.49	4.93	-1.4	-0.2	116	91.7
2015	SLU	A+	29	0	0	0	2	2	10¹	9	0	0.0	10.5	12	59%	.333	0.87	0.87	0.84	2.11	3.4	0.4	77	
2015	NYN	MLB	29	0	3	0	8	7	39²	55	5	2.5	5.7	25	53%	.355	1.66	5.90	4.45	4.78	1.2	0.1	111	92.2
2015	LVG	AAA	29	8	3	0	14	14	88¹	105	7	1.8	6.4	63	45%	.338	1.39	4.58	3.88	3.64	16.3	1.7	96	
2016	KCA	MLB	30	8	9	0	33	14	125	146	24	2.7	6.4	89	42%	.309	1.46	4.68	5.21	6.01	-11.3	-1.2	116	92.5
2017	*KCA*	*MLB*	*31*	*6*	*8*	*0*	*19*	*19*	*113*	*128*	*17*	*3.0*	*6.7*	*84*	*48%*	*.311*	*1.46*	*4.68*	*4.71*	*5.24*	*2.9*	*0.3*	*123*	
2018	*KCA*	*MLB*	*32*	*5*	*6*	*0*	*15*	*15*	*87²*	*97*	*13*	*3.4*	*7.6*	*74*	*48%*	*.316*	*1.49*	*4.50*	*4.67*	*5.04*	*4.2*	*0.4*	*117*	

Breakout: 20%   Improve: 43%   Collapse: 16%   Attrition: 22%   MLB: 76%   *Comparables: Charlie Morton, Randy Wells, Tim Stauffer*

Seeking insurance for a suspect back of the rotation, the Royals picked up Gee. His value lies in his ability to throw strikes and eat innings, small portions at a time. As a reliever, he was trusted with a lead only three times all year and one of those was a 10-run cushion. As a fifth starter, he was nearly average. Which, for the right price, was exactly what the Royals needed.

Kelvin Herrera   RHP

Born: 12/31/89   Age: 27   Bats: R   Throws: R   Height: 5'10"   Weight: 200   Entered Pro Ball: International Free Agent, 2006

YEAR	TEAM	LVL	AGE	W	L	SV	G	GS	IP	H	HR	BB/9	K/9	K	GB%	BABIP	WHIP	ERA	FIP	DRA	VORP	WARP	cFIP	MPH
2014	KCA	MLB	24	4	3	0	70	0	70	54	0	3.3	7.6	59	52%	.274	1.14	1.41	2.72	3.80	5.3	0.6	100	101.0
2015	KCA	MLB	25	4	3	0	72	0	69²	52	5	3.4	8.3	64	46%	.249	1.12	2.71	3.41	3.72	7.7	0.8	98	101.0
2016	KCA	MLB	26	2	6	12	72	0	72	57	6	1.5	10.8	86	46%	.290	0.96	2.75	2.43	2.79	17.5	1.8	73	99.7
2017	*KCA*	*MLB*	*27*	*3*	*3*	*25*	*55*	*0*	*58*	*52*	*7*	*2.8*	*9.4*	*61*	*48%*	*.292*	*1.19*	*3.39*	*3.66*	*3.83*	*7.5*	*0.8*	*83*	
2018	*KCA*	*MLB*	*28*	*3*	*1*	*20*	*60*	*0*	*64*	*55*	*7*	*2.7*	*9.3*	*66*	*48%*	*.283*	*1.16*	*3.40*	*3.55*	*3.84*	*8.5*	*0.9*	*84*	

Breakout: 25%   Improve: 44%   Collapse: 36%   Attrition: 11%   MLB: 99%   *Comparables: Joakim Soria, Huston Street, Tug McGraw*

The hardest thrower in the Royals' bullpen, Herrera lost a tick off his fastball velocity in 2016, but still enjoyed the most productive season of his career. The slider he developed at the end of the 2015 season remains a weapon, throwing it to same side batters 16 percent of the time. Once he jumped ahead in the count, he unleashed it nearly a quarter of the time. Pro tip to batters: Don't fall behind. Opponents hit only .133 against his slider with a paltry .067 ISO. As the Royals' bullpen continues to percolate with quality arms, he's the next in line for the closer role.

Luke Hochevar   RHP

Born: 9/15/83   Age: 33   Bats: R   Throws: R   Height: 6'5"   Weight: 225   Entered Pro Ball: Round 1, 2006 Draft (#1 overall)

YEAR	TEAM	LVL	AGE	W	L	SV	G	GS	IP	H	HR	BB/9	K/9	K	GB%	BABIP	WHIP	ERA	FIP	DRA	VORP	WARP	cFIP	MPH
2015	OMA	AAA	31	0	1	0	9	4	10¹	16	2	7.0	8.7	10	47%	.438	2.32	7.84	6.50	5.25	-0.1	0.0	109	
2015	KCA	MLB	31	1	1	1	49	0	50²	49	7	2.8	8.7	49	38%	.298	1.28	3.73	3.97	4.49	1.2	0.1	104	96.6
2016	KCA	MLB	32	2	3	0	40	0	37¹	31	6	2.2	9.6	40	38%	.269	1.07	3.86	4.02	3.50	6.1	0.6	94	96.3
2017	*KCA*	*MLB*	*33*	*2*	*1*	*1*	*33*	*0*	*35*	*34*	*5*	*3.0*	*9.0*	*35*	*50%*	*.304*	*1.31*	*4.04*	*4.18*	*4.55*	*2.0*	*0.2*	*104*	
2018	*KCA*	*MLB*	*34*	*2*	*1*	*1*	*45*	*0*	*49²*	*48*	*8*	*3.1*	*8.6*	*47*	*50%*	*.295*	*1.32*	*4.21*	*4.38*	*4.74*	*1.7*	*0.2*	*110*	

Breakout: 17%   Improve: 43%   Collapse: 20%   Attrition: 17%   MLB: 83%   *Comparables: Tom Gorzelanny, Darren Dreifort, Alfredo Simon*

Some journeys are complicated. The only no. 1 overall draft pick in Royals franchise history, Hochevar scuffled as a starter, flourished in the bullpen, sat out the first run to an AL pennant recovering from Tommy John surgery, returned to reestablish himself as a key component of the lockdown bullpen in their title run in '15 and then missed the final half of last year after undergoing a procedure to relieve Thoracic Outlet syndrome. Whew. When healthy, as seen in '15 and part of '16, the velocity and three-pitch mix out of the bullpen translates to a strong strikeout-to-walk ratio. Those injuries have cost him, though, as Hochevar has thrown just 158 innings since 2013. There's still life—and value—in that right arm.

Greg Holland   RHP

Born: 11/20/85 Age: 31   Bats: R   Throws: R   Height: 5'10"   Weight: 205   Entered Pro Ball: Round 10, 2007 Draft (#306 overall)

YEAR	TEAM	LVL	AGE	W	L	SV	G	GS	IP	H	HR	BB/9	K/9	K	GB%	BABIP	WHIP	ERA	FIP	DRA	VORP	WARP	cFIP	MPH
2014	KCA	MLB	28	1	3	46	65	0	62¹	37	3	2.9	13.0	90	49%	.268	0.91	1.44	1.86	1.85	18.3	2.0	62	98.4
2015	KCA	MLB	29	3	2	32	48	0	44²	39	2	5.2	9.9	49	51%	.319	1.46	3.83	3.24	3.64	5.3	0.6	96	96.7
2017	KCA	MLB	31	2	1	24	33	0	35¹	30	5	3.8	11.7	46	39%	.308	1.27	3.52	3.72	3.96	3.9	0.4	86	
2018	KCA	MLB	32	3	1	38	54	0	51²	46	7	4.0	11.4	66	39%	.312	1.34	3.70	3.85	4.16	5.2	0.5	91	

Breakout: 22%   Improve: 34%   Collapse: 33%   Attrition: 12%   MLB: 90%   *Comparables: Jonathan Papelbon, Sean Marshall, Sergio Romo*

One of baseball's elite relievers in 2013 and 2014, Holland missed the end of 2015 and all of 2016 following Tommy John surgery. Never blessed with particularly good command, he'll need to rediscover mid-90s heat to be a late-inning option again. Despite just 320 career innings, the former All-Star closer is already 31 years old. He'll be a risky, high-upside flier.

Ian Kennedy   RHP

Born: 12/19/84 Age: 32   Bats: R   Throws: R   Height: 6'0"   Weight: 200   Entered Pro Ball: Round 1, 2006 Draft (#21 overall)

YEAR	TEAM	LVL	AGE	W	L	SV	G	GS	IP	H	HR	BB/9	K/9	K	GB%	BABIP	WHIP	ERA	FIP	DRA	VORP	WARP	cFIP	MPH
2014	SDN	MLB	29	13	13	0	33	33	201	189	16	3.1	9.3	207	42%	.315	1.29	3.63	3.18	4.21	14.0	1.5	101	94.4
2015	SDN	MLB	30	9	15	0	30	30	168¹	166	31	2.8	9.3	174	41%	.301	1.30	4.28	4.54	4.39	12.9	1.4	99	93.8
2016	KCA	MLB	31	11	11	0	33	33	195²	173	33	3.0	8.5	184	34%	.268	1.22	3.68	4.63	4.71	14.2	1.5	110	94.5
2017	KCA	MLB	32	9	13	0	30	30	180	178	29	3.3	9.0	180	50%	.298	1.37	4.52	4.52	4.93	6.4	0.7	100	
2018	KCA	MLB	33	10	11	0	29	29	175	169	29	3.3	9.3	181	50%	.297	1.33	4.27	4.43	4.79	12.7	1.3	111	

Breakout: 15%   Improve: 49%   Collapse: 25%   Attrition: 8%   MLB: 88%   *Comparables: Ervin Santana, Tim Lincecum, Edwin Jackson*

Bombs away, right? Kennedy has become synonymous with the long ball, perhaps a surprising development given his last two home addresses are among the more difficult parks for hitters to leave the yard. Hidden in his homer rate from last summer is that it actually decreased as the season progressed. He coughed up 19 dingers in the first three months, for an abysmal 1.9 HR/9. He followed that up with 14 homers the rest of the way, good for a 1.2 HR/9. Regression? Perhaps. Yet a sustained decrease in home run rate given his recent track record is cause for celebration. Otherwise, he's the same pitcher we've come to expect: a durable strike-thrower who has an ability to miss bats in the zone. Kennedy is entering the second year of a five-year contract signed in the winter of 2015 and holds an opt out following this season. The Royals are surely hoping he exercises that or they'll be paying a hefty price for the back side of his aging curve.

Kevin McCarthy   RHP

Born: 2/22/92 Age: 25   Bats: R   Throws: R   Height: 6'3"   Weight: 200   Entered Pro Ball: Round 16, 2013 Draft (#474 overall)

YEAR	TEAM	LVL	AGE	W	L	SV	G	GS	IP	H	HR	BB/9	K/9	K	GB%	BABIP	WHIP	ERA	FIP	DRA	VORP	WARP	cFIP	MPH
2015	LEX	A	23	1	1	2	6	0	12	10	0	0.8	6.0	8	60%	.263	0.92	1.50	2.40	3.69	1.5	0.2	93	
2015	WIL	A+	23	3	3	4	16	0	33	24	2	1.4	6.3	23	57%	.232	0.88	1.64	3.10	3.26	5.3	0.6	91	
2015	NWA	AA	23	1	0	0	11	0	17¹	24	1	4.2	4.7	9	48%	.348	1.85	5.71	4.39	7.49	-5.3	-0.6	109	
2016	NWA	AA	24	3	2	11	22	0	34²	26	3	2.1	7.5	29	53%	.245	0.98	3.12	3.41	3.56	4.5	0.5	91	
2016	OMA	AAA	24	2	4	5	25	0	33¹	28	4	4.3	8.1	30	56%	.270	1.32	2.97	5.01	4.36	2.2	0.2	94	
2016	KCA	MLB	24	1	0	0	10	0	8¹	11	1	5.4	7.6	7	55%	.357	1.92	6.48	4.79	4.87	0.1	0.0	109	96.1
2017	KCA	MLB	25	2	3	0	50	0	53	58	6	3.6	5.7	34	52%	.297	1.49	5.21	4.66	5.31	-1.9	-0.2	100	
2018	KCA	MLB	26	1	0	0	20	0	20²	20	3	5.2	8.9	21	52%	.304	1.56	4.68	4.85	5.24	-0.4	0.0	120	

Breakout: 15%   Improve: 18%   Collapse: 14%   Attrition: 29%   MLB: 33%   *Comparables: Jake Dunning, Jose Ortega, Fernando Abad*

A member of the 2013 draft class, McCarthy competed at three levels for the Royals, reaching the majors as a September call-up. Featuring an easy delivery and a fastball that resides in the low 90s, along with an average slider and change, he's always going to be facing long odds to stick in a pen as strong as the one they have in Kansas City.

Kris Medlen   RHP

Born: 10/7/85 Age: 31   Bats: B   Throws: R   Height: 5'10"   Weight: 190   Entered Pro Ball: Round 10, 2006 Draft (#310 overall)

YEAR	TEAM	LVL	AGE	W	L	SV	G	GS	IP	H	HR	BB/9	K/9	K	GB%	BABIP	WHIP	ERA	FIP	DRA	VORP	WARP	cFIP	MPH
2015	OMA	AAA	29	1	0	0	3	3	15¹	16	6	0.6	5.3	9	51%	.222	1.11	4.11	8.10	5.07	0.4	0.0	101	
2015	NWA	AA	29	0	1	0	3	3	15	13	2	2.4	6.6	11	67%	.250	1.13	3.00	4.76	3.51	2.6	0.3	95	
2015	KCA	MLB	29	6	2	0	15	8	58¹	56	6	2.8	6.2	40	51%	.282	1.27	4.01	4.10	4.28	4.6	0.5	104	93.5
2016	KCA	MLB	30	1	3	0	6	6	24¹	30	2	7.4	6.7	18	49%	.354	2.05	7.77	5.16	5.74	-1.0	-0.1	119	92.9
2016	OMA	AAA	30	0	3	0	8	5	19²	25	9	3.2	8.2	18	41%	.281	1.63	8.69	9.06	3.84	3.2	0.3	102	
2017	KCA	MLB	31	3	4	0	10	10	52¹	55	7	3.7	7.0	41	49%	.301	1.45	4.59	4.62	5.16	1.8	0.2	121	
2018	KCA	MLB	32	8	10	0	26	26	155¹	168	21	4.2	7.1	122	49%	.311	1.55	4.66	4.84	5.24	3.6	0.4	121	

Breakout: 16%   Improve: 37%   Collapse: 23%   Attrition: 18%   MLB: 86%   *Comparables: Alexi Ogando, Bronson Arroyo, Jaret Wright*

Returning from a second Tommy John surgery, the Royals took a chance on Medlen ahead of the 2015 season and found a handsome reward in limited action coming out of the bullpen. Penciled in to pick up some starts at the back of the rotation, his 2016 was filled with setbacks and roadblocks. He failed to record an out in the third inning in each of his final two starts before he was shut down with a rotator cuff strain on May 12. Medlen never found his way back to Kansas City, twice being pulled from minor-league rehab assignments.

Alec Mills   RHP

Born: 11/30/91 Age: 25   Bats: R   Throws: R   Height: 6'4"   Weight: 190   Entered Pro Ball: Round 22, 2012 Draft (#673 overall)

YEAR	TEAM	LVL	AGE	W	L	SV	G	GS	IP	H	HR	BB/9	K/9	K	GB%	BABIP	WHIP	ERA	FIP	DRA	VORP	WARP	cFIP	MPH
2014	LEX	A	22	2	1	0	7	7	38	25	0	2.4	7.8	33	58%	.263	0.92	1.18	2.72	2.58	12.1	1.2	80	
2015	WIL	A+	23	7	7	0	21	21	113¹	122	3	1.1	8.8	111	52%	.350	1.20	3.02	2.09	1.67	42.9	4.6	69	
2016	NWA	AA	24	1	2	0	12	12	67²	57	2	1.6	9.0	68	44%	.314	1.02	2.39	2.13	1.06	30.3	3.3	67	
2016	OMA	AAA	24	4	3	0	12	11	58	62	8	2.9	8.4	54	47%	.323	1.40	4.19	4.74	2.91	15.6	1.6	87	
2016	KCA	MLB	24	0	0	0	3	0	3¹	3	0	13.5	10.8	4	44%	.333	2.40	13.50	6.11	4.68	0.1	0.0	105	94.2
2017	KCA	MLB	25	4	5	0	38	8	74¹	76	8	2.9	7.2	59	50%	.303	1.36	4.04	4.07	4.39	6.1	0.6	100	
2018	KCA	MLB	26	5	4	0	47	9	93¹	84	10	4.2	10.0	104	50%	.307	1.36	3.75	3.90	4.21	10.3	1.1	94	

Breakout: 18%   Improve: 35%   Collapse: 26%   Attrition: 43%   MLB: 73%   *Comparables: Tyler Lyons, Michael Clevinger, Kyle Gibson*

Do you like strikeouts? Do you have disdain for the walk? If the answer to both of these questions is yes, Mills is the pitcher for you. Splitting time between Double and Triple-A, the former 22nd-round pick issued just 1.5 BB/9 while punching out 8.7 K/9 in just over 125 minor-league innings. He features a swing-and-miss fastball with arm-side run and a developing change, along with a curve that's a work in progress. He got knocked around in a couple of appearances in the show, but it's not out of the realm of possibility he could develop into a mid-to-back-of-the-rotation starter.

Mike Minor   LHP

Born: 12/26/87 Age: 29   Bats: R   Throws: L   Height: 6'4"   Weight: 210   Entered Pro Ball: Round 1, 2009 Draft (#7 overall)

YEAR	TEAM	LVL	AGE	W	L	SV	G	GS	IP	H	HR	BB/9	K/9	K	GB%	BABIP	WHIP	ERA	FIP	DRA	VORP	WARP	cFIP	MPH
2014	ATL	MLB	26	6	12	0	25	25	145¹	165	21	2.7	7.4	120	43%	.323	1.44	4.77	4.36	4.45	6.2	0.7	106	92.9
2016	OMA	AAA	28	0	4	0	8	8	34²	38	7	4.4	8.6	33	37%	.333	1.59	6.23	5.91	5.72	-1.4	-0.1	104	
2017	KCA	MLB	29	4	4	0	46	6	74	71	9	3.3	7.7	63	52%	.287	1.30	4.39	4.26	4.67	3.5	0.4	100	
2018	KCA	MLB	30	6	4	0	71	8	115²	107	14	3.3	7.9	101	52%	.283	1.29	3.99	4.14	4.44	9.4	1.0	101	

Breakout: 24%   Improve: 44%   Collapse: 18%   Attrition: 11%   MLB: 89%   *Comparables: Travis Wood, Dave Bush, Scott Baker*

There's risk. And with that risk, there's sometimes a reward. Other times, it just doesn't work out like you draw it up on the white board. There was no reward for the Royals in Minor's first season in the organization. Even though he was recovering from shoulder surgery, he was signed with the intent he would complete his rehab, throw a handful of innings in the minors and then arrive in Kansas City around the All-Star break to provide a stable reinforcement in the back of the rotation. Except he never made it to Kansas City. Setback after setback cut his season short. He's back for at least one more season to try again. They may yet realize a reward. It's just risky to count on it.

Franklin Morales   LHP

Born: 1/24/86 Age: 31   Bats: L   Throws: L   Height: 6'1"   Weight: 210   Entered Pro Ball: International Free Agent, 2002

YEAR	TEAM	LVL	AGE	W	L	SV	G	GS	IP	H	HR	BB/9	K/9	K	GB%	BABIP	WHIP	ERA	FIP	DRA	VORP	WARP	cFIP	MPH
2014	COL	MLB	28	6	9	0	38	22	142¹	166	24	4.1	6.3	100	45%	.315	1.62	5.37	5.39	5.78	-15.9	-1.8	118	93.9
2015	KCA	MLB	29	4	2	0	67	0	62¹	58	4	2.0	5.9	41	51%	.277	1.16	3.18	3.49	4.77	-0.4	0.0	104	95.0
2016	TOR	MLB	30	0	1	0	5	0	4	3	1	4.5	4.5	2	25%	.182	1.25	9.00	6.86	5.80	-0.4	0.0	122	92.9
2017	KCA	MLB	31	2	2	0	19	4	34	35	5	3.7	7.1	27	56%	.297	1.45	4.79	4.86	5.38	-0.4	0.0	125	
2018	KCA	MLB	32	4	4	0	51	8	93²	101	15	3.9	7.1	73	56%	.303	1.51	4.89	5.06	5.49	-2.2	-0.2	126	

Breakout: 26%   Improve: 49%   Collapse: 23%   Attrition: 25%   MLB: 81%   *Comparables: Jorge Sosa, Brian Duensing, Todd Wellemeyer*

This is a man who knows about efficiency. Despite a modest $2 million salary, Morales managed to earn just under $34,000 per pitch in 2016. Every time he threw the ball off a major-league mound, Morales could afford to buy a brand new mid-level luxury sedan. We should all strive for this level of professional prowess. Sure, he lost five miles per hour on his fastball during the season (down to 88 mph) and will struggle to find a guaranteed contract in 2017, but those are going to be some smooth rides.

Peter Moylan   RHP

Born: 12/2/78 Age: 38   Bats: R   Throws: R   Height: 6'2"   Weight: 225   Entered Pro Ball: International Free Agent, 1996

YEAR	TEAM	LVL	AGE	W	L	SV	G	GS	IP	H	HR	BB/9	K/9	K	GB%	BABIP	WHIP	ERA	FIP	DRA	VORP	WARP	cFIP	MPH
2015	GWN	AAA	36	2	0	6	27	0	28²	22	1	2.8	7.5	24	57%	.269	1.08	3.14	3.19	2.77	6.8	0.7	98	
2015	ATL	MLB	36	1	0	0	22	0	10¹	12	1	0.0	7.0	8	69%	.314	1.16	3.48	2.87	3.41	1.5	0.2	94	92.6
2016	OMA	AAA	37	1	1	5	12	0	12²	8	0	3.6	7.1	10	59%	.235	1.03	0.71	3.80	4.45	0.7	0.1	99	
2016	KCA	MLB	37	2	0	0	50	0	44²	42	4	3.2	6.9	34	63%	.281	1.30	3.43	3.96	3.80	5.8	0.6	98	92.6
2017	KCA	MLB	38	2	1	0	42	0	44²	47	5	3.5	7.0	35	49%	.304	1.45	4.43	4.29	5.01	0.2	0.0	114	
2018	KCA	MLB	39	2	1	0	43	0	41²	43	6	3.6	7.7	36	49%	.303	1.42	4.36	4.54	4.93	0.6	0.1	112	

Breakout: 16%   Improve: 31%   Collapse: 14%   Attrition: 7%   MLB: 57%   *Comparables: Hideki Okajima, J.C. Romero, Scott Atchison*

It's all about the worms these days. In this era of power arms out of the bullpen, Moylan is something of an anomaly. Averaging just around 90 mph on his two-seamer, it comes in with some heavy sink. He's no Zack Britton when it comes to generating ground balls, but just the same, worms should be very afraid when he toes the slab. Those worms get a reprieve when he features his second pitch, a slider that comes in below 80 mph. Even though batters can get the barrel on his off-speed stuff, it's a pitch that features some depth, so he limits the hard contact. Moylan already stepped away from the game once to coach and pitched more major-league innings last season than the previous five years combined. What happens next is anyone's guess.

A.J. Puckett   RHP

Born: 5/27/95   Age: 22   Bats: R   Throws: R   Height: 6'4"   Weight: 200   Entered Pro Ball: Round 2, 2016 Draft (#67 overall)

YEAR	TEAM	LVL	AGE	W	L	SV	G	GS	IP	H	HR	BB/9	K/9	K	GB%	BABIP	WHIP	ERA	FIP	DRA	VORP	WARP	cFIP	MPH
2016	LEX	A	21	2	3	0	11	11	51²	42	4	2.6	6.4	37	52%	.264	1.10	3.66	3.96	5.00	0.1	0.0	106	
2017	KCA	MLB	22	1	3	0	8	8	35	46	6	4.8	3.7	14	63%	.309	1.84	6.41	6.36	7.03	-6.1	-0.6	167	
2018	KCA	MLB	23	5	10	0	24	24	140	168	23	6.1	6.5	101	63%	.320	1.87	5.88	6.06	6.45	-12.0	-1.2	151	

Breakout: 0%   Improve: 1%   Collapse: 0%   Attrition: 1%   MLB: 1%   Comparables: Michael Ynoa, Josh Wall, Sugar Ray Marimon

The Royals love them some athletes, so it wasn't a surprise when they selected Puckett in the second round of the 2016 draft. While splitting time between the mound and the gridiron as a prep, Puckett suffered a freak brain injury that forced him into a medically induced coma for two weeks and ultimately pushed him to baseball full time. He was drafted by the A's out of high school, but chose to attend Pepperdine, where he threw 45 consecutive scoreless frames and was the WAC pitcher of the year. Puckett's fastball sits in the mid-to-low 90s and he complements it with a plus change, along with a slider and a developing overhand curve. His command improved once he developed a simple, repeatable delivery with a low leg kick. With one of the higher floors in the system, he's off to a promising start.

Joakim Soria   RHP

Born: 5/18/84   Age: 33   Bats: R   Throws: R   Height: 6'3"   Weight: 200   Entered Pro Ball: International Free Agent, 2001

YEAR	TEAM	LVL	AGE	W	L	SV	G	GS	IP	H	HR	BB/9	K/9	K	GB%	BABIP	WHIP	ERA	FIP	DRA	VORP	WARP	cFIP	MPH
2014	TEX	MLB	30	1	3	17	35	0	33¹	25	0	1.1	11.3	42	42%	.291	0.87	2.70	1.09	2.23	8.4	0.9	78	92.6
2014	DET	MLB	30	1	1	1	13	0	11	13	2	1.6	4.9	6	52%	.289	1.36	4.91	5.25	2.23	2.8	0.3	79	92.8
2015	DET	MLB	31	3	1	23	43	0	41	32	8	2.4	7.9	36	46%	.222	1.05	2.85	4.84	4.21	2.3	0.2	96	95.2
2015	PIT	MLB	31	0	0	1	29	0	26²	23	0	2.7	9.4	28	41%	.329	1.16	2.03	1.96	4.11	1.8	0.2	96	94.7
2016	KCA	MLB	32	5	8	1	70	0	66²	70	10	3.6	9.2	68	52%	.323	1.46	4.05	4.32	4.08	6.6	0.7	95	95.2
2017	KCA	MLB	33	3	3	2	60	0	63	63	9	3.2	8.7	62	44%	.297	1.34	4.46	4.23	4.73	1.8	0.2	100	
2018	KCA	MLB	34	1	0	1	24	0	25	25	4	3.6	8.5	24	44%	.301	1.41	4.40	4.58	4.97	0.2	0.0	113	

Breakout: 17%   Improve: 41%   Collapse: 25%   Attrition: 9%   MLB: 86%   Comparables: John Axford, Pedro Feliciano, Scott Linebrink

It wasn't supposed to be like this. The plan was for Soria to make a triumphant return to Kansas City, his home from 2006-2012 and the place where he made a name for himself. Instead, he suffered through the worst full season of his major-league career. While Dayton Moore and his staff have an outstanding track record of putting together a quality bullpen from internal options and scrapheap arms, they decided to go after an option with a high sticker price. Instead of a dependable seventh- or eighth-inning guy, they got a wildly inconsistent reliever. One who was at times unlucky, but who also didn't help himself when his control would inexplicably disappear in the midst of an outing. Ned Yost, stubborn by nature, stuck by his old reliever to the bitter end, calling on Soria for more high-leverage situations than any reliever but Kelvin Herrera. By the end of the year, the carnage was undeniable. Twelve blown leads. Five other games he entered with the score tied and left with a deficit. In the Royals' pennant-winning years, their success was built on a trio of quality arms coming out of the back end of the pen. They're sticking to that blueprint, so they'll either need a rebound season here or they'll need to cast in the old waters to find a replacement for those high-leverage, late-inning situations.

Josh Staumont   RHP

Born: 12/21/93   Age: 23   Bats: R   Throws: R   Height: 6'3"   Weight: 200   Entered Pro Ball: Round 2, 2015 Draft (#64 overall)

YEAR	TEAM	LVL	AGE	W	L	SV	G	GS	IP	H	HR	BB/9	K/9	K	GB%	BABIP	WHIP	ERA	FIP	DRA	VORP	WARP	cFIP	MPH
2016	WIL	A+	22	2	10	0	18	15	73	62	3	8.3	11.6	94	46%	.328	1.77	5.05	4.55	7.22	-14.5	-1.5	121	
2016	NWA	AA	22	2	1	0	11	11	50¹	42	2	6.6	13.1	73	42%	.364	1.57	3.04	3.24	3.57	8.5	0.9	94	
2017	KCA	MLB	23	4	6	1	36	16	90¹	95	12	7.2	8.7	88	53%	.321	1.85	5.45	5.53	5.98	-7.8	-0.8	139	
2018	KCA	MLB	24	2	3	0	16	9	66²	65	9	7.9	10.7	79	53%	.329	1.86	5.20	5.37	5.71	-1.9	-0.2	132	

Breakout: 3%   Improve: 5%   Collapse: 2%   Attrition: 2%   MLB: 8%   Comparables: Ethan Martin, Jae Kuk Ryu, Michael Ynoa

His triple-digit fastball comes in so hot it has fried an egg. His hammer curve has caused the tectonic plates to shift. His command is so suspect, it was picked up on charges of petty theft, but was later thrown out of court for insufficient evidence. He once struck out a hitter just by looking at him. He's Josh Staumont, the most interesting pitcher in the Royals' system.

Matt Strahm   LHP

Born: 11/12/91   Age: 25   Bats: R   Throws: L   Height: 6'3"   Weight: 185   Entered Pro Ball: Round 21, 2012 Draft (#643 overall)

YEAR	TEAM	LVL	AGE	W	L	SV	G	GS	IP	H	HR	BB/9	K/9	K	GB%	BABIP	WHIP	ERA	FIP	DRA	VORP	WARP	cFIP	MPH
2015	LEX	A	23	2	1	4	14	0	26	12	1	4.2	13.2	38	48%	.234	0.92	2.08	2.68	1.69	9.1	1.0	80	
2015	WIL	A+	23	1	6	1	15	11	68	48	7	2.5	11.0	83	37%	.255	0.99	2.78	3.21	1.26	28.4	3.1	73	
2016	NWA	AA	24	3	8	0	22	18	102¹	102	14	2.0	9.4	107	40%	.320	1.22	3.43	3.72	2.53	28.9	3.1	87	
2016	KCA	MLB	24	2	2	0	21	0	22	13	0	4.5	12.3	30	50%	.283	1.09	1.23	2.02	2.91	5.0	0.5	80	96.8
2017	KCA	MLB	25	5	7	0	18	18	90	93	12	3.3	7.7	77	52%	.301	1.41	4.42	4.46	4.80	4.5	0.5	100	
2018	KCA	MLB	26	9	10	0	30	30	187²	170	26	4.3	10.7	223	52%	.306	1.38	4.03	4.20	4.51	16.0	1.6	103	

Breakout: 36%   Improve: 47%   Collapse: 19%   Attrition: 28%   MLB: 78%   Comparables: Scott Elbert, Jae Kuk Ryu, Antonio Bastardo

What if we told you there was a pitcher in the Royals' system who threw in the mid-90s, featured swing-and-miss stuff and generated an above-average number of ground-ball outs? Is that something that would interest you? Look no further than Strahm, the first player from the 21st round of the 2012 draft to make the show. He made the transition from the Texas League to the majors with aplomb. The next question is, how will the Royals deploy the young left-hander going forward? He excelled in relief, but the Royals can use the help in the rotation, which is where he worked for most of the last two seasons.

Jason Vargas   LHP

Born: 2/2/83   Age: 34   Bats: L   Throws: L   Height: 6'0"   Weight: 215   Entered Pro Ball: Round 2, 2004 Draft (#68 overall)

YEAR	TEAM	LVL	AGE	W	L	SV	G	GS	IP	H	HR	BB/9	K/9	K	GB%	BABIP	WHIP	ERA	FIP	DRA	VORP	WARP	cFIP	MPH
2014	KCA	MLB	31	11	10	0	30	30	187	197	19	2.0	6.2	128	41%	.299	1.27	3.71	3.87	4.30	11.2	1.2	105	89.7
2015	KCA	MLB	32	5	2	0	9	9	43	46	5	2.5	5.7	27	41%	.297	1.35	3.98	4.27	4.39	3.3	0.4	113	90.3
2016	OMA	AAA	33	0	2	0	3	3	13²	16	3	0.7	11.9	18	35%	.382	1.24	5.93	4.16	2.22	4.7	0.5	79	
2016	KCA	MLB	33	0	0	0	3	3	12	8	1	2.2	8.2	11	36%	.219	0.92	2.25	3.11	4.54	1.1	0.1	103	89.0
2017	KCA	MLB	34	6	8	0	19	19	114	118	16	2.4	7.2	91	46%	.294	1.30	4.36	4.29	4.76	6.2	0.6	100	
2018	KCA	MLB	35	10	10	0	28	28	172²	185	27	2.3	7.2	139	46%	.302	1.33	4.27	4.45	4.81	12.1	1.3	112	

Breakout: 20%   Improve: 45%   Collapse: 20%   Attrition: 11%   MLB: 83%   *Comparables: Kyle Lohse, Johan Santana, Joel Pineiro*

Vargas underwent Tommy John surgery in August 2015, meaning he missed out on the Royals' title run. Maybe that motivated him in his recovery, because he was throwing simulated games in July, a mere 11 months after getting a new UCL. He made his return to the major-league rotation in September. The irony here is Vargas does nothing with haste. Prior to his surgery, on his best fastballing days, he would hit the double eights on the radar gun. Around the time his ligament tore in 2015, his velocity dipped to 86 mph, which is where it sat in his return. Maybe a normal offseason throwing regimen help him find his missing mph. Will anyone notice? Or maybe he'll finally win the Jered Weaver Award for slowest average fastball speed, non-knuckleballer division. As Vargas enters the final year of a four-year contract, the Royals will count on him to provide some innings and some tortoise-like stability in the back of the rotation.

Yordano Ventura   RHP

Born: 6/3/91   Age: 26   Bats: R   Throws: R   Height: 6'0"   Weight: 195   Entered Pro Ball: International Free Agent, 2008

YEAR	TEAM	LVL	AGE	W	L	SV	G	GS	IP	H	HR	BB/9	K/9	K	GB%	BABIP	WHIP	ERA	FIP	DRA	VORP	WARP	cFIP	MPH
2014	KCA	MLB	23	14	10	0	31	30	183	168	14	3.4	7.8	159	48%	.288	1.30	3.20	3.63	3.18	33.6	3.7	100	100.3
2015	KCA	MLB	24	13	8	0	28	28	163¹	154	14	3.2	8.6	156	53%	.307	1.30	4.08	3.54	3.48	29.0	3.1	88	99.8
2016	KCA	MLB	25	11	12	0	32	32	186	190	23	3.8	7.0	144	51%	.297	1.44	4.45	4.55	4.44	19.1	2.0	106	99.5
2017	KCA	MLB	26	9	12	0	30	30	180	177	20	3.6	7.9	158	51%	.299	1.39	4.21	4.19	4.60	13.0	1.3	100	
2018	KCA	MLB	27	11	10	0	30	30	189¹	181	22	3.7	8.8	186	51%	.302	1.36	3.91	4.07	4.41	20.9	2.2	100	

Breakout: 23%   Improve: 55%   Collapse: 14%   Attrition: 8%   MLB: 88%   *Comparables: Brandon McCarthy, Jarrod Parker, Max Scherzer*

Let's take a moment to focus on the positives for the enigmatic Ventura. To begin, at 96.1 mph, he throws the fastest average heater of any starting pitcher not nicknamed Thor. Next, there's his hammer curve that breaks on a 12-6 plane and features an above-average spin rate. Opponents swung and missed over 16 percent of the time he offered the curve and hit just .172 against it last year. The negatives? His fastball will flatten out at times and hitters were able to tee off it to the tune of a .333 AVG with a .586 SLG. His walk rate threatened to career out of control early in the season, before he got it back on track. Conversely, his strikeouts are down and he got a swing and miss on only five percent of his fastballs, down from 11 percent two years ago. The stuff is still there, but inconsistencies continue to bedevil the young right-hander and time is running out if he's to fulfill his potential.

Chris Young   RHP

Born: 5/25/79   Age: 38   Bats: R   Throws: R   Height: 6'10"   Weight: 255   Entered Pro Ball: Round 3, 2000 Draft (#89 overall)

YEAR	TEAM	LVL	AGE	W	L	SV	G	GS	IP	H	HR	BB/9	K/9	K	GB%	BABIP	WHIP	ERA	FIP	DRA	VORP	WARP	cFIP	MPH
2014	SEA	MLB	35	12	9	0	30	29	165	143	26	3.3	5.9	108	25%	.238	1.23	3.65	5.04	8.12	-60.2	-6.7	148	88.0
2015	KCA	MLB	36	11	6	0	34	18	123¹	91	16	3.1	6.1	83	28%	.209	1.09	3.06	4.49	6.00	-13.6	-1.5	129	88.9
2016	KCA	MLB	37	3	9	1	34	13	88²	104	28	4.4	9.5	94	31%	.318	1.66	6.19	6.58	5.05	1.7	0.2	119	90.2
2017	KCA	MLB	38	4	5	0	56	6	87	83	14	3.8	8.3	80	39%	.281	1.36	5.05	4.80	5.24	-1.5	-0.2	100	
2018	KCA	MLB	39	2	2	0	32	3	50²	52	8	5.1	8.2	46	39%	.299	1.59	5.09	5.26	5.70	-2.6	-0.3	131	

Breakout: 8%   Improve: 22%   Collapse: 14%   Attrition: 21%   MLB: 49%   *Comparables: Randy Wolf, Freddy Garcia, Ted Lilly*

Ignoring a fly-ball rate higher than the sun and a BABIP that was 20,000 leagues under the sea, the Royals decided to award Young with a two year, $11.5 million contract last offseason. Regression can sometimes be a costly lesson. While his fly-ball rate dropped below 50 percent for the first time since 2005, his home run rate spiked to a ghastly 2.8 HR/9. Couple with a BABIP that's suddenly above league average and you have a mess on your hands. The initial thought was Young could serve as a swingman over the duration of his contract. Now in the final year of the deal, it's likely he'll pitch the remainder of his Royals tenure out of the bullpen.

Kyle Zimmer   RHP

Born: 9/13/91   Age: 25   Bats: R   Throws: R   Height: 6'3"   Weight: 225   Entered Pro Ball: Round 1, 2012 Draft (#5 overall)

YEAR	TEAM	LVL	AGE	W	L	SV	G	GS	IP	H	HR	BB/9	K/9	K	GB%	BABIP	WHIP	ERA	FIP	DRA	VORP	WARP	cFIP	MPH
2015	LEX	A	23	1	0	0	9	0	16	11	1	3.4	11.8	21	49%	.278	1.06	1.12	2.80	2.28	4.6	0.5	83	
2015	NWA	AA	23	2	5	3	15	7	48	42	4	2.6	9.6	51	48%	.299	1.17	2.81	3.13	1.42	18.9	2.0	79	
2017	KCA	MLB	25	1	2	0	5	5	25	26	3	3.7	7.1	20	47%	.298	1.51	4.47	4.45	4.89	1.0	0.1	100	
2018	KCA	MLB	26	9	10	0	29	29	180²	168	23	5.0	10.0	200	47%	.307	1.48	4.20	4.38	4.73	12.0	1.2	108	

Breakout: 12%   Improve: 21%   Collapse: 28%   Attrition: 45%   MLB: 60%   *Comparables: Chase Anderson, Cody Martin, George Kontos*

Stop us if you've heard this one before: Zimmer should be ready to go by spring training. Along with Truck Day and traffic jams in suburban Phoenix, the Royals' insistence that *this* is going to be the year we see a healthy Zimmer has become a rite of spring. No one disputes his stuff as being worthy of the front of the rotation. The reality is he simply can't find a way to stay out of the doctor's office and on the field. Shut down in July after throwing just 5.2 innings—fewer than the 64 he tossed in 2014, but more than the 4.2 he tallied in 2013—he underwent thoracic outlet surgery. The procedure was deemed a success and he completed a four-week throwing program to prepare for a normal offseason conditioning routine. Whether he makes an impact in Kansas City is anyone's guess.

LINEOUTS

Hitters

NAME	POS	TEAM	LVL	AGE	PA	R	2B	3B	HR	RBI	BB	K	SB	CS	AVG/OBP/SLG	TAv	VORP	BABIP	BRR	FRAA	WARP
D.J. Burt	2B	LEX	A	20	542	74	16	5	4	59	51	108	43	17	.257/.335/.338	.261	22.1	.322	7.0	2B(113): -14.7, SS(11): 0.8	0.9
Samir Duenez	1B	LEX	A	20	285	30	15	3	6	49	15	40	14	2	.272/.312/.419	.264	5.1	.297	1.4	1B(58): 1.5	0.7
	1B	WIL	A+	20	235	30	13	2	7	42	19	34	10	2	.300/.363/.479	.301	14.3	.331	1.6	1B(52): -5.0	1.0
	1B	NWA	AA	20	59	4	5	0	0	9	5	12	2	0	.278/.339/.370	.249	0.3	.357	0.4	1B(1): -0.0	0.0
Alfredo Escalera-Maldonado	OF	WIL	A+	21	311	37	10	1	3	30	21	75	5	3	.269/.334/.343	.257	4.9	.356	-0.4	LF(56): 2.6, RF(3): -0.1	0.7
	OF	NWA	AA	21	218	25	14	0	2	23	6	51	5	1	.277/.299/.376	.262	6.9	.353	1.6	CF(19): 0.3, LF(18): -1.9	0.5
Cam Gallagher	C	NWA	AA	23	346	23	16	1	4	24	37	52	2	2	.259/.348/.359	.264	11.1	.300	-3.9	C(80): 19.7	3.3
Marten Gasparini	SS	LEX	A	19	429	35	12	2	7	42	31	134	14	10	.196/.256/.293	.227	2.9	.278	0.1	SS(107): -5.9	-0.3
Ryan O'Hearn	1B	WIL	A+	22	98	13	7	0	7	18	8	27	0	0	.352/.408/.670	.384	13.7	.436	-0.3	1B(21): -0.6	1.3
	1B	NWA	AA	22	466	49	25	2	15	60	48	131	3	5	.258/.339/.437	.284	14.8	.342	-2.8	1B(61): 2.0, LF(39): -3.3	1.5
Ramon Torres	SS	NWA	AA	23	185	20	5	1	1	8	18	18	9	4	.268/.339/.329	.253	6.1	.295	1.9	2B(22): 1.2, SS(17): 1.2	0.9
	SS	OMA	AAA	23	315	35	12	1	2	21	15	61	12	3	.259/.295/.327	.242	8.3	.321	2.7	SS(50): -3.2, 2B(23): -0.5	0.5
Corey Toups	SS	WIL	A+	23	179	21	10	5	2	11	22	35	6	1	.252/.352/.419	.279	9.6	.314	0.9	2B(30): 0.9, SS(9): -0.6	1.0
	SS	NWA	AA	23	394	61	25	2	10	38	36	96	16	3	.275/.358/.450	.303	25.6	.352	-1.3	2B(83): 11.1, SS(1): 0.9	4.1
Chase Vallot	C	LEX	A	19	330	37	20	0	13	44	39	118	0	0	.246/.367/.463	.300	22.8	.372	0.4	C(53): -4.3	2.0

A speedy Royals minor leaguer isn't particularly notable, but **D.J. Burt** also has impressive plate discipline that allows him to leverage his wheels. ❖ Young for every level he's played, the Royals were aggressive with 20-year-old **Samir Duenez**, promoting him twice during the season. A strong contact rate and developing power give the organization confidence he can handle the fast track. ❖ At 17 years and four months in 2012, **Alfredo Escalera-Maldonado** was the youngest player ever drafted. Debuting at Double-A last year, he struggled to make necessary adjustments; his instincts and makeup have the Royals hopeful a repeat turn through the Texas League will find him back on track. ❖ When finally eclipsing a .700 OPS at Double-A is considered a step forward, you'd better be able to cut it defensively, and **Cam Gallagher** still has enough chops there to forge a path toward a backup catcher destiny. ❖ In his first taste of Low-A, **Marten Gasparini** struggled with pitch recognition and, in the rare event he reached base, his raw skills on the paths were exposed as well. ❖ The Royals signed **Jeison Guzman** for $1.5 million in 2015 and he didn't disappoint in his first taste of pro ball, showing plate discipline along with a line-drive bat. With a quick release and strong footwork around the bag, he could move over to second. ❖ Signed for $2 million last summer, **Seuly Matias** led the Arizona Rookie League in home runs while showing off a strong arm that will eventually land him in right field. ❖ A new wrinkle was added to **Ryan O'Hearn**'s profile, as the budding slugger tacked on opposite-field power to his arsenal. Nearly half his home run production last year was to the left of center. ❖ Shades of Salvador Perez, the Royals signed 17-year-old backstop **Sebastian Rivero** from Venezuela for $450,000. ❖ **Esteury Ruiz** flashed some power potential in the Dominican Summer League as a 17-year-old. ❖ Defense and speed have been the calling cards for **Ramon Torres** as he's progressed through the system. The bat? Not so much a calling card as a "While You Were Out" note. ❖ **Corey Toups** wasn't supposed to pack power in his tool kit, but showed flashes as he's moved through the system. He could have a productive utility role in his future. ❖ The power plays to all fields for **Chase Vallot**. The issue always has been his inability to consistently introduce bat to ball. ❖ A powerful swing that generates pop to all fields defines catcher **Meibrys Viloria**. So does his strong arm and what the Royals see as his leadership skills, so it's time for him to move up the ladder.

Pitchers

NAME	TEAM	LVL	AGE	W	L	SV	G	GS	IP	H	HR	BB/9	K/9	K	GB%	BABIP	WHIP	ERA	FIP	DRA	VORP	WARP	cFIP	MPH
Andrew Edwards	NWA	AA	24	0	0	2	10	0	18	14	0	2.0	11.5	23	60%	.350	1.00	0.50	1.46	1.76	5.9	0.6	72	
	OMA	AAA	24	0	1	5	32	0	43¹	44	7	6.0	10.6	51	43%	.336	1.68	5.40	5.54	5.81	-4.1	-0.4	101	
Gerson Garabito	LEX	A	20	2	11	0	18	18	80²	78	9	3.9	6.8	61	38%	.284	1.40	4.80	4.90	7.08	-18.5	-2.0	116	
Foster Griffin	LEX	A	20	1	4	0	7	7	37¹	35	3	2.2	7.0	29	60%	.281	1.18	3.38	3.61	4.60	1.7	0.2	101	
	WIL	A+	20	5	10	0	20	20	95¹	130	9	4.1	7.2	76	47%	.376	1.81	6.23	4.72	5.53	-0.6	-0.1	106	
Jake Junis	NWA	AA	23	9	7	0	21	21	119	110	12	2.0	8.8	117	43%	.302	1.15	3.25	3.36	3.21	24.9	2.7	90	
	OMA	AAA	23	1	3	0	6	6	30	39	6	2.1	7.8	26	41%	.367	1.53	7.20	5.69	3.90	4.8	0.5	98	
Eric Skoglund	NWA	AA	23	7	10	0	27	27	156¹	135	19	2.2	7.7	134	44%	.263	1.11	3.45	3.85	2.45	45.9	5.0	97	
Nolan Watson	LEX	A	19	3	11	0	24	24	96¹	125	19	4.1	5.6	60	36%	.323	1.75	7.57	6.40	9.89	-52.2	-5.7	126	

After missing all of 2015 following Tommy John surgery, **Tim Collins** sat out all of 2016 when he needed a second procedure. ❖ It's about projectability for **Garrett Davila**, who's on the prospect radar as a potential starter for the back end of the rotation. ❖ Big right-hander **Andrew Edwards** was on the fast track to Kansas City at the end of July, having found success as a reliever in the upper minors, but hit a wall in August—a very, very large wall. ❖ Signed out of the Dominican for $50,000 in 2012, getting walks under control will be key for **Gerson Garabito**, as he struggled at times in his first taste of full-season ball. ❖ **Foster Griffin** struggled with command upon his promotion to High-A and none of his pitches profile as a plus, but there's still time for the young lefty. ❖ With plus potential on his fastball and curve, right-hander **Jake Junis** consistently pounds the strike zone and has improved in each of his three seasons. ❖ Throwing in the mid-90s when drafted in 2015, **Ashe Russell** spent the summer barely moving the needle above 88 mph. Couple that with command and delivery issues, and the shine has quickly dulled for the former first-round pick. ❖ He lacks a plus pitch, but **Eric Skoglund** uses his tall frame to his advantage, keeping hitters off balance with extreme downward plane coming from a three-quarters delivery. ❖ **Jace Vines** seemed to wear down as his collegiate season at Texas A&M progressed, but that didn't deter the Royals from taking him in the fourth round. He had difficulty missing bats in his debut. ❖ Command issues and the long ball plagued former first-round pick **Nolan Watson** in his first taste of full-season competition.

LOS ANGELES ANGELS

Essay by Meg Rowley

*Player comments by Matthew Kory, Ken Funck
and BP staff*

A few things to know about Mike Trout. On Opening Day of the 2017 season, Trout will have five years and 70 days of major-league service time. His current contract with the Los Angeles Angels of Anaheim expires at the end of the 2020 season. He has a full no-trade clause. The Angels have Trout for four more years. Four. More. Years.

Time functions strangely in baseball. In normal life, time progresses linearly. You turn two before you turn six, and you learn to read before you learn to drive a car. You don't hit home runs before you hit off of a tee. We run into moments of déjà vu that eddy us through time as it passes. We briefly wonder "have I been here before?" but give a little shake of the head and carry on. A season before the right now may have been like this season, but it is not this same one exactly. Routine isn't time travel.

Time matters for all of the obvious reasons of mortality, but in baseball it has a bit of funk to it. Seasons plod along and observe well-worn beats so that they can feel almost predictable. It invites the suggestion that it's all a little bit of history repeating, from slightly different seats. Franchises plod along, too. They observe overlapping cycles of player development and contention, frustration and optimism, denouement and derision. Their little twists and stages make us think we are observing time more like Friedrich Nietzsche may have understood it, as a series of returns, finite players and energies and outcomes destined to recur over an infinite number of seasons.

There's something comforting to that notion, even if it means franchises are doomed to repeated run-ins with failed executives and bad contracts. Our boys will get another shot. Summer comes again. Baseball becomes the thing our linear lives cling to for a few months each year. Knowing where in the return a franchise is, and acting accordingly, is perhaps the most important task for a front office. No one wants to pay a premium to acquire an ace when you ought to be playing for draft picks.

Our own lives move along linearly, held in pleasant tension with the looping recurrences of our favorite franchises. The problem comes when you have a Mike Trout. Just one Mike Trout gums up the whole thing. You aren't exactly on linear time, and you're not on ol' Friedrich's time. You're on Mike Trout's time, and boy, are you blowing it.

ANGELS PROSPECTUS
2016 W-L: 74-88, 4TH IN AL WEST

Pythag	.494	15th	DER	.699	21st
RS/G	4.43	17th	B-Age	28.5	14th
RA/G	4.49	18th	P-Age	28.6	19th
TAv	.258	18th	Salary	$164.7M	7th
BRR	-0.25	16th	M$/MW	$6M	3rd
TAv-P	.272	23rd	DL Days	1254	25th
FIP	4.58	29th	$ on DL	22%	25th

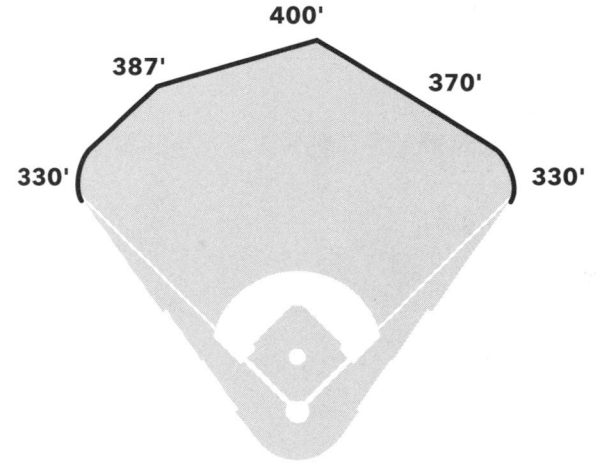

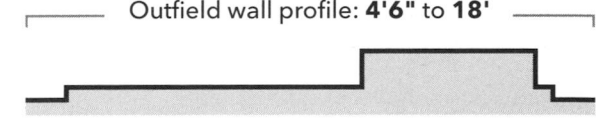

Outfield wall profile: **4'6" to 18'**

Three-Year Park Factors

Runs	Runs/RH	Runs/LH	HR/RH	HR/LH
100	102	98	98	94

Top Hitter WARP	8.7	Mike Trout
Top Pitcher WARP	4.6	Matt Shoemaker
Top Prospect		Jahmai Jones

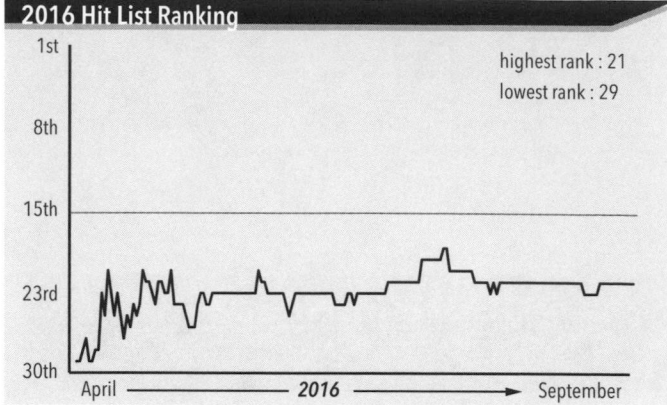

2016 Hit List Ranking

highest rank : 21
lowest rank : 29

April — 2016 → September

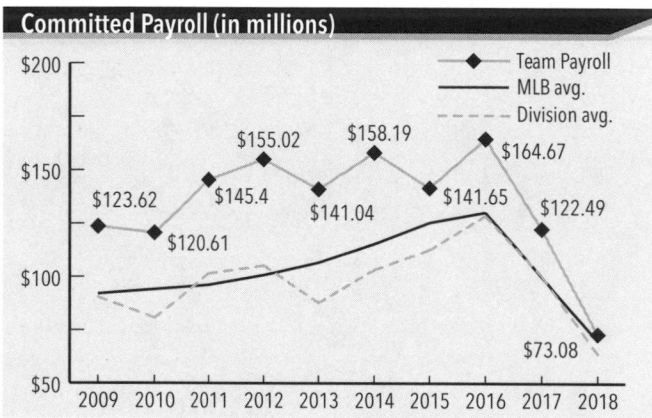

Committed Payroll (in millions)

- ◆ Team Payroll
- — MLB avg.
- --- Division avg.

$123.62
$120.61
$145.4
$155.02
$141.04
$158.19
$141.65
$164.67
$122.49
$73.08

2009 2010 2011 2012 2013 2014 2015 2016 2017 2018

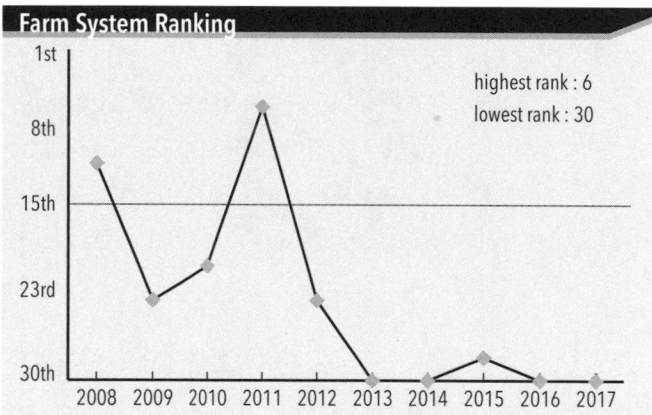

Farm System Ranking

highest rank : 6
lowest rank : 30

2008 2009 2010 2011 2012 2013 2014 2015 2016 2017

Personnel

President:
John Carpino

General Manager:
Billy Eppler

Assistant General Manager:
Steve Martone

Assistant General Manager:
Jonathan Strangio

Manager:
Mike Scioscia

BP Alumni:
Chris Mosch

Any season in which you employ the best player in baseball and flounder is a failure of a sort. It's a very baseball sort of failure, the kind that teaches us that baseball is like life, and that life isn't just or fair, and that we sometimes want to move faster and further than our circumstances allow, and that a man can occupy only one bit of physical space at a time, and that human cloning is a ways off. The particular contours of last year's Angels failure felt different than they had, which might count as something, but that something would also feel like failure.

The Angels' starting rotation was decimated by injury. The Angels had no depth. The Angels employed Johnny Giavotella and Tim Lincecum for a time, and Cliff Pennington and Jered Weaver for longer. The Angels didn't employ Josh Hamilton, but had to pay him anyway. They had a lousy bullpen. Albert Pujols got older. Matt Shoemaker had a run-in with a screaming line drive, and now has a titanium plate in his head. That's the sort of failure 2016 was for the Angels; airport security will always take Matt Shoemaker 15–20 minutes longer because of it.

BP ranked the Angels' farm system dead last coming into the season. The team's only major bright spot was Trout, on his way to another MVP-caliber performance that was, shockingly, rewarded with an actual piece of MVP hardware. But even Trout caused stomachs to knot, as every day the Angels slipped from contention more smart baseball people wondered aloud if he would be traded. It was clear the Angels were in a spot, a bad way, a bind, and that the easiest way to get out of it was perhaps to trade Trout. Trout wasn't ever really available, because if you trade the best player in baseball all the other facts of your biography get second paragraph billing in your obituary, but Angels fans still had to contend with the rumors. The thought of having your heart stolen is an unpleasant one.

Last season was a failure, but its ending was a success. Time helped the Angels out a little in that respect. Time helped out the Angels a little in that respect. After years of discord between Mike Scioscia and Jerry Dipoto, the longtime manager's working relationship with new general manager Billy Eppler seems more civil or at least less publically discordant. Eppler even described Scioscia as an "information savant" at a SABR Analytics Conference, and Scioscia let him.

Weaver and C.J. Wilson are free agents. This will be the last year the Angels pay Hamilton. Tyler Skaggs and Garrett Richards' elbows are a year healthier. Andrelton Simmons and Kole Calhoun will again lend the team services. Cameron Maybin will roam left field instead of Daniel Nava or Jefry Marté or Nick Buss. If you squint hard enough, and imagine a healthy rotation, and a few savvy pickups and some luck, you can see the Angels as a contender.

You could talk yourself into the idea that they're in the phase of the return we'd call "coming out of it." That time is, as the old song says, on their side. But they aren't in a normal return. A normal return ignores Mike Trout.

✦ ✦ ✦

Your trouble starts once you have a Mike Trout, because once you have a Mike Trout you're expected to do something with him. That something can't just be getting swept in the 2013 ALDS by the Royals, or finishing a game out of the second Wild Card spot in 2015. Trout somethings should be like Trout. They should make you gape, they should make you goggle. They should make you swoon. They should make you feel sort of sad for the fans who came before and didn't live long enough to see a Trout. They should be marvelous, because that's what Trout is. They should be big sweeping moves, like pairing your Trout with Albert Pujols, only they should work better. They should work as well as Trout does.

In linear time, we tend to think of the future as progressive, hopeful. What comes tomorrow is unknown, so it may well be terrific. Maybe there is another Mike Trout out there! Franchise time is hopeful too, because the part of the cycle that comes after rebuilding is contention. A prospect could show unexpected promise. Eppler could make good trades. The Astros could decide to become youth pastors, or cobble shoes. The Angels could be good or healthy, or enough of each to fool us.

But Trout's time isn't unknown. Trout's time is set and he is going to leave. Not maybe, not some day. In four years—in 2021. In 2021, Mike Trout will be a free agent and in almost every instance of the future, in whatever version of time we observe, he is going to leave. Maybe for New York or Boston or Washington D.C. or up the freeway to L.A. proper. For a lot of money, that part is certain. He is going to leave and play very good baseball—maybe even the *best* baseball—somewhere else.

Long before his company would own the Angels, Walt Disney described the allure of Disneyland:

"Fantasy, if it's really convincing, can't become dated, for the simple reason that it represents a flight into a dimension that lies beyond the reach of time. In this new dimension, whatever it is, nothing corrodes or gets run down at the heel or gets to look ridiculous like, say, the celluloid collar or the bustle. And nobody gets any older."

Any other franchise with any other guy, this would be fine. Eppler and Maybin and a maybe healthy rotation—these are good moves. Taking your breath after you get out from under bad contracts is a good move. For the Angels, in franchise time, it is good. But in Mike Trout's time? These four years? They scream for more. Trout's time demands you be awesome. Trout's time demands that you take full advantage of the Trout you have. That you not look run down in the heel or ridiculous. That you somehow not get any older in four years. That you avoid becoming dated.

The smart baseball observer in all of us understands what the Angels are doing and christens it good. Sturdy. Lasting. But the part of us that wants to be convinced of fantasy? That wants to find a new dimension, somewhere out there in center field? We're painfully aware of Mike Trout's time. And boy, are you blowing it. ■

—*Meg Rowley is an author*
of Baseball Prospectus

HITTERS

Jett Bandy C

Born: 3/26/90 Age: 27 Bats: R Throws: R Height: 6'4" Weight: 235 Entered Pro Ball: Round 31, 2011 Draft (#945 overall)

YEAR	TEAM	LVL	AGE	PA	R	2B	3B	HR	RBI	BB	K	SB	CS	AVG/OBP/SLG	TAv	VORP	BABIP	BRR	FRAA	WARP
2014	ARK	AA	24	363	38	12	0	13	40	33	63	2	4	.250/.348/.413	.304	28.9	.273	-3.4	C(91): 7.8	3.9
2015	SLC	AAA	25	344	47	21	0	11	60	16	63	0	0	.291/.347/.466	.272	17.6	.329	-1.5	C(84): 0.7	1.9
2015	ANA	MLB	25	2	1	0	0	1	1	0	0	0	0	.500/.500/2.000	.770	1.1	.000	0.0	C(1): -0.0	0.1
2016	SLC	AAA	26	105	13	7	0	2	21	2	19	2	1	.274/.314/.411	.262	1.8	.312	-2.7	C(21): 1.3	0.3
2016	ANA	MLB	26	231	23	9	0	8	25	11	38	1	0	.234/.281/.392	.242	4.2	.246	-2.0	C(68): 0.9	0.5
2017	*MIL*	*MLB*	*27*	*248*	*28*	*11*	*0*	*9*	*30*	*14*	*52*	*1*	*0*	*.243/.302/.415*	*.252*	*8.7*	*.273*	*-0.5*	*C -1*	*0.1*
2018	*MIL*	*MLB*	*28*	*273*	*33*	*11*	*0*	*10*	*33*	*15*	*59*	*1*	*0*	*.235/.299/.399*	*.248*	*5.4*	*.267*	*-1.3*	*C -2*	*0.4*

Breakout: 7%   Improve: 27%   Collapse: 22%   Attrition: 38%   MLB: 65%   Comparables: *Jason Jaramillo, Adam Moore, Tim Federowicz*

The injuries and ineffectiveness that plagued Geovany Soto and Carlos Perez allowed Bandy to drink their milkshakes and stake out his tract behind the Anaheim dish last season. His long swing guarantees low batting averages and he'll never be an OBP, but Bandy can put a serious dent in a fastball and is a threat to launch 20-plus bombs in a full season. He's worked hard to improve his receiving skills and is an average pitch framer, and while his offensive numbers wilted down the stretch last year his infectious enthusiasm never did. Bandy will never be a star, but he has the makeup, arm and power to be a league-average backstop.

YEAR	TEAM	P. COUNT	FRM RUNS	BLK RUNS	THRW RUNS	TOT RUNS
2014	ARK	12392	4.5	1.1	2.6	8.2
2015	ANA	16	0.0	0.1	0.0	0.0
2015	SLC	11935	2.1	0.4	-1.0	1.5
2016	ANA	8749	-1.3	1.6	1.7	2.0
2017	*ANA*	*9316*	*-2.1*	*0.8*	*0.4*	*-1.0*
2018	*ANA*	*10251*	*-2.8*	*0.8*	*0.4*	*-1.6*

Kole Calhoun   RF

Born: 10/14/87 Age: 29 Bats: L Throws: L Height: 5'10" Weight: 205 Entered Pro Ball: Round 8, 2010 Draft (#264 overall)

YEAR	TEAM	LVL	AGE	PA	R	2B	3B	HR	RBI	BB	K	SB	CS	AVG/OBP/SLG	TAv	VORP	BABIP	BRR	FRAA	WARP
2014	SLC	AAA	26	22	7	2	1	1	5	0	3	0	1	.500/.500/.818	.391	3.4	.556	-0.3	RF(4): -0.4	0.3
2014	ANA	MLB	26	537	90	31	3	17	58	38	104	5	3	.272/.325/.450	.293	29.1	.313	3.9	RF(123): -1.2 • 1B(2): -0.0	3.1
2015	ANA	MLB	27	686	78	23	2	26	83	45	164	4	1	.256/.308/.422	.267	13.8	.304	-2.3	RF(157): 13.9 • 1B(1): 0.0	3.0
2016	ANA	MLB	28	672	91	35	5	18	75	67	118	2	3	.271/.348/.438	.277	23.5	.309	0.1	RF(154): -7.8	1.6
2017	*ANA*	*MLB*	*29*	*666*	*84*	*29*	*4*	*22*	*75*	*57*	*138*	*4*	*3*	*.261/.326/.432*	*.270*	*24.4*	*.301*	*-0.9*	*RF 3*	*2.2*
2018	*ANA*	*MLB*	*30*	*594*	*75*	*26*	*3*	*20*	*74*	*53*	*131*	*3*	*2*	*.256/.324/.430*	*.264*	*15.1*	*.300*	*0.7*	*RF 3*	*1.9*

Breakout: 3%   Improve: 40%   Collapse: 4%   Attrition: 7%   MLB: 95%   Comparables: *Seth Smith, Nate Schierholtz, Juan Rivera*

As he nears his thirties Calhoun is what he is, which may sound like a pejorative until you realize what he is makes him a very good major-league right fielder. He wasn't able to replicate his Gold Glove defense last year but made up for it at the plate, making more contact and drawing more walks to post a solid OBP along with his usual above-average lefty power. The Red Baron even managed to strafe same-side pitching last year, making him an everyday force near the top of the Angels' lineup. Offseason core muscle surgery shouldn't jeopardize his spring, so expect Calhoun to continue providing value-priced production again.

Ji-Man Choi   1B

Born: 5/19/91 Age: 26 Bats: L Throws: R Height: 6'1" Weight: 230 Entered Pro Ball: International Free Agent, 2009

YEAR	TEAM	LVL	AGE	PA	R	2B	3B	HR	RBI	BB	K	SB	CS	AVG/OBP/SLG	TAv	VORP	BABIP	BRR	FRAA	WARP
2014	TAC	AAA	23	281	41	7	2	5	30	36	42	2	2	.283/.381/.392	.277	9.9	.323	0.2	1B(40): -0.4 • LF(25): -2.3	0.7
2015	TAC	AAA	24	67	8	4	0	1	16	10	14	0	1	.298/.403/.421	.279	0.8	.381	-1.2	1B(14): -1.7	-0.1
2016	SLC	AAA	25	227	31	17	1	5	31	31	34	4	3	.346/.434/.527	.321	12.8	.390	-4.7	1B(28): 1.6 • LF(15): -1.1	1.4
2016	ANA	MLB	25	129	9	4	0	5	12	16	27	2	4	.170/.271/.339	.217	-3.6	.173	-0.1	1B(27): 2.1 • LF(20): 0.2	-0.1
2017	*ANA*	*MLB*	*26*	*250*	*29*	*10*	*1*	*7*	*29*	*30*	*51*	*3*	*2*	*.244/.340/.392*	*.258*	*5.1*	*.285*	*-0.7*	*1B 0, LF -1*	*0.4*
2018	*ANA*	*MLB*	*27*	*308*	*39*	*12*	*1*	*8*	*34*	*38*	*64*	*3*	*3*	*.241/.339/.387*	*.259*	*4.3*	*.283*	*-0.8*	*1B 0, LF -2*	*0.3*

Breakout: 3%   Improve: 22%   Collapse: 13%   Attrition: 20%   MLB: 48%   Comparables: *David Cooper, Travis Shaw, Eric Campbell*

While Choi has demonstrated a talent for getting on base in the minor leagues, that ability can sometimes translate to the majors as excessive passivity. Choi hasn't had a real chance to disprove that theory yet and his lack of power at an offense-first position means we may never find out. If he brought anything more to the table defensively he might get more of a chance, but despite hitting well at Triple-A he may just not have the resume to convince the skeptics.

Kaleb Cowart   3B

Born: 6/2/92 Age: 25 Bats: B Throws: R Height: 6'3" Weight: 225 Entered Pro Ball: Round 1, 2010 Draft (#18 overall)

YEAR	TEAM	LVL	AGE	PA	R	2B	3B	HR	RBI	BB	K	SB	CS	AVG/OBP/SLG	TAv	VORP	BABIP	BRR	FRAA	WARP
2014	ARK	AA	22	487	48	18	4	6	54	43	99	26	7	.223/.295/.324	.234	3.3	.272	1.7	3B(120): -2.3	0.1
2015	INL	A+	23	221	32	14	4	2	23	22	43	10	2	.242/.326/.387	.273	10.9	.298	1.7	3B(42): 6.1 • SS(4): -0.1	1.8
2015	SLC	AAA	23	253	35	13	3	6	45	29	64	2	1	.323/.395/.491	.296	17.0	.422	0.3	3B(49): -1.7 • LF(5): 0.4	1.7
2015	ANA	MLB	23	52	8	2	0	1	4	5	19	1	1	.174/.255/.283	.195	-1.7	.269	0.0	3B(33): 1.2	-0.1
2016	SLC	AAA	24	458	58	34	5	9	58	37	100	18	4	.280/.340/.452	.269	16.2	.347	-1.1	3B(65): 1.4 • 1B(15): -0.8	1.6
2016	ANA	MLB	24	87	8	4	0	1	8	0	23	0	0	.176/.184/.259	.148	-6.9	.226	0.5	3B(21): 1.0 • 2B(15): -0.0	-0.6
2017	*ANA*	*MLB*	*25*	*161*	*17*	*7*	*1*	*3*	*15*	*12*	*43*	*4*	*1*	*.220/.281/.349*	*.229*	*0.6*	*.284*	*0.3*	*2B -1, 3B 1*	*-0.1*
2018	*ANA*	*MLB*	*26*	*321*	*35*	*14*	*2*	*8*	*33*	*25*	*87*	*7*	*2*	*.223/.287/.361*	*.231*	*-0.1*	*.288*	*0.7*	*2B -3, 3B 1*	*-0.2*

Breakout: 3%   Improve: 7%   Collapse: 5%   Attrition: 11%   MLB: 16%   Comparables: *Ryan Rohlinger, Matt Mangini, Carlos Rivero*

You know that different sound you hear when a true offensive prodigy makes hard contact? The switch-hitting Kowart pretty much never makes that sound, which is why he's never profiled as having anywhere near enough stick to carry the hot corner despite his defensive wizardry there. Hence the decision last year to groom him for utility work, leading to a late-season MLB stint at second base. He proved capable if uninspiring at the keystone, which leaves the Angels with the following story problem: is your team better off with an average glove and a subpar bat in the middle infield, or a vacuum glove and a dismal bat at third base? If you saw this on your college boards, your best answer would probably be "None Of The Above."

C.J. Cron   1B

Born: 1/5/90 Age: 27 Bats: R Throws: R Height: 6'4" Weight: 235 Entered Pro Ball: Round 1, 2011 Draft (#17 overall)

YEAR	TEAM	LVL	AGE	PA	R	2B	3B	HR	RBI	BB	K	SB	CS	AVG/OBP/SLG	TAv	VORP	BABIP	BRR	FRAA	WARP
2014	SLC	AAA	24	213	30	14	1	7	33	18	40	2	1	.316/.385/.511	.299	13.4	.368	1.7	1B(42): -0.4	1.3
2014	ANA	MLB	24	253	28	12	1	11	37	10	61	0	0	.256/.289/.450	.265	2.0	.300	-1.6	1B(36): -0.9	0.1
2015	SLC	AAA	25	98	15	10	2	6	23	4	14	0	0	.323/.347/.667	.314	5.0	.324	-1.4	1B(16): -1.3	0.4
2015	ANA	MLB	25	404	37	17	1	16	51	17	82	3	1	.262/.300/.439	.262	6.3	.293	1.4	1B(58): -0.5	0.6
2016	SLC	AAA	26	24	0	1	0	0	2	3	5	1	0	.150/.250/.200	.183	-1.6	.188	0.1	1B(4): -0.3	-0.2
2016	ANA	MLB	26	445	51	26	1	16	69	24	75	2	3	.278/.325/.467	.282	12.4	.302	-2.0	1B(97): 2.4	1.5
2017	*ANA*	*MLB*	*27*	*556*	*63*	*27*	*2*	*22*	*75*	*31*	*113*	*3*	*2*	*.261/.309/.449*	*.268*	*13.0*	*.294*	*-1.0*	*1B -1*	*1.0*
2018	*ANA*	*MLB*	*28*	*481*	*62*	*23*	*2*	*20*	*65*	*29*	*101*	*2*	*1*	*.259/.310/.451*	*.264*	*8.3*	*.293*	*-0.8*	*1B -1*	*0.8*

Breakout: 4%   Improve: 54%   Collapse: 5%   Attrition: 8%   MLB: 92%   Comparables: *Adam Lind, Matt Adams, Mike Jacobs*

The Angels were happy to have Cron man first base last year, and not just because playing without a first baseman would seriously inflate their pitching staff's BABIP. He's adequate defensively, but Cron's calling card has long been right-handed power, which is prodigious compared to weekend softball players and minor-league shortstops but a little underweight in the context of big-league sluggers. A free-swinger who makes contact but rarely walks, Cron underwent offseason surgery to reduce thumb pain in the same hand that cost him a month of work last summer. He's expected to be fine this spring, and a healthy Cron should do more than enough to earn his modest pre-arbitration salary, but his out-making ways will likely keep him from growing into a true middle-of-the-order force.

Yunel Escobar   3B

Born: 11/2/82   Age: 34   Bats: R   Throws: R   Height: 6'2"   Weight: 215   Entered Pro Ball: Round 2, 2005 Draft (#75 overall)

YEAR	TEAM	LVL	AGE	PA	R	2B	3B	HR	RBI	BB	K	SB	CS	AVG/OBP/SLG	TAv	VORP	BABIP	BRR	FRAA	WARP
2014	TBA	MLB	31	529	33	18	0	7	39	43	60	1	1	.258/.324/.340	.257	19.9	.282	1.5	SS(136): -13.9 • LF(1): -0.0	0.7
2015	WAS	MLB	32	591	75	25	1	9	56	45	70	2	2	.314/.375/.415	.284	30.7	.347	-0.8	3B(134): -21.7	1.0
2016	ANA	MLB	33	567	68	28	1	5	39	40	67	0	3	.304/.355/.391	.260	18.2	.339	-0.1	3B(129): -5.6	1.3
2017	ANA	MLB	34	569	60	22	1	7	47	42	74	2	2	.266/.322/.355	.251	10.5	.293	-1.8	3B -15	-1.2
2018	ANA	MLB	35	486	54	21	0	7	45	39	67	1	1	.261/.325/.357	.245	3.5	.290	0.1	3B -13	-1.0

Breakout: 1%   Improve: 27%   Collapse: 13%   Attrition: 26%   MLB: 82%   Comparables: Billy Goodman, Spike Owen, Kevin Seitzer

As he's slid down the defensive spectrum from sure-handed shortstop to immobile, error-prone third baseman, Escobar's bat has somehow managed to keep cashing his checks. A free-swinging contact hitter with infrequent power and little speed, his offensive value is tied to his ability to bat .300, which is chained to posting a favorable BABIP, which is shackled to his high ground-ball rate, which is duct-taped to his astronomical rate of bouncing into twin killings, which is hitched to the razor line on which his career is poised. As long as enough safeties bleed through, Escobar can set the table often enough to overcome his toxic glove and penchant for rally-ending two-hoppers. Once they stop, the resulting .250/.300/.350 line from a defensive liability will no longer cut it.

Danny Espinosa   2B

Born: 4/25/87   Age: 30   Bats: B   Throws: R   Height: 6'0"   Weight: 205   Entered Pro Ball: Round 3, 2008 Draft (#87 overall)

YEAR	TEAM	LVL	AGE	PA	R	2B	3B	HR	RBI	BB	K	SB	CS	AVG/OBP/SLG	TAv	VORP	BABIP	BRR	FRAA	WARP
2014	WAS	MLB	27	364	31	14	3	8	27	18	122	8	1	.219/.283/.351	.233	-1.1	.319	-1.3	2B(89): -0.4 • SS(12): -0.0	-0.2
2015	WAS	MLB	28	412	59	21	1	13	37	33	106	5	2	.240/.311/.409	.264	15.5	.299	3.1	2B(81): 9.0 • 3B(16): -0.2	2.6
2016	WAS	MLB	29	601	66	15	0	24	72	54	174	9	2	.209/.306/.378	.258	25.0	.261	1.4	SS(157): 7.1	3.3
2017	ANA	MLB	30	417	45	15	1	12	43	29	126	6	1	.211/.282/.354	.230	3.6	.278	0.2	2B 7	0.8
2018	ANA	MLB	31	503	59	20	1	16	57	39	158	6	1	.212/.290/.367	.239	5.4	.281	0.8	2B 9	1.5

Breakout: 2%   Improve: 47%   Collapse: 4%   Attrition: 15%   MLB: 91%   Comparables: Jose Valentin, Brandon Inge, Ronny Cedeno

There's a peculiarity about Espinosa, where folks tend to see a guy they'd rather replace instead of the guy who's kind of an alright little ballplayer when left to his own devices. He lost his job in July of 2015 just as he was starting to kick into gear at the dish. Then his GM went out and signed Stephen Drew—fresh off consecutive negative WARP seasons—to compete with him for at-bats. Espinosa's proclivity for the strikeout is the biggest wart on his game, and in severity it is more akin to a gangrenous limb. But after bouncing around the dirt for most of his career he revealed himself as one of the best defensive shortstops in the majors last season, and coupled with solid pop and enough patience to override his batting average woes, he ended up nearly posting a top-ten season at the position by WARP. If he can manage to do it again in his walk year, he may just find himself a bit more stability for the next few seasons, warts and all.

Nolan Fontana   SS

Born: 6/6/91   Age: 26   Bats: L   Throws: R   Height: 5'11"   Weight: 195   Entered Pro Ball: Round 2, 2012 Draft (#61 overall)

YEAR	TEAM	LVL	AGE	PA	R	2B	3B	HR	RBI	BB	K	SB	CS	AVG/OBP/SLG	TAv	VORP	BABIP	BRR	FRAA	WARP
2014	CCH	AA	23	305	33	21	1	1	26	61	76	5	8	.262/.418/.376	.304	20.7	.383	-2.7	2B(41): -0.2 • SS(25): 1.3	2.3
2015	FRE	AAA	24	456	56	21	6	3	40	74	99	6	11	.241/.369/.357	.278	24.1	.317	0.1	SS(57): -6.1 • 2B(31): -0.9	1.9
2016	CCH	AA	25	44	4	4	0	0	4	8	5	1	0	.278/.409/.389	.280	2.4	.323	-0.1	SS(9): 1.2	0.4
2016	FRE	AAA	25	407	35	15	0	3	27	32	108	4	3	.195/.268/.262	.208	-4.4	.266	2.5	SS(77): -5.4 • 2B(27): 1.7	-0.8
2017	ANA	MLB	26	250	25	10	1	3	20	33	71	2	2	.204/.314/.306	.223	0.9	.278	-0.8	SS -2, 2B 0	-0.1
2018	ANA	MLB	27	230	25	9	1	3	20	29	65	2	2	.207/.315/.312	.227	-0.7	.280	-0.6	SS -2, 2B 0	-0.2

Breakout: 2%   Improve: 11%   Collapse: 6%   Attrition: 13%   MLB: 20%   Comparables: Oswaldo Navarro, Jonathan Diaz, Tommy Field

Fontana was keeping his prospect status afloat through making decent contact and drawing a ton of walks. In 2016, that all deflated. Fontana turned into a whiff machine with subpar discipline. While he can hack it at shortstop, Fontana's glove isn't good enough to forgive his almost complete lack of pop. At age 26, it's a critical year for Fontana, who has dug himself a hole he'll need to hit his way out of to reach the major leagues.

Johnny Giavotella   2B

Born: 7/10/87   Age: 29   Bats: R   Throws: R   Height: 5'8"   Weight: 185   Entered Pro Ball: Round 2, 2008 Draft (#49 overall)

YEAR	TEAM	LVL	AGE	PA	R	2B	3B	HR	RBI	BB	K	SB	CS	AVG/OBP/SLG	TAv	VORP	BABIP	BRR	FRAA	WARP
2014	OMA	AAA	26	493	66	33	2	7	61	47	36	20	4	.308/.373/.440	.293	32.4	.321	0.5	2B(65): -4.9 • 3B(29): 0.4	2.8
2014	KCA	MLB	26	41	8	1	0	1	5	1	5	0	1	.216/.268/.324	.259	1.8	.219	0.8	2B(12): 0.5	0.2
2015	ANA	MLB	27	502	51	25	5	4	49	32	59	2	1	.272/.318/.375	.257	12.6	.301	1.0	2B(128): -3.3 • SS(1): -0.0	1.0
2016	ANA	MLB	28	367	44	20	1	6	31	13	39	4	3	.260/.287/.376	.237	2.0	.276	0.7	2B(97): -16.1	-1.5
2016	SLC	AAA	28	30	2	3	0	0	1	3	3	1	0	.296/.367/.407	.275	1.7	.333	0.3	2B(7): 1.4	0.3
2017	ANA	MLB	29	376	37	18	1	6	38	28	52	5	2	.259/.317/.373	.245	9.9	.285	1.0	2B -7, 3B -0	0.4
2018	ANA	MLB	30	471	51	21	1	8	45	36	68	5	2	.253/.312/.361	.242	6.7	.279	1.3	2B -8, 3B 0	-0.2

Breakout: 5%   Improve: 28%   Collapse: 12%   Attrition: 18%   MLB: 77%   Comparables: Eric Sogard, Russ Adams, Angel Sanchez

It's easy for fans to get upset at players when they fail. "Two in scoring position and the guy strikes out?" "How did he not get to that ball?" These are understandable thoughts to have, but the real fault isn't with the guy who fails to make those plays, it's with the team for asking him to make them in the first place. Which brings us to Giavotella. He doesn't hit right-handers well. He doesn't hit left-handers well. He doesn't play the field particularly well. He has no power. He has no patience. Yet the Angels kept trotting him out there on the daily until August, when he was finally relocated to Triple-A after an unclaimed wander through assignment-designated waters.

Jahmai Jones   CF

Born: 8/4/97   Age: 19   Bats: R   Throws: R   Height: 6'0"   Weight: 215   Entered Pro Ball: Round 2, 2015 Draft (#70 overall)

YEAR	TEAM	LVL	AGE	PA	R	2B	3B	HR	RBI	BB	K	SB	CS	AVG/OBP/SLG	TAv	VORP	BABIP	BRR	FRAA	WARP
2016	BUR	A	18	70	8	1	0	1	10	5	13	1	0	.242/.294/.306	.219	-0.8	.286	0.2	CF(8): -0.7 • LF(4): -0.1	-0.2
2017	ANA	MLB	19	250	27	8	1	6	21	15	73	4	2	.203/.256/.317	.203	-5.7	.266	0.0	CF -1, RF -0	-0.8
2018	ANA	MLB	20	369	40	12	1	10	39	24	101	6	3	.221/.277/.352	.225	-3.5	.279	0.3	CF -2, RF 0	-0.6

Breakout: 0%   Improve: 8%   Collapse: 2%   Attrition: 6%   MLB: 13%   *Comparables: Engel Beltre, Nomar Mazara, Elvis Andrus*

Every rookie-league field is stuffed to the gills with tremendous raw physical talent, so despite his plus speed, quick bat and instincts it isn't Jones' athleticism that stands out. What makes him more likely than most to carve a path to the big leagues is his off-the-charts makeup. A baseball player born into a football family, Jones receives top marks for his work ethic, baseball acumen, leadership and coachability—traits that will help him get the most out of his gifts. He's a natural center fielder who shows an advanced approach at the plate and on the bases, and a swing that should eventually produce at least average power. In a relatively thin Angels system, Jones has the greatest likelihood of surviving the long bus rides, soul-crushing slumps and endless injury rehabs of the minors to blossom into a star.

Brandon Marsh   OF

Born: 12/18/97   Age: 19   Bats: L   Throws: R   Height: 6'2"   Weight: 190   Entered Pro Ball: Round 2, 2016 Draft (#60 overall)

YEAR	TEAM	LVL	AGE	PA	R	2B	3B	HR	RBI	BB	K	SB	CS	AVG/OBP/SLG	TAv	VORP	BABIP	BRR	FRAA	WARP
2017	ANA	MLB	19	250	28	8	1	6	25	29	42	4	1	.227/.322/.353	.243	5.0	.251	-0.1		0.5

Breakout: 0%   Improve: 22%   Collapse: 9%   Attrition: 16%   MLB: 38%   *Comparables: Wayne Causey, Ed Kranepool, Jurickson Profar*

Despite not actually debuting yet, Marsh had himself an up-and-down first summer as a professional. The Angels thought they'd drafted a slam dunk in the second round, but he left the ball rattling around the iron after his team visit following the draft led to second thoughts about honoring his college commitment instead. He eventually capitulated and signed at slot value, but a back injury kept him off the grass until instructs. When healthy he'll show a couple of plus tools in his speed and arm, and the raw power won't be far behind at maturity. But will he hit? Can he hang in center? Those will have to be the questions for another day.

Jefry Marte   1B

Born: 6/21/91   Age: 26   Bats: R   Throws: R   Height: 6'1"   Weight: 220   Entered Pro Ball: International Free Agent, 2007

YEAR	TEAM	LVL	AGE	PA	R	2B	3B	HR	RBI	BB	K	SB	CS	AVG/OBP/SLG	TAv	VORP	BABIP	BRR	FRAA	WARP
2014	MID	AA	23	460	50	17	0	10	53	45	69	9	3	.259/.333/.375	.268	15.3	.286	-1.4	3B(91): 6.5 • 1B(3): 0.3	2.3
2015	TOL	AAA	24	399	49	25	3	15	65	31	64	8	5	.275/.341/.487	.284	21.9	.294	-0.4	3B(91): 0.4 • 1B(4): -0.1	2.2
2015	DET	MLB	24	90	9	4	0	4	11	8	22	0	0	.213/.284/.413	.250	0.8	.241	0.2	1B(22): 0.7 • 3B(7): 0.6	0.2
2016	SLC	AAA	25	189	22	12	1	3	24	22	35	3	3	.265/.354/.407	.284	7.1	.315	-0.2	1B(36): 4.1 • 3B(6): -0.3	1.1
2016	ANA	MLB	25	284	38	14	0	15	44	18	59	2	2	.252/.310/.481	.273	9.8	.267	0.2	1B(29): -0.2 • LF(27): 0.6	1.1
2017	ANA	MLB	26	378	43	16	1	14	48	29	81	4	3	.240/.304/.417	.260	8.1	.270	-0.8	1B 2, 3B 2	1.0
2018	ANA	MLB	27	463	59	20	1	18	60	38	101	5	3	.240/.310/.423	.259	8.3	.271	0.3	1B 2, 3B 2	1.4

Breakout: 4%   Improve: 32%   Collapse: 11%   Attrition: 20%   MLB: 65%   *Comparables: Kendrys Morales, Nick Evans, Travis Shaw*

During a sunless and brooding Angels season wracked with injury and ineffectiveness, Marte's emergence as a useful fill-in and surprising power source was a shining exception. The minor-league veteran hit his way to The Show last May and never let up, filling in at the infield corners and surviving a baptism by fire in left field. Marte doesn't draw walks but is finally showing the thump that's long been expected from him, although he's unlikely to again turn nearly 20 percent of his fly balls into souvenirs. Still, power is power, and now that he's proven he can hit big-league pitching he should continue to find work as a platoon corner man and bench bat.

Cameron Maybin   CF

Born: 4/4/87   Age: 30   Bats: R   Throws: R   Height: 6'3"   Weight: 215   Entered Pro Ball: Round 1, 2005 Draft (#10 overall)

YEAR	TEAM	LVL	AGE	PA	R	2B	3B	HR	RBI	BB	K	SB	CS	AVG/OBP/SLG	TAv	VORP	BABIP	BRR	FRAA	WARP
2014	ELP	AAA	27	61	8	2	1	1	6	6	10	1	0	.264/.328/.396	.241	-0.5	.295	-0.7	CF(15): -0.8	-0.1
2014	SDN	MLB	27	272	24	13	4	1	15	19	56	4	3	.235/.290/.331	.233	1.9	.297	1.1	CF(86): -4.7	-0.3
2015	ATL	MLB	28	555	65	18	2	10	59	45	102	23	6	.267/.327/.370	.264	22.2	.316	3.5	CF(139): 0.8	2.5
2016	TOL	AAA	29	100	14	9	0	2	11	14	17	4	1	.188/.310/.365	.236	0.0	.212	0.8	CF(9): 0.4	0.0
2016	DET	MLB	29	391	65	14	5	4	43	36	69	15	6	.315/.383/.418	.277	23.9	.383	5.1	CF(91): -0.8	2.4
2017	ANA	MLB	30	557	63	20	3	10	51	47	108	20	7	.249/.314/.363	.251	15.6	.295	1.4		1.0
2018	ANA	MLB	31	493	56	18	3	11	50	41	101	15	6	.246/.311/.369	.247	8.8	.293	3.7	LF 0, RF 0	1.0

Breakout: 1%   Improve: 44%   Collapse: 9%   Attrition: 19%   MLB: 94%   *Comparables: Ryan Sweeney, Angel Pagan, Franklin Gutierrez*

Throughout Maybin's career, the mantra has always been *man, if he could just stay healthy, he'd be so good*. The narrative took a 90-degree turn as the lusciously-locked center fielder missed over 60 games to injuries, including a broken wrist to start the season; a second DL trip for a sprained thumb, and numerous day-to-day maladies, mostly involving the extremities. But after a month of rehab games, Maybin flew out of the gates with seven multi-hit games in his first nine starts. He's your favorite streaming TV app;

when he fails, it's just so helpless and frustrating. But when it works, it constantly shows you why a team was willing to trade you Miguel Cabrera for it.

Cliff Pennington   SS

Born: 6/15/84   Age: 33   Bats: B   Throws: R   Height: 5'11"   Weight: 195   Entered Pro Ball: Round 1, 2005 Draft (#21 overall)

YEAR	TEAM	LVL	AGE	PA	R	2B	3B	HR	RBI	BB	K	SB	CS	AVG/OBP/SLG	TAv	VORP	BABIP	BRR	FRAA	WARP
2014	ARI	MLB	30	201	21	5	3	2	10	20	36	6	1	.254/.340/.350	.272	8.7	.309	0.2	SS(23): 0.2 • 2B(18): 0.4	1.1
2015	ARI	MLB	31	157	15	3	0	1	10	16	29	3	0	.237/.314/.281	.216	-2.4	.290	-0.6	SS(24): 2.9 • 3B(12): -0.1	0.1
2015	TOR	MLB	31	92	9	3	0	2	11	11	20	0	0	.160/.270/.280	.218	-0.9	.182	0.5	2B(22): 1.6 • 3B(6): -0.0	0.1
2016	SLC	AAA	32	26	3	2	1	0	3	3	4	0	0	.304/.385/.478	.266	0.7	.368	-0.1	2B(2): 0.2 • SS(2): -0.1	0.1
2016	ANA	MLB	32	188	18	4	2	3	10	13	55	1	0	.209/.265/.308	.202	-5.3	.289	0.1	2B(58): -2.3 • SS(17): 1.1	-0.7
2017	*ANA*	*MLB*	*33*	*191*	*18*	*6*	*1*	*2*	*16*	*17*	*41*	*2*	*0*	*.223/.292/.312*	*.227*	*1.1*	*.274*	*0.1*	*2B 1, SS 1*	*0.1*
2018	*ANA*	*MLB*	*34*	*225*	*23*	*7*	*1*	*3*	*19*	*21*	*49*	*2*	*0*	*.222/.300/.311*	*.224*	*-1.0*	*.274*	*-0.1*	*2B 1, SS 1*	*0.1*

Breakout: 2%   Improve: 30%   Collapse: 8%   Attrition: 27%   MLB: 93%   *Comparables: Ramon Santiago, Ted Kubiak, Casey Candaele*

It's easy now to scoff at the two-year deal lavished on Pennington before last season, wondering about the need for a rebuilding team to bring in a glove-first veteran utility man to soak up innings that could otherwise go to a prospect. How soon we forget that a) the Angels were actually aspirational last spring and b) they had no middle-infield prospects for Pennington to block. The former Oakland draftee can still pick it all over the field but with his anemic bat no longer scaring anyone pitchers continually work him in the zone and refuse to walk him, excising his last vestige of offensive value.

Carlos Perez   C

Born: 10/27/90   Age: 26   Bats: R   Throws: R   Height: 6'0"   Weight: 210   Entered Pro Ball: International Free Agent, 2008

YEAR	TEAM	LVL	AGE	PA	R	2B	3B	HR	RBI	BB	K	SB	CS	AVG/OBP/SLG	TAv	VORP	BABIP	BRR	FRAA	WARP
2014	OKL	AAA	23	340	33	16	2	6	34	29	54	3	0	.259/.323/.385	.254	11.4	.295	-0.5	C(74): 7.7 • 1B(5): -0.2	1.9
2015	SLC	AAA	24	79	11	8	0	2	12	7	7	1	0	.361/.418/.556	.330	9.6	.381	0.4	C(16): 2.5	1.2
2015	ANA	MLB	24	283	20	13	0	4	21	19	49	2	0	.250/.299/.346	.249	6.8	.292	-2.2	C(80): 2.2 • 1B(2): -0.6	0.9
2016	SLC	AAA	25	40	9	4	0	3	10	1	7	0	2	.359/.375/.692	.354	4.9	.379	-0.6	C(9): -0.2	0.5
2016	ANA	MLB	25	291	25	16	0	5	31	12	49	1	0	.209/.244/.325	.198	-5.4	.236	0.0	C(82): 2.2 • 1B(1): -0.0	-0.3
2017	*ANA*	*MLB*	*26*	*184*	*18*	*9*	*0*	*4*	*18*	*12*	*33*	*1*	*0*	*.242/.289/.369*	*.239*	*4.3*	*.273*	*-0.3*	*C 1*	*0.3*
2018	*ANA*	*MLB*	*27*	*268*	*30*	*12*	*1*	*7*	*29*	*19*	*50*	*1*	*0*	*.240/.296/.382*	*.240*	*3.4*	*.267*	*-0.9*	*C 1*	*0.5*

Breakout: 12%   Improve: 45%   Collapse: 12%   Attrition: 24%   MLB: 91%   *Comparables: Jonathan Lucroy, Francisco Cervelli, Devin Mesoraco*

Perez's 2015 season was moderately interesting in that, if you squinted, you might have seen worthwhile production. His 2016 season was probably best viewed from behind very dark glasses. Perez performed slightly worse all around and did it while being a year older. Catchers are notoriously late offensive bloomers, so Perez could blossom, chrysanthemum-like, later in his career. But if he's lying dormant under the dirt, there aren't many signs of it from above. His hitting was worse in 2016 and any above-average framing ability remained speculative. He did throw out exactly 38 percent of runners for the second straight season, so if you see fans with "38%!" t-shirts around Angels Stadium, that's why.

YEAR	TEAM	P. COUNT	FRM RUNS	BLK RUNS	THRW RUNS	TOT RUNS
2014	OKL	9874	8.6	0.0	-0.7	7.9
2015	ANA	10676	-0.5	-0.7	1.2	-0.1
2015	SLC	2392	2.7	0.0	0.1	2.9
2016	ANA	11140	-2.5	1.4	1.4	0.3
2017	*ANA*	*7015*	*-0.7*	*0.3*	*0.4*	*0.0*
2018	*ANA*	*10235*	*-1.3*	*0.5*	*0.5*	*-0.4*

Albert Pujols   DH/1B

Born: 1/16/80   Age: 37   Bats: R   Throws: R   Height: 6'3"   Weight: 240   Entered Pro Ball: Round 13, 1999 Draft (#402 overall)

YEAR	TEAM	LVL	AGE	PA	R	2B	3B	HR	RBI	BB	K	SB	CS	AVG/OBP/SLG	TAv	VORP	BABIP	BRR	FRAA	WARP
2014	ANA	MLB	34	695	89	37	1	28	105	48	71	5	1	.272/.324/.466	.295	27.2	.265	-2.1	1B(116): -1.6 • 3B(1): 0.0	2.8
2015	ANA	MLB	35	661	85	22	0	40	95	50	72	5	3	.244/.307/.480	.279	17.9	.217	-1.0	1B(95): 6.2 • 3B(1): -0.0	2.6
2016	ANA	MLB	36	650	71	19	0	31	119	49	75	4	0	.268/.323/.457	.274	11.8	.260	-3.8	1B(28): -1.2	1.1
2017	*ANA*	*MLB*	*37*	*604*	*73*	*26*	*1*	*27*	*84*	*46*	*75*	*4*	*1*	*.256/.315/.451*	*.273*	*16.7*	*.251*	*-0.9*	*1B 0*	*1.9*
2018	*ANA*	*MLB*	*38*	*450*	*58*	*18*	*0*	*20*	*61*	*32*	*60*	*2*	*1*	*.243/.300/.433*	*.257*	*8.1*	*.239*	*-1.6*	*1B 0*	*0.9*

Breakout: 0%   Improve: 19%   Collapse: 8%   Attrition: 7%   MLB: 72%   *Comparables: Carlos Lee, Victor Martinez, Vladimir Guerrero*

Halfway through his 10-year mega-contract Pujols has settled into the sort of consistency that has long been a hallmark of his career, but at a far less Olympian level than in his Cardinals heyday. You can expect him to be healthy enough to play 150 games, but he'll always be either willing himself through foot pain or recovering from the surgeries needed to relieve it. He'll post the counting stats (say, 30/100) of a legitimate run producer, but without the walks and doubles of a truly premium bat. He'll be a good hitter, but not a great one; a solid fielder, but an increasingly infrequent one; a contender to lead the league in both home runs and double-play groundouts. If you ignore the money, you can be happy with that type of production from your DH. If you can't ignore the money, remember that the league is currently swimming in lucre and signing Pujols to a five-year, $140 million contract starting today would be a very bad idea, but not necessarily a franchise crippler.

Andrelton Simmons   SS

Born: 9/4/89   Age: 27   Bats: R   Throws: R   Height: 6'2"   Weight: 200   Entered Pro Ball: Round 2, 2010 Draft (#70 overall)

YEAR	TEAM	LVL	AGE	PA	R	2B	3B	HR	RBI	BB	K	SB	CS	AVG/OBP/SLG	TAv	VORP	BABIP	BRR	FRAA	WARP
2014	ATL	MLB	24	576	44	18	4	7	46	32	60	4	5	.244/.286/.331	.230	9.3	.263	3.6	SS(146): 10.3	2.2
2015	ATL	MLB	25	583	60	23	2	4	44	39	48	5	3	.265/.321/.338	.248	17.0	.285	0.7	SS(147): 10.5	2.9
2016	ANA	MLB	26	483	48	22	2	4	44	28	38	10	1	.281/.324/.366	.249	15.3	.298	0.8	SS(124): 6.5	2.2
2017	*ANA*	*MLB*	*27*	*575*	*55*	*23*	*3*	*11*	*59*	*36*	*53*	*6*	*3*	*.260/.308/.375*	*.250*	*20.2*	*.269*	*-0.4*	*SS 5*	*1.9*
2018	*ANA*	*MLB*	*28*	*534*	*59*	*22*	*3*	*11*	*55*	*33*	*53*	*5*	*2*	*.262/.309/.382*	*.246*	*12.3*	*.271*	*1.4*	*SS 5*	*1.9*

Breakout: 2%   Improve: 50%   Collapse: 5%   Attrition: 12%   MLB: 98%   *Comparables: Elvis Andrus, Dick Groat, Felix Millan*

Round 1 went to Francisco Lindor, who edged out Simmons for the Gold Glove in the first of many likely battles between the Ali and Frazier of American League run prevention. A torn thumb ligament that cost Simmons a month didn't help, but when he played he was his normal, transcendental self, displaying intercontinental range, accuracy and explosiveness. At the plate he maintained the contact-oriented, gap-to-gap approach that serves him best, sacrificing power to make sure he posts a credible on-base percentage. Simmons will never match the gaudy offensive numbers of the new-wave shortstop prospects now entering the game, but his newfound ability to avoid becoming a serial out-maker should allow him to remain one of the game's most valuable infielders.

Matt Thaiss   1B

Born: 5/6/95   Age: 22   Bats: L   Throws: R   Height: 6'0"   Weight: 195   Entered Pro Ball: Round 1, 2016 Draft (#16 overall)

YEAR	TEAM	LVL	AGE	PA	R	2B	3B	HR	RBI	BB	K	SB	CS	AVG/OBP/SLG	TAv	VORP	BABIP	BRR	FRAA	WARP
2016	BUR	A	21	226	24	12	3	4	31	22	28	1	0	.276/.351/.427	.293	5.8	.302	-3.6	1B(43): 5.3	1.2
2017	ANA	MLB	22	250	24	10	1	7	29	17	58	1	0	.226/.285/.372	.230	-3.0	.269	-0.3	1B 5	0.2
2018	ANA	MLB	23	281	33	12	1	9	32	21	66	1	0	.231/.292/.388	.241	-2.3	.274	-0.5	1B 6	0.4

Breakout: 5%   Improve: 18%   Collapse: 2%   Attrition: 20%   MLB: 24%   *Comparables: Nick Evans, James Loney, Chris Marrero*

Questions swirled before the draft as to whether Thaiss could stay behind the plate, but it appeared the Angels had answered them with an emphatic "we think so!" when they tapped him 16th overall in June. Or not? The club instead made the curious decision to immediately move him to first base, where the Cavalier will have a significantly higher bar to clear in order to justify his first-round pedigree.

Mike Trout   CF

Born: 8/7/91   Age: 25   Bats: R   Throws: R   Height: 6'2"   Weight: 235   Entered Pro Ball: Round 1, 2009 Draft (#25 overall)

YEAR	TEAM	LVL	AGE	PA	R	2B	3B	HR	RBI	BB	K	SB	CS	AVG/OBP/SLG	TAv	VORP	BABIP	BRR	FRAA	WARP
2014	ANA	MLB	22	705	115	39	9	36	111	83	184	16	2	.287/.377/.561	.352	84.6	.349	4.7	CF(149): -1.7	9.2
2015	ANA	MLB	23	682	104	32	6	41	90	92	158	11	7	.299/.402/.590	.353	83.5	.344	1.6	CF(156): 9.9	10.0
2016	ANA	MLB	24	681	123	32	5	29	100	116	137	30	7	.315/.441/.550	.355	90.7	.371	4.8	CF(148): -7.5	8.6
2017	ANA	MLB	25	653	100	30	7	31	102	90	143	19	5	.301/.404/.553	.335	75.6	.351	1.7	CF 3	7.7
2018	ANA	MLB	26	592	97	27	5	31	99	86	132	17	5	.302/.409/.566	.335	64.3	.350	3.3	CF 3	7.3

Breakout: 5%   Improve: 68%   Collapse: 1%   Attrition: 2%   MLB: 100%   *Comparables: Mickey Mantle, Giancarlo Stanton, Frank Thomas*

Previous Trout comments in BP Annuals have compared him to an angelfish, discussed his preternatural abilities low in the strike zone and measured the difficulty of projecting his career with that of Jamie Moyer. All of that is great and true and good, but this year we're not beating around any bushes: Mike Trout is the greatest baseball player in the game and quite possibly one of the 10 best ever. Through his age-24 season there is a sound and, really, correct argument that he should have five MVP awards. If Trout continues to average 9.38 WARP per season, which would be a ridiculous assumption for everyone but the player currently being discussed, he'll pass Mickey Mantle's career total at age 31. He'll pass Willie Mays, the greatest center fielder of all time, in his age-37 season. And Trout hasn't even yet reached what we know to be a hitter's peak. So while we could compare Trout to the fastest hyper-car or the best-tasting ice cream ever or Elon Musk, maybe for a season let's not do that. Instead, let's be direct and recognize we are in the presence of the greatest of true greatness. Trout is the best player of several generations and worth the price of admission on his own — a fact that, given the Angels' roster, they seem to have noticed.

Taylor Ward   C

Born: 12/14/93   Age: 23   Bats: R   Throws: R   Height: 6'1"   Weight: 185   Entered Pro Ball: Round 1, 2015 Draft (#26 overall)

YEAR	TEAM	LVL	AGE	PA	R	2B	3B	HR	RBI	BB	K	SB	CS	AVG/OBP/SLG	TAv	VORP	BABIP	BRR	FRAA	WARP
2015	BUR	A	21	103	10	3	0	1	12	10	15	1	1	.348/.412/.413	.296	7.8	.408	0.1	C(20): -0.6	0.8
2016	INL	A+	22	529	61	11	0	10	56	48	81	0	0	.249/.323/.337	.240	9.4	.279	1.4	C(90): 4.1	1.4
2017	ANA	MLB	23	250	24	8	0	6	27	20	55	0	0	.225/.292/.345	.225	2.6	.266	-0.5	C 0	0.3
2018	ANA	MLB	24	268	31	8	0	7	28	22	56	0	0	.233/.300/.356	.235	1.9	.271	-0.7	C 0	0.2

Breakout: 3%   Improve: 11%   Collapse: 1%   Attrition: 33%   MLB: 40%   *Comparables: Tucker Barnhart, Steve Clevenger, Carlos Perez*

Ward is a lineout player trapped in the full-comment section, and if he were employed by pretty much any other team we'd merely tell you he's a strong-armed catcher with raw-but-improving receiving skills and a fringy bat. Since he's an Angel, however, we're blessed with the opportunity to enlighten you about the improvements he made at the plate last year, as Ward started to pull the ball with more authority as the season went on

YEAR	TEAM	P. COUNT	FRM RUNS	BLK RUNS	THRW RUNS	TOT RUNS
2017	ANA	8456	0.0	0.0	0.0	0.0
2018	ANA	9061	0.0	0.0	0.0	0.0

and flashed what may become average power to go with a reasonably solid feel for the strike zone. Catchers often need to spend more time in the hatchery than other prospects, but there's a chance Ward could eventually grow into a reasonable big-league backup.

PITCHERS

Jose Alvarez   LHP

Born: 5/6/89   Age: 28   Bats: L   Throws: L   Height: 5'11"   Weight: 190   Entered Pro Ball: International Free Agent, 2005

YEAR	TEAM	LVL	AGE	W	L	SV	G	GS	IP	H	HR	BB/9	K/9	K	GB%	BABIP	WHIP	ERA	FIP	DRA	VORP	WARP	cFIP	MPH
2014	ANA	MLB	25	0	0	0	2	0	0²	1	0	0.0	13.5	1	0%	.500	1.50	0.00	0.16	4.75	0.0	0.0	103	91.0
2014	SLC	AAA	25	0	2	0	6	6	30²	35	8	4.4	5.0	17	55%	.276	1.63	6.75	7.84	6.15	-1.3	-0.1	115	
2015	ANA	MLB	26	4	3	0	64	0	67	58	5	3.1	7.9	59	52%	.277	1.21	3.49	3.57	3.94	5.7	0.6	100	93.3
2016	ANA	MLB	27	1	3	0	64	0	57¹	71	4	2.4	8.0	51	46%	.362	1.50	3.45	3.07	4.15	5.3	0.5	98	92.9
2017	*ANA*	*MLB*	*28*	*3*	*3*	*0*	*57*	*0*	*60*	*56*	*5*	*2.9*	*7.5*	*50*	*54%*	*.287*	*1.24*	*3.68*	*3.73*	*4.08*	*6.0*	*0.6*	*90*	
2018	*ANA*	*MLB*	*29*	*3*	*1*	*0*	*62*	*0*	*65¹*	*52*	*6*	*3.6*	*9.3*	*68*	*54%*	*.273*	*1.19*	*3.61*	*3.63*	*3.95*	*7.9*	*0.8*	*84*	

Breakout: 19%   Improve: 39%   Collapse: 20%   Attrition: 32%   MLB: 85%   Comparables: *Troy Patton, Phil Coke, Dustin Moseley*

Alvarez doesn't overpower hitters, making him less than the 2017 platonic ideal of relievers. Even so, 2016 showed him to be entirely rosterable and thus a perfectly cromulent reliever (Note: Angels comments officially meet requirement for *Simpsons* references). He maintains reasonable-to-good ground-ball and home run rates, and last year continued to tighten up his control. It's not an overwhelming profile, but he gets his outs consistently, and in a bullpen that posted the second-worst DRA in baseball last year that ain't bad.

Andrew Bailey   RHP

Born: 5/31/84   Age: 33   Bats: R   Throws: R   Height: 6'3"   Weight: 240   Entered Pro Ball: Round 6, 2006 Draft (#188 overall)

YEAR	TEAM	LVL	AGE	W	L	SV	G	GS	IP	H	HR	BB/9	K/9	K	GB%	BABIP	WHIP	ERA	FIP	DRA	VORP	WARP	cFIP	MPH
2015	TRN	AA	31	1	0	2	11	0	14¹	6	0	3.8	10.7	17	42%	.194	0.84	0.63	2.15	2.45	3.6	0.4	88	
2015	SWB	AAA	31	0	0	4	9	0	12¹	12	1	2.2	9.5	13	35%	.333	1.22	2.19	2.83	2.96	2.7	0.3	90	
2015	NYA	MLB	31	0	1	0	10	0	8²	9	2	5.2	6.2	6	43%	.286	1.62	5.19	6.45	4.48	0.2	0.0	109	95.5
2016	PHI	MLB	32	3	1	0	33	0	32¹	32	6	4.2	9.2	33	41%	.292	1.45	6.40	5.04	4.67	1.1	0.1	106	94.4
2016	ANA	MLB	32	0	0	6	12	0	11¹	9	1	1.6	6.4	8	46%	.235	0.97	2.38	3.64	4.49	0.6	0.1	107	94.5
2017	*ANA*	*MLB*	*33*	*2*	*3*	*5*	*47*	*0*	*50*	*51*	*8*	*3.6*	*8.1*	*45*	*50%*	*.295*	*1.42*	*5.06*	*4.77*	*5.17*	*-1.1*	*-0.1*	*100*	
2018	*ANA*	*MLB*	*34*	*2*	*1*	*2*	*37*	*0*	*39¹*	*36*	*6*	*3.9*	*8.9*	*39*	*50%*	*.282*	*1.35*	*4.68*	*4.72*	*5.12*	*-0.3*	*0.0*	*118*	

Breakout: 18%   Improve: 26%   Collapse: 24%   Attrition: 22%   MLB: 64%   Comparables: *Joel Peralta, David Aardsma, Tyler Walker*

Everybody loves a redemption tale and nothing in baseball holds quite the baptismal power of ninth-inning success. That explains why Bailey's 10 clean closes in 11 tries last September earned him a million-dollar re-up from the Angels, washing away the sins of a failed season in Philadelphia, four years of injury and ineffectiveness and even that Piggly Wiggly he knocked over in Yazoo. Sure, Bailey's velocity is down a few ticks from his previous glory and he doesn't miss as many bats as he used to, but at least he kept his walk rate low for a month. It's possible he's found something and can resurrect his career as a solid late-innings option, but even Angels eventually run out of forgiveness.

Cam Bedrosian   RHP

Born: 10/2/91   Age: 25   Bats: R   Throws: R   Height: 6'0"   Weight: 230   Entered Pro Ball: Round 1, 2010 Draft (#29 overall)

YEAR	TEAM	LVL	AGE	W	L	SV	G	GS	IP	H	HR	BB/9	K/9	K	GB%	BABIP	WHIP	ERA	FIP	DRA	VORP	WARP	cFIP	MPH
2014	ARK	AA	22	1	0	15	30	0	32¹	10	1	2.8	15.9	57	57%	.196	0.62	1.11	0.92	0.66	15.1	1.6	42	
2014	ANA	MLB	22	0	1	0	17	0	19¹	23	2	5.6	9.3	20	43%	.356	1.81	6.52	4.30	5.02	-1.1	-0.1	109	97.2
2015	SLC	AAA	23	1	1	3	24	0	35²	32	0	3.5	10.6	42	54%	.348	1.29	2.78	2.51	2.27	10.5	1.1	88	
2015	ANA	MLB	23	1	0	0	34	0	33¹	40	3	5.1	9.2	34	45%	.378	1.77	5.40	4.12	5.55	-3.1	-0.3	106	97.0
2016	ANA	MLB	24	2	0	1	45	0	40¹	30	1	3.1	11.4	51	52%	.309	1.09	1.12	2.09	2.55	10.8	1.1	75	97.6
2017	*ANA*	*MLB*	*25*	*2*	*3*	*0*	*47*	*0*	*50*	*47*	*6*	*3.6*	*9.6*	*54*	*52%*	*.303*	*1.35*	*4.01*	*3.88*	*4.37*	*3.4*	*0.4*	*99*	
2018	*ANA*	*MLB*	*26*	*2*	*1*	*0*	*44*	*0*	*47*	*39*	*6*	*4.2*	*11.3*	*59*	*52%*	*.299*	*1.30*	*3.67*	*3.71*	*4.03*	*5.3*	*0.5*	*87*	

Breakout: 39%   Improve: 51%   Collapse: 25%   Attrition: 29%   MLB: 86%   Comparables: *Macay McBride, Jose Arredondo, Jordan Walden*

He always had the fastball, but it was the growth of Bedrosian's slider that turned the former first-round pick and son of former Cy Young winner Steve into the Angels' best reliever. Bedrosian ditched the changeup and used the slider both in and out of the zone to generate swings and misses. His strikeout rate jumped as a result. Pair that with a high-90s fastball and even if he misses his spot with it, batters often can't catch up. Even when batters did make contact it resulted in a ground ball half the time. Bedrosian had Tommy John surgery in 2010 and missed a significant chunk of 2016 with blood clots in his pitching arm, but if healthy the potential is there for a late-inning impact reliever.

Jesse Chavez   RHP

Born: 8/21/83   Age: 33   Bats: R   Throws: R   Height: 6'2"   Weight: 175   Entered Pro Ball: Round 42, 2002 Draft (#1252 overall)

YEAR	TEAM	LVL	AGE	W	L	SV	G	GS	IP	H	HR	BB/9	K/9	K	GB%	BABIP	WHIP	ERA	FIP	DRA	VORP	WARP	cFIP	MPH
2014	OAK	MLB	30	8	8	0	32	21	146	142	17	3.0	8.4	136	43%	.302	1.31	3.45	3.92	3.70	17.7	2.0	95	93.6
2015	OAK	MLB	31	7	15	1	30	26	157	164	18	2.8	7.8	136	45%	.312	1.35	4.18	3.82	4.19	15.3	1.6	97	94.1
2016	TOR	MLB	32	1	2	0	39	0	41¹	43	9	2.2	9.1	42	46%	.309	1.28	4.57	4.78	4.38	2.7	0.3	101	95.6
2016	LAN	MLB	32	1	0	0	23	0	25²	28	3	2.8	7.4	21	39%	.325	1.40	4.21	4.00	4.23	2.1	0.2	101	94.9
2017	*ANA*	*MLB*	*33*	*9*	*11*	*0*	*29*	*29*	*165¹*	*167*	*24*	*3.1*	*8.1*	*150*	*41%*	*.300*	*1.37*	*4.35*	*4.38*	*4.74*	*9.3*	*1.0*	*100*	
2018	*ANA*	*MLB*	*34*	*10*	*11*	*0*	*30*	*30*	*188²*	*191*	*28*	*3.2*	*8.5*	*177*	*41%*	*.303*	*1.36*	*4.36*	*4.39*	*4.75*	*13.6*	*1.4*	*109*	

Breakout: 12%   Improve: 40%   Collapse: 17%   Attrition: 17%   MLB: 80%   Comparables: *Carlos Torres, Claudio Vargas, Scott Downs*

Innings are important—even at a league-average (or thereabout) rate. Chavez can give you those, either in the rotation or from the bullpen. He didn't start a game in 2016 after beginning 47 the previous two seasons, and became more of a two-pitch guy as a result, leaning on his four-seamer and cutter. That alteration wasn't enough to improve his performance, as his DRA and cFIP both continued their slow creep in the wrong direction. Chavez registered a four-plus ERA as a reliever in both Toronto and Los Angeles, so he should double-up, strike "fit" seamlessly into the Angels rotation.

Joe Gatto   RHP

Born: 6/14/95   Age: 22   Bats: R   Throws: R   Height: 6'3"   Weight: 220   Entered Pro Ball: Round 2, 2014 Draft (#53 overall)

YEAR	TEAM	LVL	AGE	W	L	SV	G	GS	IP	H	HR	BB/9	K/9	K	GB%	BABIP	WHIP	ERA	FIP	DRA	VORP	WARP	cFIP	MPH
2016	BUR	A	21	3	8	0	15	15	64	88	5	4.6	7.6	54	56%	.379	1.89	7.03	4.35	7.33	-16.4	-1.8	116	
2017	ANA	MLB	22	2	5	0	12	12	50²	72	10	6.1	3.5	19	61%	.323	2.09	7.09	7.13	7.51	-11.5	-1.2	175	
2018	ANA	MLB	23	4	9	0	22	22	131²	163	23	6.0	6.0	89	61%	.322	1.91	6.17	6.21	6.54	-10.9	-1.1	154	

Breakout: 0%   Improve: 0%   Collapse: 0%   Attrition: 0%   MLB: 0%   Comparables: Madison Younginer, Luis Perdomo, Jairo Diaz

They say you can't scout stats, which is good for Gatto because if you could he'd have been cut. As it stood, the team's no. 1 prospect going into the season was so bad that he was pulled from Single-A and sent back to the practice fields of Arizona to start over. The athleticism and velocity are still there, but his ability to pitch at anything approaching a pro level is increasingly dubious.

Deolis Guerra   RHP

Born: 4/17/89   Age: 28   Bats: R   Throws: R   Height: 6'5"   Weight: 245   Entered Pro Ball: International Free Agent, 2005

YEAR	TEAM	LVL	AGE	W	L	SV	G	GS	IP	H	HR	BB/9	K/9	K	GB%	BABIP	WHIP	ERA	FIP	DRA	VORP	WARP	cFIP	MPH
2014	ROC	AAA	25	2	2	0	36	1	52	51	5	3.1	9.3	54	30%	.315	1.33	4.33	3.57	1.96	19.7	2.0	87	
2015	IND	AAA	26	2	1	4	25	0	36²	21	1	2	9.1	37	38%	.220	0.79	1.23	2.15	1.41	14.3	1.5	76	
2015	PIT	MLB	26	2	0	0	10	0	16²	26	5	1.6	9.2	17	40%	.438	1.74	6.48	5.74	4.51	0.4	0.0	103	93.3
2016	ANA	MLB	27	3	0	0	44	0	53¹	52	6	1.2	6.1	36	42%	.272	1.11	3.21	3.72	4.90	0.4	0.0	110	92.8
2017	ANA	MLB	28	2	3	3	52	0	55	57	8	2.5	6.9	42	45%	.293	1.31	4.53	4.45	4.78	1.2	0.1	100	
2018	ANA	MLB	29	2	1	1	44	0	47	43	7	3.2	9.2	48	45%	.287	1.26	4.18	4.21	4.59	2.4	0.2	105	

Breakout: 20%   Improve: 37%   Collapse: 12%   Attrition: 23%   MLB: 60%   Comparables: Edgmer Escalona, Brad Brach, Craig Breslow

The Angels nabbed Guerra in the Rule 5 draft before last season, tinkered with his mechanics and were rewarded with a solid year of relief and a possible bullpen cog on the cheap. The former Mets, Twins and Pirates farmhand lives off his changeup, throwing it nearly half the time in an effort to keep hitters from sitting on his mundane four-seamer. Guerra doesn't miss many bats but posted one of the lowest walk rates in the league, allowing him to mostly survive the inevitable bouts of gopheritis that will always plague him. The one-time top prospect has soldiered on through years of heightened expectations, disappointment and diminishing stuff, so it's a pleasant surprise to see him emerge from the gloom and find success, however fleeting.

Andrew Heaney   LHP

Born: 6/5/91   Age: 26   Bats: L   Throws: L   Height: 6'2"   Weight: 195   Entered Pro Ball: Round 1, 2012 Draft (#9 overall)

YEAR	TEAM	LVL	AGE	W	L	SV	G	GS	IP	H	HR	BB/9	K/9	K	GB%	BABIP	WHIP	ERA	FIP	DRA	VORP	WARP	cFIP	MPH
2014	JAX	AA	23	4	2	0	9	8	53²	45	2	2.2	8.7	52	47%	.285	1.08	2.35	2.46	2.47	16.1	1.7	81	
2014	NWO	AAA	23	5	4	0	15	15	83²	75	9	2.5	9.8	91	45%	.296	1.17	3.87	3.89	1.53	39.3	3.9	72	
2014	MIA	MLB	23	0	3	0	7	5	29¹	32	6	2.1	6.1	20	48%	.289	1.33	5.83	5.42	4.33	1.5	0.2	107	93.8
2015	SLC	AAA	24	6	2	0	14	14	78¹	95	2	2.9	8.5	74	48%	.372	1.53	4.71	3.11	3.31	17.3	1.8	92	
2015	ANA	MLB	24	6	4	0	18	18	105²	99	9	2.4	6.6	78	41%	.284	1.20	3.49	3.70	5.06	0.2	0.0	113	94.1
2016	ANA	MLB	25	0	1	0	1	1	6	7	2	0.0	10.5	7	44%	.312	1.17	6.00	5.11	4.03	0.9	0.1	98	94.3
2017	ANA	MLB	26	2	2	0	6	6	34²	35	4	3.0	7.7	30	60%	.299	1.33	4.02	4.11	4.38	4.2	0.4	100	
2018	ANA	MLB	27	10	10	0	30	30	186¹	169	21	4.1	9.6	198	60%	.297	1.36	4.03	4.06	4.39	19.7	2.0	100	

Breakout: 25%   Improve: 50%   Collapse: 25%   Attrition: 23%   MLB: 90%   Comparables: Dillon Gee, Brett Oberholtzer, Lance Lynn

In September 2015 we learned Heaney had become the first baseball player to sell part of his future earnings to a company that sold shares of those earnings to speculators. Flash forward seven months to the 2016 season: Heaney started one game before going on the disabled list with what was initially described as a strained flexor muscle. After months of diagnoses and re-diagnoses, including attempts to treat the issue with rest and stem-cell therapy, Heaney underwent Tommy John Surgery in July. He'll likely miss the 2017 season. Say this for Heaney, he's learned the most important lesson about being a pitcher: always take the money as soon as it's offered.

Kyle Kendrick   RHP

Born: 8/26/84   Age: 32   Bats: R   Throws: R   Height: 6'3"   Weight: 220   Entered Pro Ball: Round 7, 2003 Draft (#205 overall)

YEAR	TEAM	LVL	AGE	W	L	SV	G	GS	IP	H	HR	BB/9	K/9	K	GB%	BABIP	WHIP	ERA	FIP	DRA	VORP	WARP	cFIP	MPH
2014	PHI	MLB	29	10	13	0	32	32	199	214	25	2.6	5.5	121	47%	.290	1.36	4.61	4.54	5.78	-20.9	-2.3	117	92.3
2015	COL	MLB	30	7	13	0	27	27	142¹	172	33	2.8	5.1	80	41%	.300	1.52	6.32	6.15	6.56	-23.4	-2.5	127	91.2
2016	SLC	AAA	31	6	5	0	16	15	93¹	101	13	1.8	6.5	67	49%	.303	1.29	4.72	4.84	3.57	18.3	1.9	97	
2017	ANA	MLB	32	5	6	0	16	16	92	101	16	2.9	6.1	63	55%	.293	1.43	5.14	5.13	5.60	-1.3	-0.1	132	
2018	ANA	MLB	33	8	11	0	28	28	169¹	189	30	3.0	6.3	119	55%	.297	1.44	5.15	5.19	5.61	-2.5	-0.3	132	

Breakout: 16%   Improve: 42%   Collapse: 8%   Attrition: 9%   MLB: 65%   Comparables: Kyle Lohse, Brian Lawrence, Jason Jennings

After Kendrick gave up a league-leading 33 homers for the Rockies in 2015, he tried and failed to make the Braves coming out of spring training. That's the 93-loss Braves. This is not a good two seasons. It didn't get better. He signed with the Angels in April, was sent to Triple-A and missed much of the season with a shoulder impingement. Well, they said it was a shoulder impingement. It could easy have been whiplash. Either way Kendrick brings his lack of stuff and recent injury history into 2017, when he might hold down a minor-league rotation spot in a sea-level park.

John Lamb   LHP

Born: 7/10/90   Age: 26   Bats: L   Throws: L   Height: 6'4"   Weight: 205   Entered Pro Ball: Round 5, 2008 Draft (#145 overall)

YEAR	TEAM	LVL	AGE	W	L	SV	G	GS	IP	H	HR	BB/9	K/9	K	GB%	BABIP	WHIP	ERA	FIP	DRA	VORP	WARP	cFIP	MPH
2014	OMA	AAA	23	8	10	0	27	26	138¹	137	19	4.4	8.5	131	41%	.303	1.48	3.97	5.26	6.82	-16.6	-1.7	117	
2015	OMA	AAA	24	9	1	0	17	17	94¹	80	7	2.8	9.2	96	36%	.297	1.16	2.67	3.58	2.69	27.3	2.8	83	
2015	LOU	AAA	24	1	1	0	3	3	17	14	0	3.7	11.1	21	23%	.326	1.24	2.65	2.10	2.78	4.8	0.5	84	
2015	CIN	MLB	24	1	5	0	10	10	49²	58	8	3.4	10.5	58	40%	.376	1.55	5.80	4.19	3.98	6.1	0.6	96	93.7
2016	CIN	MLB	25	1	7	0	14	14	70	84	14	4.0	7.5	58	45%	.327	1.64	6.43	5.50	5.66	-2.3	-0.2	109	92.2
2016	LOU	MLB	25	2	2	0	6	6	29¹	35	1	2.8	8.0	26	38%	.370	1.50	5.22	2.96	3.54	5.9	0.6	101	
2017	*ANA*	*MLB*	*26*	*5*	*6*	*0*	*18*	*18*	*91*	*95*	*13*	*3.6*	*8.1*	*82*	*49%*	*.309*	*1.44*	*4.54*	*4.50*	*4.96*	*5.2*	*0.5*	*115*	
2018	*ANA*	*MLB*	*27*	*6*	*7*	*0*	*21*	*21*	*122¹*	*115*	*19*	*4.7*	*10.2*	*138*	*49%*	*.304*	*1.46*	*4.65*	*4.68*	*5.08*	*4.6*	*0.5*	*118*	

Breakout: 22%   Improve: 49%   Collapse: 21%   Attrition: 30%   MLB: 82%   *Comparables: Bobby Parnell, Brandon Workman, Jonny Venters*

Beset by elbow trouble early in his pro career and shoulder trouble lately, Lamb has lost the velocity that used to provide him with substantial margin for error. He's left with a heater that relies on location, and a trio of secondary weapons that might allow him to get by with it: a changeup, a curveball and a cutter, all capable of missing bats. For reasons of durability, he might end up in relief, and if he doesn't, he's going to need a way to lessen his vulnerability to the long ball.

Tim Lincecum   RHP

Born: 6/15/84   Age: 33   Bats: L   Throws: R   Height: 5'11"   Weight: 170   Entered Pro Ball: Round 1, 2006 Draft (#10 overall)

YEAR	TEAM	LVL	AGE	W	L	SV	G	GS	IP	H	HR	BB/9	K/9	K	GB%	BABIP	WHIP	ERA	FIP	DRA	VORP	WARP	cFIP	MPH
2014	SFN	MLB	30	12	9	1	33	26	155²	154	19	3.6	7.7	134	49%	.299	1.39	4.74	4.28	4.91	-1.6	-0.2	108	92.2
2015	SFN	MLB	31	7	4	0	15	15	76¹	75	7	4.5	7.1	60	45%	.300	1.48	4.13	4.31	6.02	-8.0	-0.9	119	90.0
2016	ANA	MLB	32	2	6	0	9	9	38¹	68	11	5.4	7.5	32	43%	.432	2.37	9.16	7.12	6.68	-5.6	-0.6	123	90.5
2016	SLC	AAA	32	0	3	0	7	7	38¹	30	2	3.3	8.7	37	48%	.267	1.15	3.76	3.80	3.35	8.5	0.9	89	
2017	*ANA*	*MLB*	*33*	*4*	*5*	*0*	*12*	*12*	*67¹*	*72*	*11*	*4.3*	*8.0*	*60*	*43%*	*.306*	*1.54*	*5.13*	*5.03*	*5.58*	*-0.8*	*-0.1*	*130*	
2018	*ANA*	*MLB*	*34*	*8*	*11*	*0*	*27*	*27*	*161¹*	*170*	*30*	*4.4*	*7.9*	*142*	*43%*	*.297*	*1.54*	*5.35*	*5.39*	*5.82*	*-5.8*	*-0.6*	*137*	

Breakout: 16%   Improve: 45%   Collapse: 14%   Attrition: 13%   MLB: 76%   *Comparables: J.A. Happ, Jorge De La Rosa, Paul Maholm*

Surgery didn't heal Lincecum's radar gun readings, and his fastball dipped into Weaverian waters in 2016. Without his heat Lincecum is a shadow of a major-league pitcher, as pinpoint location was never a strength even during his Cy Young heyday. He's still "Tim Lincecum," so he may get another chance somewhere in 2017, but unless there's an incredibly large trampoline at the bottom of this cliff, the only thing he has left is name recognition.

Grayson Long   RHP

Born: 5/27/94   Age: 23   Bats: R   Throws: R   Height: 6'5"   Weight: 230   Entered Pro Ball: Round 3, 2015 Draft (#104 overall)

YEAR	TEAM	LVL	AGE	W	L	SV	G	GS	IP	H	HR	BB/9	K/9	K	GB%	BABIP	WHIP	ERA	FIP	DRA	VORP	WARP	cFIP	MPH
2016	BUR	A	22	3	3	0	8	8	40	27	2	3.6	10.1	45	40%	.258	1.08	1.58	3.08	2.41	11.6	1.3	87	
2016	INL	A+	22	2	1	0	3	3	14	14	5	2.6	9.6	15	32%	.281	1.29	5.14	7.07	2.83	4.1	0.4	89	
2017	*ANA*	*MLB*	*23*	*2*	*4*	*0*	*12*	*12*	*42²*	*50*	*8*	*5.1*	*6.2*	*30*	*67%*	*.303*	*1.72*	*6.09*	*5.99*	*6.67*	*-5.7*	*-0.6*	*155*	
2018	*ANA*	*MLB*	*24*	*5*	*9*	*0*	*27*	*27*	*166¹*	*168*	*29*	*5.3*	*8.3*	*154*	*67%*	*.296*	*1.60*	*5.44*	*5.48*	*5.96*	*-5.2*	*-0.5*	*139*	

Breakout: 1%   Improve: 1%   Collapse: 0%   Attrition: 1%   MLB: 1%   *Comparables: Steven Matz, Mike McClendon, Kyle McPherson*

Unlike the opponent-tripping Duke guard who was wrongly awarded free throws after charging straight into stationary defensive players, this Grayson is a prospect you can root for with pride. Long cut a wide swath through the Midwest league, using his polished fastball/slider/change arsenal to dominate less experienced hitters. His stuff is more workmanlike than filthy, but if the former Aggie can pass the Double-A test this year he has the frame and approach to grow into a fourth starter and innings eater. And if you need anything else to find him more endearing than other athletes named Grayson, check out his profile on the TAMU website: Long looks nearly as natty in a bowtie as our old friends Ben Lindbergh and Jason Wojciechowski. So there's that.

Greg Mahle   LHP

Born: 4/17/93   Age: 24   Bats: L   Throws: L   Height: 6'2"   Weight: 230   Entered Pro Ball: Round 15, 2014 Draft (#449 overall)

YEAR	TEAM	LVL	AGE	W	L	SV	G	GS	IP	H	HR	BB/9	K/9	K	GB%	BABIP	WHIP	ERA	FIP	DRA	VORP	WARP	cFIP	MPH
2014	BUR	A	21	0	1	1	18	0	29¹	20	1	3.7	11.7	38	46%	.250	1.09	3.38	2.77	3.71	4.4	0.5	92	
2015	INL	A+	22	0	1	9	21	0	22²	26	1	1.2	12.3	31	46%	.446	1.28	3.57	2.28	1.45	8.2	0.9	71	
2015	ARK	AA	22	3	3	16	31	0	35¹	34	1	2.8	9.2	36	55%	.333	1.27	3.06	2.56	2.69	8.0	0.9	85	
2016	ANA	MLB	23	1	0	0	24	0	18¹	23	4	4.9	6.9	14	57%	.339	1.80	5.40	6.38	5.00	-0.1	0.0	107	92.0
2016	SLC	AAA	23	1	1	2	30	0	32²	48	7	3.3	6.6	24	53%	.380	1.84	7.71	6.32	4.27	2.5	0.3	105	
2017	*ANA*	*MLB*	*24*	*1*	*2*	*0*	*33*	*0*	*35*	*38*	*4*	*3.6*	*6.4*	*25*	*47%*	*.305*	*1.52*	*4.92*	*4.61*	*5.04*	*-0.2*	*0.0*	*100*	
2018	*ANA*	*MLB*	*25*	*2*	*1*	*0*	*39*	*0*	*41¹*	*39*	*5*	*4.6*	*9.5*	*44*	*47%*	*.307*	*1.45*	*4.27*	*4.30*	*4.63*	*1.9*	*0.2*	*106*	

Breakout: 13%   Improve: 16%   Collapse: 1%   Attrition: 12%   MLB: 21%   *Comparables: Kevin Chapman, Chasen Shreve, Donnie Joseph*

His minor-league strikeout rate is outstanding, and when you watch him you can see why. This is a comment and not a video though, so here's a description: Mahle throws three pitches from the left side, all from a variety of arm slots, but centered around a sidearm delivery. None are overpowering in velocity or movement. It's easy to see right-handed hitters injuring themselves rushing to the plate to face him, which is why of the 86 batters he faced last season, 47 were lefties. Problem was, both righties and lefties crushed him equally (over a .900 OPS for both) Perhaps with better sheltering and increased command there's a big league-caliber LOOGY here.

Alex Meyer   RHP

Born: 1/3/90   Age: 27   Bats: R   Throws: R   Height: 6'9"   Weight: 225   Entered Pro Ball: Round 1, 2011 Draft (#23 overall)

YEAR	TEAM	LVL	AGE	W	L	SV	G	GS	IP	H	HR	BB/9	K/9	K	GB%	BABIP	WHIP	ERA	FIP	DRA	VORP	WARP	cFIP	MPH
2014	ROC	AAA	24	7	7	0	27	27	130¹	116	10	4.4	10.6	153	49%	.321	1.38	3.52	3.66	2.96	40.4	4.0	91	
2015	MIN	MLB	25	0	0	0	2	0	2²	4	2	10.1	10.1	3	22%	.286	2.62	16.88	13.98	5.93	-0.4	0.0	113	98.6
2015	ROC	AAA	25	4	5	0	38	8	92	101	4	4.7	9.8	100	47%	.372	1.62	4.79	3.28	4.85	2.4	0.2	97	
2016	ROC	AAA	26	1	1	1	3	2	17¹	11	0	2.1	9.9	19	54%	.268	0.87	1.04	1.67	1.85	6.6	0.7	78	
2016	MIN	MLB	26	0	1	0	2	1	3²	8	1	9.8	12.3	5	36%	.538	3.27	12.27	7.20	4.70	0.3	0.0	104	97.6
2016	ANA	MLB	26	1	2	0	5	5	21²	17	2	5.4	10.0	24	40%	.273	1.38	4.57	3.89	4.93	1.0	0.1	105	97.7
2017	ANA	MLB	27	4	5	0	35	11	83	81	9	4.3	8.5	79	55%	.302	1.47	4.26	4.26	4.59	5.4	0.6	100	
2018	ANA	MLB	28	6	6	0	51	15	126¹	111	15	5.7	11.4	160	55%	.313	1.52	4.20	4.24	4.58	9.7	1.0	103	

Breakout: 20%   Improve: 43%   Collapse: 22%   Attrition: 32%   MLB: 71%   *Comparables: Nate Karns, Matt Maloney, Eric Surkamp*

A top-25 prospect before the 2015 season, Meyer was relegated to being part of last summer's fabled Ricky Nolasco-for-Hector Santiago deal as a quasi-throw-in. This shows both how well the Twins develop their minor-league talent and how desperate the Angels are for anyone who can throw a baseball from a mound. Meyer's size and stuff are as intriguing as ever, but his penchant for injuries and losing his mechanics make him difficult to rely on. Beggars can't be choosers, so the Angels will take their shot.

Mike Morin   RHP

Born: 5/3/91   Age: 26   Bats: R   Throws: R   Height: 6'4"   Weight: 220   Entered Pro Ball: Round 13, 2012 Draft (#417 overall)

YEAR	TEAM	LVL	AGE	W	L	SV	G	GS	IP	H	HR	BB/9	K/9	K	GB%	BABIP	WHIP	ERA	FIP	DRA	VORP	WARP	cFIP	MPH
2014	ANA	MLB	23	4	4	0	60	0	59	51	3	2.9	8.2	54	48%	.287	1.19	2.90	3.11	3.50	6.5	0.7	97	94.7
2015	SLC	AAA	24	4	2	1	14	0	17¹	25	3	3.1	9.9	19	39%	.415	1.79	6.23	5.04	2.95	3.8	0.4	96	
2015	ANA	MLB	24	4	2	1	47	0	35¹	36	3	2.3	10.4	41	41%	.344	1.27	6.37	2.82	3.71	3.9	0.4	92	95.0
2016	SLC	AAA	25	0	1	2	11	0	10	8	2	0.9	9.9	11	44%	.261	0.90	3.60	4.72	2.44	2.8	0.3	88	
2016	ANA	MLB	25	2	2	0	60	0	55²	52	6	2.4	7.9	49	41%	.295	1.20	4.37	3.61	3.84	7.0	0.7	102	93.9
2017	ANA	MLB	26	1	2	0	33	0	35	36	6	3.1	8.2	32	59%	.299	1.38	4.84	4.69	4.99	0.0	0.0	100	
2018	ANA	MLB	27	2	1	0	48	0	51¹	48	8	3.5	9.1	52	59%	.291	1.33	4.37	4.40	4.75	1.7	0.2	108	

Breakout: 31%   Improve: 48%   Collapse: 22%   Attrition: 20%   MLB: 78%   *Comparables: Kevin Jepsen, Manny Delcarmen, Bill Bray*

The 2016 season saw Morin's promising 2015 jump in strikeout rate dip down to his more pedestrian 2014 levels. An explanation? Opposing batters no longer feared (or were fooled by) his signature changeup. In fact, batters hit it harder than ever before—managing a .388 slugging percentage on the pitch, compared to .188 and .175 the previous two seasons. As a fly-ball pitcher, the fact that Angel Stadium favored home runs for the first time in his career didn't help things, but for Morin to be more than just a guy he has to reverse this negative trend.

Ricky Nolasco   RHP

Born: 12/13/82   Age: 34   Bats: R   Throws: R   Height: 6'2"   Weight: 235   Entered Pro Ball: Round 4, 2001 Draft (#108 overall)

YEAR	TEAM	LVL	AGE	W	L	SV	G	GS	IP	H	HR	BB/9	K/9	K	GB%	BABIP	WHIP	ERA	FIP	DRA	VORP	WARP	cFIP	MPH
2014	MIN	MLB	31	6	12	0	27	27	159	203	22	2.2	6.5	115	44%	.351	1.52	5.38	4.32	4.20	11.2	1.2	97	92.8
2015	MIN	MLB	32	5	2	0	9	8	37¹	50	3	3.4	8.4	35	42%	.392	1.71	6.75	3.48	4.00	4.4	0.5	98	93.5
2016	MIN	MLB	33	4	8	0	21	21	124²	139	18	2.1	6.7	93	43%	.315	1.35	5.13	4.26	4.12	17.2	1.8	102	93.7
2016	ANA	MLB	33	4	6	0	11	11	73	63	8	1.8	6.3	51	46%	.257	1.07	3.21	3.83	3.87	12.1	1.2	102	93.0
2017	ANA	MLB	34	11	13	0	33	33	198	206	29	2.6	7.7	170	46%	.302	1.34	4.32	4.34	4.70	12.1	1.2	100	
2018	ANA	MLB	35	10	11	0	30	30	185¹	201	31	2.6	7.6	157	46%	.309	1.38	4.54	4.58	4.96	10.0	1.0	116	

Breakout: 25%   Improve: 52%   Collapse: 16%   Attrition: 12%   MLB: 88%   *Comparables: Kevin Millwood, A.J. Burnett, Josh Beckett*

Nolasco was exactly what a decimated rotation needed in 2016, namely someone who wasn't immediately in need of surgery. Acquired midseason from the Twins, who are graciously covering $4 million of the $12 million owed to him in 2017, Nolasco can be a bargain for the Angels by merely breaking the 1.0-WARP barrier. However, this is less like Chuck Yeager breaking the sound barrier and more like watching an old guy with a walker cross the highway and wondering whether or not he'll make it before the light turns. At best, Nolasco is a back-end starter at free agent money for one season. [Shruggy emoji.] Still, the potential for injury is real—elbow soreness derailed his 2015 season—and his 2018 option becomes a player option with 202.1 more innings, so even a "good" season from Nolasco comes with a price most teams would likely rather not pay.

Brett Oberholtzer   LHP

Born: 7/1/89   Age: 27   Bats: L   Throws: L   Height: 6'1"   Weight: 225   Entered Pro Ball: Round 8, 2008 Draft (#250 overall)

YEAR	TEAM	LVL	AGE	W	L	SV	G	GS	IP	H	HR	BB/9	K/9	K	GB%	BABIP	WHIP	ERA	FIP	DRA	VORP	WARP	cFIP	MPH
2014	OKL	AAA	24	1	2	0	5	5	31	35	9	0.9	9.0	31	44%	.306	1.23	4.65	5.86	2.00	12.9	1.3	83	
2014	HOU	MLB	24	5	13	0	24	24	143²	170	12	1.8	5.9	94	39%	.325	1.38	4.39	3.58	5.22	-6.1	-0.7	110	91.8
2015	HOU	MLB	25	2	2	0	8	8	38¹	44	4	4.0	6.3	27	49%	.328	1.59	4.46	4.46	5.10	-0.1	0.0	111	90.9
2015	FRE	AAA	25	7	4	0	12	12	70	71	9	1.5	6.7	52	41%	.284	1.19	3.86	4.30	3.34	15.3	1.6	90	
2016	PHI	MLB	26	2	2	1	26	0	50¹	58	11	3.6	6.8	38	46%	.299	1.55	4.83	5.71	5.27	-1.6	-0.2	116	91.9
2016	ANA	MLB	26	1	1	0	11	0	20	27	7	4.1	7.2	16	36%	.323	1.80	8.55	7.56	5.17	-0.4	0.0	118	91.6
2017	TOR	MLB	27	1	2	0	5	5	25	27	4	3.1	6.6	18	42%	.296	1.48	4.87	5.02	5.22	0.1	0.0	100	
2018	TOR	MLB	28	8	10	0	29	29	177	188	30	3.5	8.0	157	42%	.305	1.45	4.81	4.86	5.25	3.5	0.4	124	

Breakout: 23%   Improve: 49%   Collapse: 16%   Attrition: 18%   MLB: 81%   *Comparables: Jake Arrieta, Jeremy Sowers, Sergio Mitre*

A lefty reliever with underwhelming stuff and an overwhelming last name, Oberholtzer (German for "overwhelming") landed in Anaheim when the Phillies, owners of one of the game's worst bullpens, decided they didn't need him. If you had to characterize this, it would not be a vote of confidence. In half the innings with Anaheim, Oberholtzer (Dutch for "twice as bad") was twice as bad as he'd been in Philadelphia. Whether he continues to strengthen his fingernails on the edge of the Angels' cliff or that of another equally desperate organization isn't something that should keep anyone but the Oberholzers (Icelandic for "don't hold the bear") up at night.

Brooks Pounders   RHP

Born: 9/26/90   Age: 26   Bats: R   Throws: R   Height: 6'5"   Weight: 265   Entered Pro Ball: Round 2, 2009 Draft (#53 overall)

YEAR	TEAM	LVL	AGE	W	L	SV	G	GS	IP	H	HR	BB/9	K/9	K	GB%	BABIP	WHIP	ERA	FIP	DRA	VORP	WARP	cFIP	MPH
2014	WIL	A+	23	0	1	0	3	3	15²	16	0	4.0	10.3	18	44%	.372	1.47	4.02	2.75	3.65	3.4	0.3	96	
2015	WIL	A+	24	0	1	0	2	2	10	12	1	0.9	9.0	10	38%	.393	1.30	5.40	3.15	3.12	2.2	0.2	90	
2015	NWA	AA	24	3	4	0	8	8	49¹	39	3	3.5	5.8	32	42%	.255	1.18	2.19	4.13	3.74	7.4	0.8	107	
2016	OMA	AAA	25	5	3	0	31	7	80¹	67	5	4.1	10.1	90	33%	.302	1.29	3.14	3.86	3.49	14.6	1.5	97	
2016	KCA	MLB	25	2	1	0	13	0	12²	19	6	2.1	9.2	13	33%	.361	1.74	9.24	7.92	4.94	0.0	0.0	107	95.4
2017	*ANA*	*MLB*	*26*	*1*	*1*	*0*	*24*	*0*	*25*	*24*	*3*	*3.8*	*8.1*	*22*	*54%*	*.292*	*1.37*	*4.23*	*4.41*	*4.57*	*1.1*	*0.1*	*100*	
2018	*ANA*	*MLB*	*27*	*2*	*1*	*0*	*35*	*0*	*37¹*	*30*	*4*	*4.8*	*10.7*	*44*	*54%*	*.285*	*1.34*	*4.02*	*4.05*	*4.43*	*2.5*	*0.3*	*98*	

Breakout: 16%   Improve: 31%   Collapse: 14%   Attrition: 34%   MLB: 51%   *Comparables: Cory Luebke, Tyler Cloyd, Hiram Burgos*

Brooks Pounders is an 80-grade baseball name. If only his arm projected to the same heights. Instead, he features four pedestrian pitches and doesn't generate a ton of swings and misses. The fastball isn't especially fast and his best off-speed pitch, a slider, doesn't feature a ton of break. He's been a starter for mot of his professional career, but if he's to make his mark in the majors it will be out of the bullpen. We're left to wonder why his comps aren't Bob Walk, Eric Plunk and Grant Balfour.

J.C. Ramirez   RHP

Born: 8/16/88   Age: 28   Bats: R   Throws: R   Height: 6'4"   Weight: 250   Entered Pro Ball: International Free Agent, 2005

YEAR	TEAM	LVL	AGE	W	L	SV	G	GS	IP	H	HR	BB/9	K/9	K	GB%	BABIP	WHIP	ERA	FIP	DRA	VORP	WARP	cFIP	MPH
2014	AKR	AA	25	1	0	1	10	0	13	5	1	5.5	9.7	14	39%	.133	1.00	2.08	4.05	5.19	-0.5	-0.1	102	
2014	COH	AAA	25	1	3	2	25	0	31¹	33	5	3.2	4.3	15	48%	.280	1.40	3.45	5.62	6.91	-5.5	-0.5	119	
2015	ARI	MLB	26	1	1	0	12	0	15¹	15	1	2.3	6.5	11	62%	.298	1.24	4.11	3.36	5.24	-0.9	-0.1	117	97.7
2015	RNO	AAA	26	0	1	1	23	0	25	22	0	3.6	6.5	18	55%	.282	1.28	2.88	3.36	4.40	1.5	0.1	102	
2015	TAC	AAA	26	1	1	0	14	0	18	17	2	3.5	9	18	40%	.312	1.33	2.50	4.38	4.41	1.0	0.1	102	
2015	SEA	MLB	26	0	1	0	8	0	8¹	10	2	7.6	5.4	5	17%	.286	2.04	7.56	7.90	5.59	-0.8	-0.1	116	99.1
2016	CIN	MLB	27	1	3	1	27	0	32¹	35	7	2.5	7.8	28	57%	.295	1.36	6.40	5.10	4.33	2.3	0.2	97	98.9
2016	ANA	MLB	27	2	1	1	43	0	46¹	42	5	2.5	6.0	31	55%	.259	1.19	2.91	4.27	4.65	1.7	0.2	97	99.6
2017	*ANA*	*MLB*	*28*	*2*	*3*	*2*	*52*	*0*	*55*	*56*	*8*	*3.0*	*6.6*	*41*	*48%*	*.285*	*1.33*	*4.82*	*4.66*	*5.00*	*-0.1*	*0.0*	*100*	
2018	*ANA*	*MLB*	*29*	*2*	*1*	*1*	*48*	*0*	*51*	*45*	*7*	*3.7*	*8.5*	*48*	*48%*	*.271*	*1.29*	*4.41*	*4.45*	*4.84*	*1.2*	*0.1*	*111*	

Breakout: 27%   Improve: 41%   Collapse: 14%   Attrition: 24%   MLB: 70%   *Comparables: Javy Guerra, Rich Thompson, Dan Jennings*

As a member of five different organizations in four years, Ramirez is an expert on those tiny packages of pretzels they give you on airplanes. In an age when mid-90s fastballs are a staple of modern bullpens, you'd think Ramirez would easily find a permanent gig. Instead the fastball/slider combo hasn't been the strikeout elixir you'd expect, and when the ball doesn't go on the ground it ends up off of or over the wall far more than teams can tolerate. Unless something drastic changes Ramirez will remain the cautionary tale about how velocity doesn't always equal success.

Cory Rasmus   RHP

Born: 11/6/87   Age: 29   Bats: R   Throws: R   Height: 6'0"   Weight: 200   Entered Pro Ball: Round 1, 2006 Draft (#38 overall)

YEAR	TEAM	LVL	AGE	W	L	SV	G	GS	IP	H	HR	BB/9	K/9	K	GB%	BABIP	WHIP	ERA	FIP	DRA	VORP	WARP	cFIP	MPH
2014	SLC	AAA	26	2	1	2	22	0	28	23	2	5.1	7.7	24	43%	.259	1.39	4.18	4.63	5.68	-1.1	-0.1	106	
2014	ANA	MLB	26	3	2	0	30	6	56	42	5	2.7	9.2	57	39%	.253	1.05	2.57	3.20	3.53	6.7	0.7	97	95.4
2015	SLC	AAA	27	0	1	1	10	3	15¹	9	0	1.2	14.7	25	44%	.281	0.72	2.35	0.73	1.64	5.9	0.6	68	
2015	ANA	MLB	27	0	0	0	16	1	20²	15	3	4.8	11.8	27	39%	.261	1.26	5.23	4.12	4.52	0.6	0.1	94	94.5
2016	ANA	MLB	28	0	2	0	19	1	24²	25	4	5.8	6.2	17	32%	.276	1.66	5.84	5.90	7.25	-6.1	-0.6	136	94.3
2017	*ANA*	*MLB*	*29*	*2*	*1*	*0*	*29*	*1*	*34²*	*32*	*5*	*3.9*	*8.2*	*31*	*41%*	*.278*	*1.36*	*4.56*	*4.60*	*4.96*	*0.6*	*0.1*	*113*	
2018	*ANA*	*MLB*	*30*	*2*	*1*	*1*	*44*	*1*	*60*	*55*	*8*	*4.6*	*9.5*	*63*	*41%*	*.290*	*1.43*	*4.50*	*4.54*	*4.90*	*1.2*	*0.1*	*112*	

Breakout: 32%   Improve: 54%   Collapse: 18%   Attrition: 23%   MLB: 80%   *Comparables: Craig Breslow, Brandon Kintzler, Jesse Carlson*

It was another lost season for Rasmus, who scuffled while pitching through a groin issue which eventually led to his second core muscle surgery, costing him three months before an uninspiring September return. When he did take the mound Rasmus couldn't find the strike zone or miss bats. His soaring walk rate nearly crossed the stream of his plummeting strikeout rate, which for a major league pitcher is "all life as we know it stopping instantaneously and every molecule in your body exploding at the speed of light"-level bad. Released at season's end, Rasmus is two years removed from his lone effective big-league season, but if he's put his injury woes in the rear-view mirror he's as likely as anyone to post a randomly solid summer in relief.

Garrett Richards   RHP

Born: 5/27/88   Age: 29   Bats: R   Throws: R   Height: 6'3"   Weight: 210   Entered Pro Ball: Round 1, 2009 Draft (#42 overall)

YEAR	TEAM	LVL	AGE	W	L	SV	G	GS	IP	H	HR	BB/9	K/9	K	GB%	BABIP	WHIP	ERA	FIP	DRA	VORP	WARP	cFIP	MPH
2014	ANA	MLB	26	13	4	0	26	26	168²	124	5	2.7	8.8	164	52%	.264	1.04	2.61	2.63	3.44	26.1	2.9	84	98.8
2015	ANA	MLB	27	15	12	0	32	32	207¹	181	20	3.3	7.6	176	56%	.274	1.24	3.65	3.83	3.64	33.1	3.5	92	97.8
2016	ANA	MLB	28	1	3	0	6	6	34²	31	2	3.9	8.8	34	47%	.302	1.33	2.34	3.28	3.78	6.1	0.6	95	98.5
2017	*ANA*	*MLB*	*29*	*11*	*11*	*0*	*29*	*29*	*182²*	*169*	*23*	*3.5*	*8.8*	*179*	*44%*	*.291*	*1.31*	*4.09*	*4.13*	*4.44*	*16.4*	*1.7*	*100*	
2018	*ANA*	*MLB*	*30*	*11*	*10*	*0*	*29*	*29*	*182²*	*167*	*22*	*3.5*	*9.2*	*186*	*44%*	*.294*	*1.30*	*3.96*	*3.99*	*4.31*	*23.4*	*2.4*	*98*	

Breakout: 15%   Improve: 47%   Collapse: 29%   Attrition: 14%   MLB: 97%   *Comparables: Clay Buchholz, Tyson Ross, Brandon Webb*

Richards pitched well in 2016, but he didn't pitch much. He left his May 1 start due to dehydration, which somehow morphed into a damaged ulnar collateral ligament. Thanks, "according to reports!" Attempts to avoid Tommy John surgery through rest and/or stem-cell treatments often serve only to postpone the inevitable, but in Richards' case the early returns allow cautious optimism and he's been cleared (for now) to rejoin the Angels' rotation in the spring. If he can stay healthy—he's had knee surgery in the recent past as well—the sinking action on his upper-90s fastball combined with the severe depth of his slider will put him at the top of the rotation for a pitching staff desperately in need of a leader.

Matt Shoemaker   RHP

Born: 9/27/86   Age: 30   Bats: R   Throws: R   Height: 6'2"   Weight: 225   Entered Pro Ball: Undrafted Free Agent, 2008

YEAR	TEAM	LVL	AGE	W	L	SV	G	GS	IP	H	HR	BB/9	K/9	K	GB%	BABIP	WHIP	ERA	FIP	DRA	VORP	WARP	cFIP	MPH
2014	SLC	AAA	27	1	0	0	5	5	25²	34	2	3.2	9.1	26	47%	.421	1.68	6.31	3.97	3.87	5.4	0.5	86	
2014	ANA	MLB	27	16	4	0	27	20	136	122	14	1.6	8.2	124	43%	.286	1.07	3.04	3.29	3.37	21.6	2.4	89	93.7
2015	ANA	MLB	28	7	10	0	25	24	135¹	135	24	2.3	7.7	116	42%	.285	1.26	4.46	4.56	4.92	2.3	0.2	104	93.5
2016	ANA	MLB	29	9	13	0	27	27	160	166	18	1.7	8.0	143	42%	.315	1.23	3.88	3.47	2.86	44.5	4.6	91	94.4
2017	ANA	MLB	30	10	10	0	29	29	174	173	23	2.3	8.2	158	44%	.297	1.26	3.94	3.95	4.30	18.3	1.9	100	
2018	ANA	MLB	31	10	10	0	28	28	172²	163	26	2.8	9.3	178	44%	.294	1.25	4.08	4.11	4.45	18.9	1.9	102	

Breakout: 13%   Improve: 33%   Collapse: 23%   Attrition: 20%   MLB: 68%   *Comparables: Philip Humber, Tom Koehler, Sam LeCure*

Shoemaker endured the most frightening moment of the 2016 season when a screamer off the bat of Kyle Seager caught him on the side of the head. It caused a small fracture to his skull and required emergency surgery to stop the bleeding in his brain, though at press time Shoemaker's recovery was coming along nicely and he was expected to be ready to take the mound in spring training. It was a disturbing end to a solid bounce-back year, as Shoemaker improved on the recipe he used during his 2014 breakout. When he leaves his fastball up in the zone it gets tattooed, so Shoemaker opted for even more liberal application of his splitter, throwing it a third of the time regardless of the count. Off-balance hitters found it hard to sit on the fastball or lay off the splitter, helping Shoemaker post the best walk and strikeout rates of his career. Home runs will always be an issue for him, but if The Cobbler can come back healthy and keep avoiding ball four he'll remain an excellent second starter.

Tyler Skaggs   LHP

Born: 7/13/91   Age: 25   Bats: L   Throws: L   Height: 6'4"   Weight: 215   Entered Pro Ball: Round 1, 2009 Draft (#40 overall)

YEAR	TEAM	LVL	AGE	W	L	SV	G	GS	IP	H	HR	BB/9	K/9	K	GB%	BABIP	WHIP	ERA	FIP	DRA	VORP	WARP	cFIP	MPH
2014	ANA	MLB	22	5	5	0	18	18	113	107	9	2.4	6.8	86	51%	.293	1.21	4.30	3.58	3.73	13.9	1.5	96	94.6
2016	SLC	AAA	24	3	2	0	7	7	32¹	19	2	2.2	12.5	45	39%	.246	0.84	1.67	2.48	1.14	15.1	1.6	62	
2016	ANA	MLB	24	3	4	0	10	10	49²	51	5	4.2	9.1	50	44%	.331	1.49	4.17	3.91	4.10	6.9	0.7	96	95.7
2017	ANA	MLB	25	9	10	0	29	29	153²	144	17	3.2	8.7	148	44%	.294	1.29	3.88	3.89	4.23	17.4	1.8	97	
2018	ANA	MLB	26	10	9	0	29	29	183	161	22	3.7	10.1	205	44%	.294	1.29	3.81	3.84	4.16	22.6	2.3	93	

Breakout: 26%   Improve: 53%   Collapse: 22%   Attrition: 17%   MLB: 95%   *Comparables: Martin Perez, Marcus Stroman, Dallas Braden*

Flashes of Brilliance would make a good name for a movie about Skaggs' career to date, though the concept itself is problematic as movies aren't typically made about average-ish, injury-prone pitchers. The former first-rounder returned in July, two years removed from Tommy John surgery, and posted three starts with a Game Score of 72 or above (50 is average), and four starts with a Game Score of 35 or below. Shakiness is good in a martini, less so in a pitcher. It's not entirely unexpected when missing so much time, though. Only 25 years young, the Angels want (and, let's be honest, need) Skaggs to be more than he's shown so far, if for no other reason than Daniel Radcliffe can't star in a movie they don't make.

Nate Smith   LHP

Born: 8/28/91   Age: 25   Bats: L   Throws: L   Height: 6'3"   Weight: 210   Entered Pro Ball: Round 8, 2013 Draft (#247 overall)

YEAR	TEAM	LVL	AGE	W	L	SV	G	GS	IP	H	HR	BB/9	K/9	K	GB%	BABIP	WHIP	ERA	FIP	DRA	VORP	WARP	cFIP	MPH
2014	INL	A+	22	6	3	0	10	10	55²	41	3	2.3	8.2	51	0%	.250	0.99	3.07	3.36					
2014	ARK	AA	22	5	3	0	11	11	62¹	48	3	4.3	9.7	67	34%	.290	1.25	2.89	3.04	4.25	6.8	0.7	100	
2015	ARK	AA	23	8	4	0	17	17	101²	82	10	2.5	7.2	81	44%	.247	1.08	2.48	3.90	3.38	19.3	2.1	92	
2015	SLC	AAA	23	2	4	0	7	7	36	48	7	3.8	5.8	23	42%	.320	1.75	7.75	6.10	5.16	0.6	0.1	109	
2016	SLC	AAA	24	8	9	0	26	26	150¹	166	18	2.6	7.3	122	40%	.324	1.40	4.61	4.61	4.77	9.6	1.0	103	
2017	ANA	MLB	25	1	1	0	7	2	15	15	2	3.2	6.3	11	54%	.291	1.36	4.58	4.64	4.86	0.5	0.1	100	
2018	ANA	MLB	26	6	5	1	50	13	118	105	16	4.9	9.5	124	54%	.285	1.44	4.59	4.63	4.98	4.0	0.4	115	

Breakout: 18%   Improve: 34%   Collapse: 8%   Attrition: 37%   MLB: 56%   *Comparables: Logan Verrett, Matt Andriese, Rudy Owens*

Smith's ERAs in Salt Lake City over the past two seasons would lead you to believe he's more of a candidate to be cut than promoted. But Salt Lake City is at 4,226 feet above sea level, which makes pitching there more difficult, a fact highlighted by his home/road splits. At home at Smith's Ballpark (that's really what it's called), a 5.52 ERA. Away: 3.74. He can drop a mean changeup, but Smith's stuff doesn't overwhelm and guys who frequently lean on fringy breaking stuff aren't at their best at high altitude. A sore elbow curtailed his potential debut in 2016, but health permitting he should get his shot at big-league hitters this year.

Huston Street   RHP

Born: 8/2/83   Age: 33   Bats: R   Throws: R   Height: 6'0"   Weight: 205   Entered Pro Ball: Round 1, 2004 Draft (#40 overall)

YEAR	TEAM	LVL	AGE	W	L	SV	G	GS	IP	H	HR	BB/9	K/9	K	GB%	BABIP	WHIP	ERA	FIP	DRA	VORP	WARP	cFIP	MPH
2014	SDN	MLB	30	1	0	24	33	0	33	18	3	1.9	9.3	34	42%	.195	0.76	1.09	2.86	3.32	4.3	0.5	96	91.7
2014	ANA	MLB	30	1	2	17	28	0	26¹	24	1	2.4	7.9	23	33%	.299	1.18	1.71	2.70	3.81	2.0	0.2	96	92.1
2015	ANA	MLB	31	3	3	40	62	0	62¹	52	7	2.9	8.2	57	36%	.263	1.16	3.18	3.70	4.59	0.8	0.1	109	91.6
2016	ANA	MLB	32	3	2	9	26	0	22¹	31	5	4.8	5.6	14	38%	.351	1.93	6.45	6.37	6.50	-3.8	-0.4	126	90.9
2017	*ANA*	*MLB*	*33*	*2*	*3*	*34*	*52*	*0*	*55*	*52*	*8*	*3.3*	*7.6*	*46*	*39%*	*.280*	*1.28*	*4.49*	*4.59*	*4.72*	*1.6*	*0.2*	*100*	
2018	*ANA*	*MLB*	*34*	*2*	*1*	*20*	*36*	*0*	*38*	*37*	*6*	*3.8*	*7.2*	*30*	*39%*	*.279*	*1.39*	*4.84*	*4.88*	*5.27*	*-0.9*	*-0.1*	*121*	

Breakout: 13%   Improve: 34%   Collapse: 31%   Attrition: 9%   MLB: 85%   Comparables: Eric Gagne, Jon Rauch, Kevin Gregg

"It's safe to say his command hasn't been quite what we've seen." Thus spoke Undersecretary of Understatement Mike Scoscia as Street went on the disabled list with a sore knee in August, ending both his season and a string of 16 appearances in which batters sprinted to the plate and lit into him to the tune of .409/.481/.682. The veteran closer had already missed a month with an oblique injury and spent much of the year watching helplessly as first Cam Bedrosian and then Andrew Bailey thrived in his place. Parsing out how much of Street's struggles were due to injury versus diminishing skill is fool's errand, as hitters will sort that out for us soon enough. In either case, the veteran slider-slinger's run of ninth-inning dominance has likely reached its expiration date.

Nick Tropeano   RHP

Born: 8/27/90   Age: 26   Bats: R   Throws: R   Height: 6'4"   Weight: 200   Entered Pro Ball: Round 5, 2011 Draft (#160 overall)

YEAR	TEAM	LVL	AGE	W	L	SV	G	GS	IP	H	HR	BB/9	K/9	K	GB%	BABIP	WHIP	ERA	FIP	DRA	VORP	WARP	cFIP	MPH
2014	OKL	AAA	23	9	5	0	23	20	124²	90	11	2.4	8.7	120	40%	.248	0.99	3.03	3.81	2.90	39.1	3.9	87	
2014	HOU	MLB	23	1	3	0	4	4	21²	19	0	3.7	5.4	13	43%	.279	1.29	4.57	3.34	4.82	0.0	0.0	113	92.7
2015	SLC	AAA	24	3	6	0	16	16	88	97	9	3.7	9.8	96	42%	.353	1.51	4.81	4.08	3.70	15.7	1.6	90	
2015	ANA	MLB	24	3	2	0	8	7	37²	40	2	2.4	9.1	38	42%	.342	1.33	3.82	2.57	3.30	7.4	0.8	94	93.4
2016	ANA	MLB	25	3	2	0	13	13	68¹	70	14	4.1	9.0	68	36%	.309	1.48	3.56	5.23	4.48	6.7	0.7	110	93.4
2017	*ANA*	*MLB*	*26*	*5*	*5*	*0*	*14*	*14*	*77²*	*75*	*11*	*3.5*	*8.5*	*73*	*54%*	*.298*	*1.36*	*4.31*	*4.36*	*4.70*	*6.6*	*0.7*	*108*	
2018	*ANA*	*MLB*	*27*	*8*	*8*	*0*	*24*	*24*	*143²*	*122*	*20*	*4.5*	*10.5*	*168*	*54%*	*.290*	*1.35*	*4.23*	*4.26*	*4.61*	*12.5*	*1.3*	*106*	

Breakout: 24%   Improve: 41%   Collapse: 30%   Attrition: 31%   MLB: 87%   Comparables: Taylor Jungmann, Erik Johnson, Jimmy Nelson

One silver lining for the Angels: All of their pitchers can't get hurt again, because they'll all still be recovering from Tommy John surgery. Tropeano was one of the unlucky lambs in that particular slaughterhouse, going under the knife late enough in the season that he isn't likely to see the field again until 2018. When he returns he'll hope his fly-ball tendencies and iffy secondary pitches are offset by enough strikeouts that he can grab one of the last spots in the Angels' rotation.

Jered Weaver   RHP

Born: 10/4/82   Age: 34   Bats: R   Throws: R   Height: 6'7"   Weight: 210   Entered Pro Ball: Round 1, 2004 Draft (#12 overall)

YEAR	TEAM	LVL	AGE	W	L	SV	G	GS	IP	H	HR	BB/9	K/9	K	GB%	BABIP	WHIP	ERA	FIP	DRA	VORP	WARP	cFIP	MPH
2014	ANA	MLB	31	18	9	0	34	34	213¹	193	27	2.7	7.1	169	35%	.267	1.21	3.59	4.22	4.70	3.3	0.4	115	89.7
2015	ANA	MLB	32	7	12	0	26	26	159	163	24	1.9	5.1	90	37%	.273	1.23	4.64	4.78	5.99	-16.1	-1.7	125	87.2
2016	ANA	MLB	33	12	12	0	31	31	178	209	37	2.6	5.2	103	30%	.301	1.46	5.06	5.58	7.97	-51.6	-5.3	144	86.2
2017	*ANA*	*MLB*	*34*	*8*	*11*	*0*	*25*	*25*	*149¹*	*159*	*33*	*2.9*	*6.6*	*109*	*48%*	*.279*	*1.38*	*5.61*	*5.61*	*6.11*	*-10.6*	*-1.1*	*148*	
2018	*ANA*	*MLB*	*35*	*7*	*10*	*0*	*22*	*22*	*131²*	*142*	*29*	*2.7*	*6.4*	*94*	*48%*	*.280*	*1.38*	*5.59*	*5.63*	*6.09*	*-9.3*	*-1.0*	*148*	

Breakout: 15%   Improve: 39%   Collapse: 24%   Attrition: 12%   MLB: 76%   Comparables: Rick Sutcliffe, Jeremy Guthrie, Bronson Arroyo

Visit the top of the CN Tower in Toronto and they will tie a line to you and let you "walk" around the edge, leaning over the 1,999-foot drop as you go. Our palms are getting sweaty at the very thought of it. This is the same feeling we get from looking at the velocity readings on Jered Weaver's fastball. How does a guy survive in the majors with a fastball that never breaks 85 mph? The answer has two parts. First, throw five different pitches and none more than a quarter of the time. Second, define "survive." Batters hit .297/.345/.517 with 37 homers off Weaver, meaning, on average, he turned every hitter into Robinson Cano. Or, if you prefer, Adrian Beltre.

C.J. Wilson   LHP

Born: 11/18/80   Age: 36   Bats: L   Throws: L   Height: 6'1"   Weight: 210   Entered Pro Ball: Round 5, 2001 Draft (#141 overall)

YEAR	TEAM	LVL	AGE	W	L	SV	G	GS	IP	H	HR	BB/9	K/9	K	GB%	BABIP	WHIP	ERA	FIP	DRA	VORP	WARP	cFIP	MPH
2014	ANA	MLB	33	13	10	0	31	31	175²	169	17	4.4	7.7	151	49%	.306	1.45	4.51	4.34	4.15	13.4	1.5	109	93.1
2015	ANA	MLB	34	8	8	0	21	21	132	118	13	3.1	7.5	110	45%	.281	1.24	3.89	3.99	4.63	6.6	0.7	105	92.6
2017	*ANA*	*MLB*	*36*	*2*	*2*	*0*	*6*	*6*	*34¹*	*33*	*5*	*4.1*	*8.6*	*33*	*67%*	*.298*	*1.42*	*4.64*	*4.67*	*5.06*	*1.6*	*0.2*	*117*	
2018	*ANA*	*MLB*	*37*	*6*	*7*	*0*	*19*	*19*	*111*	*107*	*16*	*4.2*	*8.6*	*106*	*67%*	*.295*	*1.43*	*4.62*	*4.66*	*5.04*	*5.5*	*0.6*	*116*	

Breakout: 14%   Improve: 41%   Collapse: 17%   Attrition: 10%   MLB: 82%   Comparables: Jose Contreras, Chuck Finley, Al Leiter

On December 8, 2011 the Angels committed $317.5 million to Albert Pujols and C.J. Wilson (only $77.5 million of that was Wilson's). Pujols' contract will end, and we're quoting, "when the lizard people run their flag up the pole at the United States Capitol," but Wilson's deal is over. It really ended after the 2015 season, as he missed all of 2016 when persistent shoulder soreness led to surgery for fraying in his rotator cuff and labrum. In the end, the Angels got 9.9 WARP from Wilson, or about two WARP per season for about $8 million per. That wasn't the going rate when he signed, but it is now. It's hardly a bargain, but the deal worked fine for the Angels and, likely, for Wilson as well. Now 36 and coming off shoulder surgery, Wilson's left arm is still attached to his torso, so he'll get a shot somewhere.

Kirby Yates RHP

Born: 3/25/87   Age: 30   Bats: L   Throws: R   Height: 5'10"   Weight: 210   Entered Pro Ball: Round 26, 2005 Draft (#798 overall)

YEAR	TEAM	LVL	AGE	W	L	SV	G	GS	IP	H	HR	BB/9	K/9	K	GB%	BABIP	WHIP	ERA	FIP	DRA	VORP	WARP	cFIP	MPH
2014	DUR	AAA	27	1	0	16	21	0	25	10	0	3.2	12.6	35	45%	.196	0.76	0.36	1.76	0.99	12.1	1.2	69	
2014	TBA	MLB	27	0	2	1	37	0	36	33	4	3.8	10.5	42	34%	.315	1.33	3.75	3.77	4.37	0.5	0.1	103	94.5
2015	DUR	AAA	28	1	2	6	23	0	25¹	27	5	4.3	12.1	34	39%	.344	1.54	5.33	4.70	2.41	7.1	0.7	89	
2015	TBA	MLB	28	1	0	0	20	0	20¹	23	10	3.1	9.3	21	30%	.245	1.48	7.97	8.61	5.00	-0.7	-0.1	113	94.7
2016	SWB	AAA	29	0	1	4	14	0	16²	12	0	3.2	10.3	19	46%	.279	1.08	1.62	2.15	2.92	3.8	0.4	91	
2016	NYA	MLB	29	2	1	0	41	0	41¹	41	5	4.1	10.9	50	44%	.340	1.45	5.23	3.93	3.51	6.7	0.7	93	95.3
2017	ANA	MLB	30	1	1	0	24	0	25	24	3	3.8	8.9	25	52%	.293	1.37	4.38	4.17	4.64	1.0	0.1	100	
2018	ANA	MLB	31	2	1	1	47	0	49¹	41	7	4.8	10.5	58	52%	.280	1.38	4.46	4.50	4.86	1.0	0.1	110	

Breakout: 15%   Improve: 31%   Collapse: 11%   Attrition: 17%   MLB: 63%   *Comparables: Chris Hatcher, Fernando Cabrera, Brandon Gomes*

The man brought scores of Kirby photos to Yankees Twitter, but also brought just as much anxiety. Though his DRA will say his season wasn't as bad as it appears on paper, it still left much to be desired. Sure, he cut down his fly-ball, homer and hard-hit rates massively, all while inducing more ground balls. And that's promising. But he still looks too much like the guy who routinely got shelled in Tampa Bay. He'll need to continue improving those numbers to earn more work in high-leverage spots.

LINEOUTS

Hitters

NAME	POS	TEAM	LVL	AGE	PA	R	2B	3B	HR	RBI	BB	K	SB	CS	AVG/OBP/SLG	TAv	VORP	BABIP	BRR	FRAA	WARP
Roberto Baldoquin	SS	INL	A+	22	255	19	6	1	0	15	21	62	3	3	.198/.274/.233	.213	-3.8	.271	0.7	SS(28): 1.5, 2B(25): -1.1	-0.4
Nick Buss	OF	SLC	AAA	29	372	49	23	8	6	46	30	66	8	5	.290/.345/.462	.278	13.2	.342	-1.2	RF(35): 1.1, CF(22): 0.3	1.7
	OF	ANA	MLB	29	90	7	7	1	1	8	6	24	2	1	.198/.247/.346	.198	-3.3	.259	0.4	LF(24): -1.3, RF(5): -0.0	-0.5
Sean Coyle	2B	PAW	AAA	24	80	6	1	0	2	4	6	30	1	0	.125/.192/.222	.163	-6.1	.175	-0.2	2B(14): 1.1, CF(7): 2.5	-0.3
	2B	PME	AA	24	170	21	9	0	3	10	19	56	1	2	.185/.296/.308	.224	-1.3	.276	0.1	3B(28): 1.0, 2B(9): -0.1	0.0
	2B	ARK	AA	24	176	20	6	1	3	13	14	56	7	3	.204/.277/.312	.233	1.8	.296	2.1	2B(38): 1.1	0.3
David Fletcher	SS	INL	A+	22	355	42	12	1	3	31	22	43	15	3	.275/.321/.346	.254	11.7	.307	1.6	SS(47): -6.0, 2B(28): -0.2	0.6
	SS	ARK	AA	22	83	10	6	0	0	6	3	13	1	0	.300/.325/.375	.277	5.0	.358	0.6	SS(18): 2.2	0.3
Ramon Flores	LF	MIL	MLB	24	289	18	8	0	2	19	31	58	3	0	.205/.294/.261	.214	-5.5	.254	1.5	RF(49): 0.6, CF(29): -2.9	-0.7
	LF	CSP	AAA	24	31	3	1	0	1	2	2	7	0	0	.250/.290/.393	.251	1.0	.286	0.7	RF(5): -0.7, LF(3): -0.0	0.0
Craig Gentry	CF	ANA	MLB	32	39	2	1	0	0	2	3	6	0	0	.147/.237/.176	.153	-3.8	.179	-0.4	LF(12): 0.8, CF(1): 0.0	-0.3
	CF	INL	A+	32	28	3	1	0	0	3	5	4	2	0	.227/.393/.273	.282	2.3	.278	1.1	LF(4): -0.1	0.2
	CF	SLC	AAA	32	37	6	1	0	0	1	5	8	4	0	.129/.243/.161	.172	-1.9	.167	0.8	LF(6): -0.7	-0.3
Ryan LaMarre	OF	BOS	MLB	27	6	1	0	0	0	0	1	2	0	0	.000/.167/.000	.061	-1.2	.000	-0.1	LF(2): -0.1, RF(1): -0.1	-0.1
	OF	PAW	AAA	27	358	44	15	0	10	41	28	80	17	6	.303/.369/.445	.299	23.6	.371	0.3	CF(46): 0.2, RF(25): -2.2	2.3
Rey Navarro	MI	SLC	AAA	26	175	12	9	2	1	13	5	28	0	0	.227/.253/.325	.208	-4.3	.267	-0.1	SS(16): -0.4, 2B(11): -1.4	-0.8
Gregorio Petit	SS	SLC	AAA	31	62	7	3	0	0	3	5	13	2	0	.327/.377/.382	.268	2.8	.419	-0.2	SS(15): 1.5, 2B(2): 0.2	0.5
	SS	ANA	MLB	31	223	21	13	1	2	17	15	51	1	1	.245/.299/.348	.221	-1.0	.316	0.5	2B(50): -2.7, SS(32): 2.1	-0.1
Shane Robinson	PH	SLC	AAA	31	80	14	4	0	0	4	3	8	4	0	.315/.346/.370	.270	5.2	.348	2.7	CF(6): -1.0, LF(4): -0.3	0.5
	PH	ANA	MLB	31	111	16	3	0	1	10	10	17	3	2	.173/.257/.235	.191	-5.3	.200	-0.2	LF(34): 4.5, CF(19): -0.9	-0.2
Brendan Ryan	SS	SYR	AAA	34	83	7	4	1	1	8	4	17	1	0	.263/.305/.382	.264	2.7	.322	-0.1	2B(8): 1.0, 3B(6): 0.5	0.3
	SS	ANA	MLB	34	14	1	0	0	0	0	0	7	0	0	.077/.077/.077	.074	-1.8	.167	0.2	SS(16): 0.7, LF(1): -0.0	-0.1
	SS	SLC	AAA	34	212	16	6	1	0	15	18	48	6	3	.232/.295/.274	.203	-5.6	.306	-1.1	SS(49): -6.1, 3B(4): -0.9	-1.3
Geovany Soto	C	SLC	AAA	33	38	2	4	0	1	8	1	7	0	0	.194/.216/.389	.199	-1.3	.214	-0.2	C(7): 0.1	-0.1
	C	ANA	MLB	33	86	11	5	0	4	9	6	21	0	0	.269/.321/.487	.270	5.0	.321	0.2	C(23): -0.9, 3B(1): 0.0	0.4

Roberto Baldoquin failed to crack the Mendoza Line in his second tour of the California League, which is a feat not unlike DiMaggio's hit streak but the exact opposite. His defense doesn't project well enough at any of the positions he plays to suggest the Angels' $8 million investment may yield so much as a utility infielder. ❖ One of three 16-year-old international signings last season, **Edwin Bisay** is a catcher from Venezuela, which isn't to say next season he won't be a first baseman from the Dominican Republic. These international teenagers are impossible to project! ❖ **Nick Buss** doesn't run like a greyhound or hit like a bolt. In fact, he trails in most ways to be a productive player, so fittingly the Angels were his last stop. ❖ **Sean Coyle** is a short, white second baseman with power who was drafted by the Red Sox, but until he learns to make more and better contact his list of Dustin Pedroia comps will end there. ❖ A grinding, scrapper of a dirt dog who grinds his way through scrappy at-bats and isn't afraid to get dirty, dog, **David Fletcher** is a quintessential plays-above-his-tools little guy. ❖ **Ramon Flores** got the first extended MLB action of his career and flopped with the Brewers, but he's a useful left-handed bat who should resurface with another organization. ❖ Everything is declining for **Craig Gentry**, making his chances of catching on with the Mariners and Astros in order to collect the entire set of AL West hats sadly minimal. ❖ **Ryan LaMarre** faced as many hitters as pitchers during his brief 2016 stint in Boston, which is not a great sign when you're trying to make it as a backup outfielder. ❖ After not hitting at a Triple-A environment made for hitters, 27-year-old **Rey Navarro** has become a bookmark on the 40-man roster. The Angels will remove him once they read that far. ❖ **Gregorio Petit** got the first extended big-league playing time of his career at age 31, which is awesome, but then he didn't hit well or control the strike zone. He lacks a standout skill, even among utility men. ❖ Re-write lyrics to "Mrs. Robinson" or joke about his "SugaShane" nickname, but in the end **Shane Robinson** is another in a hoarder's collection of sixth outfielders. ❖ **Brendan Ryan**'s once-great fielding has disappeared. Considering his bat never appeared, rostering him has become a bit of magic called "the great disappearing wins trick." ❖ The only Angels catcher to contribute anything with his bat in 2016, **Geovanny Soto** showed some power in between knee injuries. ❖ The Angels plunked an extra 300 grand over slot to nab **Nonie Williams** in the third round because his combination of blazing speed and tantalizing pop was enough to overlook suspect potential at shortstop.

Pitchers

NAME	TEAM	LVL	AGE	W	L	SV	G	GS	IP	H	HR	BB/9	K/9	K	GB%	BABIP	WHIP	ERA	FIP	DRA	VORP	WARP	cFIP	MPH
A.J. Achter	SLC	AAA	27	2	2	3	29	1	46¹	31	9	2.7	6.4	33	43%	.175	0.97	3.50	5.79	5.72	-3.8	-0.4	110	
	ANA	MLB	27	1	0	0	27	0	37²	43	7	2.9	3.3	14	45%	.286	1.46	3.11	5.81	7.21	-9.4	-1.0	129	93.9
Austin Adams	ARK	AA	25	0	1	4	32	0	41¹	29	2	5.2	13.3	61	42%	.321	1.28	3.05	2.82	2.36	10.9	1.2	83	
Manny Banuelos	GWN	AAA	25	0	2	0	9	9	30¹	31	2	6.5	6.2	21	48%	.305	1.75	4.75	4.82	8.20	-9.6	-1.0	120	
	MIS	AA	25	0	2	0	4	4	18¹	23	4	3.9	9.3	19	40%	.352	1.69	5.40	5.39	5.15	-0.1	0.0	103	
Jaime Barria	BUR	A	19	8	6	0	25	25	117	133	6	1.6	6.0	78	44%	.323	1.32	3.85	3.42	4.26	9.8	1.1	98	
Vicente Campos	TAM	A+	23	4	2	0	10	10	59¹	50	3	3.5	8.5	56	40%	.292	1.23	3.49	3.39	3.93	10.2	1.0	99	
	TRN	AA	23	5	1	0	9	9	56²	45	1	2.2	7.6	48	42%	.277	1.04	3.02	2.74	3.73	8.6	0.9	96	
	MOB	AA	23	1	2	0	4	4	20	22	0	2.2	6.8	15	56%	.355	1.35	3.60	2.87	3.98	2.5	0.3	100	
	ARI	MLB	23	0	0	0	1	0	5²	4	2	3.2	6.4	4	33%	.125	1.06	3.18	7.42	5.61	-0.4	0.0	117	91.3
Abel De Los Santos	SYR	AAA	23	1	1	0	15	0	20¹	25	0	5.8	11.5	26	31%	.431	1.87	3.54	2.53	4.11	1.9	0.2	102	
	HAR	AA	23	0	0	5	14	0	14	9	2	6.4	8.4	13	34%	.194	1.36	3.86	5.72	6.72	-3.1	-0.3	115	
	PEN	AA	23	1	2	3	17	0	23¹	11	1	2.7	9.6	25	38%	.175	0.77	1.54	2.63	2.46	5.9	0.6	89	
	CIN	MLB	23	0	0	0	5	0	5²	7	1	6.4	3.2	2	33%	.300	1.94	11.12	7.42	6.87	-1.2	-0.1	128	94.2
Cody Ege	MIA	MLB	25	0	0	0	5	0	3	8	1	6.0	6.0	2	21%	.538	3.33	12.00	9.19	5.39	-0.1	0.0	109	87.6
	NWO	AAA	25	4	3	5	36	0	44	42	1	5.5	7.2	35	49%	.306	1.57	4.50	4.68	6.71	-8.5	-0.9	111	
	ANA	MLB	25	1	0	0	13	0	8²	8	1	3.1	9.3	9	54%	.304	1.27	1.04	3.57	4.92	0.0	0.0	110	90.8
Jake Jewell	INL	A+	23	2	15	0	28	27	137	191	10	4.3	6.8	104	52%	.389	1.87	6.31	4.81	8.84	-51.5	-5.3	118	
Keynan Middleton	INL	A+	22	1	1	0	25	0	36¹	22	7	5.0	13.9	56	42%	.227	1.16	3.72	4.79	1.62	14.0	1.4	78	
	ARK	AA	22	0	0	6	13	0	15	11	1	2.4	10.8	18	42%	.270	1.00	1.20	2.45	2.99	2.9	0.3	84	
	SLC	AAA	22	0	1	2	8	0	14²	14	1	2.5	8.6	14	48%	.302	1.23	4.91	3.52	3.90	1.7	0.2	94	
Eduardo Paredes	INL	A+	21	1	2	4	19	0	22	18	2	2.5	13.1	32	47%	.327	1.09	3.27	3.21	1.59	8.5	0.9	75	
	ARK	AA	21	0	3	8	35	0	48¹	46	6	2.6	8.0	43	40%	.284	1.24	3.35	3.88	2.84	10.1	1.1	100	
Daniel Wright	PEN	AA	25	2	0	0	8	2	20	10	0	1.8	9.9	22	55%	.213	0.70	0.45	1.72	2.25	6.0	0.6	79	
	CIN	MLB	25	0	2	0	4	2	13	25	2	1.4	4.2	6	39%	.426	2.08	7.62	4.72	7.03	-2.5	-0.3	122	92.1
	LOU	AAA	25	6	5	0	17	12	83²	109	10	2.7	7.0	65	40%	.350	1.60	6.13	4.21	4.47	7.3	0.8	109	
	ANA	MLB	25	1	3	0	5	5	26²	32	5	2.0	5.1	15	42%	.321	1.42	5.40	5.66	6.65	-4.0	-0.4	125	92.2

A.J. Achter threw the equivalent of four full games for the Angels despite posting a strikeout rate that would embarrass mid-80s Jeff Ballard. ❖ **Austin Adams** has struck out or walked 47 percent of the batters he's faced in five seasons as a minor leaguer. He has the raw stuff to be a late-inning reliever, but his control is nowhere near good enough to capitalize on it. ❖ **Manny Banuelos**, the former hard-throwing Yankees prospect, is a now a soft-throwing back-of-the-rotation hopeful. Thanks, Tommy John surgery! ❖ **Jaime Barria** earned organizational pitcher of the year honors after commanding a moving fastball and showing feel for a sweet cambio at Low-A. ❖ **Jose Campos** made his MLB debut with the Diamondbacks in August and was claimed off waivers by the Angels in November. His control is lacking, but he could carve out a middle-relief niche. ❖ **Abel De Los Santos** has (narrowly) secured the distinction of being the best Abel De Los Santos ever to pitch in the Reds organization—there was another one, a mere six months older, who never made it out of A-Ball. ❖ A skinny left-hander with a multitude of mechanics, **Cody Ege** got himself (and his mid-80s fastball) to the majors seemingly by pure will. ❖ **Jake Jewell** got crowned by Cal League hitters, surrendering the most earned runs in the league and tying for the most losses in all of minor-league baseball. A solid sinker and change give him a chance, but poor control has thus far usurped the stuff. ❖ **Matt Koch** is your typical uninteresting fifth-starter type. He mixes a four-seamer and cutter for most of his repertoire, and may fit best in the bullpen. ❖ **Keynan Middleton**'s fastball jumped into the high 90s after a move to the bullpen and his delivery—which involves turning his back to the hitter—adds potential to the late-inning setup profile. ❖ **Eduardo Paredes**' great low-minors numbers predictably took a hit in his first action above Single-A, but he throws strikes with a low-90s fastball and decent off-speed stuff. ❖ **Daniel Wright** made his big-league debut in 2016, pitching for both the Reds and the Angels, but he appears destined to organizational depth long term.

LOS ANGELES DODGERS

Essay by Andy McCullough

Player comments by Craig Goldstein and BP staff

In the fall of 1920, with the sport still reeling from the Black Sox scandal, the swells of Major League Baseball voted to appoint a judge from Illinois named Kenesaw Mountain Landis as the head of the sport. Landis refused anything except absolute power, so the sport dissolved its leadership committee and handed him a gavel over the game. The man who cracked John D. Rockefeller and Standard Oil would now be in charge of policing the sport.

The next summer, a jury in Chicago cleared the accused Black Sox on charges of conspiracy to defraud. Landis was less kind. He banned eight members of the team, starting the chain of human events that would lead to Ray Liotta's movie stardom. He also issued a series of smaller decrees, including telling teams not to announce their starting pitcher until the day of the game. He wanted to discourage gamblers from capitalizing on information ahead of time.

I am not sure how much Landis would enjoy about baseball today. There is a designated hitter now, and replay can mess with the flow of the evening. The meddling of interleague play has reduced some of the World Series' spectacle. Wrigley Field has a scoreboard and Fenway Park has an elevator. The money! My goodness, the money. When Landis went after Rockefeller in 1906, the judge ordered the tycoon to pay a fine of $29.24 million. In 2016, Ryan Howard made $25 million. Actually, given Landis' despicable protection of the color line, Ryan Howard would probably really bug him. Landis seems like a bad guy.

But let me tell you this. Kenesaw Mountain Landis would fucking love the "starting rotation" of the 2016 Los Angeles Dodgers.

✦ ✦ ✦

Throughout the summer, the reporters surrounding Dodgers manager Dave Roberts engaged in a daily ritual. After a few questions about various issues, someone inevitably tried to fill in the pitching for the rest of the week. Let's say it's a Wednesday, and Kenta Maeda was starting. That meant that Scott Kazmir, most likely, was pitching on Thursday.

But the weekend? The conversation usually went something like this (the details have been invented, so don't bother wasting your time looking it up on B-Ref).

DODGERS PROSPECTUS
2016 W-L: 91-71, 1ST IN NL WEST

Pythag	.559	6th	DER	.712	4th
RS/G	4.48	14th	B-Age	28.8	21st
RA/G	3.94	5th	P-Age	28.7	21st
TAv	.271	5th	Salary	$249.8M	1st
BRR	0.47	14th	M$/MW	$5.6M	4th
TAv-P	.249	6th	DL Days	1941	29th
FIP	3.65	3rd	$ on DL	30%	30th

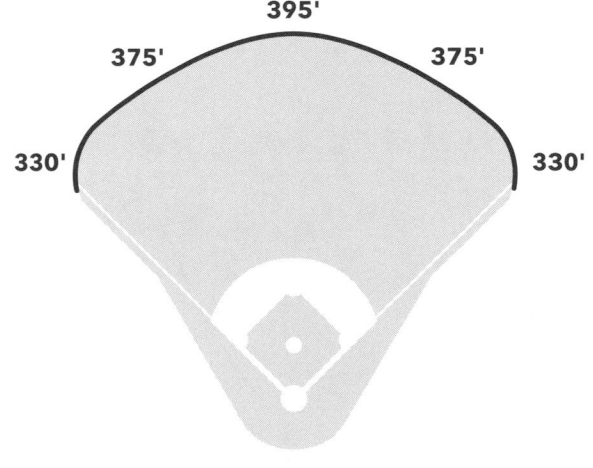

Outfield wall profile: **4' to 8'**

Three-Year Park Factors

Runs	Runs/RH	Runs/LH	HR/RH	HR/LH
92	86	90	95	97

Top Hitter WARP	6.8	Yasmani Grandal
Top Pitcher WARP	5.7	Clayton Kershaw
Top Prospect		Yadier Alvarez

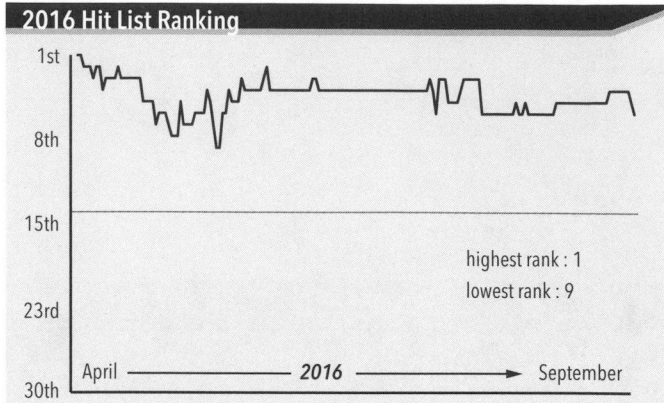

2016 Hit List Ranking

highest rank : 1
lowest rank : 9

April — 2016 → September

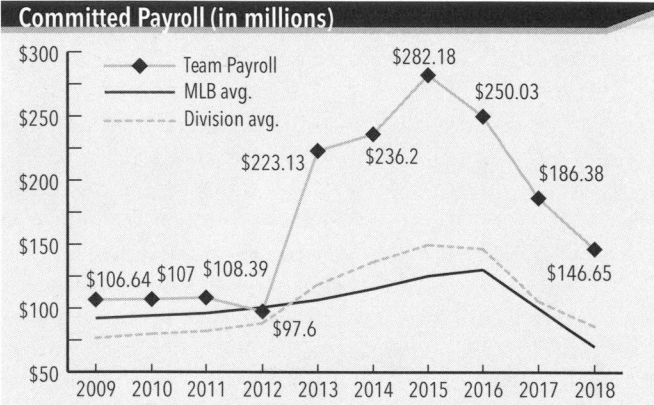

Committed Payroll (in millions)

Team Payroll
MLB avg.
Division avg.

$282.18
$250.03
$223.13
$236.2
$186.38
$146.65
$106.64 $107 $108.39
$97.6

2009 2010 2011 2012 2013 2014 2015 2016 2017 2018

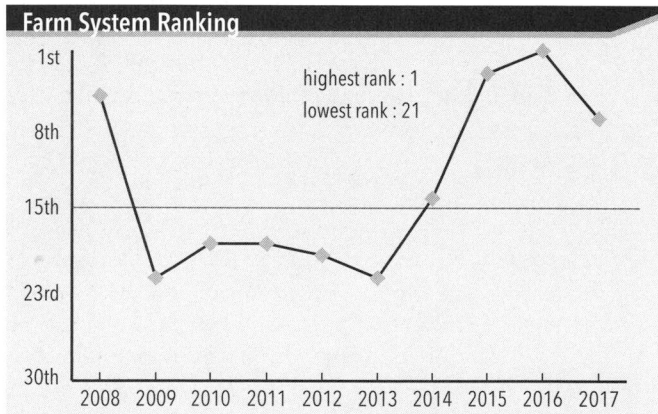

Farm System Ranking

highest rank : 1
lowest rank : 21

2008 2009 2010 2011 2012 2013 2014 2015 2016 2017

Personnel

**President,
Baseball Operations:**
Andrew Friedman

General Manager:
Farhan Zaidi

SVP, Baseball Operations:
Josh Byrnes

Manager:
Dave Roberts

BP Alumni:
Josh Herzenberg

Q: Dave, do you have starters for the weekend?
Roberts: The weekend … the weekend. Yeah. On Friday, we're going with Ross Stripling.
Q: Saturday?
Roberts: Saturday … Saturday. Yeah. We haven't gotten that far yet.
Q: Sunday?
Roberts: Sunday … Sunday. Yeah. We've got a lot of options, but we haven't decided just yet.

This was my seventh season covering Major League Baseball. I have covered good teams and I have covered bad teams. I've never seen anything like the Dodgers this past season, when a good baseball team operated with a rotation seemingly based on chaos, and Roberts maneuvered the spinning plates with enough dexterity to become the National League Manager of the Year in his first season on the job.

Fifteen different men started for the Dodgers in 2016. The best was Clayton Kershaw, who saw perhaps the finest season of his career derailed by his back injury. The worst was Hyun-Jin Ryu, who missed all of 2015 due to shoulder surgery, returned in July of 2016 with his fastball hovering in the mid-80s, made one start in which he got his head kicked in by San Diego and never pitched again.

The only member of the Opening Day rotation to last the entire season without landing on the disabled list was Maeda. A rookie who pitched in Japan before 2016, he had flunked his physical when he left the Hiroshima Carp due to irregularities with his elbow and shoulder. The Dodgers protected him by using him on four days of rest in only 13 of his 32 starts.

The youngest pitcher was Julio Urias, who was 19 when he arrived in May and became the second pitcher this century to debut as a teenager. The oldest was 36-year-old Rich Hill, who was acquired on August 1 but did not pitch until September due to blisters, then earned a spot in infamy when Roberts removed him after seven perfect innings in Miami. The second-oldest was Brandon McCarthy, who returned from Tommy John surgery only four days before his 33rd birthday, then suffered a mysterious case of the yips that left him unable to throw strikes.

Five rookies debuted as starters. Bud Norris was around for a while. I'm trying to say there was a lot of weird shit going on. And sometimes I wondered if they were doing it on purpose.

✦ ✦ ✦

A week after the final game of the World Series, Dodgers general manager Farhan Zaidi stood inside a ballroom of his peers and admitted to the obvious.

"This notion of being a little preemptive the third time through the order has been around a little while," Zaidi said. "But at the same time, every GM in here would say they'd take seven good innings whenever they can get it. Because it has a lot of spillover effects as you go through the rest of your rotation, you've rested your bullpen. There's still a ton of value in that."

Before we proceed, let's make this clear: The Dodgers would prefer to fill a rotation with five excellent starters. But finding five excellent starters has always been hard, and assembling a more affordable, more efficient, more flexible alternative has become easier for a team with resources like the Dodgers.

Because you are a human being reading this book, I assume I do not need to tell you that free-agent contracts for pitchers can be catastrophic. The Dodgers are neither unaware of this phenomenon nor are they immune to it. During the first two offseasons after Andrew Friedman took over the baseball operations department, the largest contract the team agreed to with a free-agent pitcher was worth $48 million. McCarthy signed a four-year deal worth that much before 2015, Kazmir signed a three-year deal worth that much before 2016.

Both of those contracts have been disastrous. McCarthy blew out in 2015 and it's unclear how he will bounce back in 2017. Kazmir logged a mediocre season, then suffered a myriad of injuries to his neck and back, which prevented him from opting into free agency, an unexpected outcome when he initially signed the deal.

The Dodgers can overcome setbacks like these, and the reasons why demonstrate how the franchise, under Friedman's leadership, has chosen to distribute its enviable array of financial resources. Despite evidence to the contrary, some observers still believe the team will operate like a financial behemoth of old, like the Yankees under George Steinbrenner. Last winter, I can recall articles suggesting the Dodgers would pursue both Zack Greinke and David Price in free agency.

The Dodgers did not sign either. On the open market, pitching has never been more expensive. It has also never been easier to get opposing hitters out. Friedman and his cohorts are trying to exploit this dissonance. Between defensive shifts, advanced scouting, pitchers willing to study the data and increasingly fungible bullpens, this is a great era for teams willing to be creative when it comes to run prevention.

And the Dodgers have dumped money into depth in recent years. They made a convoluted trade that involved taking on millions of dollars in order to acquire Alex Wood.

They paid $1.5 million to Brandon Beachy last season even though he was on a minor-league deal. They refused to part with prospects like Urias or Jose De Leon. The surplus allowed the club to survive a hellish season in 2016.

The Dodgers started losing pitchers before last season even started: Brett Anderson underwent back surgery in March. On the day the team planned to name Mike Bolsinger as the fifth starter, he popped an oblique muscle and was never the same. Kazmir was shaky all year. Neither McCarthy nor Ryu became reliable. And the loss of Kershaw in June sent a seismic shock through the organization.

Kershaw's injury forced the team to scramble, and forced Roberts to embrace a style that became his calling card in the second half. It's quite difficult to find a starter who can go seven. But a starter who can go five? The Dodgers thrived on finding pitchers capable of doing just that. The club operated for a significant portion of 2016 with an eight-man bullpen, and subjected every pitcher not named "Kershaw" to strict monitoring during the third time through the order.

We see versions of managing like this every October, when the margins for error are so slim. The Dodgers found a way to run their ballclub like this all season, which allowed the club to overcome a record-setting year in which 28 different players landed on the disabled list and the team used 55 different players. Some veterans chafed at the restrictions. But most of the rookies didn't know any better, and the Dodgers capitalized on their willingness to be flexible.

"I actually think it's pretty easy to explain," Zaidi said. "There is an intuition to [the idea that] the pitcher gets tired over the course of the game, and hitters get to see the pitcher multiple times. I actually think it creates an incentive for players to work on their durability and work on their pitch mixes. If you want to throw seven innings in a game, perform well the third time through the order, and it's not an issue."

Zaidi mentioned how the team talks about creating a "162-game rotation" not a "five-man rotation." The Dodgers entered the offseason after 2016 with nine pitchers on the 40-man roster capable of being in the Opening Day rotation. After Kershaw, they were all men with question marks, based on either inexperience or ineffectiveness. But the team will continue to seek volume, believing that an excess of quantity can produce enough quality to survive. ■

—Andy McCullough covers the Dodgers for the Los Angeles Times

HITTERS

Cody Bellinger   1B

Born: 7/13/95   Age: 21   Bats: L   Throws: L   Height: 6'4"   Weight: 210   Entered Pro Ball: Round 4, 2013 Draft (#124 overall)

YEAR	TEAM	LVL	AGE	PA	R	2B	3B	HR	RBI	BB	K	SB	CS	AVG/OBP/SLG	TAv	VORP	BABIP	BRR	FRAA	WARP
2015	RCU	A+	19	544	97	33	4	30	103	52	150	10	2	.264/.336/.538	.315	39.9	.314	2.5	1B(91): 8.9, CF(26): -0.1	5.3
2016	TUL	AA	20	465	61	17	1	23	65	59	94	8	2	.263/.359/.484	.313	32.0	.287	1.0	1B(81): 0.7, CF(13): -0.3	3.6
2017	LAN	MLB	21	250	32	10	1	13	38	24	71	2	0	.236/.314/.465	.267	7.6	.279	-0.2	1B 2, CF 0	1.1
2018	LAN	MLB	22	450	65	19	1	24	69	48	124	3	1	.241/.325/.477	.291	20.7	.284	-0.5	1B 4, CF 0	2.8

Breakout: 5%   Improve: 23%   Collapse: 7%   Attrition: 12%   MLB: 41%   *Comparables: Matt Olson, Jon Singleton, Travis Snider*

Bellinger entered the year coming off a 30-homer season at High-A, but saddled with questions regarding his strikeout rate and the validity of his Cal League power outburst. Asked and answered. Bellinger cut his strikeout rate by seven percentage points while moving up a level, yet much of the power came with him to Tulsa. He will still sell out to get to said power, but his hands and the leverage in his swing suggests the power can continue to translate up the chain. Bellinger isn't your standard first baseman no matter how you slice it. Every once in a Lance Berkman can a guy who mans the cold corner also patrol center field, but Bellinger can play there in a pinch and would be playable in either corner outfield spot as well. He's so good at first, though, that the Dodgers might be tempted to not test him further up the defensive spectrum. He enjoyed a taste of Triple-A by season's end and should spend the full season there in 2017. Whatever you do please don't call him "baellinger," even to your friends.

Willie Calhoun   2B

Born: 11/4/94   Age: 22   Bats: L   Throws: R   Height: 5'8"   Weight: 187   Entered Pro Ball: Round 4, 2015 Draft (#132 overall)

YEAR	TEAM	LVL	AGE	PA	R	2B	3B	HR	RBI	BB	K	SB	CS	AVG/OBP/SLG	TAv	VORP	BABIP	BRR	FRAA	WARP
2015	GRL	A	20	66	9	3	0	1	8	5	7	0	0	.393/.439/.492	.346	7.3	.434	0.0	2B(12): -1.6	0.6
2015	RCU	A+	20	82	11	7	0	3	14	7	13	0	0	.329/.390/.548	.321	8.1	.362	0.9	2B(20): -1.3	0.7
2016	TUL	AA	21	560	75	25	1	27	88	45	65	0	0	.254/.318/.469	.282	26.1	.242	0.3	2B(119): -9.3	1.8
2017	LAN	MLB	22	250	30	12	0	12	37	18	45	0	0	.252/.310/.460	.262	10.0	.264	-0.5	2B -4	0.7
2018	LAN	MLB	23	345	47	16	1	17	51	25	64	0	0	.255/.312/.469	.281	17.2	.268	-0.8	2B -5	1.3

Breakout: 5%   Improve: 34%   Collapse: 8%   Attrition: 25%   MLB: 61%   *Comparables: Lonnie Chisenhall, Jonathan Schoop, Dilson Herrera*

The Dodgers got aggressive with their pint-sized power hitter, jumping him to Double-A despite just 20 games at High-A in 2015. He responded by bashing his way through the Texas League roping 53 extra base hits, of which more than half were home runs. Calhoun didn't match the stellar averages he recorded in the lower minors, but he showed a solid approach at the plate and was more than acceptable for a 21-year-old getting his first taste of the upper minors. He continued his offensive tour de force in the Arizona Fall League, earning MVP honors in the Fall Stars game by showing his affinity for barreling that ball to the tune of three hits in three at bats with a homer. The lingering questions with Calhoun rest on the defensive side of the ball. There was talk of his having to shift to left field, but he spent the entire season at the keystone in Tulsa. He's not graceful there, committing 21 errors last year, but did improve his fielding percentage substantially from 2015. Incidentally, at 5-foot-9 and with a below-average arm, the outfield might not be a noticeably better fit either. The Dodgers hope he'll continue to improve with instruction and focus, and there's optimism that he'll be passable enough defensively to allow his bat to carry him.

Yusniel Diaz   CF

Born: 10/7/96   Age: 20   Bats: R   Throws: R   Height: 6'1"   Weight: 195   Entered Pro Ball: International Free Agent, 2015

YEAR	TEAM	LVL	AGE	PA	R	2B	3B	HR	RBI	BB	K	SB	CS	AVG/OBP/SLG	TAv	VORP	BABIP	BRR	FRAA	WARP
2016	RCU	A+	19	348	47	8	7	8	54	29	71	7	8	.272/.333/.418	.269	8.7	.326	-2.1	CF(34): -5.6, RF(15): -0.7	0.4
2017	LAN	MLB	20	250	25	9	2	7	28	16	67	3	2	.226/.279/.372	.228	-0.1	.285	-0.3	CF -2, RF -0	-0.2
2018	LAN	MLB	21	337	39	12	3	10	39	24	85	4	3	.235/.293/.391	.252	5.5	.291	-0.2	CF -2, RF 0	0.3

Breakout: 3%   Improve: 13%   Collapse: 0%   Attrition: 5%   MLB: 15%   *Comparables: Anthony Gose, Cedric Hunter, Caleb Gindl*

While he may not have the flashiest tools in the system, Diaz shows a diverse skillset with relative safety—a combination that netted him a $15.5 million bonus after defecting from Cuba. Yet polish and upside are not always strangers in a Venn diagram. Aggressively assigned to High-A, Diaz was solid, flashing five average or better tools throughout the season. He displayed his raw talent early before struggling through some adjustments and a shoulder injury. He returned to form later in the season, refining his approach and smoking line drives to all fields, and hitting .287/.330/.491 across his final 26 games. Diaz saw the majority of his action up the middle, but if he must move to a corner, he'll need to maintain a semblance of the power he showed down the stretch. Don't ignore the cultural and language barriers Diaz had to overcome when putting his success in context this season. As he gets more comfortable, the on-field elements of his game should blossom.

Andre Ethier   OF

Born: 4/10/82   Age: 35   Bats: L   Throws: L   Height: 6'2"   Weight: 210   Entered Pro Ball: Round 2, 2003 Draft (#62 overall)

YEAR	TEAM	LVL	AGE	PA	R	2B	3B	HR	RBI	BB	K	SB	CS	AVG/OBP/SLG	TAv	VORP	BABIP	BRR	FRAA	WARP
2014	LAN	MLB	32	380	29	17	6	4	42	31	74	2	2	.249/.322/.370	.263	6.2	.307	-4.3	CF(68): -3.0, LF(16): -2.1	0.1
2015	LAN	MLB	33	445	54	20	7	14	53	43	75	2	3	.294/.366/.486	.314	29.0	.330	-2.7	RF(80): -2.3, LF(51): -0.1	2.8
2016	RCU	A+	34	35	7	4	0	0	3	1	6	0	0	.290/.343/.419	.291	2.0	.346	0.3	RF(3): 0.0, LF(2): -0.2	0.2
2016	LAN	MLB	34	26	2	1	0	1	2	2	6	0	0	.208/.269/.375	.235	-0.2	.235	-0.1	LF(4): -0.7	-0.1
2017	LAN	MLB	35	365	39	17	2	9	42	33	72	2	2	.259/.333/.413	.270	12.1	.304	-0.7	RF -1, LF -2	1.0
2018	LAN	MLB	36	212	26	10	1	6	25	20	44	1	1	.255/.332/.411	.277	7.2	.301	-1.2	RF 0, LF -1	0.6

Breakout: 1%   Improve: 27%   Collapse: 6%   Attrition: 23%   MLB: 90%   *Comparables: Aubrey Huff, Mike Sweeney, Lyle Overbay*

Ethier fractured his tibia in March and missed the majority of the season. Like a penguin returning home to find his mate had chosen another, he found himself frozen out of playing time by better options when he did make his way back to Chavez Ravine in September. Despite what can charitably be described as "mild production," Ethier was included on the postseason roster and made a last-ditch plea for his inclusion in any long-term plans, going 2-for-6 in postseason pinch-hitting appearances, including a home run. Long discussed in trade rumors, it's likely Ethier will see his name on the block once more, as the Dodgers carry significant depth in the outfield. After all, penguins are only monogamous during mating season... if that.

Adrian Gonzalez   1B

Born: 5/8/82   Age: 35   Bats: L   Throws: L   Height: 6'2"   Weight: 215   Entered Pro Ball: Round 1, 2000 Draft (#1 overall)

YEAR	TEAM	LVL	AGE	PA	R	2B	3B	HR	RBI	BB	K	SB	CS	AVG/OBP/SLG	TAv	VORP	BABIP	BRR	FRAA	WARP
2014	LAN	MLB	32	660	83	41	0	27	116	56	112	1	1	.276/.335/.482	.301	26.0	.294	-5.3	1B(157): 10.9	4.1
2015	LAN	MLB	33	643	76	33	0	28	90	62	107	0	1	.275/.350/.480	.302	30.8	.294	-2.1	1B(149): 11.0	4.5
2016	LAN	MLB	34	633	69	31	0	18	90	55	117	0	2	.285/.349/.435	.293	28.1	.328	0.3	1B(151): -1.5	2.7
2017	LAN	MLB	35	613	67	31	0	21	79	48	110	1	1	.270/.329/.440	.272	15.8	.299	-1.8	1B 7	2.1
2018	LAN	MLB	36	529	68	26	0	19	68	44	100	0	0	.262/.326/.438	.278	14.8	.292	-1.6	1B 6	2.2

Breakout: 0%   Improve: 27%   Collapse: 5%   Attrition: 24%   MLB: 92%   Comparables: Aubrey Huff, Don Baylor, Ted Kluszewski

The Dodgers "butter-and-egg man" (boy do we already miss Vin...) pinched his pennies at the dish this year, failing to pay his first-half electric bill and suffering a power outage as a result. The generator finally wheezed back online in the second half, but Newton's Third Law was in full effect at the three in L.A. Those 50 additional points of slugging were met with the equal but opposite reaction of Gonzalez's on-base percentage, leaving him with nearly identical OPS tallies. The hope is that Gonzalez can reacquire his ability to blend the two approaches rather than trade one for the other. If he can't, he might consider legally changing his name to Adroam Gpmza;ez so it'll at least be harder for people to complain about him.

Yasmani Grandal   C

Born: 11/8/88   Age: 28   Bats: B   Throws: R   Height: 6'1"   Weight: 235   Entered Pro Ball: Round 1, 2010 Draft (#12 overall)

YEAR	TEAM	LVL	AGE	PA	R	2B	3B	HR	RBI	BB	K	SB	CS	AVG/OBP/SLG	TAv	VORP	BABIP	BRR	FRAA	WARP
2014	SDN	MLB	25	443	47	19	1	15	49	58	115	3	0	.225/.327/.401	.286	21.2	.277	-3.1	C(76): 11.5, 1B(37): -1.2	3.5
2015	LAN	MLB	26	426	43	12	0	16	47	65	92	0	1	.234/.353/.403	.276	20.4	.268	-4.0	C(107): 25.3, 1B(6): -0.1	4.9
2016	LAN	MLB	27	457	49	14	1	27	72	64	116	1	3	.228/.339/.477	.299	33.1	.250	-5.1	C(115): 32.0, 1B(4): 0.4	6.8
2017	LAN	MLB	28	524	65	20	1	21	70	73	121	2	1	.239/.347/.431	.279	31.0	.278	-1.3	C 36	6.4
2018	LAN	MLB	29	424	60	15	0	18	56	61	104	1	1	.230/.344/.423	.284	22.6	.271	-3.3	C 28	5.5

Breakout: 2%   Improve: 38%   Collapse: 1%   Attrition: 6%   MLB: 97%   Comparables: Chris Iannetta, Carlos Santana, Ryan Doumit

From April 12 through June 30, Grandal "hit" .179/.292/.347. From July 1 through the end of the season, he **hit** .267/.376/.581. Grandal was a contender for down-ballot MVP votes thanks to elite defense driven by framing so good that it should be on display at LACMA. Despite being a switch-hitter, the Dodgers shielded him from left-handed pitchers, amassing fewer than 100 plate appearances against southpaws. Grandal's slow start could be attributed to his offseason A/C joint surgery, and at only 28 years old, it wouldn't be a surprise to see him shoulder a heavier workload next season. If he can step up his performance as a right-handed batter in 2017—for his career, he doesn't have a remarkable platoon split—it will be difficult for the Dodgers to keep him out of the lineup.

YEAR	TEAM	P. COUNT	FRM RUNS	BLK RUNS	THRW RUNS	TOT RUNS
2014	SDN	9898	14.5	-1.1	-2.7	10.8
2015	LAN	13767	25.6	-0.8	0.0	24.8
2016	LAN	15887	26.7	0.4	0.4	27.5
2017	LAN	18703	34.2	-0.4	0.0	33.8
2018	LAN	15138	26.7	-0.4	-0.1	26.2

Enrique Hernandez   OF

Born: 8/24/91   Age: 25   Bats: R   Throws: R   Height: 5'11"   Weight: 200   Entered Pro Ball: Round 6, 2009 Draft (#191 overall)

YEAR	TEAM	LVL	AGE	PA	R	2B	3B	HR	RBI	BB	K	SB	CS	AVG/OBP/SLG	TAv	VORP	BABIP	BRR	FRAA	WARP
2014	CCH	AA	22	43	9	3	0	1	5	3	5	3	0	.325/.372/.475	.298	2.9	.333	0.1	2B(10): 0.7	0.4
2014	OKL	AAA	22	289	41	17	2	8	31	18	25	6	5	.337/.380/.508	.295	22.0	.346	1.7	2B(26): -0.4, 3B(14): 0.7	2.4
2014	HOU	MLB	22	89	10	4	2	1	8	8	11	0	0	.284/.348/.420	.283	4.5	.319	0.3	CF(11): 0.3, LF(8): 1.0	0.6
2014	NWO	AAA	22	84	8	5	0	2	6	10	13	0	1	.250/.345/.403	.286	4.9	.276	-0.5	2B(11): 0.1, SS(8): -0.3	0.5
2014	MIA	MLB	22	45	3	2	1	2	6	4	10	0	0	.175/.267/.425	.267	1.5	.179	0.0	CF(7): 0.9, RF(3): 1.2	0.4
2015	OKL	AAA	23	64	6	2	0	1	9	4	14	1	0	.169/.219/.254	.187	-2.2	.200	0.6	SS(8): -0.4, CF(4): -0.2	-0.3
2015	LAN	MLB	23	218	24	12	2	7	22	11	46	0	2	.307/.346/.490	.315	18.2	.364	0.1	2B(20): 1.1, CF(19): -1.4	2.0
2016	LAN	MLB	24	244	25	8	0	7	18	28	64	0	5	.190/.283/.324	.240	0.5	.234	-0.9	LF(41): 0.1, CF(22): -0.5	0.1
2017	LAN	MLB	25	520	57	24	2	15	58	39	103	4	2	.250/.309/.405	.257	17.7	.288	-0.9	2B 1, SS 0	1.6
2018	LAN	MLB	26	444	54	22	2	14	53	35	87	3	2	.250/.312/.415	.266	16.6	.285	0.0	2B 1, SS 0	1.9

Breakout: 3%   Improve: 57%   Collapse: 7%   Attrition: 14%   MLB: 94%   Comparables: Matt Murton, Michael Brantley, Lastings Milledge

A spark plug for the team in 2015, Hernandez short-circuited in 2016. The Dodgers had big plans for the lefty-mashing, multi-position-playing Puerto Rican as the weak-side platoon at the keystone, and possibly in center field. The plan started off well, as Hernandez belted two home runs off Madison Bumgarner in a mid-April game and finished the night hitting .440 batting average on the young season. Over the next 22 games, he hit .047/.180/.047. Thereafter, he spent the rest of the season hovering around the Mendoza Line. A ham both on-screen and off, the closest thing to a star turn that Hernandez pulled was a guest spot on The Bold and the Beautiful in September. Hernandez will hope for another crack at the role—and improved results—in 2017. Otherwise, his lines will get cut.

Gavin Lux SS

Born: 11/23/97 Age: 19 Bats: L Throws: R Height: 6'2" Weight: 190 Entered Pro Ball: Round 1, 2016 Draft (#20 overall)

YEAR	TEAM	LVL	AGE	PA	R	2B	3B	HR	RBI	BB	K	SB	CS	AVG/OBP/SLG	TAv	VORP	BABIP	BRR	FRAA	WARP
2017	LAN	MLB	19	250	24	9	1	5	21	16	82	0	0	.195/.248/.302	.195	-5.6	.274	-0.3	SS -3	-0.9
2018	LAN	MLB	20	338	35	12	2	8	33	24	105	0	0	.209/.268/.335	.222	-1.8	.285	-0.4	SS -4	-0.6

Breakout: 0%   Improve: 4%   Collapse: 1%   Attrition: 5%   MLB: 9%   Comparables: Raul Mondesi, Elvis Andrus, Carlos Triunfel

Tagged as a potential first-rounder, the Wisconsin prep product was never bound to be a Royal—Kansas City lost their first rounder as penance for signing Ian Kennedy. Still, 19 other teams craved a different kind of buzz, and decided that this kind of Lux just wasn't for them. Their loss was the Dodgers gain; he stood out as a true shortstop in a class that lacked them, impressing evaluators with his professional attitude and ability to draw the most out of his solid tools. He packs a smooth, left-handed stroke at the plate, and while he may never have significant pop, he's shown the ability to drive the ball thanks to added weight. He's a high-floor prospect who has a good shot at reaching the majors; something his uncle and 1982 second-overall pick Augie Schmidt never accomplished.

Johan Mieses OF

Born: 7/13/95 Age: 21 Bats: R Throws: R Height: 6'2" Weight: 185 Entered Pro Ball: International Free Agent, 2013

YEAR	TEAM	LVL	AGE	PA	R	2B	3B	HR	RBI	BB	K	SB	CS	AVG/OBP/SLG	TAv	VORP	BABIP	BRR	FRAA	WARP
2015	GRL	A	19	181	16	10	1	5	20	11	31	7	4	.277/.320/.440	.292	9.3	.308	-0.8	CF(24): 0.1, RF(18): 1.0	1.1
2015	RCU	A+	19	214	35	18	1	6	19	13	57	3	1	.245/.299/.439	.258	5.3	.316	0.6	CF(25): 3.2, LF(15): -0.5	1.1
2016	RCU	A+	20	514	72	31	3	28	78	36	147	3	7	.247/.314/.510	.295	33.8	.297	1.1	CF(78): 0.4, LF(21): 3.1	3.7
2017	LAN	MLB	21	250	27	12	1	11	33	13	80	1	1	.216/.264/.409	.231	0.9	.273	-0.5	CF 2, LF 1	0.5
2018	LAN	MLB	22	387	48	19	1	18	53	22	119	2	2	.223/.275/.429	.254	6.7	.278	-0.8	CF 4, LF 2	1.4

Breakout: 7%   Improve: 11%   Collapse: 3%   Attrition: 12%   MLB: 22%   Comparables: Greg Halman, Trayce Thompson, Christian Yelich

After spending the second half of the 2015 season in High-A, Mieses returned to Rancho Cucamonga looking like a different player. Looking is the operative word here, because while he *did* hit for more power, Mieses was—for all intents and purposes—the same style of player. He doesn't get cheated at the plate, and that type of approach will always come with its share of strikeouts. Still, his improved physique helped him generate more power and take advantage of his above-average straight-line speed. Double-A will be a big test as advanced arms will be more willing to exploit his free-swinging ways. The realistic outlook casts him as a platoon outfielder who can fill in at any outfield position, but a jump to everyday player status is within reach if he can refine his approach and curtail the swings-and-Mieses.

Joc Pederson CF

Born: 4/21/92 Age: 25 Bats: L Throws: L Height: 6'1" Weight: 220 Entered Pro Ball: Round 11, 2010 Draft (#352 overall)

YEAR	TEAM	LVL	AGE	PA	R	2B	3B	HR	RBI	BB	K	SB	CS	AVG/OBP/SLG	TAv	VORP	BABIP	BRR	FRAA	WARP
2014	ABQ	AAA	22	553	106	17	4	33	78	100	149	30	13	.303/.435/.582	.329	63.4	.385	3.7	CF(99): -2.6, LF(12): 1.9	6.4
2014	LAN	MLB	22	38	1	0	0	0	0	9	11	0	0	.143/.351/.143	.210	-1.2	.235	-0.4	CF(7): 0.8, RF(5): -0.2	-0.1
2015	LAN	MLB	23	585	67	19	1	26	54	92	170	4	1	.210/.346/.417	.287	32.9	.262	0.3	CF(147): -21.6	1.2
2016	LAN	MLB	24	476	64	26	0	25	68	63	130	6	2	.246/.352/.495	.310	35.5	.296	-3.6	CF(132): -1.3	3.5
2017	LAN	MLB	25	588	82	21	1	29	84	89	170	9	6	.233/.355/.456	.288	35.7	.290	-1.2	CF -8	2.4
2018	LAN	MLB	26	539	82	20	1	27	79	84	157	8	5	.233/.361/.464	.302	36.5	.290	-1.1	CF -7	3.2

Breakout: 3%   Improve: 62%   Collapse: 2%   Attrition: 2%   MLB: 100%   Comparables: Ike Davis, Grady Sizemore, Oswaldo Arcia

Yung Joc has been damn near everything throughout his brief career. 11th-round draft pick. Overslot signee. Sum-of-his-tools grinder. Flashy top prospect. 30/30 man at Triple-A. Rookie of the Year front-runner. Second-half flameout. All of that gets us to 2016 and his age-24 season. Pederson was more Jekyll than Hyde, registering the second-best TAv on the team thanks in part to a .260/.380/.520 slash line in the second half that proved he won't be a perennial fader. While several steps forward were taken, it's worth noting that Pederson continues to flail against southpaws, recording a paltry .469 OPS against them last season. His defense improved, to where an everyday role is within reach if he can be merely bad against lefties. He's addressed many of the questions scouts had on him as a prospect, but one aspect of his game has all but left as his baserunning notes now read: CF don't run.

Yasiel Puig RF

Born: 12/7/90 Age: 26 Bats: R Throws: R Height: 6'2" Weight: 240 Entered Pro Ball: International Free Agent, 2012

YEAR	TEAM	LVL	AGE	PA	R	2B	3B	HR	RBI	BB	K	SB	CS	AVG/OBP/SLG	TAv	VORP	BABIP	BRR	FRAA	WARP
2014	LAN	MLB	23	640	92	37	9	16	69	67	124	11	7	.296/.382/.480	.322	53.6	.356	3.5	RF(91): 0.4, CF(53): 1.8	6.2
2015	LAN	MLB	24	311	30	12	3	11	38	26	66	3	3	.255/.322/.436	.286	14.7	.296	1.4	RF(78): -0.2	1.6
2016	OKL	AAA	25	75	12	3	1	4	12	6	8	0	1	.348/.400/.594	.348	5.2	.351	-3.0	RF(17): -0.0	0.5
2016	LAN	MLB	25	368	45	14	2	11	45	24	74	5	2	.263/.323/.416	.274	13.6	.306	1.4	RF(90): 5.6, LF(5): -0.0	2.0
2017	LAN	MLB	26	502	66	23	4	19	65	44	103	8	5	.279/.353/.474	.293	31.3	.323	-0.6	RF 4, CF -0	3.1
2018	LAN	MLB	27	415	57	19	2	16	57	38	86	6	4	.276/.353/.473	.302	28.0	.320	1.5	RF 3, CF 0	3.4

Breakout: 5%   Improve: 55%   Collapse: 3%   Attrition: 6%   MLB: 99%   Comparables: Vladimir Guerrero, Hunter Pence, Andrew McCutchen

We saw Puig fail for the first time in 2015, and we saw him fail again in 2016. Or at least we think we did. Was Puig's ride on the struggle bus as intense as his narrative or his season totals would indicate? You be the judge: from Opening Day through June 2, Puig slashed .237/.283/.360, and subsequently landed on the disabled list with a strained left hamstring (sound familiar?). He returned on June 21, and from then until the trade deadline, he was Good Yasiel Puig, batting .308/.390/.440. Naturally, he was sent to the minors to make room for Josh Reddick's .396 August OPS (yes, OPS). Puig was then brought back in September, and hit .281/.338/.561 the rest of the way. It's hard to draw meaning from the smaller samples, but there's at least something to suggest that, when healthy, Puig is still a highly valuable commodity. Given the rumors flying since late July, it's possible we find out just *how* valuable the market sees him this winter.

Edwin Rios   3B

Born: 4/21/94   Age: 23   Bats: L   Throws: R   Height: 6'3"   Weight: 220   Entered Pro Ball: Round 6, 2015 Draft (#192 overall)

YEAR	TEAM	LVL	AGE	PA	R	2B	3B	HR	RBI	BB	K	SB	CS	AVG/OBP/SLG	TAv	VORP	BABIP	BRR	FRAA	WARP
2016	GRL	A	22	128	17	8	1	6	13	8	44	3	1	.252/.305/.487	.297	7.6	.348	0.0	3B(20): -0.1 • 1B(9): 0.6	0.9
2016	RCU	A+	22	188	37	11	1	16	46	8	35	0	0	.367/.394/.712	.387	30.3	.383	1.0	3B(20): 1.2 • 1B(18): 0.9	3.3
2016	TUL	AA	22	135	14	7	0	5	17	8	31	0	0	.254/.304/.434	.271	5.3	.292	0.1	3B(28): 0.8 • 1B(4): 0.2	0.7
2017	LAN	MLB	23	250	29	11	1	13	38	11	76	1	0	.240/.279/.457	.250	4.1	.294	-0.4	3B -0, 1B 1	0.6
2018	LAN	MLB	24	348	46	16	1	18	52	17	104	1	0	.244/.285/.465	.269	9.2	.299	-0.7	3B 0, 1B 2	1.2

Breakout: 3%   Improve: 20%   Collapse: 3%   Attrition: 14%   MLB: 43%   Comparables: *Brandon Wood, Alex Liddi, Juan Francisco*

The Dodgers' minor leaguer player of the year, Rios burst onto the scene by slamming 27 home runs across three different levels, ultimately ending the season in Double-A Tulsa. The 2015 sixth-rounder makes up for average bat speed with enough strength that there are rumors Brut is looking into a sponsorship deal. Don't be fooled by his Cal League-inflated batting average: Rios' game is predicated on power, as his long swing features enough holes that Shia Labeouf could star in it. A third baseman by trade, his likely home is at the cold corner thanks to plodding feet, which negatively affect his range. There will be always be bushels of strikeouts, but if he can somehow manage to make patience second nature—to go walking in his sleep—a move across the diamond would would hardly matter.

Darin Ruf   1B/OF

Born: 7/28/86   Age: 30   Bats: R   Throws: R   Height: 6'3"   Weight: 250   Entered Pro Ball: Round 20, 2009 Draft (#617 overall)

YEAR	TEAM	LVL	AGE	PA	R	2B	3B	HR	RBI	BB	K	SB	CS	AVG/OBP/SLG	TAv	VORP	BABIP	BRR	FRAA	WARP
2014	LEH	AAA	27	91	6	6	0	1	10	6	16	1	0	.265/.308/.373	.252	-0.3	.309	-1.1	LF(14): -1.0 • 1B(8): 0.3	-0.1
2014	PHI	MLB	27	117	13	8	0	3	8	8	32	0	0	.235/.310/.402	.270	3.5	.304	0.5	1B(20): 0.5 • LF(15): -0.7	0.4
2015	LEH	AAA	28	28	3	1	0	0	6	0	2	0	0	.308/.321/.346	.239	-0.9	.320	-0.6	1B(5): -0.3 • LF(2): -0.2	-0.1
2015	PHI	MLB	28	297	30	12	0	12	39	21	69	1	0	.235/.300/.414	.264	3.8	.268	-1.7	1B(66): -2.1 • LF(22): -1.5	0.0
2016	LEH	AAA	29	390	56	18	2	20	65	29	78	0	0	.294/.356/.529	.312	25.3	.324	-1.0	1B(47): -0.4 • LF(23): -0.3	2.5
2016	PHI	MLB	29	89	8	2	0	3	9	4	25	0	1	.205/.236/.337	.199	-3.6	.246	0.1	1B(14): -0.3 • LF(13): -1.3	-0.5
2017	LAN	MLB	30	138	17	6	0	6	18	11	36	0	0	.246/.315/.445	.268	5.4	.293	-0.3	LF -0, 1B -0	0.4
2018	LAN	MLB	31	202	27	9	0	9	28	17	55	0	0	.238/.310/.435	.272	6.5	.287	-0.3	LF -1, 1B 0	0.6

Breakout: 0%   Improve: 20%   Collapse: 9%   Attrition: 17%   MLB: 60%   Comparables: *Bryan LaHair, Micah Hoffpauir, Brandon Moss*

On June 10, 2016, Darin Ruf hit a triple while wearing a uniform with a cheesesteak on it. What thoughts were going through Ruf's head as he was chugging around the bases, digging in for his first three-bagger since 2012? Was he wistfully thinking that he could have been digging for third in a Phillies' uniform instead of a novelty uniform the IronPigs rolled out to ostensibly sell more meat-related concessions? Was he laughing inside, struck by the absurdity of what was happening, realizing that moments like this are extremely rare and wonderful? Or was he just getting hungry thinking about all of the delicious meat-related concessions available at Coca-Cola Park?

It is easy to get bogged down in value judgments of what players are and especially of what they should have been, but these are the kind of magical moments that non-athletes do not experience. Ruf is 30 years old. It is entirely possible that he never gets another big league at-bat again. But 35 times in his life, he experienced the joy of socking a home run out of a major league ball park. Oh yeah, and then there was that one time he hit a triple while wearing a uniform that featured a cheesesteak—a far more endearing symbol of Philadelphia than the Phillies could ever hope to be.

Corey Seager   SS

Born: 4/27/94   Age: 23   Bats: L   Throws: R   Height: 6'4"   Weight: 215   Entered Pro Ball: Round 1, 2012 Draft (#18 overall)

YEAR	TEAM	LVL	AGE	PA	R	2B	3B	HR	RBI	BB	K	SB	CS	AVG/OBP/SLG	TAv	VORP	BABIP	BRR	FRAA	WARP
2014	RCU	A+	20	365	61	34	2	18	70	30	76	5	1	.352/.411/.633	.355	52.0	.411	2.4	SS(64): 10.2, SS(7): 10.2	7.3
2014	CHT	AA	20	161	28	16	3	2	27	10	39	1	1	.345/.381/.534	.305	15.0	.450	1.4	SS(35): -1.0	1.5
2015	TUL	AA	21	86	17	7	1	5	15	5	11	1	1	.375/.407/.675	.393	15.2	.385	0.5	SS(15): 0.1 • 3B(4): -0.2	1.6
2015	OKL	AAA	21	464	64	30	2	13	61	32	65	3	0	.278/.332/.451	.285	32.4	.298	2.2	SS(90): 8.1 • 3B(15): 0.9	4.2
2015	LAN	MLB	21	113	17	8	1	4	17	14	19	2	0	.337/.425/.561	.356	15.3	.387	0.4	SS(21): 1.6 • 3B(6): 0.7	1.9
2016	LAN	MLB	22	687	105	40	5	26	72	54	133	3	3	.308/.365/.512	.320	73.1	.355	2.7	SS(155): -8.4	6.7
2017	LAN	MLB	23	633	84	37	3	25	80	44	130	2	1	.283/.335/.483	.288	46.8	.324	-1.2	SS 0	4.1
2018	LAN	MLB	24	604	83	34	2	25	87	48	123	2	1	.287/.347/.496	.306	50.3	.327	1.3	SS 0	5.5

Breakout: 3%   Improve: 58%   Collapse: 5%   Attrition: 9%   MLB: 94%   Comparables: *Evan Longoria, Pablo Sandoval, David Wright*

The Good: Seager lived up to enormous hype. He entered 2016 as the top-ranked prospect in baseball and showed he could avoid a shift down the defensive spectrum for at least for a few years. He also set a Dodgers record for home runs by a shortstop in his first full season and, along with Justin Turner, was the lifeblood of the Dodgers offense. He finished just a few shades of WARP behind his brother despite the age and experience gap between them, and was edged out of a top-10 WARP season by teammate Yasmani Grandal.

The Bad: Time is a slow and inexorable march towards death. Every day that we delight in the pleasures of Seager's athletic prowess is another day closer to having him no longer.

The Ugly: Not Seager. That's a handsome man. Damn.

Rob Segedin   4C

Born: 11/10/88 Age: 28 Bats: R Throws: R Height: 6'2" Weight: 220 Entered Pro Ball: Round 3, 2010 Draft (#112 overall)

YEAR	TEAM	LVL	AGE	PA	R	2B	3B	HR	RBI	BB	K	SB	CS	AVG/OBP/SLG	TAv	VORP	BABIP	BRR	FRAA	WARP
2014	SWB	AAA	25	85	7	2	0	1	11	4	14	0	0	.143/.188/.208	.129	-9.9	.154	0.0	3B(20): 3.1	-0.7
2014	TRN	AA	25	394	46	21	1	8	49	52	60	1	0	.283/.398/.428	.298	26.9	.322	0.8	3B(73): 7.4 • 1B(5): 0.2	3.7
2015	TRN	AA	26	103	8	4	0	3	19	11	17	1	1	.303/.379/.449	.298	4.1	.338	-1.3	1B(16): -0.5 • 3B(4): -0.0	0.4
2015	SWB	AAA	26	181	24	8	1	4	15	15	34	2	0	.278/.350/.414	.297	8.0	.331	-2.2	1B(24): -0.9 • 3B(16): 1.1	0.9
2016	OKL	AAA	27	424	71	23	9	21	69	40	81	3	4	.319/.392/.598	.351	50.5	.356	0.0	3B(58): 0.4 • 1B(36): -4.0	4.9
2016	LAN	MLB	27	83	9	2	1	2	12	6	22	0	0	.233/.301/.370	.246	0.9	.294	0.2	1B(9): -0.5 • RF(7): 0.3	0.1
2017	LAN	MLB	28	143	17	6	1	5	17	13	33	0	0	.247/.325/.426	.269	5.2	.292	-0.2	3B 1, 1B -0	0.5
2018	LAN	MLB	29	274	34	11	2	9	33	25	66	0	0	.233/.317/.405	.268	7.6	.281	-0.4	3B 2, 1B -1	0.9

Breakout: 3%   Improve: 14%   Collapse: 9%   Attrition: 15%   MLB: 33%   Comparables: Zach Lutz, Zelous Wheeler, Jack Hannahan

Hard to believe that an MLB debut including four RBI wouldn't top Segedin's list of best memories, but so went 2016 for the 27-year-old rookie. Following his debut on August 7, Segedin hit his first career home run in Cincinnati, and then made it back-to-back games when he clocked one off Madison Bumgarner the following day. As if that wasn't enough, he raced from the Giants game to the hospital, as his wife Robin gave birth to their son, Robinson. If his first game, first homer, and first child didn't do it for him, Segedin also became the answer to a trivia question on October 2, as he was the bookend out of Vin Scully's Hall-of-Fame career. Here's to (the) Segedin(s) for making us feel inadequate for all that we've accomplished in a two-month span.

Trayce Thompson   CF

Born: 3/15/91 Age: 26 Bats: R Throws: R Height: 6'3" Weight: 225 Entered Pro Ball: Round 2, 2009 Draft (#61 overall)

YEAR	TEAM	LVL	AGE	PA	R	2B	3B	HR	RBI	BB	K	SB	CS	AVG/OBP/SLG	TAv	VORP	BABIP	BRR	FRAA	WARP
2014	BIR	AA	23	595	86	34	6	16	59	65	151	20	5	.237/.324/.419	.269	25.2	.301	4.0	CF(81): 4.1 • LF(48): 0.7	3.2
2015	CHR	AAA	24	417	53	23	4	13	39	23	79	11	5	.260/.304/.441	.259	13.1	.295	1.5	CF(94): 2.2 • RF(5): 2.4	1.7
2015	CHA	MLB	24	135	17	8	3	5	16	13	26	1	0	.295/.363/.533	.308	10.6	.341	1.5	RF(18): 0.2 • LF(12): 0.8	1.1
2016	LAN	MLB	25	262	31	11	0	13	32	26	66	5	1	.225/.302/.436	.271	11.8	.255	2.5	CF(32): 0.2 • RF(28): -2.5	0.7
2017	LAN	MLB	26	285	36	13	2	10	32	22	76	5	2	.229/.290/.411	.250	8.0	.280	0.3	LF 1, CF 1	0.7
2018	LAN	MLB	27	397	48	19	2	15	50	31	105	7	2	.228/.294/.416	.258	11.3	.277	2.2	LF 1, CF 1	1.4

Breakout: 9%   Improve: 42%   Collapse: 13%   Attrition: 24%   MLB: 76%   Comparables: Trayvon Robinson, Wladimir Balentien, Brennan Boesch

Acquired in the three-team trade that sent Jose Peraza and others to the Reds, Thompson has delivered the most value of the trio of players received, at least at the big-league level. He recorded a prodigious slash line in May, thanks mostly to a .600-plus slugging percentage and some notable late-game heroics. This made him seem like an able-bodied fill-in for the weak-side platoon role that Scott Van Slyke left vacant, but obscured the fact that he struggled to slug .400 in any other month. Two stress fractures in his back sidelined him for the second half of the season, and his roster spot was usurped by a combination of Josh Reddick and Andrew Toles. He could still factor into the 2017 outfield rotation—a platoon with Toles might be ideal—but first he'll need to prove that he's back at full health, and that May wasn't merely a mirage.

Andrew Toles   OF

Born: 5/24/92 Age: 25 Bats: L Throws: R Height: 5'10" Weight: 185 Entered Pro Ball: Round 3, 2012 Draft (#119 overall)

YEAR	TEAM	LVL	AGE	PA	R	2B	3B	HR	RBI	BB	K	SB	CS	AVG/OBP/SLG	TAv	VORP	BABIP	BRR	FRAA	WARP
2014	PCH	A+	22	218	28	10	1	1	13	12	31	18	10	.261/.302/.337	.233	2.4	.300	1.7	CF(46): -1.4	0.1
2016	RCU	A+	24	100	22	8	2	0	9	6	13	9	3	.370/.414/.500	.331	-0.8	.430	2.6	LF(9): -0.8 • CF(7): 0.8	1.3
2016	TUL	AA	24	190	27	14	3	5	22	12	30	13	3	.314/.363/.514	.323	18.2	.355	1.6	CF(24): -0.1 • RF(19): 2.7	2.3
2016	OKL	AAA	24	59	6	5	0	2	7	2	8	1	5	.321/.339/.518	.301	3.2	.340	-0.8	CF(7): 1.0 • LF(5): -0.2	0.4
2016	LAN	MLB	24	115	19	9	1	3	16	8	25	1	1	.314/.365/.505	.303	9.5	.385	1.8	LF(18): 2.4 • CF(9): -0.2	1.2
2017	LAN	MLB	25	414	54	22	2	10	40	22	88	15	7	.259/.300/.409	.251	9.2	.306	0.4	LF 3	1.1
2018	LAN	MLB	26	495	58	27	3	14	59	30	108	18	9	.260/.308/.423	.265	15.3	.308	1.2	LF 4	2.1

Breakout: 12%   Improve: 47%   Collapse: 12%   Attrition: 41%   MLB: 78%   Comparables: Jeff Fiorentino, Shane Victorino, Kevin Pillar

Perhaps the best current example of the prospect mantra "development isn't linear," Toles took the long route to the majors, if such a thing exists for a 24-year-old. The Rays—then helmed by Andrew Friedman—selected Toles out of Chipola Junior College, where he attended after being dismissed from the University of Tennessee in 2011. He went on to swipe 62 bases during his first year in full-season ball, but missed two months in 2014 due to personal reasons—later reported as anxiety—and was released in early 2015. Toles spent most of that year out of organized baseball, at one point bagging groceries at a local Kroger. The Dodgers signed him to a minor league deal after the 2015 season, and he was assigned to High-A to open season one of his career's second act. It took him three months to breeze through Double- and Triple-A, and he was electrifying in his debut season both on offense and defense (he recorded six outfield assists in only 48 games). His whirlwind ride culminated in eight postseason starts and an .878 postseason OPS. The son of New Orleans Saints first-rounder Alvin, Toles spent some of his time away from baseball accompanying his father on one of his long-haul truck routes in an effort to gain some clarity. The Dodgers hope the message turns out to be as figurative as it was literal: keep on trucking.

Justin Turner 3B

Born: 11/23/84 Age: 32 Bats: R Throws: R Height: 5'11" Weight: 205 Entered Pro Ball: Round 7, 2006 Draft (#204 overall)

YEAR	TEAM	LVL	AGE	PA	R	2B	3B	HR	RBI	BB	K	SB	CS	AVG/OBP/SLG	TAv	VORP	BABIP	BRR	FRAA	WARP
2014	LAN	MLB	29	322	46	21	1	7	43	28	58	6	1	.340/.404/.493	.340	34.4	.404	1.0	3B(59): 3.1 • SS(15): -0.2	4.0
2015	LAN	MLB	30	439	55	26	1	16	60	36	71	5	2	.294/.370/.491	.321	39.9	.321	1.2	3B(100): -0.9 • 1B(10): -0.1	4.2
2016	LAN	MLB	31	622	79	34	3	27	90	48	107	4	1	.275/.339/.493	.309	49.1	.293	-1.7	3B(144): -4.5 • 1B(1): -0.0	4.6
2017	LAN	MLB	32	608	70	33	2	19	77	45	105	5	2	.278/.341/.448	.283	31.4	.310	-0.8	3B -0	2.9
2018	LAN	MLB	33	548	71	30	1	18	69	44	100	3	1	.275/.342/.448	.293	30.5	.310	-0.1	3B 0	3.3

Breakout: 3% Improve: 46% Collapse: 2% Attrition: 7% MLB: 96% Comparables: Edgar Martinez, Nomar Garciaparra, Bill Madlock

Having missed significant time in each of the last two seasons, it was expected that Turner would miss more in 2016, following offseason microfracture surgery. Instead, he produced his greatest season (by WARP) to date on the back of a career-high in games played. While there was a slight decline in his level of play, most of that came via a slow start, as he slashed .247/.330/.325 in April, but recorded an .861 OPS the rest of the way. Coming off a walk-year performance that kicked it into overdrive, it's difficult to imagine a balanced Dodgers lineup without Turner it. Now that the former Titan and seventh-round pick has gotten his big payday, we'll finally learn the answer to the age-old question: who got the hooch?

Chase Utley 2B

Born: 12/17/78 Age: 38 Bats: L Throws: R Height: 6'1" Weight: 195 Entered Pro Ball: Round 1, 2000 Draft (#15 overall)

YEAR	TEAM	LVL	AGE	PA	R	2B	3B	HR	RBI	BB	K	SB	CS	AVG/OBP/SLG	TAv	VORP	BABIP	BRR	FRAA	WARP
2014	PHI	MLB	35	664	74	36	6	11	78	53	85	10	1	.270/.339/.407	.287	35.9	.295	2.8	2B(147): 4.7 • 1B(1): -0.0	4.5
2015	PHI	MLB	36	282	23	12	1	5	30	22	35	3	0	.217/.284/.333	.240	0.5	.227	-1.1	2B(62): -2.0 • 1B(4): -0.1	-0.2
2015	LAN	MLB	36	141	14	9	1	3	9	10	29	1	0	.202/.291/.363	.241	0.6	.237	-0.4	2B(26): 1.8 • 3B(3): -0.1	0.2
2016	LAN	MLB	37	565	79	26	3	14	52	40	115	2	2	.252/.319/.396	.273	21.6	.299	-1.1	2B(134): 1.3 • 3B(1): -0.0	2.4
2017	LAN	MLB	38	504	53	23	3	13	57	40	85	4	1	.244/.315/.390	.246	12.8	.271	0.1	2B 3, 3B 0	1.7
2018	LAN	MLB	39	378	42	16	2	9	40	28	66	2	1	.234/.301/.370	.248	6.7	.262	0.0	2B 2, 3B 0	1.0

Breakout: 1% Improve: 25% Collapse: 14% Attrition: 19% MLB: 66% Comparables: Lou Whitaker, Marco Scutaro, Jamey Carroll

Utley supplanted Howie Kendrick as the team's regular at the keystone, and produced a 95 OPS+ in over 500 at-bats. That might not sound like much, but it was one of the top-25 offensive seasons of all-time for a second baseman age 37 or older. That list is filled with the likes of Nap Lajoie, Eddie Collins, Lou Whitaker, Jeff Kent and more... but he also slots in behind Marco Scutaro (14th) and Jamey Carroll (19th), so it's something of a mixed bag. The Dodgers loved Utley's intensity on the field and leadership off of it, and he showed some attitudinal flexibility when he agreed to dye his peppered hair brown after Corey Seager smashed two home runs in Philadelphia. It wouldn't be a surprise to see The Man return to the Dodgers (who originally drafted him a score ago), but if he does, it's likely as a mentor to The Boy Wonder rather than as an everyday player.

Alex Verdugo OF

Born: 5/15/96 Age: 21 Bats: L Throws: L Height: 6'0" Weight: 205 Entered Pro Ball: Round 2, 2014 Draft (#62 overall)

YEAR	TEAM	LVL	AGE	PA	R	2B	3B	HR	RBI	BB	K	SB	CS	AVG/OBP/SLG	TAv	VORP	BABIP	BRR	FRAA	WARP
2015	GRL	A	19	444	50	23	2	5	42	17	53	13	5	.295/.325/.394	.258	10.9	.326	-0.7	CF(89): 16.7 • RF(11): 1.4	3.1
2015	RCU	A+	19	96	20	9	2	4	19	4	12	1	0	.385/.406/.659	.372	14.1	.408	0.4	CF(23): 2.2	1.8
2016	TUL	AA	20	529	58	23	1	13	63	44	67	2	6	.273/.336/.407	.275	20.8	.292	-1.2	CF(91): -4.1 • RF(30): -0.1	1.8
2017	LAN	MLB	21	250	25	12	1	7	30	14	47	1	1	.253/.296/.405	.241	3.3	.286	-0.5	CF -0, RF -1	0.3
2018	LAN	MLB	22	393	48	19	2	13	49	25	73	1	1	.260/.309/.429	.267	12.0	.290	-0.8	CF 0, RF -1	1.2

Breakout: 4% Improve: 25% Collapse: 2% Attrition: 19% MLB: 32% Comparables: Manuel Margot, Joc Pederson, Melky Cabrera

Tackling Double-A at age 20 is no small feat, and Verdugo was up to the task. Don't let the numbers fool you—this kid can hit. He has a potential plus-plus hit tool, though it comes with only average expected power. He's played center field for the most part as a pro, but his future belongs in right. Verdugo has added some weight, which will slow him a bit in the field, and his powerful arm (he was a two-way player before turning pro) should be plenty for a corner. He could be a high-end regular if the bat plays to its potential, but falling short of it could leave him as more of a tweener.

PITCHERS

Yadier Alvarez RHP

Born: 3/7/96 Age: 21 Bats: R Throws: R Height: 6'3" Weight: 175 Entered Pro Ball: International Free Agent, 2015

YEAR	TEAM	LVL	AGE	W	L	SV	G	GS	IP	H	HR	BB/9	K/9	K	GB%	BABIP	WHIP	ERA	FIP	DRA	VORP	WARP	cFIP	MPH
2016	GRL	A	20	3	2	0	9	9	39¹	31	1	2.5	12.6	55	50%	.326	1.07	2.29	1.85	1.38	15.9	1.7	72	
2017	LAN	MLB	21	3	3	0	9	9	40¹	40	5	4.3	7.6	34	48%	.314	1.46	4.72	4.62	5.46	0.5	0.0	128	
2018	LAN	MLB	22	7	9	0	27	27	158¹	136	19	4.9	9.5	167	48%	.309	1.40	4.32	4.69	5.00	7.3	0.8	117	

Breakout: 6% Improve: 6% Collapse: 0% Attrition: 2% MLB: 7% Comparables: Carl Edwards Jr, Wilking Rodriguez, Luis Severino

One of the farm system's crown jewels, Alvarez signed for $16 million, and the Dodgers paid nearly double that due to overage penalties. When you watch him throw, you suddenly understand their willingness to do so, as he peppers the zone with upper-90s fastballs that meander into the triple digits on occasion. He pairs this low-effort, high-velo offering with a slider that flashes plus and has gained consistency as he's found stability in his mechanics. His change lags significantly, but that's not uncommon at this stage of development. Given the potency of his top two offerings, it would be easy to think he's destined for the bullpen. However, his potential as a starter merits a lengthy rope for the development of a third pitch, something that will likely be a focus going forward. His ceiling is a top-of-the-rotation starter, making him a quality prospect the likes of which Dodgers fans haven't seen since...Julio Urias.

Luis Avilan   LHP

Born: 7/19/89   Age: 27   Bats: L   Throws: L   Height: 6'2"   Weight: 225   Entered Pro Ball: International Free Agent, 2005

YEAR	TEAM	LVL	AGE	W	L	SV	G	GS	IP	H	HR	BB/9	K/9	K	GB%	BABIP	WHIP	ERA	FIP	DRA	VORP	WARP	cFIP	MPH
2014	GWN	AAA	24	0	1	0	9	0	11²	13	0	8.5	4.6	6	50%	.342	2.06	5.40	5.16	10.18	-6.3	-0.6	130	
2014	ATL	MLB	24	4	1	0	62	0	43¹	47	2	4.4	5.2	25	58%	.317	1.57	4.57	4.21	5.07	-2.8	-0.3	114	95.7
2015	ATL	MLB	25	2	4	0	50	0	37²	35	4	2.4	7.4	31	49%	.284	1.19	3.58	3.69	4.37	1.4	0.2	94	95.8
2015	LAN	MLB	25	0	1	0	15²	13	2	2.9	10.3	18	55%	.275	1.15	5.17	3.67	4.35	0.6	0.1	94	95.5
2016	OKL	AAA	26	0	3	4	33	0	34	35	3	4.2	9.8	37	49%	.337	1.50	4.24	4.37	4.94	0.1	0.0	98	
2016	LAN	MLB	26	3	0	0	27	0	19²	12	0	4.6	12.8	28	55%	.286	1.12	3.20	2.17	2.84	4.7	0.5	80	94.4
2017	LAN	MLB	27	2	1	0	33	0	34	32	4	3.4	8.2	31	51%	.290	1.31	4.20	4.10	4.68	0.9	0.1	100	
2018	LAN	MLB	28	2	1	0	46	0	48²	40	7	3.6	9.0	49	51%	.284	1.21	4.13	4.46	4.83	1.6	0.2	109	

Breakout: 33%   Improve: 64%   Collapse: 15%   Attrition: 8%   MLB: 89%   Comparables: Bryan Shaw, Darren O'Day, Renyel Pinto

Who knows what could have been if the Dodgers received this year's version of Avilan in 2015, when they were attempting to bolster their bullpen at the trade deadline. He was hit to high heaven post-trade last year, but rebounded nicely to produce a nice ERA and nicer-still DRA. His strikeout and walk rates both ticked up significantly, so it's fair to wonder whether this type of production could conceivably hold over the course of a full season, or whether some well-timed hits could blow it all up. It's also worth noting the small sample we're discussing, as Avilan compiled fewer than 20 innings in Los Angeles, and was never considered more than the second lefty in the bullpen.

Pedro Baez   RHP

Born: 3/11/88   Age: 29   Bats: R   Throws: R   Height: 6'0"   Weight: 235   Entered Pro Ball: International Free Agent, 2007

YEAR	TEAM	LVL	AGE	W	L	SV	G	GS	IP	H	HR	BB/9	K/9	K	GB%	BABIP	WHIP	ERA	FIP	DRA	VORP	WARP	cFIP	MPH
2014	CHT	AA	26	2	1	6	17	0	19¹	15	0	4.2	8.4	18	35%	.278	1.24	2.79	2.88	6.97	-4.5	-0.5	102	
2014	ABQ	AAA	26	0	0	6	23	0	22²	27	4	1.6	7.9	20	46%	.343	1.37	4.76	5.02	4.23	2.8	0.3	96	
2014	LAN	MLB	26	0	0	0	20	0	24	16	3	1.9	6.8	18	38%	.197	0.88	2.62	3.85	5.59	-2.9	-0.3	112	98.4
2015	LAN	MLB	27	4	2	0	52	0	51	47	4	1.9	10.6	60	41%	.326	1.14	3.35	2.53	3.75	5.4	0.6	89	99.8
2016	LAN	MLB	28	3	2	0	73	0	74	52	11	2.7	10.1	83	44%	.233	1.00	3.04	3.85	3.65	10.9	1.1	90	99.2
2017	LAN	MLB	29	3	2	3	51	0	54	51	7	3.1	9.3	56	43%	.294	1.27	3.83	3.95	4.39	3.2	0.3	100	
2018	LAN	MLB	30	3	1	2	58	0	62	49	8	3.4	10.6	73	43%	.300	1.17	3.58	3.86	4.19	6.4	0.7	94	

Breakout: 29%   Improve: 60%   Collapse: 15%   Attrition: 22%   MLB: 92%   Comparables: Shawn Kelley, Matt Lindstrom, Vinnie Pestano

You know those nature documentaries that track members of the big cat family? Where the British voiceover speaks in hushed tones and says something like "here now we see the *felidae panthera*, more commonly known as the *Jaguar*, lie patiently in wait of its prey. It will wait up to six hours, barely moving, as to keep its impending victim unaware." That's the approach announcers need to take with Baez, who registered the slowest pace in the majors, averaging over 30 seconds between pitches. It was an effective plan of attack, at least in 2016, as Baez would lull batters to sleep before unleashing an upper-90s fastball. The downside? He continues to give up too many long balls and he's borderline unwatchable—unlike those nature docs.

Joe Blanton   RHP

Born: 12/11/80   Age: 36   Bats: R   Throws: R   Height: 6'3"   Weight: 225   Entered Pro Ball: Round 1, 2002 Draft (#24 overall)

YEAR	TEAM	LVL	AGE	W	L	SV	G	GS	IP	H	HR	BB/9	K/9	K	GB%	BABIP	WHIP	ERA	FIP	DRA	VORP	WARP	cFIP	MPH
2014	SAC	AAA	33	1	0	0	2	2	10²	13	1	2.5	8.4	10	36%	.375	1.50	5.06	3.89	3.15	3.1	0.3	98	
2015	OMA	AAA	34	3	2	0	7	6	39¹	34	7	2.3	6.9	30	42%	.239	1.12	3.89	5.30	2.23	13.3	1.4	92	
2015	KCA	MLB	34	2	2	2	15	4	41²	43	6	1.5	8.6	40	50%	.311	1.20	3.89	3.56	3.17	7.6	0.8	82	93.2
2015	PIT	MLB	34	5	0	0	21	0	34¹	26	1	2.4	10.2	39	50%	.287	1.02	1.57	2.14	3.24	5.9	0.6	83	93.1
2016	LAN	MLB	35	7	2	0	75	0	80	55	7	2.9	9.0	80	34%	.240	1.01	2.47	3.37	4.36	5.4	0.6	103	93.4
2017	LAN	MLB	36	4	3	0	40	7	74	65	9	2.8	9.3	76	44%	.307	1.19	3.70	3.71	4.33	9.3	1.0	96	
2018	LAN	MLB	37	3	3	0	31	6	70²	63	9	2.7	9.4	74	44%	.308	1.19	3.73	4.02	4.36	7.6	0.8	97	

Breakout: 21%   Improve: 43%   Collapse: 14%   Attrition: 13%   MLB: 71%   Comparables: Bartolo Colon, Roy Oswalt, Brett Tomko

The question heading into the season was whether Blanton's prowess as a reliever was a short-lived success or something more sustainable. We got our answer in a big way. He solidified what had been a previously shaky Dodgers bullpen, throwing more innings than all but five relievers, most often setting up for the dominant Kenley Jansen. A Google Image Search of "Joe Blanton" will lead one to the varied, surprised faces of their searchee; almost as if he is the embodiment of our collective reaction to such a high-quality season. Perhaps we shouldn't have been surprised, though. A recent trend in baseball has been to take one's best pitch and simply throw it more often, and Blanton continued what he started in 2015 by hurling his slider nearly 40 percent of the time. This worked wonders for Blanton all the way up until the NLCS, when he badly hung a hook to Miguel Montero that produced exactly the kind of season-defining moment he'd built a second career to avoid. As another JB smoothly intones, 'Heaven's a heartbreak away."

Grant Dayton LHP

Born: 11/25/87 Age: 29 Bats: L Throws: L Height: 6'2" Weight: 195 Entered Pro Ball: Round 11, 2010 Draft (#347 overall)

YEAR	TEAM	LVL	AGE	W	L	SV	G	GS	IP	H	HR	BB/9	K/9	K	GB%	BABIP	WHIP	ERA	FIP	DRA	VORP	WARP	cFIP	MPH
2014	JAX	AA	26	0	1	3	11	0	16¹	17	0	2.2	9.9	18	41%	.347	1.29	1.10	1.72	3.82	1.9	0.2	88	
2014	NWO	AAA	26	2	2	1	39	0	55²	53	10	3.6	9.9	61	39%	.299	1.35	3.72	5.08	2.57	17.1	1.7	98	
2015	NWO	AAA	27	2	1	0	25	0	35	25	1	1.3	9	35	33%	.270	0.86	2.83	2.49	2.56	9.2	0.9	80	
2015	OKL	AAA	27	1	1	0	9	0	11²	16	1	2.3	10	13	33%	.429	1.63	9.26	3.51	2.40	3.3	0.3	81	
2015	TUL	AA	27	0	2	1	8	0	10²	9	0	5.9	14.3	17	56%	.391	1.50	2.53	2.08	2.88	2.2	0.2	80	
2016	TUL	AA	28	3	0	1	12	0	15²	8	0	1.7	16.1	28	46%	.308	0.70	2.30	0.37	0.84	6.8	0.7	54	
2016	OKL	AAA	28	2	2	4	26	0	36¹	22	2	2.0	15.6	63	34%	.303	0.83	2.48	1.71	0.64	17.4	1.8	48	
2016	LAN	MLB	28	0	1	0	25	0	26¹	14	4	2.1	13.3	39	29%	.196	0.76	2.05	3.00	2.79	6.4	0.7	82	94.6
2017	LAN	MLB	29	3	2	1	47	0	49	44	6	3.0	10.2	56	50%	.303	1.25	3.22	3.58	3.87	5.7	0.6	85	
2018	LAN	MLB	30	3	1	1	60	0	63²	48	7	3.8	12.2	86	50%	.315	1.17	3.26	3.52	3.81	9.2	1.0	82	

Breakout: 18%   Improve: 26%   Collapse: 24%   Attrition: 36%   MLB: 60%   Comparables: Zach Phillips, Jairo Asencio, Michael Broadway

The Dodgers made a trade on July 15, 2015 that was notable mostly because it signified their lack of hope for former first-round pick Chris Reed. The return? A 27-year-old left-handed reliever who had yet to register even a single major league inning. Reed still hasn't cracked an MLB roster, but Dayton made quite the impact with Los Angeles. He struck out a higher percentage of batters during his time in the majors than he ever did on the farm, helping fortify the bullpen in the wake of J.P. Howell's ineffectiveness and Adam Liberatore's injury. Dayton attacks hitters with pedestrian fastball velocity but impressive spin rates, and he's not afraid to challenge hitters up in the zone, which helps set up his curveball nicely. He wore down towards the end of the season and (notably) in the playoffs, but Dayton earned the trust of Dave Roberts and set himself up well for next season.

Jose De Leon RHP

Born: 8/7/92 Age: 24 Bats: R Throws: R Height: 6'2" Weight: 190 Entered Pro Ball: Round 24, 2013 Draft (#724 overall)

YEAR	TEAM	LVL	AGE	W	L	SV	G	GS	IP	H	HR	BB/9	K/9	K	GB%	BABIP	WHIP	ERA	FIP	DRA	VORP	WARP	cFIP	MPH
2014	GRL	A	21	2	0	0	4	4	22²	14	1	0.8	16.7	42	31%	.317	0.71	1.19	0.62	0.41	12.7	1.3	42	
2015	RCU	A+	22	4	1	0	7	7	37²	26	1	1.9	13.9	58	45%	.325	0.90	1.67	2.00	0.76	18.1	2.0	55	
2015	TUL	AA	22	2	6	0	16	16	76²	61	11	3.4	12.3	105	36%	.294	1.17	3.64	3.64	1.32	32.1	3.5	62	
2016	OKL	AAA	23	7	1	0	16	16	86¹	61	9	2.1	11.6	111	36%	.259	0.94	2.61	3.23	1.67	35.2	3.6	72	
2016	LAN	MLB	23	2	0	0	4	4	17	19	5	3.7	7.9	15	46%	.280	1.53	6.35	7.01	5.25	0.2	0.0	111	94.5
2017	LAN	MLB	24	3	2	0	11	6	36²	32	4	3.0	9.6	39	48%	.293	1.20	3.31	3.53	3.92	5.0	0.5	86	
2018	LAN	MLB	25	10	9	0	30	30	188²	124	17	3.9	12.2	256	48%	.290	1.09	2.96	3.20	3.52	35.4	3.7	72	

Breakout: 27%   Improve: 48%   Collapse: 14%   Attrition: 21%   MLB: 74%   Comparables: Eric Surkamp, Tyler Thornburg, Alex Cobb

De Leon burst onto the scene with a virtuoso performance to close out 2014, before laying waste to the high-octane environs of the California League and stymying Double-A hitters down the stretch. 2016 brought more of a lurch, as he toiled away in Oklahoma City and saw Julio Urias leapfrog him on the depth chart. He finally debuted in September, whiffing nine Padres in the process—but we already knew he could pitch against Triple-A lineups. He'll continue to be homer-prone if he leaves his heater up, as it lacks the elite velocity needed to skirt that kind of trouble. His changeup, however, is a swing-and-miss offering, and he could become a mid-rotation starter if he can find more consistency with his slider. He figures to be a significant part of the Dodgers rotation going forward...or the chip that brings it in via trade.

Josh Fields RHP

Born: 8/19/85 Age: 31 Bats: R Throws: R Height: 6'0" Weight: 195 Entered Pro Ball: Round 1, 2008 Draft (#20 overall)

YEAR	TEAM	LVL	AGE	W	L	SV	G	GS	IP	H	HR	BB/9	K/9	K	GB%	BABIP	WHIP	ERA	FIP	DRA	VORP	WARP	cFIP	MPH
2014	HOU	MLB	28	4	6	4	54	0	54²	50	2	2.8	11.5	70	33%	.343	1.23	4.45	2.12	3.34	7.0	0.8	86	96.9
2015	HOU	MLB	29	4	1	0	54	0	50²	39	2	3.4	11.9	67	37%	.308	1.14	3.55	2.16	3.21	8.5	0.9	83	97.1
2016	HOU	MLB	30	0	0	0	15	0	15²	23	2	1.7	11.5	20	31%	.457	1.66	6.89	2.79	4.42	1.0	0.1	98	97.0
2016	FRE	AAA	30	1	0	1	23	0	27¹	19	0	2.3	10.5	32	46%	.279	0.95	1.65	2.15	2.03	8.9	0.9	82	
2016	LAN	MLB	30	1	0	0	22	0	19¹	20	2	3.7	10.2	22	41%	.333	1.45	2.79	3.65	4.27	1.5	0.2	97	97.4
2017	LAN	MLB	31	3	2	0	47	0	49	45	6	3.2	9.8	54	45%	.299	1.27	3.43	3.78	4.05	4.8	0.5	89	
2018	LAN	MLB	32	3	1	0	59	0	62²	52	7	3.1	10.0	70	45%	.302	1.17	3.47	3.73	4.05	7.5	0.8	87	

Breakout: 26%   Improve: 36%   Collapse: 22%   Attrition: 15%   MLB: 74%   Comparables: Vinnie Pestano, Scott Dohmann, Bobby Seay

Consider the child star that never quite made it. Someone who was clearly supposed to be something big, was sold as something big and wasn't a flameout, but also wasn't as advertised. Perhaps it's Jonathan Silverman for you. Or Breckin Meyer. Or maybe even Mena Suvari. Expected to be a quick mover as a first-round reliever with big heat and a wipeout slider, Fields stalled. Consider it the failed pilot of his career. He wasn't heard from for a bit, but he was honing his craft, and he got a background part for his MLB debut in 2013. He's since established himself as reliable filler, chewing a scene or some innings if need be, and everyone knows his name (even if it's mostly because of who he never became). Fittingly acquired by Hollywood's team midseason, Fields flourished under the bright lights, posting the best ERA of his career and outperforming his FIP for the second time. The success came in a lower-leverage role, and his flyball tendencies mean he might never be suited for the bullpen's starring role. But good character actors never lack for work.

Rich Hill   LHP

Born: 3/11/80   Age: 37   Bats: L   Throws: L   Height: 6'5"   Weight: 220   Entered Pro Ball: Round 4, 2002 Draft (#112 overall)

YEAR	TEAM	LVL	AGE	W	L	SV	G	GS	IP	H	HR	BB/9	K/9	K	GB%	BABIP	WHIP	ERA	FIP	DRA	VORP	WARP	cFIP	MPH
2014	PAW	AAA	34	3	3	2	25	0	39	29	0	3.9	10.4	45	50%	.299	1.18	3.23	2.51	1.53	16.5	1.6	76	
2014	ANA	MLB	34	0	0	0	2	0	0	1	0			0	0%	1.000				4.54		0.0	88	94.7
2014	NYA	MLB	34	0	0	0	14	0	5¹	6	0	5.1	15.2	9	42%	.500	1.69	1.69	2.03	4.54	0.0	0.0	102	91.8
2015	SYR	AAA	35	2	2	0	25	0	21²	12	1	8.7	13.3	32	54%	.262	1.52	2.91	4.40	3.32	4.4	0.4	97	
2015	PAW	AAA	35	3	2	0	5	5	32¹	27	3	2.5	8.1	29	48%	.282	1.11	2.78	3.59	3.53	5.8	0.6	99	
2015	BOS	MLB	35	2	1	0	4	4	29	14	2	1.6	11.2	36	51%	.197	0.66	1.55	2.24	2.35	8.8	0.9	66	92.7
2016	OAK	MLB	36	9	3	0	14	14	76	55	2	3.3	10.7	90	51%	.290	1.09	2.25	2.50	2.57	23.6	2.4	75	93.0
2016	LAN	MLB	36	3	2	0	6	6	34¹	22	2	1.3	10.2	39	38%	.244	0.79	1.83	2.11	2.54	10.7	1.1	76	92.2
2017	*LAN*	*MLB*	*37*	*10*	*6*	*0*	*23*	*23*	*131*	*111*	*14*	*3.1*	*10.6*	*154*	*70%*	*.296*	*1.20*	*3.27*	*3.41*	*3.81*	*19.9*	*2.1*	*85*	
2018	*LAN*	*MLB*	*38*	*9*	*8*	*0*	*24*	*24*	*143¹*	*115*	*15*	*3.1*	*10.7*	*171*	*70%*	*.313*	*1.15*	*3.28*	*3.54*	*3.84*	*26.1*	*2.7*	*83*	

Breakout: 20%   Improve: 39%   Collapse: 19%   Attrition: 9%   MLB: 78%   *Comparables: Randy Choate, Scott Atchison, R.A. Dickey*

With Tal's extinction in Houston, Rich becomes one of only two remaining Hills in the majors—and by far the most effective one (sorry, Aaron). His late-2015 resurgence continued into 2016, allowing the A's to cash him in at the deadline when the Dodgers came calling. Hill's arrival in L.A. paired him with Kershaw, giving the Dodgers a 1-2 punch comprising the two best ERAs in baseball since the former returned from those other leagues. Known for his picturesque curveball as a prospect, Hill's feel for the pitch has waxed rather than waned. He throws multiple iterations of the pitch from different arm slots, and it accounted for a plurality of his pitches thrown this year. Blisters conspired to keep him off the mound for extended stretches, and are an ever-present threat to an aging and brittle pitcher—exemplified in Dave Roberts' decision to pull him from a perfect game for fear that they were developing in the thick Miami heat. Still, despite looking more like Upper-Middle-Class Knoll in the playoffs, he timed his entrance into a free agent market thinner than the Angels rotation perfectly, and walked away $48 million heavier for his troubles.

J.P. Howell   LHP

Born: 4/25/83   Age: 34   Bats: L   Throws: L   Height: 6'0"   Weight: 180   Entered Pro Ball: Round 1, 2004 Draft (#31 overall)

YEAR	TEAM	LVL	AGE	W	L	SV	G	GS	IP	H	HR	BB/9	K/9	K	GB%	BABIP	WHIP	ERA	FIP	DRA	VORP	WARP	cFIP	MPH
2014	LAN	MLB	31	3	3	0	68	0	49	31	2	4.6	8.8	48	59%	.236	1.14	2.39	3.27	3.38	6.0	0.7	97	88.7
2015	LAN	MLB	32	6	1	1	65	0	44	47	3	2.9	8.0	39	60%	.333	1.39	1.43	3.37	3.54	5.7	0.6	97	89.2
2016	LAN	MLB	33	1	1	0	64	0	50²	56	4	2.7	7.8	44	60%	.338	1.40	4.09	3.54	4.40	3.2	0.3	98	87.4
2017	*LAN*	*MLB*	*34*	*2*	*1*	*1*	*42*	*0*	*44²*	*40*	*6*	*3.1*	*8.1*	*40*	*63%*	*.296*	*1.23*	*4.17*	*4.23*	*4.88*	*1.0*	*0.1*	*112*	
2018	*LAN*	*MLB*	*35*	*1*	*1*	*1*	*28*	*0*	*22²*	*20*	*3*	*3.0*	*7.6*	*19*	*63%*	*.294*	*1.24*	*4.21*	*4.54*	*4.93*	*0.5*	*0.1*	*113*	

Breakout: 11%   Improve: 29%   Collapse: 36%   Attrition: 8%   MLB: 83%   *Comparables: Scot Shields, Dennys Reyes, J.C. Romero*

Last year's comment began with an ode to Howell's reliability, but while his peripherals remained largely intact, he dialed up his worst ERA since a 30-inning stint in 2011—and that was his first action back from shoulder surgery. It was poor timing for the impending free agent, who once again worked a yeoman's load despite losing around two ticks on his fastball. Perhaps the decline in velocity is to blame for the slight uptick in his home run rate, which could in turn be blamed for the elevated ERA. Or perhaps this is the penance one pays for parlaying Rumspringa into an MLB career. Either way, last year's comment may have missed the mark in foreshadowing Howell's consistency, but it was eerily prescient in predicting the downfall of the Pitt-Jolie clan.

Kenley Jansen   RHP

Born: 9/30/87   Age: 29   Bats: B   Throws: R   Height: 6'5"   Weight: 270   Entered Pro Ball: International Free Agent, 2004

YEAR	TEAM	LVL	AGE	W	L	SV	G	GS	IP	H	HR	BB/9	K/9	K	GB%	BABIP	WHIP	ERA	FIP	DRA	VORP	WARP	cFIP	MPH
2014	LAN	MLB	26	2	3	44	68	0	65¹	55	5	2.6	13.9	101	36%	.350	1.13	2.76	1.88	2.19	16.7	1.8	67	97.4
2015	LAN	MLB	27	2	1	36	54	0	52¹	33	6	1.4	13.8	80	36%	.260	0.78	2.41	2.17	2.26	14.3	1.5	63	95.6
2016	LAN	MLB	28	3	2	47	71	0	68²	35	4	1.4	13.6	104	33%	.238	0.67	1.83	1.48	1.95	23.1	2.4	58	96.6
2017	*LAN*	*MLB*	*29*	*4*	*2*	*40*	*61*	*0*	*64¹*	*48*	*9*	*2.2*	*12.8*	*92*	*40%*	*.290*	*1.00*	*2.45*	*2.96*	*3.12*	*12.8*	*1.3*	*62*	
2018	*LAN*	*MLB*	*30*	*4*	*2*	*49*	*80*	*0*	*85¹*	*59*	*11*	*1.8*	*12.3*	*117*	*40%*	*.287*	*0.89*	*2.67*	*2.88*	*3.12*	*18.8*	*1.9*	*63*	

Breakout: 19%   Improve: 49%   Collapse: 28%   Attrition: 7%   MLB: 98%   *Comparables: David Robertson, Francisco Rodriguez, Huston Street*

Performing in a walk year, Jansen walked all over the competition. He recorded career-bests in innings pitched, ERA, WHIP, DRA and TAv allowed. He regained a tick of lost velocity on his cutter and used it to cut swaths through the league writ large. He also showcased a newfound durability in the playoffs, going two-plus innings on more than one occasion. He'll be remembered most for his valiant efforts in Game 5 of the NLDS, entering with none out in the seventh and laboring for more than 50 pitches to cobble together seven crucial outs beore turning things over to the best pitcher on the planet. Still, it was his Game 6 performance in the NLCS that will appeal to teams in free agency. Jansen stared down a potent Cubs lineup and faced the minimum over three innings, ringing up four and barely breaking a sweat—in stark contrast to Clayton Kershaw's struggles preceding him. If he wasn't already the best reliever in baseball, becoming a multi-inning monster might just get him to the top.

Scott Kazmir   LHP

Born: 1/24/84   Age: 33   Bats: L   Throws: L   Height: 6'0"   Weight: 195   Entered Pro Ball: Round 1, 2002 Draft (#15 overall)

YEAR	TEAM	LVL	AGE	W	L	SV	G	GS	IP	H	HR	BB/9	K/9	K	GB%	BABIP	WHIP	ERA	FIP	DRA	VORP	WARP	cFIP	MPH
2014	OAK	MLB	30	15	9	0	32	32	190¹	171	16	2.4	7.8	164	44%	.285	1.16	3.55	3.38	3.40	30.4	3.4	93	94.3
2015	OAK	MLB	31	5	5	0	18	18	109²	84	7	2.9	8.3	101	48%	.262	1.09	2.38	3.13	3.76	16.0	1.7	99	94.7
2015	HOU	MLB	31	2	6	0	13	13	73¹	78	13	2.9	6.6	54	40%	.288	1.39	4.17	5.16	3.67	11.5	1.2	99	94.4
2016	LAN	MLB	32	10	6	0	26	26	136¹	133	21	3.4	8.8	134	42%	.298	1.36	4.56	4.52	4.84	7.8	0.8	109	94.4
2017	*LAN*	*MLB*	*33*	*9*	*6*	*0*	*21*	*21*	*126*	*117*	*17*	*3.0*	*9.1*	*127*	*50%*	*.293*	*1.26*	*3.90*	*4.03*	*4.50*	*9.5*	*1.0*	*100*	
2018	*LAN*	*MLB*	*34*	*10*	*10*	*0*	*28*	*28*	*166²*	*146*	*24*	*2.9*	*9.1*	*168*	*50%*	*.299*	*1.20*	*4.01*	*4.33*	*4.69*	*15.6*	*1.6*	*109*	

Breakout: 8%   Improve: 45%   Collapse: 23%   Attrition: 18%   MLB: 89%   *Comparables: Johan Santana, Josh Beckett, Kevin Millwood*

The 2012 science fiction book *The Long Earth*, penned by authors Terry Pratchett and Stephen Baxter, conceives of a world very much like our own, with one crucial difference. Much of our population has departed thanks to the discovery of nearby earths, not within our solar system or galaxy, but rather "a thought away." Travel there is achieved via a potato-powered device called a "Stepper," allowing those who use them to "step" into a similar earth, from which they can continue on stepping or return back to the more familiar earth. All of these "stepwise" earths have carried on over the years, unfettered by human existence, though earlier hominid species do appear. "What does this have to do with Kazmir?" you might be asking, and the answer is precious little, but that it's nice to conceive of a frame for a world in which he was productive during 2016.

Clayton Kershaw   LHP

Born: 3/19/88   Age: 29   Bats: L   Throws: L   Height: 6'4"   Weight: 225   Entered Pro Ball: Round 1, 2006 Draft (#7 overall)

YEAR	TEAM	LVL	AGE	W	L	SV	G	GS	IP	H	HR	BB/9	K/9	K	GB%	BABIP	WHIP	ERA	FIP	DRA	VORP	WARP	cFIP	MPH
2014	LAN	MLB	26	21	3	0	27	27	198¹	139	9	1.4	10.8	239	53%	.278	0.86	1.77	1.78	1.60	71.4	7.9	54	95.2
2015	LAN	MLB	27	16	7	0	33	33	232²	163	15	1.6	11.6	301	52%	.281	0.88	2.13	2.02	1.86	83.2	8.9	54	95.8
2016	LAN	MLB	28	12	4	0	21	21	149	97	8	0.7	10.4	172	51%	.254	0.72	1.69	1.84	2.03	55.1	5.7	57	95.1
2017	*LAN*	*MLB*	*29*	*15*	*7*	*0*	*28*	*28*	*196*	*144*	*21*	*1.6*	*11.5*	*250*	*45%*	*.279*	*0.89*	*2.47*	*2.63*	*2.92*	*49.2*	*5.1*	*59*	
2018	*LAN*	*MLB*	*30*	*16*	*10*	*0*	*34*	*34*	*227*	*153*	*22*	*1.5*	*11.5*	*290*	*45%*	*.281*	*0.84*	*2.40*	*2.57*	*2.78*	*71.6*	*7.4*	*53*	

Breakout: 14%   Improve: 44%   Collapse: 22%   Attrition: 6%   MLB: 98%   *Comparables: CC Sabathia, Brandon Webb, Erik Bedard*

It's easy to be at a loss for words when it comes to Kershaw because it is hard to describe an athlete, a man buried under mountains of accomplishment that are in turn entombed under a crush of expectations, which have been subsumed by praise. He's a Russian Nesting Doll of achievement, operating on the peripheries of what we consider humanly possible.

Kershaw debuted as a full-time starter in 2009 and has pitched at a Cy Young level from that point on, garnering three awards and amassing more black ink than a tattoo parlor in the process. He ascended a staircase built on the astonished giggles of Vin Scully describing "public enemy number one," shedding the lofty comparisons draped on him as a top prospect and emerging into his own light. He is one of the historic greats, operating in real time.

What once took on an ethereal quality looks far more recognizable these days. Not the results, goodness no, those are still pristine, but rather the process. His curveball, which once arced so effortlessly towards the heavens before snapping down and alighting in the catcher's glove, now rises furiously and descends with purpose, driven hard by the force of gravity to which it had previously seemed immune.

Where he once seemed to glide, Kershaw grinds, with remarkable effectiveness. Staggeringly, the more mortal he looks the more godly his performance becomes, with 2016 representing a career-best ERA, albeit in limited innings. To quote Robert O'Connell "[Kershaw] is, principally, a worker." In this way it is easier to relate to him, to recognize ourselves in him, but perhaps just a better, more competent version of ourselves. Which might be why it is so tempting for managers to lean on him longer than necessary come playoff time. It's not that Kershaw can't pitch in the playoffs (4.55 ERA), but rather because he appears so often to be limitless that he is extended well beyond what would be asked of others.

This is not to excuse his playoff performance so much as to ascertain a reason. Some would have you believe there's an allergy to the big stage, an aversion to the later innings. Reason would tell you he has his breaking points, distant though they may be, and he's pushed both to and past them in the biggest moments. A most human trait indeed. Perhaps then, we can celebrate Kershaw The Man for making the spectacular become routine, rather than knock Kershaw The Narrative for his humanity.

Adam Liberatore   LHP

Born: 5/12/87   Age: 30   Bats: L   Throws: L   Height: 6'3"   Weight: 240   Entered Pro Ball: Round 21, 2010 Draft (#641 overall)

YEAR	TEAM	LVL	AGE	W	L	SV	G	GS	IP	H	HR	BB/9	K/9	K	GB%	BABIP	WHIP	ERA	FIP	DRA	VORP	WARP	cFIP	MPH
2014	DUR	AAA	27	6	1	4	54	0	65	43	1	2.1	11.9	86	46%	.292	0.89	1.66	1.65	1.30	29.2	2.9	54	
2015	OKL	AAA	28	0	1	3	19	0	21²	18	2	4.2	7.5	18	44%	.267	1.29	3.74	4.66	4.34	1.4	0.1	106	
2015	LAN	MLB	28	2	2	0	39	0	29²	26	3	2.7	8.8	29	45%	.284	1.18	4.25	3.43	4.01	2.3	0.2	96	96.3
2016	LAN	MLB	29	2	2	0	58	0	42²	34	2	3.6	9.9	47	40%	.296	1.20	3.38	2.93	4.11	4.1	0.4	98	94.3
2017	*LAN*	*MLB*	*30*	*2*	*2*	*0*	*37*	*0*	*39*	*37*	*5*	*3.1*	*8.6*	*38*	*50%*	*.294*	*1.28*	*3.86*	*4.10*	*4.42*	*2.2*	*0.2*	*100*	
2018	*LAN*	*MLB*	*31*	*3*	*1*	*0*	*57*	*0*	*60¹*	*44*	*7*	*4.1*	*11.2*	*75*	*50%*	*.292*	*1.18*	*3.67*	*3.96*	*4.30*	*5.5*	*0.6*	*95*	

Breakout: 13%   Improve: 22%   Collapse: 12%   Attrition: 14%   MLB: 40%   *Comparables: Blake Parker, Rob Wooten, Tim Wood*

In 2014, Childish Gambino dropped a freestyle on HOT97 with Rosenberg that accomplished something heretofore thought impossible: positive YouTube comments. It was four minutes of straight fire, kicked off with the refrain "I've been grindin' my whole life." Liberatore knows a little something about grinding—as do most 28-year-old rookies. A 21st-round pick by the Rays from Tennessee Technological University in 2010, Liberatore wasn't handed anything on the diamond, including a check. But as Gambino croons, "they gave the wrong [pitchers] money." Liberatore didn't post an ERA over 3.74 in his minor league career, yet he didn't earn many chances due to his low-90s fastball, even as a lefty. Finally afforded an opportunity to get that paper in 2016, he reeled off a string as epic as the aforementioned freestyle, recording a 42-game, 33-inning stretch from April to July where he allowed two earned runs and struck out 38 against only 10 walks. Liberatore struggled down the stretch and was ultimately surpassed by Grant Dayton as the go-to lefty—likely due to an elbow that needed arthroscopic surgery after the season. As a result, he'll enter Spring Training just trying to make the team. That's nothing new for Liberatore, of course. He's been grindin' his whole life.

Kenta Maeda   RHP

Born: 4/11/88   Age: 29   Bats: R   Throws: R   Height: 6'1"   Weight: 175   Entered Pro Ball: International Free Agent, 2016

YEAR	TEAM	LVL	AGE	W	L	SV	G	GS	IP	H	HR	BB/9	K/9	K	GB%	BABIP	WHIP	ERA	FIP	DRA	VORP	WARP	cFIP	MPH
2016	LAN	MLB	28	16	11	0	32	32	175²	150	20	2.6	9.2	179	45%	.283	1.14	3.48	3.62	3.41	38.0	3.9	93	92.5
2017	LAN	MLB	29	12	8	0	29	29	165¹	143	19	2.7	9.5	175	41%	.289	1.16	3.39	3.58	3.94	22.8	2.3	88	
2018	LAN	MLB	30	10	9	0	30	30	186	153	20	2.4	9.2	191	41%	.294	1.09	3.37	3.64	3.96	29.8	3.1	87	

Breakout: 16%   Improve: 40%   Collapse: 17%   Attrition: 5%   MLB: 95%   *Comparables: Tim Lincecum, Gio Gonzalez, Zack Greinke*

The unimpeachable Wikipedia informs us that Kenta means "one who has health and is well-formed." That's perhaps some nominative determinism for the one Dodgers starter to make it through the season unscathed, though it is worth noting he frequently received extra days of rest. Maeda came to Los Angeles via an unusual, incentive-laden contract. His gamble on himself paid off, as he earned $8.75 million in bonuses on top of his $3-million base salary en route to a third-place finish in NL Rookie of the Year voting. Lacking impact stuff, Maeda is the type of pitcher who benefits from an early hook, as opponents tagged him for an .887 OPS the third time through the order. The Dodgers recognized this, which explains how he accrued fewer than 180 innings in 32 starts. If you're wondering what Wikipedia has to say about "Maeda," it means "front rice paddy." We don't have anything on that.

Dustin May   RHP

Born: 9/6/97   Age: 19   Bats: R   Throws: R   Height: 6'6"   Weight: 180   Entered Pro Ball: Round 3, 2016 Draft (#101 overall)

Dodgers fans will miss Vin Scully in the years to come, but perhaps even more so if-and-when May takes the mound for the first time. You can almost hear Scully's syrupy drawl describing May as a tall drink of water with ginger locks and a slinger's arm slot. In reality, May won't touch the majors for a few years but his consistency is benefitting from professional coaching, allowing his potent fastball-slider combination to flourish. Both his fastball and breaking ball have produced excellent spin rates, with the former topping the list at the World Wood Bat Association World Championships. And at 6-foot-6, May's lanky frame might not be done adding good weight. Once he does, he'll not only be long, but strong, which will help him get his spin rate on.

Brandon McCarthy   RHP

Born: 7/7/83   Age: 33   Bats: R   Throws: R   Height: 6'7"   Weight: 235   Entered Pro Ball: Round 17, 2002 Draft (#510 overall)

YEAR	TEAM	LVL	AGE	W	L	SV	G	GS	IP	H	HR	BB/9	K/9	K	GB%	BABIP	WHIP	ERA	FIP	DRA	VORP	WARP	cFIP	MPH
2014	ARI	MLB	30	3	10	0	18	18	109²	131	15	1.6	7.6	93	56%	.345	1.38	5.01	3.79	3.10	21.2	2.3	84	95.2
2014	NYA	MLB	30	7	5	0	14	14	90¹	91	10	1.3	8.2	82	51%	.307	1.15	2.89	3.25	2.87	19.7	2.2	82	95.1
2015	LAN	MLB	31	3	0	0	4	4	23	24	9	1.6	11.3	29	39%	.288	1.22	5.87	6.25	3.59	3.8	0.4	90	96.0
2016	RCU	A+	32	0	2	0	4	4	14	21	6	1.3	7.7	12	48%	.326	1.64	7.07	8.00	5.56	-0.1	0.0	96	
2016	LAN	MLB	32	2	3	0	10	9	40	29	2	5.8	9.9	44	35%	.278	1.38	4.95	3.74	6.93	-7.0	-0.7	118	94.7
2017	LAN	MLB	33	7	5	0	29	15	100¹	99	12	3.1	8.6	95	44%	.304	1.35	3.83	3.97	4.37	8.6	0.9	100	
2018	LAN	MLB	34	10	10	0	29	29	181	172	23	2.8	8.3	167	44%	.315	1.26	3.87	4.18	4.49	19.4	2.0	103	

Breakout: 9%   Improve: 42%   Collapse: 16%   Attrition: 14%   MLB: 84%   *Comparables: Freddy Garcia, Jake Peavy, John Lackey*

McCarthy suffered through yet another forgettable campaign in 2016, missing all of April, May and June with injuries. He returned to the field with an impressive run in July, but as Cormac McCarthy has written "many a pitch in many a mudded field is unspeakable and calamitous beyond reckoning." This was never more true in August when, in three consecutive starts, McCarthy walked exactly five batters and uncorked multiple wild pitches, lasting fewer than four innings each time out. He returned late in September, but couldn't lock down a roster spot for the playoffs after allowing six runs without recording an out in relief against the Giants. A healthy McCarthy is one of the Dodgers better starters, but it's getting harder to recall what a healthy McCarthy looks like. He'll vie for a rotation spot in Spring Training, hoping to leave 2016 behind as "a fevered dream, a trance bepopulate with chimeras having neither analogue nor precedent."

Bud Norris   RHP

Born: 3/2/85   Age: 32   Bats: R   Throws: R   Height: 6'0"   Weight: 215   Entered Pro Ball: Round 6, 2006 Draft (#189 overall)

YEAR	TEAM	LVL	AGE	W	L	SV	G	GS	IP	H	HR	BB/9	K/9	K	GB%	BABIP	WHIP	ERA	FIP	DRA	VORP	WARP	cFIP	MPH
2014	BAL	MLB	29	15	8	0	28	28	165¹	149	20	2.8	7.6	139	44%	.279	1.22	3.65	4.25	3.52	24.2	2.7	101	95.8
2015	BAL	MLB	30	2	9	0	18	11	66¹	84	14	3.4	6.8	50	44%	.329	1.64	7.06	5.61	4.89	0.5	0.0	105	96.3
2015	SDN	MLB	30	1	2	0	20	0	16²	16	1	3.2	11.3	21	61%	.349	1.32	5.40	2.68	4.72	0.4	0.0	104	97.8
2016	ATL	MLB	31	3	7	0	22	10	70¹	68	6	3.6	7.7	60	53%	.302	1.36	4.22	3.87	4.39	7.0	0.7	104	96.0
2016	LAN	MLB	31	3	3	0	13	9	42²	48	8	4.4	8.9	42	45%	.328	1.62	6.54	5.20	4.61	3.2	0.3	103	95.8
2017	LAN	MLB	32	6	6	0	18	18	99¹	94	15	3.3	8.7	96	55%	.313	1.31	4.39	4.37	5.13	4.8	0.5	120	
2018	LAN	MLB	33	6	7	0	19	19	111¹	106	18	3.1	8.9	110	55%	.313	1.30	4.40	4.76	5.14	4.8	0.5	121	

Breakout: 20%   Improve: 50%   Collapse: 24%   Attrition: 13%   MLB: 86%   *Comparables: Gavin Floyd, Nate Robertson, Jason Hammel*

Sometimes you just need something to get by. To get you through a day. Sure, there are top shelf options available, but it's hard to consistently stomach the cost. Enter Norris. He's not going to wow you. He's always there; reliably present; rarely more or less than advertised. He'll fill some innings, get the job done. Oh sure, sometimes he debuts a new wrinkle, an All-American rebrand, but the content remains the same; just slightly different packaging for the empty calories you're consuming. A new pitch for the same product. Of course, if the product changed it wouldn't be so reliable, would it? That's part of the charm. If you find it appealing... this Bud's for you.

Vidal Nuno   LHP

Born: 7/26/87   Age: 29   Bats: L   Throws: L   Height: 5'11"   Weight: 210   Entered Pro Ball: Round 48, 2009 Draft (#1445 overall)

YEAR	TEAM	LVL	AGE	W	L	SV	G	GS	IP	H	HR	BB/9	K/9	K	GB%	BABIP	WHIP	ERA	FIP	DRA	VORP	WARP	cFIP	MPH
2014	NYA	MLB	26	2	5	0	17	14	78	86	15	3.0	6.9	60	39%	.301	1.44	5.42	5.20	5.04	-1.8	-0.2	113	91.4
2014	ARI	MLB	26	0	7	0	14	14	83²	71	10	2.2	7.4	69	39%	.257	1.09	3.76	3.87	5.01	-1.7	-0.2	112	91.4
2015	RNO	AAA	27	3	3	0	8	8	50²	51	7	1.4	7.3	41	54%	.288	1.16	3.38	4.31	2.00	18.6	1.9	69	
2015	ARI	MLB	27	0	1	0	3	0	14¹	10	1	3.1	11.9	19	44%	.273	1.05	1.88	2.46	3.82	1.8	0.2	94	91.4
2015	SEA	MLB	27	1	4	0	32	10	74²	80	14	2.0	7.5	62	43%	.300	1.30	4.10	4.77	3.94	8.2	0.9	96	91.8
2016	SEA	MLB	28	1	1	0	55	1	58²	67	11	1.7	7.8	51	38%	.326	1.33	3.53	4.47	4.10	5.7	0.6	107	92.1
2017	LAN	MLB	29	1	1	0	23	0	24²	22	3	2.5	8.5	23	49%	.288	1.16	3.45	3.86	4.06	2.3	0.2	91	
2018	LAN	MLB	30	3	1	1	66	0	70	53	8	2.8	9.6	75	49%	.278	1.06	3.42	3.69	3.99	8.7	0.9	87	

Breakout: 26%   Improve: 50%   Collapse: 19%   Attrition: 18%   MLB: 89%   Comparables: Aaron Heilman, J.A. Happ, Rich Hill

Nuno spent 2016 like a *Westworld* host stuck on a tragic loop; almost a third of his appearances came when the Mariners were down three or more runs. His role was to be roughed up a bit when a lefty was required, only to be trotted back out a few turns later for lack of other options. He'll hope such violent delights have Hollywood ends after being shipped to the Dodgers for Carlos Ruiz.

Hyun-jin Ryu   LHP

Born: 3/25/87   Age: 30   Bats: R   Throws: L   Height: 6'3"   Weight: 250   Entered Pro Ball: International Free Agent, 2013

YEAR	TEAM	LVL	AGE	W	L	SV	G	GS	IP	H	HR	BB/9	K/9	K	GB%	BABIP	WHIP	ERA	FIP	DRA	VORP	WARP	cFIP	MPH
2014	LAN	MLB	27	14	7	0	26	26	152	152	8	1.7	8.2	139	50%	.319	1.19	3.38	2.59	3.65	20.1	2.2	85	94.3
2016	RCU	A+	29	1	1	0	5	5	18	15	2	0.5	7.0	14	45%	.241	0.89	2.00	3.77	3.15	4.7	0.5	90	
2016	LAN	MLB	29	0	1	0	1	1	4²	8	1	3.9	7.7	4	50%	.412	2.14	11.57	5.54	4.93	0.2	0.0	111	92.7
2017	LAN	MLB	30	2	2	0	6	6	30	29	4	2.2	8.4	28	42%	.296	1.22	3.74	3.84	4.26	3.1	0.3	100	
2018	LAN	MLB	31	7	7	0	22	22	132¹	123	20	2.0	8.3	123	42%	.304	1.16	3.92	4.24	4.54	12.8	1.3	107	

Breakout: 14%   Improve: 44%   Collapse: 21%   Attrition: 14%   MLB: 90%   Comparables: Roberto Hernandez, Doug Fister, Mark Buehrle

Following a lost season due to a shoulder injury, Ryu nearly doubled down (don't call him Trent), appearing in fewer than five innings in 2016—and clearly diminished ones at that. He succumbed to elbow tendinitis and later an elbow debridement, though he'll supposedly be ready for the start of the 2017 season. Sounds familiar, right? The Dodgers won't be able to rely on Ryu for 2017 even if he is healthy—missing damn near two seasons will do that to you—but that is hardly an obstacle for a team with this kind of pitching depth. He's clearly a fighter, but given his injury history one wonders how much more time Ryu can miss before the Dodgers tell him to hit the streets.

Yaisel Sierra   RHP

Born: 6/5/91   Age: 26   Bats: R   Throws: R   Height: 6'1"   Weight: 170   Entered Pro Ball: International Free Agent, 2016

YEAR	TEAM	LVL	AGE	W	L	SV	G	GS	IP	H	HR	BB/9	K/9	K	GB%	BABIP	WHIP	ERA	FIP	DRA	VORP	WARP	cFIP	MPH
2016	RCU	A+	25	5	5	0	20	13	74	87	9	3.0	7.9	65	48%	.344	1.51	6.20	4.84	5.01	3.2	0.3	105	
2016	TUL	AA	25	1	2	0	10	0	14²	14	0	3.1	12.9	21	60%	.368	1.30	4.30	1.34	2.14	4.2	0.5	77	
2017	LAN	MLB	26	4	3	1	29	9	65²	72	10	3.7	6.1	44	58%	.316	1.51	5.21	5.14	5.97	-4.6	-0.5	142	
2018	LAN	MLB	27	4	4	1	30	11	98²	95	15	5.1	8.8	96	58%	.319	1.53	4.98	5.41	5.71	-2.6	-0.3	135	

Breakout: 2%   Improve: 2%   Collapse: 2%   Attrition: 3%   MLB: 5%   Comparables: Matt Fox, Sammy Solis, Dirk Hayhurst

Things that Sierra has in common with Aroldis Chapman: 1) He is Cuban. 2) He signed for $30 million. 3) He flamed out as a starter. This could all start to sound like good news for Dodgers fans since, y'know, Chapman just won a World Series ring. The problem? The things they don't have in common are more important. To wit, Sierra lacks Chapman's fastball, slider, athleticism, left-handedness and velocity. What began with hype, and quickly turned to bust, could be salvaged thanks to Sierra's uptick in velo upon shifting to the pen. Still, that's not exactly what you're looking for when you drop that kind of cheddar on a signing bonus.

Brock Stewart   RHP

Born: 10/3/91   Age: 25   Bats: L   Throws: R   Height: 6'3"   Weight: 210   Entered Pro Ball: Round 6, 2014 Draft (#189 overall)

YEAR	TEAM	LVL	AGE	W	L	SV	G	GS	IP	H	HR	BB/9	K/9	K	GB%	BABIP	WHIP	ERA	FIP	DRA	VORP	WARP	cFIP	MPH
2015	GRL	A	23	2	2	0	7	7	38	38	4	1.4	9.0	38	36%	.324	1.16	2.84	3.32	2.05	13.4	1.4	77	
2015	RCU	A+	23	2	4	0	18	12	63	75	6	2.6	9.3	65	42%	.365	1.48	5.43	4.00	3.31	11.9	1.3	94	
2016	RCU	A+	24	2	0	0	2	2	11	5	0	1.6	8.2	10	44%	.185	0.64	0.82	2.44	3.28	2.7	0.3	93	
2016	OKL	AAA	24	4	0	0	9	9	50²	41	4	1.1	9.6	54	44%	.278	0.93	2.49	2.97	1.53	21.5	2.2	77	
2016	TUL	AA	24	3	4	0	10	10	59¹	41	0	1.7	9.9	65	46%	.275	0.88	1.37	1.65	1.44	24.1	2.6	72	
2016	LAN	MLB	24	2	2	0	7	5	28	33	7	3.9	8.0	25	44%	.317	1.61	5.79	5.94	4.69	1.9	0.2	111	95.9
2017	LAN	MLB	25	2	2	0	30	2	40¹	39	5	3.2	8.0	36	56%	.294	1.32	4.05	4.19	4.57	1.9	0.2	100	
2018	LAN	MLB	26	4	3	1	65	4	88	69	10	4.1	10.3	100	56%	.297	1.24	3.84	4.14	4.48	7.0	0.7	100	

Breakout: 2%   Improve: 2%   Collapse: 2%   Attrition: 3%   MLB: 5%   Comparables: Matt Fox, Sammy Solis, Cristhian Martinez

It could be hard to reconcile Stewart's minor league performance with his major league stats. Then again, it could be hard to remember who Stewart is. The first player from the Dodgers' 2014 draft class to reach the majors, he pitched at three minor league levels in 2016 and didn't record an ERA over 2.49 at any stop, including stints of more than 50 innings at Double- and Triple-A. So how does *that* guy end up with a 5.79 ERA in the majors? Perhaps it's as simple as "the minors aren't the majors" and "his stuff just doesn't fool MLB hitters". Then again, 14 of his 18 earned runs allowed came in three isolated innings over his first two starts, so it's clear his stuff works just fine much of the time. He lacks the pedigree and the arsenal to be more than a back-end starter, but should see plenty of time as a spot starter/mop-up man in his career.

Ross Stripling   RHP

Born: 11/23/89 Age: 27   Bats: R   Throws: R   Height: 6'3"   Weight: 210   Entered Pro Ball: Round 5, 2012 Draft (#176 overall)

YEAR	TEAM	LVL	AGE	W	L	SV	G	GS	IP	H	HR	BB/9	K/9	K	GB%	BABIP	WHIP	ERA	FIP	DRA	VORP	WARP	cFIP	MPH
2015	TUL	AA	25	3	6	0	13	13	67¹	61	7	2.5	7.4	55	55%	.281	1.19	3.88	3.86	2.97	15.9	1.7	88	
2016	OKL	AAA	26	0	2	0	5	4	16²	20	2	1.1	9.2	17	38%	.360	1.32	3.78	3.60	3.95	2.5	0.3	98	
2016	LAN	MLB	26	5	9	0	22	14	100	96	10	2.7	6.7	74	52%	.283	1.26	3.96	3.94	4.32	10.5	1.1	105	93.3
2017	LAN	MLB	27	4	3	0	42	5	64	64	7	3.0	7.1	51	45%	.294	1.33	4.04	4.07	4.58	3.1	0.3	100	
2018	LAN	MLB	28	4	3	0	51	5	78²	68	9	3.6	8.7	76	45%	.300	1.25	3.89	4.20	4.56	5.9	0.6	103	

Breakout: 25%   Improve: 52%   Collapse: 19%   Attrition: 27%   MLB: 82%   *Comparables: David Phelps, Josh Tomlin, Burke Badenhop*

There's nothing like a first impression. Stripling seeped into the collective consciousness of Dodgers fans when plans A, B and C for the fifth-starter spot tanked. He showed up on April 8 for his first major-league start and proceeded to throw 7 1/3 hitless innings. Nothing like putting your rookie manager in a bind *immediately*. Stripling was pulled after allowing a baserunner who came around to score, and the Dodgers ultimately lost the game. His pitches are plain yogurt: an entirely competent and utterly bland mixture that can fill a void when needed. He's a fine back-end/sixth-starter option who should be able to shoulder a bigger workload as his Tommy John surgery drifts further into the rearview.

Julio Urias   LHP

Born: 8/12/96 Age: 20   Bats: L   Throws: L   Height: 6'0"   Weight: 215   Entered Pro Ball: International Free Agent, 2012

YEAR	TEAM	LVL	AGE	W	L	SV	G	GS	IP	H	HR	BB/9	K/9	K	GB%	BABIP	WHIP	ERA	FIP	DRA	VORP	WARP	cFIP	MPH
2014	RCU	A+	17	2	2	0	25	20	87²	60	4	3.8	11.2	109	46%	.314	1.11	2.36	3.35	2.27	31.7	3.2	85	
2015	TUL	AA	18	3	4	0	13	13	68¹	53	4	2.0	9.7	74	47%	.282	1.00	2.77	2.60	1.82	24.9	2.7	65	
2016	OKL	AAA	19	5	1	0	11	7	45	31	2	1.6	9.8	49	54%	.269	0.87	1.40	2.72	1.63	18.3	1.9	70	
2016	LAN	MLB	19	5	2	0	18	15	77	81	5	3.6	9.8	84	45%	.358	1.45	3.39	3.21	3.97	11.6	1.2	97	95.4
2017	LAN	MLB	20	8	5	0	19	19	108¹	102	12	3.0	9.1	109	45%	.299	1.28	3.52	3.71	4.07	13.3	1.4	94	
2018	LAN	MLB	21	11	9	0	30	30	189²	149	20	3.7	11.3	238	45%	.314	1.20	3.30	3.56	3.86	31.9	3.3	86	

Breakout: 11%   Improve: 18%   Collapse: 7%   Attrition: 9%   MLB: 25%   *Comparables: Tyler Skaggs, Madison Bumgarner, Jose Fernandez*

Mound so empty, need a centerpiece
20-year-old pitcher and a young lefty

Cut minor leaguers down with backdoor freezes
Then he'd clear em with his heat, kid is still a baby
You talking curveballs, it's 70 grade
You talking stats, check his DRA
Switch up his style, he'll throw any pitch
Try and touch his change n' he'll make you whiff

Look what he's done
He's another lefty star boy
Look what he's done
He's another lefty star boy

Tell a hitta "go sit"
Legend of July 2012, he's well rested
Took a little time, with a stint in the Cal League
Now he's in the bigs and the team's lookin savvy
Still cannot throw a complete season
Might not matter if he's the one
200 innings pitched we can hope to god
We don't pray for WARs, we just pray for stars

Look what he's done
He's another lefty star boy
Look what he's done
He's another lefty star boy

Alex Wood   LHP

Born: 1/12/91   Age: 26   Bats: R   Throws: L   Height: 6'4"   Weight: 215   Entered Pro Ball: Round 2, 2012 Draft (#85 overall)

YEAR	TEAM	LVL	AGE	W	L	SV	G	GS	IP	H	HR	BB/9	K/9	K	GB%	BABIP	WHIP	ERA	FIP	DRA	VORP	WARP	cFIP	MPH
2014	ATL	MLB	23	11	11	0	35	24	171²	151	16	2.4	8.9	170	48%	.295	1.14	2.78	3.22	3.05	33.6	3.7	86	92.5
2015	ATL	MLB	24	7	6	0	20	20	119¹	132	8	2.7	6.8	90	49%	.332	1.41	3.54	3.48	3.98	14.5	1.6	101	91.9
2015	LAN	MLB	24	5	6	0	12	12	70¹	66	7	2.9	6.3	49	57%	.280	1.27	4.35	4.13	4.11	7.6	0.8	101	91.0
2016	LAN	MLB	25	1	4	0	14	10	60¹	56	5	3.0	9.8	66	55%	.319	1.26	3.73	3.22	3.36	13.2	1.4	90	92.7
2017	LAN	MLB	26	4	3	0	27	8	59	56	6	2.9	8.7	58	38%	.299	1.27	3.50	3.59	4.08	6.7	0.7	93	
2018	LAN	MLB	27	7	5	0	58	15	136	114	14	2.7	9.3	141	38%	.304	1.14	3.33	3.59	3.88	20.6	2.1	85	

Breakout: 23%   Improve: 61%   Collapse: 15%   Attrition: 8%   MLB: 94%   Comparables: Matt Garza, Nathan Eovaldi, Johnny Cueto

The Dodgers finally got the Wood they thought they acquired at the deadline in 2015, only they got way less of him than anticipated. Despite being on the team for a full season, Wood threw 10 fewer innings for the boys in blue than he did in just two months the season prior, with an elbow injury that resulted in an arthroscopic debridement keeping him on the shelf from late May through late September. He was largely the same pitcher as 2015, only he saw an extra three strikeouts per nine, perhaps aided by the slightly smaller sample size and a few relief appearances. With a plethora of injury-prone and ineffective starters in front of him, it's possible he opens 2017 in the bullpen, but we woodn't (sorry) be surprised if he makes more starts than relief appearances next year.

LINEOUTS

Hitters

NAME	POS	TEAM	LVL	AGE	PA	R	2B	3B	HR	RBI	BB	K	SB	CS	AVG/OBP/SLG	TAv	VORP	BABIP	BRR	FRAA	WARP
Stetson Allie	RF	ALT	AA	25	414	53	20	2	16	63	42	110	1	2	.247/.324/.444	.272	10.5	.303	-1.2	RF(93): -6.4	0.4
Austin Barnes	C	OKL	AAA	26	385	59	22	5	6	39	43	53	18	3	.295/.380/.443	.308	38.3	.335	3.3	C(63): 17.0, 2B(15): 1.2	5.7
	C	LAN	MLB	26	37	3	1	0	0	2	5	9	0	0	.156/.270/.188	.187	-1.0	.217	0.3	C(9): 0.2, 2B(7): -0.2	-0.1
Carl Crawford	LF	LAN	MLB	34	87	8	2	1	0	6	4	11	0	1	.185/.230/.235	.175	-5.9	.211	-0.1	LF(21): -0.7	-0.7
Charlie Culberson	MI	OKL	AAA	27	285	32	17	2	4	33	18	61	6	5	.260/.310/.385	.248	6.4	.325	-1.1	SS(57): 4.7, 3B(5): -0.3	1.2
	MI	LAN	MLB	27	68	6	3	0	1	7	1	13	1	0	.299/.309/.388	.260	3.8	.358	1.6	SS(11): -0.9, 2B(10): -0.7	0.2
Brendon Davis	SS	GRL	A	18	436	51	18	2	5	49	29	118	8	3	.241/.295/.334	.239	8.1	.326	1.1	SS(80): -2.5, 3B(19): 1.5	0.8
Omar Estevez	2B	GRL	A	18	508	46	32	2	9	61	26	121	3	6	.255/.298/.389	.255	8.8	.322	-2.8	2B(58): 3.9, SS(41): 6.2	2.1
Kyle Farmer	C	TUL	AA	25	297	31	18	2	5	31	25	44	2	0	.256/.323/.395	.261	10.9	.286	-1.0	C(56): -0.0, 3B(16): -1.4	1.0
Ibandel Isabel	1B	GRL	A	21	98	17	5	1	7	15	9	41	1	2	.273/.347/.591	.331	8.1	.425	0.4	1B(15): 0.3	0.9
Micah Johnson	2B	OKL	AAA	25	516	72	23	3	5	37	41	105	26	11	.261/.321/.356	.253	16.1	.327	6.1	2B(84): 5.3, LF(25): -0.3	2.3
	2B	LAN	MLB	25	6	1	0	0	0	0	0	1	0	0	.167/.167/.167	.112	-0.6	.200	0.2	2B(3): -0.1, LF(1): -0.0	-0.1
Jacob Scavuzzo	OF	TUL	AA	22	459	59	21	2	10	39	28	100	4	2	.266/.318/.397	.270	12.4	.324	-1.0	LF(87): 1.6, CF(7): -1.1	1.4
Will Smith	C	GRL	A	21	97	12	1	0	1	7	11	18	2	1	.256/.371/.305	.264	6.3	.317	2.0	C(18): -0.0, 2B(3): -0.2	0.6
	C	RCU	A+	21	115	13	4	0	2	12	14	31	1	0	.216/.330/.320	.248	1.8	.292	-1.3	C(16): 0.4, 3B(6): 1.0	0.3
Chris Taylor	SS	SEA	MLB	25	3	0	0	0	0	0	0	2	0	0	.333/.333/.333	.234	0.0	1.000	0.0	SS(1): -0.3	0.0
	SS	TAC	AAA	25	280	41	19	4	3	29	29	49	12	5	.312/.387/.457	.294	20.7	.378	0.0	SS(50): 2.2, 2B(7): -1.2	2.2
	SS	OKL	AAA	25	64	7	6	2	0	8	6	16	5	0	.368/.438/.544	.345	9.2	.512	1.0	SS(13): -1.2, 3B(2): -0.1	0.8
	SS	LAN	MLB	25	62	8	2	2	1	7	4	13	0	0	.207/.258/.362	.207	-0.7	.250	0.7	3B(10): -0.1, 2B(7): -0.5	-0.2
Scott Van Slyke	LF	OKL	AAA	29	31	5	1	0	1	5	2	5	1	0	.207/.258/.345	.234	0.4	.217	0.7	LF(2): -0.8, RF(2): 0.1	0.0
	LF	LAN	MLB	29	113	10	6	0	1	7	5	24	1	2	.225/.292/.314	.218	-3.0	.282	-0.5	LF(19): -0.3, RF(10): -0.5	-0.4
Will Venable	CF	LEH	AAA	33	149	12	7	0	2	19	17	28	2	2	.205/.304/.307	.232	0.4	.242	1.6	RF(14): 2.8, CF(13): 0.1	0.3
	CF	LAN	MLB	33	19	2	1	0	0	0	0	5	0	0	.056/.105/.111	.083	-2.9	.077	0.1	RF(4): -0.2, LF(1): 0.1	-0.3
	CF	OKL	AAA	33	172	23	6	1	4	25	15	32	3	2	.276/.343/.404	.265	7.6	.325	2.7	CF(17): -4.1, LF(11): -1.3	0.2
Shawn Zarraga	C	TUL	AA	27	99	9	7	0	0	14	12	13	0	1	.306/.384/.388	.293	3.9	.351	-3.2	C(23): 1.5, 1B(1): 0.0	0.6
	C	OKL	AAA	27	53	5	2	0	0	2	4	10	0	0	.167/.226/.208	.202	-1.4	.205	-0.3	C(11): 1.1, 1B(5): -0.2	-0.1

Stetson Allie's third stint in Altoona went better than his second, but worse than his first. Has anyone thought to try this guy's arm on the mound? ❖ Known for his positional flexibility—he can play catcher, second and third—**Austin Barnes** should spend more time getting acquainted with first base, a spot he rarely reached as a major-league hitter. ❖ Some believe that a hefty contract can earn a bad player extra chances, playing time, etc. If that were the case for those of us at Baseball Prospectus, **Carl Crawford** would receive a full comment. ❖ In the span of 18 days **Charlie Culberson** went from hitting a game-winning, division-clinching home run in Vin Scully's last home game to striking out on a failed bunt attempt in Game 5 of the NLCS. ❖ An overslot fifth-rounder in 2015, **Brendon Davis** is a projectable infielder who is in dire need of some muscle mass if he is going to start earning that "o" in his name. ❖ It's hard to believe that a 19-year-old with an advanced bat and a six million dollar bonus could be overlooked, but **Omar Estevez** is Pulling. It. Off. ❖ **Kyle Farmer** was on his way to a breakout season, hitting .296/.342/.465 before breaking his wrist right before Memorial Day, but struggled upon his return in late July. ❖ When he hits, **Mitch Hansen** is one of those vaunted five-tool prospects. It's no sure thing he will, though. ❖ With approach issues, a first-base profile, and a long swing, there is a lot stacked against **Ibandel Isabel**, but he's got enough power that it could conceivably be a carrying tool. ❖ The only thing more blinding than **Micah Johnson**'s speed is the pace at which he is becoming irrelevant. ❖ Signed for $140,000, switch-hitting backstop **Keibert Ruiz** will be given every shot to stay behind the plate, and he showcases a promising future at it. ❖ **Jacob Scavuzzo** continues to alternate good years with bad, and will need to show more power if he's going to hack it as a corner outfielder. ❖ Not to be confused with the actor, the pitcher, or the sentence fragment, **Will Smith** is an athletic backstop with a polished defensive skill set. He won't offer much pop, but he could profile as a starter if his average and on-base skills translate to wood. ❖ The acquisition of **Chris Taylor** has to be considered a wild success on the basis of how Not Zach Lee he is. ❖ **Cody Thomas** spurned baseball for the Texas A&M gridiron in 2013, but signed for a shade under $300,000 in the 13th round last year. His big-time athleticism fuels good range, a plus arm and ample power at the dish. ❖ The lefty-heavy Dodgers could've used a southpaw-smasher like **Scott Van Slyke** in the postseason. Unfortunately, the actual Van Slyke was too busy recovering from wrist surgery. ❖ The worst part about **Will Venable**'s putrid offensive performance was that it recalled Eugenio Velez's somehow worse 2011 season. ❖ It's not entirely clear what Andrew Friedman saw when he acquired Aruban native **Shawn Zarraga** in the winter of 2014, but you know what they say—zirriga when others zarraga.

Pitchers

NAME	TEAM	LVL	AGE	W	L	SV	G	GS	IP	H	HR	BB/9	K/9	K	GB%	BABIP	WHIP	ERA	FIP	DRA	VORP	WARP	cFIP	MPH
Imani Abdullah	GRL	A	19	4	4	0	16	16	72¹	70	10	1.5	7.3	59	39%	.282	1.13	3.61	4.14	2.82	17.7	1.9	87	
Brett Anderson	LAN	MLB	28	1	2	0	4	3	11¹	25	4	3.2	4.0	5	51%	.429	2.56	11.91	7.95	6.19	-1.1	-0.1	118	94.2
Louis Coleman	LAN	MLB	30	2	1	0	61	0	48	45	5	4.5	8.4	45	37%	.299	1.44	4.69	4.35	5.30	-1.8	-0.2	119	91.9
Chase DeJong	TUL	AA	22	14	5	0	25	25	141²	106	15	2.5	7.9	125	38%	.239	1.02	2.86	3.68	3.58	23.8	2.6	104	
Caleb Ferguson	GRL	A	19	1	4	0	10	10	50¹	49	3	0.5	7.3	41	60%	.309	1.03	2.68	2.92	2.83	12.2	1.3	85	
Carlos Frias	OKL	AAA	26	3	3	0	8	4	36¹	37	2	2.7	6.7	27	55%	.315	1.32	4.46	3.86	4.33	3.3	0.3	104	
	LAN	MLB	26	0	0	0	1	0	4	2	0	2.2	6.8	3	36%	.182	0.75	0.00	2.44	5.27	-0.1	0.0	116	94.8
Yimi Garcia	LAN	MLB	25	0	0	0	9	0	8¹	9	0	1.1	4.3	4	41%	.310	1.20	3.24	2.95	4.96	0.0	0.0	108	95.5
Chris Hatcher	LAN	MLB	31	5	4	0	37	0	40²	40	8	4.6	9.5	43	45%	.296	1.50	5.53	5.25	4.10	3.9	0.4	104	97.8
Josh Ravin	LAN	MLB	28	0	0	0	10	0	9²	2	1	3.7	12.1	13	33%	.059	0.62	0.93	3.08	3.81	1.2	0.1	92	98.9
Jacob Rhame	OKL	AAA	23	1	7	7	54	0	63	53	5	4.0	10.0	70	36%	.298	1.29	3.29	3.86	3.63	9.3	1.0	102	
Josh Sborz	RCU	A+	22	8	4	0	20	19	108¹	82	8	2.5	9.0	108	44%	.261	1.03	2.66	3.59	2.55	34.9	3.6	85	
	TUL	AA	22	0	1	1	10	0	16²	17	2	3.2	9.2	17	52%	.312	1.38	3.78	3.78	4.30	0.8	0.1	95	
Jordan Schafer	TUL	AA	29	1	1	0	31	1	40	41	4	3.8	10.4	46	47%	.330	1.45	3.15	3.46	3.10	7.4	0.8	93	
Jordan Sheffield	GRL	A	21	0	1	0	7	7	11	11	2	4.9	10.6	13	43%	.346	1.55	4.09	5.39	4.34	0.8	0.1	104	
Mitchell White	GRL	A	21	0	0	0	8	4	16	3	0	3.4	11.2	20	65%	.100	0.56	0.00	2.10	2.58	3.9	0.4	82	

An 11th-round draft pick in 2015, **Imani Abdullah** netted just under $650,000 to forego his college commitment. The projectable right-hander has size (6-foot-4) and showcases a low-90s fastball, an inconsistent curve and a nascent change. ❖ It's hard to decide whether the worst part of **Brett Anderson**'s season was his ERA, or the fact that his ERA exceeded his innings total. ❖ One can only imagine that **Walker Buehler**'s arduous return from Tommy John surgery was made worse by persistent refrains of "Buehler...Buehler..." The 2015 first-round pick finally answered the call, returning to the mound this summer and throwing five healthy innings. ❖ The Dodgers thought they found a diamond in the rough with **Louis Coleman**, but his name is still two characters from Trading Places and they can't take that away from him. ❖ A solid pitcher's frame and a general ability to throw strikes will make it somewhat difficult for patient hitters to **Chase De Jong** from the game. ❖ A 38th-round pick, **Caleb Ferguson** can run his heavy fastball with plus life up to 93 mph from the left side, with a breaking ball that could get to average. There have been lengthy careers built on less. ❖ The combination of added pitching depth and a back injury left **Carlos Frias** out in the cold. ❖ A healthy **Yimi Garcia** would have provided valuable bullpen depth for the Dodgers. This Garcia missed most of the year with a biceps injury and later required knee surgery. ❖ **Chris Hatcher** throws hard enough to deserve an MLB role, but a combination of poor control and a Grade-3 oblique strain cost him his season. ❖ It's hard to decide if **Josh Ravin**'s biggest impact this year was when the picture of his broken arm went viral, when he got into it on Twitter with Enrique Hernandez, or when he relieved Jesse Chavez at home against the Diamondbacks on September 5, allowing the box score to read Chavez, Ravin at Chavez Ravine. ❖ **Jacob Rhame** has the stuff of a closer and the command of a middle reliever, which makes him a future middle reliever. He pitched well but walked too many in Triple-A. ❖ A fastball/slider pitcher with good command, **Josh Sborz** showed he could handle the lower minors. The question is whether he can handle a long-term role in the rotation. ❖ **Jordan Schafer** tried to reinvent himself as a LOOGY, and he wasn't bad at Double-A. Of course, he also wasn't good enough to avoid being converted to a pinch-runner later in the year. ❖ **Jordan Sheffield** is a short right-hander with a high-effort delivery, a scar from Tommy John surgery and a hot fastball-breaker combination. You're expecting us to say his future is in the bullpen, right? Well, his future might be in the bullpen. ❖ **Mitchell White** is an athletic, well-built right-hander whose three-pitch mix (led by a cutter) makes him an intriguing starting pitching prospect.

MIAMI MARLINS

Essay by Emma Baccellieri

Player comments by Bryan Joiner and BP staff

The concept of "meaningful baseball" relies on a very one-dimensional view both of meaning and of baseball. But it's a convenient—if overly simplistic—way to describe September games with playoff implications, and so people use it and will keep using it. By this standard, last year was the first time in more than a decade that the Marlins were playing meaningful baseball in the last week of the season. But using "meaningful baseball" to describe the Marlins' final week of September is either a cruel way of underscoring how meaningless that baseball was, or a gross understatement of how meaningful it felt.

The team began the season with the basic building blocks in place to be at least somewhat competitive, but success was far from guaranteed. To earn a playoff berth would require that just about everything go right. And for the first half of the year, it did. Injuries were minimal. Several players, including outfielders Marcell Ozuna and Christian Yelich, got off to remarkably hot starts. There was none of the baseball operations meddling that has become custom from owner Jeffrey Loria, such as the 2015 decision to switch general manager Dan Jennings from the front office to the dugout by appointing him manager.

Instead, the Marlins were six games over .500 at the All-Star break, and as late as mid-August they were still holding onto a Wild Card spot. But injuries down the stretch exposed a lack of depth, and by September they had been pushed to the fringes of a crowded playoff race. To be in the running at all, though, was legitimate progress for a franchise that hadn't boasted a winning record in seven years.

This was the Marlins' backdrop for the death of their ace, José Fernández, killed in a boat crash at age 24 exactly one week before the final game of the regular season.

Baseball's framework offers no space to accommodate this sort of tragedy. This is most obviously true in that Fernández's death was without precedent in baseball's living memory—one of a generation's greatest pitchers, possibly greater still than that, suddenly gone. It is most painfully true in that there is no real space in *any* framework to accommodate this sort of tragedy. There is no consideration of reason or fairness in this sort of grief, only the void of grief itself. It destroys our ideas of what is constant and what is safe and, most plainly, what is here. To say that there are layers to this heartache expresses its

MARLINS PROSPECTUS
2016 W-L: 79-82, 3RD IN NL EAST

Pythag	.478	20th	DER	.697	22nd
RS/G	4.07	27th	B-Age	28.1	10th
RA/G	4.24	8th	P-Age	27.7	8th
TAv	.267	8th	Salary	$74.4M	28th
BRR	4.67	8th	M$/MW	$2M	29th
TAv-P	.271	22nd	DL Days	964	15th
FIP	4.01	11th	$ on DL	13%	17th

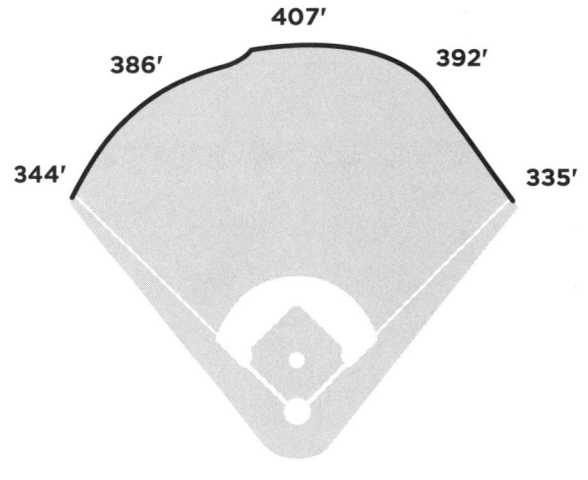

— Outfield wall profile: **7'** to **11.5'** —

Three-Year Park Factors

Runs	Runs/RH	Runs/LH	HR/RH	HR/LH
90	80	91	84	90

Top Hitter WARP	5.2	Christian Yelich
Top Pitcher WARP	6.5	Jose Fernandez
Top Prospect		Braxton Garrett

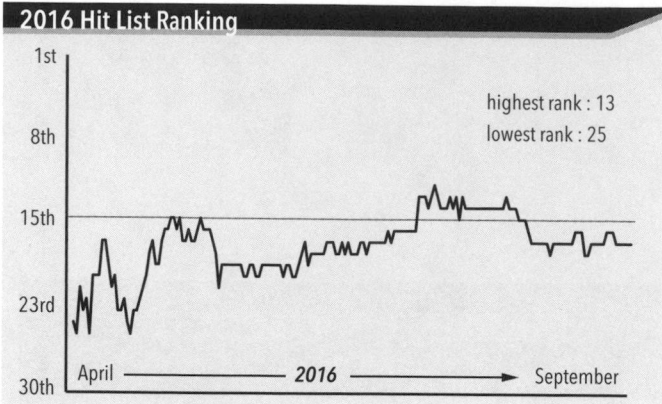

2016 Hit List Ranking

highest rank : 13
lowest rank : 25

April ——— *2016* ——→ September

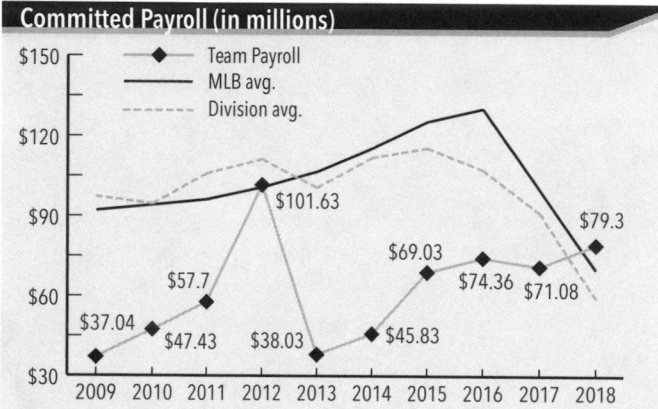

Committed Payroll (in millions)

◆ Team Payroll
— MLB avg.
--- Division avg.

$101.63
$57.7
$37.04
$47.43 $38.03
$45.83
$69.03 $74.36 $71.08
$79.3

2009 2010 2011 2012 2013 2014 2015 2016 2017 2018

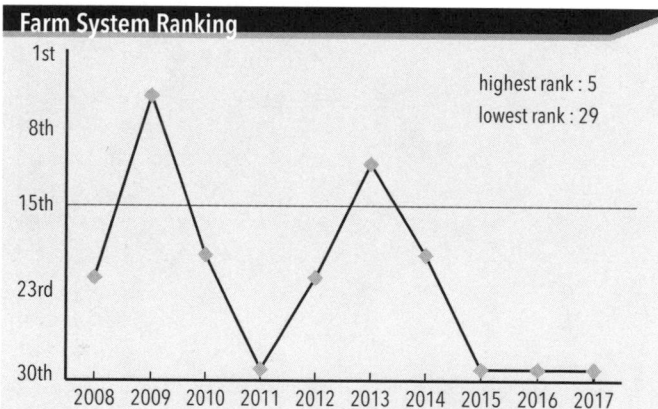

Farm System Ranking

highest rank : 5
lowest rank : 29

2008 2009 2010 2011 2012 2013 2014 2015 2016 2017

Personnel

President:
Michael Hill

Assistant General Manager:
Mike Berger

VP, Player Development:
Marc DelPiano

Manager:
Don Mattingly

BP Alumni:
Bryan Holcomb
Jason Paré

depth but not its chaos; these are impossible knots, not simple sheets.

Mourning Fernández as a person was inextricably tied to mourning Fernández as a ballplayer, to say nothing of baseball's more dangerous and distant collective act of mourning him as how we imagined he might have been. This, then, was the psychological setting for the Marlins' final week of 2016 baseball—a week with the team technically still in contention for a playoff spot. "Meaningful baseball," suddenly made to look miserably shallow and cheap. The relationship between grief and the search for meaning in something, anything, is often intimate; to label baseball as meaningful in this context felt woefully inadequate at best and cruelly mocking at worst.

That is, at least if one subscribes strictly to the standard of "meaningful" that is accepted as the foundation of "meaningful baseball." This is meaning derived from a simplistic moral calculus—from winning and nothing else, the idea that baseball matters only in the service of achieving a playoff spot. This is meaning that operates only within the absolute states of victory and defeat, with no recognition of aesthetic or emotion within the corresponding wins and losses. It is the meaning that franchises exist to chase, though some chase it more distantly and abstractly—and the Marlins, under ownership driven by naked greed far more brazen than that of most franchises, consistently chase it with zero abstraction but limited success.

By this standard, the Marlins had only an outside shot at meaning to begin with. On the day of Fernández's death they sat five games out of the National League's second Wild Card spot, not yet mathematically eliminated but only barely so. Meaning is more nuanced than this, though. And so is baseball. There was little "meaningful baseball" left for the Marlins, but the baseball that was left held meaning of a deeper and more complicated sort. The final week of the season was baseball as routine, baseball as a return to the outlines of normalcy, baseball as a dependable structure with rules that make sense.

It was, essentially, baseball as everything that grief is not. It was, one day after Fernández's death, Dee Gordon leading off by taking the first pitch from the right side of the plate in tribute to his teammate and then taking the second pitch deep for a home run. And there was, in that at-bat, a far more meaningful catharsis than anything possible in the construct of "meaningful baseball." The Marlins won that first game after Fernández's death; they lost four of the five that followed and came up just short of their first winning record since 2009. In a twist of circumstance almost too brazenly on the nose to be tragic, their chances for "meaningful baseball" officially ended when they were eliminated with a loss on September 28th—the same day that Fernández's funeral procession wound through the streets of Miami and past Marlins Park, pallbearers wearing his jersey as they carried his casket.

✦✦✦

The baseball Fernández played was most obviously meaningful because it was excellent—meaningful because of the triple-digit heat, meaningful because of that dazzling curveball, meaningful because how could someone this spectacularly good *not* mean something? But it was also meaningful in how clearly he loved it. Of all the video clips and highlights put on an endless loop of grieving after his death, one that showed up again and again was Fernández celebrating a home run from the dugout, going completely wild, just iridescently and ridiculously *happy*.

His joy is so pure and so wholly earnest that it's almost impossible to describe it in terms that aren't cloying or cheesy. The home run in question did not win a game and the game was not one that mattered. It was mid-July, in Fernández's rookie year of 2013, and the Marlins were in last place. This was a team that had no chance at "meaningful baseball" and knew it would not likely have one in the near future, and Fernández still loved baseball simply and purely enough to give meaning to an ordinary home run anyway.

How the Marlins managed to play anything at all in the days after Fernández's death was a question of humanity far more than it was a question of baseball. While those games were a setting for grief and a channel to navigate it, the loss to process was a human one and not a baseball one. How the Marlins might manage not just to play again, but to play "meaningful baseball" again, is an entirely different question and a far more uncomfortable one. To ask how the Marlins can now play "meaningful baseball"—to ask how the Marlins try to win from here—requires addressing Fernández's death as a baseball loss rather than a human one. Here, there are no satisfying answers.

It is quite easy for front offices to dehumanize players, simply by virtue of the vocabulary. They are assets, they are team-controlled, their value is determined only by their production and maximizing that value is finding a way to pay them less than the market should demand. Such is the language of the system. But even in a structure as ruthless as this, an answer to the question of how to "replace" Fernández seems unthinkable to the point of gross indecency. The fact that this is a task the Marlins must shoulder at all is a painful reminder of just how irreplaceable Fernández was—primarily and most significantly as a person, but as a ballplayer, too.

There is no way to replace Jose Fernández on the free agent market or in a trade or with prospects from your farm system. The emotional response is that none of those sources can possibly yield anyone with the childlike joy of Fernández, the relentless passion of his play, the simple fun of watching him pitch. The rational response is just as bleak. Strip away the humanity and the sentimentality and leave bare the cold unfeelingness of stat lines and projection systems—still no source can possibly yield a pitcher as good as Fernández, because no pitcher available is that good.

Without Fernández, the Marlins' rotation is a haphazard collection of bets with questionable payoff (Wei-Yin Chen, Edinson Volquez) and homegrown arms with the most

limited of successes (Tom Koehler, Adam Conley). But rather than focus on upgrading starting pitching this winter, the team targeted its bullpen. After being rebuffed with big offers to the two best closers on the market, Aroldis Chapman and Kenley Jansen, the Marlins instead settled for a pair of cheaper and less talented alternatives: Brad Ziegler and Junichi Tazawa. On its surface, this strategy makes little sense; there is no good reason for a team to so heavily focus on improving its relief pitching when its starting rotation is in near shambles. But, then again, what strategy makes sense when the task at hand is replacing José Fernández?

✦✦✦

The deeply human tragedy of Fernández's death is set against the cheap and comparatively absurd baseball tragedy of the Marlins and their ownership. The history of the franchise is relatively brief, not yet three decades old, but its pattern is clear. It's one of sudden, fitful teardowns and reconstruction that may or may not follow. Every team experiences cycles of success and failure (or at least of comparatively up-and-down periods scaled to the standards of the team itself), but the Marlins experience these differently. Their cycles are faster and more unpredictable, with the swing from up to down more dramatic because their cycles are not the product of the team's performance itself.

Instead, their cycles are triggered by the whims of an owner whose involvement in team activity long crossed the point of reason. The Marlins' operating principle is one of greed streaked with incompetence, and the result is a team invested neither in its players nor its fans nor its community, because its owner considers himself beholden to none of them. This is all to say that the Marlins have something of a tradition built around the need to start over. They are a franchise accustomed to dysfunction, to hopelessness, to the seemingly random and ultimately pointless. And this tradition collectively provides a cheap, hollow background for a painfully human tragedy.

Strictly in terms of baseball, the loss of Fernández does not put the Marlins nearly so far back as they have traditionally found themselves when forced to start over. But even with Fernández, the Marlins were only just hovering on the border of being competitive, and with him gone and a weak rotation behind the chances of a successful season are not good. The Marlins' concept of "meaningful baseball" has always been slightly apart from that of other teams, because there is no indication that one year of "meaningful baseball" will beget another. Everything is at the mercy of Loria's impatience and imagination; another fire sale could always be around the corner, another move to ratchet up the dysfunction in a way that pushes them once more into a punchline.

And now their concept of meaningful baseball is something different, too—something deeper and more complex, in its understanding both of meaning and of baseball. ■

—Emma Baccellieri is an author
of Baseball Prospectus

HITTERS

Brian Anderson   3B

Born: 5/19/93   Age: 24   Bats: R   Throws: R   Height: 6'3"   Weight: 185   Entered Pro Ball: Round 3, 2014 Draft (#76 overall)

YEAR	TEAM	LVL	AGE	PA	R	2B	3B	HR	RBI	BB	K	SB	CS	AVG/OBP/SLG	TAv	VORP	BABIP	BRR	FRAA	WARP
2014	BAT	A-	21	85	11	3	1	3	12	6	11	1	1	.273/.333/.455	.271	2.9	.286	-0.1	2B(17): -1.8	0.1
2014	GRB	A	21	172	27	7	0	8	37	13	28	0	0	.314/.378/.516	.324	15.0	.336	-1.6	3B(26): 2.0 • 2B(9): 0.4	1.8
2015	JUP	A+	22	530	50	22	2	8	62	40	109	2	2	.235/.304/.340	.269	19.3	.287	-0.9	3B(121): 4.1	2.5
2016	JUP	A+	23	207	27	12	2	3	25	22	38	3	0	.302/.377/.440	.300	13.9	.364	-1.5	3B(47): 8.1	2.3
2016	JAX	AA	23	345	38	9	1	8	40	36	59	0	0	.243/.330/.359	.268	13.7	.274	0.2	3B(85): 12.5	2.8
2017	MIA	MLB	24	250	25	10	1	7	29	20	63	0	0	.230/.297/.379	.240	2.2	.283	-0.4	3B 5, 1B 0	0.8
2018	MIA	MLB	25	389	46	16	1	12	44	31	101	0	0	.230/.297/.384	.254	5.3	.284	-0.8	3B 8, 1B 0	1.5

Breakout: 2%   Improve: 9%   Collapse: 6%   Attrition: 13%   MLB: 18%   *Comparables:* Andrew Burns, Adam Duvall, Eric Campbell

As years go, 2016 was a rough one, but it was pretty good for Brian Anderson, who won the Marlins' minor league player of the year award. For Anderson's sake and our collective sanity, we'll call it a draw. Anderson started the season at High-A Jupiter, where he mashed through the end of May. At Double-A Jacksonville, he hit respectably and put his power and pitch selection on display. He's also got glove to spare, totaling nearly 20 FRAA across the minors. It would be a surprise not to see him in the show this year, and in the best-case scenario he becomes a solid, beloved Marlin for a long time. It doesn't usually end that way, but dare to dream.

Justin Bour   1B

Born: 5/28/88   Age: 29   Bats: L   Throws: R   Height: 6'3"   Weight: 265   Entered Pro Ball: Round 25, 2009 Draft (#770 overall)

YEAR	TEAM	LVL	AGE	PA	R	2B	3B	HR	RBI	BB	K	SB	CS	AVG/OBP/SLG	TAv	VORP	BABIP	BRR	FRAA	WARP
2014	NWO	AAA	26	430	59	27	0	18	72	39	57	3	1	.306/.372/.517	.320	32.6	.319	-1.6	1B(91): 5.0	3.7
2014	MIA	MLB	26	83	10	3	0	1	11	9	19	0	0	.284/.361/.365	.278	1.9	.370	-0.6	1B(15): 1.0	0.3
2015	NWO	AAA	27	62	8	1	0	1	5	11	6	1	0	.275/.403/.353	.283	2.3	.295	0.2	1B(13): -0.1	0.2
2015	MIA	MLB	27	446	42	20	0	23	73	34	101	0	0	.262/.321/.479	.289	13.2	.294	-4.1	1B(111): -6.3	0.7
2017	MIA	MLB	29	502	59	22	1	20	68	46	99	1	0	.257/.328/.444	.275	13.7	.286	-1.1	1B -2	1.1
2018	MIA	MLB	30	423	57	18	0	18	58	40	87	0	0	.253/.326/.445	.283	12.6	.282	-2.4	1B -1	1.2

Breakout: 7%   Improve: 43%   Collapse: 13%   Attrition: 13%   MLB: 84%   *Comparables:* Gaby Sanchez, Ryan Garko, Lyle Overbay

During the press conference following Ichiro Suzuki's 3,000th hit, a reporter asked the legend who the most famous person to congratulate him had been, presumably angling for the name of some political or cultural leader who had sent a text. Without hesitation Ichiro responded "Justin Bour" and the room broke out laughing at the continuation of a long-running inside joke between the two. This is good for Bour. Sometimes game recognizes game in the strangest ways. On the bad side, Bour missed the fat middle of last season with a busted ankle. When he played he banged right-handers to a .268/.361/.496 clip, which was almost completely in tune with his season line. He doesn't need to improve against lefties to have a solid career, but he does if he wants to play every day. Either way, he'll be around. His white-hot fame doesn't flame out easily.

Derek Dietrich   2B

Born: 7/18/89   Age: 27   Bats: L   Throws: R   Height: 6'0"   Weight: 205   Entered Pro Ball: Round 2, 2010 Draft (#79 overall)

YEAR	TEAM	LVL	AGE	PA	R	2B	3B	HR	RBI	BB	K	SB	CS	AVG/OBP/SLG	TAv	VORP	BABIP	BRR	FRAA	WARP
2016	MIA	MLB	28	321	35	12	1	15	51	38	56	0	0	.264/.349/.475	.307	17.7	.278	-1.1	1B(82): -5.2	1.3
2014	MIA	MLB	24	183	31	6	2	5	17	13	38	1	0	.228/.326/.386	.277	10.4	.270	2.9	2B(44): 1.4 • 3B(1): -0.3	1.3
2014	NWO	AAA	24	92	15	3	0	7	16	4	18	1	0	.317/.391/.610	.360	13.2	.333	0.0	2B(21): -0.4	1.3
2015	NWO	AAA	25	224	25	13	2	7	27	15	45	0	2	.260/.357/.458	.305	15.2	.303	-0.7	2B(35): -4.7 • 1B(8): -0.8	1.2
2015	MIA	MLB	25	289	38	14	3	10	24	23	65	0	2	.256/.346/.456	.301	19.3	.303	0.8	LF(46): -3.9 • 3B(26): 0.5	1.7
2016	JAX	AA	26	22	2	0	0	0	0	2	7	0	0	.167/.318/.167	.225	-0.2	.273	0.0	2B(4): 0.0 • 1B(1): -0.0	0.0
2016	MIA	MLB	26	412	39	20	5	7	42	32	84	1	0	.279/.374/.425	.308	29.7	.343	-1.1	2B(75): -0.2 • 1B(16): -0.1	3.0
2017	MIA	MLB	27	296	34	13	2	10	36	22	70	1	0	.245/.331/.426	.274	13.1	.294	-0.4	1B -1, 3B -0	1.1
2018	MIA	MLB	28	393	51	18	3	14	50	29	91	1	0	.249/.338/.437	.289	20.2	.297	0.8	1B -1, 3B 0	2.2

Breakout: 3%   Improve: 43%   Collapse: 6%   Attrition: 8%   MLB: 95%   *Comparables:* Chase Utley, Logan Forsythe, Neil Walker

One man's trash, etc. Thrust into a starting role in the wake of Dee Gordon's 80-game suspension for PEDs, Dietrich acquitted himself well enough that the Marlins moved him all over the field to keep his bat in the lineup once Gordon returned. He's a perfect platoon player, hitting .297/.397/.455 against righties last year compared to .200/.264/.292 against lefties, while playing multiple defensive positions. He was the living definition of what happens when preparation meets opportunity.

A.J. Ellis   C

Born: 4/9/81   Age: 36   Bats: R   Throws: R   Height: 6'2"   Weight: 225   Entered Pro Ball: Round 18, 2003 Draft (#541 overall)

YEAR	TEAM	LVL	AGE	PA	R	2B	3B	HR	RBI	BB	K	SB	CS	AVG/OBP/SLG	TAv	VORP	BABIP	BRR	FRAA	WARP
2014	LAN	MLB	33	347	21	9	0	3	25	53	57	0	0	.191/.323/.254	.227	-0.5	.225	-4.1	C(92): -14.8	-1.7
2015	LAN	MLB	34	217	24	9	0	7	21	32	38	0	0	.238/.355/.403	.293	13.6	.265	-2.7	C(62): -2.1	1.2
2016	LAN	MLB	35	161	8	5	0	1	13	16	24	1	1	.194/.285/.252	.202	-2.5	.226	-0.1	C(46): 0.1	-0.2
2016	PHI	MLB	35	35	3	3	0	1	9	3	7	1	0	.313/.371/.500	.328	3.1	.375	-0.9	C(11): -0.8	0.2
2017	MIA	MLB	36	121	12	4	0	2	11	15	23	0	0	.227/.326/.341	.251	3.4	.265	-0.3	C -3	0.0
2018	MIA	MLB	37	84	10	3	0	2	8	11	17	0	0	.217/.323/.329	.251	1.4	.255	-0.7	C -2	-0.1

Breakout: 0%   Improve: 23%   Collapse: 9%   Attrition: 25%   MLB: 78%   *Comparables:* Tim McCarver, Gregg Zaun, Ramon Hernandez

The loudest reaction to a baseball trade last year came when Ellis—a 35-year-old career backup catcher—was traded to the Phillies for Carlos Ruiz in a swap of venerable backstops. The consternation centered around Clayton Kershaw's close relationship with Ellis, but also with the Dodgers' possible lack of concern with team chemistry. The impact of the Ellis trade on either of these aspects is impossible to prove, but it did shine a light on how easy it is to forget that there can be collateral damage when relationships that players forge over the course of multiple seasons are disrupted. In the long-term, all of this will be forgotten. Eddie Perez eventually stopped caddying Greg Maddux and the Hall-of-Famer-to-be endured. Clayton Kershaw will survive.

YEAR	TEAM	P. COUNT	FRM RUNS	BLK RUNS	THRW RUNS	TOT RUNS
2014	LAN	12138	-12.3	-0.9	-0.8	-14.0
2015	LAN	7583	-5.9	0.0	1.0	-4.9
2016	LAN	6050	-0.8	-1.0	-0.2	-2.0
2016	PHI	1303	-0.9	0.0	0.0	-0.9
2017	*MIA*	*3377*	*-2.6*	*-0.3*	*0.0*	*-2.9*
2018	*MIA*	*2335*	*-2.1*	*-0.3*	*0.0*	*-2.4*

Jeff Francoeur   RF

Born: 1/8/84   Age: 33   Bats: R   Throws: R   Height: 6'4"   Weight: 225   Entered Pro Ball: Round 1, 2002 Draft (#23 overall)

YEAR	TEAM	LVL	AGE	PA	R	2B	3B	HR	RBI	BB	K	SB	CS	AVG/OBP/SLG	TAv	VORP	BABIP	BRR	FRAA	WARP
2014	SDN	MLB	30	28	2	0	0	0	1	3	7	0	0	.083/.179/.083	.141	-2.3	.111	0.2	RF(7): -0.1	-0.3
2014	ELP	AAA	30	487	55	22	3	15	69	21	95	11	2	.289/.320/.450	.275	11.6	.331	0.7	RF(103): -14.2 • P(8): -0.1	-0.2
2015	PHI	MLB	31	343	34	16	1	13	45	13	77	0	2	.258/.286/.433	.258	4.1	.297	-1.4	RF(85): 0.4 • LF(20): -2.1	0.2
2016	ATL	MLB	32	276	29	13	0	7	33	16	75	2	0	.249/.290/.381	.260	5.9	.320	0.0	LF(53): -5.2 • RF(10): 0.7	0.1
2016	MIA	MLB	32	55	4	2	1	0	1	4	15	0	2	.280/.333/.360	.261	0.2	.400	-1.0	LF(10): -0.5 • RF(7): 0.6	0.0
2017	*MIA*	*MLB*	*33*	*314*	*29*	*13*	*1*	*8*	*34*	*16*	*77*	*2*	*1*	*.228/.272/.359*	*.222*	*-2.2*	*.281*	*-0.3*	*LF -8, RF -2*	*-1.3*
2018	*MIA*	*MLB*	*34*	*294*	*30*	*11*	*1*	*7*	*29*	*17*	*74*	*1*	*1*	*.221/.269/.344*	*.229*	*-3.0*	*.276*	*-0.3*	*LF -7, RF -1*	*-1.3*

Breakout: 0%   Improve: 28%   Collapse: 11%   Attrition: 19%   MLB: 76%   *Comparables: Corey Patterson, Gary Varsho, Dick Williams*

Frenchy was made for baseball and baseball for Frenchy, and they can't get enough of each other. Dubbed "The Natural" by *Sports Illustrated* in a garish 2005 cover story, Francouer has been an obvious anachronism from day one, the archetype at the center of the myth that Baseball Prospectus was created to destroy regarding what makes a player good versus what makes him *seem* good. BP and others successfully did that on a macro level insofar as it's possible, but Frenchy turned out to be revolution-proof. He's always ready to play the game his way and teams keep employing him even if the on-field product has been basically the same not-all-that-good for a decade, save for some built-in gradual decline getting worse. He has played for six teams in the last three seasons, and you imagine he could have six teams left before it's all done.

Stone Garrett   LF

Born: 11/22/95 Age: 21   Bats: R   Throws: R   Height: 6'2"   Weight: 195   Entered Pro Ball: Round 8, 2014 Draft (#227 overall)

YEAR	TEAM	LVL	AGE	PA	R	2B	3B	HR	RBI	BB	K	SB	CS	AVG/OBP/SLG	TAv	VORP	BABIP	BRR	FRAA	WARP
2015	BAT	A-	19	247	36	18	6	11	46	19	60	8	5	.297/.352/.581	.339	26.7	.355	-1.0	CF(58): -2.1	2.6
2016	GRB	A	20	212	21	9	2	6	16	11	71	1	2	.213/.265/.371	.226	-2.2	.300	0.6	LF(33): -2.3 • CF(7): 1.6	-0.3
2017	*MIA*	*MLB*	*21*	*250*	*22*	*9*	*1*	*8*	*28*	*13*	*91*	*1*	*1*	*.195/.241/.341*	*.203*	*-6.9*	*.277*	*-0.4*	*LF 0, RF -0*	*-0.7*
2018	*MIA*	*MLB*	*22*	*290*	*30*	*11*	*1*	*9*	*32*	*15*	*104*	*1*	*1*	*.198/.246/.353*	*.217*	*-6.5*	*.277*	*-0.5*	*LF 0, RF 0*	*-0.7*

Breakout: 0%   Improve: 0%   Collapse: 0%   Attrition: 2%   MLB: 2%   *Comparables: Marcell Ozuna, Trayce Thompson, Yorman Rodriguez*

You can draw blood from him after all. Garrett was sidelined in June when fellow Marlins blue chipper Josh Naylor played a prank on his roommate that ended the with Garrett suffering nerve damage, for which he received three stitches and sat out six weeks. Naylor was traded to San Diego in the Andrew Cashner deal shortly thereafter; draw your own conclusions. Upon his return Garrett wasn't quite as effective at High-A Greensboro as he'd been at Batavia in 2015, but despite that and the perma-terror associated with hand injuries it's probably best to just give him a mulligan on 2016. This is his age-21 season and when he hits the ball it still goes very, very far. Patience, (Greenboro) Grasshopper.

Dee Gordon   2B

Born: 4/22/88   Age: 29   Bats: L   Throws: R   Height: 5'11"   Weight: 170   Entered Pro Ball: Round 4, 2008 Draft (#127 overall)

YEAR	TEAM	LVL	AGE	PA	R	2B	3B	HR	RBI	BB	K	SB	CS	AVG/OBP/SLG	TAv	VORP	BABIP	BRR	FRAA	WARP
2014	LAN	MLB	26	650	92	24	12	2	34	31	107	64	19	.289/.326/.378	.268	25.0	.346	4.0	2B(144): -2.8	2.4
2015	MIA	MLB	27	653	88	24	8	4	46	25	91	58	20	.333/.359/.418	.292	41.1	.383	4.1	2B(145): -0.6	4.3
2016	NWO	AAA	28	36	7	1	1	0	2	1	5	3	0	.257/.278/.343	.235	0.4	.300	0.4	2B(9): -2.0	-0.2
2016	MIA	MLB	28	345	47	7	6	1	14	18	55	30	7	.268/.305/.335	.244	7.1	.319	3.4	2B(78): -6.0	0.1
2017	*MIA*	*MLB*	*29*	*639*	*82*	*21*	*8*	*4*	*41*	*39*	*109*	*51*	*16*	*.272/.316/.355*	*.247*	*17.7*	*.323*	*5.9*	*2B -4*	*1.4*
2018	*MIA*	*MLB*	*30*	*495*	*51*	*17*	*5*	*4*	*43*	*30*	*88*	*38*	*13*	*.273/.320/.360*	*.254*	*15.6*	*.325*	*3.6*	*2B -3*	*1.4*

Breakout: 2%   Improve: 46%   Collapse: 5%   Attrition: 12%   MLB: 91%   *Comparables: Emilio Bonifacio, Alexi Casilla, Chris Getz*

The Hall of Fame is not a monolithic entity. The National Baseball Hall of Fame and Museum, as clearly stated, features both the Hall of Fame—a cold, quiet, historically underwhelming *plaque locker*—and the museum, a vibrant multimedia exhibit dedicated to the best, coolest and most touching moments in baseball history. Now Gordon will be represented there, even if he evokes hysteria elsewhere. Yes, he was busted for using PEDs at the outset of 2016, but even if you're the lovechild of Buster Olney and Joe McCarthy, you can hopefully still recognize that what Gordon did on September 26, 2016 was a miracle on this earth. Dee's dinger to open the first game after Jose Fernandez's death, his only homer of the year, is one of the transcendent, moving moments in the game's history, and the most obviously emotionally devastating one since Mike Piazza's homer in the first game in New York City after 9/11. It was historic, but unfortunately it can't totally obscure the mess of his season. He should be back to normal now, whatever that entails.

Albert Guaimaro   C

Born: 1/17/99   Age: 18   Bats: R   Throws: R   Height: 6'0"   Weight: 180   Entered Pro Ball: International Free Agent, 2016

YEAR	TEAM	LVL	AGE	PA	R	2B	3B	HR	RBI	BB	K	SB	CS	AVG/OBP/SLG	TAv	VORP	BABIP	BRR	FRAA	WARP
2017	MIA	MLB	18	250	22	10	0	5	23	12	80	3	2	.197/.238/.306	.192	-7.8	.272	-0.3	CF -0, C 0	-0.9
2018	MIA	MLB	19	246	23	10	1	5	23	11	80	3	2	.199/.237/.318	.203	-7.4	.272	-0.1	CF 0, C 0	-0.8

Breakout: 0%   Improve: 0%   Collapse: 0%   Attrition: 0%   MLB: 0%   *Comparables: Raul Mondesi, Wilmer Flores*

Life comes at you fast. Once an outfielder in Boston's system, Guaimaro is now a catcher in the Marlins' organization, and he's still only 18. One of the five Red Sox prospects removed from the organization for violating international signing rules, he signed with the Marlins in July with the idea of playing him behind the dish. He hit .250/.302/.420 in the Dominican Summer League before the change and .194/.256/.222 afterward, but it's probably best to allow Guaimaro some breathing room. He now gets a drama-free year to adjust and improve while the rest of us wait to see if all that fuss was worth it.

Adeiny Hechavarria   SS

Born: 4/15/89   Age: 28   Bats: R   Throws: R   Height: 6'0"   Weight: 195   Entered Pro Ball: International Free Agent, 2010

YEAR	TEAM	LVL	AGE	PA	R	2B	3B	HR	RBI	BB	K	SB	CS	AVG/OBP/SLG	TAv	VORP	BABIP	BRR	FRAA	WARP
2014	MIA	MLB	25	574	53	20	10	1	34	26	86	7	5	.276/.308/.356	.243	15.9	.323	3.6	SS(146): 9.2	2.8
2015	MIA	MLB	26	499	54	17	6	5	48	23	78	7	2	.281/.315/.374	.249	17.4	.325	3.2	SS(130): 6.2	2.5
2016	MIA	MLB	27	547	52	17	6	3	38	33	73	1	0	.236/.283/.311	.223	8.5	.269	6.5	SS(153): 2.6	1.1
2017	MIA	MLB	28	547	48	19	5	6	46	31	95	5	3	.248/.289/.340	.231	10.5	.290	0.0	SS 5	0.7
2018	MIA	MLB	29	479	48	16	4	6	43	30	85	4	2	.247/.295/.346	.237	8.5	.288	3.2	SS 4	1.4

Breakout: 1%   Improve: 36%   Collapse: 11%   Attrition: 18%   MLB: 95%   *Comparables: Donovan Solano, Alex Cintron, Yuniesky Betancourt*

Hechavarria turned in a modest, ultimately positive season despite being what the MarlinManiac blog called "The Worst Offensive Player in Baseball (Again)." Ouch—but hey, more hardware! Maybe the backhanded encomia are why the Marlins keep him around, but with Miguel Rojas and J.T. Riddle waiting in the wings he's ostensibly trade bait. His glove is forever as real as a heart attack, even if he notched a modest 2.6 FRAA last year. If the Marlins are all mixed up at what to do at shortstop, it's likely Hechevarria's .311 slugging line bringing them down, down.

Chris Johnson   1B/3B

Born: 10/1/84   Age: 32   Bats: R   Throws: R   Height: 6'3"   Weight: 225   Entered Pro Ball: Round 4, 2006 Draft (#129 overall)

YEAR	TEAM	LVL	AGE	PA	R	2B	3B	HR	RBI	BB	K	SB	CS	AVG/OBP/SLG	TAv	VORP	BABIP	BRR	FRAA	WARP
2014	ATL	MLB	29	611	43	27	0	10	58	23	159	6	0	.263/.292/.361	.239	5.4	.345	-0.3	3B(150): -22.6 • 1B(1): -0.0	-1.9
2015	ATL	MLB	30	162	12	7	0	2	11	7	49	2	1	.235/.272/.320	.228	-2.5	.330	-0.8	3B(23): -1.0 • 1B(20): 0.9	-0.3
2015	CLE	MLB	30	93	6	4	0	1	7	3	25	0	0	.289/.312/.367	.232	-1.2	.391	0.1	1B(10): -0.3 • 3B(4): -0.0	-0.2
2016	MIA	MLB	31	264	20	11	0	5	24	19	78	0	0	.222/.281/.329	.218	-8.2	.306	-0.9	1B(81): -1.6 • 3B(11): -0.4	-1.1
2017	MIA	MLB	32	250	24	12	0	5	27	14	65	1	0	.258/.301/.381	.239	-0.2	.334	-0.4	1B -1, 3B -1	-0.3
2018	MIA	MLB	33	254	27	12	0	5	26	15	68	1	0	.253/.299/.372	.247	-0.4	.331	-0.6	1B -2, 3B -1	-0.3

Breakout: 9%   Improve: 28%   Collapse: 18%   Attrition: 35%   MLB: 82%   *Comparables: Frank Thomas, John Ellis, Jeff Baker*

Johnson was nervous to come to the Marlins because, as S.L. Price wrote in a heartbreaking *Sports Illustrated* profile of Jose Fernandez, as a member of the Braves he'd started a near-brawl with Fernandez after the latter pimped his first career home run. The fun part about this, from a consumer's perspective, has always been that by the time Fernandez got back to the plate after circling the bases, the benches had cleared, and a photo taken at the moment of confrontation shows everyone bracing for impact, except for the beaming Fernandez. This isn't war. It's fun. Johnson didn't get it, but he does now. After the ace's death Johnson told Price he had learned so much about Fernandez simply by talking to him that he immediately understood the error of his ways. On the internet, baseball's culture war is always raging; in the case of Johnson it's a reminder that every changed mind helps. Good for him, even (especially) if he looks like he's on the way out of the game he loves.

Thomas Jones   OF

Born: 12/9/97   Age: 19   Bats: R   Throws: R   Height: 6'4"   Weight: 195   Entered Pro Ball: Round 3, 2016 Draft (#84 overall)

YEAR	TEAM	LVL	AGE	PA	R	2B	3B	HR	RBI	BB	K	SB	CS	AVG/OBP/SLG	TAv	VORP	BABIP	BRR	FRAA	WARP
2017	MIA	MLB	19	250	21	9	1	4	22	17	88	3	1	.183/.244/.284	.190	-8.8	.269	-0.1		-1.0

Breakout: 0%   Improve: 6%   Collapse: 2%   Attrition: 5%   MLB: 12%   *Comparables: Nomar Mazara, Engel Beltre, Raul Mondesi*

The front office loves Jones, a big third-round pick who was a three-star football recruit out of a South Carolina high school and can scorch the basepaths. He hit an especially nice .420 in his last prep season, which probably was the death knell for his football dreams. Still, given Jones' gridiron pedigree it's no surprise that Vanderbilt lost him to the Marlins (because they're bad at football, see). He's still got a long way to go by virtue of being extremely young, but he showed a great eye in rookie-ball and there's a lot to like here.

Marcell Ozuna   CF

Born: 11/12/90 Age: 26 Bats: R Throws: R Height: 6'1" Weight: 225 Entered Pro Ball: International Free Agent, 2008

YEAR	TEAM	LVL	AGE	PA	R	2B	3B	HR	RBI	BB	K	SB	CS	AVG/OBP/SLG	TAv	VORP	BABIP	BRR	FRAA	WARP
2014	MIA	MLB	23	612	72	26	5	23	85	41	164	3	1	.269/.317/.455	.285	30.3	.337	-1.0	CF(140): -6.1 • LF(11): 4.3	3.1
2015	NWO	AAA	24	132	21	12	1	5	11	11	23	1	0	.317/.379/.558	.360	18.3	.359	0.7	CF(29): -1.8	1.7
2015	MIA	MLB	24	494	47	27	0	10	44	30	110	2	3	.259/.308/.383	.255	15.2	.320	3.8	CF(111): -11.3 • RF(15): 0.8	0.5
2016	MIA	MLB	25	608	75	23	6	23	76	43	115	0	5	.266/.321/.452	.292	39.4	.296	1.6	CF(123): -6.6 • LF(11): -1.4	3.5
2017	MIA	MLB	26	583	63	28	3	20	74	39	132	2	2	.260/.313/.435	.269	27.0	.308	-1.2	CF -9	1.0
2018	MIA	MLB	27	545	69	26	2	20	72	39	127	2	2	.262/.317/.447	.282	28.5	.311	1.3	CF -8	2.2

Breakout: 4%   Improve: 62%   Collapse: 2%   Attrition: 4%   MLB: 100%   Comparables: Adam Jones, Austin Jackson, Matt Kemp

Ozuna hit everything he saw in May, batting .411/.450/.705, but otherwise replicated his disastrous 2015 heading into his first arbitration year. He's represented by Scott Boras, and you best bet the super agent has May's highlight reel at the ready. Ozuna isn't a free agent until 2020, which makes him the perfect trade chit for the resource-strapped Marlins, especially when the alternative is almost certainly and erratically productive player who may very well be happier elsewhere. It's either that or take your chances with Boras. Good luck, friend.

Martin Prado   3B

Born: 10/27/83 Age: 33 Bats: R Throws: R Height: 6'0" Weight: 215 Entered Pro Ball: International Free Agent, 2001

YEAR	TEAM	LVL	AGE	PA	R	2B	3B	HR	RBI	BB	K	SB	CS	AVG/OBP/SLG	TAv	VORP	BABIP	BRR	FRAA	WARP
2014	ARI	MLB	30	436	44	17	4	5	42	23	57	2	1	.270/.317/.370	.246	7.5	.301	0.7	3B(99): -6.7 • 2B(4): -1.0	0.0
2014	NYA	MLB	30	137	18	9	0	7	16	3	23	1	0	.316/.336/.541	.327	12.1	.340	0.3	2B(17): 1.7 • 3B(11): 1.3	1.5
2015	MIA	MLB	31	551	52	22	2	9	63	37	68	1	0	.288/.338/.394	.283	29.2	.313	0.2	3B(124): 0.0 • 2B(11): -0.2	3.1
2016	MIA	MLB	32	658	70	37	3	8	75	49	69	2	2	.305/.359/.417	.288	39.9	.331	0.2	3B(150): -2.8	3.8
2017	MIA	MLB	33	620	67	30	2	10	56	43	76	2	1	.275/.327/.389	.263	19.3	.299	-1.2	3B -2	1.2
2018	MIA	MLB	34	532	60	24	1	9	53	40	70	0	0	.269/.326/.380	.267	15.7	.296	0.2	3B -2	1.5

Breakout: 2%   Improve: 25%   Collapse: 4%   Attrition: 15%   MLB: 91%   Comparables: Yunel Escobar, George Kell, Harvey Kuenn

Prado's 2016 wasn't merely his best season in five years, capping a slow, steady four-year stream of improvements after his career cratered in 2013. It was more than that. The Marlins wouldn't leave the field until Prado had the ball at the end of every inning, and it was Prado who spoke to the media following the death of Jose Fernandez on behalf of the bereaved team. He was their leader. On the final day of the season, as if to cement this, Prado served as player/manager. Signed to a three-year, $40 million extension in September, it's clear that the team loves Prado and vice versa. This is a beautiful friendship.

J.T. Realmuto   C

Born: 3/18/91 Age: 26 Bats: R Throws: R Height: 6'1" Weight: 210 Entered Pro Ball: Round 3, 2010 Draft (#104 overall)

YEAR	TEAM	LVL	AGE	PA	R	2B	3B	HR	RBI	BB	K	SB	CS	AVG/OBP/SLG	TAv	VORP	BABIP	BRR	FRAA	WARP
2014	JAX	AA	23	423	66	25	6	8	62	41	59	18	5	.299/.369/.461	.302	41.7	.333	5.6	C(88): 18.3	6.4
2014	MIA	MLB	23	30	4	1	1	0	9	1	8	0	0	.241/.267/.345	.227	0.3	.333	0.0	C(9): -0.6	0.0
2015	MIA	MLB	24	467	49	21	7	10	47	19	70	8	4	.259/.290/.406	.260	20.4	.285	0.5	C(118): -15.8	0.5
2016	MIA	MLB	25	545	60	31	0	11	48	28	100	12	4	.303/.343/.428	.282	38.0	.357	1.6	C(129): -6.5	3.3
2017	MIA	MLB	26	519	57	26	3	12	54	30	94	10	4	.269/.314/.411	.262	26.6	.310	0.3	C -12	1.2
2018	MIA	MLB	27	525	62	26	4	15	62	32	99	10	4	.265/.314/.425	.275	28.2	.303	1.0	C -12	1.7

Breakout: 9%   Improve: 45%   Collapse: 8%   Attrition: 21%   MLB: 99%   Comparables: Wilson Ramos, Francisco Cervelli, Miguel Montero

At the right angle, Jacob Tyler Realmuto looks like the most underrated player on the Marlins and perhaps one of the more underrated players in the game. He finished third among major-league catchers with a .303 batting average and posted a strong .282 TAv despite a near-total inability to hit lefties. Don Mattingly handed him 80 percent of his plate appearances versus righties, so it worked out and figures to work out in the future. However, Realmuto's pitch framing is awful and hurts the Marlins in ways his stout offensive numbers will never reflect.

YEAR	TEAM	P. COUNT	FRM RUNS	BLK RUNS	THRW RUNS	TOT RUNS
2014	JAX	11404	17.3	-0.4	1.4	18.4
2014	MIA	996	-0.5	0.1	0.0	-0.4
2015	MIA	16187	-15.7	-0.2	0.2	-15.8
2015	NWO	416	0.1	0.0	0.0	0.0
2016	MIA	18935	-13.5	2.0	2.0	-9.5
2017	MIA	18567	-13.5	1.0	0.9	-11.6
2018	MIA	18771	-14.4	1.1	0.8	-12.5

Miguel Rojas   SS

Born: 2/24/89 Age: 28 Bats: R Throws: R Height: 5'11" Weight: 195 Entered Pro Ball: International Free Agent, 2005

YEAR	TEAM	LVL	AGE	PA	R	2B	3B	HR	RBI	BB	K	SB	CS	AVG/OBP/SLG	TAv	VORP	BABIP	BRR	FRAA	WARP
2014	ABQ	AAA	25	173	27	9	0	4	13	10	21	7	3	.302/.353/.434	.273	10.1	.326	1.2	SS(23): -0.6 • 3B(16): 0.5	1.1
2014	LAN	MLB	25	162	16	3	0	1	9	10	28	0	0	.181/.242/.221	.174	-6.9	.217	0.5	SS(66): 3.3 • 3B(19): -0.0	-0.4
2015	NWO	AAA	26	275	32	15	4	3	23	13	26	2	5	.301/.343/.430	.285	17.9	.324	-0.4	SS(63): 7.3 • 3B(1): 0.2	2.6
2015	MIA	MLB	26	157	13	7	1	1	17	11	16	0	1	.282/.329/.366	.273	9.4	.307	1.9	SS(32): -1.9 • 2B(9): -0.6	0.8
2016	MIA	MLB	27	214	27	12	0	1	14	11	27	2	1	.247/.288/.325	.217	-2.1	.280	0.7	2B(45): -0.6 • 1B(41): 1.7	0.2
2017	MIA	MLB	28	249	25	11	1	3	20	15	37	2	2	.250/.296/.353	.238	4.9	.278	-0.5	SS 1, 2B 1	0.5
2018	MIA	MLB	29	305	33	13	2	5	30	18	49	2	2	.253/.306/.370	.249	7.0	.283	0.9	SS 2, 2B 2	1.1

Breakout: 4%   Improve: 36%   Collapse: 9%   Attrition: 18%   MLB: 82%   Comparables: Eduardo Nunez, Jonathan Herrera, Angel Sanchez

Everyone knows "life is like a box of chocolates," per Forrest Gump. What our theory presupposes is: maybe it isn't. Maybe life is like the single-serving candies on Halloween night. The world tears us open, devours us and discards our physical packaging into the ground. We just don't know who or what is going to eat us. So it is with Rojas, an all-glove, no-bat shortstop who could take the starter's job from Adeiny Hechavarria or be passed by utility hero J.T. Riddle, and it won't change a dang thing about what he is. He's a Krackel, and the only question is when the game decides to swallow him whole.

Giancarlo Stanton   RF

Born: 11/8/89   Age: 27   Bats: R   Throws: R   Height: 6'6"   Weight: 245   Entered Pro Ball: Round 2, 2007 Draft (#76 overall)

YEAR	TEAM	LVL	AGE	PA	R	2B	3B	HR	RBI	BB	K	SB	CS	AVG/OBP/SLG	TAv	VORP	BABIP	BRR	FRAA	WARP
2014	MIA	MLB	24	638	89	31	1	37	105	94	170	13	1	.288/.395/.555	.342	61.3	.353	2.3	RF(143): 13.6	8.3
2015	MIA	MLB	25	318	47	12	1	27	67	34	95	4	2	.265/.346/.606	.353	34.8	.294	0.5	RF(71): 7.7	4.6
2016	MIA	MLB	26	470	56	20	1	27	74	50	140	0	0	.240/.326/.489	.307	31.2	.290	0.4	RF(106): 2.4	3.5
2017	MIA	MLB	27	561	83	25	1	35	95	69	163	5	1	.256/.352/.527	.307	42.3	.308	-0.6	RF 8	4.8
2018	MIA	MLB	28	486	77	22	0	30	83	60	139	3	1	.256/.353/.525	.320	40.4	.306	0.6	RF 7	5.1

Breakout: 2%   Improve: 59%   Collapse: 2%   Attrition: 1%   MLB: 100%   Comparables: Jose Canseco, Darryl Strawberry, Harmon Killebrew

A generation's avatar of pure power, Stanton took a roller coaster ride in 2016. He followed a good April with a horrendous May and June only to turn July into his personal punching bag. Then he got hurt and slowly cooled to the finish. Can we call this a typical season at this point? His overall line was a little low, but injuries are always around the corner and it's probably safe to say 600 plate appearances are generally out of the picture going forward. Between that and his iconically long swing, Stanton seems likely to continue to vacillate between periods of sinewy futility and searing white heat. The best thing you can say about Stanton is that you can never, ever look away, even in a lower-bound year like 2016. It should get a little better now, but the forecast never changes.

Ichiro Suzuki   RF

Born: 10/22/73   Age: 43   Bats: L   Throws: R   Height: 5'11"   Weight: 175   Entered Pro Ball: International Free Agent, 2000

YEAR	TEAM	LVL	AGE	PA	R	2B	3B	HR	RBI	BB	K	SB	CS	AVG/OBP/SLG	TAv	VORP	BABIP	BRR	FRAA	WARP
2014	NYA	MLB	40	385	42	13	2	1	22	21	68	15	3	.284/.324/.340	.252	6.1	.346	2.6	RF(119): -4.0 • LF(9): -0.3	0.2
2015	MIA	MLB	41	438	45	5	6	1	21	31	51	11	5	.229/.282/.279	.218	-6.1	.257	3.5	RF(73): 8.5 • LF(30): -0.1	0.2
2016	MIA	MLB	42	365	48	15	5	1	22	30	42	10	2	.291/.354/.376	.266	8.5	.329	-1.7	RF(54): -1.5 • LF(14): 1.4	0.8
2017	MIA	MLB	43	335	32	11	3	1	20	19	47	9	3	.244/.285/.302	.219	-3.1	.280	1.0	RF 2, LF 0	-0.3
2018	MIA	MLB	44	285	25	9	2	0	19	17	42	7	2	.234/.278/.285	.211	-6.7	.272	0.8	RF 1, LF 0	-0.5

Breakout: 5%   Improve: 15%   Collapse: 19%   Attrition: 19%   MLB: 52%   Comparables: Omar Vizquel, Enos Slaughter, Bob Boone

Suzuki found the fountain of youth in the first half, hitting .335 after several rough seasons in a row seemingly put him on the edge of retirement. He faded in the second half, but reached 3,000 career MLB hits on August 7 and finished the year with his highest AVG, OBP and OPS since 2010 in Seattle. It's very possible that if Suzuki had played his entire professional career in America he'd have already surpassed Pete Rose as the all-time MLB hits leader, and his combined total between Japan and America may wind up closer to 4,500 than Rose's final tally of 4,256. Miami exercised its $2 million option on Suzuki for 2017, so Ichiro! will spend age 43 in a part-time role while continuing to be one of the best, coolest and most interesting players in baseball history.

Tomas Telis   C

Born: 6/18/91   Age: 26   Bats: B   Throws: R   Height: 5'8"   Weight: 220   Entered Pro Ball: International Free Agent, 2007

YEAR	TEAM	LVL	AGE	PA	R	2B	3B	HR	RBI	BB	K	SB	CS	AVG/OBP/SLG	TAv	VORP	BABIP	BRR	FRAA	WARP
2014	FRI	AA	23	295	31	16	2	2	33	17	29	7	1	.303/.339/.401	.274	11.1	.325	-2.7	C(46): -0.3 • 3B(1): 0.5	1.2
2014	ROU	AAA	23	147	18	7	2	3	17	6	12	1	1	.345/.377/.489	.296	10.3	.363	0.2	C(19): -1.7 • 1B(9): 0.5	0.9
2014	TEX	MLB	23	71	7	2	0	0	8	1	10	0	0	.250/.271/.279	.234	1.0	.293	-0.1	C(17): -8.0	-0.8
2015	ROU	AAA	24	300	43	15	1	5	25	14	31	1	2	.291/.327/.404	.251	6.2	.313	-1.3	C(50): -0.9 • 1B(3): 0.1	0.6
2015	TEX	MLB	24	12	1	0	0	0	2	0	1	0	0	.182/.250/.182	.194	-0.6	.200	-0.3	C(4): -1.3	-0.2
2015	NWO	AAA	24	55	3	0	0	0	4	5	6	2	0	.333/.389/.333	.284	4.3	.372	0.5	C(12): -8.8	-0.5
2015	MIA	MLB	24	29	1	0	0	0	0	1	3	0	0	.148/.207/.148	.171	-2.3	.167	-0.7	C(7): -2.1	-0.5
2016	NWO	AAA	25	368	46	16	3	6	45	27	42	4	2	.310/.362/.429	.292	24.3	.338	0.5	C(55): -23.8 • 1B(25): 0.1	0.1
2016	MIA	MLB	25	13	1	0	0	1	4	0	2	0	0	.308/.308/.538	.311	0.7	.300	-0.4	C(3): -0.3	0.0
2017	MIA	MLB	26	93	9	4	0	1	9	5	14	0	0	.265/.304/.373	.249	1.3	.297	-0.1	1B 1, C -2	-0.1
2018	MIA	MLB	27	207	23	9	1	4	21	11	33	1	0	.264/.308/.381	.258	3.4	.296	-0.3	1B 2, C -5	0.0

Breakout: 6%   Improve: 20%   Collapse: 11%   Attrition: 25%   MLB: 53%   Comparables: Robinzon Diaz, Ramon Cabrera, Humberto Quintero

Co-Mr. October? Telis, who actually debuted in the majors in 2014, hit his first home run in Game 162 last year. J.T. Realmuto has the starting catcher job on lock, but Telis figures to be a pretty solid backup if he can harness improvements he's made on the defensive end throughout his long, steady rise to the majors. FRAA detests the work he did at Triple A last year, thanks largely to some really terrible framing numbers, but his arm is OK. He threw out 25 percent of runners in New Orleans, down from 43 percent in 2015. He should try for 43 percent again. Or, you know, even higher!

YEAR	TEAM	P. COUNT	FRM RUNS	BLK RUNS	THRW RUNS	TOT RUNS
2014	FRI	6004	-0.7	0.0	-0.1	-0.8
2014	ROU	2202	-1.0	0.0	-0.5	-1.4
2014	TEX	2268	-7.2	-1.0	-0.4	-8.7
2015	ROU	7286	-5.4	0.3	2.3	-2.8
2015	TEX	402	-1.3	0.3	0.0	-1.0
2015	MIA	557	-2.0	0.2	0.0	-1.8
2015	NWO	1789	-8.1	-0.2	-0.2	-8.5
2016	MIA	213	-0.1	0.1	0.0	-0.1
2017	MIA	1118	-2.3	0.0	0.0	-2.3
2018	MIA	2493	-5.3	0.0	0.0	-5.3

Christian Yelich   LF

Born: 12/5/91   Age: 25   Bats: L   Throws: R   Height: 6'3"   Weight: 195   Entered Pro Ball: Round 1, 2010 Draft (#23 overall)

YEAR	TEAM	LVL	AGE	PA	R	2B	3B	HR	RBI	BB	K	SB	CS	AVG/OBP/SLG	TAv	VORP	BABIP	BRR	FRAA	WARP
2014	MIA	MLB	22	660	94	30	6	9	54	70	137	21	7	.284/.362/.402	.286	32.0	.356	2.6	LF(138): -5.2 • CF(12): -1.7	2.8
2015	MIA	MLB	23	525	63	30	2	7	44	47	101	16	5	.300/.366/.416	.288	27.8	.370	1.4	LF(103): 4.9 • CF(36): -3.3	3.1
2016	MIA	MLB	24	659	78	38	3	21	98	72	138	9	4	.298/.376/.483	.318	56.6	.356	2.2	LF(120): -6.2 • CF(31): 0.2	5.2
2017	MIA	MLB	25	647	76	33	3	16	74	67	142	15	5	.277/.355/.428	.283	37.3	.341	0.3	LF 1, CF -1	3.3
2018	MIA	MLB	26	572	74	30	2	15	67	61	124	13	5	.279/.358/.434	.296	36.6	.341	1.9	LF 1, CF -1	4.0

Breakout: 2%   Improve: 53%   Collapse: 0%   Attrition: 1%   MLB: 99%   Comparables: Gary Matthews, Roy Foster, Don Baylor

In early August, Miami-area radio host Brendan Tobin said on-air that he'd "literally" eat crow if Yelich, who then had 11 homers but had never previously topped nine in a year, reached the 20-tater mark. One scorching September later Yelich did just that, and Tobin pledged to make good on his bet. To see what he might eat, visit crowbusters.com for real, crowd-sourced crow recipes, including Summer Crow Kabobs and Crow in a Blanket. (We wish we were kidding.) No longer a star in the making, Yelich is a bona fide stud, and the South Florida sky's the limit. His slugging percentage hasn't gone down through four seasons, and Don Mattingly says he wants Yelich to get to 30 round-trippers in 2017. Even if he doesn't get there, he's one of the game's brightest stars.

PITCHERS

Kyle Barraclough RHP

Born: 5/23/90 Age: 27 Bats: R Throws: R Height: 6'3" Weight: 225 Entered Pro Ball: Round 7, 2012 Draft (#240 overall)

YEAR	TEAM	LVL	AGE	W	L	SV	G	GS	IP	H	HR	BB/9	K/9	K	GB%	BABIP	WHIP	ERA	FIP	DRA	VORP	WARP	cFIP	MPH
2014	PMB	A+	24	1	1	1	16	0	18²	28	0	5.3	8.7	18	57%	.459	2.09	5.30	3.39	6.41	-2.5	-0.3	108	
2014	PEO	A	24	1	1	10	32	0	40	21	0	5.2	13.5	60	51%	.259	1.10	1.12	2.21	2.26	12.4	1.3	86	
2015	PMB	A+	25	1	0	4	11	0	15	9	0	5.4	13.8	23	32%	.290	1.20	0.60	1.90	2.70	3.3	0.4	90	
2015	SFD	AA	25	2	0	8	23	0	24²	19	0	7.3	10.2	28	49%	.302	1.58	3.28	3.70	4.96	-0.6	-0.1	115	
2015	MIA	MLB	25	2	1	0	25	0	24¹	12	1	6.7	11.1	30	34%	.224	1.23	2.59	3.45	4.34	1.0	0.1	102	97.8
2016	MIA	MLB	26	6	3	0	75	0	72²	45	1	5.4	14.0	113	55%	.301	1.22	2.85	2.15	2.35	21.1	2.2	70	98.0
2017	*MIA*	*MLB*	*27*	*3*	*2*	*3*	*50*	*0*	*53*	*43*	*5*	*4.9*	*11.8*	*70*	*42%*	*.301*	*1.35*	*3.51*	*3.51*	*4.00*	*5.4*	*0.6*	*89*	
2018	*MIA*	*MLB*	*28*	*3*	*1*	*3*	*61*	*0*	*65*	*44*	*6*	*5.1*	*13.0*	*94*	*42%*	*.309*	*1.23*	*3.10*	*3.43*	*3.72*	*10.1*	*1.0*	*80*	

Breakout: 36%   Improve: 54%   Collapse: 21%   Attrition: 20%   MLB: 89%   Comparables: *Tanner Scheppers, Brian Wilson, A.J. Ramos*

A year after performing well in his first 24 career innings Barraclough was sterling, blistering the National League to a tune of 113 strikeouts in 72.2 innings in 2016. We live in the age of the super-reliever, so Barraclough and his 97 mph four-seamer might not be mentioned alongside the Chapmans, Millers, Kimbrels, Brittons or Betancii of the world, but he's closer to them than you might think. So, are the Marlins ready for this jelly? He looks like Miami's closer of the future, or if A.J. Ramos goes down with an injury, the present. He could also be nice trade bait at the 2017 deadline, but that's looking at the glass half-empty, and we prefer our coffee cups bottomless when talkin' donuts.

Jeff Brigham RHP

Born: 2/16/92 Age: 25 Bats: R Throws: R Height: 6'0" Weight: 200 Entered Pro Ball: Round 4, 2014 Draft (#129 overall)

YEAR	TEAM	LVL	AGE	W	L	SV	G	GS	IP	H	HR	BB/9	K/9	K	GB%	BABIP	WHIP	ERA	FIP	DRA	VORP	WARP	cFIP	MPH
2015	RCU	A+	23	4	5	0	17	14	68	78	8	4.8	8.5	64	57%	.340	1.68	5.96	5.28	6.67	-12.4	-1.3	116	
2015	JUP	A+	23	2	2	0	6	5	33²	34	0	2.4	5.9	22	52%	.324	1.28	1.87	2.75	3.76	4.7	0.5	97	
2016	JUP	A+	24	7	8	1	27	23	122²	115	6	3.4	8.2	112	41%	.307	1.32	4.04	3.43	3.48	26.6	2.7	96	
2017	*MIA*	*MLB*	*25*	*6*	*7*	*1*	*34*	*20*	*104¹*	*114*	*14*	*4.3*	*6.3*	*73*	*56%*	*.323*	*1.57*	*5.02*	*5.06*	*5.92*	*-6.7*	*-0.7*	*141*	
2018	*MIA*	*MLB*	*26*	*4*	*6*	*0*	*22*	*17*	*118*	*115*	*16*	*5.6*	*8.7*	*114*	*56%*	*.328*	*1.60*	*4.76*	*5.31*	*5.61*	*-1.1*	*-0.1*	*132*	

Breakout: 5%   Improve: 7%   Collapse: 0%   Attrition: 5%   MLB: 7%   Comparables: *Jake Esch, Garrett Mock, Sammy Solis*

Brigham depends on a fastball that touches the upper 90s, and the question has always been whether or not he could control it. The answer has generally been no, but baby steps: the right-hander acquired in the Mat Latos trade has cut more than a walk-and-a-half off his BB/9 since he got to the organization. It's still not great, but Rome wasn't built in a day. Neither were any of the cities attempting to rival Rome that fizzled out shortly after they got started, of course, but who cares about those?

Luis Castillo RHP

Born: 12/12/92 Age: 24 Bats: R Throws: R Height: 6'2" Weight: 170 Entered Pro Ball: International Free Agent, 2012

YEAR	TEAM	LVL	AGE	W	L	SV	G	GS	IP	H	HR	BB/9	K/9	K	GB%	BABIP	WHIP	ERA	FIP	DRA	VORP	WARP	cFIP	MPH
2014	AUG	A	21	2	2	10	48	0	58²	56	6	3.8	10.1	66	46%	.316	1.38	3.07	4.00	2.59	16.1	1.7	87	
2015	GRB	A	22	4	3	4	25	7	63¹	59	1	2.7	9.0	63	53%	.326	1.23	2.98	2.74	2.20	20.1	2.1	82	
2015	JUP	A+	22	2	3	0	10	9	43²	44	2	2.9	6.4	31	50%	.308	1.33	3.50	3.67	4.50	2.7	0.3	101	
2016	JUP	A+	23	8	4	0	23	23	117²	95	2	1.4	7.0	91	50%	.271	0.96	2.07	2.46	2.17	42.8	4.4	81	
2016	JAX	AA	23	0	2	0	3	3	14	12	1	4.5	7.7	12	42%	.262	1.36	3.86	4.25	5.68	-0.9	-0.1	106	
2017	*MIA*	*MLB*	*24*	*6*	*5*	*1*	*47*	*14*	*104²*	*112*	*13*	*3.2*	*6.1*	*71*	*52%*	*.319*	*1.43*	*4.54*	*4.59*	*5.40*	*-0.1*	*0.0*	*127*	
2018	*MIA*	*MLB*	*25*	*4*	*4*	*1*	*31*	*10*	*90²*	*86*	*12*	*4.3*	*8.3*	*84*	*52%*	*.316*	*1.43*	*4.30*	*4.79*	*5.11*	*2.6*	*0.3*	*119*	

Breakout: 5%   Improve: 8%   Collapse: 2%   Attrition: 7%   MLB: 15%   Comparables: *Mayckol Guaipe, Chase Anderson, Randy Wells*

Not that one. Originally acquired from San Francisco in the Casey McGehee deal, the Marlins shipped the right-hander to San Diego as part of the Andrew Cashner trade in July, and that was that. Except it wasn't, because Colin Rea was damaged goods and was later shipped back to San Diego for Castillo. When the Marlins got him back they heaped praise on the young righty as if the whole thing never happened. He's got a fastball that can hit triple digits and could eventually command three plus pitches, but the important part is that he's still improving. He earned the Marlins' minor league pitcher of the year award last season and enters 2017 with loads of potential, and not just to confuse people because of his name and where he plays.

Wei-Yin Chen LHP

Born: 7/21/85   Age: 31   Bats: R   Throws: L   Height: 6'0"   Weight: 200   Entered Pro Ball: International Free Agent, 2012

YEAR	TEAM	LVL	AGE	W	L	SV	G	GS	IP	H	HR	BB/9	K/9	K	GB%	BABIP	WHIP	ERA	FIP	DRA	VORP	WARP	cFIP	MPH
2014	BAL	MLB	28	16	6	0	31	31	185²	193	23	1.7	6.6	136	42%	.296	1.23	3.54	3.92	4.39	9.2	1.0	100	94.4
2015	BAL	MLB	29	11	8	0	31	31	191¹	192	28	1.9	7.2	153	43%	.290	1.22	3.34	4.13	4.00	23.0	2.5	100	94.3
2016	MIA	MLB	30	5	5	0	22	22	123¹	134	22	1.8	7.3	100	42%	.302	1.28	4.96	4.54	4.74	8.5	0.9	104	93.5
2017	MIA	MLB	31	10	11	0	29	29	182¹	175	25	2.2	8.2	167	56%	.291	1.19	3.97	3.94	4.44	15.0	1.5	100	
2018	MIA	MLB	32	12	11	0	31	31	200¹	180	26	1.9	8.1	180	56%	.296	1.11	3.58	3.97	4.30	27.1	2.8	99	

Breakout: 16%   Improve: 48%   Collapse: 22%   Attrition: 19%   MLB: 88%   *Comparables: Gil Meche, Josh Johnson, Freddy Garcia*

Have you ever had a reverse commute? Chen's 2016 is what happens when the reverse commute screws you much, much harder than the commute proper. Expected to improve on his above-average line by virtue moving to the NL, he got hurt and put up a stinker of a season caused mostly by a drastically increased HR/9 and a slight drop in velocity. This year should be better. Chen is basically your league-average starter and we'll find out whether his injury caused systemic or merely temporary problems. If he's healthy he should return to his sweet spot of "good enough" and the Marlins could use it. At $15.5 million with pricier options through 2021 he's not exactly cheap by the team's standards, though that probably says more about them than him.

Adam Conley LHP

Born: 5/24/90   Age: 27   Bats: L   Throws: L   Height: 6'3"   Weight: 200   Entered Pro Ball: Round 2, 2011 Draft (#72 overall)

YEAR	TEAM	LVL	AGE	W	L	SV	G	GS	IP	H	HR	BB/9	K/9	K	GB%	BABIP	WHIP	ERA	FIP	DRA	VORP	WARP	cFIP	MPH
2014	NWO	AAA	24	3	5	0	12	11	60	65	3	3.9	7.2	48	53%	.333	1.52	6.00	4.20	4.22	10.1	1.0	102	
2015	NWO	AAA	25	9	3	0	19	18	107	85	4	3.4	6.8	81	48%	.265	1.17	2.52	3.83	4.12	14.0	1.4	94	
2015	MIA	MLB	25	4	1	0	15	11	67	65	7	2.8	7.9	59	41%	.304	1.28	3.76	3.83	4.20	6.2	0.7	104	95.2
2016	MIA	MLB	26	8	6	0	25	25	133¹	125	13	4.2	8.4	124	41%	.300	1.40	3.85	4.24	5.14	3.3	0.3	109	94.3
2017	MIA	MLB	27	7	8	0	24	24	120	111	11	3.5	8.3	111	60%	.296	1.32	3.90	3.84	4.37	10.8	1.1	100	
2018	MIA	MLB	28	9	9	0	29	29	181²	142	17	4.2	10.0	202	60%	.300	1.25	3.53	3.93	4.26	21.2	2.2	95	

Breakout: 26%   Improve: 49%   Collapse: 26%   Attrition: 30%   MLB: 88%   *Comparables: Jimmy Nelson, Josh Outman, Justin Germano*

Conley was slated to return from the DL on Sunday, September 25, and to get him work right away the Marlins pushed back Jose Fernandez's scheduled start to a Monday he'd never see. After Fernandez's death and a canceled Sunday game, Conley threw 45 pitches over three shutout innings that Monday and said afterward he had "never been more tired in his life." Conley started 25 games for the Fish and escaped with a sub-4.00 ERA. He could stand to walk fewer guys, but otherwise he's good.

Odrisamer Despaigne RHP

Born: 4/4/87   Age: 30   Bats: R   Throws: R   Height: 6'0"   Weight: 200   Entered Pro Ball: International Free Agent, 2014

YEAR	TEAM	LVL	AGE	W	L	SV	G	GS	IP	H	HR	BB/9	K/9	K	GB%	BABIP	WHIP	ERA	FIP	DRA	VORP	WARP	cFIP	MPH
2014	ELP	AAA	27	1	3	0	5	5	23²	36	3	4.9	11.0	29	0%	.440	2.07	7.61	4.67					
2014	SDN	MLB	27	4	7	0	16	16	96¹	85	6	3.0	6.1	65	55%	.267	1.21	3.36	3.72	4.82	0.1	0.0	113	93.8
2015	SDN	MLB	28	5	9	0	34	18	125²	142	17	2.3	4.9	69	53%	.298	1.38	5.80	4.80	5.31	-4.2	-0.5	117	94.1
2016	BAL	MLB	29	0	2	0	16	0	27¹	32	3	4.9	5.6	17	38%	.337	1.72	5.60	5.05	6.89	-5.8	-0.6	132	95.2
2016	NOR	AAA	29	1	9	0	18	17	88¹	91	5	2.8	7.1	70	53%	.319	1.34	3.87	3.44	4.50	8.1	0.8	99	
2016	MIA	MLB	29	0	0	0	3	0	3	4	0	3.0	0.0	0	50%	.333	1.67	9.00	4.19	6.28	-0.4	0.0	128	94.3
2017	MIA	MLB	30	1	1	0	25	0	26²	27	3	3.6	6.7	20	50%	.294	1.40	4.71	4.48	4.99	-0.2	0.0	100	
2018	MIA	MLB	31	2	1	0	35	0	36²	35	4	3.6	7.4	30	50%	.307	1.34	4.11	4.57	4.94	0.8	0.1	112	

Breakout: 10%   Improve: 34%   Collapse: 17%   Attrition: 16%   MLB: 61%   *Comparables: Jaret Wright, Shawn Hill, Brian Duensing*

It ultimately cannot be a great sign that the perpetually disappointing Marlins and Padres are constantly exchanging players, both directly—as in the Andrew Cashner deal—and indirectly—as in the case of Despaigne. Despaigne started the calendar year with the Padres, was traded to the Orioles in February and was claimed off waivers by the Marlins in late September. His is a fringe big-league arm, albeit one under club control until 2021. A sinker/cutter specialist, he's a Marlin for now, at least until A.J. Preller calls again.

Brian Ellington RHP

Born: 8/4/90   Age: 26   Bats: R   Throws: R   Height: 6'3"   Weight: 215   Entered Pro Ball: Round 16, 2012 Draft (#497 overall)

YEAR	TEAM	LVL	AGE	W	L	SV	G	GS	IP	H	HR	BB/9	K/9	K	GB%	BABIP	WHIP	ERA	FIP	DRA	VORP	WARP	cFIP	MPH
2014	JUP	A+	23	2	2	0	35	0	47¹	51	2	4.6	10.6	56	32%	.371	1.58	4.75	3.29	3.08	11.1	1.1	92	
2015	JAX	AA	24	4	1	0	25	0	43	28	0	2.7	9.8	47	37%	.259	0.95	2.51	2.09	2.55	10.4	1.1	83	
2015	MIA	MLB	24	2	1	0	23	0	25	17	1	4.7	6.5	18	39%	.225	1.20	2.88	4.04	4.99	-0.8	-0.1	118	99.5
2016	NWO	AAA	25	1	0	2	32	0	34²	17	2	6.8	14.0	54	31%	.238	1.24	3.12	3.78	2.60	9.1	0.9	85	
2016	MIA	MLB	25	4	2	0	32	0	33	27	2	4.4	8.7	32	31%	.281	1.30	2.45	3.67	4.81	0.6	0.1	113	100.4
2017	MIA	MLB	26	2	2	0	35	0	37	34	4	4.2	8.9	37	49%	.294	1.38	4.32	4.11	4.68	1.0	0.1	100	
2018	MIA	MLB	27	2	1	0	39	0	41	31	5	4.4	10.6	48	49%	.291	1.24	3.71	4.11	4.46	3.0	0.3	100	

Breakout: 31%   Improve: 43%   Collapse: 10%   Attrition: 29%   MLB: 64%   *Comparables: Preston Claiborne, Warner Madrigal, Travis Schlichting*

The Luke Skywalker to Craig Breslow's Ben Kenobi, Ellington credits the itinerant Red Sox castoff with saving his career thanks to three pearls of wisdom: a) "Be as simple as you can," b) "Don't try to do anything more," and c) "Don't be anybody else but yourself." It's boilerplate, but just as it was for Luke with Obi-Wan it's as much about the messenger as about the message. Breslow made Ellington feel like he belonged in the majors, and that was all Ellington needed. He enters 2017 potentially having figured that out, though he'll face the future without his mentor.

Jake Esch   RHP

Born: 3/27/90   Age: 27   Bats: R   Throws: R   Height: 6'3"   Weight: 205   Entered Pro Ball: Round 11, 2011 Draft (#343 overall)

YEAR	TEAM	LVL	AGE	W	L	SV	G	GS	IP	H	HR	BB/9	K/9	K	GB%	BABIP	WHIP	ERA	FIP	DRA	VORP	WARP	cFIP	MPH
2014	JUP	A+	24	6	6	0	25	24	135²	147	7	2.3	7.0	105	53%	.326	1.33	4.05	3.38	3.47	32.0	3.2	90	
2015	JAX	AA	25	6	5	0	15	15	85¹	69	5	3.5	7.2	68	47%	.263	1.20	3.48	3.70	4.26	7.9	0.9	100	
2015	NWO	AAA	25	1	3	0	6	6	30	41	3	2.7	6	20	42%	.369	1.67	5.40	4.67	5.39	-0.3	0.0	110	
2016	JAX	AA	26	10	9	0	22	22	118¹	117	8	2.8	6.2	82	45%	.296	1.30	4.03	3.88	6.69	-21.0	-2.3	109	
2016	NWO	AAA	26	2	1	0	4	4	23²	26	2	3.4	5.3	14	42%	.320	1.48	5.70	4.90	5.19	0.4	0.0	109	
2016	MIA	MLB	26	0	1	0	3	3	13	17	4	4.2	6.9	10	50%	.342	1.77	5.54	7.26	5.01	0.5	0.1	107	92.9
2017	MIA	MLB	27	0	1	0	2	2	10	11	1	3.4	6.1	7	61%	.296	1.47	4.75	4.27	5.27	-0.1	0.0	100	
2018	MIA	MLB	28	6	8	0	21	21	124	109	17	4.6	8.9	123	61%	.303	1.39	4.46	4.97	5.34	2.6	0.3	125	

Breakout: 3%   Improve: 7%   Collapse: 1%   Attrition: 11%   MLB: 13%   Comparables: Travis Chick, Matt Fox, Virgil Vasquez

Esch sketched a 4.31 ERA in the minors before being was promoted to Miami at the end of August to replace an injured David Phelps. He wasn't great in the majors, though his ERA improved at every level as he was rushed through the system in the fabled, disheveled "Marlins Manner," flying to the big-league club as fast as possible.

Jose Fernandez   RHP

Born: 7/31/92   Age: 24   Bats: R   Throws: R   Height: 6'3"   Weight: 240   Entered Pro Ball: Round 1, 2011 Draft (#14 overall)

YEAR	TEAM	LVL	AGE	W	L	SV	G	GS	IP	H	HR	BB/9	K/9	K	GB%	BABIP	WHIP	ERA	FIP	DRA	VORP	WARP	cFIP	MPH
2014	MIA	MLB	21	4	2	0	8	8	51²	36	4	2.3	12.2	70	50%	.271	0.95	2.44	2.15	1.88	17.0	1.9	67	98.6
2015	JUP	A+	22	1	1	0	4	4	19²	18	1	1.8	11.4	25	38%	.370	1.12	3.20	1.89	1.90	6.9	0.8	72	
2015	MIA	MLB	22	6	1	0	11	11	64²	61	4	1.9	11.0	79	44%	.343	1.16	2.92	2.26	3.03	14.7	1.6	77	99.2
2016	MIA	MLB	23	16	8	0	29	29	182¹	149	13	2.7	12.5	253	44%	.332	1.12	2.86	2.34	2.23	63.3	6.5	61	98.6

Jose Fernandez was the absolute value of baseball. He wasn't just good at it; he was the best. He wasn't just pleased with his work, in concept and execution, he was the most joyful player in the game. His story wasn't just breathtaking, terrifying and inspiring, it was incredible and uplifting toward the limits of both imagination and creative license. He was also baseball's avatar of positivity, the rare fire-breathing righty who wasn't also a fire-breathing jerk. He did everything right. And we lost him. However Fernandez is judged going forward, baseball now has its James Dean, Grace Kelly, Jimi Hendrix or to whomever you want to compare him. It's tempting so say these are cases of unrealized potential, but that's not right. Like those legends, Fernandez's potential was fully realized. He didn't leave anything on the table. He just left us sitting alone at the same table, forced to contemplate life without him.

Jarlin Garcia   LHP

Born: 1/18/93   Age: 24   Bats: L   Throws: L   Height: 6'3"   Weight: 215   Entered Pro Ball: International Free Agent, 2010

YEAR	TEAM	LVL	AGE	W	L	SV	G	GS	IP	H	HR	BB/9	K/9	K	GB%	BABIP	WHIP	ERA	FIP	DRA	VORP	WARP	cFIP	MPH
2014	GRB	A	21	10	5	0	25	25	133²	152	13	1.4	7.5	111	49%	.332	1.29	4.38	3.77	3.25	32.5	3.4	86	
2015	JUP	A+	22	3	5	0	18	18	97	96	4	2.1	6.4	69	41%	.303	1.23	3.06	3.05	3.73	14.5	1.6	96	
2015	JAX	AA	22	1	3	0	7	7	36²	38	4	4.2	8.6	35	41%	.324	1.50	4.91	4.20	4.34	3.1	0.3	104	
2016	JAX	AA	23	1	3	0	9	9	39²	38	4	2.5	6.1	27	48%	.274	1.24	4.54	4.25	4.87	1.0	0.1	104	
2017	MIA	MLB	24	3	4	0	11	11	54	61	8	3.4	5.5	33	61%	.321	1.51	4.99	5.06	5.91	-2.1	-0.2	141	
2018	MIA	MLB	25	5	6	0	18	18	104²	101	14	4.7	8.3	97	61%	.318	1.48	4.54	5.07	5.38	1.8	0.2	127	

Breakout: 3%   Improve: 4%   Collapse: 10%   Attrition: 17%   MLB: 20%   Comparables: Bruce Billings, Justin Marks, Erik Davis

Talk about a tease. Garcia was called up to Miami in May after a particularly rough stretch for the bullpen, but was sent back to Double-A days later without getting into a game. One of Miami's top pitching prospects, he figures to make the roster coming out of spring training on the strength of a mid-90s four-seamer and secondary offerings of a hard slider and changeup. He's still only 24, so there's ample reason for the Fish to like him even outside of the fact he's a fire-breathing lefty.

Braxton Garrett   LHP

Born: 8/5/97   Age: 19   Bats: L   Throws: L   Height: 6'3"   Weight: 190   Entered Pro Ball: Round 1, 2016 Draft (#7 overall)

A lefty curveballer on his best day is near the top of the list of the sport's aesthetic marvels. These are your Barry Zitos, Cliff Lees and Rich Hills at the peak of their powers, spitting medium-hot fire, bending pitches to perfect spots or freezing batters with the mildest of cheeses and never letting up. Garrett, the seventh overall pick in last year's draft, is a budding curveball artist. The Scott Boras client signed above slot a few hours before the deadline rather than attend Vanderbilt. In the wake of the slow-moving Tyler Kolek first-round-pick disaster, the team has said Garrett depends on a pitch that's less taxing on the arm than that of a power repertoire. Maybe they're a tad snakebitten, but you can't blame them for becoming infected with Garrett-type. If even a fraction of the purple prose on Garrett's bender is the real deal there's a lot to like here.

Tom Koehler   RHP

Born: 6/29/86   Age: 31   Bats: R   Throws: R   Height: 6'3"   Weight: 235   Entered Pro Ball: Round 18, 2008 Draft (#538 overall)

YEAR	TEAM	LVL	AGE	W	L	SV	G	GS	IP	H	HR	BB/9	K/9	K	GB%	BABIP	WHIP	ERA	FIP	DRA	VORP	WARP	cFIP	MPH
2014	MIA	MLB	28	10	10	0	32	32	191¹	177	16	3.3	7.2	153	46%	.290	1.30	3.81	3.81	4.27	12.1	1.3	108	95.6
2015	MIA	MLB	29	11	14	0	32	31	187¹	180	22	3.7	6.6	137	49%	.283	1.37	4.08	4.56	4.93	3.0	0.3	113	94.6
2016	MIA	MLB	30	9	13	0	33	33	176²	176	22	4.2	7.5	147	44%	.298	1.47	4.33	4.64	5.22	2.8	0.3	115	94.4
2017	MIA	MLB	31	8	10	0	28	28	148	138	16	3.8	8.0	133	47%	.291	1.35	4.27	4.16	4.76	6.9	0.7	100	
2018	MIA	MLB	32	8	9	0	26	26	156¹	137	17	3.9	8.9	155	47%	.312	1.31	3.79	4.20	4.55	15.6	1.6	103	

Breakout: 21%   Improve: 42%   Collapse: 16%   Attrition: 17%   MLB: 73%   Comparables: Tim Stauffer, Sergio Mitre, Randy Wells

His name anagrams to "Let homer? Ok!" which is unfortunate. He gave up 1.1 HR/9 in 2016, which is neither great nor terrible, and was basically the exact same rate at which the aging and revered King Felix Hernandez let up long balls last season. In fact, Koehler's and Hernandez's lines were shockingly similar all the way down last year, and Koehler logged more innings. At $3.5 million, it was a lot cheaper than Hernandez's $25 million, and while it's hard to get excited about a player like this he's an example of the Marlins doing something right without getting royally screwed.

Tyler Kolek   RHP

Born: 12/15/95 Age: 21   Bats: R   Throws: R   Height: 6'5"   Weight: 260   Entered Pro Ball: Round 1, 2014 Draft (#2 overall)

YEAR	TEAM	LVL	AGE	W	L	SV	G	GS	IP	H	HR	BB/9	K/9	K	GB%	BABIP	WHIP	ERA	FIP	DRA	VORP	WARP	cFIP	MPH
2015	GRB	A	19	4	10	0	25	25	108²	108	7	5.1	6.7	81	51%	.298	1.56	4.56	4.87	8.26	-36.6	-3.9	123	
2017	MIA	MLB	21	2	3	0	8	8	32²	38	5	6.1	4.7	17	59%	.320	1.85	6.33	6.29	7.45	-6.8	-0.7	175	
2018	MIA	MLB	22	5	10	0	26	26	153¹	152	23	7.3	7.7	132	59%	.315	1.81	5.84	6.52	6.87	-15.0	-1.6	161	

Breakout: 1%   Improve: 1%   Collapse: 0%   Attrition: 1%   MLB: 1%   *Comparables: Edgar Olmos, Parker Bridwell, Elvis Araujo*

The former no. 2 overall pick hasn't had anything go right since signing with the Marlins for $6 million in 2014, the third most-ever for a high school pitcher. He capped off a disappointing 2015 season at Greensboro by having Tommy John surgery in early April. It would be an understatement to say things look dicey and you have to imagine that the Marlins will throw good money after bad to make it better given where Kolek was drafted, even if they're ultimately just buying lottery tickets. Hey, you gotta be in it to win it.

Raudel Lazo   LHP

Born: 4/12/89 Age: 28   Bats: L   Throws: L   Height: 5'9"   Weight: 180   Entered Pro Ball: International Free Agent, 2011

YEAR	TEAM	LVL	AGE	W	L	SV	G	GS	IP	H	HR	BB/9	K/9	K	GB%	BABIP	WHIP	ERA	FIP	DRA	VORP	WARP	cFIP	MPH
2015	JUP	A+	26	1	1	1	8	0	12	7	0	1.5	9.0	12	43%	.233	0.75	1.50	1.67	2.49	3.0	0.3	83	
2015	JAX	AA	26	3	2	0	18	0	29¹	29	2	2.1	9.8	32	39%	.351	1.23	2.15	2.83	2.90	6.0	0.6	89	
2015	MIA	MLB	26	0	0	0	7	0	5²	5	1	3.2	7.9	5	29%	.250	1.24	3.18	4.75	5.19	-0.3	0.0	110	92.3
2016	JAX	AA	27	0	1	2	10	0	11²	10	0	0.8	6.2	8	31%	.286	0.94	3.09	2.46	4.25	0.6	0.1	100	
2016	NWO	AAA	27	2	0	2	24	0	30¹	28	1	3.0	8.0	27	52%	.297	1.25	1.78	3.56	3.58	4.7	0.5	95	
2017	MIA	MLB	28	2	1	0	40	0	42¹	44	5	3.2	6.9	32	52%	.319	1.38	4.34	4.36	5.24	-0.6	-0.1	120	
2018	MIA	MLB	29	2	1	1	43	0	57	45	7	4.5	9.5	60	52%	.290	1.30	4.00	4.46	4.83	1.9	0.2	110	

Breakout: 5%   Improve: 10%   Collapse: 8%   Attrition: 15%   MLB: 20%   *Comparables: Josh Judy, Joe Bisenius, Justin Freeman*

Lazo's natural talent is beyond dispute, but his body hasn't let him harness it. He had two Tommy John surgeries before finally landing in the majors last September. He was his live-armed self throughout the year at Double and Triple A, using a low-90s four-seamer and a nasty 80 mph slider, but didn't pitch for the big-league club. He's 27 years old and he's a lefty, so you have to figure he's Miami-bound at some point.

Brett Lilek   LHP

Born: 8/10/93 Age: 23   Bats: L   Throws: L   Height: 6'4"   Weight: 220   Entered Pro Ball: Round 2, 2015 Draft (#50 overall)

YEAR	TEAM	LVL	AGE	W	L	SV	G	GS	IP	H	HR	BB/9	K/9	K	GB%	BABIP	WHIP	ERA	FIP	DRA	VORP	WARP	cFIP	MPH
2015	BAT	A-	21	1	2	0	11	10	35	30	1	1.8	11.1	43	44%	.333	1.06	3.34	2.20	1.65	14.1	1.5	68	
2016	GRB	A	22	0	1	0	7	5	16	19	1	9.0	7.3	13	43%	.348	2.19	5.06	6.15	10.34	-9.6	-1.0	134	
2017	MIA	MLB	23	2	3	0	9	9	32²	39	6	5.9	5.7	21	72%	.325	1.84	6.48	6.44	7.62	-7.5	-0.8	180	
2018	MIA	MLB	24	3	7	0	19	19	113	120	22	7.0	7.7	97	72%	.321	1.84	6.29	7.03	7.40	-14.5	-1.5	174	

Breakout: 2%   Improve: 2%   Collapse: 0%   Attrition: 2%   MLB: 2%   *Comparables: Tim Adleman, Josh Wall, Joseph Biagini*

Lilek pitched a grand total of 16 innings early in 2016, ineffectually fighting through the strained shoulder that would shelve him through the final four months. He's a big lefty with a fastball/curveball/changeup mix out of Arizona, and triples as a certified sneakerhead and accomplished tweeter. He's not just baseball-young, he's just young overall. He is, however, baseball-young, so there could be a bright future here unless the league can effectively stand their ground against his arsenal.

Jeff Locke   LHP

Born: 11/20/87 Age: 29   Bats: L   Throws: L   Height: 6'0"   Weight: 200   Entered Pro Ball: Round 2, 2006 Draft (#51 overall)

YEAR	TEAM	LVL	AGE	W	L	SV	G	GS	IP	H	HR	BB/9	K/9	K	GB%	BABIP	WHIP	ERA	FIP	DRA	VORP	WARP	cFIP	MPH
2014	IND	AAA	26	3	1	0	9	9	50	51	5	4.0	6.7	37	55%	.299	1.46	4.14	4.62	4.05	9.4	0.9	100	
2014	PIT	MLB	26	7	6	0	21	21	131¹	127	16	2.7	6.1	89	53%	.278	1.27	3.91	4.34	4.18	9.6	1.1	108	93.1
2015	PIT	MLB	27	8	11	0	30	30	168¹	179	15	3.2	6.9	129	53%	.312	1.42	4.49	3.98	4.56	9.7	1.0	109	93.9
2016	PIT	MLB	28	9	8	0	30	19	127¹	151	17	3.1	5.2	73	51%	.315	1.53	5.44	4.88	5.73	-6.2	-0.6	119	94.2
2017	MIA	MLB	29	8	10	0	24	24	144	145	17	3.2	6.9	110	48%	.292	1.36	4.43	4.37	4.95	3.7	0.4	100	
2018	MIA	MLB	30	11	12	0	32	32	202²	183	23	3.3	7.6	171	48%	.296	1.27	3.99	4.43	4.80	15.7	1.6	111	

Breakout: 31%   Improve: 45%   Collapse: 32%   Attrition: 23%   MLB: 90%   *Comparables: John Lannan, Charlie Morton, Sergio Mitre*

It's sort of astounding that Locke made it through the entire season on the Pirates' roster. He was atrocious as a starter, posting a 5.86 ERA in 19 starts. He was awful as a reliever, allowing batters to hit .322/.365/.500 in 21 innings. Southpaws hit .274/.329/.423 against him. Folks, the last time a Locke looked this *LOST*, Jacob got stabbed in the back. Locke is no longer terribly young, no longer terribly cheap (he made $3 million last season) and no longer terribly close to his All-Star 2013 campaign. He's just terrible, and the Smoke Monster killed his Pirates career.

Dustin McGowan   RHP

Born: 3/24/82   Age: 35   Bats: R   Throws: R   Height: 6'3"   Weight: 235   Entered Pro Ball: Round 1, 2000 Draft (#33 overall)

YEAR	TEAM	LVL	AGE	W	L	SV	G	GS	IP	H	HR	BB/9	K/9	K	GB%	BABIP	WHIP	ERA	FIP	DRA	VORP	WARP	cFIP	MPH
2014	TOR	MLB	32	5	3	1	53	8	82	80	13	3.6	6.7	61	39%	.275	1.38	4.17	5.05	5.36	-6.4	-0.7	119	97.6
2015	PHI	MLB	33	1	2	0	14	1	23¹	29	7	7.7	8.1	21	42%	.314	2.10	6.94	7.83	6.05	-3.3	-0.4	118	97.3
2015	LEH	AAA	33	2	2	15	31	1	39²	41	2	5.4	6.4	28	45%	.300	1.64	4.08	4.29	9.93	-21.9	-2.2	125	
2016	MIA	MLB	34	1	3	1	55	0	67	49	7	4.4	8.5	63	55%	.241	1.22	2.82	4.23	3.85	8.4	0.9	95	97.7
2017	MIA	MLB	35	2	2	0	45	0	48	45	5	4.1	8.3	44	49%	.288	1.37	4.52	4.19	4.84	0.4	0.0	100	97.7
2018	MIA	MLB	36	2	1	0	45	0	47²	42	5	4.0	9.2	49	49%	.308	1.33	3.85	4.27	4.62	2.7	0.3	104	

Breakout: 23%   Improve: 31%   Collapse: 20%   Attrition: 14%   MLB: 62%   *Comparables: Joel Peralta, Randy Flores, Luis Ayala*

There was a moment around the time *Tyler Perry's Meet the Browns* opened in theaters when it looked like McGowan might turn into a top-line starter with the Blue Jays. From then until last year, things were more or less dumps for McGowan. In last year's annual we wrote: "To watch McGowan pitch is to be absolutely convinced that he has the stuff to be a major-league reliever. To watch him pitch is to be absolutely unconvinced that he'll rein in any of it enough to be effective in any role." Well, he did it! McGowan pitched 67 innings with a 2.45 ERA over 55 games, which is exactly what you'd expect his best self at this point of his career. Even if he doesn't do it again, kudos to him for proving us wrong. Between his injury history and his public struggle with Type-1 diabetes—he wears an insulin pump during games—it's amazing that he's still here at all, let alone thriving at age 34.

Justin Nicolino   LHP

Born: 11/22/91   Age: 25   Bats: L   Throws: L   Height: 6'3"   Weight: 195   Entered Pro Ball: Round 2, 2010 Draft (#80 overall)

YEAR	TEAM	LVL	AGE	W	L	SV	G	GS	IP	H	HR	BB/9	K/9	K	GB%	BABIP	WHIP	ERA	FIP	DRA	VORP	WARP	cFIP	MPH
2014	JAX	AA	22	14	4	0	28	28	170¹	162	10	1.1	4.3	81	49%	.267	1.07	2.85	3.44	3.35	35.6	3.8	98	
2015	NWO	AAA	23	7	7	0	20	20	115	134	11	2.3	4.9	63	52%	.324	1.42	3.52	4.61	4.17	14.5	1.5	101	
2015	MIA	MLB	23	5	4	0	12	12	74	72	8	2.4	2.8	23	46%	.259	1.24	4.01	4.88	6.67	-13.0	-1.4	129	91.8
2016	NWO	AAA	24	7	6	0	14	14	85	87	10	1.4	5.2	49	54%	.282	1.18	4.13	4.56	2.56	26.3	2.7	90	
2016	MIA	MLB	24	3	6	0	18	13	79¹	96	8	2.3	4.2	37	49%	.317	1.46	4.99	4.43	5.96	-5.6	-0.6	122	92.4
2017	MIA	MLB	25	2	2	0	5	5	28	30	3	2.4	5.4	17	46%	.295	1.32	4.19	4.29	4.69	1.5	0.2	100	
2018	MIA	MLB	26	10	10	0	30	30	190²	168	19	3.2	8.0	169	46%	.302	1.24	3.74	4.17	4.52	19.0	2.0	103	

Breakout: 19%   Improve: 36%   Collapse: 26%   Attrition: 38%   MLB: 80%   *Comparables: Justin Germano, Cody Anderson, Yorman Bazardo*

Talisman: The Magical Quest Game is a largely forgotten fantasy board game that's exactly what it sounds like: a battle to the death between orcs, maidens, fireballs and all that. The coolest thing about it is while every character has a fighting score, they also have a craft score, and a player can always choose to battle with craft instead of strength. This is the nerd's dream: to be able to slay giants using one's wiles instead of their muscles. Nicolino, one of several Marlins on the fifth starter/bullpen fringe, has the craft. He pitched out of the bullpen in September after being a starter at every level of the minor leagues. Now he'll fight for a rotation spot, boasting a four-pitch arsenal, the breadth of which makes up for the fact that none of those pitches is particularly fast. He's a junkballer. He's the nerd's dream.

Nefi Ogando   RHP

Born: 6/3/89   Age: 28   Bats: R   Throws: R   Height: 6'0"   Weight: 230   Entered Pro Ball: International Free Agent, 2010

YEAR	TEAM	LVL	AGE	W	L	SV	G	GS	IP	H	HR	BB/9	K/9	K	GB%	BABIP	WHIP	ERA	FIP	DRA	VORP	WARP	cFIP	MPH
2014	REA	AA	25	5	1	7	48	0	56	64	6	4.5	9.2	57	51%	.352	1.64	6.27	4.53	4.29	3.5	0.4	98	
2015	REA	AA	26	2	3	2	24	0	34²	25	2	4.9	8.6	33	44%	.258	1.27	2.86	3.85	5.59	-3.3	-0.4	107	
2015	LEH	AAA	26	2	2	1	21	0	28¹	27	1	3.8	7	22	46%	.295	1.38	2.86	3.76	5.92	-3.2	-0.3	106	
2015	PHI	MLB	26	0	0	0	4	0	4	7	0	4.5	4.5	2	47%	.412	2.25	9.00	3.66	4.61	0.0	0.0	110	97.6
2016	NWO	AAA	27	0	0	2	22	0	24¹	18	2	4.1	7.0	19	56%	.235	1.19	3.33	4.95	5.84	-2.4	-0.2	105	
2016	MIA	MLB	27	0	0	0	14	0	15²	10	0	4.6	4.6	8	61%	.204	1.15	2.30	3.70	5.24	-0.5	0.0	111	97.6
2017	MIA	MLB	28	2	1	0	39	0	41¹	41	5	3.9	6.8	31	50%	.310	1.42	4.50	4.66	5.41	-1.5	-0.2	125	
2018	MIA	MLB	29	1	1	0	28	0	37¹	31	4	4.6	10.0	42	50%	.312	1.33	3.72	4.13	4.47	2.7	0.3	101	

Breakout: 4%   Improve: 7%   Collapse: 10%   Attrition: 11%   MLB: 17%   *Comparables: Frank Mata, Leyson Septimo, Cody Hall*

Ogando ping-ponged between Triple A and the majors in 2016, and ping-pong diplomacy dictates we say he did OK. It sure looks like he did, with an ERA in a handful of innings not markedly different from the ERA he put up in two handfuls in New Orleans. You don't have to dig deep to see that what Ogando is doing isn't sustainable, though. In the Big Easy, his DRA was 5.84, not terribly different from his 5.24 mark in his Marlins cameo. That's not good, and no amount of spin can change that.

David Phelps   RHP

Born: 10/9/86   Age: 30   Bats: R   Throws: R   Height: 6'2"   Weight: 200   Entered Pro Ball: Round 14, 2008 Draft (#440 overall)

YEAR	TEAM	LVL	AGE	W	L	SV	G	GS	IP	H	HR	BB/9	K/9	K	GB%	BABIP	WHIP	ERA	FIP	DRA	VORP	WARP	cFIP	MPH
2014	NYA	MLB	27	5	5	1	32	17	113	115	13	3.7	7.3	92	44%	.301	1.42	4.38	4.43	4.46	4.1	0.4	114	92.7
2015	MIA	MLB	28	4	8	0	23	19	112	119	11	2.7	6.2	77	43%	.303	1.36	4.50	4.05	5.08	-0.3	0.0	114	93.0
2016	MIA	MLB	29	7	6	4	64	5	86²	61	5	3.9	11.8	114	48%	.286	1.14	2.28	2.84	2.85	21.4	2.2	73	96.1
2017	MIA	MLB	30	4	5	0	48	8	85	75	10	3.5	9.8	92	48%	.294	1.27	3.93	3.81	4.38	6.3	0.7	100	
2018	MIA	MLB	31	6	5	0	69	11	124¹	102	14	3.3	9.6	132	48%	.300	1.18	3.55	3.93	4.26	13.9	1.4	95	

Breakout: 18%   Improve: 47%   Collapse: 23%   Attrition: 11%   MLB: 92%   *Comparables: C.J. Wilson, Clay Buchholz, Jason Hammel*

Phelps has bounced from the rotation to the bullpen for much of his career, but last season may keep him as a reliever because he was so dominant in a late-inning role. In relief he can fully harness his wily electricity in whatever voltage is needed. For his career Phelps has a 3.30 ERA with 10.6 strikeouts per nine innings as a reliever, compared to a 4.21 ERA with 7.3 strikeouts per nine innings as a starter. He has value in either role, but only relief work gives him a chance to be an impact arm.

A.J. Ramos   RHP

Born: 9/20/86   Age: 30   Bats: R   Throws: R   Height: 5'10"   Weight: 200   Entered Pro Ball: Round 21, 2009 Draft (#638 overall)

YEAR	TEAM	LVL	AGE	W	L	SV	G	GS	IP	H	HR	BB/9	K/9	K	GB%	BABIP	WHIP	ERA	FIP	DRA	VORP	WARP	cFIP	MPH
2014	MIA	MLB	27	7	0	0	68	0	64	36	1	6.0	10.3	73	45%	.233	1.23	2.11	3.18	3.74	5.3	0.6	101	94.4
2015	MIA	MLB	28	2	4	32	71	0	70¹	45	6	3.3	11.1	87	44%	.252	1.01	2.30	3.03	2.98	13.5	1.4	82	95.8
2016	MIA	MLB	29	1	4	40	67	0	64	52	1	4.9	10.3	73	44%	.309	1.36	2.81	2.94	3.41	11.1	1.1	98	95.4
2017	MIA	MLB	30	3	3	30	55	0	58²	48	6	4.3	10.6	69	42%	.285	1.27	3.72	3.68	4.18	4.8	0.5	92	
2018	MIA	MLB	31	3	1	26	61	0	64¹	47	7	4.1	10.7	76	42%	.285	1.17	3.52	3.88	4.21	6.5	0.7	92	

Breakout: 26%   Improve: 46%   Collapse: 32%   Attrition: 14%   MLB: 90%   *Comparables: Michael Gonzalez, Darren O'Day, Jose Valverde*

Are 40 saves good? Yes, they're probably good. Like RBIs, the save stat tells us very little about exactly how much each one is worth, but get a lot of them and mom's gonna be proud no matter what. Ramos beat out both Proven Closer Fernando Rodney and Ideal Closer Kyle Barraclough for his job, and acquitted himself nicely. He may not keep the gig and control issues will always loom, but Ramos has proven himself to be a high-leverage arm no matter the role.

Drew Steckenrider   RHP

Born: 1/10/91   Age: 26   Bats: R   Throws: R   Height: 6'5"   Weight: 215   Entered Pro Ball: Round 8, 2012 Draft (#257 overall)

YEAR	TEAM	LVL	AGE	W	L	SV	G	GS	IP	H	HR	BB/9	K/9	K	GB%	BABIP	WHIP	ERA	FIP	DRA	VORP	WARP	cFIP	MPH
2015	GRB	A	24	1	3	0	10	5	39¹	38	2	3.9	7.8	34	47%	.316	1.40	2.75	3.71	3.62	6.4	0.7	99	
2015	JUP	A+	24	4	3	1	15	8	56²	59	2	4.0	7.0	44	56%	.324	1.48	3.18	3.50	5.23	-1.9	-0.2	109	
2016	JUP	A+	25	0	0	1	6	0	10	2	0	1.8	15.3	17	64%	.143	0.40	0.00	0.45	1.64	3.8	0.4	70	
2016	JAX	AA	25	1	0	6	24	0	30¹	12	0	3.0	11.6	39	54%	.197	0.73	1.48	1.84	1.59	10.6	1.1	68	
2016	NWO	AAA	25	0	1	7	10	0	11²	11	1	5.4	11.6	15	52%	.333	1.54	5.40	4.06	2.30	3.5	0.4	87	
2017	MIA	MLB	26	3	2	1	31	5	48²	48	6	4.1	7.8	42	51%	.317	1.43	4.39	4.49	5.20	0.6	0.1	122	
2018	MIA	MLB	27	1	1	0	13	3	34	30	4	4.9	10.3	39	51%	.323	1.42	3.99	4.43	4.73	1.9	0.2	109	

Breakout: 18%   Improve: 23%   Collapse: 7%   Attrition: 23%   MLB: 31%   *Comparables: Mike Fiers, Darin Downs, Jose Valdez*

Steckenrider had a busy 2016. The power-relieving righty started off dominating at High-A Jupiter and Double-A Jacksonville before running into trouble at Triple-A New Orleans, a not uncommon occurrence in a Marlins organization that likes to rush its players up the ladder. The good news for Steckenrider is that his ratios were consistent, so while his ERA ballooned his DRA barely budged. A converted outfielder—he *volunteered* to help a beleaguered bullpen at the University of Tennessee—his four-seamer tops out at 95 mph and he features a hard slider as his main secondary option.

Junichi Tazawa   RHP

Born: 6/6/86   Age: 31   Bats: R   Throws: R   Height: 5'11"   Weight: 200   Entered Pro Ball: International Free Agent, 2008

YEAR	TEAM	LVL	AGE	W	L	SV	G	GS	IP	H	HR	BB/9	K/9	K	GB%	BABIP	WHIP	ERA	FIP	DRA	VORP	WARP	cFIP	MPH
2014	BOS	MLB	28	4	3	0	71	0	63	58	5	2.4	9.1	64	38%	.303	1.19	2.86	2.97	3.84	4.5	0.5	95	96.2
2015	BOS	MLB	29	2	7	3	61	0	58²	65	5	2.0	8.6	56	42%	.349	1.33	4.14	3.02	4.08	4.1	0.4	96	95.9
2016	BOS	MLB	30	3	2	0	53	0	49²	47	9	2.5	8.6	54	40%	.292	1.23	4.17	4.19	3.80	6.5	0.7	95	95.0
2017	MIA	MLB	31	3	3	0	55	0	58²	56	8	2.8	9.1	59	39%	.303	1.30	4.00	4.01	4.42	3.2	0.3	100	
2018	MIA	MLB	32	2	1	0	46	0	48²	44	6	2.7	8.9	48	39%	.311	1.22	3.99	4.02	4.35	4.2	0.4	98	

Breakout: 34%   Improve: 44%   Collapse: 24%   Attrition: 22%   MLB: 87%   *Comparables: Tyler Yates, Mike MacDougal, Wilton Lopez*

For every action there is an equal and opposite reaction. For every David Ortiz finale, there is a (potential) Junichi Tazawa finale. Big Papi's farewell stole all the headlines, and rightfully so, but Tazawa has likely thrown his last pitch as a Red Sox, and he deserved a better fate than what he got last year. The long-time Red Sox setup man was treated with all the care of a crash test dummy from 2012-2016, logging 283.2 innings. We saw the effects of his workload start to eat away at his effectiveness and durability in 2015, and those trends continued last year when Tazawa posted his lowest average fastball velocity since 2011 and threw his fewest innings since 2012. Given his age and resume it's likely that Tazawa gets several more chances to stick in someone's pen. His home run rate, percentage of hard-hit balls and injury history are all trending in the wrong direction, though. It seems like just yesterday he was blowing fastballs past Miguel Cabrera, but time waits for no reliever.

Jose Urena   RHP

Born: 9/12/91   Age: 25   Bats: R   Throws: R   Height: 6'2"   Weight: 200   Entered Pro Ball: International Free Agent, 2008

YEAR	TEAM	LVL	AGE	W	L	SV	G	GS	IP	H	HR	BB/9	K/9	K	GB%	BABIP	WHIP	ERA	FIP	DRA	VORP	WARP	cFIP	MPH
2014	JAX	AA	22	13	8	0	26	25	162	155	14	1.6	6.7	121	48%	.290	1.14	3.33	3.39	4.04	21.2	2.3	87	
2015	NWO	AAA	23	6	1	0	11	11	67²	65	4	2.5	5.5	41	54%	.292	1.24	2.66	4.13	4.37	7.0	0.7	98	
2015	MIA	MLB	23	1	5	0	20	9	61²	73	5	3.6	4.1	28	49%	.319	1.59	5.25	4.67	5.93	-6.4	-0.7	127	97.1
2016	NWO	AAA	24	3	3	0	12	12	48¹	41	4	3.9	7.6	41	46%	.278	1.28	3.17	4.71	5.29	0.3	0.0	105	
2016	MIA	MLB	24	4	9	1	28	12	83²	91	11	3.1	6.2	58	49%	.297	1.43	6.13	4.76	5.81	-5.0	-0.5	113	97.7
2017	MIA	MLB	25	4	6	0	28	13	84	88	8	3.3	6.1	58	54%	.297	1.40	4.44	4.27	4.92	2.0	0.2	100	
2018	MIA	MLB	26	8	9	0	27	27	163²	140	17	3.7	8.6	156	54%	.301	1.27	3.80	4.23	4.60	15.2	1.6	104	

Breakout: 12%   Improve: 39%   Collapse: 28%   Attrition: 31%   MLB: 84%   *Comparables: Justin Germano, Jake Arrieta, Eddie Butler*

Urena trouble? Urena luck! Hope springs eternal for the young righty, whose ETA in the rotation is this year. He transmuted from the bullpen into a starter's role last season and seems likely to stick, given how his incandescent fastball didn't lose much, if anything in the switch. He throws serious gas, in the form of 95 mph sinkers and fastballs, and has an 80-grade hat game. Stands out even on a team with a host of potential starters, even if predicting how this plays out is something of an infinite ... joke.

Edinson Volquez   RHP

Born: 7/3/83   Age: 33   Bats: R   Throws: R   Height: 6'0"   Weight: 220   Entered Pro Ball: International Free Agent, 2001

YEAR	TEAM	LVL	AGE	W	L	SV	G	GS	IP	H	HR	BB/9	K/9	K	GB%	BABIP	WHIP	ERA	FIP	DRA	VORP	WARP	cFIP	MPH
2014	PIT	MLB	30	13	7	0	32	31	192²	166	17	3.3	6.5	140	53%	.263	1.23	3.04	4.12	4.03	17.1	1.9	110	96.0
2015	KCA	MLB	31	13	9	0	34	33	200¹	190	16	3.2	7.0	155	47%	.290	1.31	3.55	3.79	4.66	9.2	1.0	103	96.3
2016	KCA	MLB	32	10	11	0	34	34	189¹	217	23	3.6	6.6	139	52%	.319	1.55	5.37	4.53	4.90	9.8	1.0	106	96.0
2017	MIA	MLB	33	9	11	0	29	29	165¹	157	17	3.5	8.1	149	53%	.294	1.34	4.07	3.99	4.54	11.7	1.2	100	
2018	MIA	MLB	34	10	10	0	29	29	175	160	19	3.3	8.2	159	53%	.307	1.29	3.80	4.22	4.57	17.7	1.8	104	

Breakout: 8%   Improve: 48%   Collapse: 14%   Attrition: 20%   MLB: 87%   *Comparables: Doug Davis, Barry Zito, Vicente Padilla*

"I feel sexy tonight." That was the famous proclamation Volquez made to his batterymate Salvador Perez prior to spinning six shutout innings in Game 1 of the 2015 ALCS. While Sexy Ed pitched himself into Royals lore that postseason, he followed it up with a spinster-like performance in 2016. The walk rate has usually been the least attractive thing on his stat line, but opponents were too busy barreling his offerings to wait out earning a free pass. His hard-contact rate was the highest it's been going back to his second season in the majors, and was largely the result of the opposition hammering both his sinker and his curve. And while Volquez threw a couple of clunkers in the first half, it was his post-break performance that was completely dreadful.

Nick Wittgren   RHP

Born: 5/29/91   Age: 26   Bats: R   Throws: R   Height: 6'2"   Weight: 210   Entered Pro Ball: Round 9, 2012 Draft (#287 overall)

YEAR	TEAM	LVL	AGE	W	L	SV	G	GS	IP	H	HR	BB/9	K/9	K	GB%	BABIP	WHIP	ERA	FIP	DRA	VORP	WARP	cFIP	MPH
2014	JAX	AA	23	5	5	20	52	0	66	73	6	1.9	7.6	56	42%	.332	1.32	3.55	3.40	3.36	11.0	1.2	94	
2015	NWO	AAA	24	1	6	19	51	0	62¹	58	6	1.2	9.2	64	35%	.302	1.06	3.03	3.23	1.37	24.6	2.5	77	
2016	NWO	AAA	25	1	0	2	10	0	12²	6	1	2.8	7.8	11	39%	.167	0.79	1.42	3.96	4.14	1.2	0.1	100	
2016	MIA	MLB	25	4	3	0	48	0	51²	50	6	1.7	7.3	42	41%	.286	1.16	3.14	3.71	4.09	5.1	0.5	100	94.6
2017	MIA	MLB	26	2	3	0	50	0	53	55	7	2.6	7.5	44	57%	.297	1.32	4.39	4.24	4.76	0.9	0.1	100	
2018	MIA	MLB	27	3	1	0	52	0	55¹	45	7	3.3	10.1	62	57%	.296	1.18	3.58	3.98	4.33	4.9	0.5	95	

Breakout: 42%   Improve: 53%   Collapse: 12%   Attrition: 21%   MLB: 72%   *Comparables: Rich Thompson, Steve Cishek, Fernando Salas*

Wittgren acquitted himself nicely as a rookie. Unlike most of the Marlins' peloton of middle relievers, he's never started a game at any level and isn't about to start now. It's good to know who you are. Wittgren relies on a four-seamer, a changeup and slider, and seems destined to be a setup man for whomever emerges as the Marlins' closer, but he's still just a member of the peloton. In Wittgren's defense, they *are* making pretty good time.

Brad Ziegler   RHP

Born: 10/10/79   Age: 37   Bats: R   Throws: R   Height: 6'4"   Weight: 220   Entered Pro Ball: Round 20, 2003 Draft (#595 overall)

YEAR	TEAM	LVL	AGE	W	L	SV	G	GS	IP	H	HR	BB/9	K/9	K	GB%	BABIP	WHIP	ERA	FIP	DRA	VORP	WARP	cFIP	MPH
2014	ARI	MLB	34	5	3	1	68	0	67	60	5	3.2	7.3	54	65%	.284	1.25	3.49	3.67	2.92	11.7	1.3	94	86.9
2015	ARI	MLB	35	0	3	30	66	0	68	48	3	2.2	4.8	36	74%	.220	0.96	1.85	3.47	3.14	11.9	1.3	93	86.4
2016	ARI	MLB	36	2	3	18	36	0	38¹	41	1	3.5	6.3	27	66%	.333	1.46	2.82	3.45	3.03	8.3	0.9	85	85.9
2016	BOS	MLB	36	2	4	4	33	0	29²	26	1	3.3	9.4	31	64%	.312	1.25	1.52	2.67	2.95	6.7	0.7	84	86.9
2017	MIA	MLB	37	3	2	3	50	0	53	48	5	3.3	7.5	45	48%	.285	1.24	3.93	3.88	4.37	3.2	0.3	96	
2018	MIA	MLB	38	2	1	2	41	0	43²	36	4	3.1	7.4	36	48%	.285	1.18	4.02	4.06	4.41	3.5	0.4	97	

Breakout: 22%   Improve: 42%   Collapse: 23%   Attrition: 9%   MLB: 84%   *Comparables: Scott Downs, Salomon Torres, Francisco Cordero*

We may be in the midst of the Golden Age of hard-throwing relievers, but Ziegler keeps finding another way to get the job done. The veteran sinkerballer ignored advice about old canines and new tricks, throwing the lowest percentage of fastballs and the highest percentage of changeups in his career to great effect. Ziegler recorded a career-best strikeout rate at the age of 36 and, while his walk rate rose, his groundball rate stayed steady. A midseason trade from Arizona to Boston saw his role downgraded from closer to setup man, but Ziegler showed he's still up to the task of pitching in the AL and in an even less favorable home ballpark than Chase Field. He's an attractive, affordable alternative to the big-money closers on the market, as he's proven yet again that older pooches can still be good dogs, Brent.

LINEOUTS

Hitters

NAME	POS	TEAM	LVL	AGE	PA	R	2B	3B	HR	RBI	BB	K	SB	CS	AVG/OBP/SLG	TAv	VORP	BABIP	BRR	FRAA	WARP
Austin Dean	OF	JAX	AA	22	536	60	23	5	11	67	48	110	1	2	.238/.307/.375	.257	8.6	.283	-0.5	LF(115): 0.5, RF(1): -0.0	1.0
Destin Hood	OF	NWO	AAA	26	522	61	29	3	15	80	37	113	11	6	.267/.316/.435	.291	28.7	.315	0.5	LF(69): -4.1, RF(31): -3.4	2.1
	OF	MIA	MLB	26	25	3	1	0	1	2	0	11	0	1	.240/.240/.400	.222	-1.1	.385	-0.7	LF(5): -0.4, RF(2): -0.1	-0.2
Adrian Nieto	C	NWO	AAA	26	129	9	4	0	1	19	15	38	1	0	.195/.287/.257	.221	-0.5	.280	-0.9	C(34): 2.0	0.1
Austin Nola	INF	NWO	AAA	26	407	34	23	1	6	44	24	56	4	1	.261/.308/.376	.248	9.0	.293	1.0	2B(56): 5.3, SS(32): 2.6	2.2
Yefri Perez	OF	JAX	AA	25	377	49	7	3	1	28	39	66	39	11	.259/.334/.308	.264	17.7	.315	5.1	CF(62): 1.1, 2B(13): -0.3	1.9
	OF	MIA	MLB	25	3	5	1	0	0	0	0	1	4	2	.667/.667/1.000	.612	1.5	1.000	0.3	SS(2): -0.0, 2B(1): -0.0	0.1
Joshua Riddle	SS	JAX	AA	24	429	49	18	4	3	51	33	72	5	1	.278/.332/.368	.269	20.0	.331	1.0	SS(71): 0.7, 2B(21): -0.2	2.2
	SS	NWO	AAA	24	57	4	2	0	1	2	1	9	1	0	.268/.281/.357	.253	1.0	.304	-0.8	SS(13): -1.7, 2B(1): -0.0	-0.1
Avery Romero	2B	JAX	AA	23	117	13	3	2	1	10	15	17	2	0	.190/.299/.290	.244	2.4	.217	1.1	2B(16): -3.1, 3B(14): 2.4	0.2
	2B	JUP	A+	23	296	28	13	0	3	27	20	39	1	0	.253/.311/.335	.242	1.8	.283	-1.9	3B(72): -6.0	-0.4
Xavier Scruggs	1B	NWO	AAA	28	382	69	24	0	21	50	58	90	4	2	.290/.408/.565	.354	44.6	.343	1.8	1B(57): -5.3, LF(30): 2.6	4.3
	1B	MIA	MLB	28	69	1	3	0	1	5	5	20	0	0	.210/.290/.306	.239	-1.8	.293	-1.2	1B(19): -1.0, LF(2): -0.3	-0.3
Isael Soto	OF	GRB	A	19	448	51	24	5	9	38	43	115	3	0	.247/.320/.399	.278	13.8	.323	-0.8	RF(101): -7.1	0.7

Austin Dean's bat is alive, but just as living beings desire contact with one another, the bat yearns for more frequent contact with pitches. ❖ Call it kismet: **Destin Hood** has been passed from the Nationals to the Indians to the Phillies to the Marlins like a platoon outfielder, which is exactly what he is. ❖ In a rationed league, it increasingly looks like the cup of coffee **Adrian Nieto** grabbed with the White Sox in 2014 will be his only one. We dare anoint his career to be in free-fall. ❖ Aaron Nola is one of the best young pitchers in baseball, but big brother **Austin Nola** is a light-hitting utility man hopeful. ❖ **Yefri Perez** was called up to be the Marlins' "designated runner" in September. You want him on your team, especially in October. You just don't want him playing very much. ❖ **J.T. Riddle** is so obviously a medium-floor, low-ceiling utility player that his otherwise wonderful, literary sounding name is unnecessarily grating. ❖ The bloom is off the rose for **Avery Romero**, whose prospect status started to wilt a year ago and hit full-on winter freeze mode at Double-A. ❖ **Xavier Scruggs**' power played extremely well at Triple-A again in 2016, but it's never translated to the majors and he's already 29 years old. ❖ As your friendly HBO Queen Regent will tell you, power is power, and **Isael Soto** has it. He's talented, but inconsistent at the plate in the field.

Pitchers

NAME	TEAM	LVL	AGE	W	L	SV	G	GS	IP	H	HR	BB/9	K/9	K	GB%	BABIP	WHIP	ERA	FIP	DRA	VORP	WARP	cFIP	MPH
Elvis Araujo	PHI	MLB	24	2	1	0	32	0	27¹	35	4	5.6	9.5	29	40%	.378	1.90	5.60	5.05	4.80	0.5	0.1	110	94.5
	LEH	AAA	24	1	0	1	18	0	20²	15	2	2.6	8.3	19	45%	.232	1.02	2.18	3.60	3.67	3.0	0.3	94	
Austin Brice	JAX	AA	24	4	7	2	27	13	93¹	79	5	2.8	7.6	79	47%	.280	1.16	2.89	3.48	3.13	19.5	2.1	94	
	MIA	MLB	24	0	1	0	15	0	14	9	2	3.2	9.0	14	53%	.194	1.00	7.07	4.54	4.07	1.4	0.1	94	96.6
Hunter Cervenka	ATL	MLB	26	1	0	0	50	0	34	20	2	6.1	9.3	35	51%	.231	1.26	3.18	4.01	4.58	1.5	0.2	104	94.9
	MIA	MLB	26	0	0	0	18	0	9¹	11	1	4.8	6.8	7	45%	.333	1.71	4.82	4.69	4.21	0.8	0.1	104	94.3
Tayron Guerrero	SDN	MLB	25	0	0	0	1	0	2	3	0	4.5	0.0	0	50%	.375	2.00	4.50	4.69	4.86	0.0	0.0	109	96.2
	ELP	AAA	25	0	0	0	13	0	12	12	1	6.8	8.2	11	43%	.286	1.75	6.00	6.30	6.71	-2.3	-0.2	113	
	SAN	AA	25	0	3	0	19	0	23²	20	1	3.8	9.5	25	48%	.300	1.27	4.94	3.43	3.53	3.2	0.3	92	
	JAX	AA	25	1	1	4	12	0	14	11	0	1.9	9.6	15	27%	.297	1.00	1.93	2.25	3.45	2.0	0.2	92	
Kevin Guzman	GRB	A	21	1	4	0	7	5	27²	22	1	2.6	9.1	28	54%	.273	1.08	3.90	3.36	3.21	5.3	0.6	92	
Justin Jacome	GRB	A	22	1	5	0	21	16	72²	69	5	4.5	5.8	47	42%	.286	1.44	3.72	4.69	9.37	-35.6	-3.9	129	
Kyle Lobstein	PIT	MLB	26	2	0	0	14	0	25	25	2	4.3	5.4	15	52%	.291	1.48	3.96	4.71	5.78	-2.3	-0.2	117	90.1
	IND	AAA	26	1	3	1	19	6	50¹	55	3	3.0	7.5	42	46%	.344	1.43	4.11	3.35	4.09	6.0	0.6	95	
Bryan Morris	MIA	MLB	29	0	0	1	24	0	17²	15	4	5.1	6.6	13	50%	.239	1.42	3.06	6.53	5.05	-0.2	0.0	111	95.4
Sam Perez	BAT	A-	21	1	1	0	16	8	48¹	41	4	2.8	6.7	36	44%	.278	1.16	3.54	4.10	3.49	8.6	0.9	95	
Chris Reed	JAX	AA	26	1	0	0	4	2	14²	12	0	3.1	6.8	11	64%	.267	1.16	3.07	3.25	4.83	0.2	0.0	94	
	NWO	AAA	26	3	4	0	20	9	66²	54	9	3.6	7.3	54	46%	.242	1.22	3.78	5.34	5.73	-3.6	-0.4	106	

Years ago, **Elvis Araujo** was a raw starting pitching prospect for Cleveland. Now he's a reliever whose potential won't be realized until he can consistently throw strikes. ❖ **Austin Brice** sipped the coffee for the first time last season, but mostly spit it out. ❖ Acquired in August from the Braves, **Hunter Cervenka** is not, as his name suggests, an enforcer for the Buffalo Sabres. He's a a LOOGY through and through. ❖ A certified flame-thrower, **Tayron Guerrero** is a *Two*-True-Outcomes pitcher. You're either walking to first or walking back to the dugout. ❖ The highest-upside piece in the Mat Latos deal, **Kevin Guzman** missed most of the 2016 season to injury and was good when he did pitch. ❖ **Justin Jacome** was hurt for the first few months of 2016, but managed to post respectable enough numbers at Single-A Greenville until the wheels came off in late August and early September. ❖ **Kyle Lobstein** is a finesse pitcher without finesse, which is why he's bounced around while posting a 5.06 ERA in 128 big-league innings thus far. ❖ **Bryan Morris** missed half the season following back surgery and was dropped by the Marlins, but latched on with the Giants as an interesting comeback candidate with a 2.80 career ERA. ❖ **Sam Perez** flashes a mid-90s fastball and clearly has the goods, and the fifth-round pick's versatility can only help him going forward. ❖ Acquired from the Dodgers in exchange for reliever Grant Dayton in mid-July, **Chris Reed** had a so-so year between Double-A and Triple-A at age 25. ❖ **Remey Reed** was part of an Oklahoma State staff that blistered its way through the season. A big righty who throws mostly a fastball and cutter, Reed said his dream was to be drafted in the first three rounds, but he signed with the Marlins anyway after waiting twice as long.

MILWAUKEE BREWERS

Essay by Jack Moore

Player comments by Nicholas Zettel, Mauricio Rubio and BP staff

When Casey Stengel brought his Yankees to town for the 1957 World Series, he called Milwaukee baseball fans "bush league." Little did he know what he was getting himself into. The fans at County Stadium rode Stengel for all three games in Milwaukee, clanging cowbells at deafening decibels and heckling the New York manager whenever he emerged from the dugout, counting out loud each of his steps whenever he headed to the mound to consult with his pitcher.

The Braves rebounded from a crushing 12-3 defeat in Game 3, the first in Milwaukee, to win the next two and take a 3-2 series lead back to New York. Game 5 was a 1-0 shutout hurled by spitballer extraordinaire Lew Burdette in front of 45,811 screaming Wisconsinites, the second of what would be three dominant wins by Burdette. It was Burdette's Game 7 win that gave the championship to little old bush league Milwaukee. "BUSHVILLE WINS!" read one sign seen in downtown Milwaukee as thousands went wild in celebration.

Milwaukee doesn't get much love when we think of the great American baseball towns, with people from the coasts like Stengel often relegating it to the level of the bush leagues. But boy, do we turn out for baseball, and we have since the Braves gave Milwaukee its first professional club in half a century in 1953. Over their first five years in the city, the club drew a ludicrous 10,225,356 fans, by a wide margin the most in the majors. The only other club to even draw six million in that five-year span was the Yankees, at a relatively paltry 7,492,038.

When Milwaukee has sported a competitive club, it has in fact proven to be one of America's great baseball towns. It will never have that reputation across the country, though, thanks to a half-century filled with losing and the overshadowing influences of the Chicago squads just 45 minutes down I-94. But throughout Milwaukee's history, the city has shown a fervor for baseball and a desire to support a franchise. Unfortunately, a whole host of structural issues have limited Milwaukee's baseball clubs—and their ability to rake in revenue—and contributed to its perception as an also-ran, bush league baseball city.

Professional baseball had already been an institution in Milwaukee before the Braves arrived. The Triple-A Brewers

BREWERS PROSPECTUS
2016 W-L: 73-89, 4TH IN NL CENTRAL

Pythag	.459	23rd	DER	.700	20th
RS/G	4.03	28th	B-Age	27.4	5th
RA/G	4.84	27th	P-Age	28.1	13th
TAv	.263	12th	Salary	$63.9M	30th
BRR	-0.19	15th	M$/MW	$2.1M	28th
TAv-P	.276	25th	DL Days	1184	23rd
FIP	4.41	23rd	$ on DL	14%	19th

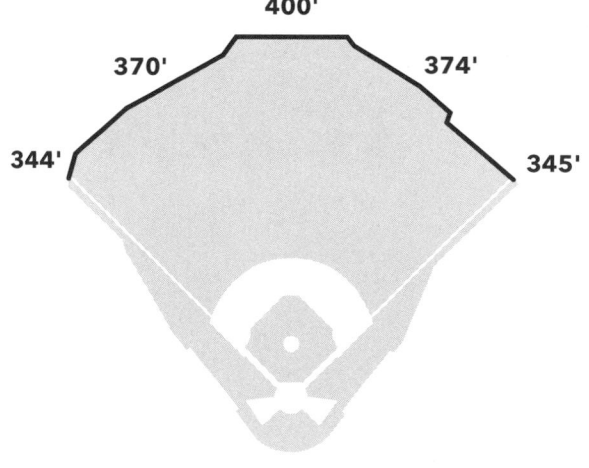

Outfield wall profile: **8'**

Three-Year Park Factors

Runs	Runs/RH	Runs/LH	HR/RH	HR/LH
102	99	104	106	124

Top Hitter WARP	4.8	Jonathan Villar
Top Pitcher WARP	3.3	Zach Davies
Top Prospect		Lewis Brinson

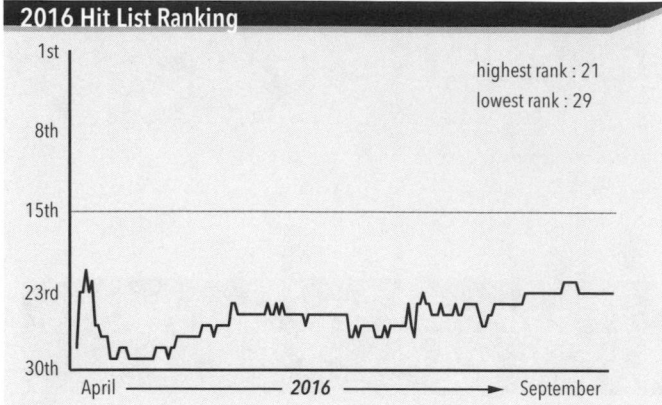

2016 Hit List Ranking

highest rank : 21
lowest rank : 29

April — 2016 → September

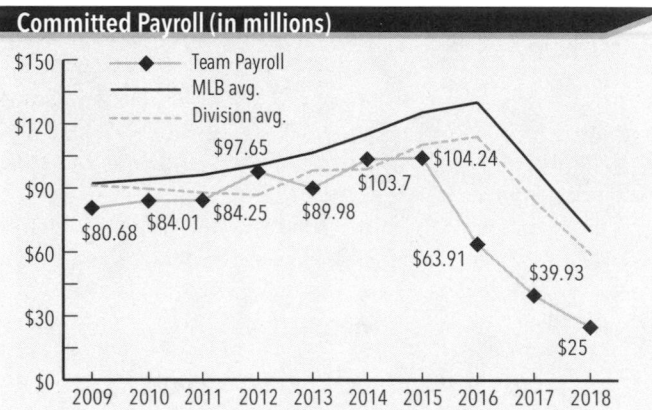

Committed Payroll (in millions)

Team Payroll
MLB avg.
Division avg.

$97.65
$80.68 $84.01 $84.25 $89.98 $103.7 $104.24
$63.91 $39.93
$25

2009 2010 2011 2012 2013 2014 2015 2016 2017 2018

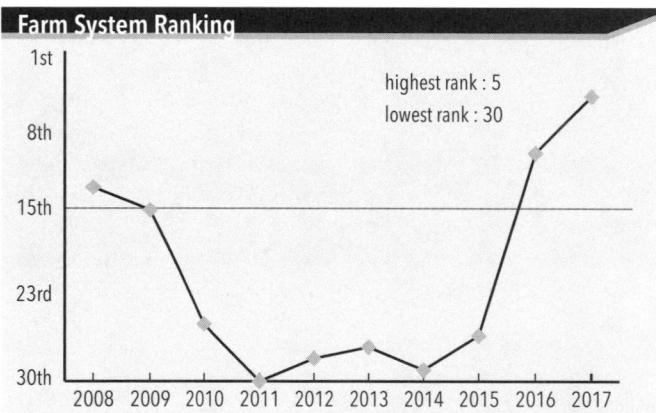

Farm System Ranking

highest rank : 5
lowest rank : 30

2008 2009 2010 2011 2012 2013 2014 2015 2016 2017

Personnel

General Manager:
David Stearns

VP, Assistant General Manager:
Matt Arnold

Senior Advisor:
Doug Melvin

Manager:
Craig Counsell

BP Alumni:
James Fisher
Adam Hayes
Matt Kleine
Dan Turkenkopf

of the American Association spent 51 seasons as the city's premier professional baseball club. County Stadium was planned to be the new home of the Brewers beginning in 1953, but the ballpark was so state of the art that the Boston Braves, then the Brewers' parent franchise, decided to pack up and make Milwaukee their new home.

Milwaukee immediately showed its enthusiasm for top-flight baseball. Over 10,000 people showed up to the park's first public event, an open house on March 15, 1953. Plans for an exhibition between Boston's former National League club and the Red Sox were thwarted by winter weather, but 60,000 people showed up for a parade welcoming the Braves to Wisconsin. On April 14, County Stadium opened for real, and 34,357 were treated to a complete game 10-inning victory over the Cardinals by Milwaukee ace Warren Spahn. They set a National League attendance record in their first season in Milwaukee at 1,826,397.

The Braves would set two more attendance records in Milwaukee, at 2,131,388 in 1954 and again at 2,215,404 in the World Championship season of 1957. But as the club lost its stars and started to fall toward the middle of the league, attendance tailed off sharply. By 1962, the Braves only drew 766,921—their first Milwaukee season in which they failed to sell a million tickets. No coincidence, that was the year Lou Perini, the man who brought the franchise from Boston to Milwaukee, sold the club to a syndicate led by an insurance broker named William Bartholomay.

Bartholomay and his group saw an American South devoid of baseball competition. The Houston Astros, a 1962 expansion team, were the only squad south of the Mason-Dixon line when Bartholomay's group snapped up the Braves. Not only could a team in Atlanta likely draw similar or better than the early 1960s Braves managed in Milwaukee, most critically they had a much bigger media market available to rake in fees for radio and television broadcasting rights.

By the 1960 census, Milwaukee was substantially larger than Atlanta—741,324 people to 487,455. But the lack of professional teams in nearby major cities in the south, such as New Orleans (15th largest, 627,525), Memphis (22nd, 497,455) and Birmingham (36th, 340,887) meant Atlanta offered a huge potential market. Atlanta's potential was even greater in comparison to Milwaukee, whose nearest major cities were already claimed by MLB teams in Chicago and Minneapolis.

Indeed, the Braves thrived in Atlanta, even though it took a cable television revolution under Ted Turner to make good on the club's gigantic media rights potential. Milwaukee, meanwhile, was left with the scrap former Braves minority owner Bud Selig was able to scoop up in the aftermath—the Seattle Pilots, which he won in a bankruptcy auction in 1970 and swiftly moved to Milwaukee to become the Brewers.

When the Braves came to Milwaukee, the pieces of a championship club were coming together. The 1953 Braves won 92 games and featured stars like Eddie Mathews, Warren Spahn, Johnny Logan and Lew Burdette, all of whom played major roles on the 1957 championship club. The 1969 Pilots won 64 games and didn't have a single pitcher with an ERA+ better than 100.

It's easy to look at the Braves' flagging attendance numbers in the early 1960s and point the finger at Milwaukee's fans for losing their enthusiasm. But that's an unfair assessment of the situation. It was clear as soon as Bartholomay's syndicate purchased the club that they had intentions of moving. Accusations flew in Milwaukee that management was not making the moves necessary to bring the club back to its competitive status in the late 1950s, if not actively tanking the squad in a downright *Major League*-esque fashion.

They were swiftly proven right when the Braves bolted for Atlanta, only playing out the 1965 season in Milwaukee because it was the last year of their lease with County Stadium. Braves ownership fought for an early exit to the bitter end and even offered a $500,000 buyout to escape. For Milwaukee's fans, the situation was simple: Why show up for a team you know isn't trying to win?

But don't misconstrue the city's disdain for the Braves and the grifters who ran them for a lack of enthusiasm for baseball. The city fought hard in court against the proposed move to Atlanta, and when a state judge ruled in the city's favor in 1966 to force Major League Baseball to keep a team in Milwaukee, fans were elated. As usual though, baseball's anti-trust exemption proved too much to overcome, and both the state and national Supreme Courts ruled in the franchise's favor.

Still, the fight to keep MLB in Milwaukee continued. The next year, Selig managed to convince the White Sox to schedule games at County Stadium. The first, a midseason exhibition in 1967 between the White Sox and Twins, drew 51,000 fans to County Stadium, a remarkable total considering the building only had 43,768 seats. The enthusiasm was enough for the White Sox to schedule nine home games there—one against each American League club—for the 1968 season.

The series was a great success, drawing an average of nearly 30,000 fans per game in a season where the dismal 67-95 White Sox pushed just over 9,000 per game through the Comiskey Park turnstiles. As their fortunes continued to stagnate in 1969, the White Sox once again hosted one home game against each American League club—now 11 games thanks to expansion. Attendance declined to just over 18,000 per game in Milwaukee, but that was still nearly triple what the White Sox drew in Chicago.

It wasn't enough to garner an expansion team—the media markets in Seattle, San Diego and Montreal were too enticing for owners. It was only due to the failure of the Pilots—who spent their sole year in Seattle playing in a decrepit building known aptly as Sicks' Stadium—that Milwaukee managed to drag Major League Baseball back. It took a decade for the Brewers to become competitive; the club's ninth season in Milwaukee was the first season they managed to finish within 10 games of first place.

Even the dreadfully mediocre teams of the mid-1970s managed to draw big crowds. The 94-loss 1975 club drew 1.2 million fans, third in the 12-team American League, and the club drew at least one million fans per season every subsequent year except for the strike-shortened 1981 campaign. The Brewers set a new city attendance record in 1983, the season after it made its first and only run to the World Series, as they drew 2.4 million fans as the reigning league champs.

But under Selig, the club consistently cried poor. In the mid-1980s, Selig became the leader of a coalition of small-market owners who fought hard for limitations to big-market spending in many forms, varying from revenue sharing to salary caps to banning cable television broadcasts. Under Selig—and later, under his daughter Wendy Selig-Prieb following his ascendancy—the Brewers routinely carried among the lowest payrolls in the league, and not coincidentally spent multiple decades under .500 as the ideal proof that small-market franchises can't win because the deck is stacked against them.

Of course teams like the Yankees and Dodgers, with all the resources of the metropolis behind them, are going to have an easier time competing than the Brewers. All the ways baseball teams make money—from gates to sponsorships to media rights—scale with population. The problem is many of the measures Selig and his small-market coalition pushed through only helped small-market teams stay profitable when they lose. Rules like draft and international spending caps and free agent compensation have cut off the best ways for small market teams to get better in a hurry.

Revenue sharing can help, but not when it offers as much incentive to continue losing with low payrolls as it does to go for the gusto and spend to bring in talent. These policies instead wind up encouraging teams like the Brewers (or Royals, or Rays, etc.) to go through long periods of rebuilding—some may prefer the term tanking—and taking a shot only when a short window of opportunity appears via a wave of hot prospects. The result is long stretches of not only losing, but hopelessness.

And thus we get to the same problem the early 1960s Braves faced. Milwaukee will turn out to watch a competitive baseball team. Milwaukee will even turn out to watch a mediocre baseball team, as long as they're giving it their all. But when Milwaukee knows there is nothing truly at stake, no championship hopes whatsoever, they will stay home. In County Stadium's final 10 seasons, from 1991-2000, the Brewers finished no higher than 10th out of 14 in attendance. And who can blame them? Baseball isn't free.

Until last year, things had been different under Mark Attanasio, who bought the Brewers before the 2005 season. The 2005 team saw the call-ups of Rickie Weeks and Prince Fielder and the first .500 season in 23 years. From that year through the 2014 season—which was brutally choked away in August and September—every team had at least a semblance of hope on Opening Day. The first 10 teams under

Attanasio all finished with at least 2.2 million in attendance despite just two playoff appearances and four seasons over .500. From 2005-2014, the Brewers ranked 11th in attendance despite the smallest market size in the league and a mediocre 821-799 record. The explanation is simple: Milwaukee hungers for baseball, if you'll just give it to them.

Having experienced the awesome energy of the 2008 and 2011 playoff runs, the knowledge that there have been so many wasted baseball seasons in Milwaukee is saddening. When the Brewers are rolling, every game spent tailgaiting in the parking lots at Miller Park feels like a giant party. While I understand the logic behind the team's current rebuilding efforts and am a fan of most of the individual moves David Stearns and company have made since taking over, I hate seeing all pretense of competition removed from Brewers games. I hate seeing Miller Park look more like a wake than a party—or worse, turned into Wrigley Field North.

I think the franchise is on the right track. But for the foreseeable future, this club is building, not competing. The Miller Park tailgates will always be great, but there will be many days of empty bleachers in 2017, and possibly beyond. It hurts to see what can be such a vibrant ballpark so down. It will be worth it in the end—when Milwaukee wins, it parties hard—but so much of what powers a great baseball town is hope, and right now it's awfully hard to find hope in Bushville. ■

—Jack Moore is an author of
Baseball Prospectus

HITTERS

Orlando Arcia   SS

Born: 8/4/94   Age: 22   Bats: R   Throws: R   Height: 6'0"   Weight: 165   Entered Pro Ball: International Free Agent, 2010

YEAR	TEAM	LVL	AGE	PA	R	2B	3B	HR	RBI	BB	K	SB	CS	AVG/OBP/SLG	TAv	VORP	BABIP	BRR	FRAA	WARP
2014	BRV	A+	19	546	65	29	5	4	50	42	65	31	11	.289/.346/.392	.263	27.0	.326	4.3	SS(90): 7.3 • 2B(36): -0.0	3.5
2015	BLX	AA	20	552	74	37	7	8	69	30	73	25	8	.307/.347/.453	.294	41.5	.343	1.3	SS(123): 15.8 • 2B(3): 0.2	6.2
2016	CSP	AAA	21	440	59	19	6	8	53	29	77	15	8	.267/.320/.403	.249	12.2	.312	-0.5	SS(92): 6.9 • 2B(7): 0.6	2.0
2016	MIL	MLB	21	216	21	10	3	4	17	15	47	8	0	.219/.273/.358	.217	-1.6	.267	-1.0	SS(53): 3.8	0.2
2017	*MIL*	*MLB*	*22*	*606*	*72*	*29*	*5*	*15*	*57*	*31*	*125*	*16*	*6*	*.248/.288/.393*	*.241*	*15.0*	*.292*	*1.1*	*SS 11*	*2.2*
2018	*MIL*	*MLB*	*23*	*581*	*67*	*28*	*5*	*16*	*68*	*34*	*117*	*16*	*6*	*.257/.303/.415*	*.260*	*21.5*	*.298*	*1.6*	*SS 11*	*3.5*

Breakout: 5%   Improve: 37%   Collapse: 7%   Attrition: 21%   MLB: 56%   *Comparables: Ketel Marte, Asdrubal Cabrera, Jorge Polanco*

The Age Of The Shortstop is upon us again, and this time it's seemingly more diverse than the turn-of-the-century big-body slugger shortstops. If front offices are valuing defensive production more than in the past, or perhaps quantifying it more effectively, it should not be surprising that this wave of shortstops may generally stick because of their gloves. Arcia's ascent to the majors was christened by midseason rebuilding trades and a chance to challenge the youngster to adjust at the highest level, so it's understandable that some found his production lacking in 2016. Still, the 21-year old was among the youngest players in the Pacific Coast League and a quick adjustment helped Arcia right the ship in Milwaukee. The glove is legit, and if the bat is anywhere near the post-adjustment .260/.302/.450 line Arcia will be lauded as a middle infield anchor.

Ryan Braun   RF

Born: 11/17/83 Age: 33   Bats: R   Throws: R   Height: 6'2"   Weight: 205   Entered Pro Ball: Round 1, 2005 Draft (#5 overall)

YEAR	TEAM	LVL	AGE	PA	R	2B	3B	HR	RBI	BB	K	SB	CS	AVG/OBP/SLG	TAv	VORP	BABIP	BRR	FRAA	WARP
2014	MIL	MLB	30	580	68	30	6	19	81	41	113	11	5	.266/.324/.453	.278	16.1	.304	-3.1	RF(134): 2.9 • CF(1): -0.0	2.1
2015	MIL	MLB	31	568	87	27	3	25	84	54	115	24	4	.285/.356/.498	.298	34.3	.322	3.5	RF(130): -11.6	2.4
2016	MIL	MLB	32	564	80	23	3	30	91	46	98	16	5	.305/.365/.538	.316	45.7	.326	1.4	LF(127): -8.2 • RF(2): -0.0	3.9
2017	*MIL*	*MLB*	*33*	*597*	*82*	*27*	*3*	*27*	*86*	*51*	*122*	*17*	*4*	*.277/.343/.489*	*.288*	*35.7*	*.310*	*1.3*	*LF -6*	*2.9*
2018	*MIL*	*MLB*	*34*	*512*	*71*	*23*	*2*	*22*	*72*	*47*	*110*	*13*	*4*	*.269/.342/.471*	*.291*	*28.8*	*.308*	*0.3*	*LF -5*	*2.6*

Breakout: 0%   Improve: 29%   Collapse: 5%   Attrition: 9%   MLB: 95%   *Comparables: Jason Bay, Sid Gordon, Matt Holliday*

Second-half discussion about a near-trade to the Dodgers derailed the serious discussion that Braun's age-32 season should have opened: can he catch Paul Molitor and Robin Yount as the best player in Brewers history? Braun overcame two serious medical ailments involving his back and thumb in consecutive seasons, improved both years and now claims 43.0 career WARP. By comparison, Molitor had 63.7 WARP in Milwaukee and 49.8 through age 32. Yount had 77.7 WARP with the Brewers and was already at 64.2 through age 32. If Braun is to catch either, he'll need to continue his steady and intriguing post-30 climb. As much as fans now clamor for a Braun trade, doing so would deprive the base of one of the more interesting narratives to follow during the rebuilding lull.

Lewis Brinson   CF

Born: 5/8/94   Age: 23   Bats: R   Throws: R   Height: 6'3"   Weight: 195   Entered Pro Ball: Round 1, 2012 Draft (#29 overall)

YEAR	TEAM	LVL	AGE	PA	R	2B	3B	HR	RBI	BB	K	SB	CS	AVG/OBP/SLG	TAv	VORP	BABIP	BRR	FRAA	WARP
2014	HIC	A	20	186	36	8	1	10	28	18	46	7	4	.335/.405/.579	.329	22.4	.413	3.0	CF(43): 5.9	2.9
2014	MYR	A+	20	199	17	8	1	3	22	15	50	5	5	.246/.307/.350	.251	2.6	.323	-0.9	CF(33): 2.7 • LF(3): 0.2	0.5
2015	HDS	A+	21	298	51	22	7	13	42	31	64	13	6	.337/.416/.628	.363	39.9	.402	0.9	CF(51): -1.4 • LF(7): 1.1	4.3
2015	FRI	AA	21	121	14	8	1	6	23	6	28	2	1	.291/.328/.545	.301	7.9	.333	-0.3	CF(22): 3.8 • LF(3): 0.4	1.3
2015	ROU	AAA	21	37	9	1	0	1	4	7	6	3	0	.433/.541/.567	.428	7.6	.522	0.3	LF(7): 0.0 • CF(1): -0.2	0.8
2016	FRI	AA	22	326	46	14	6	11	40	17	64	11	4	.237/.280/.431	.244	3.5	.264	-0.4	CF(65): -0.6 • RF(5): -1.1	0.1
2016	CSP	AAA	22	93	14	9	0	4	20	2	21	4	2	.382/.387/.618	.323	8.9	.455	-0.1	CF(23): 6.3	1.6
2017	*MIL*	*MLB*	*23*	*156*	*19*	*7*	*1*	*6*	*19*	*10*	*42*	*4*	*2*	*.247/.296/.438*	*.255*	*4.7*	*.302*	*0.2*	*CF 3*	*0.7*
2018	*MIL*	*MLB*	*24*	*379*	*47*	*17*	*3*	*15*	*50*	*24*	*103*	*9*	*4*	*.246/.299/.439*	*.263*	*12.4*	*.302*	*0.8*	*CF 8*	*2.2*

Breakout: 4%   Improve: 25%   Collapse: 4%   Attrition: 18%   MLB: 48%   *Comparables: Michael Choice, Franklin Gutierrez, Kirk Nieuwenhuis*

The main piece coming back in the Jonathan Lucroy trade, Brinson offers a bucket full of average-or-better tools in his profile and tore it up at Triple-A Colorado Springs following the deal. Brinson plays a smooth center field, utilizing his plus speed to the fullest and tracking fly balls well. He also has plus power in the profile, and while there's some swing-and-miss present in his bat Brinson has the potential for an average hit tool.

Keon Broxton   CF

Born: 5/7/90   Age: 27   Bats: R   Throws: R   Height: 6'3"   Weight: 195   Entered Pro Ball: Round 3, 2009 Draft (#95 overall)

YEAR	TEAM	LVL	AGE	PA	R	2B	3B	HR	RBI	BB	K	SB	CS	AVG/OBP/SLG	TAv	VORP	BABIP	BRR	FRAA	WARP
2014	ALT	AA	24	471	67	22	9	15	52	59	122	25	6	.275/.369/.484	.299	36.1	.357	4.4	CF(80): 1.3 • LF(43): 4.0	4.4
2015	ALT	AA	25	204	35	12	4	3	26	19	51	11	6	.302/.365/.464	.292	16.0	.395	3.5	CF(43): 4.5 • RF(1): -0.3	2.2
2015	IND	AAA	25	367	51	15	8	7	42	47	105	28	9	.256/.352/.423	.275	14.8	.356	0.1	LF(46): 3.9 • CF(31): -3.0	1.8
2015	PIT	MLB	25	2	3	0	0	0	0	0	1	1	1	.000/.000/.000	.001	-0.1	.000	0.1	RF(1): -0.0 • CF(1): -0.0	0.0
2016	CSP	AAA	26	199	30	11	7	8	26	20	60	18	8	.287/.362/.562	.306	15.5	.391	0.3	CF(38): 3.4 • LF(4): -0.5	2.0
2016	MIL	MLB	26	244	28	10	1	9	19	36	88	23	4	.242/.354/.430	.278	13.2	.373	1.3	CF(68): 0.9	1.5
2017	*MIL*	*MLB*	*27*	*352*	*50*	*13*	*4*	*12*	*38*	*39*	*117*	*22*	*7*	*.229/.318/.412*	*.256*	*10.7*	*.323*	*2.9*	*CF 3 • LF 1*	*1.5*
2018	*MIL*	*MLB*	*28*	*450*	*57*	*18*	*5*	*16*	*56*	*50*	*152*	*27*	*8*	*.230/.318/.419*	*.264*	*15.1*	*.327*	*1.3*	*CF 4 • LF 1*	*2.2*

Breakout: 5%   Improve: 18%   Collapse: 8%   Attrition: 24%   MLB: 54%   *Comparables: Justin Maxwell, Chris Dickerson, Jonathan Van Every*

Behind top prospect Orlando Arcia, Broxton was the MVP at Triple-A Colorado Springs. The power/speed/patience torrent eventually showed in Milwaukee, as Broxton leaned on an unsustainably high .425 batting average on balls in play to hit .294/.399/.538 in the second half and overcome early struggles. That surge was strong enough to place Broxton in the NL's top 25 for power/speed number, and the walks show a refined eye. The strikeout rate will be singular for Broxton, who packs as extreme a profile as one could desire within his 6-foot-3 frame.

Chris Carter   1B

Born: 12/18/86   Age: 30   Bats: R   Throws: R   Height: 6'4"   Weight: 245   Entered Pro Ball: Round 15, 2005 Draft (#455 overall)

YEAR	TEAM	LVL	AGE	PA	R	2B	3B	HR	RBI	BB	K	SB	CS	AVG/OBP/SLG	TAv	VORP	BABIP	BRR	FRAA	WARP
2014	HOU	MLB	27	572	68	21	1	37	88	56	182	5	2	.227/.308/.491	.293	23.8	.267	0.3	1B(14): -0.5 • LF(6): 0.1	2.6
2015	HOU	MLB	28	460	50	17	0	24	64	57	151	1	2	.199/.307/.427	.266	4.5	.244	-2.7	1B(115): 0.0	0.4
2016	MIL	MLB	29	644	84	27	1	41	94	76	206	3	1	.222/.321/.499	.288	20.1	.260	-4.9	1B(155): -12.1	0.8
2017	*MIL*	*MLB*	*30*	*569*	*77*	*22*	*1*	*32*	*89*	*68*	*186*	*3*	*1*	*.223/.320/.470*	*.267*	*13.6*	*.277*	*-1.8*	*1B -4*	*1.0*
2018	*MIL*	*MLB*	*31*	*537*	*78*	*21*	*1*	*30*	*82*	*66*	*175*	*2*	*1*	*.216/.317/.459*	*.276*	*13.5*	*.266*	*-1.8*	*1B -4*	*1.0*

Breakout: 1%   Improve: 48%   Collapse: 4%   Attrition: 10%   MLB: 98%   *Comparables: Mark Reynolds, Chris Davis, Cecil Fielder*

Carter versus Coin Flip, 2016: 50.2 percent of the first baseman's plate appearances ended in a home run, a walk or a strikeout, coordinating the laws of the Three True Outcomes and the laws of probability with beautiful orchestration. To dream of those 10 sacrifice flies, seven of which came before July, 10 fly balls now filed under "RBI" or "what could have been." Those flies were twinkles in Carter's eye, a little glimpse of September before the masher was ready to unleash his power to its fullest extent. Poor Spencer Patton knows that feeling, as he saw Carter destroy a baseball and the new Wrigley Field scoreboard in one swift September swing, in a certain demonstration that projected distances and game log descriptions are an injustice to the game. So here goes: "Flyball, would have crossed Waveland and Sheffield had the Ricketts foregone renovation expenses." That ball hit the scoreboard so hard it was tough to tell if Carter hit a homer or the rooftop owners filed another lawsuit.

Trent Clark   CF

Born: 11/1/96   Age: 20   Bats: L   Throws: L   Height: 6'0"   Weight: 205   Entered Pro Ball: Round 1, 2015 Draft (#15 overall)

YEAR	TEAM	LVL	AGE	PA	R	2B	3B	HR	RBI	BB	K	SB	CS	AVG/OBP/SLG	TAv	VORP	BABIP	BRR	FRAA	WARP
2016	WIS	A	19	262	27	15	2	2	24	37	68	5	10	.231/.346/.344	.250	0.8	.325	-4.0	CF(49): -0.6 • LF(10): -1.3	-0.1
2017	*MIL*	*MLB*	*20*	*250*	*29*	*9*	*1*	*5*	*20*	*27*	*77*	*3*	*4*	*.199/.289/.318*	*.212*	*-4.0*	*.276*	*-1.1*	*CF -2 • LF -1*	*-0.7*
2018	*MIL*	*MLB*	*21*	*316*	*36*	*12*	*1*	*7*	*30*	*37*	*93*	*4*	*6*	*.205/.303/.332*	*.235*	*-0.8*	*.278*	*-1.0*	*CF -2 • LF -1*	*-0.4*

Breakout: 1%   Improve: 6%   Collapse: 0%   Attrition: 3%   MLB: 8%   *Comparables: Joe Benson, Cedric Hunter, Ramon Flores*

Clark is a little deceiving in that he has a physically stacked body, but doesn't produce much in-game power due to the linear nature of his swing. He struggled with contact all year, as he was dealing with a hamstring injury. There are the makings of an above-average hit tool here, and he's an above-average runner who shows excellent instincts on the basepaths. It was a down year for sure, but Clark has the potential be a solid player and earns extra marks for hitting without batting gloves.

Isan Diaz   SS

Born: 5/27/96   Age: 21   Bats: L   Throws: R   Height: 5'10"   Weight: 185   Entered Pro Ball: Round 2, 2014 Draft (#70 overall)

YEAR	TEAM	LVL	AGE	PA	R	2B	3B	HR	RBI	BB	K	SB	CS	AVG/OBP/SLG	TAv	VORP	BABIP	BRR	FRAA	WARP
2016	WIS	A	20	587	71	34	5	20	75	72	148	11	8	.264/.358/.469	.286	37.6	.332	2.5	SS(90): -0.7 • 2B(41): 1.2	4.2
2017	MIL	MLB	21	250	28	10	1	10	32	23	79	1	1	.216/.293/.397	.235	4.0	.283	-0.4	SS -1 • 2B 0	0.4
2018	MIL	MLB	22	438	57	19	1	18	58	44	131	2	2	.229/.310/.424	.262	14.7	.294	-0.8	SS -1 • 2B 0	1.5

Breakout: 5%   Improve: 12%   Collapse: 4%   Attrition: 10%   MLB: 25%   Comparables: Corey Seager, Addison Russell, Trevor Story

Have you ever driven a car around the main drag in your city, just blasting your favorite jam with all the windows down and not a care in the world? That feeling is what it's like to watch Diaz play. There's danger in the swing, as Diaz generates hard contact when he squares the baseball up and it creates lofty fly balls that land safely over the fence. Diaz led the Midwest League in home runs and pairs that power potential with a solid approach at the plate and some feel for the barrel. There's swing-and-miss in the profile, but he has the tools to overcome that.

Mauricio Dubon   SS

Born: 7/19/94   Age: 22   Bats: R   Throws: R   Height: 6'0"   Weight: 160   Entered Pro Ball: Round 26, 2013 Draft (#773 overall)

YEAR	TEAM	LVL	AGE	PA	R	2B	3B	HR	RBI	BB	K	SB	CS	AVG/OBP/SLG	TAv	VORP	BABIP	BRR	FRAA	WARP
2014	LOW	A-	19	274	40	8	1	3	34	9	26	7	8	.320/.337/.395	.266	14.6	.341	1.6	SS(64): -1.4	1.4
2015	GRN	A	20	262	43	12	3	4	29	18	34	18	4	.301/.354/.428	.294	23.3	.337	6.3	2B(38): 9.0 • SS(18): 1.0	3.5
2015	SLM	A+	20	269	27	9	0	1	18	23	38	12	3	.274/.343/.325	.240	6.6	.320	2.1	SS(52): -2.1 • 2B(5): 0.1	0.5
2016	SLM	A+	21	279	53	11	3	0	29	33	25	24	4	.306/.387/.379	.289	25.6	.338	5.5	SS(61): -11.4	1.5
2016	PME	AA	21	270	48	20	6	6	40	11	36	6	3	.339/.371/.538	.301	25.7	.374	4.1	SS(62): -6.0	2.1
2017	MIL	MLB	22	250	31	10	2	6	25	14	50	7	2	.256/.302/.398	.236	5.8	.295	0.5	SS -5	0.1
2018	MIL	MLB	23	388	45	15	2	11	45	23	75	10	3	.261/.309/.409	.256	12.9	.297	1.1	SS -8 • CF 0	0.5

Breakout: 6%   Improve: 33%   Collapse: 9%   Attrition: 22%   MLB: 51%   Comparables: Tyler Pastornicky, Jorge Polanco, Jean Segura

For the better part of a decade, the Red Sox couldn't develop a shortstop better than Nick Green. Yet over the past few years we've seen them produce Xander Bogaerts, Jose Iglesias, Javier Guerra and now Dubon. A steal of a 26th round pick, Dubon has quick wrists and great hand-eye coordination and he's an above-average runner to boot. The native Honduran (he'd be just the second to reach the majors) is a solid defender at short, but started playing some center field in the AFL. It's easy to understand the Red Sox thoughts behind that move; if Dubon stays in this org, it's likely as a utility player. He might be starter material on a second-division team, though, making Dubon the Red Sox most likely to be traded since Manny Margot headed west.

Lucas Erceg   3B

Born: 5/1/95   Age: 22   Bats: L   Throws: R   Height: 6'3"   Weight: 200   Entered Pro Ball: Round 2, 2016 Draft (#46 overall)

YEAR	TEAM	LVL	AGE	PA	R	2B	3B	HR	RBI	BB	K	SB	CS	AVG/OBP/SLG	TAv	VORP	BABIP	BRR	FRAA	WARP
2016	WIS	A	21	180	17	9	3	7	29	12	38	1	3	.281/.328/.497	.295	10.4	.325	-0.8	3B(37): -0.6	1.1
2017	MIL	MLB	22	250	25	10	1	9	31	13	71	1	1	.224/.269/.389	.222	-2.4	.279	-0.4	3B -2	-0.5
2018	MIL	MLB	23	253	30	10	1	10	32	15	72	1	1	.226/.275/.403	.241	0.2	.280	-0.5	3B -2	-0.2

Breakout: 6%   Improve: 14%   Collapse: 7%   Attrition: 23%   MLB: 27%   Comparables: Mat Gamel, Renato Nunez, Brandon Laird

Erceg was impressive across two levels in 2016, providing power, more contact than expected and double-plus arm strength at the hot corner. In spite of the high averages, Erceg did strike out a fair amount as he loves his power to the pull side and constantly tries to tap into it by attempting to pull everything that comes his way. That stuff works in the lower minors to an extent, but his approach will have to mature as he progresses levels.

Jake Gatewood   3B

Born: 9/25/95   Age: 21   Bats: R   Throws: R   Height: 6'5"   Weight: 190   Entered Pro Ball: Round 1, 2014 Draft (#41 overall)

YEAR	TEAM	LVL	AGE	PA	R	2B	3B	HR	RBI	BB	K	SB	CS	AVG/OBP/SLG	TAv	VORP	BABIP	BRR	FRAA	WARP
2015	WIS	A	19	193	16	5	1	4	16	14	65	5	0	.209/.275/.316	.226	0.3	.306	-0.8	SS(52): -3.9	-0.4
2016	WIS	A	20	524	70	33	0	14	64	18	141	3	2	.240/.268/.391	.242	4.8	.303	0.6	3B(93): -1.9 • 1B(26): 0.5	0.4
2017	MIL	MLB	21	250	21	10	0	8	28	8	90	0	0	.197/.228/.343	.193	-10.5	.273	-0.4	3B -0 • 1B 0	-1.2
2018	MIL	MLB	22	397	42	17	0	14	46	15	141	0	0	.204/.238/.363	.214	-11.5	.278	-0.9	3B -1 • 1B 0	-1.3

Breakout: 0%   Improve: 0%   Collapse: 0%   Attrition: 2%   MLB: 2%   Comparables: Josh Bell, Juan Francisco, Renato Nunez

Gatewood was moved from shortstop to third base after it became clear his defensive prowess there was comparable to Kanye West's singing ability. Then he was moved to first base after Lucas Erceg came up and pushed Gatewood off the position, placing an extreme amount of pressure on a bat that hasn't exactly lit the world on fire yet. Gatewood still has that prodigious raw power and he's grown into his frame impressively, which is part of the reason he had to move off third base. But the contact and approach still aren't there, and they will have to be if he's going to be manning the cold corner.

Scooter Gennett   2B

Born: 5/1/90   Age: 27   Bats: L   Throws: R   Height: 5'10"   Weight: 185   Entered Pro Ball: Round 16, 2009 Draft (#496 overall)

YEAR	TEAM	LVL	AGE	PA	R	2B	3B	HR	RBI	BB	K	SB	CS	AVG/OBP/SLG	TAv	VORP	BABIP	BRR	FRAA	WARP
2014	MIL	MLB	24	474	55	31	3	9	54	22	67	6	3	.289/.320/.434	.269	14.5	.321	-1.1	2B(119): -11.1 • RF(1): -0.0	0.4
2015	CSP	AAA	25	79	12	7	1	2	11	4	10	0	1	.307/.342/.507	.276	2.7	.333	-0.7	2B(17): -0.2	0.3
2015	MIL	MLB	25	391	42	18	4	6	29	12	68	1	3	.264/.294/.381	.233	0.8	.309	1.1	2B(108): -2.8	-0.2
2016	MIL	MLB	26	542	58	30	1	14	56	38	114	8	1	.263/.317/.412	.262	14.6	.315	-0.8	2B(127): 5.0	2.0
2017	MIL	MLB	27	335	39	17	2	8	34	18	62	4	2	.268/.307/.412	.251	9.2	.307	-0.2	2B -3	0.5
2018	MIL	MLB	28	453	53	23	3	13	54	26	85	5	2	.267/.311/.425	.262	14.3	.303	-0.2	2B -4	1.1

Breakout: 6%   Improve: 50%   Collapse: 8%   Attrition: 15%   MLB: 97%   Comparables: Donovan Solano, Hector Luna, Luis Gonzalez

Is there anything better, as an empiricist, than to encounter cases that consistently disprove hypotheses or outlast expectations or even call into question measurement assumptions and tools? Stat-heads throw around the small-sample-size moniker and love regressions to the mean, but they infrequently bask in the total glory of falsifiability, paradigm shifts or the social constructions of their measurements. And so there's this air of inevitability that creeps through even some of the most methodologically smooth writing: Gennett can't hit lefties (and then he significantly adjusts his approach at the plate to hit lefties); Gennett can't field (and then he improves his FRAA two consecutive seasons); Gennett is a borderline bench player (and then he posts solidly average production during his best season of his career). Revisit those hypotheses, revisit those methods, and consider the alternate interpretations of your prospect grades: Gennett is one player who demonstrates the joy in being wrong within your own worldview. Who's next? Or, when do you change your worldview?

Monte Harrison   CF

Born: 8/10/95   Age: 21   Bats: R   Throws: R   Height: 6'3"   Weight: 220   Entered Pro Ball: Round 2, 2014 Draft (#50 overall)

YEAR	TEAM	LVL	AGE	PA	R	2B	3B	HR	RBI	BB	K	SB	CS	AVG/OBP/SLG	TAv	VORP	BABIP	BRR	FRAA	WARP
2015	WIS	A	19	184	18	6	2	2	11	14	77	6	4	.148/.246/.247	.184	-8.0	.265	1.0	CF(42): -5.8 • RF(4): 0.0	-1.5
2016	WIS	A	20	298	34	11	1	6	37	20	97	8	3	.221/.294/.337	.233	1.1	.321	1.0	CF(48): -1.7 • RF(14): 0.2	1.0
2017	MIL	MLB	21	250	26	7	1	6	21	15	100	3	2	.174/.239/.294	.185	-10.3	.270	-0.1	CF 0 • RF 0	-1.0
2018	MIL	MLB	22	243	24	8	1	7	24	15	98	3	2	.170/.239/.306	.199	-8.9	.262	0.1	CF 0 • RF 0	-0.9

Breakout: 0%   Improve: 0%   Collapse: 0%   Attrition: 1%   MLB: 1%   Comparables: Keon Broxton, Joe Benson, Daniel Fields

You know, between Lucas Erceg, Brett Phillips and Monte Harrison it's starting to seem like the Brewers are trying to corner the market on heat-throwing outfielders. Harrison has double-plus arm strength and plus run. He was hurt a lot in 2016, which is really cutting into his development. There are tools here, but he has to start showing more hit ability in game to unlock them.

Martin Maldonado   C

Born: 8/16/86   Age: 30   Bats: R   Throws: R   Height: 6'0"   Weight: 230   Entered Pro Ball: Round 27, 2004 Draft (#803 overall)

YEAR	TEAM	LVL	AGE	PA	R	2B	3B	HR	RBI	BB	K	SB	CS	AVG/OBP/SLG	TAv	VORP	BABIP	BRR	FRAA	WARP
2014	MIL	MLB	27	126	14	5	0	4	16	11	32	0	0	.234/.320/.387	.257	4.9	.293	0.3	C(42): 8.1 • 1B(2): -0.1	1.4
2015	MIL	MLB	28	256	19	7	0	4	22	23	65	0	1	.210/.282/.293	.208	-2.6	.272	-0.5	C(74): 4.4 • 1B(1): -0.0	0.2
2016	MIL	MLB	29	253	21	7	0	8	21	35	56	1	0	.202/.332/.351	.245	6.5	.234	-1.1	C(69): 3.9	1.1
2017	ANA	MLB	30	451	45	15	0	11	45	39	114	1	1	.210/.287/.336	.228	5.7	.258	-1.0	C 9	1.5
2018	ANA	MLB	31	356	42	13	0	10	38	33	91	0	0	.216/.300/.357	.237	3.8	.264	-0.8	C 7	1.1

Breakout: 3%   Improve: 31%   Collapse: 12%   Attrition: 18%   MLB: 92%   Comparables: Yorvit Torrealba, Gerald Laird, Landon Powell

When Jonathan Lucroy started for the Brewers, many people had the chance to ask, "Could Martin Maldonado start?" After Lucroy left, Maldonado provided the ultimate gift to Brewers fans: 10 extra-base hits and 20 walks (seven of them intentional) in 152 plate appearances. Baseball is fun for its superstars, and it's even better when the role players like Maldonado have their chance to shine. The strong glove reputation will stick, and so the once-trusty veteran has ascended to the next level of challenges to answer.

YEAR	TEAM	P. COUNT	FRM RUNS	BLK RUNS	THRW RUNS	TOT RUNS
2014	MIL	4528	7.3	0.3	-0.1	7.4
2014	MIL	4528	7.3	0.3	-0.1	7.4
2015	MIL	10023	5.8	0.6	0.7	7.1
2016	MIL	9275	2.1	1.4	1.8	5.4
2017	MIL	17424	7.0	1.6	1.9	10.5
2018	MIL	13760	4.5	1.0	1.4	6.9

Kirk Nieuwenhuis   OF

Born: 8/7/87   Age: 29   Bats: L   Throws: R   Height: 6'3"   Weight: 225   Entered Pro Ball: Round 3, 2008 Draft (#100 overall)

YEAR	TEAM	LVL	AGE	PA	R	2B	3B	HR	RBI	BB	K	SB	CS	AVG/OBP/SLG	TAv	VORP	BABIP	BRR	FRAA	WARP
2014	LVG	AAA	26	229	34	13	3	11	32	15	56	3	3	.265/.319/.512	.274	9.7	.310	-0.3	LF(31): 8.5 • CF(25): -0.8	1.7
2014	NYN	MLB	26	130	16	14	1	3	16	16	39	4	0	.259/.346/.482	.306	9.3	.361	0.6	LF(17): 0.6 • CF(14): 0.2	1.0
2015	ANA	MLB	27	24	4	2	0	0	1	2	9	0	1	.136/.208/.227	.194	-0.9	.231	0.1	LF(9): 0.6 • CF(3): -0.2	-0.1
2015	LVG	AAA	27	119	21	6	3	8	29	10	21	2	0	.324/.381/.667	.341	14.2	.333	1.0	CF(20): -3.1 • RF(3): 0.6	1.2
2015	NYN	MLB	27	117	17	9	0	4	13	9	40	2	1	.208/.282/.406	.268	3.8	.290	-0.1	LF(25): 0.1 • CF(13): 1.8	0.6
2016	MIL	MLB	28	392	38	18	1	13	44	56	133	8	9	.209/.324/.385	.264	12.9	.302	0.5	CF(83): -3.6 • RF(28): -3.3	0.6
2017	MIL	MLB	29	175	21	8	1	6	21	18	54	3	2	.221/.303/.403	.248	4.0	.289	-0.3	LF 1 • CF -0	0.3
2018	MIL	MLB	30	297	37	13	1	11	37	33	92	5	4	.219/.310/.404	.257	7.1	.289	0.6	LF 2 • CF -1	0.9

Breakout: 8%   Improve: 34%   Collapse: 7%   Attrition: 13%   MLB: 81%   Comparables: Chris Dickerson, Rick Ankiel, Casper Wells

The Beatles' rooftop concert taught its viewing public that Ringo Starr was absolutely the most talented of the Fab Four, and probably the most revolutionary to boot. Yet Starr willingly, even dutifully, took his place at the kit so his bandmates could take the more obvious spotlight. Astute listeners probably knew from the beginning that Ringo was indeed the most talented Beatles player, and absolutely the best Beatles member for his ability to take on a role that assured him less notoriety throughout his career. What the uber-talented like Starr knew—and this most certainly applies to the most patient and multifaceted fourth outfielders as well—is that sometimes you need to take the back seat so that George, John and Paul can have their chances. So it goes with Nieuwenhuis and Hernan, Jake, Ramon and Alex.

Jacob Nottingham   C

Born: 4/3/95   Age: 22   Bats: R   Throws: R   Height: 6'2"   Weight: 230   Entered Pro Ball: Round 6, 2013 Draft (#167 overall)

YEAR	TEAM	LVL	AGE	PA	R	2B	3B	HR	RBI	BB	K	SB	CS	AVG/OBP/SLG	TAv	VORP	BABIP	BRR	FRAA	WARP
2015	QUD	A	20	253	34	18	1	10	46	18	51	1	2	.326/.387/.543	.316	20.3	.385	-2.4	C(39): 1.0 • 1B(10): -0.2	2.2
2015	LNC	A+	20	76	14	6	1	4	14	3	10	0	0	.324/.368/.606	.328	7.8	.333	-0.5	C(16): 0.1 • 1B(1): 0.0	0.9
2015	STO	A+	20	182	25	9	0	3	22	12	38	1	0	.299/.352/.409	.292	12.6	.365	0.4	C(34): -1.0 • 1B(7): -0.1	1.2
2016	BLX	AA	21	456	46	14	0	11	37	29	138	9	2	.234/.295/.347	.248	12.2	.320	0.0	C(98): 4.7 • 1B(3): 0.1	1.8
2017	*MIL*	*MLB*	*22*	*250*	*26*	*10*	*0*	*9*	*31*	*13*	*77*	*1*	*0*	*.232/.282/.394*	*.230*	*4.3*	*.303*	*-0.3*	*C -4 • 1B 0*	*0.0*
2018	*MIL*	*MLB*	*23*	*328*	*40*	*14*	*1*	*13*	*42*	*20*	*100*	*2*	*1*	*.236/.290/.413*	*.252*	*8.7*	*.305*	*-0.4*	*C -5 • 1B 0*	*0.4*

Breakout: 1%   Improve: 9%   Collapse: 8%   Attrition: 20%   MLB: 27%   *Comparables: Jorge Alfaro, Gary Sanchez, Hank Conger*

YEAR	TEAM	P. COUNT	FRM RUNS	BLK RUNS	THRW RUNS	TOT RUNS
2017	*MIL*	8618	-3.0	-0.8	-0.4	-4.2
2018	*MIL*	11304	-3.8	-0.8	-0.6	-5.2

Catchers exist on their own defensive spectrum. Some catchers have enough athleticism to play an up-the-middle position or a corner-outfield spot, some have just enough to make it work at third base and then there are guys like Nottingham who are stuck at first base if the whole catching thing doesn't work out. There are concerns with Nottingham; his approach collapsed last year against more advanced competition and opinions on his catching ability are varied. He's a large adult, so he has his issues blocking balls down in the plate and doesn't set a good target. None of it really matters if he doesn't tap into his prodigious strength, however. He doesn't have the kind of defensive profile that compels you to eat the bad offensive production even if you are a Nottingham-stan.

Hernan Perez   3B/OF

Born: 3/26/91   Age: 26   Bats: R   Throws: R   Height: 6'1"   Weight: 215   Entered Pro Ball: International Free Agent, 2007

YEAR	TEAM	LVL	AGE	PA	R	2B	3B	HR	RBI	BB	K	SB	CS	AVG/OBP/SLG	TAv	VORP	BABIP	BRR	FRAA	WARP
2014	TOL	AAA	23	596	69	32	7	6	53	36	65	21	6	.287/.331/.404	.247	22.2	.315	5.8	SS(118): -2.5 • 2B(14): 0.9	2.1
2014	DET	MLB	23	6	1	0	0	0	0	1	1	0	0	.200/.333/.200	.225	-0.1	.250	-0.1	2B(5): 0.0 • 3B(2): -0.0	0.0
2015	DET	MLB	24	34	1	0	0	0	0	1	11	1	0	.061/.088/.061	.039	-6.6	.091	-0.3	3B(8): -0.0 • 2B(5): -0.1	-0.7
2015	MIL	MLB	24	238	13	15	2	1	21	4	48	4	1	.270/.281/.365	.227	-1.9	.335	-1.3	3B(72): 0.6 • 2B(14): -1.0	-0.3
2016	CSP	AAA	25	67	10	4	1	1	11	3	10	2	0	.339/.364/.484	.289	4.4	.385	0.4	2B(10): -0.7 • 3B(6): 0.1	0.4
2016	MIL	MLB	25	430	50	18	2	13	56	18	94	34	7	.272/.302/.428	.273	19.8	.322	3.0	3B(60): -0.4 • RF(36): 3.7	2.4
2017	*MIL*	*MLB*	*26*	*351*	*39*	*15*	*2*	*7*	*33*	*13*	*66*	*16*	*4*	*.254/.279/.378*	*.229*	*-1.4*	*.291*	*2.3*	*RF 9 • 3B -0*	*0.9*
2018	*MIL*	*MLB*	*27*	*512*	*55*	*23*	*3*	*13*	*56*	*23*	*99*	*23*	*6*	*.256/.289/.393*	*.242*	*2.4*	*.292*	*0.3*	*RF 14 • 3B 0*	*1.8*

Breakout: 6%   Improve: 24%   Collapse: 11%   Attrition: 27%   MLB: 49%   *Comparables: Charlie Culberson, Brent Morel, Matt Dominguez*

When does a utility player prove they can start, as opposed to simply continuing to serve as a utility player? Perez is this living, breathing question, as the former infield gloveman from the Tigers' system stuck with the Brewers on a minor-league contract and established himself as a fringe-power/speed depth option while moving to right field and playing nearly everywhere else. Perhaps his ugly K/BB ratio answers the utility-or-starter question, which only leads one to say that Perez keeps a role and has his work cut out for himself.

Brett Phillips   CF

Born: 5/30/94   Age: 23   Bats: L   Throws: R   Height: 6'0"   Weight: 185   Entered Pro Ball: Round 6, 2012 Draft (#189 overall)

YEAR	TEAM	LVL	AGE	PA	R	2B	3B	HR	RBI	BB	K	SB	CS	AVG/OBP/SLG	TAv	VORP	BABIP	BRR	FRAA	WARP
2014	QUD	A	20	443	68	21	12	13	58	36	76	18	10	.302/.362/.521	.320	41.2	.341	2.3	RF(60): 7.9 • CF(44): -3.2	4.7
2014	LNC	A+	20	128	19	8	2	4	10	14	20	5	4	.339/.421/.560	.320	11.4	.384	0.3	CF(20): -2.5 • CF(4): -2.5	0.6
2015	LNC	A+	21	322	68	19	7	15	53	22	64	8	6	.320/.379/.588	.328	11.6	.368	3.0	CF(53): 1.5 • RF(9): 0.3	3.8
2015	CCH	AA	21	145	22	8	4	1	18	8	26	7	2	.321/.372/.463	.294	11.6	.393	2.6	CF(28): 6.3 • RF(3): 0.7	2.0
2015	BLX	AA	21	98	14	7	3	0	6	14	30	2	1	.250/.361/.413	.286	6.3	.385	0.8	CF(22): 4.0	1.1
2016	BLX	AA	22	517	60	14	6	16	62	67	154	12	7	.229/.332/.397	.278	24.9	.311	1.5	CF(102): -3.0 • RF(19): 0.3	2.4
2017	*MIL*	*MLB*	*23*	*250*	*32*	*10*	*3*	*8*	*28*	*20*	*72*	*4*	*2*	*.235/.302/.418*	*.242*	*4.2*	*.299*	*0.2*	*CF 0 • RF 1*	*0.7*
2018	*MIL*	*MLB*	*24*	*373*	*44*	*14*	*4*	*12*	*45*	*31*	*107*	*6*	*3*	*.234/.301/.411*	*.252*	*7.0*	*.298*	*0.5*	*CF 1 • RF 2*	*1.1*

Breakout: 1%   Improve: 17%   Collapse: 3%   Attrition: 12%   MLB: 34%   *Comparables: Kirk Nieuwenhuis, Michael Choice, Franklin Gutierrez*

There are guns, there are cannons and then there are the kind of ultralight beam arms Phillips possesses. His arm is double-plus with the kind of strength and carry that ends up on YouTube videos everyone shares if he gets to the highest level. The "if" is a new one for Phillips, as his season at the plate was abysmal and put a ding on his overall profile. He still has the potential for an above-average hit tool and he profiles to produce average home run totals, which would work very well with his plus run tool. He'll have to improve his approach, as his contact rates took a scary downturn in 2016.

Michael Reed   OF

Born: 11/18/92   Age: 24   Bats: R   Throws: R   Height: 6'0"   Weight: 215   Entered Pro Ball: Round 5, 2011 Draft (#161 overall)

YEAR	TEAM	LVL	AGE	PA	R	2B	3B	HR	RBI	BB	K	SB	CS	AVG/OBP/SLG	TAv	VORP	BABIP	BRR	FRAA	WARP
2014	BRV	A+	21	457	50	20	5	5	47	78	79	33	13	.255/.396/.378	.292	24.2	.310	-0.3	RF(99): 0.0 • CF(2): -0.2	2.4
2015	BLX	AA	22	377	43	20	5	5	49	53	80	25	7	.278/.379/.422	.309	22.5	.347	-3.0	RF(76): 4.0 • CF(8): 0.1	2.9
2015	CSP	AAA	22	148	19	13	2	0	21	20	31	1	0	.246/.351/.381	.246	2.1	.323	1.4	RF(31): -3.5 • CF(5): -1.5	-0.3
2015	MIL	MLB	22	6	2	1	0	0	0	0	3	0	0	.333/.333/.500	.304	-0.6	.667	-1.0	RF(3): -0.1	-0.1
2016	CSP	AAA	23	492	68	20	2	8	45	74	124	20	8	.248/.366/.365	.259	11.7	.333	0.9	CF(50): -5.7 • RF(42): -8.0	-0.1
2016	MIL	MLB	23	24	3	0	0	0	0	2	7	1	0	.182/.250/.182	.167	-1.2	.267	0.4	CF(5): 0.5 • LF(2): -0.2	-0.1
2017	*MIL*	*MLB*	*24*	*71*	*8*	*3*	*0*	*1*	*7*	*9*	*19*	*2*	*1*	*.220/.325/.350*	*.246*	*1.7*	*.293*	*0.1*	*CF -1*	*0.1*
2018	*MIL*	*MLB*	*25*	*305*	*37*	*13*	*1*	*7*	*32*	*38*	*84*	*10*	*4*	*.225/.329/.369*	*.258*	*8.2*	*.299*	*0.8*	*CF -3*	*0.6*

Breakout: 6%   Improve: 15%   Collapse: 11%   Attrition: 21%   MLB: 34%   *Comparables: Jaff Decker, Brian Goodwin, Joey Rickard*

This is not sour grapes, but rather a recognition that one needs to properly assemble and age the very best grapes to produce World Series wine. Milwaukee rested Ryan Braun systematically for 35 starts, Domingo Santana missed 105 starts, Ramon Flores and Keon Broxton struggle mightily in April and May, and yet Reed only earned seven starts? One could certainly say that Reed is too young for this to matter, that he may have nursed an injury or that he hadn't expanded on his strengths at Triple-A Colorado Springs or that it was worth looking at other outfield options first or that Reed will have plenty of options to work in the 2017 outfield. You can't have everything, but if you can have anything, it should be ample playing time for your most intriguing organizational depth or breakthrough prospects during a rebuilding year.

Domingo Santana   RF

Born: 8/5/92   Age: 24   Bats: R   Throws: R   Height: 6'5"   Weight: 220   Entered Pro Ball: International Free Agent, 2009

YEAR	TEAM	LVL	AGE	PA	R	2B	3B	HR	RBI	BB	K	SB	CS	AVG/OBP/SLG	TAv	VORP	BABIP	BRR	FRAA	WARP
2014	HOU	MLB	21	18	1	0	0	0	0	0	14	0	0	.000/.056/.000	.066	-2.8	.000	0.1	LF(3): -0.8 • RF(2): -0.1	-0.4
2014	OKL	AAA	21	513	63	27	2	16	81	64	149	6	4	.296/.384/.474	.304	36.9	.408	0.7	RF(59): -0.3 • LF(49): -0.0	3.6
2015	HOU	MLB	22	42	6	2	0	2	8	2	17	2	1	.256/.310/.462	.256	0.9	.400	0.3	RF(9): -0.2 • LF(3): -0.8	0.0
2015	FRE	AAA	22	326	62	18	3	16	59	48	91	1	4	.320/.426/.582	.348	36.0	.429	0.6	RF(59): -6.8 • LF(1): 0.2	3.0
2015	CSP	AAA	22	85	13	5	1	2	18	6	17	1	1	.380/.424/.544	.319	6.9	.467	-0.1	LF(14): -1.6 • RF(4): -0.4	0.5
2015	MIL	MLB	22	145	14	5	0	6	18	18	46	2	0	.231/.345/.421	.299	9.6	.310	0.6	CF(23): -2.9 • RF(16): -1.4	0.5
2016	WIS	A	23	28	4	0	0	1	3	4	5	0	0	.174/.321/.304	.245	-0.1	.176	0.0	RF(4): -0.1	0.0
2016	MIL	MLB	23	281	34	14	0	11	32	32	91	2	3	.256/.345/.447	.287	14.8	.359	1.6	RF(62): -4.7 • LF(4): -0.3	1.0
2017	*MIL*	*MLB*	*24*	*485*	*59*	*20*	*1*	*19*	*63*	*55*	*157*	*4*	*3*	*.246/.338/.433*	*.273*	*21.3*	*.342*	*-1.2*	*RF -5 • CF -0*	*0.9*
2018	*MIL*	*MLB*	*25*	*497*	*69*	*20*	*1*	*21*	*68*	*58*	*162*	*4*	*3*	*.249/.343/.448*	*.287*	*26.0*	*.344*	*2.0*	*RF -5 • CF 0*	*2.2*

Breakout: 3%   Improve: 39%   Collapse: 16%   Attrition: 23%   MLB: 80%   *Comparables: Wil Myers, Oswaldo Arcia, Pedro Alvarez*

Santana's overall production remained remarkably similar from 2015 to 2016, but the big change came in the expectations through which his performance was viewed. He failed to take the hoped-for step forward at the plate, missed big chunks of time with injuries and struggled defensively in right field after seeing action in center field as a rookie. He did finish on a high note with a big September and Santana has the Three True Outcomes skill set to be an above-average hitter, including huge power from a 6-foot-5 frame. However, even as the Brewers trudge on in rebuilding mode, he's no sure thing to be part of the long-term plan.

Travis Shaw   3B

Born: 4/16/90   Age: 27   Bats: L   Throws: R   Height: 6'4"   Weight: 230   Entered Pro Ball: Round 9, 2011 Draft (#292 overall)

YEAR	TEAM	LVL	AGE	PA	R	2B	3B	HR	RBI	BB	K	SB	CS	AVG/OBP/SLG	TAv	VORP	BABIP	BRR	FRAA	WARP
2014	PME	AA	24	208	35	8	1	11	37	29	23	5	3	.305/.406/.548	.319	13.4	.301	-1.8	1B(35): -3.3 • 3B(6): -0.4	1.0
2014	PAW	AAA	24	346	43	21	1	10	41	28	76	2	0	.262/.321/.431	.260	2.1	.312	-2.1	1B(75): 4.6 • 3B(6): -0.4	0.6
2015	PAW	AAA	25	322	29	12	2	5	30	26	54	0	1	.249/.318/.356	.251	2.8	.289	-1.3	3B(43): 4.2 • 1B(31): -2.8	0.5
2015	BOS	MLB	25	248	31	10	0	13	36	18	57	0	1	.270/.327/.487	.278	6.2	.304	-1.0	1B(55): -0.2 • 3B(8): 0.4	0.7
2016	BOS	MLB	26	530	63	34	2	16	71	43	133	5	1	.242/.306/.421	.246	5.7	.299	-0.8	3B(105): 7.4 • 1B(50): 2.2	1.6
2017	*MIL*	*MLB*	*27*	*556*	*62*	*25*	*2*	*21*	*72*	*46*	*130*	*3*	*1*	*.244/.309/.426*	*.256*	*11.9*	*.286*	*-0.8*	*3B 9 • 1B 0*	*1.9*
2018	*MIL*	*MLB*	*28*	*543*	*70*	*25*	*2*	*21*	*72*	*48*	*125*	*3*	*1*	*.249/.319/.439*	*.270*	*16.2*	*.290*	*-1.0*	*3B 9 • 1B 0*	*2.8*

Breakout: 4%   Improve: 39%   Collapse: 10%   Attrition: 15%   MLB: 80%   *Comparables: Andy Marte, Trevor Plouffe, Luis Valbuena*

After their trip to the Star Market left them with Pablo Sandoval and a big bill, the Red Sox didn't Stop & Shop for hot corner help again last offseason. Instead they let Sandoval, Brock Holt and Shaw battle it out in spring training, and it was Shaw's performance that earned him the starting nod. Shaw was a Whole Foods-quality product at a Market Basket price in April and May, hitting .292/.358/.508. Then he morphed into Two-Buck Chuck, batting just .207/.270/.361 from June 1 onward. The Mayor of Ding Dong City retains some usefulness as a strong-side platoon bat who can adequately play both corner infield spots, but he's clearly overmatched as a first-division starter. He won't have to be that now, after being shipped to the Milwaukee in December, and he'll attempt to Piggly Wiggly his way into a role on the next good Brewers team.

Andrew Susac   C

Born: 3/22/90   Age: 27   Bats: R   Throws: R   Height: 6'1"   Weight: 215   Entered Pro Ball: Round 2, 2011 Draft (#86 overall)

YEAR	TEAM	LVL	AGE	PA	R	2B	3B	HR	RBI	BB	K	SB	CS	AVG/OBP/SLG	TAv	VORP	BABIP	BRR	FRAA	WARP
2014	FRE	AAA	24	253	34	9	0	10	32	34	50	0	0	.268/.379/.451	.295	21.8	.305	0.4	C(56): 15.0	3.7
2014	SFN	MLB	24	95	13	8	0	3	19	7	28	0	0	.273/.326/.466	.291	7.1	.368	0.5	C(29): -2.2	0.5
2015	SAC	AAA	25	32	6	3	0	1	2	3	10	0	0	.321/.406/.536	.334	3.4	.471	-0.3	C(7): -0.4	0.3
2015	SFN	MLB	25	148	14	7	2	3	14	14	43	0	0	.218/.297/.368	.254	4.5	.299	-0.8	C(40): 0.9	0.6
2016	SAC	AAA	26	239	28	12	1	8	36	24	45	0	0	.273/.343/.455	.306	19.0	.304	-2.3	C(50): 9.4	2.9
2016	CSP	AAA	26	43	2	1	0	0	3	2	16	0	0	.125/.163/.150	.124	-4.5	.200	-0.2	C(10): 0.3	-0.4
2016	MIL	MLB	26	19	3	1	0	1	2	2	5	0	0	.235/.316/.471	.274	1.4	.273	0.3	C(6): -0.9	0.1
2017	*MIL*	*MLB*	*27*	*303*	*34*	*13*	*1*	*11*	*36*	*30*	*80*	*0*	*0*	*.233/.314/.408*	*.255*	*12.8*	*.289*	*-0.6*	*C 4*	*1.0*
2018	*MIL*	*MLB*	*28*	*234*	*30*	*10*	*1*	*8*	*29*	*23*	*62*	*0*	*0*	*.229/.312/.405*	*.260*	*8.4*	*.282*	*-0.1*	*C 3*	*1.2*

Breakout: 7%   Improve: 30%   Collapse: 16%   Attrition: 32%   MLB: 74%   *Comparables: Curtis Casali, Roberto Perez, Rob Bowen*

The next Jonathan Villar could very well sit on the Brewers' 40-man roster. Consider players who made at least two organizational Top 10 lists (but preferably three), have played two part-time seasons in the majors, are (or were) blocked by another starter or surpassed by an advanced prospect and have enough scouting question marks to make a breakout a surprise. By the way, it's kind of stunning how many players one can find, sitting on organizational top-10 lists year after year, maybe stalling a bit, leaving many chances for teams to snatch up their own personal Jonathan Villars. All Susac needs is time, and one can raise those question marks about the bat or the glove. In limited

YEAR	TEAM	P. COUNT	FRM RUNS	BLK RUNS	THRW RUNS	TOT RUNS
2014	FRE	6308	13.3	-0.2	1.2	14.3
2014	SFN	3009	-1.9	-0.8	0.1	-2.6
2015	SAC	869	0.4	0.0	0.0	0.4
2015	SFN	4737	0.4	0.5	-0.7	0.1
2016	MIL	577	-0.8	0.0	0.0	-0.8
2017	*MIL*	*10719*	*4.2*	*-0.1*	*-0.5*	*3.6*
2018	*MIL*	*8292*	*2.8*	*-0.1*	*-0.5*	*2.3*

time behind the plate in San Francisco, Susac's throwing and framing fluctuated, and the same can be said for plate discipline and power. But this is just the belly of the whale for this saga. In the book version, Susac and Villar converge to lead a stellar middle of the diamond in Milwaukee; we'll see how the silver screen adapts that plot.

Eric Thames   1B

Born: 11/10/86   Age: 30   Bats: L   Throws: R   Height: 6'0"   Weight: 210   Entered Pro Ball: Round 7, 2008 Draft (#219 overall)

YEAR	TEAM	LVL	AGE	PA	R	2B	3B	HR	RBI	BB	K	SB	CS	AVG/OBP/SLG	TAv	VORP	BABIP	BRR	FRAA	WARP
2017	MIL	MLB	30	585	62	24	4	17	68	44	159	7	3	.238/.298/.396	.244	0.7	.302	0.0	1B 0	-0.3
2018	MIL	MLB	31	350	41	14	2	10	40	28	99	4	2	.233/.298/.392	.248	0.1	.300	0.0	-	0.0

Breakout: 1%   Improve: 25%   Collapse: 6%   Attrition: 21%   MLB: 67%   Comparables: Travis Ishikawa, Xavier Paul, Jesus Guzman

There are a lot of discussions around league translations or equivalents and what they mean. Lots of math. Lots of assumptions. Lots of variables. Thames, on the other hand, is a walking translation. A nearly average major-league hitter when he set off for Korea in 2013, he's spent the last three years putting up Barry Bonds-type numbers in the KBO, including a 40/40 season two years ago in which he hit .381/.497/.790. He outproduced every Korean import we've ever seen come to the United States, which should say (and, really, has always said) a ton about those hitters. He'll play first base in Milwaukee and even though his former life was as an outfielder, that's the right decision—don't let those stolen base numbers fool you. Even if he returns simply as the nearly average hitter he was back in 2012, he should be well worth the three-year, $16 million contract he signed. And if he ends up declining that $7.5 million player option for 2020 in order to hit free agency as a 33-year-old, maybe we'll start seeing more baseball detours through Korea than Japan.

Jonathan Villar   SS

Born: 5/2/91   Age: 26   Bats: B   Throws: R   Height: 6'1"   Weight: 215   Entered Pro Ball: International Free Agent, 2008

YEAR	TEAM	LVL	AGE	PA	R	2B	3B	HR	RBI	BB	K	SB	CS	AVG/OBP/SLG	TAv	VORP	BABIP	BRR	FRAA	WARP
2014	OKL	AAA	23	225	34	2	3	3	27	31	61	24	6	.258/.363/.347	.269	16.1	.362	4.4	SS(48): 1.0	1.7
2014	HOU	MLB	23	289	31	13	2	7	27	19	80	17	4	.209/.267/.354	.228	6.1	.271	4.0	SS(82): 4.9	1.2
2015	FRE	AAA	24	313	59	13	5	5	32	27	77	35	9	.271/.342/.407	.276	24.0	.359	6.7	SS(59): -4.3 • 3B(6): -0.4	1.9
2015	HOU	MLB	24	128	18	7	1	2	11	10	29	7	2	.284/.339/.414	.270	5.2	.360	-0.4	SS(22): 1.3 • 3B(12): 1.1	0.8
2016	MIL	MLB	25	679	92	38	3	19	63	79	174	62	18	.285/.369/.457	.291	44.9	.373	-2.4	SS(108): 5.6 • 3B(42): -4.0	4.8
2017	MIL	MLB	26	626	92	26	4	15	55	59	169	48	14	.249/.318/.394	.250	16.5	.321	5.5	2B -2 • SS 1	1.7
2018	MIL	MLB	27	552	65	24	4	13	60	54	149	41	13	.249/.325/.395	.257	16.6	.322	1.5	2B -2 • SS 1	1.6

Breakout: 3%   Improve: 59%   Collapse: 11%   Attrition: 19%   MLB: 96%   Comparables: Felipe Lopez, Josh Rutledge, Bobby Crosby

If you read BP's top-10 prospects list for the Astros in 2013, last season's breakout for Villar is all there: the plus hit tool, the big arm, the ability to drive the ball, 70 speed, the "loose play," the all-out profile that made Villar a dream to watch with the Brewers. The best part is that Villar improved his plate approach and showed that he can get on base many different ways; he can work a count for a walk, he can drive the ball, bunt for a hit and he can beat out grounders (Villar out-hit the NL by 70 points in the infield). Moreover, the switch-hitter yields power to different parts of the park, depending on which batter's box he occupied. That power plays pull, center field and opposite field. The next three years may look different for Villar, but he has enough tools to ensure that's more of a positive statement than a negative one. If the home run power takes a step back, Villar can still drive the ball and beat out infield hits; if the speed isn't as effective, Villar still has that plate discipline and power; as the power and speed decline, the meticulous discipline suggests that Villar may be able to morph along with it. For now, fans can dream on those four-plus wins and imagine those endless tools hitting the diamond.

PITCHERS

Chase Anderson   RHP

Born: 11/30/87   Age: 29   Bats: R   Throws: R   Height: 6'1"   Weight: 200   Entered Pro Ball: Round 9, 2009 Draft (#276 overall)

YEAR	TEAM	LVL	AGE	W	L	SV	G	GS	IP	H	HR	BB/9	K/9	K	GB%	BABIP	WHIP	ERA	FIP	DRA	VORP	WARP	cFIP	MPH
2014	MOB	AA	26	4	2	0	6	6	39	22	1	1.4	8.8	38	48%	.212	0.72	0.69	2.19	1.99	14.0	1.5	74	
2014	ARI	MLB	26	9	7	0	21	21	114¹	117	16	3.1	8.3	105	42%	.313	1.37	4.01	4.19	4.81	0.3	0.0	106	93.6
2015	ARI	MLB	27	6	6	0	27	27	152²	158	18	2.4	6.5	111	44%	.302	1.30	4.30	4.16	4.81	4.5	0.5	108	94.3
2016	MIL	MLB	28	9	11	0	31	30	151²	155	28	3.1	7.1	120	38%	.287	1.37	4.39	5.13	5.66	-5.1	-0.5	122	93.6
2017	MIL	MLB	29	7	9	0	24	24	136	136	20	3.1	7.7	118	45%	.292	1.34	4.53	4.52	4.80	5.8	0.6	100	
2018	MIL	MLB	30	8	10	0	26	26	154²	135	23	3.3	8.6	147	45%	.291	1.24	4.44	4.61	5.00	9.2	0.9	118	

Breakout: 21%   Improve: 40%   Collapse: 23%   Attrition: 23%   MLB: 77%   Comparables: Armando Galarraga, J.A. Happ, Josh Tomlin

According to Brooks Baseball, Anderson shelved his cutter while thriving down the stretch. The right-hander gained more whiffs from his primary and secondary fastball and more ground balls from his secondary fastball, changeup and curveball. It's tempting to say that Anderson needs to work deep into games, but he's proven to serve as valuable rotational depth with his extended hot streaks and in-season adjustments. Will the cutter dare return in 2017?

Jacob Barnes   RHP

Born: 4/14/90   Age: 27   Bats: R   Throws: R   Height: 6'2"   Weight: 220   Entered Pro Ball: Round 14, 2011 Draft (#431 overall)

YEAR	TEAM	LVL	AGE	W	L	SV	G	GS	IP	H	HR	BB/9	K/9	K	GB%	BABIP	WHIP	ERA	FIP	DRA	VORP	WARP	cFIP	MPH
2014	HUN	AA	24	2	6	0	23	21	105²	94	9	3.2	6.4	75	40%	.274	1.25	4.26	4.24	5.75	-6.2	-0.7	114	
2015	BLX	AA	25	4	5	0	39	6	75	74	2	3.6	10.1	84	53%	.362	1.39	3.36	2.69	2.11	23.0	2.5	78	
2016	CSP	AAA	26	2	1	1	17	0	22¹	14	1	2.8	9.3	23	54%	.245	0.94	1.21	3.18	2.40	6.4	0.7	82	
2016	MIL	MLB	26	0	1	1	27	0	26²	24	1	2.0	8.8	26	49%	.315	1.12	2.70	2.40	3.87	3.3	0.3	89	97.9
2017	*MIL*	*MLB*	*27*	*2*	*2*	*0*	*45*	*0*	*47¹*	*45*	*5*	*3.4*	*7.9*	*42*	*50%*	*.295*	*1.33*	*4.11*	*4.04*	*4.33*	*3.1*	*0.3*	*98*	
2018	*MIL*	*MLB*	*28*	*2*	*1*	*0*	*46*	*0*	*49*	*39*	*6*	*4.0*	*10.3*	*56*	*50%*	*.300*	*1.24*	*4.03*	*4.17*	*4.52*	*3.3*	*0.3*	*102*	

Breakout: 9%   Improve: 16%   Collapse: 21%   Attrition: 28%   MLB: 42%   *Comparables: Francisco Cruceta, Chad Reineke, Carlos Torres*

Barnes took a big step forward in 2015, joining several other prospects scouted and drafted during the late Bruce Seid's regime in doing so. Last season he reached the majors for the first time at age 26 and looked good enough to think he may not be going back to the minors. There are no secrets with Barnes' 95-plus mph fastball and 40 percent slider frequency, which yields plenty of whiffs for the righty. Better yet, Barnes stumbled with a midseason injury, but returned strong in September to leave a good final impression.

Phil Bickford   RHP

Born: 7/10/95   Age: 21   Bats: R   Throws: R   Height: 6'4"   Weight: 200   Entered Pro Ball: Round 1, 2015 Draft (#18 overall)

YEAR	TEAM	LVL	AGE	W	L	SV	G	GS	IP	H	HR	BB/9	K/9	K	GB%	BABIP	WHIP	ERA	FIP	DRA	VORP	WARP	cFIP	MPH
2016	AUG	A	20	3	4	0	11	11	60	49	2	2.2	10.4	69	34%	.308	1.07	2.70	2.38	2.26	18.4	2.0	82	
2016	SJO	A+	20	2	2	0	6	6	33	21	3	3.3	9.8	36	35%	.237	1.00	2.73	3.99	2.78	9.8	1.0	91	
2016	BRV	A+	20	2	1	0	6	5	27	26	1	5.0	10.0	30	38%	.333	1.52	3.67	3.40	4.42	3.1	0.3	105	
2017	*MIL*	*MLB*	*21*	*4*	*7*	*0*	*18*	*18*	*81²*	*87*	*15*	*4.3*	*6.9*	*63*	*70%*	*.311*	*1.54*	*5.61*	*5.52*	*6.28*	*-6.5*	*-0.7*	*149*	
2018	*MIL*	*MLB*	*22*	*5*	*8*	*0*	*23*	*23*	*132²*	*119*	*23*	*5.1*	*9.4*	*138*	*70%*	*.301*	*1.47*	*5.30*	*5.55*	*5.93*	*-4.1*	*-0.4*	*142*	

Breakout: 8%   Improve: 9%   Collapse: 1%   Attrition: 4%   MLB: 10%   *Comparables: Keyvius Sampson, Trevor May, Miguel Almonte*

The changeup is going to be the determining factor for which innings Phil Bickford ultimately calls home in the majors. If he finds a feel for the changeup, the former first-round pick acquired from the Giants for Will Smith has the delivery and arm strength to work through a lineup multiple times as a starter, and the third pitch will give him another offering to sprinkle in there. If it doesn't, Bickford will still have the stuff to pitch in the majors, albeit in a relief role where his slider could play up. His development will be on hold for 50 games following a "drug of abuse" suspension.

Michael Blazek   RHP

Born: 3/16/89   Age: 28   Bats: R   Throws: R   Height: 6'0"   Weight: 205   Entered Pro Ball: Round 35, 2007 Draft (#1068 overall)

YEAR	TEAM	LVL	AGE	W	L	SV	G	GS	IP	H	HR	BB/9	K/9	K	GB%	BABIP	WHIP	ERA	FIP	DRA	VORP	WARP	cFIP	MPH
2014	NAS	AAA	25	4	4	1	37	17	102¹	106	9	3.5	7.7	87	49%	.317	1.43	4.13	4.40	6.19	-6.2	-0.6	102	
2015	MIL	MLB	26	5	3	0	45	0	55²	40	3	2.9	7.6	47	49%	.242	1.04	2.43	3.20	4.57	0.9	0.1	101	95.8
2016	MIL	MLB	27	3	1	0	41	0	41¹	52	7	5.9	7.8	36	44%	.349	1.91	5.66	5.75	4.94	0.1	0.0	117	96.2
2017	*MIL*	*MLB*	*28*	*2*	*1*	*0*	*30*	*0*	*31*	*30*	*4*	*3.9*	*7.5*	*26*	*48%*	*.290*	*1.40*	*4.67*	*4.60*	*4.78*	*0.5*	*0.0*	*100*	
2018	*MIL*	*MLB*	*29*	*2*	*1*	*0*	*30*	*0*	*32¹*	*26*	*4*	*4.4*	*9.6*	*35*	*48%*	*.291*	*1.29*	*4.31*	*4.48*	*4.86*	*1.0*	*0.1*	*111*	

Breakout: 20%   Improve: 35%   Collapse: 16%   Attrition: 22%   MLB: 63%   *Comparables: Esmerling Vasquez, Troy Patton, Edgmer Escalona*

DRA didn't like Blazek in 2015 (4.57) despite what was largely viewed as a breakthrough campaign, and then his ERA was actually worse than his DRA in a 2016 to forget. Placing faith in the common mantra that relievers are volatile, one might look at that riding fastball and suggest Blazek is an asset, especially to a rebuilding club. So frequently, the volatility line is placed on relievers to justify trading a good one while their value is high, so this line is in favor of a bullish take on the player to be named later now that his value has hit a low point.

Tyler Cravy   RHP

Born: 7/13/89   Age: 27   Bats: R   Throws: R   Height: 6'2"   Weight: 220   Entered Pro Ball: Round 17, 2009 Draft (#526 overall)

YEAR	TEAM	LVL	AGE	W	L	SV	G	GS	IP	H	HR	BB/9	K/9	K	GB%	BABIP	WHIP	ERA	FIP	DRA	VORP	WARP	cFIP	MPH
2014	HUN	AA	24	8	1	0	14	12	73¹	47	7	1.8	7.9	64	48%	.212	0.85	1.72	3.54	2.50	22.0	2.3	84	
2015	CSP	AAA	25	7	7	0	17	17	95¹	92	6	2.9	7.1	75	41%	.303	1.29	3.97	3.95	5.23	0.8	0.1	109	
2015	MIL	MLB	25	0	8	0	14	7	42_	47	5	4.6	7.4	35	42%	.326	1.62	5.70	4.73	5.72	-3.5	-0.4	119	93.7
2016	CSP	AAA	26	3	3	0	21	9	56¹	56	5	4.5	10.4	65	46%	.338	1.49	5.91	4.11	2.66	16.0	1.6	86	
2016	MIL	MLB	26	0	1	0	20	2	28¹	21	3	3.8	7.0	22	28%	.231	1.16	2.86	4.39	6.00	-3.0	-0.3	126	94.5
2017	*MIL*	*MLB*	*27*	*2*	*2*	*0*	*28*	*3*	*43*	*42*	*6*	*3.6*	*7.6*	*37*	*53%*	*.289*	*1.36*	*4.61*	*4.66*	*4.74*	*1.3*	*0.1*	*100*	
2018	*MIL*	*MLB*	*28*	*6*	*4*	*0*	*73*	*8*	*114²*	*88*	*14*	*4.5*	*9.7*	*124*	*53%*	*.281*	*1.27*	*4.40*	*4.56*	*4.93*	*4.4*	*0.5*	*113*	

Breakout: 23%   Improve: 45%   Collapse: 20%   Attrition: 39%   MLB: 76%   *Comparables: Pat Misch, Phil Coke, Zach Jackson*

Top 10 Brewers fly-ball pitchers during the Miller Park era, by WARP: Marco Estrada (3.5), Shaun Marcum (2.9), Matt Kinney (1.9), Mike Fiers (1.7), Jim Henderson (1.6), Chad Fox (1.0), Luis Vizcaino (0.6), Julio Santana (0.6), Rick Helling (0.6), Mark DiFelice (0.5). Among all National League pitchers with at least 70 innings from 2015-2016, Cravy's ground-ball rate of 34.3 percent ranked ninth-lowest. Tyler Thornburg was in the eighth spot and he worked out OK, so let's focus on that instead of Cravy beginning his career with a 0-9 record in 34 appearances.

Zach Davies RHP

Born: 2/7/93 Age: 24 Bats: R Throws: R Height: 6'0" Weight: 155 Entered Pro Ball: Round 26, 2011 Draft (#785 overall)

YEAR	TEAM	LVL	AGE	W	L	SV	G	GS	IP	H	HR	BB/9	K/9	K	GB%	BABIP	WHIP	ERA	FIP	DRA	VORP	WARP	cFIP	MPH
2014	BOW	AA	21	10	7	0	21	20	110	106	8	2.6	8.9	109	54%	.314	1.25	3.35	3.30	2.02	39.2	4.2	75	
2015	NOR	AAA	22	5	6	0	19	18	101¹	91	4	2.9	7.2	81	54%	.290	1.22	2.84	3.08	3.69	18.0	1.8	94	
2015	CSP	AAA	22	1	2	0	5	5	27	38	2	4	7	21	57%	.391	1.85	5.00	4.45	2.57	8.2	0.8	97	
2015	MIL	MLB	22	3	2	0	6	6	34	26	2	4.0	6.4	24	58%	.245	1.21	3.71	3.84	4.14	3.5	0.4	107	90.9
2016	MIL	MLB	23	11	7	0	28	28	163¹	166	20	2.1	7.4	135	47%	.302	1.25	3.97	3.93	3.58	32.2	3.3	99	91.4
2017	MIL	MLB	24	8	10	0	26	26	148	147	18	2.7	7.7	128	47%	.296	1.29	4.01	4.04	4.23	15.6	1.6	98	
2018	MIL	MLB	25	10	10	0	28	28	173	147	21	3.2	9.5	182	47%	.306	1.21	3.87	3.99	4.34	21.6	2.2	99	

Breakout: 24% Improve: 55% Collapse: 18% Attrition: 16% MLB: 94% *Comparables: Gio Gonzalez, Vance Worley, Matt Harvey*

In 2016, 14 different Brewers posted at least 1.0 WARP. Six of those players were homegrown, five were acquired via trade, two were signed as free agents and one was a waiver claim. Among the traded-for players, only two came from true rebuilding deals in which a veteran was swapped for prospects: Zach Davies (3.3) and Domingo Santana (1.0). Davies is the face of the Brewers' rebuilding effort so far, an unlikely ace with a fascinating changeup, an exceptional ability to adjust strategy and approach, and a stubborn attitude to stick with his plan. Last season Davies also worked on a variation of his sinker, and more prominently featured a cutter to keep batters off balance. Watching Davies work lends an excellent argument in favor of replacing the common sinker/slider arsenal with a sinker/changeup approach, as going off-speed on the same plane as the sinking fastball is a beautiful and devastating occurrence.

Matt Garza RHP

Born: 11/26/83 Age: 33 Bats: R Throws: R Height: 6'4" Weight: 220 Entered Pro Ball: Round 1, 2005 Draft (#25 overall)

YEAR	TEAM	LVL	AGE	W	L	SV	G	GS	IP	H	HR	BB/9	K/9	K	GB%	BABIP	WHIP	ERA	FIP	DRA	VORP	WARP	cFIP	MPH
2014	MIL	MLB	30	8	8	0	27	27	163¹	143	12	2.8	6.9	126	46%	.268	1.18	3.64	3.51	4.43	7.5	0.8	113	95.2
2015	MIL	MLB	31	6	14	0	26	25	148²	176	23	3.5	6.3	104	47%	.319	1.57	5.63	4.96	5.89	-13.5	-1.5	118	95.1
2016	WIS	A	32	0	2	0	3	3	11¹	13	1	0.8	7.9	10	56%	.364	1.24	4.76	3.39	3.57	1.8	0.2	94	
2016	MIL	MLB	32	6	8	0	19	19	101²	117	11	3.2	6.2	70	57%	.311	1.50	4.51	4.37	4.29	12.1	1.3	103	94.7
2017	MIL	MLB	33	6	9	0	23	23	121	125	19	3.4	7.2	98	43%	.292	1.39	4.83	4.81	5.09	1.2	0.1	100	
2018	MIL	MLB	34	6	8	0	21	21	124²	122	19	3.2	7.7	106	43%	.306	1.33	4.72	4.92	5.31	3.1	0.3	125	

Breakout: 7% Improve: 50% Collapse: 12% Attrition: 22% MLB: 85% *Comparables: Vicente Padilla, Doug Davis, Gavin Floyd*

Entering the final season of a four-year, $50 million contract, the fact that Garza remains in Milwaukee shows he simply hasn't pitched well enough to be traded for any value. At age 32 his average fastball velocity fell to a career-low and he hasn't whiffed 7.0 batters per nine innings since 2013. Garza's lone saving grace last season was pushing his ground-ball rate above 50 percent for the first time, which could be a recipe for hanging around somewhere as a back-of-the-rotation starter once his contract is up. If the fly-ball tendencies return, Garza simply doesn't have the command to live on as a low-90s, low-strikeout starter.

Steven Geltz RHP

Born: 11/1/87 Age: 29 Bats: R Throws: R Height: 5'10" Weight: 210 Entered Pro Ball: Undrafted Free Agent, 2008

YEAR	TEAM	LVL	AGE	W	L	SV	G	GS	IP	H	HR	BB/9	K/9	K	GB%	BABIP	WHIP	ERA	FIP	DRA	VORP	WARP	cFIP	MPH
2014	DUR	AAA	26	3	3	1	29	0	41²	27	3	3.7	13.0	60	32%	.276	1.06	2.38	2.71	1.50	17.8	1.8	67	
2014	TBA	MLB	26	0	1	0	11	0	8¹	6	3	5.4	15.1	14	25%	.231	1.32	3.24	7.00	3.36	1.0	0.1	94	95.0
2015	TBA	MLB	27	2	6	2	70	2	67¹	45	8	3.5	8.2	61	36%	.216	1.05	3.74	4.08	4.89	-1.2	-0.1	110	94.5
2016	DUR	AAA	28	0	2	3	31	0	35²	30	3	4.3	10.1	40	27%	.297	1.32	3.03	3.53	4.95	0.0	0.0	108	
2016	TBA	MLB	28	0	2	0	27	0	26²	24	11	3.0	7.8	23	22%	.191	1.24	5.74	7.87	7.12	-6.4	-0.7	131	94.6
2017	MIL	MLB	29	3	1	1	54	0	57²	48	9	3.4	8.5	54	47%	.275	1.22	4.58	4.54	5.16	-0.2	-0.1	121	
2018	MIL	MLB	30	2	1	0	33	0	39	32	7	3.9	9.7	42	47%	.286	1.27	4.70	4.88	5.30	-0.7	-0.1	124	

Breakout: 18% Improve: 30% Collapse: 22% Attrition: 22% MLB: 60% *Comparables: Cory Wade, Leo Rosales, Anthony Varvaro*

There's no way to sugarcoat Geltz's 2016 season. Always homer-prone, the diminutive right-hander aired everything out last year—no relief pitcher with 20+ innings even came close to his nearly four home runs per nine innings. For perspective, he possessed the second-highest rate of bombs allowed in the past five seasons, only surpassed by former teammate Kirby Yates in 2015. He was undoubtedly his team's worst reliever, a tough task given how sketchy the replacement-level Tampa bullpen was. Things took an even darker turn later in the season; no amount of homers allowed or runs relinquished excuse the death threats he received via social media. Trust Geltz to remain resilient—his career story arc includes climbing to the majors after going undrafted, battling through a mysterious allergic reaction during the season, and now fighting through five months of awful performance and extreme negativity. Setbacks? Pshaw. He'll be back in the big leagues grinding out innings again this year.

Junior Guerra RHP

Born: 1/16/85 Age: 32 Bats: R Throws: R Height: 6'0" Weight: 205 Entered Pro Ball: International Free Agent, 2001

YEAR	TEAM	LVL	AGE	W	L	SV	G	GS	IP	H	HR	BB/9	K/9	K	GB%	BABIP	WHIP	ERA	FIP	DRA	VORP	WARP	cFIP	MPH
2015	BIR	AA	30	2	3	0	5	3	19²	15	2	1.8	11.9	26	48%	.325	0.97	2.29	2.90	1.42	7.9	0.9	65	
2015	CHA	MLB	30	0	0	0	3	0	4	7	1	2.2	6.8	3	57%	.462	2.00	6.75	5.60	4.45	0.1	0.0	103	96.7
2015	CHR	AAA	30	2	4	7	26	8	63²	44	5	4.1	11.2	79	44%	.260	1.15	3.39	3.11	2.21	20.9	2.1	79	
2016	CSP	AAA	31	0	2	0	5	5	26²	18	2	3.7	8.4	25	40%	.235	1.09	4.05	4.06	3.24	6.2	0.6	95	
2016	MIL	MLB	31	9	3	0	20	20	121²	94	10	3.2	7.4	100	47%	.250	1.13	2.81	3.75	4.43	12.6	1.3	101	95.5
2017	MIL	MLB	32	6	7	0	18	18	108	99	15	3.4	8.5	102	40%	.287	1.28	4.26	4.31	4.50	8.1	0.8	100	
2018	MIL	MLB	33	11	11	0	32	32	204¹	167	27	3.8	10.0	228	40%	.297	1.24	4.10	4.25	4.61	19.6	2.0	105	

Breakout: 14% Improve: 22% Collapse: 16% Attrition: 10% MLB: 61% *Comparables: Carlos Torres, Jason Grilli, Rich Hill*

By now you already know it, but it's worth repeating: "age ain't nothing but a number." Guerra joined rare company by making his starting debut during his age-31 season. Initially a praiseworthy pitcher for his amazing backstory, Guerra stormed the scene with an ace-worthy DRA throughout the first half. Command might be the scouting question mark for this righty, but Guerra adjusted by working on a moving fastball to accompany his wicked knuckling splitter. The wild splitter places Guerra among the company of other age-31 debuts, such as Hisashi Iwakuma and Jose Contreras, and both of those righties suggest different career trajectories for the intriguing Guerra. He has ample tools to make it happen, be it in the rotation or the bullpen, carving out his own uncanny career arc.

Josh Hader   LHP

Born: 4/7/94 Age: 23 Bats: L Throws: L Height: 6'3" Weight: 185 Entered Pro Ball: Round 19, 2012 Draft (#582 overall)

YEAR	TEAM	LVL	AGE	W	L	SV	G	GS	IP	H	HR	BB/9	K/9	K	GB%	BABIP	WHIP	ERA	FIP	DRA	VORP	WARP	cFIP	MPH
2014	LNC	A+	20	9	2	2	22	15	103¹	76	9	3.3	9.8	112	41%	.254	1.10	2.70	4.10	3.47	23.3	2.4	97	
2014	CCH	AA	20	1	1	0	5	4	20	16	2	7.2	10.8	24	35%	.286	1.60	6.30	4.87	5.77	-1.3	-0.1	112	
2015	CCH	AA	21	3	3	1	17	10	65¹	60	5	3.3	9.5	69	42%	.301	1.29	3.17	3.47	3.31	12.5	1.4	90	
2015	BLX	AA	21	1	4	0	7	7	38²	27	3	2.6	11.6	50	47%	.282	0.98	2.79	2.81	1.90	13.5	1.5	66	
2016	BLX	AA	22	2	1	0	11	11	57	38	1	3.0	11.5	73	41%	.291	1.00	0.95	2.14	1.57	22.4	2.4	70	
2016	CSP	AAA	22	1	7	0	14	14	69	63	5	4.7	11.5	88	43%	.345	1.43	5.22	3.81	2.86	19.1	2.0	83	
2017	MIL	MLB	23	1	1	0	25	0	26¹	23	2	4.0	9.2	27	47%	.287	1.27	3.66	3.59	3.95	2.8	0.3	88	
2018	MIL	MLB	24	2	1	0	30	0	31²	21	3	5.2	11.9	42	47%	.293	1.25	3.62	3.74	4.03	3.8	0.4	86	

Breakout: 13%   Improve: 23%   Collapse: 22%   Attrition: 37%   MLB: 64%   *Comparables: Rafael Montero, Jess Todd, Gio Gonzalez*

There's a pretty good argument that you should never send a top pitching prospect to Colorado Springs, as Hader became the latest victim of the high-altitude, high-offense environment. Hader's fastball clocks in the upper 90s and he has a plus slider, but his command has always been an issue and it went backward in 2016. His potential upside is still a fair distance from where he currently is as a player, but that upside is the kind of thing you whisper in your dreams at night hoping it comes true. If he ever gets his command to acceptable levels he's going to be a monster, and if he doesn't he will be one of the most infuriating pitchers in the majors.

Taylor Jungmann   RHP

Born: 12/18/89 Age: 27 Bats: R Throws: R Height: 6'6" Weight: 210 Entered Pro Ball: Round 1, 2011 Draft (#12 overall)

YEAR	TEAM	LVL	AGE	W	L	SV	G	GS	IP	H	HR	BB/9	K/9	K	GB%	BABIP	WHIP	ERA	FIP	DRA	VORP	WARP	cFIP	MPH
2014	HUN	AA	24	4	4	0	9	9	52	52	4	2.6	8.0	46	60%	.316	1.29	2.77	3.46	2.40	16.3	1.7	81	
2014	NAS	AA	24	8	6	0	19	18	101²	88	7	4.1	8.9	101	57%	.301	1.32	3.98	4.32	3.29	27.7	2.8	84	
2015	CSP	AAA	25	2	3	0	11	9	59¹	61	2	4.4	8.2	54	60%	.349	1.52	6.37	3.89	2.93	15.2	1.6	90	
2015	MIL	MLB	25	9	8	0	21	21	119¹	106	11	3.5	8.1	107	48%	.290	1.28	3.77	3.95	4.30	10.4	1.1	105	94.5
2016	CSP	AAA	26	1	3	0	8	8	31	39	6	10.2	7.0	24	43%	.337	2.39	9.87	8.85	18.06	-43.8	-4.5	144	
2016	BLX	AA	26	3	4	0	13	13	75¹	53	2	4.2	9.7	81	55%	.273	1.17	2.51	2.99	3.18	16.0	1.7	82	
2016	MIL	MLB	26	0	5	0	8	6	26²	30	4	5.7	6.1	18	47%	.310	1.76	7.76	6.04	5.30	0.1	0.0	121	92.3
2017	MIL	MLB	27	2	2	0	15	5	39	38	5	4.4	7.5	32	61%	.295	1.47	4.76	4.82	4.92	0.8	0.1	100	
2018	MIL	MLB	28	7	7	0	50	16	132	103	16	5.9	9.4	138	61%	.285	1.44	4.88	5.07	5.48	-0.5	-0.1	128	

Breakout: 24%   Improve: 36%   Collapse: 21%   Attrition: 40%   MLB: 66%   *Comparables: Taylor Jordan, Chris Rusin, Michael Kirkman*

Bob Uecker is a national treasure not because of his self-sabotaging sense of humor, but because the man calls a proper change-up curveball in all of its glory. One benefit of listening to Uecker is that his upbringing in mid-20th Century baseball culture ensures that he's best suited to discuss topics like crossfire pitching deliveries. The topic appeared in 2016 because Jungmann lost the timing mechanism in his delivery, which produced a crucial flaw in his carefully balanced, levers-and-pulleys crossfire. Calling it a herky-jerky delivery does not do it justice and Uecker is right to place Jungmann in the category of that historical delivery. Jungmann has already advanced from potential bust, long-brewing player development to top-20 value among 2011 first rounders, which is simply to say that if you think this is already a journey, Jungmann undoubtedly will have more twists and turns in mind.

Corey Knebel   RHP

Born: 11/26/91 Age: 25 Bats: R Throws: R Height: 6'4" Weight: 220 Entered Pro Ball: Round 1, 2013 Draft (#39 overall)

YEAR	TEAM	LVL	AGE	W	L	SV	G	GS	IP	H	HR	BB/9	K/9	K	GB%	BABIP	WHIP	ERA	FIP	DRA	VORP	WARP	cFIP	MPH
2014	ERI	AA	22	3	0	1	11	0	15	8	1	4.8	13.8	23	53%	.241	1.07	1.20	2.75	1.94	4.9	0.5	74	
2014	TOL	AAA	22	1	1	2	14	0	18¹	6	0	4.4	9.8	20	55%	.158	0.82	1.96	2.98	3.18	4.4	0.4	90	
2014	DET	MLB	22	0	0	0	8	0	8²	11	0	3.1	11.4	11	56%	.440	1.62	6.23	1.66	3.39	1.1	0.1	89	96.6
2014	ROU	AAA	22	1	0	0	9	0	12	9	2	3.8	15.0	20	42%	.318	1.17	3.75	4.03	1.41	5.2	0.5	75	
2015	CSP	AAA	23	1	2	6	16	0	15¹	14	1	4.1	12.9	22	42%	.371	1.37	4.70	2.95	1.92	5.1	0.5	82	
2015	MIL	MLB	23	0	0	0	48	0	50¹	44	8	3.0	10.4	58	50%	.290	1.21	3.22	4.06	3.22	8.3	0.9	86	97.5
2016	CSP	AAA	24	1	0	2	11	2	13²	5	0	2.0	9.2	14	66%	.172	0.59	1.32	2.33	1.82	4.9	0.5	78	
2016	MIL	MLB	24	1	4	2	35	0	32²	32	3	4.4	10.5	38	43%	.333	1.47	4.68	3.61	3.77	4.4	0.5	95	97.7
2017	MIL	MLB	25	3	3	35	55	0	57	53	8	3.5	9.2	59	48%	.291	1.30	4.13	4.23	4.35	3.6	0.4	96	
2018	MIL	MLB	26	3	1	30	55	0	58	48	7	3.6	10.1	65	48%	.301	1.22	3.89	4.04	4.39	4.7	0.5	98	

Breakout: 36%   Improve: 52%   Collapse: 24%   Attrition: 18%   MLB: 85%   *Comparables: Rex Brothers, Joey Devine, Cody Allen*

Scouting reports have branded Knebel a potential back-end reliever, and 2016 stands as his first trial by fire. Knebel entered 40 percent of his appearances when the game was within one run and another 31 percent with two or three-run leads. This proved to be a big test for Knebel, who was often spelled by manager Craig Counsell in favor of Jhan Marinez, Carlos Torres, Blaine Boyer or Tyler Thornburg when trouble showed. For this reason, six of Knebel's 20 runs allowed were inherited runners scored, which leads one to ask whether the righty should have been allowed to work out of his own jams. Oddly enough, Knebel ratcheted up his big-rising fastball with more velocity and arm-side run in 2016, but could not draw more whiffs. If the trend holds, go bullish on Knebel taking his next step as a high-leverage reliever.

Kodi Medeiros   LHP

Born: 5/25/96   Age: 21   Bats: L   Throws: L   Height: 6'2"   Weight: 180   Entered Pro Ball: Round 1, 2014 Draft (#12 overall)

YEAR	TEAM	LVL	AGE	W	L	SV	G	GS	IP	H	HR	BB/9	K/9	K	GB%	BABIP	WHIP	ERA	FIP	DRA	VORP	WARP	cFIP	MPH
2015	WIS	A	19	4	5	1	25	16	93¹	79	0	3.9	9.1	94	65%	.307	1.27	4.44	2.96	3.74	14.4	1.5	97	
2016	BRV	A+	20	4	12	0	23	22	85	102	4	6.7	6.8	64	55%	.356	1.94	5.93	4.79	11.97	-61.4	-6.3	137	
2017	MIL	MLB	21	4	6	0	28	16	76²	91	12	6.2	5.1	44	49%	.328	1.88	6.20	6.25	6.87	-13.4	-1.4	161	
2018	MIL	MLB	22	3	5	0	18	12	85	82	12	7.8	8.3	79	49%	.319	1.83	6.03	6.34	6.68	-7.9	-0.8	156	

Breakout: 1%   Improve: 1%   Collapse: 0%   Attrition: 1%   MLB: 1%   Comparables: Edgar Olmos, Elvin Ramirez, Blake Snell

Now that we're somewhat removed from the 2014 draft we can focus more on what Medeiros can be instead of what he can't be. Medeiros is stretched as a starter, as he has issues repeating his mechanics. He can get rotational with his delivery, which causes his stuff to lose effectiveness and causes some nasty command issues. His fastball works in the low-to-mid-90s and he pairs it with a plus slider, so there are major-league qualities here. It's just probably not going to work well in the rotation.

Jimmy Nelson   RHP

Born: 6/5/89   Age: 28   Bats: R   Throws: R   Height: 6'6"   Weight: 250   Entered Pro Ball: Round 2, 2010 Draft (#64 overall)

YEAR	TEAM	LVL	AGE	W	L	SV	G	GS	IP	H	HR	BB/9	K/9	K	GB%	BABIP	WHIP	ERA	FIP	DRA	VORP	WARP	cFIP	MPH
2014	NAS	AAA	25	10	2	0	17	16	111	70	3	2.6	9.2	114	62%	.241	0.92	1.46	2.97	1.37	53.8	5.4	62	
2014	MIL	MLB	25	2	9	0	14	12	69¹	82	6	2.5	7.4	57	50%	.344	1.46	4.93	3.75	4.45	2.9	0.3	107	96.0
2015	MIL	MLB	26	11	13	0	30	30	177¹	163	18	3.3	7.5	148	52%	.285	1.29	4.11	4.13	4.89	3.7	0.4	104	96.0
2016	MIL	MLB	27	8	16	0	32	32	179¹	186	25	4.3	7.0	140	51%	.299	1.52	4.62	5.16	5.71	-6.9	-0.7	113	95.5
2017	MIL	MLB	28	8	10	0	26	26	156	150	20	3.7	7.9	136	73%	.291	1.37	4.46	4.53	4.73	7.8	0.8	100	
2018	MIL	MLB	29	11	12	0	31	31	200¹	171	24	4.0	8.8	197	73%	.296	1.29	4.30	4.46	4.85	14.6	1.5	112	

Breakout: 11%   Improve: 34%   Collapse: 32%   Attrition: 25%   MLB: 88%   Comparables: Roberto Hernandez, Randy Wells, Dana Eveland

There is no end to the pitch-tinkering for Nelson, who has spent the past three seasons swimming in the Brewers' middle-to-low rotation while working with a few different arsenals. The rising star, sinker/slider Nelson of 2013-2014 did not find ample success with those pitches, and instead of honing them further, decided to work on those offerings while expanding to a new curveball and primary fastball for 2015. That just didn't fit, so the righty doubled down on both his primary and sinking fastballs throughout a rough 2016. Nelson's struggles nearly escape explanation, as the hard sinker in 2016 drops and rides arm side more than his 2014 version, back when he primarily worked sinker/slider. Perhaps some nostalgia is in order for Nelson to succeed by returning to those roots and reconstructing his approach.

Luis Ortiz   RHP

Born: 9/22/95   Age: 21   Bats: R   Throws: R   Height: 6'3"   Weight: 230   Entered Pro Ball: Round 1, 2014 Draft (#30 overall)

YEAR	TEAM	LVL	AGE	W	L	SV	G	GS	IP	H	HR	BB/9	K/9	K	GB%	BABIP	WHIP	ERA	FIP	DRA	VORP	WARP	cFIP	MPH
2015	HIC	A	19	4	1	0	13	13	50	45	1	1.6	8.3	46	45%	.306	1.08	1.80	2.50	2.81	13.4	1.4	87	
2016	HDS	A+	20	3	2	0	7	6	27²	23	4	2.0	9.1	28	51%	.264	1.05	2.60	4.22	2.80	8.2	0.8	86	
2016	FRI	AA	20	1	4	1	9	8	39²	47	3	1.6	7.7	34	47%	.352	1.36	4.08	3.36	2.78	10.1	1.1	94	
2016	BLX	AA	20	2	2	0	6	6	23¹	26	2	3.9	6.2	16	33%	.316	1.54	1.93	4.35	6.44	-3.5	-0.4	122	
2017	MIL	MLB	21	4	6	0	18	18	71¹	80	12	3.3	6.0	48	62%	.319	1.49	5.23	5.19	5.83	-2.1	-0.2	138	
2018	MIL	MLB	22	6	10	0	29	29	177¹	171	28	4.2	8.6	169	62%	.314	1.43	4.99	5.20	5.56	0.0	0.0	132	

Breakout: 8%   Improve: 10%   Collapse: 2%   Attrition: 11%   MLB: 13%   Comparables: Patrick Corbin, Randall Delgado, Vicente Campos

Acquired by the Brewers alongside Lewis Brinson in the Jonathan Lucroy trade, Ortiz works with a fastball that runs in the 92-97 range and a slider that projects to miss bats at the highest level. He pairs it with plus command, which he didn't show in his brief stint with Biloxi last year, but his ability to hit the strike zone is in there. Scouts frequently worry about his body, as he's got a soft midsection already and projects to add bad weight.

Blake Parker   RHP

Born: 6/19/85   Age: 32   Bats: R   Throws: R   Height: 6'3"   Weight: 225   Entered Pro Ball: Round 16, 2006 Draft (#479 overall)

YEAR	TEAM	LVL	AGE	W	L	SV	G	GS	IP	H	HR	BB/9	K/9	K	GB%	BABIP	WHIP	ERA	FIP	DRA	VORP	WARP	cFIP	MPH
2014	IOW	AAA	29	0	1	25	35	0	35²	28	3	3.3	13.1	52	44%	.325	1.15	1.77	2.97	1.19	16.5	1.6	64	
2014	CHN	MLB	29	1	1	0	18	0	21	24	3	1.7	10.3	24	32%	.350	1.33	5.14	3.25	4.09	0.9	0.1	93	92.8
2016	TAC	AAA	31	1	2	19	38	0	39²	24	4	2.5	12.7	56	44%	.256	0.88	2.72	3.12	0.92	17.8	1.8	64	
2016	SEA	MLB	31	0	0	0	1	0	1	1	0	9.0	0.0	0	75%	.250	2.00	0.00	6.11	4.25	0.1	0.0	107	94.4
2016	NYA	MLB	31	1	0	1	16	0	16¹	16	1	4.4	8.3	15	49%	.312	1.47	4.96	3.90	4.84	0.2	0.0	107	94.2
2017	MIL	MLB	32	2	2	0	40	0	42	38	6	3.4	8.9	42	50%	.288	1.29	4.32	4.31	4.61	1.7	0.2	100	
2018	MIL	MLB	33	2	1	0	46	0	48²	42	7	3.7	9.9	53	50%	.277	1.27	4.11	4.26	4.26	2.2	0.2	105	

Breakout: 26%   Improve: 38%   Collapse: 18%   Attrition: 27%   MLB: 67%   Comparables: Jason Bulger, Clay Rapada, Mike Adams

He imploded in a late-September game in Toronto, but after coming over from the Mariners, the catcher-turned-journeyman pitcher was quietly one of the Yankees' best relievers. That certainly says something about where their bullpen was at, but there was little to complain about with the job Parker did. The right-hander, who broke in at age 27, seemed to do enough to hang around in the league, which is cool, because we need more Blakes in the bigs.

Wily Peralta   RHP

Born: 5/8/89   Age: 28   Bats: R   Throws: R   Height: 6'1"   Weight: 255   Entered Pro Ball: International Free Agent, 2005

YEAR	TEAM	LVL	AGE	W	L	SV	G	GS	IP	H	HR	BB/9	K/9	K	GB%	BABIP	WHIP	ERA	FIP	DRA	VORP	WARP	cFIP	MPH
2014	MIL	MLB	25	17	11	0	32	32	198²	198	23	2.8	7.0	154	56%	.295	1.30	3.53	4.08	3.62	26.9	3.0	102	98.5
2015	MIL	MLB	26	5	10	0	20	20	108²	130	14	3.1	5.0	60	53%	.320	1.54	4.72	4.86	5.99	-11.0	-1.2	118	97.1
2016	CSP	AAA	27	1	3	0	10	10	41¹	55	5	3.7	8.5	39	56%	.391	1.74	6.31	4.64	4.03	6.0	0.6	89	
2016	MIL	MLB	27	7	11	0	23	23	127²	152	19	3.0	6.6	93	52%	.336	1.53	4.86	4.75	4.47	12.7	1.3	109	97.6
2017	MIL	MLB	28	7	9	0	24	24	136	144	19	3.3	7.3	111	46%	.303	1.43	4.52	4.57	4.76	6.4	0.7	100	
2018	MIL	MLB	29	9	10	0	28	28	170²	162	22	3.3	8.4	159	46%	.317	1.31	4.27	4.43	4.79	13.5	1.4	112	

Breakout: 18%   Improve: 52%   Collapse: 15%   Attrition: 15%   MLB: 85%   Comparables: Vance Worley, Manny Parra, Ivan Nova

When the alchemists devised The Philosopher's Stone, their goal was nothing short of balancing the universe in order to attain immortality. Modern science followed suit, with such a luminary as René Descartes declaring on his deathbed that this problem of death would soon be solved by science. Unfortunately, neither science nor alchemy have proven effective in the search for immortality, so they turned to the pursuit of MLB player development and scouting. Peralta has baffled the modern universe by making considerable adjustments at the MLB level, first between his 2013 and 2014 campaigns, and now within the 2016 season. The sheer audacity of Peralta's second half resurgence is a shot in favor of the philosopher's stone, a resounding demonstration of immortality via player development and the perpetual convergence between non-tender candidate and mid-rotation stalwart.

Cody Ponce   RHP

Born: 4/25/94   Age: 23   Bats: R   Throws: R   Height: 6'6"   Weight: 240   Entered Pro Ball: Round 2, 2015 Draft (#55 overall)

YEAR	TEAM	LVL	AGE	W	L	SV	G	GS	IP	H	HR	BB/9	K/9	K	GB%	BABIP	WHIP	ERA	FIP	DRA	VORP	WARP	cFIP	MPH
2015	WIS	A	21	2	1	3	12	7	46	43	1	1.8	7.0	36	52%	.300	1.13	2.15	2.77	3.36	8.9	0.9	93	
2016	BRV	A+	22	2	8	0	17	17	72	84	6	2.1	8.6	69	47%	.345	1.40	5.25	3.21	2.88	20.8	2.1	85	
2017	MIL	MLB	23	3	4	0	20	13	61¹	70	10	3.1	5.9	40	57%	.322	1.48	5.09	5.07	5.58	-0.8	-0.1	134	
2018	MIL	MLB	24	5	8	0	28	22	146¹	146	23	4.0	8.1	131	57%	.316	1.45	5.02	5.23	5.50	0.2	0.0	132	

Breakout: 1%   Improve: 2%   Collapse: 0%   Attrition: 2%   MLB: 3%   Comparables: Vidal Nuno, Adam Conley, Bryan Price

Like just about every big-name Brewers pitching prospect, Ponce had a rough ride in 2016, including forearm tightness that downed him at the start of the year. When he's on, Ponce shows three plus pitches, plus command and some insane upside. When he's not on, he can cut off his delivery and overcompensates with his hips to decreased effectiveness. He should be right more often in 2017.

Brent Suter   LHP

Born: 8/29/89   Age: 27   Bats: L   Throws: L   Height: 6'5"   Weight: 195   Entered Pro Ball: Round 31, 2012 Draft (#965 overall)

YEAR	TEAM	LVL	AGE	W	L	SV	G	GS	IP	H	HR	BB/9	K/9	K	GB%	BABIP	WHIP	ERA	FIP	DRA	VORP	WARP	cFIP	MPH
2014	HUN	AA	24	10	10	0	28	27	152¹	144	14	3.1	7.0	118	44%	.297	1.29	3.96	4.01	3.28	32.8	3.5	101	
2015	BLX	AA	25	5	3	0	20	11	83	71	2	3.6	6.9	64	48%	.296	1.25	1.95	3.45	3.14	17.1	1.8	103	
2015	CSP	AAA	25	3	1	0	6	6	35¹	35	4	1.5	4.8	19	48%	.277	1.16	3.31	4.51	4.18	4.4	0.4	99	
2016	CSP	AAA	26	6	6	2	26	15	110²	129	5	1.1	6.1	75	41%	.348	1.29	3.50	3.41	2.99	27.7	2.9	98	
2016	MIL	MLB	26	2	2	0	14	2	21²	25	3	2.1	6.2	15	44%	.328	1.38	3.32	4.43	4.54	1.5	0.1	111	86.9
2017	MIL	MLB	27	2	2	0	35	0	36	38	5	2.8	6.3	26	57%	.295	1.36	4.60	4.68	4.71	0.8	0.1	100	
2018	MIL	MLB	28	1	0	0	27	0	29	25	4	3.8	9.1	29	57%	.302	1.29	4.45	4.61	5.00	0.4	0.0	114	

Breakout: 9%   Improve: 16%   Collapse: 14%   Attrition: 27%   MLB: 36%   Comparables: Shane Komine, Fabio Castro, Graham Godfrey

Is a "replacement-level player" actually a replacement-level player, or does the organization create the replacement-level player? How does replacement-level value change across organizations? Would a team's replacement-level value be higher if they opened the floodgates and allowed more advanced-minors players into MLB or would that diminish value in the name of depth? This is worth asking in a Brent Suter comment, because he's one of those advanced minor-league players who's pretty good and—BAM!—suddenly he's in the show with fringe-average peripherals and an 84 mph fastball thrown 63 percent of the time. The southpaw makes the Brewers better by providing serviceable depth from within the organization, especially working as a classic swingman reliever. How many Brent Suters are MLB teams missing?

Devin Williams   RHP

Born: 9/21/94   Age: 22   Bats: R   Throws: R   Height: 6'3"   Weight: 165   Entered Pro Ball: Round 2, 2013 Draft (#54 overall)

YEAR	TEAM	LVL	AGE	W	L	SV	G	GS	IP	H	HR	BB/9	K/9	K	GB%	BABIP	WHIP	ERA	FIP	DRA	VORP	WARP	cFIP	MPH
2015	WIS	A	20	3	9	0	22	13	89	75	3	3.6	9.0	89	40%	.295	1.25	3.44	3.28	3.90	12.0	1.3	94	
2016	WIS	A	21	6	3	2	17	10	72¹	64	4	4.2	9.2	74	48%	.309	1.35	3.61	3.60	4.63	2.1	0.2	105	
2016	BRV	A+	21	1	2	0	5	2	25	27	2	4.3	7.2	20	36%	.329	1.56	4.32	4.25	5.55	-0.9	-0.1	110	
2017	MIL	MLB	22	4	5	1	39	11	79²	90	14	5.3	5.9	52	65%	.317	1.72	6.09	5.99	6.79	-21.8	-2.2	160	
2018	MIL	MLB	23	2	4	0	18	9	82²	82	14	6.3	8.7	80	65%	.320	1.69	5.84	6.13	6.51	-8.5	-0.9	153	

Breakout: 3%   Improve: 3%   Collapse: 0%   Attrition: 3%   MLB: 3%   Comparables: Anthony Bass, Wily Peralta, Andrew Faulkner

From mid-June to mid-July it looked like Williams was finally going to figure out his command. It all collapsed after that, as he started losing his release spot and the ball ended up all over the place. Williams' fastball is heavy and when he stays on top of his slider it's a nice pitch. He repeats his delivery well and he generates easy velocity, so it comes down to maintaining a consistent release point.

LINEOUTS

Hitters

NAME	POS	TEAM	LVL	AGE	PA	R	2B	3B	HR	RBI	BB	K	SB	CS	AVG/OBP/SLG	TAv	VORP	BABIP	BRR	FRAA	WARP
Garin Cecchini	3B	CSP	AAA	25	469	50	21	5	5	52	33	64	13	5	.271/.325/.380	.244	2.1	.305	1.1	1B(64): 0.6, 3B(52): -6.0	-0.4
Ryan Cordell	CF	FRI	AA	24	445	69	22	5	19	70	32	97	12	4	.264/.319/.484	.291	24.7	.299	0.6	CF(42): 3.7, LF(35): 4.4	3.8
Jake Elmore	SS	CSP	AAA	29	182	25	3	0	2	19	26	19	13	4	.320/.428/.380	.298	11.2	.354	-0.6	2B(32): -3.1, LF(17): -1.8	0.6
	SS	MIL	MLB	29	99	7	2	0	0	4	17	17	2	3	.218/.371/.244	.242	-0.1	.279	-0.8	LF(14): -1.6, 3B(4): 0.4	-0.2
Gilbert Lara	INF	HEL	Rk	18	246	30	10	0	2	28	12	59	2	1	.250/.293/.320	.220	0.9	.324	1.6	SS(52): 5.3, 3B(2): -0.1	0.6
Manny Pina	C	CSP	AAA	29	262	35	21	3	5	43	17	39	1	1	.329/.371/.506	.296	17.8	.371	-3.4	C(57): -8.2	1.0
	C	MIL	MLB	29	81	4	4	0	2	12	10	15	0	1	.254/.346/.394	.263	2.4	.296	-1.2	C(17): -0.8	0.2
Josmil Pinto	C	CSP	AAA	27	315	46	21	3	11	51	26	67	0	0	.308/.362/.517	.275	14.3	.365	0.6	C(41): -10.4, 1B(31): 0.6	0.5
	C	MIL	MLB	27	6	1	0	0	0	0	1	4	0	0	.000/.167/.000	.111	-0.7	.000	0.0		-0.1
Corey Ray	OF	BRV	A+	21	254	24	13	2	5	17	20	54	9	5	.247/.307/.385	.268	3.9	.299	-1.9	CF(28): -3.7	0.0
Yadiel Rivera	SS	CSP	AAA	24	326	38	7	8	2	41	10	78	4	3	.227/.262/.322	.196	-11.3	.294	-0.4	SS(41): 3.6, 2B(32): 4.1	-0.3
	SS	MIL	MLB	24	71	12	4	0	0	3	2	20	0	0	.212/.235/.273	.179	-2.3	.304	1.3	3B(15): -0.6, 2B(13): 0.1	-0.3

In an alternate universe, **Garin Cecchini** had Jonathan Villar's 2016. Perhaps in this one he snatches Villar's 2017. ❖ Improving plate discipline and power likely spiked **Ryan Cordell**'s prospect stock and made it likely that 2016 was his last season in Double-A, but it's cool because there's also an IKEA in Round Rock. ❖ Jon Lester is one of 13 pitchers to allow both a hit and a walk to **Jake Elmore**, and he's one of only four pitchers to walk Elmore twice. ❖ Signed out of the Dominican Republic for $3.1 million in 2014, **Gilbert Lara** draws praise for his offensive upside despite not hitting at all in the low minors yet. ❖ Behind Jonathan Lucroy and Martin Maldonado, the Brewers' catching depth did not have many chances to prove their defensive prowess. In **Manny Pina**'s case, the bat helps to speak for those lacking defensive chances, as the veteran saw his first real playing time in the majors. ❖ The TAv in Colorado Springs improved from 2015's Rochester marks for **Josmil Pinto**, but the catcher/designated hitter could not find his way to extended playing time in Milwaukee even after the Jonathan Lucroy trade. ❖ Drafted as a potential power/speed player out of Louisville, **Corey Ray** had a rather pedestrian first crack at professional baseball in 2016. Ray underwent surgery to repair a torn meniscus in October, which can be a scary thing for a speedster. ❖ **Yadiel Rivera** was up and down several times in 2016, filling a utility role for the Brewers when not struggling at Triple-A.

Pitchers

NAME	TEAM	LVL	AGE	W	L	SV	G	GS	IP	H	HR	BB/9	K/9	K	GB%	BABIP	WHIP	ERA	FIP	DRA	VORP	WARP	cFIP	MPH
Blaine Boyer	MIL	MLB	34	2	4	1	61	0	66	80	4	2.3	3.5	26	51%	.325	1.47	3.95	4.00	5.81	-6.1	-0.6	119	95.1
Chris Capuano	MIL	MLB	37	1	1	0	16	0	24	23	7	5.6	10.1	27	44%	.286	1.58	4.12	6.73	4.60	1.0	0.1	101	91.4
David Goforth	MIL	MLB	27	0	0	0	10	0	10²	18	3	3.4	7.6	9	55%	.385	2.06	10.97	6.28	5.24	-0.3	0.0	102	95.4
	CSP	AAA	27	3	4	2	42	0	51¹	56	3	6.1	6.7	38	51%	.331	1.77	4.91	5.16	10.04	-29.0	-3.0	121	
Preston Guilmet	TOL	AAA	28	3	3	0	65	0	68¹	71	4	1.6	10.8	82	43%	.372	1.21	2.77	2.14	1.74	24.4	2.5	69	
Adrian Houser	BLX	AA	23	3	7	0	13	13	70¹	76	5	2.8	7.2	56	62%	.326	1.39	5.25	3.68	3.39	13.3	1.4	92	
Jorge Lopez	CSP	AAA	23	1	7	0	17	16	79¹	101	12	6.2	7.5	66	58%	.355	1.97	6.81	6.29	6.89	-13.8	-1.4	111	
	BLX	AA	23	2	4	0	8	8	45¹	45	5	3.2	9.3	47	48%	.323	1.35	3.97	3.81	2.97	10.7	1.2	85	
Damien Magnifico	CSP	AAA	25	6	7	18	52	0	62	57	2	4.8	8.9	61	63%	.314	1.45	4.06	3.82	5.72	-5.2	-0.5	93	
	MIL	MLB	25	0	0	0	3	0	3	2	0	9.0	0.0	0	64%	.182	1.67	6.00	7.19	5.53	-0.2	0.0	110	98.5
Jhan Marinez	TBA	MLB	27	0	0	0	3	0	3²	2	1	0.0	7.4	3	70%	.111	0.55	2.45	5.02	4.19	0.3	0.0	103	97.0
	MIL	MLB	27	0	1	0	43	0	58²	60	3	3.2	7.2	47	52%	.318	1.38	3.22	3.63	4.74	1.5	0.2	103	97.0
Ben Rowen	BUF	AAA	27	0	4	1	37	0	47¹	46	1	2.1	6.3	33	65%	.306	1.20	2.47	2.75	2.89	10.9	1.1	92	
	CSP	AAA	27	0	0	0	8	0	10²	11	0	2.5	10.1	12	34%	.379	1.31	1.69	2.31	1.83	3.7	0.4	93	
	MIL	MLB	27	0	0	0	4	0	3	10	0	0.0	6.0	2	71%	.588	3.33	15.00	1.85	3.86	0.4	0.0	102	82.1
Rob Scahill	PIT	MLB	29	0	0	0	15	0	16¹	18	1	3.3	7.2	13	58%	.347	1.47	4.41	3.86	4.00	1.8	0.2	97	96.1
	IND	AAA	29	0	2	3	13	0	18	23	0	4.0	9.0	18	58%	.371	1.72	4.00	2.50	3.59	2.7	0.3	95	
	MIL	MLB	29	0	0	0	16	0	18¹	16	1	1.5	6.9	14	67%	.268	1.04	2.45	3.19	4.05	1.9	0.2	97	94.7
Carlos Torres	MIL	MLB	33	3	3	2	72	0	82¹	65	8	3.3	8.5	78	46%	.260	1.15	2.73	3.79	4.22	6.9	0.7	96	94.1

Yhonathan Barrios is on the Brewers' list of power arms either injured or returning from injury, and if it gets any longer we're going to have to print a second edition. ❖ If **Blaine Boyer** were an investment banker, his boutique would be Soft Contact, LLC. DRA need not apply. ❖ FIP hated **Chris Capuano** in 2016, but that's okay: DRA agrees with ERA that the veteran southpaw still has some gas left in the tank if healthy. ❖ Command simply has not followed **David Goforth** to the advanced minors, as the right-hander walked 62 of 436 Triple-A batters between cups of coffee in 2015 and 2016. ❖ Keep an eye on dollar-store reliever **Preston Guilmet**, who piled up these Triple-A numbers since July 1: 30 innings, 50 strikeouts, eight walks, one homer. With three decent pitches, he's an uncommon righty who's even tougher on left-handers. ❖ **Adrian Houser** has had an eventful stint in the Brewers' organization: Quick to the majors in 2015, underrated in 2016 beneath surface minor-league struggles and derailed by a Tommy John surgery. ❖ **Jorge Lopez** looked like a solid bet to become a mid-rotation starter following a perceived breakout in 2015, but he took a huge step backward in 2016 thanks to awful control. ❖ **Damien Magnifico** was mostly Above-Averagico at Triple-A, but given all of the relievers the Brewers dealt away in 2016, expect him to carve out a role this season. ❖ Most Valuable Garbageman? **Jhan Marinez** entered 52 percent of his 2016 appearances when his team faced a deficit of two or more runs. ❖ If you want to know whether you're an optimist, ask yourself: "If healthy, would **Sean Nolin** have cracked the starting rotation of the 2016 Brewers?" ❖ Is a submarine fastball a screwball? **Ben Rowen**'s is 80-82 mph, "drops" six inches compared to a spin-less ball and runs seven inches armside. ❖ GM David Stearns landed 1.6 pitching WARP from waiver claims in 2016; 1.3 of that was Junior Guerra and 0.2 belonged to **Rob Scahill**, the Brewers' most effective waiver reliever. ❖ A sneaky-good reliever, **Carlos Torres** is an extremely thrifty GM's Mariano Rivera, complete with a big cutter and ERAs that out-perform DRA. ❖ After missing all of the last two seasons with an elbow injury that eventually led to Tommy John surgery, **Taylor Williams** will look to harness the potential that once landed him fourth on the Brewers' top 10.

MINNESOTA TWINS

Essay by Parker Hageman

Player comments by Aaron Gleeman and BP staff

It was a watershed offseason for the Minnesota Twins. The keys to the house—as well as all the pine tar, sunflower seeds and Diamond Dust—have been handed over to a pair of new-school executives with impressive recommendations in chief baseball officer Derek Falvey and general manager Thad Levine. Falvey comes to Minnesota from Cleveland, where he gained a reputation as a pitching development guru who helped turn the Indians into one of the best staffs in the game. His new right-hand man, Levine, arrives from Texas, where he was instrumental to all things Rangers for more than a decade.

There's no doubt that Terry Ryan is a well-respected baseball man who has forgotten more about the game than the people reading and writing this book could hope to learn, but when it comes to upgrading the Twins have finally gone from flip phone to iPhone. But in how bad of shape is the organization that Ryan left behind and how quickly can Falvey and Levine turn things around after the worst stretch in Twins history?

Normally assuming control of a 103-loss organization means a complete tear down, but the Twins actually have plenty of positives and a solid foundation that could translate into sustained success in the not-too-distant future. Architects who rehab old buildings often refer to the ones that are perfect for renovation as having "good bones" and the Twins arguably have really good bones. Consider:

- The major-league roster has a core of young, high-end talent like Miguel Sano, Byron Buxton and Jose Berrios around which to build.
- Only Phil Hughes and Byungho Park are under contract beyond 2018, giving them some payroll flexibility.
- The farm system includes respectable prospect talent such as Nick Gordon, Tyler Jay, Alex Kirilloff and Kohl Stewart.
- They have the pleasure of making the no. 1 overall pick in the 2017 draft, which will provide a huge long-term boost to the talent stockpile.

Just picture Falvey and Levine looking up and seeing the blimp scrolling "The World Is Yours."

Recent track record notwithstanding the Twins also have the tools in place to develop those young players

TWINS PROSPECTUS
2016 W-L: 59-103, 5TH IN AL CENTRAL

Pythag	.401	29th	DER	.681	29th
RS/G	4.46	16th	B-Age	26.9	4th
RA/G	5.49	29th	P-Age	28.4	16th
TAv	.251	28th	Salary	$105.3M	18th
BRR	11.18	5th	M$/MW	$8.8M	1st
TAv-P	0.270	21st	DL Days	638	5th
FIP	4.53	26th	$ on DL	16%	20th

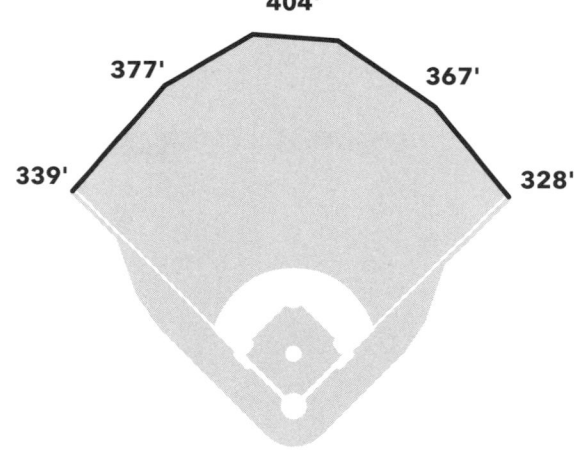

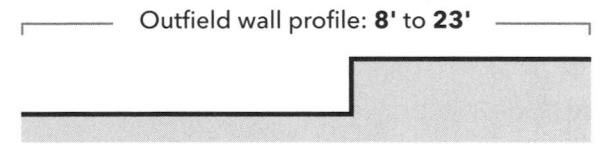

Outfield wall profile: **8' to 23'**

Three-Year Park Factors

Runs	Runs/RH	Runs/LH	HR/RH	HR/LH
101	102	100	103	97

Top Hitter WARP	4.1	Brian Dozier
Top Pitcher WARP	3.1	Ervin Santana
Top Prospect		Nick Gordon

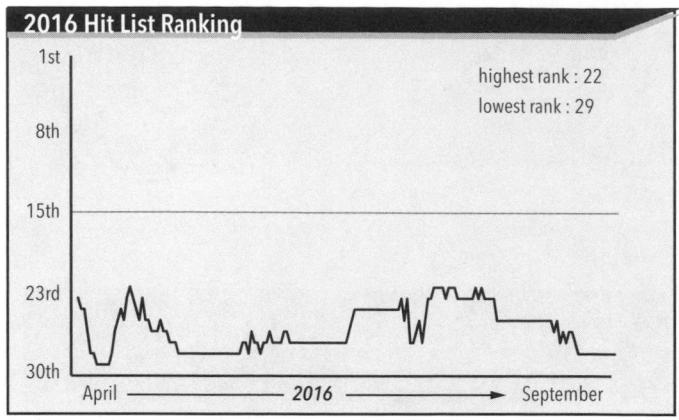

2016 Hit List Ranking

highest rank : 22
lowest rank : 29

April ——— **2016** ——→ September

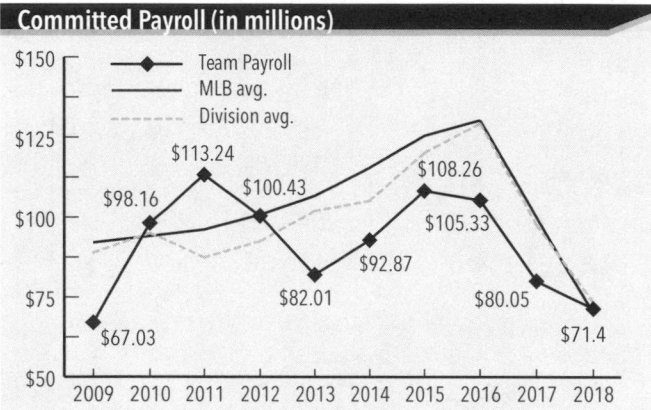

Committed Payroll (in millions)

- Team Payroll
- MLB avg.
- Division avg.

$113.24
$98.16
$100.43
$108.26
$105.33
$92.87
$82.01
$67.03
$80.05
$71.4

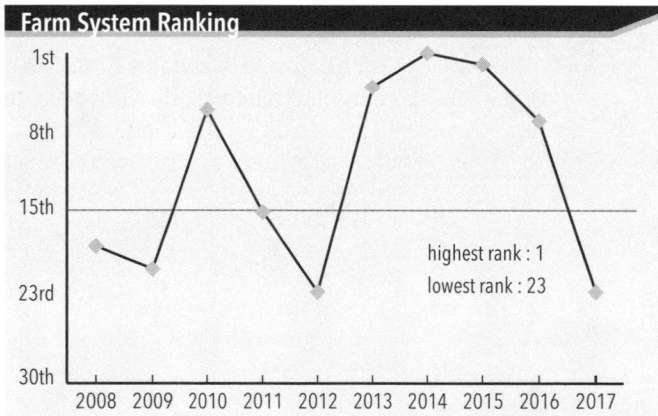

Farm System Ranking

highest rank : 1
lowest rank : 23

Personnel

EVP, Chief Baseball Officer:
Derek Falvey

SVP, General Manager:
Thad Levine

Assistant General Manager:
Rob Antony

VP, Player Personnel:
Mike Radcliff

Manager:
Paul Molitor

properly, but they need a fresh mindset on how to get the most out of them. The organization just invested in building state-of-the-art player development facilities in Florida, providing a competitive advantage over teams that lack the ability to house, nourish, educate and train their minor leaguers. The Twins also placed Trackman radar—the same devices that spit out all that fascinating StatCast data—at all of their minor-league ballparks. If leveraged properly, the development team will no longer discuss hitters and pitchers in terms of batting averages and strikeouts, but rather launch angles, exit velocities and spin rates.

There's a scene in the movie *Friday* where Smokey (Chris Tucker) says Craig's (Ice Cube) house "ain't never got two things that match" and rattles off examples like "peanut butter, no jelly" and "ham, no burger." (Smokey punctuates his rant with a "daayaam," the delivery of which apparently landed Tucker an unlimited amount of work in the early 2000s for no clear reason, sort of like the movie industry's version of Denny Hocking.) In many ways, Terry Ryan's roster planning felt a lot like this: Nothing seemed to match.

When the Ryan-led Twins finally reached into the free agent market for pitching, all of their auxiliary moves did little to enhance their hefty investments. For example, with catching a significant need they eschewed targeting anyone with strong framing numbers, instead settling on Kurt Suzuki, who had no discernable defensive advantages whatsoever. His strength, Ryan said, was his ability to handle a staff. One quick glance at the team's ERA over the last three years will tell you how little that mattered, even without factoring in Suzuki's awful framing numbers.

Meanwhile, planning for the outfield was a dumpster fire rolled in cluster**** smothered in a hot mess. Rather than reinforce the outfield with speedy fly-ball killers to support a contact-oriented staff, they filled the space with statutes and frying pan hands such as Josh Willingham, Oswaldo Arcia, Chris Colabello, Torii Hunter, Robbie Grossman and whichever banjo-hitter was available off the waiver wire. The lack of planning for the outfield spiraled so far out of control that career-long infielders—like Eduardo Nunez, Eduardo Escobar, Danny Santana and, most infamously, Jason Bartlett—were asked to trudge to the outfield to apparently fulfill the *Benny Hill* theme song highlight video quota.

Perhaps the biggest shruggy-guy-emoji moment of the Ryan administration came when the Twins decided to move Miguel Sano to the outfield. At Torii Hunter's retirement press conference manager Paul Molitor announced that Sano would prepare to take over right field in place from the departing veteran. Molitor tried to assuage fears by saying that Sano's participation in the upcoming Dominican winter league would allow him to familiarize himself with the intricacies of the job, but each box score revealed that Sano was only playing third base on the island.

When this was pointed out to the Twins, their response was that Sano was taking reps in the outfield during batting practice and shagging fly balls—which is kind of like saying he's going to learn how to be a pilot by running around the room with his arms spread making airplane noises. Shortly after that, depending on whom you ask, either Sano was told by the Twins to shut it down or Sano decided on his own to stop playing and focus on conditioning. The conditioning efforts resulted in a modest five-pound decrease, about which the organization was not shy in expressing their disappointment.

The Twins gave themselves the out. If Sano failed in right field (which he predictably did), it was because he didn't lose weight and commit himself enough, not because he was ill-suited for an outfield position or because the original idea was bananas to begin with. Players certainly deserve culpability but decision-makers should take on more of the responsibility. This, after all, was a premeditated disaster.

Outside of the curious maneuvering, Ryan seemed to eschew simple advantages that are often so vital for mid-market teams. When he was asked about using platoons, Ryan bristled. "I think we need players out there that can get 600 plate appearances," he said. Meanwhile, the AL Central rival Indians made shrewd offseason signings and midseason trades to play those same matchups on both sides of the ball, and went all the way to the World Series. Acquiring a full-time player often takes up too many resources for low-payroll teams, so it makes sense to target complementary players at a lower cost. That's nothing new, bold or innovative, but it will be all of those things for the Twins.

Improving how players come out of the development system will certainly be a focus of the new front office as well. When asked how he planned to improve the organization's longstanding pitching woes, Falvey said the Twins would scour the free agent market, explore trades and even consider "unique development philosophies." One such "unique" philosophy that Falvey introduced in Cleveland was the implementation of weighted ball training at every level of the minor leagues in an effort to improve velocity and arm strength. Tactics like that may help end the pattern of Twins pitching prospects stalling out before reaching Minnesota.

Ryan's player development system, which once provided so generously for the Twins in the early 2000s, spurted out incomplete and flawed talent in his second tenure. Buxton was promoted without ever seeing what a great slider is or how to bunt. Kepler's defense in the outfield was a work in progress. Santana didn't know how to play shortstop with an instruction manual. Berrios located fastballs with the precision of a presidential pollster. And plate discipline was severely lacking in nearly every position player prospect.

Players like Arcia and Aaron Hicks performed well in the minors, possessed quality tools and posted solid numbers, but fell flat upon their introduction to major-league competition. In the case of Arcia, his left-handed power potential was drool-worthy but early struggles against left-handed pitching caused the coaching staff to reinvent his swing. They tried to eliminate his leg kick. They tried to get him to keep his hands still. They tried to get him to focus on driving the ball middle-away to the opposite field.

By 2016, with so much triage performed on his approach, Arcia was eventually unable to hit against lefties *or* righties and was unceremoniously discarded midway through the year. Similar stories have played out with Twins prospects for years, dating back to now-familiar names like David Ortiz and Carlos Gomez. Too often they took a strength and reducing the player to a pile of trembling jelly in a jersey, all in the name of making mold-fitting improvements.

It's getting hard to remember that there was a time when the Twins were viewed as a model franchise, thriving despite small payrolls. Those days are gone with along with the Metrodome, but the mindset remained as the game changed around them. With new leadership in place, the Twins hope to return to those days. We'll see. ■

—Parker Hageman covers the
Twins for Twins Daily

HITTERS

Travis Blankenhorn   3B

Born: 8/3/96   Age: 20   Bats: L   Throws: R   Height: 6'2"   Weight: 208   Entered Pro Ball: Round 3, 2015 Draft (#80 overall)

YEAR	TEAM	LVL	AGE	PA	R	2B	3B	HR	RBI	BB	K	SB	CS	AVG/OBP/SLG	TAv	VORP	BABIP	BRR	FRAA	WARP
2016	CDR	A	19	102	11	5	2	1	12	8	28	2	1	.286/.356/.418	.291	3.6	.403	-1.1	2B(8): 0.4 • 3B(1): -0.3	0.4
2017	MIN	MLB	20	250	26	9	1	7	24	13	81	0	0	.211/.256/.349	.204	-5.2	.285	-0.3	2B 1 • 3B -0	-0.5
2018	MIN	MLB	21	323	36	13	2	10	36	18	102	1	0	.221/.272/.373	.221	-3.9	.294	-0.5	2B 1 • 3B 0	-0.3

Breakout: 1%   Improve: 11%   Collapse: 0%   Attrition: 8%   MLB: 14%   *Comparables: Dilson Herrera, Delino DeShields, Nick Noonan*

When the Twins drafted Blankenhorn, scouting director Deron Johnson explained: "We really like his swing and think he has [a] chance [to hit] for power." He was a prep shortstop but moved to third base in his pro debut, and played mostly second base last year. He may end up in left field, in which case Johnson better be right about his swing. Blankenhorn's nine homers tied for sixth in the Appalachian League despite playing only half the schedule before a promotion to Low-A. He was mostly a singles hitter there, and both his strikeout rate and plate discipline require a little work, but Blankenhorn will try to tap into more of that upside as he takes on his first full year in full-season ball.

Byron Buxton   CF

Born: 12/18/93   Age: 23   Bats: R   Throws: R   Height: 6'2"   Weight: 190   Entered Pro Ball: Round 1, 2012 Draft (#2 overall)

YEAR	TEAM	LVL	AGE	PA	R	2B	3B	HR	RBI	BB	K	SB	CS	AVG/OBP/SLG	TAv	VORP	BABIP	BRR	FRAA	WARP
2014	FTM	A+	20	134	19	4	2	4	16	10	33	6	2	.240/.313/.405	.254	4.8	.298	1.5	CF(28): 6.0 • RF(2): -0.4	1.0
2015	CHT	AA	21	268	44	7	12	6	37	26	51	20	2	.283/.351/.489	.305	22.4	.332	2.4	CF(59): 14.3	4.0
2015	ROC	AAA	21	59	11	3	1	1	8	4	12	2	1	.400/.441/.545	.377	9.7	.500	0.9	CF(11): 1.3	1.1
2015	MIN	MLB	21	138	16	7	1	2	6	6	44	2	2	.209/.250/.326	.214	-0.9	.301	1.3	CF(44): 6.5	0.6
2016	ROC	AAA	22	209	41	11	3	11	24	14	58	7	0	.305/.359/.568	.327	23.7	.382	2.9	CF(47): -2.3	2.2
2016	MIN	MLB	22	331	44	19	6	10	38	23	118	10	2	.225/.284/.430	.246	10.3	.329	4.9	CF(92): 6.5	1.7
2017	MIN	MLB	23	500	61	21	7	17	59	32	153	16	3	.244/.296/.434	.252	17.6	.321	2.8	CF 15	2.8
2018	MIN	MLB	24	546	65	23	8	18	68	36	165	18	3	.241/.297/.428	.244	11.5	.317	5.5	CF 17	3.1

Breakout: 5%   Improve: 47%   Collapse: 6%   Attrition: 15%   MLB: 77%   Comparables: *Melvin Upton, Adam Jones, Cameron Maybin*

One of the best and most-hyped prospects of the past decade, Buxton struggled like few other hitters in Twins history through his first 110 games, batting .199 with 124 strikeouts and only 19 walks. The same story played out several times. He dominated the minors using a pronounced leg kick, got called up, ditched those mechanics for a toned-down toe-tap, and hit like a pitcher. By the time he rejoined the roster on September 1, the "bust" label was being thrown around far too freely for a 22-year-old with his tools and pedigree. Buxton showed how premature that was by batting .287/.357/.653 with nine homers in the final month, totaling 17 extra-base hits—the most by a Twins hitter in September since Harmon Killebrew in 1967. He still whiffed way too much but Buxton's power was eye-opening as he stuck with the leg kick and crushed upper-deck bombs. He looked every bit like the drooled-over stud prospect who hit .303 with 18 homers and a .524 slugging percentage in 122 games at Double-A and Triple-A.

One of MLB's fastest players, he's already an elite center fielder who combines limitless range with a fearlessness bordering on recklessness and a plus arm. His speed and position makes it seem natural for Buxton to be a leadoff man, but viewing him through that stereotypical lens ignores an offensive skill set more suited for big swings and extra bases. One great month doesn't wipe away 110 games of awful approaches and worse results, but September gave a much-needed glimpse of the type of impact player Buxton could be if he can just control the strike zone enough to live in attack mode. Buxton can be an All-Star even if his bat never really clicks, but the potential is there for him to develop into a 30-30 hitter with Gold Glove defense. There just aren't a whole lot of comps for that ceiling.

Jason Castro   C

Born: 6/18/87   Age: 30   Bats: L   Throws: R   Height: 6'3"   Weight: 215   Entered Pro Ball: Round 1, 2008 Draft (#10 overall)

YEAR	TEAM	LVL	AGE	PA	R	2B	3B	HR	RBI	BB	K	SB	CS	AVG/OBP/SLG	TAv	VORP	BABIP	BRR	FRAA	WARP
2014	HOU	MLB	27	512	43	21	2	14	56	34	151	1	0	.222/.286/.366	.245	10.1	.294	-2.3	C(114): 9.3	2.1
2015	HOU	MLB	28	375	38	19	0	11	31	33	115	0	0	.211/.283/.365	.231	4.5	.280	-1.2	C(103): 11.5	1.7
2016	HOU	MLB	29	376	41	16	3	11	32	45	123	2	1	.210/.307/.377	.239	7.4	.297	-1.3	C(111): 17.2 • 1B(3): -0.2	2.5
2017	MIN	MLB	30	484	53	25	2	15	55	45	133	2	1	.239/.313/.405	.249	16.1	.307	-0.8	C 15	1.8
2018	MIN	MLB	31	369	43	19	1	10	42	35	104	1	0	.230/.307/.388	.237	3.6	.299	-1.3	C 11	1.6

Breakout: 3%   Improve: 41%   Collapse: 7%   Attrition: 14%   MLB: 94%   Comparables: *John Buck, Chris Snyder, Geovany Soto*

Back in 2013, Castro made the All-Star team as a 26-year-old with uncanny power and plate discipline for such a fine defensive backstop. If he could get over his strikeout problem, the sky looked like the limit. Instead, three years later, Castro has only turned into a bigger whiff machine and the power has never returned. His defense has become his finest asset, as he consistently ranks among the best pitch framers in the league. Castro wasn't supposed to be one of those all-glove no-bat veteran catchers who flood the free agent market every year, but unfortunately the dynamic bat he showed in 2013 looks like it's nothing but history these days. The Twins, eager to improve on years of subpar framing, signed him to a three-year, $24.5 million free agent contract.

YEAR	TEAM	P. COUNT	FRM RUNS	BLK RUNS	THRW RUNS	TOT RUNS
2014	HOU	16021	11.5	2.2	-1.6	12.2
2015	HOU	14019	11.0	-1.0	1.0	11.0
2016	HOU	14976	17.0	-0.1	-0.7	16.2
2017	MIN	18001	16.2	-0.2	-0.3	15.7
2018	MIN	13715	11.2	-0.4	-0.3	10.6

Juan Centeno   C

Born: 11/16/89   Age: 27   Bats: L   Throws: R   Height: 5'9"   Weight: 195   Entered Pro Ball: Round 32, 2007 Draft (#991 overall)

YEAR	TEAM	LVL	AGE	PA	R	2B	3B	HR	RBI	BB	K	SB	CS	AVG/OBP/SLG	TAv	VORP	BABIP	BRR	FRAA	WARP
2014	LVG	AAA	24	202	19	5	0	1	17	15	26	2	0	.291/.343/.335	.266	7.6	.329	-3.5	C(52): -2.8	0.5
2014	BIN	AA	24	83	8	5	0	0	8	6	11	0	1	.286/.337/.351	.229	0.7	.333	-0.3	C(21): -1.4	-0.1
2014	NYN	MLB	24	33	1	0	0	0	2	3	5	0	0	.200/.273/.200	.173	-1.5	.240	-0.1	C(9): -0.9	-0.3
2015	MIL	MLB	25	23	0	1	0	0	0	2	7	0	0	.048/.130/.095	.107	-2.2	.071	0.3	C(7): -1.3	-0.4
2015	CSP	AAA	25	187	11	6	3	0	24	5	19	2	2	.295/.312/.364	.228	2.7	.323	0.9	C(46): -9.6	-0.7
2016	ROC	AAA	26	55	5	1	0	1	5	4	4	1	0	.245/.315/.327	.240	1.0	.250	-0.1	C(14): -0.1	0.1
2016	MIN	MLB	26	192	16	12	1	3	25	12	38	0	0	.261/.312/.392	.237	3.2	.319	-1.0	C(53): -11.6	-0.9
2017	MIN	MLB	27	250	23	10	1	3	23	13	42	1	0	.254/.296/.353	.220	1.9	.291	-0.3	C -14	-1.3
2018	MIN	MLB	28	246	25	10	1	4	23	13	46	0	0	.253/.297/.355	.225	-0.2	.294	-0.4	C -14	-1.5

Breakout: 10%   Improve: 17%   Collapse: 18%   Attrition: 30%   MLB: 55%   Comparables: *Drew Butera, Bryan Holaday, Rob Johnson*

John Ryan Murphy's ineptitude forced Centeno into an expanded role, and the 26-year-old journeyman showed a decent bat and a terrible glove. He looks the part of a catcher at a stocky 5-foot-9 and has the contact skills to produce the empty .260 or so batting average necessary to carve out a niche as a left-handed-hitting backup, but it's hard to imagine any team living with his defense behind the plate. Centeno threw out just 14 percent of attempted base-stealers, and there were 38 combined passed balls and wild pitches in his 439 innings—73 percent higher than the league average. He even tossed in six errors for good measure.

YEAR	TEAM	P. COUNT	FRM RUNS	BLK RUNS	THRW RUNS	TOT RUNS
2014	BIN	2691	-0.9	-0.1	0.0	-1.0
2014	LVG	6583	-1.2	-0.5	-0.7	-2.3
2014	NYN	1229	-1.0	-0.9	-0.1	-1.9
2015	CSP	6471	-8.1	-1.1	-0.4	-9.6
2015	MIL	876	-1.2	-0.1	0.0	-1.3
2016	MIN	7221	-10.1	-2.6	-0.4	-13.1
2017	*MIN*	*9188*	*-11.0*	*-2.3*	*-0.5*	*-13.8*
2018	*MIN*	*9043*	*-11.3*	*-2.3*	*-0.5*	*-14.1*

Brian Dozier   2B

Born: 5/15/87   Age: 30   Bats: R   Throws: R   Height: 5'11"   Weight: 200   Entered Pro Ball: Round 8, 2009 Draft (#252 overall)

YEAR	TEAM	LVL	AGE	PA	R	2B	3B	HR	RBI	BB	K	SB	CS	AVG/OBP/SLG	TAv	VORP	BABIP	BRR	FRAA	WARP
2014	MIN	MLB	27	707	112	33	1	23	71	89	129	21	7	.242/.345/.416	.279	34.0	.269	4.3	2B(156): 5.5	4.4
2015	MIN	MLB	28	704	101	39	4	28	77	61	148	12	4	.236/.307/.444	.260	23.1	.261	4.8	2B(157): -8.5	1.6
2016	MIN	MLB	29	691	104	35	5	42	99	61	138	18	2	.268/.340/.546	.291	41.4	.280	1.1	2B(151): -1.8	4.1
2017	*MIN*	*MLB*	*30*	*674*	*92*	*33*	*3*	*25*	*78*	*61*	*134*	*15*	*4*	*.244/.316/.437*	*.261*	*28.3*	*.270*	*0.9*	*2B -3*	*2.1*
2018	*MIN*	*MLB*	*31*	*551*	*72*	*26*	*2*	*22*	*74*	*52*	*115*	*11*	*3*	*.240/.317/.440*	*.256*	*17.0*	*.266*	*2.2*	*2B -2*	*1.6*

Breakout: 0%   Improve: 48%   Collapse: 2%   Attrition: 6%   MLB: 95%   *Comparables: Kelly Johnson, Neil Walker, Marcus Giles*

A high-contact/low-power college shortstop, and $30,000 senior sign as an eighth-round pick, Dozier was still in A-ball at 24 and hit 16 homers in 1,613 total plate appearances as a minor leaguer. Last season he hit 13 homers in August on the way to a single-season record of 42 for AL second basemen. Dozier is baseball's unlikeliest slugger although he was building up to last year's breakout by slowly trending up in each of the previous three seasons. His transformation from utility man to slugger began in mid-2013 as he changed his approach at the plate to become one of MLB's most pull-heavy fly-ball artists. It leaves him susceptible to lengthy slumps—before his insane power binge Dozier hit .205 and slugged .354 in 127 games from July 1, 2015 through May 31, 2016—but any fastball left up is a souvenir. He won't hit 40 homers again but Dozier is an All-Star with 25 homers and under team control for two more years at a bargain bin salary.

Eduardo Escobar   SS

Born: 1/5/89   Age: 28   Bats: B   Throws: R   Height: 5'10"   Weight: 185   Entered Pro Ball: International Free Agent, 2006

YEAR	TEAM	LVL	AGE	PA	R	2B	3B	HR	RBI	BB	K	SB	CS	AVG/OBP/SLG	TAv	VORP	BABIP	BRR	FRAA	WARP
2014	MIN	MLB	25	465	52	35	2	6	37	24	93	1	1	.275/.315/.406	.252	13.3	.336	0.7	SS(98): -8.7 • 3B(25): -1.4	0.5
2015	MIN	MLB	26	446	48	31	4	12	58	28	86	2	3	.262/.309/.445	.266	15.4	.301	-1.4	SS(71): -5.9 • LF(35): 4.0	1.5
2016	MIN	MLB	27	377	32	14	2	6	37	21	72	1	3	.236/.280/.338	.209	-3.3	.280	1.7	SS(71): 1.1 • 3B(23): -1.1	-0.4
2017	*MIN*	*MLB*	*28*	*294*	*28*	*16*	*2*	*6*	*30*	*18*	*58*	*1*	*1*	*.253/.298/.391*	*.238*	*3.4*	*.297*	*-0.7*	*3B -3 • SS -1*	*-0.5*
2018	*MIN*	*MLB*	*29*	*300*	*34*	*17*	*2*	*7*	*34*	*21*	*59*	*1*	*1*	*.259/.311/.414*	*.244*	*3.3*	*.300*	*0.1*	*3B -3 • SS -1*	*-0.2*

Breakout: 2%   Improve: 33%   Collapse: 9%   Attrition: 18%   MLB: 95%   *Comparables: Zack Cozart, Ronny Cedeno, Donovan Solano*

Escobar thrived in a part-time role for two years, playing all over the field and outproducing his punchless minor-league track record with surprising pop from both sides of the plate. Handed the starting shortstop job last season, he struggled early before getting hurt and returned to find himself looking up at Eduardo Nunez, and later Jorge Polanco, on the depth chart. Escobar never got on track, as his defense slipped and career-long issues controlling the strike zone became the focus when not attached to any power. As a switch-hitter capable of 50 extra-base hits and passable shortstop defense, he is a starting-caliber talent, but players like him tend to find their way to the bench, where the ever-present platoon advantage and versatility can best be leveraged, and 2016 brought him closer to that destiny.

Mitch Garver   C

Born: 1/15/91   Age: 26   Bats: R   Throws: R   Height: 6'1"   Weight: 220   Entered Pro Ball: Round 9, 2013 Draft (#260 overall)

YEAR	TEAM	LVL	AGE	PA	R	2B	3B	HR	RBI	BB	K	SB	CS	AVG/OBP/SLG	TAv	VORP	BABIP	BRR	FRAA	WARP
2014	CDR	A	23	504	65	29	1	16	79	61	65	7	5	.298/.399/.481	.323	47.3	.320	-0.9	C(63): -0.0 • 1B(4): 1.1	5.0
2015	FTM	A+	24	520	46	24	1	4	58	69	82	5	3	.245/.356/.333	.275	24.7	.287	1.1	C(77): -0.2 • 1B(14): -0.8	2.6
2016	CHT	AA	25	407	44	25	0	11	66	43	86	1	3	.257/.334/.419	.278	18.4	.305	0.3	C(46): 8.4 • 1B(14): -1.0	2.8
2016	ROC	AAA	25	84	6	5	0	1	8	7	21	0	0	.329/.381/.434	.305	7.0	.436	0.4	C(14): 0.1 • 1B(2): -0.1	0.7
2017	*MIN*	*MLB*	*26*	*29*	*3*	*1*	*0*	*1*	*3*	*3*	*7*	*0*	*0*	*.240/.317/.392*	*.249*	*1.0*	*.290*	*-0.1*	*C 0*	*0.1*
2018	*MIN*	*MLB*	*27*	*262*	*32*	*13*	*0*	*8*	*30*	*26*	*62*	*0*	*0*	*.238/.319/.397*	*.246*	*5.1*	*.288*	*-0.8*	*C 0*	*0.5*

Breakout: 3%   Improve: 9%   Collapse: 10%   Attrition: 19%   MLB: 34%   *Comparables: Dan Butler, Johnny Monell, Tony Sanchez*

He's too old to be a prospect and his offensive production isn't going to force any issues, but Minnesota's system-wide catching dearth could open the door for Garver. He draws walks and controls the strike zone well, isn't totally without power and graded out very well in pitch framing last year—a skill of heightened importance in the new Twins' regime. Garver should get his first shot at becoming the most generic backup catcher in baseball at some point in 2017.

YEAR	TEAM	P. COUNT	FRM RUNS	BLK RUNS	THRW RUNS	TOT RUNS
2017	*MIN*	*1060*	*0.2*	*-0.1*	*0.0*	*0.1*
2018	*MIN*	*9572*	*1.2*	*-1.0*	*0.0*	*0.2*

Nick Gordon SS

Born: 10/24/95 Age: 21 Bats: L Throws: R Height: 6'0" Weight: 160 Entered Pro Ball: Round 1, 2014 Draft (#5 overall)

YEAR	TEAM	LVL	AGE	PA	R	2B	3B	HR	RBI	BB	K	SB	CS	AVG/OBP/SLG	TAv	VORP	BABIP	BRR	FRAA	WARP
2015	CDR	A	19	535	79	23	7	1	58	39	88	25	8	.277/.336/.360	.258	23.0	.333	2.9	SS(118): 8.1	3.3
2016	FTM	A+	20	494	56	23	6	3	52	23	87	19	13	.291/.335/.386	.277	25.2	.353	-2.9	SS(103): 4.3 • 2B(2): -0.1	3.0
2017	*MIN*	*MLB*	*21*	*250*	*28*	*12*	*2*	*5*	*22*	*11*	*61*	*5*	*3*	*.245/.285/.370*	*.224*	*1.9*	*.310*	*-0.1*	*SS 4 • 2B -0*	*0.6*
2018	*MIN*	*MLB*	*22*	*320*	*34*	*15*	*3*	*7*	*33*	*15*	*76*	*6*	*4*	*.250/.292/.384*	*.233*	*2.3*	*.312*	*0.2*	*SS 5 • 2B 0*	*0.8*

Breakout: 4%   Improve: 8%   Collapse: 0%   Attrition: 6%   MLB: 11%   *Comparables: Yamaico Navarro, Nick Franklin, Orlando Arcia*

Tom Gordon's son and Dee Gordon's little brother was the fifth overall pick in the 2014 draft, as the Twins bet big on his ability to stick at shortstop while putting some meat on his bones. It's been a mixed bag so far. Gordon has hit .285 through three pro seasons and is still generally regarded as a lock to stay at the position, but it's come with little power or plate discipline to speak of. His overall prospect profile is somewhat similar to Dee's when he was coming up through the Dodgers' system, albeit with nowhere near as much speed. Dee never developed power and ended up moving to second base, but turned elite wheels and contact skills into plenty of value. Nick won't be able to follow that exact path, which is why staying at shortstop is the key to his career.

Zach Granite CF

Born: 9/17/92 Age: 24 Bats: L Throws: L Height: 6'1" Weight: 175 Entered Pro Ball: Round 14, 2013 Draft (#410 overall)

YEAR	TEAM	LVL	AGE	PA	R	2B	3B	HR	RBI	BB	K	SB	CS	AVG/OBP/SLG	TAv	VORP	BABIP	BRR	FRAA	WARP
2014	CDR	A	21	85	9	2	2	0	2	4	8	1	4	.291/.321/.367	.255	0.7	.319	-1.2	CF(14): -2.2 • LF(7): -1.2	-0.3
2015	CDR	A	22	83	17	5	1	0	5	12	6	7	1	.358/.463/.463	.358	11.9	.393	1.8	LF(13): 2.3 • CF(4): 0.1	1.5
2015	FTM	A+	22	441	59	10	4	1	26	41	63	21	12	.249/.328/.304	.250	8.5	.294	1.7	CF(64): 6.4 • LF(39): 5.9	2.3
2016	CHT	AA	23	584	86	18	8	4	52	42	43	56	14	.295/.347/.382	.276	33.8	.312	8.2	CF(108): 4.5 • LF(18): 1.0	4.2
2017	*MIN*	*MLB*	*24*	*250*	*34*	*9*	*2*	*5*	*22*	*17*	*40*	*14*	*4*	*.262/.313/.393*	*.236*	*4.6*	*.290*	*1.4*	*CF 1 • LF 1*	*0.7*
2018	*MIN*	*MLB*	*25*	*398*	*46*	*14*	*4*	*9*	*43*	*28*	*63*	*23*	*7*	*.265/.319/.400*	*.244*	*7.1*	*.290*	*3.2*	*CF 2 • LF 1*	*1.1*

Breakout: 6%   Improve: 22%   Collapse: 5%   Attrition: 29%   MLB: 44%   *Comparables: J.B. Shuck, Matt Szczur, Todd Cunningham*

It's difficult to have a breakout season while hitting four homers in 127 games, but Granite came pretty close. He entered the season as a marginal prospect whose speed was his lone tool of note, but the former 14th-round pick controlled the strike zone exceptionally well at Double-A, quadrupled his career homer total and drove more balls into the gaps on the way to being named Twins minor league player of the year. His speed is still the headliner, as Granite swiped 56 bases at an 80 percent clip and graded out very well in center field, but for the first time in his career he looks like a potential regular rather than strictly a reserve with good wheels.

Robbie Grossman LF

Born: 9/16/89 Age: 27 Bats: B Throws: L Height: 6'0" Weight: 215 Entered Pro Ball: Round 6, 2008 Draft (#174 overall)

YEAR	TEAM	LVL	AGE	PA	R	2B	3B	HR	RBI	BB	K	SB	CS	AVG/OBP/SLG	TAv	VORP	BABIP	BRR	FRAA	WARP
2014	OKL	AAA	24	199	30	16	0	4	15	22	38	10	8	.337/.417/.497	.319	20.2	.414	0.9	CF(35): -3.1 • LF(7): -0.7	1.6
2014	HOU	MLB	24	422	42	14	2	6	37	55	105	9	3	.233/.337/.333	.258	5.3	.311	-2.0	LF(67): -4.5 • RF(32): 0.1	-0.1
2015	HOU	MLB	25	54	7	2	0	1	5	5	17	0	0	.143/.222/.245	.182	-2.6	.194	0.4	LF(17): -2.2 • RF(4): -0.1	-0.5
2015	FRE	AAA	25	408	54	16	1	5	37	55	85	14	8	.254/.354/.349	.252	3.8	.318	-1.3	LF(75): 0.5 • CF(7): 1.3	0.6
2016	COH	AAA	26	139	14	5	0	6	13	21	25	3	1	.256/.370/.453	.285	5.4	.279	-1.6	CF(19): -1.5 • LF(10): 1.9	0.6
2016	MIN	MLB	26	389	49	19	1	11	37	55	96	2	3	.280/.386/.443	.287	18.0	.364	-0.2	LF(75): -8.4 • CF(1): -0.0	1.0
2017	*MIN*	*MLB*	*27*	*276*	*34*	*12*	*1*	*6*	*25*	*33*	*66*	*5*	*3*	*.251/.341/.378*	*.256*	*6.8*	*.320*	*-0.6*	*LF -2 • CF -1*	*0.2*
2018	*MIN*	*MLB*	*28*	*360*	*44*	*15*	*1*	*7*	*37*	*45*	*91*	*6*	*4*	*.250/.345/.376*	*.250*	*4.3*	*.325*	*-0.7*	*LF -2 • CF -1*	*0.1*

Breakout: 6%   Improve: 38%   Collapse: 6%   Attrition: 20%   MLB: 89%   *Comparables: Bryan Petersen, Ryan Langerhans, David DeJesus*

Released by the Indians in spring training, Grossman signed a minor-league deal with the Twins in mid-May and was in the majors 48 hours later. He got off to a roaring start and remained productive all year, settling in as Minnesota's second-best hitter. Extreme plate discipline made him a stat-head favorite as a prospect with Pittsburgh and Houston, but Grossman's initial struggles in the big leagues laid bare a lack of power and an approach that was more passive than patient. He showed plenty of pop with the Twins, but his overall plan at the plate was still more about coaxing walks than getting into damage-doing counts. Offensively he's definitely worthy of at least a part-time role, but Grossman is a brutal defensive corner outfielder and may always be a slump away from losing a gig.

Max Kepler CF

Born: 2/10/93 Age: 24 Bats: L Throws: L Height: 6'4" Weight: 205 Entered Pro Ball: International Free Agent, 2009

YEAR	TEAM	LVL	AGE	PA	R	2B	3B	HR	RBI	BB	K	SB	CS	AVG/OBP/SLG	TAv	VORP	BABIP	BRR	FRAA	WARP
2014	FTM	A+	21	407	53	20	6	5	59	34	62	6	2	.264/.333/.393	.273	15.3	.304	-1.0	CF(61): -6.9 • RF(18): -0.7	0.7
2015	FTM	A+	22	26	4	2	0	0	0	2	5	1	0	.250/.308/.333	.277	1.2	.316	0.4	RF(5): -0.1	0.1
2015	CHT	AA	22	482	76	32	13	9	71	67	63	18	4	.322/.416/.531	.341	55.7	.359	8.0	1B(37): -0.2 • RF(31): 3.5	6.9
2015	MIN	MLB	22	7	0	0	0	0	0	0	3	0	0	.143/.143/.143	.114	-0.9	.250	0.0	RF(2): 0.1	-0.1
2016	ROC	AAA	23	128	16	4	6	1	19	16	14	1	1	.282/.367/.455	.292	7.5	.309	0.7	RF(26): 2.0 • CF(6): 0.5	1.0
2016	MIN	MLB	23	447	52	20	2	17	63	42	93	6	2	.235/.309/.424	.254	6.3	.261	0.9	RF(108): -1.7 • CF(4): -0.0	0.5
2017	*MIN*	*MLB*	*24*	*582*	*65*	*28*	*7*	*17*	*71*	*54*	*114*	*8*	*2*	*.256/.327/.435*	*.264*	*18.3*	*.294*	*0.8*	*RF 4*	*2.0*
2018	*MIN*	*MLB*	*25*	*570*	*73*	*29*	*7*	*18*	*73*	*54*	*109*	*7*	*2*	*.264/.337/.457*	*.266*	*16.6*	*.301*	*1.2*	*RF 4*	*2.3*

Breakout: 5%   Improve: 42%   Collapse: 13%   Attrition: 17%   MLB: 84%   *Comparables: Ryan Sweeney, Domonic Brown, Elijah Dukes*

Coming off an MVP season at Double-A, the plan was for Max Kepler to spend at least a couple months at Triple-A. Instead he was called up a week into the 2016 season as an injury replacement and then again on June 1. In his second engagement, he played too well to send back down, showing far more power than he ever did in the minors, although his production shrunk following a three-homer game on August 1. Kepler was very raw when the Twins signed him out of Germany as a 16-year-old and injuries further kept him from breaking through prior to 2015, but there was never much doubt about his physical tools and even the power development wasn't a shock given his athletic 6-foot-4 frame. Kepler is still somewhat raw, which shows up most in the field, but his range and arm are both plus in a corner spot. He has superstar upside if the power sticks, and can still be an All-Star if he settles into the 20-homer range thanks to above-average contributions across the board.

Alex Kirilloff   OF

Born: 11/9/97   Age: 19   Bats: L   Throws: L   Height: 6'2"   Weight: 195   Entered Pro Ball: Round 1, 2016 Draft (#15 overall)

YEAR	TEAM	LVL	AGE	PA	R	2B	3B	HR	RBI	BB	K	SB	CS	AVG/OBP/SLG	TAv	VORP	BABIP	BRR	FRAA	WARP
2017	MIN	MLB	19	250	21	10	1	7	27	10	74	0	0	.210/.242/.340	.193	-9.9	.272	-0.4	RF 1 • CF -0	-1.1
2018	MIN	MLB	20	333	36	13	1	10	38	15	92	0	0	.230/.266/.378	.218	-7.3	.289	-0.6	RF 1 • CF 0	-0.7

Breakout: 0%   Improve: 5%   Collapse: 2%   Attrition: 4%   MLB: 9%   *Comparables: Nomar Mazara, Engel Beltre, Rougned Odor*

The last prep outfielder drafted in the first round by a front office regime that fetishized them for two decades, Kirilloff was a line-drive machine in his pro debut, and showed impressive power in a league where homers are relatively rare. He also swung at everything—a potential stumbling block as he moves up the organizational ladder—and because Kirilloff looks destined for a corner spot the bar for his offensive development is high. If things go well he'd fit nicely in right field around 2020 or so, but there's a lot of polishing that needs to take place first.

Joe Mauer   1B

Born: 4/19/83   Age: 34   Bats: L   Throws: R   Height: 6'5"   Weight: 225   Entered Pro Ball: Round 1, 2001 Draft (#1 overall)

YEAR	TEAM	LVL	AGE	PA	R	2B	3B	HR	RBI	BB	K	SB	CS	AVG/OBP/SLG	TAv	VORP	BABIP	BRR	FRAA	WARP
2014	MIN	MLB	31	518	60	27	2	4	55	60	96	3	0	.277/.361/.371	.261	9.6	.342	4.2	1B(100): 2.8	1.4
2015	MIN	MLB	32	666	69	34	2	10	66	67	112	2	1	.265/.338/.380	.258	2.7	.309	-2.6	1B(137): -1.6	0.1
2016	MIN	MLB	33	576	68	22	4	11	49	79	93	2	0	.261/.363/.389	.259	3.1	.301	-2.2	1B(95): -2.8	0.0
2017	MIN	MLB	34	608	63	30	2	9	63	72	106	2	1	.275/.360/.394	.267	14.2	.326	-0.8	1B -0	1.1
2018	MIN	MLB	35	487	59	24	2	8	49	56	92	0	0	.269/.354/.389	.257	4.7	.324	-0.5	1B 0	0.5

Breakout: 0%   Improve: 41%   Collapse: 9%   Attrition: 21%   MLB: 86%   *Comparables: Dan Driessen, Rusty Staub, Doug Mientkiewicz*

The former first overall pick has not been the same since suffering a concussion on August 19, 2013. There are lots of ways to examine his decline, but anything that fails to start with the brain injury as the driving force is ignoring the obvious. Mauer was a 30-year-old career .323/.405/.468 hitter in the middle of a typically outstanding year, batting .324/.404/.476. He missed the rest of 2013, came back in 2014 as a first baseman, and has hit just .267/.353/.380 since. There have been stretches—like the beginning of last season—in which Mauer looks like his old self, but his reflexes simply are not the same and he's admitted to ongoing blurred vision among other common post-concussion symptoms. Mauer's trademark patience at the plate has allowed him to remain an average player, but there's a constant, inescapable sadness that comes with watching a once-amazing catcher on a Hall of Fame path limp to the finish line far too soon.

J.R. Murphy   C

Born: 5/13/91   Age: 26   Bats: R   Throws: R   Height: 5'11"   Weight: 205   Entered Pro Ball: Round 2, 2009 Draft (#76 overall)

YEAR	TEAM	LVL	AGE	PA	R	2B	3B	HR	RBI	BB	K	SB	CS	AVG/OBP/SLG	TAv	VORP	BABIP	BRR	FRAA	WARP
2014	SWB	AAA	23	196	17	9	0	6	28	13	42	0	0	.246/.292/.397	.238	5.1	.284	1.0	C(46): 9.8	1.5
2014	NYA	MLB	23	85	7	4	0	1	9	4	22	0	0	.284/.318/.370	.267	2.8	.379	-1.1	C(30): 1.0	0.4
2015	NYA	MLB	24	172	21	9	1	3	14	12	43	0	0	.277/.327/.406	.258	7.2	.357	0.2	C(65): -1.8	0.6
2016	ROC	AAA	25	290	24	14	0	3	39	21	51	0	0	.236/.286/.323	.229	2.0	.274	-1.4	C(80): 18.8	2.2
2016	MIN	MLB	25	90	4	3	0	1	3	5	19	0	0	.146/.193/.220	.162	-5.2	.175	-0.3	C(25): 0.2	-0.5
2017	MIN	MLB	26	126	12	6	0	3	13	9	27	0	0	.247/.297/.386	.238	3.0	.290	-0.3	C 1	0.2
2018	MIN	MLB	27	174	20	8	0	5	19	13	38	0	0	.239/.295/.381	.230	0.8	.283	-0.3	C 2	0.3

Breakout: 6%   Improve: 22%   Collapse: 22%   Attrition: 21%   MLB: 70%   *Comparables: Tony Cruz, Rob Brantly, James McCann*

Last offseason the Twins set out to find a long-term answer at catcher and decided on Murphy, the Yankees backup at the time, acquiring him for former top prospect Aaron Hicks. It took less than a month for Murphy to play his way back to the minors with a 3-for-40 start and he stayed there until September, returning when rosters expanded despite being terrible at Triple-A. Hicks' lack of development keeps the trade from looking like a true blunder, but Murphy has a career .620 OPS in the majors and .687 OPS at Triple-A through age 25. Murphy's one standout skill might be pitch framing, so the front office regime change could give him a second chance—especially since they've now acknowledged it's an important trait by signing Jason Castro.

YEAR	TEAM	P. COUNT	FRM RUNS	BLK RUNS	THRW RUNS	TOT RUNS
2014	NYA	3213	1.7	-0.7	-0.2	0.8
2014	SWB	6727	11.7	-0.2	-0.8	10.7
2015	NYA	6891	-0.7	-1.7	-0.1	-2.5
2016	MIN	3340	0.9	-1.8	0.1	-0.9
2017	MIN	4870	3.4	-1.4	-0.2	1.7
2018	MIN	6725	4.4	-1.9	-0.4	2.2

Daniel Palka   1B

Born: 10/28/91   Age: 25   Bats: L   Throws: L   Height: 6'2"   Weight: 220   Entered Pro Ball: Round 3, 2013 Draft (#88 overall)

YEAR	TEAM	LVL	AGE	PA	R	2B	3B	HR	RBI	BB	K	SB	CS	AVG/OBP/SLG	TAv	VORP	BABIP	BRR	FRAA	WARP
2014	SBN	A	22	521	63	23	5	22	82	56	129	9	3	.248/.332/.466	.288	19.9	.294	-1.4	1B(93): 8.9 • RF(11): 4.9	3.5
2015	VIS	A+	23	576	95	36	3	29	90	56	164	24	7	.280/.352/.532	.329	49.4	.353	1.1	RF(69): 3.5 • 1B(37): -0.7	5.4
2016	CHT	AA	24	345	42	12	4	21	65	38	100	7	4	.270/.348/.547	.321	25.4	.324	-1.4	RF(66): -11.3 • 1B(3): -0.5	1.5
2016	ROC	AAA	24	223	31	12	0	13	25	18	86	2	1	.232/.296/.483	.279	5.9	.324	-2.3	RF(47): -5.2	0.1
2017	MIN	MLB	25	250	32	10	1	13	37	21	84	3	1	.230/.297/.460	.252	4.9	.296	-0.1	RF -3 • LF -0	0.2
2018	MIN	MLB	26	329	46	14	1	18	50	30	110	4	2	.233/.304/.468	.256	5.4	.300	-0.1	RF -4 • LF 0	0.1

Breakout: 3%   Improve: 18%   Collapse: 8%   Attrition: 24%   MLB: 45%   *Comparables: Kyle Jensen, Peter O'Brien, Jabari Blash*

Acquired from Arizona last offseason for light-hitting catcher Chris Herrmann in a "good trade, who'd we get?" scenario, Palka bashed 34 homers between Double-A and Triple-A. His power potential is immense, but his strikeout rate is firmly in red-flag territory and he doesn't balance it with a strong walk rate. That he's also already a poor corner outfielder defensively means the standard for offense will be high enough that smacking 20-25 homers alone will not cut it, although it'll probably get him to the majors no matter what. There are hitters who thrive in the big leagues while striking out in one-third of their plate appearances, but those same hitters generally didn't whiff one-third of the time in the minors. That's the challenge ahead of Palka, who has one tool in his box.

Byung-ho Park   1B

Born: 7/10/86   Age: 30   Bats: R   Throws: R   Height: 6'1"   Weight: 220   Entered Pro Ball: International Free Agent, 2015

YEAR	TEAM	LVL	AGE	PA	R	2B	3B	HR	RBI	BB	K	SB	CS	AVG/OBP/SLG	TAv	VORP	BABIP	BRR	FRAA	WARP
2016	MIN	MLB	29	244	28	9	1	12	24	21	80	1	0	.191/.275/.409	.234	-3.2	.230	0.7	1B(24): 0.2	-0.3
2016	ROC	AAA	29	128	18	5	0	10	19	6	32	0	0	.224/.297/.526	.290	4.9	.216	-0.4	1B(14): 0.0	0.5
2017	MIN	MLB	30	275	33	10	1	14	40	21	85	1	0	.221/.295/.438	.252	3.1	.271	-0.4	1B 0	0.2
2018	MIN	MLB	31	219	28	7	0	11	30	18	69	0	0	.204/.282/.407	.235	-0.6	.249	0.2	1B 0	0.0

Breakout: 2%   Improve: 34%   Collapse: 8%   Attrition: 20%   MLB: 86%   Comparables: Josh Phelps, J.P. Arencibia, Carlos Pena

Minnesota had little need for a designated hitter last offseason, but liked Park's power potential enough to invest $25 million in the Korean slugger and misguidedly send Miguel Sano to the outfield. Sano was predictably brutal in right field and, after a solid first month, Park was even worse at the plate. His power is for real, as Park hit tape-measure bombs from foul pole to foul pole, but he couldn't make consistent contact against anything above 90 miles per hour or anything with spin. It's possible he was doomed anyway, as the Twins eventually revealed that he played most of the season with a hand injury before undergoing surgery in August while in the minors. Park has two years left on an inexpensive deal, but the Twins still have plenty of other DH options and he will likely have to settle for the Kennys Vargas scenic route back to Minnesota.

Trevor Plouffe   3B

Born: 6/15/86   Age: 31   Bats: R   Throws: R   Height: 6'2"   Weight: 215   Entered Pro Ball: Round 1, 2004 Draft (#20 overall)

YEAR	TEAM	LVL	AGE	PA	R	2B	3B	HR	RBI	BB	K	SB	CS	AVG/OBP/SLG	TAv	VORP	BABIP	BRR	FRAA	WARP
2014	MIN	MLB	28	582	69	40	2	14	80	53	109	2	1	.258/.328/.423	.272	22.5	.299	-0.6	3B(127): 0.0	2.5
2015	MIN	MLB	29	632	74	35	4	22	86	50	124	2	1	.244/.307/.435	.261	13.5	.274	-5.4	3B(140): 5.2 • 1B(17): 0.7	2.1
2016	ROC	AAA	30	20	4	2	0	1	2	1	5	0	0	.316/.350/.579	.329	2.5	.385	0.7	3B(2): 0.9 • 1B(1): 0.1	0.4
2016	MIN	MLB	30	344	35	13	1	12	47	19	60	1	0	.260/.303/.420	.241	1.8	.284	-0.7	3B(63): -1.7 • 1B(13): -0.2	0.0
2017	MIN	MLB	31	385	43	19	1	14	50	30	79	1	0	.250/.312/.431	.251	6.6	.284	-1.4	3B -0 • 1B 1	0.8
2018	MIN	MLB	32	341	43	17	1	13	44	25	72	0	0	.248/.308/.433	.253	3.2	.280	-1.4	3B 0 • 1B 1	0.4

Breakout: 0%   Improve: 34%   Collapse: 10%   Attrition: 13%   MLB: 85%   Comparables: Joe Crede, Adrian Beltre, Eric Soderholm

Trevor Plouffe reached the majors as a light-hitting shortstop in 2010 and looked as if he'd never played the position, endangering fans along the first-base line despite logging 5,000 innings at the position in the minors. His transformation to power-hitting third baseman took place at Triple-A in 2011, and turned him from a marginal prospect to a five-year starter in Minnesota. It's quite a story, although Brian Dozier did basically the same thing in the same organization and then kept improving while Plouffe stalled out. There's no shame in that—Plouffe made huge strides on both sides of the ball just to establish himself as an everyday asset—but the Twins clearly believed that he had another gear. Instead his mediocrity has been remarkably consistent. The same .250 average, .750 OPS, and decent defense that was a source of excitement from a minimum-salaried rookie became a source of frustration from a well-paid veteran and punched his ticket out of town.

Jorge Polanco   SS

Born: 7/5/93   Age: 23   Bats: B   Throws: R   Height: 5'11"   Weight: 200   Entered Pro Ball: International Free Agent, 2009

YEAR	TEAM	LVL	AGE	PA	R	2B	3B	HR	RBI	BB	K	SB	CS	AVG/OBP/SLG	TAv	VORP	BABIP	BRR	FRAA	WARP
2014	FTM	A+	20	432	61	17	6	6	45	46	60	10	8	.291/.364/.415	.282	28.9	.327	1.0	SS(86): 0.1 • 2B(6): -1.3	2.8
2014	MIN	MLB	20	8	2	1	1	0	3	2	2	0	0	.333/.500/.833	.452	1.9	.500	0.1	SS(4): 0.2	0.2
2014	NBR	AA	20	157	13	6	0	1	16	9	28	7	3	.281/.323/.342	.244	4.4	.342	0.8	SS(33): 1.0 • 2B(4): -0.1	0.6
2015	ROC	AAA	21	94	7	6	0	0	6	4	10	1	0	.284/.309/.352	.231	0.8	.313	0.2	SS(19): -0.5	0.0
2015	MIN	MLB	21	12	1	0	0	0	1	2	1	1	0	.300/.417/.300	.270	0.9	.333	0.3	SS(4): -0.5	0.0
2015	CHT	AA	21	431	55	17	3	6	47	35	63	18	10	.289/.346/.393	.261	18.0	.330	1.5	SS(83): 2.5 • 2B(8): -0.5	2.2
2016	ROC	AAA	22	325	32	14	6	9	39	27	51	5	4	.276/.335/.457	.287	17.5	.304	0.3	2B(64): 5.5 • 3B(2): 0.2	2.4
2016	MIN	MLB	22	270	24	15	4	4	27	17	46	4	3	.282/.332/.424	.259	9.3	.328	-0.7	SS(47): -1.8 • 3B(9): -0.7	0.7
2017	MIN	MLB	23	606	73	27	6	14	59	40	114	11	6	.265/.313/.410	.249	18.4	.306	-0.1	SS 3 • 2B 0	1.7
2018	MIN	MLB	24	573	69	27	5	16	69	42	112	10	6	.268/.323/.433	.253	15.5	.309	0.3	SS 3 • 2B 0	2.0

Breakout: 7%   Improve: 38%   Collapse: 6%   Attrition: 16%   MLB: 55%   Comparables: Luis Valbuena, Enrique Hernandez, Steve Lombardozzi

Minnesota's player development issues have been plentiful, but the handling of Polanco has been particularly odd. He was called up from Single-A in 2014 and 2015 just to sit on the bench when short-term infield help was needed. Last year at Triple-A he was moved from shortstop to second base, logging zero innings at his old position for four months, at which point the Twins turned to him as their starting shortstop down the stretch. Polanco's athleticism enabled him to avoid being a disaster, but his lack of arm strength makes him better-suited for the keystone. There's more pop in his bat than modest minor-league homer totals and a rail-thin frame would suggest. His contact skills are already strong and he's not impatient, so more walks may be coming, too. There are lots of prospects with higher ceilings, but it's tough to imagine Polanco not developing into at least a valuable regular… somewhere.

Ben Rortvedt C

Born: 9/25/97 Age: 19 Bats: L Throws: R Height: 5'10" Weight: 190 Entered Pro Ball: Round 2, 2016 Draft (#56 overall)

YEAR	TEAM	LVL	AGE	PA	R	2B	3B	HR	RBI	BB	K	SB	CS	AVG/OBP/SLG	TAv	VORP	BABIP	BRR	FRAA	WARP
2017	MIN	MLB	19	250	22	10	1	5	23	14	74	-1	0	.205/.252/.320	.193	-4.8	.272	-0.3	C 0	-0.5
2018	MIN	MLB	20	263	28	10	1	6	27	17	74	1	0	.227/.280/.355	.219	-1.8	.296	-0.4	C 0	-0.2

Breakout: 0% Improve: 5% Collapse: 2% Attrition: 5% MLB: 10% Comparables: Francisco Pena, Rougned Odor, Nomar Mazara

High school catchers from cold weather states generally aren't great draft-day bets, although the Twins can be excused for thinking otherwise after snagging Joe Mauer first overall in 2001. Last year's second-rounder, Rortvedt draws praise for having above-average potential on both sides of the ball. He struggled offensively in his pro debut, but did control the strike zone well at age 18. Minnesota lacks catching prospects with long-term promise, but a prep catcher from Wisconsin simply isn't going to move quickly through any system, and he'll likely need significant reps in the low minors.

YEAR	TEAM	P. COUNT	FRM RUNS	BLK RUNS	THRW RUNS	TOT RUNS
2017	MIN	9059	0.0	0.0	0.0	0.0
2018	MIN	9527	0.0	0.0	0.0	0.0

Eddie Rosario OF

Born: 9/28/91 Age: 25 Bats: L Throws: R Height: 6'1" Weight: 180 Entered Pro Ball: Round 4, 2010 Draft (#135 overall)

YEAR	TEAM	LVL	AGE	PA	R	2B	3B	HR	RBI	BB	K	SB	CS	AVG/OBP/SLG	TAv	VORP	BABIP	BRR	FRAA	WARP
2014	FTM	A+	22	34	5	0	0	0	4	4	5	1	1	.300/.382/.300	.265	0.1	.360	-1.1	CF(7): -0.7 • 2B(2): 0.1	0.0
2014	NBR	AA	22	336	40	20	3	8	36	17	68	8	4	.237/.277/.396	.237	-1.2	.277	-1.9	CF(43): 2.8 • LF(18): 3.3	0.5
2015	ROC	AAA	23	100	11	2	1	3	12	5	17	1	1	.242/.280/.379	.248	0.5	.267	-0.5	CF(11): -1.0 • RF(10): -0.5	-0.1
2015	MIN	MLB	23	474	60	18	15	13	50	15	118	11	6	.267/.289/.459	.252	9.8	.332	4.1	LF(86): 12.4 • RF(34): -0.3	2.4
2016	ROC	AAA	24	169	26	14	0	7	25	7	25	5	3	.319/.343/.538	.303	13.3	.338	1.1	CF(29): 0.5 • RF(9): 3.0	1.7
2016	MIN	MLB	24	354	52	17	2	10	32	12	91	5	2	.269/.295/.421	.248	9.0	.338	4.4	LF(57): 0.6 • CF(37): -1.7	0.8
2017	MIN	MLB	25	548	62	25	7	17	64	22	130	10	5	.257/.286/.433	.243	11.0	.308	0.6	LF 3 • RF -1	0.6
2018	MIN	MLB	26	491	58	24	6	18	65	22	118	9	5	.257/.291/.450	.245	7.7	.304	3.9	LF 3 • RF -1	1.0

Breakout: 1% Improve: 44% Collapse: 9% Attrition: 19% MLB: 94% Comparables: Laynce Nix, Jake Marisnick, Felix Pie

Paul Molitor became convinced Rosario was ready for the big leagues in his first spring as Twins manager, repeatedly praising his swing and campaigning for his early call-up. Rosario was 23 and coming off an underwhelming Double-A season that included a suspension for marijuana and a hideous strikeout-to-walk ratio. Molitor was perhaps technically right about Rosario's swing, as he hit .267 with plenty of power as a rookie, but his hacktastic approach was anything but ready. Last year's awful start washed away any rookie shine, leading to a Triple-A demotion. Rosario took it in stride, hit his way back to Minnesota, and finished on a high note, but 209 strikeouts and 22 unintentional walks through 214 career games is so absurdly undisciplined that it's impossible to focus on any strengths. His power, speed and defense are strong enough that he could become a standout regular despite a poor walk rate, but Rosario's strike-zone control would need to win the lottery just to qualify as poor—and the Gopher 5 has been about as friendly to him as major league curveballs thus far.

Miguel Sano 3B

Born: 5/11/93 Age: 24 Bats: R Throws: R Height: 6'4" Weight: 260 Entered Pro Ball: International Free Agent, 2009

YEAR	TEAM	LVL	AGE	PA	R	2B	3B	HR	RBI	BB	K	SB	CS	AVG/OBP/SLG	TAv	VORP	BABIP	BRR	FRAA	WARP
2015	CHT	AA	22	286	55	18	1	15	48	38	68	5	1	.274/.374/.544	.332	30.4	.315	1.0	3B(63): -1.1	3.2
2015	MIN	MLB	22	335	46	17	1	18	52	53	119	1	1	.269/.385/.530	.314	17.7	.396	-4.0	3B(9): -0.4 • 1B(2): 0.0	1.9
2016	ROC	AAA	23	30	3	1	0	2	2	5	10	0	0	.160/.300/.440	.239	0.3	.154	0.2	3B(5): -0.5 • RF(1): -0.2	0.0
2016	MIN	MLB	23	495	57	22	1	25	66	54	178	1	0	.236/.319/.462	.262	13.5	.329	2.0	3B(42): 6.5 • RF(38): -1.7	1.9
2017	MIN	MLB	24	596	78	26	2	31	90	72	201	2	1	.240/.334/.473	.277	25.6	.322	-1.0	3B 3	2.7
2018	MIN	MLB	25	556	83	25	1	30	86	72	184	2	1	.241/.341/.485	.275	20.1	.320	-1.1	3B 3	2.5

Breakout: 6% Improve: 67% Collapse: 7% Attrition: 9% MLB: 98% Comparables: Kris Bryant, Eddie Mathews, Mark Reynolds

Sano's rookie season was a Three True Outcomes revelation for an organization that has shied away from strikeouts—and power—to absurd degrees, as he constantly dragged pitchers deep into counts and punished them with homers and walks. His sophomore season was a mess, as he rarely took advantage of those same counts—his OPS with the count full plummeted from 1.281 to .660—and made it easy for strikeout-phobic criticism to land. It also didn't help that the Twins misguidedly sent him to right field, where the 6-foot-5, 275-pound Sano looked as out of place as Steven Seagal in a Coen Brothers movie. He may not be suited for third base long-term either, but Sano's value is in his bat, and with Trevor Plouffe moving on it's his position to lose. For all the flaws he showed in 2016, a .781 OPS and 25 homers in 116 games is promising from a 23-year-old. Sano hit .277 in the minors, including .255 at Double-A, so his .269 rookie mark probably set the bar too high for one of the most strikeout-prone sluggers ever. If left alone to simply hit he's a near-lock for 40-homer, 100-walk seasons, but reaching superstar heights will require finding a path to more contact without losing the bad-intentioned swing.

Danny Santana CF

Born: 11/7/90 Age: 26 Bats: B Throws: R Height: 5'11" Weight: 185 Entered Pro Ball: International Free Agent, 2007

YEAR	TEAM	LVL	AGE	PA	R	2B	3B	HR	RBI	BB	K	SB	CS	AVG/OBP/SLG	TAv	VORP	BABIP	BRR	FRAA	WARP
2014	ROC	AAA	23	105	15	7	2	0	7	6	28	4	1	.268/.311/.381	.239	0.9	.377	-0.7	SS(20): -2.5	-0.2
2014	MIN	MLB	23	430	70	27	7	7	40	19	98	20	4	.319/.353/.472	.291	27.5	.405	2.0	CF(69): 0.2 • SS(34): -7.0	2.3
2015	ROC	AAA	24	162	24	10	4	3	15	7	25	6	3	.322/.348/.500	.309	13.8	.365	-0.5	SS(30): 2.5 • CF(2): -0.1	1.7
2015	MIN	MLB	24	277	30	10	5	0	21	6	68	8	4	.215/.241/.291	.194	-6.0	.290	1.4	SS(66): -0.6 • CF(5): -0.0	-0.7
2016	MIN	MLB	25	248	29	10	2	2	14	12	55	12	9	.240/.279/.326	.207	-7.2	.305	-0.9	CF(40): 1.1 • LF(17): -0.7	-0.8
2017	MIN	MLB	26	66	8	3	1	1	6	3	15	3	1	.264/.296/.396	.239	1.2	.328	0.2	SS -0 • CF 0	0.0
2018	MIN	MLB	27	222	23	11	3	4	24	10	51	8	4	.264/.302/.406	.238	2.5	.325	0.6	SS -2 • CF 1	0.2

Breakout: 7% Improve: 64% Collapse: 11% Attrition: 19% MLB: 97% Comparables: Corey Patterson, Carlos Gomez, Juan Lagares

Instead of merely regressing following his out-of-nowhere, BABIP-driven rookie excellence in 2014, Santana has been one of baseball's worst players. He's not without tools, but speed and athleticism haven't turned him into an asset on the bases or in the field and his bat is an undisciplined mess. Among the 299 major leaguers with at least 500 plate appearances over the last two seasons, Santana ranks 296th in on-base percentage and 297th in slugging percentage, all while posting an abysmal 123/18 K/BB ratio. He's still relatively young, and coaches seem to see promise in him, but through three seasons his .268/.302/.382 line matches his .276/.318/.399 mark in the minors and it's unclear where he'd be a plus defensively.

Kurt Suzuki   C

Born: 10/4/83   Age: 33   Bats: R   Throws: R   Height: 5'11"   Weight: 205   Entered Pro Ball: Round 2, 2004 Draft (#67 overall)

YEAR	TEAM	LVL	AGE	PA	R	2B	3B	HR	RBI	BB	K	SB	CS	AVG/OBP/SLG	TAv	VORP	BABIP	BRR	FRAA	WARP
2014	MIN	MLB	30	503	37	34	0	3	61	34	46	0	1	.288/.345/.383	.265	17.9	.310	-4.7	C(119): -18.3	0.0
2015	MIN	MLB	31	479	36	17	0	5	50	29	59	0	0	.240/.296/.314	.216	-1.7	.265	-1.8	C(130): -12.3	-1.5
2016	MIN	MLB	32	373	34	24	1	8	49	18	48	0	0	.258/.301/.403	.238	6.9	.276	-0.9	C(99): -9.4	-0.3
2017	MIN	MLB	33	372	35	19	1	6	36	23	50	0	0	.253/.306/.368	.227	4.5	.276	-1.6	C -12	-0.8
2018	MIN	MLB	34	360	37	18	0	6	34	22	54	0	0	.242/.296/.351	.223	-2.2	.269	-1.7	C -12	-1.6

Breakout: 8%   Improve: 38%   Collapse: 8%   Attrition: 26%   MLB: 84%   *Comparables: John Stephenson, Einar Diaz, Mike Redmond*

Kurt Suzuki has a sterling defensive reputation, with coaches and pitchers singing his praises every year, but the numbers tell a very different story. Advanced metrics show Suzuki as one of the worst pitch framers in baseball each season since 2009 (he gave back 97.7 runs in those eight years), which is even more unfortunate since it negates almost all of the meager offensive production he put together. He also struggles to corral pitches in the dirt and control the running game, throwing out just 19 percent of attempted base-stealers from 2014-2016. Thanks to a high contact rate and decent gap power, Suzuki's bat has been acceptable on the surface level, but—perhaps more so than any other catcher—the ability to better quantify what should go into a defensive reputation has left his looking like an artfully constructed counterfeit.

YEAR	TEAM	P. COUNT	FRM RUNS	BLK RUNS	THRW RUNS	TOT RUNS
2014	MIN	16027	-19.5	1.2	-0.9	-19.2
2015	MIN	17433	-8.8	1.0	-3.6	-11.4
2016	MIN	13825	-7.1	1.7	-1.9	-7.2
2017	MIN	13388	-10.2	1.1	-2.7	-11.8
2018	MIN	12969	-11.2	0.9	-2.7	-13.1

Kennys Vargas   DH

Born: 8/1/90   Age: 26   Bats: B   Throws: R   Height: 6'5"   Weight: 290   Entered Pro Ball: Undrafted Free Agent, 2009

YEAR	TEAM	LVL	AGE	PA	R	2B	3B	HR	RBI	BB	K	SB	CS	AVG/OBP/SLG	TAv	VORP	BABIP	BRR	FRAA	WARP
2014	NBR	AA	23	405	50	17	0	17	63	43	68	0	2	.281/.360/.472	.297	18.2	.303	-1.0	1B(81): 6.3	2.6
2014	MIN	MLB	23	234	26	10	1	9	38	12	63	0	0	.274/.316/.456	.275	5.7	.340	0.1	1B(13): -0.3	0.6
2015	CHT	AA	24	151	20	3	2	7	24	26	32	0	0	.287/.417/.516	.339	13.0	.333	-0.7	1B(27): 2.3	1.7
2015	ROC	AAA	24	151	20	6	0	6	22	26	39	0	0	.279/.411/.475	.325	10.8	.359	-1.0	1B(26): 0.9	1.2
2015	MIN	MLB	24	184	18	4	0	5	17	9	54	0	0	.240/.277/.349	.212	-7.7	.319	-1.1	1B(18): 0.2	-0.8
2016	ROC	AAA	25	402	41	16	1	15	58	66	89	1	0	.233/.361/.424	.296	16.1	.270	-3.1	1B(77): -2.2	1.4
2016	MIN	MLB	25	177	27	11	0	10	20	24	57	0	0	.230/.333/.500	.275	2.9	.291	-1.7	1B(32): -2.1	0.1
2017	MIN	MLB	26	438	53	17	1	19	61	47	116	0	0	.247/.332/.444	.270	11.1	.301	-0.9	1B 0	1.2
2018	MIN	MLB	27	439	60	18	1	19	60	49	120	0	0	.242/.329/.438	.260	8.6	.299	-1.5	1B 0	1.0

Breakout: 4%   Improve: 38%   Collapse: 8%   Attrition: 21%   MLB: 80%   *Comparables: Brandon Allen, Chris Shelton, Chris Carter*

Kennys Vargas was so far down the Twins' designated hitter/first baseman depth chart that he was nearly exported to Korea during spring training. Instead he spent most of the season at Triple-A, returning to Minnesota for 47 games spread over multiple stints and outperforming the Korean import who helped bury him in the first place. He totaled 25 homers and 90 walks in 143 games between the majors and minors, but Vargas likely maxes out as a .250 hitter and, even after shedding a few pounds from a massive 6-foot-5 frame, lacks the mobility to play first base every day. If given 500 at-bats he'll produce enough to be an asset offensively, but Vargas fits best as a platoon designated hitter, and teams don't line up for that skill set in a 26-year-old.

PITCHERS

Jose Berrios   RHP

Born: 5/27/94   Age: 23   Bats: R   Throws: R   Height: 6'0"   Weight: 185   Entered Pro Ball: Round 1, 2012 Draft (#32 overall)

YEAR	TEAM	LVL	AGE	W	L	SV	G	GS	IP	H	HR	BB/9	K/9	K	GB%	BABIP	WHIP	ERA	FIP	DRA	VORP	WARP	cFIP	MPH
2014	FTM	A+	20	9	3	0	16	16	96¹	78	4	2.1	10.2	109	38%	.297	1.05	1.96	2.51	1.35	45.4	4.6	69	
2014	NBR	AA	20	3	4	0	8	8	40²	33	2	2.7	6.2	28	45%	.261	1.11	3.54	3.65	4.84	1.8	0.2	107	
2015	CHT	AA	21	8	3	0	15	15	90²	77	6	2.4	9.1	92	49%	.296	1.11	3.08	3.09	1.72	34.0	3.7	75	
2015	ROC	AAA	21	6	2	0	12	12	75²	59	6	1.7	9.9	83	40%	.277	0.96	2.62	2.79	1.44	32.5	3.3	64	
2016	ROC	AAA	22	10	5	0	17	17	111¹	74	8	2.9	10.1	125	45%	.254	0.99	2.51	2.91	1.89	42.7	4.4	82	
2016	MIN	MLB	22	3	7	0	14	14	58¹	74	12	5.4	7.6	49	39%	.344	1.87	8.02	6.16	7.55	-14.2	-1.5	125	95.9
2017	MIN	MLB	23	8	8	0	23	23	131	131	16	3.6	7.7	112	50%	.297	1.41	4.32	4.40	4.70	8.0	0.8	100	
2018	MIN	MLB	24	8	8	0	23	23	135²	118	17	4.8	10.3	156	50%	.296	1.41	4.27	4.26	4.63	12.1	1.2	105	

Breakout: 20%   Improve: 38%   Collapse: 20%   Attrition: 24%   MLB: 83%   *Comparables: David Price, Robbie Erlin, Gio Gonzalez*

Minnesota has stockpiled an assortment of high-end young hitting talent, but Jose Berrios stands alone as the singular pitching prospect with frontline-starter upside. He appeared to be ready for a call-up in late 2015, but stayed at Triple-A and was asked to repeat the level last season. He dominated there again, giving him a 2.79 ERA and 211/53 K/BB ratio in 190 total innings versus International League hitters, but when the Twins finally gave him a shot he was the Oxford Dictionary definition of not ready. Berrios couldn't command his fastball, couldn't get hitters to chase his breaking ball and couldn't get in enough favorable counts to rely on his change. And big leaguers knocked all three offerings around amid talk of Berrios tipping his pitches. He's still very young and his velocity was as advertised, but rumblings about a flat fastball and better control than command will need to be dispelled. Minnesota desperately needs Berrios to lead the rotation's turnaround.

Buddy Boshers   LHP

Born: 5/9/88   Age: 29   Bats: L   Throws: L   Height: 6'3"   Weight: 205   Entered Pro Ball: Round 4, 2008 Draft (#139 overall)

YEAR	TEAM	LVL	AGE	W	L	SV	G	GS	IP	H	HR	BB/9	K/9	K	GB%	BABIP	WHIP	ERA	FIP	DRA	VORP	WARP	cFIP	MPH
2014	SLC	AAA	26	1	0	0	11	0	13	10	1	9.0	8.3	12	56%	.290	1.77	6.23	5.85	6.78	-2.1	-0.2	111	
2014	ARK	AA	26	2	3	0	29	8	61	47	1	4.0	10.3	70	56%	.295	1.21	2.66	2.42	3.28	11.9	1.3	83	
2016	ROC	AAA	28	1	1	2	22	0	26	18	1	3.8	10.0	29	48%	.266	1.12	1.04	2.71	3.30	4.8	0.5	88	
2016	MIN	MLB	28	2	0	0	37	0	36	35	3	1.8	9.2	37	48%	.308	1.17	4.25	2.80	2.93	8.2	0.8	87	94.2
2017	MIN	MLB	29	2	3	0	49	0	51	51	6	3.4	8.2	47	50%	.301	1.38	4.16	4.07	4.46	3.0	0.3	100	
2018	MIN	MLB	30	1	0	0	18	0	18²	17	3	4.7	10.3	21	50%	.310	1.46	4.38	4.37	4.75	0.6	0.1	106	

Breakout: 18%   Improve: 32%   Collapse: 22%   Attrition: 33%   MLB: 60%   *Comparables: Chaz Roe, Donnie Veal, Chris Leroux*

Originally the Angels' fourth-round pick in the 2008 draft, Boshers was released following a walk-filled 2014 split between Double-A and Triple-A. He spent 2015 playing independent ball, harnessing his above-average raw stuff enough to get a minor-league deal from the Twins. One ugly outing in mid-August accounted for 35 percent of his earned runs allowed, but Boshers looked like a big leaguer (and before that looked too good for Triple-A). He works in the low-90s with his fastball and relies heavily on a low-80s curveball that's his best pitch, giving him a usable weapon versus right-handed hitters.

Nick Burdi   RHP

Born: 1/19/93   Age: 24   Bats: R   Throws: R   Height: 6'5"   Weight: 220   Entered Pro Ball: Round 2, 2014 Draft (#46 overall)

YEAR	TEAM	LVL	AGE	W	L	SV	G	GS	IP	H	HR	BB/9	K/9	K	GB%	BABIP	WHIP	ERA	FIP	DRA	VORP	WARP	cFIP	MPH
2014	CDR	A	21	0	0	4	13	0	13	8	0	5.5	18.0	26	55%	.400	1.23	4.15	1.33	1.54	5.1	0.5	73	
2015	FTM	A+	22	2	2	2	13	0	20	12	1	1.4	13.1	29	44%	.275	0.75	2.25	1.37	1.24	7.7	0.8	63	
2015	CHT	AA	22	3	4	2	30	0	43²	40	3	6.6	11.1	54	49%	.322	1.65	4.53	3.99	3.89	4.1	0.4	98	
2017	MIN	MLB	24	1	1	1	31	0	32¹	37	5	4.9	8.1	29	54%	.326	1.68	4.97	5.11	5.29	-1.0	-0.1	124	
2018	MIN	MLB	25	1	0	1	27	0	35²	34	5	5.6	11.0	43	54%	.318	1.56	4.59	4.58	4.89	0.6	0.1	113	

Breakout: 3%   Improve: 3%   Collapse: 7%   Attrition: 11%   MLB: 11%   *Comparables: Ben Heller, Hector Neris, James Pazos*

As a hard-throwing college reliever, there was talk of Nick Burdi reaching the big leagues within months of the Twins drafting him in the second round of the 2014 draft. This clearly did not happen. Instead his control problems stalled a rapid rise, and then an arm injury the team repeatedly called "minor" knocked him out for nearly all of 2016. Burdi touches triple-digits and has whiffed 13 batters per nine, so if healthy it won't take much for him to get back on the fast track. In the meantime, his little brother Zack, drafted two years later by the White Sox, may get to the majors first.

J.T. Chargois   RHP

Born: 12/3/90   Age: 26   Bats: B   Throws: R   Height: 6'3"   Weight: 200   Entered Pro Ball: Round 2, 2012 Draft (#72 overall)

YEAR	TEAM	LVL	AGE	W	L	SV	G	GS	IP	H	HR	BB/9	K/9	K	GB%	BABIP	WHIP	ERA	FIP	DRA	VORP	WARP	cFIP	MPH
2015	FTM	A+	24	1	0	4	16	0	15	12	0	3.0	11.4	19	48%	.286	1.13	2.40	1.63	2.62	3.5	0.4	86	
2015	CHT	AA	24	1	1	11	32	0	33	26	1	5.5	9.3	34	56%	.298	1.39	2.73	3.64	3.62	4.1	0.4	97	
2016	CHT	AA	25	0	0	7	11	0	11²	8	1	3.9	10.8	14	38%	.250	1.11	1.54	3.32	2.83	2.5	0.3	93	
2016	ROC	AAA	25	2	1	9	28	0	35	27	1	2.1	10.5	41	54%	.286	1.00	1.29	1.88	2.71	8.7	0.9	78	
2016	MIN	MLB	25	1	1	0	25	0	23	25	0	4.7	6.7	17	54%	.357	1.61	4.70	3.32	4.64	0.9	0.1	106	98.7
2017	MIN	MLB	26	1	2	0	29	0	31	32	4	3.7	7.2	25	50%	.301	1.49	4.79	4.60	4.93	0.2	0.0	100	
2018	MIN	MLB	27	1	0	0	27	0	28²	28	4	4.7	9.1	29	50%	.306	1.50	4.70	4.69	5.07	0.0	0.0	117	

Breakout: 27%   Improve: 38%   Collapse: 10%   Attrition: 27%   MLB: 54%   *Comparables: Preston Claiborne, Travis Schlichting, Andrew McKiraha*

One of the worst debuts in Twins history got Chargois immediately sent back to the minors, but he returned in August and fared well in September with 13 strikeouts against just three walks. Chargois' high-90s fastball gets most of the attention, but a high-80s slider may prove to be his best weapon. His changeup is mostly a work in progress, but he clearly has the raw stuff to make a two-pitch repertoire work in a one-inning role. Chargois was thought to be on the fast track when the Twins drafted him in 2012, but injuries cost him all of 2013 and 2014. He's racked up 125 strikeouts in 118 innings since then while allowing just three homers, but Chargois' command comes and goes.

Tyler Duffey   RHP

Born: 12/27/90   Age: 26   Bats: R   Throws: R   Height: 6'3"   Weight: 220   Entered Pro Ball: Round 5, 2012 Draft (#160 overall)

YEAR	TEAM	LVL	AGE	W	L	SV	G	GS	IP	H	HR	BB/9	K/9	K	GB%	BABIP	WHIP	ERA	FIP	DRA	VORP	WARP	cFIP	MPH
2014	FTM	A+	23	3	0	0	4	4	22¹	22	0	2.0	5.2	13	36%	.286	1.21	2.82	2.90	4.16	3.6	0.4	99	
2014	NBR	AA	23	8	3	0	18	18	111¹	104	14	1.5	6.8	84	47%	.274	1.10	3.80	4.13	3.09	26.5	2.8	96	
2014	ROC	AAA	23	2	0	0	3	3	16	16	3	3.4	9.0	16	28%	.302	1.38	3.94	5.11	3.25	4.4	0.4	95	
2015	CHT	AA	24	2	2	0	8	8	52²	46	2	2.1	9.2	54	54%	.322	1.10	2.56	1.99	1.62	20.3	2.2	70	
2015	ROC	AAA	24	5	6	0	14	14	85¹	73	1	1.9	7.2	68	47%	.276	1.07	2.53	2.38	2.80	23.7	2.4	84	
2015	MIN	MLB	24	5	1	0	10	10	58	56	4	3.1	8.2	53	51%	.315	1.31	3.10	3.21	3.52	10.1	1.1	89	93.3
2016	ROC	AAA	25	1	1	0	5	5	30²	24	4	3.5	7.3	25	35%	.238	1.17	2.93	4.41	5.42	-0.2	0.0	114	
2016	MIN	MLB	25	9	12	0	26	26	133	167	25	2.2	7.7	114	49%	.339	1.50	6.43	4.69	4.05	19.4	2.0	92	93.2
2017	MIN	MLB	26	8	8	0	26	26	130	134	15	2.6	7.2	103	46%	.298	1.32	4.02	4.08	4.36	12.8	1.3	100	
2018	MIN	MLB	27	9	10	0	30	30	190²	179	24	3.5	9.1	193	46%	.299	1.33	4.12	4.11	4.46	17.0	1.8	101	

Breakout: 27%   Improve: 54%   Collapse: 15%   Attrition: 14%   MLB: 92%   *Comparables: Tommy Milone, Anthony DeSclafani, Carlos Carrasco*

Duffey entered 2015 as a mid-level prospect and ended it as the Twins' second-best starter, but he turned back into a pumpkin last season. A college reliever who served as Rice's co-closer with J.T. Chargois, he's handled the move to starting from a workload standpoint, but the lack of a consistent third pitch looms over him. His advanced stats didn't change much from 2015 to 2016, and in fact he sliced his walk rate considerably, but Duffey went from five homers allowed in 196 innings to serving up 29 homers in 164 innings. Normalizing his flyball and homer rates leaves Duffey looking like a mid-rotation starter, and even within last year's struggles there were a half-dozen starts in which he looked like a rotation building block. Yet because he's already 26 and was never viewed as a high-end prospect, the leash won't be very long if another Home Run Derby breaks out. Giving the bullpen another chance is a viable fallback plan.

Kyle Gibson   RHP

Born: 10/23/87 Age: 29   Bats: R   Throws: R   Height: 6'6"   Weight: 215   Entered Pro Ball: Round 1, 2009 Draft (#22 overall)

YEAR	TEAM	LVL	AGE	W	L	SV	G	GS	IP	H	HR	BB/9	K/9	K	GB%	BABIP	WHIP	ERA	FIP	DRA	VORP	WARP	cFIP	MPH
2014	MIN	MLB	26	13	12	0	31	31	179¹	178	12	2.9	5.4	107	57%	.287	1.31	4.47	3.82	3.68	23.1	2.6	100	94.1
2015	MIN	MLB	27	11	11	0	32	32	194²	186	18	3.0	6.7	145	56%	.287	1.29	3.84	3.93	3.74	29.0	3.1	93	94.5
2016	MIN	MLB	28	6	11	0	25	25	147¹	175	20	3.4	6.4	104	50%	.330	1.56	5.07	4.66	4.69	11.1	1.1	105	93.6
2017	MIN	MLB	29	10	10	0	29	29	165¹	170	21	3.2	7.2	131	45%	.300	1.40	4.29	4.43	4.65	11.0	1.1	100	
2018	MIN	MLB	30	8	9	0	25	25	150	153	20	3.6	7.6	127	45%	.303	1.42	4.46	4.46	4.83	10.2	1.1	111	

Breakout: 22%   Improve: 44%   Collapse: 29%   Attrition: 18%   MLB: 94%   *Comparables: Tyson Ross, Brandon McCarthy, Clay Buchholz*

For his entire career, any time Kyle Gibson has turned in a strong start it's been treated locally as if a breakout is taking place. Perhaps it's because he's a former first-rounder or because Tommy John surgery delayed what was supposed to be a rapid rise to the majors. Or maybe it's just that he does look the part of a top-of-the-rotation starter once every six weeks. Realistically though, it's just not happening. Gibson is a 29-year-old with a career 4.59 ERA and 4.09 DRA. He induces groundballs and, in theory, has the velocity and movement to generate missed bats, too. However, no AL starter threw fewer pitches in the strike zone and he's never topped 6.7 strikeouts per nine. Gibson isn't a bad pitcher, especially if he ever got to pitch in front of an infield defense that was more Jarlsberg than Swiss, and if everything he does wasn't framed within long-expired expectations, his lack of command and inconsistency wouldn't be so frustrating. But it is and they are.

Stephen Gonsalves   LHP

Born: 7/8/94   Age: 22   Bats: L   Throws: L   Height: 6'5"   Weight: 213   Entered Pro Ball: Round 4, 2013 Draft (#110 overall)

YEAR	TEAM	LVL	AGE	W	L	SV	G	GS	IP	H	HR	BB/9	K/9	K	GB%	BABIP	WHIP	ERA	FIP	DRA	VORP	WARP	cFIP	MPH
2014	CDR	A	19	2	3	0	8	8	36²	31	1	2.7	10.8	44	36%	.326	1.15	3.19	2.50	2.37	12.5	1.3	84	
2015	CDR	A	20	6	1	0	9	9	55	29	2	2.5	12.6	77	41%	.243	0.80	1.15	2.11	1.02	25.7	2.7	65	
2015	FTM	A+	20	7	2	0	15	15	79¹	66	4	4.3	6.2	55	39%	.270	1.31	2.61	3.58	6.44	-12.0	-1.3	120	
2016	FTM	A+	21	5	4	0	11	11	65²	43	2	2.7	9.0	66	48%	.248	0.96	2.33	2.55	2.56	21.3	2.2	87	
2016	CHT	AA	21	8	1	0	13	13	74¹	43	1	4.5	10.8	89	38%	.255	1.08	1.82	2.76	3.20	15.7	1.7	89	
2017	MIN	MLB	22	6	7	0	20	20	104¹	112	16	4.7	7.2	84	58%	.304	1.59	5.14	5.18	5.52	-0.6	-0.1	130	
2018	MIN	MLB	23	5	7	0	17	17	100²	90	16	6.4	10.1	113	58%	.293	1.61	5.25	5.23	5.64	-1.7	-0.2	132	

Breakout: 7%   Improve: 23%   Collapse: 7%   Attrition: 19%   MLB: 38%   *Comparables: Mauricio Robles, Jake Odorizzi, Robbie Ray*

From the moment the Twins drafted Gonsalves out of a California high school in 2013 his numbers have been excellent, but his fastball command has been singled out as a long-term worry. Last season he held opponents to a .179 batting average and just three homers in 549 plate appearances, while reaching Double-A as a 21-year-old. All of that, along with struggling to keep a walk rate under 4.0 at every level, usually comes attached to a fire-baller's profile, but Gonsalves' fastball resides in the low-90s. He's a good prospect—arguably the best the Twins have remaining in the high minors—but an uncommon stuff/stats mix makes him tough to project with confidence.

Phil Hughes   RHP

Born: 6/24/86   Age: 31   Bats: R   Throws: R   Height: 6'5"   Weight: 240   Entered Pro Ball: Round 1, 2004 Draft (#23 overall)

YEAR	TEAM	LVL	AGE	W	L	SV	G	GS	IP	H	HR	BB/9	K/9	K	GB%	BABIP	WHIP	ERA	FIP	DRA	VORP	WARP	cFIP	MPH
2014	MIN	MLB	28	16	10	0	32	32	209²	221	16	0.7	8.0	186	38%	.324	1.13	3.52	2.68	2.96	43.7	4.8	81	94.6
2015	MIN	MLB	29	11	9	0	27	25	155¹	184	29	0.9	5.4	94	37%	.304	1.29	4.40	4.67	5.92	-14.6	-1.6	114	93.1
2016	MIN	MLB	30	1	7	0	12	11	59	76	11	2.0	5.2	34	36%	.323	1.51	5.95	5.04	7.88	-16.6	-1.7	133	92.5
2017	MIN	MLB	31	8	9	0	23	23	138	156	24	1.8	6.9	106	41%	.303	1.35	4.53	4.60	4.88	5.6	0.6	100	
2018	MIN	MLB	32	8	9	0	24	24	142	165	25	1.8	6.9	108	41%	.313	1.37	4.65	4.61	4.99	7.6	0.8	117	

Breakout: 14%   Improve: 50%   Collapse: 16%   Attrition: 16%   MLB: 84%   *Comparables: Aaron Harang, Freddy Garcia, Ervin Santana*

In true Twins fashion, they signed Phil Hughes to a three-year, $24 million free-agent contract, got a career year out of him in the first season, immediately signed him to an unnecessary three-year, $42 million extension, and then watched him struggle before breaking down. His status for 2017 is uncertain following thoracic outlet syndrome surgery and a busted knee cap, so the new front office inherits a broken-down 31-year-old with a career 4.41 ERA under contract through 2019. As an extreme fly-ball pitcher committed to pounding the strike zone with low-90s velocity his margin for error is slim. It worked brilliantly in 2014, as he broke the all-time K/BB record, but as the health issues piled up and Hughes' velocity dipped he was essentially throwing batting practice.

Tyler Jay   LHP

Born: 4/19/94   Age: 23   Bats: L   Throws: L   Height: 6'1"   Weight: 185   Entered Pro Ball: Round 1, 2015 Draft (#6 overall)

YEAR	TEAM	LVL	AGE	W	L	SV	G	GS	IP	H	HR	BB/9	K/9	K	GB%	BABIP	WHIP	ERA	FIP	DRA	VORP	WARP	cFIP	MPH
2015	FTM	A+	21	0	1	1	19	0	18¹	18	0	3.9	10.8	22	41%	.353	1.42	3.93	2.07	2.88	3.7	0.4	92	
2016	FTM	A+	22	5	5	0	13	13	69²	64	5	2.7	8.8	68	51%	.311	1.22	2.84	3.31	2.87	20.1	2.1	89	
2016	CHT	AA	22	0	0	0	5	2	14	13	2	3.2	5.8	9	50%	.262	1.29	5.79	4.96	4.73	0.4	0.0	107	
2017	*MIN*	*MLB*	*23*	*3*	*3*	*0*	*20*	*8*	*56¹*	*68*	*8*	*3.9*	*6.1*	*38*	*51%*	*.325*	*1.65*	*5.10*	*5.06*	*5.41*	*-0.2*	*0.0*	*128*	
2018	*MIN*	*MLB*	*24*	*7*	*7*	*1*	*46*	*18*	*132²*	*136*	*20*	*4.8*	*8.5*	*125*	*51%*	*.311*	*1.56*	*4.97*	*4.95*	*5.27*	*1.4*	*0.1*	*124*	

Breakout: 1%   Improve: 1%   Collapse: 0%   Attrition: 3%   MLB: 3%   *Comparables: Tyler Duffey, Matthew Bowman, Bud Norris*

The culmination of the Twins' half-decade pattern of drafting college relievers and attempting to turn them into starters, Jay was a bullpen stud at Illinois, earning first-team All-American honors amid speculation that he could be in the big leagues within months of the draft. Instead the Twins took him sixth overall and sent him to Single-A. He remained there to begin last year, moved up to Double-A in July, and was shut down after just 14 innings with neck problems. Jay's numbers as a starter are more good than great, with his once-deadly fastball/slider pairing playing down a tick, and the slight left-hander may simply not be able to handle the workload anyway. At age 23 the clock is ticking, but for now the Twins still see him as a starter.

Felix Jorge   RHP

Born: 1/2/94   Age: 23   Bats: R   Throws: R   Height: 6'2"   Weight: 170   Entered Pro Ball: International Free Agent, 2011

YEAR	TEAM	LVL	AGE	W	L	SV	G	GS	IP	H	HR	BB/9	K/9	K	GB%	BABIP	WHIP	ERA	FIP	DRA	VORP	WARP	cFIP	MPH
2014	CDR	A	20	2	5	0	12	8	39	57	9	4.6	5.3	23	43%	.358	1.97	9.00	7.00	10.89	-23.9	-2.5	128	
2015	CDR	A	21	6	7	0	23	22	142	118	11	2.0	7.2	114	47%	.267	1.06	2.79	3.54	3.38	29.0	3.1	93	
2016	FTM	A+	22	9	3	0	14	14	93	76	3	1.1	7.5	77	52%	.280	0.94	1.55	2.50	2.22	33.7	3.5	80	
2016	CHT	AA	22	3	5	0	11	11	74¹	83	7	1.5	3.9	32	52%	.306	1.28	4.12	4.21	5.51	-3.4	-0.4	110	
2017	*MIN*	*MLB*	*23*	*6*	*9*	*0*	*21*	*21*	*121*	*158*	*21*	*3.1*	*4.0*	*54*	*61%*	*.317*	*1.65*	*5.58*	*5.66*	*5.94*	*-6.3*	*-0.7*	*142*	
2018	*MIN*	*MLB*	*24*	*7*	*9*	*0*	*22*	*22*	*130¹*	*146*	*23*	*4.3*	*6.8*	*98*	*61%*	*.305*	*1.59*	*5.55*	*5.51*	*5.91*	*-6.3*	*-0.7*	*140*	

Breakout: 9%   Improve: 14%   Collapse: 1%   Attrition: 12%   MLB: 19%   *Comparables: Dillon Gee, Kyle Lobstein, Cody Anderson*

Initially put on the fast track, Jorge struggled with full-season competition at age 20 and was demoted back to rookie-ball. He gave it a second try in 2015 and fared well, following it up by dominating High-A to begin last season. His strikeout rate vanished after a midseason promotion to Double-A, but Jorge's excellent control kept him afloat. While not a soft-tosser, his strength is definitely in pounding the strike zone with a low-90s fastball and good offspeed stuff. He walked just 23 of 656 batters faced last season, which is remarkable for a 22-year-old. Jorge could be in the mix as a back-of-the-rotation starter for the Twins as soon as late this season, although the lack of missed bats will be a red flag until it's not.

Brandon Kintzler   RHP

Born: 8/1/84   Age: 32   Bats: R   Throws: R   Height: 6'0"   Weight: 190   Entered Pro Ball: Round 40, 2004 Draft (#1182 overall)

YEAR	TEAM	LVL	AGE	W	L	SV	G	GS	IP	H	HR	BB/9	K/9	K	GB%	BABIP	WHIP	ERA	FIP	DRA	VORP	WARP	cFIP	MPH
2014	MIL	MLB	29	3	3	0	64	0	58¹	62	8	2.5	4.8	31	59%	.293	1.34	3.24	4.65	4.31	1.2	0.1	111	94.4
2015	MIL	MLB	30	0	1	0	7	0	7	12	1	6.4	9.0	7	67%	.478	2.43	6.43	5.16	3.98	0.6	0.1	101	92.9
2015	CSP	AAA	30	1	1	0	17	0	19	23	0	1.9	6.6	14	71%	.365	1.42	5.21	2.76	3.90	2.2	0.2	88	
2016	ROC	AAA	31	4	1	0	10	0	15¹	15	0	1.8	6.5	11	56%	.326	1.17	3.52	2.52	3.39	2.7	0.3	96	
2016	MIN	MLB	31	0	2	17	54	0	54¹	59	5	1.3	5.8	35	63%	.310	1.23	3.15	3.57	3.89	6.5	0.7	92	95.2
2017	*MIN*	*MLB*	*32*	*3*	*3*	*25*	*54*	*0*	*57*	*63*	*7*	*2.8*	*5.9*	*38*	*48%*	*.304*	*1.43*	*4.55*	*4.43*	*4.75*	*1.5*	*0.2*	*100*	
2018	*MIN*	*MLB*	*33*	*2*	*1*	*15*	*42*	*0*	*44*	*47*	*6*	*3.4*	*6.6*	*32*	*48%*	*.305*	*1.45*	*4.63*	*4.61*	*4.98*	*0.4*	*0.0*	*113*	

Breakout: 26%   Improve: 43%   Collapse: 21%   Attrition: 24%   MLB: 72%   *Comparables: Jared Burton, Joe Beimel, Fernando Rodriguez*

Cut loose by the Brewers following a 2015 wrecked by injury, Kintzler failed to make the Twins' bullpen out of spring training as a non-roster invite...and finished the season as their closer. He's not really suited for that role, but Kintzler's heavy, low-90s fastball generates grounders in bunches and he really committed to pounding the strike zone. Among all relievers with 50-plus innings, only Andrew Miller and Deolis Guerra had a lower walk rate, and Kintzler ranked eighth in groundball percentage. Prior to the knee and shoulder problems, Kintzler had a 3.08 ERA for the Brewers from 2011-2014, and while he's BABIP dependent, it's a skill set that should fit nicely in middle relief.

Patrick Light   RHP

Born: 3/29/91   Age: 26   Bats: R   Throws: R   Height: 6'5"   Weight: 220   Entered Pro Ball: Round 1, 2012 Draft (#37 overall)

YEAR	TEAM	LVL	AGE	W	L	SV	G	GS	IP	H	HR	BB/9	K/9	K	GB%	BABIP	WHIP	ERA	FIP	DRA	VORP	WARP	cFIP	MPH
2014	GRN	A	23	2	0	0	3	3	17¹	15	1	2.1	9.9	19	60%	.304	1.10	4.15	2.84	2.80	5.1	0.5	86	
2014	SLM	A+	23	6	6	0	22	22	115	135	10	2.6	4.5	57	45%	.311	1.46	4.93	4.67	7.35	-22.4	-2.3	115	
2015	PME	AA	24	1	1	3	21	0	29²	18	3	3.3	9.7	32	63%	.208	0.98	2.43	3.54	3.98	2.5	0.3	92	
2015	PAW	AAA	24	2	4	2	26	0	33	31	2	7.1	9.5	35	53%	.322	1.73	5.18	4.28	10.59	-20.8	-2.1	119	
2016	BOS	MLB	25	0	0	0	2	0	2²	7	2	3.4	6.8	2	50%	.417	3.00	23.62	13.61	5.25	-0.1	0.0	108	98.0
2016	PAW	AAA	25	1	1	7	25	0	31	21	1	4.9	10.5	36	44%	.260	1.23	2.32	2.91	4.64	1.1	0.1	96	
2016	MIN	MLB	25	0	1	0	15	0	14	15	2	9.6	9.0	14	59%	.310	2.14	9.00	6.18	5.08	-0.2	0.0	107	97.3
2017	*MIN*	*MLB*	*26*	*1*	*1*	*0*	*24*	*0*	*25*	*28*	*3*	*4.5*	*6.7*	*19*	*54%*	*.298*	*1.57*	*5.13*	*4.83*	*5.18*	*-0.6*	*-0.1*	*100*	
2018	*MIN*	*MLB*	*27*	*2*	*1*	*0*	*37*	*0*	*39*	*37*	*5*	*5.9*	*9.7*	*42*	*54%*	*.303*	*1.59*	*4.84*	*4.82*	*5.20*	*-0.6*	*-0.1*	*117*	

Breakout: 23%   Improve: 35%   Collapse: 4%   Attrition: 26%   MLB: 43%   *Comparables: Alberto Cabrera, Adam Russell, Mike Ekstrom*

Acquired from the Red Sox in exchange for middle reliever Fernando Abad at the trade deadline, Light was called up four weeks later despite walking 4.5 batters per nine at Triple-A. Paul Molitor kept turning to him in relatively tight spots and he was a disaster, showing zero ability to command his high-90s fastball. What's odd about Light's awful control is that, prior to converting to the bullpen in 2015, he walked half as many batters as a Single-A starter. He didn't throw 98 mph then, of course. So far the big-time velocity hasn't equaled big-time strikeouts.

Trevor May   RHP

Born: 9/23/89   Age: 27   Bats: R   Throws: R   Height: 6'5"   Weight: 240   Entered Pro Ball: Round 4, 2008 Draft (#136 overall)

YEAR	TEAM	LVL	AGE	W	L	SV	G	GS	IP	H	HR	BB/9	K/9	K	GB%	BABIP	WHIP	ERA	FIP	DRA	VORP	WARP	cFIP	MPH
2014	ROC	AAA	24	8	6	0	18	18	98¹	75	4	3.6	8.6	94	38%	.270	1.16	2.84	3.16	3.51	24.5	2.4	93	
2014	MIN	MLB	24	3	6	0	10	9	45²	59	7	4.3	8.7	44	39%	.377	1.77	7.88	4.80	4.47	1.8	0.2	106	94.7
2015	MIN	MLB	25	8	9	0	48	16	114²	127	11	2.0	8.6	110	41%	.340	1.33	4.00	3.22	3.28	21.6	2.3	91	96.8
2016	MIN	MLB	26	2	2	0	44	0	42²	39	7	3.6	12.7	60	32%	.317	1.31	5.27	3.76	3.14	8.7	0.9	87	96.7
2017	*MIN*	*MLB*	*27*	*3*	*3*	*0*	*54*	*0*	*57*	*51*	*6*	*3.2*	*9.7*	*61*	*47%*	*.299*	*1.25*	*3.21*	*3.55*	*3.67*	*8.3*	*0.9*	*79*	
2018	*MIN*	*MLB*	*28*	*3*	*1*	*0*	*49*	*0*	*51²*	*43*	*5*	*3.6*	*11.1*	*64*	*47%*	*.302*	*1.24*	*3.36*	*3.36*	*3.66*	*7.9*	*0.8*	*77*	

Breakout: 29%   Improve: 58%   Collapse: 19%   Attrition: 17%   MLB: 90%   *Comparables: Chad Bettis, Liam Hendriks, Jacob deGrom*

Faced with a mid-2015 logjam of mediocre veteran starters, the Twins did a very Twins-like thing by sending the least-experienced, highest-upside pitcher to the bullpen. May had shown a decent amount of promise starting and unsurprisingly looked even better relieving, boosting his strikeout rate by 40 percent to 11.7 punchouts per nine. However, he broke down physically several times after being durable as a starter, and Minnesota's rotation remained a mess. May has always said he wants to rejoin the rotation and his 115/38 strikeout-to-walk ratio in 127 innings as a starter makes it odd to give up on him as a 180-inning contributor. He's absolutely capable of being a late-inning bullpen asset, but the Twins of all teams shouldn't be in the business of prematurely tossing aside potential mid-rotation starters.

Adalberto Mejia   LHP

Born: 6/20/93   Age: 24   Bats: R   Throws: L   Height: 6'3"   Weight: 195   Entered Pro Ball: International Free Agent, 2011

YEAR	TEAM	LVL	AGE	W	L	SV	G	GS	IP	H	HR	BB/9	K/9	K	GB%	BABIP	WHIP	ERA	FIP	DRA	VORP	WARP	cFIP	MPH
2014	RIC	AA	21	7	9	0	22	21	108	119	9	2.6	6.8	82	36%	.326	1.39	4.67	3.78	5.16	0.6	0.1	102	
2015	RIC	AA	22	5	2	0	12	9	51¹	38	2	3.2	6.7	38	46%	.238	1.09	2.45	3.41	3.73	7.6	0.8	102	
2016	RIC	AA	23	3	2	0	11	11	65	48	4	2.2	8.0	58	48%	.251	0.98	1.94	3.16	2.45	19.1	2.1	78	
2016	SAC	AAA	23	4	1	0	7	7	40²	42	5	2.4	9.5	43	42%	.327	1.30	4.20	4.02	2.51	12.8	1.3	87	
2016	MIN	MLB	23	0	0	0	1	0	2¹	5	0	3.9	0.0	0	42%	.417	2.57	7.71	4.39	5.97	-0.3	0.0	110	93.2
2016	ROC	AAA	23	2	2	0	4	4	26¹	28	3	1.0	8.5	25	33%	.329	1.18	3.76	3.21	3.67	4.9	0.5	92	
2017	*MIN*	*MLB*	*24*	*2*	*2*	*0*	*15*	*5*	*35*	*37*	*4*	*3.1*	*6.6*	*26*	*53%*	*.297*	*1.41*	*4.33*	*4.27*	*4.64*	*2.1*	*0.2*	*100*	
2018	*MIN*	*MLB*	*25*	*5*	*5*	*0*	*38*	*12*	*96¹*	*89*	*13*	*4.9*	*9.2*	*99*	*53%*	*.295*	*1.47*	*4.67*	*4.65*	*5.04*	*2.8*	*0.3*	*116*	

Breakout: 23%   Improve: 30%   Collapse: 16%   Attrition: 37%   MLB: 55%   *Comparables: Jay Jackson, Carlos Rosa, Zach Lee*

Rob Antony's biggest splash as interim general manager, Mejia was acquired from the Giants at the trade deadline in exchange for infielder Eduardo Nunez. Mejia shed enough weight to go from bad-bodied to big-bodied, but the lefty lacks the fastball velocity to match his frame. Mejia tops out in the low 90s, but locates well and draws positive reviews for both his changeup and slider. Reaching his modest ceiling is no sure thing because of a high flyball rate, but Mejia is a decent bet to become a useful back-of-the-rotation starter. He should get an opportunity soon in Minnesota.

Tommy Milone   LHP

Born: 2/16/87   Age: 30   Bats: L   Throws: L   Height: 6'0"   Weight: 220   Entered Pro Ball: Round 10, 2008 Draft (#301 overall)

YEAR	TEAM	LVL	AGE	W	L	SV	G	GS	IP	H	HR	BB/9	K/9	K	GB%	BABIP	WHIP	ERA	FIP	DRA	VORP	WARP	cFIP	MPH
2014	OAK	MLB	27	6	3	0	16	16	96¹	91	12	2.4	5.7	61	39%	.262	1.21	3.55	4.45	4.52	3.3	0.4	117	88.6
2014	SAC	AAA	27	1	1	0	4	4	21	28	5	3.9	7.3	17	46%	.343	1.76	6.43	6.46	6.53	-1.8	-0.2	122	
2014	MIN	MLB	27	0	1	0	6	5	21²	37	4	4.6	5.8	14	46%	.393	2.22	7.06	5.93	5.09	-0.6	-0.1	115	88.7
2015	ROC	AAA	28	4	0	0	5	5	38²	25	2	0.7	10.9	47	47%	.261	0.72	0.70	1.63	0.74	19.6	2.0	50	
2015	MIN	MLB	28	9	5	1	24	23	128²	128	17	2.5	6.4	91	44%	.279	1.27	3.92	4.27	4.43	9.3	1.0	105	90.0
2016	ROC	AAA	29	4	0	0	7	7	48²	41	4	0.7	7.6	41	48%	.268	0.92	1.66	2.86	1.67	19.9	2.0	84	
2016	MIN	MLB	29	3	5	0	19	12	69¹	84	15	2.9	6.4	49	48%	.308	1.53	5.71	5.50	4.66	5.0	0.5	106	89.7
2017	*MIL*	*MLB*	*30*	*4*	*4*	*0*	*55*	*5*	*77*	*75*	*10*	*3.0*	*8.1*	*70*	*45%*	*.291*	*1.29*	*4.22*	*4.16*	*4.43*	*4.9*	*0.5*	*100*	
2018	*MIL*	*MLB*	*31*	*5*	*3*	*0*	*69*	*5*	*99²*	*90*	*13*	*2.7*	*8.4*	*92*	*45%*	*.299*	*1.20*	*4.27*	*4.26*	*4.62*	*6.7*	*0.7*	*105*	

Breakout: 17%   Improve: 49%   Collapse: 15%   Attrition: 11%   MLB: 85%   *Comparables: Dillon Gee, Nick Blackburn, Jeff Karstens*

To spend a half-dozen years in big-league rotations as a flyball pitcher with an 87 mph fastball and mediocre control is a remarkable accomplishment for which Tommy Milone deserves credit. It's tempting to look at Milone's raw stuff or Triple-A dominance and deem him a Quadruple-A pitcher, which is why multiple teams have quickly lost faith following rough patches. However, he's been a valuable back-end starter in the majors for 700 innings now, which is why those same teams ended up turning back to him before long. Milone is both so much better than he ought to be and still not very good, like a so-so dinner out that remains exactly as edible when you pull it out of the fridge three days later. You won't be leaving a favorable Yelp review, but you know you'll be back eventually.

Ryan O'Rourke LHP

Born: 4/30/88   Age: 29   Bats: R   Throws: L   Height: 6'3"   Weight: 230   Entered Pro Ball: Round 13, 2010 Draft (#405 overall)

YEAR	TEAM	LVL	AGE	W	L	SV	G	GS	IP	H	HR	BB/9	K/9	K	GB%	BABIP	WHIP	ERA	FIP	DRA	VORP	WARP	cFIP	MPH
2014	NBR	AA	26	2	4	4	50	0	40²	36	5	3.5	11.5	52	41%	.307	1.28	3.98	3.58	3.43	6.4	0.7	82	
2015	ROC	AAA	27	0	0	0	20	0	13²	13	1	4.6	14.5	22	22%	.387	1.46	5.93	2.43	2.16	4.2	0.4	84	
2015	MIN	MLB	27	0	0	0	28	0	22	16	3	6.1	9.8	24	43%	.236	1.41	6.14	4.74	4.21	1.2	0.1	102	92.8
2016	ROC	AAA	28	1	1	1	33	0	28	26	1	1.9	9.3	29	51%	.338	1.14	1.93	2.31	3.53	4.5	0.5	84	
2016	MIN	MLB	28	0	1	0	26	0	25	18	3	3.6	8.6	24	50%	.238	1.12	3.96	4.07	3.98	2.8	0.3	97	92.3
2017	*MIN*	*MLB*	*29*	*1*	*1*	*0*	*24*	*0*	*25*	*26*	*3*	*3.7*	*8.0*	*23*	*46%*	*.302*	*1.44*	*4.24*	*4.28*	*4.51*	*1.4*	*0.1*	*100*	
2018	*MIN*	*MLB*	*30*	*2*	*1*	*0*	*37*	*0*	*39¹*	*35*	*5*	*4.9*	*10.4*	*46*	*46%*	*.306*	*1.43*	*4.11*	*4.10*	*4.44*	*2.6*	*0.3*	*98*	

Breakout: 14%   Improve: 20%   Collapse: 20%   Attrition: 27%   MLB: 52%   Comparables: *Mike Zagurski, Evan Reed, C.C. Lee*

A former 13th-round draft pick and non-prospect, O'Rourke got his first call-up at 27 after consistently shutting down left-handed hitters in the minors. He's shown it was no fluke by holding big-league lefties to a .134/.244/.239 line in 80 plate appearances, combining a deceptive delivery with a low-90s fastball and sharp slider. His early results against righties are better than insinuated from a minor-league track record full of extreme splits, but it's difficult to see him thriving in a role beyond southpaw specialist.

Glen Perkins LHP

Born: 3/2/83   Age: 34   Bats: L   Throws: L   Height: 6'0"   Weight: 205   Entered Pro Ball: Round 1, 2004 Draft (#22 overall)

YEAR	TEAM	LVL	AGE	W	L	SV	G	GS	IP	H	HR	BB/9	K/9	K	GB%	BABIP	WHIP	ERA	FIP	DRA	VORP	WARP	cFIP	MPH
2014	MIN	MLB	31	4	3	34	63	0	61²	62	7	1.6	9.6	66	36%	.316	1.18	3.65	3.13	3.15	9.2	1.0	85	95.6
2015	MIN	MLB	32	3	5	32	60	0	57	58	9	1.6	8.5	54	34%	.297	1.19	3.32	3.79	4.40	2.0	0.2	98	96.1
2016	MIN	MLB	33	0	0	0	2	0	2	5	0	4.5	13.5	3	38%	.625	3.00	9.00	1.61	4.36	0.1	0.0	100	93.5
2017	*MIN*	*MLB*	*34*	*2*	*2*	*10*	*39*	*0*	*41*	*42*	*7*	*2.3*	*8.7*	*40*	*49%*	*.299*	*1.27*	*4.10*	*4.37*	*4.40*	*2.7*	*0.3*	*100*	
2018	*MIN*	*MLB*	*35*	*2*	*1*	*6*	*39*	*0*	*41²*	*43*	*7*	*2.7*	*8.5*	*39*	*49%*	*.299*	*1.32*	*4.55*	*4.53*	*4.91*	*0.7*	*0.1*	*112*	

Breakout: 16%   Improve: 35%   Collapse: 30%   Attrition: 14%   MLB: 91%   Comparables: *Francisco Rodriguez, Rafael Betancourt, Damaso Marte*

Shifting to the bullpen in late 2010 resurrected Perkins' career, bumping his velocity into the mid-90s and transforming him from a below-average starter to one of the best closers in the league. Perkins saved back-to-back All-Star games for the AL and was one of the few consistent bright spots for some very bad Twins teams from 2011-2015, but then he broke down. First he tried to pitch through back, shoulder and neck problems, but the results weren't pretty and he eventually underwent surgery in June to repair a torn labrum. He signed an under-market extension in 2014, which will pay $6.5 million in the final guaranteed year, with the hope being that he'll be ready to contribute in the first half. Perkins is from Minnesota, starred for the Gophers in college and is one of the most fan-friendly, tweet-posting athletes around. The Twins' bullpen could desperately use even a lesser version of the 2011-2015 standout, but at this point Perkins' outlook is very uncertain.

Ryan Pressly RHP

Born: 12/15/88   Age: 28   Bats: R   Throws: R   Height: 6'3"   Weight: 210   Entered Pro Ball: Round 11, 2007 Draft (#354 overall)

YEAR	TEAM	LVL	AGE	W	L	SV	G	GS	IP	H	HR	BB/9	K/9	K	GB%	BABIP	WHIP	ERA	FIP	DRA	VORP	WARP	cFIP	MPH
2014	ROC	AAA	25	1	4	6	35	0	60¹	55	1	3.1	9.4	63	44%	.318	1.26	2.98	2.58	3.26	14.0	1.4	88	
2014	MIN	MLB	25	2	0	0	25	0	28¹	30	3	2.5	4.4	14	50%	.281	1.34	2.86	4.50	4.80	-1.0	-0.1	108	95.5
2015	ROC	AAA	26	0	2	0	7	0	10	6	1	5.4	13.5	15	35%	.263	1.20	4.50	3.26	2.71	2.5	0.3	88	
2015	MIN	MLB	26	3	2	0	27	0	27²	27	0	3.9	7.2	22	49%	.318	1.41	2.93	2.82	4.40	0.9	0.1	104	97.0
2016	MIN	MLB	27	6	7	1	72	0	75¹	79	8	2.7	8.0	67	41%	.311	1.35	3.70	3.70	5.00	-0.2	0.0	102	98.0
2017	*MIN*	*MLB*	*28*	*3*	*3*	*0*	*59*	*0*	*62*	*59*	*7*	*3.0*	*7.5*	*52*	*49%*	*.300*	*1.36*	*4.04*	*4.07*	*4.36*	*4.3*	*0.4*	*99*	
2018	*MIN*	*MLB*	*29*	*2*	*1*	*1*	*48*	*0*	*51*	*49*	*6*	*3.5*	*9.0*	*51*	*49%*	*.308*	*1.35*	*3.85*	*3.84*	*4.17*	*5.0*	*0.5*	*92*	

Breakout: 23%   Improve: 45%   Collapse: 23%   Attrition: 24%   MLB: 82%   Comparables: *Wesley Wright, Joey Devine, Kevin Jepsen*

This is what a realistic Rule 5 success story looks like. After snagging him from the Red Sox in 2013, the Twins brought Pressly along slowly—first as a long reliever/mop-up man and then as a low-leverage middle reliever—before entrusting him with late-inning work in 2016. It didn't always go well and he's never going to be a star, but with a 3.55 ERA through 208 career innings, Pressly is now an established big-league reliever. His strikeout rate has always lagged behind his mid-90s fastball velocity, which is odd considering Pressly's slider and curveball have both been solid offerings. His raw stuff makes him a candidate for rapid improvement, although given that his ERA hasn't lined up with his DRA, the end result may not look very different.

Taylor Rogers LHP

Born: 12/17/90   Age: 26   Bats: L   Throws: L   Height: 6'3"   Weight: 170   Entered Pro Ball: Round 11, 2012 Draft (#340 overall)

YEAR	TEAM	LVL	AGE	W	L	SV	G	GS	IP	H	HR	BB/9	K/9	K	GB%	BABIP	WHIP	ERA	FIP	DRA	VORP	WARP	cFIP	MPH
2014	NBR	AA	23	11	6	0	24	24	145	150	4	2.3	7.0	113	50%	.327	1.29	3.29	3.04	2.60	42.4	4.5	90	
2015	ROC	AAA	24	11	12	0	28	27	174	190	9	2.3	6.5	126	53%	.330	1.34	3.98	3.21	2.37	56.5	5.8	92	
2016	ROC	AAA	25	0	1	0	7	2	18	24	1	3.0	7.5	15	44%	.365	1.67	4.50	3.22	3.53	3.2	0.3	102	
2016	MIN	MLB	25	3	1	0	57	0	61¹	63	7	2.3	9.4	64	51%	.326	1.29	3.96	3.53	3.30	11.4	1.2	82	95.0
2017	*MIN*	*MLB*	*26*	*2*	*2*	*0*	*44*	*0*	*46²*	*47*	*4*	*2.8*	*7.3*	*38*	*44%*	*.304*	*1.34*	*3.55*	*3.75*	*3.95*	*5.4*	*0.6*	*87*	
2018	*MIN*	*MLB*	*27*	*2*	*1*	*0*	*35*	*0*	*37²*	*34*	*4*	*4.1*	*9.4*	*39*	*44%*	*.306*	*1.36*	*3.95*	*3.95*	*4.27*	*3.2*	*0.3*	*94*	

Breakout: 20%   Improve: 40%   Collapse: 25%   Attrition: 36%   MLB: 77%   Comparables: *P.J. Walters, Adam Conley, Roberto Hernandez*

Minnesota's collection of soft-tossing starters has been second-to-none for decades and once in awhile someone emerges from the low-velocity pack to become a valued reliever. As a starter in the minors, Rogers was nothing special, getting knocked around by right-handed hitters on the way to marginal-prospect status, but he shifted to the bullpen full-time last season and is now viewed in a new light. He still struggles too much versus righties to be a dependable late-inning option, but his stuff plays up a bit as a reliever and he can be mostly spotted versus lefties, whom he held to .202/.261/.286 with 27 strikeouts and six walks in 92 plate appearances. He misses enough bats and throws enough strikes to be a contributor in the middle innings.

Fernando Romero RHP

Born: 12/24/94 Age: 22 Bats: R Throws: R Height: 6'0" Weight: 215 Entered Pro Ball: International Free Agent, 2011

YEAR	TEAM	LVL	AGE	W	L	SV	G	GS	IP	H	HR	BB/9	K/9	K	GB%	BABIP	WHIP	ERA	FIP	DRA	VORP	WARP	cFIP	MPH
2014	CDR	A	19	0	0	0	3	3	12	13	1	3.8	6.8	9	44%	.343	1.50	3.00	4.32	5.13	0.4	0.0	106	
2016	CDR	A	21	4	1	0	5	5	28	18	0	1.6	8.0	25	53%	.250	0.82	1.93	2.33	3.26	5.5	0.6	91	
2016	FTM	A+	21	5	2	0	11	11	62¹	48	1	1.4	9.4	65	58%	.288	0.93	1.88	2.00	1.67	26.3	2.7	72	
2017	*MIN*	*MLB*	*22*	*3*	*3*	*0*	*16*	*9*	*54¹*	*64*	*8*	*3.2*	*6.4*	*38*	*50%*	*.322*	*1.54*	*4.75*	*4.86*	*5.09*	*2.0*	*0.2*	*119*	
2018	*MIN*	*MLB*	*23*	*5*	*5*	*0*	*19*	*15*	*100*	*100*	*13*	*3.9*	*8.8*	*98*	*50%*	*.309*	*1.43*	*4.40*	*4.37*	*4.71*	*6.8*	*0.7*	*109*	

Breakout: 14%   Improve: 22%   Collapse: 1%   Attrition: 14%   MLB: 25%   *Comparables: Andre Rienzo, Liam Hendriks, Alec Asher*

Tommy John surgery just 88 innings into his pro career cost Romero most of 2014 and all of 2015, but he returned last year with a bigger fastball and dominated two levels of Single-A. Romero works in the mid-90s, compared to the low-90s when he signed for $260,000 out of the Dominican Republic as a 16-year-old, and his slider is a swing-and-miss pitch with bite. He's a diminutive right-hander with more time on the disabled list than on the mound, so expectations should be held in check, but despite the setbacks Romero is now on track to reach Double-A at age 22 and has as much upside as any prospect in the Twins' system.

Ervin Santana RHP

Born: 12/12/82 Age: 34 Bats: R Throws: R Height: 6'2" Weight: 175 Entered Pro Ball: International Free Agent, 2000

YEAR	TEAM	LVL	AGE	W	L	SV	G	GS	IP	H	HR	BB/9	K/9	K	GB%	BABIP	WHIP	ERA	FIP	DRA	VORP	WARP	cFIP	MPH
2014	ATL	MLB	31	14	10	0	31	31	196	193	16	2.9	8.2	179	45%	.319	1.31	3.95	3.36	4.05	17.1	1.9	97	95.8
2015	ROC	AAA	32	3	0	0	3	3	20²	17	2	1.7	4.8	11	41%	.242	1.02	1.74	4.08	5.08	0.5	0.1	101	
2015	MIN	MLB	32	7	5	0	17	17	108	104	12	3.0	6.8	82	43%	.285	1.30	4.00	4.14	4.67	4.9	0.5	106	95.8
2016	MIN	MLB	33	7	11	0	30	30	181¹	168	19	2.6	7.4	149	44%	.285	1.22	3.38	3.77	3.85	30.5	3.1	97	95.6
2017	*MIN*	*MLB*	*34*	*11*	*10*	*0*	*28*	*28*	*176*	*171*	*26*	*3.0*	*8.0*	*156*	*43%*	*.289*	*1.30*	*4.29*	*4.40*	*4.65*	*11.7*	*1.2*	*100*	
2018	*MIN*	*MLB*	*35*	*11*	*11*	*0*	*30*	*30*	*191²*	*192*	*29*	*2.8*	*8.2*	*175*	*43%*	*.298*	*1.32*	*4.35*	*4.34*	*4.71*	*15.9*	*1.6*	*109*	

Breakout: 19%   Improve: 41%   Collapse: 23%   Attrition: 15%   MLB: 85%   *Comparables: Roy Oswalt, Johan Santana, John Lackey*

Suspended for PEDs in the spring of 2015 before his four-year, $54 million contract even began, Ervin Santana fared well following his 50-game absence and then carried the Twins' rotation last year. Essentially a two-pitch starter who occasionally mixes in a changeup to complement a good fastball/slider combination, Santana is a flyball pitcher who falls apart when they clear the fence and looks like a no. 2 starter when they don't. His velocity and strikeout rate haven't slipped any after more than 2,000 innings of work, and the remaining two seasons and $27 million left on his deal now look like a relative bargain.

Hector Santiago LHP

Born: 12/16/87 Age: 29 Bats: R Throws: L Height: 6'0" Weight: 215 Entered Pro Ball: Round 30, 2006 Draft (#915 overall)

YEAR	TEAM	LVL	AGE	W	L	SV	G	GS	IP	H	HR	BB/9	K/9	K	GB%	BABIP	WHIP	ERA	FIP	DRA	VORP	WARP	cFIP	MPH
2014	SLC	AAA	26	1	1	0	3	3	14	23	0	4.5	5.8	9	48%	.426	2.14	6.43	4.13	7.20	-2.2	-0.2	113	
2014	ANA	MLB	26	6	9	0	30	24	127¹	120	15	3.7	7.6	108	32%	.288	1.36	3.75	4.31	6.48	-23.6	-2.6	125	94.6
2015	ANA	MLB	27	9	9	0	33	32	180²	156	29	3.5	8.1	162	31%	.252	1.26	3.59	4.74	6.01	-18.9	-2.0	122	93.8
2016	ANA	MLB	28	10	4	0	22	22	120²	104	20	4.3	8.0	107	40%	.257	1.33	4.25	5.00	5.84	-6.4	-0.7	124	95.3
2016	MIN	MLB	28	3	6	0	11	11	61¹	65	13	3.2	5.4	37	28%	.264	1.42	5.58	5.78	5.38	-0.1	0.0	125	93.8
2017	*MIN*	*MLB*	*29*	*9*	*11*	*0*	*28*	*28*	*159*	*162*	*29*	*3.9*	*7.9*	*140*	*48%*	*.290*	*1.45*	*5.07*	*5.21*	*5.49*	*-4.3*	*-0.4*	*100*	
2018	*MIN*	*MLB*	*30*	*7*	*10*	*0*	*25*	*25*	*146²*	*152*	*28*	*4.0*	*7.8*	*127*	*48%*	*.290*	*1.48*	*5.38*	*5.34*	*5.80*	*-5.1*	*-0.5*	*137*	

Breakout: 16%   Improve: 37%   Collapse: 17%   Attrition: 9%   MLB: 87%   *Comparables: John Danks, Daisuke Matsuzaka, Odrisamer Despaigne*

Every year, like clockwork, Hector Santiago out-performed his secondary numbers on the way to a nice-looking ERA. Despite a high-80s fastball, awful control and an extreme fly-ball rate he posted a sub-4.00 ERA each year from 2011 to 2015. His magic powers began to vanish for the Angels last year and then his deal with the devil expired following a trade to Minnesota, as Santiago coughed up 13 homers and 39 total runs in 61 innings. Santiago's past success was built on inducing weak contact and wriggling out of jams with runners on base, both of which can certainly be skills, but the chasm between his solid ERA and ghastly DRA has been so consistent—and watching him last season was so maddening—that it takes wishful thinking to buy into him as more than a serviceable back-of-the-rotation arm.

Kohl Stewart RHP

Born: 10/7/94 Age: 22 Bats: R Throws: R Height: 6'3" Weight: 195 Entered Pro Ball: Round 1, 2013 Draft (#4 overall)

YEAR	TEAM	LVL	AGE	W	L	SV	G	GS	IP	H	HR	BB/9	K/9	K	GB%	BABIP	WHIP	ERA	FIP	DRA	VORP	WARP	cFIP	MPH
2014	CDR	A	19	3	5	0	19	19	87	75	4	2.5	6.4	62	57%	.270	1.14	2.59	3.73	5.47	-0.3	0.0	107	
2015	FTM	A+	20	7	8	0	22	22	129¹	134	2	3.1	4.9	71	59%	.308	1.38	3.20	3.45	8.53	-49.5	-5.4	121	
2016	FTM	A+	21	3	2	0	9	9	51²	39	2	3.3	7.7	44	52%	.255	1.12	2.61	3.27	3.91	9.0	0.9	99	
2016	CHT	AA	21	9	6	0	16	16	92	91	4	4.3	4.6	47	54%	.291	1.47	3.03	4.49	9.08	-40.7	-4.4	127	
2017	*MIN*	*MLB*	*22*	*5*	*9*	*0*	*21*	*21*	*109*	*142*	*17*	*4.7*	*3.6*	*44*	*53%*	*.314*	*1.83*	*6.02*	*6.05*	*6.34*	*-10.5*	*-1.1*	*151*	
2018	*MIN*	*MLB*	*23*	*3*	*6*	*0*	*13*	*13*	*76*	*90*	*13*	*6.1*	*6.4*	*54*	*53%*	*.314*	*1.86*	*6.29*	*6.24*	*6.62*	*-8.7*	*-0.9*	*156*	

Breakout: 6%   Improve: 7%   Collapse: 1%   Attrition: 7%   MLB: 9%   *Comparables: Ryan Webb, Anthony Ortega, Shawn Morimando*

High school pitchers are like a story that gets exaggerated in front of strangers at a party and the beginning of their pro career is what happens when someone who actually bore witness joins the circle to clarify a few things. It's not so much that the dramatized version is a flat-out lie, but the person telling the tale is aware some details are being fudged. Stewart's story was that he threw in the mid-90s and had ace potential, which is why the Twins picked him fourth overall in the 2013 draft. Then he took a minor-league mound throwing in the low-90s and struck out just 5.9 batters per nine through his first 70 starts. It's still a story that might be worth telling some day because Stewart induces tons of grounders and is young enough to develop more bat-missing ability, but the version told at the party sounded a lot better before the fact-checking buzzkill.

Michael Tonkin   RHP

Born: 11/19/89 Age: 27   Bats: R   Throws: R   Height: 6'7"   Weight: 220   Entered Pro Ball: Round 30, 2008 Draft (#906 overall)

YEAR	TEAM	LVL	AGE	W	L	SV	G	GS	IP	H	HR	BB/9	K/9	K	GB%	BABIP	WHIP	ERA	FIP	DRA	VORP	WARP	cFIP	MPH
2014	ROC	AAA	24	3	4	10	39	0	45	41	2	2.4	9.2	46	48%	.305	1.18	2.80	2.82	1.80	17.7	1.8	79	
2014	MIN	MLB	24	0	0	0	25	0	19	23	2	2.8	7.6	16	50%	.350	1.53	4.74	4.11	4.14	0.7	0.1	102	96.2
2015	ROC	AAA	25	2	1	14	33	0	41	25	2	1.1	10.1	46	54%	.240	0.73	1.10	1.99	1.09	17.5	1.8	61	96.7
2015	MIN	MLB	25	0	0	0	26	0	23¹	21	4	3.5	7.3	19	57%	.258	1.29	3.47	4.99	3.93	2.0	0.2	99	96.7
2016	MIN	MLB	26	3	2	0	65	0	71²	80	13	3.0	10.0	80	36%	.344	1.45	5.02	4.36	3.70	10.1	1.0	97	96.6
2017	MIN	MLB	27	2	3	0	49	0	49	52	7	3.1	8.6	49	48%	.304	1.37	4.22	4.19	4.51	2.7	0.3	100	
2018	MIN	MLB	28	3	1	0	50	0	53	49	7	3.7	10.3	61	48%	.303	1.33	4.03	4.03	4.39	3.8	0.4	97	

Breakout: 30%   Improve: 53%   Collapse: 20%   Attrition: 21%   MLB: 82%   *Comparables: Jerry Blevins, Brian Wilson, Justin De Fratus*

Known to Twins' fans first as Jason Kubel's brother-in-law and then for posting huge strikeout rates in the minors, Tonkin's minor-league options expiring finally got him an extended stay in Minnesota after three dominant years at Triple-A. He looks the part of a late-inning reliever at 6-foot-5 with a mid-90s fastball, but Paul Molitor never trusted him in anything resembling a high-leverage role despite constantly changing the bullpen pecking order all season. Tonkin is better than his bloated ERA, but without an improved slider it'll be tough for him to be trusted in the late innings.

LINEOUTS

Hitters

NAME	POS	TEAM	LVL	AGE	PA	R	2B	3B	HR	RBI	BB	K	SB	CS	AVG/OBP/SLG	TAv	VORP	BABIP	BRR	FRAA	WARP
Luis Arraez	INF	CDR	A	19	514	67	31	3	3	66	31	51	3	3	.347/.386/.444	.314	34.8	.382	-3.3	2B(82): 6.9 • 3B(3): 0.2	4.6
James Beresford	INF	ROC	AAA	27	516	63	14	3	0	35	43	78	2	1	.269/.330/.312	.244	6.8	.321	2.5	3B(52): -4.0 • 2B(42): -2.6	0.3
	INF	MIN	MLB	27	24	0	1	0	0	0	1	6	0	0	.227/.261/.273	.197	-1.1	.313	0.0	1B(6): 1.0 • 3B(3): -0.1	0.0
Tanner English	CF	FTM	A+	23	142	24	3	4	4	10	20	47	10	0	.235/.348/.429	.286	9.2	.348	1.3	CF(28): -2.4	0.7
Engelb Vielma	SS	FTM	A+	22	30	5	0	0	0	0	5	8	2	0	.200/.333/.200	.247	0.1	.294	-0.6	SS(4): 0.9 • 2B(3): -0.5	0.0
	SS	CHT	AA	22	367	47	7	4	0	21	34	62	10	8	.271/.345/.318	.254	12.0	.333	1.6	SS(57): -0.3 • 3B(21): 2.8	1.4
LaMonte Wade	OF	CDR	A	22	261	32	6	3	4	27	44	27	5	3	.280/.410/.396	.306	20.3	.298	2.0	CF(31): -0.3 • LF(21): 2.1	2.4
	OF	FTM	A+	22	127	17	8	1	4	24	10	17	1	1	.318/.386/.518	.348	14.9	.337	-0.2	CF(18): -0.4 • LF(6): 0.2	1.5

Luis Arraez has the power you'd expect from a 160-pound second baseman, but he led the Midwest League in batting average (.347) as a 19-year-old and has nearly as many walks as strikeouts through 202 pro games. ❖ Last year's second-round draft pick struggled at rookie-ball in his 38-game pro debut, but **Akil Baddoo** drew plenty of walks for a raw 17-year-old and has plus speed in the outfield. ❖ One of several organizational soldiers rewarded with a call-up in a 103-loss season, **James Beresford** lacks the range to be a trusted shortstop and lacks the bat to contribute much anywhere else. ❖ A massive teenager signed for $1.4 million strictly because of his power potential, **Lewin Diaz** has looked the part so far with 18 homers and 36 doubles through 136 rookie-ball games. ❖ He's tiny and injuries derailed his 2016 season, but **Tanner English** has standout speed and range with enough power and plate discipline to reach the majors by 2018. ❖ Signed out of the Dominican Republic for $4 million as a 16-year-old in 2015, **Wander Javier** will try to avoid wandering down the defensive spectrum from shortstop, but should have enough offensive upside to thrive at another position if needed. ❖ Considered the best defensive shortstop in the Twins' farm system, **Engelb Vielma** has a Ben Revere-like lack of power, but can slap enough singles to carve out a role anyway. ❖ **LaMonte Wade** is an outfield tweener, lacking the range for center and the power for a corner, but a .410 on-base percentage with more walks (101) than strikeouts (80) in the low minors makes him worth watching.

Pitchers

NAME	TEAM	LVL	AGE	W	L	SV	G	GS	IP	H	HR	BB/9	K/9	K	GB%	BABIP	WHIP	ERA	FIP	DRA	VORP	WARP	cFIP	MPH
Andrew Albers	ROC	AAA	30	10	6	0	21	21	124¹	150	10	2.2	6.1	84	41%	.346	1.45	3.69	3.68	3.57	24.5	2.5	110	
	MIN	MLB	30	0	0	0	6	2	17	27	5	3.2	8.5	16	49%	.379	1.94	5.82	6.11	4.07	2.0	0.2	102	90.5
D.J. Baxendale	CHT	AA	25	6	7	0	14	14	81	82	4	1.8	6.6	59	42%	.308	1.21	3.44	3.17	3.21	17.0	1.8	96	
	ROC	AAA	25	2	1	0	23	0	35	28	1	2.1	10.3	40	47%	.297	1.03	1.29	2.03	1.87	12.0	1.2	84	
Pat Dean	ROC	AAA	27	5	7	0	16	16	87¹	113	10	2.0	5.0	49	45%	.332	1.51	5.56	4.26	5.73	-3.7	-0.4	112	
	MIN	MLB	27	1	6	0	19	9	67¹	88	13	3.1	6.7	50	45%	.350	1.65	6.28	5.16	5.12	0.8	0.1	107	92.3
Justin Haley	PME	AA	25	5	4	0	12	12	61¹	49	1	2.8	8.7	59	40%	.293	1.11	2.20	2.67	2.60	17.0	1.8	89	
	PAW	AAA	25	8	6	0	15	14	85¹	70	8	2.7	7.1	67	45%	.264	1.12	3.59	3.80	4.42	8.5	0.9	102	
Trevor Hildenberger	CHT	AA	25	2	3	16	32	0	38²	21	2	1.4	10.5	45	61%	.211	0.70	0.70	2.21	1.20	15.2	1.6	62	
Mason Melotakis	CHT	AA	25	1	2	0	36	0	33¹	36	3	3.2	11.3	42	43%	.384	1.44	2.97	3.14	2.95	6.6	0.7	81	
Brandon Peterson	FTM	A+	24	3	0	4	22	0	34	20	1	3.7	11.6	44	37%	.264	1.00	2.65	2.37	2.03	11.5	1.2	83	
	CHT	AA	24	1	2	0	16	0	26	20	1	5.2	10.7	31	28%	.288	1.35	4.15	3.28	3.39	3.9	0.4	104	
Neil Ramirez	CHN	MLB	27	0	0	0	8	0	7²	5	1	9.4	11.7	10	29%	.250	1.70	4.70	5.40	5.58	-0.5	-0.1	123	94.3
	MIL	MLB	27	0	0	0	2	0	1²	2	2	0.0	16.2	3	25%	.000	1.20	10.80	15.19	6.30	-0.2	0.0	125	94.1
	MIN	MLB	27	0	0	0	8	0	14²	15	5	6.1	6.8	11	25%	.256	1.70	6.14	8.08	6.50	-2.5	-0.3	125	94.5
	ROC	AAA	27	0	0	0	16	0	20¹	14	2	3.1	12.0	27	26%	.267	1.03	3.10	2.97	2.88	4.7	0.5	90	
Jake Reed	CHT	AA	23	3	3	3	41	0	60	51	2	3.3	9.6	64	47%	.314	1.22	3.90	3.02	2.40	15.6	1.7	91	
	ROC	AAA	23	1	1	0	9	0	10²	8	0	1.7	6.8	8	71%	.258	0.94	1.69	2.51	4.07	1.1	0.1	92	
Randy Rosario	FTM	A+	22	6	6	1	21	16	94¹	102	3	3.2	6.5	68	58%	.330	1.44	3.34	3.37	5.96	-5.5	-0.6	109	
Lachlan Wells	CDR	A	19	6	4	0	12	12	71¹	57	4	2.0	7.9	63	43%	.272	1.02	1.77	3.28	2.59	19.2	2.1	85	
Alex Wimmers	ROC	AAA	27	2	1	11	39	0	49²	42	2	4.3	9.1	50	47%	.294	1.33	3.62	3.25	5.77	-4.5	-0.5	107	
	MIN	MLB	27	1	3	0	16	0	17¹	14	2	5.7	7.3	14	55%	.267	1.44	4.15	4.89	4.20	1.5	0.2	103	93.8

Andrew Albers came back to Minnesota for a second go-around after a pilgrimage across the northern border, but the soft-tossing lefty simply doesn't have the arsenal to keep big-league hitters from teeing off. ❖ **D.J. Baxendale** fell off the prospect radar as a starting pitcher, but a midseason move to the bullpen saw him tick up both his fastball and his chances of becoming a big leaguer. ❖ **Pat Dean** was a surprise addition to the 40-man roster in 2015 and a surprise midseason call-up in 2016, but him getting knocked around was certainly not a surprise after failing to miss bats throughout his tour through the minors. ❖ **Justin Haley** served as a solid if unremarkable starter in both Portland and Pawtucket last season. He's close enough to the majors that he could warrant a full writeup in the next Annual, marking the first time anyone under the age of 30 will have seen Haley's comment. ❖ **Trevor Hildenberger's** minor-league numbers are incredible, including a 1.47 ERA, 165 strikeouts and just 18 walks in 141 innings of relief, and he was shredding Double-A with a heavy low-90s fastball before a late-season elbow injury. ❖ After nearly two years on the sidelines following Tommy John surgery, **Mason Melotakis** showed better velocity and more bat-missing ability than before in a 36-appearance stint at Double-A. ❖ Shaky command may keep **Brandon Peterson** from reaching his potential, but the Minnesota native has topped 11 strikeouts per nine in all four pro seasons and could be a bullpen option in 2017. ❖ Missing bats has never been a problem for **Neil Ramirez**, but staying off the disabled list and throwing the ball over the plate are career-long issues that may keep him bouncing around bullpens. ❖ **Jake Reed** has the raw stuff and groundball rate to succeed as a late-inning reliever, but the former fifth-round pick out of Oregon hasn't been able to find an out pitch against left-handed hitters yet. ❖ Surprisingly added to the 40-man roster prior to the 2016 season despite barely pitching above rookie-ball, **Randy Rosario** was unimpressive at High-A and could be destined for the bullpen. ❖ **Lewis Thorpe** was a highly touted $500,000 signing as a 16-year-old out of Australia and dominated in the low minors to establish himself as a top prospect, but the southpaw missed all of 2015 and 2016 following Tommy John surgery. ❖ It's tough to disprove conspiracy theories, but the fact remains that **Lachlan Wells** and fellow Australian southpaw Lewis Thorpe have never pitched in the United States during the same season. ❖ Simply reaching the majors is a helluva story for **Alex Wimmers**, who fought through major injuries and a prolonged battle with the yips, but the former first-round pick likely tops out as a middle reliever.

NEW YORK METS

Essay by Ted Berg

Player comments by Jarrett Seidler and BP staff

It thunders down from the mountaintops, rustles through the forests and echoes through the city streets. A name whispered in fear, chanted in exultation or shouted in glory: Syndergaard.

Syndergaard. It's almost too perfect. The sound of it alone evokes only the epic. Syndergaard is a towering explosion or a nightmarish tempest or the massive volcano quaking on the outskirts of the village. The name could solely describe something devastating and awesome, some freakish and unforeseen force wreaking havoc on the mundane world we thought we knew.

Then you look at the guy, and he's absolutely all those things: Noah Syndergaard, 6'6" and 240 pounds of pure lightning, with bolts blistering from his arm, his eyes and the back of his cap. The Mets' 24-year-old righty operates with all the subtlety of a sledgehammer, mixing the hardest fastball of any big-league starter with a speed-metal slider and a curveball Terry Collins long ago named "the hook from hell." He looks like a create-a-player borne of a heavy-thumbed gamer indiscriminate with the attributes, or an emissary from some post-human species evolved to master baseball.

And he comes, of course, with perhaps the majors' most perfect nickname: Noah Syndergaard is Thor, the hammer-wielding Norse god of thunder, in scale, in appearance and in bravado. His mortal form, somehow available to the Mets as only one part of the deal that put R.A. Dickey on the Blue Jays after the 2012 season, pitches among us now for as long as we can stave off Ragnarok.

Only, and obviously, there's a catch: Noah Syndergaard is not actually immortal, hard as that sometimes is to believe. He is a pathetic human like the rest of us, bigger and stronger certainly, but impervious to neither pain nor injury nor all the impossibly small fluctuations in execution that account for fairly large swings in on-field performance. And so after Syndergaard steamrolled the National League for most of 2016's first half, he appeared, due to regression or fatigue or impairment or exposure or just plain bad luck, at least a bit more mortal in the second. It might require some squinting – Syndergaard had an excellent season, all told – but his walk rate ticked up and the strikeouts ticked down. With that came murmurs again of some nebulous arm issue: A bone spur, specifically, though one the Mets downplayed

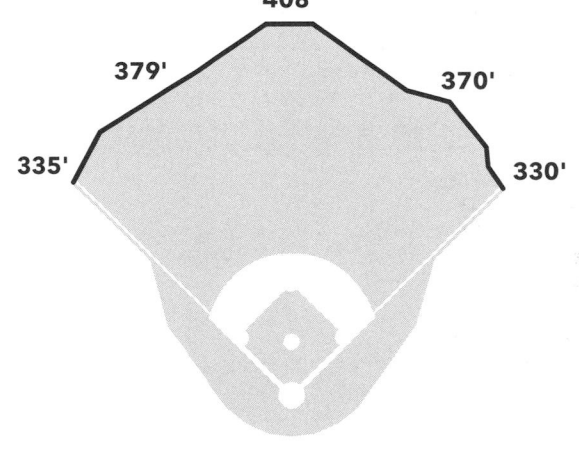

METS PROSPECTUS
2016 W-L: 87-75, 2ND IN NL EAST

Pythag	.538	10th	DER	.692	27th
RS/G	4.14	26th	B-Age	29.7	26th
RA/G	3.81	3rd	P-Age	28.5	18th
TAv	.274	4th	Salary	$135.2M	14th
BRR	-10.17	26th	M$/MW	$3.2M	20th
TAv-P	.263	16th	DL Days	832	11th
FIP	3.61	1st	$ on DL	19%	22nd

Outfield wall profile: **8'**

Three-Year Park Factors

Runs	Runs/RH	Runs/LH	HR/RH	HR/LH
90	89	88	103	102

Top Hitter WARP	5.3	Yoenis Cespedes
Top Pitcher WARP	5.6	Noah Syndergaard
Top Prospect		Amed Rosario

2016 Hit List Ranking

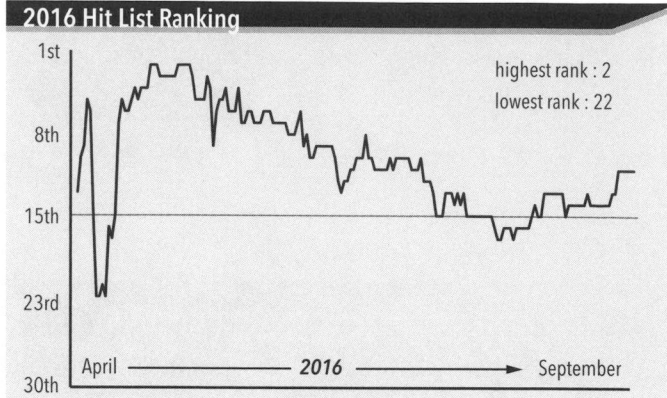

highest rank : 2
lowest rank : 22

April ——— **2016** ——→ September

Committed Payroll (in millions)

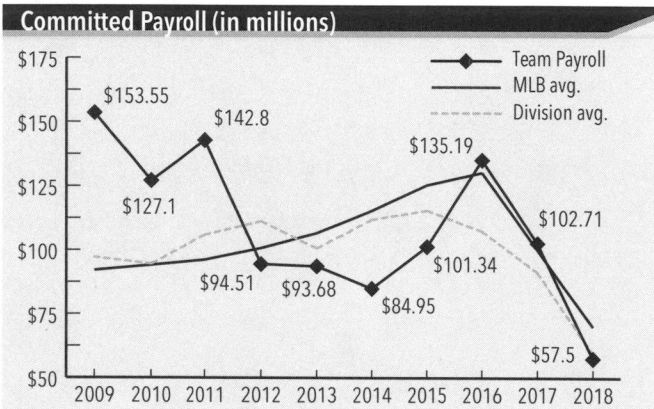

- Team Payroll
- MLB avg.
- Division avg.

$153.55
$127.1
$142.8
$94.51
$93.68
$84.95
$135.19
$101.34
$102.71
$57.5

2009 2010 2011 2012 2013 2014 2015 2016 2017 2018

Farm System Ranking

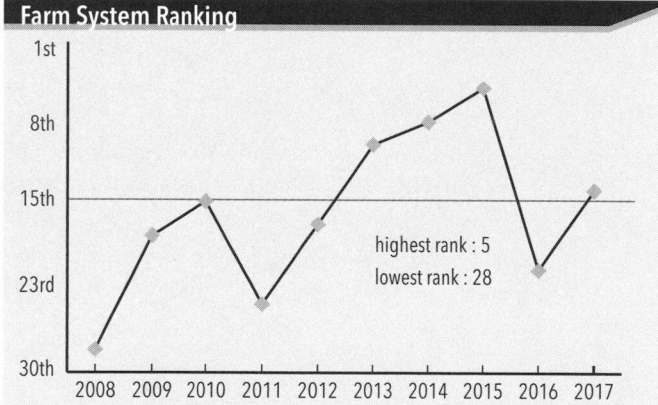

highest rank : 5
lowest rank : 28

2008 2009 2010 2011 2012 2013 2014 2015 2016 2017

Personnel

General Manager:
Sandy Alderson

SVP, Baseball Operations:
John Ricco

VP, International and Amateur Scouting:
Tommy Tanous

Manager:
Terry Collins

BP Alumni:
Jesse Behr

and have continued to downplay.

Perhaps it's true. Maybe whatever irregularity exists in Syndergaard's right elbow did not limit him in any way last season. Maybe it never will, as there's no conclusive way to distinguish the impact of injury from the myriad other factors that might affect a pitcher's performance. But given the Mets' recent history, and the nature of pitching in general, it'd seem downright silly to assume Syndergaard's full and uncompromised health in 2017 and dismiss any worried whispers.

No fan who followed the Mets in 2016 should need any reminder of the pattern, which typically goes something like this:

1. Immensely talented pitcher endures a handful of shaky, bad or short starts.
2. Pitcher and team diminish possibility of injury.
3. Pitcher gets an MRI, which finds "no structural damage" and pitcher is declared day-to-day.
4. Pitcher hits the disabled list.
5. Pitcher undergoes season-ending arm surgery.

Matt Harvey, after a successful 2015 return from the Tommy John surgery that cost him all of 2014, slogged through 17 starts last season before eventually needing surgery to alleviate thoracic outlet syndrome in his right shoulder. Steven Matz, whose professional debut was delayed by his own Tommy John procedure for more than two full years after the Mets drafted him in 2009, pitched through bone spurs in his elbow for most of 2016. He finally hit the disabled list in mid-August with a rotator cuff strain, and ultimately underwent a procedure to remove the spurs. Jacob deGrom, another Tommy John survivor, made his final start on September 1, then underwent surgery in the middle of that month to move the ulnar nerve in his pitching elbow. Zack Wheeler, initially expected to return around the All-Star Break after a Tommy John surgery all his own, faced complications in his recovery and never saw the Citi Field mound in 2016.

The spate of injuries left Syndergaard and the ageless (and now departed) Bartolo Colon as the last men standing from the club's vaunted Opening Day rotation by season's end. Had Madison Bumgarner not shut down the Mets in the NL Wild Card game, the New York team faced a postseason journey—earned largely on the strength of a stellar pitching staff—almost entirely undone by the time they needed them most. The Mets entered 2016 stacked to go four-deep with ace-caliber starters in a potential playoff rotation, and exited it with unheralded (though still surprisingly effective) arms like Robert Gsellman and Seth Lugo entrenched in their starting staff. Pitching will do that.

It's easy to assign blame, but far more difficult to determine any actual issue beyond the risks and tolls inherent in throwing baseballs at unnatural speeds. The Mets, in one of the lone traits carried forward into Sandy Alderson's tenure from Omar Minaya's, certainly appear to have some sort of top-down communication issue when it comes to injuries (and not just to their pitchers). But it's impossible to believe any club—no less a generally well-managed one like the Mets under Alderson—wouldn't be doing absolutely everything in its power to keep its best pitchers on the mound. It's 2017 and baseball is a multi-billion-dollar industry staffed throughout by smart and gifted people at the top of their fields. The Mets training staff will again, inevitably, face a chorus of boos come Opening Day, but the idea that a team with the Mets' resources and wherewithal would happily continue to put the health of their prized arms in the hands of some ham-fisted stooges seems too ridiculous to examine any further.

✦ ✦ ✦

The Mets aim to open camp in 2017 with all five of their ballyhooed fireballers standing as tall and healthy as Syndergaard did last season. And if that's the case, it's practically an embarrassment of riches. None of the 29 other teams, no matter their offseason machinations, can come close to matching the Mets' staff for upside. In Syndergaard, deGrom and Harvey, the club has three starters who have already established their ability to dominate opposing hitters when healthy. For his career, deGrom's stellar 2.88 FIP and 4.21 strikeout-to-walk ratio somehow rank as the *worst* of the trio. And Syndergaard, at 24 and armed with the aforementioned dazzling arsenal of pitches, confidence and hair, appears primed to somehow get even better.

Matz, at 25, has yet to throw more than 140 innings in a professional season, but has also yet to post anything short of excellent numbers at any level. Wheeler, now 26, can't match the rest of the expected rotation in recent big-league results, but maintains the capacity for high-90s heat that made him a mega-prospect in the Mets' and Giants' systems. (It's easy to forget he had a 3.32 DRA in over 185 innings during the 2014 season.) And because the Mets now just mint 23-year-old starters with beautiful flowing hair and sharp sliders that touch the low 90s, Gsellman becomes the insurance option. Even Lugo, a 27-year-old former 34th-round pick out of Division III Centenary College of Louisiana who sits seventh on the depth chart, boasts some bodacious stuff: His 12-to-6 curveball blew away previous Statcast records for spin rate during his debut season in 2016.

But uncertainty looms. By fostering incredible depth in their rotation, Alderson and the Mets' front office have established a strong hedge in the case of an injury or two. But the plain truth is that the Mets aim to open 2017 with four starting pitchers in their rotation coming off season-ending surgeries on their pitching arms, and a pair of insurance policies with only 108 2/3 big-league innings between them. And anyone thinking, "well, heck, they can't *all* get hurt," need to look back no further than last season for evidence of all that could go wrong.

So the Mets enter 2017 with perhaps baseball's broadest error bar. Their everything-goes-right scenario appears a spectacular one, with stud pitchers on the mound every night, workloads managed and injuries avoided. An incredible rotation intact for October. But the darker side seems just as likely. Pitchers get hurt, so too many Mets pitchers get hurt. The club fails to capitalize on its wealth of pitching talent beyond its 2015 World Series run, and a window with two divisional rivals in rebuilding mode closes.

Simply put: No matter what collection of position players takes the field behind the Mets' starting staff this season, the club's fate rests on the success and health of Syndergaard, Harvey, deGrom, Matz and Wheeler. Every one of those guys has demonstrated reason for unbridled optimism, but practically everything we know about pitching offers a bleaker outlook. The pitches look supernatural, but the arms that throw them, sadly, remain of this earth. ∎

—*Ted Berg is the lead baseball writer at For The Win*

HITTERS

Jay Bruce   RF

Born: 4/3/87   Age: 30   Bats: L   Throws: L   Height: 6'3"   Weight: 225   Entered Pro Ball: Round 1, 2005 Draft (#12 overall)

YEAR	TEAM	LVL	AGE	PA	R	2B	3B	HR	RBI	BB	K	SB	CS	AVG/OBP/SLG	TAv	VORP	BABIP	BRR	FRAA	WARP
2014	CIN	MLB	27	545	71	21	1	18	66	44	149	12	3	.217/.281/.373	.244	4.7	.269	4.2	RF(131): 1.4 • 1B(3): -0.1	0.7
2015	CIN	MLB	28	649	72	35	4	26	87	58	145	9	5	.226/.294/.434	.261	9.0	.251	-2.7	RF(150): 3.0	1.3
2016	CIN	MLB	29	402	60	22	6	25	80	27	83	4	2	.265/.316/.559	.301	24.4	.275	0.5	RF(95): -8.3 • CF(1): -0.0	1.7
2016	NYN	MLB	29	187	14	5	0	8	19	17	43	0	0	.219/.294/.391	.251	-0.5	.246	-2.1	RF(43): -2.0	-0.3
2017	NYN	MLB	30	558	67	25	2	24	76	49	143	7	3	.231/.300/.436	.262	14.9	.270	-0.3	RF 0	1.1
2018	NYN	MLB	31	532	69	24	1	23	72	49	141	6	3	.227/.300/.430	.266	14.2	.268	-0.1	RF 0	1.6

Breakout: 4%   Improve: 55%   Collapse: 4%   Attrition: 10%   MLB: 100%   Comparables: Mark Trumbo, Jason Kubel, Johnny Blanchard

If there's a remaining divide between traditional baseball men and the sabermetrically-inclined, the rubber really meets the road at a thin subsection of players like Jay Bruce. Traditionalists still consider Bruce to be a star because of his 30-plus home run power and consistently high RBI totals. Advanced statistics have generally shown Bruce to be a fringe starter at best since 2014—a player whose mediocre on-base skills and indifferent outfield defense outweigh his power. If you drill deeper, Bruce's high RBI totals are thanks to the great fortune of spending a career batting behind Joey Votto.

Despite their reputation for leaning on sabermetrics, the Mets have planted their flag on the "star" side of the Jay Bruce divide, showing repeated interest in trading for him over the years, leading to his August 1st acquisition. Bruce rewarded that faith with one of the worst slumps of his career, a two-month-long car crash of strikeouts and stranded runners that he only escaped in the last week of the season. His reward was a Wild Card Game start and the world's most predictable 0-for-3 against Madison Bumgarner, the exact type of tough lefty Bruce should never face.

Asdrubal Cabrera   SS

Born: 11/13/85   Age: 31   Bats: B   Throws: R   Height: 6'0"   Weight: 205   Entered Pro Ball: International Free Agent, 2002

YEAR	TEAM	LVL	AGE	PA	R	2B	3B	HR	RBI	BB	K	SB	CS	AVG/OBP/SLG	TAv	VORP	BABIP	BRR	FRAA	WARP
2014	CLE	MLB	28	416	54	22	2	9	40	27	79	7	2	.246/.305/.386	.252	11.5	.286	-0.7	SS(92): -2.0	1.1
2014	WAS	MLB	28	200	20	9	2	5	21	22	29	3	0	.229/.312/.389	.274	8.3	.245	0.7	2B(48): -2.8 • SS(1): 0.0	0.6
2015	TBA	MLB	29	551	66	28	5	15	58	36	107	6	3	.265/.315/.430	.261	21.4	.306	-0.4	SS(136): -8.2	1.4
2016	NYN	MLB	30	568	65	30	1	23	62	38	103	5	1	.280/.336/.474	.298	45.7	.310	0.1	SS(135): -3.9	4.3
2017	NYN	MLB	31	531	59	26	2	15	59	40	103	6	2	.248/.309/.406	.258	21.3	.282	-0.3	SS -5	1.1
2018	NYN	MLB	32	509	61	24	1	15	59	39	101	5	2	.242/.307/.399	.261	18.0	.275	-0.2	SS -5	1.4

Breakout: 2%   Improve: 42%   Collapse: 6%   Attrition: 6%   MLB: 92%   Comparables: Jhonny Peralta, Stephen Drew, J.J. Hardy

A year ago, Sandy Alderson jumped quickly into the free agent class to ink Asdrubal Cabrera to a two-year, $18.5 million contract with a team option, ending the much-maligned Ruben Tejada/Wilmer Flores shortstop era. Cabrera was expected to provide a limited but steady glove and adequate offensive production until something better came along, with the flexibility to shift around the infield in a utility role if, needed. Instead, Cabrera locked down the shortstop position and put up the best season of his long career, even while struggling all year with a knee injury suffered in spring training. He hit for average, he hit for power, he fielded shortstop well enough and he even earned plaudits as a leader in the clubhouse. Amed Rosario could push him to another position or even another team at some point soon, but Cabrera's already been worth every penny of his contract and then some.

Eric Campbell   4C

Born: 4/9/87   Age: 30   Bats: R   Throws: R   Height: 6'3"   Weight: 215   Entered Pro Ball: Round 8, 2008 Draft (#254 overall)

YEAR	TEAM	LVL	AGE	PA	R	2B	3B	HR	RBI	BB	K	SB	CS	AVG/OBP/SLG	TAv	VORP	BABIP	BRR	FRAA	WARP
2014	LVG	AAA	27	163	39	15	0	3	24	20	20	3	1	.355/.442/.525	.309	15.3	.398	2.2	1B(17): 1.9 • 2B(13): -0.1	1.7
2014	NYN	MLB	27	211	16	9	0	3	16	17	55	3	0	.263/.322/.358	.264	4.4	.348	-0.7	LF(20): 1.9 • 3B(19): -1.5	0.5
2015	LVG	AAA	28	142	28	9	1	5	18	25	20	7	2	.363/.493/.593	.372	20.2	.409	-0.1	3B(22): -0.8 • LF(8): -0.2	1.9
2015	NYN	MLB	28	206	28	8	0	3	19	26	37	5	3	.197/.312/.295	.227	-0.7	.230	0.1	3B(48): -4.8 • 1B(5): 0.0	-0.5
2016	LVG	AAA	29	354	63	15	4	7	47	41	55	7	3	.301/.390/.447	.274	12.2	.343	1.3	1B(44): 1.7 • LF(17): 1.5	1.4
2016	NYN	MLB	29	88	9	1	0	1	9	10	24	1	0	.173/.284/.227	.210	-2.6	.235	0.2	1B(21): -1.0 • 3B(7): -0.3	-0.4
2017	NYN	MLB	30	250	28	10	1	6	27	29	56	4	2	.239/.336/.369	.252	4.2	.292	-0.3	1B 2 • 3B -1	0.6
2018	NYN	MLB	31	264	33	10	0	6	28	30	61	4	2	.238/.335/.370	.268	6.4	.294	-0.2	1B 2 • 3B -1	0.9

Breakout: 1%   Improve: 29%   Collapse: 7%   Attrition: 18%   MLB: 66%   Comparables: Steve Pearce, Travis Ishikawa, Stephen Vogt

The Mets have talked up Campbell's exit velocity and bad BABIP luck for years, but he's now compiled nearly a full season's worth of MLB playing time with a career slugging percentage of .311, a beautiful disaster for a player at any of the four corners. Yet even a player this marginal to a major-league roster—his stats scream "good in the clubhouse"—is one of the thousand or so best baseball players on the planet. Baseball is really hard and this former Boston College standout spent many years honing his craft to get incredibly good at it compared to the rest of the world. Just not compared to the rest of the majors. Maybe he'll fare better in Japan, where he has joined the Hanshin TIgers for 2017.

Gavin Cecchini   MI

Born: 12/22/93 Age: 23   Bats: R   Throws: R   Height: 6'2"   Weight: 200   Entered Pro Ball: Round 1, 2012 Draft (#12 overall)

YEAR	TEAM	LVL	AGE	PA	R	2B	3B	HR	RBI	BB	K	SB	CS	AVG/OBP/SLG	TAv	VORP	BABIP	BRR	FRAA	WARP
2014	SAV	A	20	259	42	17	4	3	25	25	41	7	1	.259/.333/.408	.276	18.4	.299	3.5	SS(53): 3.4	2.2
2014	SLU	A+	20	271	36	10	1	5	31	32	40	3	3	.236/.325/.352	.246	6.7	.259	0.3	SS(59): -5.1	0.2
2015	BIN	AA	21	485	64	26	4	7	51	42	55	3	4	.317/.377/.442	.300	36.2	.348	-2.3	SS(109): 2.4	4.2
2016	LVG	AAA	22	499	71	27	2	8	55	48	55	4	1	.325/.390/.448	.274	25.2	.357	-2.1	SS(105): -11.5, 2B(3): 1.2	1.5
2016	NYN	MLB	22	7	2	2	0	0	2	0	2	0	0	.333/.429/.667	.642	2.5	.500	0.0	SS(2): -0.0	0.3
2017	NYN	MLB	23	62	6	3	0	1	6	5	12	0	0	.248/.311/.376	.251	2.0	.289	-0.1	SS -0	0.1
2018	NYN	MLB	24	334	39	14	2	8	37	28	65	1	0	.252/.318/.393	.265	12.5	.292	-0.6	SS -1	1.3

Breakout: 6%   Improve: 33%   Collapse: 4%   Attrition: 19%   MLB: 46%   Comparables: Brad Miller, Greg Garcia, Chris Taylor

Sometimes the line between being a good player and a fringe player can be quite thin. Cecchini possesses nearly all of the skills and physical tools necessary to be a very good major-league shortstop, but he's missing the one that you can't survive without at the position—teams are just not willing to accept an inability to make the basic throws from the six spot. Cecchini's arm doesn't play there, and there is little hope it ever will. A brief Vegas trial late in the season at second base should provide a big hint as to Cecchini's ultimate defensive destination, but there's only so far he can slide down the positional spectrum given his offensive profile.

Yoenis Cespedes   LF

Born: 10/18/85 Age: 31   Bats: R   Throws: R   Height: 5'10"   Weight: 220   Entered Pro Ball: International Free Agent, 2012

YEAR	TEAM	LVL	AGE	PA	R	2B	3B	HR	RBI	BB	K	SB	CS	AVG/OBP/SLG	TAv	VORP	BABIP	BRR	FRAA	WARP
2014	OAK	MLB	28	432	62	26	3	17	67	28	80	3	2	.256/.303/.464	.290	21.7	.278	1.7	LF(82): 7.0 • CF(9): -0.4	3.1
2014	BOS	MLB	28	213	27	10	3	5	33	7	48	4	0	.269/.296/.423	.269	5.7	.325	-0.1	LF(43): 4.3	1.1
2015	DET	MLB	29	427	62	28	2	18	61	19	87	3	4	.293/.323/.506	.293	23.1	.331	0.6	LF(99): 12.6	3.8
2015	NYN	MLB	29	249	39	14	4	17	44	14	54	4	1	.287/.337/.604	.334	25.1	.306	0.6	CF(40): -2.3 • LF(35): 1.0	2.6
2016	NYN	MLB	30	543	72	25	1	31	86	51	108	3	1	.280/.354/.530	.326	48.3	.298	-1.9	LF(80): 7.7 • CF(63): -4.7	5.3
2017	NYN	MLB	31	602	74	27	3	28	87	41	134	5	3	.261/.317/.475	.282	32.1	.294	-0.8	LF 11	4.1
2018	NYN	MLB	32	531	70	23	2	24	75	38	125	4	2	.254/.311/.457	.282	24.6	.291	0.0	LF 9	3.7

Breakout: 0%   Improve: 41%   Collapse: 2%   Attrition: 4%   MLB: 96%   Comparables: Alfonso Soriano, Josh Hamilton, Ron Gant

Cespedes is simply one of the most entertaining players in the game. For a few otherwise boring weeks of spring training, Cespedes provided daily amusement by arriving to camp in a rotation of awesomely tricked-out cars and trucks. He then topped it off by riding into camp one day on his favorite horse, Candy. (Yes, he trotted to his parking spot on a real, live horse. Noah Syndergaard followed along on a second horse from the Cespedes ranch.) Once real baseball got underway, Cespedes consolidated and even added to his 2015 offensive gains, with a noticeably improved approach. As always, he hit the usual jaw-dropping homers and uncorked some incredible throws along the way. If there's a slight blemish here, it's that trying to fit Cespedes in center stretched the Mets' outfield defense, and may have led to a lingering quad injury. He's far better-suited—and just far better—in left.

Michael Conforto   OF

Born: 3/1/93 Age: 24   Bats: L   Throws: R   Height: 6'1"   Weight: 215   Entered Pro Ball: Round 1, 2014 Draft (#10 overall)

YEAR	TEAM	LVL	AGE	PA	R	2B	3B	HR	RBI	BB	K	SB	CS	AVG/OBP/SLG	TAv	VORP	BABIP	BRR	FRAA	WARP
2014	BRO	A-	21	186	30	10	0	3	19	16	29	3	0	.331/.403/.448	.315	16.5	.383	1.9	LF(41): 0.8	1.8
2015	SLU	A+	22	206	25	12	0	7	28	17	26	0	1	.283/.350/.462	.292	9.0	.294	-1.7	LF(41): 7.0	1.7
2015	BIN	AA	22	197	21	12	3	5	26	23	35	1	0	.312/.396/.503	.312	12.0	.368	-2.4	LF(45): -0.1	1.3
2015	NYN	MLB	22	194	30	14	0	9	26	17	39	0	1	.270/.335/.506	.315	15.0	.297	0.6	LF(50): 2.8	1.9
2016	LVG	AAA	23	144	30	8	2	9	28	13	18	2	2	.422/.483/.727	.381	20.1	.446	-1.1	LF(18): 0.2 • RF(6): 0.9	2.0
2016	NYN	MLB	23	348	38	21	1	12	42	36	89	2	1	.220/.310/.414	.271	12.6	.267	1.2	LF(73): -1.6 • RF(9): 0.8	1.2
2017	NYN	MLB	24	324	39	16	1	13	44	30	74	2	1	.253/.329/.454	.279	16.2	.294	-0.7	LF 1 • 1B 0	1.3
2018	NYN	MLB	25	446	60	22	1	19	62	42	103	2	1	.252/.330/.460	.290	23.7	.291	0.8	LF 1 • CF -1	2.5

Breakout: 3%   Improve: 43%   Collapse: 9%   Attrition: 15%   MLB: 92%   Comparables: Adam Lind, Travis Snider, Dayan Viciedo

The sequel to Michael Conforto's blockbuster rookie campaign resembled *The Two Towers* from the Peter Jackson adaptation of *The Lord of the Rings*: at times brilliant, at times painful and meandering, and by the end nothing was where you expected it to be. When you walked out, it felt incomplete and unsatisfying, but when you took a step back you realized, hey, that was pretty good and got us where we needed to be for the next movie.

Conforto was one of the best hitters in baseball early in the season before falling into a dreadful slump, while battling a wrist injury and inconsistent playing time, stemming from a lack of confidence from his manager—sadly, a recurring storyline in Queens. The organization seemingly lost faith as well, shipping him back and forth between the minors and the majors and ultimately blocking him with the acquisition of Jay Bruce. But heroes never bow out so easily and Conforto quietly put together 33 games of complete domination in Triple-A, followed by a productive part-time role in September. Andúril in hand, 2017 could see *The Return of the King*—if he can just convince Terry Collins and Sandy Alderson to follow him into the light.

Travis d'Arnaud   C

Born: 2/10/89   Age: 28   Bats: R   Throws: R   Height: 6'2"   Weight: 210   Entered Pro Ball: Round 1, 2007 Draft (#37 overall)

YEAR	TEAM	LVL	AGE	PA	R	2B	3B	HR	RBI	BB	K	SB	CS	AVG/OBP/SLG	TAv	VORP	BABIP	BRR	FRAA	WARP
2014	LVG	AAA	25	59	13	8	0	6	16	3	5	0	0	.436/.475/.909	.412	12.1	.409	-0.5	C(10): 2.3	1.4
2014	NYN	MLB	25	421	48	22	3	13	41	32	64	1	0	.242/.302/.416	.268	20.1	.259	-0.3	C(105): 5.7	2.9
2015	BIN	AA	26	20	3	1	0	0	1	0	2	0	0	.300/.300/.350	.220	-0.4	.333	-0.3	C(4): 0.2	0.0
2015	NYN	MLB	26	268	31	14	1	12	41	23	49	0	0	.268/.340/.485	.312	25.0	.289	-0.1	C(64): 12.0	4.0
2016	SLU	A+	27	38	3	2	0	0	5	9	5	1	0	.310/.474/.379	.311	2.7	.375	-0.2	C(3): 0.0	0.3
2016	NYN	MLB	27	276	27	7	0	4	15	19	50	0	0	.247/.307/.323	.239	6.2	.293	-0.3	C(73): 7.4	1.4
2017	*NYN*	*MLB*	*28*	*416*	*47*	*19*	*1*	*13*	*49*	*38*	*75*	*0*	*0*	*.249/.321/.414*	*.265*	*21.6*	*.276*	*-0.8*	*C 11*	*2.9*
2018	*NYN*	*MLB*	*29*	*305*	*39*	*13*	*1*	*10*	*37*	*29*	*59*	*0*	*0*	*.245/.320/.414*	*.271*	*14.2*	*.274*	*-0.5*	*C 8*	*2.4*

Breakout: 0%   Improve: 40%   Collapse: 9%   Attrition: 15%   MLB: 95%   Comparables: *Victor Martinez, Kurt Suzuki, Devin Mesoraco*

YEAR	TEAM	P. COUNT	FRM RUNS	BLK RUNS	THRW RUNS	TOT RUNS
2014	BIN	94	0.0	0.0	0.0	0.0
2014	LVG	1338	2.6	0.0	-0.2	2.4
2014	NYN	14765	8.8	-4.8	-2.4	1.6
2015	BIN	438	0.3	0.0	0.0	0.3
2015	LVG	249	0.1	0.0	0.0	0.1
2015	NYN	9002	12.6	0.4	0.1	13.2
2016	NYN	10281	7.5	1.1	-2.1	6.5
2017	*NYN*	*14936*	*13.1*	*-0.1*	*-1.6*	*11.4*
2018	*NYN*	*10964*	*8.9*	*-0.2*	*-1.2*	*7.5*

Will the real Travis d'Arnaud please stand up? His 2015 level of production was a half-season of MVP-level performance on both sides of the ball. By the end of 2016, however, he'd lost most of his playing time to a journeyman defensive specialist who started the season in Triple-A.

The conundrum facing the Mets is that d'Arnaud seems unable to stay healthy while catching—2016's major injury was a strained rotator cuff that cost him two months and seemed to hamper his hitting and throwing after his return—but he's also one of baseball's most valuable pitch-framers. Confiscating d'Arnaud's tools of ignorance initially feels like a good option, but might only keep him healthy enough for his bat to disappoint in a corner. Moving him out from behind the plate also eliminates the upside of getting a full year of that 2015 goodness, but it's hard to trust that he can catch 120 games when he's only come close once in the last five seasons. Time is closer to running out than you might think, because while d'Arnaud still seems vaguely prospecty and young, he actually turns 28 before Opening Day.

Alejandro De Aza   OF

Born: 4/11/84   Age: 33   Bats: L   Throws: L   Height: 6'0"   Weight: 195   Entered Pro Ball: International Free Agent, 2001

YEAR	TEAM	LVL	AGE	PA	R	2B	3B	HR	RBI	BB	K	SB	CS	AVG/OBP/SLG	TAv	VORP	BABIP	BRR	FRAA	WARP
2014	CHA	MLB	30	439	45	19	5	5	31	33	100	15	7	.243/.309/.354	.245	0.8	.311	-2.0	LF(112): -0.1 • CF(14): 3.3	0.4
2014	BAL	MLB	30	89	11	5	3	3	10	6	19	2	3	.293/.341/.537	.312	4.8	.350	-1.3	LF(20): 2.0 • CF(2): -0.1	0.7
2015	BAL	MLB	31	112	16	4	1	3	7	7	34	2	2	.214/.277/.359	.229	-2.2	.288	-1.0	LF(19): 1.7 • RF(13): -0.0	-0.1
2015	BOS	MLB	31	178	23	9	5	4	25	12	36	3	1	.292/.347/.484	.298	10.9	.352	0.9	LF(33): -0.8 • RF(24): -1.6	0.9
2015	SFN	MLB	31	75	12	4	1	0	3	12	14	2	2	.262/.387/.361	.285	2.9	.333	-0.5	LF(17): 0.6	0.4
2016	NYN	MLB	32	267	31	9	0	6	25	26	67	4	3	.205/.297/.321	.234	-1.9	.259	-2.1	CF(46): -3.1 • LF(22): -0.3	-0.5
2017	*NYN*	*MLB*	*33*	*271*	*30*	*11*	*2*	*6*	*26*	*22*	*64*	*6*	*4*	*.243/.313/.375*	*.242*	*3.4*	*.301*	*-1.2*	*CF 1 • LF 1*	*0.5*
2018	*NYN*	*MLB*	*34*	*244*	*27*	*10*	*2*	*5*	*25*	*20*	*61*	*5*	*3*	*.239/.310/.369*	*.253*	*3.6*	*.303*	*-0.8*	*CF 1 • LF 1*	*0.5*

Breakout: 1%   Improve: 33%   Collapse: 9%   Attrition: 17%   MLB: 95%   Comparables: *Reed Johnson, Michael Bourn, Will Venable*

In one of the odder moves the of 2015-16 offseason, the Mets signed Alejandro De Aza just before Christmas to serve as the long side of a centerfield platoon with Juan Lagares. De Aza hadn't spent significant time in center since 2013, and the Mets already had Brandon Nimmo in Triple-A to provide the same profile for the minimum. Things only got more complicated when the Mets re-signed Yoenis Cespedes, demoting De Aza to a $5.75-million fifth outfielder with no real role. Or so we thought. Terry Collins inexplicably played him a ton anyway, and De Aza ended up having the fourth-most games played on the entire roster. Every few weeks, Collins would give some variation on the quote "we have to get De Aza going," talking up his veteranness and professional hitterness—while conveniently leaving out his below replacement levelness. At any sign that his bat was heating up, Collins would start shoveling more and more playing time at him. Suffice it to say, De Aza never got going.

Lucas Duda   1B

Born: 2/3/86   Age: 31   Bats: L   Throws: R   Height: 6'4"   Weight: 255   Entered Pro Ball: Round 7, 2007 Draft (#243 overall)

YEAR	TEAM	LVL	AGE	PA	R	2B	3B	HR	RBI	BB	K	SB	CS	AVG/OBP/SLG	TAv	VORP	BABIP	BRR	FRAA	WARP
2014	NYN	MLB	28	596	74	27	0	30	92	69	135	3	2	.253/.349/.481	.311	31.9	.283	-2.4	1B(146): -6.9 • LF(1): -0.2	2.7
2015	NYN	MLB	29	554	67	33	0	27	73	66	138	0	2	.244/.352/.486	.320	38.9	.285	1.0	1B(129): -8.0	3.3
2016	NYN	MLB	30	172	20	7	0	7	23	15	36	0	0	.229/.302/.412	.281	6.3	.250	0.7	1B(45): -3.5	0.3
2017	*NYN*	*MLB*	*31*	*571*	*69*	*23*	*0*	*24*	*77*	*67*	*145*	*2*	*2*	*.233/.333/.426*	*.272*	*16.6*	*.276*	*-1.8*	*1B -7*	*0.4*
2018	*NYN*	*MLB*	*32*	*398*	*54*	*16*	*0*	*17*	*52*	*48*	*104*	*0*	*0*	*.227/.331/.419*	*.278*	*12.0*	*.271*	*-0.1*	*1B -5*	*0.7*

Breakout: 2%   Improve: 41%   Collapse: 8%   Attrition: 17%   MLB: 93%   Comparables: *Kevin Youkilis, Ryan Zimmerman, Paul Konerko*

The loss of Duda to a back injury for most of the season hurt the Mets badly on the field, as they struggled to find even replacement-level production at first in his stead. It might have hurt even worse off the field, where the extremely entertaining @wefollowlucasduda Instagram "fan" account—actually run by teammate Curtis Granderson, having fun with Duda's well-known aversion to the spotlight—went dormant. Despite his excellent production in 2014 and 2015 after he finally won the regular first base job, the Mets have never seemed willing to commit to Duda, even leading to rumors that he might be non-tendered this offseason. Instead, he'll go into his walk year looking to get back to form, with an array of younger options lurking if he doesn't.

Wilmer Flores   INF

Born: 8/6/91   Age: 25   Bats: R   Throws: R   Height: 6'3"   Weight: 205   Entered Pro Ball: International Free Agent, 2007

YEAR	TEAM	LVL	AGE	PA	R	2B	3B	HR	RBI	BB	K	SB	CS	AVG/OBP/SLG	TAv	VORP	BABIP	BRR	FRAA	WARP
2014	LVG	AAA	22	241	43	11	2	13	57	16	39	0	2	.323/.367/.568	.311	22.8	.339	-0.3	SS(32): 6.2 • 2B(12): 0.3	2.9
2014	NYN	MLB	22	274	28	13	1	6	29	12	31	1	0	.251/.286/.378	.249	6.3	.265	-0.2	SS(51): 2.4 • 2B(19): -1.4	0.8
2015	NYN	MLB	23	510	55	22	0	16	59	19	63	0	1	.263/.295/.408	.262	19.2	.273	-0.1	SS(103): -1.2 • 2B(37): 2.4	2.2
2016	NYN	MLB	24	335	38	14	0	16	49	23	48	1	1	.267/.319/.469	.305	21.9	.268	-2.4	3B(51): -3.8 • 1B(27): 0.4	2.0
2017	NYN	MLB	25	226	25	10	0	8	28	11	35	0	0	.262/.300/.432	.264	8.2	.276	-0.6	2B 0 • 3B -2	0.6
2018	NYN	MLB	26	319	40	14	0	12	42	18	51	1	0	.259/.304/.434	.272	11.6	.273	-0.7	2B 0 • 3B -3	1.0

Breakout: 2%   Improve: 58%   Collapse: 6%   Attrition: 9%   MLB: 98%   Comparables: Lonnie Chisenhall, Matt Duffy, Matt Dominguez

The One Where Wilmer Finally Developed turned into The One Where Wilmer Got Hurt. New York's resident *Friends* expert was in the midst of an offensive breakout when Terry Collins thought the game was on a break and forgot to pinch-run for him in a key September tilt. Flores ended up in a bad plate collision, and after weeks of asking Wilmer how he was doing, the Mets discovered Flores had a broken hamate bone. Flores was there when the injury rains began to pour, filling in at all four infield positions and often kicking the Met offense out of second gear. He's still young enough to hope that The One Where Wilmer Hits Righties airs, but being a good platoon/utility player and general cultural icon isn't so bad either.

Andres Gimenez   SS

Born: 9/4/98   Age: 18   Bats: L   Throws: R   Height: 6'0"   Weight: 165   Entered Pro Ball: International Free Agent, 2015

YEAR	TEAM	LVL	AGE	PA	R	2B	3B	HR	RBI	BB	K	SB	CS	AVG/OBP/SLG	TAv	VORP	BABIP	BRR	FRAA	WARP
2017	NYN	MLB	18	250	24	9	1	6	25	20	73	2	1	.208/.276/.331	.217	-0.3	.274	-0.4	SS 0 • 2B 0	0.0
2018	NYN	MLB	19	263	28	10	1	7	27	20	78	2	2	.209/.275/.345	.231	0.6	.273	-0.3	SS 0 • 2B 0	0.1

Breakout: 0%   Improve: 0%   Collapse: 0%   Attrition: 0%   MLB: 0%   Comparables: Raul Mondesi, Wilmer Flores

Andres Gimenez represents a category of players who we simply don't have much information on: international signees who haven't shown up in the States yet. Since signing, Gimenez has played in extended spring training at the Mets' Dominican complex, and rotated between the two Met affiliates in the Dominican Summer League. What we know about Gimenez is that he was *Baseball America*'s number two international prospect for the 2015-16 signing period, and his $1.2 million bonus ended up looking like a bargain between the time it was "agreed upon" and the day on which he signed. He hit a ton in the Dominican Summer League as one of the youngest players on both rosters he graced. The reports are pretty basic at this point: smooth swing, smooth actions at short, good speed. Past that, you can dream on everything else.

Curtis Granderson   OF

Born: 3/16/81   Age: 36   Bats: L   Throws: R   Height: 6'1"   Weight: 200   Entered Pro Ball: Round 3, 2002 Draft (#80 overall)

YEAR	TEAM	LVL	AGE	PA	R	2B	3B	HR	RBI	BB	K	SB	CS	AVG/OBP/SLG	TAv	VORP	BABIP	BRR	FRAA	WARP
2014	NYN	MLB	33	654	73	27	2	20	66	79	141	8	2	.227/.326/.388	.275	19.6	.265	-0.9	RF(142): -5.0 • CF(15): -0.4	1.8
2015	NYN	MLB	34	682	98	33	2	26	70	91	151	11	6	.259/.364/.457	.314	49.2	.305	1.3	RF(149): 1.3 • CF(2): 0.7	5.5
2016	NYN	MLB	35	633	88	24	5	30	59	74	130	4	2	.237/.335/.464	.296	37.7	.254	1.3	RF(110): 3.5 • CF(36): -5.8	3.7
2017	NYN	MLB	36	524	71	19	2	21	62	61	130	6	3	.227/.323/.419	.266	20.9	.266	-0.4	CF -6 • RF 0	1.0
2018	NYN	MLB	37	510	66	18	2	20	65	58	130	5	2	.222/.315/.407	.267	17.2	.262	0.3	CF -6 • RF 0	1.3

Breakout: 0%   Improve: 24%   Collapse: 5%   Attrition: 9%   MLB: 77%   Comparables: J.D. Drew, Jermaine Dye, Matt Stairs

The Grandyman still can. The 13-year veteran kept chugging along with his big smile, staving off that pesky aging curve with another classic Curtis Granderson season. Years after he moved off center except for token appearances, the Mets asked Granderson to play center semi-regularly down the stretch. He battled the position to somewhat of a draw—a large victory for the Mets in turn—even making a spectacular catch in the Wild Card Game. The once-questionable $60 million contract the Mets signed him to prior to 2014 now looks like a huge bargain with only a single year remaining.

In addition to his excellence on the field, Granderson won the Roberto Clemente Award for his sportsmanship and community service. Always quick to brighten a fan's day with an autograph, a tossed baseball, or a wave from the field, Granderson is active in all kinds of youth initiatives in Chicago, New York and elsewhere. Most notably, he donated $5 million to build Curtis Granderson Stadium at his alma mater University of Illinois-Chicago, and perhaps more importantly, an associated baseball academy for underprivileged kids. He remains one of the easiest guys in baseball to root for.

Kelly Johnson   UT

Born: 2/22/82   Age: 35   Bats: L   Throws: R   Height: 6'1"   Weight: 200   Entered Pro Ball: Round 1, 2000 Draft (#38 overall)

YEAR	TEAM	LVL	AGE	PA	R	2B	3B	HR	RBI	BB	K	SB	CS	AVG/OBP/SLG	TAv	VORP	BABIP	BRR	FRAA	WARP
2014	NYA	MLB	32	227	21	9	2	6	22	23	50	2	1	.219/.304/.373	.256	-1.0	.260	-4.8	3B(41): -0.0 • 1B(27): 2.8	0.2
2014	BOS	MLB	32	25	1	1	0	0	1	0	10	0	0	.160/.160/.200	.120	-2.7	.267	0.2	1B(5): -0.1 • 3B(2): 0.3	-0.3
2014	BAL	MLB	32	45	7	4	0	1	4	6	11	0	1	.231/.333/.410	.304	2.3	.296	-0.9	3B(17): -1.3 • 2B(3): -0.1	0.1
2015	ATL	MLB	33	197	20	5	0	9	34	13	43	1	1	.275/.321/.451	.286	5.9	.313	-2.8	LF(27): 1.3 • 1B(20): 1.9	0.8
2015	NYN	MLB	33	138	18	6	0	5	13	10	38	1	0	.250/.304/.414	.271	5.5	.318	0.6	2B(27): 0.9 • 1B(5): 0.3	0.7
2016	ATL	MLB	34	132	8	6	0	1	10	10	25	1	0	.215/.273/.289	.225	-2.2	.260	-1.0	2B(26): -0.5 • LF(6): -0.5	-0.3
2016	NYN	MLB	34	201	17	8	0	9	24	15	40	3	0	.268/.328/.459	.285	10.6	.296	-0.3	2B(26): -3.7 • 3B(21): -0.8	0.6
2017	NYN	MLB	35	314	34	11	1	10	37	28	81	3	1	.226/.299/.376	.239	2.5	.278	-2.2	2B -2 • 3B -0	0.1
2018	NYN	MLB	36	178	20	6	0	5	19	16	47	1	0	.211/.285/.348	.238	-0.4	.262	-1.3	2B -1 • 3B 0	-0.2

Breakout: 0%   Improve: 24%   Collapse: 14%   Attrition: 19%   MLB: 71%   Comparables: Tim Teufel, Jay Bell, Ronnie Belliard

If you look at Kelly Johnson's transaction history, it sure looks like the Mets have been using the hapless Atlanta Braves as a quasi-farm team to stash spare players until needed, much like the Yankees and the Athletics circa the late-1950s. In reality, it's all quite benign. Kelly Johnson keeps signing with the Braves because he lives outside of Atlanta and the Mets keep trading for Kelly Johnson because they love his versatility and veteran presence. After an indifferent two months in Atlanta, Johnson turned in a great two-thirds of a season's worth of super-utility work with the Mets, fueled by newfound pull power. There's at least a little reason to believe that might be more than a sample size quirk, as Johnson is now intentionally emulating Daniel Murphy's pull-happy approach.

Juan Lagares   CF

Born: 3/17/89   Age: 28   Bats: R   Throws: R   Height: 6'1"   Weight: 215   Entered Pro Ball: International Free Agent, 2006

YEAR	TEAM	LVL	AGE	PA	R	2B	3B	HR	RBI	BB	K	SB	CS	AVG/OBP/SLG	TAv	VORP	BABIP	BRR	FRAA	WARP
2014	NYN	MLB	25	452	46	24	3	4	47	20	87	13	4	.281/.321/.382	.275	20.0	.341	1.0	CF(112): 10.9	3.4
2015	NYN	MLB	26	465	47	16	5	6	41	16	87	7	3	.259/.289/.358	.245	8.0	.308	1.4	CF(137): -0.7 • RF(2): -0.3	0.7
2016	NYN	MLB	27	160	15	7	2	3	9	11	27	4	2	.239/.301/.380	.245	2.4	.274	0.1	CF(68): 2.0 • RF(2): 0.1	0.5
2017	NYN	MLB	28	191	19	8	1	3	18	9	39	4	1	.255/.296/.373	.244	3.6	.305	0.2	CF 2	0.4
2018	NYN	MLB	29	223	24	10	2	4	23	12	45	4	2	.255/.300/.383	.252	4.7	.300	0.4	CF 3	0.8

Breakout: 4%   Improve: 53%   Collapse: 3%   Attrition: 9%   MLB: 96%   Comparables: Mike Devereaux, Coco Crisp, Brian McRae

When the Mets signed Juan Lagares to a long-term extension in the spring of 2015, it was viewed as a reasonable move (if not a steal), locking up one of baseball's best defenders at a bargain price through his arbitration years, with a cheap option covering his first year of free agency. Lagares had made some improvements offensively in 2014, and looked like a building block for a Mets team entering its contention cycle. Jump ahead two seasons and guaranteeing Lagares $23 million seems like a bad misstep. He's no longer a standout defender in center, even when healthy, and he's rarely been healthy of late. Hitting was never the strongest part of his game, but he's backslid far enough that it's difficult to justify playing him regularly without the Kiermaier-level defense. Lagares is young enough that he could yet rebound on either side of the ball, but another season like the last two will mark him as a cautionary tale about players who peak early.

Desmond Lindsay   OF

Born: 1/15/97   Age: 20   Bats: R   Throws: R   Height: 6'0"   Weight: 200   Entered Pro Ball: Round 2, 2015 Draft (#53 overall)

YEAR	TEAM	LVL	AGE	PA	R	2B	3B	HR	RBI	BB	K	SB	CS	AVG/OBP/SLG	TAv	VORP	BABIP	BRR	FRAA	WARP
2015	BRO	A-	18	53	3	3	0	0	7	7	19	0	1	.200/.308/.267	.240	-0.6	.346	-1.0	CF(14): -3.8	-0.5
2016	BRO	A-	19	134	18	5	0	4	17	20	26	3	1	.297/.418/.450	.345	15.4	.358	-0.1	CF(29): -3.3	1.3
2017	NYN	MLB	20	250	23	8	1	6	26	22	84	1	0	.195/.270/.318	.211	-3.6	.275	-0.4	CF -4	-0.8
2018	NYN	MLB	21	295	33	10	1	8	30	29	95	1	0	.200/.285/.332	.233	-0.7	.275	-0.6	CF -4	-0.5

Breakout: 1%   Improve: 5%   Collapse: 0%   Attrition: 3%   MLB: 7%   Comparables: Joe Benson, Caleb Gindl, Anthony Gose

The Mets were very happy to nab Out-of-Door Academy's Lindsay with their first pick in the 2015 draft, viewing him as a first-round talent who fell because of nagging leg injuries. A season-and-a-half later, he's proven both that he was a first-round talent and that his leg injuries are perilously close to being described as chronic. Despite the latter, he's such a good athlete that the Mets have moved him up the defensive spectrum, converting him from a high school corner infielder to a pro centerfielder. He'll make his full-season debut in 2017, and could rise quickly given his advanced bat.

James Loney   1B

Born: 5/7/84   Age: 33   Bats: L   Throws: L   Height: 6'3"   Weight: 235   Entered Pro Ball: Round 1, 2002 Draft (#19 overall)

YEAR	TEAM	LVL	AGE	PA	R	2B	3B	HR	RBI	BB	K	SB	CS	AVG/OBP/SLG	TAv	VORP	BABIP	BRR	FRAA	WARP
2014	TBA	MLB	30	651	59	27	0	9	69	41	80	4	0	.290/.336/.380	.271	7.4	.319	-5.5	1B(152): -5.3	0.2
2015	TBA	MLB	31	388	25	16	0	4	32	23	34	2	4	.280/.322/.357	.243	-8.3	.298	-5.7	1B(101): 1.1	-0.8
2016	ELP	AAA	32	169	22	7	0	2	28	9	12	0	0	.342/.373/.424	.257	-0.7	.356	-2.0	1B(35): 1.1 • RF(1): 0.0	0.0
2016	NYN	MLB	32	366	30	16	1	9	34	16	37	0	0	.265/.307/.397	.257	1.7	.275	-0.9	1B(97): -5.8	-0.4
2017	NYN	MLB	33	375	37	16	0	8	40	24	49	1	1	.269/.317/.381	.244	-1.2	.293	-2.7	1B -4 • LF -0	-0.6
2018	NYN	MLB	34	333	37	13	0	6	33	21	46	0	0	.261/.309/.366	.249	-2.0	.286	-2.4	1B -3 • LF 0	-0.6

Breakout: 4%   Improve: 34%   Collapse: 8%   Attrition: 27%   MLB: 85%   Comparables: Jesus Alou, Sean Casey, Brayan Pena

The danger with acquiring James Loney is that your manager might fall in love with the skills listed on LinkedIn, though it hasn't been updated since he forgot his password back in 2011. After being released by the Rays in spring training, Loney couldn't find a major-league gig and landed in Triple-A. The Mets got him at the end of May for the proverbial bag of baseballs, thus making him the literal definition of a replacement player. And, sure enough, that overrated defensive reputation and empty batting average established him as such once again. Terry Collins, the farm director for the Dodgers when Loney was their top prospect over a decade ago, pretended he got a legitimate regular instead of the 2016 version and played him in 100 of the Mets' remaining 112 games, often at the expense of better, younger players. Loney did contribute an amazing, KBO-style bat flip after hitting the game-winning home run in the playoff-clincher in Philadelphia, at least.

Brandon Nimmo   OF

Born: 3/27/93   Age: 24   Bats: L   Throws: R   Height: 6'3"   Weight: 205   Entered Pro Ball: Round 1, 2011 Draft (#13 overall)

YEAR	TEAM	LVL	AGE	PA	R	2B	3B	HR	RBI	BB	K	SB	CS	AVG/OBP/SLG	TAv	VORP	BABIP	BRR	FRAA	WARP
2014	SLU	A+	21	279	59	9	5	4	25	50	51	9	3	.322/.448/.458	.318	27.7	.401	1.5	CF(56): -4.3	2.4
2014	BIN	AA	21	279	38	12	4	6	26	36	54	5	1	.238/.339/.396	.258	7.2	.283	0.1	CF(44): -0.1 • LF(21): -3.5	0.4
2015	SLU	A+	22	20	3	1	0	0	2	4	3	0	0	.125/.300/.188	.211	-1.0	.154	-0.4	CF(2): -0.4	-0.2
2015	BIN	AA	22	302	26	12	3	2	16	26	55	0	0	.279/.354/.368	.266	6.1	.343	-3.9	CF(57): -2.6 • RF(10): 0.9	0.4
2015	LVG	AAA	22	112	19	3	1	3	8	18	20	5	4	.264/.393/.418	.284	6.3	.304	0.9	CF(17): 3.9 • RF(13): -0.1	1.0
2016	LVG	AAA	23	444	72	25	8	11	61	46	73	7	8	.352/.423/.541	.304	35.3	.411	2.8	CF(65): 1.0 • LF(23): 1.5	3.9
2016	NYN	MLB	23	80	12	1	0	1	6	6	20	0	0	.274/.338/.329	.267	2.0	.365	-0.4	LF(13): -0.2 • RF(7): -0.0	0.2
2017	NYN	MLB	24	107	11	4	1	2	11	11	26	1	1	.244/.330/.377	.259	3.0	.308	-0.2	RF 1	0.4
2018	NYN	MLB	25	336	41	12	2	9	37	35	84	3	3	.248/.333/.393	.272	11.3	.313	-0.3	RF 3	1.6

Breakout: 5%   Improve: 24%   Collapse: 17%   Attrition: 27%   MLB: 55%   Comparables: Desmond Jennings, Jaff Decker, Jackie Bradley

Nimmo has yet to discover his in-game power stroke, and time is running out. Drafted out of American Legion ball in Wyoming (yes, we're still mentioning this every year), Nimmo was expected to grow into a power-hitting corner guy. Instead, he's stuck in center way longer than expected and turned into a contact machine, finishing only a point behind teammate T.J. Rivera for the PCL batting crown. The Mets were curiously unwilling to let Nimmo play center in the majors even when running out a parade of corner guys late in the season, which throws some cold water on the idea that he might have an MLB future there. But he's got a shot at being the new Nick Markakis, a comp that is cliché but too on the nose not to use.

Kevin Plawecki C

Born: 2/26/91 Age: 26 Bats: R Throws: R Height: 6'2" Weight: 210 Entered Pro Ball: Round 1, 2012 Draft (#35 overall)

YEAR	TEAM	LVL	AGE	PA	R	2B	3B	HR	RBI	BB	K	SB	CS	AVG/OBP/SLG	TAv	VORP	BABIP	BRR	FRAA	WARP
2014	BIN	AA	23	249	33	18	0	6	43	16	27	0	0	.326/.378/.487	.304	22.5	.344	0.8	C(54): 6.2	3.1
2014	LVG	AAA	23	170	25	6	0	5	21	14	21	0	0	.283/.345/.421	.266	8.6	.299	-0.3	C(40): 7.1 • 1B(1): -0.0	1.6
2015	LVG	AAA	24	90	7	5	1	1	9	3	12	0	0	.224/.267/.341	.198	-3.8	.250	-1.7	C(20): -0.3 • 1B(1): -0.0	-0.4
2015	NYN	MLB	24	258	18	9	0	3	21	17	60	0	0	.219/.280/.296	.241	4.7	.277	-1.6	C(70): 12.0	1.8
2016	LVG	AAA	25	207	27	11	0	8	40	13	19	0	1	.300/.348/.484	.278	9.9	.297	-1.9	C(41): 4.4 • 1B(5): 0.2	1.5
2016	NYN	MLB	25	151	6	6	0	1	11	17	33	0	0	.197/.298/.265	.228	2.3	.255	0.3	C(45): 5.7	0.8
2017	*NYN*	*MLB*	*26*	*98*	*10*	*4*	*0*	*2*	*10*	*7*	*19*	*0*	*0*	*.236/.297/.361*	*.245*	*3.0*	*.273*	*-0.2*	*C 3*	*0.4*
2018	*NYN*	*MLB*	*27*	*187*	*22*	*7*	*0*	*5*	*20*	*14*	*38*	*0*	*0*	*.230/.298/.367*	*.253*	*5.1*	*.265*	*-0.4*	*C 5*	*1.1*

Breakout: 8%   Improve: 40%   Collapse: 15%   Attrition: 29%   MLB: 88%   *Comparables: JD Closser, Lou Marson, Tony Cruz*

Sometimes a player's profile is very different from what you expect it to be. Kevin Plawecki was supposed to be average at pretty much everything. In our 2015 Mets prospect list, he was graded as a 50 or 50-plus on every tool except speed, and gave his realistic outcome as a Role 5 average big-league catcher. Plawecki was one of the least controversial prospects in the game, with large-scale agreement that this is what he'd become. Now, of course, the Plawecki that has emerged is a superlative defensive catcher who can't hit a lick. What the heck happened here? Entering 2016, the theory was that sinus-related vertigo issues crippled his 2015 offensive output...and then he was even worse in the majors in 2016. Catchers are freaking weird.

YEAR	TEAM	P. COUNT	FRM RUNS	BLK RUNS	THRW RUNS	TOT RUNS
2014	BIN	7326	5.1	0.6	0.1	5.8
2014	LVG	5051	7.8	0.2	-1.4	6.6
2015	LVG	2811	0.0	0.0	-0.0	-0.1
2015	NYN	9093	12.3	0.4	-0.3	12.4
2016	NYN	5670	6.2	1.0	-0.1	7.1
2017	*NYN*	*3588*	*2.4*	*0.3*	*-0.2*	*2.4*
2018	*NYN*	*6844*	*4.2*	*0.6*	*-0.4*	*4.4*

Jose Reyes 3B

Born: 6/11/83 Age: 34 Bats: B Throws: R Height: 6'0" Weight: 195 Entered Pro Ball: International Free Agent, 1999

YEAR	TEAM	LVL	AGE	PA	R	2B	3B	HR	RBI	BB	K	SB	CS	AVG/OBP/SLG	TAv	VORP	BABIP	BRR	FRAA	WARP
2014	TOR	MLB	31	655	94	33	4	9	51	38	73	30	2	.287/.328/.398	.274	39.7	.312	6.4	SS(142): -12.7	3.0
2015	TOR	MLB	32	311	36	17	0	4	34	17	38	16	2	.285/.322/.385	.252	12.5	.315	2.6	SS(69): -2.8	1.0
2015	COL	MLB	32	208	21	8	2	3	19	9	24	8	4	.259/.291/.368	.224	1.4	.281	0.4	SS(47): 0.6	0.2
2016	ABQ	AAA	33	40	7	0	0	2	2	7	4	3	0	.303/.425/.485	.311	4.0	.296	0.2	SS(9): -0.9	0.3
2016	BIN	AA	33	33	6	1	0	0	2	3	3	1	1	.207/.273/.241	.230	-0.3	.222	-0.3	3B(7): -0.4	-0.1
2016	NYN	MLB	33	279	45	13	4	8	24	23	49	9	2	.267/.326/.443	.285	18.2	.302	1.6	3B(50): -2.5 • SS(13): 0.1	1.6
2017	*NYN*	*MLB*	*34*	*479*	*60*	*20*	*3*	*9*	*41*	*34*	*64*	*20*	*4*	*.265/.315/.382*	*.255*	*14.6*	*.288*	*2.4*	*3B -0 • SS -1*	*1.1*
2018	*NYN*	*MLB*	*35*	*324*	*36*	*15*	*1*	*6*	*33*	*25*	*46*	*12*	*3*	*.260/.318/.382*	*.261*	*10.0*	*.285*	*1.9*	*3B 0 • SS 0*	*1.0*

Breakout: 1%   Improve: 27%   Collapse: 12%   Attrition: 23%   MLB: 90%   *Comparables: Jerry Hairston, Billy Goodman, Kevin Seitzer*

After David Wright went down yet again, the Mets signed this departed franchise legend off the scrap heap to fill in at third base for the remainder of the season. As you can see above, Reyes performed fairly well in that role. In an alternate universe, this could have been a feel-good story chronicling the journey home for one of the Mets' brightest homegrown stars. Despite the best efforts of many involved to create that narrative, the truth was far more complicated.

Jose Reyes was available to the Mets for the league minimum because of serious domestic abuse allegations, for which Major League Baseball suspended him for the first 51 games of the season. And while this wasn't the first or only instance of domestic violence arbitrage in New York last season, repetition did not make this an easier or more pleasant pill to swallow. Please consider supporting victims of domestic violence through your local women's shelter, or a charity such as RAINN or Joe Torre's Safe At Home Foundation.

Rene Rivera C

Born: 7/31/83 Age: 33 Bats: R Throws: R Height: 5'10" Weight: 215 Entered Pro Ball: Round 2, 2001 Draft (#49 overall)

YEAR	TEAM	LVL	AGE	PA	R	2B	3B	HR	RBI	BB	K	SB	CS	AVG/OBP/SLG	TAv	VORP	BABIP	BRR	FRAA	WARP
2014	SDN	MLB	30	329	27	18	1	11	44	27	76	0	0	.252/.319/.432	.276	17.0	.301	-1.3	C(89): 27.0 • 1B(3): -0.1	4.9
2015	TBA	MLB	31	319	16	14	0	5	26	11	86	0	0	.178/.213/.275	.176	-15.5	.230	-2.8	C(107): 5.9 • 1B(7): -0.1	-1.0
2016	LVG	AAA	32	29	3	1	0	0	5	2	3	0	0	.280/.357/.320	.290	0.7	.318	-1.5	C(8): 0.3	0.1
2016	NYN	MLB	32	207	12	4	0	6	26	16	54	0	0	.222/.291/.341	.239	3.8	.276	-1.0	C(59): 11.1 • 1B(1): 0.0	1.5
2017	*NYN*	*MLB*	*33*	*123*	*11*	*5*	*0*	*3*	*12*	*8*	*30*	*0*	*0*	*.225/.276/.348*	*.226*	*1.0*	*.275*	*-0.3*	*C 5*	*0.5*
2018	*NYN*	*MLB*	*34*	*177*	*18*	*7*	*0*	*4*	*18*	*10*	*45*	*0*	*0*	*.217/.268/.337*	*.220*	*-1.5*	*.265*	*-0.8*	*C 7*	*0.5*

Breakout: 1%   Improve: 29%   Collapse: 18%   Attrition: 24%   MLB: 85%   *Comparables: Vance Wilson, John Baker, Humberto Quintero*

Rene Rivera raises one of the emerging philosophical questions of current sabermetrics: if a catcher is this good defensively, does he need to be able to hit at all? All evidence points to Rivera being an otherworldly defender, brilliant at all the aspects we have a firm measure on calculating, like framing and throwing, and even a step beyond that to some we're still working on, like calling games and handling pitchers. He also can't hit a lick outside of the occasional home run, and doesn't take enough advantage of opposite-handed pitching to create easy role compartmentalization—his career .671

YEAR	TEAM	P. COUNT	FRM RUNS	BLK RUNS	THRW RUNS	TOT RUNS
2014	SDN	11771	22.5	2.6	2.9	27.9
2015	TBA	12905	5.2	-0.5	1.3	6.0
2016	NYN	7602	8.2	-0.7	1.0	8.5
2017	*NYN*	*4798*	*3.9*	*-0.1*	*0.4*	*4.2*
2018	*NYN*	*6922*	*5.0*	*-0.3*	*0.6*	*5.3*

OPS against lefties doesn't scream "oh man, we have to get him in there against Gio Gonzalez" with much volume.* He also seemed overexposed on both sides of the ball when assigned regular duty in Tampa Bay in early 2015. Sabermetricians used to call Gregg Zaun the "Practically Perfect Backup Catcher." In current times, that title might fall to Rivera—if you don't decide his defense is so good that you should start him altogether.

*In his two at-bats against Gonzalez, Rivera has a sacrifice fly and a single, but as arguably the best left-handed starter in the NL East, the point still holds.

T.J. Rivera   2B

Born: 10/27/88 Age: 28 Bats: R Throws: R Height: 6'1" Weight: 205 Entered Pro Ball: Undrafted Free Agent, 2011

YEAR	TEAM	LVL	AGE	PA	R	2B	3B	HR	RBI	BB	K	SB	CS	AVG/OBP/SLG	TAv	VORP	BABIP	BRR	FRAA	WARP
2014	SLU	A+	25	274	42	16	0	4	47	14	37	2	1	.341/.383/.452	.285	12.1	.383	-0.7	1B(25): -1.0 • 2B(18): -2.7	0.7
2014	BIN	AA	25	221	28	13	0	1	28	11	27	1	0	.358/.394/.438	.291	13.8	.399	-1.0	SS(29): -2.1 • 3B(15): -0.0	1.2
2015	LVG	AAA	26	196	26	17	1	2	21	7	25	0	0	.306/.345/.443	.260	5.0	.346	-0.8	3B(31): 2.3 • 2B(17): -2.9	0.4
2015	BIN	AA	26	234	37	10	0	5	27	12	22	1	1	.341/.380/.455	.290	15.6	.363	1.2	2B(22): 0.4 • SS(17): 1.7	2.0
2016	LVG	AAA	27	442	67	31	1	11	85	23	54	3	3	.353/.393/.516	.301	32.1	.383	1.1	3B(69): -0.0 • 2B(14): 0.2	3.4
2016	NYN	MLB	27	113	10	4	1	3	16	3	17	0	0	.333/.345/.476	.325	10.1	.360	-0.5	2B(26): -1.0 • 3B(9): -0.5	0.9
2017	NYN	MLB	28	106	11	5	0	2	11	5	20	0	0	.275/.312/.400	.258	3.6	.318	-0.3	2B -1	0.2
2018	NYN	MLB	29	291	33	13	0	7	32	14	58	0	0	.267/.311/.397	.263	8.4	.311	-0.8	2B -2	0.7

Breakout: 3%   Improve: 15%   Collapse: 8%   Attrition: 17%   MLB: 32%   Comparables: Zelous Wheeler, Glenn Williams, Terry Tiffee

In the grand tradition of Mike from Whitestone, Steven from Stony Brook, Nelson from Coney Island, and Johnny from Bensonhurst comes our latest local hero: T.J. from Throgs Neck. Few things grab the collective attention of the Mets' fanbase more than a local kid with a story, and Rivera has quite a humdinger. An undrafted senior out of Troy University in 2011, Rivera got into the organization through a dash of analytics—his college stats piqued the interest of then-analytics guru Ian Levin—and a pinch of old-fashioned word-of-mouth scouting, coming in the form of a recommendation from former Met catcher Mackey Sasser. The Mets never prioritized his development, shifting him between positions and levels as organizational needs warranted. But he always showed off a strong batting average—hitting over .300 at every level of the minors except Rookie ball, where he hit .290—and "played the game the right way." Rivera finally made it to Double-A in mid-2014, and then he *really* started to hit. He hasn't stopped yet.

One of the cool things about baseball is that if you hit .350 long enough anywhere, even as an organizational player in Las Vegas, you're going to get the call. Perhaps that hit tool will ultimately carry Rivera's profile—it sure did in limited time in 2016—or perhaps it won't. But even if it was only a charmed month, Rivera's timely hitting in September was a big part of lifting the Mets into the playoffs, and that's a heck of an accomplishment for a guy with his background.

Amed Rosario   SS

Born: 11/20/95 Age: 21 Bats: R Throws: R Height: 6'2" Weight: 190 Entered Pro Ball: International Free Agent, 2012

YEAR	TEAM	LVL	AGE	PA	R	2B	3B	HR	RBI	BB	K	SB	CS	AVG/OBP/SLG	TAv	VORP	BABIP	BRR	FRAA	WARP
2014	SAV	A	18	31	2	0	1	1	4	1	11	0	0	.133/.161/.300	.157	-2.8	.167	-0.1	SS(2): 0.1 • 3B(1): -0.2	-0.3
2014	BRO	A-	18	290	39	11	5	1	23	17	47	7	3	.289/.337/.380	.274	16.4	.345	0.7	SS(64): 2.6	2.0
2015	SLU	A+	19	417	41	20	5	0	25	23	73	12	4	.257/.307/.335	.240	8.8	.316	0.9	SS(102): 13.9	2.5
2016	SLU	A+	20	290	27	10	8	3	40	21	36	13	6	.309/.359/.442	.299	24.0	.345	0.5	SS(60): -0.2	2.4
2016	BIN	AA	20	237	38	14	5	2	31	19	51	6	2	.341/.392/.481	.302	20.9	.433	1.7	SS(53): -5.2	1.7
2017	NYN	MLB	21	250	24	10	2	5	26	14	65	4	1	.238/.284/.367	.230	3.9	.305	0.2	SS 1	0.6
2018	NYN	MLB	22	357	39	14	4	8	38	22	90	6	2	.247/.297/.385	.253	10.1	.312	0.5	SS 2	1.3

Breakout: 4%   Improve: 10%   Collapse: 1%   Attrition: 9%   MLB: 17%   Comparables: Nick Franklin, Alen Hanson, Yamaico Navarro

Rosario emerged as one of the top prospects in baseball during 2016, finally turning projection and potential into production. Better yet, he's grown into his offense without sliding down the defensive spectrum as it was feared he might early on in his pro career, instead adding at least a full grade of speed to the package. He's yet to hit for much in-game power, but his wrists and bat speed suggest that's coming next. Rosario's favorite phrase on social media is "Don't be surprised, be ready," and don't be surprised—with an unsettled infield filled with health risks—if Rosario is making his debut in the majors this year. He's certainly pretty close to ready.

Justin Ruggiano   OF

Born: 4/12/82 Age: 35 Bats: R Throws: R Height: 6'1" Weight: 210 Entered Pro Ball: Round 25, 2004 Draft (#748 overall)

YEAR	TEAM	LVL	AGE	PA	R	2B	3B	HR	RBI	BB	K	SB	CS	AVG/OBP/SLG	TAv	VORP	BABIP	BRR	FRAA	WARP
2014	IOW	AAA	32	25	3	1	0	0	0	3	6	0	0	.143/.280/.190	.194	-1.2	.200	0.3	RF(5): -0.5	-0.2
2014	CHN	MLB	32	250	29	13	1	6	28	18	70	2	4	.281/.337/.429	.290	12.8	.375	0.5	RF(34): -2.9 • CF(18): -0.9	1.1
2015	SEA	MLB	33	81	8	4	0	2	3	11	27	3	2	.214/.321/.357	.245	0.3	.317	-0.5	CF(15): -1.4 • RF(11): -0.4	-0.2
2015	TAC	AAA	33	205	27	9	0	10	29	23	51	6	4	.296/.385/.514	.306	13.1	.364	-0.5	LF(17): -3.1 • CF(11): -0.8	0.9
2015	LAN	MLB	33	60	12	4	1	4	12	3	14	2	0	.291/.350/.618	.354	8.4	.324	1.6	LF(16): -1.4 • RF(2): -0.2	0.7
2016	TEX	MLB	34	4	0	1	0	0	1	0	1	0	0	.250/.250/.500	.232	0.0	.333	0.0	LF(1): 0.1	0.0
2016	ROU	AAA	34	190	26	10	1	7	23	23	53	3	1	.226/.321/.427	.295	8.2	.283	-2.2	LF(31): -0.7	0.8
2016	NYN	MLB	34	22	4	0	0	2	6	2	9	0	1	.350/.409/.650	.368	2.3	.556	-0.8	CF(6): 0.4 • RF(1): -0.0	0.3
2017	SFN	MLB	35	126	16	5	0	5	15	12	36	2	2	.236/.311/.415	.262	4.4	.301	-0.2	LF 1 • CF -0	0.4
2018	SFN	MLB	36	92	12	4	0	3	11	8	27	2	1	.232/.307/.406	.264	2.8	.299	0.2	LF 1 • CF 0	0.4

Breakout: 1%   Improve: 29%   Collapse: 10%   Attrition: 18%   MLB: 84%   Comparables: Marcus Thames, Josh Hamilton, Andruw Jones

The Mets picked up Ruggiano as a free agent in late July following his release from Texas' Triple-A club. In the fourth inning of his Met debut, he sprained his shoulder diving for a ball in the right-center gap. In an attempt to fit in with his teammates, he played through it for a couple games before finally going on the disabled list. In an attempt to fit in with the organization's reputation, Ruggiano came back for a handful more games, and then went on the DL again for the rest of the season.

Dominic Smith 1B

Born: 6/15/95 Age: 22 Bats: L Throws: L Height: 6'0" Weight: 250 Entered Pro Ball: Round 1, 2013 Draft (#11 overall)

YEAR	TEAM	LVL	AGE	PA	R	2B	3B	HR	RBI	BB	K	SB	CS	AVG/OBP/SLG	TAv	VORP	BABIP	BRR	FRAA	WARP
2014	SAV	A	19	518	52	26	1	1	44	51	77	5	4	.271/.344/.338	.261	0.9	.321	-4.8	1B(110): -3.1	-0.2
2015	SLU	A+	20	497	58	33	0	6	79	35	75	2	1	.305/.354/.417	.279	7.6	.351	-6.5	1B(104): 9.2	1.8
2016	BIN	AA	21	542	64	29	2	14	91	50	74	2	1	.302/.367/.457	.292	17.6	.329	-5.3	1B(106): 1.1	2.0
2017	NYN	MLB	22	250	25	11	0	7	29	18	56	0	0	.247/.302/.386	.242	-0.1	.295	-0.5	1B 1	0.1
2018	NYN	MLB	23	380	46	18	0	12	45	29	84	0	0	.253/.312/.407	.267	6.5	.300	-1.0	1B 2	0.9

Breakout: 6% Improve: 23% Collapse: 5% Attrition: 24% MLB: 35% *Comparables: Nick Evans, Dan Vogelbach, Chris Marrero*

A square peg in a round hole, Smith possesses excellent hitting ability to all fields, but has yet to show the power expected of a first baseman. Still, value is value, even if his spray chart looks more like it was induced by an up-the-middle player. It remains to be seen whether Smith's hitting approach will hold up in the majors, or whether he'll develop more power as he matures, but as long as he keeps hitting .300, it'll play.

Tim Tebow OF

Born: 8/14/87 Age: 29 Bats: L Throws: L Height: 6'3" Weight: 255 Entered Pro Ball: Round 1, 2010 NFL Draft (#25 overall)

"Was he born in Cuba? OK, then our interest is probably not as high as it would be. We'll make a decision on that. I don't want to be too cavalier about it. Probably not going to have an impact on us in a material way in the next two months."
—Sandy Alderson on Tim Tebow, August 9, 2016

"I have to tell you, the notion that we're going to spend $100,000-plus on a player so we can sell a couple of hundred dollars worth of T-shirts in Kingsport, those economics don't work. This was not about making money."
—Sandy Alderson after signing Tim Tebow, September 9, 2016

By mid-September, an agreement was signed letting the Mets, and MLB jersey supplier Majestic, market Tebow as if he were a member of the major-league team. Tebow Mets jerseys and t-shirts were made available at major sporting goods chains and websites, along with the Mets clubhouse shops at Citi Field, and of course at Tebow's first destination: Port St. Lucie. He quickly became one of baseball's best sellers.

As for things related to baseball, reports out of the Arizona Fall League indicated Tebow couldn't touch even fringe pitching. At 29, he'll have to stop rolling over to the right side on everything and start hitting quickly to have a shot at anything more than a token famous guy run. But hey, at least most of the low-level Met affiliates are in prime SEC Country, right?

Neil Walker 2B

Born: 9/10/85 Age: 31 Bats: B Throws: R Height: 6'3" Weight: 210 Entered Pro Ball: Round 1, 2004 Draft (#11 overall)

YEAR	TEAM	LVL	AGE	PA	R	2B	3B	HR	RBI	BB	K	SB	CS	AVG/OBP/SLG	TAv	VORP	BABIP	BRR	FRAA	WARP
2014	PIT	MLB	28	571	74	25	3	23	76	45	88	2	2	.271/.342/.467	.294	32.6	.288	0.4	2B(135): -2.6	3.3
2015	PIT	MLB	29	603	69	32	3	16	71	44	110	4	1	.269/.328/.427	.274	25.7	.306	1.8	2B(146): 4.7	3.3
2016	NYN	MLB	30	458	57	9	1	23	55	42	84	3	1	.282/.347/.476	.300	31.2	.302	0.3	2B(111): 2.7	3.5
2017	NYN	MLB	31	518	59	21	1	19	66	45	100	3	1	.255/.325/.426	.269	24.7	.284	-0.8	2B 0	2.2
2018	NYN	MLB	32	427	55	17	1	15	54	37	85	1	1	.249/.320/.418	.272	18.7	.278	0.4	2B 0	2.1

Breakout: 2% Improve: 41% Collapse: 4% Attrition: 5% MLB: 95% *Comparables: Davey Johnson, Orlando Hudson, Aaron Hill*

Walker was well on his way to the best season of his career—and a sizable haul in free agency—but he became a True Met instead. Walker spent the last two weeks of August battling a theoretically minor, day-to-day back injury. In a midday press availability session on August 31, Sandy Alderson finally revealed that Walker was playing through a herniated disc in his back, but assured everyone that Walker would be fine to continue doing so. In his pre-game press availability session that evening, Terry Collins brought up the possibility of surgery and Walker only being able to handle a limited role in September and October. By Collins' post-game press conference, Walker had been ruled out for the rest of the season. Instead of a lucrative multi-year deal, Walker accepted the qualifying offer to return to the Mets on a one-year, $17.2 million deal. He'll try to repeat 2016, except without all the injury-related Metsing. Problem is, he's still a Met.

David Wright 3B

Born: 12/20/82 Age: 34 Bats: R Throws: R Height: 6'0" Weight: 205 Entered Pro Ball: Round 1, 2001 Draft (#38 overall)

YEAR	TEAM	LVL	AGE	PA	R	2B	3B	HR	RBI	BB	K	SB	CS	AVG/OBP/SLG	TAv	VORP	BABIP	BRR	FRAA	WARP
2014	NYN	MLB	31	586	54	30	1	8	63	42	113	8	5	.269/.324/.374	.258	13.8	.325	-2.2	3B(133): -3.2	1.2
2015	SLU	A+	32	33	5	0	0	0	1	5	6	0	0	.321/.424/.321	.330	3.5	.409	0.2	3B(7): -2.1	0.2
2015	NYN	MLB	32	174	24	7	0	5	17	22	36	2	1	.289/.379/.434	.315	17.1	.351	2.5	3B(38): -4.0	1.4
2016	NYN	MLB	33	164	18	8	0	7	14	26	55	3	2	.226/.350/.438	.298	10.8	.320	-0.8	3B(36): -0.7	1.0
2017	NYN	MLB	34	260	35	12	1	7	28	28	53	5	2	.268/.348/.423	.278	12.6	.316	-0.3	3B -3	0.9
2018	NYN	MLB	35	129	16	6	0	4	15	14	27	2	1	.262/.344/.413	.283	5.7	.310	0.0	3B -1	0.5

Breakout: 0% Improve: 44% Collapse: 7% Attrition: 11% MLB: 98% *Comparables: Scott Rolen, Melvin Mora, Aramis Ramirez*

Could this be the end for "Captain America?" Wright returned from a career-threatening 2015 diagnosis of spinal stenosis only to suffer a season-ending and career-threatening herniated disc in his neck in 2016. Wright plans to give it another shot in 2017, but unless he's hiding some Super Soldier Serum, it's hard to see him as much more than a part-time player until the next serious injury comes. Wright will likely fall a bit short of the Hall of Fame trajectory he was on through age 30, but he's still had a hell of a career. When on the field, through it all, Wright somehow remained a legitimate threat at the plate. Defensively, injuries have robbed him of range and the ability to make a strong throw, and it's been tough to watch at times. Given his defense, health and the four years left on contract, Wright is the best argument this side of Kyle Schwarber for the National League to implement the designated hitter rule.

PITCHERS

Jerry Blevins LHP

Born: 9/6/83 Age: 33 Bats: L Throws: L Height: 6'6" Weight: 190 Entered Pro Ball: Round 17, 2004 Draft (#516 overall)

YEAR	TEAM	LVL	AGE	W	L	SV	G	GS	IP	H	HR	BB/9	K/9	K	GB%	BABIP	WHIP	ERA	FIP	DRA	VORP	WARP	cFIP	MPH
2014	WAS	MLB	30	2	3	0	64	0	57¹	48	3	3.6	10.4	66	41%	.306	1.24	4.87	2.74	3.28	7.7	0.9	92	93.0
2015	NYN	MLB	31	1	0	0	7	0	5	0	0	0.0	7.2	4	55%	.000	0.00	0.00	1.56	3.80	0.5	0.1	93	92.0
2016	NYN	MLB	32	4	2	2	73	0	42	36	4	3.2	11.1	52	47%	.302	1.21	2.79	3.09	2.96	9.4	1.0	82	91.5
2017	NYN	MLB	33	2	1	1	36	0	38¹	29	5	3.4	10.5	45	54%	.293	1.14	3.62	3.73	4.21	3.0	0.3	91	
2018	NYN	MLB	34	4	2	2	78	0	60²	48	8	3.4	10.0	68	54%	.288	1.17	3.83	4.11	4.46	4.7	0.5	98	

Breakout: 18%   Improve: 43%   Collapse: 31%   Attrition: 10%   MLB: 94%   *Comparables: Damaso Marte, Hideki Okajima, J.J. Putz*

Hello, Jerry. 2016 was surprisingly the first time in Blevins' long career that he was deployed as a strict LOOGY. We've regularly predicted in past annuals that he would drift to the role as his career progressed, as it's a natural fit for his middling fastball velocity and big loopy curve and he was finally shepherded in as the alpha southpaw by Terry Collins. Blevins posted a career-high strikeout rate and a career-low DRA, but in a bit of BABIP-driven small sample trivia, he was actually slightly worse against left-handed hitters than righties on the year. Now that he's a card-carrying member of the Effective Lefty Specialists of America, only health will stop him from pitching for another decade.

Jacob deGrom RHP

Born: 6/19/88 Age: 29 Bats: L Throws: R Height: 6'4" Weight: 180 Entered Pro Ball: Round 9, 2010 Draft (#272 overall)

YEAR	TEAM	LVL	AGE	W	L	SV	G	GS	IP	H	HR	BB/9	K/9	K	GB%	BABIP	WHIP	ERA	FIP	DRA	VORP	WARP	cFIP	MPH
2014	LVG	AAA	26	4	0	0	7	7	38¹	39	2	2.3	6.8	29	60%	.311	1.28	2.58	3.73	2.74	12.8	1.3	87	
2014	NYN	MLB	26	9	6	0	22	22	140¹	117	7	2.8	9.2	144	47%	.297	1.14	2.69	2.64	3.24	24.9	2.8	87	96.4
2015	NYN	MLB	27	14	8	0	30	30	191	149	16	1.8	9.7	205	48%	.271	0.98	2.54	2.73	3.23	39.2	4.2	81	97.7
2016	NYN	MLB	28	7	8	0	24	24	148	142	15	2.2	8.7	143	47%	.312	1.20	3.04	3.36	3.48	31.0	3.2	92	96.3
2017	NYN	MLB	29	12	10	0	30	30	180	157	20	2.8	9.4	189	45%	.291	1.18	3.51	3.55	3.87	26.2	2.7	88	
2018	NYN	MLB	30	12	10	0	32	32	210¹	167	23	3.1	10.3	241	45%	.302	1.14	3.37	3.61	3.91	35.0	3.6	86	

Breakout: 21%   Improve: 46%   Collapse: 24%   Attrition: 17%   MLB: 94%   *Comparables: Doug Fister, Collin McHugh, Jeff Niemann*

As good as deGrom's 2016 was on the surface, it's even better when you consider that he rushed back from a lat injury to start the season, and was in Cy Young contention with an ERA of 2.29 in mid-August. Three awful starts while trying to pitch through numbness and discomfort—caused by the ulnar nerve injury that would ultimately end his season—sullied the overall line. When healthy, his arsenal of four average-or-better pitches, combined with top-notch command, deceives hitters like few others in baseball can.

While deGrom was an incredibly late bloomer, even that has a sensible narrative supporting it: his "pitching age" has always been much younger than his actual age. He was a college shortstop, and only began his starting pitching career as a junior at Stetson. He showed enough promise in that short period to be a ninth-round draft pick, but missed most of his first two pro seasons with Tommy John surgery. By the time he really got going in the minors, he was the oddball combination of overaged and inexperienced for his levels, and thus became easy to overlook. The huge consolidations all came at once, and he's been an ace-level pitcher for nearly 500 innings now. Occam's razor suggests that deGrom is simply an ace.

Justin Dunn RHP

Born: 9/22/95 Age: 21 Bats: R Throws: R Height: 6'2" Weight: 185 Entered Pro Ball: Round 1, 2016 Draft (#19 overall)

YEAR	TEAM	LVL	AGE	W	L	SV	G	GS	IP	H	HR	BB/9	K/9	K	GB%	BABIP	WHIP	ERA	FIP	DRA	VORP	WARP	cFIP	MPH
2016	BRO	A-	20	1	1	0	11	8	30	25	1	3.0	10.5	35	46%	.320	1.17	1.50	2.87	2.89	7.6	0.8	90	
2017	NYN	MLB	21	2	3	0	14	7	34²	38	6	4.5	7.2	27	65%	.322	1.59	5.58	5.47	6.37	-3.6	-0.4	153	
2018	NYN	MLB	22	5	7	1	38	21	160²	148	26	4.1	8.7	155	65%	.301	1.37	4.76	5.16	5.43	0.6	0.1	131	

Breakout: 0%   Improve: 0%   Collapse: 0%   Attrition: 0%   MLB: 0%   *Comparables: T.J. McFarland, Vincent Velasquez, Adrian Sampson*

Shortly after the draft, a video went viral of Mets first-rounder Justin Dunn, his Boston College teammates, and his family in a Duffy's Sports Grill in Florida going absolutely crazy celebrating his selection. Was the slender righty thrilled because he got picked by a team well-suited to develop a pitcher often sitting in the mid-90s with a potentially wicked slider? Was the Long Island native thrilled to be drafted by his hometown team? Or was Dunn just looking forward to many more visits to Duffy's, the social center of life in Port St. Lucie, the spring training home of the Mets? (Unless you prefer The Vine and Barley for its superior drink selection.)

Jeurys Familia RHP

Born: 10/10/89 Age: 27 Bats: R Throws: R Height: 6'3" Weight: 240 Entered Pro Ball: International Free Agent, 2007

YEAR	TEAM	LVL	AGE	W	L	SV	G	GS	IP	H	HR	BB/9	K/9	K	GB%	BABIP	WHIP	ERA	FIP	DRA	VORP	WARP	cFIP	MPH
2014	NYN	MLB	24	2	5	5	76	0	77¹	59	3	3.7	8.5	73	59%	.264	1.18	2.21	3.04	3.08	12.1	1.3	92	98.6
2015	NYN	MLB	25	2	2	43	76	0	78	59	6	2.2	9.9	86	61%	.272	1.00	1.85	2.76	2.47	19.4	2.1	76	100.1
2016	NYN	MLB	26	3	4	51	78	0	77²	63	1	3.6	9.7	84	66%	.304	1.21	2.55	2.43	3.60	11.8	1.2	80	98.8
2017	NYN	MLB	27	2	2	27	38	0	39²	36	4	3.4	9.6	42	49%	.298	1.28	3.37	3.65	3.86	4.7	0.5	82	
2018	NYN	MLB	28	3	1	37	57	0	60¹	46	6	3.4	10.6	71	49%	.300	1.14	3.31	3.54	3.85	8.5	0.9	83	

Breakout: 34%   Improve: 59%   Collapse: 16%   Attrition: 11%   MLB: 92%   *Comparables: Bryan Shaw, Renyel Pinto, Alexi Ogando*

On October 5th, New York City Council Speaker Melissa Mark-Viverito announced a campaign against domestic violence in partnership with the National Coalition Against Domestic Violence. Most of the major New York sports teams joined the campaign. The Mets' representative, closer Jeurys Familia, filmed a public service announcement declaring he was "not a fan of domestic violence." It debuted before the Wild Card Game that night, a few hours before Familia gave up a season-ending home run to Conor

Gillaspie. As it turns out, that home run was not nearly the most disappointing event of 2016 for the Mets' closer, who led the league in saves a year after bursting onto the scene as one of the most dominant and awe-inspiring relievers in the game. On October 31, Jeurys Familia was arrested in Fort Lee, New Jersey on suspicion of domestic violence. He pled not guilty, and Major League Baseball is still investigating the incident.

Robert Gsellman   RHP

Born: 7/18/93   Age: 23   Bats: R   Throws: R   Height: 6'4"   Weight: 205   Entered Pro Ball: Round 13, 2011 Draft (#402 overall)

YEAR	TEAM	LVL	AGE	W	L	SV	G	GS	IP	H	HR	BB/9	K/9	K	GB%	BABIP	WHIP	ERA	FIP	DRA	VORP	WARP	cFIP	MPH
2014	SAV	A	20	10	6	0	20	20	116¹	122	2	2.6	7.1	92	56%	.331	1.34	2.55	3.34	4.41	13.3	1.4	101	
2015	SLU	A+	21	6	0	0	8	8	51	37	1	1.9	6.5	37	61%	.250	0.94	1.76	2.79	3.84	7.0	0.8	96	
2015	BIN	AA	21	7	7	0	16	16	92¹	89	4	2.5	4.8	49	54%	.277	1.25	3.51	3.65	4.62	4.9	0.5	105	
2016	BIN	AA	22	3	4	0	11	11	66¹	57	2	2.0	6.5	48	57%	.282	1.09	2.71	3.25	3.27	13.4	1.5	92	
2016	LVG	AAA	22	1	5	0	9	9	48²	56	8	3.0	7.4	40	55%	.318	1.48	5.73	5.20	4.31	5.6	0.6	90	
2016	NYN	MLB	22	4	2	0	8	7	44²	42	1	3.0	8.5	42	57%	.325	1.28	2.42	2.67	4.13	6.0	0.6	93	95.9
2017	NYN	MLB	23	9	9	0	26	26	148	146	16	3.2	6.7	111	45%	.289	1.33	4.22	4.27	4.62	9.2	0.9	100	
2018	NYN	MLB	24	9	9	0	27	27	159²	124	17	4.5	9.6	171	45%	.290	1.27	3.94	4.23	4.56	16.7	1.7	104	

Breakout: 15%   Improve: 28%   Collapse: 25%   Attrition: 36%   MLB: 65%   Comparables: Aaron Poreda, Archie Bradley, Gio Gonzalez

As a skinny, moderately-heralded righty with great flow, Gsellman received constant Jacob deGrom comps coming up through the Mets system. These comps weren't fair to Gsellman, because precious few prospects have the jump in velocity, stuff and command that deGrom had. It was just a visual resemblance...right? Well, in 2016, Gsellman's fastball velocity jumped more than a couple ticks, he added a vicious hard slider that immediately became his best secondary offering and his command tightened. He still doesn't possess the elite fastball command or change, but "slightly worse than Jacob deGrom" is still pushing into the top-of-the-rotation pitcher discussion. Gsellman has to prove he can hold up under a full season's workload in the rotation, but the Mets might have developed *another* good one here.

Matt Harvey   RHP

Born: 3/27/89   Age: 28   Bats: R   Throws: R   Height: 6'4"   Weight: 215   Entered Pro Ball: Round 1, 2010 Draft (#7 overall)

YEAR	TEAM	LVL	AGE	W	L	SV	G	GS	IP	H	HR	BB/9	K/9	K	GB%	BABIP	WHIP	ERA	FIP	DRA	VORP	WARP	cFIP	MPH
2015	NYN	MLB	26	13	8	0	29	29	189¹	156	18	1.8	8.9	188	49%	.273	1.02	2.71	3.08	3.13	41.0	4.4	86	98.8
2016	NYN	MLB	27	4	10	0	17	17	92²	111	8	2.4	7.4	76	44%	.353	1.47	4.86	3.51	4.96	4.1	0.4	104	97.4
2017	NYN	MLB	28	10	9	0	26	26	156	142	19	2.6	8.9	154	44%	.291	1.20	3.74	3.74	4.14	18.0	1.9	96	
2018	NYN	MLB	29	11	10	0	31	31	195	168	24	2.7	9.3	201	44%	.304	1.16	3.64	3.90	4.24	26.6	2.7	96	

Breakout: 20%   Improve: 47%   Collapse: 30%   Attrition: 11%   MLB: 92%   Comparables: Alex Cobb, Clay Buchholz, Ricky Romero

Well, *The Dark Knight Rises* was a pretty lousy movie by the end. Gotham's former savior was brutal for half the season, and all involved claimed he was healthy, which was alarming because a healthy Matt Harvey should never be that bad. It was almost a relief to find out there was an underlying medical diagnosis—except the diagnosis turned out to be thoracic outlet syndrome, a nerve and blood vessel issue in the chest and shoulder that has been the bane of many good pitchers' existence.

Research by Craig Edwards of FanGraphs and Carl Triano of Beyond the Box Score shows that the range of outcomes for pitchers suffering from thoracic outlet syndrome varies wildly. Some pitchers, like Kenny Rogers and Aaron Cook, have returned healthy and nearly as effective as before, while others never pitched well again, like Chris Carpenter. Overall, the group was a bit worse than their career marks on ERA- and FIP- upon returning, and many had their careers ultimately shortened. But no pitcher has ever had thoracic outlet syndrome as an ace in his twenties, like Harvey. We'll start finding out in spring training whether Harvey can return to being Christian Bale in 2017, as the Mets certainly need him to be more than Ben Affleck.

Jim Henderson   RHP

Born: 10/21/82   Age: 34   Bats: L   Throws: R   Height: 6'5"   Weight: 220   Entered Pro Ball: Round 26, 2003 Draft (#777 overall)

YEAR	TEAM	LVL	AGE	W	L	SV	G	GS	IP	H	HR	BB/9	K/9	K	GB%	BABIP	WHIP	ERA	FIP	DRA	VORP	WARP	cFIP	MPH
2014	MIL	MLB	31	2	1	0	14	0	11¹	14	3	3.2	13.5	17	38%	.423	1.59	7.15	4.60	2.85	2.1	0.2	90	96.5
2015	CSP	AAA	32	1	1	2	29	1	29²	31	4	5.2	7.6	25	34%	.314	1.62	4.55	5.39	6.76	-6.0	-0.6	119	
2016	NYN	MLB	33	2	2	0	44	0	35	34	7	3.6	10.3	40	29%	.293	1.37	4.11	4.87	5.02	-0.2	0.0	111	96.3
2017	NYN	MLB	34	2	1	1	40	0	42²	41	7	3.8	8.9	42	45%	.311	1.39	4.81	4.70	5.63	-2.2	-0.2	130	
2018	NYN	MLB	35	2	1	1	35	0	34¹	33	7	4.3	9.3	36	45%	.311	1.44	5.07	5.48	5.94	-3.1	-0.3	138	

Breakout: 17%   Improve: 27%   Collapse: 15%   Attrition: 6%   MLB: 58%   Comparables: Justin Miller, Jason Bulger, Tim Byrdak

One of the more fascinating developments over the last decade or two has been the increasing prevalence of "free talent" quality relief options who throw in the mid-90s with a good slider. Henderson has now been that "95-and-a-slider" guy coming out of nowhere twice, rising out of Milwaukee's system in 2012 to become an effective closer by 2013, and rising from minor-league free agent to dominant setup man in April with the 2016 Mets. Unfortunately, the chronic shoulder problems that caused his fall from grace in 2014-15 returned when the Mets started leaning on Henderson to pitch multiple innings and on back-to-back days. He looked better again in September though, and is still young enough to go for the "95-and-a-slider" hat trick.

Seth Lugo   RHP

Born: 11/17/89   Age: 27   Bats: R   Throws: R   Height: 6'4"   Weight: 225   Entered Pro Ball: Round 34, 2011 Draft (#1032 overall)

YEAR	TEAM	LVL	AGE	W	L	SV	G	GS	IP	H	HR	BB/9	K/9	K	GB%	BABIP	WHIP	ERA	FIP	DRA	VORP	WARP	cFIP	MPH
2015	BIN	AA	25	6	5	0	19	19	109	108	8	2.5	8	97	44%	.307	1.27	3.80	3.41	3.35	21.1	2.3	86	
2015	LVG	AAA	25	2	2	0	5	5	27	27	3	1.7	10	30	43%	.324	1.19	4.00	3.60	1.75	10.7	1.1	79	
2016	LVG	AAA	26	3	4	0	21	14	73¹	103	10	2.5	7.6	62	46%	.375	1.68	6.50	4.66	2.36	23.9	2.5	93	
2016	NYN	MLB	26	5	2	0	17	8	64	49	7	3.0	6.3	45	46%	.230	1.09	2.67	4.37	5.06	1.4	0.1	114	95.9
2017	*NYN*	*MLB*	*27*	*4*	*4*	*0*	*34*	*6*	*64*	*65*	*8*	*3.4*	*7.1*	*51*	*48%*	*.296*	*1.40*	*4.44*	*4.47*	*4.75*	*2.2*	*0.2*	*100*	
2018	*NYN*	*MLB*	*28*	*7*	*5*	*0*	*70*	*12*	*131²*	*112*	*17*	*4.1*	*9.4*	*137*	*48%*	*.301*	*1.31*	*4.18*	*4.49*	*4.82*	*7.5*	*0.8*	*111*	

Breakout: 18%   Improve: 37%   Collapse: 16%   Attrition: 20%   MLB: 61%   Comparables: *Pat Misch, Mike Bolsinger, Tyler Cloyd*

Well, that came so out of nowhere that he didn't even claim a Vogelsong Award for being one of the best players missed in last year's annual—he lost the September nod to rotation-mate Robert Gsellman. Lugo came up the chain as an unheralded, overaged swingman reliant on his curveball. The Mets looked past an unsightly Triple-A ERA to call him up a few times for low-leverage relief work, mostly because he was a warm body on the 40-man. Lugo showed enough to stay in the major-league picture, and started making some waves with his curve's outrageous spin rate. He made a solid spot start for Steven Matz on one day of rest in mid-August, and he would never give the rotation spot back. Ultimately, Lugo made eight starts, pitching at least five innings and allowing three or fewer runs each time out. He's obviously not quite *that* good and he might still profile best in the bullpen, but with Colon departing and question marks around the health of Harvey and Wheeler, the Mets will likely need him to keep pitching over his head in 2017.

Steven Matz   LHP

Born: 5/29/91   Age: 26   Bats: R   Throws: L   Height: 6'2"   Weight: 200   Entered Pro Ball: Round 2, 2009 Draft (#72 overall)

YEAR	TEAM	LVL	AGE	W	L	SV	G	GS	IP	H	HR	BB/9	K/9	K	GB%	BABIP	WHIP	ERA	FIP	DRA	VORP	WARP	cFIP	MPH
2014	SLU	A+	23	4	4	0	12	12	69¹	66	0	2.7	8.0	62	59%	.328	1.25	2.21	2.73	3.43	16.7	1.7	94	
2014	BIN	AA	23	6	5	0	12	12	71¹	66	3	1.8	8.7	69	48%	.317	1.12	2.27	2.64	1.48	29.7	3.2	73	
2015	LVG	AAA	24	7	4	0	15	14	90¹	69	6	3.1	9.4	94	57%	.278	1.11	2.19	3.44	0.95	43.4	4.4	58	
2015	BIN	AA	24	1	0	0	2	2	11¹	2	0	1.6	7.9	10	56%	.080	0.35	0.00	2.03	1.98	3.9	0.4	82	
2015	NYN	MLB	24	4	0	0	6	6	35²	34	4	2.5	8.6	34	49%	.300	1.23	2.27	3.64	3.27	7.2	0.8	92	96.6
2016	NYN	MLB	25	9	8	0	22	22	132¹	129	14	2.1	8.8	129	54%	.312	1.21	3.40	3.43	3.41	28.6	3.0	86	96.0
2017	*NYN*	*MLB*	*26*	*9*	*7*	*0*	*23*	*23*	*131*	*117*	*12*	*2.8*	*8.8*	*128*	*40%*	*.292*	*1.19*	*3.47*	*3.43*	*3.84*	*19.5*	*2.0*	*86*	
2018	*NYN*	*MLB*	*27*	*12*	*10*	*0*	*32*	*32*	*210¹*	*156*	*19*	*3.5*	*10.7*	*249*	*40%*	*.297*	*1.13*	*3.21*	*3.43*	*3.73*	*36.9*	*3.8*	*82*	

Breakout: 30%   Improve: 60%   Collapse: 20%   Attrition: 15%   MLB: 94%   Comparables: *Lance Lynn, Kyle Hendricks, Carlos Carrasco*

Matz was hot out of the gate in 2016, an early contender for Rookie of the Year before Corey Seager decided there were no other plausible contenders. He reported an elbow problem after a start on May 9, which turned out to be a large bone spur that wasn't publicly revealed for another month and a half, as the Mets danced around the phrase "structural damage." Jon Heyman of FanRag reported around that time that the Mets convinced Matz to continue pitching through pain, and he did with decreasing effectiveness until his shoulder joined the chorus of barking in August. After another month of unsuccessfully trying to get him back on the mound, the Mets finally gave in and shut Matz down at the end of September. Surgery to remove the bone spur followed a few days later.

You've probably noticed by now that a lot of these comments follow the same formula: When healthy, such-and-such Met is good/great, but in 2016, that Met wasn't healthy much/at all and the Mets pushed the situation too far. Honestly, this isn't the first Annual in which that's been the case, and you might think at some point, the Mets would consider changes to their medical and training staff. Instead, trainer Ray Ramirez will get booed by the diehards at his umpteenth consecutive Opening Day.

Rafael Montero   RHP

Born: 10/17/90   Age: 26   Bats: R   Throws: R   Height: 6'0"   Weight: 185   Entered Pro Ball: International Free Agent, 2011

YEAR	TEAM	LVL	AGE	W	L	SV	G	GS	IP	H	HR	BB/9	K/9	K	GB%	BABIP	WHIP	ERA	FIP	DRA	VORP	WARP	cFIP	MPH
2014	LVG	AAA	23	6	4	0	16	16	80	69	4	3.8	9.0	80	44%	.297	1.29	3.60	3.66	2.10	32.4	3.2	90	
2014	NYN	MLB	23	1	3	0	10	8	44¹	44	8	4.7	8.5	42	36%	.298	1.51	4.06	5.11	5.60	-3.8	-0.4	118	94.8
2015	NYN	MLB	24	0	1	0	5	1	10	9	0	4.5	11.7	13	50%	.321	1.40	4.50	2.06	3.46	1.6	0.2	92	95.0
2016	LVG	AAA	25	4	6	0	16	16	80	111	12	4.5	7.7	68	46%	.375	1.89	7.20	5.47	4.84	4.5	0.5	102	
2016	BIN	AA	25	4	3	0	9	9	49	35	4	3.5	7.3	40	51%	.233	1.10	2.20	4.19	3.83	6.9	0.7	100	
2016	NYN	MLB	25	0	1	0	9	3	19	23	4	7.6	9.5	20	37%	.358	2.05	8.05	6.34	5.51	-0.7	-0.1	118	95.0
2017	*NYN*	*MLB*	*26*	*2*	*2*	*0*	*26*	*3*	*39*	*38*	*4*	*4.2*	*7.6*	*34*	*48%*	*.288*	*1.39*	*4.42*	*4.36*	*4.72*	*1.3*	*0.1*	*100*	
2018	*NYN*	*MLB*	*27*	*2*	*2*	*0*	*32*	*3*	*49*	*39*	*6*	*5.0*	*10.0*	*54*	*48%*	*.293*	*1.36*	*4.33*	*4.65*	*5.00*	*1.4*	*0.1*	*114*	

Breakout: 15%   Improve: 33%   Collapse: 29%   Attrition: 38%   MLB: 74%   Comparables: *Mike Montgomery, Alex Colome, Scott Lewis*

Montero's nickname might as well be "The Exception," because he's the one recent Mets pitching prospect of note who has been a straight-up bust. Perhaps instead we should go with "Dune," because his outings are about as unwatchable and nonsensical as the David Lynch film adaptation. Once upon a time, Montero's strength was his preternatural command, but that's totally vanished over the last few years. Now usually unable or unwilling to throw strikes, all that's left are the memories. If he doesn't build around his raw velocity and occasionally useful change, this may well be the last time you read about him in the Annual.

Jon Niese   LHP

Born: 10/27/86 Age: 30 Bats: L Throws: L Height: 6'3" Weight: 215 Entered Pro Ball: Round 7, 2005 Draft (#209 overall)

YEAR	TEAM	LVL	AGE	W	L	SV	G	GS	IP	H	HR	BB/9	K/9	K	GB%	BABIP	WHIP	ERA	FIP	DRA	VORP	WARP	cFIP	MPH
2014	NYN	MLB	27	9	11	0	30	30	187²	193	17	2.2	6.6	138	50%	.304	1.27	3.40	3.64	4.36	10.0	1.1	102	91.3
2015	NYN	MLB	28	9	10	0	33	29	176²	192	20	2.8	5.8	113	57%	.300	1.40	4.13	4.44	4.67	7.8	0.8	110	91.8
2016	PIT	MLB	29	8	6	0	23	18	110	132	21	3.1	6.2	76	55%	.314	1.55	4.91	5.40	5.24	0.9	0.1	109	91.8
2016	NYN	MLB	29	0	1	0	6	2	11	13	4	7.4	9.8	12	35%	.300	2.00	11.45	8.19	5.21	0.1	0.0	110	91.4
2017	NYN	MLB	30	7	7	0	20	20	115¹	118	17	3.1	7.4	95	51%	.317	1.36	4.61	4.55	5.37	2.5	0.3	126	
2018	NYN	MLB	31	9	11	0	29	29	175³	180	27	3.0	7.4	145	51%	.318	1.36	4.55	4.90	5.30	4.9	0.5	125	

Breakout: 21%   Improve: 51%   Collapse: 22%   Attrition: 17%   MLB: 91%   Comparables: Joe Blanton, Paul Maholm, Nate Robertson

Just when you thought the Mets were free of Jon Niese, they dealt for him at the trade deadline. Like many back-end starter types, Niese's performance is cursed by his "ability" to provide fairly consistent innings. For his career, batters have hit just .260/.319/.369 against Niese the first time through the order, and .300/.360/.469 against him third time around. As baseball has started to recognize that pitchers deteriorate more during games than we'd previously thought, some teams have gotten more out of pitchers like Niese in relief or more lightly-structured starting roles. Indeed, the Mets used Niese effectively as a reliever in the 2015 playoffs and had planned to do so upon reacquiring him in 2016, a plan quickly stymied by injuries to seemingly every other starter, and then to Niese himself.

Cameron Planck   RHP

Born: 3/5/98 Age: 19 Bats: R Throws: R Height: 6'3" Weight: 210 Entered Pro Ball: Round 11, 2016 Draft (#340 overall)

In the zero-sum game of draft pools, one draft pick's misfortune is often another draft pick's windfall. The Kentucky prep pitcher was a target of the Mets early in the 2016 draft, tantalizing the team with his low-to-mid-90s fastball, but Planck wouldn't agree to a pre-draft deal. The Mets took him anyway in the 11th round. After Anthony Kay's bonus was slashed, opening up more money, the Mets met Planck's number, a cool million and one dollars. He's raw and a long, long way from the majors, but worth keeping tabs on.

Addison Reed   RHP

Born: 12/27/88 Age: 28 Bats: L Throws: R Height: 6'4" Weight: 230 Entered Pro Ball: Round 3, 2010 Draft (#95 overall)

YEAR	TEAM	LVL	AGE	W	L	SV	G	GS	IP	H	HR	BB/9	K/9	K	GB%	BABIP	WHIP	ERA	FIP	DRA	VORP	WARP	cFIP	MPH
2014	ARI	MLB	25	1	7	32	62	0	59¹	57	11	2.3	10.5	69	28%	.295	1.21	4.25	4.00	3.85	4.2	0.5	102	95.0
2015	RNO	AAA	26	1	1	5	11	0	10¹	8	1	4.4	9.6	11	48%	.250	1.26	1.74	4.18	3.60	1.5	0.2	97	
2015	ARI	MLB	26	2	2	3	38	0	40²	47	2	3.1	7.5	34	41%	.344	1.50	4.20	3.16	4.23	2.2	0.2	99	94.8
2015	NYN	MLB	26	1	1	1	17	0	15¹	11	1	2.9	10.0	17	50%	.270	1.04	1.17	2.77	4.24	0.8	0.1	99	95.0
2016	NYN	MLB	27	4	2	1	80	0	77²	60	4	1.5	10.5	91	42%	.286	0.94	1.97	2.01	2.31	22.9	2.4	77	94.8
2017	NYN	MLB	28	3	2	3	52	0	54	51	9	2.8	9.9	60	57%	.292	1.24	4.16	4.16	4.54	2.3	0.2	100	
2018	NYN	MLB	29	2	1	2	45	0	47²	41	8	2.6	9.7	52	57%	.292	1.15	4.00	4.30	4.68	2.4	0.2	105	

Breakout: 23%   Improve: 47%   Collapse: 25%   Attrition: 9%   MLB: 88%   Comparables: Drew Storen, Jordan Walden, Hector Rondon

Mets pitching coach Dan Warthen has worked some miracles during his time in Flushing, but none may be bigger than turning Addison Reed into a top reliever. Previously a wildly-overrated closer for the White Sox and Diamondbacks, the Mets picked up Reed as a postseason non-tender candidate in a minor August 2015 waiver trade after falling out of favor in Arizona. Right before the trade, he made a mechanical adjustment to his leg kick, and upon arriving in Queens he was reborn with an unhittable slider and elite fastball command. An elevated release point in 2016 caused batters to have even more trouble distinguishing his pitches and kept his slider out of the air—his 60 percent groundball rate on the pitch was easily a career-high, and not a single one left the yard. Reed himself is proof that relievers can be highly volatile, but nothing about this seems unsustainable.

Hansel Robles   RHP

Born: 8/13/90 Age: 26 Bats: R Throws: R Height: 5'11" Weight: 185 Entered Pro Ball: International Free Agent, 2008

YEAR	TEAM	LVL	AGE	W	L	SV	G	GS	IP	H	HR	BB/9	K/9	K	GB%	BABIP	WHIP	ERA	FIP	DRA	VORP	WARP	cFIP	MPH
2014	BIN	AA	23	7	6	0	30	18	110²	107	10	3.5	8.6	106	38%	.312	1.36	4.31	3.97	3.96	14.7	1.6	103	
2015	NYN	MLB	24	4	3	0	57	0	54	37	8	3.0	10.2	61	34%	.227	1.02	3.67	3.94	4.18	3.2	0.3	101	98.7
2016	NYN	MLB	25	6	4	1	68	0	77²	69	7	4.2	9.8	85	31%	.307	1.35	3.48	3.60	5.02	-0.4	0.0	111	98.8
2017	NYN	MLB	26	3	2	10	52	0	54	48	6	4.0	9.3	57	43%	.289	1.32	4.02	3.94	4.41	3.1	0.3	98	
2018	NYN	MLB	27	3	1	6	57	0	61	45	7	4.4	10.9	74	43%	.289	1.23	3.79	4.07	4.42	4.8	0.5	98	

Breakout: 26%   Improve: 47%   Collapse: 24%   Attrition: 27%   MLB: 91%   Comparables: Dan Straily, Tyler Clippard, James McDonald

The extra velocity Robles found a few years ago got him to the majors, but two years in, his future role is still unclear. Oddly, he's at his best when used in a true long-man role, and forced to throw (and locate) his entire fastball/slider/change mix instead of just trying to blow everyone away with ol' number one. This was most apparent when forced into an impressive quasi-start behind an injured Bartolo Colon in June. However, despite significant need down the stretch and a long, sometimes successful history starting in the minors, the Mets never went back to Robles in a starting role. In the bullpen, the stuff often makes you think he is destined for high-leverage work, but the command rarely does.

Fernando Salas   RHP

Born: 5/30/85   Age: 32   Bats: R   Throws: R   Height: 6'2"   Weight: 200   Entered Pro Ball: International Free Agent, 2007

YEAR	TEAM	LVL	AGE	W	L	SV	G	GS	IP	H	HR	BB/9	K/9	K	GB%	BABIP	WHIP	ERA	FIP	DRA	VORP	WARP	cFIP	MPH
2014	ANA	MLB	29	5	0	0	57	0	58²	50	5	2.1	9.4	61	32%	.285	1.09	3.38	2.96	4.03	2.9	0.3	99	93.9
2015	ANA	MLB	30	5	2	0	72	0	63²	61	8	1.7	10.5	74	38%	.308	1.15	4.24	3.12	3.22	10.5	1.1	87	93.6
2016	ANA	MLB	31	3	6	6	58	0	56¹	52	9	3.0	7.2	45	42%	.272	1.26	4.47	4.60	4.08	5.6	0.6	105	93.8
2016	NYN	MLB	31	0	1	0	17	0	17¹	11	3	0.0	9.9	19	30%	.200	0.63	2.08	3.24	3.97	1.9	0.2	105	93.6
2017	*NYN*	*MLB*	*32*	*3*	*1*	*2*	*59*	*0*	*62²*	*55*	*9*	*2.8*	*9.3*	*65*	*43%*	*.301*	*1.19*	*3.93*	*3.98*	*4.57*	*3.7*	*0.4*	*102*	
2018	*NYN*	*MLB*	*33*	*2*	*1*	*1*	*34*	*0*	*32²*	*28*	*5*	*2.8*	*9.2*	*33*	*43%*	*.293*	*1.18*	*4.01*	*4.31*	*4.66*	*1.7*	*0.2*	*105*	

Breakout: 20%   Improve: 34%   Collapse: 34%   Attrition: 11%   MLB: 81%   *Comparables: Tony Sipp, Darren O'Day, Frank Francisco*

As bullpens have become increasingly specialized over the past few years, an entirely new role has emerged from what used to be the generic blob of middle relief: The Seventh Inning Guy. The Seventh Inning Guy role is an extension of The Eighth Inning Guy, pitching the seventh inning when eligible for a hold, plus the occasional eighth or ninth in non-save scenarios, minus the occasional obvious LOOGY situations. It's a great role for Salas, an adequate-to-good reliever who gets lefties out just as well as righties, but gives up too many homers to pitch in your highest-leverage situations. The journeyman phase of his career—where he ends up doing this on a new team every year or two—awaits.

Josh Smoker   LHP

Born: 11/26/88   Age: 28   Bats: L   Throws: L   Height: 6'2"   Weight: 250   Entered Pro Ball: Round 1, 2007 Draft (#31 overall)

YEAR	TEAM	LVL	AGE	W	L	SV	G	GS	IP	H	HR	BB/9	K/9	K	GB%	BABIP	WHIP	ERA	FIP	DRA	VORP	WARP	cFIP	MPH
2015	SLU	A+	26	1	0	6	14	0	21¹	12	1	2.5	11.0	26	50%	.216	0.84	1.69	2.18	1.89	6.7	0.7	77	
2015	BIN	AA	26	1	0	0	21	0	21	16	0	4.7	11.1	26	50%	.308	1.29	3.00	2.36	3.53	2.8	0.3	91	
2016	LVG	AAA	27	3	2	3	52	0	57	66	5	2.8	12.8	81	46%	.409	1.47	4.11	2.97	0.97	25.3	2.6	62	
2016	NYN	MLB	27	3	0	0	20	0	15¹	16	4	2.3	14.7	25	31%	.387	1.30	4.70	4.30	2.94	3.5	0.4	84	98.1
2017	*NYN*	*MLB*	*28*	*3*	*2*	*0*	*52*	*0*	*54*	*51*	*6*	*3.3*	*10.0*	*61*	*46%*	*.309*	*1.32*	*3.53*	*3.57*	*3.97*	*5.7*	*0.6*	*89*	
2018	*NYN*	*MLB*	*29*	*3*	*1*	*0*	*59*	*0*	*62²*	*49*	*7*	*3.9*	*11.4*	*80*	*46%*	*.315*	*1.21*	*3.35*	*3.58*	*3.86*	*8.8*	*0.9*	*84*	

Breakout: 28%   Improve: 41%   Collapse: 11%   Attrition: 26%   MLB: 61%   *Comparables: Henry Owens, Zac Rosscup, Mike Zagurski*

A 2009 first-round pick by the Nationals, Smoker has had a long and winding road to the big leagues that is equal parts perseverance and blind luck. Shoulder injuries of increasing severity robbed him of velocity and ultimately his prospectdom with Washington, and Smoker was out of organized baseball by the end of the 2013 season. He caught on as a reliever with the Rockford Aviators of the independent Frontier League after an open tryout in 2014, but wasn't good enough there to catch any eyes. Through happenstance, Smoker's usual bullpen catcher was unavailable one day early in 2015, so an independent league coach named Paul Fletcher filled in. Fletcher also happened to be doing bird dog scout work for the Mets on the side, and tipped the organization off that he had found a lefty throwing in the mid-90s. Smoker, once again possessing an electric fastball along with a quality splitter and slider, got a tryout and was signed shortly thereafter. He opened the 2015 season as a 26-year-old reliever in the the Sally League. By the end of 2015, he'd conquered Double-A and made it onto the 40-man roster. By the end of 2016, he was averaging 96 on that fastball and his strikeout rate sat between Andrew Miller's and Craig Kimbrel's. That's a long way from Rockford.

Noah Syndergaard   RHP

Born: 8/29/92   Age: 24   Bats: L   Throws: R   Height: 6'6"   Weight: 240   Entered Pro Ball: Round 1, 2010 Draft (#38 overall)

YEAR	TEAM	LVL	AGE	W	L	SV	G	GS	IP	H	HR	BB/9	K/9	K	GB%	BABIP	WHIP	ERA	FIP	DRA	VORP	WARP	cFIP	MPH
2014	LVG	AAA	21	9	7	0	26	26	133	154	11	2.9	9.8	145	47%	.378	1.48	4.60	3.70	1.91	56.7	5.7	76	
2015	LVG	AAA	22	3	0	0	5	5	29²	20	2	2.4	10.3	34	52%	.261	0.94	1.82	2.99	1.65	12.0	1.2	76	
2015	NYN	MLB	22	9	7	0	24	24	150	126	19	1.9	10.0	166	48%	.279	1.05	3.24	3.28	2.98	35.0	3.7	80	99.5
2016	NYN	MLB	23	14	9	0	31	30	183²	168	11	2.1	10.7	218	52%	.334	1.15	2.60	2.33	2.71	54.0	5.6	70	100.5
2017	*NYN*	*MLB*	*24*	*12*	*9*	*0*	*29*	*29*	*182²*	*156*	*17*	*2.6*	*10.4*	*211*	*41%*	*.300*	*1.15*	*3.04*	*3.03*	*3.37*	*36.7*	*3.8*	*72*	
2018	*NYN*	*MLB*	*25*	*13*	*10*	*0*	*32*	*32*	*206²*	*156*	*20*	*3.0*	*11.5*	*265*	*41%*	*.312*	*1.09*	*2.91*	*3.11*	*3.37*	*48.0*	*5.0*	*71*	

Breakout: 32%   Improve: 62%   Collapse: 15%   Attrition: 16%   MLB: 95%   *Comparables: Marcus Stroman, Carlos Martinez, Patrick Corbin*

The John Smoltz to Madison Bumgarner's Jack Morris in the epic National League Wild Card Game, "Thor" already seems like a long-established ace of aces. But 2016 was actually his first full major-league season, and he's clearly still developing new super powers. For example, in spring training, Syndergaard concentrated on refining a hard slider that he'd occasionally thrown with flashes of brilliance in the latter parts of 2015. By the time the regular season came around, that new slider was one of the most devastating pitches in baseball, sitting in the low-90s and touching 95. The only restrictions on how good Syndergaard can be are those of the human body, because he's doing things with a baseball that nobody else has ever done.

Thomas Szapucki   LHP

Born: 6/12/96   Age: 21   Bats: R   Throws: L   Height: 6'2"   Weight: 205   Entered Pro Ball: Round 5, 2015 Draft (#149 overall)

YEAR	TEAM	LVL	AGE	W	L	SV	G	GS	IP	H	HR	BB/9	K/9	K	GB%	BABIP	WHIP	ERA	FIP	DRA	VORP	WARP	cFIP	MPH
2016	BRO	A-	20	2	2	0	4	4	23	10	0	4.3	15.3	39	46%	.256	0.91	2.35	1.58	1.27	10.1	1.1	74	
2017	*NYN*	*MLB*	*21*	*2*	*2*	*0*	*6*	*6*	*35²*	*32*	*4*	*5.0*	*9.5*	*38*	*48%*	*.322*	*1.46*	*4.44*	*4.31*	*5.05*	*2.0*	*0.2*	*119*	
2018	*NYN*	*MLB*	*22*	*5*	*6*	*0*	*16*	*16*	*94²*	*76*	*11*	*4.9*	*10.5*	*110*	*48%*	*.307*	*1.34*	*4.00*	*4.31*	*4.55*	*10.1*	*1.0*	*107*	

Breakout: 2%   Improve: 2%   Collapse: 0%   Attrition: 1%   MLB: 3%   *Comparables: Carl Edwards Jr, Wilking Rodriguez, Nick Tropeano*

Every year a few lower-minors pitching prospects of little note bust out into top-101 arms out of nowhere. This year, the Mets won the lottery with Szapucki. He entered 2016 as an indistinguishable fifth-round prep arm with minimal separation from the plethora of six-figure bonus prep arms dotting the low-minors. He showed up in the Appalachian League in the summer, mowing hitters down with a very lively fastball (now suddenly touching 97), an advanced curveball and an interesting change. This is the type of arsenal that will get you noticed post-haste, especially when combined with the obscene video game stats Szapucki compiled at Kingsport and Brooklyn. He's now firmly entrenched as one of the game's best left-handed pitching prospects.

Zack Wheeler RHP

Born: 5/30/90   Age: 27   Bats: L   Throws: R   Height: 6'4"   Weight: 195   Entered Pro Ball: Round 1, 2009 Draft (#6 overall)

YEAR	TEAM	LVL	AGE	W	L	SV	G	GS	IP	H	HR	BB/9	K/9	K	GB%	BABIP	WHIP	ERA	FIP	DRA	VORP	WARP	cFIP	MPH
2014	NYN	MLB	24	11	11	0	32	32	185¹	167	14	3.8	9.1	187	55%	.304	1.33	3.54	3.52	3.32	31.3	3.5	95	97.9
2017	NYN	MLB	27	6	6	0	41	13	98²	86	10	4.2	9.4	103	62%	.289	1.32	3.98	3.95	4.35	8.2	0.8	100	
2018	NYN	MLB	28	7	5	0	51	15	125²	92	12	4.5	10.8	151	62%	.294	1.23	3.59	3.86	4.15	16.3	1.7	93	

Breakout: 19%   Improve: 42%   Collapse: 24%   Attrition: 9%   MLB: 87%   *Comparables: Edinson Volquez, Wade Davis, Garrett Richards*

Wheeler's 2016 is a reminder that, for as routine as we consider Tommy John surgery to be now, it's not routine at all. The Mets originally set him up to return around July 1, over fifteen months out from his surgery, but his rehab assignment was delayed for several months due to nerve complications in his surgically-repaired elbow. He pitched one inning on August 6 for High-A Port St. Lucie, and then came down with another complication, this time with his flexor muscle. He was quietly shut down for the season about a month later. He'll try again in the spring, but it's impossible to say whether Wheeler will look anything like the top-of-the-rotation starter we last saw in the second half of 2014.

Gabriel Ynoa RHP

Born: 5/26/93   Age: 24   Bats: R   Throws: R   Height: 6'2"   Weight: 205   Entered Pro Ball: International Free Agent, 2009

YEAR	TEAM	LVL	AGE	W	L	SV	G	GS	IP	H	HR	BB/9	K/9	K	GB%	BABIP	WHIP	ERA	FIP	DRA	VORP	WARP	cFIP	MPH
2014	SLU	A+	21	8	2	0	14	14	82	95	7	1.4	7.0	64	44%	.330	1.32	3.95	3.45	2.43	28.8	2.9	83	
2014	BIN	AA	21	3	2	0	11	11	66¹	74	9	1.6	5.7	42	40%	.304	1.30	4.21	4.53	6.38	-8.5	-0.9	107	
2015	BIN	AA	22	9	9	0	25	24	152¹	157	14	1.8	4.8	82	47%	.283	1.23	3.90	4.12	4.41	11.5	1.2	103	
2016	LVG	AAA	23	12	5	0	25	25	154¹	170	15	2.3	4.5	78	48%	.300	1.36	3.97	4.87	5.55	-3.6	-0.4	114	
2016	NYN	MLB	23	1	0	0	10	3	18¹	26	0	3.4	8.3	17	51%	.413	1.80	6.38	2.64	5.16	0.1	0.0	107	95.4
2017	NYN	MLB	24	3	4	0	34	6	61	65	6	3.0	5.1	35	47%	.289	1.37	4.64	4.47	4.94	0.8	0.1	100	
2018	NYN	MLB	25	4	3	0	42	7	78	67	8	4.3	8.0	69	47%	.292	1.34	4.29	4.60	4.97	3.0	0.3	114	

Breakout: 14%   Improve: 20%   Collapse: 19%   Attrition: 34%   MLB: 47%   *Comparables: Chaz Roe, Adam Wilk, Kendry Flores*

As a group, Mets pitching prospects sure do get a lot of velocity jumps and good new sliders relatively late in the player development process. Common theories to explain this phenomenon include pitching coach Dan Warthen secretly being a warlock, COO Jeff Wilpon practicing human sacrifice to the Lord of Light a la Stannis Baratheon, or a developmental philosophy that emphasizes maximizing arm strength and adding a hard slider with a deeper, looser grip at the higher levels. The latest contestant in this great game is Ynoa, a solid but generic command-and-control prospect brought up in August to provide emergency innings. Ynoa's velocity on the fastball did tick up a little and he did tighten up the slider, but it wasn't quite the crazy, drastic improvement others in the system have shown. At the very least, he's a major league quality arm, but the role and value is still far from clear.

LINEOUTS

Hitters

NAME	POS	TEAM	LVL	AGE	PA	R	2B	3B	HR	RBI	BB	K	SB	CS	AVG/OBP/SLG	TAv	VORP	BABIP	BRR	FRAA	WARP
Pete Alonso	1B	BRO	A-	21	123	20	12	1	5	21	11	22	0	1	.321/.382/.587	.366	14.1	.357	-0.5	1B(27): 2.3	1.7
Wuilmer Becerra	RF	SLU	A+	21	263	27	17	0	1	34	9	52	7	1	.312/.341/.393	.268	5.5	.388	0.0	RF(13): -0.0	0.6
Luis Carpio	MI	BRO	A-	18	52	4	2	0	0	1	8	10	0	0	.140/.288/.186	.217	-2.7	.182	-0.9		-0.3
Phillip Evans	INF	SLU	A+	23	33	3	0	0	0	2	5	3	0	0	.143/.273/.143	.186	-1.9	.160	0.1	3B(3): 0.1 • 2B(2): 0.5	-0.1
	INF	BIN	AA	23	386	50	30	0	8	39	19	60	1	1	.335/.374/.485	.304	30.4	.384	0.7	SS(39): 0.6 • 2B(32): -3.8	3.1
Luis Guillorme	MI	SLU	A+	21	505	47	16	2	1	46	43	63	4	2	.263/.332/.315	.246	9.9	.303	0.1	SS(72): -1.4 • 2B(52): 3.8	1.3
Ty Kelly	UT	LVG	AAA	27	316	45	21	1	2	35	38	42	5	6	.328/.409/.435	.294	17.9	.378	-1.4	LF(35): 1.0 • 2B(24): -1.6	2.0
	UT	NYN	MLB	27	71	9	1	1	1	7	11	9	0	0	.241/.352/.345	.261	2.5	.260	0.5	3B(10): 0.7 • LF(8): 0.2	0.3
Johnny Monell	C	LVG	AAA	30	461	69	22	1	19	75	37	76	2	0	.276/.336/.470	.260	11.9	.294	-2.4	C(62): -11.3 • 1B(22): -1.3	-0.1
Tomas Nido	C	SLU	A+	22	370	38	23	2	7	46	19	42	0	1	.320/.357/.459	.294	27.8	.344	-2.4	C(88): 4.9	3.4
Matt Reynolds	INF	LVG	AAA	25	299	43	15	2	2	24	26	64	9	2	.264/.336/.357	.229	0.9	.340	0.5	3B(30): 0.3 • SS(29): -1.9	0.1
	INF	NYN	MLB	25	96	11	8	0	3	13	4	34	0	1	.225/.266/.416	.256	3.4	.327	0.2	SS(21): 0.2 • 3B(7): -0.1	0.4
Ali Sanchez	C	BRO	A-	19	181	15	10	0	0	11	10	26	2	0	.216/.260/.275	.221	-1.4	.255	-0.5	C(33): -0.5	-0.2
Champ Stuart	OF	SLU	A+	23	315	49	9	6	6	24	31	95	25	3	.265/.347/.407	.275	20.9	.383	6.2	CF(70): -6.1	1.5
	OF	BIN	AA	23	203	23	3	1	2	10	14	73	15	3	.201/.264/.261	.193	-6.5	.318	1.1	CF(43): 1.5	-0.5

Second-round pick **Pete Alonso** beat the stuffing out of the ball in Brooklyn until his season ended with wrist problems, and is the one former Florida Gator the Mets signed this year who might be a major-league player some day. ❖ The Mets picked up toolsy outfielder **Wuilmer Becerra** as a flier in the R.A. Dickey trade (that's quickly becoming the Noah Syndergaard trade), and between a string of injuries and a baffling lack of game power, it's still unclear what they've got in him. ❖ Preseason sleeper prospect **Luis Carpio** was felled by a shoulder injury in spring training. Initially projected to miss the season, he showed up in Brooklyn in late-August for some DH at-bats, but his ability to continue playing shortstop remains in some doubt. ❖ 2011 bonus baby **Phillip Evans** started the season with a tenuous grip on a roster spot as the backup infielder at High-A. A few weeks into the season, injuries opened up some Double-A playing time, where Evans won the Eastern League batting title and reclaimed his prospect status. ❖ **Gregory Guerrero**, nephew of Vlad, was born in 1999, the year his uncle made his first All-Star team. Congratulations on feeling old. ❖ **Luis Guillorme** is the best defensive infielder in the system, and his father (@lguillorme) is a genuinely entertaining Mets Twitter follow. ❖ Kudos to career minor-league utilityman **Ty Kelly** for hiring an agent smart enough to place him with the Mets. A shiny early-season batting average at the Triple-A Las Vegas launching pad bought Ty his major-league debut, several months of per diem in The Show, and even a hit in the playoffs. ❖ It's a little surprising that **Johnny Monell** never found his way back to the majors in 2016. As a card-carrying member of the Fraternal Order of Backup Catchers, he's liable to keep popping up in this section for another eight years or so. ❖ **Tomas Nido** has always been a quality defender with some offensive potential, and he hit his way up prospect lists in 2016 by winning the Florida State League batting title. ❖ After collecting a 2015 playoff share as Ruben Tejada's emergency replacement who never played, **Matt Reynolds** settled into his likely ten-year career as an up-and-down utility player in 2016. You can do far worse, and the Mets often have. ❖ Deposed minor-league skipper Wally Backman once called **Ali Sanchez** the best pitch-framer in the Mets organization, but the jury is still out on whether he'll hit. ❖ **Champ Stuart**, speed demon from the Bahamas, is perfectly qualified to be the Mets' Terrance Gore, right down to the inability to hit upper-minors pitching. Yet, instead of filling a need during September, Stuart was sent to the WBC qualifying tournament, where his .525 OPS in Double-A earned him the cleanup spot for runner-up Great Britain.

Pitchers

NAME	TEAM	LVL	AGE	W	L	SV	G	GS	IP	H	HR	BB/9	K/9	K	GB%	BABIP	WHIP	ERA	FIP	DRA	VORP	WARP	cFIP	MPH
Nabil Crismatt	BRO	A-	21	0	1	1	8	3	31	26	4	1.2	10.2	35	52%	.272	0.97	3.19	3.08	2.76	7.9	0.8	85	
	COL	A	21	1	2	0	4	3	28²	20	1	0.6	10.0	32	45%	.264	0.77	1.88	2.04	1.64	10.4	1.1	72	
Josh Edgin	LVG	AAA	29	2	2	2	37	0	33¹	35	2	5.4	10.3	38	50%	.375	1.65	3.24	4.29	4.48	1.8	0.2	96	
	NYN	MLB	29	1	0	0	16	0	10¹	10	1	5.2	9.6	11	43%	.333	1.55	5.23	4.06	4.41	0.6	0.1	103	93.2
Chris Flexen	SLU	A+	21	10	9	0	25	25	134	125	6	3.4	6.4	95	50%	.287	1.31	3.56	3.69	5.76	-4.3	-0.4	111	
Sean Gilmartin	LVG	AAA	26	9	7	0	19	18	107¹	122	12	2.6	7.9	94	47%	.331	1.43	4.86	4.29	3.21	25.1	2.6	89	
	NYN	MLB	26	0	1	0	14	1	17²	21	4	3.6	5.6	11	53%	.304	1.58	7.13	6.24	5.08	-0.2	0.0	111	90.4
Erik Goeddel	LVG	AAA	27	1	1	1	24	1	28²	28	2	4.7	10.7	34	44%	.333	1.50	4.08	3.93	3.16	5.8	0.6	90	
	NYN	MLB	27	2	2	0	36	0	35²	33	5	3.5	9.1	36	29%	.277	1.32	4.54	4.25	4.75	0.9	0.1	118	94.6
Kevin McGowan	SLU	A+	24	1	0	2	15	2	33	20	1	1.1	9.0	33	45%	.235	0.73	0.82	2.01	1.99	11.7	1.2	76	
	BIN	AA	24	4	1	0	26	2	49²	48	2	3.1	8.7	48	42%	.317	1.31	3.26	3.10	4.03	4.1	0.4	98	
Paul Sewald	LVG	AAA	26	5	3	19	56	0	65²	58	9	2.9	11.0	80	38%	.295	1.20	3.29	4.07	2.06	21.2	2.2	78	

Nabil Crismatt has spent the last few years on a tour of rookie- and A-ball affiliates, breezing through each level on the strength of a good change and a looping curve, and could spend the next few years turning into a useful reliever. ❖ After missing all of 2015 with Tommy John surgery, **Josh Edgin** finally made it back to the majors in August, where he had trouble finding both his command and the plate. ❖ **Chris Flexen** might not look that interesting on his stat page, but he's a projectable righty in the Mets system with some idea of how to pitch and a breaking ball that flashes—a profile the Mets have done curiously well with, even among prospects they've traded. ❖ The high point of **Sean Gilmartin**'s season was his July engagement to CNN's conservative talking head Kayleigh McEnany—which doubled as the best, and possibly only, story of someone hurling junk from the left and someone hurling junk from the right coming together in 2016. ❖ **Erik Goeddel** has battled so many elbow problems in his career that he once had a MRI labeled "dirty" because the doctors couldn't separate the old injuries from new ones, but when healthy, he's a perfectly adequate middle reliever. ❖ The Mets took **Anthony Kay**, the *other* lefty out of Ward Melville High School on Long Island (via UConn), with the Daniel Murphy compensation draft pick. Kay failed his post-draft physical, had his bonus cut nearly in half and underwent Tommy John surgery, while Murphy turned into the reincarnation of Rogers Hornsby. Advantage: Nationals. ❖ **Kevin McGowan**'s stuff and command made huge strides with a move to shorter stints, and he could factor into a major-league bullpen as soon as this year. ❖ **Marcos Molina** was developing into one of the top prospects in the system before Tommy John surgery and two mostly lost seasons, but he looked good in the Arizona Fall League and could yet be an impact arm if he stays healthy. ❖ **Paul Sewald** has pitched well at every level, and was by far the most effective pitcher for Las Vegas in 2016, but he never got a chance to add some major league per diem to his $1,000 signing bonus out of the draft.

NEW YORK YANKEES

Essay by Jared Diamond

Player comments by Kenny Ducey and BP staff

Unless you grew up in or around the New York metropolitan area, happen to have a particular sartorial affinity for pinstriped clothing or pray at the Church of the Holy Jeter, you probably hate the Yankees.

Don't feel bad about it. You're certainly not alone. The Yankees themselves practically want you to hate them. They long ago cast themselves as the undisputed villains of the baseball galaxy, spending exorbitant amounts of cash and raiding the farm systems of their small-market rivals to dominate the competition for years. They even went to court to protect their rights to the phrase "Evil Empire," fully embracing their role as an organization to be feared, not adored.

But starting in the middle of last summer, as Gary Sanchez commenced to transform Yankee Stadium into his personal launching pad, something strange happened: The Yankees—the joyless, win-or-die, soul-sucking Yankees—showed glimpses of becoming … well, sort of likable.

Sure, the Yankees' recent performance on the field has helped improve their national reputation, as the vitriol usually hurtled their direction dissipated in favor of apathy. They missed the playoffs for the third time in four years in 2016 and haven't appeared in a postseason series since 2012. The familiar complaints about the Yankees buying championships gave way to undying rage over Cardinals Devil Magic and the Giants' Even Year B.S.

It's difficult to truly despise a team that doesn't actually win. That, however, doesn't tell the entire story of the changing optics surrounding the perception of the Yankees.

It almost goes without saying at this point that the best way to build a successful franchise has evolved in recent years, moving away from sheer dollars and toward homegrown talent. An emphasis on player development has emerged as the safest pathway to October over the brute-force approach that rich big-market teams used to their benefit for so long.

Even the Cubs, with their not-insubstantial payroll, only put themselves in the position to win their first World Series since 1908 because of smart drafting (Kris Bryant, Javy Baez) and shrewd trades (Anthony Rizzo, Jake Arrieta). Only after the Cubs assembled a young core with their own ingenuity did Theo Epstein and his braintrust seriously open their wallets to add the final pieces of the puzzle.

YANKEES PROSPECTUS
2016 W-L: 84-78, 4TH IN AL EAST

Pythag	.485	17th	DER	.708	8th
RS/G	4.2	22nd	B-Age	30.2	28th
RA/G	4.33	10th	P-Age	27.9	10th
TAv	.249	29th	Salary	$227.9M	2nd
BRR	-2.85	20th	M$/MW	$6.1M	2nd
TAv-P	.248	5th	DL Days	1153	21st
FIP	4.16	13th	$ on DL	11%	11th

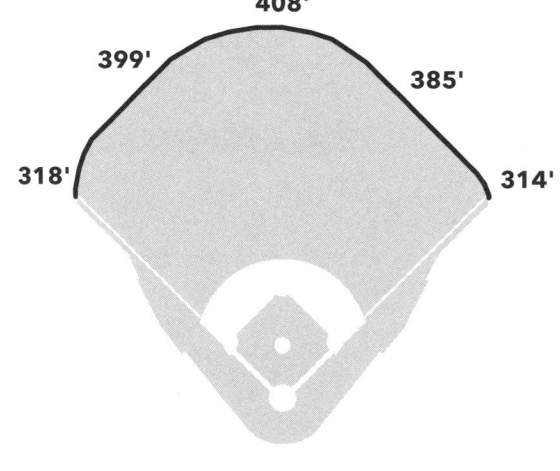

Outfield wall profile: **8'**

Three-Year Park Factors

Runs	Runs/RH	Runs/LH	HR/RH	HR/LH
108	110	111	116	117

Top Hitter WARP	2.7	Brett Gardner
Top Pitcher WARP	5.6	Michael Pineda
Top Prospect		Gleyber Torres

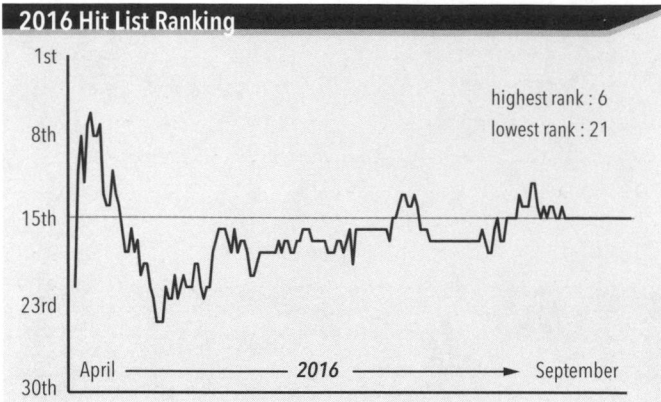

2016 Hit List Ranking

highest rank : 6
lowest rank : 21

April ——— *2016* ——→ September

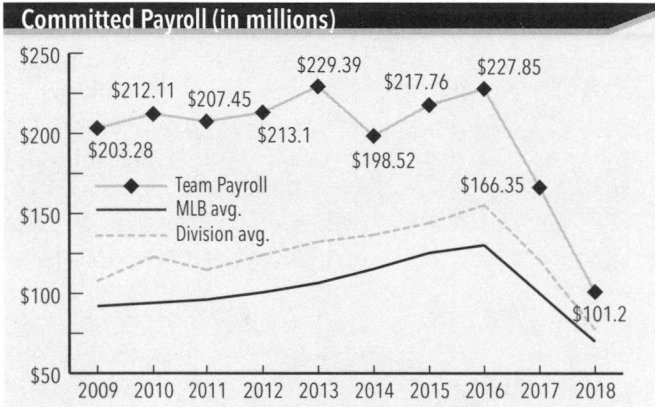

Committed Payroll (in millions)

$229.39
$227.85
$212.11
$207.45
$217.76
$203.28
$213.1
$198.52
$166.35
$101.2

◆ Team Payroll
— MLB avg.
--- Division avg.

2009 2010 2011 2012 2013 2014 2015 2016 2017 2018

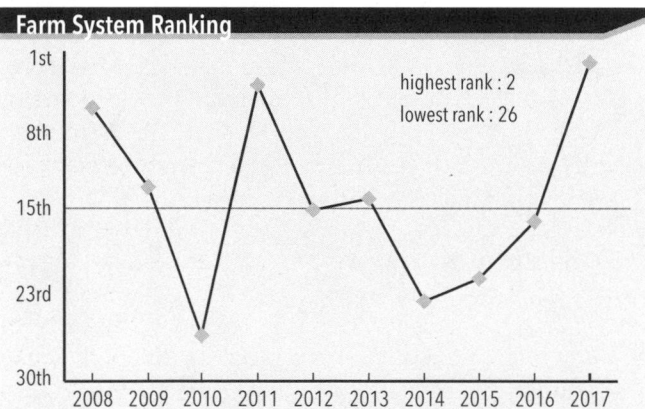

Farm System Ranking

highest rank : 2
lowest rank : 26

2008 2009 2010 2011 2012 2013 2014 2015 2016 2017

Personnel

General Manager:
Brian Cashman

Manager:
Joe Girardi

SVP, Assistant General Manager:
Jean Afterman

Assistant General Manager:
Michael Fishman

Vice President of Baseball Operations:
Tim Naehring

Over time, the Yankees--a club with just one title to its name since defeating the Mets in the 2000 Subway Series--came to understand that their money doesn't carry nearly as much weight as it once did. That realization, coupled with Hal Steinbrenner's stated desire to slash his team's budget under the luxury tax threshold, has forced the Yankees into a new era. George Steinbrenner saw no problem a lavish check couldn't fix. His son has opted for a more measured plan of attack.

By doing so, the Yankees have begun the process of constructing a roster that all fans—not just fans who bleed in white and midnight blue—can appreciate. Accomplishing that goal took a purge of historic proportions, a full-blown Yankees fire sale for the first time in a generation.

They cut Alex Rodriguez, suddenly beloved as a television analyst but still mostly reviled as a baseball player. They traded closer Aroldis Chapman, whose violation of MLB's domestic violence policy made him a controversial figure even among Yan zkees diehards. They bid farewell to first baseman Mark Teixeira, who rode off into retirement largely as an expensive, injury-ravaged reminder that high-priced free agents don't guarantee multiple rings.

In their place, the Yankees promoted a group of farmhands who grew to be known as the Baby Bombers. Sanchez led the charge, bashing 20 home runs in 53 games and shattering plenty of rookie records along the way. He enters his first full major-league season already viewed as perhaps the Yankees' premier slugger at age 24.

Meanwhile, before an oblique strain sidelined him in mid-September, 24-year-old outfielder Aaron Judge demonstrated the immense power that has made him such an exciting prospect. Though he struggled to adjust to major-league pitching, striking out 42 times in 84 at-bats, he hit two home runs that traveled farther than 440 feet, including a 457-foot moonshot in his first big-league plate appearance. (Even that paled in comparison to the ridiculous bomb he hit during one already-famous spring-training batting-practice session, when Judge blasted a ball *over* the scoreboard.)

And, if all goes well, there is more on the way. Infielder Gleyber Torres, the prize of the Chapman deal, will open the year at Double-A Trenton and could climb the ladder quickly. Outfielder Clint Frazier, whom the Yankees acquired from Cleveland for reliever Andrew Miller in July, is already at Triple-A. The fifth overall pick in the 2013 draft, the 22-year-old Frazier appears on track for his debut sometime in 2017. All told, in the span of about a week in July in which they traded Chapman, Miller and Carlos Beltran for 10 prospects, the Yankees turned a barren farm system into one of baseball's most fertile. (Chapman has since returned to New York, signing a five-year, $86 million contract in December, the largest deal for a reliever in baseball history.)

Almost immediately, the Yankees' youth movement sparked a new, fresh vibe in the clubhouse, bringing real attitude and enthusiasm to a team that at times seemed to confuse "professionalism" with "conformity." Gone was the businesslike atmosphere that was so prevalent when Rodriguez and Beltran presided over the locker room, an ethos they no doubt inherited from Derek Jeter and Mariano Rivera before them.

In its place, there was loud music, earnest energy and a renewed sense of fun. It's that last part that makes the current crop of Yankees so tough to resist compared to many of their predecessors. They have personality. They aren't robots. These are players even the most ardent Yankee haters can at least find intriguing, if not lovable.

Consider Sanchez: His nickname, bestowed upon him by general manager Brian Cashman, is "The Kraken"--the legendary sea monster. He signs his tweets with the hashtag #IamGary or #ElGary, which has already inspired a robust online t-shirt business. At least one shirt features a cartoon image of Pablo Sanchez, the all-around superstar of the "Backyard Baseball" video game series. (Suffice it to say that one is appealing to the millennial demographic.)

Judge, a 6-foot-7 behemoth of a man, has already proven himself to be a gentle giant, boasting a broad, boyish smile that rarely leaves his face. Then there's Frazier, whose persona is decidedly un-Yankee-like—in the best possible way. Though he had to trim much of his bushy red hair to comply with Yankee policy, Frazier has ingratiated himself to fans by living up to his moniker of "Red Thunder."

He flaunted his new ties to New York on Twitter in a very public effort to land a date with a popular social-media personality. He used the internet to shame his roommate for inadvertently locking him out of his house and then invited fans to follow his offseason exploits on Instagram. In other words, Frazier has shared more with his fans in a few months than Jeter did in two decades. If Frazier's bat develops the way the Yankees expect, he has all the makings of a star.

Cashman, the Yankees' GM since 1998, has made no secret of his desire to model the roster after the late-90s teams. Speaking with reporters after shipping Miller to the Indians, he said, "I think our system that currently now is in play is starting to hopefully mirror what that system started to produce."

After all, the Yankees appeared in six World Series from 1996-2003 and won four, one of the most fruitful periods for any team in history. They achieved this remarkable feat by flexing their financial muscles, yes, but also with a star-studded crop of homegrown talent (Jeter, Rivera) and a consistent group of key contributors acquired in trades (Paul O'Neill, Tino Martinez).

Writing as someone born and raised in the New York metropolitan area, I can say with certainty that those Yankees teams weren't hated. That's not to say most of the country rooted for them to keep winning championships—these were still the Yankees—but they were respected. (The massive standing ovations Jeter and Rivera received at Fenway Park before they retired says all you need to know.)

For lifelong Yankees fans unaccustomed to outsiders reacting to their favorite team with anything but intense scorn, all of this has led to a bit of an existential crisis: If the Yankees aren't detested by everybody, do they lose their inherent Yankee-ness? What are the New York Yankees—the Evil Empire itself—if fans find themselves … not hating them?

These are fair questions that are forcing the Yankees and their fans to face their own fallibility. When I posted them to my own Twitter followers, many of the responses echoed a similar refrain: "If you have no haters, you're not popping champagne." There's no doubt at least some of the hatred directed toward the Yankees stems from jealousy. That hasn't been much of an issue these past few years, and it has resulted in the Yankees embarking on a near-unprecedented rebuilding process.

But fear not: This period of the Yankees playing nice with the global community might not last long. Sure, in 2017 fans everywhere will keep their eye on Sanchez's progress and could very well fall in love with Frazier whenever he reaches New York. But eventually, the honeymoon will end. The earth will return to its axis.

Again, remember: These are still the Yankees we're talking about, in spite of their current makeup. At any moment, no matter what Cashman says, they could abandon their entire plan and dip into their well of prospects to trade for whichever superstar hits the open market.

Even if they stick to their convictions, the winter of 2018 is rapidly approaching. Bryce Harper, Matt Harvey, Manny Machado and so many others will be free agents. The Yankees—not coincidentally, mind you—will have plenty of money to spend after many of their big contracts finally expire. Knowing them, they will probably pony up close to a billion dollars, bring in a bunch of big-time players and infuriate everybody else again.

Sooner or later, the Yankees will reaffirm their place as the Yankees and start to win. Fans everywhere will remember why they hate the Yankees. Balance in the baseball universe will be restored. ∎

—Jared Diamond covers the Yankees for the Wall Street Journal

HITTERS

Dustin Ackley   LF

Born: 2/26/88   Age: 29   Bats: L   Throws: R   Height: 6'1"   Weight: 205   Entered Pro Ball: Round 1, 2009 Draft (#2 overall)

YEAR	TEAM	LVL	AGE	PA	R	2B	3B	HR	RBI	BB	K	SB	CS	AVG/OBP/SLG	TAv	VORP	BABIP	BRR	FRAA	WARP
2014	SEA	MLB	26	542	64	27	4	14	65	32	90	8	4	.245/.293/.398	.262	11.6	.273	0.3	LF(133): 1.8	1.5
2015	SEA	MLB	27	207	22	8	1	6	19	14	38	2	2	.215/.270/.366	.240	0.6	.234	-0.2	LF(63): -4.4 • CF(21): 0.0	-0.4
2015	NYA	MLB	27	57	6	3	2	4	11	4	7	0	0	.288/.333/.654	.358	5.3	.262	-1.4	2B(9): -0.8 • 1B(4): 0.0	0.4
2016	NYA	MLB	28	70	6	0	0	0	4	8	9	0	0	.148/.243/.148	.176	-4.6	.170	0.4	1B(13): 0.6 • RF(9): -0.5	-0.5
2017	*NYA*	*MLB*	*29*	*250*	*29*	*11*	*1*	*7*	*28*	*22*	*43*	*3*	*2*	*.253/.321/.410*	*.247*	*2.9*	*.279*	*-0.3*	*1B 3 • RF -0*	*0.5*
2018	*NYA*	*MLB*	*30*	*110*	*13*	*5*	*1*	*3*	*13*	*10*	*20*	*1*	*1*	*.250/.317/.409*	*.247*	*0.5*	*.277*	*-0.1*	*1B 1 • RF 0*	*0.1*

Breakout: 2%   Improve: 42%   Collapse: 15%   Attrition: 18%   MLB: 94%   Comparables: *Norm Larker, Chip Hale, David Segui*

After a rough beginning to 2016, a torn labrum ended Ackley's season early and sent his name into oblivion. It wouldn't be shocking if some general managers forgot the former no. 2 overall draft pick and one-time top prospect was in the league. He was decent for 23 games with the Yankees in 2015, which sadly might lead his resume at this point, right above consistent batted-ball numbers.

Tyler Austin   1B/RF

Born: 9/6/91   Age: 25   Bats: R   Throws: R   Height: 6'2"   Weight: 220   Entered Pro Ball: Round 13, 2010 Draft (#415 overall)

YEAR	TEAM	LVL	AGE	PA	R	2B	3B	HR	RBI	BB	K	SB	CS	AVG/OBP/SLG	TAv	VORP	BABIP	BRR	FRAA	WARP
2014	TRN	AA	22	437	56	20	5	9	47	36	80	3	2	.275/.336/.419	.274	11.1	.323	-1.9	RF(59): 1.1 • 1B(19): -1.6	1.3
2015	SWB	AAA	23	299	33	8	0	4	27	26	81	8	1	.235/.309/.311	.227	-3.5	.317	1.8	RF(54): -1.6 • LF(10): -1.1	-0.6
2015	TRN	AA	23	86	8	5	2	2	8	8	16	3	2	.260/.337/.455	.260	2.2	.305	0.8	RF(17): 3.3	0.6
2016	TRN	AA	24	210	22	10	1	4	29	30	46	1	1	.260/.367/.395	.277	7.2	.326	1.2	1B(37): 0.1 • LF(7): -1.5	0.6
2016	SWB	AAA	24	234	39	24	0	13	49	32	59	5	0	.323/.415/.637	.359	26.9	.400	-0.2	1B(39): -3.4 • RF(4): -0.3	2.4
2016	NYA	MLB	24	90	7	3	0	5	12	7	36	1	0	.241/.300/.458	.261	1.4	.357	0.3	1B(27): 1.8 • RF(3): -0.0	0.3
2017	*NYA*	*MLB*	*25*	*149*	*18*	*6*	*1*	*5*	*18*	*14*	*42*	*1*	*0*	*.241/.316/.418*	*.256*	*2.1*	*.307*	*-0.1*	*1B -1 • RF -0*	*0.0*
2018	*NYA*	*MLB*	*26*	*351*	*45*	*16*	*1*	*13*	*45*	*34*	*99*	*3*	*1*	*.242/.319/.428*	*.253*	*3.2*	*.309*	*-0.2*	*1B -2 • RF 0*	*0.1*

Breakout: 6%   Improve: 23%   Collapse: 5%   Attrition: 22%   MLB: 43%   Comparables: *Travis Ishikawa, Christian Walker, Tommy Medica*

The 25-year-old hit the cover off the ball at Triple-A, earning a spot in the big leagues after the emotional departure of Alex Rodriguez, and he made noise right away by going deep in his first at-bat, just before Aaron Judge did the same. After the dust settled Austin proved to be a capable hitter at the major-league level, though his power wasn't as immediately present as many had hoped. Still, he put together good at bats, with an impressive 45.7 percent zone rate for a rookie, and he did post a respectable 34 percent hard-hit rate. The sample size is small, but Austin appears to be a big-league hitter, and that's without the power numbers he's capable of.

Greg Bird   1B

Born: 11/9/92   Age: 24   Bats: L   Throws: R   Height: 6'4"   Weight: 220   Entered Pro Ball: Round 5, 2011 Draft (#179 overall)

YEAR	TEAM	LVL	AGE	PA	R	2B	3B	HR	RBI	BB	K	SB	CS	AVG/OBP/SLG	TAv	VORP	BABIP	BRR	FRAA	WARP
2014	TAM	A+	21	325	36	22	1	7	32	45	70	1	0	.277/.375/.442	.297	15.5	.342	-1.2	1B(61): 1.1	1.7
2014	TRN	AA	21	116	16	8	0	7	11	18	27	0	0	.253/.379/.558	.329	8.3	.274	-1.0	1B(24): -1.2	0.8
2015	TRN	AA	22	212	29	16	0	6	29	24	30	1	1	.258/.358/.445	.302	12.4	.279	1.2	1B(41): 2.2	1.6
2015	SWB	AAA	22	150	15	7	1	6	23	11	27	0	0	.301/.353/.500	.304	7.1	.333	-1.3	1B(29): 0.3	0.8
2015	NYA	MLB	22	178	26	9	0	11	31	19	53	0	0	.261/.343/.529	.312	9.3	.319	-1.4	1B(46): 1.0	1.1
2017	*NYA*	*MLB*	*24*	*496*	*62*	*24*	*1*	*22*	*68*	*52*	*128*	*0*	*0*	*.244/.328/.457*	*.270*	*12.7*	*.291*	*-1.2*	*1B 0*	*1.1*
2018	*NYA*	*MLB*	*25*	*496*	*70*	*25*	*1*	*23*	*72*	*56*	*131*	*0*	*0*	*.245/.335/.468*	*.268*	*9.0*	*.293*	*-1.3*	*1B 0*	*1.0*

Breakout: 3%   Improve: 23%   Collapse: 19%   Attrition: 29%   MLB: 64%   Comparables: *Kennys Vargas, Jon Singleton, Joey Votto*

Offseason shoulder surgery held Bird out for all of 2016, which only seemed to add to his legend. The cult hero who blasted tantalizing homers as a rookie in 2015 after an injury to Mark Teixeira is finally set to take on a starting role as he turns 24. His long absence will have his followers breaking down stadium gates and shoving folks out of the way like Zack Hample to get a look at him this spring. In 2017, this Bird will be … uncaged.

Billy Butler   DH

Born: 4/18/86   Age: 31   Bats: R   Throws: R   Height: 6'0"   Weight: 260   Entered Pro Ball: Round 1, 2004 Draft (#14 overall)

YEAR	TEAM	LVL	AGE	PA	R	2B	3B	HR	RBI	BB	K	SB	CS	AVG/OBP/SLG	TAv	VORP	BABIP	BRR	FRAA	WARP
2014	KCA	MLB	28	603	57	32	0	9	66	41	96	0	0	.271/.323/.379	.256	-0.4	.310	-3.7	1B(37): 0.1	0.0
2015	OAK	MLB	29	601	63	28	1	15	65	52	101	0	0	.251/.323/.390	.255	-6.2	.282	-9.1	1B(7): 0.2	-0.6
2016	OAK	MLB	30	242	24	16	0	4	31	19	34	0	0	.276/.331/.403	.254	0.2	.308	-1.2	1B(22): -1.1	-0.1
2016	NYA	MLB	30	32	3	2	0	1	4	2	8	0	0	.345/.375/.517	.314	2.0	.429	-0.2	1B(3): 1.0	0.3
2017	*NYA*	*MLB*	*31*	*323*	*37*	*15*	*0*	*10*	*41*	*30*	*58*	*0*	*0*	*.273/.345/.435*	*.263*	*5.2*	*.308*	*-2.6*	*1B 1*	*0.7*
2018	*NYA*	*MLB*	*32*	*297*	*38*	*13*	*0*	*9*	*36*	*27*	*55*	*0*	*0*	*.265/.336/.418*	*.256*	*1.4*	*.300*	*-2.5*	*1B 1*	*0.2*

Breakout: 1%   Improve: 43%   Collapse: 4%   Attrition: 9%   MLB: 91%   Comparables: *Ed Kranepool, Aubrey Huff, Richie Hebner*

"Country Breakfast" was renamed "Big City Brunch" in 2016. Butler's once-powerful bat continued its sharp decline, landing him on waivers by the end of the year to be claimed by the Yankees. For a player slower than 3G download speeds who lacks a capable glove in the field, five home runs just doesn't cut it. The power seems to be gone. There's still time for another name change, but it's likely going to be something lame, like "Lunch By The Beach, But Not Really By The Beach, Actually A Few Blocks Inland, Sorry For Deceiving You."

Starlin Castro 2B

Born: 3/24/90   Age: 27   Bats: R   Throws: R   Height: 6'2"   Weight: 230   Entered Pro Ball: International Free Agent, 2006

YEAR	TEAM	LVL	AGE	PA	R	2B	3B	HR	RBI	BB	K	SB	CS	AVG/OBP/SLG	TAv	VORP	BABIP	BRR	FRAA	WARP
2014	CHN	MLB	24	569	58	33	1	14	65	35	100	4	4	.292/.339/.438	.278	28.4	.337	-2.6	SS(133): 3.8	3.6
2015	CHN	MLB	25	578	52	23	2	11	69	21	91	5	5	.265/.296/.375	.243	9.2	.298	-2.2	SS(109): 2.8 • 2B(38): 1.7	1.5
2016	NYA	MLB	26	610	63	29	1	21	70	24	118	4	0	.270/.300/.433	.250	8.1	.305	-2.1	2B(150): 1.5 • SS(3): -0.5	0.9
2017	*NYA*	*MLB*	*27*	*588*	*61*	*27*	*3*	*16*	*69*	*30*	*102*	*5*	*3*	*.268/.308/.416*	*.253*	*15.5*	*.301*	*-0.9*	*2B 1*	*1.5*
2018	*NYA*	*MLB*	*28*	*528*	*63*	*24*	*2*	*16*	*63*	*29*	*94*	*4*	*2*	*.264/.310/.418*	*.249*	*8.9*	*.296*	*-1.4*	*2B 1*	*1.1*

Breakout: 3%   Improve: 54%   Collapse: 5%   Attrition: 11%   MLB: 99%   *Comparables: Frank Catalanotto, Dave Stapleton, Frank Bolling*

To most people hearing the word "project" brings about great angst. Somehow, though, it sends Brian Cashman into a state of exhilaration. The Yankees GM took on a 25-year-old middle infielder who had fallen out of favor in Chicago last offseason in hopes of unlocking the player who once appeared destined for the 3,000-hit club, to mixed results. Castro proved that he can he can be a perfectly average hitter and capitalize on a hitters' park—shattering his career-high with 21 dingers in the cozy Yankee Stadium—but still has something left to prove on defense. At age 26 his FRAA dropped off significantly, though he did play second base, a position he did not know much about before relocating to New York. He's still a relatively young, controllable middle infielder, but it's beginning to look like he will never be anything more than average.

Jacoby Ellsbury CF

Born: 9/11/83   Age: 33   Bats: L   Throws: L   Height: 6'1"   Weight: 195   Entered Pro Ball: Round 1, 2005 Draft (#23 overall)

YEAR	TEAM	LVL	AGE	PA	R	2B	3B	HR	RBI	BB	K	SB	CS	AVG/OBP/SLG	TAv	VORP	BABIP	BRR	FRAA	WARP
2014	NYA	MLB	30	635	71	27	5	16	70	49	93	39	5	.271/.328/.419	.278	26.9	.296	-1.2	CF(141): 5.1	3.5
2015	NYA	MLB	31	501	66	15	2	7	33	35	86	21	9	.257/.318/.345	.249	13.3	.301	4.2	CF(110): -7.8	0.6
2016	NYA	MLB	32	626	71	24	5	9	56	54	84	20	8	.263/.330/.374	.246	12.3	.295	2.3	CF(148): -14.5	-0.2
2017	*NYA*	*MLB*	*33*	*632*	*81*	*25*	*4*	*12*	*54*	*49*	*99*	*28*	*8*	*.263/.322/.382*	*.247*	*14.7*	*.297*	*2.8*	*CF -2*	*0.9*
2018	*NYA*	*MLB*	*34*	*557*	*64*	*21*	*3*	*11*	*57*	*46*	*89*	*22*	*7*	*.262/.325/.383*	*.243*	*7.1*	*.297*	*1.7*	*CF -2*	*0.6*

Breakout: 2%   Improve: 26%   Collapse: 14%   Attrition: 21%   MLB: 88%   *Comparables: Ruben Amaro, Eddie Milner, Mark Kotsay*

The best thing that ever happened to Ellsbury was the dismal season that Jason Heyward had in Chicago, because it gave the media a new horrible contract to discuss. Ellsbury is owed around $85 million over the next four years, an unsightly dollar amount to pay a declining outfielder who played *terrible* defense and once again underwhelmed at the plate. The 33-year-old is falling fast, but on the bright side, his hard-hit rate was back up six points from 2015 at 26.6 percent. He's still making outs, but at least he's making good contact. That would give the impression that there's a chance he turns things around, but he'll never come close to being worth his salary.

Clint Frazier OF

Born: 9/6/94   Age: 22   Bats: R   Throws: R   Height: 6'1"   Weight: 190   Entered Pro Ball: Round 1, 2013 Draft (#5 overall)

YEAR	TEAM	LVL	AGE	PA	R	2B	3B	HR	RBI	BB	K	SB	CS	AVG/OBP/SLG	TAv	VORP	BABIP	BRR	FRAA	WARP
2014	LKC	A	19	542	70	18	6	13	50	56	161	12	6	.266/.349/.411	.277	26.6	.372	0.8	CF(111): -18.9 • RF(1): 0.0	0.8
2015	LYN	A+	20	588	88	36	3	16	72	68	125	15	7	.285/.377/.465	.297	34.5	.348	-2.3	CF(93): -5.1 • RF(35): 0.4	3.2
2016	AKR	AA	21	391	56	25	1	13	48	41	86	13	4	.276/.356/.469	.298	24.3	.331	1.4	RF(31): -2.7 • LF(26): 2.4	2.7
2016	COH	AAA	21	21	2	0	1	0	0	0	6	0	0	.238/.238/.333	.237	-0.2	.333	-0.1	RF(3): 0.2 • LF(2): 0.4	0.0
2016	SWB	AAA	21	108	17	2	3	3	7	7	30	0	0	.228/.278/.396	.248	1.6	.294	0.8	LF(13): -0.7 • RF(6): 1.5	0.2
2017	*NYA*	*MLB*	*22*	*250*	*32*	*10*	*1*	*9*	*28*	*22*	*76*	*3*	*1*	*.233/.307/.407*	*.244*	*3.8*	*.305*	*-0.1*	*RF 0 • LF 1*	*0.5*
2018	*NYA*	*MLB*	*23*	*344*	*42*	*14*	*1*	*11*	*41*	*31*	*105*	*4*	*2*	*.229/.304/.397*	*.242*	*1.7*	*.302*	*0.0*	*RF 0 • LF 2*	*0.3*

Breakout: 1%   Improve: 22%   Collapse: 1%   Attrition: 15%   MLB: 40%   *Comparables: Joel Guzman, Thomas Neal, Nick Castellanos*

Imagine if Air Bud played baseball. That's Clint Frazier: An adorable golden retriever who's incredible at a sport and plays fearlessly with unmatched intensity and passion. He's quick, he's full of energy and he'll fetch almost any baseball hit to him in the outfield. At the dish he has what Brian Cashman called "legendary" bat speed. Unfortunately, Frazier had to cut his 80-grade hair to move to New York, but perhaps it will make him even faster. At the very least it seemed to revive his bat, which had been slumping in Triple-A Columbus.

Brett Gardner LF

Born: 8/24/83   Age: 33   Bats: L   Throws: L   Height: 5'11"   Weight: 195   Entered Pro Ball: Round 3, 2005 Draft (#109 overall)

YEAR	TEAM	LVL	AGE	PA	R	2B	3B	HR	RBI	BB	K	SB	CS	AVG/OBP/SLG	TAv	VORP	BABIP	BRR	FRAA	WARP
2014	NYA	MLB	30	636	87	25	8	17	58	56	134	21	5	.256/.327/.422	.278	28.8	.305	4.5	LF(126): -0.6 • CF(25): -0.6	3.1
2015	NYA	MLB	31	656	94	26	3	16	66	68	135	20	5	.259/.343/.399	.264	22.6	.312	4.7	LF(119): 0.6 • CF(40): -2.2	2.2
2016	NYA	MLB	32	634	80	22	6	7	41	70	106	16	4	.261/.351/.362	.254	14.8	.310	5.2	LF(147): 11.1 • CF(3): -0.1	2.7
2017	*NYA*	*MLB*	*33*	*643*	*80*	*25*	*6*	*12*	*58*	*63*	*132*	*18*	*4*	*.256/.331/.389*	*.253*	*19.1*	*.305*	*2.2*	*LF 6*	*2.0*
2018	*NYA*	*MLB*	*34*	*527*	*63*	*20*	*5*	*11*	*56*	*54*	*111*	*13*	*4*	*.250/.334/.390*	*.248*	*9.3*	*.297*	*3.3*	*LF 5*	*1.5*

Breakout: 3%   Improve: 36%   Collapse: 8%   Attrition: 13%   MLB: 91%   *Comparables: Frank Catalanotto, Delino DeShields, Don Buford*

Unlike his outfield-mate Jacoby Ellsbury, Brett Gardner has stood the test of time to this point. The 33-year-old turned in a spectacular season of defensive play in left field while remaining stagnant on offense and on the basepaths. The power numbers have dissipated, but Gardner continues to hit the ball hard (25.8 percent in 2016) and spray it to all field, putting a career-high 28.2 percent of his batted balls up the middle. The offense barely slipped, and the defense looked as good as ever. At $12 million per year over the next two seasons, Gardner is a valuable left fielder.

Didi Gregorius   SS

Born: 2/18/90   Age: 27   Bats: L   Throws: R   Height: 6'3"   Weight: 205   Entered Pro Ball: International Free Agent, 2007

YEAR	TEAM	LVL	AGE	PA	R	2B	3B	HR	RBI	BB	K	SB	CS	AVG/OBP/SLG	TAv	VORP	BABIP	BRR	FRAA	WARP
2014	RNO	AAA	24	260	42	14	4	3	25	24	26	3	0	.310/.389/.447	.280	15.5	.338	1.0	2B(38): -2.8 • SS(19): 1.8	1.4
2014	ARI	MLB	24	299	35	9	5	6	27	22	52	3	0	.226/.290/.363	.245	10.9	.257	4.5	SS(67): 0.3 • 2B(11): 1.2	1.4
2015	NYA	MLB	25	578	57	24	2	9	56	33	85	5	3	.265/.318/.370	.251	18.8	.297	1.0	SS(155): 1.2	2.2
2016	NYA	MLB	26	597	68	32	2	20	70	19	82	7	1	.276/.304/.447	.257	26.8	.290	4.2	SS(153): -5.3	2.2
2017	NYA	MLB	27	573	58	24	4	14	64	35	90	5	2	.259/.309/.401	.249	20.8	.283	-0.1	SS 2	1.5
2018	NYA	MLB	28	516	61	20	4	15	60	33	87	4	1	.254/.309/.408	.244	11.7	.278	2.6	SS 2	1.5

Breakout: 6%   Improve: 43%   Collapse: 4%   Attrition: 12%   MLB: 98%   *Comparables: Daniel Descalso, Eduardo Nunez, Adeiny Hechavarria*

With all the twists and turns that Gregorius has taken over the past two seasons there is really no telling what will happen to him next. He began his time with the Yankees in 2015 as a defensive-minded shortstop with lots to learn on offense, and by the end of 2016 he was an incredible reverse-splits hitter with a questionable glove. How does that happen? Well, it's probably because he was growing up. Gregorius will be 27 on Opening Day, and—as the cliche goes—he has learned a lot about himself over the past two seasons. He's cracked the code on how to hit breaking pitches and figured out how to capitalize on the short porch in right field at Yankee Stadium. In the process, though, he lost focus on his fielding, finishing 2016 with a dismal FRAA that was six runs lower than the previous season. The hope going forward with Gregorius is that he pieces his game together entering his prime years. Can he remember how to field and hit righties again (.272 in 2015) while retaining his power and success against lefties? Or will he have yet another off-the-rails season and turn into a completely different player? Given his age, odds are that volatility is a thing of the past, but it's impossible to say for sure.

Chase Headley   3B

Born: 5/9/84   Age: 33   Bats: B   Throws: R   Height: 6'2"   Weight: 215   Entered Pro Ball: Round 2, 2005 Draft (#66 overall)

YEAR	TEAM	LVL	AGE	PA	R	2B	3B	HR	RBI	BB	K	SB	CS	AVG/OBP/SLG	TAv	VORP	BABIP	BRR	FRAA	WARP
2014	SDN	MLB	30	307	27	12	1	7	32	22	73	4	1	.229/.296/.355	.243	5.0	.285	0.8	3B(76): -2.6	0.3
2014	NYA	MLB	30	224	28	8	0	6	17	29	49	3	2	.262/.371/.398	.286	12.4	.324	0.9	3B(51): 6.2 • 1B(7): 1.3	2.2
2015	NYA	MLB	31	642	74	29	1	11	62	51	135	0	2	.259/.324/.369	.245	9.6	.317	-0.8	3B(155): 3.8 • 1B(1): -0.0	1.4
2016	NYA	MLB	32	529	58	18	1	14	51	51	118	8	2	.253/.331/.385	.248	10.7	.306	0.1	3B(140): 4.9	1.6
2017	NYA	MLB	33	553	64	23	1	16	61	56	128	5	2	.251/.334/.400	.259	15.2	.307	-1.0	3B 7	1.9
2018	NYA	MLB	34	488	63	19	0	15	56	54	115	3	2	.248/.339/.399	.255	8.3	.305	0.1	3B 6	1.6

Breakout: 3%   Improve: 40%   Collapse: 8%   Attrition: 14%   MLB: 91%   *Comparables: Robin Ventura, Wayne Gross, Mike Lamb*

At first glance Headley's 2016 was as unspectacular as Justin Guarini's pop career. Upon looking at his monthly splits, though, there's some hope. Sandwiched between two miserable months to bookend his season was steady offensive production—Headley hit .277 from May through August with 12 homers at the bottom of the Yankees' lineup. The key? A mid-May adjustment he made in his swing to unlock his hands. Sure, he wasn't worth his $13 million salary, but those four months of hitting plus an improved glove (FRAA doesn't do justice how bad he was in the field in 2015) make for a palatable season. A repeat would be considered a success.

Aaron Hicks   OF

Born: 10/2/89   Age: 27   Bats: B   Throws: R   Height: 6'1"   Weight: 205   Entered Pro Ball: Round 1, 2008 Draft (#14 overall)

YEAR	TEAM	LVL	AGE	PA	R	2B	3B	HR	RBI	BB	K	SB	CS	AVG/OBP/SLG	TAv	VORP	BABIP	BRR	FRAA	WARP
2014	NBR	AA	24	178	30	11	1	4	21	28	27	2	3	.297/.404/.466	.311	15.6	.336	1.9	CF(27): 0.3 • RF(9): 0.6	1.8
2014	ROC	AAA	24	84	9	5	0	1	8	9	13	1	1	.278/.349/.389	.247	0.6	.317	-0.6	CF(16): -3.2 • LF(4): 0.3	-0.2
2014	MIN	MLB	24	225	22	8	0	1	18	36	56	4	3	.215/.341/.274	.245	2.3	.300	-0.8	CF(57): 6.8 • LF(6): -0.5	0.9
2015	ROC	AAA	25	168	26	13	4	3	20	17	30	2	1	.342/.405/.544	.344	20.3	.407	1.4	CF(24): 4.4 • RF(9): -0.3	2.5
2015	MIN	MLB	25	390	48	13	3	11	33	34	66	13	3	.256/.323/.398	.253	7.4	.285	-0.9	CF(88): 6.5 • RF(16): -0.6	1.5
2016	NYA	MLB	26	361	32	13	1	8	31	30	68	3	4	.217/.281/.336	.220	-6.8	.248	0.3	RF(86): 0.0 • LF(25): 0.0	-0.5
2017	NYA	MLB	27	308	35	12	2	8	32	32	67	6	3	.236/.315/.381	.247	4.3	.281	0.0	RF -3 • LF 1	0.2
2018	NYA	MLB	28	390	47	15	2	11	44	42	85	7	3	.237/.321/.391	.245	2.7	.281	-0.3	RF -3 • LF 1	0.3

Breakout: 7%   Improve: 41%   Collapse: 3%   Attrition: 20%   MLB: 89%   *Comparables: Jose Tabata, Angel Pagan, David DeJesus*

The only highlight of Hicks' season was his at-bat song—"Highlights" by Kanye West. In all seriousness, Hicks failed to take the step forward offensively that many hope he would, and outside of a Statcast-record-shattering throw from right field in April he was surprisingly mediocre in the field. The switch-hitter actually managed to hit righties better than lefties, contrary to the strengths indicated by his history. Perhaps this proven success—seasons apart—against both righties and lefties will eventually culminate in Hicks being an average offensive player with a strong arm. A solid finish to the season lights a candle of hope, but a larger sample size does its best to extinguish that flame.

Matt Holliday   LF

Born: 1/15/80   Age: 37   Bats: R   Throws: R   Height: 6'4"   Weight: 240   Entered Pro Ball: Round 7, 1998 Draft (#210 overall)

YEAR	TEAM	LVL	AGE	PA	R	2B	3B	HR	RBI	BB	K	SB	CS	AVG/OBP/SLG	TAv	VORP	BABIP	BRR	FRAA	WARP
2014	SLN	MLB	34	667	83	37	0	20	90	74	100	4	1	.272/.370/.441	.292	36.0	.298	3.2	LF(150): -12.4	2.6
2015	SLN	MLB	35	277	24	16	1	4	35	39	49	2	1	.279/.394/.410	.299	14.7	.335	-1.4	LF(64): -6.5	0.9
2016	SLN	MLB	36	426	48	20	1	20	62	35	71	0	0	.246/.322/.461	.279	15.4	.253	-1.1	LF(84): -5.3 • 1B(10): 0.7	1.1
2017	NYA	MLB	37	566	69	26	1	21	75	61	104	3	1	.262/.352/.447	.279	21.6	.291	-1.1	1B 2	2.4
2018	NYA	MLB	38	410	54	19	0	14	52	43	80	1	0	.252/.341/.428	.262	10.8	.284	0.0	1B 1	1.3

Breakout: 0%   Improve: 20%   Collapse: 9%   Attrition: 9%   MLB: 85%   *Comparables: Jayson Werth, Monte Irvin, Luis Gonzalez*

Nagging injuries and advancing age have robbed Holliday of his defensive utility and finally conspired to end his streak of seasons posting a .290-plus TAv at 10, a record of consistent production exceeded only by Miguel Cabrera's 11 straight (and counting). Big Daddy still displays the plus approach that has long underpinned his success, but his numbers were dragged down by a career-low batting average on balls in play. Holliday can still sting the ball—his average exit velocity trailed only Nelson Cruz and Giancarlo Stanton last year—but his launch angle dropped and he traded line-drive singles for hard-hit ground outs. It's not crazy to think that one of the best pure hitters of his generation can rediscover some loft and provide a few more years of solid production.

Aaron Judge   RF

Born: 4/26/92   Age: 25   Bats: R   Throws: R   Height: 6'7"   Weight: 275   Entered Pro Ball: Round 1, 2013 Draft (#32 overall)

YEAR	TEAM	LVL	AGE	PA	R	2B	3B	HR	RBI	BB	K	SB	CS	AVG/OBP/SLG	TAv	VORP	BABIP	BRR	FRAA	WARP
2014	CSC	A	22	278	36	15	2	9	45	39	59	1	0	.333/.428/.530	.341	25.9	.408	-2.8	RF(55): 2.1	2.9
2014	TAM	A+	22	285	44	9	2	8	33	50	72	0	0	.283/.411/.442	.302	19.9	.377	1.8	RF(61): 8.7	2.9
2015	TRN	AA	23	280	36	16	3	12	44	24	70	1	0	.284/.350/.516	.316	23.0	.345	2.6	RF(52): 10.8	3.7
2015	SWB	AAA	23	260	27	10	0	8	28	29	74	6	2	.224/.308/.373	.247	0.8	.289	-0.2	RF(50): 7.6 • CF(8): -0.5	0.8
2016	SWB	AAA	24	410	62	18	1	19	65	47	98	5	0	.270/.366/.489	.311	31.4	.319	2.8	RF(66): 11.8 • LF(7): -0.6	4.3
2016	NYA	MLB	24	95	10	2	0	4	10	9	42	0	1	.179/.263/.345	.222	-2.5	.282	-0.5	RF(27): -3.0	-0.6
2017	NYA	MLB	25	532	67	20	2	23	70	57	165	3	1	.235/.323/.434	.264	14.3	.306	-0.7	RF 8	2.1
2018	NYA	MLB	26	515	72	20	1	23	72	58	163	3	1	.237/.331/.443	.261	10.9	.313	-0.8	RF 8	2.0

Breakout: 5%   Improve: 23%   Collapse: 7%   Attrition: 25%   MLB: 57%   Comparables: Jabari Blash, Kyle Jensen, Scott Schebler

For all the hype surrounding this massive human being entering the season, Judge was Trinidad James in 2016—a one-hit wonder (aside: "Female$ Welcomed" is a very underrated song). After punishing a changeup 446 feet into center field in his first career at-bat, Judge carried the worrisome contact rates that plagued him at Triple-A into the bigs, where he was easily fooled at the plate. He's proven he can hit baseballs very far, but it's time for the 24-year-old to prove he can make consistent contact.

Jorge Mateo   SS

Born: 6/23/95   Age: 22   Bats: R   Throws: R   Height: 6'0"   Weight: 190   Entered Pro Ball: International Free Agent, 2012

YEAR	TEAM	LVL	AGE	PA	R	2B	3B	HR	RBI	BB	K	SB	CS	AVG/OBP/SLG	TAv	VORP	BABIP	BRR	FRAA	WARP
2015	CSC	A	20	409	51	18	8	2	33	36	80	71	15	.268/.338/.378	.277	25.5	.338	4.1	SS(79): -0.9	2.6
2015	TAM	A+	20	91	15	5	3	0	7	7	18	11	2	.321/.374/.452	.313	10.6	.409	2.3	SS(20): -0.0	1.1
2016	TAM	A+	21	507	65	16	9	8	47	33	108	36	15	.254/.306/.379	.244	11.8	.313	3.2	SS(62): -4.8 • 2B(40): -0.7	0.6
2017	NYA	MLB	22	250	35	9	3	7	22	15	70	15	5	.225/.273/.371	.216	1.2	.289	1.7	SS -0 • 2B 0	0.1
2018	NYA	MLB	23	381	43	14	5	11	44	25	103	24	8	.236/.289/.399	.233	5.9	.298	3.9	SS 0 • 2B 0	0.6

Breakout: 1%   Improve: 15%   Collapse: 5%   Attrition: 10%   MLB: 22%   Comparables: Tim Beckham, Chris Nelson, Jonathan Villar

Things could have gone better for Mateo, who entered 2016 as the team's "shortstop of the future," struggled to get on base at High-A Tampa and saw his team trade for a more exciting player at his position who happens to be two years younger. Now second banana to Gleyber Torres, there is considerably less pressure on Mateo's shoulders, which could potentially help him regain form. His calling card is his speed, but with poor on-base skills he won't have much of a chance to showcase it.

Rob Refsnyder   RF

Born: 3/26/91   Age: 26   Bats: R   Throws: R   Height: 6'0"   Weight: 200   Entered Pro Ball: Round 5, 2012 Draft (#187 overall)

YEAR	TEAM	LVL	AGE	PA	R	2B	3B	HR	RBI	BB	K	SB	CS	AVG/OBP/SLG	TAv	VORP	BABIP	BRR	FRAA	WARP
2014	TRN	AA	23	244	35	19	5	6	30	14	38	5	5	.342/.385/.548	.329	21.5	.391	-2.2	2B(58): 4.9	2.8
2014	SWB	AAA	23	333	47	19	1	8	33	41	67	4	4	.300/.389/.456	.288	18.7	.364	-0.8	2B(64): -4.5 • RF(9): -1.1	1.3
2015	SWB	AAA	24	525	66	28	2	9	56	56	73	12	2	.271/.359/.402	.283	29.0	.302	3.1	2B(107): 7.8	3.8
2015	NYA	MLB	24	47	3	3	0	2	5	3	7	2	0	.302/.348/.512	.268	0.7	.324	-0.8	2B(15): 0.5	0.1
2016	SWB	AAA	25	230	25	10	1	2	20	17	30	6	0	.316/.365/.402	.286	9.5	.356	-2.8	3B(26): -1.9 • 2B(16): -0.7	0.7
2016	NYA	MLB	25	175	25	9	0	0	12	18	30	2	1	.250/.328/.309	.227	-4.7	.304	-1.7	1B(25): -2.0 • RF(23): 0.8	-0.6
2017	NYA	MLB	26	64	7	3	0	2	8	6	13	1	0	.268/.340/.427	.268	2.4	.313	0.0	2B 0 • 3B -0	0.2
2018	NYA	MLB	27	311	39	15	1	9	37	28	61	4	1	.267/.339/.429	.262	7.6	.310	-1.2	2B 1 • 3B -2	0.7

Breakout: 3%   Improve: 34%   Collapse: 12%   Attrition: 22%   MLB: 60%   Comparables: James Darnell, Brendan Harris, Taylor Green

It's beginning to look like Refsnyder is a Quadruple-A player entering his age-26 season. After all that he did at the plate in Triple-A during the 2015 season, the second baseman fumbled a larger dose of plate appearances in 2016 and his production was pretty even with that of a replacement-level player. That could be what he is at this point, though we still haven't seen what he can do with a hefty bunch of at-bats. On the bright side, he appeared to be a somewhat capable defender at a few different positions, which was one of the biggest knocks on him as he rose through the Yankees' system. It could take a change of scenery to figure out what he's made of.

Austin Romine   C

Born: 11/22/88   Age: 28   Bats: R   Throws: R   Height: 6'1"   Weight: 220   Entered Pro Ball: Round 2, 2007 Draft (#94 overall)

YEAR	TEAM	LVL	AGE	PA	R	2B	3B	HR	RBI	BB	K	SB	CS	AVG/OBP/SLG	TAv	VORP	BABIP	BRR	FRAA	WARP
2014	SWB	AAA	25	313	33	17	0	6	33	24	54	1	0	.242/.300/.365	.223	-1.5	.279	-0.7	C(62): -2.5 • 1B(13): -0.6	-0.5
2014	NYA	MLB	25	13	2	1	0	0	1	0	4	0	0	.231/.231/.308	.189	-0.6	.333	-0.1	C(3): -0.2 • 1B(1): -0.0	-0.1
2015	SWB	AAA	26	366	38	19	0	7	49	22	53	0	1	.260/.311/.379	.254	13.2	.289	1.3	C(75): 6.0 • 1B(10): -0.7	1.9
2015	NYA	MLB	26	2	0	0	0	0	0	0	0	0	0	.000/.000/.000	.020	-0.4	.000	0.0	1B(1): 0.2	0.0
2016	NYA	MLB	27	176	17	11	0	4	26	7	31	1	0	.242/.269/.382	.217	-0.6	.271	-0.1	C(50): -3.0 • 1B(6): -0.2	-0.4
2017	NYA	MLB	28	124	12	6	0	3	13	7	26	0	0	.238/.285/.380	.230	1.9	.277	-0.3	C -2	-0.1
2018	NYA	MLB	29	240	27	11	0	7	27	14	52	0	0	.235/.283/.383	.226	-0.1	.271	-0.6	C -4	-0.4

Breakout: 5%   Improve: 29%   Collapse: 18%   Attrition: 39%   MLB: 76%   Comparables: Bryan Holaday, Jason Jaramillo, Mike Rabelo

In hindsight, the fact that Romine beat out Gary Sanchez—the greatest player of his generation—for the backup catcher spot out of spring training is incredible. All kidding aside, the 28-year-old went from a Quadruple-A catcher to a legitimate bench player in 2016, producing at an above-average rate for his position and providing fine defense. His most valuable trait last season? Quietly hitting .364 in 48 plate appearances with runners in scoring position. Somehow the Yankees continue to produce an abundance of catchers year in and year out. If only they could do that other positions.

YEAR	TEAM	P. COUNT	FRM RUNS	BLK RUNS	THRW RUNS	TOT RUNS
2014	NYA	244	-0.2	0.1	0.0	-0.1
2014	SWB	8934	0.0	-0.4	-2.0	-2.3
2015	SWB	10657	7.9	-0.1	-0.3	7.5
2016	NYA	5754	-1.9	-0.1	-0.3	-2.4
2017	NYA	4598	-0.7	-0.2	-0.4	-1.3
2018	NYA	8907	-2.0	-0.4	-0.9	-3.3

Blake Rutherford   OF

Born: 5/2/97   Age: 20   Bats: L   Throws: R   Height: 6'3"   Weight: 195   Entered Pro Ball: Round 1, 2016 Draft (#18 overall)

YEAR	TEAM	LVL	AGE	PA	R	2B	3B	HR	RBI	BB	K	SB	CS	AVG/OBP/SLG	TAv	VORP	BABIP	BRR	FRAA	WARP
2017	NYA	MLB	20	250	25	9	1	6	23	15	85	0	0	.198/.249/.326	.195	-8.1	.276	-0.4	CF 0 • LF -0	-0.8
2018	NYA	MLB	21	268	29	9	1	7	28	19	87	1	0	.206/.266/.342	.211	-6.8	.281	-0.5	CF 0 • LF 0	-0.7

Breakout: 1%   Improve: 3%   Collapse: 0%   Attrition: 2%   MLB: 4%   *Comparables: Joe Benson, Chris Parmelee, Engel Beltre*

It's rare that you see baseball fans thrown into a frenzy over a tweet from a rookie-league team, yet many fans won't forget where they were on the night of August 27, 2016 when the Pulaski Yankees tweeted: "RE: Blake Rutherford. The Pulaski Yankees have no comment. All questions may be directed to Yankees Player Development Complex in Tampa." They later erased the message. Rutherford, a five-tool outfielder once projected to be drafted in the top five picks, fell all the way to no. 18 for the Yankees amid concerns he wouldn't sign. When he *did* sign, fans fell so deeply in love with his bat after a torrid start in rookie-ball that they panicked when the aforementioned cryptic message appeared and disappeared (it turned out to be a minor hamstring issue). Rutherford is capable of hitting for contact from the left side, spraying the ball and seeing pitches with a careful eye. He has the potential to hit a lot of dingers at the next level once he develops his swing a bit more. The 19-year-old looks like a raw, special talent.

Gary Sanchez   C

Born: 12/2/92   Age: 24   Bats: R   Throws: R   Height: 6'2"   Weight: 230   Entered Pro Ball: International Free Agent, 2009

YEAR	TEAM	LVL	AGE	PA	R	2B	3B	HR	RBI	BB	K	SB	CS	AVG/OBP/SLG	TAv	VORP	BABIP	BRR	FRAA	WARP
2014	TRN	AA	21	477	48	19	0	13	65	43	91	1	1	.270/.338/.406	.283	27.3	.314	-2.6	C(93): 8.0	3.8
2015	TRN	AA	22	254	33	14	0	12	36	18	50	6	0	.262/.319/.476	.297	19.2	.285	-0.6	C(54): 4.6	2.6
2015	SWB	AAA	22	146	17	9	0	6	26	11	28	1	2	.295/.349/.500	.292	10.3	.330	-0.2	C(29): 2.8	1.3
2015	NYA	MLB	22	2	0	0	0	0	0	0	1	0	0	.000/.000/.000	.033	-0.4	.000	0.0		0.0
2016	SWB	AAA	23	313	39	21	1	10	50	21	45	7	1	.282/.339/.468	.299	25.1	.302	-0.9	C(64): 11.4	3.8
2016	NYA	MLB	23	229	34	12	0	20	42	24	57	1	0	.299/.376/.657	.332	23.5	.317	-1.2	C(36): 3.1	2.7
2017	NYA	MLB	24	613	79	28	1	31	92	49	143	5	1	.260/.323/.480	.278	36.7	.294	-0.7	C 4	2.6
2018	NYA	MLB	25	558	79	26	0	28	85	46	127	4	1	.262/.328/.484	.273	25.4	.295	-1.8	C 4	3.1

Breakout: 1%   Improve: 27%   Collapse: 27%   Attrition: 31%   MLB: 81%   *Comparables: Ryan Lavarnway, Devin Mesoraco, Travis d'Arnaud*

Brian Cashman called Sanchez "a real high-end catcher" at the end of 2015, which the majority of the public saw as yet another attempt on the Yankees' part to overhype one of their prospects. Well, those people ate it last season, big time. Sanchez finally got a chance in the majors and became a household name in just 53 games. There is little question that he can mash, taking all types of pitches deep at a record rate and scaring pitchers into avoiding the strike zone in the process. Even Sanchez's work behind the plate, which has long been the knock on him, was superb. He was an adequate blocker and threw out 41 percent of baserunners—12 points higher than the league average—to inspire the #DROG (Don't Run On Gary) hashtag on Twitter. He does it all, and looks the part of a budding superstar.

YEAR	TEAM	P. COUNT	FRM RUNS	BLK RUNS	THRW RUNS	TOT RUNS
2014	TRN	13230	6.6	-1.4	1.9	7.0
2015	SWB	3954	2.9	0.1	0.1	3.1
2015	TRN	7918	3.1	0.4	1.2	4.6
2016	NYA	5290	1.7	-1.6	1.0	1.1
2017	NYA	19097	4.2	-2.8	1.3	2.8
2018	NYA	17385	3.6	-2.3	1.2	2.4

Mark Teixeira   1B

Born: 4/11/80   Age: 37   Bats: B   Throws: R   Height: 6'3"   Weight: 225   Entered Pro Ball: Round 1, 2001 Draft (#5 overall)

YEAR	TEAM	LVL	AGE	PA	R	2B	3B	HR	RBI	BB	K	SB	CS	AVG/OBP/SLG	TAv	VORP	BABIP	BRR	FRAA	WARP
2014	NYA	MLB	34	508	56	14	0	22	62	58	109	1	1	.216/.313/.398	.265	7.3	.233	0.3	1B(117): -3.6	0.4
2015	NYA	MLB	35	462	57	22	0	31	79	59	85	2	0	.255/.357/.548	.313	24.5	.246	-3.8	1B(108): 3.3	3.0
2016	NYA	MLB	36	438	43	16	0	15	44	47	105	2	0	.204/.292/.362	.231	-12.3	.238	-4.1	1B(110): -6.2	-1.9
2017	NYA	MLB	37	418	52	16	0	19	59	47	89	2	0	.229/.322/.436	.256	4.9	.247	-1.9	1B -1	0.5
2018	NYA	MLB	38	333	45	12	0	15	45	37	73	0	0	.220/.313/.418	.249	-1.3	.239	-1.7	1B 0	-0.2

Breakout: 1%   Improve: 20%   Collapse: 9%   Attrition: 13%   MLB: 66%   *Comparables: Ryan Klesko, Lyle Overbay, Travis Hafner*

Teixeira decided in June that it would be his final season, walking away from the game after 14 years and giving way to a new generation of Yankees corner infielders like Greg Bird and Tyler Austin. He'll likely get some consideration on the Hall of Fame ballot in 2022, but it doesn't seem likely that he'll last more than a year. The switch-hitter didn't dazzle at the plate with his counting stats, but he was solid during his peak and he supplied elite defense through his final season. There's a chance Teixeira, who had a very vanilla personality and style of play, goes down as one of the generation's forgotten players, which is a shame given how good he was in his prime. You'll also likely win a bar bet in eight years on the fact that he played for the Angels during his career. Whatever happened to Casey Kotchman?

Gleyber Torres   SS

Born: 12/13/96 Age: 20 Bats: R Throws: R Height: 6'1" Weight: 175 Entered Pro Ball: International Free Agent, 2013

YEAR	TEAM	LVL	AGE	PA	R	2B	3B	HR	RBI	BB	K	SB	CS	AVG/OBP/SLG	TAv	VORP	BABIP	BRR	FRAA	WARP
2014	BOI	A-	17	32	4	2	3	1	4	4	7	2	0	.393/.469/.786	.373	5.7	.500	0.6	SS(7): 0.4	0.6
2015	SBN	A	18	514	53	24	5	3	62	43	108	22	13	.293/.353/.386	.266	22.1	.373	-2.0	SS(119): -9.3	1.4
2015	MYR	A+	18	24	1	0	0	0	2	1	7	0	1	.174/.208/.174	.151	-2.0	.250	-0.3	SS(7): 0.3	-0.2
2016	MYR	A+	19	409	62	23	3	9	47	42	87	19	10	.275/.359/.433	.282	26.0	.341	0.2	SS(87): 0.9	2.8
2016	TAM	A+	19	138	19	6	2	2	19	16	23	2	3	.254/.341/.385	.279	5.2	.299	-2.9	SS(27): -0.8 • 2B(1): 0.0	0.5
2017	NYA	MLB	20	250	31	10	1	7	24	18	71	5	3	.230/.291/.375	.226	2.2	.300	-0.3	SS -3 • 2B 0	0.0
2018	NYA	MLB	21	396	47	18	2	12	46	30	113	8	5	.240/.302/.400	.239	4.9	.312		SS -4 • 2B 0	0.1

Breakout: 2%   Improve: 11%   Collapse: 0%   Attrition: 5%   MLB: 14%   *Comparables: Trevor Story, Alen Hanson, Addison Russell*

The young shortstop got quite the introduction to New York after coming over in the Aroldis Chapman trade, struggling in his first week in High-A Tampa and drawing the hottest of takes from the city's tabloids. He quickly turned things around at the plate, proving why he's one of baseball's top prospects, and continued to mash in the Arizona Fall League. With the way he's hitting, Torres—profiled just a couple of years ago as a defensive shortstop—could rise quickly through the organization. Now out of Chicago, Torres isn't blocked by a handful of uber-talented young infielders and can see the light at the end of the tunnel.

Ronald Torreyes   2B

Born: 9/2/92 Age: 24 Bats: R Throws: R Height: 5'10" Weight: 150 Entered Pro Ball: International Free Agent, 2010

YEAR	TEAM	LVL	AGE	PA	R	2B	3B	HR	RBI	BB	K	SB	CS	AVG/OBP/SLG	TAv	VORP	BABIP	BRR	FRAA	WARP
2014	OKL	AAA	21	519	65	20	5	2	46	25	26	12	9	.298/.345/.376	.272	27.2	.310	3.9	2B(73): 0.6 • 3B(24): -0.8	3.1
2015	FRE	AAA	22	72	7	1	0	0	5	1	9	0	1	.200/.211/.214	.157	-6.4	.230	-0.7	2B(13): -1.2 • SS(5): -0.5	-0.8
2015	NHP	AA	22	54	4	2	0	0	9	4	2	2	0	.140/.204/.180	.134	-5.6	.146	-0.1	2B(14): -0.7 • SS(1): -0.0	-0.7
2015	TUL	AA	22	274	39	13	2	4	19	20	23	3	3	.293/.348/.410	.289	19.7	.308	1.6	SS(48): 0.3 • 2B(7): -0.9	2.0
2015	OKL	AAA	22	53	10	2	1	0	3	2	4	0	0	.306/.340/.388	.281	2.8	.326	-0.1	2B(7): -0.7 • SS(5): 1.4	0.4
2015	LAN	MLB	22	8	1	1	0	0	1	1	1	0	0	.333/.429/.500	.328	0.8	.400	0.0	2B(4): 0.2 • 3B(3): -0.0	0.1
2016	NYA	MLB	23	168	20	7	4	1	12	10	20	2	1	.258/.305/.374	.249	4.6	.289	0.9	3B(34): 4.3 • SS(15): -1.2	0.7
2017	NYA	MLB	24	165	16	7	1	3	15	8	19	2	1	.261/.299/.373	.239	2.1	.276	-0.2	SS -0 • 3B 1	0.1
2018	NYA	MLB	25	323	36	13	3	6	33	18	38	3	2	.264/.313/.392	.242	3.1	.277	-0.2	SS 0 • 3B 2	0.5

Breakout: 4%   Improve: 22%   Collapse: 8%   Attrition: 14%   MLB: 45%   *Comparables: Joe Panik, Rey Navarro, Josh Harrison*

This super-utility player, nicknamed "Toe" by manager Joe Girardi—something no man should be called—was a spectacular find by the team's front office. Just 24, he's already been signed by the Reds, traded to the Cubs, acquired by the Astros, Blue Jays and Dodgers, traded to the Yankees, claimed off waivers by the Angels and claimed back by the Yankees. That's some way to begin your twenties! Torreyes proved he can be plugged in almost anywhere and provide slightly-above-average defense with a steady bat.

Tyler Wade   MI

Born: 11/23/94 Age: 22 Bats: L Throws: R Height: 6'1" Weight: 185 Entered Pro Ball: Round 4, 2013 Draft (#134 overall)

YEAR	TEAM	LVL	AGE	PA	R	2B	3B	HR	RBI	BB	K	SB	CS	AVG/OBP/SLG	TAv	VORP	BABIP	BRR	FRAA	WARP
2014	CSC	A	19	576	77	24	6	1	51	57	118	22	13	.272/.350/.349	.260	21.6	.349	1.3	SS(94): 5.7, 2B(15): -1.1	2.7
2015	TAM	A+	20	418	51	11	5	2	28	39	65	31	15	.280/.349/.353	.274	23.1	.331	2.3	SS(72): 5.8, 2B(24): -0.9	3.0
2015	TRN	AA	20	117	6	4	0	1	3	2	24	2	1	.204/.224/.265	.198	-2.6	.265	0.3	SS(28): -1.3	-0.4
2016	TRN	AA	21	583	90	16	7	5	27	66	103	27	8	.259/.352/.349	.271	37.6	.317	11.0	SS(91): -6.0, 2B(38): -0.1	3.4
2017	NYA	MLB	22	250	30	8	2	5	22	21	61	7	3	.233/.302/.353	.225	2.0	.292	0.4	SS -0 • 2B -0	0.1
2018	NYA	MLB	23	404	46	13	3	9	42	34	98	12	5	.235/.305/.363	.231	2.4	.293	1.2	SS -1 • 2B -1	0.1

Breakout: 6%   Improve: 18%   Collapse: 6%   Attrition: 15%   MLB: 26%   *Comparables: Jose Pirela, Ehire Adrianza, Ivan De Jesus*

The 2013 fourth-round pick has quickly worked his way through the Yankees' farm system by leaning on a strong glove and plus speed. He's a rather interesting prospect, given that he came out of nowhere in a system well-stocked with talent in the middle infield. Neither of his two best skills are good enough to make him stand out—especially his defensive production, which dipped—but if his bat continues to trend in the right direction he'll have just enough to crack an organizational top 10. Now 22, he'll likely get a shot in the major leagues by the end of 2017, where the world will see whether he can get on base enough to be a capable big leaguer.

Mason Williams   CF

Born: 8/21/91 Age: 25 Bats: L Throws: R Height: 6'1" Weight: 185 Entered Pro Ball: Round 4, 2010 Draft (#145 overall)

YEAR	TEAM	LVL	AGE	PA	R	2B	3B	HR	RBI	BB	K	SB	CS	AVG/OBP/SLG	TAv	VORP	BABIP	BRR	FRAA	WARP
2014	TRN	AA	22	563	67	18	4	5	40	47	68	21	8	.223/.290/.304	.216	-7.1	.248	2.9	CF(106): 4.5 • RF(11): -0.7	-0.3
2015	TRN	AA	23	144	14	7	0	0	11	19	17	11	6	.317/.407/.375	.304	8.4	.365	-1.4	LF(14): 0.3 • CF(13): -1.0	0.8
2015	SWB	AAA	23	91	12	7	1	0	11	8	6	2	1	.321/.382/.432	.298	7.3	.347	1.0	CF(20): 2.0	1.0
2015	NYA	MLB	23	22	3	3	0	1	3	1	3	0	0	.286/.318/.571	.300	1.5	.294	0.0	CF(8): -1.0	0.1
2016	TAM	A+	24	43	2	2	1	0	1	1	4	0	0	.333/.349/.429	.281	0.6	.368	-1.1	CF(4): 0.3	0.1
2016	SWB	AAA	24	138	19	8	1	0	23	5	21	1	1	.296/.313/.376	.260	4.1	.343	0.8	CF(18): -1.5 • RF(3): -0.1	0.3
2016	NYA	MLB	24	29	4	1	0	0	2	1	12	0	0	.231/.321/.333	.231	0.1	.533	0.3	RF(7): -0.2 • LF(2): 0.4	0.1
2017	NYA	MLB	25	64	7	3	0	1	6	5	12	1	1	.243/.295/.362	.229	0.0	.278	0.0	LF 0 • CF 0	0.0
2018	NYA	MLB	26	265	30	12	1	6	28	22	49	6	3	.248/.311/.381	.234	-0.1	.281	0.2	LF 2 • CF 1	0.2

Breakout: 3%   Improve: 16%   Collapse: 6%   Attrition: 20%   MLB: 30%   *Comparables: Shane Robinson, Matt Szczur, Daniel Robertson*

The former top prospect had a tumultuous year recovering from right shoulder surgery, which derailed a promising 2015 season. When he returned at Triple-A he resumed production at nearly the same level, and when he got a late-season call to the big leagues in wake of Aaron Judge's injury he made the most of it and helped the Yankees win several key games. Williams doesn't have the "franchise center fielder" pedigree he once did, but at 25 he still has a chance to make some impact. The disheartening struggles with weak minor-league pitching seem buried in the past, and the focus for Williams now is just staying on the field.

PITCHERS

Albert Abreu   RHP

Born: 9/26/95   Age: 21   Bats: R   Throws: R   Height: 6'2"   Weight: 175   Entered Pro Ball: International Free Agent, 2013

YEAR	TEAM	LVL	AGE	W	L	SV	G	GS	IP	H	HR	BB/9	K/9	K	GB%	BABIP	WHIP	ERA	FIP	DRA	VORP	WARP	cFIP	MPH
2016	QUD	A	20	2	8	4	21	14	90	62	5	4.9	10.4	104	49%	.264	1.23	3.50	3.85	3.68	12.4	1.4	102	
2016	LNC	A+	20	1	0	0	3	2	11²	12	2	6.9	8.5	11	41%	.312	1.80	5.40	6.37	5.61	-0.3	0.0	113	
2017	*NYA*	*MLB*	*21*	*3*	*5*	*0*	*27*	*12*	*70²*	*79*	*12*	*6.5*	*6.4*	*50*	*56%*	*.297*	*1.83*	*6.31*	*6.25*	*6.54*	*-13.4*	*-1.4*	*154*	
2018	*NYA*	*MLB*	*22*	*4*	*6*	*0*	*21*	*14*	*108¹*	*101*	*17*	*7.7*	*9.7*	*117*	*56%*	*.294*	*1.80*	*6.02*	*5.86*	*6.24*	*-8.1*	*-0.8*	*146*	

Breakout: 2%   Improve: 2%   Collapse: 0%   Attrition: 2%   MLB: 3%   Comparables: Zach Braddock, Austin Brice, Jose Ceda

Between a mid-90s fastball and a plus changeup and curveball, Abreu's stuff is as nasty as it gets in the low minors. Unfortunately for Abreu, a number of opponents have figured out one simple trick to get on base against him: just keep the bat on the shoulder. Abreu's walk rate has escalated every year as he has progressed up the ladder. He already has such a nasty and versatile arsenal that it's very easy to imagine Abreu in the upper half of a rotation a few years down the line. But Abreu has some trouble repeating his delivery, and he's going to have to figure that out if he's ever going to develop the command he'll need to succeed at the upper levels of the minors, much less the majors.

John Barbato   RHP

Born: 7/11/92   Age: 24   Bats: R   Throws: R   Height: 6'1"   Weight: 235   Entered Pro Ball: Round 6, 2010 Draft (#184 overall)

YEAR	TEAM	LVL	AGE	W	L	SV	G	GS	IP	H	HR	BB/9	K/9	K	GB%	BABIP	WHIP	ERA	FIP	DRA	VORP	WARP	cFIP	MPH
2014	SAN	AA	21	2	2	16	27	0	31¹	26	3	2.9	9.5	33	42%	.280	1.15	2.87	3.31	2.92	6.7	0.7	91	
2015	TRN	AA	22	2	2	0	26	0	42¹	42	4	3	9.4	44	41%	.330	1.32	4.04	3.62	2.28	11.5	1.2	86	
2015	SWB	AAA	22	4	0	3	14	0	25	13	1	4	9.4	26	47%	.211	0.96	0.36	2.92	3.77	3.2	0.3	94	
2016	NYA	MLB	23	1	2	0	13	0	13	13	2	3.5	10.4	15	46%	.333	1.38	7.62	4.41	3.98	1.4	0.1	99	96.6
2016	SWB	AAA	23	3	2	3	31	1	48¹	38	3	4.3	9.1	49	47%	.276	1.26	2.61	3.44	4.32	3.5	0.4	103	
2017	*NYA*	*MLB*	*24*	*1*	*2*	*0*	*29*	*0*	*30*	*31*	*4*	*4.1*	*7.5*	*25*	*51%*	*.295*	*1.47*	*4.95*	*4.73*	*4.93*	*0.2*	*0.0*	*100*	
2018	*NYA*	*MLB*	*25*	*2*	*1*	*0*	*37*	*0*	*39²*	*35*	*5*	*5.3*	*10.6*	*47*	*51%*	*.298*	*1.46*	*4.53*	*4.39*	*4.79*	*1.1*	*0.1*	*109*	

Breakout: 31%   Improve: 43%   Collapse: 6%   Attrition: 32%   MLB: 54%   Comparables: Edgmer Escalona, Mark Melancon, Chase Whitley

The 24-year-old was brilliant in the beginning of his first big-league season, but things went downhill after his fifth appearance. As a result, Barbato only saw one more chance with the Yankees after May 8. His slider still needs some work, but the youngster showed impressive control in the bigs. He has done enough at Triple-A the past two seasons to place him firmly on the radar for 2017.

Dellin Betances   RHP

Born: 3/23/88   Age: 29   Bats: R   Throws: R   Height: 6'8"   Weight: 265   Entered Pro Ball: Round 8, 2006 Draft (#254 overall)

YEAR	TEAM	LVL	AGE	W	L	SV	G	GS	IP	H	HR	BB/9	K/9	K	GB%	BABIP	WHIP	ERA	FIP	DRA	VORP	WARP	cFIP	MPH
2014	NYA	MLB	26	5	0	1	70	0	90	46	4	2.4	13.5	135	49%	.241	0.78	1.40	1.67	1.43	30.5	3.4	52	99.5
2015	NYA	MLB	27	6	4	9	74	0	84	45	6	4.3	14.0	131	49%	.257	1.01	1.50	2.45	2.07	24.6	2.6	57	99.7
2016	NYA	MLB	28	3	6	12	73	0	73	54	5	3.5	15.5	126	56%	.353	1.12	3.08	1.74	1.57	27.6	2.8	45	100.8
2017	*NYA*	*MLB*	*29*	*3*	*3*	*5*	*62*	*0*	*65*	*45*	*4*	*3.4*	*13.5*	*99*	*55%*	*.298*	*1.06*	*2.03*	*2.20*	*2.22*	*20.2*	*2.1*	*37*	
2018	*NYA*	*MLB*	*30*	*4*	*2*	*4*	*77*	*0*	*82*	*48*	*5*	*3.5*	*14.7*	*134*	*55%*	*.284*	*0.98*	*2.12*	*2.06*	*2.23*	*25.4*	*2.6*	*36*	

Breakout: 30%   Improve: 60%   Collapse: 20%   Attrition: 16%   MLB: 99%   Comparables: Brett Cecil, Mark Melancon, Adam Ottavino

It's hard to classify 2016 as anything but a step in the wrong direction for Betances, who worked the eighth inning better than anyone in baseball for most of 2015. The menacing right-hander wasn't necessarily *bad*—and much of his issues stemmed from a massive increase in BABIP—but he simply wasn't as dominant, spending most of the season with an ERA in the mid-twos. He did finally settle down in the second half, but was an absolute disaster in September, allowing 13 runs in 8.1 innings as the Yankees chased a playoff spot. Brian Cashman broke up "No-Runs DMC" thinking he still had a dominant closer, but entered free agency having second thoughts. Betances is still a great reliever, but the hype train lost some of its steam last year.

Luis Cessa   RHP

Born: 4/25/92   Age: 25   Bats: R   Throws: R   Height: 6'0"   Weight: 205   Entered Pro Ball: International Free Agent, 2008

YEAR	TEAM	LVL	AGE	W	L	SV	G	GS	IP	H	HR	BB/9	K/9	K	GB%	BABIP	WHIP	ERA	FIP	DRA	VORP	WARP	cFIP	MPH
2014	SLU	A+	22	7	8	0	20	20	114²	110	7	2.1	6.5	83	50%	.293	1.19	4.00	3.52	3.64	24.9	2.5	93	
2015	BIN	AA	23	7	4	0	13	13	77¹	77	2	2	7.1	61	50%	.315	1.22	2.56	2.69	2.05	26.1	2.8	83	
2015	LVG	AAA	23	0	3	0	5	5	24¹	40	3	1.5	8.9	24	56%	.425	1.81	8.51	3.85	2.05	8.8	0.9	80	
2015	TOL	AAA	23	1	3	0	7	7	37²	46	2	3.6	8.1	34	49%	.376	1.62	5.97	3.40	4.42	3.7	0.4	102	
2016	SWB	AAA	24	6	3	0	15	14	77¹	66	8	2.7	8.0	69	47%	.278	1.15	3.03	3.62	3.30	17.5	1.8	96	
2016	NYA	MLB	24	4	4	0	17	9	70¹	64	16	1.8	5.9	46	45%	.233	1.11	4.35	5.48	5.69	-3.4	-0.4	113	97.5
2017	*NYA*	*MLB*	*25*	*7*	*8*	*0*	*43*	*19*	*126*	*138*	*18*	*3.2*	*6.5*	*91*	*45%*	*.300*	*1.46*	*4.77*	*4.78*	*4.85*	*4.8*	*0.5*	*100*	
2018	*NYA*	*MLB*	*26*	*7*	*8*	*0*	*49*	*20*	*150¹*	*146*	*23*	*4.7*	*9.0*	*150*	*45%*	*.298*	*1.49*	*5.01*	*4.84*	*5.22*	*2.4*	*0.3*	*121*	

Breakout: 25%   Improve: 38%   Collapse: 38%   Attrition: 46%   MLB: 91%   Comparables: Andre Rienzo, Brandon Workman, T.J. House

PECOTA may hate Cessa's chances of transforming into an effective back-end starter, but PECOTA didn't watch any of Cessa's games because PECOTA doesn't have eyes. Sure, the 24-year-old struggled with the longball when given a shot to start, which isn't great when you pitch at Yankee Stadium, but that was pretty much the extent of his flaws. Cessa flashed decent strikeout potential, limited his walks and proved he can pitch in meaningful games, getting the Yankees a big win over the Red Sox in his second-to-last start of the year as they chased a Wild Card spot. He's got work to do, but Cessa could fill a cookie-cutter fifth-inning/long-reliever role, following in the footsteps of Yankee greats from Chase Whitley to David Phelps. At the very least, he is already making his general manager look good by coming over from Detroit with Chad Green in exchange for Justin Wilson last offseason.

Aroldis Chapman   LHP

Born: 2/28/88   Age: 29   Bats: L   Throws: L   Height: 6'4"   Weight: 215   Entered Pro Ball: International Free Agent, 2010

YEAR	TEAM	LVL	AGE	W	L	SV	G	GS	IP	H	HR	BB/9	K/9	K	GB%	BABIP	WHIP	ERA	FIP	DRA	VORP	WARP	cFIP	MPH
2014	CIN	MLB	26	0	3	36	54	0	54	21	1	4.0	17.7	106	44%	.290	0.83	2.00	0.86	1.06	20.5	2.3	38	103.2
2015	CIN	MLB	27	4	4	33	65	0	66¹	43	3	4.5	15.7	116	38%	.331	1.15	1.63	1.97	2.04	19.6	2.1	63	103.0
2016	NYA	MLB	28	3	0	20	31	0	31¹	20	2	2.3	12.6	44	38%	.273	0.89	2.01	1.89	1.95	10.5	1.1	57	104.1
2016	CHN	MLB	28	1	1	16	28	0	26²	12	0	3.4	15.5	46	59%	.261	0.82	1.01	0.86	2.16	8.3	0.9	58	104.2
2017	NYA	MLB	29	3	3	40	57	0	60	45	9	3.5	13.9	94	52%	.295	1.12	2.83	3.22	3.18	12.2	1.3	65	
2018	NYA	MLB	30	4	2	44	67	0	70²	51	10	3.3	13.7	108	52%	.289	1.10	3.04	3.19	3.46	12.3	1.3	74	

Breakout: 22%   Improve: 52%   Collapse: 29%   Attrition: 8%   MLB: 98%   *Comparables: David Robertson, Greg Holland, Francisco Rodriguez*

Fastest pitches thrown in MLB, 2016: (1) A. Chapman; (2) A. Chapman; (3) A. Chapman; (4) A. Chapman; (5) A. Chapman; (6) A. Chapman; (7) A. Chapman; (8) A. Chapman; (9) A. Chapman; (10) A. Chapman; (11) A. Chapman; (12) A. Chapman; (13) A. Chapman; (14) A. Chapman; (15) A. Chapman; (16) A. Chapman; (17) A. Chapman; (18) A. Chapman; (19) A. Chapman; (20) A. Chapman; (21) A. Chapman; (22) A. Chapman; (23) A. Chapman; (24) A. Chapman; (25) A. Chapman.

Chapman also throws a slider.

Ian Clarkin   LHP

Born: 2/14/95   Age: 22   Bats: L   Throws: L   Height: 6'2"   Weight: 190   Entered Pro Ball: Round 1, 2013 Draft (#33 overall)

YEAR	TEAM	LVL	AGE	W	L	SV	G	GS	IP	H	HR	BB/9	K/9	K	GB%	BABIP	WHIP	ERA	FIP	DRA	VORP	WARP	cFIP	MPH
2014	CSC	A	19	3	3	0	16	15	70	64	6	2.8	9.1	71	44%	.319	1.23	3.21	3.74	2.91	19.6	2.0	90	
2016	TAM	A+	21	6	9	0	18	18	98	100	4	2.8	6.6	72	51%	.313	1.33	3.31	3.26	4.77	7.6	0.8	104	
2017	NYA	MLB	22	3	5	0	13	13	62²	79	12	4.2	4.6	32	58%	.308	1.73	6.02	6.08	6.21	-5.1	-0.5	148	
2018	NYA	MLB	23	4	8	0	20	20	117	136	23	5.6	7.3	95	58%	.316	1.79	6.29	6.10	6.49	-10.7	-1.1	154	

Breakout: 1%   Improve: 2%   Collapse: 0%   Attrition: 2%   MLB: 3%   *Comparables: Jose Ramirez, Alex Colome, Adrian Sampson*

Have you ever given an important speech or presentation only to feel an eyelash on your cheek mid-way through? You try to power through the slight irritation, but you can't shake it. It's just noticeable enough for you to think about it during your presentation. That's Ian Clarkin. He's just good enough that the Yankees can't help but notice him. Nothing spectacular, but an arm nonetheless, and one that has been simply "fine" all the way through the minors. Soon a big-league team will wipe this eyelash off their face and into the majors. He's probably a long-man out of the bullpen or a back-end starter at the next level, and could follow in the footsteps of David Phelps, Chase Whitley, Adam Warren and Ivan Nova, the next in a long line of swingmen mass-produced in the Yankees' factory.

Tyler Clippard   RHP

Born: 2/14/85   Age: 32   Bats: R   Throws: R   Height: 6'3"   Weight: 200   Entered Pro Ball: Round 9, 2003 Draft (#274 overall)

YEAR	TEAM	LVL	AGE	W	L	SV	G	GS	IP	H	HR	BB/9	K/9	K	GB%	BABIP	WHIP	ERA	FIP	DRA	VORP	WARP	cFIP	MPH
2014	WAS	MLB	29	7	4	1	75	0	70¹	47	5	2.9	10.5	82	38%	.251	1.00	2.18	2.72	2.25	17.5	1.9	87	94.1
2015	OAK	MLB	30	1	3	17	37	0	38²	25	3	4.9	8.8	38	22%	.214	1.19	2.79	3.93	6.29	-6.8	-0.7	130	93.6
2015	NYN	MLB	30	4	1	2	32	0	32¹	24	5	2.8	7.2	26	24%	.209	1.05	3.06	4.68	6.18	-5.3	-0.6	132	93.9
2016	ARI	MLB	31	2	3	1	40	0	37²	34	7	3.6	11.0	46	34%	.310	1.30	4.30	4.35	3.94	4.3	0.4	98	93.3
2016	NYA	MLB	31	2	3	2	29	0	25¹	20	3	3.9	9.2	26	32%	.258	1.22	2.49	4.01	3.66	3.7	0.4	99	93.8
2017	NYA	MLB	32	3	3	3	57	0	60	53	11	3.7	9.6	65	39%	.272	1.26	4.70	4.73	4.73	1.7	0.2	100	
2018	NYA	MLB	33	2	1	2	50	0	53²	48	10	3.7	9.2	55	39%	.265	1.30	4.94	4.81	5.21	-0.9	-0.1	122	

Breakout: 29%   Improve: 51%   Collapse: 25%   Attrition: 13%   MLB: 92%   *Comparables: Brian Fuentes, Rafael Soriano, Craig Breslow*

After eight-plus years away from the Yankees, Clippard made his triumphant return to the team that drafted him back in 2003. No one was particularly eager to see what the 31-year-old would do, considering he was acquired just as the Yankees traded away two of the best relievers on earth and essentially gave up on the season, but he did leave a positive impression at the end of 2016. Clippard had a miserable beginning to the season in Arizona, but turned things around in New York and proved he can still pitch effectively in the eighth inning.

Nathan Eovaldi   RHP

Born: 2/13/90   Age: 27   Bats: R   Throws: R   Height: 6'2"   Weight: 225   Entered Pro Ball: Round 11, 2008 Draft (#337 overall)

YEAR	TEAM	LVL	AGE	W	L	SV	G	GS	IP	H	HR	BB/9	K/9	K	GB%	BABIP	WHIP	ERA	FIP	DRA	VORP	WARP	cFIP	MPH
2014	MIA	MLB	24	6	14	0	33	33	199²	223	14	1.9	6.4	142	46%	.323	1.33	4.37	3.34	4.46	8.3	0.9	104	98.9
2015	NYA	MLB	25	14	3	0	27	27	154¹	175	10	2.9	7.1	121	53%	.337	1.45	4.20	3.39	3.75	22.8	2.4	94	100.2
2016	NYA	MLB	26	9	8	0	24	21	124²	123	23	2.9	7.0	97	50%	.275	1.31	4.76	4.94	4.63	9.7	1.0	101	99.9
2017	NYA	MLB	27	6	7	0	19	19	108²	116	17	3.1	7.9	95	38%	.309	1.41	4.51	4.52	4.73	9.0	0.9	108	
2018	NYA	MLB	28	7	7	0	20	20	118¹	124	19	3.2	8.3	109	38%	.308	1.40	4.71	4.56	4.94	6.8	0.7	114	

Breakout: 37%   Improve: 61%   Collapse: 22%   Attrition: 22%   MLB: 96%   *Comparables: Edwin Jackson, Trevor Cahill, Anibal Sanchez*

A second Tommy John surgery awaits Eovaldi, who partially tore the UCL in his right elbow and tore his flexor tendon off the bone in his right forearm. He'll likely return in 2018 at age 28, which is troublesome considering he's very much still a work in progress as a starter. During his time with the Yankees, he increased his fastball velocity and added a cutter and splitter to his repertoire. While this equated in more swings outside the zone he still struggled as a starter, and very much earned a disastrous 5.08 ERA in the role.

A move to the bullpen late in the season seemed to benefit Eovaldi, who tossed 7.2 scoreless frames as a reliever, and that could be his home when he finally heals.

Chad Green RHP

Born: 5/24/91   Age: 26   Bats: L   Throws: R   Height: 6'3"   Weight: 210   Entered Pro Ball: Round 11, 2013 Draft (#336 overall)

YEAR	TEAM	LVL	AGE	W	L	SV	G	GS	IP	H	HR	BB/9	K/9	K	GB%	BABIP	WHIP	ERA	FIP	DRA	VORP	WARP	cFIP	MPH
2014	WMI	A	23	6	4	0	23	23	130¹	121	8	1.9	8.6	125	53%	.315	1.14	3.11	3.08	2.55	41.9	4.3	81	
2015	ERI	AA	24	5	14	0	27	27	148²	170	9	2.6	8.3	137	51%	.351	1.43	3.93	3.22	3.05	33.7	3.7	88	
2016	SWB	AAA	25	7	6	0	16	16	94²	68	3	2.0	9.5	100	50%	.271	0.94	1.52	2.16	1.90	36.2	3.7	74	
2016	NYA	MLB	25	2	4	1	12	8	45²	49	12	3.0	10.2	52	44%	.314	1.40	4.73	5.30	3.79	7.5	0.8	92	97.1
2017	NYA	MLB	26	8	9	0	24	24	136	146	21	3.3	7.7	117	57%	.304	1.46	4.68	4.69	4.84	6.2	0.6	100	
2018	NYA	MLB	27	7	9	0	24	24	138²	132	21	4.7	10.0	154	57%	.306	1.48	4.80	4.65	5.04	6.3	0.7	116	

Breakout: 18%   Improve: 42%   Collapse: 23%   Attrition: 39%   MLB: 75%   *Comparables: Jeff Manship, Gonzalez Germen, Matt Barnes*

Normally hearing a player's success attributed to hard work causes eyes to roll and televisions to turn dark. But that was actually the case with Green, who admitted that his slider was "nonexistent" in spring training. The young right-hander put in work like his name was A$AP Ferg, developing the pitch enough over the course of a few months to induce whiff after whiff at the big-league level. Green's 84 mph slider mixed in with his 96 mph fastball breaks enough vertically to torment even the league's best hitters. He's got two solid pitches and a pretty good cutter, which will make him a solid bullpen option if all else fails. But the potential is there for Green to be a mid-rotation starter.

Ben Heller RHP

Born: 8/5/91   Age: 25   Bats: R   Throws: R   Height: 6'3"   Weight: 205   Entered Pro Ball: Round 22, 2013 Draft (#651 overall)

YEAR	TEAM	LVL	AGE	W	L	SV	G	GS	IP	H	HR	BB/9	K/9	K	GB%	BABIP	WHIP	ERA	FIP	DRA	VORP	WARP	cFIP	MPH
2014	LKC	A	22	4	1	4	28	0	37	19	3	3.9	15.6	64	46%	.254	0.95	2.43	2.54	0.74	17.7	1.8	59	
2014	CAR	A+	22	1	0	1	17	0	16	8	1	7.3	9.6	17	49%	.194	1.31	2.25	5.21	6.48	-2.3	-0.2	118	
2015	LYN	A+	23	0	2	12	36	0	34¹	30	0	3.4	11.3	43	37%	.333	1.25	4.46	2.06	2.14	9.8	1.1	82	
2016	AKR	AA	24	1	0	7	15	0	16¹	3	1	2.8	12.7	23	53%	.069	0.49	0.55	2.62	1.18	6.4	0.7	71	
2016	COH	AAA	24	2	2	5	28	0	25¹	20	1	2.5	8.9	25	46%	.284	1.07	2.49	3.01	2.39	7.2	0.7	89	
2016	NYA	MLB	24	1	0	0	10	0	7	11	3	5.1	7.7	6	43%	.320	2.14	6.43	9.53	6.45	-1.2	-0.1	115	98.0
2017	NYA	MLB	25	1	1	0	14	0	15	15	2	3.8	7.7	13	54%	.293	1.44	5.02	4.55	4.93	0.1	0.0	100	
2018	NYA	MLB	26	2	1	0	32	0	34	29	5	5.0	10.7	40	54%	.284	1.40	4.52	4.39	4.71	1.3	0.1	106	

Breakout: 21%   Improve: 27%   Collapse: 18%   Attrition: 40%   MLB: 49%   *Comparables: Pedro Strop, R.J. Swindle, John Gaub*

The 25-year-old, who was sent to the Yankees in the Andrew Miller trade, looked the part of a rookie reliever in 2016. Heller struggled to find the visitor's clubhouse following a game at Fenway, becoming mixed up in a sea of fans, and also struggled to put away hitters in his short time with the big-league club. The former late-round pick is still plenty exciting with a dominant fastball and steadily-improving slider, and is poised to turn into an impact reliever in the bigs. He'll get a handle on how to navigate a lineup, and the path to his locker, in time.

Jonathan Holder RHP

Born: 6/9/93   Age: 24   Bats: R   Throws: R   Height: 6'2"   Weight: 235   Entered Pro Ball: Round 6, 2014 Draft (#182 overall)

YEAR	TEAM	LVL	AGE	W	L	SV	G	GS	IP	H	HR	BB/9	K/9	K	GB%	BABIP	WHIP	ERA	FIP	DRA	VORP	WARP	cFIP	MPH
2014	STA	A-	21	1	2	0	10	7	32²	35	1	2.8	8.3	30	47%	.327	1.38	3.03	2.92	3.59	6.4	0.7	97	
2015	TAM	A+	22	7	5	0	19	18	103¹	92	3	1.8	6.8	78	42%	.281	1.09	2.44	2.79	3.25	20.9	2.3	93	
2016	TRN	AA	23	3	1	10	28	0	41	27	2	1.5	13.0	59	45%	.298	0.83	2.20	1.85	1.41	15.1	1.6	58	
2016	SWB	AAA	23	2	0	6	12	0	20¹	7	1	0.0	15.5	35	42%	.188	0.34	0.89	0.36	0.64	9.8	1.0	42	
2016	NYA	MLB	23	0	0	0	8	0	8¹	8	1	4.3	5.4	5	37%	.269	1.44	5.40	4.91	6.09	-1.0	-0.1	121	94.7
2017	NYA	MLB	24	1	1	0	24	0	25¹	24	3	3.3	8.1	23	56%	.289	1.31	4.31	4.08	4.36	1.7	0.2	100	94.7
2018	NYA	MLB	25	3	1	1	54	0	57²	46	8	4.3	10.4	66	56%	.273	1.28	4.28	4.15	4.42	3.9	0.4	102	

Breakout: 28%   Improve: 44%   Collapse: 12%   Attrition: 28%   MLB: 62%   *Comparables: Brandon Beachy, Travis Chick, Jae Kuk Ryu*

It takes a lot to get attention as a reliever in just one season, but Holder managed to do that in 2016. He turned a decent season at High-A in 2015 into a ridiculous 2016 season that saw him climb up to Triple-A, where he struck out 11 batters in a row during an appearance. The only level he didn't dominate in 2016 was the majors, but if last season is any indication he should prove himself rather quickly, and could even find a spot in the middle innings.

James Kaprielian RHP

Born: 3/2/94   Age: 23   Bats: R   Throws: R   Height: 6'4"   Weight: 200   Entered Pro Ball: Round 1, 2015 Draft (#16 overall)

YEAR	TEAM	LVL	AGE	W	L	SV	G	GS	IP	H	HR	BB/9	K/9	K	GB%	BABIP	WHIP	ERA	FIP	DRA	VORP	WARP	cFIP	MPH
2016	TAM	A+	22	2	1	0	3	3	18	8	1	1.5	11.0	22	70%	.179	0.61	1.50	2.03	1.68	7.6	0.8	72	
2017	NYA	MLB	23	2	2	0	7	7	34	35	5	3.7	7.9	30	46%	.301	1.43	4.60	4.60	4.77	2.7	0.3	111	
2018	NYA	MLB	24	8	9	0	29	29	177	170	26	3.6	9.2	181	46%	.302	1.37	4.48	4.34	4.65	12.3	1.3	108	

Breakout: 3%   Improve: 3%   Collapse: 2%   Attrition: 3%   MLB: 6%   *Comparables: Elih Villanueva, Juan Nicasio, Zach McAllister*

Last year's annual said Kaprielian "is unlikely to bust completely," so naturally he strained his elbow flexor and missed most of the season. The Yankees drafted Kaprielian no. 16 overall in 2015 with the expectation that he would help the team in 2016, and he surely would have if he'd stayed healthy. It's a shame given that reports out of Tampa early in the year called him "unbelievably good," and at one point he was consistently hitting 99 with his fastball. We'll have to wait a little longer to see it at the big-league level.

Bryan Mitchell   RHP

Born: 4/19/91   Age: 26   Bats: L   Throws: R   Height: 6'3"   Weight: 210   Entered Pro Ball: Round 16, 2009 Draft (#495 overall)

YEAR	TEAM	LVL	AGE	W	L	SV	G	GS	IP	H	HR	BB/9	K/9	K	GB%	BABIP	WHIP	ERA	FIP	DRA	VORP	WARP	cFIP	MPH
2014	TRN	AA	23	2	5	0	14	13	61¹	64	6	4.3	8.8	60	55%	.328	1.52	4.84	4.09	5.42	-1.5	-0.2	92	
2014	SWB	AAA	23	4	2	0	9	8	41²	45	5	3.5	7.3	34	52%	.325	1.46	3.67	4.44	6.40	-3.1	-0.3	103	
2014	NYA	MLB	23	0	1	0	3	1	11	10	0	2.5	5.7	7	56%	.312	1.18	2.45	3.25	4.11	0.7	0.1	102	96.4
2015	SWB	AAA	24	5	5	0	15	15	75	63	1	4.4	7.3	61	54%	.286	1.33	3.12	3.18	7.27	-16.4	-1.7	111	
2015	NYA	MLB	24	0	2	1	20	2	29²	37	4	4.9	8.8	29	50%	.359	1.79	6.37	4.72	4.37	1.3	0.1	105	98.2
2016	NYA	MLB	25	1	2	0	5	5	25	26	1	4.3	4.0	11	49%	.301	1.52	3.24	4.19	6.22	-2.4	-0.2	119	96.9
2017	*NYA*	*MLB*	*26*	*6*	*7*	*0*	*19*	*19*	*95*	*103*	*13*	*4.1*	*6.7*	*70*	*46%*	*.302*	*1.58*	*4.94*	*4.97*	*5.10*	*1.6*	*0.2*	*100*	
2018	*NYA*	*MLB*	*27*	*6*	*9*	*0*	*24*	*24*	*139*	*134*	*20*	*5.2*	*9.0*	*139*	*46%*	*.301*	*1.54*	*5.12*	*4.94*	*5.35*	*1.6*	*0.2*	*124*	

Breakout: 21%   Improve: 38%   Collapse: 23%   Attrition: 35%   MLB: 71%   *Comparables: Kyle Lobstein, Hayden Penn, Garrett Mock*

Mitchell was the talk of spring training until a foot injury killed most of his season. Then, just as everyone forgot he was even in the organization, the 25-year-old was pretty damn good in the rotation, with the exception of one miserable outing against the Dodgers. He's had worse luck with injuries over the past two seasons than George Costanza had with women, and if that ever turns around, he'll make his manager very happy with his contributions as a back-end starter or middle-inning reliever.

Michael Pineda   RHP

Born: 1/18/89   Age: 28   Bats: R   Throws: R   Height: 6'7"   Weight: 260   Entered Pro Ball: International Free Agent, 2005

YEAR	TEAM	LVL	AGE	W	L	SV	G	GS	IP	H	HR	BB/9	K/9	K	GB%	BABIP	WHIP	ERA	FIP	DRA	VORP	WARP	cFIP	MPH
2014	NYA	MLB	25	5	5	0	13	13	76¹	56	5	0.8	7.0	59	42%	.233	0.83	1.89	2.74	3.67	9.9	1.1	95	95.7
2015	NYA	MLB	26	12	10	0	27	27	160²	176	21	1.2	8.7	156	50%	.332	1.23	4.37	3.31	3.04	36.4	3.9	75	95.7
2016	NYA	MLB	27	6	12	0	32	32	175²	184	27	2.7	10.6	207	46%	.340	1.35	4.82	3.76	2.58	54.3	5.6	78	96.9
2017	*NYA*	*MLB*	*28*	*11*	*9*	*0*	*28*	*28*	*168*	*158*	*21*	*2.6*	*9.8*	*182*	*38%*	*.303*	*1.24*	*3.56*	*3.59*	*3.67*	*29.5*	*3.0*	*82*	
2018	*NYA*	*MLB*	*29*	*11*	*10*	*0*	*31*	*31*	*194*	*186*	*25*	*2.6*	*9.8*	*212*	*38%*	*.309*	*1.25*	*3.77*	*3.64*	*3.95*	*30.5*	*3.1*	*88*	

Breakout: 22%   Improve: 56%   Collapse: 16%   Attrition: 7%   MLB: 90%   *Comparables: Derek Holland, Ricky Nolasco, James Shields*

Woof. Has there been a more confusing/frustrating pitcher over the past three seasons than Pineda? He's become famous for lasting around five innings, giving up five runs and striking out a hearty bunch of batters. Many thought he would finally stay healthy and break out in 2016, and while he did manage to miraculously throw a career-high 175.2 innings, he was not good in most of them. With his age-28 season approaching it appears we sadly know now what this once-exciting pitching talent is. If there's one thing Pineda is elite at, though, it's confusing the hell out of evaluators. So who knows, maybe he'll turn around and pitch like a no. 2 starter in 2017.

CC Sabathia   LHP

Born: 7/21/80   Age: 36   Bats: L   Throws: L   Height: 6'6"   Weight: 300   Entered Pro Ball: Round 1, 1998 Draft (#20 overall)

YEAR	TEAM	LVL	AGE	W	L	SV	G	GS	IP	H	HR	BB/9	K/9	K	GB%	BABIP	WHIP	ERA	FIP	DRA	VORP	WARP	cFIP	MPH
2014	NYA	MLB	33	3	4	0	8	8	46	58	10	2.0	9.4	48	50%	.350	1.48	5.28	4.81	2.88	10.0	1.1	87	91.6
2015	NYA	MLB	34	6	10	0	29	29	167¹	188	28	2.7	7.4	137	48%	.317	1.42	4.73	4.65	3.56	28.3	3.0	96	93.0
2016	NYA	MLB	35	9	12	0	30	30	179²	172	22	3.3	7.6	152	52%	.288	1.32	3.91	4.24	3.87	29.7	3.1	98	93.4
2017	*NYA*	*MLB*	*36*	*10*	*9*	*0*	*24*	*24*	*160*	*165*	*23*	*3.4*	*8.1*	*144*	*54%*	*.301*	*1.41*	*4.44*	*4.49*	*4.60*	*11.6*	*1.2*	*100*	
2018	*NYA*	*MLB*	*37*	*10*	*10*	*0*	*27*	*27*	*160*	*164*	*22*	*3.4*	*8.0*	*141*	*54%*	*.302*	*1.40*	*4.60*	*4.46*	*4.84*	*12.2*	*1.3*	*111*	

Breakout: 17%   Improve: 41%   Collapse: 15%   Attrition: 13%   MLB: 76%   *Comparables: Ryan Dempster, Jose Contreras, A.J. Burnett*

One of the best stories of 2016 was the 36-year-old former Cy Young winner overcoming addiction and years of injury woes to pitch like a legit rotation arm. Many thought Sabathia should have begun the year in the bullpen, with Ivan Nova impressing in spring training, and now he's a consensus starter entering 2017. He's finally figured out how to pitch without the velocity he once had, and he's still striking out hitters around the same pace as his entire career. It seems CC will have the graceful finish to his long, accomplished career that we never thought possible.

Luis Severino   RHP

Born: 2/20/94   Age: 23   Bats: R   Throws: R   Height: 6'2"   Weight: 215   Entered Pro Ball: International Free Agent, 2011

YEAR	TEAM	LVL	AGE	W	L	SV	G	GS	IP	H	HR	BB/9	K/9	K	GB%	BABIP	WHIP	ERA	FIP	DRA	VORP	WARP	cFIP	MPH
2014	CSC	A	20	3	2	0	14	14	67²	62	2	2.0	9.3	70	53%	.321	1.14	2.79	2.70	2.12	25.0	2.6	77	
2014	TAM	A+	20	1	1	0	4	4	20²	11	0	2.6	12.2	28	59%	.239	0.82	1.31	1.55	1.76	8.8	0.9	75	
2014	TRN	AA	20	2	2	0	6	6	25	20	1	2.2	10.4	29	48%	.297	1.04	2.52	2.27	2.07	8.8	0.9	78	
2015	TRN	AA	21	2	2	0	8	8	38	32	2	2.4	11.4	48	46%	.319	1.11	3.32	2.37	1.47	15.3	1.7	68	
2015	SWB	AAA	21	7	0	0	11	11	61¹	40	0	2.5	7.3	50	42%	.237	0.93	1.91	2.51	2.59	18.4	1.9	90	
2015	NYA	MLB	21	5	3	0	11	11	62¹	53	9	3.2	8.1	56	51%	.265	1.20	2.89	4.34	3.43	11.4	1.2	89	97.8
2016	SWB	AAA	22	8	1	0	13	12	77¹	75	4	2.1	9.1	78	46%	.321	1.20	3.49	2.60	2.67	22.9	2.4	85	
2016	NYA	MLB	22	3	8	0	22	11	71	78	11	3.2	8.4	66	45%	.324	1.45	5.83	4.44	4.49	5.8	0.6	100	99.0
2017	*NYA*	*MLB*	*23*	*5*	*6*	*0*	*29*	*15*	*90*	*91*	*13*	*3.3*	*8.0*	*80*	*51%*	*.296*	*1.37*	*4.45*	*4.46*	*4.60*	*6.0*	*0.6*	*100*	
2018	*NYA*	*MLB*	*24*	*8*	*9*	*0*	*27*	*27*	*161*	*145*	*24*	*4.0*	*9.7*	*174*	*51%*	*.292*	*1.35*	*4.52*	*4.38*	*4.76*	*10.6*	*1.1*	*110*	

Breakout: 28%   Improve: 62%   Collapse: 20%   Attrition: 20%   MLB: 96%   *Comparables: Aaron Nola, Rubby De La Rosa, Shelby Miller*

The top prospect's second season in the majors didn't quite go as planned, leaving questions about his future. After coming close to dominating as a very young rookie starter in 2015, Severino came back in 2016 with the same exact stuff—a fastball in the high 90s and a good slider—but failed to get it done in the rotation. After a demotion, and a second chance as a reliever, Severino appeared to be much more effective in his new role. He's still got the talent and repertoire to be an above-average pitcher, but the question is just what he'll be above average at. The upcoming season may make or break his future as a starter.

Chasen Shreve   LHP

Born: 7/12/90   Age: 26   Bats: L   Throws: L   Height: 6'4"   Weight: 195   Entered Pro Ball: Round 11, 2010 Draft (#344 overall)

YEAR	TEAM	LVL	AGE	W	L	SV	G	GS	IP	H	HR	BB/9	K/9	K	GB%	BABIP	WHIP	ERA	FIP	DRA	VORP	WARP	cFIP	MPH
2014	MIS	AA	23	3	2	7	36	0	54¹	42	4	1.5	12.6	76	46%	.336	0.94	2.48	1.42	1.11	22.6	2.4	44	
2014	ATL	MLB	23	0	0	0	15	0	12¹	10	0	2.2	10.9	15	50%	.312	1.05	0.73	1.40	3.21	1.8	0.2	86	93.8
2015	NYA	MLB	24	6	2	0	59	0	58¹	49	10	5.1	9.9	64	47%	.273	1.41	3.09	4.89	3.77	6.1	0.7	97	93.5
2016	SWB	AAA	25	0	0	0	13	1	16²	4	1	3.8	10.8	20	46%	.094	0.66	1.62	2.81	3.44	2.9	0.3	86	
2016	NYA	MLB	25	2	1	1	37	0	33	29	8	3.5	9.0	33	44%	.247	1.27	5.18	5.71	4.45	1.9	0.2	105	93.8
2017	*NYA*	*MLB*	*26*	*2*	*2*	*0*	*33*	*0*	*35*	*33*	*5*	*3.8*	*8.9*	*35*	*46%*	*.295*	*1.37*	*4.26*	*4.38*	*4.39*	*2.3*	*0.2*	*100*	
2018	*NYA*	*MLB*	*27*	*2*	*1*	*0*	*45*	*0*	*47²*	*42*	*6*	*4.6*	*10.5*	*56*	*46%*	*.300*	*1.39*	*4.20*	*4.08*	*4.43*	*3.2*	*0.3*	*98*	

Breakout: 30%   Improve: 42%   Collapse: 18%   Attrition: 23%   MLB: 74%   *Comparables: Wes Littleton, David Aardsma, Aaron Loup*

Last season proved that Shreve's exciting few months as a 24-year-old rookie were a flash in the pan. The Yankees can take some consolation in the fact that Manny Banuelos, whom they traded to Atlanta in exchange for Shreve, hasn't worked out with his new club, but they would have loved it if he filled the hole lefty Justin Wilson left last offseason. There's still time for the 26-year-old to improve, but he just doesn't look like a major leaguer given his two-year body of work.

Masahiro Tanaka   RHP

Born: 11/1/88   Age: 28   Bats: R   Throws: R   Height: 6'3"   Weight: 215   Entered Pro Ball: International Free Agent, 2014

YEAR	TEAM	LVL	AGE	W	L	SV	G	GS	IP	H	HR	BB/9	K/9	K	GB%	BABIP	WHIP	ERA	FIP	DRA	VORP	WARP	cFIP	MPH
2014	NYA	MLB	25	13	5	0	20	20	136¹	123	15	1.4	9.3	141	48%	.299	1.06	2.77	3.07	2.04	42.4	4.7	75	94.4
2015	NYA	MLB	26	12	7	0	24	24	154	126	25	1.6	8.1	139	48%	.243	0.99	3.51	3.96	2.86	37.9	4.1	81	94.6
2016	NYA	MLB	27	14	4	0	31	31	199²	179	22	1.6	7.4	165	49%	.271	1.08	3.07	3.47	3.55	40.3	4.2	87	93.6
2017	*NYA*	*MLB*	*28*	*11*	*9*	*0*	*28*	*28*	*176*	*164*	*24*	*2.1*	*8.4*	*164*	*35%*	*.286*	*1.15*	*3.84*	*3.86*	*3.96*	*25.2*	*2.6*	*91*	
2018	*NYA*	*MLB*	*29*	*12*	*11*	*0*	*31*	*31*	*200*	*186*	*30*	*2.0*	*8.2*	*182*	*35%*	*.279*	*1.15*	*4.13*	*4.00*	*4.33*	*24.5*	*2.5*	*100*	

Breakout: 23%   Improve: 52%   Collapse: 25%   Attrition: 8%   MLB: 94%   *Comparables: Justin Verlander, Tim Lincecum, David Price*

Tanaka's fastball velocity dropped a tad at the beginning of last year, causing some uneasiness in the Bronx, but his production on the season did not. In fact, the Japanese import's third year in the big leagues was nearly as good as his first; he cracked the Cy Young conversation, came an out away from cracking the 200-inning mark and limited home runs in a big way. All this seemed unattainable in 2014, when Tanaka was diagnosed with a partially-torn ulnar collateral ligament in his right elbow, an injury that more often than not leads to Tommy John surgery. As the months pass, the decision to forgo Tommy John surgery is looking like a good one. Tanaka has learned how pitch with his slightly-damaged elbow, delivering sinkers at a career-high 30.2 percent clip in 2016. That pitch has been vital to his positive results in the states, and the amount of times he threw it last year is a good indicator of how often he got in front of hitters. The Yankees have tried to piece together a good rotation to negative results recently, but that's not on Tanaka. None of the team's shortcomings—even a disappointing loss in the 2015 Wild Card game—have been his fault. He's been as consistent a performer as Kenan Thompson on "Saturday Night Live."

Dillon Tate   RHP

Born: 5/1/94   Age: 23   Bats: R   Throws: R   Height: 6'2"   Weight: 165   Entered Pro Ball: Round 1, 2015 Draft (#4 overall)

YEAR	TEAM	LVL	AGE	W	L	SV	G	GS	IP	H	HR	BB/9	K/9	K	GB%	BABIP	WHIP	ERA	FIP	DRA	VORP	WARP	cFIP	MPH
2016	HIC	A	22	3	3	0	17	16	65	78	5	3.7	7.6	55	44%	.378	1.62	5.12	4.37	7.21	-16.4	-1.8	117	
2016	CSC	A	22	1	0	0	7	0	17¹	21	1	3.1	7.8	15	61%	.347	1.56	3.12	3.46	6.11	-2.2	-0.2	118	
2017	*NYA*	*MLB*	*23*	*2*	*5*	*0*	*21*	*11*	*51²*	*72*	*12*	*5.6*	*3.7*	*21*	*70%*	*.315*	*2.01*	*7.39*	*7.37*	*7.56*	*-13.8*	*-1.4*	*178*	
2018	*NYA*	*MLB*	*24*	*3*	*6*	*0*	*26*	*16*	*115¹*	*143*	*26*	*6.6*	*6.4*	*82*	*70%*	*.315*	*1.98*	*7.35*	*7.14*	*7.52*	*-17.6*	*-1.8*	*178*	

Breakout: 1%   Improve: 1%   Collapse: 0%   Attrition: 1%   MLB: 1%   *Comparables: Carlos Frias, Jairo Diaz, Kelvin Marte*

The fourth overall pick in the 2015 draft, Tate struggled mightily for most of his first pro season due to a serious drop off in velocity on his best pitch, the fastball. Without the upper-90s velocity that made him such an exciting prospect, he became a bit more expendable and was eventually dealt during the season. With the Yankees he quickly regained form and velocity, reportedly due to a better workout regimen. The 22-year-old still has years ahead of him, and appears poised to make people forget about a concerning beginning to his career with a bounceback 2017. Regaining the fastball is Tate's primary goal, and the next step would be developing his curveball and changeup further.

Adam Warren RHP

Born: 8/25/87 Age: 29 Bats: R Throws: R Height: 6'1" Weight: 225 Entered Pro Ball: Round 4, 2009 Draft (#135 overall)

YEAR	TEAM	LVL	AGE	W	L	SV	G	GS	IP	H	HR	BB/9	K/9	K	GB%	BABIP	WHIP	ERA	FIP	DRA	VORP	WARP	cFIP	MPH
2014	NYA	MLB	26	3	6	3	69	0	78²	63	4	2.7	8.7	76	48%	.272	1.11	2.97	2.92	3.35	9.9	1.1	96	96.4
2015	NYA	MLB	27	7	7	1	43	17	131¹	114	10	2.7	7.1	104	46%	.278	1.16	3.29	3.56	4.28	10.3	1.1	101	95.4
2016	CHN	MLB	28	3	2	0	29	1	35	31	7	4.9	6.9	27	44%	.242	1.43	5.91	5.87	5.13	-0.5	-0.1	115	95.3
2016	NYA	MLB	28	4	2	0	29	0	30¹	28	4	3.0	7.4	25	45%	.282	1.25	3.26	4.26	5.04	-0.1	0.0	116	94.9
2017	*NYA*	*MLB*	*29*	*3*	*4*	*0*	*56*	*3*	*70²*	*70*	*9*	*3.5*	*7.6*	*60*	*48%*	*.294*	*1.38*	*4.49*	*4.40*	*4.57*	*3.7*	*0.4*	*100*	
2018	*NYA*	*MLB*	*30*	*3*	*1*	*0*	*42*	*2*	*53¹*	*50*	*7*	*4.0*	*8.5*	*50*	*48%*	*.291*	*1.39*	*4.55*	*4.40*	*4.77*	*2.1*	*0.2*	*108*	

Breakout: 38%   Improve: 56%   Collapse: 22%   Attrition: 23%   MLB: 89%   *Comparables:* J.P. Howell, Mitchell Boggs, Randy Wells

He was sent to Chicago straight-up for Starlin Castro last winter, and after struggling mightily out of the Cubs' bullpen, he returned as a throw-in in the Aroldis Chapman trade—and returned back to his old self. All it took to reverse his fortune, the right-hander claims, was a short session with his old pitching coach Larry Rothschild, which helped him fix his slider. With that pitch back in the fold, his short time with the Yankees in 2016 was nearly identical to his 2015 season. Upon his re-acquisition, Brian Cashman bragged about Warren's ability to transition into a starter seamlessly, though he was exclusively used as a reliever. It seems as if the bullpen will be where he spends most of his time moving forward.

LINEOUTS

Hitters

NAME	POS	TEAM	LVL	AGE	PA	R	2B	3B	HR	RBI	BB	K	SB	CS	AVG/OBP/SLG	TAv	VORP	BABIP	BRR	FRAA	WARP
Miguel Andujar	INF	TAM	A+	21	251	34	10	2	10	41	18	30	1	3	.283/.343/.474	.287	14.6	.289	0.0	3B(51): 4.0	1.9
	INF	TRN	AA	21	319	28	16	2	2	42	21	42	2	1	.266/.323/.358	.269	12.3	.296	0.5	3B(64): -2.6	1.1
Jake Cave	OF	TRN	AA	23	116	12	8	3	3	17	10	28	3	4	.288/.353/.510	.310	7.7	.365	-0.6	LF(24): -0.3 • CF(3): -0.1	0.8
	OF	SWB	AAA	23	354	47	18	6	5	38	26	78	3	3	.261/.323/.401	.263	8.5	.329	-1.0	LF(43): -0.7 • CF(28): 1.6	1.1
Dustin Fowler	OF	TRN	AA	21	574	67	30	15	12	88	22	86	25	11	.281/.311/.458	.277	29.1	.313	3.5	CF(119): -9.6 • LF(3): -0.3	2.0
Kyle Higashioka	C	TRN	AA	26	256	31	15	0	11	51	26	42	0	1	.293/.355/.509	.313	22.4	.305	-2.0	C(61): 14.1	3.9
	C	SWB	AAA	26	160	24	9	0	10	30	12	31	0	1	.250/.306/.514	.275	7.3	.252	-1.9	C(36): 4.5	1.2
Billy McKinney	OF	TEN	AA	21	349	37	12	3	1	31	47	68	2	4	.252/.355/.322	.259	5.4	.320	-0.1	RF(74): -0.0 • LF(3): -0.4	0.5
	OF	TRN	AA	21	142	15	7	1	3	13	12	29	2	2	.234/.310/.375	.273	3.5	.281	-0.8	RF(32): 1.4 • CF(1): 0.2	0.5
Nick Solak	2B	STA	A-	21	279	48	13	1	3	25	30	39	8	0	.321/.412/.421	.308	23.8	.372	-3.0	2B(57): -3.0	2.2
Donovan Solano	2B	SWB	AAA	28	546	64	33	3	7	67	25	79	2	1	.319/.349/.436	.287	27.9	.361	-3.4	3B(65): 4.3 • 2B(55): -0.2	3.4
	2B	NYA	MLB	28	23	5	2	0	1	2	1	3	0	0	.227/.261/.455	.258	0.6	.222	0.0	2B(6): -0.1 • 3B(2): -0.1	0.0
Eric Young	LF	CSP	AAA	31	329	48	9	2	3	30	31	51	23	6	.263/.338/.339	.253	6.6	.308	1.9	LF(44): 1.1 • RF(36): -1.4	0.5
	LF	NYA	MLB	31	1	2	0	0	0	0	0	0	1	0	.000/.000/.000	.016	-0.1	.000	0.1	CF(2): 0.1	0.0

Miguel Andujar has some exciting tools—plus bat speed, raw power and arm strength—but is still sanding the rough edges out of his game. ❖ The Yankees' prodigal son **Jake Cave** went to Cincinnati and returned last year, and hit a home run so far it landed on top of an apartment building. That was representative of his larger success at Triple-A. ❖ **Dustin Fowler** has surprised many with his play in the minors thus far, and has the potential to be a solid big-league regular if he can unlock more power in his bat. ❖ **Kyle Higashioka** finally put together a healthy year, flashing strong defense and pop, and moving from an organizational player to the 40-man roster. ❖ **Billy McKinney** has hit at every level and the 2015 first-round pick could get a shot to conquer big-league pitching in 2017. Scouts love his slow clock at the plate. ❖ **Nick Solak**, the Yankees' second-round pick in 2016, is the proud owner of a Derek Jeter replica jersey and a line-drive hitter who hit a ton in college at Louisville. ❖ **Donovan Solano** was basically Ian Kinsler at Triple-A last year, and then he was back to being Donovan Solano in the bigs by the end of the season. ❖ **Eric Young Jr.** is the one player you couldn't name in the Yankees' 2016 Sporcle quiz, and will probably be a professional pinch-runner from here on out.

Pitchers

NAME	TEAM	LVL	AGE	W	L	SV	G	GS	IP	H	HR	BB/9	K/9	K	GB%	BABIP	WHIP	ERA	FIP	DRA	VORP	WARP	cFIP	MPH
Domingo Acevedo	CSC	A	22	3	1	0	8	8	42²	34	1	1.5	10.1	48	48%	.300	0.96	1.90	2.02	2.24	13.2	1.4	80	
	TAM	A+	22	2	3	0	10	10	50¹	49	3	2.7	9.7	54	42%	.343	1.27	3.22	2.89	2.51	16.6	1.7	83	
Chance Adams	TAM	A+	21	5	0	0	12	12	57²	41	4	2.3	11.4	73	42%	.276	0.97	2.65	2.51	1.36	26.4	2.7	70	
	TRN	AA	21	8	1	0	13	12	69²	35	5	3.1	9.2	71	47%	.181	0.85	2.07	3.33	2.34	21.1	2.3	87	
Richard Bleier	SWB	AAA	29	2	3	1	12	10	58	66	2	1.7	3.9	25	64%	.318	1.33	3.72	3.38	5.14	1.0	0.1	101	
	NYA	MLB	29	0	0	0	23	0	23	20	0	1.6	5.1	13	55%	.270	1.04	1.96	2.63	5.04	-0.2	0.0	108	91.7
Dietrich Enns	TRN	AA	25	7	2	0	12	12	70	55	3	3.9	9.5	74	35%	.297	1.21	1.93	3.13	3.76	10.4	1.1	98	
	SWB	AAA	25	7	2	1	14	10	65	47	3	3.6	6.9	50	42%	.253	1.12	1.52	3.52	4.35	6.9	0.7	109	
J.P. Feyereisen	AKR	AA	23	4	3	5	33	0	40¹	30	3	4.5	12.5	56	42%	.300	1.24	2.23	3.04	2.01	12.2	1.3	77	
	TRN	AA	23	3	0	0	9	0	18	8	0	3.0	11.0	22	47%	.211	0.78	0.50	2.58	1.75	6.0	0.6	76	
Giovanny Gallegos	TRN	AA	24	2	1	2	17	0	33	20	1	1.9	14.5	53	44%	.302	0.82	1.09	1.18	0.97	13.8	1.5	52	
	SWB	AAA	24	5	1	2	25	0	45	28	4	2.0	10.6	53	32%	.235	0.84	1.40	2.70	2.60	11.8	1.2	82	
Domingo German	CSC	A	23	1	1	0	5	5	26	15	2	0.7	6.2	18	43%	.186	0.65	3.12	3.48	3.39	4.7	0.5	91	
	TAM	A+	23	0	2	0	5	5	23²	26	1	3.4	7.6	20	45%	.342	1.48	3.04	3.38	4.16	3.5	0.4	100	
Nick Goody	SWB	AAA	24	0	1	5	18	0	23¹	12	4	1.5	13.5	35	33%	.182	0.69	1.93	2.91	1.06	10.1	1.0	64	
	NYA	MLB	24	0	0	0	27	0	29	30	7	3.7	10.6	34	25%	.311	1.45	4.66	5.24	4.32	2.1	0.2	112	93.1
J.R. Graham	MIN	MLB	26	0	0	0	1	0	1²	3	0	5.4	10.8	2	50%	.500	2.40	10.80	2.51	4.15	0.2	0.0	101	96.1
	TRN	AA	26	2	1	5	17	0	29²	26	1	2.7	10.0	33	51%	.321	1.18	1.82	2.58	2.64	6.9	0.7	86	
Ronald Herrera	TRN	AA	21	10	7	0	23	23	132	131	9	2.4	8.4	123	44%	.323	1.26	3.75	3.27	2.67	35.7	3.9	88	
Tommy Layne	BOS	MLB	31	0	1	0	34	0	28²	27	1	4.4	7.8	25	55%	.329	1.43	3.77	3.39	4.37	1.9	0.2	105	92.6
	NYA	MLB	31	2	0	1	29	0	16	10	2	3.9	7.3	13	49%	.186	1.06	3.38	4.79	4.28	1.2	0.1	104	92.3
Zack Littell	CLN	A	20	5	5	0	16	16	97²	94	5	1.9	8.8	95	51%	.332	1.18	2.76	2.96	2.72	24.9	2.7	85	
	BAK	A+	20	8	1	0	12	11	68	64	3	1.7	8.1	61	49%	.311	1.13	2.51	3.20	2.87	19.4	2.0	88	
Jordan Montgomery	TRN	AA	23	9	4	0	19	19	102¹	94	5	3.2	8.5	97	45%	.299	1.27	2.55	3.21	3.05	23.2	2.5	91	
	SWB	AAA	23	5	1	0	6	6	37	28	0	2.2	9.0	37	56%	.286	1.00	0.97	1.90	2.25	12.7	1.3	77	
Branden Pinder	NYA	MLB	27	0	0	0	1	0	1	3	0	9.0	9.0	1	75%	.750	4.00	18.00	4.11	4.85	0.0	0.0	107	95.9
Yefrey Ramirez	CSC	A	22	4	2	0	11	11	61	48	4	2.1	9.7	66	41%	.255	1.02	2.80	2.92	1.95	20.8	2.3	78	
	TAM	A+	22	3	7	0	11	11	63¹	34	5	2.6	9.4	66	42%	.195	0.82	2.84	3.33	2.19	23.1	2.4	83	
Justus Sheffield	LYN	A+	20	7	5	0	19	19	95¹	91	6	3.8	8.8	93	45%	.321	1.37	3.59	3.80	3.03	25.8	2.7	93	
	TAM	A+	20	3	1	0	5	5	26	14	0	3.5	9.3	27	45%	.226	0.92	1.73	2.33	3.13	6.8	0.7	96	
Anthony Swarzak	SWB	AAA	30	1	4	7	15	6	46²	47	4	1.5	8.3	43	45%	.323	1.18	3.86	2.95	2.85	12.3	1.3	90	
	NYA	MLB	30	1	2	0	26	0	31	28	10	2.0	9.0	31	46%	.240	1.13	5.52	6.07	3.38	5.5	0.6	94	95.8

Domingo Acevedo is a young, 6-foot-7 starting pitcher who can throw 103 mph, so you may want to file that name away somewhere in your mind. ❖ Aside from having the name of a Vine star, **Chance Adams** possesses an incredible fastball at 97 mph and dazzled at Double-A last year. ❖ **Richard Bleier** went from totally made-up name to surprisingly effective middle reliever by the end of the season, a productive campaign for the 30-year-old journeyman. ❖ Coming into 2016, **Dietrich Enns** was an advanced four-pitch lefty who blew through the low minors. He blew through the high-minors with similar ease, stamping him as a real prospect. ❖ **J.P. Feyereisen** says the player in the major leagues he'd like to strike out the most is Josh Donaldson. He'll likely get that chance sooner rather than later, using his power slider to try to put him away. ❖ **Giovanny Gallegos** has rocketed through the system since his conversion to relief. He'll present a tongue-twister for announcers in the majors pretty soon. ❖ The NFL can only hope its Sundays make a comeback quite like **Domingo German**'s. He reached High-A in his first season back from Tommy John. ❖ Best known for looking like Mike Trout, **Nick Goody** had his moments in 2016, but the two-pitch reliever was once again rather uninspiring and easily lost in the shuffle of Quadruple-A relievers. ❖ A former top-100 prospect, **J.R. Graham** is still hanging around and had an encouraging season in the minors after an atrocious beginning to the season in the majors. ❖ Previously traded for the likes of Kyle Blanks and Jose Pirela, pint-sized righty **Ronald Herrera** keeps proving doubters wrong with excellent command and deception. ❖ Metrics say that luck was behind **Tommy Layne**'s short, surprisingly steady stint with the Yankees in 2016. He memorably raced toward home to field a dribbler, and dove to tag the plate to record a crucial out in a big game during the team's playoff push. ❖ **Zack Littell** has always had a decent curve and an average fastball, but he took a legitimate step forward in 2016 and could truly emerge with a big 2017 season. ❖ Signed for $1.15 million as a third-round pick, **Nolan Martinez** is a skinny right-hander with a plus fastball. ❖ This should be the season we finally get to see **Jordan Montgomery**, who's been toying with minor-league hitters by using his plus breaking ball. ❖ After the Yankees swiped right on **Branden Pinder** a good amount in 2015, Tommy John cut his 2016 season short. ❖ Just when we thought we couldn't see any new spellings of the classic first name, **Yefrey Ramirez** comes along and surprises us all, much like he surprised with his run through Charleston and Tampa. ❖ **Nick Rumbelow** was one of many Yankees lost to Tommy John surgery, a step in the wrong direction after a promising 2015 campaign for the upper-level relief prospect. ❖ Triple-A could be in the cards in 2017 for **Justus Sheffield**, who has one of the best sliders around, but is unfortunately not related to Gary Sheffield. ❖ For three games, **Anthony Swarzak** was a revelation. Then, he returned to mediocrity. BP writer Kenny Ducey will always remember him saying Gary Sanchez was "real good" the day before his call-up. Maybe he's still a revelation.

OAKLAND ATHLETICS

Essay by Erik Malinowski

Player comments by Ashley Varela and BP staff

"*It is a complicated situation because of the obvious governmental limitations and then you lay on that the fact that you have a football team and a baseball team who desperately need new facilities and you lay on top of that the fact that they play in the same facility right now. You have to work out the logistics of that, so it is very, very complicated.*"

— *MLB commissioner Rob Manfred, Oct. 10, 2016*

Here's a confession: The Oakland-Alameda County Coliseum is one of my absolute favorite places to watch baseball. If you've ever set foot inside the building, then you know how ludicrous that sentiment seems. Yes, the architecture, as currently constituted, represents little more than postmodern concrete ugliness at its worst. Its aesthetic can best be classified as "practical," yet even a stadium whose primary job is to merely function would likely have some semblance of reliable plumbing, which the Coliseum does not. I once walked into a weekday night game during the second inning, sat down in my seat and realized that the upper deck lighting encircling us had inexplicably gone dark. Enveloped in twilight and surrounded by perhaps 10,000 similarly befuddled fans, I could only sit and wait, hoping the light would soon return.

Sometimes the metaphors slap you right in the face, but that's how it is with this franchise. There is no subtlety; what you see is what you get, and what you get these days is a subpar team struggling to keep its nostrils above a cresting wave. But the Coliseum? That place is the real article. It's authentic. The crowds expect both nothing and everything, but unrepressed enthusiasm lives down deep in their marrow. On the micro-level, it's often a hell of a fun time, no matter your rooting interest.

And when the A's make good on their habit of sneaking up on unsuspecting AL West opponents, you then start to hear variations on that old narrative about Billy Beane and how the hell he keeps winning time and again. Beane built his reputation by forging rosters that contained some unholy hodgepodge of cost-controlled stars and players possessing undervalued skill sets. Starters who could eat innings. Hitters who would get on base, one after another like lemmings toward the cliff's edge. Relievers who could accumulate outs, no matter the method.

ATHLETICS PROSPECTUS
2016 W-L: 69-93, 5TH IN AL WEST

Pythag	.429	25th	DER	.701	17th
RS/G	4.03	28th	B-Age	28.7	19th
RA/G	4.7	23rd	P-Age	27.4	6th
TAv	.252	26th	Salary	$86.8M	26th
BRR	-7.03	23rd	M$/MW	$3.6M	14th
TAv-P	.268	19th	DL Days	1966	30th
FIP	4.2	14th	$ on DL	25%	28th

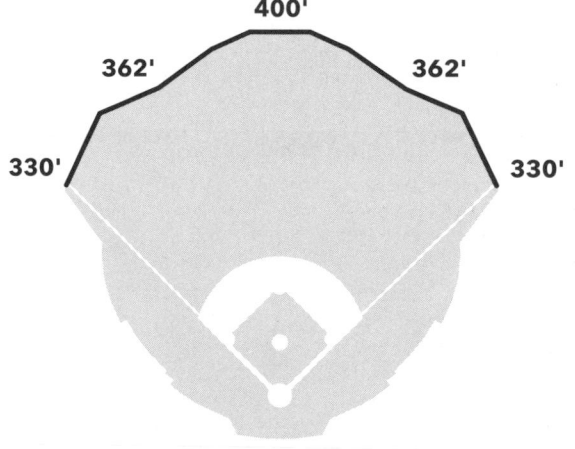

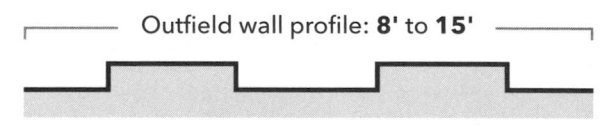

Outfield wall profile: **8'** to **15'**

Three-Year Park Factors

Runs	Runs/RH	Runs/LH	HR/RH	HR/LH
96	98	94	89	81

Top Hitter WARP	3.5	Marcus Semien
Top Pitcher WARP	2.6	Sean Manaea
Top Prospect		Franklin Barreto

2016 Hit List Ranking

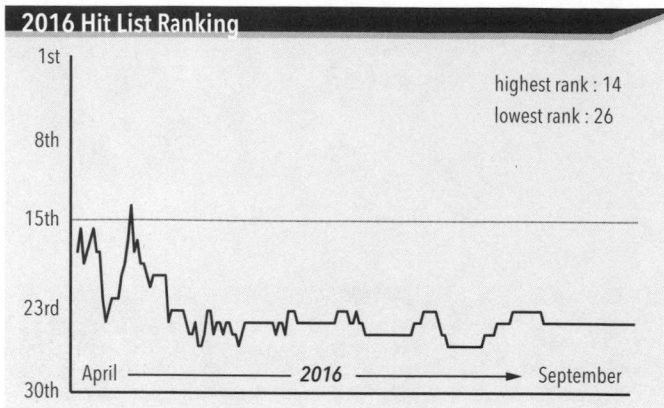

highest rank : 14
lowest rank : 26

1st · 8th · 15th · 23rd · 30th

April — 2016 → September

Committed Payroll (in millions)

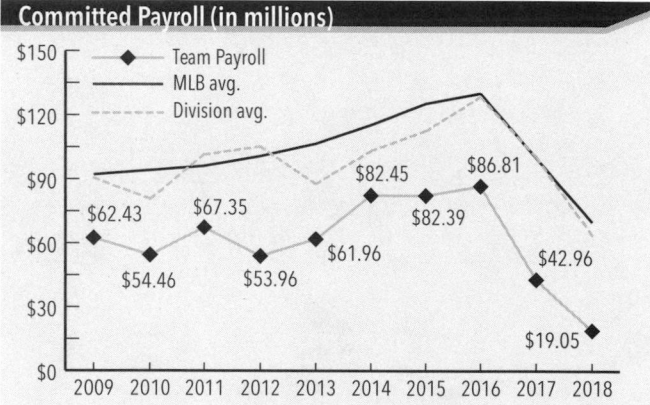

- ◆ Team Payroll
- — MLB avg.
- --- Division avg.

$150 · $120 · $90 · $60 · $30 · $0

$62.43 · $54.46 · $67.35 · $53.96 · $61.96 · $82.45 · $82.39 · $86.81 · $42.96 · $19.05

2009 2010 2011 2012 2013 2014 2015 2016 2017 2018

Farm System Ranking

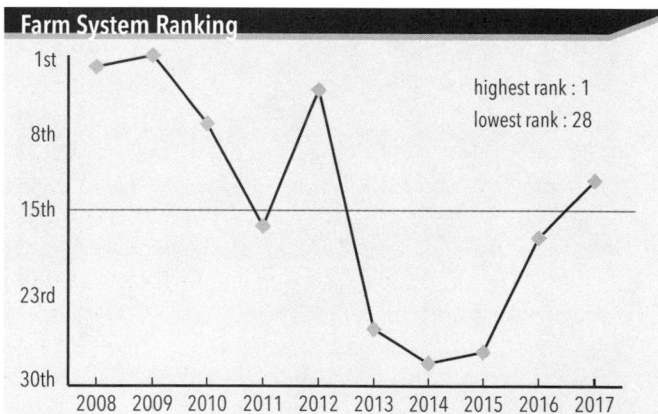

highest rank : 1
lowest rank : 28

1st · 8th · 15th · 23rd · 30th

2008 2009 2010 2011 2012 2013 2014 2015 2016 2017

Personnel

EVP, Baseball Operations:
Billy Beane

General Manager:
David Forst

Assistant General Manager:
Dan Kantrovitz

Assistant General Manager:
Billy Owens

Manager:
Bob Melvin

BP Alumni:
Al Skorupa

Problem is, that's not what the A's are anymore. Their collective team on-base percentage in 2016 was .304, the third-lowest mark in baseball. They stole the fifth-fewest bases, drew the fourth-fewest walks and posted an OPS+ (93) worse than the Marlins, Rays and Twins. Sure, they had a 42-dinger surprise in Khris Davis, but he also struck out 166 times. (That's 60 more than Jason Giambi ever had as an Athletic.) Oakland's largest comeback win of the year? Four runs. And who was tops in WARP among position players? Marcus Freakin' Semien (3.5).

The pitching was just as unimpressive. Sonny Gray suffered through a lost season of 22 mostly frustrating starts (1.9 WARP), and Rich Hill, their most reliable starter, made just 14 starts before shipping off to the Dodgers along with Josh Reddick on deadline day. As a whole, A's pitchers struck out the fourth-fewest batters and posted an ERA+ (88) worse than the Phillies, Padres and Braves. From innings seven through nine A's pitchers had the fifth-lowest K/9, and Oakland's ninth-inning ERA (4.78) was appreciably worse than its mark in all other innings (4.48). Just seeing an A's game through to its natural end became a soul-crushing chore.

Of course, there are valid reasons Oakland only won 69 games. One is that the A's were decimated by injuries. According to ManGamesLost.com, Oakland accrued the second-most games lost to injury—a whopping 1,907. Only the Dodgers (1,964 games) suffered more. But Oakland's estimated WAR lost was in the *negative*. The A's forfeited an estimated –9.4 WAR due to those absent players. In other words, based on the quality of the players relegated to the disabled list, one could posit that Oakland was better off without them. And yet, they still lost 93 games.

But just as worrisome for the A's is not just the glaring dearth of talent but of personalities as well. In those halcyon years of 2000-2003, Oakland not only played superlative, playoff-quality ball but had the egos to match the stats. Leaner times followed, but the A's were almost always more interesting than they deserved to be. There are remaining vestiges of that culture dotted throughout the 25-man roster—Sean Doolittle, Stephen Vogt and John Axford come to mind first—but the skilled and fun reserves with which this organization used to be flooded have reached critically low levels.

"We had to find the best site that served the majority of our fans for the very long term. … We intend to build the most spectacular arena in the country. … It doesn't get any better than this."

— *Golden State Warriors co-owner Joe Lacob in San Francisco, May 22, 2012*

Instead, all good cheer has emigrated just a couple hundred yards to the southwest into the covered confines of Oracle Arena, home to the Golden State Warriors, a team that was, for the better part of two decades, among the

NBA's bottom-feeding franchises. Heading into the 2012-2013 season, the Warriors had made the playoffs *once* in 19 seasons. But that year, they won 47 games and upset the heavily favored Nuggets in the playoffs. The next year, Golden State won 51 games and made the playoffs again. The year after that, they won their first championship in 40 years, back when the A's were winning a trio of World Series titles in the mid-70s. Last season, the Warriors won an all-time record 73 games before—actually, let's stop there.

My point is two-fold. First is that these things can turn around remarkably quickly, so long as management is willing to *invest* in young talent. This has long been the A's big bugaboo: they can develop talent but are loathe to keep it around too long. (I maintain that the Eric Chavez contract still awakens some A's folk into a late-night cold sweat.) But there was a cavalcade of ex-A's parading through last fall's playoffs—the World Series-winning trio of Jon Lester, Ben Zobrist and Addison Russell chief among them—and you can't build anything lasting if you keep turning the roster over every couple of seasons.

But the Warriors also matter in this discussion because they're ditching Oakland. They too need a new arena and their cash-infused owners decided years ago to privately finance said construction … but to do so across the bay in San Francisco. Chase Center is slated to open in the fall of 2019. With each passing Golden State victory, the organization is one game closer to packing up and moving out.

That emerging reality should be enough to spur some momentum on the part of the city and county for a new A's stadium, the logic going something like "well, we can't lose the A's too!" The problem is that they play in northern California, where taxpayer financing of stadiums has become anathema to said tax-paying public. Besides, there has always been the parallel problem of what to do with the Oakland Raiders, their Coliseum roommate who *also* happens to need a new stadium.

"I would like to thank Governor Sandoval, the Southern Nevada Tourism Infrastructure Committee, and the members of the Nevada Legislature on this historic day. All parties have worked extremely hard to develop and approve this tremendous stadium project that will serve as a proud new home for the entire Raider Nation."
— *Raiders owner Mark Davis, Oct. 14, 2016*

Thanks to Las Vegas, the issue with the Raiders may finally be solved. And if that agreement falls through, Los Angeles can still potentially house this prodigal son, clad in black and silver, for the foreseeable future.

The A's, however, remain faithful to Oakland. They flirted with Fremont some years ago (RIP Cisco Field schematics) but that never materialized and now Oakland remains their best option. With the Warriors and Raiders both looking like lame ducks, the city should have no choice but to go all-in on the A's. Mayor Libby Schaaf has said as much, commissioner Rob Manfred wants the A's to stay put and co-owner John Fisher, normally so hermetic in his official dealings, has taken on a surprisingly visible role in the search for a new stadium site within Oakland city limits.

When the A's finally move into new digs some years from now, it's anyone's guess what that team will resemble. At the moment, the A's are defined by their plainness and utter lack of identity. They have no projected superstars on their roster or in the system; Sonny Gray may be the closest thing they've got to such a franchise face, but neither he nor the A's can afford another doomed season like he endured last year. Alas, the A's still need a ton of help across the roster and Gray remains their most prized asset, so he'll likely be gone by next trading deadline. The song, as ever, remains the same.

In a way, Beane has a chance to start fresh in 2017. It's his 20th season at the decision-making helm, and while David Forst, his longtime right-hand man, remains entrenched as general manager, it's still Beane's team for now. There's no reason to think 2017 is his last best chance to recapture, say, the peak-*Moneyball* success of 2002, but Beane should approach this year as such. Entering the 2015 season, a Beane team had never topped 90 losses in a year. They may do so in 2017 for a third straight season, which could prove catastrophic not just to the team (of which he's also a minority owner) but his legacy.

"There is a real desire to find a way to get something done here in Oakland. I think that that doesn't always seem like that was always the case. There seems to be a commitment."
— *Beane, Sept. 23, 2016*

There's a real chance that in five years the A's will not only be Oakland's lone professional team but will finally be playing in a new home of its own. That will feel cosmically correct, since the team and city identities are so inextricably tied to each other. Oakland doesn't have the wealth or sheen of San Francisco and its outlying tech-centric areas, which will now fully cater to the Warriors. They can't match the innate allure of Vegas neon or the strobe lights of Hollywood. Nor do they possess the cachet and operations resources of the Giants just across the bay.

What the A's do cling to is that aforementioned flicker of authenticity. Maybe that's why I prefer going to the Coliseum, which wears its history in every frayed, load-bearing pillar. Now, that doesn't mean it shouldn't see the shiny side of a wrecking ball as quickly as possible, but I'll savor every remaining chance I can to be there. Until that last day, the A's will remain the most legit ticket in town, a throwback to a bygone era of sports that, for reasons both fair and not, doesn't truly exist anywhere else around here. ■

—*Erik Malinowski is a writer and editor based in the Bay Area*

HITTERS

Yonder Alonso   1B

Born: 4/8/87   Age: 30   Bats: L   Throws: R   Height: 6'1"   Weight: 230   Entered Pro Ball: Round 1, 2008 Draft (#7 overall)

YEAR	TEAM	LVL	AGE	PA	R	2B	3B	HR	RBI	BB	K	SB	CS	AVG/OBP/SLG	TAv	VORP	BABIP	BRR	FRAA	WARP
2014	SDN	MLB	27	288	27	19	1	7	27	17	36	6	1	.240/.285/.397	.253	2.2	.251	1.3	1B(77): 2.1 • 3B(3): 0.0	0.5
2015	SDN	MLB	28	402	50	18	1	5	31	42	48	2	1	.282/.361/.381	.271	6.3	.313	-2.0	1B(102): 3.8 • 3B(2): -0.0	1.1
2016	OAK	MLB	29	532	52	34	0	7	56	45	74	3	1	.253/.316/.367	.245	-2.0	.284	0.2	1B(145): 6.2 • 3B(7): -0.5	0.4
2017	*OAK*	*MLB*	*30*	*479*	*46*	*24*	*1*	*7*	*47*	*41*	*64*	*4*	*2*	*.258/.323/.367*	*.256*	*6.2*	*.286*	*-1.0*	*1B 2*	*0.4*
2018	*OAK*	*MLB*	*31*	*433*	*49*	*22*	*0*	*8*	*43*	*40*	*61*	*3*	*2*	*.258/.326/.375*	*.253*	*2.3*	*.285*	*0.1*	*1B 1*	*0.4*

Breakout: 0%   Improve: 35%   Collapse: 9%   Attrition: 18%   MLB: 93%   *Comparables: Casey Kotchman, Norm Larker, Conor Jackson*

Experiments are fun, but there are only so many times you can shove a handful of Mentos into a liter of Diet Coke and expect something other than a geyser of soda to come shooting out. Alonso's 2016 season was no less predictably explosive, bringing career-low numbers as he transferred his sub-.400 SLG from the expansive Petco Park to an even roomier Oakland Coliseum. He delivered an uncharacteristically high FRAA during his first fully healthy season since 2010, but no amount of rest and rehab could resuscitate the power potential he once flashed in the Reds' system. Those who cannot remember the past—in this case, Alonso's limited range and middling production value—are condemned to repeat it, which means we could see a lot more of the sluggish infielder at first base.

Franklin Barreto   SS

Born: 2/27/96   Age: 21   Bats: R   Throws: R   Height: 5'10"   Weight: 190   Entered Pro Ball: International Free Agent, 2012

YEAR	TEAM	LVL	AGE	PA	R	2B	3B	HR	RBI	BB	K	SB	CS	AVG/OBP/SLG	TAv	VORP	BABIP	BRR	FRAA	WARP
2014	VAN	A-	18	328	65	23	4	6	61	26	64	29	5	.311/.384/.481	.314	34.1	.378	2.9	SS(68): -4.5	3.1
2015	STO	A+	19	364	50	22	3	13	47	15	67	8	3	.302/.333/.500	.318	35.7	.337	0.6	SS(86): -14.6	2.3
2016	MID	AA	20	507	63	25	3	10	50	36	90	30	15	.281/.340/.413	.274	27.5	.330	3.1	SS(81): -11.3 • 2B(33): -2.9	1.4
2017	*OAK*	*MLB*	*21*	*250*	*32*	*11*	*1*	*6*	*24*	*12*	*57*	*9*	*4*	*.249/.292/.392*	*.243*	*6.8*	*.299*	*0.1*	*SS -4 • 2B -1*	*0.2*
2018	*OAK*	*MLB*	*22*	*414*	*47*	*19*	*2*	*11*	*48*	*22*	*91*	*15*	*8*	*.255/.301/.407*	*.254*	*12.2*	*.303*	*1.0*	*SS -7 • 2B -2*	*0.4*

Breakout: 7%   Improve: 18%   Collapse: 4%   Attrition: 16%   MLB: 35%   *Comparables: Alen Hanson, Addison Russell, Nick Franklin*

Acquired in the Josh Donaldson trade, Barreto is a solid hitting prospect coming off a successful first foray at Double-A. Fueled by an aggressive plate approach, his cold start evaporated with double-digit home runs and a career-high 30 stolen bases. His glovework still leaves something to be desired, but with some refining of his fundamentals and a few more reps at Triple-A he'll be a stable enough defender to earn looks at both short and second base when the A's call him up in the next year or two.

Matt Chapman   3B

Born: 4/28/93   Age: 24   Bats: R   Throws: R   Height: 6'0"   Weight: 210   Entered Pro Ball: Round 1, 2014 Draft (#25 overall)

YEAR	TEAM	LVL	AGE	PA	R	2B	3B	HR	RBI	BB	K	SB	CS	AVG/OBP/SLG	TAv	VORP	BABIP	BRR	FRAA	WARP
2014	BLT	A	21	202	22	8	3	5	20	7	46	2	1	.237/.282/.389	.221	-0.8	.288	0.4	3B(21): 2.4	0.2
2015	STO	A+	22	352	60	21	3	23	57	39	79	4	1	.250/.341/.566	.335	37.5	.257	0.6	3B(77): 11.2	5.3
2016	MID	AA	23	504	78	26	4	29	83	59	147	7	4	.244/.335/.521	.297	35.4	.293	1.8	3B(100): 14.3 • SS(10): 3.6	5.8
2016	NAS	AAA	23	85	14	1	1	7	13	9	26	0	0	.197/.282/.513	.302	6.7	.186	0.2	3B(18): 2.0	0.9
2017	*OAK*	*MLB*	*24*	*250*	*31*	*10*	*1*	*13*	*38*	*23*	*77*	*1*	*1*	*.218/.294/.451*	*.258*	*7.2*	*.262*	*-0.2*	*3B 6 • SS 0*	*1.5*
2018	*OAK*	*MLB*	*25*	*315*	*43*	*12*	*2*	*17*	*46*	*30*	*99*	*2*	*1*	*.213/.292/.446*	*.259*	*6.6*	*.257*	*-0.3*	*3B 8 • SS 0*	*1.6*

Breakout: 4%   Improve: 20%   Collapse: 18%   Attrition: 27%   MLB: 48%   *Comparables: Mike Olt, Chris Carter, Xavier Scruggs*

Power potential? Check. Above-average defense at the hot corner? Check. An arm powerful enough to make you question your previously-held beliefs about the known universe? Check. Solid contact rate? We'll stop you right there. Chapman impressed in his first full season at Double-A, flashing enough raw power and improved mechanics at third base to merit a late-season promotion to Triple-A. He profiles as a versatile plus-defender off the bench due to chronic contact issues, but if he can replicate a .500-plus slugging percentage he'll find a way into the starting lineup.

Khris Davis   LF

Born: 12/21/87   Age: 29   Bats: R   Throws: R   Height: 5'10"   Weight: 195   Entered Pro Ball: Round 7, 2009 Draft (#226 overall)

YEAR	TEAM	LVL	AGE	PA	R	2B	3B	HR	RBI	BB	K	SB	CS	AVG/OBP/SLG	TAv	VORP	BABIP	BRR	FRAA	WARP
2014	MIL	MLB	26	549	70	37	2	22	69	32	122	4	1	.244/.299/.457	.281	21.1	.275	-0.6	LF(134): 3.3	2.7
2015	WIS	A	27	24	1	0	0	0	2	3	2	0	1	.100/.208/.100	.152	-2.3	.105	0.0	LF(3): -0.0	-0.2
2015	MIL	MLB	27	440	54	16	2	27	66	44	122	6	2	.247/.323/.505	.286	19.0	.285	-1.3	LF(108): -5.2	1.5
2016	OAK	MLB	28	610	85	24	2	42	102	42	166	1	2	.247/.307/.524	.287	23.9	.270	-3.3	LF(93): -5.1	1.9
2017	*OAK*	*MLB*	*29*	*594*	*75*	*26*	*2*	*31*	*89*	*45*	*148*	*5*	*2*	*.240/.305/.468*	*.277*	*25.1*	*.270*	*-0.8*	*LF 2*	*2.7*
2018	*OAK*	*MLB*	*30*	*556*	*78*	*24*	*1*	*29*	*85*	*46*	*141*	*3*	*2*	*.240/.310/.472*	*.277*	*21.4*	*.270*	*-1.7*	*LF 2*	*2.6*

Breakout: 2%   Improve: 53%   Collapse: 1%   Attrition: 3%   MLB: 95%   *Comparables: Mark Trumbo, Jonny Gomes, Jason Bay*

As disparate as apples and oranges, oil and water, the emerald-tarped Mount Davis and the scenic vistas of the East Bay, Davis paired a career-best TAv with the league's second-most-unforgiving run environment for right-handed batters. The slugger was acquired from the Brewers in a preseason trade that cost the A's multiple top-shelf prospects, and any initial reservations about his ability to translate his power numbers in a pitchers' park dissipated on the way to 42 homers. Davis might be a one-trick pony, but as long as that pony can routinely clear the fences in Oakland (and doesn't try fielding too many balls in left field) there isn't much worth complaining about.

Brett Eibner   CF

Born: 12/2/88   Age: 28   Bats: R   Throws: R   Height: 6'4"   Weight: 225   Entered Pro Ball: Round 2, 2010 Draft (#54 overall)

YEAR	TEAM	LVL	AGE	PA	R	2B	3B	HR	RBI	BB	K	SB	CS	AVG/OBP/SLG	TAv	VORP	BABIP	BRR	FRAA	WARP
2014	WIL	A+	25	51	5	3	0	1	3	10	16	3	2	.220/.373/.366	.299	3.3	.333	0.2	RF(9): -0.8 • CF(1): -0.1	0.2
2014	OMA	AAA	25	311	42	13	2	7	27	30	78	5	2	.241/.317/.380	.245	4.1	.307	0.6	CF(50): -3.2 • RF(16): 1.2	0.2
2015	OMA	AAA	26	431	65	23	1	19	81	38	79	10	0	.303/.364/.514	.312	36.8	.338	3.0	CF(53): -6.7 • RF(34): -4.8	2.8
2016	OMA	AAA	27	219	37	7	1	11	32	30	48	5	1	.288/.385/.516	.308	18.1	.328	1.3	CF(34): -3.2 • RF(11): -0.8	1.5
2016	KCA	MLB	27	85	11	6	0	3	10	6	23	0	0	.231/.286/.423	.250	0.8	.288	0.0	RF(9): 1.1 • LF(9): 0.2	0.2
2016	OAK	MLB	27	123	10	4	1	3	12	13	27	0	0	.165/.252/.303	.211	-3.8	.188	-0.8	CF(19): -0.9 • RF(19): -1.0	-0.6
2017	*OAK*	*MLB*	*28*	*337*	*38*	*13*	*1*	*11*	*38*	*31*	*83*	*3*	*1*	*.232/.302/.393*	*.254*	*9.3*	*.279*		*CF -6 • RF -1*	*-0.1*
2018	*OAK*	*MLB*	*29*	*397*	*49*	*17*	*1*	*14*	*48*	*37*	*101*	*3*	*1*	*.232/.304/.404*	*.253*	*7.6*	*.280*	*-0.2*	*CF -7 • RF -1*	*0.0*

Breakout: 4%   Improve: 20%   Collapse: 14%   Attrition: 28%   MLB: 56%   *Comparables: Thomas Pham, Matt Den Dekker, John Mayberry*

Even the death rattle of a deflating balloon generates some buzz, not unlike Eibner's .165 batting average at the end of 2016. Acquired from the Royals in exchange for Billy Burns in late July, he's too old to be a prospect but intriguing enough to warrant an opportunity in the majors. Defensively, he's well-versed in all angles of the outfield, but his offensive profile appears to be inextricably linked to modest power potential.

Ryon Healy   1B/3B

Born: 1/10/92   Age: 25   Bats: R   Throws: R   Height: 6'5"   Weight: 225   Entered Pro Ball: Round 3, 2013 Draft (#100 overall)

YEAR	TEAM	LVL	AGE	PA	R	2B	3B	HR	RBI	BB	K	SB	CS	AVG/OBP/SLG	TAv	VORP	BABIP	BRR	FRAA	WARP
2014	STO	A+	22	600	73	29	2	16	83	28	79	0	1	.285/.318/.428	.256	7.3	.304	-1.0	3B(46): 2.3 • 1B(29): 0.3	1.0
2015	MID	AA	23	543	63	31	1	10	62	30	82	0	1	.302/.339/.426	.254	6.6	.341	-3.2	3B(84): -1.4 • 1B(24): -0.0	0.6
2016	MID	AA	24	164	27	12	3	8	34	18	35	1	0	.338/.409/.628	.362	18.6	.398	-0.5	1B(25): 0.6 • 3B(7): -0.5	2.0
2016	NAS	AAA	24	210	33	16	1	6	30	13	40	0	1	.318/.362/.505	.324	17.5	.369	0.0	1B(19): -1.2 • 3B(15): -3.4	1.3
2016	OAK	MLB	24	283	36	20	0	13	37	12	60	0	0	.305/.337/.524	.303	19.0	.352	-2.4	3B(72): -0.1	2.0
2017	*OAK*	*MLB*	*25*	*575*	*54*	*28*	*2*	*16*	*67*	*24*	*119*	*0*	*0*	*.259/.290/.404*	*.252*	*9.3*	*.302*	*-1.3*	*3B -4*	*0.2*
2018	*OAK*	*MLB*	*26*	*557*	*63*	*27*	*2*	*16*	*65*	*25*	*118*	*0*	*0*	*.258/.293/.409*	*.249*	*3.7*	*.302*	*-2.4*	*3B -4*	*0.0*

Breakout: 9%   Improve: 22%   Collapse: 16%   Attrition: 38%   MLB: 63%   *Comparables: Ryan Wheeler, Brandon Laird, Joel Guzman*

Tweaked swing mechanics unlocked the door to the majors for Healy, who was selected in the third round of the 2013 draft but failed to crack the Athletics' top-prospect rankings in any season. He obliterated the Double-A and Triple-A circuits in 2016, forcing a well-deserved promotion midseason. While his .200-plus ISO appeared inflated in the hitter-friendly Pacific Coast League, it survived the jump to the majors with minimal damage. Healy was stationed at third base for the majority of his breakout season in Oakland, but profiles better on the opposite side of the infield with a below-average glove.

Matt Joyce   RF/LF

Born: 8/3/84   Age: 32   Bats: L   Throws: R   Height: 6'2"   Weight: 205   Entered Pro Ball: Round 12, 2005 Draft (#360 overall)

YEAR	TEAM	LVL	AGE	PA	R	2B	3B	HR	RBI	BB	K	SB	CS	AVG/OBP/SLG	TAv	VORP	BABIP	BRR	FRAA	WARP
2014	TBA	MLB	29	493	51	23	2	9	52	62	111	2	5	.254/.349/.383	.278	16.0	.316	-0.3	LF(81): 2.1 • RF(15): -1.3	1.9
2015	SLC	AAA	30	43	3	1	0	2	6	5	9	0	0	.333/.419/.528	.328	3.8	.385	0.1	LF(7): -0.6	0.3
2015	ANA	MLB	30	284	17	12	1	5	21	30	67	0	3	.174/.272/.291	.217	-6.1	.215	0.5	LF(64): -0.3 • RF(2): -0.1	-0.7
2016	PIT	MLB	31	293	45	10	1	13	42	59	67	1	1	.242/.403/.463	.306	22.6	.285	2.6	RF(43): -1.4 • LF(26): -0.3	2.2
2017	*OAK*	*MLB*	*32*	*493*	*55*	*19*	*2*	*13*	*52*	*62*	*106*	*3*	*3*	*.229/.330/.379*	*.263*	*15.0*	*.271*	*-1.5*	*RF -1*	*0.8*
2018	*OAK*	*MLB*	*33*	*348*	*42*	*14*	*1*	*9*	*37*	*44*	*77*	*1*	*2*	*.224/.325/.368*	*.254*	*6.0*	*.268*	*0.9*	*RF -1*	*0.5*

Breakout: 2%   Improve: 32%   Collapse: 5%   Attrition: 9%   MLB: 92%   *Comparables: Bobby Murcer, Jim King, Johnny Grubb*

Coming off the least successful career as an Angel since Lucifer, Joyce was a bit of a longshot to function as a productive Pirate. But sometimes longshots pay off, and Joyce did in a smallish sample for Pittsburgh last season. Lefties are to Matt what perfect games are to Jim or simple sentences are to James, but our Joyce was once again in platoon heaven against righties, reaching base at a .400-plus clip and hitting for solid power. Having exorcised the Angels and Demons of his 2015 campaign, Joyce seems well positioned to spend the next few seasons as the 22nd- or 23rd-best player on some team's roster. Life could be worse.

Jed Lowrie   2B

Born: 4/17/84   Age: 33   Bats: B   Throws: R   Height: 6'0"   Weight: 180   Entered Pro Ball: Round 1, 2005 Draft (#45 overall)

YEAR	TEAM	LVL	AGE	PA	R	2B	3B	HR	RBI	BB	K	SB	CS	AVG/OBP/SLG	TAv	VORP	BABIP	BRR	FRAA	WARP
2014	OAK	MLB	30	566	59	29	3	6	50	51	79	0	0	.249/.321/.355	.260	18.7	.281	-1.9	SS(130): -8.0	1.2
2015	HOU	MLB	31	263	35	14	0	9	30	28	43	1	0	.222/.312/.400	.263	10.6	.233	1.2	3B(47): -6.3 • SS(17): 1.0	0.6
2016	OAK	MLB	32	369	30	12	1	2	27	26	65	0	0	.263/.314/.322	.229	-2.9	.316	-1.1	2B(82): 2.1 • SS(2): -0.0	-0.1
2017	*OAK*	*MLB*	*33*	*501*	*47*	*24*	*1*	*9*	*51*	*42*	*78*	*1*	*0*	*.250/.315/.368*	*.254*	*14.7*	*.281*	*-1.0*	*2B 3*	*1.6*
2018	*OAK*	*MLB*	*34*	*365*	*39*	*16*	*1*	*6*	*35*	*29*	*59*	*0*	*0*	*.244/.306/.352*	*.240*	*2.8*	*.275*	*-0.7*	*2B 2*	*0.6*

Breakout: 1%   Improve: 32%   Collapse: 7%   Attrition: 14%   MLB: 94%   *Comparables: Mark Ellis, Aaron Hill, Red Schoendienst*

So this is how the career of a 30-something middle infielder with limited defensive range and occasional power dies: with a bunionectomy and a deviated septum. Lowrie has transformed the disabled list into a regular vacation spot, and his latest trips likely won't be his last. A shin contusion and injured foot ligament brought a quick end to his return season in Oakland, though with another year on his contract he'll compete for a gig in spring training. Despite a modest spike in average and on-base percentage, he lost some power at the plate during the first half. With Danny Valencia and Ryon Healy platooning at third, a switch to the keystone helped skew his defensive stats in a positive direction for the first time in four years, though Lowrie still doesn't rate anywhere close to an elite defender. Predicting any kind of positive output for the veteran is a fool's errand this late in his career, as he'll need to prove he can stay healthy enough to stick out a full season first.

Richie Martin INF

Born: 12/22/94 Age: 22 Bats: R Throws: R Height: 5'11" Weight: 190 Entered Pro Ball: Round 1, 2015 Draft (#20 overall)

YEAR	TEAM	LVL	AGE	PA	R	2B	3B	HR	RBI	BB	K	SB	CS	AVG/OBP/SLG	TAv	VORP	BABIP	BRR	FRAA	WARP
2015	VER	A-	20	226	31	6	4	2	16	25	47	7	7	.237/.353/.342	.280	12.8	.305	-0.3	SS(46): -0.5	1.3
2016	STO	A+	21	382	46	14	2	3	31	36	73	12	8	.230/.322/.312	.247	10.8	.284	0.7	SS(82): -11.0	0.0
2017	*OAK*	*MLB*	*22*	*250*	*27*	*9*	*1*	*3*	*18*	*18*	*60*	*5*	*3*	*.211/.282/.308*	*.217*	*0.2*	*.268*	*-0.2*	*SS -3*	*-0.4*
2018	*OAK*	*MLB*	*23*	*339*	*35*	*12*	*2*	*5*	*30*	*26*	*80*	*7*	*4*	*.217/.289/.324*	*.226*	*0.0*	*.272*	*0.2*	*SS -5*	*-0.5*

Breakout: 6% Improve: 11% Collapse: 7% Attrition: 12% MLB: 19% Comparables: *Ehire Adrianza, Cristhian Adames, Pete Kozma*

Martin slugged below .400 in three seasons as the Florida Gators' shortstop, but the A's drafted him 20th overall in 2015 for his glove. He remains a standout defender after two pro seasons, but he's hit just .236 with five homers in 142 games against low-minors competition. The good news is that Martin's college patience has carried over somewhat, as he's coaxed a walk in more than 10 percent of his trips to the plate, but Single-A walk rates tend to evaporate quickly when attached to punchless bats. His defense, speed, and plate discipline can get him to the majors, but Martin's lack of hitting ability will likely keep him from being more than a utility man.

Bruce Maxwell C

Born: 12/20/90 Age: 26 Bats: L Throws: R Height: 6'1" Weight: 250 Entered Pro Ball: Round 2, 2012 Draft (#62 overall)

YEAR	TEAM	LVL	AGE	PA	R	2B	3B	HR	RBI	BB	K	SB	CS	AVG/OBP/SLG	TAv	VORP	BABIP	BRR	FRAA	WARP
2014	STO	A+	23	334	33	11	1	6	35	41	58	0	1	.273/.365/.381	.266	16.7	.322	-0.2	C(73): 0.1	1.7
2014	MID	AA	23	94	8	3	0	0	2	9	32	0	1	.141/.223/.176	.145	-7.6	.226	-0.5	C(24): 4.1	-0.4
2015	MID	AA	24	381	32	16	0	2	48	39	54	0	1	.243/.321/.308	.220	-3.0	.282	-1.4	C(78): 15.6	1.4
2016	NAS	AAA	25	219	27	12	0	10	41	24	38	1	0	.321/.393/.539	.334	25.8	.354	-1.1	C(60): 16.4	4.3
2016	OAK	MLB	25	101	8	6	1	1	14	8	24	0	0	.283/.337/.402	.265	4.9	.368	0.3	C(29): -0.8	0.4
2017	*OAK*	*MLB*	*26*	*416*	*37*	*16*	*1*	*7*	*37*	*35*	*94*	*0*	*0*	*.223/.289/.326*	*.231*	*-0.7*	*.276*	*-0.9*	*C 3*	*-0.2*
2018	*OAK*	*MLB*	*27*	*410*	*43*	*16*	*1*	*8*	*39*	*34*	*97*	*0*	*0*	*.220/.287/.333*	*.227*	*-2.5*	*.272*	*-0.9*	*C 3*	*0.1*

Breakout: 4% Improve: 14% Collapse: 11% Attrition: 17% MLB: 42% Comparables: *Sandy Leon, Chris Herrmann, Roberto Perez*

Maxwell's transformation from humble, defense-oriented backup backstop to productive major-league hitter appeared as effortless as it was instantaneous. He renounced his flirtations with the Mendoza line at Double-A Midland and instead courted a .300-plus TAv at Triple-A Nashville before spring-boarding to the majors in August. Whatever fairy godmother magic dusted his bat during the 2015 offseason, it would behoove the rookie catcher to preserve it when he gets a second look in 2017.

YEAR	TEAM	P. COUNT	FRM RUNS	BLK RUNS	THRW RUNS	TOT RUNS
2014	MID	3299	3.4	-0.1	-0.1	3.2
2015	MID	10748	17.0	1.3	-0.9	17.4
2016	OAK	3366	-0.5	-0.1	-0.1	-0.7
2017	*OAK*	*6139*	*3.8*	*-0.2*	*-0.1*	*3.5*
2018	*OAK*	*6049*	*3.5*	*-0.2*	*-0.1*	*3.2*

Renato Nunez 3B

Born: 4/4/94 Age: 23 Bats: R Throws: R Height: 6'1" Weight: 220 Entered Pro Ball: International Free Agent, 2010

YEAR	TEAM	LVL	AGE	PA	R	2B	3B	HR	RBI	BB	K	SB	CS	AVG/OBP/SLG	TAv	VORP	BABIP	BRR	FRAA	WARP
2014	STO	A+	20	563	75	28	3	29	96	34	113	2	0	.279/.336/.517	.280	24.4	.303	-1.6	3B(80): -0.4 • 3B(3): -0.4	2.4
2015	MID	AA	21	416	62	23	0	18	61	28	66	1	0	.278/.332/.480	.277	14.9	.293	-0.9	3B(49): -0.8 • 1B(16): -0.5	1.5
2016	NAS	AAA	22	550	61	20	2	23	75	31	119	2	0	.228/.278/.412	.262	16.8	.249	0.9	3B(89): -1.2 • LF(12): -0.5	1.6
2016	OAK	MLB	22	15	0	0	0	0	1	0	3	0	0	.133/.133/.133	.089	-3.1	.167	-0.7		-0.3
2017	*OAK*	*MLB*	*23*	*189*	*20*	*7*	*1*	*8*	*24*	*8*	*45*	*0*	*0*	*.225/.265/.402*	*.242*	*0.6*	*.254*	*-0.4*	*3B -0 • 1B 1*	*0.0*
2018	*OAK*	*MLB*	*24*	*428*	*52*	*17*	*1*	*18*	*56*	*20*	*101*	*0*	*0*	*.227/.272/.411*	*.243*	*1.0*	*.255*	*-0.9*	*3B 0 • 1B 1*	*0.2*

Breakout: 0% Improve: 21% Collapse: 4% Attrition: 18% MLB: 42% Comparables: *Brandon Laird, Mat Gamel, Jedd Gyorko*

After manhandling opposing pitchers at Double-A the year before, Nunez opened 2016 at Triple-A and made the final jump to the majors when rosters expanded in the fall. He didn't look comfortable in either environment, however, and his above-average power and speed were overmatched by an overly aggressive approach and an inflated strikeout rate. His youth and flexibility around the horn play in his favor, but unless he can solve major-league pitchers with the same puissance he displayed in the Texas League, he'll find it difficult to stick in the majors.

Matt Olson 1B

Born: 3/29/94 Age: 23 Bats: L Throws: R Height: 6'5" Weight: 230 Entered Pro Ball: Round 1, 2012 Draft (#47 overall)

YEAR	TEAM	LVL	AGE	PA	R	2B	3B	HR	RBI	BB	K	SB	CS	AVG/OBP/SLG	TAv	VORP	BABIP	BRR	FRAA	WARP
2014	STO	A+	20	634	111	31	1	37	97	117	137	2	0	.262/.404/.543	.326	50.8	.287	0.3	1B(102): -0.6 • RF(6): 0.5	5.1
2015	MID	AA	21	585	82	37	0	17	75	105	139	5	1	.249/.388/.438	.285	22.2	.311	-0.4	1B(62): 12.5 • RF(59): 15.5	5.4
2016	NAS	AAA	22	540	69	34	1	17	60	71	132	1	0	.235/.335/.422	.279	15.5	.289	-2.9	RF(81): -3.2 • 1B(49): 3.8	1.7
2016	OAK	MLB	22	28	3	1	0	0	0	7	4	0	0	.095/.321/.143	.194	-1.6	.118	-0.2	RF(5): -0.7 • 1B(4): -0.1	-0.2
2017	*OAK*	*MLB*	*23*	*134*	*15*	*6*	*0*	*5*	*16*	*18*	*36*	*0*	*0*	*.214/.325/.392*	*.262*	*2.9*	*.265*	*-0.3*	*LF -0 • 1B 1*	*0.3*
2018	*OAK*	*MLB*	*24*	*405*	*52*	*20*	*0*	*14*	*48*	*54*	*109*	*0*	*0*	*.218/.327/.397*	*.262*	*8.4*	*.272*	*-1.1*	*LF 0 • 1B 2*	*1.1*

Breakout: 3% Improve: 17% Collapse: 13% Attrition: 20% MLB: 46% Comparables: *Jaff Decker, Wladimir Balentien, Kyle Parker*

An abundance of patience and the ability to take a walk might come in handy during political discourse around the holiday season, but their benefits are insufficient for a prospect on the cusp of a major-league career. Olson's high walk rate was the only thing skewing in his favor during his first taste of Triple-A, and his lackluster performance continued to fuel lingering concerns about a propensity to sacrifice above-average power potential in favor of a high on-base percentage. He joined the cadre of September call-ups and flailed his way to a sub-.100 AVG with the Athletics, and while immense power still lurks underneath a high strikeout rate, his defensive limitations could hold him back from a starting role.

Chad Pinder   SS/2B

Born: 3/29/92   Age: 25   Bats: R   Throws: R   Height: 6'2"   Weight: 195   Entered Pro Ball: Round 2, 2013 Draft (#71 overall)

YEAR	TEAM	LVL	AGE	PA	R	2B	3B	HR	RBI	BB	K	SB	CS	AVG/OBP/SLG	TAv	VORP	BABIP	BRR	FRAA	WARP
2014	STO	A+	22	436	61	32	5	13	55	22	99	12	9	.288/.336/.489	.286	23.2	.352	-1.0	2B(70): -4.4 • SS(12): 1.5	1.7
2015	MID	AA	23	522	71	32	2	15	86	28	103	7	5	.317/.361/.486	.288	34.4	.374	-0.1	SS(112): -18.7	1.7
2016	NAS	AAA	24	465	72	23	3	14	51	25	108	5	1	.258/.310/.425	.278	31.4	.312	4.5	SS(98): -4.1 • 2B(4): -0.9	2.7
2016	OAK	MLB	24	55	4	4	0	1	4	3	14	0	0	.235/.273/.373	.230	0.4	.297	0.4	2B(13): 0.1 • SS(7): -0.2	0.0
2017	OAK	MLB	25	188	19	9	1	5	20	7	48	1	1	.241/.279/.389	.246	4.6	.299	-0.3	SS -1 • 2B -2	-0.1
2018	OAK	MLB	26	403	46	19	1	13	48	18	104	2	1	.242/.285/.401	.248	7.3	.298	-0.6	SS -3 • 2B -4	0.0

Breakout: 6%   Improve: 19%   Collapse: 16%   Attrition: 37%   MLB: 49%   Comparables: Trevor Plouffe, Charlie Culberson, Juan Diaz

The Athletics got a sneak peek at Pinder's versatility when Jed Lowrie hit the disabled list with a season-ending foot injury in August. The rookie posted a .230 TAv while holding down the fort at second base and mixing in a few starts at shortstop and DH. His patience and power have yet to blossom in Oakland's run-suppressing environment, but an impressive showing at Triple-A could convince the club to give him a second look in 2017 if Lowrie is unable to return at full capacity. As the kids say, get you a middle infielder who can do both (in this case, sustain a steady contact rate and provide an occasional burst of power).

Rangel Ravelo   1B

Born: 4/24/92   Age: 25   Bats: R   Throws: R   Height: 6'1"   Weight: 225   Entered Pro Ball: Round 6, 2010 Draft (#188 overall)

YEAR	TEAM	LVL	AGE	PA	R	2B	3B	HR	RBI	BB	K	SB	CS	AVG/OBP/SLG	TAv	VORP	BABIP	BRR	FRAA	WARP
2014	BIR	AA	22	551	72	37	4	11	66	56	77	10	6	.309/.386/.473	.310	33.7	.343	-0.2	1B(108): 5.2 • 3B(2): 0.3	4.2
2015	MID	AA	23	98	13	6	1	2	17	9	17	0	1	.318/.378/.477	.279	2.4	.371	-0.5	1B(15): 0.4	0.3
2015	NAS	AAA	23	112	10	5	1	1	18	7	22	0	0	.277/.324/.376	.267	1.6	.338	-0.4	1B(13): -0.9 • LF(1): -0.0	0.1
2016	NAS	AAA	24	416	60	23	1	8	54	34	63	1	1	.262/.334/.395	.275	9.8	.293	-1.2	1B(71): -4.2 • RF(7): -0.4	0.4
2017	OAK	MLB	25	250	25	12	1	6	28	18	49	1	0	.251/.315/.390	.252	3.4	.294	-0.4	1B 0 • RF -0	0.3
2018	OAK	MLB	26	318	36	15	1	7	34	23	64	1	1	.249/.310/.383	.250	1.2	.293	-0.7	1B 0 • RF -1	0.1

Breakout: 4%   Improve: 11%   Collapse: 3%   Attrition: 15%   MLB: 20%   Comparables: Jordan Brown, Matt Hague, Gaby Sanchez

Ravelo isn't your prototypical first baseman, and we don't mean that in a good way. His instincts and defense present as passable with no obvious defects, but his total lack of power forces him to depend entirely on his plate discipline and hit tools. At best he looks like the slap-happy platoon partner of a lefty power hitter. At worst? Failing to develop a viable power stroke could leave him with limited options against major-league pitching.

Marcus Semien   SS

Born: 9/17/90   Age: 26   Bats: R   Throws: R   Height: 6'0"   Weight: 195   Entered Pro Ball: Round 6, 2011 Draft (#201 overall)

YEAR	TEAM	LVL	AGE	PA	R	2B	3B	HR	RBI	BB	K	SB	CS	AVG/OBP/SLG	TAv	VORP	BABIP	BRR	FRAA	WARP
2014	CHR	AAA	23	366	57	20	3	15	52	53	59	7	2	.267/.380/.502	.282	24.8	.282	2.8	SS(42): 0.9 • 3B(17): 3.4	3.1
2014	CHA	MLB	23	255	30	10	2	6	28	21	70	3	0	.234/.300/.372	.248	2.5	.310	-1.3	3B(33): 2.3 • 2B(26): 0.4	0.6
2015	OAK	MLB	24	601	65	23	7	15	45	42	132	11	5	.257/.310/.405	.253	20.5	.312	0.8	SS(152): -4.2	1.7
2016	OAK	MLB	25	621	72	27	2	27	75	51	139	10	2	.238/.300/.435	.266	32.2	.268	2.6	SS(159): 1.4	3.5
2017	OAK	MLB	26	636	81	26	4	20	67	58	136	11	4	.246/.317/.410	.267	32.5	.287	0.6	SS 0	2.8
2018	OAK	MLB	27	563	70	24	4	18	68	53	121	9	3	.243/.317/.414	.264	22.5	.283	0.7	SS 0	2.5

Breakout: 2%   Improve: 54%   Collapse: 6%   Attrition: 11%   MLB: 97%   Comparables: Khalil Greene, Bobby Crosby, Jhonny Peralta

Semien's defensive transformation was nothing short of miraculous during his late-season resurgence in 2015. He's not a standout among the stacked class of up-and-coming shortstops, but his newfound confidence in the field and refined approach at the plate helped his value trend upward in his second full season. Nearly doubling his home run count didn't hurt either, and some have speculated that his success was closely tied to a newfound habit of going to the opposite field.

Jake Smolinski   LF

Born: 2/9/89   Age: 28   Bats: R   Throws: R   Height: 5'11"   Weight: 205   Entered Pro Ball: Round 2, 2007 Draft (#70 overall)

YEAR	TEAM	LVL	AGE	PA	R	2B	3B	HR	RBI	BB	K	SB	CS	AVG/OBP/SLG	TAv	VORP	BABIP	BRR	FRAA	WARP
2014	FRI	AA	25	307	43	15	3	10	35	32	54	6	2	.267/.349/.459	.305	19.0	.295	-0.7	LF(49): 2.4 • RF(4): 0.0	2.3
2014	ROU	AAA	25	34	7	6	0	0	6	4	5	0	0	.267/.353/.467	.290	2.9	.320	1.0	LF(7): -0.6 • CF(1): -0.4	0.2
2014	TEX	MLB	25	92	12	5	0	3	12	3	24	0	0	.349/.391/.512	.337	7.6	.458	-0.6	LF(12): -2.2 • RF(9): -0.6	0.5
2015	ROU	AAA	26	50	9	5	0	4	14	4	7	0	1	.422/.480/.800	.426	9.9	.441	0.3	RF(9): 0.1 • LF(1): 0.9	1.1
2015	TEX	MLB	26	74	12	1	0	1	6	11	20	1	0	.133/.270/.200	.204	-0.2	.171	2.4	LF(25): 0.5 • RF(6): 0.1	0.0
2015	NAS	AAA	26	97	16	9	0	5	17	8	9	2	1	.349/.402/.628	.423	18.3	.338	-0.2	LF(18): 0.4 • RF(7): -1.0	1.8
2015	OAK	MLB	26	118	12	6	2	5	20	8	19	0	1	.226/.288/.462	.295	6.5	.226	0.1	LF(27): -1.4 • RF(10): 2.8	0.9
2016	NAS	AAA	27	159	20	14	0	3	15	11	23	6	1	.248/.310/.407	.282	9.2	.277	1.2	CF(27): -2.2 • LF(8): 0.1	0.7
2016	OAK	MLB	27	319	28	6	2	7	27	19	44	1	2	.238/.299/.345	.237	-0.1	.257	-1.0	CF(49): 0.4 • RF(29): -2.9	-0.3
2017	OAK	MLB	28	410	46	19	2	12	46	30	74	4	2	.249/.313/.410	.268	17.0	.278	-0.5	CF -2 • RF 1	1.2
2018	OAK	MLB	29	384	46	18	1	12	46	28	73	3	2	.242/.308/.409	.260	10.6	.270	0.6	CF -2 • RF 1	1.0

Breakout: 2%   Improve: 48%   Collapse: 9%   Attrition: 21%   MLB: 90%   Comparables: Lorenzo Cain, Roger Bernadina, Ryan Spilborghs

The Athletics plugged Smolinski into center field down the stretch after gutting their outfield with a pair of midseason trades. The veteran journeyman yanked his TAv over the Mendoza line by several points, but his defense took a significant hit and an aggressive approach at the plate exacerbated an already-dismal walk rate. By season's end only one response felt appropriate: "You're killing us, Smols."

Eric Sogard 2B

Born: 5/22/86   Age: 31   Bats: L   Throws: R   Height: 5'9"   Weight: 180   Entered Pro Ball: Round 2, 2007 Draft (#81 overall)

YEAR	TEAM	LVL	AGE	PA	R	2B	3B	HR	RBI	BB	K	SB	CS	AVG/OBP/SLG	TAv	VORP	BABIP	BRR	FRAA	WARP
2014	OAK	MLB	28	329	38	10	0	1	22	31	37	11	4	.223/.298/.268	.225	-1.7	.251	0.3	2B(102): 8.2 • SS(14): 0.2	0.7
2015	OAK	MLB	29	401	40	12	3	1	37	23	50	6	1	.247/.294/.304	.224	-0.9	.283	2.2	2B(96): 5.7 • SS(17): -0.0	0.5
2017	OAK	MLB	31	250	24	10	1	2	20	19	33	5	2	.248/.307/.333	.234	4.6	.276	0.5	SS 0 • 2B 1	0.7
2018	OAK	MLB	32	22	2	1	0	0	2	2	3	0	0	.243/.302/.327	.230	0.1	.270	0.0	SS 0 • 2B 0	0.0

Breakout: 0%   Improve: 37%   Collapse: 6%   Attrition: 22%   MLB: 92%   *Comparables: Ryan Theriot, Jerry Hairston, Jonathan Herrera*

The Nerd Power that fueled Sogard's six-year run with the A's ran out in April when the infielder succumbed to a shoulder injury and underwent season-ending surgery to remove loose bodies from his left knee. His bat has been a non-starter for several years, but the potential damage to his defensive range could be cause for concern if he returns to the major-league stage in 2017.

Stephen Vogt 1B

Born: 11/1/84   Age: 32   Bats: L   Throws: R   Height: 6'0"   Weight: 225   Entered Pro Ball: Round 12, 2007 Draft (#365 overall)

YEAR	TEAM	LVL	AGE	PA	R	2B	3B	HR	RBI	BB	K	SB	CS	AVG/OBP/SLG	TAv	VORP	BABIP	BRR	FRAA	WARP
2014	SAC	AAA	29	97	18	8	2	3	19	8	8	1	0	.364/.412/.602	.374	18.2	.372	1.3	C(19): 2.1 • LF(1): -0.2	2.0
2014	OAK	MLB	29	287	26	10	2	9	35	16	39	1	0	.279/.321/.431	.287	11.9	.297	0.4	1B(47): -1.4 • RF(17): -0.7	1.1
2015	OAK	MLB	30	511	58	21	3	18	71	56	97	0	2	.261/.341/.443	.286	23.7	.290	-7.0	C(99): -11.9 • 1B(25): -1.1	1.1
2016	OAK	MLB	31	532	54	30	2	14	56	35	83	0	0	.251/.305/.406	.262	19.0	.275	-3.0	C(113): -12.9 • 1B(1): -0.0	0.6
2017	OAK	MLB	32	543	62	24	3	15	56	43	92	1	1	.253/.312/.404	.261	19.2	.281	-1.0	C -15 • 1B -0	0.8
2018	OAK	MLB	33	495	57	20	3	13	55	38	90	0	0	.247/.306/.391	.249	7.8	.279	-3.0	C -14 • 1B 0	-0.8

Breakout: 1%   Improve: 27%   Collapse: 8%   Attrition: 17%   MLB: 88%   *Comparables: Dioner Navarro, Robinson Chirinos, John Baker*

J.M. Barrie once implored children to resurrect fairies by way of shouting and clapping, and perhaps the same holds true for Vogt's stat line in 2016. The "I believe in Stephen Vogt" chant that swept through the right field bleachers of the Oakland Coliseum appears to have died down since its inception in 2014, but given Vogt's career-worst BABIP and FRAA he could benefit from the extra mojo. The decline shouldn't fully compromise his trade value or starting role, however, and all things considered 14 homers and another .250-plus TAv isn't too shabby for a catcher.

YEAR	TEAM	P. COUNT	FRM RUNS	BLK RUNS	THRW RUNS	TOT RUNS
2014	OAK	1315	0.7	0.0	0.1	0.9
2014	SAC	2392	2.2	0.0	0.3	2.5
2015	OAK	13004	-9.8	-0.7	0.7	-9.8
2016	OAK	15068	-11.2	-1.9	0.1	-13.1
2017	OAK	14222	-11.8	-1.7	0.0	-13.5
2018	OAK	12963	-12.0	-1.7	-0.1	-13.9

PITCHERS

Raul Alcantara RHP

Born: 12/4/92   Age: 24   Bats: R   Throws: R   Height: 6'4"   Weight: 220   Entered Pro Ball: International Free Agent, 2009

YEAR	TEAM	LVL	AGE	W	L	SV	G	GS	IP	H	HR	BB/9	K/9	K	GB%	BABIP	WHIP	ERA	FIP	DRA	VORP	WARP	cFIP	MPH
2014	MID	AA	21	2	0	0	3	3	19²	17	0	2.3	4.6	10	54%	.288	1.12	2.29	3.17	4.57	1.4	0.2	103	
2015	STO	A+	22	0	2	0	15	15	48²	54	3	1.5	5.4	29	46%	.319	1.27	3.88	4.00	6.14	-5.7	-0.6	112	
2016	MID	AA	23	5	6	0	17	17	90	100	11	2.7	7.3	73	50%	.322	1.41	4.80	4.15	3.67	14.3	1.5	101	
2016	NAS	AAA	23	4	0	0	8	8	45²	38	1	0.6	6.3	32	39%	.272	0.90	1.18	2.80	2.79	12.9	1.3	96	
2016	OAK	MLB	23	1	3	0	5	5	22¹	31	9	1.6	5.6	14	41%	.306	1.57	7.25	8.17	5.56	-0.5	-0.1	118	95.7
2017	OAK	MLB	24	3	5	0	52	5	75	79	8	3.0	5.4	45	58%	.293	1.38	4.71	4.47	4.98	0.8	0.1	100	
2018	OAK	MLB	25	5	3	0	66	5	95²	88	11	4.4	8.6	91	58%	.293	1.41	4.18	4.37	4.71	4.7	0.5	107	

Breakout: 17%   Improve: 31%   Collapse: 13%   Attrition: 29%   MLB: 49%   *Comparables: Yorman Bazardo, Brandon Workman, David Phelps*

Theater superstition holds that a bad dress rehearsal precedes a good opening night. In Alcantara's case the opposite might be true. Two years removed from Tommy John surgery, Alcantara stunned the A's after a midseason promotion to Triple-A ended with a 1.18 ERA and K/BB ratio of 10.6 in 46 innings. On the big stage, however, Alcantara froze in the spotlight with a swollen ERA and command issues that fed into a cringeworthy 3.6 HR/9 rate. Then again, if his major-league flub was just the watery-eyed, sweaty-palmed dress rehearsal for his spot in the 2017 rotation, he's doing everything right.

Henderson Alvarez RHP

Born: 4/18/90   Age: 27   Bats: R   Throws: R   Height: 6'0"   Weight: 205   Entered Pro Ball: International Free Agent, 2006

YEAR	TEAM	LVL	AGE	W	L	SV	G	GS	IP	H	HR	BB/9	K/9	K	GB%	BABIP	WHIP	ERA	FIP	DRA	VORP	WARP	cFIP	MPH
2014	MIA	MLB	24	12	7	0	30	30	187	198	14	1.6	5.3	111	56%	.304	1.24	2.65	3.55	3.74	22.9	2.5	99	96.4
2015	MIA	MLB	25	0	4	0	4	4	22¹	28	1	2.8	3.6	9	60%	.318	1.57	6.45	3.88	5.01	0.2	0.0	112	93.6
2015	JUP	A+	25	0	1	0	3	3	11¹	11	0	1.6	6.4	8	57%	.297	1.15	1.59	2.28	3.90	1.5	0.2	97	
2016	NAS	AAA	26	1	0	0	5	5	18²	17	3	2.9	8.2	17	48%	.275	1.23	3.86	5.11	3.56	3.7	0.4	95	
2016	STO	A+	26	0	1	0	5	5	13¹	17	1	1.4	4.7	7	55%	.348	1.42	4.72	4.09	5.31	0.2	0.0	106	
2017	OAK	MLB	27	2	2	0	7	7	35²	37	4	2.3	5.7	23	49%	.290	1.28	4.29	4.14	4.82	2.6	0.3	114	
2018	OAK	MLB	28	9	9	0	27	27	160¹	164	17	2.2	5.9	104	49%	.291	1.27	3.89	4.08	4.37	18.0	1.9	101	

Breakout: 25%   Improve: 58%   Collapse: 19%   Attrition: 18%   MLB: 97%   *Comparables: Matt Harrison, Mike Pelfrey, Anibal Sanchez*

It takes two to make a thing go right, and in Alvarez's case those two things were a major-league platform and a functional biceps tendon. He got neither in 2016 and his A's career was outta sight before it even began. He's still just 27 years old and not that far removed from a no-hitter in 2013 and an All-Star selection in 2014, but the ex-Marlins sinkerballer has logged a grand total of 22 innings since then.

John Axford   RHP

Born: 4/1/83   Age: 34   Bats: R   Throws: R   Height: 6'5"   Weight: 220   Entered Pro Ball: Round 42, 2005 Draft (#1259 overall)

YEAR	TEAM	LVL	AGE	W	L	SV	G	GS	IP	H	HR	BB/9	K/9	K	GB%	BABIP	WHIP	ERA	FIP	DRA	VORP	WARP	cFIP	MPH
2014	CLE	MLB	31	2	3	10	49	0	43²	34	6	6.2	10.5	51	55%	.259	1.47	3.92	4.74	3.28	5.8	0.6	97	97.1
2014	PIT	MLB	31	0	1	0	13	0	11	9	0	4.9	9.8	12	54%	.321	1.36	4.09	2.83	3.10	1.7	0.2	95	97.4
2015	COL	MLB	32	4	5	25	60	0	55²	56	4	5.2	10.0	62	56%	.342	1.58	4.20	3.59	2.84	11.6	1.2	86	99.0
2016	OAK	MLB	33	6	4	3	68	0	65²	65	6	4.1	8.2	60	56%	.311	1.45	3.97	3.97	4.37	4.4	0.5	97	98.3
2017	*OAK*	*MLB*	*34*	*3*	*3*	*0*	*63*	*0*	*66*	*66*	*9*	*4.2*	*8.6*	*64*	*48%*	*.299*	*1.45*	*5.01*	*4.54*	*5.15*	*-1.3*	*-0.1*	*100*	
2018	*OAK*	*MLB*	*35*	*1*	*0*	*0*	*20*	*0*	*21¹*	*22*	*3*	*4.9*	*8.2*	*19*	*48%*	*.302*	*1.56*	*4.77*	*4.96*	*5.37*	*-0.7*	*-0.1*	*120*	

Breakout: 21%   Improve: 40%   Collapse: 26%   Attrition: 16%   MLB: 84%   *Comparables: Brad Lidge, Kyle Farnsworth, Michael Gonzalez*

Axford has two primary tools in his wheelhouse: consistent velocity on his heater and an uncanny ability to correctly predict Oscar winners. During the first year of his two-year deal with the A's, Axford's fastball velocity registered a slight uptick from 2015, but failed to generate the high strikeout rate and sub-3.00 DRA of seasons past. A move from the high-octane environment of Coors Field to the temperate climate of Oakland Coliseum did wonders for his walk rate, but his poor location led to seven blown saves—one for each incorrect prediction he made during the 2016 Academy Awards.

Jharel Cotton   RHP

Born: 1/19/92   Age: 25   Bats: R   Throws: R   Height: 5'11"   Weight: 195   Entered Pro Ball: Round 20, 2012 Draft (#626 overall)

YEAR	TEAM	LVL	AGE	W	L	SV	G	GS	IP	H	HR	BB/9	K/9	K	GB%	BABIP	WHIP	ERA	FIP	DRA	VORP	WARP	cFIP	MPH
2014	RCU	A+	22	6	10	0	25	20	126²	113	18	2.4	9.8	138	45%	.291	1.16	4.05	4.24	1.71	54.3	5.5	71	
2015	RCU	A+	23	1	0	0	4	2	22¹	14	1	2.8	11.3	28	30%	.265	0.94	1.61	2.79	2.10	6.9	0.7	79	
2015	TUL	AA	23	5	2	0	11	8	62²	49	4	3.0	10.2	71	49%	.296	1.12	2.30	2.87	2.67	16.3	1.8	71	
2016	OKL	AAA	24	8	5	0	22	16	97¹	80	17	3.0	11.0	119	42%	.268	1.15	4.90	4.53	2.27	32.9	3.4	77	
2016	NAS	AAA	24	3	1	0	6	6	38¹	28	3	1.6	8.5	36	43%	.248	0.91	2.82	3.41	2.63	11.4	1.2	78	
2016	OAK	MLB	24	2	0	0	5	5	29¹	20	4	1.2	7.1	23	36%	.198	0.82	2.15	3.72	4.59	2.5	0.3	103	94.5
2017	*OAK*	*MLB*	*25*	*7*	*8*	*0*	*24*	*24*	*120*	*112*	*12*	*2.9*	*7.5*	*100*	*50%*	*.285*	*1.23*	*4.01*	*3.88*	*4.38*	*11.6*	*1.2*	*100*	
2018	*OAK*	*MLB*	*26*	*7*	*7*	*0*	*24*	*24*	*141¹*	*112*	*15*	*4.4*	*10.2*	*160*	*50%*	*.277*	*1.28*	*3.72*	*3.90*	*4.21*	*16.8*	*1.7*	*95*	

Breakout: 11%   Improve: 35%   Collapse: 22%   Attrition: 34%   MLB: 72%   *Comparables: Rafael Montero, Tim Cooney, Steven Matz*

A prototypical back-end starter acquired from the Dodgers for Rich Hill at the trade deadline, Cotton boasts a dynamic fastball/changeup combo that, when paired with an effective command of the strike zone, immobilized most bats in the highest rungs of the minors. Although his secondary offerings lack the same bite and movement that would bump the right-hander to the top of the rotation, his cutter garnered an uncharacteristically high whiff rate during his September debut. It'll take more than improved command to unseat Sean Manaea, Kendall Graveman and Sonny Gray, but tweaking his control and developing a working curveball might help Cotton secure a more stable position within the Athletics' pitching staff.

Ross Detwiler   LHP

Born: 3/6/86   Age: 31   Bats: R   Throws: L   Height: 6'3"   Weight: 210   Entered Pro Ball: Round 1, 2007 Draft (#6 overall)

YEAR	TEAM	LVL	AGE	W	L	SV	G	GS	IP	H	HR	BB/9	K/9	K	GB%	BABIP	WHIP	ERA	FIP	DRA	VORP	WARP	cFIP	MPH
2014	WAS	MLB	28	2	3	1	47	0	63	68	5	3.0	5.6	39	47%	.309	1.41	4.00	4.13	5.41	-6.5	-0.7	116	95.6
2015	TEX	MLB	29	0	5	0	17	7	43	62	9	4.2	5.9	28	38%	.358	1.91	7.12	6.13	6.22	-6.2	-0.7	125	94.8
2015	ATL	MLB	29	1	0	0	24	0	15¹	20	1	9.4	7.6	13	71%	.404	2.35	7.63	6.03	6.64	-2.9	-0.3	126	95.2
2016	CLE	MLB	30	0	0	0	7	0	4²	3	1	7.7	5.8	3	57%	.154	1.50	5.79	7.18	6.31	-0.5	-0.1	126	93.2
2016	COH	AAA	30	2	4	0	12	12	62²	64	6	3.0	5.9	41	46%	.297	1.36	4.60	4.25	7.71	-16.6	-1.7	110	
2016	NAS	AAA	30	4	0	0	4	3	23¹	20	4	1.5	9.3	24	41%	.258	1.03	3.86	4.54	1.98	8.7	0.9	83	
2016	OAK	MLB	30	2	4	0	9	7	44	56	4	3.1	4.7	23	42%	.333	1.61	6.14	4.33	6.72	-7.1	-0.7	125	94.4
2017	*OAK*	*MLB*	*31*	*5*	*6*	*1*	*45*	*13*	*103²*	*112*	*13*	*3.5*	*6.2*	*71*	*59%*	*.301*	*1.47*	*4.78*	*4.72*	*5.40*	*-0.8*	*-0.1*	*126*	
2018	*OAK*	*MLB*	*32*	*3*	*3*	*1*	*27*	*8*	*69¹*	*77*	*9*	*4.1*	*6.8*	*53*	*59%*	*.315*	*1.56*	*4.57*	*4.77*	*5.16*	*1.2*	*0.1*	*118*	

Breakout: 22%   Improve: 37%   Collapse: 13%   Attrition: 19%   MLB: 64%   *Comparables: Sergio Mitre, Randy Wells, Tim Stauffer*

Modern slot machines recreate the fun of cranking an old-fashioned lever to generate finite odds that, to the optimistic mind, conceal a sizable and obtainable jackpot. In reality, the odds they calculate keep that big payday well out of reach for even the most tenacious gambler, while simulating the high of a win with smaller payouts that distract the player from the negative sum in their wallet. Oakland gambled with Detwiler in mid-July, sending cash considerations to Cleveland in exchange for a left-hander who exhibited flashes of inconsistency, poor command and velocity issues. Manager Bob Melvin kept cranking the lever for nearly 50 innings expecting better results, but the payout (a 5.50 DRA and abysmal walk and strikeout rates) did little to offset the lefty's drain on an injury-weakened staff.

Sean Doolittle   LHP

Born: 9/26/86   Age: 30   Bats: L   Throws: L   Height: 6'2"   Weight: 210   Entered Pro Ball: Round 1, 2007 Draft (#41 overall)

YEAR	TEAM	LVL	AGE	W	L	SV	G	GS	IP	H	HR	BB/9	K/9	K	GB%	BABIP	WHIP	ERA	FIP	DRA	VORP	WARP	cFIP	MPH
2014	OAK	MLB	27	2	4	22	61	0	62²	38	5	1.1	12.8	89	24%	.246	0.73	2.73	1.74	2.15	16.3	1.8	68	96.5
2015	OAK	MLB	28	1	0	4	12	0	13²	12	1	3.3	9.9	15	35%	.306	1.24	3.95	2.96	4.33	0.6	0.1	100	95.0
2016	OAK	MLB	29	2	3	4	44	0	39	33	6	1.8	10.4	45	33%	.281	1.05	3.23	3.41	3.25	7.5	0.8	87	97.5
2017	*OAK*	*MLB*	*30*	*2*	*2*	*0*	*37*	*0*	*39*	*34*	*5*	*2.3*	*9.7*	*42*	*43%*	*.287*	*1.13*	*3.72*	*3.53*	*4.09*	*3.9*	*0.4*	*94*	
2018	*OAK*	*MLB*	*31*	*3*	*1*	*0*	*53*	*0*	*56¹*	*48*	*9*	*2.2*	*9.5*	*59*	*43%*	*.270*	*1.10*	*3.70*	*3.86*	*4.16*	*5.5*	*0.6*	*94*	

Breakout: 30%   Improve: 47%   Collapse: 26%   Attrition: 13%   MLB: 88%   *Comparables: Frank Francisco, Jose Valverde, Hong-Chih Kuo*

Doolittle may be Oakland's preferred closer, but chronic shoulder issues have now kept him from a full workload in back-to-back seasons when his 2016 campaign was derailed midseason with another shoulder strain. His second stint on the disabled list was preceded by a promising run of improved peripherals and a sizable spike in fastball velocity, both of which worked in the southpaw's favor as the Athletics inched toward the trade deadline. Poor timing kept him out of the limelight until September, however, and he capped his last nine outings of the year with a 15 percent whiff rate and .364 BABIP. Barring future setbacks, he'll start back at square one again next season.

Ryan Dull   RHP

Born: 10/2/89   Age: 27   Bats: R   Throws: R   Height: 5'9"   Weight: 175   Entered Pro Ball: Round 32, 2012 Draft (#979 overall)

YEAR	TEAM	LVL	AGE	W	L	SV	G	GS	IP	H	HR	BB/9	K/9	K	GB%	BABIP	WHIP	ERA	FIP	DRA	VORP	WARP	cFIP	MPH
2014	MID	AA	24	5	5	6	40	0	56¹	52	6	2.4	9.7	61	40%	.299	1.19	2.88	3.30	2.47	14.9	1.6	84	
2015	MID	AA	25	3	1	12	35	0	45	29	1	2.6	10.4	52	44%	.262	0.93	0.60	2.14	1.59	15.7	1.7	73	
2015	NAS	AAA	25	0	1	0	12	0	16	10	1	1.7	11.8	21	35%	.250	0.81	1.12	2.35	2.15	4.9	0.5	77	
2015	OAK	MLB	25	1	2	1	13	0	17	12	4	3.2	8.5	16	39%	.200	1.06	4.24	5.34	4.59	0.2	0.0	100	92.9
2016	OAK	MLB	26	5	5	3	70	0	74¹	50	10	1.8	8.8	73	34%	.209	0.87	2.42	3.54	3.71	10.4	1.1	93	92.9
2017	OAK	MLB	27	3	3	3	58	0	61¹	56	7	2.5	8.2	56	54%	.281	1.16	3.86	3.75	4.25	5.0	0.5	94	
2018	OAK	MLB	28	3	1	2	61	0	64¹	52	7	3.2	10.0	72	54%	.275	1.16	3.40	3.57	3.89	8.2	0.8	82	

Breakout: 29%   Improve: 45%   Collapse: 19%   Attrition: 21%   MLB: 75%   *Comparables: A.J. Ramos, Alex Hinshaw, Santiago Casilla*

Dull's sophomore season was anything but lackluster, and not just because he carries a puntastic surname. While he isn't poised to supplant closers Sean Doolittle or Ryan Madson, the right-hander dominated in a setup role with an electric fastball-slider combo and exceptional strand rate. He experienced a slight slump over the second half as hitters made the adjustments they are wont to do, but his consistency and good health should keep him locked into the bullpen for the foreseeable future.

Kendall Graveman   RHP

Born: 12/21/90   Age: 26   Bats: R   Throws: R   Height: 6'2"   Weight: 200   Entered Pro Ball: Round 8, 2013 Draft (#235 overall)

YEAR	TEAM	LVL	AGE	W	L	SV	G	GS	IP	H	HR	BB/9	K/9	K	GB%	BABIP	WHIP	ERA	FIP	DRA	VORP	WARP	cFIP	MPH
2014	LNS	A	23	2	0	0	4	4	26¹	11	0	2.1	8.5	25	68%	.175	0.65	0.34	2.27	2.99	7.2	0.7	89	
2014	DUN	A+	23	8	4	0	16	16	96²	89	1	1.7	6.0	64	59%	.287	1.11	2.23	2.88	3.89	18.4	1.9	94	
2014	BUF	AAA	23	3	2	0	6	6	38¹	34	1	1.2	5.2	22	66%	.282	1.02	1.88	2.94	3.94	7.7	0.8	100	
2014	TOR	MLB	23	0	0	0	5	0	4²	4	0	0.0	7.7	4	64%	.286	0.86	3.86	1.45	3.98	0.3	0.0	97	95.2
2015	NAS	AAA	24	2	1	0	4	4	24¹	20	1	3.3	5.2	14	64%	.241	1.19	1.85	4.09	4.40	2.4	0.2	112	
2015	OAK	MLB	24	6	9	0	21	21	115²	126	15	3.0	6.0	77	51%	.302	1.42	4.05	4.57	4.71	4.7	0.5	107	93.3
2016	OAK	MLB	25	10	11	0	31	31	186	196	22	2.3	5.2	108	53%	.290	1.31	4.11	4.35	5.01	7.2	0.7	102	95.3
2017	OAK	MLB	26	8	12	0	30	30	159	162	17	2.5	5.7	101	46%	.290	1.29	4.37	4.23	4.82	7.6	0.8	100	
2018	OAK	MLB	27	10	10	0	31	31	195¹	185	23	2.9	7.5	163	46%	.287	1.27	3.97	4.16	4.52	17.1	1.8	103	

Breakout: 27%   Improve: 66%   Collapse: 11%   Attrition: 12%   MLB: 90%   *Comparables: Homer Bailey, Tommy Hunter, Chris Tillman*

The Jekyll and Hyde routine that characterized Graveman's 2015 season returned to torment the A's again in 2016. At times, he looked like a solid no. 3 starter, upping his use of a nasty sinker to induce a higher whiff rate, chewing through six innings of a perfect game and joining Babe Ruth as one of several starters to double as cleanup hitters in Yankee Stadium. At other times, the right-hander appeared on the cusp of another demotion, leaning too hard on an ineffective cutter and watching increased home run and walk rates feed into a 5.01 DRA. A lack of significant rotation depth gave Graveman much-needed job security, but if his 2017 begins the way Robert Louis Stevenson's famed novella ends, it's unlikely he'll find himself in the heart of the rotation for much longer.

Sonny Gray   RHP

Born: 11/7/89   Age: 27   Bats: R   Throws: R   Height: 5'10"   Weight: 190   Entered Pro Ball: Round 1, 2011 Draft (#18 overall)

YEAR	TEAM	LVL	AGE	W	L	SV	G	GS	IP	H	HR	BB/9	K/9	K	GB%	BABIP	WHIP	ERA	FIP	DRA	VORP	WARP	cFIP	MPH
2014	OAK	MLB	24	14	10	0	33	33	219	187	15	3.0	7.5	183	58%	.277	1.19	3.08	3.49	3.03	44.0	4.9	87	95.7
2015	OAK	MLB	25	14	7	0	31	31	208	166	17	2.6	7.3	169	53%	.255	1.08	2.73	3.42	3.43	38.1	4.1	88	95.6
2016	OAK	MLB	26	5	11	0	22	22	117	133	18	3.2	7.2	94	54%	.319	1.50	5.69	4.63	3.92	18.7	1.9	94	95.1
2017	OAK	MLB	27	9	11	0	29	29	174	163	18	2.9	7.7	148	41%	.290	1.26	4.04	3.88	4.42	16.0	1.7	100	
2018	OAK	MLB	28	11	10	0	30	30	184	168	21	3.5	8.8	180	41%	.293	1.30	3.78	3.96	4.29	22.9	2.4	98	

Breakout: 18%   Improve: 41%   Collapse: 26%   Attrition: 8%   MLB: 91%   *Comparables: Ricky Romero, Ubaldo Jimenez, Clay Buchholz*

What a difference a year makes. An injury-ravaged season sent Gray's stock plummeting, demoting him from a front-of-the-line ace to a mid-rotation piece. Gray's presence on the team was felt in sporadic bursts between disabled list stints for food poisoning, a back strain and forearm tightness, and the only outing in which he did not get shelled was a one-inning trial after he returned from his forearm injury. By all other measures, he was abysmal, posting career-high walk and home run rates and a career-low strikeout rate. The location issues didn't help, even in the gaping maw of the Coliseum, where opposing hitters batted .291. If there's something more sinister lurking beneath his poor command and an unlucky streak of injuries, Gray's days as Oakland's ace could be numbered.

Jesse Hahn RHP

Born: 7/30/89 Age: 27 Bats: R Throws: R Height: 6'4" Weight: 215 Entered Pro Ball: Round 6, 2010 Draft (#191 overall)

YEAR	TEAM	LVL	AGE	W	L	SV	G	GS	IP	H	HR	BB/9	K/9	K	GB%	BABIP	WHIP	ERA	FIP	DRA	VORP	WARP	cFIP	MPH
2014	SAN	AA	24	2	1	0	13	10	42¹	34	1	3.2	8.1	38	66%	.282	1.16	1.91	2.77	2.97	10.3	1.1	89	
2014	SDN	MLB	24	7	4	0	14	12	73¹	57	4	3.9	8.6	70	52%	.270	1.21	3.07	3.38	3.94	7.2	0.8	102	93.9
2015	OAK	MLB	25	6	6	0	16	16	96²	88	5	2.3	6.0	64	53%	.273	1.17	3.35	3.48	4.38	7.6	0.8	101	94.8
2016	OAK	MLB	26	2	4	0	9	9	46¹	57	8	3.7	4.5	23	51%	.320	1.64	6.02	5.59	6.28	-4.7	-0.5	122	96.4
2016	NAS	AAA	26	1	7	0	15	15	66²	72	4	4.6	6.2	46	55%	.318	1.59	4.32	4.79	7.67	-17.2	-1.8	117	
2017	OAK	MLB	27	3	5	0	11	11	66	70	7	3.6	5.7	42	57%	.293	1.47	4.86	4.65	5.34	-0.7	-0.1	100	
2018	OAK	MLB	28	7	8	0	22	22	129²	127	15	4.2	7.3	105	57%	.289	1.44	4.42	4.62	5.00	6.7	0.7	116	

Breakout: 31%   Improve: 57%   Collapse: 12%   Attrition: 20%   MLB: 86%   *Comparables: Dana Eveland, Ross Detwiler, Zach Britton*

The Ghost of Injuries Past returned to haunt Hahn on multiple occasions, amputating both ends of his season with a blister on his pitching hand and a shoulder strain that cost him the better part of the second half. He sought solace at Triple-A Nashville, where he approached Pacific Coast League batters with unfettered generosity, gifting them a career-worst DRA and walk rate during his four-month rehab fever dream. A major-league rotation spot is still within reach in 2017, but Hahn will need to look both consistent and healthy to earn a place in lieu of the Athletics' younger, healthier options.

Liam Hendriks RHP

Born: 2/10/89 Age: 28 Bats: R Throws: R Height: 6'0" Weight: 200 Entered Pro Ball: International Free Agent, 2007

YEAR	TEAM	LVL	AGE	W	L	SV	G	GS	IP	H	HR	BB/9	K/9	K	GB%	BABIP	WHIP	ERA	FIP	DRA	VORP	WARP	cFIP	MPH
2014	TOR	MLB	25	1	0	0	3	3	13¹	12	3	2.7	5.4	8	35%	.225	1.20	6.07	6.23	4.76	0.0	0.0	112	93.2
2014	BUF	AAA	25	8	1	0	18	16	108¹	92	6	0.6	7.6	91	54%	.279	0.91	2.33	2.67	1.45	51.7	5.1	70	
2014	OMA	AAA	25	4	1	0	5	5	35	33	1	1.5	9.0	35	49%	.337	1.11	2.83	2.59	0.88	18.9	1.9	72	
2014	KCA	MLB	25	0	2	0	6	3	19¹	26	0	1.4	7.0	15	46%	.388	1.50	4.66	2.23	4.57	0.4	0.0	111	94.2
2015	TOR	MLB	26	5	0	0	58	0	64²	59	3	1.5	9.9	71	49%	.322	1.08	2.92	2.11	3.01	12.2	1.3	80	97.8
2016	OAK	MLB	27	0	4	0	53	0	64²	69	6	1.9	9.9	71	42%	.344	1.28	3.76	2.81	3.04	13.9	1.4	84	96.8
2017	OAK	MLB	28	3	3	0	63	0	66	59	6	2.2	8.5	63	46%	.291	1.13	3.18	3.25	3.67	9.7	1.0	79	
2018	OAK	MLB	29	2	1	0	45	0	47²	38	4	2.6	10.1	53	46%	.286	1.08	2.81	2.96	3.22	9.6	1.0	63	

Breakout: 21%   Improve: 53%   Collapse: 18%   Attrition: 27%   MLB: 91%   *Comparables: Doug Fister, Jacob deGrom, Burke Badenhop*

Hendriks had his *Eat, Pray, Love* breakthrough in 2015, when a switch to the bullpen and a revitalized fastball-slider combo pulled his career out of a rut. The Blue Jays swapped him for Jesse Chavez, hoping to sacrifice some bullpen depth in order to patch an ailing rotation. While the pitcher-friendly confines of Oakland Coliseum should have underscored Hendriks' sub-4.00 DRA and suppressed his below-average BABIP, things didn't go quite according to plan. The Aussie experimented with a fastball-heavy approach early in the season, bulking up an 8.27 ERA and inducing a pitiful 10 percent whiff rate before hitting the disabled list with an elbow strain. Post-DL, he reverted to the three-pronged arsenal that helped him steamroll opposing batters in Toronto and found similar success out of the 'pen in Oakland. It's a promising look for the Athletics' middle-relief options, but whether the new-and-improved Hendriks is here to stay or just on an extended vacation from his nagging command issues remains to be seen.

Grant Holmes RHP

Born: 3/22/96 Age: 21 Bats: L Throws: R Height: 6'1" Weight: 215 Entered Pro Ball: Round 1, 2014 Draft (#22 overall)

YEAR	TEAM	LVL	AGE	W	L	SV	G	GS	IP	H	HR	BB/9	K/9	K	GB%	BABIP	WHIP	ERA	FIP	DRA	VORP	WARP	cFIP	MPH
2015	GRL	A	19	6	4	0	24	24	103¹	86	6	4.7	10.2	117	44%	.307	1.35	3.14	3.48	3.48	20.0	2.1	98	
2016	RCU	A+	20	8	4	1	20	18	105¹	103	6	3.7	8.5	100	53%	.316	1.39	4.02	3.84	4.32	13.0	1.3	102	
2016	STO	A+	20	3	3	0	6	5	28²	44	4	3.1	7.5	24	60%	.408	1.88	6.91	5.00	4.24	3.8	0.4	102	
2017	OAK	MLB	21	6	8	0	22	22	105²	122	13	4.8	5.4	64	52%	.307	1.69	5.31	5.22	5.87	-4.7	-0.5	139	
2018	OAK	MLB	22	4	5	0	15	15	88²	86	10	6.8	8.6	85	52%	.304	1.72	4.87	5.09	5.38	0.7	0.1	127	

Breakout: 12%   Improve: 12%   Collapse: 2%   Attrition: 11%   MLB: 16%   *Comparables: Giovanni Soto, Zach Eflin, Mike Foltynewicz*

To quote another famous Holmes, there is nothing more deceptive than an obvious fact. Applied to Grant Holmes' High-A stat line, the obvious facts look like an inflated walk rate and sub par DRA, highlighted by a three-point dip in his strikeout rate after the right-hander was shipped to the A's in the Rich Hill trade. Spotty command and a slow adjustment to the extremely hitter-friendly California League disguised Holmes' upside, which relies on a mid-90s fastball paired with a power curve and a serviceable change-up. When his command is on point, he projects as a front-end starter, but as often as he misses bats he also misses the strike zone. Without a drastic adjustment off the mound he profiles better at the back end of the bullpen.

Ryan Madson RHP

Born: 8/28/80 Age: 36 Bats: L Throws: R Height: 6'6" Weight: 225 Entered Pro Ball: Round 9, 1998 Draft (#254 overall)

YEAR	TEAM	LVL	AGE	W	L	SV	G	GS	IP	H	HR	BB/9	K/9	K	GB%	BABIP	WHIP	ERA	FIP	DRA	VORP	WARP	cFIP	MPH
2015	KCA	MLB	34	1	2	3	68	0	63¹	47	5	2.0	8.2	58	56%	.249	0.96	2.13	3.06	2.96	12.3	1.3	83	97.0
2016	OAK	MLB	35	6	7	30	63	0	64²	63	7	2.8	6.8	49	48%	.292	1.28	3.62	4.02	4.41	4.0	0.4	100	96.9
2017	OAK	MLB	36	3	3	30	58	0	61¹	59	8	2.7	7.5	51	46%	.290	1.27	4.27	4.18	4.58	2.7	0.3	100	
2018	OAK	MLB	37	2	1	20	50	0	53	52	7	2.9	6.8	40	46%	.281	1.31	4.35	4.56	4.95	0.6	0.1	115	

Breakout: 29%   Improve: 49%   Collapse: 24%   Attrition: 7%   MLB: 78%   *Comparables: Trever Miller, Mike Adams, Scott Eyre*

Madson has hardly been the picture of health, but he stabilized with the Royals during their 2015 run and made himself an enviable target for teams seeking bullpen depth the following year. The A's were first to the party, inking Madson to a three-year deal in hopes that the right-hander would return the above-average output he generated in Kansas City. The veteran reliever focused on refining his four-pitch arsenal, mixing in a curveball and bringing a little more heat off the mound, but velocity issues began to erode his stat line during the second half. Bouncing back will be no simple feat at age 36 and he'll need more than a clean bill of health to retain his closer role.

Sean Manaea   LHP

Born: 2/1/92   Age: 25   Bats: R   Throws: L   Height: 6'5"   Weight: 245   Entered Pro Ball: Round 1, 2013 Draft (#34 overall)

YEAR	TEAM	LVL	AGE	W	L	SV	G	GS	IP	H	HR	BB/9	K/9	K	GB%	BABIP	WHIP	ERA	FIP	DRA	VORP	WARP	cFIP	MPH
2014	WIL	A+	22	7	8	0	25	25	121²	102	5	4.0	10.8	146	45%	.319	1.28	3.11	3.11	2.78	38.1	3.8	88	
2015	WIL	A+	23	1	0	0	4	4	19²	22	0	1.8	10.1	22	44%	.407	1.32	3.66	1.78	2.08	6.6	0.7	83	
2015	MID	AA	23	6	0	0	7	7	42²	34	3	3.2	10.8	51	40%	.301	1.15	1.90	2.95	2.80	10.9	1.2	84	
2016	NAS	AAA	24	2	0	0	3	3	18	16	1	2.0	10.5	21	54%	.319	1.11	1.50	2.78	2.30	6.1	0.6	78	
2016	OAK	MLB	24	7	9	0	25	24	144²	135	20	2.3	7.7	124	46%	.281	1.19	3.86	4.04	3.76	25.6	2.6	92	95.2
2017	OAK	MLB	25	7	9	0	24	24	127	124	14	2.7	7.9	111	48%	.297	1.29	3.97	3.87	4.35	12.7	1.3	100	
2018	OAK	MLB	26	9	9	0	29	29	182¹	165	22	3.4	9.1	185	48%	.293	1.28	3.75	3.93	4.25	20.9	2.2	97	

Breakout: 35%   Improve: 66%   Collapse: 12%   Attrition: 14%   MLB: 91%   *Comparables: Danny Duffy, Felix Doubront, Patrick Corbin*

Manaea obliterated left-handed batters during his first MLB foray, using more brute strength than delicate finesse to execute an above-average strikeout rate. Against right-handed opponents, he shed his Hulk-like tendencies to reveal a mortal form, and inflated walk and home run rates might have bumped him to the back end of the rotation if Jesse Hahn had not been sidelined with a blister issue. The left-hander's own health issues surfaced on multiple occasions, once when he suffered a forearm strain in June and again in September when he missed two starts with a back strain. He skirted any serious threats to his pitching arm, however, and capitalized on the Athletics' weak rotation to get a full season's worth of starts. Thanks to a fortunate intersection of talent and opportunity, Manaea emerged as a front-end starter, no small feat for a pitcher whose last three seasons have been gutted by a string of serious injuries. His control, though spotty at times, stabilized with increased usage of his changeup, and an uptick in velocity on his off-speed pitches catalyzed a much-needed resurgence in the second half. While he still struggled to command his fastball within the strike zone, his slider and changeup missed enough bats to balance out his stat line. In a season when the Athletics found themselves at the bottom of the leaderboards in both defense and pitching, Manaea's breakout not only helped him Hulk-smash his way into a starting role, but solidified his place in the rotation.

Daniel Mengden   RHP

Born: 2/19/93   Age: 24   Bats: R   Throws: R   Height: 6'2"   Weight: 190   Entered Pro Ball: Round 4, 2014 Draft (#106 overall)

YEAR	TEAM	LVL	AGE	W	L	SV	G	GS	IP	H	HR	BB/9	K/9	K	GB%	BABIP	WHIP	ERA	FIP	DRA	VORP	WARP	cFIP	MPH
2015	QUD	A	22	4	1	0	8	6	38²	30	1	1.9	8.4	36	49%	.274	0.98	1.16	2.65	2.65	10.7	1.1	87	
2015	LNC	A+	22	2	1	1	10	8	49²	59	4	3.3	8.7	48	46%	.367	1.55	5.26	4.10	3.62	7.9	0.9	97	
2015	STO	A+	22	4	2	0	8	8	42¹	39	6	2.1	8.7	41	53%	.275	1.16	4.25	4.53	3.68	6.5	0.7	97	
2016	MID	AA	23	2	0	0	4	4	23	15	0	4.7	11.0	28	51%	.283	1.17	0.78	2.31	2.84	5.8	0.6	86	
2016	NAS	AAA	23	8	2	0	13	13	75¹	54	4	2.0	8.0	67	50%	.246	0.94	1.67	3.43	1.92	28.7	3.0	78	
2016	OAK	MLB	23	2	9	0	14	14	72	83	9	4.1	8.9	71	42%	.344	1.61	6.50	4.30	4.32	8.4	0.9	105	95.5
2017	OAK	MLB	24	2	3	0	21	5	45	43	5	3.5	7.4	37	54%	.291	1.35	4.43	4.23	4.75	2.0	0.2	100	
2018	OAK	MLB	25	6	5	0	51	12	111¹	97	12	4.2	9.4	116	54%	.289	1.34	3.86	4.04	4.34	11.3	1.2	99	

Breakout: 28%   Improve: 58%   Collapse: 12%   Attrition: 17%   MLB: 90%   *Comparables: Rubby De La Rosa, Vance Worley, Robbie Ray*

Mengden may have looked like the second coming of Rollie Fingers, but the resemblance didn't extend much further than the curled tips of their handlebar mustaches. After stunning opposing batters in the minors, the right-hander broke into the majors when Billy Beane's rotation suffered a midseason collapse. His command issues offset an otherwise impressive fastball-changeup combo, and if he manages to replicate his DRA he could carve a prominent spot for himself within the Athletics' staff.

Frankie Montas   RHP

Born: 3/21/93   Age: 24   Bats: R   Throws: R   Height: 6'2"   Weight: 255   Entered Pro Ball: International Free Agent, 2009

YEAR	TEAM	LVL	AGE	W	L	SV	G	GS	IP	H	HR	BB/9	K/9	K	GB%	BABIP	WHIP	ERA	FIP	DRA	VORP	WARP	cFIP	MPH
2014	WNS	A+	21	4	0	0	10	10	62	45	2	2.0	8.1	56	54%	.256	0.95	1.60	2.90	2.51	21.2	2.1	84	
2015	BIR	AA	22	5	5	0	23	23	112	89	3	3.9	8.7	108	43%	.282	1.22	2.97	3.03	4.61	6.0	0.7	90	
2015	CHA	MLB	22	0	2	0	7	2	15	14	1	5.4	12.0	20	38%	.361	1.53	4.80	3.10	3.71	2.0	0.2	96	99.8
2016	OKL	AAA	23	0	0	0	4	3	11¹	12	0	1.6	11.9	15	63%	.400	1.24	2.38	1.60	2.17	3.9	0.4	76	
2017	OAK	MLB	24	2	3	0	47	0	50	45	4	3.7	7.8	43	51%	.287	1.30	3.90	3.86	4.29	3.9	0.4	96	
2018	OAK	MLB	25	3	1	0	50	0	52²	39	4	4.8	10.3	60	51%	.273	1.28	3.46	3.63	3.94	6.4	0.7	84	

Breakout: 20%   Improve: 35%   Collapse: 15%   Attrition: 29%   MLB: 55%   *Comparables: Sean Nolin, Felix Doubront, Jeurys Familia*

With sharper command and a working changeup, Montas profiles well as a back-end starter. Without it, his lethal fastball-slider combo fits best in middle relief, where he can absorb some innings while retaining the deception that has proven key to his approach. The kicker? The right-hander acquired from the Dodgers in the Rich Hill swap will need to stay healthy long enough to see either scenario play out at the big-league level.

Zachary Neal   RHP

Born: 11/9/88   Age: 28   Bats: R   Throws: R   Height: 6'3"   Weight: 220   Entered Pro Ball: Round 17, 2010 Draft (#527 overall)

YEAR	TEAM	LVL	AGE	W	L	SV	G	GS	IP	H	HR	BB/9	K/9	K	GB%	BABIP	WHIP	ERA	FIP	DRA	VORP	WARP	cFIP	MPH
2014	STO	A+	25	0	0	0	2	2	15²	8	0	0.0	10.9	19	42%	.222	0.51	0.57	1.51	2.77	4.9	0.5	76	
2014	MID	AA	25	3	0	0	5	5	31	25	0	1.2	7.3	25	53%	.269	0.94	0.58	2.18	2.35	9.9	1.1	81	
2014	SAC	AAA	25	7	7	0	20	19	119¹	137	15	1.2	6.0	80	44%	.317	1.28	4.07	4.50	4.01	22.9	2.3	100	
2015	MID	AA	26	3	3	0	7	7	36¹	43	7	3.7	5.4	22	47%	.313	1.60	6.44	5.91	5.88	-3.2	-0.3	115	
2015	NAS	AAA	26	7	10	0	21	20	131¹	151	10	1.4	5.3	78	48%	.320	1.30	4.18	3.97	3.44	26.9	2.7	93	
2016	NAS	AAA	27	7	2	0	11	11	61²	62	5	1.2	4.7	32	53%	.274	1.14	3.21	4.17	4.76	4.0	0.4	111	
2016	OAK	MLB	27	2	4	2	24	6	70	72	9	0.8	3.5	27	53%	.265	1.11	4.24	4.31	5.57	-3.3	-0.3	109	91.9
2017	*OAK*	*MLB*	*28*	*4*	*5*	*0*	*26*	*10*	*73²*	*81*	*8*	*2.0*	*4.1*	*33*	*52%*	*.290*	*1.32*	*4.62*	*4.51*	*5.00*	*1.5*	*0.2*	*100*	
2018	*OAK*	*MLB*	*29*	*6*	*7*	*0*	*43*	*17*	*125²*	*129*	*17*	*3.6*	*6.8*	*96*	*52%*	*.293*	*1.43*	*4.54*	*4.78*	*5.17*	*2.7*	*0.3*	*121*	

Breakout: 7%   Improve: 18%   Collapse: 10%   Attrition: 20%   MLB: 35%   Comparables: *Philip Humber, Charles Brewer, Kevin Mulvey*

After seven seasons as a minor-league starter Neal finally made his MLB debut at age 27 and finished a solid rookie year with a strong September in Oakland's bullpen. Neal tops out in the low 90s, but features good off-speed stuff and pounds the strike zone. And no pitcher missed fewer bats in 2016, as Neal managed a minuscule 3.47 strikeouts per nine innings. That's the fifth-lowest strikeout rate by any pitcher with 70 or more innings since 2010, and each of the four lower rates belonged to starters (Aaron Cook, Justin Nicolino, Jake Westbrook, Derek Lowe). Neal generated more whiffs in the minors, but just barely, averaging 5.5 K/9 at Double-A and Triple-A. He has the potential to be a useful low-leverage arm, but more than that he has the potential to make for a really weird viewing experience.

Dillon Overton   LHP

Born: 8/17/91   Age: 25   Bats: L   Throws: L   Height: 6'2"   Weight: 175   Entered Pro Ball: Round 2, 2013 Draft (#63 overall)

YEAR	TEAM	LVL	AGE	W	L	SV	G	GS	IP	H	HR	BB/9	K/9	K	GB%	BABIP	WHIP	ERA	FIP	DRA	VORP	WARP	cFIP	MPH
2014	VER	A-	22	0	1	0	5	5	15	11	0	0.6	13.2	22	47%	.324	0.80	2.40	0.91	1.19	6.9	0.7	65	
2015	STO	A+	23	2	4	0	14	12	61¹	62	7	1.8	8.7	59	34%	.331	1.21	3.82	4.07	2.38	18.1	2.0	84	
2015	MID	AA	23	5	2	0	13	13	64²	65	4	2.1	6.5	47	34%	.305	1.24	3.06	3.34	3.30	12.9	1.4	97	
2016	NAS	AAA	24	13	5	0	21	20	125²	132	6	2.2	7.5	105	37%	.326	1.30	3.29	3.46	3.94	19.3	2.0	103	
2016	OAK	MLB	24	1	3	0	7	5	24¹	48	12	2.6	6.3	17	24%	.396	2.26	11.47	9.11	8.21	-7.8	-0.8	136	91.1
2017	*OAK*	*MLB*	*25*	*2*	*3*	*0*	*22*	*6*	*50*	*56*	*6*	*2.8*	*5.8*	*33*	*61%*	*.299*	*1.43*	*4.79*	*4.46*	*5.13*	*0.2*	*0.0*	*100*	
2018	*OAK*	*MLB*	*26*	*4*	*3*	*0*	*30*	*8*	*71²*	*71*	*9*	*3.6*	*8.3*	*66*	*61%*	*.302*	*1.38*	*4.02*	*4.21*	*4.55*	*5.8*	*0.6*	*103*	

Breakout: 11%   Improve: 30%   Collapse: 11%   Attrition: 31%   MLB: 49%   Comparables: *Pedro Hernandez, Tony Pena, Joe Wieland*

Overton allowed a dozen home runs during his first major-league run and not, as one might hope, over a ton of innings. It's to the left-hander's credit that he vaulted to the big leagues just three years after undergoing Tommy John surgery, but unless he brings up his fastball velocity or develops his cutter into a viable pitch, he's unlikely to make much headway within the Athletics' 2017 rotation.

A.J. Puk   LHP

Born: 4/25/95   Age: 22   Bats: L   Throws: L   Height: 6'7"   Weight: 220   Entered Pro Ball: Round 1, 2016 Draft (#6 overall)

YEAR	TEAM	LVL	AGE	W	L	SV	G	GS	IP	H	HR	BB/9	K/9	K	GB%	BABIP	WHIP	ERA	FIP	DRA	VORP	WARP	cFIP	MPH
2016	VER	A-	21	0	4	0	10	10	32²	23	0	3.3	11.0	40	46%	.277	1.07	3.03	1.92	2.08	11.5	1.2	80	
2017	*OAK*	*MLB*	*22*	*2*	*3*	*0*	*8*	*8*	*33*	*36*	*5*	*4.5*	*7.1*	*26*	*54%*	*.306*	*1.58*	*5.08*	*5.16*	*5.57*	*-0.4*	*0.0*	*133*	
2018	*OAK*	*MLB*	*23*	*6*	*8*	*0*	*29*	*29*	*179²*	*168*	*23*	*4.2*	*8.4*	*169*	*54%*	*.291*	*1.41*	*4.29*	*4.46*	*4.70*	*9.8*	*1.0*	*112*	

Breakout: 2%   Improve: 2%   Collapse: 1%   Attrition: 3%   MLB: 4%   Comparables: *Patrick Light, Tyler Wilson, Andrew Heaney*

There are more questions than answers when it comes to first rounder and former Florida Gators standout A.J. Puk. Will he be able to pair a lethal fastball-slider combo with the requisite delicacy and command to strike out major-league competition? Will his imposing windup erode his efficiency out of the stretch or help him bear down on hitters with increasing speed and precision? Will he flame out in the minors or rise to meet his ceiling at the top of a big-league rotation? Can too much be made of 30-odd innings and a sub-3.00 DRA from the stomping grounds of the New York-Penn League? Is there really, or has there ever been, such a thing as a pitching prospect?

Chris Smith   RHP

Born: 4/9/81   Age: 36   Bats: R   Throws: R   Height: 6'0"   Weight: 190   Entered Pro Ball: Round 4, 2002 Draft (#118 overall)

YEAR	TEAM	LVL	AGE	W	L	SV	G	GS	IP	H	HR	BB/9	K/9	K	GB%	BABIP	WHIP	ERA	FIP	DRA	VORP	WARP	cFIP	MPH
2014	ELP	AAA	33	2	1	0	14	6	43¹	44	5	3.9	9.6	46	38%	.330	1.45	5.61	4.67	4.47	4.4	0.4	111	
2015	SAN	AA	34	0	0	0	2	2	10	5	0	1.8	9.9	11	50%	.227	0.70	0.90	1.70	2.73	2.6	0.3	90	
2015	ELP	AAA	34	5	7	0	22	22	127²	121	11	3	8.5	121	44%	.309	1.28	3.60	3.86	1.87	48.7	5.0	75	
2016	NAS	AAA	35	6	8	0	22	22	130²	120	11	3.1	8.3	121	46%	.292	1.26	3.93	4.04	2.90	35.5	3.7	96	
2016	OAK	MLB	35	0	0	0	13	0	24²	14	2	4.7	10.6	29	47%	.214	1.09	2.92	3.39	3.52	4.0	0.4	93	89.8
2017	*OAK*	*MLB*	*36*	*7*	*7*	*0*	*39*	*18*	*126²*	*122*	*14*	*3.5*	*7.3*	*102*	*42%*	*.286*	*1.35*	*4.23*	*4.21*	*4.80*	*9.0*	*0.9*	*110*	
2018	*OAK*	*MLB*	*37*	*7*	*6*	*0*	*27*	*18*	*126²*	*119*	*16*	*4.2*	*9.2*	*129*	*42%*	*.300*	*1.41*	*4.05*	*4.26*	*4.60*	*10.8*	*1.1*	*105*	

Breakout: 8%   Improve: 19%   Collapse: 7%   Attrition: 4%   MLB: 32%   Comparables: *Matt Palmer, Stephen Randolph, Eric Junge*

Smith is more familiar with the ruts and back roads of the minor-league and independent-ball circuits than the manicured mounds of the big leagues, but his return to the majors after a grueling six years yielded respectable dividends. A fastball that sits just this side of 88 mph and an average slider should keep him relevant at Triple-A Nashville, even if he remains blocked from a full-time gig on the 25-man roster.

J.B. Wendelken   RHP

Born: 3/24/93   Age: 24   Bats: R   Throws: R   Height: 6'0"   Weight: 220   Entered Pro Ball: Round 13, 2012 Draft (#421 overall)

YEAR	TEAM	LVL	AGE	W	L	SV	G	GS	IP	H	HR	BB/9	K/9	K	GB%	BABIP	WHIP	ERA	FIP	DRA	VORP	WARP	cFIP	MPH
2014	WNS	A+	21	7	10	0	27	27	145²	181	15	2.0	8.0	129	39%	.356	1.47	5.25	3.87	2.81	45.1	4.6	87	
2015	BIR	AA	22	6	2	5	27	0	43	36	4	2.3	11.7	56	28%	.305	1.09	2.72	2.67	1.57	15.1	1.6	75	
2015	CHR	AAA	22	0	0	0	12	0	16	14	2	2.8	7.3	13	42%	.250	1.19	4.50	4.09	3.91	1.8	0.2	99	
2016	NAS	AAA	23	1	4	5	39	0	46²	48	5	5.1	12.7	65	35%	.368	1.61	4.11	4.26	3.78	6.0	0.6	94	
2016	OAK	MLB	23	0	0	0	8	0	12²	18	3	6.4	8.5	12	35%	.375	2.13	9.95	6.42	5.13	-0.2	0.0	117	95.5
2017	OAK	MLB	24	3	2	0	33	4	53¹	58	7	3.6	7.6	45	56%	.317	1.49	4.41	4.44	4.95	1.8	0.2	114	
2018	OAK	MLB	25	3	2	0	27	5	64	60	8	4.4	10.1	72	56%	.312	1.43	3.87	4.04	4.34	5.9	0.6	98	

Breakout: 5%   Improve: 11%   Collapse: 2%   Attrition: 14%   MLB: 22%   *Comparables: Preston Guilmet, Jesse Chavez, Noe Ramirez*

Acquired from the White Sox for Brett Lawrie during the 2015 winter meetings, Wendleken arrived in Oakland with an above-average changeup and little else. Even that was taken from him during his first foray into the majors, when an acute case of *invisiblestrikezonitis* inflated his DRA beyond the reasonable limit for a rookie pitcher.

LINEOUTS

Hitters

NAME	POS	TEAM	LVL	AGE	PA	R	2B	3B	HR	RBI	BB	K	SB	CS	AVG/OBP/SLG	TAv	VORP	BABIP	BRR	FRAA	WARP
Jaycob Brugman	OF	MID	AA	24	176	27	7	3	5	20	16	33	2	3	.261/.335/.439	.272	5.9	.300	-1.0	CF(31): -7.0 • RF(7): 0.2	-0.1
	OF	NAS	AAA	24	433	50	26	4	7	67	36	88	5	3	.295/.352/.438	.294	29.2	.358	1.7	CF(72): -2.3 • RF(17): 2.2	3.0
Mark Canha	1B	OAK	MLB	27	44	4	0	0	3	6	0	20	0	1	.122/.140/.341	.164	-3.6	.105	-0.1	1B(5): 0.1 • 3B(3): -0.1	-0.4
Jaff Decker	PH	DUR	AAA	26	417	55	18	2	12	35	59	79	18	7	.255/.366/.421	.277	19.5	.295	0.5	CF(74): -3.8 • RF(15): -0.5	1.6
	PH	TBA	MLB	26	57	1	1	0	0	1	4	14	1	0	.154/.211/.173	.158	-4.6	.205	0.1	RF(13): -0.4 • LF(3): 0.3	-0.5
Tyler Ladendorf	INF	NAS	AAA	28	137	17	5	0	1	6	7	26	0	0	.234/.274/.297	.242	4.9	.287	3.4	CF(15): 0.1 • LF(8): 1.3	0.6
	INF	OAK	MLB	28	50	6	0	0	0	1	1	13	2	0	.083/.102/.083	.053	-8.8	.114	0.3	2B(30): 0.7 • 3B(3): 0.0	-0.8
Andrew Lambo	PH	OAK	MLB	27	1	0	0	0	0	0	0	0	0	0	.000/.000/.000	-.016	-0.3	.000	0.0		0.0
	PH	NAS	AAA	27	240	29	10	3	4	30	21	43	1	0	.255/.321/.384	.270	4.4	.298	-1.9	LF(27): -0.9	0.4
Matt McBride	C	NAS	AAA	31	274	33	20	1	7	30	26	49	0	1	.267/.339/.441	.306	21.1	.309	-2.0	C(46): 6.9 • RF(12): 0.3	3.0
	C	OAK	MLB	31	44	4	3	0	0	2	1	10	0	0	.209/.227/.279	.184	-1.7	.273	0.0	C(16): -0.8 • RF(1): -0.0	-0.3
Maxwell Muncy	INF	NAS	AAA	25	268	34	7	2	8	26	35	54	5	0	.251/.360/.408	.295	15.1	.291	-0.5	LF(28): -1.4 • 3B(13): -1.3	1.2
	INF	OAK	MLB	25	133	13	2	0	2	8	20	24	0	0	.186/.308/.257	.217	-2.5	.218	0.3	2B(21): 0.3 • RF(17): 0.1	-0.2
Yairo Munoz	SS	MID	AA	21	414	44	16	3	9	39	23	76	6	7	.240/.286/.367	.234	1.1	.278	-1.0	SS(41): 0.8 • 2B(27): 0.5	0.5
Chris Parmelee	RF	NYA	MLB	28	8	4	1	0	2	4	0	3	0	0	.500/.500/1.375	.569	2.7	.667	0.1	1B(6): 0.2	0.3
	RF	SWB	AAA	28	245	29	10	0	11	29	29	42	0	0	.248/.335/.449	.288	9.0	.258	-0.7	1B(48): 6.0 • LF(2): 0.2	1.6
Josh Phegley	C	NAS	AAA	28	23	2	1	0	0	1	4	6	0	0	.316/.435/.368	.313	2.3	.462	0.3	C(3): 0.1	0.2
	C	OAK	MLB	28	86	11	6	0	1	10	5	13	0	0	.256/.314/.372	.260	2.8	.292	-1.1	C(25): -4.7 • P(1): -0.0	-0.2
Colin Walsh	2B	MIL	MLB	26	63	4	1	0	0	2	15	22	0	0	.085/.317/.106	.194	-2.2	.160	0.2	3B(11): 0.0 • LF(2): 0.2	-0.2
	2B	NAS	AAA	26	245	31	12	1	4	26	41	63	0	0	.259/.384/.388	.295	14.8	.353	1.1	LF(25): 0.9 • 3B(7): 0.6	1.6
Joe Wendle	2B	NAS	AAA	26	526	81	31	9	12	61	26	112	14	4	.279/.324/.452	.275	25.4	.340	3.2	2B(122): 4.4	3.1
	2B	OAK	MLB	26	104	11	1	0	1	11	6	16	2	0	.260/.298/.302	.245	0.5	.296	-0.7	2B(28): 1.5	0.2

Yet another prized July 2 signing for San Diego, **Luis Almanzar** has impressive tools at the plate with some question marks about where he'll end up defensively. ❖ **Jaycob Brugman** lacks power for a corner outfielder, but the former BYU standout had a solid year between Double-A and Triple-A to put himself on the A's radar. ❖ **Mark Canha**'s rise from Triple-A to second-string MLB infielder in 2015 read like a Cinderella story for any Rule 5 draftee. Living happily ever after, however, proved more of an issue in 2016 when Canha underwent hip surgery in May. ❖ **Jaff Decker**'s name is pronounced "Jeff," which makes about as much sense as putting him on a 40-man roster. ❖ Shoulder problems put the brakes on **Sam Fuld**'s season well before it gained any traction. When healthy, his defense-first approach offered the A's some outfield depth despite a bat that never quite warmed up to major-league pitching. ❖ Acquired by the A's for Orlando Cabrera way back in 2009, **Tyler Ladendorf** finally received more than a cup of coffee at age 28 and showed why he'd been in the minors for so long. ❖ It didn't look like a comeback was in the cards for **Andrew Lambo** after the outfielder underwent surgery to combat testicular cancer halfway through the season. He'll return to Oakland on a minor-league contract and hopefully with a clean bill of health. ❖ **Matt McBride** is a journeyman catcher/first baseman who's spent parts of four seasons in the majors while totaling just 194 at-bats. His bat is above-average for a catcher if given a chance, but teams are unlikely to trust him there. ❖ **Max Muncy** was a first baseman/third baseman in the minors, logging zero innings at second base, but he was thrust into action there by the A's during his debut and will need the versatility to stick in the majors. ❖ **Yairo Munoz** saw plenty of time around the horn in 2016, but it's his offensive positioning that needs refining if he's going to turn a slap-happy stroke into a viable home run rate. ❖ **Chris Parmelee** went deep twice in his first start as a Yankee, then got hurt the next game and was never heard from again. At least he's got a couple clips for the highlight reel. ❖ **Josh Phegley** played second fiddle to Stephen Vogt behind the plate, and a cyst in his right knee plus a bout of strep throat limited him to 86 plate appearances. ❖ If on-base percentage took human form, it would be shaped something like **Colin Walsh**, whose zen approach piles up walks but offers little else. ❖ **Joe Wendle** is the charming second-string bachelor in your favorite romantic comedy, the one who won't sweep you off your feet with grand displays of speed or power, but will be quietly waiting to take center stage when the leading man (read: Coco Crisp) steps out of the limelight.

Pitchers

NAME	TEAM	LVL	AGE	W	L	SV	G	GS	IP	H	HR	BB/9	K/9	K	GB%	BABIP	WHIP	ERA	FIP	DRA	VORP	WARP	cFIP	MPH
Chris Bassitt	OAK	MLB	27	0	2	0	5	5	28	35	5	4.5	7.4	23	47%	.330	1.75	6.11	5.28	4.73	2.0	0.2	106	96.0
Paul Blackburn	TEN	AA	22	6	4	0	18	18	102¹	96	6	2.3	6.3	72	56%	.285	1.19	3.17	3.47	3.95	12.9	1.4	92	
	WTN	AA	22	3	1	0	8	7	40²	42	2	2.0	6.0	27	58%	.312	1.25	3.54	3.30	4.07	4.6	0.5	94	
Simon Castro	ABQ	AAA	28	0	5	10	50	0	53¹	52	5	2.0	9.8	58	49%	.324	1.20	3.38	3.72	1.77	18.9	1.9	79	
Dakota Chalmers	VER	A-	19	5	4	0	15	13	67	55	8	5.0	8.3	62	44%	.253	1.37	4.70	4.90	5.25	-0.4	0.0	111	
	NAS	AAA	26	0	0	0	20	0	25	18	0	2.2	12.6	35	60%	.327	0.96	1.08	1.64	1.57	9.4	1.0	65	
	OAK	MLB	26	3	1	0	35	0	47²	37	6	3.2	10.2	54	64%	.267	1.13	4.53	3.55	3.03	10.3	1.1	78	92.7
Casey Meisner	STO	A+	21	1	14	1	28	19	117	126	12	4.5	7.7	100	37%	.325	1.58	4.85	5.00	6.48	-14.3	-1.5	116	
Fernando Rodriguez	OAK	MLB	32	2	0	0	34	0	40²	30	3	3.8	8.2	37	37%	.257	1.16	4.20	3.57	4.34	2.8	0.3	105	95.1
Logan Shore	VER	A-	21	0	2	0	7	7	21	17	1	3.0	9.0	21	50%	.262	1.14	2.57	2.89	3.46	4.1	0.4	95	
Josh Smith	LOU	AAA	28	4	4	0	9	8	45	44	5	2.6	7.6	38	50%	.307	1.27	3.80	3.86	3.62	8.5	0.9	92	
	CIN	MLB	28	3	3	0	32	2	59²	57	11	3.9	7.2	48	43%	.264	1.39	4.68	5.33	5.83	-5.3	-0.6	115	93.2
Tyler Sturdevant	TBA	MLB	30	0	1	0	16	0	18¹	18	1	2.9	6.9	14	39%	.321	1.31	3.93	3.43	5.06	-0.2	0.0	111	93.6
	DUR	AAA	30	3	2	4	34	0	39¹	39	6	2.7	11.2	49	46%	.344	1.30	3.66	3.73	2.19	12.1	1.2	75	
Andrew Triggs	NAS	AAA	27	2	1	2	16	0	18¹	16	0	2.5	10.3	21	59%	.314	1.15	2.95	2.90	2.74	4.5	0.5	85	
	OAK	MLB	27	1	1	0	24	6	56¹	56	5	2.1	8.8	55	52%	.315	1.22	4.31	3.16	3.45	10.6	1.1	82	92.6
Bobby Wahl	MID	AA	24	0	1	10	33	0	40²	26	3	3.8	10.6	48	55%	.256	1.06	2.21	3.11	3.21	6.9	0.7	80	

Chris Bassitt played through a month of elbow pain before receiving a proper diagnosis, ending with Tommy John surgery. ❖ Last summer, the Cubs traded **Paul Blackburn** for the man who recorded the final out in their first World Series win since 1908. Three months later, Seattle traded him for the guy who punched Billy Butler in the face. ❖ **Simon Castro** has 17 career major league innings and archeologists may never truly know why. ❖ Considered a first-round talent who dropped to the third round in 2015, **Dakota Chalmers**' big fastball has been sidetracked by his lack of command. ❖ **Daniel Coulombe** eviscerated Triple-A competition with a merciless K/BB ratio, but despite improved command and a slight uptick in fastball velocity he registered middling numbers with the A's again. ❖ Were Professor Trelawney to interpret the tea leaves in **Felix Doubront**'s cup, she might find something resembling the Grim—or, at the very least, a lengthy and grueling recovery process from Tommy John surgery. ❖ Mechanical problems and the aerodynamic atmosphere of the California League bruised **Casey Meisner**'s ERA. While he boasts decent fastball command and a crude three-pitch repertoire, he might need a rain check on his projected 2017 call-up. ❖ One elbow injury can spell disaster for any pitcher, but two Tommy John surgeries followed by two additional elbow fractures in a three-year span is something straight out of a Stephen King novel. **Jarrod Parker** hasn't seen a mound in three seasons. ❖ A steady if unremarkable presence in the A's bullpen, **Fernando Rodriguez** was waylaid by a lat tear halfway through the year. He underwent shoulder surgery in September, bringing an injury-riddled ride through the AL West to a final stop. ❖ Rotation-mates with A.J. Puk at Florida, **Logan Shore** was more often the Gators' top starter and joined the A's as a second rounder. He has an average fastball, good control and a projected quick path to the back of a rotation. ❖ **Josh Smith** got better at getting ahead of hitters in 2016, but still lacks the stuff to dominate in relief, the command to start and any ability to shoot from beyond the arc. ❖ Back in 2012, former BP author and current Astros Pro Scouting Director Kevin Goldstein called **Tyler Sturdevant** a "sleeper" thanks to his plus cutter, but today he doesn't flash any plus pitches and he's only a sleeper, in the sense that he's a somnambulant replacement-level relief arm. ❖ **Andrew Triggs**' extreme sidearm delivery disguised sub par offerings, but improved command and a successful migration to the rotation helped convert his career trajectory from journeyman reliever to potential back-end starter. ❖ **Bobby Wahl**'s signature triple-digit velocity got him to Triple-A, but some late-season control issues cast a shadow over his future as a major-league reliever.

PHILADELPHIA PHILLIES

Essay by Corinne Landrey

Player comments by Mike Gianella and BP staff

I f there's a sport that lends itself to the poetic more than baseball, I'm not familiar with it. I won't pretend to know all the reasons why baseball is so innately literary, but I imagine it has something to do with the cadence of the game and the contemplative nature brought on by the natural pauses that allow us to take in atmosphere and situation before each play. There's also the endearingly intimate relationship between baseball and its history. We all tuned in this summer for the last season of Vin Scully stories about baseball years gone by, and listened with rapt attention to the man who could tell first-hand accounts of everyone from Jackie Robinson to Corey Seager.

Whatever the reasons, though, there's a natural tendency to look to the sport for deeper meaning and symbolism. Now, I don't know if the symbolism is real or if it's merely something we impose upon a game which is so inextricably driven by narrative. However, whether it's meaningful or merely coincidental, I do know that the facts presented in the following story are very much true.

The sky was the deepest color of dusk—that faint blue color the sky turns each night as it desperately clings to the day's final rays of sunshine. The sun may have been setting on the day, but Citizens Bank Park was as alive as it has ever been. The Phillies were trailing the Cardinals 3-1 in the bottom of the sixth inning, but two singles and a strikeout brought Ryan Howard to the plate representing the go-ahead run.

The right-hander on the mound clearly wanted nothing to do with the slugger in front of him. Howard laid off three fastballs nowhere near the zone and battled four changeups which—while still out of the zone—were close enough for swings. A whiff and three fouls on those offspeed pitches left the count 3-2 with the eighth pitch of the at-bat on the way. Finally, the pitcher missed and left a changeup right over the heart of the plate. Howard unleashed his mighty swing and deposited the baseball in the upper deck of the right-field stands. Citizens Bank Park erupted and Ryan Howard trotted around the bases—as he's done so many times in his career—under the twilight sky. The Phillies tacked on runs throughout the final three innings and ultimately won the game, 11-6.

The date of that game was October 1, 2011, and that go-ahead shot was the last of eight postseason home runs Ryan

PHILLIES PROSPECTUS
2016 W-L: 71-91, 4TH IN NL EAST

Pythag	.379	30th	DER	.696	23rd
RS/G	3.77	30th	B-Age	26.8	3rd
RA/G	4.91	26th	P-Age	26	1st
TAv	.253	25th	Salary	$88.8M	25th
BRR	-3.35	22nd	M$/MW	$3.4M	18th
TAv-P	.285	29th	DL Days	1103	19th
FIP	4.39	22nd	$ on DL	26%	29th

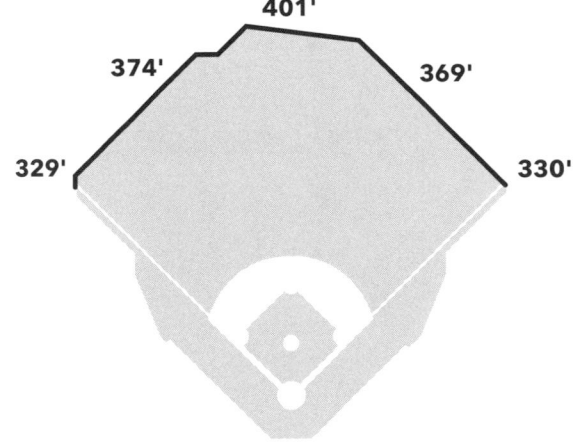

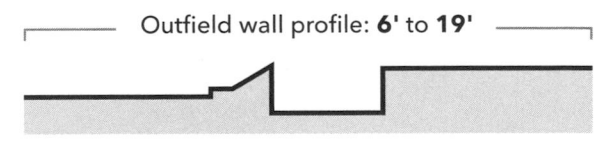

Outfield wall profile: **6'** to **19'**

Three-Year Park Factors

Runs	Runs/RH	Runs/LH	HR/RH	HR/LH
97	98	95	113	103

Top Hitter WARP	5.1	Odubel Herrera
Top Pitcher WARP	3.9	Aaron Nola
Top Prospect		J.P. Crawford

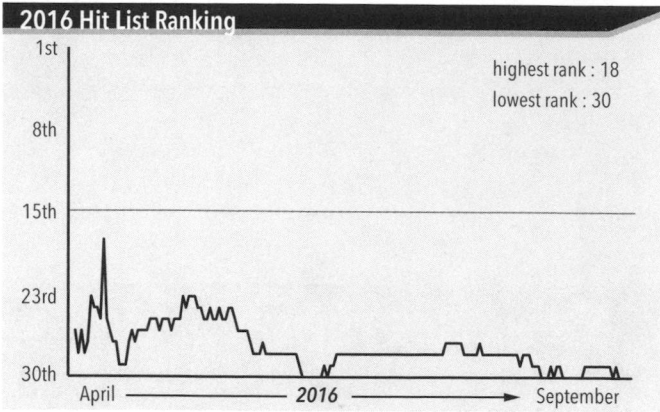

2016 Hit List Ranking

highest rank : 18
lowest rank : 30

April ——— *2016* ——→ September

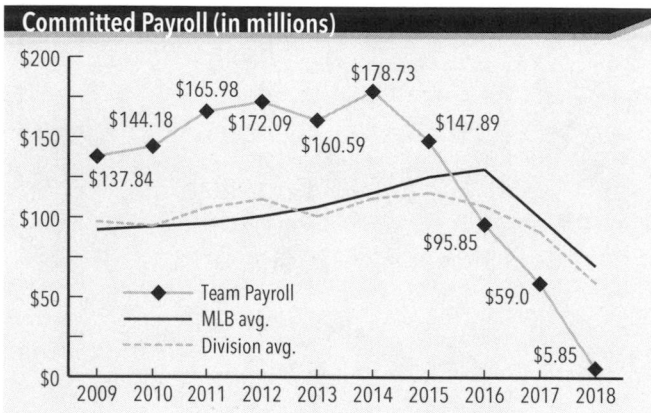

Committed Payroll (in millions)

$178.73
$165.98
$172.09
$144.18
$160.59
$147.89
$137.84
$95.85
$59.0
$5.85

◆ Team Payroll
— MLB avg.
-- Division avg.

2009 2010 2011 2012 2013 2014 2015 2016 2017 2018

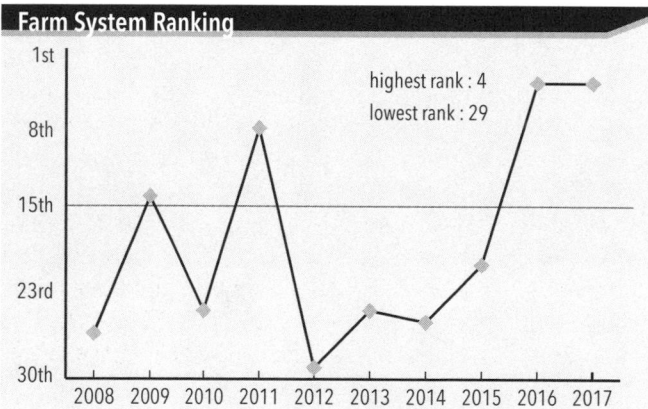

Farm System Ranking

highest rank : 4
lowest rank : 29

2008 2009 2010 2011 2012 2013 2014 2015 2016 2017

Personnel

President:
Andy MacPhail

VP, General Manager:
Matt Klentak

Assistant General Manager:
Scott Proefrock

Assistant General Manager:
Ned Rice

Manager:
Pete Mackanin

BP Alumni:
Lewie Pollis

Howard would hit for the Phillies. It was a heroic moment to which Philadelphia fans had become accustomed but, unbeknownst to anyone in that stadium, Howard's career as a productive baseball player was about to be extinguished as irrevocably as that day's sunlight.

Six days later, in the fifth and final game of the series, Ryan Howard grounded out for the final out in the 1-0 loss only to blow out his Achilles tendon while running down the first base line. That moment, as Howard lay collapsed in the basepath with the Cardinals celebrating around him, was the end. It was the end of the Phillies' dynastic run of five straight division titles. It was the end of Howard's reign as *the* dominant slugger in the majors—from 2006 to 2011 Howard hit 262 homers, a figure only two players were within *fifty* home runs of: Albert Pujols (244) and Prince Fielder (228). It was the end of an era.

Five years *to the day* after that triumphant twilight three-run homer, Howard dug into the batter's box at Citizens Bank Park once again. With the Phillies trailing 2-0 in the fifth, he represented the tying run against a right-hander named Bartolo Colon. Once again, he unleashed that majestic swing and deposited the ball in the right-field seats. The crowd gave him a standing ovation and insisted he take a curtain call. In 2011, the people in the stadium were blissfully unaware they were witnessing the figurative end of an era, but there was no such naiveté in 2016. This was the literal end—Ryan Howard's 390th and final home run in a Phillies uniform—and everybody knew it.

✦ ✦ ✦

Five weeks earlier, the Phillies traded their long-time catcher Carlos Ruiz to the Dodgers, leaving Howard as the sole remaining icon of the franchise's most recent glory years. With the $23-million team option for 2017 on Howard's contract certain to be declined at the end of the season, there was no mistaking that this concluded the final chapter of a momentous era of Phillies baseball.

The uncertain realities of the rest of the current Phillies roster surrounding Howard during that final weekend of the 2016 season, however, provided a glaring contrast to the certainty of his farewell. The book of the last great Phillies team is bound, written, footnoted and on the shelf. The book of the next great Phillies team is currently a swath of blank pages.

The 2016 Phillies finished the season with a 71-91 record which, while far from good, did represent an eight-game improvement over their record the previous summer. They are a team whose worst days are ostensibly behind them. So much so that it no longer feels wholly accurate to refer to the Phillies as a rebuilding team. They've made their big moves and developed their big prospects. If all goes according to plan, key pieces of their future core are in the high minors, if not already on the major league roster. The foundational act of rebuilding is already in the rearview mirror, but that doesn't necessarily make the future all that clear.

Like Schrödinger's cat, the Phillies are currently in an unknown state where the rebuild is simultaneously alive and dead—or, perhaps more accurately, it's a success and a failure. Naturally, the future is unwritten for every team, but something about the true absence of established major-league talent makes the uncertainty all the more palpable in Philadelphia.

Aaron Nola is both a healthy no. 2 starter and a pitcher whose career is felled by injury. Jorge Alfaro is both an All-Star catcher and a player who can't hit his weight. J.P. Crawford is a franchise player and a frustratingly inconsistent major leaguer. Vince Velasquez is a top-of-the-rotation starter and a relief pitcher. The millions upon millions of dollars in available payroll space is invested wisely and it's squandered on devastatingly disappointing free agent contracts.

The unanswered questions for Philadelphia are seemingly endless, but that doesn't mean we didn't learn anything in 2016. We may not know nearly enough to confidently predict whether or not the rebuild is ultimately a success or a failure, but a few aspects of the big picture outlook are slowly coming into clearer focus. Let's take a moment to consider three things we learned last summer about the newest iteration of the Phillies.

First and foremost, this was the first season under the Andy MacPhail/Matt Klentak administration. At the very least, it's fair to say they didn't move to town and go full A.J. Preller on their new team. The moves they made last winter were, by and large, minimal. They made a few low-profile trade acquisitions—Charlie Morton and Jeremy Hellickson—to shore up the starting rotation and scoured the waiver wire to secure relief pitching depth and an extra outfielder in Peter Bourjos.

There was, of course, one glaring exception to their otherwise quiet offseason: the Ken Giles trade. In a market where elite relief pitching is fetching high returns, the Phillies new front office flipped Giles and Jonathan Arauz, a rookie-league shortstop, to the Astros for an impressive looking return of four prospects—Vince Velasquez, Mark Appel, Harold Arauz, Thomas Eshelman—and Brett Oberholtzer, a major-league swing arm who has already been removed from the Phillies roster.

Aside from that one major deal, the actions (and inactions) of this administration make it clear that they have no qualms about being patient. There was no quick fix available for a Phillies roster so depressingly devoid of talent. They are demonstrating a commitment to giving their emerging prospects the time and opportunity necessary to develop. As their current crop of prospects pans out (and doesn't), the front office will have a clearer idea of the reinforcements needed and unexpected holes that will need to be filled by long-term investments. Presumably as that occurs over the 2017 and 2018 seasons, they will forgo their bargain-bin hunting, but time will tell. As of this writing, acquisitions of reliever Pat Neshek and the qualifying-offer-aided retention of Jeremy Hellickson are early indicators that it will be another relatively quiet offseason in Philadelphia…with one significant exception. The Phillies made their first long-term commitment to a member of their new core by locking former Rule 5 Draftee Odubel Herrera into a five-year extension with club options for 2022 and 2023.

Another takeaway from the 2016 Phillies season is that the team has legitimate pitching talent. Jerad Eickhoff, acquired from Texas in the Cole Hamels trade, has emerged as a true mid-rotation workhorse. Vince Velasquez's 16-strikeout performance in his second start dazzled the baseball world and showed the undeniable potential of his stellar fastball. During much of the first half Aaron Nola looked like a front-of-the-rotation starter, but command and injury woes sullied the end of his season. Seeing all three of these young pitchers fulfill their potential at various points last season was undeniably encouraging even as questions about future health and developmental steps remain unanswered.

Lastly (and least importantly) we re-learned that the fungible bullpen theory has merit. Jeanmar Gomez was acquired as a minor-league free agent in January 2015 and put together a shockingly effective performance as the Phillies closer this past summer. He wore down in September, but at the end of August, he had 34 saves and 2.97 ERA. How should the Phillies apply the knowledge that reliever performance is maddeningly unpredictable as they continue building for the future? Declining to invest significant resources in the bullpen until a more established core is in place is an appealing proposition.

The frustrating truth, though, is that we didn't learn much more than that. You'll note the Phillies' offense went unmentioned in the "what we learned" discussion. Many of their top position player prospects—J.P. Crawford, Nick Williams, Jorge Alfaro—spent the vast majority of their seasons in the minor leagues. Tommy Joseph did emerge as a surprisingly productive first baseman after being outrighted off the roster last winter, but his incredible comeback raises more questions than it answers. Outside of Odubel Herrera cementing his status as the starting center fielder, the future lineup is riddled with question marks.

✦ ✦ ✦

One of the biggest questions at the end of the 2016 season, however, was what to make of Ryan Howard's legacy now that his Phillies career is complete. Outside of Philadelphia—and inside it, to a degree—his name has become synonymous with disastrous contracts, but the ill-fated and ill-conceived five-year, $125 million extension is no more. It stands as a warning to future baseball front offices, but in time Howard's specific legacy in Philadelphia will transition back to the seemingly inevitable hero time and time again. WARP says he was the least valuable of the most iconic contributors to the Phillies glory years—Howard, Jimmy Rollins, Chase Utley, Cole Hamels—and by more than half on average. But nearly 400 home runs and a championship ring say the disappointing end of Howard's career will soon be forgotten as he finally resumes his standing as one of the most beloved figures in Philly sports.

No matter how overdue it may or may not have been, Ryan Howard's final home run was a cathartic moment for Phillies fans. It bid an official goodbye to arguably the greatest era in Phillies baseball anyone has ever known, and inarguably the greatest for anyone under the age of 35.

For the past five years, much of the Phillies' present revolved around its past. The full focus of the team and its fans is now on the unwritten future represented by the current team. Will these new dawn Phillies be as successful as the last era? Will any of them join Howard and his former teammates in Philly sports lore one day?

Only time can tell. ∎

—Corinne Landrey is a baseball analyst living in the great state of Delaware who has previously written for MLB.com, FanGraphs, The Hardball Times, and Crashburn Alley

HITTERS

Jorge Alfaro   C

Born: 6/11/93   Age: 24   Bats: R   Throws: R   Height: 6'2"   Weight: 225   Entered Pro Ball: International Free Agent, 2010

YEAR	TEAM	LVL	AGE	PA	R	2B	3B	HR	RBI	BB	K	SB	CS	AVG/OBP/SLG	TAv	VORP	BABIP	BRR	FRAA	WARP
2014	MYR	A+	21	437	63	22	5	13	73	23	100	6	5	.261/.318/.440	.268	18.7	.315	-1.7	C(75): -1.0 • 1B(17): 0.0	1.8
2014	FRI	AA	21	99	12	4	0	4	14	6	23	0	0	.261/.343/.443	.271	4.7	.311	0.1	C(15): -1.0 • 1B(1): -0.2	0.4
2015	FRI	AA	22	207	22	15	2	5	21	9	61	2	1	.253/.314/.432	.250	5.5	.347	0.6	C(35): -0.3 • 1B(1): -0.0	0.6
2016	REA	AA	23	435	68	21	2	15	67	22	105	3	2	.285/.325/.458	.268	20.9	.347	-1.5	C(95): 16.5	4.0
2016	PHI	MLB	23	17	0	0	0	0	0	1	8	0	0	.125/.176/.125	.079	-2.5	.250	-0.1	C(4): -0.1	-0.3
2017	*PHI*	*MLB*	*24*	*30*	*3*	*1*	*0*	*1*	*3*	*1*	*10*	*0*	*0*	*.220/.261/.374*	*.228*	*0.4*	*.294*	*-0.1*	*C -0*	*-0.1*
2018	*PHI*	*MLB*	*25*	*251*	*28*	*10*	*1*	*9*	*29*	*12*	*81*	*0*	*0*	*.216/.266/.377*	*.236*	*2.4*	*.289*	*-0.5*	*C -2*	*0.1*

Breakout: 4%   Improve: 10%   Collapse: 5%   Attrition: 19%   MLB: 20%   *Comparables: Lucas May, Max Stassi, Luke Montz*

Although it may not have showed up in the stat line, 2016 was a big step forward for Alfaro in that he showed that he has the defensive chops to stick behind the plate in the majors. In retrospect the Ivan Rodriguez comps were ill-conceived (duh), but Alfaro's cannon behind the dish combined with the refinement of his game calling and receiving skills make him a legit prospect in his own right. His free-swinging approach will cost Alfaro some batting average in the majors, but the raw power combined with a newfound ability to go the opposite way at times will more than make up for that. Even if Alfaro doesn't live up to the Texas-sized hype, he could still be a cornerstone for the Phillies for years to come.

YEAR	TEAM	P. COUNT	FRM RUNS	BLK RUNS	THRW RUNS	TOT RUNS
2014	FRI	2077	-0.4	-0.1	0.1	-0.4
2015	FRI	5306	-0.3	-0.8	0.2	-0.9
2016	PHI	576	0.0	-0.6	0.0	-0.6
2017	*PHI*	*1101*	*0.1*	*-0.3*	*0.0*	*-0.2*
2018	*PHI*	*9197*	*0.4*	*-2.3*	*-0.1*	*-2.1*

Aaron Altherr   OF

Born: 1/14/91   Age: 26   Bats: R   Throws: R   Height: 6'5"   Weight: 215   Entered Pro Ball: Round 9, 2009 Draft (#287 overall)

YEAR	TEAM	LVL	AGE	PA	R	2B	3B	HR	RBI	BB	K	SB	CS	AVG/OBP/SLG	TAv	VORP	BABIP	BRR	FRAA	WARP
2014	CLR	A+	23	33	6	1	2	0	2	5	8	1	0	.250/.364/.429	.278	1.9	.350	0.3	CF(6): 2.6 • RF(1): -0.3	0.4
2014	PHI	MLB	23	5	0	0	0	0	0	0	2	0	0	.000/.000/.000	.005	-1.1	.000	0.0	LF(1): 0.1	-0.1
2014	REA	AA	23	492	54	27	2	14	57	26	110	12	6	.236/.287/.399	.242	1.7	.279	-2.9	CF(100): 1.0 • LF(12): 2.4	0.5
2015	REA	AA	24	260	29	19	3	6	29	28	40	8	3	.293/.371/.480	.302	16.0	.332	-0.4	RF(42): 3.9 • RF(16): 1.3	2.3
2015	LEH	AAA	24	229	36	13	2	8	38	21	44	8	1	.294/.362/.495	.303	18.0	.338	1.7	CF(35): 3.2 • RF(9): 0.2	2.2
2015	PHI	MLB	24	161	25	11	4	5	22	16	41	6	2	.241/.338/.489	.300	9.8	.301	0.0	LF(23): 0.5 • RF(11): 0.6	1.4
2016	PHI	MLB	25	227	23	6	0	4	22	23	69	7	2	.197/.300/.288	.235	-0.7	.280	0.3	RF(42): -2.5 • LF(20): 0.7	-0.3
2017	*PHI*	*MLB*	*26*	*527*	*60*	*24*	*3*	*15*	*56*	*40*	*144*	*13*	*4*	*.225/.293/.385*	*.246*	*6.9*	*.286*	*1.2*	*RF -1 • CF 0*	*0.3*
2018	*PHI*	*MLB*	*27*	*504*	*59*	*22*	*3*	*16*	*59*	*40*	*142*	*12*	*4*	*.227/.298/.392*	*.256*	*9.1*	*.290*	*0.8*	*RF -1 • CF 0*	*0.9*

Breakout: 6%   Improve: 31%   Collapse: 12%   Attrition: 18%   MLB: 57%   *Comparables: Clete Thomas, Brennan Boesch, Wladimir Balentien*

Entering spring training, Altherr was one of the more intriguing players in the projected 2016 Opening Day lineup, but a torn tendon sheath in his left wrist in early March put him out of commission until late July. For about a week after he returned, Altherr looked like he hadn't missed a beat, stealing two bases and swatting two homers, including a shot off of Madison Bumgarner. The rest of his campaign looked like what you might expect from a toolsy hitter who missed spring training and had yet to play a full season in the majors. Altherr slashed .193/.289/.257 from August 5 through the end of the season. The rust was prominent more often than not, and the long swing—combined with subpar plate coverage that had hounded him as a prospect—reemerged down the stretch. Like a lot of Phillies, Altherr is not as young as you'd expect for a team that is in the middle of a rebuilding effort.

Cody Asche   3B

Born: 6/30/90   Age: 27   Bats: L   Throws: R   Height: 6'1"   Weight: 205   Entered Pro Ball: Round 4, 2011 Draft (#151 overall)

YEAR	TEAM	LVL	AGE	PA	R	2B	3B	HR	RBI	BB	K	SB	CS	AVG/OBP/SLG	TAv	VORP	BABIP	BRR	FRAA	WARP
2014	PHI	MLB	24	434	43	25	0	10	46	33	102	0	1	.252/.309/.390	.260	12.3	.315	-0.3	3B(112): 0.4	1.4
2015	LEH	AAA	25	67	7	3	0	1	3	6	9	0	0	.295/.358/.393	.270	1.1	.333	-1.0	LF(15): -1.3	0.0
2015	PHI	MLB	25	456	41	22	3	12	39	26	111	1	2	.245/.294/.395	.248	4.1	.304	-2.1	LF(63): -2.9 • 3B(51): -2.4	-0.1
2016	LEH	AAA	26	123	20	8	0	6	15	11	26	1	0	.279/.350/.514	.306	9.2	.316	0.7	LF(16): 2.8 • 3B(7): -0.5	1.2
2016	PHI	MLB	26	218	22	15	0	4	18	18	54	3	1	.213/.284/.350	.239	0.7	.271	0.5	LF(57): 1.6	0.2
2017	*PHI*	*MLB*	*27*	*284*	*31*	*14*	*1*	*10*	*36*	*21*	*71*	*2*	*1*	*.244/.302/.416*	*.249*	*5.8*	*.296*	*-0.3*	*LF 0 • 3B -0*	*0.7*
2018	*PHI*	*MLB*	*28*	*292*	*35*	*14*	*1*	*9*	*35*	*22*	*74*	*2*	*1*	*.241/.301/.407*	*.259*	*6.2*	*.296*	*-0.4*	*LF 0 • 3B 0*	*0.7*

Breakout: 7%   Improve: 43%   Collapse: 6%   Attrition: 15%   MLB: 90%   *Comparables: Brennan Boesch, Felix Pie, Domonic Brown*

Ryan Howard is often viewed as the face of the franchise's post-2011 failures, but in many ways Cody Asche is more emblematic. Drafted in the fourth round of the 2011 draft, Asche rolled through the minor leagues and gave Phillies fans a misguided sense of how good he would be at a time when it felt like Ruben Amaro Jr. could do no wrong and the fun times would last forever. Asche didn't turn into a pumpkin, but he played out like the second-division regular you might have expected him to be based on the scouting reports coming out of college and his advanced age in the low minors. After being pushed off of third base by Maikel Franco, Asche is now a below-average corner outfielder, with both the glove and the bat. The Phillies rebuild is about to bear fruit, and Asche is weeks—maybe even days—away from being pushed aside by some of the younger, more talented players in the pipeline.

Andres Blanco   3B

Born: 4/11/84   Age: 33   Bats: B   Throws: R   Height: 5'10"   Weight: 195   Entered Pro Ball: International Free Agent, 2000

YEAR	TEAM	LVL	AGE	PA	R	2B	3B	HR	RBI	BB	K	SB	CS	AVG/OBP/SLG	TAv	VORP	BABIP	BRR	FRAA	WARP
2014	LEH	AAA	30	155	16	6	0	0	11	13	25	3	5	.241/.314/.285	.213	-0.7	.292	1.2	SS(39): 1.6 • 2B(5): -0.4	0.1
2014	PHI	MLB	30	53	4	5	0	1	3	2	6	0	0	.277/.306/.447	.267	1.4	.300	-0.6	3B(10): 0.5 • SS(6): 0.2	0.3
2015	PHI	MLB	31	261	32	22	3	7	25	21	44	1	1	.292/.360/.502	.303	19.8	.335	1.1	3B(36): -2.3 • 2B(22): 0.8	2.0
2016	PHI	MLB	32	209	26	15	1	4	21	11	41	2	3	.253/.316/.405	.260	7.7	.301	1.5	3B(21): -0.7 • 2B(20): -1.6	0.5
2017	*PHI*	*MLB*	*33*	*240*	*25*	*13*	*1*	*5*	*25*	*16*	*47*	*2*	*2*	*.249/.307/.393*	*.253*	*7.1*	*.290*	*-0.6*	*3B -0 • SS 0*	*0.4*
2018	*PHI*	*MLB*	*34*	*168*	*19*	*9*	*1*	*4*	*18*	*11*	*34*	*1*	*1*	*.247/.311/.385*	*.256*	*4.3*	*.289*	*0.4*	*3B 0 • SS 0*	*0.5*

Breakout: 2%   Improve: 33%   Collapse: 9%   Attrition: 18%   MLB: 85%   *Comparables: Don Kelly, Jack Hannahan, Mike Lamb*

A month into the 2016 season it looked like Blanco was going to inexplicably prolong the magic that carried him to a .303 TAv as an infield sub the year before. Alas, he turned back into what he has been throughout most of his career: a subpar hitter who can play every infield position adequately, if not spectacularly. Like a number of Phillies throughout their rebuild, Blanco has served the team like one of those faithful old retainers in a turn-of-the-century British novel about the juxtaposition between the serving and ruling classes. Blanco has done his job admirably, but when the time comes for the Phillies to compete again, he is fairly interchangeable with a number of other big league backups.

Peter Bourjos   CF

Born: 3/31/87   Age: 30   Bats: R   Throws: R   Height: 6'1"   Weight: 185   Entered Pro Ball: Round 10, 2005 Draft (#313 overall)

YEAR	TEAM	LVL	AGE	PA	R	2B	3B	HR	RBI	BB	K	SB	CS	AVG/OBP/SLG	TAv	VORP	BABIP	BRR	FRAA	WARP
2014	SLN	MLB	27	294	32	9	5	4	24	20	78	9	3	.231/.294/.348	.242	6.7	.311	3.5	CF(104): 1.3	0.9
2015	SLN	MLB	28	225	32	8	3	4	13	19	59	5	8	.200/.290/.333	.228	0.2	.263	0.7	CF(93): -2.4	-0.2
2016	PHI	MLB	29	383	40	20	7	5	23	17	91	6	4	.251/.292/.389	.251	4.3	.323	0.8	RF(115): -2.7 • CF(10): -0.3	0.1
2017	*PHI*	*MLB*	*30*	*331*	*36*	*12*	*4*	*7*	*32*	*22*	*88*	*7*	*5*	*.229/.291/.367*	*.229*	*0.7*	*.290*	*1.3*	*RF 1 • CF 0*	*0.2*
2018	*PHI*	*MLB*	*31*	*360*	*38*	*12*	*4*	*8*	*37*	*23*	*99*	*7*	*5*	*.225/.286/.361*	*.237*	*1.2*	*.287*	*1.9*	*RF 1 • CF 0*	*0.3*

Breakout: 4%   Improve: 42%   Collapse: 14%   Attrition: 27%   MLB: 90%   *Comparables: Roger Bernadina, Ed Stroud, Gabe Kapler*

Last year, the Phillies did what you expect teams in a rebuild to do. They picked up castoffs from other organizations who were extremely unlikely to amount to anything in the hopes that one or two of these players could turn useful once again. One of those players was Bourjos, whose only halfway-decent season was way back in 2011 for the Los Angeles Angels. Absent of an inexplicable 30-day stretch (June 6-July 5) where Bourjos slashed .440/.481/.707, he performed like the marginal fourth outfielder he has been for the last five seasons. He didn't work out, but given where the Phillies started, you certainly can't blame them for trying. Bourjos is an outfield tweener, and even by this modest standard is going to have a difficult time finding a big league bench job.

Dylan Cozens   RF

Born: 5/31/94   Age: 23   Bats: L   Throws: L   Height: 6'6"   Weight: 235   Entered Pro Ball: Round 2, 2012 Draft (#77 overall)

YEAR	TEAM	LVL	AGE	PA	R	2B	3B	HR	RBI	BB	K	SB	CS	AVG/OBP/SLG	TAv	VORP	BABIP	BRR	FRAA	WARP
2014	LWD	A	20	556	69	25	6	16	62	40	147	23	7	.248/.303/.415	.251	3.1	.314	-1.5	RF(110): -4.7 • LF(8): 0.2	-0.2
2015	CLR	A+	21	397	52	22	5	5	46	26	79	18	5	.282/.335/.411	.279	16.1	.346	2.1	RF(70): 2.0 • LF(12): -1.8	1.8
2015	REA	AA	21	44	6	2	0	3	9	3	7	2	1	.350/.386/.625	.369	4.1	.355	-1.6	RF(11): -0.9	0.3
2016	REA	AA	22	586	106	38	3	40	125	61	186	21	1	.276/.350/.591	.303	36.7	.348	0.3	RF(89): 5.1 • LF(29): -0.4	4.2
2017	*PHI*	*MLB*	*23*	*250*	*31*	*11*	*1*	*11*	*34*	*17*	*86*	*5*	*1*	*.223/.277/.427*	*.242*	*3.6*	*.297*	*0.6*	*RF 1 • LF -0*	*0.5*
2018	*PHI*	*MLB*	*24*	*388*	*48*	*18*	*2*	*17*	*53*	*27*	*128*	*9*	*2*	*.233/.287/.436*	*.261*	*10.2*	*.309*	*1.2*	*RF 2 • LF 0*	*1.3*

Breakout: 2%   Improve: 16%   Collapse: 1%   Attrition: 11%   MLB: 32%   *Comparables: Jamie Romak, Steven Moya, Bryce Brentz*

Double-A Reading's FirstEnergy Stadium plays like a bandbox, but Cozens is a big dude whose power would show up in nearly any park. The problem is that Cozens' stiff, arm-heavy approach is likely to be exposed by more advanced pitching. He can be beat by hard pitches up and in or off-speed pitches down and away. He is a smart baserunner, which is reflected in his high stolen-base totals despite his lack of foot speed, but this is also something that won't translate to the majors. Cozens will be fun to watch if he defies the scouting reports, but the lack of overall athleticism makes this unlikely.

J.P. Crawford   SS

Born: 1/11/95   Age: 22   Bats: L   Throws: R   Height: 6'2"   Weight: 180   Entered Pro Ball: Round 1, 2013 Draft (#16 overall)

YEAR	TEAM	LVL	AGE	PA	R	2B	3B	HR	RBI	BB	K	SB	CS	AVG/OBP/SLG	TAv	VORP	BABIP	BRR	FRAA	WARP
2014	LWD	A	19	267	37	16	0	3	19	37	37	14	7	.295/.398/.405	.291	21.1	.342	1.2	SS(59): 0.8	2.3
2014	CLR	A+	19	271	32	7	0	8	29	28	37	10	7	.275/.352/.407	.284	15.8	.292	-2.9	SS(62): 0.2	1.6
2015	CLR	A+	20	95	15	1	0	1	8	14	9	5	2	.392/.489/.443	.369	15.1	.435	1.1	SS(20): 0.9	1.7
2015	REA	AA	20	405	53	21	7	5	34	49	45	7	2	.265/.354/.407	.272	21.9	.289	1.0	SS(86): 6.7	3.1
2016	REA	AA	21	166	23	8	0	3	13	30	21	5	3	.265/.398/.390	.283	11.7	.295	1.3	SS(36): 6.1	1.9
2016	LEH	AAA	21	385	40	11	1	4	30	42	59	7	4	.244/.328/.318	.241	10.4	.284	2.1	SS(87): -3.0	0.8
2017	*PHI*	*MLB*	*22*	*186*	*20*	*7*	*1*	*4*	*18*	*20*	*37*	*3*	*1*	*.237/.319/.366*	*.251*	*6.0*	*.277*	*-0.2*	*SS 2*	*0.6*
2018	*PHI*	*MLB*	*23*	*419*	*51*	*16*	*2*	*11*	*46*	*44*	*82*	*6*	*3*	*.244/.325/.383*	*.264*	*15.9*	*.283*	*-0.2*	*SS 4*	*2.1*

Breakout: 9%   Improve: 31%   Collapse: 10%   Attrition: 25%   MLB: 47%   *Comparables: Ivan De Jesus, Joe Panik, Gavin Cecchini*

After the big club got off to a 24-17 start, many dreamed of the possibility that Crawford would be a midseason call-up who would spark the team the way that shortstops like Addison Russell and Carlos Correa did in 2015. Denizens of Philadelphia were so excited that they spent a grand total of five minutes on local sports talk radio not talking about the Eagles' season opener four months in the future. But the Phillies crashed and burned (as expected) while Crawford didn't break out at Triple-A and spent the entire season in the minors. The latter outcome shouldn't have come as a surprise. Crawford played his entire 2016 campaign as a 21-year-old, and while the raw ability is tremendous, there still is some work to do on his approach and positioning in the batter's box. There is no doubt that Crawford is inevitably going to man the six for the Fightin' Klentaks, but given the Phillies' current position there is zero reason to rush him to Philadelphia. Whether it is on Opening Day or sometime later in the year, there is an excellent chance that Crawford both surfaces in 2017 for the Phillies and cements his place as a key part of their future.

Maikel Franco   3B

Born: 8/26/92   Age: 24   Bats: R   Throws: R   Height: 6'1"   Weight: 215   Entered Pro Ball: International Free Agent, 2010

YEAR	TEAM	LVL	AGE	PA	R	2B	3B	HR	RBI	BB	K	SB	CS	AVG/OBP/SLG	TAv	VORP	BABIP	BRR	FRAA	WARP
2014	LEH	AAA	21	556	64	33	4	16	78	30	81	3	1	.257/.299/.428	.247	10.6	.276	2.4	3B(107): -3.2 • 1B(23): 0.3	0.8
2014	PHI	MLB	21	58	5	2	0	0	5	1	13	0	0	.179/.190/.214	.147	-4.1	.227	0.5	3B(12): 1.5 • 1B(5): -0.3	-0.3
2015	LEH	AAA	22	151	15	12	1	4	24	8	25	2	0	.355/.384/.539	.323	15.5	.404	1.3	3B(29): -2.0 • 1B(4): -0.2	1.4
2015	PHI	MLB	22	335	45	22	1	14	50	26	52	1	0	.280/.343/.497	.305	25.5	.297	0.8	3B(75): -6.0 • 1B(2): 0.2	2.1
2016	PHI	MLB	23	630	67	23	1	25	88	40	106	1	1	.255/.306/.427	.267	23.3	.271	-1.6	3B(148): -6.8	1.7
2017	*PHI*	*MLB*	*24*	*600*	*66*	*29*	*2*	*23*	*80*	*34*	*107*	*2*	*1*	*.256/.303/.441*	*.266*	*20.7*	*.278*	*-1.0*	*3B -8*	*0.7*
2018	*PHI*	*MLB*	*25*	*568*	*74*	*26*	*2*	*25*	*80*	*37*	*104*	*1*	*1*	*.257/.309/.457*	*.281*	*24.9*	*.275*	*0.0*	*3B -8*	*1.9*

Breakout: 1%   Improve: 55%   Collapse: 0%   Attrition: 3%   MLB: 97%   *Comparables: Nolan Arenado, Mike Moustakas, Nick Castellanos*

There is no way to sugarcoat it: 2016 was a significant step back for Franco, the young slugger who was supposed to be the center-piece of the new and exciting Phillies offense. Franco is an odd duck: a free-swinger who doesn't strike out a lot and doesn't miss as much as you would expect given his high swing rates. It isn't the lack of contact but the quality when Franco does connect that is the issue. This is part of a larger problem when it comes to approach, losing focus and getting too pull-happy despite a bat that is capable of going the other way. It is far too soon to write off a 24-year-old slugger with the talent that Franco has, and it is possible that with a better lineup around him, he might be less inclined to press. Without sustained improvements, Franco is likely to be more of a solid albeit inconsistent regular than a future star.

Freddy Galvis   SS

Born: 11/14/89   Age: 27   Bats: B   Throws: R   Height: 5'10"   Weight: 185   Entered Pro Ball: International Free Agent, 2006

YEAR	TEAM	LVL	AGE	PA	R	2B	3B	HR	RBI	BB	K	SB	CS	AVG/OBP/SLG	TAv	VORP	BABIP	BRR	FRAA	WARP
2014	CLR	A+	24	20	4	0	2	1	3	0	2	0	0	.200/.200/.550	.248	0.6	.176	0.2	SS(2): -0.0 • 2B(2): 0.0	0.1
2014	LEH	AAA	24	149	22	14	1	3	15	11	25	1	1	.267/.322/.452	.261	7.4	.308	1.1	SS(30): -2.0 • 2B(3): 0.7	0.6
2014	PHI	MLB	24	128	14	3	1	4	12	8	30	1	0	.176/.227/.319	.215	-1.5	.198	-0.4	SS(25): 1.1 • 3B(11): -0.0	-0.1
2015	PHI	MLB	25	603	63	14	5	7	50	30	103	10	1	.263/.302/.343	.241	15.8	.309	3.4	SS(146): -4.0 • 2B(4): 0.1	1.3
2016	PHI	MLB	26	624	61	26	3	20	67	25	136	17	6	.241/.274/.399	.239	8.6	.280	-3.5	SS(156): 0.8	1.0
2017	*PHI*	*MLB*	*27*	*439*	*45*	*17*	*3*	*11*	*45*	*21*	*89*	*7*	*2*	*.236/.271/.377*	*.230*	*4.3*	*.268*	*0.5*	*SS -1 • 2B 1*	*0.0*
2018	*PHI*	*MLB*	*28*	*535*	*59*	*22*	*3*	*16*	*62*	*27*	*112*	*8*	*3*	*.239/.279/.392*	*.241*	*7.4*	*.271*	*-0.3*	*SS -2 • 2B 1*	*0.7*

Breakout: 1%   Improve: 39%   Collapse: 12%   Attrition: 20%   MLB: 98%   *Comparables: Adeiny Hechavarria, Marwin Gonzalez, Ronny Cedeno*

As transitional players go, Galvis is fun. If you are not a Phillies fan, you can be forgiven for missing out on the fact that Galvis was one of three major league shortstops to hit at least 15 home runs and steal at least 15 bases. The problem for the Phillies and Galvis is that the other two—Francisco Lindor and Jonathan Villar—were just a wee bit better. Anyone who had the intestinal fortitude to watch the Phillies day in and day out knows that despite the pretty raw counting stats, Galvis isn't more than a semi-passable regular, and even this is somewhat generous. But to be fair, asking him to be the everyday shortstop for two full seasons was a lot. Galvis was an understudy who has waited far longer than anyone could have expected for the lead actor to show up. When J.P. Crawford is ready at some point in 2017, Galvis gives the Phillies a pretty solid backup infielder, provided that arbitration doesn't make him a prohibitively expensive one.

Tyler Goeddel   OF

Born: 10/20/92   Age: 24   Bats: R   Throws: R   Height: 6'4"   Weight: 180   Entered Pro Ball: Round 1, 2011 Draft (#41 overall)

YEAR	TEAM	LVL	AGE	PA	R	2B	3B	HR	RBI	BB	K	SB	CS	AVG/OBP/SLG	TAv	VORP	BABIP	BRR	FRAA	WARP
2014	PCH	A+	21	479	41	25	8	6	61	46	98	20	9	.269/.349/.408	.277	21.5	.335	-2.9	3B(106): 7.6	2.9
2015	MNT	AA	22	533	68	17	10	12	72	48	98	28	9	.279/.350/.433	.297	32.8	.326	1.9	LF(61): -5.9 • RF(25): -2.0	2.7
2016	PHI	MLB	23	234	17	3	3	4	16	17	52	3	0	.192/.258/.291	.216	-4.9	.234	0.5	LF(69): -5.6 • RF(12): -0.6	-1.2
2017	PHI	MLB	24	164	18	5	2	4	16	11	41	4	1	.228/.286/.369	.239	1.6	.282	0.5	RF -0	0.1
2018	PHI	MLB	25	373	43	13	4	11	42	29	95	9	3	.231/.297/.387	.254	6.8	.285	0.4	RF -1	0.7

Breakout: 4%   Improve: 19%   Collapse: 7%   Attrition: 14%   MLB: 34%   *Comparables: Kelly Johnson, Matt Murton, Bryan Petersen*

Expectations were that Goeddel—the first overall pick in last winter's Rule 5 draft—would get a long look at a corner outfield spot, but it didn't quite work out that way. A slow start in April quickly pushed Goeddel to the bench and even though he did have a strong May, he was overmatched in the majors. Of course, Goeddel has always had a toolsy profile and jumped Triple-A entirely, so his struggles should not have come as a big surprise. The former Ray will head to the minors to open the 2017 campaign, and while last year was a disappointment, good years from Rule 5 picks who spend the entire year in the majors are still the exception and not the rule, even in Philadelphia.

Cesar Hernandez   2B

Born: 5/23/90   Age: 27   Bats: B   Throws: R   Height: 5'10"   Weight: 160   Entered Pro Ball: International Free Agent, 2006

YEAR	TEAM	LVL	AGE	PA	R	2B	3B	HR	RBI	BB	K	SB	CS	AVG/OBP/SLG	TAv	VORP	BABIP	BRR	FRAA	WARP
2014	REA	AA	24	117	13	4	1	3	14	13	13	1	3	.340/.410/.485	.311	10.2	.364	0.3	3B(18): -0.4 • SS(8): -0.2	1.1
2014	LEH	AAA	24	171	23	6	3	0	10	15	34	7	4	.256/.322/.333	.230	-0.3	.328	-0.4	2B(21): -2.5 • SS(16): -0.3	-0.3
2014	PHI	MLB	24	125	13	2	0	1	4	9	33	1	1	.237/.290/.281	.234	0.2	.321	-0.2	3B(14): -0.6 • 2B(11): -1.1	-0.2
2015	PHI	MLB	25	452	57	20	4	1	35	40	86	19	5	.272/.339/.348	.261	14.5	.342	1.7	2B(88): 8.8 • SS(12): -0.1	2.5
2016	PHI	MLB	26	622	67	14	11	6	39	66	116	17	13	.294/.371/.393	.287	33.4	.363	-0.9	2B(149): -0.2 • SS(4): -0.2	3.4
2017	PHI	MLB	27	629	75	20	7	8	50	56	129	20	10	.268/.331/.368	.258	22.0	.330	0.9	2B -1	1.9
2018	PHI	MLB	28	535	59	16	6	7	50	47	113	16	8	.263/.327/.366	.261	17.6	.323	1.0	2B -1	1.8

Breakout: 6%   Improve: 44%   Collapse: 3%   Attrition: 13%   MLB: 94%   *Comparables: Dee Gordon, Alexi Casilla, Chris Getz*

Stop us if you have heard this one before, but for the third year in a row Hernandez exceeded expectations. Granted, those expectations have always been somewhere between "modest" and "practically nothing," but Hernandez has gone from a fringe utility infielder to a solid major league second baseman in the span of three seasons. While maligned at times for mental miscues both on the field and on the bases, Hernandez is one of the more teachable players in the organization. His numbers picked up in the second half when the coaching staff worked with him to cut back on his swing and take advantage of his speed on grounders. If Hernandez can keep up this level of production, he will be part of the next great Phillies team, even if he won't be one of their greats.

Odubel Herrera   CF

Born: 12/29/91   Age: 25   Bats: L   Throws: R   Height: 5'11"   Weight: 205   Entered Pro Ball: International Free Agent, 2008

YEAR	TEAM	LVL	AGE	PA	R	2B	3B	HR	RBI	BB	K	SB	CS	AVG/OBP/SLG	TAv	VORP	BABIP	BRR	FRAA	WARP
2014	MYR	A+	22	137	26	3	1	0	11	23	21	9	3	.297/.412/.342	.293	10.0	.359	2.4	LF(8): -1.6 • 2B(6): -1.4	0.7
2014	FRI	AA	22	408	47	16	4	2	48	29	70	12	7	.321/.373/.402	.290	21.5	.389	-1.6	2B(91): -8.3 • LF(3): -0.3	1.4
2015	PHI	MLB	23	537	64	30	3	8	41	28	129	16	8	.297/.344/.418	.274	27.9	.387	4.6	CF(136): -2.0	2.8
2016	PHI	MLB	24	656	87	21	6	15	49	63	134	25	7	.286/.361/.420	.293	45.7	.349	3.1	CF(155): 4.3	5.2
2017	PHI	MLB	25	581	64	23	4	12	61	44	131	17	7	.273/.331/.399	.264	24.4	.337	0.7	CF 3	2.1
2018	PHI	MLB	26	541	65	22	3	13	60	43	120	16	7	.272/.336/.407	.275	25.8	.332	2.8	CF 3	3.1

Breakout: 1%   Improve: 59%   Collapse: 2%   Attrition: 9%   MLB: 97%   *Comparables: Austin Jackson, Dexter Fowler, Adam Jones*

PECOTA does a lot of things well, but one thing it doesn't do is project continued growth for a 24-year-old Rule 5 success story. After a breakout season in 2015, Herrera came flying out of the blocks in 2016, slashing .320/.428/.438 in his first 243 plate appearances. Increased plate discipline led to a bushel of walks and an improved contact rate on pitches both in and out of the zone. Herrera struggled for a couple of months after his quick start, giving back some of the gains he made with his batting eye and frustrating his manager, leading to a brief benching. On the positive side, Herrera added some over-the-fence power and improved his center-field defense, making him even more of a well-rounded player. Herrera has been so good that it is easy to forget that he was an unfinished product in the Rangers system prior to hearing his name at the 2014 Winter Meetings. Maybe this is as good as it gets for him, but a five-WARP outfielder under team control through 2023? That'll play.

Rhys Hoskins   1B

Born: 3/17/93   Age: 24   Bats: R   Throws: R   Height: 6'4"   Weight: 225   Entered Pro Ball: Round 5, 2014 Draft (#142 overall)

YEAR	TEAM	LVL	AGE	PA	R	2B	3B	HR	RBI	BB	K	SB	CS	AVG/OBP/SLG	TAv	VORP	BABIP	BRR	FRAA	WARP
2014	WPT	A-	21	273	30	15	0	9	40	21	54	3	3	.237/.311/.408	.260	1.2	.268	-0.2	1B(37): 0.3	0.2
2015	LWD	A	22	290	39	17	4	9	51	26	50	2	4	.322/.397/.525	.351	28.2	.369	-1.6	1B(64): -0.7	2.9
2015	CLR	A+	22	277	47	19	2	8	39	29	49	2	0	.317/.394/.510	.336	22.1	.367	-1.7	1B(58): 1.3	2.5
2016	REA	AA	23	589	95	26	1	38	116	71	125	8	3	.281/.377/.566	.317	38.3	.297	-1.1	1B(129): -0.6	4.1
2017	PHI	MLB	24	250	32	10	1	13	38	23	69	1	0	.245/.323/.470	.274	8.3	.293	-0.4	1B 1	1.0
2018	PHI	MLB	25	367	51	16	1	18	54	36	103	1	0	.243/.324/.463	.289	14.6	.295	-0.7	1B 1	1.7

Breakout: 3%   Improve: 19%   Collapse: 19%   Attrition: 25%   MLB: 47%   *Comparables: Chris Carter, Paul Goldschmidt, Matt Clark*

The gap between scouting and sabermetrics is often a canard, but once in a while it still rears its ugly head. Hoskins is a great example. The scouting reports see a player with a low ceiling who is going to get eaten alive by advanced pitching, while a more stat-minded view sees a hitter who could survive at higher levels. In particular, Hoskins' strikeout-to-walk rates haven't been as bad as you would expect given his scouting profile. If he can continue to make decent contact he could make it in the bigs as a platoon starter with a big power bat. All guys like Hoskins can do is keep mashing until the scouts are ultimately proven wrong or wash out trying.

Ryan Howard   1B

Born: 11/19/79   Age: 37   Bats: L   Throws: L   Height: 6'4"   Weight: 250   Entered Pro Ball: Round 5, 2001 Draft (#140 overall)

YEAR	TEAM	LVL	AGE	PA	R	2B	3B	HR	RBI	BB	K	SB	CS	AVG/OBP/SLG	TAv	VORP	BABIP	BRR	FRAA	WARP
2014	PHI	MLB	34	648	65	18	1	23	95	67	190	0	0	.223/.310/.380	.260	4.7	.288	-1.5	1B(141): -7.7	-0.3
2015	PHI	MLB	35	503	53	29	1	23	77	27	138	0	0	.229/.277/.443	.250	-2.4	.272	-2.6	1B(116): -2.0	-0.5
2016	PHI	MLB	36	362	35	10	0	25	59	27	114	0	1	.196/.257/.453	.255	1.3	.205	-1.1	1B(83): -3.0	-0.2
2017	PHI	MLB	37	368	41	14	1	16	50	29	116	0	0	.214/.279/.407	.237	-2.2	.269	-1.0	1B -2	-0.4
2018	PHI	MLB	38	238	29	9	0	10	30	18	76	0	0	.210/.274/.394	.242	-2.0	.266	-0.8	1B -1	-0.3

Breakout: 3%   Improve: 23%   Collapse: 9%   Attrition: 27%   MLB: 75%   *Comparables: Dave Kingman, Tony Clark, Olmedo Saenz*

It isn't worth wasting 211 words lamenting what Howard is: a faintly flickering ember of the player he was, a hitter who can blast a mistake pitch 400-plus feet but can do little else. It is worth remembering the player that Ryan Howard was. From 2006-2011, Howard was one of only three major hitters with a .307 TAv in five or more seasons; Albert Pujols and Matt Holliday were the others. Howard wasn't the greatest player on the Phillies during their five-year playoff streak, but he was one of their most exciting ones. Every Howard at-bat felt like it had the potential to end with a monstrous blast over the right field wall, and while the idea of a "feared" hitter is antiquated and perhaps silly, having that kind of power in the middle of a strong Phillies lineup made Howard an asset. Yet for all of Howard's on-the-field accomplishments, the greatest memories of Howard might be his smile and the joy that radiated from his face every time he took the field in his prime. Howard will never be considered an all-time great, but history is likely to be kinder to him from a distance and remember him for what he was, rather than what he could have been.

Tommy Joseph   1B

Born: 7/16/91   Age: 25   Bats: R   Throws: R   Height: 6'1"   Weight: 255   Entered Pro Ball: Round 2, 2009 Draft (#55 overall)

YEAR	TEAM	LVL	AGE	PA	R	2B	3B	HR	RBI	BB	K	SB	CS	AVG/OBP/SLG	TAv	VORP	BABIP	BRR	FRAA	WARP
2014	REA	AA	22	87	8	4	1	5	19	5	13	0	0	.282/.345/.551	.303	7.3	.279	-0.3	C(21): -1.9	0.6
2015	LEH	AAA	23	175	9	9	0	3	18	3	33	0	0	.193/.220/.301	.187	-1.2	.221	-1.1	1B(22): -1.0 • C(19): -0.0	-1.1
2016	LEH	AAA	24	100	11	7	0	6	17	4	12	0	1	.347/.370/.611	.339	7.2	.346	-2.1	1B(17): -0.4	0.7
2016	PHI	MLB	24	347	47	15	0	21	47	22	75	1	1	.257/.308/.505	.293	16.3	.267	0.7	1B(97): -5.8	1.1
2017	PHI	MLB	25	588	72	26	1	31	89	32	127	2	1	.252/.299/.475	.272	17.8	.271	-1.2	1B -9	0.3
2018	PHI	MLB	26	526	74	23	1	30	84	31	115	2	1	.255/.305/.491	.287	21.8	.272	0.6	1B -8	1.5

Breakout: 3%   Improve: 49%   Collapse: 4%   Attrition: 14%   MLB: 90%   *Comparables: Jesus Montero, Justin Morneau, Joey Votto*

If all Joseph did in 2016 was make the majors, hit a home run or two before failing miserably, and then disappear into the proverbial sunset, it still would have been a feel-good story because of Joseph's health struggles and sputtering developmental path. Instead, he went from being a player the Phillies were looking at simply because the roster was thin to someone who has a legitimate chance of being a productive major

YEAR	TEAM	P. COUNT	FRM RUNS	BLK RUNS	THRW RUNS	TOT RUNS
2014	REA	2939	-0.3	0.2	-2.1	-2.2
2015	LEH	2879	0.5	0.0	0.1	0.5

league regular. During the course of the season, Joseph improved his batting eye, increased his walk rate while decreasing his whiff rate and started showing substantial gains against right-handed pitching. It remains to be seen how well Joseph would do with regular at-bats but he has earned the chance to get them. It is possible the concussions that held him back and eventually stripped him of his pads are in the rearview mirror and we are just now seeing the powerful prospect he once was emerge offensively.

Howie Kendrick   LF/2B

Born: 7/12/83   Age: 33   Bats: R   Throws: R   Height: 5'11"   Weight: 220   Entered Pro Ball: Round 10, 2002 Draft (#294 overall)

YEAR	TEAM	LVL	AGE	PA	R	2B	3B	HR	RBI	BB	K	SB	CS	AVG/OBP/SLG	TAv	VORP	BABIP	BRR	FRAA	WARP
2014	ANA	MLB	30	674	85	33	5	7	75	48	110	14	5	.293/.347/.397	.278	25.2	.347	-2.2	2B(154): 0.8	2.9
2015	LAN	MLB	31	495	64	22	2	9	54	27	82	6	2	.295/.336/.409	.272	21.4	.342	3.1	2B(113): -1.2	2.2
2016	LAN	MLB	32	543	65	26	2	8	40	50	96	10	2	.255/.326/.366	.255	14.6	.301	4.9	LF(94): -0.6 • 2B(32): 0.6	1.4
2017	PHI	MLB	33	504	58	22	3	9	46	32	97	8	3	.269/.317/.389	.258	15.7	.317	0.2	LF 3	1.6
2018	PHI	MLB	34	469	51	20	3	9	48	30	92	6	2	.261/.310/.381	.260	12.3	.309	1.2	LF 3	1.7

Breakout: 2%   Improve: 38%   Collapse: 7%   Attrition: 9%   MLB: 94%   *Comparables: Jay Payton, Eric Byrnes, Vernon Wells*

Burdened by a qualifying offer, Kendrick found a limited market and returned to the Dodgers on a two-year, $20 million deal. Robbed of his position by Chase Utley, Kendrick spent most of his time in left field, and even expressed a preference for it when he had the choice. A dismal April (.151/.182/.151) dragged down his season totals (.734 OPS from that point on), and resulted in his first career batting average below .279, including the minor leagues. Despite getting playoff starts against left-handed pitchers, Kendrick read the writing on the wall and let management know he wasn't going to be happy with a reduced role, precipitating a trade to Philadelphia and a likely role as the team's regular left fielder in 2017.

Scott Kingery   2B

Born: 4/29/94   Age: 23   Bats: R   Throws: R   Height: 5'10"   Weight: 180   Entered Pro Ball: Round 2, 2015 Draft (#48 overall)

YEAR	TEAM	LVL	AGE	PA	R	2B	3B	HR	RBI	BB	K	SB	CS	AVG/OBP/SLG	TAv	VORP	BABIP	BRR	FRAA	WARP
2015	LWD	A	21	282	43	9	2	3	21	18	43	11	1	.250/.314/.337	.251	7.4	.287	2.6	2B(65): 0.6	0.8
2016	CLR	A+	22	420	60	29	3	3	28	33	54	26	5	.293/.360/.411	.290	26.0	.334	1.6	2B(88): 7.4	3.4
2016	REA	AA	22	166	16	7	0	2	18	5	36	4	2	.250/.273/.333	.220	-0.5	.306	1.9	2B(37): -1.3	-0.2
2017	PHI	MLB	23	250	29	11	1	6	23	12	61	6	2	.231/.275/.359	.223	0.8	.284	0.4	2B 3	0.4
2018	PHI	MLB	24	361	39	16	1	9	38	19	86	9	2	.235/.283/.368	.241	4.8	.286	0.8	2B 4	0.9

Breakout: 11%   Improve: 17%   Collapse: 3%   Attrition: 11%   MLB: 24%   *Comparables: Eric Young, Micah Johnson, Odubel Herrera*

While he isn't a top-flight prospect, Kingery offers the kind of reliability that could keep him employed in the major leagues for years to come. What Kingery lacks in raw power he makes up for with good contact skills and a sound batting eye. His speed and baserunning acumen should mostly translate to the majors, giving him 20-steal potential. The challenge with a profile like Kingery's is that the defense makes him either a major league second baseman or a poor use of a roster spot, as the defense wouldn't survive for long at short or third. Kingery could make for an adequate double-play partner for J.P. Crawford on that next great Phillies team, but it is more likely that he is either a stopgap or trade bait if the Phillies decide to keep Cesar Hernandez at the keystone.

Andrew Knapp   C

Born: 11/9/91   Age: 25   Bats: B   Throws: R   Height: 6'1"   Weight: 195   Entered Pro Ball: Round 2, 2013 Draft (#53 overall)

YEAR	TEAM	LVL	AGE	PA	R	2B	3B	HR	RBI	BB	K	SB	CS	AVG/OBP/SLG	TAv	VORP	BABIP	BRR	FRAA	WARP
2014	CLR	A+	22	90	7	1	0	1	7	5	26	1	0	.157/.222/.205	.163	-9.7	.214	-1.1	.	-1.0
2014	LWD	A	22	314	39	19	4	5	25	27	71	3	3	.290/.354/.438	.287	19.6	.368	1.0	C(42): -3.4	1.7
2015	CLR	A+	23	281	38	14	3	2	28	29	63	0	1	.262/.356/.369	.282	14.2	.344	-1.7	C(46): 0.3	1.6
2015	REA	AA	23	241	39	21	4	11	56	22	43	1	0	.360/.419/.631	.356	33.1	.405	0.0	C(48): -4.9	3.0
2016	LEH	AAA	24	443	55	24	1	8	46	37	107	2	2	.266/.330/.390	.264	22.3	.343	0.9	C(104): 12.9 • 1B(1): -0.0	3.6
2017	PHI	MLB	25	250	25	12	1	8	30	19	73	0	0	.238/.303/.397	.245	8.4	.314	-0.4	C -2 • 1B -0	0.7
2018	PHI	MLB	26	310	36	15	1	9	36	24	91	0	0	.235/.298/.392	.255	9.0	.311	-0.7	C -3 • 1B 0	0.6

Breakout: 7%   Improve: 15%   Collapse: 13%   Attrition: 28%   MLB: 40%   Comparables: Johnny Monell, Michael McKenry, Josh Donaldson

Knapp didn't have a bad year, but he did take a few steps back from his breakout campaign in 2015. The power dropped somewhat, and while some of this was a product of moving from a hitter-happy ballpark to a pitcher-friendly one, more of this had to do more experienced arms exploiting Knapp's approach. The bigger issue is that Knapp's defense is flawed in an era where more and more teams are willing to sacrifice offense at catcher in favor of a strong pitch framer with good receiving skills. He's far too young to simply write-off as a career backup, but the presence of Jorge Alfaro and the emergence of Cameron Rupp are going to make it difficult for Knapp to establish himself barring an injury or a trade.

YEAR	TEAM	P. COUNT	FRM RUNS	BLK RUNS	THRW RUNS	TOT RUNS
2015	REA	6622	-3.5	-0.8	0.2	-4.1
2017	PHI	9026	-1.1	-1.3	-0.3	-2.6
2018	PHI	11193	-1.6	-1.4	-0.4	-3.4

Mickey Moniak   OF

Born: 5/13/98   Age: 19   Bats: L   Throws: R   Height: 6'2"   Weight: 185   Entered Pro Ball: Round 1, 2016 Draft (#1 overall)

YEAR	TEAM	LVL	AGE	PA	R	2B	3B	HR	RBI	BB	K	SB	CS	AVG/OBP/SLG	TAv	VORP	BABIP	BRR	FRAA	WARP
2017	PHI	MLB	19	250	22	9	1	6	24	11	83	4	2	.192/.234/.309	.190	-8.8	.266	0.0	CF 2 • LF 0	-0.8
2018	PHI	MLB	20	322	33	11	2	8	33	16	100	6	3	.209/.256/.341	.219	-4.6	.280	0.3	CF 2 • LF 0	-0.3

Breakout: 0%   Improve: 5%   Collapse: 2%   Attrition: 4%   MLB: 10%   Comparables: Engel Beltre, Nomar Mazara, Rougned Odor

Moniak wasn't considered the best player on the board in the 2016 draft. The Phillies made him the number one pick overall in part because he was the best high school bat available, but primarily to save on slot and redistribute money later in the draft. Moniak's long-term projection is as a starting center fielder with above-average defense and good baserunning ability, but it is his potential with the bat that generates the most excitement. Scouts have fawned over his hit tool and approach at the plate, both of which are extremely polished for an 18-year-old. If the power doesn't develop, Moniak can still be a very capable starting outfielder, but if he grows into 15-20 homers annually, he has a chance to live up to that top-of-the-draft billing.

Roman Quinn   OF

Born: 5/14/93   Age: 24   Bats: B   Throws: R   Height: 5'10"   Weight: 170   Entered Pro Ball: Round 2, 2011 Draft (#66 overall)

YEAR	TEAM	LVL	AGE	PA	R	2B	3B	HR	RBI	BB	K	SB	CS	AVG/OBP/SLG	TAv	VORP	BABIP	BRR	FRAA	WARP
2014	CLR	A+	21	382	51	10	3	7	36	36	80	32	12	.257/.343/.370	.259	15.4	.316	3.1	CF(69): 0.9 • SS(17): -3.1	1.3
2015	REA	AA	22	257	44	6	6	4	15	18	42	29	10	.306/.356/.435	.283	19.6	.360	6.2	CF(58): 3.4	2.5
2016	REA	AA	23	322	58	14	6	6	25	30	68	31	8	.287/.361/.441	.278	24.5	.357	9.6	CF(62): -7.3 • LF(4): -0.8	2.0
2016	PHI	MLB	23	69	10	4	0	0	6	8	19	5	1	.263/.373/.333	.282	3.9	.395	0.8	LF(12): -0.0 • RF(4): 0.1	0.5
2017	PHI	MLB	24	91	12	3	1	2	8	7	24	6	2	.235/.295/.363	.239	1.9	.303	0.8	CF -0	0.1
2018	PHI	MLB	25	322	37	11	3	8	35	23	88	22	7	.238/.302/.380	.249	8.2	.304	3.3	CF -1	0.8

Breakout: 12%   Improve: 25%   Collapse: 2%   Attrition: 15%   MLB: 41%   Comparables: Reymond Fuentes, Gorkys Hernandez, Kevin Kiermaier

In the time it took you to read this sentence, Quinn either stole a base or got injured. Maybe both. The frequent injuries are a shame, because they mask a player who has the potential to be an electrifying, top-of-the-lineup force who—oh by the way—is a fleet-of-foot centerfielder with a decent arm. Despite missing a month and a half in the minors with an oblique strain, Quinn found his way up to Philadelphia in September and gave fans a tantalizing glimpse of what might be. Quinn is one of the fastest players in organized ball this side of Billy Hamilton but has the potential to offer a little more offense than the preeminent speedster does. Quinn will be 23 on Opening Day, but 2017 is a big year for him as the Phillies as to try figure out if he's a game-changing leadoff hitter or a fourth outfielder who makes opponents miserable in the late innings with his speed. Either way, when he's healthy, Quinn is going to be fun to watch.

Cornelius Randolph   LF

Born: 6/2/97   Age: 20   Bats: L   Throws: R   Height: 5'11"   Weight: 205   Entered Pro Ball: Round 1, 2015 Draft (#10 overall)

YEAR	TEAM	LVL	AGE	PA	R	2B	3B	HR	RBI	BB	K	SB	CS	AVG/OBP/SLG	TAv	VORP	BABIP	BRR	FRAA	WARP
2016	LWD	A	19	276	33	12	1	2	27	26	57	5	4	.274/.355/.357	.297	16.8	.346	1.5	LF(53): 0.6	1.9
2017	PHI	MLB	20	250	23	10	1	5	25	19	72	1	0	.213/.281/.333	.220	-2.4	.283	-0.5	LF 2	0.0
2018	PHI	MLB	21	372	41	15	1	9	38	30	101	1	1	.223/.295/.352	.244	1.9	.290	-0.8	LF 3	0.5

Breakout: 1%   Improve: 7%   Collapse: 0%   Attrition: 4%   MLB: 9%   Comparables: Ramon Flores, Jeimer Candelario, Caleb Gindl

There are many roads to prospect success or failure, but nothing speaks to potential failure like being locked in at a position before you turn 20. Randolph's hit tool is impressive, and even a down year riddled with shoulder and back injuries didn't diminish his long-term projection with the bat. The problem is that he has already been administered a left-field-only profile. This can lead to an actual career in left field but it can also lead to a DH-only track or a long life riding buses in the minor leagues and impressing everyone with lights-out Triple-A power for years and years. Cornelius Randolph is a legendary name, so regardless of where he eventually lands, people will likely tell stories of a man who was taller than the upper deck and launched home runs into the sun.

Cameron Rupp   C

Born: 9/28/88   Age: 28   Bats: R   Throws: R   Height: 6'2"   Weight: 260   Entered Pro Ball: Round 3, 2010 Draft (#108 overall)

YEAR	TEAM	LVL	AGE	PA	R	2B	3B	HR	RBI	BB	K	SB	CS	AVG/OBP/SLG	TAv	VORP	BABIP	BRR	FRAA	WARP
2014	LEH	AAA	25	219	19	8	0	6	19	21	76	0	0	.165/.256/.299	.208	-3.3	.230	-0.7	C(56): -1.5	-0.5
2014	PHI	MLB	25	64	4	4	0	0	6	4	20	0	0	.183/.234/.250	.161	-3.5	.275	-0.2	C(18): -1.2	-0.5
2015	PHI	MLB	26	299	24	9	1	9	28	24	71	0	1	.233/.301/.374	.242	5.3	.281	-2.4	C(80): -5.8	-0.1
2016	PHI	MLB	27	419	36	26	1	16	54	24	114	1	0	.252/.303/.447	.270	22.3	.315	-1.0	C(104): -3.7	1.9
2017	PHI	MLB	28	531	53	23	1	18	64	35	153	1	1	.223/.280/.384	.239	12.5	.283	-1.2	C -8	-0.7
2018	PHI	MLB	29	489	59	21	0	18	60	34	142	0	0	.225/.285/.396	.249	11.0	.283	-1.7	C -8	0.3

Breakout: 7%   Improve: 39%   Collapse: 12%   Attrition: 27%   MLB: 83%   *Comparables: Welington Castillo, Rob Bowen, Michael McKenry*

Rupp was supposed to be a transitional player: the bridge between team legend Carlos Ruiz and inevitable-catcher-of-the-future Jorge Alfaro. But somewhere along the way, Rupp became a little bit more than that: a decent if unspectacular backstop whose size finally translated into some over-the-fence pop. Oh those catchers and their non-linear developmental curves. The package certainly isn't perfect: Rupp was in the bottom third among catchers in pitch framing and his contact rate leaves much to be desired. At a minimum, Rupp should start 2017 as the Phillies' starter while Alfaro puts the finishing touches on his game in Triple-A. In an era when some teams have difficulty finding even one decent catcher, having Rupp as a backup plan is a nice option to have if Alfaro isn't everything he is supposed to be.

YEAR	TEAM	P. COUNT	FRM RUNS	BLK RUNS	THRW RUNS	TOT RUNS
2014	LEH	7335	-0.3	0.0	-0.3	-0.6
2014	PHI	2409	-1.2	0.2	0.2	-0.9
2015	PHI	11024	-5.6	0.3	0.8	-4.5
2016	PHI	14903	-3.3	0.7	-0.7	-3.4
2017	PHI	19316	-7.7	0.7	-0.2	-7.3
2018	PHI	17802	-8.2	0.5	-0.3	-8.1

Nick Williams   LF

Born: 9/8/93   Age: 23   Bats: L   Throws: L   Height: 6'3"   Weight: 195   Entered Pro Ball: Round 2, 2012 Draft (#93 overall)

YEAR	TEAM	LVL	AGE	PA	R	2B	3B	HR	RBI	BB	K	SB	CS	AVG/OBP/SLG	TAv	VORP	BABIP	BRR	FRAA	WARP
2014	MYR	A+	20	408	61	28	4	13	68	19	117	5	7	.292/.343/.491	.285	19.2	.391	-1.3	LF(44): -0.3 • CF(25): -3.5	1.5
2014	FRI	AA	20	64	4	2	1	0	4	2	21	1	1	.226/.250/.290	.205	-2.0	.341	0.1	LF(11): -1.5 • CF(4): 0.1	-0.4
2015	FRI	AA	21	415	56	21	4	13	45	32	77	10	8	.299/.357/.479	.291	22.6	.346	0.3	LF(45): -0.1 • CF(38): -1.7	2.2
2015	REA	AA	21	100	21	5	2	4	10	3	20	3	0	.320/.340/.536	.320	10.4	.370	1.5	CF(21): 1.1	1.2
2016	LEH	AAA	22	527	78	33	6	13	64	19	136	6	4	.258/.287/.427	.258	10.7	.325	-0.7	LF(50): 1.8 • CF(38): 0.7	1.4
2017	PHI	MLB	23	98	10	5	1	3	12	4	29	1	1	.240/.272/.412	.244	1.3	.311	-0.1	LF -0	0.1
2018	PHI	MLB	24	340	40	17	3	12	43	14	98	4	2	.251/.288/.432	.262	8.7	.322	-0.1	LF 0	0.9

Breakout: 4%   Improve: 13%   Collapse: 0%   Attrition: 8%   MLB: 19%   *Comparables: Corey Dickerson, Zoilo Almonte, Marc Krauss*

While local curmudgeons took notice of Williams' multiple benchings in June for "failing to hustle" out a couple of grounders on two separate occasions, the real issue for Williams was his abysmal walk rate. Williams has the plate discipline of a man devouring his last meal, and while the raw talent was able to overcome this during the first half of his minor league campaign, he finished with a putrid .221/.236/.383 slash from July 1 until the end of the season. However, Williams is young and is likely to make it to Philadelphia and get an opportunity based on his tools alone—which are among the best in the organization. Whether he becomes a strong first-division regular or a fourth outfielder in the long term is going to depend entirely on pitch recognition and learning to lay off of breaking balls in the dirt. There is still a lot to like in Williams' profile, but 2016 was a clear and significant step back.

PITCHERS

Mark Appel   RHP

Born: 7/15/91   Age: 25   Bats: R   Throws: R   Height: 6'5"   Weight: 220   Entered Pro Ball: Round 1, 2013 Draft (#1 overall)

YEAR	TEAM	LVL	AGE	W	L	SV	G	GS	IP	H	HR	BB/9	K/9	K	GB%	BABIP	WHIP	ERA	FIP	DRA	VORP	WARP	cFIP	MPH
2014	LNC	A+	22	2	5	0	12	12	44¹	74	9	2.2	8.1	40	54%	.373	1.92	9.74	5.32	3.78	8.9	0.9	92	
2014	CCH	AA	22	1	2	0	7	6	39	35	2	3.0	8.8	38	46%	.300	1.23	3.69	2.99	4.09	4.8	0.5	92	
2015	CCH	AA	23	5	1	0	13	13	63¹	68	7	3.3	7.0	49	46%	.314	1.44	4.26	4.37	5.33	-1.6	-0.2	104	
2015	FRE	AAA	23	5	2	0	12	12	68¹	67	6	3.7	8	61	47%	.303	1.39	4.48	4.36	5.41	-0.8	-0.1	102	
2016	LEH	AAA	24	3	3	0	8	8	38¹	40	3	4.7	8.0	34	45%	.325	1.57	4.46	4.06	5.67	-1.4	-0.1	110	
2017	PHI	MLB	25	1	1	0	3	3	15	16	2	3.6	7.2	13	49%	.295	1.43	4.76	4.48	5.01	0.3	0.0	100	
2018	PHI	MLB	26	8	9	0	26	26	153¹	124	19	5.1	9.7	166	49%	.296	1.38	4.40	4.72	5.07	7.3	0.8	118	

Breakout: 11%   Improve: 17%   Collapse: 16%   Attrition: 27%   MLB: 37%   *Comparables: Phil Irwin, Gus Schlosser, Alex Wilson*

2016 was supposed to deliver a new lease on life for the former no. 1 overall pick. Part of the blockbuster trade that sent Ken Giles to the Astros, the Phillies knew that Appel was going to be a project, but didn't anticipate shoulder and elbow injuries limiting him to eight starts before the team had to pull the plug on his season. There were some signs of life before the injury, but now the Phillies are looking at a 25-year-old pitcher who has never had sustained success as a professional. The team has had moderate success working with projects like this, but Appel offers one of the greatest challenges the new regime has faced to date.

Alec Asher   RHP

Born: 10/4/91   Age: 25   Bats: R   Throws: R   Height: 6'4"   Weight: 230   Entered Pro Ball: Round 4, 2012 Draft (#156 overall)

YEAR	TEAM	LVL	AGE	W	L	SV	G	GS	IP	H	HR	BB/9	K/9	K	GB%	BABIP	WHIP	ERA	FIP	DRA	VORP	WARP	cFIP	MPH
2014	FRI	AA	22	11	11	0	28	28	154	139	18	1.9	7.1	122	36%	.265	1.11	3.80	3.74	3.16	35.4	3.8	102	
2015	FRI	AA	23	1	4	0	8	8	43	39	3	3.8	9.0	43	32%	.308	1.33	3.98	3.60	3.89	5.8	0.6	97	
2015	ROU	AAA	23	3	6	0	12	12	64²	71	16	2.6	7.5	54	35%	.293	1.39	4.73	6.03	3.50	12.9	1.3	91	
2015	LEH	AAA	23	2	0	0	4	4	26	27	3	1	4.2	12	36%	.273	1.15	2.08	4.08	4.85	1.3	0.1	103	
2015	PHI	MLB	23	0	6	0	7	7	29	42	8	3.1	5.0	16	40%	.330	1.79	9.31	6.78	6.77	-5.4	-0.6	126	94.5
2016	LEH	AAA	24	3	0	0	4	4	29¹	15	4	0.9	5.8	19	48%	.136	0.61	1.53	3.95	3.60	5.7	0.6	96	
2016	REA	AA	24	1	2	0	5	5	29¹	29	1	1.5	6.4	21	53%	.292	1.16	3.38	2.88	3.03	6.7	0.7	89	
2016	PHI	MLB	24	2	1	0	5	5	27²	22	1	1.3	4.2	13	38%	.231	0.94	2.28	3.37	5.74	-1.2	-0.1	125	91.9
2017	*PHI*	*MLB*	*25*	*3*	*5*	*0*	*11*	*11*	*62²*	*62*	*8*	*2.5*	*6.8*	*47*	*53%*	*.287*	*1.23*	*4.40*	*4.24*	*4.66*	*3.6*	*0.4*	*100*	
2018	*PHI*	*MLB*	*26*	*7*	*8*	*0*	*22*	*22*	*127*	*100*	*16*	*3.5*	*9.3*	*131*	*53%*	*.279*	*1.18*	*4.05*	*4.33*	*4.69*	*11.5*	*1.2*	*108*	

Breakout: 19%   Improve: 37%   Collapse: 24%   Attrition: 36%   MLB: 67%   Comparables: Michael Bowden, Scott Lewis, Keyvius Sampson

The great Branch Rickey once said that "luck is the residue of design." In Asher's case, it's difficult to figure out what the designer intended. He somehow posted a 2.28 ERA in five September starts, but a 5.74 DRA does a better job of telling the tale. Asher does not generate enough swinging strikes to survive in the majors. The problem is not that he doesn't throw hard—which he certainly doesn't—but that his secondary offerings aren't anything special. It is possible that Asher gets another opportunity for the Phillies but if they have to count on him for a significant number of innings in 2017, it will likely be because of multiple injuries. A PED suspension cost Asher 80 games in 2016, but losing a half-season of development time only really matters if there is room for him to develop, which is unlikely to happen either as a starter or a non-fungible reliever.

Joaquin Benoit   RHP

Born: 7/26/77   Age: 39   Bats: R   Throws: R   Height: 6'4"   Weight: 250   Entered Pro Ball: International Free Agent, 1996

YEAR	TEAM	LVL	AGE	W	L	SV	G	GS	IP	H	HR	BB/9	K/9	K	GB%	BABIP	WHIP	ERA	FIP	DRA	VORP	WARP	cFIP	MPH
2014	SDN	MLB	36	4	2	11	53	0	54¹	28	3	2.3	10.6	64	38%	.203	0.77	1.49	2.29	3.09	8.4	0.9	85	96.9
2015	SDN	MLB	37	6	5	2	67	0	65¹	36	7	3.2	8.7	63	48%	.182	0.90	2.34	3.77	3.96	5.4	0.6	95	96.8
2016	SEA	MLB	38	1	1	0	26	0	24¹	20	4	5.5	10.4	28	43%	.254	1.44	5.18	4.91	3.91	2.9	0.3	99	96.8
2016	TOR	MLB	38	2	0	1	25	0	23²	17	1	3.4	9.1	24	38%	.271	1.10	0.38	2.77	3.72	3.3	0.3	98	96.5
2017	*PHI*	*MLB*	*39*	*3*	*3*	*35*	*64*	*0*	*67*	*55*	*9*	*3.6*	*9.8*	*74*	*38%*	*.273*	*1.21*	*4.17*	*4.00*	*4.39*	*3.9*	*0.4*	*99*	
2018	*PHI*	*MLB*	*40*	*3*	*1*	*26*	*58*	*0*	*61¹*	*48*	*8*	*3.6*	*9.4*	*64*	*38%*	*.273*	*1.18*	*4.06*	*4.34*	*4.70*	*2.9*	*0.3*	*108*	

Breakout: 15%   Improve: 36%   Collapse: 24%   Attrition: 10%   MLB: 72%   Comparables: Joe Nathan, Arthur Rhodes, Rafael Betancourt

Benoit had quite the up-and-down 2016. Despite almost no change in his stuff from his very solid years in San Diego (and an excellent strikeout rate), he began Joaquin hitters to an insane degree in Seattle (5.5 BB/9). He became so unreliable that he was eventually traded straight up for Drew Storen—a man who was DFA'd by the Blue Jays. He turned his year around in Toronto, as Benoit allowed just one run in 23.2 post-trade innings. However, his season ended when he fell and tore his calf while running in from the bullpen for a brawl. At age 40, any more "down" periods could be the end.

Clay Buchholz   RHP

Born: 8/14/84   Age: 32   Bats: L   Throws: R   Height: 6'3"   Weight: 190   Entered Pro Ball: Round 1, 2005 Draft (#42 overall)

YEAR	TEAM	LVL	AGE	W	L	SV	G	GS	IP	H	HR	BB/9	K/9	K	GB%	BABIP	WHIP	ERA	FIP	DRA	VORP	WARP	cFIP	MPH
2014	PAW	AAA	29	0	1	0	2	2	10²	6	2	1.7	8.4	10	42%	.167	0.75	2.53	4.76	3.72	2.4	0.2	91	
2014	BOS	MLB	29	8	11	0	28	28	170¹	182	17	2.9	7.0	132	48%	.315	1.39	5.34	4.03	4.34	9.3	1.0	103	93.9
2015	BOS	MLB	30	7	7	0	18	18	113¹	114	6	1.8	8.5	107	49%	.329	1.21	3.26	2.65	3.00	26.2	2.8	80	94.3
2016	BOS	MLB	31	8	10	0	37	21	139¹	130	21	3.6	6.0	93	42%	.263	1.33	4.78	5.02	6.08	-12.1	-1.3	121	94.4
2017	*PHI*	*MLB*	*32*	*5*	*7*	*0*	*19*	*19*	*100²*	*92*	*13*	*2.9*	*8.3*	*92*	*52%*	*.287*	*1.22*	*4.32*	*4.13*	*4.60*	*6.5*	*0.7*	*100*	
2018	*PHI*	*MLB*	*33*	*6*	*7*	*0*	*21*	*21*	*122²*	*103*	*16*	*2.9*	*7.8*	*107*	*52%*	*.279*	*1.16*	*4.48*	*4.50*	*4.89*	*8.2*	*0.8*	*115*	

Breakout: 22%   Improve: 42%   Collapse: 23%   Attrition: 9%   MLB: 84%   Comparables: Scott Downs, Salomon Torres, Francisco Cordero

After 10 seasons and 1,167 innings in the majors, here's what we can say we know about Buchholz: ¯_(ツ)_/¯. He's one of the game's most frustrating, talented and inconsistent pitchers, and 2016 was turbulent even by his standards. Through his first 10 starts, Buchholz was so atrocious (6.35 ERA) that the Sox bumped him to the bullpen despite a paper-thin back-half of their rotation. He spent all of June, July and August throwing in relief or spot starting, pitching to a modest 4.00 ERA, but was cast back into a full-time starting role in September. What'd Buchholz do? He pitched great, of course, dominating in four of his five final starts and earning starting rights in Game 3 of the ALDS. It's a testament to just how bad he was in the early going that his $13.5 million option for 2017 wasn't a complete no-brainer, but Boston did pick it up. High school relationships have fewer ups and downs, and the Red Sox finally ended things right before winter break, sending The Clay Buchholz Experience to Philadelphia in exchange for infield prospect Josh Tobias. It's a great fit because everyone knows that Philly fans are super accepting of inconsistency.

Zach Eflin RHP

Born: 4/8/94   Age: 23   Bats: R   Throws: R   Height: 6'6"   Weight: 215   Entered Pro Ball: Round 1, 2012 Draft (#33 overall)

YEAR	TEAM	LVL	AGE	W	L	SV	G	GS	IP	H	HR	BB/9	K/9	K	GB%	BABIP	WHIP	ERA	FIP	DRA	VORP	WARP	cFIP	MPH
2014	LEL	A+	20	10	7	0	24	24	128	138	9	2.2	6.5	93	52%	.338	1.32	3.80	4.02	3.96	23.2	2.3	95	
2015	REA	AA	21	8	6	0	23	23	131²	136	12	1.6	4.6	68	44%	.286	1.21	3.69	4.04	4.69	5.9	0.6	105	
2016	LEH	AAA	22	5	2	0	11	11	68¹	49	2	1.4	7.2	55	47%	.245	0.88	2.90	2.55	2.94	18.2	1.9	89	
2016	PHI	MLB	22	3	5	0	11	11	63¹	67	12	2.4	4.4	31	37%	.261	1.33	5.54	5.52	7.68	-16.3	-1.7	132	96.0
2017	PHI	MLB	23	3	5	0	31	10	75	79	11	2.7	5.9	50	57%	.289	1.33	4.96	4.78	5.14	-0.3	0.0	100	
2018	PHI	MLB	24	8	8	0	63	18	156²	136	23	3.7	8.4	146	57%	.290	1.28	4.49	4.82	5.21	3.4	0.4	122	

Breakout: 18%   Improve: 37%   Collapse: 17%   Attrition: 36%   MLB: 69%   *Comparables: Blake Beavan, Jeanmar Gomez, Alex Sanabia*

Sometimes it takes a few years for a pitcher's results to sync up with his stuff, and there's no better example of this on the Phillies than with Eflin. His fastball sits in the mid-90s, and he can ramp it up to 97 with ease. The problem comes with all of his secondary offerings, which are inconsistent and lack command. A two-pitch pitcher with Eflin's talent can thrive in the minors and can even have great outings in the majors, but for the most part what you get is what Eflin delivered in 2016: poor results without a lot of whiffs as hitters sat on his fastball. A knee injury may have been a blessing in disguise; it gives Philadelphia a chance to pull the throttle back and send Eflin to Triple-A for more seasoning.

Jerad Eickhoff RHP

Born: 7/2/90   Age: 26   Bats: R   Throws: R   Height: 6'4"   Weight: 245   Entered Pro Ball: Round 15, 2011 Draft (#474 overall)

YEAR	TEAM	LVL	AGE	W	L	SV	G	GS	IP	H	HR	BB/9	K/9	K	GB%	BABIP	WHIP	ERA	FIP	DRA	VORP	WARP	cFIP	MPH
2014	FRI	AA	23	10	9	0	27	26	154¹	129	17	3.0	8.4	144	39%	.269	1.17	4.08	3.83	4.40	14.1	1.5	101	
2015	FRI	AA	24	1	0	0	2	2	10	7	2	2.7	12.6	14	36%	.250	1.00	2.70	4.30	3.48	1.8	0.2	86	
2015	ROU	AAA	24	9	4	0	18	17	101²	95	12	2.9	8.2	93	35%	.291	1.26	4.25	4.40	3.13	24.4	2.5	90	
2015	LEH	AAA	24	2	1	0	3	3	21²	17	1	1.2	7.9	19	28%	.254	0.92	2.49	2.42	3.21	5.0	0.5	88	
2015	PHI	MLB	24	3	3	0	8	8	51	40	5	2.3	8.6	49	38%	.257	1.04	2.65	3.28	4.25	4.7	0.5	97	93.6
2016	PHI	MLB	25	11	14	0	33	33	197¹	187	30	1.9	7.6	167	43%	.278	1.16	3.65	4.23	3.98	30.4	3.1	98	93.4
2017	PHI	MLB	26	8	10	0	27	27	153	138	19	2.2	8.3	143	52%	.282	1.12	3.90	3.78	4.13	17.9	1.9	95	
2018	PHI	MLB	27	11	11	0	33	33	214¹	158	27	2.9	10.1	240	52%	.276	1.05	3.57	3.81	4.13	29.3	3.0	94	

Breakout: 24%   Improve: 43%   Collapse: 25%   Attrition: 28%   MLB: 87%   *Comparables: James McDonald, Dan Straily, Dillon Gee*

If teen romantic comedies have taught us anything at all, it's that sometimes the person you've been looking for all along was right in front of you the entire time. Considered an afterthought in the blockbuster trade that sent Cole Hamels to Texas last year, Eickhoff has emerged as one of the best prospects from that haul, as he built on his promising 2015 with another solid campaign. Eickhoff couldn't get his feel for the curve in 2015 because he was having difficulty adjusting to the seams on a major league ball. Once he did start throwing it, it was like that moment when the love interest takes off her glasses, and another character creepily whispers "go to her." Eickhoff still needs a few more finishing touches, but Phillies fans will be initiating an odd, slow clap in appreciation of him for years to come.

Jeanmar Gomez RHP

Born: 2/10/88   Age: 29   Bats: R   Throws: R   Height: 6'3"   Weight: 215   Entered Pro Ball: International Free Agent, 2005

YEAR	TEAM	LVL	AGE	W	L	SV	G	GS	IP	H	HR	BB/9	K/9	K	GB%	BABIP	WHIP	ERA	FIP	DRA	VORP	WARP	cFIP	MPH
2014	PIT	MLB	26	2	2	1	44	0	62	70	6	3.3	5.5	38	48%	.318	1.50	3.19	4.34	5.48	-6.8	-0.8	117	93.6
2015	PHI	MLB	27	2	3	0	65	0	74²	82	4	2.0	6.0	50	51%	.317	1.33	3.01	3.28	4.58	1.1	0.1	103	94.0
2016	PHI	MLB	28	3	5	37	70	0	68²	78	6	2.9	6.2	47	54%	.327	1.46	4.85	4.00	5.08	-0.8	-0.1	105	94.2
2017	PHI	MLB	29	3	3	5	59	0	62	63	8	2.9	7.0	48	46%	.294	1.33	4.51	4.37	4.66	1.8	0.2	100	
2018	PHI	MLB	30	3	1	2	52	0	54²	50	6	2.7	7.5	45	46%	.298	1.21	3.89	4.15	4.50	3.8	0.4	100	

Breakout: 43%   Improve: 57%   Collapse: 23%   Attrition: 23%   MLB: 91%   *Comparables: Matt Albers, Casey Janssen, Seth McClung*

Of the many idioms in the English language, "the wheels came off" is one of the most counterintuitive. Of all of the problems a vehicle can have, the wheels coming off is at the bottom of a very long list of things that can and will go wrong. Idiomatic (and perhaps idiotic) pedantry aside, throughout most of the first half it felt like only a matter of time before the wheels came off for Gomez. He doesn't light up the radar gun, doesn't have a pitch that features any especially nasty movement and doesn't even offer enough variety with his pitches to keep hitters off balance for all that long. Gomez belongs in a big league bullpen, but there was nothing sustainable in his glittering first half numbers, and nothing to suggest that he'll take a step further this year or beyond.

Kevin Gowdy RHP

Born: 11/16/97 Age: 19   Bats: R   Throws: R   Height: 6'4"   Weight: 170   Entered Pro Ball: Round 2, 2016 Draft (#42 overall)

The word "polish" is often associated with Gowdy, and with good reason. The 18-year-old sports clean mechanics, throws in the low-90s with ease and has the potential to grow into his frame and add more velocity as he matures. The slider is already a decent pitch and Gowdy's change should develop in time. Part of the reason the Phillies "settled" on Mickey Moniak was to move that slot money to Gowdy, who received a $3.5 million bonus (nearly $2 million over slot) that lured him away from a commitment to UCLA. So far so good, but as is always the case with recently-drafted 18-year-old prep arms, Gowdy hasn't really been tested yet.

Jeremy Hellickson RHP

Born: 4/8/87 Age: 30 Bats: R Throws: R Height: 6'1" Weight: 190 Entered Pro Ball: Round 4, 2005 Draft (#118 overall)

YEAR	TEAM	LVL	AGE	W	L	SV	G	GS	IP	H	HR	BB/9	K/9	K	GB%	BABIP	WHIP	ERA	FIP	DRA	VORP	WARP	cFIP	MPH
2014	DUR	AAA	27	1	4	0	5	5	18²	38	1	2.4	7.7	16	41%	.493	2.30	7.23	3.46	4.53	2.5	0.3	97	
2014	TBA	MLB	27	1	5	0	13	13	63²	71	8	3.0	7.6	54	38%	.321	1.45	4.52	4.18	4.42	2.9	0.3	111	92.3
2015	ARI	MLB	28	9	12	0	27	27	146	151	22	2.7	7.5	121	45%	.291	1.33	4.62	4.47	4.22	14.0	1.5	105	92.2
2016	PHI	MLB	29	12	10	0	32	32	189	173	24	2.1	7.3	154	43%	.274	1.15	3.71	4.02	4.34	21.4	2.2	101	92.2
2017	PHI	MLB	30	8	11	0	30	30	159	149	22	2.4	8.5	151	45%	.291	1.20	4.09	3.98	4.35	14.6	1.5	100	
2018	PHI	MLB	31	10	10	0	32	.32	202¹	180	27	2.3	8.6	193	45%	.300	1.15	3.80	4.07	4.41	21.3	2.2	101	

Breakout: 18%   Improve: 40%   Collapse: 21%   Attrition: 14%   MLB: 85%   *Comparables: Gil Meche, Jason Vargas, Ervin Santana*

In the world of player analysis, expectation and perception are brothers-in-arms. The combination of Hellickson's 2.95 ERA and Rookie of the Year Award in 2011 led to the inevitable belief that Hellickson has been a profound disappointment. In reality, it is the same as it ever was for Helly. He is a solid-if-unspectacular back-end starting pitcher who can eat 170-180 innings, while even putting together the odd gem now and again. The Phillies grabbed him in the offseason prior to 2016 with these modest returns in mind and Hellickson delivered, posting the highest WARP of his career. He is at his best when he is mixing up his arsenal of four pitches and pounding the zone. It's a tried-and-true formula for most pitchers of Hellickson's ilk, and as long he stays healthy he should be able to keep on trucking with this approach well into his 30s.

David Hernandez RHP

Born: 5/13/85 Age: 32 Bats: R Throws: R Height: 6'3" Weight: 245 Entered Pro Ball: Round 16, 2005 Draft (#483 overall)

YEAR	TEAM	LVL	AGE	W	L	SV	G	GS	IP	H	HR	BB/9	K/9	K	GB%	BABIP	WHIP	ERA	FIP	DRA	VORP	WARP	cFIP	MPH
2015	ARI	MLB	30	1	5	0	40	0	33²	33	6	2.9	8.8	33	40%	.297	1.31	4.28	4.77	4.32	1.5	0.2	104	96.9
2016	PHI	MLB	31	3	4	1	70	0	72²	77	11	4.0	9.9	80	40%	.337	1.50	3.84	4.36	4.05	7.4	0.8	98	96.3
2017	PHI	MLB	32	3	1	0	59	0	62¹	55	10	3.2	9.9	69	49%	.305	1.24	4.28	4.16	5.00	0.9	0.1	114	
2018	PHI	MLB	33	2	1	0	31	0	30²	28	5	3.3	9.5	32	49%	.307	1.27	4.41	4.74	5.15	0.0	0.0	119	

Breakout: 17%   Improve: 31%   Collapse: 29%   Attrition: 7%   MLB: 78%   *Comparables: John Axford, Frank Francisco, Joel Hanrahan*

Once again, Hernandez started the year as the presumptive closer, this time around for the Phillies. Once again, Hernandez quickly lost the job, this time due to a shaky initial outing against the Reds. While that hardly seems fair, such is life for the itinerant closer without a long-term guaranteed contract. Hernandez could use a third pitch and a lot more sink on his fastball, but as long as he is dealing in the mid-90s, he should have a job in a major league bullpen for years to come barring injury.

Franklyn Kilome RHP

Born: 6/25/95 Age: 22 Bats: R Throws: R Height: 6'6" Weight: 175 Entered Pro Ball: International Free Agent, 2013

YEAR	TEAM	LVL	AGE	W	L	SV	G	GS	IP	H	HR	BB/9	K/9	K	GB%	BABIP	WHIP	ERA	FIP	DRA	VORP	WARP	cFIP	MPH
2015	WPT	A-	20	3	2	0	11	11	49¹	41	1	3.8	6.6	36	57%	.282	1.26	3.28	4.02	5.76	-2.6	-0.3	113	
2016	LWD	A	21	5	8	0	23	23	114²	113	6	3.9	10.2	130	49%	.346	1.42	3.85	3.28	4.23	10.0	1.1	101	
2017	PHI	MLB	22	4	8	0	18	18	86²	100	15	5.1	6.1	58	60%	.328	1.73	5.88	5.88	6.70	-10.9	-1.1	158	
2018	PHI	MLB	23	5	8	0	20	20	120	117	21	6.5	8.5	113	60%	.314	1.70	5.78	6.26	6.59	-11.0	-1.1	157	

Breakout: 0%   Improve: 0%   Collapse: 0%   Attrition: 0%   MLB: 0%   *Comparables: Brian Flynn, Michael Belfiore, Michael Stutes*

Kilome continued to impress, taking a big step forward in the South Atlantic League. Command had always been an issue for him, but he improved significantly in the second half, seeing his walk rate plummet from 5.0 walks per nine in his first 12 starts to 2.8 in his last 12. When everything's working for Kilome, he has a mid-90s heater with good sink, a power curve and a change with good fade and deception. That being said, Kilome's mechanics have been more inconsistent than the ones at the garage that was investigated by the award-winning local news "I-Team" last year. The upside is that of a frontline starter, but there is plenty of washout potential as well.

Ben Lively RHP

Born: 3/5/92 Age: 25 Bats: R Throws: R Height: 6'4" Weight: 190 Entered Pro Ball: Round 4, 2013 Draft (#135 overall)

YEAR	TEAM	LVL	AGE	W	L	SV	G	GS	IP	H	HR	BB/9	K/9	K	GB%	BABIP	WHIP	ERA	FIP	DRA	VORP	WARP	cFIP	MPH
2014	BAK	A+	22	10	1	0	13	13	79	57	6	1.8	10.8	95	35%	.281	0.92	2.28	2.97	1.40	36.9	3.7	72	
2014	PEN	AA	22	3	6	0	13	13	72	60	7	4.5	9.5	76	37%	.290	1.33	3.88	4.01	4.05	9.4	1.0	103	
2015	REA	AA	23	8	7	0	25	25	143²	160	14	2.8	7	111	40%	.336	1.43	4.13	4.08	4.00	17.4	1.9	103	
2016	REA	AA	24	7	0	0	9	9	53	35	1	2.5	8.3	49	39%	.241	0.94	1.87	2.60	2.24	16.8	1.8	88	
2016	LEH	AAA	24	11	5	0	19	19	117²	83	10	2.1	6.9	90	41%	.221	0.93	3.06	3.51	3.30	26.7	2.8	105	
2017	PHI	MLB	25	2	2	0	19	3	32	32	4	3.4	7.2	26	59%	.287	1.32	4.82	4.37	4.98	0.2	0.0	100	
2018	PHI	MLB	26	6	5	0	69	10	121²	95	16	4.6	10.0	135	59%	.287	1.29	4.30	4.61	4.99	4.3	0.4	115	

Breakout: 18%   Improve: 28%   Collapse: 11%   Attrition: 34%   MLB: 49%   *Comparables: Logan Verrett, Mike Montgomery, Matt Andriese*

It isn't often looked at this way, but the success of a rebuilding movement can often be viewed based on the players a team doesn't need to use. Before the Phillies replenished their farm system, Lively appeared to be an important part of the rebuild, or at the very least a future member of the team's rotation. In 2016, Lively looked more like a future reliever, Triple-A insurance or a trade chip for the team to improve its depth. The numbers were great, particularly at Double-A, but Lively's stuff won't play up in the majors as deception can only take a pitcher so far as a carrying tool. Pitching injuries being as ubiquitous as they are, Lively will likely stumble his way into a handful of major league starts this year, but barring an unforeseen step forward, he isn't more than a back-end arm.

Adonis Medina   RHP

Born: 12/18/96   Age: 20   Bats: R   Throws: R   Height: 6'1"   Weight: 185   Entered Pro Ball: International Free Agent, 2014

YEAR	TEAM	LVL	AGE	W	L	SV	G	GS	IP	H	HR	BB/9	K/9	K	GB%	BABIP	WHIP	ERA	FIP	DRA	VORP	WARP	cFIP	MPH
2016	WPT	A-	19	5	3	0	13	13	64²	47	5	3.3	4.7	34	57%	.214	1.10	2.92	4.66	7.66	-17.4	-1.8	121	
2017	PHI	MLB	20	2	4	0	16	8	48²	59	10	4.7	4.2	22	65%	.315	1.75	6.54	6.69	7.46	-12.0	-1.2	178	
2018	PHI	MLB	21	5	8	0	30	19	138	147	26	5.1	6.6	101	65%	.308	1.63	5.91	6.41	6.74	-15.4	-1.6	162	

Breakout: 0%   Improve: 0%   Collapse: 0%   Attrition: 0%   MLB: 0%   *Comparables: Brett Marshall, Alex Cobb, Alberto Cabrera*

Medina's strikeout rate is unimpressive, but it is difficult to argue against the raw stuff to date. He sits in the low 90s with his fastball and can touch 96 and 97 at times. His secondary stuff is advanced for a 19-year-old arm, and it is entirely possible Medina was willing to generate weak contact rather than go for the punch out. His size will always be a potential concern, but he already looks bigger than his listed height and weight. Short-season results are seldom instructive, but Medina will move another rung up the ladder in 2017 and has an opportunity to emerge as a mid-tier starting pitcher.

Adam Morgan   LHP

Born: 2/27/90   Age: 27   Bats: L   Throws: L   Height: 6'1"   Weight: 200   Entered Pro Ball: Round 3, 2011 Draft (#120 overall)

YEAR	TEAM	LVL	AGE	W	L	SV	G	GS	IP	H	HR	BB/9	K/9	K	GB%	BABIP	WHIP	ERA	FIP	DRA	VORP	WARP	cFIP	MPH
2015	LEH	AAA	25	0	6	0	13	13	68¹	81	7	3.6	4.3	33	39%	.307	1.58	4.74	4.75	9.27	-30.1	-3.1	134	
2015	PHI	MLB	25	5	7	0	15	15	84¹	88	14	1.8	5.2	49	31%	.276	1.25	4.48	4.90	6.66	-14.8	-1.6	133	91.6
2016	LEH	AAA	26	6	1	0	8	7	50¹	43	4	1.8	9.3	52	42%	.293	1.05	3.06	2.85	2.15	17.6	1.8	78	
2016	PHI	MLB	26	2	11	0	23	21	113¹	141	23	2.3	7.5	95	40%	.331	1.50	6.04	5.02	5.01	4.3	0.4	112	93.6
2017	PHI	MLB	27	3	3	0	46	3	60	59	7	2.6	7.9	53	55%	.296	1.28	4.20	3.87	4.43	3.7	0.4	100	
2018	PHI	MLB	28	5	3	0	73	4	97²	81	12	3.1	9.5	103	55%	.297	1.17	3.76	4.03	4.37	8.9	0.9	97	

Breakout: 33%   Improve: 56%   Collapse: 8%   Attrition: 17%   MLB: 80%   *Comparables: Craig Stammen, Vidal Nuno, Nick Blackburn*

Fastball velocity is just like money. It isn't everything, but having it makes life a lot easier. Once a hard throwing lefty, Morgan can't nearly throw as hard as he used to and has to rely on guile and witchcraft in order to succeed. This wasn't on display for the Phillies in 2016 as, more often than not, Morgan was a pitching version of a piñata. Home runs are more common than they used to be, but even by today's standards while pitching in a park suited for right-handed power, Morgan's 23 jacks allowed in less than 120 innings was discouraging. Even more problematic than the lack of velocity were a short stride and poor extension that made Morgan's already compromised stuff play even worse. By the end of the season, Morgan had moved away from the four-seamer in favor of a sinker. Whether this is a permanent change remains to be seen, but on a team with a number of young arms, Morgan runs the risk of being left behind or banished to the bullpen.

Hector Neris   RHP

Born: 6/14/89   Age: 28   Bats: R   Throws: R   Height: 6'2"   Weight: 215   Entered Pro Ball: International Free Agent, 2010

YEAR	TEAM	LVL	AGE	W	L	SV	G	GS	IP	H	HR	BB/9	K/9	K	GB%	BABIP	WHIP	ERA	FIP	DRA	VORP	WARP	cFIP	MPH
2014	REA	AA	25	2	0	0	11	0	19¹	12	3	4.7	5.6	12	44%	.176	1.14	1.86	5.68	5.09	-0.5	-0.1	111	
2014	PHI	MLB	25	1	0	0	1	0	1	0	0	0.0	9.0	1	50%	.000	0.00	0.00	1.10	4.17	0.0	0.0	99	94.4
2014	LEH	AAA	25	4	3	2	37	1	58	50	5	2.9	9.0	58	43%	.287	1.19	4.19	3.77	4.08	8.2	0.8	88	
2015	LEH	AAA	26	1	3	1	27	0	37¹	38	1	5.8	8.4	35	36%	.327	1.66	3.62	3.56	6.30	-5.7	-0.6	113	
2015	PHI	MLB	26	2	2	0	32	0	40¹	38	8	2.2	9.1	41	39%	.280	1.19	3.79	4.75	4.18	2.4	0.3	100	95.5
2016	PHI	MLB	27	4	4	2	79	0	80¹	59	9	3.4	11.4	102	44%	.272	1.11	2.58	3.34	3.43	13.8	1.4	77	96.9
2017	PHI	MLB	28	3	3	5	59	0	62	52	7	3.2	9.9	68	45%	.289	1.20	3.56	3.61	3.89	7.1	0.7	85	
2018	PHI	MLB	29	3	1	3	56	0	59¹	40	7	3.6	11.7	77	45%	.282	1.09	3.35	3.58	3.88	8.2	0.8	84	

Breakout: 23%   Improve: 39%   Collapse: 19%   Attrition: 23%   MLB: 70%   *Comparables: Brad Brach, Evan Scribner, Craig Breslow*

While Jeanmar Gomez was the closer for the Phillies nearly all season long, Neris was by far their best reliever. Abandoning his slider almost entirely, Neris moved to a two-pitch repertoire, featuring his low-to-mid-90s fastball and a splitter that became a signature pitch as the season progressed. Free from worrying about trying to mix in pitches he didn't seem that confident in in the past, Neris evolved into one of those flame-throwing relievers who simply rears back, fires and dares batters to hit him. The result was not only a big spike in his strikeout rate, but more grounders and weaker contact when hitters did manage to get a piece. Neris certainly isn't invincible—his home-run rate is too high to consider him an elite reliever—but if the Phillies decide to give Neris the ball in the ninth, he's more than capable of doing the job.

Pat Neshek   RHP

Born: 9/4/80   Age: 36   Bats: B   Throws: R   Height: 6'3"   Weight: 220   Entered Pro Ball: Round 6, 2002 Draft (#182 overall)

YEAR	TEAM	LVL	AGE	W	L	SV	G	GS	IP	H	HR	BB/9	K/9	K	GB%	BABIP	WHIP	ERA	FIP	DRA	VORP	WARP	cFIP	MPH
2014	SLN	MLB	33	7	2	6	71	0	67¹	44	4	1.2	9.1	68	37%	.233	0.79	1.87	2.35	3.21	9.6	1.1	87	93.5
2015	HOU	MLB	34	3	6	1	66	0	54²	49	8	2.0	8.4	51	34%	.273	1.12	3.62	3.91	3.60	6.7	0.7	106	93.1
2016	HOU	MLB	35	2	2	0	60	0	47	33	6	2.1	8.2	43	37%	.216	0.94	3.06	3.64	4.26	3.7	0.4	99	92.0
2017	PHI	MLB	36	3	3	0	59	0	62	57	9	2.5	8.8	61	46%	.284	1.19	4.17	4.01	4.38	3.7	0.4	99	
2018	PHI	MLB	37	3	1	0	52	0	55¹	47	8	2.4	9.2	57	46%	.287	1.10	3.80	4.06	4.38	4.6	0.5	98	

Breakout: 21%   Improve: 37%   Collapse: 25%   Attrition: 7%   MLB: 68%   *Comparables: Hideki Okajima, Neal Cotts, Joel Peralta*

At this point in his career, Neshek should probably be a right-handed specialist—no surprise considering the 36-year-old's lack of velocity and awkward arm angle. Neshek held 130 right-handed opponents to two home runs and a .172/.209/.254 mark, whereas just 55 left-handed batters managed four home runs and a .250/.321/.646 line against him. Luckily for Neshek, there will never be a shortage of right-handed batters to retire late in baseball games. It would be inadvisable to rely on Neshek in a closer or setup role, but he has shown that he has plenty to provide to a manager who's willing and able to play matchups around him.

Aaron Nola   RHP

Born: 6/4/93   Age: 24   Bats: R   Throws: R   Height: 6'2"   Weight: 195   Entered Pro Ball: Round 1, 2014 Draft (#7 overall)

YEAR	TEAM	LVL	AGE	W	L	SV	G	GS	IP	H	HR	BB/9	K/9	K	GB%	BABIP	WHIP	ERA	FIP	DRA	VORP	WARP	cFIP	MPH
2014	CLR	A+	21	2	3	0	7	6	31¹	24	4	1.4	8.6	30	34%	.247	0.93	3.16	3.61	1.74	13.2	1.3	76	
2014	REA	AA	21	2	0	0	5	5	24	25	4	1.9	5.6	15	49%	.284	1.25	2.62	4.90	3.14	5.6	0.6	96	
2015	REA	AA	22	7	3	0	12	12	76²	59	4	1.1	6.9	59	45%	.259	0.89	1.88	2.88	1.40	31.5	3.4	76	
2015	LEH	AAA	22	3	1	0	6	6	32²	38	3	2.5	9.1	33	52%	.365	1.44	3.58	3.16	1.13	15.2	1.5	81	
2015	PHI	MLB	22	6	2	0	13	13	77²	74	11	2.2	7.9	68	50%	.289	1.20	3.59	4.06	3.38	14.7	1.6	91	93.5
2016	PHI	MLB	23	6	9	0	20	20	111	116	10	2.4	9.8	121	57%	.334	1.31	4.78	3.12	2.33	37.3	3.9	75	93.0
2017	PHI	MLB	24	8	9	0	26	26	137	123	15	2.4	9.4	144	45%	.293	1.15	3.59	3.38	3.80	21.1	2.2	85	
2018	PHI	MLB	25	11	10	0	33	33	212¹	170	23	2.6	10.4	245	45%	.305	1.09	3.24	3.46	3.76	34.3	3.5	82	

Breakout: 32%   Improve: 62%   Collapse: 11%   Attrition: 14%   MLB: 95%   Comparables: Gerrit Cole, Carlos Martinez, Brett Cecil

Early in 2016, a good deal of media attention was lavished on how the curveball was the "signature" pitch of the organization. No one's curve received more attention than Nola's. The combination of a three-quarters arm slot and nasty horizontal break made Nola's bender one of the hardest pitches to hit in the league during the first two months of the season, and made his decent-but-not-dominant low-90s heater more difficult to adjust to by comparison. Then in June, Nola looked like a different pitcher, as he lost command of everything. Despite the continued high swing-and-miss rates, Nola started walking more batters and looking far more hittable. There was some BABIP bad luck mixed in there, but the ultimate culprit turned out to be a UCL sprain and low-grade flexor sprain in his throwing elbow. The Phillies played it safe and shut Nola down with the hopes that he returns in 2017 as what he appeared to be in April and May: a legitimate ace who doesn't need oodles of velocity to knock the bats out of hitters' hands.

Nick Pivetta   RHP

Born: 2/14/93   Age: 24   Bats: R   Throws: R   Height: 6'5"   Weight: 220   Entered Pro Ball: Round 4, 2013 Draft (#136 overall)

YEAR	TEAM	LVL	AGE	W	L	SV	G	GS	IP	H	HR	BB/9	K/9	K	GB%	BABIP	WHIP	ERA	FIP	DRA	VORP	WARP	cFIP	MPH
2014	HAG	A	21	13	8	0	26	25	132¹	142	15	2.7	6.7	98	44%	.309	1.37	4.22	4.60	4.58	12.5	1.3	101	
2015	POT	A+	22	7	4	0	15	14	86¹	70	4	3.0	7.5	72	46%	.274	1.15	2.29	3.26	3.73	12.7	1.4	100	
2015	HAR	AA	22	0	2	0	3	3	15	19	4	5.4	3.6	6	34%	.294	1.87	7.20	7.74	7.69	-4.3	-0.5	134	
2015	REA	AA	22	2	2	0	7	7	28¹	32	4	6	7.9	25	41%	.341	1.80	7.31	5.67	8.10	-9.5	-1.0	137	
2016	REA	AA	23	11	6	0	22	22	124	108	10	3.0	8.1	111	45%	.283	1.20	3.41	3.75	3.78	18.1	2.0	96	
2016	LEH	AAA	23	1	2	0	5	5	24²	20	2	3.6	9.9	27	48%	.300	1.22	2.55	3.49	2.86	6.8	0.7	88	
2017	PHI	MLB	24	6	9	0	23	23	122	124	18	3.8	6.9	93	57%	.310	1.43	4.91	4.90	5.65	-1.2	-0.1	134	
2018	PHI	MLB	25	6	8	0	21	21	120²	107	17	5.3	9.5	127	57%	.311	1.48	4.80	5.16	5.52	0.5	0.1	130	

Breakout: 10%   Improve: 22%   Collapse: 15%   Attrition: 33%   MLB: 45%   Comparables: Andrew Chafin, Adam Ottavino, Ty Blach

Pivetta isn't quite as highly regarded as some of the Phillies' minor league arms, but still has the potential to crack the team's rotation eventually. A repeat trip to Double-A in 2016 saw better results, most notably with improved feel for and command of his fastball. Pivetta needs a third pitch to make it in the majors as a starter; otherwise it is likely that he will get locked into a bullpen role. It is too early for Philadelphia to make that call, so he will start 2017 in a minor league rotation, either at Reading or Lehigh Valley.

Edubray Ramos   RHP

Born: 12/19/92 Age: 24   Bats: R   Throws: R   Height: 6'0"   Weight: 160   Entered Pro Ball: International Free Agent, 2010

YEAR	TEAM	LVL	AGE	W	L	SV	G	GS	IP	H	HR	BB/9	K/9	K	GB%	BABIP	WHIP	ERA	FIP	DRA	VORP	WARP	cFIP	MPH
2014	WPT	A-	21	1	0	2	11	1	22²	12	0	0.8	9.5	24	41%	.214	0.62	0.79	1.72	1.78	8.2	0.9	72	
2015	CLR	A+	22	3	4	8	29	0	49¹	31	2	1.1	8.6	47	46%	.232	0.75	1.46	2.21	2.19	13.8	1.5	75	
2015	REA	AA	22	1	2	0	18	0	20¹	17	0	4.4	8	18	19%	.288	1.33	3.54	3.27	5.10	-0.8	-0.1	106	
2016	REA	AA	23	1	1	7	11	0	15	9	1	0.6	9.0	15	51%	.211	0.67	2.40	2.62	2.09	4.4	0.5	78	
2016	LEH	AAA	23	1	0	3	15	0	23²	15	0	1.1	9.9	26	32%	.250	0.76	0.38	1.48	2.31	7.0	0.7	86	
2016	PHI	MLB	23	1	3	0	42	0	40	36	5	2.5	9.0	40	38%	.298	1.17	3.83	3.64	4.22	3.3	0.3	94	98.0
2017	PHI	MLB	24	3	3	0	53	0	56¹	53	8	2.9	8.3	52	53%	.289	1.26	4.52	4.24	4.68	1.5	0.2	100	
2018	PHI	MLB	25	2	1	0	48	0	51	39	7	3.4	10.4	59	53%	.288	1.16	3.91	4.17	4.54	3.3	0.3	103	

Breakout: 39%   Improve: 55%   Collapse: 8%   Attrition: 28%   MLB: 75%   Comparables: Cody Allen, Stephen Pryor, Josh Spence

Cobbling together a good bullpen isn't necessarily a priority during a rebuilding movement, but ideally having two or three solid arms emerge as useful components helps. Ramos is a good example of where the Phillies' approach with pitching has worked well. Ramos was capably throwing four pitches for strikes, but the Phillies had him focus on his mid-90s fastball and slider. The result was a strong season marred only by a poor September that may have been the result of elbow soreness that sidelined Ramos at the end of the regular season. If healthy, Ramos will be a key cog in the Phillies' 2017 bullpen.

Sixto Sanchez   RHP

Born: 7/29/98   Age: 18   Bats: R   Throws: R   Height: 6'0"   Weight: 185   Entered Pro Ball: International Free Agent, 2015

The Phillies have more than a few young pitchers who have excited scouts, so it isn't whistling Dixie to say that Sanchez is arguably the highest-ceiling arm of the lot. He doesn't have much in the way of size, but makes up for that with a fastball that sits in the mid-90s and flirted with triple digits in a few starts. As an 18-year-old in the GCL, Sanchez still has a long way to go before getting to the majors. His curveball and change are raw and, like every young pitcher since the dawn of time, he will need further development on those secondaries before the jury reaches a verdict.

Jake Thompson   RHP

Born: 1/31/94   Age: 23   Bats: R   Throws: R   Height: 6'4"   Weight: 235   Entered Pro Ball: Round 2, 2012 Draft (#91 overall)

YEAR	TEAM	LVL	AGE	W	L	SV	G	GS	IP	H	HR	BB/9	K/9	K	GB%	BABIP	WHIP	ERA	FIP	DRA	VORP	WARP	cFIP	MPH
2014	LAK	A+	20	6	4	0	16	16	83	75	3	2.7	8.6	79	44%	.316	1.20	3.14	3.11	2.40	29.4	3.0	86	
2014	ERI	AA	20	1	0	0	2	2	11	10	0	3.3	5.7	7	40%	.286	1.27	2.45	3.45	2.54	3.3	0.3	107	
2014	FRI	AA	20	3	1	0	7	6	35²	28	3	4.5	11.1	44	46%	.305	1.29	3.28	3.34	2.87	9.2	1.0	86	
2015	FRI	AA	21	6	6	0	17	17	87²	94	7	3.1	8.0	78	46%	.330	1.41	4.72	3.82	3.70	13.5	1.5	96	
2015	REA	AA	21	5	1	0	7	7	45	33	3	2.4	6.8	34	52%	.256	1.00	1.80	3.42	3.63	7.3	0.8	91	
2016	LEH	AAA	22	11	5	0	21	21	129²	105	10	2.6	6.0	87	48%	.252	1.10	2.50	3.82	5.45	-1.5	-0.2	108	
2016	PHI	MLB	22	3	6	0	10	10	53²	53	10	4.7	5.4	32	49%	.264	1.51	5.70	6.20	6.43	-6.4	-0.7	123	93.8
2017	PHI	MLB	23	2	3	0	22	6	46	48	6	3.6	6.5	34	53%	.290	1.40	5.04	4.74	5.22	-0.7	-0.1	100	
2018	PHI	MLB	24	5	4	0	45	11	100²	82	13	4.7	9.2	103	53%	.291	1.34	4.48	4.80	5.21	1.9	0.2	121	

Breakout: 16%   Improve: 30%   Collapse: 21%   Attrition: 35%   MLB: 67%   *Comparables: Archie Bradley, Casey Coleman, Brad Hand*

At a glance, Thompson's 2016 looks like a step in the wrong direction. The strikeout rate dropped precipitously, mostly due to his difficulty locating his slider—his bread-and-butter pitch that must be tip-top in order for Thompson to survive as a quality major league pitcher. Thompson was hit hard after he was promoted to Philadelphia, and for the first time in his career had a propensity for surrendering the long ball. What is easy to forget in this calculus is that Thompson is only 23 and possesses the ability to throw all four of his pitches for strikes. If the Phillies can coax some consistency out of his slider, as well as his other secondary offerings, Thompson has the potential to survive as a mid-tier starter at a minimum.

Alberto Tirado   RHP

Born: 12/10/94   Age: 22   Bats: R   Throws: R   Height: 6'0"   Weight: 180   Entered Pro Ball: International Free Agent, 2011

YEAR	TEAM	LVL	AGE	W	L	SV	G	GS	IP	H	HR	BB/9	K/9	K	GB%	BABIP	WHIP	ERA	FIP	DRA	VORP	WARP	cFIP	MPH
2014	LNS	A	19	1	2	1	13	7	40	45	3	8.8	9.0	40	55%	.359	2.10	6.30	5.61	10.70	-24.1	-2.5	133	
2014	VAN	A-	19	1	0	0	17	3	35²	25	1	7.1	9.1	36	58%	.255	1.49	3.53	4.77	7.22	-8.5	-0.9	120	
2015	DUN	A+	20	4	3	3	31	0	61¹	45	4	5.1	9.0	61	52%	.272	1.30	3.23	4.08	7.27	-17.4	-1.9	126	
2015	CLR	A+	20	1	0	0	9	0	16	6	0	10.1	9.0	16	61%	.182	1.50	0.56	4.92	7.31	-4.6	-0.5	126	
2016	LWD	A	21	7	1	0	20	11	61¹	48	3	5.3	14.1	96	37%	.352	1.37	3.23	3.11	2.51	16.7	1.8	94	
2017	PHI	MLB	22	3	3	1	37	6	57²	58	9	6.6	7.7	49	59%	.319	1.74	5.80	5.80	6.62	-12.4	-1.3	156	
2018	PHI	MLB	23	2	3	1	30	6	83	69	11	7.5	10.5	97	59%	.314	1.68	5.27	5.71	6.01	-5.5	-0.6	141	

Breakout: 4%   Improve: 4%   Collapse: 1%   Attrition: 3%   MLB: 5%   *Comparables: Phillippe Aumont, Mauricio Cabrera, Patrick Schuster*

The inconsistency in Tirado's command and delivery make it likely that he'll land in the majors as a reliever, but you can't blame the Phillies for trying to exploit his ceiling and use him as a starting pitcher. Tirado started 2016 as a reliever before being sent back to instructional league ball to stretch out for the rotation. The results in a 12-start stretch were impressive. The combination of 14 strikeouts per nine and a 2.12 ERA opened a lot of eyes and gave Tirado new life as a starter. The concerns remain about consistency, not only from game to game, but from pitch to pitch—yet if Tirado can get the command together and keep his walks to a merely below-average rate, he's got a shot.

Vincent Velasquez   RHP

Born: 6/7/92   Age: 25   Bats: R   Throws: R   Height: 6'3"   Weight: 205   Entered Pro Ball: Round 2, 2010 Draft (#58 overall)

YEAR	TEAM	LVL	AGE	W	L	SV	G	GS	IP	H	HR	BB/9	K/9	K	GB%	BABIP	WHIP	ERA	FIP	DRA	VORP	WARP	cFIP	MPH
2014	LNC	A+	22	7	4	0	15	10	55¹	45	6	3.7	11.7	72	44%	.243	1.23	3.74	3.96	2.48	18.6	1.9	79	
2015	CCH	AA	23	4	0	0	9	5	33	20	2	3.5	12.3	45	35%	.246	1.00	1.91	2.63	2.36	9.7	1.0	77	
2015	HOU	MLB	23	1	1	0	19	7	55²	50	5	3.4	9.4	58	31%	.310	1.28	4.37	3.43	4.87	0.6	0.1	107	97.5
2016	PHI	MLB	24	8	6	0	24	24	131	129	21	3.1	10.4	152	37%	.325	1.33	4.12	4.00	3.95	20.5	2.1	91	96.8
2017	PHI	MLB	25	7	9	0	24	24	136	118	18	3.0	10.3	156	53%	.293	1.19	3.86	3.70	4.11	16.3	1.7	94	
2018	PHI	MLB	26	11	10	0	30	30	190²	138	23	3.4	11.2	238	53%	.292	1.10	3.38	3.62	3.94	30.6	3.2	88	

Breakout: 28%   Improve: 59%   Collapse: 16%   Attrition: 16%   MLB: 91%   *Comparables: Carlos Marmol, Edinson Volquez, Brandon Beachy*

Recency bias is definitely a thing in baseball analysis, but never is it more of a thing than it is in April. Four months of waiting for spring training combined with a month of meaningless March contests have a way of twisting even the sharpest baseball minds into overemphasizing the results of a tiny handful of games. This blind spot was on full display on April 14, 2016, when Velasquez struck out 16 Padres in a complete game shutout at Citizens Bank Park. Combined with Ken Giles' early struggles and loss of the closer's job in Houston, many in Philadelphia concluded that trading too much for relief pitching is bad and that the Phillies Won The Trade®. Six months later, Velasquez came down to earth, Giles was once again dominant in the ninth for the Astros and Aroldis Chapman and Andrew Miller were facing off in the World Series. This isn't to say that the Phillies did the wrong thing by flipping Giles for Velasquez and a boatload of prospects, but rather that the concept behind the trade was not bad for either team. Both squads got what they wanted, but in the Phillies case it's more likely that they received a solid no. 3 starter with some long-term health risk than a future ace in the making.

LINEOUTS

Hitters

NAME	POS	TEAM	LVL	AGE	PA	R	2B	3B	HR	RBI	BB	K	SB	CS	AVG/OBP/SLG	TAv	VORP	BABIP	BRR	FRAA	WARP
Emmanuel Burriss	2B	LEH	AAA	31	187	21	6	1	0	13	9	25	6	1	.263/.296/.309	.231	0.2	.303	-0.2	2B(25): 2.7 • SS(14): -1.5	0.1
	2B	PHI	MLB	31	50	3	1	1	0	0	2	10	1	0	.111/.184/.178	.135	-4.0	.143	1.1	2B(5): -0.6 • LF(3): -0.8	-0.5
Taylor Featherston	INF	PHI	MLB	26	28	2	1	0	0	1	2	11	2	0	.115/.179/.154	.122	-3.1	.200	0.1	2B(4): -0.7	-0.4
	INF	LEH	AAA	26	439	56	23	4	13	37	25	98	6	3	.254/.311/.428	.271	21.6	.304	3.1	3B(50): -0.0 • 2B(28): 0.8	2.4
Andrew Pullin	OF	CLR	A+	22	153	21	11	2	4	19	5	19	0	0	.293/.320/.476	.291	8.3	.315	0.3	LF(24): -0.6 • RF(7): -0.9	0.7
	OF	REA	AA	22	206	32	10	0	10	32	13	36	0	0	.346/.393/.559	.319	14.5	.382	-1.8	LF(35): -2.1 • RF(11): 1.9	1.6
Darnell Sweeney	2B	LEH	AAA	25	447	48	17	5	6	35	38	100	12	11	.233/.299/.345	.234	1.5	.293	0.9	2B(54): 5.0 • 3B(40): -3.1	0.2
Joshua Tobias	2B	LWD	A	23	415	49	24	3	7	55	31	59	6	4	.304/.375/.444	.319	32.1	.343	-1.9	2B(80): 8.9 • LF(5): -1.4	4.3
	2B	CLR	A+	23	146	21	7	0	2	14	12	30	4	1	.254/.324/.357	.274	5.1	.306	-0.7	2B(29): 1.1 • LF(2): -0.3	0.6
Carlos Tocci	OF	CLR	A+	20	556	66	26	2	3	50	34	76	13	6	.284/.331/.362	.263	20.6	.324	1.7	CF(122): -3.2 • RF(4): -0.2	1.8
Jesmuel Valentin	2B	REA	AA	22	388	59	17	5	5	38	38	56	4	3	.276/.346/.399	.270	15.4	.313	0.9	2B(80): -5.7 • SS(9): -1.5	0.9
	2B	LEH	AAA	22	123	17	2	0	4	14	12	24	0	1	.248/.325/.381	.253	3.4	.286	1.0	2B(36): 2.3	0.6

Emmanuel Burriss had a .361 OPS in his three and a half months on the Phillies roster, making him the fourth-best hitting pitcher on his own team. ❖ It was more of the same in 2016 for **Taylor Featherston**: flashes of power in the minors, but completely over-matched in the majors. He might be out of chances. ❖ Ignore the raw numbers, **Jhailyn Ortiz** is an athletic teenager with massive power potential who could be a fixture in the heart of the Phillies order by the time you realize your kids don't call you as much as they used to. ❖ **Andrew Pullin** missed a month of the season due to a personal matter, then made up for lost time with the best OPS of his career. His smallish size and pull-heavy approach may not work in the majors. ❖ **Darnell Sweeney** was a sleeper for playing time in Philadelphia entering the 2016 season, but he spent the entire year at Triple-A before being reacquired by the Dodgers in November. ❖ **Joshua Tobias** is one of those weird middle infield tweeners whose bat could play at second but probably doesn't have the defensive chops to stay on the grass. ❖ **Carlos Tocci** has many promising aspects to his game, but has spent enough time at each level of full-season ball to have sandwiches named after him at local Lakewood and Clearwater restaurants. ❖ It feels like **Jesmuel Valentin** has been a fringy prospect for longer than his dad was a major leaguer. The Phillies must really value bloodlines; they added Valentin to their 40-man in November.

Pitchers

NAME	TEAM	LVL	AGE	W	L	SV	G	GS	IP	H	HR	BB/9	K/9	K	GB%	BABIP	WHIP	ERA	FIP	DRA	VORP	WARP	cFIP	MPH
Andrew Anderson	LWD	A	22	1	3	0	7	7	37¹	29	3	2.9	9.9	41	46%	.286	1.10	3.38	3.29	2.92	8.7	1.0	91	
	CLR	A+	22	2	1	0	8	8	32²	26	0	2.8	10.2	37	39%	.313	1.10	1.93	2.00	2.33	11.4	1.2	84	
Victor Arano	CLR	A+	21	4	1	4	35	0	63	52	4	2.1	10.1	71	38%	.296	1.06	2.29	2.59	1.97	21.8	2.2	78	
	REA	AA	21	1	1	1	11	0	16²	11	2	2.2	13.0	24	47%	.250	0.90	2.16	2.76	1.63	5.7	0.6	71	
David Buchanan	LEH	AAA	27	10	9	0	27	26	167¹	163	15	2.2	5.1	95	48%	.277	1.21	3.98	3.95	6.99	-30.8	-3.2	112	
Elniery Garcia	CLR	A+	21	12	4	0	20	19	117²	94	8	2.8	7.0	91	46%	.254	1.10	2.68	3.58	4.57	11.7	1.2	103	
Luis Garcia	LEH	AAA	29	6	3	13	48	0	54²	38	3	4.0	8.7	53	63%	.261	1.13	2.14	3.53	4.39	3.5	0.4	93	
	PHI	MLB	29	1	1	0	17	0	15¹	21	2	4.7	8.2	14	55%	.373	1.89	6.46	4.82	4.33	1.1	0.1	101	99.0
Severino Gonzalez	REA	AA	23	2	0	0	6	0	10²	9	0	1.7	7.6	9	39%	.273	1.03	1.69	2.23	3.66	1.3	0.1	95	
	LEH	AAA	23	0	1	0	15	1	35¹	37	3	1.5	6.6	26	49%	.301	1.22	3.31	3.48	3.32	6.6	0.7	98	
	PHI	MLB	23	1	2	0	27	0	35¹	40	4	1.8	8.7	34	27%	.343	1.33	5.60	3.41	5.35	-1.5	-0.2	111	95.9
Dalier Hinojosa	PHI	MLB	30	0	1	0	10	0	11	10	1	2.5	6.5	8	52%	.281	1.18	3.27	3.73	4.39	0.7	0.1	107	95.7
	LEH	AAA	30	1	3	1	22	0	24¹	25	2	5.2	8.5	23	34%	.333	1.60	2.96	4.07	5.79	-2.2	-0.2	114	
Phil Klein	TEX	MLB	27	0	1	0	8	0	8²	8	2	2.1	12.5	12	24%	.316	1.15	5.19	4.03	4.58	0.5	0.1	107	94.2
	ROU	AAA	27	0	0	0	8	1	12²	14	2	3.6	8.5	12	42%	.316	1.50	4.26	5.06	3.66	2.2	0.2	100	
	LEH	AAA	27	5	1	0	14	10	65¹	44	4	1.8	10.5	76	42%	.261	0.87	1.52	2.46	1.45	27.6	2.8	69	
	PHI	MLB	27	0	0	0	4	2	10²	15	0	5.9	5.9	7	39%	.417	2.06	8.44	4.12	4.87	0.3	0.0	108	94.1
Michael Mariot	LEH	AAA	27	1	2	1	26	0	32¹	16	3	3.6	6.7	24	43%	.160	0.90	2.23	4.19	4.77	0.7	0.1	110	
	PHI	MLB	27	1	0	2	25	0	21²	18	5	5.8	9.6	23	31%	.245	1.48	5.82	6.00	4.85	0.3	0.0	114	95.4
Ricardo Pinto	REA	AA	22	7	6	0	27	25	156	150	20	2.9	5.8	101	46%	.268	1.29	4.10	4.86	7.49	-41.9	-4.5	114	
Joely Rodriguez	REA	AA	24	7	0	2	33	0	49	46	3	2.9	7.5	41	63%	.312	1.27	2.57	3.46	3.27	8.0	0.9	88	
	LEH	AAA	24	0	0	0	13	0	19¹	16	0	2.8	8.4	18	42%	.302	1.14	2.79	2.24	4.30	1.4	0.1	96	
	PHI	MLB	24	0	0	0	12	0	9²	8	0	3.7	6.5	7	59%	.296	1.24	2.79	3.29	4.98	0.0	0.0	101	98.0
David Rollins	TAC	AAA	26	5	0	2	37	0	45¹	39	4	1.2	6.4	32	42%	.265	0.99	3.77	3.85	3.40	7.9	0.8	101	
	SEA	MLB	26	1	0	0	11	0	9¹	12	2	6.8	5.8	6	44%	.312	2.04	7.71	6.86	6.40	-1.5	-0.2	122	94.3
James Russell	PHI	MLB	30	0	0	0	7	0	4¹	9	2	10.4	8.3	4	33%	.438	3.23	18.69	10.80	6.22	-0.6	-0.1	124	91.9
	LEH	AAA	30	3	5	0	29	13	79²	88	11	2.1	5.5	49	34%	.288	1.34	4.29	4.52	6.87	-14.3	-1.5	122	

Drew Anderson impressed in limited innings coming off Tommy John surgery, with his fastball suddenly flashing in the mid-90s. With improved command and consistency, he could be a mid-rotation starter in a few years. ❖ In his first full season as a reliever, **Victor Arano** impressed, amping his fastball up into the mid-90s and continuing to display good control. ❖ After spending parts of two seasons in the Phillies' rotation, **David Buchanan** spent all of 2016 as the "oh man, *he's* starting this game" guy at Lehigh Valley. ❖ **Elniery Garcia** added a little velocity to his three-pitch arsenal, but his diminutive stature may limit him to a bullpen role in the long term. ❖ **Luis Garcia** sits in the high-90s and touches 100. Despite that, he hasn't solidified a bullpen spot for the Phillies in four years of opportunities, which tells you all you need to know about the rest. ❖ The idea of using **Severino Gonzalez** as a starter was a short-lived one, and while he did pick up some additional velocity out of the bullpen, he didn't pick up any additional effectiveness. ❖ **Matt Harrison** didn't pitch at all for the Phillies last year and has logged just 44 innings in the majors since signing a five-year contract extension in 2013 with the Rangers to avoid arbitration. His career may be over. ❖ **Dalier Hinojosa** started the season as a closer candidate for the Phillies, which said more about the sad state of the team's bullpen in April than it did about Hinojosa's ability. ❖ Nabbed on waivers from Texas in June, **Phil Klein** has been used as a starter throughout most of his career, but is better suited to relief work in the long run. ❖ **Michael Mariot** and his fringe major league stuff slipped quietly into the Philadelphia bullpen without anyone noticing last season, and will likely slip out with the same aplomb. ❖ His potential earned **Ricardo Pinto** a trip to the Futures Game, but his breaking ball and command are still raw. Without a working curve, his future is likely in the bullpen. ❖ **Joely Rodriguez** transitioned to the bullpen and quickly made his way to the majors. This is the Philadelphia chapter of Teach Your Kids How To Throw Left-Handed International reminding you to teach your kids how to throw left-handed. ❖ **David Rollins** was drafted four times before it finally stuck, and each time a sliver of his effectiveness split off—left behind in Los Angeles, Seattle (twice) and Toronto like horcruxes. ❖ Formerly a lefty specialist for the Cubs, **James Russell** was stretched out in the minors in the hopes of making him an innings-eating starting pitcher. It went about as well as you'd imagine.

PITTSBURGH PIRATES

Essay by Russell A. Carleton

Player comments by Ben Carsley and BP staff

And then, it fell apart.

The Pirates weren't supposed to do *that*. This was a team that won 98 games in 2015 and returned much of the same core. And it wasn't like they had been a band of geriatric warriors the year before. In theory, this was a team that should have at least challenged for a playoff spot. But, 78 wins?

For a while, the Pirates were the new A's. They hired someone from BP to run their stats department before it was cool (Dan Fox, Director of Baseball Informatics). They hired a former Indians assistant general manager before it was cool (Neal Huntington). They were even the subject of a behind-the-scenes book that focused on their data gathering and analyzing chops (Travis Sawkchik's excellent *Big Data Baseball*).

They played in a small market with a beautiful ballpark in a division where they had to compete against the mighty Cubs and Cardinals, and yet they still managed to have a run of excellence. They had Andrew McCutchen, who was described in last year's Annual as "the perfect franchise player." How does a team like that returning the core from a 98-win season have a 20-game fall in the standings?

First off, it's worth pointing out that while the Pirates won 98 actual games in 2015, we know that a team's overall quality is typically better assessed by their run differential and Pythagorean record. In 2015, the Pirates had a Pythagorean record much more aligned with a 93-win team. Obviously that's nothing to be ashamed of, but the Pirates are a case study in how fragile it all can be, and it started with A.J. Burnett's retirement the day after the 2015 season ended.

Burnett had admirably filled a very necessary role by reliably providing around 180 non-embarrassing innings. He was no longer a star, but in his final year he made a mere $8.5 million as an oft-overlooked cog in the machine. If only Burnett could have stayed around forever. J.A. Happ, who pitched brilliantly for the Pirates in 2015 following a midseason trade, hit the open market and signed a three-year, $36 million contract with the Blue Jays rather than returning to the Pirates as Burnett's quasi-replacement. He had a career year in Toronto, receiving Cy Young votes for the first time at age 33.

PIRATES PROSPECTUS
2016 W-L: 78-83, 3RD IN NL CENTRAL

Pythag	.482	18th	DER	.693	25th
RS/G	4.5	13th	B-Age	28.9	22nd
RA/G	4.68	22nd	P-Age	28.4	16th
TAv	.265	9th	Salary	$99.9M	20th
BRR	-3.15	21st	M$/MW	$2.9M	23rd
TAv-P	.276	25th	DL Days	552	4th
FIP	4.34	19th	$ on DL	4%	1st

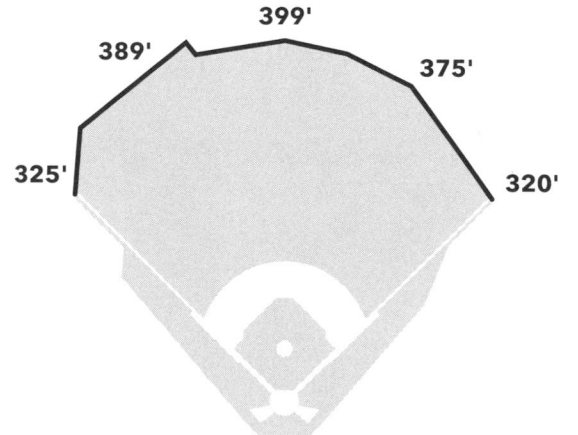

Outfield wall profile: **6'** to **21'**

Three-Year Park Factors

Runs	Runs/RH	Runs/LH	HR/RH	HR/LH
97	95	99	85	100

Top Hitter WARP	3.8	Starling Marte
Top Pitcher WARP	2.5	Juan Nicasio
Top Prospect		Austin Meadows

2016 Hit List Ranking

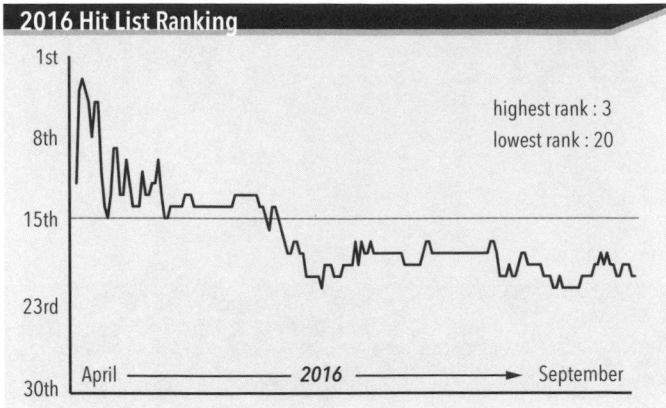

highest rank : 3
lowest rank : 20

April — 2016 → September

Committed Payroll (in millions)

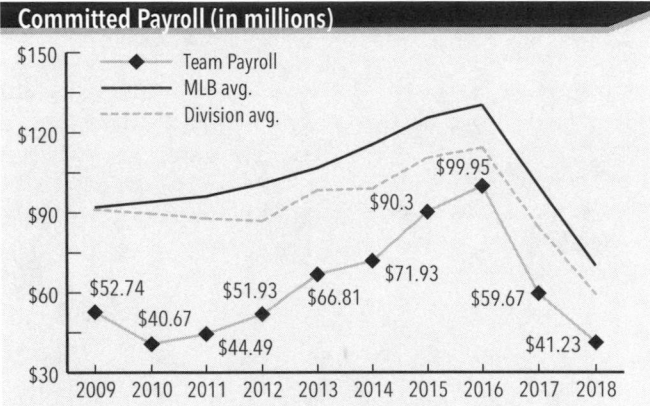

- ◆ Team Payroll
- — MLB avg.
- --- Division avg.

$99.95
$90.3
$52.74
$40.67
$51.93
$44.49
$66.81
$71.93
$59.67
$41.23

2009 2010 2011 2012 2013 2014 2015 2016 2017 2018

Farm System Ranking

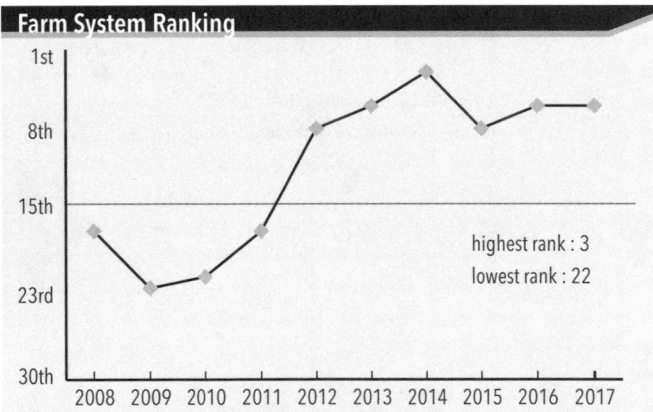

highest rank : 3
lowest rank : 22

2008 2009 2010 2011 2012 2013 2014 2015 2016 2017

Personnel

President:
Frank Coonelly

EVP, General Manager:
Neal Huntington

Assistant General Manager:
Kevan Graves

Assistant General Manager:
Greg Smith

Assistant General Manager:
Kyle Stark

Manager:
Clint Hurdle

BP Alumni:
Dan Fox
Grant Jones
Stuart Wallace

Signing Happ is the sort of move that the Blue Jays and their $140 million payroll could make much more easily than the Pirates and their $100 million payroll. And in trying to replace Burnett/Happ, the Pirates got creative. Neil Walker, another necessary cog player who was entering the last year of his contract, got dealt to the Mets for left-hander Jon Niese. It wasn't a bad idea. Niese wasn't a star, but his $9 million salary was reasonable and he'd thrown at least 175 innings in three of the four previous seasons with middle-of-the-road results.

The trade was enabled by the idea that the Pirates could install longtime super-utility man Josh Harrison into the everyday second base role. While Walker was boringly consistent, Harrison was more of a gamble. He'd had an All-Star season in his first foray into regular playing time in 2014, but was merely average in 2015. Walker was a slightly-above-average player, so to hold serve the Pirates only needed Harrison to be somewhere between the 2014 and 2015 versions.

David Freese was brought aboard to fill the Harrison role of being the team's ninth position player, manning the corner infield spots and demanding only $3 million in return. And while the Pirates might miss Harrison's ability to play anywhere, Sean Rodriguez was already on the roster as a play-everywhere bench option. In theory, the gambit to replace Burnett was a success. The Pirates traded Walker's salary, replaced Burnett's innings, used some on-hand surplus in the form of Harrison to patch the hole left by Walker and added Freese to patch the hole left by Harrison.

It was entirely reasonable to believe that they would not be worse for the wear in 2016. The only other major change that the Pirates made was a *Moneyball*-era throwback move, saving a bit of cash by signing OBP darling and former catcher Scott Hatt … sorry, John Jaso to replace Pedro Alvarez at first base. When you're a low-payroll team, it sometimes takes four paragraphs to replace one retiring starting pitcher.

Everyone knew the Cubs were going to be very good, but there was honest hope in Pittsburgh for another wonderful summer at the prettiest park in MLB. On paper, the Pirates had done everything right. Sure, there was risk, but there's risk in everything. It didn't work out. Niese was bad enough that the Pirates put a "return to sender" label on him and shipped him back to the Mets. Francisco Liriano's improved control disappeared and he was dealt to the Blue Jays. Gerrit Cole got hurt. Jeff Locke pitched a team-high 127.1 innings. Stud closer Mark Melancon was swapped for long-term help before leaving as a free agent.

Harrison was even worse than the 2015 version. Francisco Cervelli, signed to an extension largely for his magical pitch-framing skills, caught 33 fewer games. According to BP's framing metrics Cervelli netted the Pirates nearly two additional wins by buying extra strikes for his pitchers in 2015 and the step down from elite to average in 2016 made an outsized difference. The Pirates bled away little bits of value here and there. Several of their dice rolls came up snake eyes. It adds up.

Oh, and McCutchen went from being a bona fide superstar to being … well, it would be wrong to call his performance flat-out *bad*. His season was like one of those days when you never quite wake all the way up. Before the season, Pirates fans were starting to get nervous because the former MVP was signed for "only" another three years. He'd recorded scarily consistent on-base percentages from 2012-2015 (.400, .404, .410, .401), but fell 75 points from his usual mark and continued to slip defensively. Even the debris from the Great McCutchen Collpase of 2016 was still an above-average player, but what happened?

The most notable discovery from a deeper dive into McCutchen's performance is that he suddenly started hitting the ball up, and not in a good way. His pop-up rate was more than double his 2015 rate. Evidence from the StatCast system shows that his exit velocity was fairly consistent from 2015 to 2016, but his launch angles were much more concentrated in excess of 35 degrees. That's a bit of a physics problem. Even if you hit with the same force, a ball launched at a higher angle is going to use more of that force to go up rather than far. A ball that goes up a long way and travels only 120 feet will be caught by the shortstop.

The 2016 Pirates are a lesson in an old maxim. "Sometimes you do everything right and it doesn't work." The decisions that they made were all tactically defensible, maybe even brilliant. They somehow assembled a team of guys who were all quietly above average and produced value in ways that weren't always fully appreciated, but they worked. The thing about the 2017 Pirates is that while some talent from the (dare I say it?) glory days has gone away, there's more in the pipeline led by Jameson Taillon, Tyler Glasnow and Austin Meadows.

Every magician eventually runs out of rabbits. The easiest seduction in baseball is to believe that a guy who was good two years ago is still every bit as good, even if he just had a bad year. And that a whole bunch of guys who were good two years ago are still just as good, even if they collectively had a bad year. The problem with projecting the Pirates isn't that they're necessarily doomed, but that a "good season" may no longer mean 90-plus victories. It's really hard to get a grasp on teams that have these sorts of drastic drop-offs, but if there's something that you need to steel yourself against in the steel city, it's the possibility that the Pirates are headed for an era of being "pretty good." ■

—Russell A. Carleton is an author
of Baseball Prospectus

HITTERS

Josh Bell   1B

Born: 8/14/92   Age: 24   Bats: B   Throws: R   Height: 6'2"   Weight: 240   Entered Pro Ball: Round 2, 2011 Draft (#61 overall)

YEAR	TEAM	LVL	AGE	PA	R	2B	3B	HR	RBI	BB	K	SB	CS	AVG/OBP/SLG	TAv	VORP	BABIP	BRR	FRAA	WARP
2014	BRD	A+	21	363	45	20	4	9	53	25	43	5	4	.335/.384/.502	.309	23.6	.364	-1.8	RF(62): -8.2	1.5
2014	ALT	AA	21	102	13	2	0	0	7	8	12	4	1	.287/.343/.309	.248	0.7	.329	0.3	RF(19): 3.1	0.4
2015	ALT	AA	22	427	47	17	6	5	60	44	50	7	4	.307/.376/.427	.299	18.9	.335	-2.1	1B(84): -7.5	1.2
2015	IND	AAA	22	145	20	7	3	2	18	21	15	2	0	.347/.441/.504	.325	11.2	.377	-0.1	1B(32): -3.2	0.8
2016	IND	AAA	23	484	57	23	4	14	60	57	74	3	7	.295/.382/.468	.306	24.1	.328	-4.0	1B(96): -3.3 • RF(4): 1.2	2.3
2016	PIT	MLB	23	152	18	8	0	3	19	21	19	0	1	.273/.368/.406	.286	6.4	.294	0.2	1B(23): -0.3 • RF(16): -2.3	0.4
2017	PIT	MLB	24	541	69	24	4	15	59	54	88	3	3	.280/.353/.440	.277	18.2	.313	-1.0	1B -3	1.3
2018	PIT	MLB	25	566	76	26	4	18	72	57	94	3	3	.285/.360/.460	.292	24.7	.316	-0.9	1B -3	2.3

Breakout: 3%   Improve: 29%   Collapse: 16%   Attrition: 21%   MLB: 66%   *Comparables: Conor Jackson, Chris Carter, Ji-Man Choi*

If you want Bell to be a prototypical first baseman, you're always going to be disappointed. Bell doesn't figure to be a plus-plus power threat despite his big frame. He'll hit some dingers, no doubt, but his swing just isn't geared to mash, especially from the right side. If you stop focusing on what Bell can't do and start appreciating what he's good at—namely getting on base—you'll live a much fuller and happier life. In his first stint in the majors, Bell posted a better TAv than Jose Abreu, Hanley Ramirez and Chris Davis. You could call him the Bell of the ball, because he walked more than he struck out, and looked dominant versus lefties. He's still a work in progress, but you weren't a finished product when you were 23, either. Don't just focus on the negatives when you could be giving Bell a ringing endorsement.

Francisco Cervelli   C

Born: 3/6/86   Age: 31   Bats: R   Throws: R   Height: 6'1"   Weight: 210   Entered Pro Ball: International Free Agent, 2003

YEAR	TEAM	LVL	AGE	PA	R	2B	3B	HR	RBI	BB	K	SB	CS	AVG/OBP/SLG	TAv	VORP	BABIP	BRR	FRAA	WARP
2014	TRN	AA	28	20	2	0	0	0	0	4	4	0	0	.133/.350/.133	.198	-0.7	.182	0.1	C(2): 0.0, 1B(1): -0.1	-0.1
2014	NYA	MLB	28	162	18	11	1	2	13	11	41	1	0	.301/.370/.432	.285	7.9	.408	-2.0	C(42): 6.1, 1B(5): -0.0	1.5
2015	PIT	MLB	29	510	56	17	5	7	43	46	94	1	1	.295/.370/.401	.281	32.2	.359	0.0	C(128): 20.5	5.7
2016	PIT	MLB	30	393	42	14	1	1	33	56	72	6	2	.264/.377/.322	.265	16.6	.329	-2.9	C(95): 10.3, 1B(2): -0.1	2.8
2017	PIT	MLB	31	525	54	20	3	6	46	54	103	4	2	.259/.347/.359	.255	20.6	.318	-0.5	C 16	3.8
2018	PIT	MLB	32	472	54	17	2	6	42	47	98	2	1	.250/.339/.347	.255	13.2	.310	-1.8	C 13	2.8

Breakout: 3%   Improve: 35%   Collapse: 12%   Attrition: 22%   MLB: 88%   *Comparables: Carlos Ruiz, Jose Lobaton, Matt Treanor*

A year-and-a-half after letting Russell Martin depart for colder pastures, the Pirates were determined to avoid suffering a similar fate with Cervelli. They signed the former Yankee to a three-year, $31 million extension, keeping him away from a free agent market in which he would've been the second- or third-most attractive backstop. That's the good news. The bad news is Cervelli was banged up for much of 2016 and his production slipped when he was healthy enough to play. A broken hamate bone forced Cervelli to miss five weeks, and he injured his foot and thumb at various points after returning. Our defensive metrics still love Cervelli, and while he lost some batting average and power from a year ago he raised his OBP. Catchers aren't generally good bets to stay on the field more often as they get older, but if he enjoys better luck than a Spinal Tap drummer next season Cervelli should be able to log more time.

YEAR	TEAM	P. COUNT	FRM RUNS	BLK RUNS	THRW RUNS	TOT RUNS
2014	NYA	5573	6.3	1.0	-0.1	7.1
2014	SWB	141	0.1	0.0	0.0	0.0
2014	TRN	265	0.1	0.0	0.0	0.1
2015	PIT	17330	19.0	-1.3	-2.6	15.1
2016	PIT	13232	11.0	-2.1	-2.0	6.9
2017	PIT	18727	17.5	-2.3	-2.2	13.0
2018	PIT	16835	14.2	-2.3	-2.1	9.8

Will Craig   3B

Born: 11/16/94 Age: 22   Bats: R   Throws: R   Height: 6'3"   Weight: 212   Entered Pro Ball: Round 1, 2016 Draft (#22 overall)

YEAR	TEAM	LVL	AGE	PA	R	2B	3B	HR	RBI	BB	K	SB	CS	AVG/OBP/SLG	TAv	VORP	BABIP	BRR	FRAA	WARP
2016	WEV	A-	21	274	28	12	0	2	23	41	37	2	0	.280/.412/.362	.319	18.8	.322	-1.9	3B(40): -0.7	1.9
2017	PIT	MLB	22	250	24	9	1	5	26	22	62	0	0	.218/.299/.339	.220	-2.8	.273	-0.3	3B -0	-0.3
2018	PIT	MLB	23	263	30	10	1	6	27	24	63	0	0	.225/.308/.359	.243	0.8	.278	-0.5	3B 0	0.1

Breakout: 3%   Improve: 14%   Collapse: 1%   Attrition: 17%   MLB: 19%   *Comparables: Rio Ruiz, Zelous Wheeler, Jeimer Candelario*

Will Craig add much-needed depth to a top-heavy Pirates farm system, or
Will Craig look like an overdraft at 22nd overall a few years down the line?
Will Craig's transition from Wake Forest to to the minors be smooth, or
Will Craig find himself overmatched due to his non-elite bat speed?
Will Craig prove those who say he can't stay at third base wrong, or
Will Craig's bat make moving to first base a non-issue anyway?
Will Craig bring back his glorious, terrifying, free-flowing mullet, or
Will Craig be content to look like a C.J. Cron/John Lackey lovechild?
Will Craig jokes at Baseball Prospectus ever be funny, or
Will Craig just make our Craig jokes that much worse?

Elias Diaz   C

Born: 11/17/90 Age: 26   Bats: R   Throws: R   Height: 6'0"   Weight: 210   Entered Pro Ball: International Free Agent, 2008

YEAR	TEAM	LVL	AGE	PA	R	2B	3B	HR	RBI	BB	K	SB	CS	AVG/OBP/SLG	TAv	VORP	BABIP	BRR	FRAA	WARP
2014	ALT	AA	23	367	41	20	0	6	54	30	51	3	2	.328/.378/.445	.293	29.2	.365	0.8	C(88): 11.8 • 1B(1): 1.1	4.5
2014	IND	AAA	23	37	4	1	0	0	3	6	6	0	1	.152/.243/.182	.172	-1.7	.185	0.2	C(9): 0.1	-0.2
2015	IND	AAA	24	363	33	16	4	4	47	29	47	1	4	.271/.330/.382	.253	8.7	.301	-1.0	C(60): 2.2	1.1
2015	PIT	MLB	24	2	0	0	0	0	0	0	1	0	0	.000/.000/.000	-.003	-0.5	.000	0.0		0.0
2016	BRD	A+	25	28	6	0	0	1	5	4	2	0	1	.391/.464/.522	.331	3.5	.381	0.2	C(6): -0.3	0.3
2016	PIT	MLB	25	4	0	0	0	0	1	0	1	0	0	.000/.000/.000	.007	-0.9	.000	0.0	C(1): 0.1	-0.1
2016	IND	AAA	25	97	4	3	0	0	10	3	17	1	0	.266/.289/.298	.216	-1.1	.325	-1.0	C(25): -2.3	-0.3
2017	PIT	MLB	26	31	3	1	0	1	3	2	6	0	0	.259/.310/.385	.244	0.9	.299	-0.1	C -0	0.0
2018	PIT	MLB	27	184	21	8	1	4	20	12	35	0	0	.251/.305/.381	.248	4.1	.289	-0.4	C -3	0.1

Breakout: 4%   Improve: 7%   Collapse: 13%   Attrition: 16%   MLB: 37%   *Comparables: Jason Jaramillo, Steve Clevenger, Caleb Joseph*

Diaz doesn't show up on top prospect lists, but he's been viewed as a potential high-quality backup for a few seasons. The Pirates certainly could've used him as such in 2016, but Elias didn't play in a game until July 4 after undergoing elbow debridement surgery in May. Diaz was then shut down for good after suffering a leg infection in September, appearing in just one game for Pittsburgh. Diaz's future is still about as bright as a future can be for a probable backup, but you can't be the backup if you need a backup yourself.

YEAR	TEAM	P. COUNT	FRM RUNS	BLK RUNS	THRW RUNS	TOT RUNS
2014	ALT	11824	9.0	-0.1	1.4	10.3
2014	IND	1322	0.4	0.0	-0.1	0.2
2015	IND	8398	2.0	0.6	0.0	2.6
2016	PIT	141	0.0	0.0	0.0	0.0
2017	PIT	1133	-0.4	0.0	0.0	-0.5
2018	PIT	6738	-2.8	0.0	-0.1	-2.9

Adam Frazier   SS

Born: 12/14/91 Age: 25   Bats: L   Throws: R   Height: 5'10"   Weight: 180   Entered Pro Ball: Round 6, 2013 Draft (#179 overall)

YEAR	TEAM	LVL	AGE	PA	R	2B	3B	HR	RBI	BB	K	SB	CS	AVG/OBP/SLG	TAv	VORP	BABIP	BRR	FRAA	WARP
2014	BRD	A+	22	540	62	21	2	1	42	37	61	14	8	.252/.307/.309	.237	12.3	.285	3.5	SS(117): 3.4	1.6
2015	ALT	AA	23	423	59	21	4	2	30	34	42	11	7	.324/.384/.416	.301	34.4	.360	2.3	SS(58): 0.1 • CF(29): -0.7	3.6
2016	IND	AAA	24	299	34	16	4	0	22	29	27	17	15	.333/.401/.425	.326	26.5	.369	-1.3	LF(44): 2.1 • CF(17): -3.3	2.6
2016	PIT	MLB	24	160	21	8	1	2	11	12	26	4	1	.301/.356/.411	.290	6.4	.353	-2.3	LF(20): -0.6 • 2B(12): -0.7	0.6
2017	PIT	MLB	25	199	24	9	1	3	17	15	30	6	4	.276/.328/.387	.254	5.4	.310	-0.3	RF -0 • 2B 0	0.5
2018	PIT	MLB	26	391	45	18	3	7	41	29	63	10	7	.276/.334/.402	.264	12.1	.310	0.0	RF 0 • 2B 0	1.4

Breakout: 7%   Improve: 20%   Collapse: 3%   Attrition: 20%   MLB: 40%   *Comparables: Erik Komatsu, Jon Jay, L.J. Hoes*

Tim Tebow picks up a bat and the economy booms in Bristol. Byron Buxton steals a base and we announce that he's arrived. Pat Venditte throws OK with two hands and earns a cult following. Yet Frazier just keeps hitting and hitting and hitting, and no one pays him any mind. Frazier led the NCAA in hits as a junior at Mississippi State back in 2013, yet fell to the sixth round. In 1,520 minor-league plate appearances, Frazier hit .299/.363/.370, but odds are you'd never heard of him until he was called up this June, or maybe even until now. Frazier has limitations; he's got less power than a freshman in a fraternity, and he went just 17-for-32 in steal attempts in Indianapolis. But he can play a decent shortstop, run a bit and has a hit tool you can believe in. Here's hoping the Pirates take notice.

David Freese 3B

Born: 4/28/83   Age: 34   Bats: R   Throws: R   Height: 6'2"   Weight: 225   Entered Pro Ball: Round 9, 2006 Draft (#273 overall)

YEAR	TEAM	LVL	AGE	PA	R	2B	3B	HR	RBI	BB	K	SB	CS	AVG/OBP/SLG	TAv	VORP	BABIP	BRR	FRAA	WARP
2014	ANA	MLB	31	511	53	25	1	10	55	38	124	1	3	.260/.321/.383	.269	18.2	.330	-0.4	3B(122): -8.5	1.1
2015	SLC	AAA	32	25	2	0	0	1	6	3	4	0	0	.286/.400/.429	.284	0.8	.313	-0.3	3B(3): -0.2	0.1
2015	ANA	MLB	32	470	53	27	0	14	56	31	107	1	1	.257/.323/.420	.268	17.8	.310	0.3	3B(113): 0.4	2.0
2016	PIT	MLB	33	492	63	23	0	13	55	45	142	0	0	.270/.352/.412	.270	16.6	.372	-0.4	3B(78): 0.3 • 1B(58): 2.9	2.0
2017	*PIT*	*MLB*	*34*	*410*	*43*	*19*	*1*	*10*	*47*	*36*	*96*	*1*	*1*	*.259/.334/.400*	*.260*	*11.5*	*.322*	*-1.1*	*3B -1 • 1B 2*	*0.9*
2018	*PIT*	*MLB*	*35*	*376*	*46*	*17*	*1*	*9*	*41*	*34*	*92*	*0*	*0*	*.253/.331/.391*	*.265*	*9.6*	*.320*	*0.0*	*3B -1 • 1B 2*	*1.1*

Breakout: 1%   Improve: 38%   Collapse: 13%   Attrition: 13%   MLB: 90%   *Comparables: Casey Blake, Ty Wigginton, Melvin Mora*

It was strange that it took Freese until March 11 to sign last year. It was even stranger that he netted just $3 million after a very solid 2015 with the Angels; the last time a Mr. Freese got this raw a deal, Uma Thurman told Arnold Schwarzenegger that George Clooney killed his wife. Freese walked and struck out more than usual last season, but all in all he was the same slightly-above-average hitter and slightly-above-average defender we've come to know. The former World Series hero was especially potent against lefties, hitting .337/.419/.543 in 105 PA. The Pirates rewarded Freese by locking him up through at least 2018 for $10.5 million.

Willy Garcia   OF

Born: 9/4/92   Age: 24   Bats: R   Throws: R   Height: 6'2"   Weight: 215   Entered Pro Ball: International Free Agent, 2010

YEAR	TEAM	LVL	AGE	PA	R	2B	3B	HR	RBI	BB	K	SB	CS	AVG/OBP/SLG	TAv	VORP	BABIP	BRR	FRAA	WARP
2014	ALT	AA	21	474	59	27	5	18	63	24	145	8	4	.271/.311/.478	.277	18.2	.361	1.2	RF(103): -1.3 • LF(19): 2.7	2.0
2015	ALT	AA	22	224	26	7	2	5	29	11	47	3	2	.314/.353/.441	.280	7.1	.381	-2.2	LF(38): 7.1 • CF(11): -0.2	1.5
2015	IND	AAA	22	291	36	11	4	10	38	12	76	1	4	.246/.285/.424	.251	-0.1	.305	-3.0	RF(47): 3.3 • CF(13): 1.8	0.8
2016	IND	AAA	23	499	53	30	4	6	43	31	131	5	9	.245/.293/.366	.244	0.8	.326	0.1	RF(124): -1.1 • CF(3): -0.5	0.4
2017	*PIT*	*MLB*	*24*	*67*	*7*	*3*	*1*	*2*	*8*	*3*	*20*	*0*	*1*	*.241/.279/.406*	*.239*	*0.2*	*.315*	*-0.1*	*RF -0*	*-0.1*
2018	*PIT*	*MLB*	*25*	*282*	*33*	*13*	*2*	*10*	*36*	*14*	*83*	*2*	*2*	*.248/.292/.429*	*.258*	*4.9*	*.319*	*-0.4*	*RF -1*	*0.4*

Breakout: 9%   Improve: 16%   Collapse: 4%   Attrition: 21%   MLB: 30%   *Comparables: Bryce Brentz, Zoilo Almonte, Hunter Renfroe*

Garcia is a 24-year-old who's yet to reach the majors, yet in many ways the book is already out on him: great arm, good raw pop and no semblance of plate discipline. Not every prospect needs to project as a future superstar to be worth our time, and there's a potential role player in here somewhere. Still, Garcia needs to sock more dingers or strike out less (or both) if he wants to hold our attention.

Alen Hanson   2B

Born: 10/22/92   Age: 24   Bats: B   Throws: R   Height: 5'11"   Weight: 175   Entered Pro Ball: International Free Agent, 2009

YEAR	TEAM	LVL	AGE	PA	R	2B	3B	HR	RBI	BB	K	SB	CS	AVG/OBP/SLG	TAv	VORP	BABIP	BRR	FRAA	WARP
2014	ALT	AA	21	527	64	21	12	11	58	31	88	25	11	.280/.326/.442	.279	29.7	.321	-0.9	SS(100): -0.0 • 2B(17): 1.5	3.3
2015	IND	AAA	22	529	66	17	12	6	43	37	91	35	12	.263/.313/.387	.254	9.3	.311	-1.6	2B(111): 10.5 • 3B(7): 0.4	2.1
2016	IND	AAA	23	478	58	15	7	8	32	32	78	36	15	.266/.318/.389	.255	12.3	.307	2.2	2B(67): -7.9 • LF(26): -0.2	0.4
2016	PIT	MLB	23	33	5	1	0	0	1	2	5	2	1	.226/.273/.258	.208	-0.4	.269	0.5	2B(8): -0.4	-0.1
2017	*PIT*	*MLB*	*24*	*160*	*20*	*6*	*2*	*4*	*16*	*9*	*32*	*9*	*4*	*.254/.294/.408*	*.243*	*3.7*	*.291*	*0.9*	*2B 0 • LF 0*	*0.4*
2018	*PIT*	*MLB*	*25*	*316*	*36*	*11*	*5*	*8*	*36*	*20*	*64*	*17*	*7*	*.252/.304/.411*	*.251*	*8.2*	*.287*	*2.3*	*2B 1 • LF 0*	*1.0*

Breakout: 4%   Improve: 17%   Collapse: 5%   Attrition: 24%   MLB: 36%   *Comparables: Ryan Brett, Micah Johnson, Taylor Featherston*

Hanson essentially repeated his 2015 performance in Triple-A, which wasn't that good. We talk often about how prospect development isn't linear, but that's usually meant to warn against highs and lows. In Hanson's case, the linear part isn't the problem; it's the development. Hanson's been the same guy for the better part of three seasons. He can hit a little bit, he's got some speed and he can play several non-premium positions. But he's got no MMMBop in his bat, he's not a great baserunner and he's a bit too reluctant to take The Walk (listen, it was a Hanson album in 2007). Add it all together and Hanson looks like a utility player through and through, something the Pirates acknowledged when they started getting him some time in the outfield. That may seem like a disappointing outcome for a former top prospect, but for an international free agent who signed for $90,000 back in 2009, it's really not.

Josh Harrison   3B

Born: 7/8/87   Age: 29   Bats: R   Throws: R   Height: 5'8"   Weight: 190   Entered Pro Ball: Round 6, 2008 Draft (#191 overall)

YEAR	TEAM	LVL	AGE	PA	R	2B	3B	HR	RBI	BB	K	SB	CS	AVG/OBP/SLG	TAv	VORP	BABIP	BRR	FRAA	WARP
2014	PIT	MLB	26	550	77	38	7	13	52	22	81	18	7	.315/.347/.490	.305	37.2	.353	0.4	3B(72): 5.0 • RF(26): 4.7	5.1
2015	IND	AAA	27	20	0	0	0	0	0	1	2	0	0	.053/.100/.053	.113	-2.5	.059	0.0	3B(3): 0.4 • RF(1): -0.5	-0.3
2015	PIT	MLB	27	449	57	29	1	4	28	19	71	10	8	.287/.327/.390	.264	15.7	.336	1.8	3B(72): 2.1 • 2B(37): -0.8	1.9
2016	PIT	MLB	28	522	57	25	7	4	59	18	76	19	4	.283/.311/.388	.254	14.2	.323	3.1	2B(128): 0.2 • RF(1): -0.2	1.5
2017	*PIT*	*MLB*	*29*	*636*	*76*	*36*	*6*	*11*	*58*	*27*	*93*	*19*	*7*	*.279/.314/.419*	*.254*	*21.1*	*.309*	*1.3*	*2B -1*	*1.7*
2018	*PIT*	*MLB*	*30*	*545*	*60*	*32*	*5*	*11*	*60*	*24*	*82*	*15*	*6*	*.278/.317/.422*	*.261*	*19.0*	*.308*	*2.0*	*2B -1*	*2.0*

Breakout: 1%   Improve: 49%   Collapse: 5%   Attrition: 11%   MLB: 98%   *Comparables: Brandon Phillips, Omar Infante, Orlando Hudson*

Harrison highlighted his 2015 season and clicked copy-paste, hitting for an OK average with no power or on-base skills again. The only real differences came in the field, where Harrison primarily manned second base instead of third, and on the bases, where he set a new career high in steals. It's safe to say Harrison's 2014 power surge was a mirage, and he continues to treat walking with more disdain than those humans that WALL-E saved. He's a down-the-order hitter, but thanks to his speed, versatility and contact abilities, Harrison is still a valuable asset. As to whether he'll be worth $18 million to a small-market team like the Pirates over the next two seasons, Harrison's back-loaded extension is one Pittsburgh probably could live without.

Ke'Bryan Hayes   3B

Born: 1/28/97   Age: 20   Bats: R   Throws: R   Height: 6'1"   Weight: 210   Entered Pro Ball: Round 1, 2015 Draft (#32 overall)

YEAR	TEAM	LVL	AGE	PA	R	2B	3B	HR	RBI	BB	K	SB	CS	AVG/OBP/SLG	TAv	VORP	BABIP	BRR	FRAA	WARP
2015	WEV	A-	18	52	8	1	0	0	7	6	7	1	1	.220/.320/.244	.296	1.9	.250	-1.7	3B(12): 3.2	0.5
2016	WVA	A	19	276	27	12	1	6	37	16	51	6	5	.263/.319/.393	.290	14.0	.304	-1.5	3B(64): 2.5	1.8
2017	PIT	MLB	20	250	24	10	1	6	27	14	62	2	1	.231/.283/.361	.220	-2.9	.285	-0.4	3B 2	-0.1
2018	PIT	MLB	21	381	43	17	1	11	43	21	90	3	2	.243/.294/.388	.245	2.2	.293	-0.6	3B 3	0.6

Breakout: 1%   Improve: 6%   Collapse: 0%   Attrition: 3%   MLB: 7%   Comparables: Cheslor Cuthbert, Jeimer Candelario, Jefry Marte

The 32nd pick in the 2015 draft, Hayes experienced plenty of ups and a few downs in his second pro season. Scouting reports express general enthusiasm over the Sally League All-Star's hit tool and glove work, which he pairs with a strong arm and impressive bloodlines (his father Charlie played 14 years in the majors). The negatives include Hayes' lack of game power, some trouble on the bases and plenty of time on the disabled list. The missed reps hurt, but Hayes is young enough that he should still reach High-A at some point in 2017.

John Jaso   1B

Born: 9/19/83   Age: 33   Bats: L   Throws: R   Height: 6'2"   Weight: 205   Entered Pro Ball: Round 12, 2003 Draft (#338 overall)

YEAR	TEAM	LVL	AGE	PA	R	2B	3B	HR	RBI	BB	K	SB	CS	AVG/OBP/SLG	TAv	VORP	BABIP	BRR	FRAA	WARP
2014	OAK	MLB	30	344	42	18	3	9	40	28	60	2	0	.264/.337/.430	.294	18.2	.300	-2.2	C(54): -13.5	0.5
2015	PCH	A+	31	23	3	2	0	0	0	2	4	0	0	.286/.348/.381	.252	-0.3	.353	-0.4	LF(1): -0.3 • 1B(1): -0.1	-0.1
2015	TBA	MLB	31	216	23	17	0	5	22	28	39	1	2	.286/.380/.459	.300	9.1	.336	-1.9	LF(7): -0.8 • RF(1): -0.0	0.9
2016	PIT	MLB	32	432	45	25	3	8	42	45	74	0	4	.268/.353/.413	.280	12.3	.314	-1.4	1B(108): -6.8 • RF(1): -0.2	0.5
2017	PIT	MLB	33	269	33	14	1	6	27	32	45	1	2	.268/.361/.418	.276	10.0	.307	-0.9	1B -3 • LF -1	0.5
2018	PIT	MLB	34	254	32	14	1	6	28	29	44	1	1	.267/.356/.415	.280	8.8	.308	-0.9	1B -3 • LF -1	0.5

Breakout: 2%   Improve: 26%   Collapse: 3%   Attrition: 11%   MLB: 96%   Comparables: Joe Mauer, Dan Driessen, Mike Sweeney

Jaso already looked like something Will Turner would have fought in the first *Pirates of the Caribbean* movie, so it's appropriate that he signed a two-year pact with the Buccos before last season. In the Dreadhead Pirate Jaso's inaugural stint with Pittsburgh, he came much as advertised, functioning as an unexpected but acceptable option against

YEAR	TEAM	P. COUNT	FRM RUNS	BLK RUNS	THRW RUNS	TOT RUNS
2014	OAK	6169	-11.3	-0.5	-1.2	-13.1

righties. Jaso looked cursed the 25 times he was allowed to face southpaws, recording just one hit and striking out seven times. With the emergence of Josh Bell and the Pirates' loaded outfield, one imagines Jaso serving in a complementary role moving forward. If it doesn't work out, the upcoming *Pirates* budget has a production cost of $320 million, so maybe Jaso can find more lucrative work elsewhere.

Jung-ho Kang   3B

Born: 4/5/87   Age: 30   Bats: R   Throws: R   Height: 6'0"   Weight: 210   Entered Pro Ball: International Free Agent, 2015

YEAR	TEAM	LVL	AGE	PA	R	2B	3B	HR	RBI	BB	K	SB	CS	AVG/OBP/SLG	TAv	VORP	BABIP	BRR	FRAA	WARP
2015	PIT	MLB	28	467	60	24	2	15	58	28	99	5	4	.287/.355/.461	.294	33.2	.344	1.7	3B(77): 5.4 • SS(60): -8.6	3.2
2016	IND	AAA	29	57	5	0	0	2	7	7	11	0	1	.146/.246/.271	.219	-0.8	.135	-0.2	3B(13): -0.7	-0.2
2016	PIT	MLB	29	370	45	19	0	21	62	36	79	3	1	.255/.354/.513	.310	26.9	.273	-3.7	3B(92): 8.5	3.7
2017	PIT	MLB	30	475	60	22	1	20	66	38	102	5	3	.261/.341/.464	.281	23.8	.297	-0.8	3B 8 • SS -1	2.9
2018	PIT	MLB	31	400	55	19	1	16	55	33	86	3	2	.259/.340/.456	.286	19.7	.298	-0.5	3B 6 • SS -1	2.7

Breakout: 3%   Improve: 56%   Collapse: 1%   Attrition: 12%   MLB: 98%   Comparables: Evan Longoria, David Wright, Eric Chavez

We're now two seasons into Kang's four-year contract, but we still don't really know what Kang can do over a full season. After missing 36 games in 2015, Kang played in just 103 last season, sitting out April as he recovered from a broken leg/torn meniscus, then missing parts of August and September with a shoulder injury. When he did play, Kang traded in some average for power. Kang walked more and struck out at about the same rate as he did in 2015, and his dip in average seems primarily to be a function of BABIP. If he can stay on the field and stay out of trouble off it—he was accused of, but not charged with, sexual assault in June and charged with an offseason DUI—Kang could be poised for a true breakout year. That'd be a gift for a Pirates infield that's light on power, if not on former West Virginia Power.

Kevin Kramer   2B

Born: 10/3/93   Age: 23   Bats: L   Throws: R   Height: 6'1"   Weight: 190   Entered Pro Ball: Round 2, 2015 Draft (#62 overall)

YEAR	TEAM	LVL	AGE	PA	R	2B	3B	HR	RBI	BB	K	SB	CS	AVG/OBP/SLG	TAv	VORP	BABIP	BRR	FRAA	WARP
2015	WEV	A-	21	209	34	7	3	0	17	25	28	9	4	.305/.390/.379	.307	18.9	.358	3.2	2B(44): 7.4 • SS(2): -1.1	2.7
2015	WVA	A	21	56	9	2	1	0	3	5	8	3	0	.240/.321/.320	.246	1.8	.286	1.2	2B(8): -0.3 • SS(2): -0.6	0.1
2016	BRD	A+	22	513	56	29	2	4	57	48	63	3	9	.277/.352/.378	.268	18.0	.312	0.8	2B(103): 9.5	2.8
2017	PIT	MLB	23	250	27	12	1	5	23	19	48	1	1	.247/.309/.377	.234	2.6	.287	-0.5	2B 3	0.6
2018	PIT	MLB	24	346	39	16	2	8	37	27	66	1	1	.249/.314/.389	.252	7.0	.287	-0.7	2B 4	1.3

Breakout: 5%   Improve: 18%   Collapse: 2%   Attrition: 10%   MLB: 26%   Comparables: Adrian Cardenas, Kyle Seager, Austin Barnes

It's nice to know the Pirates have a sense of humor; after drafting (Kevin) Newman with their first pick in 2015, they popped Kramer in the second round, directly appealing to the niche of *Seinfeld* fans who also follow the minor leagues. A shortstop at UCLA, Kramer justified his selection in his first full professional season by posting a solid TAv at High-A and earning positive defensive reviews at second base. Power and speed aren't big parts of Kramer's game, but he can hit, has a good approach at the plate and "a nose for the ball," as one scouting report put it. Kramer's upside isn't sky-high, but there are enough tools here that he should make it to The Show (about nothing).

Starling Marte   LF

Born: 10/9/88   Age: 28   Bats: R   Throws: R   Height: 6'1"   Weight: 190   Entered Pro Ball: International Free Agent, 2007

YEAR	TEAM	LVL	AGE	PA	R	2B	3B	HR	RBI	BB	K	SB	CS	AVG/OBP/SLG	TAv	VORP	BABIP	BRR	FRAA	WARP
2014	PIT	MLB	25	545	73	29	6	13	56	33	131	30	11	.291/.356/.453	.312	39.5	.373	1.5	LF(114): -6.5 • CF(28): -2.9	3.3
2015	PIT	MLB	26	633	84	30	2	19	81	27	123	30	10	.287/.337/.444	.281	25.4	.333	-1.3	LF(141): -5.2 • CF(18): 2.7	2.5
2016	PIT	MLB	27	529	71	34	5	9	46	23	104	47	12	.311/.362/.456	.289	32.2	.380	4.9	LF(114): 4.6 • CF(16): -0.3	3.8
2017	PIT	MLB	28	585	77	28	7	16	66	30	129	37	11	.280/.334/.446	.274	27.4	.338	4.0	LF -2	2.5
2018	PIT	MLB	29	523	64	27	6	15	64	27	117	30	10	.275/.332/.450	.282	26.0	.332	2.0	LF -2	2.6

Breakout: 1%   Improve: 49%   Collapse: 9%   Attrition: 14%   MLB: 97%   Comparables: Chris Heisey, Hunter Pence, Yoenis Cespedes

Is Marte now the Pirates' best player? Andrew McCutchen has the history, Gerrit Cole the pedigree and Gregory Polanco the upside, but Marte out-produced them all last season. Marte set career highs in batting average and stolen bases, and turned in his best defensive season per FRAA. He missed nearly all of September with lingering back issues, but when Marte was on the field he performed as one of the better outfielders in baseball. There are already rumors that Marte will bump McCutchen from center field next season, and that would be as smart for Pittsburgh's defense as it would be symbolic of time's ceaseless march. Marte's six-year, $31 million extension remains the yin to the Jose Tabata extension yang, proving that all in this universe is balanced.

Andrew McCutchen   CF

Born: 10/10/86   Age: 30   Bats: R   Throws: R   Height: 5'10"   Weight: 195   Entered Pro Ball: Round 1, 2005 Draft (#11 overall)

YEAR	TEAM	LVL	AGE	PA	R	2B	3B	HR	RBI	BB	K	SB	CS	AVG/OBP/SLG	TAv	VORP	BABIP	BRR	FRAA	WARP
2014	PIT	MLB	27	648	89	38	6	25	83	84	115	18	3	.314/.410/.542	.350	73.8	.355	1.1	CF(146): -15.9	6.4
2015	PIT	MLB	28	685	91	36	3	23	96	98	133	11	5	.292/.401/.488	.326	62.1	.339	-1.9	CF(152): -17.1	4.8
2016	PIT	MLB	29	675	81	26	3	24	79	69	143	6	7	.256/.336/.430	.275	30.5	.297	-0.3	CF(151): -8.7	2.3
2017	PIT	MLB	30	657	89	32	4	25	91	78	122	12	6	.292/.382/.494	.302	49.9	.330	-0.5	CF -11	3.5
2018	PIT	MLB	31	589	84	29	3	21	81	73	113	10	5	.287/.380/.485	.307	44.0	.328	-0.4	CF -10	3.7

Breakout: 2%   Improve: 54%   Collapse: 2%   Attrition: 6%   MLB: 100%   Comparables: Andy Pafko, Carlos Beltran, Willie Mays

Few baseball players have earned universal love throughout the sport the way McCutchen has. Twitter eggs from St. Louis aside, does *anyone* dislike this guy? That's what made McCutchen's 2016 so hard to watch; all the great ones inevitably fade, but not all fade so fast and not all were so damn easy to root for to begin with. Despite the injury issues and stark decline in performance, all is not lost for Cutch. He still hit for decent power, some of his decline in average is likely a function of BABIP and he was much better in the second half. We're not here to sugarcoat, though: McCutchen struck out more, walked and made hard contact less and continued his decline on the basepaths and especially in the field. Will McCutchen's performance ever return to the halcyon levels of 2011-2014? Probably not, but it seems even less likely that he'll be just a two-win player moving forward. A move out of center field and a modest rebound at the plate both seem in order.

Austin Meadows   OF

Born: 5/3/95   Age: 22   Bats: L   Throws: L   Height: 6'3"   Weight: 200   Entered Pro Ball: Round 1, 2013 Draft (#9 overall)

YEAR	TEAM	LVL	AGE	PA	R	2B	3B	HR	RBI	BB	K	SB	CS	AVG/OBP/SLG	TAv	VORP	BABIP	BRR	FRAA	WARP
2014	WVA	A	19	167	18	13	1	3	15	14	30	2	3	.322/.388/.486	.293	10.7	.383	-0.3	CF(38): 1.1	1.2
2015	BRD	A+	20	556	72	22	4	7	54	41	79	20	7	.307/.357/.407	.289	32.0	.351	-0.1	CF(114): -14.6	1.9
2015	ALT	AA	20	28	5	2	3	0	1	2	5	1	0	.360/.429/.680	.375	3.9	.450	-0.2	CF(6): -0.3	0.4
2016	ALT	AA	21	190	33	16	8	6	23	16	32	9	3	.311/.365/.611	.332	19.7	.343	0.8	CF(39): 2.5 • LF(2): -0.6	2.3
2016	IND	AAA	21	145	16	7	3	6	24	15	34	8	2	.214/.297/.460	.291	9.6	.236	0.9	CF(23): -3.4 • LF(11): -0.2	0.6
2017	PIT	MLB	22	64	8	3	1	2	7	4	14	2	1	.257/.310/.432	.256	1.8	.304	0.2	CF -0	0.1
2018	PIT	MLB	23	332	41	16	4	11	42	26	76	10	3	.258/.321/.445	.270	12.7	.308	1.3	CF -2 • RF 0	1.2

Breakout: 4%   Improve: 26%   Collapse: 1%   Attrition: 21%   MLB: 56%   Comparables: Joc Pederson, Colby Rasmus, Brett Jackson

It can be hard to discern when a player is injury-prone or just unlucky. Unfortunately, Meadows seems to be both. He didn't appear in a game until April 24 after suffering an orbital fracture during a workout. Meadows then missed nearly all of July with a hamstring injury. It wasn't the same hamstring that cost him most of his 2014 season, but add it all together and he managed just 352 plate appearances all year. When on the field, he remains among the most well-rounded prospects in the game. He's proven twice that Double-A is no challenge for him, and the Pirates have the outfield depth to let Meadows bloom in Indy before (STOP READING HERE, PIRATES FANS) he replaces Andrew McCutchen.

Jordy Mercer   SS

Born: 8/27/86   Age: 30   Bats: R   Throws: R   Height: 6'3"   Weight: 205   Entered Pro Ball: Round 3, 2008 Draft (#79 overall)

YEAR	TEAM	LVL	AGE	PA	R	2B	3B	HR	RBI	BB	K	SB	CS	AVG/OBP/SLG	TAv	VORP	BABIP	BRR	FRAA	WARP
2014	PIT	MLB	27	555	56	27	2	12	55	35	89	4	1	.255/.305/.387	.256	22.8	.285	3.9	SS(144): 10.5 • RF(1): -0.0	3.7
2015	IND	AAA	28	26	3	0	0	1	3	1	5	0	0	.240/.269/.360	.241	0.3	.263	-0.2	SS(7): 0.5	0.1
2015	PIT	MLB	28	430	34	21	0	3	34	27	73	3	2	.244/.293/.320	.228	5.4	.290	2.1	SS(115): 2.8	0.9
2016	PIT	MLB	29	584	66	22	3	11	59	51	83	1	1	.256/.328/.374	.258	25.8	.286	3.0	SS(146): -7.1	1.9
2017	PIT	MLB	30	536	54	26	2	11	54	38	89	3	1	.257/.312/.384	.245	17.4	.289	-0.9	SS 1	1.0
2018	PIT	MLB	31	510	57	23	1	11	53	38	89	2	1	.249/.309/.376	.246	12.6	.281	2.3	SS 1	1.5

Breakout: 1%   Improve: 42%   Collapse: 4%   Attrition: 14%   MLB: 94%   Comparables: Cliff Pennington, Zack Cozart, Brendan Ryan

What is there to say about Mercer that hasn't been said about a plain bagel, a store-bought tomato sauce or an egg white omelette? He's perfectly serviceable and utterly unremarkable. Thanks in large part to Jung-ho Kang's injury, Mercer saw a full season's worth of playing time. He rebounded from a down 2015 offensively, posting the highest walk rate and driving in the most runs of his career, but his defense took a turn for the worse, a bad sign for a 30-year-old without real offensive skills. Mercer is a fine spare tire for a Pirates infield that tends to get plenty of flats, but if you need to use him every day you might want to change your driving habits.

Max Moroff   IF

Born: 5/13/93   Age: 24   Bats: B   Throws: R   Height: 5'10"   Weight: 185   Entered Pro Ball: Round 16, 2012 Draft (#496 overall)

YEAR	TEAM	LVL	AGE	PA	R	2B	3B	HR	RBI	BB	K	SB	CS	AVG/OBP/SLG	TAv	VORP	BABIP	BRR	FRAA	WARP
2014	BRD	A+	21	534	57	30	6	1	50	54	129	21	15	.244/.324/.340	.257	10.2	.332	-3.1	2B(123): 6.1 • SS(5): -0.2	1.6
2015	ALT	AA	22	612	79	28	6	7	51	70	111	17	13	.293/.374/.409	.294	36.6	.356	-0.7	2B(109): 3.4 • SS(13): 1.3	4.6
2016	PIT	MLB	23	2	0	0	0	0	0	0	2	0	0	.000/.000/.000	-.014	-0.5	--	0.0		-0.1
2016	IND	AAA	23	520	61	18	4	8	45	90	129	9	7	.230/.367/.349	.272	20.9	.311	-1.3	2B(61): 1.5 • 3B(43): -1.5	2.3
2017	PIT	MLB	24	250	31	10	2	5	23	30	65	4	3	.237/.333/.369	.243	4.6	.308	-0.4	2B 1 • 3B -0	0.6
2018	PIT	MLB	25	340	41	14	2	7	35	41	88	5	4	.237/.333/.377	.258	8.6	.305	-0.2	2B 2 • 3B 0	1.1

Breakout: 3%   Improve: 11%   Collapse: 3%   Attrition: 20%   MLB: 32%   *Comparables: Logan Forsythe, Logan Watkins, Colin Walsh*

Pittsburgh's minor league player of the year in 2015 was unable to do Moroff the same in 2016. The 23-year-old struggled mightily at Triple-A, walking frequently but also striking out a lot, hitting for a low average and running into outs on the bases. Moroff made his first MLB appearance in July, but was with the club for less than a week and then got passed over during September call-ups. Likely eyeing a future as a utility infielder, Moroff played 61 games at second, 43 at third and 20 at short in Indianapolis. That versatility will help, but not as much as rediscovering the stroke that made Moroff an Eastern League All-Star in 2015.

Kevin Newman   SS

Born: 8/4/93   Age: 23   Bats: R   Throws: R   Height: 6'1"   Weight: 180   Entered Pro Ball: Round 1, 2015 Draft (#19 overall)

YEAR	TEAM	LVL	AGE	PA	R	2B	3B	HR	RBI	BB	K	SB	CS	AVG/OBP/SLG	TAv	VORP	BABIP	BRR	FRAA	WARP
2015	WEV	A-	21	173	25	10	1	2	9	10	22	7	1	.226/.281/.340	.260	5.9	.252	-1.0	SS(38): -6.3	0.0
2015	WVA	A	21	110	14	4	1	0	8	9	8	6	1	.306/.376/.367	.289	7.3	.333	-0.4	SS(23): 0.3	0.8
2016	BRD	A+	22	189	24	10	1	3	24	17	12	4	1	.366/.394/.494	.355	28.1	.375	1.4	SS(38): 1.5	3.0
2016	ALT	AA	22	268	41	11	2	2	28	26	24	6	3	.288/.361/.378	.268	14.8	.308	2.3	SS(60): 0.2	1.6
2017	PIT	MLB	23	250	30	11	1	6	25	18	38	2	1	.267/.327/.404	.250	8.8	.294	-0.1	SS 0	1.0
2018	PIT	MLB	24	355	42	16	2	9	40	26	54	4	1	.269/.329/.414	.268	15.0	.295	-0.1	SS 1	1.7

Breakout: 6%   Improve: 34%   Collapse: 5%   Attrition: 19%   MLB: 49%   *Comparables: Greg Garcia, Chris Taylor, Brad Miller*

Tebowing. Planking. The Mannequin Challenge. Teens and millennials have no shortage of silly trends that burn hot and then fizzle out, but the Pirates have to put a stop to the Broken Orbital Bone craze their prospects love so much. Austin Meadows suffered his facial fracture in March, and Newman missed three weeks in May following suit. When healthy, Newman did what Newman does: he hit the crap out of the ball. Newman may take Kanye West's treatise on power a little too seriously, but what he lacks in pop he makes up for with a plus, potentially plus-plus hit tool and a universally lauded feel for the game. Some scouts doubt his ability to stick at short, but if he can he's a potential first-division regular.

Gregory Polanco   RF

Born: 9/14/91   Age: 25   Bats: L   Throws: L   Height: 6'5"   Weight: 230   Entered Pro Ball: International Free Agent, 2009

YEAR	TEAM	LVL	AGE	PA	R	2B	3B	HR	RBI	BB	K	SB	CS	AVG/OBP/SLG	TAv	VORP	BABIP	BRR	FRAA	WARP
2014	IND	AAA	22	305	51	17	5	7	51	28	49	16	6	.328/.390/.504	.300	20.5	.377	0.7	RF(69): 10.2	3.1
2014	PIT	MLB	22	312	50	9	0	7	33	30	59	14	5	.235/.307/.343	.245	3.2	.272	2.3	RF(83): 10.8	1.5
2015	PIT	MLB	23	652	83	35	6	9	52	55	121	27	10	.256/.320/.381	.264	15.2	.308	1.3	RF(144): 11.1 • LF(8): 0.2	2.8
2016	PIT	MLB	24	587	79	34	4	22	86	53	119	17	6	.258/.323/.463	.276	19.6	.291	-1.0	RF(111): 3.5 • LF(29): 0.1	2.4
2017	PIT	MLB	25	605	72	30	4	17	69	53	114	21	8	.259/.324/.422	.260	16.0	.297	1.1	RF 6 • CF -0	1.9
2018	PIT	MLB	26	572	70	28	4	17	69	51	110	19	8	.258/.324/.427	.269	18.1	.294	1.1	RF 6 • CF 0	2.6

Breakout: 7%   Improve: 52%   Collapse: 3%   Attrition: 7%   MLB: 99%   *Comparables: Jeremy Hermida, Tony Tarasco, Jeff Francoeur*

We got a glimpse of who Polanco could truly be in 2016 when the 24-year-old posted a career-best TAv, hitting for more power without sacrificing on-base ability. He was especially dominant in the first half, when he hit .287/.362/.500 and the internet was flooded with "Gregory Polanco Has Arrived" columns. That hot start made Polanco's second half (.220/.267/.414) all the more disappointing, as he battled shoulder and knee injuries—getting PRP injections just to play—and then suffered a facial fracture in the season's final week. Those boo-boos, combined with added bulk, hurt Polanco in the field and on the bases, so much so that our numbers indicate he was actually more valuable in 2015 despite his improvements at the plate. Polanco was a top prospect and has already earned an extension, so you can understand the air of impatience that surrounds Pirates fans when they discuss him. But look closely and you'll see a player who seems poised for a breakout and one who'll be just 25 for most of 2017.

Jason Rogers   1B

Born: 3/13/88   Age: 29   Bats: R   Throws: R   Height: 6'1"   Weight: 260   Entered Pro Ball: Round 32, 2010 Draft (#969 overall)

YEAR	TEAM	LVL	AGE	PA	R	2B	3B	HR	RBI	BB	K	SB	CS	AVG/OBP/SLG	TAv	VORP	BABIP	BRR	FRAA	WARP
2014	HUN	AA	26	324	42	18	2	7	43	31	56	5	1	.282/.355/.432	.281	18.3	.326	2.0	3B(66): 2.4	2.2
2014	NAS	AAA	26	232	36	11	4	11	39	22	38	0	0	.316/.379/.568	.335	26.3	.338	-1.3	3B(56): 5.6	3.2
2014	MIL	MLB	26	10	0	1	0	0	0	1	1	0	0	.111/.200/.222	.171	-0.7	.125	0.0	1B(4): -0.1	-0.1
2015	CSP	AAA	27	147	25	8	0	8	24	24	23	0	0	.344/.449/.607	.349	15.6	.370	-0.2	1B(24): 0.9 • 3B(6): 0.6	1.7
2015	MIL	MLB	27	169	22	6	2	4	16	15	34	0	0	.296/.367/.441	.294	8.8	.360	0.3	1B(24): -1.8 • LF(3): -0.4	0.7
2016	IND	AAA	28	420	38	18	2	6	40	43	78	1	0	.263/.338/.371	.257	6.2	.315	-1.2	3B(49): -0.7 • 1B(10): -0.5	0.5
2016	PIT	MLB	28	33	2	0	1	0	2	7	9	0	0	.080/.303/.160	.186	-1.7	.125	0.0	1B(5): -0.3 • 3B(4): -0.1	-0.2
2017	*PIT*	*MLB*	*29*	*250*	*28*	*11*	*2*	*7*	*31*	*25*	*52*	*0*	*0*	*.260/.338/.424*	*.259*	*6.9*	*.306*	*0.3*	*3B 1 • 1B -1*	*0.8*
2018	*PIT*	*MLB*	*30*	*256*	*32*	*10*	*1*	*8*	*30*	*25*	*53*	*0*	*0*	*.257/.334/.415*	*.269*	*7.7*	*.302*	*0.1*	*3B 1 • 1B -1*	*0.8*

Breakout: 1%   Improve: 15%   Collapse: 9%   Attrition: 20%   MLB: 39%   *Comparables: Scott Moore, Steve Pearce, Matt Hague*

Look, we all have weird hobbies. Some of us collect stamps or postcards or bottle caps. Some of us respond "nice" to any tweet with the numbers 69 or 420 in them. Others watch Skip Bayless on purpose. For the Pirates, their weird thing is an obsession with replacement-level first basemen. That's why they shipped Trey Supak and Keon Broxton to the Brewers for Rogers in December of 2015. It hasn't worked out, as Rogers regressed in Indianapolis and flopped in brief cameos in Pittsburgh. With Josh Bell entrenching himself as the Pirates' first baseman of the present and future, Rogers is likely to be stuck back in Indy.

Jacob Stallings   C

Born: 12/22/89   Age: 27   Bats: R   Throws: R   Height: 6'5"   Weight: 220   Entered Pro Ball: Round 7, 2012 Draft (#226 overall)

YEAR	TEAM	LVL	AGE	PA	R	2B	3B	HR	RBI	BB	K	SB	CS	AVG/OBP/SLG	TAv	VORP	BABIP	BRR	FRAA	WARP
2014	BRD	A+	24	249	22	11	0	4	30	28	52	1	2	.241/.332/.349	.255	8.6	.297	-1.9	C(68): 4.0	1.3
2015	ALT	AA	25	292	25	14	1	3	32	15	64	4	1	.275/.313/.370	.249	6.6	.340	-2.8	C(74): 0.6 • P(1): -0.0	0.8
2016	IND	AAA	26	275	23	17	0	6	28	11	66	0	1	.214/.252/.350	.215	-2.9	.265	-2.5	C(80): -10.0	-1.3
2016	PIT	MLB	26	15	0	1	0	0	2	0	4	1	0	.400/.400/.467	.300	0.9	.545	-0.4	C(4): -0.4	0.0
2017	*PIT*	*MLB*	*27*	*250*	*24*	*12*	*1*	*6*	*26*	*15*	*66*	*0*	*0*	*.230/.281/.367*	*.216*	*1.1*	*.289*	*-0.4*	*C -10*	*-0.9*
2018	*PIT*	*MLB*	*28*	*163*	*17*	*7*	*0*	*4*	*16*	*10*	*46*	*0*	*0*	*.220/.269/.343*	*.217*	*-1.6*	*.282*	*-0.4*	*C -7*	*-0.9*

Breakout: 2%   Improve: 12%   Collapse: 6%   Attrition: 13%   MLB: 21%   *Comparables: Craig Tatum, Brett Nicholas, Cody Stanley*

It's appropriate that Stallings is a backup catcher, because his job is to bide his time until a better option comes along. That being said, his lack of upside shouldn't detract from a season full of milestones for the former Tar Heel. In 2016, Stallings received his first call to the majors, earned his first MLB hit and even notched a walk-off RBI against former Pirate Mark Melancon. Stallings is 27 and struggled at Triple-A a year ago, so we might've already seen his best. But as any 7-year-old trying to push back their bedtime knows, Stallings about making the most of your time, and our hero's certainly done that.

YEAR	TEAM	P. COUNT	FRM RUNS	BLK RUNS	THRW RUNS	TOT RUNS
2015	ALT	9682	-1.9	1.3	1.1	0.5
2015	ALT	9682	-1.9	1.3	1.1	0.5
2016	PIT	563	-0.4	0.2	0.0	-0.2
2017	*PIT*	*9244*	*-10.9*	*0.9*	*0.1*	*-9.8*
2018	*PIT*	*6027*	*-7.4*	*0.6*	*0.0*	*-6.8*

Chris Stewart   C

Born: 2/19/82   Age: 35   Bats: R   Throws: R   Height: 6'4"   Weight: 205   Entered Pro Ball: Round 12, 2001 Draft (#373 overall)

YEAR	TEAM	LVL	AGE	PA	R	2B	3B	HR	RBI	BB	K	SB	CS	AVG/OBP/SLG	TAv	VORP	BABIP	BRR	FRAA	WARP
2014	PIT	MLB	32	154	9	5	0	0	10	12	27	0	1	.294/.362/.331	.261	6.6	.364	0.1	C(46): 4.4	1.2
2015	PIT	MLB	33	172	9	8	0	0	15	6	29	0	0	.289/.320/.340	.243	4.7	.348	0.2	C(52): 6.7	1.2
2016	ALT	AA	34	35	6	0	0	0	3	8	1	0	0	.200/.400/.200	.234	-0.9	.200	-1.5	C(10): 1.2	0.0
2016	PIT	MLB	34	113	10	4	0	1	7	12	15	0	0	.214/.319/.286	.236	2.9	.244	0.6	C(31): -2.9 • 1B(1): 0.0	0.0
2017	*PIT*	*MLB*	*35*	*94*	*8*	*3*	*0*	*1*	*7*	*7*	*14*	*0*	*0*	*.245/.311/.315*	*.228*	*1.5*	*.281*	*-0.2*	*C 0*	*0.4*
2018	*PIT*	*MLB*	*36*	*99*	*10*	*4*	*0*	*1*	*8*	*8*	*16*	*0*	*0*	*.238/.307/.307*	*.228*	*0.5*	*.275*	*0.1*	*C 0*	*0.1*

Breakout: 1%   Improve: 26%   Collapse: 13%   Attrition: 29%   MLB: 78%   *Comparables: Mike Lavalliere, Bob Boone, Gerald Laird*

If you bet the over on Stewart posting a .340-plus BABIP for the third straight season, you got a little too greedy. The bubble finally burst on Stewart's batted-ball luck, and he posted his worst TAv since 2013. In addition to his predictable regression at the plate, Stewart's defensive skills declined again, and the longtime backup dipped into negative FRAA territory for the first time in nine years. The Pirates inked Stewart to a two-year, $3 million contract before last season, but given the short money involved and Pittsburgh's plethora of backups, Stewart had best prove he's got something left in the tank.

YEAR	TEAM	P. COUNT	FRM RUNS	BLK RUNS	THRW RUNS	TOT RUNS
2014	IND	533	0.4	0.0	0.0	0.4
2014	PIT	5743	4.6	0.3	-0.2	4.7
2015	ALT	188	0.0	0.0	0.0	0.0
2015	IND	455	0.1	0.0	0.0	0.1
2015	PIT	5779	6.8	-0.3	-0.6	5.9
2016	PIT	4077	-2.3	-1.7	0.0	-4.0
2017	*PIT*	*3485*	*0.9*	*-0.7*	*-0.1*	*0.1*
2018	*PIT*	*3660*	*0.5*	*-0.8*	*-0.2*	*-0.4*

Cole Tucker   SS

Born: 7/3/96   Age: 20   Bats: B   Throws: R   Height: 6'3"   Weight: 185   Entered Pro Ball: Round 1, 2014 Draft (#24 overall)

YEAR	TEAM	LVL	AGE	PA	R	2B	3B	HR	RBI	BB	K	SB	CS	AVG/OBP/SLG	TAv	VORP	BABIP	BRR	FRAA	WARP
2015	WVA	A	18	329	46	13	3	2	25	16	49	25	6	.293/.322/.377	.269	18.7	.336	3.0	SS(69): 2.8	2.3
2016	WVA	A	19	67	9	4	2	1	2	4	9	1	1	.262/.308/.443	.312	6.5	.294	0.5	SS(15): 2.7	1.0
2016	BRD	A+	19	304	36	12	1	1	25	29	62	5	6	.238/.312/.301	.236	3.1	.306	-1.1	SS(61): 12.6	1.6
2017	*PIT*	*MLB*	*20*	*250*	*27*	*10*	*1*	*4*	*21*	*13*	*60*	*5*	*2*	*.233/.276/.347*	*.211*	*-1.3*	*.288*	*-0.1*	*SS 4*	*0.3*
2018	*PIT*	*MLB*	*21*	*372*	*39*	*15*	*3*	*7*	*38*	*21*	*86*	*7*	*4*	*.244/.289/.369*	*.236*	*3.8*	*.297*	*0.3*	*SS 6*	*1.0*

Breakout: 1%   Improve: 10%   Collapse: 0%   Attrition: 2%   MLB: 13%   *Comparables: Ruben Tejada, Orlando Arcia, Tim Beckham*

We already knew that Tucker was fast, strong-armed and adept with a glove, but in 2016 we learned that he has some Wolverine-esque healing powers, too. The former first rounder underwent surgery for a torn labrum in August of 2015 and was scheduled to miss 10-12 months. Turns out Tucker could teach George R.R. Martin a thing or two about deadlines, because he made his 2016 debut on May 8. He stayed healthy for the remainder of the season, but he didn't produce at the plate, and questions about the future utility of his hit tool remain unanswered. Is Tucker a legit first-division shortstop or a Jordy Mercer rerun with a bit more speed? A full, injury-free season back at High-A should help give us a clearer picture.

PITCHERS

Antonio Bastardo   LHP

Born: 9/21/85   Age: 31   Bats: R   Throws: L   Height: 5'11"   Weight: 205   Entered Pro Ball: International Free Agent, 2005

YEAR	TEAM	LVL	AGE	W	L	SV	G	GS	IP	H	HR	BB/9	K/9	K	GB%	BABIP	WHIP	ERA	FIP	DRA	VORP	WARP	cFIP	MPH
2014	PHI	MLB	28	5	7	0	67	0	64	43	4	4.8	11.4	81	32%	.260	1.20	3.94	3.07	3.55	6.7	0.7	97	94.2
2015	PIT	MLB	29	4	1	1	66	0	57¹	39	4	4.1	10.0	64	34%	.246	1.13	2.98	3.35	4.44	1.7	0.2	105	95.3
2016	NYN	MLB	30	0	0	0	41	0	43²	41	8	4.3	9.5	46	38%	.282	1.42	4.74	5.11	5.19	-1.1	-0.1	113	93.6
2016	PIT	MLB	30	3	0	0	28	0	24	19	3	4.1	10.5	28	18%	.271	1.25	4.12	3.98	5.54	-1.5	-0.2	114	93.7
2017	*PIT*	*MLB*	*31*	*2*	*3*	*0*	*50*	*0*	*52*	*49*	*8*	*4.1*	*9.4*	*55*	*51%*	*.293*	*1.39*	*4.67*	*4.56*	*4.83*	*0.5*	*0.1*	*100*	
2018	*PIT*	*MLB*	*32*	*2*	*1*	*0*	*49*	*0*	*51²*	*44*	*8*	*3.8*	*9.5*	*54*	*51%*	*.295*	*1.29*	*4.50*	*4.69*	*5.08*	*0.3*	*0.0*	*116*	

Breakout: 33%   Improve: 42%   Collapse: 28%   Attrition: 19%   MLB: 92%   *Comparables: Joel Hanrahan, David Hernandez, Rod Scurry*

In the *A Song of Ice and Fire* universe, bastards in high-born houses earn surnames based on the nine regions of Westeros in which their "legitimate" families live. That's why Jon Snow isn't Jon Stark or Jon Targaryen. If we're going to follow ASOAIF rules for Bastardo, his name has to tie into Pennsylvania, because he just can't stay away. Maybe Antonio Bridges? Tony Keystone? Anthony Swingstate? After signing a two-year deal with the Mets last offseason, Bastardo was shipped back to the Pirates when Jon Niese went back to the Mets. He was better in Pittsburgh, but Bastardo still had the worst season of his career with dramatic uptick in homers and BABIP. Aside from the increase in taters there were no real red flags in Bastardo's performance, so we can chalk this one up to reliever volatility.

Steven Brault   LHP

Born: 4/29/92   Age: 25   Bats: L   Throws: L   Height: 6'0"   Weight: 200   Entered Pro Ball: Round 11, 2013 Draft (#339 overall)

YEAR	TEAM	LVL	AGE	W	L	SV	G	GS	IP	H	HR	BB/9	K/9	K	GB%	BABIP	WHIP	ERA	FIP	DRA	VORP	WARP	cFIP	MPH
2014	DEL	A	22	9	8	0	22	21	130	107	4	1.9	8.0	115	50%	.286	1.04	3.05	3.09	2.47	42.7	4.4	86	
2014	FRD	A+	22	2	0	0	3	3	16¹	7	0	1.1	5.0	9	56%	.152	0.55	0.55	2.78	3.52	3.8	0.4	92	
2015	BRD	A+	23	4	1	0	13	13	65²	62	3	2.9	6.2	45	52%	.292	1.26	3.02	3.44	4.82	1.9	0.2	105	
2015	ALT	AA	23	9	3	0	15	15	90	72	1	1.9	8.0	80	51%	.273	1.01	2.00	2.37	1.99	31.1	3.4	74	
2016	IND	AAA	24	2	7	0	16	15	71¹	66	6	4.4	10.2	81	39%	.319	1.42	3.91	3.59	2.71	20.7	2.1	89	
2016	PIT	MLB	24	0	3	0	8	7	33¹	45	5	4.6	7.8	29	47%	.354	1.86	4.86	5.11	6.21	-3.2	-0.3	117	93.8
2017	*PIT*	*MLB*	*25*	*6*	*6*	*0*	*16*	*16*	*96*	*96*	*11*	*3.6*	*7.0*	*75*	*52%*	*.295*	*1.40*	*4.38*	*4.41*	*4.70*	*5.1*	*0.5*	*100*	
2018	*PIT*	*MLB*	*26*	*8*	*9*	*0*	*24*	*24*	*143²*	*115*	*17*	*5.1*	*9.9*	*158*	*52%*	*.298*	*1.37*	*4.45*	*4.65*	*5.01*	*8.7*	*0.9*	*116*	

Breakout: 16%   Improve: 30%   Collapse: 34%   Attrition: 42%   MLB: 77%   *Comparables: Brandon Workman, Mike Kickham, Andre Rienzo*

Heading into last season, Brault looked every bit like a traditional back-end lefty starter. He features a low-90s fastball, a slider, a sinker and a changeup just to keep hitters honest. Now that you know his repertoire, it's perhaps not a surprise that Brault didn't miss many bats or allow many free passes in Altoona in 2015, but he flipped the script in Indy last season, setting career-highs in strikeout and walk rates. Despite a hamstring strain that knocked him out for a bit mid-season, Brault made seven underwhelming starts for the Pirates. The Pirates tend to get the most out of guys like Brault, but they also buy in bulk. As such, Brault is likely to serve as Triple-A depth unless something goes really right for him or really wrong for Pittsburgh.

Phil Coke   LHP

Born: 7/19/82   Age: 34   Bats: L   Throws: L   Height: 6'1"   Weight: 210   Entered Pro Ball: Round 26, 2002 Draft (#786 overall)

YEAR	TEAM	LVL	AGE	W	L	SV	G	GS	IP	H	HR	BB/9	K/9	K	GB%	BABIP	WHIP	ERA	FIP	DRA	VORP	WARP	cFIP	MPH
2014	DET	MLB	31	5	2	1	62	0	58	69	5	3.1	6.4	41	56%	.340	1.53	3.88	4.00	3.93	3.6	0.4	102	96.4
2015	CHN	MLB	32	0	0	0	16	0	10	14	1	2.7	8.1	9	64%	.406	1.70	6.30	3.56	3.99	0.8	0.1	97	95.8
2015	TOR	MLB	32	0	0	0	2	0	2²	1	1	6.8	10.1	3	33%	.000	1.12	3.38	7.98	3.95	0.2	0.0	97	95.9
2015	NAS	AAA	32	0	3	0	10	0	14²	24	1	4.3	8.6	14	44%	.451	2.11	9.82	4.21	4.53	0.6	0.1	101	
2016	NYA	MLB	33	0	0	0	3	0	6	7	1	6.0	1.5	1	44%	.273	1.83	6.00	7.44	7.52	-1.7	-0.2	124	95.5
2016	SWB	AAA	33	5	3	0	20	11	70	68	3	2.7	7.8	61	49%	.308	1.27	2.96	2.97	3.92	10.5	1.1	91	
2016	PIT	MLB	33	0	0	0	3	0	4	3	0	6.8	6.8	3	40%	.300	1.50	0.00	3.94	6.50	-0.7	-0.1	121	95.3
2017	*PIT*	*MLB*	*34*	*3*	*2*	*0*	*48*	*3*	*63²*	*71*	*8*	*3.7*	*7.1*	*50*	*52%*	*.341*	*1.53*	*4.61*	*4.56*	*5.19*	*0.4*	*0.0*	*116*	
2018	*PIT*	*MLB*	*35*	*2*	*1*	*0*	*35*	*2*	*44*	*50*	*6*	*4.3*	*7.1*	*35*	*52%*	*.343*	*1.61*	*5.05*	*5.28*	*5.68*	*-2.1*	*-0.2*	*127*	

Breakout: 24%   Improve: 33%   Collapse: 15%   Attrition: 9%   MLB: 59%   *Comparables: Mike MacDougal, Oliver Perez, Dustin McGowan*

The second episode of *Narcos* is titled "The Sword of Simon Bolivar," and it chronicles Pablo Escobar's strikes against the communist militant group M-19 in the jungles of Columbia. It also pays homage to our protagonist's career, because it's 46 minutes of lefties getting slaughtered by Coke men. Phil has held southpaws to a .240/.300/.356 line, but he's up against two enemies that make the Medellin Cartel look soft: right-handed batters and Father Time. The former have smoked Coke to the tune of .295/.377/.449, and the latter has led to a steady decline in velocity.

Gerrit Cole   RHP

Born: 9/8/90   Age: 26   Bats: R   Throws: R   Height: 6'4"   Weight: 220   Entered Pro Ball: Round 1, 2011 Draft (#1 overall)

YEAR	TEAM	LVL	AGE	W	L	SV	G	GS	IP	H	HR	BB/9	K/9	K	GB%	BABIP	WHIP	ERA	FIP	DRA	VORP	WARP	cFIP	MPH
2014	IND	AAA	23	3	1	0	4	4	22¹	21	1	2.0	6.4	16	51%	.294	1.16	2.01	3.31	2.83	7.2	0.7	96	
2014	PIT	MLB	23	11	5	0	22	22	138	127	11	2.6	9.0	138	52%	.311	1.21	3.65	3.20	3.24	24.5	2.7	90	98.5
2015	PIT	MLB	24	19	8	0	32	32	208	183	11	1.9	8.7	202	49%	.304	1.09	2.60	2.69	3.53	35.9	3.8	87	98.6
2016	PIT	MLB	25	7	10	0	21	21	116	131	7	2.8	7.6	98	48%	.345	1.44	3.88	3.37	4.56	10.3	1.1	99	98.3
2017	*PIT*	*MLB*	*26*	*11*	*10*	*0*	*29*	*29*	*174*	*166*	*19*	*2.7*	*8.3*	*160*	*55%*	*.298*	*1.26*	*3.74*	*3.79*	*4.04*	*22.0*	*2.3*	*92*	
2018	*PIT*	*MLB*	*27*	*12*	*10*	*0*	*32*	*32*	*202¹*	*175*	*22*	*2.7*	*9.0*	*203*	*55%*	*.307*	*1.16*	*3.65*	*3.78*	*4.11*	*30.0*	*3.1*	*93*	

Breakout: 26%   Improve: 62%   Collapse: 14%   Attrition: 7%   MLB: 90%   *Comparables: Jon Lester, Rich Harden, David Price*

Are we really to believe these are the acts of loving baseball gods? A just god? A wise god? We'd been waiting for Gerrit Cole, Ace since his UCLA days, and he finally delivered in 2015. "That's great," we said. "Now show us you're a *True* Ace. Do it again." But Cole didn't get the chance to enter the upper echelon of year-in, year-out alpha dogs, because for the umpteenth time, the baseball powers-that-be decided we didn't deserve to see a fun, young pitcher in his prime. Cole started strong, sporting a 2.77 ERA through his first 12 starts. Then he hit the DL with a triceps strain in June, missing more than a month. He looked good through four outings upon his return, but that's when the baseball gods, those feckless thugs, really struck. The big right-hander got torched by the Reds, Dodgers and Astros with only one good start in between, and it was back to the DL, this time with elbow inflammation. A visit to famed Dr. Neal ElAttrache revealed no structural damage, but Cole made just one more start before being shut down for good, opting for a full offseason of rest and recovery. It's entirely possible the Cole Train gets right back on track at age 26. He's about to get expensive, though, and given his previous contract gripes and his Scott Boras ties, a long-term future in Pittsburgh seems like a longshot. That gives the Pirates a narrow window to win with Cole, a window in which he should be dominant on the mound, if his west wing stays healthy. But if injuries deprive us of Cole's prime, feel free to march into one or Two Cathedrals and unleash on the baseball deities, full President Bartlet style.

Neftali Feliz   RHP

Born: 5/2/88   Age: 29   Bats: R   Throws: R   Height: 6'3"   Weight: 235   Entered Pro Ball: International Free Agent, 2005

YEAR	TEAM	LVL	AGE	W	L	SV	G	GS	IP	H	HR	BB/9	K/9	K	GB%	BABIP	WHIP	ERA	FIP	DRA	VORP	WARP	cFIP	MPH
2014	ROU	AAA	26	1	1	7	24	0	28²	19	6	2.5	9.7	31	30%	.203	0.94	3.14	5.20	4.07	4.0	0.4	104	
2014	TEX	MLB	26	2	1	13	30	0	31²	20	5	3.1	6.0	21	29%	.176	0.98	1.99	4.93	6.14	-5.8	-0.6	124	97.2
2015	ROU	AAA	27	0	1	0	10	0	11	15	1	3.3	9	11	23%	.368	1.73	7.36	4.14	5.04	-0.1	0.0	97	
2015	TEX	MLB	27	1	2	6	18	0	19²	24	2	4.1	7.3	16	36%	.344	1.68	4.58	4.17	5.80	-2.4	-0.3	109	97.1
2015	DET	MLB	27	2	2	4	30	0	28¹	33	3	2.9	7.3	23	40%	.353	1.48	7.62	3.92	5.81	-3.5	-0.4	110	98.6
2016	PIT	MLB	28	4	2	2	62	0	53²	40	10	3.5	10.2	61	38%	.240	1.14	3.52	4.57	3.76	7.2	0.7	93	99.3
2017	*PIT*	*MLB*	*29*	*2*	*1*	*4*	*46*	*0*	*49*	*42*	*6*	*3.2*	*8.8*	*48*	*42%*	*.297*	*1.22*	*4.09*	*3.99*	*4.59*	*2.8*	*0.3*	*104*	
2018	*PIT*	*MLB*	*30*	*2*	*1*	*3*	*37*	*0*	*37¹*	*31*	*6*	*3.7*	*9.2*	*38*	*42%*	*.285*	*1.24*	*4.52*	*4.70*	*5.07*	*0.3*	*0.0*	*119*	

Breakout: 30%   Improve: 49%   Collapse: 25%   Attrition: 24%   MLB: 87%   *Comparables: Neal Cotts, Bill Bray, David Aardsma*

Somehow, Feliz is still just 29. Last season was a good one for Feliz, who posted the second-best strikeout rate and third-best DRA of his career. Better yet, the former Rookie of the Year technically avoided the DL all season, though his last appearance came on September 3, when he was sidelined with a vague "arm injury." That's part of the inherent risk of signing Feliz, but he proved that he still has the talent to pitch late in games.

Yeudy Garcia RHP

Born: 10/6/92 Age: 24 Bats: R Throws: R Height: 6'2" Weight: 203 Entered Pro Ball: International Free Agent, 2013

YEAR	TEAM	LVL	AGE	W	L	SV	G	GS	IP	H	HR	BB/9	K/9	K	GB%	BABIP	WHIP	ERA	FIP	DRA	VORP	WARP	cFIP	MPH
2015	WVA	A	22	12	5	1	30	21	124¹	92	4	3.0	8.1	112	54%	.259	1.07	2.10	3.33	3.74	19.3	2.1	99	
2016	BRD	A+	23	6	8	1	26	25	127¹	122	7	3.8	9.0	127	50%	.317	1.38	2.76	3.41	3.62	26.1	2.7	98	
2017	PIT	MLB	24	6	7	0	31	21	109¹	119	13	4.7	5.9	72	48%	.320	1.61	5.14	5.06	5.79	-4.2	-0.4	136	
2018	PIT	MLB	25	3	5	0	15	13	83	77	11	6.2	8.7	80	48%	.313	1.61	5.26	5.53	5.93	-3.0	-0.3	138	

Breakout: 6%   Improve: 7%   Collapse: 3%   Attrition: 9%   MLB: 11%   *Comparables: Andrew Bailey, Brad Mills, Erik Davis*

The Pirates signed Garcia out of the Dominican Republic at the relatively old age of 20, but the hard-throwing righty has made up for lost time. Working off of a plus-plus fastball and a slider that's better than what they serve at Applebee's, Garcia carved up High-A hitters, fanning 22.7 percent of them while posting a solid ERA. The drawbacks? Garcia lacks a meaningful third pitch, allows too many walks and has a delivery that some scouts argue portends a future in the bullpen. That's sort of the default loadout for "talented mid-minors right-hander," so as good as Garcia has looked at times, he needs to learn a new trick if he wants to start long term.

Tyler Glasnow RHP

Born: 8/23/93 Age: 23 Bats: L Throws: R Height: 6'8" Weight: 220 Entered Pro Ball: Round 5, 2011 Draft (#152 overall)

YEAR	TEAM	LVL	AGE	W	L	SV	G	GS	IP	H	HR	BB/9	K/9	K	GB%	BABIP	WHIP	ERA	FIP	DRA	VORP	WARP	cFIP	MPH
2014	BRD	A+	20	12	5	0	23	23	124¹	74	3	4.1	11.4	157	40%	.260	1.05	1.74	2.63	1.30	59.4	6.0	73	
2015	ALT	AA	21	5	3	0	12	12	63	41	2	2.7	11.7	82	42%	.269	0.95	2.43	1.98	1.33	26.3	2.8	58	
2015	IND	AAA	21	2	1	0	8	8	41	33	1	4.8	10.5	48	39%	.314	1.34	2.20	2.82	3.95	6.2	0.6	91	
2016	IND	AAA	22	8	3	0	20	20	110²	65	4	5.0	10.8	133	43%	.255	1.15	1.87	2.92	2.95	29.5	3.0	87	
2016	PIT	MLB	22	0	2	0	7	4	23¹	22	2	5.0	9.3	24	49%	.317	1.50	4.24	4.30	5.07	0.4	0.0	102	96.8
2017	PIT	MLB	23	6	6	0	30	15	95	82	9	4.7	9.0	96	45%	.288	1.37	4.06	4.08	4.35	8.3	0.9	100	
2018	PIT	MLB	24	7	7	0	23	23	135²	92	12	5.6	11.3	170	45%	.287	1.30	3.86	4.02	4.33	16.6	1.7	98	

Breakout: 19%   Improve: 35%   Collapse: 23%   Attrition: 23%   MLB: 74%   *Comparables: Gio Gonzalez, Henry Owens, Matt Moore*

When you watch Glasnow pitch, you can't help but come away both optimistic and frustrated. It's clear that Glasnow is capable of utter dominance. When he was first summoned to the majors in July, he left behind a wake of devastation at Triple-A. Why the angst? Glasnow's career-long command issues were exacerbated in his brief stints in the majors. In Glasnow's four starts for Pittsburgh, he was excellent once, terrible once, average once and once left hurt. Such has been the Glasnow experience to date, each tantalizing glimpse of a potential front-line starter marred by something much uglier. The Pirates will likely have to live with those ups and downs early in Glasnow's career, but he's a half-grade of command away from at least serving as a functional mid-rotation starter. Should Pittsburgh find a way to do for Glasnow what they've done for so many of their reclamation projects, the future might have something special in store for him yet.

Clay Holmes RHP

Born: 3/27/93 Age: 24 Bats: R Throws: R Height: 6'5" Weight: 230 Entered Pro Ball: Round 9, 2011 Draft (#272 overall)

YEAR	TEAM	LVL	AGE	W	L	SV	G	GS	IP	H	HR	BB/9	K/9	K	GB%	BABIP	WHIP	ERA	FIP	DRA	VORP	WARP	cFIP	MPH
2015	BRD	A+	22	0	2	0	6	6	23	18	0	2.7	6.3	16	67%	.273	1.09	2.74	3.21	5.18	-0.3	0.0	106	
2016	ALT	AA	23	10	9	0	26	26	136¹	138	10	4.2	6.7	101	63%	.314	1.48	4.22	4.55	4.77	4.9	0.5	105	
2017	PIT	MLB	24	6	7	0	21	21	100¹	109	10	4.2	5.0	56	38%	.318	1.55	4.85	4.87	5.51	0.6	0.1	128	
2018	PIT	MLB	25	5	7	0	20	20	115	108	13	5.6	7.9	101	38%	.315	1.56	5.00	5.26	5.68	-1.2	-0.1	131	

Breakout: 6%   Improve: 12%   Collapse: 10%   Attrition: 22%   MLB: 29%   *Comparables: Manny Banuelos, D.J. Mitchell, Andrew Chafin*

Unlike with most Clay Holmes, the foundation isn't the problem here. Every scouting report on the big right-hander uses phrases like "power frame" or "workhouse build" or "broad shoulders." Holmes' issue lies instead in his lack of control, as evidenced by the 10.7 percent walk rate he posted in Altoona. Last season was Holmes' first full one since undergoing Tommy John surgery, so perhaps we should cut him some slack, but some scouts think Holmes is starting to fit the mold of a power reliever rather than a back-end starter. The good news is he throws hard and flashes a power curve, so maybe, just maybe, we'll someday say that Clay Holmes is kiln it out of the pen.

Jared Hughes RHP

Born: 7/4/85 Age: 31 Bats: R Throws: R Height: 6'7" Weight: 240 Entered Pro Ball: Round 4, 2006 Draft (#110 overall)

YEAR	TEAM	LVL	AGE	W	L	SV	G	GS	IP	H	HR	BB/9	K/9	K	GB%	BABIP	WHIP	ERA	FIP	DRA	VORP	WARP	cFIP	MPH
2014	PIT	MLB	28	7	5	0	63	0	64¹	51	4	2.7	5.0	36	66%	.246	1.09	1.96	3.96	3.90	4.2	0.5	106	94.7
2015	PIT	MLB	29	3	1	0	76	0	67	70	3	2.6	4.8	36	65%	.306	1.33	2.28	3.83	4.74	-0.3	0.0	112	95.2
2016	PIT	MLB	30	1	1	1	67	0	59¹	62	6	3.3	5.2	34	59%	.295	1.42	3.03	4.72	5.11	-0.9	-0.1	109	95.6
2017	PIT	MLB	31	2	3	0	50	0	52	56	6	3.4	5.3	31	69%	.294	1.44	5.02	4.81	5.11	-1.1	-0.1	100	
2018	PIT	MLB	32	2	1	0	45	0	47²	46	5	3.0	5.6	30	69%	.296	1.30	4.39	4.60	4.98	0.8	0.1	114	

Breakout: 35%   Improve: 48%   Collapse: 21%   Attrition: 19%   MLB: 85%   *Comparables: Burke Badenhop, Rafael Perez, Kevin Gregg*

Hughes increased his strikeout rate in 2016. The problem is he increased it to just 13.2 percent, and that "jump" was mitigated by a rise in walks and homers and a decline in ground balls. Hughes threw his heavy, sinking two-seamer exactly as often as he did in 2015, but swapped out some sliders for a few more changeups. It didn't matter much, namely because batters hit .294 against his sinker. Hughes induced eight more double plays—his specialty—and finished with a solid ERA, but DRA and WARP tell a less encouraging story. He's durable and youngish enough that he'll get more chances, but maybe what he really needs is a change of scenery to a team with a big home ballpark that specializes in working with ground-ball pitchers. Ah, crap ...

Drew Hutchison   RHP

Born: 8/22/90   Age: 26   Bats: L   Throws: R   Height: 6'3"   Weight: 205   Entered Pro Ball: Round 15, 2009 Draft (#460 overall)

YEAR	TEAM	LVL	AGE	W	L	SV	G	GS	IP	H	HR	BB/9	K/9	K	GB%	BABIP	WHIP	ERA	FIP	DRA	VORP	WARP	cFIP	MPH
2014	TOR	MLB	23	11	13	0	32	32	184²	173	23	2.9	9.0	184	37%	.293	1.26	4.48	3.87	3.55	26.4	2.9	96	95.2
2015	TOR	MLB	24	13	5	0	30	28	150¹	179	22	2.6	7.7	129	40%	.343	1.48	5.57	4.39	4.99	1.4	0.1	108	95.3
2016	TOR	MLB	25	1	0	0	3	2	12²	13	4	2.8	8.5	12	36%	.281	1.34	4.97	6.50	5.55	-0.5	0.0	117	94.7
2016	BUF	AAA	25	6	5	0	18	18	102	78	11	3.1	9.7	110	42%	.264	1.11	3.26	3.65	2.90	27.6	2.8	97	
2016	IND	AAA	25	1	1	0	7	6	36	37	5	3.8	7.0	28	35%	.288	1.44	4.50	4.75	4.15	4.7	0.5	97	
2016	PIT	MLB	25	0	0	0	6	1	11¹	15	2	2.4	7.9	10	35%	.371	1.59	5.56	4.77	5.60	-0.5	0.0	115	94.3
2017	PIT	MLB	26	4	5	0	25	10	75²	78	11	3.4	8.3	70	53%	.303	1.42	4.47	4.48	4.74	3.2	0.3	100	
2018	PIT	MLB	27	9	9	0	53	21	162²	155	23	3.4	9.0	163	53%	.320	1.33	4.40	4.58	4.95	9.1	0.9	115	

Breakout: 19%   Improve: 45%   Collapse: 16%   Attrition: 9%   MLB: 96%   Comparables: Mike Minor, Drew Smyly, Kyle Davies

All any of us truly desires in life is to feel wanted, whether we're seeking the affection of an admirer or the love of a parent or the adoration of an MLB team that will give us one more shot at sticking in a rotation. Hutchison must feel like the belle of the ball after the Pirates gave up Francisco Liriano, Reese McGuire and Harold Ramirez for him last August in a trade that definitely had nothing to do with salary relief. Really, how could you not want a pitcher with a career 4.93 ERA? The Pirates have had plenty of success with reclamation project pitchers—Liriano himself was one—so maybe you think they deserve the benefit of the doubt. Even if the Pirates succeed in turning Hutchison's career around, it's disappointing they punted on two good prospects for a potential back-end starter and $18 million in savings.

Mitch Keller   RHP

Born: 4/4/96   Age: 21   Bats: R   Throws: R   Height: 6'3"   Weight: 195   Entered Pro Ball: Round 2, 2014 Draft (#64 overall)

YEAR	TEAM	LVL	AGE	W	L	SV	G	GS	IP	H	HR	BB/9	K/9	K	GB%	BABIP	WHIP	ERA	FIP	DRA	VORP	WARP	cFIP	MPH
2016	WVA	A	20	8	5	0	23	23	124¹	96	4	1.3	9.5	131	50%	.282	0.92	2.46	2.41	1.65	46.5	5.1	71	
2017	PIT	MLB	21	5	6	0	19	19	85²	96	12	3.2	5.9	56	56%	.324	1.47	4.94	4.87	5.64	-0.7	-0.1	131	
2018	PIT	MLB	22	6	9	0	24	24	144¹	139	20	4.0	8.1	130	56%	.316	1.41	4.72	4.94	5.39	2.2	0.2	125	

Breakout: 17%   Improve: 21%   Collapse: 2%   Attrition: 11%   MLB: 25%   Comparables: Robert Stephenson, Alex Reyes, Luis Severino

After generating buzz as an over-slot signee in 2014, Keller doused his own prospect flame in 2015, throwing just 19 innings as he nursed a strained forearm. Consider the flames rekindled after a 2016 campaign in which Keller was arguably the most dominant and consistent starter at Low-A. Using a heavy, downhill fastball and a curveball that can miss bats, Keller crushed his opponents in West Virginia, striking out 26.8 percent of the batters he faced and posting 33 consecutive scoreless innings. The normally conservative Pirates promoted Keller to Bradenton for a playoff start, and he acquitted himself well there too. There's no ace upside here, but Keller has the frame, fastball and fluid delivery of a mid-rotation asset. The Pirates just grow these guys on trees, it seems.

Chad Kuhl   RHP

Born: 9/10/92   Age: 24   Bats: R   Throws: R   Height: 6'3"   Weight: 220   Entered Pro Ball: Round 9, 2013 Draft (#269 overall)

YEAR	TEAM	LVL	AGE	W	L	SV	G	GS	IP	H	HR	BB/9	K/9	K	GB%	BABIP	WHIP	ERA	FIP	DRA	VORP	WARP	cFIP	MPH
2014	BRD	A+	21	13	5	0	28	28	153¹	141	9	2.5	5.9	100	59%	.287	1.19	3.46	3.96	4.59	17.2	1.7	103	
2015	ALT	AA	22	11	5	0	26	26	152²	133	10	2.4	6	101	57%	.265	1.14	2.48	3.68	2.42	45.3	4.9	94	
2016	IND	AAA	23	6	3	0	16	16	83²	81	9	1.7	7.1	66	48%	.295	1.16	2.37	3.71	2.86	23.1	2.4	89	
2016	PIT	MLB	23	5	4	0	14	14	70²	73	7	2.5	6.8	53	46%	.304	1.32	4.20	3.99	5.22	1.1	0.1	109	96.1
2017	PIT	MLB	24	6	6	0	19	19	95	98	10	2.8	6.1	64	49%	.293	1.33	4.25	4.24	4.60	6.1	0.6	100	
2018	PIT	MLB	25	8	9	0	27	27	165	142	19	3.6	8.7	160	49%	.301	1.26	4.10	4.29	4.65	13.9	1.4	108	

Breakout: 20%   Improve: 40%   Collapse: 20%   Attrition: 28%   MLB: 80%   Comparables: Erik Johnson, Alex Sanabia, Robbie Ross

Every organization needs players like Kuhl; affordable, competent and with plenty of remaining minor-league options. Kuhl has quietly ascended the organizational ladder, flying under the radar as Tyler Glasnow, Jameson Taillon and others stole the spotlight. After earning spot starts in June and July, the Pirates put Kuhl in their rotation for good on August 9. He spun six quality starts in his next 10, but allowed plenty of baserunners, and DRA suggests he was lucky to escape the season with a ... ohh of course the Kuhl kid finishes with a 4.20 ERA. As a sinker-throwing lefty without inspiring secondary pitches, Kuhl's ceiling is lower than Bag End's. We've already seen his useful floor, though, and if the Pirates need someone to soak up innings, they could use Kuhl For The Summer once more.

Wade LeBlanc   LHP

Born: 8/7/84   Age: 32   Bats: L   Throws: L   Height: 6'3"   Weight: 210   Entered Pro Ball: Round 2, 2006 Draft (#61 overall)

YEAR	TEAM	LVL	AGE	W	L	SV	G	GS	IP	H	HR	BB/9	K/9	K	GB%	BABIP	WHIP	ERA	FIP	DRA	VORP	WARP	cFIP	MPH
2014	NYA	MLB	29	0	0	0	1	0	1	2	0	9.0	0.0	0	60%	.400	3.00	18.00	9.16	5.38	-0.1	0.0	108	90.5
2014	SLC	AAA	29	10	4	0	22	22	128	143	11	3.0	8.4	119	41%	.352	1.45	4.43	4.04	2.77	42.5	4.2	86	
2014	ANA	MLB	29	1	1	0	10	3	28²	25	2	1.9	6.6	21	42%	.274	1.08	3.45	3.33	4.12	1.7	0.2	106	90.2
2016	BUF	AAA	31	7	2	0	14	14	89²	84	3	2.1	8.5	85	43%	.315	1.17	1.71	2.51	1.96	33.7	3.5	85	
2016	SEA	MLB	31	3	0	1	11	8	50	52	14	1.6	7.4	41	34%	.264	1.22	4.50	5.65	5.04	1.2	0.1	109	89.0
2016	PIT	MLB	31	1	0	1	8	0	12	7	0	1.5	7.5	10	41%	.219	0.75	0.75	2.02	5.03	0.3	0.0	104	88.7
2017	PIT	MLB	32	3	3	0	47	2	57	57	6	2.8	7.8	49	46%	.300	1.31	3.83	3.87	4.18	5.0	0.5	93	
2018	PIT	MLB	33	4	2	0	60	2	74	65	9	3.4	9.3	77	46%	.312	1.26	3.95	4.11	4.47	5.8	0.6	99	

Breakout: 12%   Improve: 13%   Collapse: 14%   Attrition: 14%   MLB: 37%   Comparables: Shawn Hill, Eric Stults, Lenny DiNardo

So no one told you life was gonna be this way [clap clap clap clap]
Fastball's a joke, arm's broke, you just got DFAAAAAAd
But then the Pirates said "we want you here,"
Though you haven't had good games, good starts, good 'pens
Or a good careeeeeer but
Seventh chance for youuuuu
Cause the Pirates are poor
Seventh chance for youuuuu
Six teams showed you the door
Seventh chance for youuuuu
This will end poorly toooooooo.

Juan Nicasio   RHP

Born: 8/31/86   Age: 30   Bats: R   Throws: R   Height: 6'4"   Weight: 255   Entered Pro Ball: International Free Agent, 2006

YEAR	TEAM	LVL	AGE	W	L	SV	G	GS	IP	H	HR	BB/9	K/9	K	GB%	BABIP	WHIP	ERA	FIP	DRA	VORP	WARP	cFIP	MPH
2014	CSP	AAA	27	3	2	1	10	4	35²	41	4	3.8	9.1	36	43%	.378	1.57	4.54	4.48	4.56	4.1	0.4	96	
2014	COL	MLB	27	6	6	0	33	14	93²	107	19	3.0	6.1	63	49%	.298	1.47	5.38	5.42	5.22	-4.8	-0.5	110	96.2
2015	LAN	MLB	28	1	3	1	53	1	58¹	59	1	4.9	10.0	65	47%	.360	1.56	3.86	2.85	4.29	2.8	0.3	100	98.1
2016	PIT	MLB	29	10	7	0	52	12	118	117	15	3.4	10.5	138	45%	.331	1.37	4.50	3.82	3.34	24.0	2.5	89	97.2
2017	*PIT*	*MLB*	*30*	*2*	*2*	*0*	*50*	*0*	*52*	*49*	*6*	*3.7*	*9.6*	*56*	*46%*	*.304*	*1.36*	*3.87*	*3.90*	*4.20*	*4.2*	*0.4*	*93*	
2018	*PIT*	*MLB*	*31*	*1*	*1*	*1*	*27*	*0*	*28²*	*26*	*3*	*3.5*	*9.5*	*30*	*46%*	*.322*	*1.30*	*3.98*	*4.14*	*4.49*	*2.0*	*0.2*	*99*	

Breakout: 22%   Improve: 41%   Collapse: 19%   Attrition: 13%   MLB: 82%   Comparables: *Jorge De La Rosa, Luke Hochevar, Carlos Villanueva*

The definition of insanity is putting Nicasio in the rotation again and again and expecting different results. Nicasio suffered a 5.05 ERA through 12 starts last season, but posted a 3.88 ERA in 56 innings of relief. That should look familiar; Nicasio's career splits now have him as the proud owner of a 5.11 ERA as a starter versus a 3.80 ERA coming out of the pen. You can't blame the Pirates for thinking Ray Searage might be able to turn water into a mid-rotation starter one more time, but the evidence is pretty clear. Nicasio induced more grounders and allowed fewer fly balls as a reliever, and batters lost more than 100 points of slugging against him in that role.

Ivan Nova   RHP

Born: 1/12/87   Age: 30   Bats: R   Throws: R   Height: 6'5"   Weight: 240   Entered Pro Ball: International Free Agent, 2004

YEAR	TEAM	LVL	AGE	W	L	SV	G	GS	IP	H	HR	BB/9	K/9	K	GB%	BABIP	WHIP	ERA	FIP	DRA	VORP	WARP	cFIP	MPH
2014	NYA	MLB	27	2	2	0	4	4	20²	32	6	2.6	5.2	12	50%	.371	1.84	8.27	6.93	5.60	-1.8	-0.2	115	94.9
2015	SWB	AAA	28	1	1	0	2	2	11	12	1	2.5	5.7	7	43%	.324	1.36	4.91	4.16	5.14	0.2	0.0	103	
2015	NYA	MLB	28	6	11	0	17	17	94	99	13	3.2	6.0	63	52%	.290	1.40	5.07	4.84	4.39	7.1	0.8	105	95.6
2016	NYA	MLB	29	7	6	1	21	15	97¹	107	19	2.3	6.9	75	56%	.297	1.36	4.90	5.06	3.79	16.6	1.7	90	95.4
2016	PIT	MLB	29	5	2	0	11	11	64²	68	4	0.4	7.2	52	55%	.318	1.10	3.06	2.66	3.83	10.8	1.1	93	95.6
2017	*PIT*	*MLB*	*30*	*10*	*10*	*0*	*28*	*28*	*168*	*175*	*20*	*2.3*	*7.2*	*135*	*66%*	*.303*	*1.31*	*4.01*	*4.04*	*4.33*	*15.9*	*1.6*	*100*	
2018	*PIT*	*MLB*	*31*	*10*	*10*	*0*	*28*	*28*	*174*	*174*	*20*	*2.1*	*7.3*	*141*	*66%*	*.318*	*1.23*	*3.95*	*4.10*	*4.46*	*20.5*	*2.1*	*102*	

Breakout: 25%   Improve: 48%   Collapse: 17%   Attrition: 15%   MLB: 89%   Comparables: *Brett Myers, Jorge De La Rosa, Wandy Rodriguez*

The headlines almost write themselves. "Ivan the Terrible No Longer; Super Nova Shines in Pittsburgh." Nova looked like he'd burned out in his 191 post-Tommy John innings in New York, flirting with a 5.00 ERA and a DRA that was only slightly more optimistic. The Pirates traded for him at the deadline nonetheless, and they once again turned Yankees trash into their treasure. Nova morphed back into a viable mid-rotation starter in Pittsburgh, dramatically cutting his walk rate while missing more bats and keeping the ball in the yard. Rather than changing Nova's repertoire, the Pirates focused on his approach, encouraging Nova to attack the zone and throw inside instead of nibbling. The result? Nova allowed three walks in 11 starts in Pittsburgh after walking 25 in 15 starts in pinstripes, and then re-signed for three years as a free agent.

Felipe Rivero   LHP

Born: 7/5/91   Age: 25   Bats: L   Throws: L   Height: 6'2"   Weight: 210   Entered Pro Ball: International Free Agent, 2008

YEAR	TEAM	LVL	AGE	W	L	SV	G	GS	IP	H	HR	BB/9	K/9	K	GB%	BABIP	WHIP	ERA	FIP	DRA	VORP	WARP	cFIP	MPH
2014	HAR	AA	22	2	7	0	10	10	43²	45	4	3.7	7.8	38	52%	.304	1.44	4.12	4.18	3.23	9.7	1.0	93	
2015	WAS	MLB	23	2	1	2	49	0	48¹	35	2	2.0	8.0	43	47%	.250	0.95	2.79	2.67	3.72	5.3	0.6	96	98.4
2016	WAS	MLB	24	0	3	1	47	0	49²	43	4	2.7	9.6	53	48%	.310	1.17	4.53	3.31	3.25	9.5	1.0	88	98.5
2016	PIT	MLB	24	1	3	0	28	0	27¹	23	3	5.9	12.8	39	48%	.317	1.50	3.29	3.84	3.71	3.8	0.4	88	99.8
2017	*PIT*	*MLB*	*25*	*3*	*3*	*5*	*59*	*0*	*62*	*58*	*5*	*3.6*	*9.0*	*63*	*51%*	*.302*	*1.32*	*3.46*	*3.54*	*3.87*	*7.3*	*0.8*	*84*	
2018	*PIT*	*MLB*	*26*	*2*	*1*	*2*	*40*	*0*	*42¹*	*31*	*3*	*4.2*	*10.8*	*51*	*51%*	*.301*	*1.19*	*3.35*	*3.48*	*3.78*	*6.3*	*0.6*	*80*	

Breakout: 41%   Improve: 63%   Collapse: 14%   Attrition: 15%   MLB: 88%   Comparables: *Jordan Walden, Will Smith, Macay McBride*

Life got a lot tougher for Rivero at the trade deadline. In Washington, he was a success story, the failed-starter-turned-dominant-reliever representative of Mike Rizzo's never-ending ability to fleece the Rays. In Pittsburgh, he's the guy who replaced Mark Melancon, and while he has the stuff to adequately fill those big shoes, he'll need a better idea of where the ball is going. Half of the 10 runs Rivero allowed as a Pirate came on September 25, when he got shellacked in one-third of an inning against, who else, the Nationals. Rivero was good otherwise, although not quite Melancon good, and he won't be until he stops giving up walks the way Tampa Bay gives up good pitchers.

A.J. Schugel RHP

Born: 6/27/89   Age: 28   Bats: R   Throws: R   Height: 6'0"   Weight: 200   Entered Pro Ball: Round 25, 2010 Draft (#774 overall)

YEAR	TEAM	LVL	AGE	W	L	SV	G	GS	IP	H	HR	BB/9	K/9	K	GB%	BABIP	WHIP	ERA	FIP	DRA	VORP	WARP	cFIP	MPH
2014	MOB	AA	25	6	4	0	26	26	147²	142	3	3.0	7.1	117	46%	.319	1.30	3.47	3.00	3.64	26.1	2.8	97	
2015	MOB	AA	26	7	2	0	12	12	77¹	74	5	1.7	6.1	52	52%	.295	1.15	2.21	3.46	3.23	16.0	1.7	90	
2015	RNO	AAA	26	2	7	0	9	9	38	65	4	4	6.4	27	44%	.427	2.16	10.18	5.05	6.67	-5.8	-0.6	111	
2015	ARI	MLB	26	0	0	0	5	0	9	17	2	5.0	5.0	5	61%	.385	2.44	5.00	6.61	4.83	-0.1	0.0	113	94.2
2016	IND	AAA	27	1	2	0	13	0	18	13	0	1.5	9.0	18	44%	.283	0.89	4.00	1.83	2.96	4.0	0.4	86	
2016	PIT	MLB	27	2	2	1	36	0	52	41	4	2.2	8.0	46	42%	.264	1.04	3.63	3.22	4.06	5.2	0.5	100	94.7
2017	PIT	MLB	28	1	1	0	20	0	21	22	2	3.2	6.8	16	43%	.299	1.38	4.03	4.03	4.32	1.4	0.1	98	
2018	PIT	MLB	29	2	1	0	40	0	42	35	4	4.5	9.4	44	43%	.311	1.33	3.99	4.17	4.48	3.0	0.3	100	

Breakout: 4%   Improve: 14%   Collapse: 8%   Attrition: 17%   MLB: 32%   Comparables: Carlos Torres, Everett Teaford, Steve Johnson

Schugel sure has moved around a lot in his brief career. Drafted by the Angels in 2010, Schugel was sent to Arizona as part of the Tyler Skaggs deal in 2013. After stalling out in the high minors, he was released last offseason and claimed by the Mariners, then released again and claimed by the Pirates. The son of former Twins catcher and current Reds scout Jeff, A.J. relied heavily on a fastball/changeup combo to keep hitters off balance during his solid Pittsburgh debut. Before you get *too* excited about the prospects of a cheap, league-average reliever, a word of caution: Schugel hit the 60-day DL with a right shoulder injury late in the season. That's not a promising sign for a player whose calling card is logging multi-inning outings, but doubt Schugel's survival skills at your own risk; the man endured stints in the Angels, D-backs and Mariners systems, after all. Bear Grylls has filmed entire episodes about less.

Jameson Taillon RHP

Born: 11/18/91   Age: 25   Bats: R   Throws: R   Height: 6'5"   Weight: 220   Entered Pro Ball: Round 1, 2010 Draft (#2 overall)

YEAR	TEAM	LVL	AGE	W	L	SV	G	GS	IP	H	HR	BB/9	K/9	K	GB%	BABIP	WHIP	ERA	FIP	DRA	VORP	WARP	cFIP	MPH
2016	IND	AAA	24	4	2	0	10	10	61²	44	2	0.9	8.9	61	49%	.253	0.81	2.04	1.95	1.44	26.8	2.8	66	
2016	PIT	MLB	24	5	4	0	18	18	104	99	13	1.5	7.4	85	55%	.287	1.12	3.38	3.75	3.55	20.9	2.2	90	96.5
2017	PIT	MLB	25	10	9	0	29	29	165¹	162	19	2.0	7.7	141	45%	.296	1.20	3.71	3.74	4.02	21.3	2.2	92	
2018	PIT	MLB	26	11	10	0	32	32	211²	189	23	1.9	8.4	198	45%	.305	1.11	3.50	3.63	3.95	32.7	3.4	88	

Breakout: 19%   Improve: 55%   Collapse: 19%   Attrition: 13%   MLB: 95%   Comparables: David Price, Gerrit Cole, Jered Weaver

So *that's* what Taillon can do when he's healthy. The second overall pick in the 2010 draft finally stayed on the mound for, well, most of a season, and logged more innings than he did from 2013-2015 combined. That's largely because he missed *all* of 2014 and 2015, and it was encouraging to see Taillon return no worse for the wear, throwing in the mid-90s with a devastating curveball and a solid changeup. It wouldn't be a Taillon season without an injury of some sort, and the Canadian-Texan did miss the better part of a month with shoulder soreness. He was even more effective upon returning though, turning "here we go agains" into "this was worth the waits." Now comes the real question: after logging a career-high in innings, can Taillon do it again this season? Let's hope so, because baseball is a little more fun when he's right.

Ryan Vogelsong RHP

Born: 7/22/77   Age: 39   Bats: R   Throws: R   Height: 6'4"   Weight: 215   Entered Pro Ball: Round 5, 1998 Draft (#158 overall)

YEAR	TEAM	LVL	AGE	W	L	SV	G	GS	IP	H	HR	BB/9	K/9	K	GB%	BABIP	WHIP	ERA	FIP	DRA	VORP	WARP	cFIP	MPH
2014	SFN	MLB	36	8	13	0	32	32	184²	178	18	2.8	7.4	151	41%	.294	1.28	4.00	3.82	5.34	-10.4	-1.1	117	92.6
2015	SFN	MLB	37	9	11	0	33	22	135	140	17	3.9	7.2	108	47%	.299	1.47	4.67	4.55	5.71	-10.3	-1.1	117	93.6
2016	ALT	AA	38	1	0	0	2	2	11	8	1	1.6	3.3	4	50%	.212	0.91	2.45	4.36	4.72	0.5	0.0	106	
2016	IND	AAA	38	0	2	0	2	2	11	9	3	0.8	3.3	4	51%	.176	0.91	3.27	6.26	3.88	1.8	0.2	101	
2016	PIT	MLB	38	3	7	0	24	14	82¹	80	11	4.4	6.7	61	43%	.277	1.46	4.81	5.04	5.71	-3.8	-0.4	123	92.4
2017	PIT	MLB	39	6	6	0	17	17	91	93	13	3.9	7.1	72	49%	.314	1.45	4.86	4.86	5.49	0.7	0.1	128	
2018	PIT	MLB	40	7	10	0	26	26	151²	150	22	3.9	6.7	114	49%	.303	1.42	5.13	5.35	5.79	-3.5	-0.4	136	

Breakout: 8%   Improve: 20%   Collapse: 8%   Attrition: 4%   MLB: 42%   Comparables: Bruce Chen, Brian Moehler, Paul Byrd

In May of 2016, BP author Rob Mains created the Vogelsong Award, an honor bestowed upon the best-performing hitter and pitcher in a given month who did not appear in the *2016 Baseball Prospectus Annual*. The award is named in memory of the four-year gap Vogelsong experienced between Annual entries from 2008-2011, during his three-year stint in Japan. The 2016 inaugural winners? Jeremy Hazelbaker and Dan Straily in April; Bobby Wilson and Joseph Biagini in May; Whit Merrifield and Buddy Boshers in June; Jett Bandy and Brandon Kintzler in July; Ryon Healy and Matt Strahm in August; and finally, T.J. Rivera and Matthew Bowman in September. Why waste your time listing the mostly anonymous recipients of a made-up award? Because we promise it's still much more interesting than Ryan Vogelsong's 2016 season.

Tony Watson LHP

Born: 5/30/85   Age: 32   Bats: L   Throws: L   Height: 6'4"   Weight: 225   Entered Pro Ball: Round 9, 2007 Draft (#278 overall)

YEAR	TEAM	LVL	AGE	W	L	SV	G	GS	IP	H	HR	BB/9	K/9	K	GB%	BABIP	WHIP	ERA	FIP	DRA	VORP	WARP	cFIP	MPH
2014	PIT	MLB	29	10	2	2	78	0	77¹	64	5	1.7	9.4	81	51%	.298	1.02	1.63	2.66	3.00	12.8	1.4	80	96.7
2015	PIT	MLB	30	4	1	1	77	0	75¹	55	3	2.0	7.4	62	50%	.251	0.96	1.91	2.87	4.70	0.1	0.0	98	96.3
2016	PIT	MLB	31	2	5	15	70	0	67²	52	10	2.7	7.7	58	46%	.232	1.06	3.06	4.41	4.23	5.6	0.6	100	95.5
2017	PIT	MLB	32	3	3	25	59	0	62	58	8	2.8	7.7	54	54%	.281	1.21	3.97	4.16	4.28	4.4	0.5	98	
2018	PIT	MLB	33	3	1	16	55	0	58²	51	7	3.0	7.1	46	54%	.280	1.20	4.37	4.53	4.91	1.5	0.2	116	

Breakout: 23%   Improve: 45%   Collapse: 23%   Attrition: 12%   MLB: 95%   Comparables: Scot Shields, Brian Fuentes, Luke Gregerson

From 2013-2015, Watson was one of the better setup men in the game. He threw 224 innings with a sub-2.00 ERA, but 2014 All-Star appearance aside, Watson remained largely anonymous, recording just five saves. In 2016—a year partially defined by positive reliever usage—Watson notched 15 saves, but he was average-ish by ERA and downright bad by DRA. It doesn't take a detective to figure out why Watson's numbers took a turn for the worse. His walk and homer rates went up while his ground-ball rate, strand rate and velocity went down. He's a Proven Closer (TM) now, though, so whether his value increased or decreased heading into his walk year … well, that's an unsolved mystery.

Trevor Williams   RHP

Born: 4/25/92   Age: 25   Bats: R   Throws: R   Height: 6'3"   Weight: 230   Entered Pro Ball: Round 2, 2013 Draft (#44 overall)

YEAR	TEAM	LVL	AGE	W	L	SV	G	GS	IP	H	HR	BB/9	K/9	K	GB%	BABIP	WHIP	ERA	FIP	DRA	VORP	WARP	cFIP	MPH
2014	JUP	A+	22	8	6	0	23	23	129	138	5	2.0	6.3	90	52%	.322	1.29	2.79	3.17	3.81	25.6	2.6	92	
2014	JAX	AA	22	0	1	0	3	3	15	22	0	3.6	8.4	14	69%	.431	1.87	6.00	2.52	2.31	4.9	0.5	89	
2015	JAX	AA	23	7	8	0	22	21	117	126	9	2.8	6.8	88	54%	.320	1.38	4.00	3.75	3.04	26.5	2.9	92	
2015	NWO	AAA	23	0	2	0	3	3	14	15	0	4.5	8.4	13	46%	.341	1.57	2.57	3.46	3.67	2.5	0.3	102	
2016	IND	AAA	24	9	6	0	20	19	110¹	103	5	2.4	6.0	74	53%	.284	1.21	2.53	3.34	3.51	22.3	2.3	95	
2016	PIT	MLB	24	1	1	0	7	1	12²	19	4	3.6	7.8	11	49%	.366	1.89	7.82	6.74	5.37	-0.4	0.0	109	96.7
2017	PIT	MLB	25	2	2	0	6	6	30	33	3	3.0	5.7	19	46%	.298	1.47	4.35	4.31	4.70	1.6	0.2	100	
2018	PIT	MLB	26	7	9	0	26	26	151²	140	19	4.4	8.5	143	46%	.313	1.41	4.52	4.74	5.12	6.3	0.7	118	

Breakout: 17%   Improve: 22%   Collapse: 27%   Attrition: 49%   MLB: 61%   *Comparables: Aaron Brooks, Mike Wright, Brad Mills*

If you're reading this you probably agree that wins are a meaningless stat, but there's an exception to every rule. On Wednesday, September 7, Williams recorded his first "W" in the majors, pitching three scoreless innings against the Cardinals. There's nothing particularly remarkable about that distinction, but baseball took notice because of who was in attendance: Williams' wife, his baby son and his dad, who was in the midst of a battle with lymphoma. Williams got to present the game ball to his father in a moment the cameras caught, and it got real dusty real fast at PNC Park. It's tough to tell exactly what the future holds for Williams on the mound. He could be a middle reliever or a back-end starter. But no matter how he fares, he gave us a very human moment in a year that was too short on them. That's a win in anyone's book.

LINEOUTS

Hitters

NAME	POS	TEAM	LVL	AGE	PA	R	2B	3B	HR	RBI	BB	K	SB	CS	AVG/OBP/SLG	TAv	VORP	BABIP	BRR	FRAA	WARP
Stephen Alemais	SS	WEV	A-	21	168	23	5	0	1	18	5	18	9	3	.263/.297/.314	.255	7.7	.290	2.4	SS(35): -4.1	0.4
	SS	WVA	A	21	42	2	1	1	0	2	2	11	1	3	.189/.244/.270	.193	-1.8	.259	-0.9	SS(11): 0.9	-0.1
Barrett Barnes	OF	ALT	AA	24	458	60	28	7	9	47	41	105	10	4	.306/.377/.477	.308	27.5	.392	-3.7	LF(105): -1.6	2.8
Chris Bostick	INF	HAR	AA	23	297	34	11	8	6	33	25	58	8	8	.290/.356/.462	.297	18.2	.347	-0.4	2B(62): -3.7 • LF(6): 0.8	1.7
	INF	SYR	AAA	23	242	27	11	2	2	18	16	67	3	2	.203/.261/.297	.214	-3.9	.279	1.0	2B(47): -4.9 • 3B(13): -1.1	-1.0
Pedro Florimon	SS	IND	AAA	29	340	36	12	4	5	36	33	87	14	4	.255/.327/.372	.255	10.7	.338	2.1	LF(33): 4.2 • SS(29): -2.6	1.5
	SS	PIT	MLB	29	25	4	1	1	0	4	1	12	0	1	.208/.240/.333	.188	-2.7	.417	-1.7	2B(8): -0.1 • SS(6): 0.2	-0.3
Eric Fryer	C	SLN	MLB	30	41	7	2	0	0	5	3	7	0	1	.368/.415/.421	.304	3.2	.452	-0.5	C(22): -1.2	0.2
	C	PIT	MLB	30	92	12	2	1	0	8	10	18	0	2	.218/.300/.269	.236	1.7	.274	-0.2	C(32): -2.1	0.0
Jin-De Jhang	C	IND	AAA	23	23	2	1	0	0	2	1	2	0	0	.200/.261/.250	.183	-0.5	.211	0.3	C(5): 1.2	0.1
	C	ALT	AA	23	204	20	13	0	1	21	11	12	1	0	.298/.338/.383	.256	8.8	.309	1.1	C(48): -7.5	0.1
Connor Joe	3B	BRD	A+	23	443	49	26	2	5	52	45	84	2	4	.277/.351/.392	.273	18.9	.337	-0.6	3B(96): -10.6	0.9
Michael Morse	LF	PIT	MLB	34	8	0	0	0	0	0	0	2	0	0	.000/.000/.000	.003	-1.9	.000	0.0	1B(1): -0.0	-0.2
Gift Ngoepe	SS	IND	AAA	26	373	40	20	1	8	27	31	130	5	2	.217/.289/.355	.237	6.5	.328	0.4	SS(99): 5.0 • 2B(3): 0.3	1.2
Jose Osuna	OF	ALT	AA	23	283	34	18	3	6	38	23	44	1	1	.269/.329/.435	.277	8.3	.298	0.3	1B(55): -3.3 • RF(9): -0.4	0.6
	OF	IND	AAA	23	234	27	19	1	7	31	13	36	2	3	.291/.333/.482	.280	8.8	.322	0.3	1B(27): 1.0 • LF(24): 4.0	1.4

The Pirates' most recent third-round pick, **Stephen Alemais** has a unique profile as a glove-first Millennial college shortstop who grew up idolizing Derek Jeter. ❖ **Barrett Barnes** had far and away the best year of his pro career, posting a .308 TAv at Double-A. The former first rounder/Mark Appel consolation prize finally stayed healthy, hit eight homers in August and was especially deadly against left-handed pitchers. ❖ There are Duke basketballers who've found warmer welcomes than the one **Chris Bostick** received. Despite his Triple-A struggles, the Pirates must like his second-division upside. ❖ To call **Pedro Florimon** a Quad-A player would be to drastically overstate the success he's enjoyed at Triple-A. Glenn Rhee had better luck with a bat. ❖ Eternal backup catcher **Eric Fryer** recorded his most career PA, which is good news for him and bad news for the two clubs that employed him. ❖ **Jin-De Jhang** just keeps hitting and keeps moving up the ladder. With Reese McGuire gone, he has an even clearer path to becoming MLB's first Taiwanese catcher. ❖ Former supplemental first rounder **Connor Joe** hit decently well in Bradenton, but lacks power and was "This Is Fine" Dog defensively at third base. ❖ Despite his solid stint with the Pirates in 2015, **Michael Morse** tapped out just eight PA before getting DFA'd on April 13. None of the other 29 teams capitalized on Morse's free agency, and there's a chance his career is ---...-. .-. ❖ **Gift Ngoepe** and fellow prospects Dovydas Neverauskas and Warwick Saupold were arrested following an altercation at a bar in Toledo. One imagines the fight began when a fourth patron glared at Ngoepe for buying a round of Kentucky Mules for everyone, quite literally looking a Gift horse in the mouth. ❖ **Jose Osuna** is a Large Adult Son who's made slow and steady progress through the Pirates' system. He lacks the power you want from a 1B/OF prospect, but he's hit reasonably well at every stop. ❖ **Kyle Waldrop** is like a Quadruple-A guy, only instead of being stuck between the talent levels of Triple-A and the majors, he's sandwiched between Double-A and Triple-A. There's no cute name for that predicament, for obvious reasons.

Pitchers

NAME	TEAM	LVL	AGE	W	L	SV	G	GS	IP	H	HR	BB/9	K/9	K	GB%	BABIP	WHIP	ERA	FIP	DRA	VORP	WARP	cFIP	MPH
Lisalverto Bonilla	TUL	AA	26	1	2	0	7	7	37¹	33	2	3.1	9.4	39	58%	.307	1.23	3.38	2.91	2.53	10.7	1.2	89	
	OKL	AAA	26	4	5	2	24	6	73²	76	4	3.3	9.7	79	53%	.346	1.40	4.28	3.42	2.37	22.8	2.4	85	
Tyler Eppler	ALT	AA	23	9	10	0	27	27	162¹	176	14	1.8	5.9	106	42%	.310	1.29	3.99	3.89	3.10	36.0	3.9	102	
Taylor Hearn	HAG	A	21	1	0	0	8	2	22²	25	3	2.8	12.3	31	39%	.389	1.41	3.18	3.31	1.92	7.2	0.8	81	
	WVA	A	21	1	1	0	8	3	22²	15	2	4.0	14.3	36	47%	.256	1.10	1.99	2.69	1.94	7.1	0.8	80	
Gage Hinsz	WVA	A	20	6	8	0	17	17	93¹	93	8	2.4	6.5	67	43%	.296	1.26	3.66	4.33	5.82	-8.4	-0.9	111	
Nick Kingham	BRD	A+	24	2	0	0	2	2	11	8	0	0.8	8.2	10	68%	.286	0.82	0.00	1.98	2.76	3.3	0.3	86	
	ALT	AA	24	1	1	0	2	2	11	6	1	3.3	8.2	10	48%	.179	0.91	5.73	3.81	3.28	2.2	0.2	98	
Justin Masterson	IND	AAA	31	2	2	0	25	5	54¹	62	3	4.3	5.3	32	52%	.339	1.62	4.97	4.70	8.37	-19.7	-2.0	124	
Dovydas Neverauskas	ALT	AA	23	1	0	1	22	0	28	12	0	3.5	10.3	32	58%	.194	0.82	2.57	2.25	2.29	7.6	0.8	80	
	IND	AAA	23	3	4	4	25	0	30	36	1	3.3	7.2	24	52%	.368	1.57	3.60	3.20	3.55	4.7	0.5	95	
Brandon Waddell	BRD	A+	22	4	0	0	5	5	29	13	1	0.6	8.1	26	46%	.154	0.52	0.93	2.11	3.48	6.4	0.7	83	
	ALT	AA	22	7	9	0	22	20	118	122	9	4.7	7.2	94	61%	.321	1.55	4.12	4.49	5.01	0.8	0.1	104	
Jon Webb	SWB	AAA	25	4	3	1	36	5	72²	67	5	2.8	10.2	82	43%	.321	1.24	3.59	2.76	2.30	22.2	2.3	82	

Lisalverto Bonilla returned from Tommy John surgery to pitch well. That puts him a long talk with Ray Searage away from becoming a 20-game winner. ❖ Presumably the first big, hard-throwing, right-handed Texan in MLB history, **Tyler Eppler** also boasts pretty good command. The only problem? Despite his stuff, size and strike-throwing ways, he didn't miss many bats in Double-A. ❖ Acquired from the Nationals as part of the Mark Melancon deal, **Taylor Hearn** is a hard-throwing lefty with a wipeout slider who only sometimes knows where the ball is going. ❖ **Gage Hinsz** has a ways to go before he lands on any top-100 prospects lists, but the big right-hander saw his velocity tick up and more than doubled his previous career-high workload. Not bad for an 11th-round pick out of Montana. ❖ Tommy John survivor **Nick Kingham** climbed back on the mound in late July, making six rehab starts in rookie-ball before rejoining the ranks of Double-A. The Monastic Pig is poised to serve as the type of asset the Pirates truly need; yet another back-end starting option. ❖ The Pirates popped high-school righty and Clemson commit **Travis MacGregor** earlier than most draft pundits expected when they took him 68th overall. He signed for almost $50,000 under slot, which is probably not a coincidence. ❖ Long known for his sinker with late downward movement, **Justin Masterson**'s career is unfortunately following a similar trajectory. The righty threw just 59 innings in the minors—mostly as a reliever—following offseason arthroscopic shoulder surgery. ❖ **Dovydas Neverauskas** a) would be the first Lithuanian-born major leaguer since 1933, b) made the Eastern League All-Star team, c) comes from a long line of Olympic discus throwers, d) allowed just two hits in 44 PA in May, e) was *not* the Pirates prospect with the best name to get arrested after a bar fight in Toledo in late August. Only one of those isn't true. ❖ Expensive fourth-round pick **Braeden Ogle** pairs a mid-90s fastball with an advanced breaking pitch, meaning many batters will get caught looking at his curves. ❖ Former College World Series star **Brandon Waddell** allowed 61 free passes in 118 innings at Double-A last season, truly making him the Minister of Silly Walks. ❖ **Tyler Webb** is a big left-hander with a decent fastball/slider combo and a deceptive delivery. He could get his feet wet as a LOOGY, but has some upside beyond that.

SAN DIEGO PADRES

Essay by Dustin Palmateer

Player comments by Matt Collins and BP staff

The date was July 29, 2016.

Matt Kemp swaggered to the plate in the bottom of the ninth, kicked at the back of the batter's box a dozen times and stared out at Reds journeyman Blake Wood. He took a couple of fastballs for strikes before eventually succumbing to a hard-biting slider, and swaggered back to a dugout he'd grown unfamiliar with. Most all the players acquired with Kemp just a year and half earlier—in A.J. Preller's frantic first offseason as general manager—were gone. Justin Upton had departed via free agency; Craig Kimbrel, Melvin Upton Jr. and a broken James Shields had left via trade; Will Middlebrooks was somewhere in the minors. Only Wil Myers and Derek Norris remained, and Norris—with an OPS hovering around .600—was there in spirit only.

It would be Kemp's last at-bat as a Padre, as he was traded to the Braves the next day for Hector Olivera in an exchange of the unwanted.

Kemp was acquired in December of 2014 for Yasmani Grandal and a few spare parts, a deal that didn't make sense then or now, but kicked off the Padres then-bold and hopeful strategy of landing every big-name vet on the market. Since the trade, Grandal has developed into one of the game's best two-way catchers with the Dodgers, combining power and patience at the plate with league-best pitch framing behind it. Kemp has dealt with arthritic hips and disinterest in right field while providing good-not-great production offensively—nowhere near enough hitting to make up for a declining set of skills and a hefty paycheck. Ultimately the deal would go on to symbolize San Diego's failure in evaluating what they had and what they wanted, along with the pratfalls of a rookie GM going all-in before knowing where the coffee machine is stationed.

When the dust settled, the Padres finished 2015 and 2016 with 182 combined losses, and were somehow, someway *worse* than the 2011–2014 squads, none of which won more than 77 games and all of which employed Alexi Amarista. The good news is that Preller's clumsy early moves and the demise of his Frankenstein roster hid the inner-workings of a greater plan: to build a player development machine driven by good, old-fashioned scouting.

✦ ✦ ✦

PADRES PROSPECTUS
2016 W-L: 68-94, 5TH IN NL WEST

Pythag	.446	24th	DER	.704	13th
RS/G	4.23	20th	B-Age	28.1	10th
RA/G	4.75	24th	P-Age	27.9	10th
TAv	.252	26th	Salary	$100.8M	19th
BRR	18	2nd	M$/MW	$4.5M	6th
TAv-P	.275	24th	DL Days	1369	26th
FIP	4.44	25th	$ on DL	16%	20th

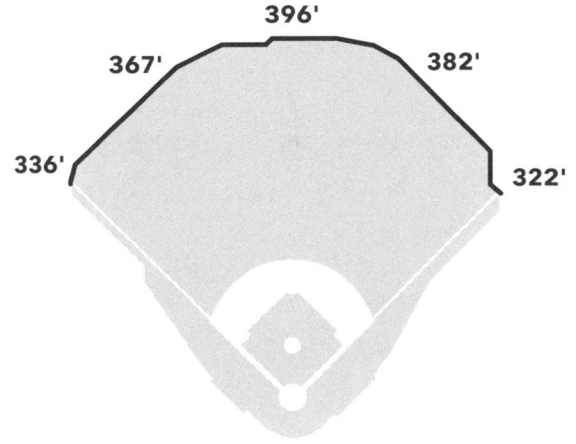

Outfield wall profile: **8'** to **11'**

Three-Year Park Factors

Runs	Runs/RH	Runs/LH	HR/RH	HR/LH
94	95	88	106	84

Top Hitter WARP	3.5	Wil Myers
Top Pitcher WARP	2.6	Drew Pomeranz
Top Prospect		Manuel Margot

2016 Hit List Ranking

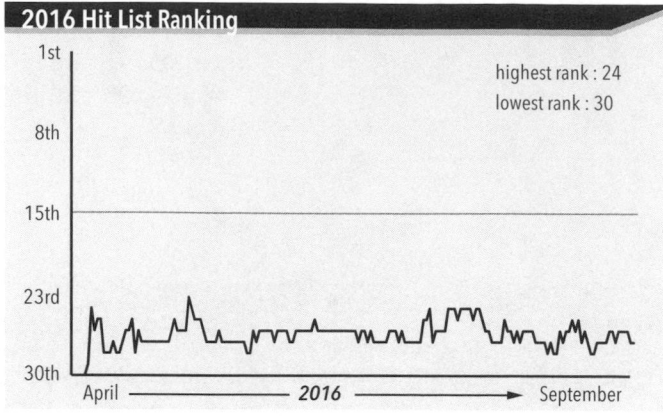

highest rank : 24
lowest rank : 30

April ——— *2016* ——→ September

Committed Payroll (in millions)

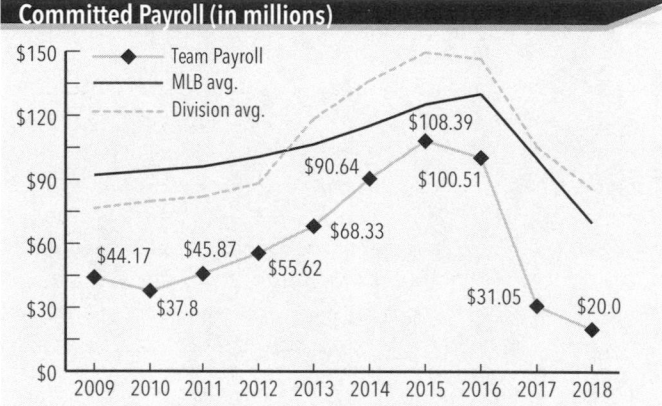

- ◆ Team Payroll
- —— MLB avg.
- ---- Division avg.

$108.39
$90.64
$100.51
$68.33
$55.62
$44.17
$45.87
$37.8
$31.05
$20.0

2009 2010 2011 2012 2013 2014 2015 2016 2017 2018

Farm System Ranking

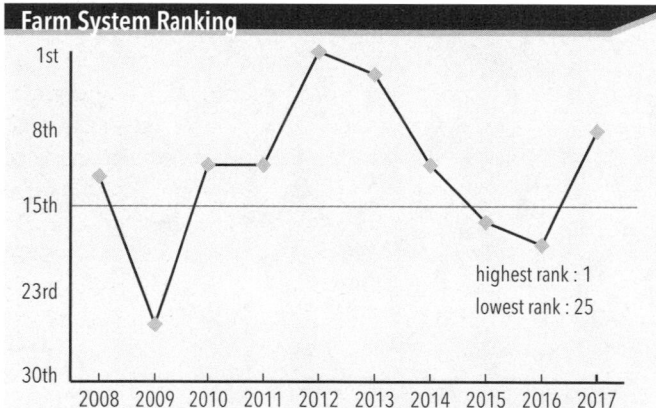

highest rank : 1
lowest rank : 25

2008 2009 2010 2011 2012 2013 2014 2015 2016 2017

Personnel

EVP, General Manager:
A.J. Preller

VP, Assistant General Manager:
Fred Uhlman Jr.

Assistant General Manager:
Josh Stein

Manager:
Andy Green

After that 2014-2015 offseason—which Rany Jazayerli once described, in a single article at Grantland, as disastrous, destructive and disturbing (cue Jackie Chiles)—Preller started to string together good move after good move. For example:

- He held Craig Kimbrel just long enough for Dave Dombrowski to get settled in Boston, dealing him to the Red Sox last offseason for Manuel Margot, the current no. 1 prospect in the farm system, and a trio of promising youngsters in Javier Guerra, Logan Allen and Carlos Asuaje.
- He moved enigmatic first baseman Yonder Alonso to the A's for Drew Pomeranz in a nondescript swap of disappointments. Of course, only one of them is either nondescript or disappointing now (unless you're hanging out at a Dunkin Donuts in Allston). Pomeranz, after posting a 2.47 first-half ERA as a starter in a decidedly not disappointing stint in San Diego, was flipped to Boston in July for diminutive right-hander Anderson Espinoza, who projects—fingers crossed—as a frontline starter on the next good Padres team. Alonso posted a career-worst .245 TAv in Oakland.
- He traded Fernando Rodney and Andrew Cashner to the Marlins last season for more notable prospects plus recovering relief ace Carter Capps.
- He even unloaded the burdensome contracts of Kemp, Shields and Upton Jr. last year without eating *all* the remaining money and netting halfway interesting prospects like Fernando Tatis Jr. and Hansel Rodriguez.

In between the front-page trades, Preller and the Padres worked tirelessly to build a foundation for future Padres success.

Early in his tenure he imported respected baseball minds like Chris Kemp and longtime friend and colleague Don Welke from Texas to his inner circle. He pried perennial GM-in-waiting Logan White away from the Dodgers and added Acey Kohrogi, who also spent large chunks of his career with White in L.A., to beef up San Diego's presence in the Pacific Rim. Sam Geaney, from the A's, was hired to head player development, and Preller also reportedly stocked up on scouts across the board, names that rarely hit the bright lights of the internet or print but remain undeniably important to sustainable success. He didn't completely clean house, either; Fred Uhlman Jr. and Mark Conner were kept on in prominent roles, not to mention Josh Stein—steadfast survivor of three regime changes—and most of the analytics department, helping to bridge the gap between fresh faces and some semblance of organizational stability. If the on-the-field team was the laundromat, *this* team was the lab.

Preller has also stayed true to himself throughout the process. Most general managers today are dissectors of data, delegators of responsibility, surveyors of the Big Picture. Preller—with the Ivy League pedigree of your typical modern-day GM—wears shirts that don't fit, seems to loathe anything that takes him away from a ballpark (like press conferences and interviews) and is far more interested in teenage baseball players from Venezuela than the most recent developments in Python. He's still working more like a glorified area scout than an info-age general manager, combing the countryside in search of the next big thing. Most GMs, today, dabble in scouting; Preller is a scout dabbling in GM-ing, too invested in the trees to give them up for a wide-angle view of the forest. It's different, of course, but perhaps more a feature than a bug, since these Padres seem hellbent on out-scouting every organization outside of Sonoma. It's Moneyball turned on its head.

Both Preller's 2015 and 2016 drafts are still in the way-too-soon-to-tell stage, but there's obvious talent there. Jacob Nix, once spurned by the Astros as part of the Brady Aiken debacle and later taken in the third round of the 2015 draft by the Padres, put together a solid full-season debut at Single-A Fort Wayne last season, generally drawing favorable reviews from scouts. Two of last year's first-round picks, Cal Quantrill and Hudson Potts—controversial selections for different reasons—both surpassed expectations in their pro debuts; Quantrill racked up 46 strikeouts in 37 healthy innings spread across three levels and Potts, then 17, held his own both offensively and defensively in rookie ball before graduating to Low-A Tri-City in August. Even Phil Maton, a 20th-round flyer from 2015, has a gaudy K:BB ratio in two professional seasons as a reliever, a run of dominance that continued through the Arizona Fall League.

Not surprisingly, given Preller's track record in Texas, it's in the foreign market where the Padres have made their greatest strides.

After a restrained 2015—outside of some serious flirtation with Yoan Moncada and unrestricted free agent Yasmany Tomas—the Padres spent north of $60 million on international amateurs last summer, a number that includes a hefty MLB-mandated tax for blowing past their comparatively puny bonus pool of $3 million and change. With perennial international powerhouses like the Red Sox, Yankees, Rangers and Cubs all sidelined for past spending sprees, the Padres inked eight of Baseball America's top 50 international prospects along with high-profile Cubans Adrian Morejon and Jorge Ona. Whether it's luck or skill, it may be most impressive that the Padres timed the market impeccably, making their all-in effort when a third of the league, and most of its big spenders, were in the penalty box. Not to mention just months before a new CBA would put an end to international spending outbursts. They didn't stop in Latin America either, signing their first international free agent from Asia, 19-year-old right-handed pitcher Wen-Hua Sung of Taiwan.

Combine the returns from the trades, the draft (including the Rule 5 one) and international expenditures and the few prospect holdovers salvaged from the pre-Preller days, and the farm system appears as well-stocked with high-upside and depth as it's ever been. Margot, Hunter Renfroe and Austin Hedges, all of whom have at least earned a cup of coffee, are ready for the majors right now—or at least when service-time rules say a permanent call-up makes most fiscal sense. After them, there's a group of players that may take a year or two, pitchers like Quantrill, Dinelson Lamet and college lefty Eric Lauer. Then there are the younger guys. Luis Urias, a 19-year-old second baseman, brought his strikeout resistant bat to High-A Lake Elsinore last year. Michael Gettys, born with five tools, had his best all-around season in 2016 at the same locale. Out of hurlers Espinoza, Nix, Allen, Morejon, Austin Smith, Jean Cosme and recent TJ casualty Chris Paddack, only Nix and Paddack can legally drink—both only able to grasp a cold one in January. Then there's the armada of 16- and 17-year old Latin players; many years away, but full of game-changing potential once scarce in the organization.

Maybe two and a half years isn't enough time to identify a new Padres' way, particularly when the first year involved a poorly timed (and poorly executed) win-now push followed by an abrupt pivot. So far, though, the one constant under Preller's reign has been a relentless, globetrotting pursuit of talented, high-ceiling players, and a scouting-centered approach that leans heavily on multiple looks and obsessive familiarity. It may not have been as loud as the teardowns around them, but the Padres have quietly built a strong organization from the top down.

John Conniff, longtime writer at Padres minor-league hub MadFriars.com, said that this is the most talented group of prospects he's seen in 10-plus years covering San Diego's affiliates, and that the group of baseball people finding them is as diligent as any. It's a blueprint—find good, young players and win major-league games someday—that seems plainly obvious in the abstract but remains hard to implement. The Padres are off on the right foot, with a farm system that's overflowing with equal parts slow-burn upside and production, and a mind-set to keep adding to it. What they've done since the end of the 2015 season, completely transforming the prospect cavalry and the direction of the organization, shows that, for a change, they're pointed the right way and moving forward with vigor.

✦ ✦ ✦

Of course, it's still the Padres, so everything is held together by antique fishing line and dollar store duct tape.

Preller was suspended for a month last September—the second suspension of his front office career— for keeping shady medical records in an issue that surfaced during his deadline maneuvers, particularly the Pomeranz-to-Boston deal, when the Red Sox discovered that their newly acquired left-hander had underwent some undocumented preventive health measures prior to the deal. That move happened before the Marlins sent Colin Rea, part of the Cashner deal, back to the Padres—a largely unprecedented move—because his elbow fell apart upon arrival in Miami, and amid persistent White Sox grumbling over Shields. The common thread among all of this isn't just rule breaking (or bending), but that many parties end up annoyed at Preller, piling on so much as to prompt a thorough MLB investigation. While a third suspension seems unlikely—even though Preller dances close to the line—he may have already done enough damage with some rival teams that they won't be so eager to deal with him, a notably negative side effect for a team as trade-happy as San Diego.

It's also possible that things fall apart more conventionally. Beyond simply finding talent, Preller & Co. still must prove they can *develop* it; that they can take toolsy athletes and turn them into good major-league baseball players. It's a mostly behind-the-scenes process that can make or break the best-laid plans of any team. The Padres have had their share of promising prospects over the years—from Sean Burroughs to Matt Bush to Donavan Tate to Anthony Rizzo—but they've been unable to convert them into big-league stars with anything approaching league-average efficiency. Then there's the fact that they've focused on the high-risk segment of the prospect population: young pitching and

16-year-old prospects. At worst, they peter out and tend to break down easily. At best, they take a *long* time to arrive.

But there is, for the first time since Jed Hoyer and Jason McLeod left for Chicago back in 2011, hope for something beyond 76-86, and an identifiable formula for getting there. Scout, scout and scout some more [mix in steady dose of analytics as needed].

✦✦✦

The date was September 28, 2016.

Hunter Renfroe swaggered to the plate in the bottom of the third, kicked at the back of the batter's box just a couple times, and stared out at Dodgers pitcher Jose De Leon. He took a breaking pitch for a ball and then clobbered a low-and-in 93 mph heater to the roof of the Western Metal Supply Co. building. There will be losing first—lots of it—but if things go as planned, these Preller-led Padres should re-emerge as legitimate NL West threats by the end of the decade; this time younger, homegrown and carefully crafted. ∎

—Dustin Palmateer is an author
of Baseball Prospectus

HITTERS

Alexi Amarista   SS

Born: 4/6/89   Age: 28   Bats: L   Throws: R   Height: 5'6"   Weight: 160   Entered Pro Ball: International Free Agent, 2007

YEAR	TEAM	LVL	AGE	PA	R	2B	3B	HR	RBI	BB	K	SB	CS	AVG/OBP/SLG	TAv	VORP	BABIP	BRR	FRAA	WARP
2014	SDN	MLB	25	466	39	13	2	5	40	29	69	12	1	.239/.286/.314	.243	9.0	.271	0.7	SS(73): 3.9 • 3B(22): 1.8	1.4
2015	SDN	MLB	26	357	28	10	4	3	30	24	55	5	1	.204/.257/.287	.205	-5.2	.232	0.9	SS(85): 3.2 • LF(11): -0.5	-0.2
2016	ELP	AAA	27	55	9	3	0	1	4	4	8	1	0	.333/.382/.458	.302	4.3	.366	-0.2	SS(9): -0.9 • 2B(2): -0.0	0.3
2016	SDN	MLB	27	150	9	2	0	0	11	8	26	9	2	.257/.295/.271	.208	-5.1	.313	-1.6	2B(28): 1.6 • SS(12): 0.4	-0.4
2017	COL	MLB	28	129	13	5	1	2	11	8	19	3	1	.241/.284/.350	.225	0.1	.265	0.4	SS 1 • 2B -0	0.0
2018	COL	MLB	29	146	15	5	1	3	14	9	22	3	1	.238/.288/.354	.232	0.1	.259	-0.1	SS 1 • 2B 0	0.1

Breakout: 0%   Improve: 42%   Collapse: 12%   Attrition: 17%   MLB: 92%   Comparables: Cesar Izturis, Cesar Gutierrez, Bucky Dent

With bullpen specialization sweeping the league, versatility among position players is becoming more and more valuable. Amarista is doing everything he can to test this theory to the fullest extremes. He did get fewer plate appearances than he's had since his career started in Anaheim, being relegated to the bench after years of playing nearly every day. However, he also continued to prove that his ability to play all over the diamond can only be matched by his inability to hit major-league pitching. On the other hand, 2016 marked the second consecutive year in which he was brought in to pitch in a blowout, as well as the second consecutive year in which he did not allow a base runner. Versatility is what will keep Amarista in the majors, and the ability to appear on the mound in garbage time can only add to his value.

Oswaldo Arcia   RF

Born: 5/9/91   Age: 26   Bats: L   Throws: R   Height: 6'0"   Weight: 225   Entered Pro Ball: International Free Agent, 2007

YEAR	TEAM	LVL	AGE	PA	R	2B	3B	HR	RBI	BB	K	SB	CS	AVG/OBP/SLG	TAv	VORP	BABIP	BRR	FRAA	WARP
2014	ROC	AAA	23	85	16	7	0	5	18	5	17	1	0	.312/.365/.597	.288	4.7	.339	0.6	RF(16): 0.4	0.5
2014	MIN	MLB	23	410	46	16	3	20	57	31	127	1	2	.231/.300/.452	.271	10.3	.292	-0.6	RF(100): -3.0	0.8
2015	MIN	MLB	24	65	6	0	0	2	8	4	15	0	0	.276/.338/.379	.245	-1.1	.333	-1.4	LF(15): 0.9 • RF(4): -0.0	0.0
2015	ROC	AAA	24	311	31	13	0	12	41	18	82	0	1	.199/.257/.372	.234	-4.4	.228	-1.0	RF(55): -5.1 • LF(5): -0.1	-1.0
2016	MIN	MLB	25	114	8	4	0	4	12	10	46	0	0	.214/.289/.369	.229	-1.3	.340	0.0	LF(16): -3.3 • RF(15): 0.1	-0.5
2016	TBA	MLB	25	61	7	2	1	2	7	6	19	1	1	.259/.328/.444	.280	2.4	.353	0.1	RF(11): -0.1 • LF(3): -0.1	0.2
2016	PCH	A+	25	30	6	0	1	3	7	2	7	0	0	.286/.333/.679	.341	3.9	.278	0.8	RF(5): 0.2	0.4
2016	MIA	MLB	25	2	0	0	0	0	0	0	1	0	0	.000/.000/.000	.010	-0.5	.000	0.0		0.0
2016	SDN	MLB	25	45	2	1	0	2	4	2	14	0	0	.116/.156/.279	.167	-3.1	.111	0.4	RF(13): -0.5	-0.4
2017	SDN	MLB	26	250	29	10	1	12	35	19	77	1	1	.232/.300/.437	.251	4.9	.295	-0.3	RF 0 • LF -1	0.5
2018	SDN	MLB	27	209	27	8	1	9	28	16	64	1	1	.229/.298/.426	.260	4.3	.292	-0.3	RF 0 • LF 0	0.4

Breakout: 6%   Improve: 55%   Collapse: 10%   Attrition: 15%   MLB: 92%   Comparables: Travis Snider, Ian Stewart, Brandon Moss

Arcia didn't get to experience much success in 2016, but he did get to experience many different parts of the country. His year started in Minnesota, where he stayed until being designated for assignment in June. He was eventually traded to Tampa Bay, lasting two months before being designated for assignment again. Next, he traveled to Miami only to be designated for assignment after just two plate appearances. Finally, he was claimed off waivers by San Diego, which kept him for the rest of the year. Through all of those uniform changes, Arcia continued to show some flashes of power potential with even more flashes of approach issues, leaving much to be desired in his overall production. But hey, at least he racked up some frequent flyer miles.

Carlos Asuaje   2B

Born: 11/2/91   Age: 25   Bats: L   Throws: R   Height: 5'9"   Weight: 160   Entered Pro Ball: Round 11, 2013 Draft (#323 overall)

YEAR	TEAM	LVL	AGE	PA	R	2B	3B	HR	RBI	BB	K	SB	CS	AVG/OBP/SLG	TAv	VORP	BABIP	BRR	FRAA	WARP
2014	GRN	A	22	383	59	24	10	11	73	41	56	7	4	.305/.391/.542	.316	33.2	.333		3B(38): -0.9 • 2B(24): 1.9	3.3
2014	SLM	A+	22	176	27	14	2	4	28	18	34	1	3	.323/.398/.516	.320	16.9	.390	1.1	LF(19): 2.2 • 2B(16): 0.1	1.9
2015	PME	AA	23	570	60	23	7	8	61	56	88	9	6	.251/.334/.374	.259	11.5	.289	-1.5	2B(106): -17.3 • 3B(9): -0.3	-0.6
2016	ELP	AAA	24	597	98	32	11	9	69	49	82	10	5	.321/.378/.473	.282	29.6	.363	0.2	2B(119): -8.8 • LF(7): -0.8	2.0
2016	SDN	MLB	24	25	2	2	0	0	2	1	4	0	0	.208/.240/.292	.199	-1.0	.250	-0.1	2B(6): 0.2	-0.1
2017	*SDN*	*MLB*	*25*	*63*	*6*	*3*	*1*	*1*	*6*	*5*	*13*	*1*	*0*	*.246/.308/.390*	*.247*	*1.5*	*.294*	*0.0*	*2B -1*	*0.0*
2018	*SDN*	*MLB*	*26*	*341*	*40*	*15*	*3*	*8*	*38*	*27*	*74*	*3*	*2*	*.252/.318/.405*	*.262*	*10.9*	*.301*	*-0.1*	*2B -7*	*0.5*

Breakout: 0%   Improve: 5%   Collapse: 13%   Attrition: 25%   MLB: 42%   Comparables: Scott Sizemore, Steve Tolleson, Travis Denker

The first thing you notice when you see Asuaje on the field is his minuscule stature. Though he's listed at 5-foot-9, it's safe to assume he's at least a couple inches shorter than that. Don't be too distracted by the height, though, because the dude can flat out hit. Carrying an impressive hit tool that allows him to spray line drives all over the place and enough speed to ensure solid power numbers despite not hitting the ball over the fence, Asuaje can be part of major-league lineups for years to come. Combine that with the ability to play multiple positions, and baby you got a stew goin'. Pretty good for arguably the fourth-best piece in the Craig Kimbrel trade.

Christian Bethancourt   C

Born: 9/2/91   Age: 25   Bats: R   Throws: R   Height: 6'2"   Weight: 210   Entered Pro Ball: International Free Agent, 2008

YEAR	TEAM	LVL	AGE	PA	R	2B	3B	HR	RBI	BB	K	SB	CS	AVG/OBP/SLG	TAv	VORP	BABIP	BRR	FRAA	WARP
2014	GWN	AAA	22	365	33	17	1	8	48	13	61	7	1	.283/.308/.408	.242	8.8	.318	0.3	C(80): 1.8	1.1
2014	ATL	MLB	22	117	7	3	0	0	9	3	26	1	1	.248/.274/.274	.210	-0.4	.322	0.2	C(31): -4.2	-0.5
2015	GWN	AAA	23	218	25	19	0	4	31	12	31	5	0	.327/.359/.480	.291	16.0	.365	-0.4	C(48): 1.6	1.8
2015	ATL	MLB	23	160	16	8	0	2	12	5	33	1	1	.200/.225/.290	.201	-2.1	.242	0.2	C(42): -2.7	-0.5
2016	SDN	MLB	24	204	20	9	0	6	25	10	56	1	2	.228/.265/.368	.220	0.0	.288	0.6	C(41): 2.1 • LF(8): -0.3	0.1
2017	*SDN*	*MLB*	*25*	*188*	*19*	*10*	*0*	*5*	*20*	*7*	*40*	*2*	*1*	*.251/.277/.393*	*.236*	*2.3*	*.294*	*-0.3*	*LF 0 • C -1*	*-0.2*
2018	*SDN*	*MLB*	*26*	*296*	*34*	*15*	*0*	*10*	*36*	*12*	*66*	*3*	*2*	*.251/.283/.414*	*.250*	*5.5*	*.291*	*0.7*	*LF 0 • C -1*	*0.3*

Breakout: 5%   Improve: 27%   Collapse: 20%   Attrition: 34%   MLB: 80%   Comparables: J.T. Realmuto, Jeff Mathis, J.R. Murphy

Bethancourt has four partial seasons under his belt and has been among MLB's worst hitters in all of them. Defense has always been his calling card, but his framing behind the dish leaves a lot to be desired. Despite all of this, he's one of the more interesting players in the game right now. After appearing in two games as a garbage-time pitcher, the Padres are considering utilizing the 25-year-old as a pitcher/catcher/outfielder hybrid. Switching him to the mound makes some sense considering his anemic bat and the fact that his arm has always been his top tool. In his limited pitching action, he hit 96 mph with his fastball and also featured a knuckleball that came in 40 mph slower. We've seen experiments like this before that haven't worked—hello Micah Owings—and it's likely Bethancourt will follow that path. Though, based on what we've seen from him thus far it's certainly worth a shot.

YEAR	TEAM	P. COUNT	FRM RUNS	BLK RUNS	THRW RUNS	TOT RUNS
2014	ATL	4221	-4.4	-0.6	0.2	-4.9
2014	GWN	11439	-0.1	-0.2	1.4	1.1
2015	ATL	5948	-4.8	-0.3	0.5	-4.6
2015	GWN	6604	1.2	0.4	0.4	2.0
2016	SDN	5383	-0.9	-1.6	0.0	-2.5
2016	SDN	5383	-0.9	-1.6	0.0	-2.5
2017	*SDN*	*2234*	*-1.0*	*-0.2*	*0.1*	*-1.2*
2018	*SDN*	*3515*	*-1.7*	*-0.3*	*0.1*	*-1.9*

Alex Dickerson   LF

Born: 5/26/90   Age: 27   Bats: L   Throws: L   Height: 6'3"   Weight: 235   Entered Pro Ball: Round 3, 2011 Draft (#91 overall)

YEAR	TEAM	LVL	AGE	PA	R	2B	3B	HR	RBI	BB	K	SB	CS	AVG/OBP/SLG	TAv	VORP	BABIP	BRR	FRAA	WARP
2014	SAN	AA	24	147	20	11	2	3	24	9	28	0	1	.321/.367/.496	.303	8.4	.387	-0.5	RF(28): -0.2	0.9
2015	ELP	AAA	25	519	82	36	9	12	71	45	96	4	0	.307/.374/.503	.308	37.1	.360	1.0	LF(96): -8.3 • RF(16): -0.2	2.9
2015	SDN	MLB	25	8	0	0	0	0	0	0	3	0	0	.250/.250/.250	.150	-0.7	.400	0.0	LF(1): 0.1	-0.1
2016	ELP	AAA	26	241	50	16	3	10	51	14	27	0	0	.382/.425/.622	.332	24.0	.397	1.6	LF(36): -4.7 • 1B(10): -0.0	2.0
2016	SDN	MLB	26	285	39	16	2	10	37	26	44	5	1	.257/.333/.455	.287	14.4	.274	0.5	LF(68): -3.4	1.1
2017	*SDN*	*MLB*	*27*	*315*	*35*	*17*	*3*	*10*	*40*	*23*	*64*	*2*	*1*	*.268/.329/.453*	*.273*	*14.6*	*.310*	*-0.1*	*LF -2*	*1.1*
2018	*SDN*	*MLB*	*28*	*396*	*50*	*22*	*3*	*13*	*51*	*28*	*80*	*2*	*1*	*.269/.329/.456*	*.281*	*18.3*	*.311*	*0.1*	*LF -3*	*1.7*

Breakout: 6%   Improve: 34%   Collapse: 15%   Attrition: 28%   MLB: 80%   Comparables: Jake Smolinski, Allen Craig, Ryan Church

After a brief and underwhelming MLB debut in 2015, Dickerson took advantage of his second run through the PCL and destroyed Triple-A pitching. He came up to the majors at the end of June, playing on something close to an everyday basis. He was able to carry some of his Triple-A performance to the majors, showing above-average discipline at the plate. More importantly, he flashed the power some scouts worried he lacked. Though his defense leaves something to be desired, he did more than enough in 2016 to raise his stock to its highest point in at least three years.

Javier Guerra   SS

Born: 9/25/95   Age: 21   Bats: L   Throws: R   Height: 5'11"   Weight: 155   Entered Pro Ball: International Free Agent, 2012

YEAR	TEAM	LVL	AGE	PA	R	2B	3B	HR	RBI	BB	K	SB	CS	AVG/OBP/SLG	TAv	VORP	BABIP	BRR	FRAA	WARP
2015	GRN	A	19	477	64	23	3	15	68	30	112	7	9	.279/.329/.449	.280	28.5	.342	0.0	SS(112): 9.4 • 2B(1): 0.0	4.0
2016	LEL	A+	20	431	49	19	1	9	41	34	141	4	4	.202/.264/.325	.228	1.1	.287	-1.9	SS(102): 2.7	0.4
2017	*SDN*	*MLB*	*21*	*250*	*23*	*9*	*1*	*8*	*28*	*14*	*86*	*1*	*1*	*.202/.249/.347*	*.203*	*-3.5*	*.279*	*-0.5*	*SS 1*	*-0.3*
2018	*SDN*	*MLB*	*22*	*359*	*40*	*14*	*1*	*12*	*41*	*22*	*120*	*1*	*1*	*.210/.262/.370*	*.227*	*-0.6*	*.284*	*-0.8*	*SS 1*	*0.1*

Breakout: 1%   Improve: 1%   Collapse: 0%   Attrition: 3%   MLB: 3%   *Comparables: Trevor Story, Orlando Calixte, Nick Franklin*

If 2015 was the breakout of all breakouts for Guerra, 2016 was the backslide of all backslides. In his first full season as a pro, the slick-fielding shortstop added previously unforeseen power that helped mask his massive strikeout problems. That performance was enough to make him the 1-A piece in a deal for Craig Kimbrel. His first year with San Diego brought about the ramifications that can come with contact issues as large as Guerra's. He struck out in nearly one-third of his plate appearances and ended up as one of the worst hitters in the batter-friendly California League. It's not all bad news, though. He'll be just 21 in 2017, and is still among the best defensive shortstops in the minors. The contact issues clearly need to be figured out, but that power is still in there somewhere.

Austin Hedges   C

Born: 8/18/92   Age: 24   Bats: R   Throws: R   Height: 6'1"   Weight: 210   Entered Pro Ball: Round 2, 2011 Draft (#82 overall)

YEAR	TEAM	LVL	AGE	PA	R	2B	3B	HR	RBI	BB	K	SB	CS	AVG/OBP/SLG	TAv	VORP	BABIP	BRR	FRAA	WARP
2014	SAN	AA	21	457	31	19	2	6	44	23	89	1	3	.225/.268/.321	.210	-5.8	.269	-1.7	C(106): 39.3	3.6
2015	ELP	AAA	22	79	12	8	0	2	15	8	8	1	0	.324/.392/.521	.313	7.3	.344	0.0	C(17): 5.5	1.3
2015	SDN	MLB	22	152	13	2	0	3	11	8	38	0	0	.168/.215/.248	.191	-2.1	.202	1.6	C(47): 8.5	0.7
2016	ELP	AAA	23	334	55	20	1	21	82	13	51	1	1	.326/.353/.597	.301	28.3	.329	-0.4	C(73): 5.5	3.5
2016	SDN	MLB	23	26	2	1	0	0	1	0	7	0	1	.125/.154/.167	.119	-2.7	.167	-0.1	C(7): -0.5	-0.3
2017	*SDN*	*MLB*	*24*	*471*	*47*	*21*	*1*	*16*	*54*	*21*	*107*	*0*	*0*	*.232/.269/.390*	*.232*	*7.9*	*.268*	*-1.0*	*C 12*	*2.4*
2018	*SDN*	*MLB*	*25*	*406*	*47*	*17*	*1*	*15*	*51*	*20*	*95*	*0*	*0*	*.235/.275/.406*	*.243*	*7.1*	*.269*	*-0.9*	*C 10*	*1.9*

Breakout: 8%   Improve: 23%   Collapse: 7%   Attrition: 23%   MLB: 38%   *Comparables: Luis Exposito, J.R. Murphy, Tony Cruz*

For catchers, defense is infinitely more important than offense. Plenty of backstops can't hit worth a lick, but if they can provide value behind the plate there's a spot for them in the majors. Hedges is trying his best to test the extremes of that theory. To be fair, the former top prospect spent most of his time at Triple-A and put up legitimately good offensive numbers. These weren't just PCL-inflated stats, either; the adjusted numbers graded out very well. However, he looked lost in a small-sample run against major-league pitching at the end of the year. His defense will continue to give him shots, but something has to give on the other side of the ball if he'll fulfill his promise as a quality everyday player.

YEAR	TEAM	P. COUNT	FRM RUNS	BLK RUNS	THRW RUNS	TOT RUNS
2014	SAN	15026	35.4	1.5	4.7	41.5
2015	ELP	2301	4.4	0.1	0.1	4.5
2015	SDN	5804	8.4	1.2	0.2	9.8
2016	SDN	901	-0.5	0.3	0.0	-0.2
2017	*SDN*	*17941*	*9.6*	*2.1*	*0.6*	*12.2*
2018	*SDN*	*15483*	*8.0*	*2.0*	*0.4*	*10.4*

Travis Jankowski   CF

Born: 6/15/91   Age: 26   Bats: L   Throws: R   Height: 6'2"   Weight: 185   Entered Pro Ball: Round 1, 2012 Draft (#44 overall)

YEAR	TEAM	LVL	AGE	PA	R	2B	3B	HR	RBI	BB	K	SB	CS	AVG/OBP/SLG	TAv	VORP	BABIP	BRR	FRAA	WARP
2014	EUG	A-	23	36	6	0	0	0	1	3	5	4	0	.182/.250/.182	.174	-1.8	.214	0.4	CF(7): -1.6	-0.4
2014	LEL	A+	23	25	2	1	0	0	1	6	3	1	0	.167/.375/.222	.271	1.0	.200	0.1	CF(3): -0.7 • CF(1): -0.7	0.0
2014	SAN	AA	23	112	14	4	1	0	10	8	14	10	2	.240/.297/.300	.227	-0.8	.273	-0.3	CF(28): -0.9	-0.2
2015	SAN	AA	24	321	50	11	5	1	13	36	40	23	8	.316/.395/.401	.281	14.1	.365	-1.3	CF(62): 2.8	1.8
2015	ELP	AAA	24	113	19	6	2	0	12	13	10	9	3	.392/.464/.495	.335	13.8	.432	1.5	CF(24): 2.7	1.7
2015	SDN	MLB	24	96	9	2	2	2	12	4	24	2	1	.211/.245/.344	.234	0.3	.266	0.2	CF(23): -2.5 • RF(11): 0.8	-0.2
2016	SDN	MLB	25	383	53	13	2	2	12	42	100	30	12	.245/.332/.313	.238	10.0	.343	7.1	CF(87): -1.8 • RF(22): -0.2	0.8
2017	*SDN*	*MLB*	*26*	*622*	*80*	*23*	*5*	*8*	*45*	*57*	*135*	*39*	*12*	*.249/.317/.350*	*.242*	*14.8*	*.309*	*4.1*	*LF 4 • CF 3*	*1.6*
2018	*SDN*	*MLB*	*27*	*533*	*59*	*19*	*4*	*8*	*50*	*52*	*116*	*33*	*11*	*.247/.325/.358*	*.251*	*15.2*	*.305*	*6.8*	*LF 3 • CF 3*	*2.3*

Breakout: 7%   Improve: 55%   Collapse: 12%   Attrition: 17%   MLB: 83%   *Comparables: Brett Gardner, Billy Burns, Emilio Bonifacio*

Built with the hair of a Hanson brother, Jankowski's speed is always going to be his calling card. There was little doubt of that in 2016, as he managed to tie for 10th in all of baseball in stolen bases despite accumulating just 383 plate appearances. The speed was on full display in August when he stole home twice in a 10-day span. He hasn't managed to translate that speed into positive defensive grades in center field. At the plate, he relies on a solid hit tool to go with patience and questionable contact skills. Although he was a fine hitter against righties in 2016, his .398 OPS vs. left-handed pitching suggests a platoon role may be in his future. He'll need the hit tool to play close to its ceiling if he's going to make it as an everyday player, particularly with the lack of MMM-Bop in his bat.

Manuel Margot   CF

Born: 9/28/94   Age: 22   Bats: R   Throws: R   Height: 5'11"   Weight: 180   Entered Pro Ball: International Free Agent, 2011

YEAR	TEAM	LVL	AGE	PA	R	2B	3B	HR	RBI	BB	K	SB	CS	AVG/OBP/SLG	TAv	VORP	BABIP	BRR	FRAA	WARP
2014	GRN	A	19	413	61	20	5	10	45	37	49	39	13	.286/.355/.449	.282	24.8	.309	2.8	CF(96): 10.3	3.6
2014	SLM	A+	19	56	4	5	0	2	14	2	5	3	2	.340/.364/.560	.320	5.4	.333	0.0	CF(16): -0.5	0.5
2015	SLM	A+	20	198	35	6	5	3	17	11	15	20	5	.282/.321/.420	.273	9.6	.289	1.5	CF(42): 5.8	1.7
2015	PME	AA	20	282	38	21	4	3	33	21	36	19	8	.271/.326/.419	.270	13.0	.303	1.9	CF(63): -2.5 • RF(1): 0.1	1.1
2016	ELP	AAA	21	566	98	21	12	6	55	36	64	30	11	.304/.351/.426	.270	30.8	.335	7.9	CF(121): 14.4 • RF(1): 0.2	4.7
2016	SDN	MLB	21	37	4	4	1	0	3	0	7	2	0	.243/.243/.405	.274	2.4	.300	0.8	CF(9): 0.6 • RF(1): 0.1	0.3
2017	*SDN*	*MLB*	*22*	*462*	*57*	*20*	*5*	*9*	*40*	*25*	*84*	*20*	*8*	*.249/.290/.385*	*.242*	*8.7*	*.285*	*2.0*	*CF 11*	*1.7*
2018	*SDN*	*MLB*	*23*	*538*	*59*	*23*	*6*	*12*	*58*	*32*	*96*	*24*	*9*	*.257/.303/.400*	*.257*	*16.0*	*.292*	*3.1*	*CF 12*	*3.1*

Breakout: 3%   Improve: 22%   Collapse: 10%   Attrition: 26%   MLB: 44%   Comparables: Ben Revere, Ryan Sweeney, Gerardo Parra

As the prized jewel for San Diego in the Craig Kimbrel deal, Margot spent the majority of last season at Triple-A prior to a late-season cup of coffee. He only played 10 games, but showed off all of the tools we can expect to see from him moving forward. His speed is his calling card, as he stole two bases in that span. More importantly he uses his legs to propel his defense to near-elite levels. At the plate, he shows off an aggressive style that can get the better of him at times, but mostly plays well with his solid bat-to-ball skills. While scouts are torn over his raw power abilities, his speed and line-drive-oriented swing will help him rack up extra-base hits even if he doesn't put the ball over the fence. The power will determine how high he can climb, but there is enough of a base here for Margot to be a solid regular as soon as 2017.

Wil Myers   1B

Born: 12/10/90   Age: 26   Bats: R   Throws: R   Height: 6'3"   Weight: 205   Entered Pro Ball: Round 3, 2009 Draft (#91 overall)

YEAR	TEAM	LVL	AGE	PA	R	2B	3B	HR	RBI	BB	K	SB	CS	AVG/OBP/SLG	TAv	VORP	BABIP	BRR	FRAA	WARP
2014	DUR	AAA	23	31	3	1	0	2	6	7	7	3	0	.250/.419/.542	.306	2.4	.267	0.2	RF(2): -0.0 • LF(2): 0.9	0.3
2014	TBA	MLB	23	361	37	14	0	6	35	34	90	6	1	.222/.294/.320	.233	-6.0	.286	-2.6	RF(78): 3.6 • 1B(2): 0.0	-0.3
2015	SDN	MLB	24	253	40	13	1	8	29	27	55	5	2	.253/.336/.427	.288	13.2	.302	0.7	CF(38): -5.5 • 1B(22): 0.3	0.8
2016	SDN	MLB	25	676	99	29	4	28	94	68	160	28	6	.259/.336/.461	.290	33.2	.305	5.2	1B(149): 1.5 • RF(7): -0.3	3.5
2017	*SDN*	*MLB*	*26*	*592*	*75*	*27*	*2*	*22*	*76*	*57*	*141*	*18*	*4*	*.256/.329/.440*	*.272*	*17.9*	*.306*	*1.5*	*1B 4*	*2.1*
2018	*SDN*	*MLB*	*27*	*551*	*75*	*25*	*1*	*23*	*76*	*57*	*132*	*16*	*4*	*.258/.335/.457*	*.287*	*22.8*	*.305*	*1.0*	*1B 3*	*2.8*

Breakout: 5%   Improve: 51%   Collapse: 1%   Attrition: 10%   MLB: 99%   Comparables: Brandon Belt, Justin Morneau, Adam Lind

There's no easier way for on-field production to go unnoticed than being in a controversial trade that involves future stars. This goes doubly for Myers. The first deal that sent him from Kansas City to Tampa Bay obviously didn't go as planned, as Wade Davis became the real prize of the famous Shields-for-Myers swap. The controversy around the move guaranteed it'd be one of the first events you think of throughout Myers' career. Then, just one year later, he was sent to San Diego in a huge three-team deal that included Trea Turner. If Turner ends up being the star he looks like he could be, it'll be just another event Myers will be remembered for over his production. Despite all that, Myers is looking like a good major-league player. He was finally shifted out of the outfield and found a home at first base, part of the reason he was able to complete his first full season. Not only did he stay on the field, he showed the same offensive potential he's shown since his rookie year. The power is legitimate, and if he can find a way to bump his AVG up above .270, maybe there's some hope he can be remembered for his talent rather than the talent for which he was traded.

Jorge Ona   OF

Born: 12/31/96   Age: 20   Bats: R   Throws: R   Height: 6'0"   Weight: 220   Entered Pro Ball: International Free Agent, 2016

YEAR	TEAM	LVL	AGE	PA	R	2B	3B	HR	RBI	BB	K	SB	CS	AVG/OBP/SLG	TAv	VORP	BABIP	BRR	FRAA	WARP
2017	*SDN*	*MLB*	*20*	*250*	*25*	*9*	*1*	*3*	*21*	*25*	*40*	*4*	*1*	*.233/.313/.329*	*.227*	*1.0*	*.265*	*0.0*		*0.1*

Breakout: 5%   Improve: 21%   Collapse: 2%   Attrition: 8%   MLB: 36%   Comparables: Rusty Staub, Bill Mazeroski, Ed Kirkpatrick

Ona is the latest Cuban outfielder to sign in the States, and while the upside of a Yasiel Puig may not exist, he's an exciting prospect in his own right. At just 19 years old, he has already shown impressive power with a strong hit tool to boot. Having yet to play at any level beyond instructs, we have yet to see how well these tools could carry over to the highest level. The Padres consider it worth the risk, giving him what would be a record signing bonus for the franchise had they not just signed Adrian Morejon for $11 million.

Hudson Potts   SS

Born: 10/28/98   Age: 18   Bats: R   Throws: R   Height: 6'3"   Weight: 205   Entered Pro Ball: Round 1, 2016 Draft (#24 overall)

YEAR	TEAM	LVL	AGE	PA	R	2B	3B	HR	RBI	BB	K	SB	CS	AVG/OBP/SLG	TAv	VORP	BABIP	BRR	FRAA	WARP
2016	TRI	A-	17	72	7	0	1	0	6	9	13	2	1	.233/.352/.267	.284	5.1	.298	0.8	SS(10): 1.1, 3B(3): -0.2	0.7
2017	*SDN*	*MLB*	*18*	*250*	*21*	*10*	*1*	*5*	*25*	*12*	*74*	*1*	*1*	*.210/.251/.324*	*.199*	*-5.9*	*.279*	*-0.3*	*SS 1 • 3B 0*	*-0.6*
2018	*SDN*	*MLB*	*19*	*261*	*26*	*10*	*1*	*6*	*27*	*11*	*80*	*1*	*1*	*.211/.249/.344*	*.214*	*-4.5*	*.279*	*-0.3*	*SS 1 • 3B 0*	*-0.4*

Breakout: 0%   Improve: 0%   Collapse: 0%   Attrition: 0%   MLB: 0%   Comparables: Raul Mondesi, Wilmer Flores

Although Potts—who formerly went by Hudson Sanchez—was the second of three first rounders taken by the Padres, he's the least exciting of the trio. He was picked with the purpose of signing an under-slot deal to allow San Diego to do more later in the draft, but Potts showed off strong defensive skills on the left side of the infield along with solid production at the plate. He's likely tabbed to be a bit piece rather than someone you build a team around. At the same time, Potts is just as likely to be remembered as merely a player who was drafted to enable the selections of other draft picks.

Hunter Renfroe   OF

Born: 1/28/92   Age: 25   Bats: R   Throws: R   Height: 6'1"   Weight: 220   Entered Pro Ball: Round 1, 2013 Draft (#13 overall)

YEAR	TEAM	LVL	AGE	PA	R	2B	3B	HR	RBI	BB	K	SB	CS	AVG/OBP/SLG	TAv	VORP	BABIP	BRR	FRAA	WARP
2014	LEL	A+	22	316	46	21	3	16	52	28	81	9	3	.295/.370/.565	.340	30.5	.359	-0.3	RF(49): 0.3 • RF(7): 0.3	3.3
2014	SAN	AA	22	251	17	12	0	5	23	25	53	2	1	.232/.307/.353	.244	1.3	.280	-0.5	LF(30): -0.3 • CF(22): -2.0	0.0
2015	SAN	AA	23	463	50	22	3	14	54	33	112	4	1	.259/.313/.425	.259	8.8	.316	1.6	RF(79): 13.3 • CF(8): -1.7	2.2
2015	ELP	AAA	23	95	15	5	2	6	24	4	20	1	0	.333/.358/.633	.314	8.0	.369	0.7	RF(18): 1.1 • CF(3): 0.1	0.9
2016	ELP	AAA	24	563	95	34	5	30	105	22	115	5	2	.306/.336/.557	.277	22.2	.339	1.8	RF(111): 2.1 • CF(12): -1.0	2.4
2016	SDN	MLB	24	36	8	3	0	4	14	1	5	0	0	.371/.389/.800	.404	6.1	.346	0.2	RF(9): 0.7	0.7
2017	SDN	MLB	25	485	54	22	2	21	67	26	132	2	1	.242/.286/.444	.253	8.8	.292	-0.6	RF 4	1.0
2018	SDN	MLB	26	490	63	23	2	23	70	31	136	2	1	.241/.293/.451	.265	12.0	.291	-0.7	RF 4	1.8

Breakout: 4%   Improve: 25%   Collapse: 10%   Attrition: 31%   MLB: 50%   Comparables: Bryce Brentz, Scott Schebler, Brett Carroll

Renfroe is both one of the more intriguing outfield prospects in baseball and one of the most frustrating. The tools are there for a longtime middle-of-the-order bat, as the power is legitimate regardless of what ballpark he calls home (he reached the top of the Western Metal Supply building with a blast in San Diego). Unfortunately, he's watched his plate discipline be further and further exploited as he's moved up the ladder. He spent the majority of 2016 at Triple-A, showing both his ability to make strong contact and his ability to widen the strike zone. He had a small cup of coffee in the majors during which he displayed the same tendencies. There is still plenty of hope for Renfroe to refine his approach enough to allow his power to play on a consistent basis, and if he can do that there is a legitimate All-Star candidate hidden in that package.

Adam Rosales   IF

Born: 5/20/83   Age: 34   Bats: R   Throws: R   Height: 6'2"   Weight: 200   Entered Pro Ball: Round 12, 2005 Draft (#362 overall)

YEAR	TEAM	LVL	AGE	PA	R	2B	3B	HR	RBI	BB	K	SB	CS	AVG/OBP/SLG	TAv	VORP	BABIP	BRR	FRAA	WARP
2014	ROU	AAA	31	307	42	16	3	7	43	28	61	3	0	.276/.349/.434	.279	16.1	.329	0.5	3B(50): 1.5 • 1B(15): 0.6	1.7
2014	TEX	MLB	31	181	20	7	0	4	19	13	42	4	2	.262/.328/.378	.272	5.2	.331	0.4	1B(32): 3.7 • 3B(7): 0.0	0.9
2015	TEX	MLB	32	125	14	4	0	3	7	10	30	4	4	.228/.296/.342	.229	-0.2	.284	0.7	1B(19): 0.5 • 2B(19): 1.6	0.1
2016	SDN	MLB	33	248	37	12	3	13	35	29	88	4	0	.229/.319/.495	.287	15.8	.308	1.2	3B(41): 3.3 • 2B(36): -1.4	1.9
2017	SDN	MLB	34	250	28	11	1	7	27	21	65	4	2	.231/.299/.383	.238	4.0	.287	0.8	3B 1 • 2B 0	0.6
2018	SDN	MLB	35	235	27	10	1	6	25	19	63	3	1	.223/.292/.367	.243	2.8	.282	0.8	3B 1 • 2B 0	0.4

Breakout: 1%   Improve: 29%   Collapse: 11%   Attrition: 26%   MLB: 73%   Comparables: Ed Lucas, Greg Norton, Darnell McDonald

It's been a while since we had this much Rosales in our lives, with 2016 representing a career-high in games and his most plate appearances since 2008. It wasn't just the frequency of his appearances that was jarring, though. Rosales turned into a completely different player with the snap of a finger. Formerly a contact-oriented hitter whose production relied on solid defense all over the infield, he suddenly transformed into a Three True Outcomes hitter in 2016. Among all players with at least 200 PA, Rosales was the only hitter with a 10 percent walk rate, a 35 percent strikeout rate and a .250 isolated power. This change in approach resulted in the most productive season of his career.

Hector Sanchez   C

Born: 11/17/89   Age: 27   Bats: B   Throws: R   Height: 6'0"   Weight: 235   Entered Pro Ball: International Free Agent, 2009

YEAR	TEAM	LVL	AGE	PA	R	2B	3B	HR	RBI	BB	K	SB	CS	AVG/OBP/SLG	TAv	VORP	BABIP	BRR	FRAA	WARP
2014	SFN	MLB	24	177	8	8	0	3	28	8	55	0	1	.196/.237/.301	.208	-2.0	.266	-0.2	C(45): 2.2 • 1B(1): -0.3	0.0
2014	FRE	AAA	24	20	1	0	0	1	3	1	3	0	0	.158/.200/.316	.187	-1.0	.133	-0.1	C(5): -0.1	-0.1
2015	SAC	AAA	25	152	18	6	0	4	14	9	25	0	0	.273/.318/.403	.256	3.3	.304	-2.1	C(30): -4.2	-0.1
2015	SFN	MLB	25	59	5	4	0	1	5	2	14	0	0	.179/.207/.304	.183	-2.9	.220	-0.8	C(16): -1.6	-0.5
2016	CHR	AAA	26	30	2	1	0	2	3	1	6	0	0	.143/.200/.393	.196	-0.7	.100	0.0	C(8): -1.2	-0.2
2016	CHA	MLB	26	8	0	0	0	0	1	1	2	0	0	.143/.250/.143	.180	-0.3	.200	0.0	C(2): -0.9	-0.1
2016	ELP	AAA	26	200	25	16	0	13	40	20	40	0	0	.324/.392/.636	.326	15.8	.352	-1.5	1B(27): -1.9 • C(10): -2.1	1.2
2016	SDN	MLB	26	46	3	1	0	3	7	3	8	0	0	.286/.348/.524	.316	4.5	.290	0.0	C(12): -2.9	0.2
2017	SDN	MLB	27	250	26	12	0	9	32	15	60	0	0	.242/.294/.412	.239	3.6	.285	-0.3	C -7 • 1B -1	-0.4
2018	SDN	MLB	28	127	15	6	0	4	15	8	31	0	0	.233/.285/.399	.244	1.2	.275	-0.2	C -3 • 1B 0	-0.3

Breakout: 5%   Improve: 44%   Collapse: 14%   Attrition: 25%   MLB: 88%   Comparables: Martin Maldonado, Hank Conger, Cameron Rupp

Think of a generic backup catcher. What qualities do they have? Probably weak at the plate, but can hold their own behind the plate. Sanchez breaks that mold, as his defensive skills leave a lot to be desired, but the power he's shown in small samples is intriguing. Combine that with solid plate discipline between Triple-A and the majors, and there could be a real offensive threat here. Sanchez will likely remain a career backup if/when he spends a full season on a major-league roster, but he's also an example of how razor thin the line between a backup and a regular can be.

YEAR	TEAM	P. COUNT	FRM RUNS	BLK RUNS	THRW RUNS	TOT RUNS
2014	FRE	440	-0.1	0.0	0.0	0.0
2014	SFN	5051	3.2	-1.2	-0.1	1.9
2015	SAC	4506	-3.6	-0.3	-0.5	-4.4
2015	SFN	1578	-1.3	-0.8	-0.1	-2.2
2016	CHA	346	-0.9	0.0	0.0	-0.9
2016	SDN	1342	-2.8	0.0	0.0	-2.8
2017	SDN	5018	-5.4	-0.8	-0.3	-6.5
2018	SDN	2542	-2.8	-0.4	-0.1	-3.4

Luis Sardinas   SS

Born: 5/16/93   Age: 24   Bats: B   Throws: R   Height: 6'1"   Weight: 180   Entered Pro Ball: International Free Agent, 2009

YEAR	TEAM	LVL	AGE	PA	R	2B	3B	HR	RBI	BB	K	SB	CS	AVG/OBP/SLG	TAv	VORP	BABIP	BRR	FRAA	WARP
2014	FRI	AA	21	90	12	5	1	0	9	3	12	1	1	.253/.278/.333	.244	3.8	.293	1.7	SS(20): -1.5 • 2B(1): -0.0	0.2
2014	ROU	AAA	21	273	39	15	2	1	28	8	39	9	4	.290/.310/.374	.238	4.1	.336	-0.9	SS(60): 0.1	0.4
2014	TEX	MLB	21	125	12	6	0	0	8	5	21	5	1	.261/.303/.313	.228	0.3	.319	0.7	2B(19): -1.9 • SS(13): 1.6	0.0
2015	CSP	AAA	22	416	51	17	5	1	33	20	54	16	4	.282/.319/.359	.230	4.1	.325	2.1	SS(74): -1.0 • 2B(30): -0.2	0.3
2015	MIL	MLB	22	105	8	0	1	0	4	6	25	0	0	.196/.240/.216	.188	-3.9	.260	-0.1	2B(16): 0.7 • SS(14): 0.3	-0.3
2016	SEA	MLB	23	77	12	0	0	2	5	1	25	1	1	.181/.203/.264	.173	-4.1	.244	-0.2	SS(18): -0.6 • 3B(3): 0.3	-0.5
2016	TAC	AAA	23	177	17	4	0	0	17	9	20	7	4	.252/.295/.276	.232	0.5	.283	-0.7	SS(30): 0.5 • 3B(5): 0.4	-0.3
2016	ELP	AAA	23	22	5	2	0	0	1	3	3	1	0	.263/.364/.368	.230	0.7	.313	0.5	SS(5): -0.7	0.0
2016	SDN	MLB	23	120	13	6	1	2	13	11	23	3	1	.287/.353/.417	.292	10.4	.349	1.6	SS(32): 2.0 • 2B(1): 0.1	1.3
2017	*SDN*	*MLB*	*24*	*529*	*49*	*21*	*3*	*6*	*43*	*23*	*100*	*12*	*4*	*.243/.276/.333*	*.219*	*1.3*	*.288*	*0.6*	*SS -0*	*-0.5*
2018	*SDN*	*MLB*	*25*	*523*	*53*	*20*	*3*	*8*	*48*	*26*	*99*	*12*	*5*	*.252/.292/.352*	*.235*	*5.9*	*.297*	*1.2*	*SS 0*	*0.6*

Breakout: 2%   Improve: 17%   Collapse: 6%   Attrition: 26%   MLB: 51%   *Comparables: Marwin Gonzalez, Freddy Galvis, Luis Hernandez*

Once upon a time, Sardinas was just another highly regarded young infielder in the Rangers' farm system. His bat has never come around and his stock had reached an all-time low halfway through the 2016 season. However, after an August trade that sent him to San Diego, his bat started flashing some potential as he provided well-rounded production. You can't ignore the long track record of being anemic at the plate, but his defense, speed and that flash of offensive potential will earn him more chances.

Ryan Schimpf   2B

Born: 4/11/88   Age: 29   Bats: L   Throws: R   Height: 5'9"   Weight: 180   Entered Pro Ball: Round 5, 2009 Draft (#160 overall)

YEAR	TEAM	LVL	AGE	PA	R	2B	3B	HR	RBI	BB	K	SB	CS	AVG/OBP/SLG	TAv	VORP	BABIP	BRR	FRAA	WARP
2014	NHP	AA	26	219	35	17	1	15	37	28	56	3	0	.270/.370/.616	.336	22.0	.299	0.4	LF(14): -1.7 • 2B(13): 1.2	2.3
2014	BUF	AAA	26	246	29	7	1	9	21	24	59	0	1	.189/.290/.358	.231	-0.7	.212	1.0	2B(38): 3.3 • RF(12): 1.4	0.5
2015	NHP	AA	27	307	43	20	0	20	56	42	54	2	1	.271/.378/.581	.325	24.0	.267	-1.9	RF(18): -2.4 • LF(14): -0.5	2.3
2015	BUF	AAA	27	122	12	6	0	3	7	11	23	0	2	.200/.270/.336	.229	-0.3	.224	1.4	RF(10): -1.5 • 3B(7): -0.3	-0.2
2016	ELP	AAA	28	190	36	17	0	15	48	21	33	0	1	.355/.432/.729	.362	26.1	.370	0.7	3B(33): -0.3 • 1B(6): 0.5	2.7
2016	SDN	MLB	28	330	48	17	5	20	51	42	105	1	1	.217/.336/.533	.315	29.7	.260	1.9	2B(68): -1.7 • 3B(14): 0.5	2.9
2017	*SDN*	*MLB*	*29*	*468*	*61*	*22*	*2*	*26*	*73*	*50*	*131*	*1*	*1*	*.229/.322/.482*	*.277*	*27.1*	*.265*	*-1.0*	*2B 3*	*2.6*
2018	*SDN*	*MLB*	*30*	*506*	*74*	*23*	*2*	*28*	*79*	*56*	*144*	*1*	*0*	*.225/.322/.480*	*.284*	*29.5*	*.261*	*1.5*	*2B 3*	*3.5*

Breakout: 6%   Improve: 25%   Collapse: 8%   Attrition: 18%   MLB: 57%   *Comparables: Luke Scott, Andrew Brown, Jeff Larish*

If he wasn't stuck on one of the worst teams in the league, Schimpf would've been a big 2016 story. Coming out of nowhere as a minor-league signing, he was arguably the top power hitter in the game in July and August, knocking 16 dingers with a .418 ISO in that time. As a 28-year-old, it appeared that he'd never be able to break through, as he put up good numbers at Double-A but could never make the leap to Triple-A. It turns out he just needed some PCL action to get him over that hump, as he finally produced above-average numbers at the level. Even if he never hits another major-league home run, his 2016 showing is far more than anyone ever expected.

Yangervis Solarte   3B

Born: 7/7/87   Age: 29   Bats: B   Throws: R   Height: 5'11"   Weight: 205   Entered Pro Ball: International Free Agent, 2005

YEAR	TEAM	LVL	AGE	PA	R	2B	3B	HR	RBI	BB	K	SB	CS	AVG/OBP/SLG	TAv	VORP	BABIP	BRR	FRAA	WARP
2014	SWB	AAA	26	21	3	3	1	0	5	1	2	0	0	.600/.619/.850	.476	5.9	.667	0.0	3B(4): -0.1 • SS(1): 0.1	0.6
2014	NYA	MLB	26	289	26	14	0	6	31	30	34	0	0	.254/.337/.381	.270	9.9	.270	-1.1	3B(66): -1.2 • 2B(17): -1.3	0.8
2014	SDN	MLB	26	246	30	5	1	4	17	23	24	0	1	.267/.336/.355	.267	8.5	.281	-0.1	3B(45): -2.4 • 2B(10): -1.4	0.4
2015	SDN	MLB	27	571	63	33	4	14	63	34	56	1	0	.270/.320/.428	.266	16.1	.279	-2.1	3B(92): -3.8 • 1B(28): -0.7	1.4
2016	SDN	MLB	28	443	55	26	1	15	71	30	63	1	1	.286/.341/.467	.289	24.9	.306	-2.2	3B(95): 6.2 • 2B(15): 0.9	3.3
2017	*SDN*	*MLB*	*29*	*597*	*63*	*31*	*3*	*16*	*72*	*47*	*70*	*1*	*1*	*.273/.334/.430*	*.269*	*19.8*	*.286*	*-1.1*	*3B -5 • 1B -0*	*1.2*
2018	*SDN*	*MLB*	*30*	*499*	*63*	*25*	*2*	*15*	*61*	*42*	*61*	*0*	*0*	*.272/.337/.435*	*.278*	*18.4*	*.284*	*-1.6*	*3B -4 • 1B 0*	*1.5*

Breakout: 0%   Improve: 40%   Collapse: 9%   Attrition: 12%   MLB: 97%   *Comparables: Alberto Callaspo, Ken Oberkfell, George Kell*

Solarte is continuing the type of career that most players can only hope for, as a long-time minor leaguer who finally got his chance at the highest level and ran with it. His latest season was the best one yet, improving in every aspect of the game. His offense benefited with a higher quality of contact that showed in both his career-high BABIP and power production. Perhaps more importantly, he graded positively at the hot corner for the first time. Against all the odds, it's looking less and less crazy that he may actually end up being as good as non-2012 Chase Headley, the man for whom he was traded at the 2014 deadline.

Cory Spangenberg   2B

Born: 3/16/91   Age: 26   Bats: L   Throws: R   Height: 6'0"   Weight: 195   Entered Pro Ball: Round 1, 2011 Draft (#10 overall)

YEAR	TEAM	LVL	AGE	PA	R	2B	3B	HR	RBI	BB	K	SB	CS	AVG/OBP/SLG	TAv	VORP	BABIP	BRR	FRAA	WARP
2014	EUG	A-	23	25	3	0	1	0	2	0	6	2	0	.200/.200/.280	.156	-1.6	.263	0.5	2B(4): 0.0 • CF(1): -0.1	-0.2
2014	SAN	AA	23	304	38	17	8	2	22	15	63	14	9	.331/.365/.470	.300	18.9	.421	-1.8	2B(48): 0.5 • CF(14): 2.6	2.3
2014	SDN	MLB	23	65	7	2	1	2	9	2	14	4	2	.290/.313/.452	.278	3.0	.348	0.2	3B(9): -0.6 • LF(4): -1.2	0.1
2015	SAN	AA	24	27	3	0	1	0	1	1	2	1	1	.192/.222/.269	.204	-0.3	.208	0.4	3B(3): 0.6 • 2B(2): 0.0	0.0
2015	SDN	MLB	24	345	38	17	5	4	21	28	75	9	4	.271/.333/.399	.268	15.9	.344	4.0	2B(70): -4.6 • 3B(19): 0.1	1.2
2016	SDN	MLB	25	53	6	1	1	1	8	4	13	1	0	.229/.302/.354	.235	-0.2	.294	-0.2	2B(13): 0.4	0.0
2017	*SDN*	*MLB*	*26*	*227*	*24*	*10*	*3*	*4*	*23*	*15*	*52*	*7*	*3*	*.260/.305/.397*	*.246*	*6.1*	*.317*	*0.5*	*2B -1 • 3B -0*	*0.3*
2018	*SDN*	*MLB*	*27*	*207*	*23*	*10*	*2*	*4*	*22*	*15*	*48*	*6*	*3*	*.262/.317/.401*	*.255*	*6.0*	*.322*	*1.2*	*2B -1 • 3B 0*	*0.5*

Breakout: 7%   Improve: 56%   Collapse: 12%   Attrition: 30%   MLB: 96%   *Comparables: Donovan Solano, Ronny Cedeno, Josh Harrison*

Last year was supposed to be an important one for Spangenberg, who showed flashes of a solid future in 2015, his first extended time in the majors. Instead, we last saw Spangenberg on April 19, and the rest of the season was a series of bad news. His original injury was a strained quadriceps, which was re-torn as he was getting ready to begin his rehab from the original injury. The promise still exists for the former first-round pick, and there's still plenty of time for him to settle in as a regular. Missing a crucial developmental year after pitchers had a chance to adjust to his talents didn't help the cause, though.

Brett Wallace   1B

Born: 8/26/86   Age: 30   Bats: L   Throws: R   Height: 6'2"   Weight: 250   Entered Pro Ball: Round 1, 2008 Draft (#13 overall)

YEAR	TEAM	LVL	AGE	PA	R	2B	3B	HR	RBI	BB	K	SB	CS	AVG/OBP/SLG	TAv	VORP	BABIP	BRR	FRAA	WARP
2014	NOR	AAA	27	374	50	12	0	10	35	29	98	0	1	.265/.329/.389	.252	0.4	.343	-0.9	1B(72): 2.5 • 3B(7): -0.4	0.2
2014	BUF	AAA	27	151	12	5	0	7	23	15	33	0	0	.323/.404/.519	.309	8.5	.387	-1.4	1B(29): 0.7	0.9
2015	ELP	AAA	28	271	34	13	0	8	37	24	56	1	0	.305/.380/.460	.289	17.0	.367	0.4	3B(60): -12.0	0.5
2015	SDN	MLB	28	107	14	6	0	5	16	10	31	0	0	.302/.374/.521	.314	7.2	.400	-0.4	1B(17): -0.5 • 3B(5): 0.2	0.7
2016	SDN	MLB	29	256	19	10	0	6	20	29	83	0	0	.189/.309/.318	.239	0.9	.271	-0.1	3B(42): -4.5 • 1B(20): -0.7	-0.4
2017	*SDN*	*MLB*	*30*	*119*	*13*	*5*	*0*	*4*	*15*	*9*	*36*	*0*	*0*	*.241/.312/.408*	*.254*	*2.4*	*.321*	*-0.3*	*1B -0*	*0.2*
2018	*SDN*	*MLB*	*31*	*240*	*29*	*9*	*0*	*8*	*29*	*19*	*76*	*0*	*0*	*.230/.303/.390*	*.252*	*2.4*	*.311*	*-0.2*	*1B 0*	*0.2*

Breakout: 5%   Improve: 19%   Collapse: 7%   Attrition: 16%   MLB: 52%   *Comparables: Chris Shelton, Josh Fields, Marcus Thames*

The former first-round pick continued a familiar career trend, taking three steps back after his step forward in 2015. Wallace was forced to the hot corner for most of his playing time, a position to which he is not well suited. Bad defense can be expected, but his performance at the plate was shockingly bad even given how disappointing his career had been to this point. His power dissipated to middle-infielder levels and his AVG fell below the Mendoza line thanks to a 32 percent strikeout rate and a career-low BABIP. Being the 13th overall pick can get you far, but at age 30 he's running out of chances.

PITCHERS

Ryan Buchter   LHP

Born: 2/13/87   Age: 30   Bats: L   Throws: L   Height: 6'4"   Weight: 250   Entered Pro Ball: Round 33, 2005 Draft (#984 overall)

YEAR	TEAM	LVL	AGE	W	L	SV	G	GS	IP	H	HR	BB/9	K/9	K	GB%	BABIP	WHIP	ERA	FIP	DRA	VORP	WARP	cFIP	MPH
2014	ATL	MLB	27	1	0	0	1	0	1	0	0	9.0	9.0	1	100%	.000	1.00	0.00	4.10	4.18	0.0	0.0	104	93.3
2014	GWN	AAA	27	3	3	1	49	0	63	51	5	5.7	9.0	63	35%	.286	1.44	3.29	4.39	5.34	0.0	0.0	121	
2015	OKL	AAA	28	0	0	3	27	0	32²	27	0	4.4	10.7	39	39%	.321	1.32	1.65	2.77	2.85	7.5	0.8	90	
2015	IOW	AAA	28	2	0	0	16	0	18	9	0	4.5	11.5	23	44%	.231	1.00	2.00	2.71	3.06	3.7	0.4	91	
2016	SDN	MLB	29	3	0	1	67	0	63	34	4	4.4	11.1	78	21%	.227	1.03	2.86	3.11	4.03	6.6	0.7	104	94.6
2017	*SDN*	*MLB*	*30*	*3*	*3*	*5*	*58*	*0*	*61¹*	*53*	*8*	*4.3*	*10.0*	*68*	*47%*	*.290*	*1.34*	*4.01*	*4.17*	*4.48*	*3.0*	*0.3*	*100*	
2018	*SDN*	*MLB*	*31*	*3*	*1*	*2*	*51*	*0*	*53²*	*40*	*7*	*4.7*	*12.1*	*72*	*47%*	*.303*	*1.26*	*3.87*	*4.15*	*4.53*	*3.6*	*0.4*	*100*	

Breakout: 13%   Improve: 22%   Collapse: 11%   Attrition: 14%   MLB: 36%   *Comparables: Blake Parker, Rob Wooten, Charlie Manning*

You can be forgiven if you hadn't heard of Buchter before the 2016 season began. As a 29-year-old with one major-league inning under his belt, there was little reason to be aware of his presence. He bucked all expectations and even flirted with San Diego's closer job in the middle of the year. There was a downward trend in his performance over the second half, and the control issues that kept him out of the majors all of those years are still present. However, as a lefty who's shown the ability to strike out more than 11 batters per nine innings, Buchter can expect to have many more appearances in his future.

Carter Capps   RHP

Born: 8/7/90   Age: 26   Bats: R   Throws: R   Height: 6'5"   Weight: 220   Entered Pro Ball: Round 2, 2011 Draft (#121 overall)

YEAR	TEAM	LVL	AGE	W	L	SV	G	GS	IP	H	HR	BB/9	K/9	K	GB%	BABIP	WHIP	ERA	FIP	DRA	VORP	WARP	cFIP	MPH
2014	NWO	AAA	23	0	1	0	7	0	11	8	0	4.9	13.9	17	56%	.348	1.27	1.64	2.24	2.21	3.8	0.4	80	
2014	MIA	MLB	23	0	0	0	17	0	20¹	19	1	2.2	11.1	25	39%	.340	1.18	3.98	2.32	3.03	3.3	0.4	87	100.4
2015	NWO	AAA	24	0	2	3	13	0	15	10	0	6	9	15	50%	.263	1.33	1.80	3.80	5.55	-1.1	-0.1	105	
2015	MIA	MLB	24	1	0	0	30	0	31	18	2	2.0	16.8	58	43%	.327	0.81	1.16	1.13	1.72	10.3	1.1	48	100.6
2017	*SDN*	*MLB*	*26*	*1*	*1*	*0*	*21*	*0*	*22¹*	*19*	*3*	*3.2*	*11.2*	*28*	*46%*	*.304*	*1.25*	*3.15*	*3.62*	*3.76*	*2.9*	*0.3*	*82*	
2018	*SDN*	*MLB*	*27*	*3*	*1*	*0*	*59*	*0*	*63*	*47*	*6*	*3.3*	*11.7*	*82*	*46%*	*.306*	*1.11*	*3.04*	*3.26*	*3.56*	*10.7*	*1.1*	*75*	

Breakout: 31%   Improve: 58%   Collapse: 20%   Attrition: 10%   MLB: 87%   *Comparables: Rex Brothers, Sean Doolittle, Jordan Walden*

The league was robbed of one of its most entertaining pitchers in 2016, as Capps was sidelined for the entire year after undergoing Tommy John surgery early in spring training. That didn't keep him out of the news, as he was sent to San Diego via trade while on the shelf, meaning the Padres *got* an injured arm in a trade for once. Regardless of which uniform he's wearing, fans have to hope the procedure did not mess with the 100-plus mph fastball that helped him post near-historic numbers in 2015. His signature crow-hop, a move that was deemed legal after much controversy, will help make up for some diminished stuff, but Capps needs to regain most of his form if he wants to get back to joining the elite relievers.

Paul Clemens   RHP

Born: 2/14/88   Age: 29   Bats: R   Throws: R   Height: 6'3"   Weight: 215   Entered Pro Ball: Round 7, 2008 Draft (#220 overall)

YEAR	TEAM	LVL	AGE	W	L	SV	G	GS	IP	H	HR	BB/9	K/9	K	GB%	BABIP	WHIP	ERA	FIP	DRA	VORP	WARP	cFIP	MPH
2014	HOU	MLB	26	0	1	0	13	0	24²	28	5	4.7	5.8	16	44%	.280	1.66	5.84	6.20	6.05	-4.3	-0.5	117	96.1
2014	OKL	AAA	26	6	3	1	19	5	46¹	37	4	4.5	8.0	41	36%	.258	1.29	4.08	4.74	7.66	-10.8	-1.1	123	
2015	LEH	AAA	27	0	3	0	6	5	24	27	3	7.5	8.2	22	44%	.333	1.96	6.00	5.45	5.75	-1.5	-0.1	117	
2015	NWA	AA	27	0	1	1	5	3	15²	15	2	3.4	5.2	9	42%	.260	1.34	7.47	4.96	5.46	-0.9	-0.1	105	
2016	NWO	AAA	28	6	4	0	14	14	75¹	66	6	3.0	7.9	66	42%	.278	1.21	4.30	4.12	3.67	14.0	1.4	96	
2016	MIA	MLB	28	1	0	0	2	2	10	11	5	7.2	5.4	6	41%	.222	1.90	6.30	11.19	6.74	-1.6	-0.2	123	93.7
2016	SDN	MLB	28	3	5	0	16	12	61¹	61	9	3.4	6.9	47	42%	.281	1.37	3.67	4.83	6.81	-10.0	-1.0	124	95.4
2017	SDN	MLB	29	3	4	0	10	10	57	59	8	3.6	7.0	44	52%	.295	1.44	4.63	4.78	5.19	-0.1	0.0	100	
2018	SDN	MLB	30	4	5	0	14	14	82	76	12	4.3	8.8	81	52%	.312	1.41	4.62	4.96	5.37	1.6	0.2	126	

Breakout: 20%   Improve: 36%   Collapse: 11%   Attrition: 18%   MLB: 55%   *Comparables: Tim Stauffer, Brian Stokes, Nate Bump*

In an otherwise lackluster August baseball game between the Padres and the Phillies, Clemens got some pine tar on his jersey during an at-bat and was forced to change into a new one. With it being throwback jersey day in San Diego, each player only had the one jersey with their name on it. He had to throw on a number 91 jersey with the word "Player" in the spot where a last name typically goes. It was a sadly poetic moment, as there may not be a more generic, up-and-down pitcher than Clemens. And the answer to the question you're asking is no, they are not related.

Jarred Cosart   RHP

Born: 5/25/90   Age: 27   Bats: R   Throws: R   Height: 6'3"   Weight: 205   Entered Pro Ball: Round 38, 2008 Draft (#1156 overall)

YEAR	TEAM	LVL	AGE	W	L	SV	G	GS	IP	H	HR	BB/9	K/9	K	GB%	BABIP	WHIP	ERA	FIP	DRA	VORP	WARP	cFIP	MPH
2014	HOU	MLB	24	9	7	0	20	20	116¹	119	7	3.9	5.8	75	58%	.302	1.46	4.41	4.05	4.06	10.0	1.1	108	96.4
2014	MIA	MLB	24	4	4	0	10	10	64	54	2	3.1	5.6	40	52%	.267	1.19	2.39	3.29	4.30	3.8	0.4	110	96.0
2015	NWO	AAA	25	0	1	0	4	4	16¹	21	2	4.4	6.1	11	53%	.339	1.78	6.06	5.31	6.18	-1.6	-0.2	111	
2015	MIA	MLB	25	2	5	0	14	13	69²	63	10	4.3	6.1	47	55%	.259	1.38	4.52	5.14	5.37	-2.5	-0.3	114	96.7
2016	NWO	AAA	26	3	4	0	10	10	50²	55	8	4.4	5.3	30	50%	.292	1.58	4.09	6.07	6.27	-5.2	-0.5	120	
2016	MIA	MLB	26	0	1	0	4	4	19²	19	0	7.3	5.0	11	66%	.292	1.78	5.95	4.51	5.38	0.0	0.0	116	95.1
2016	SDN	MLB	26	0	3	0	9	9	37¹	42	4	5.5	6.5	27	60%	.317	1.74	6.03	5.14	4.93	1.8	0.2	115	94.8
2017	SDN	MLB	27	7	10	0	26	26	137	141	15	4.1	6.8	104	39%	.291	1.43	4.41	4.53	4.53	3.8	0.4	100	
2018	SDN	MLB	28	8	9	0	25	25	146²	121	14	4.4	8.5	139	39%	.291	1.32	4.07	4.37	4.71	12.4	1.3	109	

Breakout: 28%   Improve: 47%   Collapse: 22%   Attrition: 21%   MLB: 84%   *Comparables: Zach Britton, Chien-Ming Wang, Garrett Richards*

If you're ever thinking about relocating for work, find a way to get advice from Cosart, who's already been dealt three times in his career despite having just finished his age-26 season. In each of those spots, he's continued to be one of the more confusing arms in baseball. Once a top prospect with undeniable talent—there's a reason so many teams have traded for him—Cosart has shown big stuff without any results. After starting his career with 6.1 no-hit innings, it's been all downhill. A move to the bullpen is likely the next step in his career, and if he can't improve his strikeout numbers there it may be over before any of us expected.

Robbie Erlin   LHP

Born: 10/8/90   Age: 26   Bats: R   Throws: L   Height: 6'0"   Weight: 190   Entered Pro Ball: Round 3, 2009 Draft (#93 overall)

YEAR	TEAM	LVL	AGE	W	L	SV	G	GS	IP	H	HR	BB/9	K/9	K	GB%	BABIP	WHIP	ERA	FIP	DRA	VORP	WARP	cFIP	MPH
2014	SAN	AA	23	0	0	0	3	3	10¹	12	1	3.5	8.7	10	42%	.367	1.55	3.48	3.60	4.67	0.6	0.1	102	
2014	ELP	AAA	23	0	1	0	2	2	10²	21	2	1.7	6.8	8	50%	.475	2.16	9.28	5.20	3.52	2.6	0.3	96	
2014	SDN	MLB	23	4	5	0	13	11	61¹	71	6	2.2	6.8	46	43%	.332	1.40	4.99	3.66	4.71	0.8	0.1	113	91.8
2015	ELP	AAA	24	7	6	0	24	24	125¹	151	22	2.7	7.5	105	47%	.329	1.50	5.60	5.24	1.80	48.8	5.0	83	
2015	SDN	MLB	24	1	2	0	3	3	17	16	1	1.1	5.3	10	52%	.294	1.06	4.76	3.28	4.61	0.9	0.1	105	92.1
2016	SDN	MLB	25	1	2	0	3	2	15²	12	3	1.7	7.5	13	43%	.231	0.96	4.02	4.59	4.33	1.6	0.2	103	91.4
2017	SDN	MLB	26	2	2	0	7	7	36¹	38	5	2.8	7.4	30	49%	.324	1.35	4.16	4.26	4.80	3.1	0.3	112	
2018	SDN	MLB	27	7	9	0	26	26	150¹	147	21	3.9	9.1	152	49%	.329	1.41	4.36	4.69	5.03	7.8	0.8	117	

Breakout: 22%   Improve: 48%   Collapse: 22%   Attrition: 28%   MLB: 85%   *Comparables: Tommy Milone, Anthony Bass, Sean O'Sullivan*

In what should have been a make-or-break season for Erlin, the soft-throwing lefty had one good start and one atrocious start before a torn UCL ended his year. When he's going well, he can mix in strong off-speed pitches to keep hitters off balance and prevent them from teeing off on his lackluster fastball. Unfortunately, that often doesn't happen and he struggles to miss bats at an acceptable rate. He'll get another chance when he's healthy, but his best shot at sticking in a rotation is seeing Henry Rowengartner's doctor for his surgery.

Anderson Espinoza   RHP

Born: 3/9/98   Age: 19   Bats: R   Throws: R   Height: 6'0"   Weight: 160   Entered Pro Ball: International Free Agent, 2014

YEAR	TEAM	LVL	AGE	W	L	SV	G	GS	IP	H	HR	BB/9	K/9	K	GB%	BABIP	WHIP	ERA	FIP	DRA	VORP	WARP	cFIP	MPH
2016	GRN	A	18	5	8	0	17	17	76	77	2	3.2	8.5	72	49%	.338	1.37	4.38	2.99	3.54	12.4	1.4	96	
2016	FTW	A	18	1	3	0	8	7	32¹	38	1	2.2	7.8	28	44%	.363	1.42	4.73	3.17	4.24	2.7	0.3	99	

Breakout: 0%   Improve: 0%   Collapse: 0%   Attrition: 0%   MLB: 0%   *Comparables: Manny Banuelos, Martin Perez, Tyler Skaggs*

Espinoza might be the most fascinating pitching prospect in baseball. After signing with the Red Sox for a massive bonus out of Venezuela, the righty lit both the DSL and the GCL on fire as a 17-year-old. After just a half a season as a professional, he was already drawing comparisons to Pedro Martinez. Comparing someone who can't even legally buy a pack of butts in the States to arguably the greatest pitcher in history is patently absurd, but the excitement was understandable. The results took a slight step back in 2016, but Espinoza continued to show off the potential for three plus offerings and strong command. He's no longer with Boston, both his original organization and the one with which Pedro reached legendary status, but don't expect the hype to lessen.

Christian Friedrich   LHP

Born: 7/8/87   Age: 29   Bats: R   Throws: L   Height: 6'4"   Weight: 215   Entered Pro Ball: Round 1, 2008 Draft (#25 overall)

YEAR	TEAM	LVL	AGE	W	L	SV	G	GS	IP	H	HR	BB/9	K/9	K	GB%	BABIP	WHIP	ERA	FIP	DRA	VORP	WARP	cFIP	MPH
2014	CSP	AAA	26	2	9	1	27	13	91¹	114	16	3.8	8.2	83	57%	.354	1.68	7.00	5.54	6.34	-7.0	-0.7	99	
2014	COL	MLB	26	0	4	0	16	3	24¹	25	3	3.7	10.0	27	38%	.324	1.44	5.92	3.97	3.88	2.2	0.2	98	94.1
2015	COL	MLB	27	0	4	0	68	0	58¹	75	5	3.9	6.9	45	49%	.361	1.71	5.25	4.07	4.96	-1.6	-0.2	108	93.4
2016	SDN	MLB	28	5	12	0	24	23	129¹	131	13	3.6	7.0	100	47%	.295	1.41	4.80	4.20	5.23	1.9	0.2	113	91.7
2017	SDN	MLB	29	7	10	0	26	26	137	143	18	3.4	7.3	111	48%	.299	1.42	4.32	4.48	4.86	4.9	0.5	100	
2018	SDN	MLB	30	8	9	0	25	25	149²	143	19	3.8	8.3	138	48%	.314	1.38	4.27	4.59	4.98	8.6	0.9	115	

Breakout: 28%   Improve: 47%   Collapse: 28%   Attrition: 27%   MLB: 89%   Comparables: Randy Wells, Kameron Loe, Jeff Niemann

A former first-round pick who never put it together in the majors, Friedrich was looking to rebound in 2016 after leaving the hell-scape that is Coors Field. Although he was brought in to work out of the bullpen, bad luck throughout San Diego's rotation turned him back into a starter. Things didn't work out as planned and he gave the world even more proof that he shouldn't be a starter regardless of which park he calls home. On the other hand, he pitched well against left-handed batters and the prospect pedigree is still there. Someone could be pleasantly surprised by what he could provide as a LOOGY.

Brad Hand   LHP

Born: 3/20/90   Age: 27   Bats: L   Throws: L   Height: 6'3"   Weight: 220   Entered Pro Ball: Round 2, 2008 Draft (#52 overall)

YEAR	TEAM	LVL	AGE	W	L	SV	G	GS	IP	H	HR	BB/9	K/9	K	GB%	BABIP	WHIP	ERA	FIP	DRA	VORP	WARP	cFIP	MPH
2014	JUP	A+	24	0	0	0	2	2	12	4	0	1.5	10.5	14	84%	.160	0.50	0.75	1.56	2.20	4.5	0.5	77	
2014	NWO	AAA	24	2	0	0	4	4	22	18	3	3.7	9.0	22	54%	.268	1.23	3.27	4.70	2.71	7.4	0.7	89	
2014	MIA	MLB	24	3	8	1	32	16	111	112	10	3.2	5.4	67	53%	.287	1.36	4.38	4.17	4.59	2.2	0.2	114	95.3
2015	MIA	MLB	25	4	7	0	38	12	93¹	107	9	3.1	6.5	67	48%	.330	1.49	5.30	4.10	5.09	-1.6	-0.2	110	95.1
2016	SDN	MLB	26	4	4	1	82	0	89¹	63	8	3.6	11.2	111	47%	.264	1.11	2.92	3.11	2.70	22.6	2.3	78	95.6
2017	SDN	MLB	27	3	3	0	63	0	66	58	6	3.3	9.0	67	49%	.286	1.22	3.42	3.59	3.97	7.0	0.7	88	
2018	SDN	MLB	28	3	1	0	66	0	70	51	6	3.7	10.4	81	49%	.289	1.14	3.29	3.53	3.83	10.0	1.0	82	

Breakout: 17%   Improve: 46%   Collapse: 22%   Attrition: 12%   MLB: 86%   Comparables: Edinson Volquez, J.P. Howell, Robbie Ross

Every year, starting pitchers convert to the bullpen with the hopes of revitalizing careers. After seeing guys like Andrew Miller and Zach Britton take the leap, the dream remains alive for fringe starters everywhere. Hand looks like he could be the next name on that list, as he excelled in his first full season as a reliever. The short outings helped mask his command issues and helped his stuff play up enough to double his previous career-high in K/9. Meanwhile, some of the stamina that comes with preparing to start all season stayed with Hand, as he led baseball in appearances and all relievers in innings. The southpaw dominated lefties and performed well enough against righties to avoid being limited to a situational role.

Edwin Jackson   RHP

Born: 9/9/83   Age: 33   Bats: R   Throws: R   Height: 6'2"   Weight: 215   Entered Pro Ball: Round 6, 2001 Draft (#190 overall)

YEAR	TEAM	LVL	AGE	W	L	SV	G	GS	IP	H	HR	BB/9	K/9	K	GB%	BABIP	WHIP	ERA	FIP	DRA	VORP	WARP	cFIP	MPH
2014	CHN	MLB	30	6	15	0	28	27	140²	168	18	4.0	7.9	123	41%	.352	1.64	6.33	4.42	5.60	-12.0	-1.3	114	95.9
2015	CHN	MLB	31	2	1	0	23	0	31	30	0	3.5	6.7	23	46%	.306	1.35	3.19	2.94	5.31	-2.1	-0.2	118	97.2
2015	ATL	MLB	31	2	2	1	24	0	24²	14	4	3.3	6.2	17	35%	.156	0.93	2.92	4.99	5.14	-1.2	-0.1	118	96.7
2016	MIA	MLB	32	0	1	0	8	0	10²	13	2	5.1	5.9	7	35%	.344	1.78	5.91	6.00	5.96	-0.8	-0.1	120	95.4
2016	ELP	AAA	32	0	1	0	3	3	12²	20	4	4.3	6.4	9	40%	.375	2.05	7.11	5.77	8.47	-4.4	-0.5	116	
2016	SDN	MLB	32	5	6	0	13	13	73¹	79	12	4.3	6.6	54	42%	.299	1.55	5.89	5.31	6.62	-10.6	-1.1	123	94.6
2017	SDN	MLB	33	4	5	0	24	13	80	84	13	3.9	7.7	69	40%	.323	1.48	4.86	4.91	5.66	-1.5	-0.2	131	
2018	SDN	MLB	34	7	9	0	42	23	158¹	164	26	4.0	7.8	136	40%	.317	1.48	4.97	5.35	5.79	-4.6	-0.5	134	

Breakout: 20%   Improve: 45%   Collapse: 17%   Attrition: 14%   MLB: 78%   Comparables: Aaron Harang, Paul Maholm, Kyle Lohse

Jackson crossed two more teams off his list in 2016, meaning he's officially played for over one-third of MLB clubs. He trails Octavio Dotel by just two uniforms for the all-time record. Unfortunately for Jackson, he's not giving teams many reasons to continue to take chances on him. After pitching to good results (albeit with bad peripherals) out of the bullpen in 2015, he was forced back to the rotation. The result was control issues that even he hadn't seen since 2007, as well as gaudy home run numbers despite calling both Miami and San Diego home. Hopefully some teams will still believe in his potential as a reliever and hopefully those teams are among the 19 who have not yet rostered Jackson. Baseball is due for another record chase.

Eric Lauer   LHP

Born: 6/3/95   Age: 22   Bats: R   Throws: L   Height: 6'3"   Weight: 205   Entered Pro Ball: Round 1, 2016 Draft (#25 overall)

YEAR	TEAM	LVL	AGE	W	L	SV	G	GS	IP	H	HR	BB/9	K/9	K	GB%	BABIP	WHIP	ERA	FIP	DRA	VORP	WARP	cFIP	MPH
2016	TRI	A-	21	1	0	0	7	7	25	17	0	2.5	10.1	28	55%	.273	0.96	1.44	2.37	2.84	6.7	0.7	89	
2017	SDN	MLB	22	2	3	0	9	9	35	38	6	4.3	6.8	26	57%	.320	1.56	5.28	5.42	6.10	-2.1	-0.2	144	
2018	SDN	MLB	23	5	8	0	28	28	168¹	161	24	4.3	8.4	156	57%	.314	1.43	4.64	5.00	5.36	2.4	0.2	126	

Breakout: 2%   Improve: 2%   Collapse: 0%   Attrition: 0%   MLB: 2%   Comparables: *Wilking Rodriguez, Braden Shipley, Juan Jaime*

Part of the Padres' trio of 2016 first-round picks, Lauer spent his college days at Kent State, but he really burst on to the scene in the summer of 2015 when he was among the best pitchers in the Cape Cod League. After being drafted, the big lefty spent time at three different levels, with most of those innings coming in the Northwest League. If you're looking for a high-ceiling arm, Lauer isn't the pick for you. If, however, you're into high-floor southpaws who have a chance to make the majors in their second professional season, well then buy your Lauer stock now.

Brandon Maurer   RHP

Born: 7/3/90   Age: 26   Bats: R   Throws: R   Height: 6'5"   Weight: 230   Entered Pro Ball: Round 23, 2008 Draft (#702 overall)

YEAR	TEAM	LVL	AGE	W	L	SV	G	GS	IP	H	HR	BB/9	K/9	K	GB%	BABIP	WHIP	ERA	FIP	DRA	VORP	WARP	cFIP	MPH
2014	TAC	AAA	23	1	0	3	12	1	19¹	18	2	3.7	11.2	24	40%	.333	1.34	2.79	3.80	4.80	1.3	0.1	103	
2014	SEA	MLB	23	1	4	0	38	7	69²	74	6	2.5	7.1	55	41%	.308	1.33	4.65	3.52	4.53	1.0	0.1	111	98.8
2015	SDN	MLB	24	7	4	0	53	0	51	39	3	2.6	6.9	39	48%	.243	1.06	3.00	3.34	4.46	1.4	0.1	103	97.9
2016	SDN	MLB	25	0	5	13	71	0	69²	65	7	3.0	9.3	72	39%	.297	1.26	4.52	3.50	4.18	6.1	0.6	96	98.4
2017	SDN	MLB	26	3	3	20	53	0	55	54	6	2.9	8.6	53	42%	.303	1.30	3.55	3.75	4.09	5.1	0.5	89	
2018	SDN	MLB	27	3	1	15	58	0	61²	52	7	3.1	9.9	67	42%	.314	1.20	3.43	3.68	4.00	7.7	0.8	86	

Breakout: 32%   Improve: 60%   Collapse: 10%   Attrition: 10%   MLB: 91%   Comparables: *Luke Hochevar, Jenrry Mejia, Felix Doubront*

Always an inconspicuous arm, Maurer may finally be setting himself up to get recognized by a large audience. He was first noticed by scouts strictly because he pitched on the same high school team as Gerrit Cole. Drafted in the 23rd round by the Mariners, he moved quickly through the system to little-to-no fanfare. After being traded to San Diego and being converted to a full-time reliever, he started to show more potential. Although the strikeouts didn't come right away, he improved his swinging-strike rate in 2015 and set himself up for a big role in 2016. The season got off to a slow start, and he was eventually surpassed in the pecking order by guys like Ryan Buchter and Brad Hand. He slowly worked his way back and Maurer ended the year as the Padres' closer.

Adrian Morejon   LHP

Born: 2/27/99   Age: 18   Bats: L   Throws: L   Height: 6'0"   Weight: 165   Entered Pro Ball: International Free Agent, 2016

The Padres blew past their international spending limit in 2016, signing many of the top Latino prospects. Morejon was the pinnacle of that outburst, as he came over from Cuba for a robust $11 million bonus. The southpaw's fastball already sits in the mid-90s, and at age 17 it's fair to expect that velocity to grow. Since his deal was technically one that started in the 2017 season, he was limited to simulated games in the Dominican Republic and we didn't get a chance to see the phenom in real games. He'll surely make his professional debut in 2017, and it could come in full-season ball. Based on all of the scouting reports, we'll be screaming for More Adrian throughout his career.

Jacob Nix   RHP

Born: 1/9/96   Age: 21   Bats: R   Throws: R   Height: 6'4"   Weight: 220   Entered Pro Ball: Round 3, 2015 Draft (#86 overall)

YEAR	TEAM	LVL	AGE	W	L	SV	G	GS	IP	H	HR	BB/9	K/9	K	GB%	BABIP	WHIP	ERA	FIP	DRA	VORP	WARP	cFIP	MPH
2016	FTW	A	20	3	7	0	25	25	105¹	115	5	1.7	7.7	90	48%	.340	1.28	3.93	3.01	3.37	19.2	2.1	91	
2017	SDN	MLB	21	4	7	0	17	17	74²	92	13	3.7	4.7	39	66%	.324	1.63	5.77	5.68	6.58	-8.4	-0.9	157	
2018	SDN	MLB	22	6	10	0	27	27	158²	161	26	4.3	7.2	127	66%	.309	1.50	5.26	5.66	6.00	-5.6	-0.6	144	

Breakout: 2%   Improve: 2%   Collapse: 2%   Attrition: 3%   MLB: 4%   Comparables: *Vance Worley, Felipe Rivero, Roman Mendez*

Chances are Nix will always be best remembered as the player whose deal with the Astros was ruined after they couldn't sign no. 1 pick Brady Aiken. Clearly, this was a rough and unfair break for Nix, who had to spend the following season with IMG Academy. The Padres ended up taking the righty in the third round and since then he's done his best to rewrite the narrative. Although the ceiling is still limited to a mid-rotation starter, he cut his walk rate by a substantial margin against Midwest League hitters. If those gains remain as he climbs the ranks, Nix's floor will begin to rise and his connection to Aiken will begin to disappear.

Luis Perdomo   RHP

Born: 5/9/93   Age: 24   Bats: R   Throws: R   Height: 6'2"   Weight: 185   Entered Pro Ball: International Free Agent, 2010

YEAR	TEAM	LVL	AGE	W	L	SV	G	GS	IP	H	HR	BB/9	K/9	K	GB%	BABIP	WHIP	ERA	FIP	DRA	VORP	WARP	cFIP	MPH
2014	SCO	A-	21	1	0	0	2	2	12	11	1	0.8	9.8	13	47%	.323	1.00	1.50	2.61	2.67	3.6	0.4	86	
2014	PEO	A	21	3	6	0	11	11	57	64	4	3.3	6.5	41	51%	.314	1.49	5.05	4.27	7.16	-10.9	-1.1	114	
2015	PEO	A	22	5	9	0	17	17	100¹	103	7	2.8	9.0	100	55%	.334	1.34	3.68	3.39	3.01	24.7	2.6	91	
2015	PMB	A+	22	1	3	0	6	5	26¹	31	1	2.1	6.2	18	49%	.345	1.41	5.13	2.98	4.29	2.3	0.2	98	
2016	SDN	MLB	23	9	10	0	35	20	146²	187	23	2.8	6.4	105	60%	.342	1.59	5.71	4.88	4.02	20.6	2.1	99	96.4
2017	SDN	MLB	24	6	10	0	26	26	130	144	16	2.9	6.7	96	47%	.309	1.47	4.31	4.40	4.80	5.5	0.6	100	
2018	SDN	MLB	25	9	10	0	29	29	180¹	176	21	3.1	8.1	162	47%	.322	1.32	3.98	4.27	4.59	15.7	1.6	105	

Breakout: 24%   Improve: 42%   Collapse: 15%   Attrition: 32%   MLB: 70%   Comparables: *Brandon Maurer, Sean O'Sullivan, Ty Taubenheim*

As a Rule 5 pick, it was crucial for Perdomo to get off to a good start for the Padres. Instead, he was thrown out in garbage time of the season's first game and promptly allowed six runs in one inning. Despite that, he survived on the active roster for the entire season, giving himself the opportunity to develop more in the minors in 2017. He'll need it, as his performance was inconsistent at best and highlighted by the rare high-grounder, high-home run combination. On the other hand, there's clearly some talent here, as his DRA and cFIP indicate, and it's important to remember he never made it past High-A prior to last season.

Kevin Quackenbush   RHP

Born: 11/28/88 Age: 28 Bats: R Throws: R Height: 6'4" Weight: 235 Entered Pro Ball: Round 8, 2011 Draft (#263 overall)

YEAR	TEAM	LVL	AGE	W	L	SV	G	GS	IP	H	HR	BB/9	K/9	K	GB%	BABIP	WHIP	ERA	FIP	DRA	VORP	WARP	cFIP	MPH
2014	ELP	AAA	25	0	0	6	13	0	14¹	9	0	2.5	7.5	12	67%	.222	0.91	1.26	2.86	4.23	1.8	0.2	100	
2014	SDN	MLB	25	3	3	6	56	0	54¹	42	2	3.0	9.3	56	41%	.278	1.10	2.48	2.62	3.83	4.0	0.4	99	93.4
2015	ELP	AAA	26	1	0	2	9	0	11²	6	0	1.5	10.8	14	39%	.261	0.69	0.77	1.71	2.91	2.6	0.3	83	
2015	SDN	MLB	26	3	2	0	57	0	58¹	52	6	3.1	8.9	58	44%	.291	1.23	4.01	3.59	4.32	2.5	0.3	101	92.8
2016	ELP	AAA	27	1	0	2	9	0	13	12	0	1.4	11.1	16	51%	.343	1.08	2.08	1.72	1.51	5.0	0.5	77	
2016	SDN	MLB	27	7	7	2	60	0	59²	55	8	3.3	6.3	42	38%	.260	1.29	3.92	4.63	6.12	-7.6	-0.8	123	92.8
2017	SDN	MLB	28	3	3	5	53	0	55	56	8	3.4	7.6	47	48%	.292	1.39	4.78	4.60	5.07	-1.0	-0.1	100	
2018	SDN	MLB	29	3	1	3	51	0	53²	47	7	3.6	9.1	54	48%	.296	1.26	4.14	4.45	4.82	1.9	0.2	110	

Breakout: 20%   Improve: 38%   Collapse: 27%   Attrition: 25%   MLB: 78%   Comparables: Joey Devine, Fernando Salas, Ryan Cook

Quackenbush is an example of the risks associated with relief prospects. For every Craig Kimbrel, there's a "closer of the future" who does not live up the hype. Quackenbush again showed off his upside at Triple-A, but took another step backward in the majors. After a lack of command had held him back in the first two years of his career, that got even worse while his strikeout ability cratered. As a righty who relies on deception rather than velocity, command is crucial. Entering his age-28 season, Quackenbush is running out of chances to live up to that potential he showed just a few years ago.

Cal Quantrill   RHP

Born: 2/10/95 Age: 22 Bats: L Throws: R Height: 6'2" Weight: 165 Entered Pro Ball: Round 1, 2016 Draft (#8 overall)

YEAR	TEAM	LVL	AGE	W	L	SV	G	GS	IP	H	HR	BB/9	K/9	K	GB%	BABIP	WHIP	ERA	FIP	DRA	VORP	WARP	cFIP	MPH
2016	TRI	A-	21	0	2	0	5	5	18²	15	0	1.0	13.5	28	56%	.333	0.91	1.93	1.26	1.38	8.0	0.8	70	
2017	SDN	MLB	22	2	3	0	9	9	34²	38	6	4.1	6.9	27	61%	.326	1.57	5.31	5.38	6.03	-1.8	-0.2	144	
2018	SDN	MLB	23	4	6	0	22	22	131	128	20	4.1	8.5	124	61%	.319	1.43	4.70	5.07	5.34	2.1	0.2	128	

Breakout: 1%   Improve: 1%   Collapse: 0%   Attrition: 0%   MLB: 1%   Comparables: Tyler Wilson, Wilking Rodriguez, Andrew Heaney

Quantrill turned down an opportunity to sign with the Yankees out of high school, instead opting for Stanford. Things started off swimmingly, as he was their first freshman to start on Opening Day since Mike Mussina. He'd eventually miss all of 2015 following Tommy John surgery, but was still set up as a potential no. 1 pick if everything went well in his return. Instead, he was shut down in March and didn't pitch in college again. The Padres were able to swipe him with the eighth overall pick, and the early returns were phenomenal. Behind strong command and a changeup that will be a real weapon, the lanky right-hander moved through three levels in his first year of professional ball. Given that he's already been under the knife once, health will always be a question. If he can stay on the mound, Quantrill's arrival in the majors could come quickly, even if he has a long way to go before reaching Mussina's heights.

Colin Rea   RHP

Born: 7/1/90 Age: 26 Bats: R Throws: R Height: 6'5" Weight: 225 Entered Pro Ball: Round 12, 2011 Draft (#383 overall)

YEAR	TEAM	LVL	AGE	W	L	SV	G	GS	IP	H	HR	BB/9	K/9	K	GB%	BABIP	WHIP	ERA	FIP	DRA	VORP	WARP	cFIP	MPH
2014	LEL	A+	23	11	9	0	28	28	139	151	11	2.4	7.6	118	56%	.332	1.35	3.88	4.02	3.17	37.5	3.8	89	
2015	SAN	AA	24	3	2	0	12	12	75	50	1	1.3	7.2	60	50%	.233	0.81	1.08	2.35	1.88	26.7	2.9	74	
2015	ELP	AAA	24	2	2	0	6	6	26²	29	2	4.1	6.8	20	48%	.321	1.54	4.39	4.65	3.87	4.3	0.4	106	
2015	SDN	MLB	24	2	2	0	6	6	31²	29	2	3.1	7.4	26	50%	.290	1.26	4.26	3.48	3.96	3.9	0.4	104	93.3
2016	SDN	MLB	25	5	5	0	19	18	99¹	101	12	4.0	6.9	76	48%	.295	1.46	4.98	4.80	5.24	1.3	0.1	111	94.8
2016	MIA	MLB	25	0	0	0	1	1	3¹	1	0	0.0	10.8	4	43%	.143	0.30	0.00	0.79	4.81	0.2	0.0	112	93.3
2017	SDN	MLB	26	5	6	0	18	18	92²	91	12	3.3	7.3	75	50%	.308	1.35	4.39	4.43	5.12	4.5	0.5	118	
2018	SDN	MLB	27	7	10	0	27	27	158	143	21	4.3	9.1	160	50%	.310	1.39	4.45	4.79	5.19	5.5	0.6	119	

Breakout: 22%   Improve: 42%   Collapse: 29%   Attrition: 36%   MLB: 83%   Comparables: Billy Buckner, Trevor Bell, Carlos Frias

It was a whirlwind of a season for Rea, who spent the first half in San Diego before being dealt to Miami. That trip didn't last long, as he left his first Marlins start after 3.1 innings, triggering them to send him back to San Diego, where he was diagnosed with a torn UCL. Understandably, Miami was upset about potentially receiving damaged goods, and the trade-back began a controversy that included multiple teams and ended with A.J. Preller's suspension. On the mound, Rea flashed improved velocity, but paired it with rough command, ensuring that his 2016 will be remembered solely for his involvement in the Padres controversy.

Clayton Richard   LHP

Born: 9/12/83 Age: 33 Bats: L Throws: L Height: 6'5" Weight: 240 Entered Pro Ball: Round 8, 2005 Draft (#245 overall)

YEAR	TEAM	LVL	AGE	W	L	SV	G	GS	IP	H	HR	BB/9	K/9	K	GB%	BABIP	WHIP	ERA	FIP	DRA	VORP	WARP	cFIP	MPH
2014	MOB	AA	30	0	2	0	3	3	15	23	2	2.4	4.2	7	59%	.375	1.80	6.60	4.79	3.76	2.4	0.3	98	
2015	IND	AAA	31	4	2	0	9	9	56	53	3	2.1	4	25	57%	.260	1.18	2.09	3.87	4.38	5.7	0.6	105	
2015	CHN	MLB	31	4	2	0	23	3	42¹	47	3	1.5	4.7	22	60%	.297	1.28	3.83	3.61	5.51	-3.0	-0.3	109	94.2
2016	CHN	MLB	32	0	1	1	25	0	14	23	0	4.5	4.5	7	73%	.411	2.14	6.43	4.11	4.38	1.4	0.1	109	94.2
2016	SDN	MLB	32	3	3	0	11	9	53²	58	4	4.0	5.7	34	64%	.314	1.53	2.52	4.23	4.11	7.0	0.7	106	93.1
2017	SDN	MLB	33	7	10	0	24	24	136	142	15	3.2	5.9	90	54%	.293	1.39	4.39	4.49	4.94	3.6	0.4	100	
2018	SDN	MLB	34	10	12	0	31	31	201²	189	22	3.2	6.5	147	54%	.296	1.29	4.23	4.54	4.93	12.4	1.3	114	

Breakout: 9%   Improve: 27%   Collapse: 15%   Attrition: 16%   MLB: 61%   Comparables: Claudio Vargas, Jamey Wright, Chien-Ming Wang

In high school, Richard was Indiana's Mr. Baseball *and* Mr. Football while also graduating as class valedictorian. To follow that up with an eight-year major-league career that looks to continue is quite a life. It's not as if he's a dominant pitcher, but he's proven himself to be solid depending on the role. Splitting last year between the Cubs and the Padres, as well as between the bullpen and rotation, Richard rode his sinker-heavy approach to a 66 percent ground-ball rate. This approach gives him a razor-thin margin for error, but it's gotten him this far.

Tyson Ross   RHP

Born: 4/22/87   Age: 30   Bats: R   Throws: R   Height: 6'6"   Weight: 245   Entered Pro Ball: Round 2, 2008 Draft (#58 overall)

YEAR	TEAM	LVL	AGE	W	L	SV	G	GS	IP	H	HR	BB/9	K/9	K	GB%	BABIP	WHIP	ERA	FIP	DRA	VORP	WARP	cFIP	MPH
2014	SDN	MLB	27	13	14	0	31	31	195²	165	13	3.3	9.0	195	59%	.291	1.21	2.81	3.22	3.08	38.1	4.2	91	96.3
2015	SDN	MLB	28	10	12	0	33	33	196	172	9	3.9	9.7	212	62%	.320	1.31	3.26	3.00	3.04	44.4	4.8	83	95.6
2016	SDN	MLB	29	0	1	0	1	1	5¹	9	0	1.7	8.4	5	47%	.474	1.88	11.81	3.00	4.09	0.8	0.1	100	95.2
2017	SDN	MLB	30	2	2	0	6	6	37	32	4	3.9	9.7	40	51%	.321	1.31	3.76	3.75	4.37	4.9	0.5	99	
2018	SDN	MLB	31	6	6	0	16	16	96¹	85	13	3.9	9.9	106	51%	.319	1.32	4.04	4.35	4.70	9.3	1.0	108	

Breakout: 16%   Improve: 50%   Collapse: 20%   Attrition: 15%   MLB: 89%   *Comparables: Doug Fister, Jeff Niemann, Jake Arrieta*

In hindsight, perhaps we should have seen Ross' season-ending injury coming. He checked all the boxes. In his two full seasons in the rotation (2014 and 2015), just 25 pitchers amassed more innings. On top of the recent mileage on his arm, Ross relies heavily on his slider, throwing it almost 40 percent of the time. It's a stressful pitch that has blown out arms before. Finally, his velocity was beginning to spike, peaking at 96 mph in 2014 before taking a step back the following year. No one can predict when a pitcher will get hurt, but seeing Ross implode in his Opening Day start and then never return perhaps shouldn't have been so surprising.

Carlos Villanueva   RHP

Born: 11/28/83   Age: 33   Bats: R   Throws: R   Height: 6'2"   Weight: 220   Entered Pro Ball: International Free Agent, 2002

YEAR	TEAM	LVL	AGE	W	L	SV	G	GS	IP	H	HR	BB/9	K/9	K	GB%	BABIP	WHIP	ERA	FIP	DRA	VORP	WARP	cFIP	MPH
2014	CHN	MLB	30	5	7	2	42	5	77²	89	6	2.2	8.3	72	45%	.342	1.39	4.64	3.10	3.24	11.5	1.3	94	92.0
2015	SLN	MLB	31	4	3	2	35	0	61	50	6	3.1	8.1	55	42%	.265	1.16	2.95	3.77	5.09	-2.5	-0.3	107	90.8
2016	SDN	MLB	32	2	2	1	51	0	74	89	17	1.7	7.4	61	44%	.319	1.39	5.96	5.21	4.85	1.0	0.1	107	90.8
2017	SDN	MLB	33	3	2	1	44	4	63	63	10	2.5	7.9	55	47%	.310	1.27	4.47	4.35	5.20	0.4	0.0	120	
2018	SDN	MLB	34	4	3	1	48	5	95	89	15	3.3	8.4	88	47%	.301	1.30	4.52	4.85	5.26	0.1	0.0	121	

Breakout: 21%   Improve: 44%   Collapse: 19%   Attrition: 17%   MLB: 81%   *Comparables: Darren Dreifort, Moe Drabowsky, Tom Gorzelanny*

The good news for Villanueva is that he has a clear role carved out, which is half the battle for a nondescript reliever. For the second year in a row, he served as a multi-inning arm bridging the gap from rough starts to the back of the bullpen. The bad news is, based on what he showed in 2016, he shouldn't appear in anything beyond blowouts. He pounded the zone more than ever before, which certainly helped his walk rate, but also led to him allowing home runs at a higher rate than all but three pitchers with at least 70 innings. There's a little more good news, though: he has the best mustache in the league.

LINEOUTS

Hitters

NAME	POS	TEAM	LVL	AGE	PA	R	2B	3B	HR	RBI	BB	K	SB	CS	AVG/OBP/SLG	TAv	VORP	BABIP	BRR	FRAA	WARP
Jabari Blash	OF	ELP	AAA	26	229	30	12	0	11	30	41	66	1	2	.260/.415/.514	.313	17.6	.340	0.6	LF(31): 0.3 • RF(18): 1.2	2.0
	OF	SDN	MLB	26	84	7	2	0	3	5	11	34	1	0	.169/.298/.324	.207	-2.4	.265	0.4	RF(18): 2.6 • LF(4): -0.1	0.0
Franchy Cordero	OF	LEL	A+	21	322	47	16	8	5	35	19	83	11	8	.286/.339/.444	.285	21.3	.381	3.1	CF(68): -4.8 • LF(2): -0.4	1.7
	OF	SAN	AA	21	264	31	8	8	6	19	17	67	12	6	.306/.356/.478	.312	20.8	.401	-0.7	CF(59): 1.2	2.4
Josh Naylor	1B	GRB	A	19	370	42	24	2	9	54	22	62	10	3	.269/.317/.430	.287	11.5	.304	-1.9	1B(81): -2.7	1.0
	1B	LEL	A+	19	144	17	5	0	3	21	3	22	1	1	.252/.264/.353	.236	-2.9	.276	-0.6	1B(32): -3.0	-0.6
Jose Pirela	2B	SDN	MLB	26	41	2	2	0	0	0	1	9	0	1	.154/.175/.205	.157	-3.9	.200	-0.7	2B(12): -1.4 • RF(1): -0.0	-0.6
	2B	ELP	AAA	26	146	19	7	3	2	16	9	21	1	1	.248/.295/.387	.211	-4.2	.281	0.4	LF(17): -1.0 • RF(8): -0.6	-0.6
Jose Rondon	INF	SAN	AA	22	409	45	21	2	5	44	15	66	13	4	.279/.310/.386	.266	19.3	.325	0.8	SS(93): -2.9	1.8
	INF	SDN	MLB	22	26	1	0	0	0	1	1	4	0	0	.120/.154/.120	.128	-2.2	.143	0.2	SS(7): -0.2	-0.2
	INF	ELP	AAA	22	82	8	4	0	1	9	1	12	0	1	.300/.305/.388	.236	1.2	.338	0.0	SS(17): 0.1 • 3B(7): 0.5	0.2
Jose Ruiz	C	LEL	A+	21	185	14	9	0	0	9	5	41	1	1	.215/.245/.266	.179	-7.7	.279	-0.2	C(49): 2.7 • P(1): -0.0	-0.5
Fernando Tatis Jr.	SS	TRI	A-	17	49	4	4	2	0	5	3	13	1	1	.273/.306/.455	.307	4.5	.364	0.4	SS(7): -1.3 • 3B(3): -0.7	0.2
Luis Torrens	C	STA	A-	20	50	6	4	0	0	5	4	7	1	1	.311/.360/.400	.277	3.1	.359	0.1	C(11): 0.0	0.3
	C	CSC	A	20	164	9	6	0	2	10	22	26	1	1	.230/.348/.317	.229	0.3	.270	-1.8	C(40): 0.3	0.1
Jemile Weeks	2B	ELP	AAA	29	42	7	1	3	0	1	6	3	2	0	.306/.405/.500	.273	2.2	.333	0.2	SS(5): -0.0 • 3B(4): -0.6	0.1
	2B	SDN	MLB	29	57	5	1	1	0	2	3	14	1	0	.140/.204/.200	.156	-3.3	.194	1.2	2B(17): 1.8 • 3B(1): -0.0	-0.2

Jabari Blash finally made it to the majors after years in the high-minors, and while he carried his walk rate and power to the highest level he also brought a detrimental strikeout rate. ❖ **Franchy Cordero** hit well at Double-A and held his own in center field, but he still makes Steak Tartare look overcooked. ❖ **Allen Cordoba** will never hit for power, but won the Appalachian League batting title and walked more than he whiffed. He's fringy at shortstop, but his advanced approach and plus speed make him one to watch. ❖ **Josh Naylor** showed off his boom-or-bust hitting style in two organizations, but his year will be better remembered for the fact that he injured a teammate with a knife in one of those classic knife pranks. ❖ The Padres and **Jose Pirela** hoped a move out west would help him discover his bat, but instead everything got worse for the former Yankees prospect in 2016. ❖ **Jose Rondon** continued to show an ability to get hits with no power and no walks in the minors, while struggling to do much of anything in a small cup of coffee in the bigs. ❖ **Jeisson Rosario** appears to be a bit ahead of most of his fellow July 2 signees, showing off a polished approach at the plate along with a chance to stay in center field. ❖ **Jose Ruiz** has a generic name, a generic backup-catcher skill set and plays for the Padres. We've already forgotten who he is. ❖ **Fernando Tatis Jr.** is young enough that the possibilities for his career are endless, but we're all just curious if he'll start a mysterious Twitter account that may or may not be his. ❖ **Luis Torrens**, who originally signed with the Yankees out of Venezuela for $1.3 million, was unprotected in the Rule 5 draft and went off the board with the second pick. He's a good defensive catcher with some pop, but has barely played due to injuries. ❖ **Jemile Weeks** continued to live in the shadow of his older brother Rickie in 2016, missing most of the year due to a knee injury and putting up a lackluster performance when he did play.

Pitchers

NAME	TEAM	LVL	AGE	W	L	SV	G	GS	IP	H	HR	BB/9	K/9	K	GB%	BABIP	WHIP	ERA	FIP	DRA	VORP	WARP	cFIP	MPH
Logan Allen	FTW	A	19	3	4	0	15	11	54	48	2	3.7	7.8	47	38%	.301	1.30	3.33	3.61	5.03	-0.6	-0.1	108	
Buddy Baumann	ELP	AAA	28	1	1	2	24	0	28²	22	3	3.8	9.7	31	34%	.271	1.19	3.14	4.28	3.01	6.2	0.6	98	
	SDN	MLB	28	1	0	0	11	0	9²	7	0	3.7	9.3	10	28%	.280	1.14	3.72	2.67	4.90	0.1	0.0	107	91.5
Enyel De Los Santos	FTW	A	20	3	2	0	11	7	52²	38	2	2.4	7.7	45	41%	.242	0.99	2.91	3.23	3.85	6.0	0.7	98	
	LEL	A+	20	5	3	0	15	15	68¹	70	11	3.2	6.8	52	38%	.291	1.38	4.35	5.56	5.37	0.8	0.1	108	
Miguel Diaz	WIS	A	21	1	8	3	26	15	94²	83	7	2.8	8.7	91	47%	.279	1.18	3.71	3.59	3.30	16.7	1.8	93	
Keith Hessler	ARI	MLB	27	0	0	0	2	0	3	5	0	6.0	6.0	2	42%	.417	2.33	9.00	4.85	8.32	-1.1	-0.1	135	92.9
	ELP	AAA	27	1	1	2	28	0	36²	32	1	2.9	10.3	42	53%	.330	1.20	2.95	2.85	3.23	7.1	0.7	81	
	SDN	MLB	27	1	0	0	15	0	18²	19	2	5.3	4.3	9	41%	.266	1.61	3.38	5.38	6.62	-3.4	-0.4	129	93.7
Erik Johnson	CHA	MLB	26	0	2	0	2	2	11²	14	5	4.6	8.5	11	44%	.290	1.71	6.94	8.33	5.57	-0.3	0.0	115	93.0
	CHR	AAA	26	2	1	0	8	8	49	44	7	3.1	6.4	35	39%	.255	1.24	2.94	4.64	4.63	3.9	0.4	114	
	SDN	MLB	26	0	4	0	4	4	19²	32	9	3.2	4.6	10	41%	.333	1.88	9.15	8.88	5.82	-1.0	-0.1	119	92.0
Walker Lockett	FTW	A	22	1	3	0	8	8	45	43	0	1.6	5.8	29	49%	.285	1.13	3.00	2.79	4.88	0.7	0.1	102	
	LEL	A+	22	4	3	0	11	10	66¹	57	3	1.6	7.6	56	59%	.274	1.04	2.98	3.34	3.13	17.1	1.8	89	
	SAN	AA	22	4	1	0	6	4	34²	27	2	0.5	6.8	26	66%	.255	0.84	2.08	2.78	2.38	10.1	1.1	84	
	ELP	AAA	22	1	2	0	3	3	18	23	2	1.0	6.0	12	44%	.344	1.39	4.50	4.50	4.38	1.9	0.2	100	
Brandon Morrow	LEL	A+	31	0	1	0	2	2	11²	15	1	2.3	6.2	8	41%	.368	1.54	6.94	4.23	4.77	0.9	0.1	104	
	SAN	AA	31	1	1	0	2	2	10¹	18	3	3.5	3.5	4	40%	.375	2.13	7.84	7.63	8.93	-4.4	-0.5	127	
	ELP	AAA	31	0	0	2	12	2	21	29	2	3.9	9.0	21	52%	.403	1.81	6.43	4.24	3.27	4.4	0.5	92	
	SDN	MLB	31	0	0	0	18	0	16	19	2	1.7	4.5	8	47%	.309	1.38	1.69	4.37	5.26	-0.5	-0.1	112	97.1
Chris Paddack	GRB	A	20	2	0	0	6	6	28¹	9	0	0.6	15.2	48	51%	.163	0.39	0.95	1.46	0.36	14.6	1.6	43	
	FTW	A	20	0	0	0	3	3	14	11	0	1.9	14.8	23	45%	.379	1.00	0.64	0.83	1.34	5.7	0.6	71	
Jacob Smith	RIC	AA	26	2	1	1	22	0	20¹	17	1	10.2	11.5	26	27%	.314	1.97	7.08	5.28	6.47	-3.9	-0.4	116	
	SDN	MLB	26	1	0	0	4	0	4	5	1	2.2	6.8	3	33%	.364	1.50	4.50	6.44	4.66	0.1	0.0	106	93.4
Jose Torres	LEL	A+	22	0	2	1	20	0	25¹	21	2	3.6	8.9	25	51%	.279	1.22	3.55	3.95	3.71	3.9	0.4	97	
	SAN	AA	22	1	2	2	25	0	36¹	20	1	3.0	8.9	36	52%	.218	0.88	1.24	2.55	3.34	5.6	0.6	82	
	SDN	MLB	22	0	0	0	4	0	3	3	0	6.0	9.0	3	22%	.333	1.67	0.00	3.19	4.46	0.2	0.0	112	96.4
Cesar Vargas	SAN	AA	24	0	0	0	2	2	12²	5	0	0.7	9.9	14	59%	.185	0.47	1.42	1.21	2.25	4.0	0.4	74	
	SDN	MLB	24	0	3	0	7	7	34	41	5	4.0	7.4	28	56%	.343	1.65	5.03	4.86	4.57	3.0	0.3	105	91.9

Logan Allen missed some of the year with elbow issues, but continued to be the rare high-floor high school draftee who could work his way to the back of a major-league rotation sooner than his classmates. ❖ After eight years in the minors and four years at Triple-A, **Buddy Baumann** finally made the leap to the majors and served as a reminder of just how hard it is to reach the highest level. ❖ **Enyel De Los Santos** was nothing but a lottery ticket for San Diego, but so fat least he's still got a chance to pay off big. ❖ San Diego traded up to snag **Miguel Diaz** with the top pick in the Rule 5 draft, plucking the hard-throwing, high-effort reliever from Milwaukee. He's unlikely to be ready for setup work, but the Padres will have plenty of mop-up duty to go around. ❖ **Jon Edwards** has struck out more than 11 batters per nine innings in his career and is still below replacement level, which feels like it should be impossible. ❖ **Keith Hessler** couldn't carry his Triple-A success to the majors, and even during his 12 scoreless outings to finish the year he walked more batters than he struck out. ❖ **Erik Johnson**, a former top-100 prospect, will probably never help San Diego more than being part of the deal that unloaded James Shields' contract. ❖ The retirement of **Josh Johnson** is the negative that can never be proven. The two-time All-Star, who hasn't pitched since 2013, signed a minor-league deal to rummage through the junk drawer that is his arm one more time. ❖ **Walker Lockett** is both a sentence with an exclamation point and a pitching prospect whose 2016 season deserves an exclamation point, after racing through four levels of the minors. ❖ The rare post-post-post-hype pitcher, **Brandon Morrow** was once again limited due to injuries and once again largely ineffective when on the mound. ❖ **Chris Paddack** came out of nowhere in the Marlins' organization, and after being traded to San Diego looks like he could be a mid-rotation arm. Unfortunately, due to injury, it'll have to wait until 2018. ❖ **Jacob Smith** has shown big stuff that makes him intriguing, but it's overshadowed by the kind of bad command that led to Hanley Ramirez hitting Smith's first career pitch out of the park. ❖ One of many young, intriguing relief arms in San Diego's organization, **Jose Torres** rocketed from High-A to the majors and could have the brightest future of the bunch. ❖ **Cesar Vargas** started his major-league career with surprising success before imploding, both metaphorically and physically, in his seventh and final start of the season.

SAN FRANCISCO GIANTS

Essay by Grant Brisbee

Player comments by Patrick Dubuque and BP staff

The even-year mythology was annoying and cutesy, obvious and unavoidable, a knock-knock joke stretched out for so long that even Giants fans were getting tired of it. It *was* a myth, of course—a product of our brains seeing patterns where none exist—but it was hard not to point out the obvious. Every other year, the Giants would reach into their bag of nonsense and share it with the rest of the world. But there wasn't really any logical reason that a team would actually do it every other year. It was a just a coincidence.

Then Conor Gillaspie hit a three-run homer to ruin the Mets' season. Gillaspie was a one-time Giants prospect who rejoined the organization after years away. He was the heir to Ryan Vogelsong and Travis Ishikawa, which meant these guys were just cycling through the same role, like the Doctor from *Doctor Who* or so many Green Lanterns. If you didn't believe in even-year nonsense before the home run, your faith was tested. It was just the second homer Jeurys Familia had allowed all season and Gillaspie wasn't much of a power hitter, but the sinker sailed high and the ball sailed higher.

"No," the rational part of you muttered, like the protagonist in the first act of a science-fiction movie. "This is all just a fluke, a coincidence." And when the Cubs hosted the Giants in the Division Series, the better team won the first two games because that's how baseball works. Sometimes.

Then Gillaspie turned around a 102 mph fastball from Aroldis Chapman to spark a dramatic Giants comeback in Game 3, and your faith was shattered. Of the 44 left-handed batters to face Chapman in the regular season, just five got a hit. Here was another Giants reject, the same one as the previous series, stunning the baseball world with a quick bat and a booming line drive. The Cubs had the weight of history crushing them and the Giants had the controlled substance of the even years propelling them. There was no mythology; there was only even-year truth; there was only Conor Gillaspie in all his forms.

A day later, the Giants' bullpen stabbed the even-year mythology in the throat. The team would probably like to move the carcass off to the side of the road, but it's there as a cautionary tale for now. The even year was strong, but the kinetic energy of an apocalyptic bullpen was stronger. It all added up to one of the lousiest, least-watchable baseball seasons a team will ever, ever, ever inflict upon its fans.

GIANTS PROSPECTUS
2016 W-L: 87-75, 2ND IN NL WEST

Pythag	.557	7th	DER	.713	3rd
RS/G	4.41	19th	B-Age	29.1	25th
RA/G	3.9	4th	P-Age	29.5	27th
TAv	.268	7th	Salary	$172.1M	5th
BRR	-12.68	28th	M$/MW	$4.1M	9th
TAv-P	.253	8th	DL Days	669	7th
FIP	3.8	4th	$ on DL	12%	14th

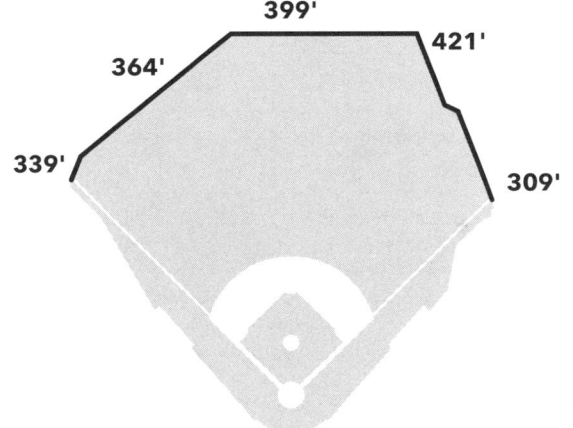

Outfield wall profile: **8' to 25'**

Three-Year Park Factors

Runs	Runs/RH	Runs/LH	HR/RH	HR/LH
94	92	92	84	73

Top Hitter WARP	7.6	Buster Posey
Top Pitcher WARP	5.5	Madison Bumgarner
Top Prospect		Tyler Beede

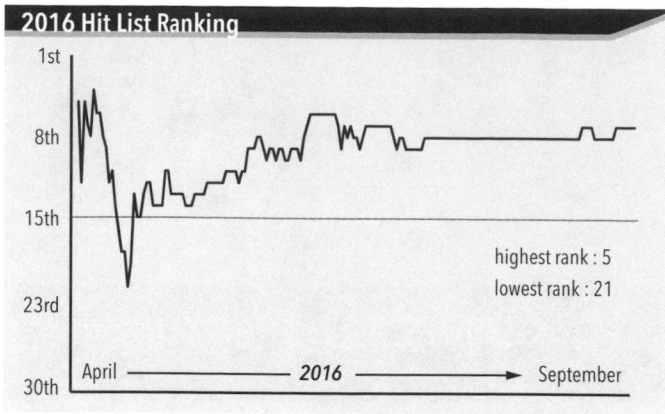

2016 Hit List Ranking

highest rank : 5
lowest rank : 21

April — *2016* → September

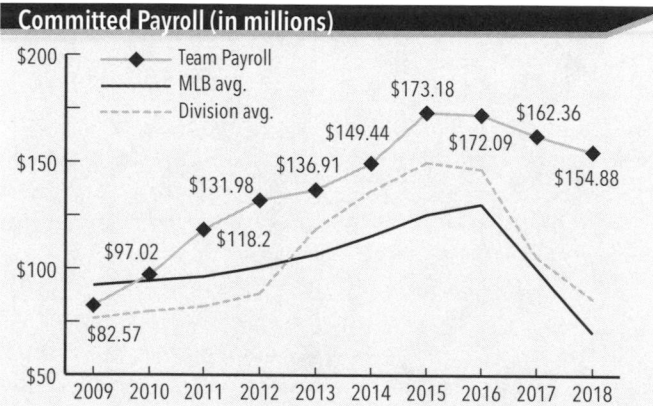

Committed Payroll (in millions)

- ◆ Team Payroll
- —— MLB avg.
- - - - Division avg.

$82.57
$97.02
$118.2
$131.98
$136.91
$149.44
$173.18
$172.09
$162.36
$154.88

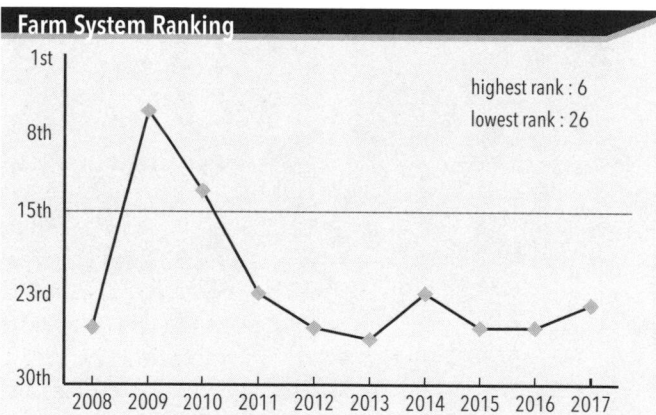

Farm System Ranking

highest rank : 6
lowest rank : 26

Personnel

EVP, Baseball Operations:
Brian Sabean

SVP, General Manager:
Bobby Evans

SVP, Player Personnel:
Dick Tidrow

VP, Assistant General Manager:
John Barr

Manager:
Bruce Bochy

Does that sound like it's coming from a spoiled brat? Probably. I'll wear it. This essay started with a description of two different postseason successes that were a week apart. There are some franchises that have trouble matching that in a decade. I'm not sure if the Expos/Nationals can do much better in 48 seasons. That's before you get into the other recent reasons Giants fans are spoiled. By that measure, the 2016 season was fine. It had some high points—more high points than other teams are guaranteed in any given season—and it ended with disappointment, just like it did for every team that wasn't the Cubs. There were eight teams that lost 90 games or more, you know. At least a couple of them started the season as contenders. Now *those* were unwatchable seasons.

And yet, I'll provide some support for my assertion. It starts with the premise that there's nothing worse than watching a game for three hours, only to have it sucked into the garbage disposal at the last second. The blown save is worse than the 200-minute game when it comes to making baseball enjoyable. All that time, most of it spent with optimism and a sense of certainty. *I don't know how this season will go, but I'm pretty sure I know how this game will end.* Then, flrrrrrmp, sucked into the gears and spit into a waste treatment plant. It's put upon you, for some reason, to watch the next game, which probably starts in a dozen hours or so.

Let's continue with the premise that there's nothing more exciting than a ninth-inning comeback. Down to your last out. Down to your last strike. Facing the other team's closer, the flamethrower, the unhittable All-Star. There's a hit, maybe, a home run. Heck, you'll always settle for an error or a balk. There are so many ways to scratch out that one run. So many ways to walk off and break the hearts of the other guys.

Here's how many wins the Giants had in 2016 when trailing after eight innings: Zero. There were 62 times they entered the ninth inning trailing. They lost all 62 of those games.

Here's how many wins other teams had against the Giants in 2016 when trailing after eight innings: Nine. The other teams snatched victory from the jaws of defeat nine times, and they did it with home runs, walks and even a walk-off balk.

Consider that the Giants had at least one win when trailing after eight innings in every season since moving to San Francisco. The 100-loss team of 1985 did it three times. Consider that the Giants hadn't lost as many games when leading after eight innings in any season since moving to San Francisco. The previous record was eight losses, in 1999, when the hitters were larger and crueler.

This would help explain why the team fared worse than their Pythagorean record. It would help explain why they were neck and neck with the Dodgers in Baseball Prospectus' First Order Winning Percentage and why the Giants were one of the five best teams in baseball according to Second and Third Order Winning Percentages. The other teams got the hits/walks/balks/injunctions at just the right time in the ninth inning. The Giants never did.

Let's finish with the premise that it's better to stink first and succeed second than it is to succeed first and stink second. Enjoying your chosen hobby has a lot to do with managed expectations. The movie you weren't expecting much from that turns out to be a classic? Golden. The movie from your favorite director that sounded like a dream project from the second it was announced, but turned out to be a dog? Extra painful.

The Giants entered the All-Star break with the best record in baseball and the starting pitcher in the All-Star game, who was only starting because the *other* Giants ace pitched a shutout the Sunday before. They didn't look like a team that needed a random Conor Gillaspie cameo to succeed in the postseason. They looked like they might have been blessed with the strongest roster of any Giants team since Barry Bonds retired.

In the second half, though, the Giants had one of the worst records in baseball, going 30-42 when merely going .500 would have locked down the division. They did this while outscoring their opponents by 11 runs, which is a pretty neat trick to pull off. The 2016 Giants, then, were masters at managing expectations, doing just enough to disappoint you in every respect. Think they're going to win? Guess what, they're not. Think they're going to come back? Guess what, they're not. Think they're good? Guess what, they're actually one of the worst teams in baseball.

And at the last second, when you thought the even-year locusts were going to devour the Cubs' crops and force a nervous Game 5 with Johnny Cueto on the mound, the Giants delivered one of the worst bullpen collapses in postseason history. It was a perfect ending for the even-year mythos, really. The bullpen is mightier, both for good and for evil. It was hard to watch, just trust me on that. Even for someone as spoiled as your typical Giants fan.

What does it mean for the 2017 Giants, though? Consider Russell Carleton's (Warning! Effusive Praise Ahead!) tremendous BP article on September 29, in which he looked at "bullpen contagion." That is, the tendency of a bullpen to struggle collectively when things started to turn, with the disastrous performances and general dread becoming a self-fulfilling prophecy. He found evidence that pitchers in doomed bullpens tended to walk more batters than they were supposed to. Maybe they were gripping the ball tighter.

Maybe they were in their own heads, worrying about the recent past. Maybe they were just trying too hard not to screw up.

It fit with the Giants. The most egregious sin from the bullpen in the game that ended their season wasn't a single, double, triple or homer. It was a walk. Javier Lopez walked Anthony Rizzo with a three-run lead in the ninth inning, even though he couldn't have tied the game. There was no reward for being that careful with him. There was only risk. Yet it still happened. The bullpen contagion was real, and it spread. However, there's no reason for it to linger into next season, especially when most of the principals aren't likely to return. The bullpen should be better, if only because it can't be worse.

The lineup should do a better job of scoring runs, which should leave more breathing room for the bullpen, which should avoid the contagion. The Giants hit far worse with runners in scoring position, in late-and-close situations and with runners in scoring position and two outs. It's possible that they feasted on mop-up pitchers when they were running away with games, skewing the overall numbers. But it's more likely that their cluster luck was just lousy.

The rotation was actually a strength last year. They spent money on two starting pitchers (Johnny Cueto and Jeff Samardzija) who probably would have gotten just as much money, if not more, this offseason. That's not always the case with free agent pitchers. And at the deadline, the Giants traded one of their cherished homegrown infielders for a rotation fix that would last beyond the season. It stung at the time, but there's no doubting the Giants were happy to have Matt Moore instead of wading into the acid ponds of the free agent market.

It's a roster that wasn't in need of an overhaul. It's a roster that just needs to avoid doing *that* again, in which *that* is defined as playing a particularly unwatchable brand of baseball at just the wrong time. The 2016 Giants weren't bereft of even-year nonsense and memorable magic. Maybe time will allow us to appreciate it more. But the good news is they failed in a way that would be exceptionally hard to repeat, even if they tried their odd-year best. The 2017 Giants still have the strong foundation that made the first half of 2016 seem completely rational. That probably means a lot more than any notions of even-year nonsense.

Probably. ▪

—Grant Brisbee covers the Giants
for McCovey Chronicles

HITTERS

Christian Arroyo   SS

Born: 5/30/95   Age: 22   Bats: R   Throws: R   Height: 6'1"   Weight: 180   Entered Pro Ball: Round 1, 2013 Draft (#25 overall)

YEAR	TEAM	LVL	AGE	PA	R	2B	3B	HR	RBI	BB	K	SB	CS	AVG/OBP/SLG	TAv	VORP	BABIP	BRR	FRAA	WARP
2014	AUG	A	19	125	10	3	1	1	14	4	22	1	2	.203/.226/.271	.189	-6.6	.237	-0.8	2B(26): 6.7 • SS(5): -0.1	0.0
2014	SLO	A-	19	267	39	14	2	5	48	18	31	6	1	.333/.378/.469	.309	24.7	.360	0.1	SS(58): 3.9	3.0
2015	SJO	A+	20	409	48	28	2	9	42	19	73	5	3	.304/.344/.459	.304	31.8	.355	-2.3	SS(88): -2.5	3.2
2016	RIC	AA	21	517	57	36	1	3	49	29	72	1	1	.274/.316/.373	.254	12.5	.313	-1.3	3B(48): 2.1 • SS(48): -1.1	1.5
2017	*SFN*	*MLB*	*22*	*250*	*25*	*14*	*1*	*5*	*23*	*11*	*52*	*0*	*0*	*.252/.287/.377*	*.227*	*0.8*	*.301*	*-0.4*	*SS 1 • 3B 1*	*0.4*
2018	*SFN*	*MLB*	*23*	*313*	*33*	*17*	*1*	*7*	*33*	*16*	*66*	*0*	*0*	*.252/.294/.389*	*.246*	*3.9*	*.300*	*-0.7*	*SS 1 • 3B 2*	*0.8*

Breakout: 1%   Improve: 12%   Collapse: 7%   Attrition: 22%   MLB: 27%   *Comparables: Neil Walker, Josh Vitters, Cheslor Cuthbert*

Imagine a Giants middle infield prospect. Now imagine a Giants middle infield prospect with a pedigree. Don't worry about the 2016 numbers, which were primarily a product of the run environment in Double-A Richmond, although if you want to worry about the low walk rates, that's acceptable. Arroyo remains what he's been: a shortstop who probably doesn't have the range to continue being a shortstop and a hitter who probably doesn't need to be a shortstop to be valuable. Despite the lack of speed he positions himself well, wields a strong arm and moves well glove side, so with Matt Duffy in Tampa Bay, Arroyo's natural destination appears to be third base. Offensively his short swing translates into a high contact rate and doubles power. In other words, he'll fit right in.

Brandon Belt   1B

Born: 4/20/88   Age: 29   Bats: L   Throws: L   Height: 6'5"   Weight: 220   Entered Pro Ball: Round 5, 2009 Draft (#147 overall)

YEAR	TEAM	LVL	AGE	PA	R	2B	3B	HR	RBI	BB	K	SB	CS	AVG/OBP/SLG	TAv	VORP	BABIP	BRR	FRAA	WARP
2014	FRE	AAA	26	20	2	3	0	2	5	1	5	0	1	.526/.550/1.000	.572	7.2	.667	-0.1	1B(4): -0.1	0.7
2014	SFN	MLB	26	235	30	8	0	12	27	18	64	3	1	.243/.306/.449	.277	5.7	.288	-0.4	1B(59): 8.6 • RF(1): -0.0	1.6
2015	SFN	MLB	27	556	73	33	5	18	68	56	147	9	3	.280/.356/.478	.317	35.4	.363	-1.5	1B(120): 8.1 • LF(14): 0.2	4.7
2016	SFN	MLB	28	655	77	41	8	17	82	104	148	0	4	.275/.394/.474	.316	37.8	.346	-6.4	1B(151): 0.6 • LF(3): 0.0	4.0
2017	*SFN*	*MLB*	*29*	*621*	*82*	*34*	*5*	*19*	*71*	*71*	*148*	*5*	*3*	*.269/.358/.456*	*.285*	*23.2*	*.336*	*-1.0*	*1B 8*	*3.2*
2018	*SFN*	*MLB*	*30*	*538*	*71*	*30*	*4*	*16*	*67*	*64*	*130*	*3*	*2*	*.269/.360/.453*	*.294*	*22.6*	*.337*	*-2.6*	*1B 7*	*3.2*

Breakout: 7%   Improve: 60%   Collapse: 5%   Attrition: 6%   MLB: 95%   *Comparables: Don Mincher, Boog Powell, Mark Teixeira*

After finishing among the NL's top 10 in True Average in 2015 and starting 2016 hot, Belt fell back to earth a little bit and wound up finishing … 10th. Baseball's Best Disappointment refined his patented formula by hitting the lowest ground-ball rate and the third-highest line-drive rate in the game, spraying doubles all over the place. The new twist: he went from having a decent eye to finishing among the leaders in walks, earning his first All-Star berth and cementing him as truly, honestly, one of the best hitters in baseball. Armed with a six-year extension, expect to see Belt finish as the runner-up on All-Star vote totals for years to come.

Gregor Blanco   CF

Born: 12/24/83   Age: 33   Bats: L   Throws: L   Height: 5'11"   Weight: 175   Entered Pro Ball: International Free Agent, 2000

YEAR	TEAM	LVL	AGE	PA	R	2B	3B	HR	RBI	BB	K	SB	CS	AVG/OBP/SLG	TAv	VORP	BABIP	BRR	FRAA	WARP
2014	SFN	MLB	30	444	51	18	6	5	38	41	77	16	5	.260/.333/.374	.271	19.6	.311	4.0	CF(72): -1.5 • LF(64): 0.1	2.0
2015	SFN	MLB	31	372	59	19	3	5	26	40	59	13	5	.291/.368/.413	.299	27.5	.338	4.3	CF(44): -3.2 • LF(38): 3.3	2.8
2016	SFN	MLB	32	274	28	10	4	1	18	29	51	6	3	.224/.309/.311	.237	-0.8	.279	-0.7	RF(34): -0.8 • LF(29): -0.2	-0.4
2017	*SFN*	*MLB*	*33*	*276*	*31*	*11*	*3*	*3*	*24*	*29*	*54*	*8*	*3*	*.255/.335/.363*	*.245*	*6.1*	*.309*	*1.2*	*RF -0 • CF -1*	*0.7*
2018	*SFN*	*MLB*	*34*	*276*	*30*	*11*	*3*	*3*	*25*	*29*	*56*	*7*	*3*	*.250/.330/.360*	*.255*	*6.7*	*.305*	*1.5*	*RF 0 • CF -1*	*0.8*

Breakout: 3%   Improve: 36%   Collapse: 9%   Attrition: 17%   MLB: 87%   *Comparables: Dave Martinez, Willie Bloomquist, Terry Puhl*

Blanco's 2016 season was one of those dark comedies where there aren't any actual jokes, just a series of misfortunes. After a quiet, Blanconian April our hapless hero was pressed into full-time service in May, right around when the locusts arrived. Each month got worse for the fourth outfielder extraordinaire, with each slump worsening into a deeper slump and each clean hit refusing to fall. Pitchers pounded him away and he flailed at anything with break, unraveling years of steady offensive progress in a matter of weeks. Finally, the Giants were forced to admit that they had half a dozen other fourth outfielders and perhaps more importantly that Blanco's shoulder, hurt early, never really healed. Despite the fact that a bounce-back age-33 season is likely, he'll probably come as a bargain for some team given his recent woes and defensive limitations in center. Still, it was a good run for Blanco and the Giants alike despite staying on the air one season too long.

Trevor Brown   C

Born: 11/15/91   Age: 25   Bats: R   Throws: R   Height: 6'2"   Weight: 195   Entered Pro Ball: Round 10, 2012 Draft (#328 overall)

YEAR	TEAM	LVL	AGE	PA	R	2B	3B	HR	RBI	BB	K	SB	CS	AVG/OBP/SLG	TAv	VORP	BABIP	BRR	FRAA	WARP
2014	SJO	A+	22	212	19	5	1	2	22	12	33	0	0	.215/.259/.282	.218	0.9	.244	2.1	C(39): -1.5 • 2B(7): -0.6	-0.4
2014	FRE	AAA	22	80	6	3	0	0	13	7	13	0	0	.319/.380/.361	.272	5.0	.390	0.0	C(22): -0.1 • 2B(1): -0.0	0.5
2015	SAC	AAA	23	314	35	17	0	2	27	21	53	1	0	.261/.319/.343	.247	10.8	.313	2.1	C(72): 8.2	1.9
2015	SFN	MLB	23	43	1	3	0	0	5	3	8	1	1	.231/.279/.308	.225	0.8	.281	0.4	C(13): -1.9	-0.1
2016	SFN	MLB	24	184	17	7	0	5	19	10	39	0	1	.237/.283/.364	.237	2.1	.279	-1.5	C(60): -6.1 • 3B(1): -0.0	-0.4
2017	*SFN*	*MLB*	*25*	*62*	*5*	*3*	*0*	*1*	*5*	*4*	*13*	*0*	*0*	*.239/.288/.340*	*.228*	*0.9*	*.289*	*-0.1*	*C -1*	*-0.1*
2018	*SFN*	*MLB*	*26*	*216*	*23*	*10*	*1*	*4*	*22*	*13*	*46*	*1*	*0*	*.239/.290/.361*	*.239*	*3.0*	*.285*	*-0.3*	*C -4*	*-0.2*

Breakout: 6%   Improve: 25%   Collapse: 19%   Attrition: 37%   MLB: 74%   *Comparables: Rob Brantly, Carlos Perez, Austin Romine*

With Andrew Susac hurt and eventually shipped off to Milwaukee as part of the Will Smith deal, Brown found himself as the official backup catcher for the Giants in 2016. In most sports, being second-string is surprisingly profitable: no one in football is more popular than the backup quarterback and the sixth man in basketball is prized for his energy and fresh legs. It's never really worked that way in baseball, particularly when the starter is Buster Posey, and particularly when the backup is Trevor Brown. The converted second baseman struggled in all aspects of the game, hitting, running and fielding with equally deleterious effect. He's only played three years at the position, so at least from a defensive standpoint, he has room for growth. And Susac was a wasted resource, blocked as he was. Still, unless the Giants find someone to take his job, Brown could make Will Smith a slightly less popular name around the Bay in 2016.

YEAR	TEAM	P. COUNT	FRM RUNS	BLK RUNS	THRW RUNS	TOT RUNS
2014	FRE	3077	0.6	0.0	-0.2	0.4
2015	SAC	9859	6.4	0.2	0.7	7.3
2015	SFN	1696	-1.8	0.2	0.0	-1.5
2016	SFN	6269	-5.4	-1.6	-0.4	-7.5
2017	SFN	2327	-1.0	-0.2	0.0	-1.3
2018	SFN	8125	-3.6	-0.8	-0.2	-4.6

Gustavo Cabrera   LF

Born: 1/23/96   Age: 21   Bats: R   Throws: R   Height: 6'2"   Weight: 190   Entered Pro Ball: International Free Agent, 2012

YEAR	TEAM	LVL	AGE	PA	R	2B	3B	HR	RBI	BB	K	SB	CS	AVG/OBP/SLG	TAv	VORP	BABIP	BRR	FRAA	WARP
2016	AUG	A	20	75	9	4	1	0	5	5	16	3	0	.232/.293/.319	.247	0.9	.302	0.4	LF(18): -0.5	0.0
2016	SLO	A-	20	130	25	9	1	4	13	5	42	1	0	.246/.285/.434	.279	4.2	.338	-0.3	LF(16): -3.6	0.1
2017	SFN	MLB	21	250	22	10	1	5	23	12	80	2	1	.206/.249/.323	.199	-7.3	.286	0.0	LF -3	-1.1
2018	SFN	MLB	22	187	18	8	1	4	18	9	60	1	0	.209/.256/.333	.215	-4.1	.290	0.0	LF -2	-0.7

Breakout: 1%   Improve: 1%   Collapse: 0%   Attrition: 2%   MLB: 2%   *Comparables: Destin Hood, Rymer Liriano, Moises Sierra*

Cabrera last got an annual comment in 2014. Mere days after it was submitted for printing, the blue-chip international signee, not yet even an adult, slipped on a wet floor in his home in the Dominican. As he fell, he put his right arm through a glass table, severing every nerve and blood vessel at the wrist. An astronomical combination of quick thinking, fortune and the efforts of his family, friends, Giants scout Pablo Peguero and staff surgeons (the team flew him to their own facility to ensure he got proper care) saved his arm and his baseball career. Every nerve in his arm had to be reconnected in order to maintain functionality and the surgery took nearly five hours. After two years of rehab, two years of follow-up surgeries and a random hamstring injury that cut short his fall-league comeback, Cabrera returned to organized baseball. He's not at full strength; who knows what that even means, now. And his talents, while exciting enough to earn him top billing during his signing period, were always raw. But for now, Cabrera is playing baseball. That's enough.

Brandon Crawford   SS

Born: 1/21/87   Age: 30   Bats: L   Throws: R   Height: 6'2"   Weight: 215   Entered Pro Ball: Round 4, 2008 Draft (#117 overall)

YEAR	TEAM	LVL	AGE	PA	R	2B	3B	HR	RBI	BB	K	SB	CS	AVG/OBP/SLG	TAv	VORP	BABIP	BRR	FRAA	WARP
2014	SFN	MLB	27	564	54	20	10	10	69	59	129	5	3	.246/.324/.389	.269	25.7	.307	-0.2	SS(149): 9.9	3.9
2015	SFN	MLB	28	561	65	33	4	21	84	39	119	6	4	.256/.321/.462	.291	38.0	.294	-0.9	SS(140): 6.1	4.7
2016	SFN	MLB	29	623	67	28	11	12	84	57	115	7	0	.275/.342/.430	.280	36.6	.322	-1.8	SS(155): 4.1	4.2
2017	SFN	MLB	30	579	59	26	6	13	63	49	118	6	2	.251/.319/.397	.252	18.7	.298	0.0	SS 5	2.1
2018	SFN	MLB	31	551	64	26	5	13	60	46	116	4	2	.250/.318/.401	.259	17.1	.299	-1.0	SS 5	2.4

Breakout: 3%   Improve: 61%   Collapse: 3%   Attrition: 6%   MLB: 97%   *Comparables: Asdrubal Cabrera, J.J. Hardy, Stephen Drew*

The year is 2089. The only elections remaining are for televised dance competitions. Eighty percent of pets are robots. All non-catcher position players are manned by pitchers, since balls in play are nearly extinct. And "is Brandon Crawford for real?" articles are still being published on the internet. The former non-prospect and non-hitter polished his game yet again in 2016, adding another Gold Glove to his resume and narrowly missing his second All-Star berth. His power waned, primarily because of an untenable 16.2 percent HR/FB rate in 2015, but he made up for it by refining his plate approach, holding up on pitches out of the zone and setting himself up for better counts. On the whole Crawford appears headed toward one of those pleasant "get better at hitting while getting worse at fielding" decline phases that all the slick shortstops hope for, one that will reward the Giants and their army of renewable not-quite-shortstop prospects. Even after he's re-made into a cyborg to fight in the oncoming Baseball Wars of the 2060s.

Steven Duggar   CF

Born: 11/4/93   Age: 23   Bats: L   Throws: R   Height: 6'2"   Weight: 195   Entered Pro Ball: Round 6, 2015 Draft (#186 overall)

YEAR	TEAM	LVL	AGE	PA	R	2B	3B	HR	RBI	BB	K	SB	CS	AVG/OBP/SLG	TAv	VORP	BABIP	BRR	FRAA	WARP
2015	SLO	A-	21	267	40	12	1	1	27	35	52	6	3	.293/.390/.367	.283	12.9	.373	1.4	RF(52): 10.0 • CF(7): -0.8	2.3
2016	SJO	A+	22	311	43	12	4	9	30	44	66	6	7	.284/.386/.462	.323	24.5	.346	-2.2	RF(60): 5.0 • CF(5): -0.1	3.0
2016	RIC	AA	22	276	35	16	4	1	24	28	51	9	7	.321/.391/.432	.327	27.7	.397	1.0	CF(59): 7.6	3.8
2017	SFN	MLB	23	250	30	11	2	5	23	25	62	4	3	.252/.330/.385	.250	5.4	.326	-0.4	CF 2 • RF 1	1.0
2018	SFN	MLB	24	379	44	16	3	8	39	38	96	6	4	.248/.325/.383	.261	9.4	.322	-0.2	CF 3 • RF 2	1.6

Breakout: 0%   Improve: 20%   Collapse: 7%   Attrition: 16%   MLB: 44%   *Comparables: Brian Goodwin, Desmond Jennings, Dexter Fowler*

When we're young, we base our identities on our greatest strengths; as we grow older, we become known primarily by our weaknesses. Luckily, Duggar is still young, so there's time to still enjoy all the positive aspects of his game: the athleticism, the range in center, the bat that seems to find every hole in the infield. But despite an excellent season overall, and the aplomb with which he handled a midseason promotion, the questions that may someday haunt him remain. Will his natural speed ever translate into baserunning skill? Will he ever refine his routes in center to truly maximize his defensive talent? Will he be able to adjust his swing mechanics to render his quick bat into an actual power stroke? If the answer is yes, Duggar could develop into a solid regular. If not, he's a suitable replacement for Gregor Blanco, with a lifetime of thinking wistfully back to when he could have been an All-Star contender.

Aramis Garcia   C

Born: 1/12/93   Age: 24   Bats: R   Throws: R   Height: 6'2"   Weight: 220   Entered Pro Ball: Round 2, 2014 Draft (#52 overall)

YEAR	TEAM	LVL	AGE	PA	R	2B	3B	HR	RBI	BB	K	SB	CS	AVG/OBP/SLG	TAv	VORP	BABIP	BRR	FRAA	WARP
2014	SLO	A-	21	76	5	3	0	2	12	5	19	0	0	.229/.289/.357	.217	-0.3	.286	-0.1	C(18): -0.3	-0.1
2015	AUG	A	22	363	42	15	1	15	61	35	77	0	1	.273/.350/.467	.313	31.1	.312	-3.4	C(72): 3.8	3.7
2015	SJO	A+	22	84	10	4	0	0	5	9	22	1	0	.227/.310/.280	.223	0.5	.321	0.1	C(19): 0.9	0.1
2016	SJO	A+	23	160	20	6	0	2	20	14	42	1	0	.257/.323/.340	.254	4.7	.350	-1.7	C(41): 1.8	0.7
2017	SFN	MLB	24	250	24	9	1	7	28	19	73	0	0	.218/.281/.358	.220	2.1	.284	-0.3	C 1	0.3
2018	SFN	MLB	25	225	25	8	1	6	24	18	66	0	0	.213/.280/.353	.231	1.2	.279	-0.4	C 1	0.2

Breakout: 8%   Improve: 18%   Collapse: 11%   Attrition: 30%   MLB: 31%   Comparables: Jose Lobaton, Adrian Nieto, Cameron Rupp

Garcia's catcher-speed march toward the majors was halted in late May after breaking his face on a second baseman's knee. He returned to High-A San Jose and wound up demonstrating some improvement over his first stab at the level, but still has a way to go. Suarez has a prospect profile out of time: His swing is built for decent power and reasonable contact by the standards of the position, and his arm (42 percent caught stealing rate) would win the admiration of any 1980s scout. But his footwork and glove still need a lot of practice, and calling him a bat-first catching prospect insinuates a bit more bat. He's still trending as a player who can help at the major-league level, but you'll need plenty of patience.

YEAR	TEAM	P. COUNT	FRM RUNS	BLK RUNS	THRW RUNS	TOT RUNS
2017	SFN	9065	0.0	0.0	0.0	0.0
2018	SFN	8160	0.0	0.0	0.0	0.0

Conor Gillaspie   3B

Born: 7/18/87   Age: 29   Bats: L   Throws: R   Height: 6'1"   Weight: 195   Entered Pro Ball: Round 1, 2008 Draft (#37 overall)

YEAR	TEAM	LVL	AGE	PA	R	2B	3B	HR	RBI	BB	K	SB	CS	AVG/OBP/SLG	TAv	VORP	BABIP	BRR	FRAA	WARP
2014	CHA	MLB	26	506	50	31	5	7	57	36	78	0	4	.282/.336/.416	.277	21.0	.325	-1.9	3B(127): -6.2	1.6
2015	CHA	MLB	27	185	10	11	1	3	15	9	34	0	1	.237/.276/.364	.227	-1.2	.275	-0.7	3B(52): 0.5 • 1B(2): 0.3	-0.1
2015	ANA	MLB	27	68	4	4	1	1	9	4	13	0	0	.203/.250/.344	.218	-1.5	.240	-0.8	3B(17): -2.5 • 2B(1): -0.0	-0.4
2016	SAC	AAA	28	52	6	3	0	1	4	1	6	1	0	.314/.327/.431	.262	0.9	.341	-0.4	3B(7): -0.5 • 1B(1): -0.1	0.0
2016	SFN	MLB	28	205	24	8	4	6	25	12	28	1	2	.262/.307/.440	.273	6.8	.278	-1.9	3B(45): 0.3 • 1B(7): 0.1	0.7
2017	SFN	MLB	29	266	26	12	3	5	27	19	43	1	1	.254/.307/.389	.246	2.7	.286	-0.4	3B -2 • 1B 1	0.1
2018	SFN	MLB	30	193	22	9	2	4	21	14	33	0	0	.254/.309/.399	.254	2.3	.286	-0.6	3B -1 • 1B 1	0.2

Breakout: 4%   Improve: 46%   Collapse: 11%   Attrition: 18%   MLB: 93%   Comparables: Casey McGehee, Andy LaRoche, Freddy Sanchez

If the utilitarians are correct that our actions should be judged by the net value of their effects on everyone involved, this means John Stuart Mill was a big fan of Win Probability Added, and that the factor of when something is done matters almost more than what is being done. Such is the case for the 29-year-old Gillaspie, whom statistics without much persuasion insist existed before October 5, 2016. And yet Gillaspie's ninth-inning, game-winning home run off Mets closer Jeurys Familia, the latest addition to the general confoundment of Giants against the natural order of the universe, will prove to be the key to free coffee and donuts the rest of his life. He may never have another moment of greatness in him; he may measure out the rest of his life in benches sat on. Even so, he deserves every cup of Starbucks, every sprinkle.

Eduardo Nunez   3B

Born: 6/15/87   Age: 30   Bats: R   Throws: R   Height: 6'0"   Weight: 195   Entered Pro Ball: International Free Agent, 2004

YEAR	TEAM	LVL	AGE	PA	R	2B	3B	HR	RBI	BB	K	SB	CS	AVG/OBP/SLG	TAv	VORP	BABIP	BRR	FRAA	WARP
2014	ROC	AAA	27	41	7	1	0	1	6	1	8	1	0	.282/.293/.385	.225	-0.6	.323	-0.2	SS(4): -0.0 • 3B(4): -0.3	-0.1
2014	MIN	MLB	27	213	26	7	4	4	24	5	31	9	3	.250/.271/.382	.226	0.1	.278	0.9	3B(20): -0.1 • SS(20): -1.4	0.3
2015	MIN	MLB	28	204	23	14	1	4	20	12	29	8	4	.282/.327/.431	.262	7.1	.314	0.8	SS(27): 2.3 • 3B(16): -1.1	0.9
2016	MIN	MLB	29	396	49	15	1	12	47	15	58	27	6	.296/.325/.439	.264	20.7	.320	4.8	SS(51): -1.7 • 3B(33): 0.0	1.9
2016	SFN	MLB	29	199	24	9	3	4	20	14	30	13	4	.269/.327/.418	.271	10.0	.302	1.4	3B(48): 3.8 • SS(4): -0.3	1.4
2017	SFN	MLB	30	573	64	24	6	9	53	31	91	31	9	.265/.306/.382	.245	10.5	.300	3.6	3B -9 • SS -0	-0.3
2018	SFN	MLB	31	531	56	23	4	8	52	31	87	26	9	.258/.305/.375	.246	8.5	.293	3.7	3B -8 • SS 0	0.0

Breakout: 3%   Improve: 39%   Collapse: 13%   Attrition: 13%   MLB: 94%   Comparables: Joaquin Arias, Chone Figgins, Lou Klimchock

None of it makes sense. Nunez made the All-Star team for the last-place Twins. He got traded to a team with solid regulars at all three positions he plays, in exchange for their third-best prospect. He then doubled his walk rate and ended up with 40(!) stolen bases. Essentially, the former King of the Infield Fly exists to confound, which makes him a perfect hitter for the Giants. Utility infielders can earn their title one of two ways: by being able to play multiple positions, or not being able to hit well enough to play any position. Until last year, Nunez was clearly the latter, so upon his arriving in the Bay the Giants gave Nunez a permanent home at Matt Duffy's position and ... it actually worked. He's the kind of league-average hitter who does absolutely nothing well, an aesthetic blight on the game. PECOTA believes that the whole season was a mirage, but knowing Nunez, next year will just bring a different one.

Angel Pagan   CF

Born: 7/2/81   Age: 35   Bats: B   Throws: R   Height: 6'2"   Weight: 200   Entered Pro Ball: Round 4, 1999 Draft (#136 overall)

YEAR	TEAM	LVL	AGE	PA	R	2B	3B	HR	RBI	BB	K	SB	CS	AVG/OBP/SLG	TAv	VORP	BABIP	BRR	FRAA	WARP
2014	SFN	MLB	32	413	56	21	2	3	27	25	53	16	6	.300/.342/.389	.277	18.6	.339	0.3	CF(91): -0.5	2.0
2015	SFN	MLB	33	551	55	21	3	3	37	32	93	12	4	.262/.303/.332	.236	3.8	.310	0.6	CF(124): -10.7	-0.7
2016	SFN	MLB	34	543	71	24	5	12	55	42	66	15	4	.277/.331/.418	.274	22.0	.298	2.7	LF(123): 7.1 • CF(4): 0.3	3.0
2017	SFN	MLB	35	514	61	24	5	7	44	36	77	14	5	.272/.323/.389	.246	10.8	.308	0.6	LF 8 • CF -0	2.0
2018	SFN	MLB	36	434	46	19	3	5	41	31	68	10	4	.263/.315/.371	.251	7.0	.302	0.7	LF 6 • CF 0	1.5

Breakout: 0%   Improve: 18%   Collapse: 12%   Attrition: 18%   MLB: 70%   Comparables: Jay Payton, Shannon Stewart, Chris Denorfia

To quote Joseph Campbell: "If you want resurrection, you need crucifixion." Baseball is, in a way, America's mythological tradition applied to modern life, an unending cycle of heroes and heroics. Pagan suffered through his own tradition of death, in the form of his abysmal 2015 season, only to be resurrected last year. He arrived intact; other than moving to left for incoming free agent Denard Span, he produced the prototypical Angel Pagan season. It's an age-old story: a handful of home runs, a handful of stolen bases, a handful of injuries and a handful of times you forgot he hadn't already retired. Entering his age-35 season, Pagan is probably not the hero of his own story anymore, but he's survived long enough to transition into the wise-old-man archetype.

Joe Panik   2B

Born: 10/30/90   Age: 26   Bats: L   Throws: R   Height: 6'1"   Weight: 190   Entered Pro Ball: Round 1, 2011 Draft (#29 overall)

YEAR	TEAM	LVL	AGE	PA	R	2B	3B	HR	RBI	BB	K	SB	CS	AVG/OBP/SLG	TAv	VORP	BABIP	BRR	FRAA	WARP
2014	FRE	AAA	23	326	50	14	4	5	45	27	33	3	2	.321/.382/.447	.289	20.2	.346	-0.6	2B(61): -5.0 • SS(10): -0.8	1.4
2014	SFN	MLB	23	287	31	10	2	1	18	16	33	0	0	.305/.343/.368	.262	8.8	.343	1.1	2B(70): -4.0	0.5
2015	SFN	MLB	24	432	59	27	2	8	37	38	42	3	2	.312/.378/.455	.314	32.6	.330	-1.1	2B(99): -6.4	2.8
2016	SFN	MLB	25	526	67	21	7	10	62	50	47	5	0	.239/.315/.379	.256	13.2	.245	1.3	2B(126): 12.7	2.7
2017	*SFN*	*MLB*	*26*	*594*	*69*	*27*	*5*	*10*	*56*	*50*	*62*	*4*	*1*	*.277/.341/.406*	*.266*	*26.2*	*.294*	*-0.2*	*2B -1*	*2.2*
2018	*SFN*	*MLB*	*27*	*527*	*64*	*23*	*5*	*12*	*59*	*48*	*57*	*3*	*1*	*.279/.348/.422*	*.280*	*27.2*	*.293*	*0.6*	*2B -1*	*2.8*

Breakout: 3%   Improve: 52%   Collapse: 7%   Attrition: 14%   MLB: 99%   *Comparables: Dustin Pedroia, Nellie Fox, Ron Hunt*

It still shouldn't work. Now that we have exit velocity data, we know that every ball Panik hits travels so slowly it has its own dotted line, as if it were traveling via one of those map-crossing cinematic montages. Yet despite the predictable drop in BABIP responsible for most of his offensive dropoff in 2016, Panik made up for it by being unpredictable in a new way, winning a Gold Glove for his work at second base. In retrospect, this telling of the Joe Panik Story is far more believable than the last one, and although PECOTA remains grumpy about missing on him, it's easy to see the non-prospect march through his career in stodgy, valuable fashion.

Jarrett Parker   LF

Born: 1/1/89   Age: 28   Bats: L   Throws: L   Height: 6'4"   Weight: 210   Entered Pro Ball: Round 2, 2010 Draft (#74 overall)

YEAR	TEAM	LVL	AGE	PA	R	2B	3B	HR	RBI	BB	K	SB	CS	AVG/OBP/SLG	TAv	VORP	BABIP	BRR	FRAA	WARP
2014	RIC	AA	25	419	52	20	6	12	58	45	103	11	4	.275/.370/.463	.293	22.5	.353	-0.5	RF(70): -3.8 • CF(30): -3.7	1.6
2014	FRE	AAA	25	89	13	5	0	3	10	9	23	1	2	.278/.360/.456	.306	7.4	.358	1.1	RF(22): 1.3	0.9
2015	SAC	AAA	26	504	74	25	3	23	74	62	164	20	7	.283/.375/.514	.321	39.8	.398	-1.8	RF(61): 1.8 • LF(48): -3.5	3.9
2015	SFN	MLB	26	54	11	2	0	6	14	5	21	1	1	.347/.407/.755	.413	9.0	.500	-0.5	RF(9): -1.2 • LF(5): 0.3	0.9
2016	SAC	AAA	27	222	44	8	2	16	35	26	66	1	1	.273/.365/.582	.332	21.4	.330	0.7	RF(39): -2.6 • LF(11): 0.2	2.0
2016	SFN	MLB	27	151	22	3	1	5	14	19	44	0	1	.236/.358/.394	.281	5.8	.321	-0.5	RF(21): -1.1 • LF(17): -0.9	0.4
2017	*SFN*	*MLB*	*28*	*353*	*46*	*13*	*2*	*15*	*45*	*38*	*116*	*5*	*3*	*.239/.330/.440*	*.270*	*14.4*	*.329*	*-0.1*	*LF -3*	*1.0*
2018	*SFN*	*MLB*	*29*	*447*	*62*	*17*	*3*	*20*	*62*	*50*	*147*	*6*	*3*	*.242/.336/.453*	*.285*	*21.3*	*.333*	*-0.6*	*LF -4*	*1.8*

Breakout: 2%   Improve: 18%   Collapse: 14%   Attrition: 22%   MLB: 52%   *Comparables: Jason Dubois, Jai Miller, Nelson Cruz*

Parker is older than Madison Bumgarner, Ruben Tejada, Camden Yards, Daniel Radcliffe, *The Simpsons* and the Game Boy. He's older than Crying Jordan. It must have been frustrating to the former 2010 second rounder to finally get his shot, following a delicious cup of 2015 coffee, only to be thwarted by the Angel Pagan Talent Reunion Tour. Parker's probably not starter-caliber anyway; he's a mistake-pitch hitter whose swing is so rough that he can strike out in the middle of another strikeout. But he has plenty of power, and his defense is acceptable enough to make him more than just a pinch-hitter. Given the slap-happiness of the Giants' current bench, Parker's virtues complement the team's needs fairly well.

Hunter Pence   RF

Born: 4/13/83   Age: 34   Bats: R   Throws: R   Height: 6'4"   Weight: 220   Entered Pro Ball: Round 2, 2004 Draft (#64 overall)

YEAR	TEAM	LVL	AGE	PA	R	2B	3B	HR	RBI	BB	K	SB	CS	AVG/OBP/SLG	TAv	VORP	BABIP	BRR	FRAA	WARP
2014	SFN	MLB	31	708	106	29	10	20	74	52	130	13	6	.277/.332/.445	.288	32.1	.318	2.0	RF(161): 2.8 • CF(1): -0.0	3.9
2015	SAC	AAA	32	20	6	0	0	2	5	2	4	0	0	.294/.350/.647	.345	1.5	.250	-0.6	RF(5): -0.4	0.1
2015	SFN	MLB	32	223	30	13	1	9	40	16	48	4	1	.275/.327/.478	.288	11.2	.320	1.2	RF(51): 9.9	2.3
2016	SAC	AAA	33	25	6	2	0	3	7	0	3	0	0	.417/.440/.875	.444	5.2	.389	-0.1	RF(7): -0.3	0.5
2016	SFN	MLB	33	442	58	23	1	13	57	43	95	1	1	.289/.357/.451	.304	25.7	.348	-1.8	RF(102): -0.8	2.6
2017	*SFN*	*MLB*	*34*	*598*	*68*	*26*	*4*	*19*	*75*	*47*	*120*	*8*	*3*	*.266/.326/.436*	*.271*	*22.2*	*.307*	*0.0*	*RF 6*	*2.6*
2018	*SFN*	*MLB*	*35*	*421*	*52*	*18*	*2*	*13*	*52*	*33*	*87*	*4*	*2*	*.266/.326/.430*	*.276*	*15.8*	*.311*	*0.3*	*RF 5*	*2.2*

Breakout: 0%   Improve: 28%   Collapse: 11%   Attrition: 23%   MLB: 94%   *Comparables: Michael Cuddyer, Scott Hairston, Andre Ethier*

After seven consecutive seasons of 150-plus games, Pence has put together 158 in the past two combined, with last year's malady arriving in the form of a torn hamstring. In between, he was his amiably goofy self, playing Magic: The Gathering at bachelor parties and having signs created in his honor. A little light on the power and a few more singles, but otherwise basic Hunter Pence. Probably.

We tend to think of the aging curve, and talent, as the accumulation and dispersal of this invisible force, like midichlorians, sealed within a person. But most of the time, that's not what old age is. Old age is doing the same thing you do every day, like going to the gym or composing a sonnet or hitting a baseball, until something goes wrong. And then it takes a little longer to get back to 100 percent, and a little longer, until you never quite make it back before the next thing, and again, until you no longer remember what 100 percent is. The problem for Pence, and for you if you're not there already, is that it's impossible to know what bad luck is and what old age is. Could he arrive back in form, put in a full season of .300 True Average and leave his freak injuries aside? Certainly. Or he could start off that way, and get tripped up by one thing, take one bad slide into second, and suddenly realize along with the rest of us that he's nearly 35 years old, that 35 is basically almost 40, that it basically is the same as 40 for some players.

There's nothing we can do about this. Sabermetrics, like science, can't tell us how we're going to die/retire. All we can do is enjoy, and hope.

Buster Posey   C

Born: 3/27/87   Age: 30   Bats: R   Throws: R   Height: 6'1"   Weight: 215   Entered Pro Ball: Round 1, 2008 Draft (#5 overall)

YEAR	TEAM	LVL	AGE	PA	R	2B	3B	HR	RBI	BB	K	SB	CS	AVG/OBP/SLG	TAv	VORP	BABIP	BRR	FRAA	WARP
2014	SFN	MLB	27	605	72	28	2	22	89	47	69	0	1	.311/.364/.490	.316	48.9	.319	-3.5	C(111): 23.8 • 1B(35): 1.4	8.2
2015	SFN	MLB	28	623	74	28	0	19	95	56	52	2	0	.318/.379/.470	.320	55.8	.320	-1.8	C(106): 17.4 • 1B(42): -1.7	7.7
2016	SFN	MLB	29	614	82	33	2	14	80	64	68	6	1	.288/.362/.434	.289	40.5	.303	-3.3	C(123): 33.9 • 1B(15): -0.7	7.6
2017	SFN	MLB	30	609	74	31	2	19	79	59	73	3	1	.301/.371/.471	.295	47.1	.316	-0.8	C 36 • 1B -0	7.2
2018	SFN	MLB	31	553	73	28	2	17	71	51	73	1	0	.292/.359/.462	.297	37.6	.309	-2.6	C 31 • 1B 0	7.5

Breakout: 0%   Improve: 49%   Collapse: 2%   Attrition: 3%   MLB: 99%   Comparables: Ted Simmons, Joe Mauer, Victor Martinez

One of the problems with great talent, from an analytical standpoint, is that people are willing to accept 80 percent of it. You could argue that Posey had a down year by his standards, despite winning his first Gold Glove, making his fourth All-Star team and earning MVP votes for the sixth time in his six full seasons. The reason: Posey hit a mere two home runs after the All-Star break, and was observed to be visibly uncomfortable swinging the bat, due to back issues. But 80 percent of Buster Posey is still better than anyone else around, and somewhat more so than backup Trevor Brown, so he gamed through it and still managed to put up the fourth-most valuable 2016 season by WARP standards. While pitch-framing value has dwindled league-wide, as Jeff Sullivan has written, as teams better understand its importance and emphasize its value with their players, Posey's deftness with the glove has grown increasingly unparalleled by any catcher in the league not named Yasmani. As long as his defense continues, ignore any talk of moving him off the position for the sake of his health. Even if catching long term has an effect on his counting stats, he'll remain more valuable behind the plate than nearly anyone.

YEAR	TEAM	P. COUNT	FRM RUNS	BLK RUNS	THRW RUNS	TOT RUNS
2014	SFN	14256	23.6	1.1	0.4	25.1
2015	SFN	13948	12.7	2.0	0.9	15.6
2016	SFN	17017	27.6	2.2	2.1	31.9
2017	SFN	18330	29.4	2.6	1.4	33.4
2018	SFN	16635	25.1	2.0	1.1	28.3

Bryan Reynolds   CF

Born: 1/27/95   Age: 22   Bats: B   Throws: R   Height: 6'3"   Weight: 200   Entered Pro Ball: Round 2, 2016 Draft (#59 overall)

YEAR	TEAM	LVL	AGE	PA	R	2B	3B	HR	RBI	BB	K	SB	CS	AVG/OBP/SLG	TAv	VORP	BABIP	BRR	FRAA	WARP
2016	SLO	A-	21	171	28	12	1	5	30	11	41	2	0	.312/.368/.500	.301	7.2	.391	0.6	CF(19): -3.4	0.4
2016	AUG	A	21	66	11	5	0	1	8	3	20	1	0	.317/.348/.444	.316	4.3	.452	0.2	CF(11): 1.5	0.6
2017	SFN	MLB	22	250	21	10	1	6	26	11	80	0	0	.214/.253/.339	.203	-5.7	.294	-0.3	CF -0	-0.6
2018	SFN	MLB	23	227	24	10	1	6	24	11	73	0	0	.221/.265/.364	.227	-1.9	.303	-0.4	CF 0	-0.2

Breakout: 2%   Improve: 4%   Collapse: 1%   Attrition: 4%   MLB: 6%   Comparables: Michael Taylor, Trayvon Robinson, Aaron Altherr

Before the 2016 draft, Reynolds was considered a potential first-round pick; instead, he had to settle for being the Giants' first pick at no. 59. So far, it looks like the other 29 teams made the mistake. The switch-hitting center fielder blew through the Northwest League and fared similarly in a stint at Single-A Augusta. He's a well-rounded athlete, with a quick bat and good power, and instincts to make up for his lack of speed. The two potential pitfalls: He swings like a Brunansky, making contact a real concern as he advances, and a weak arm could make him a dreaded left-field prospect if he can't hold his ground in center. Despite these concerns, Reynolds could prove to be the best outfield prospect the Giants have developed in a quarter century, given that the bar is Fred Lewis.

Chris Shaw   1B

Born: 10/20/93   Age: 23   Bats: L   Throws: R   Height: 6'4"   Weight: 235   Entered Pro Ball: Round 1, 2015 Draft (#31 overall)

YEAR	TEAM	LVL	AGE	PA	R	2B	3B	HR	RBI	BB	K	SB	CS	AVG/OBP/SLG	TAv	VORP	BABIP	BRR	FRAA	WARP
2015	SLO	A-	21	200	22	11	0	12	30	19	41	0	0	.287/.360/.551	.305	9.5	.310	-1.8	1B(31): 1.4	1.1
2016	SJO	A+	22	305	47	22	0	16	55	28	70	0	0	.285/.357/.544	.333	24.7	.326	-2.4	1B(52): -0.7	2.5
2016	RIC	AA	22	256	26	16	4	5	30	20	55	0	0	.246/.309/.414	.270	1.6	.299	-3.5	1B(48): -2.3	-0.1
2017	SFN	MLB	23	250	27	12	2	9	33	18	68	0	0	.239/.299/.430	.248	1.7	.296	-0.3	1B -1 • 3B 0	0.1
2018	SFN	MLB	24	322	41	16	2	13	43	25	85	0	0	.246/.310/.443	.271	7.2	.302	-0.6	1B -1 • 3B 0	0.7

Breakout: 8%   Improve: 22%   Collapse: 4%   Attrition: 18%   MLB: 37%   Comparables: Ike Davis, Jesus Aguilar, Ryan Lavarnway

Shaw's short stride at the plate recalls a kid making his way across an icy parking lot. He runs like he has to control each muscle in his legs consciously. And yet when bat hits ball, you can tell why he's a prospect. AT&T Park is the worst ballpark in baseball for left-handed power, so it's fortunate that Shaw has enough strength to hit a ball 400 feet underwater, even if he runs under the same aquatic conditions. The first baseman will begin 2017 repeating Double-A, but with the hitting so advanced—and the rest of his game so uncoachable—it won't be long before he's pinch-hitting for major-league pitchers in the fifth inning. Whether he graduates to full-time labor will depend on his ability to make consistent contact.

Denard Span   CF

Born: 2/27/84   Age: 33   Bats: L   Throws: L   Height: 6'0"   Weight: 210   Entered Pro Ball: Round 1, 2002 Draft (#20 overall)

YEAR	TEAM	LVL	AGE	PA	R	2B	3B	HR	RBI	BB	K	SB	CS	AVG/OBP/SLG	TAv	VORP	BABIP	BRR	FRAA	WARP
2014	WAS	MLB	30	668	94	39	8	5	37	50	65	31	7	.302/.355/.416	.288	42.8	.330	6.8	CF(147): 8.1	5.6
2015	WAS	MLB	31	275	38	17	0	5	22	25	26	11	0	.301/.365/.431	.305	22.4	.318	2.3	CF(61): 2.2	2.6
2016	SFN	MLB	32	637	70	23	5	11	53	53	79	12	7	.266/.331/.381	.263	21.5	.291	-0.2	CF(137): -15.7	0.6
2017	SFN	MLB	33	642	73	31	7	6	50	51	77	19	5	.274/.330/.381	.256	21.9	.302	2.1	CF -1	1.4
2018	SFN	MLB	34	520	56	25	5	5	48	44	67	14	4	.269/.331/.375	.260	16.3	.299	2.4	CF -1	1.7

Breakout: 1%   Improve: 26%   Collapse: 13%   Attrition: 19%   MLB: 91%   Comparables: Johnny Damon, Mark Kotsay, Coco Crisp

After watching a successful 2015 season get cut down by a hip injury, Span whiled away the holiday season before signing with the Giants at a fairly significant injury discount of $31 million over three years. Without looking at the numbers, it was a strong move: Span was healthy before that season and he proved to be once again while filling a major defensive hole. Only, it just didn't work out. Span's contact ability showed signs of erosion, particularly on pitches out of the zone, and a career-low BABIP rendered him a league-average bat despite converting a bunch of his doubles into home runs. Which would be fine! League-average center fielders are worth $10 million easy these days. Only, yet again, the defensive metrics detect a more troubling decline in his range. He's no Aaron Rowand, but unless he can reverse the aging process, it's likely that Span's contract will turn out to be a bit of a disappointment.

Kelby Tomlinson   2B

Born: 6/16/90   Age: 27   Bats: R   Throws: R   Height: 6'3"   Weight: 180   Entered Pro Ball: Round 12, 2011 Draft (#387 overall)

YEAR	TEAM	LVL	AGE	PA	R	2B	3B	HR	RBI	BB	K	SB	CS	AVG/OBP/SLG	TAv	VORP	BABIP	BRR	FRAA	WARP
2014	RIC	AA	24	494	63	9	6	1	32	44	82	49	12	.268/.340/.323	.251	12.4	.325	1.0	2B(73): 0.5 · SS(50): -2.1	1.2
2015	RIC	AA	25	289	43	18	3	1	28	25	37	16	6	.324/.387/.431	.316	28.4	.372	3.3	2B(49): 2.3 · SS(25): -1.9	3.1
2015	SAC	AAA	25	149	21	1	1	2	15	7	22	5	3	.316/.354/.382	.266	5.9	.360	0.2	2B(16): 2.1 · SS(15): 0.6	0.9
2015	SFN	MLB	25	193	23	6	3	2	20	14	40	5	4	.303/.358/.404	.294	12.7	.382	1.3	2B(50): -1.1 · SS(1): -0.0	1.2
2016	SAC	AAA	26	213	28	8	1	0	20	22	26	12	3	.286/.370/.341	.278	12.8	.331	1.7	SS(20): -1.0 · 2B(16): 1.0	1.4
2016	SFN	MLB	26	120	13	4	0	0	6	12	18	5	1	.292/.370/.330	.261	5.8	.352	2.2	2B(19): -0.5 · SS(7): -0.4	0.6
2017	SFN	MLB	27	61	7	2	1	1	5	5	12	3	1	.265/.326/.352	.245	1.8	.323	0.2	2B 0	0.2
2018	SFN	MLB	28	283	31	10	2	3	25	23	56	11	4	.263/.328/.356	.251	7.8	.319	2.4	2B 0	0.9

Breakout: 5%   Improve: 24%   Collapse: 12%   Attrition: 27%   MLB: 67%   Comparables: Ryan Theriot, Johnny Giavotella, Jake Elmore

It's not often you see a ballplayer get his first annual comment as a major leaguer, but if it were going to happen, you'd be wise to bet on it being a Giants infielder. After a shockingly successful 2015 filling in for Joe Panik, the unheralded Tomlinson was expected to round out his utility resume by getting some outfield experience in 2016. It didn't work out that way; instead, he got pressed into Panik-imitating again until a sprained thumb took him out of service and lost him his job as the team was forced to acquire rentals. The outfield experiment may not happen—he didn't play an inning out there in his minor-league stint—but he'll have plenty of work, subbing in and slapping balls into the hole as often as he can.

Mac Williamson   RF

Born: 7/15/90   Age: 26   Bats: R   Throws: R   Height: 6'4"   Weight: 240   Entered Pro Ball: Round 3, 2012 Draft (#115 overall)

YEAR	TEAM	LVL	AGE	PA	R	2B	3B	HR	RBI	BB	K	SB	CS	AVG/OBP/SLG	TAv	VORP	BABIP	BRR	FRAA	WARP
2014	SJO	A+	23	100	16	7	0	3	11	13	14	6	1	.318/.420/.506	.325	9.1	.353	0.9		0.9
2015	RIC	AA	24	290	41	16	2	5	42	25	53	3	1	.293/.366/.429	.303	15.4	.351	-1.8	RF(55): 1.1	1.8
2015	SAC	AAA	24	227	35	12	0	8	31	26	55	1	0	.249/.370/.439	.317	19.4	.307	1.6	LF(30): -3.4 · RF(16): 1.2	1.8
2015	SFN	MLB	24	34	2	0	1	0	1	0	8	0	0	.219/.235/.281	.189	-2.1	.280	-0.4	LF(6): -0.4 · RF(3): -0.1	-0.3
2016	SAC	AAA	25	226	35	14	0	11	42	12	53	2	1	.269/.314/.495	.303	14.9	.306	0.5	LF(25): 1.8 · RF(23): -1.0	1.6
2016	SFN	MLB	25	127	14	3	0	6	15	13	35	0	1	.223/.315/.411	.254	1.8	.268	0.0	RF(23): -0.9 · LF(13): 2.2	0.3
2017	SFN	MLB	26	356	41	16	2	12	43	29	92	1	1	.246/.321/.420	.265	12.5	.306	-0.6	LF 1 · RF 1	1.3
2018	SFN	MLB	27	428	55	19	2	14	53	37	112	1	1	.250/.329/.425	.275	16.1	.315	-0.7	LF 2 · RF 1	2.0

Breakout: 7%   Improve: 32%   Collapse: 18%   Attrition: 30%   MLB: 74%   Comparables: Todd Linden, Chris Heisey, Aaron Cunningham

Some men are born at the right time. There was an era, not long ago, when there wasn't room in the game for men like Williamson and their mandated month-long slumps. But now we live in an enlightened age, one in which men are free, free to swing through every sixth pitch and roll over another 50 percent, and hit with just enough power to compensate. The hit-or-miss prospect spent half the year on San Francisco's bench, thriving early before joining in the team's communal late-season swoon. He'll never be great and he probably won't even be a starter. But on average, he'll do enough to help the team. Just try to watch him on the right days.

PITCHERS

Tyler Beede   RHP

Born: 5/23/93   Age: 24   Bats: R   Throws: R   Height: 6'3"   Weight: 210   Entered Pro Ball: Round 1, 2014 Draft (#14 overall)

YEAR	TEAM	LVL	AGE	W	L	SV	G	GS	IP	H	HR	BB/9	K/9	K	GB%	BABIP	WHIP	ERA	FIP	DRA	VORP	WARP	cFIP	MPH
2015	SJO	A+	22	2	2	0	9	9	52¹	51	2	1.5	6.4	37	64%	.295	1.15	2.24	3.43	4.54	3.2	0.3	97	
2015	RIC	AA	22	3	8	0	13	13	72¹	62	4	4.4	6.1	49	60%	.269	1.34	5.23	4.21	7.34	-18.0	-2.0	113	
2016	RIC	AA	23	8	7	0	24	24	147¹	136	9	3.2	8.2	135	49%	.309	1.28	2.81	3.48	3.28	29.8	3.2	89	
2017	SFN	MLB	24	7	7	0	22	22	120²	119	11	3.7	6.6	88	43%	.313	1.40	4.19	4.20	5.00	7.5	0.8	117	
2018	SFN	MLB	25	8	9	0	26	26	157	141	15	5.1	9.2	161	43%	.326	1.46	4.01	4.47	4.78	12.6	1.3	110	

Breakout: 13%   Improve: 27%   Collapse: 20%   Attrition: 33%   MLB: 55%   Comparables: Esmil Rogers, Daniel Wright, Mike Kickham

If Beede were a character in a sitcom, he'd be the reliable married friend who gives the main character advice they never listen to. If he were a country, he'd be one of those European nations that's always way up on the list for education and low crime rates. If he were a type of plant he'd be a very healthy, thriving plant, maybe some kind of fern. There's just nothing wrong with Beede's profile: he looks like a solid starter, wields the repertoire of a solid starter and displays the advanced feel of a solid starter. He's going to be a solid starter, is what we're saying: locating his low-90s fastball well and mixing up his secondaries at just the right times, wielding a two-seamer with heavy run to fend off those pesky lefties. He may not be quite as exciting as when he was drafted in the first round, but that combination of ground balls and strikeouts will be more than enough, perhaps as early as this year.

Ty Blach   LHP

Born: 10/20/90   Age: 26   Bats: R   Throws: L   Height: 6'2"   Weight: 200   Entered Pro Ball: Round 5, 2012 Draft (#178 overall)

YEAR	TEAM	LVL	AGE	W	L	SV	G	GS	IP	H	HR	BB/9	K/9	K	GB%	BABIP	WHIP	ERA	FIP	DRA	VORP	WARP	cFIP	MPH
2014	RIC	AA	23	8	8	0	25	25	141	142	8	2.5	5.8	91	47%	.295	1.28	3.13	3.70	3.14	32.8	3.5	98	
2015	SAC	AAA	24	11	12	0	27	27	165¹	189	16	1.7	5.1	93	49%	.311	1.33	4.46	4.33	3.40	35.0	3.6	93	
2016	SAC	AAA	25	14	7	0	26	26	162²	147	9	2.1	6.3	113	50%	.280	1.14	3.43	3.79	2.05	59.6	6.1	92	
2016	SFN	MLB	25	1	0	0	4	2	17	8	1	2.6	5.3	10	60%	.152	0.76	1.06	3.66	3.97	2.4	0.2	103	93.1
2017	SFN	MLB	26	3	2	0	8	8	40	41	3	2.6	5.7	25	42%	.295	1.30	3.68	3.80	4.35	3.7	0.4	100	
2018	SFN	MLB	27	7	8	0	24	24	142¹	120	13	3.7	8.4	133	42%	.300	1.26	3.64	4.07	4.40	15.6	1.6	100	

Breakout: 8%   Improve: 23%   Collapse: 22%   Attrition: 29%   MLB: 52%   Comparables: D.J. Mitchell, Eric Jokisch, Logan Verrett

It's a good thing his last name is so close to the letter A, because Blach is the platonic ideal of Giants pitching prospects. Go ahead and fill out your bingo cards now: he's an unnaturally healthy pitcher who throws in the low 90s with excellent fastball command, which in turn prevents large platoon splits. His secondaries are generally weak, but he can get by on them as long as he hits his targets. He lives with contact by inducing scads of ground balls. And he wants to banish all poetry from the nation. It says something that the Giants let the 25-year-old Blach rot at Triple-A while handing 50 starts to the Law Offices of Peavy, Cain & Suarez, although it's hard to say exactly what. Blach looked competent in his brief opportunity to start, and he's not going to be any more or less Ty Blach than he is right now. It's not an exciting profile by any means, but every Kirk Rueter deserves his day.

Clayton Blackburn   RHP

Born: 1/6/93   Age: 24   Bats: L   Throws: R   Height: 6'3"   Weight: 230   Entered Pro Ball: Round 16, 2011 Draft (#507 overall)

YEAR	TEAM	LVL	AGE	W	L	SV	G	GS	IP	H	HR	BB/9	K/9	K	GB%	BABIP	WHIP	ERA	FIP	DRA	VORP	WARP	cFIP	MPH
2014	RIC	AA	21	5	6	0	18	18	93	94	1	1.9	8.2	85	57%	.341	1.23	3.29	2.54	1.56	37.9	4.0	78	
2015	SAC	AAA	22	10	4	0	23	20	123	127	6	2.3	7.2	99	52%	.323	1.29	2.85	3.55	2.44	38.8	4.0	90	
2016	SAC	AAA	23	7	10	0	25	23	136¹	142	18	2.3	6.7	101	46%	.292	1.30	4.36	4.86	3.78	23.6	2.4	102	
2017	SFN	MLB	24	1	1	0	3	3	15	17	1	2.7	6.2	11	44%	.296	1.35	3.74	3.73	4.42	1.3	0.1	100	
2018	SFN	MLB	25	9	10	0	30	30	187	165	18	3.9	9.2	191	44%	.319	1.31	3.63	4.06	4.40	19.8	2.0	100	

Breakout: 10%   Improve: 23%   Collapse: 31%   Attrition: 43%   MLB: 68%   Comparables: Dallas Keuchel, P.J. Walters, Jake Buchanan

Blackburn has long divided scouts, but in 2016 his lack of an out pitch appeared to finally catch up with him. He was never overpowering even at his zenith, but his strikeout rate has dropped in five straight seasons and his margin for error has dwindled. Blackburn has to be nearly perfect to even rate as a back-of-the-rotation starter, and in 2016 he was far from perfect. The possibility of eating innings and ranking third among major-league Claytons remains, but he's been leapfrogged in the organization by more tantalizing arms.

Madison Bumgarner   LHP

Born: 8/1/89   Age: 27   Bats: R   Throws: L   Height: 6'5"   Weight: 250   Entered Pro Ball: Round 1, 2007 Draft (#10 overall)

YEAR	TEAM	LVL	AGE	W	L	SV	G	GS	IP	H	HR	BB/9	K/9	K	GB%	BABIP	WHIP	ERA	FIP	DRA	VORP	WARP	cFIP	MPH
2014	SFN	MLB	24	18	10	0	33	33	217¹	194	21	1.8	9.1	219	46%	.296	1.09	2.98	3.02	2.56	55.0	6.1	83	94.1
2015	SFN	MLB	25	18	9	0	32	32	218¹	181	21	1.6	9.6	234	43%	.282	1.01	2.93	2.90	2.80	55.1	5.9	81	94.3
2016	SFN	MLB	26	15	9	0	34	34	226²	179	26	2.1	10.0	251	41%	.267	1.03	2.74	3.28	3.25	53.2	5.5	89	92.6
2017	SFN	MLB	27	14	11	0	33	33	207	176	21	2.5	9.8	227	52%	.288	1.12	3.16	3.26	3.74	33.2	3.4	84	
2018	SFN	MLB	28	13	10	0	33	33	215²	167	22	2.3	9.6	230	52%	.287	1.03	2.99	3.33	3.61	44.1	4.5	78	

Breakout: 26%   Improve: 56%   Collapse: 18%   Attrition: 10%   MLB: 98%   Comparables: Yovani Gallardo, Hyun-jin Ryu, Cole Hamels

Bumgarner spent the first half as the best starter outside of Los Angeles; when Clayton Kershaw went down, Bumgarner caught a very light case of the West Bay Virus that waylaid the rest of the team and wound up finishing fourth in Cy Young voting. His season only reinforced all of his pre-established qualities; as one of the most consistent aces in the game, and of postseason mastery following a shutout against the Mets in the Wild Card game. It's rare that you hear folks talk about the Hall of Fame candidacies of age-26 players, but rarely do people who can barely rent a car have so much of their legacy in place. The most common comp is Curt Schilling, and perhaps an unfortunate one given that Schilling did his best work after his 30th birthday, and that he'd easily have his own plaque if not for a certain lack of charisma. Bumgarner obviously still has numbers to compile, and at least one aging curve to navigate, but even though it's irresponsible to talk about his enshrinement as inevitable it's growing equally irresponsible not to appreciate how strong his case is compared to his age-related peers.

Matt Cain   RHP

Born: 10/1/84   Age: 32   Bats: R   Throws: R   Height: 6'3"   Weight: 230   Entered Pro Ball: Round 1, 2002 Draft (#25 overall)

YEAR	TEAM	LVL	AGE	W	L	SV	G	GS	IP	H	HR	BB/9	K/9	K	GB%	BABIP	WHIP	ERA	FIP	DRA	VORP	WARP	cFIP	MPH
2014	SFN	MLB	29	2	7	0	15	15	90¹	81	13	3.2	7.0	70	46%	.265	1.25	4.18	4.55	5.60	-7.7	-0.9	112	93.8
2015	SAC	AAA	30	1	2	0	5	3	19²	18	2	1.8	10.1	22	38%	.296	1.12	3.20	3.45	2.34	6.3	0.6	79	
2015	SFN	MLB	30	2	4	0	13	11	60²	71	12	3.0	6.1	41	36%	.304	1.50	5.79	5.57	6.64	-10.7	-1.1	130	93.2
2016	SAC	AAA	31	1	1	0	2	2	10²	11	1	3.4	5.1	6	42%	.286	1.41	5.06	5.22	6.75	-1.7	-0.2	117	
2016	SFN	MLB	31	4	8	0	21	17	89¹	103	16	3.2	7.3	72	41%	.321	1.51	5.64	5.18	6.37	-10.3	-1.1	119	92.5
2017	SFN	MLB	32	9	10	0	26	26	156	155	20	3.4	7.2	125	49%	.290	1.35	4.35	4.47	5.05	2.2	0.2	100	
2018	SFN	MLB	33	9	10	0	27	27	164¹	149	22	3.0	7.5	136	49%	.288	1.24	4.15	4.61	4.98	10.4	1.1	117	

Breakout: 16%   Improve: 47%   Collapse: 15%   Attrition: 9%   MLB: 77%   Comparables: Kyle Lohse, Marco Estrada, Gil Meche

In case you missed how the second half of the Giants' season lay dying, here's a quick recap: after a long illness, Cain strained his lower back and the team spent the autumn dragging him in a wagon to his hometown of Jefferson, Mississippi, to give him a proper burial. Jake Peavy hurt his arm and the team had to make an impromptu cast out of concrete, Brian Sabean sold the rights to Phil Bickford in order to buy himself new false teeth and Santiago Casilla burned down a house and was taken away. It was all very confusing and the narrators were all pretty unreliable and Madison Bumgarner's mules all drowned, for some reason. It's hard to explain. All we know for certain going into 2017 is that Matt Cain is, in fact, a fish.

Santiago Casilla   RHP

Born: 7/25/80   Age: 36   Bats: R   Throws: R   Height: 6'0"   Weight: 210   Entered Pro Ball: International Free Agent, 2000

YEAR	TEAM	LVL	AGE	W	L	SV	G	GS	IP	H	HR	BB/9	K/9	K	GB%	BABIP	WHIP	ERA	FIP	DRA	VORP	WARP	cFIP	MPH
2014	SFN	MLB	33	3	3	19	54	0	58¹	35	3	2.3	6.9	45	57%	.211	0.86	1.70	3.15	3.22	8.2	0.9	96	96.6
2015	SFN	MLB	34	4	2	38	67	0	58	51	6	3.6	9.6	62	48%	.298	1.28	2.79	3.66	3.65	6.8	0.7	95	95.9
2016	SFN	MLB	35	2	5	31	62	0	58	50	8	2.9	10.1	65	50%	.292	1.19	3.57	3.98	3.31	10.7	1.1	89	96.0
2017	SFN	MLB	36	3	1	28	50	0	52²	43	5	3.4	9.1	53	57%	.294	1.19	3.73	3.61	4.48	3.5	0.4	100	
2018	SFN	MLB	37	2	1	18	33	0	31¹	27	3	3.5	8.6	30	57%	.302	1.26	3.78	4.20	4.54	2.1	0.2	101	

Breakout: 26%   Improve: 44%   Collapse: 30%   Attrition: 7%   MLB: 80%   *Comparables: Brian Fuentes, Matt Belisle, Mike Adams*

If Casilla's ERA were the subject of the "One Bid" game from The Price is Right, and the contestants were four Giants fans, they would have all gone over. The age-35 closer held onto the job for most of the year by his fingernails, despite posting pretty average peripherals by Casilla standards. The trick: he made his runs count, leading the league in blown saves with nine. Between April and June 1, Casilla gave up five runs, and four of them resulted in coughing up one-run leads. After that Bruce Bochy started tightening the leash, to the point at which he'd pull the closer mid-inning at the first sign of trouble. It's probably best for all parties that he's moving on; he's not really good enough to close anymore, but his reputation for pyrotechnics will obscure a fine setup man if given a short-term deal.

Samuel Coonrod   RHP

Born: 9/22/92   Age: 24   Bats: R   Throws: R   Height: 6'2"   Weight: 225   Entered Pro Ball: Round 5, 2014 Draft (#148 overall)

YEAR	TEAM	LVL	AGE	W	L	SV	G	GS	IP	H	HR	BB/9	K/9	K	GB%	BABIP	WHIP	ERA	FIP	DRA	VORP	WARP	cFIP	MPH
2015	AUG	A	22	7	5	0	23	22	111²	103	3	2.7	9.2	114	50%	.319	1.23	3.14	2.97	2.25	36.9	3.9	87	
2016	SJO	A+	23	5	3	0	11	11	63²	46	3	3.1	5.9	42	46%	.235	1.07	1.98	4.14	5.60	-0.9	-0.1	112	
2016	RIC	AA	23	4	3	0	13	13	77¹	59	7	4.4	6.1	52	39%	.231	1.25	3.03	5.05	8.50	-29.3	-3.2	124	
2017	SFN	MLB	24	6	8	0	22	22	112¹	118	15	4.3	5.2	65	60%	.300	1.53	5.34	5.31	6.35	-9.8	-1.0	151	
2018	SFN	MLB	25	4	7	0	15	15	87¹	86	15	6.1	7.9	77	60%	.308	1.66	5.59	6.21	6.65	-9.3	-1.0	156	

Breakout: 4%   Improve: 4%   Collapse: 6%   Attrition: 10%   MLB: 12%   *Comparables: Henry Sosa, Donnie Veal, Cody Anderson*

The big story for Coonrod coming out of 2015 was his improved control; the former Southern Illinois Saluki was drafted for the hornets in his arm with the hope that they could be tamed later, and early results appeared promising. However, he took a step back in 2016, watching his walk rate climb over two levels. This put more weight on his changeup, which despite moderate improvement appears to lack the tumble necessary to be anything more than a decoy. There's time enough for reform and if he recovers his pre-2016 fastball, along with his whip-like slider, it may not even be necessary for a starting role. If not, he's in a good position for late-inning relief work on a team that would gratefully accept it.

Johnny Cueto   RHP

Born: 2/15/86   Age: 31   Bats: R   Throws: R   Height: 5'11"   Weight: 220   Entered Pro Ball: International Free Agent, 2004

YEAR	TEAM	LVL	AGE	W	L	SV	G	GS	IP	H	HR	BB/9	K/9	K	GB%	BABIP	WHIP	ERA	FIP	DRA	VORP	WARP	cFIP	MPH
2014	CIN	MLB	28	20	9	0	34	34	243²	169	22	2.4	8.9	242	48%	.238	0.96	2.25	3.28	2.56	61.6	6.8	86	95.9
2015	CIN	MLB	29	7	6	0	19	19	130²	93	11	2.0	8.3	120	45%	.234	0.93	2.62	3.22	3.73	19.6	2.1	95	95.3
2015	KCA	MLB	29	4	7	0	13	13	81¹	101	10	1.9	6.2	56	43%	.343	1.45	4.76	4.03	3.69	12.6	1.3	95	95.0
2016	SFN	MLB	30	18	5	0	32	32	219²	195	15	1.8	8.1	198	52%	.293	1.09	2.79	3.00	3.54	44.5	4.6	90	94.3
2017	SFN	MLB	31	11	10	0	29	29	174	157	18	2.6	8.6	166	51%	.289	1.17	3.46	3.56	4.08	21.2	2.2	94	
2018	SFN	MLB	32	11	10	0	30	30	192¹	160	19	2.4	8.5	181	51%	.291	1.10	3.29	3.65	3.95	32.2	3.3	88	

Breakout: 8%   Improve: 33%   Collapse: 30%   Attrition: 7%   MLB: 90%   *Comparables: Roy Oswalt, Justin Verlander, Erik Bedard*

Cueto's season was a definitive success for all parties. The right-handed ace signed to essentially a two-year contract (he will surely opt out, at this rate) after a strangely disappointing rental stint with the champion Royals. He went on to finish sixth in the Cy Young voting and had what could be seen, depending on your metrics of choice, as his finest year to date. If anything he's underrated, first toiling in Cincinnati, then struggling on the big stage and now receiving second billing to Madison Bumgarner. He's never had the raw stuff or the gaudy numbers that inspire listicles. He's been on a third of a *Sports Illustrated* cover.

   But you're smart. You can read a stat line, and you know who Cueto is. So instead, let's devote the rest of this comment to talking about what a *treasure* he is to watch. Not just the precision of his pitches, but the beforehand: the hesitations, the shimmies, the twitches in his delivery that disrupt the timing of hitters and baserunners. The quick pitches. Even the seemingly useless little acts, like shaking off Buster Posey before he's even put down a sign. Baseball needs these little pockets of chaos, and it's particularly rewarding when combined with such performative excellence.

Jose Dominguez   RHP

Born: 8/7/90   Age: 26   Bats: R   Throws: R   Height: 6'0"   Weight: 200   Entered Pro Ball: International Free Agent, 2007

YEAR	TEAM	LVL	AGE	W	L	SV	G	GS	IP	H	HR	BB/9	K/9	K	GB%	BABIP	WHIP	ERA	FIP	DRA	VORP	WARP	cFIP	MPH
2014	LAN	MLB	23	0	0	0	5	0	6¹	7	2	4.3	11.4	8	33%	.312	1.58	11.37	6.58	4.83	-0.2	0.0	104	99.4
2014	ABQ	AAA	23	1	2	10	31	0	33¹	31	1	4.9	10.5	39	51%	.337	1.47	3.24	3.73	4.15	4.4	0.4	96	
2015	TBA	MLB	24	1	0	0	4	0	5²	2	0	3.2	7.9	5	75%	.167	0.71	0.00	2.40	3.67	0.7	0.1	94	95.5
2015	DUR	AAA	24	0	2	1	30	2	27²	36	5	6.5	8.1	25	32%	.365	2.02	6.18	5.87	8.28	-10.3	-1.0	123	
2016	ELP	AAA	25	3	3	6	27	0	35²	28	1	6.3	9.1	36	51%	.290	1.49	3.79	4.51	5.57	-2.4	-0.2	107	
2016	SDN	MLB	25	1	0	0	34	0	35²	34	5	4.3	5.0	20	49%	.266	1.43	5.05	5.65	5.96	-3.9	-0.4	122	98.6
2017	*SFN*	*MLB*	*26*	*3*	*1*	*2*	*55*	*0*	*57²*	*57*	*7*	*4.1*	*6.9*	*44*	*53%*	*.312*	*1.45*	*4.63*	*4.64*	*5.58*	*-2.9*	*-0.3*	*130*	
2018	*SFN*	*MLB*	*27*	*2*	*1*	*1*	*31*	*0*	*34*	*30*	*4*	*4.6*	*9.1*	*34*	*53%*	*.314*	*1.40*	*4.04*	*4.49*	*4.87*	*1.0*	*0.1*	*110*	

Breakout: 20%   Improve: 31%   Collapse: 7%   Attrition: 25%   MLB: 45%   *Comparables: Preston Claiborne, Rhiner Cruz, Josh Spence*

In a way, Dominguez is a pitcher we've seen a thousand times before. He's a reliever with some notable pedigree and an upper-90s fastball. Accompanying that velocity is the lack of a strong second offering and an even more alarming lack of command. In 2016, he received more run support in the majors than ever before and he walked almost as many batters as he struck out while allowing an abundance of home runs in a pitchers' park. On the bright side, Dominguez's cousin, Alex Colomé, has some experience in mastering a secondary offering to turn into a dominant reliever. There is plenty of hope remaining for Dominguez, but he needs to start showing it soon.

Cory Gearrin   RHP

Born: 4/14/86   Age: 31   Bats: R   Throws: R   Height: 6'3"   Weight: 200   Entered Pro Ball: Round 4, 2007 Draft (#138 overall)

YEAR	TEAM	LVL	AGE	W	L	SV	G	GS	IP	H	HR	BB/9	K/9	K	GB%	BABIP	WHIP	ERA	FIP	DRA	VORP	WARP	cFIP	MPH
2015	SAC	AAA	29	2	2	0	33	0	43	38	4	2.9	9.6	46	46%	.293	1.21	2.72	3.86	3.00	9.2	0.9	84	
2015	SFN	MLB	29	0	0	0	7	0	3²	1	0	2.5	12.3	5	100%	.143	0.55	4.91	1.25	3.45	0.5	0.1	88	94.4
2016	SFN	MLB	30	3	2	3	56	0	48¹	42	4	2.6	8.4	45	56%	.286	1.16	4.28	3.33	4.03	5.1	0.5	92	94.0
2017	*SFN*	*MLB*	*31*	*2*	*2*	*0*	*44*	*0*	*46*	*46*	*5*	*3.3*	*7.9*	*41*	*47%*	*.304*	*1.37*	*3.88*	*4.03*	*4.51*	*2.1*	*0.2*	*100*	
2018	*SFN*	*MLB*	*32*	*2*	*1*	*0*	*40*	*0*	*42*	*35*	*5*	*3.7*	*8.9*	*41*	*47%*	*.295*	*1.24*	*3.73*	*4.15*	*4.51*	*2.9*	*0.3*	*101*	

Breakout: 21%   Improve: 26%   Collapse: 18%   Attrition: 13%   MLB: 54%   *Comparables: Mitch Stetter, Chris Hatcher, Doug Slaten*

We're each special little snowflakes. No one has, on the cellular level, your exact eyelashes or your encyclopedic knowledge of The Baby-Sitter's Club canon. That's what makes writing middle relief comments hard: we know each of them is an individual, with individual hopes and dreams and Netflix histories. But they're all righties who throw in the low-to-mid 90s with sharp sliders and struggle occasionally with control. All of them, even the lefties. But not Gearrin. Gearrin is more than that, because once in the 12th inning of a game against the Diamondbacks he played one-third of an inning in the field. He struck out a batter, swapped to left to watch Javier Lopez walk a batter, then came back to get the final two outs. A good old Waxahachie Swap, and a save, something that hasn't happened in 25 years.

Joan Gregorio   RHP

Born: 1/12/92   Age: 25   Bats: R   Throws: R   Height: 6'7"   Weight: 180   Entered Pro Ball: International Free Agent, 2010

YEAR	TEAM	LVL	AGE	W	L	SV	G	GS	IP	H	HR	BB/9	K/9	K	GB%	BABIP	WHIP	ERA	FIP	DRA	VORP	WARP	cFIP	MPH
2014	SJO	A+	22	2	2	0	6	5	22²	27	2	5.2	10.7	27	23%	.370	1.76	6.75	4.23	4.57	2.6	0.3	106	
2014	AUG	A	22	2	7	1	13	12	68	50	2	3.6	8.6	65	41%	.259	1.13	3.57	3.47	4.30	8.5	0.9	97	
2015	RIC	AA	23	3	2	1	37	9	78²	64	6	3.7	8.2	72	38%	.272	1.22	3.09	3.69	4.33	5.2	0.6	97	
2016	RIC	AA	24	0	2	0	5	5	27	15	1	2.0	10.0	30	48%	.222	0.78	2.33	2.28	1.92	9.5	1.0	77	
2016	SAC	AAA	24	6	8	0	21	21	107¹	112	13	3.6	10.2	122	37%	.343	1.44	5.28	4.34	3.52	21.8	2.2	94	
2017	*SFN*	*MLB*	*25*	*1*	*1*	*0*	*18*	*0*	*18*	*18*	*2*	*4.1*	*8.4*	*17*	*54%*	*.299*	*1.42*	*3.81*	*4.35*	*4.41*	*1.0*	*0.1*	*100*	
2018	*SFN*	*MLB*	*26*	*2*	*1*	*0*	*30*	*0*	*31²*	*25*	*3*	*4.9*	*10.4*	*36*	*54%*	*.311*	*1.35*	*3.63*	*4.04*	*4.35*	*2.7*	*0.3*	*96*	

Breakout: 9%   Improve: 23%   Collapse: 20%   Attrition: 36%   MLB: 45%   *Comparables: Michael Clevinger, Matt Shoemaker, Tyler Lyons*

"Shorter Chris R. Young" may not be the sexiest prospect profile around, but you have to admit it worked for Chris R. Young. The six-foot-seven Gregorio built up his numbers in 2016, both on the innings count and on the bathroom scale, and in the process has made himself back into an interesting starting pitching prospect for a team that could sure use an interesting starting pitching prospect. Expect to hear the words "perceived velocity" a lot, as Gregorio relies heavily on the wingspan to enhance a live, low-90s fastball, but his slider also started getting connected to the words "flashes" and "plus," not a terrible thing. Don't get caught up in the bad ERA at Triple-A Sacramento: there's something here, as long as health and command maintain their current trendlines.

George Kontos   RHP

Born: 6/12/85   Age: 31   Bats: R   Throws: R   Height: 6'3"   Weight: 215   Entered Pro Ball: Round 5, 2006 Draft (#164 overall)

YEAR	TEAM	LVL	AGE	W	L	SV	G	GS	IP	H	HR	BB/9	K/9	K	GB%	BABIP	WHIP	ERA	FIP	DRA	VORP	WARP	cFIP	MPH
2014	FRE	AAA	29	3	3	4	30	0	47²	41	4	2.1	11.0	58	41%	.303	1.09	2.08	3.05	2.43	15.4	1.5	77	
2014	SFN	MLB	29	4	0	0	24	0	32¹	24	1	3.1	7.5	27	39%	.267	1.08	2.78	2.86	4.68	-0.7	-0.1	108	93.2
2015	SFN	MLB	30	4	4	0	73	0	73¹	57	9	1.5	5.4	44	44%	.219	0.94	2.33	4.05	4.88	-1.4	-0.1	112	93.5
2016	SFN	MLB	31	3	2	0	57	0	53¹	42	3	3.4	5.9	35	45%	.244	1.16	2.53	3.84	6.18	-7.2	-0.7	118	92.8
2017	*SFN*	*MLB*	*32*	*3*	*2*	*0*	*48*	*0*	*51¹*	*53*	*6*	*3.2*	*6.3*	*36*	*43%*	*.288*	*1.37*	*4.64*	*4.46*	*5.12*	*-1.2*	*-0.1*	*100*	
2018	*SFN*	*MLB*	*33*	*2*	*1*	*0*	*49*	*0*	*52*	*50*	*6*	*3.2*	*6.7*	*39*	*43%*	*.296*	*1.31*	*4.19*	*4.67*	*5.07*	*0.4*	*0.0*	*116*	

Breakout: 26%   Improve: 41%   Collapse: 30%   Attrition: 17%   MLB: 85%   *Comparables: Geoff Geary, Jared Burton, Casey Fien*

Kontos completed his fifth tour of duty in the Giants' bullpen, and his fourth successful one. Still, PECOTA (and its new confidant, DRA) remain skeptical. A little of it is pitch framing; Buster Posey can make almost everyone look better than they are. But the majority of the discrepancy stems from Kontos' flagging peripherals, with strikeout and walk rates heading on a collision course. He does inspire plenty of weak contact, and Giants fans have decades of experience in watching pitchers defy advanced statistics. He's danced this dance for a while now, so the computers will continue to be wrong about Kontos until the moment they're right. After that they won't have the chance anymore, because he'll most likely be out of the league.

Matt Krook   LHP

Born: 10/21/94 Age: 22   Bats: L   Throws: L   Height: 6'2"   Weight: 205   Entered Pro Ball: Round 4, 2016 Draft (#125 overall)

YEAR	TEAM	LVL	AGE	W	L	SV	G	GS	IP	H	HR	BB/9	K/9	K	GB%	BABIP	WHIP	ERA	FIP	DRA	VORP	WARP	cFIP	MPH
2017	SFN	MLB	22	2	3	0	8	8	32²	35	2	7.1	5.4	20	20%	.325	1.85	5.25	5.27	6.18	-2.2	-0.2	143	
2018	SFN	MLB	23	5	8	0	27	27	158²	155	11	6.3	6.0	105	20%	.309	1.68	4.77	5.34	5.62	-0.7	-0.1	132	

Breakout: 4%   Improve: 4%   Collapse: 1%   Attrition: 4%   MLB: 6%   Comparables: Daniel Hudson, Wilking Rodriguez, Marc Rzepczynski

In a system lousy with pitchability, where every starter has six pitches that barely make it to the plate, Krook stands out for his amplitude alone. Miami drafted him in the first round in 2013, but a physical revealed shoulder problems and sent him packing to the University of Oregon. There he fell to Tommy John surgery and returned with even more wildness than the usual recovering patient. He finally got drafted in the fourth round in 2016 and you can see what happened after that. But oh, what might be: the flashes of brilliance he showed in college weren't done justice by the word "brilliant." He has the potential for a plus fastball/slider combo and a terrifying curve. There's a nonzero chance that this is the Matt Krook the world gets. There is a much higher chance that it is not.

Derek Law   RHP

Born: 9/14/90 Age: 26   Bats: R   Throws: R   Height: 6'2"   Weight: 210   Entered Pro Ball: Round 9, 2011 Draft (#297 overall)

YEAR	TEAM	LVL	AGE	W	L	SV	G	GS	IP	H	HR	BB/9	K/9	K	GB%	BABIP	WHIP	ERA	FIP	DRA	VORP	WARP	cFIP	MPH
2014	RIC	AA	23	2	0	13	27	0	28	19	1	4.5	9.3	29	51%	.265	1.18	2.57	3.35	3.20	5.1	0.5	94	
2015	RIC	AA	24	0	1	13	28	0	25²	31	1	2.8	11.2	32	45%	.400	1.52	4.56	2.22	1.87	8.2	0.9	81	
2016	SFN	MLB	25	4	2	1	61	0	55	44	3	1.5	8.2	50	50%	.270	0.96	2.13	2.57	3.70	7.8	0.8	92	96.2
2017	SFN	MLB	26	2	2	3	44	0	46	48	5	3.0	7.9	41	48%	.307	1.38	3.91	3.90	4.52	2.0	0.2	100	
2018	SFN	MLB	27	2	1	2	42	0	44¹	38	5	3.6	10.1	50	48%	.315	1.25	3.53	3.94	4.26	4.2	0.4	95	

Breakout: 34%   Improve: 47%   Collapse: 14%   Attrition: 23%   MLB: 72%   Comparables: Michael Kohn, Rich Thompson, Mychal Givens

Most of us are not who we were at 23. We get married, have children, get our hearts broken, fall into a career or a bottle, or get consumed by editing Wikipedia entries on bronze-age comic books. Some, like Derek Law, have Tommy John surgery. So when the man who somewhat famously struck out 45 batters and walked one at High-A tore the last of his bandages off and emerged as a major-league pitcher in 2016, it was a revelation. The control, never quite aligned with his violent motion, was back, and he ran with it. It took Bruce Bochy some time to trust a pitcher who wasn't born when *DuckTales* went on the air, but eventually Law worked his way into late-inning situations. As long as he can stave off injuries and the horrors of the suburban aging curve, there are plenty of medium-leverage innings in his future.

Javier Lopez   LHP

Born: 7/11/77 Age: 39   Bats: L   Throws: L   Height: 6'4"   Weight: 220   Entered Pro Ball: Round 4, 1998 Draft (#133 overall)

YEAR	TEAM	LVL	AGE	W	L	SV	G	GS	IP	H	HR	BB/9	K/9	K	GB%	BABIP	WHIP	ERA	FIP	DRA	VORP	WARP	cFIP	MPH
2014	SFN	MLB	36	1	1	0	65	0	37²	31	2	4.5	5.3	22	68%	.238	1.33	3.11	4.30	3.67	3.4	0.4	112	88.2
2015	SFN	MLB	37	1	0	0	77	0	39¹	19	1	3.7	5.9	26	69%	.173	0.89	1.60	3.39	3.97	3.2	0.3	103	86.8
2016	SFN	MLB	38	1	3	1	68	0	26²	24	3	5.1	5.1	15	64%	.253	1.46	4.05	5.44	5.26	-0.8	-0.1	117	86.7
2017	SFN	MLB	39	2	1	1	34	0	36	33	4	4.2	6.6	27	58%	.289	1.39	4.74	4.66	5.71	-1.2	-0.1	129	
2018	SFN	MLB	40	3	1	2	70	0	35²	37	5	4.2	6.5	26	58%	.314	1.52	4.90	4.90	5.90	-3.4	-0.3	133	

Breakout: 11%   Improve: 36%   Collapse: 26%   Attrition: 7%   MLB: 71%   Comparables: Matt Thornton, Scott Downs, Al Worthington

The Giants' relief corps witnessed unhealthy amounts of turmoil in 2016, but none of it touched Lopez, whose bullpen role was established in the Magna Carta. The Lord Protector over the Kingdom of LOOGYs, in his age-38 season, finally showed signs of the heaviness of his crown: His walks matched his strikeouts and the few righties he did dare to face torched him for .333/.448/.500. Even lefties were able to solve him to a level that hadn't been seen since his unmentionable days with the Red Sox. As retirement looms, questions arise. How much adjustment will it take for Lopez to exist in a suddenly righty-dominated world? When he plays checkers in the park, will he instinctively seek out like-handed opponents?

Mark Melancon   RHP

Born: 3/28/85 Age: 32   Bats: R   Throws: R   Height: 6'2"   Weight: 210   Entered Pro Ball: Round 9, 2006 Draft (#284 overall)

YEAR	TEAM	LVL	AGE	W	L	SV	G	GS	IP	H	HR	BB/9	K/9	K	GB%	BABIP	WHIP	ERA	FIP	DRA	VORP	WARP	cFIP	MPH
2014	PIT	MLB	29	3	5	33	72	0	71	51	4	1.4	9.0	71	60%	.258	0.87	1.90	2.06	2.35	16.8	1.9	76	94.4
2015	PIT	MLB	30	3	2	51	78	0	76²	57	4	1.6	7.3	62	58%	.251	0.93	2.23	2.85	3.32	11.9	1.3	91	93.7
2016	PIT	MLB	31	1	1	30	45	0	41²	31	2	1.9	8.2	38	49%	.257	0.96	1.51	2.71	2.85	9.8	1.0	82	93.3
2016	WAS	MLB	31	1	1	17	30	0	29²	21	1	0.9	8.2	27	65%	.263	0.81	1.82	2.11	2.99	6.5	0.7	82	93.7
2017	SFN	MLB	32	3	2	39	53	0	55	51	5	2.4	8.2	51	45%	.292	1.18	3.02	3.41	3.75	7.2	0.7	82	
2018	SFN	MLB	33	3	1	41	58	0	62	54	6	2.6	7.6	52	45%	.292	1.16	3.44	3.84	4.16	6.6	0.7	94	

Breakout: 22%   Improve: 44%   Collapse: 27%   Attrition: 9%   MLB: 96%   Comparables: Scot Shields, Francisco Cordero, Eric Gagne

Melancon doesn't throw quite as hard as he used to, but he's managed to mitigate the velocity migration with more movement and pinpoint precision. His cutter stays on plane longer and wanders farther than it used to and batters had a devil of a time trying to barrel it in 2016. He controlled contact as well as any hurler in the game, generating an average exit velocity lower than all but six other hurlers with a hundred pitches tracked. A good bit of that contact bounced its way around the infield, and he continued a now four-year run of model stinginess with the free pass. One would think that given his recent run and job security, he'd be a near lock to lead his alma mater in saves, yet he's still nearly 450 shy of fellow Arizona alum Trevor Hoffman.

Matt Moore   LHP

Born: 6/18/89   Age: 28   Bats: L   Throws: L   Height: 6'3"   Weight: 210   Entered Pro Ball: Round 8, 2007 Draft (#245 overall)

YEAR	TEAM	LVL	AGE	W	L	SV	G	GS	IP	H	HR	BB/9	K/9	K	GB%	BABIP	WHIP	ERA	FIP	DRA	VORP	WARP	cFIP	MPH
2014	TBA	MLB	25	0	2	0	2	2	10	10	1	4.5	5.4	6	42%	.281	1.50	2.70	4.76	4.83	0.0	0.0	111	94.4
2015	PCH	A+	26	0	0	0	3	3	11	9	1	3.3	7.4	9	50%	.258	1.18	1.64	4.07	4.09	1.2	0.1	100	
2015	DUR	AAA	26	2	3	0	7	7	40¹	35	6	2.7	12.9	58	46%	.330	1.17	3.57	3.26	1.50	17.0	1.7	64	
2015	TBA	MLB	26	3	4	0	12	12	63	74	9	3.3	6.6	46	42%	.332	1.54	5.43	4.79	5.53	-3.2	-0.3	116	94.7
2016	TBA	MLB	27	7	7	0	21	21	130	125	20	2.8	7.5	109	38%	.280	1.27	4.08	4.47	4.83	7.7	0.8	109	95.3
2016	SFN	MLB	27	6	5	0	12	12	68¹	59	5	4.2	9.1	69	42%	.297	1.33	4.08	3.57	5.12	1.8	0.2	107	95.4
2017	*SFN*	*MLB*	*28*	*9*	*9*	*0*	*26*	*26*	*148*	*139*	*17*	*3.4*	*8.9*	*146*	*52%*	*.298*	*1.32*	*3.83*	*3.95*	*4.48*	*11.5*	*1.2*	*100*	
2018	*SFN*	*MLB*	*29*	*9*	*9*	*0*	*26*	*26*	*155¹*	*139*	*18*	*3.3*	*8.8*	*152*	*52%*	*.309*	*1.26*	*3.72*	*4.13*	*4.48*	*17.7*	*1.8*	*102*	

Breakout: 19%   Improve: 52%   Collapse: 22%   Attrition: 13%   MLB: 90%   *Comparables: Matt Garza, Jonathan Sanchez, Matt Harrison*

The Giants' refusal to accept their ill-fated season is perhaps best symbolized by their trade for Moore, the former no. 2 prospect in baseball. The lefty didn't come cheap, costing them the no. 2 prospect in their own organization, Lucius Fox. Moore supplied a dozen non-Peavy/Cain starts and matched his pre-trade ERA exactly, while doing so in a nearly-opposite way: After the trade he looked, in the best and worst terms, a little more like Matt Moore again. He became a more volatile pitcher overall, striking out and walking more batters, following up quality starts with disasters. His velocity showed signs of repair, although they'll (and he'll) never be what he was before Olympus struck him down. But with three years of somewhat modest salary left from that stunning, not-quite-a-bargain extension he signed in 2012, he'll probably remain on the periphery of San Francisco's plans for a while.

Steven Okert   LHP

Born: 7/9/91   Age: 25   Bats: L   Throws: L   Height: 6'3"   Weight: 210   Entered Pro Ball: Round 4, 2012 Draft (#148 overall)

YEAR	TEAM	LVL	AGE	W	L	SV	G	GS	IP	H	HR	BB/9	K/9	K	GB%	BABIP	WHIP	ERA	FIP	DRA	VORP	WARP	cFIP	MPH
2014	SJO	A+	22	1	2	19	33	0	35¹	33	2	2.8	13.8	54	46%	.308	1.25	1.53	2.52	1.28	15.4	1.5	74	
2014	RIC	AA	22	1	0	5	24	0	33	24	3	3.0	10.4	38	43%	.266	1.06	2.73	3.23	1.74	11.4	1.2	79	
2015	SAC	AAA	23	5	3	3	52	0	61¹	62	7	4.3	10.1	69	46%	.337	1.48	3.82	4.35	3.58	9.2	0.9	92	
2016	SAC	AAA	24	4	3	3	41	0	47¹	53	2	2.1	11.4	60	42%	.370	1.35	3.80	2.43	2.04	15.4	1.6	74	
2016	SFN	MLB	24	0	0	0	16	0	14	14	2	2.6	9.0	14	42%	.316	1.29	3.21	3.90	4.04	1.4	0.1	99	94.4
2017	*SFN*	*MLB*	*25*	*2*	*2*	*0*	*40*	*0*	*42*	*44*	*4*	*3.4*	*8.2*	*38*	*49%*	*.312*	*1.44*	*3.81*	*3.89*	*4.43*	*2.3*	*0.2*	*100*	
2018	*SFN*	*MLB*	*26*	*2*	*1*	*0*	*47*	*0*	*49¹*	*42*	*5*	*4.6*	*10.9*	*60*	*49%*	*.327*	*1.36*	*3.61*	*4.03*	*4.35*	*4.2*	*0.4*	*97*	

Breakout: 30%   Improve: 38%   Collapse: 14%   Attrition: 43%   MLB: 56%   *Comparables: Donnie Joseph, Anthony Zych, Shawn Armstrong*

After a couple rough outings in April, Okert returned to Sacramento and watched a parade of his colleagues get promoted before him. A workable September call-up, as well as the impending departure of long-time obstacle Javier Lopez, offer a ray of hope for the lefty. The 2014 version of Okert was a late-inning reliever with a nasty slider and a changeup to deal with right-handed hitters; the 2016 version lost a little bite on his pitches, and dumped the change for a cutter that doesn't have enough cut. That combination is still LOOGY-caliber, so at minimum the Giants have a new Lopez.

Joshua Osich   LHP

Born: 9/3/88   Age: 28   Bats: L   Throws: L   Height: 6'2"   Weight: 230   Entered Pro Ball: Round 6, 2011 Draft (#207 overall)

YEAR	TEAM	LVL	AGE	W	L	SV	G	GS	IP	H	HR	BB/9	K/9	K	GB%	BABIP	WHIP	ERA	FIP	DRA	VORP	WARP	cFIP	MPH
2014	RIC	AA	25	1	0	0	28	0	33¹	28	4	5.4	7.3	27	56%	.264	1.44	3.78	5.18	6.69	-6.8	-0.7	101	
2015	RIC	AA	26	0	1	19	31	0	34	23	1	2.6	9	34	60%	.242	0.97	1.59	2.62	3.25	5.6	0.6	87	
2015	SFN	MLB	26	2	0	0	35	0	28²	24	4	2.5	8.5	27	49%	.247	1.12	2.20	3.93	4.33	1.2	0.1	100	97.8
2016	SFN	MLB	27	1	3	0	59	0	36¹	31	7	4.7	6.2	25	65%	.226	1.38	4.71	6.13	6.13	-2.5	-0.3	109	98.5
2017	*SFN*	*MLB*	*28*	*1*	*1*	*0*	*22*	*0*	*23¹*	*24*	*3*	*3.8*	*6.7*	*17*	*48%*	*.297*	*1.47*	*4.65*	*4.81*	*5.13*	*-0.6*	*-0.1*	*100*	
2018	*SFN*	*MLB*	*29*	*1*	*0*	*0*	*28*	*0*	*29²*	*25*	*3*	*4.6*	*8.8*	*29*	*48%*	*.294*	*1.36*	*4.15*	*4.62*	*5.02*	*0.4*	*0.0*	*115*	

Breakout: 19%   Improve: 36%   Collapse: 11%   Attrition: 26%   MLB: 57%   *Comparables: Craig Breslow, Josh Roenicke, Alex Hinshaw*

Someone must have whispered "future Giants closer" regarding Osich at some point, because the fireballing lefty came down with a case of Hunter Strickland Disease that lasted so long he might have renamed it. Command was a concern heading into the season, but things fell apart in spectacular fashion: He was unable to get his offspeed stuff over the plate, missing with his changeup more than half the time. This led to hitters sitting on the fastball in fastball counts, which led to a sudden decrease in Osich's self-esteem. The Giants sent him to the DL with a forearm strain, which they may have actually done to him themselves just for the rehab. There's still time and material left here for another retooling, but the Giants would probably prefer to allow the fireworks to take place in Sacramento.

Jake Peavy   RHP

Born: 5/31/81   Age: 36   Bats: R   Throws: R   Height: 6'1"   Weight: 195   Entered Pro Ball: Round 15, 1999 Draft (#472 overall)

YEAR	TEAM	LVL	AGE	W	L	SV	G	GS	IP	H	HR	BB/9	K/9	K	GB%	BABIP	WHIP	ERA	FIP	DRA	VORP	WARP	cFIP	MPH
2014	BOS	MLB	33	1	9	0	20	20	124	131	20	3.3	7.3	100	42%	.301	1.43	4.72	4.83	4.42	5.7	0.6	113	92.4
2014	SFN	MLB	33	6	4	0	12	12	78²	65	3	1.9	6.6	58	40%	.270	1.04	2.17	3.00	4.61	2.0	0.2	112	92.1
2015	SAC	AAA	34	0	3	0	6	6	32¹	39	5	2.5	7.8	28	34%	.340	1.48	6.12	4.90	6.79	-5.3	-0.5	103	
2015	SFN	MLB	34	8	6	0	19	19	110²	99	12	2.0	6.3	78	40%	.263	1.12	3.58	3.89	5.32	-3.0	-0.3	113	92.4
2016	SFN	MLB	35	5	9	0	31	21	118²	134	18	2.7	7.7	102	38%	.320	1.43	5.54	4.40	5.93	-7.9	-0.8	114	90.8
2017	*SFN*	*MLB*	*36*	*6*	*6*	*0*	*18*	*18*	*107*	*101*	*14*	*3.0*	*7.6*	*91*	*46%*	*.301*	*1.28*	*4.31*	*4.25*	*5.17*	*4.7*	*0.5*	*122*	
2018	*SFN*	*MLB*	*37*	*5*	*6*	*0*	*14*	*14*	*84¹*	*88*	*12*	*3.1*	*7.6*	*71*	*46%*	*.324*	*1.39*	*4.33*	*4.80*	*5.19*	*3.5*	*0.4*	*121*	

Breakout: 18%   Improve: 43%   Collapse: 14%   Attrition: 13%   MLB: 70%   Comparables: Freddy Garcia, Roy Oswalt, Bronson Arroyo

Here's what kind of season it was for the former Cy Young winner: before losing his rotation spot at the end of July, he had nearly as many starts with six or more runs allowed (5) as he did one or zero (6). He also saw the seventh inning only five times in 21 tries. And that wasn't even the worst of it: On the first day of spring training, he learned that he'd been defrauded out of $15 million in investments. Given how difficult it would be to go to work knowing that your next two days' salary will be devoted to a speeding ticket earned on your commute, it's unfathomable to estimate the effect of Peavy's disaster on his concentration. It's possible, sadly, to combine his fly-ball propensity with a dwindling fastball and estimate his ability to earn enough for future capitalist endeavors.

Sergio Romo   RHP

Born: 3/4/83   Age: 34   Bats: R   Throws: R   Height: 5'11"   Weight: 185   Entered Pro Ball: Round 28, 2005 Draft (#852 overall)

YEAR	TEAM	LVL	AGE	W	L	SV	G	GS	IP	H	HR	BB/9	K/9	K	GB%	BABIP	WHIP	ERA	FIP	DRA	VORP	WARP	cFIP	MPH
2014	SFN	MLB	31	6	4	23	64	0	58	43	9	1.9	9.2	59	38%	.233	0.95	3.72	3.91	3.08	9.0	1.0	95	90.0
2015	SFN	MLB	32	0	5	2	70	0	57¹	51	3	1.6	11.1	71	39%	.331	1.06	2.98	1.94	2.33	15.2	1.6	74	89.4
2016	SFN	MLB	33	1	0	4	40	0	30²	26	5	2.1	9.7	33	39%	.292	1.08	2.64	3.84	3.64	4.5	0.5	94	87.8
2017	*SFN*	*MLB*	*34*	*2*	*1*	*1*	*36*	*0*	*38¹*	*32*	*5*	*2.8*	*9.7*	*41*	*47%*	*.302*	*1.15*	*3.56*	*3.71*	*4.28*	*3.0*	*0.3*	*96*	
2018	*SFN*	*MLB*	*35*	*3*	*1*	*1*	*57*	*0*	*50*	*44*	*7*	*3.1*	*9.3*	*52*	*47%*	*.302*	*1.22*	*3.73*	*4.13*	*4.48*	*3.7*	*0.4*	*100*	

Breakout: 16%   Improve: 31%   Collapse: 32%   Attrition: 12%   MLB: 89%   Comparables: Francisco Rodriguez, Damaso Marte, Rafael Betancourt

Imagine how much easier the world would be if we all were offered the platoon advantage: introvert teachers could call in salesman types to deliver parent-teacher conferences. Parents struggling with toddlers could call in experts to get them to eat their peas. All of our flaws and weaknesses glossed over, minimized. So it went yet again with Romo, who was a flexor strain and a tick off his fastball away from being his usual excellent, limited self. Expect all of the above trends to continue, as Romo leans more heavily on his slider than ever, transforming into more of a specialist to maintain success in those specialized situations.

Jeff Samardzija   RHP

Born: 1/23/85   Age: 32   Bats: R   Throws: R   Height: 6'5"   Weight: 225   Entered Pro Ball: Round 5, 2006 Draft (#149 overall)

YEAR	TEAM	LVL	AGE	W	L	SV	G	GS	IP	H	HR	BB/9	K/9	K	GB%	BABIP	WHIP	ERA	FIP	DRA	VORP	WARP	cFIP	MPH
2014	CHN	MLB	29	2	7	0	17	17	108	99	7	2.6	8.6	103	54%	.306	1.20	2.83	3.07	2.68	25.8	2.9	80	96.8
2014	OAK	MLB	29	5	6	0	16	16	111²	92	13	1.0	8.0	99	49%	.262	0.93	3.14	3.33	2.81	25.1	2.8	79	97.3
2015	CHA	MLB	30	11	13	0	32	32	214	228	29	2.1	6.9	163	41%	.303	1.29	4.96	4.20	5.00	1.9	0.2	106	96.8
2016	SFN	MLB	31	12	11	0	32	32	203¹	190	24	2.4	7.4	167	47%	.285	1.20	3.81	3.89	4.37	22.3	2.3	101	96.7
2017	*SFN*	*MLB*	*32*	*12*	*11*	*0*	*29*	*29*	*194¹*	*189*	*23*	*2.6*	*8.2*	*178*	*46%*	*.299*	*1.27*	*3.74*	*3.87*	*4.39*	*17.0*	*1.8*	*100*	
2018	*SFN*	*MLB*	*33*	*13*	*12*	*0*	*32*	*32*	*204²*	*189*	*26*	*2.4*	*8.1*	*183*	*46%*	*.305*	*1.19*	*3.70*	*4.11*	*4.45*	*25.7*	*2.6*	*102*	

Breakout: 13%   Improve: 44%   Collapse: 30%   Attrition: 5%   MLB: 87%   Comparables: Ted Lilly, Anibal Sanchez, Dan Haren

Some types of sharks must keep moving in order to stay alive. The fact is equally true regarding aging starting pitchers. The Giants made a very large bet ($90 million over five years) that Samardzija would return to form, and he did return to a form, just not one anyone recognized. Instead he settled firmly in between his disastrous 2015 and his previous high-water mark, providing 200 nearly league-average innings. Ordinarily pitchers in their thirties have to keep an eye on the radar gun, but velocity hasn't been a problem for Samardzija; batters are simply making more contact than they used to. His splitter, once his out-pitch, went from generating 20 percent whiffs in the Good Old Days to less than 15 percent in 2015-16. He's been forced to use it less and less, and instead pulled his curveball out of mothballs as a backup. It's worked, if only for now. Once the velocity declines, as it does for all of us, the former footballer will be forced to further reimagine himself.

Will Smith   LHP

Born: 7/10/89   Age: 27   Bats: R   Throws: L   Height: 6'5"   Weight: 265   Entered Pro Ball: Round 7, 2008 Draft (#229 overall)

YEAR	TEAM	LVL	AGE	W	L	SV	G	GS	IP	H	HR	BB/9	K/9	K	GB%	BABIP	WHIP	ERA	FIP	DRA	VORP	WARP	cFIP	MPH
2014	MIL	MLB	24	1	3	1	78	0	65²	62	6	4.2	11.8	86	46%	.350	1.42	3.70	3.22	3.08	10.3	1.1	85	96.2
2015	MIL	MLB	25	7	2	0	76	0	63¹	52	5	3.4	12.9	91	48%	.329	1.20	2.70	2.50	2.90	12.7	1.4	70	95.8
2016	MIL	MLB	26	1	3	0	27	0	22	18	3	3.7	9.0	22	42%	.263	1.23	3.68	4.32	3.73	3.0	0.3	95	94.2
2016	SFN	MLB	26	1	1	0	26	0	18¹	13	0	4.4	12.8	26	40%	.325	1.20	2.95	1.82	3.40	3.2	0.3	94	95.0
2017	*SFN*	*MLB*	*27*	*2*	*2*	*3*	*44*	*0*	*46*	*41*	*4*	*3.7*	*10.6*	*55*	*49%*	*.311*	*1.31*	*2.94*	*3.27*	*3.67*	*6.5*	*0.7*	*79*	
2018	*SFN*	*MLB*	*28*	*3*	*1*	*2*	*47*	*0*	*50*	*39*	*4*	*3.7*	*11.4*	*63*	*49%*	*.324*	*1.19*	*2.75*	*3.06*	*3.32*	*9.9*	*1.0*	*68*	

Breakout: 31%   Improve: 57%   Collapse: 16%   Attrition: 12%   MLB: 93%   Comparables: Ryan Madson, Aaron Crow, Tony Pena

It's both a blessing and a curse to be left-handed. At the bottom of the ladder, being left-handed can keep you off unemployment all by itself; at the top, it can weigh you down like a graduate degree on an entry-level resume. After missing the start of the year with an injury and yielding a prospective closing role to Jeremy Jeffress, Smith recovered just in time to earn the Brewers a nice haul in prospects from the Giants. Bruce Bochy took his excellent, expensive new reliever and basically made him a LOOGY. Even as the rest of the bullpen disintegrated around him, even as Game 4 of the NLCS got away, Bochy could never find the courage to trust Smith. The lesson: avoid being typecast. The human brain is driven to compartmentalize, to sort, to simplify. Not everything is under your control, but do whatever you can to avoid getting lumped in with the Javier Lopezes of life.

Hunter Strickland   RHP

Born: 9/24/88   Age: 28   Bats: R   Throws: R   Height: 6'4"   Weight: 220   Entered Pro Ball: Round 18, 2007 Draft (#564 overall)

YEAR	TEAM	LVL	AGE	W	L	SV	G	GS	IP	H	HR	BB/9	K/9	K	GB%	BABIP	WHIP	ERA	FIP	DRA	VORP	WARP	cFIP	MPH
2014	RIC	AA	25	1	1	11	38	0	35²	25	3	1.0	12.1	48	41%	.275	0.81	2.02	2.09	1.16	14.6	1.6	59	
2014	SFN	MLB	25	1	0	1	9	0	7	5	0	0.0	11.6	9	56%	.312	0.71	0.00	0.53	3.09	1.1	0.1	86	100.1
2015	SAC	AAA	26	1	1	5	15	0	21²	14	0	1.2	10.4	25	69%	.275	0.78	1.66	1.85	1.54	8.1	0.8	65	
2015	SFN	MLB	26	3	3	0	55	0	51¹	34	4	1.8	8.8	50	40%	.240	0.86	2.45	2.93	3.96	4.3	0.5	95	99.3
2016	SFN	MLB	27	3	3	3	72	0	61	50	4	2.8	8.4	57	47%	.274	1.13	3.10	3.20	3.88	7.4	0.8	98	99.5
2017	SFN	MLB	28	3	2	0	48	0	51¹	50	6	3.0	8.1	46	47%	.298	1.31	3.89	4.01	4.50	2.4	0.2	100	
2018	SFN	MLB	29	3	1	0	57	0	60²	47	7	3.3	10.0	67	47%	.294	1.14	3.41	3.79	4.12	6.7	0.7	91	

Breakout: 29%   Improve: 45%   Collapse: 23%   Attrition: 22%   MLB: 82%   Comparables: Mark Melancon, Pedro Strop, Zach Putnam

Talk about red herrings. The Giants and manager Bruce Bochy had one of the league's most unconventional bullpen-usage patterns, wielding one of the game's most combustible closers. So naturally Strickland, long considered the franchise's closer of the future, wound up with just the three saves. The arsenal, a double-barrel shotgun of plus fastball and slider, is intact, and his infamous home run woes of the 2014 playoffs are growing distant on the horizon. His overall numbers, and the peripherals beneath them, were more than acceptable. Strickland's season is a microcosm of the Giants' bullpen as a whole, which ranked near the top of the ERA leaderboards and yet led the league in blown saves. The relievers, as a whole, performed very well in low- and medium-leverage situations, then choked at the worst possible moment. Bochy wielded an itchy hook with everyone, pulling them at the first sign of trouble, and yet with every move, he seemed to pick the wrong guy. The question: Was Bochy responding to a group of unreliable headcases, or was he, through his tinkering, creating them? It's impossible to prove which, but given the impending turnover, and a winter to rest and collect thoughts, the remaining firemen in black and orange will almost certainly regain some of their clutchiness in 2017. And Strickland will be one of the leaders of that corps.

Albert Suarez   RHP

Born: 10/8/89   Age: 27   Bats: R   Throws: R   Height: 6'3"   Weight: 235   Entered Pro Ball: International Free Agent, 2006

YEAR	TEAM	LVL	AGE	W	L	SV	G	GS	IP	H	HR	BB/9	K/9	K	GB%	BABIP	WHIP	ERA	FIP	DRA	VORP	WARP	cFIP	MPH
2014	PCH	A+	24	1	0	0	3	3	14	14	0	0.6	6.4	10	44%	.304	1.07	0.64	2.18	3.38	3.4	0.3	90	
2014	MNT	AA	24	3	6	0	11	11	56	67	4	3.1	5.1	32	44%	.330	1.54	4.34	4.10	5.36	-0.8	-0.1	113	
2015	ARK	AA	25	11	9	0	27	27	163	142	14	2.2	6.7	121	41%	.269	1.12	2.98	3.68	3.33	31.9	3.5	93	
2016	SAC	AAA	26	4	3	0	9	7	45²	46	3	2.8	7.7	39	45%	.314	1.31	4.34	3.92	3.03	11.4	1.2	97	
2016	SFN	MLB	26	3	5	0	22	12	84	84	11	2.8	5.8	54	50%	.281	1.31	4.29	4.67	5.66	-3.8	-0.4	111	94.9
2017	SFN	MLB	27	3	2	0	34	3	47	50	4	3.2	6.2	33	49%	.298	1.39	4.13	4.07	4.73	1.4	0.1	100	
2018	SFN	MLB	28	3	2	0	46	4	65²	58	6	4.4	8.8	64	49%	.311	1.37	3.86	4.31	4.66	4.1	0.4	104	

Breakout: 15%   Improve: 25%   Collapse: 17%   Attrition: 25%   MLB: 52%   Comparables: Josh Banks, Josh Geer, Tyler Cloyd

Suarez Mk. 1 (see below for patch notes on upcoming Mk. 2 below) fought his way through Tommy John surgery, knee issues, and Lyme disease to reach the majors at 27. Acquired as a minor-league free agent, he was called up to replace Vin Mazzaro in the long-relief role, then took over a starting role as the back of the Giants' rotation fell apart. He's no warm, buttered piece of toast (again, see below), but rather a five-inning starter with four below-average pitches who gives up copious amounts of contact. It's great that he made it, after all the work and the pain. It also wouldn't be surprising to see a "Demoted: A Suarez, recalled A Suarez from Triple-A Sacramento" on the transaction wire sometime next season.

Andrew Suarez   LHP

Born: 9/11/92   Age: 24   Bats: L   Throws: L   Height: 6'2"   Weight: 205   Entered Pro Ball: Round 2, 2015 Draft (#61 overall)

YEAR	TEAM	LVL	AGE	W	L	SV	G	GS	IP	H	HR	BB/9	K/9	K	GB%	BABIP	WHIP	ERA	FIP	DRA	VORP	WARP	cFIP	MPH
2015	SLO	A-	22	1	0	0	5	5	19¹	17	2	0.9	7.0	15	53%	.273	0.98	1.40	3.70	3.43	4.0	0.4	91	
2015	SJO	A+	22	1	0	0	3	3	15	13	2	1.2	9.6	16	46%	.297	1.00	1.80	3.78	2.56	4.2	0.5	87	
2016	SJO	A+	23	2	1	0	5	5	29²	25	2	1.5	10.3	34	61%	.299	1.01	2.43	2.91	2.02	11.4	1.2	78	
2016	RIC	AA	23	7	7	0	19	19	114	129	11	1.9	7.1	90	48%	.332	1.34	3.95	3.72	2.94	27.4	3.0	87	
2017	SFN	MLB	24	6	6	0	19	19	106	116	11	2.6	6.3	74	50%	.326	1.38	4.13	4.08	4.93	7.5	0.8	115	
2018	SFN	MLB	25	8	9	0	25	25	149	146	17	3.8	9.1	150	50%	.336	1.40	3.82	4.27	4.56	15.5	1.6	105	

Breakout: 14%   Improve: 24%   Collapse: 11%   Attrition: 27%   MLB: 39%   Comparables: Cory Mazzoni, Hector Noesi, Dillon Overton

"Won't always miss this many bats," read nearly every scouting profile written about Suarez in 2016, and yet he wound up doing just that. That's good news, because it was the only thing he really needed. Suarez already wields an arsenal of four acceptable pitches, all capable of finding their way to the edge of the plate. Add some of those swinging strikes into the formula and you have yourself a useful third or fourth starter prospect. No, he's not exciting. Think of him as a warm, buttered piece of toast, or a lesser Wodehouse novel, or a *Psych* rerun.

LINEOUTS

Hitters

NAME	POS	TEAM	LVL	AGE	PA	R	2B	3B	HR	RBI	BB	K	SB	CS	AVG/OBP/SLG	TAv	VORP	BABIP	BRR	FRAA	WARP
Ehire Adrianza	2B	SJO	A+	26	36	8	3	0	5	11	2	4	0	0	.333/.361/.879	.353	4.4	.240	-0.2	SS(5): 0.2 • 3B(1): -0.0	0.5
	2B	SAC	AAA	26	37	6	2	0	1	3	2	4	1	3	.257/.297/.400	.262	1.2	.267	-0.2	3B(5): -0.8 • SS(3): -0.1	0.0
	2B	SFN	MLB	26	71	3	2	0	2	7	2	13	0	1	.254/.299/.381	.250	0.9	.292	-0.8	SS(13): 0.8 • 2B(7): 0.3	0.2
Gordon Beckham	3B	ATL	MLB	29	273	25	16	1	5	30	26	50	1	0	.217/.300/.354	.241	1.9	.250	-0.8	2B(51): -0.1 • 3B(15): -1.7	0.1
	3B	SFN	MLB	29	6	0	0	0	0	1	0	2	0	0	.000/.000/.000	.074	-0.9	.000	0.0	3B(3): 0.1	-0.1
Wynton Bernard	OF	TOL	AAA	25	163	18	5	1	1	11	10	30	10	3	.235/.286/.302	.233	0.2	.286	1.0	CF(16): -0.2 • LF(15): 1.6	0.0
	OF	ERI	AA	25	263	38	8	4	6	22	27	39	13	2	.308/.381/.458	.291	15.5	.348	2.0	LF(23): -0.8 • CF(20): -1.2	1.5
Orlando Calixte	INF	NWA	AA	24	152	26	9	0	2	14	9	31	14	3	.295/.333/.403	.290	7.7	.361	0.4	RF(32): 3.5 • 2B(3): -0.3	1.1
	INF	OMA	AAA	24	367	48	17	5	9	29	28	68	5	6	.265/.320/.428	.281	16.7	.307	-2.0	CF(34): 3.0 • 2B(17): 0.4	1.7
Dylan Davis	RF	AUG	A	22	269	38	17	4	8	43	30	58	3	1	.288/.368/.496	.347	26.2	.349	1.9	RF(32): -4.5 • LF(17): -2.4	2.1
	RF	SJO	A+	22	276	36	10	1	18	49	22	61	1	0	.278/.344/.544	.316	22.4	.298	1.3	RF(45): -8.1 • LF(5): 0.0	1.5
Miguel Gomez	INF	AUG	A	23	285	41	17	1	8	43	12	25	3	2	.371/.401/.532	.334	20.2	.386	-2.6	3B(31): -1.6 • 1B(7): -0.0	2.0
	INF	SJO	A+	23	182	25	9	2	9	24	8	28	1	0	.267/.302/.500	.303	11.8	.272	-0.7	3B(20): -2.4 • 1B(7): -0.4	0.8
Gorkys Hernandez	CF	SAC	AAA	28	503	74	22	3	8	51	52	77	20	13	.302/.382/.421	.294	35.6	.349	2.1	CF(113): -2.3	3.4
	CF	SFN	MLB	28	57	7	5	0	2	4	3	11	0	1	.259/.298/.463	.273	2.2	.293	-0.1	CF(14): 0.1 • RF(6): 1.1	0.4
C.J. Hinojosa	INF	SJO	A+	21	302	45	14	3	6	34	36	46	1	4	.296/.378/.442	.314	31.2	.336	1.1	SS(68): 5.0	3.7
	INF	RIC	AA	21	251	27	7	2	3	19	20	43	1	0	.248/.312/.336	.244	4.8	.291	-1.0	SS(55): 4.3	1.0
Travis Ishikawa	1B	CHR	AAA	32	175	24	4	0	6	18	14	54	0	1	.201/.277/.344	.217	-6.0	.260	-0.2	1B(18): 1.4 • LF(3): 0.0	-0.5
	1B	SAC	AAA	32	308	31	13	0	12	55	29	81	0	0	.257/.344/.440	.285	10.7	.320	-0.9	1B(57): 5.6 • LF(6): 0.1	1.7
Jalen Miller	SS	AUG	A	19	500	65	20	5	5	44	26	107	11	5	.223/.271/.322	.237	5.6	.277	3.8	2B(104): -5.9 • SS(7): -0.6	-0.1
Miguel Olivo	C	SAC	AAA	37	313	41	12	4	10	34	18	90	1	0	.246/.289/.419	.254	11.2	.318	0.4	C(65): 4.2 • 1B(1): -0.0	0.7
Juniel Querecuto	INF	DUR	AA	23	129	11	8	0	0	11	6	31	3	1	.242/.289/.308	.209	-3.0	.326	0.0	3B(21): -0.7 • 2B(15): -0.7	-0.5
	INF	MNT	AA	23	246	26	11	3	3	27	21	43	0	0	.241/.303/.359	.252	6.7	.282	1.5	3B(24): 1.2 • 2B(18): 4.0	1.3
	INF	TBA	MLB	23	11	1	0	1	0	2	0	6	0	0	.091/.091/.273	.118	-1.1	.200	0.1	2B(2): -0.2 • SS(1): -0.0	-0.1
Heath Quinn	LF	SLO	A-	21	239	37	19	1	9	34	26	50	3	0	.337/.423/.571	.352	27.3	.405	1.6	RF(47): 8.3	3.8
Austin Slater	OF	RIC	AA	23	172	20	8	1	5	25	24	36	6	1	.317/.413/.490	.339	19.5	.387	1.1	CF(33): -9.6 • LF(7): -0.3	1.0
	OF	SAC	AAA	23	278	36	12	0	13	42	33	53	2	6	.298/.381/.506	.329	26.1	.335	-0.5	LF(48): 0.3 • CF(15): -1.4	2.6
Ruben Tejada	SS	SLN	MLB	26	40	6	2	0	0	3	2	8	0	0	.176/.225/.235	.199	-0.9	.207	0.2	3B(10): 0.4 • SS(7): 0.7	-0.1
	SS	SFN	MLB	26	38	3	3	0	0	2	5	5	0	0	.156/.237/.250	.204	-1.7	.185	-0.1	3B(13): -0.2 • 1B(1): -0.0	-0.1
	SS	SAC	AAA	26	155	18	11	1	1	21	7	21	0	1	.301/.338/.413	.268	7.0	.341	-0.5	SS(37): -0.3 • 3B(2): 0.5	0.8
Angel Villalona	1B	RIC	AA	25	64	4	2	0	1	5	6	20	0	0	.143/.250/.232	.194	-4.3	.200	-0.8	1B(5): 0.1	-0.4

The phrase "utility player" probably started off as a compliment for guys like **Ehire Adrianza**, but in these dark modern times it's really just an indictment on the heartless corporation who wrings every drop of value, every moment of service time out before discarding the husk onto the free agent market. ❖ Congratulations! You found the lineout for **Gordon Beckham**, which might just be the world's worst treasure hunt. The Giants traded for him a week before the end of the season, to cover for an ailing Eduardo Nunez. He went hitless. ❖ **Wynton Bernard** can fly and is relatively inexperienced for his age. It might've seemed like a long shot a few years ago, but his work ethic could push him to a major-league niche. ❖ **Kyle Blanks** is the sort of player who finally gets left out of an annual and then hits 25 home runs. So here he is, which now means it won't happen, which means he didn't need to be mentioned here. ❖ **Orlando Calixte** has mastered Double-A, but still finds Triple-A perplexing. Perhaps 2017 is the year we'll see Orlando bloom, but as any *Pirates of the Caribbean* fan knows, that's not always worth the wait. ❖ It was a heck of a year for **Dylan Davis** at High-A San Jose, but he'll need to prove that he can do more than clobber mistake pitches at the higher levels. His defense is ponderous and he's prone to getting beaten by good sequencing. ❖ We're talking about an 18-year-old corner outfielder in rookie ball, but **Sandro Fabian**'s bat-to-ball skill is interesting enough to make his name worth filing away for 2020. ❖ A career .314 hitter across five minor-league seasons, **Miguel Gomez** has more minor hits than the former Roc La Familia artist with whom he shares a name. ❖ Once a fabled prospect, **Gorkys Hernandez** is now one of baseball's ronin, wandering from one hamlet to the next, catching the pop flies that would otherwise roll to the wall. Someone has to stand there, after all, to oppose the next batch of heroes. ❖ **C.J. Hinojosa** is trapped halfway between the raw talent he flashed in high school and the poor work ethic that tarnished his college career. He lacks polish or instincts, but has the potential to make it as a reserve infielder. ❖ Like a listless millennial, **Travis Ishikawa** keeps moving back in with his folks, signing a minor-league contract with the Giants in June. Unfortunately, the Giants fell just short of the NLCS Game 5 necessary to deploy him. ❖ With teammate Lucius Fox out of town, **Jalen Miller** takes over his role as the team's high-profile disappointing shortstop. Scouts still believe the hit tool will come around, though now the concern is that his fringe-to-average arm will force him to second. ❖ Like Poe's Tell-Tale Heart, **Miguel Olivo** never goes away, never rests. Hidden in the minor leagues, like clockwork, you can hear it: the whiff of a bat at a pitch out of the zone. Again. And again. It will never stop, until at last you succumb to madness. ❖ Was it a dream? Minor-league utility infielder **Juniel Querecuto** woke up one morning at his home in Venezuela and found himself summoned to Tampa for the last week in September to fill out a decimated infield. ❖ **Heath Quinn** is a Three True Outcomes guy whose potential will depend on that third outcome. His defense is acceptable in the corners, but the hit tool is a concern. ❖ Nearly every team has an outfielder dreaded by their fans, a canary in the metaphorical coal mine: the guy whose presence in the lineup means things have gone wrong. The Giants never seem to have one of those, because they always have a guy like **Austin Slater** at Triple-A. ❖ **Ruben Tejada** appeared to play his cards right, signing with St. Louis just as starting shortstop Jhonny Peralta went down with injury. Instead he got hurt enough to watch Aledmys Diaz incinerate the world, and played intermittently and inconsistently enough to get cut twice. ❖ This is the 10th time **Angel Villalona** has appeared in the BP Annual, surely a record among players who never reached Triple-A. This is all that there is left to say about him.

Pitchers

NAME	TEAM	LVL	AGE	W	L	SV	G	GS	IP	H	HR	BB/9	K/9	K	GB%	BABIP	WHIP	ERA	FIP	DRA	VORP	WARP	cFIP	MPH
Ray Black	RIC	AA	26	1	4	6	35	0	31¹	17	1	9.2	15.2	53	39%	.286	1.56	4.88	3.55	5.39	-2.3	-0.2	100	
Kyle Crick	RIC	AA	23	4	11	0	23	23	109	110	8	5.5	7.1	86	46%	.311	1.62	5.04	4.85	7.34	-27.2	-2.9	122	
Chase Johnson	RIC	AA	24	1	4	5	24	7	52¹	47	2	3.1	6.4	37	56%	.285	1.24	3.27	3.64	4.11	5.1	0.6	99	
Jordan Johnson	SJO	A+	22	8	9	0	22	22	120	133	24	2.9	8.3	111	43%	.311	1.43	5.32	5.56	3.83	21.9	2.2	97	
Rodolfo Martinez	SJO	A+	22	1	1	21	32	0	30²	23	1	2.9	9.7	33	51%	.275	1.08	0.88	2.96	3.10	6.8	0.7	91	
	RIC	AA	22	0	3	3	25	0	23	29	1	5.9	6.7	17	41%	.364	1.91	6.65	4.66	6.87	-5.5	-0.6	122	
Vin Mazzaro	SFN	MLB	29	1	0	0	2	0	1	7	0	9.0	0.0	0	46%	.636	8.00	54.00	9.19	10.21	-0.6	-0.1	115	94.0
	SAC	AAA	29	2	2	1	38	4	67	61	4	3.6	5.8	43	54%	.284	1.31	3.22	4.56	5.76	-5.3	-0.5	112	
Reyes Moronta	SJO	A+	23	0	3	14	60	0	59	43	7	3.1	14.2	93	34%	.295	1.07	2.59	3.17	0.77	28.3	2.9	60	
Joe Nathan	CHN	MLB	41	1	0	0	3	0	2	2	0	9.0	18.0	4	0%	.500	2.00	0.00	2.19	4.85	0.0	0.0	102	94.3
	SFN	MLB	41	1	0	0	7	0	4¹	3	0	4.2	10.4	5	27%	.273	1.15	0.00	2.26	4.99	0.0	0.0	102	93.0
Daniel Slania	RIC	AA	24	7	6	0	27	10	82²	68	6	2.4	8.6	79	39%	.277	1.09	2.50	3.23	2.74	20.7	2.2	89	
	SJO	A+	24	2	2	0	5	4	24	27	3	3.4	6.8	18	56%	.316	1.50	5.25	5.21	5.20	0.7	0.1	106	
	SAC	AAA	24	2	0	0	2	2	13	8	0	2.8	9.7	14	24%	.242	0.92	1.38	2.49	4.04	1.9	0.2	94	
Chris Stratton	SFN	MLB	25	1	0	0	7	0	10	11	1	4.5	5.4	6	38%	.323	1.60	3.60	4.79	5.21	-0.3	0.0	117	94.1
	SAC	AAA	25	12	6	0	21	20	125²	120	6	2.8	7.4	103	45%	.305	1.27	3.87	3.73	3.84	20.8	2.1	96	

Ray Black still possesses a fastball measurable only in parsecs, but he went on the 60-day DL in June for an undisclosed arm injury, assumed to be "too good for this world." ❖ It was a rough year for **Kyle Crick**, the pitching equivalent of a sawed-off shotgun. It may be time to disassemble the whole package and try to put the parts back together as a reliever. ❖ Any year in which you're placed on waivers to make room for Vin Mazzaro can't be a good one, but at least **Ian Gardeck** should return from Tommy John surgery in 2017. ❖ The Great **Chase Johnson** Starting Experiment finally got canceled in season four, and like most shows it probably went a year too long. The strikeouts worryingly vanished in 2016, but his ground-ball rate returned and that's his hypothetical bread and butter. ❖ One of the rare 2015 breakout stories of the Giants' system, former 22nd rounder **Jordan Johnson** was a popular sleeper on last year's prospect lists. He will be less popular this year. The hope is that his diminished arsenal was brought on by fatigue caused by a rare injury-free workload. ❖ **Rodolfo Martinez** can hit triple-digits on his fastball! Unfortunately, that doesn't mean he always does, in the same sense that you can hit half-court shots. ❖ If it's better to burn out than fade away, **Vin Mazzaro** took the advice literally, giving up nine runs in one-third of an inning before getting outrighted to Triple-A. He's only 29, though, so like Neil Young, he'll find a way to stick around forever. ❖ **Reyes Moronta** may not sound like a person or look like a pitcher, but he struck out more than 14 per nine in the Cal League on the strength of a mid-90s fastball and a biting slider. ❖ After missing most of two years to Tommy John, 41-year-old **Joe Nathan** pitched 4.1 innings of scoreless middle relief in September. If this proves to be the end (he vows to take another shot at age 42), it's not a fitting end to a great career, but it's a fine one. ❖ **Daniel Slania** comes equipped with a low-90s fastball, a quick whip-like slider, an anonymous changeup and a permanent day-old stubble. His is a life destined for middle relief, but he'll get to wear a big-league uniform soon. ❖ **Chris Stratton**'s ancestry may or may not link back to a small village in southwest England called Stratton-on-the-Fosse. In case there's a connection: It's a quiet, unspectacular village that once housed a thriving coal mining industry, but is no longer productive.

SEATTLE MARINERS

Essay by Kate Preusser

*Player comments by Meg Rowley, Brendan Gawlowski
and BP staff*

MARINERS PROSPECTUS
2016 W-L: 86-76, 2ND IN AL WEST

Pythag	.539	9th	DER	.708	8th
RS/G	4.74	6th	B-Age	30.5	30th
RA/G	4.36	12th	P-Age	28.9	25th
TAv	.265	9th	Salary	$142.3M	12th
BRR	-15.3	29th	M$/MW	$3.4M	16th
TAv-P	.259	13th	DL Days	1094	17th
FIP	4.26	17th	$ on DL	10%	10th

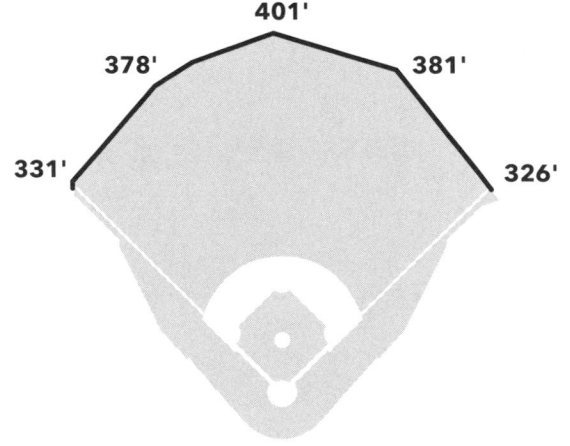

Outfield wall profile: **8'**

Three-Year Park Factors

Runs	Runs/RH	Runs/LH	HR/RH	HR/LH
95	95	95	101	105

Top Hitter WARP	6.9	Kyle Seager
Top Pitcher WARP	3.1	James Paxton
Top Prospect		Tyler O'Neill

Tolstoy said there are only two stories. Either someone goes on a journey, or a stranger comes to town. Jerry Dipoto's arrival in Seattle echoes this ur-narrative. After years of being stranded in the deserts of ineptitude like the baserunners the Mariners love to leave behind, a handsome, charismatic stranger came to town, speaking a new language of advanced stats and defensive shifts, promising to lead Seattle to the playoffs.

The three eternal truths of Seattle: Umbrellas are for tourists; the 405 is undriveable during daylight hours; the Mariners are bad. In the first four seasons of their existence, the Mariners lost 400 games. They once had a manager who left a spring training game mid-game to take a vacation to California. They followed five years of Gargamel cosplayer Bill Bavasi with eight years of missing *Guess Who?* game piece Jack Zduriencik, which left the team with little depth, no real farm system and several unwieldy contracts, including one that consistently rates as one of the biggest albatrosses in baseball. After a 2015 season in which the core aged another year and underachieved in spectacular fashion, Dipoto was given the keys to the franchise and the charge of rebuilding the team while at the same time making the most of a window that isn't so much closing as it is being sucked into another dimension, *Dr. Who*-style.

Dipoto moved quickly upon his arrival in Seattle; in this version of the story, a stranger comes to town and sets it on fire. Dipoto attacked the old roster like MacArthur at Inchon, and when the dust settled, Jack Z's creaky-kneed right-hand power hitters and fringy infielders had been replaced by younger, cheaper, more athletic players who fit Jerry's saber-friendly mindset. Offloading Mark Trumbo, who went on to have a career year in Baltimore, for backup catcher Steve Clevenger, who went on to tweet his way out of a job, looks like the worst misstep of Dipoto's early season trades, but from a process standpoint—Dipoto's mantra of "younger, cheaper, more athletic" especially applies to the Mariners outfield—the move made sense. He addressed the team's lack of depth by signing players on the cheap, whether they were bounceback candidates like closer Steve Cishek or fringe arms like Nick Vincent from the Padres, and traded to get the Mariners' first athletically competent center fielder

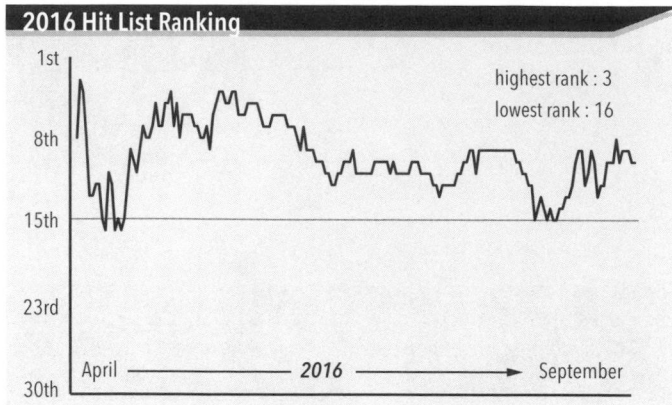

2016 Hit List Ranking

highest rank : 3
lowest rank : 16

April ——— *2016* ——→ September

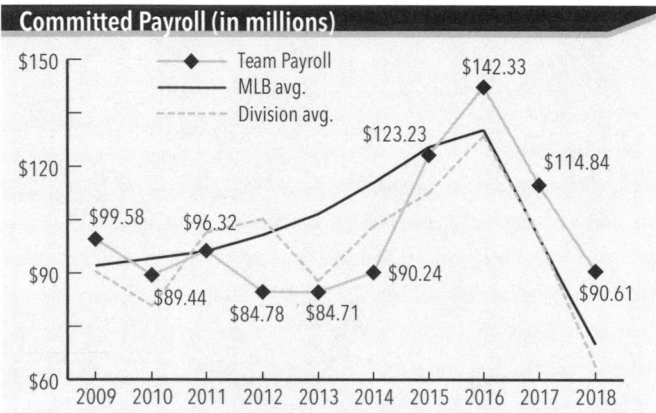

Committed Payroll (in millions)

◆ Team Payroll
— MLB avg.
--- Division avg.

$142.33
$123.23
$114.84
$99.58
$96.32
$90.24
$90.61
$89.44
$84.78 $84.71

2009 2010 2011 2012 2013 2014 2015 2016 2017 2018

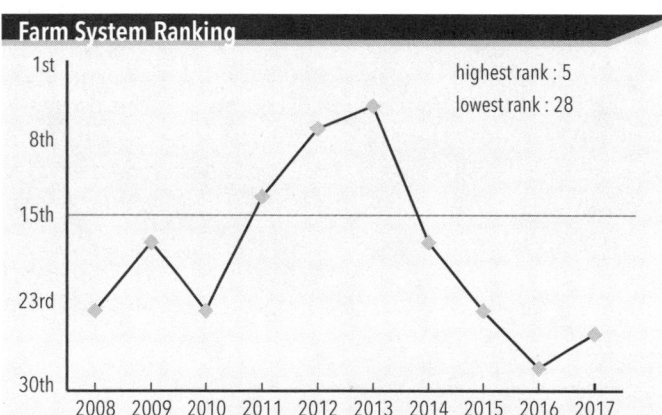

Farm System Ranking

highest rank : 5
lowest rank : 28

2008 2009 2010 2011 2012 2013 2014 2015 2016 2017

Personnel

EVP, General Manager:
Jerry Dipoto

**VP, Assistant General
Manager:**
Jeff Kingston

VP, Player Personnel:
Tom Allison

Manager:
Scott Servais

BP Alumni:
John Choiniere

in years. The team instituted the slogan "Control the Zone" and began preaching improving walks and cutting down on strikeouts across levels to improve on-base percentage (and improve it did, fifteen points above last year's mark and twenty-five points better than the 2014 team, which just missed the playoffs). One hallmark of Dipoto's leadership is a commitment to state things clearly, and then follow through on that. He identifies a need, he moves to fill the need and he moves on.

Most importantly, Dipoto looked at maximizing the assets the team did have. Along with new manager Scott Servais, Dipoto instituted a clubhouse culture that focused on building team chemistry through friendly hitting competitions, pool tournaments and daily getting-to-know-you meetings during Spring Training. The team kept up those activities throughout the season, with things like the Mariners Olympics, "dress where you're from" day and the Swelmet—a Darth Vader helmet painted in vintage Mariners colors that Robinson Canó bought off a fan which became a totem for the season, awarded after each win by new third base coach Manny Acta to the game's MVP. Dipoto doesn't get credit for signing Canó and Nelson Cruz, but he and Servais do get credit for maximizing the pair's leadership abilities, doing things like assigning each to captain a team for a situational hitting drill (losers buy dinner). Good clubhouse culture is often a byproduct of success; Dipoto and Servais attempted to reverse-engineer success by instilling that culture early on. Dysfunction often works in silence; Dipoto and Servais emphasized communication and clarity. This also addressed problems that had cropped up in the clubhouse previously, whether it was Mike Zunino hearing disjointed messaging about how to fix his plate approach—leading to a finish below the Mendoza line—or former third base coach Andy Van Slyke upbraiding Cano for his attempt to help struggling shortstop Brad Miller. The tension in the "stranger comes to town" narrative is based on taboo, an outsider intruding and upsetting the status quo, but by definition it takes a stranger to problematize that status quo in the first place.

After an injury-plagued and personally devastating 2015, Canó rebounded in 2016 to be the Mariners' second-most valuable player by WARP, hitting a career-best 39 home runs. The Mariners saw tremendous offensive production from their "big three" of Cano, Cruz and Kyle Seager, and new signing Leonys Martin complemented his above-average defense with a triple-slash line that was a significant improvement on his black hole of a 2015. Norichika Aoki posted a dreadful first half and spent some time in the minors before re-joining the team and hitting well after the All-Star Break, helping solidify an outfield with a history of offensive underachievement.

Other signings didn't work out as well. Adam Lind, brought in to replace Logan Morrison, was an unmitigated disaster at the plate, even if he provided some memorable walk-off moments. Wade Miley handed out home runs like free samples at Costco and was flipped to Baltimore late in the season for Ariel Miranda, who had the same home run issues but at a much cheaper price tag. New closer Steve Cishek struggled down the stretch and lost his job to phenom Edwin Diaz.

One thing Dipoto showed was an ability to be flexible and react quickly to problems using all of his admittedly limited organizational depth. There was little hesitation in spelling underachieving players in Triple-A, or promoting young talent straight from Double-A, as in the case of Diaz or stocky fireballer Dan Altavilla, both of whom helped solidify a sagging bullpen. There was only so much he could do, however, with a pitching rotation that was marked by inconsistency and poor health, even as James Paxton emerged as a legitimate ace, flashing a big fastball and nasty cutter. Thanks mostly to uneven pitching performances, the Mariners again fell short of their postseason ambitions, a reminder that change might come quickly when a stranger comes to town, but preparing a journey into October takes time.

However, time is not on Dipoto's side. Paxton's performance was exciting, but thanks to nagging injuries he enters his age-28 season having started 20 games in the majors just once. Of the big three only Seager is under 30, and he is teetering on the brink of having that crystal in his hand light up red. Félix Hernández is only 30, but his best years may be behind him barring a radical new approach to his arsenal. After all, declining velocity and failing command make for interesting bedfellows. If literature only has two stories, baseball has three: the so-called "success cycle," in which teams are either competing, building or rebuilding. Thanks to this strong core, the Mariners should be a competing team, but this core has has been unable yet to drive the Mariners into the playoffs. They came close in 2014 and 2016, but even a Wild Card berth has remained out of reach. The Mariners, then, find themselves in a middle place. Theoretically, they are a competing team, but they are still searching for the right combination of pieces on the MLB roster to keep pace with the juggernaut Astros or Rangers. However, they also lack sufficient prospects to be considered a building or rebuilding team. Dipoto has done much to address the Mariners' weak farm, but growing crops takes time, as does reversing a cycle of failure that saw the system register a combined .400 winning percentage in 2015.

But maybe Tolstoy was wrong. Maybe there are more than two stories. Maybe someone goes on a trip, but the destination won't be clear for months or years, if there is a clear-cut destination at all. Maybe a stranger doesn't come to town so much as the town comes to the stranger. Maybe a team isn't always in a defined stage of the success cycle, but sitting uncomfortably in that middle place. Maybe that's okay. Comfort can be the enemy of innovation. After the aristocratic, cosseted Tolstoy would come writers violently repressed by their government, and their relation to narrative was much more tenuous. Joseph Brodsky, one of these writers, notes, "In the business of writing, what one accumulates is not experience but uncertainties."

Life offers no guarantees, and our greatest arts—and certainly baseball is one of them—attest to that. If there are more than two stories in literature, maybe there are also more stories in baseball. You acquire a glove-first centerfielder and he hits 15 home runs; you sign a contact-oriented OBP machine and he posts the first double-digit strikeout rate of his career. Reliable arms fail; others emerge from nowhere flashing tongues of flame. In every season, storms arise, but a team that's been solidly built is ready to withstand those storms and re-direct their season's story. Uncertainties pile up and in that lack of easy answers, new answers emerge. The power of rejecting narrative structures is the power of rejecting those who would tell your story for you, and it's a power Dipoto & Co. must harness if they want to claim for baseball a city that has lived too long with its nose pressed to the glass of other teams' successes. ■

—Kate Preusser is the managing editor
at Lookout Landing

HITTERS

Braden Bishop   CF

Born: 8/22/93   Age: 23   Bats: R   Throws: R   Height: 6'1"   Weight: 190   Entered Pro Ball: Round 3, 2015 Draft (#94 overall)

YEAR	TEAM	LVL	AGE	PA	R	2B	3B	HR	RBI	BB	K	SB	CS	AVG/OBP/SLG	TAv	VORP	BABIP	BRR	FRAA	WARP
2015	EVE	A-	21	248	34	8	1	2	22	5	33	13	3	.320/.367/.393	.285	14.9	.368	1.2	CF(51): 9.8 • LF(2): -0.2	2.6
2016	CLN	A	22	284	38	5	1	1	21	25	48	6	1	.290/.363/.331	.284	15.4	.355	1.5	CF(40): -0.4 • LF(14): -0.9	1.5
2016	BAK	A+	22	184	19	6	0	2	22	11	39	2	0	.247/.300/.319	.262	4.6	.310	-1.1	CF(34): -3.1 • RF(7): -0.7	0.1
2017	SEA	MLB	23	250	26	8	1	5	22	12	62	1	0	.230/.279/.337	.217	-2.4	.285	-0.3	CF -1 • LF -0	-0.4
2018	SEA	MLB	24	306	33	10	1	7	30	16	74	1	0	.233/.285/.347	.225	-3.6	.285	-0.5	CF -1 • LF 0	-0.5

Breakout: 2%   Improve: 6%   Collapse: 2%   Attrition: 5%   MLB: 8%   *Comparables: Travis Jankowski, Josh Anderson, Ryan LaMarre*

On the field, Bishop is a 70 runner with good instincts and a strong arm. In other words, he's a natural center fielder. At the plate, he's an aggressive—if not ill-disciplined—hitter with a short cut built to hit line drives. He has enough strength to knock a few mistakes out of the yard, but he's rapped fewer and fewer line drives at each passing level. Bishop is still a decent bet to reach the big leagues, but it's getting harder to imagine him settling in as a starter.

Away from the diamond, Bishop's grassroots 4Mom foundation—part charity, part Alzheimer's awareness movement—makes him an easy prospect to root for. He started 4Mom in college on behalf of his ailing mother and the movement has only gained steam over the past few years.

Robinson Cano   2B

Born: 10/22/82   Age: 34   Bats: L   Throws: R   Height: 6'0"   Weight: 210   Entered Pro Ball: International Free Agent, 2001

YEAR	TEAM	LVL	AGE	PA	R	2B	3B	HR	RBI	BB	K	SB	CS	AVG/OBP/SLG	TAv	VORP	BABIP	BRR	FRAA	WARP
2014	SEA	MLB	31	665	77	37	2	14	82	61	68	10	3	.314/.382/.454	.317	54.1	.335	2.8	2B(150): 2.7	6.3
2015	SEA	MLB	32	674	82	34	1	21	79	43	107	2	6	.287/.334/.446	.285	30.8	.316	-2.6	2B(149): -2.0	3.1
2016	SEA	MLB	33	715	107	33	2	39	103	47	100	0	1	.298/.350/.533	.299	46.0	.299	-1.7	2B(157): 4.4	5.2
2017	SEA	MLB	34	690	84	35	1	26	95	55	98	4	3	.293/.354/.478	.294	48.0	.311	-1.8	2B 0	4.7
2018	SEA	MLB	35	595	81	30	1	21	80	48	86	2	2	.291/.353/.470	.285	33.2	.311	-0.2	2B 0	3.6

Breakout: 0%   Improve: 42%   Collapse: 6%   Attrition: 13%   MLB: 98%   *Comparables: Chase Utley, Ben Zobrist, Paul Molitor*

And, breathe. The back end of Cano's contract was always going to look bad, but the first half of 2015 raised the troubling specter that it was going to look bad right now, another unfortunate Mariners contract and another hitter eventually swallowed by Safeco. 2015 Cano was sapped of much of his power; 2016 Cano set a personal best for home runs. 2015 Cano was obviously limited in the field; 2016 Cano returned to virtuoso form, rendering the hustle in smooth and casual flicks of the wrist. 2015 Cano inspired worried talk of "cliffs" and "decline" and conflict with former Seattle coaches; 2016 Cano finished 8th in AL MVP voting, flashing that smile throughout. Regaining his health and home run stroke gave the Mariners their first taste of the Cano they expected in 2014, all iridescent cool and bat drops that couldn't help but recall another left-handed bat of yore, though he wore *his* cap forward. If he was slightly off the pace of the New York Cano Show, no one really minded. It was nice to breathe again.

Nelson Cruz   DH

Born: 7/1/80   Age: 36   Bats: R   Throws: R   Height: 6'2"   Weight: 230   Entered Pro Ball: International Free Agent, 1998

YEAR	TEAM	LVL	AGE	PA	R	2B	3B	HR	RBI	BB	K	SB	CS	AVG/OBP/SLG	TAv	VORP	BABIP	BRR	FRAA	WARP
2014	BAL	MLB	33	678	87	32	2	40	108	55	140	4	5	.271/.333/.525	.313	38.8	.288	-4.0	LF(60): -0.5 • RF(11): -0.4	4.2
2015	SEA	MLB	34	655	90	22	1	44	93	59	164	3	2	.302/.369/.566	.331	54.0	.350	-0.2	RF(80): -4.0	5.4
2016	SEA	MLB	35	667	96	27	1	43	105	62	159	2	0	.287/.360/.555	.316	41.4	.320	-5.1	RF(48): -5.3	3.7
2017	SEA	MLB	36	640	84	26	1	35	101	52	155	2	2	.264/.329/.496	.290	30.2	.299	-1.5	RF -2	3.0
2018	SEA	MLB	37	489	70	20	1	26	76	41	122	1	1	.255/.323/.483	.279	19.4	.292	-1.9	RF -2	1.9

Breakout: 0%   Improve: 27%   Collapse: 11%   Attrition: 7%   MLB: 88%   *Comparables: Carlos Delgado, David Ortiz, Joe Adcock*

There is a moment in *A Charlie Brown Christmas* when a nonplussed Sally, dictating a Christmas list full of $10s and $20s, explains to her brother, "All I want is what I have coming to me…all I want is my fair share." For years all Mariners management wanted was right-handed power, and all Mariners fans wanted was a designated hitter who actually hit. With Edgar Martinez's glory days in the rear view and the intervening years littered with failed experiments and Jesus Montero, surely they had it coming to them. Cruz proved to be an answer to both wishes, shifting primarily to DH in 2016 and managing the transition just fine. He posted his third straight season with 40 or more home runs and if his numbers dipped a bit, they were still impressive enough so as not to suggest a looming swoon. His boomstick is no small part of what's keeping the Mariners' window for contention wedged open, and Mariners fans and brass alike hope their Christmas gifts come a bit early, say in October.

Benjamin Gamel   OF

Born: 5/17/92   Age: 25   Bats: L   Throws: L   Height: 5'11"   Weight: 185   Entered Pro Ball: Round 10, 2010 Draft (#325 overall)

YEAR	TEAM	LVL	AGE	PA	R	2B	3B	HR	RBI	BB	K	SB	CS	AVG/OBP/SLG	TAv	VORP	BABIP	BRR	FRAA	WARP
2014	TRN	AA	22	586	58	31	3	2	51	36	88	13	5	.261/.308/.340	.238	-0.3	.306	1.0	LF(99): -4.5 • CF(16): -1.7	-0.7
2015	SWB	AAA	23	551	77	28	14	10	64	46	108	13	5	.300/.348/.472	.293	34.6	.364	1.8	CF(74): 0.9 • LF(33): 3.8	4.4
2016	NYA	MLB	24	10	1	0	0	0	0	1	1	0	0	.125/.222/.125	.184	-0.4	.143	0.2	RF(5): -0.5	-0.1
2016	SWB	AAA	24	533	80	26	5	6	51	43	94	19	8	.308/.365/.420	.289	34.1	.370	4.6	CF(70): -7.7 • LF(25): 0.2	2.6
2016	SEA	MLB	24	47	8	2	0	1	5	5	15	0	0	.200/.289/.325	.246	0.5	.292	0.1	RF(24): -1.2 • LF(2): -0.4	-0.1
2017	SEA	MLB	25	331	36	15	3	7	34	23	75	6	3	.255/.308/.394	.250	7.1	.312	0.2	LF 1 • CF -0	0.6
2018	SEA	MLB	26	462	53	21	4	12	52	34	109	8	4	.254/.313/.405	.249	6.4	.313	0.5	LF 2 • CF 0	0.9

Breakout: 11%   Improve: 43%   Collapse: 9%   Attrition: 43%   MLB: 64%   *Comparables: Reymond Fuentes, Ben Francisco, Shane Victorino*

Gamel, acquired from the Yankees after the All-Star break, is going to get a shot to anchor a corner outfield spot with Dipoto and Co. seemingly confident in his ability to transfer his minor league success to Safeco's expanse. Gamel shows good instincts in the outfield, which makes up for a lack of plus speed, and can conceivably play across the grass. He doesn't hit for much power, and what there is will come in the form of doubles and triples. The mishmash of Seth Smith, Danny Valencia and fellow youngster Guillermo Heredia is there if he falters, but if Gamel can pull off that hair, holding down an outfield spot seems doable.

Franklin Gutierrez   RF

Born: 2/21/83   Age: 34   Bats: R   Throws: R   Height: 6'2"   Weight: 200   Entered Pro Ball: International Free Agent, 2000

YEAR	TEAM	LVL	AGE	PA	R	2B	3B	HR	RBI	BB	K	SB	CS	AVG/OBP/SLG	TAv	VORP	BABIP	BRR	FRAA	WARP
2015	TAC	AAA	32	209	34	12	0	7	31	23	43	2	0	.317/.402/.500	.315	16.8	.379	1.2	LF(29): -0.5 • CF(1): 0.3	1.7
2015	SEA	MLB	32	189	27	11	0	15	35	14	54	0	0	.292/.354/.620	.334	16.8	.340	-0.7	LF(42): 3.7 • RF(4): -0.1	2.2
2016	SEA	MLB	33	283	33	9	0	14	39	29	85	1	0	.246/.329/.452	.272	9.9	.309	1.2	RF(64): -4.2 • LF(9): 0.1	0.6
2017	SEA	MLB	34	272	32	12	0	12	38	21	77	1	0	.242/.307/.439	.257	7.3	.297	0.2	RF -2 • LF 0	0.7
2018	SEA	MLB	35	250	32	11	0	11	33	19	71	0	0	.236/.300/.423	.251	3.2	.292	0.1	RF -2 • LF 0	0.2

Breakout: 3%   Improve: 33%   Collapse: 11%   Attrition: 24%   MLB: 84%   *Comparables: Justin Ruggiano, Jermaine Dye, Aaron Guiel*

Given almost 100 more plate appearances in 2016, Gutierrez wasn't quite able to replicate his 2015 success, but he remains a useful player. With the addition of Danny Valencia, an upgrade over the player Gutierrez has aged into, he sets off for his fourth organization—bet you forgot he was part of the Milton Bradley-to-L.A. deal too. After a parade of maladies that would have made a Greek chorus accuse the baseball gods of being a bit too on the nose, the man once known as "Death to Flying Things" might be happy just to escape with all his limbs intact.

Mitch Haniger   CF

Born: 12/23/90   Age: 26   Bats: R   Throws: R   Height: 6'2"   Weight: 215   Entered Pro Ball: Round 1, 2012 Draft (#38 overall)

YEAR	TEAM	LVL	AGE	PA	R	2B	3B	HR	RBI	BB	K	SB	CS	AVG/OBP/SLG	TAv	VORP	BABIP	BRR	FRAA	WARP
2014	HUN	AA	23	271	41	7	1	10	34	19	41	4	0	.255/.316/.416	.281	11.3	.267	-0.4	RF(47): -3.2 • CF(25): 0.0	0.9
2014	MOB	AA	23	30	5	3	0	0	5	3	4	0	0	.333/.433/.458	.362	4.6	.381	0.9	RF(7): 0.6	0.6
2015	MOB	AA	24	174	23	10	1	1	19	16	32	4	4	.281/.351/.379	.281	8.6	.341	0.2	CF(38): -1.9 • LF(12): 1.6	0.9
2015	VIS	A+	24	226	40	16	3	12	36	17	39	8	2	.332/.381/.619	.368	30.7	.353	1.4	RF(24): 2.1 • CF(21): -0.8	3.4
2016	MOB	AA	25	236	21	14	2	5	30	30	37	4	3	.294/.407/.462	.317	17.9	.340	-0.9	LF(32): -2.6 • CF(16): -1.2	1.5
2016	RNO	AAA	25	312	58	20	3	20	64	39	62	8	1	.341/.428/.670	.360	43.5	.373	3.4	RF(34): 1.5 • CF(34): -0.4	4.6
2016	ARI	MLB	25	123	9	2	1	5	17	12	27	0	0	.229/.309/.404	.250	2.3	.256	0.2	CF(22): 1.6 • LF(9): 0.1	0.4
2017	SEA	MLB	26	229	28	9	1	9	31	20	52	2	1	.253/.326/.448	.276	10.7	.290	-0.2	LF -2	0.8
2018	SEA	MLB	27	395	53	16	2	16	54	36	93	4	2	.255/.333/.452	.273	14.4	.298	-0.2	LF -3	1.2

Breakout: 4%   Improve: 35%   Collapse: 16%   Attrition: 28%   MLB: 74%   *Comparables: Casper Wells, Ben Francisco, Chip Ambres*

Haniger's breakout was the surprise of Arizona's season. He orchestrated his 2015 demotion to the California League to rework his swing and the results speak for themselves. Now with a bigger stride, Haniger raked across two levels before he earned a big-league cup of coffee and acquitted himself well with an average exit velocity well above average. He gets on base, can cover center field and projects as a plus defender in a corner. He's a late bloomer, but Haniger has the tools to be an average everyday player just a year after it appeared his career might be all but over.

Guillermo Heredia   OF

Born: 1/31/91   Age: 26   Bats: R   Throws: L   Height: 5'10"   Weight: 180   Entered Pro Ball: International Free Agent, 2016

YEAR	TEAM	LVL	AGE	PA	R	2B	3B	HR	RBI	BB	K	SB	CS	AVG/OBP/SLG	TAv	VORP	BABIP	BRR	FRAA	WARP
2016	WTN	AA	25	260	39	7	2	2	34	36	32	2	5	.293/.405/.376	.306	17.7	.322	-1.0	CF(41): -2.3 • RF(12): -0.0	1.6
2016	TAC	AAA	25	157	27	6	1	2	13	12	15	3	0	.312/.378/.413	.323	17.1	.333	2.1	CF(32): 0.5 • LF(3): 0.1	1.9
2016	SEA	MLB	25	107	12	3	0	1	12	12	15	1	1	.250/.349/.315	.248	0.4	.289	-0.6	LF(35): 3.8 • RF(14): -0.2	0.4
2017	SEA	MLB	26	295	33	11	1	6	30	30	48	2	1	.261/.348/.387	.270	9.4	.295	-0.6	RF 2 • LF 1	1.2
2018	SEA	MLB	27	334	42	12	1	8	36	34	57	2	1	.258/.348/.388	.265	9.0	.292	-0.7	RF 2 • LF 1	1.4

Breakout: 3%   Improve: 40%   Collapse: 16%   Attrition: 26%   MLB: 69%   *Comparables: Brett Gardner, L.J. Hoes, Bryan Petersen*

What a difference a year makes. Entering last spring training Heredia had a lot of catching up to do after nearly two years out of baseball following his defection from Cuba in 2015, and it showed. Now he's one of the young, athletic, defensively-minded outfielders Jerry Dipoto mentions as potential anchors. Heredia has good speed and instincts in the field, which should allow him to cover a lot of Safeco grass, but he still has work to do offensively. The swing is short and a bit stiff, although he didn't hit terribly over 45 games last year. He's probably a fourth outfielder, but the good defensive profile—combined with a more workable bat—is that of someone who could find his way to a larger role.

Chris Iannetta   C

Born: 4/8/83   Age: 34   Bats: R   Throws: R   Height: 6'0"   Weight: 230   Entered Pro Ball: Round 4, 2004 Draft (#110 overall)

YEAR	TEAM	LVL	AGE	PA	R	2B	3B	HR	RBI	BB	K	SB	CS	AVG/OBP/SLG	TAv	VORP	BABIP	BRR	FRAA	WARP
2014	ANA	MLB	31	373	41	22	0	7	43	54	91	3	0	.252/.373/.392	.298	28.3	.329	-0.3	C(104): -9.5	2.1
2015	ANA	MLB	32	317	28	10	0	10	34	41	83	0	1	.188/.293/.335	.230	3.3	.225	-0.8	C(85): 14.2 • 1B(2): 0.0	1.9
2016	SEA	MLB	33	338	23	14	0	7	24	38	83	0	0	.210/.303/.329	.231	0.2	.266	-5.1	C(93): -15.6	-1.6
2017	*SEA*	*MLB*	*34*	*314*	*36*	*12*	*0*	*9*	*34*	*43*	*82*	*1*	*0*	*.220/.331/.364*	*.248*	*10.7*	*.279*	*-1.5*	*C -6*	*0.5*
2018	*SEA*	*MLB*	*35*	*258*	*31*	*9*	*0*	*7*	*26*	*35*	*69*	*0*	*0*	*.213/.323/.347*	*.243*	*3.8*	*.274*	*-1.3*	*C -6*	*-0.2*

Breakout: 0%   Improve: 38%   Collapse: 18%   Attrition: 18%   MLB: 90%   *Comparables: Bob Brenly, Ernie Whitt, Darrell Porter*

Every exercise in Jerry Dipoto regime building features two things: trading Mark Trumbo and acquiring Iannetta. Mariners Jerry proved to be no different, with Dipoto signing the veteran backstop to spell Mike Zunino's re-education in Tacoma. The 2015 version of Iannetta was one of baseball's best framers; the 2016 version of Iannetta was one of the very worst. That sort of variation will likely pique the interest of many a sabermetric hobbyist trying to unpack the mysteries of framing, but after a season spent hovering around the Mendoza line the Mariners were thoroughly disinterested in participating in any such experimentation, declining Iannetta's $4.25 million option for 2017.

YEAR	TEAM	P. COUNT	FRM RUNS	BLK RUNS	THRW RUNS	TOT RUNS
2014	ANA	13871	-7.3	-0.9	0.2	-8.0
2015	ANA	11581	14.4	-0.8	-0.6	13.1
2016	SEA	13011	-14.4	-1.5	0.7	-15.2
2017	*SEA*	*11911*	*-4.6*	*-1.2*	*0.0*	*-5.8*
2018	*SEA*	*9775*	*-4.8*	*-1.2*	*-0.1*	*-6.0*

Dae-Ho Lee   1B

Born: 6/21/82   Age: 35   Bats: R   Throws: R   Height: 6'4"   Weight: 250   Entered Pro Ball: International Free Agent, 2016

YEAR	TEAM	LVL	AGE	PA	R	2B	3B	HR	RBI	BB	K	SB	CS	AVG/OBP/SLG	TAv	VORP	BABIP	BRR	FRAA	WARP
2016	TAC	AAA	34	29	3	4	0	2	6	2	2	0	0	.519/.552/.889	.518	7.5	.522	-0.6	1B(3): 0.1	0.8
2016	SEA	MLB	34	317	33	9	0	14	49	20	74	0	0	.253/.312/.428	.264	2.1	.294	-2.9	1B(84): -4.0	-0.2
2017	*SEA*	*MLB*	*35*	*250*	*29*	*10*	*0*	*10*	*34*	*17*	*58*	*0*	*0*	*.255/.314/.437*	*.260*	*4.0*	*.297*	*-1.1*	*1B -4*	*0.0*
2018	*SEA*	*MLB*	*36*	*182*	*23*	*7*	*0*	*7*	*24*	*13*	*44*	*0*	*0*	*.244/.305/.419*	*.254*	*0.2*	*.286*	*-0.9*	*1B -3*	*-0.3*

Breakout: 0%   Improve: 19%   Collapse: 12%   Attrition: 19%   MLB: 84%   *Comparables: Jeff Baker, Olmedo Saenz, Cliff Johnson*

Back when the Mariners played in the Kingdome, there was a mid-tier department store called the Bon Marché known for its catchy jingles and deep discounts. One such jingle was set to the tune of "The Banana Boat Song." *Day-o, One Day Sale, One day only at The Bon Marché! Save 20, 30, 40 percent! Saturday only at the Bon Marché.* Lee's year was a tale of two halves. Through June the corpulent Korean slugger was mashing, with almost a third of his hits going for extra bases. After June he stopped hitting almost entirely. He's one of the slowest players in the game and while his defense at first was good for someone who looks like Dae-Ho Lee, it was pretty uninspiring by normal first base standards. So not hitting isn't going to cut it.

Why the digression into department store jingles? Dae-Ho walked up to Harry Belafonte's song and with every drop in OBP you could almost hear the Safeco crowd filling in the blanks after the Dae-o. *Down 20, 30, 40 percent!* We never do rid ourselves of those childhood earworms.

Kyle Lewis   OF

Born: 7/13/95   Age: 21   Bats: R   Throws: R   Height: 6'4"   Weight: 210   Entered Pro Ball: Round 1, 2016 Draft (#11 overall)

YEAR	TEAM	LVL	AGE	PA	R	2B	3B	HR	RBI	BB	K	SB	CS	AVG/OBP/SLG	TAv	VORP	BABIP	BRR	FRAA	WARP
2016	EVE	A-	20	135	26	8	5	3	26	16	22	3	0	.299/.385/.530	.342	12.8	.344	-1.2	CF(25): 0.1	1.4
2017	*SEA*	*MLB*	*21*	*250*	*23*	*9*	*1*	*7*	*27*	*16*	*71*	*1*	*0*	*.209/.266/.345*	*.212*	*-3.1*	*.268*	*-0.2*	*CF 1*	*-0.2*
2018	*SEA*	*MLB*	*22*	*299*	*33*	*11*	*2*	*9*	*33*	*20*	*82*	*1*	*0*	*.218/.276/.369*	*.226*	*-2.5*	*.274*	*-0.3*	*CF 1*	*-0.1*

Breakout: 2%   Improve: 5%   Collapse: 0%   Attrition: 3%   MLB: 5%   *Comparables: Abraham Almonte, Domonic Brown, Daniel Fields*

One of the most pernicious aspects of Lewis's major knee injury—a torn ACL with all the trimmings—is that he had little reason for being in Everett at all on that fateful July day. It's not uncommon for a first-round pick to spend a couple of weeks in short season ball, where he can get his feet wet at the professional level and adjust to using a wood bat consistently. But Lewis was long past that point. He had hit homers, roped line drives to all fields, stolen bases and proved that Everett's cozy ballpark was too small to test his range in the outfield. Even before he got hurt, evaluators were mixed on whether he could stick in center long term and, sadly, the injury probably forces him to right field sooner rather than later. With plus power potential—he'll need to fill out a bit to get there, but he has a great frame for adding productive weight—and a decent idea of what he's doing at the plate, Lewis still has the ingredients needed to be a first-division regular. It might take a little longer than we thought, though, and we won't know for sure until he's back on the field.

Luis Liberato   OF

Born: 12/18/95   Age: 21   Bats: L   Throws: L   Height: 6'1"   Weight: 175   Entered Pro Ball: International Free Agent, 2013

YEAR	TEAM	LVL	AGE	PA	R	2B	3B	HR	RBI	BB	K	SB	CS	AVG/OBP/SLG	TAv	VORP	BABIP	BRR	FRAA	WARP
2015	CLN	A	19	32	3	1	1	0	0	2	10	1	0	.133/.188/.233	.161	-1.8	.200	0.5	CF(7): -0.6	-0.3
2015	EVE	A-	19	215	34	10	5	5	31	24	47	10	3	.260/.341/.453	.287	12.8	.318	1.9	CF(21): 1.9 • LF(18): 1.3	1.7
2016	CLN	A	20	432	65	19	8	2	29	47	100	4	2	.258/.340/.368	.285	19.9	.347	-0.4	CF(45): 2.5 • LF(27): 3.6	2.9
2017	*SEA*	*MLB*	*21*	*250*	*26*	*9*	*2*	*5*	*22*	*19*	*76*	*1*	*0*	*.206/.271/.331*	*.210*	*-4.1*	*.276*	*-0.1*	*CF 2 • LF 1*	*-0.1*
2018	*SEA*	*MLB*	*22*	*354*	*38*	*13*	*3*	*9*	*37*	*28*	*105*	*1*	*0*	*.215/.280/.358*	*.224*	*-4.4*	*.281*	*-0.2*	*CF 3 • LF 2*	*0.0*

Breakout: 2%   Improve: 4%   Collapse: 0%   Attrition: 3%   MLB: 6%   *Comparables: Joe Benson, Daniel Fields, Xavier Avery*

Playing in cold temperatures for the first time and facing the best competition of his life, Liberato struggled to get going in the Midwest league. He warmed with the weather though, and his second half surge was enough to remind everyone why he's one of the few toolsy youngsters with upside in Seattle's system. He's an above-average runner with a throwing arm a tick better than that. He can hit the ball hard to all fields and there's just enough loft in his swing to keep pitchers honest. Liberato's future hinges on his response to the classic Jack Sprat Conundrum: if he bulks up he might develop enough power for a corner, whereas if he stays lean there's a shot he could handle center and earn a job as a fourth outfielder. Either way, if he doesn't close the holes in his swing he might not make it out of Double-A.

Adam Lind   1B

Born: 7/17/83   Age: 33   Bats: L   Throws: L   Height: 6'2"   Weight: 195   Entered Pro Ball: Round 3, 2004 Draft (#83 overall)

YEAR	TEAM	LVL	AGE	PA	R	2B	3B	HR	RBI	BB	K	SB	CS	AVG/OBP/SLG	TAv	VORP	BABIP	BRR	FRAA	WARP
2014	TOR	MLB	30	318	38	24	2	6	40	28	48	0	0	.321/.381/.479	.306	19.6	.369	2.9	1B(47): -1.2	2.0
2015	MIL	MLB	31	572	72	32	0	20	87	66	100	0	0	.277/.360/.460	.294	24.6	.309	-0.2	1B(138): -6.9	1.9
2016	SEA	MLB	32	430	48	17	0	20	58	26	89	0	1	.239/.286/.431	.240	-4.7	.259	-0.7	1B(101): -3.3	-0.8
2017	SEA	MLB	33	433	50	19	1	16	58	39	87	0	0	.266/.332/.444	.267	12.3	.302	0.7	1B -5	0.8
2018	SEA	MLB	34	316	41	13	0	11	40	28	65	0	0	.259/.325/.422	.261	4.6	.296	0.4	1B -4	0.1

Breakout: 2%   Improve: 27%   Collapse: 3%   Attrition: 12%   MLB: 95%   Comparables: Mike Sweeney, Justin Morneau, Ryan Doumit

The list of things the Mariners wanted Adam Lind to do in 2016: punish right-handed pitching, knock some home runs and play a competent first base. You know, good Adam Lind things. The list of things Adam Lind actually did in 2016: posted an on-base percentage of .287...vs. right-handed pitching, knocked some home runs, wore pants that looked uncomfortably tight and had odd little wisps of hair stick out of his cap and batting helmet. You know, bad Adam Lind things.

Leonys Martin   CF

Born: 3/6/88   Age: 29   Bats: L   Throws: R   Height: 6'2"   Weight: 200   Entered Pro Ball: International Free Agent, 2011

YEAR	TEAM	LVL	AGE	PA	R	2B	3B	HR	RBI	BB	K	SB	CS	AVG/OBP/SLG	TAv	VORP	BABIP	BRR	FRAA	WARP
2014	TEX	MLB	26	583	68	13	7	7	40	39	114	31	12	.274/.325/.364	.259	20.0	.336	4.3	CF(152): 18.4	4.3
2015	ROU	AAA	27	43	7	3	0	2	4	5	4	2	1	.297/.372/.541	.343	5.8	.281	0.8	CF(8): 2.3 • RF(1): -0.0	0.8
2015	TEX	MLB	27	310	26	12	0	5	25	16	69	14	5	.219/.264/.313	.210	-4.6	.270	1.4	CF(92): 11.6	0.7
2016	SEA	MLB	28	576	72	17	3	15	47	44	149	24	6	.247/.306/.378	.244	10.7	.313	2.5	CF(143): 5.6	1.7
2017	SEA	MLB	29	584	69	21	4	13	56	40	133	26	9	.249/.302/.379	.242	11.6	.300	2.4	CF 10	1.7
2018	SEA	MLB	30	535	61	21	3	13	58	40	125	22	8	.248/.309/.387	.241	7.0	.300	2.8	CF 9	1.8

Breakout: 1%   Improve: 50%   Collapse: 8%   Attrition: 18%   MLB: 96%   Comparables: Aaron Rowand, Cameron Maybin, Angel Pagan

Our degree of satisfaction is often a function of our expectations. To wit, when your recent expectations of center field range from James Jones to Austin Jackson, Martin is a dramatic upgrade. As buy-low trades go, it is especially pleasing when competent outfield defense is acquired *for* James Jones. Martin's output in the early going raised expectations further, as he rediscovered his power and thumped nine home runs through the end of May. Pre-2015 WARP sang a siren song and Mariners fans began to crow about pulling one over on a division rival, but a hamstring injury and DL stint seemed to derail Martin's progress. Even when he returned it was obvious the injury nagged at times, and the power dried up as his bat regressed. Martin without significant power looks a lot more like the guy the Mariners thought they were acquiring, and while that's a useful player, whether fans will be satisfied with that given new expectations remains to be seen.

Taylor Motter   UT

Born: 9/18/89   Age: 27   Bats: R   Throws: R   Height: 6'1"   Weight: 195   Entered Pro Ball: Round 17, 2011 Draft (#540 overall)

YEAR	TEAM	LVL	AGE	PA	R	2B	3B	HR	RBI	BB	K	SB	CS	AVG/OBP/SLG	TAv	VORP	BABIP	BRR	FRAA	WARP
2014	MNT	AA	24	506	60	19	3	16	61	34	71	15	7	.274/.326/.436	.268	16.8	.289	1.8	RF(87): 10.5 • 2B(16): 0.6	3.2
2015	DUR	AAA	25	558	74	43	1	14	72	57	95	26	8	.292/.366/.471	.304	38.5	.332	-0.7	RF(62): 2.2 • 3B(25): 1.1	4.1
2016	TBA	MLB	26	93	11	3	0	2	9	11	19	0	1	.188/.290/.300	.228	-0.4	.217	-0.1	SS(9): -0.4 • LF(7): 0.6	0.0
2016	DUR	AAA	26	387	44	17	0	13	46	33	65	19	4	.229/.297/.389	.240	3.7	.245	-1.0	SS(37): -3.0 • 3B(25): -1.2	-0.3
2017	SEA	MLB	27	92	12	4	0	3	11	7	19	3	1	.241/.304/.411	.253	2.5	.271	0.1	LF -1 • 2B 0	0.1
2018	SEA	MLB	28	313	38	13	0	11	38	25	66	9	3	.235/.301/.403	.245	4.0	.263	0.6	LF -4 • 2B 1	0.1

Breakout: 2%   Improve: 11%   Collapse: 21%   Attrition: 25%   MLB: 42%   Comparables: Steve Tolleson, Ryan Rohlinger, Tommy Field

There's a new one almost every day: a fringe prospect that came up as a middle infielder with a bit of pop, but something breaks wrong. Maybe he's blocked, or maybe he doesn't have the footwork or arm to stick at short. But the bat might play! Our guy hits a bit at High-A or Double-A or even–in Motter's case–at Triple-A, and shows a little pop, a little speed, a little discipline. Of course, the team tries him out in both the infield and the outfield, and **bam!** All of a sudden you've got "The Next Ben Zobrist." (This happens with even more frequency for Rays, Cubs and Athletics players.) PECOTA thinks he could eventually be a slightly below-average MLB hitter, which means he could be "The Next Chris Taylor." Get over it.

Shawn O'Malley   UT

Born: 12/28/87   Age: 29   Bats: B   Throws: R   Height: 5'11"   Weight: 175   Entered Pro Ball: Round 5, 2006 Draft (#139 overall)

YEAR	TEAM	LVL	AGE	PA	R	2B	3B	HR	RBI	BB	K	SB	CS	AVG/OBP/SLG	TAv	VORP	BABIP	BRR	FRAA	WARP
2014	ARK	AA	26	41	3	0	1	0	5	6	8	1	0	.188/.308/.250	.275	1.5	.240	0.2	CF(3): -0.1 • 2B(1): 0.1	0.2
2014	SLC	AAA	26	376	60	19	9	3	38	39	44	13	4	.330/.411/.475	.302	35.5	.372	3.9	SS(56): -4.4 • 2B(13): 3.5	3.6
2014	ANA	MLB	26	16	3	0	0	0	1	0	8	2	0	.188/.188/.188	.167	-0.7	.375	0.3	LF(5): -0.8 • 2B(1): 0.0	-0.2
2015	TAC	AAA	27	344	50	11	5	5	39	19	47	20	7	.297/.345/.413	.267	13.1	.335	1.1	2B(57): -7.3 • CF(11): -1.6	0.3
2015	SEA	MLB	27	57	10	1	0	1	7	12	14	3	0	.262/.418/.357	.320	5.9	.357	1.0	CF(14): -1.4 • LF(4): 0.2	0.5
2016	TAC	AAA	28	100	15	5	1	1	13	13	18	5	1	.317/.412/.439	.327	11.9	.391	2.1	2B(13): -1.7 • SS(5): -0.7	1.0
2016	SEA	MLB	28	232	24	9	2	2	17	18	59	6	2	.229/.299/.319	.223	-2.4	.309	-1.5	SS(36): -0.5 • RF(19): 0.1	-0.4
2017	*SEA*	*MLB*	*29*	*187*	*20*	*6*	*2*	*2*	*16*	*16*	*40*	*6*	*2*	*.246/.312/.350*	*.242*	*0.3*	*.300*	*0.6*	*SS -1 • 2B -0*	*0.0*
2018	*SEA*	*MLB*	*30*	*351*	*38*	*12*	*3*	*5*	*32*	*31*	*77*	*10*	*3*	*.241/.318/.350*	*.238*	*1.8*	*.294*	*-0.8*	*SS -2 • 2B -1*	*-0.3*

Breakout: 2%   Improve: 22%   Collapse: 12%   Attrition: 25%   MLB: 61%   *Comparables:* Andrew Romine, Ezequiel Carrera, Elian Herrera

On August 6, 2016, O'Malley hit a go-ahead three-run jack, triggering a heretofore unknown clause in the Mariners bylaws that any player with a winning hit during Ken Griffey Jr. Hall of Fame Weekend automatically becomes mayor of his hometown. So Kennewick's own will have something to do when his career as a useful bench piece comes to a close, which is nice since versatile slap-hitting utility players rarely stumble into movie careers.

Tyler O'Neill   RF

Born: 6/22/95   Age: 22   Bats: R   Throws: R   Height: 5'11"   Weight: 210   Entered Pro Ball: Round 3, 2013 Draft (#85 overall)

YEAR	TEAM	LVL	AGE	PA	R	2B	3B	HR	RBI	BB	K	SB	CS	AVG/OBP/SLG	TAv	VORP	BABIP	BRR	FRAA	WARP
2014	CLN	A	19	245	31	9	0	13	38	20	79	5	0	.247/.322/.466	.294	13.7	.320	0.3	LF(36): -2.6 • RF(13): 1.4	1.3
2015	BAK	A+	20	449	68	21	2	32	87	29	137	16	5	.260/.316/.558	.322	34.6	.303	-0.7	RF(39): -0.5 • LF(35): 0.0	3.5
2016	WTN	AA	21	575	68	26	4	24	102	62	150	12	2	.293/.374/.508	.327	47.3	.364	-0.8	RF(108): -8.4 • LF(5): -0.2	4.2
2017	*SEA*	*MLB*	*22*	*250*	*32*	*9*	*1*	*14*	*38*	*18*	*84*	*3*	*1*	*.235/.299/.461*	*.260*	*7.0*	*.303*	*0.0*	*RF -2 • LF 0*	*0.6*
2018	*SEA*	*MLB*	*23*	*339*	*47*	*13*	*1*	*18*	*52*	*26*	*111*	*4*	*1*	*.238/.306/.466*	*.265*	*8.9*	*.304*	*-0.1*	*RF -3 • LF 0*	*0.7*

Breakout: 2%   Improve: 38%   Collapse: 3%   Attrition: 13%   MLB: 61%   *Comparables:* Domingo Santana, Oswaldo Arcia, Javier Baez

By any reasonable expectation 2016 should have been a difficult year for O'Neill. The jump from High-A to Double-A is notoriously difficult and many promising hitters have been stifled by the advanced arms loitering in the upper minors. O'Neill, a very young, power-first prospect with severe strikeout problems, seemed destined to struggle. He didn't. Not only did he translate his 70 raw power into games, but he did so while nearly doubling his walk rate and making more contact than he did in Bakersfield. It was a truly impressive season that firmly placed him into the discussion of baseball's best corner outfield prospects. That's not to say that O'Neill is without his warts. He doesn't recognize spin out of the hand well. He is still lured out of the strike zone too often. Despite a strong arm, he won't be an asset in the outfield. At the end of the day though, it's starting to look like O'Neill will hit just enough for the power to play as a starter in right field. Just 22 years old, he'll begin 2017 in Triple-A and could see time in the major leagues by the end of the season. He's the rare Mariners prospect to get legitimately excited about.

D.J. Peterson   1B

Born: 12/31/91   Age: 25   Bats: R   Throws: R   Height: 6'1"   Weight: 210   Entered Pro Ball: Round 1, 2013 Draft (#12 overall)

YEAR	TEAM	LVL	AGE	PA	R	2B	3B	HR	RBI	BB	K	SB	CS	AVG/OBP/SLG	TAv	VORP	BABIP	BRR	FRAA	WARP
2014	HDS	A+	22	299	51	23	1	18	73	23	65	6	0	.326/.381/.615	.318	26.4	.372	1.3	3B(37): -1.8 • 1B(8): 1.1	2.5
2014	WTN	AA	22	248	32	8	0	13	38	22	51	1	1	.261/.335/.473	.286	12.5	.283	-0.8	3B(45): -1.1 • 1B(9): 0.5	1.3
2015	WTN	AA	23	393	39	19	2	7	44	31	90	5	0	.223/.290/.346	.238	-3.6	.279	-0.9	1B(57): 1.3 • 3B(28): -2.1	-0.5
2016	WTN	AA	24	312	31	21	0	11	43	27	68	1	1	.271/.340/.466	.299	13.8	.317	-1.6	1B(62): -2.6	1.2
2016	TAC	AAA	24	192	26	7	1	8	35	11	51	0	1	.253/.307/.438	.267	3.4	.311	-0.4	1B(32): 3.9 • 3B(7): -0.2	0.7
2017	*SEA*	*MLB*	*25*	*250*	*28*	*10*	*0*	*11*	*34*	*15*	*71*	*0*	*0*	*.230/.284/.419*	*.243*	*0.3*	*.282*	*-0.5*	*1B 1 • 3B -0*	*0.1*
2018	*SEA*	*MLB*	*26*	*339*	*42*	*15*	*1*	*15*	*45*	*22*	*98*	*0*	*0*	*.229/.285/.420*	*.246*	*-1.2*	*.282*	*-0.8*	*1B 1 • 3B 0*	*0.0*

Breakout: 6%   Improve: 14%   Collapse: 4%   Attrition: 17%   MLB: 23%   *Comparables:* Andrew Brown, Brock Peterson, Garrett Jones

Few hitters in Seattle's system enjoyed a bigger rebound last year than Peterson, a bat-first prospect who forgot how to hit in 2015. He recommended hitting for power, homering 19 times across two levels before a late-summer finger injury truncated his season. Despite the bounceback it's difficult to imagine Peterson hitting enough to justify a full-time job at first base. His swing is geared more for doubles in the gap than towering fly balls, and his strikeout rate soared in Triple-A where pitchers with quality off-speed offerings exploited his tendency to chase spin out of the zone. For their part, the Mariners don't seem convinced that he'll cut it at first base either; had Peterson stayed healthy, he'd have been given time in left field to close out the season. Realistically, the upside here is a guy who can handle the short side of a cold corner platoon and fake it in an outfield corner when starters need a day off.

Herschel Powell   OF

Born: 1/14/93   Age: 24   Bats: L   Throws: L   Height: 5'10"   Weight: 185   Entered Pro Ball: Round 20, 2012 Draft (#619 overall)

YEAR	TEAM	LVL	AGE	PA	R	2B	3B	HR	RBI	BB	K	SB	CS	AVG/OBP/SLG	TAv	VORP	BABIP	BRR	FRAA	WARP
2014	BLT	A	21	312	43	7	4	3	17	53	49	16	13	.335/.452/.429	.327	29.4	.404	-2.0	CF(66): -0.2	3.0
2014	STO	A+	21	69	11	3	1	0	11	8	4	0	2	.377/.449/.459	.316	6.6	.404	0.3	CF(11): -0.6 • RF(3): 1.8	0.8
2015	MNT	AA	22	276	44	6	6	1	22	29	38	11	8	.328/.408/.416	.302	19.8	.385	1.6	CF(34): -0.2 • RF(17): 3.6	2.5
2015	DUR	AAA	22	246	22	10	3	2	18	32	41	7	6	.257/.360/.364	.259	3.4	.309	-2.3	CF(29): 3.0 • LF(22): -0.9	0.5
2016	TAC	AAA	23	277	39	9	2	3	27	22	42	10	6	.270/.326/.359	.249	5.8	.311	0.5	CF(61): -0.2	0.6
2017	*SEA*	*MLB*	*24*	*250*	*32*	*8*	*2*	*5*	*22*	*24*	*50*	*6*	*4*	*.258/.335/.379*	*.247*	*5.5*	*.307*	*-0.4*	*CF 3 • LF -0*	*0.9*
2018	*SEA*	*MLB*	*25*	*377*	*45*	*12*	*3*	*8*	*39*	*35*	*76*	*9*	*7*	*.260/.334/.385*	*.249*	*6.0*	*.306*	*0.1*	*CF 4 • LF 0*	*1.0*

Breakout: 7%   Improve: 17%   Collapse: 4%   Attrition: 21%   MLB: 43%   *Comparables:* Ezequiel Carrera, J.B. Shuck, Gary Brown

Off the field Powell had a busy year. First came his second substance-related suspension, this time an 80-game ban for taking chlorodehydromethyltestosterone. Just one of many in a head-scratching run of players caught taking long-banned anabolic steroids in 2016, Powell passionately claimed his innocence, vowing that he would "not rest until there is a full explanation for this result, which will vindicate me." Whether Powell and the rest of his dumbfounded counterparts are eventually exonerated or (more likely) not, Boog the Younger wasn't done making headlines. In winter ball he got into a fight with Phillies prospect Dylan Cozens, supposedly after poking fun of Cozens's inability to hit a breaking ball.

On the field Powell hit an empty .270. For the first time pitchers consistently exploited his willingness to work the count, and he earned the dreaded "passive, not patient" label. There's a poor man's Denard Span in here, but between a lost year developmentally and more than a few whispers about his coachability, Powell has a lot to prove in 2017. But then again, he's always been somewhat comfortable with two strikes.

Joe Rizzo   3B

Born: 3/31/98   Age: 19   Bats: L   Throws: R   Height: 5'9"   Weight: 194   Entered Pro Ball: Round 2, 2016 Draft (#50 overall)

YEAR	TEAM	LVL	AGE	PA	R	2B	3B	HR	RBI	BB	K	SB	CS	AVG/OBP/SLG	TAv	VORP	BABIP	BRR	FRAA	WARP
2017	SEA	MLB	19	250	21	8	0	6	25	15	84	0	0	.193/.244/.311	.194	-9.4	.268	-0.4	3B -4	-1.4
2018	SEA	MLB	20	320	34	11	1	9	34	21	102	1	0	.210/.265/.345	.216	-7.9	.282	-0.5	3B -5	-1.4

Breakout: 0%   Improve: 6%   Collapse: 2%   Attrition: 6%   MLB: 12%   *Comparables: Nomar Mazara, Raul Mondesi, Rougned Odor*

Rizzo isn't the world's best athlete—he's a rare big-money high school draftee with no shot to stick up the middle—but he can knock the crap out of the ball, and the scouts who know him best are impressed with his work ethic and the improvements he made defensively over the last year. Of course, he won't turn 19 until close to Opening Day and we're years from knowing if he can hang at third or have to shift to the cold corner. According to stories from his high school days, he's also the latest in a long line of baseball players who enjoy a good practical joke, having once sent a JV player on a thirty-minute hunt for left-handed curveballs. Should he reach the majors someday, he'll presumably be a club asset on social media.

Carlos Ruiz   C

Born: 1/22/79   Age: 38   Bats: R   Throws: R   Height: 5'10"   Weight: 215   Entered Pro Ball: International Free Agent, 1998

YEAR	TEAM	LVL	AGE	PA	R	2B	3B	HR	RBI	BB	K	SB	CS	AVG/OBP/SLG	TAv	VORP	BABIP	BRR	FRAA	WARP
2014	PHI	MLB	35	445	43	25	1	6	31	46	60	4	2	.252/.347/.370	.281	23.2	.281	-4.1	C(109): -8.2	1.7
2015	PHI	MLB	36	320	23	13	1	2	22	28	43	1	1	.211/.290/.285	.219	1.1	.242	0.0	C(83): -19.1	-1.9
2016	PHI	MLB	37	193	18	6	0	3	12	24	28	3	1	.261/.368/.352	.280	10.4	.299	-2.3	C(47): -4.4	0.6
2016	LAN	MLB	37	40	3	2	0	0	3	3	5	0	0	.278/.350/.333	.264	2.2	.323	0.3	C(9): -1.0	0.1
2017	SEA	MLB	38	168	16	8	0	3	17	14	24	1	1	.247/.322/.362	.249	5.3	.272	-0.3	C -7	-0.4
2018	SEA	MLB	39	115	13	5	0	2	11	9	17	1	0	.239/.316/.349	.239	1.2	.266	-0.6	C -5	-0.4

Breakout: 0%   Improve: 23%   Collapse: 13%   Attrition: 25%   MLB: 69%   *Comparables: Gregg Zaun, Mike Redmond, Scott Hatteberg*

Acquired in exchange for clubhouse leader and longest-tenured Dodger A.J. Ellis, Ruiz made his presence felt quickly, gifting a Louis Vuitton watch to Brock Stewart after he voluntarily gave up his number so Ruiz could don his no. 51. While the trade frustrated many fans, Chooch did his part against left-handed pitching after the trade, slashing .308/.379/.346 against southpaws and bashing a pinch-hit home run in the postseason. Playoff heroics and gift-giving preferences aside, Ruiz's uptick in age and downtick in power tell us that time is not on his side, and it's likely that Stewart's watch lasts longer than Ruiz's impact.

YEAR	TEAM	P. COUNT	FRM RUNS	BLK RUNS	THRW RUNS	TOT RUNS
2014	PHI	15509	-13.0	3.9	0.5	-8.6
2015	PHI	12505	-18.8	-0.1	-1.3	-20.3
2016	PHI	6968	-7.0	1.3	0.7	-4.9
2016	LAN	1291	-0.7	0.0	0.0	-0.7
2017	SEA	6195	-8.1	0.6	-0.2	-7.8
2018	SEA	4253	-6.2	0.4	-0.2	-6.0

Kyle Seager   3B

Born: 11/3/87   Age: 29   Bats: L   Throws: R   Height: 6'0"   Weight: 210   Entered Pro Ball: Round 3, 2009 Draft (#82 overall)

YEAR	TEAM	LVL	AGE	PA	R	2B	3B	HR	RBI	BB	K	SB	CS	AVG/OBP/SLG	TAv	VORP	BABIP	BRR	FRAA	WARP
2014	SEA	MLB	26	654	71	27	4	25	96	52	118	7	5	.268/.334/.454	.306	46.6	.296	-0.8	3B(157): 20.7	7.4
2015	SEA	MLB	27	686	85	37	0	26	74	54	98	6	6	.266/.328/.451	.279	31.3	.278	-2.3	3B(160): 12.9 · SS(1): 0.0	4.7
2016	SEA	MLB	28	676	89	36	3	30	99	69	108	3	1	.278/.359/.499	.293	46.4	.295	1.8	3B(156): 21.3	7.0
2017	SEA	MLB	29	673	82	32	2	26	91	60	113	6	3	.266/.337/.457	.280	32.6	.286	-1.4	3B 20	5.1
2018	SEA	MLB	30	543	73	28	1	21	73	50	94	3	2	.264/.338/.457	.275	20.4	.287	0.0	3B 16	3.9

Breakout: 2%   Improve: 51%   Collapse: 4%   Attrition: 9%   MLB: 100%   *Comparables: Richie Hebner, Aramis Ramirez, Pablo Sandoval*

You can't imagine New York without the Empire State Building, or L.A. without the Hollywood Sign and increasingly, you can't imagine the Mariners without Kyle Seager. Seager the Elder ranked fifth in position player WARP in 2016 and second in the AL behind the category's automatic quarterback. He gets overlooked in part because of the balance in his game. Despite a spike in errors he displays excellent defense at third, albeit quietly. He set career bests in all three pillars of the "triple slash" and thumped 30 home runs for the first time. And like Felix before him, he stayed. In the face of the failed prospects and poor player development that defined the Jack Zduriencik era, the third-rounder persevered, the lone home-grown position player whose jersey you didn't worry about buying. While Seattle basked in the fading glow of its King, its Prince kept working, coming back year after year a little better than before, somehow underappreciated despite the $100 million contract. You get the sense that's just how he likes it.

Jean Segura   SS

Born: 3/17/90   Age: 27   Bats: R   Throws: R   Height: 5'10"   Weight: 205   Entered Pro Ball: International Free Agent, 2007

YEAR	TEAM	LVL	AGE	PA	R	2B	3B	HR	RBI	BB	K	SB	CS	AVG/OBP/SLG	TAv	VORP	BABIP	BRR	FRAA	WARP
2014	MIL	MLB	24	557	61	14	6	5	31	28	70	20	9	.246/.289/.326	.233	11.9	.275	4.8	SS(144): 22.2	3.8
2015	MIL	MLB	25	584	57	16	5	6	50	13	93	25	6	.257/.281/.336	.217	4.0	.298	5.3	SS(140): 12.6	1.8
2016	ARI	MLB	26	694	102	41	7	20	64	39	101	33	10	.319/.368/.499	.300	54.8	.353	6.5	2B(142): 5.5 • SS(23): 0.3	6.2
2017	*SEA*	*MLB*	*27*	*648*	*82*	*22*	*5*	*13*	*57*	*30*	*99*	*29*	*9*	*.268/.306/.388*	*.251*	*26.1*	*.297*	*3.1*	*SS 17*	*3.8*
2018	*SEA*	*MLB*	*28*	*583*	*67*	*21*	*5*	*14*	*64*	*31*	*91*	*25*	*8*	*.267/.313/.400*	*.252*	*20.3*	*.295*	*5.1*	*SS 15*	*3.8*

Breakout: 6%   Improve: 47%   Collapse: 10%   Attrition: 13%   MLB: 97%   *Comparables: Erick Aybar, Juan Bonilla, Dee Gordon*

Segura saw himself reborn in the desert. "The Hit Machine" changed his stance a bit over the winter, lowering his hands which helped him be more direct to the ball in the process. The changes paid off, as he set career-highs in hits (an NL-high 204), batting average, on-base percentage, doubles and homers. His move to second base was relatively smooth defensively, as one would expect from a career shortstop. Even counting on some regression to the mean—his BABIP alone screams lowered expectations in Seattle—Segura's poised to continue being a well-rounded contributor entering 2017.

Richie Shaffer   3B

Born: 3/15/91   Age: 26   Bats: R   Throws: R   Height: 6'3"   Weight: 220   Entered Pro Ball: Round 1, 2012 Draft (#25 overall)

YEAR	TEAM	LVL	AGE	PA	R	2B	3B	HR	RBI	BB	K	SB	CS	AVG/OBP/SLG	TAv	VORP	BABIP	BRR	FRAA	WARP
2014	MNT	AA	23	491	58	28	4	19	64	56	119	4	0	.222/.318/.440	.267	17.5	.261	-0.5	3B(109): -2.7	1.6
2015	MNT	AA	24	175	22	10	0	7	27	23	49	3	0	.262/.362/.470	.305	10.4	.340	-2.5	3B(34): -5.6	0.5
2015	DUR	AAA	24	282	42	17	1	19	45	31	74	1	1	.270/.355/.582	.324	24.0	.303	-1.3	3B(42): -4.4 • 1B(19): -0.5	2.0
2015	TBA	MLB	24	88	11	3	0	4	6	10	32	0	1	.189/.307/.392	.266	1.5	.256	-0.4	1B(10): 0.1 • 3B(8): 0.3	0.1
2016	DUR	AAA	25	496	49	27	0	11	48	65	135	4	1	.227/.329/.367	.250	5.2	.303	-1.3	3B(67): -0.5 • RF(28): -1.7	0.3
2016	TBA	MLB	25	54	5	6	0	1	4	5	18	0	1	.250/.315/.438	.271	0.9	.367	-0.4	1B(11): -0.1 • 3B(4): -0.2	0.1
2017	*PHI*	*MLB*	*26*	*54*	*7*	*2*	*0*	*2*	*7*	*6*	*16*	*0*	*0*	*.221/.310/.424*	*.254*	*1.7*	*.279*	*-0.1*		*0.2*
2018	*PHI*	*MLB*	*27*	*288*	*38*	*13*	*0*	*12*	*38*	*31*	*89*	*1*	*0*	*.220/.310/.420*	*.254*	*8.1*	*.281*	*-0.6*	*-*	*0.9*

Breakout: 3%   Improve: 15%   Collapse: 9%   Attrition: 29%   MLB: 49%   *Comparables: Ryan Schimpf, Mike Olt, Alex Liddi*

After bombing 30 dingers across three levels during a breakout 2015, this was supposed to be *The Year* for Shaffer. Sure, he was blocked by players like Evan Longoria and, er, James Loney in the past, but he'd built up enough versatility where he could fit in at any corner. To win a regular job with the Rays all he needed was to get off to his expected solid start in Durham…which never happened. Instead he backslid at the plate and rarely made contact enough to tap into his prodigious power from the previous season. Going into his age-26 year he's exactly at the point where bat-first corner prospects tend to earn the dreaded "Quad-A" label, and an offseason trade to Seattle makes him perhaps an understudy for a player that represents one of his best-case scenarios: Danny Valencia. That makes 2017 *The Year* for Shaffer again, but in a much more ominous sense.

Seth Smith   LF/RF

Born: 9/30/82   Age: 34   Bats: L   Throws: L   Height: 6'3"   Weight: 210   Entered Pro Ball: Round 2, 2004 Draft (#50 overall)

YEAR	TEAM	LVL	AGE	PA	R	2B	3B	HR	RBI	BB	K	SB	CS	AVG/OBP/SLG	TAv	VORP	BABIP	BRR	FRAA	WARP
2014	SDN	MLB	31	521	55	31	5	12	48	69	87	1	1	.266/.367/.440	.310	32.3	.305	-1.6	LF(102): 0.5 • RF(43): -2.0	3.4
2015	SEA	MLB	32	452	54	31	5	12	42	47	99	0	0	.248/.330/.443	.281	20.0	.298	2.6	LF(65): 0.2 • RF(55): -1.8	2.0
2016	SEA	MLB	33	438	62	15	0	16	63	48	89	0	0	.249/.342/.415	.262	8.0	.282	-1.2	RF(74): -3.5 • LF(35): -1.6	0.3
2017	*SEA*	*MLB*	*34*	*485*	*59*	*24*	*2*	*14*	*51*	*53*	*104*	*0*	*0*	*.246/.335/.409*	*.267*	*15.4*	*.292*	*-1.0*	*RF -0*	*1.1*
2018	*SEA*	*MLB*	*35*	*330*	*41*	*16*	*1*	*9*	*38*	*37*	*73*	*0*	*0*	*.243/.334/.404*	*.260*	*6.9*	*.291*	*-0.1*	*RF 0*	*0.7*

Breakout: 0%   Improve: 26%   Collapse: 19%   Attrition: 26%   MLB: 92%   *Comparables: Shawn Green, Trot Nixon, Andy Pafko*

Mariners fans have taken to calling Seth Smith "Dad" and, as nicknames go, it's fitting. Dads get you practical gifts, like hitting .256/.351/.431 against righties. It's the gift-of-socks slash line but dang it, you do need good socks. Dads teach you life lessons, like how to work the count and have professional at-bats. Dads play uninspiring defense in right, causing you to wonder if you and your siblings shouldn't buy Dad a riding mower or a Ben Gamel for Father's Day. Mostly, Dads are reliable. They let you know, in the constantly shifting world of Jerry Dipoto's outfield, that someone will always pick you up, and if you're very good, might let you get ice cream or a home run on the way home. But not both.

Jesus Sucre   C

Born: 4/30/88   Age: 29   Bats: R   Throws: R   Height: 6'0"   Weight: 225   Entered Pro Ball: International Free Agent, 2005

YEAR	TEAM	LVL	AGE	PA	R	2B	3B	HR	RBI	BB	K	SB	CS	AVG/OBP/SLG	TAv	VORP	BABIP	BRR	FRAA	WARP
2014	TAC	AAA	26	181	13	7	1	2	16	4	29	0	1	.274/.293/.360	.232	3.2	.317	0.3	C(47): 12.5	1.6
2014	SEA	MLB	26	64	4	2	0	0	5	0	17	0	0	.213/.213/.246	.175	-2.7	.295	-0.3	C(21): 2.5	0.0
2015	TAC	AAA	27	26	4	0	0	0	2	3	8	0	0	.261/.346/.261	.297	2.4	.400	0.2	C(6): -0.4	0.2
2015	SEA	MLB	27	142	9	6	0	1	7	6	21	0	0	.157/.195/.228	.165	-6.7	.181	0.4	C(50): 3.5 • P(2): -0.0	-0.3
2016	TAC	AAA	28	104	7	4	1	0	11	3	15	0	1	.273/.301/.333	.220	-0.7	.321	-0.9	C(28): -0.1	-0.1
2016	SEA	MLB	28	29	4	2	0	1	5	2	5	0	0	.480/.552/.680	.404	5.0	.579	-0.5	C(9): -0.3	0.5
2017	SEA	MLB	29	90	7	3	0	1	8	4	16	0	0	.238/.273/.329	.218	0.4	.276	-0.2	C 1	0.1
2018	SEA	MLB	30	140	13	5	0	2	12	6	28	0	0	.227/.265/.321	.209	-2.3	.264	-0.1	C 1	-0.1

Breakout: 2%   Improve: 25%   Collapse: 13%   Attrition: 28%   MLB: 63%   Comparables: Omir Santos, Humberto Quintero, Craig Tatum

Considering that Sucre's 2016 started with him badly fracturing his fibula during winter ball any amount of production would have been a success for the backup, including his usual trick of barely hitting at all. Instead, he rejoined the big league club in September and went on a hellacious tear. Sure, it was only 29 plate appearances, but when you think about it, doesn't it sort of figure a guy whose name is literally Sugar Jesus would have at least one sweet resurrection in him?

YEAR	TEAM	P. COUNT	FRM RUNS	BLK RUNS	THRW RUNS	TOT RUNS
2014	SEA	2576	2.3	0.3	0.0	2.6
2014	TAC	5608	10.8	0.2	1.8	12.8
2015	SEA	6224	2.7	1.0	0.6	4.3
2015	SEA	6224	2.7	1.0	0.6	4.3
2015	TAC	895	-0.3	0.0	0.0	-0.3
2016	SEA	1022	-0.1	0.1	-0.1	-0.1
2017	SEA	3545	0.5	0.3	0.2	1.0
2018	SEA	5519	0.4	0.5	0.3	1.1

Danny Valencia   3B

Born: 9/19/84   Age: 32   Bats: R   Throws: R   Height: 6'2"   Weight: 210   Entered Pro Ball: Round 19, 2006 Draft (#576 overall)

YEAR	TEAM	LVL	AGE	PA	R	2B	3B	HR	RBI	BB	K	SB	CS	AVG/OBP/SLG	TAv	VORP	BABIP	BRR	FRAA	WARP
2014	KCA	MLB	29	119	8	5	0	2	11	7	27	0	0	.282/.328/.382	.276	2.3	.354	-2.8	3B(26): 0.4 • 2B(6): -0.6	0.2
2014	TOR	MLB	29	165	12	11	1	2	19	7	35	1	1	.240/.273/.364	.225	-2.5	.292	-1.3	3B(40): 1.1 • 1B(20): -0.3	-0.2
2015	TOR	MLB	30	173	26	13	0	7	29	9	40	2	1	.296/.331/.506	.281	6.9	.353	-0.6	LF(32): -1.7 • 3B(10): -1.0	0.5
2015	OAK	MLB	30	205	33	10	1	11	37	20	40	0	1	.284/.356/.530	.310	16.7	.308	0.5	3B(45): -2.1	1.6
2016	OAK	MLB	31	517	72	22	1	17	51	41	115	1	1	.287/.346/.446	.287	24.4	.346	-2.5	3B(68): -3.7 • RF(37): -0.1	2.1
2017	SEA	MLB	32	481	51	23	1	17	62	29	108	1	1	.259/.306/.431	.262	7.0	.302	-1.2	1B 8	1.4
2018	SEA	MLB	33	488	58	23	1	16	59	29	113	1	1	.253/.299/.414	.249	-1.4	.299	-2.1	1B 8	0.7

Breakout: 3%   Improve: 34%   Collapse: 5%   Attrition: 12%   MLB: 88%   Comparables: Ty Wigginton, Greg Dobbs, Mike Lamb

Valencia returned to the A's on a waiver claim in 2015, but came into his own with a career-high WARP and home run total in 2016. He was demoted to a utility role after the All-Star break when Ryon Healy lassoed a starting job at third base, but the only sign of real conflict with his teammates reared its head during a clubhouse altercation with Billy Butler over a product endorsement gone sour. Butler got the boot by the end of August, while Valencia bid adieu several months later when he was shipped to the Mariners for a new platoon opportunity with Dan Vogelbach.

Dan Vogelbach   1B

Born: 12/17/92   Age: 24   Bats: L   Throws: R   Height: 6'0"   Weight: 250   Entered Pro Ball: Round 2, 2011 Draft (#68 overall)

YEAR	TEAM	LVL	AGE	PA	R	2B	3B	HR	RBI	BB	K	SB	CS	AVG/OBP/SLG	TAv	VORP	BABIP	BRR	FRAA	WARP
2014	DAY	A+	21	560	71	28	1	16	76	66	91	4	4	.268/.357/.429	.280	15.3	.296	-3.1	1B(103): -9.9	0.6
2015	TEN	AA	22	313	41	16	1	7	39	57	61	1	1	.272/.403/.425	.310	16.0	.330	-3.0	1B(75): 1.4	1.9
2016	IOW	AAA	23	365	53	18	2	16	64	55	67	0	0	.318/.425/.548	.349	35.7	.362	-1.8	1B(76): -3.0	3.4
2016	TAC	AAA	23	198	26	7	0	7	32	42	34	0	0	.240/.404/.422	.308	8.9	.263	-3.1	1B(25): -0.9	0.8
2016	SEA	MLB	23	13	0	0	0	0	0	1	6	0	0	.083/.154/.083	.102	-2.3	.167	-0.4	1B(4): -0.3	-0.3
2017	SEA	MLB	24	237	28	9	0	9	31	32	55	0	0	.242/.347/.424	.275	7.3	.285	-0.6	1B -2	0.4
2018	SEA	MLB	25	454	64	18	1	19	61	59	107	0	0	.248/.350/.441	.276	12.5	.293	-1.2	1B -4	0.9

Breakout: 2%   Improve: 15%   Collapse: 14%   Attrition: 24%   MLB: 47%   Comparables: Chris Carter, Ji-Man Choi, Travis Shaw

The arc of the moral universe is long, but it bends toward Dan Vogelbach hitting designatedly. That's not a dig at Vogelbach's, shall we say, healthy frame—although in his few at-bats at Safeco his walk-up song was "Brick House," a testament either to the Safeco DJ's cruelty or Vogelbach's self-awareness. The path to DH is easier to visualize with the trade to Seattle, but as the Mariners still employ Nelson Cruz, Vogelbach will need something else to do for now, so he'll try his hand at first. The defense and speed will never dazzle, but his patient approach and power should play and the Mariners bought a nice insurance policy in the form of Danny Valencia should the big man prove to be less than mighty-mighty.

Mike Zunino   C

Born: 3/25/91   Age: 26   Bats: R   Throws: R   Height: 6'2"   Weight: 220   Entered Pro Ball: Round 1, 2012 Draft (#3 overall)

YEAR	TEAM	LVL	AGE	PA	R	2B	3B	HR	RBI	BB	K	SB	CS	AVG/OBP/SLG	TAv	VORP	BABIP	BRR	FRAA	WARP
2014	SEA	MLB	23	476	51	20	2	22	60	17	158	0	3	.199/.254/.404	.241	12.8	.248	1.5	C(130): 19.5	3.6
2015	SEA	MLB	24	386	28	11	0	11	28	21	132	0	1	.174/.230/.300	.196	-8.4	.239	-1.1	C(112): 6.8	-0.2
2015	TAC	AAA	24	43	7	2	0	3	8	0	8	0	0	.317/.349/.585	.290	2.2	.333	-0.2	C(4): -0.3	0.2
2016	TAC	AAA	25	327	47	15	0	17	57	35	69	0	1	.286/.376/.521	.320	29.7	.318	-2.5	C(57): 18.9	5.0
2016	SEA	MLB	25	192	16	7	0	12	31	21	65	0	0	.207/.318/.470	.289	12.6	.250	-1.7	C(52): 1.9	1.5
2017	*SEA*	*MLB*	*26*	*384*	*44*	*14*	*1*	*17*	*50*	*27*	*117*	*1*	*1*	*.215/.286/.412*	*.247*	*13.4*	*.264*	*-1.0*	*C 12*	*1.8*
2018	*SEA*	*MLB*	*27*	*376*	*48*	*14*	*1*	*18*	*52*	*26*	*118*	*0*	*0*	*.211/.283/.415*	*.242*	*7.0*	*.260*	*-0.1*	*C 12*	*2.0*

Breakout: 4%   Improve: 56%   Collapse: 6%   Attrition: 14%   MLB: 96%   *Comparables: Jarrod Saltalamacchia, Mike Napoli, Wilson Betemit*

For two weeks in August, Mike Zunino was exactly what the Mariners thought they were drafting in 2012. He came back from Triple-A a new man, no longer tempted by junk low and away, content to wait for a pitch to drive or to take a walk. From August 1 to the 20th, he slashed .310/.434/.714 with five home runs. This was the version of Mike Zunino who was worth a first-round pick; an offensive powerhouse, and a guy who could clear Safeco. The prodigious defense was just a bonus. On August 21, the league started adjusting to Mike's adjustment and things got harder. He still punished mistakes and—perhaps more encouragingly—kept walking, despite a mounting strikeout rate. Jerry Dipoto declared 2016 "The Year of Mike Zunino," a chance to go back and fix what the prior regime had so badly broken. If the young backstop wants to keep earning big league meal money and hitting white balls for batting practice, he'll need to make 2017 "The Year of Mike Zunino's Next Adjustment."

YEAR	TEAM	P. COUNT	FRM RUNS	BLK RUNS	THRW RUNS	TOT RUNS
2014	SEA	17328	20.4	-2.0	0.4	18.7
2015	SEA	14437	9.7	-1.6	0.5	8.6
2015	TAC	577	-0.2	0.0	0.0	-0.2
2016	SEA	6955	2.1	1.7	-0.1	3.8
2017	*SEA*	*14187*	*12.9*	*0.1*	*0.1*	*13.1*
2018	*SEA*	*13900*	*12.1*	*0.2*	*0.0*	*12.3*

PITCHERS

Dan Altavilla   RHP

Born: 9/8/92   Age: 24   Bats: R   Throws: R   Height: 5'11"   Weight: 200   Entered Pro Ball: Round 5, 2014 Draft (#141 overall)

YEAR	TEAM	LVL	AGE	W	L	SV	G	GS	IP	H	HR	BB/9	K/9	K	GB%	BABIP	WHIP	ERA	FIP	DRA	VORP	WARP	cFIP	MPH
2014	EVE	A-	21	5	3	0	14	14	66	74	7	4.4	9.0	66	47%	.310	1.61	4.36	4.83	3.27	15.3	1.6	90	
2015	BAK	A+	22	6	12	0	28	28	148¹	138	11	3.2	8.1	134	37%	.300	1.29	4.07	4.15	4.43	10.7	1.2	102	
2016	WTN	AA	23	7	3	16	43	0	56²	40	3	3.5	10.3	65	48%	.261	1.09	1.91	3.04	2.70	12.8	1.4	88	
2016	SEA	MLB	23	0	0	0	15	0	12¹	11	0	0.7	7.3	10	50%	.306	0.97	0.73	1.97	4.05	1.3	0.1	97	99.2
2017	*SEA*	*MLB*	*24*	*2*	*3*	*0*	*47*	*0*	*49¹*	*50*	*7*	*4.1*	*7.1*	*39*	*66%*	*.289*	*1.46*	*5.21*	*4.90*	*5.25*	*-1.5*	*-0.2*	*100*	
2018	*SEA*	*MLB*	*25*	*2*	*1*	*0*	*42*	*0*	*44²*	*40*	*7*	*5.3*	*10.1*	*50*	*66%*	*.290*	*1.49*	*4.80*	*4.89*	*5.15*	*-0.5*	*0.0*	*121*	

Breakout: 16%   Improve: 25%   Collapse: 11%   Attrition: 23%   MLB: 44%   *Comparables: Daryl Thompson, Josh Outman, Felipe Paulino*

In 2016, Dan Altavilla was converted to reliever, pitched well in Jackson, skipped Tacoma and threw high-leverage innings in Seattle, where his fastball played up in the bullpen and his slider continued to improve and impress. Only time will tell just how viable he is as the set-up man in front of Edwin Diaz, but what we really ought to investigate is whether Altavilla is one big muscle or several muscles standing on each other's shoulders, wearing a trench coat and a set of blindingly white teeth.

Jonathan Aro   RHP

Born: 10/10/90   Age: 26   Bats: R   Throws: R   Height: 6'0"   Weight: 235   Entered Pro Ball: International Free Agent, 2011

YEAR	TEAM	LVL	AGE	W	L	SV	G	GS	IP	H	HR	BB/9	K/9	K	GB%	BABIP	WHIP	ERA	FIP	DRA	VORP	WARP	cFIP	MPH
2014	GRN	A	23	1	3	7	25	0	67¹	52	3	2.9	9.9	74	49%	.278	1.10	2.27	3.04	2.14	21.8	2.2	83	
2014	SLM	A+	23	2	0	1	7	1	20	12	1	3.2	10.8	24	39%	.244	0.95	1.80	2.97	2.50	6.2	0.6	86	
2015	PME	AA	24	3	2	0	8	0	22¹	15	0	3.2	7.7	19	41%	.227	1.03	2.82	2.78	3.64	2.7	0.3	102	
2015	PAW	AAA	24	0	1	2	26	0	51²	43	2	1.7	9.2	53	37%	.297	1.03	3.14	2.42	1.77	18.1	1.8	75	
2015	BOS	MLB	24	0	1	0	6	0	10¹	15	2	3.5	7.0	8	19%	.371	1.84	6.97	5.23	6.44	-2.0	-0.2	128	94.6
2016	SEA	MLB	25	0	0	0	1	0	0²	1	0	13.5	0.0	0	33%	.333	3.00	0.00	7.61	4.99	0.0	0.0	106	94.4
2016	TAC	AAA	25	3	2	1	24	1	36¹	29	2	2.5	6.2	25	36%	.250	1.07	2.48	3.89	4.62	1.6	0.2	114	
2017	*SEA*	*MLB*	*26*	*1*	*1*	*0*	*19*	*0*	*19²*	*21*	*3*	*3.4*	*6.5*	*14*	*55%*	*.292*	*1.42*	*5.00*	*4.96*	*5.21*	*-0.5*	*-0.1*	*100*	
2018	*SEA*	*MLB*	*27*	*1*	*0*	*0*	*21*	*0*	*22²*	*20*	*3*	*5.0*	*10.1*	*25*	*55%*	*.292*	*1.46*	*4.62*	*4.71*	*5.11*	*-0.1*	*0.0*	*118*	

Breakout: 9%   Improve: 15%   Collapse: 5%   Attrition: 17%   MLB: 23%   *Comparables: Mauro Zarate, Hector Neris, Noe Ramirez*

In social choice theory Arrow's Impossibility Theorem tells us that if voters are presented with three or more options, ranked voting systems can't convert the ranked preferences of individuals into a single, communal preference. In Mariners bullpen theory, Aro's Impossibility Theorem tells us that if fans are presented with three or more pitchers, ranked voting systems can't convert the ranked preferences of fans into a single, communal preference for Jonathan Aro.

Arquimedes Caminero   RHP

Born: 6/16/87   Age: 30   Bats: R   Throws: R   Height: 6'4"   Weight: 245   Entered Pro Ball: International Free Agent, 2006

YEAR	TEAM	LVL	AGE	W	L	SV	G	GS	IP	H	HR	BB/9	K/9	K	GB%	BABIP	WHIP	ERA	FIP	DRA	VORP	WARP	cFIP	MPH
2014	MIA	MLB	27	0	1	0	6	0	6²	8	2	5.4	10.8	8	37%	.353	1.80	10.80	6.40	4.20	0.2	0.0	105	98.2
2014	NWO	AAA	27	4	1	10	42	0	63	70	7	4.3	11.3	79	41%	.362	1.59	4.86	4.40	3.73	11.3	1.1	89	
2015	PIT	MLB	28	5	1	0	73	0	74²	63	7	3.5	8.8	73	48%	.276	1.23	3.62	3.83	3.91	6.6	0.7	104	100.8
2016	PIT	MLB	29	1	2	1	39	0	41	46	4	4.8	7.0	32	48%	.336	1.66	3.51	4.80	6.40	-6.5	-0.7	118	101.4
2016	SEA	MLB	29	1	1	0	18	0	19²	21	3	5.0	8.2	18	40%	.300	1.63	3.66	5.09	6.74	-3.9	-0.4	119	101.1
2017	*SEA*	*MLB*	*30*	*3*	*1*	*0*	*54*	*0*	*57*	*59*	*9*	*4.1*	*7.9*	*50*	*55%*	*.299*	*1.49*	*4.76*	*4.95*	*5.28*	*-1.6*	*-0.2*	*121*	
2018	*SEA*	*MLB*	*31*	*1*	*0*	*0*	*25*	*0*	*29¹*	*29*	*4*	*4.4*	*8.8*	*29*	*55%*	*.298*	*1.48*	*4.63*	*4.73*	*5.14*	*-0.3*	*0.0*	*117*	

Breakout: 16%   Improve: 39%   Collapse: 13%   Attrition: 22%   MLB: 67%   Comparables: Bobby Seay, Louis Coleman, Jesse Carlson

During a Pirates' loss in late 2015, Vin Scully filled part of Caminero's appearance with a geometry lesson. "Euclid is the father of geometry. Mmmm didn't we all love that? And Archimedes devised a formula, determines the volume of an irregular shaped object using water displacement. Yeah, I didn't do too well in that either." Much like Vin attempting geometry, Caminero fared poorly in 2016. His home run rate, FIP and ERA all climbed when he got to Safeco after an August waiver trade, finishing the year with a DRA north of six. Caminero is toting his high-90s fastball to Japan this summer, where his new employers will try to calculate the limit of BB as his command approaches zero.

Steve Cishek   RHP

Born: 6/18/86   Age: 31   Bats: R   Throws: R   Height: 6'6"   Weight: 215   Entered Pro Ball: Round 5, 2007 Draft (#166 overall)

YEAR	TEAM	LVL	AGE	W	L	SV	G	GS	IP	H	HR	BB/9	K/9	K	GB%	BABIP	WHIP	ERA	FIP	DRA	VORP	WARP	cFIP	MPH
2014	MIA	MLB	28	4	5	39	67	0	65¹	58	3	2.9	11.6	84	46%	.331	1.21	3.17	2.14	1.92	18.6	2.1	75	94.6
2015	MIA	MLB	29	2	6	3	32	0	32	37	4	3.9	7.9	28	49%	.350	1.59	4.50	3.54	5.02	-1.1	-0.1	107	93.1
2015	SLN	MLB	29	0	0	1	27	0	23¹	18	2	5.0	7.7	20	43%	.254	1.33	2.31	4.36	4.97	-0.7	-0.1	107	93.2
2016	SEA	MLB	30	4	6	25	62	0	64	44	8	3.0	10.7	76	45%	.242	1.02	2.81	3.53	2.69	16.2	1.7	83	93.9
2017	*SEA*	*MLB*	*31*	*1*	*1*	*0*	*23*	*0*	*24²*	*22*	*3*	*3.4*	*9.9*	*27*	*47%*	*.292*	*1.27*	*3.77*	*3.78*	*4.21*	*2.1*	*0.2*	*95*	
2018	*SEA*	*MLB*	*32*	*3*	*1*	*1*	*52*	*0*	*55*	*50*	*8*	*3.4*	*10.0*	*61*	*47%*	*.291*	*1.27*	*3.97*	*4.09*	*4.37*	*4.1*	*0.4*	*98*	

Breakout: 29%   Improve: 40%   Collapse: 29%   Attrition: 15%   MLB: 88%   Comparables: Francisco Rodriguez, Nick Masset, Jesse Crain

In *A Room with a View*, Lucy Honeychurch's dour chaperone Charlotte Bartlett bemoans not getting what she expected: "The signora distinctly wrote 'south rooms, with a view and close together,' instead of which she has given us north rooms without a view and a long way apart." Going into 2016 Jerry Dipoto told Mariners fans he had acquired a closer who could get righties and lefties out, instead of which he gave them a righty specialist with splits a long way apart. Things started well enough, but hardly any good can come from a reliever with a career-high 13.1 percent HR/FB rate, and by August he was supplanted by Edwin Diaz. Cishek is still plenty useful against right-handed hitters, but with offseason hip surgery likely to sideline him through the beginning of spring training and possibly longer it's unclear whether expectations and reality will be close together or a long way apart.

Edwin Diaz   RHP

Born: 3/22/94   Age: 23   Bats: R   Throws: R   Height: 6'3"   Weight: 165   Entered Pro Ball: Round 3, 2012 Draft (#98 overall)

YEAR	TEAM	LVL	AGE	W	L	SV	G	GS	IP	H	HR	BB/9	K/9	K	GB%	BABIP	WHIP	ERA	FIP	DRA	VORP	WARP	cFIP	MPH
2014	CLN	A	20	6	8	0	24	24	116¹	96	5	3.2	8.6	111	44%	.289	1.19	3.33	3.48	3.24	28.5	2.9	94	
2015	BAK	A+	21	2	0	0	7	7	37	21	3	2.2	10.2	42	52%	.217	0.81	1.70	3.62	2.14	12.1	1.3	82	
2015	WTN	AA	21	5	10	0	20	20	104¹	102	5	3.2	8.9	103	42%	.333	1.33	4.57	3.22	3.11	23.0	2.5	89	
2016	WTN	AA	22	3	3	1	16	6	40²	32	3	1.5	12.0	54	58%	.302	0.96	2.21	2.29	1.40	16.2	1.8	57	
2016	SEA	MLB	22	0	4	18	49	0	51²	45	6	2.6	15.3	88	45%	.377	1.16	2.79	2.00	1.43	20.3	2.1	51	101.0
2017	*SEA*	*MLB*	*23*	*2*	*2*	*28*	*47*	*0*	*49¹*	*42*	*5*	*3.1*	*10.2*	*56*	*53%*	*.293*	*1.20*	*3.02*	*3.36*	*3.58*	*7.7*	*0.8*	*75*	
2018	*SEA*	*MLB*	*24*	*3*	*1*	*27*	*55*	*0*	*57²*	*41*	*6*	*4.1*	*12.6*	*81*	*53%*	*.281*	*1.15*	*3.13*	*3.22*	*3.48*	*9.9*	*1.0*	*72*	

Breakout: 29%   Improve: 58%   Collapse: 19%   Attrition: 22%   MLB: 91%   Comparables: David Price, Aroldis Chapman, Matt Moore

Scroll through a single-season reliever K/9 leaderboard and you'll see some familiar names. Aroldis Chapman leads the way with a 17.67 in 2014 followed by your Jansens and Betanceses and Kimbrels, with Chapman thrown in a few more times for good measure. And then sitting at eighth all-time for a reliever with at least 40 innings pitched is Diaz. Nicknamed "Sugar," his performance last year rendered any lingering concerns about his conversion from starter moot and left Seattle fans lifted and feeling so gifted and wondering how Diaz got so fly. His fastball sits in the high 90s and can touch 100, but his hard, late-breaking slider—thrown with a new grip Diaz learned from Joaquin Benoit—that has elevated the 22-year-old from an intriguing piece to a potential star. If he seemed to fatigue a bit at season's end, you'd be well-served to remember he's young and skipped Triple-A on his way to the majors. If Diaz continues on this path he should be a staple of the Mariners bullpen, and reliever leaderboards, for years to come.

Charlie Furbush   LHP

Born: 4/11/86   Age: 31   Bats: L   Throws: L   Height: 6'5"   Weight: 215   Entered Pro Ball: Round 4, 2007 Draft (#151 overall)

YEAR	TEAM	LVL	AGE	W	L	SV	G	GS	IP	H	HR	BB/9	K/9	K	GB%	BABIP	WHIP	ERA	FIP	DRA	VORP	WARP	cFIP	MPH
2014	SEA	MLB	28	1	5	1	67	0	42¹	40	4	1.9	10.8	51	39%	.327	1.16	3.61	2.83	3.09	6.5	0.7	89	94.2
2015	SEA	MLB	29	1	1	0	33	0	21²	9	2	2.1	7.1	17	50%	.125	0.65	2.08	3.70	4.08	1.5	0.2	100	93.8
2017	*SEA*	*MLB*	*31*	*2*	*1*	*1*	*33*	*0*	*35*	*33*	*6*	*3.2*	*9.0*	*35*	*59%*	*.281*	*1.28*	*4.37*	*4.56*	*4.73*	*0.9*	*0.1*	*110*	
2018	*SEA*	*MLB*	*32*	*3*	*1*	*1*	*59*	*0*	*44²*	*42*	*7*	*3.3*	*8.9*	*44*	*59%*	*.285*	*1.32*	*4.43*	*4.53*	*4.79*	*1.4*	*0.1*	*112*	

Breakout: 30%   Improve: 41%   Collapse: 24%   Attrition: 19%   MLB: 89%   Comparables: Jesse Crain, Kevin Gregg, Fernando Rodney

Anton Chekhov once wrote: "If you say in the first chapter that there is a rifle hanging on the wall, in the second or third chapter it absolutely must go off." Chekhov would have hated Furbush, whose 2016 season was a series of promised returns that never fired and ended with surgery to repair a torn rotator cuff. The talented lefty is not expected to pitch again until 2018, leaving many to wonder if he's a rifle that may eventually come to hang on someone else's bullpen wall.

Luiz Gohara   LHP

Born: 7/31/96   Age: 20   Bats: L   Throws: L   Height: 6'3"   Weight: 210   Entered Pro Ball: International Free Agent, 2012

YEAR	TEAM	LVL	AGE	W	L	SV	G	GS	IP	H	HR	BB/9	K/9	K	GB%	BABIP	WHIP	ERA	FIP	DRA	VORP	WARP	cFIP	MPH
2014	EVE	A-	17	0	6	0	11	11	37¹	46	6	5.8	8.9	37	60%	.348	1.88	8.20	6.25	7.61	-9.4	-1.0	114	
2015	EVE	A-	18	3	7	0	14	14	53²	67	4	5.4	10.4	62	53%	.404	1.84	6.20	4.27	4.35	5.5	0.6	102	
2016	EVE	A-	19	2	0	0	3	3	15¹	13	1	1.8	12.3	21	68%	.333	1.04	1.76	2.47	1.65	6.1	0.6	74	
2016	CLN	A	19	5	2	0	10	10	54¹	44	1	3.3	9.9	60	52%	.314	1.18	1.82	2.61	2.61	14.5	1.6	89	
2017	SEA	MLB	20	3	4	0	12	12	51²	61	8	5.2	6.2	36	52%	.314	1.76	5.58	5.66	5.99	-3.0	-0.3	142	
2018	SEA	MLB	21	5	7	0	21	21	124²	129	19	5.8	8.3	114	52%	.307	1.68	5.27	5.38	5.66	-1.9	-0.2	135	

Breakout: 1%   Improve: 1%   Collapse: 0%   Attrition: 1%   MLB: 1%   *Comparables: Tyrell Jenkins, Randall Delgado, Jarrod Parker*

If a movie director wanted to dramatize a minor leaguer's developmental path to the big leagues, Gohara would make great source material for the lead character. He's basically the ultimate pitching prospect: Young? Check. Left-handed? Check. Throws hard? You betcha. Immensely obvious developmental hurdles to clear? Uh huh. From an exotic country? For baseball standards, Brazil qualifies.

It took three spins through short-season ball before Gohara passed the test, which just obscures the fact that when he left he was *still* one of the youngest players in the circuit. And boy did he look good. He comfortably sat in the mid-90s with his fastball, touching higher while working in a curve and a changeup that both flashed plus. His off-speed pitches were much improved and while the changeup in particular remains a work in progress, it's years ahead of where it was in 2015. But despite his tantalizing stuff and dominant statistics, there are still plenty of concerns in Gohara's profile. Just 20 years old, he looks closer to 300 pounds than the 210 he's listed at and conditioning has been a real problem for him. Stemming in part from that, Gohara has trouble repeating his mechanics, with his command often drifting noticeably over the course of an outing. Ultimately, he has more upside than all but a handful of minor league arms, but more work ahead of him than many with his raw physical skills.

Felix Hernandez   RHP

Born: 4/8/86   Age: 31   Bats: R   Throws: R   Height: 6'3"   Weight: 225   Entered Pro Ball: International Free Agent, 2002

YEAR	TEAM	LVL	AGE	W	L	SV	G	GS	IP	H	HR	BB/9	K/9	K	GB%	BABIP	WHIP	ERA	FIP	DRA	VORP	WARP	cFIP	MPH
2014	SEA	MLB	28	15	6	0	34	34	236	170	16	1.8	9.5	248	57%	.258	0.92	2.14	2.59	1.73	81.3	9.0	65	94.9
2015	SEA	MLB	29	18	9	0	31	31	201²	180	23	2.6	8.5	191	58%	.289	1.18	3.53	3.69	2.73	52.5	5.6	77	94.5
2016	SEA	MLB	30	11	8	0	25	25	153¹	138	19	3.8	7.2	122	52%	.271	1.32	3.82	4.59	4.71	11.1	1.1	101	92.9
2017	SEA	MLB	31	13	10	0	28	28	196	179	25	3.2	9.0	196	49%	.293	1.27	3.85	4.03	4.29	20.9	2.2	100	
2018	SEA	MLB	32	13	12	0	31	31	193	179	26	3.3	8.9	190	49%	.292	1.30	4.07	4.17	4.49	22.7	2.3	104	

Breakout: 11%   Improve: 40%   Collapse: 28%   Attrition: 6%   MLB: 90%   *Comparables: Adam Wainwright, CC Sabathia, A.J. Burnett*

On October 1, Felix Hernandez sat in the dugout at Safeco, leaning his head against the padded rail after a late-inning loss ushered in the end of another year without a playoff run. Felix didn't pitch that night. He couldn't have changed the outcome any more than he could have gone back and changed his own lost starts. But it was clear he felt it like he was marked by every bad fastball, every hung changeup. Baseball is an exploration of mortality and an exercise in decay. Not the abrupt, violent mortality of a car crash, but the slow march into uselessness. We will all one day be less useful than we are now, and be left to ask who we are.

The Felix we know is gone. Mariners fans still look forward to the King's starts, but the exclamations of "Happy Felix Day" are more tempered. For the first time in his career, you really don't know what you're going to get. Last year we saw the King hobbled and humbled, as a strained right calf landed him on the disabled list, and poor location led to walks, runs and a DRA that finally started to look like his mounting ERA. He's always been a smart pitcher, and he's dealt with declining velocity for years. His secondary stuff still loops and dives, leaving batters looking silly and us to wonder if perhaps Felix will go back to Felix-ing. And really, it could all still play if he could just command it better.

It might be fine, except that Felix has never been just fine. He could take the road most recently traveled by Justin Verlander, rediscovering forgotten parts of himself and grafting on new ones until he resembles something familiar, yet foreign. We might witness a triumphant return or a slow crawl into decay. Whatever the next iteration of Felix, we imagine it will have to be wilier and more precise, with each move anticipating the resulting counter riposte and responding with guile in turn. It will remind us of Felix, but not be him. Because the Felix we knew, the Ace, the best pitcher in baseball, is gone.

The King is dead, long live the King.

Chris Heston   RHP

Born: 4/10/88   Age: 29   Bats: R   Throws: R   Height: 6'3"   Weight: 195   Entered Pro Ball: Round 12, 2009 Draft (#357 overall)

YEAR	TEAM	LVL	AGE	W	L	SV	G	GS	IP	H	HR	BB/9	K/9	K	GB%	BABIP	WHIP	ERA	FIP	DRA	VORP	WARP	cFIP	MPH
2014	FRE	AAA	26	12	9	0	28	28	173	152	16	2.7	6.5	125	51%	.266	1.17	3.38	4.50	2.59	60.8	6.1	97	
2014	SFN	MLB	26	0	0	0	3	1	5¹	6	0	5.1	6.8	4	53%	.353	1.69	5.06	3.29	4.42	0.2	0.0	108	92.5
2015	SFN	MLB	27	12	11	0	31	31	177²	169	16	3.2	7.1	141	54%	.299	1.31	3.95	4.05	4.63	8.8	0.9	107	91.7
2016	SFN	MLB	28	1	1	0	4	0	5	9	0	10.8	5.4	3	50%	.450	3.00	10.80	5.59	6.27	-0.7	-0.1	118	89.3
2016	SAC	AAA	28	2	9	1	15	14	81¹	82	8	3.5	5.9	53	52%	.288	1.40	4.54	5.02	5.40	-0.7	-0.1	107	
2017	SEA	MLB	29	4	4	0	36	8	69	69	8	3.7	6.6	51	64%	.287	1.30	4.51	4.63	4.90	1.8	0.2	100	
2018	SEA	MLB	30	6	5	0	61	12	121²	113	16	5.0	8.9	120	64%	.294	1.48	4.71	4.80	5.21	0.8	0.1	119	

Breakout: 8%   Improve: 24%   Collapse: 13%   Attrition: 13%   MLB: 44%   *Comparables: Samuel Deduno, Brad Mills, Philip Humber*

After a promising rookie season, Heston's sophomore effort never got off the ground, as he struggled in long relief and then severely strained his oblique. He's on track to return by Opening Day, but then he'll discover a horrible truth about life: that there are millions of Chris Hestons, all of them identical and identically bloodthirsty, and at least one of them luckier than the original. The Mariners rotation offers more hope than San Francisco's, but Heston will still have to claw past a host of younger, healthier command specialists for a rotation spot. Pity him, because someday the same will be true for you.

Hisashi Iwakuma   RHP

Born: 4/12/81   Age: 36   Bats: R   Throws: R   Height: 6'3"   Weight: 210   Entered Pro Ball: International Free Agent, 2012

YEAR	TEAM	LVL	AGE	W	L	SV	G	GS	IP	H	HR	BB/9	K/9	K	GB%	BABIP	WHIP	ERA	FIP	DRA	VORP	WARP	cFIP	MPH
2014	SEA	MLB	33	15	9	0	28	28	179	167	20	1.1	7.7	154	52%	.287	1.05	3.52	3.28	2.62	44.2	4.9	81	92.1
2015	SEA	MLB	34	9	5	0	20	20	129²	117	18	1.5	7.7	111	53%	.271	1.06	3.54	3.71	2.87	31.8	3.4	80	92.1
2016	SEA	MLB	35	16	12	0	33	33	199	218	28	2.1	6.6	147	42%	.311	1.33	4.12	4.23	4.29	23.6	2.4	102	90.6
2017	*SEA*	*MLB*	*36*	*12*	*10*	*0*	*29*	*29*	*182²*	*178*	*28*	*2.2*	*7.9*	*161*	*38%*	*.290*	*1.22*	*4.05*	*4.23*	*4.52*	*14.8*	*1.5*	*100*	
2018	*SEA*	*MLB*	*37*	*11*	*11*	*0*	*29*	*29*	*183*	*175*	*29*	*2.1*	*8.1*	*166*	*38%*	*.285*	*1.19*	*4.11*	*4.21*	*4.56*	*18.4*	*1.9*	*106*	

Breakout: 16%   Improve: 40%   Collapse: 16%   Attrition: 12%   MLB: 77%   *Comparables: Josh Beckett, Hiroki Kuroda, Chris Carpenter*

Just as he was an Oakland Athletic in 2012 until he wasn't, Iwakuma was a Los Angeles Dodger, and then suddenly the Bear was back in Seattle. After his deal with L.A. fell through over concerns with his physical, the Mariners brought him back on a team-friendly, one-year deal with options for two more, and things proceeded even more oddly from there. His outings lacked their characteristic elegance, leading to career worsts in almost every statistical category. Like a KISS cover band, what Iwakuma's performances lacked in quality he made up for with volume; despite the Dodgers' medical concerns, he was the only Mariners starter to avoid the disabled list and make 30-plus starts. Iwakuma's season demonstrates two things: you can be very useful without being great, and counting on starters signed to other teams' staffs is a trick almost certain not to work a third time.

Nate Karns   RHP

Born: 11/25/87   Age: 29   Bats: R   Throws: R   Height: 6'3"   Weight: 225   Entered Pro Ball: Round 12, 2009 Draft (#352 overall)

YEAR	TEAM	LVL	AGE	W	L	SV	G	GS	IP	H	HR	BB/9	K/9	K	GB%	BABIP	WHIP	ERA	FIP	DRA	VORP	WARP	cFIP	MPH
2014	DUR	AAA	26	9	9	0	27	27	145¹	142	16	3.8	9.5	153	47%	.323	1.40	5.08	4.03	3.74	32.5	3.2	89	
2014	TBA	MLB	26	1	1	0	2	2	12	7	3	3.0	9.8	13	47%	.148	0.92	4.50	5.74	3.60	1.6	0.2	94	96.2
2015	TBA	MLB	27	7	5	0	27	26	147	132	19	3.4	8.9	145	43%	.285	1.28	3.67	4.06	3.92	18.9	2.0	97	94.6
2016	SEA	MLB	28	6	2	1	22	15	94¹	95	11	4.3	9.6	101	43%	.327	1.48	5.15	4.01	4.58	7.6	0.8	96	95.8
2017	*SEA*	*MLB*	*29*	*9*	*8*	*0*	*24*	*24*	*136*	*125*	*16*	*3.7*	*9.1*	*139*	*49%*	*.294*	*1.32*	*3.82*	*4.02*	*4.29*	*14.6*	*1.5*	*98*	
2018	*SEA*	*MLB*	*30*	*10*	*10*	*0*	*29*	*29*	*175*	*147*	*22*	*4.5*	*10.7*	*209*	*49%*	*.292*	*1.35*	*3.98*	*4.09*	*4.44*	*18.3*	*1.9*	*100*	

Breakout: 20%   Improve: 43%   Collapse: 19%   Attrition: 16%   MLB: 78%   *Comparables: Tom Koehler, Dustin Nippert, Marco Estrada*

The good: When he commands them well, Karns' curveball/fastball combo isn't just good, it's very, very good, getting batters to look silly in a way their mothers wouldn't enjoy.

The bad: Karns was shut down at the end of July with a lower back strain.

The ugly: Trips to the bullpen generally aren't a reward for good behavior. Karns often struggled to work through the order a third time, and the problem only got more pronounced over time. In the five starts before being relegated to relief, Karns failed to go more than five innings, walking 17 batters in 23.1 innings and posting a 7.33 ERA.

The outlook: Someone has to produce the tantalizing-yet-ultimately-unsatisfying innings now vacated by Taijuan Walker, and Karns is the ideal candidate.

Dean Kiekhefer   LHP

Born: 6/7/89   Age: 28   Bats: L   Throws: L   Height: 6'0"   Weight: 175   Entered Pro Ball: Round 36, 2010 Draft (#1099 overall)

YEAR	TEAM	LVL	AGE	W	L	SV	G	GS	IP	H	HR	BB/9	K/9	K	GB%	BABIP	WHIP	ERA	FIP	DRA	VORP	WARP	cFIP	MPH
2014	SFD	AA	25	0	2	7	15	0	14²	18	2	0.6	6.1	10	46%	.333	1.30	4.30	3.73	3.95	1.5	0.2	98	
2014	MEM	AAA	25	2	3	1	40	0	56²	48	7	0.8	8.3	52	44%	.265	0.94	2.54	3.89	1.79	22.4	2.2	81	
2015	MEM	AAA	26	2	1	2	50	1	59²	68	5	1.1	5.6	37	52%	.317	1.26	2.41	3.80	3.05	12.5	1.3	94	
2016	MEM	AAA	27	6	1	2	29	0	34²	32	2	2.1	5.2	20	46%	.280	1.15	2.08	4.01	6.07	-4.3	-0.4	111	
2016	SLN	MLB	27	0	0	0	26	0	22	24	2	2.9	5.7	14	48%	.301	1.41	5.32	4.32	5.06	-0.2	0.0	110	89.7
2017	*SEA*	*MLB*	*28*	*2*	*1*	*0*	*44*	*0*	*46²*	*51*	*7*	*2.7*	*5.7*	*29*	*48%*	*.296*	*1.40*	*4.64*	*4.86*	*5.15*	*-0.6*	*-0.1*	*117*	
2018	*SEA*	*MLB*	*29*	*1*	*0*	*0*	*16*	*0*	*20²*	*21*	*3*	*4.4*	*8.2*	*19*	*48%*	*.304*	*1.50*	*4.62*	*4.72*	*5.13*	*-0.2*	*0.0*	*116*	

Breakout: 3%   Improve: 5%   Collapse: 13%   Attrition: 15%   MLB: 21%   *Comparables: Jorge Rondon, Kenneth Roberts, Ross Wolf*

When you're a 26-year-old career minor-league reliever you're allowed a little *schadenfreude*, so excuse Kiekhefer if the sore elbows, knees, shoulders and *varicella*-infected skin of various Cardinals pitchers brought him joy. Injuries and illness allowed the former 36th-round pick to ride the shuttle from Memphis to St. Louis five times, giving him a platform to impress the rest of the league with his nascent LOOGY potential. Kiekhefer's low-velo assortment held lefties to a .200/.248/.295 line last year between MLB and Triple-A, numbers good enough to earn him another shot this spring in Seattle.

Zach Lee   RHP

Born: 9/13/91   Age: 25   Bats: R   Throws: R   Height: 6'4"   Weight: 227   Entered Pro Ball: Round 1, 2010 Draft (#28 overall)

YEAR	TEAM	LVL	AGE	W	L	SV	G	GS	IP	H	HR	BB/9	K/9	K	GB%	BABIP	WHIP	ERA	FIP	DRA	VORP	WARP	cFIP	MPH
2014	ABQ	AAA	22	7	13	0	28	27	150²	177	18	3.2	5.8	97	52%	.323	1.53	5.38	5.16	4.36	23.0	2.3	103	
2015	LAN	MLB	23	0	1	0	1	1	4²	11	1	1.9	5.8	3	55%	.526	2.57	13.50	5.30	4.71	0.2	0.0	113	92.2
2015	OKL	AAA	23	11	6	0	19	19	113¹	107	5	1.5	6.4	81	50%	.298	1.11	2.70	3.35	2.54	34.8	3.5	85	
2016	OKL	AAA	24	7	5	0	13	13	73²	95	11	1.8	7.0	57	53%	.353	1.49	4.89	4.73	3.90	11.8	1.2	106	
2016	TAC	AAA	24	0	9	0	14	14	74¹	98	11	2.9	6.1	50	49%	.343	1.64	7.39	5.43	4.10	10.3	1.1	105	
2017	*SDN*	*MLB*	*25*	*4*	*5*	*0*	*34*	*8*	*73*	*82*	*8*	*2.9*	*5.4*	*44*	*47%*	*.303*	*1.46*	*4.37*	*4.49*	*4.80*	*2.3*	*0.2*	*100*	
2018	*SDN*	*MLB*	*26*	*6*	*5*	*0*	*51*	*12*	*111*	*102*	*12*	*4.1*	*8.5*	*105*	*47%*	*.316*	*1.38*	*4.43*	*4.51*	*4.87*	*6.2*	*0.6*	*111*	

Breakout: 29%   Improve: 38%   Collapse: 10%   Attrition: 38%   MLB: 57%   Comparables: *Ty Blach, Rudy Owens, Logan Verrett*

In his first at-bat for the Dodgers, Chris Taylor tripled. In his first inning for the Mariners, Lee #REF! Okay, he didn't pitch for the Mariners in 2016 and earned his release, but he's a useful depth piece and if enough goes wrong with the Padre arms in front of him next year, he might prove to be exzachlee what the doctor ordered. It'll be far from ideal, but then again so was that pun.

Ariel Miranda   LHP

Born: 1/10/89   Age: 28   Bats: L   Throws: L   Height: 6'2"   Weight: 190   Entered Pro Ball: International Free Agent, 2015

YEAR	TEAM	LVL	AGE	W	L	SV	G	GS	IP	H	HR	BB/9	K/9	K	GB%	BABIP	WHIP	ERA	FIP	DRA	VORP	WARP	cFIP	MPH
2015	FRD	A+	26	1	1	0	5	5	22	16	2	3.3	9.8	24	18%	.255	1.09	4.09	3.48	2.47	6.4	0.7	89	
2015	BOW	AA	26	5	2	0	8	8	45	40	1	3.6	8.2	41	37%	.298	1.29	3.60	3.07	4.13	4.8	0.5	97	
2016	BAL	MLB	27	0	0	0	1	0	2	4	0	0.0	18.0	4	43%	.571	2.00	13.50	-0.89	7.18	-0.4	0.0	125	95.4
2016	NOR	AAA	27	4	7	0	19	19	100²	95	11	2.8	7.8	87	38%	.291	1.25	3.93	3.84	4.06	14.3	1.5	101	
2016	SEA	MLB	27	5	2	0	11	10	56	43	12	2.9	6.4	40	31%	.205	1.09	3.54	5.43	6.32	-6.1	-0.6	124	95.5
2017	*SEA*	*MLB*	*28*	*9*	*10*	*0*	*29*	*29*	*153²*	*156*	*24*	*3.3*	*7.2*	*123*	*60%*	*.288*	*1.37*	*4.66*	*4.82*	*5.17*	*1.3*	*0.1*	*100*	
2018	*SEA*	*MLB*	*29*	*9*	*11*	*0*	*30*	*30*	*185*	*175*	*31*	*4.0*	*9.1*	*187*	*60%*	*.290*	*1.39*	*4.64*	*4.74*	*5.12*	*6.1*	*0.6*	*120*	

Breakout: 21%   Improve: 30%   Collapse: 13%   Attrition: 28%   MLB: 51%   Comparables: *Radhames Liz, Michael O'Connor, Darrell Rasner*

Acquired at the deadline for Wade Miley, Miranda is still pretty raw two years after defecting from Cuba. Coaches in Seattle have noted how keen he is to learn and improve. If his slider and splitter develop into solid secondary options to pair with his fastball, Miranda's a good back-of-the-rotation piece. If they don't, you have another lefty to try out in the 'pen. Either way, it's clear he wishes he could be where the people are, up where they walk, up where they run, up where they stay all day in the sun.

Andrew Moore   RHP

Born: 6/2/94   Age: 23   Bats: R   Throws: R   Height: 6'0"   Weight: 185   Entered Pro Ball: Round 2, 2015 Draft (#72 overall)

YEAR	TEAM	LVL	AGE	W	L	SV	G	GS	IP	H	HR	BB/9	K/9	K	GB%	BABIP	WHIP	ERA	FIP	DRA	VORP	WARP	cFIP	MPH
2015	EVE	A-	21	1	1	0	14	8	39	37	2	0.5	9.9	43	46%	.340	1.00	2.08	2.29	1.36	16.3	1.7	62	
2016	BAK	A+	22	3	1	0	9	9	54²	36	2	2.1	7.7	47	45%	.230	0.90	1.65	3.18	3.09	14.5	1.5	92	
2016	WTN	AA	22	9	3	0	19	19	108¹	112	9	1.5	7.1	86	36%	.320	1.20	3.16	3.34	3.41	20.2	2.2	99	
2017	*SEA*	*MLB*	*23*	*7*	*7*	*0*	*22*	*22*	*110²*	*122*	*17*	*2.8*	*5.8*	*71*	*56%*	*.295*	*1.41*	*4.80*	*4.87*	*5.16*	*3.8*	*0.4*	*124*	
2018	*SEA*	*MLB*	*24*	*7*	*8*	*0*	*23*	*23*	*135*	*135*	*22*	*4.3*	*8.4*	*127*	*56%*	*.299*	*1.48*	*4.86*	*4.96*	*5.22*	*3.3*	*0.3*	*126*	

Breakout: 8%   Improve: 12%   Collapse: 1%   Attrition: 20%   MLB: 29%   Comparables: *Kendry Flores, Jeff Manship, Dan Straily*

Given that Moore has already succeeded in Double-A, he has a case as the top starter in Seattle's minor league system. The right-hander works off of a low-90s fastball and mixes in a changeup, curve and a show-me slider. While his change and curve could be average pitches or a tick better at full maturity it's not clear that either will be a bat-misser at the highest level. Moore compensates somewhat with his control, but against big league bats he'll have to be very precise to get by with his stuff, and evaluators aren't sold on him as a rotation arm. His ceiling is as a no. 4 starter and if he pitches well in Tacoma next spring, he should get a big league shot in 2017.

James Paxton   LHP

Born: 11/6/88   Age: 28   Bats: L   Throws: L   Height: 6'4"   Weight: 235   Entered Pro Ball: Round 4, 2010 Draft (#132 overall)

YEAR	TEAM	LVL	AGE	W	L	SV	G	GS	IP	H	HR	BB/9	K/9	K	GB%	BABIP	WHIP	ERA	FIP	DRA	VORP	WARP	cFIP	MPH
2014	TAC	AAA	25	0	1	0	3	3	10¹	13	2	5.2	12.2	14	53%	.393	1.84	4.35	5.25	3.78	2.3	0.2	92	
2014	SEA	MLB	25	6	4	0	13	13	74	60	3	3.5	7.2	59	57%	.270	1.20	3.04	3.31	3.04	14.8	1.6	95	97.8
2015	SEA	MLB	26	3	4	0	13	13	67	67	8	3.9	7.5	56	50%	.289	1.43	3.90	4.28	5.13	-0.4	0.0	103	97.2
2016	TAC	AAA	27	4	3	0	11	11	50²	43	6	2.7	9.4	53	52%	.285	1.14	3.73	4.06	2.82	14.2	1.5	80	
2016	SEA	MLB	27	6	7	0	20	20	121	134	9	1.8	8.7	117	49%	.347	1.31	3.79	2.76	3.09	30.5	3.1	79	99.7
2017	*SEA*	*MLB*	*28*	*12*	*9*	*0*	*31*	*31*	*176²*	*173*	*21*	*2.8*	*8.5*	*167*	*44%*	*.302*	*1.30*	*3.66*	*3.86*	*4.09*	*22.7*	*2.3*	*93*	
2018	*SEA*	*MLB*	*29*	*10*	*10*	*0*	*30*	*30*	*190²*	*182*	*24*	*3.5*	*9.6*	*203*	*44%*	*.309*	*1.34*	*3.87*	*3.97*	*4.29*	*22.3*	*2.3*	*96*	

Breakout: 18%   Improve: 38%   Collapse: 29%   Attrition: 29%   MLB: 86%   Comparables: *Dana Eveland, Roberto Hernandez, Zach Britton*

If Paxton's 2016 were a teen movie, it would be the sort where the purportedly mousy heroine takes off her glasses, shakes loose her ponytail and realizes she was actually beautiful all along. A slimmed down Paxton started the year in Triple-A, where his transformation began with a simple throw to first to find his natural arm slot (the baseball equivalent of taking off your glasses); affording him more comfortable mechanics and increased velocity. Suddenly he was throwing a high-90s fastball that could touch 100. For strikes. From the left side. Consistently. That, coupled with a good cutter and curveball, made him very tough to face; he ended the season with a career-best FIP and barely-over-three DRA. His durability remains a question—no Paxton season would be complete without a stint on the DL—but if he can stay healthy and sustain his 2016 form, his transformation will be complete. You were beautiful all along, James. You just had to see it in yourself.

Marc Rzepczynski   LHP

Born: 8/29/85   Age: 31   Bats: L   Throws: L   Height: 6'2"   Weight: 220   Entered Pro Ball: Round 5, 2007 Draft (#175 overall)

YEAR	TEAM	LVL	AGE	W	L	SV	G	GS	IP	H	HR	BB/9	K/9	K	GB%	BABIP	WHIP	ERA	FIP	DRA	VORP	WARP	cFIP	MPH
2014	CLE	MLB	28	0	3	1	73	0	46	42	1	3.7	9.0	46	61%	.323	1.33	2.74	2.88	3.02	7.5	0.8	92	94.1
2015	CLE	MLB	29	2	3	0	45	0	20¹	23	1	4.4	10.6	24	73%	.379	1.62	4.43	3.01	2.64	4.7	0.5	83	94.7
2015	SDN	MLB	29	0	1	0	27	0	14²	17	2	2.5	10.4	17	66%	.385	1.43	7.36	3.84	2.48	3.6	0.4	80	94.3
2016	OAK	MLB	30	1	0	0	56	0	36	38	1	6.0	9.2	37	71%	.352	1.72	3.00	3.58	4.20	3.1	0.3	90	93.5
2016	WAS	MLB	30	0	0	0	14	0	11²	8	0	3.9	6.9	9	63%	.267	1.11	1.54	3.44	3.71	1.6	0.2	90	94.2
2017	SEA	MLB	31	2	2	0	47	0	49¹	47	5	4.0	8.7	47	62%	.300	1.39	3.89	4.10	4.33	3.6	0.4	94	
2018	SEA	MLB	32	2	1	0	38	0	40¹	38	4	3.8	8.6	38	62%	.302	1.38	3.88	3.98	4.30	3.3	0.3	92	

Breakout: 29%   Improve: 45%   Collapse: 20%   Attrition: 16%   MLB: 80%   *Comparables: Joe Thatcher, Rafael Perez, Casey Janssen*

It's true, Rzepczynski lost a tiny piece of his fastball this year. But mediocre early-season results could be chalked up to poor situational execution and luck against left-handers. He yielded a leadoff baserunner in more than 40 percent of his appearances for Oakland. And his typically robust split against southpaws came tumbling on its head, weighed down by an inflated BABIP in spite of weaker contact. Fans mangled his name with unseasonably vile efforts. Another change of scenery was needed, and it occurred in late August when the Nats bought him and promptly reintroduced him to his left-on-left mojo. His combination of elite ground-ball rate, successful track record and southpawitude made him an attractive bullpen asset in free agency.

Evan Scribner   RHP

Born: 7/19/85   Age: 31   Bats: R   Throws: R   Height: 6'3"   Weight: 190   Entered Pro Ball: Round 28, 2007 Draft (#853 overall)

YEAR	TEAM	LVL	AGE	W	L	SV	G	GS	IP	H	HR	BB/9	K/9	K	GB%	BABIP	WHIP	ERA	FIP	DRA	VORP	WARP	cFIP	MPH
2014	SAC	AAA	28	4	1	16	40	0	47	39	4	1.7	13.8	72	38%	.337	1.02	3.06	2.38	0.27	26.5	2.6	50	
2014	OAK	MLB	28	1	0	0	13	0	11²	11	4	0.0	8.5	11	37%	.226	0.94	4.63	5.99	4.59	-0.1	0.0	103	93.6
2015	OAK	MLB	29	2	2	0	54	0	60	58	14	0.6	9.6	64	40%	.286	1.03	4.35	4.30	3.01	11.4	1.2	83	93.3
2016	SEA	MLB	30	0	0	0	12	0	14	5	0	1.3	9.6	15	32%	.161	0.50	0.00	1.61	3.34	2.5	0.3	93	92.2
2017	SEA	MLB	31	3	3	0	51	0	54	50	8	2.3	9.1	55	51%	.288	1.18	3.79	3.94	4.28	4.2	0.4	98	
2018	SEA	MLB	32	3	1	0	57	0	60¹	52	10	2.7	9.9	66	51%	.270	1.15	4.08	4.20	4.58	3.1	0.3	105	

Breakout: 25%   Improve: 33%   Collapse: 20%   Attrition: 11%   MLB: 72%   *Comparables: Casey Fien, Mike Adams, George Sherrill*

Scribner continued his trend of treating walks like treason in 2016, partly because of preternatural command but mostly because of an almost season-long stint on the disabled list, punctuated by lengthy stretches of staring out the window at a brick wall. The fastball still sits around 90 and he only pitched 14 innings when he returned in September, but hey, at least they were 14 good innings! Looking ahead to 2017, Scribner would no doubt love to see a repeat of his home run rate (he gave up none) but if asked to repeat the injuries, he'd no doubt say, "I would prefer not to."

Drew Storen   RHP

Born: 8/11/87   Age: 29   Bats: B   Throws: R   Height: 6'1"   Weight: 195   Entered Pro Ball: Round 1, 2009 Draft (#10 overall)

YEAR	TEAM	LVL	AGE	W	L	SV	G	GS	IP	H	HR	BB/9	K/9	K	GB%	BABIP	WHIP	ERA	FIP	DRA	VORP	WARP	cFIP	MPH
2014	WAS	MLB	26	2	1	11	65	0	56¹	44	2	1.8	7.3	46	54%	.259	0.98	1.12	2.68	3.24	7.8	0.9	93	95.6
2015	WAS	MLB	27	2	2	29	58	0	55	45	4	2.6	11.0	67	44%	.301	1.11	3.44	2.82	3.36	8.3	0.9	85	96.3
2016	TOR	MLB	28	1	3	3	38	0	33¹	43	6	2.7	8.6	32	48%	.363	1.59	6.21	4.97	3.99	3.6	0.4	97	94.1
2016	SEA	MLB	28	3	0	0	19	0	18¹	13	1	1.5	7.9	16	54%	.235	0.87	3.44	2.72	4.16	1.7	0.2	97	94.0
2017	SEA	MLB	29	2	1	8	44	0	46²	44	7	2.8	8.9	46	57%	.292	1.26	4.07	4.20	4.51	2.5	0.3	102	
2018	SEA	MLB	30	3	1	11	60	0	54²	51	8	3.0	9.0	55	57%	.292	1.27	4.01	4.11	4.44	3.7	0.4	101	

Breakout: 28%   Improve: 52%   Collapse: 26%   Attrition: 19%   MLB: 94%   *Comparables: Jesse Crain, Bobby Jenks, Frank Francisco*

Storen didn't regain the closer form he once showed with the Nationals, but he pitched much better for the Mariners after the super rare Disappointing Reliever Challenge Trade. He walked fewer guys, increased his ground-ball rate and gave up fewer home runs. It all added up to a FIP just under half of what he posted for Toronto. He's not a 43-save guy anymore, to cite a gauche stat, but he's not unemployable either. That's something, right?

Nick Vincent   RHP

Born: 7/12/86   Age: 30   Bats: R   Throws: R   Height: 6'0"   Weight: 185   Entered Pro Ball: Round 18, 2008 Draft (#555 overall)

YEAR	TEAM	LVL	AGE	W	L	SV	G	GS	IP	H	HR	BB/9	K/9	K	GB%	BABIP	WHIP	ERA	FIP	DRA	VORP	WARP	cFIP	MPH
2014	SDN	MLB	27	1	2	0	63	0	55	44	5	1.8	10.1	62	38%	.289	1.00	3.60	2.74	3.23	7.7	0.8	90	91.5
2015	ELP	AAA	28	5	3	1	40	0	50¹	48	5	2.7	12.2	68	44%	.355	1.25	3.04	3.08	1.15	21.1	2.2	71	
2015	SDN	MLB	28	0	1	0	26	0	23	25	0	3.9	8.6	22	34%	.368	1.52	2.35	2.55	5.05	-0.9	-0.1	112	91.3
2016	SEA	MLB	29	4	4	3	60	0	60¹	53	11	2.2	9.7	65	34%	.271	1.13	3.73	4.12	3.88	7.3	0.8	96	92.0
2017	SEA	MLB	30	3	3	5	51	0	54	51	8	2.8	9.3	56	41%	.295	1.25	3.81	4.07	4.28	4.2	0.4	96	
2018	SEA	MLB	31	2	1	2	44	0	46²	43	7	3.2	10.0	52	41%	.293	1.26	3.97	4.09	4.42	3.2	0.3	98	

Breakout: 33%   Improve: 58%   Collapse: 18%   Attrition: 23%   MLB: 88%   *Comparables: Tony Watson, Brad Brach, Jason Motte*

If we applied the Anna Karenina principle to relievers, we'd say that all happy relievers are alike and each unhappy reliever is unhappy in his own way. With all due respect to Tolstoy, it seems that many unhappy relievers follow a pattern. Case in point: Nick Vincent, who was traded to a Mariners team willing to give him the innings the Padres wouldn't, pitched well in April and May with a good K/9 and FIP before trying to pitch through a mid-back sprain and landing on the disabled list. He rejoined the club in August with mixed results. He'll hope to be one of the happy relievers in 2017; healthy and keeping plenty of distance between him and any oncoming trains.

Ryan Weber   RHP

Born: 8/12/90   Age: 26   Bats: R   Throws: R   Height: 6'1"   Weight: 180   Entered Pro Ball: Round 22, 2009 Draft (#658 overall)

YEAR	TEAM	LVL	AGE	W	L	SV	G	GS	IP	H	HR	BB/9	K/9	K	GB%	BABIP	WHIP	ERA	FIP	DRA	VORP	WARP	cFIP	MPH
2014	MIS	AA	23	5	6	0	32	13	101¹	129	7	1.4	5.5	62	58%	.349	1.43	4.53	3.36	2.62	27.6	2.9	92	
2015	MIS	AA	24	0	2	1	11	3	26¹	23	1	0.3	8.2	24	43%	.293	0.91	2.73	2.09	1.48	9.9	1.1	80	
2015	GWN	AAA	24	6	3	3	27	6	73¹	60	7	1.1	4.3	35	61%	.233	0.94	2.21	3.93	2.56	20.5	2.1	94	
2015	ATL	MLB	24	0	3	0	5	5	28¹	25	3	1.9	6.0	19	66%	.278	1.09	4.76	4.04	3.83	3.9	0.4	98	91.5
2016	GWN	AAA	25	2	3	1	26	5	62	65	1	2.0	6.0	41	56%	.308	1.27	2.76	2.93	2.80	15.7	1.6	97	
2016	ATL	MLB	25	1	1	0	16	2	36¹	46	7	1.2	5.7	23	50%	.325	1.40	5.45	5.00	5.25	-0.8	-0.1	105	92.8
2017	SEA	MLB	26	5	4	1	44	10	83¹	95	11	2.4	5.4	50	52%	.302	1.41	4.49	4.58	4.98	3.1	0.3	114	
2018	SEA	MLB	27	3	3	1	25	8	82¹	83	11	3.7	7.7	70	52%	.301	1.43	4.44	4.53	4.92	2.8	0.3	112	

Breakout: 22%   Improve: 36%   Collapse: 17%   Attrition: 33%   MLB: 59%   Comparables: Doug Fister, Roberto Hernandez, Geno Espineli

After making 21 appearances over two seasons with Atlanta, Weber's eight-year stint in the Braves' organization came to an end when the Mariners claimed him off of waivers. If he's going to keep on earning major league meal money he'll have to figure out a way to keep the ball out of the air. His fly-ball rate was nearly 30 percent, and his HR/FB rate was 20 percent. That's a recipe for disaster as certain as sharpies, freshly-painted walls and unsupervised toddlers.

Robert Whalen   RHP

Born: 1/31/94   Age: 23   Bats: R   Throws: R   Height: 6'2"   Weight: 220   Entered Pro Ball: Round 12, 2012 Draft (#380 overall)

YEAR	TEAM	LVL	AGE	W	L	SV	G	GS	IP	H	HR	BB/9	K/9	K	GB%	BABIP	WHIP	ERA	FIP	DRA	VORP	WARP	cFIP	MPH
2014	SAV	A	20	9	1	0	11	10	62²	44	2	2.7	7.6	53	58%	.239	1.01	2.01	3.46	4.28	7.9	0.8	98	
2015	SLU	A+	21	4	5	0	15	14	83	72	4	3.7	6.6	61	51%	.273	1.28	3.36	3.84	6.30	-11.4	-1.2	113	
2015	CAR	A+	21	1	2	0	3	3	13²	11	2	2.6	4.6	7	60%	.225	1.10	3.29	5.01	4.86	0.3	0.0	104	
2016	MIS	AA	22	7	5	0	18	18	101¹	87	4	3.3	8.3	94	55%	.292	1.22	2.49	3.19	2.03	34.5	3.7	89	
2016	GWN	AAA	22	0	1	0	3	3	18²	12	0	3.4	8.7	18	45%	.255	1.02	1.93	2.53	3.60	3.6	0.4	93	
2016	ATL	MLB	22	1	2	0	5	5	24²	20	4	4.4	9.1	25	44%	.242	1.30	6.57	5.09	4.91	1.2	0.1	105	91.8
2017	SEA	MLB	23	4	5	0	33	10	74²	73	9	3.9	6.8	57	55%	.286	1.40	4.60	4.70	4.95	1.7	0.2	100	
2018	SEA	MLB	24	7	6	0	61	16	144	118	17	5.3	10.1	162	55%	.281	1.41	4.27	4.37	4.68	9.1	0.9	107	

Breakout: 25%   Improve: 44%   Collapse: 15%   Attrition: 40%   MLB: 66%   Comparables: Trevor Rosenthal, Blake Snell, David Holmberg

Whalen joined the Braves' season-long parade of overmatched young starters in early August and took his share of lumps. He did show flashes of potential that suggest he's got a future as a back-of-the-rotation starter, despite the fact that he doesn't have the stuff to blow hitters away. It'll take a whale of an effort in camp to see him make an Opening Day roster, but don't be surprised to see him pitching in the majors again in 2017.

Tom Wilhelmsen   RHP

Born: 12/16/83   Age: 33   Bats: R   Throws: R   Height: 6'6"   Weight: 220   Entered Pro Ball: Round 7, 2002 Draft (#199 overall)

YEAR	TEAM	LVL	AGE	W	L	SV	G	GS	IP	H	HR	BB/9	K/9	K	GB%	BABIP	WHIP	ERA	FIP	DRA	VORP	WARP	cFIP	MPH
2014	SEA	MLB	30	3	2	1	57	2	79¹	47	6	4.1	8.2	72	53%	.204	1.05	2.27	3.76	3.95	4.9	0.5	100	98.0
2015	SEA	MLB	31	2	2	13	53	0	62	56	3	4.2	8.7	60	45%	.308	1.37	3.19	3.30	3.95	5.2	0.6	102	97.5
2016	TEX	MLB	32	2	3	0	21	0	21¹	38	7	3.8	4.6	11	49%	.387	2.20	10.55	7.89	5.86	-2.1	-0.2	115	96.8
2016	SEA	MLB	32	0	1	1	29	0	25	22	4	3.6	6.1	17	53%	.261	1.28	3.60	5.03	5.84	-2.4	-0.2	115	97.6
2017	SEA	MLB	33	2	1	3	48	0	51	49	8	3.9	7.8	44	48%	.284	1.40	4.73	4.85	5.24	-1.1	-0.1	120	
2018	SEA	MLB	34	1	0	1	24	0	27¹	28	5	4.2	7.7	23	48%	.293	1.49	5.08	5.21	5.63	-1.7	-0.2	130	

Breakout: 24%   Improve: 42%   Collapse: 24%   Attrition: 9%   MLB: 79%   Comparables: Santiago Casilla, Matt Wise, Matt Lindstrom

The Bartender started 2016 in Texas after being dealt with a couple of chasers for Leonys Martin. He racked up a FIP equivalent to a second grader's punch line in 21.3 innings, leaving Rangers fans wanting one bourbon, one scotch and one beer, but fared better after returning to Seattle. Sometimes you want to go where everybody knows your name. Despite the return to form Wilhelmsen was DFA'ed when the Mariners acquired James Pazos from the Yankees, proving that if you're a 32-year-old, inconsistent reliever likely due more than $3 million in arbitration, you don't have to go home but you can't stay here.

Ryan Yarbrough   LHP

Born: 12/31/91   Age: 25   Bats: R   Throws: L   Height: 6'5"   Weight: 205   Entered Pro Ball: Round 4, 2014 Draft (#111 overall)

YEAR	TEAM	LVL	AGE	W	L	SV	G	GS	IP	H	HR	BB/9	K/9	K	GB%	BABIP	WHIP	ERA	FIP	DRA	VORP	WARP	cFIP	MPH
2014	EVE	A-	22	0	1	0	12	10	38²	25	1	0.9	12.3	53	60%	.263	0.75	1.40	1.87	2.69	11.4	1.2	71	
2015	BAK	A+	23	4	7	0	16	16	81¹	86	7	2.0	8.2	74	55%	.321	1.28	3.76	3.93	3.16	17.4	1.9	93	
2016	WTN	AA	24	12	4	0	25	25	128¹	112	7	2.2	6.9	99	50%	.276	1.11	2.95	3.30	2.99	30.1	3.2	96	
2017	SEA	MLB	25	6	7	0	21	21	97²	110	15	3.2	5.5	59	52%	.295	1.48	4.96	5.14	5.37	1.1	0.1	128	
2018	SEA	MLB	26	5	7	0	21	21	123	120	19	4.5	8.3	114	52%	.289	1.48	4.98	5.07	5.39	0.9	0.1	128	

Breakout: 15%   Improve: 20%   Collapse: 7%   Attrition: 26%   MLB: 32%   Comparables: Heath Phillips, Yohan Flande, Robert Ray

Among the potential back-end starters in Seattle's system, Yarbrough might have the profile that best fits his organization. As a lefty with decent command Yarbrough is well-suited for Safeco Field, and as a 25-year-old with more than 250 professional innings under his belt, he's the club's most polished high-minors arm. His delivery looks a little stiff at a glance, but he repeats well and he gets a little deception out of his rock-and-fire motion. At this point, his success will be determined by whether he can improve his breaking ball. His curve isn't good enough right now to get whiffs consistently, and unless it takes a step forward he probably won't crack the rotation.

Anthony Zych RHP

Born: 8/7/90 Age: 26 Bats: R Throws: R Height: 6'3" Weight: 190 Entered Pro Ball: Round 4, 2011 Draft (#129 overall)

YEAR	TEAM	LVL	AGE	W	L	SV	G	GS	IP	H	HR	BB/9	K/9	K	GB%	BABIP	WHIP	ERA	FIP	DRA	VORP	WARP	cFIP	MPH
2014	TEN	AA	23	4	5	2	45	0	58¹	75	3	2.8	5.4	35	56%	.369	1.59	5.09	3.74	4.53	2.1	0.2	100	
2015	WTN	AA	24	0	0	5	15	0	16²	11	0	0.0	9.7	18	54%	.268	0.66	2.16	1.68	2.15	4.8	0.5	72	
2015	TAC	AAA	24	1	2	4	25	0	31²	34	2	2.6	10.5	37	54%	.376	1.36	3.41	3.13	2.00	10.3	1.0	84	
2015	SEA	MLB	24	0	0	0	13	1	18¹	17	1	1.5	11.8	24	53%	.348	1.09	2.45	2.01	2.87	3.9	0.4	79	98.6
2016	SEA	MLB	25	1	0	0	12	0	13²	10	0	6.6	13.8	21	50%	.357	1.46	3.29	2.45	2.57	3.6	0.4	82	97.3
2017	*SEA*	*MLB*	*26*	*1*	*1*	*0*	*19*	*0*	*19²*	*19*	*2*	*3.3*	*8.5*	*19*	*53%*	*.303*	*1.39*	*3.95*	*3.78*	*4.39*	*1.3*	*0.1*	*100*	
2018	*SEA*	*MLB*	*27*	*2*	*1*	*0*	*40*	*0*	*42²*	*36*	*5*	*4.6*	*11.1*	*52*	*53%*	*.306*	*1.37*	*3.78*	*3.88*	*4.21*	*3.9*	*0.4*	*93*	

Breakout: 33% Improve: 42% Collapse: 16% Attrition: 27% MLB: 62% *Comparables: Cory Burns, Pedro Strop, R.J. Swindle*

Zych had all the makings of a great story coming into 2016: acquired from the Cubs for $1 (literally one dollar), he tweaked his delivery and was throwing strikes with a good fastball and an above-average slider. The contract made him an intriguing hero and the improved control gave him the pitches for the part. Sadly, he was sidelined for much of the year with right rotator cuff tendinitis. Zych underwent right shoulder biceps tendon transfer surgery, which sounds like a smattering of Mary Shelley prose but apparently puts you on a path to be ready for spring training.

LINEOUTS

Hitters

NAME	POS	TEAM	LVL	AGE	PA	R	2B	3B	HR	RBI	BB	K	SB	CS	AVG/OBP/SLG	TAv	VORP	BABIP	BRR	FRAA	WARP
Bryson Brigman	MI	EVE	A-	21	318	51	6	1	0	19	41	43	17	12	.260/.369/.291	.256	10.9	.308	0.8	SS(51): -1.1 • 2B(15): -0.2	1.0
Michael Freeman	SS	RNO	AAA	28	384	56	17	6	1	24	38	75	11	1	.317/.387/.411	.283	23.2	.402	3.8	2B(71): 6.7 • CF(11): -0.4	2.9
	SS	ARI	MLB	28	11	0	0	0	0	0	2	5	0	0	.000/.182/.000	.081	-1.7	.000	0.0	RF(1): -0.1 • LF(1): -0.0	-0.2
	SS	TAC	AAA	28	119	15	6	0	3	15	13	19	1	0	.305/.378/.448	.298	8.1	.345	-0.1	2B(21): -0.4 • SS(3): 0.0	0.9
	SS	SEA	MLB	28	13	1	1	0	0	1	0	2	0	0	.385/.385/.462	.277	0.1	.455	-0.5	2B(5): 0.1 • SS(2): -0.0	0.0
Drew Jackson	SS	BAK	A+	22	596	87	24	2	6	47	50	105	16	8	.258/.332/.345	.253	22.1	.310	2.4	SS(120): 13.7	3.7
Stefen Romero	RF	SEA	MLB	27	19	1	1	0	0	3	1	4	0	0	.235/.263/.294	.257	-0.5	.286	-0.8	LF(6): 0.0 • RF(2): -0.0	-0.1
	RF	TAC	AAA	27	462	70	24	6	21	85	36	67	1	1	.304/.361/.541	.324	37.2	.317	-0.9	RF(52): -5.7 • 1B(18): -0.6	3.3
Nick Zammarelli	3B	EVE	A-	21	284	44	18	1	5	43	25	67	3	2	.329/.391/.467	.303	16.7	.427	-2.7	3B(42): 0.8 • 1B(8): 0.1	1.8

Seattle's third rounder last year, **Bryson Brigman** doesn't have the arm for short or the bat to play second. ❖ **Michael Freeman** played well enough in limited opportunities to start at second base the day after the Mariners were eliminated from the playoffs. ❖ **Brayan Hernandez** is an excellent athlete with electric bat speed and great range in center, but also gets eaten alive by good spin and needs to work on his approach—just a typical teenager getting good grades but flaking on his chores. ❖ **Drew Jackson**'s offensive numbers plummeted after a two-level jump in 2016, but defense is his calling card here and the attributes that made him attractive last winter—plus speed, plus-plus arm and good instincts in the field—were on display in the California League. ❖ Stubborn analysts insist that there is no such thing as a Quad-A player. **Stefen Romero** has defied that perspective for years, and now he'll try to cement the label in Japan. ❖ **Christopher Torres** was a bright spot at short for the AZL Mariners last summer, and he has a chance to be the organization's best middle infield prospect since…man, the Mariners have not had a lot of good ones lately. ❖ The sleeper to watch from last year's draft, **Nick Zammarelli** isn't a budding star, but the Elon product showed he could do a bit of everything in the Northwest League last summer.

Pitchers

NAME	TEAM	LVL	AGE	W	L	SV	G	GS	IP	H	HR	BB/9	K/9	K	GB%	BABIP	WHIP	ERA	FIP	DRA	VORP	WARP	cFIP	MPH
Al Alburquerque	ANA	MLB	30	0	0	0	2	0	2	2	1	9.0	4.5	1	67%	.125	2.00	4.50	11.61	5.08	0.0	0.0	109	93.7
	SLC	AAA	30	1	0	8	24	0	23²	24	0	4.9	9.9	26	37%	.353	1.56	3.80	3.17	3.68	3.4	0.3	107	
Zac Curtis	VIS	A+	23	1	0	2	8	0	10¹	12	0	4.4	19.2	22	48%	.571	1.65	5.23	1.20	1.20	4.5	0.5	74	
	ARI	MLB	23	0	1	0	21	0	13¹	13	2	8.8	6.8	10	39%	.282	1.95	6.75	7.24	7.23	-3.3	-0.3	124	93.3
	MOB	AA	23	0	1	4	19	0	19²	17	3	2.7	13.7	30	33%	.326	1.17	3.20	3.17	1.35	7.4	0.8	76	
Casey Fien	MIN	MLB	32	1	0	0	14	0	13²	21	5	2.0	7.9	12	29%	.372	1.76	7.90	6.76	4.72	0.4	0.0	109	94.4
	OKL	AAA	32	1	0	1	8	0	10¹	11	1	1.7	11.3	13	33%	.385	1.26	4.35	3.04	2.48	2.9	0.3	89	
	LAN	MLB	32	0	1	0	25	0	25²	24	8	2.5	8.1	23	42%	.235	1.21	4.21	6.26	4.81	0.5	0.0	110	95.6
Paul Fry	TAC	AAA	23	3	1	0	48	1	55	48	1	5.1	10.6	65	57%	.329	1.44	2.78	3.50	2.55	14.9	1.5	91	
Steve Johnson	SEA	MLB	28	1	0	0	16	0	16²	13	3	5.9	9.2	17	30%	.227	1.44	4.32	5.39	5.65	-1.3	-0.1	118	91.9
	TAC	AAA	28	3	0	0	11	0	22	14	1	2.5	10.6	26	46%	.265	0.91	2.05	3.04	1.59	8.2	0.8	80	
Cody Martin	TAC	AAA	26	10	7	0	25	20	114¹	106	6	2.6	9.0	114	37%	.322	1.22	3.62	3.41	1.92	43.1	4.4	92	
	SEA	MLB	26	1	2	0	9	2	25²	28	5	3.2	5.3	15	49%	.299	1.44	3.86	5.64	4.86	0.7	0.1	110	90.4
Brandon Miller	EVE	A-	21	4	2	0	14	13	56¹	47	3	1.1	8.1	51	50%	.266	0.96	2.72	3.24	2.09	19.6	2.1	79	
Nick Neidert	CLN	A	19	7	3	0	19	19	91	75	7	1.3	6.8	69	41%	.262	0.97	2.57	3.59	3.33	17.0	1.9	92	
Emilio Pagan	WTN	AA	25	4	1	9	18	0	30²	19	1	3.2	13.2	45	32%	.269	0.98	1.17	1.98	1.54	10.9	1.2	74	
	TAC	AAA	25	1	2	1	23	0	34¹	28	6	4.7	10.2	39	32%	.268	1.34	3.67	5.29	5.04	-0.3	0.0	104	
James Pazos	SWB	AAA	25	2	2	1	23	0	27¹	19	1	6.3	13.5	41	57%	.316	1.39	2.63	2.73	2.25	8.2	0.9	83	
	NYA	MLB	25	1	0	0	7	0	3¹	7	2	2.7	8.1	3	46%	.455	2.40	13.50	10.01	4.56	0.2	0.0	110	97.9
Tyler Pike	BAK	A+	22	6	5	0	25	25	125²	99	11	4.9	9.6	134	47%	.284	1.33	4.01	4.49	4.21	17.7	1.8	106	
Pat Venditte	TOR	MLB	31	0	0	0	8	0	8²	11	1	4.2	7.3	7	41%	.323	1.73	5.19	4.72	5.05	-0.1	0.0	108	88.0
	BUF	AAA	31	2	1	0	25	2	35	39	3	3.3	13.4	52	34%	.400	1.49	4.37	2.68	2.67	9.1	0.9	108	
	SEA	MLB	31	0	0	0	7	0	13¹	13	4	4.7	8.1	12	40%	.265	1.50	6.07	7.01	4.66	0.5	0.0	109	88.2
Thyago Vieira	BAK	A+	22	1	0	8	34	0	44¹	37	1	3.7	10.8	53	53%	.313	1.24	2.84	2.97	2.83	11.1	1.1	90	
Nick Wells	CLN	A	20	1	9	0	18	18	84¹	95	9	4.1	6.4	60	42%	.312	1.58	5.55	4.86	7.86	-26.7	-2.9	119	

Al Alburquerque tosses six wholly unremarkable innings for Tacoma last summer, placing him exactly 1173.96 miles and one "r" from Albuquerque. ❖ **Ryan Cook** spent the entire season on the 60-day disabled list, and while the stated reason was a strained right latissimus dorsi muscle, the real reason was the universe course correcting for all of the "Too Many Cooks" jokes. ❖ Called up early in the season from High-A Visalia, **Zac Curtis** really did come out of nowhere to join the D-backs' bullpen. Problem is, he's not very good and doesn't have much left in the way of projection. ❖ **Casey Fien** allowed three homers per nine, which somehow isn't as bad as the spelling of his surname. ❖ A career-long reliever and former 17th-round pick, left-hander **Paul Fry** has racked up 289 strikeouts in 235 pro innings along with very shaky control. ❖ **Steve Johnson's** curveball bottomed out at 60.2 mph last season. He elected free agency rather than be optioned to Tacoma, after which his name was lost to the winds. ❖ **Cody Martin** has started two games in each of the last two seasons. If he gets there in a third straight year, something will have again gone terribly wrong. ❖ The Mariners have done well scouting players from small colleges in Pennsylvania, but plucking **Brandon Miller** from Millersville University in the sixth round last year may be as prescient as it is precious. ❖ He may not be done growing, but **Nick Neidert** is already throwing in the low-90's and flashing two average or better secondary offerings. That's promising, but his curve needs to take a step forward if he's going to miss bats. ❖ Upon hearing that **Emilio Pagan** was not among two arms recalled from Pulaski to Everett back in 2013, the club's pitching coach snapped "they're gonna give me two more guys but they can't send me Pagan?" Unlike the previous sentence's implication Pagan isn't a savior, but he could do a tidy job in the seventh inning someday. ❖ After another year to remember at Triple-A, **James Pazos** will spend his winter sipping tea and aggressively trying to forget a discouraging end to the season that saw him give up two homers in just 3.1 big-league innings. ❖ **Tyler Pike** throws *just* hard enough and *just* enough strikes to keep him on the fringes of prospect lists. Yes, he throws left-handed; why did you ask? ❖ **Pat Venditte**, now it's time to get funky / To the left / Strike 'em out now y'all / One walk this time / Right hand they BOMP / Left hand less BOMP / Cha cha real smooth / Take him out ❖ **Thyago Viera's** slider is a work in progress and he may never have more than 20 command, but when you can hit 102 on the gun you get your name in the paper anyway. ❖ **Nick Wells** stopped missing bats and lost his feel for the zone, but he hits the low-90s on the gun and spins a decent, if soft, breaking ball. Yes, he throws left-handed; why did you ask?

ST. LOUIS CARDINALS

Essay by Will Leitch

Player comments by Ken Funck and BP staff

Less than 12 hours after the Cubs finished off one of the most exciting Game 7s in sports history and—oh, by the way—ended the longest, most notorious drought since the first 40 years of A.C. Green's life, their rivals in St. Louis decided to make an announcement.

With most Cubs players and fans still partying, the Cardinals released a statement that they were extending the contract of manager Mike Matheny through the 2020 season. They could have chosen any time in November to make the announcement. They chose mere hours after the Cubs won the World Series, an occurrence most Cardinals fans had assumed would mean the earth careening off its axis and crashing into the sun. "Our hope was trying to resolve this quickly," general manager John Mozeliak said.

There was a reason for that and Mozeliak expanded on it in an interview with the *St. Louis Post-Dispatch* a week later:

> *"Any time I'm asked about Mike, I feel like I'm always having to defend him. ... I know if you read Twitter or the blogs, [Matheny] definitely takes a black eye out there, but when you watch even the most recent World Series, two of the most highly respected managers in the game were being second-guessed and I think what it really tells you is managing is hard. ... With Mike, whether you agree with how he calls a game or not, he certainly has the respect of his players and he gets the most out of them."*

The Cubs winning the World Series was a massive achievement that shook the Cardinals' franchise and fan base in ways that are still being felt. The Cubs have built what appears to be an unstoppable machine. The Cardinals' immediate, almost instantaneous response was to extend Matheny, whose tactical shortcomings have led him to become perhaps the most lambasted manager in team history. "Early on, when I got the job, I knew it was going to be like drinking from a fire hose that first year," Matheny said at the press conference. "And I still feel like it. There's just so much to learn."

This season will be Matheny's sixth as Cardinals manager, which makes him the fourth-longest-tenured manager in the National League (behind Bruce Bochy, Clint Hurdle and Terry Collins). In modern terms, he's almost a grizzled vet. If he finishes out the contract, he'll have

CARDINALS PROSPECTUS
2016 W-L: 86-76, 2ND IN NL CENTRAL

Pythag	.542	8th	DER	.696	23rd
RS/G	4.81	4th	B-Age	28.6	18th
RA/G	4.4	13th	P-Age	27.9	10th
TAv	.278	2nd	Salary	$145.6M	10th
BRR	-10.56	27th	M$/MW	$3.5M	15th
TAv-P	.263	16th	DL Days	1228	24th
FIP	3.92	8th	$ on DL	21%	23rd

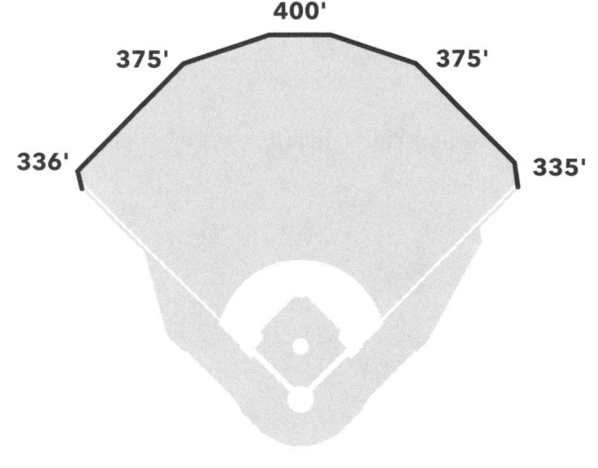

Outfield wall profile: **8'**

Three-Year Park Factors

Runs	Runs/RH	Runs/LH	HR/RH	HR/LH
95	93	93	94	104

Top Hitter WARP	4.2	Matt Carpenter
Top Pitcher WARP	3.6	Carlos Martinez
Top Prospect		Alex Reyes

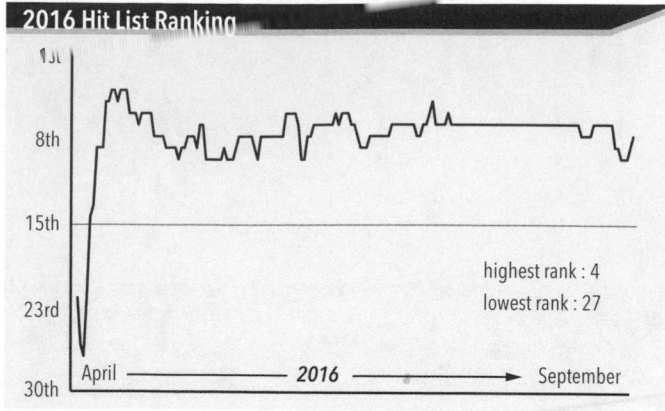

2016 Hit List Ranking

highest rank : 4
lowest rank : 27

April — 2016 → September

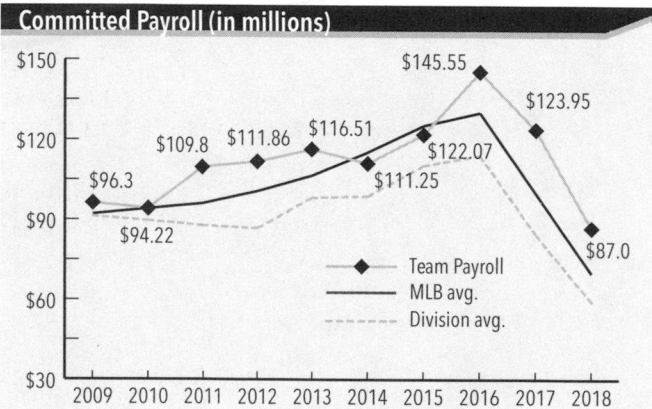

Committed Payroll (in millions)

$96.3
$94.22
$109.8
$111.86
$116.51
$111.25
$122.07
$145.55
$123.95
$87.0

◆ Team Payroll
— MLB avg.
- - - Division avg.

2009 2010 2011 2012 2013 2014 2015 2016 2017 2018

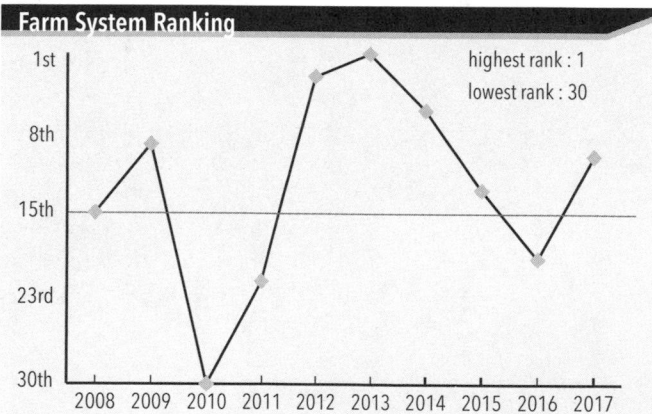

Farm System Ranking

highest rank : 1
lowest rank : 30

2008 2009 2010 2011 2012 2013 2014 2015 2016 2017

Personnel

SVP, General Manager:
John Mozeliak

Assistant General Manager:
Mike Girsch

Manager:
Mike Matheny

BP Alumni:
Zach Mortimer
Mauricio Rubio

managed the Cardinals longer than all but Tony La Russa, Red Schoendienst and Whitey Herzog, and only one fewer season than Joe Torre managed the Yankees. Which leads to these questions: What, if anything, has Matheny learned? And what have we learned about him? And perhaps most importantly, why are the Cardinals so committed to him?

In a widely discussed and shared article on popular Cardinals blog Viva El Birdos last August, managing editor Craig Edwards—hardly known as a hot-taker or bomb-thrower—laid out the case against Matheny in a post titled, helpfully: "Mike Matheny should be fired." The piece is far more aggressive than the passive voice of its headline would suggest, but it's also meticulously measured and sober.

The primary cases against Matheny, according to Edwards (and most Cardinals fans who have watched the team for the past five years):

- Bullpen mismanagement.
- Inability to trust young players on a franchise (and a sport, really) in which youth is the foundation of the whole organization's strategy.
- Obsession with long-discredited stats like wins and saves.
- Resistance to analytics, either in a philosophical sense or a practical, on-field sense.
- Dogged refusal to listen to criticism and learn from it, culminating in a relationship with the generally friendly St. Louis media that's far more contentious than it ever was with the infamously acerbic La Russa.
- After the first few years of harmonious clubhouses, there were incidents in 2016 of spring training discord and late-season low morale.

All of these issues have been consistent, and persistent, since Matheny was hired. The pivot point has always been Matheny's still-inexplicable decision to put Michael Wacha, who hadn't pitched for a month, in a decisive Game 5 in the 2014 NLCS against San Francisco (Travis Ishikawa settled it with a walk-off homer). It was a Grady Little-esque faceplant that still hasn't been fully explained, and managers have been fired for less.

Matheny had been criticized before that, but the drumbeat—even with a subsequent 100-win season—has been incessant since. There isn't a single outlet for Cardinals-related discussion—high-brow or low-brow, radio, print, online, Snapchat—in which frustration with Matheny is not at the center of most conversations. But at Cardinals offices in Busch Stadium, everything is fine. "I've always taken the position that the best way to operate a franchise and maintain continuity is to maintain the core personnel responsible for our success," Cardinals chairman Bill DeWitt Jr. said.

The Cardinals, more than anything, value stability. But the thing about stability is that it quickly becomes inertia:

Sometimes you worry so much about stability that you don't notice you're slowly sinking. What Edwards zeroed in on most in his piece was that while Mozeliak and the much-respected Cardinals front office has given Matheny a replenishing amount of talent during his tenure, they've had to work almost as hard to make up for Matheny's deficiencies.

In 2014, Mozeliak traded a clearly injured Allen Craig, whom Matheny refused to stop playing despite obvious ineffectiveness, just to get him out of the lineup and get Oscar Taveras in. Matheny responded by benching Taveras, which is similar to how the Mark Ellis vs. Kolten Wong story played out. In 2015, Mozeliak tried to fix the problem by giving him clearer options at each position, but Matheny responded by wearing out his regulars. In 2016, Mozeliak adjusted by giving Matheny more depth again, but Matheny couldn't figure that out either, forcing Wong and Randal Grichuk to spend time in the minors and not trusting Aledmys Diaz to play shortstop until he had no other choice.

In a late-in-season reflection, Mozeliak admitted: "I'm wondering if we created too much roster flexibility as opposed to stability." Each of these times, Mozeliak has a plan, Matheny thwarts the plan, Mozeliak adjusts the plan, Matheny thwarts the adjustment. So why is Mozeliak not only keeping Matheny around but giving him an extension? Mozeliak says he has "the respect of his players," which is the sort of statement that's true when a manager is winning but turns out to be irrelevant when the tide turns. (And last year, the first season missing the playoffs since 2010, was not coincidentally the first we heard occasional clubhouse grumblings.)

And "respect of the players" seems less a vital attribute—or at least not enough to make up for obvious tactical shortcomings—and more a fundamental minimum, entry-level requirement of the managerial position. If you can't do that, you're not a manager, no matter how smart you are tactically. That this has not changed—that Matheny has shown these same shortcomings year after year—is perhaps not surprising: Humans are impressively resistant to change, baseball manager or otherwise.

But what's most concerning about the Cardinals' commitment to Matheny is that they are falling into the same trap: If it's worked so far—and it's a matter of debate as to how much it's "worked"—just keep doing it. But the landscape of baseball, and specifically the National League Central, has changed dramatically since Matheny was hired in 2012. Shifts have taken over. Bullpen management seems to revolutionize every postseason. Five years in baseball thinking is like dog years. The front office hasn't stayed put in that time—for better and for worse, as Chris Correa can attest—but Matheny has. And by staying put, he has put the Cardinals behind.

The Cardinals are obsessed with keeping what they have and boosting the status quo. So far, because the talent has offset his managerial issues, Matheny has been able to benefit from this. The team hasn't fallen back too far, not yet. But changes are coming, whether the Cardinals want to admit to them or not. The Cubs are here. The Pirates are here. The Brewers and Reds are coming. The Dodgers, Giants and Nationals have already passed them.

The Cardinals think of themselves as this perpetual empire. But they're not. They are a historical anomaly, a small-market team that, because of smart management and a dedicated fan base, has been able to swing with the big boys. But the margin is thinner than ever. Matheny is right: He still has a lot to learn. And the Cardinals are running out of time for him to catch up. The day after the Cubs won the World Series, the Cardinals sent a message to their fans about their understanding of the seriousness of the threat they faced. The message was received, but not in the way it was intended. ■

—Will Leitch is a senior writer at Sports on Earth, a contributing editor at New York *magazine and a film critic at* New Republic

HITTERS

Matt Adams 1B

Born: 8/31/88   Age: 28   Bats: L   Throws: R   Height: 6'3"   Weight: 260   Entered Pro Ball: Round 23, 2009 Draft (#699 overall)

YEAR	TEAM	LVL	AGE	PA	R	2B	3B	HR	RBI	BB	K	SB	CS	AVG/OBP/SLG	TAv	VORP	BABIP	BRR	FRAA	WARP
2014	SLN	MLB	25	563	55	34	5	15	68	26	114	3	2	.288/.321/.457	.281	13.6	.338	-2.6	1B(133): -2.5	1.2
2015	SLN	MLB	26	186	14	9	0	5	24	10	41	1	0	.240/.280/.377	.242	-1.1	.285	0.1	1B(46): -0.6	-0.2
2016	MEM	AAA	27	20	4	1	0	1	2	4	3	0	0	.188/.350/.438	.326	1.7	.167	0.1	1B(4): 0.4	0.2
2016	SLN	MLB	27	327	37	18	0	16	54	25	81	0	1	.249/.309/.471	.281	8.5	.286	-2.4	1B(86): 9.1	1.8
2017	*SLN*	*MLB*	*28*	*265*	*30*	*14*	*1*	*11*	*37*	*16*	*60*	*1*	*1*	*.263/.308/.458*	*.264*	*5.8*	*.303*	*-0.6*	*1B 2*	*0.7*
2018	*SLN*	*MLB*	*29*	*263*	*34*	*14*	*0*	*11*	*36*	*18*	*62*	*1*	*0*	*.261/.311/.456*	*.272*	*6.3*	*.306*	*-1.0*	*1B 2*	*0.9*

Breakout: 4%   Improve: 45%   Collapse: 4%   Attrition: 9%   MLB: 96%   *Comparables: Mike Jacobs, Adam Lind, Mark Trumbo*

Back and shoulder woes cost Adams yet another half-season, but between trips to the whirlpool he produced his usual brand of walk-deficient, power-rich offensive mediocrity and surprisingly solid defense. Big City has always been able to put a charge into a fastball, and last year he even managed to hang in well against lefties, but he's never learned to lay off pitches he can't handle. Just a touch more discipline would up his walk rate and force pitchers to spend more time in his launch zone, but Adams is now likely beyond the age of learning new tricks. As long as he can stay on the field and produce light-tower power for a light paycheck he can be a nice complementary piece, but never the star.

Harrison Bader   OF

Born: 6/3/94   Age: 23   Bats: R   Throws: R   Height: 6'0"   Weight: 195   Entered Pro Ball: Round 3, 2015 Draft (#100 overall)

YEAR	TEAM	LVL	AGE	PA	R	2B	3B	HR	RBI	BB	K	SB	CS	AVG/OBP/SLG	TAv	VORP	BABIP	BRR	FRAA	WARP
2015	SCO	A-	21	30	6	2	0	2	4	0	5	2	0	.379/.400/.655	.356	4.0	.409	0.5	LF(4): -0.1 • RF(3): -0.4	0.4
2015	PEO	A	21	228	34	11	2	9	28	15	44	15	6	.301/.364/.505	.310	21.3	.344	3.4	CF(42): 8.9 • LF(7): 4.0	3.7
2016	MEM	AAA	22	161	22	7	1	3	17	11	38	2	3	.231/.298/.354	.249	2.5	.292	-0.1	CF(26): 1.5 • LF(16): 0.7	0.5
2016	SFD	AA	22	356	48	12	4	16	41	25	93	11	10	.283/.351/.497	.312	29.5	.349	0.7	CF(77): -1.3 • RF(4): -0.4	3.0
2017	SLN	MLB	23	250	35	10	1	10	30	16	67	5	4	.246/.306/.433	.252	6.4	.302	-0.5	CF 3 • LF 1	1.1
2018	SLN	MLB	24	346	43	13	2	13	44	22	94	7	5	.240/.300/.420	.261	9.0	.296	-0.1	CF 5 • LF 1	1.5

Breakout: 4%   Improve: 26%   Collapse: 4%   Attrition: 21%   MLB: 54%   *Comparables: Michael Choice, Joe Benson, Brett Jackson*

Bader started his first full pro season as one of the youngest players in the Texas League and vaulted his way up prospect charts by ranking among the circuit's leaders in batting average, on-base percentage, slugging percentage and dirty uniform percentage. His aggressive style makes him stand out, as the former third-round pick flies around the bases, charges fly balls, crashes into walls, swings from the heels and makes loud contact when he gets a fastball he can handle. There's a downside to that aggression, as Bader can be fooled by spin and there's plenty of swing-and-miss in his game, but the Cardinals have worked to focus that aggression by batting him leadoff. He doesn't have the raw speed of a prototypical center fielder and would be average at best in that role, but there's enough juice in his bat to carry an outfield corner. Don't be surprised if Bader shows up in the majors later this summer and grows into a solid regular.

Matt Carpenter   3B

Born: 11/26/85   Age: 31   Bats: L   Throws: R   Height: 6'3"   Weight: 205   Entered Pro Ball: Round 13, 2009 Draft (#399 overall)

YEAR	TEAM	LVL	AGE	PA	R	2B	3B	HR	RBI	BB	K	SB	CS	AVG/OBP/SLG	TAv	VORP	BABIP	BRR	FRAA	WARP
2014	SLN	MLB	28	709	99	33	2	8	59	95	111	5	3	.272/.375/.375	.288	37.8	.318	-1.6	3B(156): -3.8 • RF(2): -0.2	3.7
2015	SLN	MLB	29	665	101	44	3	28	84	81	151	4	3	.272/.365/.505	.317	56.3	.321	-0.6	3B(146): -11.4 • 2B(11): -0.1	4.8
2016	SLN	MLB	30	566	81	36	6	21	68	81	108	0	4	.271/.380/.505	.313	45.7	.307	1.2	3B(54): -3.7 • 1B(45): 0.1	4.2
2017	SLN	MLB	31	615	70	36	3	17	75	74	111	3	3	.273/.362/.449	.283	27.0	.311	-1.5	1B -1 • 2B -1	2.3
2018	SLN	MLB	32	534	68	31	2	14	63	62	101	2	2	.266/.355/.436	.285	21.4	.307	-0.3	1B 0 • 2B -1	2.2

Breakout: 0%   Improve: 38%   Collapse: 5%   Attrition: 5%   MLB: 97%   *Comparables: Sal Bando, Eric Chavez, Chase Headley*

No one in the National League is a tougher out or makes pitchers work harder than Carpenter—and we mean that literally, as the veteran infielder has faced 11,252 pitches since the start of the 2013 season, 417 more than Paul Goldschmidt, the next man on the list. He's also been one of the most versatile, both defensively and at the plate, as Carpenter has filled in all over the diamond and his selectively aggressive approach allows him to draw walks to set the table, line RBI singles the other way or launch bombs into the upper deck, depending on the team's most pressing need. Last year he proved that his recent power surge was no fluke, and with his glove declining at the hot corner, the Cardinals are planning to install their top-of-the-lineup hitter at first base. The optics of that may seem odd in a "Ned Flanders as Stanley Kowalski" sort of way, but Carpenter's bat is full-on Brando and can absolutely carry the role.

Tony Cruz   C

Born: 8/18/86   Age: 30   Bats: R   Throws: R   Height: 5'11"   Weight: 215   Entered Pro Ball: Round 26, 2007 Draft (#802 overall)

YEAR	TEAM	LVL	AGE	PA	R	2B	3B	HR	RBI	BB	K	SB	CS	AVG/OBP/SLG	TAv	VORP	BABIP	BRR	FRAA	WARP
2014	SLN	MLB	27	150	11	5	0	1	17	13	28	0	3	.200/.270/.259	.190	-3.9	.245	-0.2	C(47): -8.9 • 1B(2): 0.0	-1.4
2015	SLN	MLB	28	151	6	7	1	2	11	6	32	0	0	.204/.235/.310	.179	-5.7	.248	0.2	C(51): -0.5 • 3B(3): 0.1	-0.7
2016	OMA	AAA	29	363	32	18	0	7	55	41	74	2	1	.264/.347/.387	.268	12.1	.321	-2.5	C(61): 1.0 • 1B(22): -0.5	1.3
2016	KCA	MLB	29	5	0	0	0	0	1	0	3	0	0	.000/.000/.000	.107	-0.6	.000	0.0	C(4): -0.1	-0.1
2017	SLN	MLB	30	250	23	12	1	5	24	18	51	1	0	.229/.286/.350	.218	0.5	.271	0.5	C -5 • 1B 0	-0.5
2018	SLN	MLB	31	151	15	6	0	3	14	11	32	0	0	.222/.278/.335	.222	-0.8	.264	0.3	C -3 • 1B 0	-0.4

Breakout: 0%   Improve: 30%   Collapse: 12%   Attrition: 27%   MLB: 80%   *Comparables: Rob Johnson, Geronimo Gil, Bobby Wilson*

For a squad that insists on catching Salvy Perez nearly every day, the Royals have a strange preoccupation with backup backstops. Always on the prowl for an understudy, Kansas City acquired Cruz in December of 2015 and kept him in Omaha for the summer while Drew Butera and his hair made cameo appearances at The K. That made him the backup to the backup to the starter who never rests. Tough gig. Cruz is what he is. A second-stringer with a bat that is best left in the rack and a glove that is passable enough he can earn a living playing this beautiful game.

YEAR	TEAM	P. COUNT	FRM RUNS	BLK RUNS	THRW RUNS	TOT RUNS
2014	SFD	109	0.0	0.0	0.0	0.0
2014	SLN	5298	-7.4	-0.5	-0.1	-8.0
2015	SLN	4705	-0.6	-0.7	-0.3	-1.5
2016	KCA	171	0.0	-0.1	0.0	-0.2
2017	SLN	7165	-4.2	-1.1	0.0	-5.2
2018	SLN	4323	-2.9	-0.7	0.0	-3.6

Aledmys Diaz   SS

Born: 8/1/90   Age: 26   Bats: R   Throws: R   Height: 6'1"   Weight: 195   Entered Pro Ball: International Free Agent, 2014

YEAR	TEAM	LVL	AGE	PA	R	2B	3B	HR	RBI	BB	K	SB	CS	AVG/OBP/SLG	TAv	VORP	BABIP	BRR	FRAA	WARP
2014	SFD	AA	23	125	15	8	1	3	18	2	24	6	2	.291/.311/.453	.280	5.4	.341	-0.7	SS(17): -3.1	0.2
2014	PMB	A+	23	54	5	2	0	2	6	7	10	1	0	.227/.352/.409	.290	3.5	.242	1.2		0.4
2015	SFD	AA	24	409	47	25	2	10	46	29	62	6	5	.264/.324/.421	.269	18.8	.294	-0.4	SS(91): -1.8	1.8
2015	MEM	AAA	24	58	12	3	0	3	6	6	5	0	1	.380/.448/.620	.380	9.7	.372	0.0	SS(14): -3.2	0.7
2016	SLN	MLB	25	460	71	28	3	17	65	41	60	4	4	.300/.369/.510	.321	48.7	.312	1.4	SS(106): -9.2 • 2B(1): 0.0	4.1
2017	SLN	MLB	26	623	81	33	3	21	73	45	101	6	4	.270/.329/.452	.275	35.8	.292	-1.1	SS -11	1.8
2018	SLN	MLB	27	535	69	29	1	19	70	41	89	5	3	.266/.330/.452	.281	30.1	.287	0.1	SS -10	2.2

Breakout: 2%   Improve: 49%   Collapse: 12%   Attrition: 16%   MLB: 95%   *Comparables: Luis Valbuena, Garrett Atkins, Logan Forsythe*

When we described Diaz in these pages last year as the closest thing to a developmental bust the Cardinals had recently endured, we should have known the baseball gods would not let such an affront stand. They reached down during spring training and broke Jhonny Peralta's thumb, strained Ruben Tejada's quad, scattered omens to remind Mike Matheny that Jedd Gyorko isn't really a shortstop and Greg Garcia isn't really a starter, and smiled beatifically as Diaz spent April hitting like vintage A-Rod. He became an All-Star and a Rookie of the Year candidate, hitting for average and power out of the two-hole. It wasn't all manna, however, as Diaz was the worst defensive shortstop in all of baseball. His iron-gloved immobility had Cardinals fans pining for Peralta's sure-handed immobility early in the season, though Diaz was making routine plays with greater consistency by season's end. Expecting him to slug at last year's rate may be a stretch, but if he can soften his glove from NC-17 to R and continue to get on base he can remain among the league's better middle infielders.

Dexter Fowler   CF

Born: 3/22/86   Age: 31   Bats: B   Throws: R   Height: 6'5"   Weight: 195   Entered Pro Ball: Round 14, 2004 Draft (#410 overall)

YEAR	TEAM	LVL	AGE	PA	R	2B	3B	HR	RBI	BB	K	SB	CS	AVG/OBP/SLG	TAv	VORP	BABIP	BRR	FRAA	WARP
2014	HOU	MLB	28	505	61	21	4	8	35	66	108	11	4	.276/.375/.399	.292	28.3	.351	-0.9	CF(111): -15.3	1.4
2015	CHN	MLB	29	690	102	29	8	17	46	84	154	20	7	.250/.346/.411	.281	33.7	.308	-1.0	CF(152): 1.1	3.7
2016	CHN	MLB	30	551	84	25	7	13	48	79	124	13	4	.276/.393/.447	.312	47.1	.350	1.1	CF(121): -11.6	3.7
2017	SLN	MLB	31	639	84	25	5	14	61	82	142	15	6	.257/.355/.403	.271	28.6	.317	0.7	CF -9	1.5
2018	SLN	MLB	32	545	70	22	4	13	60	72	123	12	5	.256/.360/.404	.280	25.4	.318	-0.4	CF -8	1.9

Breakout: 0%   Improve: 41%   Collapse: 6%   Attrition: 8%   MLB: 93%   *Comparables: Amos Otis, Chet Lemon, Bernie Williams*

Fowler had a weird season. While FRAA rated his defense about 12 runs worse than in the previous season, his offensive profile—patient, smart, leveraged, with a little pop—blossomed and gave him the highest TAv (.312) of his nine-year career. The two balanced out, and his WARP (3.7) stayed exactly even. Go figure. Now, given what we know about the volatility of even the best defensive measures, if you're inclined to say that Fowler's 2016 was an improvement over his 2015, go right ahead. In fact, even at age 31, there's nothing all that concerning in Fowler's profile. He probably won't surprise you with his power any more, but 10-15 home runs is a totally reasonable expectation to go along with a .360s OBP and a solid clubhouse presence.

Greg Garcia   INF

Born: 8/8/89   Age: 27   Bats: L   Throws: R   Height: 6'0"   Weight: 190   Entered Pro Ball: Round 7, 2010 Draft (#229 overall)

YEAR	TEAM	LVL	AGE	PA	R	2B	3B	HR	RBI	BB	K	SB	CS	AVG/OBP/SLG	TAv	VORP	BABIP	BRR	FRAA	WARP
2014	MEM	AAA	24	441	60	12	3	8	40	41	95	7	5	.272/.358/.382	.274	18.8	.342	-1.6	2B(90): 4.7 • SS(13): -0.9	2.2
2014	SLN	MLB	24	18	2	1	0	0	1	1	6	0	0	.143/.333/.214	.230	-0.3	.250	-0.2	2B(4): -0.5 • SS(1): 0.0	-0.1
2015	MEM	AAA	25	389	47	19	2	0	36	48	55	16	3	.294/.391/.364	.287	28.8	.351	3.6	SS(69): -5.2 • 2B(19): -0.9	2.3
2015	SLN	MLB	25	87	7	5	0	2	4	10	12	0	0	.240/.337/.387	.278	5.1	.262	0.9	SS(12): 0.7 • 2B(10): -1.7	0.4
2016	MEM	AAA	26	120	13	4	1	0	8	11	20	2	2	.269/.350/.327	.256	2.4	.333	-1.6	SS(24): -0.1 • 2B(2): -0.1	0.2
2016	SLN	MLB	26	257	33	11	0	3	17	38	50	1	1	.276/.393/.369	.289	17.5	.346	1.0	3B(31): -0.9 • SS(30): -0.8	1.5
2017	SLN	MLB	27	125	13	5	0	2	11	13	25	2	1	.251/.338/.355	.252	4.1	.306	-0.1	2B -1 • SS -0	0.2
2018	SLN	MLB	28	352	41	14	1	5	33	36	72	4	2	.249/.339/.356	.257	10.8	.304	1.1	2B -1 • SS -1	0.9

Breakout: 6%   Improve: 24%   Collapse: 19%   Attrition: 29%   MLB: 71%   *Comparables: Justin Sellers, Ben Zobrist, Cliff Pennington*

Garcia finally spent last summer grinding out big league at-bats and fulfilling his destiny to become the Practically Perfect Utility Infielder. He hits left-handed, makes contact, draws a few walks, is an adequate shortstop and generally goes about his business with the quiet competency that leads to managerial trust. He also lacks the loud tools and flashy personality that lead to sports radio arguments and managerial second-guessing. As long as he gets on base, makes the routine play, stays out of the papers and doesn't need a multi-year contract, Garcia will remain a useful low-cost cog.

Randal Grichuk   CF

Born: 8/13/91   Age: 25   Bats: R   Throws: R   Height: 6'1"   Weight: 205   Entered Pro Ball: Round 1, 2009 Draft (#24 overall)

YEAR	TEAM	LVL	AGE	PA	R	2B	3B	HR	RBI	BB	K	SB	CS	AVG/OBP/SLG	TAv	VORP	BABIP	BRR	FRAA	WARP
2014	MEM	AAA	22	472	73	23	2	25	71	28	108	8	5	.259/.311/.493	.280	21.3	.289	-0.9	LF(53): -2.0 • CF(36): -5.3	1.4
2014	SLN	MLB	22	116	11	6	1	3	8	5	31	0	2	.245/.278/.400	.244	-1.0	.316	-1.5	RF(28): -0.1 • CF(5): 1.0	0.0
2015	SLN	MLB	23	350	49	23	7	17	47	22	110	4	2	.276/.329/.548	.316	25.9	.365	-1.5	LF(49): -2.7 • CF(37): 1.5	2.6
2016	MEM	AAA	24	86	12	4	1	6	18	2	14	0	0	.272/.302/.568	.301	6.4	.258	0.4	CF(17): -0.2	0.6
2016	SLN	MLB	24	478	66	29	3	24	68	28	141	5	4	.240/.289/.480	.275	24.0	.294	2.2	CF(115): -0.2 • LF(4): 0.6	2.5
2017	SLN	MLB	25	560	71	29	4	27	79	31	153	6	4	.246/.292/.473	.264	19.3	.293	-0.6	LF -4 • RF 0	1.1
2018	SLN	MLB	26	532	71	27	3	28	81	33	143	5	4	.246/.298/.482	.277	21.7	.288	-0.1	LF -4 • RF 0	2.0

Breakout: 2%   Improve: 57%   Collapse: 6%   Attrition: 10%   MLB: 99%   *Comparables: Oswaldo Arcia, Wily Mo Pena, Hunter Pence*

The three most frequent comments written in this book over the years involve: a) young pitchers needing to improve command; b) young hitters needing a more selective approach; and c) an awkward reference to an animated television show. So it was refreshing to watch a power-packed free-swinger like Grichuk make a concerted effort early in the year to improve his pitch recognition and lay off sliders out of the zone. Of course, sometimes when you teach Mr. Burns to recycle he winds up making Li'l Lisa's Patented Animal Slurry. While Grichuk's more patient approach led to more walks and fewer strikeouts, it also short-circuited his power. He was twice sent down to Memphis, and when he returned in August he resumed his hacking ways and rediscovered his boom stick. He's unlikely to ever become a solid on-base threat and is fringy in center field, but Grichuk has enough power to be an average bat and a plus glove in an outfield corner.

Jedd Gyorko   INF

Born: 9/23/88   Age: 28   Bats: R   Throws: R   Height: 5'10"   Weight: 215   Entered Pro Ball: Round 2, 2010 Draft (#59 overall)

YEAR	TEAM	LVL	AGE	PA	R	2B	3B	HR	RBI	BB	K	SB	CS	AVG/OBP/SLG	TAv	VORP	BABIP	BRR	FRAA	WARP
2014	ELP	AAA	25	28	7	2	0	1	5	4	4	0	0	.292/.393/.500	.310	0.0	.316	0.2	2B(6): 0.2	0.0
2014	SDN	MLB	25	443	37	17	1	10	51	36	100	3	2	.210/.280/.333	.243	4.2	.253	0.2	2B(109): -4.4	0.0
2015	ELP	AAA	26	69	8	1	0	4	9	7	11	0	1	.279/.362/.492	.271	2.8	.283	0.2	2B(16): -0.1	0.3
2015	SDN	MLB	26	458	34	15	0	16	57	27	107	0	1	.247/.297/.397	.252	8.5	.290	-1.1	2B(93): -0.5 • SS(29): -1.5	0.7
2016	SLN	MLB	27	438	58	9	1	30	59	37	96	0	0	.243/.306/.495	.292	28.3	.244	0.6	2B(46): 5.0 • 3B(39): -1.5	3.4
2017	SLN	MLB	28	400	46	15	0	18	55	30	86	1	1	.243/.303/.433	.258	12.2	.268	-1.0	3B -2 • 2B 0	0.7
2018	SLN	MLB	29	425	56	15	0	20	59	34	96	0	0	.239/.303/.433	.266	12.9	.265	-0.2	3B -3 • 2B 0	1.2

Breakout: 0%   Improve: 47%   Collapse: 1%   Attrition: 6%   MLB: 100%   *Comparables: Kelly Johnson, Ryan Flaherty, Luis Aguayo*

Last season, Gyorko finally posted the sort of numbers the Padres envisioned when they bought out his arbitration years and signed him to an extension, just not in San Diego. A grip-it-and-rip-it student of the low-contact, high-voltage school, Gyorko launched more than a quarter of his fly balls into the bleachers, a rate that placed him fourth in the National League and was nearly double his career mark. It would be foolish to expect him to duplicate that feat, but 20-plus bombs from a guy who can provide a solid glove at the corners or the keystone and serve as a donut tire at shortstop is something most any team will take.

Carson Kelly   C

Born: 7/14/94   Age: 22   Bats: R   Throws: R   Height: 6'2"   Weight: 220   Entered Pro Ball: Round 2, 2012 Draft (#86 overall)

YEAR	TEAM	LVL	AGE	PA	R	2B	3B	HR	RBI	BB	K	SB	CS	AVG/OBP/SLG	TAv	VORP	BABIP	BRR	FRAA	WARP
2014	PEO	A	19	415	41	17	4	6	49	37	54	1	0	.248/.326/.366	.264	15.9	.274	-2.2	C(79): -0.7	1.6
2015	PMB	A+	20	419	30	18	1	8	51	22	64	0	0	.219/.263/.332	.223	1.2	.239	-1.0	C(104): 1.3	0.3
2016	SFD	AA	21	236	29	7	0	6	18	14	46	0	1	.287/.338/.403	.283	14.4	.339	-0.9	C(60): 8.7	2.5
2016	MEM	AAA	21	126	14	10	0	0	14	11	17	0	0	.292/.352/.381	.261	5.8	.340	-0.1	C(32): 2.5	0.9
2016	SLN	MLB	21	14	1	1	0	0	1	0	2	0	0	.154/.214/.231	.204	-0.4	.182	-0.2	C(10): -0.2	-0.1
2017	SLN	MLB	22	250	23	11	1	6	28	15	49	0	0	.236/.287/.372	.226	3.2	.270	-0.5	C 1	0.4
2018	SLN	MLB	23	294	34	13	1	9	34	18	59	0	0	.244/.297/.396	.249	6.7	.278	-0.7	C 1	0.8

Breakout: 6%   Improve: 17%   Collapse: 10%   Attrition: 21%   MLB: 32%   *Comparables: Bryan Anderson, J.R. Murphy, Hector Sanchez*

It all started coming together for Kelly last summer, as the converted third baseman flashed enough behind the dish and at the plate to have St. Louis fans thinking they've finally found an eventual heir to Yadier Molina. Kelly has made himself into a plus receiver, with a strong arm, quiet glove and excellent agility, and he gets solid marks for his toughness, leadership and game-calling ability. His bat isn't as advanced, but Kelly has started making solid contact and can stroke line drives to all fields with a swing

YEAR	TEAM	P. COUNT	FRM RUNS	BLK RUNS	THRW RUNS	TOT RUNS
2016	SLN	539	-0.1	0.2	0.0	0.1
2017	SLN	8903	2.3	-0.1	-0.8	1.4
2018	SLN	10486	2.8	0.1	-0.9	1.9

that some scouts feel will eventually generate more power. It may be tempting to let him earn the job as Yadi's backup this spring, but Kelly's bat would benefit from a full season marinating at Triple-A before he starts his internship with the master.

Yadier Molina   C

Born: 7/13/82   Age: 34   Bats: R   Throws: R   Height: 5'11"   Weight: 205   Entered Pro Ball: Round 4, 2000 Draft (#113 overall)

YEAR	TEAM	LVL	AGE	PA	R	2B	3B	HR	RBI	BB	K	SB	CS	AVG/OBP/SLG	TAv	VORP	BABIP	BRR	FRAA	WARP
2014	SLN	MLB	31	445	40	21	0	7	38	28	55	1	1	.282/.333/.386	.256	14.0	.307	-2.5	C(107): 2.1 • 1B(1): 0.0	1.8
2015	SLN	MLB	32	530	34	23	2	4	61	32	59	3	1	.270/.310/.350	.239	7.3	.295	-4.9	C(134): 10.8	1.9
2016	SLN	MLB	33	581	56	38	1	8	58	39	63	3	2	.307/.360/.427	.278	29.0	.335	-7.7	C(146): 10.5 • 1B(2): 0.0	4.1
2017	SLN	MLB	34	480	50	26	0	10	50	31	55	3	1	.284/.331/.412	.262	19.5	.302	-1.1	C 6	2.8
2018	SLN	MLB	35	431	49	22	0	8	45	27	51	1	1	.275/.322/.394	.258	11.5	.294	-3.6	C 4	1.7

Breakout: 0%   Improve: 37%   Collapse: 8%   Attrition: 13%   MLB: 83%   *Comparables: Kenji Johjima, Mike Lieberthal, Paul Lo Duca*

Molina's Gold Glove streak may have ended at eight, but it's time for MLB to create an Adamantium Glove award specifically for him. Last year the indestructible one lapped the field in innings caught and enjoyed a BABIP-fueled offensive renaissance, putting the lie to rumors of his impending demise. Molina's arm isn't the weapon it once was, but he's still a plus defender, a master of pitch sequencing, a leader on the field and in the clubhouse, and one of the most indispensable players in the game. It may be a while yet before Father Time screws up the courage to finally stare him down and take his shin guards away.

YEAR	TEAM	P. COUNT	FRM RUNS	BLK RUNS	THRW RUNS	TOT RUNS
2014	SFD	166	-0.1	0.0	0.0	-0.1
2014	SLN	14449	0.5	1.4	2.2	4.1
2015	SLN	18104	7.8	1.5	2.4	11.6
2016	SLN	19667	9.4	1.8	-0.2	11.0
2017	SLN	16508	5.5	1.3	-0.1	6.7
2018	SLN	14824	3.2	0.9	-0.3	3.9

Brandon Moss   OF

Born: 9/16/83   Age: 33   Bats: L   Throws: R   Height: 6'1"   Weight: 210   Entered Pro Ball: Round 8, 2002 Draft (#238 overall)

YEAR	TEAM	LVL	AGE	PA	R	2B	3B	HR	RBI	BB	K	SB	CS	AVG/OBP/SLG	TAv	VORP	BABIP	BRR	FRAA	WARP
2014	OAK	MLB	30	580	70	23	2	25	81	67	153	1	0	.234/.334/.438	.290	25.2	.283	0.7	1B(67): -3.2 • LF(56): -1.5	2.6
2015	CLE	MLB	31	375	36	17	1	15	50	32	106	0	0	.217/.288/.407	.244	-3.2	.265	-3.4	RF(79): 2.3 • 1B(10): 1.2	0.0
2015	SLN	MLB	31	151	11	7	1	4	8	17	42	0	1	.250/.344/.409	.271	2.1	.337	-1.7	1B(32): -0.3 • LF(10): -0.3	0.1
2016	SLN	MLB	32	464	66	19	2	28	67	39	141	1	0	.225/.300/.484	.279	16.2	.261	-0.3	1B(64): 1.6 • LF(58): -1.9	1.6
2017	SLN	MLB	33	450	58	19	1	24	69	43	125	1	0	.240/.321/.472	.267	14.3	.283	-1.2	LF -0 • 1B 1	1.7
2018	SLN	MLB	34	422	57	16	1	20	60	39	121	0	0	.230/.309/.444	.269	10.3	.278	-1.3	LF 0 • 1B 1	1.2

Breakout: 1%   Improve: 27%   Collapse: 5%   Attrition: 9%   MLB: 89%   *Comparables: Marcus Thames, Ryan Howard, Richie Sexson*

Few players in history have struggled as badly as Moss did last fall while still being penciled into the lineup most every day. The burly lefty slashed .099/.178/.209 in September and October, becoming the first player ever to post a batting average below .100 down the stretch with over 100 plate appearances. Whether due to random chance, fatigue, age or the lingering effects of his bum hip, Moss has faded badly in the second half each of the last three seasons. When he's going well he's a Three True Outcomes threat who can lay the wood to right-handed pitching, but as he enters his mid-thirties Moss has become a defensive liability and occasional strikeout machine that is better suited to platoon and pinch-hit.

Brayan Pena   C

Born: 1/7/82   Age: 35   Bats: B   Throws: R   Height: 5'9"   Weight: 240   Entered Pro Ball: International Free Agent, 2000

YEAR	TEAM	LVL	AGE	PA	R	2B	3B	HR	RBI	BB	K	SB	CS	AVG/OBP/SLG	TAv	VORP	BABIP	BRR	FRAA	WARP
2014	CIN	MLB	32	372	23	18	1	5	26	20	42	2	3	.253/.291/.353	.240	-4.4	.273	-6.5	1B(53): -1.7 • C(46): 0.6	-0.6
2015	CIN	MLB	33	367	17	17	0	0	18	29	34	2	0	.273/.334/.324	.242	5.3	.303	-3.5	C(86): -8.4 • 1B(5): -0.1	-0.4
2016	MEM	AAA	34	22	1	0	0	0	1	1	2	0	0	.200/.227/.200	.195	-0.7	.211	0.0	C(4): 0.2 • 1B(1): 0.1	-0.1
2016	SFD	AA	34	33	2	0	0	0	0	1	4	0	0	.188/.212/.188	.146	-4.3	.214	-1.6	C(5): -0.5 • 1B(1): -0.0	-0.5
2016	PMB	A+	34	21	1	0	0	0	5	0	3	0	0	.263/.238/.263	.199	-0.9	.278	-0.1	C(2): -0.0 • 1B(1): -0.0	-0.1
2016	SLN	MLB	34	14	0	1	0	0	0	1	2	0	0	.154/.214/.231	.176	-0.7	.182	0.0	C(3): -0.4 • 1B(1): 0.0	-0.1
2017	*SLN*	*MLB*	*35*	*250*	*21*	*12*	*0*	*3*	*23*	*13*	*27*	*1*	*1*	*.257/.298/.348*	*.222*	*-0.7*	*.276*	*-2.3*	*C -6 • 1B -0*	*-0.8*
2018	*SLN*	*MLB*	*36*	*86*	*8*	*4*	*0*	*1*	*7*	*5*	*10*	*0*	*0*	*.248/.289/.331*	*.226*	*-0.9*	*.268*	*-0.8*	*C -2 • 1B 0*	*-0.4*

Breakout: 2%   Improve: 28%   Collapse: 16%   Attrition: 30%   MLB: 81%   *Comparables: Mike Lavalliere, Bob Boone, Gerald Laird*

Pena was bitten by the injury bug that haunted the Cardinals last spring, slipping on a wet step in the dugout and tearing up his knee. That led to a surgical cleanup, a long rehab, an aborted return to St. Louis and eventually a lost season. The longtime backup was released at the end of the year and may not have much left in the tank, but the affable Cuban earns high marks in the clubhouse and in the community—witness his attempts to join the Army Reserve last July—which should help earn him more chances than his fading physical talent would otherwise guarantee.

YEAR	TEAM	P. COUNT	FRM RUNS	BLK RUNS	THRW RUNS	TOT RUNS
2014	CIN	5854	0.0	0.0	1.0	0.9
2015	CIN	12480	-6.8	0.4	-2.0	-8.5
2016	SLN	277	-0.3	-0.9	-0.1	-1.3
2017	*SLN*	*7304*	*-4.4*	*-0.6*	*-0.8*	*-5.8*
2018	*SLN*	*2508*	*-1.8*	*-0.2*	*-0.3*	*-2.3*

Jhonny Peralta   3B

Born: 5/28/82   Age: 35   Bats: R   Throws: R   Height: 6'2"   Weight: 225   Entered Pro Ball: International Free Agent, 1999

YEAR	TEAM	LVL	AGE	PA	R	2B	3B	HR	RBI	BB	K	SB	CS	AVG/OBP/SLG	TAv	VORP	BABIP	BRR	FRAA	WARP
2014	SLN	MLB	32	628	61	38	0	21	75	58	112	3	2	.263/.336/.443	.285	34.9	.292	-3.1	SS(152): 5.2	4.4
2015	SLN	MLB	33	640	64	26	1	17	71	50	111	3	4	.275/.334/.411	.273	31.6	.311	-1.7	SS(148): 6.6	4.1
2016	SLN	MLB	34	313	37	17	1	8	29	20	56	0	0	.260/.307/.408	.255	5.2	.294	-3.4	3B(67): -6.0 • SS(7): -1.9	-0.3
2017	*SLN*	*MLB*	*35*	*591*	*59*	*30*	*1*	*15*	*67*	*46*	*111*	*2*	*2*	*.254/.314/.398*	*.253*	*11.2*	*.291*	*-1.8*	*3B -7 • SS 0*	*0.1*
2018	*SLN*	*MLB*	*36*	*388*	*45*	*19*	*0*	*10*	*43*	*30*	*76*	*1*	*1*	*.247/.308/.389*	*.255*	*5.6*	*.285*	*-1.6*	*3B -4 • SS 0*	*0.2*

Breakout: 0%   Improve: 31%   Collapse: 9%   Attrition: 16%   MLB: 82%   *Comparables: Juan Uribe, Mark DeRosa, Scott Spiezio*

It's been years since Peralta looked like a normal shortstop, and last summer he finally stopped fielding like one, as the husky veteran looked stiff and immobile and spent most of his time at third base leaking puddles of value onto the infield dirt. Even worse, the thumb injury that cost him most of the first half seemed to affect his swing and his approach, as Peralta's walk rate plummeted and he posted a .248/.283/.403 line through August before righting the ship somewhat down the stretch. At age 35 he may never again be a viable answer at shortstop or swing enough lumber for the hot corner, but Peralta has long defied expectations and his career descent may well follow the long, slow Juan Uribe glide path.

Delvin Perez   SS

Born: 11/24/98   Age: 18   Bats: R   Throws: R   Height: 6'3"   Weight: 175   Entered Pro Ball: Round 1, 2016 Draft (#23 overall)

YEAR	TEAM	LVL	AGE	PA	R	2B	3B	HR	RBI	BB	K	SB	CS	AVG/OBP/SLG	TAv	VORP	BABIP	BRR	FRAA	WARP
2017	*SLN*	*MLB*	*18*	*250*	*25*	*10*	*1*	*5*	*20*	*11*	*76*	*4*	*1*	*.204/.243/.314*	*.190*	*-6.2*	*.274*	*0.2*	*SS -1 • CF -0*	*-0.7*
2018	*SLN*	*MLB*	*19*	*247*	*24*	*10*	*1*	*6*	*24*	*10*	*78*	*3*	*1*	*.205/.241/.333*	*.205*	*-5.1*	*.274*	*0.3*	*SS 0 • CF 0*	*-0.6*

Breakout: 0%   Improve: 0%   Collapse: 0%   Attrition: 0%   MLB: 0%   *Comparables: Raul Mondesi, Wilmer Flores*

The Cardinals are competitive every year because their front office makes a concerted effort to avoid stepping on their own, um, plans. So when Perez—one of last spring's top prep prospects—failed a PED test and went into freefall on draft day, St. Louis didn't hesitate to scoop him up late in the first round. A pure shortstop with drool-worthy athleticism, game-changing speed, soft hands and a cannon arm, Perez projects to be a plus defender once the rough edges are sanded away. He has a quick bat, makes hard contact and will add size and strength as he matures, although his approach (like most teenagers) has a long way to go.

Thomas Pham   OF

Born: 3/8/88   Age: 29   Bats: R   Throws: R   Height: 6'1"   Weight: 210   Entered Pro Ball: Round 16, 2006 Draft (#496 overall)

YEAR	TEAM	LVL	AGE	PA	R	2B	3B	HR	RBI	BB	K	SB	CS	AVG/OBP/SLG	TAv	VORP	BABIP	BRR	FRAA	WARP
2014	MEM	AAA	26	390	63	16	6	10	44	38	81	20	2	.324/.395/.491	.318	35.8	.397	-1.3	CF(59): -1.0 • LF(29): 0.0	3.5
2014	SLN	MLB	26	2	0	0	0	0	0	0	2	0	0	.000/.000/.000	-.003	-0.4	--	0.0	LF(2): -0.0 • RF(1): -0.0	-0.1
2015	MEM	AAA	27	196	29	10	1	6	39	22	36	9	0	.327/.398/.503	.337	23.8	.379	2.2	CF(42): -5.1 • LF(2): 0.5	2.0
2015	SLN	MLB	27	173	28	7	5	5	18	19	41	2	0	.268/.347/.477	.298	13.3	.333	2.1	CF(33): -2.7 • LF(18): -0.7	1.0
2016	MEM	AAA	28	128	15	5	1	3	17	18	29	8	2	.236/.344/.382	.272	7.1	.295	1.9	CF(24): -3.0 • LF(4): 0.2	0.4
2016	SLN	MLB	28	183	26	7	0	9	17	20	71	2	1	.226/.324/.440	.270	7.7	.342	0.7	CF(34): -3.3 • LF(30): -2.1	0.2
2017	*SLN*	*MLB*	*29*	*276*	*34*	*11*	*2*	*9*	*32*	*28*	*72*	*7*	*2*	*.252/.330/.420*	*.264*	*11.5*	*.319*	*0.7*	*LF 1 • CF -1*	*1.0*
2018	*SLN*	*MLB*	*30*	*309*	*39*	*12*	*2*	*10*	*37*	*32*	*83*	*7*	*2*	*.247/.330/.417*	*.271*	*12.7*	*.316*	*1.7*	*LF 1 • CF -1*	*1.4*

Breakout: 3%   Improve: 18%   Collapse: 11%   Attrition: 18%   MLB: 63%   *Comparables: John Mayberry, Clete Thomas, John Rodriguez*

There's injury prone, there's cursed and then there's Pham, who has yet to stay healthy enough to log 400 at-bats in a season 11 years into his pro career. Last spring, for the first time, the Sin City native earned a spot on the Opening Day roster, but within hours of the first pitch he strained his oblique. Pham missed a month, was forced back to Memphis while the big club was mesmerized by the Jeremy Hazelbaker Experience, and finally returned in June to do what he always does: tantalize with his raw power, stack strikeouts like a Norwegian woodcutter on *National Firewood Night* and play a fringy center field. He's a somewhat older, significantly more fragile version of Randal Grichuk, which makes him either a very good fourth outfielder or a sub par starter.

Stephen Piscotty   RF

Born: 1/14/91   Age: 26   Bats: R   Throws: R   Height: 6'3"   Weight: 210   Entered Pro Ball: Round 1, 2012 Draft (#36 overall)

YEAR	TEAM	LVL	AGE	PA	R	2B	3B	HR	RBI	BB	K	SB	CS	AVG/OBP/SLG	TAv	VORP	BABIP	BRR	FRAA	WARP
2014	MEM	AAA	23	556	70	32	0	9	69	43	61	11	5	.288/.355/.406	.277	20.3	.313	-1.0	RF(113): 1.7 • LF(8): 0.1	2.2
2015	MEM	AAA	24	372	54	28	2	11	41	46	62	5	6	.272/.366/.475	.309	23.2	.304	-2.3	RF(61): 4.8 • LF(10): -1.2	2.8
2015	SLN	MLB	24	256	29	15	4	7	39	20	56	2	1	.305/.359/.494	.314	16.4	.372	-1.9	LF(55): -5.6 • RF(15): -0.9	1.0
2016	SLN	MLB	25	649	86	35	3	22	85	51	133	7	5	.273/.343/.457	.291	30.1	.319	-2.1	RF(146): -4.4 • CF(10): 0.2	2.7
2017	*SLN*	*MLB*	*26*	*600*	*67*	*33*	*2*	*17*	*72*	*48*	*121*	*7*	*4*	*.265/.332/.430*	*.272*	*20.3*	*.303*	*-1.2*	*RF 4*	*2.2*
2018	*SLN*	*MLB*	*27*	*567*	*71*	*32*	*2*	*17*	*69*	*47*	*107*	*6*	*4*	*.265/.334/.434*	*.281*	*22.1*	*.303*	*-1.8*	*RF 4*	*2.8*

Breakout: 5%   Improve: 49%   Collapse: 10%   Attrition: 16%   MLB: 90%   Comparables: *Travis Buck, Josh Reddick, Corey Hart*

Piscotty doesn't have the loudest tools, but his well-rounded game should make him a valuable commodity for years to come. The Stanford product has a solid approach, gets on base, is growing into the plus power that may lead to 30 bombs at his peak and has reworked his throwing mechanics to turn his arm into a weapon in right field. More importantly, he's applying his engineering degree to help his brother bring to market the Beer Bit, a magnetic rod designed to keep craft beer in pint glasses at the optimal quaffing temperature for its style. So we ask you, the Cardinals-hating, *BeerAdvocate*-quoting hipsters out there: is this not a man you can root for?

Magneuris Sierra   CF

Born: 4/7/96   Age: 21   Bats: L   Throws: L   Height: 5'11"   Weight: 160   Entered Pro Ball: International Free Agent, 2012

YEAR	TEAM	LVL	AGE	PA	R	2B	3B	HR	RBI	BB	K	SB	CS	AVG/OBP/SLG	TAv	VORP	BABIP	BRR	FRAA	WARP
2015	PEO	A	19	190	19	1	3	1	7	7	52	4	4	.191/.219/.247	.177	-11.8	.260	-1.2	CF(50): 5.9	-0.6
2016	PEO	A	20	562	78	29	4	3	60	22	97	31	17	.307/.335/.395	.284	31.4	.367	1.7	CF(121): 2.2	3.7
2017	*SLN*	*MLB*	*21*	*250*	*27*	*10*	*1*	*5*	*20*	*8*	*64*	*6*	*4*	*.230/.255/.338*	*.202*	*-6.0*	*.289*	*-0.3*	*CF 1*	*-0.5*
2018	*SLN*	*MLB*	*22*	*364*	*37*	*14*	*2*	*7*	*36*	*14*	*92*	*9*	*6*	*.242/.273/.358*	*.226*	*-2.9*	*.303*	*0.2*	*CF 2 • LF 0*	*-0.1*

Breakout: 4%   Improve: 6%   Collapse: 0%   Attrition: 4%   MLB: 6%   Comparables: *Reymond Fuentes, Engel Beltre, Gorkys Hernandez*

Sporting tremendous tools and a first name befitting a Roman politician, Sierra's biggest challenge was summed up by Cicero more than two millennia ago: "It is not by muscle, speed or physical dexterity that great things are achieved, but by reflection, force of character and judgment." His paint-peeling speed, excellent defensive instincts, strong arm and contact-oriented line-drive stroke could make Sierra a plus center fielder and table-setter, but only if he learns better judgement at the plate and on the bases. Sierra would seemingly rather take poison than ball four, and when he does hit his way on base he's thrown out stealing far too often. Whether he can improve his approach or not will spell the difference between becoming a regular or a fifth outfielder.

Edmundo Sosa   SS

Born: 3/6/96   Age: 21   Bats: R   Throws: R   Height: 5'11"   Weight: 170   Entered Pro Ball: International Free Agent, 2012

YEAR	TEAM	LVL	AGE	PA	R	2B	3B	HR	RBI	BB	K	SB	CS	AVG/OBP/SLG	TAv	VORP	BABIP	BRR	FRAA	WARP
2016	PEO	A	20	378	42	13	1	3	30	19	71	5	4	.268/.307/.336	.254	11.7	.325	-1.1	SS(85): 4.6 • 2B(1): -0.0	1.8
2016	PMB	A+	20	35	3	0	2	0	4	1	8	0	0	.294/.314/.412	.290	2.2	.385	-0.3	SS(9): -0.3 • 3B(1): 1.1	0.3
2017	*SLN*	*MLB*	*21*	*250*	*25*	*9*	*1*	*6*	*23*	*10*	*64*	*0*	*0*	*.226/.262/.349*	*.209*	*-1.9*	*.282*	*-0.3*	*SS 1 • 2B -0*	*-0.1*
2018	*SLN*	*MLB*	*22*	*267*	*28*	*10*	*1*	*7*	*28*	*12*	*67*	*0*	*0*	*.230/.267/.358*	*.226*	*-0.6*	*.283*	*-0.5*	*SS 1 • 2B 0*	*0.1*

Breakout: 2%   Improve: 4%   Collapse: 0%   Attrition: 3%   MLB: 5%   Comparables: *Orlando Calixte, Yamaico Navarro, Tim Beckham*

Sosa was a Midwest League All-Star at age 20 despite slashing .266/.308/.324 at the time, which says a lot about the young Panamanian's defensive chops. A smooth and instinctive shortstop with great range and plenty of arm for the left side of the diamond, Sosa scuffled at the plate in his first taste of full-season ball. The mature approach he flashed in the rookie leagues seemed to desert him, as he continually expanded the zone and had trouble with spin. If Sosa can refine his approach and get back to lining fastballs into the gaps, his glove could earn him a job as a second-division starter.

Kolten Wong   UT

Born: 10/10/90   Age: 26   Bats: L   Throws: R   Height: 5'9"   Weight: 185   Entered Pro Ball: Round 1, 2011 Draft (#22 overall)

YEAR	TEAM	LVL	AGE	PA	R	2B	3B	HR	RBI	BB	K	SB	CS	AVG/OBP/SLG	TAv	VORP	BABIP	BRR	FRAA	WARP
2014	MEM	AAA	23	80	16	4	0	3	13	5	9	6	0	.360/.400/.533	.351	11.5	.381	1.0	2B(18): 1.4	1.3
2014	SLN	MLB	23	433	52	14	3	12	42	21	71	20	4	.249/.292/.388	.241	9.5	.275	6.7	2B(107): -4.3	0.6
2015	SLN	MLB	24	613	71	28	4	11	61	36	95	15	8	.262/.321/.386	.259	17.8	.296	2.3	2B(147): 11.0	3.1
2016	MEM	AAA	25	34	10	0	1	4	11	4	6	1	0	.429/.529/.929	.521	11.0	.444	0.7	2B(4): 0.1 • CF(3): 0.2	1.2
2016	SLN	MLB	25	361	39	7	7	5	23	34	52	7	0	.240/.327/.355	.269	14.5	.268	1.4	2B(88): 12.5 • CF(8): -0.5	2.7
2017	*SLN*	*MLB*	*26*	*462*	*52*	*18*	*4*	*12*	*52*	*31*	*70*	*12*	*3*	*.258/.316/.405*	*.255*	*17.8*	*.282*	*1.4*	*2B 5*	*2.1*
2018	*SLN*	*MLB*	*27*	*422*	*51*	*17*	*3*	*13*	*50*	*29*	*67*	*11*	*3*	*.254/.315/.415*	*.264*	*17.3*	*.275*	*2.9*	*2B 5*	*2.4*

Breakout: 2%   Improve: 49%   Collapse: 8%   Attrition: 20%   MLB: 96%   Comparables: *Dustin Ackley, Jemile Weeks, Daniel Descalso*

If Cardinals Magic™ were actually a thing, at this point the diminutive Wong would be a few years into his role as the Pedroia of the Heartland. Instead, the young second baseman has proven out as one of the league's slickest defenders but has struggled to find consistency at the plate. Last year Wong scuffled early on, was sent to Memphis to shag fly balls and rediscover hard contact, and spent a few bizarre weeks patrolling center field in St. Louis before moving back to the keystone in July and slashing a more representative .250/.339/.434 the rest of the way. His range, hands and flair for the dramatic would go a long way toward shoring up the Cardinals' shoddy infield defense, and if he's given enough rope he's still likely to become an above-average lefty spark plug.

PITCHERS

Sandy Alcantara   RHP

Born: 9/7/95   Age: 21   Bats: R   Throws: R   Height: 6'4"   Weight: 170   Entered Pro Ball: International Free Agent, 2013

YEAR	TEAM	LVL	AGE	W	L	SV	G	GS	IP	H	HR	BB/9	K/9	K	GB%	BABIP	WHIP	ERA	FIP	DRA	VORP	WARP	cFIP	MPH
2016	PEO	A	20	5	7	0	17	17	90¹	78	4	4.5	11.9	119	46%	.333	1.36	4.08	3.21	2.78	22.5	2.5	92	
2016	PMB	A+	20	0	4	0	6	6	32¹	25	0	3.9	9.5	34	52%	.294	1.21	3.62	2.54	3.61	6.7	0.7	97	
2017	SLN	MLB	21	5	7	0	18	18	95	103	13	5.3	6.5	69	54%	.323	1.67	5.52	5.38	6.15	-6.2	-0.6	143	
2018	SLN	MLB	22	5	7	0	19	19	112²	102	16	5.8	9.4	118	54%	.317	1.55	5.12	5.31	5.70	-1.5	-0.2	134	

Breakout: 5%   Improve: 5%   Collapse: 1%   Attrition: 5%   MLB: 6%   *Comparables: Edwin Diaz, Daniel Norris, Reynaldo Lopez*

A fastball that can make radar guns flinch isn't quite the rarity it once was, but even in today's velo-rrific pitching landscape Alcantara stands out. Long and lean with a projectable frame, he maintains his upper-90s moving heat deep into starts, and flashes a burgeoning ability to command it low in the zone and induce swinging strikes above it. That pitch alone was enough for him to carve up the Midwest League as a 20-year-old, but his curveball and changeup are already weapons, making him a possible future front-line starter. The figurative road from Peoria to St. Louis is long, winding and full of minefields (whereas the literal one is short, straight and full of cornfields), but if Alcantara can maintain his health and improve his command, the sky's the limit.

Matthew Bowman   RHP

Born: 5/31/91   Age: 26   Bats: R   Throws: R   Height: 6'0"   Weight: 175   Entered Pro Ball: Round 13, 2012 Draft (#410 overall)

YEAR	TEAM	LVL	AGE	W	L	SV	G	GS	IP	H	HR	BB/9	K/9	K	GB%	BABIP	WHIP	ERA	FIP	DRA	VORP	WARP	cFIP	MPH
2014	BIN	AA	23	7	6	0	17	17	98¹	102	7	2.5	8.4	92	63%	.331	1.31	3.11	3.35	1.50	40.7	4.3	77	
2014	LVG	AAA	23	3	2	0	7	6	36¹	38	1	2.2	7.9	32	59%	.333	1.29	3.47	3.04	2.64	12.6	1.3	84	
2015	LVG	AAA	24	7	16	0	28	26	140	184	15	3.3	4.9	77	56%	.339	1.68	5.53	5.03	4.36	14.5	1.5	100	
2016	SLN	MLB	25	2	5	0	59	0	67²	59	4	2.7	6.9	52	64%	.270	1.17	3.46	3.35	3.89	8.1	0.8	96	94.3
2017	SLN	MLB	26	2	2	0	45	0	47	49	4	3.2	5.8	31	39%	.294	1.37	4.14	4.16	4.27	3.4	0.4	96	
2018	SLN	MLB	27	2	1	0	31	0	33	28	3	4.0	8.2	30	39%	.298	1.30	4.14	4.25	4.57	2.0	0.2	104	

Breakout: 20%   Improve: 35%   Collapse: 25%   Attrition: 30%   MLB: 72%   *Comparables: Adam Warren, Matt Andriese, Jimmy Nelson*

The Cardinals picked the struggling Bowman from the Mets in the Rule 5 draft, plugged the former starter into the bullpen and quickly learned they had unearthed a surprisingly effective multi-inning reliever. The Princeton product uses a full-extension delivery to serve up a sinker/slider/splitter mix that generates bushels of ground-ball outs and is effective against both righties and lefties. A human-scaled former shortstop, Bowman ended his first big-league outing in April by snaring a comebacker to start an inning-ending double play, then charmingly violated baseball's unwritten rules by not quite suppressing an unbelieving smile as he strode back to the dugout. By September, he had made everyone a believer.

Jonathan Broxton   RHP

Born: 6/16/84   Age: 33   Bats: R   Throws: R   Height: 6'4"   Weight: 285   Entered Pro Ball: Round 2, 2002 Draft (#60 overall)

YEAR	TEAM	LVL	AGE	W	L	SV	G	GS	IP	H	HR	BB/9	K/9	K	GB%	BABIP	WHIP	ERA	FIP	DRA	VORP	WARP	cFIP	MPH
2014	CIN	MLB	30	4	2	7	51	0	48¹	32	3	3.2	6.9	37	46%	.221	1.01	1.86	3.50	3.98	2.7	0.3	102	96.0
2014	MIL	MLB	30	0	1	0	11	0	10¹	9	1	1.7	10.5	12	54%	.296	1.06	4.35	2.62	3.99	0.6	0.1	102	97.4
2015	MIL	MLB	31	1	2	0	40	0	36²	41	5	2.5	9.1	37	52%	.346	1.39	5.89	3.73	3.81	3.6	0.4	89	97.1
2015	SLN	MLB	31	3	3	0	26	0	23²	20	2	4.6	9.9	26	62%	.295	1.35	2.66	3.58	3.76	2.5	0.3	90	97.3
2016	SLN	MLB	32	4	2	0	66	0	60²	52	7	3.6	8.5	57	50%	.268	1.25	4.30	4.14	4.25	4.9	0.5	99	97.6
2017	SLN	MLB	33	2	3	0	50	0	52	52	7	3.4	7.9	46	47%	.293	1.36	4.72	4.41	4.72	1.1	0.1	100	
2018	SLN	MLB	34	1	1	0	30	0	31¹	28	4	3.6	7.6	26	47%	.292	1.30	4.67	4.77	5.15	0.0	0.0	119	

Breakout: 23%   Improve: 52%   Collapse: 24%   Attrition: 11%   MLB: 88%   *Comparables: Fernando Rodney, Jeremy Affeldt, Pedro Feliciano*

A full season with Derek Lilliquist didn't result in any miracles, but Broxton managed to post another solid if unspectacular year. His fastball can still sit in the mid-90s, his slider can still fool righties and his control can still frustratingly disappear without prior written consent, making him most effective when given a clean inning to pitch. Most importantly for his bank account, Broxton still has a name and a frame that conjure images of past dominance and afford him a little more leeway and perceived upside than other, similar pitchers.

Brett Cecil   LHP

Born: 7/2/86   Age: 30   Bats: R   Throws: L   Height: 6'3"   Weight: 235   Entered Pro Ball: Round 1, 2007 Draft (#38 overall)

YEAR	TEAM	LVL	AGE	W	L	SV	G	GS	IP	H	HR	BB/9	K/9	K	GB%	BABIP	WHIP	ERA	FIP	DRA	VORP	WARP	cFIP	MPH
2014	TOR	MLB	27	2	3	5	66	0	53¹	46	2	4.6	12.8	76	55%	.344	1.37	2.70	2.37	1.95	15.0	1.7	72	95.4
2015	TOR	MLB	28	5	5	5	63	0	54¹	39	4	2.2	11.6	70	54%	.280	0.96	2.48	2.31	2.09	15.8	1.7	67	94.8
2016	TOR	MLB	29	1	7	0	54	0	36²	39	6	2.0	11.0	45	43%	.344	1.28	3.93	3.60	3.32	6.7	0.7	88	94.4
2017	SLN	MLB	30	2	3	0	50	0	52	48	5	3.0	9.8	57	55%	.302	1.24	3.28	3.37	3.55	8.0	0.8	76	
2018	SLN	MLB	31	2	1	0	39	0	41¹	35	5	3.1	9.8	45	55%	.312	1.20	3.71	3.74	4.04	4.9	0.5	89	

Breakout: 36%   Improve: 63%   Collapse: 18%   Attrition: 16%   MLB: 87%   *Comparables: Charlie Furbush, Chad Qualls, Joel Hanrahan*

Let's hope the Cardinals four-year, $30.5 million deal for man they call "Squints" comes with a prescription check. In back-to-back seasons Cecil was awful for long stretches and nearly unhittable for others, with nothing in between. He posted a 6.75 ERA through July 20, including a month-and-a-half on the sidelines, but dominated the rest of the way with a 1.74 ERA and 38 percent strikeout rate. His curveball took a small step backward last year in whiff rate (43 percent vs. 54 percent in 2015), but it's still an absolutely lethal pitch that makes him a valuable bullpen weapon, especially against lefties.

Zach Duke   LHP

Born: 4/19/83   Age: 34   Bats: L   Throws: L   Height: 6'2"   Weight: 210   Entered Pro Ball: Round 20, 2001 Draft (#594 overall)

YEAR	TEAM	LVL	AGE	W	L	SV	G	GS	IP	H	HR	BB/9	K/9	K	GB%	BABIP	WHIP	ERA	FIP	DRA	VORP	WARP	cFIP	MPH
2014	MIL	MLB	31	5	1	0	74	0	58²	49	3	2.6	11.4	74	60%	.322	1.12	2.45	2.11	1.85	17.2	1.9	71	92.2
2015	CHA	MLB	32	3	6	1	71	0	60²	47	9	4.7	9.8	66	59%	.264	1.30	3.41	4.59	3.23	10.0	1.1	91	92.0
2016	CHA	MLB	33	2	0	1	53	0	37²	31	2	3.8	10.0	42	65%	.299	1.25	2.63	3.00	2.94	8.5	0.9	81	92.4
2016	SLN	MLB	33	0	1	1	28	0	23¹	17	0	5.0	10.0	26	60%	.293	1.29	1.93	2.89	3.44	4.0	0.4	81	92.1
2017	SLN	MLB	34	3	1	1	53	0	55²	47	5	3.5	9.1	56	61%	.311	1.24	3.64	3.64	4.00	5.7	0.6	87	
2018	SLN	MLB	35	2	1	1	48	0	41¹	34	5	4.1	9.9	45	61%	.304	1.27	4.10	4.17	4.51	2.9	0.3	101	

Breakout: 15%   Improve: 28%   Collapse: 16%   Attrition: 8%   MLB: 61%   *Comparables: D.J. Carrasco, Neal Cotts, John Bale*

The Cardinals acquired Duke from the White Sox at last year's deadline, and the converted low-velo starter did what he's usually done since lowering his arm slot and moving to the 'pen: dominate same-side hitters and perform acts of worm genocide. Frustrated hitters continually beat his sinker into the ground and flail away at his curveball. Duke's propensity to work outside the zone leads to a lot of walks, but his high strikeout rate and ability to keep the ball in the yard limits the damage. While there were no indications Duke had been injured during the season, he surprisingly underwent Tommy John surgery in October, shelving him until at least 2018 when he'll be a 35-year-old with a scar and the need to prove himself all over again.

Junior Fernandez   RHP

Born: 3/2/97   Age: 20   Bats: R   Throws: R   Height: 6'1"   Weight: 180   Entered Pro Ball: International Free Agent, 2014

YEAR	TEAM	LVL	AGE	W	L	SV	G	GS	IP	H	HR	BB/9	K/9	K	GB%	BABIP	WHIP	ERA	FIP	DRA	VORP	WARP	cFIP	MPH
2016	PEO	A	19	6	5	0	14	14	78¹	71	3	3.9	7.2	63	52%	.296	1.34	3.33	3.86	6.01	-8.6	-0.9	113	
2016	PMB	A+	19	2	2	0	10	6	43²	48	4	4.1	5.2	25	47%	.297	1.56	5.36	4.88	7.00	-8.0	-0.8	116	
2017	SLN	MLB	20	5	7	0	28	16	92²	112	16	5.0	4.2	43	62%	.320	1.77	6.30	6.29	7.05	-19.2	-2.0	165	
2018	SLN	MLB	21	4	8	0	22	18	119¹	123	19	6.6	6.8	91	62%	.312	1.77	6.31	6.59	7.06	-17.0	-1.8	166	

Breakout: 0%   Improve: 0%   Collapse: 0%   Attrition: 0%   MLB: 0%   *Comparables: Wilmer Font, Alex Sanabia, Mike Foltynewicz*

Fernandez bullied his way through the Midwest League as a teenager, determined to throw mid-90s thunderbolts straight through any glove, catcher, umpire, backstop or peanut vendor foolish enough to get in his way. His high-effort delivery erodes his fastball command, and at this point his breaking ball is far more theory than property. On the plus side, Fernandez has a promising changeup that flashes plus, and his fastball seems to have more jump and wiggle than hitters expect. The Cardinals will give him every chance to get on top of his stuff and stay in the rotation, but his frame, arsenal and command profile seem best suited to late-inning relief.

Jack Flaherty   RHP

Born: 10/15/95   Age: 21   Bats: R   Throws: R   Height: 6'4"   Weight: 205   Entered Pro Ball: Round 1, 2014 Draft (#34 overall)

YEAR	TEAM	LVL	AGE	W	L	SV	G	GS	IP	H	HR	BB/9	K/9	K	GB%	BABIP	WHIP	ERA	FIP	DRA	VORP	WARP	cFIP	MPH
2015	PEO	A	19	9	3	0	18	18	95	92	2	2.9	9.2	97	37%	.330	1.29	2.84	2.83	3.05	22.9	2.4	89	
2016	PMB	A+	20	5	9	0	24	23	134	129	8	3.0	8.5	126	49%	.316	1.30	3.56	3.20	2.69	41.2	4.2	88	
2017	SLN	MLB	21	6	7	0	21	21	107²	122	17	3.9	6.2	75	61%	.326	1.56	5.24	5.18	5.75	-2.3	-0.2	136	
2018	SLN	MLB	22	7	10	0	25	25	147¹	146	23	4.7	8.4	138	61%	.322	1.52	5.19	5.36	5.69	-1.8	-0.2	135	

Breakout: 9%   Improve: 12%   Collapse: 4%   Attrition: 13%   MLB: 16%   *Comparables: Daniel Corcino, Yohander Mendez, German Marquez*

There's nothing wrong with a prospect putting in a workmanlike season, since work means health, repetition and learning to survive the grind, which usually leads to progress. And for a 20-year-old like Flaherty to post solid numbers in the Florida State League is a positive sign. Flaherty doesn't have a big fastball or a hammer curve, but he has a projectable frame, four pitches that can be at least average and the possibility of a plus changeup. If he can start missing a few more bats as he climbs the prospect ladder he could grow into the mid-rotation workhorse his stuff projects; if not, he can append "Detective Sergeant" to the front of his business card and grow into the police procedural cast member his name projects.

John Gant   RHP

Born: 8/6/92   Age: 24   Bats: R   Throws: R   Height: 6'3"   Weight: 200   Entered Pro Ball: Round 21, 2011 Draft (#642 overall)

YEAR	TEAM	LVL	AGE	W	L	SV	G	GS	IP	H	HR	BB/9	K/9	K	GB%	BABIP	WHIP	ERA	FIP	DRA	VORP	WARP	cFIP	MPH
2014	SAV	A	21	11	5	0	21	21	123	107	5	2.9	8.3	114	51%	.293	1.20	2.56	3.31	2.95	34.0	3.5	90	
2015	SLU	A+	22	2	0	0	6	6	40¹	27	4	2.2	10.7	48	50%	.232	0.92	1.79	2.89	1.26	17.1	1.9	72	
2015	BIN	AA	22	4	5	0	11	11	59¹	67	2	3.9	6.5	43	47%	.337	1.57	4.70	3.62	5.19	-0.6	-0.1	108	
2015	MIS	AA	22	4	0	0	7	7	40²	28	1	3.1	9.5	43	43%	.273	1.03	1.99	2.54	3.16	8.7	0.9	80	
2016	GWN	AAA	23	3	3	0	12	10	56	58	5	3.5	9.2	57	49%	.329	1.43	4.18	3.47	3.20	13.0	1.3	87	
2016	ATL	MLB	23	1	4	0	20	7	50	54	7	3.8	8.8	49	45%	.329	1.50	4.86	4.43	3.93	7.1	0.7	101	94.4
2017	SLN	MLB	24	2	2	0	26	3	38	40	5	3.8	7.4	32	54%	.298	1.45	4.67	4.59	4.72	1.3	0.1	100	
2018	SLN	MLB	25	3	2	0	36	4	56¹	49	6	4.8	9.4	59	54%	.308	1.40	4.37	4.50	4.85	2.5	0.3	110	

Breakout: 28%   Improve: 50%   Collapse: 13%   Attrition: 30%   MLB: 69%   *Comparables: Felipe Rivero, Jason Hammel, Marco Gonzales*

Even though Gant somehow managed to make the Opening Day roster in 2016, he spent a lot of time bouncing around from Triple-A to the bigs. His role remained the same for the most part—he was pegged as a spot starter and long reliever, and that was the spot he filled for the Braves over 50 innings of work. In addition to filling that role, he also filled the Braves' annual "Wonky Delivery" role that Jordan Walden abdicated when he was traded. It takes a lot of getting used to when you see it in action, but there's a very good chance you'll continue to see it at the big-league level.

Marco Gonzales   LHP

Born: 2/16/92   Age: 25   Bats: L   Throws: L   Height: 6'1"   Weight: 195   Entered Pro Ball: Round 1, 2013 Draft (#19 overall)

YEAR	TEAM	LVL	AGE	W	L	SV	G	GS	IP	H	HR	BB/9	K/9	K	GB%	BABIP	WHIP	ERA	FIP	DRA	VORP	WARP	cFIP	MPH
2014	PMB	A+	22	2	2	0	6	6	37²	34	1	1.9	7.6	32	53%	.303	1.12	1.43	2.67	3.18	10.1	1.0	90	
2014	SFD	AA	22	3	2	0	7	7	38²	33	2	2.3	10.7	46	45%	.304	1.11	2.33	2.19	1.88	14.4	1.5	75	
2014	MEM	AAA	22	4	1	0	8	8	45²	43	7	1.8	7.7	39	43%	.279	1.14	3.35	4.77	2.37	17.2	1.7	98	
2014	SLN	MLB	22	4	2	0	10	5	34²	32	4	5.5	8.0	31	39%	.283	1.53	4.15	4.72	6.12	-5.3	-0.6	123	91.9
2015	SLN	MLB	23	0	0	0	1	1	2²	7	1	3.4	3.4	1	43%	.462	3.00	13.50	8.41	5.75	-0.2	0.0	113	91.7
2015	MEM	AAA	23	1	5	0	14	14	69¹	91	10	3.1	6.6	51	40%	.358	1.66	5.45	5.08	5.74	-3.5	-0.4	106	
2017	SLN	MLB	25	1	1	0	14	0	14¹	14	2	3.6	7.0	11	57%	.295	1.42	4.73	4.93	4.74	0.3	0.0	100	
2018	SLN	MLB	26	2	1	0	50	0	52²	45	6	4.2	9.1	53	57%	.301	1.33	4.31	4.43	4.80	1.9	0.2	108	

Breakout: 26%   Improve: 44%   Collapse: 31%   Attrition: 47%   MLB: 92%   Comparables: Zach Miner, Taylor Jordan, T.J. House

Things have gone from bad to worse for Gonzales, as the former top pick had his comeback from shoulder woes cut short last spring by a sore elbow. Tommy John surgery ensued, and Gonzales is expected back on the mound sometime this summer, with his command to follow at least a few months after that. Health has proven to be the trapdoor in his low-ceiling/high-floor projection, but if his killer changeup survived the knife Gonzales still has a chance to become a solid fourth starter.

Mike Leake   RHP

Born: 11/12/87   Age: 29   Bats: R   Throws: R   Height: 5'10"   Weight: 170   Entered Pro Ball: Round 1, 2009 Draft (#8 overall)

YEAR	TEAM	LVL	AGE	W	L	SV	G	GS	IP	H	HR	BB/9	K/9	K	GB%	BABIP	WHIP	ERA	FIP	DRA	VORP	WARP	cFIP	MPH
2014	CIN	MLB	26	11	13	0	33	33	214¹	217	23	2.1	6.9	164	55%	.298	1.25	3.70	3.85	3.14	40.4	4.5	93	93.2
2015	CIN	MLB	27	9	5	0	21	21	136²	123	14	2.2	5.9	90	53%	.262	1.15	3.56	3.97	4.57	7.8	0.8	105	93.2
2015	SFN	MLB	27	2	5	0	9	9	55¹	51	8	2.4	4.7	29	53%	.254	1.19	4.07	4.86	4.54	3.3	0.4	104	93.0
2016	SLN	MLB	28	9	12	0	30	30	176²	203	20	1.5	6.4	125	55%	.318	1.32	4.69	3.87	3.65	33.6	3.5	96	93.0
2017	SLN	MLB	29	10	12	0	31	31	186	190	23	2.1	6.5	135	47%	.292	1.25	4.22	4.15	4.36	16.9	1.7	100	
2018	SLN	MLB	30	11	11	0	31	31	197	195	24	2.0	6.7	146	47%	.306	1.21	4.16	4.26	4.61	19.3	2.0	107	

Breakout: 22%   Improve: 43%   Collapse: 15%   Attrition: 9%   MLB: 94%   Comparables: Joe Blanton, Jeff Francis, Edwin Jackson

Leake's first season in St. Louis after signing a five-year, $80 million deal was a rousing success, unless you pay attention to those pesky "runs allowed" metrics. The longtime command-and-control specialist posted one of his lowest FIPs and best walk and ground-ball rates, upped his strikeout rate and generally pitched as well or better than he ever has. All that good work was undone by a sky-high BABIP, however, and since Statcast didn't show him giving up any more screamers than usual, a lot of that was due to the Cardinals' woeful infield defense. Leake thrives by avoiding walks and generating ground-ball outs, but when the fielders behind him show the instincts and range of an unmanned foosball table, he's bound to struggle.

Lance Lynn   RHP

Born: 5/12/87   Age: 30   Bats: R   Throws: R   Height: 6'5"   Weight: 280   Entered Pro Ball: Round 1, 2008 Draft (#39 overall)

YEAR	TEAM	LVL	AGE	W	L	SV	G	GS	IP	H	HR	BB/9	K/9	K	GB%	BABIP	WHIP	ERA	FIP	DRA	VORP	WARP	cFIP	MPH
2014	SLN	MLB	27	15	10	0	33	33	203²	185	13	3.2	8.0	181	46%	.290	1.26	2.74	3.32	3.99	19.1	2.1	102	95.4
2015	SLN	MLB	28	12	11	0	31	31	175¹	172	13	3.5	8.6	167	46%	.319	1.37	3.03	3.47	4.31	15.1	1.6	101	95.1
2017	SLN	MLB	30	7	9	0	24	24	136	133	19	3.5	8.6	130	47%	.297	1.37	4.43	4.35	4.56	9.4	1.0	100	
2018	SLN	MLB	31	8	9	0	26	26	152²	142	21	3.2	8.5	144	47%	.309	1.28	4.37	4.47	4.83	11.8	1.2	113	

Breakout: 12%   Improve: 36%   Collapse: 30%   Attrition: 13%   MLB: 94%   Comparables: Ubaldo Jimenez, Yovani Gallardo, Gavin Floyd

Lynn's impending return after a season lost to elbow surgery is good news for the Cardinals, as the big right-hander has been a rock in their rotation for years. It will also be interesting as a data point on Tommy John recovery, as his fastball-heavy approach differs from most starters. When last we saw him, Lynn was throwing his heater more than 80 percent of the time, eschewing his sketchy slider and changeup in favor of varying the speed, movement and location of his fastball. With command traditionally taking longer to recover than health for TJ survivors, will Lynn be ahead of the game by needing to only reclaim mastery over one pitch or will his need for exceptional command of that one pitch make his path more difficult? Stay tuned.

Tyler Lyons   LHP

Born: 2/21/88   Age: 29   Bats: L   Throws: L   Height: 6'4"   Weight: 210   Entered Pro Ball: Round 9, 2010 Draft (#289 overall)

YEAR	TEAM	LVL	AGE	W	L	SV	G	GS	IP	H	HR	BB/9	K/9	K	GB%	BABIP	WHIP	ERA	FIP	DRA	VORP	WARP	cFIP	MPH
2014	MEM	AAA	26	8	2	0	14	14	81¹	94	9	2.0	8.3	75	44%	.348	1.38	4.43	3.96	3.79	17.7	1.8	87	
2014	SLN	MLB	26	0	4	0	11	4	36²	33	4	2.7	8.8	36	43%	.284	1.20	4.42	3.62	4.36	1.4	0.2	101	92.9
2015	MEM	AAA	27	9	5	0	16	16	94²	104	12	1.2	9.1	96	42%	.336	1.24	3.14	3.69	0.95	45.8	4.7	57	
2015	SLN	MLB	27	3	1	0	17	8	60	59	12	2.2	9.0	60	42%	.281	1.23	3.75	4.56	5.03	-0.4	0.0	98	92.8
2016	SLN	MLB	28	2	0	0	30	0	48	35	9	2.6	8.6	46	41%	.220	1.02	3.38	4.58	4.42	3.0	0.3	102	93.4
2017	SLN	MLB	29	3	3	0	18	8	56²	54	7	2.6	7.9	49	46%	.313	1.24	3.98	3.96	4.39	7.4	0.8	100	
2018	SLN	MLB	30	4	4	0	19	11	80	72	11	3.5	9.4	84	46%	.316	1.29	4.35	4.42	4.80	5.8	0.6	111	

Breakout: 21%   Improve: 40%   Collapse: 15%   Attrition: 17%   MLB: 76%   Comparables: Matt Shoemaker, Sam LeCure, Yusmeiro Petit

Lyons began last season trying to change his spots, making a conscious effort to cut down on the gopher balls that have plagued him. He ended last season with knee surgery after missing two months with a stress reaction that never seemed to improve. In between Lyons was his typical self, drinking the tears of fellow lefties while letting righties take him deep at an alarming rate. His fly-ball tendencies and platoon issues will keep him out of the rotation and away from high-leverage situations, but if he's healthy this spring he's perfectly cast as a swingman who can save other bullpen arms and get some key outs in the middle innings.

Seth Maness RHP

Born: 10/14/88 Age: 28   Bats: R   Throws: R   Height: 6'0"   Weight: 190   Entered Pro Ball: Round 11, 2011 Draft (#350 overall)

YEAR	TEAM	LVL	AGE	W	L	SV	G	GS	IP	H	HR	BB/9	K/9	K	GB%	BABIP	WHIP	ERA	FIP	DRA	VORP	WARP	cFIP	MPH
2014	SLN	MLB	25	6	4	3	73	0	80¹	77	7	1.2	6.2	55	57%	.289	1.10	2.91	3.35	3.68	7.2	0.8	95	91.6
2015	SLN	MLB	26	4	2	3	76	0	63¹	77	7	1.8	6.5	46	58%	.345	1.42	4.26	3.81	3.92	5.5	0.6	100	91.6
2016	SLN	MLB	27	2	2	0	29	0	31²	34	2	2.3	4.5	16	58%	.296	1.33	3.41	3.75	5.11	-0.5	0.0	110	90.2
2017	*SLN*	*MLB*	*28*	*2*	*1*	*0*	*35*	*0*	*37*	*38*	*5*	*2.5*	*6.0*	*25*	*47%*	*.310*	*1.32*	*4.48*	*4.43*	*4.95*	*0.7*	*0.1*	*113*	
2018	*SLN*	*MLB*	*29*	*3*	*1*	*1*	*58*	*0*	*57*	*56*	*7*	*3.0*	*7.6*	*48*	*47%*	*.315*	*1.31*	*4.34*	*4.43*	*4.79*	*2.2*	*0.2*	*108*	

Breakout: 19%   Improve: 46%   Collapse: 18%   Attrition: 26%   MLB: 87%   *Comparables: Wesley Wright, Sean Burnett, Zach Miner*

Expecting exciting news from your doctor when you wake up from Tommy John surgery is as foolish as expecting that sketchy hole-in-the-wall with one review on Yelp to really have "the most kick-ass Thai food anywhere." Yet Maness can attest that good surprises sometimes happen, as his surgeons last August decided they wouldn't need to replace his ulnar collateral ligament and could instead repair it, slicing his likely recovery time in half. Instead of missing an entire season or more, Maness and his low-velo, low-altitude repertoire should be back in the middle innings sometime this summer doing what he always does: filling the strike zone, coaxing double-play grounders and studiously ignoring culinary advice from westworldrulz93.

Carlos Martinez   RHP

Born: 9/21/91 Age: 25   Bats: R   Throws: R   Height: 6'0"   Weight: 190   Entered Pro Ball: International Free Agent, 2009

YEAR	TEAM	LVL	AGE	W	L	SV	G	GS	IP	H	HR	BB/9	K/9	K	GB%	BABIP	WHIP	ERA	FIP	DRA	VORP	WARP	cFIP	MPH
2014	MEM	AAA	22	1	0	0	2	2	10¹	6	0	0.9	6.1	7	48%	.207	0.68	0.00	2.63	3.42	2.7	0.3	94	
2014	SLN	MLB	22	2	4	1	57	7	89¹	90	4	3.6	8.5	84	55%	.333	1.41	4.03	3.15	3.63	9.7	1.1	93	100.3
2015	SLN	MLB	23	14	7	0	31	29	179²	168	13	3.2	9.2	184	56%	.318	1.29	3.01	3.24	3.30	35.4	3.8	89	99.0
2016	SLN	MLB	24	16	9	0	31	31	195¹	169	15	3.2	8.0	174	58%	.286	1.22	3.04	3.65	3.73	35.4	3.7	92	99.6
2017	*SLN*	*MLB*	*25*	*10*	*11*	*0*	*28*	*28*	*176*	*167*	*20*	*3.3*	*8.1*	*159*	*42%*	*.293*	*1.31*	*4.19*	*4.07*	*4.33*	*16.6*	*1.7*	*100*	
2018	*SLN*	*MLB*	*26*	*11*	*11*	*0*	*30*	*30*	*190*	*161*	*21*	*3.2*	*9.1*	*191*	*42%*	*.302*	*1.20*	*3.90*	*3.98*	*4.32*	*25.7*	*2.7*	*98*	

Breakout: 26%   Improve: 55%   Collapse: 19%   Attrition: 12%   MLB: 96%   *Comparables: Gerrit Cole, David Price, Jered Weaver*

There are many recipes for pitching success, but one of the tastiest involves strikeouts, ground balls and enough velocity to overcome occasional bouts of shaky command. Martinez blended all those ingredients through 30 occasionally overpowering starts last season, firmly establishing himself as a front-line starter. Hitters have trouble barreling his mid-90s heat, slider and changeup, although learning another trick to use against lefties should be high on his to-do list. "Tsunamy" changes his hairstyle as often as his underwear and approaches everything from public appearances to dugout water cup celebrations with the open enthusiasm of a tail-wagging Labrador, making him a fan and clubhouse favorite. Health and success are never guaranteed, but Martinez may very well be on his way to becoming the eventual face of the post-Molina Cardinals.

Seung Hwan Oh   RHP

Born: 7/15/82 Age: 34   Bats: R   Throws: R   Height: 5'10"   Weight: 205   Entered Pro Ball: International Free Agent, 2016

YEAR	TEAM	LVL	AGE	W	L	SV	G	GS	IP	H	HR	BB/9	K/9	K	GB%	BABIP	WHIP	ERA	FIP	DRA	VORP	WARP	cFIP	MPH
2016	SLN	MLB	33	6	3	19	76	0	79²	55	5	2.0	11.6	103	40%	.270	0.92	1.92	2.17	2.49	21.9	2.3	71	95.7
2017	*SLN*	*MLB*	*34*	*3*	*3*	*20*	*54*	*0*	*57*	*50*	*8*	*2.4*	*10.7*	*68*	*40%*	*.294*	*1.13*	*3.43*	*3.49*	*3.67*	*7.9*	*0.8*	*78*	
2018	*SLN*	*MLB*	*35*	*3*	*1*	*15*	*60*	*0*	*63²*	*54*	*9*	*2.5*	*9.9*	*70*	*40%*	*.299*	*1.12*	*3.91*	*3.93*	*4.27*	*6.1*	*0.6*	*95*	

Breakout: 16%   Improve: 34%   Collapse: 34%   Attrition: 7%   MLB: 91%   *Comparables: Jonathan Papelbon, Francisco Cordero, Matt Thornton*

Having already proven to be the Final Boss while dominating the ninth inning in Japan and Korea, Oh can now add another league to his list of vanquished foes. The Cardinals had hoped the veteran reliever could succeed in a setup role, but his slider proved to be untouchable early on, so when Trevor Rosenthal struggled they plugged the surprisingly incombustible former Samsung Lion into the closer role and never looked back. Compact and powerful, the Stone Buddha has an unflappable mound demeanor and can reach back for mid-90s heat when he needs it. His plus change and wipeout slider are even better, helping him tame both righties and lefties and miss bats at a rate that rests comfortably among baseball's best. There's nothing fluky here, and Oh should leave overmatched hitters weepin' like a willow again this summer.

Alex Reyes RHP

Born: 8/29/94 Age: 22   Bats: R   Throws: R   Height: 6'3"   Weight: 175   Entered Pro Ball: International Free Agent, 2012

YEAR	TEAM	LVL	AGE	W	L	SV	G	GS	IP	H	HR	BB/9	K/9	K	GB%	BABIP	WHIP	ERA	FIP	DRA	VORP	WARP	cFIP	MPH
2014	PEO	A	19	7	7	0	21	21	109¹	82	6	5.0	11.3	137	40%	.295	1.31	3.62	3.45	3.26	26.5	2.7	94	
2015	PMB	A+	20	2	5	0	13	13	63²	49	0	4.4	13.6	96	46%	.371	1.26	2.26	1.75	1.16	27.7	3.0	72	
2015	SFD	AA	20	3	2	0	8	8	34²	21	1	4.7	13.5	52	44%	.286	1.12	3.12	2.32	1.83	12.6	1.4	67	
2016	MEM	AAA	21	2	3	0	14	14	65¹	63	6	4.4	12.8	93	42%	.365	1.45	4.96	3.72	2.68	19.3	2.0	78	
2016	SLN	MLB	21	4	1	1	12	5	46	33	1	4.5	10.2	52	44%	.283	1.22	1.57	2.71	3.72	7.7	0.8	94	100.1
2017	*SLN*	*MLB*	*22*	*7*	*8*	*0*	*23*	*23*	*121*	*112*	*13*	*4.2*	*9.5*	*128*	*46%*	*.301*	*1.40*	*4.04*	*3.96*	*4.13*	*14.2*	*1.5*	*95*	
2018	*SLN*	*MLB*	*23*	*10*	*9*	*0*	*31*	*31*	*195¹*	*151*	*19*	*4.5*	*11.2*	*243*	*46%*	*.313*	*1.27*	*3.65*	*3.72*	*4.00*	*28.1*	*2.9*	*90*	

Breakout: 24%   Improve: 41%   Collapse: 9%   Attrition: 23%   MLB: 65%   *Comparables: Trevor Bauer, Luis Severino, Arodys Vizcaino*

Reyes has taken the road less traveled from New Jersey, passing through the Dominican Republic (to live with his grandparents and avoid the draft), minor-league cities, the doghouse of a 50-game marijuana suspension and the Cardinals' bullpen before arriving at the front of the rotation. His raw stuff—a fastball that can hit triple digits, a jaw-dropping 12-6 curve and a Bugs Bunny changeup—grades out among the best in the game, but his ability to repeat his delivery and develop command will spell the difference between a multi-time All-Star and, say, Arquimedes Caminero. It's nearly impossible to thrive in a starting role while walking 12 percent of the batters you face, but if Reyes can spend a little more time in the strike zone he could grow into a *bonafide* ace.

Trevor Rosenthal   RHP

Born: 5/29/90   Age: 27   Bats: R   Throws: R   Height: 6'2"   Weight: 230   Entered Pro Ball: Round 21, 2009 Draft (#639 overall)

YEAR	TEAM	LVL	AGE	W	L	SV	G	GS	IP	H	HR	BB/9	K/9	K	GB%	BABIP	WHIP	ERA	FIP	DRA	VORP	WARP	cFIP	MPH
2014	SLN	MLB	24	2	6	45	72	0	70¹	57	2	5.4	11.1	87	39%	.318	1.41	3.20	2.96	3.88	4.7	0.5	100	99.7
2015	SLN	MLB	25	2	4	48	68	0	68²	62	3	3.3	10.9	83	47%	.337	1.27	2.10	2.45	3.25	11.2	1.2	84	100.3
2016	SLN	MLB	26	2	4	14	45	0	40¹	48	3	6.5	12.5	56	53%	.425	1.91	4.46	3.76	4.25	3.3	0.3	93	99.9
2017	SLN	MLB	27	2	2	5	36	0	38	36	5	4.4	9.8	42	46%	.302	1.44	4.51	4.24	4.56	1.5	0.2	100	
2018	SLN	MLB	28	2	1	4	49	0	51²	43	7	4.2	9.9	57	46%	.298	1.29	4.36	4.44	4.82	1.8	0.2	112	

Breakout: 37%   Improve: 59%   Collapse: 19%   Attrition: 10%   MLB: 98%   *Comparables: Manny Delcarmen, Sean Doolittle, Bobby Jenks*

Two years ago in this space, we said this about the Cardinals fire-baller: "Control problems will likely always be just a few outings away for Rosenthal, which is why he's destined for a long career as a second-tier closer rather than a mid-rotation starter." Rosenthal's inability to avoid ball four was temporarily cured in 2015, but came back with a vengeance last summer, costing him the closer gig before shoulder woes shelved him for most of the stretch run. He earned his sky-high BABIP last year—the highest in baseball since 1950—as hitters laid off pitches out of the zone, got ahead in the count and roped Rosenthal's fastball to center or bounced it through the immobile Cardinals infield. His top-shelf heat will always rack up whiffs, but Rosenthal's spectral control will likely keep him floating from dominance to combustibility and back again.

Kevin Siegrist   LHP

Born: 7/20/89   Age: 27   Bats: L   Throws: L   Height: 6'5"   Weight: 230   Entered Pro Ball: Round 41, 2008 Draft (#1235 overall)

YEAR	TEAM	LVL	AGE	W	L	SV	G	GS	IP	H	HR	BB/9	K/9	K	GB%	BABIP	WHIP	ERA	FIP	DRA	VORP	WARP	cFIP	MPH
2014	SLN	MLB	24	1	4	0	37	0	30¹	32	5	4.7	11.0	37	33%	.338	1.58	6.82	4.59	4.88	-1.3	-0.1	106	96.6
2015	SLN	MLB	25	7	1	6	81	0	74²	53	4	4.1	10.8	90	32%	.271	1.17	2 17	2.93	4.06	5.4	0.6	98	96.5
2016	SLN	MLB	26	6	3	3	67	0	61²	42	10	3.8	9.6	66	35%	.221	1.10	2.77	4.47	4.19	5.4	0.6	101	95.9
2017	SLN	MLB	27	2	3	0	54	0	57	50	8	3.6	9.2	58	49%	.277	1.25	4.53	4.27	4.60	2.0	0.2	100	
2018	SLN	MLB	28	3	1	1	54	0	57	42	8	3.9	9.6	61	49%	.264	1.17	4.43	4.51	4.92	1.4	0.1	115	

Breakout: 37%   Improve: 61%   Collapse: 18%   Attrition: 12%   MLB: 93%   *Comparables: Manny Delcarmen, Jeremy Accardo, Carlos Marmol*

Siegrist is that rarest of baseball birds: a middle reliever who consistently overcomes the tyranny of small samples to put up solid numbers every year. The lanky lefty shelved his slider for a new curveball last season, but still posted his familiar reverse platoon splits while striking out more than a batter per inning. His extreme fly-ball tendencies helped him overcome the Cardinals' leaky infield defense, but home runs were (and always will be) an occasional problem. Just now entering his arbitration years, Siegrist is a niche player but an important one to keep around.

Miguel Socolovich   RHP

Born: 7/24/86   Age: 30   Bats: R   Throws: R   Height: 6'1"   Weight: 205   Entered Pro Ball: International Free Agent, 2004

YEAR	TEAM	LVL	AGE	W	L	SV	G	GS	IP	H	HR	BB/9	K/9	K	GB%	BABIP	WHIP	ERA	FIP	DRA	VORP	WARP	cFIP	MPH
2014	LVG	AAA	27	2	2	3	51	0	59¹	68	5	2.9	10.3	68	42%	.375	1.47	3.64	3.46	3.27	13.7	1.4	84	
2015	MEM	AAA	28	2	2	0	21	0	32²	18	1	3.3	9.9	36	49%	.224	0.92	2.48	2.99	2.88	7.4	0.8	89	
2015	SLN	MLB	28	4	1	0	28	0	29²	25	1	3.0	8.2	27	50%	.276	1.18	1.82	2.79	4.12	1.9	0.2	99	93.3
2016	MEM	AAA	29	2	6	5	45	0	51²	42	2	2.8	10.3	59	46%	.294	1.12	3.14	2.93	2.22	15.7	1.6	79	
2016	SLN	MLB	29	1	0	0	15	0	18	5	2	2.5	8.0	16	54%	.073	0.56	2.00	3.69	3.60	2.7	0.3	95	93.2
2017	SLN	MLB	30	2	3	0	45	0	47	46	6	3.2	7.5	40	42%	.287	1.31	4.39	4.33	4.48	2.3	0.2	100	
2018	SLN	MLB	31	3	1	0	53	0	56¹	45	7	4.1	9.9	62	42%	.290	1.26	4.30	4.39	4.76	2.3	0.2	109	

Breakout: 14%   Improve: 23%   Collapse: 11%   Attrition: 12%   MLB: 39%   *Comparables: Blake Parker, Rob Wooten, Mike Ekstrom*

The only people who seem to take Socolovich seriously are the Triple-A and MLB batters he sends mumbling back to the dugout. The former Hiroshima Carp afterthought features a low-velo assortment indistinguishable from countless other organizational arms, yet no one seems able to solve him. Last year Socolovich held right-handed hitters to a .171/.242/.199 line overall and if he wasn't money against lefties he was at least barter goods. He's a riddle inside a mystery wrapped in a batting practice hurler's cloak, and we'd love to see Socolovich get a real shot at big-league relevance.

Sam Tuivailala   RHP

Born: 10/19/92 Age: 24 Bats: R Throws: R Height: 6'3" Weight: 225 Entered Pro Ball: Round 3, 2010 Draft (#106 overall)

YEAR	TEAM	LVL	AGE	W	L	SV	G	GS	IP	H	HR	BB/9	K/9	K	GB%	BABIP	WHIP	ERA	FIP	DRA	VORP	WARP	cFIP	MPH
2014	PMB	A+	21	0	1	3	29	0	37²	29	1	4.3	15.3	64	47%	.364	1.25	3.58	1.93	0.82	18.3	1.8	65	
2014	SFD	AA	21	2	1	1	17	0	21	18	0	3.9	12.9	30	56%	.375	1.29	2.57	1.69	2.74	4.9	0.5	77	
2014	SLN	MLB	21	0	0	0	2	0	1	5	2	18.0	9.0	1	0%	.600	7.00	36.00	33.10	14.44	-1.1	-0.1	125	99.8
2015	MEM	AAA	22	3	1	17	43	0	45	28	2	5.2	8.6	43	43%	.228	1.20	1.60	4.20	4.23	3.4	0.4	106	
2015	SLN	MLB	22	0	1	0	14	0	14²	13	2	4.9	12.3	20	49%	.314	1.43	3.07	3.84	3.63	1.8	0.2	92	99.3
2016	MEM	AAA	23	3	2	17	42	0	46²	47	3	4.2	13.9	72	43%	.393	1.48	5.21	2.95	1.22	19.4	2.0	71	
2016	SLN	MLB	23	0	0	0	12	0	9	12	0	6.0	7.0	7	44%	.375	2.00	6.00	4.30	5.90	-0.9	-0.1	117	98.3
2017	SLN	MLB	24	1	2	0	27	0	28²	29	3	4.1	8.6	27	48%	.307	1.49	4.50	4.11	4.58	1.1	0.1	100	
2018	SLN	MLB	25	2	1	0	39	0	41¹	35	5	4.7	10.6	49	48%	.320	1.38	4.29	4.39	4.77	1.6	0.2	107	

Breakout: 22%   Improve: 33%   Collapse: 4%   Attrition: 20%   MLB: 43%   *Comparables: Nick Rumbelow, Shae Simmons, Shawn Tolleson*

Velocity isn't everything, and it isn't the only thing. It's a very good thing, and it can help overcome other things, but to thrive in a big-league bullpen you need a second thing: control. Velocity is Sam's thing. His fastball is past you before you can say his last name, but he often doesn't know where it's going. Too many hitters just stand and watch and then walk to first base. That makes his friends sad. If Sam ever learns to match Thing 1 with Thing 2 he'll rampage through the late innings. Until then, he's just another cat in a hat.

Michael Wacha   RHP

Born: 7/1/91 Age: 25 Bats: R Throws: R Height: 6'6" Weight: 215 Entered Pro Ball: Round 1, 2012 Draft (#19 overall)

YEAR	TEAM	LVL	AGE	W	L	SV	G	GS	IP	H	HR	BB/9	K/9	K	GB%	BABIP	WHIP	ERA	FIP	DRA	VORP	WARP	cFIP	MPH
2014	SLN	MLB	22	5	6	0	19	19	107	95	6	2.8	7.9	94	44%	.288	1.20	3.20	3.14	4.23	7.2	0.8	105	96.3
2015	SLN	MLB	23	17	7	0	30	30	181¹	162	19	2.9	7.6	153	48%	.272	1.21	3.38	3.90	4.55	10.6	1.1	103	97.1
2016	SLN	MLB	24	7	7	0	27	24	138	159	15	2.9	7.4	114	48%	.334	1.48	5.09	3.95	4.61	11.3	1.2	105	96.3
2017	SLN	MLB	25	7	9	0	41	18	131	134	19	3.1	7.1	105	51%	.290	1.36	4.81	4.60	4.92	3.1	0.3	100	
2018	SLN	MLB	26	9	11	0	28	28	167	156	23	2.9	7.4	138	51%	.294	1.26	4.53	4.64	5.03	9.6	1.0	117	

Breakout: 14%   Improve: 59%   Collapse: 21%   Attrition: 8%   MLB: 98%   *Comparables: Matt Cain, Mat Latos, Yovani Gallardo*

Making Wacha Great Again, A Play In One Act:

He: "Man, Wacha was awful last year. Look at his ERA!"

She: "Yeah, he had a bad year, but that doesn't worry me too much going forward. He just gave up more hits than he normally does."

He: "Are you crazy? Why doesn't that worry you? His main job is to not give up hits."

She: "That's part of his job, but a lot of that is beyond his control. Did you see how bad the Cardinals' infield was? The things he has more control over—walks, strikeouts, home runs, grounders, how often batters swing and miss, how hard balls are hit when they don't miss—were a little worse than previous years, but not that much. All that information is out there, if you just look. If Wacha's healthy, and that's a big if, he's probably still a solid third starter."

He: "Yeah, but still. You're overthinking this. Wacha is a bad pitcher now because he gives up too many hits. It's just common sense. All my Facebook friends agree, so it must be true." [Awkward pause.] "Wanna get some tacos?"

Adam Wainwright   RHP

Born: 8/30/81 Age: 35 Bats: R Throws: R Height: 6'7" Weight: 235 Entered Pro Ball: Round 1, 2000 Draft (#29 overall)

YEAR	TEAM	LVL	AGE	W	L	SV	G	GS	IP	H	HR	BB/9	K/9	K	GB%	BABIP	WHIP	ERA	FIP	DRA	VORP	WARP	cFIP	MPH
2014	SLN	MLB	32	20	9	0	32	32	227	184	10	2.0	7.1	179	49%	.267	1.03	2.38	2.85	3.25	40.1	4.4	94	92.8
2015	SLN	MLB	33	2	1	0	7	4	28	25	0	1.3	6.4	20	52%	.287	1.04	1.61	2.16	4.16	2.7	0.3	99	93.1
2016	SLN	MLB	34	13	9	0	33	33	198²	220	22	2.7	7.3	161	45%	.330	1.40	4.62	3.97	4.49	19.2	2.0	105	93.2
2017	SLN	MLB	35	10	11	0	26	26	174	174	22	2.6	7.3	141	47%	.295	1.29	4.30	4.18	4.43	14.5	1.5	100	
2018	SLN	MLB	36	12	12	0	31	31	201²	182	24	2.6	7.4	166	47%	.295	1.20	4.20	4.30	4.64	21.0	2.2	108	

Breakout: 10%   Improve: 34%   Collapse: 28%   Attrition: 16%   MLB: 82%   *Comparables: Bob Veale, Jason Schmidt, C.J. Wilson*

There were times last summer when Wainwright seemed to have found himself, as he snapped off his signature hook with aplomb. But more frequently Waino was just another arm, struggling with his mechanics and command while trying to feel his way through an opposing lineup that was consistently barreling him up. His only black ink last year was for leading the league in hits and earned runs allowed, but if anyone deserves the benefit of the doubt and the chance to rediscover his form, it's Wainwright. The talent and moxie are still there, but it's an open question whether the old pro can still make his body bend to his will.

Luke Weaver   RHP

Born: 8/21/93 Age: 23 Bats: R Throws: R Height: 6'2" Weight: 170 Entered Pro Ball: Round 1, 2014 Draft (#27 overall)

YEAR	TEAM	LVL	AGE	W	L	SV	G	GS	IP	H	HR	BB/9	K/9	K	GB%	BABIP	WHIP	ERA	FIP	DRA	VORP	WARP	cFIP	MPH
2015	PMB	A+	21	8	5	0	19	19	105¹	98	2	1.6	7.5	88	46%	.303	1.11	1.62	2.28	2.32	32.3	3.5	84	
2016	SFD	AA	22	6	3	0	12	12	77	63	4	1.2	10.3	88	40%	.289	0.95	1.40	2.04	1.28	32.6	3.5	66	
2016	SLN	MLB	22	1	4	0	9	8	36¹	46	7	3.0	11.1	45	37%	.386	1.60	5.70	4.37	4.22	4.6	0.5	99	94.9
2017	SLN	MLB	23	2	3	0	15	6	41	43	5	2.9	7.7	36	54%	.300	1.38	4.37	4.09	4.47	3.0	0.3	100	
2018	SLN	MLB	24	8	7	0	50	19	143²	127	18	3.4	9.6	153	54%	.311	1.26	4.05	4.13	4.45	14.5	1.5	102	

Breakout: 27%   Improve: 53%   Collapse: 14%   Attrition: 27%   MLB: 77%   *Comparables: Daniel Norris, Danny Duffy, Mike Minor*

Given his college pedigree, first-round draft position, impressive command, plus changeup and instant dominion over minor-league bats, Weaver has long seemed to be Michael Wacha's willowy little brother. Thus it felt inevitable that when Wacha's shoulder went sproing last August in the midst of a pennant race, the Cardinals would hand the ball to Weaver, and the former Seminole ace would contribute eight promising starts down the stretch. Weaver's fastball can reach the mid-90s, and he throws strikes, avoids walks and sequences well, setting 'em up with the heater and sitting 'em down with the change. The polish needed by his curve and slider is still on backorder and may never be shipped, but he's added a promising cutter to fill out his arsenal. He doesn't look the part, but Weaver might just have enough pitchability to earn his living in the middle of a big-league rotation.

Jerome Williams RHP

Born: 12/4/81 Age: 35 Bats: R Throws: R Height: 6'3" Weight: 260 Entered Pro Ball: Round 1, 1999 Draft (#39 overall)

YEAR	TEAM	LVL	AGE	W	L	SV	G	GS	IP	H	HR	BB/9	K/9	K	GB%	BABIP	WHIP	ERA	FIP	DRA	VORP	WARP	cFIP	MPH
2014	HOU	MLB	32	1	4	0	26	0	47²	59	7	3.0	7.2	38	48%	.335	1.57	6.04	4.67	4.13	3.0	0.3	107	93.8
2014	ROU	AAA	32	0	1	0	2	2	10¹	16	3	0.9	2.6	3	43%	.317	1.65	6.10	7.76	8.88	-3.6	-0.4	126	
2014	TEX	MLB	32	1	1	0	2	2	10	18	0	2.7	5.4	6	41%	.462	2.10	9.90	2.86	4.14	0.6	0.1	107	93.8
2014	PHI	MLB	32	4	2	0	9	9	57¹	48	5	2.7	6.0	38	48%	.257	1.13	2.83	3.96	4.40	1.9	0.2	108	93.2
2015	REA	AA	33	1	0	0	2	2	11²	9	1	0	6.2	8	56%	.229	0.77	2.31	3.01	3.56	2.0	0.2	90	
2015	PHI	MLB	33	4	12	1	33	21	121	161	22	2.5	5.5	74	49%	.333	1.61	5.80	5.27	5.10	-1.0	-0.1	115	92.5
2016	MEM	AAA	34	5	3	0	9	9	57	64	11	2.4	5.4	34	45%	.293	1.39	4.89	5.93	6.89	-9.8	-1.0	115	
2016	SLN	MLB	34	0	0	0	11	0	17¹	22	4	3.1	4.2	8	38%	.295	1.62	5.71	6.65	6.83	-3.6	-0.4	125	91.5
2017	SLN	MLB	35	4	4	0	26	11	74²	82	11	2.9	6.0	49	49%	.316	1.42	4.98	4.82	5.54	-1.0	-0.1	130	
2018	SLN	MLB	36	4	4	0	20	11	80¹	88	12	2.9	6.3	56	49%	.317	1.41	4.99	5.13	5.55	-0.7	-0.1	130	

Breakout: 12%   Improve: 35%   Collapse: 13%   Attrition: 12%   MLB: 68%   *Comparables:* Shawn Estes, Mark Redman, Roberto Hernandez

Last September, Williams threw his final pitch of the year (and the 16,176th of his MLB career) to retire Hernan Iribarren and complete a scoreless inning of meaningless relief that kept the Cardinals within 13 runs of the Reds going into the bottom of the ninth. The big right-hander strode purposefully off the mound with his head down, the pink glove he wears in honor of the mother he lost much too soon to breast cancer swinging in front of him. After three straight seasons with a WHIP over 1.60 we may have seen the last of the Waipahu High School product on a big-league mound. Williams washed out in the middle of his career, reinvented himself in Taiwan and returned for a second act that was no more successful than the first. He never earned a multi-year contract, an award vote or any black ink, but when he's gone we'll miss him more than most, since each of his outings was a reminder that life is short and nothing is guaranteed and every day that we're able to do the things we love is a blessing.

LINEOUTS

Hitters

NAME	POS	TEAM	LVL	AGE	PA	R	2B	3B	HR	RBI	BB	K	SB	CS	AVG/OBP/SLG	TAv	VORP	BABIP	BRR	FRAA	WARP
Eliezer Alvarez	2B	PEO	A	21	499	70	36	6	6	59	53	96	36	15	.323/.404/.476	.329	45.7	.400	-0.4	2B(113): 0.7	5.1
Dean Anna	UT	MEM	AAA	29	383	48	17	1	2	39	42	55	4	3	.266/.344/.341	.252	6.6	.309	-0.2	2B(96): -11.3 • SS(2): 0.0	-0.5
Paul DeJong	3B	SFD	AA	22	552	62	29	2	22	73	40	144	3	2	.260/.324/.460	.289	31.1	.318	-1.8	3B(112): -4.4 • SS(11): 1.0	3.0
Anthony Garcia	RF	SFD	AA	24	137	17	6	0	3	16	11	24	2	2	.254/.331/.377	.269	3.5	.295	-0.1	RF(32): -0.8 • LF(1): -0.1	0.3
	RF	MEM	AAA	24	247	25	12	0	8	27	20	44	1	1	.229/.296/.394	.274	5.8	.244	-2.4	LF(40): -0.5 • RF(16): 1.8	0.7
Jose Martinez	RF	OMA	AAA	27	160	18	10	0	3	18	14	24	2	0	.298/.356/.433	.297	9.6	.331	1.1	1B(20): -1.6 • LF(12): -0.9	0.8
	RF	MEM	AAA	27	329	34	18	1	8	42	25	50	9	1	.269/.326/.415	.257	3.4	.299	-1.2	LF(30): -0.2 • RF(29): 0.2	0.3
	RF	SLN	MLB	27	18	4	1	0	0	1	2	1	0	0	.438/.500/.500	.358	2.6	.467	0.4	LF(4): 0.3 • 1B(1): 0.0	0.3
Rafael Ortega	CF	SLC	AAA	25	341	47	18	7	4	31	15	39	14	8	.317/.348/.453	.269	9.4	.350	-1.4	LF(40): 2.2 • CF(22): -0.9	1.1
	CF	ANA	MLB	25	202	24	8	0	1	16	13	23	8	3	.232/.283/.292	.210	-5.5	.261	0.1	LF(46): 0.7 • CF(10): -0.6	-0.5
Alberto Rosario	C	MEM	AAA	29	124	8	5	0	0	13	6	20	0	0	.281/.323/.325	.236	1.7	.333	-0.7	C(35): 2.9 • P(2): -0.0	0.5
	C	SLN	MLB	29	41	3	2	0	0	2	2	5	0	0	.184/.225/.237	.174	-1.9	.212	-0.1	C(17): 0.4 • 3B(1): 0.0	-0.2
Breyvic Valera	UT	SFD	AA	24	192	16	5	1	0	12	9	18	3	1	.258/.289/.298	.216	-2.0	.282	0.8	SS(26): 1.0 • 2B(15): 1.2	-0.1
	UT	MEM	AAA	24	257	32	14	1	0	31	31	22	8	4	.341/.417/.415	.331	28.5	.370	1.6	2B(32): -1.7 • 3B(21): 0.6	2.8
Louis Voit	1B	SFD	AA	25	546	70	20	5	19	74	52	83	1	2	.297/.372/.477	.308	34.1	.323	1.9	1B(104): 2.2 • LF(12): 1.3	4.0
Austin Wilson	OF	BAK	A+	24	435	56	14	1	13	49	48	157	7	3	.226/.338/.375	.267	12.0	.348	-0.3	RF(72): -1.0 • CF(27): 0.0	1.1

Eliezer Alvarez leveraged his plus speed, on-base skills and gap power into a tremendous year in the Midwest League and onto the Cardinals' 40-man roster. ❖ Quad-A utility man **Dean Anna** accurately describes himself on LinkedIn as "a line drive hitter that makes great contact" whose versatility allows him to play his game "efficiently and effectively all over the field." ❖ Late first-round pick **Dylan Carlson** has an attractive stroke from both sides of the plate, power potential, iffy center field tools, and a birth date shared with the Wye River agreement, which promised to trade "land for peace" in Palestine. At this point both have an uncertain future. ❖ Illinois State product **Paul DeJong** has soft hands and obvious thunder in his bat, but his strikeout rate spiked in his first taste of the high minors. The Cardinals have been working him out at shortstop to add positional flexibility. ❖ **Anthony Garcia** struggled all summer to make hard contact, and as an uninspiring glove man in the outfield corners that's his Prime Directive. He'll need to rediscover his patience and power stroke if he wants a career that lasts beyond the first commercial break. ❖ After more than 4,500 plate appearances in the minors and winter leagues, **Jose Martinez** earned a September cup of coffee, but the former PCL batting champ has little to offer a big-league club beyond height, persistence and well-honed packing skills. ❖ **Rafael Ortega** has some speed and has been an average bat in the minors before, but the fact that he got more than 200 plate appearances in 2016 speaks to the misery that was the Angels. ❖ After swimming for a decade in the warm little pond from which bullpen catchers evolve, **Alberto Rosario** is finally able to show off some welts from major-league foul tips. They're most likely his last, but it gives him another story to tell years from now while warming up Carl Edwards III. ❖ Switch-hitting sparkplug **Breyvic Valera** is a tough out who walks more than he whiffs, showed some unexpected pop this winter and can be slotted virtually anywhere on the field. ❖ **Louis Linwood "Luke" Voit** sounds like he should be the 19-year-old flame-thrower with a million-dollar arm and 10-cent head, but he's actually the 25-year-old first baseman who tears up Double-A while dispensing life lessons, dissing Susan Sontag and maintaining that Oswald acted alone. ❖ **Austin Wilson** repeated the Cal League as a 24-year-old, and the only thing he proved was that the "Stanford swing" is still not a compliment.

Pitchers

NAME	TEAM	LVL	AGE	W	L	SV	G	GS	IP	H	HR	BB/9	K/9	K	GB%	BABIP	WHIP	ERA	FIP	DRA	VORP	WARP	cFIP	MPH
Kendry Flores	MIA	MLB	24	0	0	0	1	1	3	1	0	9.0	3.0	1	11%	.111	1.33	0.00	5.52	5.00	0.1	0.0	115	94.7
	NWO	AAA	24	3	6	0	18	16	91¹	103	8	3.8	7.3	74	41%	.337	1.55	4.53	4.72	6.23	-9.3	-1.0	112	
Austin Gomber	PMB	A+	22	6	8	0	17	17	107²	91	5	2.0	8.4	101	42%	.287	1.07	2.93	2.76	2.43	36.5	3.7	85	
	SFD	AA	22	1	0	0	4	4	19¹	11	0	4.2	7.0	15	38%	.212	1.03	1.40	3.03	3.89	2.6	0.3	107	
Ryan Helsley	PEO	A	21	10	2	0	17	17	95	77	3	1.8	10.3	109	41%	.301	1.01	1.61	2.22	1.42	38.0	4.2	71	
Jordan Hicks	SCO	A-	19	4	1	0	6	6	30²	25	1	4.7	6.5	22	66%	.269	1.34	1.76	3.60	5.92	-2.3	-0.2	113	
Corey Littrell	SFD	AA	24	1	0	1	13	0	15²	8	2	0.6	8.0	14	51%	.154	0.57	1.72	3.24	2.78	3.4	0.4	88	
	MEM	AAA	24	1	4	1	40	1	51¹	51	5	5.1	8.6	49	49%	.303	1.56	4.56	5.01	5.43	-2.5	-0.3	111	
Mike Mayers	SFD	AA	24	5	2	0	9	9	54²	47	4	2.8	7.1	43	50%	.270	1.17	2.30	3.55	5.03	0.4	0.0	101	
	MEM	AAA	24	4	8	0	16	16	89¹	87	8	3.1	8.5	84	43%	.315	1.32	3.73	4.21	4.08	12.5	1.3	99	
	SLN	MLB	24	1	1	0	4	1	5¹	16	3	5.1	3.4	2	48%	.500	3.56	27.00	12.00	8.35	-1.9	-0.2	122	96.1
Matt Pearce	PMB	A+	22	8	8	0	20	20	136²	114	9	1.0	5.3	81	39%	.245	0.94	2.37	3.34	3.25	33.8	3.5	91	
	SFD	AA	22	1	2	0	3	3	16	21	3	3.9	6.0	16	31%	.375	1.75	7.88	5.12	4.47	1.1	0.1	106	
	MEM	AAA	22	0	2	0	2	2	11	12	2	3.3	4.9	6	32%	.263	1.45	4.91	6.08	4.95	0.5	0.1	124	
Zach Phillips	NOR	AAA	29	9	3	1	49	0	60²	60	3	4.5	12.5	84	52%	.388	1.48	4.45	2.62	2.34	17.7	1.8	77	
	PIT	MLB	29	0	0	0	8	0	6²	8	1	1.4	8.1	6	33%	.350	1.35	2.70	3.79	4.94	0.0	0.0	106	92.2
Ryan Sherriff	MEM	AAA	26	7	1	3	49	0	66²	66	4	3.1	7.4	55	61%	.301	1.34	2.84	3.89	3.23	12.8	1.3	95	
Rowan Wick	PMB	A+	23	2	0	6	23	0	24²	16	0	2.2	13.5	37	43%	.302	0.89	1.09	0.98	1.13	10.8	1.1	65	
	SFD	AA	23	0	0	0	21	0	19²	14	1	6.4	9.2	20	34%	.250	1.42	4.12	4.10	7.90	-6.9	-0.7	114	
Ronnie Williams	SCO	A-	20	4	2	0	7	7	46¹	37	1	1.4	6.4	33	59%	.254	0.95	2.72	2.90	2.84	12.4	1.3	88	
	PEO	A	20	1	3	0	6	6	35²	31	7	4.3	9.1	36	43%	.261	1.35	4.29	5.78	4.52	2.0	0.2	105	
Jake Woodford	PEO	A	19	5	5	0	21	21	108²	104	7	3.1	6.8	82	46%	.297	1.30	3.31	3.99	5.37	-4.4	-0.5	109	

Once a potentially useful piece, **Kendry Flores** looks like he's headed in the wrong direction at age 26 after a disappointing season at Triple-A. ❖ **Austin Gomber**'s mundane stuff and middling velocity won't make you randy, but his command, deception and pitchability helped him succeed at High-A and dominate the Arizona Fall League on his way to an eventual fifth starter or swing-man role. ❖ Dominating the Midwest League last summer with a high-90s fastball and surprisingly solid control was an excellent first step toward **Ryan Helsley**'s goal of becoming the first member of the Cherokee Nation to reach the majors. ❖ **Jordan Hicks** can be a mechanical mess and hasn't learned to control his moving mid-90s fastball, hard slider and changeup, but if he ever does his raw stuff will work in the late innings. ❖ With 13 professional innings under his belt we can now definitively state that late first rounder **Dakota Hudson** is tall. Whether the former Mississippi State ace can command his mid-90s fastball and hammer curve is yet to be seen. ❖ Both the Golden Corral and **Corey Littrell** have a wide array of offerings with questionable provenance and forgettable flavor. Yet last summer's move to the bullpen proved both the Golden Corral and Corey Littrell might very well contain a LOOGY. ❖ **Mike Mayers** worked his way back from thoracic outlet surgery only to flop worse than *The Love Guru* in his major-league debut, but the young righty showed just enough stuff and moxie to earn his keep as a Triple-A insurance policy. ❖ **Matt Pearce** succeeded in the low minors by avoiding walks and using a plus changeup and a variety of breakers to protect his low-velo fastball, but his rough first exposure to advanced hitters has scouts wondering how long that trick can last. ❖ Stuck in the minors for past two seasons, **Zach Phillips** made a brief cameo in the bigs after getting traded from the Orioles to the Pirates. He promptly allowed four of the eight southpaws he faced to reach base, making him more of a LGY than a LOOGY. ❖ Veteran minor-league Pokemon enthusiast **Ryan Sherriff** lowered his arm slot in the Memphis 'pen and caught himself a dominating sinker that reduces every left-handed Charizard into a flailing Magikarp. ❖ After missing nearly two full seasons to shoulder woes, **Jordan Walden** is back with the Braves, hoping to rediscover the mid-90s heat that makes him a seventh-inning weapon and avoid the mid-90s heat of re-habilitative hydrotherapy. ❖ Converted outfielder **Rowan Wick** was a revelation in his first year on the mound, flashing a high-90s fastball and striking out more than a man per inning out of the bullpen. ❖ Undersized sinkerballer **Ronnie Williams** missed plenty of bats in his first taste of full-season ball and flashed a solid changeup and developing curveball, making some scouts think he could survive in a big-league rotation. ❖ **Jake Woodford** lost time to a sore shoulder and didn't generate much swing-and-miss, but solid command of a surprisingly advanced four-pitch mix helped him survive in the Midwest League as a teenager.

TAMPA BAY RAYS

Essay by David Roth

Player comments by Bryan Grosnick and BP staff

"**H**ope Is Not A Plan" is a crowdfunded 2013 documentary about the movement to extend civil rights to people with disabilities in Canada. It is also the title of a 2007 book about the roiling adolescent years of the war in Iraq. It is emblazoned on a poster of a sneering cartoon rhino—side-eye, cigarette, handgun, cigarette, frankly redundant helmet—illustrated in a sarcastic echo of Shepard Fairey's iconic "Hope" posters, that's available for $9.99, before shipping, from a website called rangerup.com. The site otherwise deals mostly in t-shirts endorsing firearms and the global war on terror; they'll sell you the Hope Is Not A Plan rhino on a t-shirt, too.

As a quote, innocent of context or object, "hope is not a plan" is variously attributed to a number of people—Dr. Atul Gawande, Anderson Cooper—who probably didn't say it first. It is the sort of expression whose original author is effectively lost to time, which is to say that it's a cliché. That this particular cliché keeps getting applied to various long and doomy struggles is an indicator of the tone in which it is generally meant to be read. So, I suppose, is the fact that you are reading it here, at the beginning of an essay about the Tampa Bay Rays.

For the first decade or so of the team's existence, the Rays didn't have much in the way of either reasonable hope or discernible plan. Those early teams were shaped like one of those tax shelter direct-to-Netflix revenge thrillers that Ray Liotta or Nicolas Cage periodically sneak off to shoot in Romania. Swap Fred McGriff or Jose Canseco for Liotta and Cage, plug Steve Cox or Joey Gathright into the role of Unfortunate Henchman and you've got a late-night slot filler on Showtime that is...still not quite as underlit or difficult to watch as those early Devil Ray teams. Though the purgatorial vibe stays the same. The team spent its first decade deep underwater in the American League East, getting out of last place only once. That was in 2004, when the team won 70 games. It would remain a franchise high until 2008, the team's 11th year in the majors, when the Rays went all the way to the World Series.

Those early teams were hopeless, but they also lost without any apparent strategy beyond paying a few guys who had been All-Stars during the previous presidential administration. For the last decade or so, though, the Rays have had a plan. You know about it, maybe because you

RAYS PROSPECTUS
2016 W-L: 68-94, 5TH IN AL EAST

Pythag	.473	22nd	DER	.702	14th
RS/G	4.15	24th	B-Age	27.8	7th
RA/G	4.4	13th	P-Age	26.8	4th
TAv	.260	16th	Salary	$66.7M	29th
BRR	-2.55	19th	M$/MW	$2.7M	26th
TAv-P	.263	16th	DL Days	779	10th
FIP	4.22	15th	$ on DL	12%	14th

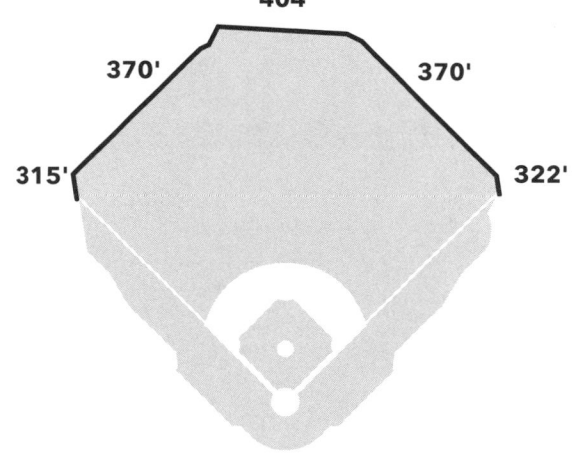

Outfield wall profile: **5' to 11'5"**

Three-Year Park Factors

Runs	Runs/RH	Runs/LH	HR/RH	HR/LH
99	101	105	98	107

Top Hitter WARP	3.8	Evan Longoria
Top Pitcher WARP	5.6	Chris Archer
Top Prospect		Willy Adames

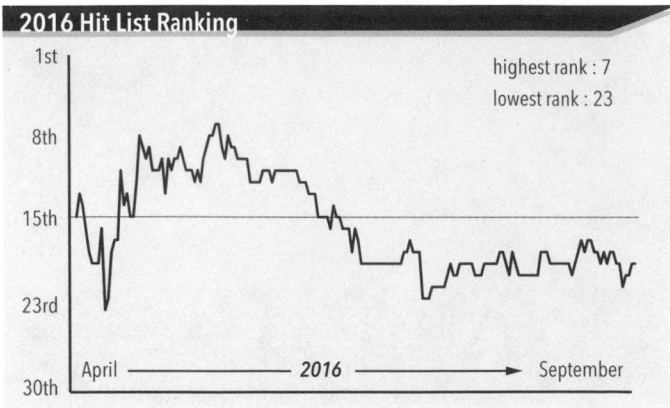

2016 Hit List Ranking

highest rank : 7
lowest rank : 23

April — *2016* → September

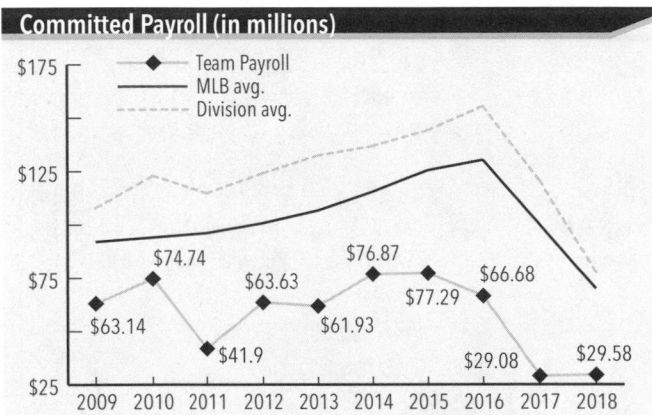

Committed Payroll (in millions)

◆ Team Payroll
— MLB avg.
- - - Division avg.

$63.14 $74.74 $41.9 $63.63 $61.93 $76.87 $77.29 $66.68 $29.08 $29.58

2009 2010 2011 2012 2013 2014 2015 2016 2017 2018

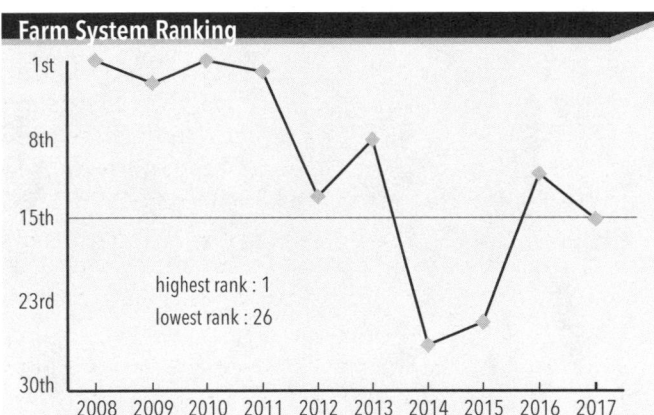

Farm System Ranking

highest rank : 1
lowest rank : 26

2008 2009 2010 2011 2012 2013 2014 2015 2016 2017

Personnel

President of Baseball Operations:
Matt Silverman

Senior Vice President:
Chaim Bloom

SVP, General Manager:
Erik Neander

Manager:
Kevin Cash

BP Alumni:
Bradley Ankrom
Chaim Bloom
James Click
Jason Cole
Shawn Hoffman
Tim Steggall

watched the Oakland Athletics do something similar last decade or maybe because you read the book that Jonah Keri wrote. Mostly you know about it because it worked: a series of better drafts around the middle of the last decade and a newfound organizational commitment to prioritizing young players over Donruss Diamond Kings brought a rich crop of young players onto the Rays' big league roster. The team was patient, smart, and lucky in all the ways good teams need to be, and they turned all that talent into some memorably spunky teams. Then as those young homegrown stars became too expensive to keep, some slightly less memorable but still notably spunky ones.

This plan, The Plan, is supremely tricky to execute, requiring the careful development and efficient deployment of low-cost players, as well as the constant cyclical cashing-in of those players on the trade market as they get more costly. This doesn't sound easy even in theory, and it is devilishly difficult in practice, but the Rays pulled it off for years. But after six straight winning campaigns and four trips to the playoffs, the Rays have finished the last three seasons below .500; a series of weak drafts (and a longer series of weaker draft position) have left the farm system mostly bereft of team-changing talent. And the budget remains the budget—at $64.1 million it was the second-lowest figure in the majors, just a shade more than what the Red Sox spent on their three most expensive starting pitchers.

The Plan is still in place, and the Rays still employ many smart people to implement it at every level of the organization. The trouble is that while The Plan has continued to do what it was designed to do, the on-field product has collapsed. For The Plan to work it has to be a perpetual motion machine with prospects cycling up and stars cycling out; in recent years, the Rays haven't produced enough from below to keep the chain moving, and have a record and roster to match. The Plan *could* still work, but it isn't. And if hope is not a plan, a plan isn't the same thing as hope. Not by itself, anyway.

At the peak of their success, the Rays were telling two compelling and perfectly parallel stories at once. One of them was a Floridian gloss on *Major League*'s ancient and demonstrably unfadeable underdog story, in which a charismatic manager and a collection of underestimated and overlooked oddballs come together to exceed expectations and kick some establishment ass. This wasn't ever a perfect fit—the core of those Rays teams were comprised of high draft picks and undervalued players swiped from other organizations in trade. The other story was more complicated, and newer. Where *Major League*'s appeal is grounded in a crew of goofs unexpectedly winning baseball games, the fable that came to be told about the Rays' rise was more a business story in the *Moneyball* vein. This one is an underdog tale too, but as with *Moneyball* it's mostly about the pursuit of efficiency and less about some raggedy dirtbags proving everyone else wrong than smart people discovering that, actually, they were indeed right. The players did the dirty work, but the smart guys made that possible by drafting right, playing the percentages, working the angles that MLB's system allows and getting 80 percent of the production at 20 percent of the price everywhere they could.

The process *is* interesting, although it was mostly only interesting because it was working in that particular moment. After the global economic crash that preceded the Rays' rise, it was natural to want to believe that things would or could be different in the future, and it was easy to look at the smart, confident young go-getters doing the impossible in St. Pete and see a future that was more hopeful than the past. These were not the amoral atavists that broke the system the last time and the time before that, the story went. These savvy, data-driven risk-takers would *remake* that system, without sentimentality but also without bias or compromise. The result would be something as ruthless and productive as before—business is business—but also exponentially more rational.

This is also a familiar story, albeit one that's more at home in fluffy profiles in *Inc* or *Wired* than the sports section. People make movies about this story, too, now: a bunch of dedicated business school types work harder and smarter than their peers, winning trade after trade and striking oil on one player after another because they alone know where to dig. It all has the shape and tenor of a heist movie, with the inefficiencies in baseball's half-free market as the security system to be hacked. The old underdog narrative is still in play, but everyone's clothes are a lot nicer and a lot less dirty.

This is sort of the same story told from two different perspectives—and the two sides are working towards the same goal—but at the same time it cannot quite be said that they are working together. At some point, these two stories cannot continue to operate in parallel. Maybe there is a clog in the pipeline delivering all that young talent to the roster to replace the ones that have left it. Maybe the big thinkers in charge start over- or under-thinking things, or fall victim to any of the many species of recursive managerial self-belief. If all that swashbuckling executive nimbleness curdles into smug habit—if fidelity to the process becomes the priority, ahead of the original object of winning games—then everything but the process will fall away.

All you have is the plan, then, which means that you are only telling one story—the one about efficiency and savvy, 80 percent of the production at 20 percent of the cost. The specifics, and the specific players involved, matter less than the bigger and more abstract thing that is acquiring and optimizing and deploying them. In 2011, Sam Miller told that story in fewer than 140 characters. "LOVE this trade for the Rays," he tweeted. "Who'd they give up? And who'd they get?"

✦ ✦ ✦

It's a strange thing to say about a team that finished with the second-worst record in baseball, but the 2016 Tampa Bay Rays executed their plan fairly well. There was bad luck, but there was so much imperfection up and down the roster that it was hard for the team to compete. A roster built around positional versatility wound up being exactly as versatile as advertised. Platoon players were platooned in ways that accentuated their strengths and protected their weaknesses. This can be true at the same time that all this is true: The Rays had fewer hits and more strikeouts than any American League team, and ranked 14th out of 15 in runs and on-base percentage.

It's simple to look at the Rays' uninspiring roster and mostly unexciting farm system, and see instance after instance in which the team's dedication to its process and belief in its own cleverness wound up being less than helpful. Steven Souza is exactly the sort of easy-to-underestimate player that the Rays assessed better than their peers back in their heyday. After his second middling season in Tampa, it still stings that he wound up being the Rays' main haul in a three-team deal that also involved Wil Myers, Joe Ross and Trea Turner. The team had ten selections in the first 61 picks of the 2011 draft, but went shockingly conservative and wound up with promising starter Blake Snell and not much else of note. Their dedication to inexpensive versatility has left it with a roster that can master a game of musical chairs, but little else. It took 89 wins to crack the American League playoffs in 2016, and 80 percent of that is 71.

However, there is some good news here. The Rays' collection of promising young starting pitchers is indeed promising; even in a down year, they were a top-10 rotation by DRA. Kevin Kiermaier is a star and remains under team control through the 2020 season. Evan Longoria finally had another offensive season in line with his career .295 TAv after two disappointing campaigns. The Rays have enough useful things on the major-league roster for their second-generation Smart Front Office Types to make an impact on its next competitive iteration.

Yet, everything continues as it's always been. In response to the howling vacuum they had at catcher in 2016, the Rays signed Wilson Ramos to a reasonable two-year deal, made possible by the fact that Ramos will still be recovering from a major knee injury when the 2017 season kicks off. It's a smart deal, which is not quite the same as saying it will help the team out much.

But a plan is not hope, and the Rays once again seem to have notably more of the former than the latter. Without the budget to pay productive players or a farm system delivering new stars, the Rays are more admirable than exciting. They remain a fascinating business school case due to the cleverness with which they've attacked the challenge of their circumstances, and their variable-heavy roster makes for an appealingly intricate thought exercise. They are possibly a few hitters away from being very good, but that's not nearly as close as it sounds.

But what's finally most deflating about the Rays, in a way that even the aimless teams of the bad old days were not, is not merely that they seem likely to lose more games than they'll win. It's that they are getting there as deftly and efficiently as possible, according to an intelligent plan crafted by intelligent people. That requires both brilliance and a deep unsentimentality, but it's tough to look past the organization's excess of sentimentality towards The Plan. This strange, insufficient, versatile and cost-effective roster is the one The Plan would create if it had been judged to be so self-evidently smart that it was allowed to operate independent of the results it produced. There are failures of imagination and discernment to be found in this organization, but it's striking that there is also nothing *unreasonable* happening here. The process and its administrators are as trustworthy as ever. The system works. It just isn't giving anyone what they want anymore. ■

—David Roth is a contributing editor at Vice Sports

HITTERS

Willy Adames   SS

Born: 9/2/95   Age: 21   Bats: R   Throws: R   Height: 6'1"   Weight: 180   Entered Pro Ball: International Free Agent, 2015

YEAR	TEAM	LVL	AGE	PA	R	2B	3B	HR	RBI	BB	K	SB	CS	AVG/OBP/SLG	TAv	VORP	BABIP	BRR	FRAA	WARP
2014	WMI	A	18	400	40	14	12	6	50	39	96	3	6	.269/.346/.428	.307	37.4	.353	0.7	SS(97): -0.7	3.8
2014	BGR	A	18	114	15	5	2	2	11	15	30	3	0	.278/.377/.433	.292	10.4	.379	2.1	SS(25): -3.0	0.8
2015	PCH	A+	19	456	51	24	6	4	46	54	123	10	1	.258/.342/.379	.275	23.1	.356	-0.6	SS(97): 4.7	3.0
2016	MNT	AA	20	568	89	31	6	11	57	74	121	13	6	.274/.372/.430	.303	47.0	.342	2.4	SS(112): 2.0	5.3
2017	TBA	MLB	21	250	25	10	2	6	27	26	77	2	1	.225/.307/.371	.243	6.8	.312	0.0	SS 1	0.8
2018	TBA	MLB	22	455	55	20	4	12	51	49	133	4	2	.237/.322/.397	.257	14.1	.321	0.0	SS 1	1.7

Breakout: 6%   Improve: 14%   Collapse: 3%   Attrition: 11%   MLB: 30%   *Comparables: Addison Russell, Corey Seager, Trevor Story*

In 2016 Adames added game power to his already intriguing tool set, and given that he's still a shortstop he's comfortably Tampa Bay's best positional farmhand. Encouragingly, his career high in dingers was the product of growth rather than a compromise at the plate. He's still a patient, disciplined hitter with a strong understanding of the strike zone, and he's now a 21-year-old man with the frame to hit doubles to all fields and knock a few balls over the fence. He's also staved off questions about his ultimate defensive home for another year. There's a chance that he grows out of the position, that his power plays down against elite competition, that the hit tool never quite reaches plus. But the odds that he falls short in all three departments is smaller now than it was a year ago, and Adames appears poised to become a functional big leaguer in short order. Well, relatively short order; we are still talking about the Rays.

Jake Bauers   1B

Born: 10/6/95   Age: 21   Bats: L   Throws: L   Height: 6'1"   Weight: 195   Entered Pro Ball: Round 7, 2013 Draft (#208 overall)

YEAR	TEAM	LVL	AGE	PA	R	2B	3B	HR	RBI	BB	K	SB	CS	AVG/OBP/SLG	TAv	VORP	BABIP	BRR	FRAA	WARP
2014	FTW	A	18	467	59	18	3	8	64	51	80	5	6	.296/.376/.414	.284	17.4	.347	0.9	1B(103): 8.6	2.7
2015	PCH	A+	19	249	33	14	2	6	38	29	33	2	3	.267/.357/.433	.298	13.1	.291	1.2	1B(52): -4.9	0.9
2015	MNT	AA	19	285	36	18	0	5	36	21	41	6	3	.276/.329/.405	.267	7.0	.307	2.3	1B(61): -1.8	0.6
2016	MNT	AA	20	581	79	28	1	14	78	73	89	10	6	.274/.370/.420	.301	33.6	.305	2.1	RF(62): 4.1 • 1B(57): 0.1	4.1
2017	TBA	MLB	21	250	27	11	0	7	29	23	56	2	1	.240/.314/.390	.249	2.8	.284	-0.5	RF 3 • 1B -0	0.6
2018	TBA	MLB	22	405	51	18	1	13	49	40	89	3	2	.250/.327/.416	.263	7.4	.293	-0.7	RF 4 • 1B 0	1.2

Breakout: 3%   Improve: 18%   Collapse: 0%   Attrition: 8%   MLB: 23%   *Comparables: Wil Myers, Nomar Mazara, Joc Pederson*

If there's a more prototypical future Rays first baseman than Bauers, I don't know who it might be. The 21-year-old lefty has terrific plate coverage, uses the whole field and possesses solid leather for a first-sacker. He can put the ball over the right-field fence, but will probably never be a middle-of-the-order masher; 20 homers may even be out of reach for him. As recent history shows, the Rays adore this profile; they targeted Bauers in the ill-advised Wil Myers-for-Steven Souza deal, and in the last few years have employed Casey Kotchman, James Loney and Logan Morrison at the three. If his hit tool and approach keep up at Durham this year—and he perhaps leans into his nascent pull power—Bauers could find his way to Tampa and push Brad Miller back across the diamond somewhere. He could even reach the heights of that top PECOTA comparable that you see up above his stat line, and transforming into a poor man's Wil Myers rather than a poor man's James Loney would make that trade look a lot more defensible in retrospect.

Tim Beckham   2B

Born: 1/27/90   Age: 27   Bats: R   Throws: R   Height: 6'0"   Weight: 195   Entered Pro Ball: Round 1, 2008 Draft (#1 overall)

YEAR	TEAM	LVL	AGE	PA	R	2B	3B	HR	RBI	BB	K	SB	CS	AVG/OBP/SLG	TAv	VORP	BABIP	BRR	FRAA	WARP
2014	DUR	AAA	24	65	8	2	0	0	4	2	14	0	2	.258/.281/.290	.191	-3.4	.333	-0.2	2B(7): -1.0 • SS(5): -0.3	-0.5
2015	DUR	AAA	25	45	5	6	0	0	4	5	10	2	1	.308/.378/.462	.285	2.2	.400	-0.3	3B(7): -0.8 • 2B(2): 0.2	0.1
2015	TBA	MLB	25	223	24	7	4	9	37	13	69	3	1	.222/.274/.429	.254	3.9	.279	-1.2	2B(38): -1.9 • SS(28): -0.1	0.0
2016	TBA	MLB	26	215	25	12	5	5	16	14	67	2	1	.247/.300/.434	.258	5.2	.349	-0.9	SS(25): 1.5 • 2B(19): -0.2	0.6
2016	DUR	AAA	26	20	0	0	0	0	0	1	7	0	1	.158/.200/.158	.170	-1.2	.250	0.0	SS(4): 0.3 • 2B(1): 0.0	-0.1
2017	TBA	MLB	27	196	19	8	2	4	20	13	54	3	2	.233/.287/.366	.239	1.4	.304	0.0	3B -2 • SS 0	-0.2
2018	TBA	MLB	28	239	25	10	3	5	24	17	69	3	2	.226/.283/.363	.231	-1.8	.301	-0.8	3B -2 • SS 0	-0.5

Breakout: 6%   Improve: 28%   Collapse: 15%   Attrition: 27%   MLB: 85%   *Comparables: Jason Donald, Zack Cozart, Pedro Florimon*

Are we supposed to be shocked that Beckham has become a just-fine utility infielder? The expectations that came with his high draft status have slowly eroded like a Pinellas County beach over time—now he's been laid bare as a post-hype fifth infielder with pop who averaged an extra-base hit every three games this past season. His ability to bang out the occasional triple or homer can paper over a fault like his iffy approach, but perhaps not his issues on the basepaths. After three miscues on the chalk in just six August games—twice failing to hustle home costing the Rays a run and once getting caught between bases—the team had enough and hucked him down to the minors. To give you some idea about the team's lack of enthusiasm for their former top pick, not even injuries to Matt Duffy and Nick Franklin caused the front office to call him back to Tampa after rosters expanded in September. Even when things start to go right, Beckham can't seem to avoid disappointment.

Curtis Casali   C

Born: 11/9/88   Age: 28   Bats: R   Throws: R   Height: 6'2"   Weight: 230   Entered Pro Ball: Round 10, 2011 Draft (#317 overall)

YEAR	TEAM	LVL	AGE	PA	R	2B	3B	HR	RBI	BB	K	SB	CS	AVG/OBP/SLG	TAv	VORP	BABIP	BRR	FRAA	WARP
2014	MNT	AA	25	96	7	5	0	1	13	16	23	0	0	.314/.500/.429	.353	11.3	.396	-1.0	C(15): -0.4	1.2
2014	DUR	AAA	25	183	11	10	0	3	15	22	50	0	0	.237/.335/.359	.233	1.0	.324	-1.5	C(41): -0.6	0.0
2014	TBA	MLB	25	84	10	3	0	0	3	8	23	0	0	.167/.268/.208	.199	-0.3	.245	1.0	C(29): 0.5	0.0
2015	DUR	AAA	26	132	14	4	0	4	13	17	29	1	0	.205/.326/.348	.276	5.4	.241	-1.6	C(24): 1.1	0.7
2015	TBA	MLB	26	113	13	6	0	10	18	8	34	0	0	.238/.304/.594	.318	10.3	.241	-0.9	C(37): 1.5	1.3
2016	DUR	AAA	27	81	5	1	0	2	15	15	12	0	0	.254/.407/.365	.285	3.6	.280	-1.1	C(13): 0.2	0.4
2016	TBA	MLB	27	256	23	10	0	8	25	25	82	0	0	.186/.273/.336	.227	-0.4	.250	-2.6	C(76): 3.2	0.3
2017	*TBA*	*MLB*	*28*	*181*	*20*	*7*	*0*	*6*	*20*	*21*	*52*	*0*	*0*	*.212/.310/.368*	*.251*	*6.4*	*.273*	*-0.4*	*C -0*	*0.1*
2018	*TBA*	*MLB*	*29*	*289*	*37*	*10*	*0*	*10*	*33*	*35*	*83*	*0*	*0*	*.213/.319/.372*	*.250*	*6.3*	*.274*	*-1.2*	*C -1*	*0.6*

Breakout: 5%   Improve: 40%   Collapse: 7%   Attrition: 27%   MLB: 77%   Comparables: *George Kottaras, Michael McKenry, Welington Castillo*

Casali started 2016 in a platoon with new teammate Hank Conger, and by September both players were toiling in Durham. There's your microcosm of Tampa's season. Of course the pressure was on, and Casali's hot hitting in 2015—a flash of surprising pop that earned him his place this past season—did feel a little unsustainable. The Vanderbilt product always had a reputation as a defense-first backstop, but "defense-first" implies that offense is around somewhere. Last year, the bat never even showed up to the park. PECOTA had him pegged for a .232 average prior to the season, and he underperformed even that measly number. He's still got decent power, and his defensive bona fides as a presenter of pitches and caller of games should keep him employed. With Wilson Ramos in town, Casali should slide into his more natural role of injury replacement and backup, in no particular order.

YEAR	TEAM	P. COUNT	FRM RUNS	BLK RUNS	THRW RUNS	TOT RUN
2014	DUR	5893	0.0	0.0	0.0	0.0
2014	MNT	1604	-0.3	0.1	-0.2	-0.5
2014	TBA	3404	1.1	-1.4	-0.1	-0.4
2015	DUR	3480	1.2	0.0	0.1	1.2
2015	TBA	4392	1.8	-1.1	-0.1	0.6
2016	TBA	9368	4.3	-1.4	0.8	3.7
2017	*TBA*	*7146*	*1.1*	*-1.1*	*0.1*	*0.1*
2018	*TBA*	*11397*	*1.1*	*-1.8*	*0.0*	*-0.6*

Hank Conger   C

Born: 1/29/88   Age: 29   Bats: B   Throws: R   Height: 6'2"   Weight: 220   Entered Pro Ball: Round 1, 2006 Draft (#25 overall)

YEAR	TEAM	LVL	AGE	PA	R	2B	3B	HR	RBI	BB	K	SB	CS	AVG/OBP/SLG	TAv	VORP	BABIP	BRR	FRAA	WARP
2014	ANA	MLB	26	260	24	12	0	4	25	22	57	0	2	.221/.293/.325	.232	4.8	.275	0.8	C(79): 23.7	3.1
2015	HOU	MLB	27	229	25	11	0	11	33	23	63	0	1	.229/.311/.448	.262	7.4	.271	-2.9	C(69): 1.8 • LF(1): -0.0	1.0
2016	TBA	MLB	28	137	6	5	0	3	10	12	40	0	0	.194/.265/.306	.204	-2.9	.259	-1.3	C(47): 1.4	-0.2
2016	DUR	AAA	28	116	7	4	1	3	11	4	24	0	0	.165/.200/.303	.175	-9.2	.181	-2.7	C(19): -3.4	-1.3
2017	*TBA*	*MLB*	*29*	*250*	*26*	*10*	*0*	*8*	*28*	*21*	*63*	*0*	*1*	*.223/.293/.376*	*.235*	*5.2*	*.270*	*-0.7*	*C 3*	*1.0*
2018	*TBA*	*MLB*	*30*	*181*	*20*	*7*	*0*	*5*	*19*	*16*	*47*	*0*	*0*	*.212/.287/.354*	*.229*	*0.3*	*.260*	*-0.5*	*C 2*	*0.3*

Breakout: 4%   Improve: 40%   Collapse: 9%   Attrition: 22%   MLB: 96%   Comparables: *Ronny Paulino, Martin Maldonado, John Baker*

All good things must come to an end, even Conger's run as one of those underrated, high-potential backups that us sabermetric types get irrationally excited about. For years he was the gold standard among backup catchers—a world-class pitch framer with switch-hitting offensive potential and a delightful way in the dugout. When those framing numbers crashed from two-plus wins per season to league average in 2015, it could've been shrugged off as a one-year blip. However, Conger produced another iffy defensive season last year, and at the same time his offensive production went from league-average to hits-for-no-average. Backup catchers with pop and clubhouse skills have more lives than a cat, so he'll ride the team-to-team catching carousel for another few seasons. Perhaps once more his pedigree will even get another set of fans irrationally excited, for old time's sake.

YEAR	TEAM	P. COUNT	FRM RUNS	BLK RUNS	THRW RUNS	TOT RUN
2014	ANA	10278	23.8	0.0	-1.3	22.5
2015	HOU	8425	3.6	0.6	-2.3	1.9
2016	TBA	5554	3.8	-0.8	-0.9	2.1
2017	*TBA*	*9437*	*5.1*	*-0.3*	*-1.0*	*3.8*
2018	*TBA*	*6827*	*3.2*	*-0.3*	*-0.7*	*2.2*

Corey Dickerson   LF

Born: 5/22/89   Age: 28   Bats: L   Throws: R   Height: 6'1"   Weight: 205   Entered Pro Ball: Round 8, 2010 Draft (#260 overall)

YEAR	TEAM	LVL	AGE	PA	R	2B	3B	HR	RBI	BB	K	SB	CS	AVG/OBP/SLG	TAv	VORP	BABIP	BRR	FRAA	WARP
2014	COL	MLB	25	478	74	27	6	24	76	24	101	8	7	.312/.364/.567	.303	26.3	.356	-2.4	LF(99): -7.0 • CF(9): -1.3	2.0
2015	ABQ	AAA	26	29	3	1	0	1	3	1	4	0	0	.286/.310/.429	.256	-0.5	.304	-0.9	LF(5): -0.9	-0.1
2015	COL	MLB	26	234	30	18	2	10	31	10	56	0	1	.304/.333/.536	.288	10.8	.367	-0.5	LF(54): -1.8 • CF(3): 0.5	1.0
2016	TBA	MLB	27	548	57	36	3	24	70	33	134	0	2	.245/.293/.469	.260	7.5	.285	-1.5	LF(76): 4.1 • RF(2): -0.3	1.2
2017	*TBA*	*MLB*	*28*	*548*	*62*	*29*	*5*	*21*	*75*	*37*	*129*	*3*	*4*	*.262/.312/.465*	*.277*	*22.5*	*.309*	*-1.3*	*LF 1 • RF -0*	*2.3*
2018	*TBA*	*MLB*	*29*	*509*	*64*	*26*	*4*	*19*	*68*	*36*	*120*	*3*	*3*	*.257/.309/.456*	*.267*	*14.6*	*.304*	*-1.3*	*LF 1 • RF 0*	*1.7*

Breakout: 1%   Improve: 54%   Collapse: 7%   Attrition: 9%   MLB: 98%   Comparables: *Khris Davis, J.D. Martinez, Chris Duncan*

Dickerson's an aggressive guy, at least when it comes to plate discipline. According to PITCHf/x data only five players swung more frequently than the lefty slugger in 2016, and no one swung at a higher percentage of pitches in the zone. That approach may have led to him spraying balls all over Coors Field, but there's a chance it doesn't quite work as well in the pitcher-friendly Trop—his BABIP dropped as precipitously as his elevation. While Dickerson's still a legit slugger despite these limitations, perhaps he'd benefit from a more selective approach *within* the strike zone, focusing on those balls in the low-inside part of the zone that he really wrecked last year. If he can get a few more balls to fall in for hits while maintaining his modest gains as a defender in left field, Dickerson might just slug his way into a three-win season.

Matt Duffy   SS

Born: 1/15/91   Age: 26   Bats: R   Throws: R   Height: 6'2"   Weight: 170   Entered Pro Ball: Round 18, 2012 Draft (#568 overall)

YEAR	TEAM	LVL	AGE	PA	R	2B	3B	HR	RBI	BB	K	SB	CS	AVG/OBP/SLG	TAv	VORP	BABIP	BRR	FRAA	WARP
2014	RIC	AA	23	417	53	24	4	3	62	42	66	20	4	.332/.398/.444	.308	38.9	.391	1.9	SS(89): 6.1 • 3B(3): -0.1	4.7
2014	SFN	MLB	23	64	5	2	0	0	8	1	14	0	1	.267/.302/.300	.242	0.3	.348	-0.5	2B(9): 1.5 • SS(7): -0.3	0.2
2015	SFN	MLB	24	612	77	28	6	12	77	30	96	12	0	.295/.334/.428	.283	35.2	.336	2.9	3B(134): 0.5 • 2B(9): -0.1	3.8
2016	SFN	MLB	25	286	32	11	2	4	21	20	40	8	4	.253/.313/.358	.259	10.0	.282	1.1	3B(69): 3.8	1.4
2016	TBA	MLB	25	80	9	3	0	1	7	3	13	0	1	.276/.300/.355	.226	0.8	.317	0.5	SS(18): 0.2 • 3B(1): -0.0	0.1
2017	TBA	MLB	26	587	62	26	3	12	63	38	106	12	4	.269/.320/.397	.263	28.6	.311	0.5	SS 1	2.4
2018	TBA	MLB	27	459	54	21	2	11	51	30	83	9	3	.271/.324/.408	.261	17.8	.310	1.5	SS 0	2.0

Breakout: 1%   Improve: 44%   Collapse: 7%   Attrition: 18%   MLB: 97%   Comparables: Lonnie Chisenhall, Andy LaRoche, Coco Crisp

There are entirely too many Matt Duffys. (Perhaps the proper term is Duffii?) The Matt Duffy that's likely to start the 2017 season at shortstop for the Rays seems like an entirely different person than the Matt Duffy that started the 2016 season at the hot corner for the Giants. (And before you ask, no, it's not because we've gotten him confused for the Matthew Duffy who was released by the Rangers this winter.) The Tampa iteration—presumably healed from the Achilles' injury that slowed him last season—probably isn't the five-win breakout rookie we saw in 2015. That power surge looks a bit like a fluke given what we've seen before and since, and he has the offensive profile of a feisty slap-hitter. The game changer is the glove that saw him slide up the defensive spectrum with relative ease, and when combined with his league-average bat would make him a better-than-average option at the six. If nothing else the skinny infielder can provide good bat control and versatility, two things that the Rays always seem to need and value.

Logan Forsythe   2B

Born: 1/14/87   Age: 30   Bats: R   Throws: R   Height: 6'1"   Weight: 205   Entered Pro Ball: Round 1, 2008 Draft (#46 overall)

YEAR	TEAM	LVL	AGE	PA	R	2B	3B	HR	RBI	BB	K	SB	CS	AVG/OBP/SLG	TAv	VORP	BABIP	BRR	FRAA	WARP
2014	TBA	MLB	27	336	32	12	1	6	26	25	71	2	0	.223/.287/.329	.240	1.3	.268	0.0	2B(74): 2.8 • 3B(6): -0.1	0.4
2015	TBA	MLB	28	615	69	33	2	17	68	55	111	9	4	.281/.359/.444	.290	29.7	.323	-2.9	2B(126): -5.0 • 1B(26): 0.6	2.8
2016	TBA	MLB	29	567	76	24	4	20	52	46	127	6	6	.264/.333/.444	.277	24.9	.314	0.6	2B(118): -7.5	1.8
2017	TBA	MLB	30	641	80	26	4	18	66	56	136	8	5	.250/.326/.402	.266	26.8	.296	-0.6	2B -3	2.2
2018	TBA	MLB	31	527	66	21	2	16	62	47	117	6	3	.246/.324/.404	.261	15.9	.291	-0.5	2B -2	1.5

Breakout: 0%   Improve: 48%   Collapse: 2%   Attrition: 6%   MLB: 95%   Comparables: Neil Walker, Marcus Giles, Aaron Hill

Steady and solid over this past two seasons, the Rays' leadoff hitter has a name out of a *nouveau-riche* trust fund prospectus and a bat straight out of baseball's old school. Forsythe refused to swing at pitches out of the zone—among batters who saw 2000+ pitches, he swung at those offerings at the fifth-lowest rate—so pitchers served up more balls in the zone to him than all but two other hitters. He had the league's fourth-smallest percentage of balls in play classified as "soft contact" to go along with that.

At the risk of going all *Green Eggs and Ham*, he hit off pitchers who threw left and pitchers who threw right. He hit at home, on the road, in the day and at night. Every single one of those splits resulted in an OPS+ that was above-average. And to his credit the guy they call "Frosty" was cool as ice in pressure-packed "close and late" appearances, slashing .329/.424/.562 in 85 chances. He has his warts—his defense at second base is crummy and we don't know if he'll continue to beat right-handers—but if you hear a loud *crack* coming from Tampa it's either the sound of Forsythe hitting a double or Tampa's front office popping a collarbone from patting themselves on the back.

Nick Franklin   2B

Born: 3/2/91   Age: 26   Bats: B   Throws: R   Height: 6'1"   Weight: 190   Entered Pro Ball: Round 1, 2009 Draft (#27 overall)

YEAR	TEAM	LVL	AGE	PA	R	2B	3B	HR	RBI	BB	K	SB	CS	AVG/OBP/SLG	TAv	VORP	BABIP	BRR	FRAA	WARP
2014	SEA	MLB	23	52	3	0	1	0	2	3	21	1	0	.128/.192/.170	.147	-4.1	.222	0.1	SS(7): 0.5 • 2B(5): 0.4	-0.4
2014	TAC	AAA	23	333	45	16	1	9	47	47	60	9	5	.294/.392/.455	.310	31.5	.340	1.2	2B(34): -5.5 • SS(34): 3.2	2.9
2014	DUR	AAA	23	113	8	2	0	2	9	10	34	2	0	.210/.288/.290	.216	-2.0	.297	0.2	2B(16): 0.4 • SS(7): 0.8	-0.1
2014	TBA	MLB	23	38	4	2	0	1	4	3	11	1	0	.206/.263/.353	.234	0.7	.261	0.1	2B(7): -0.4 • SS(3): -0.2	0.0
2015	DUR	AAA	24	221	26	10	1	11	30	27	48	4	3	.266/.353/.500	.294	11.5	.296	-2.2	2B(24): -0.6 • SS(17): -1.9	0.9
2015	TBA	MLB	24	109	11	4	1	3	7	7	37	1	0	.158/.213/.307	.175	-6.0	.213	0.3	2B(17): 0.1 • SS(11): -0.7	-0.7
2016	DUR	AAA	25	270	26	16	1	5	28	26	56	10	1	.254/.322/.392	.254	5.5	.306	0.1	2B(54): -3.5 • 3B(4): -0.4	0.3
2016	TBA	MLB	25	191	18	10	1	6	26	12	42	6	1	.270/.328/.443	.275	6.0	.325	-1.0	LF(18): 1.0 • 1B(9): -0.2	0.6
2017	TBA	MLB	26	506	59	21	2	15	54	51	129	11	3	.231/.310/.385	.252	8.1	.286	0.7	LF 4 • 2B -1	1.2
2018	TBA	MLB	27	453	55	19	1	13	51	47	115	10	3	.227/.310/.381	.245	4.3	.281	-0.5	LF 4 • 2B -1	0.8

Breakout: 8%   Improve: 59%   Collapse: 11%   Attrition: 24%   MLB: 90%   Comparables: Jason Kipnis, Logan Forsythe, Luis Valbuena

Franklin has been a boom or bust hitter ever since his 2013 season with the Mariners. For long stints in Triple-A he displayed power, speed and an advanced approach, while in short MLB bursts all three skills disappeared entirely. Things finally started to turn around this past season, as Franklin's balls in play started falling in for hits and he provided a welcome boost to the team's low on-base percentage. With that kind of offensive production baseline established, Franklin can perhaps settle into the role he was built for: dropping the hammer on right-handed pitchers while playing serviceable-to-poor defense at a myriad of positions. It's certainly not the sexy profile he had as a top-100 prospect half a decade ago—and the days of imagining him as the true and rightful heir to Ben Zobrist are long dead—but "decent utility guy" is a hell of a lot better than toiling in baseball purgatory.

Casey Gillaspie   1B

Born: 1/25/93   Age: 24   Bats: B   Throws: L   Height: 6'4"   Weight: 240   Entered Pro Ball: Round 1, 2014 Draft (#20 overall)

YEAR	TEAM	LVL	AGE	PA	R	2B	3B	HR	RBI	BB	K	SB	CS	AVG/OBP/SLG	TAv	VORP	BABIP	BRR	FRAA	WARP
2014	HUD	A-	21	308	27	16	1	7	42	42	65	2	3	.262/.364/.411	.268	2.8	.321	-2.5	1B(63): 0.2	0.3
2015	BGR	A	22	268	37	11	0	16	44	28	43	4	0	.278/.358/.530	.307	12.5	.275	-3.1	1B(60): 1.5	1.5
2015	PCH	A+	22	45	3	0	1	1	4	4	9	0	0	.146/.222/.268	.181	-3.8	.161	-0.7	1B(12): -0.6	-0.5
2016	MNT	AA	23	357	51	21	0	11	41	58	79	5	1	.270/.387/.454	.314	20.4	.327	-2.6	1B(77): 2.0	2.4
2016	DUR	AAA	23	203	27	13	2	7	23	22	38	0	1	.307/.389/.520	.313	14.5	.358	1.2	1B(45): -0.3	1.5
2017	*TBA*	*MLB*	*24*	*138*	*16*	*6*	*0*	*5*	*18*	*16*	*36*	*0*	*0*	*.232/.322/.417*	*.266*	*3.2*	*.282*	*-0.3*	*1B 0*	*0.3*
2018	*TBA*	*MLB*	*25*	*376*	*50*	*16*	*1*	*15*	*49*	*42*	*102*	*0*	*0*	*.235/.324/.427*	*.265*	*8.4*	*.290*	*-0.8*	*1B 1*	*1.0*

Breakout: 1%   Improve: 12%   Collapse: 13%   Attrition: 20%   MLB: 33%   *Comparables: Travis Shaw, Jesus Aguilar, Andy Wilkins*

Perhaps we should have seen this coming given his first-round pedigree, but Gillaspie just kind of parachuted into the upper minors and unexpectedly started wreaking havoc this past season. His production spread among Montgomery and Durham was eye-opening, even as his offensive tools don't shine particularly bright. He's locked into first base (or designated hitter, if you dream big!), but PECOTA thinks there's a chance he's already able to be a league-average switch-hitter. Of course, you need to be more than average with the lumber to be valuable at first base, so while there's a chance he could eventually become the "famous" Gillaspie and outstrip his brother Conor's big-league achievement(s), a life as a backup first baseman with a choice memory or two shouldn't surprise.

Desmond Jennings   CF

Born: 10/30/86   Age: 30   Bats: R   Throws: R   Height: 6'2"   Weight: 210   Entered Pro Ball: Round 10, 2006 Draft (#289 overall)

YEAR	TEAM	LVL	AGE	PA	R	2B	3B	HR	RBI	BB	K	SB	CS	AVG/OBP/SLG	TAv	VORP	BABIP	BRR	FRAA	WARP
2014	TBA	MLB	27	542	64	30	2	10	36	47	108	15	6	.244/.319/.378	.263	17.7	.296	1.1	CF(118): -1.2	1.8
2015	DUR	AAA	28	25	2	2	0	0	0	4	5	0	0	.143/.280/.238	.183	-1.5	.188	0.1	LF(4): -0.2	-0.2
2015	TBA	MLB	28	108	9	2	1	1	7	8	17	5	3	.268/.324/.340	.254	1.1	.309	-0.7	LF(21): 1.7 • CF(10): -0.9	0.2
2016	TBA	MLB	29	225	22	7	1	7	20	21	58	2	0	.200/.281/.350	.226	-1.7	.243	0.4	LF(33): 0.5 • CF(30): -4.1	-0.5
2017	*TBA*	*MLB*	*30*	*250*	*32*	*11*	*2*	*6*	*24*	*24*	*55*	*6*	*2*	*.241/.318/.387*	*.250*	*6.4*	*.286*	*0.1*	*LF 2 • CF 0*	*0.9*
2018	*TBA*	*MLB*	*31*	*162*	*19*	*7*	*1*	*4*	*18*	*16*	*38*	*4*	*2*	*.239/.318/.388*	*.253*	*3.0*	*.291*	*0.2*	*LF 1 • CF 0*	*0.5*

Breakout: 0%   Improve: 45%   Collapse: 8%   Attrition: 20%   MLB: 97%   *Comparables: Bobby Kielty, David DeJesus, Hideki Matsui*

Jennings has warranted a comment in every edition of this Annual since 2008, and in all but two the words "injury," "injuries" or–in one case—"shoulder and back issues" appeared in the first three sentences. The slings and arrows of outrageous fortune—and, reportedly, the turf in Tampa—have finally cut his startling athleticism and skill down to size. Once a top-10 worldwide prospect and pegged as a transformational leadoff hitter, today he's just a middling fourth outfielder. And maybe he's not even that, as it is possible that you've seen Jennings on the side of a milk carton more recently than you've seen him in a baseball game. Despite having the eighth-most plate appearances in Rays franchise history, the team released him in August and no one picked him up. Radio silence. No contender took a flyer, no team snagged him as a reclamation project. This season, finally removed from Carl Crawford's extended shadow in Tampa, perhaps he'll again flash some of the talent that once brought him so much hype.

Kevin Kiermaier   CF

Born: 4/22/90   Age: 27   Bats: L   Throws: R   Height: 6'1"   Weight: 215   Entered Pro Ball: Round 31, 2010 Draft (#941 overall)

YEAR	TEAM	LVL	AGE	PA	R	2B	3B	HR	RBI	BB	K	SB	CS	AVG/OBP/SLG	TAv	VORP	BABIP	BRR	FRAA	WARP
2014	DUR	AAA	24	143	28	7	2	3	13	12	23	11	1	.305/.362/.461	.280	9.5	.350	1.5	CF(33): 4.8	1.4
2014	TBA	MLB	24	364	35	16	8	10	35	23	71	5	4	.263/.315/.450	.286	15.0	.306	-1.4	RF(68): 6.7 • CF(42): 3.9	2.8
2015	TBA	MLB	25	535	62	25	12	10	40	24	95	18	5	.263/.298/.420	.259	17.7	.306	2.5	CF(148): 31.3 • RF(2): -0.1	5.2
2016	TBA	MLB	26	414	55	20	2	12	37	40	74	21	3	.246/.331/.410	.266	18.3	.278	2.8	CF(104): 11.9	3.1
2017	*TBA*	*MLB*	*27*	*614*	*80*	*27*	*8*	*16*	*61*	*44*	*116*	*23*	*5*	*.257/.314/.420*	*.266*	*26.6*	*.295*	*3.3*	*CF 24*	*5.0*
2018	*TBA*	*MLB*	*28*	*506*	*59*	*23*	*7*	*14*	*59*	*37*	*97*	*17*	*4*	*.253/.312/.422*	*.260*	*15.4*	*.289*	*1.8*	*CF 20*	*3.8*

Breakout: 8%   Improve: 52%   Collapse: 5%   Attrition: 12%   MLB: 99%   *Comparables: Vernon Wells, Chris Coghlan, Bobby Thomson*

The Rays' unbelievable center fielder might be the Barry Bonds of outfield defense, excelling at a level that's an order of magnitude higher than even his most talented peers. He has the total package of defensive skills: he positions himself well, runs tight routes to the ball, possesses speed and athleticism to cover the gaps and fires off assists with a cannon arm. As the lynchpin of Tampa's run prevention strategy—and all those fly-ball pitchers the team employs—Kiermaier's presence allows the Rays to turn about one hit per game into an out compared to games where he doesn't play. Averaging nearly two wins per season *simply due to defense* over the past three years, he has a case as the most impactful defensive player in baseball (non-catcher division). On the flip side, Kiermaier was also the Barry Bonds of pop-ups. His 25.2 percent infield fly rate in 2016 meant that he squibbed almost a quarter of his fly balls, far surpassing anyone else in the league. (Jose Bautista—the second place infield-fly-er—only popped up at a 18.2 percent rate.) Still, he can hit as many lazy flies as he wants, so long as he keeps tracking them down all over the outfield.

Evan Longoria   3B

Born: 10/7/85   Age: 31   Bats: R   Throws: R   Height: 6'2"   Weight: 210   Entered Pro Ball: Round 1, 2006 Draft (#3 overall)

YEAR	TEAM	LVL	AGE	PA	R	2B	3B	HR	RBI	BB	K	SB	CS	AVG/OBP/SLG	TAv	VORP	BABIP	BRR	FRAA	WARP
2014	TBA	MLB	28	700	83	26	1	22	91	57	133	5	0	.253/.320/.404	.284	37.2	.285	1.7	3B(155): 3.6	4.5
2015	TBA	MLB	29	670	74	35	1	21	73	51	132	3	1	.270/.328/.435	.275	29.8	.309	0.5	3B(148): 9.3	4.2
2016	TBA	MLB	30	685	81	41	4	36	98	42	144	0	3	.273/.318/.521	.292	41.6	.298	-2.3	3B(152): -5.1	3.8
2017	TBA	MLB	31	644	74	30	2	25	87	54	141	2	1	.258/.323/.448	.277	29.2	.296	-1.2	3B 4	3.0
2018	TBA	MLB	32	552	70	26	1	20	70	45	125	1	0	.254/.318/.430	.265	14.7	.297	-0.2	3B 3	2.0

Breakout: 0%   Improve: 33%   Collapse: 8%   Attrition: 8%   MLB: 96%   Comparables: Eric Chavez, Chase Headley, Vern Stephens

In literature, the monomyth, or "hero's journey," is one of the most common templates for a story: the hero embarks on his quest, faces trial and tribulations, is cast down and rises forth again, claiming a great victory or prize and returning home after being transformed. Now Longoria—already the greatest player in the Rays' short history—may be at something of a transformational point in his quest through baseball, the midpoint of his journey. After two years in which he was "cast down" to the level of a merely good third baseman rather than a superstar, he revived his myth somewhat last season. With the Battle of 2016 behind him his skill set certainly has transformed; Longoria put the ball in the air more than all but four major-league regulars, revitalizing his power stroke and ennobling his batting line. At the same time his once-exceptional defense seems to be failing him, and a move across the diamond is starting to look inevitable.

Today our protagonist is on the other side of 30 and nearing his ultimate conquest, which is yet to be determined. Is it a Hall-of-Fame career? If so he may want to consider sticking with the Rays, and perhaps a renewed commitment to defense, so he can remain a hot corner stalwart. But if the ultimate goal is a championship, one would have to think that it's time for Longoria to strike out for new lands, continuing his journey beyond Tampa. Either way, despite being a different player than he once was, rumors of his demise have been exaggerated; this hero's tale has not yet reached its denouement.

Joshua Lowe   3B

Born: 2/2/98   Age: 19   Bats: L   Throws: R   Height: 6'4"   Weight: 190   Entered Pro Ball: Round 1, 2016 Draft (#13 overall)

YEAR	TEAM	LVL	AGE	PA	R	2B	3B	HR	RBI	BB	K	SB	CS	AVG/OBP/SLG	TAv	VORP	BABIP	BRR	FRAA	WARP
2017	TBA	MLB	19	250	21	7	1	6	24	22	93	0	0	.177/.253/.290	.196	-8.9	.266	-0.4	3B -2	-1.2
2018	TBA	MLB	20	334	36	10	1	9	33	32	118	0	0	.193/.274/.325	.216	-8.1	.281	-0.6	3B -3	-1.2

Breakout: 0%   Improve: 7%   Collapse: 3%   Attrition: 8%   MLB: 15%   Comparables: Nomar Mazara, Domingo Santana, Raul Mondesi

Lowe was drafted out of Pope High School in Florida, but unlike the HBO series The Young Pope you should be paying attention to this. The Rays bought him out of a commitment to Florida State for two and a half million dollars back in June and their tithe brings them a great gift: raw power. Lowe looks the part of a future slugger—he's tall, long and features plus bat speed and good athleticism. And, though he's new to third base, he's blessed with a tremendous arm that saw him get consideration as a two-way player before his confirmation as an everyday hitter. Sure, the swing may be a bit hole-y and he's further away than the Second Coming, but finally hitting on a first-round pick would be the answer to the Rays' front office's prayers.

Mikie Mahtook   RF

Born: 11/30/89   Age: 27   Bats: R   Throws: R   Height: 6'1"   Weight: 200   Entered Pro Ball: Round 1, 2011 Draft (#31 overall)

YEAR	TEAM	LVL	AGE	PA	R	2B	3B	HR	RBI	BB	K	SB	CS	AVG/OBP/SLG	TAv	VORP	BABIP	BRR	FRAA	WARP
2014	DUR	AAA	24	550	56	33	6	12	68	46	137	18	5	.292/.362/.458	.272	25.5	.380	3.2	CF(74): -1.1 • RF(41): 3.6	3.0
2015	DUR	AAA	25	418	35	27	3	4	45	22	98	10	1	.249/.304/.366	.251	3.1	.323	-2.0	RF(43): -2.5 • CF(34): 6.8	0.6
2015	TBA	MLB	25	115	22	5	1	9	19	6	31	4	3	.295/.351/.619	.352	12.2	.338	-0.6	LF(16): 0.3 • CF(13): -0.8	1.4
2016	DUR	AAA	26	120	16	5	3	1	7	12	24	5	1	.305/.383/.438	.288	6.9	.383	0.6	CF(11): -1.1 • RF(9): 1.0	0.7
2016	TBA	MLB	26	196	16	9	0	3	11	7	68	0	1	.195/.231/.292	.184	-11.6	.287	-1.2	LF(26): -0.7 • CF(23): 0.6	-1.3
2017	TBA	MLB	27	305	33	14	2	8	31	19	88	6	2	.235/.293/.382	.244	4.8	.312	0.4	LF 2 • CF 1	0.5
2018	TBA	MLB	28	406	46	18	3	11	45	26	118	7	2	.235/.297/.387	.242	2.9	.312	0.5	LF 3 • CF 1	0.7

Breakout: 4%   Improve: 29%   Collapse: 11%   Attrition: 26%   MLB: 65%   Comparables: Will Venable, Matt Den Dekker, Aaron Cunningham

If Mahtook had grown a goatee for this past season you might've believed he'd swapped places with his mirror universe counterpart. The "good" Mahtook—the version from 2015—had at long last tapped into some of the power that had eluded him through his minor-league career, belting nine homers in just 115 plate appearances. His evil twin in 2016 couldn't top a .300 slugging percentage and looked completely overmatched before having his left hand shattered on an inside pitch. Perhaps his struggles had something to do with overuse against right-handed pitching—after all, he's never been projected as much more than a platoon hitter—but he should get every opportunity again this year in Tampa. Perhaps the two versions of Mahtook—the breakout star and his ineffective doppelganger—are merely two sides of the same coin: a perfectly acceptable and inexpensive fourth outfielder.

Luke Maile   C

Born: 2/6/91   Age: 26   Bats: R   Throws: R   Height: 6'3"   Weight: 225   Entered Pro Ball: Round 8, 2012 Draft (#272 overall)

YEAR	TEAM	LVL	AGE	PA	R	2B	3B	HR	RBI	BB	K	SB	CS	AVG/OBP/SLG	TAv	VORP	BABIP	BRR	FRAA	WARP
2014	MNT	AA	23	393	43	19	4	5	37	35	76	1	1	.268/.341/.387	.259	13.3	.327	-1.4	C(80): 17.4	3.3
2015	DUR	AAA	24	337	38	9	1	5	29	35	50	1	1	.207/.298/.296	.215	-0.6	.231	0.8	C(84): 16.1	1.6
2015	TBA	MLB	24	35	2	3	0	0	2	0	8	0	0	.171/.171/.257	.128	-2.9	.222	0.1	C(15): 0.0	-0.3
2016	DUR	AAA	25	214	13	13	0	2	12	16	36	0	1	.242/.310/.340	.241	1.9	.288	-1.9	C(46): 9.5	1.2
2016	TBA	MLB	25	126	10	7	0	3	15	4	36	0	0	.227/.252/.361	.215	0.6	.300	0.9	C(37): 0.9 • 1B(4): 0.4	0.2
2017	TBA	MLB	26	325	29	13	1	6	31	24	75	0	0	.220/.282/.337	.229	4.7	.271	-0.8	C 6	0.7
2018	TBA	MLB	27	333	36	14	1	8	33	24	82	0	0	.218/.283/.346	.226	0.0	.269	-0.8	C 6	0.7

Breakout: 4%   Improve: 17%   Collapse: 12%   Attrition: 24%   MLB: 49%   Comparables: Chris Herrmann, Curtis Thigpen, Bryan Holaday

Taupe paint. One bag of dead leaves. Weak tea. The 3-0 fastball down the heart of the plate, taken for a strike. Uncle John's well-regarded accounting practice. Verb conjugations. Not *that* old warehouse, but the other one further back. Breaking tax code updates. A perfectly normal toenail clipping. 3:30pm, waiting for that work e-mail to arrive. Unbuttered wheat toast. Six tarnished pennies in the car ashtray. Your local state senator. The Padres' home uniforms. Kenny G's *Breathless*. The Padres' road uniforms. Dirt. One cinder block, sitting askew on a curb in your hometown. Two peanuts. Unscented soap. Someone else's fantasy baseball team. Iowa. The FBI warning at the start of a rented movie. The Department of Motor Vehicles. The fine print. The upcoming shrubbery convention. Tap water. Luke Maile.

YEAR	TEAM	P. COUNT	FRM RUNS	BLK RUNS	THRW RUNS	TOT RUNS
2014	MNT	10222	18.4	-0.7	0.2	17.8
2015	DUR	11553	13.6	-0.7	0.7	13.5
2015	TBA	1380	0.0	-0.6	0.0	-0.6
2016	TBA	4942	1.3	0.1	0.1	1.4
2017	TBA	12625	6.6	-1.0	-0.1	5.4
2018	TBA	12954	6.3	-1.0	-0.2	5.1

Brad Miller   SS

Born: 10/18/89   Age: 27   Bats: L   Throws: R   Height: 6'2"   Weight: 200   Entered Pro Ball: Round 2, 2011 Draft (#62 overall)

YEAR	TEAM	LVL	AGE	PA	R	2B	3B	HR	RBI	BB	K	SB	CS	AVG/OBP/SLG	TAv	VORP	BABIP	BRR	FRAA	WARP
2014	SEA	MLB	24	411	47	15	4	10	36	34	95	4	2	.221/.288/.365	.263	17.0	.268	0.9	SS(107): 0.4 • 2B(13): 0.1	1.9
2015	SEA	MLB	25	497	44	22	4	11	46	47	101	13	4	.258/.329/.402	.273	20.2	.307	-2.6	SS(89): -0.1 • CF(20): -1.4	2.0
2016	TBA	MLB	26	601	73	29	6	30	81	47	149	6	4	.243/.304/.482	.280	31.7	.277	0.4	SS(105): -7.5 • 1B(39): 0.4	2.5
2017	TBA	MLB	27	603	70	24	5	20	75	54	131	10	5	.249/.317/.428	.269	15.7	.288	0.2	1B / • SS -0	2.2
2018	TBA	MLB	28	565	71	23	5	20	72	52	126	8	4	.245/.316/.431	.264	9.9	.283	-0.4	1B 6 • SS 0	1.8

Breakout: 1%   Improve: 52%   Collapse: 3%   Attrition: 7%   MLB: 100%   Comparables: Stephen Drew, Asdrubal Cabrera, Jhonny Peralta

Thirty home runs. You have to lead with that because anything else buries the lede and obscures just how strangely a player's path can wind. Miller hit more homers over his 601 plate appearances last season than the 29 he smacked over the 1243 he took during the three seasons before that. He hit more homers in a season than anyone in franchise history not named Pena, Huff, Longoria, Canseco or McGriff. How does a shortstop put his name in that kind of company? First, you follow the Josh Donaldson plan of closing off your stance at the plate and increasing your leg kick. Then you stop being a shortstop; Miller's defense at the position was and is pretty horrible. Now he hits with the power of a first baseman and plays the position to match. It's been a winding road but something feels right about Miller settling in, embracing his strengths and hiding his glove-side weakness. You may have never imagined Brad Miller the power-hitting first baseman, but we all eventually become what we were meant to be.

Logan Morrison   1B

Born: 8/25/87   Age: 29   Bats: L   Throws: L   Height: 6'2"   Weight: 240   Entered Pro Ball: Round 22, 2005 Draft (#666 overall)

YEAR	TEAM	LVL	AGE	PA	R	2B	3B	HR	RBI	BB	K	SB	CS	AVG/OBP/SLG	TAv	VORP	BABIP	BRR	FRAA	WARP
2014	TAC	AAA	26	77	13	2	0	3	8	11	8	2	0	.308/.416/.477	.324	6.7	.315	0.3	1B(6): 0.3	0.7
2014	SEA	MLB	26	365	41	20	0	11	38	24	59	5	2	.262/.315/.420	.282	8.8	.287	-2.5	1B(79): -3.8 • RF(8): 0.8	0.6
2015	SEA	MLB	27	511	47	15	3	17	54	47	81	8	4	.225/.302/.383	.254	-0.8	.238	-3.2	1B(140): -5.1 • RF(3): 0.0	-0.7
2016	TBA	MLB	28	398	45	18	1	14	43	37	89	4	2	.238/.319/.414	.260	4.5	.278	0.4	1B(83): -1.6	0.3
2017	TBA	MLB	29	399	47	16	2	14	50	39	75	5	2	.239/.320/.410	.257	5.4	.265	-1.4	1B -4	0.2
2018	TBA	MLB	30	430	54	18	1	15	53	41	81	4	2	.240/.319/.409	.258	3.4	.266	-1.4	1B -4	-0.1

Breakout: 4%   Improve: 54%   Collapse: 13%   Attrition: 17%   MLB: 98%   Comparables: James Loney, Bruce Bochte, Yonder Alonso

Ask any accountant—some Aprils are just terrible. LoMo kicked off his stint with the Rays with one of the most putrid first months in recent memory: in 64 plate appearances he whiffed 25 times and stumbled to a .100/.156/.133 slash line. This was rock bottom, and he couldn't go any MoLo. His performance ticked up over the course of the season, yet his final slash line for 2016 hewed close to his disappointing career mark despite Tampa heavily leveraging his platoon advantage. Morrison is far enough removed from his prospect potential and productive first two seasons to be considered a veteran, and a disappointing one at that. The Rays used him sparingly in the second half of the season in favor of younger, better options, and in October he submitted to wrist surgery. All this sets him up for another dismal April, albeit for a slightly different reason: he's now nothing more than a typical Triple-A first baseman.

Kevin Padlo   3B

Born: 7/15/96   Age: 20   Bats: R   Throws: R   Height: 6'2"   Weight: 205   Entered Pro Ball: Round 5, 2014 Draft (#143 overall)

YEAR	TEAM	LVL	AGE	PA	R	2B	3B	HR	RBI	BB	K	SB	CS	AVG/OBP/SLG	TAv	VORP	BABIP	BRR	FRAA	WARP
2015	ASH	A	18	99	11	5	0	2	7	14	26	2	1	.145/.273/.277	.209	-2.0	.179	0.2	3B(25): 3.6	0.2
2015	BOI	A-	18	308	44	22	2	9	46	45	62	33	5	.294/.404/.502	.325	30.6	.353	1.3	3B(59): 0.3	3.2
2016	BGR	A	19	509	71	22	3	16	66	79	134	14	9	.229/.358/.413	.289	25.0	.293	-4.7	3B(109): -9.8	1.7
2017	TBA	MLB	20	250	28	9	1	8	28	29	82	3	2	.194/.295/.354	.232	0.3	.262	-0.3	3B -1	-0.1
2018	TBA	MLB	21	410	51	16	1	14	48	50	131	6	3	.203/.307/.374	.244	2.0	.271	-0.3	3B -2	0.0

Breakout: 4%   Improve: 15%   Collapse: 0%   Attrition: 5%   MLB: 17%   *Comparables: Matt Dominguez, Matt Davidson, Miguel Sano*

Padlo, a power-hitting third baseman, will need several minor-league seasons to discover whether he'll reach his full potential as an adequate big-league regular. He too could one day be traded from one bad team to another, much like the Jake McGee-for-Corey Dickerson deal that brought him into Tampa's system. Let that be a lesson to the kids out there. Never give up on your dreams.

Alexei Ramirez   SS

Born: 9/22/81   Age: 35   Bats: R   Throws: R   Height: 6'2"   Weight: 180   Entered Pro Ball: International Free Agent, 2008

YEAR	TEAM	LVL	AGE	PA	R	2B	3B	HR	RBI	BB	K	SB	CS	AVG/OBP/SLG	TAv	VORP	BABIP	BRR	FRAA	WARP
2014	CHA	MLB	32	657	82	35	2	15	74	24	81	21	4	.273/.305/.408	.253	20.0	.292	-0.1	SS(158): 9.8	3.3
2015	CHA	MLB	33	622	54	33	0	10	62	31	68	17	7	.249/.285/.357	.236	5.4	.264	-4.4	SS(152): 4.4 • P(1): -0.0	1.0
2016	SDN	MLB	34	444	33	19	2	5	41	17	56	6	9	.240/.275/.330	.224	-0.5	.265	-1.8	SS(111): -7.4 • RF(3): -0.5	-0.9
2016	TBA	MLB	34	62	5	3	0	1	7	4	7	2	0	.246/.295/.351	.226	0.9	.265	0.6	SS(16): -0.2 • RF(1): -0.1	0.1
2017	TBA	MLB	35	498	48	23	1	7	46	20	69	13	6	.249/.282/.350	.225	2.9	.275	-2.0	SS 1 • RF -0	0.4
2018	TBA	MLB	36	448	44	20	1	6	41	19	64	10	6	.245/.279/.343	.226	-1.9	.273	-1.4	SS 1 • RF 0	-0.1

Breakout: 1%   Improve: 37%   Collapse: 7%   Attrition: 23%   MLB: 80%   *Comparables: Neifi Perez, Larry Bowa, John McDonald*

Last year's Annual warned that Ramirez's BABIP dip might have heralded the beginning of the end for the steady Cuban shortstop. In hindsight, Nostradamus has nothing on those portentous words. Ramirez was an unholy terror with the bat in 2016; among all MLB players with at least 400 plate appearances Ramirez had the fourth-worst OBP, the sixth-worst slugging percentage and the fourth-worst True Average. But Ramirez's once-competent offense was only supposed to be the frosting where his steady defense represented the moist, fluffy cake. He was *supposed* to be a defensive anchor for the revamped Padres infield, but wasn't. Both his career-worst FRAA and the eye test indicated that his days as a regular are over. The only two everyday players with a worse WARP over the 2016 season were Mark Teixeira, who retired, and Adam Lind—two other players with diminished bats and no defensive value. He probably only has one more shot before he follows Teixeira out of the league.

Daniel Robertson   SS

Born: 3/22/94   Age: 23   Bats: R   Throws: R   Height: 6'1"   Weight: 205   Entered Pro Ball: Round 1, 2012 Draft (#34 overall)

YEAR	TEAM	LVL	AGE	PA	R	2B	3B	HR	RBI	BB	K	SB	CS	AVG/OBP/SLG	TAv	VORP	BABIP	BRR	FRAA	WARP
2014	STO	A+	20	642	110	37	3	15	60	72	94	4	4	.310/.402/.471	.308	61.0	.349	3.0	SS(115): 0.8 • 2B(7): -0.7	6.2
2015	MNT	AA	21	347	49	20	5	4	41	33	58	2	3	.274/.363/.415	.306	29.7	.324	0.8	SS(69): 3.7	3.6
2016	DUR	AAA	22	511	50	21	3	5	43	58	100	2	1	.259/.358/.356	.260	18.5	.322	-0.3	SS(75): 1.8 • 2B(21): 2.0	2.5
2017	TBA	MLB	23	250	28	10	1	5	23	24	56	0	0	.239/.326/.366	.251	7.9	.296	-0.3	SS 1 • 2B 0	1.0
2018	TBA	MLB	24	387	45	16	2	8	39	33	90	0	0	.240/.322/.371	.252	8.4	.300	-0.6	SS 1 • 2B 0	1.1

Breakout: 4%   Improve: 25%   Collapse: 4%   Attrition: 16%   MLB: 36%   *Comparables: Greg Garcia, Chris Taylor, Tyler Saladino*

The only thing Robertson does really well is draw a walk, and that only means so much when you barely have enough power to push your slugging percentage past your OBP. So when one takes away the approach what are you left with? A shortstop who's not all that great at the position and being asked to learn second, third and the outfield on the fly? A hitter with the dreaded "doubles power" and not much more? Or is Robertson the rare sort of guy with average tools who just seems to turn into something greater than the sum of his parts? If you squint you can see a do-it-all super-utility type, but if you open wider what you see may not be more than a replacement-level regular.

Adrian Rondon   SS

Born: 7/7/98   Age: 18   Bats: R   Throws: R   Height: 6'1"   Weight: 190   Entered Pro Ball: International Free Agent, 2014

YEAR	TEAM	LVL	AGE	PA	R	2B	3B	HR	RBI	BB	K	SB	CS	AVG/OBP/SLG	TAv	VORP	BABIP	BRR	FRAA	WARP
2017	TBA	MLB	18	250	18	8	1	5	23	13	101	0	0	.170/.215/.273	.175	-10.9	.267	-0.5	SS -2	-1.4
2018	TBA	MLB	19	274	24	9	1	6	25	13	112	0	0	.172/.214/.285	.178	-14.1	.266	-0.6	SS -2	-1.8

Breakout: 0%   Improve: 0%   Collapse: 0%   Attrition: 0%   MLB: 0%   *Comparables: Raul Mondesi, Wilmer Flores*

The term "raw" can be both good and bad. *Eddie Murphy Raw* = good. "This catfish tastes like sushi" = bad. Rondon is both kinds of raw, possessing huge potential thanks to power and athleticism, but he's already sliding down the offensive spectrum—the defensive spectrum might be next—and hasn't broken free from Rookie ball. To be continued.

Steven Souza RF

Born: 4/24/89 Age: 28 Bats: R Throws: R Height: 6'4" Weight: 225 Entered Pro Ball: Round 3, 2007 Draft (#100 overall)

YEAR	TEAM	LVL	AGE	PA	R	2B	3B	HR	RBI	BB	K	SB	CS	AVG/OBP/SLG	TAv	VORP	BABIP	BRR	FRAA	WARP
2014	SYR	AAA	25	407	62	25	2	18	75	52	75	26	7	.350/.432/.590	.347	49.6	.398	0.0	RF(63): 5.0 • CF(27): 2.5	5.7
2014	WAS	MLB	25	26	2	0	0	2	2	3	7	0	0	.130/.231/.391	.225	-0.3	.071	0.0	RF(8): -0.1 • LF(4): -0.3	-0.1
2015	TBA	MLB	26	426	59	15	1	16	40	46	144	12	6	.225/.318/.399	.259	8.9	.318	2.2	RF(103): -1.8	0.8
2016	TBA	MLB	27	468	58	17	1	17	49	31	159	7	6	.247/.303/.409	.252	6.8	.348	2.3	RF(111): -2.9 • CF(3): 0.2	0.4
2017	TBA	MLB	28	499	64	19	1	19	59	48	155	13	6	.239/.318/.414	.266	17.5	.321	-0.2	RF -1	1.2
2018	TBA	MLB	29	502	65	19	1	18	62	50	157	12	7	.237/.320/.408	.260	13.1	.320	2.4	RF -1	1.3

Breakout: 2%   Improve: 52%   Collapse: 11%   Attrition: 20%   MLB: 94%   Comparables: Brad Hawpe, J.D. Martinez, Will Venable

For those of you who think Souza's greatest crime is simply not being Trea Turner or Wil Myers—the two stars that emerged from the Rays' infamous three-team-deal that brought him to Tampa—you're mistaken. The real felony here is Souza's unconscionable contract rate. In addition to being one of the 10 worst in baseball at making contact last season, he struck out at a higher rate than everyone in baseball except for Miguel Sano and walked only once for every *five* strikeouts. If you want to make excuses for his poor performance you can point to the injuries to his finger and waist that slowed him down (and eventually led to offseason hip surgery), but the maladies just keep piling up and the Rays didn't bring him in to be a replacement-level outfielder. He'll get another chance this year—PECOTA is still bullish on his future—but until he does the Rays will feel a twinge every time Myers goes yard and Souza swings over a breaking pitch.

Bobby Wilson C

Born: 4/8/83 Age: 34 Bats: R Throws: R Height: 6'0" Weight: 230 Entered Pro Ball: Round 48, 2002 Draft (#1417 overall)

YEAR	TEAM	LVL	AGE	PA	R	2B	3B	HR	RBI	BB	K	SB	CS	AVG/OBP/SLG	TAv	VORP	BABIP	BRR	FRAA	WARP
2014	RNO	AAA	31	299	29	11	0	3	38	23	45	0	2	.267/.324/.341	.232	0.3	.308	-4.6	C(74): 21.6	2.2
2014	ARI	MLB	31	4	0	0	0	0	0	0	0	0	0	.250/.250/.250	.188	-0.1	.250	0.0	C(2): 0.0	0.0
2015	TBA	MLB	32	59	3	0	0	0	4	4	20	0	0	.145/.203/.145	.145	-4.4	.229	-0.3	C(24): 1.4	-0.3
2015	DUR	AAA	32	55	3	1	0	0	0	6	11	0	0	.184/.273/.204	.184	-2.3	.237	-0.2	C(16): 0.1	-0.2
2015	TEX	MLB	32	88	5	5	0	1	10	7	19	0	1	.221/.291/.325	.231	1.3	.276	0.0	C(31): 4.0	0.6
2016	DET	MLB	33	15	0	0	0	0	2	1	3	0	0	.154/.200/.154	.144	-1.1	.182	0.0	C(5): -0.9	-0.2
2016	TEX	MLB	33	141	11	4	0	3	22	5	33	0	0	.250/.277/.352	.225	1.5	.305	0.1	C(42): 1.7	0.3
2016	TBA	MLB	33	95	14	2	0	4	9	5	28	0	0	.230/.272/.391	.225	1.4	.291	0.4	C(28): -2.7	-0.1
2017	TBA	MLB	34	250	22	8	0	4	22	17	61	0	0	.213/.271/.306	.203	-2.0	.261	0.0	C 3	0.1
2018	TBA	MLB	35	246	23	8	0	4	20	16	60	0	0	.207/.262/.295	.198	-6.5	.256	0.0	C 2	-0.5

Breakout: 6%   Improve: 37%   Collapse: 10%   Attrition: 31%   MLB: 78%   Comparables: John Baker, Chad Moeller, Gary Bennett

He's not the *best* backup catcher in baseball, but Wilson might be the *most* backup catcher in the game. To wit: he was drafted in the 48th round of the 2002 amateur draft, just two spots ahead of fellow second-string backstop Drew Butera. (That's backup catcher territory.) He's fluttered between orgs like a brick-shaped butterfly; during the 2016 season he went from the Rangers to the Tigers, then back to the Rangers before finally landing with his hometown Rays. And of course he hits poorly—even for a catcher—but gets raves for his game-calling and has posted good minor-league framing numbers. Best of all this is the first time he's appeared in this Annual in four years, ostensibly because third-string catchers fail to put the "fun" in fungible.

YEAR	TEAM	P. COUNT	FRM RUNS	BLK RUNS	THRW RUNS	TOT RUNS
2014	ARI	189	0.0	0.2	0.0	0.2
2014	RNO	9382	14.5	0.2	4.7	19.5
2015	DUR	1988	0.1	0.0	0.2	0.3
2015	TBA	2549	1.5	1.3	-0.1	2.7
2015	TEX	3594	4.7	0.8	-0.3	5.2
2016	DET	640	0.2	1.8	-1.4	0.6
2016	TEX	5515	2.8	0.0	0.0	2.8
2016	TBA	4222	-2.3	0.0	0.0	-2.3
2017	TBA	10026	2.3	1.4	-0.7	3.1
2018	TBA	9853	1.3	1.3	-0.8	1.9

PITCHERS

Matt Andriese RHP

Born: 8/28/89 Age: 27 Bats: R Throws: R Height: 6'3" Weight: 215 Entered Pro Ball: Round 3, 2011 Draft (#112 overall)

YEAR	TEAM	LVL	AGE	W	L	SV	G	GS	IP	H	HR	BB/9	K/9	K	GB%	BABIP	WHIP	ERA	FIP	DRA	VORP	WARP	cFIP	MPH
2014	DUR	AAA	24	11	8	0	28	25	162¹	153	18	2.7	7.2	129	53%	.291	1.24	3.77	4.24	3.79	34.8	3.5	96	
2015	DUR	AAA	25	3	3	0	13	12	65	65	2	1.4	9.6	69	50%	.344	1.15	2.35	1.94	1.12	30.1	3.1	65	
2015	TBA	MLB	25	3	5	2	25	8	65²	69	8	2.5	6.7	49	50%	.298	1.32	4.11	4.11	4.00	6.6	0.7	101	93.9
2016	DUR	AAA	26	1	2	0	6	6	34¹	32	2	1.8	11.5	44	48%	.345	1.14	3.41	2.15	0.92	16.9	1.7	65	
2016	TBA	MLB	26	8	8	1	29	19	127²	131	17	1.8	7.7	109	44%	.305	1.22	4.37	3.74	4.25	14.8	1.5	94	93.8
2017	TBA	MLB	27	6	5	0	33	13	94	92	11	2.6	8.2	86	43%	.296	1.26	3.68	3.84	4.25	9.9	1.0	98	
2018	TBA	MLB	28	8	7	0	48	19	141²	126	19	3.6	9.8	155	43%	.293	1.29	3.81	4.00	4.35	15.3	1.6	97	

Breakout: 31%   Improve: 53%   Collapse: 21%   Attrition: 32%   MLB: 89%   Comparables: Jimmy Nelson, Joe Saunders, Adam Warren

During the 2016 ALCS, it seemed like all anyone could talk about was Andrew Miller and the idea of the multi-inning relief ace. Perhaps the Rays' best chance to replicate that success is their up-and-down swingman. Used in a variety of roles over the past two years—starter, reliever, majors and minors—last season Andriese thrived in relief between starting stints, holding hitters to a .171/.198/.306 slash line. Granted this was only 10 appearances, but he hung in for at least five outs in all but one of those stints. The second time through the order is the UC Riverside product's Achilles' heel; during hitters' second look strikeouts crater and extra-base hits surge. While he's been an acceptable back-of-the-rotation starter over the past two seasons, perhaps leaning more on his grounder-inducing cutter and change in two- or three-inning bursts could unlock something more rare and special than just a competent no. 5 starter.

Chris Archer   RHP

Born: 9/26/88   Age: 28   Bats: R   Throws: R   Height: 6'3"   Weight: 190   Entered Pro Ball: Round 5, 2006 Draft (#161 overall)

YEAR	TEAM	LVL	AGE	W	L	SV	G	GS	IP	H	HR	BB/9	K/9	K	GB%	BABIP	WHIP	ERA	FIP	DRA	VORP	WARP	cFIP	MPH
2014	TBA	MLB	25	10	9	0	32	32	194²	177	12	3.3	8.0	173	48%	.296	1.28	3.33	3.42	4.14	15.1	1.7	99	97.5
2015	TBA	MLB	26	12	13	0	34	34	212	175	19	2.8	10.7	252	47%	.295	1.14	3.23	2.87	2.56	59.3	6.3	70	98.2
2016	TBA	MLB	27	9	19	0	33	33	201¹	183	30	3.0	10.4	233	49%	.297	1.24	4.02	3.77	2.92	54.7	5.6	77	97.1
2017	TBA	MLB	28	12	10	0	30	30	189	157	22	3.2	10.7	225	41%	.291	1.18	3.35	3.46	3.88	28.7	3.0	88	
2018	TBA	MLB	29	12	10	0	31	31	196	165	24	3.4	11.1	241	41%	.296	1.22	3.37	3.56	3.86	34.1	3.5	85	

Breakout: 18%   Improve: 44%   Collapse: 34%   Attrition: 9%   MLB: 94%   *Comparables: Alex Cobb, Jon Lester, Ubaldo Jimenez*

Keep calm and slide on. Archer is an elite starting pitcher even if his ERA looks a bit off. If those early-season struggles with home runs put you off, take solace in the advanced metrics that still peg him as a top-tier starter with world-class stuff. Hitters simply don't make contact against him; he was top-five in baseball among starters when it came to contact percentage, with names like Fernandez, Syndergaard and Scherzer ahead of him. When hitters do put wood on him Archer is also able to avoid line drives, the most dangerous kind of contact—and though this was his best season of suppressing liners he's showed a talent for it since his debut.

Sure, his fastball is imposing, but the slider is *special*. It's a breaker that rates as one of the best and filthiest pitches in baseball because of its high velocity and break. So by the end of the season, when Archer was most on his game, he started throwing it more and more often; his usage of the bender finally overtook that of his fastball, even as his walk rate continued to drop. Sure, he could benefit from finding a way to limit those homers—especially if the Rays eventually deal him to a more homer-happy park—but if you're worried about performance take a page out of Archer's cool-and-confident book and just relax.

Brad Boxberger   RHP

Born: 5/27/88   Age: 29   Bats: R   Throws: R   Height: 6'2"   Weight: 225   Entered Pro Ball: Round 1, 2009 Draft (#43 overall)

YEAR	TEAM	LVL	AGE	W	L	SV	G	GS	IP	H	HR	BB/9	K/9	K	GB%	BABIP	WHIP	ERA	FIP	DRA	VORP	WARP	cFIP	MPH
2014	TBA	MLB	26	5	2	2	63	0	64²	34	9	2.8	14.5	104	44%	.227	0.84	2.37	2.87	1.73	19.8	2.2	58	95.6
2015	TBA	MLB	27	4	10	41	69	0	63	54	9	4.6	10.6	74	37%	.292	1.37	3.71	4.23	3.97	5.1	0.6	97	95.1
2016	TBA	MLB	28	4	3	0	27	0	24¹	23	3	7.0	8.1	22	49%	.294	1.73	4.81	5.49	5.11	-0.4	0.0	112	94.5
2017	TBA	MLB	29	2	2	5	49	0	52	48	8	4.1	10.3	59	45%	.298	1.37	4.27	4.40	4.73	1.5	0.2	100	
2018	TBA	MLB	30	2	1	2	41	0	43	36	7	4.7	11.4	55	45%	.291	1.36	4.19	4.39	4.74	1.5	0.2	108	

Breakout: 21%   Improve: 48%   Collapse: 13%   Attrition: 19%   MLB: 85%   *Comparables: Junichi Tazawa, David Carpenter, Mike Dunn*

Core muscles weren't kind to Boxberger last season when he lost the first two months to adductor repair surgery, made one appearance and then lost the next two months to a strained oblique. He returned a day before the trade deadline—costing himself the ninth-inning role and the front office the chance to dangle a Proven Closer ™ for prospects—and spent the second half searching futilely for his control. The news wasn't all bad for Boxberger, who saw an intriguing increase in his ground-ball rate after trading some fastballs for changeups and sliders, but it'd be hard to classify 2016 as anything but a lost season. Having already slipped from the ninth to the eighth he'll have to rein in the walks to avoid another stumble on the bullpen depth chart.

Xavier Cedeno   LHP

Born: 8/26/86   Age: 30   Bats: L   Throws: L   Height: 6'0"   Weight: 215   Entered Pro Ball: Round 31, 2004 Draft (#920 overall)

YEAR	TEAM	LVL	AGE	W	L	SV	G	GS	IP	H	HR	BB/9	K/9	K	GB%	BABIP	WHIP	ERA	FIP	DRA	VORP	WARP	cFIP	MPH
2014	SYR	AAA	27	5	1	4	35	0	39¹	22	3	2.7	13.0	57	61%	.247	0.86	2.29	2.37	0.86	19.6	2.0	54	
2014	WAS	MLB	27	0	0	0	9	0	7	10	1	0.0	6.4	5	40%	.375	1.43	3.86	3.53	4.94	-0.4	0.0	108	93.5
2015	WAS	MLB	28	0	0	0	5	0	3	3	1	6.0	12.0	4	25%	.286	1.67	6.00	7.83	2.88	0.6	0.1	89	91.3
2015	TBA	MLB	28	4	1	1	61	0	43	37	3	2.5	9.0	43	56%	.296	1.14	2.09	2.92	3.08	7.8	0.8	87	91.1
2016	TBA	MLB	29	3	4	0	54	0	41¹	36	2	2.8	9.4	43	51%	.296	1.19	3.70	2.60	3.48	6.8	0.7	91	90.7
2017	TBA	MLB	30	3	3	0	54	0	57¹	51	5	3.3	9.1	58	54%	.294	1.26	3.26	3.47	3.90	6.9	0.7	85	
2018	TBA	MLB	31	3	1	1	56	0	59²	52	5	3.7	9.9	66	54%	.296	1.28	3.35	3.54	3.85	7.9	0.8	81	

Breakout: 33%   Improve: 59%   Collapse: 17%   Attrition: 19%   MLB: 89%   *Comparables: Tony Watson, Adam Ottavino, Heath Bell*

Cedeno had a season of graduation this past year, as posting a second consecutive solid campaign allowed him to shift from the Rays' second lefty to the top of the southpaw food chain. It wasn't all champagne and caviar—Cedeno struggled in close and late situations and was a coin flip between shutting down the opposition and melting down—but leaning on his cut fastball even more as part of his cutter-and-curve package led to solid peripherals. Most interesting of all is that for a pitcher who was a LOOGY in 2015, he was barely even *LOOGish* in 2016. He split his innings and batters faced equally between lefties and righties, faring admirably against both of them in terms of strikeout and walk rates. He's likely not a star, but if you're looking for a season of perfectly acceptable southpaw relief pitching, X gon' give it to ya.

Alex Cobb   RHP

Born: 10/7/87   Age: 29   Bats: R   Throws: R   Height: 6'3"   Weight: 205   Entered Pro Ball: Round 4, 2006 Draft (#109 overall)

YEAR	TEAM	LVL	AGE	W	L	SV	G	GS	IP	H	HR	BB/9	K/9	K	GB%	BABIP	WHIP	ERA	FIP	DRA	VORP	WARP	cFIP	MPH
2014	TBA	MLB	26	10	9	0	27	27	166¹	142	11	2.5	8.1	149	56%	.282	1.14	2.87	3.26	3.11	31.9	3.5	88	94.0
2016	DUR	AAA	28	0	1	0	4	4	15	24	3	3.0	6.0	10	44%	.389	1.93	6.60	5.63	4.73	1.0	0.1	112	
2016	TBA	MLB	28	1	2	0	5	5	22	32	5	2.9	6.5	16	52%	.355	1.77	8.59	5.56	4.99	0.9	0.1	107	92.5
2017	TBA	MLB	29	8	8	0	23	23	121	119	14	3.3	7.9	107	52%	.297	1.35	3.95	4.11	4.48	10.4	1.1	100	
2018	TBA	MLB	30	9	10	0	29	29	182¹	174	21	3.8	8.3	169	52%	.297	1.38	3.95	4.15	4.44	17.7	1.8	102	

Breakout: 22%   Improve: 40%   Collapse: 26%   Attrition: 12%   MLB: 91%   *Comparables: Wade Miley, Edinson Volquez, Gavin Floyd*

For almost 24 months, between the last two even Septembers, Cobb didn't pitch in a big league game. Instead he worked diligently to recover from Tommy John surgery, reportedly wearing the same rank t-shirt for good luck during each agonizing outing. His first game back should have been glorious, just for being able to stand atop a mound and face MLB hitters. Instead, he was gifted with the monstrous Blue Jays lineup, and things just kind of got worse from there. No, he didn't reinjure his UCL, just the retinas of Rays fans hoping to see their ace return to form. Cobb's velocity was down almost two miles per hour, barely squeaking over 90 mph. His vaunted splitter—a pitch he could rely on in the past to get grounders 60 percent of the time—now just looks like a slightly-slower version of his sinker. It's a long layoff and a short sample, but there's also enough here to worry we may not see that same pitcher again.

Alex Colome   RHP

Born: 12/31/88 Age: 28   Bats: R   Throws: R   Height: 6'2"   Weight: 220 Entered Pro Ball: International Free Agent, 2007

YEAR	TEAM	LVL	AGE	W	L	SV	G	GS	IP	H	HR	BB/9	K/9	K	GB%	BABIP	WHIP	ERA	FIP	DRA	VORP	WARP	cFIP	MPH
2014	PCH	A+	25	0	1	0	3	3	11	7	0	4.1	8.2	10	45%	.241	1.09	1.64	2.94	4.28	1.6	0.2	100	
2014	DUR	AAA	25	7	6	0	15	15	86	84	2	3.1	7.6	73	42%	.319	1.33	3.77	3.25	4.82	8.9	0.9	102	
2014	TBA	MLB	25	2	0	0	5	3	23²	19	1	3.8	4.9	13	40%	.247	1.23	2.66	3.88	5.83	-2.8	-0.3	123	96.2
2015	TBA	MLB	26	8	5	0	43	13	109²	112	9	2.5	7.2	88	41%	.317	1.30	3.94	3.52	4.95	-0.1	0.0	104	96.6
2016	TBA	MLB	27	2	4	37	57	0	56²	43	6	2.4	11.3	71	49%	.280	1.02	1.91	2.88	2.45	15.9	1.6	72	96.7
2017	TBA	MLB	28	3	3	30	54	0	57¹	49	6	3.1	9.5	60	49%	.290	1.21	3.17	3.59	3.81	7.5	0.8	81	
2018	TBA	MLB	29	2	1	15	32	0	33²	26	4	3.7	11.1	42	49%	.282	1.18	3.26	3.43	3.71	5.0	0.5	78	

Breakout: 18%   Improve: 44%   Collapse: 21%   Attrition: 29%   MLB: 90%   *Comparables: Joe Saunders, Wade LeBlanc, Adam Warren*

A vicious cutter is the quickest route to bullpen prominence these days for pitchers without triple-digit heat, and Colome is the latest to take it. Brad Boxberger's injury afforded the Santo Domingo native the opportunity to secure full-time closer duty and Colome rose to the occasion, almost immediately emerging as one of the very best door-slammers in baseball. His cutter, which averages less than 90 mph and comprises nearly half of his pitch mix, registered a whiff or a foul ball on nearly 75 percent of the swings taken against it—just one point below Kenley Jansen's, which comes in five miles-per-hour harder. Beyond the usual caveats about reliever volatility there's no reason to expect anything less from Colome in 2017.

Jacob Faria   RHP

Born: 7/30/93 Age: 23   Bats: R   Throws: R   Height: 6'4"   Weight: 200 Entered Pro Ball: Round 10, 2011 Draft (#330 overall)

YEAR	TEAM	LVL	AGE	W	L	SV	G	GS	IP	H	HR	BB/9	K/9	K	GB%	BABIP	WHIP	ERA	FIP	DRA	VORP	WARP	cFIP	MPH
2014	BGR	A	20	7	9	0	23	23	119²	113	9	2.4	8.0	107	44%	.300	1.21	3.46	3.55	3.51	25.7	2.7	92	
2015	PCH	A+	21	10	1	0	12	10	74¹	51	1	2.7	7.6	63	40%	.253	0.98	1.33	2.53	2.74	18.8	2.0	90	
2015	MNT	AA	21	7	3	0	13	13	75¹	52	5	3.6	11.5	96	33%	.278	1.09	2.51	2.85	1.72	28.2	3.1	74	
2016	MNT	AA	22	1	6	0	14	14	83¹	64	5	3.9	10.0	93	42%	.282	1.20	4.21	3.20	2.17	27.1	2.9	83	
2016	DUR	AAA	22	4	4	0	13	13	67²	46	7	4.3	8.5	64	40%	.227	1.15	3.72	4.08	4.93	3.1	0.3	105	
2017	TBA	MLB	23	2	2	0	32	3	46	41	5	4.2	8.2	42	58%	.283	1.34	4.28	4.31	4.75	1.6	0.2	100	
2018	TBA	MLB	24	5	3	0	65	5	94²	74	11	6.2	11.4	119	58%	.284	1.47	4.20	4.38	4.73	4.4	0.5	106	

Breakout: 11%   Improve: 21%   Collapse: 21%   Attrition: 32%   MLB: 51%   *Comparables: Jake Odorizzi, Robert Stephenson, Neil Ramirez*

Perhaps the most big-league-ready arm in Tampa Bay's system, Faria will likely make his debut in 2017. He works with a mid-90s fastball, an effective sinking change and a 12-6 curve that flashes average often enough for evaluators to project him as a potential mid-rotation contributor. There are warts in the profile, though: he often spikes his curve and his upright, mechanical delivery can fall out of alignment, inhibiting his inability to pitch to the lower part of the strike zone. There's a lot to like here, but he has a bit more developmental work ahead than your typical upper minors Tampa Bay arm.

Danny Farquhar   RHP

Born: 2/17/87 Age: 30   Bats: R   Throws: R   Height: 5'9"   Weight: 185 Entered Pro Ball: Round 10, 2008 Draft (#309 overall)

YEAR	TEAM	LVL	AGE	W	L	SV	G	GS	IP	H	HR	BB/9	K/9	K	GB%	BABIP	WHIP	ERA	FIP	DRA	VORP	WARP	cFIP	MPH
2014	SEA	MLB	27	3	1	1	66	0	71	58	5	2.8	10.3	81	45%	.298	1.13	2.66	2.89	3.23	9.9	1.1	89	95.1
2015	TAC	AAA	28	1	1	3	27	1	38	40	3	2.4	9.7	41	38%	.359	1.32	3.08	3.26	2.41	10.8	1.1	86	
2015	SEA	MLB	28	1	8	1	43	0	51	53	9	3.0	8.5	48	40%	.306	1.37	5.12	4.58	4.38	1.9	0.2	106	95.2
2016	DUR	AAA	29	4	2	2	32	0	38	33	2	2.1	5.7	24	48%	.270	1.11	3.32	3.38	6.48	-6.4	-0.7	107	
2016	TBA	MLB	29	1	0	0	35	0	35¹	33	8	3.8	11.7	46	41%	.294	1.36	3.06	5.06	3.56	5.5	0.6	91	94.7
2017	TBA	MLB	30	3	2	0	49	0	52	49	6	3.5	8.9	51	46%	.296	1.34	3.98	3.98	4.49	2.8	0.3	100	
2018	TBA	MLB	31	3	1	0	50	0	53	49	6	4.0	9.5	56	46%	.300	1.36	3.79	3.99	4.30	4.4	0.5	95	

Breakout: 27%   Improve: 49%   Collapse: 16%   Attrition: 22%   MLB: 81%   *Comparables: Jose Veras, Jason Motte, Matt Lindstrom*

This past year was a season of change for this former Mariners' setup man. First to Tampa, then to Durham. After rinsing and repeating in June Farquhar finally had success in his third run, which lasted through the end of the season—reemerging with a vengeance and commanded a role as one of the Rays' most effective setup men. Why, you ask? Farquhar's changeup has almost always been a swing-and-miss pitch against left-handed hitters, so in 2016 he just started throwing it more often, to no small success. He nearly doubled its usage against lefties, and it didn't get any less menacing with increased frequency. He also started throwing it to right-handed hitters—something he'd barely done in the past—and it got the job done there, too. Yes, Lord Farquhar is still liege to a throng of homers, but his late-season renaissance means that he could have a second reign in the late innings, provided that the more things change the more that particular pitch stays the same.

Eddie Gamboa   RHP

Born: 12/21/84   Age: 32   Bats: R   Throws: R   Height: 6'1"   Weight: 215   Entered Pro Ball: Round 21, 2008 Draft (#626 overall)

YEAR	TEAM	LVL	AGE	W	L	SV	G	GS	IP	H	HR	BB/9	K/9	K	GB%	BABIP	WHIP	ERA	FIP	DRA	VORP	WARP	cFIP	MPH
2014	NOR	AAA	29	4	5	0	14	12	77²	70	7	3.2	8.6	74	44%	.289	1.26	4.06	3.90	3.35	20.4	2.0	92	
2014	BOW	AA	29	1	2	0	5	5	31	19	1	5.2	8.7	30	31%	.220	1.19	3.19	3.68	6.42	-4.1	-0.4	112	
2015	NOR	AAA	30	8	11	0	26	19	113¹	94	6	6.7	6.3	79	43%	.267	1.57	4.61	4.91	12.08	-86.4	-8.8	141	
2016	DUR	AAA	31	6	4	0	27	12	94	65	0	3.7	8.5	89	46%	.264	1.11	2.68	2.65	3.00	22.8	2.4	96	
2016	TBA	MLB	31	0	2	0	7	0	13¹	9	1	5.4	7.4	11	49%	.235	1.27	1.35	4.23	4.30	1.0	0.1	106	89.4
2017	TBA	MLB	32	2	2	0	28	3	41	38	4	4.8	7.4	34	56%	.284	1.44	4.57	4.54	5.01	0.3	0.0	100	
2018	TBA	MLB	33	4	3	0	60	6	91¹	78	13	6.4	9.3	95	56%	.272	1.56	4.99	5.19	5.62	-4.0	-0.4	130	

Breakout: 9%   Improve: 10%   Collapse: 8%   Attrition: 17%   MLB: 20%   Comparables: Angel Castro, Matt Fox, Willie Collazo

The Rays have been collecting knuckleball pitchers—or random former Rays who perhaps can learn to throw a knuckler—since hiring Charlie Haeger to be a minor-league coordinator. While the 31-year-old Gamboa doesn't have the Tampa Bay bona fides of knuckleball converts Dan Johnson or Andy Sonnanstine, he did get the opportunity to finally ply his trade in the majors last season. After the Orioles called him up but never let him into a game during a two-day stint with the big club in April 2015 a heart-warming video of his call-up made the rounds, making him as much a fan favorite as any returning veteran. Though he scattered just a handful of runs during his debut, it will take improvement on Gamboa's nearly even dispersement of strikeouts and walks to keep him collecting a big-league per diem. Until he can tame his dancer he'll flit between Triple-A and the bigs, and between starting and relieving, in a manner befitting his primary offering.

Taylor Guerrieri   RHP

Born: 12/1/92   Age: 24   Bats: R   Throws: R   Height: 6'3"   Weight: 195   Entered Pro Ball: Round 1, 2011 Draft (#24 overall)

YEAR	TEAM	LVL	AGE	W	L	SV	G	GS	IP	H	HR	BB/9	K/9	K	GB%	BABIP	WHIP	ERA	FIP	DRA	VORP	WARP	cFIP	MPH
2015	PCH	A+	22	2	2	0	12	10	42	37	0	2.4	9.4	44	63%	.322	1.14	2.14	2.00	2.28	12.8	1.4	82	
2015	MNT	AA	22	3	1	0	8	8	36	28	2	2.0	7.0	28	67%	.241	1.00	1.50	3.39	2.71	9.5	1.0	82	
2016	MNT	AA	23	12	6	1	28	26	146	130	11	2.8	5.5	89	58%	.266	1.21	3.76	4.23	4.20	14.2	1.5	103	
2017	TBA	MLB	24	1	2	0	5	5	25	28	3	3.4	4.8	13	54%	.292	1.44	4.96	4.90	5.62	-1.0	-0.1	100	
2018	TBA	MLB	25	8	11	0	29	29	178²	169	25	4.9	8.2	162	54%	.287	1.49	4.79	4.98	5.37	1.6	0.2	126	

Breakout: 16%   Improve: 27%   Collapse: 12%   Attrition: 33%   MLB: 47%   Comparables: Edwin Escobar, Tyler Duffey, Simon Castro

Guerrieri's rise as a first-round draft pick and Top 101 pitcher bring to mind the Greek myth of Icarus, who flew too close to the sun and was destroyed for his hubris. It also brings to mind *Kid Icarus*, the old-school Nintendo game that was flashy and fun, until frustrations left the cartridge dusty. So goes the groundball specialist's career, lost in the middle levels and fading after a healthy but uninspiring season in Double-A. His visible drop in velocity 3.5 years removed from Tommy John surgery was his version of replaying the same levels over and over again, watching reflexes diminish and patterns of the Eggplant Wizard remain unlocked. There's still hope that he'll reach the final boss—in Guerrieri's case that means making the majors as a starter—but perhaps it's time to boot up a new game.

Brent Honeywell   RHP

Born: 3/31/95   Age: 22   Bats: R   Throws: R   Height: 6'2"   Weight: 180   Entered Pro Ball: Round 2, 2014 Draft (#72 overall)

YEAR	TEAM	LVL	AGE	W	L	SV	G	GS	IP	H	HR	BB/9	K/9	K	GB%	BABIP	WHIP	ERA	FIP	DRA	VORP	WARP	cFIP	MPH
2015	BGR	A	20	4	4	0	12	12	65	53	3	1.7	10.5	76	39%	.299	1.00	2.91	2.40	1.40	27.6	2.9	70	
2015	PCH	A+	20	5	2	0	12	12	65¹	57	2	2.1	7.3	53	49%	.291	1.10	3.44	2.72	2.63	17.7	1.9	87	
2016	PCH	A+	21	4	1	0	10	10	56	43	5	1.8	10.3	64	33%	.279	0.96	2.41	2.77	1.25	26.3	2.7	68	
2016	MNT	AA	21	3	2	0	10	10	59¹	51	4	2.1	8.0	53	29%	.287	1.10	2.28	3.17	3.12	13.0	1.4	97	
2017	TBA	MLB	22	5	6	0	18	18	92	96	14	3.3	7.6	77	60%	.297	1.41	4.61	4.67	5.15	3.3	0.3	122	
2018	TBA	MLB	23	9	10	0	29	29	181²	158	26	4.5	10.2	206	60%	.287	1.37	4.17	4.36	4.66	13.8	1.4	108	

Breakout: 13%   Improve: 27%   Collapse: 2%   Attrition: 18%   MLB: 35%   Comparables: Trevor May, Rafael Montero, Derek Holland

Part Ginny Baker from *Pitch* and part Kenny Powers from *Eastbound and Down*, the Rays' mercurial pitching prospect is even more fantastical than your average prospect. Like Baker his signature offering is a plus screwball—a pitch that's rarer than a Shiny Articuno and capable of ripping up left-handed hitters. Like Powers his on-field demeanor is, uh, let's go with "colorful." When on the bump, he displays enough self-confidence to make Tony Robbins blush. Comparing Honeywell to actual prospects rather than fictional hurlers and motivational speakers is tougher—there's no one quite like him on the come-up. His 2016 season was strong, tearing up High-A then holding his own in Montgomery before opening even more eyes in the AFL. With three plus pitches but no world-beater, there's a rare legitimate third-starter profile that's not just a hedge between the extreme outcomes of top-of-the-rotation starter or high-leverage reliever.

Chih-Wei Hu   RHP

Born: 11/4/93   Age: 23   Bats: R   Throws: R   Height: 6'1"   Weight: 230   Entered Pro Ball: International Free Agent, 2012

YEAR	TEAM	LVL	AGE	W	L	SV	G	GS	IP	H	HR	BB/9	K/9	K	GB%	BABIP	WHIP	ERA	FIP	DRA	VORP	WARP	cFIP	MPH
2014	CDR	A	20	7	2	0	10	9	55	40	0	2.1	7.9	48	47%	.260	0.96	2.29	2.50	3.62	10.9	1.1	97	
2015	FTM	A+	21	5	3	0	15	15	84²	79	5	2.0	7.8	73	40%	.303	1.16	2.44	2.99	2.73	22.0	2.4	86	
2015	PCH	A+	21	0	3	1	5	4	18¹	23	1	3.9	9.8	20	55%	.407	1.69	7.36	3.00	2.68	4.9	0.5	86	
2016	MNT	AA	22	7	8	0	24	24	142²	128	7	2.3	6.8	107	44%	.283	1.15	2.59	3.28	3.63	23.2	2.5	95	
2017	TBA	MLB	23	6	8	0	21	21	113¹	123	17	3.2	6.2	78	58%	.296	1.45	4.82	4.89	5.37	1.3	0.1	128	
2018	TBA	MLB	24	6	7	0	19	19	109²	104	17	4.4	8.9	109	58%	.294	1.44	4.53	4.73	5.05	4.7	0.5	119	

Breakout: 13%   Improve: 19%   Collapse: 10%   Attrition: 25%   MLB: 35%   Comparables: Ryan Merritt, John Gant, Max Scherzer

Born in Taiwan, Hu signed as an international free agent with the Twins in August of 2012. Four years and a Kevin Jepsen trade later he finds himself on the cusp of the majors. Hu works with five pitches, including a low-to-mid-90s fastball with good movement and a 90-mph palmball that just plummets out of the zone when he throws it properly. Despite that baseline and a good command profile most evaluators see him as a back-end starter. That's because the palmball—his only pitch that projects as plus—comes and goes and his command and deception won't allow him to miss enough bats to be anything more than a no. 4 starter. Ceiling aside, Hu closed the 2016 season in Durham meaning we're getting a lot closer to some very unfortunate puns.

Kevin Jepsen   RHP

Born: 7/26/84   Age: 32   Bats: R   Throws: R   Height: 6'3"   Weight: 235   Entered Pro Ball: Round 2, 2002 Draft (#53 overall)

YEAR	TEAM	LVL	AGE	W	L	SV	G	GS	IP	H	HR	BB/9	K/9	K	GB%	BABIP	WHIP	ERA	FIP	DRA	VORP	WARP	cFIP	MPH
2014	ANA	MLB	29	0	2	2	74	0	65	45	4	3.2	10.4	75	50%	.263	1.05	2.63	2.81	2.68	13.0	1.4	84	98.2
2015	TBA	MLB	30	2	5	5	46	0	41²	34	4	4.3	7.3	34	50%	.254	1.30	2.81	4.16	4.50	1.0	0.1	104	97.4
2015	MIN	MLB	30	1	1	10	29	0	28	18	1	2.2	8.0	25	42%	.224	0.89	1.61	2.53	4.54	0.5	0.1	104	97.0
2016	MIN	MLB	31	2	5	7	33	0	30²	42	7	3.5	6.5	22	31%	.350	1.76	6.16	5.81	6.82	-6.3	-0.7	133	96.4
2016	TBA	MLB	31	0	1	0	25	0	19	20	5	4.3	6.2	13	33%	.268	1.53	5.68	6.58	6.73	-3.7	-0.4	135	95.0
2017	*TBA*	*MLB*	*32*	*2*	*1*	*4*	*45*	*0*	*47*	*45*	*7*	*3.8*	*8.4*	*44*	*43%*	*.290*	*1.38*	*4.52*	*4.60*	*5.12*	*-0.3*	*0.0*	*118*	
2018	*TBA*	*MLB*	*33*	*2*	*1*	*5*	*50*	*0*	*43²*	*41*	*7*	*3.6*	*8.7*	*42*	*43%*	*.288*	*1.35*	*4.42*	*4.63*	*5.01*	*0.2*	*0.0*	*114*	

Breakout: 21%   Improve: 55%   Collapse: 23%   Attrition: 13%   MLB: 87%   Comparables: *Will Ohman, Ramon Ramirez, Aaron Heilman*

Losing command doesn't always mean gaudy walk rates. Sometimes a lack of precision can manifest in a far more sinister way. After spending years working down in the zone, eliciting grounders and limiting balls in the air, Jepsen left his bread-and-butter four-seamer up in the zone too often during 2016. That correlated with one of the worst seasons of any full-time reliever and a mid-season DFA and release. While the Rays moved to pick up the pieces after his Twins career shattered to bits, he's no longer the pitcher he once was, or even the pitcher he was before that. It is possible he could still be of some use against righties. It is also possible he's toast.

Jake Odorizzi   RHP

Born: 3/27/90   Age: 27   Bats: R   Throws: R   Height: 6'2"   Weight: 190   Entered Pro Ball: Round 1, 2008 Draft (#32 overall)

YEAR	TEAM	LVL	AGE	W	L	SV	G	GS	IP	H	HR	BB/9	K/9	K	GB%	BABIP	WHIP	ERA	FIP	DRA	VORP	WARP	cFIP	MPH
2014	TBA	MLB	24	11	13	0	31	31	168	156	20	3.2	9.3	174	32%	.295	1.28	4.12	3.78	5.18	-6.3	-0.7	107	92.8
2015	TBA	MLB	25	9	9	0	28	28	169¹	149	18	2.4	8.0	150	40%	.271	1.15	3.35	3.58	4.03	19.7	2.1	96	93.6
2016	TBA	MLB	26	10	6	0	33	33	187²	170	29	2.6	8.0	166	38%	.271	1.19	3.69	4.27	4.04	27.5	2.8	103	94.1
2017	*TBA*	*MLB*	*27*	*12*	*11*	*0*	*31*	*31*	*186*	*168*	*26*	*3.0*	*9.0*	*186*	*39%*	*.284*	*1.22*	*3.91*	*4.08*	*4.51*	*15.3*	*1.6*	*100*	
2018	*TBA*	*MLB*	*28*	*11*	*11*	*0*	*31*	*31*	*194*	*168*	*29*	*3.4*	*10.2*	*221*	*39%*	*.285*	*1.24*	*3.84*	*4.04*	*4.38*	*21.9*	*2.3*	*100*	

Breakout: 15%   Improve: 40%   Collapse: 23%   Attrition: 10%   MLB: 84%   Comparables: *Joe Blanton, Homer Bailey, Alex Cobb*

Right-handed starters who can hold left-handed batters to a .210 True Average are a rarity. The three who did it in 2016 were the AL Cy Young Award winner, the runner-up and Odorizzi, who didn't get a vote. What separates Rick Porcello and Justin Verlander from their less-decorated colleague is a weapon to neutralize fellow righties. While Odorizzi learned a devastating split-fingered change-up from teammate Alex Cobb, he's never picked up a consistent, quality breaking ball, instead toying with a curve and slider—both of which ranked bottom five in whiffs per swing last year. Scouts often say that by their 20s pitchers either have feel for spin or they don't, and Odorizzi may not. That's okay: He's sustained mid-rotation form for two years nonetheless. But if it comes late you need only to look back four sentences to see the sort of company he might keep.

Erasmo Ramirez   RHP

Born: 5/2/90   Age: 27   Bats: R   Throws: R   Height: 5'11"   Weight: 200   Entered Pro Ball: International Free Agent, 2007

YEAR	TEAM	LVL	AGE	W	L	SV	G	GS	IP	H	HR	BB/9	K/9	K	GB%	BABIP	WHIP	ERA	FIP	DRA	VORP	WARP	cFIP	MPH
2014	TAC	AAA	24	6	5	0	15	14	86¹	92	8	1.4	7.0	67	41%	.313	1.22	3.65	3.94	3.03	26.1	2.6	96	
2014	SEA	MLB	24	1	6	0	17	14	75¹	82	13	4.1	7.2	60	40%	.307	1.54	5.26	5.40	5.86	-8.9	-1.0	118	94.0
2015	TBA	MLB	25	11	6	0	34	27	163¹	145	16	2.2	6.9	126	49%	.272	1.13	3.75	3.74	3.81	22.6	2.4	95	94.1
2016	TBA	MLB	26	7	11	2	64	1	90²	90	14	2.6	6.3	63	55%	.280	1.28	3.77	4.72	4.87	1.3	0.1	101	94.3
2017	*TBA*	*MLB*	*27*	*3*	*2*	*0*	*49*	*0*	*52*	*47*	*6*	*3.0*	*8.1*	*47*	*55%*	*.283*	*1.22*	*3.79*	*3.96*	*4.35*	*3.7*	*0.4*	*99*	
2018	*TBA*	*MLB*	*28*	*3*	*1*	*0*	*59*	*0*	*62¹*	*53*	*7*	*3.3*	*9.3*	*65*	*55%*	*.279*	*1.21*	*3.65*	*3.82*	*4.15*	*6.2*	*0.6*	*91*	

Breakout: 17%   Improve: 44%   Collapse: 21%   Attrition: 8%   MLB: 84%   Comparables: *Joe Blanton, Wade Davis, Homer Bailey*

Erasmus the humanist scholar advocated a "Via Media" or "middle road" philosophy; his psuedo-namesake used the past season to follow the middle road between two roles: starter and reliever. Despite a surprisingly solid starting season the previous year he was dumped from the rotation thanks to Tampa's talent surplus, and found the second-most relief innings in baseball despite being the definition of pedestrian. In more of a statement about the Rays' bullpen than about Ramirez's skill, many of these appearances were in moderate- to high-leverage situations, and in about a quarter of them he recorded a "meltdown"—meaning he lowered the Rays' chances of winning the game by five percent or more according to Win Probability Added. So goes Erasmo, whose personal middle road seems to smack of swingman mediocrity, interesting usage aside.

Drew Smyly   LHP

Born: 6/13/89   Age: 28   Bats: L   Throws: L   Height: 6'3"   Weight: 190   Entered Pro Ball: Round 2, 2010 Draft (#68 overall)

YEAR	TEAM	LVL	AGE	W	L	SV	G	GS	IP	H	HR	BB/9	K/9	K	GB%	BABIP	WHIP	ERA	FIP	DRA	VORP	WARP	cFIP	MPH
2014	DET	MLB	25	6	9	0	21	18	105¹	111	14	2.6	7.6	89	40%	.313	1.35	3.93	4.11	4.78	0.5	0.1	97	92.6
2014	TBA	MLB	25	3	1	0	7	7	47²	25	4	2.1	8.3	44	36%	.184	0.76	1.70	3.10	4.52	1.6	0.2	98	92.6
2015	DUR	AAA	26	0	2	0	3	3	10²	13	2	5.1	11	13	34%	.367	1.78	8.44	5.13	4.20	1.3	0.1	95	
2015	TBA	MLB	26	5	2	0	12	12	66²	58	11	2.7	10.4	77	39%	.283	1.17	3.11	3.88	3.00	15.4	1.7	81	92.8
2016	TBA	MLB	27	7	12	0	30	30	175¹	174	32	2.5	8.6	167	33%	.291	1.27	4.88	4.45	4.35	19.7	2.0	108	92.7
2017	TBA	MLB	28	10	10	0	29	29	165¹	155	26	2.7	9.4	172	54%	.293	1.24	3.98	4.15	4.57	12.5	1.3	100	
2018	TBA	MLB	29	9	10	0	28	28	169²	161	29	2.7	9.2	173	54%	.288	1.25	4.12	4.34	4.69	13.6	1.4	110	

Breakout: 26%   Improve: 59%   Collapse: 18%   Attrition: 13%   MLB: 87%   Comparables: Jordan Zimmermann, Ervin Santana, Wei-Yin Chen

There are two best possible results for a pitcher most of the time: strike a guy out or pop him up. Smyly is terrific at both of these things. Both his curveball and his molasses-slow changeup—an off-speed pitch a full 10 miles per hour slower than his heater—get regular swings and misses. And the tall lefty's infield fly rate of 16 percent was better than all but three starers last season. But Smyly is a pitcher of extremes, and to offset all the whiffs and squibs there are dingers and doubles aplenty. The southpaw had the third-lowest groundball rate among starters with over 100 innings, and the only two pitchers who gave up more air contact were the twin garbage fires of Jered Weaver and A.J. Griffin. Homers continue to be a problem for Smyly, and the play of extremes between those powerfully-hit balls and easy outs creates a pitcher decidedly in the middle ground: an effective no. 3 or no. 4 starter.

Blake Snell   LHP

Born: 12/4/92   Age: 24   Bats: L   Throws: L   Height: 6'4"   Weight: 180   Entered Pro Ball: Round 1, 2011 Draft (#52 overall)

YEAR	TEAM	LVL	AGE	W	L	SV	G	GS	IP	H	HR	BB/9	K/9	K	GB%	BABIP	WHIP	ERA	FIP	DRA	VORP	WARP	cFIP	MPH
2014	BGR	A	21	3	2	0	8	8	40¹	26	1	4.2	9.4	42	69%	.253	1.12	1.79	3.14	3.93	6.8	0.7	101	
2014	PCH	A+	21	5	6	0	16	16	75¹	69	1	4.4	9.2	77	54%	.325	1.41	3.94	3.19	4.48	9.4	0.9	101	
2015	PCH	A+	22	3	0	0	4	2	21	10	0	4.7	11.6	27	59%	.227	1.00	0.00	2.17	2.40	5.8	0.6	90	
2015	MNT	AA	22	6	2	0	12	12	68²	45	5	3.8	10.4	79	48%	.260	1.08	1.57	3.26	2.24	21.8	2.4	75	
2015	DUR	AAA	22	6	2	0	9	9	44¹	29	2	2.6	11.6	57	55%	.276	0.95	1.83	2.12	1.67	17.9	1.8	65	
2016	DUR	AAA	23	3	5	0	12	12	63	56	4	4.0	12.9	90	51%	.356	1.33	3.29	2.57	1.52	26.8	2.8	62	
2016	TBA	MLB	23	6	8	0	19	19	89	93	5	5.2	9.9	98	39%	.356	1.62	3.54	3.35	4.58	7.7	0.8	105	96.2
2017	TBA	MLB	24	8	7	0	23	23	121	109	13	4.5	9.9	134	45%	.300	1.41	3.82	3.98	4.41	11.4	1.2	100	
2018	TBA	MLB	25	10	9	0	30	30	188²	149	19	5.3	12.1	253	45%	.305	1.38	3.47	3.64	3.96	26.5	2.7	86	

Breakout: 25%   Improve: 54%   Collapse: 16%   Attrition: 20%   MLB: 83%   Comparables: Dana Eveland, Will Smith, Tyler Skaggs

A son of two parents with strong German heritage might occasionally have had *macht schnell* barked at him, which translates to "hurry up" but more often than not would mean "walk faster." *Blake Snell* makes it easy to remember this phrase even without the near rhyme—after all, no starting pitcher in baseball was likely to walk opposing hitters faster than he did last season. The Rays' highly-touted young southpaw's rookie season was peppered with short outings and balls that didn't catch the plate: he led all big-league starters in walks per nine, offering up one free pass for every five outs he recorded. The vaunted 94 mph left-side four-seamer that profiled as both a swing-and-miss offering and a pitch that'd elicit weak contact didn't do much of either, but his slider was devastating and induced a whiff almost half the time hitters swung at it. While his ERA and FIP looked worthy of his top-25 prospect status, DRA hints that he could see a spike in runs allowed this coming year without corralling his wicked stuff. But if he can start throwing more strikes he and the Rays might become familiar with a very different German phrase: the *schadenfreude* they'll feel towards opposing American League hitters.

Chase Whitley   RHP

Born: 6/14/89   Age: 28   Bats: R   Throws: R   Height: 6'3"   Weight: 215   Entered Pro Ball: Round 15, 2010 Draft (#475 overall)

YEAR	TEAM	LVL	AGE	W	L	SV	G	GS	IP	H	HR	BB/9	K/9	K	GB%	BABIP	WHIP	ERA	FIP	DRA	VORP	WARP	cFIP	MPH
2014	SWB	AAA	25	3	2	0	10	6	31¹	22	0	2.3	10.6	37	56%	.286	0.96	2.01	1.76	1.65	13.9	1.4	68	
2014	NYA	MLB	25	4	3	0	24	12	75²	94	10	2.1	7.1	60	46%	.353	1.48	5.23	4.16	4.14	5.2	0.6	104	93.1
2015	SWB	AAA	26	2	0	0	3	3	17	13	0	3.2	6.9	13	35%	.265	1.12	2.12	2.69	3.51	3.4	0.3	98	
2015	NYA	MLB	26	1	2	0	4	4	19¹	20	3	2.3	7.4	16	51%	.293	1.29	4.19	4.55	4.26	1.8	0.2	100	91.5
2016	MNT	AA	27	2	1	0	6	6	27²	17	3	2.6	7.2	22	28%	.194	0.90	2.93	4.22	4.44	2.0	0.2	112	
2016	TBA	MLB	27	0	0	0	5	1	14¹	13	2	1.9	9.4	15	42%	.268	1.12	2.51	3.46	3.73	2.1	0.2	96	92.7
2017	TBA	MLB	28	1	1	0	2	2	10	10	1	3.1	7.3	8	51%	.294	1.36	4.32	3.77	4.95	0.3	0.0	100	
2018	TBA	MLB	29	9	10	0	30	30	192¹	167	25	3.8	9.3	199	51%	.281	1.29	4.02	4.21	4.57	15.2	1.6	105	

Breakout: 23%   Improve: 39%   Collapse: 13%   Attrition: 27%   MLB: 74%   Comparables: Phil Coke, Troy Patton, Dustin Nippert

Here's an incredibly banal trivia question: Who started the final game of last season for the Rays? Here's an incredibly banal answer: it was the unassuming Whitley, who made his return from Tommy John surgery. A cursory look at his 14-inning return at the back end of the season may have you thinking it was a great comeback, but that's just your mind and the stats playing tricks on you. The 2.51 ERA is shiny but three unearned runs snuck into his season, which makes his ERA a little shinier than it should be. The velocity and stuff don't appear to have changed much from where he was before the surgery, when he was a guy with fifth-starter potential thanks to his signature offering, a sweet changeup that can get swings and misses. But with both his fastball and durability still falling into iffy territory, Whitley is most likely an incredibly banal swingman.

LINEOUTS

Hitters

NAME	POS	TEAM	LVL	AGE	PA	R	2B	3B	HR	RBI	BB	K	SB	CS	AVG/OBP/SLG	TAv	VORP	BABIP	BRR	FRAA	WARP
J.P. Arencibia	C	LEH	AAA	30	48	3	2	0	1	2	0	11	0	0	.167/.167/.271	.123	-5.0	.194	0.0	C(10): 0.4	-0.5
	C	DUR	AAA	30	324	34	14	0	15	47	9	93	1	1	.252/.284/.443	.255	5.2	.312	-2.2	C(42): 0.3 • 1B(11): -0.6	0.5
Chris Betts	C	HUD	A-	19	90	2	4	0	0	7	17	23	0	0	.157/.333/.214	.218	0.0	.229	0.0		0.0
Ryan Boldt	OF	HUD	A-	21	186	17	5	1	1	15	10	24	8	9	.218/.280/.276	.225	-5.7	.247	-3.0	CF(14): -1.8 • LF(13): -0.3	-0.9
Lucius Fox	OF	AUG	A	18	331	46	6	4	2	16	37	76	25	7	.207/.305/.277	.252	12.5	.273	4.4	SS(61): -2.8	1.1
Jake Fraley	OF	HUD	A-	21	239	34	9	7	1	18	26	34	33	9	.238/.339/.344	.285	13.6	.279	1.2	CF(35): -3.4 • LF(15): 0.9	1.2
Jonah Heim	C	FRD	A+	21	329	30	14	1	7	30	33	51	2	0	.216/.300/.344	.229	3.0	.239	0.6	C(72): -2.0	0.1
	C	PCH	A+	21	47	4	1	0	1	3	2	11	0	0	.222/.255/.311	.211	-0.7	.273	-0.2	C(12): 0.2	0.0
Patrick Leonard	3B	DUR	AAA	23	145	10	5	1	0	6	13	54	0	1	.198/.276/.252	.195	-7.0	.338	0.0	1B(14): -1.0 • 3B(10): 0.7	-0.8
	3B	MNT	AA	23	307	48	24	0	9	47	20	82	8	1	.286/.345/.471	.304	25.5	.370	3.6	3B(56): -3.5 • LF(3): -0.2	2.6
Justin O'Conner	C	MNT	AA	24	26	2	0	0	1	3	0	9	0	0	.160/.154/.280	.165	-1.3	.188	0.1	C(8): -0.4	-0.2
Garrett Whitley	OF	HUD	A-	19	292	38	12	7	1	31	30	75	21	5	.266/.356/.379	.293	14.9	.372	-1.7	LF(31): 2.8 • CF(23): -0.1	1.9
Justin Williams	OF	PCH	A+	20	203	23	11	0	4	31	6	26	0	1	.330/.350/.448	.299	8.5	.361	-3.3	RF(43): 2.5	1.1
	OF	MNT	AA	20	155	20	7	2	6	28	5	30	0	1	.250/.277/.446	.262	3.7	.274	0.8	RF(34): -1.7	0.2

The Rays used four catchers last season, none of whom performed much better than replacement-level, and they were never tempted to bring **J.P. Arencibia** back to the majors. ❖ The track record of pro catchers who miss time with Tommy John surgery isn't great, but at least **Chris Betts** got his out of the way early—costing him his first pro season. Though he finally debuted in 2016, we're still waiting for the power that made him a second-round pick to follow suit. ❖ **Ryan Boldt**'s inclusion in this book is a lesson in making a good first impression. He was a rad prep prospect who kinda sucked at Nebraska, then kinda sucked at Low-A after being drafted by the Rays in the second round last year. ❖ All **Ryan Brett** needed last season was to stay healthy and prove that his hot hitting in the minors wasn't a mirage. Instead the diminutive second baseman missed the entire year with Tommy John surgery. ❖ Toolsy **Lucius Fox** needs more offensive verve in order to break into the upper echelon of prospects, and no the irony is not lost that he needs to become more of a *bat*man. ❖ **Jake Fraley** sprinted from a College World Series berth with the LSU Tigers all the way to the Hudson Valley Renegades last summer, finishing his season as the Rays' minor-league baserunner of the year with 33 steals and seven triples in just 55 games. ❖ Offensive skills tend to develop later for catchers than players at other positions. At this rate, **Jonah Heim**'s bat will be ready to contribute in the majors by the time the 2035 Annual rolls around. ❖ **Patrick Leonard** started multiple games at five different positions—third base, first base and all three outfield spots—in the minors last season. Given his offensive struggles during his call-up to Durham, he's more likely to be the next Allan Dykstra than the next Ben Zobrist. ❖ Former first-rounder **Justin O'Conner** barely played in 2016, and still hasn't been able to hit his way out of Montgomery. Given his tremendous arm and smarts—not to mention his propensity for injury—perhaps he's miscast as a catcher when he so closely resembles a pitcher. ❖ In his first professional stateside season, Venezuelan catcher **Rene Pinto** unleashed a homer barrage on the Appy League in his limited time at the level. At 19 he has a cannon arm, solid offensive tools and enough time to make us all look foolish, one way or another. ❖ Youthful outfield prospect **Garrett Whitley** is so far away from the majors that Elon Musk is building a rocket to reach him. If he keeps his athleticism and approach while improving his hit tool in High-A this year, the rocket metaphor will apply in a different, more positive way. ❖ Possessed of an everyman name and an all-too-common offensive profile, good luck remembering young **Justin Williams**, whose corner outfield bat hasn't translated his raw power into game action yet and has an extreme aversion to free passes.

Pitchers

NAME	TEAM	LVL	AGE	W	L	SV	G	GS	IP	H	HR	BB/9	K/9	K	GB%	BABIP	WHIP	ERA	FIP	DRA	VORP	WARP	cFIP	MPH
Jose Alvarado	BGR	A	21	2	0	2	10	0	24²	12	0	6.2	12.4	34	74%	.245	1.18	1.46	2.91	3.68	2.7	0.3	103	
	PCH	A+	21	2	1	0	27	0	46	38	1	7.4	10.0	51	57%	.306	1.65	3.91	3.80	7.78	-13.8	-1.4	124	
Dana Eveland	DUR	AAA	32	1	0	0	20	1	29²	16	1	1.8	6.4	21	65%	.190	0.74	0.30	3.20	2.92	6.9	0.7	86	
	TBA	MLB	32	0	1	0	33	0	23	32	3	7.4	8.2	21	49%	.397	2.22	9.00	5.85	6.21	-3.2	-0.3	117	91.7
Dylan Floro	TBA	MLB	25	0	1	0	12	0	15	23	0	3.0	8.4	14	55%	.434	1.87	4.20	2.24	3.72	2.1	0.2	98	95.1
	DUR	AAA	25	1	2	7	32	0	50	53	6	1.6	7.2	40	56%	.313	1.24	2.88	3.73	3.96	5.5	0.6	91	
Kevin Gadea	CLN	A	21	3	0	1	10	6	50¹	41	4	2.0	12.9	72	47%	.327	1.03	2.15	2.54	0.94	22.2	2.4	63	
Ryan Garton	DUR	AAA	26	4	0	2	22	0	32	31	1	2.8	11.0	39	49%	.345	1.28	3.09	2.17	2.69	8.1	0.8	81	
	TBA	MLB	26	1	2	1	37	0	39¹	44	5	2.5	7.6	33	47%	.320	1.40	4.35	3.92	4.51	2.0	0.2	101	94.2
Justin Marks	DUR	AAA	28	7	11	0	25	23	140	125	14	3.4	8.2	127	44%	.287	1.27	3.86	3.88	2.62	42.1	4.3	93	
	TBA	MLB	28	0	0	0	4	0	9	7	1	9.0	6.0	6	41%	.231	1.78	1.00	6.22	6.23	-1.3	-0.1	123	92.1
Jayson McKinley	HUD	A-	22	0	0	7	11	0	22¹	9	1	1.2	11.7	29	50%	.250	0.54	1.21	1.66	1.83	7.5	0.8	67	
Austin Pruitt	DUR	AAA	26	8	11	0	28	28	162²	166	21	1.5	8.2	149	45%	.316	1.19	3.76	3.53	2.20	56.8	5.9	77	
Enny Romero	TBA	MLB	25	2	0	1	52	0	45²	42	7	5.5	9.9	50	38%	.294	1.53	5.91	4.75	4.81	0.8	0.1	112	98.8
Jaime Schultz	DUR	AAA	25	5	7	0	27	27	130²	113	12	4.7	11.2	163	43%	.327	1.39	3.58	3.45	4.26	15.7	1.6	88	
Joe Serrapica	HUD	A-	22	1	0	8	16	0	22¹	13	0	2.0	11.3	28	39%	.195	0.81	0.00	1.44	1.86	7.5	0.8	73	
Ryne Stanek	MNT	AA	24	2	6	2	18	11	78¹	64	6	4.0	10.5	91	53%	.307	1.26	3.79	3.41	2.97	17.8	1.9	78	
	DUR	AAA	24	2	4	1	16	0	24¹	22	3	4.8	8.1	22	47%	.284	1.44	5.92	4.81	6.37	-3.8	-0.4	105	
Hunter Wood	PCH	A+	22	3	3	0	11	9	63²	34	5	3.4	7.9	56	48%	.194	0.91	1.70	3.08	3.49	13.7	1.4	96	
	MNT	AA	22	6	2	0	10	9	49¹	36	5	3.6	8.9	49	25%	.250	1.14	3.28	3.93	4.16	5.0	0.5	106	

Having one of the best fastballs in the minors is great, but **Jose Alvarado** pairs it with poor secondaries and command, which is like having Learjet with beanbag chairs for seats and no wings. ❖ **Andrew Bellatti** made some waves for the Rays in 2015 as a middle reliever with loads of movement on both his plus slider and fastball, but unfortunately movement was the order of the day last season too, as he slid all the way down to Double-A and off the Rays' 40-man roster. ❖ It takes a special kind of player to pitch in 33 games despite giving up a run per inning. **Dana Eveland** is that type of special, as trips from Triple-A to the majors somehow caused his walk rate to spike as violently as Kerri Walsh. ❖ Rising middle reliever and groundball specialist **Dylan Floro** shares just one similarity with the Norwegian island fishing town of Florø: both are unremarkable. (No man is an island.) ❖ Right-hander **Austin Franklin** is off to a great start—he already seems to have two plus pitches—but there are plenty of places where things could go askew for the 2016 third rounder. ❖ A converted third baseman with zero experience above Low-A, **Kevin Gadea** caught the Rays' eye in the Rule 5 draft because he's a rare high-velocity arm with plus control. ❖ Clearwater native **Ryan Garton** was patient zero for Tampa's weighted-ball training and it seems to have worked—his velocity jumped back up after drooping below 90 miles per hour a few seasons back. Life imitates art; much like his velocity numbers, he'll be up-and-down between Durham and Tampa. ❖ Journeyman lefty **Justin Marks** captured rare glory when he threw a 130-pitch no-hitter for Durham last season. He'll likely have a chance to duplicate the feat next season, when he'll be pitching for his fifth different Triple-A ballclub. ❖ **Jayson McKinley** mounted an exciting debut with 29 strikeouts to just three walks in the New York-Penn League, but let's hope that the undrafted free agent hasn't already peaked. ❖ **Austin Pruitt** opened the 2016 season with two straight 11-strikeout, zero-walk starts in Triple-A and has been durable his entire pro career, but the diminutive right-hander still falls into the "and others" section of the Rays' depth chart. ❖ The top prospect in the Rays' system just three years ago, **Enny Romero** still hasn't been able to harness the power of his upper-90s fastball from the left side, and he allowed same-side hitters to get on base at a near 40 percent clip in 2016. ❖ Your deep bullpen sleeper for 2017 is…**Jamie Schultz**! He's had success as a starter in the upper minors thanks to his blistering strikeout rate, but the Rays' rotation depth and his own inability to avoid the free pass make middle (or late) relief a likely eventual destination. ❖ **Joe Serrapica**'s affiliated-ball career consists of 22.3 innings and zero runs allowed. The Fordham grad was named Rays Relief Pitcher of the Year, but still hasn't sizzled enough to be dubbed a prospect. ❖ For a few weeks in June, it looked like a move to the bullpen might spark **Ryne Stanek**'s development, but a shelling in the Futures Game and two rough months in Durham has gotten him even further away from his amateur glory. ❖ Pop-up starter prospect **Hunter Wood**'s parents really, really wanted you to know they like the outdoors, which probably means they consider Tropicana Field a special kind of hell. Don't we all.

TEXAS RANGERS

Essay by Robert O'Connell

Player comments by Cat Garcia and BP staff

I don't know anybody who dislikes Adrian Beltre. Admittedly we all curate the types of baseball fans we hang out with, but the entrenched third baseman of the Texas Rangers seems to be enjoyed by all and outright beloved by most. His appeal checks off all categories. You watch for expertise? Beltre has four Gold Gloves and a Hall of Fame plaque already in commission. For daily examples of grit and fortitude? Beltre has been injured, in one form or another, since he stubbed his toe kicking at the bars of his crib at two weeks old. For wild personal histories? The Dodgers signed Beltre when he was 15, a year before they were legally allowed to do so, and he's still at it at age 38.

It doesn't hurt that he is immensely fun to watch in a way that has nothing to do with back-story or statistical excellence, or even the drama of whatever game he's participating in at the moment. The Rangers more or less had the American League West sewn up by the time they hosted the Seattle Mariners on August 30, 2016, and their 8-7 win that night came on a walk-off Rougned Odor homer, but it was Beltre who shaped everything that came before, as it often is. In the third, Seattle's Guillermo Heredia hit the worst kind of chopper down the line, the sort that loses no speed for taking thigh-high hops, but Beltre dropped to one knee, snared it clean and made the throw to first in plenty of time. In the ninth, he busted out his signature move: charging in and barehanding a Dae-Ho Lee dribbler—though he didn't quite need to—before letting go of a side-armed sinker that crossed the diamond like a homing missile. That Odor's homer won the game instead of tying it also owed something to Beltre; he had just reached base by way of a leadoff single.

The point here is that even if you were unlucky enough to have never heard of Adrian Beltre before you watched a game he played in, you would understand exactly what he was all about by the end of it. He participates insistently; he announces his entire being every time he fields a grounder or takes a swing. He is a virtuoso—"the master at work," cooed Rangers announcer Tom Grieve after he robbed Heredia—but not a bloodless one. He moves urgently, as if he were not one of the greatest third basemen in the game's history but some hanger-on, and from time to time he'll arch his eyebrows and huff with relief after making a play everyone knew he would.

RANGERS PROSPECTUS
2016 W-L: 95-67, 1ST IN AL WEST

Pythag	.505	14th	DER	.708	8th
RS/G	4.72	7th	B-Age	28.5	14th
RA/G	4.67	21st	P-Age	28.9	25th
TAv	.258	18th	Salary	$158M	8th
BRR	-9.38	25th	M$/MW	$3.1M	21st
TAv-P	.258	12th	DL Days	1485	28th
FIP	4.54	27th	$ on DL	24%	27th

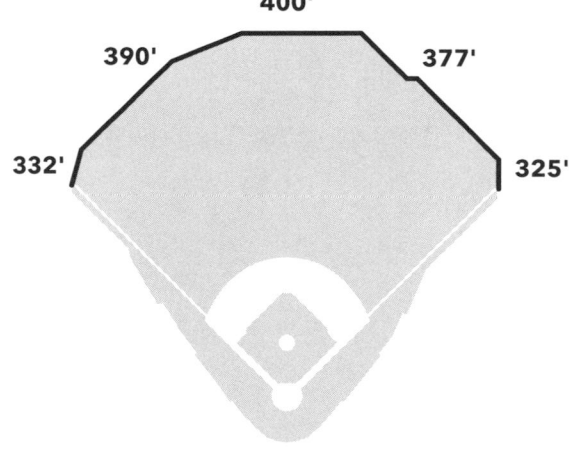

Outfield wall profile: **8'** to **14'**

Three-Year Park Factors

Runs	Runs/RH	Runs/LH	HR/RH	HR/LH
107	114	107	102	105

Top Hitter WARP	4.6	Adrian Beltre
Top Pitcher WARP	6.2	Cole Hamels
Top Prospect		Yohander Mendez

2016 Hit List Ranking

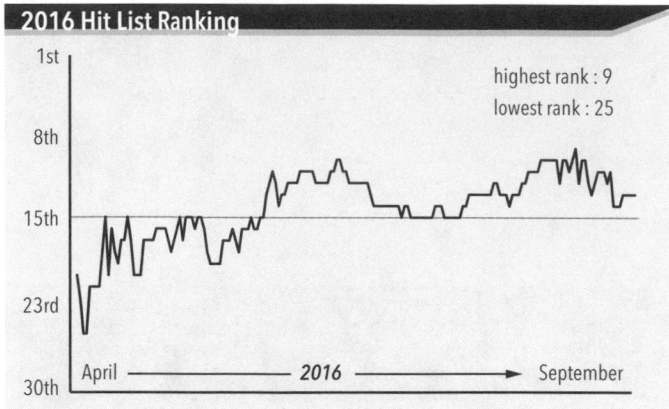

highest rank : 9
lowest rank : 25

April — 2016 → September

Committed Payroll (in millions)

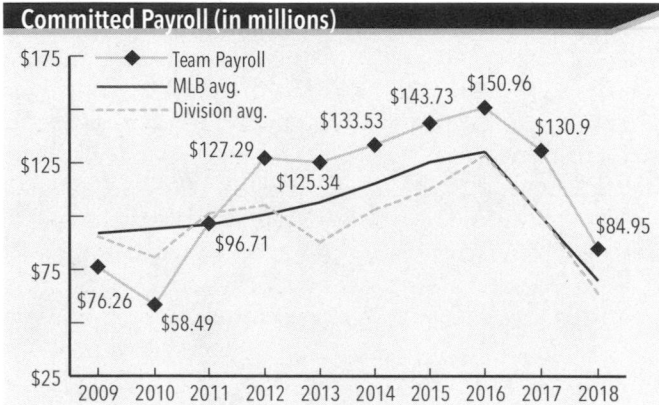

- Team Payroll
- MLB avg.
- Division avg.

$175
$125
$75
$25

$76.26
$58.49
$96.71
$127.29
$125.34
$133.53
$143.73
$150.96
$130.9
$84.95

2009 2010 2011 2012 2013 2014 2015 2016 2017 2018

Farm System Ranking

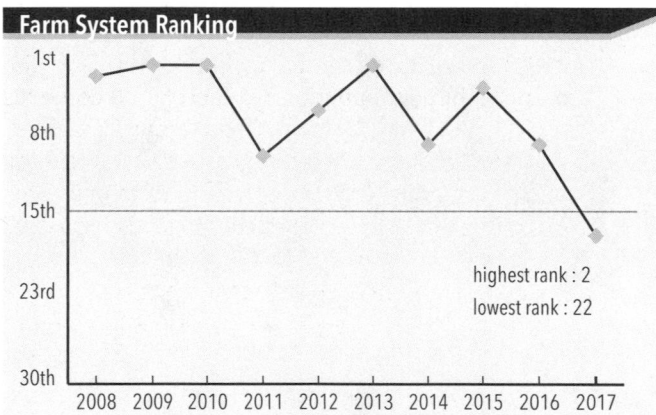

1st
8th
15th
23rd
30th

highest rank : 2
lowest rank : 22

2008 2009 2010 2011 2012 2013 2014 2015 2016 2017

Personnel

President, General Manager:
Jon Daniels

Assistant General Manager:
Mike Daly

Assistant General Manager:
Josh Boyd

Assistant General Manager:
Jayce Tingler

Manager:
Jeff Banister

So: baseball fans, as a rule, like Adrian Beltre. They perk up when an *MLB Tonight* anchor says, "And now, a Capital One Premier Play from Arlington…" and retweet videos of the homers he hits from one knee. They laugh when he gets all pissed at his teammates for touching his head. I would guess, though, that Rangers fans appreciate him even more than the rest, and not just out of loyalty or familiarity. The Rangers have been this decade's perpetual bridesmaids, a team that has turned over once or twice but managed to keep a consistent identity: talented, Achilles-heeled, built bravely but never quite fully, prone to very good summer months and very bad fall nights. On his own, Beltre is delightful. In Texas, on a team always shifting itself around and ending up at the same place, he is a necessity.

After a decade-long postseason drought coinciding with the transition from Pudge to Alex Rodriguez, the Rangers reached the 2010 World Series and lost to the San Francisco Giants in five games (even in their present diminished forms, if you put Tim Lincecum and Josh Hamilton on a diamond somewhere, Lincecum could still spot his splitter low and away, and Hamilton would still swing beautifully but five inches too high). The pathos of the team, though, was installed the next November, at the tail end of Beltre's first season in Texas, when David Freese and the St. Louis Cardinals came back from the edge of defeat to win Game 6 and walloped the Rangers in Game 7. Neftali Feliz couldn't get outs, Nelson Cruz couldn't make catches and Texas fell victim to either bad timing (twice they were one strike away) or inevitability (Cruz had a glove made of wet papier-mâché; Feliz was no sure thing himself).

That defeat became a template. Though Cruz, Feliz, Hamilton, C.J. Wilson and Ian Kinsler have given way over the years to Odor, Yu Darvish, Cole Hamels and Jonathan Lucroy, a house style of season-ending Texas losses remains. Darvish surrendered two earned runs over six and two-thirds innings of the 2012 Wild Card game, Joe Nathan gave up two more and the offense couldn't touch Baltimore's Joe Saunders. In a 2013 tie-breaker against Tampa Bay, the Rangers succumbed to what would have been the best postseason start of David Price's career, had it come in the official postseason. Their loss in the fifth game of the 2015 ALDS to Toronto, of course, was pure baseball cacophony: obscure rules, flung beers, errors and more errors. All of that set the stage for Jose Bautista's home-run-and-bat-toss combination that would win him a straight right to the cheekbone from Odor seven months later.

The 2016 Rangers fell a little more meekly than some of their forebears, swept by the Blue Jays in the division series, but in a much more significant way they carried on the tradition. Following the season, the old questions remained. The Rangers had talented up-and-comers like Nomar Mazara and Jurickson Profar joining the known-quantity vets. However, their ability to put a player ranging from intriguing to superb at most every spot on the diamond, and their solid record, covered up a miniscule run differential. They won 95 games; their Pythagorean win percentage says they should have won 82. They don't know, in other words, whether they were unlucky to lose a pair of close games in the division series or lucky to be there in the first place.

Entering 2017, the team is a Rorschach test. Elvis Andrus is due to either build on or slide back from a career year in 2016. Hamels might contend for a Cy Young or look suddenly like a 33-year-old who has thrown a ton of pitches, most recently in 100-degree Texas heat. Odor could hit 35 homers and put up a sub-.300 OBP. Darvish will be healthy or hurt; if it's the former, his space-time-shaking stuff will either find the strike zone or miss it. With general manager Jon Daniels at the helm—importer, over the years, of Cliff Lee, Prince Fielder, Hamels, Lucroy and Carlos Beltran—there's no assurance that the Rangers' roster at year end will even resemble today's, except in being just as hard to figure.

✦ ✦ ✦

In many ways, third base in Arlington is the exception, not the rule. If the players around him are inkblots, Beltre is a photograph of a cow grazing in a field or a subway train approaching a station; a vision containing crystal-clear certainty mixed into a pile of interpretation. However, even with his sustained performance over the past few seasons, Beltre may soon join this list of unknowns. He turns 39 shortly after Opening Day; he is nearing, if not reaching, the point where he will start to slip. It's remarkable that he hasn't already, given that the attributes that generally let older players hang on—smooth mechanics and flexible frames—are so absent in him. He looks like he's made of vacuum-packed stones, and he plays…well, like he's made of vacuum-packed stones. If ever someone was designed to start dropping limbs right on the damn field, it is the two-and-a-half-decade professional who wrenches his spine with every swing and unloads on every throw to first.

The magic of Beltre, though, is such that even his slowing down will captivate, whenever it comes. Unlike with most players, the version of him that sticks in the mind is not the apex, the 48 homers in 2004 with the Dodgers or the career turnaround campaign in Boston or the near-MVP second season in Texas. Rather, he seems even more himself, and more impressive, when he's scuffling. Here is the best Beltre: he is three for his last 30, his thumb hurts and he has just swung twice and pounded two pitches into his shinbone, hard. Maybe he's committed a rare error earlier in the game.

At this moment, Beltre—batting helmet tugged down low over his eyes—seems somehow to shrug off the usual process of playing professional baseball. It's as if he's not really trying to escape the slump, instead recognizing it as tied up in the success to either side. The way to make good plays, his bearing suggests as he knocks the dirt from his cleats with his bat handle, is to get the bad ones out of the way. He pulls a grounder through the hole for a single, but the result doesn't much matter. The show was the hanging in.

On the whole, the Rangers require optimism to watch. That's true for every team to some degree, but this one specifically has the air of a gamble waiting to work out or fall flat. They make big trades and laud young players; they come up short one autumn and go all-in the next. Watch them in June and your head rings with hypotheticals: *if Darvish stays healthy, if Profar takes a leap* … They hit four homers and win 9-2 on some steamy Texas afternoon, and you wonder if it will work the same way later.

The only Ranger who doesn't prompt that wondering is Beltre, the least speculative player in the game. Seeing him snap his glove around a line drive or take a big cut makes you forget about projections and age curves. Watching him stomp around at third, impatient for something to come his way, is its own kind of treat; a reminder of baseball's smaller, daily scales of time. Texas fans might be conditioned to think in terms of the era—as in, the one that could very well come and go with only a string of heartbreaking postseason losses to show for it—but at least, in Adrian Beltre, they have a player who can bring them back to the moment. ■

*—Robert O'Connell is a contributor
at Vice Sports*

HITTERS

Hanser Alberto SS

Born: 10/17/92 Age: 24 Bats: R Throws: R Height: 5'11" Weight: 215 Entered Pro Ball: International Free Agent, 2009

YEAR	TEAM	LVL	AGE	PA	R	2B	3B	HR	RBI	BB	K	SB	CS	AVG/OBP/SLG	TAv	VORP	BABIP	BRR	FRAA	WARP
2014	MYR	A+	21	285	37	15	3	5	43	10	25	10	4	.271/.301/.408	.248	9.4	.280	1.3	SS(64): 0.8 • 3B(5): 0.3	1.0
2014	FRI	AA	21	190	23	6	1	2	15	6	17	6	4	.275/.314/.354	.259	8.5	.296	1.1	SS(50): 8.3	1.8
2015	ROU	AAA	22	330	42	19	4	4	32	9	33	5	5	.310/.331/.435	.280	21.7	.335	2.2	SS(65): 4.3 • 2B(10): -1.1	2.4
2015	TEX	MLB	22	104	12	2	1	0	4	2	17	1	0	.222/.238/.263	.197	-3.1	.268	0.4	2B(24): 2.1 • SS(8): -0.0	-0.1
2016	ROU	AAA	23	277	32	13	1	7	36	8	29	2	2	.275/.302/.411	.266	10.9	.288	-1.9	SS(57): 1.0 • 2B(6): -0.0	1.2
2016	TEX	MLB	23	58	2	1	0	0	5	0	17	1	0	.143/.143/.161	.096	-1.4	.205	-2.6	3B(11): 0.3 • SS(9): 2.4	-0.8
2017	*TEX*	*MLB*	*24*	*60*	*6*	*3*	*0*	*1*	*6*	*1*	*9*	*1*	*0*	*.257/.277/.379*	*.229*	*0.4*	*.281*	*-0.1*	*SS 1 • 2B 0*	*0.1*
2018	*TEX*	*MLB*	*25*	*303*	*33*	*13*	*2*	*7*	*33*	*9*	*47*	*4*	*2*	*.263/.291/.397*	*.235*	*2.0*	*.287*	*-0.1*	*SS 3 • 2B 1*	*0.6*

Breakout: 4%   Improve: 19%   Collapse: 8%   Attrition: 26%   MLB: 54%   Comparables: Hernan Perez, Luis Hernandez, Adeiny Hechavarria

Alberto will never impress with the bat, but thankfully, his glove makes up for the lack of pop at the plate. He made just a single error while fielding over 150 innings this season at all four different positions on the infield, and it wasn't for a lack of range. And while its value may not be quantifiable, Alberto brings a bevy of cheer to the Rangers dugout, including batting cage play-by-play and making a bubble gum friend to keep him company.

Elvis Andrus SS

Born: 8/26/88 Age: 28 Bats: R Throws: R Height: 6'0" Weight: 200 Entered Pro Ball: International Free Agent, 2005

YEAR	TEAM	LVL	AGE	PA	R	2B	3B	HR	RBI	BB	K	SB	CS	AVG/OBP/SLG	TAv	VORP	BABIP	BRR	FRAA	WARP
2014	TEX	MLB	25	685	72	35	1	2	41	46	96	27	15	.263/.314/.333	.240	18.5	.305	5.8	SS(153): -5.4	1.5
2015	TEX	MLB	26	661	69	34	2	7	62	46	78	25	9	.258/.309/.357	.246	23.0	.283	5.7	SS(160): 12.8	3.8
2016	TEX	MLB	27	568	75	31	7	8	69	47	70	24	8	.302/.362/.439	.277	34.6	.333	1.4	SS(147): -3.7	3.2
2017	*TEX*	*MLB*	*28*	*600*	*66*	*27*	*4*	*6*	*50*	*47*	*79*	*26*	*10*	*.274/.329/.372*	*.252*	*23.7*	*.304*	*1.5*	*SS -2*	*1.5*
2018	*TEX*	*MLB*	*29*	*526*	*59*	*24*	*3*	*6*	*49*	*47*	*73*	*21*	*9*	*.273/.340/.374*	*.249*	*16.1*	*.303*	*3.9*	*SS -2*	*1.6*

Breakout: 2%   Improve: 39%   Collapse: 9%   Attrition: 10%   MLB: 99%   Comparables: Bobby Valentine, Dave Chalk, Mark Loretta

Albatross was the word on the lips of Rangers fans all over The Metroplex when Andrus failed to boost his offensive numbers after being signed to a massive eight-year, $118-million extension in 2013. But patience is a virtue, and one that paid off for Andrus in 2016. Andrus posted his career-best season offensively across the board in 2016, and added nearly 100 points to his slugging average. The home run power didn't increase much, but Andrus beefed up the triples and kept his strikeout rate at a modest number. If Andrus can keep up whatever magic it is he's working at the plate, he'll stay among the top offensive shortstops in the league (seriously!), making that contract look palatable, if not enviable, for the Rangers.

Adrian Beltre 3B

Born: 4/7/79 Age: 38 Bats: R Throws: R Height: 5'11" Weight: 220 Entered Pro Ball: International Free Agent, 1994

YEAR	TEAM	LVL	AGE	PA	R	2B	3B	HR	RBI	BB	K	SB	CS	AVG/OBP/SLG	TAv	VORP	BABIP	BRR	FRAA	WARP
2014	TEX	MLB	35	614	79	33	1	19	77	57	74	1	1	.324/.388/.492	.319	49.8	.345	-1.5	3B(136): -6.0	4.8
2015	TEX	MLB	36	619	83	32	4	18	83	41	65	1	0	.287/.334/.453	.279	33.1	.295	3.0	3B(142): -2.3	3.3
2016	TEX	MLB	37	640	89	31	1	32	104	48	66	1	1	.300/.358/.521	.297	39.8	.293	-3.5	3B(141): 4.9	4.6
2017	*TEX*	*MLB*	*38*	*639*	*76*	*30*	*2*	*24*	*88*	*44*	*78*	*1*	*1*	*.294/.346/.474*	*.286*	*33.3*	*.304*	*-1.3*	*3B -2*	*2.9*
2018	*TEX*	*MLB*	*39*	*523*	*69*	*24*	*1*	*20*	*71*	*35*	*69*	*0*	*0*	*.287/.338/.466*	*.273*	*18.1*	*.298*	*-0.6*	*3B -1*	*1.8*

Breakout: 0%   Improve: 19%   Collapse: 13%   Attrition: 14%   MLB: 73%   Comparables: Aramis Ramirez, Sid Gordon, Scott Rolen

The 19-year veteran is not of this baseball age: As aging curves continue to trend younger and younger, Beltre is a relic of a bygone era. At age 37, he was the oldest hitter aside from David Ortiz to rank among the top 50 in TAv. As contact rates league-wide plummet toward unthinkable depths, Beltre still keeps opposing defenses on their toes. His strikeout rate dipped for the second consecutive season, and was good enough to place sixth in baseball in 2016. And even a stinted viewing of the Rangers last season would be enough for the most casual baseball fans to notice the joy that Beltre brings on a daily basis. It's infectious and it's far too rare. He has been happy and healthy in Texas, and resolute in his pursuit of a championship—and it was further rewarded last April with a two-year, $38 million extension that will start this season. That's not too bad for a future Hall of Famer who has to actively filter through the AARP spam in his mailbox.

Robinson Chirinos C

Born: 6/5/84 Age: 33 Bats: R Throws: R Height: 6'1" Weight: 210 Entered Pro Ball: International Free Agent, 2000

YEAR	TEAM	LVL	AGE	PA	R	2B	3B	HR	RBI	BB	K	SB	CS	AVG/OBP/SLG	TAv	VORP	BABIP	BRR	FRAA	WARP
2014	TEX	MLB	30	338	36	15	0	13	40	17	71	0	1	.239/.290/.415	.267	15.9	.265	-0.3	C(91): -5.2	1.2
2015	TEX	MLB	31	273	33	16	1	10	34	28	62	0	0	.232/.325/.438	.265	11.8	.270	-1.3	C(78): -6.4	0.6
2016	TEX	MLB	32	170	21	11	0	9	20	15	44	0	1	.224/.314/.483	.268	9.1	.250	0.2	C(54): -7.3	0.2
2017	*TEX*	*MLB*	*33*	*90*	*10*	*4*	*0*	*3*	*11*	*8*	*21*	*0*	*0*	*.232/.306/.403*	*.248*	*3.1*	*.270*	*-0.2*	*C -2*	*-0.1*
2018	*TEX*	*MLB*	*34*	*153*	*19*	*6*	*0*	*5*	*19*	*12*	*37*	*0*	*0*	*.228/.301/.400*	*.240*	*2.3*	*.266*	*-0.2*	*C -4*	*-0.2*

Breakout: 3%   Improve: 33%   Collapse: 11%   Attrition: 22%   MLB: 82%   Comparables: Chris Snyder, Geovany Soto, John Baker

Between suffering a broken forearm in April and having to hold the fort down behind the plate in July while the Rangers openly shopped for his replacement, being Robinson Chirinos in the first half of 2016 was rough. His framing numbers were poor, and for a team that was suffering a crisis in the rotation, having a backup catcher attempting to lead a band of revolving-door starters was putting Chirinos between a rock and a place that didn't yet have Jonathan Lucroy. Offensively, he was overexposed playing nearly every day, save for erratic appearances of power. Yet when returned to his natural backup role in August, he hit .302/.404/.512 over the remainder of the season. With Lucroy under contract for one more turn, the Rangers will hope to see more of the less-needed version of Chirinos in 2017.

YEAR	TEAM	P. COUNT	FRM RUNS	BLK RUNS	THRW RUNS	TOT RUNS
2014	TEX	13110	-9.3	1.9	2.9	-4.4
2015	ROU	472	-0.1	0.0	0.0	-0.1
2015	TEX	10786	-5.7	1.6	0.4	-3.8
2016	TEX	6797	-8.1	2.1	0.1	-5.9
2017	TEX	3508	-3.0	0.6	0.1	-2.3
2018	TEX	5978	-5.7	0.9	0.1	-4.7

Shin-Soo Choo   LF

Born: 7/13/82   Age: 34   Bats: L   Throws: L   Height: 5'11"   Weight: 210   Entered Pro Ball: International Free Agent, 2000

YEAR	TEAM	LVL	AGE	PA	R	2B	3B	HR	RBI	BB	K	SB	CS	AVG/OBP/SLG	TAv	VORP	BABIP	BRR	FRAA	WARP
2014	TEX	MLB	31	529	58	19	1	13	40	58	131	3	4	.242/.340/.374	.266	11.5	.308	0.3	LF(64): -8.3 • RF(12): 0.7	0.4
2015	TEX	MLB	32	653	94	32	3	22	82	76	147	4	2	.276/.375/.463	.295	36.0	.335	2.7	RF(148): 6.5	4.6
2016	FRI	AA	33	24	0	1	0	0	0	3	7	0	1	.300/.417/.350	.299	1.2	.462	0.0	RF(3): -0.3	0.1
2016	TEX	MLB	33	210	27	7	0	7	17	25	46	6	3	.242/.357/.399	.273	5.8	.288	-0.6	RF(43): -0.4	0.6
2017	TEX	MLB	34	560	75	24	2	15	58	69	125	8	5	.262/.368/.415	.278	24.6	.323	-1.1	RF 5	2.7
2018	TEX	MLB	35	342	44	14	1	8	37	41	79	4	3	.256/.362/.397	.265	9.6	.321	0.5	RF 3	1.4

Breakout: 0%   Improve: 30%   Collapse: 13%   Attrition: 16%   MLB: 93%   *Comparables: Bobby Abreu, J.D. Drew, Andre Ethier*

Long gone are the days in which the famed leadoff man would be a threat on the basepaths at every stadium he toured, though he never quite stole bags like a kleptomaniac in a department store. Now entering his age-34 season, one probably wouldn't be surprised that Choo has become a shell of what he once was. Of course, the Rangers were surely not expecting him to be a five-win player into his wine appreciation years. Almost like clockwork, since his arrival in Texas, Father Time has stolen the array of tools he once possessed, leaving behind just the bat and the approach. His 2015 campaign may have left his contract's apologists hopeful for the future, but it is now sandwiched between two almost identical seasons of expensive mediocrity. With four years left on his contract, one for each trip Choo took to the disabled list this season, the Rangers appear to be lapping the field in money spent on left-handed designated hitters.

Delino DeShields   2B

Born: 8/16/92   Age: 24   Bats: R   Throws: R   Height: 5'9"   Weight: 200   Entered Pro Ball: Round 1, 2010 Draft (#8 overall)

YEAR	TEAM	LVL	AGE	PA	R	2B	3B	HR	RBI	BB	K	SB	CS	AVG/OBP/SLG	TAv	VORP	BABIP	BRR	FRAA	WARP
2014	CCH	AA	21	507	75	14	2	11	57	61	112	54	14	.236/.346/.360	.274	29.7	.293	8.7	CF(78): -5.1 • LF(29): -3.0	2.3
2015	ROU	AAA	22	27	2	3	0	0	2	1	6	0	0	.308/.333/.423	.296	0.4	.400	-1.2	CF(2): -0.1 • LF(1): -0.2	0.0
2015	TEX	MLB	22	492	83	22	10	2	37	53	101	25	8	.261/.344/.374	.259	17.2	.334	4.3	CF(87): -0.7 • LF(35): -0.4	1.7
2016	ROU	AAA	23	249	37	10	0	3	17	35	60	21	7	.261/.367/.353	.284	15.5	.349	2.4	CF(42): -6.1 • LF(7): -1.9	0.8
2016	TEX	MLB	23	203	36	7	0	4	13	15	54	8	3	.209/.275/.313	.219	-0.9	.272	2.0	CF(33): 1.3 • LF(26): -1.2	-0.1
2017	TEX	MLB	24	168	20	6	1	3	14	17	40	10	3	.242/.321/.361	.243	3.7	.302	0.9	CF -0 • LF -1	0.1
2018	TEX	MLB	25	340	40	14	3	6	34	36	81	19	6	.246/.335/.377	.246	6.6	.306	2.8	CF 0 • LF -3	0.4

Breakout: 9%   Improve: 50%   Collapse: 4%   Attrition: 9%   MLB: 72%   *Comparables: Dexter Fowler, Anthony Gose, Billy Hamilton*

With the arrival of last-minute center fielder Ian Desmond on Leap Day, the surprising 2015 starter DeShields was surprisingly back on the bench. The speedy outfielder did manage to make an appearance in 74 games, mostly in center, which is more in line with what a first-place team might envision. The two steps forward he took in sticking after the Rule 5 draft last season bottomed out in his sophomore season, as his plate discipline cratered. When you couple that with the questionable defense and nonexistent power he's always had, he'd be wise to keep a bag marked "Round Rock" packed and in his locker at all times.

Prince Fielder   1B

Born: 5/9/84   Age: 33   Bats: L   Throws: R   Height: 5'11"   Weight: 275   Entered Pro Ball: Round 1, 2002 Draft (#7 overall)

YEAR	TEAM	LVL	AGE	PA	R	2B	3B	HR	RBI	BB	K	SB	CS	AVG/OBP/SLG	TAv	VORP	BABIP	BRR	FRAA	WARP
2014	TEX	MLB	30	178	19	8	0	3	16	25	24	0	0	.247/.360/.360	.256	-0.3	.274	-1.2	1B(39): -2.9	-0.4
2015	TEX	MLB	31	693	78	28	0	23	98	64	88	0	0	.305/.378/.463	.289	21.8	.323	-4.7	1B(18): -0.6	2.3
2016	TEX	MLB	32	370	29	16	0	8	44	32	63	0	0	.212/.292/.334	.226	-12.2	.235	-3.0	1B(9): 0.5	-1.2
2017	TEX	MLB	33	412	50	18	1	14	54	44	63	0	0	.276/.364/.444	.275	12.5	.299	-2.3	1B -2	1.1
2018	TEX	MLB	34	359	48	16	0	11	44	36	56	0	0	.272/.354/.431	.269	8.1	.297	-2.2	1B -2	0.7

Breakout: 2%   Improve: 24%   Collapse: 4%   Attrition: 14%   MLB: 96%   *Comparables: Joe Mauer, Victor Martinez, Bill Freehan*

Stretching your career as long as father time and your own pride will let you is one thing. Being told by a doctor point blank that you cannot play Major League baseball anymore is another. After having two spinal fusions in his neck, that's what it came down to for Fielder, who was visibly torn up at his abrupt retirement press conference this past August. He went out as a Ranger, but he will be remembered for a storied career stealing nachos from fans in the stands in Detroit, and being a cornerstone of Brewers history in Milwaukee. He's also still the only player to hit more than 50 homers in a season while under the age of 25 since Mickey Mantle in 1956. Goodnight, sweet-swinging Prince.

Joey Gallo   3B

Born: 11/19/93   Age: 23   Bats: L   Throws: R   Height: 6'5"   Weight: 235   Entered Pro Ball: Round 1, 2012 Draft (#39 overall)

YEAR	TEAM	LVL	AGE	PA	R	2B	3B	HR	RBI	BB	K	SB	CS	AVG/OBP/SLG	TAv	VORP	BABIP	BRR	FRAA	WARP
2014	MYR	A+	20	246	53	9	3	21	50	51	64	5	3	.323/.463/.735	.400	46.6	.370	1.0	3B(54): 4.9	5.2
2014	FRI	AA	20	291	44	10	0	21	56	36	115	2	0	.232/.334/.524	.306	20.3	.322	-1.3	3B(53): -0.8 • 1B(7): -0.1	2.1
2015	FRI	AA	21	146	21	10	1	9	31	24	49	1	0	.314/.425/.636	.359	18.3	.453	0.6	3B(19): 1.4 • LF(6): 0.6	2.2
2015	ROU	AAA	21	228	20	9	0	14	32	27	90	1	0	.195/.289/.450	.267	5.7	.258	-1.9	3B(33): 0.1 • LF(14): 0.7	0.6
2015	TEX	MLB	21	123	16	3	1	6	14	15	57	3	0	.204/.301/.417	.246	1.8	.356	0.4	LF(19): 0.2 • 3B(15): 0.0	0.2
2016	ROU	AAA	22	433	71	17	6	25	66	68	150	2	0	.240/.367/.529	.325	40.0	.330	2.1	3B(44): 4.2 • 1B(32): 1.4	4.7
2016	TEX	MLB	22	30	2	0	0	1	1	5	19	1	0	.040/.200/.160	.153	-2.8	.000	-0.1	3B(5): 0.2 • 1B(1): 0.0	-0.3
2017	*TEX*	*MLB*	*23*	*561*	*78*	*17*	*3*	*33*	*86*	*72*	*222*	*2*	*0*	*.216/.322/.470*	*.272*	*16.9*	*.309*	*-0.3*	*1B -0*	*1.6*
2018	*TEX*	*MLB*	*24*	*507*	*76*	*17*	*3*	*30*	*80*	*69*	*198*	*2*	*0*	*.219/.331/.475*	*.270*	*15.1*	*.316*	*-0.4*	*1B 0*	*1.6*

Breakout: 4%   Improve: 41%   Collapse: 5%   Attrition: 15%   MLB: 79%   Comparables: *Kris Bryant, Miguel Sano, Domingo Santana*

Jon Daniels was certainly living well by managing to pull of a cornucopia of meaningful deals around the deadline while also keeping a tight grip on the treasured Gallo. Serving his first full season at Triple-A, coaches impressed upon Gallo the value of moderation: that to combat his atrocious strikeout rate, he might have to aim for the first deck of bleachers. He wore those subsequent walks as a badge of honor and raised his on-base percentage almost 80 points over his first stint in Round Rock. However, though the minor-league improvement was noticeable, he was abysmal in a very short run in Texas—and as the icing on the cake, he lost his rookie eligibility for 2017 in the season's final weekend. With a superstar blocking him at third, along with the combination of a soon-to-be star and a pimped-out bullpen cart filled with bags of money likely blocking him in the outfield corners, his road to redemption could run straight through the role Prince Fielder was supposed to occupy on this team.

Carlos Gomez   CF

Born: 12/4/85   Age: 31   Bats: R   Throws: R   Height: 6'3"   Weight: 220   Entered Pro Ball: International Free Agent, 2002

YEAR	TEAM	LVL	AGE	PA	R	2B	3B	HR	RBI	BB	K	SB	CS	AVG/OBP/SLG	TAv	VORP	BABIP	BRR	FRAA	WARP
2014	MIL	MLB	28	644	95	34	4	23	73	47	141	34	12	.284/.356/.477	.300	43.5	.339	1.7	CF(145): 3.6	5.2
2015	MIL	MLB	29	314	42	20	1	8	43	23	70	7	6	.262/.328/.423	.273	13.2	.322	0.0	CF(72): -0.2 • 2B(1): -0.0	1.4
2015	HOU	MLB	29	163	19	9	0	4	13	8	31	10	3	.242/.288/.383	.241	3.8	.278	2.0	CF(39): 4.4	0.9
2016	CCH	AA	30	21	3	0	0	1	1	0	6	0	1	.250/.286/.400	.254	0.7	.308	0.4	CF(3): 0.8	0.2
2016	HOU	MLB	30	323	27	16	1	5	29	21	100	13	2	.210/.272/.322	.210	-3.1	.300	3.9	CF(78): -4.5	-0.8
2016	TEX	MLB	30	130	18	6	0	8	24	13	36	5	3	.284/.362/.543	.307	9.5	.347	0.4	LF(28): 1.0 • CF(7): -0.0	1.1
2017	*TEX*	*MLB*	*31*	*581*	*74*	*27*	*4*	*19*	*69*	*38*	*140*	*26*	*9*	*.258/.317/.433*	*.260*	*22.6*	*.311*	*2.3*	*CF 1*	*1.9*
2018	*TEX*	*MLB*	*32*	*485*	*61*	*22*	*3*	*17*	*61*	*33*	*120*	*20*	*8*	*.256/.319/.434*	*.255*	*13.4*	*.311*	*2.7*	*CF 1*	*1.6*

Breakout: 0%   Improve: 46%   Collapse: 6%   Attrition: 8%   MLB: 97%   Comparables: *Aaron Rowand, Torii Hunter, Ellis Burks*

Did anyone in baseball have a stranger year on the field than Carlos Gomez? He continued his defensive decline at breakneck speed, finally pairing his offensive dip with his first year of below-average defense (per FRAA) since 2010. A firing, an intermission. And then, magic. Gomez was on pace to have the highest ground-ball rate of his career with the Astros, but after Jeff Luhnow essentially gave him away both within the division and up the standings, he was hitting fly balls at a career-high rate. Gomez picked it up with the Rangers in a way that paralleled how Rangers had picked themselves up all season, and he became just another part of a mystical and charming Texas success story—until the postseason, that is. At age 31, Gomez continues to show the confidence of a superstar, taking a pillow-ish contract with the Rangers, even with multi-year offers supposedly on the table.

Ronald Guzman   1B

Born: 10/20/94   Age: 22   Bats: L   Throws: L   Height: 6'5"   Weight: 205   Entered Pro Ball: International Free Agent, 2011

YEAR	TEAM	LVL	AGE	PA	R	2B	3B	HR	RBI	BB	K	SB	CS	AVG/OBP/SLG	TAv	VORP	BABIP	BRR	FRAA	WARP
2014	HIC	A	19	492	46	32	0	6	63	37	107	6	3	.218/.283/.330	.226	-14.4	.270	-1.5	1B(115): -10.5 • LF(2): 0.3	-2.5
2015	HIC	A	20	104	10	3	0	3	14	6	15	2	0	.309/.346/.433	.287	3.8	.338	-0.2	1B(24): -0.5	0.3
2015	HDS	A+	20	452	54	25	7	9	73	27	101	3	0	.277/.319/.434	.257	2.0	.343	-1.2	1B(106): 0.2	0.2
2016	FRI	AA	21	416	51	16	5	15	56	33	82	2	1	.288/.348/.477	.296	16.6	.331	-2.5	1B(95): 4.0	2.2
2016	ROU	AAA	21	95	9	5	1	1	11	6	23	0	1	.216/.266/.330	.211	-5.4	.281	-1.6	1B(20): -1.6	-0.7
2017	*TEX*	*MLB*	*22*	*33*	*3*	*1*	*0*	*1*	*3*	*2*	*8*	*0*	*0*	*.225/.272/.356*	*.218*	*-0.9*	*.284*	*0.0*	*1B -0*	*-0.1*
2018	*TEX*	*MLB*	*23*	*317*	*35*	*14*	*2*	*9*	*35*	*21*	*82*	*0*	*0*	*.234/.288/.381*	*.229*	*-6.7*	*.293*	*-0.6*	*1B -2*	*-0.9*

Breakout: 3%   Improve: 5%   Collapse: 1%   Attrition: 8%   MLB: 9%   Comparables: *Brandon Snyder, Russ Canzler, Nick Evans*

A first base prospect coming off a single-digit home run season in the Cal League certainly falls under the "has a lot to prove" umbrella, but Guzman did just that in 2016. He had his best offensive season yet in his first taste of the upper minors, blasting through Double-A and ending up in Round Rock to close the season. With Mitch Moreland moving on to New England, Guzman is positioning himself well to step into that role—the average-hitting first baseman with strong defensive skills—perhaps even in 2017, should the Rangers' Plan A falter.

Josh Hamilton LF

Born: 5/21/81 Age: 36 Bats: L Throws: L Height: 6'4" Weight: 240 Entered Pro Ball: Round 1, 1999 Draft (#1 overall)

YEAR	TEAM	LVL	AGE	PA	R	2B	3B	HR	RBI	BB	K	SB	CS	AVG/OBP/SLG	TAv	VORP	BABIP	BRR	FRAA	WARP
2014	ANA	MLB	33	381	43	21	0	10	44	32	108	3	3	.263/.331/.414	.287	13.6	.350	-3.3	LF(68): 5.5 • CF(7): 0.7	2.2
2015	FRI	AA	34	21	10	3	0	1	4	2	2	0	0	.526/.571/.842	.454	4.3	.563	-0.2	CF(2): -0.5	0.4
2015	ROU	AAA	34	38	1	3	0	0	5	1	10	0	0	.270/.289/.351	.233	-0.3	.370	-0.1	CF(5): -1.4 • LF(3): -0.4	-0.2
2015	TEX	MLB	34	182	22	8	0	8	25	10	52	0	0	.253/.291/.441	.262	4.9	.313	0.9	LF(35): -1.2 • RF(11): 0.7	0.5
2017	TEX	MLB	36	250	30	12	1	10	35	20	67	1	1	.256/.320/.455	.260	7.9	.313	-0.6	LF 2	1.1

Breakout: 1% Improve: 24% Collapse: 6% Attrition: 10% MLB: 75% Comparables: Alfonso Soriano, Andruw Jones, Bob Allison

On May 25, the Rangers announced that Josh Hamilton would miss the entire 2016 season after undergoing his third knee surgery in less than a year. It ultimately led the Rangers to release him in August. The move was made prior to September in order to ensure that should the Rangers decide to resign the 35-year-old in 2017, he would be able to attend spring training as a non-roster invitee. This feels like a long shot right now, but the offseason will tell us whether or not Hamilton will receive one last chance or if he will be left wondering who will remember his name, who will keep his flame, and who will tell his story.

Andy Ibanez 2B

Born: 4/3/93 Age: 24 Bats: R Throws: R Height: 5'10" Weight: 170 Entered Pro Ball: International Free Agent, 2015

YEAR	TEAM	LVL	AGE	PA	R	2B	3B	HR	RBI	BB	K	SB	CS	AVG/OBP/SLG	TAv	VORP	BABIP	BRR	FRAA	WARP
2016	HIC	A	23	220	28	18	1	7	35	29	28	10	8	.324/.413/.546	.375	27.4	.346	-2.2	2B(40): -0.7	2.9
2016	FRI	AA	23	343	39	18	2	6	31	25	47	5	2	.261/.318/.391	.255	7.9	.288	0.8	2B(63): -5.1 • 3B(14): 0.6	0.4
2017	TEX	MLB	24	250	27	12	1	7	30	20	48	3	2	.255/.318/.414	.248	6.2	.289	-0.3	2B -3 • 3B 0	0.4
2018	TEX	MLB	25	301	37	15	1	9	36	25	58	3	2	.257/.321/.421	.254	6.6	.292	-0.3	2B -4 • 3B 0	0.3

Breakout: 8% Improve: 23% Collapse: 3% Attrition: 26% MLB: 43% Comparables: Devon Travis, Jose Pirela, Eric Sogard

A Cuban infielder, whose power will be more to the gaps than over the fences, Ibanez has defensive tools that won him Gold Glove honors at second base in Serie Nacional. At the plate, he came out raking in Low-A, but crashed pretty hard back down to Earth once he was no longer the Ian Ziering of Beverly Hills High. He's a heady player who could get by on grit and versatility if necessary, but Ibanez also doesn't need to be an everyday player for the Rangers to make good on the $1.6 million bonus they handed him in 2015.

Jonathan Lucroy C

Born: 6/13/86 Age: 31 Bats: R Throws: R Height: 6'0" Weight: 200 Entered Pro Ball: Round 3, 2007 Draft (#101 overall)

YEAR	TEAM	LVL	AGE	PA	R	2B	3B	HR	RBI	BB	K	SB	CS	AVG/OBP/SLG	TAv	VORP	BABIP	BRR	FRAA	WARP
2014	MIL	MLB	28	655	73	53	2	13	69	66	71	4	4	.301/.373/.465	.305	54.1	.324	2.1	C(136): 16.7 • 1B(19): 0.2	7.9
2015	MIL	MLB	29	415	51	20	3	7	43	36	64	1	0	.264/.326/.391	.254	12.0	.297	-2.4	C(86): 0.8 • 1B(7): 0.1	1.4
2016	MIL	MLB	30	376	48	17	3	13	50	33	70	5	0	.299/.359/.482	.297	32.1	.340	2.0	C(82): 6.9 • 1B(6): -0.6	4.0
2016	TEX	MLB	30	168	19	7	0	11	31	14	30	0	0	.276/.345/.539	.297	12.8	.279	-1.1	C(44): 0.1	1.3
2017	TEX	MLB	31	590	66	30	4	16	72	51	83	5	1	.281/.345/.442	.275	36.5	.305	-0.3	C 8	4.8
2018	TEX	MLB	32	518	64	26	3	14	61	44	79	3	1	.273/.338/.431	.263	20.4	.301	0.4	C 6	2.9

Breakout: 0% Improve: 28% Collapse: 5% Attrition: 8% MLB: 96% Comparables: Brian McCann, Yadier Molina, Victor Martinez

In a year of historically awful takes, baseball's worst offender was the seemingly never-ending second-guessing of Lucroy's decision to veto a trade to the eventual American League Champion Indians. Yes, he expressed his vocal desire to be traded to a contending team, but Lucroy used the leverage he had negotiated just a few years earlier to try and improve his contract situation, something every one of us either has done or would do in a heartbeat. The handwringing, much like Billy Madison discussing the Industrial Revolution, caused everyone who read it to be dumber than they were before.

YEAR	TEAM	P. COUNT	FRM RUNS	BLK RUNS	THRW RUNS	TOT RUNS
2014	MIL	18951	16.4	5.2	-1.5	20.1
2015	MIL	12038	1.2	0.6	-1.0	0.7
2016	MIL	11622	3.8	2.0	3.7	9.4
2016	TEX	5788	0.5	0.0	0.0	0.5
2017	TEX	18627	5.5	2.3	1.4	9.2
2018	TEX	16342	3.3	1.7	1.1	6.1

On the field, Lucroy was not the otherworldly defender in Texas that he was in Milwaukee, but he was still an immense upgrade from the parade of backup catchers that came before him. The largest impact Lucroy made in Texas was helping to stabilize a rotation that was in dire need of a consistent and strong leader behind the plate. Which is saying a lot, as the .885 OPS he posted for the Rangers would have been his career high. Though Texas' World Series pursuit was halted at the Canadian border for the second year in a row, the Louisiana native will lead the charge towards avoiding a three-peat in 2017.

Nomar Mazara RF

Born: 4/26/95 Age: 22 Bats: L Throws: L Height: 6'4" Weight: 215 Entered Pro Ball: International Free Agent, 2011

YEAR	TEAM	LVL	AGE	PA	R	2B	3B	HR	RBI	BB	K	SB	CS	AVG/OBP/SLG	TAv	VORP	BABIP	BRR	FRAA	WARP
2014	HIC	A	19	461	68	21	2	19	73	57	99	4	3	.264/.358/.470	.291	19.5	.304	-3.5	RF(91): -7.5	1.2
2014	FRI	AA	19	97	10	7	1	3	16	9	22	0	0	.306/.381/.518	.313	3.8	.377	-3.1	RF(23): -3.0	0.1
2015	FRI	AA	20	470	57	22	2	13	56	47	92	2	0	.284/.357/.443	.280	13.0	.329	-4.5	RF(63): 0.4 • LF(32): 0.1	1.5
2015	ROU	AAA	20	88	11	4	0	1	13	5	10	0	0	.358/.409/.444	.321	7.1	.400	0.1	RF(14): 1.1 • LF(1): 0.3	0.9
2016	TEX	MLB	21	568	59	13	3	20	64	39	112	0	2	.266/.320/.419	.256	4.6	.299	-4.1	RF(112): 5.8 • LF(38): -1.4	0.9
2017	TEX	MLB	22	624	76	23	3	21	70	47	136	1	1	.258/.320/.420	.259	16.1	.303	-1.2	LF 7 • RF 0	2.1
2018	TEX	MLB	23	625	81	24	3	22	80	50	135	1	1	.267/.332/.439	.263	13.7	.312	-2.8	LF 7 • RF 0	2.2

Breakout: 5% Improve: 43% Collapse: 2% Attrition: 16% MLB: 68% Comparables: Fernando Martinez, Billy Butler, Tyler Austin

"I wanted to see what you'd do. And you didn't disappoint," the Joker uttered to Batman in the 2009 classic *The Dark Knight*. Jon Daniels could easily recreate that scene with Mazara on the other end of the dimly lit table after the 2016 campaign the rookie put together—though without the sinister disposition and cheap clown makeup—because Mazara surely didn't disappoint the Rangers. Putting up offensive marks that crushed his pre-season PECOTA projections, Mazara's above-average production at the plate was almost boringly competent. Of course, he was also a plus defender in the outfield and he was too young to buy himself a congratulatory drink after he homered off Jered Weaver in his major league debut. It's OK, though—he'll have a lot more to celebrate throughout his career.

Rougned Odor   2B

Born: 2/3/94   Age: 23   Bats: L   Throws: R   Height: 5'11"   Weight: 195   Entered Pro Ball: International Free Agent, 2011

YEAR	TEAM	LVL	AGE	PA	R	2B	3B	HR	RBI	BB	K	SB	CS	AVG/OBP/SLG	TAv	VORP	BABIP	BRR	FRAA	WARP
2014	FRI	AA	20	138	21	2	1	6	17	7	22	6	3	.279/.314/.450	.274	5.5	.294	0.0	2B(31): 2.9	0.9
2014	TEX	MLB	20	417	39	14	7	9	48	17	71	4	7	.259/.297/.402	.255	9.9	.294	1.6	2B(110): 2.8	1.4
2015	ROU	AAA	21	124	26	12	2	5	19	12	10	3	1	.352/.426/.639	.343	15.0	.355	1.0	2B(28): -1.1	1.4
2015	TEX	MLB	21	470	54	21	9	16	61	23	79	6	7	.261/.316/.465	.278	24.5	.283	4.2	2B(119): 4.5	3.1
2016	TEX	MLB	22	632	89	33	4	33	88	19	135	14	7	.271/.296/.502	.269	22.4	.297	-0.2	2B(146): 5.9	2.9
2017	*TEX*	*MLB*	*23*	*618*	*76*	*28*	*7*	*25*	*84*	*29*	*113*	*12*	*8*	*.271/.312/.474*	*.270*	*31.3*	*.296*	*-0.2*	*2B 3*	*3.1*
2018	*TEX*	*MLB*	*24*	*575*	*76*	*27*	*5*	*25*	*83*	*29*	*105*	*11*	*7*	*.274/.319/.487*	*.269*	*25.8*	*.295*	*2.7*	*2B 3*	*3.1*

Breakout: 9%   Improve: 62%   Collapse: 3%   Attrition: 0%   MLB: 97%   *Comparables: Ryan Zimmerman, Manny Machado, Paul Molitor*

Whether it be hitting a grand slam four days into his MLB career, throwing the punch heard around the world, or being charged with a throwing error that scored the Blue Jays winning run in extras during Game 3 of the ALDS, Odor has left quite the mark on Arlington in just three seasons. He made different kind of splash in 2016 by surprisingly leading the Rangers in homers, and posting the highest slugging percentage of his career. Unfortunately, it came at the same time as his lowest on-base percentage, which prevented him from taking that next step forward into the game's keystone elites. Odor's approach to every aspect of the game continues to get more aggressive from asserting himself as more of a team leader to relishing in his status as a mild villain to swinging more than ever. To that end, his approval ratings in Texas are so disproportionate to his approval ratings outside the state, you'd think he was Ted Cruz.

Jurickson Profar   2B

Born: 2/20/93   Age: 24   Bats: B   Throws: R   Height: 6'0"   Weight: 190   Entered Pro Ball: International Free Agent, 2009

YEAR	TEAM	LVL	AGE	PA	R	2B	3B	HR	RBI	BB	K	SB	CS	AVG/OBP/SLG	TAv	VORP	BABIP	BRR	FRAA	WARP
2015	HIC	A	22	35	2	1	0	1	5	1	9	0	0	.273/.314/.394	.262	0.3	.348	-0.1		0.0
2016	ROU	AAA	23	189	28	9	0	5	26	16	26	4	3	.284/.356/.426	.296	13.9	.312	0.2	SS(31): 2.9 • 2B(6): 0.0	1.7
2016	TEX	MLB	23	307	35	6	3	5	20	30	61	2	1	.239/.321/.338	.221	-6.0	.291	-1.5	3B(25): -1.2 • 2B(19): 1.8	-0.6
2017	*TEX*	*MLB*	*24*	*579*	*63*	*22*	*4*	*14*	*60*	*52*	*105*	*5*	*4*	*.252/.324/.390*	*.253*	*6.9*	*.287*	*-1.0*	*1B 4 • 3B -1*	*1.2*
2018	*TEX*	*MLB*	*25*	*520*	*64*	*21*	*3*	*14*	*59*	*47*	*96*	*4*	*3*	*.258/.331/.406*	*.254*	*4.6*	*.294*	*-1.7*	*1B 4 • 3B -1*	*1.1*

Breakout: 6%   Improve: 46%   Collapse: 9%   Attrition: 15%   MLB: 86%   *Comparables: Aaron Hill, Didi Gregorius, Enrique Hernandez*

After missing two full seasons with a shoulder injury, Profar was finally awarded his recall to the majors when Rougned Odor punched his way to a seven-game suspension. Profar impressed the Texas brass while his former double-play partner watched from the bench, earning him a permanent roster spot, but he had to ride the super-utility train to get there. The line Profar put up after a two-year hiatus was menial, but his mere presence on the roster was not. Though Profar's thin frame and relative unwillingness to put the ball in the air is unlikely to spurn much production in the power department, his patient approach and ability to hit to all fields remains and will serve as the building blocks of his offensive game going forward. Counting out the former top prospect in baseball just a few short years ago would be a poor choice.

Ryan Rua   LF

Born: 3/11/90   Age: 27   Bats: R   Throws: R   Height: 6'2"   Weight: 205   Entered Pro Ball: Round 17, 2011 Draft (#534 overall)

YEAR	TEAM	LVL	AGE	PA	R	2B	3B	HR	RBI	BB	K	SB	CS	AVG/OBP/SLG	TAv	VORP	BABIP	BRR	FRAA	WARP
2014	FRI	AA	24	288	34	13	1	10	38	30	55	5	3	.300/.375/.475	.309	21.2	.349	-0.7	3B(50): -4.2 • 1B(6): -0.3	1.7
2014	ROU	AAA	24	241	31	13	2	8	36	21	42	1	2	.313/.382/.505	.310	19.2	.355	-1.2	3B(27): -0.4 • LF(24): -2.8	1.6
2014	TEX	MLB	24	109	11	7	0	2	14	2	18	1	0	.295/.321/.419	.269	3.6	.341	0.9	LF(17): -2.2 • 1B(9): 0.3	0.2
2015	ROU	AAA	25	165	15	5	0	6	22	18	45	3	0	.197/.303/.359	.254	1.4	.239	-1.0	LF(10): 1.2 • 3B(9): 0.6	0.2
2015	TEX	MLB	25	86	10	5	0	4	7	3	32	0	0	.193/.221/.398	.223	-1.4	.255	0.0	LF(22): -0.0 • RF(4): -0.9	-0.2
2016	TEX	MLB	26	269	40	8	1	8	22	21	76	9	0	.258/.331/.400	.252	6.2	.342	3.3	LF(60): -3.9 • 1B(31): 0.5	0.2
2017	*TEX*	*MLB*	*27*	*344*	*38*	*14*	*1*	*11*	*41*	*26*	*87*	*5*	*1*	*.250/.316/.408*	*.256*	*8.8*	*.311*	*0.0*	*RF -4 • LF -2*	*0.0*
2018	*TEX*	*MLB*	*28*	*326*	*41*	*14*	*1*	*11*	*40*	*25*	*84*	*4*	*1*	*.252/.319/.421*	*.254*	*5.9*	*.314*	*1.4*	*RF -4 • LF -2*	*0.2*

Breakout: 5%   Improve: 35%   Collapse: 12%   Attrition: 21%   MLB: 80%   *Comparables: John Bowker, Ben Francisco, Seth Smith*

After only participating in 28 games during 2015, Rua finally got the most playing time of his short Rangers career this past season. Playing mostly the short-side of a platoon in left field—along with some starts peppered in at first base—Rua not only proved worthy of his roster spot, but even showed competence in hitting same-side pitching with a .714 OPS against righties. He may be a bit vanilla compared to some of the more exciting talents the Rangers possess, but sometimes the versatility of vanilla is highly underrated. Should he stay healthy, Rua is a solid notch on the Rangers depth chart.

Leody Taveras   OF

Born: 9/8/98   Age: 18   Bats: B   Throws: R   Height: 6'1"   Weight: 170   Entered Pro Ball: International Free Agent, 2015

YEAR	TEAM	LVL	AGE	PA	R	2B	3B	HR	RBI	BB	K	SB	CS	AVG/OBP/SLG	TAv	VORP	BABIP	BRR	FRAA	WARP
2016	SPO	A-	17	133	14	6	1	0	9	8	26	3	1	.228/.271/.293	.253	2.4	.283	-0.3	CF(26): 1.2 • LF(1): 0.0	0.3
2017	TEX	MLB	18	250	26	9	1	5	20	11	72	4	2	.209/.247/.321	.193	-8.1	.276	-0.1	CF -1 • RF -0	-1.0
2018	TEX	MLB	19	280	27	10	2	6	27	11	82	4	2	.211/.245/.334	.202	-9.0	.275	0.2	CF -2 • RF 0	-1.2

Breakout: 0%   Improve: 0%   Collapse: 0%   Attrition: 0%   MLB: 0%   *Comparables: Raul Mondesi, Wilmer Flores*

When your older cousin Willy stole 195 bases in his seven-year career, there are going to be expectations about your speed. Yet despite possessing enough to be regarded as plus, it's the speed at which he might fly through the minors that's even more impressive. After signing a mere 18 months ago and debuting in the Dominican Summer League in June, Taveras reached and blew through the Arizona League before finishing the season as the youngest player in the Northwest League. The 18-year-old has the potential for five average-to-plus tools and showed them off even while struggling against competition four years his senior. Only time will tell for Taveras, but if time continues to move as quickly for him as it did in 2016, the next great Rangers prospect might not be far away from the national spotlight.

Anderson Tejeda   SS

Born: 5/1/98   Age: 19   Bats: L   Throws: R   Height: 5'11"   Weight: 160   Entered Pro Ball: International Free Agent, 2014

YEAR	TEAM	LVL	AGE	PA	R	2B	3B	HR	RBI	BB	K	SB	CS	AVG/OBP/SLG	TAv	VORP	BABIP	BRR	FRAA	WARP
2016	SPO	A-	18	99	15	0	1	8	19	5	33	1	0	.277/.313/.553	.285	6.6	.340	0.5	SS(17): -1.7 • 2B(3): -0.4	0.5
2017	TEX	MLB	19	250	23	9	2	8	28	12	84	1	1	.206/.247/.354	.202	-3.9	.281	-0.1	SS -0 • 2B 0	-0.4
2018	TEX	MLB	20	369	42	13	3	13	44	20	119	2	1	.221/.267/.391	.225	-1.2	.293	-0.1	SS 0 • 2B 0	-0.2

Breakout: 0%   Improve: 6%   Collapse: 2%   Attrition: 6%   MLB: 13%   *Comparables: Raul Mondesi, Nomar Mazara, Carlos Correa*

Just what the rest of the AL West needs: another athletic Rangers middle infield prospect. Tejeda finished razing the DSL and moved to Low-A Spokane, where he continued to swing with authority, if not always on the actual plane of the ball. Scouts are torn on whether he'll stick at short, given a fair share of fielding miscues, but he wields the arm to play elsewhere and the snap to his swing to render the question moot.

Yeyson Yrizarri   SS

Born: 2/2/97   Age: 20   Bats: R   Throws: R   Height: 6'0"   Weight: 175   Entered Pro Ball: International Free Agent, 2013

YEAR	TEAM	LVL	AGE	PA	R	2B	3B	HR	RBI	BB	K	SB	CS	AVG/OBP/SLG	TAv	VORP	BABIP	BRR	FRAA	WARP
2015	ROU	AAA	18	34	2	1	1	0	4	1	5	0	1	.273/.294/.364	.196	-1.4	.321	-0.5	SS(9): -1.2	-0.3
2015	SPO	A-	18	257	27	10	1	2	29	6	46	8	6	.265/.290/.339	.240	4.8	.318	0.0	SS(57): 0.3 • 2B(5): -0.7	0.5
2016	HIC	A	19	479	53	27	3	7	53	9	91	20	15	.269/.292/.389	.266	20.4	.318	-1.5	SS(116): 13.8	3.8
2017	TEX	MLB	20	250	24	11	1	5	25	5	64	5	4	.229/.253/.351	.203	-3.6	.286	-0.5	SS 3	-0.1
2018	TEX	MLB	21	394	40	17	2	9	42	9	97	8	7	.243/.268/.377	.221	-2.2	.298	-0.2	SS 5	0.3

Breakout: 1%   Improve: 7%   Collapse: 0%   Attrition: 2%   MLB: 13%   *Comparables: Chris Owings, Raul Mondesi, Tim Beckham*

The idea of the "triple threat" appears in many fields. It could refer to those entertainers who could move audiences through their acting, dancing and singing—like Gene Kelly or Jamie Foxx. For baseball's position players, it's someone who can contribute to the three pillars of WARP—offense, defense and baserunning—and Yrizarri has the raw ingredients to be just that. Unfortunately they are raw enough that there's a pop-up restaurant in New York specifically devoted to them. His plate discipline might unravel his offensive potential, as he shows off his sweet and powerful swing early and often. His instincts on the bases currently hold his natural speed hostage. And despite having an absolute cannon of an arm, his actions in the field need to improve in order to be considered one of the top defensive shortstops in the minors. On the bright side, if one or more aspects of his game stall out, he'll always be able to fall back on being a different type of triple threat—as the only player in organized baseball whose name includes the letter Y as a consonant, a vowel and as part of a diphthong.

PITCHERS

Dario Alvarez   LHP

Born: 1/17/89   Age: 28   Bats: L   Throws: L   Height: 6'1"   Weight: 170   Entered Pro Ball: International Free Agent, 2007

YEAR	TEAM	LVL	AGE	W	L	SV	G	GS	IP	H	HR	BB/9	K/9	K	GB%	BABIP	WHIP	ERA	FIP	DRA	VORP	WARP	cFIP	MPH
2014	SAV	A	25	7	1	1	20	6	61^1	43	2	2.1	13.9	95	55%	.315	0.93	1.32	1.70	0.70	30.8	3.2	53	
2014	NYN	MLB	25	0	0	0	4	0	1^1	4	1	0.0	6.8	1	43%	.500	3.00	13.50	11.35	4.33	0.0	0.0	106	93.1
2015	BIN	AA	26	1	1	0	32	0	31	21	2	4.6	12.5	43	46%	.271	1.19	3.19	3.17	2.02	9.3	1.0	85	
2015	LVG	AAA	26	2	1	0	16	0	11	6	0	4.1	15.5	19	47%	.353	1.00	2.45	2.33	2.08	3.5	0.4	82	
2015	NYN	MLB	26	1	0	0	6	0	3^2	5	2	2.5	4.9	2	21%	.250	1.64	12.27	11.62	5.85	-0.5	0.0	111	94.0
2016	LVG	AAA	27	0	1	0	17	0	15^1	22	3	5.9	15.8	27	54%	.500	2.09	9.98	4.89	1.24	6.3	0.7	76	
2016	ATL	MLB	27	3	1	0	16	0	15	11	3	3.0	16.8	28	33%	.333	1.07	3.00	3.25	2.56	4.0	0.4	72	95.5
2016	TEX	MLB	27	0	0	0	10	0	11^2	17	3	1.5	10.0	13	46%	.438	1.63	7.71	5.25	2.47	3.2	0.3	72	95.1
2017	TEX	MLB	28	1	1	0	24	0	25^1	23	3	3.6	9.8	28	54%	.305	1.37	3.57	3.80	3.94	2.9	0.3	88	
2018	TEX	MLB	29	3	1	1	52	0	55^2	47	6	4.6	11.4	71	54%	.309	1.36	3.67	3.67	3.97	6.5	0.7	86	

Breakout: 24%   Improve: 40%   Collapse: 11%   Attrition: 25%   MLB: 60%   *Comparables: Zac Rosscup, Doug Slaten, Jack Taschner*

While the rest of the market was selling off their farms, souls and first borns for proven relievers at the trade deadline, the Rangers took a gamble on a high-strikeout, high-velocity lefty with almost no track record. Alvarez's ERA is misleading, because though FIP didn't favor him much more, DRA loved him—overlooking his astronomical home run rate and BABIP, while focusing on his ability to make hitters come up empty more often than an eight-year-old at a ring toss game. The strikeouts were a direct result of Alvarez loading up on sliders like Harold and Kumar, throwing the pitch nearly 60 percent of the time. If the advanced metrics are right, the Rangers smartly helped stack their bullpen for the meager price of slowly-falling-out-of-favor infield prospect Travis Demeritte.

Tony Barnette   RHP

Born: 11/9/83   Age: 33   Bats: R   Throws: R   Height: 6'1"   Weight: 190   Entered Pro Ball: Round 10, 2006 Draft (#297 overall)

YEAR	TEAM	LVL	AGE	W	L	SV	G	GS	IP	H	HR	BB/9	K/9	K	GB%	BABIP	WHIP	ERA	FIP	DRA	VORP	WARP	cFIP	MPH
2016	TEX	MLB	32	7	3	0	53	0	60^1	54	4	2.4	7.3	49	48%	.289	1.16	2.09	3.34	3.60	9.2	1.0	97	94.2
2017	TEX	MLB	33	3	3	0	53	0	55	56	7	2.7	7.7	47	51%	.299	1.31	3.98	4.19	4.31	4.1	0.4	99	
2018	TEX	MLB	34	1	1	0	29	0	30^2	33	4	3.2	7.4	25	51%	.311	1.42	4.34	4.34	4.72	1.1	0.1	106	

Breakout: 17%   Improve: 41%   Collapse: 29%   Attrition: 9%   MLB: 87%   *Comparables: Brandon Lyon, Craig Breslow, Fernando Rodney*

It's been a full US Senate term since Barnette has appeared in this book, but if Baseball Prospectus put out a comprehensive guide to the NPB, he'd have graced those pages. After being drafted by the Diamondbacks in 2006 and making it as far as Reno, Barnette traded a minor league rotation for a Central League bullpen, eventually locking down 41 saves with a 1.29 ERA for the Yakult Swallows in 2015. Following the Colby Lewis Pipeline to the Rangers, the native Alaskan adjusted quickly. In April, he threw four-seamers and sliders 65 percent of the time. In May, he unlocked a cutter and began throwing it a third of the time—eventually ramping it up to more than half the time in the second half. This led to his success against right-handers, who hit .186 and slugged .220 against the pitch, to the tune of a .523 OPS. Even if neutralizing lefties remains an issue, Barnette can earn his meager $1.75 million salary just by being the second ROOGY in town.

Matt Bush   RHP

Born: 2/8/86   Age: 31   Bats: R   Throws: R   Height: 5'9"   Weight: 180   Entered Pro Ball: Round 1, 2004 Draft (#1 overall)

YEAR	TEAM	LVL	AGE	W	L	SV	G	GS	IP	H	HR	BB/9	K/9	K	GB%	BABIP	WHIP	ERA	FIP	DRA	VORP	WARP	cFIP	MPH
2016	FRI	AA	30	0	2	5	12	0	17	9	2	2.1	9.5	18	42%	.184	0.76	2.65	3.47	2.34	4.5	0.5	90	
2016	TEX	MLB	30	7	2	1	58	0	61^2	44	4	2.0	8.9	61	45%	.245	0.94	2.48	2.70	3.05	13.2	1.4	85	99.7
2017	TEX	MLB	31	2	3	0	48	0	50	47	6	2.7	8.6	48	42%	.290	1.22	3.83	3.82	4.18	4.5	0.5	96	
2018	TEX	MLB	32	2	1	0	45	0	48^1	44	6	2.9	8.7	46	42%	.288	1.24	3.94	3.95	4.29	4.0	0.4	96	

Breakout: 28%   Improve: 39%   Collapse: 28%   Attrition: 15%   MLB: 88%   *Comparables: Craig Breslow, Kevin Jepsen, John Axford*

For the Rangers, Bush certainly arrived on their doorstep in the nick of time as Shawn Tolleson went from closing gig to Triple-A to outrighted off the 40-man in the span of seven months. Bush emerged as an elite and surprising force for the Rangers bullpen after they picked him up off the scrap heap in December 2015. Bush flashes double nines on the regular, and augments it using a curveball with a 41 percent whiff rate and a slider that touches 93. Finding a relief pitcher that has this type of stuff with good control is a rare gem.

Unfortunately, there's far more to this story than what has happened on the field. Unlike the last time the Rangers found themselves with a former no. 1 overall pick in search of redemption, Bush isn't just struggling with his inner demons. He had been shown the door by three different organizations—the Padres, Blue Jays and Rays—after serious run-ins with the law. The last of these incidents was in 2012 when he nearly killed a motorcyclist in Florida while driving under the influence. The Rangers didn't just sign him off the scrap heap, they signed him out of prison—he was released in October 2015 after serving over three years of a 51-month sentence.

All of this creates no shortage of uncomfortability when Bush steps onto the mound—both from the batters he faces and from the throngs who watch him. This is not a simple story about overcoming odds and adversity, or about a former top draft pick finally realizing his talent. It's a dark and complex one that needs to be told and shared in full. Incredibly, even with flaming out as a shortstop prospect and spending what should have been the peak years of his career behind bars, Bush is still on track to be the third-most valuable player to be selected in the top 10 of the 2004 draft.

Andrew Cashner   RHP

Born: 9/11/86   Age: 30   Bats: R   Throws: R   Height: 6'6"   Weight: 235   Entered Pro Ball: Round 1, 2008 Draft (#19 overall)

YEAR	TEAM	LVL	AGE	W	L	SV	G	GS	IP	H	HR	BB/9	K/9	K	GB%	BABIP	WHIP	ERA	FIP	DRA	VORP	WARP	cFIP	MPH
2014	SDN	MLB	27	5	7	0	19	19	123¹	110	7	2.1	6.8	93	50%	.275	1.13	2.55	3.06	4.20	8.7	1.0	106	97.8
2015	SDN	MLB	28	6	16	0	31	31	184²	200	19	3.2	8.0	165	50%	.330	1.44	4.34	3.88	4.31	15.8	1.7	101	98.1
2016	SDN	MLB	29	4	7	0	16	16	79¹	80	13	3.4	7.6	67	49%	.291	1.39	4.76	4.99	4.64	6.3	0.6	108	97.2
2016	MIA	MLB	29	1	4	0	12	11	52²	62	6	5.1	7.7	45	47%	.352	1.75	5.98	4.72	4.42	5.5	0.6	108	96.6
2017	*TEX*	*MLB*	*30*	*8*	*8*	*0*	*23*	*23*	*131*	*138*	*18*	*3.8*	*7.5*	*110*	*48%*	*.302*	*1.49*	*4.66*	*4.68*	*5.02*	*3.3*	*0.3*	*100*	
2018	*TEX*	*MLB*	*31*	*9*	*11*	*0*	*29*	*29*	*176¹*	*192*	*26*	*3.7*	*7.7*	*150*	*48%*	*.313*	*1.49*	*4.71*	*4.71*	*5.10*	*6.6*	*0.7*	*118*	

Breakout: 14%   Improve: 42%   Collapse: 25%   Attrition: 15%   MLB: 91%   *Comparables: Jason Vargas, Cliff Lee, Yovani Gallardo*

Tolstoy would be proud: pretty much everyone in the Andrew Cashner-to-Miami trade was miserable in their own special way last season, the centerpiece included. The one-time Grizzly Adams understudy was having the worst season of his career in San Diego when he was shipped to Miami with Colin Rea for Marlins' top prospects Josh Naylor and Luis Castillo. In Florida, things got worse. Pitching for a new contract, he did so on tilt, tossing a 5.98 ERA. Worse yet, the beard had to go, because while you can take Don Mattingly away from the Yankees' anachronistic and patently stupid no-facial-hair policy, the opposite isn't true. A free agent, Cashner signed a one-year deal with the Rangers, who won't care what he does with his face as long it's not being metaphorically beaten in by opposing hitters.

Alex Claudio   LHP

Born: 1/31/92   Age: 25   Bats: L   Throws: L   Height: 6'3"   Weight: 180   Entered Pro Ball: Round 27, 2010 Draft (#826 overall)

YEAR	TEAM	LVL	AGE	W	L	SV	G	GS	IP	H	HR	BB/9	K/9	K	GB%	BABIP	WHIP	ERA	FIP	DRA	VORP	WARP	cFIP	MPH
2014	MYR	A+	22	4	0	4	17	2	49¹	38	2	1.6	10.2	56	64%	.298	0.95	1.09	2.44	1.43	21.1	2.1	64	
2014	FRI	AA	22	2	2	0	8	6	37¹	31	1	0.5	5.3	22	52%	.246	0.88	2.17	2.53	3.08	8.7	0.9	92	
2014	TEX	MLB	22	0	0	0	15	0	12¹	14	0	2.9	10.2	14	58%	.389	1.46	2.92	1.48	2.81	2.3	0.3	90	86.9
2015	TEX	MLB	23	1	1	0	18	0	15²	12	4	3.4	7.5	13	52%	.190	1.15	2.87	6.10	3.52	2.1	0.2	97	86.2
2015	ROU	AAA	23	3	1	0	29	0	40	43	2	1.6	7.9	35	57%	.347	1.25	2.92	3.10	2.36	11.4	1.2	88	
2016	ROU	AAA	24	0	0	1	6	0	16¹	7	0	2.2	4.4	8	71%	.156	0.67	0.55	3.48	3.10	3.4	0.3	96	
2016	TEX	MLB	24	4	1	0	39	0	51²	55	2	1.7	5.9	34	63%	.312	1.26	2.79	2.93	3.73	7.1	0.7	92	88.2
2017	*TEX*	*MLB*	*25*	*3*	*3*	*0*	*53*	*0*	*55*	*57*	*6*	*2.6*	*6.5*	*40*	*43%*	*.295*	*1.32*	*4.08*	*4.10*	*4.39*	*3.7*	*0.4*	*100*	
2018	*TEX*	*MLB*	*26*	*2*	*1*	*0*	*40*	*0*	*42²*	*40*	*4*	*3.6*	*8.8*	*42*	*43%*	*.300*	*1.33*	*3.89*	*3.90*	*4.25*	*3.8*	*0.4*	*93*	

Breakout: 28%   Improve: 42%   Collapse: 17%   Attrition: 30%   MLB: 70%   *Comparables: Daniel Herrera, Josh Spence, Yimi Garcia*

Low velocity isn't something that baseball folks are programmed to find appealing, but when it comes to Claudio's changeup, it becomes a different story. And it's not just because he throws the pitch at a mind-bending 69 mph. Claudio sets up the change with a sinker that literally hit 90 mph just once the entire season and mixes in a slider that he probably should throw less often. He struggled with serving up too many long balls last season, but his answer to that seems to have been to get more grounders—a reasonable approach to a reasonable problem. Because the change is his go-to secondary offering, Claudio hasn't been used like a LOOGY and probably profiles best in bimanous fashion despite his massive splits in 2016.

Yu Darvish   RHP

Born: 8/16/86   Age: 30   Bats: R   Throws: R   Height: 6'5"   Weight: 220   Entered Pro Ball: International Free Agent, 2012

YEAR	TEAM	LVL	AGE	W	L	SV	G	GS	IP	H	HR	BB/9	K/9	K	GB%	BABIP	WHIP	ERA	FIP	DRA	VORP	WARP	cFIP	MPH
2014	TEX	MLB	27	10	7	0	22	22	144¹	133	13	3.1	11.3	182	37%	.334	1.26	3.06	2.87	2.47	37.9	4.2	76	95.6
2016	FRI	AA	29	1	1	0	5	5	20	14	1	3.2	10.8	24	50%	.277	1.05	2.25	2.48	2.58	5.6	0.6	82	
2016	TEX	MLB	29	7	5	0	17	17	100¹	81	12	2.8	11.8	132	40%	.290	1.12	3.41	3.05	2.56	31.2	3.2	71	97.1
2017	*TEX*	*MLB*	*30*	*12*	*8*	*0*	*29*	*29*	*174*	*147*	*24*	*3.1*	*11.2*	*217*	*42%*	*.295*	*1.20*	*3.59*	*3.62*	*3.86*	*26.8*	*2.8*	*88*	
2018	*TEX*	*MLB*	*31*	*11*	*9*	*0*	*29*	*29*	*178*	*149*	*25*	*3.0*	*11.1*	*220*	*42%*	*.291*	*1.17*	*3.63*	*3.62*	*3.92*	*29.3*	*3.0*	*88*	

Breakout: 15%   Improve: 46%   Collapse: 27%   Attrition: 6%   MLB: 94%   *Comparables: David Price, Randy Johnson, Zack Greinke*

Starting the season on the disabled list while still recovering from 2015 Tommy John surgery would be the first small dent that Darvish would put in the Rangers plans for 2016. Making three starts before going back on the disabled list for five weeks with neck and shoulder discomfort would be the second. But with a return announced just hours before he took the mound at Wrigley Field after the All-Star Break, Darvish sought to undo that damage with a vengeance. Not only did he post the second-highest strikeout rate among starters in 2016, but he also brought his walk rate to a career low and added a tick of velocity across the board for good measure. A full season of the now-30-year-old ace would go a long way towards helping the Rangers prove that their 2016 success was not a Pythagorean fluke.

Jake Diekman   LHP

Born: 1/21/87   Age: 30   Bats: L   Throws: L   Height: 6'4"   Weight: 200   Entered Pro Ball: Round 30, 2007 Draft (#923 overall)

YEAR	TEAM	LVL	AGE	W	L	SV	G	GS	IP	H	HR	BB/9	K/9	K	GB%	BABIP	WHIP	ERA	FIP	DRA	VORP	WARP	cFIP	MPH
2014	PHI	MLB	27	5	5	0	73	0	71	66	4	4.4	12.7	100	44%	.363	1.42	3.80	2.62	2.83	13.1	1.4	77	99.5
2015	PHI	MLB	28	2	1	0	41	0	36²	40	3	5.9	12.0	49	55%	.381	1.75	5.15	3.68	2.99	7.0	0.8	88	99.0
2015	TEX	MLB	28	0	0	0	26	0	21²	13	2	2.9	8.3	20	60%	.200	0.92	2.08	3.57	3.14	3.8	0.4	86	99.5
2016	TEX	MLB	29	4	2	4	66	0	53	36	4	4.4	10.0	59	50%	.248	1.17	3.40	3.50	3.65	7.8	0.8	89	97.7
2017	*TEX*	*MLB*	*30*	*3*	*3*	*3*	*57*	*0*	*60²*	*55*	*6*	*4.2*	*10.2*	*69*	*58%*	*.308*	*1.38*	*3.43*	*3.71*	*3.84*	*7.7*	*0.8*	*83*	
2018	*TEX*	*MLB*	*31*	*2*	*1*	*1*	*40*	*0*	*42*	*37*	*4*	*4.2*	*10.5*	*49*	*58%*	*.307*	*1.34*	*3.68*	*3.68*	*3.99*	*4.9*	*0.5*	*86*	

Breakout: 38%   Improve: 59%   Collapse: 22%   Attrition: 20%   MLB: 88%   *Comparables: Marc Rzepczynski, Brian Wilson, Steve Cishek*

Dialing up the fastball has always been easy for Diekman, but knowing where it's going hasn't. He came out of the gates untouchable, yielding only three baserunners in April over 11 appearances. Self-proclaimed issues with mechanics caused his performance to waver over the next four months. By the season's final month, he was a shell of himself, walking eight batters in 5.2 September innings and sliding further away from high-leverage innings. Things went from bad to worse as he allowed more than twice as many baserunners in the ALDS (seven) than he got outs (three). However, Diekman has shown the ability to snap his control back into shape throughout his career—something the Rangers will hope he can do once more in 2017.

Sam Dyson   RHP

Born: 5/7/88   Age: 29   Bats: R   Throws: R   Height: 6'1"   Weight: 205   Entered Pro Ball: Round 4, 2010 Draft (#126 overall)

YEAR	TEAM	LVL	AGE	W	L	SV	G	GS	IP	H	HR	BB/9	K/9	K	GB%	BABIP	WHIP	ERA	FIP	DRA	VORP	WARP	cFIP	MPH
2014	NWO	AAA	26	2	1	1	13	0	25¹	21	0	3.6	7.1	20	66%	.296	1.22	2.49	3.54	4.63	2.0	0.2	93	
2014	MIA	MLB	26	3	1	0	31	0	42	41	1	3.2	7.1	33	67%	.310	1.33	2.14	3.13	3.01	6.9	0.8	94	98.8
2015	MIA	MLB	27	3	3	0	44	0	44	41	3	3.5	8.4	41	65%	.302	1.32	3.68	3.55	2.84	9.1	1.0	82	98.5
2015	TEX	MLB	27	2	1	2	31	0	31¹	24	1	1.1	8.6	30	76%	.277	0.89	1.15	2.08	2.77	6.8	0.7	78	98.6
2016	TEX	MLB	28	3	2	38	73	0	70¹	63	5	2.9	7.0	55	65%	.291	1.22	2.43	3.58	4.05	7.2	0.7	87	98.2
2017	TEX	MLB	29	3	3	35	57	0	60²	58	6	3.2	7.6	52	53%	.295	1.31	3.62	3.93	4.00	6.6	0.7	87	
2018	TEX	MLB	30	3	1	28	54	0	57²	52	6	3.5	9.1	58	53%	.295	1.29	3.80	3.80	4.12	5.9	0.6	90	

Breakout: 32%   Improve: 50%   Collapse: 26%   Attrition: 33%   MLB: 84%   *Comparables: Xavier Cedeno, Bryan Morris, Chad Qualls*

Dyson allowed his team's season to end on the famous three-run bomb, and subsequent epic bat flip, in Game 5 of the 2015 ALDS—a home run that would become the cornerstone of puns, punches and even t-shirts all over East Texas. But if it got to him, he shook it off well. The former Sunbelt Player of the Year took over the closer role for an ailing (and failing) Shawn Tolleson in 2016, but if he hopes to hold off his predecessor's fate, he'll have to amp back up his strikeout rate, which did not hold the gains from 2015. He was a microcosm of the season in Arlington—everything looked dandy on the surface, but the peripherals proved ominous. Both Dyson and the Rangers will set out to prove they belong in their current roles—the former as closer, the latter as the team to beat in the AL West.

Chi Chi Gonzalez   RHP

Born: 1/15/92   Age: 25   Bats: R   Throws: R   Height: 6'3"   Weight: 215   Entered Pro Ball: Round 1, 2013 Draft (#23 overall)

YEAR	TEAM	LVL	AGE	W	L	SV	G	GS	IP	H	HR	BB/9	K/9	K	GB%	BABIP	WHIP	ERA	FIP	DRA	VORP	WARP	cFIP	MPH
2014	MYR	A+	22	5	2	0	11	11	65¹	56	3	2.2	6.8	49	55%	.262	1.10	2.62	3.62	4.18	10.3	1.0	98	
2014	FRI	AA	22	7	4	0	15	14	73¹	67	3	3.1	7.9	64	55%	.300	1.25	2.70	3.09	3.29	15.5	1.7	88	
2015	ROU	AAA	23	8	7	0	16	16	88¹	95	3	3.2	5.7	56	54%	.325	1.43	3.57	3.96	4.55	7.4	0.8	108	
2015	TEX	MLB	23	4	6	0	14	10	67	49	6	4.3	4.0	30	50%	.206	1.21	3.90	4.94	5.66	-4.6	-0.5	123	94.3
2016	TEX	MLB	24	0	2	0	3	3	10¹	21	1	7.8	6.1	7	46%	.444	2.90	8.71	5.62	6.19	-0.9	-0.1	119	94.4
2016	ROU	AAA	24	8	10	0	25	24	138	154	8	2.9	5.9	91	57%	.330	1.43	4.70	4.20	4.72	9.5	1.0	95	
2017	TEX	MLB	25	3	4	0	10	10	53	60	7	3.6	5.3	31	52%	.297	1.54	4.98	5.03	5.37	-0.7	-0.1	100	
2018	TEX	MLB	26	8	11	0	29	29	176²	173	24	4.7	8.3	163	52%	.299	1.50	4.83	4.84	5.24	3.9	0.4	122	

Breakout: 13%   Improve: 31%   Collapse: 24%   Attrition: 35%   MLB: 79%   *Comparables: Dallas Keuchel, Allen Webster, Kyle Hendricks*

After making only three appearances—one of them a bloodbath demanding a ritual sacrifice of 124 pitches to get through 4.2 innings—Gonzalez was shipped back to Round Rock at the height of the Rangers' rotation crisis in early July. That's quite the statement considering how badly the Rangers needed anyone with a pulse to eat innings. The 2013 first round pick's control and command issues were the ultimate culprit for him, but his 2016 season was like an experiment in seeing just how far you can push someone with paper cuts. Of the 21 hits he allowed, only three went for extra bases. For those of you counting at home, that's 18 singles allowed in 10.1 innings. That just seems impossibly cruel, and gives quite a middle finger to DIPS theory.

A.J. Griffin   RHP

Born: 1/28/88   Age: 29   Bats: R   Throws: R   Height: 6'5"   Weight: 230   Entered Pro Ball: Round 13, 2010 Draft (#395 overall)

YEAR	TEAM	LVL	AGE	W	L	SV	G	GS	IP	H	HR	BB/9	K/9	K	GB%	BABIP	WHIP	ERA	FIP	DRA	VORP	WARP	cFIP	MPH
2016	FRI	AA	28	0	1	0	3	3	10¹	12	0	3.5	11.3	13	50%	.400	1.55	3.48	1.83	3.16	2.2	0.2	88	
2016	TEX	MLB	28	7	4	0	23	23	119	116	28	3.5	8.1	107	31%	.274	1.36	5.07	5.70	5.91	-7.3	-0.8	119	90.4
2017	TEX	MLB	29	6	7	0	19	19	95	93	18	3.4	8.1	86	56%	.285	1.33	4.98	5.12	5.38	-1.4	-0.1	100	
2018	TEX	MLB	30	6	8	0	21	21	126¹	120	25	4.0	8.2	116	56%	.270	1.40	5.36	5.35	5.81	-4.0	-0.4	138	

Breakout: 22%   Improve: 43%   Collapse: 25%   Attrition: 12%   MLB: 86%   *Comparables: Brian Bannister, Josh Collmenter, David Phelps*

There are generally two camps that pitchers who struggle upon returning from Tommy John surgery fall into. There are the big stuff, small command pitchers whose ability to locate becomes untenable for the level, and there are the small stuff, big command pitchers who have historically relied on plus and above command to overcome a lack of high-end raw materials. Griffin fell into the latter category as he sputtered to a 23-start diminuendo with the Rangers—which probably would have been shorter if not for the dearth of starting pitching depth the Rangers had during 2016. In golf, there's the often-used concept of "missing on the pro side," which is when someone misses a putt but it ends up below the hole, leaving a relatively straight and uphill stroke back to the hole. The baseball equivalent is missing your spot, but leaving it off the plate. Griffin did the opposite of that far too much last season and may find himself missing from the Rangers rotation this year because of it. Then again, you might not have even realized he was in it last year.

Cole Hamels LHP

Born: 12/27/83 Age: 33 Bats: L Throws: L Height: 6'4" Weight: 205 Entered Pro Ball: Round 1, 2002 Draft (#17 overall)

YEAR	TEAM	LVL	AGE	W	L	SV	G	GS	IP	H	HR	BB/9	K/9	K	GB%	BABIP	WHIP	ERA	FIP	DRA	VORP	WARP	cFIP	MPH
2014	CLR	A+	30	0	1	0	3	3	17	12	3	0.5	6.4	12	67%	.214	0.76	2.12	4.63	3.27	4.4	0.4	88	
2014	PHI	MLB	30	9	9	0	30	30	204²	176	14	2.6	8.7	198	50%	.295	1.15	2.46	3.04	2.95	43.0	4.7	85	95.0
2015	PHI	MLB	31	6	7	0	20	20	128²	113	12	2.7	9.6	137	51%	.294	1.18	3.64	3.29	3.18	27.2	2.9	82	94.8
2015	TEX	MLB	31	7	1	0	12	12	83²	77	10	2.5	8.4	78	48%	.294	1.20	3.66	3.76	3.04	18.9	2.0	81	95.5
2016	TEX	MLB	32	15	5	0	32	32	200²	185	24	3.5	9.0	200	50%	.299	1.31	3.32	3.94	2.65	60.4	6.2	86	94.9
2017	TEX	MLB	33	13	9	0	29	29	194¹	178	22	3.2	9.3	200	55%	.299	1.28	3.70	3.78	3.99	27.2	2.8	91	
2018	TEX	MLB	34	12	11	0	30	30	186²	178	24	3.4	9.2	190	55%	.303	1.33	4.08	4.09	4.42	22.8	2.4	101	

Breakout: 12% Improve: 40% Collapse: 38% Attrition: 26% MLB: 94% *Comparables: A.J. Burnett, Josh Beckett, Erik Bedard*

Late in his excellent Phillies tenure Hamels' reputation unfairly took a hit when his win-loss record was dragged down by a poor supporting cast. His performance has changed remarkably little since a mid-2015 trade to the Rangers, but Hamels' record once again matches his ace-caliber pitching. As a fly-ball pitcher on the wrong side of 30 there were worries about Hamels' transition to the American League and a power-inflating ballpark, but he made some key adjustments to keep chugging along. Hamels relied less on his changeup in 2016 than ever before, focusing on sinking and cutting his fastball to induce more ground balls. His change-up remains a swing-and-miss weapon, but he uses it more sparingly to avoid long balls in Texas and dance around the outskirts of the strike zone. It's a recipe that worked wonders, as Hamels posted the second-best DRA of his career. He faded down the stretch and struggled in his lone playoff start, but Hamels topped 200 innings for the seventh straight year and still sports a 3.48 postseason ERA. He's one of the best (and most underrated) pitchers of this generation and has proven capable of changing his approach to thrive in tough environments for his skill set. He's shown no signs of slowing down with two seasons left on his contract.

Lucas Harrell RHP

Born: 6/3/85 Age: 32 Bats: B Throws: R Height: 6'2" Weight: 205 Entered Pro Ball: Round 4, 2004 Draft (#119 overall)

YEAR	TEAM	LVL	AGE	W	L	SV	G	GS	IP	H	HR	BB/9	K/9	K	GB%	BABIP	WHIP	ERA	FIP	DRA	VORP	WARP	cFIP	MPH
2014	HOU	MLB	29	0	3	0	3	3	12¹	19	2	6.6	6.6	9	50%	.370	2.27	9.49	6.00	4.65	0.3	0.0	108	93.5
2014	RNO	AAA	29	6	4	0	22	20	106²	115	12	6.5	5.7	67	63%	.311	1.80	5.15	6.21	6.80	-12.6	-1.3	118	
2016	ERI	AA	31	2	1	0	5	5	24²	24	1	5.1	5.8	16	60%	.295	1.54	3.28	4.41	4.72	1.0	0.1	106	
2016	GWN	AAA	31	2	1	0	9	5	32	35	1	5.3	7.6	27	61%	.347	1.69	2.81	3.76	4.31	3.4	0.4	100	
2016	ATL	MLB	31	2	2	0	5	5	29¹	25	1	3.7	6.4	21	43%	.276	1.26	3.38	3.73	5.69	-1.1	-0.1	115	94.1
2016	TEX	MLB	31	1	0	0	4	4	17²	21	3	6.6	7.6	15	47%	.346	1.92	5.60	5.99	5.73	-0.7	-0.1	116	92.9
2017	TEX	MLB	32	4	5	0	22	12	73	78	10	4.8	6.8	55	52%	.304	1.60	5.04	5.17	5.48	-1.0	-0.1	127	
2018	TEX	MLB	33	3	4	0	13	10	67¹	74	10	5.2	7.8	59	52%	.319	1.67	5.19	5.20	5.64	-1.4	-0.1	129	

Breakout: 13% Improve: 25% Collapse: 15% Attrition: 11% MLB: 55% *Comparables: Ryan Drese, John Maine, Dontrelle Willis*

Yet another fleeting character in the great tale of the Rangers pitching staff in 2016, Harrell added another team—but not another state—to his MLB tour. The 31-year-old ripped through three organizations, just one year after walking over 100 batters in Korea, and somehow held it together for long enough for the Braves to actually get something in return for him. Harrell's days of being anything more than a backup emergency starter are long gone, but worse pitchers have resurfaced in shallow bullpens.

Derek Holland LHP

Born: 10/9/86 Age: 30 Bats: B Throws: L Height: 6'2" Weight: 215 Entered Pro Ball: Round 25, 2006 Draft (#748 overall)

YEAR	TEAM	LVL	AGE	W	L	SV	G	GS	IP	H	HR	BB/9	K/9	K	GB%	BABIP	WHIP	ERA	FIP	DRA	VORP	WARP	cFIP	MPH
2014	ROU	AAA	27	2	1	0	4	4	15¹	20	5	4.7	11.2	19	52%	.349	1.83	5.87	7.03	2.40	5.7	0.6	89	
2014	TEX	MLB	27	2	0	0	6	5	37	34	0	1.2	6.1	25	42%	.296	1.05	1.46	2.21	3.90	3.8	0.4	96	94.9
2015	TEX	MLB	28	4	3	0	10	10	58²	59	11	2.6	6.3	41	43%	.281	1.30	4.91	5.27	4.83	1.6	0.2	114	95.8
2016	ROU	AAA	29	0	0	0	3	3	10	11	1	3.6	7.2	8	58%	.312	1.50	4.50	4.92	4.22	1.3	0.1	99	
2016	TEX	MLB	29	7	9	0	22	20	107¹	116	15	2.9	5.6	67	38%	.295	1.41	4.95	4.71	5.40	-0.6	-0.1	119	94.5
2017	CHA	MLB	30	5	7	0	19	19	100²	104	14	2.9	7.2	81	51%	.295	1.36	4.54	4.44	4.93	3.6	0.4	100	
2018	CHA	MLB	31	9	11	0	30	30	187	196	29	2.7	7.3	152	51%	.299	1.35	4.53	4.53	4.90	10.0	1.0	114	

Breakout: 13% Improve: 38% Collapse: 25% Attrition: 14% MLB: 86% *Comparables: Jason Vargas, John Maine, Brian Bannister*

After an eight-year run with the Rangers, the organization decided it was time to part ways with Holland and gave him $1.5 million to avoid picking up his $11 million option. It was a decision borne not so much out of age as injury, or perhaps the Samson-like shaving of his mustache. Shoulder issues have limited him to barely over 200 innings over the past three years and have robbed him of both velocity and his slider, a pitch that has driven his performance. In 2013, his last good season, he threw his slider about a quarter of the time to right-handers and they slugged .246 against it. Last season, those numbers were 10 percent and .500—and throwing his curve more didn't help matters either. He can still roundup lefties with ease (allowing a .578 OPS against them in 2016), so there's always a second career to fall back on here, but Holland is running out of time to prove his status as a starter can be salvaged.

Jeremy Jeffress RHP

Born: 9/21/87 Age: 29 Bats: R Throws: R Height: 6'0" Weight: 205 Entered Pro Ball: Round 1, 2006 Draft (#16 overall)

YEAR	TEAM	LVL	AGE	W	L	SV	G	GS	IP	H	HR	BB/9	K/9	K	GB%	BABIP	WHIP	ERA	FIP	DRA	VORP	WARP	cFIP	MPH
2014	TOR	MLB	26	0	0	0	3	0	3¹	8	0	8.1	10.8	4	33%	.667	3.30	10.80	5.26	4.56	0.0	0.0	95	97.8
2014	NAS	AAA	26	4	1	5	30	0	41²	33	0	3.9	9.7	45	64%	.317	1.22	1.51	2.84	1.98	15.6	1.6	75	
2014	MIL	MLB	26	1	1	0	29	0	28²	27	1	2.2	7.8	25	65%	.321	1.19	1.88	2.54	3.34	3.7	0.4	93	98.8
2015	MIL	MLB	27	5	0	0	72	0	68	64	5	2.9	8.9	67	60%	.314	1.26	2.65	3.25	3.25	11.0	1.2	86	97.7
2016	MIL	MLB	28	2	2	27	47	0	44²	45	2	2.2	7.1	35	59%	.312	1.25	2.22	3.21	4.04	4.6	0.5	95	98.3
2016	TEX	MLB	28	1	0	0	12	0	13¹	10	0	4.7	4.7	7	70%	.270	1.27	2.70	3.63	4.34	0.9	0.1	95	96.9
2017	*TEX*	*MLB*	*29*	*2*	*2*	*3*	*43*	*0*	*45*	*46*	*5*	*3.3*	*7.4*	*37*	*60%*	*.304*	*1.39*	*3.98*	*4.22*	*4.31*	*3.4*	*0.4*	*96*	
2018	*TEX*	*MLB*	*30*	*3*	*1*	*2*	*52*	*0*	*54²*	*51*	*6*	*3.6*	*8.8*	*53*	*60%*	*.301*	*1.33*	*3.98*	*3.98*	*4.33*	*4.3*	*0.4*	*95*	

Breakout: 43%   Improve: 65%   Collapse: 21%   Attrition: 28%   MLB: 95%   *Comparables: Pedro Strop, Evan Meek, Bryan Morris*

A former first-round pick, Jeffress ended up in the bullpen due to a lack of effective secondaries and ended up in Texas because the new-look Brewers are allergic to relievers. When the Rangers acquired Jeffress as part of the Jonathan Lucroy trade last July, they were really letting Sam Dyson know how much they loved him. At the time of his acquisition, Jeffress owned a 3.94 DRA (Dyson's was 3.84), 18.4 percent strikeout rate (Dyson's was 18.2 percent) and 57.7 ground-ball rate (Dyson's was 60.9 percent). He still packs a fastball that can make hitters…well…nervous. Unfortunately, Jeffress made waves this season for a bladder-evacuating incident all his own when he was pulled over on suspicion of DUI. He was in such bad shape that he reportedly relieved himself in the presence of an officer during his sobriety test. That meant he couldn't relieve for the Rangers for nearly a month, though Jeffress did rejoin the team in late September after entering rehab.

Strong seasonal numbers disguised the fact that Jeffress shouldn't be allowed to face any decent left-handed hitters—the .906 OPS he allowed against them last year was an exaggeration of an existing trend, highlighted by his lack of a usable change. In fact, he only got one swing-and-miss on the pitch all season. At 29, he's unlikely to improve as he gets more expensive, and he's about to get a lot more expensive.

Tyrell Jenkins RHP

Born: 7/20/92 Age: 24 Bats: R Throws: R Height: 6'4" Weight: 210 Entered Pro Ball: Round 1, 2010 Draft (#50 overall)

YEAR	TEAM	LVL	AGE	W	L	SV	G	GS	IP	H	HR	BB/9	K/9	K	GB%	BABIP	WHIP	ERA	FIP	DRA	VORP	WARP	cFIP	MPH
2014	PMB	A+	21	6	5	0	13	13	74	74	6	2.8	5.0	41	50%	.286	1.31	3.28	4.31	5.89	-2.4	-0.2	110	
2015	MIS	AA	22	5	5	0	16	16	93	84	3	4.0	5.7	59	53%	.278	1.34	3.00	3.84	5.33	-2.4	-0.3	110	
2015	GWN	AAA	22	3	4	0	9	9	45¹	43	4	4	5.8	29	55%	.277	1.39	3.57	4.48	7.56	-11.4	-1.2	114	
2016	GWN	AAA	23	9	3	0	17	12	83²	86	3	3.8	5.9	55	46%	.316	1.45	2.47	3.61	6.45	-10.8	-1.1	116	
2016	ATL	MLB	23	2	4	0	14	8	52	55	11	5.7	4.5	26	51%	.265	1.69	5.88	6.90	7.42	-12.4	-1.3	133	94.4
2017	*ATL*	*MLB*	*24*	*2*	*3*	*0*	*6*	*6*	*34*	*38*	*5*	*4.1*	*5.4*	*21*	*55%*	*.295*	*1.56*	*5.46*	*5.34*	*5.56*	*-1.4*	*-0.1*	*100*	
2018	*ATL*	*MLB*	*25*	*9*	*12*	*0*	*30*	*30*	*187²*	*168*	*27*	*4.8*	*8.1*	*170*	*55%*	*.294*	*1.43*	*5.27*	*5.28*	*5.72*	*-2.9*	*-0.3*	*135*	

Breakout: 19%   Improve: 30%   Collapse: 10%   Attrition: 26%   MLB: 47%   *Comparables: Luke French, Tyler Clippard, Anthony Swarzak*

Jenkins was one of many young pitchers the Braves threw to the wolves during the tumultuous first half of 2016. While some of those youngsters were able to avoid being devoured by the ravenous pack of major-league hitters, Jenkins wasn't one of them. He floundered as a starter and finished the season as one of Atlanta's middle-relief arms. Traded to the Rangers last winter, Jenkins could still possibly make it as a fourth or fifth starter—especially if he can work out his mechanics and continue to stay healthy. But for now the bullpen appears to be in his future.

Ariel Jurado RHP

Born: 1/30/96 Age: 21 Bats: R Throws: R Height: 6'1" Weight: 180 Entered Pro Ball: International Free Agent, 2002

YEAR	TEAM	LVL	AGE	W	L	SV	G	GS	IP	H	HR	BB/9	K/9	K	GB%	BABIP	WHIP	ERA	FIP	DRA	VORP	WARP	cFIP	MPH
2015	HIC	A	19	12	1	0	22	15	99	92	5	1.1	8.6	95	61%	.314	1.05	2.45	2.62	1.82	36.5	3.9	71	
2016	HDS	A+	20	7	2	0	16	16	79¹	83	4	2.7	8.1	71	64%	.342	1.35	3.86	3.53	3.61	16.5	1.7	95	
2016	FRI	AA	20	1	4	0	8	6	43²	44	3	2.1	7.2	35	53%	.315	1.24	3.30	3.29	3.11	9.2	1.0	86	
2017	*TEX*	*MLB*	*21*	*6*	*5*	*1*	*35*	*15*	*94²*	*110*	*10*	*3.5*	*5.3*	*55*	*36%*	*.314*	*1.54*	*4.55*	*4.64*	*4.87*	*5.9*	*0.6*	*114*	
2018	*TEX*	*MLB*	*22*	*6*	*7*	*0*	*31*	*19*	*146²*	*150*	*17*	*4.6*	*7.9*	*129*	*36%*	*.311*	*1.54*	*4.56*	*4.58*	*4.88*	*6.9*	*0.7*	*114*	

Breakout: 8%   Improve: 12%   Collapse: 2%   Attrition: 10%   MLB: 15%   *Comparables: Zach Davies, Jarrod Parker, Jameson Taillon*

Jurado took a big step forward on the organization's prospect list this year, due to both his own development and the whims of Jon Daniels and company. The right-hander built off his strong campaign in Low-A by blowing through two levels last season, finishing as one of the youngest starting pitchers in the Texas League. What Jurado lacks in natural plane, he makes up for with good run and sink on his fastball—allowing him to get grounders in spades. He repeats his delivery very well and litters the zone with strikes, but he'll have to make some progress with one of his breakers—both his slider and curve are currently below average—to accompany his potential plus change. He's got a great chance to fulfill a no. 4 starter destiny, and could take over the mantle as Panama's Starting Pitcher from, you guessed it, Bruce Chen.

Keone Kela RHP

Born: 4/16/93   Age: 24   Bats: R   Throws: R   Height: 6'1"   Weight: 215   Entered Pro Ball: Round 12, 2012 Draft (#396 overall)

YEAR	TEAM	LVL	AGE	W	L	SV	G	GS	IP	H	HR	BB/9	K/9	K	GB%	BABIP	WHIP	ERA	FIP	DRA	VORP	WARP	cFIP	MPH
2014	MYR	A+	21	0	1	5	8	0	10¹	9	0	3.5	11.3	13	37%	.333	1.26	2.61	2.16	3.24	2.2	0.2	91	
2014	FRI	AA	21	2	1	5	36	0	38²	22	1	6.3	12.8	55	50%	.259	1.27	1.86	2.86	3.15	7.3	0.8	87	
2015	TEX	MLB	22	7	5	1	68	0	60¹	52	4	2.7	10.1	68	54%	.314	1.16	2.39	2.61	2.74	13.2	1.4	76	98.6
2016	TEX	MLB	23	5	1	0	35	0	34	30	6	4.5	11.9	45	46%	.304	1.38	6.09	4.52	3.19	6.7	0.7	86	98.0
2017	*TEX*	*MLB*	*24*	*3*	*3*	*0*	*53*	*0*	*55*	*50*	*6*	*3.7*	*9.8*	*60*	*40%*	*.302*	*1.33*	*3.58*	*3.81*	*3.98*	*6.2*	*0.6*	*90*	
2018	*TEX*	*MLB*	*25*	*3*	*1*	*0*	*57*	*0*	*60²*	*50*	*7*	*4.0*	*11.2*	*75*	*40%*	*.301*	*1.27*	*3.52*	*3.53*	*3.84*	*8.1*	*0.8*	*84*	

Breakout: 38%   Improve: 62%   Collapse: 16%   Attrition: 20%   MLB: 93%   *Comparables: Mike Morin, Corey Knebel, Tim Collins*

Kela missed nearly three months of the season after having bone chips removed from his elbow in April, and when he rejoined the Rangers in mid-July, he brought an awful lot of unfortunate luck with him. Despite struggling with command post-surgery, Kela was mostly the same pitcher he was in his breakout 2015 season per DRA. He had difficulty getting hitters to offer at his curveball, leaving right-handers sitting on his fastball—which, despite sitting at 97 and touching 99, they took full advantage of. Even this version of Kela is still the best pitcher in the Rangers' bullpen and if he can close that ERA/DRA gap, he can reassume his status as the closer of the future—or whenever Sam Dyson hiccups.

Colby Lewis RHP

Born: 8/2/79   Age: 37   Bats: R   Throws: R   Height: 6'4"   Weight: 240   Entered Pro Ball: Round 1, 1999 Draft (#38 overall)

YEAR	TEAM	LVL	AGE	W	L	SV	G	GS	IP	H	HR	BB/9	K/9	K	GB%	BABIP	WHIP	ERA	FIP	DRA	VORP	WARP	cFIP	MPH
2014	TEX	MLB	34	10	14	0	29	29	170¹	211	25	2.5	7.0	133	35%	.339	1.52	5.18	4.49	5.43	-11.2	-1.2	111	91.3
2015	TEX	MLB	35	17	9	0	33	33	204²	211	26	1.8	6.2	142	35%	.290	1.24	4.66	4.15	5.30	-5.0	-0.5	116	90.8
2016	TEX	MLB	36	6	5	0	19	19	116¹	103	19	2.2	5.6	73	36%	.241	1.13	3.71	4.77	5.06	3.9	0.4	121	90.1
2017	*TEX*	*MLB*	*37*	*7*	*7*	*0*	*20*	*20*	*116¹*	*127*	*21*	*2.7*	*7.3*	*95*	*50%*	*.303*	*1.39*	*4.80*	*4.85*	*5.18*	*3.8*	*0.4*	*122*	
2018	*TEX*	*MLB*	*38*	*4*	*5*	*0*	*13*	*13*	*77¹*	*86*	*14*	*2.8*	*8.0*	*69*	*50%*	*.313*	*1.43*	*4.84*	*4.84*	*5.22*	*2.1*	*0.2*	*121*	

Breakout: 5%   Improve: 33%   Collapse: 15%   Attrition: 18%   MLB: 59%   *Comparables: Wandy Rodriguez, Kevin Millwood, Esteban Loaiza*

Colby Lewis was on the fast track to a strong campaign, dropping his ERA to a season-low 2.81 after a mid-June complete game in Oakland, before a strained lat muscle sidelined him for 11 weeks. He returned to rust and diminished velocity, peaking with a late-September return engagement in Oakland in which he gave up seven runs in less than two innings. Then to make matters worse, Lewis threw a clunker in Game 3 of the ALDS, allowing five earned runs including two long balls over just two innings of work. Unfortunately, the post-injury Lewis was closer to the true version, and there's only so long you can drive with the gas light on.

Kyle Lohse RHP

Born: 10/4/78   Age: 38   Bats: R   Throws: R   Height: 6'2"   Weight: 215   Entered Pro Ball: Round 29, 1996 Draft (#862 overall)

YEAR	TEAM	LVL	AGE	W	L	SV	G	GS	IP	H	HR	BB/9	K/9	K	GB%	BABIP	WHIP	ERA	FIP	DRA	VORP	WARP	cFIP	MPH
2014	MIL	MLB	35	13	9	0	31	31	198¹	183	22	2.0	6.4	141	42%	.268	1.15	3.54	3.92	5.28	-9.7	-1.1	118	91.7
2015	MIL	MLB	36	5	13	2	37	22	152¹	180	29	2.5	6.4	108	41%	.314	1.46	5.85	5.14	4.61	6.7	0.7	120	91.5
2016	ROU	AAA	37	3	5	0	10	10	58²	60	8	2.1	6.3	41	40%	.294	1.26	5.06	5.02	5.06	1.9	0.2	111	
2016	TEX	MLB	37	0	2	0	2	2	9¹	15	4	4.8	2.9	3	35%	.306	2.14	12.54	9.64	5.77	-0.4	0.0	127	90.2
2017	*TEX*	*MLB*	*38*	*4*	*4*	*0*	*12*	*12*	*69²*	*74*	*11*	*3.1*	*6.4*	*49*	*47%*	*.291*	*1.41*	*4.90*	*4.94*	*5.29*	*1.4*	*0.1*	*126*	
2018	*TEX*	*MLB*	*39*	*8*	*10*	*0*	*24*	*24*	*139*	*154*	*22*	*3.7*	*6.3*	*97*	*47%*	*.299*	*1.51*	*5.19*	*5.19*	*5.60*	*-2.0*	*-0.2*	*132*	

Breakout: 12%   Improve: 30%   Collapse: 10%   Attrition: 11%   MLB: 61%   *Comparables: Al Leiter, Kevin Millwood, Ted Lilly*

After the Rangers desperately needed rotation help in any usable form at the beginning of July, they called up veteran Lohse to see what he had left in his 37-year-old tank after stashing him away in Triple-A for this exact purpose. What Lohse did was strand them on a desert highway. With an ERA north of 12 in just two starts, the Rangers decided it wasn't even worth trying to keep the remnants of Kyle Lohse on the mound to eat innings, and cut ties quickly just before the trade deadline. It didn't hurt to try, right?

Nick Martinez RHP

Born: 8/5/90   Age: 26   Bats: L   Throws: R   Height: 6'1"   Weight: 200   Entered Pro Ball: Round 18, 2011 Draft (#564 overall)

YEAR	TEAM	LVL	AGE	W	L	SV	G	GS	IP	H	HR	BB/9	K/9	K	GB%	BABIP	WHIP	ERA	FIP	DRA	VORP	WARP	cFIP	MPH
2014	TEX	MLB	23	5	12	0	29	24	140¹	150	18	3.5	4.9	77	35%	.289	1.46	4.55	4.97	9.12	-67.3	-7.4	136	93.7
2015	ROU	AAA	24	1	1	0	6	6	31	32	1	2	5.2	18	43%	.320	1.26	2.90	3.73	5.36	-0.2	0.0	103	
2015	TEX	MLB	24	7	7	0	24	21	125	135	16	3.3	5.5	77	44%	.293	1.45	3.96	4.95	5.94	-12.2	-1.3	120	92.3
2016	ROU	AAA	25	7	6	0	18	16	99	109	7	1.5	6.1	67	51%	.321	1.27	3.91	3.98	3.69	18.1	1.9	92	
2016	TEX	MLB	25	2	3	0	12	5	38²	45	8	4.4	3.7	16	50%	.282	1.66	5.59	6.83	6.83	-7.0	-0.7	122	94.2
2017	*TEX*	*MLB*	*26*	*4*	*4*	*0*	*20*	*10*	*67*	*73*	*10*	*3.2*	*5.8*	*43*	*54%*	*.295*	*1.44*	*4.99*	*5.09*	*5.28*	*-0.5*	*-0.1*	*100*	
2018	*TEX*	*MLB*	*27*	*8*	*10*	*0*	*25*	*25*	*149¹*	*149*	*22*	*4.1*	*7.2*	*119*	*54%*	*.289*	*1.45*	*4.98*	*4.98*	*5.39*	*1.3*	*0.1*	*126*	

Breakout: 24%   Improve: 59%   Collapse: 13%   Attrition: 31%   MLB: 90%   *Comparables: Garrett Olson, Gavin Floyd, David Huff*

Martinez gave up at least one homer in every game he started last year (except for one), and he gave up no homers in every game he entered as a reliever (except for one). Martinez was used as a substitute when Texas needed bodies in the rotation, but 2016 proved that he's an enfeebling option even when a team is already in dire straits. With his ERA as a reliever less than a third of what it was in the rotation, Martinez can see his future brightly and he can take solace in the fact that it might actually be good enough to keep in Texas for the majority of 2017.

Yohander Mendez　LHP

Born: 1/17/95　Age: 22　Bats: L　Throws: L　Height: 6'5"　Weight: 200　Entered Pro Ball: International Free Agent, 2011

YEAR	TEAM	LVL	AGE	W	L	SV	G	GS	IP	H	HR	BB/9	K/9	K	GB%	BABIP	WHIP	ERA	FIP	DRA	VORP	WARP	cFIP	MPH
2014	HIC	A	19	3	0	0	7	6	31	26	4	0.6	8.1	28	52%	.268	0.90	2.32	3.65	2.80	9.1	0.9	81	
2015	HIC	A	20	3	3	3	21	8	66¹	57	2	2.0	10.0	74	54%	.312	1.09	2.44	2.41	2.14	21.4	2.3	80	
2016	HDS	A+	21	4	1	0	7	7	33	21	2	3.0	12.3	45	51%	.264	0.97	2.45	2.77	1.69	13.9	1.4	77	
2016	FRI	AA	21	4	1	0	10	10	46²	39	2	2.7	8.9	46	47%	.296	1.14	3.09	2.92	2.55	13.2	1.4	87	
2016	ROU	AAA	21	4	1	0	7	4	31¹	12	0	4.6	6.3	22	40%	.150	0.89	0.57	3.94	5.64	-1.5	-0.2	111	
2016	TEX	MLB	21	0	0	0	2	0	3	5	0	6.0	0.0	0	33%	.333	2.33	18.00	5.11	6.96	-0.7	-0.1	123	95.0
2017	*TEX*	*MLB*	*22*	*3*	*3*	*0*	*30*	*6*	*57*	*58*	*6*	*3.8*	*6.3*	*40*	*49%*	*.291*	*1.44*	*4.70*	*4.56*	*4.93*	*1.3*	*0.1*	*100*	
2018	*TEX*	*MLB*	*23*	*3*	*3*	*0*	*35*	*6*	*68²*	*59*	*8*	*6.1*	*9.4*	*71*	*49%*	*.283*	*1.54*	*4.88*	*4.88*	*5.28*	*0.0*	*0.0*	*122*	

Breakout: 16%　Improve: 35%　Collapse: 13%　Attrition: 26%　MLB: 56%　Comparables: *Aaron Poreda, Johnny Cueto, Jake Thompson*

A 21-year-old lefty with three pitches, a thick sheen of polish and two major-league outings isn't a bad thing for a top prospect to be. Still, that Mendez ranks atop the Rangers list at the end of the 2016 season speaks to the amount of talent they've shipped elsewhere over the last two years, as well as the job done by their international scouting department. Long an intriguing but frustrating blend of pitchability and projectability, Mendez finally stayed healthy this year, and rocketed through the system as a result. There are still doubts as to whether he can handle a starter's workload (2016 brought about a career-high 111 innings), but he's already begun to fill out his 6-foot-5 frame. He can get whiffs with the changeup thanks to impressive arm speed and more tumble than a Toronto Raptors mascot roller-skating down a flight of stairs. Mendez will need to refine his breaking ball if he's going to turn the lineup over consistently, but the long-term outlook looks fun.

Martin Perez　LHP

Born: 4/4/91　Age: 26　Bats: L　Throws: L　Height: 6'0"　Weight: 200　Entered Pro Ball: International Free Agent, 2007

YEAR	TEAM	LVL	AGE	W	L	SV	G	GS	IP	H	HR	BB/9	K/9	K	GB%	BABIP	WHIP	ERA	FIP	DRA	VORP	WARP	cFIP	MPH
2014	TEX	MLB	23	4	3	0	8	8	51¹	50	3	3.3	6.1	35	53%	.315	1.34	4.38	3.72	3.50	7.6	0.8	98	93.4
2015	ROU	AAA	24	0	1	0	4	4	20	27	2	0.9	7.7	17	55%	.397	1.45	4.95	3.50	2.84	5.5	0.6	89	
2015	TEX	MLB	24	3	6	0	14	14	78²	88	3	2.7	5.5	48	60%	.326	1.42	4.46	3.37	3.92	10.2	1.1	99	94.3
2016	TEX	MLB	25	10	11	0	33	33	198²	205	18	3.4	4.7	103	54%	.286	1.41	4.39	4.46	4.52	18.5	1.9	110	95.4
2017	*TEX*	*MLB*	*26*	*10*	*10*	*0*	*28*	*28*	*159*	*169*	*18*	*3.3*	*5.9*	*104*	*44%*	*.297*	*1.43*	*4.47*	*4.54*	*4.83*	*7.4*	*0.8*	*100*	
2018	*TEX*	*MLB*	*27*	*10*	*11*	*0*	*30*	*30*	*187*	*189*	*21*	*3.5*	*7.1*	*149*	*44%*	*.299*	*1.40*	*4.31*	*4.31*	*4.68*	*14.8*	*1.5*	*107*	

Breakout: 32%　Improve: 65%　Collapse: 14%　Attrition: 11%　MLB: 88%　Comparables: *Mike Pelfrey, Daniel Cabrera, Henderson Alvarez*

Pitching his first full season after undergoing Tommy John surgery in 2014, Perez was nothing spectacular, but he gave the Rangers what they needed most in 2016: innings. The biggest concern for Perez is that he's only gone further right on the strikeout spectrum—becoming far too conservative with his whiffs. On the bright side, his velocity has not only bounced back from where it was prior to surgery, but he's throwing as hard as ever. He may not carry the ceiling that he once had when he was a 17-year-old in the Northwest League, but with a good defense behind him, he can still have plenty of success in the back of a rotation. WIth a team-friendly contract that will pay him nearly $27 million through 2020 (assuming his options are all picked up), that's a still a strong win.

Tanner Scheppers　RHP

Born: 1/17/87　Age: 30　Bats: R　Throws: R　Height: 6'4"　Weight: 200　Entered Pro Ball: Round 1, 2009 Draft (#44 overall)

YEAR	TEAM	LVL	AGE	W	L	SV	G	GS	IP	H	HR	BB/9	K/9	K	GB%	BABIP	WHIP	ERA	FIP	DRA	VORP	WARP	cFIP	MPH
2014	TEX	MLB	27	0	1	0	8	4	23	31	6	3.9	6.7	17	54%	.333	1.78	9.00	6.77	4.23	1.4	0.2	109	97.6
2015	ROU	AAA	28	0	2	2	13	0	14	11	0	5.1	7.1	11	51%	.282	1.36	1.93	3.96	5.81	-1.4	-0.1	106	
2015	TEX	MLB	28	4	1	0	42	0	38¹	37	6	5.4	7.5	32	40%	.274	1.57	5.63	5.43	5.55	-3.6	-0.4	117	97.3
2016	TEX	MLB	29	1	1	1	10	0	8²	6	0	3.1	5.2	5	48%	.222	1.04	4.15	2.99	4.86	0.1	0.0	108	97.4
2017	*TEX*	*MLB*	*30*	*0*	*1*	*0*	*10*	*0*	*10*	*10*	*1*	*4.1*	*7.0*	*8*	*56%*	*.295*	*1.48*	*4.95*	*4.68*	*5.06*	*-0.1*	*0.0*	*100*	
2018	*TEX*	*MLB*	*31*	*2*	*1*	*0*	*43*	*0*	*45²*	*46*	*6*	*4.0*	*7.8*	*40*	*56%*	*.299*	*1.45*	*4.61*	*4.62*	*5.02*	*0.2*	*0.0*	*113*	

Breakout: 21%　Improve: 45%　Collapse: 14%　Attrition: 24%　MLB: 68%　Comparables: *Vinnie Chulk, Brian Bruney, Manny Delcarmen*

Scheppers was sidelined for five months of 2016 after undergoing microfracture surgery on his knee, and his brief return was nondescript for anything other than his pure velocity. Then again, velocity has never been an issue for the former first-rounder. His fastball-heavy approach, including both a four- and two-seamer, isn't necessarily a bad thing, but it becomes a bad thing when combined with his struggles to command his secondaries. As always, Scheppers has the raw ingredients for success as a reliever, but can't quite seem to find the recipe.

Shawn Tolleson   RHP

Born: 1/19/88   Age: 29   Bats: R   Throws: R   Height: 6'2"   Weight: 225   Entered Pro Ball: Round 30, 2010 Draft (#922 overall)

YEAR	TEAM	LVL	AGE	W	L	SV	G	GS	IP	H	HR	BB/9	K/9	K	GB%	BABIP	WHIP	ERA	FIP	DRA	VORP	WARP	cFIP	MPH
2014	TEX	MLB	26	3	1	0	64	0	71²	56	10	3.5	8.7	69	40%	.245	1.17	2.76	4.26	3.72	6.1	0.7	99	94.8
2015	TEX	MLB	27	6	4	35	73	0	72¹	66	9	2.1	9.5	76	44%	.294	1.15	2.99	3.41	3.32	11.2	1.2	85	95.3
2016	TEX	MLB	28	2	2	11	37	0	36¹	53	8	2.5	7.2	29	52%	.372	1.73	7.68	5.20	3.95	4.1	0.4	98	95.2
2017	TEX	MLB	29	2	1	13	40	0	42¹	43	8	3.0	8.5	40	41%	.297	1.35	4.64	4.83	5.02	0.2	0.0	115	
2018	TEX	MLB	30	1	0	8	27	0	28¹	29	5	3.2	8.6	27	41%	.295	1.37	4.88	4.89	5.28	-0.7	-0.1	121	

Breakout: 26%   Improve: 45%   Collapse: 18%   Attrition: 13%   MLB: 86%   *Comparables:* Edward Mujica, Mark Lowe, Rafael Soriano

You don't go from being an above-average closer to peddling an ERA so high you'd think twice about paying it for lunch without a confluence of reasons—and they existed in spades for Tolleson. First, the luck. A sky-high BABIP, along with an elevated home run rate, caused him to have one of the most extreme ERA/DRA splits in baseball. Second, the injury. It wasn't just that Tolleson was shut down with a back injury in August, but reports are that he was pitching through it earlier in the year as well. Finally, the personal. Tolleson's father was diagnosed with cancer in 2015, and he even spent a week in May on the family medical emergency list in order to spend time with him. After being optioned and then outrighted, Tolleson elected free agency and will try to right his ship on all fronts in 2017.

LINEOUTS

Hitters

NAME	POS	TEAM	LVL	AGE	PA	R	2B	3B	HR	RBI	BB	K	SB	CS	AVG/OBP/SLG	TAv	VORP	BABIP	BRR	FRAA	WARP
Jairo Beras	RF	HDS	A+	21	441	71	28	4	22	78	24	121	5	5	.262/.306/.511	.270	13.7	.315	1.6	RF(74): -7.3 • CF(8): 0.1	0.7
Michael De Leon	SS	HDS	A+	19	491	54	25	1	9	54	24	57	7	5	.267/.308/.385	.263	16.0	.287	-4.7	SS(111): 0.5 • 2B(19): -0.7	1.6
Jared Hoying	OF	ROU	AAA	27	435	62	20	6	16	66	37	78	18	4	.269/.336/.474	.291	24.7	.297	0.1	CF(55): -0.7 • RF(28): 0.2	2.6
	OF	TEX	MLB	27	49	8	2	0	0	5	3	8	1	0	.217/.265/.261	.215	-2.0	.263	-0.8	RF(17): 0.1 • LF(13): -0.4	-0.3
Eric Jenkins	CF	HIC	A	19	563	72	13	9	8	40	40	154	51	15	.221/.279/.330	.241	17.3	.297	11.2	CF(117): -4.5 • RF(1): -0.0	1.4
Will Middlebrooks	3B	CSP	AAA	27	264	38	22	2	10	47	9	59	1	1	.282/.308/.508	.262	10.3	.328	2.3	3B(54): 4.1 • 1B(7): 0.1	1.5
	3B	MIL	MLB	27	31	2	0	0	0	1	4	13	0	0	.111/.226/.111	.163	-1.8	.214	0.3	3B(8): -0.3	-0.2
Josh Morgan	3B	HDS	A+	20	533	74	19	2	7	64	44	61	4	2	.300/.367/.394	.264	20.0	.328	-0.3	3B(84): 1.4 • SS(29): 3.8	2.5
Brett Nicholas	C	ROU	AAA	27	447	57	27	1	13	58	38	88	2	2	.288/.351/.458	.303	33.0	.338	-2.9	C(70): -6.1 • 1B(19): 0.2	2.8
	C	TEX	MLB	27	45	5	5	0	2	4	4	9	0	0	.275/.356/.550	.276	2.7	.310	-0.1	C(15): -1.2	0.2
Drew Robinson	OF	ROU	AAA	24	539	76	24	10	20	67	66	148	17	5	.257/.350/.480	.312	45.5	.332	3.5	RF(38): 5.2 • 2B(27): -1.1	5.1
Jose Trevino	C	HDS	A+	23	465	67	30	0	9	68	26	49	2	1	.303/.342/.434	.275	26.3	.322	-1.3	C(100): 8.9	3.6

The in-game power finally showed up for **Jairo Beras** in the Carolina League last year, but that extra year on his birth certificate is going to be tougher to summon. ❖ High-A was kind to **Michael De Leon** as he saw a hike in his offensive stats, but when the Cal League only gets you to a .693 OPS, you better be a damn good defensive shortstop. ❖ Taken in the third round of the 2016 draft, **Kole Enright** shows off potential plus power and a solid approach at the plate, along with enough athleticism to hack it at the hot corner. ❖ At just 16 years old, Venezuelan **David Garcia** was signed to an $800,000 bonus last July, and he projects to be a catcher who can sting the ball around. Then again, what were *you* going to be at that age? ❖ At 27 years old, **Jared Hoying** finally got his moment in the sun when he made his MLB debut in May to help cover a rash of injuries in the Rangers' outfield, which probably left a better taste in his mouth than striking out in his only postseason at-bat. ❖ **Eric Jenkins** will burn up the basepaths like a pyromanic someday, that is, if he can find them in the first place. ❖ Once a top prospect and, briefly even, a promising young major leaguer, **Will Middlebrooks** is now destined to be a Triple-A slugger hopping from one minor-league deal to another. ❖ There's a path to major-league relevance for **Josh Morgan** that winds through both his hit tool and ability to pick it at multiple positions, but it's unlikely to be in a full-time role. ❖ **Brett Nicholas** was part of the catcher-by-committee team that held the Rangers together before the arrival of Jonathan Lucroy, and despite his framing numbers being as red as the team's alternate jerseys, he can hit enough to ride the shuttle once again in 2017. ❖ **Drew Robinson** has played everywhere defensively in the minors and has 15-homer power with a good eye, but may not possess the hit tool to make it in the majors. ❖ It's rare that a prospect in High-A is thought of as a potential future manager, but that says a fair amount about **Jose Trevino**'s leadership, his baseball IQ and (unfortunately) his bat.

Pitchers

NAME	TEAM	LVL	AGE	W	L	SV	G	GS	IP	H	HR	BB/9	K/9	K	GB%	BABIP	WHIP	ERA	FIP	DRA	VORP	WARP	cFIP	MPH
Kyle Cody	SPO	A-	21	2	5	0	12	9	47¹	56	4	2.5	10.1	53	58%	.381	1.46	5.13	3.71	2.47	14.3	1.5	85	
Brady Dragmire	NHP	AA	23	4	6	1	45	0	72	78	10	3.5	5.1	41	63%	.297	1.47	4.38	5.36	6.52	-14.3	-1.5	109	
Andrew Faulkner	ROU	AAA	23	5	3	4	41	1	45¹	39	3	4.0	7.7	39	46%	.279	1.30	3.97	4.51	4.78	1.0	0.1	108	
	TEX	MLB	23	0	0	0	9	0	6²	8	3	5.4	1.4	1	41%	.208	1.80	6.75	10.46	5.89	-0.7	-0.1	123	94.6
Mike Hauschild	FRE	AAA	26	9	10	0	24	24	139²	138	7	2.6	7.7	119	55%	.316	1.27	3.22	3.63	2.94	37.3	3.8	85	
Jose Leclerc	FRI	AA	22	0	5	1	10	2	23	17	1	3.9	11.0	28	30%	.291	1.17	3.52	2.75	4.52	0.9	0.1	94	
	ROU	AAA	22	2	2	1	29	0	43	23	3	5.9	10.5	50	39%	.211	1.19	2.72	4.26	5.03	-0.3	0.0	97	
	TEX	MLB	22	0	0	0	12	0	15	11	0	7.8	9.0	15	29%	.289	1.60	1.80	3.71	5.29	-0.5	-0.1	116	97.1
Brett Martin	HIC	A	21	2	3	0	9	9	43²	58	3	2.9	9.9	48	53%	.404	1.65	4.53	3.06	3.58	7.0	0.8	95	
	HDS	A+	21	2	1	0	6	6	23¹	24	3	2.7	6.2	16	55%	.292	1.33	4.24	4.91	4.92	1.4	0.1	105	
Adam Parks	FRI	AA	23	1	0	6	17	0	19¹	9	3	1.4	14.0	30	37%	.171	0.62	1.86	2.71	1.81	6.3	0.7	64	
Pedro Payano	HIC	A	21	3	3	0	15	13	73²	59	2	3.5	10.0	82	44%	.303	1.19	2.08	2.91	3.35	13.4	1.5	96	
Connor Sadzeck	FRI	AA	24	10	8	0	25	23	140²	127	18	3.3	8.5	133	47%	.292	1.27	4.16	4.34	3.71	21.3	2.3	97	
Adrian Sampson	TAC	AAA	24	7	4	0	13	13	80¹	81	5	1.3	6.8	61	49%	.310	1.16	3.25	3.50	3.20	19.2	2.0	92	
	SEA	MLB	24	0	1	0	1	1	4²	8	2	1.9	3.9	2	33%	.375	1.93	7.71	8.46	5.56	-0.1	0.0	115	94.4
Tyler Wagner	ARI	MLB	25	1	0	0	3	0	10	9	0	1.8	6.3	7	52%	.290	1.10	1.80	2.39	4.05	1.0	0.1	99	91.4
	RNO	AAA	25	1	4	0	5	5	26²	29	1	3.7	5.1	15	52%	.326	1.50	3.04	4.32	5.61	-0.8	-0.1	109	

Jose Almonte was half of the return from Boston for Brad Ziegler and the young righty took to the scenery change well. None of his pitches are plus at present, but he has a chance for three average offerings down the road. ❖ The third time was a charm for **Kyle Cody**, who was previously drafted by the Phillies and Twins and will attempt to harness his height and his upside in Texas. ❖ After a disappointing showing in his first taste of Double-A, **Brady Dragmire** was told to walk the plank in October, but resurfaced in December and will continue to rack up groundballs with average stuff in the Pirates' system. ❖ Past annuals have warned that should **Andrew Faulkner** not improve his breaking pitch his dreams of being a starter may die, and it looks like we have now seen that play out in front of our televisions and mobile devices. ❖ **Mike Hauschild** is a run-of-the-mill high-minors starter with mediocre raw stuff, decent results and little upside. ❖ **Jose Leclerc** impressed during his major league debut, touching 98 and striking out a batter per inning—and while his change needs work, he could be another potential late-inning option for the Rangers. Please note that this is the first and final Leclerc comment not to feature a pun. ❖ A sprained elbow ligament sidelined **Brett Martin** for half of the 2016 season, but he went out on the highest of notes—throwing seven hitless innings and striking out 15 in the Cal League playoffs. Don't let that line fool you though: He's a potential back-end starter. ❖ Bounding height, a fastball that touches the high 90s and two good breaking pitches can make **Michael Matuella** look exceptionally attractive as a future major leaguer, but after a major back injury and Tommy John already on his resume, he's as risky as investment advice from Jordan Belfort. ❖ **Adam Parks** sounds like the Cake Eater from *The Mighty Ducks*, but isn't. With a four-pitch mix and a strong frame, he sounds like a potential starter, but also isn't. ❖ **Pedro Payano** and his killer changeup struck out 82 batters in 73 innings at Low-A last season, and is now the next big prospect to come out of the Rangers' clown car of 2011 international signings. ❖ Taken in the first round of the 2016 draft, lefty **Cole Ragans** shows a lot of potential with a three-pitch mix that looks quite polished for a prep arm. ❖ After pitching 160 innings in Frisco, the question at hand is whether **Connor Sadzeck** can refine the control and command of his secondaries—as his fastball velocity has improved since his return from Tommy John surgery. ❖ Before **Adrian Sampson**'s second major league start, a rowdy fan yelled "Yo Adrian!" in an uninspired homage to Rocky Balboa. Distressed by so obvious a joke, Sampson threw one warmup pitch from the mound and hurt his elbow, requiring surgery to reattach his flexor bundle. ❖ Raw is the first word that comes to mind when you think of **Alex Speas**, but last year's second rounder is super projectable and might already have the highest upside of any pitching prospect in the Rangers' system. ❖ On a rate basis, **Tyler Wagner** was the D-backs' best pitcher in 2016, his bowling-ball sinker leading the way for a 1.80 ERA in 10 innings.

TORONTO BLUE JAYS

Essay by Stacey May Fowles

Player comments by Joshua Howsam, Matthew Gwin and BP staff

In a recent bout of nostalgia, I sat down and watched an old clip of beloved former Blue Jay Carlos Delgado hitting his 300th home run. The milestone blast happened back in September of 2003. At the time Rogers Centre was still called SkyDome, there was a female Blue Jays mascot named "Diamond," and Delgado—then 31 years old—was in his 11th season with the Blue Jays.

Tampa Bay Devil Rays pitcher Jorge Sosa gave up that particular monster blast in the bottom of the first inning, sparking a standing ovation and literal in-stadium fireworks. But Delgado wasn't done making history for the day, as the Canadian Baseball Hall of Famer became the 15th player in MLB history to hit four home runs in a game.

While it's easy to be amazed by nine innings that give you home runs 300, 301, 302 and 303, the thing that really astounds me about that decades-old replay is not Delgado's incredible feats, but how each blast sails over the outfield wall into almost completely empty stands. As the camera pans around the stadium for a reaction, and then follows Delgado as he proudly tours the bases victorious, there's a certain degree of absurdity to the entire celebratory tableau—*it feels like no one is there.*

I know baseball memory tends to be short, but after all the triumph and fervor of the last two glorious years of Blue Jays fandom it's hard to believe there was a time when the ballpark was so consistently less than half full. Annual attendance is up close to 1.5 million since Delgado's glory days, and getting a seat to even regular season games is now a challenge. The most recent incarnation of this team has undoubtedly electrified the city of Toronto; our status as a bona fide baseball town has been solidified, and has even threatened to topple the very Canadian game of hockey as its citizens' sport of choice.

Things now feel decidedly different than they did during that long playoff drought. The Blue Jays bandwagon is bursting at the seams, and the team's identity has shifted from the out-of-nowhere, previously ignored underdog to a fierce (and hey, maybe even strongly disliked) legitimate contender. "Canada's Team" actually matters again on the grand stage and the burgeoning community doesn't have any plans to stop cheering. With two playoff runs in a row, both of which made it all the way to the League Championship

BLUE JAYS PROSPECTUS
2016 W-L: 89-73, 2ND IN AL EAST

Pythag	.561	5th	DER	.717	2nd
RS/G	4.69	9th	B-Age	30.2	28th
RA/G	4.11	6th	P-Age	30	29th
TAv	.256	22nd	Salary	$136.8M	13th
BRR	1.92	10th	M$/MW	$3.1M	22nd
TAv-P	.241	3rd	DL Days	716	9th
FIP	4	10th	$ on DL	9%	8th

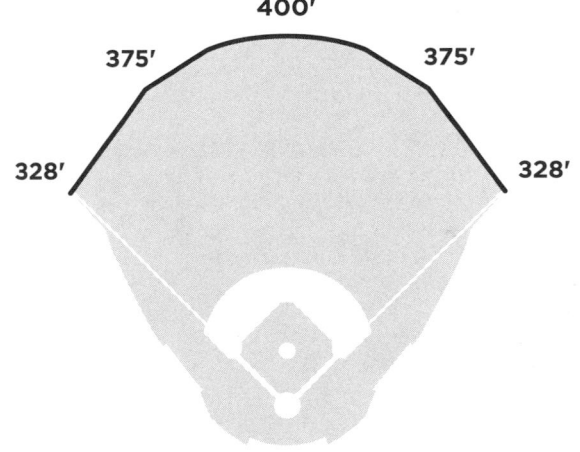

Outfield wall profile: **10'**

Three-Year Park Factors

Runs	Runs/RH	Runs/LH	HR/RH	HR/LH
102	102	102	106	105

Top Hitter WARP	5.4	Josh Donaldson
Top Pitcher WARP	4.5	Marcus Stroman
Top Prospect		Sean Reid-Foley

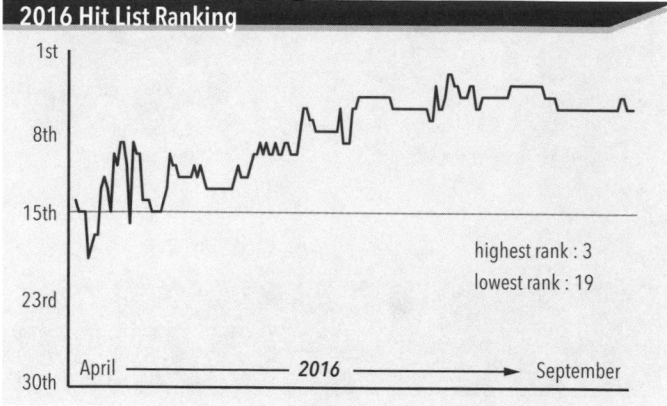

2016 Hit List Ranking

highest rank : 3
lowest rank : 19

April — 2016 → September

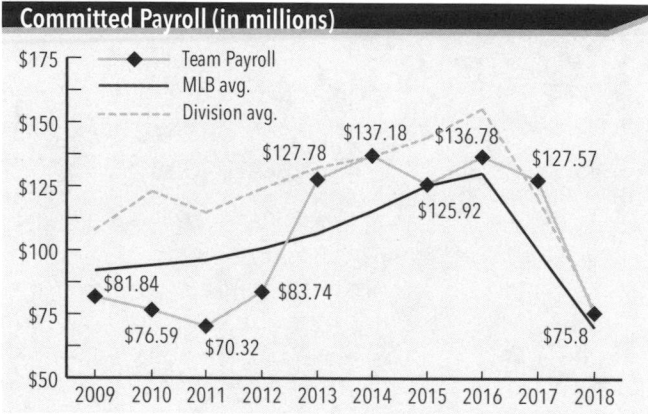

Committed Payroll (in millions)

- ◆ Team Payroll
- —— MLB avg.
- ----- Division avg.

$81.84
$76.59
$70.32
$83.74
$127.78
$137.18
$136.78
$125.92
$127.57
$75.8

2009 2010 2011 2012 2013 2014 2015 2016 2017 2018

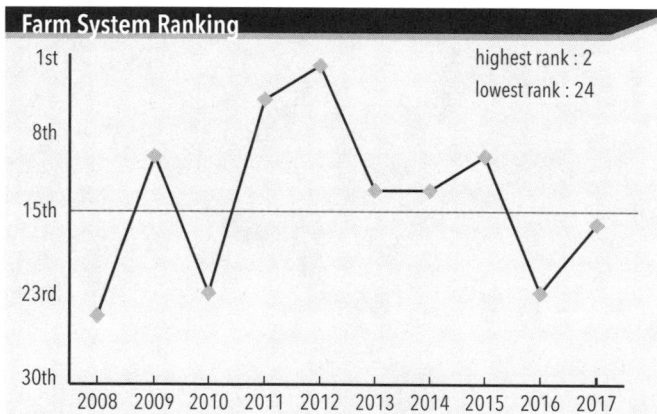

Farm System Ranking

highest rank : 2
lowest rank : 24

2008 2009 2010 2011 2012 2013 2014 2015 2016 2017

Personnel

President:
Mark Shapiro

General Manager:
Ross Atkins

VP, Baseball Operations:
Ben Cherington

Assistant General Manager:
Tony LaCava

Assistant General Manager:
Andrew Tinnish

Assistant General Manager:
Joe Sheehan

Manager:
John Gibbons

BP Alumni:
Matt Bishoff
Dan Evans

Series, we have been nothing short of transformed.

As a lifelong Blue Jays fan, I had grown accustomed to the art of losing. As a teen I watched my team triumphantly capture back-to-back World Series championships. I watched outfielder Devon White execute "The Catch" and I watched Joe Carter "touch 'em all." But those days eventually became a distant memory and it wouldn't be a stretch to say that my entire adult life has been a bit of a baseball letdown. Though I always enjoyed the game to varying degrees of intensity, for a long time I never found myself personally invested in the outcome of any of baseball's beautiful Octobers.

Cheering for a consistently mediocre team can certainly be disappointing drudgery, but there was actually some comfort to be found in the dire. My adult fandom was formed not by the lauded glory of a top-notch legendary team like the Yankees, but instead by the idea that baseball could just be loved for its own sake. A healthy perspective was something forced upon me, with every year bringing the same necessarily low expectations. I did my best to revel in the simple, sunny pleasures of the ballpark and would even go as far as to say that I felt lucky—living in the only Canadian city that offered an MLB team (RIP Expos,) it was a gift that I even got to watch live baseball at all.

And then the 2015 season changed all of that. After finishing third in the American League East in 2014 and dead last the year prior, the Blue Jays "suddenly" got good in the most champagne-popping and Bud Light-dumping of ways. (That goodness was the result of some incredibly shrewd moves on the part of former general manager Alex Anthopolous, but from a fan's perspective having one of the best teams in baseball felt like a pretty sudden, dramatic shift.) Somewhere in the summer of that year, we had to get used to the idea of backing a winner.

The 2015 season ushered in a kind of Toronto renaissance where it felt like everyone in town was donning a blue cap and had a baseball opinion to share. The rebirth was aided by a crop of new heroes like Josh Donaldson, David Price and Troy Tulowitzki. It was held up by old standbys like Jose Bautista and Edwin Encarnacion. And it was all punctuated by a now legendary Game 5, seventh-inning bat flip that became fodder for thousands of baseball conversations. Not only were we filling our once-empty ballpark, we were filling other teams' ballparks as well, booking spontaneous baseball road trips and cheering loud and proud in faraway stands.

After that first incredible ride to October, expectations going into 2016 were rightfully high with a largely intact roster and plenty of star power. In those first sweet days of spring, Blue Jays devotees were full of limitless optimism, but were also all too aware of how many favorites were destined for free agency following what might be the last chance for greatness in a long time.

✦ ✦ ✦

✦ ✦ ✦

Every season of baseball tells a story. If the Blue Jays' 2015 narrative was about an invigorating sense of sudden relevancy, the season that followed was more about hanging on to that feeling for as long as possible. When I think back on the moments that mattered, they all involve some degree of incredible cold sweat anxiety or nausea, everything hanging precariously on the fine edge between delirious victory and being forced to go home.

In early September, when the mighty Red Sox knocked the Jays out of their spot atop the AL East, the entire month became a desperate quest to squeeze into contention. The concept of "meaningful baseball" was amped right up—I have never felt more stressed, more terrified and more absolutely thrilled by a season. Every game mattered, right until that final regular season matchup with the aforementioned Red Sox, when it was decided that Toronto would be facing Baltimore in the Wild Card game.

I had long felt sympathy for fans subjected to the agony of a one-game playoff. I had seen their terrified faces on broadcasts, each one wishing their team would have a chance to fight on valiantly through October. I couldn't fathom the blistering intensity of that setup until I was there myself, in the stands at the Rogers Centre, watching 25-year-old Marcus Stroman say a private pregame prayer while kneeling at the outfield wall. The ever-optimistic wunderkind had his own unique struggles and the choice to start him in such a pivotal game came with its own gift-wrapped redemption story. (As it turned out, Stroman's strong start didn't even crack the top five when it came to the day's memorable details.)

That Wild Card game was the epitome of everything that is beautiful—and excruciatingly painful—about baseball. We lived and died by every pitch, white-knuckling it as steadfast closer Roberto Osuna managed to make it out of the ninth inning unscathed. Into the 10th and into the 11th it felt like that game would never end, that we were doomed to live in our debilitating baseball purgatory forever. And then, in one of the most dramatic moments I've ever witnessed, Encarnacion hit that miraculous three-run walk-off blast into the packed stands in left field. There were no literal fireworks for this particular occasion, but the sold-out crowd was more than happy to make their own.

We all know how this particular baseball story ends. The Jays went on to the ALDS and handily swept their old Bautista-bat-flip-hating rivals, the Rangers. The series started with a blowout and gave Bautista a chance to get his ultimate revenge against face-punching Rougned Odor after the Rangers' second baseman gave up the series-winning run on an error. In the ALCS the Jays' offense fizzled against Cleveland's pitching might.

It was hard to be genuinely devastated when Cleveland kicked the Jays around and advanced to the World Series. In some ways, and despite lofty expectations, Toronto had gotten more baseball than it could have imagined, or maybe more than it rightly deserved. Sometimes I think that loving baseball is really an exercise in coming to terms with loss. I don't just mean weathering the loss of a meaningful game or series or chance to go to the World Series for the first time in decades. Going into every year we know that only one team can take it all, so that kind of inevitable disappointment comes as no surprise.

But being a baseball devotee also means understanding that beloved players will come and go, and that a team's makeup is endlessly precarious and continually shifting. It means you can endure years of being no one, then suddenly matter, and then go back to being no one all over again. It's in this way that baseball is a gift. It forces us to understand that it's healthier to live in the moment than lament the failures of the past or the ambiguity of the future. It asks us to hold tightly to the incredible elation we feel during that herculean home run, because we know that joy is rare and fleeting. It demands that we wring every drop of pleasure out of the moment and refuse to regret what never was.

If the 2016 season was indeed a last chance to see the Blue Jays get this far for a long time, I'm happy we filled the stadium with gratitude. Sure, the immediate and long-term future of the Blue Jays feels precarious, but with uncertainty there is always hope. And after all we have seen and all we have learned, we now know that anything—including baseball greatness—is possible. ■

—Stacey May Fowles is a columnist at the Globe and Mail *and Blue Jays Nation*

Hitters

Anthony Alford   CF

Born: 7/20/94   Age: 22   Bats: R   Throws: R   Height: 6'1"   Weight: 215   Entered Pro Ball: Round 3, 2012 Draft (#112 overall)

YEAR	TEAM	LVL	AGE	PA	R	2B	3B	HR	RBI	BB	K	SB	CS	AVG/OBP/SLG	TAv	VORP	BABIP	BRR	FRAA	WARP
2014	LNS	A	19	25	3	1	0	1	3	0	8	4	0	.320/.320/.480	.287	2.2	.438	0.8	CF(4): -0.4	0.2
2015	LNS	A	20	232	49	14	1	1	16	39	60	12	1	.293/.418/.394	.287	19.7	.419	6.5	CF(47): -3.7	1.7
2015	DUN	A+	20	255	42	11	6	3	19	28	49	15	6	.302/.380/.444	.299	21.3	.374	4.1	CF(55): 0.5	2.4
2016	DUN	A+	21	401	53	17	2	9	44	53	117	18	6	.236/.344/.378	.261	15.0	.327	2.3	CF(84): 0.7 • LF(6): 0.2	1.6
2017	TOR	MLB	22	250	31	10	1	6	23	28	80	7	2	.219/.312/.359	.232	2.2	.311	0.3	CF 2 • RF 0	0.4
2018	TOR	MLB	23	336	39	14	2	8	35	38	108	9	3	.219/.313/.361	.235	0.8	.313	0.8	CF 2 • RF 0	0.4

Breakout: 1%   Improve: 18%   Collapse: 0%   Attrition: 12%   MLB: 34%   Comparables: Michael Saunders, Brett Jackson, Chris Young

Alford is one of the odder prospects in the minors. He's toolsy as can be, but has actualized on the cerebral points of the game. After 2015, he was praised for his approach at the plate in what was a breakout year. However, while the approach was still good, Alford seemed to struggle with contact in 2016. Given that he was a two-way star until 2015—splitting time between the Blue Jays and college football—he hasn't had as many reps as other prospects at his level. Yet, because of his age and tools, he'll likely be at Double-A in 2017. Two-way athlete be damned, he'll have to start improving his contact to succeed in the upper minors and then the majors.

Darwin Barney   IF

Born: 11/8/85   Age: 31   Bats: R   Throws: R   Height: 5'10"   Weight: 180   Entered Pro Ball: Round 4, 2007 Draft (#127 overall)

YEAR	TEAM	LVL	AGE	PA	R	2B	3B	HR	RBI	BB	K	SB	CS	AVG/OBP/SLG	TAv	VORP	BABIP	BRR	FRAA	WARP
2014	CHN	MLB	28	217	18	10	2	2	16	9	31	1	0	.230/.265/.328	.228	1.3	.262	2.4	2B(67): -1.2	0.0
2014	ABQ	AAA	28	38	5	1	0	0	1	3	5	0	0	.257/.316/.286	.219	0.7	.300	0.9	SS(6): 0.0 • 3B(3): -0.2	0.1
2014	LAN	MLB	28	45	6	1	0	1	7	8	3	0	0	.303/.467/.424	.364	5.4	.300	0.0	2B(12): -0.5 • SS(2): 0.1	0.6
2015	LAN	MLB	29	4	0	0	0	0	0	0	0	0	0	.000/.000/.000	-.011	-0.9	.000	0.0	3B(1): -0.0 • SS(1): 0.1	-0.1
2015	OKL	AAA	29	379	52	15	0	4	31	22	44	7	4	.277/.325/.354	.262	16.6	.306	4.4	2B(58): -3.9 • SS(18): 0.2	1.3
2015	TOR	MLB	29	26	4	1	0	2	4	1	2	0	0	.304/.333/.609	.342	2.8	.263	0.1	2B(15): 0.8	0.4
2016	TOR	MLB	30	306	35	13	2	4	19	22	48	2	2	.269/.322/.373	.234	0.7	.310	-0.9	2B(40): 1.9 • 3B(32): -0.2	0.2
2017	TOR	MLB	31	125	12	6	0	2	11	8	17	1	1	.245/.297/.354	.230	0.6	.266	-0.2	3B 0 • SS 0	-0.1
2018	TOR	MLB	32	163	17	7	0	3	16	11	23	1	1	.240/.295/.353	.224	-1.2	.263	0.4	3B 0 • SS 0	-0.1

Breakout: 0%   Improve: 35%   Collapse: 6%   Attrition: 23%   MLB: 89%   Comparables: Jonathan Herrera, Aaron Miles, Ryan Theriot

The stalwart middle infielder, of relative Cubs defensive fame, Barney had a solid year as the Blue Jays' go-to backup infield option. Of note, his defense seemed to return to form a bit after a few seasons in which FRAA rated him closer to average. That'll be important for Darwin, who is progressing through his 30s as a light-hitting infielder with mediocre speed.

Jose Bautista   RF

Born: 10/19/80   Age: 36   Bats: R   Throws: R   Height: 6'0"   Weight: 205   Entered Pro Ball: Round 20, 2000 Draft (#599 overall)

YEAR	TEAM	LVL	AGE	PA	R	2B	3B	HR	RBI	BB	K	SB	CS	AVG/OBP/SLG	TAv	VORP	BABIP	BRR	FRAA	WARP
2014	TOR	MLB	33	673	101	27	0	35	103	104	96	6	2	.286/.403/.524	.332	53.1	.287	-2.8	RF(131): 6.7 • CF(12): -0.5	6.5
2015	TOR	MLB	34	666	108	29	3	40	114	110	106	8	2	.250/.377/.536	.316	47.0	.237	0.3	RF(118): -4.8	4.5
2016	TOR	MLB	35	517	68	24	1	22	69	87	103	2	2	.234/.366/.452	.270	11.3	.255	-2.0	RF(91): -5.6 • 1B(1): -0.0	0.6
2017	TOR	MLB	36	518	75	22	1	27	81	80	89	4	2	.255/.374/.498	.294	31.6	.260	-0.8	RF -4 • 1B -0	3.0
2018	TOR	MLB	37	418	62	16	1	20	60	62	74	2	1	.244/.360/.464	.278	15.7	.253	-0.8	RF -3 • 1B 0	1.4

Breakout: 1%   Improve: 25%   Collapse: 2%   Attrition: 9%   MLB: 90%   Comparables: Lance Berkman, Gary Sheffield, Carlos Beltran

Bautista's TAv in 2016 was closer to his 2006 season in Pittsburgh than it was to any of his full seasons with the Blue Jays. That's concerning. Bautista's a smart hitter and the initial inclination would be to think that he'll be set for a rebound, but there were reasons for his poor performance beyond bad luck. Notably, Bautista wasn't hitting the ball quite as hard. Per Home Run Tracker online, the average "true distance" of his home runs was 384 feet; it hadn't been below 400 feet in any other full season with the Jays. On top of that his defense has clearly declined in the outfield, limiting his likely positions to 1B or DH. Adjusting to a lesser defensive position was already going to hurt Bautista's value and now he may have to adjust to a declining bat too.

Bo Bichette   SS

Born: 3/5/98   Age: 19   Bats: R   Throws: R   Height: 6'0"   Weight: 200   Entered Pro Ball: Round 2, 2016 Draft (#66 overall)

YEAR	TEAM	LVL	AGE	PA	R	2B	3B	HR	RBI	BB	K	SB	CS	AVG/OBP/SLG	TAv	VORP	BABIP	BRR	FRAA	WARP
2017	TOR	MLB	19	250	22	10	1	7	27	14	82	1	0	.204/.253/.342	.199	-4.8	.278	-0.3	SS 0 • 2B 0	-0.5
2018	TOR	MLB	20	316	35	13	1	10	36	20	99	1	0	.219/.273/.378	.221	-2.3	.290	-0.4	SS 0 • 2B 0	-0.2

Breakout: 0%   Improve: 5%   Collapse: 1%   Attrition: 6%   MLB: 10%   Comparables: Raul Mondesi, Elvis Andrus, Nomar Mazara

Even as the son of former Rockies slugger Dante Bichette and brother to current Yankees prospect Dante Bichette Jr., Bo could be the best Bichette around. His father and brother were restricted to the infield and outfield corners, but Bo looks like a legitimate up-the-middle talent. Scouts doubt his ability to stick at shortstop, but see second base as a likely landing spot. He has a quick bat and developing power, but he'll need to refine his swing to reach his true talent level once he's promoted beyond the lower minors. His Twitter handle also has "Bo Knows" in it. So, he's got that going for him.

Ezequiel Carrera   OF

Born: 6/11/87 Age: 30 Bats: L Throws: L Height: 5'11" Weight: 185 Entered Pro Ball: International Free Agent, 2005

YEAR	TEAM	LVL	AGE	PA	R	2B	3B	HR	RBI	BB	K	SB	CS	AVG/OBP/SLG	TAv	VORP	BABIP	BRR	FRAA	WARP
2014	TOL	AAA	27	434	68	15	5	6	41	48	65	43	13	.307/.387/.422	.281	24.3	.355	1.5	CF(69): -0.6 • RF(25): -1.0	2.2
2014	DET	MLB	27	73	12	4	1	0	2	3	14	7	1	.261/.301/.348	.244	1.9	.327	0.9	CF(38): 0.1 • LF(1): -0.4	0.2
2015	BUF	AAA	28	133	18	5	0	1	10	12	16	6	2	.276/.349/.345	.266	3.6	.313	-1.0	CF(25): -2.7 • RF(4): 0.6	0.3
2015	TOR	MLB	28	192	27	8	0	3	26	11	45	2	1	.273/.321/.372	.253	3.8	.349	1.4	LF(46): -1.6 • RF(35): -1.1	0.0
2016	TOR	MLB	29	310	47	9	1	6	23	27	70	7	4	.248/.323/.356	.238	-0.4	.311	0.2	RF(65): 4.2 • LF(45): -1.4	0.2
2017	*TOR*	*MLB*	*30*	*456*	*51*	*18*	*4*	*7*	*40*	*35*	*94*	*19*	*6*	*.254/.311/.367*	*.238*	*2.5*	*.304*	*1.7*	*RF 3 • CF -0*	*0.2*
2018	*TOR*	*MLB*	*31*	*509*	*56*	*19*	*3*	*9*	*50*	*42*	*110*	*20*	*7*	*.249/.316/.364*	*.234*	*-1.1*	*.301*	*1.8*	*RF 3 • CF 0*	*0.2*

Breakout: 0%   Improve: 14%   Collapse: 14%   Attrition: 33%   MLB: 61%   *Comparables:* Jason Ellison, Paulo Orlando, Elian Herrera

Carrera had the greatest season of his career as the left-handed fourth outfielder who could sometimes take a walk and was available when Jose Bautista was injured. Nothing extraordinary, but always around and playing a much bigger role than expected in the playoffs. That should serve him well as he continues to battle for playing time on the Blue Jays.

Chris Colabello   1B

Born: 10/24/83 Age: 33 Bats: R Throws: R Height: 6'4" Weight: 210 Entered Pro Ball: Undrafted Free Agent, 2012

YEAR	TEAM	LVL	AGE	PA	R	2B	3B	HR	RBI	BB	K	SB	CS	AVG/OBP/SLG	TAv	VORP	BABIP	BRR	FRAA	WARP
2014	MIN	MLB	30	220	17	13	0	6	39	14	66	0	2	.229/.282/.380	.245	-0.4	.308	0.2	1B(23): -0.4 • RF(19): -0.9	-0.2
2014	ROC	AAA	30	238	28	13	0	10	38	21	55	0	0	.268/.336/.469	.266	3.6	.313	-0.6	1B(54): 4.7 • RF(2): -0.1	0.8
2015	BUF	AAA	31	95	14	3	0	5	18	11	19	0	0	.337/.421/.554	.366	11.4	.390	-0.2	1B(12): -0.9 • RF(2): 0.2	1.1
2015	TOR	MLB	31	360	55	19	1	15	54	22	96	2	0	.321/.367/.520	.304	22.0	.411	1.0	1B(34): -0.0 • LF(33): -3.6	1.9
2016	TOR	MLB	32	32	0	0	0	0	1	2	9	0	0	.069/.156/.069	.088	-5.3	.100	-0.1	1B(8): -0.5 • LF(1): -0.0	-0.6
2016	DUN	A+	32	20	2	2	0	0	1	2	5	0	0	.222/.300/.333	.180	-1.6	.308	-0.2	LF(2): 0.1 • 1B(2): -0.2	-0.2
2016	BUF	AAA	32	153	14	0	0	5	11	11	46	0	0	.180/.248/.288	.178	-11.3	.225	-0.1	1B(24): -1.4 • RF(7): -0.5	-1.3
2017	*TOR*	*MLB*	*33*	*250*	*30*	*11*	*0*	*10*	*35*	*21*	*72*	*1*	*0*	*.253/.322/.444*	*.258*	*5.6*	*.323*	*0.4*	*1B -1 • RF -1*	*0.4*
2018	*TOR*	*MLB*	*34*	*158*	*21*	*6*	*0*	*6*	*21*	*13*	*46*	*0*	*0*	*.247/.316/.432*	*.253*	*1.4*	*.316*	*0.2*	*1B -1 • RF -1*	*0.0*

Breakout: 2%   Improve: 23%   Collapse: 12%   Attrition: 22%   MLB: 76%   *Comparables:* Randy Ruiz, Marcus Thames, Shelley Duncan

So it turns out there *is* a magic elixir that can help a career journeyman become an everyday big-league first baseman. It's called dehydrochlormethyltestosterone. Or Turinabol for those of us who have trouble with 10-syllable words. Colabello was already expected to fall back just due to his insanely high BABIP in 2015, but his suspension and subsequent fall from grace may have ended his MLB career completely. The projections think he could be useful going forward, but there aren't many Colabelievers left.

Josh Donaldson   3B

Born: 12/8/85 Age: 31 Bats: R Throws: R Height: 6'1" Weight: 210 Entered Pro Ball: Round 1, 2007 Draft (#48 overall)

YEAR	TEAM	LVL	AGE	PA	R	2B	3B	HR	RBI	BB	K	SB	CS	AVG/OBP/SLG	TAv	VORP	BABIP	BRR	FRAA	WARP
2014	OAK	MLB	28	695	93	31	2	29	98	76	130	8	0	.255/.342/.456	.305	46.1	.278	-2.5	3B(150): 16.2	6.9
2015	TOR	MLB	29	711	122	41	2	41	123	73	133	6	0	.297/.371/.568	.324	69.5	.314	4.0	3B(150): 1.3	7.6
2016	TOR	MLB	30	700	122	32	5	37	99	109	119	7	1	.284/.404/.549	.315	64.6	.300	4.8	3B(136): -12.2	5.4
2017	*TOR*	*MLB*	*31*	*664*	*100*	*34*	*3*	*30*	*91*	*77*	*124*	*6*	*1*	*.278/.367/.506*	*.299*	*46.5*	*.304*	*-0.2*	*3B 5*	*5.0*
2018	*TOR*	*MLB*	*32*	*557*	*80*	*28*	*2*	*24*	*81*	*64*	*108*	*3*	*1*	*.270/.359/.486*	*.282*	*25.8*	*.298*	*1.0*	*3B 5*	*3.3*

Breakout: 1%   Improve: 38%   Collapse: 4%   Attrition: 2%   MLB: 99%   *Comparables:* David Wright, Aramis Ramirez, Scott Rolen

After winning the MVP award, it's incredibly hard for any player to improve or even match it in the next season. An MVP season is where it all comes together; where luck, health, skill and narrative combine for something truly magical. That was Donaldson's reality in 2015, and there's an argument that it should've been his reality in 2016 too. He didn't have as many homers, nor did he bat in as many runners, but Donaldson's overall offensive profile graded out the same. Why? Because even at 31 he's still working to improve. In 2016, that improvement came in his approach, where he got fewer pitches in the strike zone, but was more patient, improving his walk rate by 50 percent and hitting more pitches hard than ever before. Not only is that incredibly impressive, but it bodes well for Donaldson as he moves in to his mid-30s. In other words, what can't he do?

Ryan Goins   2B/SS

Born: 2/13/88 Age: 29 Bats: L Throws: R Height: 5'10" Weight: 180 Entered Pro Ball: Round 4, 2009 Draft (#130 overall)

YEAR	TEAM	LVL	AGE	PA	R	2B	3B	HR	RBI	BB	K	SB	CS	AVG/OBP/SLG	TAv	VORP	BABIP	BRR	FRAA	WARP
2014	BUF	AAA	26	402	36	21	2	0	30	28	64	4	4	.284/.337/.353	.248	9.1	.342	0.2	SS(51): 0.7 • 2B(49): 2.1	1.2
2014	TOR	MLB	26	193	14	6	3	1	15	5	42	0	1	.188/.209/.271	.191	-8.0	.237	-0.7	2B(57): 2.1 • SS(15): -0.3	-0.7
2015	BUF	AAA	27	21	1	1	0	0	3	0	5	0	0	.350/.333/.400	.261	0.8	.438	0.0	SS(4): 0.1 • 2B(2): -0.1	0.1
2015	TOR	MLB	27	428	52	16	4	5	45	39	83	2	1	.250/.318/.354	.238	8.2	.304	3.9	2B(66): -3.5 • SS(58): 0.4	0.5
2016	BUF	AAA	28	110	9	6	0	2	10	8	23	0	1	.265/.318/.388	.258	4.3	.324	1.0	SS(14): 1.0 • 2B(10): 2.4	0.8
2016	TOR	MLB	28	196	13	9	2	3	12	9	48	1	1	.186/.228/.306	.179	-1.2	.235	-0.1	2B(37): -1.0 • SS(28): 3.3	-0.9
2017	*TOR*	*MLB*	*29*	*226*	*20*	*10*	*1*	*3*	*20*	*14*	*49*	*1*	*1*	*.239/.285/.347*	*.221*	*0.2*	*.290*	*-0.4*	*SS 2 • 2B 0*	*-0.1*
2018	*TOR*	*MLB*	*30*	*322*	*33*	*14*	*1*	*5*	*30*	*22*	*73*	*1*	*1*	*.234/.287/.346*	*.218*	*-3.0*	*.284*	*0.2*	*SS 3 • 2B 0*	*0.0*

Breakout: 2%   Improve: 28%   Collapse: 21%   Attrition: 25%   MLB: 64%   *Comparables:* Matt Tolbert, Alberto Gonzalez, Ramiro Pena

It turns out that not swinging isn't the best strategy for drawing a walk. We probably should've known this, but Goins fooled the world in 2015, when he put up the highest walk rate in the AL for the month of August. That single fact led to some optimism heading in to 2016, but Goins was as baffling offensively as always. He's still not arbitration eligible, and the Blue Jays seem to like him, so you can expect to see him return as the 26th man on the roster, shuffling back and forth from Buffalo.

Vladimir Guerrero 3B

Born: 3/16/99 Age: 18 Bats: R Throws: R Height: 6'1" Weight: 200 Entered Pro Ball: International Free Agent, 2015

YEAR	TEAM	LVL	AGE	PA	R	2B	3B	HR	RBI	BB	K	SB	CS	AVG/OBP/SLG	TAv	VORP	BABIP	BRR	FRAA	WARP
2017	TOR	MLB	18	250	24	10	1	6	26	18	73	4	2	.208/.267/.339	.205	-6.6	.272	-0.1	3B -4	-1.1
2018	TOR	MLB	19	261	28	11	1	7	27	18	77	4	2	.209/.266/.351	.213	-6.8	.272	0.0	3B -4	-1.2

Breakout: 0% Improve: 0% Collapse: 0% Attrition: 0% MLB: 0% *Comparables: Raul Mondesi, Wilmer Flores*

In general, it's hard to live up to a father who was a Hall of Fame talent. It's even harder when you're his full namesake, but Vladimir Guerrero Jr. has started out on the right foot. The 17-year-old began his minor-league career in rookie ball, starting all 50 of his games at the hot corner. He displayed some of the raw power that led to his $3.9 million bonus in 2015, and showed off the advanced approach that his advocates touted. However, while third base is the position that Guerrero Jr. wants to play, he's still relatively new to it. If he were more defensively experienced, his advanced approach would have pushed him very swiftly through the minors.

Lourdes Gurriel SS

Born: 10/19/93 Age: 23 Bats: R Throws: R Height: 6'2" Weight: 185 Entered Pro Ball: International Free Agent, 2016

YEAR	TEAM	LVL	AGE	PA	R	2B	3B	HR	RBI	BB	K	SB	CS	AVG/OBP/SLG	TAv	VORP	BABIP	BRR	FRAA	WARP
2017	TOR	MLB	23	250	28	11	2	5	26	27	36	4	2	.261/.344/.397	.253	9.6	.285	0.0	SS 0	1.1

Breakout: 3% Improve: 48% Collapse: 9% Attrition: 12% MLB: 94% *Comparables: Tony Fernandez, Elvis Andrus, Enzo Hernandez*

The latest in what is soon to be a dried-up pipeline of Serie Nacional talent coming to the majors, Gurriel is the last link in one of the great Cuban baseball families. His father was one of the country's greats, both domestically and internationally, in the 80s and 90s. His brother, Yulieski, was one of the best hitters of this decade and stands to be the Astros' first baseman in 2017. But bloodlines aren't the only thing this Gurriel brings to the table. His $22 million contract was less than many anticipated, but it's likely because he's not the type of player who shines with tools or showcases. The now-23-year-old has an above-average hit tool, a great approach at the plate, some pop and the ability to play all over the dirt (though asking him to be an everyday shortstop is likely asking too much). He'll probably need at least a half-season in the minors before the Blue Jays summon him up north, but there's a good chance he leaves other teams wondering why they let him sign for such a meager amount.

Russell Martin C

Born: 2/15/83 Age: 34 Bats: R Throws: R Height: 5'10" Weight: 205 Entered Pro Ball: Round 17, 2002 Draft (#511 overall)

YEAR	TEAM	LVL	AGE	PA	R	2B	3B	HR	RBI	BB	K	SB	CS	AVG/OBP/SLG	TAv	VORP	BABIP	BRR	FRAA	WARP
2014	PIT	MLB	31	460	45	20	0	11	67	59	78	4	4	.290/.402/.430	.309	38.8	.336	-1.1	C(107): 20.8	6.6
2015	TOR	MLB	32	507	76	23	2	23	77	53	106	4	5	.240/.329/.458	.275	27.7	.262	-0.9	C(117): 13.9 • 2B(2): -0.2	4.4
2016	TOR	MLB	33	535	62	16	0	20	74	64	148	2	1	.231/.335/.398	.252	19.3	.291	0.3	C(127): 12.0 • 3B(1): 0.0	3.2
2017	TOR	MLB	34	551	65	22	1	19	68	65	123	4	3	.236/.338/.407	.264	27.9	.276	-1.6	C 16	4.1
2018	TOR	MLB	35	484	64	20	1	16	58	58	112	3	2	.235/.337/.403	.256	15.5	.279	-0.3	C 13	3.1

Breakout: 0% Improve: 37% Collapse: 11% Attrition: 16% MLB: 94% *Comparables: John Wockenfuss, Darren Daulton, Bob Brenly*

Martin was freed of having to catch a knuckleball in 2016, but it didn't save him from issues both at the plate and behind it. He's still an elite framer and he fixed his blocking issues from 2015 (which were likely heavily attributed to the knuckleball), but his ability to control the running game disappeared. Yes, some of that is on the pitchers, but Martin still fell from a league-best 44 percent caught stealing to a league-worst 15 percent. That being said, he's still clearly an above-average defensive catcher. The worries going forward are stronger on the offensive side. Martin's contact rate fell to a career-worst 69.9 percent, which was almost six percentage points off his previous career-low. As a

YEAR	TEAM	P. COUNT	FRM RUNS	BLK RUNS	THRW RUNS	TOT RUNS
2014	PIT	14470	14.9	0.3	3.9	19.2
2015	TOR	15667	11.6	-3.6	2.6	10.6
2016	TOR	16738	14.2	0.2	-2.3	12.1
2017	TOR	18284	16.1	-1.7	0.2	14.5
2018	TOR	16059	12.2	-1.8	-0.1	10.4

result, his batting average fell to .231 and he struck out 40 times more than his previous high. He was still plenty useful as a hitter, as his power and walks remained, but there are definite reasons to worry. The hope is that a better backup and more rest will help Martin rebound, as at age 34 his best days are likely behind him.

Reese McGuire C

Born: 3/2/95 Age: 22 Bats: L Throws: R Height: 5'11" Weight: 215 Entered Pro Ball: Round 1, 2013 Draft (#14 overall)

YEAR	TEAM	LVL	AGE	PA	R	2B	3B	HR	RBI	BB	K	SB	CS	AVG/OBP/SLG	TAv	VORP	BABIP	BRR	FRAA	WARP
2014	WVA	A	19	428	46	11	4	3	45	24	44	7	2	.262/.307/.334	.232	4.7	.284	0.2	C(84): 3.7	0.9
2015	BRD	A+	20	412	32	15	0	0	34	26	39	14	7	.254/.301/.294	.228	2.8	.280	-0.8	C(90): -0.2	0.3
2016	ALT	AA	21	304	29	16	2	1	37	29	26	4	4	.259/.337/.346	.251	8.5	.282	-1.8	C(73): 3.0	1.2
2016	NHP	AA	21	61	5	2	0	0	5	7	8	2	2	.226/.328/.264	.205	-0.2	.267	0.7	C(13): -8.0	-0.9
2017	TOR	MLB	22	250	23	11	1	4	24	16	42	3	2	.234/.287/.345	.211	-0.3	.264	-0.4	C -9	-1.0
2018	TOR	MLB	23	277	30	12	1	6	28	18	45	3	2	.240/.293/.361	.224	-0.5	.265	-0.4	C -10	-1.1

Breakout: 9% Improve: 11% Collapse: 4% Attrition: 13% MLB: 17% *Comparables: Josh Thole, Carlos Perez, Bryan Anderson*

In 2016, McGuire represented an example in the trend of teams taking on salary in return for a little more prospect might. In Reese's case, he, along with outfielder Harold Ramirez, was exchanged in addition to Francisco Liriano as part of Pittsburgh's salary dump. The former first rounder has ranked as high as 59th on BP's top prospects list. Evaluators praise his defensive prowess, but the bat has never been there. He might be

YEAR	TEAM	P. COUNT	FRM RUNS	BLK RUNS	THRW RUNS	TOT RUNS
2017	TOR	9063	-8.6	0.2	-0.5	-8.9
2018	TOR	10050	-9.4	0.5	-0.6	-9.6

able fill in as the Blue Jays' backup catcher right now, but there's more potential. He'll likely get a full season at Triple-A with the starter vs. backup conversation to resume thereafter. But, even then, with Russell Martin in Toronto 'til 2019, McGuire might have some trouble getting full-time at-bats.

Kendrys Morales   DH

Born: 6/20/83   Age: 34   Bats: B   Throws: R   Height: 6'1"   Weight: 225   Entered Pro Ball: International Free Agent, 2005

YEAR	TEAM	LVL	AGE	PA	R	2B	3B	HR	RBI	BB	K	SB	CS	AVG/OBP/SLG	TAv	VORP	BABIP	BRR	FRAA	WARP
2014	MIN	MLB	31	162	12	11	0	1	18	6	27	0	0	.234/.259/.325	.223	-4.4	.273	-0.3	1B(13): -1.0	-0.6
2014	SEA	MLB	31	239	16	9	0	7	24	21	41	0	0	.207/.285/.347	.251	-1.1	.222	-1.2	1B(14): -1.1	-0.2
2015	KCA	MLB	32	639	81	41	2	22	106	58	103	0	0	.290/.362/.485	.294	22.2	.319	-5.5	1B(9): -0.4	2.3
2016	KCA	MLB	33	618	65	24	0	30	93	48	120	0	0	.263/.327/.468	.270	11.7	.283	-1.2	1B(7): -0.1 • RF(5): -0.2	1.2
2017	TOR	MLB	34	601	68	24	1	22	80	49	114	0	0	.264/.329/.446	.269	14.1	.294	-1.4	1B -1	1.6
2018	TOR	MLB	35	497	64	25	1	18	64	42	99	0	0	.256/.325/.434	.258	9.1	.289	-2.4	1B -1	0.9

Breakout: 1%   Improve: 35%   Collapse: 6%   Attrition: 20%   MLB: 94%   Comparables: Raul Ibanez, Aubrey Huff, Tino Martinez

Sometimes you make a bad decision. Like eating that week-old slice of pizza you left out on the counter. Sometimes, you get a second chance. Like when you survive after eating that week-old slice. After turning down a qualifying offer from the Mariners in 2013, Morales floundered before he got a second chance in Kansas City and found a new baseball life. He took a mild step back last summer, but his contact and line-drive rates remained static from 2014 and his ISO increased. Without the qualifying offer to dampen his value, and coming off a pair of productive seasons, he finally landed the free agent deal he missed out on last time around as the Blue Jays will pay him $33 million over the next three years for the pleasure of watching him rake.

Dioner Navarro   C

Born: 2/9/84   Age: 33   Bats: B   Throws: R   Height: 5'9"   Weight: 215   Entered Pro Ball: International Free Agent, 2000

YEAR	TEAM	LVL	AGE	PA	R	2B	3B	HR	RBI	BB	K	SB	CS	AVG/OBP/SLG	TAv	VORP	BABIP	BRR	FRAA	WARP
2014	TOR	MLB	30	520	40	22	6	12	69	32	76	3	0	.274/.317/.395	.260	17.2	.301	-1.3	C(112): -20.9	-0.4
2015	TOR	MLB	31	192	17	7	0	5	20	17	29	0	0	.246/.307/.374	.255	4.7	.262	-1.2	C(39): -3.3	0.2
2016	CHA	MLB	32	298	25	13	2	6	32	20	63	1	2	.210/.267/.339	.216	-4.9	.249	-4.8	C(83): -19.3	-2.5
2016	TOR	MLB	32	36	1	0	0	0	3	3	8	0	0	.182/.250/.182	.209	-0.4	.240	0.2	C(7): -2.9	-0.3
2017	TOR	MLB	33	288	31	12	1	8	34	22	48	1	1	.263/.321/.409	.244	8.4	.289	-1.6	C -18	-1.0
2018	TOR	MLB	34	245	29	10	0	7	28	17	43	0	0	.250/.304/.389	.235	1.4	.276	-1.4	C -16	-1.5

Breakout: 1%   Improve: 38%   Collapse: 7%   Attrition: 19%   MLB: 89%   Comparables: Josh Bard, Robert Fick, Johnny Estrada

Dioner Navarro is proof that game calling is about as important as anything else a catcher can do. In 2015, he used his sorcery on Marco Estrada, aiding in his transition from a homerful freak to a pop-up machine. But, after 2015, Navarro's work in Toronto was done. He took his talents (and a $4 million paycheck) to the South Side. However, it became clear that, with R.A. Dickey floundering, the Jays could use a backup catcher who could do more than catch the knuckleball. Not only had Navarro previously caught most of the Blue Jays' starters, manager John Gibbons seems to believe his bat is god-like. The tale of Navarro's return didn't end with a World Series, but he kept the Jays alive for another game in the ALCS. That'll always mean something.

YEAR	TEAM	P. COUNT	FRM RUNS	BLK RUNS	THRW RUNS	TOT RUNS
2014	TOR	14932	-19.8	1.3	-0.6	-19.1
2015	BUF	372	-0.1	0.0	0.0	-0.1
2015	TOR	4992	-3.6	0.1	0.3	-3.2
2016	CHA	11287	-16.8	-0.9	-0.5	-18.1
2016	TOR	868	-2.8	0.0	0.0	-2.8
2017	TOR	10422	-15.8	-0.4	-0.4	-16.6
2018	TOR	8883	-14.4	-0.4	-0.4	-15.2

Steve Pearce   1B

Born: 4/13/83   Age: 34   Bats: R   Throws: R   Height: 5'11"   Weight: 200   Entered Pro Ball: Round 8, 2005 Draft (#241 overall)

YEAR	TEAM	LVL	AGE	PA	R	2B	3B	HR	RBI	BB	K	SB	CS	AVG/OBP/SLG	TAv	VORP	BABIP	BRR	FRAA	WARP
2014	BAL	MLB	31	383	51	26	0	21	49	40	76	5	0	.293/.373/.556	.346	33.8	.322	-2.1	1B(51): 7.5 • LF(35): 4.1	5.0
2015	BAL	MLB	32	325	42	13	1	15	40	23	69	1	1	.218/.289/.422	.244	2.6	.232	2.0	LF(41): -0.5 • 1B(28): 1.0	0.3
2016	TBA	MLB	33	232	26	11	1	10	29	26	40	0	3	.309/.388/.520	.323	18.3	.342	0.0	1B(30): 1.7 • 2B(14): 0.4	2.1
2016	BAL	MLB	33	70	9	2	0	3	6	8	14	0	0	.217/.329/.400	.268	0.3	.233	1.5	1B(10): -0.3 • LF(7): -0.2	0.3
2017	TOR	MLB	34	515	63	27	1	21	71	53	103	3	2	.261/.347/.463	.281	22.1	.293	-1.4	1B 6 • RF -1	2.6
2018	TOR	MLB	35	353	49	17	1	14	48	38	73	1	1	.254/.344/.454	.270	10.0	.286	0.3	1B 4 • RF 0	1.6

Breakout: 0%   Improve: 32%   Collapse: 5%   Attrition: 11%   MLB: 89%   Comparables: Paul Konerko, Troy Glaus, Mark Teixeira

Despite a rough 2015, Pearce has proven himself a more than capable hitter with above-average power, good plate discipline and enough athleticism to play average or better defense in left field or at first base. That, at least, was true through his age-33 season. Blooming late doesn't guarantee a late decline, and Pearce's injury history might even hint at an early one. He can help any team in need of a good bat off the bench, but the less you're counting on him, the better.

Max Pentecost   C

Born: 3/10/93   Age: 24   Bats: R   Throws: R   Height: 6'2"   Weight: 191   Entered Pro Ball: Round 1, 2014 Draft (#11 overall)

YEAR	TEAM	LVL	AGE	PA	R	2B	3B	HR	RBI	BB	K	SB	CS	AVG/OBP/SLG	TAv	VORP	BABIP	BRR	FRAA	WARP
2014	VAN	A-	21	87	15	2	3	0	9	2	18	2	1	.313/.322/.410	.265	2.6	.388	0.3	C(6): -0.1	0.3
2016	LNS	A	23	267	36	15	3	7	34	21	51	4	2	.314/.375/.490	.318	19.1	.370	1.5		2.1
2016	DUN	A+	23	52	6	2	0	3	7	3	17	1	1	.245/.288/.469	.258	0.3	.310	-0.2		0.0
2017	TOR	MLB	24	250	25	11	1	9	31	14	70	1	0	.232/.281/.400	.227	-3.3	.290	-0.3		-0.4
2018	TOR	MLB	25	241	29	10	1	9	30	15	68	1	0	.232/.285/.407	.234	-2.4	.289	-0.4	-	-0.3

Breakout: 1%   Improve: 3%   Collapse: 2%   Attrition: 8%   MLB: 9%   Comparables: Joey Terdoslavich, Tyler Moore, Ben Paulsen

The Blue Jays are still waiting for the "catcher of the future" to get behind the plate. After two years of inactivity due to injury, Pentecost finally made it back into games in 2016, but only as a designated hitter. The former first-round pick showed little rust in that area, as he torched Florida State League pitching before a short call-up to New Hampshire. The next step will be to see if he can handle the job defensively and provide some return on the Blue Jays' significant draft investment. If so, Pentecost still has all the tools that made him a top-15 pick.

Kevin Pillar   CF

Born: 1/4/89   Age: 28   Bats: R   Throws: R   Height: 6'0"   Weight: 205   Entered Pro Ball: Round 32, 2011 Draft (#979 overall)

YEAR	TEAM	LVL	AGE	PA	R	2B	3B	HR	RBI	BB	K	SB	CS	AVG/OBP/SLG	TAv	VORP	BABIP	BRR	FRAA	WARP
2014	BUF	AAA	25	434	57	39	3	10	59	21	48	27	6	.323/.359/.509	.296	31.6	.345	3.2	LF(47): 1.2 • CF(31): -3.0	3.3
2014	TOR	MLB	25	122	19	9	0	2	7	4	28	1	2	.267/.295/.397	.261	2.7	.333	-0.1	LF(30): -0.8 • CF(16): 0.6	0.3
2015	TOR	MLB	26	628	76	31	2	12	56	28	85	25	4	.278/.314/.399	.257	22.3	.306	6.1	CF(142): 9.1 • LF(14): 4.2	3.8
2016	TOR	MLB	27	584	59	35	2	7	53	24	90	14	6	.266/.303/.376	.232	4.2	.306	2.7	CF(146): 2.4	0.7
2017	TOR	MLB	28	562	63	34	2	11	56	26	89	18	6	.274/.312/.410	.250	16.2	.309	1.2	CF 3	1.3
2018	TOR	MLB	29	569	65	35	2	13	65	28	94	16	6	.277/.319/.426	.251	13.2	.312	3.2	CF 4	1.8

Breakout: 3%   Improve: 42%   Collapse: 3%   Attrition: 14%   MLB: 87%   Comparables: Leonys Martin, Endy Chavez, Jeremy Reed

Pillar is living proof that you don't need an approach at the plate in order to be a good major-league player. In 2016, he somehow swung at fewer pitches, but walked a lot less and struck out a lot more. That's hard to do. But, of course, he makes up for it on defense, where his questionable diving tactics rarely fail to work out for him. He's the Cosmo Kramer of the baseball world: He does so many things wrong, but it manages to work out for him in the end. This year will be Pillar's third full season in center field and we'll get our best look yet at seeing if his defensive trends will continue.

Dalton Pompey   OF

Born: 12/11/92   Age: 24   Bats: B   Throws: R   Height: 6'2"   Weight: 195   Entered Pro Ball: Round 16, 2010 Draft (#486 overall)

YEAR	TEAM	LVL	AGE	PA	R	2B	3B	HR	RBI	BB	K	SB	CS	AVG/OBP/SLG	TAv	VORP	BABIP	BRR	FRAA	WARP
2014	DUN	A+	21	317	49	12	6	6	34	35	56	29	2	.319/.397/.471	.306	32.8	.380	6.6	CF(70): 3.4	3.6
2014	NHP	AA	21	127	20	5	3	3	12	14	18	8	5	.295/.378/.473	.304	11.8	.330	2.3	CF(30): 0.5	1.3
2014	BUF	AAA	21	56	15	5	0	0	5	3	10	6	0	.358/.393/.453	.300	4.9	.442	0.7	CF(11): -0.4	0.5
2014	TOR	MLB	21	43	5	1	2	1	4	4	12	1	0	.231/.302/.436	.257	1.6	.308	0.8	LF(9): -0.5 • CF(5): -0.2	0.1
2015	NHP	AA	22	148	26	2	3	6	22	11	23	7	3	.351/.405/.545	.342	18.3	.387	2.0	CF(22): -1.5 • LF(7): -0.5	1.8
2015	BUF	AAA	22	295	44	7	4	1	18	36	41	16	7	.285/.372/.356	.271	13.4	.332	2.1	CF(43): -3.4 • LF(22): 1.5	1.2
2015	TOR	MLB	22	103	17	8	0	2	6	7	23	5	1	.223/.291/.372	.233	-0.3	.275	-0.4	CF(21): 0.2 • LF(6): 0.2	0.0
2016	BUF	AAA	23	383	48	14	1	4	28	40	72	18	7	.270/.349/.353	.255	13.9	.331	5.2	CF(67): -3.1 • LF(24): -0.3	1.1
2016	TOR	MLB	23	2	3	0	0	0	0	0	1	2	1	.000/.000/.000	.001	-0.4	.000	0.1	LF(2): 0.0	0.0
2017	TOR	MLB	24	192	24	8	2	4	19	19	42	8	3	.262/.336/.405	.258	6.0	.320	0.7	LF 1 • RF -0	0.5
2018	TOR	MLB	25	393	48	17	4	10	45	39	87	16	6	.265/.341/.422	.257	10.2	.323	1.9	LF 1 • RF -1	1.1

Breakout: 7%   Improve: 34%   Collapse: 12%   Attrition: 21%   MLB: 68%   Comparables: Jacoby Ellsbury, Desmond Jennings, Adam Eaton

In April of 2015, Pompey was the Blue Jays' center fielder of the future and the present. Kevin Pillar's magnet for a glove and the fact that Pompey was playing somewhat scared changed that paradigm rather quickly. In 2016, Pompey was a repeat of his past: a limited power walking machine playing a great center field. That may be enough to get him more at-bats in 2017, but it'll be hard to provide value with Pillar's locked down center field leaving only the corners to contribute. Pompey is still just 24 and has enough talent to garner another shot. Will that come with the Blue Jays? Google "Kevin Pillar GIF" and you'll probably find out for yourself.

Harold Ramirez   OF

Born: 9/6/94   Age: 22   Bats: R   Throws: R   Height: 5'10"   Weight: 220   Entered Pro Ball: International Free Agent, 2011

YEAR	TEAM	LVL	AGE	PA	R	2B	3B	HR	RBI	BB	K	SB	CS	AVG/OBP/SLG	TAv	VORP	BABIP	BRR	FRAA	WARP
2014	WVA	A	19	226	30	14	1	1	24	11	35	12	3	.309/.364/.402	.283	13.5	.365	2.5	CF(24): 1.4 • RF(23): -1.4	1.4
2015	BRD	A+	20	344	45	13	6	4	47	25	48	22	15	.337/.399/.458	.330	29.0	.385	-0.9	RF(72): 3.3 • CF(1): -0.1	3.5
2016	ALT	AA	21	414	58	16	7	2	49	21	66	7	10	.306/.354/.401	.271	17.2	.363	2.4	CF(67): -7.3 • LF(14): 1.4	1.1
2017	TOR	MLB	22	250	26	12	2	5	27	13	55	4	4	.266/.317/.401	.244	4.1	.324	-0.6	CF -3 • LF 0	0.2
2018	TOR	MLB	23	374	42	18	3	7	40	21	81	7	6	.270/.324/.408	.250	5.3	.329	-0.3	CF -4 • LF 1	0.2

Breakout: 6%   Improve: 22%   Collapse: 3%   Attrition: 21%   MLB: 45%   Comparables: Andrew McCutchen, Gregory Polanco, Austin Jackson

Since cracking professional ball, all Ramirez has done is hit the ball. He'll even take a walk every now and then. However, he doesn't have much power, he doesn't have the speed to play center field and he was included as a throw-in in a trade to make the Blue Jays eat Francisco Liriano's contract. He'll likely never be a star, but if he can make consistent contact, he should at least have a future role. He doesn't need to look much further than current Blue Jays center fielder Kevin Pillar to know how tough it can be to maintain batting average, but Ramirez's better walk rate suggests it shouldn't be impossible.

Michael Saunders   OF

Born: 11/19/86   Age: 30   Bats: L   Throws: R   Height: 6'4"   Weight: 225   Entered Pro Ball: Round 11, 2004 Draft (#333 overall)

YEAR	TEAM	LVL	AGE	PA	R	2B	3B	HR	RBI	BB	K	SB	CS	AVG/OBP/SLG	TAv	VORP	BABIP	BRR	FRAA	WARP
2014	TAC	AAA	27	71	11	3	1	1	9	16	15	0	0	.327/.479/.473	.372	11.0	.436	1.0	RF(10): -0.9	1.0
2014	SEA	MLB	27	263	38	11	3	8	34	26	59	4	5	.273/.341/.450	.318	19.1	.327	0.1	RF(68): -2.9 • CF(12): -0.3	1.8
2015	DUN	A+	28	33	2	3	0	0	2	3	8	0	0	.233/.303/.333	.218	-1.3	.318	-0.5	LF(4): -0.4 • RF(2): -0.5	-0.2
2015	TOR	MLB	28	36	2	0	0	0	3	5	10	0	0	.194/.306/.194	.210	-1.8	.286	-0.7	RF(6): 1.3 • LF(3): -0.4	-0.1
2016	TOR	MLB	29	558	70	32	3	24	57	59	157	1	2	.253/.338/.478	.273	17.5	.321	-1.5	LF(106): -1.7 • RF(22): -0.4	1.6
2017	TOR	MLB	30	424	50	22	3	15	55	47	107	3	3	.252/.337/.446	.265	15.8	.310	-0.5	LF -5 • RF -1	1.1
2018	TOR	MLB	31	403	53	19	2	14	51	48	105	3	2	.246/.338/.434	.263	10.2	.306	-0.3	LF -4 • RF -1	0.5

Breakout: 3%   Improve: 52%   Collapse: 5%   Attrition: 8%   MLB: 98%   Comparables: Milton Bradley, Johnny Briggs, Jonny Gomes

Had the season ended in August, Saunders would've finished with 23 home runs, an .871 OPS and a breakout. However, September exists, and it was not kind. He capped off the season as one of baseball's worst hitters in the final month. In some cases one can be forgiven a single month, but in Saunders' case he was simply poor. When you combine that with his well-below-average defense in left field, you get a player who performed well given his 2015 knee injury, but not well enough to call 2016 a breakout.

Justin Smoak   1B

Born: 12/5/86   Age: 30   Bats: B   Throws: L   Height: 6'4"   Weight: 220   Entered Pro Ball: Round 1, 2008 Draft (#11 overall)

YEAR	TEAM	LVL	AGE	PA	R	2B	3B	HR	RBI	BB	K	SB	CS	AVG/OBP/SLG	TAv	VORP	BABIP	BRR	FRAA	WARP
2014	TAC	AAA	27	249	29	13	0	7	40	33	41	0	2	.337/.422/.502	.353	27.8	.376	-0.9	1B(42): -1.8	2.6
2014	SEA	MLB	27	276	28	13	0	7	30	24	66	0	1	.202/.275/.339	.235	-4.2	.243	-0.4	1B(79): -3.3	-0.8
2015	TOR	MLB	28	328	44	16	1	18	59	29	86	0	0	.226/.299/.470	.267	3.5	.254	-2.4	1B(110): 2.2	0.6
2016	TOR	MLB	29	341	33	10	0	14	34	40	112	1	0	.217/.314/.391	.242	-3.8	.295	-1.3	1B(111): -2.4	-0.6
2017	TOR	MLB	30	363	42	15	1	13	44	40	88	0	0	.235/.323/.412	.257	4.1	.280	-0.9	1B -2	0.0
2018	TOR	MLB	31	388	51	16	0	14	48	45	96	0	0	.232/.325/.408	.251	0.5	.278	-1.3	1B -2	-0.2

Breakout: 0%   Improve: 36%   Collapse: 3%   Attrition: 15%   MLB: 83%   *Comparables: Ben Broussard, Mitch Moreland, Lyle Overbay*

Smoak turned 30 this offseason. In general, you'd think a player's prospect sheen would've worn off by that point. But for Smoak, the man who was once a consensus top-25 prospect, that doesn't seem to be the case. There's no other explanation for the two year, $8.5 million extension the Blue Jays gave him in July. Smoak had walked a lot at the beginning of the season, but was a roughly league-average hitter overall; not particularly special from a first baseman. The Blue Jays' saving grace is that, at $8.5 million guaranteed, the contract is by no means insurmountable. It did, however, leave them with a lame duck first baseman for an offseason in which they had to redefine part of the lineup.

Rowdy Tellez   1B

Born: 3/16/95   Age: 22   Bats: L   Throws: L   Height: 6'4"   Weight: 220   Entered Pro Ball: Round 30, 2013 Draft (#895 overall)

YEAR	TEAM	LVL	AGE	PA	R	2B	3B	HR	RBI	BB	K	SB	CS	AVG/OBP/SLG	TAv	VORP	BABIP	BRR	FRAA	WARP
2014	LNS	A	19	49	6	0	0	2	7	7	10	0	0	.357/.449/.500	.369	6.5	.433	0.3	1B(8): -0.1	0.7
2015	LNS	A	20	299	36	19	0	7	49	24	56	2	2	.296/.351/.444	.290	7.7	.346	-4.4	1B(51): 2.0	1.0
2015	DUN	A+	20	148	17	5	0	7	28	14	28	3	0	.275/.338/.473	.275	4.2	.293	0.6	1B(24): 0.7	0.5
2016	NHP	AA	21	514	71	29	2	23	81	63	92	4	3	.297/.387/.530	.310	29.8	.324	-0.9	1B(101): -5.0	2.7
2017	TOR	MLB	22	34	4	2	0	1	5	3	8	0	0	.250/.326/.451	.266	0.7	.293	-0.1	1B -0	0.0
2018	TOR	MLB	23	293	41	15	1	13	42	31	72	0	0	.250/.333/.467	.266	4.7	.292	-0.7	1B -2	0.3

Breakout: 2%   Improve: 33%   Collapse: 5%   Attrition: 19%   MLB: 62%   *Comparables: Anthony Rizzo, Greg Bird, Jon Singleton*

The entire Blue Jays organization is rowdy over Tellez, as he's taken over as arguably the top upper-level hitting prospect in the system. As one of the league's youngest players, he absolutely tore it up for Double-A New Hampshire while increasing his walk rate and decreasing his strikeout rate. He has also done great work with conditioning, making it possible he can handle first base defensively in the big leagues. There are still some questions about his future, however. Scouts are torn on whether he can handle big velocity, and much of his power came at home where there was a very short porch in right field. The results thus far are very encouraging and he could crack the big leagues at some point in 2017.

Josh Thole   C

Born: 10/28/86   Age: 30   Bats: L   Throws: R   Height: 6'1"   Weight: 205   Entered Pro Ball: Round 13, 2005 Draft (#389 overall)

YEAR	TEAM	LVL	AGE	PA	R	2B	3B	HR	RBI	BB	K	SB	CS	AVG/OBP/SLG	TAv	VORP	BABIP	BRR	FRAA	WARP
2014	TOR	MLB	27	150	11	4	0	0	7	14	25	0	3	.248/.320/.278	.224	-0.1	.306	-1.2	C(53): 0.5	0.0
2015	BUF	AAA	28	170	12	5	0	0	17	20	20	0	0	.228/.320/.262	.243	2.9	.264	-1.6	C(45): 11.8	1.5
2015	TOR	MLB	28	52	5	2	0	0	2	3	9	0	0	.204/.250/.245	.174	-2.0	.250	0.1	C(18): 0.6	-0.1
2016	TOR	MLB	29	136	7	3	0	1	7	13	28	0	0	.169/.254/.220	.178	-6.5	.209	-1.3	C(50): 4.9	-0.2
2017	TOR	MLB	30	250	24	10	1	4	23	23	43	1	1	.238/.311/.342	.221	2.3	.273	-0.5	C 9	1.2
2018	TOR	MLB	31	111	12	4	0	2	10	10	20	0	0	.231/.307/.333	.222	-0.4	.267	-0.2	C 4	0.4

Breakout: 1%   Improve: 33%   Collapse: 17%   Attrition: 23%   MLB: 87%   *Comparables: Ron Brand, Bob Boone, Johnny Oates*

With R.A. Dickey heading to free agency, last season was Thole's opportunity to prove that he could do more than catch the knuckleball. Needless to say, he was unable to take advantage. Finishing with a sub .200 TAv for the third time in his career, Thole might be better off trying to learn to throw the knuckleball. Either that, or he'll have to take a trip to Boston. We hear that Steven Wright guy is pretty good.

YEAR	TEAM	P. COUNT	FRM RUNS	BLK RUNS	THRW RUNS	TOT RUNS
2014	TOR	5839	0.7	0.9	-0.6	0.9
2015	BUF	5996	11.6	0.3	-0.1	11.8
2015	TOR	1983	0.5	1.1	-0.1	1.5
2016	TOR	5590	4.8	2.9	-0.2	7.5
2017	TOR	9794	6.7	2.9	-0.5	9.0
2018	TOR	4332	2.6	1.2	-0.3	3.6

Devon Travis   2B

Born: 2/21/91   Age: 26   Bats: R   Throws: R   Height: 5'9"   Weight: 190   Entered Pro Ball: Round 13, 2012 Draft (#424 overall)

YEAR	TEAM	LVL	AGE	PA	R	2B	3B	HR	RBI	BB	K	SB	CS	AVG/OBP/SLG	TAv	VORP	BABIP	BRR	FRAA	WARP
2014	ERI	AA	23	441	68	20	7	10	52	37	60	16	5	.298/.358/.460	.276	21.2	.327	2.7	2B(95): 2.8 • CF(3): -0.6	2.5
2015	BUF	AAA	24	38	5	1	0	0	6	9	9	1	0	.219/.342/.250	.236	0.6	.304	0.8	2B(5): -0.1	0.1
2015	TOR	MLB	24	238	38	18	0	8	35	18	43	3	1	.304/.361/.498	.307	18.5	.347	1.4	2B(62): -0.3	1.9
2016	BUF	AAA	25	22	2	2	0	0	3	0	2	0	0	.273/.273/.364	.230	-0.1	.300	0.1	2B(4): -0.5	-0.1
2016	TOR	MLB	25	432	54	28	1	11	50	20	87	4	1	.300/.332/.454	.266	15.7	.358	1.6	2B(99): -0.3	1.6
2017	TOR	MLB	26	606	75	34	3	16	64	42	116	7	2	.276/.327/.434	.264	26.5	.320	-0.2	2B 1	2.3
2018	TOR	MLB	27	511	62	30	2	14	62	37	100	6	2	.275/.329/.439	.259	16.8	.320	1.5	2B 0	1.9

Breakout: 5%   Improve: 57%   Collapse: 6%   Attrition: 18%   MLB: 99%   *Comparables: Josh Harrison, Jason Kipnis, Neil Walker*

It's nice to see Travis learning from veteran double-play partner Troy Tulowitzki. He's taken to heart the lessons of being really, really good early in your career, but injured a bit too often for it to have the proper impact. After returning in late May from offseason shoulder surgery, Travis had another excellent year at the plate, eventually finding his way to the top of the Blue Jays' lineup. However, he suffered yet another big injury in the postseason and was once again recovering from surgery (this time to his knee) during the offseason. The talent to be a first-division player is clearly there, but he's going to have to stay on the field in 2017 or people will start to give up.

Troy Tulowitzki   SS

Born: 10/10/84 Age: 32 Bats: R Throws: R Height: 6'3" Weight: 205 Entered Pro Ball: Round 1, 2005 Draft (#7 overall)

YEAR	TEAM	LVL	AGE	PA	R	2B	3B	HR	RBI	BB	K	SB	CS	AVG/OBP/SLG	TAv	VORP	BABIP	BRR	FRAA	WARP
2014	COL	MLB	29	375	71	18	1	21	52	50	57	1	1	.340/.432/.603	.331	36.8	.355	-2.1	SS(89): -1.1	3.9
2015	COL	MLB	30	351	46	19	0	12	53	24	72	0	0	.300/.348/.471	.274	19.3	.351	0.7	SS(82): -2.9	1.8
2015	TOR	MLB	30	183	31	8	0	5	17	14	42	1	0	.239/.317/.380	.258	7.1	.291	0.5	SS(39): 3.0	1.1
2016	TOR	MLB	31	544	54	21	0	24	79	43	101	1	0	.254/.318/.443	.253	16.6	.272	-1.6	SS(128): 2.9	2.0
2017	TOR	MLB	32	578	71	26	1	24	81	56	110	1	0	.270/.346/.464	.277	34.1	.298	-1.2	SS 4	3.4
2018	TOR	MLB	33	493	69	21	0	21	69	50	98	0	0	.267/.347/.462	.270	20.9	.298	-0.9	SS 3	2.6

Breakout: 1% Improve: 37% Collapse: 3% Attrition: 8% MLB: 97% Comparables: Carlos Guillen, Miguel Tejada, Derek Jeter

Coming off a down 2015, especially in Toronto, the hope was that Tulowitzki would rebound and once again become the star player he'd been for his entire Rockies career. It didn't quite happen, as the shortstop's TAv actually fell slightly from the year before. But the numbers don't tell the whole story. After returning from the DL in June with a quad injury, Tulowitzki hit .280/.333/.474 the rest of the way. Those aren't exactly the numbers he was putting up in Colorado, and with Tulowitzki you always have to take his health into account, but if he can hit like that with his defensive skill, that's still a very valuable player. At age 32, he should be able to fight off heavy decline for a couple more years.

Melvin Upton, Jr.   OF

Born: 8/21/84 Age: 32 Bats: R Throws: R Height: 6'3" Weight: 185 Entered Pro Ball: Round 1, 2002 Draft (#2 overall)

YEAR	TEAM	LVL	AGE	PA	R	2B	3B	HR	RBI	BB	K	SB	CS	AVG/OBP/SLG	TAv	VORP	BABIP	BRR	FRAA	WARP
2014	ATL	MLB	29	582	67	19	5	12	35	57	173	20	7	.208/.287/.333	.243	13.0	.286	6.1	CF(139): -2.7	1.1
2015	ELP	AAA	30	55	10	2	0	1	6	4	12	4	0	.280/.333/.380	.244	1.8	.351	1.4	CF(10): 0.7	0.3
2015	SDN	MLB	30	228	23	12	4	5	17	21	62	9	3	.259/.327/.429	.283	13.3	.348	1.5	CF(63): 2.3	1.7
2016	SDN	MLB	31	374	46	11	2	16	45	23	106	20	5	.256/.304/.439	.273	16.4	.320	2.8	LF(83): 1.9 • CF(11): -1.0	1.8
2016	TOR	MLB	31	165	18	4	1	4	16	14	49	7	3	.196/.261/.318	.209	-3.6	.255	0.9	LF(38): -0.9 • CF(16): 1.0	-0.4
2017	TOR	MLB	32	582	69	23	3	18	64	51	168	23	8	.224/.292/.382	.235	6.7	.289	2.3	LF 0 • RF 0	0.1
2018	TOR	MLB	33	445	51	17	2	13	50	39	132	16	6	.216/.286/.371	.226	-1.7	.280	3.4	LF 0 • RF 0	-0.2

Breakout: 4% Improve: 32% Collapse: 15% Attrition: 36% MLB: 90% Comparables: Preston Wilson, Jim Russell, Eli Marrero

No matter which name he goes by, it seems Upton will continue to baffle teams and fans alike. After nice gains in 2015, Upton once again held baseball's lowest contact rate (69.6 percent) on pitches in the zone among qualified hitters in 2016. It really is hard to imagine a player who swings through more mediocre fastballs down the middle. And yet Upton's overall numbers were actually pretty decent despite his awful performance in Toronto, and he still looks like a viable big leaguer on the surface. The power definitely seems to have returned, and he remains a threat on the basepaths. He can't hit righties much, but he raked lefties to the tune of .275/.341/.533 and can play all three outfield spots. If used in a platoon and as a defensive sub, Upton can add value.

Richard Urena   SS

Born: 2/26/96 Age: 21 Bats: B Throws: R Height: 6'0" Weight: 185 Entered Pro Ball: International Free Agent, 2012

YEAR	TEAM	LVL	AGE	PA	R	2B	3B	HR	RBI	BB	K	SB	CS	AVG/OBP/SLG	TAv	VORP	BABIP	BRR	FRAA	WARP
2014	VAN	A-	18	37	3	2	1	0	5	3	5	1	0	.242/.297/.364	.261	1.2	.276	0.0	2B(5): -0.2 • 3B(3): -0.9	0.0
2015	DUN	A+	19	128	9	3	1	1	8	3	26	3	1	.250/.268/.315	.228	0.9	.309	0.0	SS(30): -2.6	-0.2
2015	LNS	A	19	408	62	13	4	15	58	13	84	5	5	.266/.289/.438	.254	15.7	.299	1.9	SS(90): -9.4	0.7
2016	DUN	A+	20	431	52	18	7	8	41	25	64	9	6	.305/.351/.447	.266	17.0	.346	-1.3	SS(79): 0.1	1.8
2016	NHP	AA	20	132	14	6	5	0	18	4	19	0	2	.266/.282/.395	.256	5.3	.306	0.7	SS(29): -0.8	0.5
2017	TOR	MLB	21	250	28	10	3	8	27	8	61	1	1	.240/.268/.402	.221	1.1	.287	-0.1	SS -2	-0.1
2018	TOR	MLB	22	356	39	15	4	11	42	15	86	2	2	.242/.276/.407	.229	0.7	.288	-0.3	SS -3	-0.2

Breakout: 6% Improve: 7% Collapse: 1% Attrition: 8% MLB: 12% Comparables: Chris Owings, Nick Franklin, Yamaico Navarro

Urena shot up prospect lists last year when he found the power to muscle out double-digit homers after totaling just three in his career previously. However, his 2016 was fraught with a little more adversity. The young Dominican is expected to stay at shortstop but is still figuring out the finer points of hitting. With a quick bat and solid contact skills, Urena has the tools to become an above-average hitter, but he needs to refine his plate discipline to be able to wait for better pitches at the higher levels. Fortunately, at age 21, he still has time to grow and, with Troy Tulowitzki occupying shortstop in Toronto, he'll be afforded that chance.

J.B. Woodman   CF

Born: 12/13/94 Age: 22 Bats: L Throws: R Height: 6'2" Weight: 195 Entered Pro Ball: Round 2, 2016 Draft (#57 overall)

YEAR	TEAM	LVL	AGE	PA	R	2B	3B	HR	RBI	BB	K	SB	CS	AVG/OBP/SLG	TAv	VORP	BABIP	BRR	FRAA	WARP
2016	VAN	A-	21	232	28	18	1	3	24	30	72	10	2	.272/.375/.421	.312	18.1	.407	1.0	CF(35): 2.6 • RF(10): -0.0	2.2
2016	LNS	A	21	39	5	2	0	1	5	4	13	0	1	.441/.487/.588	.380	5.2	.667	-0.3	RF(5): -1.0 • CF(4): -0.6	0.4
2017	TOR	MLB	22	250	23	10	1	6	25	20	89	1	1	.197/.267/.324	.201	-6.8	.289	-0.4	CF -0 • RF -0	-0.8
2018	TOR	MLB	23	196	21	8	1	5	20	16	70	1	1	.201/.272/.341	.212	-5.0	.292	-0.3	CF 0 • RF 0	-0.6

Breakout: 1%   Improve: 2%   Collapse: 0%   Attrition: 1%   MLB: 4%   *Comparables: Thomas Pham, Michael Taylor, Daniel Fields*

At this point in his young career, Woodman looks like a young Michael Saunders. He's a big guy with a long swing, but hasn't turned it into much in-game power. Despite his size, he's found a way to play an OK center field. Woodman won't end up there, but it's nice to know that he can play up the middle if need be. Instead, as he moves through the minors, his calling card should be a lot of gap power and a little bit of speed. At present, that long swing and the many resulting strikeouts are holding him back, but he's got a lot of time and a strong player development staff to help him iron things out.

PITCHERS

Danny Barnes   RHP

Born: 10/21/89 Age: 27 Bats: L Throws: R Height: 6'1" Weight: 195 Entered Pro Ball: Round 35, 2010 Draft (#1056 overall)

YEAR	TEAM	LVL	AGE	W	L	SV	G	GS	IP	H	HR	BB/9	K/9	K	GB%	BABIP	WHIP	ERA	FIP	DRA	VORP	WARP	cFIP	MPH
2014	DUN	A+	24	0	5	7	36	0	38²	36	4	2.8	11.4	49	35%	.327	1.24	4.19	3.21	1.74	14.8	1.5	77	
2015	NHP	AA	25	3	2	4	40	1	60²	64	5	2.8	11	74	32%	.362	1.37	2.97	2.89	2.44	15.6	1.7	79	
2016	NHP	AA	26	2	1	1	24	0	35²	17	3	1.0	10.1	40	30%	.177	0.59	1.01	2.55	2.36	9.4	1.0	86	
2016	BUF	AAA	26	1	0	5	17	0	25²	6	0	0.7	13.0	37	32%	.128	0.31	0.35	0.75	1.06	11.1	1.1	60	
2016	TOR	MLB	26	0	0	0	12	0	13²	14	0	3.3	9.2	14	44%	.359	1.39	3.95	2.16	4.37	0.9	0.1	102	94.1
2017	TOR	MLB	27	1	1	0	23	0	24	25	3	3.4	8.2	23	55%	.296	1.38	4.36	4.10	4.60	1.1	0.1	100	
2018	TOR	MLB	28	1	1	0	30	0	31¹	27	5	4.4	11.2	39	55%	.297	1.36	4.44	4.35	4.73	1.1	0.1	107	

Breakout: 17%   Improve: 23%   Collapse: 16%   Attrition: 28%   MLB: 48%   *Comparables: R.J. Swindle, Anthony Slama, Craig Breslow*

It's tough to stand out as a right-handed reliever in the minors, but damn did Barnes try. He stepped up to Triple-A for the first time and struck out more than 10 batters per nine innings, as he's done at every level of the minors. The strikeouts, combined with the fact that he was just one of six Triple-A pitchers to not give up a homer last season, made him an ideal September call-up. However, with a Blue Jays bullpen that became quite crowded down the stretch, Barnes missed out on pitching in the playoffs. He'll be one to watch heading in to spring training.

Joseph Biagini   RHP

Born: 5/29/90 Age: 27 Bats: R Throws: R Height: 6'5" Weight: 240 Entered Pro Ball: Round 26, 2011 Draft (#807 overall)

YEAR	TEAM	LVL	AGE	W	L	SV	G	GS	IP	H	HR	BB/9	K/9	K	GB%	BABIP	WHIP	ERA	FIP	DRA	VORP	WARP	cFIP	MPH
2014	SJO	A+	24	10	9	0	23	23	128	133	5	3.2	7.2	103	51%	.338	1.40	4.01	3.86	4.30	18.4	1.9	100	
2015	RIC	AA	25	10	7	0	23	22	130¹	112	5	2.3	5.8	84	54%	.264	1.12	2.42	3.35	3.98	16.0	1.7	97	
2016	TOR	MLB	26	4	3	1	60	0	67²	69	3	2.5	8.2	62	54%	.320	1.30	3.06	2.91	3.86	8.3	0.9	94	96.6
2017	TOR	MLB	27	3	4	0	55	3	69	72	7	3.5	6.8	52	46%	.298	1.42	4.23	4.27	4.49	4.2	0.4	100	
2018	TOR	MLB	28	3	2	1	46	2	58²	52	7	5.2	9.0	59	46%	.284	1.47	4.70	4.61	4.99	0.9	0.1	114	

Breakout: 19%   Improve: 34%   Collapse: 19%   Attrition: 34%   MLB: 64%   *Comparables: Pat Misch, Jeremy Hefner, Dustin Nippert*

Don't ask Biagini about pitching. He'll probably start talking about his singing or some other tangent. He can't (or won't) talk straight about his job, but that's just fine because it turns out he's pretty good at keeping his pitches from going straight as well. The Rule 5 pick surprised a lot of people by emerging as a damn good and trusted reliever. Perhaps the Giants could have used that. Biagini's role may change going forward, however. He went more than an inning in 22 of his 60 outings, and all four of his pitches (fastball, curve, slider, changeup) have above-average swing-and-miss rates and generate ground balls. That's a starter's repertoire, even if it likely will play down a little over multiple innings.

Mike Bolsinger   RHP

Born: 1/29/88 Age: 29 Bats: R Throws: R Height: 6'1" Weight: 215 Entered Pro Ball: Round 15, 2010 Draft (#451 overall)

YEAR	TEAM	LVL	AGE	W	L	SV	G	GS	IP	H	HR	BB/9	K/9	K	GB%	BABIP	WHIP	ERA	FIP	DRA	VORP	WARP	cFIP	MPH
2014	ARI	MLB	26	1	6	0	10	9	52¹	66	7	2.9	8.3	48	54%	.355	1.59	5.50	3.98	4.04	4.5	0.5	99	90.5
2014	RNO	AAA	26	8	3	0	17	16	91²	92	6	3.1	8.6	88	55%	.331	1.35	3.93	3.78	1.29	45.3	4.5	71	
2015	OKL	AAA	27	3	3	0	10	8	46²	30	2	3.5	11.8	61	47%	.272	1.03	2.31	2.89	1.96	17.0	1.7	67	
2015	LAN	MLB	27	6	6	0	21	21	109¹	104	11	3.7	8.1	98	56%	.299	1.36	3.62	3.94	3.96	13.5	1.4	101	89.7
2016	LAN	MLB	28	1	4	0	6	6	27²	33	7	2.9	8.1	25	37%	.329	1.52	6.83	5.86	5.21	0.4	0.0	114	90.2
2016	OKL	AAA	28	2	1	0	13	2	29	32	2	3.1	10.6	34	56%	.385	1.45	3.41	3.31	2.88	7.5	0.8	83	
2016	BUF	AAA	28	1	4	0	6	6	25¹	29	4	3.9	9.6	27	48%	.352	1.58	6.04	4.51	3.46	4.9	0.5	93	
2017	TOR	MLB	29	3	4	0	55	3	69	66	6	4.0	8.2	63	44%	.302	1.41	3.72	3.94	4.07	7.5	0.8	90	
2018	TOR	MLB	30	2	1	0	32	2	41²	38	4	5.1	10.1	47	44%	.310	1.47	4.21	4.13	4.48	2.9	0.3	99	

Breakout: 15%   Improve: 35%   Collapse: 20%   Attrition: 19%   MLB: 66%   *Comparables: Yusmeiro Petit, Chris Rusin, Pat Misch*

In 2015, as a 27-year-old, Bolsinger came out of nowhere and forced his way into the Dodgers' rotation. How, you ask? A shiny new cutter, of course. That cutter worked well for him until midseason, when he hit a rough patch and lost the Dodgers' trust. Then in 2016, he became the Blue Jays' return in a deadline deal that sent reliever Jesse Chavez to the Dodgers. Given his recent rotational struggles, and the Jays' relatively good rotational depth, don't expect to see him start regularly anytime soon. However, his stuff will play up in the bullpen, and you may see the Jays consider him for the long-reliever role.

Ryan Borucki   LHP

Born: 3/31/94   Age: 23   Bats: L   Throws: L   Height: 6'4"   Weight: 175   Entered Pro Ball: Round 15, 2012 Draft (#475 overall)

YEAR	TEAM	LVL	AGE	W	L	SV	G	GS	IP	H	HR	BB/9	K/9	K	GB%	BABIP	WHIP	ERA	FIP	DRA	VORP	WARP	cFIP	MPH
2014	VAN	A-	20	1	1	1	5	4	23²	13	1	1.1	8.4	22	56%	.197	0.68	1.90	3.01	2.77	6.6	0.7	84	
2016	DUN	A+	22	1	4	0	6	6	20	40	10	5.4	4.5	10	48%	.395	2.60	14.40	10.55	9.83	-9.7	-1.0	125	
2016	LNS	A	22	10	4	0	20	20	115²	105	1	2.0	8.3	107	51%	.322	1.13	2.41	2.54	2.83	28.0	3.1	86	
2017	TOR	MLB	23	5	7	0	18	18	86²	108	15	4.5	4.5	43	58%	.308	1.74	6.00	6.01	6.22	-7.2	-0.7	149	
2018	TOR	MLB	24	5	8	0	20	20	118¹	134	20	5.4	7.0	91	58%	.312	1.73	5.83	5.73	6.04	-6.2	-0.6	145	

Breakout: 2%   Improve: 5%   Collapse: 0%   Attrition: 3%   MLB: 6%   *Comparables: Matt Purke, Luis Perdomo, Tyler Anderson*

After an injury-plagued 2015 that saw him throw just 5.2 minor-league innings, the Blue Jays challenged Borucki with an assignment to High-A Dunedin, skipping Low-A Lansing. He got hammered, and was demoted after just six starts. As soon as he put on a Lugnuts jersey, Borucki hit the ground running, dominating the Midwest League until the end of the season. Despite his low level, the Blue Jays chose to add Borucki to the 40-man and protect him from the Rule 5 draft. As a 6-foot-4 lefty with a 95 mph fastball, good control and a plus-plus changeup he'd have been appealing to many clubs looking for bullpen help. It wouldn't be at all surprising if Borucki finishes 2017 with Double-A New Hampshire.

Marco Estrada   RHP

Born: 7/5/83   Age: 33   Bats: R   Throws: R   Height: 6'0"   Weight: 200   Entered Pro Ball: Round 6, 2005 Draft (#174 overall)

YEAR	TEAM	LVL	AGE	W	L	SV	G	GS	IP	H	HR	BB/9	K/9	K	GB%	BABIP	WHIP	ERA	FIP	DRA	VORP	WARP	cFIP	MPH
2014	MIL	MLB	30	7	6	0	39	18	150²	137	29	2.6	7.6	127	34%	.257	1.20	4.36	4.85	5.67	-15.7	-1.7	124	91.1
2015	TOR	MLB	31	13	8	0	34	28	181	134	24	2.7	6.5	131	34%	.216	1.04	3.13	4.38	5.20	-2.8	-0.3	119	91.4
2016	TOR	MLB	32	9	9	0	29	29	176	132	23	3.3	8.4	165	35%	.234	1.12	3.48	4.11	4.40	18.8	1.9	113	90.2
2017	TOR	MLB	33	10	11	0	29	29	165¹	156	28	3.8	8.0	147	39%	.277	1.33	4.79	4.96	5.17	1.4	0.1	100	
2018	TOR	MLB	34	8	11	0	26	26	153¹	148	30	3.8	7.6	130	39%	.269	1.39	5.49	5.39	5.85	-6.1	-0.6	141	

Breakout: 9%   Improve: 41%   Collapse: 24%   Attrition: 16%   MLB: 92%   *Comparables: Jered Weaver, Chris Young, Johan Santana*

"Hey girl, are you a Marco Estrada changeup? Because I thought we were going somewhere fast and now I'm over-committed and look silly." It's amazing the kind of success a guy can have when he can't even crack 90 mph. Over the last two years, Estrada has used a four-seam fastball that fights gravity at the greatest rate in baseball (+13" in 2016) and combined it with one of the best changeups (fifth in swing-and-miss rate) to lead the American League in opponents' batting average. It's true that he only throws 89 mph, but the unusual movement and the presence of that changeup make it too tough for hitters to adjust properly. In fact, he's so good at generating weak popups—he led all qualified starters by a gigantic margin at 16.2 percent—that instead of posting "Ks" for strikeouts, a group of fans started hanging photos of Pizza Pops every time a hitter skied one. The year wasn't without its flaws; Estrada suffered through back issues that limited him to 176 innings and lost another mile per hour on his fastball. Going forward, there are still some reasons for concern with the higher-than-average home run rate and the league-best BABIP, but back-to-back excellent seasons suggest he might really have the skill to out-pitch his fielding-independent metrics. Don't expect any changes from Estrada in his second free agent year.

Scott Feldman   RHP

Born: 2/7/83   Age: 34   Bats: L   Throws: R   Height: 6'7"   Weight: 210   Entered Pro Ball: Round 30, 2003 Draft (#886 overall)

YEAR	TEAM	LVL	AGE	W	L	SV	G	GS	IP	H	HR	BB/9	K/9	K	GB%	BABIP	WHIP	ERA	FIP	DRA	VORP	WARP	cFIP	MPH
2014	HOU	MLB	31	8	12	0	29	29	180¹	185	16	2.5	5.3	107	49%	.291	1.30	3.74	4.14	4.77	1.4	0.2	108	90.9
2015	HOU	MLB	32	5	5	0	18	18	108¹	115	13	2.2	5.1	61	51%	.291	1.31	3.90	4.29	5.28	-2.4	-0.3	109	92.6
2016	HOU	MLB	33	5	3	0	26	5	62	64	8	1.9	6.1	42	49%	.281	1.24	2.90	4.20	4.37	5.0	0.5	102	92.8
2016	TOR	MLB	33	2	1	0	14	0	15	23	2	3.6	8.4	14	66%	.412	1.93	8.40	4.17	4.62	0.8	0.1	103	93.1
2017	TOR	MLB	34	5	4	0	12	12	72²	75	10	3.1	6.7	54	52%	.292	1.38	4.68	4.59	4.97	4.0	0.4	115	
2018	TOR	MLB	35	9	11	0	27	27	159	180	25	3.1	6.7	119	52%	.309	1.48	5.01	4.92	5.32	2.7	0.3	124	

Breakout: 14%   Improve: 42%   Collapse: 24%   Attrition: 12%   MLB: 88%   *Comparables: Mark Buehrle, Tim Hudson, Johan Santana*

As a cheap trade deadline pickup, Feldman seemed like he'd be a great candidate to bolster the Jays' depth. As a cheap trade deadline pickup, Feldman did not one bit bolster the Jays' depth. Despite being touted as a solid swingman, Feldman made zero starts for the Blue Jays and was hardly even considered for the playoff roster. With a history of starting but recently turbulent relief and starting experiences, it'll be interesting to see how Feldman's 2017 team uses the 34-year-old.

Gavin Floyd   RHP

Born: 1/27/83   Age: 34   Bats: R   Throws: R   Height: 6'4"   Weight: 245   Entered Pro Ball: Round 1, 2001 Draft (#4 overall)

YEAR	TEAM	LVL	AGE	W	L	SV	G	GS	IP	H	HR	BB/9	K/9	K	GB%	BABIP	WHIP	ERA	FIP	DRA	VORP	WARP	cFIP	MPH
2014	GWN	AAA	31	1	1	0	5	5	19¹	17	3	4.2	5.1	11	52%	.241	1.34	3.26	5.79	5.63	0.3	0.0	112	
2014	ATL	MLB	31	2	2	0	9	9	54¹	55	6	2.2	7.5	45	53%	.302	1.25	2.65	3.77	3.78	6.4	0.7	95	94.2
2015	CLE	MLB	32	0	0	0	7	0	13¹	11	0	2.7	4.7	7	46%	.256	1.12	2.70	3.18	5.18	-0.7	-0.1	112	95.1
2016	TOR	MLB	33	2	4	0	28	0	31	23	4	2.3	8.7	30	41%	.241	1.00	4.06	3.91	4.04	3.2	0.3	99	96.1
2017	*TOR*	*MLB*	*34*	*2*	*2*	*0*	*15*	*5*	*35*	*34*	*5*	*3.3*	*8.1*	*31*	*56%*	*.294*	*1.35*	*4.43*	*4.50*	*4.73*	*2.5*	*0.3*	*108*	
2018	*TOR*	*MLB*	*35*	*6*	*6*	*0*	*46*	*16*	*131*	*138*	*21*	*3.3*	*8.1*	*118*	*56%*	*.309*	*1.42*	*4.77*	*4.68*	*5.09*	*3.1*	*0.3*	*118*	

Breakout: 16%   Improve: 41%   Collapse: 22%   Attrition: 14%   MLB: 83%   *Comparables: Johan Santana, C.J. Wilson, A.J. Burnett*

For the first few weeks, it looked like the Blue Jays had actually found something in Floyd; he posted a 1.65 ERA with 18 strikeouts through his first 16.1 innings. That ended quickly, as he then gave up 12 runs in his next 20 innings. However, it was at this point that Floyd's no. 1 skill finally shone through. He got injured. He had trouble with his shoulder and missed the rest of the season. The man who can't stay healthy once again failed to stay healthy. It really is nice to know that there are some things in life we can count on.

Conner Greene   RHP

Born: 4/4/95   Age: 22   Bats: R   Throws: R   Height: 6'3"   Weight: 185   Entered Pro Ball: Round 7, 2013 Draft (#205 overall)

YEAR	TEAM	LVL	AGE	W	L	SV	G	GS	IP	H	HR	BB/9	K/9	K	GB%	BABIP	WHIP	ERA	FIP	DRA	VORP	WARP	cFIP	MPH
2015	LNS	A	20	7	3	0	14	14	67¹	75	4	2.5	8.7	65	38%	.364	1.40	3.88	3.22	2.99	16.7	1.8	90	
2015	DUN	A+	20	2	3	0	7	7	40	36	1	1.8	7.9	35	55%	.297	1.10	2.25	2.34	2.80	10.1	1.1	87	
2015	NHP	AA	20	3	1	0	5	5	25	25	1	4.3	5.4	15	55%	.304	1.48	4.68	4.15	6.64	-4.3	-0.5	115	
2016	DUN	A+	21	4	4	0	15	15	77²	74	5	4.4	5.9	51	53%	.283	1.44	2.90	4.36	6.94	-12.7	-1.3	117	
2016	NHP	AA	21	6	5	0	12	12	68²	57	5	4.3	6.3	48	50%	.256	1.31	4.19	4.48	5.79	-5.3	-0.6	110	
2017	*TOR*	*MLB*	*22*	*6*	*9*	*0*	*23*	*23*	*115¹*	*133*	*19*	*4.9*	*4.9*	*63*	*59%*	*.296*	*1.70*	*5.98*	*5.97*	*6.31*	*-10.7*	*-1.1*	*149*	
2018	*TOR*	*MLB*	*23*	*4*	*6*	*0*	*14*	*14*	*84*	*85*	*13*	*6.7*	*8.2*	*76*	*59%*	*.303*	*1.75*	*5.89*	*5.80*	*6.21*	*-5.9*	*-0.6*	*146*	

Breakout: 8%   Improve: 13%   Collapse: 2%   Attrition: 10%   MLB: 18%   *Comparables: Scott Barnes, Matt Harrison, Alex Cobb*

At 6-foot-3 with a fastball that can touch the upper 90s, Greene had always been projectable but hadn't gotten the results. He caught fire in 2015 with an incredibly strong full-season debut but then struggled in 2016 at Double-A level. He really only has two pitches: a fastball and a changeup. At the lower levels of the minors, Greene could utilize his plus velocity to blow by hitters. Now, he's going to have to develop a curveball or find an intensive sinker à la Aaron Sanchez. If that doesn't work, he'll always have his modelling career to fall back on. As former BP head prospect writer Jason Parks would say: "Great body."

Jason Grilli   RHP

Born: 11/11/76   Age: 40   Bats: R   Throws: R   Height: 6'5"   Weight: 235   Entered Pro Ball: Round 1, 1997 Draft (#4 overall)

YEAR	TEAM	LVL	AGE	W	L	SV	G	GS	IP	H	HR	BB/9	K/9	K	GB%	BABIP	WHIP	ERA	FIP	DRA	VORP	WARP	cFIP	MPH
2014	PIT	MLB	37	0	2	11	22	0	20¹	22	4	4.9	9.3	21	28%	.321	1.62	4.87	5.36	4.04	1.0	0.1	103	95.7
2014	ANA	MLB	37	1	3	1	40	0	33²	29	0	2.7	9.6	36	42%	.312	1.16	3.48	2.18	4.08	1.5	0.2	103	95.4
2015	ATL	MLB	38	3	4	24	36	0	33²	28	2	2.7	12.0	45	27%	.313	1.13	2.94	2.15	3.59	4.2	0.4	87	96.0
2016	ATL	MLB	39	1	2	2	21	0	17	16	2	6.9	12.2	23	20%	.333	1.71	5.29	4.48	4.04	1.8	0.2	99	93.7
2016	TOR	MLB	39	6	4	2	46	0	42	28	8	4.1	12.4	58	35%	.238	1.12	3.64	4.25	4.04	4.3	0.4	100	94.7
2017	*TOR*	*MLB*	*40*	*2*	*3*	*2*	*47*	*0*	*49*	*46*	*8*	*4.4*	*10.8*	*60*	*46%*	*.300*	*1.42*	*4.43*	*4.42*	*4.65*	*1.8*	*0.2*	*100*	
2018	*TOR*	*MLB*	*41*	*1*	*1*	*1*	*28*	*0*	*30*	*26*	*5*	*5.0*	*11.1*	*37*	*46%*	*.291*	*1.43*	*4.70*	*4.61*	*5.00*	*0.2*	*0.0*	*115*	

Breakout: 19%   Improve: 24%   Collapse: 21%   Attrition: 9%   MLB: 56%   *Comparables: Octavio Dotel, Joel Peralta, Joe Nathan*

Remember Howard Dean's infamous yell? He has nothing on Grilli when he walks off the mound after a big strikeout. There is nobody who gets more fired up after a big moment than the veteran hurler, so it's a good thing he turned his season around when he was traded to the Blue Jays. After missing the end of 2015 with an Achilles' injury, Grilli came out of the gates slow in 2016. He couldn't throw strikes at all, walking a career-high 6.9 batters per nine innings and posting a 5.29 ERA in Atlanta. There were signs that his skills hadn't waned completely, as he was still striking out 12.2 batters per nine, so the Jays bet on a rebound. They were handsomely rewarded as Grilli stabilized the eighth-inning setup role and was nearly untouchable until a late-September swoon. His $3 million team option was a no-brainer for Toronto.

J.A. Happ   LHP

Born: 10/19/82   Age: 34   Bats: L   Throws: L   Height: 6'5"   Weight: 205   Entered Pro Ball: Round 3, 2004 Draft (#92 overall)

YEAR	TEAM	LVL	AGE	W	L	SV	G	GS	IP	H	HR	BB/9	K/9	K	GB%	BABIP	WHIP	ERA	FIP	DRA	VORP	WARP	cFIP	MPH
2014	TOR	MLB	31	11	11	0	30	26	158	160	22	2.9	7.6	133	42%	.297	1.34	4.22	4.29	4.16	11.6	1.3	102	95.2
2015	SEA	MLB	32	4	6	0	21	20	108²	121	13	2.7	6.8	82	44%	.319	1.41	4.64	4.09	4.09	11.9	1.3	98	94.7
2015	PIT	MLB	32	7	2	0	11	11	63¹	52	3	1.8	9.8	69	44%	.299	1.03	1.85	2.21	4.12	6.7	0.7	97	94.8
2016	TOR	MLB	33	20	4	0	32	32	195	168	22	2.8	7.5	163	44%	.268	1.17	3.18	3.92	4.42	20.4	2.1	105	94.3
2017	*TOR*	*MLB*	*34*	*10*	*10*	*0*	*29*	*29*	*165¹*	*168*	*25*	*3.4*	*8.0*	*147*	*44%*	*.299*	*1.40*	*4.46*	*4.62*	*4.81*	*8.0*	*0.8*	*100*	
2018	*TOR*	*MLB*	*35*	*9*	*11*	*0*	*29*	*29*	*181²*	*190*	*29*	*3.2*	*8.2*	*165*	*44%*	*.308*	*1.41*	*4.68*	*4.59*	*4.99*	*8.8*	*0.9*	*116*	

Breakout: 19%   Improve: 45%   Collapse: 19%   Attrition: 11%   MLB: 85%   *Comparables: John Lackey, A.J. Burnett, Ted Lilly*

When the Blue Jays signed Happ to a three year, $36 million contract prior to 2016, the universal reaction was that the team had greatly overpaid in years, if not dollars. Now Toronto is probably wishing they'd signed him for longer. Happ set career-highs in almost every category, leading a pitching staff that topped the AL in ERA. People look at Happ and wonder how he gets outs without a single plus pitch and with good-but-not-great command. It turns out, the Blue Jays did their homework. Happ's two-seam and four-seam fastballs are mediocre offerings on their own, but when combined together they click. The two fastballs have the largest difference in vertical movement among all qualified starters in baseball (5.1 inches), which makes it extremely difficult for hitters to adjust from one to the next. When combined with a full complement of off-speed pitches that can be thrown for strikes, Happ becomes pretty darn tough to hit. He may not be in Cy Young conversations going forward, but Happ has definitely turned himself into a new, better pitcher.

Jonathan Harris   RHP

Born: 10/16/93 Age: 23 Bats: R Throws: R Height: 6'4" Weight: 175 Entered Pro Ball: Round 1, 2015 Draft (#29 overall)

YEAR	TEAM	LVL	AGE	W	L	SV	G	GS	IP	H	HR	BB/9	K/9	K	GB%	BABIP	WHIP	ERA	FIP	DRA	VORP	WARP	cFIP	MPH
2015	VAN	A-	21	0	5	0	12	11	36	48	1	5.2	8.0	32	43%	.388	1.92	6.75	4.02	6.19	-3.8	-0.4	114	
2016	LNS	A	22	8	2	0	16	16	84²	74	1	2.6	7.8	73	50%	.296	1.16	2.23	2.93	4.23	7.4	0.8	99	
2016	DUN	A+	22	3	2	0	8	8	45	37	2	2.8	5.2	26	51%	.252	1.13	3.60	3.67	5.44	0.2	0.0	107	
2017	TOR	MLB	23	5	7	0	18	18	85¹	105	16	4.9	4.1	39	62%	.299	1.78	6.38	6.41	6.63	-11.0	-1.1	159	
2018	TOR	MLB	24	5	9	0	23	23	134	145	23	6.5	7.1	105	62%	.298	1.80	6.25	6.18	6.50	-12.5	-1.3	155	

Breakout: 3%   Improve: 4%   Collapse: 0%   Attrition: 3%   MLB: 4%   Comparables: Joseph Colon, Bryan Mitchell, Taylor Jungmann

Jon Harris is a fittingly unremarkable name for an unremarkable pitcher. The 2015 first rounder pitched much better in 2016 than in his first, tired appearance in pro ball, but it still looks like his realistic ceiling is as a no. 4 starter. He has decent command of a fastball that sits 90-94 and touches 97, and a decent curveball and changeup, but his slider/cutter is nothing special. Harris has good command and keeps the ball down, so his floor is higher than others at High-A. This season is going to be a big year for Harris pitching at Double-A New Hampshire. He'll be facing better prospects, which will put more pressure on the development of his off-speed pitches.

Francisco Liriano   LHP

Born: 10/26/83 Age: 33 Bats: L Throws: L Height: 6'2" Weight: 225 Entered Pro Ball: International Free Agent, 2000

YEAR	TEAM	LVL	AGE	W	L	SV	G	GS	IP	H	HR	BB/9	K/9	K	GB%	BABIP	WHIP	ERA	FIP	DRA	VORP	WARP	cFIP	MPH
2014	PIT	MLB	30	7	10	0	29	29	162¹	130	13	4.5	9.7	175	57%	.280	1.30	3.38	3.56	3.47	24.6	2.7	91	95.3
2015	PIT	MLB	31	12	7	0	31	31	186²	155	15	3.4	9.9	205	54%	.293	1.21	3.38	3.22	3.12	40.6	4.3	85	95.4
2016	PIT	MLB	32	6	11	0	21	21	113²	115	19	5.5	9.2	116	54%	.308	1.62	5.46	3.78	3.78	19.9	2.1	98	95.5
2016	TOR	MLB	32	2	2	0	10	10	49¹	42	7	2.9	9.5	52	52%	.267	1.18	2.92	3.94	3.67	9.2	1.0	97	95.9
2017	TOR	MLB	33	10	10	0	28	28	168	153	21	4.6	9.5	177	48%	.296	1.43	4.22	4.35	4.54	13.2	1.4	100	
2018	TOR	MLB	34	9	10	0	26	26	157²	150	22	4.6	9.5	166	48%	.301	1.47	4.66	4.57	4.95	9.0	0.9	115	

Breakout: 7%   Improve: 42%   Collapse: 25%   Attrition: 21%   MLB: 89%   Comparables: CC Sabathia, A.J. Burnett, Wandy Rodriguez

When Liriano re-signed with the Pirates after 2014, Pittsburgh's front office probably never imagined that a year and a half later they'd have to send off two decent prospects just to dump the contract. Their loss was the Blue Jays' gain, as the southpaw's career outlier walk rate stabilized, and he put up a 2.92 ERA in 10 post-trade outings (eight starts) for Toronto. His presence gave the Blue Jays flexibility to rest starters down the stretch, and gives them plenty of options for 2017. Liriano will also be chasing history, as he's only 21 starts behind Clarence Mitchell for the most career starts without throwing 200 innings in a season. As long as he stays healthy, Liriano will either reach 200 innings for the first time ever or get to say he holds a major-league record. Win-win.

Aaron Loup   LHP

Born: 12/19/87 Age: 29 Bats: L Throws: L Height: 5'11" Weight: 210 Entered Pro Ball: Round 9, 2009 Draft (#280 overall)

YEAR	TEAM	LVL	AGE	W	L	SV	G	GS	IP	H	HR	BB/9	K/9	K	GB%	BABIP	WHIP	ERA	FIP	DRA	VORP	WARP	cFIP	MPH
2014	TOR	MLB	26	4	4	4	71	0	68²	50	4	3.9	7.3	56	56%	.246	1.17	3.15	3.86	3.34	8.8	1.0	98	95.0
2015	TOR	MLB	27	2	5	0	60	0	42¹	47	6	1.5	9.8	46	59%	.339	1.28	4.46	3.70	2.90	8.5	0.9	81	96.1
2016	BUF	AAA	28	3	0	1	20	0	19²	21	0	1.4	11.9	26	54%	.404	1.22	1.83	0.98	1.07	8.5	0.9	67	
2016	TOR	MLB	28	0	0	0	21	0	14¹	15	2	2.5	9.4	15	40%	.342	1.33	5.02	4.29	4.41	0.9	0.1	104	94.8
2017	TOR	MLB	29	2	2	0	42	0	44	44	5	3.5	8.2	41	38%	.303	1.38	3.95	4.13	4.24	3.7	0.4	96	
2018	TOR	MLB	30	2	1	0	42	0	44²	41	5	3.8	8.9	44	38%	.295	1.34	4.15	4.06	4.37	3.3	0.3	99	

Breakout: 37%   Improve: 60%   Collapse: 20%   Attrition: 22%   MLB: 91%   Comparables: Kevin Jepsen, Juan Oviedo, Neal Cotts

The good news is that the lefty specialist only hit two left-handed batters in 2016, down from six in 2015. The bad news he only faced 28 lefties overall on the season, down from 77, so he actually only "improved" from 7.8 percent HBPs to 7.1 percent. That's bad. He also gave up two home runs to lefties in 28 plate appearances. That's worse. It's probably not great for your career prospects when you struggle with the one thing that would guarantee long-term employment.

Justin Maese   RHP

Born: 10/24/96 Age: 20 Bats: R Throws: R Height: 6'3" Weight: 190 Entered Pro Ball: Round 3, 2015 Draft (#91 overall)

YEAR	TEAM	LVL	AGE	W	L	SV	G	GS	IP	H	HR	BB/9	K/9	K	GB%	BABIP	WHIP	ERA	FIP	DRA	VORP	WARP	cFIP	MPH
2016	VAN	A-	19	2	2	0	5	5	26¹	20	1	0.3	6.8	20	68%	.241	0.80	2.05	2.86	2.88	6.9	0.7	85	
2016	LNS	A	19	2	4	0	10	10	56¹	59	2	2.2	7.0	44	57%	.331	1.30	3.36	3.33	4.01	6.3	0.7	96	
2017	TOR	MLB	20	3	4	0	16	9	56	69	9	4.1	3.9	25	53%	.303	1.70	5.91	5.88	6.13	-5.3	-0.5	148	
2018	TOR	MLB	21	6	9	0	27	22	146	161	24	4.5	6.3	102	53%	.300	1.60	5.60	5.52	5.81	-5.3	-0.5	141	

Breakout: 1%   Improve: 1%   Collapse: 0%   Attrition: 1%   MLB: 1%   Comparables: Randall Delgado, Tyrell Jenkins, Gabriel Ynoa

Maese has performed well since being drafted out of high school in the third round in 2015. Despite being nearly three years younger than the average player, he managed a 3.34 ERA at Low-A Lansing. He's a ground-ball pitcher who doesn't miss a ton of bats despite a lively fastball in the mid-90s and a hard slider. He'll be 20 for the entirety of 2017, so there's lots of time for him to improve his arsenal and grow as a pitcher.

Roberto Osuna   RHP

Born: 2/7/95   Age: 22   Bats: R   Throws: R   Height: 6'2"   Weight: 215   Entered Pro Ball: International Free Agent, 2011

YEAR	TEAM	LVL	AGE	W	L	SV	G	GS	IP	H	HR	BB/9	K/9	K	GB%	BABIP	WHIP	ERA	FIP	DRA	VORP	WARP	cFIP	MPH
2014	DUN	A+	19	0	2	0	7	7	22	28	3	3.7	12.3	30	37%	.446	1.68	6.55	4.07	2.13	8.5	0.9	84	
2015	TOR	MLB	20	1	6	20	68	0	69²	48	7	2.1	9.7	75	36%	.238	0.92	2.58	2.99	3.73	7.6	0.8	89	98.3
2016	TOR	MLB	21	4	3	36	72	0	74	55	9	1.7	10.0	82	35%	.256	0.93	2.68	3.16	3.52	11.9	1.2	91	98.3
2017	*TOR*	*MLB*	*22*	*3*	*3*	*35*	*56*	*0*	*59*	*54*	*8*	*2.7*	*9.6*	*63*	*46%*	*.293*	*1.21*	*3.49*	*3.80*	*3.88*	*7.3*	*0.8*	*83*	
2018	*TOR*	*MLB*	*23*	*3*	*1*	*26*	*49*	*0*	*52*	*46*	*7*	*2.8*	*10.2*	*59*	*46%*	*.293*	*1.19*	*3.77*	*3.70*	*4.01*	*5.9*	*0.6*	*87*	

Breakout: 32%   Improve: 64%   Collapse: 11%   Attrition: 6%   MLB: 94%   *Comparables: Jose Fernandez, Chris Sale, Carter Capps*

With a fastball that touches 100 mph and a slider that makes even the best hitters look silly, it's easy to forget that Osuna is still just 21. For the second straight season he was the youngest pitcher in the American League and it's entirely possible that he'll hold that title again in 2017. The Blue Jays will likely trot out Osuna as the fire-baller at the back of the bullpen, but there's a question that always comes up for the young gun who went straight to relief in the major leagues: can he start? He's possibly the only closer in the league with a true three-plus-pitch mix. As a minor leaguer, Osuna had the fastball and slider, but his changeup always flashed plus too. However, when the Blue Jays had a relief need heading in to Opening Day 2015, Osuna was fast tracked. So fast that he's yet to start a game above A-ball. That makes the starter question perplexing. Could he succeed as a starter? Probably, but the Jays would lose their best bullpen arm in a season when they will sorely need him.

Sean Reid-Foley   RHP

Born: 8/30/95   Age: 21   Bats: R   Throws: R   Height: 6'3"   Weight: 220   Entered Pro Ball: Round 2, 2014 Draft (#49 overall)

YEAR	TEAM	LVL	AGE	W	L	SV	G	GS	IP	H	HR	BB/9	K/9	K	GB%	BABIP	WHIP	ERA	FIP	DRA	VORP	WARP	cFIP	MPH
2015	DUN	A+	19	1	5	0	8	8	32²	25	1	6.6	9.6	35	45%	.279	1.50	5.23	3.81	7.68	-9.4	-1.0	121	
2015	LNS	A	19	3	5	0	17	17	63¹	57	3	6.1	12.8	90	46%	.355	1.58	3.69	3.44	2.89	16.5	1.8	97	
2016	LNS	A	20	4	2	0	11	11	58	43	2	3.4	9.2	59	52%	.277	1.12	2.95	3.08	3.44	10.1	1.1	97	
2016	DUN	A+	20	6	2	0	10	10	57¹	35	2	2.5	11.1	71	49%	.254	0.89	2.67	2.12	1.33	26.4	2.7	69	
2017	*TOR*	*MLB*	*21*	*5*	*6*	*0*	*19*	*19*	*85*	*88*	*12*	*5.4*	*7.1*	*67*	*53%*	*.296*	*1.64*	*5.37*	*5.33*	*5.60*	*-1.2*	*-0.1*	*133*	
2018	*TOR*	*MLB*	*22*	*6*	*10*	*0*	*27*	*27*	*162¹*	*149*	*24*	*6.7*	*9.8*	*177*	*53%*	*.297*	*1.66*	*5.40*	*5.32*	*5.63*	*-2.1*	*-0.2*	*134*	

Breakout: 9%   Improve: 12%   Collapse: 0%   Attrition: 7%   MLB: 13%   *Comparables: Trevor May, Jose Berrios, Jake Thompson*

Reid-Foley is not only the Blue Jays' best pitching prospect, he's also on track to be the best player born in Guam in MLB history. His only competition is John Hattig (another former Blue Jays farmhand), who had 29 plate appearances. Reid-Foley still has some work to do since he's yet to reach Double-A, but if his lower-minors results are any indication, he should get the job done. After making hitters look foolish in the Midwest league for the first half of 2016, Reid-Foley made High-A Florida State League hitters look even worse, striking out 71 batters in 57 innings. With a fastball that sits 92-94 and touches 97, which he combines with a curve/slider combo that both flash plus, Reid-Foley could be a solid no. 2 starter.

Aaron Sanchez   RHP

Born: 7/1/92   Age: 24   Bats: R   Throws: R   Height: 6'4"   Weight: 220   Entered Pro Ball: Round 1, 2010 Draft (#34 overall)

YEAR	TEAM	LVL	AGE	W	L	SV	G	GS	IP	H	HR	BB/9	K/9	K	GB%	BABIP	WHIP	ERA	FIP	DRA	VORP	WARP	cFIP	MPH
2014	NHP	AA	21	3	4	0	14	14	66	52	2	5.5	7.8	57	69%	.279	1.39	3.82	4.16	5.39	-1.2	-0.1	98	
2014	BUF	AAA	21	0	3	0	8	6	34¹	36	4	4.5	7.1	27	62%	.317	1.54	4.19	4.87	7.07	-5.1	-0.5	110	
2014	TOR	MLB	21	2	2	3	24	0	33	14	1	2.5	7.4	27	67%	.157	0.70	1.09	2.83	2.92	5.7	0.6	86	99.4
2015	TOR	MLB	22	7	6	0	41	11	92¹	74	9	4.3	5.9	61	62%	.247	1.28	3.22	4.58	4.51	4.7	0.5	107	98.2
2016	TOR	MLB	23	15	2	0	30	30	192	161	15	3.0	7.5	161	55%	.267	1.17	3.00	3.51	3.77	33.9	3.5	94	97.5
2017	*TOR*	*MLB*	*24*	*10*	*10*	*0*	*29*	*29*	*174*	*165*	*20*	*3.9*	*7.2*	*139*	*40%*	*.285*	*1.36*	*4.35*	*4.48*	*4.70*	*10.6*	*1.1*	*100*	
2018	*TOR*	*MLB*	*25*	*10*	*11*	*0*	*30*	*30*	*190²*	*169*	*24*	*4.3*	*8.5*	*180*	*40%*	*.281*	*1.36*	*4.55*	*4.46*	*4.84*	*12.5*	*1.3*	*113*	

Breakout: 22%   Improve: 50%   Collapse: 21%   Attrition: 23%   MLB: 96%   *Comparables: Jaime Garcia, Carlos Martinez, Marcus Stroman*

Aaron Sanchez vs. Noah Syndergaard is the age-old debate for Blue Jays fans. In his first full season as a major-league starter, Sanchez dominated in an incredibly tough division for pitchers. Had he not been held back due to an innings limit, Sanchez may have even had a chance at the Cy Young award; he ended the season as the ERA leader. However, what's most fascinating about Sanchez isn't that he dominated, but how he dominated. While previously pitching out of the bullpen Sanchez developed a sinker so strong that, in some ways, it's the only pitch he needs. There were games during 2016 in which he used it for three out of every four pitches. It'll be interesting to see if he'll need to vary his pitch mix as batters begin to adjust.

Bo Schultz   RHP

Born: 9/25/85   Age: 31   Bats: R   Throws: R   Height: 6'3"   Weight: 230   Entered Pro Ball: Undrafted Free Agent, 2008

YEAR	TEAM	LVL	AGE	W	L	SV	G	GS	IP	H	HR	BB/9	K/9	K	GB%	BABIP	WHIP	ERA	FIP	DRA	VORP	WARP	cFIP	MPH
2014	ARI	MLB	28	0	1	0	4	0	8	13	1	1.1	5.6	5	50%	.414	1.75	7.88	3.85	3.49	0.9	0.1	102	98.1
2014	RNO	AAA	28	10	8	0	28	23	135¹	174	17	3.1	5.5	82	56%	.334	1.63	6.18	5.23	4.71	15.3	1.5	108	
2015	BUF	AAA	29	2	1	7	16	0	21¹	15	1	3	7.6	18	47%	.246	1.03	1.69	3.06	3.14	4.2	0.4	94	
2015	TOR	MLB	29	0	1	1	31	0	43	32	7	2.9	6.5	31	48%	.208	1.07	3.56	4.83	4.35	1.7	0.2	109	98.2
2016	BUF	AAA	30	3	2	2	26	0	33²	30	2	1.9	5.6	21	52%	.283	1.10	3.74	3.41	4.63	1.2	0.1	104	
2016	TOR	MLB	30	0	1	0	16	0	16¹	17	3	1.7	5.5	10	55%	.269	1.22	5.51	4.82	5.42	-0.8	-0.1	108	98.6
2017	*TOR*	*MLB*	*31*	*1*	*2*	*0*	*28*	*0*	*29*	*31*	*3*	*3.6*	*5.9*	*19*	*45%*	*.292*	*1.44*	*4.72*	*4.53*	*4.87*	*0.4*	*0.0*	*100*	
2018	*TOR*	*MLB*	*32*	*1*	*2*	*0*	*20*	*0*	*21*	*23*	*3*	*4.7*	*7.3*	*17*	*45%*	*.313*	*1.60*	*4.93*	*4.85*	*5.25*	*-0.4*	*0.0*	*119*	

Breakout: 3%   Improve: 9%   Collapse: 5%   Attrition: 11%   MLB: 25%   *Comparables: Justin Lehr, Mike Burns, Shane Loux*

Schultz had a 5.51 ERA in limited big-league action last season, but that probably still led the league among former bar league softball players. The flame-throwing reliever's bizarre ascent to the majors included time in independent ball and as a submariner, meaning that despite his age, his career as an MLB reliever is still very much in its infancy. His power sinker still generates a lot of ground balls, and if he can harness the splitter the team is asking him to learn, he could become a useful middle reliever.

Marcus Stroman   RHP

Born: 5/1/91   Age: 26   Bats: R   Throws: R   Height: 5'8"   Weight: 180   Entered Pro Ball: Round 1, 2012 Draft (#22 overall)

YEAR	TEAM	LVL	AGE	W	L	SV	G	GS	IP	H	HR	BB/9	K/9	K	GB%	BABIP	WHIP	ERA	FIP	DRA	VORP	WARP	cFIP	MPH
2014	BUF	AAA	23	2	4	0	7	7	35²	32	1	2.3	11.4	45	54%	.348	1.15	3.03	2.12	1.18	18.1	1.8	74	
2014	TOR	MLB	23	11	6	1	26	20	130²	125	7	1.9	7.6	111	55%	.306	1.17	3.65	2.87	2.77	29.6	3.3	82	95.9
2015	TOR	MLB	24	4	0	0	4	4	27	20	2	2.0	6.0	18	64%	.237	0.96	1.67	3.51	3.71	4.1	0.4	92	94.4
2016	TOR	MLB	25	9	10	0	32	32	204	209	21	2.4	7.3	166	62%	.309	1.29	4.37	3.67	3.43	43.7	4.5	86	94.6
2017	TOR	MLB	26	12	11	0	31	31	195¹	201	24	2.9	7.5	163	43%	.303	1.37	4.06	4.19	4.37	19.1	2.0	100	
2018	TOR	MLB	27	11	11	0	30	30	190	190	25	3.2	8.7	183	43%	.308	1.36	4.23	4.14	4.49	20.3	2.1	103	

Breakout: 29%   Improve: 62%   Collapse: 18%   Attrition: 8%   MLB: 91%   *Comparables: Sonny Gray, Jon Lester, Ubaldo Jimenez*

In fewer than three full seasons, we've seen four different versions of Stroman. Most pitchers will tinker—they'll adjust their grip on a pitch or change how they try to locate it—but they don't always overhaul their entire approach. As a minor leaguer, Stroman was somewhat standard; a three-pitch pitcher with a four-seam fastball, changeup and slurvy slider. That's the first Stroman. By the time he'd reached the major leagues in 2014, the Blue Jays had taught him a cutter distinctly different from the slurve. In his first few starts it was four-seam fastballs and a mix of all the secondary stuff; standard, but different. That's the second Stroman. He'd had some success in his first foray in the majors, but was averaging under six innings per start. Stroman wanted to be a workhorse and an ace. In order to do that he was going to have to get deeper into games, which meant a greater focus on quick outs. Stroman had played around with a sinker early in 2014, but started making it a priority by the middle of the season. After being a four-seam fastball pitcher his entire career, he entirely cannibalized it with the grounder-heavy sinker. That's the third Stroman. He grew to love the sinker, throwing it as much as 70 percent of the time in a start. However, by mid-2016 the ground outs that had made Stroman superb were starting to turn into singles. He started tinkering with the cutter that he'd added in 2014, developing it into a true out-pitch again. By the end of 2016, between the slider and cutter, upward of 35 percent of Stroman's pitches were hard breaking stuff. That's the fourth Stroman. Each iteration has had success, just in different ways. As he changes he improves in some ways, but falters in others. The hope would be that he manages to combine the best results of all Stromans, but it's not clear if that'll happen. Alternatively, he may remain as baseball's Many-Faced God, with his six-pitch arsenal as his devoted followers.

T.J. Zeuch   RHP

Born: 8/1/1995   Age: 21   Bats: R   Throws: R   Height: 6'7"   Weight: 225   Entered Pro Ball: Round 1, 2016 Draft (#21 overall)

YEAR	TEAM	LVL	AGE	W	L	SV	G	GS	IP	H	HR	BB/9	K/9	K	GB%	BABIP	WHIP	ERA	FIP	DRA	VORP	WARP	cFIP	MPH
2016	VAN	A-	20	0	1	0	6	6	23	21	1	2.0	8.6	22	70%	.302	1.13	3.52	3.08	2.51	7.0	0.7	82	
2017	TOR	MLB	21	2	2	0	8	8	32²	37	5	4.4	6.0	22	44%	.308	1.63	5.22	5.42	5.41	0.2	0.0	129	
2018	TOR	MLB	22	5	7	0	23	23	135²	138	17	4.7	8.2	123	44%	.309	1.54	4.78	4.70	4.95	5.6	0.6	118	

Breakout: 2%   Improve: 2%   Collapse: 0%   Attrition: 1%   MLB: 2%   *Comparables: Nick Tropeano, Carl Edwards Jr, Wilking Rodriguez*

The Blue Jays used their first-round pick on a college starter for the second year in a row, following the selection of Jon Harris in 2015. Selected 21st overall out of Pittsburgh, Zeuch is 6-foot-7, but surprisingly seems to be able repeat his delivery reasonably well. He possesses a power sinker that will touch 97, a solid 12-6 curveball and a mediocre changeup and slider. He's likely to start the 2017 season in Lansing or Dunedin, with a chance to move up if he continues to develop. If he doesn't reach his no. 3 starter ceiling, he could be a very good late-inning reliever with the fastball-curveball combo.

LINEOUTS

Hitters

NAME	POS	TEAM	LVL	AGE	PA	R	2B	3B	HR	RBI	BB	K	SB	CS	AVG/OBP/SLG	TAv	VORP	BABIP	BRR	FRAA	WARP
Domonic Brown	LF	BUF	AAA	28	509	37	24	0	7	41	38	99	5	3	.239/.303/.336	.232	-1.0	.289	-4.4	RF(75): -13.6 • LF(42): -0.3	-2.5
Andrew Burns	UT	TOR	MLB	25	7	2	0	0	0	0	0	2	0	0	.000/.143/.000	.091	-0.5	.000	0.5	3B(4): 0.4 • 1B(1): -0.0	0.0
	UT	BUF	AAA	25	454	42	25	1	8	38	33	82	13	5	.230/.285/.352	.236	3.4	.267	2.0	2B(55): 5.3 • LF(22): 1.7	1.0
Darrell Ceciliani	OF	BUF	AAA	26	334	40	17	3	10	40	26	52	11	5	.266/.323/.441	.276	12.2	.290	-1.3	LF(39): 3.3 • CF(28): 0.5	1.6
	OF	TOR	MLB	26	29	2	2	0	0	1	1	14	0	0	.111/.172/.185	.139	-3.1	.231	-0.2	LF(8): -0.3 • RF(4): -1.0	-0.5
Matt Dominguez	3B	TOR	MLB	26	12	0	0	0	0	0	1	3	0	0	.000/.083/.000	.056	-2.2	.000	0.1	3B(3): -0.1 • 1B(1): 0.1	-0.2
	3B	BUF	AAA	26	514	47	18	0	18	67	29	70	1	0	.269/.315/.421	.260	8.8	.281	-6.3	3B(111): 13.9 • 1B(16): 0.5	2.4
A.J. Jimenez	C	BUF	AAA	26	248	24	17	1	4	28	13	33	1	1	.241/.290/.377	.243	6.0	.263	-0.8	C(67): -6.4	0.0
Junior Lake	LF	TOR	MLB	26	39	5	3	0	1	2	4	11	1	0	.200/.282/.371	.238	0.1	.261	0.3	RF(19): -1.5 • 1B(1): -0.0	-0.2
	LF	BUF	AAA	26	318	33	12	2	6	31	33	77	10	4	.231/.314/.352	.247	3.0	.295	0.2	RF(46): -1.9 • CF(29): -0.3	0.1
Jesus Montero	DH	BUF	AAA	26	518	46	24	1	11	60	23	78	1	0	.317/.349/.438	.288	14.3	.357	-6.3	1B(25): -0.1	1.5
Michael Ohlman	C	SFD	AA	25	96	9	3	0	1	16	10	19	0	2	.301/.365/.373	.300	5.3	.364	-0.4	1B(12): 0.0 • C(8): -0.4	0.5
	C	MEM	AAA	25	186	34	9	2	6	28	15	53	1	0	.280/.333/.464	.298	18.0	.366	2.5	C(49): -1.3 • 1B(2): -0.0	1.7

Once among the best prospects in baseball, **Domonic Brown**'s various issues have made him nothing but minor-league depth at this point. ❖ **Andrew Burns** can play all positions other than catcher, but still hasn't found a path that leads to a bench spot. He'll have to hit better if he's going to overtake others on the depth chart. ❖ Now that Brett Cecil is gone to St. Louis, at least **Darrell Ceciliani** should be able to reclaim his usual title of "Best Last Name Beginning with Cecil" in the organization. ❖ **Matt Dominguez** can still play third base with the best of them, but his struggles to make consistent contact have left him looking for an opening on a big-league bench. ❖ Glove-first backup catcher **A.J. Jimenez** improved his Triple-A TAv last season. Unfortunately he improved it to .243. ❖ **Junior Lake** is like an everything bagel: he has all of the toppings you might want, but each one is spread so thin, the combination leaves an adverse taste in your mouth. ❖ After a couple of rough seasons in the majors, **Jesus Montero** spent all of 2016 in the minors and put up decent numbers. It wouldn't be a shock to see him crack a big-league bench to hit against lefties in 2017. ❖ Towering **Mike Ohlman** hits well enough when judged against other catchers, plays catcher well enough when judged against first basemen and crushes lefties well enough that he could yet carve out a career as a platoon bat.

Pitchers

NAME	TEAM	LVL	AGE	W	L	SV	G	GS	IP	H	HR	BB/9	K/9	K	GB%	BABIP	WHIP	ERA	FIP	DRA	VORP	WARP	cFIP	MPH
Leonel Campos	ELP	AAA	28	2	1	1	37	0	50	47	2	5.4	11.2	62	48%	.363	1.54	4.32	3.56	4.74	1.2	0.1	90	
	SDN	MLB	28	1	0	0	18	0	22	18	3	5.7	9.8	24	51%	.268	1.45	5.73	4.82	4.11	2.1	0.2	98	95.3
Matthew Dermody	DUN	A+	25	1	1	3	16	0	18¹	21	0	0.5	9.8	20	49%	.396	1.20	1.96	1.23	2.04	6.2	0.6	78	
	NHP	AA	25	2	0	0	16	0	19²	12	1	0.9	9.6	21	43%	.229	0.71	0.92	2.19	2.29	5.3	0.6	80	
	BUF	AAA	25	0	0	0	15	0	16¹	22	0	2.8	3.3	6	45%	.344	1.65	2.76	3.35	7.96	-5.4	-0.6	122	
	TOR	MLB	25	0	0	0	5	0	3	6	1	0.0	15.0	5	60%	.556	2.00	12.00	5.11	3.68	0.4	0.0	95	93.1
Scott Diamond	TOR	MLB	29	0	0	0	1	0	1	2	0	18.0	0.0	0	40%	.400	4.00	27.00	9.11	5.00	0.0	0.0	108	90.1
	BUF	AAA	29	9	15	0	28	28	166	191	11	1.7	5.4	100	50%	.329	1.34	4.50	3.49	4.52	15.2	1.6	98	
Chad Girodo	TOR	MLB	25	0	0	0	14	0	10¹	11	3	1.7	4.4	5	69%	.242	1.26	4.35	6.78	4.94	0.0	0.0	104	89.0
	BUF	AAA	25	2	1	1	29	0	35²	45	5	3.3	6.1	24	52%	.354	1.63	3.79	4.74	6.11	-4.6	-0.5	109	
Arnold Leon	TOR	MLB	27	0	0	0	2	0	2¹	3	1	3.9	7.7	2	50%	.286	1.71	7.71	8.25	4.95	0.0	0.0	105	93.8
	BUF	AAA	27	1	0	0	3	2	12	11	1	1.5	12.0	16	36%	.333	1.08	2.25	2.08	2.72	3.3	0.3	84	
Dominic Leone	RNO	AAA	24	5	2	1	33	0	35	25	4	2.8	9.3	36	36%	.247	1.03	3.34	4.18	3.02	7.5	0.8	84	
	ARI	MLB	24	0	1	0	25	0	27	45	7	4.0	7.7	23	47%	.432	2.11	6.33	6.30	5.24	-0.8	-0.1	109	95.2
Angel Perdomo	LNS	A	22	5	7	1	27	25	127	101	4	3.8	11.1	156	41%	.309	1.22	3.19	2.89	1.96	42.8	4.7	84	
Chris Smith	NHP	AA	27	1	2	15	43	0	57	44	2	3.3	12.0	76	42%	.302	1.14	1.89	2.31	2.11	16.6	1.8	76	
Glenn Sparkman	LEX	A	24	0	2	0	3	3	14¹	21	2	1.9	11.9	19	49%	.500	1.67	6.91	3.19	1.75	5.2	0.6	73	
	WIL	A+	24	1	0	0	2	2	11²	9	1	0.8	6.9	9	46%	.235	0.86	3.86	3.89	3.96	2.0	0.2	94	
	NWA	AA	24	0	2	0	4	4	17²	21	2	2.5	10.2	20	30%	.373	1.47	4.58	3.24	4.35	1.5	0.2	101	
Ryan Tepera	BUF	AAA	28	1	2	18	37	0	45¹	33	3	3.2	9.5	48	47%	.265	1.08	2.58	3.04	3.97	5.0	0.5	89	
	TOR	MLB	28	0	1	0	20	0	18¹	17	1	3.9	8.8	18	59%	.291	1.36	2.95	3.65	4.11	1.8	0.2	97	97.3

A former Venezuelan soccer star, **Leonel Campos** continued to show off the big stuff that makes him so enticing as well as the utter lack of command that threatens to hold him back. ❖ The velocity isn't elite, but 6-foot-5 lefty **Matt Dermody** had an elite minor-league relief season. ❖ **Scott Diamond** has a name made for the big leagues, but unfortunately doesn't quite have the skills to match. He's a control lefty, so he makes for quality minor-league depth. ❖ The sidewinding lefty has dominated left-handed hitters in the minor leagues, but struggled a bit in his first taste of big-league ball. Look for **Chad Girodo** to make a few more appearances for the Jays in 2017. ❖ Most remembered for his role in a WBC brawl, **Arnold Leon** managed to have an impact on the Jays despite only making two appearances. He served up a game-winning homer in his debut and was released after his second outing. ❖ It's been a deep struggle for **Dominic Leone** to replicate his 2014 success with diminished velocity, and he'll continue to shuttle back and forth between Triple-A and the majors until something changes. ❖ It's tough to say what you're going to get start-to-start from the 6-foot-6 **Angel Perdomo**, but the 22-year-old lefty has the stuff to dominate at times. ❖ A late add to the 40-man roster, **Chris Smith** impressed with an improved fastball that reached 98 mph as he dominated the Eastern League. ❖ **Glenn Sparkman** came back strong from Tommy John surgery and has a chance to be a back-end starter with three solid pitches and plus control. ❖ **Ryan Tepera** actually seems to have taken steps to become a viable major-league reliever, trading control and missed bats, but is still far down on the bullpen pecking order.

WASHINGTON NATIONALS

Essay by Brendan Gawlowski

Player comments by Wilson Karaman and BP staff

If the decision to prematurely end Stephen Strasburg's season hadn't been made in July, perhaps the ensuing hullabaloo would have been long forgotten by now. After all, baseball is never more in its element than in mid-summer, when the game fittingly dominates the sports calendar. July is when the All-Star Game is played, when fans begin checking the wild card standings in earnest, when baseball's rumor mill enjoys top billing on SportsCenter and talk radio.

So when Nationals general manager Mike Rizzo announced in July of 2012 that he was just trying to do right by his young phenom—"When we signed Stephen I made a promise to him and to his parents that I would take care of him, and that's what we are going to do"—people noticed and they talked. Many talked about how Rizzo was making a mistake. Some talked about how to best manage Strasburg's innings count. Others thought Rizzo would walk back his comments if Washington stayed in the 2012 pennant race.

Nobody particularly *liked* Rizzo's decision, not that that was surprising in and of itself. As Rocky Bridges once said, "There are three things that the average man thinks he can do better than anybody else. Build a fire, run a hotel and manage a baseball team." But the response around the league was swift and a bit coarse, given the mutual respect teams usually show for each other. Even players in Rizzo's clubhouse chimed in; utility man Mark DeRosa lamented that Strasburg would be "like a Christmas present that you can't open."

It's difficult to overstate how jarring the decision was. The Nationals, doormats since moving to the nation's capital in 2005, were comfortably and surprisingly ensconced in first place. To shut down Strasburg, to fundamentally reduce the team's chance of winning a title, went against every competitive instinct baseball observers have been conditioned to expect from major league teams. And it wasn't just that Rizzo yanked Strasburg from his team's rotation, but the *way* he did so that affronted many throughout the game. Amidst his review of Strasburg's health, Rizzo justified the move by saying that "we are not only competing for the playoffs this season, but also in 2013, 2014, 2015 and beyond."

NATIONALS PROSPECTUS
2016 W-L: 95-67, 1ST IN NL EAST

Pythag	.600	3rd	DER	.712	4th
RS/G	4.71	8th	B-Age	28.7	19th
RA/G	3.78	2nd	P-Age	28.7	21st
TAv	.276	3rd	Salary	$145.2M	11th
BRR	15.64	3rd	M$/MW	$2.8M	25th
TAv-P	.249	6th	DL Days	465	2nd
FIP	3.62	2nd	$ on DL	5%	2nd

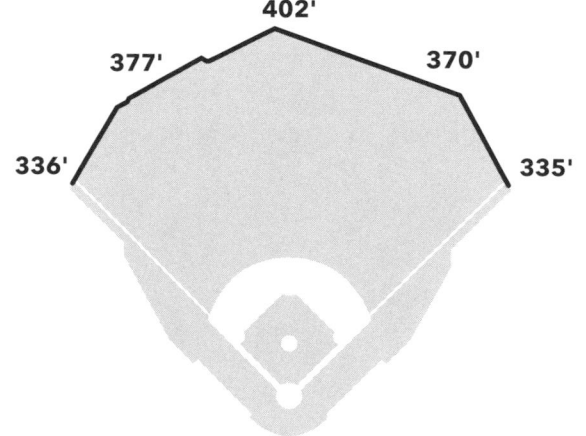

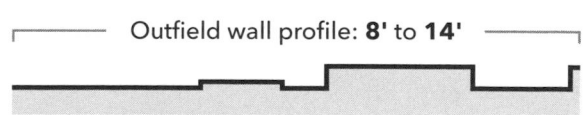

Outfield wall profile: **8'** to **14'**

Three-Year Park Factors

Runs	Runs/RH	Runs/LH	HR/RH	HR/LH
92	88	86	101	94

Top Hitter WARP	6.8	Daniel Murphy
Top Pitcher WARP	6.2	Max Scherzer
Top Prospect		Victor Robles

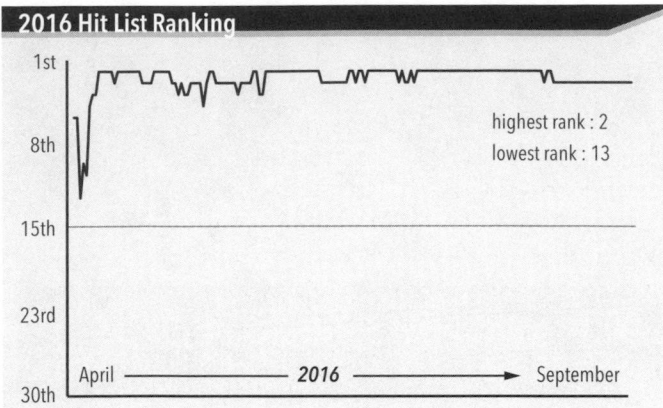

2016 Hit List Ranking

highest rank : 2
lowest rank : 13

April — *2016* → September

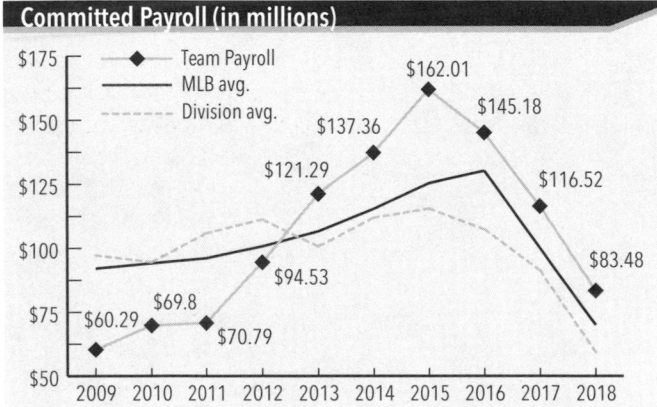

Committed Payroll (in millions)

- ◆ Team Payroll
- — MLB avg.
- -- Division avg.

$162.01
$145.18
$137.36
$121.29
$116.52
$94.53
$83.48
$60.29 $69.8
$70.79

2009 2010 2011 2012 2013 2014 2015 2016 2017 2018

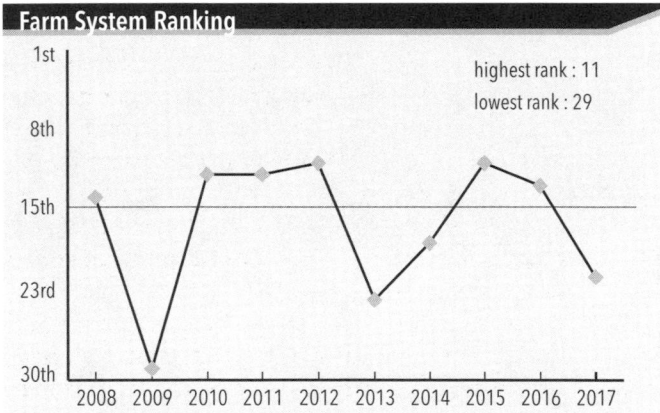

Farm System Ranking

highest rank : 11
lowest rank : 29

2008 2009 2010 2011 2012 2013 2014 2015 2016 2017

Personnel

General Manager:
Mike Rizzo

Assistant General Manager:
Doug Harris

Assistant General Manager:
Bob Miller

Manager:
Dusty Baker

Superstition is stitched into the fabric of baseball's culture and Rizzo's expressed foresight was taboo in a sport where you are taught to "focus on the next play," to "never show up your opponent" and to "take things one game at a time." Throwing away a bird in the hand for ones in 2015 and beyond jangled many throughout the industry. Executives practically rushed to comment anonymously to *USA Today*'s Bob Nightengale. Off the record, one general manager said "If we don't win the World Series, I don't care who does as long as it's not those guys. They don't deserve to win it. Not after what they did." Said another: "I hope they go down in flames. I hope it takes another 79 years before they get back to the playoffs."

The executives got their wish, and in painful fashion, as the Nationals blew a big lead in Game 5 of the NLDS. But even after a first round exit, a heartbreaking five-game loss to St. Louis where Strasburg could have tipped the series, Rizzo never wavered, saying "I stand by my decision. We'll take the criticism as it comes."

To be fair, Rizzo's thinking was hardly irrational. The 2012 season was arguably Strasburg's best full campaign, and—less than two years removed from Tommy John surgery—Rizzo understandably wanted to protect his ace. Moreover, the Nationals *were* well-positioned to compete for several years. Along with Strasburg and Harper, the Nationals had years to win before Ian Desmond, Jordan Zimmermann, Drew Storen, Wilson Ramos and several other key pieces reached free agency. A new downtown ballpark had increased Washington's spending power and with more homegrown players on the way, it appeared that destiny wore a red cap with a curvy, white 'W'. The Nationals had Harper under contract for six years, Strasburg for four and nearly every key player for at least two. October baseball and a World Series in Washington seemed inevitable.

✦ ✦ ✦

Fast forward four years and few would call the interim period a rousing success. The Nationals did win two NL East crowns, but sandwiched in between were disappointing campaigns where Washington's talented roster couldn't coalesce into a winner. Three division titles in five years begat five measly playoff victories and only 14 postseason games total. Strasburg started just one of them.

Think back to Rizzo's quote for a second, the desire to compete in "2013, '14, '15 and beyond." The Nationals have reached "beyond." Since the shutdown, Zimmermann started 100 ballgames and signed a $100 million contract with Detroit. Desmond just made his second All-Star team, but he did it in Texas and as an outfielder. Ramos, who in many ways has lived a fuller baseball life than most players ten years his senior, is now 28 and rehabbing from an ACL tear. Werth is still here but he hasn't been productive in two years. Ryan Zimmerman hasn't been good in three. Washington's two best players last year, comparatively recent imports Max Scherzer and Daniel Murphy, will both be 32 on Opening

Day. Five years and a few missed opportunities into the Strasburg/Harper core, the Nationals have to be feeling a sense of urgency.

The good news is that Washington might have the best baseball team this side of Chicago. Even with a bit of tinkering, the Nationals are loaded up and down the lineup and throughout their pitching staff. The 2016 unit might be the best team Washington has fielded since Walter Johnson's day, and that's high praise for a franchise that won more than 95 games three times in the last five seasons. They're the rare club with both a handful of stars and plenty of depth, and to be fair, the core isn't entirely composed of aging veterans. Washington isn't doomed to irrelevance in a post-Harper landscape.

Trea Turner and Anthony Rendon will likely form the backbone of Washington's lineup through the early 2020's. Turner is a promising young player who will shift back to his preferred shortstop position this season. Out of necessity, he filled in capably in center last year, but it was his bat that catapulted him into Rookie of the Year conversations. He hit .340/.377/.567, loudly rebuking critics who doubted his ability to be more than a slap hitter at the big league level. Rendon, meanwhile, has struggled with injuries throughout his collegiate and professional career, but when he's healthy, he's a star. He's as likely to help Washington win with a homer, a steal, a diving catch or a ten-pitch walk. Rendon hit .270/.348/.450 last season, and combined with excellent defense at the hot corner, he again looks like one of the best third basemen in the league.

And of course, Strasburg is no geezer either. Even if he isn't quite the world-beater he looked like in his debut season, when he awed fans across the country with a 100-mph fastball and the world's sharpest curve, the Nationals were happy to fork over $175 million to keep him in D.C. through 2023. Strasburg hasn't posted a DRA north of 2.87 since 2011, and while injuries scuttled what could have been a breakout 2016 season he should be ready for Spring Training and poised for a big year.

Beyond that group though, Washington looks a little long in the tooth. There are impact players up and down the roster, but a quick review of the rest of the squad reveals why the Nationals should be focused on winning now.

It starts with their best pitcher, and despite Strasburg's pedigree he's not the leader of the staff. That title belongs to Scherzer, the 2016 National League Cy Young winner and arguably the best pitcher alive not named Clayton Kershaw. Longtime baseball men say that there are fewer than ten aces in the league at any given time; even if there were only five, Scherzer would undoubtedly be one of them. His age and stature only reinforces the importance of winning now, though. Nobody would argue that Scherzer is on the decline—but nobody was saying that about CC Sabathia or Tim Lincecum five years ago either, or Brandon Webb back in 2007, or countless other pitchers who reached the peak of their dominance before swiftly tumbling backwards. Baseball's most frustrating truth is that great pitchers are great until they aren't, and there's no pattern warning us when one of the titans is about to fall. For the Nationals, the urgency to win isn't just to do so with Harper, but to also get a ring while Scherzer—a 32-year-old who has fired plenty of bullets in recent years—remains at the peak of his powers.

The rest of Washington's talented roster is just as ripe. Tanner Roark is 30 years old, and his 4.45 career DRA suggests that he's been fooling the National League with smoke and mirrors. Gio Gonzalez has been really good for Washington, accruing 20 WARP since arriving in 2012, but he's lost a tick off his fastball. Depending on how many innings he throws this year, he'll either be a free agent after this season or next. Murphy will also be free to walk after 2018. Nobody knows whether he can carry his breakout season into 2017, but if he's 90 percent of what he was in 2016, he's a star, and even if he reverts back to being a league average regular, the Nationals will be strong up the middle until he too requires replacement. It won't be easy for Rizzo to find suitable alternatives once the older part of the core starts to age.

Rizzo further doubled down on this window by trading for Adam Eaton over the winter. Eaton, a borderline star depending on how much you trust corner outfield defensive metrics, is in the peak of his career and he fits well on the roster. He'll probably be a tick better than Turner defensively in center field and a massive upgrade over Danny Espinosa at the plate. He didn't come cheap, though. To acquire Eaton, Rizzo dealt top pitching prospect Lucas Giolito—one of the few arms in baseball who some scouts project as a true no. 1 starter—along with promising right-handers Reynaldo Lopez and Dane Dunning. Many analysts felt that Rizzo overpaid; perhaps Rizzo simply felt the need to pay retail after missing out on the chance to obtain Andrew McCutchen. Eaton is under team control through 2021, but the move was clearly much more about present upgrades than future considerations.

Ultimately, that's because of Harper. Harper is the prodigy, the generational talent who this team has been assembled his team around. Last year was a down season by his standards, but it's worth reminding ourselves that most players in the league would kill to walk 100 times, knock 50 extra base hits and produce 4.5 WARP in any year, much less a bad one. Harper's career production thus far is remarkable and it's fair to forecast more seasons like his 2015 campaign—when he hit .330 and led the league in homers, OBP and slugging—going forward. He will terrorize National League pitching again, and he'll probably do it in 2017.

✦✦✦

With every postseason disappointment, the spectre of Rizzo's call looms larger and, in 2017, the pressure on his ballclub will be as high as it has ever been. Rizzo may have his best team but observers in and out of the organization are acutely aware that the sand at the top of the hourglass is dissipating. For just two more years, the Nationals will enjoy the artificially-deflated services of one of the few players in the world capable of producing a 10-win season. Rizzo is painfully aware of the expiration date; the Eaton trade will presumably not be the final time he pushes his minor league chips to the middle of the table.

For however good Turner becomes at peak maturity, and forever how long Scherzer, Rendon and Strasburg stay productive, Harper is the golden ticket. In two years, he will be manning right field for some other team and the Nationals will be just another outfit with a ten-year old park and a couple of good players. They are two years from becoming the late 90's Mariners, a team that turned the combined prime seasons of Alex Rodriguez, Randy Johnson, Edgar Martinez and Ken Griffey Jr. into nothing more than a couple of early-October exits.

The expectations aren't exactly fair. Of all teams, the Nationals are well aware of how the best team on paper in March can flop for six months and how an October favorite can get bounced in a week. No team, no matter how good, is ever "likely" to win the World Series; there's just too much variance in the playoffs. But that only ratchets the temperature up another degree. The stakes are clear and, fair or not, the Nationals will play the 2017 and 2018 seasons in the shadow of squandered opportunity. Rizzo has assembled an immensely talented team, and anything but a championship will be a disappointment. Washington has to win, and they have to do it now. The window is closing. The clock is ticking. ■

—Brendan Gawlowski is an author
of Baseball Prospectus

HITTERS

Yasel Antuna   SS

Born: 10/26/99 Age: 17   Bats: B   Throws: R   Height: 6'0"   Weight: 170   Entered Pro Ball: International Free Agent, 2016

The Nationals plunked a club-record $3.9 million bonus in the teenager's lap in spite of some mixed reviews about the precocious shortstop's ultimate projection. Some see a five-tool wunderkind with enough range and instinct to stick at short long-term. Others see a bat-first third-base prospect who lacks the explosiveness to develop a quality glove. Others, if they look just right, see a sailboat. One or more of these opinions may ultimately prove correct, but given that Antuna just turned 17, the verdict likely won't be in until well into the next decade.

Nick Banks   OF

Born: 11/18/94 Age: 22   Bats: L   Throws: L   Height: 6'1"   Weight: 215   Entered Pro Ball: Round 4, 2016 Draft (#124 overall)

YEAR	TEAM	LVL	AGE	PA	R	2B	3B	HR	RBI	BB	K	SB	CS	AVG/OBP/SLG	TAv	VORP	BABIP	BRR	FRAA	WARP
2016	AUB	A-	21	249	18	8	1	0	19	11	37	7	2	.277/.310/.320	.276	7.7	.327	-0.3	RF(38): 0.1 • LF(14): -1.1	0.7
2017	WAS	MLB	22	250	21	9	1	5	25	11	69	1	0	.213/.251/.328	.200	-8.1	.271	-0.3	RF 1 • LF 0	-0.8
2018	WAS	MLB	23	217	22	8	1	5	22	9	59	1	0	.215/.252/.341	.215	-5.6	.269	-0.3	RF 1 • LF 0	-0.5

Breakout: 4%   Improve: 5%   Collapse: 0%   Attrition: 5%   MLB: 5%   *Comparables: Socrates Brito, Lorenzo Cain, Scott Schebler*

A former Team USA star, Banks went from projected first-rounder entering his draft season to marginally-above-slot fourth-rounder for the Nats after a pedestrian, injury-abbreviated spring. It was more longhand, actually; Banks has sustained a litany of annual injuries dating back to high school. When healthy, he'll show solid tools across the board, with an arm strong enough for right field and enough hit, power and speed tools to profile as an average offensive contributor. He displayed quality bat-to-ball ability and a nice opposite-field approach in the age-appropriate New York-Penn League after signing, and a healthy and productive 2017 could turn him into one of the better early values of the draft class.

Rafael Bautista   CF

Born: 3/8/93   Age: 24   Bats: R   Throws: R   Height: 6'2"   Weight: 165   Entered Pro Ball: International Free Agent, 2012

YEAR	TEAM	LVL	AGE	PA	R	2B	3B	HR	RBI	BB	K	SB	CS	AVG/OBP/SLG	TAv	VORP	BABIP	BRR	FRAA	WARP
2014	HAG	A	21	543	97	20	5	5	54	33	72	69	15	.290/.341/.382	.267	28.3	.328	8.5	CF(117): 3.0 • RF(16): 3.3	3.6
2015	AUB	A-	22	34	6	3	0	0	4	1	7	3	0	.273/.294/.364	.224	0.7	.346	1.0	CF(7): 0.3	0.1
2015	POT	A+	22	226	23	7	2	0	8	11	22	23	4	.272/.318/.325	.253	5.0	.301	0.0	CF(52): -3.0	0.2
2016	HAR	AA	23	607	77	12	4	4	39	45	94	56	10	.282/.344/.341	.257	21.9	.333	7.8	CF(102): -5.2 • RF(32): 0.3	1.8
2017	WAS	MLB	24	250	32	8	1	4	19	14	53	16	3	.243/.292/.345	.222	1.3	.291	2.0	CF -1 • RF 0	0.1
2018	WAS	MLB	25	378	41	11	2	7	37	23	78	25	5	.247/.301/.354	.240	5.9	.292	3.9	CF -1 • RF 0	0.5

Breakout: 9%   Improve: 15%   Collapse: 6%   Attrition: 13%   MLB: 28%   *Comparables: Denard Span, Jose Constanza, Quintin Berry*

Gandhi once warned that there is more to life than simply increasing its speed, though Bautista may disagree. Plus-plus run times, instinctual feel on the bases and rangy centerfield defense have been his calling cards to date, and his 56 stolen bases tied for the Double-A lead last season. Most importantly, he took a step forward with the bat, making contact and getting on base at an interesting clip against more advanced pitching. If the refined approach and contact skills hold, he could enter the mix for a call-up next summer.

Wilmer Difo   SS

Born: 4/2/92   Age: 25   Bats: B   Throws: R   Height: 5'11"   Weight: 200   Entered Pro Ball: International Free Agent, 2010

YEAR	TEAM	LVL	AGE	PA	R	2B	3B	HR	RBI	BB	K	SB	CS	AVG/OBP/SLG	TAv	VORP	BABIP	BRR	FRAA	WARP
2014	HAG	A	22	610	91	31	7	14	90	37	65	49	9	.315/.360/.470	.294	49.2	.333	6.5	SS(70): 1.1 • 2B(66): 3.7	5.6
2015	POT	A+	23	83	13	7	0	3	14	8	13	4	1	.320/.386/.533	.337	10.1	.356	0.4	SS(19): -2.7	0.8
2015	HAR	AA	23	381	48	21	6	2	39	12	79	26	1	.279/.312/.387	.251	11.7	.349	0.7	SS(77): 4.9 • 2B(11): -0.7	1.7
2015	WAS	MLB	23	11	1	0	0	0	0	0	2	0	0	.182/.182/.182	.141	-1.7	.222	-0.8	2B(2): 0.0	-0.2
2016	HAR	AA	24	451	59	15	3	6	41	34	59	28	11	.259/.318/.354	.252	13.9	.288	-0.1	SS(103): -2.7	1.2
2016	WAS	MLB	24	66	14	3	0	1	7	8	12	3	0	.276/.364/.379	.261	3.1	.333	1.0	2B(9): 0.2 • SS(5): 0.3	0.4
2017	*WAS*	*MLB*	*25*	*352*	*40*	*19*	*2*	*8*	*33*	*19*	*76*	*15*	*4*	*.241/.286/.366*	*.234*	*5.6*	*.289*	*1.8*	*2B 2 • SS 0*	*0.6*
2018	*WAS*	*MLB*	*26*	*452*	*49*	*19*	*2*	*11*	*49*	*25*	*98*	*18*	*5*	*.242/.288/.378*	*.242*	*8.0*	*.287*	*2.6*	*2B 2 • SS 1*	*1.2*

Breakout: 6%   Improve: 29%   Collapse: 8%   Attrition: 32%   MLB: 55%   *Comparables: Anderson Hernandez, Nick Ahmed, Trevor Plouffe*

A season removed from forging his big-league debut, Difo spent the entirety of the season's first half on a return trip to Double-A before riding the shuttle bus back and forth to the Promised Land a couple times later in the year. He was okay on the farm, though the raw production was down. His quick wrists continued to get bat to ball at an appealing rate, and his high-contact approach held up. But his A-ball pop again failed to play against the more seasoned arms of the high minors, and his 70-grade speed didn't translate quite as well on the bases, either. Still, versatility is a key ingredient, and his ability to hold steady on both sides of the second-base bag while taking quality at-bats from both sides of the plate can prevent him from forever being that guy who struck out against Clayton Kershaw in the final at-bat of the NLDS.

Stephen Drew   2B/SS

Born: 3/16/83   Age: 34   Bats: L   Throws: R   Height: 6'0"   Weight: 200   Entered Pro Ball: Round 1, 2004 Draft (#15 overall)

YEAR	TEAM	LVL	AGE	PA	R	2B	3B	HR	RBI	BB	K	SB	CS	AVG/OBP/SLG	TAv	VORP	BABIP	BRR	FRAA	WARP
2014	BOS	MLB	31	145	11	6	1	4	11	14	39	1	1	.176/.255/.328	.212	-1.4	.216	-0.4	SS(39): 1.4	0.0
2014	NYA	MLB	31	155	7	8	0	3	15	13	36	0	1	.150/.219/.271	.195	-7.0	.175	-1.7	2B(34): -1.0 • SS(12): -0.3	-0.9
2015	NYA	MLB	32	428	43	16	1	17	44	37	71	0	2	.201/.271/.381	.236	-1.4	.201	-2.7	2B(123): -2.9 • SS(15): 0.7	-0.4
2016	WAS	MLB	33	165	24	11	1	8	21	16	31	0	1	.266/.339/.524	.318	13.8	.278	-1.1	2B(21): 1.8 • SS(12): -0.3	1.6
2017	*WAS*	*MLB*	*34*	*250*	*27*	*11*	*1*	*8*	*28*	*25*	*58*	*1*	*1*	*.218/.297/.384*	*.236*	*2.3*	*.254*	*-1.1*	*2B -1 • 3B 0*	*0.2*
2018	*WAS*	*MLB*	*35*	*113*	*13*	*5*	*0*	*3*	*12*	*11*	*26*	*0*	*0*	*.206/.287/.364*	*.240*	*0.4*	*.241*	*-0.5*	*2B 0 • 3B 0*	*0.0*

Breakout: 2%   Improve: 32%   Collapse: 14%   Attrition: 18%   MLB: 79%   *Comparables: Tadahito Iguchi, Mark DeRosa, Mark Ellis*

That ol' "Uncle Dirt" managed to generate his highest WARP since 2013 in less than 200 plate appearances tells you both how dark a turn his career had taken and how surprisingly bright his light shined in limited exposure this season. Sure, he logged his requisite time on the shelf—six weeks lost to another inner ear issue—but after scraping Mendoza's floor in 2015 he managed to reinvent himself in Washington as a righty-mashing utility infielder with unimpeachable clubhouse credentials. These days his power is almost entirely the product of pitches he can extend on, but there's still enough juice in his glove for the occasional bouts of pop to justify his continued inclusion on a 40-man roster.

Adam Eaton   CF

Born: 12/6/88   Age: 28   Bats: L   Throws: L   Height: 5'8"   Weight: 185   Entered Pro Ball: Round 19, 2010 Draft (#571 overall)

YEAR	TEAM	LVL	AGE	PA	R	2B	3B	HR	RBI	BB	K	SB	CS	AVG/OBP/SLG	TAv	VORP	BABIP	BRR	FRAA	WARP
2014	CHA	MLB	25	538	76	26	10	1	35	43	83	15	9	.300/.362/.401	.283	27.3	.359	0.6	CF(121): 0.0	3.0
2015	CHA	MLB	26	689	98	28	9	14	56	58	131	18	8	.287/.361/.431	.282	40.6	.345	5.9	CF(145): 2.1	4.6
2016	CHA	MLB	27	706	91	29	9	14	59	63	115	14	5	.284/.362/.428	.276	32.9	.329	5.9	RF(121): 24.3 • CF(48): 4.9	6.4
2017	*WAS*	*MLB*	*28*	*607*	*75*	*27*	*6*	*10*	*55*	*53*	*106*	*14*	*6*	*.277/.350/.406*	*.271*	*30.5*	*.323*	*0.3*	*CF 5*	*2.9*
2018	*WAS*	*MLB*	*29*	*566*	*68*	*25*	*5*	*11*	*60*	*49*	*103*	*11*	*5*	*.274/.350/.411*	*.279*	*29.3*	*.320*	*3.2*	*CF 5*	*3.7*

Breakout: 2%   Improve: 45%   Collapse: 4%   Attrition: 16%   MLB: 91%   *Comparables: Brett Gardner, Shane Victorino, A.J. Pollock*

The Napoleon complex routinely works in favor of the vertically-challenged baseballer. For Eaton, he's constantly proving his worth as more than a scrappy Eckstein, but rather that he is a legitimate leadoff hitter who can smack any type of base hit. That he can provide premium defense in right field. That his offense is also good enough to be a corner outfielder. That he'll successfully dive for balls that a 6-foot-2 person could reach. That he's not the other guy named Adam Eaton. That he's number one. (This one was easy, it's his uniform number.) And one of the most fascinating parts of his stat line is he basically replicated his 2015 numbers, which probably means he thought someone out there thought he couldn't do *that* either. Invest in short people, the Nationals did.

Bryce Harper   RF

Born: 10/16/92   Age: 24   Bats: L   Throws: R   Height: 6'3"   Weight: 215   Entered Pro Ball: Round 1, 2010 Draft (#1 overall)

YEAR	TEAM	LVL	AGE	PA	R	2B	3B	HR	RBI	BB	K	SB	CS	AVG/OBP/SLG	TAv	VORP	BABIP	BRR	FRAA	WARP
2014	WAS	MLB	21	395	41	10	2	13	32	38	104	2	2	.273/.344/.423	.290	17.0	.352	-1.9	LF(90): 1.6 • RF(10): -0.6	1.9
2015	WAS	MLB	22	654	118	38	1	42	99	124	131	6	4	.330/.460/.649	.386	97.4	.369	5.1	RF(140): 6.3 • CF(13): 0.8	11.2
2016	WAS	MLB	23	627	84	24	2	24	86	108	117	21	10	.243/.373/.441	.305	42.1	.264	2.3	RF(143): 2.5	4.6
2017	*WAS*	*MLB*	*24*	*575*	*82*	*25*	*3*	*27*	*85*	*81*	*120*	*11*	*5*	*.270/.375/.501*	*.305*	*42.6*	*.302*	*-0.3*	*RF 0*	*4.0*
2018	*WAS*	*MLB*	*25*	*561*	*86*	*24*	*2*	*27*	*85*	*82*	*115*	*11*	*5*	*.269/.378/.502*	*.316*	*45.9*	*.298*	*2.0*	*RF 0*	*5.0*

Breakout: 1%   Improve: 69%   Collapse: 2%   Attrition: 4%   MLB: 100%   *Comparables: Jason Heyward, Kal Daniels, Albert Pujols*

It's not every day that a player coming off a 4.5 WARP campaign in his *age-23 season* musters whispered tones of regret and underachievement in retrospectives, but here we are with the former MVP. Harper's decline was about as well-rounded as he is. His offensive production fell by half, his defensive effort slipped to "merely solid" and even though he stole a bunch more bases, his efficiency remained highly suspect. In fact, the only aspect of his production not to take a step back in 2016 was his bat decal game, seamlessly ranging from platform-driven ("Make Baseball Fun Again") to remembrance-driven ("Rumble Young Man Rumble," paying tribute to Muhammad Ali) to meme-driven (flashing an #RIPHarambe sticker in his season's final game). A BABIP that cratered by triple digits was one culprit, driven by weaker contact against stronger shift tendencies; his OPS against the shift dropped by more than 300 points. A whispered shoulder injury may or may not have played into his limited effectiveness, but whatever the cause, Harper will enter 2017 in search of a return to best-player-in-the-NL form.

Carter Kieboom   SS

Born: 9/3/97   Age: 19   Bats: R   Throws: R   Height: 6'2"   Weight: 190   Entered Pro Ball: Round 1, 2016 Draft (#28 overall)

YEAR	TEAM	LVL	AGE	PA	R	2B	3B	HR	RBI	BB	K	SB	CS	AVG/OBP/SLG	TAv	VORP	BABIP	BRR	FRAA	WARP
2017	WAS	MLB	19	250	24	8	1	6	22	14	92	0	0	.182/.232/.304	.187	-7.9	.265	-0.4	SS 0	-0.8
2018	WAS	MLB	20	315	33	11	1	9	33	19	111	1	0	.197/.253/.337	.214	-4.5	.278	-0.5	SS 0	-0.4

Breakout: 0%   Improve: 5%   Collapse: 2%   Attrition: 5%   MLB: 10%   *Comparables: Raul Mondesi, Nomar Mazara, Elvis Andrus*

After tapping Carter with the 28th pick in June, Washington is now just one Kieboom brother shy of the entire collector's set. And in a potential victory for beleaguered middle children everywhere, this Kieboom may just have the highest ceiling in the family. Early professional reports were cautiously optimistic about his ability to stick at shortstop, and despite battling some nagging injuries throughout the summer, he showed intriguing pop for a middle infielder. The sum of the parts projects as a solid if unspectacular option at the six spot.

Jose Lobaton   C

Born: 10/21/84   Age: 32   Bats: B   Throws: R   Height: 6'1"   Weight: 205   Entered Pro Ball: International Free Agent, 2002

YEAR	TEAM	LVL	AGE	PA	R	2B	3B	HR	RBI	BB	K	SB	CS	AVG/OBP/SLG	TAv	VORP	BABIP	BRR	FRAA	WARP
2014	WAS	MLB	29	230	18	9	0	2	12	15	61	0	0	.234/.287/.304	.224	0.8	.318	-1.0	C(64): 4.0	0.5
2015	WAS	MLB	30	155	11	4	0	3	20	15	40	0	0	.199/.279/.294	.226	1.1	.253	-0.5	C(42): 4.1	0.6
2016	WAS	MLB	31	114	10	3	1	3	8	12	18	0	0	.232/.319/.374	.257	3.4	.253	-1.4	C(38): 1.3	0.5
2017	WAS	MLB	32	166	15	7	0	3	16	16	40	0	0	.225/.300/.341	.235	3.1	.282	-0.3	C 3	0.4
2018	WAS	MLB	33	144	16	6	0	3	14	15	36	0	0	.226/.310/.346	.245	2.5	.286	-0.6	C 3	0.6

Breakout: 2%   Improve: 38%   Collapse: 13%   Attrition: 18%   MLB: 95%   *Comparables: Yorvit Torrealba, Gerald Laird, Jeff Reed*

Lobaton's playing time dwindled as Wilson Ramos broke out, but when he did get the call, he continued to perform pretty well behind the dish, particularly as a framer of pitches. More notably, he also managed a stellar offensive improvement to sniff league-average production just one year removed from looking up at the Mendoza Line. A flatter launch angle and more aggressive approach combined to help him make dramatically more contact against pitches of all shapes and sizes, helping him shave a full ten percentage points off an uncomfortable strikeout rate. Thrust into late-season duty, he added a second signature moment of postseason heroism as well, hitting a three-run moonshot against Rich Hill, which would prove to be the needed margin in Game 2 of the NLDS. He's a Super Two guy, so he'll play out his fourth and final year on arbitrated terms before embarking on what could be a nice run of for-hire backup catching well into his thirties.

YEAR	TEAM	P. COUNT	FRM RUNS	BLK RUNS	THRW RUNS	TOT RUNS
2014	WAS	8464	2.5	1.2	0.7	4.4
2015	WAS	5681	5.0	-0.1	-0.3	4.5
2016	WAS	4509	2.5	0.4	0.1	2.9
2017	WAS	6211	3.2	0.2	0.1	3.5
2018	WAS	5390	2.3	0.1	0.0	2.4

Daniel Murphy   2B

Born: 4/1/85   Age: 32   Bats: L   Throws: R   Height: 6'1"   Weight: 220   Entered Pro Ball: Round 13, 2006 Draft (#394 overall)

YEAR	TEAM	LVL	AGE	PA	R	2B	3B	HR	RBI	BB	K	SB	CS	AVG/OBP/SLG	TAv	VORP	BABIP	BRR	FRAA	WARP
2014	NYN	MLB	29	642	79	37	2	9	57	39	86	13	5	.289/.332/.403	.277	24.9	.322	-1.3	2B(126): -4.1 • 3B(16): -0.9	2.2
2015	NYN	MLB	30	538	56	38	2	14	73	31	38	2	2	.281/.322/.449	.283	24.7	.278	-0.9	2B(69): -2.1 • 3B(42): -2.2	2.1
2016	WAS	MLB	31	582	88	47	5	25	104	35	57	5	3	.347/.390/.595	.352	70.6	.348	1.4	2B(117): -5.0 • 1B(21): 0.6	6.8
2017	WAS	MLB	32	638	68	39	2	15	75	37	79	8	3	.288/.330/.440	.270	29.0	.307	-0.6	2B -7 • 3B -1	1.8
2018	WAS	MLB	33	515	60	31	1	12	59	30	68	5	2	.281/.322/.426	.270	20.3	.303	-0.1	2B -5 • 3B -1	1.5

Breakout: 1%   Improve: 35%   Collapse: 5%   Attrition: 6%   MLB: 97%   *Comparables: Brandon Phillips, Aaron Hill, Orlando Hudson*

We spend a lot of time and energy trying to educate people about the dangers of buying into small sample sizes, and then every now and again a guy like Murphy has to go and ruin everything. He kept his 2015 postseason party raging for another six months, clearing his career OPS by 200 points—good enough to lead the Senior Circuit. (He also paced it in doubles and slugging percentage.) Sure he was still one of the poorest defenders at second base that Major League Baseball had to offer, but after he posted the fourth-highest VORP in the game, the glove wasn't exactly the doomsday instrument of impending bench relegation that it once appeared to be. Murphy is living proof that mechanical and approach changes well into established careers can sometimes unlock wondrous new worlds, and his three-year deal with the Nats is on pace to comfortably pay for itself before Memorial Day—even with the draft pick accounted for.

Derek Norris   C

Born: 2/14/89   Age: 28   Bats: R   Throws: R   Height: 6'0"   Weight: 230   Entered Pro Ball: Round 4, 2007 Draft (#130 overall)

YEAR	TEAM	LVL	AGE	PA	R	2B	3B	HR	RBI	BB	K	SB	CS	AVG/OBP/SLG	TAv	VORP	BABIP	BRR	FRAA	WARP
2014	OAK	MLB	25	442	46	19	1	10	55	54	86	2	2	.270/.361/.403	.289	24.2	.324	-4.8	C(114): -11.6	1.4
2015	SDN	MLB	26	557	65	33	2	14	62	35	131	4	1	.250/.305/.404	.263	18.6	.310	-5.0	C(128): 13.3 • 1B(17): -1.6	3.3
2016	SDN	MLB	27	458	50	17	0	14	42	36	139	9	2	.186/.255/.328	.214	0.8	.238	1.9	C(116): 8.5 • 1B(3): -0.0	1.0
2017	WAS	MLB	28	442	50	20	1	14	49	41	110	5	2	.232/.307/.390	.252	15.6	.284	-0.3	C 6	1.3
2018	WAS	MLB	29	441	54	20	1	14	52	42	113	4	1	.231/.309/.395	.263	15.3	.284	-2.0	C 5	2.3

Breakout: 8%   Improve: 46%   Collapse: 14%   Attrition: 19%   MLB: 98%   *Comparables: John Buck, Jason Castro, Nick Hundley*

Coming off a season in which he turned into a dynamic framer but lost plenty of offensive value, 2016 was an important campaign for Norris. On the plus side, he continued to provide plenty of value behind the plate with his framing skills. Unfortunately, there weren't many other positives. He started throwing from his knees on steal attempts, which worked for a while but ended with him giving up the most value of his career in throwing. Even worse, his offensive woes reached a critical point, as he was literally the worst hitter in baseball with at least 400 plate appearances. While some of that was BABIP-related, his plate discipline was the bigger issue. Norris' contact issues matched the likes of Chris Davis and Pedro Alvarez, but came without the power those bats can provide.

YEAR	TEAM	P. COUNT	FRM RUNS	BLK RUNS	THRW RUNS	TOT RUNS
2014	OAK	13348	-9.9	-1.4	-1.7	-13.0
2015	SDN	17344	12.1	1.9	2.0	16.0
2016	SDN	16407	9.2	0.2	-3.0	6.5
2017	WAS	15781	6.3	0.5	-0.9	6.0
2018	WAS	15748	5.3	0.4	-1.0	4.8

Wilson Ramos   C

Born: 8/10/87   Age: 29   Bats: R   Throws: R   Height: 6'1"   Weight: 255   Entered Pro Ball: International Free Agent, 2004

YEAR	TEAM	LVL	AGE	PA	R	2B	3B	HR	RBI	BB	K	SB	CS	AVG/OBP/SLG	TAv	VORP	BABIP	BRR	FRAA	WARP
2014	WAS	MLB	26	361	32	12	0	11	47	17	57	0	0	.267/.299/.399	.250	13.2	.290	1.9	C(87): -1.0	1.4
2015	WAS	MLB	27	504	41	16	0	15	68	21	101	0	0	.229/.258/.358	.231	5.8	.256	-1.4	C(125): 4.6	1.1
2016	WAS	MLB	28	523	58	25	0	22	80	35	79	0	0	.307/.354/.496	.305	43.2	.327	-4.3	C(128): 7.8	5.3
2017	TBA	MLB	29	158	18	6	0	6	20	10	29	0	0	.255/.300/.422	.262	5.6	.277	-0.4	C 1	0.5
2018	TBA	MLB	30	334	43	12	0	14	45	21	63	0	0	.260/.307/.436	.271	13.7	.283	-0.9	C 1	1.6

Breakout: 2%   Improve: 41%   Collapse: 8%   Attrition: 9%   MLB: 100%   *Comparables: A.J. Pierzynski, John Wockenfuss, Rich Gedman*

It's been a long quest for Ramos to finally stay on the field and put it all together, and on the eve of his free agency he came *so close* to doing it. For five-and-a-half months he toiled, grinding on the daily at a breakneck pace he'd never before managed to sustain. The effort produced stellar results on both sides of the ball. Offensively, he stayed in the zone better, cut down on his whiffs and hit balls consistently harder and farther to drive significant increases in both his BABIP and ISO. Behind the dish, he remained an above-average defender, highlighted by stellar framing and throwing numbers. He was a top-five catcher by WARP. Then, a week shy of season's end, his ACL exploded for a second time. Once poised to cruise into nine cool figures, he'll instead enter the market with a half-season ahead on the shelf and both his future catching and earnings potential subject to the whims of the shruggy guy.

YEAR	TEAM	P. COUNT	FRM RUNS	BLK RUNS	THRW RUNS	TOT RUNS
2014	HAR	347	-0.2	0.0	0.0	-0.2
2014	WAS	11905	-2.6	-0.4	1.0	-2.0
2015	WAS	16690	0.4	2.8	2.0	5.1
2016	WAS	17715	7.4	-1.3	1.7	7.8
2017	WAS	3245	0.5	0.0	0.3	0.9
2018	WAS	6856	0.6	0.0	0.6	1.2

Anthony Rendon   3B

Born: 6/6/90   Age: 27   Bats: R   Throws: R   Height: 6'1"   Weight: 210   Entered Pro Ball: Round 1, 2011 Draft (#6 overall)

YEAR	TEAM	LVL	AGE	PA	R	2B	3B	HR	RBI	BB	K	SB	CS	AVG/OBP/SLG	TAv	VORP	BABIP	BRR	FRAA	WARP
2014	WAS	MLB	24	683	111	39	6	21	83	58	104	17	3	.287/.351/.473	.301	50.5	.314	4.9	3B(134): 1.3 • 2B(28): -2.4	5.4
2015	HAR	AA	25	27	1	3	0	0	0	3	4	0	0	.250/.333/.375	.271	0.7	.300	-0.2	2B(5): 0.6 • 3B(1): 0.4	0.2
2015	POT	A+	25	20	2	2	0	0	1	3	2	0	0	.471/.550/.588	.398	3.2	.533	0.0	3B(4): -0.1	0.3
2015	WAS	MLB	25	355	43	16	0	5	25	36	70	1	2	.264/.344/.363	.262	10.0	.321	-0.2	2B(59): -1.7 • 3B(28): 0.8	1.0
2016	WAS	MLB	26	647	91	38	2	20	85	65	117	12	6	.270/.348/.450	.296	45.1	.304	0.8	3B(155): -8.7	3.8
2017	WAS	MLB	27	553	65	29	2	16	67	55	100	9	4	.263/.341/.433	.274	24.6	.296	-0.4	3B 0	2.1
2018	WAS	MLB	28	521	68	29	1	17	65	54	94	7	3	.262/.343/.440	.285	26.3	.293	1.4	3B 0	2.9

Breakout: 2%   Improve: 39%   Collapse: 7%   Attrition: 13%   MLB: 98%   *Comparables: Edwin Encarnacion, Kyle Seager, Puddin Head Jones*

On sheer handsomeness alone, Rendon is a perennial MVP candidate, but his four-year career has seen a distinct lack of consistency thanks largely to an unattractive medical file. He managed to stay healthy for the entirety of 2016, however, and it turns out that yes, he is indeed a very good baseball player when he plays. Like his breakout 2014 campaign, he was good in just about every facet of the game. He was well above-average offensively against righties and lefties alike. His baserunning was an asset despite not being as efficient with the stolen base as he's historically been. FRAA didn't love him at third, though other defensive metrics liked him a lot more, and he was likely in the neighborhood of a solid-average hot corner denizen to boot. If it sounds boring, well, you probably haven't seen him smile.

Ben Revere   CF

Born: 5/3/88   Age: 29   Bats: L   Throws: R   Height: 5'9"   Weight: 175   Entered Pro Ball: Round 1, 2007 Draft (#28 overall)

YEAR	TEAM	LVL	AGE	PA	R	2B	3B	HR	RBI	BB	K	SB	CS	AVG/OBP/SLG	TAv	VORP	BABIP	BRR	FRAA	WARP
2014	PHI	MLB	26	626	71	13	7	2	28	13	49	49	8	.306/.325/.361	.261	24.5	.330	6.5	CF(141): -7.5	1.9
2015	PHI	MLB	27	388	49	13	6	1	26	19	36	24	5	.298/.334/.374	.268	18.0	.328	5.9	LF(56): 2.7 • CF(42): -0.1	2.0
2015	TOR	MLB	27	246	35	9	1	1	19	13	28	7	2	.319/.354/.381	.268	10.9	.355	3.9	LF(56): -7.1 • CF(1): -0.1	0.4
2016	WAS	MLB	28	375	44	9	7	2	24	18	34	14	5	.217/.260/.300	.201	-8.5	.234	3.0	CF(74): -2.2 • LF(25): 0.1	-1.1
2017	ANA	MLB	29	188	22	5	2	1	13	9	19	10	3	.278/.310/.347	.243	4.3	.301	1.3	LF 1 • CF -0	0.3
2018	ANA	MLB	30	317	33	9	3	3	29	16	34	16	4	.282/.319/.365	.253	8.6	.304	3.1	LF 1 • CF 0	1.0

Breakout: 1%   Improve: 48%   Collapse: 1%   Attrition: 14%   MLB: 92%   *Comparables: Juan Pierre, Lance Johnson, Doug Glanville*

An oblique strain cost Revere the season's first month and, apparently, his proper swing mechanics for a lot longer. He again posted an elite contact rate—the most elite of all who appeared at the plate as often as he did, in fact—but the quality of that contact declined precipitously. He spent the next four months after his return popping harmless fly balls at a career-worst rate, helping drive a putrid BABIP that was a full 80 points shy of his career average and knocking his on-base percentage into a territory even his speed couldn't salvage. His is an interesting candidacy for non-tender, trade or expensive back-up outfielder, with any and all outcomes possible.

Victor Robles   CF

Born: 5/19/97   Age: 20   Bats: R   Throws: R   Height: 6'0"   Weight: 185   Entered Pro Ball: International Free Agent, 2013

YEAR	TEAM	LVL	AGE	PA	R	2B	3B	HR	RBI	BB	K	SB	CS	AVG/OBP/SLG	TAv	VORP	BABIP	BRR	FRAA	WARP
2015	AUB	A-	18	167	29	5	4	2	16	8	21	12	4	.343/.424/.479	.334	18.9	.383	1.1	CF(37): 2.6 • RF(1): -0.2	2.2
2016	HAG	A	19	285	48	9	6	5	30	18	38	19	8	.305/.405/.459	.334	33.8	.346	6.2	CF(63): 10.4	4.9
2016	POT	A+	19	198	24	8	2	3	11	14	32	18	5	.262/.354/.387	.284	10.3	.304	-1.0	CF(40): 6.0	1.7
2017	*WAS*	*MLB*	*20*	*250*	*34*	*9*	*2*	*7*	*24*	*12*	*59*	*10*	*4*	*.239/.309/.388*	*.241*	*5.1*	*.285*	*0.6*	*CF 6*	*1.2*
2018	*WAS*	*MLB*	*21*	*403*	*49*	*15*	*3*	*12*	*47*	*21*	*93*	*17*	*7*	*.247/.319/.410*	*.265*	*14.7*	*.291*	*1.9*	*CF 10*	*2.7*

Breakout: 6%   Improve: 17%   Collapse: 0%   Attrition: 5%   MLB: 20%   *Comparables: Byron Buxton, Jose Tabata, Anthony Gose*

We debated writing "VICTOR ROBLES" just like that, all caps. Maybe an exclamation point or three and some fire emojis thrown in there before calling it a day on this comment. But given the sizable gap that remains between theoretical future and realistic present, some further elaboration is probably still warranted. Robles boasts 70-grade wheels with an arm to match, and his improving routes in center portend a plus glove at a premium position. But wait, there's more! A borderline unfair combination of advanced approach, remarkable bat speed and sublime plate coverage gives him a realistic chance to toss a third plus-plus tool into his box. This is where the raw meets the road, however. His production slowed appropriately against much more experienced competition during a second-half trial at High-A, and the power remains nascent. He'll enter 2017 numbering among the game's top prospects, with a chance to vault to the top of the pile by season's end if his bat shows further signs of actualizing. *triple fire emoji*

Pedro Severino   C

Born: 7/20/93   Age: 23   Bats: R   Throws: R   Height: 6'0"   Weight: 215   Entered Pro Ball: International Free Agent, 2010

YEAR	TEAM	LVL	AGE	PA	R	2B	3B	HR	RBI	BB	K	SB	CS	AVG/OBP/SLG	TAv	VORP	BABIP	BRR	FRAA	WARP
2014	POT	A+	20	326	41	15	1	9	36	21	57	2	0	.247/.306/.399	.256	13.3	.276	-0.7	C(93): 2.8	1.6
2015	HAR	AA	21	357	33	13	0	5	34	19	51	1	2	.246/.288/.331	.232	3.8	.276	-1.5	C(91): -0.1	0.4
2015	WAS	MLB	21	4	1	1	0	0	0	0	1	0	0	.250/.250/.500	.233	0.1	.333	0.1	C(2): 0.1	0.0
2016	SYR	AAA	22	317	25	13	0	2	21	19	45	3	4	.271/.316/.337	.238	4.8	.310	-2.0	C(81): -2.2	0.3
2016	WAS	MLB	22	34	6	2	0	2	4	5	3	0	0	.321/.441/.607	.377	6.5	.304	0.9	C(15): -0.2	0.7
2017	*WAS*	*MLB*	*23*	*31*	*3*	*1*	*0*	*1*	*3*	*2*	*6*	*0*	*0*	*.239/.287/.372*	*.237*	*0.7*	*.276*	*-0.1*	*C -1*	*-0.1*
2018	*WAS*	*MLB*	*24*	*260*	*30*	*11*	*0*	*7*	*29*	*17*	*54*	*1*	*1*	*.244/.298/.385*	*.249*	*6.0*	*.281*	*-0.6*	*C -6*	*0.0*

Breakout: 3%   Improve: 25%   Collapse: 4%   Attrition: 18%   MLB: 44%   *Comparables: J.T. Realmuto, J.R. Murphy, Austin Romine*

The Nats' ostensible "backup catcher of the future" rapped on the door a couple times more in 2016, logging another 34 (startlingly productive) plate appearances across three different stints with the big club. The bat continued to play light for his minor-league level, however, and questions persist as to whether there'll be enough juice in it to carry him into his expected role. His physicality behind the plate continued to impress, though his defensive numbers didn't exactly jive with the consistent plus grades evaluators hang on his glove, thus adding another layer of uncertainty to the profile.

YEAR	TEAM	P. COUNT	FRM RUNS	BLK RUNS	THRW RUNS	TOT RUNS
2015	HAR	12147	-1.8	0.3	1.1	-0.4
2016	WAS	1422	-0.7	0.3	0.1	-0.3
2017	*WAS*	*1171*	*-0.7*	*0.0*	*0.0*	*-0.7*
2018	*WAS*	*9837*	*-5.6*	*-0.2*	*-0.3*	*-6.2*

Juan Soto   RF

Born: 10/25/98   Age: 18   Bats: L   Throws: L   Height: 6'1"   Weight: 185   Entered Pro Ball: International Free Agent, 2015

YEAR	TEAM	LVL	AGE	PA	R	2B	3B	HR	RBI	BB	K	SB	CS	AVG/OBP/SLG	TAv	VORP	BABIP	BRR	FRAA	WARP
2016	AUB	A-	17	24	3	3	0	0	1	3	4	0	0	.429/.500/.571	.409	4.0	.529	-0.1	RF(6): 0.6 • CF(1): -0.1	0.5
2017	*WAS*	*MLB*	*18*	*250*	*22*	*10*	*1*	*6*	*27*	*14*	*77*	*0*	*0*	*.209/.256/.340*	*.206*	*-7.0*	*.279*	*-0.4*	*RF -0 • CF -0*	*-0.8*
2018	*WAS*	*MLB*	*19*	*240*	*25*	*9*	*1*	*7*	*25*	*13*	*74*	*0*	*0*	*.212/.256/.351*	*.220*	*-5.4*	*.279*	*-0.5*	*RF 0 • CF 0*	*-0.6*

Breakout: 0%   Improve: 0%   Collapse: 0%   Attrition: 0%   MLB: 0%   *Comparables: Raul Mondesi, Wilmer Flores*

"Let us dream for today and for tomorrow," the great Maya Angelou once recited. "Let us dare to dream." We don't *think* she was talking about Soto when she penned that verse, but she never did confirm that she wasn't. It was another year, and it was another teenaged J2 breakout for the Nationals, who appeared to hit a potential jackpot when Victor Robles punished short-season pitching in 2015. This season it was Soto's turn, as he racked up the Gulf Coast League's fourth-best OPS despite playing in his stateside debut as one of the league's youngest regulars. Both his hit and power tools whisper of plus potential, though if big-league pitchers are having a hard time confirming it with their own ears it is because we'll likely endure the next presidential election before any of them make his acquaintance in Nationals Park.

Andrew Stevenson   OF

Born: 6/1/94   Age: 23   Bats: L   Throws: L   Height: 6'0"   Weight: 185   Entered Pro Ball: Round 2, 2015 Draft (#58 overall)

YEAR	TEAM	LVL	AGE	PA	R	2B	3B	HR	RBI	BB	K	SB	CS	AVG/OBP/SLG	TAv	VORP	BABIP	BRR	FRAA	WARP
2015	AUB	A-	21	80	11	1	2	0	9	7	12	7	3	.361/.413/.431	.294	6.3	.426	1.2	CF(16): 3.0 • LF(3): 1.6	1.1
2015	HAG	A	21	153	28	3	2	1	16	8	16	16	4	.285/.338/.358	.282	10.7	.311	2.7	CF(35): 0.7	1.2
2016	POT	A+	22	300	37	12	8	1	18	24	44	27	9	.304/.359/.418	.287	20.8	.358	3.1	CF(60): 1.9 • LF(6): -0.9	2.2
2016	HAR	AA	22	280	38	11	2	2	16	20	51	12	5	.246/.302/.328	.237	-2.3	.299	-2.9	CF(36): 4.3 • LF(28): 2.0	0.4
2017	*WAS*	*MLB*	*23*	*250*	*31*	*9*	*2*	*5*	*21*	*15*	*59*	*10*	*4*	*.237/.286/.357*	*.225*	*0.9*	*.292*	*0.8*	*CF 3 • LF 1*	*0.5*
2018	*WAS*	*MLB*	*24*	*318*	*34*	*12*	*3*	*6*	*32*	*19*	*72*	*13*	*5*	*.242/.291/.366*	*.242*	*3.9*	*.294*	*1.6*	*CF 4 • LF 1*	*1.0*

Breakout: 2%   Improve: 7%   Collapse: 1%   Attrition: 5%   MLB: 9%   *Comparables: Logan Schafer, Charlie Blackmon, Matt Szczur*

Stevenson's glove got him drafted in the second round, and it remains his calling card as a pro. His 70-grade speed, athleticism and body control give him all the tools to thrive as an above-average defender at the highest level. That is, if his bat allows it. A steep path and lack of lower-half oomph cripples his swing's potential to produce any power, though he's got the wheels and bat-to-ball to slash and dash with reasonable effectiveness. His future role will be heavily tied to his BABIP and "quality reserve outfielder" currently occupies the fattest part of his possible outcomes bell curve as he likely heads back to Double-A in 2017.

Michael Taylor   CF

Born: 3/26/91   Age: 26   Bats: R   Throws: R   Height: 6'3"   Weight: 210   Entered Pro Ball: Round 6, 2009 Draft (#172 overall)

YEAR	TEAM	LVL	AGE	PA	R	2B	3B	HR	RBI	BB	K	SB	CS	AVG/OBP/SLG	TAv	VORP	BABIP	BRR	FRAA	WARP
2014	HAR	AA	23	441	74	17	2	22	61	50	130	34	8	.313/.396/.539	.324	44.9	.421	3.5	CF(87): 20.5 • RF(1): 0.6	7.0
2014	SYR	AAA	23	52	7	3	1	1	3	7	14	3	1	.227/.333/.409	.259	2.4	.310	0.8	CF(12): 2.5	0.5
2014	WAS	MLB	23	43	5	3	0	1	5	3	17	0	2	.205/.279/.359	.235	-0.8	.333	-0.8	CF(10): -0.2 • RF(5): 0.4	-0.1
2015	SYR	AAA	24	32	4	1	0	1	4	4	10	2	1	.385/.452/.538	.372	4.9	.563	0.2	CF(6): -1.5 • RF(1): 0.1	0.4
2015	WAS	MLB	24	511	49	15	2	14	63	35	158	16	3	.229/.282/.358	.240	3.5	.311	-0.4	CF(96): 0.9 • LF(38): 4.2	0.9
2016	SYR	AAA	25	130	17	5	1	1	9	12	33	7	1	.205/.285/.291	.234	2.3	.277	2.2	CF(28): 0.4	0.3
2016	WAS	MLB	25	237	28	11	0	7	16	14	77	14	3	.231/.278/.376	.243	3.7	.319	0.7	CF(64): 3.4 • RF(5): -0.3	0.7
2017	WAS	MLB	26	292	37	11	1	10	32	24	94	12	3	.230/.296/.387	.245	5.2	.314	1.4	CF 2 • LF 2	1.1
2018	WAS	MLB	27	347	43	13	1	12	42	31	111	15	4	.230/.302/.396	.256	7.8	.310	0.4	CF 3 • LF 2	1.5

Breakout: 7%   Improve: 56%   Collapse: 11%   Attrition: 21%   MLB: 91%   Comparables: Drew Stubbs, Curtis Granderson, Junior Lake

Handed the keys to center field by Ben Revere's crotchety oblique in April, Taylor crashed his everyday playing time into a ditch somewhere in the outskirts of Bethesda. He hit just .183/.218/.298 during Revere's absence, posting a bottom-of-the-barrel whiff rate on pitches in the zone en route to a strikeout in nearly a third of his trips to the batter's box. He was able to do some damage when he lofted one, but his contact was both too rare and too often rolled-over to generate consistent positive outcomes. A brief run of coherence in June wasn't enough to forestall demotion in July, and his subsequent International League effort yielded more of the same. The speed, semi-interesting pop and solid glove up the middle all combine to give him a big-league profile, but at 26 the bat still looks too soft for everyday play.

Trea Turner   SS

Born: 6/30/93   Age: 24   Bats: R   Throws: R   Height: 6'1"   Weight: 185   Entered Pro Ball: Round 1, 2014 Draft (#13 overall)

YEAR	TEAM	LVL	AGE	PA	R	2B	3B	HR	RBI	BB	K	SB	CS	AVG/OBP/SLG	TAv	VORP	BABIP	BRR	FRAA	WARP
2014	EUG	A-	21	105	14	2	0	1	2	11	19	9	1	.228/.324/.283	.271	4.9	.278	0.7	SS(14): 1.4	0.7
2014	FTW	A	21	216	31	14	2	4	22	24	48	14	3	.369/.447/.529	.338	28.1	.478	2.8	SS(36): 0.8	3.0
2015	SAN	AA	22	254	31	13	3	5	35	24	48	11	4	.322/.385/.471	.297	20.9	.389	1.6	SS(57): 5.5	2.9
2015	HAR	AA	22	41	6	4	1	0	4	1	8	4	0	.359/.366/.513	.303	3.6	.438	0.2	SS(10): -1.0	0.3
2015	SYR	AAA	22	205	31	7	3	3	15	13	41	14	2	.314/.353/.431	.291	16.7	.381	2.0	SS(44): 4.9 • 2B(2): -0.3	2.2
2015	WAS	MLB	22	44	5	1	0	1	1	4	12	2	2	.225/.295/.325	.259	1.3	.296	0.1	2B(12): 0.6 • SS(6): -0.1	0.2
2016	SYR	AAA	23	371	61	22	8	6	33	37	72	25	2	.302/.370/.471	.310	40.0	.369	6.1	SS(71): 8.7 • CF(6): 0.9	5.1
2016	WAS	MLB	23	324	53	14	8	13	40	14	59	33	6	.342/.370/.567	.341	42.1	.388	5.9	CF(45): -1.9 • 2B(30): -1.0	4.0
2017	WAS	MLB	24	594	86	26	7	18	64	43	138	34	6	.283/.333/.456	.281	43.9	.344	5.5	SS 13	5.5
2018	WAS	MLB	25	573	73	26	7	18	74	44	134	33	6	.284/.341/.464	.294	46.4	.347	6.7	SS 13	6.4

Breakout: 3%   Improve: 39%   Collapse: 15%   Attrition: 23%   MLB: 91%   Comparables: Josh Rutledge, Starling Marte, Brad Miller

Nuke don't know, man. What Trea Turner just did there? That is how you announce your presence with authority. The shortstop-turned-second-baseman-turned-center-fielder raked at Triple-A to start the season, then just kept right on raking like it was nothing once he got the call. He proved surprisingly adept at turning on inside pitches with authority, crushing one fewer homer in his 324 big-league plate appearances than he'd hit in over 900 as a professional before 2016. His double-plus speed translated, too, driving the best rate of steals-per-plate-appearance of anyone in the majors not named Billy Hamilton. Inconsistent routes while learning center field on the fly and some mild vulnerability to curveballs made for just about the only notable chinks in this rookie's armor. The Rookie of the Year runner-up will head into 2017 as one of the most dynamic young players in the National League—even if he's not quite as young as you'd think.

Drew Ward   3B

Born: 11/25/94 Age: 22   Bats: L   Throws: R   Height: 6'3"   Weight: 215   Entered Pro Ball: Round 3, 2013 Draft (#105 overall)

YEAR	TEAM	LVL	AGE	PA	R	2B	3B	HR	RBI	BB	K	SB	CS	AVG/OBP/SLG	TAv	VORP	BABIP	BRR	FRAA	WARP
2014	HAG	A	19	478	45	26	3	10	73	42	121	2	1	.269/.341/.413	.260	8.5	.353	-5.0	3B(92): -0.8	0.8
2015	POT	A+	20	426	47	19	2	6	47	39	110	2	1	.249/.327/.358	.256	9.2	.333	-0.9	3B(95): -3.1	0.7
2016	POT	A+	21	268	36	16	0	11	32	34	70	0	1	.278/.377/.491	.310	19.7	.353	-2.1	3B(49): 1.6	2.2
2016	HAR	AA	21	203	19	7	0	3	24	22	51	0	1	.219/.310/.309	.230	1.0	.288	0.9	3B(51): -3.9	-0.3
2017	WAS	MLB	22	250	24	10	0	7	28	20	82	0	0	.212/.282/.350	.222	-2.7	.294	-0.5	3B -1 • 1B 0	-0.4
2018	WAS	MLB	23	353	41	14	1	11	40	29	115	0	0	.218/.289/.373	.242	0.4	.299	-0.9	3B -1 • 1B 0	0.0

Breakout: 4%   Improve: 14%   Collapse: 3%   Attrition: 18%   MLB: 20%   Comparables: Mat Gamel, Will Middlebrooks, Alex Liddi

Ward took some baby steps in the first half towards alleviating some of the concerns scouts have long harbored about his ability to bring raw power into games. The production earned him a promotion to Double-A, but as babies are wont to do, he tumbled hard back down to the turf. He's a stiff defender at third, and while the will isn't in question, there's a general consensus that moving off the cold corner is a when, not an if. The offensive ceiling remains up in the air as well, and it'll determine whether there's a big-league future here or not. His struggles against southpaws snowballed to the tune of a .197/.286/.279 line across both levels, and the rainmakers he hit at High-A dried up quickly against more advanced arms. Just 22 when play resumes, the former third-rounder will likely head back to Harrisburg with something to prove in 2017.

Jayson Werth   LF

Born: 5/20/79   Age: 38   Bats: R   Throws: R   Height: 6'5"   Weight: 235   Entered Pro Ball: Round 1, 1997 Draft (#22 overall)

YEAR	TEAM	LVL	AGE	PA	R	2B	3B	HR	RBI	BB	K	SB	CS	AVG/OBP/SLG	TAv	VORP	BABIP	BRR	FRAA	WARP
2014	WAS	MLB	35	629	85	37	1	16	82	83	113	9	1	.292/.394/.455	.319	47.1	.343	2.5	RF(139): -1.4	5.1
2015	SYR	AAA	36	26	2	2	0	0	5	1	2	1	0	.391/.423/.478	.343	2.8	.409	0.0	LF(5): -0.5	0.2
2015	WAS	MLB	36	378	51	16	1	12	42	38	84	0	1	.221/.302/.384	.254	7.2	.253	1.9	LF(76): -8.6 • RF(14): -2.0	-0.4
2016	WAS	MLB	37	606	84	28	0	21	69	71	139	5	1	.244/.335/.417	.271	23.9	.288	4.1	LF(131): -7.8 • RF(2): 0.0	1.7
2017	WAS	MLB	38	548	72	25	1	17	60	63	118	5	1	.251/.342/.415	.271	25.5	.296	-0.5	LF -11	0.7
2018	WAS	MLB	39	482	62	21	0	15	58	54	107	3	1	.244/.333/.408	.273	19.6	.288	1.8	LF -10	1.0

Breakout: 0%   Improve: 20%   Collapse: 11%   Attrition: 20%   MLB: 74%   Comparables: Raul Ibanez, Mark DeRosa, Monte Irvin

The thing about werewolves, if you're in the market for a new look and moniker, is that they're kind of not the awesomest monsters. They're scary for a while and all, but just like the rest of us they get old and they get weak. Werth rebounded back into positive WARP territory in 2016, but it looked more like a dead-dog bounce than anything to howl about. After creeping down into the teens for a few years there, his whiff rate has jumped back up over twenty percent over the past couple seasons, albeit as a product of working increasingly deep counts—nobody saw more than his 4.6 pitches per plate appearance last year—rather than uptick in fruitless flails at hittable heaters. While the on-base ability remains an overall asset, and he did hit 20 homers again (who didn't?), Werth has slunk into extremely-well-paid, lefty-mashing, fourth-outfielder territory. His performance against right-handers continued a frolic in the gutter that began in earnest in 2015, and his defense, while better than the prior season's Willinghamiam effort, still cost the team more than eight runs. He'll pull down his final $21 million paycheck this season before stepping out into the pale moonlight of free agency at 39.

Ryan Zimmerman   1B

Born: 9/28/84   Age: 32   Bats: R   Throws: R   Height: 6'3"   Weight: 225   Entered Pro Ball: Round 1, 2005 Draft (#4 overall)

YEAR	TEAM	LVL	AGE	PA	R	2B	3B	HR	RBI	BB	K	SB	CS	AVG/OBP/SLG	TAv	VORP	BABIP	BRR	FRAA	WARP
2014	WAS	MLB	29	240	26	19	1	5	38	22	37	0	0	.280/.342/.449	.294	10.0	.313	-3.1	LF(30): -0.3 • 3B(23): 0.9	1.2
2015	WAS	MLB	30	390	43	25	1	16	73	33	79	1	0	.249/.308/.465	.283	12.8	.268	0.3	1B(93): -8.4 • LF(1): -0.0	0.5
2016	WAS	MLB	31	467	60	18	1	15	46	29	104	4	1	.218/.272/.370	.240	-0.5	.248	4.1	1B(114): -2.3	-0.3
2017	WAS	MLB	32	545	62	25	1	21	71	47	117	3	1	.247/.312/.430	.263	11.4	.279	-0.8	1B -6	0.1
2018	WAS	MLB	33	441	56	20	1	17	58	38	97	1	0	.244/.310/.431	.271	10.4	.276	0.2	1B -5	0.6

Breakout: 4%   Improve: 34%   Collapse: 5%   Attrition: 11%   MLB: 87%   Comparables: Michael Cuddyer, Kendrys Morales, Xavier Nady

Outside of a brief power surge in May, Zimmerman never quite managed to get it going in the season's first half. And then, well, things got typical. He missed time with an oblique issue. He came back for a half-dozen games, took a fastball off the wrist and missed more time. By the time the dust settled, he'd posted a below-average TAv for the first time in his dozen-year career. And he earned it the ugly way: he chased more secondary stuff out of the zone and he swung through more heaters inside of it. It's not a combination that portends good things for a bat-dependent and injury-prone hitter hurtling towards his mid-30s, especially one on the hook for another three years and $48 million.

PITCHERS

Bronson Arroyo   RHP

Born: 2/24/77   Age: 40   Bats: R   Throws: R   Height: 6'4"   Weight: 190   Entered Pro Ball: Round 3, 1995 Draft (#69 overall)

YEAR	TEAM	LVL	AGE	W	L	SV	G	GS	IP	H	HR	BB/9	K/9	K	GB%	BABIP	WHIP	ERA	FIP	DRA	VORP	WARP	cFIP	MPH
2014	ARI	MLB	37	7	4	0	14	14	86	92	10	2.0	4.9	47	55%	.295	1.29	4.08	4.29	4.91	-0.7	-0.1	111	88.5
2017	WAS	MLB	40	2	2	0	6	6	37	37	6	2.9	6.1	25	50%	.293	1.32	4.86	4.94	5.72	-0.6	-0.1	135	
2018	WAS	MLB	41	7	10	0	23	23	133²	135	23	3.0	6.1	91	50%	.294	1.34	5.01	5.41	5.90	-5.2	-0.5	140	

Breakout: 16%   Improve: 30%   Collapse: 14%   Attrition: 8%   MLB: 64%   Comparables: Derek Lowe, Tim Hudson, R.A. Dickey

Not many players can lay claim to receiving a paycheck from four different organizations since throwing their most recent big-league pitch. Well, not many players can tickle a guitar string as sensually as Bronson Arroyo, either. A coincidence, you say? Hairs from opposite corners of the right-hander's coiffure? Not so fast. A good busker can hustle upwards of $40 an hour—roughly five-and-a-half times the minimum wage—during a prime time subway set in our nation's capital. And if you prorate things into baseball's economic scale you're looking at something in the range of $2.8 million a year. Not bad!

Admittedly, he who was once cornrowed racked up quite the medical bill this year. There was the final push of his Tommy John recovery when he first signed. There were the associated tests to diagnose, and subsequent physical therapies to treat, a torn rotator cuff suffered in spring training. Then, finally, the stem cell injection to which he treated his pitching elbow in the summer's waning days—after just 9 2/3 innings of Rookie ball. But given the paltry minor-league contract he signed, we may still comfortably deduce that the Nats got themselves some quality aural clubhouse chemistry on the relative cheap. In an era of finding value at the margins, that's a decisive win. Little is known about what the soon-to-be 40-year-old's waning days have in store, but a cushy armchair in a big-league clubhouse beats the morbid futurism of L'Enfant Plaza station any way you slice it.

Matt Belisle   RHP

Born: 6/6/80   Age: 37   Bats: R   Throws: R   Height: 6'3"   Weight: 230   Entered Pro Ball: Round 2, 1998 Draft (#52 overall)

YEAR	TEAM	LVL	AGE	W	L	SV	G	GS	IP	H	HR	BB/9	K/9	K	GB%	BABIP	WHIP	ERA	FIP	DRA	VORP	WARP	cFIP	MPH
2014	COL	MLB	34	4	7	0	66	1	64²	74	5	2.6	6.0	43	48%	.322	1.44	4.87	3.71	4.97	-3.4	-0.4	110	94.2
2015	SLN	MLB	35	1	1	0	34	0	33²	34	1	4.0	6.7	25	55%	.314	1.46	2.67	3.67	4.46	0.9	0.1	108	93.5
2016	WAS	MLB	36	0	0	0	40	0	46	43	2	1.4	6.3	32	49%	.285	1.09	1.76	2.88	4.60	1.9	0.2	104	93.9
2017	WAS	MLB	37	2	1	1	43	0	45²	46	7	2.9	7.2	37	46%	.307	1.33	4.65	4.62	5.45	-1.5	-0.2	125	
2018	WAS	MLB	38	2	1	0	33	0	34	36	6	3.0	6.8	26	46%	.308	1.38	4.89	5.28	5.73	-2.2	-0.2	132	

Breakout: 17%   Improve: 31%   Collapse: 34%   Attrition: 19%   MLB: 76%   *Comparables: Joe Borowski, Jason Isringhausen, LaTroy Hawkins*

After a nice run as the model of durable middle relief in Colorado, Belisle has now missed significant chunks of consecutive seasons since returning to sea level. This time, a strained calf knocked him out for nearly two months, but when the cruel ravages of time weren't feasting on his aging lower half, he looked sharp. He started throwing his slider harder, tighter and much more often to left-handed hitters, and his usual equal-opportunity production evolved into a surprising grounder-heavy reverse split. However, his situational deployment didn't keep up with the progression, and right-handers teed off to force one of the largest DRA-ERA splits of any pitcher in the majors. Still, the old dog's new trick may just be enough to extend his innings-eating career, provided his body can withstand the rigors of at least part of another season.

Sean Burnett   LHP

Born: 9/17/82   Age: 34   Bats: L   Throws: L   Height: 5'11"   Weight: 185   Entered Pro Ball: Round 1, 2000 Draft (#19 overall)

YEAR	TEAM	LVL	AGE	W	L	SV	G	GS	IP	H	HR	BB/9	K/9	K	GB%	BABIP	WHIP	ERA	FIP	DRA	VORP	WARP	cFIP	MPH
2014	ANA	MLB	31	0	0	0	3	0	0²	1	0	0.0	0.0	0	67%	.333	1.50	13.50	3.16	3.90	0.0	0.0	100	88.4
2016	ROC	AAA	33	0	3	3	29	0	29¹	20	1	2.1	5.5	18	66%	.218	0.92	2.15	3.10	4.05	3.0	0.3	92	
2016	WAS	MLB	33	0	0	0	10	0	5²	5	1	1.6	4.8	3	44%	.235	1.06	3.18	4.95	5.04	0.0	0.0	108	90.0
2017	WAS	MLB	34	2	1	1	35	0	36²	37	6	3.3	6.5	27	50%	.301	1.38	4.88	5.01	5.74	-2.1	-0.2	132	
2018	WAS	MLB	35	2	0	1	35	0	30²	33	6	3.9	7.1	24	50%	.315	1.52	5.36	5.79	6.31	-4.1	-0.4	144	

Breakout: 19%   Improve: 30%   Collapse: 12%   Attrition: 4%   MLB: 54%   *Comparables: Mike MacDougal, Blaine Boyer, Dale Thayer*

Tenacity, thy name is Sean Burnett. Since his first stint in Washington ended after a successful 2012 campaign, Burnett missed almost an entire year with bone spurs in his pitching elbow, then most of the next two seasons recovering from a second Tommy John surgery. A rousing game of organizational hopscotch ensued, as he pulled Triple-A duty in Oklahoma City, Gwinnett and Rochester before journeying to Syracuse in August. Then, finally, incredibly, he once again toed a big-league rubber ten times following a September call-up. Minor-league lefties compiled a measly .164/.203/.236 line against him and he flashed a more frequent slider to better battle the ones he saw in The Show. He's 34 now, but a spring training invite and battle royale for the coveted LOOGY role in someone's bullpen is a likely next stop on his most recent comeback tour.

A.J. Cole   RHP

Born: 1/5/92   Age: 25   Bats: R   Throws: R   Height: 6'5"   Weight: 215   Entered Pro Ball: Round 4, 2010 Draft (#116 overall)

YEAR	TEAM	LVL	AGE	W	L	SV	G	GS	IP	H	HR	BB/9	K/9	K	GB%	BABIP	WHIP	ERA	FIP	DRA	VORP	WARP	cFIP	MPH
2014	HAR	AA	22	6	3	0	14	14	71	79	1	1.9	7.7	61	40%	.342	1.32	2.92	2.58	2.82	19.0	2.0	91	
2014	SYR	AAA	22	7	0	0	11	11	63	69	9	2.4	7.1	50	40%	.316	1.37	3.43	4.48	3.82	13.5	1.3	100	
2015	WAS	MLB	23	0	0	1	3	1	9¹	14	1	1.0	8.7	9	41%	.394	1.61	5.79	2.95	4.37	0.4	0.0	100	93.5
2015	SYR	AAA	23	5	6	0	21	19	105²	91	9	2.9	6.5	76	36%	.256	1.18	3.15	3.90	6.45	-13.7	-1.4	115	
2016	SYR	AAA	24	8	8	0	22	22	124²	131	16	2.5	7.9	109	43%	.310	1.33	4.26	3.95	4.20	15.8	1.6	98	
2016	WAS	MLB	24	1	2	0	8	8	38¹	37	7	3.3	9.2	39	32%	.283	1.33	5.17	4.78	4.93	1.8	0.2	114	93.4
2017	WAS	MLB	25	5	6	0	36	13	89	93	12	3.4	7.2	72	59%	.296	1.42	4.69	4.55	4.99	1.2	0.1	100	
2018	WAS	MLB	26	6	6	0	51	16	133	114	18	4.3	10.0	148	59%	.310	1.34	4.23	4.55	4.93	6.6	0.7	112	

Breakout: 16%   Improve: 26%   Collapse: 30%   Attrition: 41%   MLB: 71%   *Comparables: Dillon Gee, Colin Rea, Manny Banuelos*

Cole's career has been an unending series of baby steps, and it wasn't until the end of the season that he was finally allowed the opportunity to prove he deserved to wander the swamps of D.C. on regular rest. Assigned to Triple-A for a third consecutive year, Cole's production at the level stagnated as he morphed into a more hittable version of himself despite modest gains with his whiff and walk rates. The softer performance was perhaps a bit misleading, however, as he appeared to take a sought-after leap forward with his slider that carried over into an above-average whiff rate against big-league hitters. He'll enter 2017 with a case to state for a season-long rotation spot.

Erick Fedde   RHP

Born: 2/25/93   Age: 24   Bats: R   Throws: R   Height: 6'4"   Weight: 180   Entered Pro Ball: Round 1, 2014 Draft (#18 overall)

YEAR	TEAM	LVL	AGE	W	L	SV	G	GS	IP	H	HR	BB/9	K/9	K	GB%	BABIP	WHIP	ERA	FIP	DRA	VORP	WARP	cFIP	MPH
2015	AUB	A-	22	4	1	0	8	8	35	38	1	2.1	9.3	36	56%	.346	1.31	2.57	2.60	1.68	14.0	1.5	82	
2015	HAG	A	22	1	2	0	6	6	29	24	1	2.5	7.1	23	52%	.274	1.10	4.34	3.48	3.57	5.3	0.6	96	
2016	POT	A+	23	6	4	0	18	17	91²	85	7	1.9	9.3	95	51%	.316	1.13	2.85	3.22	1.61	39.2	4.0	73	
2016	HAR	AA	23	2	1	0	5	5	29¹	33	1	3.1	8.6	28	46%	.360	1.47	3.99	3.02	4.09	3.3	0.4	94	
2017	WAS	MLB	24	6	6	0	19	19	95²	96	13	3.3	7.2	76	52%	.314	1.38	4.48	4.53	5.08	5.1	0.5	121	
2018	WAS	MLB	25	8	10	0	29	29	179²	170	25	4.5	9.2	184	52%	.325	1.45	4.54	4.90	5.15	6.7	0.7	122	

Breakout: 13%   Improve: 17%   Collapse: 12%   Attrition: 23%   MLB: 32%   *Comparables: Dillon Overton, Sean Manaea, Steven Matz*

The Nationals operate with a loose hand around looser elbow ligaments, and Fedde's on the increasingly not-so-short list of home-grown Tommy John survivors poised to join Washington's pitching staff. More than two years removed from the scalpel, Fedde not only pitched a full season, but put an exclamation point on it by striking out 12 in his final start for Double-A Harrisburg. His plus fastball hops late, and he commands both a slider and change startlingly well for a pitcher so recently shelved. It's a complimentary three-pitch mix that can hoist him and his durable frame into the middle of a big-league rotation for a long time to come—and he could be reunited with his high school teammate, Bryce Harper, in Washington by the middle of the 2017 season.

Gio Gonzalez   LHP

Born: 9/19/85   Age: 31   Bats: R   Throws: L   Height: 6'0"   Weight: 205   Entered Pro Ball: Round 1, 2004 Draft (#38 overall)

YEAR	TEAM	LVL	AGE	W	L	SV	G	GS	IP	H	HR	BB/9	K/9	K	GB%	BABIP	WHIP	ERA	FIP	DRA	VORP	WARP	cFIP	MPH
2014	WAS	MLB	28	10	10	0	27	27	158²	134	10	3.2	9.2	162	48%	.294	1.20	3.57	3.00	3.89	16.7	1.8	92	94.5
2015	WAS	MLB	29	11	8	0	31	31	175²	181	8	3.5	8.7	169	55%	.341	1.42	3.79	3.08	3.40	32.8	3.5	93	94.4
2016	WAS	MLB	30	11	11	0	32	32	177¹	179	19	3.0	8.7	171	49%	.316	1.34	4.57	3.80	3.26	41.4	4.3	95	93.7
2017	WAS	MLB	31	12	10	0	29	29	182²	164	21	3.3	9.3	189	51%	.293	1.26	3.78	3.80	4.09	22.1	2.3	94	
2018	WAS	MLB	32	12	11	0	31	31	199	167	22	3.1	9.0	199	51%	.296	1.18	3.70	3.97	4.30	27.0	2.8	98	

Breakout: 10%   Improve: 37%   Collapse: 31%   Attrition: 10%   MLB: 92%   *Comparables: Clay Buchholz, John Lackey, Adam Wainwright*

Gonzalez's spring training pirate shag portended a mutiny against his peripherals, though to be fair to the numbers, he earned at least some of the not-so-jolly rogerin'. He maintained two-seam dominance, but probably could have ramped up the pitch's deployment all the more. Batters crushed his four-seam fastball—down two full ticks at the season's outset—and made better, more frequent contact against his secondaries. His groundball rate retreated, and more of his pitches found the bleachers than ever before. Coupled with a poor effort out of the stretch, his DRA and ERA wound up diverging by a full run and a quarter. The Nats made the no-brainer decision to pick up his $12 million option for 2017, and another 180 innings would trigger a vesting clause to guarantee that same salary in 2018. However, that threshold may prove elusive even in another campaign of tip-top health. His inefficiency helped drive a career-worst 5.5 innings per start in 2016.

Shawn Kelley   RHP

Born: 4/26/84   Age: 33   Bats: R   Throws: R   Height: 6'2"   Weight: 230   Entered Pro Ball: Round 13, 2007 Draft (#405 overall)

YEAR	TEAM	LVL	AGE	W	L	SV	G	GS	IP	H	HR	BB/9	K/9	K	GB%	BABIP	WHIP	ERA	FIP	DRA	VORP	WARP	cFIP	MPH
2014	NYA	MLB	30	3	6	4	59	0	51²	45	5	3.5	11.7	67	36%	.315	1.26	4.53	3.04	3.15	7.7	0.8	88	95.6
2015	SDN	MLB	31	2	2	0	53	0	51¹	41	4	2.6	11.0	63	44%	.301	1.09	2.45	2.60	2.93	10.2	1.1	82	94.4
2016	WAS	MLB	32	3	2	7	67	0	58	41	9	1.7	12.4	80	37%	.258	0.90	2.64	3.01	2.29	17.3	1.8	71	95.2
2017	WAS	MLB	33	3	3	38	56	0	59	51	9	3.1	11.2	74	39%	.294	1.20	3.51	3.82	3.92	6.5	0.7	82	
2018	WAS	MLB	34	3	1	37	59	0	62²	50	9	3.0	11.1	77	39%	.303	1.13	3.52	3.77	4.10	7.1	0.7	87	

Breakout: 19%   Improve: 42%   Collapse: 27%   Attrition: 12%   MLB: 88%   *Comparables: Glen Perkins, Frank Francisco, Sergio Romo*

Kelley dodged a bullet after leaving the regular season finale with a bad-looking injury that didn't turn out too bad after all. And that's good for the Nationals on two fronts: he's under contract for two more years, and he's evolved into a damn dependable reliever to boot. He posted career-best whiff and walk rates last season, turning in a top-ten performance by DRA among pitchers who either matched or bettered his 58 innings. Righties in particular felt his wrath, struggling mightily to find his fastball and whiffing in nearly 40 percent of their plate appearances. Sure he'll give up an ill-timed dinger on occasion, and durability has never been a strong suit—last year's modest innings tally marked a career high, after all—but he seemed to take well to the stability of his first multi-year deal. Kelley figures to handle high-leverage situations, whether they are in the ninth or not, for the Nats again in 2017.

Mat Latos   RHP

Born: 12/9/87   Age: 29   Bats: R   Throws: R   Height: 6'6"   Weight: 245   Entered Pro Ball: Round 11, 2006 Draft (#333 overall)

YEAR	TEAM	LVL	AGE	W	L	SV	G	GS	IP	H	HR	BB/9	K/9	K	GB%	BABIP	WHIP	ERA	FIP	DRA	VORP	WARP	cFIP	MPH
2014	LOU	AAA	26	2	0	0	4	4	19¹	17	1	3.3	6.1	13	43%	.281	1.24	2.33	3.77	5.22	1.2	0.1	102	
2014	CIN	MLB	26	5	5	0	16	16	102¹	92	9	2.3	6.5	74	41%	.269	1.15	3.25	3.62	5.31	-5.4	-0.6	116	94.1
2015	MIA	MLB	27	4	7	0	16	16	88¹	85	8	2.5	8.0	79	45%	.297	1.25	4.48	3.43	4.16	8.8	0.9	99	94.8
2015	LAN	MLB	27	0	3	0	6	5	24¹	31	3	2.2	6.7	18	52%	.354	1.52	6.66	4.02	4.25	2.2	0.2	100	95.3
2015	ANA	MLB	27	0	0	0	2	0	3²	4	2	2.5	7.4	3	42%	.200	1.36	4.91	9.38	4.33	0.3	0.0	99	96.2
2016	CHA	MLB	28	6	2	0	11	11	60¹	63	10	3.7	4.8	32	46%	.269	1.46	4.62	5.49	5.74	-2.7	-0.3	119	93.3
2016	SYR	AAA	28	1	0	0	3	3	17	16	1	3.7	5.3	10	52%	.283	1.35	1.06	3.99	6.95	-3.0	-0.3	109	
2016	WAS	MLB	28	1	1	0	6	1	9²	11	1	4.7	9.3	10	38%	.357	1.66	6.52	4.01	5.01	0.3	0.0	119	94.7
2017	WAS	MLB	29	5	6	0	16	16	91²	86	14	3.2	7.7	78	41%	.296	1.30	4.59	4.59	5.36	2.1	0.2	125	
2018	WAS	MLB	30	7	9	0	23	23	133	131	22	3.7	7.7	114	41%	.305	1.39	4.86	5.24	5.68	-1.7	-0.2	133	

Breakout: 16%   Improve: 35%   Collapse: 24%   Attrition: 12%   MLB: 89%   *Comparables: Andrew Cashner, Gavin Floyd, Daniel Cabrera*

After receiving his walking papers from the White Sox in June, Latos joined the Nats as his seventh team in an eight-year career, putting him on pace to rack up more lives than Cat Latos. The four-year run in which he averaged north of four WARP annually continues to fade further into the rearview, as it's been barely a blip in his past three seasons. He managed to find a couple missing ticks on his fastball after converting to the pen, but it didn't help his effectiveness. His stuff continued a broad decline, with fewer empty swings against each pitch in his arsenal. He's got cool tattoos and age still somehow on his side, but it's unclear if that combination will be enough to overcome the performance and character issues that have become pre-existing conditions of late.

Jonathan Papelbon   RHP

Born: 11/23/80 Age: 36 Bats: R Throws: R Height: 6'5" Weight: 230 Entered Pro Ball: Round 4, 2003 Draft (#114 overall)

YEAR	TEAM	LVL	AGE	W	L	SV	G	GS	IP	H	HR	BB/9	K/9	K	GB%	BABIP	WHIP	ERA	FIP	DRA	VORP	WARP	cFIP	MPH
2014	PHI	MLB	33	2	3	39	66	0	66¹	45	2	2.0	8.5	63	44%	.247	0.90	2.04	2.50	3.67	6.1	0.7	93	93.8
2015	PHI	MLB	34	2	1	17	37	0	39²	31	3	1.8	9.1	40	53%	.267	0.98	1.59	3.04	3.47	5.5	0.6	90	93.8
2015	WAS	MLB	34	2	2	7	22	0	23²	22	4	1.5	6.1	16	50%	.250	1.10	3.04	4.89	3.29	3.7	0.4	91	94.3
2016	WAS	MLB	35	2	4	19	37	0	35	37	3	3.6	8.0	31	36%	.327	1.46	4.37	3.73	4.71	1.0	0.1	113	94.1
2017	*WAS*	*MLB*	*36*	*2*	*1*	*13*	*37*	*0*	*39¹*	*35*	*6*	*2.8*	*8.6*	*38*	*52%*	*.293*	*1.20*	*4.33*	*4.25*	*5.04*	*0.4*	*0.0*	*117*	
2018	*WAS*	*MLB*	*37*	*2*	*1*	*15*	*44*	*0*	*45*	*45*	*8*	*2.8*	*8.1*	*41*	*52%*	*.313*	*1.31*	*4.61*	*4.97*	*5.37*	*-1.2*	*-0.1*	*125*	

Breakout: 25%   Improve: 43%   Collapse: 31%   Attrition: 6%   MLB: 81%   Comparables: *Francisco Cordero, Brendan Donnelly, Brian Fuentes*

Even before an intercostal strain shelved the Proven Closer for a few weeks in June, Papelbon's stuff was looking as dodgy as ever. His four-seamer continued to lose spin, "rise" and velocity, and his signature splitter induced 30 percent fewer fishing expeditions. Forced to stay in the zone and work from behind more often, he struggled to do the former and paid—dearly at times—for doing the latter. The Nats cut ties in August after revoking his end-game credentials in July, and he flirted with a few organizations as the summer waned before deciding he needed some "me time." Or so his agent might say.

Oliver Perez   LHP

Born: 8/15/81 Age: 35 Bats: L Throws: L Height: 6'3" Weight: 225 Entered Pro Ball: International Free Agent, 1999

YEAR	TEAM	LVL	AGE	W	L	SV	G	GS	IP	H	HR	BB/9	K/9	K	GB%	BABIP	WHIP	ERA	FIP	DRA	VORP	WARP	cFIP	MPH
2014	ARI	MLB	32	3	4	0	68	0	58²	50	5	3.7	11.7	76	47%	.312	1.26	2.91	3.20	2.85	10.7	1.2	87	94.0
2015	ARI	MLB	33	2	1	0	48	0	29	25	2	3.4	11.5	37	45%	.311	1.24	3.10	3.06	4.18	1.7	0.2	93	94.8
2015	HOU	MLB	33	0	3	0	22	0	12	14	2	3.0	10.5	14	32%	.343	1.50	6.75	3.94	4.18	0.7	0.1	93	94.6
2016	WAS	MLB	34	2	3	0	64	0	40	38	4	4.5	10.4	46	43%	.324	1.45	4.95	4.21	4.41	2.5	0.3	101	94.3
2017	*WAS*	*MLB*	*35*	*3*	*3*	*0*	*51*	*0*	*54*	*51*	*7*	*3.9*	*10.0*	*60*	*73%*	*.308*	*1.40*	*4.24*	*4.08*	*4.51*	*2.4*	*0.3*	*100*	
2018	*WAS*	*MLB*	*36*	*1*	*1*	*0*	*28*	*0*	*30*	*27*	*4*	*3.7*	*9.6*	*32*	*73%*	*.321*	*1.32*	*3.94*	*4.24*	*4.58*	*1.8*	*0.2*	*102*	

Breakout: 22%   Improve: 33%   Collapse: 33%   Attrition: 20%   MLB: 81%   Comparables: *Brad Lidge, Michael Gonzalez, Kerry Wood*

In the town of Blue Hill, Maine, there is a Twinkie. Shrouded by glass, it remains in outward appearance today exactly as it did on a fateful afternoon in 1976, when a chemistry teacher first encased it in an ultimately futile effort to teach his students about the violence of decay. Perhaps if he had attempted the experiment in this millennium, he would have instead opted for Perez's left arm as his test subject. Fifteen years after first breaking into the majors, and five since his merciful conversion to full-time relief, the southpaw can still spin a slider that misses big-league bats. Yet much like that ill-fated Twinkie, the pitch—along with the rest of Perez's arsenal—is a lot less appealing nowadays under the surface. You can bet he'll get another chance next year, though. And likely the year after, and the year after that. Polysorbate 60 is a hell of a drug, but, as Perez can most assuredly attest to, so is being left-handed.

Yusmeiro Petit   RHP

Born: 11/22/84 Age: 32 Bats: R Throws: R Height: 6'1" Weight: 255 Entered Pro Ball: International Free Agent, 2001

YEAR	TEAM	LVL	AGE	W	L	SV	G	GS	IP	H	HR	BB/9	K/9	K	GB%	BABIP	WHIP	ERA	FIP	DRA	VORP	WARP	cFIP	MPH
2014	SFN	MLB	29	5	5	0	39	12	117	97	12	1.7	10.2	133	36%	.290	1.02	3.69	2.75	3.41	16.6	1.8	84	91.2
2015	SFN	MLB	30	1	1	1	42	1	76	75	11	1.8	7.0	59	34%	.278	1.18	3.67	4.12	5.07	-2.8	-0.3	118	90.7
2016	WAS	MLB	31	3	5	1	36	1	62	67	12	2.2	7.1	49	44%	.291	1.32	4.50	4.85	4.32	4.7	0.5	106	90.9
2017	*WAS*	*MLB*	*32*	*3*	*2*	*0*	*30*	*5*	*57*	*53*	*9*	*2.5*	*8.0*	*51*	*40%*	*.297*	*1.21*	*4.24*	*4.34*	*4.93*	*3.1*	*0.3*	*114*	
2018	*WAS*	*MLB*	*33*	*6*	*5*	*1*	*47*	*12*	*132¹*	*123*	*22*	*3.0*	*9.3*	*137*	*40%*	*.309*	*1.26*	*4.27*	*4.58*	*4.96*	*5.8*	*0.6*	*113*	

Breakout: 13%   Improve: 27%   Collapse: 13%   Attrition: 15%   MLB: 61%   Comparables: *Carlos Torres, Cristhian Martinez, Scott Downs*

Petit has thrown nearly 1,800 professional innings in a career that started with top-prospect shine but has unfolded with the drab of so many Motel 6 bedspreads under which he's rested his weary body over the years. He has typically struggled to solve lefties, and though he coaxed a career-best groundball rate out of them with more changeups, they still teed off on him to the tune of a near-.600 slugging percentage. Meanwhile, his good-but-not-great whiff rate against righties limited his utility beyond soaking up the occasional lopsided inning. He turned in a quality effort in his lone emergency start, but that was about it for the highlight reel in a season that ended with a declined option and an uncertain future.

Tanner Roark   RHP

Born: 10/5/86 Age: 30 Bats: R Throws: R Height: 6'2" Weight: 235 Entered Pro Ball: Round 25, 2008 Draft (#753 overall)

YEAR	TEAM	LVL	AGE	W	L	SV	G	GS	IP	H	HR	BB/9	K/9	K	GB%	BABIP	WHIP	ERA	FIP	DRA	VORP	WARP	cFIP	MPH
2014	WAS	MLB	27	15	10	0	31	31	198²	178	16	1.8	6.3	138	42%	.270	1.09	2.85	3.44	4.40	9.6	1.1	109	93.8
2015	WAS	MLB	28	4	7	1	40	12	111	119	17	2.1	5.7	70	49%	.293	1.31	4.38	4.73	5.03	-1.2	-0.1	110	95.6
2016	WAS	MLB	29	16	10	0	34	33	210	173	17	3.1	7.4	172	51%	.269	1.17	2.83	3.83	4.45	21.0	2.2	103	94.7
2017	*WAS*	*MLB*	*30*	*10*	*10*	*0*	*29*	*29*	*165¹*	*156*	*20*	*3.1*	*7.5*	*138*	*56%*	*.287*	*1.28*	*4.25*	*4.24*	*4.60*	*10.6*	*1.1*	*100*	
2018	*WAS*	*MLB*	*31*	*9*	*10*	*0*	*29*	*29*	*176¹*	*146*	*23*	*3.2*	*8.4*	*164*	*56%*	*.281*	*1.18*	*4.15*	*4.46*	*4.82*	*13.3*	*1.4*	*113*	

Breakout: 10%   Improve: 34%   Collapse: 22%   Attrition: 19%   MLB: 73%   Comparables: *Bronson Arroyo, Rich Hill, Alfredo Aceves*

If a hundred people predicted a hundred pitchers apiece for potential Cy Young votes before 2016 began, it's entirely probable that Tanner Roark's name would not have graced a single ballot. He was a league-average swingman in 2015, after all, with no clear path to an innings increase. Yet there he was at year's end, the proud owner of a tenth-place finish after a second season in which he'd dramatically outperformed his peripherals to log around 200 innings of sub-3.00 ERA ball. He generates outsized results with a delicious mix of deception and arsenal depth. The stuff doesn't feature exceptional movement, but it has enough, and batters struggle to pick up on his pitches. He stole the fifth-most called strikes of any pitcher in the game and ran yet another well above-average BABIP on the back of unsure swings and weak contact. With a recipe perfected and three more years of club control, he offers plenty of affordable value for the foreseeable future.

Joe Ross   RHP

Born: 5/21/93   Age: 24   Bats: R   Throws: R   Height: 6'4"   Weight: 225   Entered Pro Ball: Round 1, 2011 Draft (#25 overall)

YEAR	TEAM	LVL	AGE	W	L	SV	G	GS	IP	H	HR	BB/9	K/9	K	GB%	BABIP	WHIP	ERA	FIP	DRA	VORP	WARP	cFIP	MPH
2014	LEL	A+	21	8	6	0	19	19	101²	101	6	2.5	7.7	87	54%	.325	1.27	3.98	3.83	2.75	32.1	3.2	89	
2014	SAN	AA	21	2	0	0	4	3	20	23	2	0.4	8.6	19	47%	.339	1.20	3.60	2.67	3.41	3.8	0.4	87	
2015	HAR	AA	22	2	2	0	9	9	51¹	46	3	2.1	9.5	54	50%	.323	1.13	2.81	2.80	2.24	16.3	1.8	72	
2015	SYR	AAA	22	3	1	0	5	5	24²	15	2	2.6	5.5	15	55%	.188	0.89	2.19	3.85	4.10	3.3	0.3	95	
2015	WAS	MLB	22	5	5	0	16	13	76²	64	7	2.5	8.1	69	54%	.265	1.11	3.64	3.45	3.68	11.8	1.3	93	96.3
2016	SYR	AAA	23	0	2	0	4	4	10¹	14	1	0.9	7.8	9	26%	.382	1.45	4.35	2.97	4.47	1.0	0.1	106	
2016	WAS	MLB	23	7	5	0	19	19	105	108	9	2.5	8.0	93	44%	.319	1.30	3.43	3.53	4.50	10.1	1.0	103	95.9
2017	*WAS*	*MLB*	*24*	*9*	*8*	*0*	*26*	*26*	*137*	*133*	*16*	*3.0*	*8.0*	*123*	*48%*	*.296*	*1.29*	*3.98*	*3.99*	*4.32*	*13.2*	*1.4*	*100*	
2018	*WAS*	*MLB*	*25*	*9*	*9*	*0*	*27*	*27*	*165*	*138*	*19*	*3.4*	*9.6*	*176*	*48%*	*.305*	*1.21*	*3.70*	*3.98*	*4.31*	*20.0*	*2.1*	*98*	

Breakout: 23%   Improve: 58%   Collapse: 17%   Attrition: 17%   MLB: 94%   *Comparables: Jarrod Parker, Vin Mazzaro, Homer Bailey*

Something about these Ross boys and their shoulders. A couple months after big brother Tyson hit the shelf it was Joe's turn, as dipping velocity and erratic command in an early July start pumped the breaks on what had been a nice little full-season debut in the Nats' rotation. His two-seamer and slider play well together, making for an especially dynamic duo against right-handed hitters and driving solid early-season production. The utility of a high-80s change continues to lag, however, with little velocity separation and even less drop. Lefties torched it again, giving him a huge platoon split (nearly 270 points of OPS) that has, along with his fragility and his familial ties, come to define the first act of his career.

Max Scherzer   RHP

Born: 7/27/84   Age: 32   Bats: R   Throws: R   Height: 6'3"   Weight: 210   Entered Pro Ball: Round 1, 2006 Draft (#11 overall)

YEAR	TEAM	LVL	AGE	W	L	SV	G	GS	IP	H	HR	BB/9	K/9	K	GB%	BABIP	WHIP	ERA	FIP	DRA	VORP	WARP	cFIP	MPH
2014	DET	MLB	29	18	5	0	33	33	220¹	196	18	2.6	10.3	252	38%	.315	1.18	3.15	2.87	2.41	59.5	6.6	76	96.3
2015	WAS	MLB	30	14	12	0	33	33	228¹	176	27	1.3	10.9	276	38%	.268	0.92	2.79	2.79	2.70	60.5	6.5	73	97.4
2016	WAS	MLB	31	20	7	0	34	34	228¹	165	31	2.2	11.2	284	35%	.255	0.97	2.96	3.28	3.01	59.7	6.2	81	97.1
2017	*WAS*	*MLB*	*32*	*12*	*9*	*0*	*28*	*28*	*187*	*150*	*26*	*2.5*	*11.4*	*238*	*39%*	*.284*	*1.06*	*3.33*	*3.35*	*3.61*	*32.7*	*3.4*	*80*	
2018	*WAS*	*MLB*	*33*	*13*	*11*	*0*	*32*	*32*	*209²*	*158*	*29*	*2.5*	*11.0*	*257*	*39%*	*.288*	*1.03*	*3.35*	*3.58*	*3.88*	*39.4*	*4.1*	*86*	

Breakout: 17%   Improve: 40%   Collapse: 26%   Attrition: 3%   MLB: 89%   *Comparables: Johan Santana, Josh Beckett, Zack Greinke*

Scherzer now boasts a Cy Young for each eye color after becoming just the 18th pitcher in history to win the award multiple times. He did, however, become the first to win it while leading the league in long balls allowed, and he did it despite posting his highest DRA since 2011. The stuff actually took a step forward, somehow, helping him generate career-best whiff rates with all three of his secondary pitches. His performance went next level against righties in particular, as they managed their way on base at just a paltry .189 clip. And perhaps most interestingly, he evolved into the rarest of power pitchers who actually *gains* velocity after his 30th birthday; he posted the highest sitting average on his four-seamer, nearly 1.5 mph harder than it had been clocked at as recently as 2014. With two years left before the escalators on his backloaded contract go off the rails, this deal might not look so bad after all.

Sammy Solis   LHP

Born: 8/10/88   Age: 28   Bats: R   Throws: L   Height: 6'5"   Weight: 250   Entered Pro Ball: Round 2, 2010 Draft (#51 overall)

YEAR	TEAM	LVL	AGE	W	L	SV	G	GS	IP	H	HR	BB/9	K/9	K	GB%	BABIP	WHIP	ERA	FIP	DRA	VORP	WARP	cFIP	MPH
2015	HAR	AA	26	0	3	2	11	1	13¹	19	0	3.4	7.4	11	39%	.413	1.80	6.75	3.19	5.08	-0.5	-0.1	104	
2015	SYR	AAA	26	0	0	2	9	0	13¹	8	0	3.4	7.4	11	50%	.222	0.98	2.03	2.86	3.39	2.3	0.2	99	
2015	WAS	MLB	26	1	1	0	18	0	21¹	25	2	1.7	7.2	17	46%	.329	1.36	3.38	3.49	5.28	-1.3	-0.1	104	96.7
2016	WAS	MLB	27	2	4	0	37	0	41	31	1	4.6	10.3	47	45%	.294	1.27	2.41	2.82	3.87	5.0	0.5	95	96.2
2017	*WAS*	*MLB*	*28*	*3*	*2*	*2*	*51*	*0*	*54*	*51*	*6*	*3.9*	*9.0*	*54*	*54%*	*.301*	*1.38*	*3.95*	*4.06*	*4.29*	*3.8*	*0.4*	*95*	
2018	*WAS*	*MLB*	*29*	*3*	*1*	*2*	*57*	*0*	*60*	*48*	*6*	*3.9*	*10.3*	*68*	*54%*	*.307*	*1.24*	*3.50*	*3.76*	*4.09*	*6.9*	*0.7*	*88*	

Breakout: 35%   Improve: 51%   Collapse: 15%   Attrition: 22%   MLB: 78%   *Comparables: Tom Mastny, Brian Bass, Phil Coke*

Solis only made two trips to the disabled list this season, and that counts as a win. When he was able to toe the rubber, the former second-rounder also finally managed to carve out a consistent big-league role for himself. He dramatically boosted deployment of one of the hardest, tightest curveballs to which any left-handed reliever can currently lay claim, and he rode the pitch's well above-average whiff rate to reasonable success against righties and lefties alike. Nats fans are likely still ruing the team's sudden playoff exit, Solis (Jersey accent) they can take Solis (southern drawl) in having a quality, cost-controlled middle man for the next several years.

Stephen Strasburg   RHP

Born: 7/20/88   Age: 28   Bats: R   Throws: R   Height: 6'4"   Weight: 235   Entered Pro Ball: Round 1, 2009 Draft (#1 overall)

YEAR	TEAM	LVL	AGE	W	L	SV	G	GS	IP	H	HR	BB/9	K/9	K	GB%	BABIP	WHIP	ERA	FIP	DRA	VORP	WARP	cFIP	MPH
2014	WAS	MLB	25	14	11	0	34	34	215	198	23	1.8	10.1	242	48%	.315	1.12	3.14	2.91	2.72	50.6	5.6	74	97.3
2015	WAS	MLB	26	11	7	0	23	23	127¹	115	14	1.8	11.0	155	45%	.311	1.11	3.46	2.84	2.87	31.3	3.4	77	98.0
2016	WAS	MLB	27	15	4	0	24	24	147²	119	16	2.7	11.2	183	40%	.294	1.10	3.60	2.96	2.85	41.2	4.2	80	97.2
2017	*WAS*	*MLB*	*28*	*12*	*9*	*0*	*29*	*29*	*174*	*142*	*21*	*2.7*	*11.0*	*213*	*40%*	*.291*	*1.12*	*3.31*	*3.28*	*3.58*	*30.9*	*3.2*	*80*	
2018	*WAS*	*MLB*	*29*	*12*	*10*	*0*	*33*	*33*	*215²*	*166*	*25*	*2.5*	*10.7*	*255*	*40%*	*.296*	*1.04*	*3.17*	*3.39*	*3.67*	*40.8*	*4.2*	*80*	

Breakout: 21%   Improve: 57%   Collapse: 22%   Attrition: 8%   MLB: 94%   *Comparables: Zack Greinke, Jake Peavy, Tim Lincecum*

There was Strasburg on August 1st, riding high off a quality start in Arizona, sitting at 15-1 with a 2.63 ERA, and feeling pretty alright about that seven-year extension he signed in May. Then Buckaroo Banzai asked if anyone out there wasn't having a good time, and the club screeched to a halt. Batters squared him up to the tune of a .414/.462/.776 line over his next three starts before his season effectively ended (aborted early-September return notwithstanding) on account of a curmudgeonly flexor-pronator mass. The good news? The injury had an indirect line to his second-string UCL, and robots confirmed he had suffered no elevated risk of a Tommy John redux. The bad news? It was yet another scenic route along the ostensible ace's career path, which has now seen him cross the 185-inning threshold just once in his five "full" seasons. The stuff was still there when he was healthy enough to deploy it, though a dramatically increased workload for his slider didn't quite take. No matter where he goes in 2017, there he'll be. Nats fans can only hope his destination is a pitcher's mound for 30-some-odd evenings.

Blake Treinen   RHP

Born: 6/30/88   Age: 29   Bats: R   Throws: R   Height: 6'5"   Weight: 225   Entered Pro Ball: Round 7, 2011 Draft (#226 overall)

YEAR	TEAM	LVL	AGE	W	L	SV	G	GS	IP	H	HR	BB/9	K/9	K	GB%	BABIP	WHIP	ERA	FIP	DRA	VORP	WARP	cFIP	MPH
2014	SYR	AAA	26	8	2	0	16	16	80²	78	4	2.2	7.1	64	58%	.301	1.21	3.35	3.31	3.20	22.9	2.3	82	
2014	WAS	MLB	26	2	3	0	15	7	50²	57	1	2.3	5.3	30	60%	.333	1.38	2.49	3.06	4.21	2.9	0.3	107	98.0
2015	SYR	AAA	27	0	0	0	5	0	12	6	0	0.8	10.5	14	71%	.214	0.58	0.00	1.07	2.14	3.7	0.4	72	
2015	WAS	MLB	27	2	5	0	60	0	67²	62	4	4.3	8.6	65	65%	.328	1.39	3.86	3.52	3.33	10.4	1.1	90	98.9
2016	WAS	MLB	28	4	1	1	73	0	67	51	5	4.2	8.5	63	67%	.280	1.22	2.28	3.66	3.50	10.9	1.1	89	98.1
2017	WAS	MLB	29	3	2	3	51	0	54	50	5	3.9	8.3	50	41%	.298	1.36	3.88	3.91	4.22	4.2	0.4	92	
2018	WAS	MLB	30	1	1	1	27	0	28¹	23	3	4.5	10.3	32	41%	.317	1.31	3.82	4.10	4.45	2.1	0.2	97	

Breakout: 21%   Improve: 39%   Collapse: 27%   Attrition: 25%   MLB: 75%   Comparables: Luis Mendoza, Sam LeCure, Philip Humber

Things happen for a reason, some people say. Exhibit A might just be Treinen, who as a kid nearly chopped off the thumb on what turned out to be his pitching hand. The ensuing lack of mobility once his mangled ligaments hardened into an improvised new world order forced him to hone a unique sinker grip, and the pitch has evolved into one of the league's deadliest. So nasty is its movement, in fact, that he often struggles to harness it in the strike zone. He walks a good number of hitters—lefties especially—and while he produces groundballs and whiffs aplenty, he'll need to Treinen improve his control if he aspires beyond his moderately-leveraged bullpen role. And yes, that pun is a metaphor for his sinker.

Austin Voth   RHP

Born: 6/26/92   Age: 25   Bats: R   Throws: R   Height: 6'2"   Weight: 215   Entered Pro Ball: Round 5, 2013 Draft (#166 overall)

YEAR	TEAM	LVL	AGE	W	L	SV	G	GS	IP	H	HR	BB/9	K/9	K	GB%	BABIP	WHIP	ERA	FIP	DRA	VORP	WARP	cFIP	MPH
2014	HAG	A	22	4	3	0	13	13	69²	51	1	2.8	9.6	74	54%	.281	1.05	2.45	2.68	2.26	24.6	2.5	84	
2014	POT	A+	22	2	1	0	6	6	37²	16	2	1.7	9.6	40	43%	.163	0.61	1.43	2.64	1.72	16.2	1.6	76	
2014	HAR	AA	22	1	3	0	5	5	19¹	22	4	4.2	8.8	19	43%	.333	1.60	6.52	5.63	4.88	0.7	0.1	102	
2015	HAR	AA	23	6	7	0	28	27	157¹	134	10	2.3	8.5	148	47%	.284	1.11	2.92	3.07	1.83	56.8	6.2	72	
2016	SYR	AAA	24	7	9	0	27	25	157	138	11	3.3	7.6	133	51%	.279	1.24	3.15	3.53	2.44	50.1	5.2	95	
2017	WAS	MLB	25	8	8	0	25	25	137	123	15	3.5	7.2	109	43%	.292	1.29	4.17	4.23	4.85	10.8	1.1	111	
2018	WAS	MLB	26	8	9	0	25	25	145²	118	17	4.9	9.8	159	43%	.300	1.35	4.26	4.58	4.96	8.9	0.9	114	

Breakout: 21%   Improve: 30%   Collapse: 21%   Attrition: 41%   MLB: 65%   Comparables: Charles Brewer, Edwar Cabrera, Matt Maloney

If you like that sexy kind of prospect upside that gets the loins a-tinglin', boy are you reading the wrong write-up. Voth leverages his height effectively with a high arm slot to generate a nice angle that helps maximize his pedestrian arsenal. Yet, as a right-hander, there's only so far a fastball that barely scrapes 90 on a good day can get you. His 12-6 curve and change are good enough to keep hitters honest and keep him in games when he has a feel for things, but the deficit of raw stuff leaves his margin for error perilously thin. Still, he has precious little remaining to prove in the minors after patching together a career DRA that sniffs two and a quarter across nearly 500 innings, and he'll enter the spring in possession of prime real estate on Washington's rotation depth chart.

LINEOUTS

Hitters

NAME	POS	TEAM	LVL	AGE	PA	R	2B	3B	HR	RBI	BB	K	SB	CS	AVG/OBP/SLG	TAv	VORP	BABIP	BRR	FRAA	WARP
Osvaldo Abreu	SS	POT	A+	22	563	86	23	4	6	52	55	108	18	10	.247/.328/.346	.256	18.3	.303	-1.6	SS(119): -1.8	1.7
Matt Den Dekker	OF	WAS	MLB	28	39	3	1	0	1	4	4	10	1	0	.176/.282/.294	.238	0.2	.217	0.0	CF(6): -0.0 • RF(4): 0.2	0.1
	OF	SYR	AAA	28	421	41	14	1	8	44	40	110	20	5	.207/.292/.315	.228	-3.5	.268	2.1	LF(49): -1.8 • RF(25): -3.1	-1.0
Brian Goodwin	CF	SYR	AAA	25	492	51	25	1	14	68	46	106	15	3	.280/.349/.438	.279	21.3	.336	-2.1	CF(85): -5.3 • RF(18): 0.3	1.9
	CF	WAS	MLB	25	44	1	4	1	0	5	2	14	0	0	.286/.318/.429	.252	0.4	.429	-0.2	RF(8): -1.5 • LF(5): -0.3	-0.1
Kelvin Gutierrez	3B	AUB	A-	21	35	5	3	0	0	6	3	5	4	0	.323/.371/.419	.304	2.9	.370	0.3	3B(8): 0.5	0.4
	3B	HAG	A	21	417	58	19	6	3	48	29	65	19	7	.300/.349/.406	.290	24.1	.349	0.2	3B(95): 3.5	3.0
	3B	POT	A+	21	44	7	1	0	1	2	3	5	2	2	.237/.326/.342	.258	1.9	.250	0.7	3B(9): -0.0	0.2
Chris Heisey	LF	WAS	MLB	31	155	18	3	1	9	17	13	44	0	1	.216/.290/.446	.269	4.0	.241	-0.9	LF(25): 1.8 • RF(16): -0.5	0.5
Spencer Kieboom	C	HAR	AA	25	359	27	11	0	5	31	43	61	0	0	.230/.324/.314	.243	6.5	.267	-2.8	C(93): -14.2	-0.8
	C	WAS	MLB	25	1	1	0	0	0	0	1	0	0	0		.560	0.5	--	0.2		0.1
Jose Marmolejos-Diaz	1B	POT	A+	23	440	72	36	5	11	59	59	84	2	3	.286/.381/.495	.319	30.1	.337	-2.3	1B(89): -5.2	2.6
	1B	HAR	AA	23	135	15	9	0	2	15	5	29	0	0	.299/.333/.417	.277	2.6	.371	-1.1	1B(29): -2.6	1.0
Sheldon Neuse	3B	AUB	A-	21	141	16	5	3	1	11	13	26	2	2	.230/.305/.341	.254	2.8	.280	-0.2	3B(23): 0.7 • SS(5): 1.1	0.5
Blake Perkins	CF	AUB	A-	19	241	31	5	1	1	16	25	39	10	3	.233/.318/.281	.277	12.5	.279	1.5	CF(49): 6.1 • LF(2): -0.1	2.0
	CF	HAG	A	19	33	4	0	0	0	2	5	6	0	1	.200/.333/.200	.258	-0.4	.263	-1.4	CF(7): -1.1	-0.2
Raudy Read	C	POT	A+	22	426	54	30	1	9	51	31	53	6	3	.262/.324/.415	.266	19.8	.281	-1.9	C(97): 0.6	2.1
Clint Robinson	PH	WAS	MLB	31	224	16	4	0	5	26	20	38	0	0	.235/.305/.332	.254	2.3	.259	0.3	1B(46): -4.2 • LF(3): 0.2	-0.2
Matt Skole	1B	SYR	AAA	26	573	67	22	1	24	78	66	119	2	0	.244/.337/.437	.278	19.1	.273	-1.2	1B(97): -0.9 • 3B(41): -1.2	1.8

Osvaldo Abreu's glove gives him a viable path to value that may be elevated above the vestiges of visible production he achieved while traversing High-A. ❖ **Matt den Dekker** again failed to gain any offensive traction when a big-league opportunity knocked in April, then struggled to maintain a pG-13 line at Triple-A before ultimately finding himself the victim of a late-season dFA. ❖ One of the youngest members of the 2013 J2 class, **Anderson Franco** boasts plus power and at least a puncher's chance to stick at third, but he's yet to reach full-season ball and logged just 24 games last season due to a back injury. ❖ A seven-figure J2 signee, **Luis Garcia** was born in the year 2000, which is a nice reminder that the icy grip of inevitable death is closer than it has ever been. ❖ **Brian Goodwin** had a nice bounceback season with the stick at Triple-A, earning a call-up in August and playing himself back into consideration for a future bench role on the strength of okay pop, some speed and solid defensive versatility on the grass. ❖ **Kelvin Gutierrez** combines solid physicality and arm strength at the hot corner with a steadily improving approach and some latent power projection to offer glimpses of a future second-division starter. ❖ **Chris Heisey** has always been an odd duck of an extra outfielder on account of his reverse right-handed splits, but he probably executed his formula of playable defense in the corners and occasional pop well enough to earn himself a couple hundred more big-league at-bats in 2017. ❖ By earning a walk in his one and only big-league plate appearance on the season's second-to-last day, **Spencer Kieboom** announced his arrival. It was a fitting result, actually, as he walks often and pairs the decent on-base profile with more-than-decent defensive chops that cry out for a long career backing up another catcher. ❖ **Jose Marmolejos-Diaz** snagged a 40-man roster spot despite playing just 33 career games above Single-A, as the lefty-hitting first baseman showed a promising line-drive stroke in the low minors. ❖ The Nats tabbed **Sheldon Neuse** in the second round after a breakout offensive season at Oklahoma, though despite the suggestion of his moniker the bat profiles as more of an average asset. ❖ The club's second-rounder a year ago, **Blake Perkins** has tools aplenty, highlighted by plus speed and defense in center, but he remains light years away after muddling through an aggressive short-season assignment. ❖ **Raudy Read** seems destined to a) constantly have people misread his first name as "Randy," and b) make a go of it as a backup catcher in a couple years. ❖ **Clint Robinson** earned 200 big-league plate appearances for a second straight year, but with his legs aging out of outfield duty and his bat backsliding, it is unclear he'll warrant that streak continuing. ❖ Slick-fielding shortstop **Jose Sanchez** signed for $950,000 on his 16th birthday, which is a much better thing to do on one's 16th birthday then, oh, say, get turned down for a junior prom date and ugly-cry into a half-eaten Beef 'n Cheddar in the alley behind an Arby's. ❖ In the days before 12- and 13-man bullpens, **Matt Skole** would have been a nice left-handed bench bat with some pop, yet in this era he has to settle for a lot of Dinosaur Bar-B-Que and a Triple-A Gold Glove. ❖ Taken in the 11th round out of a Florida junior college, switch-hitting **Armond Upshaw** wowed the organization's scouts with true 80-grade speed and a generally impressive tool set.

Pitchers

NAME	TEAM	LVL	AGE	W	L	SV	G	GS	IP	H	HR	BB/9	K/9	K	GB%	BABIP	WHIP	ERA	FIP	DRA	VORP	WARP	cFIP	MPH
Joan Baez	HAG	A	21	9	7	0	27	27	125²	120	5	4.6	8.5	119	42%	.324	1.46	3.94	3.81	5.70	-9.6	-1.1	112	
Jimmy Cordero	REA	AA	24	1	1	1	11	0	13	13	0	0.7	4.2	6	51%	.289	1.08	3.46	2.90	5.03	-0.4	0.0	103	
Koda Glover	HAR	AA	23	2	0	4	17	0	22¹	20	1	2.8	11.7	29	46%	.339	1.21	3.22	2.28	1.99	6.8	0.7	80	
	SYR	AAA	23	1	1	2	16	0	24	16	2	1.1	8.2	22	52%	.233	0.79	2.25	2.92	2.71	6.0	0.6	83	
	WAS	MLB	23	2	0	0	19	0	19²	15	3	3.2	7.3	16	42%	.214	1.12	5.03	4.76	4.12	1.9	0.2	111	99.0
Trevor Gott	SYR	AAA	23	3	3	1	33	0	39¹	44	2	3.0	7.1	31	59%	.336	1.45	4.35	3.47	3.43	6.7	0.7	99	
	WAS	MLB	23	0	0	0	9	0	6	6	0	4.5	9.0	6	44%	.333	1.50	1.50	3.19	4.61	0.2	0.0	107	96.5
Matt Grace	SYR	AAA	27	1	3	0	35	0	47¹	54	1	1.7	6.1	32	66%	.338	1.33	2.85	2.66	2.90	10.8	1.1	87	
	WAS	MLB	27	0	0	0	5	0	3	1	0	0.0	12.0	4	67%	.167	0.33	0.00	0.52	3.58	0.5	0.0	91	91.6
Rafael Martin	SYR	AAA	32	2	4	22	50	0	49¹	43	7	4.6	9.1	50	28%	.273	1.38	4.56	4.57	5.93	-5.3	-0.5	116	
	WAS	MLB	32	0	0	0	8	0	3²	0	0	2.5	12.3	5	33%	.000	0.27	2.45	1.28	4.27	0.3	0.0	102	90.9

Though he started 27 games in Low-A with reasonable success, it remains unlikely **Joan Baez** will overcome the control issues that have plagued his young career, and his inconsistent combination of diamond fastball and rusty mechanics appears better suited to a bullpen future. ❖ If you're ever feeling blue, just think of **Aaron Barrett** and remember that at least your arm has never snapped mid-pitch as you were just finishing up your year-long rehab from reconstructive elbow surgery. ❖ **Jimmy Cordero**'s ability to generate triple-digit radar gun readings excites everyone, but all of his other pitches are unrefined and separate bicep and shoulder injuries aren't a good omen for his future. ❖ **Koda Glover** started the year at High-A and ended it with his feet firmly planted on big-league soil, thanks to a 98-mph fastball and two solid offspeed offerings that appear poised to keep him occupying prime bullpen real estate for a long time. ❖ The Nats brought **Trevor Gott** into the bullpen mix with big plans for his big fastball, but an inflamed elbow meant that he missed more time than bats in Triple-A. ❖ The career of an organizational depth reliever certainly isn't the most glamorous of gigs, but after a second straight season logging big-league innings we bet **Matt Grace**'d tell you it beats a desk job. ❖ In a passé and entirely formulaic plot twist, the Nats bought **Jesus Luzardo** and his mid-90's fastball out of a Miami commitment while the young left-hander recovered from pre-draft Tommy John surgery. ❖ **Rafael Martin** saw his already-slow fastball lose two full ticks this year, yet he once again managed to miss a metric ton of big-league bats in a tiny sample after posting mediocre numbers at Triple-A.

The Modern Manager

by Matthew Trueblood

Last season's World Series was the best thing to happen to MLB in at least a decade. It was brilliant baseball, a story told fluidly and with perfect pace. It lasted seven games—and extra innings in the decisive one—between two teams whose title droughts, laid end to end, stretched back to the presidency of Martin Van Buren. Three of the contests lived up to the Series' favorite sobriquet and the two teams split the four drubbings evenly. There were young superstars, beloved veteran leaders and rich threads of human interest. Two of the biggest blockbuster trades of the summer had paid off and now stood as evidence of each team's skillful team building: Andrew Miller for Cleveland and Aroldis Chapman for Chicago. And an undercurrent was the battle of wits between the two managers.

Joe Maddon and Terry Francona are among the half-dozen most famous, most experienced and (arguably) best managers in baseball. Francona has two World Series rings, and entered last year's Fall Classic with a perfect 8-0 record in World Series games. What little time he hasn't spent managing winning baseball teams for the last 15 years he spent on television, calling games for FOX and ESPN. It's hard to build a bigger national and local profile than Francona has. Maddon, meanwhile, is the beloved eccentric, the mad scientist, and has become famous for stunts on and off the field. The pair also had a longer history of managing against one another than the structure of the modern game usually permits. In terms of stature, tactics and personality they couldn't have cast much longer shadows onto the field from their stations in the dugouts. That wouldn't have registered as unusual in the days of Casey Stengel, Walter Alston, Earl Weaver and Whitey Herzog, but things have changed.

One of the few managers who might be as recognizable as Maddon or Francona to the casual fan is Buck Showalter. He watched the World Series from home, his Orioles having lost in the Wild Card game when Showalter failed to call upon his relief ace, Zach Britton, as the game dragged into the late (and eventually extra) innings. Showalter has been managing longer than either Francona or Maddon—since the 1980s in the minors and as far back as 1992 in the big leagues—and has seen the job change radically during all that time, taking on higher stakes and increased overall responsibility.

However, the manager's job has also lost some autonomy and been forced to delegate more of its nominal power. Whatever authority they have is more diffuse. They're bureaucrats now. They belong to an increasingly complex organization and they have to operate under different directives than they used to. Guiding a team as far as the World Series in the modern game takes a different kind of leader, a different kind of tactician and a different kind of cooperative effort than it used to take. It's become an exercise in parallel management of very disparate priorities—sometimes competing, or even diametrically opposed priorities. It's become too big of a job for one person, which is why no one person is asked to do it anymore. The lines between the front office and the field staff are getting blurrier all the time, and for that matter so is the line between the manager and his coaches.

The Mariners hired Scott Servais as their manager prior to last season. Front office boss Jerry Dipoto brought Servais along after leaving Anaheim, where he'd kept the former big-league catcher as an assistant general manager for four years. Perhaps Dipoto had pegged Servais as a managerial candidate from the beginning. Angels owner Arte Moreno allowed Mike Scioscia to amass so much power, and invited such a dysfunctional relationship between his skipper and the front office, that we can't really know for certain. What we do know is that Servais' only post-playing experience prior to being hired was in the front office.

As soon as Servais was hired, it was clear that he would be a conduit for the free flow of information between the front office and the dugout staff. He didn't have the usual bona fides of a manager or a bench coach, from the perspective of tactical decisions or management of a clubhouse. That's fine, as modern managers often get hired without that kind of experience. Dipoto set about doing what teams across the league have done when they've hired similarly green skippers: He surrounded him with guys who could fill in the gaps. Tim Bogar, a longtime coach whose name has popped up in any number of managerial searches over the last half-decade, signed on as bench coach, and Manny Acta, the former Nationals and Indians manager with a known penchant for sabermetric analysis, got the job of third base coach.

Both of those experienced dugout hands could help Servais steer the ship straight, but there were more considerations in play. Acta's primary responsibility, more so than giving signs and coaching a base, was to design and communicate the Mariners' defensive positioning plans. That's become one of the most complex and crucial jobs performed by any member of the field staff in today's MLB. It's not merely about shifting, as the noteworthy cases of Dexter Fowler and Andrew McCutchen proved. It's about putting every player on the field in the best possible position to make a play on a batted ball from any given batter and about ensuring that the team defense is aligned optimally as a unit. (Notably, the Mariners saved an AL-best 21 runs via shifts in 2016, per Baseball Info Solutions.)

In Los Angeles, rookie manager Dave Roberts got veteran big-league manager Bob Geren for a bench coach. His staff also included Juan Castro, a longtime utility infielder who'd spent time in a front office role and as a minor-league coach. Castro's role included on-field instruction before games, but he moved to a box upstairs during them. His biggest responsibility might have been as the lone Spanish speaker on the field staff. In Roberts, Geren and Castro the Dodgers had three coaches positioned to provide players with valuable performance-centered information generated by the front office, but also to create meaningful relationships with the players who made up their first constituency.

The most important job of the modern field staff might be putting the resources provided by the front office (information, talent and facilities) to the highest possible use. It's become clear that shouldn't take the form of a hardcore stat-head standing on the top step and doing things by the sabermetric book without communicating the reasons for his decisions to his players. Acta was previously that kind of manager, or at least was placed in that kind of situation. That objective also can't be accomplished through the strong-arming of an ambivalent manager by his front office, which is how Bo Porter's stint with the Astros was sometimes portrayed.

One reason why being a big-league manager is harder than ever is that it's a lot more a matter of managing in both directions. There must be openness and trust in the relationships between the players and the field staff, and between the field staff and the front office. When that chain of communication breaks down it can hold back good teams. The Mets tumbled from contention for the NL East title last season as Terry Collins failed to get the most out of a strange amalgam of talent, especially in his outfield. They also faced the challenge of winning without most of their top-flight young pitchers after a failure to design and communicate a comprehensive plan to protect them.

On the other hand, when that communication process works especially well it can help a team overachieve. The Rangers won 95 games last season despite being one of the league's most injury-riddled teams. Jeff Banister was able to get the most out of a patchwork starting rotation, keep young players afloat in varying roles and accommodate a barrage of talented veterans (Ian Desmond, Jonathan Lucroy, Carlos Gomez) who brought their egos and expectations into the clubhouse midstream and in odd situations. Banister is a good conversation point because Texas' baseline talent, at least to the extent that we can estimate it, doesn't explain the degree of success they enjoyed over the past two seasons. They went 36-11 in one-run games last year and for the second straight season their record far outstripped their Pythagorean mark.

If you go to BP's sortable statistics menu and select the "Managers - Overall" report, what you get is a simple table. All 30 teams are listed. Their wins, losses, winning percentage, runs scored, runs allowed and Pythagorean winning percentage are shown. To the right of those six columns is one labeled "Diff%," which is simply the difference between the team's winning percentage and its Pythagorean record. It's a vestigial apparatus, an artifact of another time. It traces back to one of the first stat-head endeavors to systematically value managers' contributions. Even then it was seen as somewhat lacking, but it was the best of what was around. Over the years, as player performance data has advanced by leaps and bounds and the collective attitude of sabermetrica toward managerial choices has softened and been burdened with more and more layers of nuance, this area of analysis has fallen by the wayside.

That doesn't need to be a permanent state of affairs. The rationale for considering the variance between actual and expected records as an indicator of managers' value makes some sense. In a nutshell, the idea is that our stats—and the more advanced they are, the truer this is—are built around runs and run elements, and are pretty good at measuring the relative value provided by players on the field. However, because runs and run elements don't predict winning percentage all that reliably, and because every manager's priority is to maximize winning percentage, there's a negative space to study and evaluate.

To study the gap between real and hypothetical results is probably the right way to go about a systematic evaluation of managers. It's just that the space we need to study isn't between expected records and actual records; it's between actual performance and possible performance. Managers influence the performances of their players and influence their numbers. Looking beyond the numbers to find their value risks looking past their primary source of value. In that way, the old joke about the Manager of the Year award—that it usually goes to whichever skipper oversaw the most unlikely contending team or replaced the worst manager from the previous season—isn't that laughable.

If we are ever able to scientifically suss out the value of managers, it may turn out that they deliver that value by helping teams manage and exceed expectations through the maximization of talent. Ned Yost has carried the Royals to better records than projection systems forecasted in four straight seasons. Maybe that's because the Royals were better than anyone thought and better in some way that statistical projection systems couldn't capture, but maybe Yost and his staff have consistently helped their players achieve more (as individuals and as a team) than they would have with average management. A methodical, holistic system that assigns tangible and discrete value to the contributions of coaching staffs is a worthwhile goal, but we need to build a new framework in order to attain it.

I'm not here to build that framework; that's too big of a job right now. Rather, I'll lay out the dimensions of managers' value in today's MLB and hopefully the ball will start to roll. The first job of a manager is to minimize the deleterious impact of The Grind. Russell Carleton has demonstrated this in multiple ways over the last few years via the electronic pages of BP. Losing, absent any managerial influence, begets more losing. Players play worse after losses. Long stretches without days off have a cumulative effect on performance. Over a long season, it gets harder to bring one's best efforts to the field every day, in ways big and small. Carleton's work helps us appreciate the real magnitude of these effects, which can be quite large even when they happen in subtle ways.

Managers can exert real influence and minimize or even reverse these small disintegrations. Erstwhile Padres and new Rockies skipper Bud Black is great at this aspect of the job. Ditto for Mike Matheny. There's no single or clear mechanism for this kind of maintenance, or at least, we haven't identified one yet. Some managers are just much better at it than others, although perhaps the better way to say it would be that some *teams* or *coaching staffs* are much better at it than others. Our vocabulary will need to catch up to our knowledge soon, in more ways than that one. Be it more discipline, fewer off-day workouts, coordinated costumed road trips or the evenness of their keel, something about certain managers helps their players bounce back better after losses or helps players manage the strike zone and maintain their energy level.

Still, managing the grind of a long season isn't enough. Baseball now has what very nearly amounts to a second season. The postseason lasts a full month, and because 10 teams now gain berths, reaching the playoffs no longer qualifies automatically as a successful season. "I don't want to sound like an asshole," Cubs ace Jon Lester said on the final Saturday of the 2016 regular season, "but we haven't really done anything yet." Lester was wrong about that in that the Cubs were the first team since the 2009 Yankees to win more than 100 games, posted one of the best run differentials in baseball history and fielded perhaps the best balls-in-play defense ever. If they'd been swept in the NLDS, none of that would have been forgotten.

There's also some truth in what Lester said, because players, fans and teams themselves value postseason success more heavily relative to regular-season success than ever before, and the ratio only inches further in that direction each year. The manager's grind-smoothing role becomes extra complex, as do all facets of the job. Managing a modern pitching staff—fraught with young arms on workload limits, Tommy John surgery survivors and relievers trained to thrive in short stints—through the six-month season is no easy task. Managing one through 15 extra playoff games is even tougher.

Here, Maddon and Francona can come back to the stage for a moment. By the time the World Series began, Maddon was working with a bullpen whose key members from the beginning of the season were virtually all gone. He proactively entrusted three relievers with high-leverage work: Chapman, Carl Edwards Jr. and Mike Montgomery. None of them were on the team in April. Meanwhile, Francona tiptoed through October without Carlos Carrasco or Danny Salazar, two-fifths of his rotation during most of the season. He also rode Corey Kluber hard through the first two rounds despite the fact that Kluber had missed time during September with a leg injury. Francona had more of his full-season bullpen intact, but whenever possible he still leaned on just three arms: Kluber, Andrew Miller and Cody Allen.

Neither team had a starting pitcher get an out in the seventh inning and that's never happened in a World Series before, but even that factoid may underrepresent the proactive managerial involvement that took place. In the 2015 Series (which lasted only five games), two starters reached the ninth inning. In each of the previous four World Series, there were three starters who reached the eighth inning. This is now what managing and building a pitching staff for a full, seven-month season looks like. Managers have to learn (and many have not yet) to save bullets for their most important pitchers at certain points throughout the season.

They have to be aggressive about changing course when a reliever who might have carried their setup efforts through the first half suddenly breaks down. There must be consistent and open communication with the front office (who might we call up as a fresh arm and what reinforcements can I expect at the trade deadline?) and the training staff (what's the right number of pitches for this guy tonight and who can I most safely go to on zero days' rest after a marathon extra-inning game?) to help minimize attrition and optimize a team's performance at the moment when, as Jon Lester would say, they have not yet done anything but now have the opportunity to change that.

The Dodgers were a model of this cooperation in 2016. Under the leadership of Roberts and his experienced staff (including pitching coach Rick Honeycutt, held over to provide institutional memory and stability), Los Angeles starters threw fewer pitches per game than all but two other teams'. Roberts went to the bullpen a record 603 times. Ross Stripling was lifted from a no-hitter because of his pitch count and Rich Hill from a perfect game because of a possible blister issue. That the Dodgers won their division despite breaking the all-time record for days lost to the disabled list is a testament to Roberts and his staff, and their good use of the players and information they had.

The Dodgers knew they were taking on a lot of injury risk. Because they knew that, they also had enough depth on hand to weather the storms. They just needed the right people on the ground to ensure that the many players shuttled between roles and levels would make the necessary adjustments and keep the work environment conducive to winning. It's not always that easy, even when teams foresee certain risks and act to minimize them. The Rays amassed considerable depth around their battered collection of talented players, enough that PECOTA projected them as AL East favorites last year. They finished last. Kevin Kiermaier, the linchpin of a strong defense, missed 48 games with an injury and Tampa Bay went 14-34 in those games.

It's unfair to blame Rays manager Kevin Cash or his staff for that implosion. However, they had some role to play in first plugging the leak and then helping the club stay steady in the face of that adversity, and they couldn't do it. Assembling a roster loaded with known injury risk is an increasingly popular front-office strategy. In addition to the Dodgers and Rays, the Cardinals, Pirates and Giants each did so to some degree in 2016. The market for talent always provides a discount on players who are likely to break down, so teams with the money to make up for whatever losses they suffer (or who have so little money that they can't afford top-shelf talent) can try to find bargains there. Crucially, though, not every field staff can navigate the choppy waters of an injury-plagued season.

The old model of roster building no longer works, so the old model of roster management doesn't either. Managers need to be able to make decisions that optimize the long-term performance and health outlook of their players, even if it means passing up a chance to optimize win expectancy within a given game. Often that means proactively resting certain players or passing over a reliever who pitched three times in the last five days. It's not a coincidence that the four-man rotation died almost exactly when divisional play began, adding an extra round of playoffs before the World Series. It's also not a coincidence that the modern paradigm of pitcher usage, with its emphasis on keeping starters' pitch counts down, took hold in the early years of the Wild Card system, which added another round. It's all part of the picture.

The managers' role in keeping pitchers healthy is a tactical, cooperative one. They need to balance the developmental plan the organization has for the player, the latest information from the training staff about the player's injury risk and the need to win the game they're managing in the moment. Some managers do it well and some do it poorly, but it's a pretty straightforward job. Doing the same with position players is harder, especially as bullpens grow and benches shrink. To give proactive and restorative days off to position players throughout the season almost requires carrying more than a full complement of big-league regulars, and at that point a problem of balancing those players' egos presents itself.

The Cubs are an example. They had such a rich collection of good position players that they were forced to trade Chris Coghlan last spring. Even minus Coghlan and following a season-ending injury to Kyle Schwarber, Maddon struggled to find consistent playing time for Jorge Soler. Meanwhile, an early back injury compromised Miguel Montero at the plate for much of the regular season, so Maddon began resting the veteran catcher aggressively. It worked, as Montero had a .902 OPS over the final six weeks, with enough left over to come up with two huge hits during the playoff run. Still, Montero was irked, bemoaning a lack of communication about what he viewed as a total benching. Keeping everyone happy is impossible. Maddon made the right choices, but

Montero was left with a beef. Convincing players that playing less is in their best interest is a tall order, but one the model of a modern manager must be able to fill.

It's important to remember that the manager is not a monolith, not even to the extent that he used to be. It might be that a hitter who needs to play five times a week, instead of six, would receive that news better from a hitting coach or a positional instructor than from the manager. A manager has to be constantly aware of the crucial connective tissue within the clubhouse. The manager's role is in identifying and availing himself of the relationships players build with certain coaches. The relationships themselves matter more than ever, which is why some coaches are now just about as important to their team's success as managers are.

For a long time, there was a premise that hitting coach had little value because they were mostly sponges for praise during the good times and for blame when things went wrong. The idea was that hitting is a nearly automatic thing for a good hitter and hitting coaches mostly added value only by shortening the occasional slump or fixing an obvious swing issue. We know much better now. The recent expansion of the field staff to include an eighth uniformed coach led many teams to hire a second assistant hitting coach, underscoring the value those instructors can really have.

Good coaches can help hitters shape and reshape their approaches; shorten adjustment curves for young hitters; and, yes, fix mechanical issues big and small. Front offices are flush with new data about hitting, about how to maximize exit velocity and optimize launch angle, about which kind of pitches a batter is most likely to be able to lift to the pull field and about how a given individual might best combat a shift. Hitting coaches need to be able to turn that information into a weapon their pupils can use. Much of the same is true for pitching coaches, though by contrast they've historically been properly valued or even overvalued.

The latest trend in pitching—identifying your best pitch and throwing it as much as you possibly can, even if it isn't a fastball—is an easy one for good coaches to address. As our understanding of the key underpinnings of good mechanics improves, pitching coaches' role as simple instructors becomes increasingly important. A trickier (but even more important) aspect of the job is to build game plans, in concert with the catchers and whichever coach is in charge of defensive positioning, that maximize weak contact and the chances that a given hitter will hit the ball into the defense the team has aligned against him while minimizing the risk of making a key mistake. The synergy involved in run prevention today is greater than it has ever been, a cooperative endeavor that requires good communication and even better information.

Coaches below the level of manager can make a team better by receiving and synthesizing information from the front office, providing exceptionally good instruction and acting as a go-between for the manager and his players. Still, the manager himself has certain jobs that remain his and that remain important. Keeping young players confident, involved and protected from catastrophic failure is a vital mission and the manager is the central figure. It's his job to make sure that any player, but especially a young player with little experience, understands the team's expectations for him. It's also his job to make sure the organization is sending a consistent message to the player.

Over the last two seasons, Byron Buxton of the Twins has gone backward developmentally. He consistently crushed minor-league pitching, but when promoted to the majors he was asked to make adjustments in both mechanics and approach. It's possible, though unwise, to excuse manager Paul Molitor for the inconsistent approach to Buxton's development. The Twins fired hitting coach Tom Brunansky last fall, perhaps because of things like this. Still, Molitor ought to have been in constant communication both with the field staff of the Twins' Triple-A affiliate and with the team's higher-level player development staff to make sure of what Buxton was hearing in the minors.

He ought to have been in touch with Brunansky, ensuring that he was following the consensus plan regarding Buxton. Perhaps these things were mostly true and Molitor simply agreed with Brunansky that what Buxton was learning in Rochester constituted something less than best practices and was contributing to his trouble. Even in that case, there was a failure to communicate and change something, and it started with the big-league field staff. Batting Buxton ninth was also a gaffe. A hitter who bats ninth infrequently gets to see an opposing starter in today's MLB. Therefore, stashing a hitter with so little experience and so many adjustments that low in the lineup reduces his chances to become familiar with his opponents and to use information gained early in games during the middle and later innings. It makes the uphill climb toward offensive success even steeper.

Managers are rarely criticized for mistrusting young players or for "keeping pressure off" by stashing them in lesser roles like middle relief or the ninth slot in the order. In truth, good managers get the most out of young players by challenging them to take on as much responsibility as possible and empowering them (through instruction, information and the confidence to stick with them through tough times) to meet that challenge. That doesn't mean never benching or demoting a player. It just means messaging. Good managers don't make players feel like it's their fault when they struggle. They also take care to encourage scuffling players and remind them that progress is never linear.

I wrote earlier that the best way to measure managers' value is to assess the gap between actual, observed performance and possible performance. The problem with that, of course, is quantifying the possible. That's even truer with regard to team cohesion and chemistry, one of the principal intangible areas in which managers are supposed to provide big value, be it positive or negative. We just don't have enough information to assess that aspect of the job or of teams themselves. We don't know the full potential of the various personalities and interactions within any given group of players and we don't know what steps the manager and his staff take to keep that group happy, productive and comfortable seeking out help or new information. We don't even know what the full possible extent of a manager's influence over all of that might be. We'll almost certainly always be flying blind in this area.

Obviously, that's not true of the tactical, on-field portion of a manager's job. That's the good news. The bad news is that portion might be one of the least important pieces of the job. Carleton's past research at BP has estimated that a manager can earn his team just one or two extra wins per season through good tactical maneuvering. Half of the skipper's tactical work has been all but eliminated. Sacrifice bunts by position players have, relatively speaking, all but disappeared over the last 20 years. Pinch-hitting options are limited by bench shrinkage. The running game (stolen bases, hit-and-runs) has lost its place. Modern offenses rely on extra-base hits. Small-ball strategies increase the value only of singles, which are becoming scarce.

That said, there's still plenty of good ground on which to fight about managerial choices. The shifting paradigm of pitcher usage means that managers begin making important moves earlier than they used to, perhaps in the fifth or sixth inning. We've learned a lot about the confluence of factors that make a starter less effective as the game goes on, and that new information (coupled with the ability to obtain granular, process-centric data even as an inning unfolds) makes the decision of when to lift a starting pitcher more dynamic than ever. Then, thanks to changing bullpen roles and the imperative for many managers to use their bullpen with seven months of work in mind, there are even more levers to pull over the final few frames.

If we ever want to objectively and quantitatively understand and express managers' value, we need to take stock of what we know and what we don't know. Teasing out the degree of responsibility various members of the coaching staff might have over various aspects of the collective job will be difficult, but let's start with an inventory of knowns and unknowns. In most cases, we know when a manager is making a glaring mistake in the day-to-day management of a young player. We know when he's abusing a starting pitcher or a reliever. We can observe things like baserunners being caught stealing or thrown out at third base too often. We have reliable tallies of shift frequency, and although StatCast data on starting defensive positioning is not yet public, we already have a sense of when players are being positioned poorly.

We don't know, or have a hard time gauging, what a team's chemistry is, what effect that is having on them and what influence the manager has over that. We don't always know which players are healthy and which aren't. We have only a passing understanding of a player's day-to-day psyche and which choices a manager might make to best serve a given player's needs. The future of managing MLB teams will be fascinating. The changing nature of the job should inform changes in the criteria teams value most when searching for new managers. Youth matters. Younger managers might be more inclined to accede to the front office's input in the first place, but just as importantly they're physiologically more capable of evolving thought than older counterparts. Open-mindedness is a personality trait and old dogs can learn new tricks, but age brings ossification.

Still, track records are important. More managers should be hired after holding the same job in the minor leagues. For too long, having held such a job has been seen as unhelpful to a big-league manager. The minor-league manager's first responsibility, the thinking goes, is development, not winning, so his job is fundamentally different than that of a big-league skipper. I reject that idea. The first responsibility of a minor-league manager is communication, that aforementioned coordination between a prized prospect, the player development staff with whom he's been in contact and the coach whose primary job will be instructing that player. The first job of a big-league manager is, in reality, the same one: communicating with the front office, with each player and with the coaches who help the manager get the most out of the resources on hand.

Even more than that, having managed previously provides a tactical track record with which to project a manager's likely in-game decisions. Managers change very little once they establish a certain set of tactical habits. Not even cataclysmic events usually lead to lasting changes. Dusty Baker, who overused and abused Mark Prior and other young pitchers, pushed Stephen Strasburg markedly harder than any manager ever had in 2016, resulting in a season-ending injury the same year the team signed Strasburg to a seven-year deal. Showalter, who lost the 1995 ALDS and his job because he elected to stick with Jack McDowell in the extra innings of Game 5 and who watched the Mariners walk off in the Kingdome while closer John Wetteland stood ready in the bullpen, nonetheless lost the Wild Card game this past season by sticking with Ubaldo Jimenez in extra innings while Zach Britton went unused.

Maddon, who in 2008 intentionally walked Josh Hamilton with the bases loaded in the ninth inning because he represented the tying run, and who in 2010 spent most of a series sweep over the Tigers walking Miguel Cabrera, upped the ante in May and walked Bryce Harper 13 times over four games at Wrigley Field (the Cubs swept). Most skippers have tactical signatures and few of them ever change their stripes. A smart team will look for the rare guy, like Clint Hurdle or Ned Yost, who does stay open to that kind of change. That will probably mean hiring younger, but it might also mean hiring in a radically different manner. Greater diversity should be a goal for the league in terms of hiring practices, but also for teams in terms of finding the best candidate in a bigger pool than they currently use to select managers.

Evolution of the game seems to accelerate all the time. The state of managing is fluid. In a year, we might have a whole new outlook on where the manager plays the biggest role. In the meantime, our goal should be to observe the interactions between player talent, front office savvy and the field staff's choices with an open mind and a big-picture perspective. Managing is a job that requires many skills. The coaching staff's role as connective tissue—maximizing development, optimizing performance and engendering a winning culture—is the one that matters most. As we widen the lens to see all of these interactions at work, it will be easier than ever not to dwell too deeply on whether or not a closer pitches in a tie game on the road. ■

—Matthew Trueblood is an author
of Baseball Prospectus

2017 Managers

At the top of most manager's statistical profiles you will see their career wRM+. Rian Watt and Rob Arthur created RM and wRM+ in order to better understand the degree to which big-league managers match their best relievers to the game's biggest moments. Every bit of evidence we have suggests that assigning relievers to granite-hewn roles ("closer"; "set-up man"; "scrub") is, generally speaking, a suboptimal way to manage a bullpen. Some moments matter more than others; when they come, you want your best man in.

We ranked the relievers on each team since 2000 from best to worst in DRA. We then ranked those same pitchers by the average leverage index at the point when they first entered the game. We correlated each team's ranking of relievers by leverage index to its ranking by DRA. Effective bullpen managers used their best relievers (those with the lowest DRAs) in the most important moments (those with the highest leverage index), which pushes the RM score toward an ideal of -1. wRM+ is RM scaled to 100.

In early testing, past RM scores were statistically significant predictors of future scores, even two years out, and we found compelling evidence that managers have collectively improved at the skill over time. There's room for improvement—to account for injuries and availability, most notably—and the overall effect on wins and losses is probably something on the order of a half a win.

In the yearly manager stat lines, Pythag +/- follows the year, team and the actual record, and lets us know by how many games the team under- or overperformed its Pythagenpat record. That isn't necessarily a reflection on the manager, but it does tell us how well a team performed compared to a less noisy assessment of the underlying talent.

AVG PC reports the average pitch count of the manager's starting pitchers; 100+P and 120+P track the number of games in which the starters exceeded those pitch count thresholds. QS is the number of quality starts—a start of at least six innings and with no more than three earned runs allowed—that a manager received from his starting pitchers. BQS is Blown Quality Starts, a Baseball Prospectus stat that measures games in which the starter delivered a quality start through six innings before losing it in the seventh inning or later. A Blown Quality Start is not necessarily an indictment of a manager's abilities or tactics—a number of factors can lead a manager to leave his starter in a game after he's thrown six quality innings. Conversely, the decision by a manager to "bank" quality starts by restricting his starters to only six innings can have downsides as well, as it increases the bullpen's workload and gives it more opportunities to blow games in which the starter was cruising.

REL tallies how many pitching changes a manager made over the course of the season. REL w Zero R shows how many times the reliever called upon didn't allow any runners, his own or inherited, to score. Bequeathed runners also count against this, meaning that relievers who exit with runners on who subsequently score prevent a manager from "padding" his tally here. IBB is the number of intentional walks the manager ordered during the given season, which can be a mark of managerial strategy so long as outlying intentional-walk recipients like Miguel Cabrera are accounted for.

Managers' usage of the bench can lead to added or lost performance. PH is the number of pinch-hitters used, and PH Avg and PH HR report the offensive statistics of pinch-hitters called upon. We then turn to the so-called small-ball tactics, starting with the running game. The manager's aggressiveness on the bases is broken down by successful steals of second and third base (SB2, SB3) and times caught (CS2, CS3). We also provide the number of sacrifices a team attempted (SAC Att) and their success rate (SAC %). Be sure to keep in mind the differences between leagues, as National League sacrifice attempts, like pinch-hitter usage, are greatly inflated by the fact that pitchers bat. To correct for this, we list the number of times a manager got a successful sacrifice from a position player (POS SAC), which allows for comparisons between the two leagues. Squeeze counts the number of successful squeeze plays the team executed over the season.

Swing is the number of times a hitter swung at a pitch while the runners were in motion, while In Play reflects how many times hitters swung and made contact while those runners were off to the races. Swings on steal attempts do not always translate to hit-and-run attempts, but managers who greatly deviate from the average can be assumed to be staunch proponents or opponents of the strategy.

MANAGERS

Brad Ausmus   wRM+: 98.8

TEAM	YEAR	W	L	Pythag +/-	Avg PC	100+ P	120+ P	QS	BQS	REL	REL w Zero R	IBB	PH	PH Avg	PH HR	SB2	CS2	SB3	CS3	SAC Att	SAC %	POS SAC	Squeeze	Swing	In Play
DET	2014	90	72	3	101	103	3	90	9	473	367	34	71	.164	1	90	34	16	7	40	60	20	1	296	83
DET	2015	74	87	6	94.1	77	2	72	10	505	396	32	74	.121	1	66	44	17	5	43	53.5	23	1	293	86
DET	2016	86	75	2	94.9	62	2	72	6	476	375	25	80	.254	6	56	26	4	3	29	58.6	16	2	185	61

Dusty Baker   wRM+: 95.5

TEAM	YEAR	W	L	Pythag +/-	Avg PC	100+ P	120+ P	QS	BQS	REL	REL w Zero R	IBB	PH	PH Avg	PH HR	SB2	CS2	SB3	CS3	SAC Att	SAC %	POS SAC	Squeeze	Swing	In Play
SFN	1993	103	59	3	—	—	—	86	6	414	342	46	246	.183	4	97	59	23	6	135	75.6	52	2	—	—
SFN	1994	55	60	-3	—	—	—	68	8	287	224	40	176	.227	3	103	34	11	6	90	72.2	37	0	—	—
SFN	1995	67	77	7	—	—	—	70	5	381	278	51	227	.210	1	125	39	13	6	100	79.0	46	1	—	—
SFN	1996	68	94	-2	—	—	—	69	18	425	314	60	247	.205	6	103	47	10	5	106	72.6	42	1	—	—
SFN	1997	90	72	10	—	—	—	81	4	481	370	57	210	.268	1	105	40	16	4	86	74.4	36	1	—	—
SFN	1998	89	74	-3	84.6	57	8	79	9	433	349	68	225	.227	10	97	41	5	7	109	74.3	38	1	—	—
SFN	1999	86	76	1	103.5	106	27	79	7	450	356	41	231	.218	4	99	50	10	6	116	75.0	38	1	—	—
SFN	2000	97	65	-1	102.3	94	26	88	9	384	292	26	231	.231	7	72	34	7	5	84	86.9	25	0	—	—
SFN	2001	90	72	4	99.6	84	9	80	11	439	338	49	258	.248	14	53	35	4	7	80	83.7	31	0	—	—
SFN	2002	95	67	-5	100.9	86	21	91	5	416	352	44	201	.197	1	70	20	4	1	87	78.2	24	0	—	—
CHN	2003	88	74	2	103.5	101	25	100	5	420	335	36	236	.155	2	66	30	7	1	105	76.2	42	0	239	77
CHN	2004	89	73	-6	98.9	81	12	95	6	461	364	33	254	.236	4	64	24	2	4	117	66.7	37	0	238	80
CHN	2005	79	83	-1	97.5	78	10	91	4	457	353	48	240	.195	2	60	34	5	3	97	71.1	42	2	302	104
CHN	2006	66	96	-3	91.8	56	7	60	4	542	423	44	270	.216	5	107	41	13	5	120	70.0	56	3	361	117
CIN	2008	74	88	3	97.8	80	3	78	2	507	379	40	282	.231	4	68	39	17	6	115	62.6	34	4	317	103
CIN	2009	78	84	3	98.5	87	1	79	3	478	385	36	251	.227	4	80	35	15	4	133	75.2	47	3	322	98
CIN	2010	91	71	-1	97.8	81	4	89	3	501	408	32	256	.236	10	79	36	14	5	100	66.0	28	3	322	99
CIN	2011	79	83	-4	95.5	67	2	90	7	502	390	47	240	.286	8	85	43	12	6	110	70.9	32	2	377	131
CIN	2012	97	65	6	97.4	74	1	98	6	425	365	33	201	.269	2	73	24	14	2	119	61.3	28	2	310	97
CIN	2013	90	72	-5	95.3	61	2	94	6	461	389	28	232	.248	5	61	32	6	2	118	72.0	37	2	314	111
WAS	2016	95	67	-4	97.4	79	1	92	2	508	419	43	218	.207	12	102	37	18	2	69	69.6	11	5	330	93

Jeff Banister   wRM+: 97.6

TEAM	YEAR	W	L	Pythag +/-	Avg PC	100+ P	120+ P	QS	BQS	REL	REL w Zero R	IBB	PH	PH Avg	PH HR	SB2	CS2	SB3	CS3	SAC Att	SAC %	POS SAC	Squeeze	Swing	In Play
TEX	2015	88	74	5	95.6	55	1	79	3	498	402	29	89	.228	1	87	34	13	4	72	59.7	42	1	292	83
TEX	2016	95	67	13	93.0	45	2	84	1	479	379	16	77	.164	0	87	34	11	1	33	54.5	17	0	283	83

Bud Black   wRM+: 103.1

TEAM	YEAR	W	L	Pythag +/-	Avg PC	100+ P	120+ P	QS	BQS	REL	REL w Zero R	IBB	PH	PH Avg	PH HR	SB2	CS2	SB3	CS3	SAC Att	SAC %	POS SAC	Squeeze	Swing	In Play
SDN	2007	89	74	-1	90.0	47	0	90	4	485	404	48	272	.188	3	50	16	5	7	93	68.8	28	1	246	90
SDN	2008	63	99	-3	90.9	49	3	76	4	490	348	61	285	.198	3	34	17	2	0	76	77.6	18	0	226	93
SDN	2009	75	87	9	91.0	46	1	77	3	528	412	58	263	.248	9	72	23	10	5	111	66.7	38	1	296	90
SDN	2010	90	72	-2	94.8	54	0	87	2	499	431	51	278	.206	9	114	47	10	1	111	71.2	44	1	359	97
SDN	2011	71	91	-8	96.7	65	1	91	4	489	416	56	283	.160	2	147	42	21	2	86	64.0	23	4	391	88
SDN	2012	76	86	2	92.2	49	1	75	5	529	449	48	278	.248	6	129	42	25	2	107	58.9	30	1	396	88
SDN	2013	76	86	5	93.9	59	2	87	2	488	402	31	266	.206	8	105	31	13	3	92	56.5	23	1	284	75
SDN	2014	77	85	2	94.4	52	1	91	2	481	417	32	311	.218	11	75	31	16	3	90	62.2	32	2	248	70
SDN	2015	32	35	0	97.7	33	0	43	0	206	160	16	119	.170	1	44	10	2	1	29	58.6	11	0	106	36

Bruce Bochy   wRM+: 104.1

TEAM	YEAR	W	L	Pythag +/-	Avg PC	100+ P	120+ P	QS	BQS	REL	REL w Zero R	IBB	PH	PH Avg	PH HR	SB2	CS2	SB3	CS3	SAC Att	SAC %	POS SAC	Squeeze	Swing	In Play
SDN	1995	70	74	-2	–	–	–	73	6	337	234	37	252	.243	10	96	40	27	5	73	76.7	19	0	–	–
SDN	1996	91	71	0	–	–	–	80	8	411	335	47	280	.227	4	87	42	22	12	74	79.7	18	2	–	–
SDN	1997	76	86	4	–	–	–	67	9	426	294	37	287	.247	7	117	50	22	7	82	76.8	22	2	–	–
SDN	1998	98	64	4	90.0	59	9	99	5	369	309	45	272	.177	2	66	33	12	2	78	71.8	22	1	–	–
SDN	1999	74	88	1	95.8	67	5	81	5	402	304	48	289	.204	7	141	56	28	9	63	57.1	8	0	–	–
SDN	2000	76	86	2	98.5	78	16	75	7	443	334	50	275	.225	7	119	48	10	3	52	75.0	16	1	–	–
SDN	2001	79	83	0	93.8	61	5	77	7	422	322	54	250	.227	2	111	35	18	3	43	67.4	9	1	–	–
SDN	2002	66	96	2	91.5	47	2	74	5	459	355	61	235	.190	6	59	40	15	3	57	78.9	23	1	–	–
SDN	2003	64	98	-1	93.6	67	2	74	3	473	339	52	288	.222	4	66	36	10	2	85	58.8	23	1	251	73
SDN	2004	87	75	-1	92.2	43	2	79	5	437	342	39	248	.204	5	45	20	7	5	86	60.5	22	0	251	90
SDN	2005	82	80	6	94.3	59	2	78	5	456	367	45	271	.211	4	94	36	4	6	108	66.7	36	0	316	118
SDN	2006	88	74	1	95.7	64	5	90	8	475	376	63	258	.260	8	111	26	12	4	86	68.6	19	0	358	114
SFN	2007	71	91	-6	98.7	78	8	86	3	497	380	41	261	.268	5	106	29	13	2	96	69.8	31	3	361	115
SFN	2008	72	90	5	99.7	90	8	86	7	479	366	59	273	.239	3	99	41	6	1	91	62.6	26	3	367	132
SFN	2009	88	74	1	97.4	74	5	84	4	457	370	49	230	.251	2	69	27	8	0	97	69.1	18	0	302	99
SFN	2010	92	70	-3	99.4	77	7	95	4	476	402	58	219	.262	6	49	28	6	3	106	71.7	28	0	264	85
SFN	2011	86	76	6	99.8	90	7	103	3	480	411	46	244	.212	4	76	42	7	6	86	72.1	29	2	395	118
SFN	2012	94	68	5	100.0	91	3	93	6	526	440	42	214	.217	3	111	35	6	2	100	69.0	27	0	382	123
SFN	2013	76	86	3	96.1	79	2	80	2	524	429	64	258	.213	4	64	24	3	1	86	76.7	25	2	329	119
SFN	2014	88	74	1	94.7	59	1	86	6	475	412	35	233	.222	4	52	24	4	2	66	68.2	20	5	268	97
SFN	2015	84	78	-5	90.8	37	0	78	3	557	474	28	224	.249	1	87	32	6	3	60	75.0	12	1	309	106
SFN	2016	87	75	-4	96.6	77	1	85	3	575	488	30	257	.225	4	70	33	9	3	64	65.6	18	3	305	104

Kevin Cash   wRM+: 98.4

TEAM	YEAR	W	L	Pythag +/-	Avg PC	100+ P	120+ P	QS	BQS	REL	REL w Zero R	IBB	PH	PH Avg	PH HR	SB2	CS2	SB3	CS3	SAC Att	SAC %	POS SAC	Squeeze	Swing	In Play
TBA	2015	80	82	-1	90.6	46	1	68	3	530	416	23	179	.219	3	62	40	25	4	29	65.5	17	0	290	82
TBA	2016	68	94	-8	96.2	67	1	74	5	485	369	25	92	.128	1	48	33	12	3	31	58.1	18	1	306	86

Terry Collins   wRM+: 102.3

TEAM	YEAR	W	L	Pythag +/-	Avg PC	100+ P	120+ P	QS	BQS	REL	REL w Zero R	IBB	PH	PH Avg	PH HR	SB2	CS2	SB3	CS3	SAC Att	SAC %	POS SAC	Squeeze	Swing	In Play
HOU	1994	66	49	-2	–	–	–	64	6	268	218	34	185	.270	6	106	41	18	2	92	79.3	32	4	–	–
HOU	1995	76	68	-3	–	–	–	80	4	394	299	52	299	.294	9	150	44	26	13	90	86.7	34	1	–	–
HOU	1996	82	80	5	–	–	–	84	11	370	254	60	248	.192	6	142	54	38	9	95	71.6	21	0	–	–
ANA	1997	84	78	0	–	–	–	76	8	400	309	34	66	.207	0	109	64	16	7	57	70.2	39	0	–	–
ANA	1998	85	77	4	93.1	79	24	77	8	415	333	23	89	.179	0	84	40	9	5	72	68.1	46	2	–	–
ANA	1999	51	82	0	95.3	53	10	62	5	315	231	14	79	.239	1	53	34	4	2	39	76.9	28	0	–	–
NYN	2011	77	85	-1	95.7	63	6	84	7	514	398	48	306	.203	8	113	32	16	4	102	63.7	26	2	347	114
NYN	2012	74	88	0	95.5	69	2	101	1	505	380	29	322	.240	10	66	35	13	3	82	78.0	19	4	321	108
NYN	2013	74	88	1	95.7	69	2	94	3	534	417	38	262	.207	4	99	31	15	4	82	64.6	26	0	310	87
NYN	2014	79	83	-3	93.7	72	3	98	3	489	411	38	240	.181	3	90	27	10	7	86	68.6	18	3	274	64
NYN	2015	90	72	0	93.1	49	2	101	6	485	401	43	247	.204	4	46	23	5	1	50	58.0	8	1	250	82
NYN	2016	87	75	-1	90.6	47	0	87	2	538	434	39	284	.221	13	32	17	10	1	66	53.0	11	0	215	69

Craig Counsell   wRM+: 100.1

TEAM	YEAR	W	L	Pythag +/-	Avg PC	100+ P	120+ P	QS	BQS	REL	REL w Zero R	IBB	PH	PH Avg	PH HR	SB2	CS2	SB3	CS3	SAC Att	SAC %	POS SAC	Squeeze	Swing	In Play
MIL	2015	61	76	-3	92.4	40	0	53	6	424	338	30	244	.259	5	67	20	9	3	59	72.9	16	1	197	63
MIL	2016	73	89	-1	90.3	30	0	62	2	513	393	33	282	.178	7	144	46	35	10	87	60.9	21	2	371	76

John Farrell   wRM+: 99.0

TEAM	YEAR	W	L	Pythag +/-	Avg PC	100+ P	120+ P	QS	BQS	REL	REL w Zero R	IBB	PH	PH Avg	PH HR	SB2	CS2	SB3	CS3	SAC Att	SAC %	POS SAC	Squeeze	Swing	In Play
TOR	2011	81	81	2	97.7	81	4	81	3	474	383	28	58	.185	0	98	43	32	6	54	57.4	31	2	372	103
TOR	2012	73	89	-1	91.9	52	0	74	3	495	396	20	80	.205	1	89	31	33	8	67	49.3	32	3	406	138
BOS	2013	97	65	-5	100.0	88	5	95	6	450	355	10	81	.235	6	104	17	17	2	38	63.2	21	0	336	104
BOS	2014	71	91	0	97.7	73	1	87	6	493	410	19	91	.231	2	43	21	19	3	34	58.8	19	1	301	79
BOS	2015	51	64	0	93.7	48	0	53	2	328	251	12	51	.244	0	40	12	9	1	29	79.3	21	0	222	98
BOS	2016	93	69	-7	96.5	78	2	87	3	463	387	16	98	.190	3	71	19	11	3	19	42.1	8	0	333	119

Terry Francona   wRM+: 100.0

TEAM	YEAR	W	L	Pythag +/-	Avg PC	100+ P	120+ P	QS	BQS	REL	REL w Zero R	IBB	PH	PH Avg	PH HR	SB2	CS2	SB3	CS3	SAC Att	SAC %	POS SAC	Squeeze	Swing	In Play
PHI	1997	68	94	5	–	–	–	80	5	409	285	42	285	.184	3	79	48	11	6	98	75.5	29	0	–	–
PHI	1998	75	87	4	95.8	74	20	77	9	386	273	27	255	.232	5	87	41	10	4	86	75.6	28	0	–	–
PHI	1999	77	85	-4	96.9	79	14	73	10	441	333	24	237	.255	5	113	32	12	2	82	85.4	23	0	–	–
PHI	2000	65	97	-3	102.6	106	23	87	10	413	273	32	271	.197	2	91	25	11	3	86	81.4	28	1	–	–
BOS	2004	98	64	0	98.9	88	3	86	9	437	335	28	99	.264	2	64	27	4	2	24	50.0	10	0	263	78
BOS	2005	95	67	4	99.6	93	3	81	6	442	337	28	98	.221	1	42	12	3	0	25	56.0	13	0	252	98
BOS	2006	86	76	5	95.3	63	2	70	7	455	332	25	87	.222	0	46	22	5	1	38	57.9	22	0	273	106
BOS	2007	96	66	-7	97.6	66	3	84	10	451	379	20	73	.217	2	83	20	13	4	52	57.7	30	2	333	100
BOS	2008	95	67	-2	95.9	69	1	82	9	466	359	17	49	.250	2	99	32	21	2	47	59.6	27	0	310	90
BOS	2009	95	67	0	99.0	81	3	82	3	463	369	24	79	.221	0	106	35	19	4	32	59.4	17	0	309	97
BOS	2010	89	73	0	102.8	112	3	89	5	443	348	30	117	.260	2	56	14	11	2	38	76.3	24	0	340	108
BOS	2011	90	72	-5	96.8	78	4	71	5	443	359	11	83	.176	2	93	40	9	1	33	66.7	22	0	366	122
CLE	2013	92	70	1	94.9	68	0	73	5	540	454	26	58	.255	3	96	33	21	3	41	75.6	30	0	332	85
CLE	2014	85	77	2	94.6	61	0	78	5	573	507	51	103	.233	0	96	23	8	4	63	81.0	49	0	290	92
CLE	2015	81	80	-3	94.5	77	2	91	4	476	391	27	106	.240	4	79	26	7	1	65	72.3	45	0	274	58
CLE	2016	94	67	2	92.0	60	0	81	6	504	428	34	106	.143	1	104	25	29	6	48	64.6	27	0	294	71

John Gibbons   wRM+: 95.4

TEAM	YEAR	W	L	Pythag +/-	Avg PC	100+ P	120+ P	QS	BQS	REL	REL w Zero R	IBB	PH	PH Avg	PH HR	SB2	CS2	SB3	CS3	SAC Att	SAC %	POS SAC	Squeeze	Swing	In Play
TOR	2004	20	30	-1	90.0	16	2	19	1	130	91	11	28	.292	2	19	10	3	2	2	100.0	2	0	113	37
TOR	2005	80	82	-9	90.4	42	1	80	5	432	355	29	120	.324	2	58	32	13	2	32	65.6	20	1	339	117
TOR	2008	35	39	-3	98.6	39	1	40	4	205	179	26	43	.368	2	38	19	7	3	25	80.0	18	0	182	59
TOR	2013	74	88	-2	92.3	56	1	67	6	487	391	33	102	.220	3	87	38	25	3	44	65.9	26	0	353	99
TOR	2014	83	79	-2	96.6	68	4	86	7	449	367	23	176	.220	9	64	16	14	5	61	57.4	34	1	309	102
TOR	2015	93	69	-10	92.8	58	1	84	5	469	384	20	88	.225	3	70	18	17	4	51	70.6	34	1	281	77
TOR	2016	89	73	-3	96.0	55	0	100	5	487	381	10	84	.167	1	45	22	9	1	39	66.7	22	0	275	81

Joe Girardi   wRM+: 105.3

TEAM	YEAR	W	L	Pythag +/-	Avg PC	100+ P	120+ P	QS	BQS	REL	REL w Zero R	IBB	PH	PH Avg	PH HR	SB2	CS2	SB3	CS3	SAC Att	SAC %	POS SAC	Squeeze	Swing	In Play
FLO	2006	78	84	-2	94.2	74	3	89	4	436	332	58	247	.242	4	95	50	13	6	110	69.1	42	3	363	105
NYA	2008	89	73	1	90.5	43	0	78	5	474	379	37	88	.280	4	107	36	11	3	39	79.5	29	0	432	134
NYA	2009	103	59	6	96.5	78	4	76	4	462	372	28	90	.232	3	99	26	12	1	48	64.6	28	0	323	108
NYA	2010	95	67	-3	97.1	78	2	83	3	431	349	37	95	.167	2	93	26	9	4	48	68.8	27	0	362	110
NYA	2011	97	65	-6	95.7	69	2	84	6	465	404	43	54	.196	0	125	42	21	3	54	66.7	29	0	357	94
NYA	2012	95	67	-1	97.9	84	3	82	7	485	409	32	129	.148	4	77	24	16	3	50	62.0	28	0	321	88
NYA	2013	85	77	7	95.7	82	1	84	11	428	356	34	99	.242	1	96	27	18	4	53	67.9	35	0	302	94
NYA	2014	84	78	7	93.3	54	0	83	6	475	399	23	95	.244	2	97	23	13	3	45	64.4	27	0	311	85
NYA	2015	87	75	-1	92.5	42	0	72	9	497	400	16	111	.250	3	60	23	3	2	33	72.7	24	1	231	75
NYA	2016	84	78	6	91.5	40	0	70	8	483	383	15	75	.191	3	64	21	5	1	38	55.3	19	0	215	65

Andy Green   wRM+: 100.5

TEAM	YEAR	W	L	Pythag +/-	Avg PC	100+ P	120+ P	QS	BQS	REL	REL w Zero R	IBB	PH	PH Avg	PH HR	SB2	CS2	SB3	CS3	SAC Att	SAC %	POS SAC	Squeeze	Swing	In Play
SDN	2016	68	94	-4	90.5	39	0	69	2	510	390	44	243	.208	4	103	40	18	5	60	60.0	11	2	304	79

A.J. Hinch   wRM+: 101.9

TEAM	YEAR	W	L	Pythag +/-	Avg PC	100+ P	120+ P	QS	BQS	REL	REL w Zero R	IBB	PH	PH Avg	PH HR	SB2	CS2	SB3	CS3	SAC Att	SAC %	POS SAC	Squee-ze	Swing	In Play
ARI	2009	58	75	-4	98.8	79	0	73	5	392	281	24	220	.185	5	68	22	13	9	69	65.2	24	1	217	66
ARI	2010	31	48	0	101.9	46	5	38	6	207	133	19	119	.213	0	42	11	3	2	21	81.0	7	0	151	48
HOU	2015	86	76	-8	98.0	74	4	94	4	482	412	17	114	.224	5	99	41	21	5	40	70.0	25	2	300	83
HOU	2016	84	78	0	93.7	52	0	77	3	500	403	19	98	.209	2	90	34	12	9	44	61.4	22	3	309	77

Clint Hurdle   wRM+: 95.2

TEAM	YEAR	W	L	Pythag +/-	Avg PC	100+ P	120+ P	QS	BQS	REL	REL w Zero R	IBB	PH	PH Avg	PH HR	SB2	CS2	SB3	CS3	SAC Att	SAC %	POS SAC	Squee-ze	Swing	In Play
COL	2002	67	73	5	93.1	45	1	61	7	437	322	38	244	.276	5	82	40	10	5	51	76.5	26	1	–	–
COL	2003	74	88	-3	89.7	38	0	68	2	500	369	51	285	.260	5	57	34	6	3	103	53.4	28	1	238	85
COL	2004	68	94	-5	95.7	60	3	65	8	473	329	84	287	.253	11	36	31	8	2	148	65.5	55	0	258	87
COL	2005	67	95	-2	94.0	52	1	68	3	459	336	54	272	.224	4	61	26	4	5	131	67.2	52	2	334	116
COL	2006	76	86	-5	95.6	55	2	81	7	499	392	81	258	.215	6	80	44	4	3	167	71.3	64	0	325	112
COL	2007	90	73	-2	90.4	50	0	79	2	529	413	61	283	.216	4	98	31	2	0	130	63.8	37	2	354	104
COL	2008	74	88	1	92.2	53	0	68	3	484	370	49	250	.239	4	116	34	25	3	124	72.6	41	0	354	82
COL	2009	18	28	-3	92.5	19	0	26	2	135	96	11	73	.306	2	24	13	6	2	29	69.0	8	0	113	45
PIT	2011	72	90	3	89.5	26	0	78	2	549	452	65	275	.201	1	95	47	13	3	110	68.2	37	1	384	114
PIT	2012	79	83	1	90.4	42	0	83	2	483	398	30	266	.173	2	66	45	7	3	93	66.7	30	2	271	94
PIT	2013	94	68	5	89.7	41	0	83	2	465	395	26	285	.207	7	83	36	10	6	93	66.7	35	1	347	100
PIT	2014	88	74	1	93.7	44	0	90	3	452	361	43	317	.218	7	99	41	5	4	101	53.5	18	1	365	135
PIT	2015	98	64	4	94.2	46	0	92	7	500	431	38	267	.237	2	89	43	8	2	81	77.8	24	0	288	87
PIT	2016	78	84	0	87.4	27	0	68	0	525	405	28	290	.230	8	100	37	10	6	64	64.1	18	1	309	79

Torey Lovullo   wRM+: –

TEAM	YEAR	W	L	Pythag +/-	Avg PC	100+ P	120+ P	QS	BQS	REL	REL w Zero R	IBB	PH	PH Avg	PH HR	SB2	CS2	SB3	CS3	SAC Att	SAC %	POS SAC	Squee-ze	Swing	In Play
BOS	2015	27	20	-2	101.1	32	0	27	3	147	118	5	11	.455	0	16	10	6	3	11	63.6	7	1	81	24

Pete Mackanin   wRM+: 100.4

TEAM	YEAR	W	L	Pythag +/-	Avg PC	100+ P	120+ P	QS	BQS	REL	REL w Zero R	IBB	PH	PH Avg	PH HR	SB2	CS2	SB3	CS3	SAC Att	SAC %	POS SAC	Squee-ze	Swing	In Play
PIT	2005	12	14	0	86.6	6	0	10	0	94	67	5	53	.133	0	17	1	0	0	20	65.0	8	0	54	16
CIN	2007	41	39	3	90.9	25	3	36	4	266	198	18	130	.204	2	38	9	12	3	49	65.3	15	0	147	50
PHI	2015	37	50	0	87.3	13	2	36	2	276	204	12	140	.213	5	44	17	6	3	55	54.5	17	0	165	48
PHI	2016	71	91	11	90.1	33	0	79	2	505	361	30	259	.157	4	83	41	12	3	78	59.0	26	3	293	74

Joe Maddon   wRM+: 98.8

TEAM	YEAR	W	L	Pythag +/-	Avg PC	100+ P	120+ P	QS	BQS	REL	REL w Zero R	IBB	PH	PH Avg	PH HR	SB2	CS2	SB3	CS3	SAC Att	SAC %	POS SAC	Squee-ze	Swing	In Play
CAL	1996	6	16	0	–	–	–	10	4	52	43	10	21	.235	0	7	7	0	0	11	36.4	4	0	–	–
ANA	1999	19	10	2	96.3	13	3	11	1	85	72	3	27	.238	1	14	9	0	0	13	84.6	11	0	–	–
TBA	2006	61	101	-3	92.8	48	1	65	6	444	303	39	76	.217	1	109	45	24	7	69	50.7	32	3	417	112
TBA	2007	66	96	0	96.9	77	0	73	8	484	320	31	68	.167	0	114	43	16	4	50	68.0	33	4	350	92
TBA	2008	97	65	5	95.9	71	0	82	3	448	365	29	90	.184	1	113	38	28	10	40	57.5	20	0	388	94
TBA	2009	84	78	-2	99.1	80	1	76	5	510	425	22	134	.164	7	167	49	26	11	41	61.0	24	6	404	101
TBA	2010	96	66	-2	98.9	90	2	95	5	491	412	34	154	.242	3	147	39	25	7	67	58.2	38	6	404	120
TBA	2011	91	71	-1	102.1	98	5	99	10	438	355	38	129	.252	1	134	54	20	8	63	58.7	35	5	441	138
TBA	2012	90	72	-6	99.9	91	7	90	2	471	415	35	135	.178	3	122	38	11	5	62	54.8	32	3	354	105
TBA	2013	92	71	4	94.9	65	2	80	2	485	399	38	169	.235	1	61	34	12	3	39	61.5	24	0	292	93
TBA	2014	77	85	-2	97.1	77	0	84	1	494	418	27	130	.218	1	52	24	11	2	73	58.9	42	3	313	106
CHN	2015	97	65	6	91.1	53	2	81	3	551	459	38	287	.201	5	82	32	13	3	53	60.4	15	2	330	105
CHN	2016	103	59	-7	94.5	56	1	100	3	502	407	24	234	.215	2	57	30	9	1	78	53.8	14	8	264	93

Mike Matheny   wRM+: 101.2

TEAM	YEAR	W	L	Pythag +/-	Avg PC	100+ P	120+ P	QS	BQS	REL	REL w Zero R	IBB	PH	PH Avg	PH HR	SB2	CS2	SB3	CS3	SAC Att	SAC %	POS SAC	Squeeze	Swing	In Play
SLN	2012	88	74	-6	94.2	49	1	99	4	506	400	28	279	.190	1	72	27	18	5	104	66.3	34	0	287	100
SLN	2013	97	65	-6	96.0	67	5	88	3	483	411	26	234	.202	3	33	20	11	2	94	59.6	17	0	242	87
SLN	2014	90	72	7	94.0	60	2	91	2	485	393	35	251	.225	2	48	25	9	7	97	66.0	24	2	306	112
SLN	2015	100	62	2	94.5	64	0	106	1	515	434	37	270	.218	4	62	33	7	5	64	60.9	12	1	297	100
SLN	2016	86	76	-2	91.2	39	1	83	4	481	381	35	274	.333	17	33	19	2	6	67	55.2	13	0	207	76

Don Mattingly   wRM+: 98.9

TEAM	YEAR	W	L	Pythag +/-	Avg PC	100+ P	120+ P	QS	BQS	REL	REL w Zero R	IBB	PH	PH Avg	PH HR	SB2	CS2	SB3	CS3	SAC Att	SAC %	POS SAC	Squeeze	Swing	In Play
LAN	2011	82	79	-3	97.8	66	3	94	4	461	369	48	229	.199	4	108	31	17	9	101	70.3	38	2	360	118
LAN	2012	86	76	0	96.2	66	0	93	5	506	426	62	241	.281	2	93	39	10	2	122	67.2	33	2	329	97
LAN	2013	92	70	2	95.1	69	2	93	2	504	424	44	208	.209	4	74	22	4	5	113	62.8	32	0	283	93
LAN	2014	94	68	1	95.1	70	1	100	1	496	395	35	235	.231	1	123	46	14	3	82	57.3	15	1	340	104
LAN	2015	92	70	2	91.3	47	2	95	3	515	408	32	269	.215	8	51	26	8	8	69	71.0	15	1	250	76
MIA	2016	79	82	2	90.8	46	0	63	1	559	443	62	277	.215	6	61	25	10	3	76	60.5	15	2	240	74

Bob Melvin   wRM+: 96.4

TEAM	YEAR	W	L	Pythag +/-	Avg PC	100+ P	120+ P	QS	BQS	REL	REL w Zero R	IBB	PH	PH Avg	PH HR	SB2	CS2	SB3	CS3	SAC Att	SAC %	POS SAC	Squeeze	Swing	In Play
SEA	2003	93	69	-6	101.9	108	6	94	8	366	305	24	62	.154	2	89	34	19	3	52	67.3	32	1	248	91
SEA	2004	63	99	-5	101.7	99	12	70	10	414	305	32	99	.276	4	92	33	18	9	63	73.0	45	0	355	112
ARI	2005	77	85	13	96.6	64	3	84	10	458	330	43	309	.232	9	64	21	3	4	107	66.4	30	1	281	86
ARI	2006	76	86	-3	94.9	68	3	81	8	461	349	44	274	.194	7	64	26	11	4	94	64.9	21	0	237	80
ARI	2007	90	72	11	94.7	68	4	84	5	469	367	38	239	.239	11	90	16	18	8	85	64.7	26	0	295	89
ARI	2008	82	80	-1	95.7	55	3	95	3	443	336	41	257	.226	3	46	16	12	5	95	71.6	29	1	261	89
ARI	2009	12	17	0	95.9	10	0	16	2	91	64	3	47	.209	3	16	7	5	1	18	50.0	6	0	61	17
OAK	2011	47	52	0	100.4	51	1	55	3	282	220	9	30	.276	2	56	26	19	2	38	57.9	20	0	229	63
OAK	2012	94	68	1	92.5	52	0	90	4	462	386	34	93	.231	3	89	26	33	5	43	62.8	26	0	307	76
OAK	2013	96	66	-1	94.8	56	0	92	2	447	370	23	130	.135	5	58	24	17	3	37	56.8	21	2	253	87
OAK	2014	88	74	-12	96.0	61	1	102	5	441	380	28	161	.201	3	67	16	16	4	41	46.3	15	2	253	83
OAK	2015	68	94	-9	92.4	61	0	83	3	487	368	19	152	.252	0	65	25	13	3	24	58.3	12	1	268	90
OAK	2016	69	93	0	87.2	40	0	69	3	492	403	28	113	.185	2	44	23	6	0	24	54.2	10	1	205	61

Paul Molitor   wRM+: 98.6

TEAM	YEAR	W	L	Pythag +/-	Avg PC	100+ P	120+ P	QS	BQS	REL	REL w Zero R	IBB	PH	PH Avg	PH HR	SB2	CS2	SB3	CS3	SAC Att	SAC %	POS SAC	Squeeze	Swing	In Play
MIN	2015	83	79	2	91.2	55	0	76	6	520	420	34	72	.129	1	59	34	11	3	57	52.6	30	3	279	100
MIN	2016	59	103	-5	91.1	46	0	59	5	533	400	26	65	.123	3	87	31	4	1	58	46.6	25	0	312	86

Bryan Price   wRM+: 103.0

TEAM	YEAR	W	L	Pythag +/-	Avg PC	100+ P	120+ P	QS	BQS	REL	REL w Zero R	IBB	PH	PH Avg	PH HR	SB2	CS2	SB3	CS3	SAC Att	SAC %	POS SAC	Squeeze	Swing	In Play
CIN	2014	76	86	-3	97.3	74	1	103	2	428	337	33	219	.246	6	103	42	19	7	103	73.8	38	1	309	77
CIN	2015	64	98	-4	91.5	44	4	68	4	521	397	42	262	.195	2	99	32	35	5	70	67.1	25	3	329	81
CIN	2016	68	94	1	90.4	42	0	67	3	484	324	31	227	.215	0	106	37	33	12	97	59.8	27	1	362	96

Rick Renteria   wRM+: 99.4

TEAM	YEAR	W	L	Pythag +/-	Avg PC	100+ P	120+ P	QS	BQS	REL	REL w Zero R	IBB	PH	PH Avg	PH HR	SB2	CS2	SB3	CS3	SAC Att	SAC %	POS SAC	Squeeze	Swing	In Play
CHN	2014	73	89	3	93.6	48	1	79	0	537	446	37	272	.185	1	58	37	7	3	93	61.3	25	3	246	82

Dave Roberts   wRM+: 97.2

TEAM	YEAR	W	L	Pythag +/-	Avg PC	100+ P	120+ P	QS	BQS	REL	REL w Zero R	IBB	PH	PH Avg	PH HR	SB2	CS2	SB3	CS3	SAC Att	SAC %	POS SAC	Squeeze	Swing	In Play
LAN	2016	91	71	0	87.6	29	0	60	2	606	503	50	323	.189	6	40	22	5	2	62	48.4	5	2	254	84

Mike Scioscia   wRM+: 97.9

TEAM	YEAR	W	L	Pythag +/-	Avg PC	100+ P	120+ P	QS	BQS	REL	REL w Zero R	IBB	PH	PH Avg	PH HR	SB2	CS2	SB3	CS3	SAC Att	SAC %	POS SAC	Squee-ze	Swing	In Play
ANA	2000	82	80	1	92.0	64	6	58	9	441	341	44	86	.231	2	80	47	13	4	57	82.5	44	4	–	–
ANA	2001	75	87	-2	97.2	73	5	83	10	385	303	47	86	.200	4	95	45	20	3	61	75.4	46	1	–	–
ANA	2002	99	63	-4	99.3	86	5	94	8	400	334	24	103	.281	2	102	42	15	8	64	76.6	47	3	–	–
ANA	2003	77	85	-3	94.2	63	1	65	5	375	310	38	97	.330	1	113	54	14	3	71	70.4	49	2	362	117
ANA	2004	92	70	1	96.8	79	3	79	7	343	269	27	81	.265	1	123	42	19	3	79	70.9	54	3	458	130
ANA	2005	95	67	0	96.9	76	1	99	4	379	306	24	78	.239	1	149	47	12	8	64	67.2	42	2	417	138
ANA	2006	89	73	4	97.0	78	2	97	6	380	292	27	87	.159	3	123	45	23	6	44	70.5	29	2	452	154
ANA	2007	94	68	4	97.2	83	0	90	1	396	310	22	91	.270	2	118	47	20	8	47	68.1	31	2	424	142
ANA	2008	100	62	11	99.4	84	0	92	3	383	302	32	67	.200	0	109	38	19	8	48	66.7	32	1	364	113
ANA	2009	97	65	4	96.9	82	1	77	7	434	340	35	65	.321	2	124	57	22	5	63	68.3	41	3	447	134
ANA	2010	80	82	1	102.1	105	3	93	6	410	325	33	86	.174	0	90	39	14	10	70	60.0	41	3	400	125
ANA	2011	86	76	1	101.0	98	11	98	8	386	313	34	75	.154	2	116	47	18	4	78	64.1	46	1	417	144
ANA	2012	89	73	1	97.4	87	4	91	3	444	365	20	68	.203	2	121	27	12	4	72	65.3	43	3	419	132
ANA	2013	78	84	-3	97.5	77	6	87	5	496	400	36	83	.214	3	71	32	10	1	54	68.5	35	0	349	110
ANA	2014	98	64	1	94.1	71	3	80	5	543	467	41	103	.233	1	72	37	9	2	42	61.9	24	1	315	88
ANA	2015	85	77	6	95.0	55	2	88	5	518	429	45	102	.217	2	45	31	6	2	50	74.0	36	3	297	91
ANA	2016	74	88	-6	90.4	39	0	64	5	527	423	27	94	.171	1	60	30	12	4	49	73.5	36	3	364	118

Scott Servais   wRM+: 99.0

TEAM	YEAR	W	L	Pythag +/-	Avg PC	100+ P	120+ P	QS	BQS	REL	REL w Zero R	IBB	PH	PH Avg	PH HR	SB2	CS2	SB3	CS3	SAC Att	SAC %	POS SAC	Squee-ze	Swing	In Play
SEA	2016	86	76	-2	92.1	43	0	74	8	477	379	31	147	.252	4	48	26	8	1	43	55.8	21	0	268	83

Buck Showalter   wRM+: 98.2

TEAM	YEAR	W	L	Pythag +/-	Avg PC	100+ P	120+ P	QS	BQS	REL	REL w Zero R	IBB	PH	PH Avg	PH HR	SB2	CS2	SB3	CS3	SAC Att	SAC %	POS SAC	Squee-ze	Swing	In Play
NYA	1992	76	86	-4	–	–	–	85	14	308	236	49	89	.247	3	65	31	13	4	36	72.2	26	1	–	–
NYA	1993	88	74	1	–	–	–	81	13	333	253	58	131	.272	4	34	31	4	4	37	59.5	22	0	–	–
NYA	1994	70	43	1	–	–	–	61	8	241	181	24	79	.232	4	48	36	7	4	37	73.0	27	1	–	–
NYA	1995	79	66	0	–	–	–	74	5	302	233	21	103	.266	1	46	24	4	5	27	74.1	20	0	–	–
ARI	1998	65	97	0	89.5	59	8	75	18	368	267	32	248	.171	3	67	32	5	4	70	64.3	16	0	–	–
ARI	1999	100	62	-4	103.2	107	27	98	7	382	298	48	216	.321	5	119	35	16	3	77	79.2	23	1	–	–
ARI	2000	85	77	0	94.9	63	18	84	8	390	294	53	248	.230	2	85	34	12	8	85	71.8	21	3	–	–
TEX	2003	71	91	3	87.9	45	4	51	7	494	347	45	72	.177	0	61	24	4	1	38	63.2	21	0	260	90
TEX	2004	89	73	2	92.3	47	3	61	6	468	381	29	75	.143	1	64	32	5	4	37	62.2	22	0	257	87
TEX	2005	79	83	-3	92.5	66	2	66	2	454	325	31	43	.238	3	61	14	6	1	12	75.0	9	0	304	92
TEX	2006	80	82	-6	91.0	46	0	74	2	489	378	18	37	.182	0	47	23	6	1	35	51.4	15	0	253	83
BAL	2010	34	23	3	98.7	31	0	36	3	144	106	10	15	.154	0	25	9	4	0	15	80.0	12	0	78	26
BAL	2011	69	93	4	91.8	50	0	60	6	478	351	42	57	.309	1	74	20	7	5	41	58.5	23	2	309	97
BAL	2012	93	69	11	95.6	66	1	78	6	492	415	36	69	.161	0	55	21	3	8	51	74.5	34	1	282	102
BAL	2013	85	77	0	95.9	75	0	78	5	473	380	32	65	.143	1	70	26	9	2	39	69.2	23	0	236	68
BAL	2014	96	66	1	97.8	78	1	78	7	479	405	25	74	.308	2	37	16	6	3	56	62.5	32	1	205	60
BAL	2015	81	81	-2	93.7	63	0	72	4	453	369	27	79	.208	1	34	22	9	2	33	60.6	18	0	191	58
BAL	2016	89	73	5	94.5	66	0	69	5	443	366	23	68	.274	2	19	11	0	2	24	70.8	14	0	175	55

Brian Snitker   wRM+: 101.0

TEAM	YEAR	W	L	Pythag +/-	Avg PC	100+ P	120+ P	QS	BQS	REL	REL w Zero R	IBB	PH	PH Avg	PH HR	SB2	CS2	SB3	CS3	SAC Att	SAC %	POS SAC	Squee-ze	Swing	In Play
ATL	2016	59	65	4	89.9	40	0	49	1	456	371	40	212	.226	4	48	21	11	3	78	61.5	14	1	208	74

Ned Yost   wRM+: 100.5

TEAM	YEAR	W	L	Pythag +/-	Avg PC	100+ P	120+ P	QS	BQS	REL	REL w Zero R	IBB	PH	PH Avg	PH HR	SB2	CS2	SB3	CS3	SAC Att	SAC %	POS SAC	Squee-ze	Swing	In Play
MIL	2003	68	94	3	95.5	70	5	66	7	460	344	43	282	.220	6	89	34	9	5	98	63.3	29	1	267	82
MIL	2004	67	94	1	93.2	60	8	82	5	423	299	27	279	.205	7	124	35	14	2	96	58.3	28	1	358	101
MIL	2005	81	81	-3	99.3	86	4	91	5	396	292	52	253	.248	6	68	30	11	3	113	58.4	41	5	298	100
MIL	2006	75	87	5	94.5	67	3	81	7	427	306	34	235	.267	4	60	33	10	4	88	65.9	20	1	294	96
MIL	2007	83	79	-1	94.0	56	3	76	9	492	368	37	253	.224	6	86	25	9	4	81	74.1	22	0	321	100
MIL	2008	83	67	2	96.3	54	6	82	3	399	311	30	217	.208	7	85	27	20	7	66	69.7	17	3	333	108
KCA	2010	55	72	4	96.4	59	1	53	7	332	257	25	52	.214	2	73	35	12	4	45	66.7	25	0	281	78
KCA	2011	71	91	-7	96.9	74	0	75	5	420	339	42	36	.152	1	130	48	23	8	75	73.3	51	2	399	113
KCA	2012	72	90	-1	90.5	55	0	69	4	500	411	44	55	.208	3	109	34	22	4	42	61.9	25	1	334	97
KCA	2013	86	76	-1	98.6	79	2	95	5	427	374	21	74	.210	1	133	30	19	2	56	66.1	36	1	369	99
KCA	2014	89	73	5	98.6	90	2	95	4	451	399	14	43	.250	2	124	29	29	7	55	60.0	30	1	344	112
KCA	2015	95	67	4	92.8	52	0	71	3	493	418	10	36	.188	0	76	30	27	2	48	70.8	32	0	257	86
KCA	2016	81	81	4	93.2	61	0	68	7	472	391	8	47	.238	0	102	31	19	4	66	57.6	35	0	300	73

The Impossible Dream, Fifty Years On

by Rob Mains

The year 1967 saw the escalation of the war in Vietnam, the world's first heart transplant operation (the patient died 18 days later), the release of *Sgt. Pepper's Lonely Hearts Club Band*, the Six-Day War, the first ATM, the debut of *Star Trek* and the confirmation of the Supreme Court's first African-American Justice, Thurgood Marshall.

It also featured one of the craziest pennant races in baseball history. And, as you may have deduced as a reader of this numerically-oriented publication, it was exactly 50 years ago. So let's look back on it from our vantage point a half century later. We may not have gotten the flying cars we were promised, but we did get sabermetrics.

Setting the Stage
The 1967 American League season began with the defending World Series champion Orioles as the leading contender, along with the 1965 AL champion Twins (nine behind in 1966) and the Tigers (10 behind). Chicago, Cleveland and California each won 80-83 games in 1966 as well. The 1964 league champion Yankees, on the other hand, slumped to a losing record in 1965 and the worst record in the league in 1966, behind perennial doormats Kansas City (by 3.5 games), Washington (by 1.0 games) and Boston (by 0.5 games).

At the Break
The American League had eight games on July 9—two single games and three doubleheaders. At the end of the day, the last before the All-Star break, half the league had a winning record. Chicago led at 47-33, followed by Detroit (2.0 games back), Minnesota (2.5), California (4.5) and Boston (6.0). The outlier was Boston, which hadn't had a winning record in a decade. The Red Sox were led by left fielder Carl Yastrzemski, whose 1.023 OPS was second in the league to Baltimore's Frank Robinson.

Yaz was also fourth in homers, sixth in runs, and third in RBI. Boston's leading pitcher was Jim Lonborg, who was leading the league in strikeouts and wins while allowing a .590 OPS, ninth-lowest in the league. The first-place White Sox were paced by a superlative pitching staff, whose 2.31 ERA was nearly a run lower than the second-place Angels' 3.11, a greater gap than that between California and the last-ranked Senators' 3.83. The Twins had the league's top offense, scoring 4.46 runs per game, while the Tigers were third with 4.36.

Heading into August
Boston was the only contender to play well immediately after the All-Star game. The Red Sox were 15-5 from the break through the end of July, enabling them to move into second place, two behind the White Sox. The other four teams played around .500, ranging from Minnesota's 8-11 to Chicago's 11-9. Chicago was two ahead of Boston, four up on Detroit and five ahead of Minnesota and California.

The Stretch Drive
In August, Pythagoras exacted his revenge on the negative run differential Angels, as they went 11-16 to fall out of the race. The punchless White Sox, scoring a league-worst 2.94 runs per game, struggled to a 15-17 record. The other three contenders had a strong month. The Twins were 21-11 despite scoring runs at the second-lowest pace in the league. The Red Sox, first in runs per game and third in run prevention, were 20-15. The Tigers, third in scoring and first in run prevention, went 21-14.

As a result, the standings at the top of American League the morning of September 1 were:

	W	L	WPct	GB
Boston	76	59	.563	--
Minnesota	74	58	.561	0.5
Detroit	74	59	.556	1.0
Chicago	73	59	.553	1.5

What happened next can best be explained by a table.

Date	First	Second/GB	Third/GB	Fourth/GB
Aug 31	Bos	Min/0.5	Det/1.0	Chi/1.5
Sep 01	Bos	Min/0.5	Det/2.0	Chi/2.5
Sep 02	Min	Bos/0.5	Chi/2.0	Det/2.5
Sep 03	Min	Bos/0.5	Chi/1.0	Det/1.5
Sep 04	Min	Bos/0.5	Chi/1.0	Det/1.5
Sep 05	Min	Bos/0.5	Chi/1.0	Det/1.5
Sep 06	T-Min	T-Bos	T-Chi	T-Det
Sep 07	T-Min	T-Bos	T-Chi/0.5	T-Det/0.5
Sep 08	T-Min	T-Det	Bos/0.5	Chi/1.0
Sep 09	T-Min	T-Det	Bos/0.5	Chi/2.0
Sep 10	Min	Bos/0.5	T-Chi/1.5	T-Det/1.5
Sep 11	Min	Bos/1.0	Det/2.0	Chi/2.5
Sep 12	T-Min	T-Bos	Det/1.0	Chi/3.0
Sep 13	T-Min	T-Bos	Det/1.0	Chi/3.0
Sep 14	T-Min	T-Bos	Det/1.0	Chi/2.5
Sep 15	T-Min	T-Bos	T-Det	Chi/1.5

Date	First	Second/GB	Third/GB	Fourth/GB
Sep 16	Det	T-Min/1.0	T-Bos/1.0	Chi/1.5
Sep 17	Det	Chi/0.5	T-Min/1.0	T-Bos/1.0
Sep 18	T-Min	T-Bos	T-Det	Chi/0.5
Sep 19	T-Min	T-Bos	Chi/0.5	Det/1.0
Sep 20	T-Min	T-Bos	Chi/0.5	Det/1.0
Sep 21	T-Min	T-Bos	Chi/1.0	Det/1.5
Sep 22	Min	Bos/0.5	Det/1.0	Chi/2.0
Sep 23	Min	T-Bos/0.5	T-Det/0.5	Chi/1.0
Sep 24	Min	Bos/0.5	Chi/1.0	Det/1.5
Sep 25	T-Min	T-Bos	Chi/0.5	Det/1.5
Sep 26	Min	T-Bos/1.0	T-Chi/1.0	Det/1.5
Sep 27	Min	T-Bos/1.0	T-Det/1.0	Chi/1.5
Sep 28	Min	T-Bos/1.0	T-Det/1.0	Chi/1.5
Sep 29	Min	T-Bos/1.0	T-Det/1.0	Chi/2.0
Sep 30	T-Min	T-Bos	Det/0.5	Chi/2.0
Oct 01	Bos	T-Min/1.0	T-Det/1.0	Chi/3.0

You can read the table, so I don't need to give you a blow-by-blow. Just note that there were four teams within a game of first place with eight days left in the season.

Over the season's final 31 days, the White Sox were 16-14, the worst record of the four contenders. Just a half-game back after play on September 25, they ended the season with five games against the last-place A's and sixth-place Senators … and lost all five, scoring only five runs.

On September 28, Minnesota was 91-69, Boston 90-70 and Detroit 89-69. The Twins and Red Sox had two off days before a two-game series in Boston, while the Tigers hosted the Angels for four games. Rain prevented play on Thursday and Friday, leaving Detroit with two straight doubleheaders to end the season. The Tigers split the Saturday twinbill, while Minnesota fell to Boston 6-4 as starter Jim Kaat (7-0 with a 1.56 ERA in September entering the game) left with an elbow injury in the third inning.

Boston's Jose Santiago took the win in only his third start in the month. That set the stage for the last day of the season, with all three teams facing elimination with a loss. Detroit took the first game of its twinbill but lost the second 8-5 as Denny McLain, John Hiller and Mike Marshall—who would go on to win three Cy Young and four Fireman of the Year awards among them—gave up seven runs before the fourth inning ended. In Boston, the Red Sox came back from a 2-0 deficit with five runs in the sixth to win the pennant with a 5-3 victory.

Analysis: What Went Wrong?

Chicago White Sox, three games behind. The White Sox had problems scoring all year, finishing with 531 runs, fewer than every team in the league but the Yankees at 522. Chicago's no. 3 hitters batted .228 with a .291 on-base percentage and .321 slugging percentage, all last in the league. Manager Eddie Stanky wound up starting 13 players in the three-hole over the course of the season. And the no. 3 hitters' .612 OPS wasn't even the worst on the team; their no. 8 hitters were at .602 and their no. 6 hitters an unfathomable .497.

In fairness, White Sox Park was the most pitcher-friendly in the league in 1967, but the team would've scored more runs by swapping, say, its no. 7 hitters (.689 OPS) for those who batted third. Using the basic version of Bill James' Run Created formula (TB x (H + BB) / (AB + BB)), White Sox no. 3 hitters created 58.0 runs, while the no. 7 hitters created 68.2 in 59 fewer plate appearances. Lineup construction doesn't matter *that* much, but with White Sox pitchers giving up just 3.03 runs per game, it wouldn't have taken many extra runs to make a difference.

Minnesota Twins, one game behind. In the average 2016 American League game, the two teams combined for 9.0 runs scored via 17.5 hits (2.4 of which were home runs) and 6.1 walks with 15.7 strikeouts. In 1967, one year before the Year of the Pitcher, there were 7.4 runs per game, 15.8 hits (1.5 homers), 6.2 walks and 12.3 strikeouts. But the biggest difference? In 1967, one of every 4.4 pitcher starts resulted in a complete game, and there were 1.6 relievers per team per game. Last year, only one of 55.2 starts was a complete game and there were 3.0 relievers per team per game.

In 2016, pitchers allowed a .741 OPS the first time through the order and a .799 OPS the third time, so OPS rose by 58 points from the first to the third time starters faced opposing hitters. That's not a modern baseball feature; it's just that nobody knew about it decades ago. In 1967, starters allowed a .634 OPS the first time through the order and .686 the third, a difference of 52 points that's almost identical to the difference in 2016.

The Twins led the league with 58 complete games in 1967, yet they were more susceptible to the times-through-the-order penalty than the other contenders. Minnesota pitchers allowed a sparkling .595 OPS the first time through the order. The second time through, it crept up to .638. The third time, it was .669. The 74-point difference between the first and third times through was the highest among the four contenders, and Twins pitchers faced more batters the third time through the order than any other American League team.

And it bit the Twins at the end of the season. On the last day, tied with the Red Sox for first, in a win-or-go-home game for each team, the Twins were leading 2-0 in the sixth. Starting pitcher Dean Chance allowed a bunt single to Lonborg and then faced the Red Sox order for a third time. Three singles and a fielder's choice later, he left the game tied 2-2. Two wild pitches and an error brought both of Chance's bequeathed runners across the plate.

Boston won the pennant by a 5-3 score. Chance was the team's best pitcher, but he'd shown signs of fatigue in September, and the Twins had a fully rested fireman, Al Worthington, as well as two dependable pitchers, starter Jim Merritt and reliever Ron Kline. A slow hook during the third time through the order may have cost them the pennant.

Detroit Tigers, one game behind. The Tigers were a strong offensive team, ranking second only to Boston in runs scored and getting average or better offense at every position but third base. But the team's pinch-hitters were astonishingly bad, batting .158/.263/.192. Jerry Lumpe, who'd posted a .566 OPS the year before as the team's primary second baseman, was for some reason the primary pinch-hitter in 1967, posting a .411 OPS in 36 games. Gates Brown, who finished his career with 499 plate appearances as a pinch-hitter, the eighth most in history, had a terrible year with a .450 OPS. The Tigers used their pinch-hitters in higher-leverage situations more than any team in the league but Chicago, so the lack of production came at key points.

It's not that the Tigers didn't have pinch-hitting options: Due in part to injuries, the team had four outfielders accumulate over 360 plate appearances and two of them—Jim Northrup, who batted left, and Willie Horton, who batted right—were often on the bench. They were above-average hitters who batted .294/.381/.353 as pinch-hitters, but were used only 21 times. One of the reasons Northrup was available was that manager Mayo Smith preferred Mickey Stanley's glove in center. Stanley was a much better fielder, but he hit .210/.273/.312 and the Tigers' pitching staff allowed the league's fourth-highest ground-ball percentage to limit outfielder's fielding opportunities.

Boston Red Sox, American League Champions. You can't really criticize a team winning its first pennant in 21 years and breaking a streak of seven straight losing seasons. But we can't talk about baseball 50 years ago without touching on the topic of position player bunting. Second baseman Mike Andrews led the league with 18 sacrifices and shortstop Rico Petrocelli was tied for 11th with eight even though both were far from automatic outs. The Red Sox were also terrible base stealers, posting a 53.5 percent success rate. Of the seven Red Sox who attempted 10 or more stolen bases, Rookie of the Year runner-up Reggie Smith succeeded in 73 percent of his attempts while the other six were caught on 48 percent of their 86 tries. Just staying put would've improved their run scoring.

The Red Sox rode two hot hands to the pennant. Carl Yastrzemski led the league in batting average (.329), on-base percentage (.416), slugging percentage (.641), home runs (25), RBI (65) and runs (62) after the All-Star break en route to a Triple Crown and a near-unanimous MVP (Twins CF/3B/2B Cesar Tovar, who was clearly not even the best player on his team, inexplicably got one first-place vote from a local writer). But as amazing as Yastrzemski was—and a 221 OPS+ in the season's second half is pretty amazing—Mike Andrews, George Scott and Reggie Smith all had strong Septembers, so Yaz had help.

Jim Lonborg, who led the league in pitching WARP and would win the Cy Young award, did not have help. We all remember Madison Bumgarner's 2014 postseason, during which he threw 52.2 innings in 17 games spread over 29 games. Beginning on September 2, Lonborg pitched 56 innings in eight starts over 30 days. No other Boston pitcher had more than five starts or 35 innings during that time. His ERA over the final month was 2.73; his teammates' was 3.84. Riding a dominant starter through a series of high-pressure games … well, let's pause in our criticism of 1967 managers through our modern lens and tip our hat to Boston skipper Dick Williams for his usage of Lonborg, which has parallels to contemporary postseasons.

It's tempting to look back at the strategic shortcomings in 1967, note their similarities today and sigh. Fifty years later, *plus ça change*. But that's simplistic. Lineups today put better hitters in a position to get more plate appearances, with the no. 2 spot undergoing a revolution of sorts in recent years. Awareness of the times-through-the-order penalty has resulted in 2016 American League starters facing nearly two fewer batters per game (despite the DH) than they did in 1967. Bullpens today are populated by talented specialists; reliever ERAs in 2016 were 13 percent lower than starter ERAs, compared to eight percent lower in 1967. Base stealers were successful on fewer than 60 percent of attempts in 1967; they're safe over 70 percent of the time now.

We may not see another pennant race like 1967, but as far as tactics go, *beaucoup a changé*. ■

—Rob Mains is an author
of Baseball Prospectus

The Modern Front Office and the Future of Public Analysis

by Jeff Quinton

At Baseball Prospectus and elsewhere, the public sector primarily has two goals: (i) expand our understanding of the many facets of baseball and its interactions with other phenomenon and (ii) further and better explain the games and decisions surrounding the game. The truly brilliant among us handle the former; from catcher framing to DRA to whatever is next, from minor leaguer labor rights to front office hiring practices to all the other social and political implications of baseball. Those of us less prolific in those areas, like the author of this essay, focus on the latter and do our best to document, explain, and ask questions about what has unfolded and what might unfold.

It was not so long ago that analyzing the decisions made by baseball teams was more straightforward—did the trade help teams compete in their competitive window? Was the player acquired at a cost that considered his aging curve and his abilities in all three aspects of the game (hitting, fielding, running)? Was the player acquired at a price based on predictive statistics (as opposed to arbitrary statistics)? Was this the most production the team could have acquired for the resources spent?

If the answer to any of these questions was no, we would point out how such an acquisition was suboptimal; perhaps we would go a step further by explaining the likely reason behind the misstep (hint: they cared about RBI). The not-smart teams would make these kinds of mistakes more frequently and the smart teams would make these kinds of mistakes less frequently. Sometimes the smart teams would do something we did not understand and we would ask, "why did they do that?" And then we would figure out why and learn something (or think we learned something). Sometimes teams would hire the people from the public sector, the people that were doing the kind of work that made the previously described analysis possible, and then those teams would start to make decisions that looked more like what we thought good decisions looked like.

Before long, all the teams were smart. Yes, even the Diamondbacks now. And we'll exclude the Marlins as they are less of a team and more of a business focused on siphoning taxpayer money. The decisions being made by teams are no longer being made by former players with no input from departments other than a scouting department made up of former players. Rather, choices involving personnel and strategy are being informed by analytics. And these analytics ain't our older brothers' sabermetrics.

These analytics are almost certainly more advanced than anything available at the major sites—some teams certainly buy data from these public sources and/or consult with analysts from the public sector, but the databases, systems and processes are likely more advanced than anything being done in a transaction analysis. Moreover, the people employed by teams to compile and analyze this information are more qualified and educated than at any point in baseball's history (sadly, these people are overwhelmingly white and male and come from wealthy families, but, alas, they are very smart and qualified).

And this makes sense, it was only a matter of time before baseball teams, which have far greater incentives to hire extremely smart people and purchase baseball data than does, say, Baseball Prospectus or Fangraphs, did just that. How, then, if teams are so smart and so informed, can our analysis of their decisions and strategies be worthwhile? If teams are so stocked with data and brains, then would it not be wise for us to avoid dissecting their decisions and say, "these people know what they are doing. I mean, they just hired another guy with a PhD in applied mathematics into an entry level position"?

The answer, although it is also the self-serving answer, is that we should continue to analyze for many reasons. First and most importantly, people enjoy reading such analysis. The other reasons need further explanation and are thus further explained below.

1. Smarter and more informed does not equal perfect

One of the biggest mistakes we can make when studying the history of something is to assume that the current is markedly different from the past. Yes, teams are smarter than before and, yes, less and less of the most cutting edge information is available to the public than before, but both of these statements hold true for each of the past 10 years, yet teams continue to make suboptimal decisions. We have seen teams push their chips in because of pressure to win now, only to mortgage a promising future for short term goals that were never going to happen. More so of late, we have seen teams follow suit in baseball's new all-out rebuilding culture, only to see rebuilds stagnate or take longer than expected. We have seen teams fall victim to cognitive biases and smarter opponents. We will thus assuredly see future mistakes; we will likely see mistakes similar to those made by groups of smart, educated, affluent white males in arenas outside of baseball. Moreover, we will miss more mistakes if we blindly give these modern front offices the benefit of the doubt, if we relax our analyses in any way.

2. There is no perfect in baseball, there is only best and what will be better

Additionally, continued analysis allows us to see or hypothesize what the future will hold for baseball decision making and strategy. Because of the way Major League Baseball and other professional sports leagues are constructed (there are rules in place for competitive balance, there are no patents and players and coaches continuously change organizations), whatever strategy or process is best practice today will soon be copied and thus fail to differentiate in the future. As the Red Queen says to Alice in Lewis Carroll's *Through the Looking Glass*, "Here, you see, it takes all the running you can do to keep in the same place." Born from this is the Red Queen hypothesis which explains that when entities are in competition, an improvement in one entity necessitates improvements in its competitors should they desire to survive. In baseball, this means that current drivers for success and differentiation will soon be needed in order to simply keep up. Consequently, the means for both keeping up and outpacing the competition in baseball are always changing. This has always held true in baseball and will always continue to hold true, which means our public analysis of the decisions teams make will continue to be critical in figuring out what is coming next.

3. There is more to learn

There is always more to learn and we have realized over the past five years that there is just as much if not more to learn about baseball from the decisions teams make as there is for which to criticize them (social issues aside). We have learned that it is easy to overrate defensive metrics and/or overrate their use as a predictor for future production (think late '00s

Mariners). Fresh from our wounds, we had to relearn the importance of defense, particularly outfield defense (think 2014 and 2015 Royals). While we found that starting pitchers were more valuable than relievers, especially mediocre relievers racking up saves, we learned from teams that roles matter to players and their performance, and we later learned that truly great relievers truly matter a great deal for playoff teams if deployed optimally.

Whereas the analysis of the last decade worked to explain decisions as suboptimal (and rightfully so), today's analysis, more than ever before, can learn by trying to figure out what we are missing by trying to figure out what teams might know that we do not. This is how the public eventually came to find pitch framing; and while learning from the decisions of teams was once limited to the few "smart" teams, we now have many more such teams to learn from.

4. There is more to create

By continuing to try and understand what we know and what front offices know, we continue to push the limits of that knowledge. In doing so, in keeping our minds active and observant, we increase our chances of asking better questions and developing better insights. While those asking these questions and finding these insights might not be the people who will discover new metrics and connections, the hope is that these ideas will find the minds of those capable of finding those true breakthroughs.

Ultimately, our discussion and analysis of the game is one of the main fuels for furthering our understanding of the game. We therefore need to keep analyzing in order to keep learning and keep pushing the discussion forward. As teams bring more and more behind the curtain, we will need to be smarter and more empathetic than ever before in order to do so. The good news is that this has always been the case and we have continued to keep continuing on. ■

—Jeff Quinton is an author
of Baseball Prospectus

Top 101 Prospects

by Jeffrey Paternostro and Jarrett Seidler

---

1. Alex Reyes, RHP, St. Louis Cardinals

Putting a pitcher at the top of your national list is the kind of risk lover's high a prospect writer could normally only get from splitting tens against a six*. And similarly, even if it works out, everyone else at the table will yell at you. Names like Todd Van Poppel and Paul Wilson will come up, but Reyes is far more of a proven commodity than those two cautionary tales. Oh yeah, he also throws 100 and has two potential plus secondaries. We can quibble about his command, and yes he needs further seasoning—he's still prospect-list-eligible after all—but if we're going to bet on one guy from this list topping out at the apex of the 20-80 scale, Reyes is our pick.

*Don't split tens against a six if I am sitting at your blackjack table.

2. Dansby Swanson, SS, Atlanta Braves

We here at Baseball Prospectus would never imply that the Braves purposefully manipulated Swanson's at-bats to keep him prospect list eligible. No matter how many extra seats Atlanta might fill in their new stadium as their still-a-rookie shortstop chases an award won by such luminaries as Butch Metzger and Pat Listach. Swanson's one of your ROY Vegas favorites to be sure, as his advanced skills both at the plate and in the field were on display in his 129 at-bats in 2016. Rookie or not, Swanson is still the best reason to head to SunTrust Park this year—not to see him chase some hardware, but to see a bonafide star shortstop in the flesh.

3. Andrew Benintendi, OF, Boston Red Sox

We are tools merchants at heart. We are Frank Thomas blithely staring off into space during the playoffs and murmuring "hardware." And Benintendi doesn't feature a surfeit of tools. He's more of a left fielder than center fielder, although he runs well. He won't show you much more than average over-the-fence power, even in Fenway. He's listed at 5'10", which suggests he is closer to 5'8". But here's the thing: Man, he hits the ball hard. We watch a lot of baseball from behind home plate. We get a feel for what balls are supposed to do off the bat. Benintendi's flight path just goes further. This was true in the minors, and it was true against major league pitching. There is another school of thought on prospect lists that says to just bet on the best hitter. That would be this guy.

4. J.P. Crawford, SS, Philadelphia Phillies

Crawford was an elite prospect from the moment he stepped on the field after being selected 16th overall in the 2013 draft. Watch him for five minutes in BP or infield drills and the talent is obvious. Well that was four years ago, and Crawford has been good at every minor league stop. He really has! But we prospect writers are not known for our patience nor our resistance to newer, shinier shortstops that catch our eye. Crawford has dealt with some minor injuries and now there are questions about how much he will hit after a prosaic 2016 campaign in the upper minors. Sigh. A closer reading of the situation reveals a plus-plus defender at the six with an advanced approach at the plate who struggled in his first go-round at Triple-A at age 21. He's still an elite prospect,

even if we have to fake some of the enthusiasm this year because he isn't a teenager the reader hasn't heard of yet. We're such hipsters.

5. Yoan Moncada, 2B/3B, Chicago White Sox

Twice now, Moncada has showed us something close to the real cost of elite pieces. The Red Sox paid $63 million to sign Moncada in spring 2015—$31.5 million to Moncada himself and a matching $31.5 million penalty to Major League Baseball. He was, of course, then traded this offseason, stock holding to slightly up, as the biggest piece in the Chris Sale deal. Since, unlike most prospects, we can put something close to a free market value on Moncada's actual worth (it's still a little deflated by teams that couldn't or wouldn't blow up their international pools), by proxy he tells you just how good and underpaid Chris Sale is right now. Moncada should be better situated with the change in sock colors, since unlike the Red Sox, the White Sox have little long-term competition at second base, his natural and best position.

6. Austin Meadows, OF, Pittsburgh Pirates

Meadows was a very good prospect coming into the season, and the jump from there to elite prospect didn't just come due to graduations in front of him. Despite an orbital fracture and a hamstring issue that cost him playing time in 2016, the 21-year-old showed more power than he had in the past and did it against the most advanced arms in the minors. The Pirates still have a bit of an outfield logjam and have indicated that Meadows may end up in a corner. He's an above-average centerfielder, but his recent power spike means the profile will now play anywhere on the grass.

7. Victor Robles, OF, Washington Nationals

Well, we are tools merchants after all and Robles does offer a surfeit of them. If you put his scouting report on a slot machine payline you'd be cashing out the super jackpot (7-7-7). He's a potential .300 hitter, a plus-plus runner with a plus-plus arm, and he's already taken well to center field. Sources disagree on how much power he will actually end up with in major league games, but you don't really have to care about that right now given everything else he brings to the table. For now, just sit back and watch the show, because on any given night in Potomac or Harrisburg, he will be the best guy on the field. There's good reason the Nats didn't want to part with him as they emptied the farm this offseason.

8. Amed Rosario, SS, New York Mets

Rosario checked in at the back of our 2016 Top 101 on the strength of his defensive tools. He's an athletic shortstop with a plus arm, but when the Mets paid $1.75 million for him as a 16-year-old in 2012, they were expecting the offensive skills to eventually bloom. That finally happened this season. Rosario blitzed High-A and Double-A, showing off a potential plus hit tool—due to his lightning quick wrists and good barrel control—and you can dream on him eventually finding average power. He even turned himself into a plus-plus runner after an intensive offseason workout program. Going from a three-tool shortstop to a potential five-tool one? Well, that moves you from the back of the list to the top of the list.

9. Eloy Jimenez, OF, Chicago Cubs

We recognize that the reader perhaps does not follow all these prospects as closely as we do. This is a perfectly viable, even preferable, life choice. However, if the only exposure you've gotten to Jimenez was the 2016 Futures Game, well, those CliffNotes are good enough to pass the GSCE. He made a spectacular catch, falling into the right field stands and then hit one off the third floor of the Western Metal Supply Building. This wasn't a "One Night Only" show either. He slugged .532 in the frigid air of the Midwest League at 19, so the best is most assuredly yet to come.

10. Lucas Giolito, RHP, Chicago White Sox

Giolito tossed 136 innings across four levels, including a cameo in the majors, so why am I about to call it a lost season for the talented righty? Well, the Nationals tweaked his mechanics early in the season and were rewarded with a regressing fastball and the same command issues that have plagued him throughout his professional career. A return to his previous delivery hasn't seen the stuff come all the way back yet, but a few minutes with White Sox pitching coach Don Cooper has been known to be a panacea for many pitching ills. And in an upset, we made it all the way through the Giolito entry without a single Twin Peaks reference.

11. Brendan Rodgers, SS, Colorado Rockies

You don't want to poo-poo the performance of a 19-year-old who posted an .821 OPS in full-season ball, but Asheville is a friend to barbecue lovers, climatologists and Rockies hitting prospects. The thin air and friendly confines can make sluggers even out of the barbecue lovers and climatologists, assuming they can get a bit of uppercut in their swing. Rodgers had a 300-point OPS split between home and road, but the "don't scout the statline" mantra applies to the splits as well. Rodgers is still a potential all-star infielder and the power should eventually play as above-average in places closer to sea level. Just don't read too much into his Cal League stats next year either.

12. Lewis Brinson, OF, Milwaukee Brewers

Speaking of not scouting the stat line, Brinson's return engagement to Frisco did not go nearly as well, but the reports haven't changed. He's a year older but still a potential five-tool center fielder, and one of those tools is a 70-grade, up-the-middle glove. This makes it a stretch to say the Brewers bought low on him in the Jonathan Lucroy trade. If Brinson hits even a little bit, he is a potential star. Just don't read too much into his post-trade Colorado Springs stats (.382/.387/.618) either. The climatologists would rake there too.

13. Rafael Devers, 3B, Boston Red Sox

Devers got off to an awful start in 2016, which caused his season line to look unpretty deep into the summer. But in the end, he nearly Xeroxed his impressive 2015 line playing the entire season as a 19-year-old in High-A. He's a bit of an anachronism in many aspects: a big-framed kid with surprising athleticism, a presently good defender at third that might end up projecting out to first anyway, an advanced bat that doesn't walk much. If this all sounds like the good, San Francisco version of Pablo Sandoval, well, that's a comp everyone in the world makes. It might undersell Devers on power potential a bit, but there's a reason it's the obvious comp.

14. Tyler Glasnow, RHP, Pittsburgh Pirates

A season can be an eternity in the life of a pitching prospect, but I could just copy and paste Glasnow's entry from last year's Annual and you would be both accurately informed and hopefully none the wiser. Upper minors bats still can't square him on the infrequent occasions they make contact at all, but they also get rewarded far too often if they keep the bat on their shoulders. Glasnow has issues keeping all of his 6'8" frame in line, but a mid-90s fastball that is as easy for batters to elevate as a bowling ball and a power 12-to-6 breaker will cover a multitude of control and command issues. Still, until he gets a bit more efficient with his stuff, he'll continue to struggle to get into the sixth inning against major league lineups.

15. Gleyber Torres, SS, New York Yankees

If you're reading the prospect section at the back of this voluminous tome, you surely know already that the Chicago Cubs won the World Series, and you probably know that the Cubs made a big trade for Aroldis Chapman at the deadline. The price for upgrading middle reliever Adam Warren to Chapman was Torres, a well-rounded potential future star at short or second, plus two lesser prospects. It was a price well paid because the Cubs won and flags fly forever, right? Well, Chapman was sensational down the stretch for Chicago, but it's not like the Cubs actually needed him to win the division by 17 1/2. They really acquired Chapman for those 15 or so key postseason innings in which Chapman pitched like, well, Adam Warren, posting a 3.45 ERA and blowing three saves in seven opportunities, including Game 7 of the World Series. The Yankees re-signed Chapman after the season, making Torres the very expensive price of a true rental.

16. Clint Frazier, OF, New York Yankees

Brian Cashman is baseball's version of The Most Interesting Man In The World from the Dos Equis commercials: he doesn't always sell; but when he does, he prefers elite prospects. In the other big reliever deal Cashman made around the trade deadline, Cashman picked up an even stronger prospect package for left-handed reliever/tactical nuclear weapon Andrew Miller, led by Frazier. To put it simply, Frazier has as much hitting potential as any player in the minors, with jaw-dropping bat speed. The fiery, aggressive red-head also has a higher risk profile than most upper-minors corner outfielders, with an occasionally alarming amount of swing-and-miss. If it comes together quickly, watch out.

17. Robert Gsellman, RHP, New York Mets

Another summer always brings another blockbuster from the same staid movie franchises. Sequelitis has set in. If you are a Mets fan though, you won't be bored with more of the same. Gsellman—whose surname already sounds like a B-team Avenger character—got his star turn this summer at the Warthen Productions backlot in Queens. Previously a solid but unspectacular back-end starting pitching prospect, he showed up in New York with a few extra ticks of velocity on his sinker and a brand new plus slider. Hmm, this sounds very familiar, but even Robert McKee would admit that the formulas are there for a reason. And if you keep producing potential top-of-the-rotation starters, there's no reason to complain if all these celluloid heroes aren't exactly breaking new cinematic ground.

18. Manuel Margot, OF, San Diego Padres

If you are a slam dunk plus center fielder, we will forgive any number of other flaws. Well below-average power? Not a problem. Occasionally susceptible to spin? Well, you're only 21, man. An army deserter from the Seven Years' War, a card cheat and general scallywag who ended up losing a duel to the stepson you abused for years? Well, nobody's perfect we guess. We might be conflating Margot with Barry Lyndon now, but there is no mistaking that center-field glove. And if Barry had Margot's instincts, maybe he could have avoided the whole tragic affair.

19. Josh Hader, LHP, Milwaukee Brewers

Look, we get it. He throws across his body from a low three-quarters slot and his delivery has so much funk, it syncs up perfectly with the opening riff of "She a Bad Mama Jama." Unlike the protagonist of Carl Carlton's 1981 hit, the lean and lanky Hader is neither built nor stacked, but he was a Bad Mama Jama in 2016, carving up the upper minors as his fastball ticked up a few miles-per-hour, and his slider took a leap forward from serviceable to wipeout. The change is still more of a B-side at this point, but the delivery does give the pitch some extra deception. It's easy to talk about why Hader won't work as a major league starter, but it's hard to argue that it hasn't worked so far.

20. Nick Senzel, 3B, Cincinnati Reds

Senzel is the highest-ranked 2016 draftee on our list and earns that accolade due to having the unconventional profile of a five-tool third baseman. He's not hyper-toolsy across the board— it's fives and sixes—but when the plus grades are hit and power, his only solid-average glove and arm at the hot corner are just gilding the lily. Senzel might not have the most upside of the 2016 draft class, but he should be an above-average regular in short order.

21. Willy Adames, SS, Tampa Bay Rays

Some organizations just have a type. Going back to Ben Zobrist, the Rays have collected well-rounded young infielders without any obvious standout tools, often with gloves just short of a regular shortstop—in recent years they've dealt for Matt Duffy, Brad Miller, Logan Forsythe and Nick Franklin. Adames came along with Franklin in the 2014 David Price trade, and he has the potential to be the best of the lot. Like the rest, Adames lacks any particular standout tool, but he's developed into a better bet to stay at shortstop, and his stock has risen every season that he's been in the Tampa Bay system. Plus, if he falls a little short, there are worse things than being an imitation Ben Zobrist.

22. Brent Honeywell, RHP, Tampa Bay Rays

Yes, he throws the screwball—one of the rarest pitches in baseball— as his out pitch. And yes, he learned it from his uncle, controversial pitching guru and 1974 National League Cy Young winner, Dr. Mike Marshall. But there's a lot more to Honeywell than his mastery of a nearly dead pitch. He's got a blazing fastball to go with a developing change and curve. He's also one of the brashest, most confident prospects you'll ever see, which manifests itself everywhere from the mound to Twitter, where he famously went after Bryce Harper and his "Make Baseball Fun Again" campaign last spring.

23. Yadier Alvarez, RHP, Los Angeles Dodgers

Alvarez will be one of the last of the Cuban bonus babies, but the Dodgers shouldn't be too concerned about getting their $16 million (plus pool penalties) worth out of the lanky 20-year-old. He's touching 100 now, and still has some projection left in his frame. He's more than just a triple-digit radar gun reading too. Alvarez has an advanced mid-80s slider that, like his fastball, got better as the season wore on. The changeup and command lag behind, but unlike the guys further down this list with those same concerns, Alvarez, uh, throws 100.

24. Anderson Espinoza, RHP, San Diego Padres

We were by far your lowest national source on Espinoza last year, but another year of throwing gas—this time over 100 innings—has assuaged some of our concerns. He's still a teenager and still listed at 6' even, but most 18-year-olds can't hit 99 mph outside of a joyride in their parents' Corvette. Espinoza already has a precocious ability to throw his fastball for strikes, and both his changeup and curve are potentially plus offerings. He's still a ways from the majors, so you'll be reading plenty more about him in this space in the coming years.

25. Josh Bell, 1B/OF, Pittsburgh Pirates

There are two types of prospects that are a pain to write about every year: The mid-rotation starter—we're not there yet, but oh boy are there a lot to come—and the first base prospect. There are usually a lot fewer first base prospects, but there are only so many ways you can write "He's really going to have to hit." Fortunately for Bell, he's really going to hit, and he did so all the way up to the bigs in 2016. He's always projected for above-average power, and that finally showed up, too. He can even play the outfield in

a pinch. The Pirates really don't have need for that though, and it might be best for all involved if they keep him at first and let him do his thing.

26. Cody Bellinger, 1B/OF, Los Angeles Dodgers

It's not unusual for your first base prospect to have a little corner outfield utility, even if it only amounts to "stand there and hope that Brandon Webb's cousin Marvin is on the mound." Bellinger has taken to popping up occasionally for various Dodgers affiliates in center field. He's probably not going to be the world's largest Ben Zobrist, but it does speak to his athleticism. 2016 proved his power wasn't just a Cal League mirage either so, like Bell, we think he's really going to hit. We're also curious to see him actually play center in Dodger Stadium because it promises to be entertaining one way or the other.

27. Mitch Keller, RHP, Pittsburgh Pirates

Imagine a blind prospect audition on a reality show, oh let's call it The Tools. "This pitcher has two potential 70-grade pitches." How fast do you hit the button to turn around? Faster than if some ingénue nailed the first few bars of Janis Joplin's version of "Summertime." There are some things to iron out here. Keller only flashed his plus-plus fastball and breaker late in the season, and your new singer can get a bit pitchy at times—minor flaws, though. In more bad news, both end up choosing Kaiser Chiefs' frontman Ricky Wilson's team. Those piercing blue eyes win them over every time. Although to be fair, "Oh My God" is still quite the banger.

28. Francis Martes, RHP, Houston Astros

We're now well into our "potential no. 2 starters with some risk" tier. Martes' risks are subtler than Keller's. His two potential 70-grade offerings are better established, and his hard curve is a true wipeout pitch when he commands it. He improved his change in 2016 too, so he isn't just a future two-pitch reliever. No, Martes' issue is command, and that can be a tricky one. It's the kind of thing that can make you a frustrating mid-rotation arm that looks like an ace one start, and way too hittable the next. He's also got a, uh, non-traditional body for a power arm at the top of a rotation, closer to 2016 Bartolo than 1996 Bartolo. Not that we here at Baseball Prospectus will quibble with any version of Bartolo.

29. Jason Groome, LHP, Boston Red Sox

The Draft can be a fickle beast, and judging picks too quickly is a good way for your area prospect analyst to look silly in a few years. But it feels like the Red Sox hit it big when Groome, one of the top prep pitching prospects of recent memory, was available at the 12th pick. Nearly everyone had Groome as one of the absolute best few talents in the draft. He was considered a tougher sign, with rumors of bonus demands that Boston simply couldn't pay given their bonus pool, but the Red Sox won a staring contest near the signing deadline, signing him for an above-slot but below-expectation $3.65 million. Groome only got into three games before the end of the minor-league season, but as an extremely well-scouted and high-profile amateur, he's not much of a mystery. Groome pairs a low-to-mid-90s fastball with a brilliant two-plane curveball that has a chance to be among baseball's best, supplemented by a change that has average promise. He'll pitch most of 2017 at age 18, but even so, he could move pretty quickly.

30. Reynaldo Lopez, RHP, Chicago White Sox

As a short fireballing righty with command issues for a Washington team with a stacked rotation and wide-open bullpen, Lopez seemed ticketed for a very promising career in high-leverage relief. Then came the Adam Eaton trade, and suddenly Lopez is in the system and with the pitching coach that seems to produce a lot of good MLB starting pitchers out of pitching prospects with red flags. Prospect rankings inherently are designed to be in a bit of a vacuum, and we'll confess that Lopez's spot on this list has been fairly static for the entire ranking process, which began when we were pondering if he'd be Washington's closer by midseason. Yet it feels like folly to totally ignore that the change in circumstances probably makes Lopez's higher-end outcomes just a little more likely.

31. Ronald Acuna, OF, Atlanta Braves

The Atlanta farm system was already an embarrassment of riches even before Acuna showed up in Rome as an 18-year-old and proceeded to flash all five tools in center field. He doesn't look the part of a prodigious home-run hitter, but there's plus power in the profile due to an explosive swing. He has an advanced approach at the plate with good tracking and pitch recognition skills, and he's a plus runner with a decent chance to stick in center. He's still a long way from the majors, and an up-the-middle spot isn't a given, but he should have the bat to be a good regular in a corner outfield spot. If the whole package comes together, there's all-star potential here. You might just have to wait for the 2020s to see him in the Midsummer Classic.

32. Amir Garrett, LHP, Cincinnati Reds

As athletic a southpaw as you will find—he was also a swingman for the St. John's basketball team—Garrett continued to improve on the mound in 2016 and is now knocking on the door of a major league role. His fastball is plus-plus from the left side, bumping 96 and showing wicked arm-side run at its best. His slider continues to improve and is a potential plus offering. This is the part where we would normally tell you about the command and changeup issues, which are issues, and call him a potential mid-rotation arm. But given his athleticism and how late he came to pitching full-time, we think there might still be a bit more there than the potential number-three starter or two-pitch late-inning arm this blurb would suggest.

33. Jorge Alfaro, C, Philadelphia Phillies

#TheLegend has been on prospect lists for so long that his exploits were first noted as a monomyth archetype in Joseph Campbell's *The Hero with a Thousand Faces*. At this point he has just about completed his road of trials. He recovered from a bad ankle injury that some thought might force him to the outfield. He's improved his catcher defense markedly, and by our minor league catching metrics was one of the better receivers in the minors. He has a plus-plus arm as well. While the bat still hasn't developed to the lofty heights imagined when he was breaking beat writer car windows in batting practice, if he ends up an above-average defensive catcher, any in-game display of his elite raw power will just be a nice bonus. And if you want to dream big, well, this blurb isn't all that different from what we wrote about Gary Sanchez last year.

34. Francisco Mejia, C, Cleveland Indians

You may have heard about Mejia's 50-game hitting streak in the minors this past summer. Sure, there's always going to be a fair bit of luck involved in those kind of stretches, but in over 102 games the 20-year-old backstop hit .342 across two levels. But is batting average really what we want to hang our hat on here at Baseball Prospectus? Well, yes … because it was three-forty-two. Okay, Mejia probably isn't a .340 hitter in the majors. (We know, we know. Stop with the hot takes.) He's a potential above-average everyday catcher that could hit in the middle of a major league lineup, and as you continue down this list, you'll see that is a rare and valuable commodity indeed.

35. Ozzie Albies, SS/2B, Atlanta Braves

"Age-relative-to-league," four words with three hyphens that every prospect writer knows well. Albies was a 19-year-old that smoked Double-A pitching and held his own against Triple-A arms. And with "shortstop" affixed to his name up there, this is the kind of profile that should have us salivating. Now, being the 35th best prospect in baseball is no mean feat, but we feel a bit like Peggy Lee. Is that all there is? Albies isn't very big or strong and although his slash-and-dash approach at the plate has worked for him so far—and the plus-plus speed helps—he feels more like a polished everyday guy up the middle than a future star. However, he should be able to fill that role before he can legally drink, and you could see him and Dansby Swanson holding down the middle infield in Atlanta for a decade. That's more than enough cause to go dancing.

36. Michael Kopech, RHP, Chicago White Sox

As guys that sit behind the backstop with all the radar guns, we're bound to be a little skeptical of the July reports that Kopech touched 105 on the Salem team gun. Even the cacophony of well-calibrated scout guns often vary by a tick or two, and often the team gun is being run by an off-rotation starting pitcher that isn't quite an expert in radar technology. But even still, Kopech is the hardest-throwing starting pitcher in organized baseball—even harder than Noah Syndergaard and Yordano Ventura—and close to the hardest-throwing pitcher period. There are quite a few "but"s here. Kopech could very easily be limited to relief by mechanics, lack of reliable off-speed stuff or inability to handle a starter's workload. Between a 2015 drug suspension and a 2016 broken pitching hand sustained in a fight with a teammate, his makeup concerns are far more tangible than most prospects. That said, you can't teach a guy to sit 99-100.

37. Kyle Tucker, OF, Houston Astros

The fifth overall pick in 2015, Tucker had a solid but unspectacular full-season debut in the Midwest League. We are still waiting for enough power to show up in games to carry a future right field profile—and no, the nice .661 slugging in 69 Cal League plate appearances at the end of the season doesn't count. Yet every time Tucker came up, internally here at BP and also within baseball, everyone was utterly sure the pop was in there and would eventually make him a middle-of-the-order force in a major league lineup. And slowly but surely he moved up every successive draft of this list. We'd like to see it actually start to show up in games though. And no, whatever he slugs in however many plate appearances in the Cal League in 2017 won't count either.

38. Jose De Leon, RHP, Los Angeles Dodgers

The 20-80 scale, the cornerstone of every prospect list, is based on normal distribution. But baseball talent is not normally distributed. Even no. 2 starters are nearly impossible to find in the wilds of the minor leagues. So we are very picky about what arms we put a future 70 on. The downside of that is, come winter, we end up having to find 30 different ways to describe a mid-rotation starter. De Leon makes our lives a little bit easier because his second-best pitch is actually his changeup! That's different from our usual Top 101 mid-rotation type. The cambio tumbles off the deck and has good separation from his low-90s fastball that he can dial up to 95 at times. The slider is the third pitch instead, and it is potentially average but not a bat misser. De Leon throws a lot of strikes, but the stuff isn't so good that major league hitters won't do damage if they aren't good strikes.

39. Yohander Mendez, LHP, Texas Rangers

And now, another way to describe a mid-rotation arm—the triolet:

The Rangers Yohander,
A future third starter?
His command does not wander,
The Rangers Yohander.
Durability we must ponder,
Plus changeup, notes charter,
The Rangers Yohander,
A future third starter?

40. Sandy Alcantara, RHP, St. Louis Cardinals

We're pretty sure that Alcantara is the lowest-ranked prospect on this list that was regularly hitting triple digits on the radar gun in 2016. It's rare even in this era of high velocity to have a potential major league starter touching 100, so even with two well-be-low-average secondary offerings at present, he easily slips into our top 50. That's well-below-average in the Midwest League though, so there is plenty of time to see improvement from his curveball and change. The curve shows more promise, and the better ones are already getting swings and misses in the zone. As ludicrous as it sounds, Alcantara's lanky 6'4" frame could still add more strength in the coming years.

41. Corey Ray, OF, Milwaukee Brewers

There is no such thing as a "high-floor" player in the draft. Every amateur player's floor is "not a major leaguer." But when taking a college bat fifth overall you might expect at least some surety in your OFP. Not so with Ray. Opinions run the gamut from "future superstar" to "future fourth outfielder." Ray might not have the power for a corner or the instincts for center. He might also hit .300 and steal 30 bases a year. Depending on which projection you believe, he could be top 20, or in the back 20. We've elected to split the baby for now.

42. Raimel Tapia, OF, Colorado Rockies

It isn't actually true that Eskimo-Aleut languages have an unusually large number of words for snow, though that point is still hotly debated among linguists (their dinner parties must be fun). It touches on the broader idea that language is built around cultural concerns. If true, we are sorely disappointed in the number of English words available to us to describe Tapia's swing. It's all we have written about in regard to the Rockies outfielder for four years now. It's preferable to gloss over the rest of the profile. He's best suited to left field, and the power will be fringy even with some help from the Rocky Mountain altitude. He's fast, but an adventure on the bases. No really, like one of those Choose Your Own Adventures where every page ends with you falling into an active volcano. But oh that swing. Schopenhauer cautions us against considering the utility of aesthetic beauty, so we will just admire Tapia's swing for what it is, and let major league pitchers sort the rest out.

43. Jorge Mateo, SS/2B/OF?, New York Yankees

Mateo had a weird 2016. On the field, he remained acceptably adequate, broadly showing off the same sorts of skills in High-A that he'd shown off in Low-A a year prior. He picked up second base, a potential long-term home, as a secondary position early in the season, and played it extensively after the trade deadline in deference to Gleyber Torres. The scouting song remains the same, with 80 speed paired with excellent bat speed and a potentially plus hit tool, but inconsistent defense. Yet there were a lot of weird whispers about Mateo in 2016, many surrounding a mysterious midseason suspension that scratched him from the Futures Game and may or may not have been due to complaining about not being promoted to Double-A along with some of his friends. He reportedly added center field to his list of positions during the fall instructional league, which may be the best long-term fit for his skill set.

44. Sean Newcomb, LHP, Atlanta Braves

In the interest of full disclosure, Newcomb shares an alma mater with our Senior Prospect Writer, and we want to acknowledge there may be the hint of partisanship at play here. He's also a strapping lefty that sits in the mid-90s and brings a power, 1-to-7 Uncle Chuck to the dinner table as well. There are no red flags in the delivery, the velocity comes easy and the mechanics are simple. However, simple mechanics don't mean repeatable mechanics, or at least they haven't for Newcomb. He should be able to throw more strikes

than he does, and you can't point to long levers or high effort as an easy culprit. And now that he's pitched in Double-A, you can't even point to his lack of experience—he's a cold weather arm that wasn't highly recruited or showcased in high school—as a reason to hope he'll suddenly figure it out. So we'll hang our hat—the one with the big red 'H' Jeffrey often wears behind the backstop—on those Jon Lester comps for one more year.

45. Cal Quantrill, RHP, San Diego Padres

Quantrill, the Stanford star righty and son of perpetually under-rated former MLB reliever Paul, was widely considered a future first-overall pick right up until he had Tommy John surgery in March 2015. Most players in this scenario rush back to get in action before the draft. Quantrill instead took a longer rehab process, skipping his junior season and not letting most teams even see his bullpen sessions. In the months leading up to the draft, industry rumors swirled that Quantrill had a pre-draft deal with the Padres that was lucrative enough to get him to try to drop off other teams' maps, and sure enough San Diego popped him with the eighth pick. (There's absolutely no pre-draft dealing of this sort in baseball, no sir.) Reports were stellar in a quick late-season tour of the lower minors, in line with his pre-surgery projections. We're not totally sold yet, but we're at least talking to the finance department about the best leasing programs.

46. Riley Pint, RHP, Colorado Rockies

One of the stars of Jeff Passan's excellent book, *The Arm*, Pint is the latest in what feels like a continual line of Hardest Throwing Prep Arms Ever, hitting 102 in both workouts and showcase events. Previous holders of the high school velocity crown include Colt Griffin, Lucas Giolito and Tyler Kolek, so it's a bit of a mixed bag to say the least. Pint's family and advisors famously attempted to avoid the pitfalls and overuse of the showcase circuit, and he still went fourth overall to Colorado, which doesn't prove much except that you can do that when you can throw 102 and flash useful secondary stuff. The upside here is as big as you can imagine. The downside is...well, Colt Griffin was a middling Double-A reliever in the end.

47. Franklin Barreto, SS, Oakland Athletics

A mainstay of these lists—often somewhere in the middle—is the almost shortstop. The guy we aren't sure is a shortstop, but we're not sure isn't either. Every team will make their own evaluations on this and have their own tolerance levels for how bad a defensive shortstop they are willing to start every day. Barreto still mostly plays at the six—although the A's have gotten him time at the keystone and he's played some center field in winter ball. But if he does have to move off short, his continued good performance at the plate in the upper minors last year makes him a more plausible regular than some other "almost shortstops" out there. And in an organization currently starting Marcus Semien there in the majors, "almost" may be just as good in Oakland as it is in horseshoes and hand grenades.

48. Nick Gordon, SS, Minnesota Twins

Gordon, on the other hand, is a solid bet to stick at shortstop. That's good, since so far he hasn't shown quite as much life in his bat as Barreto. He's a potential plus hitter and added a bit of pop as he's filled out, but the power projection remains below-average. He's still a plus runner, which he uses to good effect in the field and on the bases. There is still some rawness on both sides of the ball however, and there may be further growing pains when he hits Double-A in 2017. A future above-average regular shortstop is worth the wait though.

49. Blake Rutherford, OF, New York Yankees

Like Jason Groome, Rutherford was widely considered one of the top prospects in the 2016 draft. Also like Groome, Rutherford floated big bonus numbers and fell. The Yankees ended his slide at the 18th pick, and were able to sign him for $3.282 million—well above the slot value. (Hey, wasn't this draft pool system designed to stop the Red Sox and Yankees from scooping the top signability guys?) Rutherford then went out and absolutely obliterated the Appalachian League. The Appy would usually be a fairly aggressive assignment for a prep bat just off signing, but Rutherford was a bit old for a high schooler, turning 19 shortly before the draft. Given his tools and polish, he could move up this list pretty quickly.

50. Jeff Hoffman, RHP, Colorado Rockies
We've spilled plenty of ink over the years lamenting the plight of the Rockies pitching prospect. Last year we compared Jon Gray's fate to those of Spinal Tap drummers. Hoffman's Coors Field debut in 2016 went about as well as Gray's two years ago. He surrendered seven home runs in 31 innings and walked almost as many batters as he struck out. There are reasons to be optimistic though. Hoffman's stuff is at least as good as Gray's, featuring a mid-90s heater and two potential plus breaking balls, and Gray bounced back to be an above-average starter—once park effects are thrown in the mix—in his first full MLB season. Past performance is not a guarantee of future results, but it is way too early to give up on a big righty with that repertoire.

51. Nick Williams, OF, Philadelphia Phillies
Early in the 2016 season it looked like Williams was right on track to graduate sometime in the summer and become entrenched in Philadelphia's outfield for years to come. Then came a series of strange clashes between Williams and the Triple-A manager, which led to repeated benchings starting in mid-June for hustle and on-field demeanor. Whether there's any causation here is hard to say, but over the 290 plate appearances from the first benching through the end of the season Williams hit just .238/.251/.401, and he wasn't even called up to the bigs in September. He'll start fresh in 2017—even if it's in Triple-A, as the Phillies organization let Lehigh Valley's manager go and replaced him with Double-A manager Dusty Wathan—but old concerns about his plate discipline are starting to pop up again.

52. Justus Sheffield, LHP, New York Yankees
Another prize from baseball's best summer sale, Sheffield came along with Clint Frazier in the Andrew Miller deal. Sheffield already possesses an impressive arsenal from the left side, with an explosive mid-90s fastball along with a change and slider that both show major-league potential. He's this far down the list because he's short with effort in his delivery and command that comes and goes. These are all red flags that portend "future reliever," and perhaps that's the ultimate destination, but his stuff is good enough that the rotation can't be ruled out either.

53. Tyler O'Neill, OF, Seattle Mariners
"We're not selling jeans here." If you remember any quote from *Moneyball*, it is that one. And it is true, we aren't selling jeans here (unless you are Kris Bryant). We aren't selling cutoff t-shirts either, but O'Neill would be pretty good at it. His 24-inch pythons generate the plus-plus raw power you'd expect given the gun show. He's a good athlete for a corner outfielder, but the hope here is that there is 30-home-run power in the majors to offset his swing-and-miss issues. Also that the Mariners introduce some sleeveless alternate jerseys before he gets called up.

54. Ian Happ, 2B/OF, Chicago Cubs
Remember, there is no such thing as a "high-floor" prospect, but Happ seems about as good a bet to be a major league regular as anyone on this list. There isn't a ton more upside than that though. Happ is a good hitter with average pop and the ability to play in either corner outfield spot and second base … probably. He's neither fast nor athletic, but he's a smart baserunner. He has

a good approach at the plate. He's also in the right organization to make the most out of his "positional flexibility," such as it is. He's a departure from our toolsy up-the-middle types and parade of third starters, but it takes all kinds to make a prospect list after all.

55. Triston McKenzie, RHP, Cleveland Indians
No, he's not the love interest of the latest Young Adult Dystopian novel series—now a major motion picture starring Jenna Coleman—but you'd be forgiven if you hadn't heard too much about McKenzie before this year. A supplemental first round pick for Cleveland in 2015, the Brooklyn-born beanpole was flat out unhittable in 2016 while facing only 13 hitters younger than him. He is still mostly projection as the fastball sits around 90 now, but he pairs that with an advanced curveball, and hoo boy there is a lot of projection left here. You just will be waiting until well after *The Maze Runner* trilogy wraps in theaters to find out how it all plays out.

56. Mickey Moniak, OF, Philadelphia Phillies
Moniak went first overall in the 2016 MLB Draft, and as a high-floor prep bat, he was a bit of an unusual 1-1 guy. We usually associate 1-1 with huge upside or near-immediate MLB readiness, and Moniak brings neither. That reflects in his ranking here, which is the lowest we've ranked a top overall pick in the following year's annual since we expanded from 50 prospects in 2007. He did, however, bring a savings of nearly $3 million, which allowed the Phillies to give touted prep righty Kevin Gowdy a hugely over-slot $3.5 million bonus with the 42nd pick. Most draft evaluators didn't have Moniak as the single best player in the draft, but he was generally considered among the top handful in a weaker draft for high-end talent. Given that this draft didn't have one consensus top talent, the Phillies reasonably manipulated the system. Early reports out of the GCL were promising enough.

57. Juan Soto, OF, Washington Nationals
Speaking of sequels, the Mets rivals down the Acela corridor have their own burgeoning franchise of exciting outfield prospects. One year after Victor Robles exploded onto the scene in short-season ball, Soto did the same. The ultimate profile here is different, Soto's bat was more advanced as a short-season prospect, but he lacks Robles' up-the-middle tools. He should be a good right fielder though, as he's an above-average runner at present with a big arm. You are at the theater for the offensive tools—unless this is one of those Brooklyn movie houses that serve brunch and booze at their matinees—and Soto offers plus hit and power projections. It's not hard to see why the Nats greenlit a seven-figure bonus for him.

58. James Kaprielian, RHP, New York Yankees
Kaprielian showed up for Spring Training in 2016 with his entire arsenal having ticked up. He made three dominant starts in the Florida State League, missed five months with a flexor strain, and came back to pitch well in the Arizona Fall League while retaining the gains of spring. So what do we do with him? Well, another half-season of this and we'll officially change his player card to The Enigmatic James Kaprielian. For now, we'll note the gains in velocity and secondary stuff while cautioning that at some point he's going to have to string some healthy starts together, lest the Chad Billingsley comps we keep throwing on him start reflecting the horribly injury-prone outro of Billingsley's career.

59. Isan Diaz, SS, Milwaukee Brewers
The holy grail of prospect writing may be the power-hitting shortstop. You've read about a lot of shortstops so far, and you will read about a lot more of them before we are through. There are some very good shortstop prospects above Diaz, and a few of them even project for average power. None of them hit 20 bombs as a 20-year-old in the unforgiving climes of the Midwest League. They still rank ahead of Diaz because they are better shortstops—and

more likely to be actual major league shortstops. A power-hitting second baseman isn't quite as alluring; he's more like the Veil of Veronica. We'll still take it, although we do also have some concerns about the swing-and-miss becoming truly untenable in the upper minors.

60. Grant Holmes, RHP, Oakland Athletics

If you want to stand out amongst the throng of mid-rotation starters on this list, it doesn't hurt to have as good a head of hair as Holmes. The boring stuff: His fastball/curve combo is plus, and there are questions about the change and command profile. That could describe any number of pitchers in this range, but none have his long, curly, muppet hair. It's something else to hang your hat on, even if the hat just sort of sits haphazardly on top of your impressive mane. Scouts might be divided on whether Holmes is a starter or reliever long-term, but he will always be a role 7 for Pantene marketing executives.

61. A.J. Puk, LHP, Oakland Athletics

Puk kicks off our "high-upside arms with back issues" portion of the list. A bit of a niché concern most years we suppose, but if he hadn't missed time in the 2016 college season with a balky back, Puk very well could have gone 1-1 in the draft. He is a towering lefty that already has a pretty good handle on his mechanics and a fastball that touches 98. His slider is a potential plus offering as well, and there's some actual feel for the change. We aren't just saying that to fill word count. Now that stuff doesn't always show up start-to-start, which coupled with the back issue kept Puk out of the Top 50, but a strong 2017 could make this ranking look a bit silly.

62. Erick Fedde, RHP, Washington Nationals

Tommy John feels almost de rigueur for prospect arms nowadays, but while it is more common, it is still not routine. Fedde has recovered well from his 2014 UCL replacement though, and his fastball velocity ticked up in his second year out from the surgery. He has a lively, mid-90s fastball, the rara avis that can be a swing-and-miss pitch on its own. And he pairs it with a potential plus slider and a split-change he is starting to get a better feel for. There's effort in the delivery, and in Year 3 ATJ he will need to show he can handle a starter's workload, but there is a solid mid-rotation arm in here if he can. If he can't, that fastball/slider combo would look pretty nice in a late-inning relief role.

63. Aaron Judge, OF, New York Yankees

The jury's still out on Judge, and that's starting to become concerning. 2016 was supposed to be the year that Judge finally established himself in the majors. Instead, he had a fine return trip to Scranton/Wilkes-Barre and then flopped hard in a September call-up. He's consistently had trouble adjusting to new levels, so here's hoping that the denouement of 2016 was the extent of that. The Yankees seem intent on giving him a real shot and he turns 25 a month into the new season, so his career as a prospect will adjourn one way or another this year.

64. Mike Soroka, RHP, Atlanta Braves

We aren't done with Braves pitching prospects on this list yet, and Soroka might be the one that gets overlooked the most. There's a reason for that. He's a right-handed A-ball pitcher with a good—but not huge—fastball, and there's not much projection left in his frame. So while not strictly a case of WYSIWYG, it's harder to get excited about Soroka than, say, a lefty who gets Jon Lester comps, or even a dude named Touki. So he's not a flashy prospect, but he has the potential for three average-or-better pitches, and he already has the command and pitchability boxes ticked off in the low-levels of the minors. The body is already major-league-inning-eater-ready, and Soroka has relatively low risk for a pitcher in the South Atlantic League. Maybe not low risk for a pitcher. All pitchers

are risky. That is why the Braves strategy of collecting all of them isn't the worst plan in the world.

65. Kevin Newman, SS, Pittsburgh Pirates

Kevin Newman can hit. Well, we're pretty sure Kevin Newman can hit. That's the thing. The hit tool is a little bit more of a moving target than the other four. Power, run, glove and arm are all pretty easy to see with the naked eye, and pretty easy to translate to higher levels. The hit tool is one of those French Laundry recipes that requires an immersion circulator and 17 distinct steps to make the garnish. You can't be absolutely sure it works until it works against major-league pitching. Still, we're pretty sure Kevin Newman can hit. He batted .320 and walked more than he struck out between High-A and Double-A. He's going to have to keep that up too, as he's a fringy shortstop and offers very little in the way of pop. But if you do hit, well, the rest of the stuff works itself out. There's a reason The French Laundry has three Michelin stars after all.

66. Alex Verdugo, OF, Los Angeles Dodgers

Calling Verdugo "a little uninteresting" seems casually cruel. But at this point in writing this list, we could really use an easy hook and we've already fired our medieval poetry bullet. Verdugo has a major-league skillset: a broad base of tools both at the plate and in the field. He was a pitcher in high school, and that plus arm may be unleashed in right field, since he's not quite athletic enough anymore to project well in center. He hit for more power this year in Double-A, which is nice to see out of a 20-year-old. There are some questions about how his unorthodox swing will play against higher level pitching still, and there isn't enough else here to carry the profile if he's "only" an average hitter. So Verdugo is not an ideal muse, but he is a pretty good baseball prospect.

67. Kolby Allard, LHP, Atlanta Braves

Offseason back surgery kept the young lefty off the mound until the summer, but Allard made up for lost time, flashing a 60 curve and a heavy fastball, which also projects as plus. This ranking might end up looking overly conservative in a year's time, but he is a long way from the majors, and like most of the arms in this range—even the ones without back issues—there are command and third pitch issues that need to be ironed out. This is the part of the blurb where I try to come up with new and somewhat-witty phrasing to describe Allard's mid-rotation OFP, but that could also look "low in" by 2018 list time.

68. Luis Ortiz, RHP, Milwaukee Brewers

Ortiz is a polished four-pitch starter with good command and stuff. He's already reached and had some success in Double-A, running a lively, shapeable fastball up into the mid-90s—and sometimes even a little higher—while mixing in an above-average slider and a usable change and curve. Yet he's down here in the Land of Projects and Future Relievers because of an elevated risk profile regardless. Persistent elbow and forearm problems have limited Ortiz for much of his pro career, and his 90 ⅔ innings in 2016 represented an uninspiring career-high. Tag on some legitimate concerns about his weight, and there's a significant chance that Ortiz just won't hold up under the rigors of a full major-league starting workload. It'd be unfortunate if he didn't, because there's number-two starter upside here, without the command and secondary offering concerns that frequently haunt pitchers of similar talent.

69. Thomas Szapucki, LHP, New York Mets

It's always nice when you get a Top 101 pitching prospect out of... well, it wasn't quite nowhere. Szapucki was on draftnik radars in 2015, and not just because Florida has more baseball scouts per square foot than anywhere other than the Kohl's clearance rack. He was your standard-issue projectable prep lefty, and hoo boy did he project. He was up to 98 this summer and comfortably sits 93-96 with a heater he can run or cut. Both his curve and change have a chance to get to plus, and the breaker already flashes there. He'd be higher if not for a back issue that ended his season a few weeks early, and an arm slot low enough to make one wonder if he's a starter long term. Of course, we love Josh Hader so we aren't going to ding Szapucki too much for that.

70. Kyle Lewis, OF, Seattle Mariners
Lewis would be much higher on this list if he didn't blow out his knee 30 games into his pro debut last summer. He was already far from a lock to stick in center, but his torn ACL may force him to right field even sooner than the most jaundiced observers expected. His bat can carry a corner outfield profile at least. There's potential above-average hit and power grades here, and Lewis has an advanced approach at the plate. His performance on the field pre-injury left evaluators agog, but until we know how his right knee recovers, the Magic 2-8 ball says "Outlook Cloudy."

71. Braxton Garrett, LHP, Miami Marlins
In a draft class without Jason Groome, Garrett may have garnered more attention. He had the second best curveball and one could argue he commands it better at present than his New Jersey counterpart. Garrett doesn't throw quite as hard as Groome, but there still is some projection left here and his fastball should eventually sit in the low-90s. The changeup needs work because why would you throw your change at 18 when your curve is that darn good. Garrett is more than just the best of a barren Marlins system, though given the organization's penchant for parting with prospects, who knows how long that will be the case.

72. Ariel Jurado, RHP, Texas Rangers
Jurado checks in some 30-plus spots behind organization mate Yohander Mendez despite a very similar projection. We've dinged him a bit for not having Mendez's size or upper minors experience. That matters. While the stuff profile is similar to Mendez's, it's less of a rarity to find that repertoire among right-handed pitching prospects. He's a potential mid-rotation starter with an above-average heater and change and has already shown remarkably advanced command for a 21-year-old. So that makes him a bit unusual among your dozens of no. 3 types that dot the back half of this list every year.

73. Leody Taveras, OF, Texas Rangers
More common in this portion of the list is the crazy, tooled-up teenaged center fielder a half-decade away from the majors. Taveras has all five tools in his bag, along with the kind of top-level athleticism that could make him a plus major league center fielder … eventually. He needs to get physically stronger, but he already flashes big bat speed that allows you to dream on average or better power … eventually. As Tom Petty sings, "the waiting is the hardest part." Double-A can be tricky too, of course.

74. Franklyn Kilome, RHP, Philadelphia Phillies
A lot of prospect writing can comfortably fit into a Hegelian Dialectic model, but Kilome might be the best example of this. (Thesis) We might see Kilome as an elite level prospect, a towering righty with a potential plus-plus fastball and plus curve. (Antithesis) You might see Kilome as a non-prospect with a fastball topping out in the low 90s and no idea where any of his pitches are going. And we both have seen the same pitcher, just on different days in Lakewood. But we must achieve synthesis, so he ends up here in the "young arm who might be a reliever" range. Hmm, no wonder Third Way politics are so unsatisfying.

75. Brett Phillips, OF, Milwaukee Brewers
Double-A is tricky of course, as Phillips found out in 2016. Southern League arms got him to whiff 30 percent of the time, which even in this era will raise a few eyebrows. On the plus side, when he did make contact, the power he flashed in Lancaster last year was still there despite less-friendly confines. He's still a solid

defender in center field with a howitzer for a right arm. There are plenty of big league examples for this profile. George Springer and Joc Pederson jump to mind. Phillips doesn't have that much pop yet, but he's potentially a better defender than either.

76. Chance Sisco, C, Baltimore Orioles
Our 101st rated prospect a year ago, Sisco continues to barrel up the ball at all levels, showing off a hit tool that projects to major-league plus. The big question in the profile is the same as it ever was: Will he'll stay at catcher? He's getting better defensively, but he's still not a finished product, and catcher development is weird. He'll get every shot to stick behind the dish with the Orioles, who keep running out indifferent defenders like later-career Matt Wieters and Welington Castillo at the position.

77. Albert Almora, OF, Chicago Cubs
Almora is the only prospect on this list who can never be called a bust, no matter what happens over the rest of his MLB career. In the 10th inning of Game 7 of the 2016 World Series, Almora pinch-ran at first as the go-ahead run. Kris Bryant lifted a deep fly to right, and Almora savvily tagged from first to second in one of the better baserunning reads you'll see. Two batters later, Ben Zobrist knocked Almora in. The Cubs, of course, went on to white-knuckle it through the bottom of the inning and win the whole thing, cementing Almora's place in history. As a player, Almora hasn't quite lived up to being a former sixth-overall pick with the bat, but he's developed into a nifty fielder and baserunner. He'd be ready for full-time duty in center with most clubs; with the 2017 Cubs, he'll likely be another cog that Joe Maddon moves around in the world's most versatile lineup.

78. Jahmai Jones, OF, Los Angeles Angels
Lately an Angels prospect making the 101 has seemed about as far-fetched as the plot of *Angels in the Outfield*. Jones didn't need an assist from Christopher Lloyd to make the list though (at least as far as we could see). He's a plus runner, and a potential above-average center fielder. The offensive skills took a step forward in 2016 as well, and he garners praise for his high baseball IQ. Just don't pay too much attention to the rest of the Angels system; it's about as depressing as the end of *Angels in the Outfield*. What can we say, we were big Tony Danza fans when we were younger.

79. Delvin Perez, SS, St. Louis Cardinals
There's no sense in dancing around the elephant in the room here: Delvin Perez tested positive for a performance-enhancing drug late in the 2016 draft process. The positive test absolutely tanked his stock; he was considered a top-five pick on talent and was connected to picks as high as second-overall to Cincinnati. Instead the Cardinals, always on the lookout for a bargain acquisition, snapped Perez up at 23. With little to no leverage, he signed for slot and had a quiet entry to pro ball, performing well in the Gulf Coast League. It's naive to pretend Perez was the only significant 2016 draft prospect taking PEDs, or even that he's the only prospect on this list that's taken PEDs. He's just the one that got caught, whether out of bad luck or bad doping. And it's not like the early reports out of the GCL came in down on his talent. So, cautiously, we're ranking him just a touch lower than where we would based on the talent alone, and hoping that next year the talent is what his blurb is about.

80. Bradley Zimmer, OF, Cleveland Indians
The rise and fall of the Zimmer family through prospectdom has been harsh and unrelenting—brother Kyle ranked on this list in 2013, 2014 and 2016, but has failed to establish himself amidst constant injuries. Bradley ranked 23rd on this list last year and while his overall seasonal line wasn't horrific, concerns that his long swing would have trouble with upper-level pitching are starting to actualize in strikeouts and lack of power. The underly-

ing physical tools, athleticism and strike-zone judgment are good enough that it's too early to give up on him completely, but he was supposed to be a polished college bat and now he's 24 and hasn't mastered Triple-A pitching.

81. Carson Kelly, C, St. Louis Cardinals

Kelly's baseball bildungsroman has taken him from prep arm to bat-first third base prospect, to good glove catcher, to well-rounded catching prospect. The defensive chops are unassailable, but Kelly started to spray line drives around the park in 2016, making him look like more than just a solid, twice-a-week, backup backstop. He's never going to generate much power, but as we mentioned earlier, the offensive bar for catcher is pretty low, and that empty .270 looks mighty attractive when it comes with a catcher's glove as advanced as Kelly's.

82. Albert Abreu, RHP, New York Yankees

The perceived value of catcher framing and leadership has increased so much in recent years—in great part due to the remarkable research of our own BP Stats group—that the Yankees were able to get the Astros, one of the game's most analytically-inclined teams, to cough up a top 101 prospect for the next two seasons of Brian McCann, aging and declining catcher. Abreu has the typical "good" A-ball pitching prospect starter kit: mid-90s velocity, good frame, a variety of promising secondaries and inconsistent command. Outcomes from this starting point vary wildly, but if things work out reasonably well there's a mid-rotation profile.

83. David Paulino, RHP, Houston Astros

Paulino has stuff the equal of pitchers 50 spots higher than him on the list. If you've read through the our team lists at Baseball Prospectus, or even the first 82 names on this list, you should be able to guess the reason why he's down here. Pitchers are risky propositions generally, and Paulino specifically has already had Tommy John surgery followed by a bout of elbow tendinitis. He set a career high in innings pitched this year with 90. He'll only be 23 in 2017, and he's already accrued major league service time, but we have no idea if his mid-90s fastball and hammer 12-6 curve will still show up 100, 150, or 200 innings into a season. Paulino ticks all the boxes on a scouting report, and we usually urge you to not scout the statline, but we have to make an exception for "innings pitched."

84. Franklin Perez, RHP, Houston Astros

Perez on the other hand, fits neatly into our seemingly endless run of potential mid-rotation arms. For this entry, we'll attempt a hamfisted, hard-boiled homage *(The cheaper the crook, the gaudier the patter, after all):* "He's as thin as a railroad tie and about as yielding to opposing bats. His fastball moves at speeds reserved for Italians trying to talk their way out of trouble, and his changeup is as trustworthy as a Yorkville barman. My old partner, Clearey, used to have a saying about men from the Midwest with an inconsistent breaking ball, let them buy you a drink, but never take their first offer."

85. Sean Reid-Foley, RHP, Toronto Blue Jays

Reid-Foley checks an unfortunately high number of boxes on the risk profile for future relief pitching. Durability and health questions? Check. Inconsistent mechanics? Check. Underdeveloped change? Check. Occasional command issues? Check. On the plus side, he also checks off "could have a wipeout fastball/slider combo," which at least means he might be a really good reliever. He does have a starter's body and progressed enough in 2016 that relief pitching is more of a possible outcome than his destiny.

86. Frankie Montas, RHP, Oakland Athletics

Writing up the game's top 101 prospects causes you to have to come up with many novel ways to say "he's probably a reliever" without outright saying "he's probably a reliever" over and over

again. We have no such compunction with Montas: he's probably a reliever, and he's probably a pretty cool one. He can sit close to or at 100 with a plus slider in relief. As a starter you've got injury concerns (missed most of 2016 with rib issues), stamina concerns, durability concerns, command concerns, changeup development concerns and mechanical concerns here. Short relief alleviates some of those, not to the point that it's all roses and saves, but it's the role where the player has the best chance to make an impact.

87. Trevor Clifton, RHP, Chicago Cubs

In 2013, the rumors that legendary comedian Andy Kaufman had faked his death from cancer in 1984 flared up once again. Perhaps it is just a coincidence that the Cubs "drafted" "Trevor Clifton" that summer, but we have our doubts. No longer content to make occasional appearances as Tony Clifton in Vegas nightclubs to keep the rumors circulating, we think Kaufman is attempting his most audacious character yet, a distant cousin no doubt. "Trevor Clifton" is a 21-year-old with a fastball he can dial up into the mid-90s with wicked arm-side run and a potential plus curve. Don't look so surprised, Kaufman was quite the athlete, just ask Jerry "The King" Lawler.

88. Matt Manning, RHP, Detroit Tigers

The Tigers are like the regulars at your local bistro. Oh, they'll make a show of looking at the menu, listen intently to the flowery description of the sweetbreads on special, but they always settle on a carafe of the Chinon and steak frites, medium-rare, béarnaise on the side. The Tigers may send scouts to see a toolsy SoCal shortstop, but as long as there is a hard-throwing prep righty on offer, that's where their eyes will land. Manning fit the bill this year, a 6'6", two-sport athlete with a fastball already sitting in the mid-90s with late life. The secondaries aren't much to write home about at present, much like the overly crispy bistro fries, but you're coming back for the red meat anyway. Manning has more upside than most of the arms in this region of the list, but Jacob Turner was once the Tigers' ninth-overall pick too.

89. Zack Collins, C, Chicago White Sox

The constant burden of the catching prospect—if he isn't a catcher, he isn't a prospect. The offensive bar for catchers is so low, that an empty .270 average is enough to make you a regular if you can have some facility with the tools of ignorance. Collins is a better at the plate than that, with plus raw power and a strong approach. Behind the dish he's a little more suspect, and while it isn't impossible to find those that think he sticks there, they are well outnumbered at present. Collins' bat just isn't as exciting at first base. Just ask Matt Thaiss, the other good-hitting catcher popped in the first round of last year's draft. The Angels moved him to first base and now you won't find his name anywhere near this list.

90. Yusniel Diaz, OF, Los Angeles Dodgers

As a teenaged Cuban that got an eight-figure bonus, you might have a picture in your head of Diaz as the outfield version of Yoan Moncada. Diaz was just as raw in his his full-season pro debut, but he lacks Moncada's monster tools. He also doesn't have any real weakness in his game, other than his fleetingly temporary youth. The lack of a standout tool could end up a problem down the line though. He doesn't really have the speed for center field, and his defense in general is still raw. The arm fits better in left field than right, so Diaz will have to hit a bunch to even be a solid regular. That said, holding his own as one of the youngest players in the Cal League is a good start on that path, and both the power and hit grades could end up above-average in the end. It's going to take a while, but one thing we have plenty of—as prospect list makers—is time.

91. Adonis Medina, RHP, Philadelphia Phillies

Our prospect team puts high value on getting as many live looks at guys as possible, but trying to birddog pitchers can be tricky business. Minor league rotations change rapidly, as does the weather. And then you can watch Medina throw 14 fastballs, the last of which is hit back up the box and off his ankle. They were 14 pretty good fastballs, though, with advanced command and good sink and run. But you don't have to take our word for it, as Medina is not a well-kept secret anymore. Oh, and if you ever find yourself in Williamsport, be sure to check out The Sawhorse Cafe for some damn fine coffee (we didn't say there would be no Twin Peaks references).

92. Hunter Renfroe, OF, San Diego Padres

Renfroe is the platonic ideal of a backend Top 101 prospect. He is a sure bet not to play up-the-middle. He's a right fielder all the way, though a good enough athlete for his size. He's close to the majors—in Renfroe's case, there's even a 2016 cup of coffee. This makes him a safer bet, and keeps him ahead of the young Turks that feel like they are a year away from making this list. There isn't a ton of ceiling. Renfroe has enough power to play everyday in a corner, but enough swing-and-miss to keep him from being an impact bat there. He also has a very good baseball name. "Hunter Renfroe" just sounds like a number five hitter on an 85-win team. The Padres might be a ways away from that right now, but Renfroe playing 150 games in right will help.

93. Anthony Alford, OF, Toronto Blue Jays

Last year was a largely lost one for the former Ole Miss defensive back. Coming off a breakout 2015, Alford was unexpectedly held back to repeat High-A to start the season. He immediately hurt his knee and missed a month, then came back and went into a brutal hitting funk. His season was interrupted again in June by a concussion suffered in a bad outfield collision, and it wasn't until the middle of the summer that he really got on track. Thankfully, the injuries haven't sapped him of his plus-plus speed or high-end athleticism. We still believe in the tools enough to see a major-league regular in center, but it's time to see how he performs in the high minors.

94. Walker Buehler, RHP, Los Angeles Dodgers

In the blink of an eye, in the summer of 2015, the former Vanderbilt ace went from the steal of the 2015 draft to needing Tommy John surgery immediately upon signing. Buehler returned late this summer, and has only thrown five regular season pro innings as of yet, but reports were simply outstanding. Buehler showed off even better stuff than when drafted, with a fastball sitting 95-97 and a hard curve and change both impressing. He's going to need to show that the spike in stuff is real in 2017 over both full starter-length outings and a full season, but the Dodgers may yet get their draft steal in Buehler.

95. Anderson Tejeda, SS, Texas Rangers

Of last year's top five prospects, the Rangers graduated two (Nomar Mazara and Joey Gallo), and dealt the other three for Jonathan Lucroy and Carlos Beltran (Lewis Brinson, Dillon Tate and Luis Ortiz). That's enough to send any system spiraling into Miami Marlins territory. But the Texas org remains respectable because they always seem to pull guys like Tejeda out of somewhere (usually the Dominican Republic). Signed for just $100k, the 18-year-old has the arm and instincts to stay at shortstop and he slugged over .500 in his stateside debut thanks to some impressive pound-for-pound strength and a swing geared for loft. Tejeda is overly aggressive at the plate right now, and not a sure thing to stick at shortstop, but the Rangers always seem to do well with this profile.

96. Ian Anderson, RHP, Atlanta Braves

Our last Braves pitching prospect—though not our last Braves prospect—is last summer's third-overall pick. Anderson has your traditional cold weather prep pitcher profile: Big fastball, developing secondaries, less mileage on his arm and strong lobster roll dressing opinions. There's plenty of upside here, but his potential future teammate Sean Newcomb offers a cautionary tale about how long it can take to find that upside. But if it doesn't work out, at least he can always go the Jethro Tull cover band route.

97. Alec Hansen, RHP, Chicago White Sox

Hansen entered his junior season at Oklahoma looking like a candidate to go first overall. Hansen exited his first pro season looking like a pitcher who had gone first overall. In between, Alec Hansen had an awful final run in college and fell to the 49th pick, where he signed for slot. It should be nearly impossible to go from signing for slot in the middle of the second round to making this list because of your first dozen pro games, but Hansen has truly special stuff when he's right, and he went back to looking right immediately upon signing. If he keeps it up for another season, he's either going to be near the top of this list next year, or off it due to graduation. Sometimes a change of scenery really is a big deal.

98. Tyler Jay, LHP, Minnesota Twins

Before Andrew Miller, there was Tyler Jay...wait, what? To the consternation of scouts and talent evaluators alike, Illinois continually used Jay, one of the top starting pitching prospects in the 2015 MLB Draft, as a fireman-style reliever. This is more common in college than pro ball—2016 Nats first rounder Dane Dunning was used similarly in his junior season at Florida—but rarely with a top-ten pick like Jay, and it was a chief cause of his slide to Minnesota with the eighth pick. The Twins' chief concern in 2016 was to get Jay stretched back out as a starter for the bulk of the season, which he navigated successfully until a season-ending neck injury in August. If all goes well, 2017 should see him handle something more like a regular workload. If it doesn't, well, we already know there's the potential for a fastball/slider multi-inning relief ace fallback.

99. Trent Clark, OF, Milwaukee Brewers

If you're the top-ranked prospect in back-to-back years, that's great. You are an elite, maybe even a generational, prospect. If you are the 37th-ranked prospect in back-to-back years, that's pretty good too. If you are 99th in back-to-back years, well, that's unusual. You expect a certain amount of churn at the back of these lists across 12 months. Players breakout, regress, graduate. Even if they just hold serve, you'd expect the 99th-best prospect in baseball to move up just on attrition alone. Instead, Clark is just another year older, and struggled in his first taste of the Midwest League when he wasn't dealing with injury issues. Given that he may end up in a corner, and there isn't a ton of power projection here, Clark's second go-round in full-season ball will have to go a bit better to even rate as the 99th best prospect next year.

100. Kevin Maitan, SS, Atlanta Braves

For several collective bargaining cycles, MLB has pushed an international draft system, in theory, to avoid Kevin Maitan scenarios. Everyone in the baseball community knew for many, many months that Atlanta was going to sign Maitan on July 2, 2016. BP alumnus and ESPN writer Keith Law reported in the summer of 2015 that the deal was done, nearly a full year ahead of when it was legal for the Braves and Maitan to come to a meeting of the minds. Of course, this happens all the time, but Maitan was an unusually high-profile J2 prospect, drawing outlandish comps like Miguel Cabrera. Sure enough, Maitan signed with Atlanta on the first day he was eligible for a $4.25 million bonus. It's almost like he was locked up well ahead of time, and it's almost like baseball turns an institutional blind eye to this problem. Given the prevalence of pre-draft deals in the domestic draft, it's a bit fanciful to assume that a draft would solve this problem. It sure would depress signing bonuses, though.

101. Tyler Wade, IF/OF, New York Yankees

The official prospect of the For All You Kids Out There podcast and a scout favorite, Tyler Wade made the list on his own merit, but also as a nod to all the exciting dudes around the minors. He combines easy plus speed with an advanced feel for hitting and good defensive actions. He'd be many spots higher on this list if we had any confidence he was a five-days-a-week shortstop in the majors, but his arm is just a bit too scattershot to project there regularly. He does have extensive experience at second already, and added the outfield to his repertoire this fall. Wade certainly could end up as a strong utility player, but there's a real chance for a good regular at second or even in center here. ▪

—Jeffrey Paternostro is an author of Baseball Prospectus;
Jarrett Seidler is an author of Baseball Prospectus.

Team Codes

CODE	TEAM	LG	AFF.	Name
ABE	Aberdeen	NYP	Orioles	IronBirds
ABQ	Albuquerque	PCL	Rockies	Isotopes
AKR	Akron	EAS	Indians	RubberDucks
ALT	Altoona	EAS	Pirates	Curve
ANA	Los Angeles	AL	-	Angels
ANG	AZL Angels	AZL	Angels	-
ARI	Arizona	NL	-	D-backs
ARK	Arkansas	TEX	Angels	Travelers
ART	Artemisa	CNS	-	
ASH	Asheville	SAL	Rockies	Tourists
AST	GCL Astros	GCL	Astros	GCL Astros
ATH	AZL Athletics	AZL	Athletics	-
ATL	Atlanta	NL	-	Braves
AUB	Auburn	NYP	Nationals	Doubledays
AUG	Augusta	SAL	Giants	GreenJackets
BAK	Bakersfield	CAL	Mariners	Blaze
BAL	Baltimore	AL	-	Orioles
BAT	Batavia	NYP	Marlins	Muckdogs
BGR	Bowling Green	MID	Rays	Hot Rods
BIL	Billings	PIO	Reds	Mustangs
BIN	Binghamton	EAS	Mets	Mets
BIR	Birmingham	SOU	White Sox	Barons
BLJ	GCL Blue Jays	GCL	Blue Jays	GCL Blue Jays
BLT	Beloit	MID	Athletics	Snappers
BLU	Bluefield	APP	Blue Jays	Blue Jays
BLX	Biloxi	SOU	Brewers	Shuckers
BNC	Burlington	APP	Royals	Royals
BOI	Boise	NWL	Rockies	Hawks
BOS	Boston	AL	-	Red Sox
BOW	Bowie	EAS	Orioles	Baysox
BRA	GCL Braves	GCL	Braves	GCL Braves
BRD	Bradenton	FSL	Pirates	Marauders
BRI	Bristol	APP	Pirates	Pirates
BRO	Brooklyn	NYP	Mets	Cyclones
BRR	AZL Brewers	AZL	Brewers	-
BRV	Brevard County	FSL	Brewers	Manatees
BUF	Buffalo	INT	Blue Jays	Bisons
BUR	Burlington	MID	Angels	Bees
CAR	Carolina	CAR	Braves	Mudcats
CCH	Corpus Christi	TEX	Astros	Hooks
CDR	Cedar Rapids	MID	Twins	Kernels
CFG	Cienfuegos	CNS	-	
CHA	Chicago	AL	-	White Sox
CHB	Chiba Lotte	NPB	-	Marines
CHN	Chicago	NL	-	Cubs
CHR	Charlotte	INT	White Sox	Knights
CHT	Chattanooga	SOU	Twins	Lookouts
CHU	Chunichi	NPB	-	Dragons
CIN	AZL Reds	AZL	Reds	-
CIN	Cincinnati	NL	-	Reds
CLE	AZL Indians	AZL	Indians	-
CLE	Cleveland	AL	-	Indians
CLN	Clinton	MID	Mariners	LumberKings
CLR	Clearwater	FSL	Phillies	Threshers
COH	Columbus	INT	Indians	Clippers
COL	Colorado	NL	-	Rockies
COL	Columbia	SAL	Mets	Fireflies
CRD	GCL Cardinals	GCL	Cardinals	GCL Cardinals
CSC	Charleston	SAL	Yankees	RiverDogs
CSP	Colorado Springs	PCL	Brewers	Sky Sox
CUB	AZL Cubs	AZL	Cubs	-
DAN	DSL Angels	DSL	Angels	DSL Angels
DAR	DSL Astros Orange	DSL	Astros	DSL Astros Orange
DAS	DSL Astros	DSL	Astros	DSL Astros
DAT	DSL Athletics	DSL	Athletics	DSL Athletics
DAY	Daytona	FSL	Reds	Tortugas
DBA	DSL Orioles2	DSL	Orioles	DSL Orioles2
DBL	DSL Blue Jays	DSL	Blue Jays	DSL Blue Jays
DBR	DSL Braves	DSL	Braves	DSL Braves
DBW	DSL Brewers	DSL	Brewers	DSL Brewers
DCA	DSL Cardinals	DSL	Cardinals	DSL Cardinals
DCH	DSL Cubs2	DSL	Cubs	DSL Cubs2
DCU	DSL Cubs	DSL	Cubs	DSL Cubs
DDB	DSL D-backs2	DSL	D-backs	DSL D-backs2
DDG	DSL Dodgers2	DSL	Dodgers	DSL Dodgers2
DDI	DSL D-backs	DSL	D-backs	DSL D-backs
DDO	DSL Dodgers	DSL	Dodgers	DSL Dodgers
DDR	DSL Rays	DSL	Rays	DSL Rays
DEL	Delmarva	SAL	Orioles	Shorebirds
DET	Detroit	AL	-	Tigers
DGI	DSL Giants	DSL	Giants	DSL Giants
DIA	AZL D-backs	AZL	D-backs	-
DIN	DSL Indians	DSL	Indians	DSL Indians
DME	DSL Mets1	DSL	Mets	DSL Mets1
DML	DSL Marlins	DSL	Marlins	DSL Marlins
DMR	DSL Mariners	DSL	Mariners	DSL Mariners
DNV	Danville	APP	Braves	Braves
DOD	AZL Dodgers	AZL	Dodgers	-
DOR	DSL Orioles1	DSL	Orioles	DSL Orioles1
DPA	DSL Padres	DSL	Padres	DSL Padres
DPH	DSL Phillies	DSL	Phillies	DSL Phillies
DPI	DSL Pirates1	DSL	Pirates	DSL Pirates1
DPL	DSL Phillies2	DSL	Phillies	DSL Phillies2
DRA	DSL Rays2	DSL	Rays	DSL Rays2
DRD	DSL Reds	DSL	Reds	DSL Reds
DRG	DSL Rangers	DSL	Rangers	DSL Rangers
DRJ	DSL Rojos	DSL	Reds	DSL Rojos
DRN	DSL Rangers2	DSL	Rangers	DSL Rangers2
DRO	DSL Rockies	DSL	Rockies	DSL Rockies
DRS	DSL Red Sox	DSL	Red Sox	DSL Red Sox
DRX	DSL Red Sox2	DSL	Red Sox	DSL Red Sox2
DRY	DSL Royals	DSL	Royals	DSL Royals
DTI	DSL Tigers	DSL	Tigers	DSL Tigers
DTW	DSL Twins	DSL	Twins	DSL Twins
DUN	Dunedin	FSL	Blue Jays	Blue Jays
DUR	Durham	INT	Rays	Bulls
DWA	DSL Nationals	DSL	Nationals	DSL Nationals
DWS	DSL White Sox	DSL	White Sox	DSL White Sox
DYA	DSL Yankees1	DSL	Yankees	DSL Yankees1
DYN	DSL Yankees2	DSL	Yankees	DSL Yankees2
DYT	Dayton	MID	Reds	Dragons
ELP	El Paso	PCL	Padres	Chihuahuas
ELZ	Elizabethton	APP	Twins	Twins
ERI	Erie	EAS	Tigers	SeaWolves
EUG	Eugene	NWL	Cubs	Emeralds
EVE	Everett	NWL	Mariners	AquaSox
FKU	Fukuoka	NPB	-	Hawks
FRD	Frederick	CAR	Orioles	Keys
FRE	Fresno	PCL	Astros	Grizzlies
FRI	Frisco	TEX	Rangers	RoughRiders
FTM	Fort Myers	FSL	Twins	Miracle
FTW	Fort Wayne	MID	Padres	TinCaps
GIA	AZL Giants	AZL	Giants	-
GJR	Grand Junction	PIO	Rockies	Rockies
GRB	Greensboro	SAL	Marlins	Grasshoppers
GRF	Great Falls	PIO	White Sox	Voyagers
GRL	Great Lakes	MID	Dodgers	Loons
GRN	Greenville	SAL	Red Sox	Drive
GRV	Greeneville	APP	Astros	Astros
GWN	Gwinnett	INT	Braves	Braves
HAB	La Habana	CNS	-	
HAG	Hagerstown	SAL	Nationals	Suns
HAR	Harrisburg	EAS	Nationals	Senators
HDS	High Desert	CAL	Rangers	Mavericks
HEL	Helena	PIO	Brewers	Brewers
HIC	Hickory	SAL	Rangers	Crawdads
HNS	Hanshin	NPB	-	Tigers
HOU	Houston	AL	-	Astros
HRO	Hiroshima Toyo	NPB	-	Carp
HUD	Hudson Valley	NYP	Rays	Renegades
IDA	Idaho Falls	PIO	Royals	Chukars
IND	Indianapolis	INT	Pirates	Indians
INL	Inland Empire	CAL	Angels	66ers
IOW	Iowa	PCL	Cubs	Cubs
JAX	Jacksonville	SOU	Marlins	Suns
JCY	Johnson City	APP	Cardinals	Cardinals
JUP	Jupiter	FSL	Marlins	Hammerheads
KAN	Kannapolis	SAL	White Sox	Intimidators
KCA	Kansas City	AL	-	Royals
KNC	Kane County	MID	D-backs	Cougars
KNG	Kingsport	APP	Mets	Mets

CODE	TEAM	LG	AFF.	Name
LAK	Lakeland	FSL	Tigers	Flying Tigers
LAN	Los Angeles	NL	-	Dodgers
LEH	Lehigh Valley	INT	Phillies	IronPigs
LEL	Lake Elsinore	CAL	Padres	Storm
LEX	Lexington	SAL	Royals	Legends
LKC	Lake County	MID	Indians	Captains
LNC	Lancaster	CAL	Astros	JetHawks
LNS	Lansing	MID	Blue Jays	Lugnuts
LOU	Louisville	INT	Reds	Bats
LOW	Lowell	NYP	Red Sox	Spinners
LTU	Las Tunas	CNS	-	
LVG	Las Vegas	PCL	Mets	51s
LWD	Lakewood	SAL	Phillies	BlueClaws
LYN	Lynchburg	CAR	Indians	Hillcats
MCO	DSL Mariners2	DSL	Mariners	DSL Mariners2
MEM	Memphis	PCL	Cardinals	Redbirds
MET	DSL Mets2	DSL	Mets	DSL Mets2
MHV	Mahoning Valley	NYP	Indians	Scrappers
MIA	Miami	NL	-	Marlins
MID	Midland	TEX	Athletics	RockHounds
MIL	Milwaukee	NL	-	Brewers
MIN	Minnesota	AL	-	Twins
MIS	Mississippi	SOU	Braves	Braves
MNT	Montgomery	SOU	Rays	Biscuits
MOB	Mobile	SOU	D-backs	BayBears
MOD	Modesto	CAL	Rockies	Nuts
MRL	GCL Marlins	GCL	Marlins	GCL Marlins
MRN	AZL Mariners	AZL	Mariners	-
MSO	Missoula	PIO	D-backs	Osprey
MTS	GCL Mets	GCL	Mets	GCL Mets
MYR	Myrtle Beach	CAR	Cubs	Pelicans
NAS	Nashville	PCL	Athletics	Sounds
NAT	GCL Nationals	GCL	Nationals	GCL Nationals
NBR	Hartford	EAS	Rockies	Yard Goats
NHP	New Hampshire	EAS	Blue Jays	Fisher Cats
NIP	Nippon Ham	NPB	-	Fighters
NOR	Norfolk	INT	Orioles	Tides
NWA	NW Arkansas	TEX	Royals	Naturals
NWO	New Orleans	PCL	Marlins	Zephyrs
NYA	New York	AL	-	Yankees
NYN	New York	NL	-	Mets
OAK	Oakland	AL	-	Athletics
OGD	Ogden	PIO	Dodgers	Raptors
OKL	Oklahoma City	PCL	Dodgers	Dodgers
OMA	Omaha	PCL	Royals	Storm Chasers
ONE	Connecticut	NYP	Tigers	Tigers
ORI	GCL Orioles	GCL	Orioles	GCL Orioles
ORM	Orem	PIO	Angels	Owlz
ORX	Orix	NPB	-	Buffaloes
PAW	Pawtucket	INT	Red Sox	Red Sox
PCH	Charlotte	FSL	Rays	Stone Crabs
PDR	AZL Padres	AZL	Padres	-
PEN	Pensacola	SOU	Reds	Blue Wahoos
PEO	Peoria	MID	Cardinals	Chiefs
PHI	Philadelphia	NL	-	Phillies
PHL	GCL Phillies	GCL	Phillies	GCL Phillies
PIR	GCL Pirates	GCL	Pirates	GCL Pirates
PIT	Pittsburgh	NL	-	Pirates
PMB	Palm Beach	FSL	Cardinals	Cardinals
PME	Portland	EAS	Red Sox	Sea Dogs
POT	Potomac	CAR	Nationals	Nationals
PRI	Princeton	APP	Rays	Rays
PUL	Pulaski	APP	Yankees	Yankees
QUD	Quad Cities	MID	Astros	River Bandits
RAK	Rakuten	NPB	-	Golden Eagles
RAY	GCL Rays	GCL	Rays	GCL Rays
RCU	Rancho Cucamonga	CAL	Dodgers	Quakes
REA	Reading	EAS	Phillies	Fightin Phils
RIC	Richmond	EAS	Giants	Flying Squirrels
RNG	AZL Rangers	AZL	Rangers	-
RNO	Reno	PCL	D-backs	Aces
ROC	Rochester	INT	Twins	Red Wings
ROM	Rome	SAL	Braves	Braves
ROU	Round Rock	PCL	Rangers	Express
ROY	AZL Royals	AZL	Royals	-
RSX	GCL Red Sox	GCL	Red Sox	GCL Red Sox
SAC	Sacramento	PCL	Giants	River Cats
SAN	San Antonio	TEX	Padres	Missions
SBN	South Bend	MID	Cubs	Cubs
SCO	State College	NYP	Cardinals	Spikes
SDN	San Diego	NL	-	Padres
SEA	Seattle	AL	-	Mariners
SEI	Seibu	NPB	-	Lions
SFD	Springfield	TEX	Cardinals	Cardinals
SFN	San Francisco	NL	-	Giants
SJO	San Jose	CAL	Giants	Giants
SLC	Salt Lake	PCL	Angels	Bees
SLM	Salem	CAR	Red Sox	Red Sox
SLN	St. Louis	NL	-	Cardinals
SLO	Salem-Keizer	NWL	Giants	Volcanoes
SLU	St. Lucie	FSL	Mets	Mets
SPO	Spokane	NWL	Rangers	Indians
STA	Staten Island	NYP	Yankees	Yankees
STO	Stockton	CAL	Athletics	Ports
SWB	Scranton/WB	INT	Yankees	RailRiders
SYR	Syracuse	INT	Nationals	Chiefs
TAC	Tacoma	PCL	Mariners	Rainiers
TAM	Tampa	FSL	Yankees	Yankees
TBA	Tampa Bay	AL	-	Rays
TCV	Tri-City	NYP	Astros	ValleyCats
TEN	Tennessee	SOU	Cubs	Smokies
TEX	Texas	AL	-	Rangers
TGR	GCL Tigers	GCL	Tigers	GCL Tigers
TGW	GCL Tigers West	GCL	Tigers	GCL Tigers West
TOL	Toledo	INT	Tigers	Mud Hens
TOR	Toronto	AL	-	Blue Jays
TRI	Tri-City	NWL	Padres	Dust Devils
TRN	Trenton	EAS	Yankees	Thunder
TUL	Tulsa	TEX	Dodgers	Drillers
TWI	GCL Twins	GCL	Twins	GCL Twins
VAN	Vancouver	NWL	Blue Jays	Canadians
VCU	VSL CHN	VSL	Cubs	VSL Cubs
VER	Vermont	NYP	Athletics	Lake Monsters
VIS	Visalia	CAL	D-backs	Rawhide
VPH	VSL PHI	VSL	Phillies	VSL Phillies
VSE	VSL SEA	VSL	Mariners	VSL Mariners
VTB	VSL TB	VSL	Rays	VSL Rays
VTI	VSL DET	VSL	Tigers	VSL Tigers
WAS	Washington	NL	-	Nationals
WEV	West Virginia	NYP	Pirates	Black Bears
WIL	Wilmington	CAR	Royals	Blue Rocks
WIS	Wisconsin	MID	Brewers	Timber Rattlers
WMI	West Michigan	MID	Tigers	Whitecaps
WNS	Winston-Salem	CAR	White Sox	Dash
WPT	Williamsport	NYP	Phillies	Crosscutters
WSX	AZL White Sox	AZL	White Sox	-
WTN	Jackson	SOU	Mariners	Generals
WVA	West Virginia	SAL	Pirates	Power
YAK	Hillsboro	NWL	D-backs	Hops
YAN	GCL Yankees1	GCL	Yankees	GCL Yankees
YAT	GCL Yankees2	GCL	Yankees	GCL Yankees2
YKL	Yakult	NPB	-	Swallows
YKO	Yokohama DeNa	NPB	-	BayStars
YOM	Yomiuri	NPB	-	Giants
YKO	Yokohama DeNa	NPB	-	BayStars
YOM	Yomiuri	NPB	-	Giants

PECOTA Leaderboards

Hitters

HR

Rank	NAME	Team	HR
1	Chris Davis	BAL	35
1	Edwin Encarnacion	CLE	35
1	Giancarlo Stanton	MIA	35
1	Nelson Cruz	SEA	35
5	Adam Duvall	CIN	34
6	Kris Bryant	CHN	33
6	Mark Trumbo	BAL	33
6	Joey Gallo	TEX	33
9	Chris Carter	MIL	32
9	Miguel Cabrera	DET	32
11	Anthony Rizzo	CHN	31
11	Mike Trout	ANA	31
11	Kyle Schwarber	CHN	31
11	Khris Davis	OAK	31
11	Tommy Joseph	PHI	31
11	Miguel Sano	MIN	31
11	Gary Sanchez	NYA	31
18	Josh Donaldson	TOR	30
18	Adam Jones	BAL	30
20	Joc Pederson	LAN	29
20	Carlos Gonzalez	COL	29
20	Nolan Arenado	COL	29

RBI

Rank	NAME	Team	RBI
1	Miguel Cabrera	DET	104
2	Mike Trout	ANA	102
3	Nelson Cruz	SEA	101
4	Edwin Encarnacion	CLE	99
5	Anthony Rizzo	CHN	98
6	Chris Davis	BAL	96
6	Kris Bryant	CHN	96
8	Robinson Cano	SEA	95
8	Giancarlo Stanton	MIA	95
10	Mark Trumbo	BAL	94
10	Paul Goldschmidt	ARI	94
12	Adam Duvall	CIN	93
13	Gary Sanchez	NYA	92
13	Jose Abreu	CHA	92
15	Carlos Gonzalez	COL	91
15	Nolan Arenado	COL	91
15	Josh Donaldson	TOR	91
15	Andrew McCutchen	PIT	91
15	Kyle Seager	SEA	91
20	Miguel Sano	MIN	90
20	Adam Jones	BAL	90

RUNS

Rank	NAME	Team	R
1	Carlos Santana	CLE	102
2	Mike Trout	ANA	100
2	Josh Donaldson	TOR	100
4	Adam Jones	BAL	95
5	George Springer	HOU	94
6	Paul Goldschmidt	ARI	93
7	Billy Hamilton	CIN	92
7	Jonathan Villar	MIL	92
7	Brian Dozier	MIN	92
10	Miguel Cabrera	DET	91
11	Anthony Rizzo	CHN	90
11	Jose Altuve	HOU	90
11	Joey Votto	CIN	90
14	Andrew McCutchen	PIT	89
14	Kyle Schwarber	CHN	89
16	Kris Bryant	CHN	88
16	Jason Kipnis	CLE	88
16	Charlie Blackmon	COL	88
19	Edwin Encarnacion	CLE	87
19	A.J. Pollock	ARI	87

STOLEN BASES

Rank	NAME	Team	SB
1	Billy Hamilton	CIN	71
2	Dee Gordon	MIA	51
3	Jonathan Villar	MIL	48
4	Travis Jankowski	SDN	39
5	Starling Marte	PIT	37
6	Jose Altuve	HOU	35
7	Trea Turner	WAS	34
8	A.J. Pollock	ARI	31
8	Rajai Davis	CLE	31
8	Eduardo Nunez	SFN	31
11	Jean Segura	SEA	29
12	Jacoby Ellsbury	NYA	28
13	Leonys Martin	SEA	26
13	Elvis Andrus	TEX	26
13	Terrance Gore	KCA	26
13	Carlos Gomez	TEX	26
17	Charlie Blackmon	COL	25
18	Lorenzo Cain	KCA	24
18	Jarrod Dyson	KCA	24
20	Melvin Upton	TOR	23
20	Jose Ramirez	CLE	23
20	Tim Anderson	CHA	23
20	Mookie Betts	BOS	23
20	Kevin Kiermaier	TBA	23

BATTING AVERAGE

Rank	NAME	Team	AVG
1	Miguel Cabrera	DET	.310
2	Mookie Betts	BOS	.308
3	Jose Altuve	HOU	.307
4	Buster Posey	SFN	.301
4	Mike Trout	ANA	.301
4	Michael Brantley	CLE	.301
7	Paul Goldschmidt	ARI	.295
8	Adrian Beltre	TEX	.294
8	DJ LeMahieu	COL	.294
8	Joey Votto	CIN	.294
11	Robinson Cano	SEA	.293
12	Andrew McCutchen	PIT	.292
13	Dustin Pedroia	BOS	.291
14	Melky Cabrera	CHA	.288
14	Daniel Murphy	WAS	.288
14	Nolan Arenado	COL	.288
17	Jose Abreu	CHA	.287
17	Xander Bogaerts	BOS	.287
19	Charlie Blackmon	COL	.286
19	Francisco Lindor	CLE	.286

ON-BASE PERCENTAGE

Rank	NAME	Team	OBP
1	Joey Votto	CIN	.424
2	Mike Trout	ANA	.404
3	Paul Goldschmidt	ARI	.397
4	Miguel Cabrera	DET	.389
5	Andrew McCutchen	PIT	.382
6	Bryce Harper	WAS	.375
7	Freddie Freeman	ATL	.374
7	Jose Bautista	TOR	.374
9	Buster Posey	SFN	.371
10	Kris Bryant	CHN	.369
11	Shin-Soo Choo	TEX	.368
12	Josh Donaldson	TOR	.367
12	Carlos Santana	CLE	.367
14	Mookie Betts	BOS	.366
15	Edwin Encarnacion	CLE	.363
16	Anthony Rizzo	CHN	.362
16	Matt Carpenter	SLN	.362
18	Michael Brantley	CLE	.360
18	Joe Mauer	MIN	.360
20	Brandon Belt	SFN	.358
20	Hyun-Soo Kim	BAL	.358

HITTERS CONT.

SLUGGING PERCENTAGE

Rank	NAME	Team	SLG
1	Mike Trout	ANA	.553
2	Miguel Cabrera	DET	.543
3	Nolan Arenado	COL	.528
4	Giancarlo Stanton	MIA	.527
5	Paul Goldschmidt	ARI	.525
6	Edwin Encarnacion	CLE	.523
7	Kris Bryant	CHN	.522
8	Josh Donaldson	TOR	.506
9	Carlos Gonzalez	COL	.505
10	Tom Murphy	COL	.504
11	Mookie Betts	BOS	.503
12	Bryce Harper	WAS	.501
13	Anthony Rizzo	CHN	.499
14	Jose Bautista	TOR	.498
15	Chris Davis	BAL	.497
16	Nelson Cruz	SEA	.496
17	Jose Abreu	CHA	.495
17	Joey Votto	CIN	.495
19	Andrew McCutchen	PIT	.494
20	Ryan Braun	MIL	.489

STRIKEOUT RATE

Rank	NAME	Team	SOR
1	Andrelton Simmons	ANA	0.092
2	Michael Brantley	CLE	0.097
3	Nori Aoki	HOU	0.102
4	Joe Panik	SFN	0.104
5	Jose Altuve	HOU	0.106
6	Jose Ramirez	CLE	0.111
7	Dustin Pedroia	BOS	0.115
7	Yadier Molina	SLN	0.115
9	Victor Martinez	DET	0.117
9	Yangervis Solarte	SDN	0.117
11	Buster Posey	SFN	0.120
11	Denard Span	SFN	0.120
13	Erick Aybar	DET	0.121
14	Adrian Beltre	TEX	0.122
15	Martin Prado	MIA	0.123
15	Ender Inciarte	ATL	0.123
15	Mookie Betts	BOS	0.123
18	Albert Pujols	ANA	0.124
18	Daniel Murphy	WAS	0.124
20	Jose Iglesias	DET	0.125

TRUE AVERAGE

Rank	NAME	Team	TAv
1	Mike Trout	ANA	.335
2	Joey Votto	CIN	.317
3	Miguel Cabrera	DET	.316
4	Kris Bryant	CHN	.312
5	Paul Goldschmidt	ARI	.309
6	Giancarlo Stanton	MIA	.307
7	Bryce Harper	WAS	.305
8	Freddie Freeman	ATL	.303
9	Anthony Rizzo	CHN	.302
9	Andrew McCutchen	PIT	.302
9	Edwin Encarnacion	CLE	.302
12	Josh Donaldson	TOR	.299
13	Mookie Betts	BOS	.296
14	Buster Posey	SFN	.295
14	Jose Abreu	CHA	.295
16	Robinson Cano	SEA	.294
16	Carlos Correa	HOU	.294
16	Jose Bautista	TOR	.294
19	Yasiel Puig	LAN	.293
20	Nelson Cruz	SEA	.290

ISOLATED SLUGGING

Rank	NAME	Team	ISO
1	Giancarlo Stanton	MIA	.271
2	Edwin Encarnacion	CLE	.255
2	Chris Davis	BAL	.255
4	Joey Gallo	TEX	.254
5	Ryan Schimpf	SDN	.253
6	Mike Trout	ANA	.252
7	Kris Bryant	CHN	.249
8	Tom Murphy	COL	.248
9	Chris Carter	MIL	.247
10	Adam Duvall	CIN	.246
11	Jose Bautista	TOR	.243
12	Nolan Arenado	COL	.240
13	Miguel Cabrera	DET	.233
13	Miguel Sano	MIN	.233
15	Brandon Moss	SLN	.232
15	Trevor Story	COL	.232
15	Nelson Cruz	SEA	.232
18	Bryce Harper	WAS	.231
19	Paul Goldschmidt	ARI	.230
20	Carlos Gonzalez	COL	.229
20	Anthony Rizzo	CHN	.229
20	Kyle Schwarber	CHN	.229

WALKS

Rank	NAME	Team	BBR
1	Joey Votto	CIN	.180
2	Jose Bautista	TOR	.154
3	Carlos Santana	CLE	.153
4	Joc Pederson	LAN	.151
5	Paul Goldschmidt	ARI	.142
6	Bryce Harper	WAS	.141
7	Yasmani Grandal	LAN	.139
8	Mike Trout	ANA	.138
9	Chris Iannetta	SEA	.137
10	Mike Napoli	CLE	.130
11	Dexter Fowler	SLN	.128
12	Joey Gallo	TEX	.128
13	Matt Joyce	OAK	.126
14	Edwin Encarnacion	CLE	.125
15	Kyle Schwarber	CHN	.124
16	Giancarlo Stanton	MIA	.123
17	Shin-Soo Choo	TEX	.123
18	Ben Zobrist	CHN	.122
19	Miguel Sano	MIN	.121
20	Chris Carter	MIL	.120

RUNS ABOVE AVERAGE

Rank	NAME	Team	RAA
1	Yasmani Grandal	LAN	33.8
2	Buster Posey	SFN	33.4
3	Jason Castro	MIN	15.7
4	Caleb Joseph	BAL	14.8
5	Russell Martin	TOR	14.5
6	Mike Zunino	SEA	13.1
7	Francisco Cervelli	PIT	13.0
8	Austin Hedges	SDN	12.2
9	Travis d'Arnaud	NYN	11.4
10	Martin Maldonado	MIL	10.5
11	Tyler Flowers	ATL	9.6
11	Roberto Perez	CLE	9.6
13	Jonathan Lucroy	TEX	9.2
14	Josh Thole	TOR	9.0
15	Brian McCann	HOU	8.0
16	Tony Wolters	COL	7.0
17	David Ross	CHN	6.7
17	Jeff Mathis	ARI	6.7
17	Yadier Molina	SLN	6.7
20	Derek Norris	WAS	6.0

Hitters cont.

AL WARP

Rank	NAME	Team	WARP
1	Mike Trout	ANA	7.7
2	George Springer	HOU	5.3
3	Kyle Seager	SEA	5.1
3	Miguel Cabrera	DET	5.1
5	Josh Donaldson	TOR	5
5	Kevin Kiermaier	TBA	5
7	Mookie Betts	BOS	4.9
8	Jonathan Lucroy	TEX	4.8
9	Manny Machado	BAL	4.7
9	Robinson Cano	SEA	4.7

NL WARP

Rank	NAME	Team	WARP
1	Buster Posey	SFN	7.2
2	Yasmani Grandal	LAN	6.4
3	Paul Goldschmidt	ARI	5.6
4	Trea Turner	WAS	5.5
5	Kris Bryant	CHN	5
6	Joey Votto	CIN	4.9
7	Giancarlo Stanton	MIA	4.8
8	Corey Seager	LAN	4.1
8	Yoenis Cespedes	NYN	4.1
10	Bryce Harper	WAS	4
10	Nolan Arenado	COL	4
10	Anthony Rizzo	CHN	4

CATCHER WARP

Rank	NAME	Team	WARP
1	Buster Posey	SFN	7.2
2	Yasmani Grandal	LAN	6.4
3	Jonathan Lucroy	TEX	4.8
4	Russell Martin	TOR	4.1
5	Francisco Cervelli	PIT	3.8
6	Travis d'Arnaud	NYN	2.9
7	Yadier Molina	SLN	2.8
8	Gary Sanchez	NYA	2.6
9	Austin Hedges	SDN	2.4
10	Brian McCann	HOU	2.2

1B WARP

Rank	NAME	Team	WARP
1	Paul Goldschmidt	ARI	5.6
2	Miguel Cabrera	DET	5.1
3	Joey Votto	CIN	4.9
4	Anthony Rizzo	CHN	4
5	Edwin Encarnacion	CLE	3.6
6	Jose Abreu	CHA	3.5
7	Freddie Freeman	ATL	3.4
8	Brandon Belt	SFN	3.2
9	Carlos Santana	CLE	2.8
10	Steve Pearce	TOR	2.6

2B WARP

Rank	NAME	Team	WARP
1	Robinson Cano	SEA	4.7
2	Jose Altuve	HOU	3.7
3	Jason Kipnis	CLE	3.3
4	Rougned Odor	TEX	3.1
4	Dustin Pedroia	BOS	3.1
6	Ben Zobrist	CHN	2.9
7	Ryan Schimpf	SDN	2.6
8	Devon Travis	TOR	2.3
8	Ian Kinsler	DET	2.3
10	Logan Forsythe	TBA	2.2
10	Joe Panik	SFN	2.2
10	Neil Walker	NYN	2.2

3B WARP

Rank	NAME	Team	WARP
1	Kyle Seager	SEA	5.1
2	Kris Bryant	CHN	5
2	Josh Donaldson	TOR	5
4	Manny Machado	BAL	4.7
5	Nolan Arenado	COL	4
6	Alex Bregman	HOU	3.6
7	Evan Longoria	TBA	3
8	Justin Turner	LAN	2.9
8	Jung-ho Kang	PIT	2.9
8	Adrian Beltre	TEX	2.9

SS WARP

Rank	NAME	Team	WARP
1	Trea Turner	WAS	5.5
2	Carlos Correa	HOU	4.6
3	Corey Seager	LAN	4.1
4	Francisco Lindor	CLE	3.8
4	Jean Segura	SEA	3.8
6	Troy Tulowitzki	TOR	3.4
7	Dansby Swanson	ATL	3.3
8	Marcus Semien	OAK	2.8
9	Matt Duffy	TBA	2.4
10	Addison Russell	CHN	2.3

LF WARP

Rank	NAME	Team	WARP
1	Andrew Benintendi	BOS	4.3
2	Yoenis Cespedes	NYN	4.1
3	Christian Yelich	MIA	3.3
4	Ryan Braun	MIL	2.9
5	Kyle Schwarber	CHN	2.8
6	Khris Davis	OAK	2.7
7	Starling Marte	PIT	2.5
8	Justin Upton	DET	2.4
8	Michael Brantley	CLE	2.4
10	Corey Dickerson	TBA	2.3

CF WARP

Rank	NAME	Team	WARP
1	Mike Trout	ANA	7.7
2	George Springer	HOU	5.3
3	Kevin Kiermaier	TBA	5
4	Andrew McCutchen	PIT	3.5
4	Ender Inciarte	ATL	3.5
6	Adam Eaton	WAS	2.9
6	Lorenzo Cain	KCA	2.9
8	Byron Buxton	MIN	2.8
9	Joc Pederson	LAN	2.4
10	A.J. Pollock	ARI	2.3

RF WARP

Rank	NAME	Team	WARP
1	Mookie Betts	BOS	4.9
2	Giancarlo Stanton	MIA	4.8
3	Bryce Harper	WAS	4
4	Jason Heyward	CHN	3.6
5	Yasiel Puig	LAN	3.1
5	Jose Bautista	TOR	3.1
7	Nelson Cruz	SEA	3
8	Shin-Soo Choo	TEX	2.7
9	Hunter Pence	SFN	2.6
10	David Peralta	ARI	2

AL ROOKIE WARP

Rank	NAME	Team	WARP
1	Andrew Benintendi	BOS	4.3
2	Aaron Judge	NYA	2.1
3	Trey Mancini	BAL	1.2
3	Guillermo Heredia	SEA	1.2
5	Colin Walsh	OAK	0.9
6	Michael Freeman	SEA	0.8
6	Mitch Haniger	SEA	0.8
8	Andrew Burns	TOR	0.7
9	Benjamin Gamel	SEA	0.6
9	Jared Hoying	TEX	0.6

NL ROOKIE WARP

Rank	NAME	Team	WARP
1	Dansby Swanson	ATL	3.3
2	Manuel Margot	SDN	1.7
3	Josh Bell	PIT	1.3
4	Hunter Renfroe	SDN	1.0
5	Max Moroff	PIT	0.7
6	Carson Kelly	SLN	0.6
7	Rob Segedin	LAN	0.5
8	Brandon Nimmo	NYN	0.4
8	Alen Hanson	PIT	0.4
10	Jordan Patterson	COL	0.3
10	Dean Anna	SLN	0.3
10	Steve Selsky	CIN	0.3

BIGGEST WARP DECLINE

Rank	NAME	Team	WARP 2016	WARP 2017	WARP DIFF
1	Daniel Murphy	WAS	6.8	1.8	-5.0
2	Wilson Ramos	TBA	5.2	0.5	-4.7
3	Kris Bryant	CHN	9.1	5.0	-4.1
4	Nolan Arenado	COL	7.8	4.0	-3.8
5	Eduardo Nunez	SFN	3.3	-0.3	-3.6
6	Charlie Blackmon	COL	5.2	1.7	-3.5
6	Adam Eaton	WAS	6.4	2.9	-3.5
6	Freddie Freeman	ATL	6.9	3.4	-3.5
9	Asdrubal Cabrera	NYN	4.3	1.1	-3.2
10	Jonathan Villar	MIL	4.8	1.7	-3.1
10	Odubel Herrera	PHI	5.2	2.1	-3.1

BIGGEST WARP IMPROVEMENT

Rank	NAME	Team	WARP 2016	WARP 2017	WARP DIFF
1	Andrew Benintendi	BOS	0.6	4.3	3.7
2	Jose Bautista	TOR	0.6	3.1	2.5
2	Alex Bregman	HOU	1.1	3.6	2.5
4	Dansby Swanson	ATL	1.1	3.3	2.2
5	Shin-Soo Choo	TEX	0.6	2.7	2.1
6	Orlando Arcia	MIL	0.2	2.2	2.0
7	David Peralta	ARI	0.5	2.4	1.9
7	Kevin Kiermaier	TBA	3.1	5.0	1.9
7	A.J. Pollock	ARI	0.4	2.3	1.9
10	Carlos Gomez	TEX	0.3	1.9	1.6

PITCHERS

WINS

Rank	NAME	Team	W
1	Clayton Kershaw	LAN	15
2	David Price	BOS	14
2	Chris Sale	BOS	14
2	Jon Lester	CHN	14
2	Corey Kluber	CLE	14
2	Madison Bumgarner	SFN	14
7	John Lackey	CHN	13
7	Jake Arrieta	CHN	13
7	Carlos Carrasco	CLE	13
7	Dallas Keuchel	HOU	13
7	Felix Hernandez	SEA	13
7	Cole Hamels	TEX	13
13	Rick Porcello	BOS	12
13	Jose Quintana	CHA	12
13	Josh Tomlin	CLE	12
13	Justin Verlander	DET	12
13	Collin McHugh	HOU	12
13	Kenta Maeda	LAN	12
13	Noah Syndergaard	NYN	12
13	Jacob deGrom	NYN	12
13	Hisashi Iwakuma	SEA	12
13	James Paxton	SEA	12
13	Jeff Samardzija	SFN	12
13	Chris Archer	TBA	12
13	Jake Odorizzi	TBA	12
13	Yu Darvish	TEX	12
13	Marcus Stroman	TOR	12
13	Gio Gonzalez	WAS	12
13	Max Scherzer	WAS	12
13	Stephen Strasburg	WAS	12

STRIKEOUTS

Rank	NAME	Team	SO
1	Clayton Kershaw	LAN	250
2	Chris Sale	BOS	238
2	Max Scherzer	WAS	238
4	Madison Bumgarner	SFN	227
5	Chris Archer	TBA	225
6	Corey Kluber	CLE	220
7	Yu Darvish	TEX	217
8	Stephen Strasburg	WAS	213
9	Noah Syndergaard	NYN	211
10	David Price	BOS	210
10	Jon Lester	CHN	210
12	Justin Verlander	DET	205
13	Carlos Carrasco	CLE	201
14	Cole Hamels	TEX	200
15	Jake Arrieta	CHN	197
16	Felix Hernandez	SEA	196
17	Jose Quintana	CHA	190
18	Zack Greinke	ARI	189
18	Carlos Rodon	CHA	189
18	Jacob deGrom	NYN	189
18	Gio Gonzalez	WAS	189

ERA, STARTERS

Rank	NAME	Team	ERA
1	Clayton Kershaw	LAN	2.47
2	Noah Syndergaard	NYN	3.04
3	Madison Bumgarner	SFN	3.16
4	Chris Sale	BOS	3.18
5	Rich Hill	LAN	3.27
6	Stephen Strasburg	WAS	3.31
7	Max Scherzer	WAS	3.33
8	Chris Archer	TBA	3.35
9	Lance McCullers	HOU	3.37
10	Kenta Maeda	LAN	3.39
11	David Price	BOS	3.40
12	Carlos Carrasco	CLE	3.44
13	Johnny Cueto	SFN	3.46
14	Steven Matz	NYN	3.47
15	Corey Kluber	CLE	3.48
16	Jacob deGrom	NYN	3.51
17	Michael Pineda	NYA	3.56
18	Dallas Keuchel	HOU	3.57
19	Aaron Nola	PHI	3.59
19	Yu Darvish	TEX	3.59

ERA, RELIEVERS

Rank	NAME	Team	ERA
1	Dellin Betances	NYA	2.03
2	Andrew Miller	CLE	2.11
3	Kenley Jansen	LAN	2.45
4	Ken Giles	HOU	2.72
5	Zach Britton	BAL	2.73
6	Aroldis Chapman	NYA	2.83
7	Craig Kimbrel	BOS	2.88
8	Will Smith	SFN	2.94
9	Cody Allen	CLE	3.02
9	James Hoyt	HOU	3.02
9	Edwin Diaz	SEA	3.02
9	Mark Melancon	SFN	3.02
13	Nate Jones	CHA	3.05
14	David Robertson	CHA	3.09
15	Wade Davis	CHN	3.11
16	Carson Smith	BOS	3.13
17	Carter Capps	SDN	3.15
18	Alex Colome	TBA	3.17
19	Liam Hendriks	OAK	3.18
20	Trevor May	MIN	3.21

WHIP

Rank	NAME	Team	WHIP
1	Clayton Kershaw	LAN	0.89
2	Max Scherzer	WAS	1.06
3	Jerad Eickhoff	PHI	1.12
3	Madison Bumgarner	SFN	1.12
3	Stephen Strasburg	WAS	1.12
6	Chris Sale	BOS	1.14
7	Jon Lester	CHN	1.15
7	Jake Arrieta	CHN	1.15
7	Masahiro Tanaka	NYA	1.15
7	Noah Syndergaard	NYN	1.15
7	Aaron Nola	PHI	1.15
12	Jason Hammel	CHN	1.16
12	Kenta Maeda	LAN	1.16
14	Kyle Hendricks	CHN	1.17
14	Johnny Cueto	SFN	1.17
16	Jacob deGrom	NYN	1.18
16	Chris Archer	TBA	1.18
18	Zack Greinke	ARI	1.19
18	Julio Teheran	ATL	1.19
18	Wei-Yin Chen	MIA	1.19
18	Steven Matz	NYN	1.19
18	Vincent Velasquez	PHI	1.19

SAVES

Rank	NAME	Team	SV
1	Wade Davis	CHN	41
2	Aroldis Chapman	NYA	40
2	Kenley Jansen	LAN	40
4	Francisco Rodriguez	DET	39
4	Mark Melancon	SFN	39
6	Fernando Rodney	ARI	38
6	Craig Kimbrel	BOS	38
6	Shawn Kelley	WAS	38
9	David Robertson	CHA	37
10	Zach Britton	BAL	35
10	Corey Knebel	MIL	35
10	Joaquin Benoit	PHI	35
10	Sam Dyson	TEX	35
10	Roberto Osuna	TOR	35
15	Huston Street	ANA	34
16	Jim Johnson	ATL	30
16	Cody Allen	CLE	30
16	Adam Ottavino	COL	30
16	Ken Giles	HOU	30
16	A.J. Ramos	MIA	30
16	Ryan Madson	OAK	30
16	Alex Colome	TBA	30

PITCHERS CONT.

STRIKEOUTS PER 9 IP

Rank	NAME	Team	SO9
1	Clayton Kershaw	LAN	11.5
2	Max Scherzer	WAS	11.4
3	Yu Darvish	TEX	11.2
4	Stephen Strasburg	WAS	11.0
5	Chris Archer	TBA	10.7
6	Rich Hill	LAN	10.6
6	Chris Sale	BOS	10.6
8	Lance McCullers	HOU	10.4
8	Noah Syndergaard	NYN	10.4
10	Robbie Ray	ARI	10.3
10	Vincent Velasquez	PHI	10.3
12	Corey Kluber	CLE	10.2
13	Danny Salazar	CLE	10.1
14	Carlos Carrasco	CLE	10.0
15	Madison Bumgarner	SFN	9.8
15	Justin Verlander	DET	9.8
15	Michael Pineda	NYA	9.8
18	Carlos Rodon	CHA	9.6
19	Kenta Maeda	LAN	9.5
19	Francisco Liriano	TOR	9.5
19	Drew Pomeranz	BOS	9.5

WALKS PER 9 IP

Rank	NAME	Team	BB9
1	Clayton Kershaw	LAN	1.6
2	Phil Hughes	MIN	1.8
3	Jameson Taillon	PIT	2.0
3	Josh Tomlin	CLE	2.0
5	Rick Porcello	BOS	2.1
5	Masahiro Tanaka	NYA	2.1
5	Mike Leake	SLN	2.1
8	Wei-Yin Chen	MIA	2.2
8	David Price	BOS	2.2
8	Bartolo Colon	ATL	2.2
8	Chris Sale	BOS	2.2
8	Hisashi Iwakuma	SEA	2.2
8	Jerad Eickhoff	PHI	2.2
14	Ivan Nova	PIT	2.3
14	Matt Shoemaker	ANA	2.3
16	Jose Quintana	CHA	2.4
16	Aaron Nola	PHI	2.4
16	Zack Greinke	ARI	2.4
16	Jeremy Hellickson	PHI	2.4
20	Kendall Graveman	OAK	2.5
20	Max Scherzer	WAS	2.5
20	Jordan Zimmermann	DET	2.5
20	Johnny Cueto	SFN	2.5

HOME RUNS PER 9 IP

Rank	NAME	Team	HR9
1	Lance McCullers	HOU	0.73
2	Steven Matz	NYN	0.82
3	Noah Syndergaard	NYN	0.84
4	Madison Bumgarner	SFN	0.91
5	Mike Montgomery	CHN	0.92
6	Edinson Volquez	MIA	0.93
6	Jake Arrieta	CHN	0.93
6	Sonny Gray	OAK	0.93
6	Johnny Cueto	SFN	0.93
10	Rich Hill	LAN	0.96
10	Kendall Graveman	OAK	0.96
10	Clayton Kershaw	LAN	0.96
13	Dallas Keuchel	HOU	0.97
13	Tom Koehler	MIA	0.97
13	Drew Pomeranz	BOS	0.97
13	Robert Gsellman	NYN	0.97
17	Aaron Nola	PHI	0.98
17	Jarred Cosart	SDN	0.98
17	Kyle Hendricks	CHN	0.98
17	Collin McHugh	HOU	0.98
17	Gerrit Cole	PIT	0.98

FIELDING INDEPENDENT PITCHING

Rank	NAME	Team	FIP
1	Clayton Kershaw	LAN	2.63
2	Noah Syndergaard	NYN	3.03
3	Chris Sale	BOS	3.25
4	Madison Bumgarner	SFN	3.26
5	Stephen Strasburg	WAS	3.28
6	Max Scherzer	WAS	3.35
7	Aaron Nola	PHI	3.38
8	Rich Hill	LAN	3.41
9	Lance McCullers	HOU	3.43
9	Steven Matz	NYN	3.43
11	David Price	BOS	3.46
11	Chris Archer	TBA	3.46
13	Jacob deGrom	NYN	3.55
14	Johnny Cueto	SFN	3.56
15	Carlos Carrasco	CLE	3.58
15	Kenta Maeda	LAN	3.58
17	Corey Kluber	CLE	3.59
17	Michael Pineda	NYA	3.59
19	Jon Lester	CHN	3.60
20	Robbie Ray	ARI	3.62
20	Yu Darvish	TEX	3.62

FIP IN CONTEXT

Rank	NAME	Team	cFIP
1	Clayton Kershaw	LAN	59
2	Noah Syndergaard	NYN	72
3	Chris Sale	BOS	76
4	Max Scherzer	WAS	80
4	Stephen Strasburg	WAS	80
6	Carlos Carrasco	CLE	82
6	Michael Pineda	NYA	82
8	David Price	BOS	83
8	Corey Kluber	CLE	83
10	Madison Bumgarner	SFN	84
11	Rich Hill	LAN	85
11	Aaron Nola	PHI	85
13	Steven Matz	NYN	86
14	Robbie Ray	ARI	87
14	Jon Lester	CHN	87
14	Lance McCullers	HOU	87
17	Zack Greinke	ARI	88
17	Jake Arrieta	CHN	88
17	Kenta Maeda	LAN	88
17	Jacob deGrom	NYN	88
17	Chris Archer	TBA	88
17	Yu Darvish	TEX	88

PITCHERS CONT.

WARP, STARTERS

Rank	NAME	Team	WARP
1	Clayton Kershaw	LAN	5.1
2	Chris Sale	BOS	4.1
3	Noah Syndergaard	NYN	3.8
4	David Price	BOS	3.5
5	Madison Bumgarner	SFN	3.4
5	Corey Kluber	CLE	3.4
5	Max Scherzer	WAS	3.4
8	Carlos Carrasco	CLE	3.2
8	Stephen Strasburg	WAS	3.2
8	Jon Lester	CHN	3.2
11	Michael Pineda	NYA	3.0
11	Chris Archer	TBA	3.0
13	Jake Arrieta	CHN	2.9
14	Zack Greinke	ARI	2.8
14	Cole Hamels	TEX	2.8
14	Yu Darvish	TEX	2.8
17	Jose Quintana	CHA	2.7
17	Justin Verlander	DET	2.7
17	Jacob deGrom	NYN	2.7
20	Masahiro Tanaka	NYA	2.6

WARP, ROOKIES AL

Rank	NAME	Team	WARP
1	Jharel Cotton	OAK	1.2
2	James Hoyt	HOU	0.7
3	Alec Mills	KCA	0.6
3	Alex Meyer	ANA	0.6
5	Matt Strahm	KCA	0.5
5	Robby Scott	BOS	0.5
5	Simon Castro	OAK	0.5
8	Reynaldo Lopez	CHA	0.4
8	Justin Marks	TBA	0.4
8	Jed Bradley	BAL	0.4
8	Adam Plutko	CLE	0.4

WARP, ROOKIES NL

Rank	NAME	Team	WARP
1	Alex Reyes	SLN	1.5
2	Jeff Hoffman	COL	1.0
3	Robert Gsellman	NYN	0.9
3	Tyler Glasnow	PIT	0.9
5	Grant Dayton	LAN	0.6
5	Josh Smoker	NYN	0.6
7	Steven Brault	PIT	0.5
7	Jose De Leon	LAN	0.5
9	Ty Blach	SFN	0.4
10	Robert Stephenson	CIN	0.3
10	Luke Weaver	SLN	0.3
10	Jorge Lopez	MIL	0.3
10	Kendry Flores	SLN	0.3

BIGGEST WARP DECLINE

Rank	NAME	Team	WARP 2016	WARP 2017	WARP DIFF
1	Justin Verlander	DET	6.8	2.7	-4.1
2	Cole Hamels	TEX	6.2	2.8	-3.4
3	David Price	BOS	6.5	3.5	-2.9
3	Rick Porcello	BOS	4.9	2.0	-2.9
3	Kevin Gausman	BAL	4.5	1.6	-2.9
6	Chris Sale	BOS	6.9	4.1	-2.8
6	Max Scherzer	WAS	6.2	3.4	-2.8
8	Matt Shoemaker	ANA	4.6	1.9	-2.7
8	Chris Archer	TBA	5.6	3.0	-2.7
10	Robbie Ray	ARI	4.8	2.2	-2.6
10	Michael Pineda	NYA	5.6	3.0	-2.6

BIGGEST WARP IMPROVEMENT

Rank	NAME	Team	WARP 2016	WARP 2017	WARP DIFF
1	Matt Harvey	NYN	0.4	1.9	1.4
2	Gerrit Cole	PIT	1.1	2.3	1.2
3	Tyler Skaggs	ANA	0.7	1.8	1.1
3	Garrett Richards	ANA	0.6	1.7	1.1
5	Felix Hernandez	SEA	1.1	2.2	1.0
5	Eduardo Rodriguez	BOS	0.3	1.3	1.0
5	Alex Cobb	TBA	0.1	1.1	1.0
8	Jharel Cotton	OAK	0.3	1.2	0.9
9	Tyler Glasnow	PIT	0.0	0.9	0.8
9	Adam Conley	MIA	0.3	1.1	0.8

Contributors and Acknowledgements

Emma Baccellieri lives and works in Washington, D.C. She is a staff author at Baseball Prospectus and also writes regularly for Deadspin, among other outlets. A recent graduate of Duke University, she enjoys bad puns and staying up too late.

Demetrius Bell joined the Baseball Prospectus team in February of 2016, which is where he can be found covering various rumors and/or hot topics that you need to know about on a weekly basis. In addition to his contributions to Baseball Prospectus, he also helps to cover the Atlanta Braves at SB Nation's Talking Chop blog and also covers baseball in general for SB Nation's MLB hub. He's a contributor to The Hardball Times and can also be found covering sports miscellany at FOX Sports' Yardbarker and Chris Creamer's sportslogos.net. If he's not writing for any of the aforementioned websites, you can find him in the Atlanta metro area where he is an avid follower of the local sports teams.

Craig Brown is Editor-in-Chief of BP Kansas City. He's taken up bandwidth writing about the Royals on one site or another since 2005. This is his fourth year contributing to the Annual. In addition to Baseball Prospectus, his work has appeared at ESPN, Sports On Earth and The Hardball Times. At this very moment, he's probably watching the 2014 AL Wild Card game at his Kansas City home while his family continues to tolerate his baseball obsession.

Russell Carleton is an author of *Baseball Prospectus* and a former consultant to two teams in MLB. He lives in Atlanta, Georgia.

Ben Carsley is the Managing Editor of BP Boston, host of the TINO podcast and a senior author on the BP Fantasy Team. When he's not writing about baseball, Ben is generally cooking, sampling IPAs, re-reading ASOIAF and ignoring Malinowski's Law on Twitter. By day, he manages a team of SEO writers and editors who are fairly convinced he's Ron Swanson.

Patrick Dubuque is a wastrel and a layabout, and writes a weekly column for Baseball Prospectus. He has also contributed to many other baseball sites, most of which are coincidentally defunct. He lives in Seattle with his wife Kjersten and his two verbose children, Sylvie and Felix.

Kenny Ducey is a writer for Sports Illustrated based in New York and the Editor-in-Chief of BP Bronx. He is a member of the Baseball Writers Association of America and a graduate of Fordham University.

Ken Funck has contributed to the Baseball Prospectus annual each year since 2009. He designs and manages Business Intelligence systems and lives outside Madison, Wisconsin with his beautiful wife Stephanie (who has finally grown tired of being described in these pages as "ever-supportive"), their son Max (on holiday breaks), their daughter Abby, two dogs, three kayaks, seven fishing poles and a fulfilled belief that the Cubs would actually win a world championship in his father's lifetime.

Catherine Garcia is a freelance baseball writer born and raised in Chicago, Illinois. She is a contributor at BP Wrigleyville, BP Southside and is a Baseball Prospectus columnist. When she isn't spending her time writing about, talking about, or watching baseball, she spends her days working at baseball's finest ballpark, located at 1060 W. Addison Street.

Eric Garcia McKinley is a historian by training, a research analyst for Minnesota Public Radio by day and an editor for the Rockies' blog Purple Row by night.

Mike Gianella has contributed to *Baseball Prospectus* since 2013. He has been writing about fantasy baseball since 2007. He lives in Pennsylvania with his wife Colleen, his daughters Lucy and Elise and his cats Sawyer, Luke and Leia. He hates puns and only makes them as a form of ironic performance art.

Aaron Gleeman is the editor-in-chief of Baseball Prospectus. He co-hosts the "Gleeman and The Geek" radio show/podcast on KFAN in Minnesota, where he lives with his girlfriend (and, she insists he add, their cat).

Craig Goldstein is an author and editor at Baseball Prospectus. His work has appeared in Vice Sports, Fox Sports MLB/JABO and SB Nation MLB. He lives and works in Washington, DC, where he spends just the right amount of time thinking about the failures of millennials.

Bryan Grosnick is the lead Transaction Analyst for Baseball Prospectus and the Editor-in-Chief of BP Mets. He lives in Rhode Island with his incredible wife Sarah and their son.

Matt Gwin is a student and digital marketer by day and the Co-Editor-in-Chief at BP Toronto by night. He may have left Toronto and the Blue Jays for Vancouver and the West Coast, but he manages to run the Dalton Pompey fan club from afar.

Joshua Howsam is the Co-Editor-in-Chief of BP Toronto and the Co-Host of BPT's official podcast, Artificial Turf Wars. He started out playing baseball with and against many current big league players. Then when his playing career fizzled, he chose to feed his passion by instead writing about the game he loves.

Bryan Joiner is a man for his time and place. A reporter-turned-magazine-editor-turned-digital-producer, he now makes his living by editing financial news for a ginormous corporation from kitchen table, where he also takes his meals. (His dad made the table, and it is quite nice.) The BP annual has been his favorite book for about 15 years, so getting to write the comments is a dream come true. He wrote them from the table. It really can do everything.

By day, **Wilson Karaman** chases around two small children, and by night (and sometimes during nap time) he is a senior writer at Baseball Prospectus, where he scouts the California League and contributes to prospect and fantasy coverage.

Matthew Kory is a city planner turned stay-at-home dad turned baseball writer. He has contributed to Baseball Prospectus, Sports on Earth, Vice Sports, Fox Sports, and FanGraphs. This is his second BP Annual. He thanks you for reading this far, and politely suggests you stop avoiding your family, finish wiping, and don't forget to wash your hands.

David Lee is a member of the Baseball Prospectus prospect team and a baseball writer for *The Augusta Chronicle* in Augusta, Georgia. Consider him the odd evaluator/storyteller combination, spending his life behind home plate at some ballpark in the Southeast.

Rob Mains (@Cran_Boy) is a former financial analyst living in upstate New York with his wife, dog, and local wines.

Jack Moore is a freelance writer based in Minneapolis, Minnesota writing for many sites, including BP Milwaukee. Find him on Twitter @jh_moore.

Ryan P. Morrison is a co-author of InsidetheZona.com, a contributor to the D-backs Insider magazine and a former columnist at BP Boston. As a False Claims Act attorney who represents whistleblowers in government fraud cases, he represented Mark McGuire in a case alleging unnecessary urine drug testing. McGuire with a "u."

Jeffrey Paternostro is the Senior Prospect Writer for Baseball Prospectus. He has written about prospects, reviewed funnel-cake-batter-fried pork roll and crafted poems about Wade LeBlanc for BP in his The View From Behind the Backstop column since 2015. He is also the co-host of the BP Mets podcast, "For All You Kids Out There." You can usually find him behind home plate at various northeast minor league parks in very warm socks and a Sheffield Wednesday hat.

Jeff Quinton is an alum of University of Delaware and New York University, a logistics professional for a consumer packaged goods company, a contributor at Baseball Prospectus and a kid from Plainsboro, New Jersey.

Meg Rowley is a writer for Baseball Prospectus. Her work has appeared at Lookout Landing, Just A Bit Outside and Vice Sports. Her parents have come to accept that making baseball jokes on the internet is almost as good as finishing that Ph.D. would have been. She lives in Seattle.

Bret Sayre is the Managing Editor at Baseball Prospectus. By day, he tells investment professionals what not to do. By night, he is a full-time family man, part-time cook, part-time nurse, full-time baseball writer and part-time musician. As an eight-year-old boy, he was knocked over by a man in his thirties as he tried to catch a dead ball thrown by Kevin Mitchell at Shea Stadium. Now, he lives in New Jersey with his wife, daughter and son—alongside all of the unicorns and trucks ever made.

Jarrett Seidler (@jaseidler) is a contributor to Baseball Prospectus, covering the minors, the FOX television show *Pitch* and saves by Clayton Kershaw. He also writes weekly for BP Mets and co-hosts the "For All You Kids Out There" podcast. In real life, he's a systems administrator living and working in New Jersey.

Trevor Strunk is a dad to Tilly Strunk, a husband to Kristin Strunk and a writer and teacher generally. He teaches composition at DeSales University and has his PhD in English from the University of Illinois at Chicago. He is a fan of the Phillies by birth and thanks his father for the geographical quirk that lets him root for this terrible, wonderful team. Also for helping him love baseball. He also thanks his daughter and wife for their patience as he takes time away to consider the philosophy of OPS+, and hopes they'll be willing to be even more patient in the future as he continues.

Matt Sussman (@suss2hyphens) is an IT Professional from Toledo, Ohio and member of the 371st-ranked (as of end of year 2016) men's curling team in the world. By comparison, in 2016 the 371th-ranked pitcher according to DRA was Jeff Manship.

Matt Trueblood writes at Baseball Prospectus, and values relief pitchers rationally.

Ashley Varela is a freelance writer based in Oakland, California. Her work has appeared online at Baseball Prospectus, SB Nation, Mashable and NBC Sports' HardballTalk, and in some paper-and-ink copies of USA Today Sports Weekly. Her most interesting day job involves testing and marketing interactive high school algebra courses. She also has a cat, but would prefer not to be identified as a cat person.

Rian Watt is an author of *Baseball Prospectus*, and served as Editor-in-Chief of BP Wrigleyville during the Cubs' championship 2016 season. He refuses to apologize for referring to it that way. Rian's freelance writing has also appeared at The Athletic, FiveThirtyEight.com, The Ringer and VICE Sports. By day, he serves as a public policy analyst for a Boston-based research and evaluation firm called Abt Associates, and by night he serves as a sleepier version of the same.

Jeff Wiser is the co-author of InsidetheZona.com, a website dedicated to SABR-oriented analysis of the Arizona Diamondbacks. Jeff does freelance work for the D-backs' game day program, occasionally publishes at ESPN's Sweetspot Blog and is a former featured writer and editor for Beyond the Box Score. He has a known affinity for Paul Goldschmidt's stolen bases and Felix Hernandez changeups.

Nicholas Zettel is Editor-in-Chief of BP Milwaukee. When he's not thinking about the perfect sinker/change combo, he works in Community Development and studies Urban Planning & Policy at University of Illinois at Chicago.

Acknowledgements

Emma Baccellieri: R.J. Anderson, Meg Rowley, Craig Goldstein, Aaron Gleeman, Bret Sayre, Sam Miller; my parents, my sister, the members of the coven and BDGT; the second season of Frasier, cran-raspberry LaCroix; no cats.

Demetrius Bell: Garry Bell, Patricia Bell, Sheretha Bell, DeRonne Floyd, Chris Creamer, Kris Willis, Eric Cole, Brad Rowland, Scott Coleman, Carlos Collazo, Grant McAuley, Marc Normandin, Ben Duronio, Franklin Rabon, Jane Hammond, J.R. Francis, Chris Barnewall, Kyle Parmley, Sean Highkin, Sarah Sprague, David Lee.

Craig Brown: Joe Hamrahi, Clark Fosler, David Lesky, Clint Scoles, Darin Watson, Michael Engel, Jeff Herr, Hunter Samuels, Cecilia Tan, Sam Miller, Jason Wojciechowski, Marc Normandin, Rob Neyer, Evan Brunell, David Schoenfield, the 2015 Kansas City Royals, C. E. Jones.

Ben Carsley: My Red Sox-crazed family, the ever-patient Allyson Clancy, Bret Sayre, Craig Goldstein, Sam Miller, R.J. Anderson, Aaron Gleeman, Joe Hamrahi, Jason Parks, Tim Britton, Brian MacPherson, Marc Normandin, Matt Collins, Alex Skillin, Mike Curtin, Eli Fredman, Xander Bogaerts, Mary Donovan, Daniel Ohman, The Young Pope and the C-4 Content Team.

Matthew Collins: To Marc Normandin, Ben Carsley, Bret Sayre, Ben Buchanan, Craig Goldstein and many others for giving me a platform and the tools, skills and advice to not embarrass myself on them. To my parents, for indulging my ridiculous obsession and helping me in every way imaginable. To my brother Bryan, for having an obsession with baseball and allowing me to copy everything he did growing up. To my sister Erin, for showing me what it looks like to chase a passion. To Pedro Martinez, for making baseball so damn easy to become obsessed with.

Patrick Dubuque: Thanks to Aaron Gleeman, Bret Sayre, Rob McQuown, Jonathan Judge, Sam Miller, Jason Wojciechowski, Brendan Gawlowski, Wilson Karaman, Trevor Strunk, Bryan Murphy, Grant Brisbee, Fung Yu-Lan, Kjersten, Sylvie and Felix.

Kenny Ducey: My parents, two sisters, grandparents, my dog Reggie, Bob Ahrens, Beth Knobel, Craig Goldstein, Bret Sayre and Sam Miller.

Ken Funck: Steph Bee, Will Carroll, Patrick Dubuque, Aaron Gleeman, Steven Goldman, Kevin Goldstein, Christina Kahrl, King Kaufman, Ben Lindbergh, Sam Miller, John Perrotto, Bret Sayre, Cecilia Tan, Jason Wojciechowski.

Catherine Garcia: First off I would like to thank Joe, Lyle and Lyndsay Brady, for introducing to me something I hadn't known was missing from my life for 15 years, the great game of baseball. Mauricio Rubio, who helped guide me down the path that I am on today. Sahadev Sharma, for being the first editor that helped shape me as the writer that I have become. James Fegan, for being a part of my first writing family. Ethan Spalding, for being by my side and supporting me in ways I am forever grateful for. Brett Taylor, for spending countless hours in seedy Wrigleyville bars encouraging my abilities, making me feel adequate and always putting a smile on my face. The entire BP Southside team, for being the brothers I never had. My best friends and their families, for always reading and supporting my work, disarming my doubts and encouraging my dreams. To my dad, for always being patient, understanding and supportive. And lastly, to my mom, whose last wish during her life was for me to become a successful writer. Here I am, thanking her for her endless encouragement, sacrifice and support in published writing.

Eric Garcia-McKinley: The Purple Row staff, whose insights and feedback improved the quality of many of the comments for which I'm credited; Bret Sayre and Aaron Gleeman, for giving me the opportunity; Sam Miller, for bringing me into BP's orbit; and all the inspiring baseball writers out there, for obvious reasons.

Mike Gianella: Colleen, Lucy and Elise, who may not understand my passion for baseball but are as supportive as any family could ever be. Everyone at Baseball Prospectus, especially Bret Sayre, George Bissell and everyone else on the fantasy team, who are some of the best baseball writers in the business. Alex Patton and Peter Kreutzer, for pushing me down this path and encouraging me to this day. Matt Winkelman, Corinne Landry, John Stolnis and so many other smart and talented writers, whose insights into the Phillies added so much to my own.

Aaron Gleeman: Judi, Becky and Rihanna for being the greatest women in the world. Bret Sayre and John Bonnes for carrying me constantly. Stephen Reichert, Sean Neugebauer and Jim Walsh for making my dream come true. Chinese food, for tasting super good.

Craig Goldstein: Laurie Gross, Harvey Goldstein, Alexis Goldstein, Katherine Pappas, Jason Wojciechowski, Sam Miller, Patrick Dubuque, Bret Sayre, Ian Miller, Riley Breckenridge, Jason Parks, The BP Prospect Team, Marc Normandin, R.J. Anderson, Chris Crawford, Ben Carsley, Jacob Raim, Zach Mortimer, Jason Cole, Tucker Blair, Ethan Purser, Mike Ferrin, Spike Lundberg, Tommy Rancel, Meg Rowley, James Fegan, Emma Baccellieri, Aaron Gleeman, Wilson Karaman.

Bryan Grosnick: Sarah Grosnick, Luke Grosnick, Edgar Grosnick, Phil and Debbie Grosnick, Bret Sayre, Aaron Gleeman, Sam Miller, Craig Goldstein, Patrick Dubuque and Jason Wojciechowski, R.J. Anderson, George Bissell, Jarrett Seidler, Matt Geer, Jeff Sullivan, Eno Sarris, August Fagerstrom, Daniel Rathman, Brendan Gawlowski, Rob McQuown, Harry Pavlidis and Jonathan Judge.

Bryan Joiner: Lisa, Lila, Sam, mom, Grant Stevens, dad, Ken Barsley, Greg Coldstein, Joe Kelly, Wesley Snipes, Liz Lemon, Serena Williams and my lord and savior, the Flying Spaghetti Monster.

Wilson Karaman: Lauren Danza, HK & CK, Jane and Joe Karaman; Bret Sayre, Craig Goldstein, Sam Miller, Aaron Gleeman, Daniel Rathman, anyone else who has ever edited me and made my work read better and smarter than it is by trade; Jason Parks, Tucker Blair, Ronit Shah and other prospect team members past and present; Spacemen Outernational, General G-Dubs and we out.

Matthew Kory: Stephanie Kory, Ross and Kaye Kory, Wyatt and Sacha Kory, Jeff Sullivan, Sam Miller and Ben Lindbergh, Marc Normandin and everyone who worked so hard to make this book a reality.

David Lee: Scouts are the lifeblood of the game, and they're also a major reason why I'm where I am today. I appreciate those willing to talk and answer questions while watching batting practice during those scorching hot summer afternoons. A big thank you also goes to my family for putting up with me during the writing process and each baseball season.

Rob Mains: My mother, Rhoda Mains, for instilling a love of baseball; my wife, Amy Durland, for encouraging me to pursue it; AM and PM for just being there; Ken Maeda, Sam Miller, Joe Rosales, Scott Spratt, Jeff Sullivan, Ryan Sullivan and John Thorn for encouragement/guidance/opportunity; Rob Arthur for all three; and special thanks to Alan for the Twitter handle.

Jeffrey Paternostro: My wife Jess for spending all of our family vacations in Appalachian and South Atlantic League towns. My father for arguing about the merits of the sacrifice bunt at the dinner table (even if he likes Baumann's stuff better than mine). My Main Man Jarrett Seidler, 80-grade co-host and co-conspirator. Toby Hyde for being an example to aspire to when I was first starting out and a sounding board over the years. Eric Simon for giving me an opportunity to find my voice and for some reason not editing me as much as he probably should have. Sam Miller for definitely not editing me as much as he probably should have. Oh, and Craig I guess.

Dave Pease & Stephen Reichert: Thank you to those who assisted us in preparing and editing the annual; this is an amazing and talented group. Xavier Alatorre, Colin Anderle, Clare Banks, Mark Barry, Ivan Baxter, George Bissell, Craig Brown, Daniel Camponovo, William Camponovo, Alex Chamberlain, Charlie Clarke, Brett Cowett, Colleen Cunningham, Bryan Davidson, Ryan Davis, Shawn Dingle, Cam Ellis, Michael Engel, Tim Finnegan, Craig Goldstein, Nate Greabe, Bryan Grosnick, Will Haines, John Hill, Bryan Holcomb, Misty Horten, Scooter Hotz, Joshua Howsam, Edward Hyer, J.J. Jansons, Wilson Karaman, Jeremy Koser, Kourage Kundahl, Domenic Lanza, Jeff Lewandowski, Ben Lindbergh, Jesse Lippin-Foster, Rob Mains, Eric Garcia McKinley, Rob McQuown, Andrew Mearns, Sam Miller, Kate Morrison, Sean Neugebauer, Duncan Primeaux, Mark Primiano, Daniel Rathman, Eric Roseberry, Emmett Rosenbaum, Andrew Salzman, Nick Schaefer, Karen Siatras, Scott D. Simon, Josh Slavin, Tim Smythe, Nick Stephens, Jared Terry, Gideon Turk, Darin Watson, Maggie Wiggin and Jared Wyllys.

Jeff Quinton: Bret Sayre, Sam Miller, Ben Lindbergh, Craig Goldstein, Ben Carsley, Mike Gianella, Aaron Gleeman and Jacqui Arce-Quinton.

Meg Rowley: My family, especially my mom for always requesting I "say more about that," and my step-mom for teaching me to love baseball. Also, R.J. Anderson, Emma Baccellieri, Christopher Crawford, Patrick Dubuque, Brendan Gawlowski, Craig Goldstein, Sam Miller, Bret Sayre and Jeff Sullivan for their kindness and guidance, which have made me a better writer and a happier baseball human.

Bret Sayre: Carolyn, Alyson and Joshua for always making me smile and keeping me sane. Lynn and Peter Sayre. The entire Baseball Prospectus family. Sam Miller, R.J. Anderson, Ben Lindbergh, Jason Parks, Joe Hamrahi, Marc Normandin and Ray Guilfoyle. Ryan Westmoreland. Howard Johnson. Jack Johnson (the boxer).

Jarrett Seidler: To my mother, who never stopped believing in me. Thanks to Bret Sayre for thinking I could do any of this, Craig Goldstein for being a great editor and friend, Kate Morrison for her invaluable friendship and encouragement, Bryan Grosnick for helping me develop as a writer, my collaborator on PITCHf/ox Meg Rowley and, last but not least, my podcast co-host and frequent partner-in-crime Jeffrey Paternostro.

Matt Sussman: Tom Sussman (1952-2016), who did not care much for baseball but thought the world of his son's wit and writing skills. Thank you for everything, dad.

Matt Trueblood: Thanks to my loving and beloved wife, Maria, for making room in our little world (soaked this year with pain and unpleasantness) for this thing you know brings me some small distraction. Thanks to my younger sons, Sorkin and Lincoln, for giving up a lot of Dad's time this year and for keeping light in my life. Thanks to my dad for bringing me to games ever since I was little, and for sharing your love of sports with me. Thanks to my mom for bringing me to the card shop so many times, and for setting me up with Sprite and Pringles to watch the Cubs on summer afternoons. Thanks to editors, especially Sam Miller, Bret Sayre and Aaron Gleeman, for supporting and encouraging me through a spring in which I found myself without anything much to say, a summer in which I found myself unable to shut up, and a fall in which I was overwhelmed by everything I wanted to say but couldn't. And thank you, Emerson, for making me a dad, and for helping my heart grow incalculably. I love you.

Ashley Varela: Daniel Zarchy, first, foremost and always. Bret Sayre, Sam Miller, Aaron Gleeman and every other person who has given me a place within Baseball Prospectus. The Baseball Reference Play Index and Brooks Baseball for lending me some semblance of credibility. Andres Torres, to whom I owe my love for baseball, and Munenori Kawasaki, to whom I owe my love for the Seattle Mariners.

Rian Watt: To Sahadev Sharma, who gave me my first shot in this industry. To my editors since then: Sam Miller, Craig Goldstein, R.J. Anderson, Bret Sayre, Aaron Gleeman, David Roth, Eric Nusbaum, Caitlin Kelly, Neil Paine, Gary Cohen, Jon Greenberg and Mallory Rubin. To the entire BP staff—and especially Mau—for keeping me in line and keeping my head up as I learned how to do this. To Brett Taylor, for good solid advice. To my siblings, Dale and Liah Watt, for watching the game with me for many years. To Jenny, for watching it with me now. To my grandmother, who loved Chipper Jones, and to my grandfather, who still does. And to my parents, for buying their kid a copy of *Baseball Prospectus* way back in 2004, and introducing me thereby to this whole world in the first place. Thank you. Thank you. Thank you.

Jeff Wiser: Ryan, my long-time partner in crime at Inside the 'Zona—this has been a great ride. Annie, thank you for understanding I need my space to write. Kelvin, it's important to have a person of your quality righting our ship. The Inside the 'Zona fan club, you know who you are (mostly because there are very few of you). Mike and Craig, for all the laughs and some, believe it or not, really good advice. Nick and Steve for your outstanding work covering the D-backs. Eno, for the opportunity to write about craft beer with you. Baseball Prospectus, for the amazing chance to contribute to this thing!

Nicholas Zettel: To Anna, my wife, for sharing a love of scrappy replacement players ("But is he a chump?"). To J.P. Breen, Jack Moore, Ryan Topp, Kyle Lesniewski, Jonathan Judge, Vineet Barot, Bret Sayre, Aaron Gleeman, James Fisher, Mauricio Rubio, James Walsh and Stephen Reichert for writing opportunities and sharing knowledge.

Index of Names

Baseball's Many Physical Dimensions

Unlike any other professional sport, baseball's contest is played upon fields that vary in size from park to park. With the exception of the infield diamond, where strict rules regulate the location and height of the pitcher's mound and distance between the bases, no two baseball fields are alike. From the geometry of the field to the distance and height of the outfield walls, the 30 cathedrals of Major League Baseball exhibit unique and distinguishing physical characteristics.

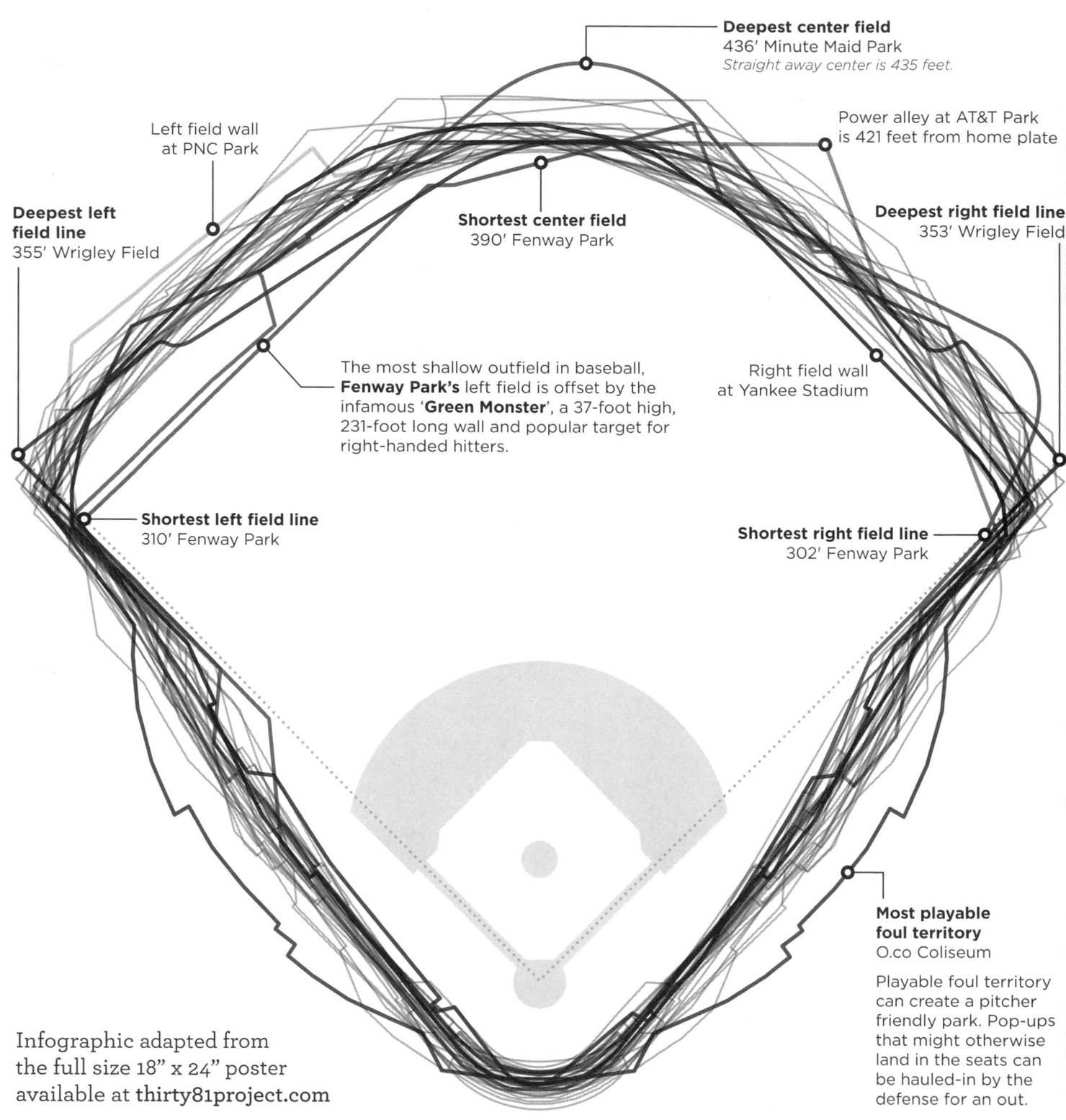

Deepest center field
436' Minute Maid Park
Straight away center is 435 feet.

Power alley at AT&T Park
is 421 feet from home plate

Left field wall
at PNC Park

**Deepest left
field line**
355' Wrigley Field

Shortest center field
390' Fenway Park

Deepest right field line
353' Wrigley Field

The most shallow outfield in baseball,
Fenway Park's left field is offset by the
infamous '**Green Monster**', a 37-foot high,
231-foot long wall and popular target for
right-handed hitters.

Right field wall
at Yankee Stadium

Shortest left field line
310' Fenway Park

Shortest right field line
302' Fenway Park

**Most playable
foul territory**
O.co Coliseum

Playable foul territory
can create a pitcher
friendly park. Pop-ups
that might otherwise
land in the seats can
be hauled-in by the
defense for an out.

Infographic adapted from
the full size 18" x 24" poster
available at thirty81project.com

THIRTY81 Project
© 2015 LOUIS J. SPIRITO | THIRTY81PROJECT.COM